A LEXICON OF THE HOMERIC DIALECT

Ἦ γάρ, ὦ φίλε, οὐ κηλῇ ὑπὸ [τῆς ποιήσεως] καὶ σύ, καὶ μάλιστα ὅταν δι' Ὁμήρου θεωρῇς αὐτήν;

PLATO, *Rep.* 607 C.

Or list'ning to the tide, with closed sight,
Be that blind bard, who on the Chian strand
By those deep sounds possessed with inward light
Beheld the ILIAD and the ODYSSEE
Rise to the swelling of the voiceful sea.

A LEXICON OF THE HOMERIC DIALECT

By Richard John Cunliffe

UNIVERSITY OF OKLAHOMA PRESS : NORMAN AND LONDON

Library of Congress Catalog Card Number: 63–17165
International Standard Book Number: 0–8061–1430–4

First published by Blackie and Son Limited, London, Glasgow, and Bombay, 1924. New edition by the University of Oklahoma Press, Publishing Division of the University, Norman, 1963. Manufactured in the U.S.A.

8 9 10 11 12 13 14 15 16 17 18 19 20 21 22 23 24 25 26

PREFACE

THIS work may claim some indulgence as the first English attempt of the kind, all the Homeric Lexicons hitherto in use in this country having been of foreign, for the most part of German, origin. It is not based on any previous Lexicon, but is the result of an independent, and, I hope, a thorough survey of the language of the two epics. I have set myself to consider together all the occurrences of all the words, and thence to deduce and classify the senses to the best of my ability, keeping as far as possible a mind open and free from preconception.

It may be useful to state here the general lines and scope of the work:—

(1) The text used is that in the Oxford Series of Classical Texts, in which the *Iliad* is edited by D. B. Monro and Mr. T. H. Allen, and the *Odyssey* by Mr. Allen. In compiling I used the first edition of the texts, that current at the time when the compilation was begun; but in reading the proofs I have used the editions current at the time when the printing was begun, *i.e.* the third of the *Iliad* and the second of the *Odyssey*. In these a number of small changes have been made. The principal variants occurring in other texts have been noted, in order that the Lexicon may be used with these texts; but the testimony of the manuscripts is remarkably uniform, and the number of important variants is not great.

(2) Proper and place names, adjectives therefrom, and patronymics have not as a rule been treated. Full *Indices Nominum* are appended to the text used.

(3) The brief etymological notes enclosed in square brackets are for the most part directed to exhibiting the interconnexion of the words and to stating cognates, chiefly in Latin and English. In the cases of the compound verbs the force of the prefixes has been indicated

by reference by number to these prefixes as classified in the list printed at the end of the book. So far as I know the prefixes have not been so treated before, although the reader is clearly entitled to know how the compiler takes them. When the prefix retains a prepositional force this is indicated by printing the corresponding English preposition in italics, the case taken being stated. The principal suffixes are referred to by number in a similar way.

(4) All parts of the verbs which are formed with any irregularity are recorded, with references to the passages in which they occur. These irregular parts, or as many of them as are required for guidance, are entered again in their alphabetical places, and are there parsed and referred to their leading verbs. An obelus (†) prefixed to a verb indicates that only the parts which are actually cited occur. In the cases of verbs not so marked, parts regularly formed occur in addition to any which are cited.

(5) In the cases of the simple verbs there is given after the citation of parts a note of all the compounds of these verbs which occur. These compounds should be referred to, as additional parts and further illustrative senses will frequently be found under them. In the few cases where compounds occur but not the simple verb references are made from the compounds to each other.

(6) In the explanations I have been solicitous to give rather exact than poetical equivalents. When the exact sense has been ascertained the reader will be able to clothe it in more poetical language for himself. I have been particularly anxious to avoid the abomination of "Wardour Street" English.

(7) The books of the epics are referred to in the usual way by the twenty-four letters of the Greek alphabet, the capital letters being used for the books of the *Iliad*, and the small for those of the *Odyssey*. The references are always to be taken as exhaustive unless the contrary is indicated by the addition of "etc." It would, of course, have been possible to make the references exhaustive in all cases; but this would have greatly increased the size (and cost) of the book, and would not after all have been of much, if indeed it would have been of any, service. It is hoped that the reader will have the satisfaction of knowing that he has before him all the occurrences of a word or use in every case where this can be thought to be of importance. It is to be noted that in this matter of reference the epics are regarded separately. Thus reference in the form Κ 192: β 363, γ 254, δ 78, τ 492,

ψ 26, etc., indicates that the word or use in question occurs once *only* in the *Iliad*, and five times *and more* in the *Odyssey*.

(8) It was found to be impossible to exhibit intelligibly in the articles the very numerous constructions under εἰ (3) (4) (5), αἴ (2), and ἤν (1) (2), and the various corresponding forms of relative and conditional relative sentences. These have accordingly been brought together in a Table printed after the List of Prefixes, etc., reference being made to the Table by number from the body of the book. It may be noted that the references in the articles εἰ, αἴ, and ἤν and in the Table are exhaustive throughout.

The commentaries of Dr. Leaf and Monro on the *Iliad*, and of Merry and Riddell on *Odyssey* I–XII, and Monro on *Odyssey* XIII–XXIV have been consulted. Of these Dr. Leaf's commentary is the fullest and has been the most helpful, and I desire to make special acknowledgements to it. My debt to Monro's *Homeric Grammar* will be obvious.

For the old *cruces* such as ἤϊος, ἠλίβατος, μέροπες, νηγάτεος, χλούνης, and the rest, I have no fresh suggestions to make; and in the cases of such words, where the context gives no guidance, I have thought it best simply to say that the meaning is unknown. There are, of course, conjectures in abundance, but these cannot be discussed in a Lexicon where space is a serious consideration. It is to be borne in mind that the Homeric language had evidently a long history when the poet received it, and that it is quite possible that he took over some of the words from his predecessors without attaching any very definite meaning to them. Similar considerations apply to words denoting arms, pieces of armour, parts of chariots, dress, utensils, and the like. The poet had, of course, no personal knowledge of the times in which he placed his scenes, and was necessarily dependent for knowledge on authorities of some kind, good or bad, of which we know nothing. It may well be that he would have found as much difficulty as we find in explaining the exact nature of, say, the μίτρη or the θόλος, or in distinguishing between, say, a ἕλιξ and a κάλυξ, or a πείρινς and an ὑπερτερίη.

My friend Mr. J. B. Douglas has very kindly gone over the work in proof, and has made many valuable suggestions. I owe and tender very grateful thanks to Mr. F. E. Webb, the printers' scholarly proof-reader, for the great care which he has bestowed on the proofs and for suggestions which he has made, and bear willing testimony to his accuracy and his untiring assiduity in a laborious task. I must, however, accept myself the ultimate responsibility for any literals that may be found. The references have all been checked by me in proof with the text, and I hope that little inaccuracy will be found.

I do not doubt that the work is open to criticism in detail. It could hardly, indeed, be otherwise in the case of a single-handed attempt to deal afresh with a vocabulary so copious and so complicated as that of the epics. I can truly say, however, that I have spared no pains, and have consciously shirked no difficulty, in the effort to make a useful book.

I did not undertake the very considerable labour which the compilation has entailed merely to help examination candidates or to assist in reading the epics as documents or as fields for philological study, although I trust that the Lexicon will be helpful for these purposes. My main hope has been, by making the reading of Homer easier, to bring to him readers who will read the epics as what above all things they are—as poems, as works of imagination. For such reading, translations being useless, an accurate and familiar knowledge of the Homeric language is the first essential. This knowledge is not to be acquired without hard, and possibly repulsive, work with grammar and dictionary; but though the way be long, the reward is sure. Let a man once acquire the power to read Homer as he reads Spenser or Milton, and he will have a possession which he would change for no other, an unfailing source of solace and of the purest pleasure. Homer is like Shakespeare in this, that he cannot be exhausted, that the more he is read the more there is found, and that while the effects are more and more felt, the means by which they are got remain more and more mysterious. The epics must be read as wholes, and not, as is too much the way, in books here and there. It will come to be realized more and more with each reading that under the smooth and apparently art-less surface there lie depths of supreme and conscious art. The man who has realized this has gone far to solve for himself the Homeric problem.

R. J. C.

ABBREVIATIONS

absol., absolute, absolutely
acc., accusative
act., active
adj., adjective
adv., adverb
advbl., adverbial
aor., aorist
app., apparently
art , article
cf., compare
comp., comparative
contr., contracted
dat., dative
encl., enclitic
Eng., English
fem., feminine
fig., figurative(ly)
fr., from
fut., future
gen., general(ly)
genit., genitive
imp., imperative
impers., impersonal(ly)
impf., imperfect
indic., indicative
infin., infinitive
int., interjection
intrans., intransitive
irreg., irregular(ly)
L., Latin
lit., literally
masc., masculine
mid., middle
neg., negative
neut., neuter
nom., nominative
opt., optative
orig., original(ly)
pa., past
pass., passive
perh., perhaps
pf., perfect
pl., plural
plupf., pluperfect
poss., possibly
ppl., participial
pple., participle
prec., the preceding word, etc.
prep., preposition
prob., probably
pron., pronoun
redup., reduplicated
sb., substantive
sc., *scilicet*
sim., similar(ly)
sing., singular
subj., subjunctive
superl., superlative
trans., transitive
vb., verb
vbl., verbal
v.l., various reading
voc., vocative
=, equivalent to

An asterisk (*) prefixed to a form indicates that the form is not actually recorded, but is assumed to have existed. For the obelus (†) see the Preface, p. vi.

A HOMERIC LEXICON

ᾶ. Ah! With voc. of *δειλός*. See *δειλός* (3) (a), (b).

ἀάατος [perh., with *ἀ-* for *ἀν-*[1], *ἀάϜατος*, fr. *ἀϜάω*. See *ἀάζω*]. Thus, not liable to *ἄτη*, that cannot be taken in vain, unimpeachable, decisive: *ἀάᾱτον Στυγὸς ὕδωρ* Ξ 271: *ἄεθλον ἀάᾰτον* φ 91, *ἄεθλος ἀάᾰτος* χ 5.

ἀᾱγής, *-ές* (*ἀϜαγής*) [*ἀ-*[1] + (*Ϝ*)*αγ-*, *ἄγνυμι*]. Unbroken, unbreakable: *ῥόπαλον* λ 575.

†***ἀάζω** (*ἀϜάζω*) [*ἀϜάτη*, *ἄτη*]. 2 sing. aor. *ἄᾰσας* (*ἄϜασας*) Θ 237. 3 *ἄᾰσε* φ 296, 297. 3 pl. *ἄᾱσαν* κ 68. Contr. 3 sing. *ᾆσε* λ 61. **Mid.** Aor. *ἀᾰσάμην* I 116, 119, T 137. 3 sing. *ἀάσατο* I 537. *ἀάσατο* Λ 340. Contr. *ἄσατο* T 95. **Pass.** Aor. *ἀάσθην* T 136. 3 sing. *ἀάσθη* Π 685, T 113: δ 503, 509. Pple. *ἀασθείς* φ 301. From *ἀ*(*Ϝ*)*άω* 3 sing. pres. mid. *ἀᾶται* T 91, 129. (**1**) To smite with blindness of the mind, infatuate, make reckless Θ 237: κ 68, λ 61, φ 296, 297.—So in mid.: *Ἄτη* (*Ἄτην*) *ἣ πάντας ἀᾶται* T 91, 129.—(**2**) In mid., to be so smitten, be made infatuated or reckless: *ἀασάμην* I 116, 119, T 137. Cf. I 537, Λ 340, T 95.—So in pass.: *μέγ' ἀάσθη* Π 685. Cf. T 113, 136: δ 503, 509, φ 301.

ἄαπτος, *-ον* [app., with *ἀ-* for *ἀν-*[1], fr. *ἅπτω*]. Thus, not to be touched, irresistible: *χεῖρες* (*χεῖρας*) A 567, Θ 450, Λ 169, N 49, Υ 503, etc.: λ 502, χ 70, 248.

ἄασε, ἀάσθη, 3 sing. aor. act. and pass. *ἀάζω*.

ἀάσχετος [an unexplained form]. = *ἄσχετος*. Not to be restrained, ungovernable: *μένος* E 892.—Of grief, uncontrollable: *πένθος* Ω 708.

ἀᾶται, 3 sing. pres. mid. *ἀάω*. See *ἀάζω*.

ἄατος [*ἀ-*[1] + (*σ*)*άω*]. Except in X 218 in contr. form *ἆτος*. Insatiate of, indefatigable in. With genit.: *πολέμοιο* E 388. Cf. E 863, Z 203, Λ 430, N 746, X 218: ν 293.

ἀβακέω [*ἀ-*[1] + *βακ-*, *βάζω*. 'To be speechless']. Hence, to be ignorant, fail in recognition δ 249.

ἀβλής, *-ῆτος* [*ἀ-*[1] + *βλη-*, *βάλλω*]. Not (yet) shot, new: *ἰόν* Δ 117.

ἄβλητος [as prec.]. Unstruck (by a missile) Δ 540.

ἀβληχρός, *-ή*, *-όν*. App., feeble, weak, gentle: *χεῖρα* E 337, *τείχεα* Θ 178: *θάνατος* λ 135, ψ 282.

ἄβρομος [*ἀ-*[2] + *βρόμος*]. With united noise N 41.

†**ἀβροτάζω** [*ἀμβροτ-*, *ἤμβροτον*. See *ἁμαρτάνω*]. 1 pl. aor. subj. *ἀβροτάξομεν*. With genit., to miss, fail of meeting: *ἀλλήλοιιν* K 65.

ἀβρότη. App. = *ἀμβροσίη*, fem. of *ἀμβρόσιος*: *νύξ* Ξ 78.

ἀγάασθε, 2 pl. *ἄγαμαι*.

ἄγαγον, aor. *ἄγω*.

ἀγαθός, *-ή*, *-όν*. (**1**) Well-born, noble Ξ 113, Φ 109: δ 611, σ 276, φ 335.—Absol.: *τοῖς ἀγαθοῖσιν* ο 324, *οὐκ ἀγαθοῖσιν* σ 383 (*v.l.* *οὐτιδανοῖσιν*).—(**2**) Warlike, soldierly, stout, skilful in fight A 131, Δ 181, Z 478, N 314, etc.—Absol.: *ἀγαθοῖσι μάχεσθαι* N 238. Cf. Φ 280 (twice), etc.—(**3**) Passing into (4): *ἀ. πάϊς Ἀλκινόοιο* θ 130, 143.—(**4**) Good, worthy, serviceable, skilled: *ἰητῆρε* B 732. Cf. Γ 179, 237, N 666, Ψ 770: *πὺξ ἀγαθόν* λ 300.—For *βοὴν ἀ.* see *βοή* (2).—(**5**) In moral sense, good, of right feeling: *ἀ. καὶ ἐχέφρων* I 341.—Of the mind, showing discretion, good judgment or discernment, well-balanced: *φρεσὶ κέχρητ' ἀγαθῇσιν* γ 266. Cf. ξ 421, π 398, ω 194.—Sim. *φρεσὶ μαίνεται οὐκ ἀγαθῇσιν* Θ 360.—(**6**) Of things or abstractions, good of their kind, good, excellent, fine, helpful, in place, or the like: *βουλάς* B 273, *ὄψιν* (his fair . . .) Ω 632. Cf. I 627, Λ 793 = O 404, Ψ 810: *βίον* (pleasant) ο 491. Cf. ι 27, ν 246, ο 405, 507, ρ 347, 352, ω 249, 286.—(**7**) Absol. in neut. *ἀγαθόν*. (**a**) A good or desirable thing B 204.—With infin.: *ἀ. νυκτὶ πιθέσθαι* H 282 = 293. Cf. Ω 130, 425: γ 196.—(**b**) What is good, good: *ἀ. τελέσειεν* β 34. Cf. δ 237, 392, θ 63.—So *εἰπεῖν εἰς ἀ.* (for the general good) I 102, *πείσεται εἰς ἀ.* (for his own good) Λ 789.—(**8**) Absol. in neut. pl. *ἀγαθά*. (**a**) In sense (7) (b) χ 209.—So *εἰς ἀ. φρονέων* Ψ 305. Cf. Ω 173: α 43.—(**b**) What is morally right: *ἀ. φρονέοντα* Z 162.—(**c**) Good things to eat ξ 441.

ἀγαίομαι = *ἄγαμαι* (5): *κακὰ ἔργα* υ 16.

ἀγακλεής, *-ές* [*ἀγα-* + *κλέος*]. Genit. *ἀγακλῆος* (for *ἀγακλεέος*) Π 738, Ψ 529. Very famous, glorious, splendid, worthy Π 738, P 716, Φ 379 Ψ 529.

ἀγακλειτός, *-ή*, *-όν* [*ἀγα-* + *κλειτός*]. = prec.

B 564, M 101, Π 463, Σ 45, Φ 530 : γ 59, η 202, ρ 370, 468, σ 351, φ 275.

ἀγακλυτός [ἀγα- + κλυτός]. = prec. Z 436 : γ 388, 428, η 3, 46, θ 502, ξ 237, φ 295, ω 103.

ἀγάλλομαι. (ἐπ-.) To exult M 114, P 473, Σ 132.—To exult in, take delight in. With dat. : πτερύγεσσιν B 462, πώλοισιν Υ 222. Cf. ε 176, ζ 272.

ἄγαλμα, -ατος, τό [ἀγάλλομαι]. (**1**) An ornament, a glory or delight Δ 144 : δ 602, σ 300, τ 257.—(**2**) Of things offered to the gods : πόλλ' ἀγάλματ' ἀνῆψεν γ 274. Cf. γ 438, θ 509, μ 347.

†**ἄγαμαι.** 1 sing. pres. ἄγαμαι ζ 168, ψ 175. 2 pl. ἀγάασθε ε 119. ἄγασθε ε 129. Infin. ἀγάασθαι π 203. 2 pl. impf. ἠγάασθε ε 122. Fut. infin. ἀγάσεσθαι θ 565, ν 173. ἀγάσσεσθαι δ 181. 3 sing. aor. ἠγάσσατο Γ 181. ἀγάσσατο P 71 : δ 658. 1 pl. ἀγασσάμεθα Γ 224 : κ 249. 3 ἀγάσαντο σ 71, ψ 211. 2 sing. subj. ἀγάσσεαι α 389. 2 pl. ἀγάσησθε Ξ 111. Pple. ἀγασσάμενος, -ου H 41, 404, Θ 29, I 51, 431, 694, 711, Ψ 639 : β 67, ψ 64. (**1**) To wonder, marvel : οἵ κ' ἀγασσάμενοι οἶον ἐπόρσειαν H 41 (admiring his chivalry ; or perh. in sense (3), grudging him honour) : ἀγάσσατο θυμός δ 658. Cf. π 203, σ 71.—(**2**) To wonder or marvel at Γ 181, 224, H 404, Θ 29, I 51, 431, 694, 711 : ζ 168, κ 249.—(**3**) To be jealous, bear a grudge Ξ 111, Ψ 639.—With dat. of person : οἱ P 71 : ε 122, ἡμῖν θ 565, ν 173.—With complementary infin. : θεαὶς ἀγάασθε παρ' ἀνδράσιν εὐνάζεσθαι ε 119. Cf. ε 129, ψ 211.—With acc. : τά δ 181.—(**4**) To be offended or hurt ψ 175.—(**5**) To be indignant or offended at : κακὰ ἔργα β 67. Cf. ψ 64.—With dat. of person : εἴ πέρ μοι ἀγάσσεαι α 389.

ἄγαμος [ἀ-[1] + γάμος]. Unmarried Γ 40.

ἀγάννιφος [ἀγα- + νίφω]. Very snowy, snow-clad. Epithet of Olympus A 420, Σ 186.

ἀγανός, -ή, -όν. (**1**) Gentle, mild, affectionate : ἐπέεσσιν B 164, 180, 189, Ω 772 : ἀ. καὶ ἤπιος β 230 = ε 8, μύθοις ο 53.—(**2**) Soothing, effecting propitiation, winning acceptance : δώροισιν I 113, εὐχωλῇσιν 499 : ν 357.—(**3**) Of the shafts of Apollo and Artemis, bringing painless death Ω 759 : γ 280 = ο 411, ε 124 = λ 173 = 199.

ἀγανοφροσύνη, -ης, ἡ [ἀγανόφρων]. Gentleness of disposition, mildness Ω 772 : λ 203.

ἀγανόφρων [ἀγανός + φρήν]. Of gentle disposition, mild : ἀνήρ Υ 467.

ἀγαπάζω [ἀγαπάω]. (ἀμφ-.) (**1**) = ἀγαπάω (1) π 17.—In mid. : οὐδ' ἀγαπαζόμενοι φιλέουσιν η 33. Cf. ρ 35 = χ 499, φ 224.—(**2**) To play the host to : ἀθάνατον θεόν Ω 464.

ἀγαπάω. (**1**) To welcome, greet, caress ψ 214. —(**2**) To be contented : οὐκ ἀγαπᾷς ὅ . . ; φ 289.

ἀγαπήνωρ, -ορος [ἀγαπάω + ἀνήρ]. Showing kindliness to fellow-men, courteous. Epithet of heroes Θ 114, N 756, O 392, Ψ 113 = 124 : η 170.

ἀγαπητός [ἀγαπάω]. Beloved, darling Z 401 : β 365, δ 727, 817, ε 18.

ἀγάρροος [ἀγα- + (σ)ρο-, ῥέω]. Strongly flowing. Epithet of the Hellespont B 845, M 30.

ἄγασθε, 2 pl. pres. ἄγαμαι.

ἀγάσσατο, 3 sing. aor. ἄγαμαι.

ἀγάστονος, -ον [ἀγα- + στον-, στένω]. Much groaning, roaring. Epithet of Amphitrite μ 97.

ἀγαυός, -ή [γαϝ-, γαίω]. Of persons, an epithet of general commendation, noble, illustrious, or the like : κήρυκες Γ 268. Cf. E 277, H 386, Λ 1, P 284, T 281, Ω 251, etc. : μνηστῆρες β 209. Cf. β 308, ζ 55, λ 213, ν 272, etc.—In superl. : ἀγαυότατον ζωόντων ο 229.

ἀγγελίη, -ης, ἡ [ἄγγελος]. A message, news, tidings : ἀλεγεινῇ B 787, ἐμὴν ἀγγελίην (about me) T 337. Cf. H 416, O 174, etc. : πατρός (about your father) α 408. Cf. α 414, β 30, ξ 374, ω 48, etc. —In cognate acc. : ἀγγελίην ἐπὶ Τυδῆ στεῖλαν (dispatched him on a message ; ἐπί advbl. (ἐπί (I) (4))) Δ 384, ἀγγελίην ἐλθόντα (having come on a message) Λ 140.—In genit. denoting scope of action : σεῦ ἕνεκ' ἀγγελίης (on a message concerning thee) Γ 206, ἀγγελίης τευ (on a message concerning someone) N 252, ἀγγελίης οἴχνεσκεν (used to go with messages) O 640. (In the last five passages the word is also taken as a masc. ἀγγελίης = ἄγγελος.)

ἀγγέλλω [ἄγγελος]. 3 pl. fut. ἀγγελέουσι I 617. Pple. ἀγγελέων, -οντος P 701 : δ 24, 528, 679. Fem. ἀγγελέουσα, -ης Θ 398, Λ 185, T 120, Ω 77, etc. : σ 186, χ 434, 496. 3 sing. aor. ἤγγειλε X 439 : ψ 22. 3 pl. subj. ἀγγείλωσι π 350. Opt. ἀγγείλαιμι ξ 120. 3 sing. ἀγγείλειε ζ 50, ο 458. Imp. ἄγγειλον Ω 145. Pple. ἀγγείλας K 448 : π 150. Infin. ἀγγεῖλαι O 159. (ἀπ-, ἐξ-, ἐπ-.) (**1**) To bear a message or order, make an announcement or communication Θ 398, 409, I 617, Λ 185, T 120, Ω 77 = 159 : π 150.—With dat. : ποιμένι λαῶν δ 24, 528. Cf. δ 679, ζ 50, ο 458, σ 186 = χ 434 = 496.—With dat. and complementary infin. : Πριάμῳ λύσασθαι Ω 145 : κείνοις οἴκονδε νέεσθαι π 350.—Without dat. : λέξασθαι Θ 517.—Sim. with dat. and ὅττι X 439.—(**2**) To announce, communicate K 448, O 159, P 701 : ψ 22.—To give news of ξ 120, 123.—To herald ν 94.

ἄγγελος, -ου, ὁ, ἡ. A messenger or envoy A 334, B 786, E 804, K 286, Λ 652, X 438, etc. : ε 29, θ 270, ο 458, π 468, ω 405, etc.—With dat. and complementary infin. : ἄμμι θωρήσσεσθαι Λ 715. Cf. Σ 167, Ω 194.—Sim. with dat. and ὅ μ 374.—Of birds of augury Ω 292, 296, 310 : ο 526.

ἄγγος, τό. A vessel or receptacle β 289.—For milk B 471 = Π 643 : ι 222, 248.—For wine π 13.

ἄγε, ἄγετε [imp. sing. and pl. of ἄγω used interjectionally]. Come ! (**1**) ἄγε. (**a**) With imp. sing. or pl. Γ 192, I 673 = K 544 : γ 475, ο 347, ψ 261.—So ἄγε δή (cf. δή (1) (a) (β)) Θ 139, Ω 407 : β 349, τ 16.—ἀλλ' ἄγε (cf. ἀλλά (3)) A 210, B 331, Δ 100, E 174, Z 340, etc. : α 169, β 212, γ 17, δ 587, ε 162, etc.—ἀλλ' ἄγε δή Φ 221, Ψ 313, Ω 137, etc. : η 162, θ 492, κ 333, μ 298.—εἰ δ(ή) ἄγε (cf. εἰ (1)) A 302, Z 376, I 167, Π 667, etc. : α 271, β 178, δ 832, μ 112, χ 391, ψ 35.—Elliptically : δεῦρ' ἄγε θ 145, 205, μ 184.—δεῦτ' ἄγε θ 11.—ἀλλ' ἄγε δεῦρο Λ 314, P 179 : ι 517, λ 561, χ 233.—

εἰ δ(ή) ἄγε δεῦρο Ρ 685, Ψ 581.—(b) With 1 sing. subj., come, I will . . . : ἀλλ' ἄγ' ἐξείπω Ι 60. Cf. υ 296, etc.—ἀλλ' ἄγε δή ν 215.—εἰ δ(ή) ἄγε ι 37, ω 336.—(c) With 1 pl, come, let us . . . : ἄγε νῆ' ἐρύσσομεν Α 141. Cf. Η 299, Ξ 314, Χ 391.—ἀλλ' ἄγε Υ 257, etc.: δ 776, θ 34, 389, κ 44, ν 13, 296, ξ 393, π 348, ρ 190.—ἀλλ' ἄγε δή Α 62, Γ 441, Δ 418, Ε 249, Λ 348, Ψ 537, Ω 356, etc. : ρ 274.—Elliptically: ἀλλ' ἄγε δεῦρο θεοὺς ἐπιδώμεθα Χ 254.—(d) With fut. : ἀλλ' ἄγε πειρήσομαι ζ 126. Cf. ν 344, 397.—ἀλλ' ἄγε δή Υ 351, Φ 60 : κ 286, ν 215.—εἰ δ(ή) ἄγε Α 524, Ψ 579 : φ 217.—(e) Introducing a question: ἀλλ' ἄγε Η 36 : τ 24.—(2) ἄγετε. (a) Absol. : ἀλλ' ἄγετε Β 72=83 : φ 73 =106.—(b) With imp. pl. : ἀλλ' ἄγετε Η 193, etc. : δ 294, κ 460=μ 23, φ 134, χ 252.—With sing.: ἀλλ' ἄγετ' ἐπαρξάσθω φ 263.—(c) With 1 pl. subj. μ 213.—ἀλλ' ἄγετε Β 139=Ι 26=704=Μ 75 =Ξ 74=370=Ο 294=Σ 297, Ε 469, Ι 165, Ρ 634, etc. : α 76, κ 176, μ 343, ν 179, π 376, ω 430.—εἰ δ(ή) ἄγετε Χ 381.—Elliptically: δεῦτ' ἄγετε δώομεν Η 350.—(d) With 1 sing.: ἀλλ' ἄγετ' ἐνείκω χ 139.

ἀγείρω. Aor. ἤγειρα Ρ 222 : β 41. ἄγειρα ξ 285. 3 sing. ἤγειρε β 28. ἄγειρε Λ 716. 3 pl. ἄγειραν γ 140. Subj. ἀγείρω Π 129. 1 pl. ἀγείρομεν Α 142 : π 349. Pple. ἀγείρας Β 664, Γ 47, Ι 338, 544 : τ 197. **Mid.** 3 pl. aor. ἀγέροντο Β 94, Σ 245 : θ 321, λ 36, υ 277. Pl. pple. ἀγρόμενοι, -ων Γ 209, Η 134, 332, Ι 74, Κ 180, Υ 166 : θ 17, 58, 172, ξ 25, π 3. Fem. -αι υ 123. Dat. -ῃσι Β 481. Infin. ἀγέρεσθαι β 385. **Pass.** 3 sing aor. ἀγέρθη Δ 152, Χ 475 : ε 458, ω 349. 3 pl. ἤγερθεν Α 57, Ω 790 : β 9, θ 24, ω 421. ἄγερθεν Ψ 287. 3 pl. plupf. ἀγηγέρατο Δ 211, Υ 13 : λ 388, ω 21. (ἀμφ-, ἐπ-, ἐσ-, συν-.) (1) To bring or gather together, cause to assemble Α 142, Β 438, Γ 47, Ι 544, Ρ 222, etc. : β 41, γ 140, π 349.—Absol. β 28.—(2) In mid. and pass., to come or gather together, assemble: ἐπεὶ ἤγερθεν Α 57. Cf. Β 52, Γ 209, Δ 211, Σ 245, Ψ 287, etc. : ἠγείροντο μάλ' ὦκα β 8. Cf. β 385, δ 686, λ 632, ξ 25 (the herd of swine), υ 123 (*v.l.* ἐγρόμεναι fr. ἐγείρω ; cf. ἐγείρω (4)), etc.—(3) In reference to things, to get together, collect: πολλά ξ 285. Cf. γ 301, τ 197.—In mid.: ἀγειρόμενοι κατὰ δῆμον ν 14.—To get by begging ρ 362.—In reference to something immaterial: θυμὸς ἀγέρθη (his spirit was rallied) Δ 152, Χ 475 : ε 458, ω 349.

ἀγελαῖος, -η [ἀγέλη]. Belonging to a or to the herd. Of oxen Λ 729, Ψ 846 : κ 410, ρ 181= υ 251, χ 299.

ἀγελείη [ἄγω + λείη = ληΐς]. That drives or carries off the spoil. Epithet of Athene Δ 128, Ε 765, Ζ 269=279, Ο 213 : ν 359, π 207.

ἀγέλη, -ης, ἡ. Locative ἀγέληφι Β 480, Π 487. A herd. Of oxen: βοῦς ἀγέληφι (in the herd) Β 480. Cf. Λ 678, 696, Ο 323, Π 487, Ρ 62, Σ 528, 573 : μ 129, 299, ξ 100.—Of horses Τ 281.

ἀγεληδόν [ἀγέλη]. In a herd Π 160.

ἄγεν, 3 pl. aor. pass. ἄγνυμι.

ἀγέραστος [ἀ-[1] + γέρας]. Meedless Α 119.

ἀγέρθη, 3 sing. aor. pass. ἀγείρω.

ἀγέροντο, 3 pl. aor. mid. ἀγείρω.

ἀγέρωχος. An epithet of commendation of peoples and persons of uncertain meaning Β 654, Γ 36, Ε 623, Η 343, Κ 430, Π 708, Φ 584 : λ 286.

ἄγετε. See ἄγε.

ἄγη[1], ἡ [ἄγαμαι]. Wonder, amazement, confusion : ἄγη μ' ἔχει Φ 221 : γ 227, π 243.

ἄγη[2], 3 sing. aor. pass. ἄγνυμι.

ἀγηγέρατο, 3 pl. plupf. pass. ἀγείρω.

ἀγηνορίη, -ης, ἡ [ἀγήνωρ]. (1) Courage, spirit Μ 46, Χ 457.—(2) The quality in excess or with arrogance. In pl. Ι 700.

ἀγήνωρ, -ορος [ἀγα- + ἀνήρ]. (1) Manly, bold, courageous Ι 398, Κ 299, Ω 42, etc. : β 103, λ 562, etc.—App. ironically (of Thersites) Β 276.—(2) Conveying at any rate a shade of blame (indicating the exhibition of the quality in excess or with arrogance) Ι 699, Φ 443 : α 106, 144, υ 160, etc.

ἀγήρως [contr. fr. ἀγήραος, fr. ἀ-[1] + γῆρας]. Nom. dual ἀγήρω Μ 323, Ρ 444. Acc. pl. ἀγήρως η 94. Not subject to old age Θ 539, Μ 323, Ρ 444 : ε 136=η 257=ψ 336, ε 218, η 94.—Of the aegis Β 447.

ἀγητός [ἄγαμαι]. To be wondered at, admirable : εἶδος ἀγητοί (*i.e.* in that only) Ε 787= Θ 228, εἶδος ἀγητόν Χ 370. Cf. Ω 376 : ξ 177.

ἀγῑνέω [lengthened fr. ἄγω]. 3 pl. pa. iterative ἀγίνεσκον ρ 294. (κατ-.) (1) In reference to domestic animals, to drive, lead, bring ξ 105, υ 213, χ 198.—To a hunting dog, to take with one ρ 294.—(2) To persons, to lead, conduct Σ 493.—(3) To things, to fetch, bring, carry Ω 784.

ἀγκάζομαι [ἀγκάς]. To take up in the arms Ρ 722.

ἀγκαλίς, ἡ [ἄγκος]. Dat. pl. ἀγκαλίδεσσι. The bent arm Σ 555, Χ 503.

ἀγκάς [ἄγκος]. Into, in, or with the arms Ε 371, Ξ 346, 353, Ψ 711, Ω 227 : η 252.

ἄγκιστρον, τό [ἄγκος]. A fish-hook (app. (at any rate sometimes) of metal ; cf. Π 408) δ 369= μ 332.

ἀγκλίνας, contr. aor. pple. ἀνακλίνω.

ἀγκοίνη, ἡ =ἀγκαλίς Ξ 213 : λ 261, 268.

ἄγκος, τό. A bend ; hence, a glen or valley Σ 321, Υ 490, Χ 190 : δ 337=ρ 128.

†ἀγκρεμάννῡμι [ἀγ-, ἀνα- (2)]. Aor. pple. fem. ἀγκρεμάσᾱσα. To hang up *on*. With dat. : χιτῶνα πασσάλῳ α 440.

ἀγκυλομήτης [ἀγκύλος + μῆτις]. Of crooked counsel, wily. Epithet of Cronos Β 205, 319, Δ 59, 75, Ι 37, Μ 450, Π 431, Σ 293 : φ 415.

ἀγκύλος [ἄγκος]. Curved. Epithet of τόξα Ε 209, Ζ 322 : φ 264.—Of ἅρμα (referring to the curved form of the front) Ζ 39.

ἀγκυλότοξος [ἀγκύλος + τόξον]. Armed with curved bows, bearing bows. Epithet of the Paeonians Β 848, Κ 428.

ἀγκυλοχείλης [ἀγκύλος + χεῖλος]. With curved lips ; hence, with hooked beak Π 428 : = χ 302, τ 538.

ἀγκών, -ῶνος, ὁ [ἄγκος]. (**1**) The bend of the arm, the elbow Ε 582, Κ 80, Λ 252, Υ 479, Ψ 395 : ξ 485, 494.—(**2**) An angle (of a wall): ἀγκῶνος τείχεος Π 702.

†**ἀγλαΐζομαι** [ἀγλαός]. Fut. infin. ἀγλαϊεῖσθαι. (ἐπ-.) To glory or take delight in something Κ 331.

ἀγλαΐη, -ης, ἡ [ἀγλαός]. Instrumental ἀγλαΐηφι Ζ 510, Ο 267. (**1**) Splendour, beauty, glory Ζ 510 = Ο 267 : ρ 310, σ 180, τ 82.—(**2**) A source of honour or distinction : κῦδός τε καὶ ἀ. ο 78 (the two words hardly to be distinguished).—(**3**) In pl., personal adornments, bravery ρ 244.

ἀγλαόκαρπος, -ον [ἀγλαός + καρπός[1]]. Bearing goodly fruit : μηλέαι η 115 = λ 589.

ἀγλαός. An epithet of commendation of somewhat indefinite meaning. (**1**) Of things or abstractions, splendid, fine, goodly, bright or the like : ἄποινα Α 23, ὕδωρ Β 307. Cf. Α 213, Β 506, Η 203, Τ 385, Ψ 262, etc. : ἱστόν β 109, ἔργα ν 289. Cf. γ 429, δ 589, ζ 291, etc.—(**2**) Of persons, goodly, fine or the like Β 736, 871, Λ 385 (see κέρας (4)), etc. : γ 190, λ 249, etc.

ἀγνοιέω [ἀγνώς]. 3 sing. aor. ἠγνοίησε Α 537, Β 807, Ν 28 : ε 78. Fem. pple. ἀγνοιήσασα υ 15. 3 sing. pa. iterative ἀγνώσασκε (contr. fr. ἀγνοήσασκε fr. ἀγνοέω) ψ 95.—(**1**) To fail to know or recognize Β 807, Ν 28 : ε 78, υ 15, ψ 95 (continually showed that she did not recognize him), ω 218.—(**2**) With dependent clause, to fail to perceive something as to (a person) : οὐδέ μιν ἠγνοίησεν ὅτι . . . Α 537.

ἁγνός, -ή. (**1**) Of goddesses, holy, pure ε 123, λ 386, σ 202, υ 71.—(**2**) Dedicated to a god, hallowed : ἑορτή φ 259.

†**ἄγνυμι** (Ϝάγνυμι). 3 dual pres. ἄγνυτον Μ 148. Fut. ἄξω Θ 403. Infin. ἀξέμεν Θ 417. 3 sing. aor. ἔαξε Η 270, Λ 175, Ρ 63 : ε 316, 385, τ 539. ἦξε Ψ 392. 3 pl. ἔαξαν γ 298. 2 sing. subj. ἄξῃς Ψ 341. 3 ἄξῃ Ε 161. Imp. ἆξον Ζ 306. Nom. dual masc. pple. ἄξαντε Ζ 40, Π 371. Infin. ἆξαι Φ 178, Ψ 467. **Pass.** Genit. pl. fem. pres. pple. ἀγνυμενάων Π 769 : κ 123. 3 sing. aor. ἐάγη Ν 162, Ρ 607 : κ 560, λ 65. ἄγη Γ 367, Π 801. 3 pl. ἄγεν Δ 214. 3 sing. pf. subj. in pass. sense ἐάγῃ Λ 559. (κατ-, περι-, συν-.) (**1**) To break, shiver, smash, shatter : αγη ξίφος Γ 367, ἆξον ἔγχος Διομήδεος Ζ 306, etc. : πρὸ κύματ' ἔαξεν ε 385 (broke their force, beat them down), αὐχὴν ἐάγη κ 560, etc.—(**2**) To wreck (a ship) γ 298.

ἀγνώς, -ῶτος [as ἄγνωστος]. Unknown ε 79.

ἀγνώσασκε, 3 sing. pa. iterative. See ἀγνοιέω.

ἄγνωστος [ἀ-[1] + γνω-, γιγνώσκω]. (**1**) Unknown β 175.—(**2**) Not to be known, unrecognizable ν 191, 397.

†**ἀγξηραίνω** [ἀγ-, ἀνα- (6)]. 3 sing. aor. subj. ἀγξηράνῃ. To dry up : ἀλωήν Φ 347.

ἄγονος [ἀ-[1] + γόνος]. App., unborn Γ 40.

ἀγοράομαι [ἀγορή]. 2 pl. ἀγοράασθε Β 337. 2 pl. impf. ἠγοράασθε Θ 230. 3 ἠγορόωντο Δ 1. (**1**) To sit in assembly, hold debate Β 337, Δ 1.—(**2**) To speak or discourse in an assembly or company Α 73, 253, etc. : β 24, δ 773, etc.—(**3**) To utter in an assembly : εὐχωλάς Θ 230.

ἀγορεύω [as prec.]. (ἐξ-.) (**1**) To hold (an assembly) : ἀγορὰς ἀγόρευον Β 788.—(**2**) To speak or discourse in an assembly or company Α 109, Β 250, Η 361, Μ 213, etc. : α 382, β 15, 36, θ 171, etc.—(**3**) To utter or say in an assembly or company : ταῦτα Η 357. Cf. Η 359, Χ 377, etc. : β 184, 210, θ 505, etc.—(**4**) To speak or tell of, make known, expound, in an assembly or company : θεοπροπίας Α 385 : δήμιόν τι β 32, 44.—(**5**) In gen., to speak, say Β 10, Ε 218, 832, Ο 53, Ρ 35, etc. : α 214, δ 76, 157, θ 570, κ 34, etc.—To counsel, advise Ε 252.—(**6**) To utter, say : ἔπεα Γ 155. Cf. Ε 274, Μ 173, Σ 95, etc. : α 307, δ 189, ε 183, λ 83, σ 15, etc.—(**7**) To speak or tell of, declare, make known, relate, recount : ταῦτα πάντα Α 365. Cf. Ι 369, Μ 176, Σ 142, Φ 99 : α 174, 179, γ 254, δ 836 (tell his fate), λ 381, etc.—To propose Χ 261.

ἀγορή, -ῆς, ἡ [ἀγείρω]. (**1**) A general assembly (cf. βουλή (1)) Β 95, 808, Δ 400, Θ 2, Ι 33, Ο 283, Σ 106, Τ 34, etc. : α 90, β 26, 257, γ 127, 137, δ 818, ι 112, etc.—In pl., of a single assembly : ἀγορὰς ἀγόρευον Β 788.—(**2**) In pl., speaking in the assembly : ἔσχ' ἀγοράων Β 275.—(**3**) The place of assembly (app. used also as a place of judgment (cf. ἀγορῆθεν) and no doubt for other public purposes) Α 490, Β 93, Η 382, 414, Ι 13, Λ 139, 807, Π 387, Σ 245, 274, 497, Τ 45, 88, 173, 249 : β 10, 37, 150, ζ 266, θ 12, 109, 503, κ 114, π 361, 377, ρ 52, υ 146, 362, ω 420.—In pl., app. of a single place : ἔμπληντ' ἀγοραί θ 16. Cf. η 44.

ἀγορῆθεν [ἀγορή + -θεν (1)]. From the place of assembly Β 264.—From the place of judgment μ 439.

ἀγορήνδε [acc. of ἀγορή + -δε (1)]. To the place of assembly Α 54, Β 51, 207, Υ 4, 16 : α 372, β 7, θ 5, ρ 72.

ἀγορητής, -οῦ, ὁ [ἀγορή]. An orator or speaker Α 248, Β 246, Γ 150, Δ 293, Η 126, Τ 82 : υ 274.

ἀγορητύς, ἡ [ἀγορή]. Oratory, eloquence θ 168.

ἀγός, -οῦ, ὁ [ἄγω]. A leader, commander, chief Γ 231, Δ 265, Ε 217, Μ 61, Ν 304, Ψ 160, etc.

ἀγοστός, -οῦ, ὁ. The palm of the hand ; or perh., one's 'grasp' Λ 425, Ν 508 = Ρ 315, Ν 520 = Ξ 452.

ἄγραυλος, -ον [ἀγρός + αὐλή]. Dwelling in the fields : βοός Κ 155, Ρ 521, Ψ 684, 780, Ω 81, ποιμένες Σ 162 : πόριες κ 410, βοός μ 253, χ 403.

†**ἀγρέω.** To take. Only in imp. ἄγρει followed by an imp. Come ! : ἀ. ἔπορσον Ε 765, ἀ. καταχεῦαι Η 459. Cf. Λ 512, Ξ 271 : φ 176.—So in pl. : ἀγρεῖτε κορήσατε υ 149.

ἄγρη, -ης, ἡ. (**1**) The chase, sport. Of birds of prey chasing smaller birds χ 306.—(**2**) The game μ 330.

ἄγριος, -η, -ον and -ος, -ον [ἀγρός]. (**1**) Of

animals, wild, untamed Γ 24, Δ 106, Θ 338, Ι 539, Ο 271 : ι 119, ξ 50.—Applied to flies Τ 30.—Absol. in neut. pl. ἄγρια, wild creatures Ε 52.—(2) Of men, fierce, savage, raging Ζ 97 = 278, Θ 96, Φ 314.—Of Scylla μ 119.—(3) Not conforming to the traditional order of society, uncivilized, barbarous, savage α 199, β 19, ζ 120 = ι 175 = ν 201, η 206, θ 575, ι 215, 494.—(4) In gen., fierce, raging, ungoverned : χόλος Δ 23, πτόλεμος Ρ 737. Cf. Θ 460, Ι 629, Ρ 398, Τ 88, Χ 313 : θ 304.—(5) Absol. in neut. pl. ἄγρια, fierceness : ἀ. οἶδεν (has fierceness in his heart) (see εἴδω (III)(12)) Ω 41.

ἀγριόφωνος [ἄγριος + φωνή]. Harsh of speech θ 294.

ἀγρόθεν [ἀγρός + -θεν (1)]. From the field or country : κατιόντ' ἀ. ν 268, ἀ. ἐρχομένην ο 428.

ἀγροιώτης, -ου [ἀγρός. Cf. ἀγρότης]. Of the country, rustic : ἀνέρες Λ 549 = Ο 272, λαοί Λ 676 : βουκόλοι λ 293.—Absol., a rustic or boor : νήπιοι ἀγροιῶται φ 85.

ἀγρόμενοι, pl. aor. pple. mid. ἀγείρω.

ἀγρόνδε [acc. of ἀγρός + -δε (1)]. To the field or country ο 370, 379, φ 370.

ἀγρονόμος, -ον [ἀγρός + νέμω]. Haunting the fields or country : νύμφαι ζ 106.

ἀγρός, -οῦ, ὁ. (1) In pl., fields, lands : πίονες ἀγροί Ψ 832. Cf. δ 757, ζ 259, θ 560, ξ 263 = ρ 432, ο 504, π 150, ρ 18, 171.—(2) In sing., a farm : ἐπ' ἀγροῦ α 190. Cf. λ 188 (at the farm), π 27, 330, 383, ρ 182, ψ 139, 359, ω 205, 212.—So in pl. : ἀγρῶν (at the farm) δ 640.—(3) In sing., the country : ἀγρῷ (in the country) Ε 137 : ἐπ' ἀγροῦ ((drawn up on the shore) in the country) α 185 = ω 308. Cf. δ 517, ε 489, σ 358, χ 47, ω 150.

ἀγρότερος, -η, -ον [in form comp. fr. ἀγρός. 'Of the country' (as opposed to the town)]. (1) Of animals, wild, untamed Β 852, Λ 293, Μ 146, Φ 486 : ζ 133, λ 611, ρ 295. — (2) Epithet of Artemis, roaming the fields, the huntress Φ 471.

ἀγρότης, ὁ [ἀγρός]. A hunter π 218.

ἀγρώσσω [ἀγρέω]. To catch, take ε 53.

ἄγρωστις, ἡ. Some kind of clover or grass ζ 90.

ἄγυια, ἡ. Acc. ἄγυιαν. Dat. ἀγυιῇ. Nom. pl. ἀγυιαί. Acc. ἀγυιάς. A street Ε 642, Ζ 391, Υ 254 : β 388 = γ 487 = 497 = λ 12 = ο 185 = 296 = 471, ο 441.

ἄγυρις, ἡ [said to be the Aeolic form of ἀγορή]. A gathering-place Π 661 (where the corpses lay heaped), Ω 141 (cf. ἀγών (3)) : γ 31.

ἀγυρτάζω [ἀγείρω]. To collect, get together τ 284.

ἀγχέμαχος [ἄγχι + μάχομαι]. Fighting at close quarters or hand to hand Ν 5, Π 248, 272, Ρ 165.

ἄγχι. (1) To within or at a short distance, near, nigh, close by : ἕστηκεν Ε 185, παρίστατο 570. Cf. Ζ 405, Η 188, Ο 442, Π 114, Ρ 338, Ψ 304, 520, etc.: σχὼν κεφαλήν α 157 = δ 70 = ρ 592, ἀ. [ἐστὶ] θύρετρα χ 136. Cf. γ 449, ε 101, ζ 56, θ 218, ι 345, π 338, υ 190, etc.—With genit. : Ἕκτορος Θ 117, θαλάσσης Ι 43. Cf. Κ 161, Λ 666, Ξ 75, 460, Ο 362, 434, Ρ 10, 300, Ω 126 : αὐτῆς β 417, ἐμεῦ δ 370. Cf. ζ 291, η 112, θ 95 = 534, ι 182, κ 400 = 455, λ 191, μ 306, τ 438, φ 433, χ 130.—With dat. : τοι Λ 362 = Υ 449, οἱ Υ 283, σφισίν Ψ 447.—(2) App., soon, shortly τ 301.

ἀγχίαλος, -ον [ἄγχι + ἅλς[1]]. By the sea Β 640, 697.

ἀγχιβαθής [ἄγχι + βαθύς]. Of the sea, deep close in shore ε 413.

ἀγχίθεος [ἄγχι + θεός]. In close intercourse with the gods : Φαίηκες ε 35 = τ 279. (Cf. ἐγγύθεν (2)(b).)

ἀγχιμαχητής [ἄγχι + μαχητής] = ἀγχέμαχος Β 604, Θ 173 = Λ 286 = Ν 150 = Ο 425 = 486 = Ρ 184.

ἀγχίμολος [ἄγχι + μολ-, βλώσκω. 'Coming near']. (1) Absol. ἐξ ἀγχιμόλοιο, from close at hand : ἰδών Ω 352.—(2) In neut. sing. ἀγχίμολον as adv. (a) To within a short distance, near, nigh, close by ξ 410, ρ 260, χ 205 = ω 502, ω 19, 386.—With dat. : ἀ. οἱ ἦλθεν Δ 529. Cf. Π 820, Ω 283 : θ 300, ο 57, 95, υ 173, ω 99, 439.—(b) Closely following : ἐδύσετο δώματα ρ 336.

ἀγχίνοος [ἄγχι + νόος]. Applying the mind closely, sagacious : ἀγχίνοος καὶ ἐχέφρων ν 332.

ἀγχιστῖνοι, -αι [perh. formed fr. *ἄγχιστις, abstract noun fr. ἄγχι. Cf. προμνηστῖνοι]. Close together, one on another, in a heap or in heaps : κέχυνται Ε 141, ἔπιπτον Ρ 361 : χ 118, ω 181, 449.

ἄγχιστος [superl. fr. ἄγχι]. (1) In neut. ἄγχιστον as adv., nearest. With dat. : ἀ. αὐτῷ ε 280.—(2) So in pl. ἄγχιστα (a) Most nearly Υ 18 (see δαίω[1] (2)).—(b) With regard to resemblance, most closely, very closely. With dat. : Νέστορι ἀ. ἐῴκει Β 58. Cf. Ξ 474 : ζ 152, ν 80.

ἀγχόθι [ἀγχοῦ + -θι]. Near, close to. With genit. : δειρῆς Ξ 412, στήθεος Ψ 762 : ἐλαίης ν 103 = 347.

ἀγχοῦ [ἄγχι]. = ἄγχι (1) Β 172, Δ 203, etc. : δ 25, ε 159, ρ 526, τ 271, etc.—With genit. : πυλάων Ω 709 : Κυκλώπων ζ 5.

ἄγχω. (ἀπ-.) To choke, throttle Γ 371.

ἄγω. Fut. ἄξω, -εις Α 139, Γ 401, Δ 239, Θ 166, Ι 429, 692, Ω 154, 183 : β 326, κ 268, π 272, ρ 22, 250. Acc. sing. masc. pple. ἄξοντα Θ 368 : λ 623. Infin. ἀξέμεναι ψ 221. ἀξέμεν Ψ 668. ἄξειν Π 832, Τ 298 : ν 212. Aor. ἤγαγον, -ες Δ 179, Ε 731, Ζ 426, Λ 480, 663, Ω 547, etc. : α 172, γ 383, δ 258, η 9, 248, ι 495, λ 509, 625, ν 323, ρ 171, 376, etc. ἄγαγον, -ες Α 346, Λ 112, Τ 118, Ω 447, 577, etc. : ξ 404, π 227. Subj. ἀγάγωμι Ω 717. ἀγάγω Β 231. 3 sing. -ησι Ω 155. -ῃ ο 311. 1 pl. -ωμεν Υ 300. 3 sing. opt. ἀγάγοι ρ 243, φ 201. Imp. ἄγαγε Ω 337. Pple. ἀγαγών, -οῦσα Δ 407, Θ 490 : δ 175, 407, ο 428, ψ 295. Aor. imp. pl. ἄξετε Γ 105, Ω 778 : ξ 414. Infin. ἀξέμεναι Ψ 50. ἀξέμεν Ψ 111, Ω 663. **Mid.** Fut. ἄξομαι Ι 367 : δ 601, φ 214. Infin. ἄξεσθαι φ 316, 322. Aor. ἠγαγόμην δ 82, ξ 211. 3 sing. -ετο Η 390, Π 190, Χ 116, 471 : ο 238. 3 sing.

subj. ἀγάγηται ζ 159. Infin. ἀγαγέσθαι Σ 87. 3 pl. aor. ἄξοντο (*v.l.* ἄξαντο) Θ 545. Imp. pl. ἄξεσθε (*v.l.* ἄξασθε) Θ 505. (ἀν-, ἀπ-, δι-, εἰσ-, εἰσαν-, ἐξ-, ἐπ-, κατ-, προσ-, συν-, ὑπ-, ὑπεξ-.) (**I**) In act. (**1**) To drive, lead, bring (an animal) Θ 368, Λ 480, Ν 572, Ρ 134, Ψ 596, 613, 654: γ 439, δ 622, λ 623, 625, ξ 27, 414, ρ 171, 213 = υ 174, ρ 600, υ 186, etc.—To take as a prize: ἵππον Ψ 577, ἡμίονον 662, 668.—To put (under the yoke) Ε 731, Κ 293, Ψ 294, 300: γ 383, 476, ο 47.—(**2**) In reference to persons, to cause to come or go, lead, conduct, take, bring, fetch Α 346, 440, Γ 105, Δ 541, Ζ 291, Η 310, Ι 89, etc.: β 326, γ 270, δ 262, ι 98, ν 134, etc.—In reference to corpses Η 418, Χ 392, etc.: ω 419.—Of an impersonal agency: τίπτε δέ σε χρειὼ δεῦρ' ἤγαγεν; δ 312.—Of fate, to lead on Β 834, Ε 614, etc. —In reference to leading astray Κ 391.—(**3**) To lead as a chief Β 557, 580, 631, Δ 179, Μ 330, Ρ 96, etc.: γ 189, ζ 7, κ 551, ξ 469, ω 427.—To take (companions) with one δ 434.—(**4**) To carry off (a horse) as spoil Π 153.—To carry off (persons) captive: υἱόν Β 231. Cf. Δ 239, Ζ 426, Θ 166, Ι 594, Λ 112, Φ 36, etc.: γυναῖκας ξ 264, etc. —Sim. with φέρω (φέρω referring to things, ἄγω to men and cattle) Ε 484.—In reference to the rape of Helen Ω 764.—To taking her back ψ 221. —To taking back her and the spoils Η 351, Χ 117.—To carrying off Briseïs Α 184, 323, 338, 391, Τ 273, etc.—To seizing and taking away (a γέρας) Α 139.—(**5**) Of a chariot, horses, etc., to bear, carry, bring Ε 839, Λ 598: ζ 37. —Of ships Ω 396: η 9, ω 299.—(**6**) In reference to things, to fetch, bring, carry, take Α 99, Η 335, Λ 632, Ο 531, Ψ 50, Ω 367, etc.: α 184, γ 312, ν 216, ξ 296, ο 159, etc.—To bring in, import: οἶνον Η 467, Ι 72, μέθυ Η 471.—To carry off as spoil Α 367.—In reference to levying compensation χ 57.—(**7**) To bring on, cause: πῆμα Ω 547: τερπωλήν σ 37.—In reference to atmospheric phenomena: νέφος ἄγει λαίλαπα Δ 278. Cf. Ψ 188. —To bring on (a period of time): ἦμαρ σ 137, Ἠῶ ψ 246.—(**8**) In various uses. In reference to conducting water in a channel Φ 262.—To direct the course of (a battle) Λ 721.—To cause (a ship) to take a certain direction ι 495.—To bring (to the birth) Τ 118.—Of hunters, to draw (a cordon) δ 792.—To bring back (intelligence) δ 258.—To keep in memory ε 311. —(**9**) In pres. pple. with a finite vb., to take and . . . (cf. αἱρέω (I) (10), εἶμι (1) (c), (6) (b), ἔρχομαι (1), (4), κίον (2), λαμβάνω (7), φέρω (6), (10)): ἀνὰ δ' εἷσεν ἄγων Α 311, στῆσεν ἄγων Β 558. Cf. Δ 392, etc.: α 130, γ 416, δ 525, 634, ο 542, etc.—(**10**) For imp. sing. and pl. ἄγε, ἄγετε, used interjectionally see these words.—(**II**) In mid. (often hardly to be distinguished from the act.). (**1**) In reference to cattle, to drive, bring Θ 505, 545.—(**2**) To carry or take, take with one: χρυσόν Ι 367. Cf. Π 223: εἵματα ζ 58. Cf. δ 82, 601, κ 35, 40.—In reference to corpses Ρ 163, Ω 139.—(**3**) To carry off captive or as spoil Β 659, Ζ 455, Η 390, Χ 116, Ψ 829.—In reference to Helen and the spoils Γ 72 = 93.—To the spoils Η 363.—To taking her back Δ 19.—To take as a prize Ψ 263.—(**4**) To take to oneself as a wife, marry. (**a**) With οἴκαδε or the like: οἴκαδ' ἄγεσθαι Γ 404, ἠγάγετο πρὸς δώματα Π 190. Cf. Ι 146, etc.: ζ 159, φ 316.—(**b**) Without such a word Σ 87, Χ 471: ξ 211, φ 322.—(**5**) To get (a wife for another). (**a**) As in (4) (a): κασιγνήτῳ γυναῖκα ἠγάγετο πρὸς δώματα ο 238.—(**b**) As in (4) (b): ἄξομαι ἀμφοτέροις ἀλόχους φ 214. Cf. δ 10.—(**6**) In reference to conducting a bride to her new home ζ 28.—(**7**) In reference to speech, to cause to pass, utter: μῦθον ὃν οὔ κεν ἀνὴρ διὰ στόμ' ἄγοιτο Ξ 91.

ἀγών, -ῶνος, ὁ. (**1**) An assembly. (**a**) θεῖον ἀγῶνα (the assemblage of the gods supposed to meet together to receive their worshippers) Η 298, Σ 376.—(**b**) An assembly brought together to view contests Ψ 258, Ω 1.—(**c**) App., the body of competitors: παντὸς ἀγῶνος ὑπέρβαλεν Ψ 847.—(**2**) A place for contests: τάδ' ἄεθλα κεῖτ' ἐν ἀγῶνι Ψ 273. Cf. Ψ 451, 495, 507, 617, 696, etc.: εὔρυναν ἀγῶνα θ 260. Cf. θ 200, 238, 259, 380, ω 86.—(**3**) In reference to the Greek ships drawn up on the beach: νεῶν (νηῶν) ἐν ἀγῶνι (in the gathering-place of the ships, *i.e.* the camp) Ο 428 = Π 500, Π 239, Τ 42.—So μετ' ἀγῶνα νεῶν Υ 33.

ἀδαημονίη [ἀδαήμων]. Ignorance, want of experience or skill. With complementary infin.: ἀμφιπολεύειν ὄρχατον ω 244.

ἀδαήμων, -ονος [ἀ-[1] + δαήμων]. Ignorant of, not experienced or versed in. With genit.: μάχης Ε 634, Ν 811; κακῶν μ 208, πληγέων ρ 283.

ἀδάκρῡτος [ἀ-[1] + δακρύω]. Not shedding tears, tearless Α 415: δ 186, ω 61.

ἀδάμαστος [ἀ-[1] + δαμασ-, δαμάζω]. Inflexible. Of Hades: ἀμείλιχος ἠδ' ἀδάμαστος Ι 158.

ἄδε, 3 sing. aor. ἁνδάνω.

ἀδεής (ἀδϜεής) [ἀ-[1] + δ(Ϝ)έος]. Also **ἀδειής** Η 117. (**1**) Fearless, without fear Η 117.—(**2**) Bold, too bold: κύον ἀδεές Θ 423, Φ 481: τ 91.

ἀδελφεός, -οῦ, ὁ. Genit. ἀδελφειοῦ (for ἀδελφεόο) Ε 21, Ζ 61, Η 120, Ν 788. A brother, one's brother Β 409, Η 2, Θ 318, Ν 695, Ο 187, etc.: δ 91, 199, 225, 512.

ἀδευκής [ἀ-[1]. Cf. ἐνδυκέως]. Harsh, untoward, unkind: ὀλέθρῳ δ 489, φῆμιν ζ 273, πότμον κ 245.

ἀδέψητος, -ον [ἀ-[1] + δέψω]. Of a hide, undressed υ 2, 142.

ἀδέω, also written **ἁδέω** [prob. ἀ(σϜ)αδέω, to be displeased, fr. ἀ-[1] + (σϜ)αδ-, ἁνδάνω]. To have too much of something. In pf. pple. ἀδηκότες, sated; hence, worn-out: καμάτῳ Κ 312 = 399. Cf. Κ 98, 471: μ 281.—Sim. μὴ δείπνῳ ἀδήσειεν (lest he should be disgusted with . . .) α 134.

ἄδην, also written **ἅδην** (ᾰ) [cf. ἄω]. To the full, to satiety Ε 203.—So ἁ. ἐλόωσι πολέμοιο (will drive him to satiety in the matter of war, give him his fill of war) Ν 315. Cf. Τ 423: ε 290.

ἀδήρῑτος [ἀ-[1] + δηρίομαι]. Free from strife: πόνος (*i.e.* unfought) Ρ 42.

ἀδινός, -ή, -όν. App. orig. expressing quick incessant motion. Hence (**1**) Of bees, flying in swarms B 87.—Sim. of flies B 469.—Of sheep, thick-thronging α 92 = δ 320.—Of the heart, beating, throbbing Π 481 : τ 516.—Of weeping, thick-coming, vehement Σ 316, X 430, Ψ 17, Ω 747.—Of the Sirens, trilling their song ψ 326.—(**2**) In neut. ἀδινόν, as adv., of the expression of grief, with thick-coming bursts, vehemently : στοναχῆσαι Σ 124 : γοόωσα δ 721.—Of the incessant lowing of calves κ 413.—So in pl. ἀδινά : στεναχίζων Ψ 225. Cf. Ω 123, 510 : η 274, ω 317.—So also in neut. comp. ἀδινώτερον : κλαῖον ἀ. ἤ τ' οἰωνοί π 216.

ἀδινῶς [adv. fr. prec.]. Of sighing, with thick-coming repetitions : ἀνενείκατο T 314.

ἀδμής, -ῆτος [ἀ-[1] + δμη-, δαμάζω]. (**1**) Not broken in : ἡμίονοι δ 637.—(**2**) Unwedded ζ 109, 228.

ἄδμητος, -η [as prec.]. Not broken in : βοῦν K 293. Cf. Ψ 266, 655 : γ 383.

ἄδοι, 3 sing. aor. opt. ἀνδάνω.

ἄδος, τό [cf. ἄδην]. Weariness Λ 88.

ἄδυτον, -ου, τό [ἀ-[1] + δύω. 'Not to be entered']. An innermost sanctuary E 448, 512.

ἀεθλεύω, also **ἀθλεύω** Ω 734 [ἄεθλος]. (**1**) To engage in a contest for a prize or as a trial of strength or skill Δ 389, Ψ 274, 737.—(**2**) To toil Ω 734.

ἀέθλιον, -ου, τό [ἄεθλον]. (**1**)=ἄεθλον I 124, 127, 266, 269, X 160, Ψ 537, 736, 748, 823.—(**2**) A contest as a trial of strength or skill θ 108, φ 117.—(**3**) In pl., the material for a contest : τόξον θέμεν σίδηρόν τε, ἀέθλια φ 4. Cf. φ 62, ω 169.

ἄεθλον, -ου, τό. A prize for a victor in a contest Λ 700, X 163, Ψ 259, 262, 273, 314, 413, 441, 511, 544, 551, 615, 620, 631, 640, 653, 700, 740, 773, 785, 849, 892, 897 : φ 73 = 106, ω 85, 89, 91.

ἄεθλος, -ου, ὁ, also **ἆθλος** θ 160. (**1**) A contest for a prize or as a trial of strength or skill Π 590 : δ 659, θ 22, 133, 160, 197, τ 576, φ 135, χ 5, etc. —A verbal contest λ 548.—(**2**) In pl., a series of contests as a part of funeral rites : ἑταῖρον ἀέθλοισι κτερέϊζε Ψ 646.—In sing., one of the contests Ψ 707, 753 = 831.—(**3**) (**a**) In pl., fights, struggles : ἀέθλους Τρώων καὶ Ἀχαιῶν Γ 126.—Feats δ 241.—Trials of endurance, hardships γ 262, δ 170.—Trials, troubles α 18, ψ 248, 350.—(**b**) A trial or trouble ψ 261.—A task imposed Θ 363, T 133 : λ 622, 624.—(**4**) The material for a contest : καταθήσω ἄεθλον, τοὺς πελέκεας τ 572. Cf. φ 91.

ἀεθλοφόρος, also **ἀθλοφόρος** I 124, 266, Λ 699 [ἄεθλον + -φορος, φέρω]. Carrying off prizes : ἵππους I 124 = 266. Cf. Λ 699, X 22, 162.

ἀεί [cf. αἰεί, αἰέν] = αἰεί M 211, Ψ 648 : ο 379.

ἀείδω. Fut. pple. in mid. form ἀεισόμενος χ 352. 3 sing. aor. ἄεισε φ 411. Imp. ἄεισον θ 492. Infin. ἀεῖσαι ξ 464. (παρ-.) (**1**) To sing : Μουσάων, αἳ ἄειδον A 604. Cf. B 598, I 191 : ἀοιδὸς ἄειδεν α 325. Cf. α 154, 155, θ 45, 87, 90, 266, κ 221, 254, ξ 464, ρ 262, 358, 385, 520, χ 331, 346, 352.—With cognate acc.: παιήονα A 473, X 391. Cf. Σ 570 : ρ 519.—Of the nightingale τ 519.—Of a bow-string φ 411.—(**2**) To sing of, tell of in song : μῆνιν A 1. Cf. I 189 : α 326, 339, 350, θ 73, 83 = 367 = 521, θ 489, 492, 538.—With infin. : πόλιν κεραϊζέμεν θ 516.—With clause : ὡς . . . θ 514.

ἀεικείη, -ης, ἡ [ἀεικής]. (**1**) Something causing marring or disfigurement Ω 19.—(**2**) In pl., unseemly conduct υ 308.

ἀεικέλιος, -η, -ον, and -ος, -ον [ἀεικής]. (**1**) Of mean personal appearance ζ 242, ν 402.—Shabby, worn : πήρης ρ 357, χιτῶνα ω 228. — Mean, wretched : κοίτῃ τ 341, δίφρον υ 259.—(**2**) Hard, grievous : ἀλαωτύν ι 503, ἄλγος ξ 32.—(**3**) Causing disfigurement : πληγῇσιν δ 244.—(**4**) Cowardly, spiritless Ξ 84.

ἀεικελίως [adv. fr. prec.]. (**1**) In unseemly wise π 109 = υ 319.—(**2**) So as to impair one's vigour θ 231.

ἀεικής, -ές (ἀϜεικής) [ἀ-[1] + (Ϝ)είκω[1]]. Dat. pl. ἀεικέσσι B 264. (**1**) Unseemly, not right or fitting Λ 142, X 395 = Ψ 24 : γ 265, δ 694, λ 429, ο 236, π 107 = υ 317, ψ 222.—Absol. : ἀεικέα μερμηρίζων δ 533. Cf. υ 394, χ 432.—In neut. in impers. construction : οὔ τοι ἀεικές [ἐστιν] I 70.—So with infin. : οὔ οἱ ἀεικὲς ἀνασσέμεν T 124. Cf. O 496.—(**2**) Inadequate in amount or value M 435, Ω 594.—(**3**) Shabby, worn : πήρην ν 437, ρ 197 = σ 108.—Absol. : ἀεικέα ἕσσο (ἕσσαι) π 199, ω 250.—(**4**) Of one's fate, hard, grievous Δ 396 : β 250, δ 339 = ρ 130, δ 340 = ρ 131, τ 550, χ 317 = 416.—(**5**) Baneful, baleful A 97, 341, 398, 456, I 495, Ξ 13, Π 32.—Horrid, horrifying : στόνος K 483, Φ 20 : χ 308, ω 184.—(**6**) Involving disgrace or degradation : πληγῇσιν B 264, ἔργον T 133, Ω 733.—(**7**) Of the mind, not giving right guidance υ 366.—(**8**) In neut. ἀεικές as adv., in unseemly wise ρ 216.

ἀεικίζω [ἀεικής]. Fut. ἀεικιῶ X 256. 3 pl. aor. subj. ἀεικίσσωσι Π 545, T 26. 1 pl. aor. opt. mid. ἀεικισσαίμεθα Π 559. Infin. ἀεικίσσασθαι X 404. Aor. infin. pass. ἀεικισθήμεναι σ 222. (καταικίζω.) (**1**) To treat in unseemly wise σ 222.—(**2**) To work despite upon, mutilate (a corpse) Π 545, 559, X 256, 404, Ω 22, 54.—Of flies marring (a corpse) T 26.

ἀείρω. Contr. acc. pl. masc. pple. αἴροντας P 724. 3 sing. aor. ἤειρε K 499. ἄειρε T 386, Ψ 730, 882. 3 pl. ἤειραν Ω 590. ἄειραν Υ 373, Ψ 362, Ω 266 : γ 312, ν 117, 120, φ 18. 3 sing. opt. ἀείραι H 130. Pple. ἀείρας, -αντος H 268, K 30, M 383, Ξ 429, Σ 615, Ω 589, etc. : α 141, β 425, γ 11, ι 240, ρ 237, ω 165, etc. Acc. pl. fem. ἀειρᾱ́σας Ω 583. Infin. ἀεῖραι Θ 424. **Mid.** Contr. 2 sing. aor. ἤραο ω 33. 3 ἤρατο Γ 373, Ξ 510, Σ 165 : α 240, δ 107, ξ 370. 1 pl. ἠράμεθα X 393. Pple. ἀειράμενος Ψ 856. Fem. ἀειραμένη Z 293 : ο 106. **Pass.** 3 sing. aor. ἀέρθη τ 540. 3 pl. ἄερθεν Θ 74. Pple. ἀερθείς θ 375, μ 432. Contr. ἀρθείς N 63 : ε 393. 3 sing. plupf. ἄωρτο (written also ἄορτο) Γ 272, Τ 253. (ἀν-, ἀπ-, ἐξ-, ἐπ-, παρ-, συν-.) (I) In act. (1) To lift, heave, raise up: στεφάνην Κ 30, δέπας Λ 637. Cf. Κ 465, 505, Τ 380, 386, Υ 325, Ψ 730, Ω 589, 590: ὑψόσε ι 240 = 340, ἀμφουδίς ρ 237.—(2) To take, lift, or pick up: λᾶαν Η 268. Cf. Μ 383, 453, Ξ 411, 429, Ρ 718: λᾶαν ι 537, σῖτον ρ 335, ἄρτους σ 120.—So with ἀνά: ἂν δ' ἄρα πελέκεας ἄειρεν Ψ 882. Cf. Χ 399.—(3) To raise for action: ἔγχος Θ 424. Cf. Υ 373, Ψ 362: ι 332.—To raise (the hands) in supplication Η 130: λ 423.—(4) To raise (a mast) to an erect position β 425 = ο 290.—To brail up (a sail) γ 11. —(5) With σύν, to harness (horses) together (cf. συναείρω) Κ 499 (in this sense perh. a different word).—(6) To carry, bear, take, bring, fetch Ζ 264, Π 678, Ρ 588, 724, Σ 615, Ω 266, 583: α 141 = δ 57, ν 117, 120, π 285, φ 18, ω 165. —Of ships, to carry (as cargo) γ 312.—(II) In mid. (1) Much like (I) (2), to take up, pick up: πέπλων ἕν' ἀειραμένη Ζ 293. Cf. Ψ 856: ο 106.—(2) To win, carry off Ξ 510.—To achieve (feats): ὅσ' ἤρατο δ 107.—To win (glory or fame) Γ 373 = Σ 165, Χ 393: α 240 = ξ 370, ω 33.—(III) In pass. (1) To be lifted or raised up, to rise, mount: πρὸς οὐρανὸν ἄερθεν Θ 74, ἴρηξ ἀπὸ πέτρης ἀρθείς (mounting and poising himself) Ν 63: ὑπὸ κύματος ἀρθείς ε 393. Cf. θ 375, μ 432, τ 540.—Of dust, to rise in a cloud Β 151, Ψ 366.—(2) Of horses, to bound: ὑψόσ' ἀειρέσθην (ἀειρόμενοι) Ψ 501: ν 83.—Of a river, to rise in a wave Φ 307.—Sim. of the water: κῦμα ποταμοῖο ἵσταт' ἀειρόμενον Φ 327.—Of the stern of a ship, to rise to the sea ν 84.—(3) To be taken up and carried off: ἑταίρων ἀειρομένων μ 249. Cf. μ 255.—(4) To be suspended, hang: μάχαιραν, ἣ πὰρ ξίφεος κουλεὸν ἄωρτο Γ 272 = Τ 253.

ἀεκαζόμενος, -η. A ppl. form = ἀέκων (1): ἀεκαζομένην μνῶνται τ 133. Cf. Ζ 458: ν 277, σ 135.

ἀεκήλιος [app. = ἀεικέλιος]. Baneful, baleful Σ 77.

ἀέκητι [ἀέκων]. With genit. (1) Against the will of, without the good will of: θεῶν ἀ. Μ 8. Cf. Ο 720: γ 28, δ 504, 665, ε 177, ζ 240, 287, μ 290, ρ 43, ω 444.—Joined with ἀντία: ἀντί' ἀθανάτων ἀ. θεῶν α 79.—(2) Doing violence to the will of, doing despite to: ἀ. σέθεν γ 213, π 94, σεῦ ἀ. ο 19.—In spite of the resistance of: Ἀργείων ἀ. Λ 667.

ἀέκων, -ουσα (ἀϜέκων) [ἀ-[1] + (Ϝ)εκών]. (1) Acting against one's will, unwilling, yielding to force, compulsion or necessity: ἀέκοντος ἐμεῖο Α 301, ἀέκοντε βάτην 327. Cf. Α 348, 430, Δ 43, Ε 164, 366, 768, Η 197, Θ 45, Κ 530, Λ 281, 519, 557, 716, Ν 367, Ξ 105, Ο 186, Π 204, 369, Ρ 112, 666, Σ 240, Τ 273, Φ 59, Χ 400: ἐρυκανόωσ' ἀέκοντα α 199. Cf. α 403, β 130, γ 484 = 494 = ο 192, δ 463, 646, η 315, ι 405, κ 266, 489, ο 200, τ 374, υ 343, φ 348.—(2) Not having one's desire, desiring something different: Τρωσὶν ἀέκουσιν ἔδυ φάος Θ 487.—(3) Acting without intention: εἰ κινήσῃ ἀ. Π 264.

ἄελλα, -ης, ἡ (ἀϜέλλη) [ἀ-[2] + Ϝελ-, (Ϝ)είλω]. (1) A whirling or stormy wind Β 293, Λ 297, Μ 40, Ν 795, Τ 377: γ 283, 320, ε 292, 304, θ 409, ξ 383, τ 189.—(2) A whirl or cloud of dust Ν 334, Π 374.

ἀελλής [app. = ἀολλής]. Crowded; hence, dense: κονίσαλος Γ 13.

ἀελλόπος [ἄελλα + πούς]. Storm-footed, swift as the winds. Epithet of Iris Θ 409 = Ω 77 = 159.

ἀελπής [as next]. Not hoped for: γαῖαν ε 408.

ἀελπτέω (ἀϜελπτέω) [ἀ-[1] + (Ϝ)έλπω]. To despair: ἀελπτέοντες σόον εἶναι (pple. of the impf.: they had been in despair of his safety) Η 310.

ἀενάων, -οντος [ἀεί + νάω]. Ever-flowing ν 109.

ἀέξω [ἀϜέξω. Cf. the later αὔξω]. (1) To increase, enlarge, strengthen: μένος Ζ 261. Cf. Μ 214, Ρ 226.—(2) To rear up to man's estate ν 360.—(3) To cherish or foster (grief) Ρ 139: λ 195, ρ 489, ω 231.—(4) To cause to prosper, bless (a farm) ξ 65, ο 372.—(5) To cause to be brought forth or produced: [οἶνον] ι 111 = 358.—(6) In pass. (a) Of spirit, to grow, wax: ἀέξεται θυμός β 315.—Of wrath, to increase in violence Σ 110. —Of a wave, to swell up, rise: οὔ ποτ' ἀέξετο κῦμα κ 93.—(b) To grow up to man's estate: νέον ἀέξετο χ 426.—(c) Of a farm, to prosper ξ 66. —(d) Of the day, to grow towards noon: ἀέξετο ἦμαρ Θ 66 = Λ 84: = ι 56.

ἀεργίη, -ης, ἡ [ἀεργός]. Idleness, laziness ω 251.

ἀεργός (ἀϜεργός) [ἀ-[1] + (Ϝ)έργον]. Not working or exerting oneself, idle, lazy Ι 320: τ 27.

ἀέρθη, 3 sing. aor. pass. ἀείρω.

ἀερσίπους, -ποδος [ἀερ-, ἀείρω + -σι- + πούς]. Lifting the feet, high-stepping. Epithet of horses: Γ 327, Ψ 475.—Applied to ἵπποι in sense 'chariot' (see ἵππος (3)) Σ 532.

ἄεσα, aor. ἰαύω.

ἀεσιφροσύνη, -ης, ἡ [ἀεσίφρων]. Thoughtlessness. In pl.: ἑπόμην ἀεσιφροσύνῃσιν (in (childish) thoughtlessness) ο 470.

ἀεσίφρων, -ονος [perh. fr. weak stem ἀϜε- of ἄ(Ϝ)ημι + -σι- + φρήν. Cf. ἄημι (3)]. Thus, subject to gusts of passion φ 302.—Blown about in mind; hence, weakened in will, volatile, flighty Υ 183, Ψ 603.

ἀζαλέος, -η, -ον [ἄζω]. Dried up, dry: βῶν Η 239, δρῦς Λ 494, οὔρεος Υ 491: ὕλης ι 234.

ἄζη, ἡ [ἄζω]. App., dry dirt or mould χ 184.

ἀζηκής, -ές [prob. for ἀδια(σ)εχής, fr. ἀ-[1] + δια- (6) + (σ)εχ-, ἔχω. Thus neg. of διεχής, separate, and = συνεχής]. (1) Incessant, continuous Ο 25, Ρ 741.—(2) In neut. ἀζηκές as adv., incessantly, continuously Δ 435, Ο 658: σ 3.

ἅζομαι. Imp. ἅζεν ρ 401. To reverence, stand in awe of, respect Α 21, Ε 434, 830: ι 200, ρ 401 (τό γε, to that point).—With infin., to shrink from *doing something*: λείβειν οἶνον Ζ 267: ξείνους ἐσθέμεναι ι 478.—With μή clause: μὴ Νυκτὶ ἀποθύμια ἕρδοι Ξ 261.

ἄζω. (καταζαίνω.) To dry up, parch Δ 487.

ἀηδών, ἡ [ἀείδω]. The nightingale τ 518.

ἀηθέσσω [ἀ-[1] + ἦθος, custom]. To be unused to. With genit.: *νεκρῶν* K 493.

†ἄημι (ἄϝημι) [cf. ἀΐω[2], ἰαύω]. 2 dual *ἄητον* I 5. Pple. *ἀείς, -έντος* E 526 : ε 478, τ 440. Infin. *ἀήμεναι* Ψ 214 : γ 176. *ἀῆναι* γ 183, κ 25. 3 sing. impf. *ἄη* μ 325, ξ 458. Pres. pple. pass. *ἀήμενος* ζ 131. 3 sing. impf. *ἄητο* Φ 386. (δι-.) (**1**) Of the winds, to blow E 526, I 5 : γ 176, 183, ε 478, κ 25, μ 325, ξ 458, τ 440.—(**2**) To blow upon (something): *πόντον ἵκανον ἀήμεναι* (so as to blow upon it) Ψ 214.—(**3**) In pass., to be blown upon: *ὑόμενος καὶ ἀήμενος* ζ 131.—Fig.: *θυμὸς ἄητο* (was blown about (by gusts of passion)) Φ 386.

ἀήρ, *ἠέρος, ἡ.* (**1**) Mist, cloud: *ἐκάλυψε ἠέρι* Γ 381 = Υ 444, *δι' ἠέρος αἰθέρ' ἵκανεν* (the hill-mist) Ξ 288. Cf. E 776, Θ 50, Λ 752, Ξ 282, Π 790, P 269, 368, 376, 644, 645, 649, Φ 6, 549, 597 : *ἠέρα χεῦεν* η 15. Cf. η 140, 143, θ 562, ι 144, λ 15, ν 189, 352.—(**2**) A body of mist, a cloud: *ἠέρι ἔγχος ἐκέκλιτο* E 356, *οἵη ἐκ νεφέων ἐρεβεννὴ φαίνεται ἀ.* (app., a dark streamer of cloud detaching itself from the main body) 864, *ἠέρα τύψεν* Υ 446.

ἀήσυλος [prob. for ἀϝίσυλος, fr. ἀ-[1] + (ϝ)ῖσος]. (Cf. *αἴσυλος.*) Unjust, unseemly, evil E 876.

ἀήτης, *-ου, ὁ* [ἄημι]. A blast or blowing (of wind) Ξ 254, O 626 (*v.l.* *ἀήτη*, fem.): δ 567, ι 139.

ἄητος [perh. fr. ἄημι]. Thus, vehement, violent, fierce: *θάρσος* Φ 395.

ἀθάνατος, *-η, -ον* [ἀ-[1] + θάνατος]. (**1**) Undying, immortal A 520, B 741, Γ 158, E 342, Θ 539, etc. : α 67, γ 346, δ 385, ε 136, μ 302, etc.—Of parts of the gods: *κρατός* A 530. Cf. N 19, Ξ 177, Π 704.—Of horses Π 154, P 444, 476, Ψ 277.—(**2**) Absol. in pl., the immortals, the gods. (**a**) Masc. (not necessarily excluding the female divinities) A 265, B 14, E 186, Θ 456, T 22, etc. : α 31, γ 47, δ 378, η 5, ξ 421, etc.—(**b**) Fem.: *ὑμῖν ἀθανάτῃσιν* H 32. Cf. Σ 86 : ε 213, ζ 16, ω 47, 55.—(**3**) Absol. in masc. sing., one of the gods: *ὥς τέ μοι ἀ. ἰνδάλλεται* γ 246. Cf. ε 73, ζ 309.—(**4**) Of a thing, of or pertaining to a god: *δόμοι* δ 79.—Of the aegis, everlasting, indestructible B 447.

ἄθαπτος [ἀ-[1] + θάπτω]. Not honoured with funeral rites: *νέκυς* X 386 : *σῶμα* λ 54, *'Ελπήνορα* 72.

ἀθεεί [ἀ-[1] + θεός]. Without the good will of the gods: *οὐκ ἀθεεὶ ἵκει* σ 353.

ἀθεμίστιος [ἀ-[1] + θέμις]. (**1**) Regardless of right σ 141.—(**2**) Absol. in neut. pl. *ἀθεμίστια*, what is wrong: *ἀ. ᾔδη* (had no regard for right in his heart, was given over to lawlessness (see εἴδω (III) (12)): ι 189. Cf. ι 428, υ 287.

ἀθέμιστος [as prec.]. (**1**) = prec. (1) ι 106, ρ 363.—(**2**) Unworthy to share in the benefits of law: *ἀφρήτωρ ἀ. ἀνέστιος* I 63.

ἀθερίζω. To slight, be indifferent to, think little of A 261 : θ 212.—Absol. ψ 174.

ἀθέσφατος, *-ον* [app. ἀ-[1] + θέσφατος]. Thus, not suited to the utterance of a (beneficent) god; hence, portentous, terrible, terrifying: *ὄμβρον* Γ 4, K 6 : *ὦρινε θάλασσαν ἀθέσφατον* (so that it became . . .) η 273.—Of winter nights, endless λ 373, ο 392.—Unlimited in amount: *σῖτος* ν 244.—In number υ 211.—Excessive in amount: *οἶνος* λ 61.

ἀθηρηλοιγός, *ὁ* [ἀθήρ, ear of corn + λοιγός. 'Consumer of ears of corn']. App., a shovel by which grain to be winnowed was thrown against the wind (= *πτύον*) λ 128 = ψ 275.

ἀθλεύω. See *ἀεθλεύω.*

ἀθλέω [ἆθλος. See ἄεθλος]. To toil H 453, O 30.

ἀθλητήρ, *-ῆρος, ὁ* [ἀθλέω]. An athlete θ 164.

ἆθλος, ἀθλοφόρος. See *ἄεθλος, ἀεθλοφόρος.*

ἀθρέω. (ἐσ-.) (**1**) To look, gaze K 11.—(**2**) To see, note, notice, observe. With complementary pple.: *βλήμενον* M 391. Cf. Ξ 334.—Absol. μ 232, τ 478.

ἀθρόοι, *-αι, -α* [app. ἀ-[2] + θρόος]. (**1**) In a body, in a mass, all together: *ἴομεν* B 439, *ἔμειναν* O 657. Cf. Ξ 38, Σ 497, T 236, Ψ 200 : α 27, β 392, γ 34, δ 405, ι 544, π 361, τ 540, χ 76, ψ 50, ω 420, 464, 468.—(**2**) In one sum: *ἀθρόα πάντ' ἀποτείσεις* X 271. Cf. α 43.—(**3**) Collected together for use or convenience: *ἀθρόα πάντα τετύχθω* β 356. Cf. β 411, ν 122.

ἄθυμος [ἀ-[1] + θυμός]. Spiritless κ 463.

ἄθυρμα, *-ατος, τό* [ἀθύρω]. A plaything O 363 : σ 323.—In pl., gewgaws ο 416.

ἀθύρω. To play, sport O 364.

αἴ [cf. εἰ]. (**1**) *αἲ γάρ* with opt. expressing a wish = εἰ (2) (b): *αἲ γὰρ μή τις φύγοι* Π 97. Cf. Δ 288, K 536, Σ 272, 464, X 346, 454 : *αἲ γὰρ δύναμιν περιθεῖεν* γ 205. Cf. δ 341, ζ 244, θ 339, ι 523, ο 156, 536, ρ 132, 163, 251, σ 235, τ 22, 309, υ 169, 236, φ 200, 402.—Of the present: *αἲ γὰρ ἡβῷμι* H 132. Cf. B 371, Δ 189 : δ 697, π 99, φ 372.—See also *αἴθε* (1).—With infin.: *αἲ γὰρ παῖδ' ἐμὴν ἐχέμεν* η 311. Cf. ω 376.—(**2**) With fut. indic. and *κεν*, subj. and *κεν*, and opt. and *κεν* in the protasis of conditional sentences = εἰ (5). For the examples and constructions see Table at end (III).—(**3**) In final clauses, if haply, in the hope that. With subj. and *κεν* = εἰ (9) (b) (β): *σπεύδειν αἴ κ' ὄφελος γενώμεθα* N 236. Cf. A 66 (reading *βούλητ'* (the indic. cannot be explained)), 207, 408, 420, B 72, 83, Z 94, 275, 277, 281, 309, H 243, Θ 282, I 172, K 55, Λ 797, 799, M 275, N 743, Π 41, 725, P 121, Σ 143, 199, 213, 457, Φ 293, Ψ 82, Ω 116, 301, 357 : α 279, 379, β 144, γ 92, δ 34, 322, μ 215, ν 182, ο 312, ρ 51, 60, χ 7, 252.—(**4**) In object clauses, whether. (**a**) With subj. and *κεν* = εἰ (10) (b) (β): *πειρήσομαι αἴ κε τύχωμι* (and see whether . . .) E 279, *εἰπέμεναι ἔπος αἴ κ' ἐθέλωσιν* (*i.e.* ask if they will agree) H 375, *πειρήσεται αἴ κε θέῃσιν* (to see whether . . .) Σ 601. Cf. Δ 249, H 394, Λ 791, P 652, 692, T 71, Υ 436 : *εἰπέ μοι, αἴ κε γνώω* (that I may see whether . . .) ξ 118. Cf. β 186, ω 217.—(**b**) With opt. and *κεν* = εἰ (10) (c) (β): *εἰπεῖν αἴ κέ περ ὔμμι φίλον γένοιτο* (and see whether . . .) H 387.

αἶα, *-ης, ἡ* [= γαῖα]. (**1**) The earth: *ὕδωρ ἐπικίδναται αἶαν* B 850. Cf. Γ 243, Θ 1, I 506, Ψ 742, Ω 695 : *κατέχει αἶα* λ 301. Cf. ω 509.—

(2) (a) A particular land or country: Θρῃκῶν αἶαν N 4: Ἀχαιΐδος αἴης ν 249.—(b) One's native land: ὁππότ' ἂν ἧς ἱμείρεται αἴης α 41.—So πατρὶς αἶα. Always in genit. πατρίδος αἴης B 162=178, Δ 172, Λ 817, Ο 740, Π 539: α 75, 203, δ 262, 521, κ 236, 472, σ 145, τ 301, ψ 353, ω 290.—(3) The surface of the earth, the earth, the ground: ὅσον τ' ὄργυι' ὑπὲρ αἴης Ψ 327.

αἰγανέη, -ης, ἡ [app. fr. αἰγ-, αἴξ. 'Goat-spear.' Used against goats in ι 156]. A hunting-spear, a spear Π 589, B 774: =δ 626=ρ 168, ι 156.

αἴγειος, -η, -ον [αἰγ-, αἴξ]. Of a goat or goats: ἀσκῷ (of goatskin) Γ 247, τυρόν (of goats' milk) Λ 639: ἀσκῷ ζ 78, κυνέην ω 231.

αἴγειρος, -ου, ἡ. The poplar Δ 482: ε 64, 239, ζ 292, η 106, ι 141, κ 510, ρ 208.

αἴγεος = αἴγειος: ἀσκόν ι 196.

αἰγιαλός, -οῦ, ὁ. A beach or shore of the sea: ὡς ὅτε κῦμα θαλάσσης αἰγιαλῷ μεγάλῳ βρέμεται B 210. Cf. Δ 422, Ξ 34: χ 385.

αἰγίβοτος, -ον [αἰγ-, αἴξ + βόσκω]. Browsed on by goats. Of Ithaca δ 606, ν 246.

αἰγίλιψ, -ιπος [sense unknown. Traditionally explained as fr. αἰγ-, αἴξ + λιπ-, λείπω, 'so steep as to be deserted (even) by goats']. Of a rock: πέτρης I 15=Π 4, N 63.

αἰγίοχος [αἰγίς + ὀχ-, ἔχω]. Aegis-bearing. Epithet of Zeus A 202, B 157, Γ 426, etc.: γ 42, δ 752, ε 103, etc.

αἰγίς, -ίδος, ἡ [perh. the orig. idea was that of a storm-cloud, whence the sense 'hurricane-wind.' Cf. ἐπαιγίζω]. The terror-striking shield of Zeus Δ 167, P 593.—Wielded by Athene B 447, E 738, Φ 400: χ 297.—By Apollo O 229, 308, 318, 361.—Lent by Athene to Achilles Σ 204.—Used to cover Hector's corpse Ω 20.

αἴγλη, -ης, ἡ. (1) The light of the sun or moon δ 45=η 84.—(2) Radiance, brightness ζ 45.—The gleam of polished metal B 458, T 362.

αἰγλήεις, -εντος [αἴγλη]. Radiant, bright. Epithet of Olympus A 532, N 243: υ 103.

αἰγυπιός, -οῦ, ὁ. App. a general name for eagles and vultures. (The αἰ. preys on live birds (P 460: χ 302), but is not represented as preying on carrion. Cf. γύψ.) H 59, N 531, Π 428, P 460: π 217, χ 302.

αἰδέομαι [αἰδώς]. Imp. αἰδεῖο Ω 503: ι 269. Fut. αἰδέσσομαι ξ 388. 3 sing. αἰδέσεται X 124, Ω 208. 3 sing. aor. αἰδέσατο φ 28. 3 sing. subj. αἰδέσεται I 508. αἰδέσσεται X 419. Imp. αἴδεσσαι I 640. 3 pl. aor. αἴδεσθεν H 93. Imp. pl. αἰδέσθητε β 65. Pple. αἰδεσθείς Δ 402, P 95. From αἰδ- 3 sing. aor. αἴδετο Φ 468: ζ 66, 329, θ 86. Imp. αἴδεο Φ 74, X 82: χ 312, 344. Pple. αἰδόμενος, -η A 331, E 531, K 237, O 563: γ 96, δ 326, π 75, τ 527. (1) To hold in reverence or honour, pay due respect to, stand in awe of, regard, fear: ἱερῆα A 23=377, βασιλῆα A 331. Cf. Δ 402, I 508, 640, Φ 74, X 82, 124, 419, Ω 208, 503: πατροκασίγνητον ζ 329. Cf. ι 269, ξ 388, π 75=τ 527, ρ 188, φ 28, χ 312=344.—Absol. K 237.—(2) To be restrained by reverence, dread or respect from *doing something*. With infin.: συλεύειν Ἀχιλῆα Ω 435. Cf. Φ 468: ξ 146, υ 343.—(3) To be moved by regard for the feelings of, spare γ 96=δ 326.—(4) To be moved by respect for the opinion of, fear what . . . may think or say: ἀλλήλους E 530=O 562. Cf. Z 442=X 105: β 65, θ 86.—Absol. E 531, O 563, P 95.—(5) To be ashamed, think shame, not to like, *to do something*. With infin.: ἀνήνασθαι H 93. Cf. Ω 90: ζ 66, 221.—Absol. σ 184.—To be shamefaced ρ 578.

ἀΐδηλος, -ον [ἀ-[1] + (F)ιδ-, εἴδω. 'Making unseen']. Destroying, working destruction or harm, baneful B 455, E 880, 897, I 436, Λ 155: θ 309, π 29, χ 165, ψ 303.

ἀϊδήλως [adv. fr. prec.]. In destructive wise, ruthlessly: κτείνεις Φ 220.

αἰδοῖος, -η, -ον [αἰδώς]. (1) Worthy to be held in reverence or honour, having a special claim to one's regard: ἑκυρός Γ 172, βασιλῆος Δ 402. Cf. B 514, Z 250, K 114, Λ 649, Ξ 210, Σ 386=425, Σ 394, Φ 75, 460, 479, X 451: παρακοίτι γ 381, ἱκέτῃσιν η 165=181. Cf. α 139=δ 55=η 175=κ 371=ο 138=ρ 94=259, γ 451, ε 88, 447, θ 22, 420, 544, ι 271, κ 11, ξ 234, ρ 152=τ 165=262=336=583, σ 314, τ 191, 254, 316.—Absol. in pl., those who have a special claim to one's regard: αἰδοίοισιν ἔδωκα ο 373.—In comp.: αἰδοιότερος πᾶσιν λ 360.—(2) In neut. pl., the private parts: αἰδοίων τε μεσηγὺ καὶ ὀμφαλοῦ N 568.—(3) Shamefaced, bashful, shy: ἀλήτης ρ 578.

αἰδοίως [adv. fr. prec.]. With due respect and regard: ἀπόπεμπον τ 243.

αἰδόμενος, aor. pple. See αἰδέομαι.

Ἄϊδόσδε [-δε (1)]. To (the house or realm) of Hades H 330, Π 856=X 362, Υ 294, Ψ 137: γ 410=ζ 11, κ 560, λ 65, 475.

ἀϊδρείη, -ης, ἡ [ἄϊδρις]. (1) Ignorance. In pl.: ἀϊδρείῃσι νόοιο λ 272.—(2) Lack of experience, heedlessness μ 41.—In pl. κ 231=257.

ἄϊδρις (ἄFιδρις) [ἀ-[1] + (F)ιδ-, εἴδω]. Ignorant, unintelligent Γ 219.—Ignorant of. With genit. κ 282.

αἰδώς, -οῦς, ἡ. (1) Reverence, respect, regard: αἰδοῖ εἴκων K 238. Cf. Ω 111: θ 480, ξ 505.—(2) Sensitiveness to the opinion of others, fear of what others may think or say, shame: ἐν φρεσὶ θέσθ' αἰδῶ N 122. Cf. O 129, 561=661, O 657, Ω 44: υ 171.—As exclam. (=ἐν φρεσὶ θέσθ' αἰδῶ): αἰ., Ἀργεῖοι E 787=Θ 228. Cf. N 95, O 502, Π 422.—(3) Something to be ashamed of P 336: γ 24.—The private parts: τά τ' αἰδῶ ἀμφικαλύπτει B 262. Cf. X 75.—(4) Modesty θ 172.—Sense of propriety, delicacy θ 324.—Shamefacedness, bashfulness γ 14, ρ 347, 352.

αἰεί [cf. ἀεί, αἰέν]. Always, ever, for ever, continually, constantly, without omission or intermission: πυραὶ καίοντο A 52, νεικεῖ με 520. Cf. A 561, B 46, 88, Γ 408, etc.: θέλγει α 56, κῆρ μοι τείρει 341. Cf. δ 353, ε 10, η 201, ι 513, etc.

αἰειγενέτης, -ου [αἰεί + γεν-, γίγνομαι]. Having being for ever, immortal. Epithet of the gods

Β 400, Γ 296, Ζ 527, Η 53, Ξ 244, 333, Π 93, Υ 104 : β 432, ξ 446, ψ 81, ω 373.

αἰέν [cf. αἰεί, ἀεί]=αἰεί Α 290, Γ 272, Ε 605, Ζ 208, Θ 361, Ι 451, etc. : α 68, β 22, δ 108, ζ 156, κ 464, ξ 21, etc.

αἰετός, -οῦ, ὁ. An eagle Θ 247=Ω 315, Μ 201=219, Ν 822, Ο 690, Ρ 674, Φ 252, Χ 308 : β 146, ο 161, τ 538, 543, υ 243, ω 538.—Joined with ὄρνις τ 548.

αἰζήϊος=αἰζηός : ἀνήρ Ρ 520 : μ 83.

ἀΐζηλος [phonetically=ἀΐδηλος]. In pass. sense, removed from sight, invisible : δράκοντ' ἀΐζηλον θῆκεν Β 318 (*v.l.* ἀρίζηλον).

αἰζηός. In full bodily strength, lusty, vigorous Π 716, Ψ 432.—Absol. in pl., such men, young men : διοτρεφέων αἰζηῶν Β 660. Cf. Γ 26, Δ 280, Ε 92, Θ 298, Κ 259, Λ 414, Ξ 4, Ο 66, 315, Ρ 282, Σ 581, Υ 167, Φ 146, 301 : μ 440.

αἴητος [sense unknown]. Of Hephaestus Σ 410.

αἰθαλόεις, -όεσσα, -όεν. (**1**) Blackened by smoke (failing to escape by the smoke-hole) Β 415 : χ 239.—(**2**) Of ashes, blackened by fire, dark Σ 23=ω 316.

αἴθε [cf. εἴθε]. Expressing a wish. (**1**) With opt.: αἰ. θεοῖσι φίλος γένοιτο Χ 41. Cf. Δ 178 : αἰ. τελευτήσειεν η 331. Cf. ξ 440=ο 341, ρ 494, σ 202, υ 61.—Of the present : αἰ. τόσον σέο φέρτερος εἴην (would that I were . . .) Π 722.—(**2**) With ὤφελλον, ὤφελον, ὄφελον. See ὀφέλλω[1] (4).

αἰθήρ, -έρος, ἡ. (**1**) The upper air, in which the clouds float and the meteorological phenomena take place : ἐν αἰθέρι καὶ νεφέλῃσιν Ο 20. Cf. Θ 556, 558=Π 300, Λ 54, Ο 686, Π 365, Σ 207, 214, Τ 379 : οὖρον ἐπαιγίζοντα δι' αἰθέρος ο 293. Cf. τ 540.—Regarded as the home and realm of Zeus : αἰθέρι ναίων Β 412. Cf. Δ 166, Ν 837, Ξ 258, Ο 192, 610 : ο 523.—As the way to or from heaven : αἴγλη δι' αἰθέρος οὐρανὸν ἷκεν Β 458. Cf. Ρ 425, Τ 351 : ἐξ αἰθέρος ἔμπεσε πόντῳ ε 50 (on the way from Olympus).—(**2**) Clear air as opposed to mist (ἀήρ) : ἐλάτη δι' ἠέρος αἰθέρ' ἵκανεν Ξ 288, πολέμιζον ὑπ' αἰθέρι Ρ 371 (cf. 368).

αἴθουσα, -ης, ἡ. (**1**) A portico or covered colonnade running round the αὐλή Ζ 243, Υ 11 (in the palace of Zeus), Ω 238 : θ 57, υ 176, 189, φ 390, χ 449.—Used as a sleeping-place for visitors : δέμνι' ὑπ' αἰθούσῃ θέμεναι Ω 644 (for Priam and the herald in the dwelling of Achilles) : =δ 297 (for Telemachus and Peisistratus in the house of Menelaus)=η 336 (for Odysseus in the palace of Alcinous), ἐν λεχέεσσι ὑπ' αἰθούσῃ γ 399 (of Telemachus in the house of Nestor)=η 345 (of Odysseus in the palace of Alcinous).—(**2**) A portico across the gateway of the αὐλή : ὑπ' αἰθούσῃ αὐλῆς Ι 472. Cf. Ω 323 : γ 493=ο 146=191.—αἰθούσης θύρας, the gate of the αὐλή σ 102 (named thus from the portico across it).

αἶθοψ, -οπος [αἴθω + ὀπ-. See ὁράω]. Epithet of οἶνος, bright, sparkling Α 462, Δ 259, Ε 341, Ζ 266, Λ 775, Ξ 5, Π 226, 230, Ψ 237, 250=Ω 791, Ω 641 : β 57=ρ 536, γ 459, η 295, ι 360, μ 19, ν 8, ξ 447, ο 500, π 14, τ 197, ω 364.—Of χαλκός, bright, flashing, gleaming Δ 495=Ε 562=681=Ρ 3=87=592=Υ 111, Ν 305, Σ 522, Υ 117 : φ 434.—Of καπνός, fire-lit (*i.e.* reflecting the light of the flame below) κ 152.

αἴθρη, -ης, ἡ [αἰθήρ]. Clear sky Ρ 646 : ζ 44, μ 75.

αἰθρηγενέτης [αἴθρη + γεν-, γίγνομαι]. Born in the upper air : Βορέης ε 296.

αἰθρηγενής=prec. : Βορέαο Ο 171, Τ 358.

αἶθρος, ὁ. App., exposure to cold air ξ 318.

αἴθυια, -ης, ἡ. Some kind of diving sea-bird : αἰθυίῃ ἐϊκυῖα ε 337, 353.

αἴθω. To set on fire, kindle. In pple. pass., burning, blazing : πυρὸς αἰθομένοιο Ζ 182. Cf. Θ 563, Κ 246, Λ 596=Ν 673=Σ 1, Λ 775, Ν 320, Ξ 396, Π 81, 293, Φ 523, Χ 135, 150 : αἰθομένας δαΐδας α 428. Cf. α 434, η 101, λ 220, μ 362, σ 343, τ 39, υ 25.

αἴθων, -ωνος [αἴθω]. (**1**) Epithet of metals and of objects made of metal, bright, shining, gleaming : σιδήρῳ Δ 485, Η 473, Υ 372, λέβητας Ι 123=265=Τ 244, τρίποδας Ω 233 : σίδηρον α 184.—(**2**) Epithet of the lion, tawny Κ 24=178, Λ 548, Σ 161.—So of oxen Π 488 : σ 372.—Of the eagle Ο 690.—(**3**) Of horses, app., sorrel or brown Β 839=Μ 97.

ἀϊκή, -ῆς, ἡ [ἀϊκ-, ἀΐσσω]. Flight, rush : τόξων Ο 709.

ἀϊκῶς [adv., with weak stem, of ἀεικής]. In unseemly wise : σὲ κύνες ἑλκήσουσ' ἀ. Χ 336.

αἷμα, -ατος, τό. (**1**) Blood : ἔρρεεν αἷμα Δ 140, μεθ' αἵματι (*i.e.* the bloody corpses) Ο 118. Cf. Α 303, Ε 100, Κ 298, Χ 70, Ψ 697, etc. : πεφυρμένον αἵματι ι 397. Cf. λ 96, 420, ν 395, σ 97, χ 19, etc.—(**2**) Race, stock : [τούτου] αἵματος εὔχομαι εἶναι Ζ 211=Υ 241. Cf. δ 611, π 300.—Blood relations collectively : κήδιστοι μεθ' αἷμα θ 583.—In genit., by blood : οἵ θ' αἵματος ἐξ ἐμεῦ εἰσίν Τ 105, οἱ σῆς ἐξ αἵματός εἰσι γενέθλης 111.

αἱμασιή, -ῆς, ἡ. A wall, app. of stones without mortar : αἱμασιὰς λέγων (λέξοντες) (*i.e.* the materials for them) σ 359, ω 224.

αἱματόεις, -όεσσα, -όεν [αἱματ-, αἷμα]. (**1**) (**a**) Covered or mingled with blood, blood-stained, bloody Ε 82, Ν 393=Π 486, Ν 617, 640, Π 841, Ρ 298, 542, Χ 369 : χ 405.—(**b**) As epithet of βρότος Η 425, Ξ 7, Σ 345, Ψ 41.—(**c**) Fig. : ἤματα Ι 326, πολέμοιο 650, πολέμου Τ 313.—(**2**) Of the colour of blood Β 267, Π 459.

αἱμοφόρυκτος [αἷμα + φορυκ-, φορύσσω]. Bedabbled with blood, exuding blood : κρέα υ 348.

αἱμύλιος. Wheedling : λόγοισιν α 56.

αἵμων, -ονος. App., wily or skilled (in something). With genit. : θήρης Ε 49.

αἰναρέτης [αἰνός + ἀρετή]. Voc. αἰναρέτη (*v.l.* αἰναρέτα). Cursed in one's valour Π 31.

αἰνέω [αἶνος]. (ἐπ-.) (**1**) To praise, commend Κ 249, Ψ 552, Ω 30.—(**2**) Absol., to approve, assent, concur : ἐπὶ δ' ᾔνεον ἄλλοι Γ 461. Cf. Θ 9 : μ 294=352, π 380 (*i.e.* will resent), 403, σ 64.

αἰνίζομαι [as prec.]. To compliment N 374 : θ 487.

αἰνόθεν [αἰνός]. Strengthening αἰνῶς by reduplication H 97. (The form has not been explained. Cf. οἰόθεν οἶος, μέγας μεγαλωστί.)

αἰνόμορος, -ον [αἰνός + μόρος]. Doomed to an evil fate X 481 : ι 53, ω 169.

αἰνοπαθής [αἰνός + παθ-, πάσχω]. Suffering dire ills σ 201.

αἶνος, -ου, ὁ. (1) Praise, commendation, compliment Ψ 795 : φ 110.—(2) A discourse or tale Ψ 652 : ξ 508.

αἰνός, -ή, -όν. (1) Dread, dire, terrible, grim Γ 20, Δ 15, E 886, P 565, Σ 465, etc. : κ 219, λ 516, μ 257, τ 568, χ 229, ω 475.—In comp. : οὐκ αἰνότερον ἄλλο γυναικός λ 427.—In superl. : στείνει ἐν αἰνοτάτῳ Θ 476. Cf. Ξ 389 : δ 441, θ 519, μ 275.—Absol. in neut. pl. : αἰνὰ παθοῦσα X 431.—In neut. pl. as adv., miserably, calamitously : τεκοῦσα A 414. Cf. π 255.—(2) Of persons. In superl., most dread : αἰνότατε Κρονίδη A 552 = Δ 25 = Θ 462 = Ξ 330 = Π 440 = Σ 361. — Beyond endurance, unbearable Θ 423.—(3) Of feelings, etc., extreme, sore, overwhelming : ἄχος Δ 169. Cf. H 215, Θ 449, K 312, X 94, etc. : κάματος ε 457. Cf. ο 342, π 87, σ 274.—In neut. pl. αἰνά as adv., grievously, bitterly : ὀλοφυρόμεναι χ 447. — In neut. superl. αἰνότατον as adv., very grievously or sorely : περιδείδια N 52.

αἴνυμαι. (ἀπο-, ἐξ-, συν-.) (1) To take hold of χ 500.—Of a feeling : πόθος μ' αἴνυται ξ 144.—(2) To take for one's use, take into one's hands : ὀϊστόν O 459 : τυρῶν (partitive genit.) ι 225, 232. Cf. ι 249, φ 53.—(3) To take away, remove, deprive of Δ 531, Λ 374, 580, N 550, Φ 490.—(4) To take, select, pick out : σύντρεις ι 429.

αἰνῶς [adv. fr. αἰνός]. (1) To such a degree as to cause apprehension χ 136.—(2) In reference to feelings, etc., in an extreme degree, strongly, sorely, deeply, heartily : δείδοικα A 555. Cf. E 352, Z 441, Θ 397, I 244, K 38, 93, 538, N 165, 481, Σ 261, T 23, Υ 29, X 454, Ω 358 : φιλέεσκεν α 264. Cf. β 327, δ 441, 597, ζ 168, ι 353, σ 80, τ 324, ω 353.—Sim. λώβη τάδε γ' ἔσσεται αἰ. (will be a sore . . .) H 97, αἰ. με μένος ἄνωγεν Ω 198.—(3) In reference to resemblance, strangely, strikingly : αἰ. θεῇς ἔοικεν Γ 158. Cf. K 547 : α 208.—(4) As a gen. intensive, in a high degree, of a surety : μοχλὸς διεφαίνετο ι 379, τάδε εἵματ' ἔχω κακά ρ 24.

αἴξ, αἰγός, ὁ, ἡ. A goat : ταύρων ἠδ' αἰγῶν A 41, ἰξάλου αἰγὸς ἀγρίου (*i.e.* of goat's horn) Δ 105. Cf. B 474, Γ 24, I 207, K 486, N 198, etc. : β 56, ι 118, ξ 101, ρ 213, 247, σ 44, etc.

ἀΐξας, aor. pple. ἀΐσσω.

αἰόλλω [αἰόλος]. To shift rapidly to and fro υ 27.

αἰολοθώρηξ [αἰόλος + θώρηξ]. With glancing θώρηξ Δ 489, Π 173.

αἰολομίτρης [αἰόλος + μίτρη]. With glancing μίτρη E 707.

αἰολόπωλος [αἰόλος + πῶλος]. Having nimble horses Γ 185.

αἰόλος, -η, -ον. (1) Glancing, gleaming, flashing E 295, H 222, Π 107.—(2) The notion of glancing light passing into that of rapid movement. (Cf. ἀργός (2).) Of wasps : σφῆκες μέσον αἰόλοι (flexible about the middle) M 167.—Of a serpent and worms, wriggling M 208 (or this might come under (1), 'glistening'), X 509.—Of the gadfly, darting χ 300.—Of the rapid motion of a horse's feet : πόδας αἰόλος ἵππος T 404.

αἰπεινός, -ή, -όν [αἰπύς]. (1) Steep, sheer : Μυκάλης κάρηνα B 869. Cf. Υ 58 : ζ 123.—Rocky, rugged : Καλυδῶνι N 217, Ξ 116.—(2) Of cities, set on a steep B 573, Z 35, I 419 = 686, N 773, O 215, 257, 558, P 328.

αἰπήεις, -εσσα [as prec.]. = prec. (2) Φ 87.

αἰπόλιον, τό [αἰπόλος]. A herd of goats B 474, Λ 679 : ξ 101, 103, ρ 213 = υ 174, φ 266.

αἰπόλος, -ου, ὁ [app. for αἰγιπόλος, fr. αἰγ-, αἴξ + -πολος, conn. with πολεύω]. A goatherd B 474, Δ 275 : ρ 247 = χ 135, ρ 369, υ 173, φ 175, 265, χ 142, 161, 182.

αἰπός, -ή, -όν [cf. next]. (1) Falling steeply down, flowing fast Θ 369, Φ 9.—(2) Of cities, set on a steep N 625 : γ 130 = ν 316, θ 516, λ 533.

αἰπύς, -εῖα, -ύ. (1) Steep, sheer : ὄρος B 603. Cf. B 811, 829, E 367, 868, Λ 711, O 84 : αἰπεῖα εἰς ἅλα πέτρη (running sheer down into the sea) γ 293. Cf. γ 287, δ 514, τ 431. —Applied to walls Z 327, Λ 181 : ξ 472.—Of a noose, hung from on high λ 278.—(2) Of cities, set on a steep B 538, I 668, O 71 : γ 485, κ 81, ο 193.—(3) Fig., difficult, hard. In impers. construction : αἰπύ οἱ ἐσσεῖται N 317.—Of ὄλεθρος (thought of as a precipice or gulf), sheer, utter Z 57, K 371, Λ 174, 441, M 345, 358, N 773, Ξ 99, 507 = Π 283, Π 859, P 155, 244, Σ 129 : α 11, 37, ε 305, ι 286, 303, μ 287, 446, ρ 47, χ 28, 43, 67.—Sim. of φόνος P 365 : δ 843, π 379.—Of the toil and moil of war, hard, daunting Λ 601, Π 651.—Of wrath, towering O 223.

αἱρέω, 3 sing. fut. αἱρήσει Φ 555, Ω 206. 2 pl. αἱρήσομεν B 141, 329, I 28. Infin. αἱρησέμεν P 488, Σ 260. αἱρήσειν B 37, N 42. Aor. εἷλον, -ες Γ 35, Δ 406, E 47, Θ 77, K 561, Φ 77, X 17, etc. : θ 330, ι 416, τ 155, φ 299, ω 377, etc. ἕλον, -ες A 197, Δ 457, E 127, Z 35, H 8, I 271, Λ 738, Π 351, P 276, etc. : α 121, β 81, γ 37, θ 106, ο 496, χ 187, etc. Subj. ἕλω, -ῃς B 228, 332, Δ 239, 416, H 71, 81, Π 128, 725. 3 sing. ἕλῃσι Ψ 345 : μ 96, ρ 323, τ 515. ἕλῃ H 77, Λ 315, etc. : φ 294. Opt. ἕλοιμι, -οις B 12, 29, 66, I 304, K 206, 345, Λ 509, O 71, etc. : δ 463, 596, τ 511. Imp. ἕλε Ξ 272. 3 sing. ἑλέτω υ 52. Pple. ἑλών, -οῦσα A 139, 501, Γ 316, Θ 13, etc. : α 318, δ 750, θ 436, ι 165, etc. Infin. ἑλέειν O 558, X 142 : λ 205, 206, 210, 426. ἑλεῖν E 118, Θ 319, O 720. Pa. iterative ἕλεσκον ξ 220. 3 sing. ἕλεσκε Ω 752 : θ 88. **Mid.** Nom. pl. pres. pple. αἱρεύμενοι Π 353. Fut. αἱρήσομαι β 357. 2 sing. αἱρήσεαι K 235. Aor. ἑλόμην E 210, Θ 108, T 60. 2 sing. εἵλευ P 206. 3 εἵλετο B 46, Γ 294, Z 472, I 344, etc. : α 99, ε 47, ζ 140, κ 363, etc. ἕλετο Δ 116, I 368, Λ 32, M 102, etc. :

δ 746, ε 121, μ 246, ξ 530. 1 pl. εἰλόμεθα ι 157, λ 21. ἑλόμεσθα Λ 730. 3 εἵλοντο Η 380, Σ 314: ζ 97. ἕλοντο Β 399, Η 122, Θ 53, Π 663, etc.: δ 786, ζ 91, θ 372, ι 86, etc. Subj. ἕλωμαι Α 137, Ρ 17, etc. 3 sing. ἕληται Μ 150, Π 650, etc.: μ 123. 3 pl. ἕλωνται Π 82, 545. Opt. ἑλοίμην, -οιο Β 127, Γ 66, Ε 317, Π 655, etc.: ξ 297, 405, π 149, 297, ρ 236, υ 62, χ 462, ω 334. 3 pl. ἑλοίατο υ 117. Imp. ἕλευ Ν 294. 3 sing. ἑλέσθω Ι 139, 391: σ 47. 2 pl. ἕλεσθε Ε 529, Η 370, Σ 298. Infin. ἑλέσθαι Ε 852, Ι 578, Ν 268, etc.: θ 68, ι 334, λ 584, etc. (ἀν-, ἀποπρο-, ἀφ-, ἐξ-, ἐξαφ-, καθ-, μεθ-, συν-.) (I) In act. (1) To take, take hold of, grasp, seize: ἡνία Θ 319, γαῖαν Λ 425. Cf. Ε 75, 353, Λ 749, Ξ 137, Φ 242, Ω 227, etc.: χεῖρα α 121. Cf. η 252, λ 205, χ 269, etc.—With genit. of a part grasped: κόμης Πηλεΐωνα (by the . . .) Α 197. Cf. Α 323, Η 108, Τ 126, Φ 71, etc.: χειρὸς Ὀδυσῆα η 168. Cf. μ 33, ρ 263, etc.—Sim. ἕλκε δουρὸς ἑλών Π 406.—With quasi-partitive genit.: μέσσου δουρὸς ἑλών Γ 78 = Η 56.—(2) Of feelings, bodily or mental states, or the like, to take hold of, come to or upon, seize, affect: μή σε λήθη αἱρείτω Β 34, χόλος μιν ᾕρει Δ 23. Cf. Γ 446, Δ 421, Ε 136, 862, Ν 581, Π 805, etc.: οἶκτος β 81, θάμβος γ 372. Cf. δ 596, θ 304, λ 43, φ 122, χ 500, etc.—Of the darkness of death Ε 47, Ν 672 = Π 607.—Of sleep Κ 193, Χ 502, Ω 5: ι 373, τ 511, υ 52.—(3) To take, capture, seize upon: ἑλὼν ἔχει γέρας Α 356, εἴ σ' αἱρήσει (get you in his power) Ω 206. Cf. Ζ 38, Κ 206, 345, Λ 315, Ρ 488, Φ 77, etc.: ἐπαΐξανθ' ἑλέτην χ 187. Cf. δ 463, μ 96, π 369.—To come upon, catch: με τ 155.—To catch up, overtake Ψ 345: θ 330.—To take (a town): πόλιν Τρώων Β 12. Cf. Β 37, 141, Δ 406, Ι 129, Π 153, etc.: ι 165, ω 377.—To take as prey: πέλειαν Χ 142.—Of Scylla μ 310.—(4) To kill, slay: ἄνδρα κορυστήν Δ 457. Cf. Ε 37, Ι 304, Κ 561, Λ 92, Ο 328, Υ 382, Φ 327, Χ 253, etc.: ξ 220, π 383.—(5) To take away, remove: ἔγχος ἀπὸ χειρός Ο 126. Cf. Β 154, Ε 127, etc.: θ 88, τ 61, φ 56, etc.—(6) To take for use or for some purpose, take into the hands: σῖτον Ι 216, σάκος Ξ 9. Cf. Ι 656, Κ 335, Ο 474, Σ 416, Ψ 839, Ω 93, etc.: τρίαιναν δ 506, ἐπὶ πήχει ἑλών (taking it and placing it on the . . .) φ 419. Cf. α 318, δ 750, θ 89, κ 145, ρ 343, τ 386, etc.—(7) To draw (a person to oneself): τὴν προτὶ οἷ εἷλεν Φ 508. Cf. ω 348.—(8) In various uses. (a) To take as one's due: λέβητα Ψ 613, βοῦν 779.—(b) To win (fame) Ρ 321.—(c) To take (wine) φ 294.—(d) Of a condition of life, to come upon (one): δούλιον ἦμαρ ρ 323.—(e) In reference to change of a person's colour: ὦχρός μιν εἷλε παρειάς Γ 35.—(f) To take up (a lay): ἔνθεν ἑλὼν [ἀοιδὴν] ὡς . . . (from the point where . . .) θ 500.—(9) With adverbs. (a) With διά, to separate, tear apart: διὰ δ' ἕλε κύκλους Υ 280.—(b) With ἐκ, to choose, select: ἐκ δ' ἕλον Χρυσηΐδα Α 369.—(c) With κατά, to lower: κὰδ δ' ἕλον ἱστόν ο 496.—To close (the eyes of the dead) λ 426.—(10) In aor. pple. with a finite vb., to take and . . . (cf. ἄγω (I) (9)): γέρας ἄξω ἑλὼν Α 139, ἑλὼν ῥίψω Θ 13. Cf. Γ 72, 316, Ζ 302, Σ 23, Τ 143, Ω 795, etc.: ξύλα δαῖον ἑλοῦσαι θ 436, δὸς ἑλών ρ 400. Cf. δ 66, θ 84, ι 382, etc.—(II) In mid. (1) To seize upon to one's own use, take away, appropriate: ἕλωμαί κε γέρας Α 137. Cf. Ι 336, Σ 445, etc.—With acc. of person deprived: τήν [μ'] ἐκ χειρῶν ἕλεθ' ὡς εἴ τινα μετανάστην Π 58.—(2) To take, capture: [Βρισηΐδα] Τ 60.—With acc. of person deprived: οὖς ἀπ' Αἰνείαν ἑλόμην Θ 108.—To take as prey: βοῶν ἐκ πῖαρ ἑλέσθαι Λ 550 = Ρ 659, [ἄρνας] αἱρεύμενοι Π 353.—Of Scylla μ 123, 246.—To carry off: Ὠρίωνα ε 121.—(3) To take away, remove: ἀπὸ κρατὸς κόρυθ' εἵλετο Ζ 472. Cf. Η 122, Κ 458, Π 663, etc.: μ 199, χ 271, etc.—In reference to life, strength, feelings, etc.: ἀπὸ μένος εἵλετο χαλκός Γ 294. Cf. Ε 317, Ι 377, Λ 381, Ρ 17, etc.: ἐκ δέος εἵλετο γυίων ζ 140. Cf. κ 363, ξ 405, etc.—Sim. in reference to one's home-coming: μὴ ἀπὸ νόστον ἕλωνται Π 82.—(4) To take for use or for some purpose, take into the hands: εἵλετο σκῆπτρον Β 46, ἐκ δ' ἕλετ' ἰόν Δ 116. Cf. Γ 338, Ζ 494, Λ 32, Ν 611, Ρ 593, Ω 343, etc.: εἵλετ' ἔγχος (ῥάβδον) (πέδιλα) α 99, ε 47, π 154. Cf. β 357, ζ 91, θ 372, ι 157, etc.—To take or carry with one: τόξον οὔ ποθ' ᾑρεῖτο φ 40.—(5) In reference to meals, to take, partake of: δεῖπνον ἕλοντο Β 399, δόρπον ἕλεσθε Η 370, etc.: δόρπον ἕλοντο δ 786, δεῖπνον εἵλοντο ζ 97, πύματον ἑλοίατο δαῖτα υ 117, etc.—In reference to drink: πιέειν οὐκ εἶχεν ἑλέσθαι λ 584.—(6) To get, obtain: ἑκὼν οὐκ ἄν τις ἕλοιτο Γ 66, οὔ πως ἅμα πάντα δυνήσεαι ἑλέσθαι Ν 729, πεῖραρ ἑλέσθαι Σ 501.—(7) To choose, select: εἴ κ' ἄνδρα ἕκαστοι ἑλοίμεθα Β 127, γυναῖκας ἐείκοσιν ἑλέσθω Ι 139. Cf. Λ 697, Μ 102, Π 282, etc.: τοὺς ἄν κε καὶ ἤθελον ἑλέσθαι ι 334. Cf. π 149, σ 47, etc.—(8) In various uses. (a) To receive, get (gifts) ω 334.—(A price) ξ 297.—(A bride-price) μυρί' ἕλοντο ο 367.—(b) To take the benefit of, take, accept: ὕπνου δῶρον ἕλοντο Η 482, Ι 713: π 481, τ 427.—(c) To agree to take, accept: ἀναίνετο μηδὲν ἑλέσθαι (refused to accept the blood-price) Σ 500.—(d) To take or exact (an oath): εἴ κε Τρωσὶν ὅρκον ἕλωμαι Χ 119. Cf. δ 746.—(e) To take (heart): ἄλκιμον ἦτορ ἕλεσθε Ε 529.

αἴροντας contr. acc. pl. masc. pple. ἀείρω.

αἶσα, -ης, ἡ. Orig. sense 'measure.' (1) αἴσῃ, in the measure of, at the value of: ἐν καρὸς αἴσῃ Ι 378.—(2) (Due) measure. (a) κατ' αἶσαν, duly, fitly, properly Γ 59 = Ζ 333, Κ 445, Ρ 716.—(b) ὑπὲρ αἶσαν, unduly, unfitly, improperly Γ 59 = Ζ 333.—Beyond measure; hence, preponderatingly: φέρτεροι ἦσαν Π 780.—(3) A share or portion: ληΐδος αἶσαν Σ 327. Cf. ε 40 = ν 138.—(4) One's portion or lot in life, one's fate or destiny: αἶσά τοι μίνυνθά περ (thy lot in life is but for a little time) Α 416, κακῇ σ' αἴσῃ τέκον (with an evil fate before thee) 418, κακῇ αἴσῃ τόξ' ἑλόμην (in an evil hour) Ε 209, ὁμῇ πεπρωμένον αἴσῃ (having his fate fixed with a like portion before him, appointed to a like portion) Ο 209, πεπρωμένον αἴσῃ (with a fate, *i.e.*

death, before him, appointed to death) Π 441 = Χ 179, οὔ τοι αἶσα πόλιν πέρθαι Π 707, ἴσῃ γιγνόμεθ' αἴσῃ (under a like fate) Χ 477, εἴ μοι αἶσα τεθνάμεναι Ω 224, ἐν θανάτοιο αἴσῃ (a lot consisting in death, i.e. death) Ω 428, 750 : κακῇ αἴσῃ οἴχετο (in an evil hour) τ 259. Cf. ε 113, 206, 288, θ 511, ν 306, ξ 359, ο 276, ψ 315.—Sim. ἔτι ἐλπίδος αἶσα ((there is) yet a portion for hope, room for hope) π 101, τ 84.—(5) Fate that comes upon or overtakes one, evil fate, doom, death : αἴσῃ ἐν ἀργαλέῃ φθίσει Χ 61. Cf. ι 52, λ 61.—(6) Fate or destiny as decreed by a god : ὑπὲρ Διὸς αἶσαν Ρ 321.—So αἶσα alone, the decrees of fate (cf. μοῖρα (7)) : ὑπὲρ αἶσαν Ζ 487.—This and (2) ((due) measure or estimation, (fitting) place in a scale of honour) app. blended : τετιμῆσθαι Διὸς αἴσῃ Ι 608.—(7) Fate personified Υ 127 : η 197.

ἀΐσθω [cf. ἄημι, ἀΐω²]. To breathe or gasp out : θυμόν Π 468, Υ 403.

αἴσιμος, -η, -ον [αἶσα]. (1) In (due) measure : ἀμείνω αἴσιμα πάντα η 310, ο 71, τίσειν αἴσιμα πάντα (all that is fitting) θ 348, ἔργα (inspired by justice) ξ 84, ταῦτ' αἴσιμα εἶπας (just, right) χ 46, φρένας αἰσίμῃ (well balanced in . . .) ψ 14.—(2) Absol. in neut. pl. αἴσιμα, what is just or right : αἰ. παρειπών Ζ 62, Η 121.—So (see εἴδω (III) (12)) ὅτ' ἄγγελος αἰ. εἰδῇ (can say the right thing) Ο 207 : αἰ. εἰδώς (having justice in his heart, just) β 231 = ε 9, αἰ. ᾔδη ξ 433.—(3) In neut. pl. as adv., in due measure φ 294.—(4) Decreed by fate, fatal : αἴσιμον ἦμαρ. See ἦμαρ (4) (a).—In neut. sing. αἴσιμον in impers. construction, (it is) fated or destined : μὴ ἡμῖν αἰ. εἴη φθίσθαι Ι 245. Cf. Ο 274, Φ 291, 495 : ο 239.

αἴσιος [αἶσα]. Showing moderation, gentle, courteous ; or perh., of good omen (cf. ἐναίσιμος (2)) : ὁδοιπόρον Ω 376.

ἀΐσσω. 3 sing. aor. ἤϊξε Δ 78, Λ 118, Ν 65, Υ 277, Φ 247, 254, Ψ 868 : ο 164. 3 pl. ἤϊξαν Ε 657 : β 154, ο 183. 3 sing. subj. ἀΐξῃ Ο 80, 580. 3 pl. ἀΐξωσι Ρ 726. Pple. ἀΐξας, -ᾶσα Β 167, Ε 81, Ζ 232, Λ 423, Μ 145, etc. : α 102, κ 117, τ 451, χ 90, 98, ω 488. 3 sing. pa. iterative ἀΐξασκε Ψ 369. Aor. infin. mid. ἀΐξασθαι Χ 195. 3 sing. aor. pass. ἠΐχθη Γ 368. 3 dual ἀϊχθήτην Ω 97. 3 pl. ἠΐχθησαν Π 404. Infin. ἀϊχθῆναι Ε 854. (ἀν-, ἀπ-, ἐπ-, μετ-, παρ-, προσ-, ὑπ-.) In all moods, to rush, fly, dart, of persons, animals, or things. (1) (a) In act. : βῆ ἀΐξασα Β 167, ἄκοντες Λ 553. Cf. Δ 78, Ε 81, 657, Ζ 232, Λ 118, Ρ 579, Ω 320, etc. : αἰετώ β 154, λικριφίς τ 451. Cf. α 102, κ 117, χ 90, etc.—(b) In mid. : ἀμφὶ δέ τ' ἀΐσσονται Λ 417, πυλάων ἀντίον ἀΐξασθαι Χ 195.—(c) In pass. : ἔγχος ἠΐχθη Γ 368, ἐτώσιον ἀϊχθῆναι Ε 854, ἐς οὐρανὸν ἀϊχθήτην Ω 97.—(2) In various shades of meaning. (a) In act., to rise to speak Σ 506 (the notion of quickness not here to be pressed).—Of disembodied spirits, to flit about κ 495.—Of the mind, to be projected in thought Ο 80.—Of chariots, to be tossed (into the air) Ψ 369.—Of light, to stream Σ 212.—Of smoke, to rise into the air κ 99.—(b) In mid., of a horse's mane, to stream Ζ 510 = Ο 267.—(c) In pass., of reins, to slip (from the hands) Π 404.

ἄϊστος [ἀ-¹ + ἰστ-, εἴδω. 'Unseen']. (1) Gone, vanished α 235, 242.—(2) Sent to destruction Ξ 258.

ἀϊστόω [ἄϊστος]. To cause to vanish or disappear υ 79.—In pass., to vanish, disappear κ 259.

αἴσυλος [prob. contr. fr. ἀ(Ϝ)ίσυλος, ἀήσυλος]. Absol. in neut. pl. αἴσυλα, what is unjust, unseemly, or evil : αἰ. ῥέζων Ε 403. Cf. Υ 202 = 433, Φ 214 : β 232 = ε 10.

αἰσυμνητήρ, -ῆρος, ὁ [app. αἶσα + μνη-, μνάομαι. 'One who is mindful of justice']. A prince Ω 347.

αἰσυμνήτης, -ου, ὁ [as prec.]. In pl., stewards of games θ 258.

αἴσχιστος [superl. fr. αἰσχ-ρός]. The most ill-favoured or ugly : ἀνήρ Β 216.

αἰσχίων, -ιον [comp. as prec.]. Shameful (as contrasted with seemly) Φ 437.

αἶσχος, τό. (1) Shame, disgrace λ 433.—A cause or occasion of shame or disgrace σ 225.—In pl., shameful deeds : αἴσχεα πόλλ' ὁρόων α 229.—(2) Insult : αἴσχεος οὐκ ἐπιδευεῖς Ν 622.—In pl., insults, reproaches Γ 242, Ζ 351, 524 : τ 373.

αἰσχρός [αἶσχος]. (1) Absol. in neut. αἰσχρόν, a shame, a disgrace Β 119, 298.—(2) Of words, insulting, reproachful Γ 38 = Ζ 325, Ν 768, Ω 238.

αἰσχρῶς [adv. fr. prec.]. With insult or reproach : ἐνένιπεν Ψ 473 : σ 321.

αἰσχύνω [αἶσχος]. 2 sing. aor. ᾔσχῦνας Ψ 571. 3 -ε Σ 24, 27 : θ 269. Pf. pple. pass. ᾐσχυμμένος Σ 180. (κατ-.) (1) To disfigure, mar, spoil the beauty of Σ 24, 27.—To mar, mutilate Σ 180, Χ 75, Ω 418.—To defile (the marriage-bed) θ 269.—(2) To bring shame upon, act unworthily of : γένος πατέρων Ζ 209.—To put to shame, discredit : ἐμὴν ἀρετήν Ψ 571.—To throw blame upon β 86.—(3) In pass., to feel shame, hesitate : δείσας αἰσχυνόμενός τε η 305. Cf. σ 12.—To feel shame at the prospect of, hesitate to incur : αἰσχυνόμενοι φάτιν ἀνδρῶν φ 323.

αἰτέω. (ἐπ-.) To ask for, request : ἵππους Ε 358. Cf. Ν 365, Ω 292 : κ 17, υ 74.—With acc. of the person from whom something is asked : ᾔτεέ με δεύτερον ι 354, αἰτήσων φῶτα ἕκαστον (to ask alms from . . .) ρ 365.—With infin., to ask *to* . . . : σῆμα ἰδέσθαι Ζ 176.—With acc. and infin. : ᾐτέομεν θεὸν φῆναι τέρας γ 173.—With double acc. of person and thing : ᾔτεέ μιν δόρυ Χ 295. Cf. β 387, ω 85, 337.—Absol., to ask alms σ 49.

†αἰτιάομαι [αἴτιος]. 3 pl. αἰτιόωνται α 32. 2 sing. opt. αἰτιόῳο υ 135. 3 αἰτιόῳτο Λ 654. Infin. αἰτιάασθαι Κ 120, Ν 775. 2 pl. impf. ᾐτιάασθε Π 202. 3 ᾐτιόωντο Λ 78. To blame Κ 120, Λ 78, 654, Ν 775, Π 202 : α 32, υ 135.

αἰτίζω [αἰτέω]. (ἀπ-.) (1) To ask for, collect : κειμήλια τ 273.—Absol., to make a request δ 651.—(2) To ask as alms : ἀκόλους ρ 222, σῖτον 558.—To ask alms from ρ 346 = 351, 502, υ 179.—Absol., to ask alms ρ 228, υ 182.

αἴτιος, -η. Blameworthy, to blame : οὔ τί μοι αἴτιοί εἰσιν Α 153. Cf. Γ 164, Ν 111, 222, Ο 137,

Τ 86, 410, Φ 275, 370 : οὐκ ἀοιδοὶ αἴτιοι, ἀλλὰ Ζεὺς αἴτιος α 348. Cf. β 87, θ 311, λ 559, χ 155.—With genit. : αἰ. πάντων (for everything) χ 48.

ἀϊχθήτην, 3 dual aor. pass. ἀΐσσω.

†αἰχμάζω [αἰχμή]. 3 pl. fut. αἰχμάσσουσι. To throw (the spear) : αἰχμὰς αἰχμάσσουσιν Δ 324.

αἰχμή, -ῆς, ἡ. (1) The point of a spear : ἀνεγνάμφθη οἱ αἰ. Γ 348. Cf. Δ 461, Ε 293, 658, Λ 237, Π 115, Ρ 600, Υ 416, etc.—(2) A spear : αἰχμὰς αἰχμάσσουσιν Δ 324, εὐήκεος Χ 319. Cf. Μ 45, Ν 504=Π 614, Ν 562, Ξ 423.—(3) Spearmanship, the spear : αἰχμῆς εὖ εἰδώς Ο 525.

αἰχμητής, -οῦ, ὁ [αἰχμάζω]. Also **αἰχμητά** Ε 197 (prob. orig. a voc. turned into a nom.). (1) A spearman as opposed to warriors otherwise armed: Ἄβαντες ἕποντο, αἰχμηταί Β 543.—(2) In gen., a warrior Α 152, Β 846, Γ 179, Δ 87, Ζ 97=278, Θ 33=464, 472, Μ 419, Ρ 588, 740 : λ 559, ω 81.—(3) With implied notion of stoutness or skill : αἰχμητὴν ἔθεσαν θεοί Α 290. Cf. Γ 49, Ε 197, 602=Π 493=Χ 269, Ε 706, Η 281, Λ 739, Μ 128, Ν 171 : χεῖρας αἰχμητὴν ἔμεναι καὶ ἐπίφρονα βουλήν (in strength of hands and wise counsel) π 242. Cf. β 19.

αἶψα. Straightway, forthwith, at once, quickly, soon : αἰ. μάλ' ἐλθέ Δ 70. Cf. Α 303, Β 664, Ε 242, Ζ 370, Θ 127, Μ 369, Ρ 116, etc. : αἰ. δεῖπνον ἕλοντο ι 86. Cf. α 392, β 292, δ 283, ο 193, π 359, etc.

αἰψηρός, -ή [αἶψα]. Quick : ἀγορήν (quick to disperse) Τ 276 : =β 257, αἰψηρὸς κόρος γόοιο (soon comes on one) δ 103.

ἀΐω[1]. 3 sing. impf. ἄϊε Κ 532, Φ 388. ἄϊε Λ 463. 3 pl. ἄϊον Σ 222. (1) To perceive, feel. With genit. : πληγῆς Λ 532.—(2) To perceive, see : οὐκ ἀΐεις ὅτι . . . ; σ 11.—(3) (a) To hear : ἄϊε Ζεύς Φ 388. Cf. Ψ 430 : κ 118, ω 415.—(b) With acc. of what is heard : κτύπον Κ 532. Cf. Ο 130, Σ 222. —(c) With genit. : φθογγῆς Π 508. Cf. Κ 189, Ο 378, Ψ 199 : βοῆς ι 401. Cf. ξ 266=ρ 435, ω 48. —(d) With genit. of person heard : ἰάχοντος Λ 463.—(4) To have seen or heard, have learned, know (cf. ἀκούω (5)) : οὐκ ἀΐεις ὡς . . . ; Κ 160. Cf. Ο 248 : α 298.

†ἀΐω[2] [cf. ἄημι]. Impf. ἄϊον. To breathe out Ο 252.

αἰών, -ῶνος, ὁ. Fem. Χ 58. (1) One's lifetime, one's life : μινυνθάδιος αἰ. ἔπλετο Δ 478=Ρ 302. Cf. Ι 415 : ε 152.—(2) Life, the state of being in life : ἀπ' αἰῶνος ὤλεο Ω 725.—(3) The animating principle, the vital spirit, the soul, the life, life, one's life (cf. θυμός (I) (1) (b)) : λίποι μ' αἰ. Ε 685. Cf. Π 453, Τ 27, Χ 58 : αἰῶνος εὔνιν ι 523. Cf. ε 160, η 224, σ 204.

ἀκάκητα [sense unknown. Traditionally explained as fr. ἀ-[1] + κακός, 'the guileless,' or fr. ἀκέομαι, 'the healer']. (Prob. orig. a voc. turned into a nom.) Epithet of Hermes Π 185 : ω 10.

ἀκαλαρρείτης [ἀκαλά, neut. pl. of ἀκαλός, cited in sense 'peaceful,' 'still' (cf. ἀκήν) + (σ)ρέω]. Silently or gently flowing. Epithet of Ocean Η 422 : τ 434.

ἀκάμας, -αντος [ἀ-[1] + καμ-, κάμνω]. Tireless. Of a river, ever-flowing, always full : Π 176.—Of a boar, untiring, steady in fight Π 823.—Of the sun, regular in his course Σ 239, 484.

ἀκάματος [as prec.]. Tireless. Epithet of fire, steadily or fiercely blazing Ε 4, Ο 598, 731, Π 122, Σ 225, Φ 13, 341, Ψ 52 : υ 123, φ 181.

ἄκανθα, -ης, ἡ. In pl., thistle-down ε 328.

†ἀκαχέω [redup. fr. ἀχέω]. 3 sing. aor. ἀκάχησε Ψ 223. Pf. pass. ἀκάχημαι θ 314, τ 95. 3 sing. ἀκάχηται ψ 360. 3 pl. ἀκηχέδαται Ρ 637. 3 pl. plupf. ἀκαχήατο Μ 179. Pple. ἀκαχήμενος, -ου Ε 24, Λ 702, Τ 312, Ω 550 : ι 62, 105, 565, κ 77, 133, 313, ν 286, ο 481, υ 84. Fem. ἀκηχεμένη Ε 364. Pl. ἀκηχέμεναι Σ 29. Infin. ἀκάχησθαι Τ 335 : δ 806. (1) To cause grief to, grieve : ἀκάχησε τοκῆας Ψ 223.—(2) In pass., to be grieved, troubled, or borne down, to grieve or sorrow : ὡς μὴ ἀκαχήμενος εἴη Ε 24, θεοὶ ἀκαχήατο Μ 179. Cf. Ε 364, Ρ 637, Σ 29, Τ 312, 335 : ὀρόων ἀκάχημαι θ 314. Cf. δ 806, ι 62 = 105 = 565 = κ 77 = 133, κ 313, ν 286, ο 481, τ 95, υ 84, ψ 360.—With genit. of what is grieved for : ἀκαχήμενον ἵππων Λ 702. Cf. Ω 550.

ἀκαχίζω [cf. prec.]. Imp. pass. ἀκαχίζευ λ 486 (1) To cause grief to, grieve, trouble, vex π 432. —(2) In pass., to be grieved or troubled, grieve, sorrow : μὴ λίην ἀκαχίζεο Ζ 486. Cf. λ 486.

ἀκαχμένος [a ppl. form fr. *ἀκή=ἀκωκή]. (1) Furnished with a sharp point : δούρατα Μ 444. Cf. Ρ 412, Φ 72.—With dat. expressing the material: ὀξέϊ χαλκῷ Κ 135=Ξ 12=Ο 482 : =α 99=ο 551= υ 127.—(2) Furnished with a sharp (double) edge : πέλεκυν (φάσγανον) ἀμφοτέρωθεν ἀκαχμένον ε 235, χ 80.

ἀκάχοντο, 3 pl. aor. mid. ἀχέω.

ἀκέομαι [ἄκος]. Also (Π 29 : ξ 383) **ἀκείομαι** (ἀκεσίομαι, fr. ἀκεσ-, ἄκος). 3 sing. aor. ἠκέσατο Ε 402, 901. Imp. ἄκεσσαι Π 523. Pl. ἀκέσασθε κ 69. (ἐξ-.) (1) To heal, cure (a) A person Ε 402, 448, 901.—(b) A wound Π 29, 523.—(2) To quench (thirst) Χ 2.—(3) To make good a blunder : ἀλλ' ἀκέσασθε κ 69.—Sim. ἀλλ' ἀκεώμεθα Ν 115 (app., let us heal the breach between Achilles and Agamemnon).—(4) To repair (a ship) ξ 383.

ἀκερσεκόμης [ἀ-[1] + κερσ-, κείρω + κόμη]. With unshorn hair. Epithet of Phoebus Υ 39.

ἄκεσμα, -ατος, τό [ἀκεσ-, ἀκέομαι]. A means of cure, a remedy : ἀκέσματ' ὀδυνάων Ο 394.

ἀκεστός, -ή [ἀκεσ-, ἀκέομαι]. That can be healed : ἀκεσταὶ φρένες ἐσθλῶν Ν 115 (app., are open to propitiation).

ἀκέων, -ουσα [a ppl. form conn. with ἀκήν]. (1) In silence, without speech : βῆ ἀ. Α 34. Cf. Α 512, 565, 569, Κ 85 : ι 427, κ 52, λ 142, ξ 110, ρ 465=491=υ 184, υ 385.—Indeclinable : ἀκέων δαίνυσθε φ 89.—Undistracted by speech of others: δαίνυσθαι ἀκέοντε ξ 195. Cf. β 311.—(2) Silent (indeclinable) : Ἀθηναίη ἀκέων ἦν Δ 22=Θ 459.

ἀκήδεστος [ἀκηδεσ-, ἀκηδής]. Without funeral rites : ἐξαπολοίατ' ἀκήδεστοι Ζ 60.

ἀκηδέστως [adv. fr. prec.]. Ruthlessly Χ 465, Ω 417.

†**ἀκηδέω** [ἀκηδής]. 2 sing. impf. ἀκήδεις Ψ 70. 3 sing. aor. ἀκήδεσε Ξ 427. To take no care for. With genit.: εὐ Ξ 427, μευ Ψ 70.

ἀκηδής, -ές [ἀ-[1] + κῆδος]. (**1**) Paying no funeral rites Φ 123.—(**2**) Not honoured with such rites Ω 554 : ω 187.—(**3**) Careless, neglectful ρ 319.—(**4**) Neglected ζ 26, τ 18, υ 130.—(**5**) Vexed by no cares Ω 526.

ἀκήλητος [ἀ-[1] + κηλέω, to bewitch. Cf. κηληθμός]. Proof against sorcery : νόος κ 329.

ἀκήν [adv. fr. acc. of *ἀκή, silence]. (**1**) In silence, without speech : ἴσαν Δ 429.—(**2**) Silent : ἔσαν β 82, δ 285, ἔμεναι φ 239 = 385.—With σιωπῇ : ἀ. ἐγένοντο σιωπῇ Γ 95 = Η 92 = 398 = Θ 28 = Ι 29 = 430 = 693 = Κ 218 = 313 = Ψ 676 : = θ 234 = λ 333 = ν 1 = π 393 = υ 320, η 154.

ἀκηράσιος [= next]. Of wine, pure, unmixed ι 205 (app. by confusion with ἄκρητος).

ἀκήρατος [app. = next]. (**1**) Unharmed, intact Ο 498 : ρ 532.—(**2**) Pure, undefiled : ὕδωρ Ω 303 (cf. prec.).

ἀκήριος[1] [ἀ-[1] + κήρ]. Unharmed μ 98, ψ 328.

ἀκήριος[2] [ἀ-[1] + κῆρ]. (**1**) Lifeless : βέλος ἀκήριον τίθησιν Λ 392. Cf. Φ 466.—(**2**) Spiritless : δέος Ε 812, 817, Ν 224, ἥμενοι ἀκήριοι Η 100.

ἀκηχέδαται, 3 pl. pf. pass. ἀκαχέω.

ἀκηχεμένη, fem. pf. pple. pass. ἀκαχέω.

ἀκιδνός. In comp. ἀκιδνότερος, -η, app., of less account, less to be regarded ε 217, θ 169, σ 130.

ἄκῑκυς [ἀ-[1] + κῖκυς]. Without strength, feeble : ὀλίγος (κακὸς) καὶ ἀ. ι 515, φ 131.

ἀκίχητος [ἀ-[1] + κιχάνω]. Not to be reached. Absol. in neut. pl. ἀκίχητα, the unattainable Ρ 75.

ἄκλαυτος [ἀ-[1] + κλαυ-, κλαίω]. (**1**) Unwept : νέκυς Χ 386. Cf. λ 54, 72.—(**2**) Not weeping δ 494.

ἀκλεής [ἀ-[1] + κλέος]. Acc. ἀκλέα (for ἀκλεέα) δ 728. Nom. pl. ἀκλεέες Μ 318.—(**1**) Without fame, inglorious Μ 318.—In neut. ἀκλεές as adv. = ἀκλειῶς (1) : ἥμενοι Η 100.—(**2**) (So as to be) the subject of no tidings : παῖδ' ἀνηρείψαντο θύελλαι ἀκλέα δ 728.

ἀκλειῶς [adv. fr. prec. Doubtless for ἀκλεεῶς]. (**1**) In inglorious wise : μὴ ἀ. ἀπολοίμην Χ 304.—(**2**) So that no tidings come : ἀ. μιν ἅρπυιαι ἀνηρείψαντο α 241 = ξ 371.

ἄκληρος [ἀ-[1] + κλῆρος]. Having no (considerable) portion of land : ἀνδρί λ 490.

ἀκμή, -ῆς, ἡ. An edge : ξυροῦ Κ 173.

ἄκμηνος. Fasting Τ 207, 346.—Not partaking of (food or drink). With genit. : σίτοιο Τ 163, πόσιος καὶ ἐδητύος 320.

ἀκμηνός [ἀκμή in sense 'highest point']. In its prime, flourishing : θάμνος ἐλαίης ψ 191.

ἀκμής, -ῆτος [ἀ-[1] + κ(α)μ-, κάμνω]. (**1**) Not tired, fresh Λ 802 = Π 44.—(**2**) Tireless Ο 697.

ἀκμόθετον, -ου, τό [ἄκμων + θε-, τίθημι]. An anvil-block Σ 410, 476 : θ 274.

ἄκμων, -ονος, ὁ. An anvil Ο 19, Σ 476 : γ 434, θ 274.

ἄκνηστις, ἡ [prob. conn. with ἄκανθα in sense 'spine,' 'prickle']. The backbone or spine κ 161.

ἀκοίτης, -ου, ὁ [ἀ-[2] + κοῖτος]. A husband, one's husband Ο 91 : ε 120, φ 88.

ἄκοιτις, ἡ [as prec.]. Acc. pl. ἀκοίτῑς κ 7. A wife, one's wife Γ 138, 447, Ζ 350, 374, Ι 397, 399, 450, Ξ 268, 353, Σ 87, Ω 537 : α 39, γ 268, η 66, κ 7, λ 266, 452, ν 42, σ 144, φ 316, 325, ω 193, 459.

ἄκολος, -ου. A scrap or morsel ρ 222.

ἀκομιστίη, -ης, ἡ [ἀ-[1] + κομίζω]. Lack of tendance or care : ἄλη τ' ἀκομιστίη τε φ 284.

ἀκοντίζω [ἄκων]. 3 sing. aor. ἀκόντισε Δ 496, Ε 533, Θ 118, Ν 183, Ρ 304, etc. 3 pl. ἠκόντισαν Π 336. ἀκόντισαν χ 255, 265, 272, 282. Imp. pl. ἀκοντίσατε χ 252. Genit. sing. masc. pple. ἀκοντίσσαντος Δ 498, Ο 575. Infin. ἀκοντίσσαι Ν 559, 585, Π 359. ἀκοντίσαι χ 263. (ἀν-.) (**1**) To throw the spear : ἀνδρὸς ἀκοντίσσαντος Δ 498 = Ο 575. Cf. Π 336, 359 : οἱ ἓξ ἀκοντίσατε χ 252. Cf. χ 255, 263.—With genit. of the person aimed at : Ἕκτορος ἀκόντισεν Θ 118. Cf. Ν 502, 559, Ρ 608.—With dat. of the weapon : δουρί Ε 533. Cf. Δ 496, Ε 611 = Ρ 347, Λ 577, Ν 403, 585, Ο 573, Π 284, Ρ 574 : θ 229.—With genit. and dat. Δ 490, Ν 183, 516, Ξ 402, 461, Ο 429, Ρ 304, 525.—(**2**) To throw (a spear) : αἰχμάς Μ 44, Ξ 422 : δοῦρα χ 265, 272, 282.

ἀκοντιστής, -οῦ, ὁ [ἀκοντίζω]. A (skilful) spearman : υἷες ἀκοντισταὶ Ἀμισωδάρου Π 328. Cf. σ 262.

ἀκοντιστύς, ἡ [as prec.]. A contest of throwing the spear : οὐδ' ἔτ' ἀκοντιστὺν ἐσδύσεαι Ψ 622.

ἀκόρητος [ἀ-[1] + κόρος]. Insatiable in, never having his or their fill of. With genit. : μόθου Η 117. Cf. Μ 335, Ν 621, 639, Ξ 479, Υ 2.

ἄκος, τό. A cure or remedy Ι 250 : χ 481.

ἄκοσμος [ἀ-[1] + κόσμος]. Disorderly, marked by turbulence : ἔπεα Β 213.

ἀκοστέω [ἀκοστή, cited as 'barley']. To have barley for food, be corn-fed : ἀκοστήσας ἐπὶ φάτνῃ Ζ 506 = Ο 263.

ἀκουάζομαι [ἀκούω]. To listen to, give ear to. With genit. : ἀοιδοῦ ι 7, ν 9.—To hear of. With double genit. of person from whom one hears of a thing and of the thing : δαιτὸς ἐμεῖο Δ 343.

ἀκουή, -ῆς, ἡ [ἀκούω]. (**1**) A sound Π 634.—(**2**) News, tidings β 308, δ 701 = ε 19, ξ 179, ρ 43.

ἄκουρος [ἀ-[1] + κοῦρος]. Without male offspring η 64.

ἀκούω. Dat. pl. masc. pres. pple. ἀκουόντεσσι α 352. 2 sing. fut. in mid. form ἀκούσεαι Ο 96. 3 pl. ἀκούσονται Ο 199. Aor. ἤκουσα -ας Α 381, Π 531, Χ 447 : λ 421, μ 265, 389, ρ 492, τ 89, χ 354, 361. ἄκουσα, -ας Α 396, Β 16, 194, Ζ 166, Η 53, Κ 276, Ρ 256, Φ 98, Ω 223, etc. : β 412, 423, γ 94, δ 281, θ 95, μ 202, ο 92, φ 210, ψ 326, etc. Subj. ἀκούσω, -ῃς Ξ 90, Ρ 245, Φ 475, 575 : α 94, 282, β 216, γ 83, λ 561, μ 41, π 32, φ 237, etc. 3 sing. opt. ἀκούσαι Η 129, Τ 81. 3 pl. ἀκούσειαν Β 98, 282. Imp. ἄκουσον Ζ 334, Ι 262 : ζ 325, μ 37, ο 318, τ 535, etc. 3 sing. ἀκουσάτω π 301. Pple. ἀκούσας, -αντος Γ 76, Δ 198, Θ 319, Κ 184, Ρ 694, etc. : δ 114, θ 491, κ 556, ο 98. Infin. ἀκοῦσαι β 375, δ 553, μ 187, ρ 115, etc. (ἐπ-, ἐσ-, ὑπ-.) (**1**) To hear : τέρπετ' ἀκούων Α 474. Cf. Δ 198, Λ 603, Ο 129,

P 245, Σ 35, etc. : ἐθέλω ἀκοῦσαι δ 553. Cf. λ 380, μ 48, ο 98, ψ 135, etc.—With dependent clause : ὡς ἐβόησας δ 281.—(2) In various constructions. (a) (α) With acc. of what is heard : μῦθον B 16. Cf. A 547, B 486, Δ 435, Z 524, K 354, Φ 575, etc. : δοῦπον ε 401. Cf. α 282, λ 421, μ 265, ψ 40, etc. —(β) With this acc. and genit. of person from whom one hears : σεῦ τὸν μῦθον T 185, σεῦ κακὸν ἔπος Ω 767 : ἄλλων μῦθον β 314. Cf. γ 94 = δ 324. —With this acc. and prep. : ἐκ δεσποίνης ἔπος ο 374.—(b) (α) With acc. of what is heard about : κακὰ ἔργα I 595. Cf. O 96, Σ 53 : πατρὸς βίοτον α 287. Cf. β 218, θ 578, π 380, τ 535.—(β) With this acc. and genit. of person from whom one hears : τόδε πατρός θ 564, ταῦτα Καλυψοῦς μ 389, [ταῦθ'] Ἑρμείαο 390.—(γ) With this acc. and acc. pple. expressing what is heard about a person : τοὺς εἰ πτώσσοντας ἀκούσαι H 129.—(δ) With infin. so expressing : τείρεσθαι Τρῶας Z 386.—(ε) With prep. : Ὀδυσῆος περὶ νόστου τ 270.—(c) With genit. of what is heard : κωκυτοῦ X 447. Cf. μ 265, φ 237 = 383, φ 290, 292.—(d) With genit. of person heard : ὁμοκλητῆρος M 273. Cf. Π 211, Ψ 452, Ω 223 : ξ 493, τ 89, χ 361.—So in reference to a beast : θηρός K 184.—(e) (α) With genit. and pple. in agreement, to hear a person doing or suffering something : ὀτρύνοντος Ἕκτορος O 506. Cf. A 396, Φ 475 : τοῦ βλημένου ρ 492. Cf. ι 497, κ 221, φ 210.—(β) With pple. alone : στενάχοντος θ 95 = 534.—So in reference to a bird : κλάγξαντος K 276.—(f) With genit. of person from whom one hears about something : ἄλλου θ 491.—(g) (α) With genit. of person heard about and pple. in agreement expressing what is heard : σέθεν ζώοντος Ω 490. Cf. λ 458, π 301.—(β) With adj. : Ὀδυσῆος ζωοῦ ρ 525.—(γ) With double genit. of person from whom one hears and of person heard about and adj. in genit. joined with pple. : Ὀδυσσῆος ζωοῦ οὐδὲ θανόντος τευ ἀκοῦσαι ρ 115.—(δ) With genit. of person heard about omitted : τεθνηῶτος α 289. Cf. β 220, 375, δ 728, 748.—(ε) With this genit. alone : πατρός δ 114.—(3) To listen, hearken, give ear : θεοὶ πάντες ἄκουον Θ 4. Cf. M 442, P 408, T 81 : ἧατ' ἀκούοντες α 326. Cf. α 352, 353, μ 37, ο 393.—(4) To listen to, give ear to. (a) With acc. of what is listened to : ἄλλων μῦθον B 200. Cf. Θ 492 : θ 429, υ 389.—(b) With genit. of person : βασιλῆων B 98. Cf. Z 334, I 262, T 79, 256 : ἀοιδοῦ α 370. Cf. η 11, ι 3, ο 318 = ω 265, π 259, ρ 520, σ 129.—(c) (α) With genit. of person, to listen to in sense of yielding or obeying : εἰπόντος Z 281. Cf. O 199 : β 423, τ 419, χ 354.—Sim., in mid., οὔ πώ σφιν ἀκούετο λαὸς ἀϋτῆς (had not attended or responded to it) Δ 331.—(β) So in reference to hearing and answering prayer : εὐξαμένου A 381. Cf. Π 531 : ζ 325 (twice).—(d) With dat. of person, to listen to favourably : ἀνέρι κηδομένῳ Π 515. Cf. οἱ with εὐξαμένοιο in Π 531 cited above.—(5) To have heard, have learned, know (cf. ἀΐω¹ (4), πεύθομαι (3)) : τὰ μέλλετ' ἀκουέμεν Ξ 125.—With infin. : καὶ σὲ ἀκούομεν ὄλβιον εἶναι (infin. of the impf.) Ω 543.—With acc. of person heard about and dependent clause : Ἀτρεΐδην ἀκούετε ὡς . . . γ 193.—With genit. of person from whom one has heard about something δ 94.—With this genit. and clause : οὐδὲ πατρῶν ἀκούεθ' οἷος . . . δ 688.—With elliptical construction β 118.—Absol. : εἴ που ἀκουεις ο 403.

ἀκράαντος [ἀ-¹ + κραιαίνω]. (1) Not accomplished, not carried out : ἔργον B 138.—(2) Not to be fulfilled : ἔπεα τ 565.—In neut. ἀκράαντον as adv., without hope of fulfilment, to no purpose β 202.

ἀκρᾱής [ἄκρος + ἄημι]. (Cf. ὑπεραής.) Acc. sing. ἀκρᾶῆ β 421. Of wind, blowing at height ; or perh., blowing with the right velocity or from the right quarter β 421, ξ 253, 299.

ἄκρη, -ης, ἡ [fem. of ἄκρος as sb.]. (1) The highest point of a city θ 508.—(2) κατ' ἄκρης, down from the top. Of a breaking wave, with full force ε 313.—Fig., utterly, to total destruction : ὤλετο N 772. Cf. O 557, X 411, Ω 728.—(3) A cape or headland Δ 425, Ξ 36 : ι 285.

ἄκρητος, -ον [ἀ-¹ + κρη-, κεράννυμι]. Unmixed : οἴνῳ ω 73. Cf. β 341, ι 297.—So σπονδαὶ ἄκρητοι (ratified by libations of unmixed wine) B 341 = Δ 159.

ἀκρίς, -ίδος, ἡ. A locust Φ 12.

ἄκρις, -ιος, ἡ [ἄκρος]. A hill-top : ἠνεμοέσσας ι 400, π 365, δι' ἄκριας κ 281, ξ 2.

ἀκριτόμῡθος [ἄκριτος + μῦθος]. (1) Indiscriminate or reckless in speech B 246.—(2) Hard to be discerned or interpreted ὄνειροι τ 560.

ἄκριτος [ἀ-¹ + κρίνω]. (1) Indiscriminate, endless : μῦθοι B 796.—Endless, never-ending : ἄχεα Γ 412, Ω 91.—Endless, never brought to reconciliation : νείκεα Ξ 205 = 304.—Absol. in neut. pl. : ἄκριτα πόλλ' ἀγόρευον θ 505 (app., held much and indiscriminate or inconsistent debate).—(2) In neut. sing. ἄκριτον as adv. (a) Indiscriminately : ἐξαγαγόντες ἀ. ἐκ πεδίου (see ἐξάγω (2)) H 337, 436.—(b) Endlessly, continually : πενθήμεναι σ 174, τ 120.

ἀκριτόφυλλος [ἄκριτος + φύλλον]. With confused or massed foliage : ὄρος B 868 (*i.e.* the separate trees are indistinguishable).

†ἀκροκελαινιάω [ἄκρος + κελαινός]. In pres. pple. ἀκροκελαινιόων, of a river, with black or dark surface Φ 249.

ἀκρόκομος [ἄκρος + κόμη]. Wearing the hair in a topknot (the hair round this being app. cut short or shaved off). Epithet of the Thracians Δ 533.

ἄκρον, -ου, τό [neut. of ἄκρος as sb.]. (1) The summit or crest of a hill λ 597.—(2) A cape or headland. Of Sunium γ 278.—(3) An end or extremity : ἐπ' ἄκρῳ δῆσε ζυγόν E 729. Cf. ι 328, 382.—(4) The extreme surface : [νύσσης] Ψ 339.

ἀκρόπολις, ἡ [ἄκρος + πόλις]. The highest part of a city, the citadel. Of Troy θ 494, 504.

ἀκρόπολος [ἄκρος. Cf. οἰόπολος]. Topmost, the topmost part of : ὄρεσσιν E 523 : τ 205.

ἀκροπόρος [ἄκρος + πείρω]. With a piercing or sharp point. Epithet of spits : ὀβελούς γ 463.

ἄκρος, -η, -ον. Extreme, at the furthest point. (**1**) Topmost, the topmost part of : πόλει Z 88 (the citadel), πρώονες Θ 557 = Π 299. Cf. E 460, Z 257, 297, 317, 512, H 345, Θ 83, I 241, Λ 351, M 282, N 523, 615, Ξ 292, 352, O 152, X 383 : σκοπέλοισιν μ 239.—(**2**) Outermost, the extremity of : πόδας Π 640. Cf. P 264 (see ἠϊών (2)), 309, 599, Υ 227 : οἰήϊον ι 483 = 540.—The edge of : χείλει M 51.—Growing on the extremity : τρίχες οὐραῖαι Ψ 519.—At the end of a row : νῆες O 653.—The base or root of : χεῖρα E 336 (cf. 458).—(**3**) The surface of : ὕδωρ Π 162 : ῥινόν χ 278.—App. in neut. ἄκρον as adv., on the surface : ἀ. ἐπὶ ῥηγμῖνος θέεσκον Υ 229 (*v.l.* ἀ. ἔπι, taking ἀ. as sb., the surface ; see ἄκρον (4)).—(**4**) In superl. ἀκρότατος, -η, -ον (in μ 11 of two terminations), much like the positive. (**a**) Topmost, the topmost part of : κορυφῇ A 499 = E 754 = Θ 3. Cf. B 793, Z 470, N 12, Ξ 157, 228, 285, O 536, Υ 52, X 172 : τύμβῳ μ 15.—Absol. : ἐπ' ἀκροτάτῃ (at the top) Δ 484.—(**b**) The extremity of : ὄζῳ B 312.—Sim. ἀκρότατον παρ' οὐδόν χ 127 (app., to one side of (and passing at right angles) one of the extremities of the threshold).—Predicatively : ὅθ' ἀκρότατος πρόεχ' ἀκτή (where the beach ran furthest out) μ 11.—(**c**) The surface of : χρόα Δ 139, χαλκόν H 246.

ἀκτή[1], -ῆς, ἡ. Corn or meal : ἀλφίτου Λ 631, Δημήτερος N 322, Φ 76 : ἀλφίτου β 355, ξ 429.

ἀκτή[2], -ῆς, ἡ. (**1**) A beach or shore of the sea : ἀκτὴν εἰσανέβαινον Σ 68. Cf. M 284, Υ 50, Ψ 125, Ω 97 : ἐπ' ἀκτῆς καθήμενος ε 82. Cf. ε 151, κ 140, 509, ν 234, ο 36, ω 378.—(**2**) A projecting part of the shore : ἀκτῇ ἐφ' ὑψηλῇ B 395 : ἀκταὶ προβλῆτες ε 405. Cf. ε 425, κ 89, μ 11, ν 98, ω 82.

ἀκτήμων [ἀ-[1] + κτῆμα]. Not possessed of, lacking. With genit. : χρυσοῖο I 126 = 268.

ἀκτίς, ἡ. Dat. pl. ἀκτῖσι ε 479, τ 441. ἀκτίνεσσι K 547 : λ 16. A ray or beam : ἠελίοιο K 547. Cf. ε 479, λ 16, τ 441.

ἄκυλος, -ου. Prob., the fruit of the ilex. Given to swine κ 242.

ἀκωκή, -ῆς, ἡ. A point : ἔγχεος E 16. Cf. E 67, K 373, Λ 253, N 251, Π 323, 478, P 295, Υ 260, Φ 60, Ψ 821, P 49 = X 327 : = χ 16, τ 453.

ἄκων, -οντος, ὁ. (**1**) A dart or javelin Δ 137, K 335, Λ 364 = Υ 451, Λ 675, Ξ 455, O 646, 709, Π 361, Υ 413, 455, 486, Φ 590 : ξ 225, 531, φ 340.—Used for guarding cattle or sheep Λ 552 = P 661, M 306 : ν 225.—(**2**) In generalized sense, the dart : ἐπιστάμενος ἄκοντι O 282.

ἅλαδε [acc. of ἅλς[1] + -δε (1)]. To or into the sea : νῆα προέρυσσεν A 308. Cf. B 165 = 181, E 598, I 358, 683, M 19, Ξ 97, 100, 106 : νῆ' εἴρυσεν β 389.—With εἰς : ποταμῶν, οἵ τ' εἰς ἁ. προρέουσιν κ 351.

ἀλάλημαι, pf. ἀλάομαι.

ἀλαλητός, -οῦ, ὁ [imitative]. A shouting B 149 : ω 463.—A shouting in distress : ἀλαλητῷ φεύγοντες Σ 149. Cf. Φ 10.—A shouting in war, the war-shout : ἀ. ἀνὰ στρατὸν ὀρώρει Δ 436. Cf. M 138, Ξ 393, Π 78.

Ἀλαλκομενηΐς [app. fr. ἄλαλκον]. Thus, the guardian or protectress. Epithet of Athene Δ 8, E 908.

ἄλαλκον, *aor.* [cf. ἀλκή, ἀλέξω]. (ἀπ-.) (**1**) To ward or keep off I 605, Φ 548, Ψ 185 : δ 167.—With dat. of person protected : κύνας οἱ P 153. Cf. T 30, Φ 138 = 250 : γ 237, ν 319.—With genit. : Τρώων λοιγόν Φ 539.—With dat. and genit. of part : κρατός τοι κακὸν ἦμαρ κ 288.—(**2**) With dat., to succour, defend, protect : οἱ X 196.

ἀλαλύκτημαι [pf. pass. fr. *ἀλυκτέω, conn. with ἀλύω]. To be distraught or sore distressed K 94.

ἀλάομαι [ἄλη]. 3 pl. ἀλόωνται γ 73, ι 254. Imp. ἀλόω ε 377. Aor. ἀλήθην ξ 120. 2 sing. ἀλήθης ξ 362. Pple. ἀληθείς ξ 380, π 205. Pf. ἀλάλημαι Ψ 74 : λ 167. 2 sing. ἀλάλησαι ο 10. 3 ἀλάληται υ 340. 2 pl. ἀλάλησθε γ 72, ι 253. Imp. ἀλάλησο γ 313. Pple. ἀλαλήμενος ν 333, ξ 122, ρ 245, φ 327. Infin. ἀλάλησθαι β 370, μ 284, ο 276, υ 206. (ἐπ-.) To wander, rove : κὰπ πεδίον ἀλᾶτο Z 201. Cf. B 667, Θ 482, K 141, Ψ 74 : μαψιδίως γ 72. Cf. β 333, 370, γ 73, δ 91, ε 336, etc.

ἀλαός. Blind : μάντιος ἀλαοῦ (for ἀλαόο) κ 493, μ 267.—Absol., a blind man θ 195.

ἀλαοσκοπιή, -ῆς, ἡ [ἀλαός + σκοπιή. 'Blind watch']. A negligent or careless watch or lookout : οὐδ' ἀλαοσκοπιὴν εἶχεν K 515, N 10, Ξ 135 : θ 285.

ἀλαόω [ἀλαός]. (ἐξ-.) To blind : ὀφθαλμοῦ (of his (my) eye) α 69, ι 516.

ἀλαπαδνός, -ή, -όν [ἀλαπάζω]. (**1**) Weak, feeble, ineffective : στίχες Δ 330, σθένος E 783 = H 257, Θ 463 : σ 373.—Comp. ἀλαπαδνότερος Δ 305.—(**2**) Having little power or influence B 675.

ἀλαπάζω. 2 sing. fut. ἀλαπάξεις B 367. Aor. ἀλάπαξα I 328, Λ 750. 3 sing. -ε ρ 424, τ 80. Infin. ἀλαπάξαι I 136, 278. (ἐξ-.) (**1**) To deprive of vigour, take the strength from : Ἀχαιούς M 67.—To ruin : Ζεὺς ἀλάπαξεν (brought all this to nought) ρ 424 = τ 80.—To work havoc in (opposed ranks) E 166, Λ 503.—(**2**) To slay Λ 750.—(**3**) To destroy or sack (a city) B 367, I 136 = 278, 328, Ω 245.

ἀλαστέω [ἄλαστος]. (ἐπ-.) To find things intolerable : ἠλάστεον θεοί (raged (impotently)) O 21.—So in aor. pple. ἀλαστήσας, giving way to such a feeling, breaking out in protest M 163.

ἄλαστος [prob. ἀ-[1] + λαθ-, λανθάνω]. Thus (**1**) Unforgettable, that never leaves one : πένθος Ω 105 : α 342, ω 423, ἄχος δ 108.—In neut. ἄλαστον as adv., of mourning, without power of forgetting, unceasingly : ὀδύρομαι ξ 174.—(**2**) Applied to a person (app. by transference of the epithet from acts to the agent), doer of deeds not to be forgotten, wretch : Ἕκτορ, ἄλαστε X 261.

ἀλαωτύς, ἡ [ἀλαόω]. A blinding ι 503.

ἀλγέω [ἄλγος]. To suffer (bodily) pain or discomfort B 269, Θ 85, M 206 : μ 27.

ἄλγιον [neut. comp. fr. ἄλγος]. So much the worse, all the harder : ἀ. τῷ ἔσσεται Σ 306. Cf.

Σ 278 : ρ 14, τ 322.—Without construction δ 292, π 147.

ἄλγιστος, -η, -ον [superl. formed as prec.]. Most difficult or hard: ἀλγίστη δαμάσασθαι Ψ 655.

ἄλγος, τό. (1) Pain, distress: ἀ. ἱκάνει θυμόν Γ 97. Cf. Z 450, 462, Σ 395, X 53, 54 : ὅπως μοι ἀ. ἀλάλκοις ν 319. Cf. β 41, 193, ο 345, τ 471.—(2) Definitely distinguished as bodily pain or suffering E 394 : ξ 32.—(3) In pl., distresses, woes, cares, hardships: Ἀχαιοῖς ἄλγε' ἔθηκεν A 2. Cf. B 667, I 321, N 346, Σ 224, Ω 568, etc. : πάθεν ἄλγεα α 4, ἄλγεσι θυμὸν ἐρέχθων ε 83 (*i.e.* expressions of grief). Cf. β 343, γ 220, θ 182, υ 339, etc.

†**ἀλδαίνω** [cf. next]. 3 sing. aor. ἤλδανε. To cause to wax or fill out: μέλεα σ 70 = ω 368.

ἀλδήσκω [cf. prec.]. To grow, increase Ψ 599.

ἀλέασθαι, aor. infin. ἀλέομαι.

ἀλεγεινός, -ή, -όν [ἄλγος]. (1) Causing pain or grief, painful, grievous, hard B 787, Δ 99, E 658, I 546, Λ 398, N 569, O 16, Σ 17, 248 = T 46 = Υ 43, Ψ 653, 701 : γ 206, θ 126, κ 78, μ 26, 226.—(2) Causing or apt to cause injury or harm: πνοιῇ Βορέω Ξ 395. Cf. P 749, Ω 8 : = θ 183 = ν 91 = 264, σ 224.—(3) Fatal, baneful: ἀγηνορίης X 457.—(4) Difficult, troublesome: δαμήμεναι K 402, P 76.—Troublesome, irksome: νηπιέῃ I 491.—(5) App., bringing repentance in its wake: μαχλοσύνην Ω 30.

ἀλεγίζω [cf. ἀλέγω]. With neg., not to care for, trouble oneself about, have regard for. With genit.: σέθεν οὐκ ἀλεγίζω A 180. Cf. A 160, Θ 477, Λ 80, M 238.—Absol. O 106.

ἀλεγύνω [cf. ἀλέγω]. To take one's part in, partake of (a meal): δαῖτας α 374. Cf. β 139, θ 38, λ 186, ν 23.

ἀλέγω. (1) To care, be concerned: οὐκ ἀλέγω Λ 389 : ρ 390.—(2) To be careful of one's duties, show due regard for another or others: ὅτις οὐκ ἀλέγει π 307. Cf. τ 154.—(3) To show concern for, busy oneself with, the right: Λιταὶ ἀλέγουσιν I 504.—(4) To attend to, busy oneself about: νηῶν ὅπλα ζ 268.—(5) With neg., not to care for or concern oneself about, regard or heed: θεῶν ὄπιν οὐκ ἀλέγοντες Π 388.—With genit.: σκυζομένης σεῦ Θ 483. Cf. ι 115, 275, υ 214.

ἀλεείνω [cf. ἀλέομαι]. (1) To escape, evade, avoid, keep out of the way, reach or influence of, avoid incurring (something coming upon or threatening one): κῆρα Γ 32 = Λ 585 = N 566 = 596 = 648 = Ξ 408, Π 817. Cf. Λ 794, N 669, Π 36, 213 = Ψ 713, P 374 : χόλον γυναικός α 433. Cf. ε 326, ζ 273, ν 148, τ 373, ω 229.—(2) To elude the notice of π 477.—Absol., to evade questioning δ 251.—(3) To shun, avoid, keep clear of or away from: πάτον ἀνθρώπων Z 202. Cf. Λ 542, Ψ 422.—(4) With infin., to shrink from *doing*, hesitate *to do*: κτεῖναι Z 167, ἀλεξέμεναι N 356.

ἀλέη[1], ἡ [ἀλέομαι]. A means of escape X 301.

ἀλέη[2], ἡ. Warmth (of the sun) ρ 23.

ἀλείατα, τά [ἀλέω]. Wheaten flour υ 108.

ἀλείς, aor. pple. pass. εἴλω.

ἄλεισον, τό. A drinking-cup (= δέπας) Λ 774, Ω 429 : γ 50, 53, δ 591, θ 430, ο 85, 469, χ 9.

ἀλείτης, -ου, ὁ [ἀλιτεῖν, aor. infin. ἀλιταίνω]. An offender: τείσεσθαι ἀλείτην Γ 28. Cf. υ 121.

ἄλειφαρ, -ατος, τό [ἀλείφω]. Unguent, oil Σ 351, Ψ 170 : γ 408 (app. here some kind of polish or varnish), ω 45, 67, 73.

†**ἀλείφω**. Aor. ἄλειψα μ 177, 200. 3 sing. ἤλειψε τ 505. ἄλειψε ζ 227. 3 pl. ἤλειψαν Σ 350. Infin. ἀλεῖψαι Ω 582 : μ 47. 3 sing. aor. mid. ἀλείψατο Ξ 171. Nom. dual masc. pple. ἀλειψαμένω K 577. Nom. fem. ἀλειψαμένη Ξ 175. (προσ-.) (1) To oil, anoint with oil Σ 350, Ω 582 : ζ 227, τ 505.—(2) To stop (the ears) with wax: ἐπ' οὔατ' ἀλεῖψαι (ἄλειψα) μ 47, 177.—To put (wax) in the ears μ 200.—(3) In mid., to anoint oneself: ἀλείψατο λίπ' ἐλαίῳ Ξ 171. Cf. K 577, Ξ 175.

ἄλεν, 3 pl. aor. pass. εἴλω.

ἀλέν, neut. aor. pple. pass. εἴλω.

ἀλεξάνεμος, -ον [ἀλέξω + ἄνεμος]. Protecting from the wind: χλαῖναν ξ 529.

ἀλεξητήρ, -ῆρος, ὁ [ἀλέξω]. One who wards off or stems: ἀλεξητῆρα μάχης Υ 396.

ἀλεξίκακος, -ον [ἀλέξω + κακόν. See κακός (11)]. Tending to avert evil: μῆτις K 20.

ἀλέξω [cf. ἄλαλκον]. 2 sing. fut. ἀλεξήσεις I 251. Acc. sing. masc. pple. ἀλεξήσοντα Z 109. Infin. ἀλεξήσειν Υ 315, Φ 374. 3 sing. aor. opt. ἀλεξήσειε γ 346. Aor. infin. mid. ἀλέξασθαι N 475, O 565, Π 562 : σ 62. (ἀπ-, ἐπ-.) (1) To ward or keep off, avert γ 346.—With dat. of person or thing protected: Δαναοῖσι κακὸν ἦμαρ I 251. Cf. I 347, 674, P 365, Υ 315 = Φ 374.—(2) With dat., to succour, defend, protect: ἀλλήλοισιν Γ 9. Cf. E 779, Z 109.—Absol., to afford succour, defence, or protection A 590, Λ 469, N 356.—(3) In mid., to ward or keep off from oneself, defend oneself against, encounter: ἀλέξασθαι κύνας N 475 : τοῦτον ἀλέξασθαι σ 62.—Absol., to defend oneself, offer resistance Λ 348 = X 231, O 565 = Π 562 : ι 57.

†**ἀλέομαι** [cf. ἀλεείνω]. 3 pl. impf. ἀλέοντο Σ 586. 3 sing. aor. ἠλεύατο N 184, 404, 503, Π 610, P 305, 526, X 274. ἀλεύατο Γ 360, H 254, Λ 360, Ξ 462 : ρ 67, υ 300, 305. 3 pl. ἀλεύαντο χ 260. 3 sing. subj. ἀλέηται δ 396. ἀλεύεται ξ 400, ω 29. 1 pl. ἀλεώμεθα E 34, Z 226. 3 sing. opt. ἀλέαιτο Υ 147 : υ 368. Imp. ἄλευαι X 285. 2 pl. ἀλέασθε δ 774. Pple. ἀλευάμενος, -ου E 28, 444, O 223, Π 711, Υ 281 : ι 277, μ 157. Infin. ἀλέασθαι N 436, 513, Υ 302, Ψ 340, 605 : ι 274, 411, π 447. ἀλεύασθαι μ 159, 269, 274. (ὑπ-, ὑπεξ-.) (1) To escape, evade, avoid, keep out of the way, reach, or influence of (something coming upon or threatening one): ἔγχεα Z 226. Cf. Γ 360, E 34, O 223, Υ 147, 281, etc. : νοῦσον ι 411. Cf. ι 274, 277, μ 157, π 447, υ 305, 368, χ 260, ω 29.—(2) Absol., to escape Υ 302.—To avoid a missile υ 300.—To flee, take to flight, take oneself off, save oneself E 28 (as it seemed to the onlookers), N 436, 513 : δ 396.—To keep out of harm's way Σ 586.—(3) To shun, avoid, keep clear of or away

from, refrain from: μύθους ὑπερφιάλους δ 774, Σειρήνων φθόγγον καὶ λειμῶνα μ 159, νῆσον 269=274, ὅμιλον ρ 67.—(4) With infin., to shrink from *doing*, hesitate *to do*: ἠπεροπεύειν Ψ 605: ξ 400.—To take care not *to do*: λίθου ἐπαυρεῖν Ψ 340.

ἅλεται, 3 sing. aor. subj. ἅλλομαι.

ἀλετρεύω [ἀλέω]. To grind: καρπόν η 104.

ἀλετρίς, ἡ [ἀλέω]. A female slave employed in grinding υ 105.

ἀλεύατο, 3 sing. aor. ἀλέομαι.

†**ἀλέω**. 3 pl. aor. ἄλεσσαν. To grind: πυρόν υ 109.

ἀλεωρή, -ῆς, ἡ [ἀλέομαι]. (1) Shrinking from the foe Ω 216.—(2) A means of defence: δηΐων ἀνδρῶν (against . . .) M 57, O 533.

ἄλη, -ης, ἡ. (Incessant) wandering κ 464, ο 342, 345, φ 284.

ἀληθείη, -ης, ἡ [ἀληθής]. The truth Ψ 361, Ω 407: η 297, λ 507, π 226=χ 420, ρ 108, 122, φ 212.

ἀλήθην, aor. ἀλάομαι.

ἀληθής, -ές [ἀ-[1] + λήθω]. (1) App., not forgetting, careful, anxious: χερνῆτις M 433.—(2) Absol. in neut. pl. ἀληθέα, the truth Z 382: γ 254=π 61, ν 254, ξ 125, ρ 15, σ 342.—(3) In neut. sing. ἀληθές as adv., truly γ 247.

ἀλήϊος [ἀ-[1] + ληΐς]. Without share of booty; hence, not rich in possessions I 125=267.

ἁλώμεναι, ἁλῆναι, aor. infin. pass. εἴλω.

ἀλήμων, -ονος, ὁ [ἄλη]. A vagrant ρ 376, τ 74.

ἅληται, 3 sing. aor. subj. ἅλλομαι.

ἀλητεύω [ἀλήτης]. (1) To wander, rove μ 330, ξ 126, π 101, σ 114.—(2) To go to and fro: κατὰ δῶμα ρ 501. Cf. χ 291.

ἀλήτης, -ου, ὁ [ἄλη]. A wanderer, vagrant ξ 124, ρ 420=τ 76, ρ 483, 576, 578, σ 18, 25, 333=393, υ 377, φ 400.

†**ἄλθομαι**. 3 sing. aor. ἄλθετο. (ἀπ-.) To become whole or sound: ἄλθετο χείρ E 417.

ἁλιαής [ἅλς[1] + ἄημι]. Blowing over the sea δ 361.

ἀλίαστος, -ον [ἀ-[1] + λιάζομαι]. (1) Unabating, unceasing B 797, M 471=Π 296, Ξ 57, Υ 31, Ω 760.—(2) In neut., ἀλίαστον as adv., without ceasing Ω 549.

ἀλίγκιος. Like, resembling. With dat.: ἀστέρι καλῷ Z 401: ἀθανάτοισιν θ 174.

ἁλιεύς, -ῆος, ὁ [ἅλιος[1]]. (1) A seaman ω 419.—With ἐρέτης π 349.—(2) A fisher μ 251, χ 384.

ἁλιμυρήεις, -εντος [ἅλς[1] + μύρω]. Seaward flowing Φ 190.—Of a river at its meeting with the sea ε 460.

ἅλιος[1], -η, -ον [ἅλς[1]]. Of the sea A 538=556, Σ 86, 139, 141, Υ 107, Ω 84, 562: γ 38, δ 349=ρ 140, δ 365, 384, 401, 438, 542, ν 96, 345, ω 47, 55, 58.—Absol. in fem. pl., sea-goddesses Σ 432.

ἅλιος[2], -η, -ον. (1) Ineffective, effecting nothing, useless, idle, vain, fruitless: πόνον Δ 26. Cf. Δ 158, 179, 498=O 575, E 18, 715, Λ 376, 380, Ξ 455, Π 480, Σ 324, Ω 92, 224: ὁδός β 273, 318.—Of a person, inefficient: σκοπός K 324.—(2) In neut. ἅλιον as adv., in vain, without result N 410, 505=Π 615.

ἁλιοτρεφής [ἅλιος[1] + τρέφω]. Sea-bred δ 442.

ἁλιόω [ἅλιος[2]]. (1) To make of no effect, frustrate: Διὸς νόον ε 104=138.—(2) To use to no effect: βέλος (did not hurl it in vain) Π 737.

ἁλίπλοος [ἅλς[1] + πλέω]. Floating on the sea, in the state of flotsam: τείχεα M 26.

ἁλιπόρφυρος [ἅλς[1] + (app.) πορφύρα, the Phoenician shell-fish called the murex, the dye got therefrom]. Thus, dyed in sea-purple: ἠλάκατα ζ 53, 306, φάρεα ν 108.

ἅλις (Ϝάλις) [ἀλ-, (Ϝ)είλω]. (1) In a throng, in swarms: μέλισσαι ἁ. πεποτήαται B 90. Cf. Γ 384, X 473.—(2) In abundance, in plenty, in great numbers: ἁ. οἱ ἦσαν ἄρουραι Ξ 122. Cf. I 137, 279, P 54, Φ 236, 319, 344, 352, X 340: χαλκὸν ἁ. δόντες ε 38=ψ 341. Cf. β 339, η 295, ν 136=π 231, ο 77=94, π 389 (with notion of excess), ρ 298, 376, ω 486.—(3) With copula to be supplied, (it is) enough: ἦ οὐχ ἁ. ὅττι . . .; E 349, Ψ 670. Cf. I 376, P 450: β 312.

†**ἁλίσκομαι** [cf. εἴλω]. 3 sing. aor. ἧλω χ 230. Subj. ἁλώω Λ 405: σ 265. 3 sing. ἁλώῃ I 592, Ξ 81: ξ 183, ο 300. 1 sing. opt. ἁλοίην X 253. 3 ἁλοίη P 506. Masc. dual pple. ἁλόντε E 487. Fem. sing. ἁλοῦσα B 374, Δ 291, N 816. Infin. ἁλώμεναι Φ 495. ἁλῶναι M 172, Φ 281: ε 312, ω 34. (1) To be taken, captured, seized: βέλτερον ὃς προφύγῃ ἠὲ ἁλώῃ Ξ 81. Cf. E 487, Λ 405, Φ 495.—With θανάτῳ, to meet one's death Φ 281: =ε 312, ω 34.—Of towns, to be taken B 374=Δ 291=N 816, I 592: χ 230.—(2) To be slain: ἠὲ κατακτάμεν ἠὲ ἁλῶναι M 172. Cf. P 506, X 253: ξ 183, ο 300, σ 265.

†**ἀλιταίνω**. 3 sing. aor. ἤλιτε I 375. Nonthematic pres. pple. mid. ἀλιτήμενος δ 807. 3 pl. aor. ἀλίτοντο ε 108. Subj. ἀλίτωμαι Ω 570. 3 sing. ἀλίτηται T 265, Ω 586. Infin. ἀλιτέσθαι δ 378. (1) In both voices, to sin or trespass against, fail in duty to: ἤλιτέ με I 375. Cf. T 265: ἀθανάτους ἀλιτέσθαι δ 378. Cf. ε 108.—(2) In mid., to transgress, infringe: Διὸς ἐφετμάς Ω 570, 586.—(3) In pres. pple. mid. ἀλιτήμενος in adjectival sense, sinning, sinful: θεοῖς (in the eyes of the gods) δ 807.

ἀλιτήμων [ἀλιταίνω]. Sinful Ω 157=186.

ἀλιτρός [as prec.]. (1)=prec.: δαίμοσιν (in the eyes of the gods) Ψ 595.—Playfully ε 182.—(2) Not showing due regard, showing ill-will Θ 361.

ἄλκαρ, τό [ἀλκή]. A means of defence, a safeguard. With dat. of person defended: Τρώεσσιν E 644.—With genit.: Ἀχαιῶν Λ 823.

ἀλκή, -ῆς, ἡ [cf. ἄλαλκον]. Dat. ἀλκί (fr. *ἄλξ) E 299, N 471, P 61, etc.: ζ 130. (1) Defence, help: οὔτε κλέος οὔτ' ἁ. E 532=O 564, οὐδέ τις ἁ. γίγνετο (γίγνεται) Φ 528: χ 305, οὐδέ τίς ἐστ' ἁ. μ 120.—(2) Prowess in defence or offence, mettle, courage, spirit: συῒ εἴκελος ἀλκήν Δ 253. Cf. Γ 45, E 299, H 164, I 706, Π 157, T 36, etc.: ἀλκὶ πεποιθώς ζ 130. Cf. ι 214, 514, ρ 315, χ 226, 237, ψ 128, ω 509.—Personified E 740.—(3) Showing of fight, resistance: οὐκ ἀπολήγει ἀλκῆς Φ 578.—Prowess displayed in action, deeds of prowess, fighting: εἰδότε ἀλκῆς Λ 710, ἔπαυσεν ἀλκῆς Ο 250. Cf. Ν 116, 197, Ο 490 (from Zeus), Υ 256, etc.: οὐ δεδαηκότες ἀλκήν β 61. Cf. δ 527.—(4) The upper hand, victory: ἀπείρητος οὐδ' ἀδήριτος ἤ τ' ἀλκῆς ἤ τε φόβοιο (whether in the matter of . . . or . . ., whether the result be . . . or . . .) Ρ 42.

ἄλκιμος [ἀλκή]. (1) Stout, courageous Ε 529, Ζ 437, Λ 483, Μ 349, Π 689, Ρ 429, Φ 586, etc.: α 302=γ 200, κ 553, χ 138, 232.—With complementary infin.: ἀ. μάχεσθαι Ο 570.—(2) Of weapons, stout, strong: ἔγχος Γ 338. Cf. Κ 135 =Ξ 12=Ο 482, Λ 43, Π 139: α 99=ο 551=υ 127, ρ 4, φ 34, χ 25, 125.

ἀλκτήρ, -ῆρος, ὁ [ἀλκ-, ἄλαλκον]. (1) A protector: ἀρῆς (against . . .) Ξ 485. Cf. Σ 100, 213. —(2) A means of protection: κυνῶν ξ 531, φ 340.

ἀλκυών, -όνος. The halcyon or kingfisher Ι 563.

ἀλλά [ἄλλος]. (1) Adversative particle, but Α 24, 25, 94, 116, 125, etc.: α 6, 16, 22, 42, 48, etc.—Elliptically: ἀλλ' οὐ γάρ σ' ἐθέλω . . . (but I say no more, for . . .) Η 242: ἀλλ' οὐ γάρ τις πρῆξις ἐγίγνετο (but they soon gave over, for . . .) κ 202=568, ἀλλ' οὐ γάρ οἱ ἔτ' ἦν ἲς ἔμπεδος (but it was of no avail, for . . .) λ 393. Cf. τ 591.—(2) Introducing an apodosis, yet, nevertheless: εἴ περ γὰρ . . . ἀλλ' οὔ πείσονται Θ 154. Cf. Α 82, Μ 349, Π 38, Ω 771, etc.: εἰ . . . ἀλλ' ἤδη παῖς τοῖος τ 86, etc.—Introducing a statement: ἀλλὰ μάλ' ὤφελλες (why . . .) δ 472.—(3) With imp. (or infin. as imp.) in command, challenge, entreaty, remonstrance, persuasion, encouragement, indignation, etc., nay but, come now! ἴθι Α 32, πίθεσθε 259. Cf. Α 393, 508, 565, Β 163, 360, etc.: μέν' αὖθι β 369, ὧδ' ἔρδειν ζ 258. Cf. γ 323, 380, δ 28, 35, 379, etc.—Sim. with subj.: ἴομεν Ζ 526, etc.: φραζώμεσθα β 167, φθεγγώμεθα κ 228, etc.—With opt.: ἐπιτρέψειας ἕκαστα δμῳάων ἤ τις . . . ο 24. —With fut.: ἐρέω μ 156.—With ἄνα. See ἄνα[1].—For ἀλλ' ἄγε (ἄγετε) see ἄγε.

ἀλλέγω [ἀλ-, ἀνα-(1)+λέγω[2]]. Aor. infin. ἀλλέξαι Φ 321. To pick up, gather up: ὀστέα Φ 321, Ψ 253.

ἄλλῃ [dat. fem. of ἄλλος as adv.]. (1) (a) Elsewhere Ν 49: γ 251, χ 140.—(b) ἄλλος ἀ., one in one quarter, one in another θ 516.—(2) (a) Elsewhither, in another direction Α 120, Ε 187, Ο 464, Φ 557: β 127=σ 288, ρ 478.—(b) In a direction other than the right: ἀ. ἀποκλίναντα (wresting the meaning) τ 556.—(c) ἄλλυδις ἀ., some or part in this direction, some or part in another ε 369, ι 458, λ 385.—(3) (a) Otherwise: εἰ βούλεται ἀ. Ο 51.—(b) ἄλλυδις ἀ.: τρέπεται χρὼς ἄλλυδις ἀ. (now to one hue, now to another) Ν 279.

ἄλληκτος [ἀ-[1]+ληκ-, λήγω]. (1) Unceasing, never still: ἄη Νότος μ 325.—Unceasing, implacable: θυμόν Ι 636.—(2) In neut. ἄλληκτον as adv, without intermission or pause: πολεμίζειν Β 452=Λ 12=Ξ 152.

ἀλλήλων [redup. fr. ἄλλος]. One another, each other: ἀλλήλοισι κέλευον Β 151. Cf. Γ 9, 15, 115, 155, Δ 449, 472, 536, etc.: ξεῖνοι ἀλλήλων α 187. Cf. α 209, β 149, δ 620, ε 79, ζ 211, ι 55, etc.

ἀλλόγνωτος [ἄλλος+γνω-, γιγνώσκω]. App., known to be other; hence, strange, foreign: δήμῳ β 366.

ἀλλοδαπός, -ή, -όν [ἄλλος. Second element doubtful]. (1) Foreign, alien Τ 324, Ω 382: θ 211, ι 36, ξ 231, ρ 485, υ 220, ψ 219.—(2) Absol., a foreigner or alien Γ 48, Π 550: γ 74=ι 255.

ἀλλοειδής, -ές [ἄλλος+εἶδος]. Of another, *i.e.* of strange, appearance: ἀλλοειδέα φαινέσκετο πάντα ν 194 (ἀ. to be scanned in three long syllables; *v.l.* ἀλλοειδέ' ἐφαίνετο).

ἄλλοθεν [ἄλλος+-θεν (1)]. (1) (a) From another place or source, from elsewhere: ἵνα μή ποθεν ἀ. αὔῃ ε 490, καλεῖ ἀ. ρ 382.—(b) ἀ. ἄλλος, some or one from one side or quarter, some or one from another Β 75, Ι 311, 671, Ν 551: ι 401, 493= κ 442, κ 119, λ 42, σ 231, ω 415.—Sim. νείκεον ἀ. ἄλλον, one beginning with one man, one with another μ 392.—(2) From another or strange land, from abroad: εἰλήλουθεν γ 318. Cf. ζ 283, η 33, 52, π 26, ρ 112, υ 360.

ἄλλοθι [ἄλλος+-θι]. (1) In another place, elsewhere δ 684, π 44, σ 401.—On his part, he too: κλαῖεν φ 83.—(2) (a) In another or strange land, abroad: ἐπὴν ἀ. ὄληται ξ 130.—ἀ. γαίης, elsewhere in the world, somewhere abroad β 131. —(b) App., with genit., elsewhere away from (one's home): ἀ. πάτρης (*i.e.* in some strange land) ρ 318.

ἀλλόθροος [ἄλλος+θρόος]. Speaking a strange tongue, foreign, alien α 183, γ 302, ξ 43, ο 453.

ἀλλοῖος [ἄλλος]. Of another sort or kind: ἔργῳ Δ 258: ἀ. φάνης π 181, ἄνδρα τ 265.

†**ἅλλομαι** [σαλ-. Cf. L. *salio*]. 2 sing. aor. ἆλσο Π 754. 3 ἆλτο Α 532, Γ 29, Δ 125, Ε 111, Ν 611, Υ 62, Ω 469, etc.: φ 388, χ 2, 80. 3 sing. subj. ἅληται Φ 536. ἅλεται Λ 192, 207. (ἀνεφ-, ἐκκατεφ-, ἐξ-, ἐσ-, ἐφ-, καθ-, κατεφ-, μεθ-, ὑπερ-.) To leap, spring, bound: εἰς ἅλα Α 532, χαμᾶζε Γ 29=Ε 494=Ζ 103=Μ 81=Ν 749, Δ 419=Π 426, Ε 111, Λ 211, Π 733, 755, Ω 469. Cf. Λ 192, 207, Μ 390, 611, Π 754, Σ 616, Υ 62, 353, Φ 174, 536, Ω 572: θύραζε φ 388. Cf. χ 2, 80.—Of an inanimate object: ἆλτ' ὀϊστός Δ 125.

ἀλλοπρόσαλλος [ἄλλος+πρός+ἄλλος]. One thing to one person, another to another, double-faced Ε 831, 889.

ἄλλος, -η, -ο. Crasis with τά gives τἄλλα Α 465, Β 428: γ 462, μ 365. (I) (1) Absol. in sing. (a) Another or additional person or thing: ἄλλο τοι ἐρέω Α 297, οἴσομεν ἄλλον Γ 104. Cf. Κ 146, Λ 663, Ξ 262, etc.: λ 454, μ 65, etc.—In apposition: ἄλλο τό γε οἶδα π 470.—(b) (α) Another or different person or thing, another, someone or something else: ἐγὼ ἢ ἄλλος Ἀχαιῶν Β 231, πείθεό τ' ἄλλῳ 360. Cf. Β 271, Ι 101, Λ 410, Ν 229, Τ 181 (in the case of another matter, *i.e.* for the future), Ω 46, etc.: ἄλλος εἴπεσκε νέων β 331, μεῖζον ἄλλο φράζονται δ 698. Cf. γ 94, δ 29, θ 202, λ 176, ν 205, ρ 404, etc.—With τις: ὡς ὄφελέν τις ἀνδρῶν ἄλλος ἔχειν Δ 316. Cf. Ν 272, Ξ 90, etc.: ἄλλο τί τοι μελέτω η 208. Cf. ξ 461, σ 334, υ 297, etc.—Predicatively: ἄλλο τι τόδε μήδεαι (it is some other thing that you are planning) ε 173.—With τίς: τίς τοι ἄλλος ὁμοῖος; P 475. Cf. P 586.—With the article, the other: ἡ ἄλλη σῖτον ἔφερεν ν 69.—With οὗτος and τις: ἄλλος τις οὗτος ἀνέστη υ 380.—(β) With the notion of difference obscured, someone. With τις: μή ποτέ τις εἴπῃσι κακώτερος ἄλλος X 106: φ 324.—(γ) ἄλλο adverbially, app., in another matter Ξ 249.—(τὸ) ἄλλο τόσον, for the rest to a certain extent, *i.e.* so far X 322, Ψ 454.—(c) In negative or conditional contexts (α) Any other or additional person or thing. With τις: οὐδέ τις ἄλλος ᾔδεεν Σ 403. Cf. Ψ 592.—(β) Another, any other or different person or thing, any one or anything else: οὐκ ἐθέλεσκες ἅμ' ἄλλῳ ἰέναι I 486, εἴ με κελεύεις οἴκοθεν ἄλλ' ἐπιδοῦναι Ψ 558. Cf. Ξ 244, Π 141, Ψ 274, etc.: οὐδέ κεν ἡμέας ἄλλο διέκρινεν (anything but death) δ 179, etc.—With τις: οὔτε σοὶ οὔτε τῳ ἄλλῳ A 299, εἴ τευ ἐξ ἄλλου γένευ E 897. Cf. B 80, E 827, I 104, M 248, Π 225, etc.: εἴ τίς μ' ἄλλη ἤγγειλεν ψ 21. Cf. ζ 68, η 67, ι 520, κ 32, etc.—Interrog.: τί σευ ἄλλος ὀνήσεται; Π 31. Cf. δ 649.—With τις: πῶς κέν τίς σ' ἄλλος ἵκοιτο; ι 351.—(γ) With the notion of difference obscured, any one, anything: οὐ σέο κύντερον ἄλλο Θ 483, οὐ δύναμαι γλυκερώτερον ἄλλο ἰδέσθαι ι 28. Cf. λ 427, ο 343, 533, υ 392.—With τις: οὔ τις σεῖο ὀλοώτερος ἄλλος Γ 365. Cf. O 569, T 321, Ψ 439, 580: οὔ τι κύντερον ἄλλο η 216. Cf. θ 32, 138, υ 201, 376.—(d) Every other, every one, any one, all: ὄφρα στυγέῃ ἄλλος A 186, ἄλλον κε σεῦ ἀπαλεξήσαιμι Ω 370, etc.: ὡς ἀπόλοιτο καὶ ἄλλος ὅτις . . . α 47, ἄλλη νεμεσῶ ἥ τις . . . ζ 286, etc.—With τις: ἵνα τις στυγέῃσιν ἄλλος Θ 515.—(2) In sing. with sb., etc. (a) (α) Another or additional: ἄλλον ὀϊστόν Θ 300. Cf. Δ 334, Θ 309, O 458, X 293, Ω 551: ἄλλην ὁδόν κ 490, 563. Cf. ο 449.—With τις: εἴ τίς μοι ἀνὴρ ἅμ' ἕποιτο καὶ ἄλλος K 222. Cf. κ 380, ο 27.—(β) Other, additional: μείζων κ' ἄλλος χόλος ἐτύχθη (*i.e.* matters would have gone further) O 121.—(γ) Besides, in addition: δόλον ἄλλον ὕφαινεν Z 187. Cf. I 365: τέρας ἄλλο φανήτω υ 101. Cf. β 93, ω 128.—With τις: σῆμ' ἄλλο τι δείξω (εἴπω) φ 217, ψ 73.—(b) (α) Another or different, some other: πρόμον ἄλλον H 116. Cf. Γ 226, H 358 = M 232, I 423, Ξ 84, Ψ 460: ῥάκος ἄλλο (other than his own raiment) ν 434, ξ 342. Cf. γ 243, κ 392, λ 127, ο 518, π 9, χ 6, ψ 186, 274.—With τις: μή τις Τρῶας ἐγείρῃσιν θεὸς ἄλλος K 511: δήμιόν τι ἄλλο β 32, 44. Cf. ν 325.—(β) With a collective sb., the other, the rest of the . . .: λαόν Λ 189, etc.: δήμῳ β 239.—(c) In negative or conditional contexts (α) Any other or additional: υἱὸν οὐ τέκετ' ἄλλον E 154. Cf. T 233.—With τις: μηδέ τις ἄλλος ἴτω ἀνήρ Ω 148 = 177. Cf. Ω 505: ε 179 = κ 344, ε 187, κ 300, σ 48.—Interrogatively: ἦέ τιν' ἄλλον ἀμύντορα μερμηρίξω π 261.—(β) Any other or different: οὐ θεὸς ἄλλος ἀνῷγεν Ξ 168. Cf. Z 411, K 330, Ψ 606: ἄλλος κ' ἀνὴρ ἵετο . . . ν 333. Cf. ε 104 = 138, λ 623, etc.—With τις: οὐδέ τις ἄλλος ἀνὴρ ἀνέτλη κ 327. Cf. φ 70, etc.—(γ) With the notion of difference obscured, merely marking a contrast. With τις: μή τί τοι ἄλλο κακὸν μελέτω ἔργον . . . ἀλλ' ἐσθιέμεν β 303.—Any: οὐκ ἂν ἐρίσσειε βροτὸς ἄλλος Γ 223. Cf. B 248: ο 69, 321.—With τις ψ 126.—(d) Every: ὄφρ' ἄλλος πτωχὸς ἀλεύεται ἠπεροπεύειν ξ 400.—(II) (1) Absol. in pl. (a) Other or additional persons or things: εἴ ποθεν ἄλλα γένοιτο I 380. Cf. H 364, X 350, etc.: τρεῖς οἱ ἄλλοι ἔσαν β 21. Cf. β 166, ρ 422, χ 62, etc.—(b) Other or different persons or things, others: πάρ' ἔμοιγε καὶ ἄλλοι A 174, ἄλλων μῦθον ἄκουε B 200. Cf. A 287, Γ 168, Δ 292, E 786, Ψ 193, etc.: ἄλλα μεμήλει α 151. Cf. β 314, δ 166, η 119, ι 188, λ 381, ξ 226, etc.—With the article: τὰ ἄλλα ἄγγελός ἐσσι (in other matters) ε 29, τὰ ἄλλα μετάλλα τ 115. Cf. ο 540, ρ 273, ψ 209.—(c) The other or different persons or things, the others: ἄτερ ἥμενον ἄλλων A 498, πρόσθ' ἄλλων Δ 304. Cf. B 211, Γ 102, E 877, M 245, 285, etc.: ἄλλοι πάντες οἴκοι ἔσαν α 11. Cf. β 209, γ 33, 58, θ 93, ι 172, etc.—With the article: τῶν ἄλλων οὔ τις ὁρᾶτο A 198. Cf. A 465, Γ 73, Δ 429, Z 41, Θ 211, etc.: οἱ ἄλλοι ἀθρόοι ἦσαν α 26. Cf. γ 427, θ 204, ι 61, 331, κ 132, etc.—(d) All others, all men or things, all: ἔξοχον ἄλλων Z 194. Cf. Γ 42, Δ 375, Z 208, H 112, N 631, etc.: περὶ ἄλλων φασὶ γενέσθαι δ 201. Cf. ε 118, θ 102, ψ 110, etc.—In genit. pl. after superl., as compared with all others: νείατος ἄλλων Z 295. Cf. A 505, K 434, Ψ 532: ὀϊζυρώτατον ἄλλων ε 105. Cf. ο 108.—(e) Men: δίκας ἠδὲ φρόνιν ἄλλων γ 244.—(2) In pl. with sb., etc. (a) (α) Other or additional: πολλοὶ ἄλλοι φῶτες ὄλοντο α 355. Cf. α 394, γ 113, ξ 200, χ 28, etc.—(β) Besides, in addition: ἦ οὐχ ἅλις ἡμῖν ἀλήμονές εἰσι καὶ ἄλλοι; ρ 376. Cf. β 65.—(b) Other or different: ἄλλα δίδου γέρα I 334. Cf. P 328, Ψ 459, 700, etc.: ἄλλα κήδεα α 244. Cf. α 374, θ 558, μ 22, etc.—(c) The other or different: Ἀτρεΐδαι τε καὶ ἄλλοι Ἀχαιοί (ye other . . .) A 17, ἄλλοι θεοί B 1. Cf. A 22, Γ 68, E 524, 709, Z 426, etc.: ἄλλους θεράποντας δ 37. Cf. α 210, θ 379, ι 543, κ 320, λ 563, etc.—With the article: τοῖς ἄλλοισι θεοῖς A 597. Cf. B 674, Λ 75, 406, Ξ 189, Π 763, Σ 103, T 83, etc.: τῶν ἄλλων ἀνέμων ε 383. Cf. ζ 176, ι 100, κ 250, λ 541, π 133, etc.—(d) All the other: Ἀχαιῶν ἔξοχον ἄλλων P 358. Cf. δ 171.—All other, all: ἄλλων νόον ἐσθλῶν I 514, etc.: εἴ τι γυναικῶν ἀλλάων περίειμι τ 326, etc.—(III) Of other kind or sort: οὐκ ἔα πόνος ἄλλος E 517 (*i.e.* it was no time for curiosity), ὄρνεον ἄλλο N 64. Cf. N 622, Φ 22: ἄλλῳ αὐτὸν φωτὶ ἤϊσκεν δ 247. Cf. λ 54.—(IV) Contextually (1) A stranger: ἄλοχοι ἄλλοισι δαμεῖεν Γ 301. Cf. Z 456, I 594, X 489, Ω 481: ἔλωρ ἄλλοισιν ν 208. Cf. ν 419, ξ 417, ο 228, υ 213, etc.—In apposition: ἄλλος τις πτωχὸς ἐλθών φ 327.—A foe: ἀδελφεὸν ἄλλος ἔπεφνεν δ 91.—(2) In contrast with something following, an ordinary man: ἄλλος μογέων ἀποκινήσασκεν Λ 636.—(3) Something not according to custom. Predicatively: ἄλλο τι τόδε περιμηχανόωνται η 200.—(4) Something other than the true: οὐκ ἂν ἄλλα παρὲξ εἴποιμι δ 348 = ρ 139.

—(5) Other than the right, the wrong: ἄλλην ὁδόν, ἄλλα κέλευθα ι 261, ἐς ἄλλην γαῖαν ν 211.—(V) Implying in terms the inclusion in a class of a person or thing not in fact included in it: αὐτὸς κάθησο καὶ ἄλλους ἵδρυε λαούς Β 191. Cf. Ε 485, 621, Λ 189, etc.: Ὀδυσσεὺς ἠδὲ καὶ ἄλλοι Φαίηκες θ 368. Cf. α 128, ε 489, ζ 84, λ 470, ο 407, etc.—(VI) (1) Correlative with ἕτερος. See ἕτερος (3) (c).—(2) Followed by ἀλλά Φ 275, Ω 697: γ 377, θ 311, φ 70, ψ 226.—By ἤ Κ 404, etc.—By εἰ μή Ρ 475, Σ 192: μ 325, ρ 383.—(3) Repeated: ἄλλος . . . ἄλλος . . . (ἄλλος . . .), one (some) . . . another (the other, others) . . . Η 473, Θ 429, Ν 730, etc.: γ 26, δ 692, θ 169, etc.—Sim.: ἄλλος ἄλλῳ ἔρεζε θεῶν Β 400. Cf. Μ 175, etc.: ξ 228, σ 301, etc.—For ἄλλος ἄλλῃ, ἄλλοθεν ἄλλος, ἄλλοτε ἄλλος, ἄλλυδις ἄλλος, see these words.—With πολλά Λ 572, etc.

ἄλλοσε [ἄλλος + -σε]. Elsewhither, elsewhere ψ 184, 204.

ἄλλοτε [ἄλλος + ὅτε]. (1) At another time, at other times Κ 120, Ν 776, Τ 200, Υ 53, Χ 171, Ω 511.—(2) Repeated: ἀ. . . . ἀ. . . ., at one time . . . at another . . ., now . . . now . . . Ε 595, Σ 159, 472, Φ 464, Ψ 368, Ω 530: δ 102, ε 331, λ 303, π 209, ψ 94.—Thrice (followed by ποτέ) Ω 10.—Sim. ὁτὲ . . . ἀ. . . . Λ 65, Σ 602, Υ 50.—ἀ. . . . ὁτὲ . . . Λ 566.—(3) With ἄλλος: ἀ. ἐπ' ἄλλον (now on to one, now on to another) Ο 684: ἀ. ἄλλῳ (now to one, now to another) δ 236.—(4) At another time, on a former occasion: ἀ. με ῥίψεν Α 590. Cf. Υ 90, 187.

ἀλλότριος, -η, -ον [ἄλλος]. (1) Of or belonging to others, not one's own Υ 298: α 160, ι 535, λ 115, σ 280, τ 119, υ 171, 221, ω 301.—As if not one's own: γναθμοῖσι γελώων ἀλλοτρίοισιν υ 347 (not expressing their real feelings).—Absol. in neut. pl., things of others, what is not one's own: ἀλλοτρίων χαρίσασθαι ρ 452. Cf. ρ 456, σ 18.—(2) Foreign, alien Ε 214: = π 102, ξ 86, σ 219.

ἄλλοφος, -ον [ἀ-^{1} + λόφος]. Having no crest: κυνέην Κ 258.

ἀλλοφρονέων, -οντος [a first element poss. conn. with ἠλεός + φρονέω]. Dazed, 'silly' Ψ 698.—Troubled or dashed in spirit κ 374.

ἄλλυδις [ἄλλος]. Elsewhither, in another direction. (1) ἀ. ἄλλος, some or part in this direction, some or part in another Λ 486, 745, Μ 461, Ρ 729, Φ 503: ε 71, ζ 138, ξ 25, 35.—(2) ἀ. ἄλλῃ. See ἄλλῃ (2) (c), (3) (b).

ἀλλύω. See ἀναλύω.

ἄλλως [ἄλλος]. (1) Otherwise, differently, so as to bring about a different result Ξ 53.—In other circumstances ο 513.—Reversing a previous decision: μετεβούλευσαν ε 286.—(2) In some other form: εἰ ἀ. δοίης δωτίνην ι 267.—For some other reason ρ 577.—In novel fashion: ἐψιάασθαι φ 429.—(3) καὶ ἀ., as it is, at the best of times, without that: ἀγήνωρ ἐστὶ καὶ ἀ. Ι 699. Cf. Υ 99: φ 87.—(4) Otherwise (connoting improvement): πάρος οὐκ ἔσσεται ἀ. Ε 218.—In other and better wise, better, more effectually: σαωσέμεν Τ 401. Cf. Λ 391: οὔ κεν ἀ. θεὸς τεύξειεν θ 176. Cf. υ 211, ω 107.—(5) Otherwise than with due regard to truth, idly, at random: ἀ. ψεύδονται ξ 124.—(6) With other result than that hoped for, in vain, fruitlessly: ἀ. ἠρήσατο Ψ 144.

ἅλμα, -ατος, τό [ἅλλομαι]. Jumping, leaping θ 128.—In pl.: περιγιγνόμεθ' ἄλλων ἅλμασιν θ 103.

ἅλμη, -ης, ἡ [ἅλς^{2}]. (1) Sea-water, brine ε 53, 322.—(2) Dried sea-spray ζ 137, 219, 225, ψ 237.

ἁλμυρός [ἅλμη]. Salt, briny: ὕδωρ δ 511, ε 100, ι 227, 470, μ 236, 240, 431, ο 294.

ἀλογέω [ἀ-^{1} + λογ-, λέγω^{2}]. To pay no heed or regard Ο 162, 178.

ἁλόθεν. See ἅλς^{1}.

ἀλοιάω. (ἀπ-.) To beat: γαῖαν Ι 568.

ἀλοίην, aor. opt. ἁλίσκομαι.

ἀλοιφή, -ῆς, ἡ [ἀλείφω]. (1) Unguent, oil ζ 220, σ 179.—Tallow applied to a bow φ 179.—(2) Oil or grease used for dressing a hide Ρ 390, 392.—(3) Hog's lard or grease: συὸς ῥάχιν τεθαλυῖαν ἀλοιφῇ Ι 208. Cf. Ι 467, Ψ 32: θ 476, ν 410.

ἁλόντε, masc. dual aor. pple. ἁλίσκομαι.

ἁλοσύδνη, -ης [sense unknown. Traditionally explained as 'daughter of the sea' (ἅλς^{1})]. Of Thetis Υ 207.—Of Amphitrite δ 404.

ἁλοῦσα, fem. aor. pple. ἁλίσκομαι.

ἄλοχος, -ου, ἡ [ἀ-^{2} + λοχ-, λέχος]. A wife, one's wife Α 114, Β 136, Ε 480, Ζ 95, Ι 336, etc.: α 36, γ 264, δ 92, ε 210, θ 243, λ 117, μ 452, etc.

ἀλόωνται, 3 pl. pres. **ἀλόω**, imp. ἀλάομαι.

ἅλς^{1}, ἁλός, ἡ [σαλ-. Cf. L. *sal*]. As genit. ἁλόθεν Φ 335. The sea Α 141, 316, 350, 358, Β 626, etc.: α 162, γ 73, δ 580, 844, ν 235, etc.

ἅλς^{2}, ἁλός, ὁ [cf. prec.]. Dat. pl. ἅλεσσι λ 123, ψ 270. (1) Salt Ι 214.—In pl.: ἅλεσσι μεμιγμένον εἶδαρ λ 123 = ψ 270.—(2) A piece of salt ρ 455.

ἆλσο, 2 sing. aor. ἅλλομαι.

ἄλσος, τό. (1) A grove Υ 8: κ 350, ρ 208.—(2) A sacred grove: Ὀγχηστόν, Ποσιδήϊον ἀ. (*i.e.* O. with its grove) Β 506: Ἀθήνης ζ 291. Cf. ζ 321, ι 200, κ 509, υ 278.

ἆλτο, 3 sing. aor. ἅλλομαι.

ἀλύξει, 3 sing. fut. ἀλύσκω.

ἀλυσκάζω [ἀλύσκω]. (1) To escape, avoid: ὕβριν ρ 581.—(2) Absol., to play the shirker Ε 253, Ζ 443.

ἀλυσκάνω [ἀλύσκω] = prec. (1): κῆρα χ 330.

ἀλύσκω. 3 sing. fut. ἀλύξει ρ 547, τ 558. Infin. ἀλύξειν Κ 371. Aor. ἤλυξα μ 335. 3 sing. ἤλυξε Λ 476. ἄλυξε ψ 332. 3 pl. ἤλυξαν γ 297. ἄλυξαν ψ 328. 2 sing. subj. ἀλύξῃς λ 113, μ 140. 3 -ῃ Κ 348: χ 66. 1 pl. opt. ἀλύξαιμεν κ 269. Pple. ἀλύξας Μ 113, Ν 395, Ο 287: β 352, ε 387, θ 353. Infin. ἀλύξαι Θ 243, Φ 565, Χ 201: δ 416, ε 345, μ 216, χ 460. (ὑπ-.) (1) To escape, evade, avoid (impending danger): ὄλεθρον Κ 371. Cf. Λ 476, Μ 113, Ν 395, Ο 287, Φ 565: κῆρας β 352 = ε 387. Cf. γ 297, κ 269, μ 216, ρ 547 = τ 558, χ 66, 363, 382, ψ 328, 332.—(2) To get away from, effect one's escape or release from (something in which one is involved): χρέος καὶ δεσμόν (getting out of the debt and freeing himself from the bonds) θ 353.—To get free from the company of: ἑταίρους μ 335.—(3) Absol., to effect one's escape, escape, save oneself Θ 243, K 348, X 201: δ 416, ε 345, λ 113 = μ 140, χ 460.

ἀλύσσω = ἀλύω: ἀλύσσοντες (maddened) X 70.

ἄλυτος, -ον [ἀ-[1] + λύω]. Not to be loosed: *πέδας* N 37, *πεῖραρ* 360: *δεσμούς* θ 275.

ἀλύω (ῡ ι 398). (1) To be beside oneself from pain or grief: ἀλύουσ' ἀπεβήσετο E 352. Cf. Ω 12.—From exultation σ 333 = 393.—(2) To manifest distraction by gestures: χερσὶν ἀλύων ι 398.

†**ἀλφάνω.** Aor. ἦλφον Φ 79. 3 sing. opt. ἄλφοι ο 453, ρ 250, υ 383. To bring in, yield (a price) (always of a human chattel): ἑκατόμβοιον Φ 79. Cf. ο 453, ρ 250, υ 383.

ἀλφεσίβοιος, -η [ἀλφε-, ἀλφάνω + -σι- + βοῦς]. Bringing (her parents many) oxen (as bride-price) Σ 593.

ἀλφηστής, -οῦ [ἀλφ-, ἀλφάνω]. Epithet of men, gain-getting, having to labour for their bread α 349, ζ 8, ν 261.

ἄλφιτον, -ου, τό. Barley (i.e. the prepared corn): ἀλφίτου ἀκτήν (barley-meal) Λ 631. Cf. β 355, ξ 429.—In pl.: ἄλφιτα λευκά Λ 640. Cf. Σ 560: β 290, 354, 380, κ 234, 520, λ 28, ξ 77, τ 197, υ 108, 119.

ἄλφοι, 3 sing. aor. opt. ἀλφάνω.

ἀλωή, -ῆς, ἡ. (1) A threshing-floor E 499, N 588, Υ 496.—(2) A piece of levelled or prepared ground, a garden, orchard, vineyard E 90, I 534, 540, Σ 57 = 438, Φ 36, 77, 346: ζ 293.—Distinguished as an orchard ω 221, 224, 226, 336.—As a vineyard Σ 561, 566 (in both cases referring to a representation in metal): α 193, η 122, λ 193.

ἀλώμεναι, ἀλῶναι, aor. infin. ἁλίσκομαι.

ἀλώω, aor. subj. ἁλίσκομαι.

ἅμα [σα-. Cf. ἁ-[2], ἅπαξ, ἅπας, ἁπλοῖς, L. *simul*]. (I) Adv. (1) With, along with, a person or persons, in his or their company: ἁ. ἕποντο A 424, φέρει ἁ. παῖδα Z 389. Cf. Γ 447, Δ 274, I 170, K 194, Λ 344, etc.: κήρυχ' ἁ. ὀπάσσας ι 90. Cf. β 287, 413, ζ 319, θ 109, ν 68, etc.—(2) All or both together, in a body, without exception: πάντες ἁ. A 495, ταῦθ' ἁ. χρὴ σπεύδειν (with united effort) N 235. Cf. A 533, Z 59, Θ 8, O 718, Σ 50, etc.: ἁ. πλέομεν γ 276. Cf. θ 121, κ 259, λ 232, μ 110, ν 82, etc.—In reference to things, all at once, without exception: ἁ. πάνθ' ἑλέσθαι N 729. Cf. Δ 320.—(3) At the same time: σκεψάμενος ἐς νῆ' ἁ. καὶ μεθ' ἑταίρους μ 247. Cf. κ 123, σ 356.—Together, at the same moment: ἁ. ἄμφω σύν ῥ' ἔπεσον H 255. Cf. N 613, T 242, etc.: ὁμαρτήσαντες ἁ. ἄμφω φ 188.—In reference to something done while others are doing other things: τῇ ἁ. 'Α. κλισίην ἔθηκεν, 'Α. δὲ . . . Φ. δὲ . . . δ 123.—(4) At the same time, besides, too, also: ἁ. δ' ἄλλ' ἀποδάσσεσθαι X 117. Cf. Ω 304: τ 376.—ἁ. . . . καὶ . . ., both . . . and . . .: ἁ. πρόσσω καὶ ὀπίσσω A 343. Cf. B 707, N 299, etc.: γ 111, τ 471, etc.—So ἁ. . . . τε . . . καὶ . . . ω 249.—ἁ. τε . . . τε N 669.—ἁ. τε . . . δὲ . . . I 519.—Other combinations in A 417, B 281, Δ 450, N 85, Ω 773, etc.: ξ 403.—(II) Prep. with dat. (freq. following the case). (1) With, along with, in company with: ἁ. ἡγεμόνεσσιν Γ 1. Cf. A 158, 226, 251, B 249, 524, etc.: τῷ ἁ. πομπὸν ἕπεσθαι δ 162. Cf. α 98, 331, 428, β 11, γ 359, etc.—(2) At the same time with, at the time of: ἁ. ἠελίῳ καταδύντι A 592. Cf. H 331, I 618, Λ 685, Σ 136, Ω 600, etc.: ἁ. ἠοῖ δ 407. Cf. ζ 31, μ 24, ξ 266, π 2, ψ 362, etc.

ἄμαθος [cf. ψάμαθος]. Loose or sandy soil E 587.

ἀμαθύνω [ἄμαθος]. To level with the dust, destroy: πόλιν I 593.

ἀμαιμάκετος, -η, -ον [perh. redup. fr. μακ-, μακρός]. Thus, of very great size or height: Χίμαιραν Z 179, Π 329: ἱστὸν νηός ξ 311.

ἀμαλδύνω. Aor. pple. ἀμαλδύνας M 32. Infin. ἀμαλδῦναι M 18. To destroy, level H 463, M 18, 32.

ἀμαλλοδετήρ, -ῆρος [ἄμαλλα, sheaf + δέω]. A binder of sheaves Σ 553, 554.

ἀμαλός, -ή. Of young animals, tender, feeble: ἄρνα X 310: σκυλάκεσσιν υ 14.

ἄμαξα, ἡ. (1) A four-wheeled cart, a waggon (app. = ἀπήνη; cf. ζ 69 with 72) H 426, M 448, Ω 150 = 179, 189, 263, 266, 711, 782: ζ 37, 72, 260, ι 241, κ 103.—(2) = ἄρκτος (2) Σ 487: = ε 273.

ἁμαξιτός [ἄμαξα]. A road X 146.

ἀμάρη, -ης, ἡ. An irrigation trench Φ 259.

†**ἁμαρτάνω.** 3 sing. impf. ἡμάρτανε K 372, Ω 68: λ 511. Fut. infin. in mid. form ἁμαρτήσεσθαι ι 512. 3 sing. aor. ἅμαρτε Δ 491, Θ 311, Λ 233, N 518, 605, O 430, P 609, Ψ 865: ζ 116. 3 sing. subj. ἁμάρτῃ I 501: ν 214. Pple. ἁμαρτών X 505, Ψ 857. Infin. ἁμαρτεῖν φ 155. Aor. ἤμβροτον φ 425, χ 154. 2 sing. -ες E 287, X 279. 3 -ε η 292, φ 421. 3 pl. -ον Π 336. (ἀφ-.) (1) To discharge a missile vainly, miss one's aim: ἤμβροτες οὐδ' ἔτυχες E 287. Cf. Θ 311, Λ 233 = N 605, N 518, X 279.—(2) To fail to hit, miss. With genit.: φωτός K 372. Cf. Δ 491, O 430, Π 336, P 609, Ψ 857, 865: σκοποῦ φ 425. Cf. φ 421.—Sim., to miss (a person) in throwing something to be caught ζ 116.—(3) To lose, be deprived of. With genit.: ὀπωπῆς ι 512.—Sim., to lose (a person) by death X 505.—(4) To fall short, be lacking or deficient in. With genit.: δώρων (failed to give in due measure) Ω 68: νοήματος ἐσθλοῦ (failed in the matter of) η 292, μύθων (failed in finding the right) λ 511.—(5) To commit wrong, sin: ὅτε κέν τις ἁμάρτῃ I 501. Cf. ν 214, φ 155.—To neglect one's duty: τόδε γ' ἤμβροτον (in this) χ 154.

ἁμαρτῇ [ἅμα + ἀρ-, ἀραρίσκω]. (1) Both or all together: δούρατ' ἤϊξαν E 656, ῥήσσοντες Σ 571.—(2) At the same moment, simultaneously Φ 162: χ 81.

ἀμαρτοεπής [ἁμαρτάνω + ἔπος. Cf. ἀφαμαρτοεπής]. Stumbling in speech. In voc. ἁμαρτοεπές N 824.

ἁματροχιή, -ῆς, ἡ [ἅμα + τροχ-, τρέχω]. A coming of wheels together, a coming of chariots abreast of each other Ψ 422.

ἀμαυρός. Dim, faint, shadowy δ 824, 835.

ἀμαχητί [ἀ-[1] + μάχη]. Without a fight Φ 437.

ἀμάω[1]. (ἀπ-, δι-.) (1) To reap, act as reaper Σ 551.—(2) To reap (a crop) ι 135.—To cut (reeds)

Ω 451.—(3) To slice off: ἀπ' οὔατ' ἀμήσαντες φ 301.

ἀμάω[2] [perh. conn. with ἅμα]. (ἐπ-, κατ-.) To collect, bring together. In mid.: ἐν ταλάροισιν ἀμησάμενος ι 247.

ἀμβαίη, contr. 3 sing. aor. opt. ἀναβαίνω.

ἀμβαλλώμεθα, contr. 1 pl. subj. mid. ἀναβάλλω.

ἀμβατός, -όν [ἀμ-, ἀνα- (1) + βα-, βαίνω]. Capable of being scaled: πόλις Z 434: οὐρανός λ 316.

ἀμβλήδην [ἀμβλη-, ἀμβάλλω = ἀναβάλλω]. Lifting up the voice X 476. (Cf. ἀνεβάλλετ' ἀείδειν under ἀναβάλλω (2).)

ἀμβολάδην [ἀμβολ-, ἀμβάλλω. See prec.]. Spirting up: λέβης ζεῖ ἀ. Φ 364.

ἀμβροσίη, -ης, ἡ [fem. of next as sb. 'Fragrance']. (1) The food of the gods ε 93, 199, ι 359, μ 63.—Introduced into Achilles T 347, 353.—Eaten by divine horses E 777.—(2) Used as a perfume δ 445.—By Here as a cleansing (and doubtless perfuming) cosmetic Ξ 170.—Applied by divine agency as a preservative or for purification to the corpse of Sarpedon Π 670, 680.—Introduced by divine agency into the corpse of Patroclus T 38.

ἀμβρόσιος, -η, -ον. Sweet-smelling, fragrant: χαῖται A 529, νύκτα B 57 (prob. referring to the fragrance of a still warm night), ὕπνος B 19 (prob. a transference of epithet from νύξ). Cf. E 338, 369, Θ 434, K 41, 142, N 35, Ξ 172, 177, 178, Σ 268, Φ 507, Ψ 187 (here no doubt with a reference to preservative properties of the divine food; cf. ἀμβροσίη (2)), Ω 341, 363: = α 97 = ε 45, δ 429 = 574, η 283, ι 404, ο 8, σ 193.

ἄμβροτος[1], -ον. = prec.: εἵματα Π 670, 680: η 260, 265, ω 59, ἐλαίῳ θ 365, νύξ λ 330.

ἄμβροτος[2] [ἀ-[1] + (μ)βροτός]. (1) Immortal Y 358, X 9, Ω 460: ω 445.—Of horses Π 381 = 867.—(2) Of or belonging to a god, divine E 339, 870: ε 347.—(3) Befitting a god P 194, 202: κ 222.—(4) App., conferring divine qualities: δῶρα σ 191.

ἀμέγαρτος, -ον [ἀ-[1] + μεγαίρω]. Not to be envied or desired. (1) Of a person in depreciation, miserable, wretched ρ 219, φ 362.—(2) Dread, dire B 420: λ 400 = 407.

ἀμείβοντες, οἱ [pres. pple. pl. of next]. The rafters, sloping to each other in pairs, of a pitched roof Ψ 712 (the wrestlers, with shoulders together but standing wide apart with their feet, being compared with a pair).

ἀμείβω. 3 sing. aor. mid. ἠμείψατο Ψ 542. ἀμείψατο Δ 403. 3 sing. subj. ἀμείψεται I 409: κ 328. Pple. ἀμειψάμενος ω 285. Infin. ἀμείψασθαι Ψ 489: β 83, δ 286, π 91. (ἀπ-, ἐπ-, παρ-.) (1) To change: ἔντεα P 192.—To exchange (with another). With genit. of what is taken in exchange: τεύχεα πρὸς Διομήδεα χρύσεα χαλκείων Z 235.—Sim., to exchange (the support of) one thing for (that of) another: γόνυ γουνός Λ 547.—(2) To cause persons to exchange: τεύχεα Ξ 381.—(3) In mid. (a) To requite: εὖ σε δώροισιν ἀμειψάμενος (making a good return to you in gifts) ω 285.—(b) To take turns with one another: ἀμειβόμενοι φυλακὰς ἔχον I 471.—So ἀμειβόμεναι ὀπὶ καλῇ (taking up the strain from each other) A 604: ω 60.—ἀμειβόμενοι κατὰ οἴκους (each in turn giving the feast in his house) α 375 = β 140.—ταρφέ' ἀμειβομένω (with frequent change (from side to side)) θ 379.—(c) To pass from one position or place to another: ἄλλοτ' ἐπ' ἄλλον [ἵππον] ἀμείβεται O 684.—(d) To pass from, leave, quit: ἕρκος ὀδόντων I 409.—(e) To enter: ἕρκος ὀδόντων κ 328.—(f) To answer, reply to A 121, 172, 292, 413, etc.: α 44, β 83, γ 102, δ 286, etc.—(g) To speak in answer, make answer N 823, Ψ 489, 492, Ω 200, 424: γ 148, δ 382, 484, ζ 67, etc.—In pres. pple. ἀμειβόμενος, -η, making answer, in answer Γ 437, H 356, Ξ 270, etc.: β 84, δ 234, 375, etc.

ἀμείλικτος, -ον [ἀ-[1] + μειλίσσω]. (Indicating) inflexible (resolve): ὄπα Λ 137, Φ 98.

ἀμείλιχος [as prec.]. Inflexible, implacable, relentless: 'Ἀΐδης I 158, ἦτορ 572, ἄνακτος Ω 734.

ἀμείνων, -ονος. Neut. ἄμεινον. Acc. sing. masc. and fem. ἀμείνω Γ 11, Δ 400, I 423. Neut. pl. ἀμείνω η 310, ο 71. Used as comp. of ἀγαθός or ἐσθλός. (1) More warlike, soldierly, or skilful in fight B 239, Δ 405, E 173, 411, Z 479, H 111, 114, O 641, Π 709, Φ 107, X 158, 333: σ 334.—So βίην ἀ. A 404, O 139.—βίῃ ἀ. Λ 787.—(2) Better, more worthy, serviceable or skilful: ἀγορῇ Δ 400. Cf. Z 350, Σ 106, Ψ 315, 479, 605 (your betters): β 180, η 51, χ 156.—In reference to personal appearance ω 374.—Of horses K 556.—(3) Of things or abstractions, better of their kind, better, more excellent, helpful or in place: ὁμίχλην νυκτὸς ἀμείνω Γ 11. Cf. A 116, H 358 = M 232, I 104, 256, 423, M 412, Ξ 107, O 509: ἀμείνω αἴσιμα πάντα η 310, ο 71. Cf. α 376 = β 141, ε 364, ξ 466, χ 374.—Impers. with infin.: πείθεσθαι ἄμεινόν [ἐστιν] A 274. Cf. Λ 469: χ 104.—Sim.: ὧς γὰρ ἄμεινον A 217.—(4) Good rather than ill: οὔ οἱ τό γ' ἄμεινον Ω 52.

ἀμείψατο, 3 sing. aor. mid. ἀμείβω.

ἀμέλγω. (ἐν-.) To milk ι 238, 244 = 341, 308.—In pass. with the milk in acc.: ἀμελγόμεναι γάλα Δ 434.

ἀμελέω [ἀ-[1] + μέλω]. With genit. (and always with neg.). (1) To disregard the claims of, fail to aid: οὐκ ἀμέλησε κασιγνήτοιο Θ 330. Cf. N 419.—In sinister sense of holding back from attempting to despoil P 9.—(2) To disregard, fail to carry out: ἐφημοσύνης P 697.

ἄμεναι, pres. infin. ἄω.

ἀμενηνός [ἀ-[1]. App. obscurely conn. with μένος]. Weak, powerless E 887.—Of ghosts, fleeting, feeble κ 521, 536, λ 29, 49.—Of dreams, fleeting, transient τ 562.

ἀμενηνόω [ἀμενηνός]. To deprive of efficiency or effect: αἰχμήν N 562.

ἀμέρδω. 3 sing. aor. ἄμερσε θ 64. Infin. ἀμέρσαι Π 53. 2 sing. aor. subj. pass. ἀμερθῇς X 58. (1) To deprive of or debar from. With genit.: αἰῶνος X 58. Cf. θ 64, φ 290.—(2) To despoil, rob Π 53.—(3) To blind (the eyes) N 340.—(4) To deprive of lustre, tarnish τ 18.

ἀμέτρητος [ἀ-[1] + μετρέω]. Immeasurable, endless: πένθος τ 512, πόνος ψ 249.

ἀμετροεπής [ἀ-[1] + μέτρον + ἔπος]. Unmeasured in words. Of Thersites B 212.

ἀμητήρ, -ῆρος, ὁ [ἀμάω [1]]. A reaper Λ 67.

ἄμητος, ὁ [as prec.]. A harvest T 223.

ἀμηχανίη, -ης, ἡ [ἀμήχανος]. Helplessness ι 295.

ἀμήχανος, -ον [ἀ-[1] + μηχανή = μῆχος]. (**1**) Without resources, helpless τ 363.—(**2**) Unmanageable, difficult to deal with: ἀ. παραρρητοῖσι πιθέσθαι (in that you will not listen to persuasion) N 726. —Of Here O 14.—Of Achilles Π 29.—Of Agamemnon T 273.—Playfully of Nestor K 167.—Against which no contrivance avails Θ 130 = Λ 310. —Impracticable, not to be attempted Ξ 262.—Difficult to deal with or expound: ὄνειροι τ 560.

ἀμιτροχίτωνες [ἀ-[1] + μίτρη + χιτών]. Wearing no μίτρη with the χιτών, not wearing the μίτρη Π 419.

ἀμιχθαλόεις, -εσσα [prob. = ὀμιχθαλόεις fr. ὀμίχλη]. Thus, misty, steaming. Of Lemnos Ω 753. (Lemnos is not volcanic. The reference may be to some jet of natural gas which has now disappeared.)

ἀμμείξας, ἀμμίξας, contr. aor. pple. ἀναμίσγω.

ἄμμες. We (= ἡμεῖς) Φ 432: ι 303, 321, χ 55. Dat. ἄμμι A 384, B 137, Δ 197, etc.: α 123, β 334, δ 770, etc. Acc. ἄμμε A 59, H 292, K 346, etc.: ι 404, κ 209, μ 221, χ 73.

ἀμμορίη, -ης, ἡ [ἄμμορος]. App., what (of good) fate does not bestow, ill fortune υ 76.

ἄμμορος, -ον [ἀ-[1] + μόρος]. (**1**) Denied the just dues of mankind, ill-fated Z 408, Ω 773. —(**2**) Having no share in, not entering. With genit.: λοετρῶν Ὠκεανοῖο Σ 489 := ε 275.

ἀμνίον, τό [app. conn. with αἷμα]. A vessel for collecting the blood of a sacrificial victim γ 444.

ἀμογητί [ἀ-[1] + μογέω]. With ease Λ 637.

ἀμόθεν [ἀμός = τις + -θεν (1)]. From any point (of a narrative): τῶν ἀ. εἰπέ α 10.

ἀμοιβάς [ἀμείβω]. Of a garment, kept for a change (= ἐπημοιβός (1)): χλαῖνα ξ 521.

ἀμοιβή, -ῆς, ἡ [ἀμείβω]. (**1**) A return or requital: ἄξιον ἔσται ἀμοιβῆς (will bring a (full) return) α 318, ἑκατόμβης (for . . .) γ 58.—(**2**) Compensation: βοῶν (for the loss of . . .) μ 382.

ἀμοιβηδίς [ἀμοιβή]. In turns Σ 506: σ 310.

ἀμοιβοί, οἱ [ἀμοιβή]. A relieving force: ἦλθον ἀμοιβοί (as a . . .) N 793.

ἀμολγός. Sense unknown. (ἐν) νυκτὸς ἀμολγῷ, gen. rendered, in the depth or gloom of night Λ 173, O 324, X 28, 317: δ 841. (But Sirius, referred to in X 27 as shining ὀπώρης, is not then seen in the depth of night; and ἀστὴρ ἕσπερος in X 317 also causes difficulty.)

ἀμός, -ή, -όν. Our (= ἡμέτερος) Z 414, Θ 178, K 448, N 96, Π 830: λ 166 = 481. (But the sense 'my' (cf. ἡμέτερος (2)) is always admissible, and in Z 414, and perh. in Θ 178, is preferable.)

ἄμοτος. In neut. ἄμοτον as adv., insatiably, continually, incessantly, without pause or intermission Δ 440, E 518, N 40, 80, T 300, X 36, Ψ 567: ζ 83, ρ 520.

†**ἀμπείρω** [ἀμ-, ἀνα- (6)]. Nom. pl. masc. aor. pple. ἀμπείραντες. To transfix, spit B 426.

ἀμπελόεις, -εσσα [ἄμπελος]. Rich in vines. Epithet of places B 561, Γ 184, I 152 = 294.

ἄμπελος, -ου, ἡ. A vine ι 110, 133, ω 246.

ἀμπεπαλών, contr. aor. pple. ἀναπάλλω.

ἀμπερές [ἀμπείρω]. Passing through. With διά (cf. διαμπερές): διὰ δ' ἀ. ἰὸς κατέπηκτο Λ 377. Cf. P 309: φ 422.

ἀμπέχω [ἀμπ-, ἀμφι- (3)]. To cover ζ 225.

ἀμπηδάω [ἀμ-, ἀνα- (1)]. To leap up, start up: ἐκ λόχου ἀμπήδησεν Λ 379.

ἀμπνεῦσαι, contr. aor. infin. ἀναπνέω.

ἄμπνυε, contr. aor. imp. ἀναπνέω.

ἀμπνύ(ν)θη, ἄμπνῦτο. See ἐμπνύνθη.

ἄμπυξ, -υκος. A diadem of metal worn over the forehead X 469.

ἄμυδις [ἅμα]. (**1**) Together, all together, in or into a body or mass: θυνόντων ἀ. K 524. Cf. I 6, K 300, M 385, N 336, 343, Υ 114, 158, 374, Ψ 217: δ 659, μ 413.—(**2**) Together, at the same time: ἀ. βρόντησε καὶ ἔμβαλε κεραυνόν μ 415 = ξ 305. Cf. ε 467.

ἀμύμων, -ονος. (**1**) An epithet of persons of general commendation, noble, illustrious, goodly, or the like: μάντις A 92, Αἰθιοπῆας 423. Cf. B 674, E 247, Z 155, Λ 835, Υ 236, etc.: Αἰγίσθοιο (app. as a merely conventional epithet) α 29, Ὀδυσῆος β 225. Cf. δ 187, η 29, θ 117, τ 332, φ 325, etc. —Of women: ἄκοιτιν Z 374. Cf. δ 4, η 303, ν 42, ο 15, etc.—Of a nymph Ξ 444.—Of a horse Π 152. —(**2**) Sim. of things or abstractions, indicating excellence or perfection: πομπῇ Z 171, ἔργα I 128, τόξῳ O 463. Cf. I 270, K 19, N 637, Π 119, T 245, Ψ 263: οἶκος α 232, μῆτις ι 414. Cf. κ 50, μ 261, ξ 508, π 237, χ 442 = 459, ψ 145, ω 80, 278.—(**3**) Absol. in neut. pl.: ὃς ἂν ἀμύμονα εἰδῇ (is of noble heart) (see εἴδω (III) (12)) τ 332.

ἀμύντωρ, -ορος, ὁ [ἀμύνω]. A defender or helper Ξ 449, O 540, 610: β 326, π 256, 261.

ἀμύνω. 3 sing. impf. ἄμυνε N 678, Ξ 71, O 731. 3 sing. aor. ἤμῦνε I 599, N 783. ἄμῦνε Δ 129, E 662, M 402, P 615. 3 sing. opt. ἀμύναι M 334, O 736. Imp. ἄμῦνον A 456, O 375: χ 208. Infin. ἀμῦναι A 67, I 576, Π 75, Ω 489, etc.: β 59, ρ 538. Aor. opt. mid. ἀμυναίμην β 62, μ 114. (ἀπ-, ἐπ-, προσ-.) (**1**) To ward off, keep off, avert: λοιγόν E 603, 662, Σ 450, Υ 98, Ω 489. Cf. Z 463, I 599, N 783, O 375, P 615: ἀρήν β 59 = ρ 538, χ 208, μνηστῆρας ω 380.—To defend oneself against, fight with: δήϊον ἄνδρα X 84.—With dat. of person or thing protected: ἡμῖν λοιγόν A 67. Cf. A 341, 398, 456, Δ 129, I 435, 495, Λ 277, 588, M 334, N 426, O 736, Π 32, 512, 835, P 511, Σ 129, Υ 124: ἄστεϊ νηλεὲς ἦμαρ θ 525.—With genit.: κῆρας παιδός M 402. Cf. Δ 11, O 731, Π 75, 80.—(**2**) To defend, protect, succour, fight for, come to the rescue of. With dat.: ὤρεσσιν E 486, σοῖσιν ἔτῃσιν Z 262. Cf. I 518, 602, Λ 674, N 464, 481, Ξ 71, 362, 369, O 73, 255, 492 (supplying αὐτοῖς), 688, Π 265, Ρ 273, 563, 703, Φ 215, 231, 414: Ἀργείοισιν λ 500, 518. Cf. π 257, φ 195, 197, χ 214.—With genit.: οὗ παιδός Π 522. Cf. Ν 109.—(**3**) Absol. to play the defender, fight, show fight: ἐξελθεῖν καὶ ἀμῦναι Ι 576. Cf. Ν 312, 678, 814, Ρ 182: οὔ τοῖοι ἀμυνέμεν β 60.—(**4**) In mid. (**a**) To ward or keep off from oneself: ἀμύνετο νηλεὲς ἦμαρ Λ 484, Ν 514. Cf. Ρ 510.—Sim. ἄνδρας θηρητῆρας ἀμύνονται περὶ τέκνων Μ 170.—To defend oneself against, fight with: Σκύλλην μ 114.—(**b**) To defend, protect, fight for. With genit.: Καλυδῶνος Ι 531. Cf. Μ 155, 179, Π 561.—With ablative: ναῦφιν Ν 700.—(**c**) Absol., to play the defender, fight: περὶ νηῶν Μ 142. Cf. Μ 227, 243, Ο 496, Π 556, 622, Σ 173, Ω 500: ἧός μοι ἀμύνεσθαι πάρ' ὀϊστοί χ 106. Cf. β 62, χ 116.

ἀμύσσω. 2 sing. fut. ἀμύξεις Α 243. (κατ-.) To tear, lacerate: χερσὶ στήθεα Τ 284.—Fig.: θυμόν Α 243.

ἀμφαγαπάζω [ἀμφ-, ἀμφι- (3)]. (**1**) To welcome (with suppressed notion of embracing) ξ 381.—(**2**) To show love to, treat with affection. In mid. Π 192.

†**ἀμφαγείρω** [ἀμφ-, ἀμφι- (3)]. 3 pl. aor. mid. ἀμφαγέροντο. In mid., to come together or gather *round*. With acc.: θεαί μιν ἀμφαγέροντο Σ 37.

ἀμφαδά [ἀμφαίνω = ἀναφαίνω]. Openly, without concealment: μὴ ἀ. ἔργα γένοιτο (disclosure should take place) τ 391.

ἀμφάδιος [as prec.]. (**1**) Open, public: γάμον ζ 288.—(**2**) Adv. of acc. fem. form ἀμφαδίην = prec. Η 196, Ν 356: ε 120.

ἀμφαδόν [as prec.]. Openly, without concealment or subterfuge: βαλέειν Η 243, ἀγορευέμεν Ι 370: ἠὲ δόλῳ ἢ ἀ. α 296, λ 120, ἢ ἀ. ἦε κρυφηδόν ξ 330 = τ 299.

ἀμφαραβέω [ἀμφ-, ἀμφι- (3)]. To rattle or ring about one: τεύχε' ἀμφαράβησεν Φ 408.

ἀμφασίη, ἡ [ἀμ- (= ἀ-[1]) + φα-, φημί]. Speechlessness: ἀ. μιν λάβεν Ρ 695: = δ 704.

†**ἀμφαφάω** [ἀμφ-, ἀμφι- (3)]. Pres. pple. ἀμφαφόων θ 196. Acc. pl. ἀμφαφόωντας τ 586. Fem. ἀμφαφόωσα δ 277. 3 pl. impf. mid. ἀμφαφόωντο ο 462. Infin. ἀμφαφάασθαι Χ 373: θ 215, τ 475. (**1**) To put the hands round, handle. In mid.: [ὅρμον] ἀμφαφόωντο ο 462. Cf. τ 475.—So μαλακώτερος ἀμφαφάασθαι (easier to deal with) Χ 373.—To handle and use: τόξον τ 586.—In mid. θ 215.—(**2**) To put the hands on in passing round: κοῖλον λόχον (the wooden horse) δ 277.—(**3**) Absol., to feel about with the hands θ 196.

ἀμφέθετο, 3 sing. aor. mid. ἀμφιτίθημι.

ἀμφεκάλυψε, 3 sing. aor. ἀμφικαλύπτω.

ἀμφέξεσα, aor. ἀμφιξέω.

ἄμφεπε, 3 sing. impf. See ἀμφιέπω.

†**ἀμφέρχομαι** [ἀμφ-, ἀμφι- (3)]. 3 sing. aor. ἀμφήλυθε. To come *round*, be diffused *round*. With acc.: ἀϋτή με ζ 122, ἀϋτμή με μ 369.

ἀμφέσταν, 3 pl. aor. ἀμφίστημι.

ἀμφέχανε, 3 sing. aor. ἀμφιχαίνω.

ἀμφεχύθη, ἀμφέχυτο, 3 sing. aor. pass. ἀμφιχέω.

ἀμφήκης. Neut. ἄμφηκες. [ἀμφ-, ἀμφι- (2) + ἀκή, point, edge.] Two-edged Κ 256, Φ 118: π 80, φ 341.

ἀμφήλυθε, 3 sing. aor. ἀμφέρχομαι.

ἀμφηρεφής [ἀμφ-, ἀμφι- (1) + ἐρέφω]. Covering on both sides: φαρέτρην (*i.e.* enclosing (the arrows)) Α 45.

ἀμφήριστος [ἀμφ-, ἀμφι- (1) + ἐρίζω]. Disputed on both sides. In neut. qualifying a vague notion 'the state of things'; hence, a dead heat: ἀμφήριστόν κ' ἔθηκεν Ψ 382, 527.

ἀμφί. (**I**) Adv. (**1**) (**a**) On both sides: ἀ. ὀβελοῖσιν ἔπειραν (so that the spits appeared on both sides) Α 465 = Β 428. Cf. Ι 210: ξύλα τ' ἀ. καὶ οἰσέμεν ὕδωρ (*i.e.* to be set on either side of the altar) γ 429. Cf. γ 462 = μ 365 = ξ 430, ξ 75.—(**b**) In reference to the two sides of the body: ἀ. ὄσσε νὺξ ἐκάλυψεν (both eyes) Ε 310 = Λ 356. Cf. Ζ 117, Κ 535, etc.: δρεψαμένω ἀ. δειράς β 153. Cf. ι 389.—Sim. in reference to the φρένες (see μέλας (1)): μένεος φρένες ἀ. μέλαιναι πίμπλαντο Α 103: = δ 661. Cf. Ρ 83, 499, 573.—From side to side: ἀ. μοι χεὶρ ὀδύνῃσιν ἐλήλαται Π 517.—(**2**) Round, about, round about: ἔστασαν Δ 330. Cf. Δ 328, Ε 194, Η 449, Λ 417, Ξ 420, etc.: χλαίνας βάλον δ 50. Cf. γ 32, δ 253, ε 72, η 14, ι 22, etc.—Joined with περί Φ 10, Ψ 191.—Fig.: ἀ. μάλα φράζεσθε (look at the matter all round, consider well) Σ 254.—(**3**) About or concerning something: τάδ' ἀ. πονησόμεθα Ψ 159. Cf. Η 316, Λ 776: τὸν δέρον ἀ. θ' ἕπον θ 61, τ 421.—(**II**) Prep. (sometimes (without anastrophe) following the case). (**1**) With dat. (**a**) On each side of: ἀ. κῦμα στείρῃ ἴαχεν Α 481, ἀ. ὤμοισιν βάλετο ξίφος (*i.e.* the belt rested on both shoulders) Β 45, θώρηκας ῥήξειν ἀ. στήθεσσιν (*i.e.* the two γύαλα) 544, ἀ. ὀχέεσσι βάλε κύκλα Ε 722, ἀ. σφοῖς ὀχέεσσιν (app., sprawling over them) Σ 231, ἀ. πυρὶ στῆσαι τρίποδα (astraddle over it) 344, etc.: ἀ. ἐνὶ δούρατι βαῖνεν (bestriding it) ε 371, ἀ. πυρὶ χαλκὸν ἵηνατε θ 426, etc.—So with locative: ἱδρώσει τελαμὼν ἀ. στήθεσφιν Β 388.—In reference to a shield protecting on both sides (cf. ἀμφίβροτος): δῄουν ἀ. στήθεσσι βοείας Ε 452. Cf. Κ 149 (across the shoulders), Λ 527, Π 108, Ρ 132, etc.—For βαίνειν ἀ. τινι see βαίνω (I) (6) (a), and cf. ἀμφιβαίνω (4).—Joined with περί λ 609.—(**b**) Round, about, round about: Τυφωέϊ Β 782, εἰδώλῳ Ε 451. Cf. Ι 654, Ν 496, Ξ 447, Ο 608, etc.: πόλει ζ 9, γούνασιν η 142. Cf. δ 245, κ 262, λ 423, ξ 23, etc.—So with locative: ἀ. κυνέην κεφαλῆφιν ἔθηκεν Κ 257. Cf. Κ 261: π 145.—In reference to something transfixing: ἀ. σιδήρῳ Ψ 30. Cf. μ 395.—With notion of protection: ἀ. βόεσσιν Ο 587. Cf. Ρ 369.—(**c**) About, concerning, for, touching, in the matter of: Ἑλένῃ Γ 70. Cf. Γ 254, Η 408, Λ 672, Ν 382, Π 647, etc.: τεύχεσιν ἀ. Ἀχιλῆος λ 546. Cf. α 48, δ 151, ξ 338, ρ 555, χ 227, etc.—(**2**) With acc. (**a**) On each side of: ἀ. κῆρ Π 481.—(**b**) Round, about, round about: ἀ. ἅλα (*i.e.* round the bay) Α 409, ἀ. Αἴαντε (with them, under their leadership) Ζ 436, τὴν ἑτέρην πόλιν ἀ. Σ 509. Cf. Β 417, Γ 231, Ε 314, Ν 335, Π 290, Ρ 290, Χ 473, etc.:

Ἰαρδάνου ἀ. ῥέεθρα γ 292. Cf. γ 163, θ 502, λ 419, ρ 65, χ 281, ω 37, etc.—Joined with *περί* B 305, P 760.—*οἱ ἀ. τινα*, a person and those with him, a group of which the person named is the chief: *οἱ δ' ἀ. Ἀτρεΐωνα ἠγερέθοντο* Ψ 233.—With several persons named Γ 146. — Sim.: *οὓς ἑτάρους στέλλοντ' ἀ. Πελάγοντα Ἀλάστορά τε . . .* Δ 295 (where P. etc. are included in *ἑτάρους*).—**(c)** About, concerning: *ἀ. ἕκαστα* τ 46.—**(3)** With genit., about, concerning: *μάχεσθον πίδακος ἀ.* Π 825. Cf. θ 267.

ἀμφίαλος, -ον [ἀμφι- (3) + ἅλς[1]]. Sea-girt. Epithet of Ithaca α 386, 395, 401, β 293, φ 252.

†ἀμφιάχω [ἀμφ-, ἀμφι- (3) + (ϝ)ι(ϝ)άχω]. Acc. fem. pf. pple. without redup. *ἀμφιαχυῖαν* (*ἀμφι-ϝακυῖαν*). Of a bird, to cry (flying) about: *τὴν λάβεν ἀμφιαχυῖαν* B 316.

†ἀμφιβαίνω [ἀμφι- (1) (3)]. 2 sing. pf. *ἀμφιβέβηκας* A 37, 451. 3 -ε Z 355, Π 66: θ 541, μ 74. 3 sing. subj. *ἀμφιβεβήκῃ* δ 400. 3 sing. plupf. *ἀμφιβεβήκει* Θ 68, Π 777: ι 198. **(1)** To be *round*, cover completely, a double (organ) (cf. *ἀμφί* (I) (1) (b)). With acc.: *πόνος* (*ἄχος*) *φρένας ἀμφιβέβηκεν* Z 355: θ 541.—**(2)** To come *round*, surround. With dat.: *Τρώων νέφος νηυσὶν* Π 66. —**(3)** To be *round*, envelop, cover up. With acc. μ 74.—**(4)** To have the feet *on each side of*, bestride (cf. *βαίνω* (I) (6) (a)). With acc. Fig.: *ἠέλιος μέσον οὐρανόν* (thought of as standing with both feet in the midst of heaven) Θ 68, Π 777: δ 400.—Hence to protect (a place) as a tutelary power A 37 = 451: ι 198.

†ἀμφιβάλλω [ἀμφι- (1) (3)]. Aor. pple. *ἀμφιβαλών, -όντος* P 742, Ψ 97: ρ 344, ψ 192. Fut. mid. *ἀμφιβαλεῦμαι* χ 103. Aor. infin. *ἀμφιβαλέσθαι* ζ 178. **(1)** To put round something: [*χεῖρας*] ρ 344.—To throw the arms *round*. With acc.: *ἀλλήλους* Ψ 97.—To put building materials *round*. With dat.: *θάμνῳ* ψ 192.—**(2)** Fig., to throw or put (strength) on both sides of something, apply (strength) vigorously: *μένος ἀμφιβαλόντες* P 742. —**(3)** In mid., to throw (a garment) round oneself ζ 178.—To put on a piece of armour χ 103.

ἀμφίβασις, ἡ [ἀμφιβαίνω]. Defence of a fallen body (cf. *ἀμφιβαίνω* (4)): *Τρώων* (by the . . .) E 623.

ἀμφιβέβηκε, 3 sing. pf. *ἀμφιβαίνω*.

ἀμφίβροτος, -η, -ον [ἀμφι- (1) + βροτός]. Protecting on both sides (as well as in front). Epithet of shields B 389, Λ 32, M 402, Υ 281.

ἀμφιγυήεις [prob. ἀμφι- (2) + γυ-, to bend, as in *γύαλον, γυρός*]. Thus, having a crooked limb on each side. Epithet or a name of Hephaestus A 607, Ξ 239, Σ 383, 393 = 462, 587, 590, 614: θ 300, 349, 357.

ἀμφίγυος [prob. as prec.]. Thus, of spears, (having a head) curved on each side, *i.e.* leaf-shaped; or perh., bending to either side, elastic N 147 = O 278 = P 731, Ξ 26 = Π 637, O 386, 712: π 474, ω 527.

†ἀμφιδαίω [ἀμφι- (3) + δαίω[1]]. 3 sing. pf. *ἀμφιδέδηε*. To burn or blaze *all round*. With acc. Fig.: *ἀϋτὴ ἄστυ ἀμφιδέδηε* Z 329.

ἀμφίδασυς, -εια [ἀμφι- (3) + δασύς]. Covered with hair: *αἰγίδα* O 309.

ἀμφιδέδηε, 3 sing. pf. *ἀμφιδαίω*.

†ἀμφιδῑνέω [ἀμφι- (3)]. 3 sing. pf. pass. *ἀμφιδεδίνηται*. (Cf. *δινωτός*.) To set round in circles, *i.e.* in strips running round: *ᾧ πέρι χεῦμα κασσιτέροιο ἀμφιδεδίνηται* Ψ 562 (the strips on the front plate being app. continued on the back plate and carried round to the front again): *κολεὸν ἐλέφαντος ἀμφιδεδίνηται* (is surrounded by (a succession of) ivory rings) θ 405.

ἀμφιδρυφής [ἀμφι- (1) + δρυφ-, δρύπτω]. Having both cheeks torn in mourning: *ἄλοχος* B 700.

ἀμφίδρυφος, -ον [as prec.]. Both torn in mourning: *παρειαί* Λ 393.

ἀμφίδυμος [ἀμφι- (2) + -δυμος as in *δίδυμος*]. Twofold, double: *λιμένες* δ 847.

ἀμφιέλισσα, -ης [ἀμφι- (1) + (ϝ)ελίσσω]. Epithet of ships, wheeling both ways; hence, easily directed, handy B 165 = 181, I 683, N 174 = O 549, P 612, Σ 260: γ 162, ζ 264, η 9, 252, ι 64, κ 91, 156 = μ 368, ξ 258 = ρ 427, ο 283, φ 390.

†ἀμφιέννῡμι [ἀμφι- (3) + (ϝ)έννυμι]. Fut. *ἀμφιέσω* ε 167. Aor. opt. *ἀμφιέσαιμι* σ 361. Fem. pple. *ἀμφιέσᾱσα* ε 264, ο 369. 3 pl. aor. mid. *ἀμφιέσαντο* ψ 142. Imp. pl. *ἀμφιέσασθε* ψ 131. **(1)** To put (garments) on a person ε 167, 264, ο 369, σ 361.—**(2)** In mid., to put (garments) on oneself ψ 131, 142.

ἀμφιέπω [ἀμφι- (3) (4) + (σ)έπω[1]]. With elision of the ι (on the loss of the σ) 3 sing. impf. *ἄμφεπε* Π 124, Σ 348: θ 437. 3 pl. -ον Σ 559, Ψ 167, Ω 622. **(1)** To handle, attend to, do what is needful to: *ἵππους* T 392. Cf. E 667, Σ 559, Ψ 167, Ω 622.—**(2)** To marshal, draw up in order B 525. —**(3)** To manage, conduct: *τάφον* Ω 804.—**(4)** In sinister sense, to employ oneself about for evil, work for the destruction of: [*Τρῶας*] γ 118.—**(5)** Of fire, to bring itself to bear upon, lap round: *πρύμνην* Π 124. Cf. Σ 348 := θ 437.

ἀμφιζάνω [ἀμφ-, ἀμφι- (3)]. To settle *about*, be deposited *upon*. With dat. Of ashes: *χιτῶνι* Σ 25.

ἀμφιθαλής [ἀμφι- (2) + θάλλω]. Absol., one who has both parents alive X 496.

ἀμφίθετος, -ον [ἀμφι- (2) + θε-, τίθημι]. Two-handled: *φιάλην* Ψ 270, *φιάλῃ* 616.

ἀμφιθέω [ἀμφι- (3)]. To run *about* or *round*. With acc.: [*πόριες*] *ἀμφιθέουσι μητέρας* κ 413.

ἀμφικαλύπτω [ἀμφι- (1) (3)]. Fut. *ἀμφικαλύψω* Ξ 343. Infin. -ειν θ 569, ν 177. 3 sing. aor. *ἀμφεκάλυψε* Γ 442, E 68, Θ 331, Π 350, etc.: δ 180, 618, ο 118. 3 sing. subj. *ἀμφικαλύψῃ* θ 511, ν 183, υ 86. Pple. *ἀμφικαλύψας* ε 493, ξ 349, ψ 17. Infin. *ἀμφικαλύψαι* ν 152, 158. **(1)** To cover both of one's . . . (cf. *ἀμφί* (I) (1) (b)). Of sleep: *βλέφαρ' ἀμφικαλύψας* ε 493. Cf. υ 86, ψ 17.—To cover completely a double (organ) (cf. *ἀμφί* (I) (1) (b)): *ἔρως φρένας ἀμφεκάλυψεν* Γ 442, Ξ 294.—**(2)** To cover up all round, enfold, conceal, contain B 262, Ψ 91.—Of a city, to receive within its walls θ 511.—Of a house, to receive as a guest δ 618 = ο 118.—Fig. of death or fate E 68, M 116, Π 350, Υ 417 : δ 180.—(3) To put *round*, cover or protect with. With dat. of what is covered or protected : σάκος οἱ Θ 331 = N 420. Cf. Ξ 343 : ξ 349.—Sim., to put *round* (something) so as to isolate (it) : ὅρος πόλει θ 569, ν 152, 158, 177, 183.

†**ἀμφικεάζω** [ἀμφι- (3)]. Aor. pple. ἀμφικεάσσας. To split off *all round* (something). With acc. : τὸ μέλαν δρυὸς ἀμφικεάσσας (splitting off (the outside wood) all round the dark heart) ξ 12.

ἀμφίκομος [ἀμφι- (3) + κόμη]. With foliage all round, thick-leafed : θάμνῳ P 677.

ἀμφικύπελλος [ἀμφι- (2) + (perh.) *κυπέλη, handle, conn. with κώπη]. Two-handled : δέπας A 584, Z 220, I 656, Ψ 219, 656, 663, 667, 699 : γ 63, θ 89, ν 57, ο 102, 120, χ 86, δέπα υ 153.

ἀμφιλαχαίνω [ἀμφι- (3) + λαχαίνω, to dig]. To dig *round about*. With acc. : φυτόν ω 242.

ἀμφιλύκη [ἀμφι- (1) (giving the notion of hesitation between two sides, hence of doubtfulness) + *λύκη = L. *lux*]. ἀ. νύξ, the (morning) twilight H 433.

†**ἀμφιμαίομαι** [ἀμφι- (3)]. Aor. imp. pl. ἀμφιμάσασθε. To carry the hands all round or over (the surface of), wipe all round or over : τραπέζας υ 152.

ἀμφιμάχομαι [ἀμφι- (3) (4)]. (1) With acc., in local sense, to fight *round* or *about* : Ἴλιον Z 461. Cf. I 412, Π 73, Σ 208.—(2) With genit., to fight *for the possession of* : τείχεος O 391. Cf. Π 496 = 533, Σ 20.

ἀμφιμέλαιναι. See μέλας (1).

†**ἀμφιμῡκάομαι** [ἀμφι- (3)]. 3 sing. pf. ἀμφιμέμῡκε. To resound or echo all round κ 227.

ἀμφινέμω [ἀμφι- (3)]. In mid., to have one's lot, dwell, *round* or *about*. With acc. With place-names B 521, 574, 585, 634, 649, 655, 835, 853, Σ 186 : τ 132.

†**ἀμφιξέω** [ἀμφι-(3)]. Aor. ἀμφέξεσα. To smooth all round : κορμόν ψ 196.

ἀμφιπέλω [ἀμφι- (3)]. Of sound, to come *round* (hearers). With dat. In mid. : ἀοιδὴ ἀκουόντεσσιν α 352.

ἀμφιπένομαι [ἀμφι- (4)]. To busy oneself about, attend to N 656, T 278.—To attend upon ο 467.—To treat surgically Δ 220, Π 28 : τ 455.—In sinister sense : Ἀστεροπαῖον ἐγχέλυες ἀμφεπένοντο (made a meal of him) Φ 203. Cf. Ψ 184.

ἀμφιπεριστέφω [ἀμφι- (3) + περι- (1)]. To put *round*. With dat. Fig., in pass., to be put *round* as a crown, adorn : οὔ οἱ χάρις ἀμφιπεριστέφεται ἐπέεσσιν θ 175.

ἀμφιπεριστρωφάω [ἀμφι- (3) + περι- (2)]. To turn about in all directions : ἵππους Θ 348.

†**ἀμφιπίπτω** [ἀμφι- (3)]. Aor. pple. fem. ἀμφιπεσοῦσα. To fall (with the arms) *round*, embrace. With acc. : πόσιν θ 523.

ἀμφιπολεύω [ἀμφίπολος]. To busy oneself about, take care of, tend : ἐμὸν βίον σ 254 = τ 127, ὄρχατον ω 244, 257.—In sinister sense : ἔδοσαν ἐρινύσιν ἀμφιπολεύειν (*i.e.* handed them over to their tender mercies) υ 78.

ἀμφίπολος, -ου, ἡ [ἀμφι- (4) + -πολος, conn. with πολεύω]. A handmaid, a female attendant or servant, hardly to be distinguished from δμῳή. (The words are sometimes used indifferently ; cf. ζ 52 with 307, and 84 with 99. But in χ 483, 484 ἀμφίπολοι seem to be personal attendants and δμῳαί the other servants.) Γ 143, 422, Z 286, 324, 372, 399, 491, 499, Σ 417 (*i.e.* representations), X 442, 461, Ω 304 : α 136, ζ 18, η 232, σ 198, τ 90, ψ 227, etc.—Of Circe's servants κ 348, 368, μ 18.—With γυνή. See γυνή (3).—With word indicating the servant's country of origin : Σικελή ω 366.—Her office : ταμίην Ω 302 : π 152.

ἀμφιπονέομαι [ἀμφι- (4)]. To busy oneself about, attend to : τάφον υ 307.—To do the offices of a 'second' to : Εὐρύαλον Ψ 681.

ἀμφιποτάομαι [ἀμφι- (3)]. To fly round and round B 315.

ἀμφίρυτος, -η [ἀμφι- (3) + ῥυ-, ῥέω]. Flowed round (by the sea), sea-girt α 50, 198, λ 325, μ 283.

ἀμφίς [ἀμφί]. (I) Adv. (1) On both sides : ᾧ ῥόπαλ' ἀ. ἐάγη (*i.e.* across his back) Λ 559, δούρασιν ἀ. [βάλεν] (with spears from both hands, with both spears at once) Φ 162.—(2) Apart, asunder : ἀ. φράζονται (have different views) B 13 = 30 = 67, ἔχουσα ἀ. (one in each scale) M 434, τόξων ἀϊκὰς ἀ. μένον (at a safe distance) O 709, ἀ. ἀρωγοί (partisans, some of one, some of the other) Σ 502, ἀ. ἀριζήλω (standing out from the others) 519, ἀ. ἄλλ' ἀποδάσσεσθαι (in addition) X 117, ἀ. ὁδοῦ Ψ 393 (see ὁδός (1)). Cf. N 345, 706 : ζυγὸν ἀ. ἔχοντες (supporting it at either end) γ 486 = ο 184, τιμὴν ἀ. ἄγοντες (in addition) χ 57. Cf. α 54.—(3) Absent : ἀ. ἐόντα ω 218.—Sim. of separation from a person τ 221.—(4) Between : ὀλίγη ἦν ἀ. ἄρουρα (between the heaps or rows) Γ 115.—(5) Round, about : τάφρος ἀ. ἐοῦσα (surrounding) H 342, Τάρταρος ἀ. [ἐστιν] Θ 481. Cf. I 464, Ξ 123, Ψ 330, Ω 488 : θ 340, 476.—(II) Prep. (1) With genit. (a) Apart from, at a distance from : Διός Θ 444. Cf. ξ 352, π 267.—(b) About, concerning : ἅρματος ἀ. ἰδών (seeing to it) B 384.—(2) With dat., round, about : ἄξονι E 723.—(3) With acc. (a) On each side of : δύο δ' ἀ. ἕκαστον [δίφρον] (one on each side of each) Λ 748.—(b) Round, about : ἕκαστον Λ 634. Cf. Ξ 274, O 225 : ζ 266, η 4, ι 399.

†**ἀμφίστημι** [ἀμφ-, ἀμφι- (3)]. 3 pl. aor. ἀμφέσταν Σ 233, Ψ 695. 3 sing. impf. mid. ἀμφίστατο Ω 712. 3 pl. -αντο Λ 733. In aor. and mid., to stand round or about Σ 233, Ψ 695, Ω 712.—To stand *round* or *about*. With acc. : ἄστυ Λ 733.

†**ἀμφιστρατόομαι** [ἀμφι- (3)]. 3 pl. impf. ἀμφεστρατόωντο. To be established *round*, besiege. With acc. : Θρυόεσσαν Λ 713.

ἀμφιστρεφής [app. ἀμφι- (3) + στρέφω]. Thus, twisted about : κεφαλαὶ τρεῖς δράκοντος ἀμφιστρεφέες Λ 40 (*i.e.* two twisted about the third).

†**ἀμφιτίθημι** [ἀμφι- (1) (3)]. 3 sing. aor. mid. ἀμφέθετο φ 431. Aor. fem. pple. pass. ἀμφιτεθεῖσα K 271. (1) To put round or about something K 271.—(2) In mid., to put on, arm oneself with : ξίφος φ 431 (*i.e.* the belt rested on both shoulders).

ἀμφιτρομέω [ἀμφι- (4)]. To tremble *for*. With genit. : τοῦ δ 820.

ἀμφίφαλος, -ον [ἀμφι- (2) + φάλος]. With two φάλοι : κυνέην E 743 = Λ 41.

ἀμφιφορεύς, -ῆος, ὁ [ἀμφι- (2) + φορ-, φέρω]. A two-handled jar Ψ 92, 170 : β 290, 349, 379, ι 164, 204, ν 105 (of natural formations in a cave), ω 74.

†**ἀμφιχαίνω** [ἀμφι- (3)]. 3 sing. aor. ἀμφέχανε. To gape *round*. With acc. : ἐμὲ κήρ (gaped for me) Ψ 79.

ἀμφιχέω [ἀμφι- (3)]. 3 sing. aor. pass. ἀμφέχυτο B 41. ἀμφεχύθη δ 716. Pple. ἀμφιχυθείς Ξ 253, Ψ 63 : π 214. Infin. ἀμφιχυθῆναι Ψ 764. (**1**) To pour or shed round or about. Of dust : πάρος κόνιν ἀμφιχυθῆναι (had settled down again) Ψ 764. —(**2**) Fig., in pass., of sound, to come *round*. With acc. : ἀμφέχυτό μιν ὀμφή B 41.—Of sleep, to be shed round one, come upon one Ξ 253, Ψ 63. —Of grief, to come *upon*. With acc. : τὴν ἄχος ἀμφεχύθη δ 716.—So of a bodily action, to embrace (a person) : ἀμφιχυθεὶς πατέρα π 214. Cf. χ 498.

ἀμφίχυτος [ἀμφιχέω]. Poured round or about ; hence of heaped-up earth : τεῖχος Υ 145.

ἀμφότερος, -η, -ον [ἄμφω]. (**1**) Both. (**a**) Of two persons, etc. In dual or (more freq.) in pl. (**α**) Absol. : ἐξαίνυτο θυμὸν ἀμφοτέρω E 156. Cf. Γ 208, Δ 38, E 261, H 3, etc. : ἀμφοτέρους ἱέρευσεν ξ 74. Cf. γ 37, λ 212, σ 17, φ 214, etc.—(**β**) With sb. or pron. : ἀμφοτέρω σφῶϊ H 280, ἐπ' ἀμφοτέρους πόδας (one after the other) N 281. Cf. Δ 521, E 163, Θ 115, M 382, etc. : ἀμφοτέρῃσιν χερσίν δ 116. Cf. γ 136, δ 282, ε 414, μ 239, etc.—With sb. to be supplied : ἀμφοτέρῃσι [χερσίν], with both hands E 416 : κ 264, λ 594, ρ 356, σ 28.—(**b**) In pl. of two groups of persons. (**α**) Absol. : ἀμφοτέρων βέλεα Θ 67. Cf. Γ 416, Δ 16, Z 120, N 303, etc. : φιλότητα μετ' ἀμφοτέροισιν ω 476. Cf. κ 204, ω 546. —(**β**) With pron. : τοὺς ἀμφοτέρους Υ 54.—(**2**) In neut. ἀμφότερον as adv., both. Followed by . . . τε . . . τε Γ 179, Δ 145.—By . . . τε καί . . . Δ 60 = Σ 365, N 166.—By . . . τε . . . δέ . . . H 418.—By καί ξ 505.—By . . . τε καί . . . καί . . . ο 78.

ἀμφοτέρωθεν [ἀμφότερος + -θεν (1)]. (**1**) From both sides : ὦρτ' ἀϋτὴ ἀ. O 313. Cf. M 431.—Of plaiting strands of a rope, across and across κ 167. —(**2**) On both sides, on either side : πλῆμναί εἰσιν ἀ. E 726. Cf. M 55, Π 563, P 440, Υ 170, Ψ 628 : χ 404.—On both edges : ἀ. ἀκαχμένον ε 235, χ 80.—At both ends : ἅψας ἀ. φ 408.—Of stating alternatives : ἐρέω ἀ. μ 58.—(**3**) In both directions : φόως γένετ' ἀ. O 669.—With περί, app., in both directions so as to meet : περὶ ἕρκος ἐλήλαται ἀ. η 113. Cf. κ 88.

ἀμφοτέρωσε [ἀμφότερος + -σε]. In both directions : γεγωνέμεν ἀ. Θ 223 = Λ 6, ἀ. λίθοι πωτῶντο M 287.

ἀμφουδίς [prob. ἀμφι- (3) + an unknown element + advbl. -δις]. App., by the middle : ἀ. ἀείρας ρ 237.

†**ἀμφράζομαι** [ἀμ-, ἀνα- (6)]. 3 sing. aor. opt. ἀμφράσσαιτο. To remark, notice : οὐλήν τ 391.

ἄμφω. Only in nom. and acc. of same form. Both. Constructed with dual or pl. (**1**) Of two persons, etc. (**a**) Absol. : ἀ. φιλέουσα A 196. Cf. A 259, B 767, Γ 148, E 153, etc. : ἀ. ἱέσθην γ 344. Cf. θ 316, κ 138, μ 424, ν 296, ο 366, σ 65, 372.—(**b**) With sb. or pron. : ἀ. χεῖρε Δ 523. Cf. E 258, Z 19, H 255, Λ 782, etc. : τοὺς ἀ. λ 301. Cf. ε 453, θ 135, π 15, σ 89, etc.—(**2**) Of two groups of persons : ἀριθμηθήμεναι ἀ. B 124.

ἄμφωτος [ἀμφ-, ἀμφι- (2) + ὠτ-, οὖς]. Having two ears (for handles) : ἄλεισον χ 10.

ἀμώμητος [ἀ-[1] + μωμάομαι]. Not to be blamed ; hence, unerring (in counsel) : Πουλυδάμαντος M 109.

ἄν[1]. Conditional or limiting particle. (Cf. κεν.) For the uses with subj., opt. and fut., aor. and impf. indic. in protasis and apodosis see (6). (**1**) With subj. : τάχ' ἂν θυμὸν ὀλέσσῃ A 205. Cf. Σ 192, X 505 : ἐγὼ ἂν ξεῖνος ἔω ι 17. Cf. δ 240, λ 328, 517, μ 81.—In X 50 (ἀπολυσόμεθα) : δ 240, λ 328, 517 (μυθήσομαι), ζ 221 (λοέσσομαι) may be aor. subj. or fut. indic.—(**2**) With opt. in potential or fut. sense : τῶν οὐκ ἄν τι φέροις A 301. Cf. B 250 (conveying an order), Γ 52 (will you not . . . ?), 66, E 32, 362, Z 141, I 77, K 204, N 741, Ξ 58, X 108, Ω 437, etc. : πῶς ἂν Ὀδυσσῆος λαθοίμην; α 65. Cf. γ 232, δ 78, ζ 57, 300, κ 573, υ 135 (do not . . .), χ 325, etc.—(**3**) In potential sense in reference to the past in suppositions contrary to fact. (**a**) With impf. or aor. indic. : ἦ τ' ἂν κέρδιον ἦεν E 201 = X 103, οὐκ ἂν θυμὸν ὤρινεν T 271. Cf. Θ 455, N 676, Π 638 : οὐκ ἂν τόσσ' ἀγόρευες (would not have . . .) β 184. Cf. ι 211, 228, 334.— (**b**) With pres. or aor. opt. : ἦ ἂν ὕστατα λωβήσαιο A 232 = B 242. Cf. A 271, Δ 223, E 85 N 127 : οὐκ ἂν ὀχλίσσειαν ι 241.—(**4**) With infin. in indirect discourse : καί δ' ἂν τοῖς ἄλλοισιν ἔφη παραμυθήσασθαι I 684.—(**5**) Joined with κεν. See κεν (5).—(**6**) For uses in protasis with εἰ and in the corresponding relative sentences see Table at end (II) (B) (a) (3) subj., (D) (7) subj., (23) opt., (III) (B) (a) (3) subj., (D) (11) fut., (34) (35) (36) (37) (38) (43) (44) subj., (49) (65) opt.—For uses in apodosis see (II) (C) (a) (2) aor. indic., (b) subj., (D) (17) (22) opt., (III) (C) (a) (3) aor. or impf. indic., (6) opt., (c) (2) opt., (D) (6) opt., (23) fut., (30) opt., (52) subj., (57) (63) opt.—For ὅτ' ἄν (not in protasis) see ὅτε (1) (a) (γ), (b) (α) (δ) (ε), (4). —For ὄφρ' ἄν (not in protasis) see ὄφρα (1) (b) (c), (5) (a) (b).—For ὡς ἄν (not in protasis) see ὡς (7) (a), (b) (β), (8) (a) (γ), (b) (γ).

ἄν[2]. See next.

ἀνά. Also in form ἄν and in assimilated form ἄμ. (**I**) Adv. (**1**) Up, upwards, in an upward direction, on to something : ἂν Χρυσηΐδα βήσομεν (put her on board) A 143, ἀνὰ δ' ἔστη B 100, ἂν δ' ἔβη (mounted) Γ 261, ἀν' ἔντεα λέγοντες (gathering them up) Λ 755. Cf. A 310, Γ 268, E 798, P 541, Φ 361, X 77, etc. : ἂν δ' αὐτοὶ βάντες (going on board) β 419 = δ 579. Cf. ζ 253, θ 3, ι 468 (see νεύω (3)), ν 56, ρ 262 (see βάλλω (II) (4)), etc.— (**2**) Back, reversal of action : ἀνά τ' ἔδραμ' ὀπίσσω

Ε 599, ἀνὰ δὲ σχέο Η 110 (see ἔχω (IV) (1) (b)): ἀνὰ πρυμνήσια λῦσαι ι 178=562=λ 637=μ 145=ο 548.—(3) Indicating extension or diffusion: ἀν' ἱστία πέτασσαν Α 480, μέλανες ἀνὰ βότρυες ἦσαν Σ 562: ἀνὰ κρητῆρα κέρασσεν γ 390. Cf. δ 41, 783=θ 54, κ 506, ω 343.—(II) Prep. (1) With dat., on, upon: ἀνὰ σκήπτρῳ Α 15=374. Cf. Ξ 352, Ο 152: ἂμ πέτρῃσιν ε 156. Cf. λ 128=ψ 275, ω 8.—In pregnant sense: ἅρματ' ἂμ βωμοῖσι τίθει Θ 441. Cf. Σ 177.—(2) With acc. (a) On to, on, upon: θῆκεν ἀνὰ μυρίκην Κ 466. Cf. Σ 278: ἂν δὲ βήσετο δίφρον γ 481. Cf. γ 492=ο 145=190, χ 176, 193, 239.—(b) Through, throughout, along, over, among, in, on: ἀνὰ στρατόν Α 10, ἂμ πεδίον Ε 87. Cf. Α 53, Δ 251, Ε 74, Ι 383, Κ 339, Ν 308, Π 349, Χ 452 (in . . .), etc.: ἂν στόμα ε 456, ἀν' ὀρσοθύρην χ 132. Cf. β 430, η 72, κ 251, σ 246, χ 18, ω 318, etc.—In reference to the mouth as the organ of speech: βασιλῆας ἀνὰ στόμ' ἔχων (having them passing through the mouth, *i.e.* talking freely of them) Β 250.—In reference to immaterial things: ἀνὰ θυμόν (in his mind) Β 36, ἀν' ἰθύν Φ 303 (see ἰθύς[2] (2)), etc. Cf. β 116, δ 638, θ 377 (see ἰθύς[2] (1)), etc.—In reference to night as a space of darkness: ἀνὰ νύκτα Ξ 80.—Indicating diffusion: ἀνὰ εἴκοσι μέτρα ι 209.—In reference to position: ἀνὰ πρόθυρον τετραμμένος (*i.e.* with his feet pointing outwards through the doorway) Τ 212.—(3) With genit., on to, upon: ἂν δὲ νηὸς βαῖνεν (went on board) β 416. Cf. ι 177, ο 284.

ἄνα[1] [ἀνά with anastrophe]. Up! get up! rouse yourself! to work! ἀλλ' ἄνα Ζ 331, Ι 247, Σ 178: σ 13.

ἄνα[2], voc. ἄναξ.

ἀναβαίνω [ἀνα- (1) (2) (5)]. (A) Contr. 1 pl. subj. ἀμβαίνωμεν ο 219. Contr. infin. ἀμβαίνειν ι 178, λ 637, etc. 3 sing. aor. ἀνέβη Α 497. 3 sing subj. ἀναβῇ β 358. 3 sing. opt. ἀναβαίη χ 132. Contr. ἀμβαίη μ 77. Pple. ἀναβάς, -άντος Α 312, 611, Ξ 287, Π 184, etc.: γ 157, ε 470, ξ 353, ο 474, etc. Fem. ἀναβᾶσα α 362, ρ 49, χ 428, etc. Infin. ἀναβήμεναι α 210. 3 sing. aor. mid. ἀνεβήσετο ψ 1. (B) Aor. pple. pl. mid. ἀναβησάμενοι ο 475. (I) *Intrans.* in all forms except (B). (1) To go up, ascend, mount: ἐς λέχος Α 611. Cf. Ξ 287, Π 184, 657, Χ 399: εἰς ὑπερῷα α 362=τ 602=φ 356, β 358, δ 751=ρ 49=ψ 364, δ 760, ψ 1. Cf. γ 483, ε 470, ξ 353.—Absol. μ 77.—In reference to leaving a room: ἀν' ὀρσοθύρην χ 132, ἀνέβαινεν ἐς θαλάμους (left the μέγαρον and took his way to . . .) 142.—Of a voyage from Ithaca to Troy α 210.—(2) To go *up to*, ascend *to*. With acc.: οὐρανόν Α 497. Cf. σ 302, τ 600, χ 428.—(3) To go on board a ship, embark: ἀναβάντες ἐπέπλεον ὑγρὰ κέλευθα Α 312: ἀναβάντες ἐλαύνομεν γ 157. Cf. δ 473, 842, ι 178=562=λ 637=μ 145=ο 548, μ 293, 401, ν 285, ξ 252, ο 209, 219, 474.—(4) Of reputation, to be spread abroad *among*. With acc.: φάτις ἀνθρώπους ἀναβαίνει ζ 29.—(II) *Trans.* in form (B), to cause to go on board a ship or embark: νὼ ἀναβησάμενοι ο 475.

ἀναβάλλω [ἀνα- (1) (3)]. Contr. 1 pl. subj. mid. ἀμβαλλώμεθα Β 436. (1) To put off, delay: ἄεθλον τ 584.—In mid.: ἔργον Β 436.—(2) In mid., to strike up, begin (to sing) (cf. βάλλω (II) (4) and ἀμβλήδην): ἀνεβάλλετ' ἀείδειν α 155, θ 266.

ἀναβέβροχε, 3 sing. pf. ἀναβρέχω.

ἀναβησάμενοι, aor. pple. pl. mid. ἀναβαίνω.

ἀνάβλησις, ἡ [ἀναβάλλω]. (1) Delay: λύσιος νεκροῖο (in . . .) Ω 655.—(2) Respite: κακοῦ (from . . .) Β 380.

†**ἀναβράχω** [ἀνα- (6)]. 3 sing. aor. ἀνέβραχε. To clash or rattle loudly: τεύχεα Τ 13.—Of a door, to creak or grate loudly φ 48.

†**ἀναβρέχω** [ἀνα- (6)+βρέχω, to wet]. 3 sing. pf. ἀναβέβροχε. To wet or moisten abundantly Ρ 54.

†**ἀναβρόχω** [ἀνα- (6)+βρόχω, to swallow]. 3 sing. aor. opt. ἀναβρόξειε μ 240. Neut. aor. pple. pass. ἀναβροχέν λ 586. (κατα-.) To swallow down, swallow λ 586, μ 240.

†**ἀναγιγνώσκω** [ἀνα- (4) (6)]. Aor. ἀνέγνων δ 250. 3 sing. ἀνέγνω Ν 734: α 216, φ 205. 3 sing. opt. ἀναγνοίη λ 144. Genit. sing. masc. pple. ἀναγνόντος ω 346. Dat. sing. fem. ἀναγνούσῃ τ 250, ψ 206. (1) To know again, recognize δ 250, λ 144, τ 250=ψ 206, ω 346.—(2) To know well, know certainly: [νόον ἐσθλόν] Ν 734 (*i.e.* best knows its value; cf. ζ 185). Cf. α 216, φ 205.

ἀναγκαίη, -ης, ἡ. Instrumental ἀναγκαίηφι Υ 143. =ἀνάγκη Ζ 85: τ 73.—In dat. ἀναγκαίῃ, of necessity Δ 300.—In instrumental, by the application of force or strength: δαμέντας Υ 143.

ἀναγκαῖος, -η, -ον [ἀνάγκη]. (1) Compelled, acting under compulsion: πολεμισταί ω 499.—Sim. of slaves ω 210.—(2) Imposing compulsion: ἦμαρ ἀναγκαῖον (see ἦμαρ (4) (b)) Π 836, μύθῳ ρ 399=υ 344.—χρειοῖ ἀναγκαίῃ, by compelling necessity, under the compulsion of necessity Θ 57.

ἀνάγκη, -ης, ἡ. (1) Necessity, compulsion: ἐπικείσετ' ἀ. Ζ 458. Cf. Ε 633, Κ 418, Υ 251, Ω 667: κ 273.—ὑπ' ἀνάγκης, under compulsion β 110=ω 146, τ 156.—(2) In dat. ἀνάγκῃ. (a) By or under compulsion or constraint: ἀ. οὔ μιν ἄξω Ι 429. Cf. Ι 692, Ο 199: ὃς ἤειδεν ἀ. α 154. Cf. δ 557, ε 154, η 217, ι 98, ξ 27, etc.—(b) Under compulsion of circumstances, of necessity, perforce: φεύγοντας Λ 150. Cf. Μ 178, Ξ 128, Ο 133, etc.: ἄγρην ἐφέπεσκον μ 330. Cf. ν 307, ο 311.

†**ἀναγνάμπτω** [ἀνα- (3)]. 3 pl. aor. ἀνέγναμψαν ξ 348. 3 sing. aor. pass. ἀνεγνάμφθη Γ 348, Η 259, Ρ 44. (1) To bend back: ἀνεγνάμφθη αἰχμή Γ 348=Η 259=Ρ 44.—(2) To unloose ξ 348.

ἀναγνοίη, 3 sing. aor. opt. ἀναγιγνώσκω.

ἀνάγω [ἀν-, ἀνα- (1)]. 1 pl. fut. ἀνάξομεν σ 115. Aor. ἀνήγαγον Ο 29. 3 sing. -ε Ζ 292, Ι 338: γ 272, δ 534. (1) To cause to go or take inland ξ 272=ρ 441.—(2) Of bringing to Troy Γ 48, Ζ 292, Ι 338, Ν 627.—To Argos Ο 29.—Of taking from Ithaca to the mainland σ 115.—(3) Of bringing gifts to temples Θ 203.—(4) Of conducting to a house: ὅνδε δόμονδε γ 272.—Without complementary words δ 534.—(5) To bring up to the mark in a contest σ 89.—(6) In mid., to put to sea, sail A 478 : τ 202.

ἀναδέδρομε, 3 sing. pf. *ἀνατρέχω.*

†**ἀναδέρκομαι** [ἀνα- (1)]. 3 sing. aor. ἀνέδρακε. To look up Ξ 436.

ἀναδέσμη, -ης, ἡ [ἀνα- (6) + δεσ-, δέω]. A woman's head-dress, app. in the form of a plaited band X 469.

†**ἀναδέχομαι** [ἀνα- (6)]. 3 sing. aor. ἀνεδέξατο E 619. 1 pl. aor. ἀνεδέγμεθα ρ 563. (1) To receive, catch : σάκος πολλὰ [δούρατα] E 619.—(2) To receive as one's portion ρ 563.

†**ἀναδύω** [ἀνα- (1) (3)]. 3 sing. aor. ἀνέδῡ A 359 : ε 322. 3 sing. opt. ἀναδύῃ (for ἀναδυίη) ι 377. Infin. ἀναδῦναι H 217. Contr. 3 sing. mid. ἀνδύεται N 225. 3 sing. aor. ἀνεδύσετο A 496 : ε 337. (1) To rise up or emerge from out of. With genit. : ἁλός A 359. Cf. ε 337.—So with acc. : κῦμα A 496.—Absol., to come to the surface ε 322.—(2) To go back, retire H 217.—To withdraw from : πόλεμον N 225.—Absol., to draw back, flinch ι 377.

ἀνάεδνος, ἡ [app. for ἀνέϝεδνος fr. ἀν-[1] + ἕϝεδνα. See ἕδνα, ἔεδνα]. Without bride-price I 146, 288, N 366.

ἀναείρω [ἀν-, ἀνα- (1)]. 3 sing. aor. ἀνάειρε Ψ 614, 725, 729, 778. Infin. ἀναεῖραι θ 298. (1) To lift up, raise θ 298.—Of a wrestler hoisting his adversary Ψ 724, 725, 729.—(2) To take up, pick up Ψ 614, 778.

ἀναθηλέω [ἀνά- (4)]. To sprout afresh A 236.

ἀνάθημα, -ατος, τό [ἀνατίθημι]. An accompaniment or accessory : δαιτός α 152, φ 430.

ἀναθήσει, 3 sing. fut. *ἀνατίθημι.*

ἀναθρῴσκω [ἀνα- (1)]. To leap or bound up. Of a stone : ἀναθρῴσκων πέτεται N 140.

ἀναιδείη, -ης, ἡ [ἀναιδής]. (1) Shamelessness, effrontery A 149, I 372.—(2) Immodesty, unchastity χ 424.

ἀναιδής [ἀν-[1] + αἰδώς]. (1) Careless of the good opinion of others, lost to all sense of decency, shameless, reckless α 254, ν 376, ρ 449, υ 29, 39, 386, ψ 37.—Absol. A 158.—(2) Of a stone or rock, reckless, careless of what mischief or trouble may ensue Δ 521. Cf. N 139 (as if the rock lent itself to the discharge of the stone) : λ 598.—Of Κυδοιμός figured as a symbol : ἀναιδέα δηϊοτῆτος (app., shamelessly insatiate of . . .) E 593.

ἀναίμων, -ονος [ἀν-[1] + αἷμα]. Bloodless E 342.

ἀναιμωτί [as prec.]. Without bloodshed P 363, 497 : σ 149, ω 532.

ἀναίνομαι. 3 sing. aor. ἀνήνατο Ψ 204 : κ 18. 3 sing. subj. ἀνήνηται I 510. Infin. ἀνήνασθαι H 93 : δ 651, ξ 239, σ 287. (ἀπ-.) (1) To refuse : δόσιν (*i.e.* to give it) δ 651, σ 287.—To refuse *to do something.* With infin. : λοιγὸν ἀμῦναι Σ 450. Cf. Σ 500, Ψ 204.—Absol. H 93, I 510, 585, Λ 647 : κ 18, ξ 239.—(2) To reject, spurn I 679.—So in reference to a course proposed : ἔργον ἀεικές γ 265.—To refuse to have to do with (a person) θ 212.—(3) To refuse to entertain an idea ; hence, to deny : ἀασάμην, οὐδ' ἀναίνομαι I 116.—To refuse to entertain expectation ξ 149.

ἀνᾱΐξας, aor. pple. *ἀναΐσσω.*

†**ἀναιρέω** [ἀν-, ἀνα- (1)]. Aor. pple. ἀνελών, -όντος A 301, Ψ 551, 736 : γ 453, σ 16. **Mid.** Fut. infin. ἀναιρήσεσθαι φ 261, χ 9. 3 sing. aor. ἀνείλετο N 296. 3 pl. ἀνέλοντο A 449, B 410 : υ 66.—3 sing. subj. ἀνέληται Π 10. Opt. ἀνελοίμην σ 357. 2 sing. ἀνέλοιο τ 22. Infin. ἀνελέσθαι Π 8, Ψ 823 : φ 117. (1) To take or pick up Ψ 551 : σ 16.—(2) To take up into the hands or arms. In mid.: οὐλοχύτας ἀνέλοντο A 449, B 410. Cf. Π 8, 10.—(3) To take up and, or in order to, carry off or appropriate : τῶν οὐκ ἄν τι φέροις ἀνελών A 301.—In mid. : [πελέκεας] φ 261.—To take up and carry off (prizes) Ψ 736.—In mid. Ψ 823.—To seize and carry off. In mid. : ὅτε κούρας ἀνέλοντο υ 66.—(4) To lift up or raise : ἀπὸ χθονός (*i.e.* the victim's head) γ 453.—In mid.: ἄλεισον ἀναιρήσεσθαι χ 9.—(5) In mid., to take for one's use : ἀνείλετ' ἔγχος N 296.—To take into service σ 357.—To take upon oneself, undertake : πατρὸς ἀέθλια φ 117.—To take into one's mind : ἐπιφροσύνας τ 22.

ἀνᾱΐσσω [ἀν-, ἀνα- (1)]. 3 pl. aor. ἀνήϊξαν O 86, Ψ 203 : σ 40, ω 463. 3 sing. opt. ἀνᾱΐξειε Γ 216. 3 pl. -ειαν Δ 114. Pple. ἀνᾱΐξας, -αντος A 584, O 6, Ψ 733, etc. : α 410, θ 186, φ 300, etc. Fem. ἀνᾱΐξᾱσα χ 240. (1) To start, spring or dart up, rise quickly or suddenly : πάντες ἀνήϊξαν O 86, Ψ 203. Cf. A 584, Δ 114, H 106, O 6, Ψ 733, Ω 621 : ἀναΐξας οἴχεται α 410. Cf. θ 186, 361, ι 288, ν 197, σ 40, τ 31, φ 119, 300, χ 240, ω 50, 463.—(2) To rush or spring *on to.* With acc. : ἅρμα Ω 440.—(3) Of springs, to gush forth X 148.—(4) To rise to speak Γ 216 (the notion of quickness not here to be pressed).

ἀναίτιος [ἀν-[1] + αἴτιος]. Not blameworthy, blameless Υ 297 : υ 135, χ 356.—Absol. Λ 654, N 775.

ἀνακαίω [ἀνα- (6)]. To light, kindle : πῦρ η 13, ι 251, 308, κ 358, υ 123, φ 181.

ἀνακηκίω [ἀνα- (1)]. To gush up, ooze forth : αἷμα H 262, ἱδρώς N 705, Ψ 507.

†**ἀνακλίνω** [ἀνα- (3)]. Aor. pple. ἀνακλῖνας σ 103. Contr. ἀγκλῖνας Δ 113 : χ 156. Infin. ἀνακλῖναι E 751, Θ 395 : λ 525. Aor. pple. pass. ἀνακλινθείς ι 371. Pl. ἀνακλινθέντες ν 78. Fem. ἀνακλινθεῖσα δ 794, σ 189. (1) To push back, open (a door) χ 156.—To remove (something covering) : νέφος E 751 = Θ 395.—App. (perh. in imitation of these lines), to suspend or delay the action of (an ambush) : ἀνακλῖναι λόχον λ 525.—(2) To cause to lean (against something) : ποτὶ ἑρκίον αὐλῆς σ 103.—To place or rest in a specified position Δ 113.—(3) In aor. pple. pass., leaning or bending back ι 371.—Reclining δ 794 = σ 189.—Of rowers swinging back to their work ν 78.

ἀνακοντίζω [ἀν-, ἀνα- (1)]. To spirt up E 113.

ἀνακόπτω [ἀνα- (3)] To thrust back φ 47.

†**ἀνακράζω** [ἀνα- (6) + κράζω in sim. sense]. Aor. ἀνέκραγον. To lift up one's voice, speak ξ 467.

ἀνακτόριος, -η, -ον [ἀνακτ-, ἄναξ]. Of a king or chief ο 397.

ἀνακυμβαλιάζω [app. ἀνα- (6) + *κυμβαλιάζω in sim. sense fr. κύμβαλον, cymbal]. Thus, of chariots, to rattle (in upsetting) Π 379.

ἀναλκείη, -ης, ἡ [ἄναλκις]. Lack of spirit, cowardice. In pl. Ζ 74 = Ρ 320, Ρ 337.

ἄναλκις, -ιδος, ὁ, ἡ [ἀν-[1] + ἀλκή]. Acc. masc. ἄναλκιν γ 375. Incapable of offering defence or resistance, spiritless, cowardly Β 201, Ε 331, 349, Θ 153, Λ 390, Ν 104, Π 355, Φ 555, etc. : γ 310, 375, δ 334 = ρ 125, ι 475.—As epithet of φύζα Ο 62.

ἄναλτος, -ον [prob. for ἄναλδτος fr. ἀν-[1] + ἀλδ-, ἀλδαίνω, ἀλδήσκω]. Thus, not to be filled out, insatiable, greedy : γαστέρα ρ 228, σ 364.—Absol. σ 114.

ἀναλύω, ἀλλύω [ἀνα- (6), ἀλ-, ἀνα- (6)]. Pa. iterative ἀλλύεσκον τ 150. 3 sing. -ε β 105, ω 140. (1) To loose, set free: ἐκ δεσμῶν (from . . .) μ 200.—(2) To undo, take down (a web) β 105 = ω 140, β 109 = ω 145, τ 150.

ἀναμαιμάω [ἀνα- (5)]. Of fire, to rage *through*. With acc. : βαθέ' ἄγκεα Υ 490.

†**ἀναμάσσω** [ἀνα- (6) + μάσσω, to handle, conn. with μαίομαι]. 2 sing. fut. ἀναμάξεις. To wipe away the stain of (a crime) τ 92.

†**ἀναμένω** [ἀνά- (6)]. Aor. ἀνέμεινα. To wait for, await : Ἠῶ τ 342.

ἀναμετρέω [ἀνα- (4)]. To measure one's way again, retrace one's course. With acc. of *terminus ad quem* : Χάρυβδιν μ 428.

†**ἀναμιμνήσκω** [ἀνα- (6)]. 2 sing. aor. ἀνέμνησας. To remind (a person of a thing). With double acc. γ 211.

ἀναμίμνω [ἀνα- (6)]. To wait for, await : ἀλλήλους Λ 171.—Absol., to stand one's ground Π 363.

ἀναμίσγω [ἀνα- (5)]. Contr. aor. pple. ἀμμείξας, ἀμμίξας Ω 529. (1) To mix up ingredients Ω 529. —(2) To mix up or mingle : σίτῳ φάρμακα (with . . .) κ 235.

ἀναμορμύρω [ἀνα- (6)]. 3 sing. pa. iterative ἀναμορμύρεσκε. To seethe or boil up μ 238.

ἀνανεύω [ἀνα- (1)]. (1) To throw up the chin in token of refusal (cf. κατανεύω) Ζ 311 (app. the statue is supposed to move its head).—(2) With infin. of what is refused : σόον ἀπονέεσθαι Π 252. —With acc. ἕτερον Π 250.—(3) To make the motion in prohibition Χ 205 : φ 129.

ἄναντα [app. a nonce-word formed fr. ἀνά by adding a termination fr. ἔναντα, ἐσάντα]. Uphill Ψ 116.

ἄναξ, -ακτος, ὁ (Ϝάναξ). Voc. (besides ἄναξ) ἄνα Γ 351, Π 233 : ρ 354. Dat. pl. ἀνάκτεσι ο 557. (1) A king (the main notion being app. that of a protecting chief rather than that of a ruler; cf. the name Ἀστυάναξ Ζ 403, and the reason for it there given. But βουληφόρος ἀ. occurs Μ 414). (a) ἀ. ἀνδρῶν (app. much like ποιμὴν λαῶν) applied to Agamemnon, gen. as a title, but sometimes as a descriptive term Α 7, 172, 442, 506, Β 402, 434, etc. : θ 77, λ 397 = ω 121. —Sim. : πολλῶν λαῶν ἀ. Ι 98.—So ἀ. alone Β 284, 360, Ι 33.—ἀ. ἀνδρῶν applied also to Anchises Ε 268.—To Aeneas Ε 311.—To Augeas Λ 701.—To Euphetes Ο 532.—To Eumelus Ψ 288.—Sim. πολέεσσ' ἄνδρεσσιν ἄνακτα of Ortilochus Ε 546.—And applied by Idomeneus to himself Ν 452.—(b) ἀ. applied to Priam Β 373, Δ 18, Ζ 451, etc. : γ 107.—To Idomeneus Β 405, Κ 112, Ο 301 : τ 181. —To Philoctetes Β 725.—To Diomedes Δ 420, Ε 794.—To Proetus Ζ 166.—To Achilles Ι 164, 276 = Τ 177, Ψ 35, 173, Ω 449, 452.—To Peleus Ι 480.—To Asius Μ 139.—To Sarpedon Μ 413, 414, Π 464.—To Helenus Ν 582, 758, 770, 781.—To Nestor Ψ 302 : γ 388.—To Menelaus Ψ 588.—To Teucrus Ψ 859.—To Odysseus γ 163, ν 194, etc. —To Teiresias λ 144, 151.—To Aias λ 561.—To Minos λ 570.—To minor heroes and personages Β 566 = Ψ 678, Β 624, 672, 679, 693, Η 8, 137, Λ 322, Ξ 489, Ο 639 : π 395 = σ 413, σ 299, τ 523, ω 305.—Applied to kings or chiefs generally : ἅρματα ἀνάκτων Β 777 : ἀνάκτων παῖδες ν 223.—To the leader of a ship's company λ 71. —With a local word : Πύλοιο Β 77. Cf. Ζ 173. —Sim. Τρώεσσιν Υ 230.—Joined with βασιλεύς υ 194.—(c) ἀ. applied to gods. To Apollo Α 36, 75, 390, etc. : θ 323, 334, 339.—To Zeus Α 502, 529, Β 102, Γ 351, Η 194, 200, Π 233, Σ 118 : ρ 354. —To Hermes Β 104.—To Sleep Ξ 233.—To Poseidon Ο 8, 57, 158, Υ 67, 404 : γ 43, 54, ι 412, 526, λ 130, ν 185, ψ 277.—To Hephaestus Ο 214, Σ 137 : θ 270.—To Hades Υ 61.—To a river ε 445, 450.—To the sun μ 176.—To the gods generally μ 290.—(2) A lord, master, owner : οὐδ' ἠγνοίησαν ἄνακτα Ν 28, τί δόμεν Πηλῆϊ ἄνακτι (to P. as your master) Ρ 443. Cf. Κ 559, Ν 38, Ο 453, Π 371, 507, Σ 417, 421, Ψ 417 = 446, 517, Ω 734 : οἴκοιο ἀ. α 397, οὔτε ἀ. οὔτε ποιμήν δ 87. Cf. ι 440, κ 216, ξ 8, 139, 170, ρ 186, 320, etc.

ἀνάξει, 3 sing. fut. ἀνάσσω.

ἀνάξομεν, 1 pl. fut. ἀνάγω.

†**ἀναοίγω** [ἀνα- (6) + οἴγω = οἴγνυμι]. 3 sing. impf. ἀνέῳγε Π 221, Ω 228. Cont. ἀνῷγε Ξ 168. 3 pl. pa. iterative ἀναοίγεσκον Ω 455. 3 sing. aor. ἀνέῳξε κ 389. (1) To open (a door) κ 389.—(2) To draw back (a bar in order to open a door) κληῖδα Ξ 168, Ω 455.—(3) To remove (a cover) Π 221, Ω 228.

ἀναπάλλω [ἀνα- (1)]. Contr. aor. pple. ἀμπεπαλών Γ 355, Ε 280, Η 244, Λ 349, Ρ 516, Υ 438, Χ 273, 289 : ω 519, 522. 3 sing. aor. pass. ἀνέπαλτο Θ 85, Ψ 694. (1) To poise and sway (a spear before throwing) Γ 355 = Ε 280 = Η 244 = Λ 349 = Ρ 516 = Χ 273 = 289, Υ 438 : ω 519 = 522. —(2) In pass., to leap or spring up : ἀναπάλλεται ἰχθύς Ψ 692. Cf. Θ 85, Ψ 694.

ἀναπαύω [ἀνα- (6)]. To cause to cease : ἔργων ἀνθρώπους ἀνέπαυσεν (from . . .) Ρ 550.

†**ἀναπετάννυμι** [ἀνα- (6)]. Acc. fem. pf. pple. pass. ἀναπεπταμένας. To open wide (a gate) Μ 122.

†**ἀναπίμπλημι** [ἀνα- (6)]. Fut. infin. ἀναπλήσειν ε 302. 2 sing. aor. subj. ἀναπλήσῃς Δ 170. Pple.

ἀναπλήσας, -αντος Θ 34, 354, 465, Λ 263, Ο 132. Infin. ἀναπλῆσαι ε 207. To fulfil (one's destiny), have full measure of (misery etc.) : πότμον Δ 170, Λ 263. Cf. Θ 34 = 354 = 465, Ο 132 : κήδεα ε 207. Cf. ε 302.

ἀναπλέω [ἀνα- (1) (5)]. Fut. infin. in mid. form ἀναπλεύσεσθαι Λ 22. (**1**) To sail upwards. Of a voyage from Greece to Troy Λ 22.—(**2**) To sail *through*, traverse. With acc. : στεινωπόν μ 234.

ἀνάπνευσις, ἡ [ἀναπνέω]. A breathing-space, a respite : ὀλίγη δέ τ' ἀ. πολέμοιο (a little (space of time) serves as a respite from . . .) Λ 801 = Π 43 = Σ 201 (ὀλίγη assimilated in gender to the predicate ; cf. Ν 237 under ἀρετή (1)).

ἀναπνέω [ἀνα- (4)]. 3 pl. aor. ἀνέπνευσαν Λ 382, Π 302. 3 pl. subj. ἀναπνεύσωσι Λ 800, Ο 235, Π 42, Σ 200, Φ 534. 3 sing. opt. ἀναπνεύσειε Τ 227. Contr. infin. ἀμπνεῦσαι Π 111. Contr. aor. imp. ἄμπνυε Χ 222. To breathe again, recover breath, draw breath, find a breathing-space or respite Λ 327, 800 = Π 42 = Σ 200, Π 111, 302, Φ 534, Χ 222. —With genit. : κακότητος (from . . .) Λ 382. Cf. Ο 235, Τ 227.

ἀνάποινος [ἀν-[1] + ἄποινα]. In neut. ἀνάποινον as adv., without ransom Α 99.

†ἀναπρήθω [ἀνα- (1)]. Aor. pple. ἀναπρήσας. To cause (tears) to well up Ι 433 : β 81.

ἀνάπτω [ἀν-, ἀνα- (1) (6)]. 3 sing. aor. ἀνῆψε γ 274. Infin. ἀνάψαι β 86, ι 137. Pf. imp. pass. ἀνήφθω μ 51, 162. (**1**) To fasten up (as an offering in a temple) γ 274.—(**2**) To tie, make fast (a rope) : πρυμνήσια ι 137. Cf. μ 51 = 162, 179.—(**3**) To fasten (blame) upon a person β 86.

ἀνάπυστος [ἀνα- (6) + πυσ-, πεύθομαι]. Discovered, revealed. Absol. in neut. pl. : ἀνάπυστα θεοὶ θέσαν (caused discovery to be made) λ 274.

ἀναροιβδέω. See ἀναρροιβδέω.

†ἀναρπάζω [ἀν-, ἀνα- (1)]. 3 sing. aor. ἀνήρπασε Ι 564. 3 pl. ἀνήρπαξαν ο 427. Pple. ἀναρπάξας Π 437. Fem. -ᾶσα δ 515, ε 419, υ 63, ψ 316. Pl. -ᾶσαι θ 409. (**1**) To snatch up and carry off Ι 564, Π 437.—Of winds δ 515, ε 419, θ 409, υ 63, ψ 316. —(**2**) To carry off as a slave ο 427.

†ἀναρρήγνῡμι [ἀνα- (6)]. 3 sing. aor. opt. ἀναρρήξειε Υ 63. Pple. ἀναρρήξας Η 461. Nom. dual masc. -αντε Σ 582. (**1**) To split, cause to open : γαῖαν Υ 63.—To tear open, rend : βοείην Σ 582.—(**2**) To tear down, demolish Η 461.

ἀναρρίπτω [ἀνα- (1)]. 3 pl. aor. ἀνέρριψαν κ 130. From ἀναρριπτέω 3 pl. impf. ἀνερρίπτουν ν 78. To throw up (the sea with the oar) : ἅλα πηδῷ η 328, ν 78.—Absol., to row vigorously κ 130.

ἀναρροιβδέω, also **ἀναροιβδέω,** μ 105. [ἀνα- (6)]. To swallow down, swallow μ 104, 105, 236, 431.

ἀνάρσιος [ἀν-[1] + ἀρ-, ἀραρίσκω. 'Not fitted, ill-fitted, ill-assorted']. Unfriendly, hostile Ω 365 : κ 459, λ 401, 408, ω 111.—Absol. : δυσμενέες καὶ ἀνάρσιοι ξ 85.

ἄναρχος [ἀν-[1] + ἀρχός]. Leaderless Β 703 = 726.

†ἀνασεύω [ἀνα- (1)]. 3 sing. aor. mid. ἀνέσσυτο. In mid., to spirt up : αἷμα Λ 458.

†ἀνασπάω [ἀνα- (3)]. 3 sing. aor. mid. ἀνεσπάσατο. To draw forth again : ἔγχος Ν 574.

ἄνασσα, -ης, ἡ (Ϝάνασσα) [fem. of ἄναξ]. Queen, protectress. Applied to Demeter Ξ 326.—In voc. addressed to Athene γ 380.—To Nausicaa ζ 149, 175.

ἀνάσσω (Ϝανάσσω) [ἄναξ]. 3 sing. fut. ἀνάξει Τ 104, 122, Υ 307. Infin. -ειν Τ 109, Υ 180. Aor. infin. mid. -ασθαι γ 245 (in mid. only here). (**1**) To protect, be patron of. With genit. : Τενέδοιο Α 38 = 452.—(**2**) To be king, chief or ruler : μετὰ τριτάτοισιν Α 252. Cf. Δ 61 = Σ 366, Π 172, Ψ 471 : η 23, 62, τ 110.—In mid. : τρὶς ἀνάξασθαι γένε' ἀνδρῶν (app., during three generations) γ 245.—With local words : ἐν Βουδείῳ Π 572. Cf. λ 276, 284, ω 26.—(**3**) To be king or chief of or ruler over. (**a**) With genit. : Ἀργείων Κ 33. Cf. λ 276.—With local words : Ἰλίου Ζ 478. Cf. γ 304, δ 602, ρ 443.—(**b**) With dat. : Μυρμιδόνεσσιν Α 180. Cf. Α 231, Β 643, Ζ 397, Ξ 85, 94, Τ 104, Ω 202, etc. : α 181, 419, β 234 = ε 12, δ 9, η 11, ι 552 = ν 25, κ 110, λ 349, 491, ο 240, υ 112, ω 26, 378.—With local words : πολλῇσιν νήσοισιν Β 108. —(**4**) In pass., to be ruled by, be under the sway of. With dat. : ἀνάσσονται ἐμοὶ αὐτῷ δ 177. —(**5**) To be lord or master of, possess, enjoy. (**a**) With genit. : τιμῆς Υ 180 : ω 30.—(**b**) With dat. : κτήμασιν οἷσιν α 117. Cf. α 402, δ 93.

ἀνασταδόν [ἀνα- (1) + στα-, ἵστημι]. Standing up : δειδέχατ' ἀ. Ι 671, ἴδεσθ' ἀ. Ψ 469.

ἀναστάς, aor. pple. ἀνίστημι (B).

ἀναστεναχίζω [ἀνα- (6)]. To groan aloud Κ 9.

ἀναστενάχω [ἀνα- (6)]. To groan aloud over, lament, bewail Ψ 211.—In mid. Σ 315, 355.

ἀναστήσας, aor. pple. ἀνίστημι (A).

ἀναστρέφω [ἀνα- (5) (6)]. Contr. 3 pl. aor. opt. ἀνστρέψειαν Ψ 436. (**1**) To upset : δίφρους Ψ 436. —(**2**) In mid., to go about *over*, find oneself in. With acc. : ἄλλην τινὰ γαῖαν ἀναστρέφομαι ν 326.

ἀναστρωφάω [ἀνα- (6)]. To keep turning about : τόξον ἐνώμα ἀναστρωφῶν φ 394.

ἀνασχέμεν, ἀνασχεῖν, aor. infin. ἀνέχω.

†ἀνατέλλω [ἀνα- (1)]. 3 sing. aor. ἀνέτειλε. To cause to spring up or be produced : ἀμβροσίην Ε 777.

†ἀνατίθημι [ἀνα- (1)]. 3 sing. fut. ἀναθήσει. To lay (reproach) *upon*. With dat. : ἐλεγχείην μοι Χ 100.

†*ἀνατλάω [ἀνα- (6)]. 2 sing. aor. ἀνέτλης ξ 47. 3 -η κ 327. 1 pl. -ημεν γ 104. To endure, suffer γ 104, ξ 47.—To withstand the operation of κ 327.

†ἀνατρέπω [ἀνα- (3)]. 3 sing. aor. mid. ἀνετράπετο. In mid., to fall supine Ζ 64, Ξ 447.

†ἀνατρέχω [ἀνα- (1) (3)]. 3 sing. aor. ἀνέδραμε Λ 354, Π 813, Ρ 297, Σ 56, 437. 3 pl. -ον Ψ 717. 3 sing. pf. ἀναδέδρομε ε 412, κ 4. (**1**) To spirt up Ρ 297.—(**2**) To run up, shoot up (like a quickly growing plant) Σ 56 = 437.—Of weals, to start up Ψ 717.—(**3**) To run, stretch, extend up : πέτρη ε 412, κ 4.—(**4**) To run back, retire Λ 354, Π 813.

ἄναυδος [ἀν-[1] + αὐδή]. Speechless ε 456.—Absol. : ἶσος ἀναύδῳ (like a dumb man) κ 378.

ἀναφαίνω [ἀνα- (6)]. Aor. infin. ἀναφῆναι δ 254. (1) To reveal, make known A 87.—To betray, denounce δ 254.—To display: ἐπεσβολίας δ 159.—To make a display of: ἀρετήν Υ 411.—(2) To afford light σ 310.—(3) In pass., to appear, be seen: οἷος ἀναφαίνεται ἀστήρ Λ 62. Cf. κ 29.—Of destruction, to be manifested, come upon one Λ 174, P 244.

ἀναφανδά [ἀναφαν-, ἀναφαίνω]. Openly, without concealment: ἀ. φιλεῦντας γ 221. Cf. γ 222, λ 455.

ἀναφανδόν [as prec.]=prec.: ἀ. ὄπυιεν (as her avowed husband) Π 178.

†**ἀναφέρω** [ἀνα- (1)]. Aor. ἀνένεικα λ 625. 3 sing. aor. mid. ἀνενείκατο Τ 314. (1) To bring or fetch up λ 625.—(2) In mid., to fetch a sigh Τ 314.

ἀναχάζομαι [ἀνα- (6)]. Aor. pple. ἀναχασσάμενος, -η Η 264, Ν 740, Φ 403: η 280, λ 97. To draw back, retire Ε 443, 600, 822, Η 264, Λ 461, Ν 740, Ο 728, Π 710, 819, Ρ 47, 108, 129, Φ 403: η 280, λ 97.

ἀναχωρέω [ἀνα- (3)]. (1) To go back, return Κ 210=411, Ν 457.—(2) To withdraw, retire ρ 453, 461.—To draw back from danger Γ 35.—Of hounds retreating from a boar Ρ 729.—To draw back or retire in fight Δ 305, Ε 107, Λ 189, 440, Ρ 30, Υ 196, 335: χ 270.

ἀνάψαι, aor. infin. ἀνάπτω.

ἀναψύχω [ἀνα- (6)]. 3 pl. aor. pass. ἀνέψυχθεν Κ 575. To cool, refresh δ 568.—Fig.: ἐπεὶ ἀνέψυχθεν ἦτορ Κ 575. Cf. Ν 84.—To cool or soothe (a wound) Ε 795.

†**ἁνδάνω** ((σ)Fανδάνω) [σFαδ-. Cf. ἡδύς, L. *suavis*]. 3 sing. ἁνδάνει β 114. 3 sing. impf. ἑήνδανε (ἐFάνδανε) Ω 25: γ 143. ἥνδανε (Fάνδανε) Α 24, 378, Ο 674, Σ 510: ε 153, θ 506, κ 373, ξ 337, 525, π 398, ρ 173. ἅνδανε γ 150. 3 sing. aor. εὔαδε (ἔFαδε) Ξ 340, Ρ 647: π 28. ἅδε (Fάδε) Μ 80, Ν 748: ω 465. 3 sing. opt. ἅδοι ζ 245, υ 327. Infin. ἁδεῖν Γ 173. Acc. sing. masc. pf. pple. ἑαδότα (FεFαδότα) Ι 173: σ 422. (ἀφ-, ἐπι-.) (1) To please, be pleasing or acceptable, find favour or acceptance ε 153, ρ 173.—With dat.: Ἕκτορι Μ 80=Ν 748. Cf. Γ 173, Ξ 340, Σ 510: β 114, γ 150, θ 506, ξ 337, 525, π 398, υ 327, ω 465.—(2) Impers. With dat.: ἐπεί τοι εὔαδεν οὕτως Ρ 647. Cf. Α 24=378, Ω 25: γ 143, κ 373.—With dat. and infin.: Αἴαντι ἑστάμεν Ο 674. Cf. ζ 245.—So ὥς τοι εὔαδε, . . . ἐσορᾶν . . . π 28.—(3) In pf. pple., pleasing, agreeable Ι 173:=σ 422.

ἄνδιχα [ἀν-, ἀνα- (6) + δίχα]. (1) In two, asunder: κεάσθη Π 412=Υ 387, Π 578.—(2) In halves, equally: δάσασθαι Σ 511, Χ 120.

ἀνδράγρια, τά [ἀνδρ-, ἀνήρ + ἄγρη. Cf. βοάγρια]. Spoils of a man, *i.e.* of a fallen foe Ξ 509.

ἀνδρακάς [ἀνδρ-, ἀνήρ]. Each man, each ν 14.

ἀνδράποδον. Dat. pl. -πόδεσσι. A slave Η 475.

ἀνδραχθής [ἀνδρ-, ἀνήρ + ἄχθος]. That is a load for a man, as heavy as a man can carry κ 121.

ἀνδρειφόντης [prob. rather ἀδριφόντης, fr. ἀδρ-, ἀνδρ-, ἀνήρ + φον-, φένω. Cf. ἀνδροτής]. Slayer of men. Epithet of Enyalius Β 651, Η 166=Θ 264=Ρ 259.

ἀνδρόκμητος [ἀνδρ-, ἀνήρ + κμη-, κάμνω]. Made by the hands of man, the work of men's hands Λ 371.

ἀνδροκτασίη, -ης, ἡ [ἀνδρ-, ἀνήρ + κτα-, κτείνω]. (1) Slaughter of men, slaughter in battle. In pl.: παύσασαι ἀνδροκτασιάων Ε 909. Cf. Η 237, Ω 548: λ 612.—In concrete sense: ὕπαγ' ἐξ ἀνδροκτασίης Λ 164.—(2) Homicide Ψ 86.

ἀνδρόμεος [ἀνδρ-, ἀνήρ]. Of man, human Λ 538 (the throng of men), Ρ 571, Υ 100, Φ 70: ι 297 (of man's flesh), 347, 374, χ 19.

ἀνδροτής, -ῆτος, ἡ [prob. rather ἀδροτής, fr. ἀδρ-, ἀνδρ-, ἀνήρ. Cf. ἀνδρειφόντης]. (1) Manhood Π 857=Χ 363.—(2) Manliness Ω 6.

ἀνδροφάγος [ἀνδρ-, ἀνήρ + φάγον]. Man-eating κ 200.

ἀνδροφόνος, -ον [ἀνδρ-, ἀνήρ + φον-, φένω]. (1) Slayer of men. Epithet of Hector Α 242, Ζ 498, Ι 351, Π 77, 840, Ρ 428, 616, 638, Σ 149, Ω 509, 724.—Of Ares Δ 441.—Of Lycurgus Ζ 134.—(2) Manslaying, fatal: χεῖρας Σ 317=Ψ 18, Ω 479.—Of a poisonous application, deadly α 261.

ἀνδύεται, contr. 3 sing. pres. mid. ἀναδύω.

ἀνέβη, 3 sing. aor. ἀναβαίνω.

ἀνεβήσετο, 3 sing. aor. mid. ἀναβαίνω.

ἀνεγείρω [ἀν-, ἀνα- (6)]. Aor. ἀνέγειρα κ 172. 3 sing. -ε Κ 138, 157: ψ 22. Infin. ἀνεγεῖραι δ 730. To wake up, cause to rise, rouse Κ 138, 157: δ 730, κ 172, ψ 16, 22.

ἀνέγναμψαν, 3 pl. aor. ἀναγνάμπτω.

ἀνέγνων, aor. ἀναγιγνώσκω.

ἀνεδέγμεθα, 1 pl. aor. ἀναδέχομαι.

ἀνεδέξατο, 3 sing. aor. ἀναδέχομαι.

ἀνέδρακε, 3 sing. aor. ἀναδέρκομαι.

ἀνέδραμε, 3 sing. aor. ἀνατρέχω.

ἀνέδυ, 3 sing. aor. ἀναδύω.

ἀνεδύσετο, 3 sing. aor. mid. ἀναδύω.

ἀνεέργω [ἀν-, ἀνα- (6)]. To keep back, restrain: φάλαγγας Γ 77=Η 55, μάχην Τρώων Ρ 752.

†**ἀνέζομαι** [ἀν-, ἀνα- (1) (4)]. 3 sing. fut. ἀνέσει σ 265. Aor. opt. ἀνέσαιμι Ξ 209. Pl. pple. ἀνέσαντες Ν 657. In the forms cited (1) To set or place upon something: ἐς δίφρον Ν 657.—Sim.: εἰς εὐνήν Ξ 209.—(2) To restore to one's place σ 265.

ἀνέηκε, 3 sing. aor. ἀνίημι.

ἀνείη, 3 sing. aor. opt. ἀνίημι.

ἀνείλετο, 3 sing. aor. mid. ἀναιρέω.

†**ἄνειμι** [ἀν-, ἀνα- (1) (3) + εἶμι]. 3 sing. ἄνεισι Χ 492, 499. Pple. ἀνιών, -όντος Ζ 480, Θ 538, Ξ 28, Σ 136, Χ 135: α 24, 259, ε 282, κ 332, μ 429, ψ 362. Fem. ἀνιοῦσα Τ 290. Acc. ἀνιοῦσαν θ 568, ν 150, 176. Impf. ἀνήϊον κ 146, 274. 3 pl. ἀνήϊον κ 446. (1) To go up κ 146.—Of the sun, to rise: ἠελίου ἀνιόντος Θ 538. Cf. Σ 136, Χ 135: Αἰθίοπες ἀνιόντος Ὑπερίονος (dwelling in the east) α 24. Cf. μ 429, ψ 362.—(2) To go inland κ 274, 446.—(3) To go up (to a person) as a suppliant: ἐς πατρὸς ἑταίρους Χ 492.—(4) To go or come back, return: ἐκ πολέμου Ζ 480. Cf. Ξ 28, Τ 290, Χ 499: α 259, ε 282, θ 568=ν 150=176, κ 332.

ἀνείμων, -ονος [ἀν-[1] + εἷμα]. Without (store of) raiment. Absol.: ἀνείμονος ἠὲ πενιχροῦ γ 348.

ἀνείρομαι [ἀν-, ἀνα- (6)]. (**1**) To ask, inquire, make inquiry Φ 508: η 21, ψ 99.—(**2**) To inquire about: τήνδε γαῖαν ν 238.—(**3**) To question (a person): σε δ 420. Cf. δ 461, 631.—(**4**) With double acc.: ὅ μ' ἀνείρεαι Γ 177: =η 243=ο 402, τ 171. Cf. α 231=ο 390.

ἀνέκραγον, aor. ἀνακράζω.

ἀνεκτός, -όν [vbl. adj. fr. ἀνέχω]. Bearable, endurable, to be endured Α 573, Κ 118, Λ 610: υ 83.—Absol. in neut. pl.: οὐκέτ' ἀνεκτὰ πέλονται (my case is now unendurable) υ 223.

ἀνεκτῶς [adv. fr. prec.]. In such wise as may be endured: μαίνεται οὐκέτ' ἀ. Θ 355. Cf. ι 350.

ἀνελθών, aor. pple. ἀνέρχομαι.

ἀνέλκω [ἀν-, ἀνα- (1) (3)]. (**1**) To draw up Μ 434.—(**2**) To draw back (*i.e.* away from one): τόξου πῆχυν Λ 375, Ν 583.—To draw back (a spear in order to recover it). In mid. χ 97.—To bend a bow φ 128, 150.

ἀνέλοντο, 3 pl. aor. mid. ἀναιρέω.

ἀνέμεινα, aor. ἀναμένω.

ἀνέμνησας, 2 sing. aor. ἀναμιμνήσκω.

ἄνεμος, -ου, ὁ. (**1**) A wind: ἐλθὼν ἀ. Ρ 57. Cf. Ε 865: ε 109, 368, μ 313.—With pl.: οἱ δ' ἄνεμοι ἔβαν (they, the winds mentioned) Ψ 229: τῶν ἄλλων ἀνέμων ε 383.—(**2**) The wind: ἀ. πρῆσεν ἱστίον Α 481. Cf. Ε 499, Ζ 147, 346, Λ 156, 308, Μ 133, 157, 207, 253, Ξ 398, Ο 383, 626, Ρ 739, Υ 492, Ψ 367, Ω 342: δεῦρ' ἀ. πέλασσεν ε 111=134. Cf. α 98, β 427, γ 300, ε 391, ι 285, λ 592, ν 276, etc.—(**3**) Joined with Βορέης Ο 26: ι 67, ξ 253, 299, τ 200.—With Ζέφυρος Π 150.—(**4**) In pl. (**a**) Winds: δύο Ι 4. Cf. Ν 795, Ξ 254, Ψ 194: ι 82, λ 400=407, μ 286, 425, ξ 313, ω 110.—(**b**) The winds: κνίσην ἄνεμοι φέρον Θ 549. Cf. Β 397, Ε 501, 525, Θ 481, Κ 437, Μ 281, Ν 334, Ξ 17, Ο 620, Π 213=Ψ 713, Ρ 56, Ψ 199, 317: πνοιὰς ἀνέμων δ 839. Cf. γ 289, ε 293, 305, 317, 330, 343, 478, ζ 43, η 272, ι 260, κ 20, 21, 47, μ 326, ν 99, τ 440.

ἀνεμοσκεπής [ἄνεμος + σκέπας]. Protecting from the wind: χλαινάων Π 224.

ἀνεμοτρεφής, -ές [ἄνεμος + τρέφω]. Of a wave, fed (*i.e.* raised) by the wind Ο 625.—Of a spear, (made of wood) toughened by (the buffeting of) the wind Λ 256.

ἀνεμώλιος [app. fr. ἄνεμος]. Thus (**1**) Like the idle blowing of the wind, idle, vain: ταῦτ' ἀνεμώλια βάζεις (what you say is idle) Δ 355.—Absol.: ἀνεμώλια βάζειν δ 837=λ 464.—(**2**) Useless, idle: τόξα Ε 216. Cf. Φ 474.—Useless, effecting nothing Υ 123.

ἀνένεικα, aor. ἀναφέρω.

ἀνέντες, aor. pple. pl. ἀνίημι.

ἀνέξομαι, fut. mid. ἀνέχω.

ἀνέπαλτο, 3 sing. aor. pass. ἀναπάλλω.

ἀνεπᾶλτο, 3 sing. aor. ἀνεφάλλομαι.

ἀνέπνευσαν, 3 pl. aor. ἀναπνέω.

ἀνερρίπτουν, 3 pl. impf. See ἀναρρίπτω.

ἀνέρριψαν, 3 pl. aor. ἀναρρίπτω.

ἀνέρχομαι [ἀν-, ἀνα- (1) (3)]. 3 sing. aor. ἀνήλυθε ζ 167. Pple. ἀνελθών κ 97, 148, 194, τ 190. (**1**) To go up κ 97=148, 194.—To go up (to a city): ἄστυδε τ 190.—Of a plant, to shoot up ζ 163, 167.—(**2**) To come back, return Δ 392, Ζ 187: α 317.

ἀνερωτάω [ἀν-, ἀνα- (6) + ἐρωτάω = εἰρωτάω]. To question (a person): ἀνηρώτων μιν δ 251.

ἄνεσαν, 3 pl. aor. ἀνίημι.

ἀνέσει, 3 sing. fut. ἀνέζομαι.

ἀνεσπάσατο, 3 sing. aor. mid. ἀνασπάω.

ἀνέσσυτο, 3 sing. aor. mid. ἀνασεύω.

ἀνέστη, 3 sing. aor. ἀνίστημι (B).

ἀνέστησε, 3 sing. aor. ἀνίστημι (A).

ἀνέστιος [ἀν-[1] + ἑστίη = ἱστίη]. Unworthy to have a home: ἀφρήτωρ ἀθέμιστος ἀ. Ι 63.

ἀνέσχε, 3 sing. aor. ἀνέχω.

ἀνέσχεθε, 3 sing. aor. ἀνέχω.

ἀνέτειλε, 3 sing. aor. ἀνατέλλω.

ἀνέτλη, 3 sing. aor. ἀνατλάω.

ἀνετράπετο, 3 sing. aor. mid. ἀνατρέπω.

ἄνευ. With genit. (**1**) Away from, aloof from: δηΐων Ν 556.—(**2**) Lacking: κέντροιο Ψ 387. Cf. ω 247.—Without need of: δεσμοῖο ν 100.—(**3**) Without the help of: ἔθεν Ρ 407.—Without the good will or permission of: ἐμέθεν Ο 213. Cf. β 372, ο 531.

ἄνευθε(ν) [ἄνευ]. (**1**) Adv. (**a**) Far away: ἀ. ἐών Β 27=64=Ω 174. Cf. Δ 277, Χ 300, Ψ 452, 474.—(**b**) Away, removed: πολλὸν ἀ. Ψ 378. Cf. δ 356, τ 575.—(**c**) Apart, aside, aloof: ἀ. ἔθηκεν Χ 368. Cf. Ψ 241, Ω 208: ι 26, λ 82.—(**2**) Prep. with genit. (**a**) Far from: πατρός Φ 78.—(**b**) Away from: νῶϊν Χ 88.—(**c**) Apart or aloof from: ἄλλων Χ 39. Cf. κ 554.—(**d**) Without, free from: πόνου η 192.—(**e**) Without the help of: ἐμεῖο Π 89. Cf. π 239.—Without the good will or permission of: θεοῦ Ε 185.—(**f**) App., in the background as regards, ready to take the place of: τοῖο ἀ. λελειμμένην Χ 333.

†**ἀνεφάλλομαι** [ἀν-, ἀνα- (1), ἐφ-, ἐπι- (11)]. 3 sing. aor. ἀνεπᾶλτο. To spring up against a person Υ 424.

ἀνέφελος, -ον [ἀ-[1] + νεφέλη]. Cloudless ζ 45.

ἀνέχω [ἀν-, ἀνα- (1) (3)]. 3 sing. aor. ἀνέσχε Ρ 310, Υ 278, Χ 80: χ 297. 3 pl. -ον Γ 318, Ζ 301, Η 177: σ 89. Pple. ἀνασχών Α 450, Γ 275, Ε 174, etc.: δ 115, 154, ν 355, ρ 239, υ 97. Infin. ἀνασχέμεν Ω 301. ἀνασχεῖν Ζ 257. 3 sing. aor. ἀνέσχεθε Η 412, Κ 461. 1 pl. -ομεν ι 294. Contr. infin. ἀνσχεθέειν ε 320. **Mid.** Fut. ἀνέξομαι Ε 895: τ 27. Contr. infin. ἀνσχήσεσθαι Ε 104, 285. 3 sing. aor. ἀνέσχετο Ε 655, Σ 430, Φ 67, 161: ψ 302. Contr. 2 sing. ἄνσχεο Ω 518. Opt. ἀνασχοίμην λ 375. Imp. ἀνάσχεο Α 586, Ε 382, Κ 321. Contr. ἄνσχεο Ψ 587, Ω 549. Pple. ἀνασχόμενος, -ου Γ 362, Λ 594, Μ 138, etc.: ξ 425, σ 95, 100, τ 448. Infin. ἀνασχέσθαι Δ 511: ν 307. (**I**) In act. (**1**) To hold up, lift up: σκῆπτρον (to the gods in testimony) Η 412, ὑψόσε (as an offering) Κ 461. Cf. Ξ 499, Υ 278, Χ 80: χεῖρας σ 89. Cf. δ 115=154, χ 297.—To lift up (the hands) in prayer Α 450, Γ 275, 318=Η 177, Ε 174, Ζ 257, 301, Σ 75, Τ 254,

Ω 301 : ι 294, ν 355, ρ 239, υ 97.—(2) To maintain, uphold : εὐδικίας τ 111.—(3) To restrain, check : ἵππους Ψ 426.—(4) To project, appear : αἰχμὴ παρ' ὦμον Ρ 310.—To come to the surface, emerge ε 320.—(II) In mid. (1) To hold up, lift up : σκῆπτρον ἀνάσχεο (in testimony) Κ 321. Cf. Μ 138 : σ 100.—To raise (a spear) for action Ε 655, Λ 594, Ο 298, Ρ 234, Φ 67, 161 : τ 448.—(2) To lift the hand Γ 362, Χ 34 : ξ 425.—Of boxers, to square up Ψ 660, 686 : σ 95.—(3) To endure, have laid upon one, suffer : κήδεα Σ 430. Cf. Ω 518 : ν 307, ψ 302.—(4) To endure, stand, withstand the action of : χαλκόν Δ 511. Cf. Ε 104, Ο 470.—(5) To endure, submit to : δουλοσύνην χ 423.—To suffer the presence or company of, bear with : ξείνους η 32. Cf. ρ 13.—(6) To endure, suffer, permit. With acc. in complementary ppl. clause: οὔ σ' ἀνέξομαι ἄλγε' ἔχοντα Ε 895. Cf. τ 27.—(7) To endure, hold up, hold out : δηρόν Ε 285. Cf. λ 375.—With complementary ppl. clause : καί κ' εἰς ἐνιαυτὸν παρὰ σοί γ' ἀνεχοίμην ἥμενος δ 595.—(8) To accept what happens, submit with patience : ἀνάσχεο Α 586. Cf. Ε 382, Ω 549.—With complementary pple. : εἰσορόων ἀνέχεσθαι π 277.—To restrain oneself, be placated : ἄνσχεο Ψ 587.

ἀνεψιός, -οῦ, ὁ. A cousin Ι 464, Κ 519, Ο 422, 554, Π 573.

ἀνέψυχθεν, 3 pl. aor. pass. ἀναψύχω.

ἄνεῳ, ἄνεω [the former app a nom. pl. masc. fr. an adj. ἄνεως. The latter (only in ψ 93 of a woman) app. to be taken as an adv.]. Silent : ἐγένεσθε Β 323. Cf. Γ 84, Ι 30 = 695 : ἧσθε β 240. Cf. η 144, κ 71, ψ 93.

ἀνέῳξε, 3 sing. aor. ἀναοίγω.

ἀνήγαγον, aor. ἀνάγω.

ἀνήῃ, 3 sing. aor. subj. ἀνίημι.

ἀνήϊξαν, 3 pl. aor. ἀναΐσσω.

ἀνήϊον, impf. ἄνειμι.

ἀνῆκε, 3 sing. aor. ἀνίημι.

ἀνήκεστος [ἀν-¹ + ἀκεσ-, ἀκέομαι]. Not to be cured or soothed Ε 394.—Not to be appeased Ο 217.

ἀνηκουστέω [ἀν-¹ + ἀκούω]. To fail to hearken to, disobey. With genit. : πατρός Ο 236 = Π 676.

ἀνήλυθε, 3 sing. aor. ἀνέρχομαι.

ἀνήμελκτος, -ον [ἀν-¹ + ἀμέλγω]. Not milked ι 439.

ἀνήνατο, 3 sing. aor. ἀναίνομαι.

†**ἀνήνοθε** [3 sing., in the first passage of a plupf. (with secondary person-ending), in the second of a pf., fr. ἀνεθ- = ἀνθ-, ἄνθος. (Cf. ἐνήνοθε)]. (ἐπ-.) To come to the surface, come forth : αἷμ' ἀ. Λ 266.—To rise up, spread upwards : κνίση ἀ. ρ 270.

ἀνήνυστος [ἀν-¹ + ἀνυσ-, ἀνύω]. Not accomplished or brought to an end : ἔργῳ π 111.

ἀνήνωρ, -ορος [ἀν-¹ + ἀνήρ]. Deprived of virility; or perh. merely, unmanly κ 301, 341.

ἀνήρ (ᾰ), ἀνδρός, ὁ. Genit. ἀνέρος Γ 61, Ε 649, etc. : α 161, 218, etc. Dat. ἀνέρι Π 516, 716, etc. : α 292, β 223, etc. Acc. ἀνέρα Ν 131, Π 215, etc. Voc. ἄνερ Ω 725. Nom. dual ἀνέρε Μ 421, 447, etc. Acc. ἀνέρε Λ 328. Nom. pl. ἀνέρες Β 1, 604, etc. : α 176, γ 471, etc. Dat. ἄνδρεσσι Ε 546, 874, etc. : α 358, κ 120, etc. Acc. ἀνέρας Α 262, Β 554, etc. : λ 630, ν 261, etc. (1) (a) A man in gen. : ἄναξ ἀνδρῶν Α 7, περὶ ἀνδρῶν (beyond all men) Φ 215. Cf. Β 198, Γ 429, Ε 37, Ι 197, etc. : ἄνδρα μοι ἔννεπε α 1, ἄνδρες ἂψ ἐγένοντο κ 395. Cf. β 91, δ 363, θ 223, ι 494, etc.—(b) Mankind, man : ὀϊζυρώτερον ἀνδρός Ρ 446.—(c) Quasi-pronominal = 'one,' 'anyone' : ὅσσον ἀ. ἴδεν Ε 770. Cf. Δ 539, Τ 183, Υ 97, etc. : νεμεσσήσαιτό κεν ἀ. α 228. Cf. γ 231, θ 139, ο 400, etc.—(d) With a qualifying sb. : ἀ. βουληφόρος (a councillor) Α 144, αἰπόλοι ἄνδρες (goatherds) Β 474. Cf. Γ 170, Δ 187, Ζ 315, Ι 524, etc. : ἀοιδὸς ἀ. γ 267. Cf. θ 584, ι 126, ξ 102, ο 427, etc.—(e) With a proper name (cf. φώς (2)) : ἀνέρος Λαομέδοντος Ε 649. Cf. Λ 92 : η 22.—(f) With ethnic words : Σίντιες ἄνδρες (the Sintians) Α 594. Cf. Γ 6, Ε 779, Κ 487, etc. : Φοῖνιξ ἀ. (a Phoenician) ξ 288. Cf. γ 31, ζ 3, ξ 263, etc.—(2) Specifically. (a) A man as distinguished from a woman : πόλεμος ἄνδρεσσι μελήσει Ζ 492. Cf. Η 139, Ι 134, Ω 707, etc. : α 358, δ 142, η 74, etc.—(b) A husband Γ 140, Ξ 504, Τ 295, etc. : α 292, ζ 181, η 68, etc.—(c) A man as distinguished from a god : Διὸς ἄγγελοι ἠδὲ καὶ ἀνδρῶν Α 334. Cf. Α 544, Ε 128, Ν 632, etc. : Ἀθήνη ἀνδρὶ ἐϊκυῖα θ 194. Cf. α 28, ν 112, π 265, etc.—Sim. ἡμιθέων ἀνδρῶν Μ 22.—With words indicative of mortality: βροτός Ε 361, Σ 85, etc. : δ 397, ε 129, etc.—θνητός Κ 403, Π 441, etc. : κ 306, π 196.—καταθνητός Κ 441.—(d) A man as distinguished from a youth: ἤδη ἀ. [ἐστιν] τ 160. Cf. λ 449.—(e) With words indicative of youthfulness, a youth : νέου ἀνδρός Ψ 589. Cf. Γ 108 : β 188, γ 24, ξ 524, φ 310, etc.—(f) A man in the full sense of the term : ἀνέρες ἔστε (quit you like men) Ε 529, Ζ 112, Θ 174, Ο 561, etc.

ἀνηρείψαντο, 3 *pl. aor. mid.* [No doubt for ἀνηρέψαντο, fr. ἀν-, ἀνα- (1) + ἀρεπ- = ἁρπ-, ἁρπάζω. Cf. ἅρπη, Ἅρπυια.] Thus, to snatch up : Γανυμήδεα ἀ. θεοί Υ 234. Cf. α 241 = ξ 371, δ 727, υ 77.

ἀνήροτος, -ον [ἀν-¹ + ἀρόω]. (1) Unploughed, untilled ι 123.—(2) Not growing as the result of tillage ι 109.

ἀνήρπαξαν, 3 pl. aor. ἀναρπάζω.

ἀνήρπασε, 3 sing. aor. ἀναρπάζω.

ἀνήσει, 3 sing. fut. ἀνίημι.

ἀνῆφθω, pf. imp. pass. ἀνάπτω.

ἀνῆψε, 3 sing. aor. ἀνάπτω.

ἀνθεμόεις, -εντος [ἄνθος]. (1) Flowery : λειμῶνι Β 467. Cf. Β 695 : μ 159.—(2) Adorned with flower-like ornaments Ψ 885 : γ 440, ω 275.

ἀνθερεών, -ῶνος, ὁ [ἀνθέω. 'The part on which the beard grows']. The chin Α 501, Γ 372, Ε 293, Ν 388.

ἀνθέριξ, -ικος. App., the stalk of corn : ἐπ' ἀνθερίκων καρπὸν θέον (the ears of the corn) Υ 227.

ἀνθέω [ἄνθος]. Of hair on the face, to sprout, grow : πρὶν ἰούλους ἀνθῆσαι λ 320.

ἄνθινος [ἄνθος]. The product of flowers, consisting of fruit : εἶδαρ ι 84.

†**ἀνθίστημι** [ἀνθ-, ἀντι- (2)]. 3 sing. aor. ἀντέστη Υ 70, 72. 3 pl. impf. mid. ἀνθίσταντο Π 305. In

aor. and mid., to face in fight. With dat.: Ἥρῃ Υ 70, Λητοῖ 72.—Absol., to make a stand Π 305.

ἄνθος, τό. (1) A flower Β 89, 468, Ι 542: ζ 231 = ψ 158, ι 51, 449.—(2) The characteristic flower of a plant: φάρμακον γάλακτι εἴκελον ἄ. (having a milk-white flower) κ 304.—(3) In collective sense, flowers, blossom: βρύει ἄνθεϊ λευκῷ Ρ 56. Cf. η 126.—(4) Fig.: ἔχει ἥβης ἄ. (is in the flower of his youth) Ν 484.

ἀνθρακιή, -ῆς, ἡ. Hot embers Ι 213.

ἄνθρωπος, -ου, ὁ. (1) (a) A human being, a man (seldom in sing. and never of a particular man): ἐσσομένοισι μετ' ἀνθρώποισιν Γ 287, μυὼν ἀνθρώπου Π 315. Cf. Ζ 14, Ι 134, Κ 213, Ν 733, etc.: πολλῶν ἀνθρώπων ἄστεα α 3, ὃς ἀνθρώπους ἐκέκαστο (all men) τ 395. Cf. α 183, γ 48, ζ 259, η 23, etc.—For μέροπες ἄνθρωποι see μέροπες.—(b) Mankind, man: οὐδὲν ἀκιδνότερον ἀνθρώπου σ 130.—(c) Quasi-pronominal = 'one,' 'anyone': ὅ κε στυγέῃσιν ἰδὼν ἄ. ἔχοντά [σε] ν 400.—(d) With a qualifying sb.: ἄ. ὁδίτης Π 263. Cf. Ω 202: η 32, ν 123.—(2) Specifically, a man as distinguished from a god: οὔτε θεῶν οὔτ' ἀνθρώπων Α 548. Cf. Β 669, Ε 442, Ζ 180, Θ 27, etc.: νέμεσις ἐξ ἀνθρώπων ἔσσεται β 136. Cf. ν 110, ξ 179, υ 112, χ 346, etc.—With words indicative of mortality: θνητός Α 339, Ξ 199, etc.: α 219, ε 32, etc.—καταθνητός Ζ 123: γ 114, ι 502, etc.

ἀνιάζω [ἀνίη]. (1) To molest, annoy τ 323.—To weary, tire Ψ 721.—(2) To be overcome by distress or pain Φ 270: χ 87.—To weary, become tired δ 460.—To become impatient δ 598.—To be oppressed, feel hampered (by the possession of something): κτεάτεσσιν Σ 300.

ἀνιάω [ἀνίη]. (1) To trouble, vex β 115.—(2) To make oneself a nuisance τ 66, υ 178.—(3) In pass., to become disgusted or disheartened: ἀνιηθέντα νέεσθαι Β 291.—To become disgusted or wearied: ὀρυμαγδῷ α 133.—To become wearied or impatient γ 117.—To be wearied or annoyed: οὔ τις ἀνιᾶται παρεόντι (by your being here) ο 335.

ἀνιδρωτί [ἀν-[1] + ἱδρώς]. Without sweat, *i.e.* without conflict: οὔ κεν ἀ. γε τελέσθη Ο 228.

ἀνίη, -ης, ἡ. (1) Trouble, inconvenience η 192.—(2) A source of danger μ 223.—A bad thing for one ο 394, υ 52.—A kill-joy: δαιτὸς ἀνίην ρ 446.

†ἀνίημι [ἀν-, ἀνα- (1) (3) + ἵημι[1]]. 3 sing. ἀνίησι δ 568, μ 105. 2 sing. opt. ἀνιείης β 185. Fem. pple. ἀνιεῖσα Ε 422. 3 sing. fut. ἀνήσει Β 276. 3 sing. aor. ἀνέηκε Ε 882. 2 sing. ἀνῆκας Φ 396. 3 -ε Β 71, Ε 405, Ζ 256, Η 25, etc.: η 289, θ 73, ξ 465, ρ 425, σ 199, τ 551, ω 440. 3 pl. aor. ἄνεσαν Φ 537. 3 sing. subj. ἀνήῃ Β 34. 3 sing. opt. ἀνείη Χ 346. Pl. pple. ἀνέντες Ε 761. From ἀνιέω 2 sing. ἀνιεῖς Ε 880. 3 sing. impf. ἀνίει Ο 24. ἀνῖει θ 359. Fem. pres. pple. mid. ἀνῑεμένη Χ 80. Acc. masc. pl. ἀνῑεμένους β 300. (1) To send up, cause to ascend: καπνόν Φ 523.—To cause to flow up: [ὕδωρ] μ 105.—(2) To stir up, set on, urge, incite, impel: σοὶ ἔπι τοῦτον Ε 405. Cf. Ε 761, Η 25, Κ 389, Π 691, Ρ 705, Φ 395, 545: β 185.—With infin.: νεικείειν βασιλῆας Β 276. Cf. Ε 422, 882, Ζ 256, Η 152, Μ 307, Ξ 362, Φ 396, Χ 252, 346: ἀειδέμεναι θ 73. Cf. ξ 465, ρ 425.—Absol. Ε 880, Υ 118.—To cause (a wind) to blow δ 568.—(3) To loose (a bond) θ 359.—To loose the fastenings of: πύλας Φ 537.—To relax hold upon, leave in peace: θυμὸν ὀδύνη Ο 24.—Of sleep, to leave, depart from Β 34, 71: η 289, σ 199, τ 551, ω 440.—(4) In mid., to loose, allow to fall away (a part of one's dress): κόλπον Χ 80.—App. by development of this sense, to take off the skin of, flay: αἶγας β 300.

ἀνῑηρός [ἀνίη]. Troublesome, tiresome: πτωχόν ρ 220. Cf. ρ 377.—In comp. in impers. construction: αὐτῷ οἱ ἀνιηρέστερον ἔσται (the worse for him) β 190.

ἀνιπτόπους, -ποδος [ἀ-[1] + νιπ-, νίζω + πούς]. With unwashen feet: ὑποφῆται Π 235.

ἄνιπτος, -ον [ἀ-[1] + νιπ-, νίζω]. Unwashen Ζ 266.

†ἀνίστημι [ἀν-, ἀνα- (1)]. (A) 3 sing. impf. ἀνίστη Ω 515, 689. 3 pl. fut. ἀναστήσουσι Η 116. Contr. 2 sing. ἀνστήσεις Ω 551. 3 -ει Ο 64. Contr. pple. ἀνστήσων Κ 32. 3 sing. aor. ἀνέστησε Ω 756. 3 sing. opt. ἀναστήσειε Α 191. Contr. imp. ἄνστησον Κ 176. Pple. ἀναστήσας Κ 179: ζ 7, η 163, 170, ξ 319. Contr. fem. ἀνστήσᾱσα Σ 358. (B) 3 sing. aor. ἀνέστη Α 68, 101, Β 76, Η 354, 365, Ι 195, Ο 287, Σ 305, 410, Ψ 635, Ω 597: β 224, ε 195, μ 439, σ 157, υ 380, φ 139, 166, 243, 392, ψ 164. 3 pl. ἀνέσταν Α 533, Η 161, Ψ 886: θ 258, κ 215. Contr. 3 dual ἀνστήτην Α 305. 3 sing. subj. ἀναστῇ σ 334. Pple. ἀναστάς, -άντος Α 387, Τ 77, 175, Ψ 542, Ω 11: δ 343, 776, π 378, ρ 134, σ 47. Contr. ἀνστάς, -άντος Β 398, Τ 269, Ψ 848: δ 674, μ 170, 195, ο 58, 96, π 358, 407, ρ 177. Fem. ἀνστᾶσα Ξ 336: τ 357. Contr. infin. ἀνστήμεναι Κ 55. **Mid.** 3 sing. impf. ἀνίστατο Η 94, 123, Ψ 491, 566, 677, 709, 734: υ 124, φ 144. Pple. ἀνιστάμενος, -ου Α 58, Ι 52, Τ 55: γ 341. 3 pl. fut. ἀναστήσονται Φ 56. Contr. infin. ἀνστήσεσθαι Β 694. (I) In impf. act. and the other forms (A) (1) To cause to rise or stand up: γέροντ' ἀνίστη Ω 515. Cf. η 163, 170, ξ 319.—To break up (an assembly) Α 191.—To cause (a people) to migrate ζ 7.—(2) To rouse from sleep Κ 32, 176, 179, Ω 689.—(3) To raise from the dead Ω 551, 756.—(4) To cause to take action, rouse to action Ο 64, Σ 358.—To put forward (a champion) Η 116.—(II) In mid. and the other forms (B) (1) To rise or stand up: Πάτροκλος ἀνέστη Ι 195. Cf. Σ 410, Ω 597: ε 195, σ 157 = φ 139 = 166 = ψ 164, φ 243 = 392.—To rise up in token of respect Α 533.—Of a beast, to stand on its hind legs κ 215.—(2) To rise up with a view to action: ἀνστάντες ἔφερον Ψ 848. Cf. γ 341, δ 674 = π 407, δ 776, θ 258, μ 170, 195, π 358, ρ 177, σ 47, τ 357.—(3) To rise to speak: ἀνιστάμενος μετέφη Α 58 = Τ 55. Cf. Α 68 = 101 = Β 76 = Η 354 = 365, Α 387, Η 94, 123, Ι 52, Τ 77, 175, 269, Ψ 491, 542, 566, 734: ἀνέστη μαντεύεσθαι υ 380. Cf. β 224, π 378.—(4) To rise at the close of an assembly Α 305, Β 398.—At the close of judicial business μ 439.—(5) To rise from bed or from sleep Κ 55, Ξ 336,

Ω 11 : ο 58, 96, υ 124.—(**6**) To rise from the dead Φ 56.—As if from the dead Ο 287.—(**7**) To rouse oneself to action Β 694, Σ 305.—To stand up to take part in a contest Ψ 709, 886 : δ 343 = ρ 134, φ 144.—To stand up as a volunteer champion Η 161.—(**8**) To stand up (to another) in a fight, etc. Ψ 635, 677 : σ 334.

ἀνίσχω [ἀν-^{1}, ἀνα- (1)]. To lift up (the hands) in prayer : *χεῖρας ἀνίσχοντες* Θ 347 = Ο 369.

ἀνιχνεύω [ἀν-, ἀνα- (6) + ἰχνεύω, to trace, fr. ἴχνος]. To trace or hunt out Χ 192.

ἀνιών, pres. pple. ἄνειμι.

ἀννέομαι [ἀν-, ἀνα- (1)]. Of the sun, to rise κ 192.

ἀνοήμων [ἀ-^{1} + νοήμων]. Lacking understanding β 270, 278, ρ 273.

ἀνόλεθρος [ἀν-^{1} + ὄλεθρος]. Unscathed Ν 761.

ἄνοος, -ον [ἀ-^{1} + νόος]. Senseless, foolish Φ 441.

ἀνοπαῖα [app. neut. pl. as adv. of an adj. ἀνοπαῖος fr. ἄνω^2 ; or poss. of such an adj. fr. ἀν-^{1} + ὀπ-. See ὁράω]. Thus, upwards, or unseen α 320. (Others write ἀνόπαια, explained as a kind of eagle.)

ἀνορούω [ἀν-, ἀνα- (1)]. (**1**) To rise or start up, spring up : *ταφὼν ἀνόρουσεν* Ι 193. Cf. Α 248, Κ 162, 519, Λ 273 = 399, 777, Ρ 130, Τ 396, Φ 246, Ψ 101 : γ 149, δ 839, κ 557, ξ 518, π 12, χ 23.—(**2**) Of the sun, to rise γ 1.

ἀνόστιμος [ἀ-^{1} + νόστιμος]. Cut off from return home : *κεῖνον ἀνόστιμον ἔθηκεν* δ 182.

ἄνοστος [ἀ-^{1} + νόστος]. = prec. ω 528.

ἄνουσος [ἀ-^{1} + νοῦσος]. Afflicted by no disease : *ἀσκηθέες καὶ ἄνουσοι* ξ 255.

ἀνούτατος [ἀν-^{1} + οὐτάω]. Not wounded (by thrust) : *ἄβλητος καὶ ἀνούτατος* Δ 540.

ἀνουτητί [as prec.]. Without inflicting a wound : *οὐδέ οἵ τις ἀνουτητί παρέστη* Χ 371.

ἀνστάς, contr. aor. pple. ἀνίστημι (Β).

ἀνστήσει, contr. 3 sing. fut. ἀνίστημι (Α).

ἀνστήτην, contr. 3 dual aor. ἀνίστημι (Β).

ἀνστρέψειαν, contr. 3 pl. aor. opt. ἀναστρέφω.

ἀνσχεθέειν, contr. aor. infin. ἀνέχω.

ἄνσχεο, contr. 2 sing. and imp. aor. mid. ἀνέχω.

ἀνσχετός [ἀν(α)σχε-, ἀνέχω]. To be endured, sufferable : *ἀνσχετὰ ἔργα* β 63.

ἀνσχήσεσθαι, contr. fut. infin. mid. ἀνέχω.

ἄντα [ἀντί]. (**I**) Adv. (**1**) Face to face : *μάχεσθαι* Τ 163, *ἀνασχομένω* Ψ 686, *θεοῖσιν ἀ. ἐῴκει* (when set face to face, when brought into comparison) Ω 630.—Facing a person : *στῆ* ζ 141.—(**2**) Straight in front of one : *ἰδών* Ν 184 = 404 = 503 = Π 610 = Ρ 305 = 526, Χ 274. Cf. φ 48, 421, χ 266, ω 181.—(**II**) Prep. with genit. (freq. following the case). (**1**) Over against, opposite : *Ἤλιδος ἀ.* Β 626.—In the presence of : *ἀ. σέθεν* δ 160.—(**2**) In hostile sense, against : *Διὸς ἀ.* Θ 424, 428. Cf. Θ 233, Ο 415, Π 621, Υ 75, 76, 355, 365, Φ 477 : χ 232.—Facing : *μευ* Ρ 29. Cf. Ρ 167, Υ 69, 73, 89.—(**3**) A (fitting) match for Φ 331.—(**4**) In front of, before : *ἀ. παρειάων* α 334 = π 416 = σ 210 = φ 65. Cf. δ 115 = 154.

ἀντάξιος [ἀντ-, ἀντι- (4) (practically as intensive) + ἄξιος]. (**1**) Worth, the equal or equivalent of. With genit. : *πολλῶν ἀ. ἄλλων* Λ 514.—(**2**) Forming a suitable equivalent Α 136.—Absol. in neut. *ἀντάξιον,* an equivalent Ι 401.

ἀντάω [ἄντα]. From ἀντέω 3 pl. impf. ἤντεον Η 423. (συν-.) (**1**) To meet, encounter. With dat. : *οἱ* Ζ 399. Cf. Η 423.—To meet a person so as to have knowledge of him Δ 375 : = δ 201.—(**2**) With genit., to encounter, come upon : *ἔνδον ἐόντων* π 254.—To light or come upon : *δαίτης* γ 44, *ὀπωπῆς* 97 = δ 327, ρ 44.—To get one's will in the matter of : *μάχης* Η 158.—(**3**) With genit., to encounter in fight : *τοῦδ' ἀνέρος* Π 423.

ἀντέστη, 3 sing. aor. ἀνθίστημι.

ἄντην [adv. fr. acc. of *ἄντη, conn. with ἀντίος]. (**1**) Face to face : *ἐσέδρακον ἀ.* Ω 223. Cf. Ο 247, Ω 464 : ε 77, θ 213.—When set face to face, when brought into comparison : *θεῷ ἐναλίγκιος ἀ.* β 5 = δ 310. Cf. χ 240, ω 371.—(**2**) To one's face : *ὁμοιωθήμεναι ἀ.* Α 187. Cf. Κ 158 : γ 120, θ 158.—(**3**) Facing the foe, man to man : *ἀ. ἵστασθε* Λ 590. Cf. Μ 152, Σ 307, Χ 109.—(**4**) Straight in front of one : *ἀ. εἰσιδέειν* Τ 15.—(**5**) Before the eyes of a company : *ἀ. οὐκ ἂν λοέσσομαι* ζ 221.—(**6**) Into one's view or presence Θ 399.

ἄντηστις, ἡ [app. abstract sb. fr. ἀντί]. Thus *κατ' ἄντηστιν,* opposite : *θεμένη δίφρον* (*i.e.* opposite the door of the *μέγαρον*) υ 387.

ἀντί [orig. sense over against, opposite]. Prep. with genit. (sometimes (without anastrophe) following the case). (**1**) Instead of, in the place of : *Ἕκτορος ἀντί* Ω 254. Cf. υ 307.—For, in exchange for : *τρεῖς ἑνὸς ἀντί* Ν 447. Cf. Ξ 471.—(**2**) As good as, the equivalent of : *πολλῶν λαῶν* Ι 116.—Entitled to the rights of : *ἱκέταο* Φ 75. Cf. θ 546.—No better than : *γυναικός* Θ 163.—(**3**) In return for : *τῶνδ' ἀντί* Ψ 650. Cf. χ 290.

ἀντιάνειραι, αἱ [ἀντι- (4) + ἀνήρ]. A match for men. Epithet of the Amazons Γ 189, Ζ 186.

†**ἀντιάω** [ἀντίος]. 3 pl. ἀντιόωσι Ζ 127, Φ 151. Acc. sing. fem. pple. ἀντιόωσαν Α 31. 3 pl. imp. ἀντιοώντων Ψ 643. Infin. ἀντιάαν Ν 215. Fut. ἀντιόω Μ 368, Ν 752. Pple. ἀντιόων, -ωντος Υ 125 : α 25. Fem. ἀντιόωσα Φ 431 : γ 436, ω 56. 2 sing. fut. ἀντιάσεις χ 28. 2 dual aor. subj. ἀντιάσητον Μ 356. 2 sing. opt. ἀντιάσειας σ 147. 3 ἀντιάσειε Ν 290 : μ 88, ν 292, φ 402. 1 pl. ἀντιάσαιμεν Η 231. Pple. ἀντιάσας, -αντος Α 67, Κ 551, Ο 297 : ζ 193, η 293, ν 312, ξ 511, ρ 442. 2 pl. impf. mid. ἀντιάασθε Ω 62. (ὑπ-.) (**1**) To meet or encounter someone : *θεὸν ἀντιάσαντα* Κ 551 : *ἱκέτην ἀντιάσαντα* (who has met one who can help him) ζ 193 = ξ 511. Cf. η 293, μ 88, ν 292, 312, ρ 442.—(**2**) To encounter in fight. With genit. : *σέθεν* Η 231.—With dat. : *ἐμῷ μένει* Ζ 127 = Φ 151, Φ 431 : *ἐκείνῳ* σ 147.—Absol. Ο 297.—(**3**) Of a missile, to reach, strike. With genit. : *στέρνων* Ν 290.—(**4**) To find, get. With genit. : *ὀνήσιος* φ 402.—(**5**) To join, come to. With genit. : *παιδὸς τεθνηότος* ω 56.—(**6**) With genit., to take part in : *πόνοιο* Μ 356. Cf. Μ 368 = Ν 752, Ν 215, Υ 125, Ψ 643 : *ἀέθλων* χ 28.—In mid. : *ἀντιάασθε γάμου* Ω 62.—

Of a god, to take part in (a sacrifice): ἑκατόμβης α 25, ἱρῶν γ 436.—To accept of (a sacrifice) A 67. —With acc., to come to share: ἐμὸν λέχος A 31.

ἀντίβιος, -η, -ον [ἀντι- (2)+βίη]. (1) Of words, wrangling, jangling A 304, B 378: σ 415=υ 323. —(2) In neut. ἀντίβιον as adv., face to face, man to man: ἀ. μαχέσασθαι Γ 20=H 40=51. Cf. Γ 435, Λ 386.—(3) Adv. of acc. fem. form ἀντιβίην. (a) Face to face, man to man E 220.—With dat.: Ἕκτορι Φ 226.—(b) To one's face: ἐριζέμεναι βασιλῆϊ ἀ. A 278.

ἀντιβολέω [ἀντι- (1) (2)+βολ-, βάλλω]. (1) To meet or encounter someone: θεὸς ἀντιβολήσας K 546. Cf. Ω 375: ζ 275, η 16.—With dat.: οἱ Λ 809, N 210, 246: η 19, μοι κ 277, ν 229.—(2) To encounter in fight. With dat.: τούτῳ H 114. Cf. Π 847: χ 360.—Absol. Λ 365=Υ 452, M 465, Π 790.—(3) To come to, fall to the lot of. With genit.: γάμος ἐμέθεν σ 272.—(4) To find, get. With genit.: ἐπητύος φ 306.—(5) To take part in. With genit.: μάχης Δ 342=M 316: τάφου δ 547.—With dat.: τάφῳ ω 87.—To be present at, witness. With dat.: φόνῳ ἀνδρῶν λ 416.

ἀντίθεος, -η [ἀντι- (4)+θεός]. Like the gods. A vague general epithet of commendation Δ 88, E 663, I 623, Λ 140, Ξ 322, Ψ 360, etc.: α 21, δ 571, ζ 241, λ 117, ξ 18 (here merely conventional), ο 90, etc.

ἀντίθυρον, τό [ἀντι- (1)+θύρη]. A space opposite a door: στῆ κατ' ἀντίθυρον κλισίης π 159 (app., from 165, in a spot opposite the door of the κλισίη and outside the gate of the αὐλή).

ἀντικρύ (ῠ E 130, 819) [ἀντί]. (1) Face to face: μάχεσθαι E 130, 819.—(2) Straight on, right on: δι' ὤμου Δ 481. Cf. Γ 359=H 253, E 67, 74, 100, 189, Λ 253, N 595, 652, Π 346, P 49=X 327, Υ 416, Ψ 876: κ 162, τ 453, χ 16.—(3) Right over: τάφρον ὑπέρθορον Π 380.—(4) (Aiming) straight in front Π 285.—(5) With genit., straight against: Ἕκτορος ἀ. Θ 301=310.—(6) Vehemently: μεμαώς N 137.—Right out, without circumlocution H 362. —(7) Utterly, completely: ἀπάραξε Π 116. Cf. Ψ 673, 867.

ἀντίος, -η, -ον [ἀντί]. (1) Opposite, facing: ἔσταν A 535.—In hostile sense Λ 94, 216, N 146, Υ 373, Φ 144: τ 445.—With genit.: ἐμεῖο P 31=Υ 197. —(2) Straight towards an object: ἀΐξας O 694: χ 90.—Straight before one: ἀθρῆσαι τ 478.— (3) To meet persons approaching: ἐξέθορεν Φ 539. —(4) In order to meet, join, encounter or intercept a person: ἦλθεν Z 54, P 257.—With genit.: Ἀγαμέμνονος ἀ. ἐλθών B 185. Cf. Λ 594, X 113: ἀ. ἦλθεν ἄνακτος π 14.—With dat.: τῇ δ' ἀ. ὄρνυτο H 20.—In hostile sense: ἀ. ἐλθών Υ 352.—With genit.: ὅς τις τοῦ γ' ἀ. ἔλθοι E 301=P 8. Cf. H 98, Υ 371, Φ 150.—With dat.: ἀ. οἱ ἦλθεν O 584. Cf. Υ 422.—In order to clasp or seize. With genit.: ἀ. ἤλυθε γούνων Υ 463.—(5) In neut. sing. ἀντίον as adv. (a) Opposite, facing: ἷζεν ξ 79, ρ 96, κατέθηκεν 334.—With genit.: Ὀδυσσῆος I 218: ε 198, π 53. Cf. ρ 257, ψ 165.—In hostile sense M 44.—With genit.: ἀλλήλων E 569.—Face to face: ἵν' ἐνίσπῃ ρ 529.—(b) Against, in contradiction. With genit.: ὅς τις σέθεν ἀ. εἴπῃ A 230.—(c) With straight aim Λ 553=P 662.— Straight before one: ἴδεν π 160.—(d) Aiming for, seeking to reach. With genit.: πυλάων X 195. —In hostile sense, in order to meet or encounter someone: ἐλθέμεναι P 67, ἐλθών T 70.—With genit.: ἀ. εἶμ' αὐτῶν E 256. Cf. H 160, Λ 219, 231, P 69, Υ 175.—(e) In reply: ἀ. ηὔδα Γ 203, Δ 265, E 217, etc.: α 213, 399, β 242, etc.— Simply in reference to addressing a person: ἔπος μιν ἀ. ηὔδα E 170. Cf. Θ 200, Ω 333: ε 28. —(6) In neut. pl. ἀντία as adv. With genit. (a) Opposite to, facing: Ἀλεξάνδροιο Γ 425.— In hostile sense: Πηλεΐωνος Υ 88=333, ἐμεῖο Φ 481, σεῖο X 253.—In the presence of: δεσποίνης ο 377.—(b) In hostile sense, in order to meet or encounter: ἀ. Πηλεΐωνος Υ 80. Cf. Υ 113, 118. —(c) Against the will of. Joined with ἀέκητι. See ἀέκητι (1).

ἀντιόω, fut. ἀντιάω.

ἀντιόωσι, 3 pl. pres. ἀντιάω.

ἀντιπέραιος [ἀντι- (1)+πέρην]. Lying opposite and beyond. Absol.: τὰ ἀντιπέραια (the opposite coast) B 635.

ἀντίσχω [ἀντ-, ἀντι- (2)]. To hold up as protection *against*. In mid. With genit.: ἀντίσχεσθε τραπέζας ἰῶν χ 74.

ἀντιτορέω [ἀντι- (3)]. To pierce: χροός E 337 (the genit. app. partitive).—To break into (a house): δόμον K 267.

ἄντιτος [ἀν-, ἀνα- (3)+τι-, τίνω]. Consisting in paying back or requital: ἄντιτα ἔργα (works of vengeance, revenge) Ω 213 (for *v.l.* see τιτός): ρ 51=60.

ἀντιφερίζω [ἀντιφέρω]. To set oneself *against*, rival. With dat.: σοί Φ 357, ὅτι μοι μένος ἀντιφερίζεις (in the matter of might) 488.

ἀντιφέρω [ἀντι- (2)]. In mid. (1) To set oneself against, rival, a person: ἀργαλέος [ἐστὶν] ἀντιφέρεσθαι (hard to set oneself against) A 589, χαλεπή [εἰμι] μένος ἀντιφέρεσθαι (to rival in the matter of might) Φ 482.—(2) To offer (successful) resistance, hold one's own E 701: π 238.

ἄντλος, -ου, ὁ. The lower part of the interior of a ship, the hold μ 411, ο 479.

ἀντολή, -ῆς, ἡ [=ἀνατολή fr. ἀνατέλλω]. A rising: ἀντολαὶ Ἠελίοιο (the pl. app. referring to the different places of rising at different seasons) μ 4.

†ἄντομαι [ἀντί]. 3 sing. aor. ἤντετο Δ 133, Π 788, Υ 415, X 203. Fem. pple. ἀντομένη Θ 412, Λ 237. Pl. ἀντόμεναι B 595. Infin. ἄντεσθαι O 698. (συν-.) (1) To meet, encounter. With dat.: ἀλλήλοισιν O 698. Cf. Π 788, X 203.—Absol. B 595, Θ 412.—Of a weapon. With dat.: ἀργύρῳ Λ 237.—(2) Of the front and back plates of the θώρηξ, to meet and overlap Δ 133=Υ 415.

ἄντρον, -ου, τό. A cave or cavern ι 216, 218, 235, 236, 298, 312, 407, ν 103=347, 363, υ 21, ω 6.

ἄντυξ, -υγος, ἡ. (1) The breastwork or rail surrounding a chariot in front and at the sides:

ὑπὲρ ἄντυγος Π 406. Cf. E 262, 322.—In pl. of a single rail Λ 535 = Υ 500, Φ 38. Cf. δοιαὶ ἄντυγες E 728 (prob. referring only to a single rail called δοιαί as terminating behind in a handle on each side).—(**2**) The rim of a shield: ἀ. ἣ πυμάτη θέεν ἀσπίδος Z 118. Cf. Ξ 412, O 645, Σ 479, 608, Υ 275.

ἄνῡμι [cf. ἀνύω]. To effect, accomplish: θοῶς ἤνυτο ἔργον ε 243.

ἄνυσις [ἀνύω]. Accomplishment, effect, result: αὐτῶν (app., on their part) B 347. Cf. δ 544.

ἀνύω [cf. next]. 3 sing. aor. ἤνῡσε δ 357, ω 71. 3 sing. opt. ἀνῡσειε ο 294. Fut. infin. pass. ἀνύσσεσθαι π 373. (ἀπ-, δι-, ἐξ-.) (**1**) To effect, accomplish: ἀνύσσεσθαι τάδε ἔργα π 373.—To effect one's purpose Δ 56.—(**2**) To consume: ἐπεί σε φλὸξ ἤνυσεν ω 71.—(**3**) To pass over, traverse: θαλάσσης ὕδωρ ο 294.—To perform a voyage δ 357.

ἄνω[1] (ᾰ Σ 473). (κατ-.) To accomplish: ὅπως ἔργον ἄνοιτο Σ 473: ἦνον ὁδόν (pursued their way, made (good) speed) γ 496.—In pass. of a period of time, to pass away, waste: νὺξ ἄνεται K 251.

ἄνω[2] [ἀνά]. (**1**) Upwards: λᾶαν ἀ. ὤθεσκεν λ 596.—(**2**) Out to sea: ὅσσον Λέσβος ἀ. ἐντὸς ἐέργει Ω 544.

ἀνῷγε, contr. 3 sing. impf. ἀναοίγω.

ἀνώγω. Fut. ἀνώξω π 404. 1 pl. aor. subj. ἀνώξομεν O 295. Infin. ἀνῶξαι κ 531. Pf. (with pres. sense) ἄνωγα K 120, Ξ 105, Ψ 245: α 269, γ 317, π 312, ρ 279, υ 43, etc. 2 sing. ἄνωγας Z 382, Ξ 262, Ω 670: μ 284, ο 346, ρ 398. 3 ἄνωγε (to be distinguished fr. 3 sing. impf.) Z 444, I 680, Ξ 195, Σ 426, Ω 90: ε 89, ρ 582, σ 409, τ 374. Imp. ἄνωχθι K 67, Λ 204, O 160, etc.: α 274, β 113, ρ 508, etc. 3 sing. ἀνώχθω Λ 189. 2 pl. ἄνωχθε χ 437. Plupf. (with impf. sense) ἠνώγεα ι 44, κ 263, ρ 55. 3 sing. ἠνώγει(ν) Z 170, H 386, K 394, M 355, Ω 190: γ 174, ε 99, 112, μ 160, ξ 336. ἀνώγει(ν) (to be distinguished fr. ἀνώγει, 3 sing. pres.) B 280, Δ 301, E 509, 899, etc.: β 385, γ 141, δ 531, θ 449, etc. From ἀνωγέω 3 pl. impf. ἠνώγεον H 394. (**1**) Of persons, to command, order, bid, give orders or injunctions. (**a**) With acc. and infin.: λαοὺς ἀπολυμαίνεσθαι A 313. Cf. I 219, Λ 15, etc.: ἐμὲ δεῦρ' ἐλθέμεν ε 99. Cf. α 274, ι 331, etc.—With neg., to forbid: οὔ τινα χάζεσθαι ἀνώγει P 357.—(**b**) With acc. alone, K 130, etc.: ε 139, τ 374, etc.—(**c**) With this acc. and acc. of what is enjoined: τίπτε με κεῖνος ἄνωγεν; Ω 90.—(**d**) With dat. and infin.: ἑτάροισι κατακῆαι κ 531. Cf. π 339, υ 139.—(**e**) With infin. alone: δεῖξαι Z 170. Cf. Z 382, H 386, Ψ 158, etc.: γ 174, δ 531, μ 284, ξ 336.—(**f**) Absol. I 690, O 725, etc.: ξ 471, σ 7, υ 282.—(**2**) Passing into milder sense, to bid, exhort, charge, desire, urge, recommend, counsel. (**a**) With acc. and infin.: δαίνυσθαί μιν E 805. Cf. I 578, 680, K 120, O 180: σὲ φράζεσθαι α 269. Cf. β 195, ε 357, ζ 216, ι 44, μ 160, etc.—With neg., to counsel or express desire against a course: οὔ τί μ' ἀνώγει θωρήσσεσθαι μ 227. Cf. υ 364.—(**b**) With acc. alone π 404.—(**c**) With infin. alone: ἐγρήγορθαι K 67. Cf. Λ 139, 646 = 778, M 355, Π 8, X 351: ἑδριάασθαι γ 35. Cf. γ 317, η 221, μ 158, π 278, 405, ρ 398, ψ 267.—With neg. as above: τύμβον οὐ μάλα πολλὸν πονέεσθαι Ψ 245.—(**d**) Absol. Ω 670.—(**3**) In sim. constructions with senses as under (2) of mental faculties and impersonal agencies: θυμός Δ 263, Z 439, H 74, Θ 189, 322, I 101, 703, Ξ 195 = Σ 426, O 43, Σ 176, T 102, Υ 77, 179, X 142, μένος καὶ θυμός Ω 198: ἦτορ α 316, θυμός ε 89, θ 70, λ 206, ξ 246, π 141, 466, σ 409, φ 194, οἶνος ξ 463, κραδίη καὶ θυμός ο 395, ἀχρημοσύνη ρ 502.—With neg. as under (2): οὐδέ με θυμὸς ἄνωγεν Z 444. Cf. Σ 90.

†**ἀνωθέω** [ἀν-, ἀνα- (1)]. Pl. aor. pple. ἀνώσαντες. To shove off, put to sea ο 553.

ἀνωϊστί [ἀνώϊστος]. At unawares: ἔπεφνεν δ 92.

ἀνώϊστος [ἀν-[1] + ὀϊσ-, ὀΐω]. Not looked for, unexpected: κακόν Φ 39.

ἀνώνυμος [ἀν-[1] + ὄνυμα, Aeolic form of ὄνομα]. Nameless, having no name: οὔ τις ἀ. ἐστιν θ 552.

ἀνώσαντες, pl. aor. pple. ἀνωθέω.

ἄνωχθι, pf. imp. ἀνώγω.

ἀξίνη, -ης, ἡ. An axe (referred to only as in warlike use) N 612, O 711 (see under πέλεκυς).

ἄξιος. (**1**) Worth, the equal or equivalent of. With genit.: οὐδ' ἑνὸς Θ 234, πολέος οἱ ἄξιος ἔσται (he will find it a thing of price) Ψ 562. Cf. O 719, Ψ 885: ἄξιον ἔσται ἀμοιβῆς (will bring a (full) return) α 318. Cf. θ 405.—(**2**) Forming a suitable equivalent, suitable, sufficient, calculated to satisfy: ἄποινα Z 46 = Λ 131. Cf. I 261: ο 388 = 429.—With infin.: Προθοήνορος ἀντὶ πεφάσθαι Ξ 472.—(**3**) Absol. in neut. ἄξιον. (**a**) An equivalent or recompense: ἦ τι ἐΐσκομεν ἀ. εἶναι τρεῖς ἑνὸς ἀντὶ πεφάσθαι; N 446.—(**b**) A suitable return: ἄξιόν κ' ἄλφοι υ 383.

ἄξυλος, -ον [prob. ἀ-[2] + ξύλον]. Thus, thickly timbered: ὕλη Λ 155.

ἄξω[1], fut. ἄγνυμι.

ἄξω[2], fut. ἄγω.

ἄξων, -ονος, ὁ. An axle E 723, 838, Λ 534, N 30, Π 378, Υ 499.

ἀοιδή, -ῆς, ἡ [ἀείδω]. (**1**) A song or lay α 328, 340, 351, θ 499, μ 44, 183, 198, ω 197.—A dirge or lament: στονόεσσαν Ω 721.—(**2**) A subject of song: ἐσσομένοισι ἀοιδήν γ 204. Cf. θ 580, ω 200.—(**3**) Singing: παῦσαν ἀοιδῆς B 595: κίθαρις καὶ ἀ. α 159. Cf. α 421 = σ 304, θ 429, ρ 605.—(**4**) The art of song: Μοῦσαι ἀοιδὴν ἀφέλοντο B 599. Cf. N 731: θ 44, 64, 253, 498, φ 406.

ἀοιδιάω [ἀοιδή]. To sing ε 61, κ 227.

ἀοίδιμος [ἀοιδή]. That is a subject of song Z 358.

ἀοιδός, -οῦ, ὁ [ἀείδω]. A minstrel or bard Σ 604: α 325, θ 43, ν 9, ρ 385, χ 376, etc.—A singer of a dirge: ἀοιδοὺς θρήνων ἐξάρχους Ω 720.

ἀολλής, -ές (ἀϜολλής) [ἀ-[2] + Ϝελ-, (Ϝ)είλω]. Only in pl. (**1**) In a body, all together: ὑπέμειναν ἀολλέες E 498. Cf. I 89, M 78, N 136, O 494, Π 601, T 190, Ψ 12, etc.: ἠγερέθοντο γ 412, λ 228. Cf. γ 427, δ 448, κ 259, υ 40, χ 446, ψ 38.—(**2**) Of inanimate objects, in a body or mass, all together: πάντα φέρωμεν ἀολλέα θ 394.—Cf. γ 165, κ 132, ξ 432.

†**ἀολλίζω** [ἀολλής]. 3 pl. aor. ἀόλλισσαν Z 287. Fem. pple. ἀολλίσσᾱσα Z 270. 3 pl. aor. pass. ἀολλίσθησαν T 54. Infin. ἀολλισθήμεναι O 588. (1) To gather together, cause to assemble: γεραιάς Z 270, 287.—(2) In pass., to come together, assemble: ἐπεὶ πάντες ἀολλίσθησαν T 54. Cf. O 588.

ἄορ, -ορος, τό. Dat. ἄορι (ᾰ). Acc. pl. in masc. form ἄορας ρ 222. A sword K 484, 489, Λ 240, 265 = 541, Ξ 385, Π 115, 473, Υ 290, 378, 462, Φ 21, 173, 179, 208: θ 403, κ 321, 333, 439 = λ 231, λ 24, ρ 222, τ 241.

ἀορτήρ, -ῆρος, ὁ [ἀορτ-, ἀείρω]. Dat. pl. ἀορτήρεσσι Λ 31. (1) A strap to support a sword, a sword-baldrick: χρυσέοισιν (app. in pl. as referring to the two ends attached to the sheath) Λ 31.—Joined with, and app. less specific than, τελαμών: περὶ στήθεσσιν ἀ. ἦν τελαμών λ 609.—(2) The shoulder-strap of a wallet ν 438 = ρ 198 = σ 109.

ἄορτο, 3 sing. plupf. pass. ἀείρω.

ἀοσσητήρ, -ῆρος, ὁ [perh. for ἀ-σοκ-jη-τηρ fr. ἀ-[2] + σεq-, (σ)έπω[2]]. (1) A helper, aider O 254, 735: δ 165, ψ 119.—(2) An avenger X 333.

ἄουτος [app. for ἄνουτος = ἀνούτατος]. Unwounded Σ 536.

ἀπαγγέλλω [ἀπ-, ἀπο- (7)]. 3 sing. pa. iterative ἀπαγγέλλεσκε P 409: σ 7. 3 sing. aor. opt. ἀπαγγείλειε P 640: π 153. Pple. ἀπαγγείλας π 133. Infin. ἀπαγγεῖλαι I 626: ι 95, ο 210. To bear a message, make a report or announcement ι 95, σ 7.—With dat.: Πηλεΐδῃ P 640. Cf. ο 210, π 133, 153, 459.—With dat. and acc., to announce or report (something) to: μῦθον Δαναοῖσιν I 626. Cf. P 409.

ἀπάγχω [ἀπ-, ἀπο- (7)]. To throttle τ 230.

ἀπάγω [ἀπ-, ἀπο- (1) (4)]. Fut. infin. ἀπάξειν Σ 326: ο 436. 3 sing. aor. ἀπήγαγε O 706: δ 289, π 370. 3 pl. -ον ν 211. (1) To drive or lead off: βόας σ 278.—To lead, conduct or bring away δ 289, ν 211.—(2) To bring or conduct back O 706, Σ 326: ο 436, π 370.

ἀπαείρω [ἀπ-, ἀπο- (1)]. In pass., to take oneself off *from*. With genit.: πόλιος Φ 563.

ἀπαίνυμαι. See ἀποαίνυμαι.

ἀπᾱΐσσω [ἀπ-, ἀπο- (1)]. Aor. pple. ἀπᾱΐξας Φ 234. (1) To spring or dart *from*. With genit.: κρημνοῦ Φ 234.—(2) Of limbs, to dart out *from*. In mid. With genit.: χεῖρες ὤμων ἀπαΐσσονται Ψ 628 (*v.l.* ἐπαΐσσονται).

ἀπαιτίζω [ἀπ-, ἀπο- (7)]. To ask for, demand: χρήματα β 78.

ἀπάλαλκον, *aor.* [ἀπ-, ἀπο- (2)]. To ward or keep off: μνηστῆρας δ 766.—To ward or keep off *from*. With genit.: σῆς κύνας κεφαλῆς X 348.

ἀπάλαμνος [ἀ-[1] + παλάμη]. Handless, shiftless, without resource: ἀνήρ E 597.

†**ἀπαλέξω** [ἀπ-, ἀπο- (2)]. Fut. infin. ἀπαλεξήσειν ρ 364. Aor. opt. ἀπαλεξήσαιμι Ω 371. (1) To ward or keep off *from*. With genit.: ἄλλον σεῦ Ω 371.—(2) To keep (a person) protected *from*. With genit.: κακότητός τινα ρ 364.

†**ἀπάλθομαι** [ἀπ-, ἀπο- (7)]. 2 and 3 dual fut. ἀπαλθήσεσθον. To be healed or cured: ἕλκεα (of the wounds) Θ 405 = 419.

ἀπαλοιάω [ἀπ-, ἀπο- (7)]. To crush, break, sever: τένοντε καὶ ὀστέα Δ 522.

ἀπαλός, -ή, -όν. (1) Soft, tender, delicate: δειρήν Γ 371. Cf. N 202, P 49 = X 327, Σ 123, 177, T 285: χεῖρας φ 151. Cf. χ 16.—Epithet of the life or vital principle: ἦτορ Λ 115.—Of the feet, stepping delicately T 92.—(2) In neut. ἀπαλόν as adv.: ἀ. γελάσαι (app., on small provocation, idly) ξ 465.

ἀπαλοτρεφής [ἀπαλός + τρέφω]. So fed as to be ἀπαλός, well-fed, plump: σιάλοιο Φ 363.

ἀπᾱμάω [ἀπ-, ἀπο- (3) + ἀμάω[1]]. To cut, cut through, sever: λαιμόν Σ 34 (for *v.l.* see ἀποτμήγω).

ἀπαμείβω [ἀπ-, ἀπο- (7)]. In mid., to answer, reply to Υ 199: η 298 = 308 = λ 347 = 362 = ν 3, θ 140 = 400, θ 158, ρ 445, τ 405, ω 327.—In pres. pple. ἀπαμειβόμενος, making answer, in reply A 84, E 814, Λ 316, etc.: α 63, η 207, ι 409, ρ 405, etc.

ἀπαμύνω [ἀπ-, ἀπο- (2)]. 3 sing. aor. ἀπήμῡνε I 597. 1 pl. aor. opt. mid. ἀπαμῡναίμεσθα O 738. Infin. ἀπαμύνασθαι Ω 369: π 72, φ 133. (1) To ward off, keep off. With dat. of person protected: Αἰτωλοῖσι κακὸν ἦμαρ I 597.—(2) In mid. (a) To ward or keep off from oneself: ἄνδρ' ἀπαμύνασθαι Ω 369 = π 72 = φ 133.—(b) Absol., to defend oneself O 738: λ 579.

†**ἀπαναίνομαι** [ἀπ-, ἀπο- (7)]. 3 pl. aor. ἀπηνήναντο H 185. Infin. ἀπανήνασθαι κ 297. (1) To refuse, reject: θεοῦ εὐνήν κ 297.—(2) To disown: [κλῆρον] H 185.

ἀπάνευθε(ν) [ἀπ-, ἀπο- (7) + ἄνευθε(ν)]. (1) Adv. (a) To far away, far away: φεῦγον I 478, ἀ. νεῶν ἐχέοντο T 356 (*i.e.* they issued from the ships and took up a position well in front of them).—From far away: ἴδεν P 198.—(Visible) from a great distance: τοῦ (*i.e.* proceeding from him) ἀ. σέλας γένετο T 374.—(b) Apart, aside, aloof: κιών A 35. Cf. B 812, Δ 227, K 425, 434, Λ 341, Σ 558, Ω 473: α 190, β 260, ζ 204, 223, 236, ι 189, ψ 86.—Apart, separately: Τειρεσίῃ ὄϊν ἱερευσέμεν κ 524 = λ 32.—(2) Prep. with genit. (a) Far from: φίλων T 378. Cf. β 164, ι 36.—(b) Away from, to a distance from: μάχης Λ 283.—(c) Apart or aloof from, at a distance from: νεῶν A 48, O 348, P 403. Cf. B 391, Λ 81, Ξ 30, 189, P 192, 426, Σ 412, 523, Υ 41, Ψ 77, 83, 141, 194, Ω 211: η 284, ρ 447.—Apart from, detaching oneself from: θεῶν Θ 10.—Apart from, without consulting: θεῶν A 549.

ἀπανήνασθαι, aor. infin. ἀπαναίνομαι.

ἀπάντῃ [ἅπας]. In all directions: φέρων ἀν' ὅμιλον ἀ. H 183, 186: χέε δέσμαθ' ἀ. θ 278.

†**ἀπανύω** [ἀπ-, ἀπο- (7)]. 3 pl. aor. ἀπήνυσαν. To perform a voyage: οἴκαδε η 326.

ἅπαξ [(σ)α- as in ἅμα]. (1) Once: θνήσκουσιν μ 22.—(2) Once for all: ἀπὸ θυμὸν ὀλέσσαι μ 350.

ἀπάξειν, fut. infin. ἀπάγω.

†**ἀπαράσσω** [ἀπ-, ἀπο- (1)]. 3 sing. aor. ἀπήραξε Ξ 497. ἀπάραξε Π 116. To smite off Ξ 497, Π 116.

†**ἀπαρέσκω** [ἀπ-, ἀπο- (7)]. Aor. infin. mid.

ἀπαρέσσασθαι. In mid., to appease: ἄνδρα Τ 183.

ἀπάρχω [ἀπ-, ἀπο- (1)]. In mid. as a word of ritual, to cut off (hairs of the victim) as the first-fruits of the sacrifice (cf. ἄρχω (1) (b)): ἀπαρχόμενος κεφαλῆς τρίχας ξ 422.—Absol. γ 446.

ἅπᾶς, -ᾶσα, -αν [(σ)α- as in ἅμα + πᾶς]. Genit. ἅπαντος, -ά̄σης, -αντος. Genit. pl. fem. ἁπᾱσέων θ 284. Strengthened form of, but hardly to be distinguished from, πᾶς. (1) In sing. (a) All the, the whole, the whole of the: ἠϊόνος Ξ 35. Cf. Ο 506, Υ 156, Φ 244, 451, etc.: οἶκον β 48. Cf. η 129, ι 6, λ 442, ν 72, etc.—Predicatively: ἐγκέφαλος ἅπας πεπάλακτο (were all spattered) Λ 98, κάρη ἅπαν ἐν κονίῃσι κεῖτο (*i.e.* was wholly defiled with dust) Χ 402, etc. Cf. δ 616, etc.—(b) All, the whole of: διέχευάν μιν ἅπαντα Η 316, Ἴλιος Χ 410. Cf. τ 421.—A whole: ἐνιαυτόν ξ 196, ο 455.—All needful: σῖτον π 83.—All possible, perfect: φιλότητος ο 158.—(2) In pl. (a) All the: φάλαγγας Ζ 83. Cf. Θ 17, Ι 159, 591, Λ 847, Ξ 79, 273, 278, Φ 260, 266, Ω 98, 237: θεοί α 19. Cf. ι 432, ξ 19, ο 17, ρ 244, σ 6, φ 260, χ 446.—(b) All: βροτῶν Ν 374. Cf. Γ 78, Ξ 332, Ρ 583: κακῶν δ 221. Cf. ζ 207, θ 284, 487, ν 157, 297, ξ 57, ρ 12, τ 372, ω 78.—(c) Absol., the whole number of specified or indicated persons or things: ἀντίοι ἔσταν ἅπαντες Α 535. Cf. Β 14, Η 153, Μ 344, Π 291, Χ 241, etc.: τελευτηθῆναι ἅπαντα β 171. Cf. β 239, γ 34, ε 262, ν 281, ρ 70 (all they had in their minds), etc.

ἄπαστος, -ον [ἀ-¹ + πασ-, πατέομαι]. Not partaking of food or drink Τ 346.—With genit.: ἐδητύος ἀ. ζ 250. Cf. δ 788.

ἀπατάω [ἀπάτη]. (ἐξ-.) (1) To speak untruthfully δ 348 = ρ 139.—(2) To trick, cheat, beguile, deal unfairly with Ι 344, 375, Ο 33, Τ 97.

ἀπάτερθε(ν) [ἀπ-, ἀπο- (7) + ἄτερθε, ἄτερ. Cf. ἄνευθε, ἄνευ]. (1) Adv., apart from others or from another: θωρήσσοντο Β 587, φθέγξατο Σ 217.—(2) Prep. with genit., separated from, at a distance from: ὁμίλου Ε 445.

ἀπάτη, -ης, ἡ. (1) An act of beguiling, a trick Β 114 = Ι 21.—A piece of unfair dealing Δ 168.—(2) In pl., wiles, trickery: ἵν' ἀπαλλάξῃς ἀπατάων Ο 31. Cf. ν 294.

ἀπατήλιος [ἀπατάω]. Cheating, beguiling. Absol. in neut. pl.: ἀπατήλια βάζει (tells lying tales) ξ 127, 157, ἀπατήλια εἰδώς (having deceit in his heart) 288 (see εἴδω (III) (12)).

ἀπατηλός [as prec.]. = prec.: οὐκ ἐμὸν ἀπατηλόν (nothing that comes from me bears deceit) Α 526.

ἀπατῑμάω [ἀπ-, ἀπο- (7)]. To lay dishonour upon: Πηλεΐωνα Ν 113.

†ἀπαυράω. Impf. ἀπηύρων Ι 131, Τ 89, Ψ 560, 808: ν 132. 2 sing. ἀπηύρᾱς Θ 237. 3 -ᾱ Ζ 17, Ι 273, Κ 495, Λ 115, 334, Ο 462, Π 828, Ρ 125, 236, Υ 290, Φ 179, 201, Ψ 291, 800, Ω 50: γ 192, δ 646, λ 203, σ 273. 3 pl. ἀπηύρων Α 430. 3 pl. fut. ἀπουρήσουσι (*v.l.* ἀπουρίσσουσι; see ἀπουρίζω) Χ 489. Aor. pple. ἀπούρας Α 356, 507, Β 240, Ζ 455, Ι 107, Λ 432, Π 831, Υ 193, Φ 296: ν 270. [For the impf. ἀπηύρων, -ας, -α should prob. be read aor. ἀπέϜραν, -ας, -α (from ἀπο- (1) + Ϝρα-, Ϝερ- as in ἀπό-(Ϝ)ερσα) with 3 pl. ἀπέϜρασαν (metrically = ἀπηύρων), pple. ἀποϜράς and fut. ἀποϜρήσουσι.] (1) To take away: γυναῖκα Α 430, θυμόν Φ 179. Cf. Α 356 = 507 = Β 240, Ζ 455, Ι 107, 131, 273, Φ 201, Ω 50.—(2) To take away from (a person), deprive (him) of. With genit. of person: Ἀχιλλῆος γέρας Τ 89. Cf. σ 273.—With dat.: πολέσσι θυμόν Ρ 236. Cf. Φ 296, Χ 489: γ 192, ν 132.—With double acc.: κῦδός μιν Θ 237. Cf. Ζ 17, Κ 495, Λ 115, 334, 432, Ο 462, Π 828, 831, Ρ 125, Υ 193, 290, Ψ 291, 560, 800, 808: νῆά σε δ 646. Cf. λ 203, ν 270.

ἀπαφίσκω. 3 sing. aor. ἤπαφε ξ 488. 3 sing. aor. opt. mid. ἀπάφοιτο ψ 216. (ἐξ-, παρ-.) To trick, cheat, beguile λ 217.—In mid. ψ 216.—With complementary infin.: οἰοχίτων' ἔμεναι ξ 488.

ἀπέβη, 3 sing. aor. ἀποβαίνω.

ἀπεβήσετο, 3 sing. aor. mid. ἀποβαίνω.

ἀπεδέξατο, 3 sing. aor. ἀποδέχομαι.

ἀπέδρυφθεν, 3 pl. aor. pass. ἀποδρύπτω.

ἀπέδῡσε, 3 sing. aor. ἀποδύω.

ἀπέδωκε, 3 sing. aor. ἀποδίδωμι.

ἀπέειπον. See ἀποεῖπον.

ἀπέεργε, 3 sing. impf. ἀποέργω.

ἀπέην, 3 sing. impf. ἄπειμι¹.

ἀπέῃσι, 3 sing. subj. ἄπειμι¹.

ἀπέθηκε, 3 sing. aor. ἀποτίθημι.

ἀπειλέω [ἀπειλή]. 3 dual non-thematic impf. ἀπειλήτην λ 313. (ἐπ-.) To declare aloud. Hence (1) To vow, promise. With fut. infin.: ῥέξειν Ψ 863, 872.—(2) To boast, vaunt Θ 150.—With pres. infin.: βητάρμονας εἶναι ἀρίστους θ 383.—With fut. infin.: διελεύσεσθαι Ν 143. Cf. λ 313.—(3) To threaten, menace. With dat.: ἀπειλήσω τοι Α 181. Cf. Β 665.—With cognate acc.: μῦθον Α 388.—With dat. and this acc. Ν 220, Π 201.—With pres. infin.: ἑλκέμεν Ι 682.—With fut. infin.: ἀφαιρήσεσθαι Α 161. Cf. Θ 415, Ο 179, Φ 453.—To threaten (an injury): ἀπειλήσω τό γε Ο 212.—Absol. in aor. pple. ἀπειλήσας, with a threatening word or gesture: προσηύδα Η 225. Cf. Υ 161, Φ 161, 452, Ψ 184: φ 368.—With dat. υ 272.

ἀπειλή, -ῆς, ἡ. In pl. (1) Boasts, vaunts Ι 244, Ξ 479.—With fut. infin.: πολεμίξειν Υ 83.—(2) Threats, menaces Ν 219, Π 200: ν 126.

ἀπειλητήρ, -ῆρος, ὁ [ἀπειλέω]. A boaster Η 96.

†ἄπειμι¹ [ἀπ-, ἀπο- (2) + εἰμί]. 3 sing. subj. ἀπέῃσι τ 169. Pple. ἀπεών, -όντος Ζ 362, Θ 522: ν 189, ξ 330, τ 299. 3 sing. impf. ἀπέην Κ 351, Υ 7. Contr. ἀπῆν ε 400, ι 473, μ 181. 1 pl. ἀπῆμεν ι 491. 3 ἄπεσαν Κ 357. Fut. ἀπέσσομαι ο 515. 3 sing ἀπέσσεται β 285, θ 150. ἀπεσσεῖται τ 302. 3 pl. ἀπέσσονται υ 155. Infin. ἀπέσσεσθαι Ρ 278: σ 146. (1) To be away, absent or distant: ἐμεῖο ἀπεόντος Ζ 362. Cf. Θ 522, Κ 351, 357, Υ 7: ὅτε τόσσον ἀπῆν ὅσσον . . . ε 400 = ι 473 = μ 181. Cf. ι 491, ν 189, ξ 330 = τ 299 (in these three lines pple. of the impf.), ο 515.—With genit.: τοῦ (*from* it) Ρ 278. Cf. σ 146, τ 169, 302, υ 155.—(2) To be unaccomplished or not brought about: ὁδὸς οὐκέτι δηρὸν ἀπέσσεται β 285, θ 150.

†**ἄπειμι**[2] [ἀπ-, ἀπο- (1) (4) + εἶμι]. Pres. ἄπειμι ρ 593. Pple. ἀπιών, -όντος K 289, M 392, N 72, 516, 567, 650, Ξ 409, 461 : ι 413. Imp. ἄπιθι ρ 478. (**1**) To go away, go off, depart : Γλαύκου ἀπιόντος M 392. Cf. N 72, 516, 567, 650, Ξ 409, 461 : ἄπιθ' ἄλλῃ ρ 478. Cf. ι 413.—(**2**) With fut. sense : ἄπειμι σύας φυλάξων ρ 593.—(**3**) To go back, return K 289.

ἀπειρέσιος, -η, -ον [ἀ-[1] + πεῖραρ]. (**1**) Boundless, endless : γαῖαν Υ 58 : ὀϊζύν λ 621.—(**2**) Numberless, countless ι 118, τ 174.

ἀπείρητος [ἀ-[1] + πειράω]. (**1**) Without making an attempt M 304.—(**2**) Not put to the issue : πόνος P 41.—(**3**) Unskilled : οὐκ ἀ. μαντεύομαι β 170.

ἀπείριτος [as ἀπειρέσιος]. Boundless κ 195.

ἀπείρων, -ονος [as prec.]. (**1**) Boundless A 350, H 446, Ω 342, 545 : α 98 = ε 46, δ 510, ο 79, ρ 386, 418, τ 107.—Of sleep, from which it might seem that one would never awake η 286.—(**2**) App., without an end by which to be unloosed, inextricable : δεσμοί θ 340.—(**3**) Numberless, countless : δῆμος Ω 776.

ἀπεκείρατο, 3 sing. aor. mid. ἀποκείρω.

†**ἀπεκλανθάνω** [ἀπ-, ἀπο- (7) + ἐκ- (1)]. Redup. pl. aor. imp. mid. ἀπεκλελάθεσθε. In mid., to put out of one's mind. With genit. : θάμβευς ω 394.

ἀπέκοψα, aor. ἀποκόπτω.

ἀπεκρέμασε, 3 sing. aor. ἀποκρεμάννυμι.

ἀπέκρυψε, 3 sing. aor. ἀποκρύπτω.

ἀπέκταμεν, 1 pl. aor. ἀποκτείνω.

ἀπέκτανε, 3 sing. aor. ἀποκτείνω.

ἀπέκτατο, 3 sing. aor. mid. ἀποκτείνω.

ἀπέκτεινε, 3 sing. aor. ἀποκτείνω.

ἀπέλεθρος, -ον [ἀ-[1] + πέλεθρον]. (**1**) Unmeasured, *i.e.* very great : ἶνα E 245, H 269 : = ι 538.—(**2**) In neut., ἀπέλεθρον as adv., to a very great distance : ἀνέδραμεν Λ 354.

ἀπελήλυθα, pf. ἀπέρχομαι.

†**ἀπεμέω** [ἀπ-, ἀπο- (1)]. 3 sing. aor. ἀπέμεσσε. To vomit forth, throw up : αἷμα Ξ 437.

ἀπεμνήσαντο, 3 pl. aor. mid. ἀπομιμνήσκω.

ἀπενάσσατο, 3 sing. aor. mid. ἀποναίω.

ἀπένεικαν, 3 pl. aor. ἀποφέρω.

ἀπέπεμψα, aor. ἀποπέμπω.

ἀπεπλάγχθη, 3 sing. aor. pass. ἀποπλάζω.

ἀπέπλω, 3 sing. aor. ἀποπλείω.

ἀπερείσιος [metathesis of ἀπειρέσιος]. Not to be reckoned, of very great amount or value : ἄποινα A 13 = 372, Z 49 = Λ 134, Z 427, I 120 = T 138, K 380, Ω 276, 502, 579, ἕδνα Π 178 : τ 529.

ἀπερρίγᾱσι, 3 pl. pf. ἀπορριγέω.

ἀπερύκω [ἀπ-, ἀπο- (2)]. To keep off or away Δ 542, P 562 : ι 119, σ 105.

ἀπέρχομαι [ἀπ-, ἀπο- (1)]. 3 sing. aor. ἀπῆλθε P 703. Pf. ἀπελήλυθα Ω 766. 3 sing. -ε τ 223, ω 310. (**1**) To go away, depart P 703.—(**2**) To depart *from*. With genit. : ἐμῆς πάτρης Ω 766 : τ 223 = ω 310, οἴκου β 136.

ἀπερωεύς, ὁ [ἀπερωέω, in causal sense. Cf. ἐρωέω[1] (4)]. A thwarter : ἐμῶν μενέων Θ 361.

ἀπερωέω [ἀπ-, ἀπο- (1) + ἐρωέω[1]]. To hold back *from*, fail to take one's part in. With genit. : πολέμου Π 723.

ἄπεσαν, 3 pl. impf. ἄπειμι[1].

ἀπεσκέδασε, 3 sing. aor. ἀποσκεδάννυμι.

ἀπέσσομαι, fut. ἄπειμι[1].

ἀπέσσυτο, 3 sing. aor. mid. ἀποσεύω.

ἀπέστη, 3 sing. aor. ἀφίστημι (B).

ἀπέστιχον, aor. ἀποστείχω.

ἀπεστυφέλιξε, 3 sing. aor. ἀποστυφελίζω.

ἀπέτῑσε, **ἀπέτεισε**, 3 sing. aor. ἀποτίνω.

ἀπέτραπε, 3 sing. aor. ἀποτρέπω.

ἀπευθής [ἀ-[1] + πεύθομαι]. (**1**) Without acquiring knowledge, uninformed : ἦλθον ἀ. γ 184.—(**2**) Unknown, hidden in mystery : ὄλεθρον γ 88.

ἀπέφθιθεν, 3 pl. aor. pass. ἀποφθίω.

ἀπέφθιτο, 3 sing. aor. pass. ἀποφθίω.

ἀπεχθαίρω [ἀπ-, ἀπο- (7)]. Aor. subj. ἀπεχθήρω Γ 415. (**1**) To hate, detest Γ 415.—(**2**) To make hateful δ 105.

ἀπεχθάνομαι [ἀπ-, ἀπο- (7)]. 3 sing. aor. ἀπήχθετο Γ 454, Z 140, 200, I 300, Ω 27. 2 sing. subj. ἀπέχθηαι I 614. 3 -ηται κ 74. 3 pl. -ωνται Δ 53. Pple. ἀπεχθόμενος, -ου κ 75, π 114, σ 165. Infin. ἀπεχθέσθαι Φ 83. (**1**) To become hateful, incur hatred or enmity β 202, σ 165.—To become hateful to, incur the hatred, disfavour, dislike or enmity of. With dat. : πᾶσιν Γ 454. Cf. Δ 53, Z 140, 200, I 300, 614, Φ 83, Ω 27 : κ 74, 75.—(**2**) To come into a state of enmity : δῆμος ἀπεχθόμενος π 114.

ἀπέχω [ἀπ-, ἀπο- (1) (2)]. Fut. ἀφέξω υ 263. 3 sing. fut. ἀποσχήσει τ 572. 3 sing. aor. subj. ἀπόσχῃ Z 96, 277. **Mid.** Fut. ἀφέξομαι τ 489. 2 sing. -εαι M 248. 1 pl. -όμεθα Θ 35, 466. 3 pl. aor. subj. ἀπόσχωνται Λ 799, Ξ 78, Π 41, Σ 199. Infin. ἀποσχέσθαι ι 211. (**1**) To keep or ward off *from*. With genit. : Τυδέος υἱὸν Ἰλίου Z 96, 277.—With dat. : ἀεικείην χροΐ Ω 19. Cf. υ 263.—To steer (a ship) so as to keep her away from a region specified : ἑκὰς νήσων ο 33.—(**2**) To cause to depart *from*. With genit. : οἴκου με τ 572.—(**3**) In mid. (**a**) To refrain *from*, hold back *from*. With genit. : πολέμου Θ 35. Cf. Θ 466, Λ 799, Ξ 78, Π 41, Σ 199.—(**b**) To keep one's hands *off*, do no harm to. With genit. : βοῶν μ 321, 328, σεῦ τ 489.—(**c**) To hold back *from* through disinclination, fail to take one's part in. With genit. : δηϊοτῆτος M 248.—(**d**) To abstain from intercourse with. With genit. : ἀλλήλων Ξ 206 = 305.—(**e**) Absol., to refrain from partaking of something ι 211.

ἀπεών, pple. ἄπειμι[1].

ἀπέωσε, 3 sing. aor. ἀπωθέω.

ἀπήγαγε, 3 sing. aor. ἀπάγω.

ἀπηλεγέως [ἀπ-, ἀπο- (6) + ἀλέγω]. Without respect of persons, without regard for consequences I 309 : α 373.

ἀπῆλθε, 3 sing. aor. ἀπέρχομαι.

ἀπήμαντος [ἀ-[1] + πημαν-, πημαίνω]. = ἀπήμων (1) τ 282.

ἀπήμβροτε, 3 sing. aor. ἀφαμαρτάνω.

ἀπῆμεν, 1 pl. impf. ἄπειμι[1].

ἀπήμων, -ονος [ἀ-[1] + πῆμα]. (1) Unharmed, unhurt, safe A 415, N 744, 761 : δ 487, ε 40 = ν 138, κ 551, ν 39, ο 436, σ 260.—(2) Doing no harm; hence (a) Convoying safely : πομποί θ 566 = ν 174.—(b) Propitious, favourable : οὖρον ε 268 = η 266. Cf. μ 167.—Profitable : μῦθος M 80 = N 748.—Bringing safety : νόστος ἀπήμων δ 519.—(c) Of sleep, gentle Ξ 164.

ἀπῆν, 3 sing. impf. ἄπειμι[1].

ἀπήνη, -ης, ἡ. A four-wheeled cart, a waggon (app. = ἅμαξα) Ω 275, 324, 447, 578, 590, 718 : ζ 57, 69, 73, 75, 78, 88, 90, 252, η 5.

ἀπηνήναντο, 3 sing. aor. ἀπαναίνομαι.

ἀπηνής, -ές [ἀπ-, ἀπο- (1) + ἠν-, face. Cf. προσηνής, ὑπηνήτης. 'With averted face']. (1) Untoward, harsh, unbending : βασιλῆος A 340. Cf. O 94, Π 35, Ψ 484, 611 : σ 381, τ 329, ψ 97, 230.—Absol. in neut. pl. : ὃς ἀπηνέα εἰδῇ (is untoward or harsh in heart) τ 329 (see εἴδω (III) (12)).—(2) Of a reply, unyielding, not conciliatory O 202.

ἀπήραξε, 3 sing. aor. ἀπαράσσω.

ἀπηύρᾱ, 3 sing. impf. ἀπαυράω.

ἀπήχθετο, 3 sing. aor. ἀπεχθάνομαι.

ἀπήωρος [ἀπ-, ἀπο- (2) + ἠωρ-, ἀείρω]. Raised far, high in air : ὄζοι μ 435.

ἀπιθέω [ἀ-[1] + πιθ-, πείθω]. (1) To refuse compliance with, disobey, disregard. With dat. : οὐδ' ἀπίθησε μύθῳ A 220.—(2) To refuse compliance with an order or injunction of. With dat. : Ἀγαμέμνονι Γ 120. Cf. Δ 198 = M 351, Z 102, K 129, Ω 300 : ψ 369.—(3) Absol., to refuse obedience or compliance B 166 = E 719 = H 43, B 441 = Ψ 895, Δ 68 = Π 458, E 767 = Θ 381 = Ξ 277 = O 78, Θ 112 = Λ 516, Θ 319, Λ 195 = O 168, M 329, 364, P 246 = 656, P 491, Ω 120, 339 : = ε 43, ο 98, χ 492.

ἄπιθι, imp. ἄπειμι[2].

ἀπινύσσω [ἀ-[1] + πινυ-, πινυτός]. (1) To lack understanding, be foolish ε 342, ζ 258.—(2) To be dazed or stupefied O 10.

ἄπιος, -η [app. fr. ἀπό]. Thus, distant, far off : ἐξ ἀπίης γαίης A 270, Γ 49 : η 25, π 18.

ἀπιστέω [ἄπιστος]. To disbelieve : τό ν 339.

ἄπιστος [ἀ-[1] + πιστός]. (1) Not to be trusted, faithless Γ 106, Ω 63, 207.—(2) Not believing, incredulous ξ 150, 391, ψ 72.

ἀπίσχω [ἀπ-, ἀπο- (2)]. To hold at a distance : ἄπισχε φάσγανον λ 95.

ἀπιών, pple. ἄπειμι[2].

ἀπλοΐς, -ΐδος [(σ)α- as in ἅμα. For the second element cf. δι-πλόος]. Worn single : χλαίνας Ω 230 : = ω 276.

ἄπνευστος [ἀ-[1] + πνευ-, πνέω]. Without breath, breathless ε 456.

ἀπό. (Commonly with anastrophe when immediately following the vb. or case-form.) (I) Adv. (1) From or away from something, away, off : ἀπὸ χλαῖναν βάλεν B 183, νίζοντες ἄπο βρότον H 425. Cf. B 261, E 308, M 83, Ξ 7, Φ 51, etc. : β 133, γ 392, κ 163, μ 199, τ 61, etc.—In reference to severing or cutting, away, off, through : ἀπὸ στομάχους τάμεν Γ 292. Cf. E 81, Λ 146, Π 587, Ψ 867, etc. : ἀπὸ πείσματ' ἔκοψα κ 127. Cf. δ 507, φ 300, χ 475, etc.—(2) Away, at a distance : ἀπὸ λοιγὸν ἀμῦναι A 67. Cf. Π 7[illegible], Ω 156, etc. : ἀπὸ κεῖνος ἔρυκεν ξ 283.—(3) Restoration, back : ἀπὸ πατρὶ δόμεναι κούρην A 98. Cf. Ω 76, etc.—(4) Requital, making up or giving compensation for something : πρίν γ' ἀπὸ πᾶσαν ἐμοὶ δόμεναι λώβην I 387. Cf. β 78.—(5) Intensive, in some cases not appreciably affecting the sense : ἀπό κε θυμὸν ὀλέσσεν Θ 90. Cf. K 186, M 52, 459, P 609, X 505, etc. : ἀπό κε ῥινοὺς δρύφθη ε 426. Cf. β 49, μ 2, ν 340, τ 81, ψ 331, etc.—(II) Prep. with genit. (1) From. (a) Indicating motion or transference : ἆλτ' ἀπ' Ὀλύμπου A 532, ἀχλὺν ἀπ' ὀφθαλμῶν ἕλον E 127. Cf. A 591, B 91, H 25, N 640, P 383, etc. : α 75, γ 307, ε 323, θ 88, ξ 129, etc.—So with ablative : στήθεσφιν Λ 374. Cf. Θ 300, K 347, N 585, Π 246, etc. : ἰκριόφιν μ 414. Cf. η 169, ξ 134, etc.—So also with forms in -θεν (1) : Τροίηθεν Ω 492 : ι 38. οὐρανόθεν Θ 365 : λ 18, μ 381. ὅθεν δ 358.—In reference to severing or cutting : ἀπ' αὐχένος ὦμον ἐέργαθεν E 147. Cf. N 202, etc.—(b) Indicating a point *from* which action takes place : ὥς φάτ' ἀπὸ πτόλιος Δ 514, εἰσεῖδεν ἀπὸ ῥίου Ξ 154 (cf. under ἐκ (II) (8)). Cf. Δ 275, 306, Π 386, Υ 5, Ω 605, etc. : ἀφ' ἵππων μάρνασθαι ι 49. Cf. δ 524, κ 121, υ 103, etc.—So with a form in -θεν (1) : οὐρανόθεν Φ 199.—In reference to a starting-point : ἀπὸ νύσσης Ψ 758 : θ 121.—(c) In reference to a vessel, source or stock *from* which something is taken or drawn : νέκταρ ἀπὸ κρητῆρος ἀφύσσων A 598. Cf. K 578, Π 160, 226 : λαχὼν ἀπὸ ληΐδος αἶσαν ε 40 = ν 138.—Sim. : ἓξ ἀφ' ἑκάστης νηός (out of . . .) ι 60.—In reference to birth : ἀπ' ἀλσέων κ 350. Cf. τ 163.—To that *from* which something proceeds or is derived : τοῖον πῦρ δαῖεν ἀπὸ κρατός E 7. Cf. M 431, Π 635, Σ 420, etc. : Χαρίτων ἄπο κάλλος ἔχουσαι ζ 18. Cf. ζ 12, μ 187, etc.—With abl. Λ 44.—To a motive or condition of action : ἀπὸ σπουδῆς H 359 = M 233 (see σπουδή (1)).—(d) In reference to that to which something is fastened : ἁψαμένη βρόχον ἀπὸ μελάθρου λ 278.—(2) (a) In reference to position, away from, far from, at a distance from, apart from : ἀπὸ πατρίδος αἴης B 162. Cf. E 322, I 437, N 696, O 33 (apart from . . .), P 301, Σ 272, Υ 261, etc. : φίλων ἄπο α 49. Cf. α 203, γ 313, ζ 40, ι 192 (apart from . . .), λ 503, ο 10, etc.—(b) In reference to warding or keeping off *from* : ἀπὸ χροὸς ὄλεθρον N 440. Cf. Δ 130, O 534 : β 59 = ρ 538.—(c) In reference to lack or want : δηρὸν ἀπὸ χροός ἐστιν ἀλοιφή ζ 220.—(d) To concealment or secrecy : κεκρυμμέν' ἀπ' ἄλλων ψ 110.—(e) Fig. : ἀπὸ θυμοῦ (out of favour) A 562 (cf. ἀποθύμιος), ἀπὸ δόξης (see δόξα) K 324 : λ 344, ἀπὸ σκοποῦ (see σκοπός (4)) λ 344.—(3) In temporal sense, immediately after : ἀπὸ δείπνου θωρήσσοντο Θ 54.

ἀποαίνυμαι, ἀπαίνυμαι [ἀπο- (1)]. (1) To take away *from* (a person), deprive (him) of. With genit. : τεύχε' Ἀπισάονος Λ 582. Cf. N 262 : ρ 322.—(2) To take off or away : τεύχεα P 85.—To withdraw, take away : κῦδος O 595 : νόστον μ 419 = ξ 309.

ἀποαίρεο, imp. mid. ἀφαιρέω.

ἀποβαίνω [ἀπο- (1)]. Fut. in mid. form ἀποβήσομαι Ε 227, Ρ 480. 3 sing. aor. ἀπέβη Ε 133, Ζ 116, 369, Θ 425, Λ 210, Μ 370, Ρ 188, 673, Σ 202, Ω 188, 468, 694 : α 319, γ 371, δ 657, 715, ε 148, ζ 41, 47, η 78, κ 307, ο 43, 454, χ 495. 3 dual ἀπεβήτην Φ 298. 3 pl. ἀπέβησαν Λ 619. Masc. pl. pple. ἀποβάντες Γ 265, Θ 492 : ν 281, ξ 346. Infin. ἀποβῆναι ε 357. 3 sing. aor. mid. ἀπεβήσετο Α 428, Β 35, Ε 352, Ψ 212 : σ 197. (**1**) To go away, depart Α 428, Β 35, Ε 133, 352, Ζ 116 = 369 = Ρ 188, Θ 425 = Λ 210 = Σ 202 = Ω 188, Μ 370, Ρ 673, Φ 298, Ψ 212, Ω 468, 694 : α 319 = ζ 41, γ 371 = η 78, δ 657, 715, ε 148, ζ 47, κ 307, ο 43, 454, σ 197, χ 495.—(**2**) To alight (from a chariot) : ἐξ ἵππων Γ 265, Θ 492, Ω 459.—To alight *from* (a chariot). With genit. : ἵππων Ε 227 = Ρ 480.—Absol. Λ 619.—(**3**) To land or disembark *from* (a ship). With genit. : νηός ν 281.—So to throw oneself *from*, quit (a raft) ε 357.—Absol., to land ξ 346.

ἀπόβλητος [ἀπο- (1) + βλη-, βάλλω]. To be thrown away or despised : ἔπος Β 361, θεῶν δῶρα Γ 65.

ἀποβλύζω [ἀπο- (1) + βλύζω, which recurs only in late Greek in sense 'to gush forth']. To send or spirt out : οἴνου ἀποβλύζων (partitive genit.) Ι 491.

†**ἀποβρίζω** [ἀπο- (7)]. Masc. pl. aor. pple. ἀποβρίξαντες. To fall asleep ι 151 = μ 7.

ἀπογυιόω [ἀπο- (7)]. To lame, cripple ; fig., to deprive (of vigour) : μή μ' ἀπογυιώσῃς μένεος Ζ 265.

ἀπογυμνόω [ἀπο- (7)]. To take the clothes off, strip : μή σ' ἀπογυμνωθέντα κακὸν θήῃ (when stripped) κ 301.

†**ἀποδατέομαι** [ἀπο- (7)]. Fut. ἀποδάσσομαι Ρ 231, Ω 595. Infin. ἀποδάσσεσθαι Χ 118. (**1**) To divide (with a person). With dat. : Ἀχαιοῖς ἄλλα Χ 118. Cf. Ω 595.—(**2**) To give as a portion : ἥμισυ ἐνάρων Ρ 231.

ἀποδειροτομέω [ἀπο- (7)]. To cut the throat of : Τρώων τέκνα Σ 336, Ψ 22 : μῆλα λ 35.

†**ἀποδέχομαι** [ἀπο- (7)]. 3 sing. aor. ἀπεδέξατο. To accept : ἄποινα Α 95.

†**ἀποδιδράσκω** [ἀπο- (7) + διδράσκω in sim. sense]. Aor. pple. ἀποδράς. To effect one's escape π 65, ρ 516.

†**ἀποδίδωμι** [ἀπο- (4) (5)]. Fut. ἀποδώσω Η 84, 362. 1 pl. -ομεν χ 58. 3 sing. aor. ἀπέδωκε Δ 478, Ε 651, Ρ 302. 3 sing. aor. subj. ἀποδῷσι θ 318. 2 pl. opt. ἀποδοῖτε χ 61. Infin. ἀποδοῦναι Α 134, Γ 285, Σ 499. (**1**) To give or pay back, restore Α 134, Γ 285, Η 84, 362 : θ 318.—(**2**) To give or pay as due or in requital : θρέπτρα Δ 478 = Ρ 302, πάντα (*i.e.* as blood-price) Σ 499. Cf. χ 58, 61.—To hand over in terms of a bargain Ε 651.

ἀποδίεμαι [ἀπο- (1)]. To chase away Ε 763.

ἀποδοῖτε, 2 pl. aor. opt. ἀποδίδωμι.

ἀποδοῦναι, aor. infin. ἀποδίδωμι.

ἀποδοχμόω [ἀπο- (7) + δοχμόω, fr. δοχμός]. To turn (something) sideways, cause (it) to droop : ἀποδοχμώσας αὐχένα ι 372.

ἀποδράς, aor. pple. ἀποδιδράσκω.

†**ἀποδρύπτω** [ἀπο- (7)]. 3 pl. aor. subj. ἀποδρύψωσι ρ 480. 3 sing. aor. opt. ἀποδρύφοι Ψ 187, Ω 21. 3 pl. aor. pass. ἀπέδρυφθεν ε 435. To tear or lacerate the skin of (a person) Ψ 187, Ω 21 : ρ 480.—In pass., of the skin, to be torn ε 435.

ἀποδύω, ἀποδύνω [ἀπο- (1)]. 3 sing. aor. ἀπέδυσε Δ 532, Σ 83. Aor. pple. ἀποδύς ε 343. (**1**) In sigmatic aor., to strip off : τεύχεα Δ 532, Σ 83.—(**2**) In impf. and non-sigmatic aor., to divest oneself of ε 343, χ 364.

ἀποδῷσι, 3 pl. aor. subj. ἀποδίδωμι.

ἀποδώσω, fut. ἀποδίδωμι.

ἀποείκω [ἀπο- (1) + εἴκω[2]]. To withdraw from, quit. With genit. : θεῶν ἀπόεικε κελεύθου Γ 406 (*v.l.* ἀπόειπε κελεύθους).

ἀποεῖπον, ἀπέειπον, *aor.* [ἀπο- (1) (7)]. Pple. ἀποειπών Τ 35. (**1**) To make refusal, refuse : ὑπόσχεο ἢ ἀπόειπε Α 515, κρατερῶς Ι 431 (or perh. this should come under (3)). Cf. Ι 510, 675.—(**2**) To renounce : θεῶν ἀπόειπε κελεύθους Γ 406 (*v.l.* ἀπόεικε κελεύθου), μῆνιν Τ 35, 75.—(**3**) To speak out, declare freely : μῦθον Ι 309 : α 373.—Absol. to speak one's mind freely α 91.—(**4**) To announce publicly, state : ἀγγελίην Η 416. Cf. Ψ 361.—To deliver (a message) π 340 (the prefix here app. giving the notion 'at full length').

ἀποέργω [ἀπο- (1) (2) + ἔργω[1]]. 3 sing. aor. ἀποέργαθε Φ 599 : φ 221. (**1**) To exclude *from*. With genit. : αἰθούσης Ω 238.—(**2**) To hold apart Θ 325.—To keep apart *from*. With genit. : Πηλεΐωνα λαοῦ Φ 599.—(**3**) To remove (a covering) *from*. With genit. : ῥάκεα οὐλῆς φ 221.—(**4**) To break the course of, shelter from : κῦμα γ 296.

ἀπόερσα, *aor.* (ἀπόϝερσα) [ἀπο- (1). For the second element cf. ἀπαυράω and L. *verro*]. 3 sing. subj. ἀποέρσῃ Φ 283. 3 sing. opt. ἀποέρσειε Φ 329. To sweep or carry away Ζ 348, Φ 283, 329.

†**ἀποθαυμάζω** [ἀπο- (7)]. 3 sing. aor. ἀπεθαύμασε. To marvel much at : ὄνειρον ζ 49.

ἀποθείομαι, aor. subj. mid. ἀποτίθημι.

ἀποθέσθαι, aor. infin. mid. ἀποτίθημι.

ἀπόθεστος [prob. fr. ἀπο- (6) + θεσ-, θέσσασθαι, to pray for. Thus 'not prayed for,' 'not desired']. Hence, cast aside, neglected ρ 296.

ἀποθνήσκω [ἀπο- (7)]. Genit. sing. masc. pf. pple. ἀποτεθνηῶτος Χ 432. 3 pl. plupf. ἀποτέθνασαν μ 393. To die λ 424, φ 33.—In pf., to be dead Χ 432 : μ 393.

ἀποθρῴσκω [ἀπο- (1)]. With genit., to leap *from* : νηός Β 702, Π 748.—Of smoke, to rise up *from* : ἧς γαίης α 58.

ἀποθύμιος [ἀπο- (2) + θυμός. 'Away from the heart.' Cf. ἀπό (II) (2) (e)]. Hence, unpleasing. Absol. in neut. pl. : μὴ Νυκτὶ ἀποθύμια ἕρδοι (do her a disfavour, offend her) Ξ 261.

†**ἀποικίζω** [ἀπ-, ἀπο- (1) + οἰκίζω fr. οἶκος]. 3 sing. aor. ἀπῴκισε. To send away from home μ 135.

ἄποινα, τά [app. ἀ-[2] (not appreciably affecting the sense) + ποινή]. A ransom. (**1**) As the price of freedom Α 13, Β 230, Ζ 49, Κ 380, Λ 106 (genit. of price), etc.—(**2**) As the price of life Ζ 46 =

Λ 131, Φ 99.—(**3**) Paid to recover a corpse Χ 349, Ω 137, 139, 276, 502, 555, 579, 594.—(**4**) Applied to gifts offered to effect a reconciliation Ι 120 = Τ 138.

ἀποίσετον, 3 dual fut. ἀποφέρω.

ἀποίχομαι [ἀπ-, ἀπο- (1)]. (**1**) To be gone or absent: πατρὸς ἀποιχομένοιο α 135, γ 77, τ 19, δηρὸν ἀποίχεται (has been long away) δ 109. Cf. α 253, ξ 8, 450, ρ 296, φ 70, 395.—(**2**) With genit., to hold aloof *from*, forsake: ἀνδρὸς ἑῆος Τ 342.—To hold aloof *from*, shrink *from*: πολέμοιο Λ 408.

ἀποκαίνυμαι [ἀπο- (7)]. To excel (another or others). With dat. of that in which one excels: παλαιμοσύνῃ πάντας θ 127. Cf. θ 219.

†**ἀποκείρω** [ἀπο- (1)]. 3 sing. aor. mid. ἀπεκείρατο. In mid., to cut off from oneself: χαίτην Ψ 141.

ἀποκηδέω [ἀπο- (6) + κῆδος]. To be careless, fail to do one's best: αἴ κ' ἀποκηδήσαντε φερώμεθα χεῖρον ἄεθλον Ψ 413 (the dual referring to the horses only, but the speaker being included in the subjects of the verb).

ἀποκῑνέω [ἀπο- (1)]. 3 sing. pa. iterative ἀποκινήσασκε Λ 636. With genit. (**1**) To lift *from*: [δέπας] τραπέζης Λ 636.—(**2**) To force away *from*: θυράων με χ 107.

†**ἀποκλίνω** [ἀπο- (1)]. Acc. sing. masc. aor. pple. ἀποκλίναντα. To bend aside: ἄλλῃ τ 556 (see ἄλλῃ (2) (b)).

†**ἀποκόπτω** [ἀπο- (1) (3)]. Fut. infin. ἀποκόψειν Ι 241. Aor. ἀπέκοψα ι 325, ψ 195. 3 sing. -ε Λ 261, Π 474: γ 449. (**1**) To cut off, strike off: κάρη Λ 261. Cf. Ι 241: ι 325, ψ 195.—(**2**) To cut through, sever: τένοντας γ 449.—To cut loose: παρήορον Π 474.

ἀποκοσμέω [ἀπο- (1)]. To clear away: ἔντεα δαιτός η 232.

†**ἀποκρεμάννῡμι** [ἀπο- (1)]. 3 sing. aor. ἀπεκρέμασε. To let hang down: αὐχένα Ψ 879.

†**ἀποκρίνω** [ἀπο- (7)]. Dual aor. pple. pass. ἀποκρινθέντε. To separate: ἀποκρινθέντε ἐναντίω ὁρμηθήτην (separating themselves from the throng) Ε 12.

†**ἀποκρύπτω** [ἀπο- (1)]. 3 sing. aor. ἀπέκρυψε Λ 718. Infin. ἀποκρύψαι Σ 465: ρ 286. To hide away, conceal Λ 718, Σ 465.—To hide away, make a secret of ρ 286.

ἀποκτείνω [ἀπο- (7)]. 3 sing. aor. ἀπέκτεινε Ι 543. Subj. ἀποκτείνω χ 167. Infin. ἀποκτεῖναι ε 18. 3 sing. aor. ἀπέκτανε Ζ 414, Ο 440, Χ 423. 3 pl. -ον ξ 271, ρ 440. 3 sing. subj. ἀποκτάνῃ μ 301. 1 pl. aor. ἀπέκταμεν ψ 121. Infin. ἀποκτάμεναι Υ 165. ἀποκτάμεν Ε 675. **Mid.** 3 sing. aor. (in pass. sense) ἀπέκτατο Ο 437, Ρ 472. Pple. (in sense of pf. pass.) ἀποκτάμενος, -ου Δ 494, Ν 660, Ψ 775. To kill, slay: πατέρ' ἀμόν Ζ 414. Cf. Δ 494, Ε 675, Θ 342 = Λ 178, Ι 543, Ν 660, Ο 437, 440, Ρ 472, Υ 165, Χ 423, Ψ 775: παῖδα ε 18. Cf. μ 301, ξ 271 = ρ 440, π 432 (go about to slay), χ 167, ψ 121.—Absol. Λ 154.

ἀπολάμπω [ἀπο- (1)]. To shine forth, gleam Τ 381, Ζ 295: = ο 108.—In mid. Ξ 183: = σ 298.—Impers. with genit.: αἰχμῆς ἀπέλαμπεν (a gleam came *from* . . .) Χ 319.

ἀπολείβω [ἀπο- (1)]. In pass., to run down *from*, trickle *off*. With genit.: ὀθονέων ἀπολείβεται ἔλαιον η 107.

ἀπολείπω [ἀπο- (7)]. (**1**) To forsake, abandon: κοῖλον δόμον Μ 169.—(**2**) To leave a remnant, not to consume all: ἤσθιε, οὐδ' ἀπέλειπεν ι 292.—(**3**) To fail, be lacking: καρπός η 117.

†**ἀπολέπω** [ἀπο- (1)]. Fut. infin. ἀπολεψέμεν. To slice off: οὔατα Φ 455.

ἀπολέσκετο, 3 sing. pa. iterative mid. ἀπόλλυμι.

ἀπόλεσσαν, 3 pl. aor. ἀπόλλυμι.

ἀπολήγω [ἀπο- (7)]. 2 sing. fut. ἀπολλήξεις τ 166. 2 sing. aor. subj. ἀπολλήξῃς Ο 31. 3 pl. -ωσι ν 151. 3 pl. opt. -ειαν μ 224. (**1**) To cease, give over, desist, stop Ν 230, Υ 99.—To fail, die out Ζ 149.—(**2**) To cease or desist *from*. With genit.: μάχης Η 263, Λ 255. Cf. Ο 31, Φ 577, Ω 475: μ 224, ν 151.—To cease or desist. With complementary pple.: δηϊόων Ρ 565. Cf. τ 166.

ἀπολιχμάομαι [ἀπο- (1) + λιχμάομαι conn. with λείχω, to lick]. To lick off. With double acc.: ὠτειλὴν αἷμ' ἀπολιχμήσονται Φ 123.

ἀπολλήξεις, 2 sing. fut. ἀπολήγω.

ἀπόλλῡμι [ἀπ-, ἀπο- (7)]. (**A**) Aor. ἀπώλεσα Σ 82: β 46, δ 95, 724, 814. 3 sing. -ε Ε 648, 758, Σ 460, Ω 44, 260: α 354, ι 265. 3 pl. -αν Ψ 280. ἀπόλεσσαν Α 268. (**B**) 3 sing. pf. ἀπόλωλε Ο 129: α 166, δ 62, 511, ξ 137, τ 85. **Mid.** 3 sing. pa. iterative ἀπολέσκετο λ 586. 2 sing. aor. ἀπώλεο λ 556. 3 -ετο Ζ 223: α 413, γ 87, ρ 253. 1 pl. -όμεθα ι 303, κ 27, λ 438, ω 186. 3 ἀπόλοντο Β 162, 178: γ 185, δ 497, λ 384. 3 sing. subj. ἀπόληται β 333. 3 pl. -ωνται Φ 459. Opt. ἀπολοίμην Χ 304: ρ 426. 3 sing. -οιτο Ε 311, 388, Ζ 170, Ξ 142, Σ 107: α 47. 3 pl. -οίατο ι 554. 3 sing. imp. ἀπολέσθω Ρ 227. Infin. ἀπολέσθαι Α 117, Γ 40, Η 390, Θ 246, etc.: γ 234, ε 347, θ 511, 563. (**I**) In aor. act. (**1**) (**a**) To destroy, kill, slay Α 268, Ε 758, Ω 260.—(**b**) To destroy, lay waste (a city) Ε 648.—(**2**) (**a**) To lose, be deprived of: Πάτροκλον Σ 82. Cf. Ψ 280: νόστιμον ἦμαρ α 354. Cf. β 46, δ 724 = 814.—(**b**) To incur the loss of under one's leadership, lose, throw away: λαοὺς πολλούς ι 265.—To lose to the foe: θώρηκα Σ 460.—(**c**) To incur the laying waste of: οἶκον δ 95.—(**d**) To lose sense of, put out of one's heart: ἔλεον Ω 44.—(**II**) In pf. act. and in mid. and pass. (**1**) To be destroyed, perish, die: πολλοὶ ἀπόλοντο Β 162 = 178. Cf. Α 117, Γ 40, Ε 311, 388, Ζ 170, 223, Η 27, 390, Θ 246, Μ 70 = Ν 227 = Ξ 70, Μ 246, Ξ 142, Ο 502, 511, Ρ 227, Φ 459, Χ 304, 474, Ψ 81: οὐ γένος ἀπόλωλεν δ 62. Cf. α 47, β 333, γ 185, 234, δ 497, 511, ε 347, θ 511, 563, ι 554, λ 384, 438, 556, ξ 137, τ 85, ω 186.—With cognate acc.: ἀπόλωλε κακὸν μόρον α 166. Cf. γ 87, ι 303.—To be undone κ 27, ρ 426.—(**2**) Of inanimate objects, to be destroyed: ἀπολέσθαι νῆας Ι 230. Cf. ι 554.—Of water, to vanish away, elude one λ 586.—(**3**) Of mental faculties, to perish, disappear:

νόος ἀπόλωλε καὶ αἰδώς O 129.—So of abstractions: ὡς ἔρις ἀπόλοιτο Σ 107. Cf. α 413, ρ 253.—(**4**) Of fruit, to perish (untimely): οὔ ποτε καρπὸς ἀπόλλυται η 117.

ἀπόλοντο, 3 pl. aor. mid. ἀπόλλυμι.

ἀπολούω [ἀπο- (1)]. In mid., to wash away *from* one's . . . With genit.: ὄφρ' ἅλμην ὤμοιϊν ἀπολούσομαι ζ 219.

ἀπολῡμαίνομαι [ἀπο- (1) + λυμαίνομαι fr. λῦμα]. To cleanse oneself from pollution A 313, 314.

ἀπολῡμαντήρ, -ῆρος, ὁ [ἀπο- (7) + λυμαίνομαι, to maltreat, fr. λύμη, outrage]. δαιτῶν ἀ., a spoiler of feasts, a kill-joy ρ 220, 377.

ἀπολύω [ἀπο- (1) (4)]. (**1**) To loose or untie *from*. With genit.: ἱμάντα κορώνης φ 46.—In mid., to undo (something) from one's person: [κρήδεμνον] ε 349.—(**2**) (**a**) To set free (a captive) on payment of ransom A 95, Z 427, K 449.—To restore (a corpse) Ω 115, 136.—(**b**) In mid., to effect the ransoming of: [Λυκάονα καὶ Πολύδωρον] χαλκοῦ (genit. of price) X 50.

ἀπόλωλε, 3 sing. pf. ἀπόλλυμι.

ἀπομηνίω [ἀπο- (7)]. To be very wroth, take deadly offence: ἀπομηνίσας Ἀγαμέμνονι (against . . .) B 772 = H 230. Cf. I 426, T 62: π 378.

†**ἀπομιμνήσκω** [ἀπο- (5)]. 3 pl. mid. ἀπεμνήσαντο. To remember a favour Ω 428.

ἀπόμνῡμι, ἀπομνύω [ἀπ-, ἀπο- (6)]. Aor. ἀπώμοσα κ 381. To swear a negative oath, swear not to do something κ 345, μ 303.—With cognate acc.: ὅρκον β 377, κ 381.

ἀπομόργνῡμι [ἀπ-, ἀπο- (1)]. 3 sing. aor. mid. ἀπομόρξατο B 269: ρ 304, σ 200. Nom. dual masc. pple. ἀπομορξαμένω Ψ 739. (**1**) To wipe off or away. With double acc.: τελαμῶνα αἷμα E 798.—(**2**) In mid., to wipe away from one's face or person: δάκρυ B 269. Cf. Ψ 739: ρ 304.—(**3**) To wipe, cleanse Σ 414.—In mid. σ 200.

ἀπομῡθέομαι [ἀπο- (1)]. To speak in dissuasion, attempt to dissuade a person I 109.

ἀπόναιο, 2 sing. aor. opt. mid. ἀπονίνημι.

†**ἀποναίω** [ἀπο- (1) + ναίω[1]]. 3 pl. aor. subj. ἀπονάσσωσι Π 86. 3 sing. aor. mid. ἀπενάσσατο B 629: ο 254. (**1**) To cause to leave one's residence; hence, to send back: κούρην Π 86.—(**2**) In mid., to leave one's home, go to . . . in order to settle there: Δουλίχιόνδε B 629. Cf. ο 254.

ἀπονέομαι [ἀπο- (1) (4)]. (Always ending a line and with ἀπ-.) (**1**) To go or come back or home, return (the infin. often as fut.; cf. νέομαι (3)): Ἴλιον ἐκπέρσαντ' ἀπονέεσθαι B 113 = 288 = E 716 = I 20, προτὶ Ἴλιον ἀπονέοντο Γ 313. Cf. M 73, Ξ 46, O 295, 305, Π 252, P 415, Υ 212, Φ 561, Ω 330: β 195, ε 27, ι 451, π 467, σ 260.—(**2**) To go away, depart: προτὶ ἄστυ ο 308 (of course in sense (1) to the speaker himself).

ἀπονήσεται, 3 sing. fut. mid. ἀπονίνημι.

ἀπόνητο, 3 sing. aor. mid. ἀπονίνημι.

ἀπονίζω [ἀπο- (1) (7)]. Aor. imp. pl. ἀπονίψατε τ 317. Masc. pl. pple. ἀπονίψαντες ω 189. Fem. pple. mid. ἀπονιψαμένη σ 172. Masc. pl. -οι χ 478. Pres. infin. mid. in form ἀπονίπτεσθαι σ 179. (**1**) To wash off or away ω 189.—(**2**) To wash (a person) τ 317.—Absol. ψ 75.—(**3**) In mid. (**a**) To wash off or away from a part of one's person. With double acc.: ἱδρῶ κνήμας K 572.—(**b**) To wash (one's person or a part thereof): χρῶτ' ἀπονιψαμένη σ 172. Cf. σ 179, χ 478.

†**ἀπονίνημι** [ἀπ-, ἀπο- (7)]. 3 sing. fut. mid. ἀπονήσεται Λ 763. 3 sing. aor. ἀπόνητο P 25: λ 324, π 120, ρ 293. 2 sing. opt. ἀπόναιο Ω 556. Pple. ἀπονήμενος ω 30. In mid., to enjoy, have the enjoyment of. With genit.: τῆς ἀρετῆς Λ 763. Cf. P 25, Ω 556: ω 30.—With the object to be supplied from the context λ 324, π 120, ρ 293.

ἀπονίπτεσθαι, pres. infin. mid. See ἀπονίζω.

ἀπονίψατε, aor. imp. pl. ἀπονίζω.

ἀπονοστέω [ἀπο- (7)]. To go or come back, return: ἄψ A 60, Θ 499 = M 115, P 406: ν 6, ω 471.

ἀπονόσφι(ν) [ἀπο- (1) (2) + νόσφι(ν)]. (**I**) Adv. (**1**) Away, far away: ἀ. ἐόντων O 548.—Away, absent σ 268.—(**2**) Apart: ἦν ἀ. κατίσχεαι B 233. —(**3**) Away, off: ἔβη Λ 555 = P 664.—In reference to direction, away, aloof: τραπέσθαι ε 350, κ 528.—(**II**) Prep. with genit. (**1**) Far from: φίλων ε 113. —(**2**) Apart from, at a distance from: ἐμεῦ ἀ. ἐόντα (keeping away from me) A 541. Cf. μ 33.—(**3**) Away from, to a distance from: ἑτάρων ἀ. καλέσσας ο 529.

ἀποξύνω [ἀπ-, ἀπο- (7) + ὀξύνω, to sharpen, fr. ὀξύς]. Aor. infin. ἀποξῦναι ι 326. (**1**) To make sharp, bring to a point: [ῥόπαλον] ι 326.—(**2**) To bring (oars (*i.e.* the blades thereof)) to the proper degree of thinness: ἐρετμά ζ 269.

ἀποξύω [ἀπο- (1)]. To scrape off. Fig.: γῆρας ἀποξύσας I 446.

†**ἀποπαπταίνω** [ἀπο- (1)]. 3 pl. fut. ἀποπαπτανέουσι. To look about away from something (*i.e.* away from the fight), look out for a chance of escape Ξ 101.

ἀποπαύω [ἀπο- (7)]. (**1**) (**a**) To stop (a person) in his course Σ 267.—To stop the operation of, curb: μένος Φ 340.—To delay: τόκον T 119.—(**b**) To cause to cease (from something). With genit.: πολέμου Λ 323.—With infin.: ἀλητεύειν σ 114.—(**c**) To restrain from *doing something*. With infin.: ὁρμηθῆναι μ 126.—(**2**) In mid., to desist, give over E 288, Φ 372.—With genit.: πολέμου A 422. Cf. Θ 473, Π 721: α 340.

ἀποπέμπω [ἀπο- (1)]. Fut. ἀποπέμψω ε 161, τ 412. Contr. 3 sing. ἀππέμψει ο 83. Aor. ἀπέπεμψα ψ 23. 3 sing. -ε ξ 334, τ 291, ω 285. Subj. ἀποπέμψω ρ 76. 3 sing. -ῃ ο 53. Imp. ἀπόπεμψον β 113. (**1**) To send away, dismiss Φ 452: β 113, ο 83, υ 133, ψ 23.—To send away or dismiss *from*. With genit.: δόμων κ 76.—(**2**) To dispatch on an errand K 72.—(**3**) To send for use: συῶν τὸν ἄριστον ξ 108.—To send to the proper quarter: δῶρα ρ 76.—(**4**) To dispatch on one's way, speed, arrange for or preside over the departure of ε 112, 146, 161, κ 65, 73, λ 339, ξ 334 = τ 291, ο 53, 65, τ 243, 316, 412, ω 285, 312.

ἀποπέσῃσι, 3 sing. aor. subj. ἀποπίπτω.

†ἀποπέτομαι [ἀπο- (1)]. Aor. pple. ἀποπτάμενος B 71. Fem. -η λ 222. To fly away B 71 : λ 222.

ἀποπίπτω [ἀπο- (1)]. 3 sing. aor. subj. ἀποπέσῃσι ω 7. To fall or drop off: ἕερσαι Ξ 351.—To fall or drop off *from*. With genit.: ὀρμαθοῦ ω 7.

†ἀποπλάζω [ἀπο- (1)]. 2 sing. aor. pass. ἀπεπλάγχθης θ 573, ο 382. 3 -η X 291. Pple. ἀποπλαγχθείς, -έντος N 592 : ι 259, μ 285. Fem. -εῖσα N 578. In pass. (1) To be driven from one's course: Τροίηθεν (*i.e.* in the course of the voyage from Troy) ι 259.—(2) To wander or rove under stress of circumstances θ 573.—(3) With genit., to be carried away *from*: πατρίδος ο 382. —App. of voluntarily steering a course *away from*: νήσου μ 285.—(4) Of a missile, to glance off (from something) N 592.—To glance off *from*. With genit.: σάκεος X 291.—(5) Of something struck, to be struck off N 578.

ἀποπλείω [ἀπο- (1)]. 3 sing. aor. ἀπέπλω ξ 339. (1) To sail away or off I 418 = 685 : θ 501, π 331. —(2) To sail away *from*. With genit.: γαίης ξ 339.

†ἀποπλύνω [ἀπο- (1)]. 3 sing. pa. iterative ἀποπλύνεσκε. Of the sea, to wash away from itself, wash up: λάϊγγας ζ 95.

ἀποπνείω [ἀπο- (1)]. To breathe forth: θυμόν Δ 524, N 654, πυρὸς μένος Z 182 : ὀδμήν δ 406.

ἀποπρό [ἀπό + πρό]. (1) Adv., to a distance: πολλὸν ἀ. φέρων Π 669, 679.—(2) Prep. with genit., at a distance from: τυτθὸν ἀ. νεῶν H 334.

†ἀποπροαιρέω [ἀπο- (1) + προ- (2) + αἱρέω]. Aor. pple. ἀποπροελών. To select or pick out: σίτου (partitive genit., 'a portion of the . . .') ρ 457.

ἀποπροέηκε, 3 sing. aor. ἀποπροΐημι.

ἀποπροελών, aor. pple. ἀποπροαιρέω.

ἀπόπροθεν [ἀπό + πρό + -θεν (2)]. (1) Far away: νῆσός τις ἀ. κεῖται η 244. Cf. ρ 408.—(2) At a distance: μένειν K 209 = 410. Cf. P 66, 501 : ζ 218. —(3) Apart from others, aloof: ποιμαίνεσκεν ι 188.

ἀπόπροθι [ἀπό + πρό + -θι]. (1) Far away: ἀ. δώματα ναίεις δ 811. Cf. Ψ 832 : ε 80, ι 18, 35.—(2) At a distance δ 757 (app., lying at a distance from the town).

†ἀποπροΐημι [ἀπο- (1) + προ- (1) + ἵημι[1]]. 3 sing. aor. ἀποπροέηκε ξ 26, χ 327. From ἀποπροϊέω 3 sing. impf. ἀποπροΐει χ 82. (1) To shoot forth, discharge (a missile) χ 82.—(2) To send from oneself, let fall from one's grasp: ξίφος χαμᾶζε χ 327. —(3) To dispatch on a mission ξ 26.

†ἀποπροτάμνω [ἀπο- (1) + προ- (2)]. Aor. pple. ἀποπροταμών. To cut off a selected portion of something: νώτου (partitive genit., 'a portion of the . . .') θ 475.

ἀποπτάμενος, aor. pple. ἀποπέτομαι.

ἀποπτύω [ἀπο- (1)]. To spit forth or out: ὄνθον Ψ 781.—Of a wave: ἁλὸς ἄχνην Δ 426.

ἀπόρθητος, -ον [ἀ-[1] + πορθέω]. Not sacked M 11.

ἀπόρνυμι [ἀπ-, ἀπο- (1)]. In mid., to set forth: ἀπορνύμενον Λυκίηθεν E 105.

ἀπορούω [ἀπ-, ἀπο- (1)]. To spring or dart away E 20, 297, 836, Λ 145, P 483, Φ 251 : χ 95.

ἀπορραίω [ἀπο- (1)]. To take away: ἦτορ π 428.—With double acc.: κτήματά σε α 404.

†ἀπορρήγνυμι [ἀπο- (1) (3)]. Aor. pple. ἀπορρήξας. (1) To break off ι 481.—(2) To break asunder: δεσμόν Z 507 = O 264.

†ἀπορριγέω [ἀπο- (1)]. 3 pl. pf. ἀπερρίγᾱσι. To shrink from *doing something*. With infin. β 52.

†ἀπορρίπτω [ἀπο- (1)]. Acc. sing. masc. aor. pple. ἀπορρίψαντα I 517. Infin. ἀπορρῖψαι Π 282. To cast away. Fig.: μῆνιν I 517, μηνιθμόν Π 282.

ἀπορρώξ, -ῶγος [ἀπορρήγνυμι]. (1) Broken off, abrupt, sheer: ἀκταί ν 98.—(2) As subst., a piece broken off. Hence (a) A specimen, something as good as (another thing specified): ἀμβροσίης ἐστὶν ἀ. ι 359.—(b) A branch stream or tributary B 755 : κ 514.

†ἀποσεύω [ἀπο- (1) (4)]. 3 sing. aor. mid. ἀπέσσυτο Z 390, O 572. 1 pl. ἀπεσσύμεθα ι 236, 396. Acc. sing. masc. pf. pple. ἀπεσσύμενον Δ 527. In mid. (1) To speed away: ἀπεσσύμενον βάλεν Δ 527. Cf. O 572.—To speed away *from*. With genit.: δώματος Z 390.—(2) To start back, retire hastily ι 236, 396.

†ἀποσκεδάννῡμι [ἀπο- (7)]. 3 sing. aor. ἀπεσκέδασε. To cause to disperse, dismiss T 309 : λ 385.

ἀποσκίδναμαι [ἀπο- (7)]. To disperse, go each his own way: οὐκ εἴα ἀποσκίδνασθαι Ψ 4.

ἀποσκυδμαίνω [ἀπο- (7)]. To be angry or wroth with. With dat.: θεοῖσιν Ω 65.

ἀποσπένδω [ἀπο- (7)]. To make libation: εὔχετ' ἀποσπένδων γ 394. Cf. ξ 331, τ 288.

ἀποσταδά [ἀπο- (2) + στα-, ἵστημι]. Standing aloof: ἢ ἀ. λίσσοιτο ζ 143. Cf. ζ 146.

ἀποσταδόν [as prec.] = prec.: μάρνασθαι O 556.

ἀποστείχω [ἀπο- (1) (4)]. Aor. ἀπέστιχον μ 333. 3 sing. -ε μ 143. Imp. ἀπόστιχε A 522. (1) To go away or off μ 143, 333.—(2) To go back, return A 522 : λ 132 = ψ 279.

ἀποστήσωνται, 3 pl. aor. subj. mid. ἀφίστημι.

ἀποστίλβω [ἀπο- (7)]. To shine or glisten: ἀλείφατος (with . . .) γ 408.

ἀπόστιχε, aor. imp. ἀποστείχω.

†ἀποστρέφω [ἀπο- (4)]. 3 sing. pa. iterative ἀποστρέψασκε X 197 : λ 597. Acc. pl. masc. fut. pple. ἀποστρέψοντας K 355. 3 sing. aor. subj. ἀποστρέψῃσι O 62. Dual pple. ἀποστρέψαντε χ 173, 190. Pl. -αντες γ 162. (1) To turn back, cause to return K 355.—To turn back from a course desired to be taken X 197.—To cause to roll back: λᾶαν λ 597.—(2) To cause to turn from the fight, put flight into the hearts of O 62.—(3) To reverse the course of (a ship), turn (her) back γ 162.—(4) To draw back (the feet and hands) in order to bind feet and hands together behind the back χ 173, 190.

†ἀποστυφελίζω [ἀπο- (1) (4)]. 3 sing. aor. ἀπεστυφέλιξε Π 703. 3 pl. -αν Σ 158. To smite so as to drive back Π 703.—So as to drive away *from*. With genit.: νεκροῦ Σ 158.

†ἀποσφάλλω [ἀπο- (1)]. 3 pl. aor. subj. ἀποσφῆλωσι γ 320. 3 sing. opt. ἀποσφήλειε Ε 567. (1) To balk of the fruits of. With genit.: πόνοιο Ε 567.—(2) To drive from one's course γ 320.

ἀπόσχῃ, 3 sing. aor. subj. ἀπέχω.

ἀποσχήσει, 3 sing. fut. ἀπέχω.

ἀποτάμνω [ἀπο- (1) (3)]. (1) To cut off. In mid. Χ 347.—(2) To cut through, sever: παρηορίας Θ 87.

ἀποτέθνασαν, 3 pl. plupf. ἀποθνήσκω.

ἀποτεθνηῶτος, genit. sing. masc. pf. pple. ἀποθνήσκω.

ἀποτείσεις, 2 sing. fut. ἀποτίνω.

ἀποτηλοῦ [ἀπο- (7) + τηλοῦ]. Far away from. With genit.: γαίης Κυκλώπων ι 117.

†**ἀποτίθημι** [ἀπο- (1)]. 3 sing. aor. ἀπέθηκε Π 254. Aor. subj. mid. ἀποθείομαι Σ 409. Infin. ἀποθέσθαι Γ 89, Ε 492. (1) To put away in the appropriate place Π 254.—In mid. Σ 409.—(2) In mid. (a) To lay aside and place somewhere Γ 89. —(b) To put away from oneself, avoid incurring: ἐνιπήν Ε 492.

ἀποτίνυμαι [ἀπο- (7)]. (1) To exact (vengeance): πολέων ποινήν (for . . .) Π 398.—(2) To punish: τῶν μ' ἀποτινύμενοι (on account of . . .) β 73.

ἀποτίνω [ἀπο- (4) (5)]. (The fut. and aor. written both -τῑ- (-τῖ-) and -τει- (-τεῖ-).) 2 sing. fut. ἀποτίσεις Χ 271. 1 pl. -ομεν Α 128. Infin. -έμεν Φ 399. 3 sing. aor. ἀπέτισε α 43, γ 195. 3 pl. -αν Δ 161. 3 sing. subj. ἀποτίσῃ Ι 512, Σ 93: χ 168. Pple. ἀποτίσας Ι 634. Infin. ἀποτῖσαι ν 193, χ 64. **Mid.** Fut. ἀποτίσομαι ν 386. 2 sing. -εαι λ 118. 3 -εται α 268, ε 24, ρ 540, ω 480. 3 sing. aor. ἀπετίσατο ψ 312. 2 sing. subj. ἀποτίσεαι π 255. 3 -εται γ 216. (1) To pay back β 132.—(2) To make requital Α 128.—(3) To make requital or return for: κομιδήν Θ 186. Cf. χ 235.—(4) To pay the penalty: ἵνα γνώῃς ἀποτίνων Ψ 487. Cf. Δ 161, Ι 512: γ 195.—(5) To pay (a penalty) Γ 286, 459, Ι 634.—(6) To pay the penalty for: Πατρόκλοιο ἕλωρα Σ 93. Cf. Φ 399, Χ 271: α 43, ν 193 = χ 64, χ 168.—(7) In mid. (a) To exact the penalty α 268.—(b) To exact (a penalty): ποινὴν ἑτάρων (for their death) ψ 312.—(c) To exact the penalty for: βίας γ 216, λ 118, π 255, ρ 540.—(d) To exact a penalty from, chastise, punish ε 24 = ω 480, ν 386.

ἀποτίσεις, 2 sing. fut. ἀποτίνω.

ἀποτμήγω [ἀπο- (1) (3)]. 3 sing. aor. opt. ἀποτμήξειε (v.l. ἀπαμήσειε) Σ 34. Pple. ἀποτμήξας, -αντος Κ 364, Λ 468, Χ 456: κ 440. (1) To cut off κ 440.—(2) To cut off, isolate Λ 468.—To cut off *from*, keep away *from*. With genit.: πόλιος Χ 456. Cf. Κ 364.—(3) To cut, cut through, sever: λαιμόν Σ 34.—(4) To cut up, cut into channels: κλιτῦς Π 390.

ἄποτμος [ἀ-[1] + πότμος. 'Bereft of a (good) lot']. Hence, unlucky, ill-starred Ω 388.—Absol.: ἀ. τις υ 140.—Superl.: ἀποτμότατος α 219.

ἀποτρέπω [ἀπο- (1) (4)]. 2 sing. fut. ἀποτρέψεις Μ 249, Υ 256. 3 sing. aor. ἀπέτραπε Λ 758, Ο 276. 3 sing. aor. mid. ἀπετράπετο Κ 200, Μ 329. (1) To cause to turn away Ο 276, Υ 109, Φ 339.—To cause to turn away *from*, divert *from*. With genit.: ἀλκῆς Υ 256.—To dissuade *from*. With genit.: πολέμοιο Μ 249.—(2) To cause to turn back or return Λ 758.—(3) In mid. (a) To turn away, pay no heed: οὐκ ἀπετράπετο Μ 329.—(b) To turn back, with pple. indicating something from which one desists: ἀπετράπετ' ὀλλὺς Ἀργείους Κ 200.

†**ἀποτρίβω** [ἀπο- (7)]. 3 pl. fut. ἀποτρίψουσι. To wear out: πολλὰ σφέλα (*i.e.*, app., will break them) ρ 232.

ἀπότροπος [ἀποτρέπω]. Living apart as if in banishment: παρ' ὕεσσιν ἀ. ξ 372.

ἀποτρωπάω [ἀπο- (1)]. (1) To cause to turn away Υ 119.—To dissuade from a course proposed π 405.—(2) In mid., with genit., to turn away *from*, avoid: λεόντων Σ 585.—To turn away *from*, delay undertaking: τόξου τανυστύος φ 112.

ἀπούρας, aor. pple. ἀπαυράω.

ἀπουρήσουσι, 3 pl. fut. ἀπαυράω.

†**ἀπουρίζω** [ἀπ-, ἀπο- (7) + οὐρίζω, to bound, fr. οὖρον]. 3 pl. fut. ἀπουρίσσουσι (v.l. ἀπουρήσουσι; see ἀπαυράω). To fix the landmarks of, mark off: ἀρούρας Χ 489 (the subject ἄλλοι giving an idea of injustice).

†**ἀποφέρω** [ἀπο- (1) (4)]. 3 dual fut. ἀποίσετον Ε 257. Infin. ἀποίσειν Κ 337. 2 sing. aor. ἀπένεικας Ξ 255, Ο 28. 3 pl. -αν π 326, 360. (1) To carry away π 326 = 360.—(2) To cause to be carried away or to go: Κόωνδέ μιν Ξ 255 = Ο 28.—(3) To bring back Ε 257.—To bring back (word): μῦθον Κ 337.

ἀπόφημι [ἀπο- (7) + φημί]. Imp. pl. mid. ἀπόφασθε Ι 422, 649. (1) To speak out, declare one's mind plainly Η 362.—(2) To deliver (a message) plainly. In mid. Ι 422, 649.

ἀποφθινύθω [ἀπο- (7)]. To waste away, perish Ε 643, Π 540 (taking θυμόν as acc. of respect).

†**ἀποφθίω** [ἀπο- (7)]. 3 pl. aor. pass. ἀπέφθιθεν ε 110, 133, η 251. 3 sing. aor. ἀπέφθιτο θ 581, ο 268, 358. Opt. ἀποφθίμην κ 51. Imp. ἀποφθίσθω Θ 429. Pple. ἀποφθίμενος, -ου Γ 322, Σ 89, 499, Τ 322, 337: ο 357, ω 88. In pass., to perish, die Γ 322, Θ 429, Σ 89, 499, Τ 322, 337: ε 110 = 133 = η 251, θ 581, κ 51, ο 268, 357, 358, ω 88.

ἀποφώλιος, -ον [app. ἀπ-, ἀπο- (6) + ὀφολ-, ὄφελος. Thus, 'useless']. Hence (1) Not fitted for action ξ 212.—Producing no result, ineffectual λ 249.—(2) Of a man in regard to mental powers, not likely to secure good results, not sagacious θ 177.—Absol. in neut. pl.: οὐκ ἀποφώλια εἰδώς (sagacious in mind) ε 182.

ἀποχάζω [ἀπο- (1)]. In mid., to retire *from*. With genit.: βόθρου λ 95.

ἀποψύχω [in (1) ἀπο- (6), in (2) ἀπο- (7) (with, in (b), admixture of ἀπο- (1)) + ψύχω in sense 'to dry']. Aor. pple. pass. ἀποψυχθείς Φ 561. (1) To lack breath, faint ω 348.—(2) To dry. In pass. (a) To get or become dry: ἱδρῶ ἀποψυχθείς (acc. of respect) Φ 561. Cf. Χ 2.—(b) Sim., to get (the sweat) dried *off* (one's garments). With genit.: χιτώνων Λ 621.

ἀππέμψει, contr. 3 sing. fut. ἀποπέμπω.

ἄπρηκτος, -ον [ἀ-[1] + πρηκ-, πρήσσω]. (1) Not accomplishing one's object Ξ 221.—(2) Leading or conducing to no result, fruitless: πόλεμον B 121. Cf. B 376: β 79.—(3) Against which nothing can be done: ἀνίην μ 223.

ἀπριάτην [adv. fr. acc. fem. of *ἀπρίατος fr. ἀ-[1] + *πρίαμαι]. Without price or payment A 99: ξ 317.

ἀπροτίμαστος, -ον [ἀ-[1] + προτι- (= προσ- (3)) + μασ-, μαίομαι]. Untouched, undefiled T 263.

ἄπτερος [ἀ-[1] + πτερόν. 'Wingless']. Hence, that does not take to itself wings: τῇ δ' ἀ. ἔπλετο μῦθος (she heard in silence) ρ 57 = τ 29 = φ 386 = χ 398.

ἀπτήν, -ῆνος [ἀ-[1] + πτη-, πέτομαι]. Unfledged: ἀπτῆσι νεοσσοῖσιν I 323.

ἀπτοεπής [prob. (F)ι-(F)άπτω as in προϊάπτω + ἔπος]. Thus, thrower about of words, reckless in speech: Ἥρη ἀπτοεπές Θ 209.

ἀπτόλεμος [ἀ-[1]]. Unwarlike B 201, I 35, 41.

ἅπτω. Aor. pple. ἅψας φ 408. 3 sing. fut. mid. ἅψεται τ 344. Infin. ἅψεσθαι ι 379. 3 sing. aor. ἥψατο A 512, E 799, O 76, 704. ἅψατο Ψ 666. 3 dual ἀψάσθην K 377. Pple. ἀψάμενος, -ου K 455, Ψ 584, Ω 357, 508: ι 386. Fem. -η λ 278, τ 473. Infin. ἅψασθαι Φ 65: ζ 169, τ 348, χ 339. (ἀν-, ἐξ-, ἐφ-, καθ-, προτι-.) (1) To fasten φ 408.—In mid. λ 278.—(2) In mid. (a) To fasten oneself to; hence, to lay hold of, seize, clasp, touch. With genit.: ἥψατο γούνων A 512. Cf. B 152, 171, 358, E 799, Θ 339, K 377, 455, O 76, 704, Π 9, 577, Υ 468, Φ 65, Ψ 584, 666, Ω 357, 508, 712: σίτου δ 60. Cf. β 423, ζ 169, κ 379, ο 288, τ 28, 344, 348, 473, χ 339.—Without construction: κύνει ἁπτόμενος ἣν πατρίδα δ 522. Cf. ι 386.—(b) Of missile weapons (as if personified), to seize their object, work mischief: βέλε' ἥπτετο Θ 67 = Λ 85 = O 319 = Π 778. Cf. P 631.—(c) To catch fire ι 379.

ἀπύργωτος, -ον [ἀ-[1] + πυργόω]. Not fortified λ 264.

ἄπυρος [ἀ-[1] + πῦρ]. Not yet put on the fire, new: τρίποδας I 122 = 264, λέβητα Ψ 267, 885.

ἀπύρωτος, -ον [ἀ-[1] + πυρόω, to expose to fire, fr. πῦρ]. = prec.: φιάλην Ψ 270.

ἄπυστος, -ον [ἀ-[1] + πυσ-, πεύθομαι]. (1) Without knowledge δ 675, ε 127.—(2) Of whom no tidings come α 242.

†ἀπωθέω [ἀπ-, ἀπο- (1) (4)]. Fut. ἀπώσω ο 280. 3 sing. -ει A 97. Infin. -έμεν N 367. 3 sing. aor. ἀπέωσε ι 81. ἀπῶσε P 649, Ω 446. 3 pl. ἀπῶσαν Φ 537. 1 pl. subj. ἀπώσομεν Θ 96: χ 76. Infin. ἀπῶσαι β 130. **Mid.** 3 sing. aor. ἀπώσατο Ω 508: ν 276. 2 sing. subj. ἀπώσεαι α 270. 3 -εται Θ 533. Pple. ἀπωσάμενος, -ου M 276, Π 301, Σ 13. Infin. ἀπώσασθαι Θ 206, O 407, 503, Π 251: ι 305. (1) To drive or thrust back. In mid.: Τρῶας ἀπώσασθαι Θ 206. Cf. Θ 533, O 407.—To drive away, expel: ἐκ Τροίης N 367.—In mid. α 270.—To thrust back, ward or keep off. In mid.: νεῖκος M 276. Cf. Σ 13.—In reference to driving away or dispersing immaterial or impalpable things: λοιγόν A 97, ὀμίχλην P 649.—(2) With genit., to drive away *from*: γέροντος ἄγριον ἄνδρα Θ 96. Cf. χ 76.—To expel *from*: δόμων β 130.—To thrust away or debar *from*: νηός ο 280.—To thrust aside *from*. In mid.: θυράων λίθον ι 305.—To ward or keep off *from*. In mid.: κακὰ νηῶν O 503. Cf. Π 251, 301.—(3) In mid., to push away from oneself Ω 508.—(4) To drive out of one's course ι 81.—In mid. ν 276.—(5) To thrust back, unfasten: ὀχῆας Φ 537, Ω 446.

ἀπῴκισε, 3 sing. aor. ἀποικίζω.

ἀπώλεσα, aor. ἀπόλλυμι.

ἀπώλετο, 3 sing. aor. mid. ἀπόλλυμι.

ἀπώμοσα, aor. ἀπόμνυμι.

ἀπώσω, fut. ἀπωθέω.

ἄρ. See next.

ἄρα, ἄρ. Also in lighter (and enclitic) form **ῥα**. (1) Expressing consequence or sequence (a) ἄρα (ἄρ): ἔκλαγξαν δ' ἄρ' ὀϊστοί A 46, διὰ μὲν ἂρ ζωστῆρος ἐλήλατο Δ 135. Cf. A 68, 148, 292, 308, 465, etc.: οἱ δ' ἄρα πάντες θαύμαζον α 381. Cf. α 106, 319, 335, 428, β 2, etc.—(b) ῥα: καί ῥα καθέζετο A 360. Cf. A 569, B 1, 48, 211, etc.: βῆ ῥ' ἴμεν α 441. Cf. α 127, 333, β 148, 321, etc.—(2) Expressing explanation, indicating a reason or cause (gen. ἄρα, but sometimes ῥα): πάντες ἄρ' οἵ γ' ἔθελον πολεμίζειν H 169, νήπιος, οὐδ' ἄρ' ἔμελλε . . . M 113. Cf. Θ 163, 558, K 46, N 191, Π 203, Ψ 670, etc.: φῆ ῥ' ἀέκητι θεῶν φυγέειν δ 504, ὡς ἄρα πυκνοὶ ἔφυν ε 480. Cf. η 301, θ 58, ο 468, τ 442, etc.—So ἐπεὶ ἄρα E 686, I 316, etc.: α 231, ψ 258, etc.—ἐπεί ῥα Λ 498, Π 206, etc.: α 263, etc.—οὕνεκ' ἄρα H 140, etc.: θ 480, etc.—τοὕνεκ' ἄρα A 96: ν 194.—γάρ ῥα A 113, 236, Λ 74, P 403, etc.: γ 143, δ 366, ε 321, etc.—(3) Amplifying, adding a circumstance. (a) ἄρα: οὐδ' ἄρ' ἔμελλε . . . K 336, ὣς ἄρα . . . M 135. Cf. B 482, Z 323, I 666, Λ 65, Ξ 18, Υ 269, etc.: πὰρ δ' ἄρ' ἔην καὶ ἀοιδὸς ἀνήρ γ 267. Cf. κ 26, ξ 421, ο 374, σ 293, ψ 29, etc.—(b) ῥα: τόν ῥ' ἔβαλεν Δ 459, etc.: καί ῥ' οὐχ ὑλάοντο π 162, etc.—(4) Summing up or resuming. ἄρα: οὗτοι ἄρ' ἡγεμόνες ἦσαν B 760, τοὺς ἄρ' ὅ γ' ἕλεν Λ 304, etc.—Sim. in enumerations B 546, 584, 615, etc.—(5) Calling attention to something: ἀλλ' ἄρα καὶ τὸν ἀπάτησεν T 96, Ἀχιλεὺς δ' ἄρ' ἐπιρρήσσεσκε καὶ οἶος Ω 456.—(6) In relative sentences, sometimes giving a certain emphasis ('mark you!' 'note this!' or the like), sometimes not appreciably affecting the sense. (a) ἄρα: ἐπεὶ ἄρα . . . Z 426, ἣν ἄρα μοι γέρας ἔξελον Π 56. Cf. Θ 177, M 295, Ξ 444, Ψ 125, etc.: οἷσιν ἄρα Ζεὺς . . . π 422. Cf. τ 55, 62, etc.—(b) ῥα: ἃ ῥ' οὐ τελέεσθαι ἔμελλον B 36, ὅτε δή ῥα . . . Π 386. Cf. A 430, B 21, Γ 61, E 70, Λ 499, etc.: τόν ῥ' ἔκταν' Ὀρέστης α 30. Cf. α 126, β 9, δ 460, η 71, π 50, etc.—Sim. in a clause introduced by ὅ, ὅ τε, ὅττι, οὕνεκα or ὡς. (a) ἄρα: ὡς εἴδονθ' ὅ τ' ἄρα . . . Θ 251: μυθήσομαι ὡς ἄρα . . . θ 498, ἐκφάσθαι οὕνεκ' ἄρα . . . ν 309.—(b) ῥα: οὐδέ τι ᾔδη ὅττι ῥα . . . N 675, γνῶ ἔργα θεῶν, ὅ ῥα . . . Π 120, etc.: ὅττι ῥά οἱ τέρας ἧκεν φ 415, γνωτὸν ἦν ὅ ῥα

. . . ω 182, etc.—(7) In the first of two related clauses. (a) ἄρα : εἴτ' ἄρα . . . εἴτε . . . A 65, οὔτ' ἄρα . . . οὔτε . . . 93. Cf. A 115, E 333, M 53, O 72, Φ 62, Ψ 632, etc. : οἱ μὲν ἄρα . . . οἱ δὲ . . . α 110. Cf. δ 566, λ 535, ν 207, ξ 166, ψ 174, etc.—(b) ῥα : τοῦ μέν ῥ' ἀφάμαρτεν, ὁ δὲ . . . Θ 119, εἰ δή ῥ' ἐθέλεις . . . ἔστι . . . Ξ 337. Cf. Δ 15, Θ 487, Λ 442, O 53, etc. : οἱ μέν ῥ' εὔχοντο . . . ὁ δὲ . . . ν 185. Cf. δ 632, ζ 120, φ 398, etc. —In the second. (a) ἄρα : ὁ μὲν . . . ὁ δ' ἄρα . . . B 621, οὐδὲ . . . ἀλλ' ἄρα . . . Z 418, οὔτε . . . οὔτ' ἄρα . . . Υ 8, etc. : ἄλλοι μὲν . . . τὸν δ' ἄρα . . . ε 111, οὔ πω . . . ἀλλ' ἔτ' ἄρα . . . χ 237, etc.— (β) ῥα Λ 419, Σ 163 : υ 16.—In both ἄρα : οὔτ' ἄρ νῦν . . . οὔτ' ἄρ' ὀπίσσω Z 352. Cf. E 89, Υ 205, Ω 337.—In the second of three θ 168.—In the third λ 124.—(8) In questions, direct or indirect. (a) ἄρα : ἦ ἄρα δή τις . . . ; Σ 429. Cf. T 56, etc. : φράσαι ἤ τις ἄρ' ἐστὶ . . . ἦ . . . χ 158. Cf. σ 357, etc.—(b) ῥα : ἦ ῥά νύ μοί τι πίθοιο ; Ξ 190. Cf. H 446, etc. : ἦ ῥά κ' ἄμ' ἡμῖν ἕποιο ; ο 431. Cf. π 462, etc.—So τ' ἄρα (τε ἄρα) and τ' ἄρ (τε ἄρ) (written also ταρ (enclitic)) A 8, B 761, Γ 226, Λ 656, M 409, N 307, Σ 6, 188, etc. : α 346, ν 417, ψ 264, etc.

ἀραβέω [ἄραβος]. (ἀμφ-.) To rattle, ring : τεύχεα Δ 504 = E 42 = 540 = N 187 = P 50 = 311, E 58, 294 = Θ 260 : ω 525.

ἄραβος, ὁ. A chattering (of the teeth) K 375.

ἀραιός, -ή, -όν (has app. lost an initial consonant). App., slender, slight, narrow : χεῖρα E 425, γλώσσῃσιν Π 161, κνῆμαι Σ 411 = Υ 37 : εἴσοδος κ 90.

ἀράξω, fut. ἀράσσω.

ἀράομαι [ἀρή¹]. 2 sing. aor. subj. ἀρήσῃ N 818. Non-thematic pres. infin. in act. form ἀρήμεναι χ 322. (κατ-.) (1) To pray. With dat. : μητρὶ ἠρήσατο A 351. Cf. A 35, Z 115, I 172, P 568, etc. : δ 761, ζ 323, μ 337, ν 355.—Absol. Γ 318, E 114, etc. : γ 62, 64, η 1.—With complementary infin. : φανήμεναι 'Ηῶ I 240. Cf. Δ 143, N 286, Ψ 209 : α 164, 366 = σ 213, δ 827, τ 533, χ 322.—With dat. and infin. N 818 : σ 176.—With dependent clause : ἧος ἵκοιο γῆρας τ 367.—(2) To invoke : ἐρινῦς β 135.—(3) To vow. With infin. : κόμην σοι κερέειν Ψ 144.—Absol. Ψ 149.

†ἀραρίσκω. (A) *Trans.* 3 sing. impf. ἀράρισκε ξ 23. 3 sing. aor. ἄρσε φ 45. Imp. ἄρσον β 289, 353. Pple. ἄρσας, -αντος A 136 : α 280. 3 sing. aor. ἤραρε Δ 110, Ψ 712 : ε 95, ξ 111. 3 pl. ἄραρον M 105. 3 sing. subj. ἀράρῃ Π 212. Pple. ἀραρών, -όντος ε 252, π 169. 3 pl. aor. pass. ἄρθεν Π 211. (B) *Intrans.* 3 sing. aor. ἤραρε δ 777. 3 pl. ἄραρον Π 214. 3 sing. pf. subj. ἀρήρῃ ε 361. Pple. ἀρηρώς, -ότος Δ 134, 213, Λ 31, N 800, O 530, 618, Ω 269 : β 342, η 45, κ 553. Fem. ἀραρυῖα, -ης Γ 331, E 744, M 134, O 737, etc. : β 344, ζ 70, 267, σ 294, 378, φ 236, 382, χ 102, 128, 155, 258, 275, ψ 42, 194. 3 sing. plupf. ἠρήρει M 56. ἀρήρει Γ 338, K 265, Π 139 : ρ 4. Aor. pple. mid. ἄρμενος, -ου Σ 600 : ε 234, 254. (ἐν-, ἐπ-, προσ-.) (I) *Trans.* (1) To fit together : κέρα Δ 110, ἀμείβοντας Ψ 712.—To fit (each other) together : ἀλλήλους βόεσσιν (with their shields, *i.e.* stood side by side with shields touching) M 105.—To fit into place : ἐν σταθμοὺς ἄρσεν φ 45.—(2) To put together, construct : τοῖχον Π 212.—(3) To fit, supply or provide (with something) : ἴκρια σταμίνεσσιν ε 252. Cf. α 280, ε 95 = ξ 111.—(4) To make fitting or suitable : γέρας A 136.—To make so as to fit : πέδιλα ξ 23.—(5) To put up for carriage (in something) : ἄγγεσιν ἅπαντα β 289.—To make tight for carriage (with something) : ἀμφιφορῆας πώμασιν β 353.—(6) To contrive, scheme to bring about : θάνατον π 169.—(7) In pass., to be formed into close array : στίχες ἄρθεν Π 211.— (II) *Intrans.* (1) To be fitted : μέσσῃ δ' ἐνὶ πῖλος ἀρήρει K 265.—To be fitted (on to something) : σανίδες ἐπὶ πύλῃσιν ἀραρυῖαι Σ 275. Cf. ε 254.— (2) To be put together or constructed : πύλας εὖ ἀραρυίας H 339, 438. Cf. I 475, M 454, Φ 535 : β 344, φ 236 = 382, χ 128, 155, 258 = 275, ψ 42, 194.—(3) To be a product of art, to be the result of applied skill : ζωστῆρι ἀρηρότι Δ 134. Cf. Δ 213, T 396.—(4) To be fitted, supplied, or provided (with something) : κνημῖδας ἐπισφυρίοις ἀραρυίας Γ 331 = Λ 18 = Π 132 = T 370, Σ 459. Cf. E 744 (ornamented with representations), Λ 31, M 56, 134, N 407, Ξ 181, O 530, 737, Ω 269, 318 : ἀπήνην ὑπερτερίῃ ἀραρυῖαν ζ 70. Cf. ζ 267 (prob., surrounded by a wall of the stones), η 45, σ 294.— (5) To be fitted closely or exactly, to be exactly adjusted (to something) : ἔγχος παλάμηφιν ἀρήρει Γ 338, κόρυθα κροτάφοις ἀραρυῖαν N 188. Cf. Π 139, Σ 600, 611 : πέλεκυν ἄρμενον ἐν παλάμῃσιν ε 234. Cf. ρ 4, σ 378, χ 102.—(6) To be pleasing : μῦθον ὃ ἤραρεν ἡμῖν δ 777.—(7) To be closely ranged together : πυργηδὸν ἀρηρότες O 618. Cf. N 800, Π 214 : πίθοι ποτὶ τοῖχον ἀρηρότες β 342.—(8) To remain in position ε 361.—(9) To be well-balanced (in mind) : φρεσὶν ἀρηρώς κ 553.

ἀράσσω. Fut. ἀράξω Ψ 673. 3 sing. aor. ἄραξε M 384, N 577, Π 324 : ι 498, μ 412, 422. 3 sing. aor. pass. ἀράχθη ε 426. (ἀπ-.) (1) To strike so as to break, shiver or smash : τρυφάλειαν N 577. Cf. M 384, Π 324, Ψ 673 : σύν κ' ὀστέ' ἀράχθη (would have had his bones smashed) ε 426. Cf. ι 498, μ 412, 422.—(2) To put together or construct by hammering : σχεδίην ε 248.

ἀράχνιον, τό [ἀράχνης, a spider]. A spider's web : εὐνῇ ἀράχνι' ἔχουσα π 35. Cf. θ 280.

ἀργαλέος, -η, -ον. (1) Hard to endure, painful, grievous, burdensome, toilsome Δ 471, K 521, Λ 278, 812, N 85, 667, 669, Ξ 87, 105, O 10, Π 109, 528, P 385, 544, 667, T 214, Φ 386, X 61 : β 199, δ 393, 483, λ 101, 293, μ 161, ο 232, 444, ω 531.— (2) Grievous or disastrous in results, baleful : χόλου K 107, χόλος Σ 119.—In comp. : ἀργαλεώτερος χόλος O 121. Cf. δ 698.—Ill-omened, presaging disaster : ἔπος φ 169.—Baneful, destructive, working disaster : Ἔριδα Λ 4.—Of Scylla μ 119.—Of winds, blowing with violence N 795, Ξ 254 : λ 400 = 407, ω 110.—Difficult to traverse : λαῖτμα θαλάσσης ε 175.—Hard to force : στόμα λαύρης χ 137.—Of a wave, dashing or breaking with violence ε 367.—

Hard to manage: βόας λ 291.—(3) In neut. ἀργαλέον, with or without copula, it is hard or difficult. With infin.: ῥῦσθαι Ο 140. Cf. Υ 368, Φ 498 : η 241.—With dat. and infin.: ἀ. μοί ἐστι θέσθαι κέλευθον Μ 410. Cf. Ρ 252, Υ 356, Ψ 791 : ν 312.—With acc. and infin.: ἀ. με ταῦτ' ἀγορεῦσαι Μ 176. Cf. π 88, τ 221.—App. rather in sense 'oppressive,' 'unfair.' With infin.: ἀ. ἀνδράσι καὶ πλεόνεσσι μαχήσασθαι (*i.e.* to have to fight with them) β 244.—Sim. with acc. and infin.: ἀ. ἕνα προικὸς χαρίσασθαι (hard, too much) ν 15.—(4) In personal construction. With infin.: ἀργαλέος Ὀλύμπιος ἀντιφέρεσθαι (is hard to set oneself against) Α 589. Cf. Μ 63 : δ 397.

ἀργεϊφόντης, ἀργειφόντης [poss. ἀργός + φαίνω]. Thus, swift appearing, the swift appearer. Epithet or a name of Hermes Β 103, Π 181, Φ 497, Ω 24, 109, 153, 182, 339, 345, 378 = 389 = 410 = 432, 445 : α 38, 84, ε 43, 49, 75, 94, 145, 148, η 137, θ 338, κ 302, 331, ω 99.

ἀργεννός, -ή, -όν [ἀργός]. White: ὀθόνῃσιν Γ 141, οἰῶν 198, Σ 529, 588, ὀΐεσσιν Ζ 424 : ρ 472.

ἀργεστής, -ᾱο [ἀργός]. App., bringing white clouds: Νότοιο Λ 306, Φ 334.

ἀργής, -ῆτος. Also -έτος Λ 818, Φ 127 [ἀργός]. (1) White: ἑανῷ Γ 419. Cf. Λ 818, Φ 127.—(2) Bright, glancing, vivid: κεραυνόν Θ 133. Cf. ε 128, 131, η 249, μ 387.

ἀργικέραυνος [ἀργός + κεραυνός]. (Wielder, the wielder) of the bright thunderbolt. Epithet or a name of Zeus Τ 121, Υ 16, Χ 178.

ἀργινόεις, -εντος [ἀργός]. White. Epithet of cities (app. from white cliffs) Β 647, 656.

ἀργιόδους, -όδοντος [ἀργός + ὀδούς]. Having white teeth or tusks: κύνας Λ 292. Cf. Ι 539, Κ 264, Ψ 32 : ὕας θ 60. Cf. θ 476, λ 413, ξ 416, 423, 438, 532.

ἀργίπους, -ποδος [ἀργός + πούς]. Swift-footed: κύνας Ω 211.

ἄργμα, -ατος [ἄρχω]. In pl., firstling pieces, portions of food offered to the gods before a meal ξ 446.

ἀργός, -ή, -όν. (1) White, bright. Of oxen, app., glistening, sleek Ψ 30.—So of a goose ο 161.—(2) The notion of brightness or gleam passing into that of rapid movement (cf. αἰόλος (2)). Of dogs, swift Α 50, Σ 283 : ρ 62 = υ 145.—Sim.: κύνες πόδας ἀργοί (swift-footed) Σ 578 : β 11.

ἀργύρεος, -η, -ον [ἄργυρος]. (1) Of silver, silver Α 49, 219, Γ 331 = Λ 18 = Π 132 = Τ 370, Ε 729, Ι 187, Λ 31, Σ 413, 563, 598, Ψ 741, Ω 605 : α 137 = δ 53 = η 173 = κ 369 = ο 136 = ρ 92, α 442, δ 125, 128, 132, 615 = ο 115, η 89, 90, 91, θ 404, κ 24 (made of strands of silver wire), 355, 357, ο 104, 123.—(2) Studded or ornamented with silver: τελαμών Λ 38. Cf. Ε 727, Σ 480.

ἀργυροδίνης [ἄργυρος + δίνη]. Silver-eddying, clear. Of the Peneus Β 753 (here app. merely conventionally, as the Peneus is (and presumably always has been) a turbid river).—Of the Xanthus (Scamander) Φ 8, 130.

ἀργυρόηλος [ἄργυρος + ἧλος]. Studded with silver nails: ξίφος (*i.e.* having the handle thus ornamented) Β 45 = Γ 334 = Π 135 = Τ 372, Γ 361 = Ν 610, Η 303, θρόνου Σ 389. Cf. Ξ 405, Ψ 807 : η 162, θ 65, 406, 416, κ 261, 314 = 366, λ 97, χ 341.

ἀργυρόπεζα [ἄργυρος + πέζα]. Silver-footed. Epithet of Thetis Α 538 = 556, Ι 410, Π 222, 574, Σ 127 = Τ 28, Σ 146, 369, 381, Ω 89, 120 : ω 92.

ἄργυρος, -ου, ὁ [ἀργός. 'The white metal']. Silver Β 857, Ε 726, Κ 438, Λ 237, Ρ 52, Σ 475 : δ 73, ζ 232 = ψ 159, κ 35, 45, τ 56, ψ 200.

ἀργυρότοξος [ἄργυρος + τόξον]. (Lord, the lord) of the silver bow. Epithet or a name of Apollo Α 37 = 451, Β 766, Ε 449, 517, 760, Η 58, Κ 515, Φ 229, Ω 56, 758 : η 64, ο 410, ρ 251.

ἀργύφεος [ἀργός]. (1) White: φᾶρος ε 230 = κ 543.—(2) Bright: σπέος Σ 50.

ἄργυφος [ἀργός]. White: ὄϊν Ω 621 : μῆλα κ 85.

ἀρδμός, -οῦ, ὁ [ἄρδω, to water (cattle)]. A watering-place Σ 521 : ν 247.

ἀρειή, -ῆς, ἡ [app. fr. ἀρή[2]]. Reviling, threats Ρ 431, Υ 109, Φ 339.

ἀρείων, -ονος. Neut. ἄρειον [ἀρε-ίων, comp. fr. ἀρε-, ἀρετή. Cf. ἄριστος]. Acc. sing. masc. ἀρείω Κ 237 : γ 250. Nom. pl. masc. ἀρείους Π 557 : β 277, ι 48. Dat. pl. masc. ἀρείοσι Α 260. (1) Better, worthier, more warlike Α 260, Β 707, Κ 237, Π 557, Φ 410, Ψ 588 : β 277, γ 250, ι 48, τ 184, υ 133.—(2) Stronger: τεῖχος Δ 407 (*i.e.* stronger than our fathers found), Ο 736 (*i.e.* stronger than this).—(3) In better condition: χρώς Τ 33.—(4) Better, the better course: τόδ' ἀμφοτέροισιν Τ 56.—Absol. in neut., anything better or more excellent: οὐ τοῦ γ' ἀ. [ἐστιν] ζ 182.—(5) App., good rather than the reverse: γῆρας ψ 286.—(6) In neut. as adv., better: φράσεται καὶ ἀ. (more clearly) ψ 114.

ἄρεκτος [ἀ-[1] + ῥεκ-, ῥέζω]. Undone, still to do: ἔτι μέγα ἔργον ἄρεκτον Τ 150.

ἀρέσθαι, aor. infin. ἄρνυμαι.

†ἀρέσκω. Aor. infin. ἀρέσαι Ι 120, Τ 138. Fut. mid. ἀρέσσομαι θ 402. 1 pl. -όμεθα Δ 362, Ζ 526. 3 aor. imp. ἀρεσάσθω Τ 179. ἀρεσσάσθω θ 396. Pple. ἀρεσσάμενος, -ου Ι 112 : θ 415, χ 55. (ἀπ-.) (1) To make atonement, effect reconciliation Ι 120 = Τ 138.—(2) In mid. (a) To conciliate, make matters up with Ι 112, Τ 179 : θ 396, 402.—Absol. θ 415.—(b) To make atonement for, make up for: ταῦτα Δ 362, τά Ζ 526.—To make up to a person for a loss by levying a contribution χ 55.

ἀρετάω [ἀρετή]. To thrive, prosper: οὐκ ἀρετᾷ κακὰ ἔργα θ 329, ἀρετῶσι λαοί τ 114.

ἀρετή, -ῆς, ἡ. (1) Manliness, valour, prowess: ἣν ἀρετὴν διαείσεται Θ 535, συμφερτὴ ἀ. πέλει Ν 237 (brought together it becomes prowess, *i.e.* union makes prowess (συμφερτή assimilated in gender to ἀ. the predicate; cf. Λ 801 under ἀνάπνευσις)). Cf. Λ 90, 763, Ν 275, 277, Ξ 118, Υ 242, Χ 268 : μ 211, ω 515.—In pl., manly or warlike qualities: ἀμείνων παντοίας ἀρετάς (in all . . .) Ο 642.—(2) Of horses, excellence in the race Ψ 276, 374.—(3) Good, creditable, serviceable qualities or character: ἠγαγόμην γυναῖκα εἵνεκ' ἐμῆς ἀρετῆς ξ 212. Cf. β 206, δ 629 = φ 187, ρ 322, σ 205, χ 244, ω 193, 197.—Sim. in pl.: παντοίῃς ἀρετῇσι κεκασμένον δ 725 = 815.—Reputation for such qualities or character: ἐϋκλείη τ' ἀ. τε ξ 402.—(4) Skill in manly exercises or pursuits Ψ 571: θ 237, 239, 244.—So ποδῶν ἀρετήν (speed) Υ 411.—(5) Majesty, dignity, rank Ι 498, Ψ 578. —(6) Good, welfare, prosperity: θεοὶ ἀρετὴν ὀπάσειαν ν 45. Cf. σ 133, 251, τ 124.

ἄρετο, 3 sing. aor. ἄρνυμαι.

ἀρή[1], -ῆς, ἡ. (1) A prayer Ο 378, 598, Ψ 199: δ 767, ρ 496.—(2) An imprecation Ι 566.

ἀρή[2], -ῆς, ἡ. Genit. ἄρεω Σ 213. Bane, harm: ὅς τις ἀρὴν ἀμύναι Μ 334, ἀρῆς ἀλκτῆρα Ξ 485 (here one who saves the family from the disgrace of a kinsman slain without reparation exacted). Cf. Π 512, Σ 100, 213, Ω 489: β 59 = ρ 538, χ 208.

ἀρήγω. Fut. infin. ἀρηξέμεν Ν 9, Ξ 265. -ειν Α 77, Ε 833. Aor. infin. ἀρῆξαι Α 408. (ἐπ-.) To help, aid, succour. With dat.: μοι Α 77. Cf. Α 408, 521, Ε 507, 833, Θ 11, Λ 242, Μ 68, Ν 9, Ξ 192, 265, 391, Ο 42, 493, Π 701, Ρ 630, Υ 25.—With a form in -φιν: φρήτρηφιν Β 363.

ἀρηγών, -όνος [ἀρήγω]. A helper, aider Δ 7, Ε 511.

ἀρηΐθοος [Ἄρηϊ, dat. of Ἄρης + θοός]. Swift in the fight: αἰζηῶν Θ 298, Ο 315, Υ 167.

ἀρηϊκτάμενος [Ἄρηϊ (see prec.) + κτάμενος (see κτείνω)]. Slain in battle: νέῳ Χ 72.

ἀρήϊος [Ἄρης]. (1) Inspired by Ares, warlike, martial Β 698, Γ 339, Δ 114, Λ 501, Μ 102, etc.: γ 109, 167, ψ 220.—(2) Used in war, warlike: τεύχεα Ζ 340. Cf. Κ 407, Ξ 381: π 284, τ 4, ψ 368, ω 219.

ἀρηΐφατος [Ἄρηϊ, dat. of Ἄρης + φα-, φένω]. Slain in battle: φῶτας Τ 31, Ω 415: ἄνδρες λ 41.

ἀρηΐφιλος [Ἄρηϊ (see prec.) + φίλος]. Dear to, favoured by Ares Β 778, Γ 21, Δ 150, etc.: ο 169.

ἀρήμεναι, non-thematic pres. infin. ἀράομαι.

ἀρημένος [a pf. pple. pass. app. formed direct fr. ἀρή[2] (the α being retained against analogy). Cf. δεδουπότος, κεκοπώς, πεφυζότες]. Worn out, impaired, broken down Σ 435: ζ 2, λ 136 = ψ 283, σ 53, 81.—App., hurt, harmed ι 403.

ἀρήξειν, fut. infin. ἀρήγω.

ἀρήρει, 3 sing. plupf. ἀραρίσκω.

ἀρηρομένῃ, dat. fem. pf. pple. pass. ἀρόω.

ἀρηρώς, pf. pple. ἀραρίσκω.

Ἄρης [use of the proper name]. Genit. Ἄρηος. Dat. Ἄρηϊ, Ἄρῃ. Acc. Ἄρηα. (1) War, battle Β 381, 385, Γ 132, Ι 532, Ν 630, Τ 142, Φ 112, etc.: π 269, υ 50.—(2) Applied to wounds inflicted in war: ἔνθα μάλιστα γίγνετ' Ἀ. ἀλεγεινός Ν 569.

ἄρηται, 3 sing. aor. subj. ἄρνυμαι.

ἀρητήρ, -ῆρος, ὁ [ἀράομαι]. A priest Α 11, 94, Ε 78.

ἀρητός [ἀράομαι]. App., prayed against; hence, accursed: γόον Ρ 37 = Ω 741 (*v.l.* ἄρρητον).

ἀρθείς, contr. aor. pple. pass. ἀείρω.

ἄρθεν, 3 pl. aor. pass. ἀραρίσκω.

ἀρθμέω [ἀρθμός, friendship, alliance]. To form friendship or alliance Η 302.

ἄρθμιος [as prec.]. Joined in friendship or alliance: ἡμῖν (with us) π 427.

ἀρίγνωτος, -ον, and -η, -ον [ἀρι- + γνωτός]. (1) Easy to be known or recognized Ν 72, Ο 490: δ 207, ζ 108, 300, ρ 265.—(2) Notorious, infamous ρ 375.

ἀριδείκετος [ἀρι- + δείκνυμι]. Distinguished, renowned λ 540.—Conspicuous, exalted: ἀνδρῶν (among . . .) Λ 248. Cf. Ξ 320: θ 382 = 401 = ι 2 = λ 355 = 378 = ν 38.

ἀρίζηλος, -η, -ον [ἀρι- + *ζῆλος, phonetically = δῆλος]. (1) Very bright, conspicuous Ν 244, Χ 27. —Standing out clearly or distinctly in representation Σ 519.—Very plain, an evident sign: δράκοντ' ἀρίζηλον θῆκεν Β 318 (*v.l.* ἀΐζηλον).—(2) Of sound, very clear or distinct Σ 219, 221.

ἀριζήλως [adv. fr. prec.]. Clearly, plainly: ἀ. εἰρημένα μ 453.

ἀριθμέω [ἀριθμός]. (1) To number, count, reckon up Β 124: δ 411, ν 215, 218, π 235.—(2) To number off: δίχα πάντας ἑταίρους κ 204.

ἀριθμός, -οῦ, ὁ. Number, the number: λέκτο δ' ἀριθμόν δ 451. Cf. π 246.—In concrete sense: μετ' ἀνδρῶν ἀριθμῷ λ 449.

ἀριπρεπής, -ές [ἀρι- + πρέπω]. (1) Very bright, conspicuous: ἄστρα Θ 556. Cf. Ο 309: ι 22.—Standing out clearly, easy to be distinguished Ψ 453.—Bright, ornamented: χηλόν θ 424.—(2) Striking, distinguished: εἶδος θ 176.—Of persons, distinguished, conspicuous, renowned: Τρώεσσιν (among the . . .) Ζ 477. Cf. Ι 441: θ 390.

ἀριστερός. Locative ἀριστερόφιν Ν 309. (1) That is on the left side, the left . . .: ὦμον Ε 16, Π 106, 478. Cf. Ε 660, Λ 321.—The left hand . . .: ἵππος Ψ 338.—(2) ἐπ' ἀριστερά. (a) To the left: νωμῆσαι βῶν Η 238, εἶτ' ἐπ' ἀ. [ἴωσιν] (from right to left of a spectator, *i.e.* in the unlucky direction) Μ 240.—To the left of. With genit.: νηῶν Μ 118. Cf. Ν 326, Ψ 336.—(b) On the left: θωρήσσοντο Β 526, λαὸν ἐέργων Μ 201 = 219 (the bird having its left to the line and passing along from the line's right to its left): Ψυρίην ἔχοντες γ 171.—Sim.: ἐπ' ἀ. χειρός ε 277.—On the left of. With genit.: μάχης Ε 355, Λ 498, Ν 765, Ρ 116 = 682, νηῶν Ν 675.—With locative: ἐπ' ἀριστερόφιν [παντὸς στρατοῦ] Ν 309.—(3) Of a bird of omen, passing as in Μ 240 above, boding ill υ 242.

ἀριστεύς, -ῆος [ἄριστος]. (1) Pre-eminent, leading, of the first rank Β 404. Cf. Γ 44, Ο 489, Ρ 203, Τ 193: ξ 218, φ 333, ω 460.—(2) Absol. in pl., the most conspicuous or distinguished, the leaders, the leading men Α 227, Ε 206, Η 73, 159, 184, 227, 327, 385 = Ψ 236, Ι 334, 396, 421, Κ 1, 117, Ο 303, Ρ 245: ζ 34, λ 227, ο 28, φ 153, 170, ω 86.

ἀριστεύω [ἀριστεύς]. 3 sing. pa. iterative ἀριστεύεσκε Ζ 460, Λ 627, 746, Π 292, 551, Ρ 351. (1) To be best, excel, take the lead Ζ 208 = Λ 784, Λ 409: δ 652.—With complementary infin.: μάχεσθαι Ζ 460, Λ 746, Π 292, 551, Ρ 351.—(2) To excel (others in something). With genit. and dat.: βουλῇ ἁπάντων Λ 627.—(3) To perform feats, do deeds of valour Η 90, Λ 506, Ο 460.

ἄριστον, τό [prob. ἀϜερ-ιστον. Cf. ἠ(Ϝ)έριος. 'The early meal']. The first meal of the day Ω 124 : π 2.

ἄριστος, -η, -ον [superl. fr. ἀρ-, ἀρετή. Cf. ἀρείων]. Crasis with ὁ gives ὤριστος Λ 288, Ν 154, 433, Π 521, Ρ 689, Τ 413, Ψ 536, Ω 384 : ρ 416. (1) The most warlike or soldierly Β 577, 817, Ζ 188, Θ 229 : δ 530, λ 500.—Absol. ω 507.—(2) The best, the best fitted to take the lead in war or peace, pre-eminent: ἀ. Ἀχαιῶν Α 91. Cf. Β 768, Ε 541, Η 50, Λ 328 (in their local community), Σ 230, Ω 255, etc. : β 51, γ 108, δ 629 = φ 187, ζ 257, ο 521, π 251, χ 29, 244, ψ 121, ω 38, 108.—Absol. (in pl., pre-eminent or leading men, chiefs): ἄριστον Ἀχαιῶν Α 244, πάντας ἀρίστους Γ 19. Cf. Γ 250, Δ 260, Ε 103, Ν 836, etc. : α 211, 245 = π 122 = τ 130, δ 272, 278, θ 78, 91, 108, 127, 512, λ 524, ρ 416, ω 429.—(3) The strongest or most powerful: κάρτεΐ τε σθένεΐ τε ἀ. Ο 108. Cf. Μ 447, Ψ 891 : γ 370.—(4) The highest in rank, dignity or power. Absol.: θεῶν ὤριστος Ν 154. Cf. Ξ 213, Σ 364, Τ 258, 413, Υ 122, Ψ 43 : ν 142, τ 303.—(5) In reference to mental powers, excelling all Τ 95.—Excelling in person or accomplishments: κούρας Ι 638.—In reference to one's person, best, excelling: εἶδος ἀρίστη (in . . .) Β 715. Cf. Γ 39 = Ν 769, Γ 124, Ζ 252, Ν 365, 378, Ρ 142 : η 57, θ 116, λ 469 = ω 17.—(6) Likely to prove the most suitable husband, the best match λ 179, π 76, σ 289, υ 335, etc.—(7) The most suitable for some purpose: φῶτας δ 778, χῶρος ε 442, η 281. Cf. δ 409, θ 36, ι 195, ο 25.—Absol. δ 666.—(8) The most skilful, versed or efficient: τέκτονες Ζ 314, βουλῇ (in . . . .) Ι 54. Cf. Ι 575, Ν 313, Χ 254, Ψ 357, 536, 659 = 802, Ψ 669 : νηυσίν (in the management of . . .) θ 247. Cf. δ 211, θ 250, 383, ν 297, ο 253, π 419.—Absol. Α 69, Ζ 76, Η 221, Ψ 483, Ω 261.—With complementary infin.: μάχεσθαί τε φρονέειν τε Ζ 78. Cf. η 327, θ 123.—(9) Of things or abstractions, the best of their kind, the most excellent, useful or helpful: βουλή Β 5 = Κ 17 = Ξ 161, Η 325 = Ι 94. Cf. Β 274, Ι 74, Μ 243, 344 = 357, Ξ 371, Ο 616, Ρ 634, 712 : νηῦς α 280, β 294, π 348. Cf. η 327, θ 424, ι 318 = 424 = λ 230, ψ 124, ω 52.—(10) Of animals, the best, the finest, swiftest, etc. Β 763, Κ 306, Ρ 62 : κ 522 = λ 30, ξ 106, σ 371, υ 163, ω 215.—Absol. Ε 266 : ι 432, μ 343, 353, 398, ξ 19, 108, 414.—(11) In neut. ἄριστον as adv., best, the best: δοκέει μοι εἶναι ἀ. ε 360.—So in neut. pl. ἄριστα: ὥς μοι δοκεῖ εἶναι ἀ. Ι 103 = 314 = Ν 735, Μ 215 : ψ 130. Cf. ν 154.—(12) In neut. pl., the best results or consequences: ὅπως ἀ. γένηται Γ 110. Cf. γ 129, ι 420, ν 365, ψ 117.—The most seemly or decent things Ζ 56.

ἀρισφαλής [ἀρι- + σφάλλω. 'Causing much stumbling']. Rough, uneven: οὐδόν ρ 196.

ἀριφραδής, -ές [ἀρι- + φραδ-, φράζομαι]. (1) Easy to be distinguished, clear, manifest: σῆμα Ψ 326 : = λ 126, φ 217, ψ 73, 273, ω 329, σήματα ψ 225.—(2) Easy to be separated or picked out from others: ὀστέα Ψ 240.

ἀρκέω. 3 sing. fut. ἀρκέσει Φ 131 : π 261. 3 sing. aor. ἤρκεσε Ζ 16, Ν 371, 397, Ο 529, 534, Υ 289 : δ 292. (ἐπ-.) (1) To ward off, keep off Ο 534.—With dat. of person protected: ὄλεθρόν οἱ Ζ 16. Cf. Υ 289 : δ 292.—Sim.: ἀπὸ χροὸς οἱ ὄλεθρον Ν 440.—(2) With dat., to defend, protect: θώρηξ οἱ Ο 529. Cf. Φ 131.—Without case Ν 371, 397.—(3) To suffice: ἥ κεν νῶϊν Ἀθήνη ἀρκέσει π 261.

ἄρκιος [ἀρκέω in sense (3)]. (1) Sufficient, ample; or perh., on which one may rely, certain, sure: μισθός Κ 304 : σ 358.—(2) In neut. ἄρκιον with infin., expressing certainty that something must happen: ἀ. ἢ ἀπολέσθαι ἠὲ . . . (it must now be settled whether we are to . . . or to . . .) Ο 502.—So οὔ οἱ ἀ. ἐσσεῖται φυγέειν (he will not be able to rely on escaping, *i.e.* he certainly will not escape) Β 393.

ἄρκτος, -ου, ἡ. (1) A bear λ 611.—(2) The constellation the Great Bear (= ἄμαξα (2)) Σ 487 : = ε 273.

ἅρμα, -ατος, τό. (1) A chariot, whether used in war, for racing or for travel (hardly to be distinguished from δίφρος) Β 384, Ε 231, Λ 528, Σ 244, Φ 38, Ψ 304, etc. : δ 8.—(2) In pl. of a single chariot: ἑσταότ' ἐν ἅρμασιν Δ 366. Cf. Δ 226, Θ 115, 441, Κ 322, Ν 537, Ψ 286, Ω 14, etc. : γ 476, 478, 492 = ο 145 = 190, δ 42, ο 47, ρ 117.

ἁρματοπηγός [ἁρματ-, ἅρμα + πήγνυμι]. That makes chariots. With ἀνήρ, a chariot-maker Δ 485.

ἁρματροχιή, ἡ [ἅρμα + τροχ-, τρέχω]. The mark or furrow left by a chariot-wheel Ψ 505.

ἄρμενος, aor. pple. mid. ἀραρίσκω.

ἁρμόζω [ἀρ-, ἀραρίσκω]. 3 sing. aor. ἥρμοσε Γ 333, Ρ 210 : ε 247. (ἐφ-.) (1) To fit or adjust (to something): [δοῦρατ'] ἀλλήλοισιν ε 247.—(2) To put together, construct. In mid.: σχεδίην ε 162.—(3) To fit well, be well adapted (to something). With dat.: θώρηξ αὐτῷ Γ 333. Cf. Ρ 210.

ἁρμονίη, -ης, ἡ [ἀρ-, ἀραρίσκω]. (1) In pl. applied to the means of fastening together the logs composing the σχεδίη of Odysseus: γόμφοισι σχεδίην καὶ ἁρμονίῃσιν ἄρασσεν ε 248 (prob. (cf. πολύδεσμος) flexible bands or cords (not pressing the sense of ἄρασσεν)). Cf. ε 361.—(2) A covenant or agreement Χ 255.

ἄρνα, τόν, τήν (Ϝάρνα) [no nom. sing. occurs. Acc. of *Ϝρήν. Cf. πολύρρην]. (1) A lamb: ἀρνῶν πρωτογόνων Δ 102 = 120 = Ψ 864 = 873, ἄρνεσσιν ἢ ἐριφοισιν Π 352, ἄρν' ἀμαλήν Χ 310. Cf. Δ 435, Ω 262 : ἄρνες κεραοὶ τελέθουσιν δ 85. Cf. ι 220, 226, ρ 242, τ 398.—(2) A sheep, a ram or ewe: ἀρνῶν αἰγῶν τε Α 66. Cf. Γ 103, 117, 119, 246, 273, 292, 310, Δ 158, Θ 131, Χ 263.

ἀρνειός, -οῦ, ὁ [ἄρνα]. A full-grown ram Β 550, Γ 197 : α 25, ι 239, 432, 444, 463, 550, λ 131 = ψ 278.—Joined with ὄϊς κ 527, 572.

ἀρνέομαι. (1) To refuse, decline: γάμον α 249

=π 126, ω 126.—To refuse to accede to: τεὸν ἔπος Ξ 212: =θ 358.—Absol., to refuse, decline to accede Ξ 191, Τ 304, Ψ 42: θ 43.—(2) To refuse to give, withhold: τόξον φ 345.

ἀρνευτήρ, -ῆρος, ὁ. A diver Π 742, Μ 385: =μ 413.

ἄρνυμαι. Aor. ἀρόμην Ψ 592. 3 sing. -ετο Ι 188, Λ 625. 3 pl. -οντο Ι 124, 266, 269. 2 sing. subj. ἄρηαι Π 84. 3 sing. -ηται Μ 435, Ξ 130, 365. 2 pl. -ησθε Λ 290. Opt. ἀροίμην Σ 121. 2 sing. -οιο Δ 95, Ι 303. 3 sing. -οιτο Ε 3, Κ 307, Υ 247, Χ 207: ν 422. 1 pl. -οίμεθα Ε 273. Infin. ἀρέσθαι Η 203, Μ 407, Π 88, Ρ 16, 287, 419, Σ 294, Υ 502, Φ 297, 543, 596: α 390, χ 253. (1) To win, achieve, gain, receive, get: τιμήν Α 159, ἀέθλια Ι 124=266, 269, οὐχ ἱερήϊον οὐδὲ βοείην (were to gain, were contending for) Χ 160. Cf. Δ 95, Ε 3, 273, 553, Ζ 446, Η 203, Ι 188, 303, Κ 307, Λ 290, 625, Μ 407, 435, Ξ 365, Π 84, 88, Ρ 16, 287, 419, Σ 121, 294, Υ 502, Φ 297, 543, 596, Χ 207, Ψ 592: α 5, 390, ν 422, χ 253.—To get (a wound) Ξ 130.—(2) To be fitted to receive the weight of: [ὀνείδεα] ἄχθος (as lading) Υ 247.

ἄρξει, 3 sing. fut. ἄρχω.

ἀρόμην, aor. ἄρνυμαι.

ἄροσις, ἡ [ἀρόω]. Arable land Ι 580: ι 134.

ἀροτήρ, -ῆρος, ὁ [ἀρόω]. A ploughman Σ 542, Ψ 835.

ἄροτος, -ου, ὁ [ἀρόω]. A cornfield ι 122.

ἄροτρον, -ου, τό [ἀρόω]. A plough Κ 353, Ν 703: ν 32, σ 374.

ἄρουρα, -ης, ἡ [ἀρόω]. (1) Arable land Ζ 195, Μ 314, Υ 185.—(2) A field: πυρῶν Λ 68. Cf. Λ 558, Μ 422, Ν 707, Ξ 122, Σ 541, 544, Φ 405, Χ 489, Ψ 599: ἐδάσσατ' ἀρούρας ζ 10.—(3) Ground, space: ὀλίγη ἦν ἀμφὶς ἀ. Γ 115.—(4) In pl., the fields, the land: ὅτε χιὼν ἐπάλυνεν ἀρούρας Κ 7. Cf. Η 421: =τ 433.—(5) The earth, the soil: καρπὸν ἀρούρης Γ 246, Ζ 142, Φ 465. Cf. Β 548, Δ 174, Θ 486, Ι 141=283, Σ 104, Φ 232: γ 3=μ 386, δ 229, ε 463, η 332, ι 357, λ 309, ν 354, τ 593, υ 379.—(6) The land as opposed to the sea Υ 226.—(7) A particular country: πατρὶς ἀ. α 407, κ 29, υ 193. Cf. β 328, ψ 311.

†ἀρόω. 3 pl. ἀρόωσι ι 108. Dat. fem. pf. pple. pass. ἀρηρομένῃ Σ 548. (1) To plough (a field) Σ 548.—(2) To use the plough, plough ι 108.

ἁρπάζω. Fut. pple. ἁρπάξων Χ 310. 3 sing. aor. ἥρπασε Ν 528, Χ 276: ο 250. ἥρπαξε Μ 305: ο 174. 3 sing. subj. ἁρπάσῃ Ρ 62, Σ 319. Pple. ἁρπάξας, -αντος Γ 444, Μ 445, Ν 199, Π 814: ε 416. Fem. -ᾱσα κ 48. (ἀν-, ἀφ-, δι-, ἐξ-.) To snatch up or away Γ 444, Ε 556, Μ 305, 445, Ν 199, 528, Π 814, Ρ 62, Σ 319, Χ 276, 310: ε 416, κ 48, ο 174, 250.

ἁρπακτήρ, -ῆρος, ὁ [ἁρπακ-, ἁρπάζω]. One who snatches, a seizer or robber Ω 262.

ἁρπαλέος [ἁρπάζω]. Greedy: κερδέων θ 164 (with transference of epithet from gainer to gains).

ἁρπαλέως [adv. fr. prec.]. Voraciously, heartily: πῖνε καὶ ἦσθεν ζ 250. Cf. ξ 110.

ἁρπάξων, fut. pple. ἁρπάζω.

ἁρπάσῃ, 3 sing. aor. subj. ἁρπάζω.

ἅρπη, -ης, ἡ [ἁρπάζω. Prob. for ἀρέπη. Cf. ἀνηρείψαντο and next]. An unknown bird of prey Τ 350.

Ἅρπυια [prob. for Ἀρέπυια. Cf. prec.]. A personification of the storm-gust: Ἁ. Ποδάργη Π 150 (here represented as a semi-divine being in the form of a mare). Cf. α 241=ξ 371, υ 77.

ἄρρηκτος, -ον [ἀ-[1]+ῥηκ-, ῥήγνυμι]. (1) Not to be broken, broken through or severed Ν 37, 360, Ξ 56=68, Ο 20: θ 275, κ 4.—(2) Not to be broken into: πόλις Φ 447.—(3) Not to be dispersed: νεφέλην Υ 150.—(4) Of the voice, tireless (cf. ἀτειρής (2), χαλκεόφωνος) Β 490.

ἄρρητος [ἀ-[1]+ῥη-, εἴρω[2]]. (1) Unspoken: ἔπος ξ 466 —(2) Unspeakable: γόον Ρ 37=Ω 741 (v.l. ἀρητόν).

ἄρσε, 3 sing. aor. ἀραρίσκω.

ἄρσην, -ενος. Male Η 315, Θ 7, Μ 451, Υ 495, Ψ 377: ι 425, 438, ν 81, τ 420.—Absol. ι 238, ξ 16.

ἀρτεμής. Dat. pl. ἀρτεμέεσσι ν 43. Safe and sound: ζωόν τε καὶ ἀρτεμέα Ε 515=Η 308: φίλοισιν ν 43.

ἀρτιεπής [ἄρτιος+ἔπος]. Glib of tongue Χ 281.

ἄρτιος [ἀρ-, ἀραρίσκω]. Fitted, exact, suitable. Absol. in neut. pl.: ἄρτια βάζειν, to speak suitably Ξ 92: =θ 240.—ἀ. οἱ ᾔδη, his character suited him, was to his taste (see εἴδω (III) (12)) Ε 326: τ 248.

ἀρτίπος [ἄρτιος+πούς]. Sound of foot θ 310.—Swift of foot Ι 505.

ἀρτίφρων [ἄρτιος+φρήν]. Well balanced in mind, sensible ω 261.

ἄρτος, -ου, ὁ. A wheaten cake ρ 343, σ 120.

ἀρτύνω [ἀρ-, ἀραρίσκω]. 3 pl. fut. ἀρτῡνέουσι α 277, β 196. Aor. pple. ἀρτύνας, -αντος Μ 43, 86, Ν 152: ξ 469, ω 153. 3 pl. aor. mid. ἠρτύναντο δ 782, θ 53. 3 sing. aor. pass. ἀρτύνθη Λ 216. (1) To make ready, prepare: ἔεδνα α 277=β 196.—(2) To set in order, array: σφέας αὐτούς Μ 43, 86, Ν 152. Cf. Λ 216, Ο 303.—To get together, muster: λόχον ξ 469.—(3) To put in position. In mid.: ἐρετμά δ 782=θ 53.—(4) To plan, contrive: θάνατον ω 153.—To devise, invent, frame: ψεύδεα λ 366.—To put into words, put forward. In mid.: ἀρτύνετο βουλήν Β 55=Κ 302.

ἀρτύω [as prec.]. (ἐπ-.) (1) To fashion, form Σ 379.—(2) To make ready, prepare: γάμον δ 771.—(3) To plan, contrive: δόλον λ 439. Cf. γ 152, π 448, υ 242.

ἀρχέκακος, -ον [ἄρχω+κακός]. Giving rise to mischief Ε 63.

ἀρχεύω [ἀρχός]. To lead, command. With dat.: Ἀργείοισιν Β 345, Τρώεσσιν Ε 200.

ἀρχή, -ῆς, ἡ [ἄρχω]. (1) A beginning, a first phase: πήματος θ 81.—(2) A beginning, origin, first cause: κακοῦ Λ 604. Cf. Χ 116: φ 4, ω 169.—ἐξ ἀρχῆς, from of old α 188, β 254, λ 438, ρ 69.—(3) Something to serve as a basis or foundation: ξεινοσύνης φ 35.—(4) An unprovoked aggression Γ 100.

ἀρχός, -οῦ, ὁ [ἄρχω]. A leader, commander,

chief A 144, 311, B 234, Δ 205, E 39, N 196, etc.: δ 496, 629 = φ 187, δ 653, θ 162, 391, κ 204.

ἄρχω. 3 sing. fut. ἄρξει δ 667. Aor. ἄρξα ξ 230. 3 pl. subj. -ωσι Δ 67, 72. 3 sing. opt. -ειε γ 106. 3 pl. -ειαν Δ 335. Genit. pl. masc. pple. ἀρξάντων Φ 437. Fut. mid. ἄρξομαι I 97. 3 sing. aor. ἄρξατο ψ 310. Pple. ἀρξάμενος, -ου T 254: φ 142. (ἀπ-, ἐξ-, ἐπ-, κατ-, ὑπ-.) **(1)** In act. and mid. **(a)** To make a beginning or start, give a lead, set an example. With complementary infin.: ἀγορεύειν (began speech, opened debate) A 571, H 347, Σ 249, νέεσθαι (lead the way) B 84, δηλήσασθαι (take the initiative in . . ., be the first to . . .) Δ 67 = 72, ὑφαίνειν μῆτιν H 324 = I 93, ἴμεν N 329: ἀγορεύειν β 15, π 345 = σ 349 = υ 359, χ 461, νέκυας φορέειν χ 437.—So ἄρξει καὶ προτέρω κακὸν ἔμμεναι (will get the start of us and do us yet further mischief) δ 667.—With pple.: χαλεπαίνων B 378.—Sim. with genit.: μύθων (cf. ἀγορεύειν above) B 433, E 420, H 445, etc.: α 28, γ 68, ε 202, etc. πολέμοιο Δ 335, Υ 154. μάχης H 232, Υ 138. μύθοιο Λ 781. φόβοιο (set the example of flight) P 597. γόοιο Ω 723. μολπῆς (led the dance) ζ 101.—To make preparations for, get ready: θεοῖσι δαιτός O 95.—With cognate acc.: ὅττι κεν ἄρχῃ I 102.—Absol.: ἀρχέτω H 286, σέο ἄρξομαι (with thee) I 97. Cf. I 69, Φ 437, 439, Ψ 12: τοῦ χώρου (from the place) φ 142, ἄρξατο ὡς . . . (by telling how . . .) ψ 310. Cf. θ 90, 499, ψ 199.—**(b)** As a word of ritual, to cut off (hairs of the victim) as the first-fruits of the sacrifice (cf. ἀπάρχω, κατάρχω): κάπρου ἀπὸ τρίχας ἀρξάμενος T 254.—Sim.: ἀρχόμενος μελέων (cutting off pieces from the limbs as first-fruits) ξ 428.—**(2)** In act. **(a)** To be the leader, commander, or chief of. With genit.: Βοιωτῶν B 494. Cf. B 517, M 93, Π 173, etc.: κ 205, ν 266.—With dat.: οἷσί περ ἄρχει B 805. Cf. ξ 230.—Absol., to be ruler, hold sway ζ 12.—**(b)** To lead the way, act as leader, take the lead A 495, Γ 420, 447, E 592, I 657, Λ 472 = O 559 = Π 632, N 136 = O 306 = P 262, N 690, 784, Ξ 134, 384, Π 65, 552, P 107, Σ 516, T 248, Φ 391: β 416, γ 12, 106, ε 237 (local genit.), ξ 471, ψ 370, ω 9, 501.—With cognate acc.: αὐτὴν ὁδόν θ 107.

ἀρωγή, -ῆς, ἡ [ἀρήγω]. Help, aid, succour: Ζηνός Δ 408, τί μοι ἀρωγῆς; (quasi-partitive genit.; 'what have I to do with . . . ?') Φ 360, ἐπ' ἀρωγῇ (showing partisanship) Ψ 574.

ἀρωγός, -οῦ, ὁ, ἡ [as prec.]. A helper, aider Δ 235, Θ 205, Σ 502 (partisans), Φ 371, 428: σ 232.

ἆσαι, aor. infin. ἄω.

ἄσαμεν, contr. 1 pl. aor. ἰαύω.

ἀσάμινθος, -ου, ἡ. A bath K 576: = δ 48, γ 468, δ 128, θ 450, 456, κ 361, ρ 87, 90, ψ 163, ω 370.

ἄσασθαι, aor. infin. mid. ἄω.

ἄσατο, contr. 3 sing. aor. mid. ἀάζω.

ἄσβεστος, -ον and **-η, -ον** [ἀ-[1] + σβέννυμι]. **(1)** Inextinguishable, unquenchable: γέλως A 599, φλόξ Π 123. Cf. Λ 50, 500, 530, N 169 = 540, Π 267, P 89, X 96: θ 326, υ 346.—**(2)** Not to be forgotten: κλέος δ 584, η 333.

ἆσε, contr. 3 sing. aor. ἀάζω.

ἄσειν, fut. infin. ἄω.

ἀσήμαντος [ἀ-[1] + σημαν-, σημαίνω]. Without a leader; hence, without a shepherd: μήλοισιν K 485.

ἆσθμα, -ατος, τό [cf. ἄημι]. Difficulty in breathing, panting: ἀργαλέῳ O 10, Π 109, ἀ. παύετο O 241.

ἀσθμαίνω [ἆσθμα]. To gasp for breath, pant E 585, K 376, 496, N 399, Π 826, Φ 182.

ἀσινής [ἀ-[1] + σίνομαι]. Unharmed λ 110 = μ 137.

ἄσις, ἡ. App. = χέραδος Φ 321.

ἄσιτος, -ον [ἀ-[1] + σῖτος]. Not partaking of food δ 788.

ἀσκελέως [adv. fr. next]. Unrelentingly T 68.

ἀσκελής, -ές [app. ἀ-[2] + σκέλλω. Thus 'dried up,' and so (1) 'withered,' (2) 'rigid' (like dried wood)]. Hence **(1)** Worn-out, wearied κ 463.—**(2)** In neut. ἀσκελές as adv., unrelentingly: κεχόλωται α 68.—Unceasingly: μηκέτ' ἀ. κλαῖε δ 543.

ἀσκέω. 3 sing. impf. ἤσκειν (for ἤσκεεν) Γ 388. (ἐπ-.) **(1)** To work on, work up, prepare or fashion with art: εἴρια Γ 388. Cf. Δ 110, K 438, Ξ 179, 240, Σ 592, Ψ 743: ἑρμῖνα ψ 198. Cf. γ 438.—**(2)** App., to smooth, adjust: χιτῶνα α 439.

ἀσκηθής [app. ἀ-[1]. Second element unknown]. Unhurt, unharmed K 212, Π 247: ε 26 = 144, 168, ι 79, λ 535, ξ 255.

ἀσκητός [ἀσκέω]. Prepared or fashioned with art: νήματος δ 134, λέχει ψ 189.

ἄσκοπος [ἀ-[1] + σκοπός. 'Not aiming']. Acting on impulse without consideration Ω 157 = 186.

ἀσκός, -οῦ, ὁ. **(1)** A leathern bag κ 19, 45, 47.—**(2)** A wine-skin Γ 247: ε 265, ζ 78, ι 196, 212.

ἄσμενος, aor. pple. ἥδομαι.

ἀσπάζομαι. To welcome, greet: δεξιῇ K 542: χερσίν γ 35, τ 415, 'Οδυσῆα χ 498.

ἀσπαίρω. **(1)** To gasp or pant in the death-struggle Γ 293, K 521, M 203, N 571, 573: θ 526, μ 254, 255, τ 229.—**(2)** Of convulsive movements of the limbs: πόδεσσιν τ 231, χ 473.—Of the heart, to throb N 443.

ἄσπαρτος, -ον [ἀ-[1] + σπαρ-, σπείρω, to sow]. **(1)** Having no seed sown in it, unsown: νῆσος ι 123.—**(2)** Not growing from (sown) seed ι 109.

ἀσπάσιος, -ον and **-η, -ον** [ἀσπάζομαι]. **(1)** Welcomed, welcome, giving gladness: ἀ. γένετ' ἐλθών K 35. Cf. Θ 488: ε 394, 397, ι 466, λ 431, ψ 233.—**(2)** Glad, well pleased: ἦλθον προτὶ ἄστυ Φ 607. Cf. ψ 238, 296.

ἀσπασίως [adv. fr. prec.]. **(1)** Welcome, giving gladness ν 33.—**(2)** Gladly H 118, Λ 327, Σ 232, 270, T 72: δ 523, θ 450, κ 131, ν 333, ξ 502.

ἀσπαστός [as ἀσπάσιος]. **(1)** = ἀσπάσιος (1): ἀ. κε φανείη ψ 60. Cf. ψ 239.—In neut. in impersonal construction: ἀσπαστόν κ' ἐμοὶ γένοιτο τ 569. Cf. η 343, θ 295.—**(2)** In neut. ἀσπαστόν as adv. = ἀσπασίως (1): ὡς 'Οδυσῆ' ἀ. ἐείσατο γαῖα ε 398. Cf. ν 35.

ἄσπερμος, -ον [ἀ-[1] + σπέρμα]. Without issue Υ 303.

ἀσπερχής, -ές [app. for ἀνσπερχής, fr. ἀν- (= ἀνα-

(6)) + σπέρχω. Thus 'hastening,' 'pressing on']. In neut. ἀσπερχές as adv., without intermission or pause Δ 32, Π 61, Σ 556, Χ 10, 188 : α 20.

ἄσπετος, -ον [ἀ-[1] + σ(ε)π-. See ἐννέπω]. (**1**) Unspeakable ; hence, boundless or immense in extent, amount, number, volume, etc.: ὕλην Β 455, κῦδος Γ 373 = Σ 165. Cf. Θ 558 = Π 300, Κ 523, Λ 245, Ν 139, Π 157, Σ 218, 403, Τ 61, Ψ 127, Ω 738, 784 : ὕδωρ ε 101, δῶρα ν 135, υ 342. Cf. ι 162 = 557 = κ 184 = 468 = 477 = μ 30, ν 395, ξ 96, 297, 412, χ 269, 407.—Absol. ν 424.—(**2**) In neut. ἄσπετον as adv., to a great (and unjustifiable) extent : τρεῖτε Ρ 332.—(**3**) In neut. pl. as adv. strengthening πολλά Λ 704 : δ 75.

ἀσπιδιώτης [ἀσπιδ-, ἀσπίς]. Shield-bearing, warlike : ἀνέρας Β 554, Π 167.

ἀσπίς, -ίδος, ἡ. A shield Β 382, Γ 347, Δ 448, Ε 437, Ν 131, etc. : α 256, τ 32, χ 25.

ἀσπιστής [ἀσπίζω fr. prec.]. Shield-bearing, warlike Δ 90 = 201, 221 = Λ 412, Ε 577, Θ 155, 214, Ν 680, Π 490, 541, 593.

ἀσπουδί [ἀ-[1] + σπουδή]. Without a struggle : μὴ ἀ. νεῶν ἐπιβαῖεν Θ 512. Cf. Ο 476, Χ 304.

ἄσσα = τινά, acc. pl. neut. of τις : ὀπποῖ' ἄσσα εἵματα ἕστο τ 218 (see τις (3) (b)).

ἅσσα = ἅ τινα, acc. pl. neut. of ὅς τις. (**1**) = ὅς τις (1) : ἅσσ' ἔλαχον Ι 367. Cf. Υ 127 : ἅσσ' ἂν μηδοίμην ε 188. Cf. η 197, λ 74.— = ὅς τις (4) Κ 208 = 409.—(**2**) With subj. or opt. in relative conditional sentences. See Table at end (III) (B) (a) (1), (D) (56).

ἆσσον [comp. of ἄγχι]. (**1**) Near (rather than far off), to within a short distance : φέρον ι 380, πάντ' ἐφόρει ν 368.—Near to, close to. With genit. : ἐμεῖο (into my presence) Ω 74 : ἔθεν τ 481.—(**2**) With εἶμι, etc., to approach, draw near : ἀ. ἴτε Α 335. Cf. Ζ 143 = Υ 429, Ι 508, Ψ 8, 667 : ι 300, τ 392.—To approach, draw near to. With genit.: Ζηνὸς οὐκ ἂν ἀ. ἱκοίμην Ξ 247. Cf. Χ 4 : κ 537 = λ 50 = 89, 148, ρ 303, ω 221.—So of something inanimate, to be brought near to : λοετρὰ καρήατος ἀ. ἱκέσθαι Ψ 44.—With dat. : ἀ. μοι στῆθι Ψ 97.—In hostile sense, to attack, make an attack : μίμν' ἀ. ἰόντα Χ 92. Cf. Α 567, Ο 105.

ἀσσοτέρω [double comp. of ἄγχι. Cf. prec.]. = prec. (1) ρ 572.—With genit. : πυρὸς τ 506.

ἄσταχυς = στάχυς Β 148.

ἀστεμφέως [adv. fr. next]. So as to prevent movement, fast, firmly : ἐχέμεν δ 419. Cf. δ 459.

ἀστεμφής, -ές [ἀ-[1] + στεμφ- as in στέμφυλον, squeezed olives. 'Not to be squeezed']. Fixed, immovable, not moving Γ 219.—Fig. : βουλήν Β 344.

ἀστερόεις, -εντος [ἀστήρ]. (**1**) Starry. Epithet of οὐρανός Δ 44, Ε 769 = Θ 46, Ζ 108, Ο 371, Τ 128, 130 : ι 527, λ 17, μ 380, υ 113.—(**2**) App., adorned with star-like ornaments (or perh., shining with star-like radiance) : θώρηκα Π 134, δόμον Σ 370.

ἀστεροπή, -ῆς, ἡ [= στεροπή]. Lightning, the lightning flash Λ 184, Ν 242, Ξ 386.

ἀστεροπητής [ἀστεροπή]. The lightener. Epithet of Zeus Α 580, 609, Η 443, Μ 275.

ἀστήρ, -έρος, ὁ [cf. ἄστρον]. (**1**) A star Ε 5, Ζ 295, 401, Λ 62, Τ 381, Χ 26, 28, 317, 318 : ν 93, ο 108.—(**2**) A falling star, a fire-ball or meteorite Δ 75.

ἀστός, -οῦ, ὁ [ἄστυ]. A (fellow-)citizen : ἀστοῖσιν ἀρήγων Λ 242 : μή μιν πρὶν γνοῖεν ἀστοί ν 192.

ἀστράγαλος, -ου, ὁ. (**1**) One of the vertebrae of the neck Ξ 466 : κ 560 = λ 65.—(**2**) In pl., a game played with the prepared bones, prob. similar to 'knuckle-bones' Ψ 88.

ἀστράπτω [cf. ἀστεροπή]. To send forth lightning, lighten. Of Zeus Β 353, Ι 237, Κ 5, Ρ 595.

ἄστρον, -ου, τό [cf. ἀστήρ]. A star. Always in pl. Θ 555, 559, Κ 252 : μ 312, ξ 483.

ἄστυ, -εος, τό (Ϝάστυ). A town or city (used as = πόλις (1) Φ 607 : ζ 177-8, θ 524-5, ξ 472-3 ; but in Ρ 144 app. the inhabited part of the city as opposed to the citadel ; see πόλις (2)) Β 332, Γ 116, Ζ 256, Η 32, etc. : α 3, γ 107, δ 9, η 40, etc.—With name of a particular town in genit. : ἀ. Ζελείης Δ 103 = 121. Cf. Ξ 281, Φ 128 : σ 1, χ 223.

ἀστυβοώτης [ἄστυ + βοάω]. That makes his voice be heard through the city : κήρυκα Ω 701.

ἄστυδε [ἄστυ + -δε (1)]. To or towards the town or city Σ 255, Ω 778 : ζ 296, κ 104, ο 503, π 331, ρ 5, τ 190.

ἀσύφηλος. App., degrading, vilifying Ω 767.—Absol. in neut., such a deed : ὥς μ' ἀσύφηλον ἔρεξεν Ι 647.

ἀσφαλέως [adv. fr. next]. (**1**) Straight on, without deviation : ὀλοοίτροχος ἀ. θέει Ν 141. Cf. ν 86.—Without hesitation, surely on to the point : ἀγορεύει θ 171.—(**2**) ἀ. μένειν, to remain or stand firm or motionless Ρ 436 : ρ 235.—Sim. ἔχει ἀ. (keeps his direction steadily) Ψ 325.

ἀσφαλής, -ές [ἀ-[1] + σφάλλω]. (**1**) Fixed, immovable : θεῶν ἕδος ζ 42.—(**2**) In neut. ἀσφαλές as adv., without stumbling or falling Ο 683.

ἀσφάραγος, -ου, ὁ (cf. λαυκανίη, φάρυξ). The wind-pipe : οὐδ' ἀπ' ἀσφάραγον τάμεν Χ 328.

ἀσφοδελός. Teeming with ἀσφόδελος or king's-spear : λειμῶνα λ 539, 573, ω 13.

†ἀσχαλάω. 3 sing. ἀσχαλάᾳ Β 293 : τ 159. 3 pl. ἀσχαλόωσι Ω 403 : α 304. Pple. ἀσχαλόων τ 534. Acc. masc. ἀσχαλόωντα Χ 412. Infin. ἀσχαλάαν Β 297. To be impatient or unable to contain oneself, chafe Β 293, 297, Χ 412, Ω 403 : α 304.—With genit. of that which causes the feeling : κτήσιος (*i.e.* the waste of it) τ 534. Cf. τ 159.

ἀσχάλλω [= prec.]. To be vexed or grieved. With complementary pple. : θωὴν τίνων β 193.

ἄσχετος [ἀ-[1] + σ(ε)χ-, ἔχω]. Not to be restrained, ungovernable : μένος ἄσχετε (in . . .) β 85 = ρ 406, β 303. Cf. γ 104, υ 19.—Of grief, uncontrollable Π 549.

ἀτάλαντος [ἀ-[2] + τάλαντον]. (**1**) Equal to, a match for. With dat. : ἀ. Ἄρηϊ Β 627. Cf. Β 169, 407, 636, 651, Ε 576, Η 47 = Λ 200, Η 166 = Θ 264 = Ρ 259, Θ 215, Κ 137, Ν 295 = 328, 500, 528, Ο 302, Π 784, Ρ 72, 536.—With a form in -φιν : θεόφιν Η 366, Ξ 318, Ρ 477 : γ 110, 409.—

(2) Like, resembling. With dat.: νυκτί M 463. Cf. N 795.

ἀταλάφρων, -ονος [ἀταλά, neut. pl. of ἀταλός + φρήν]. Of a child, with the mind just budding Z 400.

ἀτάλλω [cf. next]. To gambol N 27.

ἀταλός, -ή [cf. prec.]. App., in an early stage of life, tender: πώλοισιν Υ 222: παρθενικαί λ 39.—Absol. in neut. pl., what is natural to such a stage of life: ἀταλὰ φρονέοντες (in childish glee) Σ 567.

ἀτάρ. See αὐτάρ.

ἀταρβής [ἀ-[1] + τάρβος]. Fearless N 299.

ἀτάρβητος [ἀ-[1] + ταρβέω]. Not to be diverted from one's course: νόος Γ 63.

ἀταρπιτός, -οῦ, ἡ [metathesis of ἀτραπιτός]. = next Σ 565: ρ 234.

ἀταρπός, -οῦ, ἡ [metathesis of ἀτραπός. See ἀτραπιτός]. A pathway or path (cf. prec.) P 743: ξ 1.

ἀταρτηρός. App., baneful, baleful, or the like: ἐπέεσσιν A 223: Μέντορ ἀταρτηρέ β 243.

ἀτασθαλίη, -ης, ἡ [ἀτάσθαλος]. Always in pl. (1) Recklessness, criminal folly: σφετέρῃσιν ἀτασθαλίῃσιν ὄλοντο Δ 409. Cf. X 104: α 7, 34, κ 437, μ 300, χ 317 = 416, ψ 67, ω 458.—(2) Such characteristics displayed in deeds: ἀτασθαλίαι οἱ ἐχθραὶ ἔσαν φ 146.

ἀτασθάλλω [ἀτάσθαλος]. To act recklessly or without regard to consequences σ 57, τ 88.

ἀτάσθαλος, -ον. (1) Reckless, careless of consequences, ungoverned X 418: η 60, θ 166, ω 282.—(2) Of character, deeds, etc., displaying such characteristics: μένος N 634. Cf. π 86, χ 314, ω 352.—(3) In neut. ἀτάσθαλον, a deed displaying such characteristics: οὔ ποτ' ἀ. ἄνδρα ἐώργει δ 693.—In neut. pl. ἀτάσθαλα, such deeds: ἀ. μηχανόωντο Λ 695. Cf. γ 207, π 93, ρ 588, σ 139, 143, υ 170, 370, χ 47.

ἀτειρής [ἀ-[1] + τείρω]. (1) Not to be worn away, hard: χαλκός E 292. Cf. H 247, Ξ 25, Σ 474, T 233, Υ 108: ν 368.—Fig., of the heart Γ 60.—(2) Not liable to fatigue O 697.—Of the voice (cf. ἄρρηκτος (4)) N 45, P 555, X 227.—Sim. of character: μένος αἰὲν ἀ. (sturdy, unwearying) λ 270.

ἀτέλεστος, -ον [ἀ-[1] + τελεσ-, τελέω]. (1) Not accomplished or performed: τὰ ἔσσεται οὐκ ἀτέλεστα Δ 168. Cf. β 273, θ 571, σ 345.—(2) To no end, resulting in nothing: πόνον Δ 26, 57.—(3) In neut. ἀτέλεστον as adv., endlessly, continually π 111.

ἀτελεύτητος [ἀ-[1] + τελευτάω]. = prec. (1): οὐκ ἐμὸν ἀτελεύτητον (my word never fails) A 527. Cf. Δ 175.

ἀτελής [ἀ-[1] + τέλος]. = prec. ρ 546.

ἀτέμβω. (1) To wrong, treat improperly or with injustice: θυμὸν 'Αχαιῶν (plays or trifles with . . .) β 90. Cf. υ 294, φ 312.—(2) With genit., to debar from (one's due): ἴσης Λ 705: ι 42 = 549.—To deprive of: ἀτέμβονται νεότητος (have been robbed (by age) of their youthful vigour) Ψ 445.—ἀτεμβόμενος σιδήρου, app., lacking Ψ 834.

ἄτερ. Prep. with genit. (1) Aloof or apart from: ἀ. ἄλλων A 498. Cf. E 753.—(2) Without: ἀ. πολέμου (not on a warlike errand) Δ 376, ἀ. λαῶν E 473, ἀ. Ζηνός (without his goodwill) O 292. Cf. I 604, Φ 50, Ψ 441: ἀ. σπείρου β 102, τ 147 = ω 137. Cf. η 325, φ 409.

ἀτέραμνος [ἀ-[1]. Second element uncertain]. Hard, stubborn: κῆρ ψ 167.

ἀτερπής [ἀ-[1] + τέρπω]. (1) Joyless: χῶρον λ 94.—(2) Causing pain or distress, painful, dangerous, gruesome: λιμός T 354: χώρῳ η 279, δαῖτα κ 124.

ἄτερπος, -ον [as prec.]. = prec. (2): ὀϊζύος Z 285.

ἀτέω (ἀϝατέω) [ἀϝάτη, ἄτη]. To act rashly or recklessly Υ 332.

ἄτη, -ης, ἡ (ἀϝάτη). (1) Stupor: ἀ. φρένας εἷλεν Π 805.—(2) Blindness of the mind sent by the gods, a divine perversion or deception of the mind leading to evil-doing or mischance: Ζεύς μ' ἄτῃ ἐνέδησεν B 111 = I 18, ὡς ὅτ' ἂν ἄνδρ' ἀ. λάβῃ Ω 480 (the time of this clause and of κατακτείνας in 481 the same; the homicide has been done under impulse of the ἄτη). Cf. A 412 = Π 274, Z 356, Θ 237, T 88, Ω 28: ἄτην μετέστενον δ 261. Cf. ο 233, φ 302, ψ 223.—In pl. I 115, T 270.—Personified I 504, 505, 512, T 91, 126, 129, 136.—(3) Such blindness or deception of human origin. In pl. K 391.—(4) Hurt, harm: εἴς μ' ἄτην κοιμήσατε (to my hurt) μ 372.

ἀτίζω [ἀ-[1] + *τίζω = τίω]. To pay no heed Υ 166.

ἀτῑμάζω [ἀτιμάω]. 3 sing. pa. iterative ἀτῑμάζεσκε I 450. (1) = ἀτιμάω A 11: ζ 283, θ 309, λ 496, ν 141, ξ 164, 506, π 317 = τ 498, σ 144, υ 167, φ 332, 427, χ 418, ψ 116, ω 459.—(2) To dishonour by conjugal unfaithfulness: ἄκοιτιν I 450.

ἀτῑμάω [ἀ-[1] + τιμή]. (ἀπ-.) To treat with dishonour or no regard, hold in contempt, show no respect or regard for, slight: A 94, 356 = 507 = B 240, Z 522, Θ 163, I 62, 111, Ξ 127: ξ 57, π 274, 307, υ 133, φ 99, ψ 28.

ἀτίμητος [ἀτιμάω]. Despised; or perh., to whose life no blood-money is attached, whom anyone may slay with impunity: μετανάστην I 648 = Π 59.

ἀτῑμίη, -ης, ἡ [ἀ-[1] + τιμή]. Dishonour: ἀτιμίῃσιν ἰάλλειν (to fling at, assail, with acts of dishonour) ν 142.

ἄτῑμος [ἀ-[1] + τιμή]. (1) Held in no respect, regard or esteem A 171.—In comp.: ἀτιμότερόν με θήσεις Π 90.—In superl.: ἀτιμοτάτη θεός A 516.—(2) In neut. ἄτιμον as adv., without making recompense π 431.

ἀτιτάλλω. Aor. ἀτίτηλα Ω 60. (1) To bring up or rear (a child) Ξ 202 = 303, Π 191, Ω 60: λ 250, ο 450, σ 323, τ 354.—(2) In reference to animals, to rear. Of horses E 271, Ω 280.—Of swine ξ 41.—Of a goose ο 174.

ἄτῑτος, -ον [ἀ-[1] + τίω]. (1) Unavenged: οὐκ ἄτιτος κεῖτ' Ἄσιος N 414.—(2) Unpaid: ἵνα μὴ ποινὴ ἄτιτος ἔῃ Ξ 484.

ἄτλητος [ἀ-[1] + τλη-, τλάω]. Unbearable: πένθεϊ I 3. Cf. T 367.

ἀτος. See ἄατος.

ἀτραπιτός, -οῦ, ἡ [ἀτραπός (prob. fr. ἀ-[2] + τραπέω) + ἰτ-, εἶμι. Thus 'a way worn by continual treading']. A pathway or path (cf. ἀταρπός) ν 195.

ἀτρεκέως [adv. fr. next]. Exactly: κατάλεξον K 384 = 405 = Ω 380 = 656. Cf. B 10, K 413, 427, O 53: α 169, 179, 214, ρ 154, ω 123, 303, etc.

ἀτρεκής. In neut. ἀτρεκές as adv. (1) = prec.: οὐ δεκὰς ἀ. (not just ten) π 245.—(2) Surely, certainly E 208.

ἀτρέμας. Before a consonant **ἀτρέμα** O 318. [ἀ-[1] + τρέμω.] Without motion, still B 200, E 524, N 280, 438, 557, Ξ 352, O 318: ν 92, τ 212.

ἄτριπτος, -ον [ἀ-[1] + τριπ-, τρίβω]. Not hardened (by work): χεῖρας φ 151.

ἄτρομος [ἀ-[1] + τρόμος]. Steady, dauntless: μένος E 126, P 157, θυμός Π 163.

ἀτρύγετος, -ον [ἀ-[1] + τρυγάω]. That yields no fruit, barren: ἁλός A 316, 327, Ω 752, θαλάσσης Ξ 204, πόντον O 27, αἰθέρος P 425: ἁλός α 72, ε 52, ζ 226, θ 49, κ 179, πόντον β 370, ε 84 = 158, ε 140, η 79, ν 419, ρ 289.

Ἀτρυτώνη [traditionally fr. ἀ-[1] + τρυ-, τρύχω]. Thus, the unwearied one. Name of Athene B 157 = E 714 = Φ 420, E 115, K 284: δ 762 = ζ 324.

ἄττα [a widely spread word for 'father,' doubtless derived from childish speech]. Used in addressing an elder I 607, P 561: π 31, 57, 130, ρ 6, 599, φ 369.

ἀτύζομαι. Aor. pple. ἀτυχθείς Z 468. (1) To be terrified or distraught, to be panic-stricken, flee scared: ἀτυζόμενοι φοβέοντο Z 41, ἀτυζομένην ἀπολέσθαι (distraught to the point of death) X 474. Cf. Z 38, Θ 183, O 90, Σ 7, Φ 4, 554: λ 606, ψ 42.—(2) To be scared or put out by: πατρὸς ὄψιν ἀτυχθείς Z 468.

αὖ. (1) Again, once more: ἔφυγες θάνατον Λ 362, νῦν αὖ μ' ἄνωγας . . . (to risk myself again) Ξ 262. Cf. Π 477, Φ 82, etc.: νῦν αὖ δεῦρ' ἱκόμην (have come again to your aid) ν 303. Cf. μ 116, υ 88, etc.—(2) In impatient or remonstrative questions, again, now, this time: τίς δὴ αὖ τοι συμφράσσατο βουλάς; A 540. Cf. H 24: ψ 264.—(3) In return or requital: τοῖσιν αὖ θάνατος ἔσσεται Δ 270. Cf. K 292, Φ 399: γ 382, φ 363.—(4) In one's turn: ἔνθ' αὖ νείκεσεν E 471. Cf. Λ 145, etc.: Νέστωρ αὖ τότ' ἐφίζεν γ 411. Cf. θ 129, etc.—(5) In reply: τὸν αὖ ἀντίον ηὔδα E 647. Cf. N 254, etc.: α 213, ο 485, etc.—(6) Adversative: ἀρχοὺς αὖ ἐρέω B 493. Cf. Λ 367, etc.: ξ 174, etc.—On the other hand, again: ὃν δ' αὖ δήμου ἄνδρα ἴδοι B 198. Cf. Γ 200, 332, Δ 17, Λ 109, P 312, etc.: χωρὶς δ' αὖ . . . δ 130. Cf. β 48, γ 425, δ 211, ε 221, etc.—(7) Particle of transition or continuation: ἔνθ' αὖ ἕλεν ἄνδρα Π 603. Cf. B 618, I 700, M 182, O 138, etc.: αἰδὼς δ' αὖ . . . γ 24. Cf. δ 727, ε 18, ι 349, λ 6, etc.—App. introducing a narrative Υ 215.

†**αὐαίνω** [αὖος]. Neut. aor. pple. pass. αὐανθέν. To dry: ὄφρα φοροίη [ῥόπαλον] αὐανθέν (when dried) ι 321.

αὐγάζομαι [αὐγή, the sense 'light' passing into that of 'sight']. To see, discern Ψ 458.

αὐγή, -ῆς, ἡ. A bright light. (1) Of fire B 456, I 206, Σ 211, 610, X 134: ζ 305, ψ 89.—(2) Of lightning. In pl. N 244.—So ἵκετο Διὸς αὐγάς (the home of lightning) N 837.—(3) Of the gleam from polished armour: αὐγὴ χαλκείη N 341.—(4) Of the sun P 371, X 134: ζ 98, μ 176.—In pl. of his rays Θ 480, Π 188: β 181, λ 498, 619, ο 349.—So of rays from a star X 27.

αὐδάω [αὐδή]. 3 sing. pa. iterative αὐδήσασκε E 786, P 420. (ἐξ-, μετ-, παρ-, προσ-.) (1) To speak: ηὔδα μάντις A 92, οὐδ' ἔκλυον αὐδήσαντος (by word of mouth) K 47. Cf. Π 76, P 420: γ 337, δ 505, ι 497.—Of shouting E 786.—(2) To say, speak, utter: ἔπος Z 54, K 377, Λ 379, M 163, etc., αὔδα ὅ τι φρονέεις Ξ 195 = Σ 426: = ε 89, ἔπος ν 199.—(3) To address (a person): τὸν (etc.) ἀντίον ηὔδα Γ 203, Δ 265, E 217, Λ 822, etc.: α 213, β 242, δ 155, ε 28, etc.—(4) With double construction of (2) and (3): ἔπος μιν ἀντίον ηὔδα E 170.

αὐδή, -ῆς, ἡ. (1) Voice, speech: Ἕκτορος αὐδήν N 757, θεῷ ἐναλίγκιος αὐδήν (in . . .) T 250. Cf. A 249, O 270, T 418: τοῦ τερπόμεθ' αὐδῇ δ 160. Cf. α 371 = ι 4, β 268 = 401 = χ 206 = ω 503 = 548, β 297, δ 831, κ 311, 481.—(2) The faculty of speech: ἔχοντ' ἐν στήθεσιν αὐδήν Δ 430. Cf. Σ 419.—(3) A rumour or report: θεοῦ αὐδήν (sent abroad by a god) ξ 89.—(4) Applied to sound produced by twitching a stretched bowstring φ 411.

αὐδήεις, -εσσα [αὐδή]. (1) Having the power of speech: αὐδήεντα ἔθηκεν T 407.—(2) Using the speech of mortals (as opposed to that of the gods): θεὸς αὐδήεσσα κ 136 = λ 8 = μ 150, μ 449.—(3) As a general epithet of human (as opposed to divine) beings ε 334, ζ 125.

αὐερύω (ἀϜϜερύω) [ἀϜ-, ἀνα- (1) (3) + Ϝερύω, ἐρύω[1]]. 3 pl. aor. αὐέρυσαν A 459, B 422. (1) To pull up, pull out of the ground: στήλας M 261.—(2) To draw back. (a) To draw one's bow Θ 325.—(b) Of drawing back the head of a sacrificial victim A 459 = B 422.

αὖθι [contr. fr. αὐτόθι]. (1) On the spot, there: αὐ. μένων A 492, ἑζόμενος δὲ κατ' αὐ. (κατά adv. with the pple.) N 653, κατ' αὐ. λίπον P 535. Cf. B 328, K 62, Λ 48, N 37, X 137, etc.: αὐ. παρ' Ἀτρεΐδῃ γ 156. Cf. δ 416, θ 275, κ 567, ρ 357, etc.—So παρ' αὐ. = παρ' αὐτόθι (see αὐτόθι (1)) Ψ 163.—(2) On the spot, here: μηκέτ' αὐ. λεγώμεθα B 435. Cf. Γ 291, Z 84, I 412, N 233, etc.: μέν' αὐ. β 369. Cf. η 314, μ 24, ν 44, υ 220, etc.—(3) On the spot, at once: αὐ. λύθη ψυχή E 296. Cf. Z 281, Λ 141, Π 331, P 298, etc.: σ 91, etc.

αὐΐαχος (ἀϜϜίϜαχος) [ἀ-[2] + ϜιϜαχ-, ἰάχω]. With united shout: ἄβρομοι αὐΐαχοι N 41.

αὔλειος, -η [αὐλή]. Of the αὐλή: οὐδοῦ (the threshold of the gateway leading into the αὐλή) α 104, θύρῃσιν (= αἰθούσης θύρῃσιν; see under αἴθουσα (2)) σ 239, ψ 49.

αὐλή, -ῆς, ἡ. (1) (a) An enclosure or steading for sheep, goats, swine, etc. Δ 433, E 142, K 183: ι 184, 239, 338, 462, ξ 5, 13, ο 555, π 165.—(b) The enclosing wall or fence thought of rather than the space enclosed: αὐλῆς ὑπεράλμενον E 138.—(2) A courtyard in front of or surrounding a house: ὑπ' αἰθούσῃ αὐλῆς I 472, ἑρκίον αὐλῆς 476.

Cf. Z 247, 316, Λ 774, Ω 161, 452, 640 : ὅθι οἱ θάλαμος αὐλῆς δέδμητο (in the αὐλή) α 425, δόμοι καὶ αὐ. ζ 303. Cf. β 300, δ 678, η 112, 130, κ 10, ο 162, π 343, ρ 266, σ 101, 102, 237, υ 355, φ 191, 240, 389, χ 137, 376, 442 = 459, 449, 474, 494.—(3) App. loosely as = δῶμα (3) (b) δ 74.

αὐλίζομαι [αὖλις]. Of cattle, etc., to be driven back to the steading, come home μ 265, ξ 412.

αὖλις, ἡ [cf. αὐλή]. (1) A bird's roosting-place χ 470.—(2) A bivouac : αὖλιν ἔθεντο I 232.

αὐλός, -οῦ, ὁ. (1) A wind-instrument resembling a flute or clarionet : αὐλῶν συρίγγων τ' ἐνοπήν (app. (to avoid asyndeton) to be rendered 'flute-pipes,' taking αὐλῶν συρίγγων as virtually a compound word) K 13, αὐλοὶ φόρμιγγές τε Σ 495.—(2) Applied (app. from resemblance to a tube) to a jet or column of blood χ 18.—(3) A hollow or socket in a spear-head to receive the end of the shaft P 297.—(4) A tube or sheath to receive a pin of a περόνη τ 227 (= the κληῖδες of σ 294 : see κληΐς (5)).

αὐλῶπις, -ιδος [αὐλός + ὦπα]. App., with tubes for the eyes, *i.e.* having a vizor furnished with eye-holes E 182, Λ 353, N 530, Π 795.

αὖος, -η, -ον [αὔω¹]. (1) Dry, dried up Ψ 327 : ε 240 (sapless), σ 309.—Made of well-dried hide M 137, P 493.—(2) In neut. αὖον as adv., with a dry, *i.e.* a harsh or grating sound (cf. καρφαλέος (2)) : κόρυθες αὖον ἀΰτευν M 160. Cf. N 441.

ἄϋπνος, -ον [ἀ-¹ + ὕπνος]. (1) Sleepless, not able to sleep ι 404.—(2) Doing without sleep κ 84, τ 591.—(3) Sleepless, in which one does not sleep : νύκτας I 325 : τ 340.

αὔρη, ἡ. A breeze : αὐ. ψυχρὴ πνέει ε 469.

αὔριον [conn. with ἠ(F)έριος]. (1) To-morrow : ὄφρα μοι ἕπηται αὐ. I 429. Cf. Θ 535, I 357, 692, Σ 269 : α 272, σ 23.—(2) As *quasi*-sb. : ἠελίου ἀνιόντος ἐς αὔριον Θ 538. Cf η 318, λ 351.

ἄϋσε, 3 sing. aor. αὔω².

ἀϋσταλέος [αὔω¹]. Dry ; hence, squalid, dirty τ 327.

αὐτάγρετος [αὐτός + ἀγρέω]. Chosen by oneself, at one's choice ; or perh., taken of itself, to be had for the taking π 148.

αὐτάρ, ἀτάρ. (1) Adversative particle, but. (a) αὐτάρ A 118, 333, 488, B 224, etc. : α 57, 200, 303, 397, etc.—(b) ἀτάρ A 166, Δ 29, E 29, Z 125, Λ 614, etc. : β 122, γ 298, δ 32, ρ 307, etc.—(2) Particle of transition or continuation. (a) αὐτάρ : οὐρῆας μὲν πρῶτον ἐπῴχετο, αὐ. ἔπειτα . . . A 51. Cf. A 282, B 103, 105, 107, etc. : α 9, 123, ζ 132, θ 38, etc.—(b) ἀτάρ : μάψ, ἀ. οὐ κατὰ κόσμον (yea) B 214. Cf. A 506, B 313, Γ 268, Δ 484, etc. : α 181, 419, β 240, γ 138, etc.—(3) ἀτάρ introducing a statement or injunction : Ἕκτορ, ἀ. σὺ πόλινδε μετέρχεο Z 86. Cf. Z 429, X 331 : δ 236.—αὐτάρ introd. an apodosis Γ 290, X 390.

αὖτε. (1) In the reverse direction, back : ὅτ' ἂν αὐ. νεώμεθα H 335. Cf. Δ 384, Θ 139, etc.—(2) Of resumption of a state or condition, again. With ἐξαῦτις : αὐ. ἐξαῦτις ἀνέστη O 287.—(3) Again, once more : ἀγορῇ νικᾷς B 370, ὅτε δὴ αὐ. Ἕκτωρ Ἀργείους ὀλέκεσκεν (*i.e.* in this second instance) T 134. Cf. B 221 (as usual), Γ 191, Θ 373, I 702, Ξ 454 (meaning that his aim is always good), Φ 421, etc. : αὐ. δύω μάρψας ι 311. Cf. ε 356, χ 165, 281, etc.—(4) In impatient or remonstrative questions, again, now, this time : τίπτ' αὐ. εἰλήλουθας ; A 202. Cf. B 225, H 448, Ξ 364, Υ 16, Φ 394 : ζ 119 = ν 200, κ 281, λ 93, υ 33.—(5) In one's turn : ὁ αὐ. δῶκ' Ἀτρεΐ B 105. Cf. A 404, E 541, K 283, N 414, Ψ 278, etc. : ἔνθ' αὐ. Εὐρυδάμαντα βάλεν (*i.e.* his turn had come) χ 283. Cf. θ 127.—(6) In reply : τὸν αὐ. προσέειπεν A 206. Cf. Γ 58, 203, Δ 265, Z 144, etc. : α 178, 221, 383, 399, etc.—(7) Adversative : νῦν μὲν . . . ὕστερον αὐ. μαχήσονται H 30. Cf. Γ 67, etc. : νῦν αὐ. πανύστατος ι 452, etc.—On the other hand, again : Τρώων αὐ. ἀγορὴ γένετο H 345. Cf. E 279, H 248, Θ 55, Λ 56, etc. : ἄλλοτε δ' αὐ. παύομαι δ 102. Cf. α 111, ε 29 (for your part), μ 282 (as we cannot do here), π 463, etc.—(8) Particle of transition or continuation : Ἕκτωρ δ' αὐ. χάρη Γ 76. Cf. A 237, B 407, Z 73, Θ 26, etc. : ἡμῖν δ' αὐ. ἐπεπείθετο θυμός β 103. Cf. β 335, 386, ι 256, λ 21, etc.—(9) Hereafter, in the future, yet : εἴ ποτε δὴ αὐ. χρειὼ ἐμεῖο γένηται A 340. Cf. A 578, E 232, I 135, O 16, Ψ 605, etc. : ἡμεῖς δ' αὐ. τισόμεθα ν 14. Cf. θ 444, σ 48.

ἀϋτέω [ἀϋτή]. 3 pl. impf. ἀΰτευν M 160. (1) To shout, cry, call Υ 50, Φ 582.—Of the sound of struck armour M 160.—(2) To shout or call to : πάντας ἀρίστους Λ 258.

ἀϋτή, -ῆς, ἡ [αὔω²]. (1) A shout or cry B 153, Λ 466 : ζ 122, ξ 265 = ρ 434.—Shouting : εἴ ποτ' ἀϋτῆς σχοίατο B 97.—(2) The battle-shout : μήστωρες ἀϋτῆς Δ 328, N 93 = 479, Π 759. Cf. Δ 331, I 547, M 338, 377, Ξ 60, O 312, 718, Υ 374.—(3) Battle : δηΐων ἐν ἀϋτῇ P 167. Cf. A 492, E 732, Z 328, Λ 802 = Π 44, N 621, Ξ 37, 96, Π 63 : Τρώων ὑπεξέφυγον ἀϋτήν λ 383.

αὐτῆμαρ [αὐτός + ἦμαρ]. (1) On the same day, on that day Σ 454 : γ 311.—(2) For that day A 81.

αὐτίκα. Forthwith, straightway, at once : αὐ. ἆλτο χαμᾶζε Γ 29. Cf. A 118, 199, 539, B 322, etc. : αὐ. μνηστῆρας ἐπῴχετο α 324. Cf. β 367, 379, γ 54, 448, etc.

αὖτις. (1) In the reverse direction, backwards, back, back again : ἴτην A 347, ἐλεύσεται 425. Cf. A 522, B 208, Γ 36, Δ 19, etc. : ὑποστρέψας θ 301, κυλίνδετο λᾶας λ 598. Cf. α 317, γ 164, δ 478, ε 430, ι 496, etc.—With πάλιν. See πάλιν (1).—(2) Back to a former state or condition, again : αὐ. ἐμπνύνθη E 697. Cf. Δ 222, H 462, I 368, M 31, O 60, etc. : αὐ. ἄρ' ἕζετο ρ 602. Cf. δ 549, κ 461, etc.—With ἄψ. See ἄψ (2).—(3) Again, once more : ἰόντα A 27. Cf. A 513, H 170, K 463 (as on former occasions), Σ 153, X 449 (giving changed orders), etc. : αὐ. οἱ πόρον οἶνον ι 360. Cf. γ 161, ι 354, μ 453, ο 439, τ 65, etc.—(4) Adversative : ὅς σ' αὐ. κτείναιμι (in spite of that) ξ 405.—(5) Particle of transition : αὐ. δ' ἐκ κολεοῖο ἐρυσσάμενος ξίφος (and then . . .) M 190. Cf. σ 60.—(6) At another time, on some future occasion, another day: *μεταφρασόμεσθα καὶ αὖ.* A 140. Cf. Γ 440.

ἀϋτμή, -ῆς, ἡ [ἀϋ-τ-μή. ἀϜ-, ἄ(Ϝ)ημι]. **(1)** Breath I 609, K 89.—**(2)** Of the wind from bellows Σ 471.—Of the blowing of the winds λ 400 = 407.—Of the 'breath' of fire Φ 366: ι 389, π 290 = τ 9, τ 20 (in these three passages referring to smoke).—Of fragrance or odour: *κνίσης αὐ.* μ 369. Cf. Ξ 174.

ἀϋτμήν, -ένος, ὁ [cf. prec.]. **(1)** Breath Ψ 765.—**(2)** Of the blowing of the winds γ 289.

αὐτοδίδακτος [αὐτός + διδακ-, διδάσκω]. Self-taught χ 347.

αὐτόδιος [αὐτός + ὁδός (with Aeolic smooth breathing). 'On or by the same way']. In neut. *αὐτόδιον* as adv., straightway: *αὐ. μιν λούσασθαι ἀνώγει* θ 449.

αὐτοέτης [αὐτός + ἔτος]. In neut. *αὐτόετες* as adv., within the same year, in a year's space γ 322.

αὐτόθεν [αὐτός + -θεν (1)]. **(1)** From the place in which one is. With complementary words: *αὐ. ἐξ ἕδρης* T 77. Cf. ν 56, φ 420.—**(2)** On the spot, at once Υ 120.

αὐτόθι [αὐτός + -θι]. **(1)** On the spot, there: *αὐ. ὀλέσθαι* Γ 428, *λιπέτην* (λεῖπε) *κατ' αὐ.* (κατά adv. with the vb.) K 273, Φ 201. Cf. E 847, Ξ 119, Π 294, 848, T 403, Υ 340, Φ 496, Ω 673, 707: *αὐ. μεῖνεν* δ 508, *κατ' αὐ. λιπόντε* (see above) φ 90. Cf. δ 302, ι 29, 496, κ 132, λ 187, μ 161, ξ 285, 525, ο 327, ρ 254, ω 464.—So *παρ' αὐ.* (app. by confusion with *αὐτόφι*, locative of *αὐτός*): *κτενέειν παρ' αὐ. πάντας ἀρίστους* N 42. Cf. Υ 140, Ψ 147, 640.—**(2)** Here: *αὐ. λέξεο* I 617. Cf. K 443, T 189: ζ 245, λ 356, ξ 67.

αὐτοκασιγνήτη, -ης, ἡ [αὐτός + κασιγνήτη]. A sister of the whole blood κ 137.

αὐτοκασίγνητος, -ου, ὁ [αὐτός + κασίγνητος]. A brother of the whole blood B 706, Γ 238, Λ 427, N 534, Ξ 156, Π 718.

αὐτόματος, -η, -ον [αὐτός. Second element obscure]. **(1)** Without being asked, of one's own accord: *ἦλθεν* B 408.—**(2)** Self-acting, self-moving, self-impelled: *αὐτόμαται πύλαι μύκον* E 749 = Θ 393. Cf. Σ 376.

αὐτονυχί [αὐτός + νυχ-, νύξ]. This very night Θ 197.

αὐτός, -ή, [-ό]. Locative *αὐτόφι* M 302. This form as ablative Λ 44. As genit. T 255. Crasis with ὁ gives *ὠυτός* E 396. **(1)** Anaphoric pronoun in emphatic use. **(a)** Myself, thyself, himself, etc.: *αὐτοὺς ἑλώρια τεῦχε κύνεσσιν* (the body being regarded as the real man) A 4, *ὄφρ' ὅρκια τάμνῃ αὐ.* Γ 106, *ἄστυ καὶ αὐτούς* (the city and the men in it) Ω 499. Cf. A 133, 270, 420, 437, 487, 577, etc.: *αὐτὴν ἐς θρόνον εἷσεν* α 130, *ἐθάμβεον αὐτόν* ρ 367 (referring especially to his bodily presence or figure). Cf. α 108, 117, 393, β 40, 53, 64, etc.—**(b)** Joined with the personal pronouns in emphatic use: *ἔμ' αὐτόν* A 271, *ἐγὼν αὐ.* H 101, *σὺ αὐ.* Ξ 145. Cf. A 338, E 459, Z 272, I 521, etc.: α 33, 251, β 190, θ 396, ν 190, etc.—With sb.: *αὐτὰς πύλας* M 469, etc.: *θεοὶ αὐτοί* α 384, etc.—With proper and place names: *αὐτὴν Χρυσηΐδα* A 143. Cf. B 827, E 51, etc.: *αὐτῆς Ἰθάκης* ξ 98. Cf. α 207, η 70, etc.—**(c)** With personal pronouns in reflexive sense: *πυργηδὸν σφέας αὐτοὺς ἀρτύναντες* M 43, *εὖ ἐντύνασαν ἓ αὐτήν* Ξ 162. Cf. Γ 51, E 64, Θ 529, K 307, Π 47, etc.: δ 244, θ 211, ι 421, etc.—**(d)** In genit. strengthening possessive pronouns: *πατρὸς κλέος ἠδ' ἐμὸν αὐτοῦ* Z 446, *τὰ σ[ὰ] αὐτῆς ἔργα* 490, *νωΐτερον λέχος αὐτῶν* O 39, etc.: *αὐτῶν σφετέρῃσιν ἀτασθαλίῃσιν* α 7, *ἑοὶ αὐτοῦ θῆτες* δ 643, etc.—**(2)** By oneself, alone: *ὄφρα καὶ αὐ. λέξομαι* ψ 171.—Left to one's own devices: *αὐ. περ ἐὼν προμάχοισιν ἐμίχθη* Θ 99.—By oneself, without aid or guidance: *αὐ. πλάγξομαι* ο 311. Cf. α 53.—By its own virtue: *αὐ. ἐφέλκεται ἄνδρα σίδηρος* π 294 = τ 13.—Without compeer: *ὄφρα βασιλεύοι αὐ.* χ 53.—At one's own will, by one's own authority: *αὐ. ἀπούρας* A 356, etc.—Of one's own accord, without bidding: *αὐτὼ λαὸν ἀνώγετον . . .* Δ 287. Cf. P 254, etc.—**(3)** Without change, the same: *αὐτὰ κέλευθα* M 225. Cf. Ψ 480: θ 107, φ 366, etc.—With the article: *ὠυτὸς ἀνήρ* E 396. Cf. Z 391: *ἐκ τοκήων τῶν αὐτῶν* η 55. Cf. π 334, etc.—So with *ὅδε*: *τοῦδ' αὐτοῦ λυκάβαντος* ξ 161 = τ 306.—The very . . .: *ἄκρον ὑπὸ λόφον αὐτόν* N 615. Cf. κ 158.—**(4)** Idiomatically with sb. in comitative dat. or instrumental, with or without *σύν*, just as it is (was), . . . and all: *αὐτῇ κεν γαίῃ ἐρύσαιμι* Θ 24, *αὐτοῖσιν ὄχεσφιν* Θ 290, Λ 699, *αὐτῇ σὺν φόρμιγγι* I 194. Cf. I 542, Ξ 498, Υ 482, Ψ 8: *αὐτῷ φάρει ἀναΐξας* θ 186. Cf. ν 118, ξ 77, υ 219, φ 54.—**(5)** As reflexive pronoun: *ἄνευ ἕθεν οὐδὲ σὺν αὐτῷ* P 407. Cf. I 342, Υ 55: *κλέος αὐτῇ ποιεῖται* β 125. Cf. δ 247.—**(6)** In unemphatic use as anaphoric pronoun of the 3rd person (never in nom. or at the beginning of a clause), he, she, it, etc.: *βούλομαι αὐτὴν οἴκοι ἔχειν* A 112, *μάλα τ' ἔκλυον αὐτοῦ* 218. Cf. A 47, 360, Γ 25, 436, E 42, 170, etc.: *κήρυκες αὐτοῖσι οἶνον ἔμισγον* α 109, *ἀπὸ δ' ἔσχισεν αὐτήν* δ 507. Cf. α 143, β 128, 154, γ 22, 249, δ 110, 522, 634, etc.

αὐτοστάδιος [αὐτός + στα-, ἵστημι]. *ἐν αὐτοσταδίῃ* [ὑσμίνῃ], in stand-up fighting N 325.

αὐτοσχεδά = *αὐτοσχεδόν*. From close at hand Π 319.

αὐτοσχέδιος [αὐτοσχεδόν]. **(1)** *αὐτοσχεδίῃ* [ὑσμίνῃ], in close combat O 510.—**(2)** Adv. of acc. fem. form *αὐτοσχεδίην* = next M 192, P 294: λ 536.

αὐτοσχεδόν [αὐτός + σχεδόν]. From close at hand, at close quarters: *αὐ. κ' οὐτάζοντο* H 273. Cf. N 496, 526, O 386, 708, 746, P 530: χ 293.

αὐτοῦ [αὐτός]. **(1)** In the same place, where one is or finds oneself: *αὐ. ἔμειναν* O 656. Cf. I 634, Σ 488, etc.: *ἔσχετ' αὐ. νηῦς* μ 204. Cf. ε 274, λ 152, etc.—(2) On that spot, there: *τὸν δὲ λίπ' αὐ.* A 428. Cf. Δ 292, E 886, Z 192, Θ 207, etc.: *αὐ. ἰχθυάᾳ* μ 95. Cf. γ 397, δ 639, ε 68, ι 194, etc.—(3) Here: *αὐ. ἐνὶ Τροίῃ* B 237. Cf. B 332, E 262, N 751, Σ 330, etc.: *αὐ. τῷδ' ἐνὶ δήμῳ* β 317. Cf. γ 427, ε 362, κ 266, λ 332, etc.—(4) On the spot, at once: *αὐ. οἱ θάνατον μητίσομαι* O 349. Cf. Π 649,

P 416, Φ 114, etc. : αὐ. κε πότμον ἐπίσποι β 250. Cf. δ 703, ι 303, σ 212, etc.

αὐτοχόωνος [app. for αὐτόχωνος = αὐτοχόανος, fr. αὐτός + χόανος]. Of a mass of iron, just as it came from the smelting furnace, *i.e.* in the condition of pig-iron : σόλον Ψ 826.

αὔτως [adv. fr. αὐτός with changed accent]. (1) Without change, as before, as ever : ἔργον αὐ. ἀκράαντόν [ἐστιν] B 138. Cf. ν 336.—(2) Just as one or it is (was) : αὐ. ἧσθαι δευόμενον A 133, ὅσσ' ἔρρεξεν αὐ. (without extraneous aid) K 50, κτενέει με αὐ. (without effort) X 125, λευκὸν ἔτ' αὐ. (fresh from the maker's hand) Ψ 268, δίδωμί τοι τόδ' ἄεθλον αὐ. (without a contest) 621. Cf. E 255, Π 117, Σ 198, 338, Ω 413 : οἴχεται αὐ. (trusting to his own resources) δ 665, αὐ. ἐκείμεθα ν 281, οὐδέ τις ἡμέας αὐ. ἀππέμψει (empty-handed) ο 83, ἧ αὐ. κεῖται ἀκηδής ; (without attention) υ 130. Cf. μ 284.—καὶ αὐ., even as it is, without that : καὶ αὐ. νεικεῖ A 520.—Strengthening ὥς Γ 339, H 430, I 195, K 25 : γ 64, ζ 166, ι 31, υ 238, φ 203, 225, χ 114, ω 409.—(3) Quite, just : ἄφρονα αὐ. Γ 220. Cf. Z 400, H 100, X 484, Ω 726.—(4) Just, merely, only, doing no more : αὐ. ἐνδίεσαν κύνας Σ 584. Cf. Ξ 18 : φαγέμεν αὐ. (has not so much as barely eaten) π 143. Cf. ζ 143, ξ 151, ρ 309.—(5) To no end or purpose, idly, uselessly, vainly : αὐ. ἐριδαίνομεν B 342, κακὸν ἤμυνε καὶ αὐ. I 599. Cf. N 104, 810, O 128, 513, P 633, Φ 474, Ψ 74 : αὐ. ἄχθος ἀρούρης (a useless cumberer of the ground) υ 379. Cf. π 313.—Just for that, idly : εὔχεαι Λ 388. Cf. P 450.—Idly, without justification : αὐ. σε κλέος ἐσθλὸν ἔχει P 143. Cf. Υ 348.—Idly, thoughtlessly, lightly : σῖτον ἔδοντας μὰψ αὐ. π 111.

αὐχένιος [αὐχήν]. Of the neck γ 450.

αὐχήν, -ένος, ὁ. The neck E 147, Λ 146, O 451, Π 339, P 49, Σ 415, etc. : θ 136, ι 372, κ 559, λ 64, σ 96, τ 539, χ 16, 328.

αὐχμέω [fr. αὐχμός, drought, fr. αὔω[1]]. To be squalid or dirty ω 250.

αὔω[1], αὔω. To get fire, get a light : ἵνα μή ποθεν ἄλλοθεν αὔῃ (αὔῃ) ε 490.

αὔω[2] [ἀF-, ἄ(F)ημι]. 3 sing. aor. ἤϋσε E 784, Θ 227, Λ 10, M 439, etc. : ω 530. ἄϋσε Γ 81, E 101, Θ 160, N 409, etc. 3 pl. ἄϋσαν ζ 117. Pple. ἀΰσας, -αντος (ῡ) B 334, Δ 508, Z 66, Λ 285, etc. Infin. ἀῦσαι ι 65. (1) To shout, cry, call : ἀϋσάντων ὑπ' Ἀχαιῶν B 334, ἤϋσεν Ἥρη E 784. Cf. Z 110, Θ 227, Λ 10, Ξ 147, Σ 217, Φ 307, etc. : ζ 117, ω 530.—Of the sound of struck armour : ἀσπὶς ἄϋσεν N 409. Cf. N 441.—(2) To shout or call to : αὖεν ἑταίρους Λ 461, N 477. Cf. ι 65.

ἀφαιρέω [ἀφ-, ἀπο- (1)]. 3 sing. aor. ἀφεῖλε ξ 455. Pple. ἀφελών ι 313. Imp. mid. with hyphaeresis and uncontracted prefix ἀποαίρεο (for ἀποαιρέεο) A 275. Infin. with uncontracted prefix ἀποαιρεῖσθαι A 230. Fut. infin. ἀφαιρήσεσθαι A 161, Ψ 544. 2 sing. aor. ἀφείλεο X 18. 3 -ετο Π 689, P 177 : α 9, τ 369. 2 pl. ἀφέλεσθε A 299. 3 -οντο B 600. Subj. ἀφέλωμαι X 257. 1 pl. -ώμεθα χ 219. 1 pl. opt. -οίμεθα Π 560. Infin. ἀφελέσθαι E 622, N 511, Π 54. (1) To take away or remove : θυρεὸν ι 313, σῖτον ξ 455.—(2) In mid. (a) To take away or remove, effect deprivation of : γέρας ἀφαιρήσεσθαι A 161. Cf. Π 54, Ψ 544 : μ 64.—With immaterial object : ἀοιδήν B 600.—Cf. Π 689 = P 177, X 257 : α 9, τ 369.—(b) To take away or remove *from*. With genit. : τεύχε' ὤμοιιν ἀφελέσθαι E 622 = N 511. Cf. Π 560 : χ 219.—(c) With double acc. of what is taken away and of the person deprived of it : ὡς ἔμ' ἀφαιρεῖται Χρυσηΐδα A 182. Cf. A 275, X 18.—With the personal acc. to be supplied : δῶρ' ἀποαιρεῖσθαι [κεῖνον] ὅς τις . . . A 230.—With this acc. alone : ἐπεί μ' ἀφέλεσθέ γε δόντες A 299.

ἄφαλος, -ον [ἀ-[1] + φάλος]. Having no φάλος K 258.

†**ἀφαμαρτάνω** [ἀφ-, ἀπο- (7)]. 3 sing. aor. ἀφάμαρτε Θ 119, 302, Λ 350, N 160, Ξ 403, Π 322, Φ 171, 591, X 290. 3 sing. aor. ἀπήμβροτε O 521, Π 466, 477. Dat. sing. fem. pple. ἀφαμαρτούσῃ Z 411. (1) To discharge a missile vainly, miss one's aim : οὐδ' ἀφάμαρτε Λ 350, N 160, Ξ 403, Π 322, Φ 591, X 290, ἀπήμβροτε δουρί Π 477.—(2) To fail to hit, miss. With genit. : τοῦ Θ 119, 302, O 521, Φ 171, αὐτοῦ Π 466.—(3) To lose, be deprived of. With genit. : σεῦ Z 411.

ἀφαμαρτοεπής [ἀφαμαρτάνω + ἔπος. Cf. ἁμαρτοεπής]. Stumbling in speech Γ 215.

ἀφανδάνω [ἀφ-, ἀπο- (6)]. To displease, be displeasing to. With dat. : ὑμῖν ὅδε μῦθος π 387.

ἄφαντος, -ον [ἀ-[1] + φαν-, φαίνω]. Caused to disappear, made away with Z 60, Υ 303.

ἄφαρ. (1) Quickly, speedily, soon, at once, forthwith : ἕζετο A 349, ἵπποισι τάθη δρόμος (*i.e.* directly they had turned) Ψ 375. Cf. A 594, B 453 = Λ 13, K 537, M 221, P 392, 750, T 405, X 270, Ω 446 : οἴχεται α 410. Cf. β 95 = ω 130, γ 456, δ 85, ε 482, ζ 49, θ 270, 409, ι 328, κ 122, λ 274, ρ 305, τ 140, φ 307.—(2) Without hesitation : μένουσιν Λ 418.—(3) Of a surety, truly : ἀ. κε δοῦναι βουλοίμην Ψ 593. Cf. N 814, P 417 : ἀ. σφι τόδε λωΐον ἐστιν β 169.—(4) In vague intensifying sense : ἔφθη ὀρεξάμενος . . . ὦμον ἀ. (right into the . . .) Π 323, ἀ. κλονέοντο πεφυζότες (in wild confusion) Φ 528.

†**ἀφαρπάζω** [ἀφ-, ἀπο- (1)]. Aor. infin. ἀφαρπάξαι. To snatch *from*. With genit. : κόρυθα κρατός N 189.

ἀφάρτερος [app. comp. from, and with sense due to the notion of speed implicit in, ἄφαρ]. Swifter Ψ 311.

ἀφαυρός. (1) Powerless, feeble : παιδός H 235.—In comp. : σέο ἀφαυρότερος H 457.—In superl. : ἀφαυρότατος Ἀχαιῶν O 11. Cf. υ 110.—(2) Of a missile, ineffective. In comp. : ἵνα μὴ οἱ ἀφαυρότερον βέλος εἴη M 458 (μὴ ἀ. = the more effective, being comp. in dependent form of οὐκ ἀφαυρός, which by litotes = effective).

†**ἀφάω.** Acc. sing. masc. pres. pple. ἀφόωντα. To handle, turn over : ἀσπίδα Z 322.

ἀφέῃ, 3 sing. aor. subj. ἀφίημι.

ἀφέηκε, 3 sing. aor. ἀφίημι.

ἀφείη, 3 sing. aor. opt. ἀφίημι.

ἀφεῖλε, 3 sing. aor. ἀφαιρέω.

ἀφέλοντο, 3 pl. aor. mid. ἀφαιρέω.

ἀφελών, aor. pple. ἀφαιρέω.

ἄφενος, τό. Riches, wealth A 171, Ψ 299 : ξ 99.

ἀφέξω, fut. ἀπέχω.

ἀφεσταίη, 3 sing. pf. opt. ἀφίστημι (B).

ἀφεσταότες, pl. pf. pple. ἀφίστημι (B).

ἀφεστᾶσι, 3 pl. pf. ἀφίστημι (B).

ἀφεστήκει, 3 sing. plupf. ἀφίστημι (B).

ἀφέτην, 3 dual aor. ἀφίημι.

ἀφήῃ, 3 sing. aor. subj. ἀφίημι.

ἀφῆκε, 3 sing. aor. ἀφίημι.

ἄφημαι [ἀφ-, ἀπο- (2)]. To sit apart O 106.

ἀφήσω, fut. ἀφίημι.

ἀφήτωρ, -ορος [ἀφ-, ἀπο- (1) + ἡ-, ἵημι[1]. 'The sender forth']. The Archer. Name of Apollo I 404.

ἄφθιτος, -ον [ἀ-[1] + φθίω]. Not liable to decay, imperishable B 46, 186, E 724, N 22, Ξ 238, Σ 370. —Never failing: ἄμπελοι ι 133.—Of immaterial things: κλέος (everlasting) I 413, μήδεα (that cannot come to nought) Ω 88.

†**ἀφίημι** [ἀφ-, ἀπο- (1) + ἵημι[1]]. Fem. pl. pres. pple. ἀφιεῖσαι η 126. Fut. ἀφήσω B 263. 3 sing. aor. ἀφέηκε M 221, Φ 115, Ψ 841. ἀφῆκε Θ 133, K 372, N 410, Φ 590, Ψ 432. 3 dual aor. ἀφέτην Λ 642. 3 sing. subj. ἀφήῃ P 631. ἀφέῃ Π 590. 3 sing. opt. ἀφείη Γ 317, Υ 464. From ἀφιέω 3 sing. impf. ἀφίει A 25, 379, Λ 702, N 444, Π 613, P 529 : ω 539. **Mid.** 3 sing. impf. ἀφίετο ψ 240. **(1)** To throw, hurl, launch (a missile): ἔγχος Γ 317. Cf. Θ 133, K 372, Π 590, P 631, Ψ 432 : ω 539.—Absol., to make one's throw Ψ 841.—With genit. of the throwing limb: ἄκοντα χειρὸς ἀφῆκεν Φ 590. Cf. N 410.—**(2)** To send from oneself, let fall: ἔγχος Φ 115. Cf. M 221.—**(3)** To send forth, cause to cease: μένος [ἔγχεος] N 444 = Π 613 = P 529.—**(4)** To get rid of, slake (thirst): δίψαν Λ 642.—**(5)** To shed (blossom) η 126.—**(6)** In mid., to loose (a part of oneself) *from.* With genit.: δειρῆς οὐκ ἀφίετο πήχεε ψ 240.—**(7)** To send away, dismiss (a person) A 25 = 379, B 263, Λ 702.—To let go, set free: ζωόν Υ 464.

ἀφικάνω [ἀφ-, ἀπο- (7)]. To be in the condition of having come to, arrived at, reached, to find oneself at, be at, a specified place: τίπτε δεῦρ' ἀφικάνεις; Ξ 43.—With prep.: πρὸς τεῖχος Z 388. —With acc.: ῥοὰς ποταμῶν ι 450. Cf. ξ 159 = ρ 156 = τ 304 = υ 231, ψ 318.

†**ἀφικνέομαι** [ἀφ-, ἀπο- (7)]. 2 sing. fut. ἀφίξεαι μ 39, 127. 3 -εται Σ 270. 2 sing. aor. ἀφίκεο α 171, ξ 188, ο 489. 3 -ετο N 645, Σ 395 : α 332, ε 55, κ 502, ο 228, π 414, σ 208, υ 55, φ 25, 42, 63, ψ 338. 1 pl. -όμεθα γ 278, ι 181, 216, 543, κ 1, 135, λ 22. 3 ἀφίκοντο Λ 618, N 329, X 208, Ω 329, 448 : ξ 344, ρ 205. Subj. ἀφίκωμαι Ω 431 : ψ 269. 2 sing. -ηαι Θ 482, Λ 208 : λ 122, ο 36. 3 -ηται Λ 193, Π 63. 1 pl. -ώμεθα π 382. 3 -ωνται P 454. Opt. ἀφικοίμην υ 81. 2 sing. -οιο ο 128. 2 pl. -οίμεθα κ 420, μ 345. Imp. pl. ἀφίκεσθε θ 202. Infin. ἀφικέσθαι K 281 : δ 255. Pf. infin. ἀφῖχθαι ζ 297. **(1)** To come to an indicated place: ὁπποίης ἐπὶ νηὸς ἀφίκεο (came here) α 171 = ξ 188.—**(2)** To go, proceed, take one's way. With preps.: ἐς Ὄλυμπον υ 55, γαῖαν ὕπο υ 81.—With acc. of the place: ἄλλων δῆμον ο 228 (fled to . . .), π 382 (be forced to flee to . . .).—**(3)** To present oneself before, come into the presence of: μνηστῆρας α 332 = σ 208 = φ 63, π 414. Cf. φ 25.—**(4) (a)** With notion of attainment prominent, to come to, arrive at, reach, find oneself at, be at, a specified place: οὐδ' ἦν ἔνθ' ἀφίκηαι Θ 482.—**(b)** With preps. **(α)** εἰς, ἐς: ἐς κλισίην Ω 431 : εἰς ἄντρον ι 216. Cf. δ 255, κ 1, 135, 420, 502, λ 22, μ 127, 345, ψ 338. —**(β)** ἐπί: νῆας K 281. Cf. X 208 : ρ 205.—**(γ)** κατά: στρατόν N 329.—**(δ)** ποτί: δώματα ζ 297.—**(c)** With acc.: νῆας Λ 193, 208, P 454. Cf. Λ 618, N 645, Σ 270, Ω 329, 448 : Σούνιον γ 278. Cf. ε 55, ι 181, 543, λ 122, μ 39, ξ 344, ο 36, 128, 489, φ 42, ψ 269. —Of sound: ὁππότ' ἂν νῆας ἐμὰς ἀφίκηται ἀϋτή Π 63.—Of reaching a mark in a contest θ 202.— **(5)** Of a feeling, to come upon, seize, affect: ὅτε μ' ἄλγος ἀφίκετο Σ 395.

†**ἀφίστημι** [ἀφ-, ἀπο- (1) (4) (5)]. **(A)** 3 pl. aor. subj. mid. ἀποστήσωνται N 745. **(B)** 3 sing. aor. ἀπέστη Γ 33. 2 pl. pf. ἀφέστατε Δ 340. 3 ἀφεστᾶσι N 738, Ξ 132. 3 sing. plupf. ἀφεστήκει λ 544. 3 pl. ἀφέστασαν O 672, 675, Φ 391. 3 sing. opt. ἀφεσταίη ψ 101, 169. Pl. pple. ἀφεσταότες P 375. 3 sing. pres. mid. ἀφίσταται Ψ 517. **(I)** In form (A) To get weighed out to oneself; hence, to exact payment of: χρεῖος N 745 (*i.e.* take their revenge for what they suffered).—**(II)** In pres. mid. and the other forms (B) **(1)** To shrink back (in alarm) Γ 33.—**(2)** To keep oneself separated (by a specified distance) *from.* With genit.: ὅσσον τροχοῦ ἵππος ἀφίσταται Ψ 517.—**(3)** In pf. and plupf. **(a)** To stand apart or aloof: νόσφιν ἀφεστήκει λ 544.—**(b)** To stand idle instead of fighting: τίπτε ἀφέστατε; Δ 340. Cf. N 738, Ξ 132, O 672, 675, Φ 391.—**(c)** To keep apart or aloof from each other: πολλὸν ἀφεσταότες P 375.—To keep aloof *from.* With genit.: ἀνδρὸς ψ 101 = 169.

ἄφλαστον, τό. A tall ornamental projection in which the stern of a ship ran up (app. = κόρυμβον) O 717.

ἀφλοισμός, ὁ [said to = ἀφρός]. Foam O 607.

ἀφνειός [ἄφενος]. Rich, wealthy B 570, 825, E 9, Z 47, I 483, N 664, P 576, Ω 318, 398, 482 : α 232, 393, λ 414, ξ 116, 200, ο 227, 426, 433, ρ 420 = τ 76, ρ 423 = τ 79, σ 127.—Absol. σ 276. —In superl. ἀφνειότατος Υ 220.—With genit.: βιότοιο (in . . .) E 544, Z 14, Ξ 122.—So in comp.: ἐλαφρότεροι πόδας εἶναι ἢ ἀφνειότεροι χρυσοῖο (light of foot rather than rich in . . .) α 165.

ἀφοπλίζομαι [ἀφ-, ἀπο- (6)]. To put off (one's armour): ἔντεα Ψ 26.

ἀφορμάω [ἀφ-, ἀπο- (1)]. In pass. **(1)** To set forth, depart: ἀφορμηθέντος ἀκοῦσαι β 375, δ 748. —**(2)** To sally forth *from.* With ablative: ναῦφιν B 794.

ἀφόωντα, acc. sing. masc. pres. pple. ἀφάω.

ἀφραδέω [ἀφραδής]. To act senselessly, foolishly or thoughtlessly I 32 : η 294.

ἀφραδέως [adv. fr. next]. Senselessly, foolishly, recklessly Γ 436, Μ 62, Ψ 320, 426.

ἀφραδής [ἀ-[1] + φραδ-, φράζομαι]. (1) Senseless, foolish, reckless: *μνηστήρων* β 282.—(2) Senseless, lacking the perceptive powers proper to the living: *νεκροί* λ 476.

ἀφραδίη, -ης, ἡ [ἀφραδής]. Senselessness, folly, recklessness, thoughtlessness, heedlessness: *πολέμοιο* (in war) Β 368.—In pl. in sim. sense: *παρέδραμεν ἀφραδίῃσιν* Κ 350. Cf. Ε 649, Κ 122, Π 354: *αὐτῶν ἀπωλόμεθ' ἀφραδίῃσιν* κ 27. Cf. ι 361, ξ 481, ρ 233, τ 523, χ 288.

ἀφραίνω [ἄφρων]. (1) To act senselessly, foolishly or recklessly Β 258, Η 109.—(2) To be out of one's mind, be beside oneself υ 360.

ἀφρέω [ἀφρός]. To be covered with foam Λ 282.

ἀφρήτωρ [ἀ-[1] + φρήτρη]. Unworthy to be a member of a clan: *ἀ. ἀθέμιστος ἀνέστιος* Ι 63.

'Αφροδίτη [use of the proper name]. Sexual love: *εἰς ὅ κ' ἐκλελάθωντ' 'Αφροδίτης* χ 444.

ἀφρονέω [ἄφρων]. To act senselessly or foolishly: *Ζηνὶ μενεαίνομεν ἀφρονέοντες* Ο 104.

ἀφρός, -οῦ, ὁ. Foam Ε 599, Σ 403, Φ 325.—Foam formed in a lion's mouth Υ 168.

ἀφροσύνη, -ης, ἡ [ἄφρων]. Senselessness, folly, recklessness Η 110.—In pl. in sim. sense π 278, ω 457.

ἄφρων, -ονος [ἀ-[1] + φρήν]. Senseless, foolish Δ 104, Ε 875, Λ 389, Π 842, Ω 157 = 186: ζ 187, θ 209, ρ 586, υ 227, φ 102, 105, ψ 12.—Absol. Γ 220, Ε 761.

ἄφυλλος, -ον [ἀ-[1] + φύλλον]. Leafless, stripped of leaves: *σχίζῃσιν* Β 425.

ἀφύξειν, fut. infin. *ἀφύσσω*.

ἀφυσγετός, ὁ. App., drift-wood; or perh., mud Λ 495.

ἀφύσσω. Fut. infin. *ἀφύξειν* Α 171. 3 sing. aor. *ἤφυσε* Ν 508, Ρ 315. *ἄφυσσε* Ξ 517: β 379. 1 pl. *ἠφύσαμεν* ι 165. Imp. *ἄφυσσον* β 349. Pple. *ἀφύσσας* ι 204. Aor. mid. *ἠφυσάμην* η 286. 3 sing. *ἀφύσσατο* Π 230. 1 pl. *-άμεθα* ι 85, κ 56. Masc. pl. pple. *ἀφυσσάμενοι* δ 359. (δι-, ἐξαφύω, ἐπ-.) (1) To draw (water). In mid. δ 359, ι 85 = κ 56.—(2) To draw off (wine etc.): *νέκταρ ἀπὸ κρητῆρος* Α 598. Cf. β 349, 379, ι 9, 165, 204.—In mid.: *ἐκ κρητῆρος ἀφυσσόμενοι δεπάεσσιν* (in cups) Γ 295. Cf. Κ 579, Π 230, Ψ 220.—In pass.: *πολλὸς ἠφύσσετο οἶνος* ψ 305.—(3) To get together, heap up (wealth) Α 171.—In mid., to bring or gather together (about one): *ἀμφὶ φύλλα ἠφυσάμην* η 286.—(4) Of a weapon, to let out (the entrails) like water: *διὰ δ' ἔντερα χαλκὸς ἤφυσεν* Ν 508 = Ρ 315. Cf. Ξ 517.

ἀχάριστος [ἀ-[1] + χαρίζομαι]. Ungracious, unpleasing. Of speech θ 236.—Unpleasant, unpleasing. In comp. *ἀχαρίστερος* (ἀ-χαρίτ-τερος) υ 392.

ἄχερδος. Some kind of prickly shrub ξ 10.

ἀχερωΐς, ἡ [conn. in popular etymology with the river Acheron, from which Heracles was said to have brought the tree]. A tree, said to be the white poplar Ν 389 = Π 482.

ἀχεύω [ἄχος]. To be grieved or troubled, grieve, sorrow. Only in pres. pple.: *θυμὸν ἀχεύων* (in his heart) Ε 869, Σ 461, Ψ 566. Cf. Ι 612, Ω 128: β 23, δ 100, λ 88, φ 318.—With genit. of person grieved for: *ἄνακτος* ξ 40. Cf. π 139.

ἀχέω [ἄχος]. 3 sing. aor. *ἤκαχε* Π 822: ο 357, π 427. 3 pl. aor. mid. *ἀκάχοντο* π 342. Opt. *ἀκαχοίμην* α 236. 3 sing. *-οιτο* Θ 207, Ν 344. 1 pl. *-οίμεθα* Π 16. (1) In aor. act., to cause to grieve, grieve, trouble Π 822: ο 357.—To molest, harry: *Θεσπρωτούς* π 427.—(2) In pres. pple. act. and aor. mid., to be grieved or troubled, be in grief or trouble, grieve, sorrow: *κῆρ ἀχέων* (in his heart) Ε 399. Cf. Β 724, Θ 207, Ν 344: *μνηστῆρες ἀκάχοντο* π 342. Cf. λ 195, ο 361.—With genit. of what is grieved for: *Βρισηΐδος* Β 694. Cf. Ι 567, Π 16, Σ 446.—With dat.: *θανόντι* α 236.

ἄχθομαι [ἄχθος]. (1) Of a ship, to be laden, have her cargo on board ο 457.—(2) To be weighed down, be in pain or grief: *ὀδύνῃσιν* Ε 354, *ἕλκος* (app. acc. of part affected, 'in the wound') 361, *κῆρ* (in his heart) Λ 274 = 400.—With pple. in acc. expressing the cause of grief: *ἤχθετο* ['Αργείους] *δαμναμένους* Ν 352.

ἄχθος, τό. (1) A weight, burden, load: *ἀ. ἀρούρης* (cumbering the earth) Σ 104. Cf. Μ 452: υ 379.—A weight or load carried: *ἀ. ὕλης* ι 233.—(2) The lading or cargo of a ship Υ 247: γ 312.

ἀχλύς, -ύος, ἡ. A mist: *ἀχλύν οἱ κατέχευεν* η 41. Cf. υ 357.—In reference to blinding or to the mist of death: *κατ' ὀφθαλμῶν κέχυτ' ἀ.* Ε 696, *ἀπ' ὀφθαλμῶν νέφος ἀχλύος ὦσεν* (the cloud of mist) Ο 668. Cf. Ε 127, Π 344, Υ 321, 341, 421: χ 88.

ἀχλύω [ἀχλύς]. To become shrouded in darkness: *ἤχλυσε πόντος* μ 406 = ξ 304.

ἄχνη, -ης, ἡ. (1) Foam, froth Δ 426, Λ 307, Ο 626: ε 403, μ 238.—(2) In pl., chaff: *καρπόν τε καὶ ἄχνας* Ε 501. Cf. Ε 499.

ἄχνυμαι [ἄχος]. To be grieved or troubled, be in grief or trouble, grieve, sorrow: *ἀνέστη ἀχνύμενος* Α 103, *ἀχνύμενοι κῆρ* (in their hearts) Η 428. Cf. Α 241, 588, Β 270, Η 431, Μ 178, Ν 419, 658, Ξ 38, Ο 133, Σ 62 = 443, Σ 112 = Τ 65, Σ 320, Τ 8, 57, Χ 424, Ψ 137, 165, 284, 443, Ω 523, 526, 584, 773: δ 104, 549, 553, 661, η 297, θ 478, κ 67, 174, 570, λ 5, 388, 466, 542, μ 12, 153 = 270, 250, ξ 170, π 147, φ 115, 250, χ 188, ω 21, 420.—With genit. of person grieved for: *ἑταίρου* Θ 125 = 317. Cf. Ν 403, Ο 651, Ρ 459: λ 558, ξ 376.—With acc. expressing the cause of grief: *τὸ δ' ἐμὸν κῆρ ἄχνυται, ὅτε . . .* Ζ 524.

ἄχολος [ἀ-[1] + χόλος]. Allaying wrath δ 221.

ἄχομαι [ἄχος]. To be in trouble σ 256 = τ 129.

ἄχος, -εος, τό. (1) Pain of the mind, grief, sorrow, trouble, distress: *Πηλεΐωνι ἀ. γένετο* Α 188, *σέθεν* (for thee) Δ 169. Cf. Β 171, Ζ 336, Θ 124, Κ 145, Ν 581, etc.: δ 108, 716, θ 541, ο 358, σ 274, etc.—In pl., sorrows, troubles: *ἄχε' ἄκριτα* Γ 412, Ω 91. Cf. Ζ 413: τ 167.—(2) A subject of grief: *ἀ. μοί ἐστιν* Π 55. Cf. Ε 759, Ι 249: χ 345.—

A subject or cause of resentment: ἕνεκ' ἀλλοτρίων ἀχέων (in a quarrel not his own) Υ 298.

ἀχρεῖος [ἀ-[1] + χρείη, use, advantage. Cf. χρεῖος]. Serving no good purpose. In neut. ἀχρεῖον as adv.: ἀ. ἰδών (looking (about him) like one dazed, with helpless look) Β 269: ἀ. ἐγέλασσεν (a forced laugh (to cover embarrassment in announcing her intention)) σ 163.

ἀχρημοσύνη, ἡ [ἀ-[1] + χρῆμα]. Lack of means ρ 502.

ἄχρι(ς). **(1)** Adv., utterly, completely: τένοντε ἀ. ἀπηλοίησεν Δ 522, ἀπ' ὀστέον ἀ. ἄραξεν Π 324, γράψεν οἱ ὀστέον ἀ. (app. implying that though the wound was a superficial one (a portion of) the bone was destroyed) Ρ 599.—**(2)** Prep. with genit., until, up to: κνέφαος σ 370.

ἀχυρμιή, -ῆς, ἡ. A heap of chaff Ε 502.

ἄψ. **(1)** In the reverse direction, backwards, back, back again: ἀπονοστήσειν Α 60, ἐς κουλεὸν ὦσε ξίφος 220. Cf. Γ 32, 35, Δ 392, Ζ 467, Κ 211, etc.: ἐς πόντον ἐδύσετο ε 352. Cf. α 276, γ 307, δ 261, ι 314, λ 18, ρ 461, etc.—In reference to the direction in which one looks, backwards: ὁρόων Γ 325.—Of a period of time completing its cycle: ἀ. περιτελλομένου ἔτεος λ 295 = ξ 294.—**(2)** Back to a former state or condition, again: ἀπέλυσεν Ζ 427, ἐνὶ χώρῃ ἕζετο Ψ 349. Cf. Π 54, 58, 86, Χ 277, etc.: ἄνδρες ἐγένοντο κ 395. Cf. π 175, σ 152.—With αὖτις Θ 335, Ο 364: σ 157 = φ 139 = 166 = ψ 164.—In reference to making atonement or effecting reconciliation: ἀρέσαι Ι 120 = Τ 138. —**(3)** Again, once more: ἐπόρουσεν Γ 379. Cf. Ε 505, Ρ 543, Φ 33: ὤσασκεν λ 599. Cf. θ 90, 92.

ἅψατο, 3 sing. aor. mid. ἅπτω.

ἁψίς, -ῖδος, ἡ [ἅπτω]. A mesh of a net Ε 487.

ἀψόρροος [ἄψ + (σ)ρέω]. Of Ocean, flowing back on himself as encircling the earth Σ 399: υ 65.

ἄψορρος [ἄψ + (perh.) ἐρσ-, L. *erro*. Cf. παλίνορσος]. **(1)** Going back, returning: ἄψορροι ἀπονέοντο Γ 313, Ω 330. Cf. Φ 456.—**(2)** In neut. ἄψορρον as adv. **(a)** Back, back again: ἀ. θυμὸς ἀγέρθη Δ 152, ἀ. ἔβη προτὶ Ἴλιον Η 413. Cf. Μ 74, Π 376, Φ 382: κ 558 = λ 63.—**(b)** In reply ι 282, 501.

ἅψος, -εος, τό [ἅπτω]. A joint δ 794 = σ 189.

†ἄω [ἀ-, ἁ-, (σ)α-. Cf. ἄδην, ἄδην and L. *satis*]. Infin. ἄμεναι Φ 70. Fut. infin. ἄσειν Λ 818. 3 sing. aor. subj. ἄσῃ Σ 281. Opt. ἄσαιμι Ι 489. Infin. ἆσαι Ε 289, Λ 574, Ο 317, Υ 78, Φ 168, Χ 267, Ψ 157, Ω 211. 2 pl. fut. mid. ἄσεσθε Ω 717. Aor. infin. ἄσασθαι Τ 307. Also a 1 pl. subj. ἕωμεν (disyllable) Τ 402, formed by metathesis of quantity fr. ἥομεν fr. ἡ- = (σ)α-. **(1)** To sate, satiate: κύνας Λ 818, Ω 211.—To sate with, give a fill of. With genit.: αἵματος Ε 289 = Υ 78 = Χ 267. Cf. Ι 489, Σ 281.—In mid. Τ 307.—**(2)** To sate oneself with, take or have one's fill of. With genit.: χροός (of spears personified) Λ 574 = Ο 317, Φ 70, 168, πολέμοιο Τ 402, γόοιο Ψ 157. —In mid.: κλαυθμοῖο Ω 717.

ἄωρος [perh. fr. αἰωρέω = ἀείρω]. Thus, pendulous: πόδες μ 89 (of Scylla).

ἄωρτο, 3 sing. plupf. pass. ἀείρω.

ἀωτέω. To sleep, slumber Κ 159: κ 548.

ἄωτος. **(1)** The wool on an animal: [ἀρνειοῦ] ι 434.—**(2)** Things made of wool. **(a)** A blanket: κεκαλυμμένος οἰὸς ἀώτῳ α 443.—App. in generalized sense: λίνοιο ἄωτον (a bed-covering of linen) Ι 661. —**(b)** οἰὸς ἀ. in sense 'sling' Ν 599.—Collectively, slings Ν 716.

βάδην [βα-, βαίνω]. Step by step: ἀπιόντος Ν 516.

βάζω. 3 sing. pf. pass. βέβακται θ 408. **(1)** To speak γ 127, λ 511, σ 168.—**(2)** To say, speak, utter: ταῦτα Δ 355, ἄρτια Ξ 92: ἔπος εἴ τι βέβακται δεινόν θ 408. Cf. δ 32, 206, 837 = λ 464, θ 240, ξ 127, 157, ρ 461, σ 332 = 392.—**(3)** With double acc. of thing said and person addressed: ταῦτά μ' ἐβάζετε Π 207. Cf. Ι 58.

βάθιστος, superl. βαθύς.

βαθυδινήεις, -εντος [βαθύς + δίνη]. Deep-eddying: Ξάνθου Φ 15, Σκάμανδρον 603.

βαθυδίνης, -ου [as prec.]. = prec.: ποταμός Υ 73, Φ 143, 212, 228, 329: Ὠκεανῷ κ 511.

βαθύζωνος, -ον [βαθύς + ζώνη]. Deep-girded, so girt that the upper part of the robe falls down in a deep fold (κόλπος) over the girdle. Epithet of women Ι 594: γ 154.

βαθύκολπος, -ον [βαθύς + κόλπος]. Whose robe falls down in a deep fold over the girdle (cf. prec.). Epithet of women Σ 122, 339, Ω 215.

βαθύλειμος, -ον [βαθύς + λειμών]. Having meadows with deep rich grass: Ἄνθειαν Ι 151 = 293.

βαθυλήϊος [βαθύς + λήϊον]. With a deep rich crop: τέμενος Σ 550 (*v.l.* βασιλήϊον).

βαθύνω [βαθύς]. To lower the surface of Ψ 421.

βαθυρρείτης [βαθύς + (σ)ρέω]. With deep, steady flow Φ 195.

βαθύρροος [as prec.]. = prec. Η 422, Ξ 311, Φ 8: λ 13, τ 434.

βαθύς, -εῖα, -ύ. Fem. -έη Ε 142, Ο 606, Π 766, Φ 213. **(1)** Deep: ἅλα Α 532. Cf. Η 341, 440, Θ 336, 481, Ν 32, Ο 356, etc.: ζ 116, μ 214.—Epithet of φρήν Τ 125.—In superl. βάθιστος Θ 14.—Where we should rather say 'high': αὐλῆς (high-walled) Ε 142: ι 239, 338.—Sim., app., of a storm, reaching from earth to heaven Λ 306.—**(2)** Deep, extending far inwards: ἠϊόνος Β 92.—Deeply indenting the land: κόλπον Β 560.—**(3)** Growing thickly, affording thick covert: ὕλης Ε 555. Cf. Λ 415, Ο 606, Π 766, Υ 491, Φ 573: ρ 316.—**(4)** Lying thick: τέφρη Ψ 251.—Forming a thick deposit: ἀμάθοιο Ε 587.—**(5)** With deep soil: νειοῖο Κ 353, Σ 547.—**(6)** Forming a deep, rich crop: λήϊον Β 147, Λ 560: ι 134.—**(7)** Thick, obstructing vision: ἠέρα Υ 446. Cf. Φ 7: ι 144.

βαθύσχοινος [βαθύς + σχοῖνος]. With banks thickly set with rushes: Ἀσωπόν Δ 383.

βαίνω. **(A)** 3 sing. fut. in mid. form βήσεται Β 339. Aor. ἔβην Ω 766: ι 177. βῆν ι 196, κ 60, 169, 407, μ 367. 2 sing. ἔβης Ι 107. 3 ἔβη

A 311, 424, B 47, 187, Γ 261, etc. : α 427, β 18, 27, 173, δ 701, etc. βῆ A 34, 44, 439, B 16, etc. : α 102, 119, 441, β 5, 10, etc. 3 dual ἐβήτην Z 40. βήτην Θ 115, M 330, Ξ 281, 285, etc. : θ 49, ρ 200, χ 202, 378. βάτην A 327, E 778, I 182, 192, etc. : ω 361. 1 pl. ἔβημεν ξ 241. βῆμεν γ 131, ι 85, 150, κ 56, etc. 3 ἔβησαν Θ 343, Λ 460, M 16, N 332, etc. : ε 107, ω 301. βῆσαν υ 158, φ 188. ἔβαν A 391, 606, B 302, Γ 113, H 429, etc. : α 211, 424, γ 11, 162, 396, etc. βάν Δ 209, K 150, 273, 297, M 106, etc. : δ 779, θ 56, 109, ο 109, 295, etc. Subj. βήω Z 113. 3 pl. βῶσι ξ 86. Opt. βαίην Ω 246. Pple. βάς, βάντος E 239, Z 65, K 576, Σ 532 : β 419, δ 48, 680, ε 56, θ 296, 314, 450, 456, etc. Infin. βήμεναι P 504 : θ 518, ξ 327, τ 296. βῆναι N 459, Ξ 24. 2 sing. pf. βέβηκας O 90. 3 βέβηκε Π 69, Ψ 481. 3 pl. βεβάᾱσι B 134. 3 sing. plupf. ἐβεβήκει Z 513, Λ 296, 446, N 156, etc. βεβήκει A 221, Z 313, 495, Π 751, 856, etc.: α 360, γ 410, ζ 11, θ 361, κ 388, etc. 3 pl. βέβασαν P 286. Pple. βεβαώς Ξ 477. Acc. sing. masc. βεβαῶτα ε 130. Fem. βεβῶσα υ 14. Infin. βεβάμεν P 359, 510. 3 sing. aor. mid. ἐβήσετο Ξ 229 : η 135, ν 63, 75, ο 284. βήσετο Γ 262, 312, E 745, Θ 389 : γ 481. **(B)** 3 sing. aor. βῆσε A 310, E 164, Π 810. 1 pl. ἐβήσαμεν λ 4. βήσαμεν Λ 756. 3 βῆσαν A 438. 1 pl. subj. βήσομεν A 144. (ἀμφι-, ἀνα-, ἀπο-, δια-, εἰσ-, εἰσανα-, ἐκ-, ἐκδια-, ἐμ-, ἐξανα-, ἐξαπο-, ἐπεμ-, ἐπι-, ἐσκατα-, κατα-, μετα-, παρα-, περι-, προ-, προσ-, ὑπερ-, ὑπερκατα-.)—**(I)** *Intrans.* in all forms except those under (B). **(1)** To go, go one's way, take one's way : παρὰ θῖνα θαλάσσης A 34. Cf. A 44, 311, 424, B 16, 47, Δ 443, 495, etc. : οἰκόνδε α 424. Cf. α 102, 119, 427, β 18, 406, γ 131, ι 196, etc.—Of something inanimate : ἰκμὰς ἔβη (*i.e.* finds its way inwards, making way for the unguent) P 392.—**(2)** Of immaterial things, to go, pass. εὐχωλαί Θ 229. Cf. B 339.—So of time : ἐννέα βεβάασιν ἐνιαυτοί (have passed) B 134.—**(3) (a)** In pf. of the state or condition of going : ἔχων εὔληρα βέβηκε (is going, *i.e.* is driving the chariot) Ψ 481 : περὶ τρόπιος βεβαῶτα (bestriding it and being carried along with it) ε 130.—**(b)** In plupf. of being in the act or attitude of going : Οὔλυμπόνδε βεβήκει (was in motion to go, *i.e.* started or set out to go, took her way) A 221. Cf. Z 313, 495, Λ 446, Π 751, 856 = X 362, Π 864, P 706, X 21, Ψ 391 : α 360 = φ 354, θ 361, κ 388, ν 164, ο 464, ρ 26, 61, σ 185 = τ 503 = χ 433, τ 47 = υ 144, ψ 292.—But in strict plupf. sense : Ἄϊδόσδε βεβήκει γ 410 = ζ 11.—Without complementary words, strode along Z 513, Λ 296, N 156, Υ 161.—**(4)** To start or set out *to go, run*, etc. : βῆ θέειν B 183, βῆ ἰέναι Δ 199. Cf. E 167, Z 296, N 27, Υ 32, Ψ 229, etc. : α 441, β 298, δ 779, ξ 87, 501, etc.—**(5)** To move oneself into a specified position, get on to, into, out of, something : ἐς ἅρματα E 239, ἐς ἀσαμίνθους K 576. Cf. E 364, 745, Z 65, P 504, Σ 532, Ψ 132, etc. : ἐξ ἀσαμίνθου γ 468. Cf. γ 481, 492, δ 48, μ 229, φ 51, etc.—So with acc. : βήσετο δίφρον (mounted it) Γ 262 = 312.—Without the acc. : ὄπιθεν βῆ Ἀχιλλεύς (mounted after him) T 397.—Of going (on board a ship) : ἐπὶ νηὸς ἔβαινεν N 665. Cf. β 416, θ 501, ι 177, λ 534, ο 284, 547.—Of disembarking (from a ship) : ἐκ νηὸς βῆ A 439. Cf. γ 12, ν 116.—Sim. : ἐπ' ἠπείρου βῆμεν ι 85 = κ 56.—**(6)** With adverbs and prepositions. **(a)** With ἀμφί as prep., to bestride : ἀμφ' ἑνὶ δούρατι βαῖνεν ε 371.—So, to bestride and protect (a fallen friend) (cf. ἀμφιβαίνω (4), περιβαίνω) : ἀμφ' αὐτῷ βαῖνεν E 299. Cf. Ξ 477, P 4, 359, 510.—Sim. with περί : περὶ Πατρόκλῳ βαῖνεν P 6. Cf. P 4, 137 : υ 14.—Of bestriding the body of a foe with a view to dragging it off : Τρῶες περὶ Πατρόκλῳ βέβασαν P 286. (For the time indicated in these cases by the pf. and plupf. cf. (3).)—**(b)** With ἀνά. **(α)** To mount a chariot, etc. : ἀν' ἔβη Πρίαμος Γ 261. Cf. Γ 311, P 541 : ζ 253.—Sim. with παρά, to mount a chariot (and stand) beside another : πὰρ Μαχάων βαινέτω (βαῖνεν) Λ 513, 518.—Also with παρά as prep. : πὰρ δέ οἱ Ἶρις ἔβαινεν E 365.—**(β)** To go on board a ship : ἀν' αὐτοὶ βάντες (βαίνομεν) β 419 = δ 579, λ 5. Cf. ν 75.—**(c)** With ἐκ. **(α)** To dismount from a chariot : ἐκ δ' ἔβαν αὐτοί Γ 113.—**(β)** To disembark from a ship : ἐξ αὐτοὶ βαῖνον A 437. Cf. γ 11, δ 785, ι 150 = 547 = μ 6, ο 499.—**(d)** With μετά of crossing an indicated line : μετὰ δ' ἄστρα βεβήκει (had crossed the meridian) μ 312, ξ 483.—**(e)** For περί, παρά see (a) (b).—**(7)** To come : τίπτε βέβηκας; (hast thou come) O 90, πόλις ἐπὶ πᾶσα βέβηκε (has come to encounter us) Π 69.—**(II)** *Trans.* in forms (B). To cause to take a specified position : ἂν Χρυσηΐδα βήσομεν (let us put her on board) A 144, ἐς ἑκατόμβην βῆσεν (put it on board) 310, ἐξ ἑκατόμβην βῆσαν (landed it) 438, τοὺς ἐξ ἵππων βῆσεν (thrust or knocked off) E 164, βήσαμεν ἵππους (brought to a stand, stopped) Λ 756, φῶτας βῆσεν ἀφ' ἵππων Π 810 : ἐν τὰ μῆλα ἐβήσαμεν (put them on board) λ 4.

βάλανος, ἡ. The fruit of the φηγός κ 242, ν 409.

βάλλω. Fut. βαλέω Θ 403. βαλῶ P 451. 3 sing. βαλέει κ 290. Dat. sing. masc. pple. βαλέοντι λ 608. Aor. ἔβαλον (βάλον), -ες A 245, 436, B 692, Γ 368, E 188, 574, 588, Θ 156, etc. : α 364, δ 41, 50, 344, κ 172, ν 267, ρ 89, 483, etc. Subj. βάλω P 17, 40. 2 sing. -ησθα μ 221. 3 -ησι Φ 104, 576. -η Υ 168, 378, Ψ 855 : β 330, ε 415, ρ 279. 1 pl. -ωμεν Δ 16. Opt. βάλοιμι Π 623 : θ 216. 2 sing. -οισθα O 571. 3 -οι Λ 389 : δ 223, ρ 251, 494, υ 65, 80. Pple. βαλών, -όντος E 145, H 270, Λ 454, P 457, X 207, Ψ 572, etc. : δ 245, ε 128, θ 501, ι 470, λ 211, ρ 567, χ 92, etc. Neut. βαλόν η 279. Fem. βαλοῦσα, -ης Ψ 462 : ζ 100, υ 62. Infin. βαλέειν B 414, H 242, K 368, N 629, etc. : δ 198, ε 349, θ 508, ι 137, ξ 399, χ 174. βαλεῖν N 387, Ξ 424. 3 sing. plupf. (in intensive impf. or aor. sense) βεβλήκει(ν) Δ 108, 492, E 66, 73, 394, 661, M 401, Ξ 412, P 606 : χ 258, 275, 286. 3 sing. opt. -οι Θ 270. **Mid.** Imp. βάλλευ μ 218. Aor. βαλόμην κ 262. 3 sing. βάλετο B 45, Γ 334, E 738, Λ 29, Π 135, T 372 : ε 231, κ 544, ξ 528, ο 61.

3 pl. *ἐβάλοντο* M 377, O 566, Ψ 352 : ξ 209. 3 sing. subj. *βάλῃται* λ 428. **Pass.** 3 sing. aor. *ἔβλητο* Λ 410, 675, M 306, Π 753. *βλῆτο* Δ 518, Π 570, P 598. 3 sing. subj. *βλήεται* ρ 472. 2 sing. opt. *βλεῖο* N 288. Pple. *βλήμενος, -ου* Δ 211, Θ 514, Λ 191, 206, M 391, O 495, 580, P 726, Φ 594 : ρ 490, 493, χ 18. Infin. *βλῆσθαι* Δ 115 : χ 253. 2 sing. pf. *βέβληαι* E 284, Λ 380, N 251. 3 *βέβληται* E 103, Λ 660, 662, Π 25, 27. 3 pl. *βεβλήαται* Λ 657 : λ 194. 3 sing. plupf. *βέβλητο* μ 423. 3 pl. *βεβλήατο* Ξ 28 : η 97. Pple. *βεβλημένος, -ου* Λ 475, 592, 659, M 2, N 764, Ξ 63, etc. : λ 535, τ 69. (*ἀμφι-, ἀνα-, ἐκ-, ἐμ-, ἐπι-, κατα-, παρα-, παρακατα-, περι-, προ-, προσ-, συμ-, ὑπερ-, ὑπο-.*) **(I)** To throw. **(1)** To throw or cast in gen. : *ποτὶ σκῆπτρον βάλε γαίῃ* A 245. Cf. B 183, Φ 51, X 468, etc. : ε 349, θ 508, τ 63, υ 65, etc.—Of winds, to beat upon so as to throw (together) : *πυρῆς ἄμυδις φλόγ' ἔβαλλον* Ψ 217.—**(2)** To throw or let fly (a missile) : *χαλκόν* E 317 = 346 : *βέλος* ι 495. Cf. ι 482, 539, υ 62.—Absol. : *μὴ βάλλετε* Γ 82. Cf. A 52, Θ 282, N 718, 721, Π 104 : ι 158, λ 608.—In mid. with reciprocal force : *βαλλομένων* (as they threw at one another) M 289.—With the missile in dat. : *λάεσσιν* Γ 80. Cf. M 155 : κ 122.—**(3)** To hurl or throw (a person down) : *κατὰ Μύνητ' ἔβαλεν* B 692. Cf. E 588, Θ 156 : χ 188.—To throw in wrestling Ψ 727 : δ 344 = ρ 135.—To hurl from something : *ἐκ δίφρου* Θ 403, 417. Cf. Λ 109.—To thrust back from something : *ἀπ' αὐτάων δηΐους* M 264.—To thrust or cause to go into a place : *ἐς θάλαμον* χ 174.—**(4)** In reference to things, to throw down, destroy : *κατὰ βαλέειν μέλαθρον* B 414. Cf. I 541.—To send flying, cause to fall : *τῆλε κάρη βάλεν* Υ 482.—To knock off from something : *ἀπὸ κρατὸς κυνέην* Π 793.—Out of something : *ἐκ χειρῶν μάστιγα* Ψ 384.—To thrust or cause to strike against something : *πρὸς ἀλλήλας ἔβαλον ὄζους* Π 768.—**(5)** To thrust or urge (one's horses in front or in advance) : *τοὺς σοὺς [ἵππους] πρόσθε βαλών* Ψ 572.—Absol. Ψ 639.—Intrans. of horses, to thrust themselves forward, rush Ψ 462.—**(6)** To put (a ship to sea) : *νῆας ἐς πόντον βάλλουσιν* δ 359.—**(7)** Of the action of the sea, to beat, drive : *ποτὶ πέτρῃ κῦμα* ε 415. Cf. η 279, ι 284, μ 71.—**(8)** To cause to be somewhere or in some position, to throw, put, place, set : *σύν ῥ' ἔβαλον ῥινούς* Δ 447, *βαλέτην ἐν χερσὶν ἑταίρων* E 574. Cf. B 376, E 722, N 36, T 394, etc. : *θρόνοις ἔνι ῥήγεα* κ 352. Cf. δ 455, η 97, ι 470, λ 194, μ 221, etc.—In mid. : *ἐν (ἐπὶ) κλήρους ἐβάλοντο* Ψ 352 : ξ 209.—In mid., to put oneself in act to do something : *σὺν δ' ἐβάλοντο μάχεσθαι* M 377.—**(9)** In reference to immaterial things, to send, set, inspire : *ἐν στήθεσσι μένος βάλεν* E 513, *σὺν δ' ἔβαλον πόλεμον* (joined battle) M 181. Cf. Δ 16, P 451, Φ 547 : *ἐν φύζαν ἑτάροισιν* ξ 269 = ρ 438.—Without expressed object : *ὡς ἐνὶ θυμῷ ἀθάνατοι βάλλουσιν* α 201 = ο 173.—**(10)** To let fall : *ποτὶ γαίῃ χεῖρας* λ 424.—To let fall or shed (tears) : *δάκρυ χαμάδις βάλεν* δ 114. Cf. δ 198, 223, ρ 490.—Of shedding sleep : *ὕπνον ἐπὶ βλεφάροισιν* α 364 = π 451 = τ 604 = φ 358.—To let hang down : *ἑτέρωσε κάρη* Θ 306, Ψ 697.—To lay on (the lash) : *ἐφ' ἵπποιϊν μάστιν* ο 182.—**(11)** To turn (the eyes) : *ἑτέρωσ' ὄμματα* π 179.—**(12)** Of a river, to carry down with it and discharge (into the sea) : *ἀφυσγετὸν εἰς ἅλα* Λ 495.—Absol., to discharge its waters, empty itself : *εἰς ἅλα βάλλων* Λ 722.—**(13)** Of throwing or putting clothes, armour, etc., on a person, enduing him with them : *ἀμφί μιν φᾶρος* Ω 588. Cf. Σ 204 : γ 467, δ 50, 440, ν 434, etc.—So of putting on oneself : *σπεῖρ' ἀμφ' ὤμοισι βαλών* δ 245.—In mid. : *περὶ βάλλετο φᾶρος* B 43, *ἀμφ' ὤμοισι βάλετο ξίφος* 45 = Γ 334 = Π 135 = T 372, Λ 29. Cf. E 738, K 333 : *περὶ ζώνην βάλετ' ἰξυῖ* ε 231 = κ 544. Cf. κ 262, ξ 528, ο 61, ρ 197 = σ 108.—**(14)** In mid., to lay (to heart) : *ἐνὶ φρεσὶ βάλλεο σῇσιν* A 297 = Δ 39 = E 259 = I 611 = Π 444 = 851 = Φ 94. Cf. O 566 : λ 454 = π 281 = 299 = ρ 548 = τ 236 = 495 = 570, μ 218.—To cherish (in the heart) : *ἐν θυμῷ βάλλονται ἐμοὶ χόλον* Ξ 50.—To think of or consider as to (in one's mind) : *εἰ νόστον μετὰ φρεσὶ βάλλεαι* I 435.—Sim. : *ὡς ἐνὶ θυμῷ βάλλεαι* (as thou (fondly) fanciest) Υ 196 : *ἤ τις τοιαῦτα μετὰ φρεσὶν ἔργα βάληται* (conceives, contrives) λ 428.—**(II)** To strike. **(1) (a)** To strike or wound (a person, etc.) with a missile, and in pass., to be so struck or wounded : *υἱὸν Πριάμοιο* Δ 499, *βεβλημένοι οὐτάμενοί τε* Λ 659. Cf. Θ 81, M 391, O 249, etc. : *ἀργῆτι κεραυνῷ* ε 128, *ὁππότ' ἀνὴρ βλήεται* ρ 472. Cf. λ 535, ν 267, ρ 279, χ 283, etc.—**(b)** With the part of the body struck as object : *αὐχένα μέσσον* E 657. Cf. N 594, Π 807, Φ 591, etc. : *δεξιὸν ὦμον* ρ 462. Cf. ρ 504, χ 82.—With the part of the armour struck as object : *Αἴαντος σάκος* H 245. Cf. N 258, Φ 164, etc.—In pass. : *πήληξ βαλλομένη καναχὴν ἔχε, βάλλετο δ' αἰεί* Π 105.—**(c)** With double acc. of the person and the part of the body struck ; *στῆθός μιν* Δ 480. Cf. N 506, O 341, Π 399, Φ 166, etc. : σ 396, υ 306, χ 277.—With acc. of the person and of the part of the armour struck ; *τὸν τελαμῶνα* M 401, *Ἕκτορα θώρηκα* P 606. Cf. E 98, etc.—**(d)** In pass. with acc. of the part struck : *βλῆτο κνήμην* Δ 518. Cf. E 284, P 598.—**(e)** With double acc. of the person and of the wound : *ἕλκος τό μιν βάλε Πάνδαρος* E 795. Cf. Π 511.—**(f)** Without object, but with words indicating where the blow falls : *βάλεν Ἀτρεΐδαο κατ' ἀσπίδα* Γ 347. Cf. Γ 356, E 305, etc.—**(g)** With the missile as subject E 17 = Π 479.—**(2)** Of striking inanimate objects : *βάλε μέσσας [σανίδας]* M 457. Cf. I 574, Φ 171, Ψ 866, etc. : *νῆα κεραυνῷ* μ 388, ψ 330, *ἐπίτονος βέβλητο* (was snapped) μ 423. Cf. υ 302, χ 258 = 275.—**(3)** Of such objects striking : *ἄντυγας (ἡνίοχον) ῥαθάμιγγες* Λ 536 = Υ 501, Ψ 502.—Of the sun : *ἀκτῖσιν ἔβαλλεν* ε 479, τ 441.—Of sound : *κτύπος οὔατα βάλλει* K 535.—**(4)** In mid. with *ἀνά*, to strike up, begin (to sing) (cf. *ἀναβάλλω* (2)) : *ἀνά σφισι βάλλετ' ἀείδειν* ρ 262.

βαμβαίνω. An imitative formation, to stammer; or perh. redup. fr. *βαίνω*, to stagger K 375.

βάν, 3 pl. aor. *βαίνω*.

βάπτω. To plunge (into water) : *πέλεκυν* ι 392.

βαρβαρόφωνος [βάρβαρος, foreign + φωνή]. App. referring to harshness of speech = ἀγριόφωνος B 867.

βάρδιστος [metathesis of βράδιστος, superl. of βραδύς]. Slowest. Of horses Ψ 310, 530.

†**βαρέω** [βαρύς]. Pf. pple. βεβαρηώς, -ότος. In this pple., weighed down, overcome γ 139, τ 122.

βαρύθω [βαρύς]. To be weighed down: βαρύθει μοι ὦμος (has lost its power) Π 519.

βαρύνω [βαρύς]. Aor. pple. pass. βαρυνθείς Υ 480. Acc. neut. βαρυνθέν Θ 308. To weigh down, oppress: γυῖα βαρύνεται Τ 165. Cf. E 664, Θ 308, Υ 480: ε 321.—Sim.: δόναξ ἐβάρυνε μηρόν (app., made it painful to move) Λ 584.

βαρύς, -εῖα, -ύ [cf. βριθύς]. **(1)** Heavy. Of the hand or arm, heavy, powerful A 89, 219, E 81, Λ 235 = P 48, N 410, Φ 590, Ψ 687: σ 56. —**(2)** Heavy to bear, grievous, dire: ἄτῃ B 111 = I 18. Cf. E 417, K 71, Υ 55: ο 233.—Giving misery, stern, dire, grim: κῆρας Φ 548. Cf. η 197. —**(3)** Of a voice, deep (as proceeding from a giant's throat) ι 257.—**(4)** In neut. βαρύ as adv., of groaning, heavily, deeply A 364 = Σ 78, Δ 153, I 16, Π 20, Σ 70, 323, Ψ 60: θ 95 = 534.—So in neut. pl. βαρέα Θ 334, N 423, 538 = Ξ 432: δ 516 = ψ 317, ε 420, κ 76.

βάς, aor. pple. βαίνω.

βασίλεια, -ης, ἡ [βασιλεύς]. **(1)** The wife of a βασιλεύς. Of Penelope δ 697, 770, π 332, 337, ρ 370 = 468 = σ 351 = φ 275, ρ 513, 583, σ 314, ψ 149. —Of Arete η 241, λ 345, ν 59.—**(2)** The daughter of a βασιλεύς. Of Nausicaa ζ 115.—**(3)** β. γυναικῶν, the peerless one among women λ 258.

βασιλεύς, -ῆος, ὁ. One in authority, a king, chief, noble. **(1)** Of men (never of gods), sometimes as a title, sometimes as a descriptive term. Of Agamemnon A 9, 231, 340, 410, Γ 179, Δ 402, H 180, Λ 23, 46, 136, 262, 283, T 256.—Of Achilles A 331, Π 211.—Of Nestor B 54.—Of Paris Δ 96.—Of Priam E 464, Ω 680, 803.—Of Proetus Z 163.—Of Rhesus K 435, 494.—Of Sarpedon Π 660.—Of Menelaus δ 44, 621.—Of Alcinous η 46, 55, 141, θ 157, 257, 469, ν 62.—Of Odysseus π 335, υ 194.—Of Antinous and Eurymachus σ 64.—Of Antinous ω 179.—Of minor heroes and personages Δ 338, N 643, Υ 219, Ψ 631, 849: δ 618 = ο 118, ξ 316, 336, σ 85 = 116 = φ 308, τ 287.—Joined with ἄναξ υ 194.—**(2)** In various contexts: κρείσσων β. ὅτε χώσεται ἀνδρὶ χέρηϊ A 80, διοτρεφέων βασιλήων 176, ὅν τινα βασιλῆα κιχείη B 188, εἷς β. [ἔστω] 205. Cf. B 86, 98, 196, 214, 247, 250, 277, 445, etc.: μὴ σέ γε βασιλῆα Κρονίων ποιήσειεν α 386, δίκη βασιλήων δ 691. Cf. α 394, β 231 = ε 9, γ 480, δ 63, ζ 54, η 49, θ 41, 390, κ 110, ν 205, ξ 278, ρ 416, τ 109, υ 196, 222, ω 88, 253.

βασιλεύτατος [superl. fr. βασιλεύς]. Most royal, supreme in rank I 69.

βασιλεύτερος [comp. fr. βασιλεύς]. More royal, higher in rank I 160, 392, K 239: ο 533.

βασιλεύω [βασιλεύς]. (ἐμ-.) **(1)** To rule, hold sway, be king, chief or ruler B 203, I 616: α 392, β 47, τ 179, χ 52, ω 483.—**(2)** To be king or chief of or ruler over. **(a)** With genit.: Ἀχαιῶν α 401. —**(b)** With dat.: Γιγάντεσσιν η 59. Cf. B 206 (*v.l.* βουλεύῃσι).—**(3)** Of a woman, to enjoy rank as the wife of a βασιλεύς Z 425.—With local genit.: Πύλου λ 285.

βασιλήϊος [βασιλεύς]. Of a king or chief: τέμενος Σ 550 (*v.l.* βαθυλήϊον).—Royal, princely π 401.

βασιληΐς, -ΐδος, ἡ [as prec.]. Royal, princely Z 193.

βάσκω [in form iterative fr. βα-, βαίνω]. (ἐπι-, παρα-.) In imp. with ἴθι, 'come! go' B 8, Θ 399, Λ 186, O 158, Ω 144, 336.

βαστάζω. **(1)** To raise. Of pushing uphill λ 594.—**(2)** To take into the hands, handle: τόξον φ 405.

βάτην, 3 dual aor. βαίνω.

βάτος, -ου. In pl., the prickles of some kind of prickly shrub or plant: βάτων ἕνεκα ω 230.

βεβάᾱσι, 3 pl. pf. βαίνω.

βέβακται, 3 sing. pf. pass. βάζω.

βεβάμεν, pf. infin. βαίνω.

βεβαρηότα, acc. sing. masc. pf. pple. βαρέω.

βέβασαν, 3 pl. plupf. βαίνω.

βεβαώς, pf. pple. βαίνω.

βέβηκε, 3 sing. pf. βαίνω.

βεβίηκε, 3 sing. pf. βιάω.

βεβλαμμένον, acc. sing. masc. pf. pple. pass. βλάπτω.

βέβληαι, 2 sing. pf. pass. βάλλω.

βεβλήαται, 3 pl. pf. pass. βάλλω.

βεβλήκει(ν), 3 sing. plupf. βάλλω.

βέβληται, 3 sing. pf. pass. βάλλω.

βεβολήατο, 3 pl. plupf. pass. βολέω.

βέβρῑθε, 3 sing. pf. βρίθω.

βέβρῡχε, 3 sing. pf. βρυχάομαι.

βεβρώθοις, 2 sing. pf. opt. βιβρώσκω.

βεβρωκώς, pf. pple. βιβρώσκω.

βεβρώσεται, 3 sing. fut. pf. pass. βιβρώσκω.

βεβυσμένον, acc. sing. masc. pf. pple. pass. βύω.

βεβῶσα, fem. pf. pple. βαίνω.

βέῃ. See next.

βείομαι, βέομαι [prob. for βίομαι, subj. fr. βι(F)-, βίος]. 2 sing. βέῃ Π 852, Ω 131 (app. for βέεαι (βέε')). To live: οὔ τι Διὸς βέομαι φρεσίν O 194 (φ. app. comitative dat., 'in company with . . .,' 'in accordance with . . .'; thus, will not live and move and have my being in his mind), οὐ δηρὸν βέῃ Π 852, Ω 131, τί νυ βείομαι; (what have I now to live for?) X 431.

βέλεμνον, -ου, τό [as next]. A spear or dart: πικρά X 206.—Of arrows O 484, 489.

βέλος, -εος, τό [βάλλω]. Dat. pl. βελέεσσι E 622, Λ 576, 589, N 511, etc.: γ 280, ε 124, λ 173, 199, ο 411. βέλεσσι A 42, N 555, Ω 759. βέλεσι Λ 657: π 277. A missile. **(1)** A spear or dart, but in pl. not necessarily excluding arrows or stones: οὐχ ἅλιον β. ἧκεν Δ 498, βελέων ἐρωήν 542. Cf. E 18, 316, 622, Θ 67, 159, etc.: π 277.—ἐκ βελέων, out of range of missiles: ὕπαγεν Λ 163. Cf. Π 122, 668, 678, 781, Σ 152.—So ὑπὲκ βελέων Δ 465, Σ 232.—Motion not implied: ἐκ βελέων (keeping out of their range) Ξ 130.—**(2)** An arrow A 42,

51, 382, Δ 99, Ε 104, Ο 444, etc.: γ 280 = ο 411, ε 124 = λ 173 = 199, φ 138 = 165, φ 148, χ 83, ω 180.—**(3)** A stone Μ 159, 458, Ξ 439, Π 737.—Of the rock thrown by the Cyclops ι 495.—**(4)** Of the θρῆνυς thrown by Antinous ρ 464.—Of the ox's foot thrown by Ktesippus υ 305.—**(5)** Applied to a weapon in gen. Ν 289.—**(6)** Metaphorically of the wound inflicted by a missile: ὥς τις β. πέσσῃ Θ 513.—Of the pains of childbirth Λ 269.

βέλτερος [comp. fr. βολ-, βόλομαι). Better. In neut. βέλτερον with or without copula, it is (would be) better: β. ὃς προφύγῃ κακόν Ξ 81 ([κείνῳ] ὃς = εἴ τις).—With complementary infin.: β. ἀπολέσθαι Ο 511. Cf. Ο 197, Σ 302, Φ 485, Χ 129.—With dat. and infin.: πτωχῷ β. ἐστι δαῖτα πτωχεύειν ρ 18.—With εἰ: β., εἰ καὐτὴ πόσιν εὗρεν ἄλλοθεν ζ 282.

βένθος, τό. **(1)** The depth or gulf (of the sea): κατὰ β. ἁλός Σ 38, 49.—In pl. in sim. sense: ἐν βένθεσσιν ἁλὸς Α 358 = Σ 36. Cf. Ν 21, 32.—**(2)** In pl., the deeps or deep recesses (of the sea): θαλάσσης πάσης βένθεα οἶδεν α 53, δ 386.—The recesses or coverts (of a wood): βαθείης βένθεσιν ὕλης ρ 316.

βένθοσδε [acc. of prec. + -δε (1)]. To the deep part (of the sea), to the deep (sea): νῆα ἁλὸς β. ἔρυσσαν δ 780, θ 51.

βέομαι. See βείομαι.

βέρεθρον, -ου, τό. A gulf or deep recess: βάθιστον ὑπὸ χθονὸς β. Θ 14.—Of Scylla's cave μ 94.

βῆ, 3 sing. aor. βαίνω.

βηλός, -οῦ, ὁ. A threshold: ῥῖψεν (ῥίπτασκον) ἀπὸ βηλοῦ (*i.e.* of Olympus) Α 591, Ο 23. Cf. Ψ 202. (There is a tradition that in the first two passages it is a distinct word = οὐρανός.)

βῆμεν, 1 pl. aor. βαίνω.

βήμεναι, βῆναι, aor. infin. βαίνω.

βῆν, 1 sing. aor. βαίνω.

βῆσαν[1], 3 pl. intrans. aor. βαίνω.

βῆσαν[2], 3 pl. trans. aor. βαίνω.

βήσεται, 3 sing. fut. in mid. form βαίνω.

βήσετο, 3 sing. aor. mid. βαίνω.

βῆσσα, -ης, ἡ. A glen or dell Γ 34, Λ 87, Ξ 397, Π 634, 766, Ρ 283, Σ 588, Χ 190: κ 210, 252, 275, τ 435.

βητάρμων, -ονος, ὁ [app. βη-, βαίνω + ἀρμ-, ἁρμόζω. 'One who goes in measure']. A dancer θ 250, 383.

βήτην, 3 dual aor. βαίνω.

βήω, aor. subj. βαίνω.

βιάζω [βίη]. **(1)** To bring one's might to bear upon, bear hard upon, press, use violence against. In mid.: βιάζεταί σε Χ 229. Cf. ι 410.—In pass., to be pressed or driven: βελέεσσιν Λ 576. Cf. Λ 589, Ο 727 = Π 102.—**(2)** To push one's advantage against, constrain: βιάζετέ με μοῦνον ἐόντα μ 297.

βίαιος [βίη]. Forceful, violent: ἔργα β 236.

βιαίως [adv. fr. prec.]. Forcefully, by force, with violence: γυναιξὶ παρευνάζεσθε β. χ 37. Cf. β 237.

βιάω [βίη]. 3 sing. pf. βεβίηκε Κ 145, 172, Π 22. 3 pl. pres. mid. βιόωνται λ 503. 3 pl. impf. βιόωντο ψ 9. 3 pl. opt. βιῴατο Λ 467. **(1)** To use violence to, lay constraint upon. In mid.: οἵ κεῖνον βιόωνται λ 503. Cf. ψ 9.—Of something immaterial: τοῖον ἄχος βεβίηκεν Ἀχαιούς Κ 145 = Π 22. Cf. Κ 172.—**(2)** To prove too strong for, force, overcome. In mid.: ὄνος ἐβιήσατο παῖδας Λ 558. Cf. Λ 467, Π 823.—**(3)** To force to act against one's will. In mid.: οὔ τίς μ' ἀέκοντα βιήσεται φ 348.—To compel in a certain direction, throw upon something: ἐκβαίνοντά κέ με βιήσατο κῦμ' ἐπὶ χέρσου η 278.—**(4)** To push one's advantage against, get the better of. In mid.: ψεύδεσσι βιησάμενος Ψ 576.—**(5)** To rob (of one's due). In mid. with double acc.: νῶϊ βιήσατο μισθόν Φ 451.

βιβάσθω [βιβάω]. To stride, stride along: μακρὰ βιβάσθων Ν 809, Ο 676, Π 534.

βιβάω [redup. fr. βα-, βαίνω]. (προ-.) = prec.: μακρὰ βιβῶντα Γ 22. Cf. Ν 371, Ο 307, 686: λ 539. (In all cases with βιβάντα, etc., from next as *v.l.*)

βίβημι [as prec.]. (προ-.) = prec.: μακρὰ βιβάντα (βιβάς) Γ 22, Η 213, Ο 307, 686, ὕψι βιβάντα Ν 371: μακρὰ βιβᾶσα λ 539.—Of a ram ι 450. (For *vv. ll.* see prec.)

†**βιβρώσκω.** 2 sing. pf. opt. βεβρώθοις Δ 35. Pf. pple. βεβρωκώς Χ 94: χ 403. 3 sing. fut. pf. pass. βεβρώσεται β 203. To eat. **(1)** In pf. forms in intensive sense: εἰ βεβρώθοις Πρίαμον (eat up, devour) Δ 35.—Sim. of χρήματα β 203 (will be consumed).—**(2)** In strict pf. sense: βεβρωκὼς φάρμακα Χ 94.—So with partitive genit.: βεβρωκὼς βοός χ 403.

βίη, -ης, ἡ. Instrumental βίηφι Π 826, Σ 341, Φ 501, Ψ 315: α 403, ζ 6, ι 406, 408, 476, μ 210, 246, φ 371, 373. With vbs. of trusting Δ 325, Μ 135, 153, 256, Χ 107: φ 315. This form as locative Ο 614. As genit. Φ 367. **(1)** Bodily strength, might, power; the exercise of this: βίην ἀμείνων (in might) Α 404, Ο 139, πεποίθασι βίηφιν (in their strength) Δ 325, οὔ τίς με βίῃ δίηται Η 197, σὴ β. λέλυται Θ 103. Cf Γ 431, Η 288, Μ 135, 341, Ν 572, Ο 106, Ρ 569, Ψ 315, etc.: δόλῳ ἠὲ βίηφιν ι 406, βίης ἐπιδευέες φ 185. Cf. δ 415, ζ 6, ν 143, σ 4, υ 379, φ 128, etc.—In pl.: βίας Τρώων Ε 521. Cf. χ 219.—**(2)** National strength or power: Φαιήκων ζ 197.—**(3)** The act of putting strength into exercise, effort: μεθῆκε βίης Φ 177. Cf. δ 422, φ 126.—**(4)** Courage, spirit: οὐκ ἔστι β. φρεσίν Γ 45.—**(5)** β. τινός, periphrasis for a person (the might of . . . = the mighty . . .) (cf. ἴς (5), μένος (6), σθένος (2)): Πριάμοιο βίην Γ 105, β. Ἑλένοιο Ν 770. Cf. Ε 781, Ν 758, 781, Ο 614, Ρ 24, 187, Σ 117, Υ 307, Φ 367, Χ 323, Ψ 859: κ 200.—Sim. with adj.: βίη Ἡρακληείη Β 658. Cf. Β 666, Δ 386, Ε 638, Λ 690, Ο 640, Τ 98: λ 290, 296, 601.—**(6) (a)** Wrongful exercise of strength or power, violence: ὕβρις τε β. τε ο 329 = ρ 565. Cf. ψ 31.—In pl., acts of wrong or violence: βίας ἀποτίσεαι λ 118, π 255. Cf. γ 216, ν 310, π 189, ρ 540.—Of an inanimate agent, violent manifestations of force: βίας ἀνέμων (the blasts) Π 213 = Ψ 713.—(b) In dat.: βίῃ, by wrongful use of force, by force, forcibly: εἴ με β. καθέξει Ο 186. Cf. Π 387: ο 231.—So βίηφι α 403, ι 476, μ 210.—With genit.: βίῃ ἀέκοντος (in spite of him unwilling) Α 430: δ 646.—(7) Might, power, authority, influence Ι 498, Ψ 578.

βιός, -οῦ, ὁ. A bow Α 49, Δ 125, Κ 260, Λ 387, Ο 468, 472, Ω 605: ζ 270, τ 577 = φ 75, φ 173, 233, 328, χ 2, 246, ω 170, 177.

βίος, -ου, ὁ [βιϝ-]. One's life, course of life, manner of living: ζώεις ἀγαθὸν βίον ο 491. Cf. σ 254 = τ 127.

βιοτή, ἡ [βίος]. = prec. δ 565.

βίοτος, -ου, ὁ [βίος]. (1) Life, existence, one's life: βιότοιο μεγήρας Ν 563. Cf. Δ 170: ε 394, μ 328, ω 536.—(2) The period of one's life: βιότοιο τελευτή Η 104, Π 787.—(3) The fact of being alive: εἴ κεν πατρὸς βίοτον ἀκούσῃς α 287. Cf. β 218.—(4) The means of living, substance, goods, chattels: ἀφνειὸς βιότοιο Ε 544. Cf. Ζ 14, Ξ 122: ἀλλότριον βίοτον ἔδουσιν α 160, σ 280. Cf. α 377, β 49, 123, 126, γ 301, δ 90, 686, etc.

†**βιόω** [βίος]. 3 sing. aor. imp. βιώτω Θ 429. Infin. βιῶναι Κ 174, Ο 511: ξ 359. 2 sing. aor. mid. ἐβιώσαο θ 468. (1) To live, continue to exist: ἄλλος βιώτω Θ 429. Cf. Κ 174, Ο 511: ξ 359.—(2) Trans. in aor. mid., to give life to, rescue from death: σύ μ' ἐβιώσαο θ 468.

βιόωνται, 3 pl. pres. mid. βιάω.

βιῴατο, 3 pl. opt. mid. βιάω.

βιῶναι, aor. infin. βιόω.

βιώτω, 3 sing. aor. imp. βιόω.

βλάβεν, 3 pl. aor. pass. βλάπτω.

βλάβω [= βλάπτω]. To cause to fail or break down: βλάβεται γούνατα Τ 166: ν 34.—To cause (a speaker) to break down: βλάβεται λιγύς περ ἐὼν ἀγορητής Τ 82.

βλάπτω. 2 sing. aor. ἔβλαψας Χ 15. βλάψας Ψ 571. 3 ἔβλαψε Ψ 782. βλάψε Η 271, Ψ 774: ξ 178. 3 pl. ἔβλαψαν ψ 14. 3 pl. aor. pass. ἐβλάφθησαν Ψ 387. Also ἔβλαβεν Ψ 461. βλάβεν Ψ 545. Pple. βλαφθείς, -έντος Ζ 39, Ι 512, Ο 484, 489, 647, Π 331. Acc. sing. masc. pf. pple. βεβλαμμένον Π 660. (1) To cause to fail or break down, make useless: γούνατα Η 271. Cf. Ο 484, 489.—To stop, cut short the course of: ἵπποι ἔβλαβεν Ψ 461. Cf. Ψ 545.—Sim.: βεβλαμμένον ἦτορ (app., brought to a stop in his life, slain) Π 660.—(2) To impede the course of: ἵππους Ψ 571.—To impede the motion of, entangle: βλαφθέντα κατὰ κλόνον Π 331.—To impede in action, be in the way of: ἑταίρων τίν' ἐλαυνόντων ν 22.—To entangle, catch: ἵππω ὄζῳ ἔνι βλαφθέντε Ζ 39. Cf. Ο 647.—(3) To trip, cause to stumble Ψ 774.—To trip up (the feet of). With double acc.: ἔβλαψέ με πόδας Ψ 782.—(4) To put at a disadvantage: [ἵπποι] ἐβλάφθησαν ἄνευ κέντροιο θέοντες Ψ 387.—(5) To hinder from. With genit.: κελεύθου α 195.—(6) Of a divine agency. (a) To affect the mind of adversely, smite with mental blindness. Of Ἄτη Ι 507, 512, Τ 94.—With φρένας as object: εἰ τότε βλάπτε φρένας Ζεύς Ο 724.—(b) To deprive of good sense, put out of one's right mind: θεοί σ' ἔβλαψαν ψ 14.—With φρένας as second acc.: τόν τις ἀθανάτων βλάψε φρένας ξ 178.—(c) To foil: ἔβλαψάς μ', ἑκάεργε Χ 15.—(7) Of wine, to drive out of one's right mind φ 294.

βλεῖο, 2 sing. aor. opt. pass. βάλλω.

βλεμεαίνω. Of unknown meaning. App., to exult, bear oneself proudly, or the like: σθένεϊ βλεμεαίνων Θ 337. Cf. Ι 237, Μ 42, Ρ 22, 135, Υ 36.

βλέφαρον, τό. Always in dual or pl. The eyelids: οὐχ ὕπνος ἐπὶ βλεφάροισιν ἐφίζανε Κ 26. Cf. Κ 187, Ξ 165, Ρ 438, Τ 17, Ω 637: δάκρυ βάλεν ἐκ βλεφάροιϊν ρ 490. Cf. α 364, β 398, δ 114, ε 493, θ 522, ι 389, etc.

βλήεται, 3 sing. aor. subj. pass. βάλλω.

βλῆτο, 3 sing. aor. pass. βάλλω.

βλῆτρον, τό [βλη-, βάλλω]. App., a clamp or clincher for fastening lengths together: ξυστὸν κολλητὸν βλήτροισιν Ο 678.

βληχή, ἡ. A bleating: οἰῶν μ 266.

βλοσυρός, -ή, -όν. App., shaggy Η 212, Ο 608.

βλοσυρῶπις [prec. + ὦπα]. App., grim-looking: Γοργώ Λ 36.

βλωθρός, -ή. App., tall, stately: πίτυς Ν 390 = Π 483: ὄγχνην ω 234.

†**βλώσκω** [μβολ-]. 3 sing. aor. subj. μόλῃ Ω 781. Pple. μολών, -όντος Λ 173: γ 44, ω 335. Fem. μολοῦσα, -ης Ζ 286, Ο 720. 3 sing. pf. μέμβλωκε ρ 190. (ἐκ-, κατα-, παρα-, προ-.) (1) To go: ποτὶ μέγαρα Ζ 286.—Of a period of time, to pass away ρ 190.—(2) To come: δεῦρο Ο 720. Cf. Λ 173: γ 44, ω 335.—Of a period of time, to come on Ω 781.

βοάγρια, τά [βο-, βοῦς + ἄγρη. 'Spoils of an ox.' Cf. ἀνδράγρια]. Shields of ox-hide Μ 22: π 296.

βοάω [βοή]. 3 sing. βοᾷ Ξ 394. 3 pl. βοόωσι Ρ 265. Pple. βοόων, -ωντος Β 97, 198, Ο 687, 732. Contr. βοῶν Β 224. Dat. sing. masc. aor. pple. βώσαντι Μ 337. (ἐπι-, προ-.) (1) To cry aloud, shout: κήρυκες βοόωντες ἐρήτυον Β 97. Cf. Β 198, 224, Θ 92, Ι 12, Λ 15, Μ 337, Ο 687 = 732, Ρ 89, 334, 607 (app. for joy on seeing Hector unharmed), Ψ 847: στὰς ἐβόησα κ 311. Cf. δ 281, ε 400 = ι 473 = μ 181, ζ 294, θ 305, ι 403, ω 537.—(2) Of things, to roar, resound: θαλάσσης κῦμα Ξ 394, ἠϊόνες Ρ 265.

βόειος, -η, -ον [βοῦς]. (1) Of an ox: δέρμα ξ 24.—(2) Made from ox-hide Δ 122: ω 228.—(3) In fem. βοείη as sb. (a) A living ox's hide Σ 582.—An ox-hide lately stripped off χ 364.—An ox-hide in process of being dressed Ρ 389.—A dressed ox-hide Λ 843: υ 96.—A piece of dressed ox-leather Μ 296.—(b) A shield of ox-hide Ε 452 = Μ 425, Χ 159.

βόεος = prec. (1) Of an ox: ὄνθου Ψ 777.—(2) Made from ox-hide Χ 397, Ψ 324.—(3) In fem. βοέη as sb. (a) An (undressed) ox-hide υ 2, 142.—(b) A shield of ox-hide Ρ 492.

βοεύς, ὁ [βοῦς]. A strap of ox-leather (used for hoisting a sail): ἕλκον ἱστία βοεῦσιν β 426 = ο 291.

βοή, -ῆς, ἡ. (1) A crying out, a shouting:

βοῆς ἀΐοντες ι 401, ξ 266 = ρ 435.—A hue-and-cry, a din: διὰ ἄστεος κ 118. Cf. χ 77, 133.—(2) A shouting in battle: Λ 50, 500, 530, Ν 169 = 540, Ξ 4, Π 267.—βοὴν ἀγαθός, good at the battle-cry, marshalling or rallying his men with loud shout. Of Menelaus Β 408, 586, Γ 96, Δ 220, Ζ 37, etc.: γ 311, δ 307, 609, ο 14, 57, 67, 92, 97, ρ 120.—Of Diomedes Β 563, Ε 114, Ζ 12, Η 399, Θ 91, etc.—Of Hector Ν 123, Ο 671.—Of Aias Ο 249, Ρ 102.—Of Polites Ω 250.—(3) A loud expression of grief Ζ 465: ω 48.—(4) The sound of musical instruments Σ 495.

βοηθόος [βοή + θέω]. Running to the battle-cry, coming swiftly to the fight Ν 477.—The epithet transferred from the warrior to his chariot Ρ 481.

βοηλασίη, -ης, ἡ [βοῦς + ἐλαύνω] A driving off of cattle: νεῖκος ἀμφὶ βοηλασίῃ Λ 672.

βοητύς, ἡ [βοάω]. Noise, disturbance α 369.

βόθρος, -ου, ὁ. (1) A hole or pit dug in the ground: βόθρον ὀρύξαι κ 517, ἀπεδειροτόμησα ἐς βόθρον (so that the blood ran into the pit) λ 36. Cf. λ 25, 42, 95.—(2) A hollow by a river used for washing clothes ζ 92.—(3) The trench in which a young tree is planted Ρ 58.

†βολέω [= βάλλω]. Pf. pple. pass. βεβολημένος Ι 9: κ 247. 3 pl. plupf. βεβολήατο Ι 3. (ἀντι-.) Of grief, to smite: πένθεϊ βεβολήατο (were in the state of having been smitten, were tossed about or agitated) Ι 3. Cf. Ι 9: κ 247.

βολή, -ῆς, ἡ [βάλλω]. (1) A blow with a missile ρ 283, ω 161.—(2) A turn or glance (of the eyes) δ 150.

βόλομαι [= βούλομαι]. (1) = βούλομαι (1): ἑτέρως ἐβόλοντο α 234.—With infin.: αὐτὸν ζώειν π 387.—(2) = βούλομαι (4). With infin. and ἤ: Τρωσὶν δοῦναι ἠέ περ ἡμῖν Λ 319.

βομβέω [imitative] To make a resounding, clanging or clashing noise Ν 530, Π 118: μ 204 (the oars knocked against each other in the wash of the sea as they hung by the τροποί), σ 397.—Of the whizzing flight of a quoit θ 190.

βοόων, pres. pple. βοάω.

βοόωσι, 3 pl. pres. βοάω.

Βορέης, ὁ. Genit. (besides Βορέαο) Βορέω Ξ 395, Ψ 692: ξ 533. Βορέης as spondee Ι 5. So Βορέῃ Ψ 195. (1) The north wind Ε 524, 697, Ι 5, Ξ 395, Ο 171, Τ 358, Υ 223, Φ 346, Ψ 195, 208, 692: ε 296, 328, 331, 385, ι 81, κ 507, ξ 475, 533.—Joined with ἄνεμος Ο 26: ι 67, ξ 253, 299, τ 200.—(2) The north: πρὸς Βορέαο ν 110.

βόσις, ἡ [βόσκω]. Food: βόσιν ἰχθύσιν Τ 268.

βόσκω. 2 sing. fut. βοσκήσεις ρ 559. 3 pl. pa. iterative pass. βοσκέσκοντο μ 355. (1) To feed, tend (cattle, etc.) Ο 548: ξ 102.—(2) To feed, nourish, support: γαῖα ἀνθρώπους λ 365. Cf. ι 124, μ 97, ξ 325 = τ 294.—To fill or stuff (one's belly) ρ 228, 559, σ 364.—(3) In pass., of cattle, etc., to feed, graze: ξύλοχον κάτα βοσκομενάων Ε 162. Cf. Π 151, Ρ 62, Υ 223: δ 338 = ρ 129, λ 108, μ 128, 355, ξ 104, φ 49.—Of birds, to feed Ο 691.

βοτά, τά [βόσκω]. Grazing beasts, beasts of the herd: ἀρδμὸς πάντεσσι βοτοῖσιν Σ 521.

βοτάνη, -ης, ἡ [βόσκω]. (1) Food, fodder κ 411.—(2) A feeding-place: ὡς εἴ θ' ἕσπετο μῆλα ἐκ βοτάνης Ν 493.

βοτήρ, -ῆρος, ὁ [βόσκω]. (Cf. βώτωρ.) A herdsman: ἀγροὺς ἐπιείσομαι ἠδὲ βοτῆρας ο 504.

βοτρυδόν [βότρυς]. In clusters Β 89.

βότρυς, -υος, ὁ. A bunch or cluster of grapes: μέλανες Σ 562.

βούβοτος, -ον [βοῦς + βόσκω]. Grazed by cattle. Of Ithaca ν 246.

βούβρωστις, ἡ [app. a compound of βοῦς]. Explained as the insect that attacks cattle, the gadfly. By others connected with βι-βρώσκω and explained as ravenous hunger (taking βου- in an intensive sense. Cf. βουγάϊος) Ω 532.

βουβών, -ῶνος, ὁ. The groin Δ 492.

βουγάϊος [app. a compound of βοῦς, perh. in intensive sense. The second element perh. γαϝ-, γαίω]. Thus, perh., braggart Ν 824: σ 79.

βουκολέω [βουκόλος]. 2 sing. pa. iterative βουκολέεσκες Φ 448. (1) To feed or tend cattle: Ἀγχίσῃ βουκολέοντι Ε 313. Cf. Ξ 445: κ 85.—(2) To feed, tend (cattle): βοῦς Φ 448.—(3) In pass., of cattle, etc., to feed, graze Υ 221.

βουκόλος, -ου, ὁ [app. for βουπόλος fr. βοῦς + -πολος, conn. with πολεύω. Cf. αἰπόλος]. A herdsman Ν 571, Ο 587, Ψ 845: λ 293.—Of Philoetius υ 227, φ 83, 189, 193, χ 104, 435, 454 = ψ 297, ψ 367, ω 359, 363.

βουλευτής, ὁ [βουλεύω]. A member of the βουλή, a councillor Ζ 114.

βουλεύω [βουλή]. 1 pl. aor. subj. βουλεύσωμεν π 234. (μετα-.) (1) To deliberate, consider, take counsel with oneself, concert measures, contrive, plan: ἵνα σφίσι βουλεύῃσθα (in their interests) Ι 99. Cf. Β 206 (v.l. βασιλεύῃ): μ 58, ξ 491.—With infin.: τὸν βούλευσα κατακτάμεν (οὐτάμεναι) (debated whether to . . .) Ι 458: ι 299.—With dependent clause: ὅπως . . . (how, in what manner) ι 420, λ 229.—(2) In dual and pl., to take counsel together: ὣς βουλεύσαντε Α 531, εἰ ἐς μίαν βουλεύσομεν (take counsel to one purpose, lay our plans in common) Β 379. Cf. ν 439, π 234.—With infin. Β 347.—(3) With cognate acc.: ὅς κεν ἀρίστην βουλὴν βουλεύσῃ (devise the best counsel) Ι 75, βουλὰς βουλεύειν (to take counsel together, hold counsel, concert measures) Κ 327. Cf. Κ 147, 415, Ψ 78, Ω 652: ζ 61.—(4) To turn over in one's mind, ponder: ὁδὸν α 444.—To meditate, purpose, propose to oneself: φύξιν Κ 311 = 398.—(5) To plan, contrive, scheme to bring about: ὄλεθρον Ξ 464. Cf. ε 179 = κ 344, ε 187 = κ 300.—To plan, contrive, devise, elaborate: ψεύδεα ξ 296. Cf. ε 23 = ω 479, ψ 217.—In mid.: ἀπάτην βουλεύσατο Β 114 = Ι 21.

βουλή, -ῆς, ἡ. (1) A select council of the most important chiefs (cf. ἀγορή (1)) Β 53, 194, 202, Κ 195, Μ 213: γ 127.—(2) The deliberation or discussion in the council: ὅσοι οὐ βουλῆς ἐπάκουσαν Β 143.—(3) The place of council Β 84: ζ 55.—(4) Counsel, concerting of measures, contriving, planning, scheming: οἱ περί ἐστε βουλὴν Δαναῶν (in . . .) A 258. Cf. I 54, K 43, Λ 627, N 728, 741, Π 630: ἐπίφρονι γ 128. Cf. δ 267, μ 211, ν 298, 305, π 242, 374, 420, χ 230.—In pl.: ὅτι οἱ συμφράσσατο βουλάς A 537. Cf. A 540, B 340, I 374, O 71, Υ 154: δ 462, 677 = π 412, λ 437, 510. —For βουλὴν (βουλὰς) βουλεύειν see βουλεύω (3).—(5) A conclusion, a resolve, a course to take: βουλήν, ἡ θεοῖσιν ἐφήνδανεν H 45. Cf. B 5 = K 17 = Ξ 161, P 469: ι 318 = 424 = λ 230, ξ 337.—(6) What one has contrived or planned. In pl.: Θέτιδος ἐξήνυσε βουλάς Θ 370.—A plan or plot: οὐχ ἡμῖν συνθεύσεται ἥδε γε βουλή υ 245.—(7) Counsel given, advice, what one proposes or puts forward: πυκινήν B 55 = K 302. Cf. B 282, Δ 323, H 325 = I 94, Θ 36 = 467, M 109, Ξ 102, Σ 313, 510: εἴ τινα βουλὴν εἴποι λ 479. Cf. γ 150, θ 506, κ 46, μ 339, ω 52.—In pl.: βουλέων μευ ξύνιεν A 273. Cf. B 273.—(8) One's will, resolve, determination: Διὸς βουλή A 5. Cf. B 344, M 241, Υ 15, 20: α 86, β 372, ε 30, λ 297, ν 127, ξ 328 = τ 297.—In pl.: Ζηνὸς βουλέων M 236. Cf. N 524, Φ 229: θ 82, λ 276, π 402.—(9) One's mind, what one has in view or is doing β 281, λ 177.

βουληφόρος [prec. + -φορος, φέρω. 'Contributing counsel']. (1) A (trusted) adviser, a leader in counsel E 180 = P 485, E 633, H 126, K 518, N 219, 255, 463, Υ 83.—(2) Specifically, a member of the βουλή, a leading chief K 414, Ω 651: ν 12. —Joined with ἀνήρ A 144, B 24 = 61.—With ἄναξ M 414.—(3) As adj.: ἀγοραὶ βουληφόροι (in which counsel is exchanged) ι 112.

βούλομαι. (προ-.) (1) To have a preference for one of two things, to wish, be minded: ἄλλῃ O 51.—(2) To wish, desire (something): Τρώεσσι βούλετο νίκην H 21, N 347, Π 121. Cf. Θ 204, Ψ 682. —With infin.: Τρώεσσι κῦδος ὀρέξαι Λ 79. Cf. M 174 = O 596: δ 275, 353 (βούλοντο here app. an aor.), ο 21, 88.—(3) To be willing or ready. With infin.: ἀπὸ λοιγὸν ἀμῦναι A 67.—(4) To prefer: τό κε βουλοίμην Γ 41: λ 358 = υ 316.—With infin.: αὐτὴν οἴκοι ἔχειν A 112. Cf. Ω 39: γ 143, ι 96, ρ 187, 228, σ 364.—With ἤ: ἡμῖν Ζεὺς βούλεται ἢ Δαναοῖσι νίκην P 331.—With infin. and ἤ: λαὸν σῶν ἔμμεναι ἢ ἀπολέσθαι A 117. Cf. Ψ 594: γ 232, λ 489, μ 350, π 106, ρ 81, 404.—Absol.: βούλομαι (I prefer it so, I accept the alternative) Ω 226.

βουλῡτόνδε [βοῦς + λύω + -δε (1). 'To the time for unyoking oxen']. To or towards early afternoon: Ἠέλιος μετενίσετο β. Π 779: = ι 58. (The time specified is fixed for Π 779, and is admissible for ι 58. The reference seems to be to a custom of stopping ploughing at or soon after mid-day.)

βουπλήξ, -ῆγος, ὁ [βοῦς + πληγ-, πλήσσω]. An ox-whip or -goad; or perh., a pole-axe: θεινόμεναι βουπλῆγι Z 135.

βοῦς, βοός, ὁ, ἡ (βοϜ-. Cf. L. *bovis*). Acc. βῶν H 238. Dat. pl. βόεσσι B 481, H 474, Λ 674, M 105, etc.: υ 219. βουσί E 161, Z 424, H 333, M 293, etc.: ζ 132, ο 386, ρ 472, υ 209, 221. Acc. βόας E 556, Θ 505, 545, M 137, etc.: λ 108, 289, μ 375, σ 278, etc. βοῦς A 154, Z 93, 174, 274, etc.: α 8, 92, β 56, θ 60, etc. (1) A bull, ox, or cow. (a) Gender not determined: βοῦς ἱέρευσεν Z 174, ἀγέλην βοῶν Λ 696, ἱμάντας βοός (*i.e.* of the hide) Ψ 684. Cf. E 556, H 333, Θ 240, 505, I 466, Σ 528, etc.: νῶτα βοός δ 65. Cf. β 56, γ 421, ζ 132, λ 402, ν 32, ο 386, etc.—(b) Masculine: ἶφι κταμένοιο Γ 375, βόε ἶσον θυμὸν ἔχοντε N 703, ἐριμύκων Υ 497 (for the gender see 495). Cf. N 571, Σ 559, Ψ 775, etc.: α 108, σ 371.—Joined with ταῦρος B 480, P 389.—Qualified by ἄρσην H 314, Υ 495: τ 420. —(c) Feminine: ἐμὰς βοῦς A 154, αὐτῇσι βόεσσιν H 474. Cf. Z 93, Θ 231, K 292, Λ 172, P 62, Σ 574, etc.: στεῖραν βοῦν κ 522, πολλαί μ 128. Cf. γ 382, κ 410, λ 108, μ 262, υ 221, etc.—Distinguished from ταῦρος B 481, Π 488.—(2) A shield of ox-hide. In this sense fem.: τυκτῇσι βόεσσιν M 105. Cf. H 238, M 137, Π 636.

βουφονέω [βοῦς + φον-, φένω]. To slay an ox or oxen for sacrifice H 466.

βοῶπις [βο-, βοῦς + ὦπα]. Ox-eyed, having large, soft eyes. Epithet of Here A 551 = Δ 50 = Π 439 = Σ 360 = Υ 309, A 568, Θ 471, Ξ 159, 222, 263, O 34, 49, Σ 239, 357.—Of Clymene (one of Helen's handmaidens) Γ 144.—Of Phylomedousa H 10.—Of the sea-nymph Halie Σ 40.

Βοώτης, ὁ [ploughman, waggoner, fr. βοῦς]. The constellation the Waggoner, containing the star Arcturus ε 272.

βραδύς. Slow Θ 104: θ 330.—Absol.: κιχάνει β. ὠκύν θ 329.—For superl. see βάρδιστος.

βραδυτής, -ῆτος, ἡ [βραδύς]. Slowness, want of speed: βραδυτῆτί τε νωχελίῃ τε T 411.

βράσσων [comp. fr. βραχ-ύς, short]. Shorter: νόος (of shorter reach) K 226.

βραχίων, -ονος, ὁ. The arm M 389, N 529, 532, Π 323, 510: σ 69.

†βράχω. 3 sing. aor. ἔβραχε, βράχε. (ἀνα-.) Of armour, to rattle, clash, ring Δ 420, M 396, N 181, Ξ 420, Π 566.—Of an axle, to creak, grate E 838. —So of a door φ 49.—Of a river, to resound under the splash of something falling into it Φ 9. —Of the earth, to give forth a sound, resound Φ 387.—Of persons, to roar, shriek E 859, 863, Π 468.

βρέμω [cf. L. *fremo*]. (ἐμ-, ἐπι-.) Of the sea or the wind, to roar Δ 425.—In mid. B 210, Ξ 399.

βρέφος, τό. Unborn offspring Ψ 266.

βρεχμός, ὁ. App., the head: ἔκπεσε ἐπὶ βρεχμόν τε καὶ ὤμους E 586.

βριαρός, -ή [βρι- as in βρίθω, ὄ-βριμος]. Stout, strong: κόρυθα Λ 375. Cf. Π 413, 579, Σ 611, T 381, Υ 162, X 112.

βρίζω. (ἀπο-.) To slumber, nod Δ 223.

βριήπυος [app. βρι- as in βριαρός + ἠπύω]. Thus, with powerful or loud voice. Epithet of Ares N 521.

βρῑθοσύνη, -ης, ἡ [βριθύς]. Weight, load: ἔβραχεν ἄξων βριθοσύνῃ E 839, πέσε λίθος εἴσω βριθοσύνῃ (by its weight) M 460.

βρῑθύς, -ύ [cf. βαρύς and next]. Heavy, weighty: ἔγχος E 746 = Θ 390, Π 141 = T 388, Π 802: α 100.

βρίθω [cf. prec.]. 3 pl. aor. ἔβρῖσαν M 346, 359, P 512. Pple. βρίσας, -αντος P 233 : ζ 159. 3 sing. pf. βέβρῖθε Π 384. 3 pl. -ᾶσι ο 334. 3 sing. plupf. βεβρίθει π 474. Fem. pple. βεβρῖθυῖα Φ 385. (ἐπι-.) **(1)** To be heavy, loaded or weighed down with something. With dat. : σταφυλῇσιν Σ 561. Cf. π 474, τ 112.—With genit. : τυρῶν ι 219. Cf. ο 334.—So in pass. With dat. : καρπῷ Θ 307.—To be oppressed : ὑπὸ λαίλαπι χθών Π 384.—**(2)** To bring one's weight to bear, bear hard : ἰθὺς Δαναῶν βρίσαντες ἔβησαν P 233. Cf. M 346 = 359, P 512.—Fig., to be grievous or distressing Φ 385. —**(3)** To prevail, achieve one's end : ἐέδνοισιν ζ 159.

βρομέω [βρόμος]. Of flies, to buzz Π 642.

βρόμος, ὁ [βρέμω]. The roaring (of fire) Ξ 396.

βροντάω [βροντή]. Of Zeus, to thunder Θ 133, Υ 56 : μ 415 = ξ 305, υ 103, 113.

βροντή, -ῆς, ἡ. Thunder N 796, Φ 199 : υ 121.

βρότεος, -ον [βροτός]. Mortal, human τ 545.

βροτόεις, -εντος [βρότος]. Gory, blood-stained : ἔναρα Z 480, Θ 534, K 528, 570, O 347, P 13, 540, X 245, ἀνδράγρια Ξ 509.

βροτολοιγός [βροτός + λοιγός]. Destroyer of men. Epithet of Ares E 31 = 455, 518, 846, 909, Θ 349, Λ 295, M 130, N 298, 802, Υ 46, Φ 421 : θ 115.

βρότος, -ου, ὁ. Shed blood, gore : αἱματόεντα H 425, Ξ 7, Σ 345, Ψ 41 : μέλανα ω 189.

βροτός, -οῦ, ὁ, ἡ [(μ)βροτός. Cf. ἄμβροτος[2]]. **(1)** Liable to death, mortal : ἀνήρ E 361. Cf. E 604, Σ 85, T 22 : δ 397, ε 129, 197, 218, μ 77.—**(2)** Absol., a mortal man, a man : θεὰ βροτῷ εὐνηθεῖσα B 821. Cf. A 272, Θ 428, I 159, Λ 2, N 244, etc. : βροτῶν θελκτήρια α 337. Cf. δ 197, ε 101, ζ 149, λ 287, μ 125, etc.—Qualified by θνητός γ 3 = μ 386, η 210, π 212.—For μέροπες βροτοί see μέροπες.

βροτόω [βρότος]. To make gory, stain with blood : βεβροτωμένα τεύχεα λ 41.

βρόχος, ὁ. A noose λ 278, χ 472.

†**βρῡχάομαι**. 3 sing. pf. βέβρῡχε P 264 : ε 412. 3 sing. plupf. βεβρύχει μ 242. Pple. βεβρῡχώς N 393, Π 486. To roar. Of a wounded hero N 393 = Π 486.—Of the sea P 264 : ε 412.—Of an echoing rock μ 242.

βρύω. To teem with. With dat. : ἄνθεϊ P 56.

βρώμη, -ης, ἡ [βι-βρώσκω]. **(1)** Food κ 379, 460 = μ 23, μ 302.—**(2)** The partaking of food : μνησόμεθα βρώμης κ 177.

βρῶσις, ἡ [as prec.]. = prec. (1) T 210 : α 191, ζ 209 = 246, 248, κ 176, μ 320, ν 72, ο 490.

βρωτύς, ἡ [as prec.]. **(1)** Food σ 407.—**(2)** The partaking of food : ἐς βρωτὺν ὀτρύνετον T 205.

βύβλινος [adj. fr. βύβλος, the Egyptian papyrus]. Made of the fibrous coat of the papyrus φ 391.

βυκτής. Prob., roaring, blustering κ 20.

βυσσοδομεύω [app. fr. βυσσός + δόμος, 'to construct in the interior of the house, away from public view']. To plan or ponder secretly δ 676, θ 273, ι 316, ρ 66, 465 = 491 = υ 184.

βυσσός, -οῦ, ὁ. The depth of the sea Ω 80.

†**βύω**. Acc. sing. masc. pf. pple. pass. βεβυσμένον. To stuff full of. With genit. : τάλαρον νήματος δ 134.

βῶλος. A clod, the clods, of earth σ 374.

βωμός, -οῦ, ὁ [prob. fr. βα-, βαίνω, 'something to or on which one mounts']. **(1)** An altar A 440, 448, B 305 (in pl., but app. of a single altar), 310, Δ 48 = Ω 69, Θ 48, 238, 249, Λ 808, Ψ 148 : γ 273, ζ 162, θ 363, ν 187, ρ 210, χ 334, 379.—**(2)** A stand on which the body of a chariot was placed after removal of the wheels. In pl. of a single stand : ἅρματ' ἂμ βωμοῖσι τίθει Θ 441 (app. assimilated to ἅρματα, which is pl. in form only). —**(3)** A pedestal η 100.

βῶν, acc. sing. βοῦς.

βώσαντι, dat. sing. masc. aor. pple. βοάω.

βῶσι, 3 pl. aor. subj. βαίνω.

βωστρέω [*βωστής = *βοηστής, agent-noun fr. βοάω]. To call to for aid : Κράταιϊν μ 124.

βωτιάνειρα, ἡ [βω-, βόσκω + -τι- + ἀνήρ]. Feeding men, rich in food : Φθίῃ A 155.

βώτωρ, -ορος, ὁ. = βοτήρ M 302 : ξ 102, ρ 200.

γαῖα, -ης, ἡ [cf. γῆ, αἶα]. **(1)** The earth : στεναχίζετο γ. B 95. Cf. B 699, 782, Z 19, 282, P 447, etc. : πείρατα γαίης δ 563. Cf. β 131, γ 16, δ 417, ζ 167, λ 239, etc.—Personified Γ 278 : λ 576.—**(2)** The earth as distinguished **(a)** From the heavens : μεσσηγὺς γαίης τε καὶ οὐρανοῦ E 769 = Θ 46. Cf. Θ 16, Ξ 174, O 193 : α 54, λ 18, μ 381.—Personified O 36 : = ε 184.—**(b)** From the sea or water : γαίης καὶ πόντοιο Θ 479. Cf. Θ 24, Ξ 204 : ἐφ' ὑγρὴν ἠδ' ἐπὶ γαῖαν α 98. Cf. ε 294, 359, λ 587, μ 282, ψ 238, etc.—**(c)** From both Σ 483 : μ 404 = ξ 302.—**(3)** The earth considered with reference to extent : πολλὴ γαῖα, many regions or countries O 81 : β 364, δ 268, ξ 380.—So πολλὴν ἐπ' ἀπείρονα γαῖαν (far and wide on the . . .) ο 79. Cf. τ 284. —**(4) (a)** A particular land or country : 'Αχαιΐδα γαῖαν A 254 = H 124. Cf. A 270, Γ 49, E 545, Ψ 206 : γαίῃ ἐν ἀλλοδαπῇ ι 36. Cf. α 407, ε 35, ζ 119, 177, θ 301, etc.—**(b)** One's native land : πάρος ἣν γαῖαν ἱκέσθαι α 21, ἐν σῇ ἐὼν γαίῃ ν 294. Cf. α 59, δ 523, θ 555, υ 99, etc.—So πατρὶς γ. : ἐς πατρίδα γαῖαν B 140. Cf. Γ 244, N 645, 696, O 505, etc. : α 290, γ 117, δ 823, θ 461, κ 49, etc. —Also γαίῃ πατρωΐῃ ν 188, 251.—**(5)** The surface of the earth, the earth, the ground : ποτὶ σκῆπτρον βάλε γαίῃ A 245. Cf. Γ 114, Δ 112, Λ 161, N 200, Υ 420, Ψ 420, etc. : κατακλίνας ἐπὶ γαίῃ κ 165. Cf. β 80, θ 190, ι 289, λ 423, σ 92, etc.—**(6)** Earth as a material, earth, soil : χυτή με κατὰ γαῖα καλύπτοι Z 464. Cf. H 99, Ξ 114, Ψ 256 : ἀμφὶ γαῖαν ἔναξεν φ 122. Cf. γ 258.—Of a corpse : κωφὴν γαῖαν (the senseless clay) Ω 54.

γαιήϊος [γαῖα]. Of the Earth : υἱόν η 324.

γαιήοχος [γαιη-, γαῖα + ὀχ-, ἔχω]. Epithet or a name of Poseidon. Prob., earth-embracing, the earth-embracer (connecting Poseidon with the earth-encircling river Ocean) N 83, 125, O 174, 201, Υ 34 : α 68, γ 55, θ 322, 350, ι 528.—Joined with ἐννοσίγαιος Ι 183, Ν 43, 59, 677, Ξ 355, Ο 222, Ψ 584 : λ 241.

γαίω [γαϝ-. Cf. ἀγαυός and L. *gaudeo*]. Only in phrase κύδεϊ γαίων, of a divinity, glorying in his splendour; or perh., brilliant or glorious with splendour Α 405, Ε 906, Θ 51, Λ 81.

γάλα, γάλακτος, τό [cf. γλάγος]. Milk Δ 434, Ε 902 : δ 88, 89, ι 246, 297, κ 304.

γαλαθηνός [γάλα + θη-, θάομαι[2]]. Still sucking the mother's milk : νεβρούς δ 336 = ρ 127.

γαλήνη, -ης, ἡ. A calm. **(1)** Of the winds ε 391, μ 168.—**(2)** Of the sea : ἐλόωσι γαλήνην (through a calm sea) η 319. Cf. ε 452, κ 94.

γάλοως, ἡ. Dat. γαλόῳ Γ 122. Nom. pl. γαλόῳ Χ 473. A sister-in-law, a sister of one's husband Γ 122, Ζ 378, 383, Χ 473, Ω 769.

γαμβρός, -οῦ, ὁ. **(1)** A son-in-law Ζ 177, 178, 249, Ι 142, 284, Λ 739, Ν 428, Ω 331 : γ 387, δ 569, η 313, θ 582 (but this might come under (2)), τ 406.—**(2)** A brother-in-law Ε 474, Ν 464, 466.

γαμέω [γάμος]. Fut. γαμέω Ι 388, 391. Infin. γαμέειν ο 522. 3 sing. aor. ἔγημε Ξ 121 : λ 179, ο 241, π 34, ψ 149. γῆμε Ν 433 : α 36, λ 274, 282. Pple γήμας, -αντος Ι 399, Λ 227. Infin. γῆμαι φ 72, 158. **Mid.** 3 sing. fut. γαμέσσεται Ι 394. 3 sing. aor. opt. γήμαιτο π 392, φ 162. Fem. pple. γημαμένη λ 273. Infin. γήμασθαι β 128, ο 17, σ 270, 289, τ 159, 531, υ 335, 342. **(1)** In act., of a man, to marry, wed : κούρην Ι 388, μιν 391, Ἀδρήστοιο θυγατρῶν (partitive genit., one of his daughters) Ξ 121. Cf. Ι 399, Λ 227, Ν 433 : ἄλοχον μνηστήν α 36 (here of another's wife), λ 179, 274, 282, ο 241, 522, π 34, φ 72, 158, ψ 149.—Absol. δ 208.—**(2)** In mid. **(a)** Of a woman, to give herself in marriage to, to wed. With dat. : Εὐρυμάχῳ ο 17. Cf. β 113, 128, λ 273, π 392 = φ 162, σ 270, 289, υ 335, 342.—Absol. α 275, τ 159, 531.—**(b)** App., to get (a wife for one's son): Πηλεύς μοι γυναῖκα γαμέσσεται Ι 394 (*v.l.* γε μάσσεται).

γάμος, -ου, ὁ. **(1)** A contracting of marriage, one's marriage : ὄφρα συνώμεθα ἀμφὶ γάμῳ Ν 382 : γάμον τεύξουσιν α 277 = β 196. Cf. α 249 = π 126, β 97 = τ 142 = ω 132, β 205, δ 7, ζ 27, 66, 288, ο 126, 524, ρ 476, σ 272, τ 137, 157, υ 341, φ 250, χ 50, ω 126.—**(2)** A marriage, a wedding, a wedding-feast : γάμοι εἰλαπίναι τε Σ 491. Cf. Τ 299, Ω 62 : δαινύντα γάμον δ 3. Cf. α 226, δ 770, λ 415, υ 307, ψ 135.—**(3)** Marriage, wedlock : ἱμερόεντα ἔργα γάμοιο Ε 429 : ἐκλελάθοιτό κε γάμοιο γ 224. Cf. υ 74.

γαμφηλαί, αἱ. The jaws of an animal. Of lions Ν 200, Π 489.—Of horses Τ 394.

γαμψῶνυξ, -υχος [γαμψ- = καμψ-, κάμπτω + ὄνυξ]. With hooked talons : αἰγυπιοί Π 428 : = χ 302, π 217.

†**γανάω** [cf. next]. Nom. pl. masc. pres. pple. γανόωντες Ν 265. Fem. γανόωσαι Τ 359 : η 128. Of polished metal, to shine, gleam Ν 265, Τ 359.—Of vegetation, to be brightly green : πρασιαί η 128.

γάνυμαι [cf. prec.]. 3 sing. fut. γανύσσεται Ξ 504. To rejoice, be glad Ν 493.—To rejoice or take delight in. With dat. Υ 405.—In reference to persons : ἀνδρὶ φίλῳ ἐλθόντι Ξ 504. Cf. μ 43.

γάρ [γ(ε) ἄρ]. **(1)** Introducing the ground or reason for something said. **(a)** The γάρ clause following, for, since, seeing that Α 55, 56, 63, 78, 81, 86, etc. : α 7, 29, 40, 78, 114, 152, etc.—**(b)** The γάρ clause coming first, since, seeing that Β 803, Μ 326, Ν 736, Ο 739, Ψ 156, etc. : α 301, 337, ε 29, κ 174, μ 154, etc.—**(2)** Introducing an explanation, reason, amplification, or analysis of something previously said (often with καί; see καί (3)) Α 9, 12, 80, 262, 295, 355, Β 119, Δ 226, 301, Θ 148, Κ 352, Μ 322, etc. : α 33, 260, β 89, γ 89, 362, δ 86, ζ 164, ι 319, 432 (the clause here introduced parenthetically), λ 69, υ 42, φ 232, etc. —**(3)** Introducing as a kind of interjection a question or expression with something of an abrupt effect (sometimes translatable, why . . ., well . . .) : πῶς γάρ τοι δώσουσι γέρας ; Α 123, ἦ γάρ κεν δειλὸς καλεοίμην 293. Cf. Κ 61, Ο 201, Σ 182, etc. : πῶς γάρ με κέλεαι . . . ; κ 337, εἰ γάρ κεν σὺ μίμνοις ο 545. Cf. θ 159, κ 383, ξ 115, ο 509, π 222, etc.—For αἲ γάρ, εἰ γάρ in wishes see αἴ (1), εἰ (2) (b).—**(4)** Idiomatically following the relative ὅς : ὃ γάρ κ' ὄχ' ἄριστον εἴη (for that . . .) Μ 344 = 357, ὃ γὰρ γέρας ἐστὶ θανόντων Ψ 9 : ὃς γὰρ δεύτατος ἦλθεν α 286. Cf. ρ 172, ω 190.—So following ἵνα : ἵνα γάρ σφιν ἐπέφραδον ἠγερέθεσθαι (for there . . .) Κ 127.—And ὡς : ὡς γὰρ ἀνώγει (for so he bade) Ι 690, ὡς γὰρ ἔμοιγε (for so he was to me) Ω 68, etc. : ὡς γάρ οἱ μοῖρ' ἐστὶ . . . (for this is his destiny, to . . .) ε 41. Cf. θ 79, υ 282, etc. (In such cases the demonstrative ὥς (ὣς) is also read.)

γαστήρ, -έρος, ἡ. Genit. γαστρός ο 344. Dat. γαστρί Ε 539, 616, Ρ 519. **(1)** The belly Δ 531, Ε 539 = Ρ 519, Ε 616, Ν 372 = 398, Ν 506, Π 163 (of wolves), 465, Ρ 313, Τ 225, Φ 180 : δ 369 = μ 332, ι 433 (of a ram).—In half-personified sense: κέλεταί ἑ γ. ζ 133. Cf. η 216, ο 344, ρ 228, 286, 473, 559, σ 2, 53, 364, 380.—**(2)** The intestine of an animal stuffed with fat and blood and forming some kind of pudding or large sausage σ 44, 118, υ 25.—**(3)** The womb Ζ 58.

γάστρη, -ης, ἡ [= prec.]. The lower and rounded part of a vessel : τρίποδος Σ 348 : = θ 437.

γαυλός, -οῦ. Some kind of vessel for milk ι 223.

γε, *enclitic.* Calling attention to a word or fact or distinguishing it from others : εἴ κε θάνατόν γε φύγοιμεν Α 60, ἐπεί μ' ἀφέλεσθέ γε δόντες 299 (δόντες being here the word emphasized). Cf. Α 81, 216, 286, 352, 393, 506, etc. : κεῖνός γε ἐοικότι κεῖται ὀλέθρῳ α 46, ὅτις τοιαῦτά γε ῥέζοι 47. Cf. α 10, 203, 222, 223, 229, 339, etc.—γ' οὖν, in any case : εἴ γ' οὖν ἕτερός γε φύγῃσιν (if indeed one does escape) Ε 258, μὴ ἐμέ γ' οὖν οὗτός γε λάβοι χόλος (far be it from me) Π 30.

γεγάᾱσι, 3 pl. pf. γίγνομαι.

γέγηθε, 3 sing. pf. γηθέω.

γέγονε, 3 sing. pf. γίγνομαι.

γέγωνα, *pf.* (with pres. sense). Infin. γεγωνέμεν Θ 223, Λ 6. 3 sing. plupf. (in impf. sense) ἐγεγώνει Χ 34, Ψ 425 : φ 368. From pres. γεγώνω 3 sing. impf. (ἐ)γέγωνε Ξ 469, Ω 703 : θ 305. From pres. γεγωνέω impf. (ἐ)γεγώνευν μ 370, ρ 161. 3 pl.

γεγώνευν ι 47. Infin. γεγωνεῖν M 337. (1) To make one's voice heard: οὔ πώς οἱ ἔην βώσαντι γεγωνεῖν M 337. Cf. Θ 223 = Λ 6: ε 400 = ι 473 = μ 181, ζ 294.—αὔειν γεγωνώς, to shout making oneself heard, *i.e.* in a sustained and loud voice Θ 227 = Λ 275 = 586 = P 247, M 439 = N 149.—(2) To shout (with implication that one makes oneself heard): ἐγέγωνε Πουλυδάμαντι Ξ 469. Cf. X 34, Ψ 425, Ω 703: θ 305, ι 47, μ 370, φ 368.—(3) To declare something aloud ρ 161.

γείνατο, 3 sing. trans. aor. γίγνομαι.

γεινόμεθα, 1 pl. aor. γίγνομαι.

γείτων, -ονος. A neighbour δ 16, ε 489, ι 48.

γελαστός [γελάω]. Tending to, conceived in a spirit of, mockery; or perh., laughable: ἔργα θ 307.

†**γελάω.** 3 sing. aor. (ἐ)γέλασσε Z 471, O 101, T 362, Φ 389, 408: ι 413, ρ 542, σ 163. 3 pl. γέλασαν Ψ 840. (ἐ)γέλασσαν B 270, Ψ 784: σ 320, υ 358, φ 376. Pple. γελάσας β 301. γελάσσας Λ 378, Φ 508. Fem. γελάσᾱσα Z 484. Infin. γελάσαι ξ 465. Also pres. γελόω φ 105. Pl. pple. γελόωντες σ 40, υ 374. γελώωντες σ 111, υ 390. (ἐκ-.) (1) To smile: δακρυόεν Z 484, χείλεσιν (*i.e.* with a forced smile) O 101. Cf. ρ 542, φ 105.—Of the earth, to be bright T 362.—Of the heart, to rejoice Φ 389: ι 413 (here app. connoting inward derisive laughter. See (2) (b)).—(2) (a) To laugh Z 471, Λ 378, Φ 408, 508: β 301, ξ 465, σ 40, 111, 163, 320, υ 390.—(b) To laugh (at a person): ἐπ' αὐτῷ B 270, Ψ 784: = υ 358 = φ 376, ἐπὶ ξείνοις υ 374.—With ἐπί advbl. Ψ 840.

γελοίϊος [γελάω]. Laughable B 215.

γελόω. See γελάω.

†**γελωάω** [γελάω]. 3 pl. impf. γελώων. = γελάω (2) (a): γναθμοῖσιν ἀλλοτρίοισιν υ 347.

γέλως, ὁ [γελάω]. Dat. γέλῳ σ 100. Acc. γέλω σ 350, υ 8, 346. Laughter A 599: = θ 326, θ 343, 344, σ 100, 350, υ 8, 346.

γελώων, 3 pl. impf. γελωάω.

γελώωντες. See γελάω.

γενεή, -ῆς, ἡ [γεν-, γίγνομαι]. Instrumental γενεῆφι I 58, Ξ 112, Φ 439. (1) Race, stock, family = γένος (1), γενέθλη (1): τίη γενεὴν ἐρεείνεις; Z 145, Φ 153, πατρόθεν ἐκ γενεῆς ὀνομάζων (by his father's, that is, his family name) K 68, γενεῇ ὑπέρτερος (in birth) Λ 786, γενεὴν Διὸς εἶναι (by race sprung from . . .) Φ 187. Cf. Z 151, 211 = Υ 241, H 128, K 239, O 141, T 105, Υ 203, 214, Φ 157, Ψ 471: γενεῇ πατρώϊον (by right of descent) α 387. Cf ο 225.—Of horses, stock, breed E 265, 268.—(2) A race or generation = γένος (3): φύλλων Z 146, ἀνδρῶν 149.—A race or family: οὐ τοι γενεὴν θεοὶ νώνυμνον θῆκαν α 222. Cf. π 117.—A body of descendants, offspring: Δαρδάνου Υ 303. Cf. Υ 306, Φ 191: δ 27.—(3) The body of persons born at about a certain time and conceived of as living for a certain period, a generation: δύο γενεαὶ ἀνθρώπων A 250. Cf. Ψ 790: ξ 325 = τ 294.—(4) App., family likeness or type: αὐτῷ γενεὴν ἐῴκει (in . . .) Ξ 474.—(5) In reference to the date of one's birth, age, one's years = γένος (7): ὁπλότερος γενεῇ (in age) B 707. Cf. Δ 60 = Σ 365, Z 24, H 153, I 161, O 166, 182: τ 184.—So with instrumental: γενεῆφι νεώτατος Ξ 112. Cf. I 58, Φ 439.—(6) One's birthplace = γένος (8) Υ 390: α 407, ο 175, υ 193.

γενέθλη, -ης, ἡ [as prec.]. (1) Race, stock = γενεή (1), γένος (1): σῆς ἐκ γενέθλης T 111: Παιήονός εἰσι γενέθλης (of the race of . . .) δ 232. Cf. ν 130.—(2) Of mares, a brood: τῶν ἒξ ἐγένοντο γ. E 270 (γ. being predicate).—(3) Source, origin = γένος (2): ὅθεν ἀργύρου ἐστὶ γ. (whence comes . . .) B 857.

γενειάς, -άδος, ἡ [γένειον]. In pl., the hair on the chin, the beard: γενειάδες ἀμφὶ γένειον π 176.

γενειάω [γενειάς]. To get a beard, *i.e.* attain manhood: παῖδα γενειήσαντα σ 176. Cf. σ 269.

γένειον, -ου, τό [γένυς]. The chin Θ 371, K 454, X 74, Ω 516: λ 583, π 176, τ 473.

γενέσθαι, aor. infin. γίγνομαι.

γένεσις, ἡ [γεν-, γίγνομαι]. Source, origin: Ὠκεανόν, θεῶν γένεσιν Ξ 201 = 302. Cf. Ξ 246.

γενέσκετο, 3 sing. pa. iterative γίγνομαι.

γενετή, -ῆς, ἡ [γεν-, γίγνομαι]. One's birth: ἐκ γενετῆς Ω 535 (from his birth (onwards)): σ 6 (to be his from his birth, *i.e.* on his birth).

γενναῖος [γεν-, γίγνομαι]. Suited to (noble) birth, seemly, honourable E 253.

γενόμην, aor. γίγνομαι.

γένος, τό [γεν-, γίγνομαι]. (1) Race, stock, family = γενεή (1), γενέθλη (1): γ. ἦν ἐκ ποταμοῖο (was by race sprung from . . .) E 544. Cf. E 896, Z 209, Ξ 113, 126, Φ 186, Ψ 347: δ 63, ξ 199, 204, ο 267, 533, π 62, 401, ρ 373, τ 116, 162, φ 335, ω 269, 508, 512.—One's descent: γ. μοι ἔνθεν ὅθεν σοί Δ 58. Cf. N 354.—(2) Source, origin = γενέθλη (3): ὅθεν ἡμιόνων γ. B 852 (whence come . . .).—(3) A race or generation = γενεή (2): ἡμιθέων ἀνδρῶν M 23. Cf. δ 62, ρ 523, υ 212.—(4) App., a generation considered as a period: τρὶς ἀνάξασθαι γένε' ἀνδρῶν (during three generations) γ 245.—(5) The members of one's family: μεθ' αἷμά τε καὶ γ. αὐτῶν θ 583.—(6) Offspring, a child: δῖον γ. I 538, σὸν γένος T 124.—So of the Chimaera: θεῖον γ. (as being of divine origin) Z 180.—(7) In reference to the date of one's birth, age, one's years = γενεή (5): γένει ὕστερος ἦεν (was the younger) Γ 215.—(8) One's birthplace = γενεή (6) ζ 35.

γέντο, *3 sing. aor.* To seize or grasp: ἱμάσθλην Θ 43 = N 25. Cf. N 241, Σ 476, 477.

γένυς, ἡ. Dat. pl. γένυσσι Λ 416. Acc. pl. γένῡς λ 320. In pl., the jaws Λ 416, Ψ 688: λ 320.

γεραιός, -ή [γέρων]. (1) Absol. in masc., an old man (always of a dignified person): ἠρᾶθ' ὁ γ. A 35. Cf. Γ 191, 225, K 77, Λ 632, 645, Ξ 39, Ω 162, 252, 279, 302, 322: γ 373.—In voc. as a term of respectful address K 164, 167, 558, Λ 648, 653, Ω 390, 433, 618.—Joined with ἄττα I 607, P 561.—Without the notion of respect β 201, ξ 131, 185.—(2) Absol. in fem., an old woman (app. referring to those of the higher classes): ξυνάγουσα γεραιάς Z 87. Cf. Z 270, 287, 296.—(3) In comp. γεραίτερος (a) Older: ὃς σεῖο γ.

εὔχομαι εἶναι I 60.—Absol. γ 24.—(b) Old rather than young, elderly: κῆρυξ Ω 149, 178. Cf. γ 362.

γεραίρω [γέρας]. To honour, show honour to: νώτοισι διηνεκέεσσιν H 321: ξ 437, ἀγαθοῖσιν 441.

γέρανος, -ου, ἡ. A crane B 460 = O 692, Γ 3.

γεραρός [γέρας]. Of dignified bearing, majestic Γ 170.—In comp. γεραρώτερος Γ 211.

γέρας, τό. Acc. pl. with hyphaeresis γέρᾰ (for γέραα) B 237, I 334: δ 66. **(1)** A meed of honour, a special prize apart from the general division of spoils (represented as assigned sometimes to the king or a chief by the general consent (as in A 118, 123, 135, 276, Π 56, Σ 444: η 10), sometimes to chiefs by the king (as in I 334, 367). (But cf. I 130, 272, Λ 696, where the king is represented as choosing his prize)) A 118, 120, 123, 133, 135, 138, 161, 163, 167, 185, 276, 356 = 507 = B 240, B 237, I 111, 334, 344, 367, Π 54, 56, Σ 444, T 89: η 10, λ 534.—**(2)** Something given by way of showing honour to a person: νῶτα βοός, τά οἱ γέρα πάρθεσαν δ 66.—**(3)** An honour paid: τὸ γὰρ λάχομεν γ. ἡμεῖς Δ 49 = Ω 70. Cf. Π 457 = 675, Ψ 9: δ 197, ω 190, 296.—**(4)** A privilege: γερόντων Δ 323, I 422.—**(5)** The dignity or honours of a king: οὔ τοι Πρίαμος γ. ἐν χερὶ θήσει Υ 182. Cf. λ 175, 184, ο 522.—App., any hereditary honour or privilege bestowed on a king or a chief by the people: γ. ὅ τι δῆμος ἔδωκεν η 150.—**(6)** A gratuity: λοετροχόῳ υ 297.

γερούσιος [γέρων]. Of an oath, taken by the elders or councillors (as representing the people) X 119.—Of wine, such as is served at assemblies of councillors Δ 259: ν 8.

γέρων, -οντος, ὁ [cf. γῆρας]. Voc. γέρον A 26, 286, B 370, 796, etc.: β 40, 178, 192, γ 226, etc. Dat. pl. γέρουσι Δ 344, Z 113, I 70. **(1)** **(a)** An old man: ἔδεισεν ὁ γ. A 33, ἠμὲν νέοι ἠδὲ γέροντες B 789. Cf. A 380, 538, Γ 109, 181, Θ 518, etc.: πείθεσθαι γέροντι β 227 (app. Laertes, as Mentor, described (225) as Ὀδυσῆος ἑταῖρος, was hardly a γ.). Cf. β 39, γ 390, δ 349, θ 570, λ 38, etc.—**(b)** In voc. in a tone of respect A 286, B 370, Δ 313, Θ 102, I 115, etc.: β 40, γ 226, 331, 357, ω 244.—Without such a tone A 26: β 178, 192, δ 465, 485, ξ 37, 45, 122, 166, 386, 508, σ 10, ω 394, 407.—**(2)** In apposition: παρὰ πατρὶ γέροντι A 358. Cf. B 793, E 149, H 125, etc.: α 188, β 157, γ 436, etc.—**(3)** As a proper adj., old, stricken by age: γ. ἐὼν πολεμιστής K 549. Cf. σ 53, 81.—Of a thing, old, worn by use: σάκος χ 184.—**(4)** A member of the βουλή, an elder or councillor: βουλὴν γερόντων B 53. Cf. B 21, 404, Δ 323, 344, Z 113, I 70, 89, 422, 574, O 721, Σ 448, T 303, 338 (here including Agamemnon, the king): γέροντας πλέονας καλέσαντες η 189. Cf. β 14, φ 21, ω 255.—**(5)** An elder acting as one of a body of judges Σ 503.

γεύομαι. With genit., to taste of, take a taste of. Fig.: δουρὸς ἀκωκῆς Φ 61. Cf. φ 98.—Also, fig., to make trial of, try one's fortune with: ἀλλήλων Υ 258: Ἀχαιῶν ρ 413, χειρῶν υ 181.

γέφῡρα, ἡ. **(1)** A dike or embankment to confine a river: ποταμὸς ἐκέδασσε γεφύρας E 88. Cf. E 89.—**(2)** π(τ)ολέμοιο γέφυραι, app., ranks of men thought of as stemming the tide of war Δ 371, Θ 378, Λ 160, Υ 427.—In Θ 553 (ἐπὶ πτολέμοιο γεφύρας ἥατο) app., preserving (more or less) the stations in which they had fought.

γεφῡρόω [γέφυρα]. **(1)** To dam (a river) Φ 245. —**(2)** To make (a way) by forming an embankment: γεφύρωσε κέλευθον O 357.

γῆ, γῆς, ἡ [cf. γαῖα]. **(1)** The earth = γαῖα (1): ὄφρ' ἂν ἵκηται γῆν O 24, φυσίζοος Φ 63.—Personified Γ 104, T 259.—**(2)** The earth as distinguished from the sea, the land = γαῖα (2) (b): ἢ ἁλὸς ἢ ἐπὶ γῆς μ 27. Cf. ψ 233.—**(3)** A particular land or country = γαῖα (4): τίς γῆ; ν 233.—One's native land: ἀμῆς γῆς λ 167, 482.—**(4)** The surface of the earth, the ground = γαῖα (5): νέρθεν γῆς λ 302, ἢ πρὸς γῆν ἐλάσειε κάρη ρ 237.

γηθέω. 3 sing. pf. (in pres. sense) γέγηθε Θ 559: ζ 106. 3 sing. plupf. (in impf. sense) γεγήθει Λ 683, N 494. **(1)** To rejoice, be glad A 255, Z 212, H 189, Θ 559, Λ 683, N 416, 494, Π 530, P 567, Ω 424: ζ 106, η 269, 329 = θ 199 = ν 250 = σ 281, θ 385, ν 353 = φ 414, υ 104, ω 382.—With complementary pple.: οὐδὲ τώ ἰδὼν γήθησεν A 330. Cf. Δ 255, 283, 311, H 214, Θ 278, K 190, N 344, Ξ 140, Ω 321: ε 486 = ω 504, μ 88, ν 226, ο 165, χ 207.—With acc. of what is rejoiced at: νῶϊ προφανέντε Θ 378, τάδε I 77.—**(2)** To take pleasure or delight *in doing something*. With pple.: Ἀργείων ἐρέων γενεήν H 127.

γηθοσύνη, -ης, ἡ [γηθέω]. Joy, delight: ἐγέλασσέ οἱ ἦτορ γηθοσύνῃ Φ 390.—Of the sea N 29.

γηθόσυνος, -η [as prec.]. Joyful, glad, rejoicing Δ 272 = 326, H 122, N 82, Σ 557: ε 269, λ 540.

γῆμε, 3 sing. aor. γαμέω.

γῆρας, -αος, τό [cf. γέρων]. Dat. γήραϊ Γ 150, E 153, Ψ 644, etc.: β 16, ο 357, ω 233. γήρᾳ λ 136, ψ 283. Old age A 29, Γ 150, Δ 315, 321, E 153, Θ 103, I 446, K 79, Σ 434, 515, T 336, X 60, 420 (my years), Ψ 623, 644, Ω 487: α 218, β 16, λ 136 = ψ 283, λ 196, 497, ν 59, ο 246, 348, 357, ψ 24, 212, ω 233, 249, 390.—The period of old age: ἐς γῆρας Ξ 86. Cf. θ 226, τ 368, ψ 286.

γηράσκω [γῆρας]. From γηράω 3 sing. impf. ἐγήρα H 148, P 197. γήρα ξ 67. Also non-thematic pres. pple. γηράς P 197. (κατα-.) To grow old: ἤδη γηράσκοντα B 663. Cf. H 148, P 197 (twice), 325, Ω 541: δ 210, ξ 67, ο 409.—Of fruit, to mellow η 120.

γῆρυς, ἡ. Voice Δ 437.

γίγνομαι [redup. fr. γ(ε)ν-]. **(A)** 3 sing. pa. iterative γενέσκετο λ 208. Aor. γενόμην Σ 102, T 219, Φ 440: θ 311, ξ 141. 2 sing. γένευ E 897. 3 γένετο A 49, Z 153, N 417, Ψ 526, etc.: β 26, δ 11, ω 292, etc. 3 dual γενέσθην E 548: λ 255, 307, 312. 1 pl. γενόμεσθα Φ 89. With metrical lengthening of the first syllable γεινόμεθα X 477 (*v.l.* γιγνόμεθα). 2 ἐγένεσθε B 323. 3 (ἐ)γένοντο Γ 84, Δ 382, E 63, H 313, etc.: η 144, θ 234, σ 345, φ 24, etc. Subj. γένωμαι Θ 180, Π 39, X 358: ε 473, λ 73, χ 167. 2 sing. -ηαι Θ 282, Λ 797:

κ 486. 3 -ηται Α 341, Ζ 489, Τ 201, etc.: β 374, θ 553, ρ 23, etc. 1 pl. -ώμεθα Κ 193, Ν 236, Ρ 636. 2 -ησθε Ε 488. 3 -ωνται Β 397, Υ 308. Opt. γενοίμην Ρ 38: ξ 338, π 103. 2 sing. -οιο ι 456, ξ 440, ο 341, σ 79. 3 -οιτο Δ 17, Θ 26, Ν 233, etc.: γ 129, θ 414, σ 161, etc. 1 pl. -οίμεθα Ν 485. 2 -οισθε Η 99. 3 -οίατο Β 340: α 266, δ 346, ρ 137. 3 sing. imp. γενέσθω Θ 181: ε 224, ρ 285, χ 491. Pple. (with metrical lengthening of the first syllable) γεινόμενος, -ου (*vv. ll.* γιγνόμενος, -ου) Κ 71, Υ 128, Ψ 79, Ω 210: δ 208, η 198. Infin. γενέσθαι Γ 323, Η 199, Ρ 151, etc.: α 220, δ 173, ο 480, etc. 3 sing. pf. γέγονε Τ 122. 3 pl. γεγάᾱσι Δ 325: ε 35, ζ 62, ι 118, κ 5, ν 160, τ 279, ω 84. 3 sing. plupf. γεγόνει Ν 355. Acc. sing. masc. pple. γεγαῶτα Ι 456: δ 112, 144, τ 400. Acc. pl. γεγαῶτας Β 866. (For these pf. forms cf. μέμαα, μέμονα under μάω.) **(B)** 2 sing. aor. ἐγείναο Ε 880. 3 (ἐ)γείνατο Α 280, Δ 476, Ε 800, Ν 777, Ο 526, Φ 85, etc.: α 223, δ 13, ζ 25, η 57, 61, λ 268, 299, ο 242, φ 172. 2 sing. subj. γείνεαι υ 202. Infin. γείνασθαι Φ 160: θ 312. (ἐγ-, ἐκ-, ἐπι-, παρα-, περι-, προ-.) **(I)** In pres. and impf. and forms (A), to come into being. **(1)** To be born, take one's being: τράφεν ἠδ' ἐγένοντο Α 251, τῶν ἓξ ἐγένοντο Ε 270, πρότερος γενόμην (am the elder) Τ 219, Φ 440. Cf. Ε 548, 897, Ζ 206, 489, Κ 71, etc.: τοῦ μ' ἔκ φασι γενέσθαι α 220, γαμέοντί τε γεινομένῳ τε δ 208. Cf. γ 28, δ 723, η 198, θ 311, κ 350, etc.—**(2)** In pf., to be in the condition of having been born; hence simply, to exist, live, be: οἳ ὁπλότεροι γεγάασιν Δ 325: ἐν αἶγες γεγάασιν ι 118, οἳ νῦν γεγάασιν ω 84. Cf. ε 35 = τ 279, ζ 62, κ 5, ν 160.—In more strict pf. sense: ἤδη ἀνὴρ γέγον' ἐσθλός (has been born, is born) Τ 122.—Sim. in plupf.: Ζεὺς πρότερος γεγόνει (had been born earlier, was the elder) Ν 355.—In pple., born Ι 456: δ 112, 144, τ 400.—So ὑπὸ Τμώλῳ γεγαῶτας (born (and dwelling) there) Β 866.—**(3)** To come into view or notice, be seen, heard, etc.: κλαγγή Α 49, ὀδμή Ξ 415, σέλας Τ 374. Cf. Δ 456, Κ 375, Λ 50, Ο 607, Χ 150, etc.: μ 87, 396, χ 77, 133, ψ 137.—**(4)** Of natural phenomena, natural products, etc., to come into being, rise, grow, be: φύλλα καὶ ἄνθεα Β 468. Cf. Β 397: ἐκ νυκτῶν ἄνεμοι γίγνονται μ 287, ἐν οἶνος γίγνεται ν 245, χιὼν γένετο (fell) ξ 476. Cf. ι 51, μ 326, ρ 23, χ 491.—**(5)** To come to or upon, fall to, befall, be the lot of, affect (a person). With dat.: Πηλεΐωνι ἄχος Α 188, αἰδώς οἱ Ω 45. Cf. Γ 323, Δ 245, 289, Ι 125, Ξ 98, Τ 274, etc.: πάντα οἱ γένοιτο ρ 355, μὴ νῶϊν ἔρις γένηται σ 13. Cf. θ 414, λ 208, σ 122 = υ 199, σ 366, τ 569, φ 412.—For ἐμὲ χρεὼ γίγνεται δ 634 see χρειώ (1) (a).—Without case: ποινὴ οὔ τις ἐγίγνετο Ν 659. Cf. Α 341, Ι 380, Φ 529: χ 306.—**(6)** To be manifested or shown, to be, come into play, take effect: οὔ τις φειδὼ γίγνεται (there is no . . .) Η 410, μνημοσύνη τις γενέσθω (let there be . . .) Θ 181. Cf. Ο 359, Ψ 505: εἰ γὰρ ἐπ' ἀρῇσιν τέλος γένοιτο ρ 496. Cf. κ 202 = 568.—**(7)** To happen, occur, come round, come to pass, take place: ἠώς Α 493, τάδε ἔργα Ζ 348, ἀγορή Η 345. Cf. Γ 110, 176, Θ 130, Ρ 686, Ω 436, etc.: νόστον γενέσθαι δ 173. Cf. α 379, β 26, 374, γ 129, 228, δ 747, ε 299, λ 537, μ 191, ω 455, 461, etc.—**(8)** To become, come to be, prove to be *so and so*: ὁμηγερέες Α 57, ἄνεῳ Β 323, ἐν πυρὶ βουλαὶ γενοίατο (be cast) 340, κλισίῃσιν ἐν Ἀτρεΐδαο γένοντο (reached the . . .) Η 313. Cf. Β 453, Γ 71, Δ 17, 466, Θ 180, Υ 497, Χ 421, etc.: λέων γένετο δ 456, ὄφρ' ἔτι δύης ἐπὶ πῆμα γενοίμην (be brought into . . .) ξ 338, φόνος οἱ γένοντο φ 24. Cf. α 266, γ 271, η 154, 316, ο 446, π 175, etc.—**(9)** Passes from this last sense into that, practically, of the copula, to be *so and so*: οὔ πώ τις ὁμοῖος γένετ' ἀνήρ (was) Β 553, ὃν κάρτιστον Ἀχαιῶν φημὶ γενέσθαι (that he is) Ζ 98, ζαχρηεῖς γίγνοντο (were wont to be) Ν 684, ἀρίγνωτος Διὸς γίγνεται ἀλκή Ο 490. Cf. Δ 375, Ζ 153, 210, Ν 569, Π 746, Υ 220, etc.: οὐ νηὸς ἐπήβολος γίγνομαι β 320, τηλύγετος δ 11 (after ἐκ δούλης in 12 supply γεγαώς). Cf. δ 201, 362, ε 224, θ 586, ι 35, ρ 223, τ 344, χ 130, etc.—**(II)** In forms (B), to give (a person) being. **(1)** Of the father, to beget: παῖδα γείνατο Τυδεύς Ε 800. Cf. Δ 400, Ε 880, Ο 526, Φ 160: υἷε κραταιώ ο 242. Cf. η 61, υ 202.—**(2)** Of the mother, to bear: θεά σε γείνατο μήτηρ Α 280. Cf. Γ 238, Δ 476, Ε 896, Ζ 24, 26, Ω 608, etc.: ἥ ῥ' Ἡρακλῆα γείνατο λ 268. Cf. α 223, δ 13, ζ 25, λ 299, φ 172.—**(3)** Of both parents Η 10, Φ 142: η 57, θ 312.

γιγνώσκω [redup. fr. γνω-]. 2 sing. fut. in mid. form γνώσεαι Β 367, Κ 88: π 310. γνώσῃ Β 365. 3 -εται Θ 17, Σ 270. 1 pl. -όμεθα ψ 109. 2 -εσθε Ψ 497, Ω 242. Aor. ἔγνων Λ 526, Ν 72: ο 532, τ 475. 2 sing. ἔγνως Υ 20, Χ 10: ν 299, ρ 273. 3 ἔγνω Α 199, Ν 66, Π 530, Ρ 32, etc.: α 3, ε 444, η 234, λ 91, etc. γνῶ Δ 357, Η 189, Κ 358, Λ 439, Π 119, 658: τ 468. 3 dual γνώτην φ 36. 3 pl. ἔγνωσαν κ 397. Subj. γνώω ξ 118, ρ 549. 2 sing. γνώῃς Ψ 487. γνῷς χ 373. 3 γνώῃ Ω 688: ρ 556. γνῷ Α 411, Π 273. 2 dual γνῶτον φ 218. 1 pl. γνώομεν π 304. γνῶμεν Χ 382. 3 γνώωσι Α 302, Ψ 610, 661, Ω 688. γνῶσι Ζ 231. Opt. γνοίην Γ 235. 2 sing. γνοίης Γ 53, Ε 85, Ξ 58: ο 537, ρ 164, τ 310, υ 237, φ 202. 3 γνοίη Ρ 630: ν 192, π 458, ρ 363. 3 pl. γνοῖεν Σ 125. Imp. pl. γνῶτε Τ 84. Infin. γνώμεναι Β 349, Φ 266, 609: α 411. γνῶναι β 159, ν 312, ω 159. (ἀνα-, δια-, ἐπι-.) **(1)** **(a)** To perceive, mark, remark, note, find, see, know: ἣν ἄτην Α 411 = Π 273, Διὸς τάλαντα Π 658. Cf. Μ 272, Π 119, 362, Τ 84.—**(b)** With acc. and complementary pple.: γιγνώσκω Ἄρηα κοιρανέοντα Ε 824. Cf. Ξ 154, Ρ 84: ο 532, ρ 549, 556.—With pple. alone: ὅτε γίγνωσκε θεοῦ γόνον ἐόντα Ζ 191: γνῶναι τὸν ἐόντα (that it was he) ω 159.—With a sim. pple. in genit.: ὡς γνῶ χωομένοιο Δ 357.—With adj.: γνῶ ἄνδρας δηΐους (that they were . . .) Κ 358.—**(c)** With acc. and dependent clause: γιγνώσκω σε, ὅττι . . . Ω 563. Cf. Ε 85.—With clause only: γνώμεναι εἰ . . . Β 349. Cf. Β 365, Γ 53, Ζ 231, Θ 17, Ξ 58, Σ 125, Φ 609, etc.: γνοίης χ' οἵη ἐμὴ δύναμις [ἐστιν] υ 237. Cf.

γ 166, θ 299, ρ 269, 363, χ 373, etc.—(d) Absol.: ἵνα γνώωσι καὶ οἴδε Α 302. Cf. Α 333 = Θ 446, Ν 66, Χ 296, Ψ 487, Ω 242: γιγνώσκω, φρονέω π 136 = ρ 193 = 281, ρ 273, τ 160.—(2) To gain knowledge of, get to know, learn: Τρώων νόον Χ 382. Cf. α 3, π 304.—To get to know, make the acquaintance of (a person) α 411.—So with genit.: ἀλλήλων φ 36.—To become aware of the presence of, discover (a person) Ω 688 (twice), 691.—To experience, find: φιλότητα ο 537 = ρ 164 = τ 310.—(3) (a) To have knowledge, know: ὅσσον ἔγωγε γιγνώσκω Ν 223.—With dependent clause: γιγνώσκων ὅ τ' ἄναλκις ἔην θεός Ε 331. Cf. Ε 433: φ 209.—(b) In aor., to know: ἔγνως ἐμὴν βουλήν (knowest) Υ 20.—To know (a person): αἴ κέ ποθι γνώω τοιοῦτον ἐόντα (in case I may find that I know him, seeing he was such a one, *i.e.* such as to be likely to be known) ξ 118.—(4) To distinguish, discern: ἠμὲν θεὸν ἠδὲ καὶ ἄνδρα Ε 128. Cf. Ν 72.—With acc. and dependent clause: ἵππους οἳ δεύτεροι οἵ τε πάροιθεν Ψ 497.—(5) To know (a person or thing) for what he or it is, know the nature of, know: εὖ σε γιγνώσκων Χ 356. Cf. Ρ 32 = Υ 198, Σ 270: ἔγνω [ποταμόν] (*i.e.* recognized him for a god) ε 444, καλάμην γιγνώσκειν (*i.e.* can judge from that what I was) ξ 215. Cf. β 159, π 310.—Sim.: θεὸν ἔγνω (knew that it was a god) α 420.—Absol., to recognize one's claim, hold it good Ψ 661.—(6) To know again, recognize, know: Ἀθηναίην Α 199. Cf. Γ 235, Ε 182, 815, Η 189, Κ 88, Λ 111, 526, 651, Ξ 475, Ο 241, Π 639, Ρ 334, Ω 698: φᾶρος η 234. Cf. κ 397, λ 91, 153, 390, 471, 615, ν 188, 192, 299, 312, π 458, τ 392, 468, 475, φ 218, χ 501, ω 102.—Absol. Η 185, Ψ 453: υ 94.—To find means of recognizing. With genit.: ἀλλήλων ψ 109.

γλάγος, τό [cf. γάλα]. Milk Β 471 = Π 643.

γλακτοφάγος [γαλακτοφάγος, fr. γαλακτ-, γάλα + φάγον]. Living on (mare's) milk Ν 6.

†**γλαυκιάω** [γλαυκός]. Pres. pple. γλαυκιόων. To have the eyes bright or glaring. Of a lion Υ 172.

γλαυκός, -ή. Bright, shining, gleaming (prob. without any notion of colour). Of the sea Π 34.

γλαυκῶπις, -ιδος [γλαυκός + ὦπα]. Acc. γλαυκώπιδα Θ 373. γλαυκῶπιν α 156. (The) bright-eyed (maid) (prob. without any notion of colour). Epithet or a name of Athene Α 206, Β 166, Ε 29, Ζ 88, Θ 373, etc.: α 44, 156, β 433, γ 13, 135, etc.

γλαφυρός, -ή, -όν [γλάφω = γλύφω. See γλυφίς, and cf. διαγλάφω]. Hollow, hollowed (for the most part as a conventional epithet). Of caves Σ 402, Ω 83: α 15 = ι 30, α 73, β 20, δ 403, ε 68, 155, 194, 226, ι 114, 476, μ 210, ψ 335.—Of rocks, having a cavity or cavities Β 88: ξ 533.—Of the lyre θ 257, ρ 262, χ 340, ψ 144.—Of a harbour (referring to the curved outline) μ 305.—Elsewhere epithet of ships Β 454, 516, Γ 119, Ε 327, Θ 180, etc.: γ 287, δ 356, 513, ι 99, κ 23, etc.

γλήνη, -ης, ἡ [app. 'something bright.' Cf. next]. (1) The eye, the eyeball Ξ 494: ι 390.—(2) A plaything, a doll or puppet: ἔρρε, κακὴ γλήνη Θ 164.

γλῆνος, τό [cf. prec.]. In pl. γλήνεα, trinkets Ω 192.

γλουτός, -οῦ, ὁ. One of the buttocks: δεξιόν Ε 66, Ν 651.—In pl., the buttocks, the rump Θ 340.

γλυκερός, -ή, -όν [cf. γλυκύς]. (1) Sweet or pleasant to the taste: σίτου Λ 89: συκέαι η 116 = λ 590 (the tree for the fruit). Cf. δ 88, ξ 194, υ 69, ω 68.—Of water, sweet, fit for drinking μ 306.—(2) Generally, sweet, pleasant, giving delight or joy: ὕπνος Κ 4, μολπῆς Ν 637. Cf. Ω 3, 636: δ 295, ε 472, π 23 = ρ 41, τ 511, χ 323, ψ 145, 255.—In comp.: ἧς γαίης γλυκερώτερον ἄλλο ι 28.

γλυκύθυμος [γλυκύς + θυμός]. Of gentle or kindly mind: ἀνήρ Υ 467.

γλυκύς, -ύ. Comp. γλυκίων, γλύκιον Α 249, Β 453, Λ 13, Σ 109: ι 34. (1) Sweet or pleasant to the taste: νέκταρ Α 598.—(2) Generally, sweet, pleasant: ὕπνος Α 610, ἵμερον Γ 139. Cf. Β 71, Γ 446, Ξ 328, Ψ 232: αἰών ε 152. Cf. β 395, η 289, θ 445, ι 333, κ 31 = ν 282, κ 548, μ 338, ο 7, σ 188, 199, τ 49, χ 500, ψ 342.—In comp. Α 249, Β 453 = Λ 13, Σ 109: ι 34.

γλυφίς, -ίδος, ἡ [γλύφω, to cut out, carve. Cf. γλαφυρός]. App., the notch in an arrow to receive the string. In pl. (poss. referring to a double notch (*i.e.* two notches at right angles)) Δ 122: φ 419.

γλῶσσα, -ης, ἡ. (1) The tongue Α 249, Β 489, Ε 74, 292, Π 161, Ρ 618, Υ 248.—Of the tongues of sacrificial victims γ 332, 341.—(2) A tongue or language Β 804: τ 175.—Language, speech: γ. ἐμέμικτο Δ 438.

γλωχίς, -ῖνος [cf. τανυγλώχις]. App., a tongue forming one of the ends of the ζυγόδεσμον or yoke-fastening, the ζ. being wound round the pole criss-cross, keeping the portion with the tongue the longer, and the tongue being tucked in under its portion after that portion had been wound over, and had so secured, the end of the other and shorter portion: ὑπὸ γλωχῖνα δ' ἔκαμψαν Ω 274 (ὑπό advbl.).

γναθμός, -οῦ, ὁ. The lower jaw Ν 671 = Π 606, Π 405, Ρ 617.—In pl., the jaws π 175, σ 29, υ 347.

γναμπτός, -ή, -όν [γνάμπτω]. (1) Bent, curved: ἕλικας Σ 401: ἀγκίστροισιν δ 369 = μ 332.—(2) Fig., that can be bent or influenced: νόημα Ω 41.—(3) As epithet of the limbs, flexible, lissom Λ 669, Ω 359: λ 394, ν 398, 430, φ 283.—Sim. of jaws, moving freely in their sockets Λ 416.

†**γνάμπτω** [= κνάμπτω]. 3 sing. aor. γνάμψε. (ἀνα-, ἐπι-, περι-.) To bend: ἐν γόνυ γνάμψεν (app., crooked his knee round the other's leg) Ψ 731.

γνήσιος [γ(ε)ν-, γίγνομαι]. (Lawfully) begotten, born in wedlock, legitimate Λ 102: ξ 202.

γνοίην, aor. opt. γιγνώσκω.

γνύξ [γ(ό)νυ]. On the knee or the knees: ἔριπεν Ε 68. Cf. Ε 309, 357, Θ 329, Λ 355, Υ 417.

γνῶ, 3 sing. aor. *γιγνώσκω*.

γνώῃ, γνῷ, 3 sing. aor. subj. *γιγνώσκω*.

γνώμεναι, γνῶναι, aor. infin. *γιγνώσκω*.

γνώριμος [*γνω-, γιγνώσκω*]. (Well-)known. Absol., a friend or acquaintance π 9.

γνώσεται, 3 sing. fut. *γιγνώσκω*.

γνωτός, *-ή, -όν* [*γνω-, γιγνώσκω*]. **(1)** Easy to be known, evident: *γνωτόν* [*ἐστιν*] *ὡς* . . . H 401 Cf. ω 182.—**(2)** As sb. **(a)** A kinsman or kinswoman: *γνωτοὺς λιποῦσα* Γ 174, *γνωτοί τε γνωταί τε* O 350. Cf. N 697 = O 336.—**(b)** More specifically, a brother (and the word may bear this sense in the passages under (a)) Ξ 485, P 35, X 234.

γνώω, aor. subj. *γιγνώσκω*.

†**γοάω** [*γόος*]. 1 pl. opt. *γοάοιμεν* Ω 664. *γοάοιεν* ω 190. Pple. *γοόων, -ωντος* κ 209, μ 234, τ 119. Contr. pl. *γοῶντες* Σ 315, 355: ι 467. Fem. *γοόωσα, -ης* E 413, Z 373, Π 857, X 363, 476, Ψ 106: δ 721, 800, τ 210, 264, 513. Non-thematic infin. *γοήμεναι* Ξ 502. 3 pl. impf. *γόων* κ 567. 3 sing. pa. iterative *γοάασκε* θ 92. 3 sing. fut. in mid. form *γοήσεται* Φ 124, X 353. 3 pl. aor. *γόον* (perh. formed fr. *γόος*) Z 500. **(1)** To weep, wail, show signs of grief: *μὴ γοόωσα οἰκῆας ἐγείρῃ* E 413. Cf. Z 373, Σ 315, 355, X 476, Ψ 106: *ἑζόμενοι γόων* κ 567. Cf. δ 721, 800, θ 92, ι 467, κ 209, μ 234, τ 119, 210, 513.—**(2)** To weep for, bewail, lament, mourn for the loss of: *Ἕκτορα* Z 500, *ὃν πότμον* Π 857 = X 363: *πόσιν* τ 264.—**(3)** To pay mourning rites to: *αὐτόν* Ω 664. Cf. Ξ 502, Φ 124, X 353: ω 190.

γόμφος, *-ου, ὁ*. A wooden peg, a treenail ε 248.

γονή, *-ῆς, ἡ* [*γον-, γεν-, γίγνομαι*]. **(1)** Offspring Ω 539.—**(2)** Progeny, descendants: *Ἀρκεισιάδαο* δ 755.

γόνος, *-ου, ὁ* [as prec.] **(1)** One sprung or born. **(a)** The offspring, a child: *Διός* E 635. Cf. Ω 59: β 274, δ 207, σ 218.—**(b)** A remoter descendant Z 191, N 449.—**(c)** In both these senses: *ὃν* (*i.e.* *Λαέρταο*) *καὶ Ὀδυσσῆος* δ 741.—**(2)** The race: *Ἀτρέος* λ 436.—**(3)** Offspring I 493: δ 12, μ 130.—One's children or family: *νεώτατος γόνοιο* Υ 409.—**(4)** One's parentage: *ὃν γόνον ἐξαγόρευεν* λ 234. Cf. α 216, τ 166.

γόνυ, *τό*. Genit. *γουνός* (for *γονF-ός*) Λ 547: τ 450. *γούνατος* Φ 591. Nom. pl. *γούνατα* Δ 314, I 610, T 166, Φ 114, etc.: δ 703, ε 297, ν 34, ψ 3, etc. *γοῦνα* Z 511, Ξ 468, Φ 611, etc.: υ 352. Genit. *γούνων* A 407, Z 45, Φ 65, X 338, etc.: ζ 142, κ 264, χ 310, 339, etc. Dat. *γούνασι* E 370, Z 92, P 514, X 500, etc.: α 267, η 142, π 443, φ 55, etc. *γούνεσσι* I 488, P 451, 569. Acc. *γούνατα* E 176, Λ 609, Φ 52, Ω 478, etc.: γ 92, ε 453, ξ 236, ω 381, etc. *γοῦνα* Ξ 437, Υ 93, X 204: ζ 147, ι 266, σ 395. **(1)** The knee of men or animals: *ῥίμφα ἑ γοῦνα φέρει* Z 511 = O 268. Cf. H 118, K 358, Λ 547, Ξ 437, 468, O 269, P 386, T 72, Υ 458, Φ 302, 591, 611, X 24, 144, 452, Ψ 731: *ἔλασε γουνὸς ὕπερ* τ 450. Cf. ε 453, υ 352, ψ 3.—**(2)** In pl., the knees regarded as the seat of strength, as symbolizing the strength (cf. *γυῖα* (3)): *βλάψε οἱ γούνατα* H 271. Cf. Δ 314, E 176 = Π 425, I 610 = K 90, Λ 477, 578 = N 412 = P 349, N 360, 711, O 291, P 451, 569, T 166, 354, Υ 93, Φ 52, 114, 270, 425, X 204, 335, 388, Ψ 444, Ω 498: *τῆς λύτο γούνατα* δ 703 = ψ 205. Cf. ε 297 = 406 = χ 147, ν 34, ξ 69, 236, σ 133, 212, υ 118, χ 68, ω 345, 381.—**(3)** Of clasping the knees in supplication: *λαβέ* [*μιν*] *γούνων* (by the knees) A 407. Cf. A 500, 512, 557, Z 45, O 76, Υ 468, Φ 65, 68, 71, X 345, Ω 357, 465, 478: *μητρὸς ποτὶ γούνασι χεῖρας βάλλειν* ζ 310. Cf. ζ 142, 147, 169, η 142, κ 264, 323, χ 310, 339, 342, 365.—So with a word of seizing to be supplied: *λισσέσκετο γούνων* I 451. Cf. κ 481, χ 337.—Sim.: *περὶ γούνατ' ἐμὰ στήσεσθαι λισσομένους* Λ 609. Cf. Σ 457, Υ 463: *σὰ γούναθ' ἱκάνω* ε 449, η 147, *Ἀμφινόμου πρὸς γοῦνα καθέζετο* (as putting himself under his protection) σ 395. Cf. γ 92 = δ 322, ι 266, ν 231.—Also *λίσσομ' ὑπὲρ γούνων* X 338.—Of kissing the knees in supplication: *ἤ οἱ γούνατ' ἔκυσσε* Θ 371. Cf. ξ 279.—**(4)** By extension, in pl., the knee(s) and thigh(s) of a sitting person: *ἐν γούνασι πῖπτε Διώνης* (on her knee) E 370, *Ἀθηναίης ἐπὶ γούνασιν* (on the lap, *i.e.*, app., of a seated statue) Z 92, 273, 303. Cf. E 408, I 455, 488, Φ 506, X 500: *ἐμὲ γούνασιν οἷσιν ἐφεσσάμενος* π 443. Cf. τ 401, φ 55.—*ταῦτα θεῶν ἐν γούνασι κεῖται*, the issue lies with the gods (perh. referring to the custom of placing gifts on the lap of a statue (cf. Z 92, 273, 303 cited above), the gifts being irrevocably dedicated, and symbolizing complete submission to divine governance) P 514 = Υ 435: = α 267 = π 129, α 400.

γόον, 3 pl. aor. *γοάω*.

γόος, *-ου, ὁ*. **(1)** Weeping, wailing, lamentation, mourning E 156, Z 499, P 37, Σ 51, Ψ 10, 14, etc.: δ 102, 113, θ 540, π 144, τ 268, φ 228, etc.—In pl.: *ὀδύνας τε γόους τε* α 242.—**(2)** Inclination to weep: *πᾶσιν ὑπέδυ γ.* κ 398.—**(3)** Mourning rites, formal mourning or lamentation: *ἦρχε γόοιο* Ω 723. Cf. Ω 747, 761.

γοόων, γοόωσα, pres. pple. *γοάω*.

γουνάζομαι [*γουν-, γόνυ*. 'To clasp the knees, clasp by the knees, in supplication.' Cf. *γόνυ* (3)]. Fut. *γουνάσομαι* A 427. To supplicate, entreat. Retaining the genitival construction of a vb. of taking hold, and with the construction extended to something appealed to: *μή με γούνων γουνάζεο μηδὲ τοκήων* X 345.—With this latter construction alone: *τῶν ὄπιθέν σε γουνάζομαι* λ 66.—With prepositional clauses indicating what is appealed to: *τῶν ὕπερ* O 665. Cf. λ 66, ν 324.—With simple acc. of the person entreated: *γουνάσομαί μιν* A 427. Absol. Λ 130.

γούνατος, γουνός, genit. *γόνυ*.

γουνός [perh. fr. *γονF-, γόνυ*, in sense 'swell,' 'knoll,' and, in reference to a vineyard, etc., the part best catching the sun, and therefore the most fruitful]. *γουνῷ* (*γουνὸν*) *ἀλωῆς* I 534, Σ 57 = 438: α 193, λ 193, *ἐς γουνὸν Ἀθηνάων* λ 323 (here perh. the reference is to the citadel).

γουνοῦμαι = *γουνάζομαι*. To supplicate, entreat: *υἱόν* I 583. Cf. O 660, Φ 74, X 240: δ 433, ζ 149, χ 312, 344.—App., to supplicate (and at the same time to vow *to do something*): νεκύων κάρηνα ῥέξειν . . . κ 521, λ 29.

γοῶντες, contr. nom. pl. masc. pres. pple. γοάω.

γραίη, -ης, ἡ. =γρηῦς: πυκιμηδέος α 438.

γραπτύς, ἡ [γραπ-, γράφω]. Acc. pl. γραπτῦς. A scratch: γραπτῦς ἀλεείνων ω 229.

†γράφω. 3 sing. aor. γράψε Ρ 599. Pple. γράψας Ζ 169. (ἐπι-.) **(1)** To scratch, cut into, incise: ὀστέον Ρ 599.—**(2)** To form by scratching or incision: θυμοφθόρα Ζ 169.

γρηΰς, γρηῦς, ἡ. Dat. γρηΐ Γ 386: α 191, σ 27, ψ 33. Voc. γρηΰ χ 395, 481. γρηῦ τ 383, χ 411. An old woman Γ 386: β 377, η 8, σ 185, τ 346, ψ 1, etc.—In apposition: γρηΐ ἀμφιπόλῳ α 191. Cf. σ 27, ω 211.

γύαλον, -ου, τό [cf. γυρός]. (ἐγγυαλίζω.) One of the two curved plates, front and back, of which the θώρηξ was formed. The front plate Ε 99, 189, Ν 507=Ρ 314, Ν 587.—In pl. of the two plates Ο 530.

γυῖα, τά [γυ-, to bend. Cf. γύαλον, γυρός]. **(1)** A joint: γ. ποδῶν Ν 512.—**(2)** The limbs: γ. ἔθηκεν ἐλαφρά Ε 122=Ν 61=Ψ 772. Cf. Τ 385, Χ 448, Ψ 691.—**(3)** The limbs regarded as the seat of strength, as symbolizing the strength (cf. γόνυ (2)): λῦσε γ. Δ 469=Λ 260, Λ 240, Π 312=400, 465, Φ 406. Cf. Δ 230, Ε 811, Ζ 27, Η 6, 12, 16, Ν 85, 435, Ο 435, 581, Π 341, 805, Ρ 524, Σ 31, Τ 165, 169, Ψ 63, 627, 726: ἐκ κάματον εἵλετο γυίων κ 363. Cf. α 192, θ 233, μ 279, σ 238, 242, 341.—As that upon which fear takes hold or which it affects: τρόμος ἔλλαβε γ. Γ 34, Θ 452, Ξ 506, Ω 170. Cf. Η 215=Υ 44, Κ 95, 390: ζ 140, λ 527, σ 88.—App. as the seat of yearning: ἦλθ' ἵμερος [γόοιο] ἀπὸ γυίων Ω 514.

γυιόω [γυιός, lame]. (ἀπο-.) To lame, cripple: γυιώσω σφωΐν ἵππους Θ 402. Cf. Θ 416.

γυμνός. **(1)** Without clothes, naked: σὲ εὐλαὶ ἔδονται γυμνόν Χ 510. Cf. ζ 136.—**(2)** Without armour, unarmed: κτενέει με γυμνὸν ἐόντα Χ 124. Cf. Π 815, Ρ 122=693, 711, Σ 21, Φ 50.—**(3)** Of a bow, out of its case λ 607.—Of an arrow, out of the quiver φ 417.

γυμνόω [γυμνός]. (ἀπο-.) To make naked. In pass. **(1)** To become naked, strip oneself: αἰδέομαι γυμνοῦσθαι ζ 222. Cf. κ 341.—To strip oneself of. With genit.: γυμνώθη ῥακέων χ 1.—**(2)** To be left unprotected by armour or shield: οὖτα γυμνωθέντα Π 312=400. Cf. Μ 389, 428.—Of a wall, to be left bare of defence Μ 399.

γυναικεῖος, -η, -ον [γυναικ-, γυνή]. Of a woman: βουλάς λ 437.

γυναιμανής [γυναι-, γυνή + μαν-, μαίνομαι]. Mad for women Γ 39=Ν 769.

γύναιος [γυνή]. Of a woman: δώρων (given to a woman) λ 521, ο 247.

γυνή, γυναικός, ἡ. Voc. γύναι (see (5) below). **(1)** A woman in gen. Α 348, Β 226, Γ 72, Δ 141, Ε 349, Ι 128, Λ 269, Μ 433, etc.: α 332, γ 154, η 57, λ 258, ν 288, ο 20, σ 248, τ 235, etc.—**(2)** The mistress of a house π 334, φ 86.—**(3)** In pl., the female servants in a house: τετυγμένα χερσὶ γυναικῶν Χ 511. Cf. Σ 559: εἰς ὅ κ' εἴπω γυναιξὶ δεῖπνον τετυκεῖν ο 76. Cf. β 108, π 304, ρ 75, σ 186, τ 16, χ 437, etc.—With ἀμφίπολος α 362, ζ 52, η 235, π 413, φ 8, etc.—With δμωή Ζ 323, Ι 477: η 103, ν 66, π 108=υ 318, ρ 505, τ 490, χ 37, etc.—In sing., one of the servants ο 417, 434, 439, τ 344, etc.—With words indicating the servant's country of origin: Φοίνισσα ο 417, Σικελή ω 211.—Her office: ταμίη Ζ 390: β 345, γ 479, ἀλετρίς υ 105.—**(4)** Specifically. **(a)** A woman as distinguished from a man: γυναικὸς ἀντὶ τέτυξο Θ 163. Cf. Η 139, 236, Ι 134, Ο 683, etc.: οὔτ' ἄνδρ' οὔτε γυναῖκα δ 142, ζ 161. Cf. η 109, ν 308, ο 163, τ 408, etc.—**(b)** A wife: σὺν γυναιξί τε καὶ τεκέεσσιν Δ 162. Cf. Γ 48, Ζ 160, Θ 57, Ι 394, Ρ 36, etc.: ἀνὴρ ἠδὲ γ. ζ 184. Cf. α 13, 433, β 249, η 347, ξ 211, ρ 152, φ 72, etc.—**(c)** A concubine as opposed to a wife Ω 497.—**(d)** A woman as distinguished from a goddess: θεᾶς οὐδὲ γυναικός Ξ 315. Cf. Π 176, Ω 58: ἢ θεὸς ἠὲ γ. κ 228, 255.—With words indicative of mortality: θνητάων Υ 305: θνητήν λ 244.—**(5)** In voc. as a term of courteous or respectful address, 'lady' Γ 204, 438, Ζ 441, Ω 300: δ 148, ζ 168, θ 424, λ 248, etc.

γῡρός [cf. γυῖα, γύαλον]. Bent, rounded τ 246.

γύψ, γῡπός, ὁ. A vulture (except in λ 578 always preying on carrion. Cf. αἰγυπιός) Δ 237, Λ 162, Π 836, Σ 271, Χ 42: λ 578, χ 30.

γωρῡτός, -οῦ, ὁ. A case for a bow φ 54.

δαείω, aor. subj. δάω.

δαήμεναι, δαῆναι, aor. infin. δάω.

δαήμων, -ονος [δάω]. Skilled, experienced Ο 411, Ψ 671.—With genit.: ἄθλων (in . . .) θ 159. Cf. θ 263, π 253.

δᾱήρ, -έρος, ὁ (δαϝήρ). Voc. δᾶερ (see below). Genit. pl. δαέρων as spondee Ω 762, 769. A brother-in-law Γ 180, Ξ 156, Ω 762, 769.—In voc. Ζ 344, 355.

δαήσεαι, 2 sing. fut. δάω.

δάηται, 3 sing. aor. subj. pass. δαίω[1].

δαί. Emphasizing particle used after interrogatives: τίς δ. ὅμιλος; α 225. Cf. Κ 408 (*v.l.* δ' αἱ): ω 299.

δαιδάλεος, -η, -ον [δαίδαλον]. Curiously wrought or ornamented Δ 135, Ζ 418, Θ 195, Ι 187, Ν 331, 719, Π 222, Ρ 448, Σ 379, 390, 612, Τ 380, Χ 314: α 131, κ 315=367, ρ 32.

δαιδάλλω [δαίδαλον]. To ornament curiously: σάκος Σ 479: χρυσῷ τε καὶ ἀργύρῳ ψ 200.

δαίδαλον, -ου, τό. Something curiously wrought, an ornament τ 227.—In pl., things curiously wrought, pieces of cunning workmanship, ornaments: χάλκεον δαίδαλα πολλά Σ 400. Cf. Ε 60, Ξ 179, Σ 482, Τ 13, 19.

δαΐζω [δαίω[2]]. Aor. infin. δαΐξαι Β 416, Π 841. Pf. pple. pass. δεδαϊγμένος, -ου Ρ 535, Σ 236, Τ 203, 211, 283, 292, 319, Χ 72: ν 320. **(1)** To rend, tear: Ἑκτόρεον χιτῶνα Β 416. Cf. Η 247, Π 841.—To tear (the hair) Σ 27.—**(2)** To rend the flesh of, wound, slay: δεδαϊγμένον ἦτορ (app., with the life killed in him) P 535, δαΐζων χαλκῷ Ω 393. Cf. Λ 497, Σ 236, T 203, 211, 283, 292, 319, Φ 147, X 72.—Absol., to do execution Φ 33.—(3) To divide (meat) into portions ξ 434.—(4) Fig., in pass., to be in two minds, be in doubt: δαϊζόμενος ἢ . . . ἦε . . . Ξ 20 —Of the mind, etc., to be troubled or distressed: ἐδαΐζετο θυμός I 8 = O 629. Cf. ν 320.

δαϊκτάμενος [δαΐ, dat. of δάϊς + κτάμενος. See κτείνω]. Slain in battle: αἰζηῶν Φ 146, 301.

δαιμόνιος, -η [δαίμων]. Under superhuman influence, 'possessed,' whose actions are unaccountable or ill-omened. In voc. (1) In stern reproof A 561, Z 326, I 40.—More gently Z 521.—(2) In more or less stern remonstrance B 190, Γ 399, Δ 31: σ 15, τ 71.—In tender or gentle remonstrance Z 407, 486: κ 472, ψ 166, 174, 264.—(3) Conveying an implication of folly or senselessness B 200, N 448, 810: δ 774, σ 406.—(4) App. indicating a degree of wonder, the person addressed showing himself superior to what his outward man would indicate: δαιμόνιε ξείνων ξ 443.—(5) App., with orig. sense lost sight of, merely in affectionate address Ω 194.

δαίμων, -ονος, ὁ, ἡ. (1) A superhuman power, with little notion of personality (sometimes difficult to distinguish from the next sense). (a) Represented as evil or maleficent: μάχης ἐπὶ μήδεα κείρει δ. ἡμετέρης O 468. Cf. I 600, Λ 480, O 418, Φ 93: στυγερός οἱ ἔχραε δ. ε 396. Cf. δ 275, ε 421, ζ 172 (cf. θεοί 174), η 248, κ 64, λ 587, μ 169, 295, ξ 488, π 194, 370 (evil to the speaker), ρ 446, τ 201, ω 149.—(b) As beneficent: ἄλλα δ. ὑποθήσεται γ 27. Cf. ι 381, ρ 243 = φ 201 (cf. θεός τις φ 196), τ 10, 138.—(c) With neither notion prominent ξ 386.—(2) In generalized sense, superhuman power, heaven, fate, the gods (sometimes difficult to distinguish from the prec. sense): σὺν δαίμονι (if heaven so wills it) Λ 792, O 403, πρὸς δαίμονα φωτὶ μάχεσθαι (against the will of the gods) P 98. Cf. H 291, 377 = 396, P 104: δαίμονος αἶσα λ 61. Cf. β 134, π 64, σ 146, 256 = τ 129, τ 512, υ 87, ω 306.—δαίμονά τοι δώσω (I will deal thee fate, *i.e.* death) Θ 166.—(3) With more marked notion of personality: ἐπέσσυτο δαίμονι ἶσος E 438 = Π 705 = 786 = Υ 447. Cf. E 459 = 884, Υ 493, Φ 18, 227.—(4) (a) In pl. = θεοί in gen.: βεβήκει μετὰ δαίμονας ἄλλους A 222. Cf. Z 115, Ψ 595.—(b) In sing. of a particular god: οὐδ' ἐπιορκήσω πρὸς δαίμονος (*i.e.* the god, or, as in the sequel, the gods, by whom he was to swear) T 188: λίσσομ' ὑπὲρ θυέων καὶ δαίμονος (*i.e.* whatever god the sacrifice was being made to) ο 261.—More definitely: γίγνωσκον ὃ κακὰ μήδετο δ. γ 166 (the context app. showing that the reference is exclusively to Zeus).—(c) Of a definite goddess present in her own person: ἦρχε δ. (*i.e.* Aphrodite) Γ 420.

δαίνῡμι [δαίω²]. Fut. infin. δαίσειν T 299. 2 sing. subj. mid. δαινύῃ θ 243. δαινῦῃ τ 328. 3 sing. opt. δαινῦτο Ω 665. 3 pl. δαινύατο σ 248. 2 sing. impf. δαίνυο Ω 63. Nom. pl. masc. aor. pple. δαισάμενοι η 188, σ 408. (μετα-.) (1) (a) To give (a meal): δαίνυ δαῖτα γέρουσιν I 70.—(b) To give (a wedding-feast): δαινύντα γάμον δ 3.—Sim. δαίσειν γάμον (app., to bring it about) T 299.—(c) To give (a funeral-feast) Ψ 29: γ 309.—(2) In mid. (a) (α) To take a meal (often with the notion of faring well or revelling): εἴ τις δαίνυται εὔφρων O 99. Cf. A 468 = 602 = B 431 = H 320 = Ψ 56, Δ 386, E 805, H 477, I 228: δαινύμενοι τερπώμεθα α 369. Cf. α 228, β 247, 311, γ 471, η 188, 203, θ 243, κ 9, 61, 452, μ 398, ξ 195, 250, ο 398, π 479 = τ 425, ρ 332, σ 248, 408, τ 328, φ 89, 290, 319.—(β) Of a wedding-feast Ω 63: δ 15, 238.—(γ) Of a funeral-feast Ω 665.—(δ) With cognate acc. As (α): εἰλαπίνην δαίνυντο Ψ 201. Cf. γ 66 = υ 280, η 50, λ 186, ν 26.—As (γ) Ω 802.—(b) To partake of: ἑκατόμβας I 535 (*i.e.* of the god's share thereof): κρέα τε καὶ μέθυ ι 162 = 557 = κ 184 = 468 = 477 = μ 30.

δαίς, δαιτός, ἡ [δαίω²]. (1) A meal (often with the notion of faring well or revelling): δαίνυ δαῖτα I 70, δαῖτα πένοντο Σ 558 (app. a meal for the King and his retainers, that for the ἔριθοι being mentioned below), πειθώμεθα δαιτί (*i.e.* to hunger) Ψ 48. Cf. A 467, 468, 575, 579, Δ 259, 343, etc.: ὄφρ' ἂν δαῖτα πτωχεύῃ (*i.e.* beg his bread) ρ 11, δαιτῶν ἀπολυμαντῆρα 220. Cf. α 152, 374, β 322, γ 33, η 232, κ 124, etc.—Of the god's share of a sacrifice: Ζεὺς ἔβη κατὰ δαῖτα A 424. Cf. Δ 48 = Ω 69: τέρπετο δαιτὶ παρήμενος α 26 (of Poseidon). Cf. γ 336, 420, θ 76.—Of what a beast devours Ω 43.—(2) A wedding-feast σ 279.—(3) A funeral-feast Ω 802.

δάϊς, ἡ. Dat. δαΐ (for δαΐ-ι). War, battle: ἐν δαΐ λυγρῇ (λευγαλέῃ) N 286, Ξ 387, Ω 739.

δαΐς, -ΐδος, ἡ [δαίω¹]. A torch Σ 492: α 428, 434, β 105 = ω 140, η 101, σ 310, 354, τ 48, 150, ψ 290.

δαίσειν, fut. infin. δαίνυμι.

δαίτη, -ης, ἡ = δαίς (1) K 217: η 50.—Of a god's share of a sacrifice γ 44.

δαίτηθεν [δαίτη + -θεν¹]. From, leaving, a meal: δαίτηθεν ἰόντα κ 216.

δαιτρεύω [δαιτρός]. (1) To carve meat ξ 433, ο 323.—(2) To make an apportionment of spoil Λ 688, 705.

δαιτρόν, τό [δαίω²]. One's portion Δ 262.

δαιτρός, ὁ [δαίω²]. One who carves meat, a carver α 141 = δ 57, ρ 331.

δαιτροσύνη, -ης, ἡ [δαιτρός]. The art of carving meat. In pl.: θεράποντε δαήμονε δαιτροσυνάων π 253.

δαιτυμών, -όνος, ὁ [δαιτύς]. Dat. δαιτυμόνεσσι η 102, χ 12. A guest at or partaker of a meal or feast δ 621, η 102, 148, θ 66 = 473, ι 7, ο 467, ρ 605, χ 12 (in the last two passages of the self-invited guests, the suitors).

δαιτύς, -ύος, ἡ = δαίς (1) X 496.

δαΐφρων, -ονος [δάω + φρήν]. Skilled, whether in war or in the arts of peace. Epithet of heroes, etc. B 23, Δ 252, Z 162, I 651, Λ 123, Ξ 459, etc.:

α 48, δ 687, ζ 256, θ 8, ο 519, φ 16, etc.—Absol. in voc. E 277.—Applied to Anticleia ο 356.

δαίω[1] [δαϝ-, δηϝ-, δαυ-]. 3 sing. pf. (in pres. sense) δέδηε N 736, P 253, Υ 18 : υ 353. 3 sing. plupf. (in impf. sense) δεδήει B 93, M 35, 466. 3 sing. aor. subj. pass. δάηται Υ 316, Φ 375. (ἀμφι-.) (1) To set on fire, kindle : ξύλα Σ 347 : θ 436.—To light (a fire) I 211 : η 7.—To cause (fire) to appear or blaze E 4, 7, Σ 206, 227.—(2) In pf. and plupf. and in pass., to burn or blaze : πῦρ δαίετο Φ 343. Cf. Θ 75, Σ 227, Υ 316 = Φ 375 : ε 61.—Of the eyes, to blaze M 466.—So of a lion's eyes ζ 132.—Fig. : Ὄσσα δεδήει (spread like wild-fire) B 93, νῦν ἄγχιστα μάχη δέδηε (app., now most nearly blazes up, *i.e.* is on the point of blazing up) Υ 18. Cf. M 35, N 736, P 253 : οἰμωγὴ δέδηε (is bursting forth) υ 353.

δαίω[2] [cf. δαΐζω, δατέομαι]. 3 pl. pf. pass. δεδαίαται α 23. To divide or apportion. (1) In mid. : κρέα δαίετο ο 140. Cf. ρ 332.—(2) In pass. : Αἰθίοπας, τοὶ διχθὰ δεδαίαται (are divided) α 23, μήλων δαιομένων (in the division of the . . .) ι 551.—Fig., to be troubled or distressed : δαίεταί μοι ἦτορ α 48.

†δάκνω. 3 sing. aor. δάκε E 493. Infin. δακέειν P 572, Σ 585. To bite. Of dogs Σ 585.—Of a fly P 572.—Fig. : δάκε φρένας μῦθος E 493 (cf. θυμοδακής).

δάκρυ, τό [cf. δάκρυον]. (1) A tear : δεύοντο δάκρυσι κόλποι I 570. Cf. Ψ 16, Ω 162 : η 260, ρ 103 = τ 596.—(κατὰ) δ. χέειν, to shed a tear, to weep A 357, 413, Γ 142, Z 405, I 14, etc. : β 24, δ 556, λ 5, μ 12, ξ 280, etc.—Sim. in various expressions : βαλέειν ἀπὸ δ. παρειῶν δ 198. Cf. δ 114, 223, ρ 490.—ἔκπεσέ οἱ δ. B 266 : π 16.—κατείβετο δ. Ω 794 : τί δ. κατείβετον ; φ 86.—δ. ἀπομόρξασθαι, to wipe away one's tears B 269 : ρ 304.—δ. ἔδευε παρειάς (his tears) θ 522.—(2) As the visible feature of weeping ; hence, in pl., tears, weeping : δάκρυσι θυμὸν ἐρέχθων ε 83 = 157.

δακρυόεις, -εντος. Fem. -εσσα. [δάκρυον.] (1) Shedding tears, weeping Z 455, Π 10, Σ 66, Φ 493, 496, 506, X 499 : κ 415.—In neut. δακρυόεν as adv. : γελάσασα (smiling through her tears) Z 484.—(2) Accompanied by tears : γόοιο δ 801, ρ 8, ω 323.—(3) Causing tears, bringing misery : πόλεμον E 737 = Θ 388, P 512. Cf. Λ 601, N 765, Π 436.

δάκρυον, τό [cf. δάκρυ]. Dat. pl. δακρύοισι σ 173. Instrumental δακρυόφι P 696, Ψ 397 : δ 705, κ 248, τ 472, υ 349. This form as ablative ε 152. (1) A tear : ὄσσε δακρυόφι πλῆσθεν (with tears) P 696 = Ψ 397 : = δ 705 = τ 472, οὐδέ ποτ' ὄσσε δακρυόφιν τέρσοντο (were free of tears) ε 152, δάκρυα κεῦθεν τ 212. Cf. κ 248 = υ 349, σ 173.—δάκρυα χέειν, to shed tears, to weep H 426, Π 3, Σ 17, 235 : ω 46.—χύτο δάκρυα Ψ 385 : δάκρυα χέοντο δ 523.—Sim. in various expressions : δάκρυ' ἀναπρήσας I 433 : β 81.—(κατὰ) δάκρυον εἴβειν, to shed a tear, to weep Π 11, T 323, Ω 9 : δ 153, θ 531, λ 391, π 219, 332, ω 234, 280.—δάκρυα λείβειν N 88, 658, Σ 32 : ε 84 = 158, θ 86, 93 = 532, π 214.—δάκρυ' ἔκβαλεν τ 362.—δάκρυον ἧκεν π 191, ψ 33.—δάκρυα πίπτει ξ 129.—δάκρυα ῥέεν P 437 : τ 204.—δάκρυ' ὀμόργνυσθαι (ὀμόρξασθαι) Σ 124 : θ 88, λ 527, 530.—(2) As the visible feature of weeping : τείσειαν Δαναοὶ ἐμὰ δάκρυα (my weeping, *i.e.* the cause thereof, my wrongs) A 42.

δᾰκρυπλώω [δάκρυ + πλώω in sense 'to flow.' Cf. L. *pluo*]. To flow with tears, be maudlin τ 122.

δακρύω [δάκρυον]. 2 sing. pf. pass. δεδάκρυσαι Π 7. 3 pl. δεδάκρυνται X 491 : υ 204, 353. (1) To shed tears, weep : δακρύσας ἕζετο (with a burst of tears) A 349. Cf. K 377, T 229 : δάκρυσα ἰδών λ 55 = 395, 87. Cf. α 336, ρ 33, 38, φ 82, ψ 207.—(2) In pf. pass., to be in tears : τίπτε δεδάκρυσαι ; Π 7.—To be covered or filled with tears : δεδάκρυνται παρειαί X 491. Cf. υ 204, 353.

δᾱλός, -οῦ, ὁ. (1) A piece of ignited material for communicating fire, a fire-brand N 320, O 421 : ε 488.—(2) A brand snatched from the fire or from a brazier τ 69.

†δαμάζω. 3 sing. fut. δαμάᾳ X 271. δαμᾷ A 61. 3 pl. δαμόωσι Z 368. Aor. ἐδάμασσα E 191. 2 sing. δάμασσας Φ 90. 3 ἐδάμασσε Z 159, N 434, Ξ 316, etc. : λ 171, χ 246, ω 109, etc. δάμασε Π 543, X 446 : ψ 310. δάμασσε E 106, I 118, Λ 98, etc. 3 pl. δάμασσαν Π 845 : ξ 367. Subj. δαμάσσω Π 438. 3 sing. δαμάσῃ ε 468, τ 488, 496, φ 213. δαμάσσῃ E 138 : ρ 24, σ 57. 1 pl. δαμάσσομεν X 176. Imp. δάμασον I 496 : λ 562. δάμασσον Γ 352. Pple. δαμάσσας δ 244. Nom. pl. δαμάσαντες Σ 113, T 66 : ι 59. **Mid.** 3 sing. aor. (ἐ)δαμάσσατο E 278 : ι 516. 3 pl. δαμάσαντο K 210, 411. 3 sing. subj. δαμάσσεται Λ 478, Φ 226. Opt. δαμασαίμην δ 637. 1 pl. δαμασαίμεθα Π 561. 3 pl. δαμασαίατο π 105. Pple. δαμασσάμενος, -ου O 476 : ι 454. Infin. δαμάσασθαι X 379, Ψ 655. **Pass.** Aor. ἐδαμάσθην θ 231. 3 sing. δαμάσθη T 9. Pple. δαμασθείς Π 816, X 55. Aor. pass. δάμην Υ 94. 3 sing. (ἐ)δάμη B 860, 874, I 545, Φ 383 : α 237, γ 90, δ 499. 1 pl. ἐδάμημεν N 812. 3 δάμεν Θ 344, M 14, O 2, Σ 103 : δ 495. Subj. δαμείω σ 54. 2 sing. δαμήῃς Γ 436. 3 δαμήῃ X 246. 2 pl. δαμήετε H 72. 3 sing. opt. δαμείη E 564, M 403 : δ 790, ρ 252. 3 pl. δαμεῖεν Γ 301. Pple. δαμείς, -έντος Γ 429, E 653, Z 74, Π 420, etc. : γ 410, ζ 11, ω 100. Infin. δαμήμεναι K 403, P 77, Υ 266, 312, Φ 291. δαμῆναι N 98, O 522, Π 434, Φ 578, etc. : γ 269, δ 397, σ 156. 3 sing. aor. imp. δμηθήτω I 158. Acc. sing. masc. pple. δμηθέντα Δ 99, E 646. 1 pl. pf. δεδμήμεσθα E 878. Plupf. δεδμήμην λ 622. 3 sing. δέδμητο γ 305, ε 454. 3 pl. δεδμήατο Γ 183. Pple. δεδμημένος, -ου K 2, Ξ 482, Ω 678 : η 318, ν 119, ξ 318, ο 6, σ 237. (1) To break in, tame. In mid. : ἡμίονον, ἥ τ' ἀλγίστη δαμάσασθαι Ψ 655. Cf. δ 637.—To control (horses) K 403 = P 77.—Fig. : Διὸς μάστιγι δαμέντες M 37. Cf. N 812.—(2) To bring into subjection : σοὶ δεδμήμεσθα E 878. Cf. λ 622.—Of political subjection Γ 183, Z 159 : γ 305.—To subject (to a man) in marriage : ἀνδρί με δάμασσεν Σ 432.—To subject (a woman to the discretion of a victor): ἄλοχοι δ' ἄλλοισι δαμεῖεν Γ 301.—(3) Of feelings, sleep, etc., to overcome: ἔρος μ' ἐδάμασσεν Ξ 316. Cf. Κ 2=Ω 678, Ξ 353: δεδμημένος ὕπνῳ η 318. Cf. ν 119, ο 6.—Of natural agencies, to have an overpowering effect upon, wear out, exhaust: ἀλὶ δέδμητο ε 454. Cf. θ 231, ξ 318.—(4) To curb or restrain (one's spirit): δάμασον θυμὸν μέγαν Ι 496. Cf. Σ 113=Τ 66: λ 562.—In pass., to be appeased or placated: δμηθήτω Ι 158.—(5) To overpower, get the better of, master: ἐπεὶ Ξάνθοιο δάμη μένος Φ 383. Cf. Π 816: δ 397.—In mid.: δαμασσάμενος οἴνῳ ι 454. Cf. ι 516.—To defeat, rout, put to flight: κλῖναν δαμάσαντες Ἀχαιούς ι 59. Cf. Ζ 74=Ρ 320, Κ 310 =397, Ν 98, Π 420, Ρ 337, Υ 143: ψ 310.—In mid. Κ 210=411, Ο 476.—(6) To put an end to, destroy, kill, slay: εἰ πόλεμος δαμᾷ Ἀχαιούς Α 61, μὴ ὑπ' αὐτοῦ δουρὶ δαμήῃς (by him with his spear) Γ 436, σοὶ δαμῆναι (by thee) Ν 603. Cf. Β 860, Δ 479, Ε 106, Λ 98, Ξ 482, Τ 203, etc.: μοῖρ' ἐπέδησε δαμῆναι γ 269 (app. referring to Aegisthus as fate-bound to (ultimate) ruin; or perh. to Clytaemnestra as yielding to passion (sense (3))), μή με στίβη δαμάσῃ ε 468. Cf. α 237, γ 90, 410, δ 495, λ 171, σ 54, etc.—In mid. Ε 278, Λ 478, Π 561, Φ 226, Χ 379: π 105.—Of a shield, in pass., to be unable to resist a blow, be pierced Υ 266.—To do violence to, disfigure (oneself): αὐτόν μιν πληγῇσι δαμάσσας δ 244.—(7) To subject to a foe, cause to be defeated Ι 118.—(8) To cause to be slain by a foe: ἐμῇς ὑπὸ χερσὶ δάμασσον [Ἀλέξανδρον] Γ 352. Cf. Ζ 368, Ν 434, Π 543, 845, Σ 119, Χ 446, etc.: τούσδε μοῖρ' ἐδάμασσεν χ 413. Cf. ξ 367, σ 57, τ 488=φ 213, τ 496.

δάμαρ, -αρτος, ἡ [δαμ-, δαμάζω]. A wife Γ 122, Ξ 503: δ 126, ν 290, ω 125.

δάμασε, δάμασσε, 3 sing. aor. δαμάζω.

δάμη, 3 sing. aor. pass. δαμάζω.

δάμνημι [cf. δαμάζω]. From δαμνάω 3 sing. δαμνᾷ λ 221. 3 sing. impf. (ἐ)δάμνα Ε 391, Ξ 439, Π 103, Φ 52, 270. 2 sing. pres. mid. δαμνᾷ Ξ 199. (ὑπο-.) (1) To control, keep in order: Ἥρην ἐπέεσσιν Ε 893.—(2) To overcome by troubling the senses. In mid.: φιλότητα καὶ ἵμερον, ᾧ τε σὺ πάντας δαμνᾷ Ξ 199.—(3) To have an overpowering effect upon, wear out, exhaust: δεσμός ἑ ἐδάμνα Ε 391. Cf. Ξ 439, Φ 52, 270.—In mid. ξ 488.—(4) To overpower, master Π 103.—(5) To defeat, rout, put to flight: Ἀχαιοὺς Τρωσὶν δαμναμένους (by the Trojans) Ν 16=353. Cf. Ε 746= Θ 390:=α 100.—(6) To kill, slay: Τρώεσσιν δάμνασθαι (by the Trojans) Θ 244=Ο 376. Cf. Λ 309.—To destroy, consume: σάρκας πυρὸς μένος δαμνᾷ λ 221.—To pierce, rend (a shield) Φ 401.

δαμόωσι, 3 pl. fut. δαμάζω.

δᾱνός [δαίω[1]] Dried, dry: ξύλα ο 322.

δάος, τό [cf. δαΐς]. A torch: δ. μετὰ χερσὶν ἔχουσα ψ 294.—Collectively, torches: δ. μετὰ χερσὶν ἔχουσαι Ω 647: =δ 300=η 339=χ 497.

δάπεδον, -ου, τό [δα- (app. referring to the work of levelling, stamping, etc.)+πέδον, the ground]. (1) A levelled and prepared surface: ἐν τυκτῷ δαπέδῳ δ 627=ρ 169.—(2) A floor of a house Δ 2: κ 227, λ 420, χ 188, 309=ω 185, χ 455.—Of the under surface of the realm of Hades λ 577.

δάπτω. 3 sing. fut. δάψει Ν 831. 2 sing. aor. ἔδαψας Φ 398. 3 ἔδαψε Ε 858. (κατα-.) (1) To devour. Of wild beasts Λ 481, Π 159.—Fig. of fire Ψ 183.—(2) Of rending flesh Ε 858, Ν 831, Φ 398.

δαρδάπτω [lengthened fr. prec.]. To devour. Of wild beasts Λ 479.—Fig.: κτήματα δαρδάπτουσιν ξ 92=π 315.

†δαρθάνω. 3 sing. aor. ἔδραθε. (κατα-, παρα-.) To sleep, go to sleep, take one's rest υ 143.

δάσασθαι, aor. infin. δατέομαι.

δασάσκετο, 3 sing. pa. iterative δατέομαι.

δάσκιος, -ον [δα- + σκιή]. Thickly shaded, with thick shades: ὕλη Ο 273: ὕλην ε 470.

δασμός, ὁ [δασ-, δατέομαι]. A division or apportionment: ἤν ποτε δασμὸς ἵκηται Α 166.

δάσονται, 3 pl. fut. δατέομαι.

δασπλῆτις [prob. fr. δασ- (=δεσ-, house, as in δέσποινα)+πλη-, πελάζω. Cf. τειχεσιπλήτης]. Thus, that approaches houses (with hostile intent), smiter of houses: Ἐρινύς ο 234.

δάσσαντο, 3 pl. aor. δατέομαι.

δασύμαλλος [δασύς + μαλλός, a lock of wool]. With thick fleece: ἄρσενες ὄϊες ι 425.

δασύς, -εῖα, -ύ. Thick with hair, hairy ξ 51.—App., spread so as to lie thickly: ῥῶπας ξ 49.

δατέομαι [δα-, δαίω[2]]. 3 sing. impf. δατεῦντο Ψ 121: α 112. 3 sing. pa. iterative δασάσκετο Ι 333. 3 pl. fut. δάσονται Χ 354: β 368. 3 sing. aor. ἐδάσσατο ζ 10. 1 pl. δασσάμεθα ι 42, 549. 3 ἐδάσαντο ξ 208. δάσσαντο Α 368: τ 423. 3 pl. subj. δάσωνται ρ 80. 1 pl. opt. δασαίμεθα β 335. Pl. pple. δασσάμενοι γ 66, 316, ο 13, π 385, υ 280. Infin. δάσασθαι Σ 511, Χ 120, Ψ 21: σ 87, χ 476. δάσσασθαι υ 216. 3 sing. pf. pass. δέδασται Α 125, Ο 189: ο 412. (ἀπο-.) (1) To divide among themselves, make mutual apportionment of: χηρωσταὶ διὰ κτῆσιν δατέοντο Ε 158. Cf. Α 368, Ι 138=280: τάδε δ' αὐτοὶ δάσονται β 368. Cf. β 335, γ 316=ο 13, ι 42, 549, ξ 208, π 385, ρ 80, υ 216.—Fig.: μένος Ἄρηος δατέονται (app., share between them, are alike filled with) Σ 264.—(2) To divide, apportion: διὰ παῦρα δασάσκετο Ι 333. Cf. Α 125, Ο 189, Σ 511, Χ 120: γ 66=υ 280, ζ 10, ο 412, τ 423.—To divide into portions: κρέα α 112.—(3) To divide among themselves as prey, to tear (and devour). Of dogs, etc. Χ 354, Ψ 21: σ 87, χ 476.—(4) To cut in pieces Υ 394—To cut up (the ground) Ψ 121.

δάφνη, -ης, ἡ. The laurel ι 183.

δαφοινεός [=next]. Red (with blood) Σ 538.

δαφοινός [δα- + φοινός]. Red or tawny: δράκων Β 308, δέρμα λέοντος Κ 23, θῶες Λ 474.

δάψει, 3 sing. fut. δάπτω.

***†δάω**. 2 sing. fut. in mid. form δαήσεαι γ 187, τ 325. Aor. ἐδάην Γ 208: δ 267. Subj. δαείω Κ 425, Π 423, Φ 61: ι 280. 1 pl. δαῶμεν Β 299. Infin. δαήμεναι Ζ 150, Υ 213, Φ 487: ν 335, ψ 262. δαῆναι δ 493. 2 sing. pf. δεδάηκας θ 146. 3

δεδάηκε θ 134. Pple. δεδαώς ρ 519. Pl. δεδαηκότες β 61. 3 sing. redup. aor. δέδαε ζ 233, θ 448, υ 72, ψ 160. From this tense is formed infin. mid. δεδάασθαι (for δεδαέσθαι) π 316. (προ-.) (1) To get to know, know, learn: ἀμφοτέρων φυήν Γ 208, πολέμοιο δαήμεναι (about war) Φ 487. Cf. Z 150 = Υ 213: γ 187, δ 267, 493. With dependent clause: ἤ . . . ἦε . . . B 299. Cf. Π 423, Φ 61: πῶς ἐμεῦ δαήσεαι εἰ . . . ; (about me) τ 325.—Absol.: ὄφρα δαείω K 425: ι 280. Cf. ν 335, ψ 262.—(2) To acquire practical knowledge of or skill in. In pf., to have such knowledge of or skill in: εἴ τιν' ἄεθλον δεδάηκεν θ 134. Cf. β 61, θ 146, ρ 519.—(3) In redup. aor., to teach (something): ἔργα δ' Ἀθηναίη δέδαεν υ 72.—With double acc. of person and thing: ὃν Ἥφαιστος δέδαεν τέχνην παντοίην ζ 233 = ψ 160. Cf. θ 448.—In mid., to have oneself taught; hence, to get to know, acquire knowledge of: γυναῖκας δεδάασθαι, αἵ τε . . . καὶ αἵ . . . π 316.

δέ. (1) Adversative particle, but, yet, on the other hand, while A 29, 83, 108, 137, 167, etc.: α 13, 19, 33, 75, 212, etc.—(2) Particle of continuation, often introducing a subordinate statement or a parenthesis: πολλὰς δὲ ψυχὰς Ἄϊδι προΐαψεν A 3, νοῦσον ὦρσεν, ὀλέκοντο δὲ λαοί 10, Μύδωνα βάλεν—ὁ δ' ὑπέστρεφε ἵππους—χερμαδίῳ E 581. Cf. A 19, 25, 33, 34, 35, etc.: α 3, 51, 53, 71, 93, etc.—(3) Giving a reason or explanation, for: πίθεσθ'· ἄμφω δὲ νεωτέρω ἐστὸν ἐμεῖο A 259, ἐμέθεν ξύνες· Διὸς δέ τοι ἄγγελός εἰμι B 26, μή τι ῥέξῃ κακόν· θυμὸς δὲ μέγας ἐστὶ βασιλήων 196. Cf. A 271, Γ 410, Δ 438, 478, H 259, etc.: α 168, 433, β 36, 41, γ 48, etc.—(4) Introducing a principal clause after a relative, temporal or conditional protasis: οἱ δ' ἐπεὶ οὖν ἤγερθεν . . . τοῖσι δὲ μετέφη A 58, εἰ δέ κε μὴ δώωσιν, ἐγὼ δέ κεν αὐτὸς ἕλωμαι 137, ὅν τινα βασιλῆα κιχείη, τὸν δ' ἀγανοῖς ἐπέεσσιν ἐρητύσασκεν B 189. Cf. B 322, Δ 262, E 261, 439, H 314, I 167, etc.: ε 425, η 109, θ 25, κ 366, λ 148, π 274, etc.—Introducing without antecedent clause B 802, Γ 229, etc.: δ 400, ε 428, etc.—(5) Introducing a question: τίς δὲ σύ ἐσσι; Z 123, τίς δ' οἶδ' εἰ . . . ; O 403. Cf. Z 55, K 82, Λ 792, Ξ 264, O 244, etc.: β 332, 363, δ 312, 681, ζ 276, etc.—(6) Before an imp. or a subj. as imp.: σὺ δὲ παῦε τεὸν μένος A 282. Cf. B 344, etc.: τῶν δὲ βοῶν ἀπεχώμεθα μ 321. Cf. γ 247, ε 346, π 130, χ 312, etc.

δέατο, 3 *sing. impf.* To seem, appear ζ 242.

δέγμενος, pf. pple. δέχομαι.

δεδάασθαι, redup. aor. infin. mid. δάω.

δέδαε, 3 sing. redup. aor. δάω.

δεδάηκε, 3 sing. pf. δάω.

δεδαίαται, 3 pl. pf. pass. δαίω[2].

δεδαϊγμένος, pf. pple. pass. δαΐζω.

δεδάκρυνται, 3 pl. pf. pass. δακρύω.

δέδασται, 3 sing. pf. pass. δατέομαι.

δεδαώς, pf. pple. δάω.

δεδεγμένος, pf. pple. δέχομαι.

δεδειπνήκει, 3 sing. plupf. δειπνέω.

δέδεξο, pf. imp. δέχομαι.

δεδέξομαι, fut. pf. δέχομαι.

δέδετο, 3 sing. plupf. pass. δέω.

δέδηε, 3 sing. pf. δαίω[1].

δεδίᾱσι, 3 pl. pf. See δείδοικα.

δεδιδάχθαι, pf. infin. pass. διδάσκω.

δεδίσκομαι = δειδίσκομαι (1) ο 150.

δεδμημένος[1], pf. pple. pass. δαμάζω.

δεδμημένος[2], pf. pple. pass. δέμω.

δεδμήμεσθα, 1 pl. pf. pass. δαμάζω.

δεδμήμην, δέδμητο[1], **δεδμήατο,** 1 and 3 sing. and 3 pl. plupf. pass. δαμάζω.

δέδμητο[2], 3 sing. plupf. pass δέμω.

δεδοκημένος, pf. pple. δέχομαι.

δέδορκε, 3 sing. pf. δέρκομαι.

δέδοται, 3 sing. pf. pass. δίδωμι.

δεδουπότος, genit. sing. masc. pf. pple. δουπέω.

δεδραγμένος, pf. pple. δράσσομαι.

δέδῡκε, 3 sing. pf. δύω.

δέελος [app. for δήελος = δῆλος]. Thus, conspicuous, easy to be distinguished: σῆμα K 466.

δεῖ [prob. fr. δέω]. It is binding on (one), behoves (one). With acc. and infin.: τί δεῖ πολεμιζέμεναι Τρώεσσιν Ἀργείους; I 337.

δείδεκτο, 3 sing. plupf. mid. δείκνυμι.

δειδέχαται, 3 pl. pf. mid. δείκνυμι.

δειδήμων, -ονος [δείδοικα]. Fearful, timid Γ 56.

δείδια, pf. See δείδοικα.

δείδιε[1], 3 sing. pf. See δείδοικα.

δείδιε[2], 3 sing. plupf. See δείδοικα.

δείδιθι, pf. imp. See δείδοικα.

δείδιμεν, 1 pl. pf. See δείδοικα.

δειδίμεν, pf. infin. See δείδοικα.

δειδίξεσθαι, fut. infin. δειδίσσομαι.

δείδισαν, 3 pl. plupf. See δείδοικα.

δειδίσκομαι [app. redup. fr. δικ-, δείκνυμι. Cf. δεικανάομαι]. (1) To pledge in drinking = δείκνυμι (5): δέπαϊ σ 121.—(2) To welcome, greet γ 41, υ 197.

δειδίσσομαι [redup. fr. δικ-, δείδοικα]. Fut. infin. δειδίξεσθαι Υ 201, 432. Aor. infin. δειδίξασθαι Σ 164. (1) To frighten, alarm, scare Δ 184, M 52, N 810 (try to . . .), Υ 201 = 432.—To scare (away from something): Ἕκτορ' ἀπὸ νεκροῦ Σ 164.—(2) To use threats to, threaten B 190, O 196.

†**δείδοικα** (δέδϝοικα), *pf. with pres. sense.* 1 sing. δείδοικα A 555, I 244, K 538, Σ 261, Ω 435: θ 230, ω 353. 2 -ας M 244. 3 -ε Φ 198. Also 1 sing. δείδια (δέδϝια) N 49, 481, Φ 536: δ 820, ζ 168, ρ 188. 2 -ας σ 80. 3 -ε π 306. 1 pl. δείδιμεν H 196, I 230: β 199. 3 δεδίᾱσι Ω 663. 3 sing. plupf. (with impf. sense) δείδιε (with secondary person-ending) Σ 34, Ω 358. 1 pl. ἐδείδιμεν Z 99. 3 (ἐ)δείδισαν E 790, H 151, O 652. Imp. δείδιθι E 827, Ξ 342: δ 825, σ 63. Pl. δείδιτε Υ 366. Pple. δειδιώς, -ότος Γ 242, Δ 431, Z 137, M 39, O 628, Υ 45, Φ 24, Ω 384: ξ 60, σ 77. Infin. δειδίμεν ι 274, κ 381. Also δείδω (app. for δείδοα (δέδϝοα)) K 39, Λ 470, N 745, Ξ 44, T 24, Υ 30, X 455: ε 300, 419, 473, μ 122. 3 sing. fut. in mid. form δείσεται Υ 130. Infin. δείσεσθαι O 299. 2 sing. aor. ἔδεισας (ἔδϝεισας) X 19, Ω 364. 3 ἔδεισε A 33, 568, Γ 418, K 240, Υ 61, Ψ 425, Ω 571, 689: κ 448. δεῖσε E 623, Θ 138, N 163. 2 pl. ἐδείσατε N 624. 3 ἔδεισαν κ 219,

ν 184. δεῖσαν H 93. 3 sing. subj. δείσῃ Ω 116. 2 pl. -ητε Ω 779. 3 sing. opt. δείσειε H 456, Ω 672. Pple. δείσας, -αντος Γ 37, E 863, Θ 136, Φ 248, etc.: δ 792, ι 72, μ 203, σ 396, etc. Fem. δείσᾱσα π 331. (περιδείδια, ὑποδείδια.) (1) To be afraid, feel fear: ἔδεισεν ὁ γέρων A 33 = Ω 571. Cf. A 568, E 233, Z 137, H 151, I 230, K 240, etc.: μὴ δείδιθι δ 825. Cf. δ 792, η 305, ι 236, 396, κ 219, 381, μ 203, 224, ν 184, ξ 60, π 331, σ 77, φ 367, ω 534.—(2) With dependent clause. (a) In reference to the fut. with μή and subj. (or after secondary tenses opt.): μὴ ἐρυσαίατο νεκρόν E 298, μὴ τελέσῃ ἔπος Ξ 44. Cf. K 39, Λ 470, N 745, Σ 34, T 24, Υ 30, 62, Φ 536, X 455: δ 820, ε 419, 473, θ 230, μ 122, φ 286, ω 353.—(b) In reference to the past with μή and indic.: μὴ πάντα νημερτέα εἶπεν ε 300.—In virtual reference to the past with μή and subj.: μή σε παρείπῃ (that she may prove to have . . ., *i.e.* that she has . . .) A 555. Cf. K 538.—(c) With infin., to be afraid *to do something*, shrink from *doing it*: ὑποδέχθαι H 93. Cf. O 299: ζ 168.—(3) To be afraid of, fear, be in fear of, dread, to anticipate with fear, shrink from: αἴσχεα Γ 242, μήτε σύ γ' Ἄρηα τό γε δείδιθι E 827 (τό γε, for that matter), Ζηνὸς μῆνιν N 624. Cf. E 790, Z 99, M 39, N 49, Σ 261, X 19, etc.: οὔ τινα β 199, ἐμὴν ἐνιπήν κ 448. Cf. ι 72, 257, κ 130, μ 244, ρ 577, σ 63, 80, 396.—With complementary infin.: οὐ δείσαντες νέμεσιν ἔσεσθαι χ 39. Cf. Ξ 342 (τό γε as in E 827 above).—In double construction with acc. and μή with subj.: ταῦτα δείδοικα, μή οἱ ἀπειλὰς ἐκτελέσωσι θεοί, ἡμῖν δ' αἴσιμον εἴη . . . I 244 (here also with opt. of remoter consequence). Cf. ρ 188.—(4) To stand in awe of, reverence, hold in awe or due respect: σημάντορας Δ 431. Cf. Ω 116, 435: ι 274, ξ 389, π 306, χ 39.

δείδω. See δείδοικα.

δειελιάω [δείελος. 'To act as befits the evening']. Hence, app., to sup: ἔρχεο δειελιήσας ρ 599.

δείελος, ὁ [cf. δείλη]. (1) The setting sun, the evening: δ. ὀψὲ δύων Φ 232.—(2) As adj.: δείελον ἦμαρ (evening) ρ 606.

†δεικανάομαι [δείκνυμι]. 3 pl. imp. δεικανόωντο. (1) To pledge in drinking = δείκνυμι (5) O 86.—(2) To welcome, greet σ 111, ω 410.

†δείκνῡμι. Pres. pple. δεικνύς N 244. Fut. δείξω ζ 194, η 29, μ 25, ν 344, φ 217. 3 sing. aor. ἔδειξε κ 303, ξ 323, τ 293, ω 147. δεῖξε E 870, H 184, K 476: γ 174, ε 241. 2 sing. opt. δείξειας T 332. 3 -ειε ζ 144. Imp. δεῖξον ζ 178. Infin. δεῖξαι Γ 452, Z 170. **Mid.** Pres. pple. δεικνύμενος I 196, Ψ 701: δ 59. 3 pl. pf. (with pres. sense) δειδέχαται η 72. 3 sing. plupf. (with impf. sense) δείδεκτο I 224. 3 pl. δειδέχατο Δ 4, I 671, X 435. (ἐν-.) (1) To manifest, exhibit, display: σῆμα βροτοῖσιν N 244. Cf. γ 174.—(2) To show, bring forward or exhibit to be looked at: αἷμα καταρρέον E 870. Cf. Z 170, H 184, T 332: ξ 323 = τ 293, φ 217, ω 147.—In mid. Ψ 701.—(3) To show, point out: Ἀλέξανδρον Γ 452. Cf. K 476: πόλιν ζ 144. Cf. ζ 178, 194, η 29, ν 344.—With dependent clause: ὅθι δένδρεα πεφύκει ε 241.—(4) To point out in words, tell, explain κ 303, μ 25.—(5) In mid., to pledge in drinking (app. from a custom of pointing to the person whose health was to be drunk): δείδεκτ' Ἀχιλῆα I 224. Cf. Δ 4, I 671.—(6) In mid., to welcome, greet: τῷ δεικνύμενος I 196. Cf. X 435: δ 59, η 72.

δείλη, ἡ [cf. δείελος]. Evening Φ 111.

δείλομαι [δείλη]. Of the sun, to decline towards evening: δείλετ' ἠέλιος η 289.

δειλός, -ή [δϜι-, δείδοικα]. (1) Cowardly, craven A 293, N 278.—(2) Sorry, worthless: δειλαί δειλῶν ἐγγύαι (given by worthless fellows) θ 351.—(3) (a) Luckless, wretched, 'poor' (in a tone of compassion or self-pity): δειλοῖσί σφι γόου κατάπαυμα P 38. Cf. E 574, P 670, T 287, Φ 464, X 31, 76, Ψ 65, 105, 221, 223, Ω 525: ἐμοὶ δειλῷ κακὰ μήδετο ξ 243. Cf. ι 65, λ 19, μ 341, ο 408, υ 115.—In voc.: ἆ δειλέ P 201, Ω 518: λ 618, ξ 361.—ἆ δειλώ P 443.—ἆ δειλοί Λ 816: κ 431, υ 351.—Sim.: ὤ μοι ἐγὼ δειλή Σ 54. Cf. X 431: ε 299.—(b) Tinged with hostility or contempt: ἆ δειλέ Λ 441, 452, Π 837: σ 389, φ 288.—ἆ δειλώ φ 86.

δεῖμα, τό [δϜι-, δείδοικα]. Fear, terror E 682.

δείματο, 3 sing. aor. mid. δέμω.

Δεῖμος, ὁ [δεῖμα]. Fear personified Δ 440, Λ 37, O 119.

δεινός, -ή, -όν [δϜι-, δείδοικα]. (1) Causing, or such as to cause, fear, fearful, terrible, awe-inspiring, dread, dire A 200, B 321, E 739, Θ 135, Λ 418, etc.: γ 145, ε 52, λ 157, μ 94, χ 405, etc.—With complementary infin.: δεινὸν γένος βασιλήϊόν ἐστι κτείνειν π 401.—Of noises, troubling the hearers, terrible, dreadful: καναχήν Π 104. Cf. A 49, Ψ 688.—Of something said, calculated to trouble the hearer, out of place, unseemly: ἔπος θ 409, φ 169.—(2) In neut. δεινόν as adv., so as to cause fear, fearfully, terribly, dreadfully: δ. δερκόμενοι Γ 342. Cf. Γ 337, Δ 420, Z 182, Θ 133, Λ 10, etc.: κῦμα δ. ἐπεσσύμενον ε 314. Cf. ε 403, λ 608, μ 85, 106, 236, χ 124, etc.—So in pl. δεινά E 439, O 13, Π 706 = Υ 448.—(3) Troubling with excessive wonder, marvellous, strange: θαῦμα N 100.—Exciting wonder, wonderful: πελώρου κ 168.—(4) To be regarded or treated with awe, reverence or respect: ὅρκου B 755, θεός Δ 514. Cf. Γ 172, E 839, Z 380 = 385, Σ 394, Φ 25: η 41, 246, 255, θ 22, κ 136 = λ 8 = μ 150, μ 322, 449, ξ 234.—In superl. δεινότατος O 38: = ε 186.—(5) Of armour, with notion of great power of resistance, proof against blows, stout: σάκος H 245, 266. Cf. K 254, 272, Υ 259.—(6) Feeling fear: ἀγορὴ δεινὴ τετρηχυῖα (in fear and disorder) H 346.

δείξω, fut. δείκνυμι.

δείους, genit. δέος.

δειπνέω [δεῖπνον]. 3 sing. plupf. δεδειπνήκει ρ 359. To take δεῖπνον (1) (a) In sense (1) (a) T 304: ι 312, ο 397.—(b) In sense (1) (b) ο 79.—(c) In sense (1) (f) δ 685, ρ 359, 506, υ 119.—(d) In sense (1) (g) ι 155.—(2) Of the meal taken by Hermes on arriving at Calypso's island ε 95.—Of that taken by the disguised Odysseus on arriving at Eumaeus's hut ξ 111.

δείπνηστος, ὁ [δεῖπνον]. The time for δεῖπνον: ὅτε δ. ἔην ρ 170 (here in sense (1) (f)).

†**δειπνίζω** [δεῖπνον]. Aor. pple. δειπνίσσας. To entertain at δεῖπνον: κατέπεφνε δειπνίσσας δ 535 = λ 411 (app. in sense (1) (f), but the time is not determined).

δεῖπνον, -ου, τό. **(1)** The principal meal of the day. **(a)** Taken before beginning the day's work, whether of fighting or of a peaceful occupation B 381 = T 275, B 399, Θ 53, T 171, 316, 346: ι 311.—**(b)** Taken by travellers before setting out ο 77 = 94.—**(c)** Taken in an interval of occupation Λ 86, Σ 560: ζ 97.—**(d)** Taken after work Ψ 158.—**(e)** Taken on returning from a nocturnal expedition K 578.—**(f)** The regular principal meal, taken in the late morning or about mid-day α 124, 134, ρ 176, τ 321, 419, υ 390, ω 215, 360, 386, 394, 412.—**(g)** A meal taken on shore by a ship's company ι 86 = κ 57, κ 155, ο 500.—**(h)** A meal taken in the evening (γ 497) by travellers arriving at a house and finding a marriage-feast in progress δ 61 (the same meal called δόρπον 213; and cf. μεταδόρπιος 194).—**(i)** Of an ἔρανος on the day after a marriage-feast δ 624.—**(2)** Simply, a meal κ 116, ο 316.—**(3)** The material for a meal: αἶγας ρ 214 = υ 175.—**(4)** A feed for horses B 383.

δείραντας, acc. pl. masc. aor. pple. δέρω.

δειρή, -ῆς, ἡ. **(1)** The neck or throat Γ 371, 396, N 202, Ξ 412, Σ 177, T 285: χ 472, ψ 208, 240.—Of the necks of Scylla μ 90.—Of an eagle's neck M 204: β 153.—**(2)** The neck-opening of a θώρηξ Λ 26.

δειροτομέω [δειρή + τομ-, τάμνω]. (ἀπο-.) To cut the throat of, to slay thus; or simply, to slay Φ 89, 555, Ψ 174: χ 349.

δεῖσε, 3 sing. aor. See δείδοικα.

δείσεται, 3 sing. fut. See δείδοικα.

δέκα, *indeclinable*. Ten B 372, 489, 618, Δ 347, I 122 = 264, Λ 24, 33, T 247, Ψ 851, 882, Ω 232: δ 129, ι 160, ω 340.—With another numeral: ἑπτὰ καὶ δ. ε 278, η 267, ω 63.

δεκάκις [δέκα]. **(1)** Ten times I 379.—**(2)** Ten times the normal, tenfold: ἄποινα X 349.

δεκάς, -άδος, ἡ [δέκα]. A body or company of ten: εἴ κ' ἐς δεκάδας διακοσμηθεῖμεν B 126. Cf. B 128: π 245.

δέκατος, -η, -ον [δέκα]. **(1)** The tenth: Ἠώς Z 175, ἐς δεκάτους ἐνιαυτούς (app. for ἐς δέκα ἐνιαυτούς by confusion with ἐς δέκατον ἐνιαυτόν) Θ 404 = 418. Cf. B 329, I 474, M 15, Ω 785: ε 107, η 253 = ξ 314, μ 447, ξ 241, 325 = τ 294, π 18, τ 192.—**(2)** δεκάτη (*sc.* ἡμέρη), the tenth day: δεκάτῃ (on the tenth day) ι 83.—So τῇ δεκάτῃ A 54, Ω 612, 665: κ 29.

δεκάχιλοι [δέκα + χίλιοι]. Ten thousand E 860 = Ξ 148.

δέκτης, ὁ [δεκ-, δέχομαι]. A beggar δ 248.

δέκτο, 3 sing. aor. δέχομαι.

δελφίς, -ῖνος, ὁ. A dolphin Φ 22: μ 96.

δέμας, τό [δέμω]. **(1)** One's bodily frame or build: οὐ δέμας οὐδὲ φυήν (the two words difficult to distinguish) A 115, μικρὸς δέμας E 801 (here app. 'stature'), δέμας εἰκυῖα θεῇσιν Θ 305. Cf. N 45, P 323, 555, Φ 285, X 227, Ω 376: δέμας ἀθανάτοισιν ὁμοῖος γ 468. Cf. β 268 = 401 = χ 206 = ω 503 = 548, δ 796, ε 212, 213, η 210, θ 14, 116, 194, λ 469 = ω 17, ν 222, 288, ξ 177, π 157, 174, σ 251, τ 124, 381, υ 31, 194, ψ 163.—Of animals: συῶν δέμας κ 240. Cf. ρ 307, 313.—**(2)** In advbl. acc. with genit., in the build of, after the similitude of, like (as our 'like' has developed fr. orig. Teutonic *lîko-, body, form): πυρός Λ 596 = N 673 = Σ 1, P 366.

δέμνια, τά [δέμω]. A bedstead, a bed. (In Ω 644 two beds are referred to. See 648. So perh. also in δ 297, 301; but from ο 45 it would rather appear that Telemachus and Peisistratus were then sleeping together): δέμνι' ὑπ' αἰθούσῃ θέμεναι Ω 644: = δ 297 = η 336, δέμνια κούρης ζ 20. Cf. δ 301, θ 277, 282, 296, 314, λ 189, τ 318, 599, υ 139.

δέμω [cf. δόμος]. Aor. ἔδειμα Φ 446. 3 sing. -ε I 349. 3 pl. -αν H 436, Ξ 32. 1 pl. subj. δείμομεν H 337. 3 sing. aor. mid. (ἐ)δείματο ζ 9, ξ 8. 3 sing. plupf. pass. (ἐ)δέδμητο N 683: α 426, ι 185, ξ 6. Pl. pple. δεδμημένοι Z 245, 249. To construct, build, form: πύργους H 337. Cf. Z 245, 249, H 436, I 349, N 683, Ξ 32, Φ 446; ὅθι οἱ θάλαμος δέδμητο (was in the state of having been built, *i.e.*; simply, stood) α 426, θάλαμον ψ 192. Cf. ι 185, ξ 6.—In mid. ζ 9, ξ 8.

δενδίλλω. App., to turn the eyes, give meaning looks: ἐς ἕκαστον I 180.

δένδρεον, -ου, τό. For dat. δενδρέῳ *v.l.* δένδρει fr. δένδρος Γ 152. A tree Γ 152, I 541, Λ 88, N 437, Φ 338: δ 458, ε 238, 241, η 114, λ 588, ν 196, σ 359, τ 112, 520, ω 336.

δενδρήεις, -εσσα [δένδρεον]. Abounding in trees: νῆσος α 51, ἄλσεϊ ι 200.

δέξατο, 3 sing. aor. δέχομαι.

δεξιός, -ή, -όν. Locative δεξιόφιν N 308. **(1)** That is on the right side, the right . . .: ὦμον E 46 = Π 343, E 98, 189, Λ 507, Ξ 450, Π 289, 468, X 133: ρ 462, 504, σ 95, τ 452. Cf. Δ 481, E 66, Λ 584, N 651.—The right-hand . . .: ἵππον Ψ 336.—**(2)** ἐπὶ δεξιά, to the right: νωμῆσαι βῶν H 238, εἴτ' ἐπὶ δ. ἴωσιν (from left to right of a spectator, *i.e.* in the lucky direction) M 239.—ἐπὶ δεξιόφιν, on the right of. With genit.: παντὸς στρατοῦ N 308.—**(3)** Of a bird of omen, passing as in M 239 above, boding well: δεξιὸν ἧκεν ἐρωδιόν K 274. Cf. N 821, Ω 294 = 312, 320: β 154, ο 160 = 525, 531, ο 164, ω 312.—**(4)** In fem. δεξιή (*sc.* χείρ), the right hand: δεξιῇ ἠσπάζοντο K 542.—A grasp or clasp of the right hand as the sign of a pledge B 341 = Δ 159.

δεξιτερός, -ή, -όν [in form comp. of prec. with changed accent]. Fem. instrumental δεξιτερῆφι τ 480. This form as locative Ω 284: ο 148. **(1)** That is on the right side, the right . . .: κνήμην Δ 519. Cf. E 393, H 108, K 373, Λ 377, Ξ 137, Φ 167, Ω 284, 672: α 121, ο 148, σ 258, 397, τ 480, υ 197, ϕ 410.—The right-hand part of, the part of on the right: *γναθμὸν δεξιτερόν* Π 405.—**(2)** In fem. *δεξιτερή* (*sc.* *χείρ*), the right hand: *δεξιτερῇ ἑλοῦσα* A 501. Cf. Φ 490, X 320.

δέξο, aor. imp. *δέχομαι*.

δέξομαι, fut. *δέχομαι*.

δέος, *τό* (*δϝέος*) [*δϝι-*, *δείδοικα*]. Genit. *δείους* K 376, O 4. **(1)** Fear, terror, affright, apprehension Δ 421, E 812, 817, H 479, Θ 77, K 376, N 224, Ξ 387, O 4, 658, P 67, 625: ζ 140, λ 43, 633, μ 243, ξ 88, χ 42, ω 450, 533.—**(2)** Reason or cause for fear or apprehension: *οὔ τοι ἔπι δ.* A 515.—With complementary infin.: *σοὶ οὐ δ. ἔστ' ἀπολέσθαι* M 246. Cf. ε 347, θ 563.

δέπας, *τό*. Dat. *δέπαϊ* Ψ 196, Ω 285: γ 41, ο 149, σ 121, υ 261. *δέπᾳ* κ 316. Pl. *δέπα* (for *δέπαα*) ο 466, τ 62, υ 153. Genit. *δεπάων* H 480. Dat. *δεπάεσσι* A 471, Γ 295, Θ 162, etc.: γ 340, η 137, σ 418, etc. *δέπασσι* O 86. A drinking-cup: *ἐπαρξάμενοι δεπάεσσιν* (locative dat., into the . . .) A 471 = I 176, *ἀμφικύπελλον* A 584. Cf. Γ 295, Δ 3, 262, H 480, I 203, etc.: γ 41, η 137, ι 10, σ 152, τ 62, etc.

δέρκομαι. 3 sing. pa. iterative *δερκέσκετο* ε 84, 158. Aor. *ἔδρακον* κ 197. 3 sing. pf. (in pres. sense) *δέδορκε* X 95. Pple. *δεδορκώς* τ 446. (*ἀνα-*, *δια-*, *ἐσ-*, *κατα-*, *προσ-*.) **(1)** To see, behold, look upon: *Τρῶας* N 86. Cf. Ξ 141.—**(2)** To have the power of sight as being alive: *ἐμεῦ* (*ἐμέθεν*) *ἐπὶ χθονὶ δερκομένοιο* A 88: π 439.—**(3)** To descry, make out: *καπνόν* κ 197.—Absol.: *ὀξύτατον δέρκεσθαι* P 675.—**(4)** To direct the sight, look: *ἐπὶ πόντον* ε 84 = 158.—**(5)** To look, glance: *δεινόν* Γ 342, Λ 37, Ψ 815. Cf. X 95, Ψ 477.—Fig., with cognate acc.: *πῦρ ὀφθαλμοῖσι δεδορκώς* τ 446.

δέρμα, *-ατος*, *τό* [*δέρω*]. **(1)** A hide or skin stripped from a beast: *συός* I 548. Cf. δ 436, 440, χ 362.—**(2)** The prepared skin of a beast: *λέοντος* K 23, 177. Cf. ν 436, ξ 50, 519.—**(3)** A piece of leather: *βόειον* ξ 24.—Used as = *ἄντυξ* (2) Z 117.—A leathern bag: *πυκινοῖσιν* β 291.—**(4)** The human skin: *ἔσχεθε δ' οἶον δέρμα* (the strip of skin not severed) Π 341. Cf. ν 431.

δερμάτινος [*δερματ-*, *δέρμα*]. Leathern: *τροποῖς* δ 782 = θ 53.

δέρτρον, *τό* [*δέρω*]. The membrane enclosing the intestines: *γῦπε δ. ἔσω δύνοντες* λ 579.

δέρω. 3 pl. aor. *ἔδειραν* A 459, B 422: μ 359. Acc. pl. masc. pple. *δείραντας* κ 533, λ 46. (*ἐκ-*.) To flay (a beast) H 316, Ψ 167, Ω 622: θ 61, κ 533 = λ 46, τ 421.—Absol. A 459 = B 422: μ 359.

δεσμός, *ὁ* [*δεσ-*, *δέω*]. Pl. *δέσματα* α 204. Acc. *δέσματα* X 468: θ 278. **(1)** Any means of securing a person, a bond, bonds: *δῆσαν κρατερῷ ἐνὶ δεσμῷ* E 386. Cf. E 391, K 443, O 19: *δεσμὸν ἀνέγναμψαν* ξ 348. Cf. θ 317, 353, 359, 360, μ 160, ο 232, 444, χ 189, 200.—In pl. (app., except where the idea of number is involved, used indifferently with the sing.): *ὑπελύσαο δεσμῶν* A 401: *ἐνὶ πλεόνεσσι δεσμοῖσι διδέντων* μ 54. Cf. α 204, θ 274, 278, 296, 336, 340, λ 293, μ 164, 196, 200.—**(2)** A halter for a horse Z 507 = O 264.—**(3)** A ship's mooring-cable ν 100.—**(4)** A knot (in a cord put round a chest to secure the lid) θ 443, 447.—**(5)** A means of securing a gate: *ἐπὶ δεσμὸν ἴῆλαι* [*θύραις*] ϕ 241 (app. not referring to a regular fastening. The gate is in fact secured with a *ὅπλον νεός*. See 390).—**(6)** A rivet Σ 379.—**(7)** In pl., articles of head-dress in gen.: *δέσματα σιγαλόεντα* X 468 (the particular articles being specified in the next line).

δέσποινα, *-ης*, *ἡ* [*δεσ-*, house + a second element conn. with *πόσις*[1]. Cf. *δεσπότης*, master, *πότνια*; also *δασπλῆτις*]. The lady of a house, a mistress η 53, ξ 9 = 451, ξ 127, ο 374, 377, τ 83, ψ 2.—Joined with *ἄλοχος* γ 403.—With *γυνή* η 347.

δετή, *-ῆς*, *ἡ* [*δέω*]. A faggot Λ 554 = P 663.

δευήσεαι, 2 sing. fut. *δεύομαι*. See *δεύω*[2].

δεῦρο. In form *δεύρω* Γ 240 (*v.l.* *δεῦρο*). Hither. **(1)** With vbs. of motion: *ἤλυθον* A 153. Cf. B 138, Γ 240, Z 426, K 406, X 12, Ψ 21, etc.: *μολόντες* γ 44. Cf. θ 424, ο 213, π 132, ρ 53, ω 299, etc.—With imp.: *δ. ἴθι* Γ 130. Cf. Γ 390, H 75, N 235.—In pregnant sense: *δ. παρέστης* Γ 405.—Elliptically (with *ἄγε*): *ἄγε δ., ὄφρα* . . . P 685. Cf. ι 517, λ 561.—**(2)** With other vbs.: *κάλεσσον* Δ 193, *ὀρόωντες* P 637. Cf. Ω 106: ρ 529.—**(3)** With imp. (with or without *ἄγε*), come! *ἄγε δ. παρ' ἔμ' ἵστασο* Λ 314, P 179. Cf. Ψ 581: *δ. ὄρσο* χ 395. Cf. θ 145, 205, μ 184, χ 233.—**(4)** With 1 pl. subj. (with or without *ἄγε*), come! let us . . . : *δ. ἐς τοὺς φύλακας καταβήομεν* K 97. Cf. P 120, X 254, Ψ 485: θ 292.

δεύτατος [superl. to *δεύτερος*]. Last, the last: *ἦλθεν* T 51: α 286, *τοῦτο δεύτατον εἶπεν ἔπος* ψ 342.

δεῦτε = *δεῦρο*. Used in dual and pl. contexts. **(1)** = *δεῦρο* (1) elliptically: *δ. καί μ' ἀμύνετε* N 481. Cf. θ 307.—**(2)** = *δεῦρο* (3): *δ. δύω μοι ἕπεσθον* X 450.—With *ἄγε* θ 11.—**(3)** = *δεῦρο* (4) (with or without *ἄγετε*): *δ. ἴομεν* Ξ 128. Cf. H 350: β 410, θ 133.

δεύτερος [prob. fr. *δεύω*[2]]. **(1)** Coming second in a contest: *γνώσεσθ' ἵππους οἳ δεύτεροι οἵ τε πάροιθεν* Ψ 498.—With ellipse of sb.: *τῷ δευτέρῳ ἵππον ἔθηκεν* Ψ 265. Cf. Ψ 750.—In neut. pl. *δεύτερα*, the prize for the second Ψ 538.—**(2)** Coming second in gaining estimation, taking a second place: *ἵνα μὴ δ. ἔλθοι* K 368. Cf. X 207.—**(3)** (except in P 45, Φ 596 strengthened by *αὖτε*) **(a)** Second in doing something, following another in doing it: *ἠρᾶτο* K 283. Cf. Ψ 729, 841.—**(b)** In fighting, coming in with one's throw or stroke after an opponent: *προΐει ἔγχος* H 248, Υ 273. Cf. E 855, H 268, P 45, Φ 169, 596.—**(4)** With genit.: *ἐμεῖο δεύτεροι* (left behind or surviving me) Ψ 248.—**(5)** In neut. *δεύτερον* as adv. **(a)** In the second place. With *αὖ*: *δ. αὖ θώρηκ' ἔδυνεν* Γ 332 = Λ 19 = Π 133 = T 371. Cf. Z 184.—**(b)** A second time, again: *ὁρμηθείς* Π 402.—With *αὖτε* Γ 191.—With *αὖτις* A 513: γ 161, τ 65 (cf. σ 321), χ 69.—Sim.: *ᾔτεέ με δ. αὖτις* (asked for a second supply) ι 354.—**(c)** Another time, for the future. With *αὖτε*: *δ. αὖτ' ἀλέασθαι ἀμείνονας ἠπεροπεύειν* Ψ 605.—Again, in the future: *οὔ μ' ἔτι δ. ὧδε ἵξετ' ἄχος* Ψ 46. Cf. σ 24.

—(d) So as to come in as in (3) (b): ὁρμηθείς Π 467. Cf. Γ 349.

δεύω[1]. Pa. iterative δεύεσκον η 260. (κατα-.) To wet, moisten Β 471 = Π 643, Ι 570, Ν 655 = Φ 119, Ρ 51, 361, Ψ 15 (twice), 220: ε 53, ζ 44, η 260, θ 522, ι 290.

δεύω[2] (δέϝω). 3 sing. aor. ἐδεύησε ι 483, 540. Also in form δῆσε Σ 100. Except in these forms as deponent **δεύομαι.** 2 sing. fut. δευήσεαι ζ 192, ξ 510. Infin. -εσθαι Ν 786: ψ 128. (ἐπιδεύομαι.) **(1)** To lack, be without, want, not to have. With genit.: ἡγεμόνος Β 709. Cf. Β 128, Δ 48 = Ω 69, Ε 202, Θ 127, Ν 786, Σ 100: ἐσθῆτος ζ 192, ξ 510. Cf. η 73, θ 137, ψ 128.—Absol.: ἧσθαι δευόμενον (with empty hands) Α 134, μηδέ τι θυμῷ δευέσθω (fail) Υ 122, δευόμενος (in his need) Χ 492.—To be in the state of having (something) fail one, be deprived of, lose. With genit.: θυμοῦ Γ 294, Υ 472.—**(2)** To fall short of (a person). With genit.: Ἀργείων Ψ 484. Cf. α 254, δ 264.—To be unequal to, unfitted for. With genit.: πολέμοιο Ν 310. Cf. Ρ 142.—**(3)** To suffer want or be stinted in the matter of. With genit.: δαιτός Α 468 = 602 = Β 431 = Η 320 = Ψ 56 := π 479 = τ 425.—**(4)** To fail *to do something*. With infin.: ἐδεύησεν οἰήϊον ἄκρον ἱκέσθαι ι 483 = 540.

δέχομαι. Fut. δέξομαι Σ 115, Χ 365. 3 sing. -εται Ρ 208, Σ 331. Fut. pf. δεδέξομαι Ε 238. 3 sing. aor. (ἐ)δέξατο Α 446, Β 186, Ε 158, Ζ 483, Ι 633, etc.: α 121, ε 462, θ 483, λ 327, φ 82, etc. Imp. δέξαι Ε 227, Ζ 46, Λ 131, Ρ 480, Ω 137, 429, 555. Pple. δεξάμενος, -ου Ι 333, 636, Ξ 203, Ρ 391, Ψ 89: θ 419, ν 72, ο 132, ρ 110. Fem. -η ξ 128, τ 355. Infin. δέξασθαι Α 112: σ 287. 3 sing. aor. δέκτο Β 420, Ο 88: ι 353. Imp. δέξο Τ 10. Infin. δέχθαι Α 23, 377. 3 pl. pf. δέχαται Μ 147. Imp. δέδεξο Ε 228, Υ 377, Χ 340. Pple. δεδεγμένος, -ου Δ 107, Θ 296, Κ 62, Λ 124, Ο 745, Ψ 273. δέγμενος, -ου Β 794, Ι 191, Σ 524: υ 385. Also pf. pple. δεδοκημένος Ο 730. Plupf. ἐδέγμην ι 513, μ 230. (ἀνα-, ἀπο-, ἐκ-, παρα-, ποτι-, ὑπο-.) **(1)** To receive or take something offered, given, handed over, etc., to accept: ἄποινα Α 20, παιδὸς κύπελλον (from him) 596, σκῆπτρόν οἱ (from him) Β 186, χαλκὸν δέδεξο (app., be minded to accept) Χ 340. Cf. Α 446, Ε 227, Ζ 483, Ι 633, Ρ 391, etc.: κρήδεμνον ε 462, δῶρα (for custody) θ 419, χρυσὸν ἀνδρός (as the price of the betrayal of . . .) λ 327, ἔγχος οἱ (relieved him of . . .) ο 282 = π 40. Cf. α 121, θ 483, ι 353, ρ 356, τ 355, etc.—Of a god, to accept (a sacrifice) Β 420.—**(2)** To receive (a child) for nurture Ξ 203.—To receive and undertake the charge of (a person) Ψ 89.—To receive, welcome Ε 158, Σ 238, 331.—To receive hospitably, entertain ξ 128, ρ 110, τ 316.—**(3)** To accept, resign oneself to: κῆρα Σ 115, Χ 365.—To accept, put up with, make the best of: μῦθον υ 271.—**(4)** In pf. and plupf. **(a)** To expect, look for: χρυσὸν Ἀλεξάνδροιο (from . . .) Λ 124.—With acc. and infin.: φῶτα μέγαν ἐδέγμην ἐλεύσεσθαι ι 513. Cf. μ 230.—**(b)** To wait. With dependent clause: ὁππότ' ἀφορμηθεῖεν (watching for the time when . . .) Β 794, εἰς ὅ κεν ἔλθῃς Κ 62. Cf. Σ 524: υ 385.—To await. With dependent clause: Αἰακίδην ὁπότε λήξειεν Ι 191.—Of things: ἱππῆας ἄεθλα δεδεγμένα Ψ 273.—Absol.: δεδεγμένος (on the watch) Δ 107.—**(c)** To await the attack of, stand up to, be ready for: Ἀχιλλῆα Υ 377. Cf. Ε 228, 238, Μ 147, Ο 745.—Absol. Θ 296, Ο 730.—**(5)** App., to succeed, come next: δέχεταί μοι κακὸν ἐκ κακοῦ Τ 290.

†**δέψω.** Aor. pple. δεψήσας. To work or knead with the hands in order to soften: κηρόν μ 48.

δέω. 3 sing. pa. iterative mid. δησάσκετο Ω 15. 3 sing. plupf. pass. δέδετο Ε 387, Ψ 866: ο 232, ω 229. 3 pl. δέδεντο Κ 475: ι 443, κ 92. (ἐκ-, ἐν-, ἐπι-, κατα-, συν-.) **(1)** To tie or secure in its place, fasten: δῆσε ζυγόν Ε 730. Cf. Ω 190, 267: β 425 = ο 290.—In mid. θ 37.—**(2)** To tie into a bundle, bind together. In mid.: δράγματα δέοντο Σ 553.—**(3)** To tie or attach by a cord, a strap, etc.: ἐκ δίφροιο ἔδησεν [Ἕκτορα] Χ 398, ποδός (by the foot) Ψ 854. Cf. Ψ 866: ι 443.—In mid. Ω 15.—To tie round (with a fastening). In mid.: [πόδα] δησάμενος τελαμῶνι Ρ 290.—**(4)** To moor (a ship) κ 92.—**(5)** To tie or secure (a rope): πρυμνήσια Α 436. Cf. Ω 273: κ 96, ο 498.—In mid. Θ 26: β 430.—**(6)** To tie or secure (a person's feet, etc.): πόδας καὶ χεῖρας Φ 454. Cf. Φ 30: χ 189.—**(7)** To bind or secure (a person), put (him) in bonds: δῆσαν κρατερῷ ἐνὶ δεσμῷ Ε 386. Cf. Α 406, Β 231, Ε 387, Κ 443: θ 352, ι 99, μ 50, 161, 178, 196, ο 232.—Fig.: ἡμέτερον μένος Ξ 73: κελεύθου με (hinders from . . .) δ 380 = 469. Cf. ξ 61.—To halter or secure (a horse or an ox) Θ 544, Κ 475, Ν 572.—**(8)** To bind up (a wound) τ 457.—**(9)** In mid., to tie on to one's person: ἐδήσατο πέδιλα Ω 340, Β 44 = Κ 22 = 132 = Ξ 186: = β 4 = δ 309 = υ 126, α 96, ε 44, ο 550, π 155, ρ 2.—Sim. in pass.: περὶ κνήμησι κνημῖδας δέδετο (had them bound about his legs) ω 229.

δή. **(1)** Temporal particle. **(a)** **(α)** By or before this (or that) time, by now, now, already, ere this: ἐννέα δὴ βεβάασιν ἐνιαυτοί Β 134. Cf. Α 394, 503, Β 117, Γ 150, Ε 383, Θ 297, etc.: ὃς δὴ γήραϊ κυφὸς ἔην β 16. Cf. α 26, 161, γ 245, δ 373, η 152, ν 10, etc.—**(β)** Indicating the arrival of a point of time, arrival at a result: ἐξ οὗ δὴ διαστήτην (from the time when the quarrel came to the point of breaking out) Α 6, εἰ δὴ ὁμοῦ πόλεμός τε δαμᾷ καὶ λοιμὸς Ἀχαιούς (if it has come to this that . . .) 61, νημερτὲς μὲν δή μοι ὑπόσχεο (you must now decide) 514. Cf. Α 161, 574, Θ 34, Ι 202, 309, 434, Τ 9, Υ 115, etc.: ἦ μάλα δή με θέσφαθ' ἱκάνει ν 172, ὅππως δὴ μνηστῆρσι χεῖρας ἐφήσει (at this crisis of his fate) υ 29, αἲ γὰρ δὴ θεοὶ τισαίατο λώβην (to such a pitch of insolence have they come) 169. Cf. ξ 333, 379, τ 510, χ 395, ψ 43, etc.—With ἄγε, ἄγετε. See ἄγε.—With ἄγρει φ 176.—**(b)** Now, at this (or that) time: καὶ δὴ τάχ' ἔμελλε . . . Ζ 52. Cf. Α 388, Β 436, Ι 245, Λ 126, 441, Ρ 261, etc.: ὃς δή σφι σχεδόν ἐστιν β 284. Cf. δ 551, 770, ε 401, 409, κ 549, π 280, etc.—**(c)** Joined with, and emphasizing or defining, other temporal words: *αἰεὶ δή* M 323, *δὴ αὖ* A 540, *δὴ αὖτε* A 340, *ἐπεὶ δή* Δ 124, *ἐπὴν δή* Π 453, *καί νυ δή* H 273, *νῦν δή* B 284, *ὁππότε δή* Π 53, *ὅτε δή* A 432, *ὀψὲ δή* H 94, *τάχα δή* N 120, *τῆμος δή* μ 441, *τότε δή* A 92, etc.—**(2)** As affirmative or emphasizing particle: *μὴ δὴ οὕτως κλέπτε νόῳ* A 131. Cf. A 286, 295, B 158, 301, Z 476, Θ 491, Λ 314, N 260, Σ 364, etc.: *εἰ δὴ ἐξ αὐτοῖο τόσος πάϊς εἰς Ὀδυσῆος* α 207. Cf. α 253, 384, γ 352, 357, δ 819, ε 23, λ 348, ξ 282, etc.—Giving a touch of scorn, forsooth, to be sure: *ὡς δὴ τοῦδ' ἕνεκά σφιν ἑκηβόλος ἄλγεα τεύχει* A 110. Cf. Γ 403, Θ 177, Ξ 88, etc.: φ 170.—Emphasizing superlatives: *κάρτιστοι δὴ κεῖνοι τράφεν* A 266. Cf. Z 98, H 155, K 436, X 76, etc.: *οἴκτιστον δὴ κεῖνο ἴδον* μ 258. Cf. θ 519, λ 309, etc.

†δήεις, 2 *sing.* *δήομεν*, 1 *pl.* *δήετε*, 2 *pl.* [Subjunctives with strong stem answering to *δᾰ-* in *ἐδάην*, etc. See *δάω*. The *-εις* of 2 sing. app. a trace of an older inflexion, *-ω*, *-εις*, *-ει*, answering to *-ομεν*, *-ετε*.] To find, to light or come upon: *δούρατα δήεις* (will find) N 260. Cf. ζ 291, η 49, ν 407.—Of immaterial things: *ἐν πήματα οἴκῳ* λ 115.—To find, get: *ἄλλοθι ἕδρην* π 44.—To find out by experience: *τέκμωρ Ἰλίου* I 418 = 685.—To attain to, bring about: *ἄνυσιν* δ 544.

δηθά [*δήν*]. For a long time, for long, long: *μηκέτι δ. λεγώμεθα* B 435, *ποταμῷ δ. ἱερεύετε ταύρους . . . καθίετε ἵππους* (the vbs. to be taken as presents, 'have long been sacrificing . . .') Φ 131. Cf. E 104, 587, K 52, Ξ 110, O 512: *δ. πήματα πάσχει* (has been suffering) α 49, δ *θύρῃσιν ἐφεστάμεν* 120. Cf. β 255, 404, γ 313, 336, δ 373, 466, η 152, θ 411, μ 351, π 313, χ 177.

δηθύνω [*δηθά*]. To tarry, delay, loiter A 27, Z 503, 519: μ 121, ρ 278.

δήϊος[1], *-ον* (the first syllable scanned ◡) [conn. with *δαίω*[1]. Perh. orig. *δᾰϝιος*. Cf. *θεσπιδαής*]. Epithet of fire, blazing, consuming B 415, Z 331, Θ 181, I 347, 674, Λ 667, Π 127, 301, Σ 13.

δήϊος[2]. (The first syllable scanned ◡ when followed by ◡—.) **(1)** Hostile, enemy: *ἄνδρα* Z 481. Cf. I 317 = P 148, K 358, M 57, O 533, X 84, Ω 684.—Epithet of *πόλεμος*, destructive, deadly Δ 281, E 117, H 119 = 174, P 189, T 73, Φ 422.—Of Ares H 241.—**(2)** As sb., an enemy, a foe: *δηΐοισι μάχεσθαι* Δ 373. Cf. B 544, Z 82, I 76, K 206, Λ 190 = 205, M 264, 276, N 395, 556, O 548, Π 591, P 167, 272, 667, Σ 208, 220.

δηϊοτής, *-ῆτος, ἡ* [*δήϊος*[2]]. **(1)** Battle, warfare, strife, struggle Γ 20, E 348, H 29, M 248, Ξ 129, Π 815, Υ 245, etc.: ζ 203, λ 516, μ 257, χ 229.—**(2)** In concrete sense, the fighters, the fighting throng: *θέων ἀνὰ δηϊοτῆτα* O 584, P 257.

†δηϊόω [*δήϊος*[2]]. 3 pl. opt. *δηϊόῳεν* δ 226. Pple. *δηϊόων* P 566, Σ 195, Ψ 176. Pl. *δηϊόωντες* Λ 153. 3 pl. impf. pass. *δηϊόωντο* N 675. Contr. forms. Pres. pple. *δηῶν* P 65. 3 pl. impf. *δῄουν* E 452, Λ 71, M 425, O 708, Π 771. Fut. infin. *δηώσειν* I 243. 3 sing. aor. subj. *δηώσῃ* Π 650. 3 pl. *-ωσι* Δ 416, M 227. Pple. *δηώσας*, *-αντος* Θ 534, Ξ 518, Π 158, Σ 83, X 218. Aor. pple. pass. *δηωθείς*, *-έντος* Δ 417: ι 66. **(1)** To treat as a foe, to wound, kill, slay Θ 534, Λ 71 = Π 771, Λ 153, M 227, O 708, Π 650, P 566, Σ 83, 195, X 218, Ψ 176: δ 226, ι 66.—To inflict slaughter upon (a hostile force): *Τρῶας* Δ 416. Cf. Δ 417, I 243, N 675.—**(2)** To rend or tear: *βοείας* E 452 = M 425. Cf. Ξ 518.—Of beasts tearing their prey Π 158, P 65.

δηλέομαι. 3 sing. aor. subj. *δηλήσηται* Γ 107. (*δια-*.) **(1)** To do harm or mischief to, hurt, injure: *μή πως ἀμφοτέρους δηλήσεαι* Ψ 428.—Absol. θ 444, ν 124.—Of warlike action Δ 67 = 72: κ 459, λ 401, 408, χ 368, ω 111.—Absol. Δ 236, 271.—Of a weapon: *ῥινὸν δηλήσατο χαλκός* χ 278.—Also, absol., to do harm, lead to mischief: *σή κε βουλὴ δηλήσεται* Ξ 102.—**(2)** To ravage, destroy: *καρπόν* A 156.—**(3)** To violate (a treaty) Γ 107.

δήλημα, *-ατος, τό* [*δηλέομαι*]. Something that brings harm, a bane: *δηλήματα νηῶν* μ 286.

δηλήμων, *-ονος* [*δηλέομαι*]. Working mischief, baneful Ω 33.—As sb., a bane σ 85 = 116 = φ 308.

δῆλος. Clear, plain, manifest υ 333.

δημιοεργός, *ὁ* [*δήμιος + ἔργον*]. One who works for the common weal, not for himself or for a private employer ρ 383, τ 135.

δήμιος, *-ον* [*δῆμος*]. **(1)** Belonging to the community, public: *οἶκος* υ 264.—**(2)** Relating to the public interests, public: *πρῆξις* γ 82.—Absol.: *ἦέ τι δήμιον πιφαύσκεται;* β 32. Cf. β 44, δ 314.—**(3)** Discharging public functions: *αἰσυμνῆται* θ 259.—**(4)** In neut. pl. *δήμια* as adv., at the public cost (cf. *δημόθεν*): *πίνουσιν* P 250.

δημοβόρος [*δῆμος* (1) + *βορ-*, *βι-βρώσκω*]. (*κατα-δημοβορέω*.) That devours the common stock: *βασιλεύς* A 231.

δημογέρων, *-οντος* [*δῆμος + γέρων*]. = *γέρων* (4) Γ 149, Λ 372.

δημόθεν [*δῆμος* (1) + *-θεν* (1)]. From the common stock: *δ. ἄλφιτα δῶκα* τ 197.

δημός, *-οῦ, ὁ*. Fat Θ 240, 380 = N 832, Λ 818, Φ 127, 204, X 501, Ψ 168, 243, 253, 750: ι 464, ξ 428, ρ 241.

δῆμος, *-ου, ὁ*. **(1)** The common stock or store: *ἐς δῆμον ἔδωκεν* Λ 704.—**(2)** A district, country, land, realm: *Ἐρεχθῆος* B 547. Cf. B 828, Γ 201, E 710, Z 158, 225, I 634, Π 437, 455, 514, 673, 683, T 324, Υ 385, Ω 481: *Ἰθάκης* α 103. Cf. α 237, β 317, γ 100, ζ 3, θ 555, ν 233, υ 210, φ 307, ω 12, etc.—**(3)** A community or people: *παντὶ δήμῳ* Γ 50, Ω 706, *θεὸς ὣς τίετο δήμῳ* (in the . . ., among the . . .) E 78, K 33, Λ 58, N 218, Π 605. Cf. I 460, Λ 328, M 447, P 577, Σ 295, 500, Υ 166: *κατὰ δῆμον* β 101, *δήμου ἡγήτορες* ν 186. Cf. β 239, 291, δ 691, η 11, 150, ξ 205, 239, π 114, 425, etc.—**(4)** A body or force of men: *ἑτεραλκέα δῆμον* O 738. Cf. P 330.—App., a multitude: *ἐπὶ δ' ἔστενε δ. ἀπείρων* Ω 776.—**(5)** The common people: *δήμου ἄνδρα* B 198.—App., one of the common people: *δῆμον ἐόντα* M 213.

δήν (δϝήν). For a long time, for long, long: ἀκέων δ. ἧστο Α 512. Cf. Α 416, Ε 412, Ζ 131, 139, Θ 126, Ι 30 = 695, Ν 573, Π 736, Ρ 695, Υ 426, Ψ 690: δ. ἀπεών (having been long . . .) ν 189, ὀϊζὺν δ. ἔχομεν (have long been suffering . . .) ξ 416. Cf. α 281, β 36, δ 494, ε 127, ζ 33, υ 155, χ 473, etc.

δηναιός [δήν]. Long-lived Ε 407.

δήνεα, τά [app. fr. δάω]. (1) Arts, wiles: ὀλοφώϊα κ 289.—(2) What one has in one's mind, thoughts, counsels: ἤπια δήνεα οἶδεν Δ 361 (see ἤπιος (1)): θεῶν ψ 82.

δῄουν, 3 pl. contr. impf. δηϊόω.

†**δηριάομαι** [δῆρις]. 3 dual δηριάασθον Μ 421. 3 pl. imp. δηριαάσθων Φ 467. Infin. δηριάασθαι Π 96, Ρ 734. 3 pl. impf. δηριόωντο θ 78. To strive, contend, struggle, in passages cited.

†**δηρίομαι** [as prec.]. 3 pl. aor. δηρίσαντο θ 76. 3 dual aor. δηρινθήτην Π 756. = prec.

δῆρις, ἡ. Strife, contention Ρ 158: ω 515.

δηρός [δήν]. (1) Of time, long Ξ 206 = 305.—Absol.: ἐπὶ δηρόν Ι 415.—(2) In neut. sing. δηρόν as adv., for a long time, for long, long: μένειν Β 298. Cf. Ε 120, Κ 371, Ν 151, Π 852, Τ 64, etc.: ἐσκοπίαζον κ 260. Cf. α 203, β 285, ε 396, π 171, φ 112, etc.

δησάσκετο, 3 sing. pa. iterative mid. δέω.

δῆσε[1], 3 sing. aor. δέω.

δῆσε[2], 3 sing. aor. δεύω[2].

δηωθείς, contr. aor. pple. pass. δηϊόω.

δηῶν, contr. pres. pple. δηϊόω.

δηώσειν, contr. fut. infin. δηϊόω.

διά. (I) Adv. (1) Through: διὰ δ' ἔπτατ' ὀϊστός Ε 99: διὰ τάφρον ὀρύξας (*i.e.* stretching in a line) φ 120.—Sim. κλέος διὰ ξεῖνοι φορέουσιν (through the lands they traverse) τ 333.—With ἀμπερές. See ἀμπερές.—(2) Severing, sundering, splitting, dividing: διὰ κτῆσιν δατέοντο Ε 158. Cf. Β 655, Ι 333, Ρ 522, Υ 280, etc.: διὰ ξύλα κεάσσαι ο 322. Cf. ι 157, 291, etc.—(3) Intensive: διὰ χρόα ἔδαψεν Ε 858. Cf. Μ 308, Ν 507, Τ 90, etc.: ἐπὴν σχεδίην διὰ κῦμα τινάξῃ ε 363.—(II) Prep. (sometimes, without anastrophe, following the case). (1) With genit. (a) Through, passing through, piercing: πέλεκυς, ὅς εἶσιν διὰ δουρός Γ 61. Cf. Γ 357, Δ 135, 481, Ε 113, etc.: κόρυθος διά ω 523. Cf. χ 16.—With a form in -φι: διὰ στήθεσφιν Χ 284, Ε 41 = 57 = Θ 259 = Λ 448 := χ 93.—In reference to pain: ὀδύνη διὰ χροὸς ἦλθεν Λ 398. — (b) Through, traversing or passing through (a space, a passage, a throng, or the like): αἰθέρος Β 458, Σκαιῶν Γ 263, προμάχων Δ 495. Cf. Ε 250, 503, Ζ 226, Η 340, Ι 478, etc.: Ὠκεανοῖο κ 508, νηός μ 206. Cf. κ 118, 391, λ 581, μ 335, etc.—With a form in -φι: δι' ὄρεσφιν Κ 185.—Of extension: σύες (ὕες) τανύοντο διὰ φλογός Ι 468 = Ψ 33. Cf. ι 298.—Among: ἔπρεπε καὶ διὰ πάντων Μ 104.—(2) With acc. (a) Through, passing through, piercing: ἔντεα Ψ 806. Cf. Η 247, Υ 269.—(b) Through, traversing or passing through (a space, a passage, a throng, or the like) or among (objects): δώματα Α 600, ἔντεα Κ 298, στόμα 375. Cf. Θ 343, Λ 118, Μ 62, Ρ 283, Ψ 122, etc.: σφέας η 40, ἄκριας κ 281. Cf. β 154, ζ 50, ι 447, κ 150, etc.—In reference to night regarded as a space: νύκτα δι' ὀρφναίην Κ 83. Cf. Β 57, Θ 510, Ω 363, 653, etc.: ι 143, 404, μ 284, etc.—During (the night): διὰ νύκτα μάχεσθαι Κ 101. Cf. ο 8, τ 66.—Of extension: διὰ κρατερὰς ὑσμίνας Β 40.—Cf. ι 400.—Among: πολέας διὰ κοιρανέοντα Δ 230.—(c) Through, by means of, by virtue of, by the help or working of: μαντοσύνην Α 72, ἰότητα Ο 41. Cf. Κ 497, Ο 71: βουλάς θ 82, Ἀθήνην 520. Cf. λ 276, 437, ν 121, τ 154, 523.—(d) On account of, because of: κάλλος λ 282, ἀτασθαλίας ψ 67.

διαβαίνω [δια- (3)]. Aor. pple. διαβάς Μ 458. Infin. διαβήμεναι δ 635. To pass *over*, cross. With acc.: τάφρον Μ 50.—Absol., to cross over: ἐς Ἤλιδα δ 635.—εὖ διαβάς, with the legs set well apart Μ 458.

διαγιγνώσκω [δια- (7)]. Aor. infin. διαγνῶναι Η 424. To distinguish, discern: ἄνδρα ἕκαστον Η 424. Cf. Ψ 240.—Absol. Ψ 470.

†**διαγλάφω** [δια- (10) + γλάφω = γλύφω, to cut out, carve. Cf. γλυφίς, γλαφυρός]. Fem. aor. pple. διαγλάψᾱσα. To hollow out, form: εὐνὰς ἐν ψαμάθοισιν δ 438.

†**διάγω** [δι-, δια- (3)]. 3 pl. aor. διήγαγον. To convey across a strait: πορθμῆες υ 187.

†**διαδέρκομαι** [δια- (10)]. 3 sing. aor. opt. διαδράκοι. To catch sight of, see Ξ 344.

διαδηλέομαι [δια- (10)]. To do sore hurt to ξ 37.

διαδράκοι, 3 sing. aor. opt. διαδέρκομαι.

διαδράμοι, 3 sing. aor. opt. διατρέχω.

διαείδω [δια- (7)]. 3 sing. fut. in mid. form διαείσεται Θ 535. (1) To distinguish, discern. In pass.: ἀρετὴ διαείδεται ἀνδρῶν Ν 277.—(2) To learn the value of, know. With acc. and dependent clause: ἣν ἀρετήν, εἰ . . . (whether . . .) Θ 535.

διαεῖπον [δια- (9)]. Contr. imp. δίειπε Κ 425. (1) To go through in talk: μῦθοι ἔσονται διαειπέμεν ἀλλήλοισιν δ 215. — (2) To tell fully, declare. Absol. Κ 425.

†**διάημι** [δι-, δια- (1)]. 3 sing. impf. διάη. To blow *through*. With acc.: θάμνους ε 478, λόχμην τ 440.

διαθειόω [δια- (10) + θειόω = θεειόω]. To fumigate thoroughly with sulphur: μέγαρον χ 494.

†**διαθρύπτω** [δια- (5) + θρύπτω, to break]. Nom. sing. neut. aor. pple. pass. διατρυφέν. To break in pieces, shiver: ξίφος διατρυφὲν ἔκπεσε χειρός Γ 363.

διαίνω. 3 sing. aor. ἐδίηνε Χ 495. To wet, moisten Ν 30, Φ 202, Χ 495.

†**διακείρω** [δια- (10)]. Aor. infin. διακέρσαι. To thwart, frustrate: ἐμὸν ἔπος Θ 8.

†**διακλάω** [δια- (5)]. Aor. pple. διακλάσσας. To break in two: τόξα Ε 216.

διακοσμέω [δια- (6) (10)]. (1) To separate out and form into suitable bodies, marshal Β 476.—To divide up and form (into bodies): ἐς δεκάδας Β 126.—(2) To put in due order. In mid.: ἐπεὶ μέγαρον διεκοσμήσαντο χ 457.

διακριδόν [διακρίνω]. Clearly, without doubt: δ. εἶναι ἄριστοι (ἄριστος) M 103, O 108.

†**διακρίνω** [δια- (6) (7)]. 3 sing. fut. διακρινέει B 387. 3 sing. aor. διέκρῖνε δ 179. 3 pl. -αν P 531. 3 sing. subj. διακρίνῃ H 292, 378, 397. 3 pl. -ωσι B 475. 3 sing. opt. διακρίνειε θ 195. **Pass.** Fut. infin. διακρινέεσθαι σ 149, υ 180. 3 pl. aor. διέκριθεν B 815. 2 pl. subj. διακρινθῆτε ω 532. 2 pl. opt. διακρινθεῖτε Γ 102. Pple. διακρινθείς, -έντος H 306, Υ 141, 212. Infin. διακρινθήμεναι Γ 98. Nom. pl. fem. pf. pple. διακεκριμέναι ι 220. (1) To separate out and form into suitable bodies, marshal B 815.—To separate out, sort out: αἰπόλια αἰγῶν B 475. Cf. ι 220.—(2) To separate, part: ἡμέας δ 179.—Of combatants Γ 98, 102, H 292 = 378 = 397, H 306, P 531, Υ 141, 212: σ 149, υ 180, ω 532.—Sim.: μένος ἀνδρῶν B 387.—(3) To distinguish, make out: τὸ σῆμα θ 195.

διάκτορος, -ου, ὁ [perh. fr. διακ-, lengthened fr. δι-α-, δι-, to run, as in δίεμαι]. Thus, the runner. Epithet or a name of Hermes B 103, Φ 497, Ω 339, 378 = 389 = 410 = 432, 445: α 84, ε 43, 75, 94, 145, θ 335, 338, μ 390, ο 319, ω 99.

†**διαλέγομαι** [δια- (9) + λέγομαι, λέγω²]. 3 sing. aor. διελέξατο. To go through, debate: ταῦτα Λ 407 = P 97 = Φ 562 = X 122 = 385.

διᾰμάω [app. fr. δια- (5) + ἀμάω¹]. To cut through: διάμησε χιτῶνα Γ 359 = H 253.

διαμετρέω [δια- (10)]. To measure off Γ 315.

διαμετρητός [διαμετρέω]. Measured off Γ 344.

διαμοιράομαι [δια- (10) + μοιράω, to divide, fr. μοῖρα]. To divide, apportion: ἕπταχα πάντα ξ 434.

διαμπερές [δι-, δια- (1) + ἀμπερές]. (1) Right through: βέλος ἐξέρυσε E 112 (*i.e.* in the direction of the arrow so as not to pull against the barbs), αἰχμὴ ἦλθεν 658. Cf. E 284, N 547.—With genit.: ἀσπίδος M 429. Cf. Υ 362.—Right through so as to make itself felt: οὐκ ὄμβρος περάασκεν ε 480, τ 442.—(2) Continuously, without break or interval: πέτρη τετύχηκεν κ 88. Cf. Π 640: ε 256 — Continuously, all the way: θρόνοι ἐρηρέδατο η 96 —Right round: σταυροὺς ἔλασσεν ξ 11. Cf. Σ 563. —Right on: ἡγεμόνευε ρ 194. Cf. K 325.—All together, in a mass M 398.—Right through a company, in turn H 171.—So as to meet, thoroughly: πόδας χεῖράς τε ἀποστρέψαντε χ 190.—(3) Of time, continuously, without intermission, break or interval K 89, 331, O 70, Π 499, T 272, X 264: δ 209, θ 245, λ 558, ν 59, ο 196, υ 47, ψ 151.—In intensive sense: ἔγχος κέ σε κατέπαυσε δ. (for good) Π 618.

διάνδιχα [δι-, δια- (10) + ἄνδιχα]. (1) By halves I 37.—(2) With divided mind: μερμήριξεν (was in two minds) A 189, N 455, (had half a mind) Θ 167.

†**διανύω** [δι-, δια- (10)]. 3 sing. aor. διήνυσε. To make an end. With pple.: κακότητ' ἀγορεύων ρ 517.

†**διαπέρθω** [δια- (10)]. 3 sing. aor. διέπερσε ι 265. 1 pl. -αμεν γ 130, λ 533, ν 316. 1 pl. subj. διαπέρσομεν I 46. Infin. διαπέρσαι Δ 53, 55. 1 pl. aor. διεπράθομεν A 367. 3 pl. -ον θ 514. Infin. διαπραθέειν H 32, I 532, Σ 511. 3 sing. aor. pass. διεπράθετο ο 384. To sack or ravage (a town) A 367, Δ 53, 55, H 32, I 46, 532, Σ 511: γ 130 = ν 316, θ 514, ι 265, λ 533, ο 384.

†**διαπέτομαι** [δια- (2)]. 3 sing. aor. διέπτατο. (1) To traverse a space by flight O 83, 172.—(2) To fly away through some opening α 320.

διαπλήσσω [δια- (5)]. Aor. infin. διαπλῆξαι θ 507. To split: δρῦς Ψ 120.—To split in pieces θ 507.

διαπορθέω [δια- (10)]. = διαπέρθω B 691.

διαπραθέειν, aor. infin. διαπέρθω.

διαπρήσσω [δια- (10)]. Aor. opt. διαπρήξαιμι ξ 197. (1) To traverse a space, pass, advance, make one's way: πεδίοιο (local genit., 'along the . . .') B 785 = Γ 14, Ψ 364.—To accomplish (a journey) A 483: = β 429, β 213.—(2) To pass or spend (time) I 326.—(3) To make an end. With pple.: λέγων ἐμὰ κήδεα ξ 197.

διαπρό [διά strengthened by πρό]. (1) Right through: ἦλυθ' ἀκωκή E 66. Cf. E 538, H 260, M 184, N 388, Υ 276, Φ 164, etc.: χ 295, ω 524.—With genit.: μίτρης Δ 138. Cf. E 281, Ξ 494.—(2) Through the whole extent: τάνυται P 393.

διαπρύσιον [app. conn. with διαμπερές]. (1) Of shouting, piercingly Θ 227 = Λ 275 = 586 = P 247, M 439 = N 149.—(2) Without a break: πεδίοιο τετυχηκώς (on the . . .) P 748.

διαπτοιέω [δια- (10)]. To terrify, scare σ 340.

διαρπάζω [δι-, δια- (10)]. To make prey of Π 355.

διαρραίω [δια- (5)]. Fut. infin. pass. διαρραίσεσθαι Ω 355. To dash in pieces, destroy, make an end of, bring to nought B 473, I 78, Λ 713, 733, P 727, Ω 355: α 251 = π 128, β 49, μ 290.

†**διαρρίπτω** [δια- (1)]. 3 sing. pa. iterative διαρρίπτασκε. To shoot (an arrow) through something τ 575.

†**διασεύω** [δια- (1) (2) (3)]. 3 sing. aor. mid. διέσσυτο. To speed or pass quickly *through* or *across*. With genit.: τάφροιο K 194: μεγάροιο X 460: δ 37.—Of a piercing weapon O 542.—With acc.: λαόν B 450.—Absol., of a weapon E 661.

†**διασκεδάννῡμι** [δια- (4)]. 3 sing. aor. διεσκέδασε ε 369, 370, η 275. 3 sing. opt. διασκεδάσειε ρ 244. To scatter, disperse ε 369, 370.—To break up into its component parts and disperse these: σχεδίην η 275.—To scatter to the winds, make an end of: ἀγλαΐας ρ 244.

διασκίδνημι. = prec. To scatter, disperse: νέφεα E 526.

διασκοπιάομαι [δια- (7) (10) + σκοπιάομαι fr. σκοπιή]. (1) To spy out K 388.—(2) To distinguish, discern P 252.

διαστήτην, 3 dual aor. διΐστημι.

†**διασχίζω** [δια- (5)]. 3 sing. aor. διέσχισε ι 71. 3 sing. aor. pass. διεσχίσθη Π 316. (1) To sever, rend: νεῦρα διεσχίσθη Π 316.—(2) To tear in pieces: ἱστία ι 71.

†**διατμήγω** [δια- (5) (6)]. Aor. pple. διατμήξας Φ 3: γ 291, ε 409, μ 174. Aor. διέτμαγον η 276. 3 pl. aor. pass. διέτμαγεν A 531, H 302, M 461, Π 354: ν 439. (1) To divide into two, sever Φ 3 (*i.e.* severing the fugitives into two bodies).—So of ships sailing together and severed into two bodies by a storm γ 291.—(2) To cleave (the sea), tra-

verse (it) ε 409, η 276.—(3) In pass., of two persons, to leave one another, part: ἐν φιλότητι διέτμαγεν H 302. Cf. A 531 := ν 439.—(4) To cut in pieces μ 173.—In pass., of the boards of a gate coming apart M 461.—Of a scattered flock Π 354.

†διατρέχω [δια- (2)]. 3 pl. aor. διέδραμον γ 177. 3 sing. opt. διαδράμοι ε 100. To run *over*, traverse. With acc.: κέλευθα γ 177. Cf. ε 100.

†διατρέω [δια- (4)]. 3 pl. aor. διέτρεσαν. To flee in all directions: θῶες Λ 481, ἄλλυδις ἄλλος 486.

διατρίβω [δια- (10)]. **(1)** To rub down into small fragments, crumble Λ 847.—**(2)** To throw obstacles in the way of, put off, delay β 265, υ 341.—To thwart, oppose: τὸν ἐμὸν χόλον Δ 42.—**(3)** To put off (a person). With double acc. of the person and of what is delayed: Ἀχαιοὺς ὃν γάμον β 204.—**(4)** To put off time, loiter, delay T 150.—With genit., to hold back from, delay in undertaking: ὁδοῖο β 404.

διατρύγιος [δια- (8) + τρύγη. See τρυγάω]. Bearing fruit through the seasons, never failing ω 342.

διατρυφέν, nom. sing. neut. aor. pple. pass. διαθρύπτω.

διαφαίνω [δια- (1) (10)]. In pass. **(1)** To appear or be seen *through*. With genit.: ὅθι νεκύων διεφαίνετο χῶρος Θ 491 = K 199.—**(2)** To glow ι 379.

†διαφθείρω [δια- (10)]. 3 sing. fut. διαφθέρσει N 625. 2 sing. pf. διέφθορας O 128. **(1)** To destroy utterly: πόλιν N 625.—**(2)** In pf., to have lost one's wits, be beside oneself O 128.

†διαφράζω [δια- (9)]. 3 sing. aor. διεπέφραδε. To go through, say, tell Υ 340: ρ 590.—Absol. Σ 9: ζ 47.

διαφύσσω [δι-, δια- (8) (10)]. 3 sing. aor. διήφυσε τ 450. **(1)** To draw off (wine) in large quantities or constantly π 110.—**(2)** To lay open or rend (flesh) (as if to draw off the life) τ 450.

†διαχέω [δια- (5)]. 3 pl. aor. διέχευαν. To dismember or divide into joints (a sacrificial victim) H 316 := τ 421, γ 456, ξ 427.

διδάσκω [redup. fr. δα-, δάω]. 3 sing. aor. (ἐ)δίδαξε E 51, Λ 832: θ 481, 488. 1 pl. διδάξαμεν χ 422. 3 ἐδίδαξαν Ψ 307. Pf. infin. pass. δεδιδάχθαι Λ 831. **(1)** To teach, instruct (a person) Λ 832, Ψ 308: θ 488.—**(2)** To teach, impart knowledge of (something) I 442, Ψ 307: χ 422 (ἐργάζεσθαι complementary).—**(3)** With double acc. of person and thing: σφέας οἴμας θ 481.—With infin. of what is taught: βάλλειν ἄγρια πάντα E 51.—With acc. of person and this infin.: ὑψαγόρην σ' ἔμεναι α 384.—**(4)** In pass., to gain knowledge of, learn: φάρμακα δεδιδάχθαι (*i.e.* their properties) Λ 831.—With genit.: διδασκόμενος πολέμοιο (concerning war, *i.e.* the art of war) Π 811.

δίδημι [redup. fr. δε-, δέω]. = δέω (7) Λ 105: μ 54.

διδυμάων [as next]. Only in dual and pl. Twin: διδυμάονε παῖδε E 548, Z 26.—(The) twins: Ὕπνῳ καὶ Θανάτῳ διδυμάοσιν Π 672 = 682.

δίδυμος [redup. fr. δύο]. **(1)** Two, two (to one) Ψ 641.—**(2)** Double: αὐλοῖσιν τ 227.

†δίδωμι [redup. fr. δο-]. 1 sing. pres. δίδωμι Ψ 620: ο 125, υ 342. 2 διδοῖς I 164. διδοῖσθα T 270. 3 δίδωσι I 261, Υ 299, Ω 528: α 348, ρ 287, 474. διδοῖ I 519: δ 237, ρ 350. 1 pl. δίδομεν B 228, Φ 297. 3 διδοῦσι B 255, T 265: α 313, θ 167, ρ 450, σ 279. 2 pl. opt. διδοῖτε λ 357. 3 διδοῖεν σ 142. 2 sing. impf. ἐδίδους τ 367. 3 (ἐ)δίδου E 165, Z 192, H 305, etc.: θ 63, 64, λ 289, σ 191, 323, χ 236. 1 pl. δίδομεν θ 545. 3 δίδοσαν δ 585, ξ 286, etc. Imp. δίδωθι γ 380. δίδου γ 58. Pple. διδούς, -όντος I 699: α 390, λ 117, ν 378. Infin. διδοῦναι Ω 425. Pa. iterative δόσκον I 331: ρ 420, τ 76. 3 sing. δόσκε Σ 546. 3 pl. δόσκον Ξ 382. Fut. δώσω Θ 166, Ξ 238, T 144, etc.: β 223, δ 589, π 80, etc. 2 sing. -εις τ 167. 3 -ει A 96, Θ 143, I 270, etc: β 135, ξ 444, ρ 11, etc. 3 pl. -ουσι A 123, 135, I 255, K 215, X 341: δ 480, ψ 358. 1 pl. διδώσομεν ν 358. Infin. δωσέμεναι K 393, N 369: δ 7. -έμεν K 323, X 117. -ειν E 654, Z 53, T 195, etc.: ω 342. διδώσειν ω 314. Aor. ἔδωκα ι 361, ο 373. δῶκα Δ 43: δ 649, ν 273, τ 185, etc. 2 sing. ἔδωκας E 285, Φ 473, Ω 685: χ 290, ω 337. δῶκας δ 647, θ 415, ω 340. 3 ἔδωκε Θ 216, O 719, Σ 456, etc.: α 67, η 150, ξ 63, etc. δῶκε A 347, Z 193, N 727, etc.: γ 40, ι 203, κ 19, etc. 3 pl. ἔδωκαν N 303, X 379, Ψ 745: θ 440, ν 369. δῶκαν ζ 215. 1 pl. aor. ἔδομεν ω 65. δόμεν P 443. 3 ἔδοσαν T 291: ν 135, ξ 216, ρ 148, etc. δόσαν A 162, Δ 320, Π 867, etc.: η 242, ι 93, ξ 39, etc. Subj. δῶ ι 356, υ 296. 2 sing. δῷς H 27. 3 δώῃσι A 324, M 275. δώῃ Z 527, Θ 287, Π 88, etc.: μ 216, σ 87, φ 338, etc. δῷσι A 129: α 379, β 144. 1 pl. δώομεν H 299, 351: π 184. δῶμεν Ψ 537: θ 389, ν 13. 3 δώωσι A 137, I 136, 278. δῶσι Γ 66. Opt. δοίην η 314, ο 449, σ 361. 2 sing. δοίης Π 625: δ 600, ι 268, ρ 223, 455. 3 δοίη I 379, 385, P 127, 562, etc.: β 54, ζ 144, ι 229, etc. 1 pl. δοῖμεν N 378: β 336, π 386. 3 δοῖεν A 18, T 264, Ψ 650, Ω 686: ζ 180, η 148, θ 411, 413, ο 316, ω 402. Imp. δός A 338, E 359, Π 524, etc.: γ 46, ζ 178, ι 355, etc. 3 sing. δότω B 383, Λ 798, Ξ 377, Σ 301: η 166. 2 pl. δότε Z 476: β 212, ζ 209, φ 281, etc. Fem. pple. δοῦσα ο 369. Nom. pl. masc. δόντες A 299: ε 38, ψ 341. Infin. δόμεναι A 98, Δ 380, I 120, etc.: α 317, ι 518, ρ 417, etc. δόμεν Δ 379, I 571, Σ 458, 508: ρ 404. δοῦναι Λ 319, O 216, Ψ 593: α 292, 316. 3 sing. aor. opt. pass. δοθείη β 78. 3 sing. pf. δέδοται E 428. (ἀπο-, ἐκ-, ἐπι-, περι-.) **(1)** To make another the owner of, give, present: τόξον ἔδωκεν B 827, δῶρα δίδωσι (offers) I 261. Cf. B 102, E 272, Z 219, H 299, etc.: τάλαρον ἔδωκεν δ 125, ἕδνα διδόντες (offering) λ 117. Cf. α 313, 316, β 336, etc.—In reference to something immaterial: τιμῆς ἥμισυ Z 193.—To assign (a share of spoil) A 162, B 228, I 334, etc.—To make over one's rights in: ἑπτὰ πτολίεθρα I 149, 291.—**(2)** To give as a reward or prize: δύω χρυσοῖο τάλαντα Σ 508. Cf. K 305, Ψ 537, 551, 560, 616, 620, 807, etc.—**(3)** To offer (a sacrifice): θεοῖς ἑκατόμβας H 450 = M 6. Cf. α 67, π 184, τ 367.—Sim. δῶρα θεοῖσιν Υ 299. Cf. Ω 425 : ν 358.—(4) To give (food or drink), put (food or drink) before a person : δέπας οἴνου Σ 546 : ξεινήϊα γ 490. Cf. ζ 209, η 166, ι 93, etc.—To see to the due providing of (a meal) : δεῖπνον ἑταίροισιν κ 155.—Of feeding horses Β 383.—Of an eagle feeding its young Μ 222.—(5) To pay (a price) α 431, ο 388=429, 449.—To pay (ransom) Φ 41, 42, Χ 341, Ψ 746, Ω 594, 685, 686.—To make over (as compensation) : ἵππους υἱὸς ποινήν Ε 266.—To pay as bride-price Λ 243, 244.—To give (μείλια) Ι 147, 289.—(6) To give in marriage : θυγατέρα ἥν Ζ 192=Λ 226. Cf. Ν 369, 378, Ξ 268, 275, Τ 291 : α 292, β 54, 223, δ 7, λ 289, ο 367.—(7) To give or confer (something immaterial) : μέγ' εὖχος Ε 285 : γέρας η 150. Cf. Ε 654=Λ 445, Π 625, Φ 473.—Sim. : δαιμονά τοι δώσω (will deal thee . . .) Θ 166 : γαστὴρ πολλὰ κακὰ δίδωσιν ρ 287, 474.—To give or utter (an oath) τ 302.—(8) To resign one's claims to : ἵππον Ψ 553, 592, 610.—(9) To give the use of, lend : φάσγανον Κ 255. Cf. Ε 359, 363, Κ 260, Λ 798, etc. : νῆα β 212=δ 669. Cf. γ 369, δ 647, 649, ε 234, 237, ζ 144, 178, etc.—To give the services of : ἐπικούρους Δ 379, 380 : β 212=δ 669.—To give as a servant or slave ρ 223, 442.—(10) To give, commit, hand over, for some purpose : σάκος χείρονι φωτί Ξ 377. Cf. Α 324, Β 205, Ι 331, Ο 455, Ρ 127, Φ 84, etc. : ἄλεισον γ 50. Cf. γ 40, 437, ε 351, κ 33, ξ 112, φ 233, etc.—Sim. : ὀδύνησί μιν (μ') ἔδωκεν Ε 397 : ρ 567, ἀχέεσσί με δώσεις τ 167.—With infin. expressing the purpose : δός σφωϊν [κούρην] ἄγειν Α 338. Cf. Ε 26, Ζ 53, Η 471, Λ 704, Π 40, etc. : δὸς τούτῳ δέπας σπεῖσαι γ 46. Cf. σ 87, υ 78.—To give (the hand) Ψ 75.—To commit (to the flames) ω 65.—(11) Of a divine power (a) To give, grant, bestow, as a boon or in answer to prayer : ναύτῃσιν οὖρον Η 4. Cf. Α 178, Γ 66, Δ 320, Ι 38, etc. : ἐπιφροσύνην ε 437. Cf. β 116, γ 58, δ 237, η 148, θ 44, etc.—(b) To send or afflict with (something evil) : ἄλγεα Α 96. Cf. Β 375, Ι 571, Τ 264, 270, Ω 241, etc. : ἄτην δ 262. Cf. β 135, δ 237, η 242, ξ 39, etc. —(c) With infin., to empower or permit *to do something*, grant *a person's doing it* or *its being done* : ἐκπέρσαι πόλιν Α 18, τὸν δῦναι δόμον Ἄϊδος Γ 322. Cf. Α 129, Ε 118, Ζ 307, Η 203, Ρ 646, etc. : παλίντιτα ἔργα γενέσθαι α 379, ἄλοχον ἰδέειν θ 411. Cf. γ 60, ζ 327, η 110, μ 216, χ 253, etc.—To appoint as one's lot : τολυπεύειν πολέμους Ξ 86. —(d) Absol. : διάνδιχα δῶκε Κρόνου πάϊς Ι 37. Cf. Χ 285, Ω 529 : Διός γε διδόντος α 390. Cf. α 348, η 35, τ 396.—(12) Absol., to accede to one's wishes : σοὶ δῶκα ἑκὼν ἀέκοντί γε θυμῷ Δ 43.—(13) To restore (cf. (14) (a) (b)) : κτήματα Η 364. Cf. Η 391, 393, Λ 125, Χ 117.—(14) Uses with adverbs. (a) With ἀπό, to restore (cf. (13)) : πρίν γ' ἀπὸ πατρὶ δόμεναι κούρην Α 98.—To make up for, give compensation for : πρίν γ' ἀπὸ πᾶσαν ἐμοὶ δόμεναι λώβην Ι 387. Cf. β 78.—(b) With πάλιν, to restore (cf. (13)) Α 116, Η 79=Χ 342, Χ 259.

διέδραμον, 3 pl. aor. διατρέχω.

διεέργω [δι-, δια- (6)]. To keep apart, separate Μ 424.

δίειπε, contr. imp. διαεῖπον.

διείπομεν, 1 pl. impf. διέπω.

διείρομαι [δι-, δια- (9)]. To ask about at length ; or simply, to ask about Α 550.—With double acc. (cf. εἴρομαι (4)) : ταῦτά με Ο 93 : δ 492, λ 463, ω 478.

διέκ [διά strengthened by ἐκ]. Right through ; or simply, through. With genit. : προθύρου Ο 124. Cf. κ 388, ρ 61, 460, σ 101, 185=τ 503=χ 433, σ 386, τ 47=υ 144, φ 299.

διέκριθεν, 3 pl. aor. pass. διακρίνω.

†διελαύνω [δι-, δια- (1) (3)] 3 sing. aor. διήλασε. (1) To drive (horses, etc.) across something Μ 120 (across the ditch).—To drive them *across*. With genit. : τάφροιο Κ 564.—(2) To drive or thrust (a weapon) *through*. With genit. : λαπάρης ἔγχος Π 318.—To drive or thrust a weapon *through*. With genit. : ἀσπίδος Ν 161.

διελέξατο, 3 sing. aor. διαλέγομαι.

διελεύσεσθαι, fut. infin. διέρχομαι.

διελθέμεν, aor. infin. διέρχομαι.

δίεμαι [cf. δίον[2], διώκω]. Aor. sub. δίωμαι φ 370. 3 sing. δίηται Η 197, Ο 681, Π 246, Χ 189, 456. 3 pl. δίωνται Ρ 110. 3 sing. opt. δίοιτο ρ 317. (ἀπο-, ἐνδίημι.) (1) To chase, pursue Χ 189 : ρ 317 —(2) To chase away, drive off or away : λῖν Ρ 110. Cf. Μ 276, Σ 162, Χ 456 : φ 370.—Sim. : ἀπὸ ναῦφι μάχην Π 246.—To cause to retire, put to flight Η 197.—(3) To send or chase away, dismiss : ξεῖνον ἀπὸ μεγάροιο ρ 398. Cf. υ 343.—(4) To drive (horses) Ο 681.—(5) As pass. (a) To be driven off or away Μ 304.—(b) Of horses, to be driven, race Ψ 475.

†διέξειμι [δι-, δια- (1) + ἐξ- (1) + εἶμι]. Infin. (in fut. sense) διεξίμεναι. To pass through and emerge from something : πύλας, τῇ ἔμελλε διεξίμεναι πεδίονδε Ζ 393.

διεξερέομαι [δι-, δια- (9), ἐξ- (9)]. To question closely about. With double acc. : ἐμὲ ταῦτα Κ 432.

διεξίμεναι, infin. διέξειμι.

διέπερσε, 3 sing. aor. διαπέρθω.

διεπέφραδε, 3 sing. aor. διαφράζω.

διέπραθον, 3 pl. aor. διαπέρθω.

διέπτατο, 3 sing. aor. διαπέτομαι.

διέπω [δι-, δια- (10) + ἕπω[1]]. (1) To bring into order or under control : στρατόν Β 207. Cf. Ω 247.—(2) To carry on, manage Α 166.—To attend to, carry through : τὰ ἕκαστα μ 16.—To attend to, arrange, settle Λ 706.

†διερέσσω [δι-, δια- (2)]. Aor. διήρεσ(σ)α. To row or propel oneself in the water through a space μ 444 (through the strait), ξ 351 (through the water between the ship and the shore).

διερός. (1) App., living : βροτός ζ 201. —(2) App., nimble : ποσὶ ι 43.

διέρχομαι [δι-, δια- (1) (2)]. Fut. infin. διελεύσεσθαι Ν 144, Υ 263. 3 sing. aor. διῆλθε Ψ 876 : τ 453. 3 pl. opt. διέλθοιεν Κ 492. Infin. διελθέμεν Υ 100, Ω 716 : ζ 304. (1) Of a weapon, to pierce its way Υ 263, Ψ 876 : τ 453.—To pierce or pass *through*. With genit. : χροός Υ 100.—(2) To pass through or traverse a space : ὅπως ἵπποι ῥεῖα διέλθοιεν Κ 492. Cf. Ω 716.—To pass *through* or traverse. With genit. : μεγάροιο ζ 304.—With acc. : ἄστυ Ζ 392. Cf. Γ 198, Ν 144.

διεσκέδασε, 3 sing. aor. διασκεδάννυμι.

διέσσυτο, 3 sing. aor. mid. διασεύω.

διέσταμεν, 1 pl. pf. διΐστημι.

διέστησαν, 3 pl. aor. διΐστημι.

διέσχε, 3 sing. aor. διέχω.

διέσχισε, 3 sing. aor. **διεσχίσθη**, 3 sing. aor. pass. διασχίζω.

διέτμαγον, aor. διατμήγω.

διέτρεσαν, 3 pl. aor. διατρέω.

διέφθορας, 2 sing. pf. διαφθείρω.

διέχευαν, 3 pl. aor. διαχέω.

†**διέχω** [δι-, δια- (1)]. 3 sing. aor. διέσχε. To pass through, hold its way : [ὀϊστός] Ε 100. Cf. Λ 253, Υ 416.

δίζημαι [prob. a non-thematic redup. pres. = ζητέω]. 2 sing. δίζηαι λ 100. 1 pl. aor. subj. διζησόμεθα π 239. (1) To seek for, try to find (a person or a strayed animal) : Πάνδαρον Δ 88. Cf. Ε 168, Κ 84, Ν 760 : ἵππους φ 22. Cf. ο 90.—To seek out, try to get the help of : ἄλλους π 239.—(2) To seek after, try to acquire or have : φάρμακον α 261. Cf. Ρ 221.—To strive after, seek to achieve : νόστον λ 100, ψ 253.—(3) To seek in marriage, woo π 391 = φ 161.

δίζυξ, -υγος [δι-, δισ- + ζυγόν]. Yoked, or meant to be yoked, in pairs : ἵπποι Ε 195, Κ 473.

δίζω [prob. thematic form answering to δίζημαι]. To be in doubt, hesitate : ἠὲ . . . ἦ . . . Π 713.

διήγαγον, 3 pl. aor. διάγω.

διηκόσιοι [δι-, δισ- + ἑκατόν]. Two hundred Ι 383.—Absol. Θ 233.

διήλασε, 3 sing. aor. διελαύνω.

διῆλθε, 3 sing. aor. διέρχομαι.

διηνεκέως [adv. fr. next]. Right through, at length : ἀγορεῦσαι η 241.—Fully, plainly, in detail δ 836, μ 56.

διηνεκής [δι-, δια- (8) + ἐνεκ-. See φέρω]. Carried straight through, straight : ὦλκα σ 375.—Without break or obstruction : ἀτραπιτοί ν 195.—Continuous : νώτοισιν (slices cut the whole length of the back) Η 321 : ξ 437 —Thrown out far, far-stretching : ῥίζῃσιν Μ 134.—Carried right round : ῥάψε ῥάβδοισι διηνεκέσιν περὶ κύκλον Μ 297.

διήνυσε, 3 sing. aor. διανύω.

διήρεσ(σ)α, aor. διερέσσω.

δίηται, 3 sing. aor. subj. δίεμαι.

διήφυσε, 3 sing. aor. διαφύσσω.

†**διικνέομαι** [δι-, δια- (9)]. Fut. διΐξομαι Ι 61. 2 sing. aor. διίκεο Τ 186. To go through in speaking : πάντα Ι 61, Τ 186.

διϊπετής [app. fr. Διί, dat. of Ζεύς + πε-, πίπτω]. Thus, falling in the sky, *i.e.* rain-fed ; or poss., falling by the power or ordinance of Zeus. Epithet of rivers Π 174, Ρ 263, Φ 268, 326 : δ 477, 581, η 284.

διΐστημι [δι-, δια- (6)]. 3 dual aor. διαστήτην Α 6, Π 470. 3 pl. διέστησαν Ω 718. Nom. pl. masc. pple. διαστάντες Μ 86, Ρ 391. 1 pl. pf. διέσταμεν Φ 436. (1) In aor. and mid. (a) To stand apart or aside : διαστάντες (severing, parting, *i.e.* in order to form themselves into bodies) Μ 86, τὼ [ἵππω] διαστήτην (wheeled apart, *i.e.* with their hind quarters) Π 470, διαστάντες (taking their stand at (regular) intervals) Ρ 391, διέστησαν καὶ εἶξαν ἀπήνῃ (stood aside, parted this way and that) Ω 718.—(b) Of the sea, to part, be cleft Ν 29.—(c) To come into variance, quarrel Α 6.—(2) In pf., to have one's stand, stand, apart : τίη διέσταμεν ; (why do we not come to close quarters ?) Φ 436.

διΐφιλος [Διί, dat. of Ζεύς + φίλος. Prob. better written thus than Διὶ φίλος. Cf. διιπετής, which is clearly a compound]. Dear to Zeus, favoured by Zeus Α 74, 86, Β 628, Ζ 318, Θ 493, 517, Ι 168, Κ 49, 527, Λ 419, 473, 611, Ν 674, Π 169, Σ 203, Χ 216, Ω 472.

δικάζω [δίκη]. Fut. δικάσω Ψ 579. 3 pl. aor. δίκασαν λ 547. Imp. pl. δικάσσατε Ψ 574. (1) To pronounce judgment, give a decision Σ 506, Ψ 574, 579 : λ 547.—(2) To form a decision, come to a resolve Α 542, Θ 431 (lay down the law for . . .).—(3) In mid., to seek a judgment or decision, plead one's cause λ 545, μ 440.

δίκαιος [δίκη]. (1) Conforming to the traditional order of society, observing the usages common to civilized men, civilized ζ 120 = ι 175 = ν 201, θ 575.—In superl. δικαιότατος Λ 832, Ν 6.—(2) Mindful of the usages of courtesy, well-bred γ 52.—(3) Acting with due regard to what is right, upright, honourable β 282, γ 133, ν 209.—In comp. δικαιότερος Τ 181.—(4) Absol. in neut. δίκαιον, something right or proper : ἐπὶ ῥηθέντι δικαίῳ (when the right word has been spoken) σ 414 = υ 322.—οὐ δ. with infin., (it is) not right or proper *to* : ἀτέμβειν υ 294, φ 312.

δικαίως [adv. fr. prec.]. In due or proper wise ξ 90.

δικασπόλος [δίκας, acc. pl. of δίκη + -πολος, conn. with πολεύω]. Busied about judgments, administering justice Α 238 : λ 186.

δίκη, -ης, ἡ. (1) Custom, usage, way : βασιλήων δ 691. Cf. σ 275, τ 43.—With notion of privilege : γερόντων ω 255.—Applied to a mode of existence or action imposed from without : δμώων ξ 59. Cf. λ 218.—Something that always happens in specified circumstances τ 168.—(2) Right, justice Π 388, Τ 180 : ξ 84.—In pl., rules of right, principles of justice : οὐ δίκας εἰδότα οὐδὲ θέμιστας (having no regard for justice or the usages of (civilized) men ; see εἴδω (III) (12)) ι 215. Cf. γ 244.—(3) A judgment or doom : ὃς Λυκίην εἴρυτο δίκῃσιν (by his (impartial) administration of justice) Π 542. Cf. Σ 508.—(4) A plea of right, a claim : δίκας εἴροντο (were asking questions about their . . . , seeking decisions in regard to them) λ 570. Cf. Ψ 542.

δικλίς, -ίδος [δι-, δισ- + κλίνω]. Of gates or

doors, double : πύλας δικλίδας M 455. Cf. β 345, ρ 268.

δίκτυον, -ου, τό. A fishing-net χ 386.

δῑνεύω [δίνη]. 3 sing. pa. iterative δινεύεσκε Ω 12. (1) To turn (one's team) this way and that Σ 543.—(2) To whirl oneself about, spin round. Of acrobats Σ 606 := δ 19.—Of a bird, to circle or wheel in flight Ψ 875.—(3) To wander, rove, roam. Δ 541, Ω 12 : τ 67.

δῑνέω [as prec.]. (ἀμφι-, ἐπι-.) (1) To whirl round (before throwing) : σόλον Ψ 840.—To cause to revolve: μοχλόν ι 384, 388.—(2) To whirl oneself about, spin round. Of dancers Σ 494.—(3) In pass. (a) To go in a circle: πόλιν πέρι δινηθήτην X 165.—(b) To wander, rove, roam ι 153, π 63.—(c) Of the eyes, to be turned in various directions, wander P 680.

δίνη, -ης, ἡ. An eddy or whirlpool (in a river) Φ 11, 132, 213, 239, 246, 353 : ζ 116.

δῑνήεις, -εντος [δίνη]. Eddying, whirling. Epithet of rivers. Of the Lycian Xanthus B 877, E 479.—Of the Trojan Xanthus (Scamander) Θ 490, Ξ 434 = Φ 2 = Ω 693, Φ 125, 206, 332, X 148.—Of other rivers Υ 392 : ζ 89, λ 242.

δῑνωτός, -ή, -όν [δινόω fr. δῖνος = δίνη]. (Cf. ἀμφιδινέω.) (1) App., adorned with inlaid circles or spirals of a precious material Γ 391 : τ 56.—(2) App., ornamented with rings or round pieces of specified materials N 407.

δῑογενής [δι-ο-, fr. Δι- of oblique cases of Ζεύς + γεν-, γίγνομαι]. Sprung from Zeus. Epithet of heroes A 337, 489, B 173, Δ 489, I 106, Λ 810, Ψ 294, etc.—In *Od.* always of Odysseus β 352, ε 203, θ 3, κ 443, etc.

Διόθεν [Δι-ο- as in prec. + -θεν (1)]. (1) From, sent by, Zeus Ω 194, 561.—(2) By his power or will O 489.

διοϊστεύω [δι-, δια- (1) (2)]. (1) To shoot an arrow *through*. With genit. : πελέκεων τ 578 = φ 76. Cf. τ 587, φ 97 = 127, φ 114.—(2) To shoot an arrow over an indicated space μ 102.

δίοιτο, 3 sing. aor. opt. δίεμαι.

†διόλλῡμι [δι-, δια- (10)]. 3 sing. pf. διόλωλε. To go to ruin : οἶκος ἐμὸς διόλωλε β 64.

δίον[1], *aor.* [δFι-, δείδοικα]. To be afraid E 566, I 433, Λ 557.—With μή and opt. P 666 : χ 96.

δίον[2], *aor.* [Cf. δίεμαι.] To flee, run X 251.

διοπτεύω [δι-, δια- (10) + ὀπτεύω fr. ὀπ-. See ὁράω]. (ἐποπτεύω.) To act the spy K 451.

διοπτήρ, -ῆρος, ὁ [cf. prec.]. A spy K 562.

δῖος, δῖα, δῖον [Δι- of oblique cases of Zeus]. (1) Of Zeus : δῖον γένος I 538 (= Διὸς κούρη 536).—(2) (a) Bright, shining. Of the sea A 141, B 152, Ξ 76, etc. : γ 153, δ 577, ε 261, etc.—Of rivers (or perh. rather = διιπετής) B 522, M 21.—Of the dawn I 240, Λ 723, Σ 255, etc. : ι 151, λ 375, π 368, etc.—Of the αἰθήρ Π 365 : τ 540.—Of the earth Ξ 347, Ω 532.—(b) (α) Of goddesses, bright, resplendent, glorious B 820, Γ 389, 413, E 370, K 290 (here, of Athene, perh. rather in sense (1) = Διὸς τέκος 284) : ε 263, 321, 372, μ 133, υ 68, 73.—Applied to Charybdis μ 104, 235.—(β) With superl. sense : δῖα θεάων, bright, etc., among goddesses (partitive genit.), brightest, etc., of goddesses (cf. (3) (b) (β)) E 381, Z 305, Ξ 184, etc. : α 14, δ 382, κ 400, etc.—(3) An epithet of general commendation. (a) Of men, noble, illustrious, goodly, or the like A 7, 145, B 57, 221, Γ 329, Δ 319, E 211, Z 31, K 285, Ξ 3, P 705, Ω 618, etc. : α 196, 284, 298, γ 439, δ 655, λ 168, 522, ξ 3, φ 240, etc.—Sim. of peoples or bodies of men : Ἀχαιοί E 451. Cf. K 429, Λ 455, 504, Σ 241, Υ 354 : γ 116, τ 177, 199.—(b) (α) Of women, noble, queenly, or the like E 70, Z 160, P 40 : γ 266.—(β) With superl. sense : δῖα γυναικῶν, pearl of women (cf. (2) (b) (β)) B 714, Γ 171, 228, 423 : α 332, δ 305, υ 147, etc.—(c) Of horses, noble, well-bred, or the like Θ 185, Ψ 346 (here perh. rather in sense (1), 'divine'; cf. 347).—(d) Of cities, etc., famed, rich, or the like B 615, 836, Λ 686, 698, Φ 43 : γ 326, δ 313, 702 = ε 20, ν 275, 440, ο 298, ρ 121, ω 431.

διοτρεφής [δι-ο- (cf. διογενής) + τρέφω]. Nourished or cherished by Zeus. Epithet of kings, chiefs, etc. A 176, B 660, E 463, H 109, Λ 648, etc. : γ 480, δ 26, ε 378, η 49, χ 136, etc.—Absol. in voc. I 229, P 685, Φ 75, etc. : δ 391, κ 266, 419, ο 155, 199, ω 122.

δίπλαξ, -ακος [δι-, δισ-. For the second element cf. next]. (1) Double, applied in two layers : δημῷ Ψ 243. Cf. Ψ 253.—(2) As fem. sb., a χλαῖνα intended to be worn double Γ 126, X 441 : τ 241.

διπλόος [δι-, δισ-. For the second element cf. ἁ-πλοΐς and prec.]. Contr. acc. sing. fem. διπλῆν K 134 : τ 226. (1) Worn double : χλαῖναν K 134 : τ 226.—(2) Of the θώρηξ, consisting of two plates : ὅθι ζωστῆρος ὀχῆες σύνεχον καὶ δ. ἤντετο θώρηξ Δ 133 = Υ 415 (*i.e.* where the two plates met (and overlapped) at the sides. But there is great confusion in these passages. The belt would naturally be fastened in front, not at the side ; and in Υ the wound is behind).

δίπτυχος, -ον [δι-, δισ- + πτυχ-, πτύξ]. From δίπτυξ acc. sing. fem. δίπτυχα (cf. ὑπόβρυξ). (1) Worn double : δίπτυχον λώπην ν 224.—(2) In a double fold : δίπτυχα [κνίσην] ποιήσαντες (*i.e.* folding it with a double fold so as to enclose the sacrificial joints) A 461 = B 424 := γ 458 = μ 361.

δίς [δύο]. Twice : δὶς τόσσον ι 491.

δισθανής [δισ- + θαν-, θνήσκω]. Dying twice μ 22 (*i.e.* with a second death to face).

δισκέω [δίσκος]. To engage in a contest of throwing the δίσκος : ἀλλήλοισιν (with . . .) θ 188.

δίσκος, -ου, ὁ. A mass of stone for distance-throwing as a trial of strength or skill Ψ 431, B 774 := δ 626 = ρ 168, θ 129, 186.

δίσκουρα, τά Ψ 523 = δίσκου οὖρα. See οὖρον (3).

δῑφάω. To seek for, search for Π 747.

δίφρος, -ου, ὁ [contr. fr. διφόρος fr. δι-, δισ- + -φορος, φέρω. 'Something that carries two,' *i.e.* (in war) the ἡνίοχος and the παραιβάτης]. (1) (a) A chariot, whether used in war, for racing, for travel or for conveyance in general (hardly to be distinguished from ἅρμα) Γ 262, 310, Ε 20, Ν 392, Ψ 335, 370, Ω 322, etc.: γ 324, 369, 481, 483, δ 590, ξ 280.—(b) The platform thereof, composed of straps plaited and strained tight Ε 727.—(2) A seat (the notion of 'two' app. lost) Γ 424, Ζ 354, Ω 578: δ 717, ρ 330, τ 97, υ 259, etc.

δίχα [δι-, δίς]. (1) In two: δ. ἑταίρους ἠρίθμεον (into two bodies) κ 203, δ. σφισὶ πάντα δέδασται (between them) ο 412.—(2) In two ways: δ. σφισὶν ἥνδανε βουλή (they were divided in opinion) Σ 510: γ 150, βάζομεν (in disagreement, at variance) γ 127.—So of favouring different sides, taking different parts: δ. θυμὸν ἔχοντες Υ 32. Cf. Φ 386.—Of doubt or hesitation: δ. μερμήριζεν (was in two minds) χ 333. Cf. π 73, τ 524.

διχθά [as prec.]. (1) = prec. (1) α 23 (into two tribes).—(2) = prec. (2). Of doubt, etc. Π 435.

διχθάδιος, -η, -ον [διχθά]. (1) Two (and different): κῆρας Ι 411.—(2) In neut. pl. διχθάδια as adv. = δίχα (2). Of doubt, etc. Ξ 21.

δίψα, -ης, ἡ. Thirst Λ 642, Τ 166, Φ 541, Χ 2.

διψάω [δίψα]. To be athirst: διψάων (in (his) thirst) λ 584.

†**διωθέω** [δι-, δια- (5)]. 3 sing. aor. διῶσε. To tear asunder, rend: κρημνὸν [πτελέη] διῶσεν Φ 244.

διώκω [cf. δίεμαι]. 3 dual impf. διώκετον Κ 364. (1) To chase, pursue Ε 65, 672, Θ 339, Κ 359, 364, Ν 64, Π 598, Ρ 463, Φ 3, 601, Χ 8, 157, 158, 168, 173, 199, 200, 230: ο 278.—In mid. Φ 602.—Absol.: διωκέμεν ἠδὲ φέβεσθαι Ε 223 = Θ 107.—(2) To send away, chase away σ 409.—In mid. σ 8.—(3) To pursue, seek to win: ἀκίχητα Ρ 75.—(4) To drive (a chariot) Θ 439.—Absol. Ψ 344, 424, 499, 547.—(5) Of a wind, to drive (a vessel) ε 332.—(6) Of rowers, to propel (a vessel). Absol.: ῥίμφα διώκοντες μ 182.—In pass., of a vessel, to be propelled by any agency, course along: ῥίμφα διωκομένη ν 162.

δίωμαι, aor. subj. δίεμαι.

διῶσε, 3 sing. aor. subj. διωθέω.

δμηθήτω, 3 sing. aor. imp. pass. δαμάζω.

δμῆσις, ἡ [δμη-, δαμάζω]. Control, handling Ρ 476.

δμήτειρα, ἡ [as prec.]. The subduer (cf. πανδαμάτωρ): Νὺξ δ. θεῶν καὶ ἀνδρῶν Ξ 259.

δμῳή, -ῆς, ἡ [δμ-, δαμάζω]. A bondwoman, a female servant (cf. ἀμφίπολος) Ζ 375, 376, Ι 658, Σ 28, Χ 449, Ψ 550, Ω 582, 587, 643: α 147, β 412, δ 49, ζ 307, ο 461, ρ 34, etc.—Of Calypso's servants ε 199.—With γυνή. See γυνή (3).

δμώς, -ωός, ὁ [as prec.]. Genit. pl. δμώων α 398, ι 206, ξ 59, ρ 402, etc. Dat. δμώεσσι ζ 71, λ 431, ο 379, ω 213, etc. δμωσί ρ 389. A bondman, a man-servant Τ 333: = η 225, δ 644, ζ 69, λ 190, ρ 299, ω 210, etc.—With ἀνήρ π 305.

δνοπαλίζω. 2 sing. fut. δνοπαλίξεις ξ 512. App., to knock aside or about, or, to shake: ἀνὴρ ἄνδρ' ἐδνοπάλιζεν Δ 472.—Of clothes, app., metaphorically, to knock them about; or perh., to flutter or flaunt them: τὰ σὰ ῥάκεα δνοπαλίξεις ξ 512.

δνοφερός, -ή, -όν [δνόφος, darkness]. (1) Dark, devoid of light ν 269, ο 50.—(2) Dark in hue Ι 15 = Π 4.

δοάσσατο, 3 *sing. aor.* [app. conn. with δοκέω]. 3 sing. subj. δοάσσεται Ψ 339. To seem, appear. With infin.: ἄκρον ἱκέσθαι Ψ 339.—Impers.: κέρδιον εἶναι Ν 458 = Ξ 23 = Π 652: = ο 204 = σ 93 = χ 338 = ω 239, ε 474 = ζ 145, κ 153.

δοθείη, 3 sing. aor. opt. pass. δίδωμι.

δοιή, -ῆς, ἡ [δοιός]. Doubt Ι 230.

δοίην, aor. opt. δίδωμι.

δοιός, -ή, -όν [δύο]. (1) Two Γ 236, Δ 7, Ε 206, 728 (see under ἄντυξ (1)), Λ 431, 634, Μ 455, 464, Ν 126, Π 326, Σ 605, Τ 310, Χ 148, Ψ 194, Ω 527, 608, 609, 648: δ 18, 129, 526, ε 476, κ 84, π 253, 296, τ 562.—(2) In neut. pl. δοιά as adv., in two ways, in double wise: κακὸν ἔμπεσεν οἴκῳ β 46.

δοκεύω [δοκ-, δέχομαι]. To watch, keep an eye upon: μεταστρεφθέντα (for his turning away) Ν 545, Ὠρίωνα Σ 488: = ε 274. Cf. Θ 340, Π 313, Ψ 325.

δοκέω. (1) To seem, appear. With infin.: ὃς δοκέει χαριέστατος εἶναι Ζ 90. Cf. Ψ 459, 470: α 227, β 33, ε 342, ζ 258, θ 388, ρ 415, σ 18, 125, υ 93.—Impers.: ὥς μοι δοκεῖ εἶναι ἄριστα Ι 103 = 314 = Ν 735. Cf. Ζ 338, Μ 215: α 376 = β 141, ε 360, ν 154, σ 354, ψ 130.—(2) To seem likely to . . . With fut. infin.: οὔ μοι δοκέει μύθοιο τελευτὴ κρανέεσθαι Ι 625.—(3) To seem or appear to oneself, think oneself. With infin.: δοκέεις τις μέγας ἔμμεναι σ 382.—(4) To think, suppose, fancy, imagine. With pres. infin.: δόκησε σφίσι θυμὸς ὣς ἔμεν ὡς εἰ . . . κ 415.—With fut. infin.: νικησέμεν Η 192.

δοκός, ἡ [δοκ-, δέχομαι]. A beam supporting a roof τ 38, χ 176, 193.—A piece of timber intended to be used as such a beam Ρ 744.

δόλιος, -η, -ον [δόλος]. (1) Characterized by or showing craft or guile δ 455, 529, ι 282.—(2) Craftily and skilfully arranged: κύκλον δ 792.

δολίχαυλος, -ον [δολιχός + αὐλός (3)]. With long αὐλός: αἰγανέας ι 156 (meaning simply 'long'; the second element not to be pressed).

δολιχεγχής [δολιχός + ἔγχος] With long spears Φ 155.

δολιχήρετμος, -ον [δολιχός + ἐρετμόν]. With long oars. Epithet of the Phaeacians θ 191 = 369 = ν 166.—Of ships δ 499, τ 339, ψ 176.

δολιχός, -ή, -όν. (1) Long Δ 533, Η 255, Ι 86, Ν 162, Ο 474, Ρ 607: γ 169, δ 393, 483, ρ 426, τ 448.—Of time: νύκτα δολιχὴν σχέθεν (so as to be . . .) ψ 243.—Of a disease, long drawn-out, protracted λ 172.—(2) In neut. sing. δολιχόν as adv., for a long time, for long, long Κ 52.

δολιχόσκιος [doubtfully explained as fr. δολιχός + σκιή, 'casting a long shadow,' 'long']. Epithet of spears: ἔγχος Γ 346, 355, Ε 15, Ζ 44, Η 213, Ν 509, Π 801, Υ 262, Φ 139, Ψ 798, etc.: τ 438, χ 95, 97, ω 519, 522.

δολόεις, -εσσα [δόλος]. (1) Crafty, wily η 245, ι 32.—(2) Craftily or cunningly made θ 281.

δολομήτης, -ου [δόλος + μῆτις]. Crafty of counsel, wily. Absol. in voc. δολομῆτα Α 540.

δολόμητις [as prec.]. =prec. α 300=γ 198= 308, γ 250, δ 525, λ 422.

δόλος, -ου, ὁ. (1) Bait for catching fish μ 252.—(2) Any cunningly made contrivance for ensnaring or bringing into one's power. Of the bonds forged by Hephaestus θ 276, 282, 317.—Of the Trojan horse θ 494.—(3) Any cunning or crafty contrivance, a trick or stratagem Γ 202, Δ 339, Z 187, Λ 430, O 14, Σ 526 : β 93, γ 119, 122, δ 437, 453, ε 356, ι 19, 422, κ 232, 258, 380, λ 439, ν 292, 293, τ 137, ω 128.—(4) Guile, craft, cunning, trickery: ἔπεφνε δόλῳ H 142. Cf. Φ 599, 604, Ψ 585 : ἠὲ δόλῳ ἢ ἀμφαδόν α 296, λ 120. Cf. β 106=ω 141, β 368, ι 406, 408, τ 212.—(The) contrivance or plotting: ὑπ' Αἰγίσθοιο δόλῳ γ 235. Cf. δ 92.—Craftiness, cunning: δόλου οὐ λήθετο Ψ 725. Cf. ψ 321.

δολοφρονέω [δόλος + φρονέω]. To have guile in one's heart, plan trickery Γ 405, Ξ 197, 300 =329=T 106 : κ 339, σ 51=φ 274.

δολοφροσύνη, -ης, ἡ [δολόφρων, fr. δόλος + φρήν]. Trickery, deceit T 112.—In pl.: δολοφροσύνῃς ἀπάτησεν T 97.

δόμεν[1], 1 pl. aor. δίδωμι.

δόμεν[2], **δόμεναι**, aor. infin. δίδωμι.

δόμονδε [acc. of δόμος + -δε (1)]. (1) To the house χ 479, ω 220.—(2) Home, to one's home Ω 717.—So ὅνδε δόμονδε Π 445 : α 83=ξ 424= υ 239=φ 204, γ 272, ρ 527, υ 329.

δόμος, -ου, ὁ [δεμ-, δέμω. Cf. δῶμα, L. *domus*]. (1) A house or abode B 513, 701, I 382, K 267, Σ 290, Ω 673, etc. : α 126, δ 43, ζ 302, π 274, σ 8, υ 361, etc.—In pl. in the same sense: δόμοις ἔνι ποιητοῖσιν E 198. Cf. Z 370, Λ 132, Ξ 202, Ψ 84, etc. : α 380, γ 313, ζ 303, ο 465, etc.—(2) Of the house or realm of Hades: δόμον Ἄϊδος Γ 322. Cf. H 131, Λ 263, Ξ 457, Υ 336, Ω 246 : ι 524, κ 512, λ 69, 150, 627, ψ 252, 322.—So in pl.: Ἀΐδαο δόμοισιν X 52, 482, Ψ 19=179, Ψ 103 : δ 834= ω 264, κ 175, 491=564, ξ 208, ο 350, υ 208, ω 204.—(3) A temple: Ἐρεχθῆος η 81. Cf. Z 89.—(4) Of a nest of wasps or bees M 169.—Of a sheepfold M 301=ζ 134.—(5) With a distinguishing word: χαλκήϊον σ 328 (see χαλκήϊος).—(6) Applied to particular parts of a house. (a) To Penelope's quarters α 330, φ 5.—(b) To the μέγαρον (sometimes difficult to say whether the word should be taken in this restricted sense): δόμον κάτα δαινυμένοισιν ρ 332. Cf. β 322, η 144, χ 199, 291, 381, 440, 455.

δονακεύς [δόναξ]. A thicket of reeds Σ 576.

δόναξ, -ακος, ὁ [δονέω]. (1) A reed K 467 : ξ 474.—(2) The shaft of an arrow: ἐκλάσθη δ. Λ 584.

δονέω. (1) To shake, cause to quiver P 55.—(2) To drive about, put in commotion: βόας οἶστρος χ 300.—Of the wind driving clouds M 157.

δόντες, nom. pl. masc. aor. pple. δίδωμι.

δόξα, -ης, ἡ [δοξ-, δοκέω]. What one expects: ἀπὸ δόξης (away from, *i.e.* such or so as to fall short of or disappoint, expectation) K 324 : λ 344.

δορός, -οῦ, ὁ [δέρω]. A leathern bag β 354, 380.

δορπέω [δόρπον]. To take δόρπον Ψ 11 : η 215, θ 539, ο 302 (twice).

δόρπον, -ου, τό. The evening meal, taken after the day's work, whether of fighting or of a peaceful occupation H 370, 380, 466, Θ 503, I 66, 88, Λ 730, Σ 245, 298, 314, T 208, Ψ 55, Ω 2, 444, 601 : β 20, δ 213 (see δεῖπνον (1) (h)), 429=574, 786, η 13, 166, θ 395, ι 291, 344, μ 283, 292, 307, 439, ν 31, 34, 280, ξ 347, 407, 408, π 453, σ 44, τ 402, υ 392, φ 428.

δόρυ, τό. Genit. δουρός (for δορϜός) Γ 61, P 295, Ψ 529, etc. : τ 453. δούρατος Λ 357. Dat. δουρί A 303, O 420, X 246, etc. : θ 229, π 441, χ 92, etc. δούρατι N 77 : ε 371. Nom. dual δοῦρε K 76 : σ 377. Acc. δοῦρε Γ 18, M 298, Φ 145, etc. : α 256, μ 228, π 295, χ 101, 125. Nom. pl. δοῦρα B 135, Λ 571, T 361, etc. : μ 441. δούρατα E 656, M 36, N 264 : ε 361. Genit. δούρων X 243 : ρ 384. Dat. δούρεσσι M 303 : θ 528. δούρασι Φ 162. Acc. δοῦρα E 495, Z 3, Ω 450, etc. : ε 243, μ 443, χ 144, etc. δούρατα E 618, N 260, P 234, etc. : ε 162, χ 110, 251, etc. (1) A shoot or stem of a tree ζ 167.—(2) A tree-trunk, a piece of timber in the rough: δοῦρα κέρσαντες Ω 450. Cf. Γ 61 : ε 162, 243.—(3) A beam, plank, or log: δοῦρα νεῶν B 135. Cf. M 36, O 410, P 744 : τέκτονα δούρων ρ 384. Cf. ε 361, 370, 371, ι 384, 498, μ 441, 443.—Something made of beams or planks. Applied to the Trojan horse θ 507.—(4) The shaft of a spear: πῆλε κόλον δ. Π 117 (perh. δ. in 114 should be taken in the same sense).—(5) A spear B 382, Δ 490, Θ 258, N 130, P 355, Φ 145, etc. : α 256, θ 229, λ 532, ξ 277, π 295, χ 101, etc.—Used in hunting Φ 577 : κ 162, 164, τ 448, 453.—In guarding a sheepfold M 303.—Personified: εἰ καὶ ἐμὸν δ. μαίνεται Θ 111.—Fig.: δουρὶ δ' ἐμῷ κτεάτισσα Π 57. Cf. Π 708, Σ 341.

δός, aor. imp. δίδωμι.

δόσαν, 3 pl. aor. δίδωμι.

δόσις, ἡ [δο-, δίδωμι]. (1) A gift: δ. ὀλίγη τε φίλη τε (*i.e.* even a small gift is welcome) ζ 208. Cf. K 213 : ξ 58, σ 287.—(2) A giving for use, a loan δ 651.

δόσκον, pa. iterative δίδωμι.

δότε, aor. imp. pl. δίδωμι.

δοτήρ, -ῆρος, ὁ [δο-, δίδωμι]. One who gives out or distributes: ταμίαι, σίτοιο δοτῆρες T 44.

δότω, 3 sing. aor. imp. δίδωμι.

δούλειος [δοῦλος, a slave. Cf. next]. Of a slave: δούλειον ἐπιπρέπει (show like a slave's) ω 252.

δούλη, -ης, ἡ [cf. prec.]. A female slave: γένετ' ἐκ δούλης (*i.e.* a captive) δ 12. Cf. Γ 409.

δούλιος = δούλειος: δούλιον ἦμαρ. See ἦμαρ (4) (c).

δουλιχόδειρος [δο(υ)λιχός + δειρή]. Long-necked: κύκνων B 460 = O 692.

δουλοσύνη, -ης, ἡ [as δούλειος]. Slavery χ 423.

δοῦναι, aor. infin. δίδωμι.

δουπέω (γδουπέω) [δοῦπος]. 3 pl. aor. ἐγδούπησαν Λ 45. Genit. sing. masc. pf. pple. δεδουπότος Ψ 679 (app. formed direct fr. δοῦπος. Cf. ἀρημένος, κεκοπώς, πεφυζότες.) (ἐν-.) (1) To give forth a sound: δούπησε πεσών (fell with a thud) Δ 504=

E 42=540=N 187=P 50=311, E 617, Λ 449, N 373, 442, O 421, 524, 578, Π 325, 401, 599, 822, P 580, Υ 388: χ 94, ω 525.—App., to thunder Λ 45.—(2) To fall in fight, be slain N 426.—App., simply, to die: δεδουπότος Οἰδιπόδαο Ψ 679.

δοῦπος, -ου, ὁ (γδοῦπος. Cf. ἐρίγδουπος). A sound or noise. Of the roaring of the sea ε 401, μ 202.—Of the roar of rushing and meeting waters Δ 455.—Of noise or din in battle: ἐς δοῦπον ἀκόντων (to where the sound is, *i.e.* to battle) Λ 364=Υ 451, δοῦπον ἀκόντων (the whiz) Π 361, τεῖχος ὕπερ δ. ὀρώρει M 289. Cf. I 573, Π 635.—Of the sound of persons approaching or moving: ἐπερχομένων δ. Ψ 234. Cf. K 354: κ 556, π 10.

δουράτεος [δουρατ-, δόρυ]. Made of beams or planks. Of the Trojan horse θ 493, 512.

δούρατος, genit. δόρυ.

δουρηνεκής [δουρ-, δόρυ + ἐνεκ-. See φέρω]. In neut. sing. δουρηνεκές as adv., as far as a spear 'carries,' a spear-throw: ἄπεσαν K 357.

δουρικλειτός [δουρί, dat. of δόρυ + κλειτός]. Famous with, *i.e.* for, the spear, renowned in fight. Epithet of Menelaus E 55, 578, K 230, Ψ 355: ο 52, ρ 116, 147.—Of Diomedes Λ 333.

δουρικλυτός [as prec. + κλυτός]. =prec. Epithet of Idomeneus B 645, 650, E 45, N 210, 467, 476.—Of Tlepolemus B 657.—Of Meges E 72.—Of Diomedes K 109, Ψ 681.—Of Agastrophus Λ 368.—Of Odysseus Λ 396, 401, 661=Π 26.—Of the Lesser Aias Ξ 446.—Of Automedon Π 472.—Of Meriones Π 619.—Of Achilles Φ 233.—Of Peiraeus ο 544, ρ 71.

δουρικτητός, -ή [as prec. + κτητός]. Won by the spear, a captive. Of Briseïs I 343.

δουροδόκη, -ης, ἡ [δουρ-, δόρυ + δοκ-, δέχομαι]. A rack or stand for holding spears α 128.

δουρός, genit. δόρυ.

δοῦσα, aor. pple. fem. δίδωμι.

δόχμιος. =next. In neut. pl. δόχμια as adv., across-hill: ἄναντα κάταντα πάραντά τε δ. τε Ψ 116 (hardly to be distinguished from πάραντα).

δοχμός (ἀποδοχμόω). Taking a slanting direction: ἀΐσσοντε (slantwise) M 148.

δράγμα, -ατος, τό [δραγ-, δράσσομαι]. An armful; in reaping, the corn cut by a sweep of the sickle, a swath Λ 69, Σ 552.

δραγμεύω [as prec.] In reaping, to pick up the cut corn in armfuls Σ 555.

δραίνω [desiderative fr. δράω]. To be for doing, be minded to do: εἴ τι δραίνεις K 96.

δράκων, -οντος, ὁ [prob. fr. δρακ-, δέρκομαι]. (With fem. reference in Z 181.) A serpent or snake B 308, Γ 33, Z 181, Λ 26, 39, M 202=220, X 93: δ 457.

δράμε, 3 sing. aor. τρέχω.

†**δράσσομαι**. Pf. pple. δεδραγμένος. To clutch at, grasp. With genit.: κόνιος δεδραγμένος N 393 =Π 486.

δρατός [metathesis of δαρτός, fr. δέρω]. Skinned, flayed: σώματα Ψ 169.

†**δράω**. Opt. δρώοιμι. (παρα-, ὑπο-.) To do, accomplish: ἄσσ' ἐθέλοιεν ο 317.

δρεπάνη, -ης, ἡ [δρέπω]. A sickle Σ 551.

δρέπανον, -ου, τό [as prec.]. =prec. σ 368.

δρέπω. To pluck, pick off. In mid. μ 357.

δρήστειρα, ἡ [fem. of next]. A female servant: αἳ δῶμα κάτα δρήστειραι ἔασιν τ 345. Cf. κ 349.

δρηστήρ, -ῆρος, ὁ [agent-noun fr. δράω]. A manservant π 248, σ 76, υ 160.

δρηστοσύνη, -ης, ἡ [δράω]. Domestic service, household work ο 321.

δρῑμύς, -εῖα, -ύ. Of the pains of childbirth, sharp, piercing Λ 270.—Of wrath, bitter, piercing Σ 322.—Of fighting, bitter, keenly contested O 696.—Applied to passion manifesting itself outwardly (and app. likened to smarting tears) ω 319.

δρίος [δρῦς. For δρϝ-ος]. A coppice ξ 353.

δρόμος, -ου, ὁ [δρομ-, δραμ-, τρέχω]. (1) Running Σ 281.—A running: δρόμου ἰσχανόωσαν (for the race) Ψ 300, ὡς μεμνέῳτο δρόμους 361 (app., the running of the various chariots. Not 'laps,' as the course seems to be only out and home. *V.l.* δρόμου, 'the running' simply), πύματον τέλεον δρόμον (the last part of the race, *i.e.* that from the turn home) 373, 768. Cf. Ψ 375, 526. 758: θ 121.—(2) A race-course Ψ 321.—(3) A piece of ground suited to horses δ 605.

δρυΐνος [δρῦς]. Oaken, or perh., wooden φ 43.

δρυμά, τά [δρῦς]. (1) Thickets, coppices (prob. not nec. of oak) Λ 118: κ 251.—(2) The pl. app. expressing vague mass or quantity rather than plurality: ἐείσατο καπνὸς διὰ δ. κ 150. Cf. κ 197.

δρύοχοι, οἱ [δρῦς + ὀχ-, ἔχω]. Stays or trestles supporting the keel of a ship under construction τ 574.

δρύπτω. (ἀπο-, περι-.) To tear away or strip off: ἀπό κε ῥινοὺς δρύφθη (would have had his skin stripped off) ε 426. Cf. Π 324.—In mid. of reciprocal action β 153 (tearing each other's . . .).

δρῦς, δρυός, ἡ [cognate with Eng. *tree*, doubtless the orig. sense. Cf. δρίος, δρυΐνος, δρυμά, δρύοχοι, δρυτόμος]. Pl. δρύες M 132. Acc. δρῦς Λ 494, Ψ 118. (1) An oak Λ 494, M 132, N 389=Π 482, Ξ 398, 414, Σ 558, Ψ 118: μ 357, ξ 328=τ 297.—(2) A felled oak or a piece thereof: ξύλον δρυός Ψ 328. Cf. ι 186, ξ 12, 425.—(3) In phrase **οὐκ ἀπὸ δρυὸς οὐδ' ἀπὸ πέτρης** X 126: τ 163, an obscure proverbial expression. In X the sense seems to be 'giving utterance to thoughts from any source as they arise,' 'with unconsidered or idle words.' In τ the sense seems to be 'for you are sprung (from men) not from . . .'

δρυτόμος, -ου, ὁ [δρῦς + τομ-, τάμνω]. A woodcutter Λ 86, Π 633, Ψ 315.

δρώοιμι, opt. δράω.

δῦ, 3 sing. aor. δύω.

†**δυάω** [δύη]. 3 pl. δυόωσι. To afflict υ 195.

δύη, -ης, ἡ. Suffering, misery: δ. μ' ἔχει ξ 215, δύης πῆμα (sorrow of suffering, sorrow and suffering) 338. Cf. σ 53, 81.

δύη, 3 sing. aor. opt. δύω.

δύῃ, 3 sing. aor. subj. δύω.

δῦθι, aor. imp. δύω.

δύμεναι, δῦναι, aor. infin. δύω.

δύναμαι. 2 sing. subj. δύνηαι Z 229. Opt. δυναίμην Σ 464 : ι 523. 2 sing. δύναιο δ 388. 3 δύναιτο δ 644. Genit. sing. masc. pple. δῡναμένοιο α 276, λ 414. Fut. δυνήσομαι A 588. 2 sing. -εαι A 241, 562, N 729. 3 -εται T 163 : α 78, β 191, κ 291, φ 403. 3 sing. aor. (ἐ)δυνήσατο E 621, N 510, 607, 647, Ξ 33, 423 : ρ 303. 1 pl. subj. δυνησόμεθα π 238. 3 sing. aor. (ἐ)δυνάσθη Ψ 465 : ε 319. (**1**) To be able, have the power, ability or strength, be in a position, *to do something*. With infin. : τεύχε' ὤμοιιν ἀφελέσθαι E 621. Cf. A 241, B 343, Γ 236, Z 101, N 634, etc. : ἐριδαινέμεν οἶος α 78. Cf. β 191, γ 89, δ 374, σ 230, φ 171, etc.—Of things : οὐδέ μοι αἷμα τερσῆναι δύναται (as if it was striving) Π 519. Cf. Ξ 33.—With ellipse of infin. : δύναται ἅπαντα δ 237. Cf. Z 229 : κ 306, ξ 445.—Absol. : εἰ δύνασαί γε A 393. Cf. T 360 : μέγα δυναμένοιο (possessed of great power or influence) α 274, λ 414, δύναμαι γάρ δ 612, δύνασαι γάρ (thou well knowest how to do it) ε 25. Cf. δ 827, π 208.—(**2**) Of moral possibility : τελευτὴν ποιῆσαι (cannot make up her mind to . . .) α 250 = π 127, προλιπεῖν σε (have not the heart to . . .) ν 331.

δύναμις, ἡ [δύναμαι]. (**1**) Power, strength, might : ὅση δ. γε πάρεστιν Θ 294, N 786. Cf. N 787, X 20, Ψ 891 : β 62, γ 205, υ 237 = φ 202, ψ 128.—(**2**) Power to do something : ἀκέσασθε· δ. γὰρ ἐν ὑμῖν κ 69.

δυνάσθη, 3 sing. aor. δύναμαι.

δύνηαι, 2 sing. subj. δύναμαι.

δυνήσατο, 3 sing. aor. δύναμαι.

δύντα, acc. sing. masc. aor. pple. δύω.

δύνω. See δύω.

δύο, δύω, *indeclinable*. (The forms about equally common. Used with both dual and pl.) Two A 16, 250, B 731, Γ 18, E 159, K 253, etc. : α 256, δ 27, 496, ε 388, θ 312, κ 515, etc.—Absol. : δύω μοι ἔπεσθον X 450. Cf. B 346, K 224, T 271, Ψ 174, etc. : β 22, ζ 63, ξ 74, etc.—With other numerals : δύω καὶ εἴκοσι B 748 : ι 241, κ 208.—δύω καὶ πεντήκοντα θ 35, 48, π 247.

δυοκαίδεκα, *indeclinable* [= δυώδεκα, δώδεκα]. Twelve B 557, Z 93 = 274, 308, K 560, Λ 228, T 225 : θ 59, ξ 13, σ 293, τ 578 = φ 76.—Absol. : δ. πάντες ἄριστοι π 251. Cf. ι 195.

δυόωσι, 3 pl. δυάω.

δυσᾱής [δυσ- (1) + ἄημι]. Genit. pl. δυσᾱήων ν 99. Of winds, blowing with violence, stormy, blustering E 865, Ψ 200 : ε 295, μ 289, ν 99.

δῦσαι, aor. infin. δύω.

δυσάμμορος, -ον [δυσ- (2) + ἄμμορος]. Dogged by persistent evil fate, most miserable T 315, X 428, 485, Ω 727.

δύσαντο, 3 pl. aor. mid. δύω.

δυσαριστοτόκεια [δυσ- (1) + ἄριστος + τοκ-, τίκτω]. That bare the noblest of sons to an evil fate Σ 54.

δύσετο, 3 sing. aor. mid. δύω.

δύσζηλος [δυσ- (2) + ζῆλος, jealousy]. Apt to put a bad construction on things, suspicious η 307.

δυσηλεγής [δυσ- (2) + ἀλεγ-, ἀλεγεινός]. Bringing much woe. Epithet of war T 154.—Of death χ 325.

δυσηχής [δυσ- (2) + ἄχος]. Bringing much woe. Epithet of war B 686, H 376 = 395, Λ 524, 590, N 535, Σ 307.—Of death Π 442 = X 180, Σ 464.

δυσθαλπής [δυσ- (1) + θάλπω]. Evil in the matter of heat, cold : χειμῶνος P 549.

δύσκε, 3 sing. pa. iterative δύω.

δυσκέλαδος [δυσ- (1) + κέλαδος]. Ill-sounding, evil to the ears : φόβοιο Π 357.

δυσκηδής [δυσ- (2) + κῆδος]. Bringing pain or discomfort : νύκτα ε 466.

δυσκλεής [δυσ- (1) + κλέος]. Acc. δυσκλέα (for δυσκλεέα). With smirched fame B 115 = I 22.

δυσμενέων, *pres. pple.* [δυσμενής]. Bearing ill-will, in enemy wise : εἰ δ. κάκ' ἔρεξεν β 72. Cf. β 73, υ 314.

δυσμενής [δυσ- (1) + μένος]. Dat. pl. δυσμενέεσσι E 488, K 193, X 403, etc. : γ 90, ξ 218, ρ 289, etc. δυσμενέσι Γ 51. (**1**) Bearing ill-will, hostile, enemy E 488, Z 453, K 40, 100, 221, 395, N 263, P 158, T 168, 232, Ω 288, 365 : γ 90, δ 246, 319, ζ 200, θ 217, ξ 221, ο 387, χ 234. — (**2**) Absol. in pl., enemies, foes, the foe : μάχεσθαι δυσμενέεσσιν Π 521. Cf. Γ 51, K 193, T 62, X 403 : δυσμενέες καὶ ἀνάρσιοι (*i.e.* pirates) ξ 85. Cf. δ 822, ζ 184, ξ 218, π 121, 234, ρ 289.

δυσμήτηρ [δυσ- (1) + μήτηρ]. In voc. δύσμητερ, mother of an ill sort ψ 97.

δύσμορος [δυσ- (1) + μόρος]. Doomed to an evil fate, ill-starred, unlucky X 60, 481 : α 49, η 270, π 139, υ 194, ω 290, 311.

δύσομαι, fut. mid. δύω.

δῡσομένου, genit. sing. masc. aor. pple. mid. δύω.

Δύσπαρις [δυσ- (1) + Πάρις]. In voc. Δύσπαρι, Paris, thou wretch Γ 39 = N 769.

δυσπέμφελος [δυσ-. Second element obscure]. Stormy : [πόντος] Π 748.

δυσπονής [δυσ- (2) + πόνος]. Distressing ε 493.

δύστηνος, -ον [δυσ-. Second element obscure]. Wretched, unhappy, miserable, unfortunate P 445, X 477 : α 55, δ 182, ε 436, λ 76, ν 331, ρ 10, 483, 501, τ 354, ω 289.—Absol. : δυστήνων παῖδες Z 127 = Φ 151. Cf. X 59 : ζ 206, η 223, 248, κ 281, λ 80, 93, υ 224.

δυσχείμερος, -ον [δυσ- (2) + χεῖμα]. Vexed by bitter weather, inclement. Of Dodona B 750, Π 234.

δύσω, fut. δύω.

δυσώνυμος, -ον [δυσ- (1) + ὄνυμα, Aeolic form of ὄνομα]. Of ill name, accursed Z 255, M 116 : τ 571.

†**δυσωρέομαι** [app. δυσ- (1) + ὤρη, care, concern]. 3 pl. aor. subj. δυσωρήσωνται (most MSS. -ονται, prob. the orig. form). To keep painful watch K 183.

δῦτε, 2 pl. aor. imp. δύω.

δύω, two. See δύο.

δύω, δύνω. 3 sing. pa. iterative δύσκε Θ 271. Fut. δύσω B 261. 3 pl. sigmatic aor. ἔδῡσαν ξ 341. Infin. δῦσαι E 435, N 182. 3 sing. aor. ἔδῡ Γ 36, Λ 63, Σ 241, Ψ 154, etc. : γ 329, ν 35, π 220, etc. δῦ Θ 85, P 210, Σ 416, Φ 118. 3 dual ἐδύτην Z 19, K 254, 272. 2 pl. ἔδῦτε ω 106. 3 ἔδῦσαν Σ 145. ἔδυν Δ 222, Λ 263. Subj. δύω Z 340, H 193, P 186, Σ 192, Φ 559, X 99, 125. 2 sing. δύῃς I 604. 3 δύῃ Λ 194, 209, P 455. 3 sing. opt. δύη (for δυίη) σ 348, υ 286. Imp. δῦθι Π 64. 3 sing. δύτω Ξ 377. Pl. δῦτε Σ 140. Acc. sing. masc. pple. δύντα T 308. Nom. dual δύντε χ 201. Infin. δύμεναι Z 185, 411, Ξ 63, T 313. δῦναι B 413, Γ 322, H 131, K 221, Λ 537, Υ 76: ν 30. 3 sing. pf. δέδῡκε E 811, I 239: μ 93. **Mid.** Fut. δύσομαι μ 383. 2 sing. -εαι I 231. 3 pl. -ονται H 298. Infin. -εσθαι η 18. 3 pl. aor. δύσαντο Ψ 739. 3 pl. opt. δῡσαίατο Σ 376. 3 sing. aor. (ἐ)δύσετο B 578, Γ 328, H 465, O 120, T 368, Φ 515, etc.: β 388, δ 425, ε 352, ζ 321, ρ 336, ψ 366, etc. Imp. δύσεο Π 129, T 36: ρ 276. Genit. sing. masc. pple. δῡσομένου α 24. (ἀνα-, ἀπο-, ἐκ-, ἐνδύνω, ἐξανα-, ἐξαποδύνω, ἐσ-, κατα-, περι-, ὑπεξανα-, ὑπο-.) **(I)** In fut. and sigmatic aor. act., with adverbs indicating deprivation, to strip off (clothes, etc.): εἰ μὴ ἀφ' εἵματα δύσω B 261. Cf. E 435, N 182: ξ 341.—Sim. in pres. subj., to put off (one's armour): ἐπεί κ' ἀπὸ τεύχεα δύω X 125.—**(II)** In the tenses other than the fut. and sigmatic aor. act. **(1)** In act. and mid., to enter, go into, make one's way into: δῦναι δόμον Ἄϊδος Γ 322, H 131, δύοντο τεῖχος O 345. Cf. Z 19, 411, Λ 263, Φ 515, X 99: δέρτρον δύνοντες (thrusting their beaks into it) λ 579, ἐδύσετο δώματα ρ 336. Cf. η 18, 81, ν 366, ω 106.—To plunge into (the sea): δῦνε πόντον O 219. Cf. Σ 140.—Of the apparent motion of a star: ἔδυ νέφεα Λ 63.—Absol., to take its inward way, pass: δύνει ἀλοιφή P 392. Cf. Π 340, Φ 118.—**(2)** In act. and mid. with preps., to go, make one's way, place oneself (*into* or *under* something): βέλος εἰς ἐγκέφαλον δῦ Θ 85. Cf. E 140, Θ 271, Φ 559: οὗς ὑπ' Ὀδυσσεὺς δύσετο ε 482, μέσσῃ κατὰ σπείους δέδυκεν (stands waist-deep) μ 93. Cf. μ 383.—So of plunging into the sea: δύσεθ' ἁλὸς κατὰ κῦμα Z 136, ὑπὸ κῦμ' ἔδυσαν Σ 145: ἐς πόντον ἐδύσετο ε 352. Cf. δ 425, 570 = λ 253.—**(3)** In act. and mid., to enter, mingle with (a throng or company, etc.): δῦναι ὅμιλον Λ 537, Υ 76. Cf. Z 185, H 298, I 604, K 221, Ξ 63, Π 729, P 552, Σ 376, T 313, Υ 379: δύσεο μνηστῆρας (go among them, mix with them) ρ 276.—Sim. with a prep.: καθ' ὅμιλον ἔδυ Γ 36.—**(4)** In act. and mid., to get into, put on (armour or clothes): ἐδύσετο χαλκόν B 578, Λ 16, ἔντε' ἔδυνεν Γ 339, δύσαντο χιτῶνας Ψ 739. Cf. Γ 328, 332 = Λ 19 = Π 133 = T 371, Z 340, H 193, Θ 43 = N 25, I 596, N 241, Ξ 382, O 120, Π 64, 129, P 186, 194, 202, Σ 192, 416, T 368: χιτῶνα δῦνεν ο 61, δυέσθην τεύχεα χ 114. Cf. χ 113, ψ 366.—Of putting on the 'cap of Hades' E 845.—Sim. with preps.: κατὰ τεύχε' ἔδυν Δ 222. Cf. K 254, 272, Ψ 131: ἐν τεύχεσσι δύοντο ω 496. Cf. χ 201, ω 498.—So ἐν ἀσπίδι δύτω Ξ 377.—Fig.: δύσεο δ' ἀλκήν T 36. Cf. I 231.—**(5)** In act. and mid., of the sun, to enter Ocean, set: δύσετ' ἠέλιος H 465, ἔδυ φάος Θ 487. Cf. B 413, Λ 194 = 209 = P 455, Σ 241, T 308, Ψ 154: Αἰθίοπες δυσομένου Ὑπερίονος (dwelling in the west) α 24. Cf. β 388 = γ 487 = 497 = λ 12 = ο 185 = 296 = 471, γ 329 = ε 225, ζ 321, θ 417, ν 30, 35, π 220 = φ 226.—So of a constellation: ὀψὲ δύοντα Βοώτην ε 272.—Sim.: δείελος ὀψὲ δύων Φ 232.—**(6)** In act., of feelings or physical or mental states, to come upon, befall: κάματος γυῖα δέδυκεν E 811, Μελέαγρον ἔδυ χόλος I 553. Cf. I 239, Λ 268, 272, T 16, 367, X 94: ὄφρ' ἔτι μᾶλλον δύῃ ἄχος κραδίην σ 348 = υ 286.—Of a god, to inspire: δῦ μιν Ἄρης P 210.

δυώδεκα, *indeclinable* [= δυοκαίδεκα, δώδεκα]. Twelve B 637, Σ 230, Φ 27: ι 159, 204, μ 89, τ 199.—Absol.: ὄφρα δ. ἔπεφνεν K 488.

δυωδεκάβοιος [δυώδεκα + βοῦς]. Of the value of twelve oxen: δυωδεκάβοιον τίον (at . . .) Ψ 703.

δυωδέκατος, -η [δυώδεκα. Cf. δωδέκατος]. **(1)** The twelfth: ἠώς A 493 = Ω 31, Φ 81, Ω 413.—**(2)** δυωδεκάτη (*sc.* ἡμέρη), the twelfth day: δυωδεκάτῃ (on the twelfth day) Φ 46: ἑνδεκάτη τε δυωδεκάτη τε β 374, δ 588.—So τῇ δυωδεκάτῃ Ω 667.

δυωκαιεικοσίμετρος [μέτρον]. Holding twenty-two measures: τρίποδα Ψ 264.

δυωκαιεικοσίπηχυς, -υ [πῆχυς in sense 'cubit']. Twenty-two cubits long: ξυστόν O 678.

δῶ, τό [app. = δῶμ = δῶμα]. **(1)** A house or abode A 426, H 363, Ξ 173, Σ 385 = 424, T 355, Φ 438, 505: α 176, 392, β 262, δ 139, 169, θ 28, 321, κ 111 = ο 424, λ 501, ν 4, ο 432, ω 115.—**(2)** Of the house or realm of Hades: Ἄϊδος δῶ Ψ 74: λ 571.

δῶ, aor. subj. δίδωμι.

δώδεκα, *indeclinable* [= δυοκαίδεκα, δυώδεκα]. Twelve Z 248, I 123 = 265 = T 244, I 328, Λ 25, 692, Σ 336, Ψ 22, 175, 181, Ω 229, 230, 603: δ 636 = φ 23, θ 390, κ 5, ν 182, ξ 100, τ 574, υ 107, χ 144, ω 276.—Absol.: δ. οὖτα O 746. Cf. β 353, χ 424.

δωδέκατος, -η [= δυωδέκατος]. **(1)** The twelfth: ἠώς Ω 781.—**(2)** δωδεκάτη (*sc.* ἡμέρη), the twelfth day: δωδεκάτῃ (on the twelfth day) A 425: πρὶν δωδεκάτην γενέσθαι δ 747.

δώῃ, δώῃσι, 3 sing. aor. subj. δίδωμι.

δῶκα, aor. δίδωμι.

δῶμα, -ατος, τό [cf. δόμος]. **(1)** A house or abode: ὑψερεφὲς μέγα δ. E 213, θάλαμον καὶ δ. καὶ αὐλήν Z 316 (app. the house in gen., a particular part, the θ., being specially mentioned; cf. χ 494). Cf. A 18, B 854, Ξ 121, O 143, Φ 44, etc.: πρὸς δ. (home) β 298, Ἀλκινόοιο δ. θ 13. Cf. γ 368, ε 208, π 276, υ 192, ψ 50, etc.—In pl. in the same sense: ἐν δώμασ' ἐμοῖσιν Z 221. Cf. A 222, Λ 77, Π 190, Ψ 89, etc.: α 116, γ 355, ρ 479, τ 194, etc.—**(2)** Of the house or realm of Hades: δ. Ἀΐδαο O 251: μ 21.—**(3)** Applied to particular parts of a house. **(a)** To Penelope's quarters. In pl. σ 314.—**(b)** To the μέγαρον (sometimes difficult to say whether the word should be taken in this restricted sense. In χ 494 μέγαρον and δ. are app. distinguished): βῆ διὰ δ. η 139. Cf. Δ 386, O 101: α 228, β 247, δ 15, 44, 46, η 85, ρ 329, 501, 541, 566, σ 153, 341, υ 149, 178, φ 378, χ 23,

307, 360, ψ 146.—So in pl.: φαίνοντες κατὰ δώματα δαιτυμόνεσσιν η 102. Cf. A 600: δ 72, ι 7, ρ 531, υ 159, φ 234, χ 22, ω 183.

δώομεν, δῶμεν, 1 pl. aor. subj. δίδωμι.

δωρέομαι [δῶρον]. To give K 557.

δωρητός [δωρέομαι]. Open to gifts, that may be appeased by gifts I 526.

δῶρον, -ου, τό [δω-, δίδωμι]. **(1)** A gift or present A 213, H 299, I 164, T 3, Ψ 745, etc.: α 311, δ 130, θ 397, ο 18, ρ 76, etc.—**(2)** Something given as a return or reward: δώρῳ ἔπι μεγάλῳ K 304. Cf. I 576, 598, Λ 124, Ξ 238, etc.: πόρε μοι δῶρα ι 201. Cf. β 186, λ 521, ο 247.—Of a share of spoil A 230.—Of ransom for a corpse X 341, Ω 76, 119 = 147 = 176 = 196, 447, 458.—**(3)** Something given or devoted to a god: δ. Ἀθήνῃ Z 293. Cf. A 390, Θ 203, Υ 299, Ω 68, 425: ν 358, π 185.—**(4)** Of what is bestowed by the gods on mortals. Of one's lot or fortune: δώρων οἷα δίδωσι [Ζεύς] Ω 528. Cf. Ω 534: σ 142.—Of personal qualities: δῶρ' Ἀφροδίτης Γ 54, 64. Cf. Γ 65: σ 191.—Of sleep: ὕπνου δ. ἕλοντο H 482, I 713: π 481, τ 427.—**(5)** Gifts more or less voluntary, 'benevolences' (cf. δωτίνη (2)): δώροισι κατατρύχω λαούς P 225.

δῶσι, 3 pl. aor. subj. δίδωμι.

δῷσι, 3 sing. aor. subj. δίδωμι.

δώσω, fut. δίδωμι.

δωτήρ, -ῆρος [δω-, δίδωμι]. A bestower θ 325.

δωτίνη, -ης, ἡ [as prec.]. **(1)** A gift or present ι 268.—Gifts collectively: εἰς ὅ κε πᾶσαν δωτίνην τελέσω λ 352.—**(2)** = δῶρον (5) I 155, 297.

δώτωρ = δωτήρ. In voc. δῶτορ θ 335.

δώωσι, 3 pl. aor. subj. δίδωμι.

ἕ, ἑ. See ἑέ.

ἔā, impf. εἰμί.

ἐάᾳς[1], 2 sing., **ἐάᾳ,** 3 sing. ἐάω.

ἐάᾳς[2], 2 sing. subj. ἐάω.

ἐάγη, 3 sing. aor. pass. ἄγνυμι.

ἐάγῃ, 3 sing. pf. subj. ἄγνυμι.

ἑāδότα, acc. sing. masc. pf. pple. ἁνδάνω.

ἑάλη, 3 sing. aor. pass. εἴλω.

ἑāνός[1], -οῦ, ὁ (Fεσανός) [Fέσνυμι, ἕννυμι]. With ἑ- lengthened to εἱ- in the first arsis Π 9. A robe or garment Γ 385, 419, Ξ 178, Π 9, Φ 507.

ἑāνός[2] [perh. fr. ἐάω]. Yielding, flexible, pliant: πέπλον E 734 = Θ 385. Cf. Σ 352, 613, Ψ 254.

ἔαξε, 3 sing. aor. ἄγνυμι.

ἔαρ, ἔαρος, τό (Fέαρ. Cf. L. *ver*). The spring: ἔαρος νέον ἱσταμένοιο τ 519. Cf. Z 148.

ἔāσι, 3 pl. pres. εἰμί.

ἔασκε, 3 sing. pa. iterative ἐάω.

ἕαται, 3 pl. pres. ἧμαι.

ἑάφθη, 3 *sing. aor. pass.* [prob. fr. (F)ι-(F)άπτω. See προϊάπτω. For the aspirate cf. ἕηκε, ἕεστο, etc.]. Thus, to be hurled or thrust N 543, Ξ 419.

ἐάω. Also **ἐῶ** Θ 428, **εἰῶ** Δ 55. 2 sing. ἐάᾳς μ 282, τ 374. 3 ἐάᾳ Θ 414. 3 pl. εἰῶσι B 132, Λ 550, P 659. 2 sing. subj. ἐάᾳς λ 110, μ 137. 1 pl. εἰῶμεν φ 260. 3 εἰῶσι Υ 139. Opt. ἐῷμι π 85. 3 sing. ἐῷ υ 12. Infin. ἐάαν θ 509. Pa. iterative εἴασκον E 802. 2 sing. ἔασκες T 295. 3 εἴασκε Λ 125, Υ 408: χ 427. ἔασκε B 832, Λ 330, Ω 17. 3 pl. fut. ἐάσουσι φ 233. 3 sing. aor. εἴᾱσε K 299. **(1) (a)** To let (a person) be, leave (him) where he is: [κούρην] A 276.—**(b)** To let be, do no harm to: σε Ω 569, 684. Cf. Π 731: δ 744. (Prob. Ω 557 should be added, omitting 558.)—With complementary adj.: εἴ κ' ἀσινέας ἐάᾳς λ 110 = μ 137.—Absol. Φ 221.—**(c)** To let alone, leave, do nothing further to E 148, Θ 317, Λ 148, 323, 426, Υ 456, Ω 17.—**(d)** To put aside, lay down: δόρυ κ 166.—To lay aside, depart from: χόλον I 260.—To give over, cease from: κλαυθμόν δ 212.—**(e)** To leave, forgo the use of: ἵππους Δ 226.—**(f)** To abandon, cease to contend for: ἔναρα P 13.—**(g)** To let be, not to mind or trouble about: ἔναρα O 347: ὅρκον ξ 171, μιν π 147.—To cease to think about, put out of one's thoughts: μνηστήρων βουλήν β 281. Cf. I 701: ξ 183.—**(h)** To disregard, pass by, put aside: ἄλλους O 87.—**(i)** Not to give, withhold: τὸ μὲν δώσει, τὸ δ' ἐάσει ξ 444.—**(2)** With infin. **(a)** To leave so as to be in a specified or indicated state, let be in such and such a state: Περίφαντα κεῖσθαι E 847. Cf. E 684, Θ 125, O 472, Π 60, Σ 112 = T 65, T 8, Ω 523: θ 509, φ 260.—**(b)** To leave *to do* or *suffer something*: Τρῶας καὶ Ἀχαιοὺς μάρνασθαι E 32, τοὺς πόνον ἐχέμεν N 2. Cf. B 236, 346, E 465, Θ 244 = O 376, O 522, Π 96, 451, Υ 311, Φ 556, X 398: σ 222.—To leave *to do something*, wait for *one's doing it*: αὐτόν μιν πατρὸς μνησθῆναι δ 118.—To turn (animals) loose *to feed*: σιάλους νέμεσθαι υ 164.—**(c)** To leave or commit *to be cared for*: τὸν ξεῖνον Τηλεμάχῳ μελέμεν σ 420.—**(d)** To give up the idea of *doing something*: κλέψαι Ἕκτορα Ω 71.—**(3)** To suffer, let, allow, permit. With infin.: νῆας ἑλκέμεν B 165, εἴ περ οὐκ εἰῶ διαπέρσαι (seek to hinder) Δ 55, εἴσω δ' οὔ μιν θυμὸς ἐφορμηθῆναι ἐάσει (will not suffice for that) Σ 282. Cf. B 132, E 717, Θ 243, 399, Λ 437, X 416, etc.: δορπῆσαι η 215, ζώειν ν 359. Cf. β 70, η 274, κ 443, 536, λ 453, μ 282, χ 427, etc.—Absol.: ἀλλά μ' ἐᾶσαι (let me have my will) Δ 42, οὐ γὰρ ἐάσω P 449, Σ 296. Cf. E 517: η 41, κ 291, υ 273.—**(4)** With neg. and infin. **(a)** Not to suffer *to do something*, bid or tell not *to do it*: οὐδ' εἴα κλαίειν H 427. Cf. B 832 = Λ 330, E 256, 802, 819, Θ 414, Λ 718, Σ 189, T 295, Υ 408, X 206, Ψ 4, Ω 395: οὐκ ἐάσουσιν δόμεναι φ 233. Cf. δ 805, ι 468, τ 25, ψ 77.—**(b)** Not to approve of *doing something*, give one's voice against *doing it*: οὐκ εἴασχ' Ἑλένην δόμεναι Λ 125. Cf. Θ 428.—**(c)** To be an obstacle or hindrance to *the doing of something*: παῖς ἐμὸς ἧος ἔην ἔτι νήπιος γήμασθ' οὔ μ' εἴα τ 531.

ἐάων, *genit. pl. fem.* [*ἐή, doubtfully connected with ἐΰς]. Good things, blessings Ω 528: θ 325, 335.

ἔβαλε, 3 sing. aor. βάλλω.

ἔβαν, 3 pl. aor. βαίνω.

ἑβδόματος, -η [ἕβδομος + superl. suff.]. (1) The seventh H 248.—(2) ἑβδομάτη (sc. ἡμέρη), the seventh day: ἑβδομάτῃ (on the seventh day) κ 81, ξ 252.

ἕβδομος [ἑπτά]. The seventh T 117, Ω 399: μ 399 = ο 477.

ἐβεβήκει, 3 sing. plupf. βαίνω.

ἔβην, aor. βαίνω.

ἐβήσαμεν, 1 pl. trans. aor. βαίνω.

ἐβήσετο, 3 sing. aor. mid. βαίνω.

ἐβιώσαο, 2 sing. aor. mid. βιόω.

ἔβλαβεν, ἐβλάφθησαν, 3 pl. aor. pass. βλάπτω.

ἔβλητο, 3 sing. aor. pass. βάλλω.

ἔβρῖσαν, 3 pl. aor. βρίθω.

†**ἐγγίγνομαι** [ἐγ-, ἐν- (1)]. 3 pl. pf. ἐγγεγάᾱσι Δ 41, Z 493, P 145; ν 233. 3 pl. trans. aor. subj. ἐγγείνωνται T 26. (1) In pf., to exist, live, be *in*. With dat.: τοὶ Ἰλίῳ ἐγγεγάασιν Z 493, P 145.—To exist, live, be, in a place: τίνες ἀνέρες ἐγγεγάασιν; ν 233. Cf. Δ 41.—(2) In trans. aor., to give being to, breed, in an indicated place: μὴ μυῖαι εὐλὰς ἐγγείνωνται T 26.

ἐγγυαλίζω [ἐγ-, ἐν- (2) + γυ- (as in γύαλον), the hollow of the hand]. To put into the hand; hence (1) To hand over, pay: ἔεδνα θ 319.—(2) To put (a person) into one's hands to be cared for: [ξεῖνόν] τοι ἐγγυαλίζω π 66.—(3) Generally, to give, grant, commit, bestow: τιμήν A 353. Cf. B 436, I 98, Λ 192, 207, 753, O 491, 644, P 206, 613, Ψ 278: ὅττι κε κέρδος ἐγγυαλίξῃ (put into our minds) ψ 140.

†**ἐγγυάω** [ἐγγύη]. Infin. mid. ἐγγυάασθαι. To accept (an undertaking) θ 351.

ἐγγύη [cf. ἐγγυαλίζω] The giving of a pledge, an undertaking θ 351.

ἐγγύθεν [ἐγγύς + -θεν (1) (2)]. (1) From close at hand: σάκος οὔτασεν N 647. Cf. N 562, O 529: μ 354.—(2) (a) Near, at hand: ἐς δ' ἐνόησ' Αἴαντε ἐ. M 337. Cf. ι 423, μ 183.—(b) Dwelling near enough to admit of regular intercourse: οὔ τινες ἐ. εἰσίν ζ 279.—With dat.: θεοῖσιν η 205 (cf. ἀγχίθεος).—(c) Following closely: ἔχ' ἐ. ἵππους Ψ 516. Cf. X 141, Ψ 763.—(d) Taking a course close to something, 'shaving' it: τέρμ' ὀρόων στρέφει ἐ. Ψ 323.—(3) Near, near to, close to. With genit.: Ἀρήνης Λ 723.—With dat.: αὐτῷ Σ 133. Cf. P 554, T 409, X 295: ω 446.—(4) With ἐλθεῖν of drawing near or approaching: ἐ. ἐλθών E 72. Cf. E 275, H 219 = Λ 485 = P 128, Λ 396, N 574, Ξ 446, Ω 360: γ 36, θ 62 = 471, θ 261.—So ἐ. ἱσταμένη K 508. Cf. O 710, P 582.—With ἐλθεῖν and dat.: ἐ. οἱ ἦλθεν Σ 16, 381. Cf. Υ 330: δ 630, ο 163, ρ 71.—So ἤντετό οἱ ἐ. X 204.

ἐγγύθι [ἐγγύς + -θι]. (1) Near, at hand: ὀρύξομεν ἐ. τάφρον H 341. Cf. Π 71.—Of a period of time: ἐ. δ' ἠώς K 251.—(2) Near, near to, close to. With genit.: νηῶν I 73, K 561. Cf. Z 317: η 29, ν 156, ω 358.—With dat.: μοι X 300.—(3) Like prec. (4): ἐ. στάς (drawing near, approaching) α 120.

ἐγγύς. (1) Near, at hand: ἐ. ἐόντα Θ 318. Cf. I 201, K 113, 221, Λ 340, 346, 464, Ξ 110, 417, P 484, Υ 425, Φ 533, Ψ 378: β 165, ι 166, 181, κ 30, ξ 484, ρ 301, χ 163, 355, ω 495.—Near or close to each other: ἐ. νυκτός τε καὶ ἤματός εἰσι κέλευθοι κ 86.—(2) Near, near to, close to. With genit.: ἁλός I 153 = 295, O 619. Cf. I 232, K 274, N 247, O 650: ν 268, ξ 518, ρ 205, φ 215.—With dat.: τοι Ω 365. Cf. X 453.—With prep.: ἐπ' αὐτάων ἐ. X 153.—(3) With ἰέναι of drawing near or approaching: ἐ. ἰών Δ 496 = E 611 = P 347, Λ 429, M 457.—So ἱστάμενοι ἐ. Σ 586.—So also of persons coming up to each other: ἐ. στήτην Γ 344.—With genit.: στῆ Ἕκτορος ἐ. H 225.—With dat.: τῷ ἐ. ἰόντε Φ 285.

ἐγδούπησαν, 3 pl. aor. δουπέω.

ἐγέγωνε, 3 sing. impf. γεγώνω. See γέγωνα.

ἐγεγώνει, 3 sing. plupf. γέγωνα.

ἐγεγώνευν, impf. γεγωνέω. See γέγωνα.

ἐγείνατο, 3 sing. trans. aor. γίγνομαι.

ἐγείρω. Aor. ἤγειρα E 208. 2 sing. -ας N 778. 3 ἔγειρε E 496, 517, Z 105, Λ 213, O 567, 603, P 544, 552, Υ 31, Ψ 234: ζ 48, ο 44, ω 164. 3 pl. ἤγειραν P 261. 3 sing. subj. ἐγείρησι K 511. -η E 413. 1 pl. -ομεν B 440, Δ 352, Θ 531, K 108, 146, Σ 304, T 237. 3 pl. opt. ἐγείρειαν K 166. Infin. ἐγεῖραι E 510. 3 pl. pf. ἐγρηγόρθᾱσι (app. fr. the mid. forms ἐγρήγορθε, ἐγρήγορθαι cited below) K 419. **Mid.** 3 sing. aor. ἔγρετο B 41, H 434, O 4, Ω 789: ζ 117, ν 187. 3 sing. opt. ἔγροιτο ζ 113. Imp. ἔγρεο K 159: ο 46, ψ 5. Pple. ἐγρόμενος κ 50. Infin. ἔγρεσθαι ν 124. Imp. pl. pf. ἐγρήγορθε H 371, Σ 299. Infin. ἐγρήγορθαι K 67. (ἀν-, ἐπ-.) (1) To rouse from sleep, waken: καὶ ὑπνώοντας ἐγείρει Ω 344 := ε 48 = ω 4. Cf. E 413, K 108, 146, 166, 511, Ψ 234: ζ 48, ο 44.—To keep awake: μελεδήματά [μιν] ἔγειρεν ο 8.—(2) To rouse, stimulate, stir to action: ἔγειρέ μιν Διὸς νόος O 242. Cf. E 208, 510, N 58, O 232, 567, 594, 603, P 552: ω 164.—Absol.: ἔγειρε κατὰ στρατόν N 357.—(3) To stir up, bring about, cause to break forth (battle, strife, etc.): ὀξὺν Ἄρηα B 440, Δ 352 = T 237, Θ 531 = Σ 304. Cf. E 496 = Z 105 = Λ 213, E 517, N 778, P 261, 544, Υ 31.—(4) In mid. (a) To rouse oneself from sleep, waken: ἔγρετο Ζεύς O 4. Cf. B 41, K 159: ἐγρόμενος μερμήριξα κ 50. Cf. ζ 113, 117, ν 124, 187, ο 46, υ 100, ψ 5.—(b) To rouse oneself to action, bestir oneself: ἔγρετο λαός H 434, Ω 789 (perh. rather ἤγρετο fr. ἀγείρω; cf. ἀγείρω (2)).—(c) In pf., to keep oneself awake, be on the alert: ἐγρήγορθε ἕκαστος H 371 = Σ 299.—So in act. form ἐγρηγόρθασι K 419.—App., merely = (a): ἐγρήγορθαι ἄνωχθι K 67.

ἐγέλασσε, 3 sing. aor. γελάω.

ἐγένοντο, 3 pl. aor. γίγνομαι.

ἔγημε, 3 sing. aor. γαμέω.

ἐγήρα, 3 sing. impf. γηράω. See γηράσκω.

ἔγκατα, τά. Dat. pl. ἔγκασι Λ 438. The entrails Λ 176 = P 64, Λ 438, Σ 583: ι 293, μ 363.

†**ἐγκαταπήγνῡμι** [ἐγ-, ἐν- (2), κατα- (1)]. Aor. ἐγκατέπηξα. To thrust down *into*. With dat.: ξίφος κουλεῷ λ 98.

†**ἐγκατατίθημι** [ἐγ-, ἐν- (2), κατα- (1)]. 3 sing. aor. mid. ἐγκάτθετο Ξ 223 : λ 614, ψ 223. Imp. ἐγκάτθεο Ξ 219. To lay down *in*; to put *in*, place *within*. With dat. : τοῦτον ἱμάντα τεῷ κόλπῳ Ξ 219. Cf. Ξ 223.—Fig.: ὃς κεῖνον τελαμῶνα ἑῇ ἐγκάτθετο τέχνῃ λ 614 (put it into his invention, *i.e.* conceived the idea of it), τὴν ἄτην ἑῷ ἐγκάτθετο θυμῷ ψ 223 (took or admitted the illusion into her heart).

†**ἔγκειμαι** [ἐγ-, ἐν- (1)]. 2 sing. fut. ἐγκείσεαι. To lie (wrapped) *in*. With dat. : εἵμασιν Χ 513.

ἐγκέκλιται, 3 sing. pf. pass. ἐγκλίνω.

†**ἐγκεράννῡμι** [ἐγ-, ἐν- (1)]. Fem. aor. pple. ἐγκεράσᾱσα. To mix or dilute in a vessel : οἶνον Θ 189.

ἐγκέφαλος, -ου, ὁ [ἐγ-, ἐν- (1) + κεφαλή]. The brain, the brains Γ 300, Θ 85, Λ 97, Μ 185, Π 347, Ρ 297, Υ 399 : ι 290, 458, ν 395.

†**ἐγκλίνω** [ἐγ-, ἐν- (3)]. 3 sing. pf. pass. ἐγκέκλιται. In pass., to rest *upon*; fig., to be laid or imposed *upon*. With dat. : πόνος ὔμμι Ζ 78.

ἐγκονέω [app. ἐγ-, ἐν-. Second element obscure]. To show activity, make haste : στόρεσαν λέχε' ἐγκονέουσαι Ω 648. Cf. η 340 = ψ 291.

ἐγκοσμέω [ἐγ-, ἐν- (1)]. To arrange or stow *in*. With dat. : τὰ τεύχεα νηΐ ο 218.

†**ἐγκρύπτω** [ἐγ-, ἐν- (1)]. 3 sing. aor. ἐνέκρυψε. To put away *in*. With dat. : δαλὸν σποδιῇ ε 488.

†**ἐγκύρω** [ἐγ-, ἐν- (2)]. 3 sing. aor. ἐνέκυρσε. To run *into*, encounter. With dat. : φάλαγξιν Ν 145.

ἔγνων, aor. γιγνώσκω.

ἔγρετο, 3 sing. aor. mid. ἐγείρω.

†**ἐγρηγοράω** [cf. the pf. forms under ἐγείρω and also ἐγρηγορτί]. Pres. pple. ἐγρηγορόων. To be in a state of wakefulness, be awake : κεῖτ' ἐγρηγορόων υ 6.

ἐγρήγορθαι, infin. pf. mid. ἐγείρω.

ἐγρηγόρθᾱσι, 3 pl. pf. ἐγείρω.

ἐγρηγορτί [cf. the pf. forms under ἐγείρω and also ἐγρηγοράω]. In a state of wakefulness, awake, on the alert : ἥατο Κ 182.

ἐγρήσσω [ἐγρ-, ἐγείρω]. To be in a state of wakefulness, be on the alert : πάννυχοι ἐγρήσσοντες Λ 551 = Ρ 660.—To lie awake υ 33, 53.

ἔγροιτο, 3 sing. aor. opt. mid. ἐγείρω.

ἐγχείη, -ης, ἡ [= ἔγχος]. **(1)** A spear Β 818, Γ 137, Ε 167, Η 261, Π 75, Φ 69, etc. : ι 55, λ 40. —**(2)** Spearmanship, the spear : κέκαστο πάντας ἐγχείῃ Ξ 125. Cf. Β 530.

ἐγχείῃ, 3 sing. subj. ἐγχέω.

ἔγχελυς, -υος. An eel Φ 203, 353.

ἐγχεσίμωρος [ἔγχεσι, dat. pl. of ἔγχος. Second element obscure. Cf. ἰόμωρος, ὑλακόμωρος]. App., eager or active with the spear Β 692, 840, Η 134 : γ 188.

ἐγχέσπαλος [ἐγχεσ-, ἔγχος + πάλλω]. Wielding, fighting with, the spear Β 131, Ξ 449, Ο 605.

†**ἐγχέω** [ἐγ-, ἐν- (2)]. 3 sing. subj. ἐγχείῃ ι 10, 3 sing. aor. mid. ἐνεχεύατο τ 387. To pour into a vessel. In mid. : ὕδωρ τ 387.—To pour *into*. With dat. : μέθυ δεπάεσσιν ι 10.

ἔγχος, -εος, τό [cf. ἐγχείη]. **(1)** A spear Β 389, Δ 282, Ζ 65, Λ 484, Ο 536, Σ 195, etc. : α 99, β 10, κ 145, ρ 62, φ 34, χ 271, etc.—**(2)** Spearmanship, the spear : ἔγχεϊ φέρτερος εἶναι Γ 431. Cf. Η 289, Π 809, 834, Σ 252, Τ 218, Φ 159.

ἐγχρίμπτω [ἐγ-, ἐν- (6)]. Aor. pple. ἐγχρίμψας Ψ 334. 3 sing. imp. aor. pass. ἐγχριμφθήτω Ψ 338. Pple. ἐγχριμφθείς Η 272 (*v.l.* ἐνιχριμφθείς (ἐνι-, ἐν-)), Ν 146. Fem. ἐγχριμφθεῖσα Ε 662. Acc. sing. masc. ἐνιχριμφθέντα Ρ 405. **(1)** To bring near to. With dat. : τέρματι ἐγχρίμψας ἅρμα ('shaving' it) Ψ 334.—**(2)** In pass., to come near to. With dat. : αἰχμὴ ὀστέῳ ἐγχριμφθεῖσα (grazing it) Ε 662, ἀσπίδι ἐγχριμφθείς (app., having it driven on him by the force of the blow) Η 272. Cf. Ρ 405.—So ἐν νύσσῃ ἵππος ἐγχριμφθήτω (let him 'shave' it) Ψ 338.—Absol. : νωλεμὲς ἐγχρίμπτοντο (fought at close quarters, pressed each other hard) Ρ 413. Cf. Ν 146.

ἐγώ(ν) [cf. L. *ego*, Eng. *I*]. Pron. of the 1st person sing., I Α 26, 29, 76, 111, 117, 137, etc. : α 65, 179, 200, 212, 214, 303, etc.—Strengthened by γε : ἐγώ γε, ἔγωγε Α 173, 282, 296, 298, etc. : α 215, 217, γ 182, 232, etc.

ἐδάην, aor. δάω.

ἐδαμάσθην, aor. pass. δαμάζω.

ἐδάμασσα, aor. δαμάζω.

ἐδάμη, 3 sing. aor. pass. δαμάζω.

ἐδανός [orig. and sense unknown. Connexion with ἡδύς doubtful. Also written (doubtfully) ἑδανός, eatable, fr. ἔδω]. Epithet of ἔλαιον Ξ 172.

ἐδάσσατο, 3 sing. **ἐδάσαντο,** 3 pl. aor. δατέομαι.

ἔδαφος, τό. The hull (of a ship) ε 249.

ἔδαψε, 3 sing. aor. δάπτω.

ἐδέγμην, plupf. δέχομαι.

ἐδέδμητο, 3 sing. plupf. pass. δέμω.

ἐδείδιμεν, 1 pl. **ἐδείδισαν,** 3 pl. plupf. See δείδοικα.

ἔδειμα, aor. δέμω.

ἔδειξε, 3 sing. aor. δείκνυμι.

ἔδειραν, 3 pl. aor. δέρω.

ἔδεισε, 3 sing. aor. See δείδοικα.

ἐδέξατο, 3 sing. aor. δέχομαι.

ἔδεσκε, 3 sing. pa. iterative ἔδω.

ἐδεύησε, 3 sing. aor. δεύω[2].

ἐδήδαται, ἐδήδεται. See ἔδω.

ἐδήδοται, 3 sing. pf. pass. ἔδω.

ἐδηδώς, pf. pple. ἔδω.

ἐδητύς, -ύος, ἡ [ἔδω]. Food, meat Λ 780, Τ 231, 320 : δ 788, ε 201, ζ 250, κ 384, ρ 603.—See also under ἵημι[1] (9).

ἐδίδαξε, 3 sing. aor. διδάσκω.

ἐδίδου, 3 sing. impf. δίδωμι.

ἐδίηνε, 3 sing. aor. διαίνω.

ἔδμεναι, infin. ἔδω.

ἔδνα, τά (Ϝέδνα) [prob. conn. with (σϜ)ανδάνω, and orig. σϜέδνα]. Also, with prothetic ἐ, **ἐέδνα** (ἐϜεδνα). **(1)** A bride-price : πορὼν ἀπερείσια ἔδνα Π 178. Cf. Π 190, Χ 472 : ἐέδνοισι βρίσας ζ 159. Cf. θ 318, λ 117 = ν 378, λ 282, ο 18, π 391 = φ 161, τ 529.—(2) App., a dowry given by her parents to the bride α 277 = β 196.

ἕδος, τό [(σ)εδ-, ἕζομαι]. (1) One's seat: λιπὼν ἑ. Ι 194. Cf. Α 534, 581.—(2) The seat of a people, etc., an abode: Θήβης ἑ. (consisting in . . .) Δ 406, ἀθανάτων ἑ. Ε 360, Θ 456. Cf. Ε 367, 868, Ω 144, 544: ζ 42, λ 263, ν 344.—(3) Sitting: οὐχ ἑ. ἐστίν (it is no time for sitting) Λ 648. Cf. Ψ 205.

ἔδοσαν, 3 pl. aor. δίδωμι.

ἔδραθε, 3 sing. aor. δαρθάνω.

ἔδρακον, aor. δέρκομαι.

ἔδραμε, 3 sing. aor. τρέχω.

ἕδρη, -ης, ἡ [as ἕδος]. (1) (a) A seat: ἄλλοθι δήομεν ἕδρην π 44. Cf. γ 429, θ 16.—(b) One's seat: αὐτόθεν ἐξ ἕδρης Τ 77. Cf. Β 99, 211: ν 56, π 42.—(2) A seat of honour: τίον σε ἕδρῃ Θ 162. Cf. Μ 311.—(3) A company sitting together: ἐννέα ἕδραι ἔσαν γ 7, 31.

†**ἑδριάομαι** [(σ)εδ-, ἕζομαι]. 3 pl. impf. ἑδριόωντο Κ 198: η 98, π 344. Infin. ἑδριάασθαι Λ 646, 778: γ 35. (1) To sit down Κ 198: γ 35, π 344.—With κατά Λ 646 = 778.—(2) To sit, be seated: ἔνθ' ἑδριόωντο πίνοντες η 98.

ἔδῦ, 3 sing. **ἔδυν,** 3 pl. aor. δύω.

ἐδυνάσθη, 3 sing. aor. δύναμαι.

ἐδυνήσατο, 3 sing. aor. δύναμαι.

ἔδῡσαν[1], 3 pl. sigmatic aor. δύω.

ἔδῡσαν[2], 3 pl. aor. δύω.

ἐδύσετο, 3 sing. aor. mid. δύω.

ἐδύτην, 3 dual. **ἔδῡτε,** 2 pl. aor. δύω.

ἔδω. Infin. ἔδμεναι Δ 345, Ε 203, Ν 36, Χ 347: ι 476, κ 243, ξ 42, π 84, ρ 260, υ 214. 3 sing. pa. iterative ἔδεσκε Χ 501. Pf. pple. ἐδηδώς Ρ 542. Subj. mid. (in fut. sense) ἔδομαι ι 369. 2 sing. ἔδεαι Ω 129. 3 pl. ἔδονται Δ 237, Π 836, Σ 271, 283, Χ 509: β 123, χ 30. 3 sing. pf. pass. ἐδήδοται χ 56 (written also ἐδήδεται (for which cf. ὀρώρεται under ὄρνυμι) and ἐδήδαται (3 pl.)). (κατα-.) (1) Of men and beasts, to eat (food): κρέα Δ 345. Cf. Ε 341, Ζ 142, Κ 569, Μ 319, Ν 322, Φ 465, Χ 501: οἷα σύες ἔδουσιν κ 243. Cf. γ 480, ε 197, θ 222, ι 89 = κ 101, ι 84, λ 123 = ψ 270, ξ 17, 81, π 110, ρ 533, τ 536.—Absol., to take food, eat: εἰωθότες ἔδμεναι ἄδην Ε 203. Cf. Ν 36: πίνοντες καὶ ἔδοντες η 99. Cf. κ 243, 427, ξ 42, π 50, 84, ρ 260, υ 214.—(2) Fig., to eat (one's heart): θυμὸν ἔδοντες ι 75 = κ 143. Cf. Ω 129: κ 379.—(3) Of beasts, etc., to eat up, devour: χρόα γῦπες ἔδονται Δ 237, λέων κατὰ ταῦρον ἐδηδώς Ρ 542. Cf. Ο 636, Π 836, Σ 271, 283, Χ 42: χ 30.—Of the cannibal Cyclops ι 297, 369, 476.—Of a man fiercely desiring vengeance: ὠμὰ κρέα ἔδμεναι Χ 347.—Of worms, to eat, gnaw: σὲ εὐλαὶ ἔδονται Χ 509: μὴ κέρα ἶπες ἔδοιεν (should be found eating or to have eaten . . .) φ 395.—(4) To eat up, devour, consume, make away with: ἀλλότριον βίοτον α 160. Cf. α 250 = π 127, α 375 = β 140, β 123, ν 419, ξ 377, 417, π 389, 431, σ 280, φ 332, χ 56, ψ 9.

ἐδωδή, -ῆς, ἡ [ἔδω]. (1) Food, meat: καταστρύχω ἐδωδῇ λαούς (*i.e.* with requisitions for it) Ρ 225, κορεσσάμενος ἐδωδῆς Τ 167. Cf. δ 105, ε 95 = ξ 111, ε 196, ζ 76, ξ 42, 193.—(2) Fodder for horses Θ 504.—(3) Eating: νέον ἀπέληγεν ἐδωδῆς Ω 475. Cf. γ 70.

ἔδωκα, aor. δίδωμι.

ἑέ (ἐϜέ). Acc. ἑέ Υ 171, Ω 134. ἕ Δ 497, Ξ 162, Ο 241, etc.: ρ 387, etc. ἑ (encl.) Α 236, 510, Β 11, 197, etc.: α 321, 434, δ 527, ζ 133, etc. Genit. εἷο Δ 400: χ 19. ἕο Β 239, Ε 343, Ν 163, etc.: ε 459, η 217, θ 211, ι 398, etc. ἑό (encl.) Ο 165: ξ 461. εὑ (encl.) Ι 377, Ξ 427, Ω 293, etc. ἕθεν Γ 128, Ε 56, Ζ 62, Μ 205, etc.: τ 481, ψ 304. ἑθέν (encl.) Α 114, Ι 419, 686, Ο 199, etc. Dat. ἑοῖ Ν 495: δ 38. οἷ Ε 64, Θ 327, Ι 306, etc.: λ 433, ρ 330, χ 14, etc. οἱ (encl.) Α 72, 79, 104, 188, etc.: α 17, 37, 62, 88, etc. (1) In the encl. forms pron. of the 3rd person sing., him, her, it: μαντοσύνην, τήν οἱ πόρεν Α 72, περὶ γάρ ῥά ἑ χαλκὸς ἔλεψε φύλλα 236. Cf. Β 217, Γ 408, Δ 534, Ε 103, etc.: α 335, β 21, ζ 133, θ 405, etc.—(2) Reflexive in the accented forms: ἀμφὶ ἓ παπτήνας Δ 497. Cf. Β 239, Γ 128, Δ 400, Ε 56, 800, Θ 327, Ν 163, Ο 241, Ρ 407, Τ 385, etc.: κρήδεμνον ἀπὸ ἕο λῦσεν ε 459. Cf. η 217, ι 398, λ 433, χ 19, etc.

ἔεδνα. See ἕδνα.

ἐεδνόομαι [ἔεδνα]. To give in marriage β 53.

ἐεδνωτής, ὁ [ἔεδνα]. A match-maker, marriage-broker: οὐκ ἐεδνωταὶ κακοί εἰμεν Ν 382.

ἐεικοσάβοιος, -ον [ἐεικοσ-, ἐείκοσι + -α- (on analogy of numerals in -α) + βοῦς]. (1) Of the value of twenty oxen: τιμήν χ 57.—(2) In neut. pl. ἐεικοσάβοια, the value of twenty oxen: ἔδωκεν α 431.

ἐείκοσι, ἐεικοστός. See εἴκοσι, εἰκοστός.

ἐεικόσορος, -ον [ἐείκοσι + ὀρ-, ἐρ-, ἐρέσσω]. Of twenty oars: νηός ι 322.

ἐείλεον, 3 pl. impf. εἰλέω. See εἴλω.

ἔειπας, 2 sing. aor. See εἶπον.

ἔειπον. See εἶπον.

εείσατο[1], 3 sing. aor. mid. εἴδω (B).

ἐείσατο[2], 3 sing. aor. mid. ἵημι[2].

ἐέλδομαι, ἐέλδωρ. See ἔλδομαι, ἔλδωρ.

ἐελμένος, pf. pple. pass. εἴλω.

ἐέλπεται. See ἔλπω.

ἐέλσαι, aor. infin. εἴλω.

ἐέργαθε, 3 sing. aor. ἔργω[1].

ἐεργμέναι, nom. pl. fem. pf. pple. pass. ἔργω[1].

ἐέργνῡ, 3 sing. impf. ἔργνυμι.

ἐέργω. See ἔργω[1].

ἐέρση, ἐερσήεις. See ἔρση, ἑρσήεις.

ἔερτο, 3 sing. plupf. pass. εἴρω[1].

ἐέρχατο, 3 pl. plupf. pass. ἔργω[1].

ἐέσσατο, 3 sing. aor. mid. See ἕζομαι.

ἐέσσατο, 3 sing. aor. mid. ἕννυμι.

ἔεστο, 3 sing. plupf. mid. ἕννυμι.

ἐζευγμέναι, nom. pl. fem. pf. pple. pass. ζεύγνυμι.

ἔζευξαν, 3 pl. aor. ζεύγνυμι.

ἕζομαι [σε-σδ-, redup. fr. σ(ε)δ-, the rough breathing representing the first σ. Cf. ἵζω, L. *sedeo*]. The pres. indic. only in 2 sing. ἕζεαι κ 378. The forms from ἑζόμην (with imp. ἕζευ Ω 522) may be regarded as aorists, with the infin. accented ἑζέσθαι. From the same root 3 sing. aor. act. εἷσε Α 311, Β 549, Γ 382, Ζ 189, Η 57, Ι 200, Ψ 359: α 130, δ 531, ζ 8, η 169, θ 472, κ 233, 314, 366, μ 34, ξ 49, ο 286, σ 103, υ 210. 3 pl. εἷσαν Δ 392, Ε 693, Ψ 698, Ω 578, 720 : γ 416, ζ 212. ἕσαν Τ 393. Imp. εἷσον η 163. Pple. ἕσας ξ 280. Fem. ἕσᾶσα κ 361. Also 3 sing. aor. in mid. form ἑέσσατο ξ 295. (ἀν-, ἐφ-, καθ-, παρ-.) (I) In pres. and in impf. (or aor. (see above)). (1) To seat oneself, sit down, take one's seat: ἕζετ' ἀπάνευθε νεῶν Α 48. Cf. Α 68, 246, 349, Γ 211, Ζ 354, etc. : ἕζοντο κατὰ κλισμούς α 145. Cf. β 14, δ 51, 136, μ 172, ρ 602, etc.—(2) To crouch down : ἕζετο προϊδών Χ 275. Cf. ξ 31.—To sink to the ground, collapse Ν 653, Ξ 495, Φ 115.—To sink (to the ground): αἱ Ἀχαιῶν κῆρες ἐπὶ χθονὶ ἑζέσθην Θ 74.—(3) To assume a sitting from a recumbent position : ἕζετο δ' ὀρθωθεὶς Β 42, Ψ 235. Cf. ζ 118. —(II) In sigmatic aor. act. and mid. (1) To cause to seat oneself, bid be seated: κὰδ δ' εἷσεν Ἀχαιούς Η 57. Cf. Ι 200, Ω 578 : ξεῖνον ἐπὶ θρόνου εἷσον η 163. Cf. α 130, γ 416, η 169, θ 472, κ 233, 314 = 366, μ 34, ξ 49, ο 286.—(2) To cause (a person) to be somewhere, place (him) there : κὰδ δ' εἷσ' ἐν θαλάμῳ Γ 382. Cf. Ε 693, Ψ 698 : ἐς ἀσάμινθον ἕσασα κ 361, ἐς Λιβύην μ' ἐπὶ νηὸς ἑέσσατο (for a voyage to Libya) ξ 295. Cf. ζ 212, ξ 280, σ 103.—(3) To lay or post (an ambush) : λόχον Δ 392, Ζ 189 : δ 531.—(4) To post, detail for a duty : σκοπὸν εἷσε Φοίνικα Ψ 359. Cf. Ω 720. —So of putting in charge : ἐπὶ βουσίν υ 210.—(5) To place, establish, settle : κὰδ δ' ἐν Ἀθήνῃς εἷσεν [Ἐρεχθῆα] Β 549.—So to settle (a people) ζ 8.—(6) With ἀνά, to put on board a ship Α 311.—(7) To put in its place, settle: ἀμφὶ λέπαδν' ἕσαν Τ 393.

ἕῃ, 3 sing. subj. εἰμί.

ἧκε, 3 sing. aor. ἵημι[1].

ἕην, 3 sing. impf. εἰμί.

ἑήνδανε, 3 sing. impf. ἁνδάνω.

ἑῆος, genit. See ἐΰς.

ἕησθα, 2 sing. impf. εἰμί.

ἕῃσι, 3 sing. subj. εἰμί.

ἔθανε, 3 sing. aor. θνήσκω.

ἔθειραι, αἱ. (1) The mane of a horse Θ 42 = Ν 24.—(2) Horse-hairs forming a crest on a helmet : μιάνθησαν ἐ. αἵματι Π 795. Cf. Τ 382, Χ 315.

ἐθείρω. App., to tend, till : ἀλωήν Φ 347.

ἐθελήσω, fut. ἐθέλω.

ἔθελξε, 3 sing. aor. θέλγω.

ἐθελοντήρ, -ῆρος, ὁ [ἐθέλω]. A volunteer β 292.

ἐθέλχθης, 2 sing. aor. pass. θέλγω.

ἐθέλω. 2 sing. pa. iterative ἐθέλεσκες Ι 486. 3 -ε Ι 353. 3 pl. -ον Ν 106. Fut. ἐθελήσω θ 223. 2 sing. -εις σ 362. 3 -ει Ο 215, Σ 262 : ρ 226. 3 dual -ετον θ 316. Aor. ἐθέλησα ν 341. 3 sing. -ε Σ 396. 2 sing. pres. subj. in shorter form θέλῃσθα Α 554. (1) (a) To be minded, have a mind, desire, wish, purpose, choose. With infin. : περὶ πάντων ἔμμεναι ἄλλων Α 287. Cf. Β 247, Γ 404, Ε 441, Ζ 150, Θ 10, etc. : τοῦτ' ἀρέσθαι α 390, οὐδ' ἤθελον ἐξαπατῆσαι (did not mean to . . .) ν 277. Cf. α 405, β 86, γ 243, δ 540, ε 205, etc.—Elliptically : ἔρξον ὅπως ἐθέλεις Δ 37, αἴ κ' ἐθέλῃσθα Τ 147 (if the infinitives be taken as depending on πάρα σοί or as imperatives). Cf. Α 554, Ι 146, Ξ 337, Φ 484, etc. : εἰ δ' ἐθέλεις πεζός (prefer) γ 324, ἔπιον ὅσον ἤθελε θυμός 342. Cf. β 54, δ 391, ξ 54, υ 136, etc.—Absol. : οὐκ εἰῶσ' ἐθέλοντα (thwart my desire) Β 132, αἴ κ' ἐθέλῃσιν (if he will have it so) Σ 306, οὐκ ἐθέλων (unintentionally) Ψ 88. Cf. Ζ 165, Κ 556, Ξ 120, Σ 473, etc. : τὴν ἐθέλων ἐθέλουσαν ἀνήγαγεν γ 272. Cf. α 349, γ 228, ο 72, ρ 424, χ 31, etc.—(b) To choose or desire (that a person shall do something). With acc. and infin. : ἔμ' ἧσθαι δευόμενον Α 133. Cf. Γ 67. —(2) (a) Without implication of desire, to be minded, willing, prepared, disposed, inclined, content. With infin. : ἄποινα δέξασθαι Α 112, ἑτάροισιν ἀμυνέμεν Ρ 702. Cf. Α 116, Γ 241, Ζ 281, Ν 743, Τ 187, etc. : κείνου ὄλεθρον ἐνισπεῖν γ 92. Cf. ι 95, κ 342, λ 105, ο 435, ρ 321, etc.—Elliptically : αἴ κ' ἐθέλῃσι, δώσει Θ 142. Cf. Ι 255, Λ 782, Τ 142, Ω 335, etc. : αἴ κ' ἐθέλῃσ', ἰήσεται ι 520. Cf. η 305, ρ 11, 19, 277, etc.—Absol. : μεθιεῖς τε καὶ οὐκ ἐθέλεις Ζ 523. Cf. Δ 300, Κ 291 (ἐθέλουσα = πρόφρασσα 290), Υ 87, Ω 289, etc. : οὐκ ἐθελούσῃ β 50. Cf. ε 99, η 315, ο 449, υ 98, etc. —(b) With acc. and infin. as under (1) (b) : εἴ μ' ἐθέλεις τελέσαι τάφον Ω 660. Cf. π 318.—(3) With οὐ, to decline, refuse. With infin. : εἰ ἂν τιμὴν οὐκ ἐθέλωσι τίνειν Γ 289. Cf. Ο 492.—(4) To have the heart, venture. With infin. : ἀντίον ἐλθέμεναι Ρ 66. Cf. Ι 353, Ν 106.—(5) Passes into the sense to be able, have the power : οὐδ' ἔθελε [ποταμὸς] προρέειν Φ 366.

ἔθεν, ἑθέν. See ἑέ.

ἔθετο, 3 sing. aor. mid. τίθημι.

ἐθηήσαντο, 3 pl. aor. θηέομαι.

ἔθηκα, aor. τίθημι.

ἔθλασε, 3 sing. aor. θλάω.

ἔθνος, τό (Ϝέθνος). (1) A body or band of men : ἑτάρων εἰς ἐ. ἐχάζετο Γ 32 = Λ 585 = Ν 566 = 596 = 648 = Ξ 408, Ν 165, 533, Π 817. Cf. Β 91 = 464, Η 115, Λ 595 = Ο 591 = Ρ 114, Λ 724, Μ 330, Ν 495, Ρ 552, 581, 680.—So ἔθνεα νεκρῶν κ 526, λ 34, 632.—(2) A swarm (of bees) Β 87.—(Of flies) Β 469.—A flight (of birds) Β 459, Ο 691.—A herd (of swine) ξ 73.

ἔθορε, 3 sing. aor. θρῴσκω.

ἔθρεψε, 3 sing. aor. τρέφω.

ἔθω [conn. with ἦθος and orig. σϜέθω. Cf. L. *suesco*]. 3 sing. pf. εἴωθε Ε 766 : ρ 394. ἔωθε Θ 408, 422. Pple. εἰωθώς, -ότος Ε 203, 231, Ζ 508, Ο 265. (1) In pres. pple., after one's wont : οὓς παῖδες ἐριδμαίνωσιν ἔθοντες Π 260.—Of a beast, after the manner of its kind Ι 540.—(2) In pf., to be wont or accustomed. With infin. : εἰωθότες ἔδμεναι ἄδην Ε 203. Cf. Ε 766, Ζ 508 = Ο 265, Θ 408, 422 : ρ 394.—Adjectivally in pple., to which one is accustomed : ἡνιόχῳ εἰωθότι Ε 231.

εἰ (cf. αἴ, ἤν). (1) Interjectionally with imp., come ! εἰ φευγόντων Ι 46, εἰ ἄκουσον 262.—For εἰ δ' ἄγε (ἄγετε) see ἄγε.—(2) With opt. introducing a wish. (a) εἴ τις τούσδε καλέσειεν Κ 111. Cf. Ο 571, Π 559, Ω 74 : εἰ βόες εἶεν σ 371. Cf.

ι 456, σ 376.—See also εἴθε.—(b) So εἰ γάρ: εἰ γὰρ Ἀθήνη δοίη κάρτος P 561. Cf. α 255, γ 218, ρ 496, 513, σ 366.—Of the present: εἰ γὰρ εἴην ἀθάνατος Θ 538. Cf. N 825.—(3) Citing a fact in corroboration or as the ground of an appeal or exhortation made or to be made, if it is certain or true that . . ., as surely as . . . For the examples see (I) of Table at end.—(4) Introducing in protasis one of two opposed clauses, even if, even though, though, granted that (such words as 'yet,' 'still,' 'nevertheless,' introducing or suppliable before the apodosis). For the examples and constructions see (II) of Table.—(5) Introducing the protasis of conditional sentences, if, on condition that, supposing that (such words as 'then,' 'consequently,' 'therefore,' introducing or suppliable before the apodosis). For the examples and constructions see (III) of Table.—(6) With ὡς (or ὡς . . . τε) expressing supposition for comparison. (a) With indic.: ὡς εἴ θ' ἕσπετο μῆλα N 492.—(b) With subj.: ὡς εἴ τε φιλήσῃ I 481.—(c) With opt.: ἴσαν ὡς εἴ τε πυρὶ χθὼν νέμοιτο B 780, οὐκ ἀλέγω, ὡς εἴ με γυνὴ βάλοι Λ 389. Cf. Λ 467, X 410: ι 314, κ 416, 420, ρ 366.—(7) Sim. without expressed vb.: ὡς εἴ τε θῶες Λ 474. Cf. E 374 = Φ 510, I 648 = Π 59, Π 192, T 17, 366, X 150, Ψ 598, Ω 328: η 36, ξ 254, ρ 111, τ 39, 211.—(8) εἰ μή without expressed vb., unless it be (were), unless, except: εἰ μὴ Πάτροκλος P 477. Cf. Σ 193, Ψ 792: μ 326, ρ 383.—(9) In final clauses, if haply, in the hope that. (a) With fut.: μενοίνεον εἰ τελέουσιν M 59.—(b) With subj. (α) Pure: ἐλθεῖν εἴ πως ὕπνον χεύῃ Ξ 163. Cf. δ 739, ε 471, μ 96.—(β) With κεν: στήομεν, εἴ κεν ἐρύξομεν O 297. Cf. χ 76.—(c) With opt.: ἐρήτυον, εἴ ποτ' ἀϋτῆς σχοίατο B 97. Cf. Γ 450, K 19, 206, M 122, Ξ 163, P 104, Σ 322, Υ 464, X 196, Ψ 40: β 342, δ 317, ε 439, ζ 144, ι 229, 267, 349, 418, λ 479, 628, μ 334, ο 316, χ 91.—(10) In object clauses, whether. (a) With indic.: φράσαι εἴ με σαώσεις A 83, οὐκ οἶδ' εἰ θεός ἐστιν E 183. Cf. B 367, Z 367, Θ 111, Ξ 125, Φ 266: α 207, θ 133, κ 193, λ 371, 458, 494, ν 328, ρ 510, τ 216, 325, ω 259. —εἴτε (εἴ τε) . . . εἴτε (εἴ τε) . . .: εἴτ' εὐχωλῆς ἐπιμέμφεται εἴθ' ἑκατόμβης A 65. Cf. B 349: γ 90.—With fut. and κεν: τὰ Ζεὺς οἶδεν, εἴ κε τελευτήσει ο 524.—(b) With subj. (α) Pure: οὐκ οἶδ' εἰ κακορραφίης ἐπαύρηαι O 16.—εἴτε . . . εἴτε . . . M 239.—(β) With κεν: ἣν ἀρετὴν διαείσεται, εἴ κ' ἐμὸν ἔγχος μείνῃ Θ 535. Cf. Θ 532, O 403, Π 860, X 244: β 332, γ 216.—(c) With opt. (α) Pure: ἐπειρᾶτο εἴ πώς οἱ εἴξειαν (to see whether . . .) N 807. Cf. Δ 88, E 168, M 333, N 760, P 681, T 385: κακὰ βυσσοδομεύων, εἴ πως τισαίμην (considering how . . .) ι 317, μῦθόν κε φαίην, εἴ σφωϊν ἅδοι (*i.e.* to see if they will agree) υ 327. Cf. α 115, β 351, ι 421, κ 147, μ 113, ν 415, ξ 460, 498, σ 375, υ 224, χ 381, ψ 91.—(β) With κεν: τίς οἶδ' εἴ κέν οἱ θυμὸν ὀρίναις; Λ 792. Cf. μ 113, ξ 120.

εἰαμενή, -ῆς, ἡ. A piece of low or flat-lying land: ἐν εἰαμενῇ ἕλεος (consisting of . . ., forming . . .) Δ 483, O 631.

εἰανός. See ἑανός[1].

εἰαρινός, -ή, -όν (Ϝειαρινός) [(Ϝ)έαρ, with the ε metrically lengthened]. Of the spring, spring . . .: ἄνθεσιν B 89. Cf. B 471 = Π 643, Θ 307: σ 367 = χ 301.

εἴασκον, pa. iterative ἐάω.

εἵαται, 3 pl. pres. **εἵατο**[1], 3 pl. impf. ἧμαι.

εἵατο[2], 3 pl. plupf. mid. ἕννυμι.

εἴβω [= λείβω]. (κατ-.) To shed (a tear) Π 11, T 323, Ω 9: δ 153, θ 531, λ 391, π 219, 332, ω 234, 280.

εἰδάλιμος, -η [εἶδος]. Fair to see, comely ω 279.

εἶδαρ, -ατος, τό [ἐδ-Ϝαρ, fr. ἐδ-, ἔδω]. (1) Food, meat ι 84, λ 123 = ψ 270.—In pl. of food of various kinds: εἴδατα πόλλ' ἐπιθεῖσα α 140 = δ 56 = η 176 = κ 372 = ο 139 = ρ 95.—Of food disposed on a table: ἀπὸ δ' εἴδατα χεῦεν ἔραζε χ 20, 85.—Of food used as bait: ἰχθύσι δόλον κατὰ εἴδατα βάλλων μ 252.—(2) Fodder for horses E 369, N 35.

εἰδήσεις, 2 sing. fut. εἴδω (C).

εἶδος (Ϝεῖδος) [εἴδω]. (One's general bodily) appearance or form (when used without qualification connoting comeliness): εἰ. ἀρίστη B 715, ἥ τε κόμη τό τε εἰ. Γ 55. Cf. B 58, Γ 39 = N 769, Γ 45, 124, 224, E 787 = Θ 228, Z 252, K 316, N 365, 378, P 142, 279, Φ 316, X 370, Ω 376: εἰ. Ἀφροδίτης δ 14. Cf. δ 264, ε 213, 217, ζ 16, 152, η 57, θ 116, 169, 174, 176, λ 337 = σ 249, λ 469 = ω 17, λ 550, ξ 177, ρ 454, σ 4, 251, τ 124, υ 71, ω 253, 374.—Of a dog ρ 308.

†**εἴδω** [Ϝιδ-. Cf. L. *video*]. (A) Aor. εἶδον (ἔϜιδον) T 292: κ 194, λ 281, 298, 576, ω 445. ἴδον (Ϝίδον) A 262, Γ 169, Λ 614, P 328, Ψ 462, etc.: α 212, δ 269, ζ 160, ν 318, ψ 40, etc. 2 sing. εἶδες λ 162. ἴδες Υ 205, X 236: λ 371. 3 εἶδε Δ 149, E 572, Λ 112, T 16, Ψ 874, etc.: δ 524, ρ 31. ἴδε Δ 151, I 195, N 495, Ω 702, etc.: α 3, ε 375, λ 615, φ 83, etc. 3 dual ἰδέτην β 152 (*v.l.* ἱκέτην). 1 pl. εἴδομεν ι 182. ἴδομεν μ 244. 3 εἶδον E 515, H 308, Φ 207: κ 453. ἴδον A 600, K 275, M 83, Π 660, Ψ 202, etc.: β 155, κ 219, ξ 29, χ 22, ω 391, etc. Subj. ἴδωμι Σ 63, X 450. ἴδω Ω 555: κ 387, π 32. 2 sing. ἴδῃς Δ 205: ο 76. 3 ἴδῃ Δ 98, 195, Ω 337. 1 pl. ἴδωμεν K 97: φ 112, 336. 2 ἴδητε Δ 249: κ 426. 3 ἴδωσι T 174. Opt. ἴδοιμι Z 284: ι 229, κ 147. 2 sing. ἴδοις Δ 223, Z 330: σ 375, 379. 3 ἴδοι B 198, Δ 232, Ω 583, etc.: ζ 113, ω 491. 3 pl. ἴδοιεν M 268: σ 246. Imp. ἴδε P 179: θ 443, χ 233. Pple. ἰδών, -οῦσα A 148, 537, Γ 224, N 184, O 12, Ω 320, etc.: γ 438, δ 43, ζ 199, η 224, ρ 215, ω 90, etc. Infin. ἰδέειν Γ 236, E 475, P 643, Ψ 463, etc.: δ 475, ζ 314, λ 567, ρ 142, etc. ἰδεῖν Θ 453, etc.: λ 143, etc. 3 sing. pa. iterative ἴδεσκε Γ 217. **Mid.** Aor. ἰδόμην K 47: ε 359, π 472, τ 185. 3 sing. ἴδετο δ 22. 3 pl. εἴδοντο Γ 154, Θ 251, Π 278, P 724. ἴδοντο Δ 374, Ω 484: η 322, σ 320. Subj. ἴδωμαι A 262, Z 365, Φ 61, etc.: ζ 126, ν 215, ψ 83. 2 sing. ἴδηαι Γ 130, N 229, Σ 135, etc.: ζ 311, σ 269, ψ 5. ἴδῃ A 203, Γ 163, N 449, O 32: λ 94, ο 432. 3 ἴδηται B 237, P 93, T 151, etc.: δ 412,

ρ 9, φ 159, etc. 1 pl. *ἰδώμεθα* κ 44. 2 *ἴδησθε* Ο 147 : δ 414, 421, θ 307. 3 sing. opt. *ἴδοιτο* Γ 453, Μ 333, Ρ 681, etc. : θ 280, κ 574, λ 366. 3 pl. *ἰδοίατο* Σ 524 : α 163, λ 361. Imp. pl. *ἴδεσθε* Ψ 469. Infin. *ἰδέσθαι* Γ 194, Ζ 176, Ξ 286, Ο 600, Σ 83, etc. : γ 233, ζ 306, ρ 265, ω 369, etc.—**(B)** 3 sing. pres. mid. *εἴδεται* Α 228, Θ 559, Ν 98, Ξ 472, Ω 197 : ι 11. Pple. *εἰδόμενος, -η* Β 280, Γ 122, Ε 462, Ν 69 : α 105, β 268, 401, γ 372, ζ 22, θ 8, χ 206, ω 503, 548. 2 sing. aor. *ἐείσαο* Ι 645. 3 *ἐείσατο* β 320, ε 398, 442, η 281, 343, θ 295, κ 149. *εἴσατο* Β 791, Ν 191 (reading *χρώς*. See below (II) (1)) Υ 81, Ω 319: ε 281, 283, θ 283, ν 352, τ 283. 3 pl. *εἴσαντο* Μ 103. 3 sing. opt. *εἴσαιτο* Β 215. Pple. *εἰσάμενος* Ν 45, Π 716, Ρ 73, Φ 213, etc. : λ 241. With prothetic *ἐ* *ἐεισάμενος* Β 22, Π 720, Ρ 326, 585, Υ 82. Fem. *εἰσαμένη* Ε 785, Ρ 555. *ἐεισαμένη* Β 795, Γ 389 : ζ 24.—**(C)** Pf. *οἶδα* (*Ϝοῖδα*) Δ 163, Η 237, Π 50, Σ 192, Τ 219, Ω 105, etc. : γ 184, ζ 176, θ 215, ξ 365, ρ 307, υ 309, etc. 2 sing. *οἶδας* α 337. *οἶσθα* Α 85, Η 358, Ο 93, Ω 662, etc. : δ 465, ο 20, ρ 573, ψ 60, etc. 3 *οἶδε* Α 343, Δ 361, Η 236, Σ 185, etc. : α 53, δ 771, ν 405, υ 46, etc. 1 pl. *ἴδμεν* Α 124, Η 281, Κ 100, Ψ 890, etc. : δ 109, κ 190, μ 189, ψ 110, etc. 2 *ἴστε* Β 485, Ψ 276 : η 211, φ 110. 3 *ἴσᾱσι* Ζ 151, Σ 420, Υ 214 : β 211, δ 379, 468, ν 239. *ἴσᾱσι* Ι 36, Ψ 312 : β 283, θ 559, λ 122, ω 188, etc. Plupf. *ᾔδεα* (in form an aor., for *ἐϜείδεσα*) Θ 366, Ξ 71: δ 745, ν 340. 2 sing. *ᾔδησθα* τ 93. *ᾐείδης* (for *ἐϜείδεας*) Χ 280. 3 *ᾔδεε* Β 409, Ρ 402, Σ 404, etc. : ψ 29. *ᾔδη* Α 70, Ε 64, Ν 355, Υ 466, etc. : β 16, γ 146, ξ 433, ψ 220, etc. *ᾐείδη* ι 206. 3 pl. *ἴσαν* Σ 405 : α 176, δ 772, ν 170, ψ 152. Subj. *εἰδέω* Α 515. *εἰδῶ* α 174, δ 645, ν 232, ξ 186, ω 258, 297, 403. *ἰδέω* Ξ 235 : π 236. 2 sing. *εἰδῇς* Α 185, Ζ 150, Υ 213, Φ 487 : β 111, η 317, λ 442. *ἰδῇς* Θ 420 : ι 348, χ 234. 3 *εἰδῇ* Ο 207, 412, Υ 122, Ψ 322 : θ 586, τ 329, 332. *ἰδῇ* Θ 406. 1 pl. *εἴδομεν* Α 363, Ν 327, Π 19, Χ 130, 244 : γ 18. 2 *εἴδετε* Θ 18, Σ 53 : ι 17. 3 *εἰδῶσι* β 112. 2 sing. opt. *εἰδείης* ε 206. 3 *εἰδείη* Μ 229, Π 73. Imp. *ἴσθι* β 356, λ 224. 3 sing. *ἴστω* Η 411, Ο 36, Τ 258, etc. : ε 184, ξ 158, π 302, etc. Pple. *εἰδώς, -υῖα* Α 385, Β 823, 345, Κ 250, Ο 527, Ρ 5, etc. : α 37, γ 277, μ 156, ω 51, etc. Fem. *ἰδυῖα, -ης* Α 365, 608, Ι 128, Σ 380, 482, Υ 12, etc. : α 428, η 92, ν 289, ο 418, ψ 182, ω 278, etc. Infin. *ἴδμεναι* Ν 273 : δ 200, 493, μ 154. *ἴδμεν* Λ 719 : θ 146, 213. 2 sing. fut. *εἰδήσεις* η 327. Infin. *εἰδησέμεν* ζ 257. *εἰδήσειν* Α 546. Fut. in mid. form *εἴσομαι* Θ 532, Ξ 8 (see (III) (1)) : τ 501, χ 7 (see (III) (10)). 2 sing. *εἴσεαι* Η 226, Φ 292 : β 40, π 246, ω 506. 3 *εἴσεται* Α 548, Θ 111, Π 243. (δια-, εἰσαν-, εἰσ-, ἐκκατ-, ἐξ-, ἐπ-, περίοιδα, προ-.) **(I)** In forms (A) in act. and mid. **(1)** To discern with the eye, catch sight of, see, perceive, behold : *τὼ ἰδὼν* Α 330. Cf. Β 198, Γ 236, Δ 255, Ζ 176, Ν 330, etc. : *ὡς ξείνους ἴδον* γ 34. Cf. α 113, δ 523, ε 41, ζ 113, ι 182, etc.—Absol. : *οὐδ' ἠγνοίησεν ἰδοῦσα* Α 537. Cf. Ε 770, Θ 397, Ρ 646, Ψ 469, etc. : *ὅθεν κέ τις οὐδὲ ἴδοιτο* (app., which dazzle the (mind's) eye, defy detection) λ 366. Cf. γ 373, ε 74, φ 122, ψ 40, etc.—**(2)** To look at, inspect, examine : *τόξον* φ 405. Cf. ν 215.—To see to, look to : *πῶμα* θ 443.—So *ἅρματος ἀμφὶς ἰδών* Β 384.—Of a surgeon, to see (a patient) Δ 195, 205.—To examine (a wound) Δ 217.—**(3)** With *ἐ(ι)σάντα*, to look at face to face, look in the face : *ἔγνω ἐσάντα ἰδών* Ρ 334. Cf. ε 217, λ 143, ο 532, π 458, ρ 239.—**(4)** To witness, see, look on at : *θέσκελα ἔργα* Γ 130. Cf. Α 203, Ν 344, Ρ 179 : θ 307, χ 233.—**(5)** To go to see, see, visit (a person) : *οἰκῆας ἄλοχόν τε* Ζ 365. Cf. Σ 63 : δ 162.—To visit, inspect : *μῆλα* Δ 476. Cf. Κ 97 : δ 412, ο 505.—To see *to*, inspect : *ἐπὶ ἔργα ἰδεῖν* π 144.—**(6)** To see so as to gain knowledge or experience of : *Φρύγας* Γ 185. Cf. Α 262, etc. : *πολλῶν ἀνθρώπων ἄστεα* α 3. Cf. δ 269, ζ 160, etc.—Sim. : *νόστιμον ἦμαρ* γ 233 = ε 220 = θ 466, ζ 311.—So *ἧς οὔ τι χάριν ἴδεν* (had no joy of her) Λ 243.—**(7)** With pple. expressing something observed in connexion with a person or thing : *μή σε ἴδωμαι θεινομένην* Α 587. Cf. Α 600, Γ 154, Ε 572, Ο 279, etc. : α 163, γ 221, θ 286, λ 528, etc.—Sim. with adj. : *ὡς ἴδε χῶρον ἐρῆμον* Κ 520. Cf. Ρ 652 : ω 371.—So *οἷον* δ 421.—With adj. and pple. : *ζωόν τε καὶ ἀρτεμέα προσιόντα* Ε 515 = Η 308.—**(8)** To see, find out, discover. With dependent clause : *αἴ κεν . . .* Δ 249. Cf. Ε 221 = Θ 105, Θ 251, 376, Τ 144, Φ 61, Χ 450 : *ὅττι τάδ' ἐστίν* κ 44. Cf. χ 234, ω 491.—With acc. and clause : *ἴδοις κέ με, εἰ . . .* σ 375.—Absol. : *ὄφρα ἴδωμεν* φ 112, 336. Cf. ζ 126, φ 159.—To see or find out to one's cost. With clause : *οἷος Ζηνὸς γόνος ἐνθάδ' ἱκάνω* Ν 449. Cf. Β 237, Ο 32.—To see or know of something happening. With infin. : *οὔ πω ἰδόμην οὐδ' ἔκλυον ἄνδρ' ἕνα τοσσάδε μητίσασθαι* Κ 47.—**(9)** To direct one's eyes, look, glance : *ὑπόδρα* Α 148, *εἰς οὐρανόν* Γ 364. Cf. Β 271, Ζ 404, Ρ 167, Ψ 143, etc. : β 152, θ 165, μ 244, π 477, ρ 304, etc.—Sim. : *ἔμοιγε εἰς ὦπα ἰδέσθαι* Ι 373. Cf. Ο 147 : ψ 107.—**(10)** The aor. infin. used epexegetically : *θαῦμα ἰδέσθαι* Ε 725, *νέκυν σαῶσαι ἢ ἀλόχῳ ἰδέειν* Ω 36. Cf. Γ 194, Κ 439, Σ 83, 212, 377 : ε 217, ζ 306, η 45, θ 20, 366, ι 143, ν 108, ρ 265, σ 195, τ 380, χ 405, ω 369, 374.—**(II)** In forms (B) **(1)** To be seen, appear, come into view : *εἴδεται ἄστρα* Θ 559, *οὔ πῃ χρὼς εἴσατο* Ν 191 (for the sense with *v.l.* *χροός* see ἵημι[2] (5)). Cf. Ω 319 : *τῇ οἱ (μοι) ἐείσατο χῶρος ἄριστος* ε 442, η 281 (app. tinged with the notion of seeming, 'where there seemed to be . . .'). Cf. ε 281, 283, 398, κ 149, ν 352.—So *εἴδεται ἦμαρ δαμῆναι* Ν 98.—**(2)** To seem, appear. With infin. : *τό τοι κὴρ εἴδεται εἶναι* Α 228, *γελοίϊον ἔμμεναι* Β 215. Cf. Ι 645, Μ 103 : ι 11.—With adj. without infin. : *οὔ μοι κακὸς εἴδεται* Ξ 472. Cf. τ 283.—Impers. with infin. : *τί τοι εἴδεται εἶναι;* Ω 197. Cf. β 320.—With adj. without infin. : *ἀσπαστὸν ἐείσατο κοιμηθῆναι* η 343, θ 295.—**(3)** To make a show of *doing something*. With infin. : *εἴσατ' ἴμεν ἐς Λῆμνον* θ 283.—**(4)** To make oneself like. With dat. : *τῷ ἐεισάμενος* Β 22, *εἴσατο φθογγὴν Πολίτῃ* (in voice) 791. Cf. Β 795, Ε 785, Ν 45, Φ 213, etc. : ζ 24, λ 241.—**(5)** To be like, resemble. With dat.: εἰδομένη κήρυκι (in the likeness of . . .) B 280. Cf. Γ 122, E 462, N 69: α 105, β 268 = 401 = χ 206 = ω 503 = 548, γ 372, ζ 22, θ 8.—(**III**) In forms (C) (**1**) To have cognizance of, be apprised of, know about: ὃς ᾔδη τὰ ἐόντα A 70, θεοπρόπιον ὅ τι οἶσθα 85. Cf. B 38, 486, E 64, Z 150, N 355, etc.: οἶδε δίκας ἄλλων γ 244, εἰδότα πολλά (with my knowledge of the world) ι 281. Cf. β 16, δ 745, θ 559, μ 154, π 246, etc.—So εἰδὼς κῆρ' ὀλοήν (the doom before him) N 665, ἠείδης τὸν ἐμὸν μόρον (had knowledge that I was doomed) X 280: οὐ εἰδότ' ὄλεθρον (not suspecting) δ 534. Cf. α 37, β 283.—With prep.: περὶ κείνου ρ 363.—To be (sufficiently) informed as to: τούτους δ 551.—Absol.: ἵνα εἴδομεν ἄμφω A 363, οἶσθα 365, τάχα εἴσομαι Ξ 8 (or the word may be referred to ἵημι[2] (4)). Cf. A 385, I 345, Σ 404, Ω 105, etc.: α 174, 216, δ 200, ρ 153, etc.—(**2**) To make the acquaintance of: Φαιήκων ὅσσοι ἄριστοι ζ 257. Cf. θ 213.—To be acquainted or familiar with: θαλάσσης βένθεα α 53, δ 386, ἴσαν ἡμέτερον δῶ α 176 (or the word may be referred to εἶμι (6) (a)). Cf. ζ 176, η 25, θ 560, ν 239.—Absol.: πρὶν εἰδότες ν 113.—To know the character of: ἑκάστην τ 501.—(**3**) To know so as to have skill in: μαντοσύνας B 832 = Λ 330, ἔργα Σ 420.—Cf. Γ 202, H 236, 237, I 128, 270, Λ 719, T 245, Ψ 263: α 337, θ 134, 146, ν 289 = π 158, ο 418, ω 278.—To be acquainted with, know the use of: νέας λ 124 = ψ 271.—To know the properties of: φάρμακα Λ 741.—(**4**) To know of the existence of, know of: ξυνήϊα A 124. Cf. T 115: ι 206, λ 122, ψ 269.—(**5**) To feel, be influenced by: νέμεσιν Z 351.—(**6**) To bear in mind: ταῦτα πάντα λ 224.—(**7**) In imp. in oaths and adjurations: ὅρκια Ζεὺς ἴστω H 411, ἴστω τόδε Γαῖα O 36. Cf. K 329, T 258: ε 184, ξ 158 = ρ 155 = υ 230, τ 303.—(**8**) With genit., to know about: πένθεος Λ 657, ἄλλου δ' οὔ τευ οἶδα τεῦ . . . Σ 192 (I do not know as to anyone whether . . . (with abrupt change to the direct interrogative)): κείνων γ 184 (or the genit. may be taken as depending on οἵ τε . . . οἵ τε . . .).—To have experience of or skill in: τόξων B 718, τόκοιο P 5. Cf. B 823, Δ 310, Z 438, Λ 710, O 412, Ψ 665, etc.: α 202, δ 818, ε 250.—With complementary infin.: τόξων εἰδότες μάχεσθαι B 720.—Absol.: φάρμακα εἰδὼς πάσσεν (skilfully) Δ 218.—The pf. pple. adjectivally: ἰδυίῃσι πραπίδεσσιν (knowing, skilful) A 608, Σ 380, 482, Υ 12: η 92.—(**9**) To know how *to do something*, to have skill or facility in *doing it*. With infin.: οὐδέ τι οἶδε νοῆσαι A 343, οἶδα νωμῆσαι βῶν H 238. Cf. H 240, 241, 358 = M 232, O 632, 679, Υ 201 = 432, Ψ 309, 312: θ 215.—(**10**) With pple. expressing something known: Πάτροκλον τεθνηότα P 402. Cf. η 211, ψ 29, ω 404.—With dependent clause: ὅσσον . . . A 515, εἰ . . . E 183. Cf. B 192, Δ 360, Θ 32, 532, K 100, Ξ 71, O 204, Υ 434, etc.: β 332, γ 18, δ 109, 712, 771, θ 28, π 424, ρ 78, etc.—With acc. and clause: ᾔδεε γὰρ ἀδελφεὸν ὡς ἐπονεῖτο B 409: σκοπὸν ἄλλον εἴσομαι, αἴ κε τύχωμι (whether . . .) χ 7 (or the word may be referred to ἵημι[2] (1)). Cf. δ 772 = ν 170 = ψ 152, ξ 365, ρ 373.—So τό γε, ὁπποτέρῳ . . . Γ 308. Cf. E 406, T 421, Υ 466: τόδε, μὴ . . . ω 506. Cf. γ 146, ν 314, ξ 119, etc.—(**11**) To know to one's cost. With clause: ὅσσον φέρτερός εἰμι A 185. Cf. H 226, Θ 111, 406, Π 243, Φ 487.—(**12**) To have (in one's mind), be endowed with: ἔπεα φρεσὶ ᾔσιν ᾔδη B 213. Cf. λ 445.—So without φρεσίν: πεπνυμένα μήδεα εἰδὼς H 278. Cf. Γ 202, Σ 363, Ψ 322, 709, Ω 88: β 38, 88, 122, δ 696, 711, ε 182, ζ 12, θ 586, ν 296, τ 286, υ 46, χ 361, ω 442.—Of character, disposition or mood: ἄγρια. See ἄγριος (5).—ἀθεμίστια. See ἀθεμίστιος (2).—αἴσιμα. See αἴσιμος (2).—ἀμύμονα. See ἀμύμων (3).—ἀπατήλια. See ἀπατήλιος.—ἀπηνέα. See ἀπηνής (1).—ἄρτια. See ἄρτιος.—δίκας, θέμιστας. See δίκη (2).—ἤπια, ἤπια δήνεα. See ἤπιος (1).—θέμιστα. See θέμις (1).—κεδνά. See κεδνός (3).—λυγρά. See λυγρός (3).—ὀλοφώϊα. See ὀλοφώϊος.—φίλα, φίλα μήδεα. See φίλος (5) (c).—κεχαρισμένα. See χαρίζομαι (2) (b).—(**13**) ἴδμεναι χάριν, to owe thanks, feel indebted: ἰδέω τοι χάριν Ξ 235.

εἴδωλον, -ου, τό [εἴδω]. An unreal image, a phantom E 449, 451.—Appearing in a dream δ 796, 824, 835.—Of the shades of the dead Ψ 104: λ 83, 213, 602.—So εἴδωλα καμόντων Ψ 72: λ 476, ω 14.—Of the shades of slain men passing below υ 355.

εἶεν, 3 pl. opt. εἰμί.

εἴῃ, 3 sing. subj. εἰμί.

εἴη, 3 sing. opt. εἰμί.

εἵη, 3 sing. aor. opt. ἵημι[1].

εἶθαρ. (**1**) Right on, right through E 337, Υ 473.—(**2**) Straightway, forthwith Λ 579 = N 412 = P 349, M 353, P 119, 707, Ψ 256.

εἴθε (cf. αἴθε). Expressing a wish. With opt.: εἰ. ἀγαθὸν τελέσειεν β 33.—Of the present: εἰ. ὣς ἡβώοιμι H 157 = Λ 670, Ψ 629: = ξ 468. Cf. Δ 313.

εἴκελος, -η, -ον (Ϝείκελος) [εἴκω[1]. Cf. ἴκελος, ἐΐσκω]. (**1**) Like, resembling. With dat.: συῒ εἰ. ἀλκήν (in . . .) Δ 253, P 281. Cf. N 53, 330, 688, Ξ 386, P 88, Σ 154, etc.: κ 304, τ 384, υ 88, φ 411, χ 240.—(**2**) In neut. sing. εἴκελον as adv., in the manner of, like. With dat.: σκιῇ εἰ. ἔπτατο λ 207.

εἰκοσάκις [εἴκοσι]. Twenty times I 379.

εἴκοσι, *indeclinable* (Ϝείκοσι). Also, with prothetic ἐ, **ἐείκοσι(ν)** (ἐϜείκοσι). Twenty A 309, Z 217, I 123 = 265 = T 244, I 139, 281, Λ 25, 34, N 260, Π 810, 847, Σ 373, 470: α 280, β 212 = δ 669, β 355, δ 360, 530, 778, ε 244, ι 209, μ 78, π 250, τ 536, υ 158.—With other numerals: δύω καὶ εἰ. B 748: ι 241, κ 208. πίσυρες καὶ εἰ. π 249. ἑκατὸν καὶ εἰ. B 510.

εἰκοσινήριτος [app. εἴκοσιν + -ηριτος, conn. with ἀριθμός. 'Twenty-counted']. Twenty times the normal, twenty-fold: ἄποινα X 349.

εἰκοστός. Also, with prothetic ἐ, **ἐεικοστός.** The twentieth Ω 765: β 175, ε 34, ζ 170, π 206 = τ 484 = φ 208 = ω 322, ρ 327, τ 222, ψ 102 = 170.

†**εἴκω**[1] (Ϝείκω) [Ϝικ-]. 3 sing. impf. εἶκε Σ 520. 3 sing. aor. opt. εἴξειε X 321. Pf. ἔοικα (ϜέϜοικα) η 209, χ 348. 2 sing. -ας O 90: α 208, θ 164,

σ 128, ω 253, etc. 3 -ε A 119, Γ 170, M 212, Ψ 493, etc. : α 278, ζ 60, π 202, υ 194, etc. 3 dual ἔϊκτον (ϜέϜικτον) δ 27. Pple. ἐοικώς, -ότος A 47, B 337, Γ 222, M 146, Φ 600, etc. : α 46, γ 124, 125, κ 390, σ 240, etc. εἰκώς (ϜεϜικώς) Φ 254. Fem. pl. ἐοικυῖαι Σ 418. Sing. ἐϊκυῖα, -ης Γ 386, Z 389, I 399, Ψ 66, etc. : β 383, θ 194, ν 222, etc. 3 sing. plupf. ἐῴκει B 58, Ξ 474, Σ 548, Ω 258, 630 : α 411, δ 654, ι 190, π 288, τ 7, ω 273, 446. 3 dual ἐΐκτην A 104, Φ 285, Ψ 379 : δ 662. 3 pl. ἐοίκεσαν N 102. 3 sing. in mid. form ἤϊκτο δ 796, ν 288, π 157, υ 31. ἔϊκτο Ψ 107. (ἐπέοικε.) (I) To seem likely. Impers. : ὅθι σφίσιν εἶκε λοχῆσαι (where there was opportunity) Σ 520, ὅπῃ εἴξειε μάλιστα (where he might find an opening) X 321.—(II) Otherwise only in pf. and plupf. (with pres. and impf. sense). (1) To seem *to be*. With infin. : οὐδὲ ἐῴκει ἀνδρὸς θνητοῦ πάϊς ἔμμεναι Ω 258.—(2) To resemble, be like. With dat. : θεῇς ἔοικεν Γ 158. Cf. A 47, B 58, E 604, Z 389, Λ 613, N 102, Ξ 136, O 90, etc. : α 208, β 383, δ 27, ε 51, ζ 187, η 209, θ 164, κ 390, etc.—With fut. pple. : ἐπιβησομένοισιν ἐΐκτην (seemed about to . . .) Ψ 379. Cf. λ 608.—Adjectivally in pple. : μῦθοί γε ἐοικότες [εἰσίν] (your speech is like your father's) γ 124, ὧδε ἐοικότα μυθήσασθαι (speech so like your father's) 125. Cf. δ 141, τ 380.—(3) To be fit or worthy *to do something*. With infin. : ἔοικά τοι παραείδειν χ 348.—Adjectivally in pple., fitting, suitable : ἐϊκυῖαν ἄκοιτιν I 399 : ἐοικότα καταλέξω (suited to the occasion) δ 239. Cf. α 46.—(4) ἔοικε impers., it is fitting, right, seemly. (a) With dat. : ἔοικέ τοι I 70.—With dat. and infin. : τὰ οὔ τι καταθνητοῖσιν ἔοικεν ἄνδρεσσιν φορέειν K 440. Cf. ζ 60.—(b) With acc. : ὥς σε ἔοικεν χ 196.—With acc. and infin. : οὐδὲ ἔοικε δῆμον ἐόντα παρὲξ ἀγορευέμεν M 212. Cf. B 233, Ψ 649 : α 278 = β 197, γ 357, ε 212, η 159, θ 146, π 202.—(c) With infin. alone : δειδίσσεσθαί σε B 190, ἥν τιν' ἔοικεν [ἀποτινέμεν] Γ 286. Cf. Γ 459, Δ 286, Ξ 212, T 79, Φ 379, 436 : [κτερεΐξαι] α 291. Cf. β 223, γ 335, θ 358, ω 273.—(d) Absol. : ἐπεὶ οὐδὲ ἔοικε A 119, Ψ 493 : φ 319, 322.

εἴκω[2] (Ϝείκω) [cf. L. *vicis*]. 3 sing. aor. εἶξε Ω 100. 3 pl. -αν Ω 718 : β 14. 3 sing. subj. εἴξῃ P 230. 3 pl. -ωσι M 224. 3 sing. opt. εἴξειε N 321 : ξ 221, χ 91. 3 pl. -ειαν N 807. Imp. pl. εἴξατε Ω 716. Pple. εἴξας, -αντος Θ 164, I 110, 598, Ω 43 : ξ 262, ρ 431. Fem. -āσα ε 126. Infin. εἶξαι Ψ 337. 3 sing. pa. iterative εἴξασκε ε 332. (ἀπο-, ὑπο-.) (1) In fighting, to retire, give way, give ground : εἰ εἴξωσιν 'Αχαιοί M 224. Cf. E 606, Θ 164, M 48, N 321, 807, P 230 : ὅ τέ μοι εἴξειε πόδεσσιν ξ 221 (app., whoever fled before me with his feet ; or perh. in sense (4) with πόδεσσιν in sense (2) of πούς).—With genit., to shrink or withdraw from (battle) : πολέμου E 348. Cf. Δ 509.—(2) To retire or withdraw from, leave, quit. With genit. : προθύρου σ 10. Cf. χ 91.—(3) To make way or room for someone or something : εἶξε δ' 'Αθήνῃ Ω 100. Cf. β 14.—With dat. : οὐρεῦσιν Ω 716, ἀπήνῃ 718.—(4) To yield, confess oneself second : τὸ ὃν μένος οὐδενὶ εἴκων (to none in . . .) X 459 : = λ 515.—Of something inanimate, to yield, give way : εἴκοι ὑπὸ βῶλος ἀρότρῳ (give the plough free passage) σ 374.—(5) To yield, give way, allow play to (a feeling, a defect of character, a personal quality, a circumstance). With dat. : σῷ θυμῷ I 110. Cf. I 598, K 122, 238, N 225, Ω 43 : πενίῃ ξ 157. Cf. ε 126, ν 143, ξ 262 = ρ 431, σ 139, χ 288.—(6) *Trans.*, to yield, give : ἵππῳ ἡνία (give him the rein) Ψ 337.—To give up, surrender, hand over ε 332.

εἰλαπινάζω [εἰλαπίνη]. To feast, revel : τῷ κεν ἐπισχοίης πόδας εἰλαπινάζων Ξ 241. Cf. β 57 = ρ 536, ρ 410.

εἰλαπιναστής, ὁ [εἰλαπίνη]. A boon-companion P 577.

εἰλαπίνη, -ης, ἡ. A feast or banquet, properly one given by a single host (cf. ἔρανος) : ἢ γάμῳ ἢ ἐράνῳ ἢ εἰλαπίνῃ λ 415. Cf. K 217, Σ 491, Ψ 201 : α 226.

εἶλαρ, τό. A means of defence or protection : νηῶν τε καὶ αὐτῶν (for . . .) H 338, 437, Ξ 56 = 68 : κύματος (against . . .) ε 257.

εἰλάτινος, -η, -ον [ἐλάτη. ἐλάτινος could not stand in the hexameter]. Of the fir : ὄζοισιν Ξ 289.—Of fir-wood : ἐπιβλής Ω 454. Cf. β 424 = ο 289, τ 38.

εἷλε, 3 sing. aor. αἱρέω.

Εἰλείθυια, -ης, ἡ [explained as fr. ἐλυθ- (see ἔρχομαι). 'The comer,' 'she who comes in the woman's hour of need' ; or, 'she who makes the child come forth']. The goddess presiding over child-birth Π 187, T 103 : τ 188.—In pl. Λ 270, T 119.

εἵλετο, 3 sing. aor. mid. αἱρέω.

εἷλευ, 2 sing. aor. mid. αἱρέω.

εἰλεῦντο, 3 pl. impf. pass. εἰλέω. See εἴλω.

εἰλέω. See εἴλω.

εἰλήλουθα, pf. ἔρχομαι.

εἰλίπους, -ποδος [εἰλ-, εἰλύω + πούς. Thus, 'rolling the feet,' the feet being but slightly lifted, and each as set forward describing a segment of a circle. Contrast with ἀερσίπους]. Dat. pl. εἰλιπόδεσσι Z 424, Π 488. Shambling. Epithet of oxen Z 424, I 466 = Ψ 166, O 547, Π 488, Φ 448 : α 92 = δ 320, θ 60, ι 46.

εἱλίσσετο, 3 sing. impf. mid. ἑλίσσω.

εἷλον, 3 pl. aor. αἱρέω.

εἴλῡμα, τό [εἰλύω]. A wrapper ζ 179.

εἰλῡφάζω [app. fr. εἰλύω]. To roll along : ἄνεμος φλόγα εἰλυφάζει Υ 492.

†**εἰλῠφάω** [app. as prec.]. Pres. pple. εἰλυφόων. = prec. : εἰλυφόων ἄνεμος φέρει [πῦρ] Λ 156.

†**εἰλύω** [ϜελϜ-, Ϝελυ-. Cf. εἴλω]. Fut. εἰλύσω Φ 319. 3 sing. pf. pass. εἴλῡται M 286. 3 pl. εἰλύαται υ 352. 3 sing. plupf. εἴλυτο Π 640 : ε 403. Pple. εἰλυμένος, -ου E 186, P 492, Σ 522 : ξ 136, 479. Also 3 sing. aor. pass. ἐλύσθη Ψ 393. Pple. ἐλυσθείς Ω 510 : ι 433. (1) In aor. pple. pass., bent upon oneself, crouching : προπάροιθε ποδῶν 'Αχιλῆος ἐλυσθείς Ω 510.—Curled up : ὑπὸ γαστέρ' [ἀρνειοῦ] ἐλυσθεὶς ι 433.—In Ψ 393 (ῥυμὸς

ἐπὶ γαῖαν ἐλύσθη) app., swung to the ground.—(2) To wrap something round (something), wrap up; hence, to cover up, cover: νεφέλῃ εἰλυμένος Ε 186. Cf. Μ 286, Π 640, Ρ 492, Σ 522, Φ 319; εἴλυτο ἁλὸς ἄχνῃ ε 403. Cf. ξ 136, 479, υ 352.

εἴλω, εἰλέω (Fείλω, Fειλέω) [Fελ-, FελF-. Cf. εἰλύω, ἑλίσσω, L. *volvo*. Conn. with ἅλις, ἁλίσκομαι, ἀολλής]. 3 pl. impf. ἐείλεον Σ 447. Acc. sing. masc. pres. pple. εἰλεῦντα λ 573. 3 pl. aor. ἔλσαν Λ 413. Pple. ἔλσας ε 132, η 250. Infin. ἔλσαι Α 409, Σ 294, Φ 225. With prothetic ἐ, ἐέλσαι Φ 295. **Pass.** 3 pl. impf. εἰλεῦντο Φ 8. 3 sing. aor. ἐάλη Ν 408, Υ 168, 278. 3 pl. ἄλεν Χ 12. Pple. ἀλείς, -έντος Π 403, Φ 534, 571, 607, Χ 47, 308: ω 538. Neut. ἀλέν Ψ 420. Infin ἀλήμεναι Ε 823, Σ 76, 286. ἀλῆναι Π 714. 1 pl. pf. ἐέλμεθα (FεFέλμεθα) Ω 662. Pple. ἐελμένος Ν 524. Pl. -οι Μ 38, Σ 287. (προτιειλέω.) (1) To hem in, pen in, coop up (a body of foes): κατὰ πρύμνας ἔλσαι Ἀχαιούς Α 409. Cf. Θ 215 (twice), Μ 38, Σ 76, 294, 447, Φ 225, 295.—Sim. of the Cyclops: εἴλει ἐνὶ σπῆϊ μ 210.—Of herding together the unfaithful handmaids χ 460.—In reference to a single person: ἔλσαν [Ὀδυσσῆα] ἐν μέσσοισιν Λ 413.—To force in a crowd (into something): ἡμίσεες ἐς ποταμὸν εἰλεῦντο Φ 8.—Of a hunter, to drive (the quarry) together λ 573.—In reference to confined water: χειμέριον ἀλὲν ὕδωρ Ψ 420.—(2) In pass. (a) To get together into a body: ἔστασαν εἰλόμενοι (massing together at bay) Ε 782. Cf. Ε 823.—To throng (into something): ἐς τεῖχος ἀλῆναι Π 714. Cf. Φ 534, Χ 12, 47.—Sim.: πόλις ἔμπλητο ἀλέντων Φ 607.—To be cooped up in limits narrow for the number: οἶσθα ὡς κατὰ ἄστυ ἐέλμεθα Ω 662. Cf. Ε 203, Σ 286, 287.—(b) To get oneself into small compass, crouch down: πᾶς ἐάλη Ν 408, ἐνὶ δίφρῳ ἧστο ἀλείς (cowering) Π 403, Ἀχιλῆα ἀλεὶς μένεν (crouching for a spring) Φ 571, οἴμησεν ἀλείς (drawing himself together) Χ 308 := ω 538. Cf. Υ 168, 278.—(3) To impede or thwart the progress of: ὅν περ ἄελλαι εἰλέωσιν Β 294.—To restrain from freedom of movement, confine: Διὸς βουλῇσιν ἐελμένος Ν 524.—Sim. of the wind making navigation impossible τ 200.—App., to stop, hold from motion, pin down: νῆα Ζεὺς ἔλσας ἐκέασσεν ε 132 = η 250.

εἷμα, -ατος, τό (Fέσ-μα) [ἕννυμι]. (1) A garment: εἷμα δ' ἔχ' ἀμφ' ὤμοισιν Σ 538. Cf. ξ 501.—(2) In pl., clothes, clothing, raiment: εἰ μὴ ἀφ' εἵματα δύσω Β 261. Cf. Γ 392, Ε 905, Π 670, 680, Σ 517, Χ 154, 510, Ψ 67, Ω 162: εἵματα ἑσσάμενος β 3, ὑφαντά ν 218. Cf. δ 750, ε 167, ζ 26, θ 249, etc.—In apposition: φᾶρός τε χιτῶνά τε εἵματα ζ 214 (for raiment), η 234 (that he had on). Cf. κ 542 = ξ 320, ξ 132, 154, 341, 396, 516, ο 338, 368, π 79 = ρ 550 = φ 339, χ 487.

εἷμαι, pf. mid. ἕννυμι.

εἵμαρτο, 3 sing. plupf. pass. μείρομαι.

εἰμέν, 1 pl. pres. indic. εἰμί.

†**εἰμί** [ἐσ-μί. Cf. L. *sum*, Eng. *am*]. (The whole of the pres. indic. except εἶς (εἴς), ἔασι may be enclitic.) 1 sing. εἰμί Α 186, 516, Β 26, Δ 58, etc.: β 286, 314, θ 214, ι 519, etc. 2 ἐσσί Α 176, 280, Γ 164, 172, etc.: α 175, 297, β 274, γ 123, etc. εἶς (εἴς) Π 515, Ω 407. εἰς Π 538, Τ 217, etc.: α 170, 207, δ 371, 611, etc. 3 ἔστι Ζ 267, 4.3, Ι 250, Μ 65, etc.: β 130, 310, δ 193, 354, etc. ἐστί Α 63, 107, 114, 169, etc.: α 50, 66, 70, 205, etc. 2 dual ἐστόν Α 259, Ι 198, Λ 138, etc.: δ 61. 1 pl. εἰμέν Ε 873, Η 231, Θ 234, Ι 640, etc.: γ 80, η 205, 307, θ 246, etc. 2 ἐστέ Α 258, Β 301, 485, etc.: γ 71, δ 63, ε 118, etc. 3 εἰσί Α 153, 272, Β 201, 227, etc.: β 29, 51, 87, 254, etc. ἔᾱσι Β 125, 131, Η 73, 295, etc.: δ 79, ε 381, θ 162, κ 349, etc. Subj. ἔω Α 119: ι 18. 3 sing. ἔῃσι Β 366: λ 434, ο 422, ω 202. ἔῃ Κ 225, Μ 300, etc.: τ 329, etc. ᾖσι Τ 202: θ 147, 163, etc. εἴῃ (*v.l.* εἴῃ) Η 340, Ι 245. 3 pl. ἔωσι Ι 140, 282, Κ 306: δ 165, ψ 119. ὦσι Ξ 274: ω 491. Opt. εἴην, -ης Β 260, Δ 189, Ε 24, Ι 57, Λ 670, Μ 345, etc.: β 74, δ 205, ε 209, ζ 244, λ 360, etc. 2 pl. εἶτε φ 195. 3 εἶεν Β 372, etc.: ι 89, etc. 2 sing. ἔοις Ι 284. 3 ἔοι Ι 142, etc.: ρ 421, etc. 3 sing. imp. ἔστω Α 144, Β 204, Η 34, etc.: α 370, β 230, 355, etc. 2 pl. ἔστε Γ 280, Ε 529, Ζ 112, etc. 3 ἔστων Α 338: α 273. Imp. in mid. form ἔσσο α 302, etc. Pple. ἐών, -όντος, ἐοῦσα, -ης, ἐόν, -όντος Α 70, 131, 290, 352, 546, 587, Γ 159, Δ 426, etc.: α 22, 202, 263, 265, 431, 435, β 200, 241, etc. Also οὔσης τ 489. ὄντας η 94. Infin. ἔμμεναι Α 117, 287, Β 129, 216, etc.: α 33, 172, 215, 217, etc. ἔμεναι Γ 40, Ε 602, Θ 193, etc.: α 385, ξ 489, etc. ἔμμεν Σ 364: ι 455, etc. ἔμεν Δ 299, Ι 35, etc.: ε 257, κ 416, etc. εἶναι Α 91, 228, 564, Β 116, etc.: α 15, 164, 180, 187, etc. 1 sing. impf. ἦα Ε 808: β 313, κ 156, λ 620, ξ 212, etc. ἔᾱ Δ 321, Ε 887: ξ 222, 352. ἔον Λ 762, Ψ 643. 2 ἔησθα Χ 435: π 420, ψ 175. ἦσθα Ε 898, Ν 228, etc.: δ 31, ν 314, π 199, etc. 3 ἦεν Β 769, Γ 41, 211, 215, etc.: α 18, 131, 233, β 47, etc. ἔην Β 217, 219, 529, 580, etc.: β 272, γ 180, 249, 267, etc. ἦν Β 77, 96, 220, 313, etc.: α 177, γ 401, ε 239, ζ 82, etc. ἤην Λ 808: τ 283, ψ 316, ω 343. 3 dual ἤστην Ε 10. 1 pl. ἦμεν Λ 689, 692: ω 171. 2 ἦτε Π 557. 3 ἦσαν Β 487, 641, 760, Γ 145, etc.: α 27, β 119, ζ 6, 86, etc. ἔσαν Α 267, 321, Β 311, 618, etc.: α 12, 126, β 21, 82, etc. Pa. iterative ἔσκον Η 153. 3 sing. ἔσκε Γ 180, Ε 536, Ζ 19, 153, etc.: β 59, 346, δ 270, ι 508, etc. Fut. ἔσσομαι, -εαι Α 239, 573, Β 347, Δ 267, Ζ 353, Κ 453, etc.: α 40, 204, β 270, 273, ζ 33, λ 137, etc. 3 sing. ἐσσεῖται Β 393, Ν 317. ἔσομαι, ἔσεαι, ἔσεται, ἔσται, etc. Α 136, 211, 546, 563, Δ 305, etc.: α 312, 397, β 61, γ 325, π 267, etc. 2 sing. ἔσῃ τ 254. Pple. ἐσσόμενος, -η, -ον Α 70, Β 119, Γ 287, etc.: γ 204, θ 580, λ 433, etc. Infin. ἔσσεσθαι Ζ 339, Λ 444, Μ 324, etc.: ξ 176, π 311. ἔσεσθαι Ε 644, Ξ 56, Φ 533, etc.: δ 108, 494, ζ 165, etc. (ἀπ-, ἐν-, ἐπ-, μετ-, παρ-, περι-, συν-, ὑπ-.) (1) To be, exist: ὅμαδος ἦν Β 96, ἡμῖν εἰνατός ἐστιν ἐνιαυτός (has been completed, has passed) 295, οὐκ ἔσθ' ὅς . . . (the man does not live who . . .) Χ 348. Cf. Β 204, 641, 642, Η 340, Ι 249, etc.: θεοὺς αἰὲν

ἐόντας α 263. Cf. β 89, δ 195, ε 239, ζ 82, 210, etc. —Impers.: ἔσται ὅτ' ἂν . . . (the day will come when . . .) Θ 373.—Absol. in fut. pple. pl., the men to come, posterity: αἰσχρὸν καὶ ἐσσομένοισι πυθέσθαι Β 119, etc.: ἐλεγχείη καὶ ἐσσομένοισι πυθέσθαι φ 255, etc.—Sim. in neut. pres. pple. pl., the present: τὰ ἐόντα Α 70 (τὰ ἐσσόμενα in the same line being 'the future,' and πρὸ ἐόντα 'the past' (pple. of the impf.)).—(**2**) Impers., to be possible: ὡς οὐκ ἔστι φυγεῖν Μ 327, οὐδ' ἄρα πως ἦν ἀσπερχὲς κεχολῶσθαι Π 60. Cf. Ζ 267, Η 239, Μ 65, Ν 114, Ξ 63, etc.: οὔ πως ἔστι δαίνυσθαι ἀκέοντα β 310, εἴ τί που ἔστιν (if it may be) δ 193. Cf. β 130, ε 103, ι 411, λ 158, ο 49, etc.—(**3**) As copula, to be: ἔχθιστός μοί ἐσσι Α 176, καὶ σὲ τὸ πρὶν ἀκούομεν ὄλβιον εἶναι Ω 543 (infin. of the impf.). Cf. Α 63, 107, 114, 153, 186, etc.: οἴκοι ἔσαν α 12. Cf. α 18, 27, 66, 70, 170, etc.—Impers.: ἐμοί κε κέρδιον εἴη . . . Ζ 410. Cf. Α 169, 211, 229, etc.: β 74, 190, ρ 191, etc.

†εἶμι [cf. L. *i-*, *eo*]. 1 sing. εἶμι Α 169, Γ 305, Ξ 200, Σ 143, Ω 92, etc.: β 214, 318, 359, κ 273, ρ 277, etc. 2 εἶσθα Κ 450: τ 69. 3 εἶσι Β 87, Λ 415, Φ 573, Ψ 226, etc.: β 89, ζ 131, λ 149, τ 571, etc. 1 pl. ἴμεν Ρ 155 (or this may be taken as infin.): β 127, κ 431, σ 288. 3 ἴασι Π 160. Subj. ἴω Π 245, Σ 188, Ω 313: γ 22, ο 509, 511. ἴωμι Ι 414 (*v.l.* ἵκωμι). 2 sing. ἴῃς Ω 295. ἴῃσθα Κ 67. 3 ἴῃ θ 395, σ 194. ἴῃσι Ι 701. 1 pl. ἴομεν Ζ 526, Κ 126, Ξ 128, Ρ 340, etc.: β 404, ζ 259, ρ 190, ψ 254, etc. ἴομεν Β 440, Ι 625, Μ 328, Ξ 374, Φ 438: ω 432. 3 ἴωσι Μ 239. 3 sing. opt. ἴοι Ξ 21. ἰείη Τ 209. Imp. ἴθι Α 32, Ζ 143, Θ 399, Ν 235, Ψ 646, etc.: γ 323, η 30, σ 171, χ 157. 3 sing. ἴτω Η 75, Μ 349, Ρ 254, Ψ 667, etc.: α 276, γ 421. Pl. ἴτε Α 335. Pple. ἰών, ἰοῦσα, ἰόν Α 138, Β 596, Γ 406, Δ 278, Κ 468, Μ 264, etc.: α 356, β 179, γ 276, δ 276, ι 88, ξ 322, etc. Infin. ἴμεναι Υ 32: θ 303, ξ 532, π 341, φ 8, etc. ἴμμεναι Υ 365. ἴμεν Α 170, Ε 167, Μ 356, Ρ 155 (but see above), Σ 14, etc.: α 441, δ 713, ζ 255, κ 537, etc. ἰέναι Α 227, Β 94, Γ 119, Ι 487, etc.: β 364, δ 483, θ 12, ι 225, etc. Impf. ἤϊα δ 427, 433, 572, κ 309. 3 sing. ἤϊε Α 47, Η 213, Ν 602, Ω 596, etc.: ε 57, η 7, π 178, φ 391, etc. ᾔει Κ 286, Ν 247: θ 290. ᾖε Μ 371: σ 253, 257, τ 126, υ 89. ἴε Β 872, Γ 383: η 82, π 41, ρ 30, ω 221, etc. 3 dual ἴτην Α 347: ι 430, φ 244. 1 pl. ᾔομεν κ 251, 570, λ 22. 3 ἤϊσαν Κ 197, Ν 305, Ρ 495: τ 436, υ 7, ω 9, 13. ἴσαν Α 494, Γ 2, Μ 88, Τ 45, etc.: α 176, β 259, δ 300, ζ 223, etc. ἤϊον ψ 370, ω 501. 2 sing. fut. εἴσῃ π 313. (ἀν-, ἀπ-, διεξ-, εἰσ-, εἰσαν-, ἐξ-, ἐπ-, κατ-, μετ-, παρ-, προσ-, συν-.) (**1**) (**a**) To go, go one's way, take one's way, proceed: κλισίηνδε Α 185, νῆας ἔπι Γ 119, ἰὼν πολέος πεδίοιο (over . . .) Ε 597, οἴκαδ' ἴμεν Ρ 155 (taking ἴμεν as infin. with ἐπιπείσεται 154, and understanding an implied apodosis ('let him go'), or taking δέ 155 as indicating the apodosis. For the alternative see (10) (a)). Cf. Β 348, Ζ 490, Η 209, Ι 487, etc.: ἐπὶ βοῦν ἴτω γ 421, ἴσαν λείην ὁδόν (traversed) κ 103. Cf. α 356, β 127, ζ 102, 259, λ 22, etc.—Absol. Α 47, Β 94, Γ 2, etc.: γ 22, ε 57, π 313 (will go about), etc.—For βῆ ἰέναι etc. see βαίνω (4).—For βάσκ' ἴθι see βάσκω.—(**b**) With fut. pple. expressing purpose: Ἑλένην καλέουσ' ἴεν Γ 383. Cf. Κ 32, Λ 652, Μ 216, Ξ 200, etc.: δ 24, ζ 31, ξ 532, ρ 365, σ 428.—(**c**) In pple. with a finite vb., to go and . . . (cf. ἄγω (I) (9)): αὐτὸς χ' ἕλωμαι ἰών Α 138. Cf. Γ 406, Ι 87, Π 729, Σ 62, etc.: οἴσετε θᾶσσον ἰοῦσαι υ 154. Cf. γ 469, θ 142, ι 88 = κ 100, ρ 70, φ 243 = 392, χ 103.—(**2**) Of the motion of a ship Α 482: = β 428.—Of birds Μ 239, Ρ 756, Χ 309.—Of bees Β 87.—Of wind Ν 796.—Of a storm-cloud Δ 278.—Of smoke Σ 207, Φ 522.—Of an axe Γ 61.—Of a heavenly body Χ 317: κ 191, μ 380.—Of time passing: τάχα δ' εἶσι τέταρτον [ἔτος] (is fast passing away) β 89.—Of a rumour or report going abroad ψ 362.—Of food passing into the body Τ 209.—(**3**) To go, depart, set out: ἀλλ' ἴθι (begone) Α 32. Cf. Ζ 221, Ι 625, 701, Π 838: ἰὼν ἐν νηυσὶν β 226. Cf. β 367, 404, κ 549, λ 72, ξ 480, ο 89, 348, ρ 190, 194, σ 257, ω 311, 313.—(**4**) To adopt a course of action: τῇ ἴμεν ᾗ κε σὺ ἡγεμονεύῃς Ο 46.—(**5**) To move oneself into a specified position, to get (on to something): ἐπ' οὐδόν Ζ 375: ρ 466, σ 110, υ 128, φ 124 = 149, ω 178, 493.—Of going (on board a ship): ἐπὶ νηὸς ἰόντι (ἰών) τ 238, 339, ψ 176.—(**6**) (**a**) To come: ὕστερον αὖτις ἰόντα Α 27, νέον κλισίηθεν ἰόντα Μ 336 (pple. of the impf., 'just come'). Cf. Β 596, Γ 130, Κ 356, Π 87, etc.: ἴσαν ἡμέτερον δῶ α 176 (or the word may be referred to εἴδω (III) (2)). Cf. γ 257, δ 670 (on the return voyage), ζ 179, ι 279 (when you arrived), ξ 153, ρ 600 (come back), ω 152 (returning), etc.—Of the appearance of a star Χ 27, Ψ 226.—(**b**) In pple. with a finite vb., to come and . . . (cf. (1) (c)): ὄψεσθ' Ἕκτορ' ἰόντες Ω 704. Cf. μ 184.—(**7**) Of hostile approach: ὑπὸ τεῖχος ἰόντας Μ 264. Cf. Δ 480, Κ 189, etc.—(**8**) Of the coming on of a period of time: ἥδε δὴ ἠὼς εἶσιν (is approaching) τ 571.—So of death Ρ 202.—(**9**) In imp. with imp., come, . . .: ἀλλ' ἴθι προκάλεσσαι Μενέλαον Γ 432. Cf. Κ 53, 175, Λ 611, Τ 347: χ 157.—Sim.: ἀλλ' ἴθι καὶ σὸν ἑταῖρον κτερέϊζε Ψ 646. Cf. σ 171.—So with fut.: ἀλλ' ἴθι, ταῦτα δ' ἀρεσσόμεθα Δ 362.—Absol.: ἀλλ' ἴθι Ξ 267.—(**10**) In pres. with fut. sense. (**a**) To go: εἶμι Φθίηνδε Α 169 (I will . . .), οἴκαδ' ἴμεν Ρ 155 (we will . . .) (but see (1) (a)). Cf. Α 420, 426, Γ 305, 410, Ε 256, Η 98, Κ 55, 325, Λ 652, Μ 368 = Ν 752, Ρ 147, Σ 63, 114, 143, 280, 333, Υ 142, 362, 365, 371, Ψ 835, Ω 92, 224: τάχ' εἶσθα θύραζε τ 69. Cf. β 214 = 359, β 318, γ 361, 367, κ 273, λ 149, ο 214, ρ 6, 277, ψ 362.—(**b**) To come: οὐδέ μιν οἴω νῦν ἰέναι Ρ 710.—With fut. pple.: ἡμέας εἶσι κυδοιμήσων Ο 136. Cf. Κ 450.

εἰν. See ἐν.

εἰνάετες [εἰνα- (prob. = ἐνϝα-, ἐννέα) + ἔτος]. For nine years Σ 400: γ 118, ε 107, ξ 240, χ 228.

εἶναι, infin. εἰμί.

εἶναι, aor. infin. ἵημι[1].

εἰνάκις [εἰνα-. See εἰνάετες]. Nine times ξ 230.

εἰνάλιος, -η, -ον [εἰν-, ἐν- (1) + ἅλς[1]]. Inhabiting the sea: κήτεϊ δ 443. Cf. ε 67, ο 479.

εἰνάνυχες [εἰνα- (see εἰνάετες) + νυχ-, νύξ]. App. an adv., for nine nights: εἰ. ἴαυον I 470 (or perh. nom. pl. in a personal construction).

εἰνατέρες, αἱ. The wives of one's husband's brothers Z 378, 383, X 473, Ω 769.

εἴνατος [prob. for ἔνϝατος fr. ἐννέα]. = ἔνατος. The ninth: ἐνιαυτός B 295, εἰ. ἦλθεν (was the ninth to . . .) Θ 266.

εἵνεκα. See ἕνεκα.

εἰνί. See ἐν.

εἰνόδιος [εἰν-, ἐν- (1) + ὁδός]. (Having their nest) by the way-side: σφήκεσσιν Π 260.

εἰνοσίφυλλος [ἐνϝοσι- (ἐν- (3) + ϝοθ-, ὠθέω) + φύλλον. Cf. ἐννοσίγαιος. 'Making its leaves to shake']. Covered with trembling leafage: Νήριτον B 632. Cf. B 757: ι 22, λ 316.

εἴξασκε, 3 sing. pa. iterative εἴκω[2].

εἶξε, 3 sing. aor. εἴκω[2].

εἴξειε, 3 sing. aor. opt. εἴκω[1] and εἴκω[2].

εἷο. See ἑέ.

εἰοικυῖαι, fem. pl. pf. pple. εἴκω[1].

εἶπον, ἔειπον, *aor.* (ϝεῖπον, ἔϝειπον) [cf. (ϝ)ἔπος]. 2 sing. subj. εἴπῃσθα Υ 250: λ 224, χ 373. Imp. εἰπέ A 85, Z 86, Λ 819, Ω 113, etc.: α 10, θ 555, ξ 118, ω 114, etc. Also 2 sing. indic. εἶπας A 106, 108: χ 46. ἔειπας (*v.l.* ἔειπες) A 286, Ω 379, etc. Imp. pl. εἴπατε γ 427, φ 198. 3 sing. pa. iterative εἴπεσκε B 271, Γ 297, P 423, X 375, etc.: β 324, δ 772, θ 328, ψ 148, etc. (ἀπο-, δια-, ἐξ-, μετέειπον, παρ-, προσέειπον.) **(1)** To utter speech, speak, say: ὣς εἰπών A 68, ἐπεὶ κατὰ μοῖραν ἔειπες I 59. Cf. A 230, B 139, Z 75, O 185, T 82, etc.: α 96, β 251, δ 772, θ 166, χ 288, etc.—Followed by what is said directly reported E 600, Z 375, H 46, Π 513, T 286, etc.: β 324, ε 298, θ 328, ι 171, etc.—**(2)** To utter, speak, say, tell: ὅττι κεν εἴπῃς A 294, ποῖον ἔειπες N 824. Cf. A 286, B 59, Δ 22, H 68, P 716, etc.: κενὰ εὔγματα χ 249. Cf. γ 227, δ 204, ε 300, ο 314, σ 422, etc.—To give (judgment): δίκην Σ 508.—**(3)** To tell, tell of or about, give information about, describe, explain: κακὸν τόσον ὅσσον ἐτύχθη P 410. Cf. I 688, K 384, Ψ 350, etc.: γαῖαν τεήν θ 555, τεὸν γένος τ 162. Cf. α 169, β 31, λ 177, ρ 106, ψ 273, etc.—With genit.: εἰπέ μοι πατρός λ 174. Cf. α 10.—Absol.: Ἀχιλῆϊ εἰπεῖν P 692: τίπτ' οὔ οἱ εἶπες; ν 417. Cf. α 282, β 216, ο 158, χ 429, etc.—Followed by a direct question: εἰπέ μοι, τί . . .; ω 474. Cf. λ 144.—**(4)** With infin. or clause in indirect discourse, to say, state, assert, tell. With infin.: νούσῳ ὑπ' ἀργαλέῃ φθίσθαι (that he would . . .) N 666. Cf. Σ 9, Ω 113.—With ὅτ(τ)ι, that P 655: π 131.—With ὡς, how χ 373.—With question: ὅ τι . . . A 64, ἤ . . . ἦ . . . I 673, ὅππως . . . K 544: ὁππόθι . . . γ 89, ἠὲ (ἦ) . . . ἦ . . . γ 214 = π 95, δ 28, λ 494, ὅς τις . . . δ 379 = 468, ὅττι . . . δ 391, ὅ τι . . . θ 577, ὅπ(π)ῃ . . . ι 279, 457, εἰ . . . λ 494, ν 328, ὅσσα . . . ν 306, ὁππόθεν . . . ξ 47, ὁπποῖα . . . τ 218, ὅπως . . . φ 198.—With acc. and dependent clause: εἰπὲ τόνδε, ὅς τις ὅδ' ἐστίν Γ 192: εἰπὲ νόστον, ὡς . . . δ 379 = 468. Cf. δ 389 = κ 539.—Sim.: τόδε εἰπέ, ἤ (ἠὲ) . . . ἦ . . . Λ 819, Ω 380, τόδε εἰπέ, ποσσῆμαρ . . . Ω 656: τόδε εἰπέ, εἰ . . . α 206, λ 370, 457, ἤ (ἠὲ) . . . ἦε (ἦ) δ 486, ο 383, ὅππῃ . . . θ 572, ἦ . . . π 137, τάδε κ' εἴποι, ὡς . . . χ 350, ἕκαστα εἰπεῖν, ὡς . . . ω 237.—So περὶ μητρός, ἤ . . . ἦ . . . ο 347.—**(5)** To bid, direct, order, recommend. With dat. and infin.: Ποσειδάωνι τὰ ἃ πρὸς δώμαθ' ἱκέσθαι O 57. Cf. Z 114, Ξ 501: δμῳῇσι δαῖτα πένεσθαι γ 427. Cf. α 37, δ 682, ο 76, φ 235, χ 262, 431.—Sim.: Νέστορι εἰπεῖν [χαίρειν] ο 152.—So μετὰ δμῳῇσιν ἔειπεν στῆσαι τρίποδα θ 433. Cf. π 151.—With dat. and clause: εἰπεῖν Ἀγαμέμνονι εἰ ἐποτρύνειε . . . ξ 497, εἰπὲ πατρὶ μή με δηλήσεται χ 367.—With dat. only: εἰπὲ μητέρι Z 86.—With acc. of what is enjoined: ἕκαστα γ 361.—**(6)** To speak of, allude to: Ἀγαμέμνονα A 90.—To speak (well) of: ἵνα τίς σ' εὖ εἴπῃ α 302 = γ 200.—To call (so and so): πολλοί μιν ἐσθλὸν ἔειπον τ 334. Cf. Θ 373.—With acc. of the person of whom something is said and what is said directly reported: εἴποι τις "πατρὸς . . . ἀμείνων" ἐκ πολέμου ἀνιόντα Z 479.—**(7)** To address (a person): Ἕκτορα M 60 = 210, N 725, P 334, Υ 375. Cf. P 237 = 651.—With double acc. of person and of what is said: ἐξαίσιόν τι εἰπών τινα δ 690. Cf. χ 314, ψ 91.—With prep. and cognate acc.: τὸν πρὸς μῦθον ἔειπεν E 632. Cf. B 59, 156, etc.: δ 803, ξ 492, π 460, etc.

εἶραι, αἱ [app. conn. with εἴρω[2]]. Thus, a speaking-place: εἰράων προπάροιθε Σ 531.

εἴργω. See ἔργω[1].

εἴρερος (σείρερος) [(σ)είρω[1]]. Slavery θ 529.

εἰρεσίη, -ης, ἡ [ἐρέσσω]. Rowing κ 78, λ 640, μ 225.

εἰρήνη, -ης, ἡ. Peace B 797, I 403 = X 156: ω 486.

εἰρήσεται[1], 3 sing. fut. εἴρομαι.

εἰρήσεται[2], 3 sing. fut. pf. pass. εἴρω[2].

εἴρηται[1], 3 sing. subj. εἴρομαι.

εἴρηται[2], 3 sing. pf. pass. εἴρω[2].

εἴριον, -ου, τό. Also **ἔριον** δ 124. [Cf. εἶρος.] Wool M 434: δ 124.—In pl.: ἤσκειν εἴρια καλά Γ 388. Cf. σ 316, χ 423.

εἰροκόμος, -ου, ἡ [εἰρ-, εἴριον + κομέω]. A wool-dresser Γ 387.

εἴρομαι. Fut. εἰρήσομαι η 237, τ 104, 509. 3 sing. -εται τ 46. 1 pl. -όμεθα δ 61. From aor. ἠρόμην 1 pl. subj. ἐρώμεθα θ 133. 3 sing. opt. ἔροιτο α 135, γ 77. Infin. ἐρέσθαι α 405, γ 69, 243, ξ 378, ο 362, π 465. From ἐρέω pres. opt. ἐρέοιμι λ 229. 1 pl. -οιμεν δ 192. Pple. ἐρέων H 128: φ 31. In mid. form. Subj. ἐρέωμαι ρ 509. 3 pl. impf. ἐρέοντο A 332, Θ 445, I 671: κ 63, 109. Imp. ἔρειο (app. for ἐρέεο) Λ 611. Infin. ἐρέεσθαι ζ 298, ψ 106. From ἔρημι 1 pl. subj. ἐρείομεν A 62. (ἀν-, δι-, διεξερέομαι, ἐξ-.) **(1)** To ask, inquire, make inquiry, ask questions: εἴρετο δεύτερον αὖτις A 513. Cf. I 671: κ 63, ξ 378, ο 263, 362, ψ 106, ω 114, 474.—With indirect question: ὁππόθεν εἰμέν γ 80. Cf. δ 423, ι 402, κ 109, ρ 120.—**(2)** To ask or inquire about: *εἰρόμεναι παῖδας* Z 239. Cf. H 128, K 416, Ω 390: *δώματα πατρὸς ἐμοῦ* ζ 298. Cf. ι 13, 503, λ 542, π 402, 465.—With indirect question: *νόστον, ὡς . . .* δ 423.—(**3**) To question (a person): *μάντιν τινά* A 62. Cf. A 332, 553, H 127, Θ 445, O 247: α 135, 188, 284, γ 77, δ 192, ι 251, λ 229, τ 46, 95, υ 137.—With indirect question: *Νέστορ' ἔρειο ὅν τινα . . .* Λ 611. Cf. γ 69, δ 61, θ 133, ρ 368, 509.—So *ἐθέλω σε περὶ ξείνοιο ἐρέσθαι, ὁππόθεν . . .* α 405.—With cognate acc.: *ἔπος ἄλλο ἐρέσθαι Νέστορα* γ 243.—(**4**) With double acc. of person questioned and of what is inquired about: *τό σε πρῶτον εἰρήσομαι* η 237 = τ 104. Cf. θ 549, λ 570 (see under *δίκη* (4)), ρ 571, τ 509.—(**5**) To ask about, look for, seek: *ἵππους* φ 31.

εἰροπόκος [*εἰρ-, εἴριον + πόκος*]. Woolly-fleeced: *ὀΐεσσιν* E 137: *ὀΐων* ι 443.

εἶρος, *τό = εἴριον*: *ἰοδνεφές* δ 135, ι 426.

εἰρῦαται[1], 3 pl. pf. pass. *ἐρύω*[1].

εἰρῦαται[2], 3 pl. pf. mid. *ἐρύω*[2].

εἰρύατο[1], 3 pl. plupf. pass. *ἐρύω*[1].

εἰρῦατο[2], 3 pl. plupf. mid. *ἐρύω*[2].

εἴρυντο[1], 3 pl. plupf. pass. *ἐρύω*[1].

εἴρυντο[2], 3 pl. plupf. mid. *ἐρύω*[2].

εἰρυόμεσθα, 1 pl. pres. mid. See *ἐρύω*[2].

εἰρυσάμην, aor. mid. *ἐρύω*[1].

εἰρύσατο, 3 sing. aor. mid. *ἐρύω*[2].

εἴρυσ(σ)ε, 3 sing. aor. *ἐρύω*[1].

εἰρύσσασθαι, aor. infin. mid. *ἐρύω*[2].

εἰρύσσατο, 3 sing. aor. mid. *ἐρύω*[1].

εἰρύσσονται, 3 pl. fut. mid. *ἐρύω*[2].

εἴρῡτο[1], 3 sing. aor. mid. *ἐρύω*[1].

εἴρῡτο[2], 3 sing. plupf. mid. *ἐρύω*[2].

†**εἴρω**[1] (*σείρω*. Cf. *σειρή*, L. *sero*). 3 sing. plupf. pass. *ἔερτο* (*σέσερτο*) ο 460. Acc. sing. masc. pple. *ἐερμένον* σ 296. To connect together by a string: [*ὅρμος*] *ἠλέκτροισιν ἔερτο* (was strung with . . .) ο 460. Cf. σ 296.

†**εἴρω**[2] (*Fείρω*. Cf. L. *verbum*, Eng. *word*). In pres. only β 162, λ 137, ν 7. Fut. *ἐρέω* A 76, Δ 39, Z 334, Ω 106, etc.: β 187, λ 126, ο 27, ψ 130, etc. 3 sing. *ἐρέει* Δ 176, 182, Z 462, H 91, I 56: γ 20, 328, π 378. 3 pl. *ἐρέουσι* X 108: ζ 285, φ 329. Pple. *ἐρέων, -οντος* Λ 652, Ξ 355, Ψ 226: κ 245, ο 41, π 329, 334. Fem. *ἐρέουσα* A 419, B 49: ψ 2, 16. Infin. *ἐρέειν* Γ 83: δ 747. **Pass.** Dat. sing. neut. aor. pple. *ῥηθέντι* σ 414, υ 322. 3 sing. pf. *εἴρηται* (*FέFρηται*) Δ 363. 3 sing. plupf. *εἴρητο* K 540: π 11, 351. Pple. *εἰρημένος, -ου* Θ 524: μ 453. 3 sing. fut. pf. *εἰρήσεται* Ψ 795. (*ἐξ-*.) (**1**) To utter speech, speak, say: *ἔκ τοι ἐρέω* A 204. Cf. Δ 182, I 56, 103, K 534, etc.: δ 140, ζ 285, μ 38, τ 224, etc.—Followed by what is said directly reported A 204, B 257, Δ 176, I 314, etc.: β 187, ο 318, ρ 229, ψ 130, etc.—(**2**) To utter, speak, say, tell: *ἄλλο* A 297, *ἀγγελίην* Ξ 355. Cf. A 419, Γ 83, Δ 363, Ψ 795, etc.: *ψεῦδος* γ 20, *οὔνομα* ζ 194. Cf. β 162, μ 453, π 11, σ 414, etc.—(**3**) To tell, tell of or about, give information about, describe, explain: *ἀρχοὺς νηῶν* B 493. Cf. Γ 177, Ψ 326: *ὀλοφώϊα γέροντος* δ 410. Cf. η 243 = ο 402, κ 289, 292, λ 126, τ 171.—With ppl. clause: *δεσποίνῃ ἐρέουσα πόσιν ἔνδον ἐόντα* ψ 2.—Absol.: *τοιγὰρ ἐγὼν ἐρέω* A 76. Cf. Z 334, I 528: *μὴ πρὶν σοὶ ἐρέειν* δ 747. Cf. μ 58, 156, π 259, 334, σ 129, 338, υ 48, 229, ω 481.—(**4**) With clause in indirect discourse, to say, state, assert, tell. With *ὡς*, that Ψ 787: δ 376.—With *οὕνεκα* π 378.—With question: *τοῦ εἵνεκα . . .* Ω 106.—(**5**) Of the dawn or the morning-star, to herald or be the harbinger of (the daylight): *φόως ἐρέουσα* B 49. Cf. Ψ 226.

εἰρωτάω. (*ἀνερωτάω*.) (**1**) To ask, inquire. With question: *εἰρώτα τίς εἴη* ο 423.—(**2**) To question (a person): *εἰρωτᾷς με* ε 97.—With double acc. of person questioned and of what is inquired about: *ταῦθ' ἅ μ' εἰρωτᾷς* δ 347 = ρ 138. Cf. ι 364.

εἰς, ἐς. (**I**) Adv. (**1**) To or towards something: *ἐς ἄλοχον ἐκαλέσσατο* (to him) Ω 193.—(**2**) Into something: *ἐς δ' ἄγε χειρὸς ἑλών* (brought him in) Λ 646 = 778. Cf. A 142, 309, Ω 447, 458, 577: *ἐς δ' ἦλθον μνηστῆρες* α 144. Cf. δ 36, π 349, φ 391, etc.—(**3**) Giving notion of a directing of the sight in a particular direction: *θεοὶ ἐς πάντες ὁρῶντο* X 166. Cf. M 335, Φ 527.—(**II**) Prep. (commonly accented when immediately following the case-form) (**1**) With acc. (**a**) To, towards: *ἄγειν ἐς Χρύσην* A 100. Cf. A 222, 366, 402, 423, 490, etc.: *ἐς Σπάρτην* α 93. Cf. α 85, 90, 172, 210, 276, etc.—With a form in *-δε* (1): *εἰς ἅλαδε* κ 351.—In reference to giving or presenting: *ἐς δῆμον ἔδωκεν* Λ 704.—(**b**) Indicating arrival at, going as far as to, reaching, a point: *ἐς Χρύσην ἵκανεν* A 431. Cf. B 667, Δ 446, Θ 509, I 354, Π 640, etc.: *ἐς Τένεδον ἐλθόντες* γ 159. Cf. γ 31, 488, δ 255, ε 115, ζ 119, etc.—Sim.: *ἐς ὁρμὴν ἔγχεος ἐλθεῖν* E 118.—Also *ἐφάνη λὶς εἰς ὁδόν* O 276, *ἐς Πηλῆ' ἱκέτευσεν* Π 574: *κάτθεσαν εἰς Ἰθάκην* (brought to . . . and set down there) π 230.—Of falling *to* one's lot: *ἐς ἑκάστην* [*νῆ'*] *ἐννέα λάγχανον αἶγες* ι 159.—(**c**) Indicating direction or position: *ἐς πῦρ ἔτρεψεν* Σ 469. Cf. γ 293, κ 528, μ 81.—Of the direction in which one looks: *ἰδὼν εἰς οὐρανόν* Γ 364. Cf. B 271, Z 404, K 11, etc.: ε 439, θ 170, κ 37, μ 247, etc.—So *εἰς ὦπα*. See *ὦπα*.—Fig. of looking *to*, attending *to*: *ἐς ἐμὰ ἔργ' ὁρόωσα* τ 514.—Of looking *to*, regarding: *ἐς γενεὴν ὁρόων* K 239. Cf. σ 219.—(**d**) In reference to purpose or intent: *ἐς πόλεμον θωρηχθῆναι* (for the fray) A 226, *εἰ ἐς μίαν βουλεύσομεν* B 379 (see *βουλεύω* (2)). Cf. I 102, O 508, T 205, etc.: *εἰς ὀρχηστὺν τρεψάμενοι* α 421. Cf. ζ 65, μ 372, τ 429, etc.—Sim.: *ἐς πόλεμον προφανέντε* P 487.—(**e**) Into: *εἰς ἅλα* A 141. Cf. A 220, B 152, E 857, Π 714, Ω 795, etc.: *ἐς ἀσαμίνθους* δ 48. Cf. γ 153, δ 220, ε 460, λ 523, χ 201, etc.—In reference to mingling with or joining persons: *οὐδ' ἐς Ἀχαιοὺς μίσγετο* Σ 215.—(**f**) In reference to division *into* sections: *ἐς δεκάδας* B 126.—(**g**) On to, on: *ἐς δίφρον ἄρνας θέτο* Γ 310. Cf. E 239, Λ 192, Ξ 287, Φ 536, Ω 332, etc: α 130, γ 483, δ 51, θ 296, ξ 280, ο 131, etc.—(**h**) As much as Ψ 523.—(**i**) In reference to time. (**α**) Up to or until (a point or period of time): *ἐς ἠέλιον καταδύντα* A 601. Cf. E 465, Ξ 86, T 162, etc. : ἐς δεκάτην γενεήν ξ 325. Cf. ι 161, λ 351, 375, etc.—For εἰς ὅ κε . . . see ὅς² (II) (9) (a).—(**β**) Indicating the beginning of a period : ἠελίου ἀνιόντος ἐς αὔριον Θ 538.—(**γ**) To the end of, during, for (a period) : εἰς ἐνιαυτόν Τ 32, Φ 444 : ἔς περ ὀπίσσω σ 122. Cf. δ 526, 595, κ 467, λ 356, ο 230, etc.—(**δ**) In reference to appointing a time : καλεσσαμένω ἐς ἠέλιον καταδύντα (for sunset) γ 138, αὔριον ἔς η 318. Cf. η 317.—Against, in view of (a time) : ἐς γάμου ὥρην ο 126.—So εἰς ὅτε κε . . . β 99 = τ 144 = ω 134.—(**ε**) Indicating the anticipated arrival of a point or period of time : εἰς ὥρας (in due season) ι 135, ἐλεύσεσθαι ἢ ἐς θέρος ἢ ἐς ὀπώρην (with the . . .) ξ 384. Cf. μ 126.—(**ζ**) Within, during the course of (a space) : τρὶς εἰς ἐνιαυτόν δ 86. Cf. Θ 404 = 418 (see δέκατος (1)) : ξ 196.—(**2**) With genit. (**a**) = (1) (a) : ἐς γαλόων Ζ 378, εἰς Ἄϊδος Ν 415, ἐς Πριάμοιο Ω 160, ἐς Ἀχιλλῆος 309, ἀνδρὸς ἐς ἀφνειοῦ 482, etc. : ἐς ἡμετέρου β 55 = ρ 534 (*v.l.* ἡμέτερον), ἐς πατρός β 195, εἰς Αἰγύπτοιο στῆσα νέας (brought them to . . .) δ 581, ἐς Ἀλκινόοιο θ 418, ἐς τώ δμῶε ἴτην Ὀδυσῆος φ 244, etc.—(**b**) = (1) (b) : εἰς Ἄϊδος οὔ πώ τις ἀφίκετο κ 502. (These uses with genit. also explained by ellipse of δῶμα ; but δ 581 and (reading the genit.) β 55, ρ 534 cannot be thus explained.)

εἷς, εἰς, 2 sing. pres. indic. εἰμί.

εἷς, μία, ἕν [σεμ-ς. Cf. L. *simplex*]. Genit. ἑνός, μιῆς, ἑνός. Fem. also ἴα, ἰῆς Δ 437, Ι 319, Λ 174, Ν 354, Π 173, Σ 251, Φ 569, Χ 477, Ω 496 : ξ 435. Dat. sing. neut. ἰῷ Ζ 422. (**1**) One, one only, a single . . . : κοίρανος Β 204. Cf. Β 205, 292, Η 336, 435, Θ 355, Κ 48, Λ 40, Μ 456, Ν 260, Ο 416, 511, Φ 569, Ω 540 : πόλιν δ 176. Cf. α 377 = β 142, ε 371, ι 209, ξ 94, φ 121, χ 138, ψ 118.—One and no other : εἷς οἰωνὸς ἄριστος Μ 243.—By oneself, left alone : μή με περιστήωσ' ἕνα πολλοί Ρ 95.—Absol. Β 346, Θ 234, Ν 447, Χ 425 : δ 105, 498, κ 116, μ 154, ν 15, υ 313.—Absol. in acc. fem. : ἐς μίαν βουλεύειν. See βουλεύω (2).—(**2**) With the article (**a**) One as distinguished from others : ἡ μί' οὔ πω παύετο υ 110. Cf. Λ 174.—Sim. in an enumeration : τὰς δύο . . . τὴν δὲ μίαν . . . Υ 272. Cf. ξ 435.—(**b**) The first : τῆς ἰῆς στιχὸς ἦρχε . . . τῆς δ' ἑτέρης . . . Π 173.—(**3**) Strengthened by οἶος : ἕνα οἶον ἴει Δ 397. Cf. Σ 565 : μίαν οἴην παῖδα η 65. Cf. β 412, ξ 514, χ 130.—Strengthening οἶος : ταμίη τε μί' οἴη (she and none other) ι 207.—Strengthened by μοῦνος : ἀμφίπολος μία μούνη ψ 227.—(**4**) Not pressing the notion of unity or singleness, one, someone : εἷς τις ἀνὴρ βουληφόρος (one of the βουλή) Α 144.—Absol. : εἷς θεῶν (one of the gods) Ε 603, Υ 98. Cf. Ζ 293, Ξ 267, 275, 411 : ὁ μὲν . . . εἷς δὲ . . . εἷς δ' αὖ . . . (one . . . another . . . another . . .) γ 421, δώσει τι ἕν (something) ο 83. Cf. α 339, ο 106, χ 117.—(**5**) One, the same, one and the same : εἰν ἑνὶ δίφρῳ Ε 160, 609, Λ 103, 127. Cf. Δ 437, 446 = Θ 60, Ζ 422, Ι 319, Ν 354, 487, Ο 710, Π 219, Ρ 267, Σ 251, Χ 477, Ω 66, 396, 496 : γ 128.—The same as. With dat. : τώ μοι μία γείνατο μήτηρ (the same as in my case, the same as my own) Γ 238. Cf. Τ 293.

εἰσάγω, ἐσάγω [εἰσ- (1) (2), ἐσ-]. 3 sing. aor. εἰσήγαγε γ 191. 3 pl. -ον Ω 719 : τ 420. Pple. εἰσαγαγών, -όντος Μ 18, Ω 620 : ξ 49. Fem. -οῦσα κ 233, 314, 366. (**1**) To bring or conduct in : Λαοδίκην ἐσάγουσα Ζ 252. Cf. κ 233, 314 = 366, ξ 49, 419, τ 420.—To bring in to one's aid : ποταμῶν μένος Μ 18.—(**2**) To bring or conduct *into*. With acc. : [παῖδα] Ἴλιον εἰσαγαγών Ω 620. Cf. Ω 719 : δ 43.—To bring or lead home *to*. With acc. : Κρήτην ἑταίρους γ 191.

εἴσαιτο, 3 sing aor. opt. mid. εἴδω (B).

εἰσάμενος, aor. pple. mid. εἴδω (B).

εἶσαν, 3 pl. aor. See ἕζομαι.

εἰσαναβαίνω [εἰσ- (1) + ἀνα- (1)]. 3 pl. aor. εἰσανέβησαν Ζ 74, Ρ 320. Fem. pple. εἰσαναβᾶσα Β 514, Ω 700 : π 449, ρ 101, τ 594. Pl. -ᾶσαι (*v.l.* ἐξαναβᾶσαι) Ω 97. Infin. εἰσαναβῆναι Ρ 337. To go *up to* or *on to*. With acc. : ὑπερώϊον Β 514, ὁμὸν λέχος Θ 291. Cf. Ζ 74 = Ρ 320, Ρ 337, Σ 68, Ω 97, 700 : π 449, ρ 101, τ 594.—Of a voyage to Troy : ὅτε Ἴλιον εἰσανέβαινον β 172, σ 252 = τ 125.

εἰσανάγω [εἰσ- (2) + ἀν-, ἀνα- (1)]. App., to carry off inland, or simply, to carry off, *into* (a condition) (cf. ἀνάγω (1)). With acc. : εἴρερον εἰσανάγουσιν θ 529.

†**εἰσανείδω** [εἰσ- (4) + ἀν-, ἀνα- (1)]. Aor. pple. εἰσανιδών. To look up *to*. With acc. : οὐρανόν Π 232, Ω 307.

†**εἰσάνειμι** [εἰσ- (1) + ἀν-, ἀνα- (1) + εἶμι]. Pple. εἰσανιών. To ascend or climb *to*. With acc. : οὐρανόν Η 423.

εἰσανιδών, aor. pple. εἰσανείδω.

εἰσανιών, pres. pple. εἰσάνειμι.

εἰσάντα (only in ε 217), **ἐσάντα** [εἰσ- (4), ἐσ- + ἄντα]. In the face, face to face : ἰδών Ρ 334. Cf. ε 217, κ 453, λ 143, ο 532, π 458, ρ 239.

εἴσατο¹, 3 sing. aor. mid. εἴδω (B).

εἴσατο², 3 sing. aor. mid. ἵημι².

εἰσαφικάνω [εἰσ- (1) + ἀφ-, ἀπο- (7)]. To come to, arrive at, reach : Λῆμνον Ξ 230. Cf. χ 99, 112.

†**εἰσαφικνέομαι** [εἰσ- (1) + ἀφ-, ἀπο- (7)]. 2 sing. subj. εἰσαφίκηαι Υ 336. 3 -ηται μ 40, π 228, υ 188. 3 sing. opt. εἰσαφίκοιτο μ 84, χ 415, ψ 66. Infin. εἰσαφικέσθαι Χ 17 : ν 404, ο 38. To come or go to, arrive at, reach : Ἴλιον Χ 17. Cf. Υ 336 : μ 40, ν 404 = ο 38, π 228 = υ 188, χ 415 = ψ 66.—Of reaching with an arrow μ 84.

εἰσβαίνω, ἐσβαίνω [εἰσ- (2) (3), ἐσ-]. 3 sing. aor. opt. ἐσβαίη Μ 59. Nom. pl. masc. pple. ἐσβάντες Κ 573. (**1**) To effect an entrance Μ 59.—(**2**) To plunge into something Κ 573.—(**3**) To go on board ship, embark : αἶψ' εἴσβαινον ι 103 = 179 = 471 = 563 = λ 638 = μ 146 = ο 549, ο 221.

εἶσε, 3 sing. aor. See ἕζομαι.

εἴσεαι, 2 sing. fut. See εἴδω (C).

†**εἰσείδω, ἐσείδω** [εἰσ- (4), ἐσ-]. Aor. ἐσεῖδον (ἐσϜ-) (*v.l.* εἰσεῖδον) λ 582, 593. ἔσιδον (*v.l.* εἴσιδον) λ 306. 3 sing. εἰσεῖδε Ξ 153, 158. εἴσιδε Ξ 13, Σ 235 : α 118, ε 392. ἔσιδε (*v.l.* εἴσιδε) ι 251, ν 197, χ 407, 408, ψ 324, ω 493. 3 dual

εἰσιδέτην φ 222. 1 pl. ἐσίδομεν (v.l. εἰσίδομεν) ι 148. 3 ἔσιδον (v.l. εἴσιδον) π 356. Fem. pple. ἐσιδοῦσα Χ 407. Infin. εἰσιδέειν Π 256, Τ 15: ζ 230. ἐσιδέειν (v.l. εἰσιδέειν) μ 446, ψ 157. 3 sing. pa. iterative ἐσίδεσκε ψ 94. 3 dual aor. mid. ἐσιδέσθην ω 101. (1) To look towards, look at ψ 94.—(2) To catch sight of, see, perceive, behold: Ζῆνα Ξ 158. Cf. Ξ 13, Χ 407: α 118, ε 392, ι 148, λ 306, 582, 593, ν 197, χ 407, 408, ψ 324.—Absol.: ἐπεὶ εἰσιδέτην φ 222. Cf. ι 251, μ 446, ω 101.—(3) To witness, see, look on at: φύλοπιν Π 256.—(4) With pple. expressing something observed in connexion with a person or thing: ἑταῖρον κείμενον ἐν φέρτρῳ Σ 235. Cf. π 356.—Sim.: τοὺς σχεδὸν ἔσιδεν ω 493.—(5) To direct one's eyes, look, glance: Ἥρη εἰσεῖδεν Ξ 153. Cf. Τ 15.—(6) The infin. used epexegetically: μείζονα εἰσιδέειν ζ 230 = ψ 157.

†εἴσειμι [εἰσ- (2) + εἶμι]. 1 sing. pres. εἴσειμι. In pres. with fut. sense. (1) To go in: μετ' ἀνέρας σ 184.—(2) To go *into*; hence, to come within the range of. With acc.: Ἀχιλῆος ὀφθαλμούς Ω 463.

†εἰσελαύνω [εἰσ- (1) (2)]. Pres. pple. εἰσελάων κ 83. 3 pl. aor. εἰσέλασαν ν 113. Nom. pl. masc. pple. εἰσελάσαντες Ο 385. (1) To drive in: ἵππους Ο 385.—To drive a flock or herd in or home κ 83.—(2) To bring a ship to land ν 113.

εἰσελθών, aor. pple. εἰσέρχομαι.

εἰσέπτατο, 3 sing. aor. εἰσπέτομαι.

†εἰσερύω [εἰσ- (2) + ἐρύω¹]. Nom. pl. masc. aor. pple. εἰσερύσαντες. To draw *into*. With acc.: νῆα σπέος εἰσερύσαντες μ 317.

εἰσέρχομαι, ἐσέρχομαι [εἰσ- (1) (2), ἐσ-]. Fut. ἐσελεύσομαι α 88, ρ 52. Aor. εἰσήλυθον Β 798, Γ 184. 3 sing. εἰσήλυθε δ 338, ρ 129. εἰσῆλθε Β 321, Δ 376, Ζ 318, Π 254: δ 802, ρ 324, φ 242, ψ 88. 3 pl. εἰσῆλθον κ 112. 3 sing. subj. εἰσέλθῃσι Θ 522. Imp. εἴσελθε Ζ 354: π 25. ἔσελθε ρ 275. Pl. ἐσέλθετε φ 230. Pple. εἰσελθών Ι 138, 280, Λ 560, Ω 465, 477. Fem. εἰσελθοῦσα Δ 34, Ξ 169. Infin. ἐσελθεῖν Μ 341. (1) To go or proceed *to*. With acc.: Ἰθάκην α 88. Cf. ρ 52.—(2) To go in, get in, enter: ἔνθ' εἰσῆλθε Ζ 318. Cf. Μ 341, Ξ 169, Ω 465, 477: ν 112, φ 230, ψ 88.—With prep.: ἐς θάλαμον δ 802.—(3) With acc. (a) To go or get *into*, enter: πόλιν Θ 522. Cf. Γ 184, Δ 376, Λ 560, Π 254: δ 338 = ρ 129, κ 112, ρ 275, 324 = φ 242.—Fig.: πενίη οὔ ποτε δῆμον ἐσέρχεται ο 407. Cf. Ρ 157.—(b) To go *within* or *behind*: πύλας καὶ τείχεα Δ 34.—(c) To enter *into*, play a part in: μάχας Β 798.—(4) To come in, enter: εἴσελθε καὶ ἕζεο Ζ 354. Cf. π 25.—(5) With acc. (a) To come *within* or *behind*: τεῖχος Χ 56.—(b) To come *in among*, mingle with: θεῶν ἑκατόμβας Β 321.—(6) To come in or present oneself to take part in a proceeding: νῆα χρυσοῦ νηησάσθω (νηήσασθαι) εἰσελθών Ι 138, 280.

εἴσεται¹, 3 sing. fut. See εἴδω (C).

εἴσεται², 3 sing. fut. mid. ἵημι².

εἴσῃ, 2 sing. fut. εἶμι.

εἰσήγαγε, 3 sing. aor. εἰσάγω.

εἰσῆλθε, 3 sing. aor. εἰσέρχομαι.

εἰσήλυθον, aor. εἰσέρχομαι.

εἶσθα, 2 sing. **εἶσι,** 3 sing. εἶμι.

εἰσί, 3 pl. εἰμί.

εἴσιδον, aor. εἰσείδω.

εἰσίθμη, ἡ [εἰσ- (2) + ἰθ-, εἶμι]. An entrance ζ 264.

ἐΐσκω (ϝεϝίσκω) [app. for ϝεϝίκσκω, fr. ϝικ-, εἴκω¹. Cf. ἴσκω, εἴκελος]. For εἴσκοντες, v.l. for ἴσκοντες, see ἴσκω (2). (1) To cause to take the likeness of, make like. With dat.: ἄλλῳ αὐτὸν φωτὶ ἤϊσκεν δ 247. Cf. ν 313.—(2) To liken to, deem like, compare with. With dat.: ἀρνειῷ μιν Γ 197. Cf. Ε 181, Ω 371: Ἀρτέμιδί σε ζ 152. Cf. θ 159, π 187, υ 362.—(3) To think, fancy, suppose, conjecture: ὡς σὺ ἐΐσκεις δ 148.—With infin.: ἄντα σέθεν Ξάνθον ἠΐσκομεν εἶναι Φ 332. Cf. Ν 446: ι 321 (infin. to be supplied), λ 363.

εἰσνοέω [εἰσ- (4)]. To note, descry, see: πατέρα Ω 700: Ὠρίωνα λ 572, βίην Ἡρακληείην 601.

εἴσοδος, ἡ [εἰσ- (2) + ὁδός]. An entrance κ 90.

†εἰσοιχνέω [εἰσ- (1)]. 3 pl. εἰσοιχνεῦσι ι 120. Acc. sing. fem. pple. εἰσοιχνεῦσαν ζ 157. With acc., to go *to*, land upon: νῆσον ι 120.—To approach in order to take part in: χορόν ζ 157.

εἴσομαι¹, fut. See εἴδω (C).

εἴσομαι², fut. mid. ἵημι².

εἶσον, aor. imp. See ἕζομαι.

εἰσοράω, ἐσοράω [εἰσ- (4), ἐσ-]. 3 pl. εἰσορόωσι Μ 312: θ 173, ο 520, υ 166. 2 pl. opt. εἰσορόῳτε θ 341. Pple. εἰσορόων Ε 183, Θ 52, Κ 123, Λ 82, 601, Χ 321, Ω 632: π 26, 277, φ 393. Dat. εἰσορόωντι Ψ 464: ω 319. Acc. εἰσορόωντα Ο 456, Ρ 687: γ 123, δ 75, ζ 161, θ 384, ξ 214. Pl. εἰσορόωντες Δ 4, Η 214, Ι 229, Ν 88, Ω 23: η 71, ι 321, λ 363, υ 311. Dat. εἰσορόωσι θ 327. Acc. εἰσορόωντας Γ 342, Δ 79, Ω 482. Fem. εἰσορόωσα Λ 73: τ 537. Dat. εἰσοροώσῃ ψ 239. Acc. εἰσορόωσαν δ 142. Pl. εἰσορόωσαι Δ 9, Ε 418. Imp. pl. mid. εἰσοράασθε Ψ 495. Infin. εἰσοράασθαι Ξ 345: γ 246, ι 324, κ 396, ω 252. 3 pl. impf. εἰσορόωντο Ψ 448. From ὀπ- fut. in mid. form ἐσόψομαι Ε 212. 3 sing. ἐσόψεται Ω 206. (1) To look at or upon, see, view, behold: Τρώων πόλιν Δ 4. Cf. Ε 183, Η 214, Θ 52 = Λ 82, Ι 229, Λ 601, Ν 88, Ψ 448, 495, Ω 632: πατέρα ω 319. Cf. θ 327, π 26, υ 311.—To set eyes upon, see: πατρίδ' ἐμήν Ε 212. Cf. Ω 206.—To look upon, be a spectator of the doings of: μνηστήρων ὅμιλον π 29, ψ 303.—To observe, survey: χρόα Χ 321.—To keep one's eyes upon, watch: Πληϊάδας ε 272.—(2) Absol., to see, behold: θάμβος ἔχεν εἰσορόωντας Γ 342. Cf. Δ 9, 79. Ε 418, Λ 73, Ξ 345, Ρ 687, Ω 23, 482: γ 123, δ 75, 142, ζ 161, θ 384, ι 321, λ 363, ξ 214, π 277, τ 537, ψ 239.—To look on, be a spectator θ 341.—To direct one's sight, look Ψ 464.—To look out, watch: σχεδὸν ἴσχειν εἰσορόωντα ἵππους ('keeping his eyes open') Ο 456.—(3) To look to for guidance or counsel Κ 123.—To look towards for aid Ν 478, 490.—To watch (a person) looking for a signal for action from him φ 393.—(4) To look up to, respect, regard:

θεοὺς ὥς M 312. Cf. η 71, θ 173, ο 520, υ 166.—(5) The infin. mid. used epexegetically: καλλίονες εἰσοράασθαι κ 396. Cf. γ 246, ι 324, ω 252.

εἴσος. See ἴσος.

†εἰσπέτομαι [εἰσ- (2)]. 3 sing. aor. εἰσέπτατο. To fly *into*. With acc.: κοίλην πέτρην Φ 494.

εἴσω, ἔσω [εἰς]. (1) Into the interior of something, inwards, in: δῦναι δόμον Ἄϊδος εἴσω Γ 322, εἴσω ἀσπίδ' ἔαξεν (broke it in) H 270, εἴσω ἐπιγράψαι χρόα (app., getting within his guard) N 553. Cf. Δ 460, M 459, Π 340, Σ 282, etc.: εἴπατ' εἴσω (go in and tell) γ 427, ἔσω κίε η 50. Cf. δ 775, η 6, κ 91, λ 579, etc.—(2) In the interior, within: εἴσω δόρπον ἐκόσμει η 13. Cf. σ 96, τ 4.—(3) With acc. of something reached and entered: Ἴλιον εἴσω P 159. Cf. Λ 44, Ξ 457, Φ 125, Ω 155, etc.: πέμψαι δόμον Ἄϊδος εἴσω ι 524. Cf. λ 150, ο 40, ψ 24, etc.—So with ellipse of δόμον (or perh. on the analogy of εἰς Ἄϊδος (see εἰς (II) (2))): κατελθόντ' Ἄϊδος εἴσω Z 284. Cf. Z 422, X 425.—In reference to a point reached, but not implying entrance: νῆεσσ' ἡγήσατο Ἴλιον εἴσω A 71. Cf. Σ 58, 439, etc.: τ 182, 193.—(4) With genit. as in (3): εἴσω δώματος ᾖει θ 290. Cf. η 135.

εἰσωπός [εἰσ- (2) + ὦπα. 'Inside-looking']. Hence, within or inside of the line of. With genit.: νεῶν O 653.

εἶται, 3 sing. pf. mid. ἕννυμι.

εἶτε, 2 pl. opt. εἰμί.

εἴτε. See εἰ (10).

εἶχον, impf. ἔχω.

εἰῶ = ἐάω.

εἴωθε, 3 sing. pf. **εἰωθώς,** pf. pple. ἔθω.

ἐκ, before a vowel **ἐξ** [cf. L. *ex*]. (I) Adv. (1) Out, forth, from, away, off: ἐκ δ' εὐνὰς ἔβαλον A 436, ἐκ πάντα θεμείλια πέμπεν (*i.e.* the water tore them from their seats) M 28, ἐκ δέ οἱ ἡνίοχος πλήγη φρένας (was struck out of, lost, his wits) N 394. Cf. A 469, B 809, Γ 113, Δ 116, etc.: ἐκ δ' ἔβαν αὐτοὶ γ 11, ἐκ τοσσῶνδ' ἀέκητι οἴχεται δ 665. Cf. α 150, γ 406, 456, δ 301, etc.—In reference to keeping out of harm's way: ἔκ τ' ἀλέοντο Σ 586.—(2) Off: ἐκ δὲ καλυψάμενοι θηήσαντο κ 179 (see καλύπτω (3)). Cf. ξ 341.—(3) In reference to selection, out of specified things: ἐκ δ' ἕλον Χρυσηΐδα A 369. Cf. Λ 696.—(4) In reference to hanging or attaching, or to being hung or attached, from or to something: ἐκ δὲ πέλειαν δῆσεν Ψ 853. Cf. Σ 480.—(5) Of speaking, etc., indicating absence of restraint, out, right out, aloud: ἔκ τοι ἐρέω A 204, ἐκ δὲ γέλασσεν Z 471. Cf. A 233, etc.: β 187, δ 278, 376, etc.—Sim. of bright reflexion of light: ἔκ τ' ἔφανεν πᾶσαι σκοπιαὶ Θ 557 = Π 299.—(6) Intensive, often not appreciably affecting the sense: ἔκ τ' ὀνόμαζεν A 361, ἐκ καὶ ὀψὲ τελεῖ Δ 161. Cf. Γ 398, E 161, I 375, M 234, etc.: β 302, γ 374, η 220, κ 63, etc.—(II) Prep. with genit. (commonly accented when immediately following the case-form). (1) Out of, out from, away from, from: ἐκ Πύλου A 269, ἐκ δ' ἄγαγε κλισίης 346, μάχης ἔκ P 207. Cf. A 194, 439, B 88, 131, 146, etc.: α 259, 327, β 147, 321, γ 12, etc.—With ablative: ἐκ παλάμηφιν Γ 367. Cf. Ξ 150, O 580: β 2, γ 405, etc.—With a form in -θεν (1): ἐξ οὐρανόθεν Θ 21.—App. with ellipse of δόμου: οὐ νίσομαι ἐξ Ἀΐδαο Ψ 76. Cf. λ 625, 635, σ 299.—In reference to deprivation: ἐκ γάρ εὐ φρένας εἵλετο I 377.—Cf. Σ 311.—To returning Z 480, etc.: π 463, etc.—In reference to immaterial things: ἔγρετ' ἐξ ὕπνου B 41, ἐκ θυμοῦ πεσέειν Ψ 595. Cf. K 107, Υ 350, etc.: δ 753, 839, etc.—(2) At a distance from, away from: ἐκ καπνοῦ κατέθηκα [τεύχεα] π 288 = τ 7. Cf. Ξ 130.—(3) In reference to acquisition or selection, out of, from: τὴν ἄρετ' ἐξ ἐνάρων I 188. Cf. Δ 96, I 641, etc.: β 433, etc.—(4) In reference to growth or development, out of, from: τοῦ κέρα ἐκ κεφαλῆς πεφύκει Δ 109. Cf. Ξ 177.—With -θεν (1) ε 477.—Sim.: ἐξ ἑτέρων ἕτερ' ἐστίν (*i.e.* one set of buildings joins on to another) ρ 266.—(5) In reference to birth, sprung from, from: γένος ἦν ἐκ ποταμοῖο E 544. Cf. E 548, Ξ 472, O 187, T 105, 111, etc.: τοῦ μ' ἔκ φασι γενέσθαι α 220. Cf. α 207, κ 139, 350, ξ 202 (by . . .), π 100, etc.—With ablative: ἐκ θεόφιν γένος ἦεν Ψ 347.—(6) In reference to a place of birth or origin: μελίην, τὴν πόρε Πηλίου ἐκ κορυφῆς Π 144 = T 391. Cf. Φ 154: ἐξ Ἰθάκης γένος εἰμί ο 267. Cf. ξ 199, ο 425, ω 418, etc.—(7) In reference to source, origin, cause, motive, in general, proceeding from, from: ὄναρ ἐκ Διός ἐστιν A 63, ἐκ θυμοῦ φίλεον (from my heart) I 343. Cf. A 525, E 4, H 111, Ξ 416, Υ 129, etc.: ἐξ ἡμέων κάκ' ἔμμεναι α 33, ἐξ ὀλιγηπελίης ε 468, ὅς τε θεῶν ἒξ ἀείδῃ (under their inspiration) ρ 518. Cf. α 40, β 134, ι 512, μ 286, τ 93, etc.—With ablative: ἐκ θεόφιν πολεμίζει P 101.—Sim.: ἐκ γενεῆς ὀνομάζων (by his family name) K 68.—In reference to a source from which one draws: ἐκ κεράμων μέθυ πίνετο I 469. Cf. Φ 312, etc.: ζ 224, ι 9, κ 361.—In reference to an agent: ἐφίληθεν ἐκ Διός B 669. Cf. η 70.—(8) In reference to a point *from* which seeing, appearing, hearing, speaking, etc., or action in gen. takes place, or which is occupied by an agent: ἐξ ἄκρης πόλιος Διὶ χεῖρας ἀνασχεῖν Z 257, στᾶσ' ἐξ Οὐλύμποιο Ξ 154 (indicating the quarter from which she appeared to an observer; cf. Φ 144 and under ἀπό (II) (1) (b)), ἄστεος ἐκ σφετέρου (*i.e.* with the city as their base) Σ 210, μετέειπεν ἐξ ἕδρης T 77. Cf. Θ 75, Λ 62, 130, T 375, Υ 377, Φ 213, etc.: ἐκ Σολύμων ὀρέων ἴδεν ε 283, ἕλκε νευρὴν ἐκ δίφροιο φ 420. Cf. ι 407, μ 83, ν 56, ξ 328, π 390, etc.—With ablative: τηλεφανὴς ἐκ ποντόφιν ω 83. Cf. I 572.—With a form in -θεν (1): ἐξ ἁλόθεν Φ 335. Cf. P 548.—Sim.: δίφροιο δ' ἐκ ῥυμὸς πέλεν (stood out) E 729.—(9) In reference to a point *from* which a beginning is made: ἐκ κεφαλῆς ἐς πόδας Π 640. Cf. Σ 353, X 397, Ψ 169: η 87, 96, ψ 196, 199.—Sim.: ἐκ ῥιζέων ἐριποῦσα Φ 243.—Also: ἐξ ἀγχιμόλοιο Ω 352.—(10) In reference to suspending, hanging, attaching, from, to: ἐξ ἄντυγος ἡνία τείνας E 262. Cf. K 475, Λ 38, Σ 598, X 398, etc.: κ 96, μ 51, τ 58, ω 8, etc.—With ablative: ἐκ πασσαλόφι κρέμασεν θ 67 = 105.—With a form in -θεν (1)

Θ 19.—In reference to a person on whom something depends or hinges: τοῦ δ' ἐκ Φαιήκων ἔχεται κάρτος ζ 197. Cf. λ 346.—**(11)** In reference to succession: δέχεταί μοι κακὸν ἐκ κακοῦ (one evil after another) Τ 290.—**(12)** In temporal sense. **(a)** From, since: ἐκ νεότητος Ξ 86. Cf. Θ 296, Ι 106, Ο 69, Ω 31, 535 (see γενετή), etc.: ἐξ ἀρχῆς α 188. Cf. α 74, 212, β 254, ρ 69, σ 6 (see γενετή), etc.—For ἐξ οὗ see ὅς² (II) (9) (b).—**(b)** After, succeeding: καύματος ἐξ Ε 865.

ἑκάεργος (Fεκάϝεργος) [ἑκάς + ἔργω²]. The far-worker, the far-shooter. Epithet or a name of Apollo Α 147, 474, 479, Ε 439, Η 34, Ι 564, Ο 243, 253 = Φ 461, Π 94, Ρ 585, Φ 472, 478, 600, Χ 15, 220: θ 323.

ἐκάη, 3 sing. aor. pass. καίω.

ἕκαθεν [ἑκάς + -θεν (1) (2)]. **(1)** From afar: ἑ. φαίνεται αὐγή (*i.e.*, as we say, to a great distance) Β 456. Cf. Ν 179, Π 634.—**(2)** Far off: ἑ. ἄστυ φάτ' εἶναι ρ 25.

ἐκάθηρε, 3 sing. aor. καθαίρω.

ἐκαλέσσατο, 3 sing. aor. mid. καλέω.

ἐκάλυψε, 3 sing. aor. καλύπτω.

ἔκαμον, aor. κάμνω.

ἐκάπυσσε, 3 sing. aor. καπύω.

ἑκάς (Fεκάς). **(1)** Far, far off or away, at a great distance: στρωφᾶσθαι Τ 422. Cf. β 40, ε 358.—Comp. ἑκαστέρω η 321.—Superl. ἑκαστάτω Κ 113.—**(2)** Far, to a great distance: ἔπτατ' ὀϊστός Ν 592. Cf. μ 435.—**(3)** Far from. With genit.: ἑ. πόλιος Ε 791 = Ν 107. Cf. Ι 246, Ν 263, Ο 740, Τ 354: νηῶν ἑ. ξ 496. Cf. γ 260, δ 99, ζ 8, ο 33, ρ 73, ω 37.—With prep.: ἑ. ἀπὸ τείχεος Σ 256.

ἑκάστοθι [ἕκαστος + -θι]. In each place, at each of the spots mentioned γ 8.

ἕκαστος, -η, -ον (Fέκαστος). **(1) (a)** Each: ἀνήρ Β 805. Cf. Β 164, 610, Η 424, Κ 68, Ν 230, Σ 375, etc.: β 91, 384, ι 60, 431, κ 173, μ 99, χ 31, etc.—**(b)** In pl., each of the, all of the: ταῦτα (τὰ) ἕκαστα (all these things, these various things) Α 550, Κ 432, Λ 706, Ψ 95, φυλακτῆρες ἕκαστοι (each detachment) Ι 66, λαοὶ ἐπὶ νῆας ἕκαστοι ἐσκίδναντο (each to his ship) Ω 1. Cf. λ 9, μ 16, 151, 165, ξ 362, ο 487.—**(2)** Absol. **(a)** In sing., each, each one, each person or thing: ἑ. ἡγεμόνων Δ 428, ὥς κ' ὀστέα παισὶν ἑ. οἴκαδ' ἄγῃ Η 334 (app. loosely expressed, and meaning that each dead man's bones were to be taken to his children). Cf. Α 607, Ε 470, Ι 203, Ξ 507, Ψ 350, etc.: δίδωσι ἑκάστῳ α 349. Cf. β 392, δ 440, ι 65, 245, κ 392, etc.—**(b)** In pl., the whole number of specified or indicated persons or things. **(α)** In masc. and fem.: εἴ κ' ἄνδρα ἕκαστοι ἑλοίμεθα (each lot of ten) Β 127, ἐπεὶ κόσμηθεν ἕκαστοι (each tribe) Γ 1. Cf. Η 100, Ι 383, Ψ 55: ἕκαστοι ἠφύσαμεν (each ship's company) ι 164, θάπτον ἕκαστοι (the relatives of each) ω 417. Cf. ι 220, ν 76.—**(β)** In neut.: διασκοπιᾶσθαι ἕκαστα (all that could be spied out) Κ 388, ἕκαστ' ἐπέτελλεν (gave full injunctions) Ψ 107. Cf. Τ 332: ἵνα εἴπω ἕκαστα (give each his orders) γ 361, πόσιν ἐρέεινεν ἕκαστα (all that she had in her mind) δ 137, τελέοιέν χ' ἕκαστα (all needful affairs) ι 127, ἐρέω ἕκαστα (all that you need to know) κ 292. Cf. δ 119, θ 259, μ 25, 130, ν 191, σ 228, φ 222, ω 261, etc.—**(γ)** With the article: τὰ ἕκαστα ἐξερέουσιν (all they have to ask about) ξ 375.—**(3) (a)** In sing. with pl. vb.: οἱ κακκείοντες ἔβαν ἕκαστος Α 606. Cf. Β 775, Ε 878, Η 175, Ι 88, Ξ 87, etc.: οὐδ' ὑμεῖς ἐνὶ φρεσὶ θέσθε ἑκάστη (none of you did so) δ 729, ἕκαστος ἐνείκατε θ 392. Cf. β 252, θ 324, κ 397, λ 542, χ 57, etc.—**(b)** In sing. in apposition with pl. sb., etc.: Τρῶας τρόμος ὑπήλυθε ἕκαστον Η 215 = Υ 44. Cf. Ε 195, Κ 473, Λ 11, Ξ 151, Ο 109: πᾶσιν ἐπίστιόν ἐστιν ἑκάστῳ ζ 265.—Sim.: ὑμέτερον ἑκάστου θυμόν Ρ 226.

ἑκάτερθε(ν) (Fεκάτερθε) [Fεκ-, ἕκαστος]. **(1)** On either side: τρεῖς ἑ. Λ 27, ἑ. καθήατο (in two parties) Υ 153, τρὶς ἑ. ἔδησαν [ζυγόδεσμον] Ω 273 (*i.e.* with three turns each way round the ὀμφαλός): ἀμφίπολος ἑ. παρέστη α 335 = σ 211 = φ 66, ἀψάμενοι ἑ. ι 386 (*i.e.* taking hold of the two ends of the strap, which made a turn round the shaft, and pulling the ends alternately). Cf. η 91, ι 430, λ 578, χ 181.—**(2)** On either side of. With genit.: ὁμίλου Γ 340 = Ψ 813 (*i.e.* each retired behind his friends). Cf. Ψ 329, Ω 319: σταθμοῖϊν ἑ. (one by each σταθμός) ζ 19. Cf. ζ 263.

ἑκατηβελέτης (Fεκατηβελέτης) [ἑκατη- (see next) + βελ-, βάλλω]. = next. Epithet of Apollo Α 75.

ἑκατηβόλος (Fεκατηβόλος) [ἑκατη-, conn. with ἑκάς + βολ-, βάλλω. Cf. ἑκηβόλος]. The far-shooter. Epithet or a name of Apollo Α 370, Ε 444 = Π 711, Ο 231, Ρ 333: θ 339, υ 278.

ἑκατόγχειρος [ἑκατόν + χείρ]. The hundred-handed. Of Briareus Α 402.

ἑκατόζυγος, -ον [ἑκατόν + ζυγόν]. With a hundred rowing-benches: νηῦς Υ 247.

ἑκατόμβη, -ης, ἡ [ἑκατόν + βοῦς. Lit., 'a sacrifice of a hundred oxen']. **(1)** A great or costly sacrifice Α 65, Β 306, Ζ 115, Η 450, Ι 535, etc.: α 25, γ 59, δ 352, ε 102, η 202, etc.—**(2)** The material for such a sacrifice: ἄγειν ἑκατόμβην ἐς Χρύσην Α 99. Cf. Α 142, 309, 431, 438, 447: υ 276.

ἑκατόμβοιος [as prec.]. **(1)** Of the value of a hundred oxen Β 449.—**(2)** Absol.: ἄμειβεν ἑκατόμβοι' ἐννεαβοίων Ζ 236.—In neut. sing., the value of a hundred oxen: ἑκατόμβοιόν τοι ἦλφον Φ 79.

ἑκατόμπεδος, -ον [ἑκατόν + πεδ- (as in πεζός), πούς, in sense, a measure of length]. Measuring a hundred feet: πυρήν Ψ 164.

ἑκατόμπολις [ἑκατόν + πόλις]. Containing a hundred cities. Epithet of Crete Β 649.

ἑκατόμπυλος, -ον [ἑκατόν + πύλη]. The hundred-gated. Epithet of the Egyptian Thebes Ι 383.

ἑκατόν, *indeclinable.* A hundred Β 448, 576, Ε 744, Ι 85, Λ 244, Ξ 181.—Absol.: ἑ. τε διηκοσίων τε Θ 233.—With another numeral: ἑ. καὶ εἴκοσι Β 510, ἑ. καὶ πεντήκοντα Λ 680.

ἕκατος (Fεκ-) [a short or 'pet' form of ἑκατηβόλος]. = ἑκατηβόλος Α 385, Η 83, Υ 71, 295.

ἐκβαίνω [ἐκ- (1)]. **(A)** Aor. imp. pl. ἔκβητε θ 38. Pple. ἐκβάς η 285. Pl. ἐκβάντες κ 103, 142. **(B)** Aor. pple. pl. ἐκβήσαντες ω 301. **(I)** *Intrans.*

in all forms except (B). (1) To come forth: ἐκβαίνοντα πλῆξα κ 161.—To leave a specified region: ἀπάνευθε ποταμοῖο ἐκβὰς κατέδραθον η 285.—(2) To come forth *from*. With genit.: πέτρης Δ 107.—(3) To come out of the sea on to dry land ε 415, η 278.—(4) To leave a ship, land θ 38, κ 103, 142.—(II) *Trans.* in form (B), to set on shore ω 301.

ἐκβάλλω [ἐκ- (1)]. Aor. ἔκβαλον Σ 324: ξ 277. 3 sing. -ε Ε 39, Ξ 419, Ο 468: δ 503, ε 244, τ 278, 362. 3 pl. -ον ο 481. (1) To throw out Φ 237.—To throw overboard ο 481.—Of the sea, to cast up (on to the shore) τ 278.—To shed (tears) τ 362. To utter: ἔπος Σ 324: δ 503.—(2) To fell (trees) (cf. ἐκτάμνω (4)) ε 244.—(3) To send forth, let fall: δόρυ ἔκτοσε χειρός ξ 277.—(4) With genit., to strike *out of* (the hand): βιὸν ἔκβαλε χειρός Ο 468. Cf. β 396.—To hurl or cause to fall *from*: ἔκβαλε δίφρου Ε 39.—(5) To send forth, let fall *from* (the hand). With genit.: χειρὸς ἔκβαλεν ἔγχος Ξ 419.

ἔκβασις, ἡ [ἐκ- (1) + βα-, βαίνω]. A means of escape from something: ἁλός ε 410.

†ἐκβλώσκω [ἐκ- (1)]. 3 sing. aor. ἔκμολε. To come out: κλισίηθεν Λ 604.

ἐκγεγάμεν, pf. infin. ἐκγίγνομαι.

ἐκγεγαῶτι, dat. sing. masc. **ἐκγεγαυῖα,** nom. sing. fem. pf. pple. ἐκγίγνομαι.

†ἐκγελάω [ἐκ- (8)]. Aor. pple. ἐκγελάσας. To laugh out, laugh aloud: ἡδύ π 354, σ 35.

†ἐκγίγνομαι [ἐκ- (2)]. 3 pl. aor. ἐξεγένοντο Ε 637, Ξ 115, Υ 231, 305. Dat. sing. masc. pf. pple. ἐκγεγαῶτι Φ 185. Nom. fem. ἐκγεγαυῖα Γ 199, 418: δ 184, 219, ζ 229, ψ 218. Infin. ἐκγεγάμεν Ε 248, Υ 106, 209. 3 dual plupf. ἐκγεγάτην κ 138. (1) To be born: Πορθεῖ τρεῖς παῖδες ἐξεγένοντο (were born to . . .) Ξ 115.—(2) With genit., to be born *of*: οἳ Διὸς ἐξεγένοντο Ε 637. Cf. Γ 199, 418, Υ 106, 231, 305, Φ 185: δ 184, 219, κ 138, ζ 229, ψ 218.—To be by birth (the son) *of*: υἱὸς Ἀγχίσαο εὔχεται (εὔχομαι) ἐκγεγάμεν Ε 248, Υ 209.

ἔκγονος [ἐκ- (2) + γον-, γεν-, γίγνομαι]. (1) The offspring, a child (=γόνος (1) (a)): Τυδέος Ε 813. Cf. Υ 206: γ 123, λ 236.—(2) A remoter descendant (=γόνος (1) (b)): Μελάμποδος ο 225 (he was his great-grandson).

†ἐκδέρω [ἐκ- (3)]. Aor. pple. ἐκδείρας. To strip off: δῶκέ μ' ἐκδείρας ἀσκὸν βοός κ 19 (*i.e.* a bag made from the stripped off skin).

ἐκδέχομαι [ἐκ- (1)]. To receive from one, relieve one of: οἵ οἱ σάκος ἐξεδέχοντο Ν 710.

ἐκδέω [ἐκ- (4)]. (1) To attach, bind on χ 174.—(2) To attach so as to hang *from*, bind on to. With genit.: δρῦς ἔκδεον ἡμιόνων Ψ 121.

ἔκδηλος [ἐκ- (9)]. Conspicuous, pre-eminent Ε 2.

†ἐκδιαβαίνω [ἐκ- (1) + δια- (3)]. Nom. pl. masc. aor. pple. ἐκδιαβάντες. To go forth and *across* (a space). With acc.: τάφρον Κ 198.

†ἐκδίδωμι [ἐκ- (1)]. Aor. imp. pl. ἔκδοτε. To give up, surrender: Ἑλένην Γ 459.

ἐκδύω, ἐκδύνω [ἐκ- (1)]. 1 pl. aor. opt. ἐκδῦμεν Π 99. Pple. ἐκδύς ξ 460, χ 334. (1) To put off (a garment) α 437, ξ 460.—So in mid., to put off (one's armour): τεύχε' ἐξεδύοντο Γ 114.—(2) To go *out of*, quit. With genit.: μεγάροιο χ 334.—To escape, avoid: ὄλεθρον Π 99.

ἐκέασσε, 3 sing. aor. κεάζω.

ἐκέδασθεν, 3 pl. aor. pass. κεδάννυμι.

ἐκέδασσε, 3 sing. aor. κεδάννυμι.

ἐκεῖθι [cf. next and κεῖθι]. There ρ 10.

ἐκεῖνος, -η, -ο [cf. κεῖνος]. (1) That person or thing, the person or thing referred to, he, she, it (with backward reference): οἷος ἐ. δεινὸς ἀνήρ Λ 653. Cf. β 183, γ 113, ξ 163, 352, ο 330, 368, π 151, σ 147, τ 322, ω 288, 312, 437.—(2) As antecedent to a relative: ἐ. ὅς . . . Ι 63.—(3) Contrasted with ὁ δ 819.—(4) With sb., that: ἐν ἐκείνῳ δήμῳ γ 103.

ἐκέκαστο, 3 sing. plupf. καίνυμαι.

ἐκεκεύθει, 3 sing. plupf. κεύθω.

ἐκέκλετο, 3 sing. aor. κέλομαι.

ἐκέκλιτο, 3 sing. plupf. pass. κλίνω.

ἔκερσε, 3 sing. aor. κείρω.

ἔκηα, aor. καίω.

ἐκηβολίη, -ης, ἡ [ἐκηβόλος]. Skill in the use of the bow. In pl. Ε 54.

ἐκηβόλος (Ϝεκηβόλος) [ἑκη-, ἑκάς + βολ-, βάλλω]. =ἑκατηβόλος Α 14=373, 21, 96, 110, 438, Π 513, Χ 302, Ψ 872.

ἕκηλος (Ϝέκηλος) [cf. ἑκών, εὔκηλος]. (1) At ease, at one's ease, taking one's ease, untroubled, undisturbed, without undue exertion: τέρπονται Ε 759, ἐρρέτω (without hindrance on my part, for all I care) Ι 376. Cf. Ζ 70, Θ 512, Λ 75, Ρ 340: β 311, λ 184, ν 423, ξ 91, 167, π 314, φ 289.—(2) Implying forbearance from action, keeping the peace, holding one's peace, restraining oneself: δαίνυσθαι Ε 805. Cf. Ο 194: μ 301, ρ 478, φ 259 (giving over for the time being), 309.

ἕκητι (Ϝέκητι) [cf. ἑκών]. By the grace or aid of. With genit. (always following the case): Ἑρμείαο ἑ. ο 319. Cf. τ 86, υ 42.

ἐκθεῖσαι, nom. pl. fem. aor. pple. ἐκτίθημι.

†ἐκθνήσκω [ἐκ- (9)]. 3 pl. aor. ἔκθανον. To die: γέλῳ ἔκθανον σ 100 (app. (nearly) killed themselves with laughter).

ἐκθρῴσκω [ἐκ- (1)]. 3 sing. aor. ἐξέθορε Φ 539. ἔκθορε Π 427. (1) To leap or spring forth Φ 539.—(2) To jump *out of*. With genit.: δίφρου Π 427.—So of the heart beating in agitation and apparently striving to burst (out of the breast): κραδίη μοι ἔξω στηθέων ἐκθρῴσκει Κ 95.

ἔκιον. See κίον.

ἔκιχε, 3 sing. aor. κιχάνω.

ἐκίχεις, 2 sing. impf. See κιχάνω.

ἐκίχημεν, 1 pl. non-thematic impf. κιχάνω.

ἐκκαθαίρω [ἐκ- (9)]. To clear out, free from obstructions: οὐρούς Β 153.

ἐκκαιδεκάδωρος [ἐκ-, ἕξ + καί + δέκα + δῶρον, a palm, four fingers' breadth, *i.e.* about three inches]. Sixteen palms in length, *i.e.* about four feet: κέρα Δ 109.

ἐκκαλέω [ἐκ- (1)]. Aor. pple. ἐκκαλέσας Ω 582.

Pl. ἐκκαλέσαντες κ 471. To call forth, summon Ω 582.—To call forth for conference: με κ 471.—Of Hermes summoning souls for their passage to the nether world. In mid. ω 1.

†**ἐκκατείδω** [ἐκ- (1) + κατ-, κατα- (1)]. Aor. pple. ἐκκατιδών. To see or descry something *from* (a height). With genit.: Περγάμου Δ 508, Η 21.

†**ἐκκατεφάλλομαι** [ἐκ- (1) + κατ-, κατα- (1) + ἐφ-, ἐπι- (5)]. 3 sing. aor. ἐκκατεπᾶλτο. To leap forth *down from* for an indicated purpose: οὐρανοῦ Τ 351 (*v.l.* οὐρανοῦ ἐκ κατεπᾶλτο).

ἐκκατιδών, aor. pple. ἐκκατείδω.

†**ἐκκλέπτω** [ἐκ- (1)]. 3 sing. aor. ἐξέκλεψε. To rescue by stealth out of something: Ἄρηα Ε 390.

†**ἐκκυλίνδω** [ἐκ- (1)]. 3 sing. aor. pass. ἐξεκυλίσθη. In pass., to be rolled, roll (headlong) from a position: ἐκ δίφροιο Ζ 42 = Ψ 394.

ἔκλαγξαν, 3 pl. aor. κλάζω.

†**ἐκλανθάνω** [ἐκ- (9)]. 3 pl. redup. aor. ἐκλέλαθον Β 600. 3 sing. aor. mid. ἐκλάθετο κ 557. 3 pl. ἐξελάθοντο Π 602. 3 pl. redup. aor. subj. ἐκλελάθωνται χ 444. 3 sing. opt. ἐκλελάθοιτο γ 224. Infin. ἐκλελαθέσθαι Ζ 285. (**1**) To cause a person to forget, deprive him of (a faculty): ἐκλέλαθον κιθαριστύν Β 600.—(**2**) In mid. (**a**) To forget, fail to remember *to do*. With infin.: καταβῆναι κ 557.—(**b**) With genit., to forget, fail to bethink oneself of: οὐδ' ἀλκῆς ἐξελάθοντο Π 602.—To forget, be freed from: ὀϊζύος Ζ 285.—To (die and) forget, cease to think of (in death): γάμοιο γ 224. Cf. χ 444.

ἐκλάσθη, 3 sing. aor. pass. κλάω.

ἐκλέλαθον, 3 pl. redup. aor. ἐκλανθάνω.

ἔκλεο, 2 sing. impf. pass. κλέω. See κλείω.

ἔκλεψε, 3 sing. aor. κλέπτω.

ἔκλησις, ἡ [ἐκ- (9) + λη-, λήθω]. A forgetting: παίδων φόνοιο ω 485 (an amnesty in regard to . . .).

ἐκλίθη, ἐκλίνθη, 3 sing. aor. pass. κλίνω.

ἔκλυον. See κλύον.

ἐκλύσθη, 3 sing. aor. pass. κλύζω.

ἐκλύω [ἐκ- (1)]. 3 sing. aor. pass. ἐξελύθη Ε 293. (**1**) To set free or rescue *from*. In mid. With genit.: κακῶν σ' ἐκλύσομαι κ 286.—(**2**) αἰχμὴ ἐξελύθη Ε 293, app., was disengaged from the flesh.

ἔκμολε, 3 sing. aor. ἐκβλώσκω.

ἐκμυζάω [ἐκ- (1) + μυζάω, in late Greek, to suck]. To suck, or perh. rather, to press or squeeze out: αἷμ' ἐκμυζήσας Δ 218.

ἐκορέσθην, aor. pass. κορέννυμι.

ἐκορέσσατο, 3 sing. aor. mid. κορέννυμι.

ἔκοψα, aor. κόπτω.

ἔκπαγλος, -ον [perh. for ἔκ-πλαγ-λος, fr. ἐκ- (9) + πλαγ-, πλήσσω]. In some way striking or remarkable. (**1**) Of persons Φ 452 (extraordinarily violent or unreasonable), 589 (wonderful, great).—In superl. Α 146 and Υ 389 (most wonderful (derisively)), Σ 170 (app., incredibly remiss).—(**2**) Of words, etc., violent, vehement: ἐπέεσσιν Ο 198: θ 77, ἐνιπήν κ 448.—Of a storm, unusually violent ξ 522.—(**3**) In neut. sing. ἔκπαγλον as adv., in striking wise, vehemently, loudly, excessively: ἐπεύξατο Ν 413, 445, Ξ 453, 478, ἀεικιῶ Χ 256. Cf. ρ 216.—So in pl. ἔκπαγλα, exceedingly, strongly, deeply: φίλησα Γ 415. Cf. Ε 423.

ἐκπάγλως [adv. fr. prec.]. In striking wise, vehemently, exceedingly, strongly, deeply Α 268, Β 223, 357, Ι 238: ε 340, λ 437, 560, ο 355.

ἐκπαιφάσσω [ἐκ- (5)]. To make oneself prominent, attract attention to oneself Ε 803.

†**ἐκπάλλω** [ἐκ- (1)]. 3 sing. aor. pass. ἔκπαλτο. In pass., app., to throb *forth from*. With genit.: μυελὸς σφονδυλίων ἔκπαλτο Υ 483.

†**ἐκπατάσσω** [ἐκ- (1)]. Pf. pple. pass. ἐκπεπαταγμένος. App., to afflict (in mind): φρένας ἐκπεπαταγμένος ἐσσί (out of your wits, stirred to madness) σ 327.

ἐκπέμπω [ἐκ- (1)]. 3 pl. aor. ἔκπεμψαν π 3. 3 sing. subj. ἐκπέμψῃσι σ 336. 3 sing. opt. ἐκπέμψειε Ω 681. Aor. imp. pl. mid. ἐκπέμψασθε υ 361. (**1**) To send forth or away Ω 381: π 3.—(**2**) With genit., to send forth *from*, cause to depart *from*: πολέμου Φ 598.—To turn *out of*: δώματος σ 336.—In mid. υ 361.—(**3**) To conduct or escort *from*. With genit.: νηῶν Ω 681.

ἐκπεπαταγμένος, pf. pple. pass. ἐκπατάσσω.

ἐκπέποται, 3 sing. pf. pass. ἐκπίνω.

†**ἐκπεράω** [ἐκ- (9) + περάω[1]]. 3 sing. ἐκπερᾷ ι 323. 3 pl. ἐκπερόωσι η 35, θ 561. 3 sing. aor. ἐξεπέρησε Ν 652, Π 346: κ 162. (**1**) To pass over, traverse: λαῖτμα η 35, θ 561, ι 323.—(**2**) Of an arrow or a spear, to make its way, pass Ν 652, Π 346: κ 162.

†**ἐκπέρθω** [ἐκ- (1) (9)]. 3 sing. fut. ἐκπέρσει Σ 283, Φ 310. 3 pl. -ουσι Ε 489. Infin. -ειν Ρ 407. 2 sing. aor. subj. ἐκπέρσῃς Ν 380. 3 pl. -ωσι Α 164. Pple. -ας, -αντος Β 113, 288, Ε 716, Ι 20, Σ 327, Φ 433. Infin. ἐκπέρσαι Α 19, Β 133, Ο 216. 1 pl. aor. ἐξεπράθομεν Α 125. (**1**) To sack or plunder (a city) Α 19, 164, Β 113 = 288 = Ε 716 = Ι 20, Β 133, Ε 489, Ν 380, Ο 216, Ρ 407, Σ 283, 327, Φ 310, 433.—(**2**) To plunder or carry off *from*. With genit.: πολίων Α 125.

ἔκπεσε, 3 sing. aor. ἐκπίπτω.

ἐκπεφυυῖαι, nom. pl. fem. pf. pple. ἐκφύω.

†**ἐκπίνω** [ἐκ- (9)] Aor. ἔκπιον κ 318. 3 sing. -ε ι 353, 361. 3 pl. -ον κ 237. 3 sing. pf. pass. ἐκπέποται χ 56. (**1**) To take a draught, quaff a cup ι 353, 361, κ 237, 318.—(**2**) In pass., to be drunk up, be consumed: ὅσσα τοι ἐκπέποται χ 56.

ἐκπίπτω [ἐκ- (1)]. 3 sing. aor. ἔκπεσε Β 266, Γ 363, Δ 493, Ε 585, Θ 329, Ν 399, Ο 421, 465, Χ 448: ξ 31, 34, π 16, χ 17. 3 pl. -ον Λ 179. Infin. ἐκπεσέειν Ψ 467. (**1**) To fall out Φ 492, Ψ 467.—To fall out of one's hand: χαμαὶ οἱ ἔκπεσε κερκίς Χ 448.—Of tears, to fall, be shed Β 266: π 16.—(**2**) With genit., to fall *out of* or *from*: δίφρου Ε 585, Ν 399, ἵππων Λ 179.—To fall *out of* (one's hand or arms): χειρός Γ 363, Δ 493, Θ 329, Ο 421, 465: ξ 31, 34, χ 17.

†**ἐκπλήσσω** [ἐκ- (1)]. 3 pl. aor. pass. ἔκπληγεν. In pass., to be driven out of one's wits, become panic-struck (cf. πλήσσω (2)) Σ 225.

ἐκποτέομαι [ἐκ- (1)]. Of snow-flakes, to fly forth, be shed abroad: νιφάδες ἐκποτέονται Τ 357.

ἐκπρεπής [ἐκ- (5) + πρέπω]. Pre-eminent B 483.

†**ἐκπροκαλέω** [ἐκ- (1) + προ- (1)]. Aor. pple. fem. mid. ἐκπροκαλεσσαμένη. To summon and cause to come forward *out of*. In mid. With genit.: μεγάρων β 400.

†**ἐκπρολείπω** [ἐκ (1) + προ- (1)]. Nom. pl. masc. aor. pple. ἐκπρολιπόντες. To quit . . . and go forward, to issue from: λόχον θ 515.

†**ἐκπτύω** [ἐκ- (1)]. 3 sing. aor. ἐξέπτυσε. To spit *out of*. With genit.: στόματος ἅλμην ε 322.

ἐκρέμω, 2 sing. impf. pass. See κρεμάννυμι.

†**ἐκρήγνῡμι** [ἐκ- (9)]. 3 sing. aor. ἐξέρρηξε. To break, cause to snap asunder O 469.—To carry away, cause to give way: ὁδοῖο (partitive genit., a part of the . . .) Ψ 421.

ἔκρῑνε, 3 sing. aor. κρίνω.

†**ἐκσαόω** [ἐκ- (1)]. 3 sing. aor. ἐξεσάωσε. To save or preserve from impending danger Δ 12.—To save or preserve *from* the power of. With genit.: θαλάσσης δ 501.

†**ἐκσεύω** [ἐκ- (1)]. 3 sing. aor. mid. ἐξέσσυτο. In mid. (**1**) To speed forth ι 438.—(**2**) With genit., to speed forth *from*: πυλέων H 1.—Of sleep, to flee away *from*, forsake: βλεφάρων μοι ἐξέσσυτο ὕπνος μ 366.—To issue or gush forth *from*: φάρυγος οἶνος ι 373.

†**ἐκσπάω** [ἐκ- (1)]. 3 sing. aor. ἐξέσπασε Z 65. Nom. dual masc. aor. pple. mid. ἐκσπασσαμένω H 255. To draw out, recover (a spear) Z 65.—So in mid.: ἔγχεα (*i.e.* from the shields in which they were stuck) H 255.

†**ἐκστρέφω** [ἐκ- (1)]. 3 sing. aor. ἐξέστρεψε. To overturn (a plant) and uproot (it) *from*. With genit.: ἔρνος βόθρου P 58.

ἔκτα, 3 sing. aor. κτείνω.

ἐκτάδιος, -η, -ον [app. conn. with ἐκτανύω]. Thus, capable of being spread out, ample, flowing: χλαῖναν K 134.

ἔκταθεν, 3 pl. aor. pass. κτείνω.

ἔκταμε, 3 sing. aor. ἐκτάμνω.

ἔκταμεν, 1 pl. aor. κτείνω.

ἐκτάμνω [ἐκ (1)]. 3 sing. aor. ἐξέταμε Δ 486. ἔκταμε ι 320. 3 pl. ἐξέταμον A 460, B 423, N 391, Π 484: μ 360. Imp. ἔκταμε Λ 829. (**1**) To cut out (a sacrificial limb), sever (it) by the joint: μηρούς A 460 = B 423: = μ 360.—Of a surgeon, to cut out, extract: ἰούς Λ 515.—To cut out or extract *from*. With genit.: μηροῦ ὀϊστόν Λ 829.—(**2**) To cut from a tree for one's use: ῥόπαλον ι 320.—(**3**) To cut pieces out of, make incision in: ὕλην M 149.—(**4**) To fell (trees) (cf. ἐκβάλλω (2)) Δ 486, N 391 = Π 484.—(**5**) To cut out, shape: νήϊον Γ 62.

ἔκταν, 3 pl. aor. κτείνω.

ἔκτανε, 3 sing. aor. κτείνω.

†**ἐκτανύω** [ἐκ- (9)]. 3 sing. aor. ἐξετάνυσσε P 58. Pple. ἐκτανύσας Λ 844, Ω 18. 3 sing. aor. pass. ἐξετανύσθη H 271. (**1**) To stretch out, cause to lie stretched out Λ 844, Ω 18.—(**2**) To stretch out, lay low P 58.—In pass., to be laid low: ὕπτιος ἐξετανύσθη H 271.

ἔκτεινε, 3 sing. aor. κτείνω.

†**ἐκτελέω** [ἐκ- (9)]. Also **ἐκτελείω.** 3 pl. pres. ἐκτελέουσι λ 280. 1 pl. subj. ἐκτελέωμεν φ 135, 180, 268. 3 pl. impf. ἐξετέλειον I 493: δ 7. Fut. ἐκτελέω Ψ 96. 3 sing. ἐκτελέει K 105. 3 pl. ἐκτελέουσι B 286. Infin. ἐκτελέειν κ 27. Aor. ἐξετέλεσσα τ 156. 3 sing. -ε Σ 79: β 110, γ 99, δ 329, ω 146. 3 pl. -αν λ 317. Subj. ἐκτελέσω β 98, τ 143, ω 133. 3 pl. -ωσι I 245. 3 sing. opt. ἐκτελέσειε θ 22. Pple. ἐκτελέσας, -αντος γ 275, κ 41. 3 pl. impf. pass. ἐξετελεῦντο λ 294, ξ 293. Fut. infin. ἐκτελέεσθαι H 353, M 217. 3 sing. pf. ἐκτετέλεσται χ 5, ψ 54. (**1**) To bring to completion, carry through, carry out, bring about, accomplish, perform: ἔργον γ 99 = δ 329. Cf. H 353, Σ 79, Ψ 96: γ 275, δ 7, θ 22, κ 41, λ 280, φ 135, 180 = 268, χ 5.—Absol. κ 27 (his aid was vain), λ 317 (would have succeeded).—In pass., to come to pass, happen. Impers.: ὧδ' ἐκτελέεσθαι ὀΐομαι (thus it will be) M 217.—(**2**) To accomplish, fulfil, carry out, bring to fruition or consummation (a promise, purpose, wish, boasts): ὑπόσχεσιν B 286. Cf. I 245, K 105: γ 99 = δ 329, ψ 54.—(**3**) To finish the making of, complete: φᾶρος β 98 = τ 143 = ω 133, β 110 = ω 146, τ 156.—(**4**) To bring into being, cause to be born: γόνον I 493.—(**5**) In pass., of periods of time, to be accomplished or completed: ὅτε μῆνές τε καὶ ἡμέραι ἐξετελεῦντο λ 294 = ξ 293.

ἐκτήσατο, 3 sing. aor. κτάομαι.

†**ἐκτίθημι** [ἐκ- (1)]. Nom. pl. fem. aor. pple. ἐκθεῖσαι. To place outside on a spot indicated: λέχος ψ 179.

ἔκτισαν, 3 pl. aor. κτίζω.

ἔκτοθεν [ἐκτός + -θεν (2)]. (Cf. ἔκτοσθε(ν).) (**1**) Outside, without: ἐ. αὐλῆς (outside in the αὐλή, taking αὐλῆς as local genit.) ι 239, 338. Cf. ν 100.—(**2**) Outside the circle of. With genit.: ἐ. ἄλλων μνηστήρων α 132.

ἔκτοθι [ἐκτός + -θι]. Outside of, beyond the line or shelter of. With genit.: νηῶν O 391, πυλάων X 439.

ἕκτος [ἐκ-, ἕξ]. The sixth B 407: γ 415.

ἐκτός [ἐκ]. (**1**) Outside: ὡς ἴδε νεῦρόν τε καὶ ὄγκους ἐ. ἐόντας Δ 151 (*i.e.* they had not entered the wound), ἐ. λέξο Ω 650 (*i.e.* in the αἴθουσα). Cf. K 151: ζ 72, ξ 11, 16, ψ 135.—(**2**) With genit. (**a**) Outside of: κλισίης Ξ 13. Cf. I 67, Υ 49, Φ 608, Ψ 451: αὐλῆς ἐ. ἐών δ 678 (*i.e.* he overheard from outside the conference which was taking place in the αὐλή). Cf. φ 191, ψ 178.—(**b**) To outside of: καλέσσατο δώματος ἐ. O 143.—(**c**) Out of the region of danger from: καπνοῦ καὶ κύματος ἐ. μ 219.—(**d**) Apart from, at a distance from the line of: ὁδοῦ ν 123.—Aside or away from the line of: ὁδοῦ Ψ 424. Cf. ρ 234.

ἔκτοσε [ἐκτός + -σε]. Out of, from. With genit.: χειρός ξ 277.

ἔκτοσθε(ν) [ἐκτός + -θεν (1) (2)]. (Cf. ἔκτοθεν.) (**1**) (**a**) From without: τέρας φανήτω υ 101.—(**b**) From out of. With genit.: θαλάσσης χ 385.—(**2**) (**a**) Outside, without: ὀρύξομεν τάφρον H 341, ἕσσατο ῥινὸν λύκοιο (as an outer covering) K 334. Cf. H 440, K 263: ἐ. πάγοι ὀξέες [εἰσίν] ε 411 (*i.e.*, app., forming an outlying range). Cf. ρ 278.—(b) Outside of. With genit.: τείχεος ἐ. I 552. Cf. η 112, ψ 148.

ἔκτυπε, 3 sing. aor. κτυπέω.

ἑκυρή, -ῆς, ἡ (σϜεκυρή). A mother-in-law X 451, Ω 770.

ἑκυρός, -οῦ, ὁ (σϜεκυρός). A father-in-law Γ 172, Ω 770.

ἔκυσ(σ)ε, 3 sing. aor. κυνέω.

†**ἐκφαίνω** [ἐκ- (1)]. 3 sing. fut. ἐκφανεῖ T 104. 3 sing. aor. pass. ἐξεφαάνθη Δ 468, N 278: μ 441. 3 pl. ἐξεφάανθεν T 17. 3 sing. aor. ἐξεφάνη Σ 248, T 46, Υ 43: κ 260. **(1)** To bring to light T 104 (to the birth).—**(2)** In pass. **(a)** To appear, come forth κ 260.—To come forth from retirement Σ 248 = T 46 = Υ 43.—To appear, come into view *from*. With genit.: δοῦρα Χαρύβδιος ἐξεφαάνθη μ 441.—**(b)** To be exposed to view, be visible Δ 468.—To be seen in one's true colours, be known for what one is N 278.—**(c)** To shine, gleam: ὡς εἰ σέλας T 17.

ἐκφάσθαι, infin. mid. ἔκφημι.

ἐκφέρω [ἐκ- (1)]. 3 pl. fut. ἐξοίσουσι Ψ 675. **(1)** To bear or carry forth or away K 505: ο 470.—To carry off (a prize) Ψ 785.—**(2)** To bear, carry, bring, forth or away *from*. With genit.: πολέμοιο E 234, 664, 669. Cf. Ψ 259: θ 439.—**(3)** To carry forth (a corpse) for funeral rites Ψ 675, Ω 786.—**(4)** To bear from the field, carry out of danger Π 368, 383 = 866.—**(5)** To bring round or on (a point of time): ὅτε μισθοῖο τέλος ὧραι ἐξέφερον Φ 451.—**(6)** *Intrans. for reflexive*, to draw away from competitors in a race, shoot ahead (cf. ὑπεκφέρω (3)) Ψ 376, 377, 759.

†**ἐκφεύγω** [ἐκ- (1)]. 3 sing. aor. ἔκφυγε E 18, I 355, Λ 376, 380, Ξ 407, Π 480, X 292: δ 502, 512, ο 235. 1 pl. ἐκφύγομεν μ 212. 3 ἐξέφυγον ψ 236. Infin. ἐκφυγέειν Φ 66: ε 289, 414, τ 157, 231. **(1)** To escape, evade, avoid (impending danger or trouble): θάνατον Φ 66. Cf. I 355: δ 502, 512, ο 235, τ 157.—**(2)** To escape from, get clear or free of (danger, etc., in which one is involved): μέγα πεῖραρ ὀϊζύος ε 289. Cf. ε 414.—Absol.: ἔνθεν ἐκφύγομεν μ 212. Cf. τ 231.—To escape *from* or *out of*. With genit.: ἁλός ψ 236.—**(3)** Of a missile weapon, to fly *from* (the hand). With genit.: βέλος ἔκφυγε χειρός E 18, Λ 376, Ξ 407 = X 292, Π 480.—Absol.: οὐδ' ἅλιον βέλος ἔκφυγεν Λ 380.

†**ἔκφημι** [ἐκ- (8)]. Infin. mid. ἐκφάσθαι. **(1)** To announce or declare openly. With dependent clause: οὕνεκα . . . ν 308.—**(2)** To utter: ἔπος κ 246.

†**ἐκφθίω** [ἐκ- (1)]. 3 sing. plupf. pass. ἐξέφθιτο. Of something stored in a place, to be consumed or perish *from* or *out of* (the place). With genit.: οὔ πω νηῶν ἐξέφθιτο οἶνος ι 163. Cf. μ 329.

ἐκφορέω [ἐκ- (1)]. **(1)** To bear or carry out χ 451.—**(2)** In pass., to be borne or advance *from*. With genit.: κόρυθες νηῶν ἐκφορέοντο T 360.

ἔκφυγε, 3 sing. aor. ἐκφεύγω.

†**ἐκφύω** [ἐκ- (2)]. Nom. pl. fem. pf. pple. ἐκπεφυυῖαι. To spring *from*. With genit.: κεφαλαὶ τρεῖς ἑνὸς αὐχένος Λ 40.

ἐκχέω [ἐκ- (1) (4)]. 3 sing. aor. mid. ἐκχεύατο χ 3, ω 178. 3 sing. aor. pass. ἐξέχυτο τ 470. ἔκχυτο τ 504. Pple. ἐκχύμενος, -ου Φ 300: θ 515. 3 pl. plupf. ἐξεκέχυντο θ 279. **(1)** To pour out (liquid) Γ 296.—Of solid objects. In mid.: ὀϊστούς χ 3, ω 178.—**(2)** In pass., of a liquid, to pour out, be spread: ὕδατος ἐκχυμένοιο Φ 300.—To be spilt: ἐξέχυθ' ὕδωρ τ 470. Cf. τ 504.—Fig., to hang suspended *from*. With ablative: [δέσματα] μελαθρόφιν ἐξεκέχυντο θ 279.—Of persons, to pour out, stream forth Π 259: θ 515.

ἑκών (Ϝεκών) [cf. ἕκηλος, ἕκητι]. **(1)** Willingly, of free will, not under compulsion: ἑ. δῶκα δ 649. Cf. δ 647, ε 100, χ 351.—**(2)** Yielding too readily to one's feelings or fears or to circumstances, giving in too easily: ἑ. μεθιεῖς Z 523. Cf. N 234: γ 214 = π 95, δ 372, 377.—**(3)** On purpose, of set purpose, intentionally, advisedly: ἑ. ἡμάρτανεν K 372. Cf. Θ 81, Ψ 434, 585.—**(4)** As a matter of choice, by one's own will: ἑ. οὐκ ἄν τις ἕλοιτο [θεῶν δῶρα] Γ 66.—**(5)** Preceding ἀέκων and serving to emphasize it by contrast: ἑ. ἀέκοντί γε θυμῷ Δ 43. Cf. H 197.—Sim. in β 133 ἑ. is used rather with reference to ἀέκουσαν in 130 than as in itself giving any distinct sense.

ἐλάαν, pres. and fut. infin. ἐλαύνω.

ἔλαβε, 3 sing. aor. λαμβάνω.

ἔλαθε, 3 sing. aor. λανθάνω.

ἐλαίη, -ης, ἡ. The olive-tree P 53: ε 477, η 116 = λ 590, ν 102, 122, 346, 372, ψ 190, 195, 204, ω 246.

ἐλάϊνεος [ἐλαίη]. Of olive-wood ι 320, 394.

ἐλάϊνος. = prec. N 612: ε 236, ι 378, 382.

ἔλαιον, -ου, τό [ἐλαίη]. Olive-oil B 754, K 577, Ξ 171, Σ 350, 596, Ψ 186, 281, Ω 587: β 339, γ 466 = κ 364, δ 49 = ρ 88, δ 252, ζ 79, 96, 215, 219, η 107, θ 364, 454, κ 450, τ 505, ψ 154, ω 366.

ἐλάσασκε, 3 sing. pa. iterative ἐλαύνω.

ἔλασ(σ)ε, 3 sing. aor. ἐλαύνω.

ἐλάσσων, -ον [comp. of ἐλαχ-ύς, small]. In neut. ἔλασσον as adv., less: δουρηνεκὲς ἢ καὶ ἐ. K 357.

ἐλαστρέω [ἐλασ-, ἐλαύνω]. To drive (one's team) Σ 543.

ἐλάτη, -ης, ἡ. **(1)** The fir-tree E 560, Ξ 287: ε 239.—Fir-wood Ω 450.—**(2)** An oar H 5: μ 172.

ἐλατήρ, -ῆρος, ὁ [ἐλα-, ἐλαύνω]. One who drives, a charioteer Δ 145, Λ 702, Ψ 369.

ἐλαύνω. Infin. ἐλάαν E 366, Θ 45, N 27, X 400, Ψ 334: γ 484, 494, ζ 82, μ 47, 109, 124, ο 50, 192. 3 pl. impf. ἔλων Ω 696: δ 2. 3 sing. pa. iterative ἐλάσασκε B 199. 3 pl. fut. ἐλόωσι N 315: η 319. Infin. ἐλάαν P 496: ε 290. Aor. ἤλασα ι 375. 3 sing. ἤλασε Δ 279, I 349, Π 338, Ψ 514, etc.: γ 449, ε 367, σ 95, χ 94, etc. ἔλασε E 80, Λ 109, Π 293, X 326, Ψ 615, Ω 323: ε 313, κ 390, ο 215, τ 449, 465, ω 332. ἔλασσε Δ 299, E 539, Π 309, Υ 269, etc.: ζ 9, ξ 11, σ 96, χ 93, 295, 328. 3 pl. ἤλασαν A 154, H 450, M 6, Ψ 13. ἔλασαν T 281: γ 493, ο 146, 191. ἔλασσαν Ω 349, 421. 3 sing.

subj. ἐλάσσῃ E 236. ἐλάσῃ γ 422, κ 293, ρ 279. 3 pl. ἐλάσωσι Π 388 : μ 55. 3 sing. opt. ἐλάσειε λ 290, ρ 237, χ 97, etc. Imp. ἔλασσον X 284. Pple. ἐλάσας, -αντος Z 529, Π 87, Φ 217 : μ 343, 353, 398, ν 164. ἐλάσσας Π 713, Ω 392. Infin. ἐλάσαι E 264, T 423 : σ 94. ἐλάσσαι N 607, 647. **Mid.** 1 pl. aor. ἠλασάμεσθα Λ 682. 2 sing. opt. ἐλάσαιο υ 51. 3 pl. ἐλασαίατο K 537. Pl. ἐλασσάμενος δ 637. **Pass.** 3 sing. pf. ἐλήλαται Π 518 : η 113. 3 sing. plupf. ἐλήλατο Δ 135, K 153, N 595. ἠλήλατο E 400. 3 pl. ἐληλέατο η 86 (*vv.ll.* ἐληλάδατο, ἐληλέδατο). (δι-, εἰσ-, ἐξ-, ἐπ-, παρ-, παρεξ-, συν-.) **(1)** To drive (cattle, etc.) Δ 279, T 281 : ι 237, 337, κ 390.—To drive in or fetch (them) for some purpose μ 343, 353, 398.—In mid. δ 637.—Absol. : ὄφρ' ἐλάσῃ ἐπιβουκόλος ἀνήρ γ 422.—**(2)** In reference to persons, to drive : κακοὺς ἐς μέσσον Δ 299. Cf. Ω 532.—To drive or chase, to drive or chase away : ἐκ Τροίης 'Αχαιούς Z 529. Cf. Π 87, 293, Φ 217, Ω 392.—To banish Z 158.—For ἄδην ἐλάαν see ἄδην.—Fig. : οἵ ἐκ δίκην ἐλάσωσιν Π 388.—**(3)** To drive off (cattle, etc., as spoil) A 154 : ι 405, 465, λ 290, ο 235.—In mid. : ῥύσι' ἐλαυνόμενος Λ 674. Cf. Λ 682 : υ 51.—To drive off (captured horses) E 165, 236, 264, 327, 589, P 496.—In mid. K 537.—**(4)** To drive (horses, a chariot, a team of oxen, etc.) : ἅρματα καὶ ἵππω E 237. Cf. B 764, Λ 289, Ψ 334, Ω 325, etc. : ο 215.—Absol. : μάστιξεν ἐλάαν (to start the horses) E 366. Cf. Λ 274, N 27, Π 713, Ψ 356, etc. : εἰ βόες εἶεν ἐλαυνέμεν σ 371. Cf. γ 484, 493, δ 2, etc.—To drive up to the rescue : ἵππους P 614.—To ride (a horse) ε 371.—Fig., to carry on, keep going : κολῳόν A 575.—**(5)** To propel (a ship) with oars, row (her) η 109, μ 109, 276, ν 155, 169, ο 503.—Absol. : ἀναβάντες ἐλαύνομεν γ 157, ἐλόωσι γαλήνην (through . . .) η 319. Cf. μ 47, 55, 124, ν 22.—**(6)** Of operations conducted in line, to drive or form (a ditch, a wall, etc.) : τάφρον H 450 = M 6, I 349, ὄγμον Λ 68. Cf. Σ 564 : τεῖχος ζ 9, σταυρούς (a line of . . .) ξ 11. Cf. η 86, 113.—**(7)** To drive or thrust (a weapon) : διαπρὸ χαλκὸν ἔλασσεν O 342. Cf. E 41, 539, Υ 259, Ω 421, etc. : χ 93, 295.—To drive (a weapon) into the ground K 153.—To drive or thrust (something into a specified position) : μοχλὸν ὑπὸ σποδοῦ ι 375.—In pass. of an arrow or a spear, to pass, take its way : διὰ ζωστῆρος ἐλήλατ' [ὀϊστός] Δ 135. Cf. E 400, N 595.—**(8)** To strike or wound (never with a missile) : 'Υψήνορα ὦμον (in the . . .) E 80, κόρυθος φάλον N 614. Cf. B 199, E 584, K 455, Λ 109, N 576, Ξ 497, O 352, Π 338, Υ 475, X 326 : πέτρην δ 507, δεξιὸν ὦμον σ 95. Cf. κ 293, ρ 279, σ 92, 96, χ 94, 97, 296, 328.—Absol. : Φ 425, X 284 : γ 449, ν 164, σ 91, 94.—To dash (against the ground) : πρὸς γῆν κάρη ρ 237.—Of a wave striking ε 313, 367.—Of a boar wounding with its tusk τ 449, 465.—With cognate acc. of the wound inflicted by it τ 393 = ψ 74, φ 219, ω 332.—With σύν, to dash (one's teeth) together σ 98.—To beat (the sea with oars) (cf. τύπτω (3)) H 6.—Fig., of pain, to pierce : χεὶρ ὀδύνῃσιν ἐλήλαται Π 518.—**(9)** To beat or hammer out (metal) H 223.—To form by beating or hammering out M 296, Υ 270.

ἐλαφηβόλος, ὁ [ἔλαφος + βολ-, βάλλω]. One who smites deer, a hunter Σ 319.

ἔλαφος, -ου, ὁ, ἡ. A deer, whether hart or hind A 225, Γ 24, Θ 248, Λ 113, 475, N 102, O 271, Π 158, 757, Φ 486, X 189 : δ 335 = ρ 126, ζ 104, 133, κ 158, 180, ν 436.

ἐλαφρός, -ή, -όν. **(1)** Light, of small weight : λᾶαν M 450.—**(2)** Moving easily, nimble : γυῖα E 122 = N 61 = Ψ 772, χεῖρες Ψ 628.—Active in movement, nimble : ἀνήρ Π 745.—Swift. In comp. ἐλαφρότερος α 164 (see ἀφνειός).—In superl. ἐλαφρότατος Ψ 749 : γ 370.—Of birds X 139 : ν 87.—Of the wind T 416.—**(3)** Light to bear, not burdensome. In comp. : ἐλαφρότερός κε πόλεμος γένοιτο X 287.

ἐλαφρῶς [adv. fr. prec.]. Buoyantly ε 240.

ἐλάχεια. See λάχεια.

ἔλαχον, aor. λαγχάνω.

ἔλδομαι (Fέλδομαι). Also, with prothetic ἐ, **ἐέλδομαι** (ἐFέλδομαι). **(1)** To wish, desire. With infin. : ἰδέσθαι σε δ 162. Cf. N 638 : ε 219, ο 66, σ 164, υ 35.—**(2)** To wish for, desire, covet : κτήματα E 481.—To long for, look eagerly forward to ψ 6.—To seek the accomplishment of, prosecute (business) α 409.—**(3)** With genit., to long for, sigh after : Πασιθέης Ξ 276 : σῆς ἀλόχου ε 210.—To be eager for : ἐλδόμεναι πεδίοιο (eager to reach the . . .) Ψ 122.—To lack : ἐδωδῆς ξ 42.—**(4)** Absol. in pple., longing, desiring, eagerly expectant H 4, 7 : μ 438, φ 209, ω 400.—**(5)** As pass. : ἐελδέσθω τοι πόλεμος (let it be thy desire) Π 494.

ἔλδωρ, τό [ἔλδομαι]. Always, with prothetic ἐ, **ἐέλδωρ.** A wish or desire A 41, 455 = Π 238, A 504, Θ 242, O 74 : γ 418, ρ 242, φ 200, ψ 54.

ἕλε, 3 sing. aor. αἱρέω.

ἐλεαίρω. 3 pl. pa. iterative ἐλεαίρεσκον Ω 23. To pity, take pity upon, feel pity for, feel for B 27 = 64 = Ω 174, Z 407, K 176, Λ 665, Ω 19, 23 : γ 96 = δ 326, ξ 389, ψ 313.—With pple. expressing the plight of the pitied : Τρῶας ἀπολλυμένους H 27. Cf. I 302, N 15 : δ 828, τ 210.—With infin. : μισγέμεναι κακότητι (in regard to . . ., so as not to . . .) υ 202.—Absol. Z 431, Φ 147 : α 19, ε 450, ζ 175, κ 399, ρ 367.

ἐλέγμην, aor. mid. λέγω[2].

ἐλεγχείη, -ης, ἡ [ἔλεγχος]. **(1)** Disgrace, reproach, blame, shame X 100, Ψ 408 : ξ 38.—**(2)** An occasion or cause thereof : ἐ. σοὶ αὐτῷ ἔσσεται Ψ 342. Cf. φ 255.

ἐλεγχής [ἔλεγχος]. Deserving of reproach : 'Αργεῖοι, ἐλεγχέες Δ 242. Cf. Ω 239.

ἐλέγχιστος [superl. fr. ἔλεγχος]. The most open of all men to reproach, the most deserving of blame or contempt B 285, Δ 171, P 26 : κ 72.

ἔλεγχος, τό [cf. next]. An occasion or cause of disgrace, reproach, blame, shame : ἐ. ἔσσεται εἴ κεν . . . Λ 314.—In pl. : ἡμῖν ἂν ἐλέγχεα ταῦτα γένοιτο φ 329. Cf. φ 333.—So of persons regarded as disgraces to their kind, 'things of shame': κάκ' ἐλέγχεα B 235, E 787 = Θ 228. Cf. τὰ δ' ἐλέγχεα πάντα λέλειπται Ω 260.

ἐλέγχω [cf. prec.]. 2 sing. aor. subj. ἐλέγξῃς I 522. (**1**) To dishonour, bring to nought, make futile: μῦθον I 522.—(**2**) To bring shame on, do no credit to: σε φ 424.

ἑλέειν, aor. infin. αἱρέω.

ἐλεεινός [ἔλεος]. (**1**) That is a fitting object of pity, pitiable, piteous: νέκυν Ψ 110. Cf. Φ 273: δάκρυον (caused by feelings worthy of pity) θ 531, π 219. Cf. τ 253.—In comp. ἐλεεινότερος Ω 504.—In superl. ἐλεεινότατος θ 530.—(**2**) Moving or finding pity: φίλον ἐλθεῖν ἠδ' ἐλεεινόν Ω 309: ζ 327.—(**3**) In neut. pl. ἐλεεινά as adv., in piteous wise B 314, X 37, 408.

ἐλεέω [ἔλεος]. To pity, take pity upon, feel pity for, feel for Z 94 = 275, 309, Θ 350, O 12, Π 431, Υ 465, Φ 74, X 59, 82, 123, 419, Ω 207, 332, 503: δ 364, ι 349, λ 55 = 395, λ 87, ξ 279, χ 312 = 344.—With pple. expressing the plight of the pitied: τὼ πεσόντε E 561, 610. Cf. O 44, P 346, 352, 441, T 340: ε 336.—Absol. Z 484, I 172, X 494, Ω 301, 357: ν 182.

ἐλεήμων [ἐλεέω]. Pitiful, compassionate ε 191.

ἐλεητύς, ἡ [ἐλεέω]. Compunction in using, sparing: οὔ τις ἐ. ἀλλοτρίων χαρίσασθαι ρ 451. Cf. ξ 82.

ἑλεῖν, aor. infin. αἱρέω.

ἔλεκτο, 3 sing. aor. mid. λέγω[1].

ἐλέλειπτο, 3 sing. plupf. pass. λείπω.

†ἐλελίζω. 3 sing. aor. ἐλέλιξε A 530, Θ 199. 3 sing. aor. pass. ἐλελίχθη X 448. 3 sing. plupf. ἐλέλικτο N 558. To shake, cause to tremble A 530, Θ 199.—In pass., to shake, quiver, tremble: ἔγχος ἐλέλικτο N 558. Cf. X 448.—For ἐλέλιξε P 278: ε 314; ἐλελιξάμενος B 316; ἐλελίχθη μ 416, ξ 306; ἐλελίχθησαν E 497, Z 106, Λ 214, P 343; ἐλέλιχθεν Z 109; ἐλελιχθέντες Λ 588; ἐλέλικτο Λ 39, see ἑλίσσω.

ἐλέλυντο, 3 pl. plupf. pass. λύω.

ἔλεξα, aor. λέγω[1] and λέγω[2].

ἐλέξατο, 3 sing. aor. mid. λέγω[1].

ἐλεόθρεπτος [ἐλε(σ)-ο-, ἕλος + θρεπ-, τρέφω]. Marshbred, growing in marshy ground B 776.

ἔλεος, -ου, ὁ. Pity, compassion Ω 44.

ἐλεός, -οῦ, ὁ. A charger, platter I 215: ξ 432.

ἑλέσθαι, aor. infin. mid. αἱρέω.

ἕλεσκον, pa. iterative αἱρέω.

ἕλετο, 3 sing. aor. mid. αἱρέω.

ἑλετός, -ή, -όν [ἑλε-. See αἱρέω]. That can be seized or grasped: ἀνδρὸς ψυχή I 409.

ἕλευ, aor. imp. mid. αἱρέω.

ἐλεύθερος. Free, not in bondage: ἐλεύθερον ἦμαρ (see ἦμαρ (4) (d)), κρητῆρα ἐλεύθερον (a bowl to celebrate deliverance) Z 528.

ἐλεύσομαι, fut. ἔρχομαι.

ἐλεφαίρομαι [poss. conn. with ὀλοφώϊος]. Aor. pple. ἐλεφηράμενος Ψ 388. To play a trick upon Ψ 388.—Absol., to deceive. Of dreams τ 565.

ἐλέφας, -αντος, ὁ. Ivory E 583: δ 73, θ 404, σ 196, τ 56, 563, 564, φ 7, ψ 200.—A piece of ivory Δ 141.

ἐλέχθην, aor. pass. λέγω[2].

ἔλειψε, 3 sing. aor. λέπω.

ἕλῃ, 3 sing. aor. subj. αἱρέω.

ἐληλάδατο, 3 pl. plupf. pass. ἐλαύνω.

ἐλήλαται, 3 sing. pf. pass. ἐλαύνω.

ἐληλέατο, ἐληλέδατο, 3 pl. plupf. pass. ἐλαύνω.

ἐληλουθώς, pf. pple. ἔρχομαι.

ἕληται, 3 sing. aor. subj. mid. αἱρέω.

ἐλθέμεναι, ἐλθέμεν, ἐλθεῖν, aor. infin. ἔρχομαι.

ἐλιάσθη, 3 sing. aor. λιάζομαι.

Ἑλικώνιος. App., of Helike in Achaea, a seat of the worship of Poseidon Υ 404.

ἑλικῶπις, -ιδος, ἡ. = next: κούρην A 98.

ἑλίκωψ, -ωπος, ὁ (Ϝελίκωψ) [prob. (Ϝ)ελικ-, ἑλίσσω + ὦπα. 'Throwing the eyes round']. Thus, quick-glancing (as indicating liveliness or vivacity of disposition). Epithet of the Achaeans A 389, Γ 190, 234, Π 569 = P 274, Ω 402.

ἕλιξ, -ικος, ἡ [ἑλικ-, ἑλίσσω]. An ornament of some kind in spiral form Σ 401.

ἕλιξ, -ικος [prob. as prec., 'with twisted or 'crumpled' horns.' Or poss. fr. (σ)ελ- as in σέλας, 'shining,' 'sleek']. Epithet of oxen I 466 = Ψ 166, M 293, O 633, Σ 524, Φ 448: α 92 = δ 320, ι 46, λ 289, μ 136, 355, χ 292, ω 66.

ἔλιπον, aor. λείπω.

ἑλίσσω (Ϝελίκ-σω) [cf. εἴλω]. Aor. pple. ἑλίξας Ψ 466. 3 sing. aor. subj. mid. ἑλίξεται P 728. Pple. ἑλιξάμενος M 408, 467, N 204, P 283. Genit. pl. masc. aor. pple. pass. ἑλιχθέντων M 74. To these should no doubt be added (cf. under ἐλελίζω) 3 sing. aor. ἐ(Ϝ)έλιξε (appearing in the MSS. as ἐλέλιξε) P 278: ε 314; aor. pple. mid. (Ϝ)ελιξάμενος (ἐλελιξάμενος) B 316; 3 sing. aor. pass. ἐ(Ϝ)ελίχθη (ἐλελίχθη) μ 416, ξ 306; 3 pl. ἐ(Ϝ)ελίχθησαν (ἐλελίχθησαν) E 497, Z 106, Λ 214, P 343, ἐ(Ϝ)έλιχθεν (ἐλέλιχθεν) Z 109; pple. pl. (Ϝ)ελιχθέντες (ἐλελιχθέντες) Λ 588; and 3 sing. plupf. (Ϝ)ε(Ϝ)έλικτο (ἐλέλικτο) Λ 39. (**1**) To form in a spiral shape, twine: ἐλέλικτο δράκων Λ 39.—(**2**) To impart a circular motion to, cause to whirl ε 314, μ 416 = ξ 306.—(**3**) To bring (troops) to face the foe, rally (them) P 278.—In pass., of troops, to rally: οἱ δ' ἐλελίχθησαν E 497 = Z 106 = Λ 214 = P 343. Cf. Z 109, Λ 588, M 74.—(**4**) Absol., to turn one's horses (round a mark): περὶ τέρμαθ' ἑλισσέμεν Ψ 309. Cf. Ψ 466.—In mid., to take the turn round a mark: ἐπὶ πολλὸν ἑλίσσεται (wheels wide) Ψ 320.—(**5**) In mid., to turn oneself, turn to bay P 283, 728.—(**6**) In mid., to turn this way and that, go or betake oneself hither and thither: ἀν' ὅμιλον ἰὼν εἰλίσσετο M 49 (*v.l.* ἐλίσσετο (λίσσομαι)). Cf. M 408, 467, Φ 11.—(**7**) In mid. in various senses. To busy oneself Σ 372.—Of a recumbent person, to turn (from side to side) υ 24, 28.—To swing one's body in preparation for a throw: ἧκε ἑλιξάμενος N 204 (or perh., whirling the thrown object in a circle).—To twist oneself about in an effort to free oneself Θ 340.—Of a snake, to coil itself X 95.—To do this for a spring

B 316.—Of the steam of sacrifice, to curl A 317. —Of a thrown object, to spin Ψ 846.

ἑλκεσίπεπλος [ἑλκεσι-, ἕλκω + πέπλος]. Trailing the πέπλος, with long flowing πέπλος. Epithet of Trojan women Z 442 = X 105, H 297.

ἑλκεχίτων, -ωνος [ἑλκε-, ἕλκω + χιτών]. Trailing the χιτών, with long flowing χιτών: Ἰάονες N 685.

ἑλκέω [= ἕλκω]. (**1**) To drag away by force, carry off: ἑλκηθείσας θύγατρας X 62 (with at least a suggestion of ravishment).—(**2**) To pull at: νέκυν εἵλκεον P 395.—To pull about, tear (a corpse) P 558, X 336.—(**3**) To lay violent hands upon: Λητὼ ἕλκησε λ 580 (cf. (1)).

ἑλκηθμός, ὁ [ἑλκέω]. A being dragged or carried away by force (cf. ἑλκέω (1)) Z 465.

ἕλκος, τό. A wound Δ 190, 217, E 361, 795, Θ 405 = 419, Λ 267, 812, 834, 848, Ξ 130, O 393, Π 29, 511, 517, 523, 528, T 49, 52, Ω 420.—Of the effect of a snake's bite B 723.

ἑλκυστάζω [frequentative fr. ἑλκυσ-, ἕλκω]. To expose to dragging or pulling about Ψ 187, Ω 21.

ἕλκω (Fέλκω). (ἀν-, ἐξ-, ἐφ-, παρ-, ὑφ-.) (**1**) To drag, haul or pull along or away: ἑλκομένας νυούς X 65 (with at least a suggestion of ravishment), ὥς θ' ἡμίονοι ἕλκωσι δοκόν P 743. Cf. Γ 370, Σ 581, Υ 404, 405, X 465, Ω 52, 417: π 276, σ 10, 12, 101, φ 300.—Of dragging the body of a foe from the fight Δ 465, N 383, P 126, 289, Σ 156, 176.—Of so dragging the body of a friend Λ 258, 259.—Of Κήρ dragging off a body Σ 537.—In pass., to drag or trail along: κάρη ἕλκεσθαι ἔασεν X 398. Cf. E 665, X 401, 464, Ω 15.—(**2**) To draw, pull, pluck, in a specified direction: ἐκ ζωστῆρος ὀϊστόν Δ 213. Cf. Λ 239, 398, 457, Π 406, 409, 504.—To pull at M 398, P 393.—(**3**) To draw down (a ship) in order to launch her B 152, 165 = 181, I 683, Ξ 76, 97, 100, 106: γ 153.—(**4**) Of mules, to draw (a waggon) Ω 324.—Of horses, to draw (a charioteer) Ψ 518.—Of a charioteer, to draw (his chariot) Ψ 533.—(**5**) To draw (a plough): νειοῖο ἄροτρον K 353 (genit. of space within which). Cf. ν 32.—(**6**) To draw (a bow): ἕλκεν νευρὴν γλυφίδας τε φ 419. Cf. Δ 122. —In mid.: τόξον ἕλκετο Λ 583.—(**7**) To hoist (sails) β 426 = ο 291.—(**8**) To draw up and poise (a balance) Θ 72, X 212.—(**9**) To apply force to: νῶτα ἑλκόμενα Ψ 715.—(**10**) Fig., to bring on (a period of time): φάος ἠελίοιο ἕλκον νύκτα Θ 486.—(**11**) In mid., to draw (one's sword) A 194, 210. —To pull out (one's hair) K 15, X 77.—To draw (down the skin of the brows): [λέων] ἐπισκύνιον κάτω ἕλκεται P 136.—To draw in (a seat) τ 506.

ἔλλαβε, 3 sing. aor. λαμβάνω.

ἐλλεδανός, ὁ [(F)ελF-, (F)ελυ- as in εἰλύω]. A band for binding a corn-sheaf Σ 553.

ἐλλισάμην, aor. λίσσομαι.

ἐλλιτάνευσα, aor. λιτανεύω.

ἐλλός, ὁ. The young of the deer, a fawn τ 228.

ἕλον, aor. αἱρέω.

ἕλος, τό. A marsh-meadow Δ 483, O 631, Υ 221. —Marshy ground ξ 474.

ἐλόωσι, 3 pl. fut. ἐλαύνω.

ἐλπίς, -ίδος, ἡ (Fελπίς) [ἔλπω]. Hope π 101, τ 84.

ἔλπω (Fέλπω). Pf. ἔολπα, -ας (FέFολπα) Υ 186, Φ 583, X 216: β 275, γ 375, ε 379, θ 315, φ 317. 3 sing. plupf. ἐώλπει T 328: υ 328, φ 96, ω 313. 3 sing. impf. mid. ἐέλπετο M 407, N 609: ψ 345. With prothetic ἐ 3 sing. pres. mid. ἐέλπεται K 105, N 813. 1 sing. opt. ἐελποίμην Θ 196, P 488. (ἐπι-.) (**I**) In pres. act., to rouse hopes in, cause to hope: πάντας ἔλπει β 91 = ν 380.—(**II**) In pf. and plupf. and in mid. (**1**) In reference to the past or present, to suppose, think, fancy. With infin.: οὐδ' ἐμὲ νήϊδά γ' οὕτως ἔλπομαι γενέσθαι H 199. Cf. I 40, N 309, O 110, Π 281, P 404: ἐπὴν ἡμέας ἔλπῃ ἀφῖχθαι ζ 297. Cf. ι 419, ψ 345.—Absol.: αὐτὸς ὅ, ἔλπομ', ἐνὶ πρώτοισιν ὁμιλεῖ Σ 194.—(**2**) In reference to the fut., to expect, think it likely or probable. With fut. infin.: χαλεπῶς σ' ἔολπα τὸ ῥέξειν Υ 186. Cf. H 353, N 8, O 504, P 239, 404, 406, 603: ὡς οὐκ ἂν ἔλποιο νεώτερον ἐρξέμεν η 293. Cf. β 275, γ 375, ε 379, θ 315, φ 314.—Absol.: οὐκ ἂν ἐμοί γε ἐλπομένῳ τὰ γένοιτο γ 228.—(**3**) To hope. With fut. infin.: ἔλποντο τεῖχος ῥήξειν M 261. Cf. Θ 196, I 371, N 41, 813, Ξ 67, 422, O 701, Π 609, P 234, 395, 488, 495, Σ 260, T 328, Υ 180, 201 = 432, Φ 583, 605, X 216, Ω 491: υ 328, φ 96, ω 313. —With the infin. to be supplied: οὐ νοήματα ἐκτελέει ὅσ' ἐέλπεται K 105. Cf. γ 275.—With aor. infin.: ἐλπόμενοι παύσασθαι πολέμοιο Γ 112 (or this might come under (4)). Cf. M 407: ὅθεν οὐκ ἔλποιτο ἐλθέμεν γ 319. Cf. φ 157.—(**4**) In reference to the past of something which it is hoped has taken place. With aor. infin.: ["Εκτορα] θανέειν O 288.—(**5**) In reference to the present of something which it is hoped is taking place. With pres. infin.: ἑταίρους ἰέναι K 355.—(**6**) To hope for: νίκην N 609, O 539. Cf. φ 317.—(**7**) To trust in. With dat.: Διί Θ 526.

ἐλπωρή, -ῆς, ἡ (Fελπωρή) [ἔλπω]. Hope. With fut. infin.: ὑπάλυξιν ἔσεσθαι ψ 287.—With aor. infin.: φίλους ἰδέειν ζ 314 = η 76. Cf. β 280.

ἕλσαν, 3 pl. aor. εἴλω.

ἐλύσθη, 3 sing. aor. pass. εἰλύω.

ἕλω, aor. subj. αἱρέω.

ἔλων, 3 pl. impf. ἐλαύνω.

ἑλών, aor. pple. αἱρέω.

ἕλωρ, τό [ἑλ-. See αἱρέω]. An object of prey or of spoiling: ἀνδράσι δυσμενέεσσιν ἑ. καὶ κύρμα E 488. Cf. E 684, P 151, 667: οἰωνοῖσιν γ 271. Cf. ε 473, ν 208, ω 292.—In pl.: Πατρόκλοιο ἕλωρα ἀποτείσῃ Σ 93 (pay the penalty for the spoiling of . . .).

ἑλώρια, τά [as prec.]. Objects of prey A 4.

ἐμαράνθη, 3 sing. aor. pass. μαραίνω.

ἔμαρψε, 3 sing. aor. μάρπτω.

ἐμβαδόν [ἐμβα-, ἐμβαίνω]. By stepping, *i.e.* by land: ἐ. ἵξεσθαι πατρίδα γαῖαν O 505.

ἐμβαίνω [ἐμ-, ἐν- (2) (3)]. 3 sing. aor. ἔμβη δ 656. 3 sing. subj. ἐμβήῃ Π 94. Imp. dual ἔμβητον Ψ 403. Acc. sing. masc. pf. pple. ἐμβεβαῶτα E 199. Nom. fem. ἐμβεβαυῖα Ω 81. 3 pl. plupf. ἐμβέβασαν B 720. (**1**) With dat., to step *upon*, put one's foot *upon*: ἐλάφῳ κ 164.—To step *upon*, put the feet *upon* in passing over: νεκροῖς Κ 493.—To go *on board of*, embark *upon* (a ship): νηΐ Πύλονδε (embarked for . . .) δ 656.—Absol.: πολέες ἔμβαινον (app., sailed therein) Β 619.—(2) To enter the fray, intervene Π 94.—(3) App., to push on, make a spurt Ψ 403.—(4) In pf. and plupf. of the state or condition of having gone upon something: ἐρέται πεντήκοντα ἐμβέβασαν (were on board, formed the complement) Β 720, ἵπποισιν καὶ ἅρμασιν ἐμβεβαῶτα (mounted upon, driving) Ε 199.—So μολυβδαίνη κατὰ βοὸς κέρας ἐμβεβαυῖα (mounted upon it) Ω 81.

ἐμβάλλω [ἐμ-, ἐν- (1) (2) (3)]. 3 sing. aor. ἔμβαλε Γ 139, Λ 11, Ν 82, Φ 47, etc.: α 438, ζ 116, σ 103, τ 10, etc. 3 pl. -ον Π 122, Σ 85, Τ 88. 3 sing. opt. ἐμβάλοι Ν 320, Ο 598. Imp. pl. ἐμβάλετε ψ 179. Infin. ἐμβαλέειν Ω 645: δ 298, η 337, ι 489, κ 129. (1) To throw into something Η 188.—To throw *into*. With dat.: πόντῳ με Ξ 258. Cf. Ν 320, Ο 598, Π 122: ε 431, ζ 116, μ 415 = ξ 305.—(2) To throw upon something or someone: ῥήγεα ἐμβαλέειν Ω 645: = δ 298 = η 337. Cf. Μ 383: ψ 179.—To throw *upon*. With dat.: ἵππους πυρῇ Ψ 172. Cf. Ψ 174.—(3) With dat., to put or place *in*: ἱμάντα χερσίν Ξ 218. Cf. α 438, β 37, σ 103.—To cause to be *in* or to fall *into*: βροτοῦ σ' ἀνέρος εὐνῇ Σ 85, χερσίν μιν 'Αχιλλῆος Φ 47.—(4) In reference to mental or physical states, to inspire, induce, bring about, suggest *in*. With dat.: φόβον σφιν Ρ 118. Cf. Γ 139, Δ 444, Κ 366, Λ 11, Ν 82, Ξ 151, Π 529, Τ 88: ὀδύνας θυμῷ β 79. Cf. τ 485 = ψ 260.—Sim.: τόδ' ἐνὶ φρεσίν τ 10.—Without case Φ 304.—(5) App., to throw oneself *upon*, ply. With dat.: ἐμβαλέειν κώπῃς ι 489 = κ 129.—(6) In mid., with dat., to take *into* (one's mind), flatter oneself with the idea of: μὴ φύξιν ἐμβάλλεο θυμῷ Κ 447.—To lay *to* (one's heart), bear in mind the need for: μῆτιν ἐμβάλλεο θυμῷ Ψ 313.

ἐμβασιλεύω [ἐμ-, ἐν- (1)]. To rule or hold sway in a place Β 572.—To rule or hold sway *in*. With dat.: τῇσιν ἀμφοτέρῃσιν ο 413.

ἐμβέβασαν, 3 pl. plupf. ἐμβαίνω.

ἐμβεβαῶτα, acc. sing. masc. pf. pple. ἐμβαίνω.

ἔμβη, 3 sing. aor. ἐμβαίνω.

ἐμβρέμω [ἐμ-, ἐν- (1)]. In mid., of the wind, to roar *in*. With dat.: ἱστίῳ Ο 627.

ἔμβρυον, τό [ἐμ-, ἐν- (1) + βρύω]. The young of an animal ι 245 = 309 = 342.

ἐμέ [cf. L. *me*, Eng. *me*]. Acc. ἐμέ Α 133, 182, 454, etc.: α 212, 215, γ 60, etc. με (encl.) Α 32, 74, 83, etc.: α 220, 231, 315, etc. Genit. ἐμεῖο Α 174, 301, 341, etc.: γ 347, δ 145, 170, etc. ἐμέο Κ 124. ἐμεῦ Α 88, 453, etc.: α 313, δ 370, etc. μευ (encl.) Α 37, 273, Γ 86, etc.: β 25, 161, 229, etc. ἐμέθεν Α 525, Β 26, etc.: δ 592, θ 241, etc. Dat. ἐμοί Α 187, 523, 563, etc.: α 242, 359, β 74, etc. μοι (encl.) Α 41, 77, 120, etc.: α 1, 48, 169, etc. Pron. of the 1st person sing., me: ἐμοὶ γέρας ἑτοιμάσατε Α 118, νεωτέρω ἐμεῖο 259, ἐμεῦ ἀπονόσφιν 541, καμέτην μοι ἵπποι Δ 27, μή με κάθιζε Ζ 360, ἔμ' ἄμμορον 408, etc.—Strengthened by γε: ἐμέ γε, ἔμεγε ι 315, etc.: ε 99, etc.—ἐμοί γε, ἔμοιγε Α 174, 295, etc.: γ 227, δ 538, etc.

ἐμέθεν, ἐμεῖο. See ἐμέ.

ἔμεινα, aor. μένω.

ἔμειξαν, 3 pl. aor. μίσγω.

ἐμέμηκον, 3 pl. thematic plupf. μηκάομαι.

ἐμέμικτο, 3 sing. plupf. pass. μίσγω.

ἔμεναι, ἔμεν, infin. εἰμί.

ἐμέο, ἐμεῦ. See ἐμέ.

ἐμέω. (ἀπ-, ἐξ-.) To vomit, throw up Ο 11.

ἐμήσατο, 3 sing. aor. μήδομαι.

ἐμητίσαντο, 3 pl. aor. μητίομαι.

ἐμίγην, aor. pass. μίσγω.

ἔμικτο, 3 sing, aor. pass. μίσγω.

ἔμιξαν, 3 pl. aor. μίσγω.

ἐμίχθη, 3 sing. aor. pass. μίσγω.

ἔμμαθε, 3 sing. aor. μανθάνω.

ἐμμαπέως. Speedily, quickly Ε 836: ξ 485.

ἐμμάω [ἐμ-, ἐν- (6)]. Only in pf. pple. ἐμμεμαώς, -υῖα. (1) With eager haste, speed, alacrity, zeal: ἐμμεμαὼς ἐπόρουσεν Υ 284, 442. Cf. Ε 142, 240, 330, 838, Ν 785, Ρ 735, 746, Χ 143: ψ 127.—(2) Adjectivally, of fiery disposition, fierce Υ 468.

ἔμμεναι, ἔμμεν, infin. εἰμί.

ἐμμενής [ἐμ-, ἐν- (1) + μένω]. Only in neut. ἐμμενές as adv., without intermission, continuously, strengthening αἰεί: Κ 361, 364, Ν 517: ι 386, φ 69.

ἔμμορε, 3 sing. pf. μείρομαι.

ἔμμορος [ἐμ-, ἐν- (1) + μορ-, μείρομαι]. Having a share of, endued with: τιμῆς θ 480.

ἔμνησας, 2 sing. aor. μιμνήσκω.

ἐμνώοντο, 3 pl. impf. μνάομαι.

ἐμοί. See ἐμέ.

ἐμός, -ή, -όν [ἐμέ]. My Α 31, 42, 154, 166, 183, etc.: α 248, 251, 264, 417, β 96, etc.—With the article: τὸν ἐμὸν χόλον Δ 42. Cf. Ζ 523, etc.: β 97, λ 452, etc.—Absol.: οὐκ ἐμὸν παλινάγρετον (nothing of mine) Α 526.—As predicative adj., mine: ἵππον δώσω ἐμήν περ ἐοῦσαν Ψ 610: εἰ ἐμός ἐσσι π 300. Cf. Η 191.

ἐμπάζομαι. (1) To care about, regard, concern oneself with, pay attention to. With genit.: θεοπροπίης Π 50: ξείνων τ 134. Cf. α 271, 305, 415, β 201, ρ 488, υ 275, 384.—(2) To receive (a sacrifice). With genit.: ἱρῶν ι 553. (3) To hold in due honour, respect: ἱκέτας π 422.

ἔμπαιος. App., expert in, possessed of: οὐδ' ἔργων ἔμπαιον (–⏑⏑) οὐδὲ βίης υ 379, κακῶν φ 400.

ἐμπάσσω [ἐμ-, ἐν- (1)]. In weaving, to insert representations of *in* a web: ἐνέπασσεν ἀέθλους (*sc.* ἱστῷ) Γ 126.

ἔμπεδος, -ον [ἐμ-, ἐν- (3) + πεδ-, ποδ-, πούς. 'Firm on the feet.' Cf. ἠπεδανός]. (1) Standing firmly in place, not overthrown, intact: τεῖχος Μ 9, 12.—(2) Maintained in place, steady: ἔμπεδον ἔχων σάκος Π 107. Cf. Π 520.—In place, not displaced Κ 94: ψ 203.—(3) Safe, intact β 227, λ 178, τ 525.—Not decayed, fresh: χρώς Τ 33, 39.—Unimpaired, retaining vigour: βίη Δ 314, Η 157 = Λ 670, Ψ 629. Cf. Ε 254, Λ 813, Ν 512, Ψ 627:

κ 240, 493, λ 393, ξ 468, 503, τ 493, φ 426, χ 226.—Unimpaired in mind Υ 183.—Well-balanced: φρένες Ζ 352: σ 215.—(4) Maintained with ceaseless vigilance: φυλακή Θ 521.—(5) Secured, not liable to confiscation: γέρα Ι 335.—(6) Assured, certain, never failing: κομιδή θ 453.—Assured, to be looked forward to with certainty: πομπήν θ 30.—In unfailing succession τ 113.—(7) Affording sure testimony, unmistakable: σήματα τ 250 = ψ 206, ω 346.—(8) In neut. ἔμπεδον as adv. (a) With firm stand: στηρίξαι μ 434.—Immovably, steadily, fixedly Ρ 434: ρ 464.—Steadfastly, unshrinkingly Ε 527 = Ο 622, Ο 406.—Without stirring Ν 37: = θ 275, λ 152, 628, μ 161.—(b) Without intermission or break, continuously Μ 281: η 259.—Continually: ἐπαΐξασκεν Σ 158.—With steady course, without break or stop Χ 192.—With steady or undeviating course Ν 141, Ψ 641, 642: ν 86.—(c) App., without hesitation or uncertainty: ἄλλοτ' ἐπ' ἄλλον ἀμείβεται Ο 683.

ἔμπεσε, 3 sing. aor. ἐμπίπτω.

ἐμπεφύᾱσι, 3 pl. pf. ἐμφύω.

ἔμπης. (1) In any case: νῦν δ' ἐ. γὰρ κῆρες ἐφεστᾶσιν (but as it is, since in any case . . .) Μ 326, τλήσομαι ἐ. (on that I am resolved) Τ 308. Cf. Ω 522 (in spite of our hearts).—(2) For certain, for sure: οὔ τινα δείδιμεν ἐ. Η 196: β 199. Cf. ο 214, ω 324.—Introducing a statement of something remarkable, of a surety τ 37.—Derisively, 'really now' σ 354.—Nay even: ἐ. δέ τοι ὅρκια δώσω (I will not hesitate to . . .) τ 302.—(3) Adversatively, nevertheless, notwithstanding, all the same, still: πρῆξαι δ' ἐ. οὔ τι δυνήσεαι Α 562. Cf. Ε 191, Θ 33 = 464, Ξ 174 (though it was in the palace of Zeus that it was stirred), Ρ 632: β 191, γ 209, δ 100, ζ 190, λ 351, ξ 214, 481 (even without the χλαῖνα), π 147, σ 12, υ 311, ψ 83.—Strengthened by καί Β 297, Τ 422: ε 205.—(4) In ppl. construction with περ, though, even though: χατέουσί περ ἐ. (in need though they be) Ι 518, ἐπικρατέουσί περ ἐ. (though as it is they are the victors) Ξ 98. Cf. Ξ 1, Ο 399, Ρ 229: ο 361, σ 165, τ 356.

†ἐμπίπλημι [ἐμ-, ἐν- (6) + πίπλημι = πίμπλημι]. Imp. ἐμπίπληθι Φ 311. Fut. infin. ἐμπλησέμεν κ 523, λ 31. 3 sing. aor. ἐνέπλησε Υ 471. 3 pl. -αν ρ 503. 2 sing. subj. ἐνιπλήσῃς (ἐνι-, ἐν-) τ 117. 3 pl. -ωσι ψ 358. Imp. ἔμπλησον β 353. Pple. ἐμπλήσας, -αντος θ 495, ι 209, 212, σ 45. 3 sing. aor. mid. ἐμπλήσατο Χ 312: ι 296. Pple. ἐμπλησάμενος Χ 504. 3 pl. aor. pass. ἐνέπλησθεν Π 348. Infin. ἐνιπλησθῆναι η 221, λ 452. 3 sing. aor. ἔμπλητο Φ 607. 3 pl. ἔμπληντο θ 16. (1) To fill (a receptacle or the like) by pouring or putting something into it: ἓν δέπας ι 209. Cf. β 353, ρ 503, ψ 358.—With a liquid as subject: αἷμα κόλπον ἐνέπλησεν Υ 471.—With genit. of material: ἐμπίπληθι ῥέεθρα ὕδατος Φ 311. Cf. θ 495, ι 212, σ 45.—Sim.: πυρὴν ἐμπλησέμεν ἐσθλῶν (to heap it with . . .) κ 523 = λ 31.—Fig.: μή μοι θυμὸν ἐνιπλήσῃς ὀδυνάων τ 117.—(2) In mid., to fill one's . . .: ἐπεὶ ἐμπλήσατο νηδύν ι 296.—Fig., with genit.: μένεος ἐμπλήσατο θυμόν Χ 312. Cf. Χ 504.—(3) In pass., to be filled, be full, be stuffed: γαστὴρ ἐνιπλησθῆναι ἀνώγει η 221.—With genit.: ἐνέπλησθεν αἵματος ὀφθαλμοί Π 348, πόλις ἔμπλητο ἀλέντων Φ 607. Cf. θ 16.—Fig.: υἷος ἐνιπλησθῆναι (to have my fill of looking upon him) λ 452.

†ἐμπίπτω [ἐμ-, ἐν- (2) (3)]. 3 sing. aor. ἔμπεσε Δ 108, 217, Ι 436, Ξ 207, 306, Ο 451, Π 113, 206, Ρ 625: β 45, δ 508, ε 50, 318, μ 266, ο 375. 3 sing. subj. ἐμπέσῃ Λ 155. Imp. ἔμπεσε Π 81. (1) To fall *into*. With dat.: πέτρῃ (*i.e.* into a cleft) Δ 108: πόντῳ δ 508, ε 318.—Of an arrow, to fall *into*, enter, strike. With dat.: αὐχένι Ο 451.—Sim.: ὅθ' ἔμπεσ' ὀϊστός Δ 217.—Of fire, to be flung *into*. With dat.: νηυσίν Π 113.—Of a feeling, to enter *into*, come upon. With dat.: χόλος θυμῷ Ι 436, Ξ 207 = 306, Π 206. Cf. Ρ 625.—To come *into* (the mind), recur to one. With dat.: ἔπος θυμῷ μ 266.—(2) To fall *on to*. With dat.: πόντῳ (lighted on it) ε 50.—(3) To attack, make an attack Π 81.—Of fire, to fall *upon*. With dat.: ὅτε πῦρ ἐμπέσῃ ὕλῃ Λ 155 —Sim.: κακὸν οἴκῳ β 45, ο 375.

ἔμπλειος, -η, -ον [ἐμ-, ἐν- (6) + πλεῖος]. Also **ἐνίπλειος** ξ 113, ρ 300, τ 580, φ 78. With genit., filled with, full of: οἴνου ξ 113. Cf. σ 119, τ 580 = φ 78, υ 26, χ 3.—Infested with: κυνοραιστέων ρ 300.

ἐμπλήγδην [ἐμπλήσσω = ἐνιπλήσσω]. In striking wise, mightily: ἐ. ἕτερόν γε τίει υ 132.

ἔμπλην [app. ἐμ-, ἐν- (6) + πλη-, πελάζω]. Near or close to. With genit.: Βοιωτῶν ἐ. Β 526.

ἐμπλήσας, aor. pple. ἐμπίπλημι.

ἔμπλητο, 3 sing. aor. pass. ἐμπίπλημι.

†ἐμπνέω [ἐμ-, ἐν- (2) (3)]. Dual pple. in form ἐμπνείοντε Ρ 502. 3 sing. aor. ἐνέπνευσε Ρ 456: ι 381, τ 138. ἔμπνευσε Κ 482, Ο 262, Υ 110: ω 520. 3 sing. subj. ἐμπνεύσῃσι Ο 60. (1) To breathe *upon*. With dat.: μεταφρένῳ Ρ 502.—(2) To breathe into one, inspire him with: μένος Ο 60. Cf. ι 381, ω 520.—To breathe *into*. With dat.: τῷ μένος Κ 482. Cf. Ο 262 = Υ 110, Ρ 456.—To put *into* (one's mind), suggest. With dat. and infin.: φᾶρός μοι ἐνέπνευσε φρεσὶν ὑφαίνειν τ 138.

†ἐμπνύνθη, ἐμπνύθη. 3 *sing. aor. pass.* Ε 697, Ξ 436. Also ἔμπνῡτο Λ 359, Χ 475: ε 458, ω 349. [Prob. ἐμ-, ἐν- (6) + πνῡ-. See πέπνυμαι. In the MSS. ἀμπνύ(ν)θη, ἄμπνυντο (ἀμ-, ἀνα- (4)).] To come to after a faint: ἐμπνύνθη καὶ ἀνέδρακεν ὀφθαλμοῖσιν Ξ 436. Cf. Ε 697, Λ 359, Χ 475: ε 458, ω 349.

ἐμποιέω [ἐμ-, ἐν- (1)]. To make or construct (in something): ἐν πύργοισι πύλας ἐνεποίεον Η 438.

†ἐμπολάομαι. 3 pl. impf. ἐμπολόωντο. To get by trafficking: βίοτον πολύν ο 456.

ἔμπορος, -ου, ὁ [ἐμ-, ἐν- (1) + πορ-, περάω[1]]. One who travels in a ship belonging to another, a passenger β 319, ω 300.

†ἐμπρήθω, ἐνιπρήθω [ἐμ-, ἐνι-, ἐν- (6)]. 3 pl. impf. ἐνέπρηθον Ι 589. 3 sing. fut. ἐνιπρήσει Θ 235. Infin. ἐμπρήσειν Ι 242. ἐνιπρήσειν Μ 198, Ο 702.

3 sing. aor. ἐνέπρησε Θ 217, Χ 374. Subj. ἐνιπρήσω Θ 182. 3 pl. -ωσι Π 82. Infin. ἐνιπρῆσαι Ν 319, Ξ 47, Ο 417, 507. To destroy by fire, burn: πυρὶ νῆας Θ 182, νῆας πυρός (genit. of material) Ι 242. Cf. Θ 217, 235, Ι 589, Μ 198, Ν 319, Ξ 47, Ο 417, 507, 702, Π 82, Χ 374.

ἐμπυριβήτης [ἐμ-, ἐν- (3) + πυρί, dat. of πῦρ + βη-, βαίνω]. Made to go or stand upon the fire: τρίποδα Ψ 702.

ἐμφορέω [ἐμ-, ἐν- (1)]. In pass., to be borne or carried about *in*. With dat.: κύμασιν ἐμφορέοντο μ 419 = ξ 309.

ἔμφῡλος [ἐμ-, ἐν- (1) + φῦλον]. Of one's own tribe: ἄνδρα ο 273.

†**ἐμφύω** [ἐμ-, ἐν- (1) (3)]. 3 sing. aor. ἐνέφῡσε χ 348. 3 pl. pf. ἐμπεφύᾱσι Θ 84. Fem. pple. ἐμπεφυυῖα Α 513. (**1**) In aor., to implant or inspire knowledge of χ 348.—(**2**) In pf., to grow or be *upon*. With dat.: ὅθι τρίχες κρανίῳ ἐμπεφύᾱσιν Θ 84.—To cling closely Α 513.

ἐν Α 14, 30, 83, etc.: α 4, 15, 50, etc. **ἐνί** Α 30, 297, Γ 240, etc.: α 27, 103, δ 272, etc. **εἰνί** Θ 199, Ο 150: ι 417, κ 310, μ 256. **εἰν** Β 783, Ε 160, 446, etc.: α 162, β 256, γ 127, etc. [Cf. L. *in*, Eng. *in*.] (**I**) Adv. (**1**) In something, therein, within, there: ἐν σκόλοπας κατέπηξαν Η 441, ἐν ἄνδρες ναίουσιν Ι 154. Cf. Α 311, Τ 16 (in him), Φ 569, Ω 472, etc.: ἐν πίθοι ἕστασαν β 340. Cf. α 51, ε 254, ζ 292, μ 85, etc.—(**2**) Into something, and, in pregnant use, in something, therein: ἐν ἐρέτας ἀγείρομεν Α 142, ἐν δ' ἔπεσον Φ 9. Cf. Α 309, Θ 70, Σ 347, Τ 366, Ψ 177, etc.: γ 479, ω 498, etc.—In hostile sense: ἐν πρῶτος ὄρουσεν (upon the foe) Λ 91. Cf. Ο 624, etc.—(**3**) On; also in pregnant use: ἐν λέπαδν' ἔβαλεν Ε 730. Cf. Ι 207, Ψ 170, etc.: ἐν στρόφος ἦεν ἀορτήρ (attached to it) ν 438. Cf. η 96, ξ 519, etc.—(**4**) Among others, in a company or assembly: ἐν αὐτὸς ἐδύσετο χαλκόν Β 578. Cf. Π 551, Σ 535, etc.: η 291.—(**II**) Prep. with dat. (ἔνι with anastrophe when immediately following the case-form). (**1**) In: ἐν χερσίν Α 14, ἐνὶ οἴκῳ, ἐν Ἄργεϊ 30, νέεσσ' ἔνι Γ 240. Cf. Α 83, 358, 396, Β 194, Γ 69, Ε 160, etc.: α 15, 110, 162, 186, 255, 386, etc.—In reference to immaterial things: ἐνὶ φρεσίν Α 333, ἐν φιλότητι Β 232. Cf. Β 223, Γ 20, Ε 117, Θ 476, Ρ 647, etc.: δ 497, ζ 313, κ 465, λ 603, ο 357, etc.—In (*i.e.* by means of) (the hands of): ὄφρ' ἀνδρῶν ἐν παλάμῃσι κατέκταθεν Ε 558, etc. Cf. α 238, etc.—Sim.: ἐν ὀφθαλμοῖσιν Α 587, Σ 135, etc.: θ 459, κ 385, etc.—ἐν ῥυτῆρσι τάνυσθεν (in the governance of . . .) Π 475.—In reference to mixing: ἐν τυρὸν οἴνῳ ἐκύκα κ 234.—To that *in* which a characteristic is displayed: γυρὸς ἐν ὤμοισιν τ 246.—To measure or degree: ἐν καρὸς αἴσῃ Ι 378.—To that in reference to which one ends speech: ἐν σοὶ λήξω Ι 97.—In the matter of, in: τοῖσίν κεν ἐν ἄλγεσιν ἰσωσαίμην η 212. Cf. ν 292.—With ellipse of δώματι: εἰν Ἀΐδαο Χ 389. Cf. Ζ 47, etc.: η 132, κ 282, λ 211, etc.—(**2**) Into, and, in pregnant use, in: ὅτε νηυσὶν ἐν ὠκυπόροισιν ἔβαινον Β 351, θῆκε Περγάμῳ εἰν ἱερῇ Ε 446. Cf. Α 433, Δ 134, 482, Ε 317, 574, etc.: α 381, β 349, γ 40, 341, κ 290, etc.—In reference to the mind: ἐνὶ φρεσὶ βάλλεο σῇσιν Α 297. Cf. Ι 459, Ο 566, Φ 547, etc.: δ 729, μ 217, etc.—To closeness of approach or position: ἐν νύσσῃ ἐγχριμφθήτω Ψ 338. Cf. Ψ 344.—In among: ἐν νήεσσι πεσόντες Β 175. Cf. Λ 311, Μ 126, etc.: ξ 268, etc.—In hostile sense: ἐν Τρώεσσι θόρεν (upon them) Υ 381. Cf. Λ 325, Ν 742, Ο 635, etc.: ω 526.—Sim. of fire Λ 155.—(**3**) On, upon: ἐν Ὀλύμπῳ Α 566, θεῶν ἐν γούνασιν Ρ 514. Cf. Δ 2, 455, Η 66, Ω 527, etc.: α 108, δ 627, μ 237, ν 141, ω 332, etc.—(**4**) On to, and, in pregnant use, on: ἐν στήθεσι βάς Ζ 65, τρίποδ' ἵστασαν ἐν πυρί Σ 346. Cf. Θ 51, Ο 150, Ψ 132, etc.: γ 38, δ 136, θ 274, etc.—(**5**) Among: ἐν Δαναοῖσιν Α 109. Cf. Α 520, Β 483, Γ 31, 209, etc.: β 46, η 62, ξ 176, σ 379, etc.—In reference to inclusion in a number: ἐν τοῖσιν Ε 395. Cf. δ 452, τ 178, χ 217.—(**6**) In reference to time, in: ὥρῃ ἐν εἰαρινῇ Β 471. Cf. Λ 173, Σ 251, etc.: μ 76, ρ 176, σ 367, etc.

ἕν, neut. εἷς.

ἕνα, acc. sing. masc. εἷς.

ἐναίρω [ἔναρα. 'To despoil']. 3 sing. aor. mid. ἐνήρατο Ε 43, 59, Ζ 32, Ξ 515: ω 424. (κατ-.) (**1**) To kill in fight Ζ 229, Θ 296, Κ 481, Λ 188 = 203, Ν 338, 483, Υ 96, Φ 26, Ω 244.—In mid. Ε 43, 59, Ζ 32, Ξ 515, Π 92: ω 424.—(**2**) To kill in the chase: θῆρας Φ 485.—(**3**) In weakened sense, to mar, impair. In mid.: μηκέτι χρόα ἐναίρεο τ 263.

ἐναίσιμος, -ον [ἐν- (6) + αἴσιμος]. (**1**) (**a**) Due, fitting, proper: δῶρα Ω 425.—Of persons, right-thinking, just Ζ 521: κ 383, ρ 363.—Of the mind, intent on the right, just Ω 40: ε 190, σ 220.—Of the result of mental effort, right, in accordance with justice: τοῦτό γ' ἐναίσιμον οὐκ ἐνόησεν β 122 (this contrivance was not . . .), η 299 (in this her judgment was at fault).—(**b**) Absol. in neut. pl. ἐναίσιμα, what is right: ἐ. ἐργάζεσθαι ρ 321.—(**c**) In neut. sing. ἐναίσιμον as adv., in due season, at the appointed time: ἦλθον Ζ 519.—(**2**) Bringing omens, charged with fate: ὄρνιθες β 182.—Boding well: σήματα Β 353.—Absol. in neut. pl., omens β 159.

ἐναλίγκιος [ἐν- (6) + ἀλίγκιος]. Like, resembling, in the likeness of. With dat.: ὄρνιθι Ξ 290, θεῷ αὐδήν (in . . .) Τ 250. Cf. Ε 5, Ν 242, Ρ 583: ἀθανάτοις η 5, θεοῖς ἐναλίγκια μήδεα (like those of the gods) ν 89. Cf. α 371 = ι 4, β 5 = δ 310, π 209, 273 = ρ 202 = ω 157, ρ 337, τ 267, ω 148, 371.—In neut. in impers. construction: τῷ ἔην ἐναλίγκιον, ὡς εἰ . . ., it was like the case or state of things as [it would be] if . . ., it was as if . . . Χ 410.

ἐναμέλγω [ἐν- (2)]. To milk *into*. With dat.: γαυλοί, τοῖς ἐνάμελγεν ι 223.

ἔναντα [ἐν- (6) + ἄντα]. Facing (in hostile sense). With genit.: Ποσειδάωνος Υ 67.

ἐναντίβιος [ἐν- (6) + ἀντίβιος]. In neut. sing. ἐναντίβιον as adv., face to face, man to man: ἐ. μαχέσασθαι Θ 168, 255, Χ 223, ὅτε κέν τις ἐ. θεὸς ἔλθῃ (in open hostility) Υ 130, στῆναι ἐ. (to face the danger) Φ 266. Cf. Κ 451, Ο 179, Ρ 490, Φ 477: ξ 270, ρ 439.—With genit.: Ἀχιλῆος Υ 85.

ἐναντίος, -η, -ον [ἐν- (6) + ἀντίος]. (1) Opposite, facing: ἔστησαν κ 391. Cf. Z 247.—With genit.: ἕζετ' Ὀδυσῆος ἐναντίη ψ 89.—With dat.: οἱ I 190, ἀλλήλοισιν (*i.e.* beginning at either end of the line and meeting in the middle) Λ 67. Cf. κ 89.—Face to face ζ 329.—In hostile sense, opposite, facing. With genit.: Ἀχαιῶν E 497 = Z 106 = Λ 214 = P 343.—(2) Meeting, in order to meet, join, encounter or intercept a person, etc.: ἐναντίη ἦλθε Z 394, O 88. Cf. ν 226.—With genit.: ἐ. ἤλυθεν ἵππων O 454.—With dat.: ἐναντίη οἱ ἤλυθεν Z 251.—Sim.: πόριες σκαίρουσιν ἐναντίαι (come frisking to meet their mothers) κ 412.—In hostile sense. With dat.: ἐναντίω οἱ ὁρμηθήτην E 12.—(3) In neut. sing. ἐναντίον as adv. (a) Opposite, facing. With genit.: σφοῦ πατρός A 534.—With dat.: ὑμῖν παράκειται ἐ. ἠὲ . . . ἦ . . . (the choice is before you) χ 65.—Face to face: εἰς ὦπα ἰδέσθαι ἐ. ψ 107.—In hostile sense, face to face, man to man: μαχέσασθαι Γ 433, Υ 257. Cf. M 377, N 106, Υ 252.—Face to face, close at hand: ὦρτο Λ 129, Υ 164.—With genit., facing, opposing, against: ἄνακτος I 559. Cf. N 448, Υ 97.—So with dat.: Ἕκτορι O 304.—(b) In order to meet or join. With genit.: ἐ. ἤλυθον ἵππων ξ 278.—Sim.: τὸν ξεῖνον ἐ. κάλεσσον ρ 544.—In hostile sense. With genit.: θηρητῆρος Φ 574.

ἔναξε, 3 sing. aor. νάσσω.

ἔναρα, τά. (1) The armour and trappings of a fallen foe Z 68, 480, Θ 534, K 528, 570, N 268, O 347, P 13, 231, 540, X 245.—(2) Booty or spoil in general: φόρμιγγα ἄρετ' ἐξ ἐνάρων I 188.

†ἐναραρίσκω [ἐν- (2)]. Nom. sing. neut. pf. pple. ἐναρηρός. To be fitted into its place ε 236.

ἐναργής [ἐν- (6) + ἀργός]. (1) In visible presence: χαλεποὶ θεοὶ φαίνεσθαι ἐναργεῖς (in respect of their appearing . . ., when they appear . . .) Υ 131: Ἀθήνην, ἥ μοι ἐ. ἦλθεν γ 420. Cf. η 201, π 161.—(2) Clear or plain to the mind's eye: ὄνειρον δ 841.

ἐναρηρός, nom. sing. neut. pf. pple. ἐναραρίσκω.

ἐναρίζω [ἔναρα]. Aor. ἐνάριξα P 187. 3 sing. ἐνάριξε X 323. (ἐξ-.) (1) To strip (a slain foe) of his armour and trappings E 844.—(2) With double acc. of the spoil and of the person despoiled: τοὺς ἐνάριζον ἀπ' ἔντεα M 195, O 343. Cf. P 187, X 323.—(3) To kill in fight E 155, I 530, Λ 337, Ξ 24, Π 731, P 413, Φ 224.—(4) To kill or slay in gen. A 191.

ἐναρίθμιος, -ον [ἐν- (1) + ἀριθμός] (1) Reckoned in the number, counted B 202.—(2) Making up the number, completing the tale μ 65.

ἔνατος, -η, -ον [ἐννέα]. = εἴνατος. The ninth: μήτηρ ἐνάτη ἦν B 313 = 327.

ἔναυλος, -ου, ὁ [app. ἐν- (1) + αὐλός. Cf. sense (3) thereof. 'A hollow in . . .']. (1) A torrent-bed, a gully Π 71.—(2) A torrent Φ 283, 312.

†ἐνδείκνῡμι [ἐν- (6)]. Fut. mid. ἐνδείξομαι. In mid., to open one's mind, declare oneself T 83.

ἕνδεκα, *indeclinable* [ἕν, neut. of εἷς + δέκα]. Eleven B 713, E 193, I 329, Φ 45: ξ 103.

ἑνδεκάπηχυς, -υ [ἕνδεκα + πῆχυς, in sense 'cubit']. Eleven cubits long: ἔγχος Z 319 = Θ 494.

ἑνδέκατος, -η, -ον [ἕνδεκα]. (1) The eleventh Φ 156: γ 391, τ 192.—(2) ἑνδεκάτη (sc. ἡμέρη), the eleventh day: ἑνδεκάτῃ (on the eleventh day) Ω 666: ἑνδεκάτη τε δυωδεκάτη τε β 374, δ 588.

ἐνδέξιος [ἐν- (5) + δεξιός]. (1) App., on the right hand of a spectator (*i.e.* in the lucky quarter): ἐνδέξια σήματα φαίνων I 236.—(2) In neut. pl. ἐνδέξια as adv., (passing round) from left to right (*i.e.* in the sun's, or the lucky, direction): ἐ. οἰνοχόει A 597. Cf. H 184: ρ 365.

ἐνδέω [ἐν- (1) (3)]. (1) To bend or tie on to something: νευρήν, ἣν ἐνέδησα O 469.—To secure or tie in something: ὑπέρας ἐν αὐτῇ (sc. ἐν νηί) ε 260.—(2) Fig., to entangle or involve *in*. With dat.: ἄτῃ με B 111 = I 18.

†ἐνδίημι [ἐν- (6) + δίημι, act. of δίεμαι]. 3 pl. impf. ἐνδίεσαν. To tar on, set on (dogs) Σ 584.

ἔνδῑνα, τά [ἐν]. App., the inward parts of the body Ψ 806.

ἔνδῖος [ἐν- (1) + δῖος. 'In full light']. At mid-day: ἐ. ἦλθεν δ 450. Cf. Λ 726.

ἔνδοθεν [ἔνδον + -θεν (1) (2)]. (1) From within: ὑπακοῦσαι δ 283. Cf. υ 101.—(2) Within: Ζηνὸς τοιῆδε ἐ. αὐλή δ 74.—With genit.: αὐλῆς Z 247, Ω 161.—(3) Within one, in one's breast: εἴ οἱ κραδίη σιδηρέη ἐ. ἦεν δ 293. Cf. δ 467.

ἔνδοθι [ἔνδον + -θι]. (1) Within Υ 271, Ψ 819: δ 678.—With genit.: πύργων Σ 287.—(2) Within, in the house, in one's house, at home: τὴν ἐ. τέτμεν ἐοῦσαν ε 58. Cf. Z 498: χ 220.—(3) Within one, in one's breast: ἐ. θυμὸν ἀμύξεις A 243. Cf. X 242: β 315, θ 577, τ 377, ω 474.

ἔνδον [ἐν]. (1) Within: ἐγκέφαλος ἐ. πεπάλακτο Λ 98 = M 186 = Υ 400. Cf. M 142, Φ 362: ἐ. τις ἀοιδιάει κ 226. Cf. φ 237 = 383 (in the μέγαρον), χ 179 (in the θάλαμος).—With genit.: Διὸς [δώματος] ἐ. Υ 13. Cf. Ψ 200.—(2) Within, in the house, in one's house, at home: οὐκ ἐ. τέτμεν ἄκοιτιν Z 374, δεινή μοι θεὸς ἐ. [ἐστίν] Σ 394. Cf. K 378, Λ 767, 771, T 320, X 50: ε 61, 81, ζ 51, η 166, ι 216, 232, κ 221, ξ 407, ο 77 = 94, π 254, τ 40, 321, υ 40, φ 178 = 183, ψ 38.—Sim., app.: Καβησόθεν ἐ. ἐόντα (who had come to the city from . . .) N 363. Cf. O 438.—(3) Returned from a journey or from travels: ἄλλοθεν ἐ. ἐόντα π 26. Cf. π 202, 301, 355, 462, τ 477, φ 207, ψ 2, 29, 71.—(4) Within one, in one's breast: κραδίη ἐ. ὑλάκτει υ 13, 16. Cf. λ 337 = σ 249, ξ 178, ω 382.—(5) In the usual place, where one would expect to find a thing: ἐ., ὀΐομαι, [τεύχεά ἐστιν] χ 140.

ἐνδουπέω [ἐν- (2)]. To make a splash or thud in falling *into*. With dat.: μέσσῳ ἐνδούπησα μ 443, ἄντλῳ ἐνδούπησε πεσοῦσα ο 479.

ἐνδυκέως [app. ἐν- (6). Cf. ἀδευκής]. (1) Kindly, in gentle wise, with care for one's well-being: ἔτραφέ με Ψ 90, ἱκέτεω πεφιδήσεται Ω 158 = 187. Cf. Ω 438: η 256, κ 65, 450, ξ 62, 337, ο 305, 491, 543 = ρ 56, ρ 111, 113, τ 195 = ω 272, ω 212, 390.—(2) App., with kindly or grateful feelings: κρέ' ἤσθιεν ξ 109.

ἐνδύνω [ἐν- (2)]. Fem. aor. pple. ἐνδῦσα E 736, Θ 387. To get into, put on (clothes): χιτῶνα B 42, E 736 = Θ 387, K 21, 131.

ἐνεγκέμεν, aor. infin. φέρω.

ἐνέηκε, 3 sing. aor. ἐνίημι.

ἐνέην, 3 sing. impf. ἔνειμι.

ἔνεικε, 3 sing. aor. φέρω.

ἐνεικέμεν, aor. infin. φέρω.

ἐνείκεσας, 2 sing. aor. νεικέω.

ἔνειμε, 3 sing. aor. νέμω.

ἔνειμεν, 1 pl. ἔνειμι.

†**ἔνειμι** [ἐν- (1) + εἰμί]. 3 sing. ἔνεστι Ω 240: κ 45. 1 pl. ἔνειμεν E 477. 3 sing. opt. ἐνείη B 490, P 156. 3 sing. impf. ἐνῆεν A 593. ἐνέην ι 164, τ 443. 3 pl. ἔνεσαν Z 244: φ 12, 60. (1) To be or exist in a specified or indicated place, to be or exist in some person or thing: ὀλίγος ἔτι θυμὸς ἐνῆεν A 593, οὐκ οἴκοι ἔνεστι γόος; Ω 240. Cf. E 477, Z 244: τ 443, φ 12, 60.—(2) To be or exist *in*. With dat.: εἰ Τρώεσσι μένος ἐνείη P 156. Cf. B 490: κ 45.—(3) To be available in an indicated place: ἐνέην [οἶνος] ι 164.

ἐνεῖσα, aor. pple. fem. ἐνίημι.

ἕνεκα. Also **ἕνεκεν** ρ 288, 310. **εἵνεκα** A 174, B 138, H 374, Σ 171, etc.: β 191, ζ 156, λ 438, etc. With genit. (1) On account of, because of, for. (a) Of causes: ἕνεκ' ἀρητῆρος A 94, τοῦδ' ἕνεκα 110, εἵνεκα κούρης 298, εἵνεκα ποινῆς (on the subject of . . .) Σ 498. Cf. A 214, Γ 100 (twice), Z 525, Π 18, Υ 21, 298, etc.: εἵνεκα σεῖο ζ 156, βάτων ἕνεκα (for protection from . . .) ω 230. Cf. β 191, λ 521, ο 233, π 31, ω 251, etc.—(b) Of objects: εἵνεκα κούρης (to fetch . . .) A 336, σεῦ ἕνεκα Γ 206, ἕνεχ' ἵππων E 640. Cf. B 138, Γ 290, I 327, 560, P 92, Σ 171, etc.: σῆς μητέρος εἵνεκα (in the course of their suit) γ 212, εἵνεκα πατρός (in quest of . . .) δ 672, εἵνεκα πομπῆς (seeking . . .) θ 33, εἵνεκα κούρης (as her bride-price) 319. Cf. ν 263, ξ 70, π 334, τ 413, φ 155, etc.—(2) For the sake of, to do pleasure or service to: ἕνεκα θνητῶν A 574. Cf. A 174, Θ 428, K 27, Π 539, Φ 380, 463, X 236, Ψ 608, Ω 501: ὑῶν ἕνεκα (in care of them) ξ 416, ἕνεκα γαστρός (to satisfy it) ο 344. Cf. δ 170, θ 544, ρ 288, τ 377.

ἐνέκρυψε, 3 sing. aor. ἐγκρύπτω.

ἐνέκυρσε, 3 sing. aor. ἐγκύρω.

ἐνενήκοντα. See ἐννήκοντα.

ἐνένῑπε, 3 sing. redup. aor. ἐνίπτω.

ἐνέπλησε, 3 sing. aor. ἐμπίπλημι.

ἐνέπνευσε, 3 sing. aor. ἐμπνέω.

ἐνέπρησε, 3 sing. aor. ἐμπρήθω.

ἐνέπω. See ἐννέπω.

ἐνερείδω [ἐν- (2)]. 3 pl. aor. ἐνέρεισαν. To press or thrust *into*. With dat.: μοχλὸν ὀφθαλμῷ ι 383.

ἔνερθε(ν) [ἐνερ-, ἐν + -θεν (2). App. on the analogy of ὕπερθε(ν)]. Also **νέρθε(ν)** H 212, Λ 282, 535, N 78, Ξ 204, Π 347, Υ 57, 500, X 452: λ 302, υ 352. (1) Beneath, below: νέρθε ποσσὶν ἤϊεν H 212 (the feet being contrasted with the face), θώρηκος ἔνερθε (app., below on the . . . , taking the genit. as partitive) Λ 234. Cf. Λ 282, 535 = Υ 500, N 75, 78, Π 347, Υ 57, X 452: ι 385, ν 163, υ 352.—With genit.: ἀγκῶνος ἔνερθε Λ 252. Cf. Θ 16, Ξ 204: λ 302.—(2) Adjectivally: οἱ ἔνερθε θεοί Ξ 274.

ἔνεροι, οἱ [ἐν + comp. suff. -ερο-]. Those beneath the earth, the dwellers below O 188, Υ 61.

ἐνέρτερος [ἐνερ-, ἐν + comp. suff. -τερο-. App. on the analogy of ὑπέρ-τερος]. (1) Lower than, beneath, below. With genit.: ἐ. Οὐρανιώνων E 898.—(2) That is beneath or below: θεοί O 225.

ἔνεσαν, 3 pl. impf. ἔνειμι.

ἐνέστακται, 3 sing. pf. pass. ἐνστάζω.

ἐνεστήρικτο, 3 sing. plupf. pass. ἐνστηρίζω.

ἔνεστι, 3 sing. ἔνειμι.

ἐνετή, -ῆς, ἡ [ἐνετός, verbal adj. of ἐνίημι. 'What is sent or thrust in']. A pin or brooch Ξ 180.

ἐνεύδω [ἐν- (1) (3)]. (1) To sleep in or upon something γ 350.—(2) To sleep *in* or *upon*. With dat.: χλαῖναν καὶ κώεα τοῖσιν ἐνεῦδεν υ 95.

ἐνεύναιος, -ον [ἐν- (1) (3) + εὐνή]. In or on the bed: αὐτοῦ ἐνεύναιον (sc. δέρμα) (his own bed-covering) ξ 51.—Absol., app., a sleeper: χήτει ἐνευναίων π 35.

ἐνεχεύατο, 3 sing. aor. mid. ἐγχέω.

ἐνηείη, -ης, ἡ [ἐνηής]. The quality of being ἐνηής: ἐνηείης τις Πατροκλῆος μνησάσθω P 670.

ἐνῆεν, 3 sing. impf. ἔνειμι.

ἐνηής. App., gentle, amiable, kindly disposed or the like: ἑταῖρον P 204, Φ 96, μέμνησαί μευ ἐνηέος (as being kindly disposed to you) Ψ 648. Cf. Ψ 252: θ 200.

ἐνῆκε, 3 sing. aor. ἐνίημι.

ἔνημαι [ἐν- (1)]. To be seated in a specified place: ἵν' ἐνήμεθα δ 272.

ἐνήνοθε ρ 270. A form difficult to explain Most MSS. read ἀνήνοθε (*q.v.*). (ἐπ-.)

ἐνήρατο, 3 sing. aor. mid. ἐναίρω.

ἐνήσει, 3 sing. fut. ἐνίημι.

ἔνθα [ἐν]. (1) There: ἐ. καθέζετο A 536. Cf. A 594, 611, B 311, 724, Γ 426, E 368, etc.: α 26, 443, β 395, γ 32, 108, 279, etc.—(2) Thither, there: ἦν ἐ. ἀφίκηαι Θ 482. Cf. Z 318, N 23, Ξ 169, etc.: α 427, γ 297, δ 8, 407, etc.—ἐ. . . . ἐ., hither . . . thither, in this direction . . . in that B 90, 397, 462, E 223, K 264 (in rows), Σ 543 (up and down the field), Ψ 164 (a hundred feet square), 320 (to right and left), etc.: β 213 (thither and back again), ε 327, η 86 (lengthwise and breadth-wise), κ 517 (a cubit square), ξ 11, τ 524, υ 24, etc.—(3) Where: ἐ. πάρος κοιμᾶτο A 610. Cf. Γ 185, E 305, 480, Z 289, 348, 433, etc.: α 128, γ 295, 367, δ 635, ε 82, ζ 86, etc.—(4) Whither: ἐς Τροίην, ἐ. περ ἔβαν α 210.—To where: βὰν δ' ἴμεν ἐ. . . . N 789. Cf. Δ 247, Ω 733.—(5) (a) Then, at that time: ἐ. ἄλλοι οἴκοι ἔσαν α 11. Cf. Δ 223, 345, etc.: α 18, etc.—(b) Then, after that, thereupon: ἐ. ἄλλοι ἐπευφήμησαν A 22. Cf. B 155, Θ 268, etc.: β 382, δ 259, ε 388, κ 538, etc.

ἐνθάδε [ἔνθα]. (1) Here: ἀπολέσθαι ἐ. Ἀχαιούς Μ 70. Cf. Α 171, Β 203, 296, 343, Ε 172, etc.: β 51, δ 178, 594, 599, 602, 655, etc.—(2) Hither: ἤγομεν ἐ. πάντα Α 367. Cf. Β 287, Δ 179, Ε 129, Ζ 256, Ν 449, etc.: α 173, ζ 179, θ 428, ι 514, ν 12, 278, etc.

ἐνθέμεναι, aor. infin. ἐντίθημι.

ἔνθεν [ἐν]. (1) Thence: τὸν ἐ. ῥυσάμην Ο 29. Cf. Η 472, Κ 179, Λ 725, Υ 191, etc.: β 329, ζ 7, ι 62, μ 211, 447, etc.—In reference to seeing: ἐ. ἐφαίνετ' Ἴδη Ν 13. Cf. μ 230.—To birth: γένος μοι ἐ. ὅθεν σοί Δ 58.—To taking up a lay from a specified point: ἐ. ἑλὼν ὡς . . . (from the point where . . .) θ 500. — (2) ἐ. . . . ἑτέρωθι . . ., on one side . . . on the other . . . μ 235.—(3) Whence: ἐ. ἀπῆλθεν Ρ 703. Cf. Ω 597: δ 220, ε 195, σ 157, etc.—(4) Then, thereupon: ἐ. ἂν ἐπιφρασσαίμεθα βουλήν Ν 741.—Sim.: ἐ. πέτραι ἐπηρεφέες (then come . . .) μ 59.

ἐνθένδε [ἔνθεν]. Hence: ἐ. χρυσὸν ἄξομαι Ι 365. Cf. Θ 527: λ 69.

ἔνθετο, 3 sing. aor. mid. ἐντίθημι.

ἐνθήσω, fut. ἐντίθημι.

†**ἐνθρῴσκω** [ἐν- (2) (3)]. 3 sing. aor. ἔνθορε. With dat. (1) To leap *into*: μέσσῳ Φ 233, πόντῳ Ω 79.—(2) To leap *in among*: ὁμίλῳ Ο 623.—(3) To leap *against*: λὰξ ἔνθορεν ἰσχίῳ (*i.e.* kicked it) ρ 233.

ἐνθύμιος [ἐν- (1) + θυμός]. Taken to heart ν 421 (a subject of anxiety).

ἐνί. See ἐν.

ἔνι [for ἔν-εστι, ἔν-εισι]. There is (are) therein (thereon). With or without dat.: φρένες οὐκ ἔνι Ψ 104. Cf. Ξ 141, 216, Σ 53, Υ 248: ᾧ ἔνι λωτός δ 603, οὔ οἱ ἔνι τρίχες σ 355. Cf. δ 846, ι 126, λ 367, φ 288.

ἐνιαύσιος [ἐνιαυτός]. A year old: σῦν π 454.

ἐνιαυτός, -οῦ, ὁ [prob. 'the time when the heavens are again ἐνὶ αὐτῷ, in the same position,' and thus properly rather an epoch than a period]. A year. (1) Considered as a point or unit of time or as one of a series: ἐννέα βεβάασιν Β 134, δεκάτῳ Μ 15 (at the tenth turn of the year, at the end of the tenth year). Cf. Β 295, 551: ὅτ' ἐ. ἔην (when the turn of the year had come) κ 469. Cf. α 16, β 175, γ 391, λ 248, π 18, ρ 327.—(2) Considered as a space of time: ἐς δεκάτους ἐνιαυτούς Θ 404 = 418 (see δέκατος (1)), πέντε ἐνιαυτούς Ψ 833. Cf. Τ 32, Φ 444: τλαίης (τλαίην) ἂν ἐνιαυτόν (for a year) α 288, β 219. Cf. δ 86, 526, 595, κ 467, λ 356, ξ 196, 292, ο 230, 455.

ἐνιαύω [ἐν- (1) (4)]. (1) To pass the night in a specified place: ἔνθ' ἀνὴρ ἐνίαυεν ι 187.—(2) To pass the night *among*. With dat.: ὕεσσιν ο 557.

ἐνιζάνω [ἐν- (1)]. To sit down *in*. With dat.: αἰθούσῃσιν ἐνίζανον Υ 11.

†**ἐνίημι** [ἐν- (1) (2) + ἵημι[1]]. 3 sing. ἐνίησι μ 65. Imp. pl. ἐντέτε Μ 441. 2 sing. fut. ἐνήσεις Π 449. 3 -ει ο 198. 1 pl. -ομεν Ξ 131: β 295, μ 293. 2 sing. aor. ἐνῆκας Ι 700. 3 ἐνέηκε Κ 89: δ 233. ἐνῆκε Π 656, Ρ 570, Τ 37, Υ 80, Ψ 390. 1 pl. ἐνήκαμεν μ 401. Aor. pple. fem. ἐνεῖσα ν 387. (1) To put or throw into a vessel: [φάρμακον] δ 233.—To send or throw *into*. With dat.: νηυσὶ πῦρ Μ 441.—To send forward into the fight Ξ 131.—To send (in order to make up a number): ἄλλην ἐνίησιν ἐναρίθμιον εἶναι μ 65.—(2) To launch one's ship *into* (the sea), put *to* (sea). With dat.: ἐνήσομεν πόντῳ β 295. Cf. μ 293, 401.—(3) With dat., to set (a person) *upon*, incline (him) *to*: ἀγηνορίῃσιν Ι 700.—To involve *in*, bring within the compass of: πόνοισιν Κ 89: ὁμοφροσύνῃσιν (will incline us to . . .) ο 198.—(4) To inspire: μένος Τ 37. Cf. Ρ 570: ν 387.—To inspire or cause *in*. With dat.: τοῖσιν κότον Π 449. Cf. Π 656, Υ 80, Ψ 390.

†**ἐνικλάω** [ἐνι-, ἐν- (6). 'To break off']. Infin. ἐνικλᾶν. To thwart, frustrate Θ 408, 422.

ἐνιπή, -ῆς, ἡ [ἐνίπτω]. (1) Rebuke or reproach as felt by the person rebuked or reproached: ἀποθέσθαι ἐνιπήν Ε 492.—An instance of this, a rebuke or reproach so considered: αἰδεσθεὶς βασιλῆος ἐνιπήν Δ 402. Cf. Ξ 104: κ 448.—(2) Abuse, contumely υ 266.—(3) App., a threat: φεύγων Ποσειδάωνος ἐνιπάς ε 446.

ἐνίπλειος. See ἔμπλειος.

ἐνιπλήξωμεν, 1 pl. aor. subj. ἐνιπλήσσω.

ἐνιπλήσῃς, 2 sing. aor. subj. ἐμπίπλημι.

†**ἐνιπλήσσω** [ἐνι-, ἐν- (3). 'To stumble upon']. 1 pl. aor. subj. ἐνιπλήξωμεν Μ 72. 3 -ωσι χ 469. Nom. pl. masc. pple. ἐνιπλήξαντες Ο 344. To fall *into*, get *into*, get caught or entangled *in*. With dat.: τάφρῳ Μ 72, Ο 344: ἕρκει χ 469.

ἐνιπρήσει, 3 sing. fut. ἐμπρήθω.

ἐνίπτω. 3 sing. aor. ἠνίπαπε Β 245, Γ 427, Ε 650, Ρ 141: υ 17, 303. 3 sing. redup. aor. ἐνένιπε Ο 546, 552, Π 626, Ψ 473: π 417, σ 78, 321, 326, τ 65, 90, φ 84, 167, 287, χ 212, ψ 96. (1) To rebuke, reprove, upbraid, reproach, scold: πόσιν Γ 427. Cf. Β 245, Γ 438, Ο 546, 552, Π 626, Ρ 141, Ψ 473: π 417, σ 78, τ 90, υ 17, 303, φ 84 = 167 = 287, χ 212, ψ 96.—(2) To abuse, revile: Ε 650, Ω 768: σ 321, 326, τ 65.

†**ἐνισκίμπτω** [ἐνι-, ἐν- (1) (3) + σκίμπτω = σκήπτω. See σκήπτομαι]. Dual aor. pple. ἐνισκίμψαντε Ρ 437. 3 sing. aor. pass. ἐνισκίμφθη Π 612, Ρ 528. (1) To fix or stick *in*. With dat.: δόρυ οὔδει ἐνισκίμφθη Π 612 = Ρ 528.—(2) To cause or allow to rest *upon*. With dat.: οὔδει ἐνισκίμψαντε καρήατα Ρ 437.

ἔνισπε[1], 3 sing. aor. ἐννέπω.

ἔνισπε[2], ἐνίσπες, aor. imp. ἐννέπω.

ἐνισπήσω, fut. ἐννέπω.

ἐνίσσω [= ἐνίπτω]. (1) = ἐνίπτω (1): θυγατέρεσσίν τε καὶ υἱάσι βέλτερον εἴη ἐνισσέμεν [αὐτούς] (it is better for them that he should scold them, *i.e.* it is better that he should scold *them*) Ο 198.—(2) = ἐνίπτω (2) Χ 497, Ω 238: ω 161, 163.

ἐνιχριμφθείς, aor. pple. pass. See ἐγχρίμπτω.

ἐνίψω, fut. ἐννέπω.

ἐννέα, *indeclinable* (ἐνFέα) [cf. L. *novem*, Eng. *nine*]. Nine Β 96, 134, 654, Ζ 174, Η 161, Π 785, Σ 578, Ψ 173, Ω 252: γ 7, 8, θ 258, ι 160, λ 577, ξ 248, ω 60.

ἐννεάβοιος [ἐννέα + βοῦς]. Of the value of nine oxen. Absol. Z 236.

ἐννεακαίδεκα, *indeclinable* [ἐννέα + καί + δέκα]. Nineteen: [υἷες] Ω 496.

ἐννεάπηχυς, -υ [ἐννέα + πῆχυς in sense 'cubit']. Nine cubits long or in extent: ζυγόδεσμον Ω 270: ἐννεαπήχεες εὖρος (in . . .) λ 311.

ἐννεάχῑλοι [ἐννέα + χίλιοι]. Nine thousand E 860 = Ξ 148.

ἔννεον, 3 pl. impf. νέω[1].

ἐννεόργυιος [ἐννέα + ὄργυια]. Nine fathoms in extent: μῆκος ἐννεόργυιοι (in . . .) λ 312.

†**ἐννέπω** (ἐνσέπω) [ἐν- (6) + σ(ε)π-]. 3 sing. impf. ἔννεπε Θ 412. Imp. ἔννεπε B 761: α 1. Also **ἐνέπω** (Λ 643: ρ 549, 556, 561, ψ 301, ω 414). Fut. ἐνισπήσω (ἐνι-, ἐν-) ε 98. ἐνίψω β 137. 3 sing. -ει H 447: λ 148. 2 sing. aor. ἔνισπες (ἐνι-) Ω 388. 3 -ε B 80, Z 438. Subj. ἐνίσπω Λ 839: ι 37. 3 sing. -ῃ γ 327, θ 101, 251, ρ 529. 2 sing. opt. ἐνίσποις δ 317. 3 -οι Ξ 107. Imp. ἔνισπε δ 642. ἐνίσπες Λ 186, Ξ 470: γ 101, 247, δ 314, 331, λ 492, μ 112, ξ 185, χ 166, ψ 35. Imp. pl. ἔσπετε (prob. for ἔνσπετε) B 484, Λ 218, Ξ 508, Π 112. Infin. ἐνισπεῖν γ 93, δ 323. (1) To say, tell, tell of or about, communicate, make known: τὸν ὄνειρον B 80. Cf. H 447, Θ 412, Λ 186, 839, Ξ 107, Ω 388: κείνου ὄλεθρον γ 93 = δ 323. Cf. β 137, δ 314, 317, ε 98, ι 37, λ 492, μ 112, ξ 185, ρ 549, 556, 561, ω 414.—To tell about, tell the tale of (a person) α 1.—(2) With dependent clause, to say, tell: οἵ τινες . . . B 484, ὅππως . . . Π 112. Cf. B 761, Λ 218, Ξ 508: θ 101, 251, χ 166, ψ 35.—(3) Absol. (a) To say, tell, speak: νημερτὲς ἐνίσπες Ξ 470. Cf. Z 438: γ 101 = δ 331, γ 247, 327, δ 642, λ 148, ρ 529.—(b) To talk, hold converse: πρὸς ἀλλήλους Λ 643: ψ 301 (exchanging tales).

ἐννεσίη, -ης, ἡ [ἐνίημι. For ἐνεσίη, which could not stand in the hexameter]. An inciting or prompting. In pl.: κείνης ἐννεσίῃσιν E 894.

ἐννέωρος [ἐννέα + ὥρη]. (1) Nine years old, at nine years old λ 311.—(2) App. (the number being taken as a round one) conveying the notion of full maturity, well matured, full-grown: ἀλείφατος Σ 351: βοός κ 19, σιάλοισιν 390.—(3) In τ 179 (Μίνως ἐ. βασίλευε Διὸς ὀαριστής) the reference seems to be to an eight-yearly tenure of kingship. See Frazer, *Golden Bough*, 3rd ed., Part iii. p. 58 foll., esp. p. 70. On the analogy of διὰ τρίτης ἡμέρας, every second day, and similar expressions, ἐ. is to be translated 'by terms of eight years,' fresh kingly power being supposed to be imparted in converse with Zeus at the end of each term.

ἐννήκοντα, *indeclinable* [ἐννέα. For ἐννε-ήκοντα. Cf. τρι-ήκοντα]. Also **ἐνενήκοντα** B 602 (a form difficult to explain). Ninety B 602: τ 174.

ἐννῆμαρ [ἐννέα + ἦμαρ. For ἐννέ-ημαρ]. For or during nine days A 53, Z 174, M 25, Ω 107, 610, 664, 784: η 253 = ξ 314, ι 82, κ 28, μ 447.

ἐννοσίγαιος (ἐνϝοσίγαιος) [ἐνϝοσι- (ἐν- (1) or (3) + ϝοθ-, ὠθέω) + γαῖα. Cf. εἰνοσίφυλλος, ἐνοσίχθων]. Epithet or a name of Poseidon. Lord of earthquakes; or perh., who is ever beating the earth with his waves H 455, Θ 201, 440, I 362, M 27, Ξ 135, 510, O 173, 184, 218, Υ 20, 310, Φ 462: ε 423, ζ 326, ι 518, λ 102, ν 140.—Joined with γαιήοχος I 183, N 43, 59, 677, Ξ 355, O 222, Ψ 584: λ 241.

†**ἕννῡμι** (ϝέσ-νυμι. Cf. L. *vestis*). Fut. ἕσσω ν 400, π 79, ρ 550, φ 339. 3 sing. -ει ο 338, ρ 557. Aor. ἕσσα δ 253. 3 sing. -ε E 905, Π 680, Σ 451: η 265, κ 542, ν 436, ξ 320, π 457. 3 pl. -αν θ 366, ω 59. Imp. ἕσσον Π 670. Pple. ἕσσας ξ 396. Infin. ἕσσαι ξ 154. **Mid.** Pres. infin. ἕννυσθαι ζ 28, ξ 514, 522. 3 sing. impf. ἕννυτο ε 229, 230, κ 543. 3 sing. aor. ἐέσσατο (ἐϝέσσατο) K 23, 177: ξ 529. ἕσατο Ξ 178. ἕσσατο H 207, K 334: ζ 228. 3 pl. ἕσαντο Υ 150. ἕσσαντο Ξ 350, 383: ω 467, 500. Pple. ἑσσάμενος, -ου Ξ 282, 372, T 233, Ψ 803: β 3, δ 308, υ 125. Infin. ἕσασθαι Ω 646: δ 299, η 338. Pf. εἷμαι (ϝέσ-μαι) τ 72, ψ 115. 2 sing. ἕσσαι ω 250. 3 εἷται λ 191. 2 sing. plupf. ἕσσο Γ 57: π 199. 3 ἕεστο M 464. ἕστο Ψ 67: ρ 203, 338, τ 218, 237, χ 363, ω 158, 227. 3 dual ἕσθην Σ 517. 3 pl. εἵατο Σ 596. Pple. εἱμένος, -ου Δ 432, O 308, 389, Υ 381: ο 331, τ 327. (ἀμφι-, ἐπι-, κατα-.) (I) In act. (1) To put (clothes) on a person, clothe him with (them): εἵματα ἕσσε E 905. Cf. Π 670, 680: δ 253, η 265, θ 366, ν 400, π 457, ω 59.—(2) To put (clothes) on (a person), clothe (him) with (them). With double acc.: ἀμφί με χλαῖναν ἕσσεν κ 542 = ξ 320. Cf. ν 436, ξ 154, 396, ο 338, π 79 = ρ 550 = φ 339, ρ 557.—So of induing with armour: Πάτροκλον περὶ τὰ ἃ τεύχεα ἕσσεν Σ 451.—(II) In mid. (1) In pres., impf. and aor. (a) To put (clothes) on oneself, put (them) on: ἀμφ' ἑανὸν ἕσατο Ξ 178. Cf. K 23, 177, 334: χλαῖναν ἕννυτο ε 229. Cf. β 3 = δ 308 = υ 125, ε 230 = κ 543, ζ 28, 228, ξ 529.—In reference to a covering other than clothes: ἠέρα ἑσσαμένω Ξ 282. Cf. Ξ 350, Υ 150.—The infin. in complementary sense: οὐ πολλαὶ χλαῖναι [εἰσι] ἕννυσθαι (to cover oneself withal) ξ 514. Cf. Ω 646: = δ 299 = η 338, ξ 522.—(b) To put on (one's armour): περὶ χροῒ ἕσσατο τεύχεα H 207. Cf. Ξ 383, T 233, Ψ 803: ω 467 = 500.—So of assuming a shield: [ἀσπίδας] ἑσσάμενοι Ξ 372.—(2) In pf. and plupf., to be in the state of having put on (clothes, etc.); hence (a) To have on (clothes), be clad in (them), wear (them): χιτῶνας εἵατο Σ 596. Cf. Σ 517, Ψ 67: κακὰ εἵματα εἷται λ 191. Cf. ο 331, π 199, ρ 203 = ω 158, ρ 338, τ 72, 218, 237, 327, χ 363, ψ 115, ω 227, 250.—In reference to a covering other than clothes: εἱμένος νεφέλην O 308.—Fig.: λάϊνον χ' ἕσσο χιτῶνα (would have been stoned) Γ 57, εἱμένος ἀλκήν Υ 381.—(b) To have on, wear (armour): χαλκῷ, τὸν ἕεστο M 464. Cf. Δ 432.—Of a weapon, to be armed or pointed (with something): ξυστὰ κατὰ στόμα εἱμένα χαλκῷ O 389.

ἐννύχιος, -η, -ον [ἐν- (1) + νυχ-, νύξ]. Doing something by night, by night, in the night-time: ἐ. προμολών Φ 37. Cf. Λ 683: γ 178.

ἔννυχος, -ον [as prec.]. = prec. Λ 716.

ἐνοπή, -ῆς, ἡ [ἐνέπω]. (1) Voice or sound κ 147.—(2) Shouting: ἐνοπῇ ἴσαν Γ 2.—The shouting of fighters, the din of battle: μάχῃ ἐ. τε Μ 35, Τρώων ἐξ ἐνοπῆς (from the shouting throng) Π 782, Ρ 714. Cf. Π 246.—(3) The sound of mourning, weeping, wailing: ἐνοπήν τε γόον τε Ω 160.—(4) The sound of musical instruments: αὐλῶν συρίγγων τ' ἐνοπήν Κ 13.

†ἐνόρνῡμι [ἐν- (1) (4)]. 2 sing. aor. ἐνῶρσας Ο 366. 3 -ε Ζ 499. Pple. ἐνόρσας Ο 62. 3 sing. aor. mid. ἐνῶρτο Α 599: θ 326. (1) To awaken or induce in a person an inclination for (something), to turn him to (something): φύζαν Ο 62.—(2) To awaken or induce an inclination for (something) *in* a person, to turn him to (something). With dat.: τῇσι γόον ἐνῶρσεν Ζ 499. Cf. Ο 366.—(3) In mid., to be caused or brought about *among*, to break out *among*. With dat.: ἐνῶρτο γέλως θεοῖσιν Α 599: = θ 326.

ἐνορούω [ἐν- (3)]. (1) To leap or spring upon the foe: τῇ ἐνόρουσεν Λ 149. Cf. Λ 747.—(2) To leap or spring *upon*. With dat.: Τρωσίν Π 783. Cf. Κ 486.

ἐνόρσας, aor. pple. ἐνόρνυμι.

ἔνορχος [ἐν- (1) + ὄρχις, testicle]. Not castrated, entire: μῆλα Ψ 147.

ἐνοσίχθων, -ονος [for ἐνϜοσίχθων, fr. ἐνϜοσι- as in ἐννοσίγαιος + χθών]. = ἐννοσίγαιος. Epithet or a name of Poseidon Η 445 = Φ 287, Θ 208, Λ 751, Ν 10, 34, 65, 89, 215, 231, 554, Ξ 150, 384, Ο 41, 205, Υ 13, 63, 132, 291, 318, 330, 405, Φ 435: α 74, γ 6, ε 282, 339, 366, 375, η 35, 56, 271, θ 354, ι 283, 525, λ 252, μ 107, ν 125, 146, 159, 162.

†ἐνστάζω [ἐν- (2)]. 3 sing. pf. pass. ἐνέστακται. To drop *into*; hence, to instil *in*. With dat.: εἴ τοι σοῦ πατρὸς ἐνέστακται μένος ἠΰ β 271.

†ἐνστηρίζω [ἐν- (2)]. 3 sing. plupf. pass. ἐνεστήρικτο. To fix *in*, stick *into*. With dat.: γαίῃ ἐνεστήρικτο Φ 168.

ἐνστρέφω [ἐν- (1)]. In mid., to turn or have movement *in* (a socket). With dat.: ἔνθα μηρὸς ἰσχίῳ ἐνστρέφεται Ε 306.

†ἐντανύω [ἐν- (6)]. 3 pl. pres. ἐντανύουσιν φ 326. Fut. infin. ἐντανύειν φ 97, 127. 3 sing. aor. ἐντάννσε φ 150. Subj. ἐντανύσω φ 114. 2 sing. -ῃς φ 306. 3 -ῃ τ 577, φ 75, 315, 338. 3 sing. opt. ἐντανύσειε φ 286. Infin. ἐντανύσαι τ 587, φ 185, 247, ω 171. Aor. infin. mid. ἐντανύσασθαι φ 403. Fut. infin. pass. ἐντανύεσθαι φ 92. (1) To bend (a bow) into the position required for stringing it, to string (it) (cf. τανύω (2)): οὐδὲ τόξον ἐντάννσεν φ 150. Cf. τ 577 = φ 75, φ 92, 247, 286, 306, 315, 326, 338, 403.—Absol. φ 114, 185.—(2) To stretch (the string) so as to string a bow: νευρήν τ 587, φ 97 = 127, ω 171.

ἐνταῦθα [ἐν]. Thither, in that direction, to an indicated course of action: μή σε δαίμων ἐ. τρέψειεν Ι 601.

ἐνταυθοῖ [ἐν]. There Φ 122: σ 105, υ 262.

ἔντεα, τά. Dat. pl. ἔντεσι Ε 220, Λ 731, Π 279, Τ 384, etc. (1) Armour, harness, warlike trappings or array (not of arms) (cf. τεύχεα): ἔντε' ἔδυνεν Γ 339. Cf. Ζ 418, Κ 34, Μ 195, Ν 640, Ρ 162, etc.: τ 17, ψ 368.—(2) Appliances, furniture: δαιτός η 232.

†ἐντείνω [ἐν- (6)]. 3 sing. pf. pass. ἐντέταται Ε 728. 3 sing. plupf. ἐντέτατο Κ 263. To strain tight (with interplaited straps): δίφρος ἱμᾶσιν ἐντέταται Ε 728. Cf. Κ 263.

ἔντερον, -ου, τό (ἐν. App. in form a comp.]. (1) An intestine; a piece of gut made therefrom φ 408.—(2) In pl. ἔντερα, the bowels or intestines Ν 507 = Ρ 314, Ξ 517, Υ 418, 420.

ἐντεσιεργός [ἔντεσι dat. of ἔντεα in sense 'a draught-beast's harness' + ἔργω[2]]. Working in harness, draught- . . . : ἡμιόνους Ω 277.

ἐντέταται, 3 sing. pf. pass. ἐντείνω.

ἐντεῦθεν [ἐν]. Thence τ 568.

†ἐντίθημι [ἐν- (1) (3)]. Fut. ἐνθήσω ε 166. Aor. infin. ἐνθέμεναι Ω 646: δ 299, η 338. 1 pl. impf. mid. ἐντιθέμεσθα γ 154. 2 sing. aor. ἔνθεο Ζ 326. 3 ἔνθετο α 361, λ 102, ν 342, φ 355. Imp. ἔνθεο Δ 410, Ι 639: ω 248. Fem. pple. ἐνθεμένη Φ 124, Χ 353. (1) To put or place upon something: χλαίνας Ω 646: = δ 299 = η 338.—(2) To put or place *upon*. With dat. In mid.: ἐνθεμένη σε λεχέεσσιν Φ 124, Χ 353.—(3) To put on board a ship: σῖτον ἐνθήσω ε 166.—In mid.: κτήματ' ἐντιθέμεσθα γ 154.—(4) In mid. (a) To lay or store up *in* (one's heart). With dat.: χόλον ἔνθεο θυμῷ Ζ 326. Cf. λ 102, ν 342, ω 248.—(b) To lay *to* (heart). With dat.: μῦθον ἔνθετο θυμῷ α 361 = φ 355.—(c) To bring (one's heart) into a specified state: ἵλαον ἔνθεο θυμόν Ι 639.—(d) To put or reckon *in* (a rank or category). With dat.: μὴ πατέρας ὁμοίῃ ἔνθεο τιμῇ Δ 410.

ἔντο, 3 pl. aor. mid. ἵημι[1].

ἐντός [ἐν]. (1) Within, inside: τρομέοντό οἱ φρένες ἐ. (in his breast) Κ 10, ἐ. ἔχον (enclosing, guarding) Μ 8, πλῆσθέν οἱ μέλε' ἐ. ἀλκῆς Ρ 211: ἐ. ἔχοντες (containing) β 341, μὴ ἐ. πυκάζοιεν σφέας αὐτούς (in the bottom of the ship) μ 225.—ἐ. ἐέργειν, to bound (so that what is bounded is) within the boundary (what is bounded being regarded from the outside) Β 617, 845, Ι 404 (shuts in, holds), Σ 512 (contained), Χ 121 (contains), Ω 544: η 88 (shut in, closed).—(2) With genit.: λιμένος ἐ. Α 432. Cf. Μ 374, 380, Χ 85: ἐ. μεγάρου υ 258. Cf. κ 125, π 324, 352, ψ 190.

ἔντοσθε(ν) [ἐντός + -θεν (2)]. (1) Within, inside: μένουσιν Χ 237. Cf. Κ 262, Μ 296, 455: μ 241, ν 100.—(2) With genit., within, inside, in: ἐ. πόλιος Ζ 364, τείχεος ἐ. Μ 416. Cf. Δ 454: α 126, 128, 380 = β 145, β 424 = ο 289, ι 235, 298, κ 92, ξ 13, 194, ρ 339, σ 238, φ 417, χ 171, 204.

ἐντρέπω [ἐν (5)]. In mid., to turn oneself towards something; hence, to heed, have regard, care: οὐ σοὶ ἐντρέπεται ἦτορ α 60.—To pay heed to, have regard or care for. With genit.: ἀνεψιοῦ Ο 554.

ἐντρέχω [ἐν- (1)]. To move freely, have free play, in something Τ 385.

ἐντροπαλίζομαι [ἐν- (5) + τροπ-, τρέπω]. (μεταtροπαλίζομαι.) To keep turning round towards or to face a person or persons Z 496, Λ 547, P 109.—App., to keep turning or twisting in another's grasp Φ 492.

ἐντύνω [cf. ἐντύω]. Aor. imp. ἔντῡνον I 203. Acc. sing. fem. pple. ἐντῡ́νᾱσαν Ξ 162. 2 sing. aor. subj. mid. ἐντῡ́νεαι ζ 33. 1 pl. -ώμεθα ρ 175. Fem. pple. ἐντῡναμένη μ 18. (ἐπ-.) (1) To make ready, prepare: δέπας I 203.—(2) In mid., to make ready (a meal) for oneself, prepare (a meal): ἐντύνοντ' ἄριστον Ω 124. Cf. γ 33, ο 500, π 2, ρ 175, 182.—(3) To array or deck (oneself): εὖ ἐντύνασαν ἓ αὐτήν Ξ 162.—In mid., to array or deck oneself, make oneself ready: ὄφρ' ἐντύνεαι ζ 33. Cf. μ 18.—(4) To strike up (a song) μ 183.

ἐντυπάς [prob. ἐν (2) + τυπ-, τύπτω. 'Beating oneself into']. Thus, closely, tightly: ἐ. ἐν χλαίνῃ κεκαλυμμένος Ω 163.

ἐντύω [cf. ἐντύνω]. (ἐπ-.) To make ready, prepare: εὐνήν ψ 289.—To get (horses) ready for yoking E 720 = Θ 382.

Ἐνῡάλιος [a name of Ares]. War or battle personified Σ 309.—As epithet of Ares P 211.

ἐνύπνιος [ἐν- (1) + ὕπνος]. In neut. sing. ἐνύπνιον as adv., in one's sleep B 56 := ξ 495.

ἐνῶπα, ἔνωπα, τό [ἐν- (3) + ὦπα. 'The face upon one']. The face in generalized sense: κατ' ἐνῶπα ἰδὼν Δαναῶν (in the face of the . . .) O 320 (see κατά (II) (2) (e)).

ἐνωπαδίως [ἐνῶπα]. In the face: ἐσίδεσκεν ψ 94.

ἐνωπή = ἐνῶπα. In dat. sing. ἐνωπῇ, openly, in the sight of all E 374 = Φ 510.

ἐνώπια, τά [ἐν- (1) + ὦπα. Cf. ὑπώπια, εἰσωπός, ἐνῶπα]. The inner face of walls, inner walls. Of the inner walls of a κλισίη N 261.—App. of one of the wall-spaces on each side of the entrance of the μέγαρον, facing the αὐλή δ 42.—Of a similar space in front of the palace of Zeus Θ 435.—App. of one of the wall-spaces on each side of the entrance of the μέγαρον within χ 121.

ἐνῶρσε, 3 sing. aor. **ἐνῶρτο,** 3 sing. aor. mid. ἐνόρνυμι.

ἐξ. See ἐκ.

ἕξ, *indeclinable* (σϝέξ) [cf. L. *sex*, Eng. *six*]. Six E 641, H 247, Ψ 741, Ω 399: ι 60, μ 90, 110, 246, π 248, ω 497.—Absol.: ἓξ ἐγένοντο E 270. Cf. Ω 604: κ 6, χ 252.

ἐξάγαγε, 3 sing. aor. ἐξάγω.

ἐξαγγέλλω [ἐξ- (1)]. 3 sing. aor. ἐξήγγειλε. To bring forth word: Ἑρμέᾳ E 390.

ἐξαγορεύω [ἐξ (9)]. To declare, tell λ 234.

ἐξάγω [ἐξ- (1)]. 3 sing. aor. ἐξήγαγε E 35. ἐξάγαγε Π 188: υ 21. 2 sing. opt. ἐξαγάγοις T 332. Nom. pl. masc. aor. pple. ἐξαγαγόντες H 336, 435, N 379: χ 441, 458. (1) To lead, bring or conduct forth A 337, Φ 29: θ 106.—Of an immaterial agency: ὄφρα σε μῆτις ἐξάγαγ' ἐξ ἄντροιο υ 21.—Of bringing to the birth Π 188.—To bring or fetch: Σκυρόθεν T 332.—To lead, bring or conduct *out of* or *from*. With genit.: μάχης E 35. Cf. E 353, Λ 487, N 535: ο 465, χ 441, 458, ψ 372.—To bring or fetch *from*. With genit.: Ἄργεος N 379.—(2) To bring or fetch (inanimate objects): τύμβον ἐξαγαγόντες ἄκριτον ἐκ πεδίου H 336, 435 (app., bringing (the materials for) it without selection from . . .).

†**ἐξαείρω** [ἐξ- (1)]. Contr. 3 sing. aor. mid. ἐξήρατο. To win, get, gain, *from*. With genit., in reference to spoil: Τροίης ε 39 = ν 137.—To gain (wages or hire) κ 84.

ἐξάετες [ἕξ + -α- (on the analogy of numerals in -α) + ἔτος]. For six years: παραμίμνων γ 115.

ἐξαίνυμαι [ἐξ- (1)]. (1) To take out (and deposit): νηῒ ἐνὶ πρύμνῃ δῶρα ο 206.—(2) To take away, deprive of: θυμόν E 848.—With double acc. of what is taken and of the person deprived: θυμὸν ἀμφοτέρω E 155. Cf. Υ 459.

ἐξαίρετος, -ον [ἐξαιρέω]. Picked out, chosen, choice: γυναῖκες B 227.—Picked out or selected *from among* (a community). With genit.: [κοῦροι] Ἰθάκης ἐξαίρετοι δ 643.

†**ἐξαιρέω** [ἐξ- (1)]. 3 sing. aor. ἔξελε Ω 229: χ 110, 144. 3 pl. -ον Λ 627, Π 56, Σ 444: η 10, ι 160. **Mid.** Impf. ἐξαιρεύμην ξ 232. Aor. ἐξελόμην I 130, 331. 3 sing. ἐξείλετο B 690, Θ 323, O 460, P 678: λ 201, χ 388. ἐξέλετο Z 234, I 272, K 267, Λ 704, P 470, T 137, Ω 754. 3 pl. ἐξείλοντο π 218. (1) To take out: ἔνθεν πέπλους Ω 229. Cf. χ 110, 144.—(2) To pick out from the spoil as guerdon to a chief: Ἑκαμήδην Λ 627. Cf. Π 56, Σ 444: η 10.—Sim. of a special share of beasts slain in hunting ι 160.—(3) In mid. (a) To take away, effect deprivation of: τέκνα ἐξείλοντο π 218.—With immaterial object: φρένας Z 234, P 470.—With double acc. O 460, P 678.—To take away *from*. With genit.: φρένας μευ ἐξέλετο T 137. Cf. Ω 754: λ 201, χ 388.—To steal K 267.—(b) To take *out of* for use. With genit.: φαρέτρης ὀϊστόν Θ 323.—(c) To pick out or select for oneself from the spoil: κειμήλια ἐξελόμην I 331 (or perh. rather, took from the cities): ἄσπετα πολλά Λ 704. Cf. B 690, I 130, 272.—To pick out or select for oneself *from* (the spoil). With genit.: τῶν ἐξαιρεύμην μενοεικέα ξ 232.

ἐξαίσιος, -ον [ἐξ- (7) + αἴσιος]. (1) Going beyond measure, unreasonable: ἀρήν O 598.—Lawless, violent ρ 577.—(2) Absol. in neut. ἐξαίσιον, something contrary to right, something unfair or arbitrary δ 690.

ἔξαιτος, -ον [perh. ἐξ- (1) + αἰτέω. 'Asked for out of']. Choice, picked M 320: β 307, ε 102, τ 366.

ἐξαίφνης [app. ἐξ- (9). Cf. ἐξαπίνης]. On a sudden, suddenly: πῦρ ὄρμενον ἐ. P 738, Φ 14.

ἐξακέομαι [ἐξ- (9)]. 2 sing. aor. opt. ἐξακέσαιο Δ 36. 3 -αιτο γ 145. (1) To bring remedy or cure I 507.—To appease (wrath) γ 145.—(2) To moderate or depart from (one's wrath) Δ 36.

ἐξαλαόω [ἐξ- (9)]. (1) To blind λ 103 = ν 343.—(2) To take the power of sight from (an eye) ι 453, 504.

†**ἐξαλαπάζω** [ἐξ- (9)]. Fut. infin. ἐξαλαπάξειν N 813. 3 sing. aor. ἐξαλάπαξε E 642. 3 pl. -αν θ 495. 3 sing. subj. ἐξαλαπάξῃ Υ 30. Pple. ἐξαλαπάξας Ξ 251: δ 176. Infin. ἐξαλαπάξαι

A 129, Δ 33, 40, Θ 241, 288: γ 85. (1) To destroy or sack (a city) A 129, Δ 33 = Θ 288, Δ 40, E 642, Θ 241, Ξ 251: γ 85, θ 495.—(2) To deport the population from (a city) δ 176.—(3) To destroy: νῆας N 813, τεῖχος Υ 30.

†ἐξάλλομαι [ἐξ- (1)]. 3 sing. ἐξάλλεται E 142. Aor. pple. ἐξάλμενος O 571, P 342, Ψ 399. (1) To spring forth from the throng O 571.—(2) To spring forth *from*. With genit.: αὐλῆς E 142. Cf. P 342.—(3) To get oneself clear *of* (competitors in a race). With genit.: τῶν ἄλλων Ψ 399.

†ἐξαναβαίνω [ἐξ- (1) + ἀνα- (2)]. Fem. pl. aor. pple. ἐξαναβᾶσαι (*v.l.* εἰσαναβᾶσαι). To go up from something *on to*. With acc.: ἀκτήν Ω 97.

†ἐξαναδύω [ἐξ- (1) + ἀνα- (1)]. Aor. pple. ἐξαναδύς ε 438. Fem. pl. ἐξαναδῦσαι δ 405. To rise up or emerge *from out of*. With genit.: ἁλός δ 405, κύματος ε 438.

ἐξαναλύω [ἐξ- (1) + ἀνα- (6)]. To set free *from* or *from the power of*. With genit.: θανάτοιο Π 442 = X 180.

†ἐξαναφανδόν [ἐξ- (9) + ἀναφανδόν]. Openly, plainly, clearly: ἐρέω τοι υ 48.

†ἐξανίημι [ἐξ- (1) + ἀν-, ἀνα- (1) + ἵημι[1]]. Fem. pple. pl. ἐξανιεῖσαι. To send up and forth, emit in an upward direction: φῦσαι ἀϋτμήν Σ 471.

†ἐξανύω [ἐξ- (9)]. Fut. ἐξανύω Λ 365, Υ 452. 3 sing. aor. ἐξήνυσε Θ 370. (1) To give accomplishment to, bring to pass: Θέτιδος βουλάς Θ 370.—(2) To make an end of, slay Λ 365 = Υ 452.

ἐξαπατάω [ἐξ- (9)]. To trick, cheat, beguile, deal unfairly with I 371, X 299.—Absol., to work deceit, induce a false belief ι 414.—To deal falsely ν 277.

†ἐξαπαφίσκω [ἐξ- (9)]. 3 sing. aor. ἐξήπαφε ξ 379. Subj. ἐξαπάφω ψ 79. 3 sing. aor. opt. mid. ἐξαπάφοιτο I 376, Ξ 160. To trick, cheat, beguile, deceive ξ 379, ψ 79. —In mid. Ξ 160. —Absol. In mid. I 376.

ἐξαπέβησαν, 3 pl. aor. ἐξαποβαίνω.

ἐξαπίνης [app. ἐξ- (9). Cf. ἐξαίφνης]. On a sudden, suddenly, unexpectedly: ἐλθόντ' ἐ. E 91. Cf. I 6, O 325, Π 598, P 57: κ 557, μ 288, ξ 29, 38, φ 196, ω 160.

†ἐξαποβαίνω [ἐξ- (1) + ἀπο- (1)]. 3 pl. aor. ἐξαπέβησαν. To land or disembark *from* (a ship). With genit.: νηός μ 306.

ἐξαποδύνω [ἐξ- (3) + ἀπο- (1)]. To strip off ε 372.

†ἐξαπόλλῡμι [ἐξ- (1) + ἀπ-, ἀπο- (7)]. 3 sing. pf. ἐξαπόλωλε Σ 290: υ 357. 3 pl. aor. opt. mid. ἐξαπολοίατο Z 60. To perish *out of*, disappear *from*. With genit.: πάντες Ἰλίου Z 60. Cf. Σ 290: υ 357.

ἐξαπονίζω [ἐξ- (1) + ἀπο- (7)]. To wash with water *from* (a vessel). With genit.: λέβητα, τοῦ πόδας ἐξαπένιζεν τ 387.

ἐξαποτίνω [ἐξ- (9) + ἀπο- (5)]. To pay the full price in respect of, suffer the consequences of Φ 412.

ἐξάπτω [ἐξ- (4)]. Aor. pple. ἐξάψας χ 466. (1) To fasten from (*i.e.* to) something indicated X 397.—(2) To fasten *from* (*i.e. to*). With genit.: Ἕκτορα ἵππων Ω 51. Cf. χ 466.—(3) In mid., to fasten oneself to something; hence, to lay hold Θ 20.

†ἐξαρπάζω [ἐξ- (1)]. 3 sing. aor. ἐξήρπαξε Γ 380, Υ 443, Φ 597. Fem. pple. ἐξαρπάξᾶσα μ 100. (1) To snatch away Γ 380, Υ 443, Φ 597.—(2) To snatch *out of*. With genit.: νεός μ 100.

ἔξαρχος, -ου, ὁ [ἐξάρχω]. A leader: θρήνων Ω 721.

ἐξάρχω [ἐξ- (9)]. (1) To take the lead in, give a lead in, begin. With genit.: γόοιο Σ 51, 316 = Ψ 17, X 430, Ω 747, 761, μολπῆς Σ 606: = δ 19.—So in mid. μ 339.—(2) To take the lead in giving (counsel): βουλὰς ἐξάρχων B 273.

ἐξαυδάω [ἐξ- (8)]. To speak out: ἐξαύδα, μὴ κεῦθε A 363 = Π 19, Σ 74.

ἐξαῦτις [ἐξ- (9) + αὖτις]. (1) In the reverse direction, back, back again: ἰών E 134, N 642.—In a direction contrary to one's proper direction, back: ἀναρπάξασα θύελλα ε 419. Cf. Π 654.—(2) Back to a former state or condition, again. With αὖτε: αὖτ' ἐ. ἀνέστη O 287.—(3) Again, once more: μαχέσασθαι Γ 433. Cf. A 223, N 531: δ 213, 234, μ 122, π 193, τ 214, φ 206, ω 350.—Of repetition of action in a similar form: ἐ. μείζονα λᾶαν ἀείρας ι 537.

†ἐξαφαιρέω [ἐξ- (1) + ἀφ-, ἀπο- (1)]. 2 pl. aor. subj. mid. ἐξαφέλησθε. To take away *from*. In mid. With genit.: πασέων ψυχάς χ 444.

ἐξαφύω [ἐξ- (9) + ἀφύω = ἀφύσσω]. To draw off (wine): οἶνον ἐξαφύοντες ξ 95.

ἐξάψας, aor. pple. ἐξάπτω.

ἐξεγένοντο, 3 pl. aor. ἐκγίγνομαι.

ἐξέθορε, 3 sing. aor. ἐκθρῴσκω.

†ἐξείδω [ἐξ- (1)]. 3 sing. aor. ἔξιδεν. To look forth, stare Υ 342.

ἑξείης [ἐξ-, ἔχω]. Also **ἑξῆς** δ 449, 580, ι 104, 180, 472, 564, μ 147. (1) In an indicated order, in a row or rows: ἵσταντο Ψ 839: ἀρηρότες β 342. Cf. α 145, δ 408, 580, ζ 94, ι 8, τ 574, χ 471, etc.—In a circle A 448.—In parallel lines ε 70.—In regular turns or convolutions: ἑξείης κατέδησαν [ζυγόδεσμον] Ω 274.—(2) In sequence, one after another: εὔχεσθαι πάσας ἑξείης Z 241. Cf. O 137, X 240: λ 134, μ 177, ρ 450, φ 141, ψ 281.

ἐξείλετο, 3 sing. aor. mid. ἐξαιρέω.

†ἔξειμι [ἐξ- (1) + εἶμι]. 1 sing. pres. ἔξειμι υ 367. 2 ἔξεισθα υ 179. Imp. pl. ἔξιτε β 139. Infin. ἐξιέναι Σ 448: α 374. ἐξίμεναι λ 531 (*v.l.* ἐξέμεναι). (1) To go forth Σ 448: λ 531.—(2) To go forth *from*. With genit.: μεγάρων α 374, β 139.—(3) In pres. with fut. sense, to go forth υ 179, 367.

ἐξείνισσα, aor. ξεινίζω.

ἐξεῖπον, *aor.* [ἐξ- (8)]. (1) To speak out, say one's say I 61.—(2) To make a disclosure, tell a thing Ω 654: ο 443.

ἐξείρομαι [ἐξ- (9)]. From ἐξερέω 3 pl. ἐξερέουσι ξ 375. 3 sing. subj. ἐξερέῃσι δ 337, ρ 128. 2 sing. opt. ἐξερέοις γ 116. Fem. pple. ἐξερέουσα τ 166. Pl. masc. -οντες κ 249. In mid. form 3 sing. subj. ἐξερέηται α 416. 3 sing. opt. ἐξερέοιτο δ 119, η 17, ω 238. Infin. ἐξερέεσθαι γ 24, ν 411, τ 99.

(1) To ask, inquire, make inquiry. With indirect question: ὅτις εἴη η 17.—(2) To ask or inquire about: Διὸς βουλήν Υ 15. Cf. γ 116, ν 127, 411, ξ 375, τ 166.—(3) To question (a person): Ζῆνα Ε 756. Cf. Ω 361: γ 24, δ 119 = ω 238, κ 249, τ 99.—(4) With double acc. of person questioned and of what is inquired about: θεοπροπίης ἤν τινα θεοπρόπον ἐξερέηται α 416.—(5) To go through in questing, traverse: κνημούς δ 337 = ρ 128.

ἐξείρυσε, ἐξείρυσσαν, 3 sing. and pl. aor. ἐξερύω.

†**ἐξείρω** [ἐξ- (8) + εἴρω[2]]. Fut. ἐξερέω. (1) To speak out, speak, say Α 212 = Θ 401 = Ψ 672, Θ 286, 454, Μ 215, Ψ 410: = π 440 = τ 487, φ 337. —(2) To give information asked for, tell ι 365.

ἔξεισθα, 2 sing. pres. ἔξειμι.

ἐξεκέχυντο, 3 pl. plupf. pass. ἐκχέω.

ἐξέκλεψε, 3 sing. aor. ἐκκλέπτω.

ἐξεκυλίσθη, 3 sing. aor. pass. ἐκκυλίνδω.

ἐξελάαν, fut. infin. ἐξελαύνω.

ἐξελάθοντο, 3 pl. aor. mid. ἐκλανθάνω.

†**ἐξελαύνω** [ἐξ- (1)]. In pres. only in pple. in form ἐξελάων κ 83. 3 sing. impf. ἐξήλαυνε Κ 499. Fut. infin. ἐξελάαν Θ 527: λ 292. 3 sing. aor. ἐξήλασε ι 312. ἐξέλασε Ε 324, Λ 360, Ν 401. 3 pl. ἐξήλασσαν Λ 562. 3 pl. subj. ἐξελάσωσι π 381. Opt.. ἐξελάσαιμι σ 29. 3 sing. -ειε Φ 360. Pple. ἐξελάσας, -αντος Ε 25: ι 227. Infin. ἐξελάσαι Θ 255, Ο 417: β 248. (1) To drive a flock or herd out to pasture κ 83.—To drive or scare (a domestic animal) off or away: [ὄνον] Λ 562.—To drive or conduct (such animals) *out of.* With genit.: ἄντρου μῆλα ι 312.—(2) In reference to persons, to drive or chase away, expel Θ 527.—To drive *out of,* expel *from.* With genit.: ἄστεος Φ 360. Cf. β 248.—To drive out or banish *from.* With genit.: γαίης ἡμετέρης π 381.—To drive or force from a position taken up Ο 417.—(3) To drive off (cattle) as spoil λ 292.—To drive (animals) as spoil *from.* With genit.: ἐρίφους σηκῶν ι 227.—To drive off (captured horses) Ε 25.—To drive off (such horses) *from.* With genit.: Τρώων Ε 324 = Ν 401. Cf. Κ 499.—(4) Absol., to drive one's chariot off Λ 360.—To drive one's chariot *beyond the line of.* With genit.: τάφρου Θ 255.—(5) To knock *out of.* With genit.: ὀδόντας κε γναθμῶν ἐξελάσαιμι σ 29.

ἔξελε, 3 sing. aor. ἐξαιρέω.

ἐξελθεῖν, aor. infin. ἐξέρχομαι.

ἐξέλκω [ἐξ- (1)]. (1) To draw out Δ 214.—(2) To draw or drag *out of.* With genit.: πουλύποδος θαλάμης ἐξελκομένοιο ε 432.—(3) To pull in a specified direction: πηνίον ἐξέλκουσα παρὲκ μίτον Ψ 762.

ἔξελον, 3 pl. aor. ἐξαιρέω.

ἐξελύθη, 3 sing. aor. pass. ἐκλύω.

ἐξέμεναι, ἐξέμεν, aor. infin. ἐξίημι.

†**ἐξεμέω** [ἐξ- (1) + ἐμέω]. 3 sing. aor. opt. ἐξεμέσειε. To disgorge, throw up. Of Charybdis: ἱστόν μ 437.—To vomit forth or throw up waters. Of the same μ 237.

ἐξεναρίζω [ἐξ- (9)]. 3 sing. fut. ἐξεναρίξει Υ 339. Pple. ἐξεναρίζων Λ 101. Aor. ἐξενάριξα Ω 521. 2 sing. -ας Π 692. 3 -ε Δ 488, Η 146, Ξ 513, Χ 376, etc. 3 pl. -αν Ε 703. 2 sing. subj. ἐξεναρίξῃς Υ 181. Pple. ἐξεναρίξας Π 573: λ 273. Infin. ἐξεναρίξαι χ 264. (1) To strip (a slain foe) of his armour and trappings: Περίφαντα Ε 842. Cf. Ζ 417, Λ 246, 368, Χ 376.—(2) To strip off (the armour and trappings): τεύχεα Η 146, Ν 619 = Ρ 537 = Φ 183.—(3) To kill or slay in fight Δ 488, Ε 151, Ζ 20, Λ 101, Μ 187, etc.: χ 264.—(4) To kill or slay in gen. Π 573: λ 273.

ἐξεπέρησε, 3 sing. aor. ἐκπεράω.

ἐξεπράθομεν, 1 pl. aor. ἐκπέρθω.

ἐξέπτυσε, 3 sing. aor. ἐκπτύω.

ἐξερεείνω [ἐξ- (9)]. (1) To ask, inquire, make inquiry Ι 672, Κ 543.—(2) To inquire about κ 14, μ 34, ρ 70, τ 116, 463.—(3) To question (a person) ψ 86.—In mid. Κ 81.—(4) To go through, traverse: πόρους ἁλός μ 259.

†**ἐξερείπω** [ἐξ- (1) (9)]. 3 sing. aor. subj. ἐξερίπῃ Ξ 414. Fem. pple. ἐξεριποῦσα Ρ 440, Τ 406. (1) To fall: ὅτ' ἐξερίπῃ δρῦς Ξ 414.—(2) To stream down *from.* With genit.: χαίτη ζεύγλης ἐξεριποῦσα Ρ 440, Τ 406.

ἐξερέω[1], fut. ἐξείρω.

ἐξερέω[2], ἐξερέομαι. See ἐξείρομαι.

ἐξερίπῃ, 3 sing. aor. subj. ἐξερείπω.

ἐξέρρηξε, 3 sing. aor. ἐκρήγνυμι.

†**ἐξερύω** [ἐξ- (1) + ἐρύω[1]]. 3 sing. opt. ἐξερύοι Κ 505. 3 sing. aor. ἐξείρυσε Ψ 870. ἐξέρυσε Ε 112, Ν 532, Π 505, Υ 323: ι 397. 3 pl. ἐξείρυσσαν Ν 194. ἐξέρυσαν χ 386, 476. Pple. ἐξερύσας σ 87. Infin. ἐξερύσαι Ε 666. 3 sing. pa. iterative ἐξερύσασκε Κ 490. (1) To draw or pull out Π 505. —To pull out or away in way of mutilation: μήδεα σ 87, χ 476.—(2) With genit., to draw or pull *out of*: βέλος ὤμου Ε 112. Cf. Ε 666, Ν 532, Υ 323: ι 397.—To snatch *out of*: χειρὸς τόξον Ψ 870.—(3) To drag, haul or pull out or away: δίφρον ῥυμοῦ (by the pole) Κ 505: ἰχθύας δικτύῳ χ 386. Cf. Κ 490.—To drag or haul out of the power of the enemy: νεκρούς Ν 194.

†**ἐξέρχομαι** [ἐξ- (1)]. Aor. ἐξῆλθον Ι 476. 3 sing. -ε υ 371. 1 pl. subj. ἐξέλθωμεν θ 100. Imp. ἔξελθε τ 68. Pple. ἐξελθών, -όντος Χ 417: δ 740, ο 396, φ 90, 229, χ 375, ω 491. Fem. -οῦσα κ 230, 256, 312. Infin. ἐξελθέμεναι δ 283. ἐξελθεῖν Ι 576, Χ 237, 413. (1) To go or issue forth or out: νῦν ἐξέλθωμεν θ 100. Cf. δ 283, ο 396, τ 68, φ 90, ω 491.—(2) To go or issue forth *from.* With genit.: πυλάων Χ 413. Cf. Χ 417: υ 371, χ 375. —(3) To come or issue forth or out: θύρας ῥήξας ἐξῆλθον Ι 476. Cf. Ι 576: δ 740 (quitting his retirement), κ 230 = 256 = 312.—(4) To come or issue forth *from.* With genit.: τείχεος Χ 237: μεγάροιο φ 229.

ἐξερωέω [ἐξ- (1) + ἐρωέω[2]]. To swerve from the course: αἱ δ' ἐξηρώησαν Ψ 468.

ἐξεσάωσε, 3 sing. aor. ἐκσαόω.

ἐξεσίη, -ης, ἡ [ἐξίημι. 'A sending forth']. An embassy or mission: ἐξεσίην ἐλθόντι (ἦλθεν) (on an . . .) Ω 235: φ 20.

ἐξέσπασε, 3 sing. aor. ἐκσπάω.

ἐξέσσυτο, 3 sing. aor. mid. ἐκσεύω.

ἐξέστρεψε, 3 sing. aor. ἐκστρέφω.

ἐξέταμε, 3 sing. aor. ἐκτάμνω.

ἐξετανύσθη, 3 sing. aor. pass. ἐκτανύω.

ἐξετάνυσσε, 3 sing. aor. ἐκτανύω.

ἐξετέλειον, 3 pl. impf. See ἐκτελέω.

ἐξετέλεσσα, 1 sing. aor. ἐκτελέω.

ἐξετελεῦντο, 3 pl. impf. pass. ἐκτελέω.

ἐξέτης [ἕξ + ἔτος]. Six years old Ψ 266, 655.

ἐξέτι [ἐξ strengthened by ἔτι. Cf. ἔτι (7)]. Even from the time of. With genit. : ἐ. πατρῶν θ 245.

†**ἐξευρίσκω** [ἐξ- (9)]. 3 sing. aor. opt. ἐξεύροι. To find, discover : εἴ ποθεν ἐξεύροι [ἄνδρα] Σ 322.

ἐξεφαάνθη, ἐξεφάνη, 3 sing. aor. pass. ἐκφαίνω.

ἐξέφθιτο, 3 sing. plupf. pass. ἐκφθίω.

ἐξέφυγον, 3 pl. aor. ἐκφεύγω.

ἐξέχυτο, 3 sing. aor. pass. ἐκχέω.

ἐξήγαγε, 3 sing. aor. ἐξάγω.

ἐξήγγειλε, 3 sing. aor. ἐξαγγέλλω.

ἐξηγέομαι [ἐξ- (1)]. To lead forth to battle. With genit. : τῶν ἐξηγείσθω Β 806.

ἐξήκοντα, *indeclinable* [ἕξ]. Sixty Β 587, 610. —With another numeral : τριηκόσιοί τε καὶ ἐ. ξ 20.

ἐξήλασε, 3 sing. **ἐξήλασσαν,** 3 pl. aor. ἐξελαύνω.

ἐξήλατος, -ον [ἐξ- (6)]. Formed by hammering out : ἀσπίδα Μ 295.

ἐξῆλθον, aor. ἐξέρχομαι.

ἐξῆμαρ [ἕξ + ἦμαρ]. For or during six days : πλέομεν κ 80 = ο 476, δαίνυντο μ 397 = ξ 249.

ἐξημοιβός [ἐξ- (9) + ἀμείβω]. Serving for a change : εἵματ' ἐξημοιβά (changes of raiment) θ 249.

ἐξήνυσε, 3 sing. aor. ἐξανύω.

ἐξήπαφε, 3 sing. aor. ἐξαπαφίσκω.

ἐξηράνθη, 3 sing. aor. pass. ξηραίνω.

ἐξήρατο, 3 sing. aor. mid. ἐξαείρω.

ἐξήρπαξε, 3 sing. aor. ἐξαρπάζω.

ἐξῆς. See ἑξείης.

ἔξιδεν, 3 sing. aor. ἐξείδω.

ἐξιέναι, infin. ἔξειμι.

†**ἐξίημι** [ἐξ- (1) + ἵημι[1]]. Aor. infin. ἐξέμεναι λ 531 (*v.l.* ἐξίμεναι). ἐξέμεν Λ 141. To send forth, allow to go forth : ἂψ ἐς Ἀχαιούς Λ 141 : ἱππόθεν λ 531.

ἐξῑθύνω [ἐξ- (9)]. To serve as a means of making straight : στάθμη δόρυ νήϊον ἐξιθύνει Ο 410.

†**ἐξικνέομαι** [ἐξ- (9)]. Aor. ἐξῑκόμην Ι 479 : ν 206, υ 223. 3 sing. ἐξῑκετο Θ 439, Ω 481 : μ 166. To arrive at, reach : Φθίην Ι 479, ἄλλων δῆμον (*i.e.* flies to . . ., takes refuge in . . .) Ω 481. Cf. Θ 439 : νῆσον μ 166, ἄλλον βασιλήων (*i.e.* betaken myself to . . .) ν 206, υ 223.

ἐξίμεναι, infin. ἔξειμι.

ἐξίσχω [ἐξ- (1)]. To hold or keep outside : ἔξω ἐξίσχει κεφαλὰς βερέθρου μ 94.

ἔξιτε, imp. pl. ἔξειμι.

ἐξοίσουσι, 3 pl. fut. ἐκφέρω.

†**ἐξοιχνέω** [ἐξ- (1)]. 3 pl. ἐξοιχνεῦσι. To go forth : σὺν ἵπποισιν καὶ ὄχεσφιν Ι 384.

ἐξοίχομαι [ἐξ- (1)]. To have gone forth : ἐς Ἀθηναίης Ζ 379, 384.

†**ἐξόλλῡμι** [ἐξ- (9)]. 3 sing. aor. opt. ἐξολέσειε. To destroy : τοὺς Ζεὺς ἐξολέσειεν ρ 597.

†**ἐξονομαίνω** [ἐξ- (9)]. 2 sing. aor. subj. ἐξονομήνῃς Γ 166. Infin. ἐξονομῆναι ζ 66. (**1**) To tell the name of : τόνδ' ἄνδρα Γ 166.—(**2**) To speak of, mention : γάμον ζ 66.

ἐξονομακλήδην [ἐξ- (9) + ὄνομα + κλη-, καλέω (cf. ὀνομακλήδην)]. By name μ 250.

ἐξόπιθε(ν) [ἐξ- (9) + ὄπιθε(ν)]. (**1**) Behind, behind one Π 611 = Ρ 527. — Behind, in rear : πεζοὺς στῆσεν Δ 298.—(**2**) With genit., behind : κεράων βοὸς Ρ 521.

ἐξοπίσω [ἐξ- (9) + ὀπίσω]. (**1**) Backwards, back Λ 461, Ν 436, Ρ 108, 357.—Falling or sinking down backwards : ἤριπε Χ 467. Cf. Ξ 438, Ψ 727.—(**2**) In after time, in time to come δ 35, ν 144.

ἐξορμάω [ἐξ- (1)]. Of a ship, to sheer off from her course : κεῖσ' ἐξορμήσασα μ 221.

ἐξοφέλλω [ἐξ- (9) + ὀφέλλω[2]]. To increase or add to (something offered) : ἐξώφελλεν ἔεδνα ο 18.

ἔξοχος, -ον [ἐξ- (5) + ὀχ-, ἔχω in intrans. sense. See ἔχω (II). 'Standing out']. (**1**) Distinguished beyond others in respect of some quality, pre-eminent Β 188, Μ 269.—With genit. : ἐ. Ἀργείων κεφαλήν (standing above them by . . .) Γ 227, ἐ. αὐτῶν (among, beyond them) Ξ 118. Cf. Σ 56 = 437 : σ 205.—So with dat. : ἡρώεσσιν Β 483. — Of superior excellence, pre-eminently fine, good or splendid : δώματα ο 227.—With genit. as above : βοῦς ἐ. πάντων Β 480. Cf. Ζ 194, Υ 184.—So with dat. : αἶγας αἳ πᾶσιν ἔξοχοι αἰπολίοισιν φ 266.—(**2**) In neut. ἔξοχον as adv., beyond. With genit. : ἐτίομεν ἐ. ἄλλων Ι 631, προμάχεσθαι ἐ. ἄλλων (advancing beyond . . .) Ρ 358. Cf. Ι 641, Ν 499 : δ 171, ε 118, ζ 158, τ 247.—(**3**) In neut. pl. ἔξοχα, especially, in a high degree, greatly, by far : ἐ. μιν ἐφίλατο Ε 61, ἐ. ἀρίστας Ι 638. Cf. Υ 158 : δ 629 = φ 187, λ 432, ο 70, 71, χ 244.—Sim. : δόσαν ἐ. (as a special meed of honour) ι 551.—Beyond. With genit. : ἔμ' ἐ. πάντων ζήτει Ξ 257. Cf. Ω 113, 134 : θ 487, ω 78.

†**ἐξυπανίστημι** [ἐξ- (1) + ὑπ-, ὑπο- (1) + ἀν-, ἀνα- (1)]. 3 sing. aor. ἐξυπανέστη. To start up *from under*. With genit. : σμῶδιξ μεταφρένου Β 267.

ἔξω [ἐξ]. (**1**) In an outward direction, out : ἴσαν Ω 247. Cf. ξ 526, ψ 138.—With genit., out of, from : μεγάροιο χ 378. Cf. Κ 94, Λ 457. —(**2**) Outside : σχέθον νῆα κ 95. Cf. Ρ 265.— With genit., outside of : βερέθρου μ 94.

ἕξω, fut. ἔχω.

ἕο, ἑό, ἑοῖ. See ἑέ.

ἔοι, 3 sing. opt. εἰμί.

ἔοικα, pf. εἴκω[1].

ἔολπα, pf. ἔλπω.

ἔοργε, 3 sing. pf. ἔρδω.

ἑορτή, ἡ. A high-day or feast : ἐ. τοῖο θεοῖο (*i.e.* Apollo) φ 258. Cf. υ 156.

ἑός, -ή, -όν, **ὅς,** ἥ, ὅν [ἑέ]. Instrumental fem. ἧφι Χ 107 : φ 315. (**1**) His (**a**) ἑός Α 83, 496, 533, Β 662, Η 190, Ι 148, etc. : α 216, 218, β 195, δ 338, θ 524, λ 282, etc.—With the article : τοὺς ἑοὺς ἵππους E 321.—Absol. with the article K 256, Ψ 295.—(b) ὅς A 72, 307, 333, 609, B 832, Γ 333, etc.: α 4, 5, 117, 240, 269, 330, etc.—Absol. Δ 428.—With the article: τὰ ἃ κῆλα M 280. Cf. O 58, etc.: ι 250, λ 515, etc.—Absol. with the article Θ 430, P 193.—(2) App. of the first person: οὔ τοι ἐγώ γε ἧς γαίης δύναμαι γλυκερώτερον ἄλλο ἰδέσθαι ι 28. Cf. ν 320.—Perh. also θάρσεϊ ᾧ H 153.

ἐπαγάλλομαι [ἐπ-, ἐπί- (4)]. To exult *in*, take delight *in*. With dat.: πολέμῳ Π 91.

†**ἐπαγγέλλω** [ἐπ-, ἐπι- (5)]. 3 sing. aor. subj. ἐπαγγείλῃσι. To tell about something, give information: εἴσω δ 775.

ἐπαγείρω [ἐπ-, ἐπι- (14)]. To go about collecting: λαοὺς οὐκ ἐπέοικε ταῦτ' ἐπαγείρειν A 126 (prob. with double acc. like ἀφαιρέω (2) (c)).

ἐπάγη, 3 sing. aor. pass. πήγνυμι.

†**ἐπαγλαΐζομαι** [ἐπ-, ἐπι- (4)]. Fut. infin. ἐπαγλαϊεῖσθαι. To exult in something Σ 133.

ἐπάγω [ἐπ-, ἐπι- (17)]. Aor. ἐπήγαγον ξ 392. (1) Of hunters and their dogs, to drive on the game: ὡς ἐπάγοντες ἐπῆσαν τ 445.—(2) To bring into an indicated state of mind, induce to believe something ξ 392.

†**ἐπαείρω** (ἐπ-, ἐπι- (4) (12)]. 3 pl. aor. ἐπάειραν H 426. Pple. ἐπαείρας I 214, K 80. (1) To raise: κεφαλήν K 80.—(2) To lift and place *upon*. With genit.: [νεκροὺς] ἁμαξάων H 426. Cf. I 214.

ἔπαθον, aor. πάσχω.

ἐπαιγίζω [ἐπ-, ἐπι- (17) + αἰγίς in sense 'hurricane-wind']. Of a wind, to rush onwards B 148: ο 293.

ἐπαινέω [ἐπ-, ἐπι- (5)]. (1) To express approval *to*, to agree or concur *with* (a person). With dat.: οὔ τοι ἐπαινέομεν Δ 29 = Π 443 = X 181. Cf. Σ 312.—To express approval of: μῦθον ἐπαινήσαντες Ὀδυσσῆος B 335.—(2) Absol., to approve, assent, concur Δ 380, H 344 = I 710, Φ 290, Ψ 539, 540: δ 673 = η 226 = θ 398 = ν 47, σ 66.

ἐπαινός, -ή [ἐπ-, ἐπι- (19) + αἰνός]. Dread, dire, terrible. Epithet of Persephoneia I 457, 569: κ 491 = 564, κ 534 = λ 47.

ἐπᾱΐσσω [ἐπ-, ἐπι- (11) (14)]. Aor. ἐπήϊξα κ 322. 3 pl. ἐπήϊξαν Ψ 817: χ 271. Pple. ἐπᾱΐξας, -αντος B 146, K 345, N 546, P 293, etc.: χ 187. Infin. ἐπᾱΐξαι E 263, H 240, M 308, N 513: κ 295. 3 sing. pa. iterative ἐπᾱΐξασκε P 462, Σ 159. Aor. infin. mid. ἐπᾱΐξασθαι Ψ 773. (1) To make a rush *for*. With genit.: Αἰνείαο ἵππων E 263, νεῶν N 687.—(2) To rush *at* (in hostile sense). With dat.: Ἕκτορι προτὶ Ἴλιον (till he drove him even to . . .) Ψ 64: Κίρκῃ κ 295, 322, μοι ξ 281.—(3) With acc., to rush *at* (in hostile sense): νῶϊ E 235, τεῖχος M 308.—To rush through, charge: μόθον ἵππων H 240.—To make a rush for: Αἰνείαο ἵππους E 323.—In mid.: ἐπαΐξασθαι ἄεθλον Ψ 773.—(4) Absol., to rush upon or towards a foe: δουρὶ ἐπαΐσσων K 369 = Λ 361. Cf. Γ 369, E 98, 584, K 345, 348, M 191, N 546, P 293, 462, Σ 159, Ψ 817: χ 187, 271.—So ἐπαΐξαι μεθ' ἑὸν βέλος N 513.—Of a hawk swooping on its prey X 142.—Of a rushing wind B 146.—(5) Absol., of limbs, to have their movements, dart forth. In mid.: χεῖρες ὤμων ἐπαΐσσονται (from the . . .) Ψ 628 (*v.l.* ἀπαΐσσονται).

ἐπαιτέω [ἐπ-, ἐπι- (6)]. To ask for besides or in addition: εἴ κ' ἄλλο ἐπαιτήσειας Ψ 593.

ἐπαίτιος [ἐπ-, ἐπι- (19) + αἴτιος]. Blameworthy, to blame: οὔ τί μοι ὔμμες ἐπαίτιοι A 335.

ἐπακούω [ἐπ-, ἐπι- (5)]. (1) To hear: πάντα Γ 277. Cf. Υ 250: λ 109 = μ 323.—With genit.: βουλῆς B 143.—(2) To hear about, learn: Διὸς βουλήν ξ 328 = τ 297.—With dependent clause: ὅττι μιν ἵκετο πένθος Σ 63.—(3) To listen to, hearken to, give ear to: ἔπος I 100. Cf. ρ 584, ω 262.—With genit. of the person to whose words one hearkens: ὄφρ' ἔπος ἐπακούσῃ ἐμέθεν τ 98.

ἐπακτήρ, -ῆρος, ὁ [ἐπακ-, ἐπάγω]. A hunter: ἄνδρες ἐπακτῆρες P 135. Cf. τ 435.

†**ἐπαλάομαι** [ἐπ-, ἐπι- (14)]. 3 sing. aor. subj. ἐπαληθῇ ο 401. Pple. ἐπαληθείς δ 81, 83, ο 176. To wander or rove *over* or *among*. With acc.: Κύπρον καὶ Αἰγυπτίους δ 83. Cf. δ 81, ο 176, 401.

ἐπαλαστέω [ἐπ-, ἐπι- (5)]. To find things intolerable: τὸν ἐπαλαστήσασα προσηύδα (breaking out) α 252.

†**ἐπαλέξω** [ἐπ-, ἐπι- (5)]. Fut. pple. ἐπαλεξήσων Λ 428. Acc. sing. fem. pple. ἐπαλεξήσουσαν Θ 365. To succour, aid, protect. With dat.: τῷ Θ 365, Λ 428.

†**ἐπαλλάσσω** [ἐπ-, ἐπι- (13) + ἀλλάσσω, to change]. Nom. pl. masc. aor. pple. ἐπαλλάξαντες. Fig., to pass and repass (a rope) over the two parties in a strife so as to knit them inseparably together N 359.

ἐπάλμενος, aor. pple. ἐφάλλομαι.

ἔπαλξις, ἡ [ἐπαλέξω]. Dat. pl. ἐπάλξεσι X 3. App., a breastwork of planks M 258, 263, 308, 375, 381, 397, 406, 424, 430, X 3.

ἐπᾶλτο, 3 sing. aor. ἐφάλλομαι.

ἐπαμάω [ἐπ-, ἐπι- (5) + ἀμάω²]. To collect, get together. In mid.: εὐνὴν ἐπαμήσατο ε 482.

ἐπαμείβω [ἐπ-, ἐπι- (5) (13)]. 1 pl. aor. subj. ἐπαμείψομεν Z 230. (1) To change (things) with another. With dat.: τεύχε' ἀλλήλοις Z 230.—(2) In mid., to pass or shift *over*. With acc.: νίκη ἐπαμείβεται ἄνδρας (goes now to one now to another) Z 339.

ἐπαμοιβαδίς [ἐπαμοιβα-, ἐπαμείβω. Cf. ἐπημοιβός]. Crossing, interlaced with. With dat.: ἀλλήλοισιν ε 481.

ἐπαμύντωρ, -ορος, ὁ [ἐπαμύνω]. A protector or helper: τῷ ἦλθ' ἐ. N 384. Cf. π 263.

ἐπαμύνω [ἐπ-, ἐπι- (5)]. Aor. subj. ἐπαμύνω Z 361, M 369. 1 pl. -ομεν N 465. Imp. ἐπάμῡνον E 685, Σ 171. Infin. ἐπαμῦναι Σ 99. To defend, protect, succour, fight for, come to the rescue of. With dat.: ἑταίρῳ Σ 99. Cf. Z 361, Θ 414, M 369, N 465, Ξ 357, Σ 171.—Absol. E 685, Π 540, Φ 311, 333.

†**ἐπανατίθημι** [ἐπ-, ἐπι- (18) + ἀνα- (4)]. Aor.

infin. ἐπανθέμεναι. To close (a gate): σανίδας Φ 535.

ἐπανέστησαν, 3 pl. aor. ἐπανίστημι.

†**ἐπανήνοθε** [ἐπ-, ἐπι- (1)]. (Cf. ἐπενήνοθε.) In θ 365 3 sing. pf. Elsewhere 3 sing. plupf. (with secondary person-ending). (1) To be on the surface of something, show itself or be on something B 219, K 134.—(2) To be *on the surface of*, cover. With acc.: οἷα θεοὺς ἐπανήνοθεν θ 365.

†**ἐπανίστημι** [ἐπ-, ἐπι- (4) + ἀν-, ἀνα- (1)]. 3 pl. aor. ἐπανέστησαν. To stand or rise up at one's bidding B 85.

ἐπαοιδή, -ῆς, ἡ [ἐπ-, ἐπι- (5) + ἀοιδή]. An incantation or charm: ἐπαοιδῇ αἷμ' ἔσχεθον τ 457.

ἐπαπειλέω [ἐπ-, ἐπι- (5)]. To threaten, menace. With dat.: ἐπαπειλήσας Ἑλένῳ (with a threatening word or gesture directed to . . .) N 582.—With infin.: ὡς ἐπηπείλησεν, μὴ πρὶν ἀπονέεσθαι, πρὶν . . . Ξ 45.—To threaten with. With acc. of what is threatened and dat. of the person: ἔριδος, τὴν ἐπηπείλησ' Ἀχιλῆϊ A 319.—So with cognate acc.: ἀπειλάων, τὰς Ὀδυσῆϊ ἐπηπείλησεν ν 127.

†**ἐπαραρίσκω** [ἐπ-, ἐπι- (3)]. 3 sing. aor. ἐπῆρσε Ξ 167, 339. 3 sing. plupf. ἐπαρήρει M 456. (1) To fit *to*, to (construct and) attach *to*. With dat.: θύρας σταθμοῖσιν Ξ 167 = 339.—(2) Intrans. in plupf., to be fitted on, be upon, something: μία κληῒς ἐπαρήρει M 456.

ἐπᾱρή, -ῆς, ἡ [ἐπ-, ἐπι- (5) + ἀρή¹]. An imprecation: θεοὶ ἐτέλειον ἐπαράς I 456.

ἐπαρήγω [ἐπ-, ἐπι- (5)] To help, aid, succour. With dat.: Ὀδυσῆϊ Ψ 783. Cf. Ω 39: ν 391.

ἐπαρήρει, 3 sing. plupf. ἐπαραρίσκω.

†**ἐπαρκέω** [ἐπ-, ἐπι- (5)]. 3 sing. aor. ἐπήρκεσε. To ward off, afford protection against ρ 568.—With dat. of person protected: ὄλεθρόν οἱ B 873.

ἐπάρουρος [ἐπ-, ἐπι- (1) + ἄρουρα]. Of a hired labourer, app. attached in some way to a particular piece of land or estate λ 489.

ἐπαρτής [ἐπ-, ἐπι- (5) + ἀρ-, ἀραρίσκω]. Equipped, ready θ 151, ξ 332 = τ 289.

ἐπαρτύω [ἐπ-, ἐπι- (3)]. To fit or fix on θ 447.

†**ἐπάρχω** [ἐπ-, ἐπι- (14)]. 3 sing. aor. imp. mid. ἐπαρξάσθω σ 418, φ 263. Pple. ἐπαρξάμενος, -ου A 471, I 176: γ 340, η 183, φ 272. In mid., as a word of ritual, to go round a company and pour a few drops taken from the κρητήρ (into the drinking-cups) to be poured out as a libation before the cups were filled for drinking: ἐπαρξάμενοι δεπάεσσιν (locatival dat.) A 471 = I 176: = γ 340 = φ 272. Cf. η 183, σ 418, φ 263.

ἐπαρωγός, ὁ [ἐπ-, ἐπι- (5) + ἀρωγός]. A protector, helper, aider λ 498.

ἐπασκέω [ἐπ-, ἐπι- (19)]. To finish off or complete (with something): ἐπήσκηται τοίχῳ ρ 266.

ἐπασσάμεθα, 1 pl. aor. πατέομαι.

ἐπασσύτερος, -η, -ον [in form a comp. Prob. fr. *ἐπασσύ(ς) (for *ἐπανσσύς, fr. ἐπ-, ἐπι- (7) + ἀν-, ἀνα- (6) + συ-, σεύω). 'Pressing on after.' Cf. πανσυδίῃ]. Thus, following one another in quick succession: θνῆσκον ἐπασσύτεροι A 383. Cf. Δ 423, 427, Θ 277 = M 194 = Π 418: π 366 (relieving each other at short intervals).

ἔπαυλος, -ου, ὁ [ἐπ' αὐλῇ]. A fold for sheep, etc. ψ 358.

†**ἐπαυρίσκω** [ἐπ-, ἐπι- (5) + *αὐρίσκω]. 2 sing. aor. subj. ἐπαύρῃς σ 107 (*v.l.* ἐπαύρῃ; see below). 3 ἐπαύρῃ Λ 391, N 649. Infin. ἐπαυρέμεν Σ 302: ρ 81. ἐπαυρεῖν Λ 573, O 316, Ψ 340. **Mid.** 3 pl. pres. ἐπαυρίσκονται N 733. Fut. infin. ἐπαυρήσεσθαι Z 353. 2 sing. aor. subj. ἐπαύρηαι O 17. ἐπαύρῃ σ 107 (*v.l.* ἐπαύρῃς; see above). 3 pl. ἐπαύρωνται A 410. (1) To touch or graze: χρόα Λ 573 = O 316, N 649.—With genit.: λίθου Ψ 340.—Absol. Λ 391.—(2) With notion of deriving from contact, to bring on oneself, incur: μή τι κακὸν ἐπαύρῃς σ 107 (*v.l.* ἐπαύρῃ, mid.).—To have benefit or profit from. With genit.: τῶν ἐπαυρέμεν Σ 302.—Absol.: αὐτόν σε βούλομ' ἐπαυρέμεν ἤ τινα τῶνδε ρ 81.—In mid. With genit.: τοῦ ἐπαυρίσκονται N 733.—Ironically: ἵνα πάντες ἐπαύρωνται βασιλῆος (have cause to bless him) A 410.—In mid., to reap the fruits of. With genit.: κακορραφίης O 17.—Absol.: ἐπαυρήσεσθαί μιν ὀΐω Z 353.

†**ἐπαφύσσω** [ἐπ-, ἐπι- (6)]. 3 sing. aor. ἐπήφυσε. To draw (water) from a vessel and add it to the contents of another vessel: θερμὸν [ὕδωρ] τ 388.

ἐπέβην, aor. ἐπιβαίνω.

ἐπέβησε, 3 sing. trans. aor. ἐπιβαίνω.

ἐπεβήσετο, 3 sing. aor. mid. ἐπιβαίνω.

ἐπέβρῑσαν, 3 pl. aor. ἐπιβρίθω.

ἐπεγείρω [ἐπ-, ἐπι- (19)] 3 sing. aor. mid. ἐπέγρετο K 124: υ 57. Pple. ἐπεγρόμενος Ξ 256. (1) To rouse from sleep, waken χ 431.—(2) In mid., to rouse oneself from sleep, waken: ἄλοχος ἐπέγρετο υ 57. Cf. K 124, Ξ 256.

ἐπέγναμψε, 3 sing. aor. ἐπιγνάμπτω.

ἐπέγραψε, 3 sing. aor. ἐπιγράφω.

ἐπέγρετο, 3 sing. aor. mid. ἐπεγείρω.

ἐπέδησε¹, 3 sing. aor. ἐπιδέω.

ἐπέδησε², 3 sing. aor. πεδάω.

ἐπέδραμε, 3 sing. aor. ἐπιτρέχω.

ἐπέδωκε, 3 sing. aor. ἐπιδίδωμι.

ἐπέην, 3 sing. impf. ἔπειμι¹.

ἐπέθηκα, aor. ἐπιτίθημι.

ἐπεί. (As spondee X 379, Ψ 2: δ 13, θ 452, φ 25, ω 482.) (1) When, after that. (a) With indic.: οἱ δ' ἐπεὶ οὖν ἤγερθεν A 57. Cf. A 458, 467, 469, 484, B 16, etc.: α 2, 238, β 155, 297, 407, etc.—From the time when: ἐπεὶ ἤγαγον Ω 547. Cf. δ 13, θ 452.—(b) (α) With subj. in relative sentences corresponding to sentences with εἰ (4). See Table at end (II) (B) (a) (2).—(β) With subj. or opt. in conditional relative sentences. For the examples and constructions see Table (III) (B) (a) (1) (2) (5), (b) (1), (D) (20) (23) (26) (27) (34) (56).—(2) Since, seeing that: ἐπεὶ πολὺ βούλομαι αὐτὴν οἴκοι ἔχειν A 112. Cf. A 114, 119, 132, Δ 307, I 304, etc.: α 37, 160, 176, 205, 223, etc.—Introducing a sentence without a regular apodosis Γ 59, N 68, etc.: γ 103, θ 236, etc.

ἐπείγω. App. 3 dual subj. (with irregular short vowel) ἐπείγετον K 361. (1) To oppress by weight, weigh down M 452.—To bear hard upon, press, oppress: ἐπειγομένοισιν ἵκοντο (in sore straits) M 374. Cf. Ψ 623.—(2) Of wind, to beat upon something, blow hard: ὁππότ' ἐπείγῃ ἲς ἀνέμου O 382.—So of wind and sea beating on (a ship) ψ 235.—Of a favourable wind, to speed (a ship) on her course μ 167, ο 297.—(3) To press in pursuit, press hard upon: κεμάδα K 361.—(4) Of fire, to assail, attack: θάμνοι ἐπειγόμενοι πυρὸς ὁρμῇ Λ 157.—To play upon Φ 362.—(5) To propel (a ship) ν 115.—(6) To ply (oars) μ 205.—(7) To hurry on with, use all diligence in regard to: ὦνον ὁδαίων ο 445.—(8) To constrain, compel: ἀναγκαίη ἐπείγει Z 85: τ 73. Cf. λ 54.—To put constraint upon, debar from freedom of action: ἐπείγετο βελέεσσιν E 622 = N 511.—(9) In pass. (a) To make haste, hasten, hurry: ἐπειγέσθω Z 363.—With infin., to be eager *to do something*: μή τις ἐπειγέσθω οἰκόνδε νέεσθαι B 354. Cf. ε 399.—To be eager *for something to happen*: δῦναι [ἠέλιον] ἐπειγόμενος ν 30.—With acc., to be set on, be eager for a decision in the matter of: ἐπειγόμενοι τὸν ἐμὸν γάμον (eager for it though you be) β 97 = τ 142 = ω 132.—Without construction: ἐπειγομένην περ (curbing her impatience) ρ 570.—(b) In pres. pple., in eager haste, hurrying, with all speed: τεῖχος ἐπειγομένη ἀφικάνει Z 388. Cf. Ξ 519, Ψ 119.—Of an impersonal agency: ὅτ' ὀπὸς γάλα ἐπειγόμενος συνέπηξεν E 902.—Of winds, blowing, blustering E 501.—In a hurry: μὴ ἐπειγόμενοι ἀποπέμπετε λ 339.—Of eager rivalry Ψ 437, 496.—With genit., eager for: Ἄρηος T 142, 189: ὁδοῖο α 309, γ 284, ο 49.

ἐπειδάν [ἐπεί + δή + ἄν]. When. With subj. in a conditional relative sentence. See Table at end (III) (B) (a) (3).

†**ἐπείδω** [ἐπ-, ἐπι- (11)]. Acc. sing. masc. aor. pple. ἐπιδόντα. To look upon, behold: κακὰ πολλά X 61.

†**ἔπειμι**[1] [ἐπ-, ἐπι- (1) (7) + εἰμί]. 3 sing. opt. ἐπείη B 259. 3 sing. impf. ἐπῆεν E 127: φ 7. ἐπέην Υ 276. 3 pl. ἔπεσαν β 344. 3 sing. fut. ἐπέσσεται δ 756. (1) To be upon, to be fitted on or to something: κώπη ἐπῆεν φ 7. Cf. E 127, Υ 276: β 344.—(2) To be *upon*. With dat.: κάρη ὤμοισιν B 259.—(3) To be in existence so as to take up an inheritance: ἐπέσσεταί τις ὅς κεν ἔχῃσι δώματα δ 756.

†**ἔπειμι**[2] [ἐπ-, ἐπι- (11) (14) + εἶμι]. 1 sing. pres. ἔπειμι ψ 359. 3 ἔπεισι A 29, N 482: δ 411. Pple. ἐπιών, -όντος E 238, N 477, 482, 836, O 164, Σ 546: π 42. 3 sing. impf. ἐπήϊε P 741. 3 pl. ἐπήϊσαν λ 233. ἐπῆσαν τ 445. (1) To approach, draw near, come, come up: προμνηστῖναι ἐπήϊσαν λ 233. Cf. π 42, τ 445.—In hostile sense: τόνδ' ἐπιόντα δεδέξομαι ὀξέϊ δουρί E 238. Cf. N 477, 482, 836, O 164.—So, to come up *to*. With dat.: ὅς μοι ἔπεισιν N 482.—Of noise, to come *to*, assail the ears of. With dat.: τοῖς ὀρυμαγδὸς ἐπήϊεν P 741.—(2) To go round a number of persons: δόσκεν ἀνὴρ ἐπιών Σ 546.—(3) In pres. with fut. sense. With acc., to go *to*, visit: ἀγρὸν ἔπειμι ψ 359.—Of a state or condition, to come *upon* one: γῆράς μιν ἔπεισιν A 29.—To go *over*, hold in review: φώκας ἔπεισιν δ 411.

ἔπειρε, 3 sing. aor. πείρω.

ἔπεισι, 3 sing. pres. ἔπειμι[2].

ἔπειτα [ἐπι- (19) + εἶτα, then]. (1) Then, thereupon, after that: πολλὰ δ' ἐ. ἠρᾶτο A 35, ἕζετ' ἐ. 48. Cf. A 121, 172, 312, 387, 440, etc.: α 44, 123, 144, 336, 363, etc.—(2) Then, at that time: ἠέλιος ἐ. νέον προσέβαλλεν ἀρούρας H 421: = τ 433. Cf. Λ 776: α 106.—(3) Then, next, afterwards: κίκλησκ' ἐ. Αἴαντε B 406. Cf. Z 260, Λ 176, Π 136, Σ 96, Ψ 755, etc.: ὄφρ' ἂν ἐ. παῖδες λίπωνται (after me) γ 354, αὐτὰρ ἐ. δώσω . . . δ 590, οὐδέ τις ἄλλος γίγνετ' ἐ. ἀνέμων (succeeding it) μ 326. Cf. γ 58, ι 203, ο 261, etc.—(4) In a contemplated case, in that case, then: οὐκ ἄν σ' ἐ. κελοίμην . . . Ω 297. Cf. A 547, K 243, Π 446, X 49, etc.: νήποινοί κεν ἐ. ὄλοισθε α 380, ἦ καὶ ἐ. λευγαλέοι ἐσόμεσθα (if we make the attempt) β 60. Cf. π 301, τ 24, υ 209, ψ 287, etc.—Then, therefore, why then: οὐ σύ γ' ἐ. Τυδέος ἔκγονός ἐσσι E 812, εὔχεο σύ γ' ἐ. Κρονίωνι (since you are set on going) Ω 290. Cf. H 360, I 444, etc.: η 200, ρ 185.—In virtue of something, therein: ἐ. δὲ πολλὸν ἀάσθη T 113.—Resuming and restating, then: ἐπόρουσε . . . τρὶς ἐ. ἐπόρουσεν E 436. Cf. Υ 445, etc.: γ 62, etc.—(5) Stating an alternative: φεύγωμεν, ἤ μιν ἐ. λιτανεύσομεν Ω 356. Cf. Z 350, N 743, Υ 120, etc.: υ 63.—Introducing a statement δ 354, ι 116, ν 106.—(6) Hereafter: ἐ. πεφήσεται O 140. Cf. Π 498, Υ 130, Φ 274, Ψ 246, 551: ι 17, π 309, ω 432.—(7) In the end, in the result: τῇ καὶ ἐ. τελευτήσεσθαι ἔμελλεν θ 510. Cf. θ 520, φ 24.—After all: ἔπρηξας καὶ ἐ. Σ 357. Cf. φ 131.

ἐπεκέκλετο, 3 sing. aor. ἐπικέλομαι.

ἐπέκελσε, 3 sing. aor. ἐπικέλλω.

ἐπέκερσε, 3 sing. aor. ἐπικείρω.

ἐπέκλυον. See ἐπίκλυον.

ἐπέκλωσε, 3 sing. aor. ἐπικλώθω.

ἐπεκραίαινε, 3 sing. impf. See ἐπικραίνω.

ἐπέλαμψε, 3 sing. aor. ἐπιλάμπω.

ἐπέλασσα, aor. πελάζω.

†**ἐπελαύνω** [ἐπ-, ἐπι- (3)]. 3 sing. plupf. pass. ἐπελήλατο. To beat or hammer out (metal) upon or on to something: ἐπελήλατο χαλκός N 804, P 493.

ἐπελεύσεσθαι, fut. infin. ἐπέρχομαι.

ἐπελήλατο, 3 sing. plupf. pass. ἐπελαύνω.

ἐπελήλυθα, pf. ἐπέρχομαι.

ἐπέλησε, 3 sing. aor. ἐπιλήθω.

ἐπελθών, aor. pple. ἐπέρχομαι.

ἐπεμάσσατο, 3 sing. aor. ἐπιμαίομαι.

†**ἐπεμβαίνω** [ἐπ-, ἐπι- (12) + ἐμ-, ἐν- (3)]. Pf. pple. ἐπεμβεβαώς. To go *on to*, mount; in pf., to stand *upon*. With genit.: οὐδοῦ I 582.

ἐπεμήνατο, 3 sing. aor. ἐπιμαίνομαι.

ἐπέμυξαν, 3 pl. aor. ἐπιμύζω.

ἔπεμψε, 3 sing. aor. πέμπω.

ἐπένεικα, aor. ἐπιφέρω.

ἐπένειμε, 3 sing. aor. ἐπινέμω.

†**ἐπενήνοθε** Β 219, Κ 134 : θ 365 [ἐπ-, ἐπι- (1)]. See ἐνήνοθε, ἐπανήνοθε.

†**ἐπεντανύω** [ἐπ-, ἐπι- (5) + ἐν- (3)]. Aor. pple. ἐπεντανύσας. To draw tight (a rope) resting upon something χ 467.

†**ἐπεντύνω** [ἐπ-, ἐπι- (5)]. 3 pl. aor. subj. mid. ἐπεντύνονται. To get ready, prepare. In mid. : ἄεθλα ω 89.

ἐπεντύω [ἐπ-, ἐπι- (5)]. To get (horses) ready for yoking : ἐπέντυε ἵππους Θ 374.

ἐπέοικε, 3 *sing. pf.* [ἐπ-, ἐπι- (19) + ἔοικε. See εἴκω[1]]. 3 sing. plupf. ἐπεῴκει ω 295. (1) To be fitting or suitable for. With dat. : ὅς τις οἷ ἐ. Ι 392.—(2) To beseem, look well in. With dat. : νέῳ πάντ' ἐ. Χ 71.—(3) Impers., it is fitting, right, seemly. (a) With dat. and infin. : σφῶϊν ἐ. ἑστάμεν Δ 341.—(b) With acc. and infin. : ὅν τ' ἐ. βουλὰς βουλεύειν Κ 146 : ὧν ἐ. ἱκέτην [μὴ δεύεσθαι] ζ 193 = ξ 511. Cf. λ 186.—(c) With infin. alone : λαοὺς οὐκ ἐ. ταῦτ' ἐπαγείρειν Α 126 (see ἐπαγείρω), ὅσσ' ἐ. [ἀποδάσσασθαι] Ω 595.—(d) Absol. : ὡς ἐ. υ 293. Cf. ω 295, 481.

ἐπεπήγει, 3 sing. plupf. πήγνυμι.

ἐπέπιθμεν, 1 pl. plupf. πείθω.

ἐπέπληγον, 3 pl. thematic plupf. πλήσσω.

ἐπέπλως, 2 sing. aor. ἐπιπλέω.

ἐπεποίθει, 3 sing. plupf. πείθω.

ἐπεπόνθει, 3 sing. plupf. πάσχω.

ἐπέπταρε, 3 sing. aor. ἐπιπταίρω.

ἐπέπτατο, 3 sing. aor. ἐπιπέτομαι.

ἐπέπυστο, 3 sing. plupf. πεύθομαι.

ἐπέρασσα, aor. περάω[2].

†**ἐπερείδω** [ἐπ-, ἐπι- (18)]. 3 sing. aor. ἐπέρεισε. (1) To thrust or press (a weapon) home Ε 856.—(2) To put (one's strength) into an effort : ἐπέρεισεν ἶν' ἀπέλεθρον Η 269 := ι 538.

ἐπέρησα, aor. περάω[1].

ἐπέρριψαν, 3 pl. aor. ἐπιρρίπτω.

ἐπερρώσαντο, 3 pl. aor. ἐπιρρώομαι.

ἔπερσε, 3 sing. aor. πέρθω.

†**ἐπερύω** [ἐπ-, ἐπι- (18) + ἐρύω[1]]. 3 sing. aor. ἐπέρυσσε. To pull to (a door) : θύρην α 441.

ἐπέρχομαι [ἐπ-, ἐπι- (11) (14)]. Fut. infin. ἐπελεύσεσθαι ι 214. Aor. ἐπῆλθον η 280. 3 sing. -ε Η 262, Μ 200, Ο 84, Σ 321 : ι 233, ξ 457, 475, ο 256. ἐπήλυθε Θ 488, Ι 474, Υ 91 : δ 793, κ 31, λ 200, ρ 170, etc. 3 pl. -ον β 107, λ 295, ξ 294, τ 152, ω 142. Subj. ἐπέλθω ξ 139. 3 sing. -ῃσι Ω 651. -ῃ ε 472, κ 175. 3 pl. -ωσι ω 354. Pple. ἐπελθών Δ 334, Κ 40, Ο 630, Ω 418, etc. : α 188, ε 73, π 197, ψ 185, etc. Pl. -όντες τ 155. Pf. ἐπελήλυθα δ 268. (1) To approach, draw near, come, come up: τοῦ υἱὸς ἐπῆλθεν ο 256. Cf. Α 535, Κ 40, Ψ 234, etc.: β 13 = ρ 64, ε 73, ι 233, π 197, σ 199, τ 155, ψ 185.—To approach, come up *to*. With dat. : σφιν Μ 200.—In hostile sense : μίμνον ἐπερχόμενον Ἄσιον Μ 136. Cf. Ν 472, Ο 406, Υ 178, Χ 252.—Applied to a weapon Θ 536.—With dat. : βουσίν Υ 91.—So of a disease λ 200.—Of lions Κ 485, Ο 630. — To approach a person for a specified purpose : εἰ γέροντ' εἴρηαι ἐπελθών α 188. Cf. ρ 382.—(2) To come or present oneself : αὐτὸς ἐπελθών β 246, ω 506. Cf. ι 214.—(3) To come to a specified place : μή τις ἐνθάδ' ἐπέλθῃσιν Ω 651. Cf. ω 354.—(4) To come to, arrive at, reach, a specified or indicated place : ἦος ἐπῆλθον ἐς ποταμόν η 280. Cf. ρ 170.—Of a weapon, to make its way *to*, reach, touch. With acc. : αὐχένα Η 262.—(5) To come *to*, visit. With acc. : ἀγρόν π 27.—(6) To come *upon*, light *upon*, find. With dat. : ὁμηγερέεσσι θεοῖσιν Ο 84.—Absol. : μή τις ἐπελθὼν δηλήσαιτο ν 124. Cf. ξ 317.—(7) Of sleep, to come *upon* (one). With dat. : κλαιόντεσσιν ἐπήλυθεν ὕπνος μ 311. Cf. ε 472.—With acc. : ἐπήλυθέ μιν ὕπνος δ 793. Cf. κ 31 = ν 282.—(8) Of a period of time, to come on, come upon one : ἐπήλυθε νύξ Θ 488, Ι 474. Cf. κ 175, ξ 457, 475, ρ 606, χ 198. —To come round : ὅτ' ἐπήλυθον ὧραι β 107 = τ 152 = ω 142, λ 295 = ξ 294.—(9) To go *over*, traverse. With acc. : ἄγκεα Σ 321. Cf. δ 268.—(10) To go, betake oneself : ὁππόσ' ἐπέλθω ξ 139.

ἔπεσαν, 3 pl. impf. ἔπειμι[1].

ἐπεσβολίη, -ης, ἡ [ἐπεσβόλος]. A throwing in of one's word, a speaking uninvited. In pl. δ 159.

ἐπεσβόλος [ἐπεσ-, ἔπος + βολ-, βάλλω]. Throwing words about at random, scurrilous Β 275.

ἔπεσε, 3 sing. aor. πίπτω.

ἐπέσπον, aor. ἐφέπω[1].

ἐπέσσεται, 3 sing. fut. ἔπειμι[1].

ἐπέσσευε, 3 sing. aor. ἐπισσεύω.

ἐπέσσυται, 3 sing. pf. mid. ἐπισσεύω.

ἐπέσσυτο, 3 sing. aor. mid. ἐπισσεύω.

ἐπεστέψαντο, 3 pl. aor. mid. ἐπιστέφω.

ἐπέστη, 3 sing. aor. ἐφίστημι.

ἐπέσχον, aor. ἐπέχω.

ἐπέτειλας, 2 sing. aor. ἐπιτέλλω.

ἐπετήσιος [ἐπ-, ἐπι- (16) + ἔτος]. Coming on all through the year : καρπός η 118.

ἐπετράπομεν, 1 pl. aor. ἐπιτρέπω.

ἐπέτρεψε, 3 sing. aor. ἐπιτρέπω.

ἐπεύξατο, 3 sing. aor. ἐπεύχομαι.

ἐπευφημέω [ἐπ-, ἐπι- (4)]. To give one's voice in approval or assent Α 22 = 376.

ἐπεύχομαι [ἐπ-, ἐπι- (5)]. 2 sing. fut. ἐπεύξεαι Λ 431. 3 sing. aor. ἐπεύξατο Λ 449, Ν 373, 413, 445, Ξ 453, 478, Υ 388, Χ 330 : υ 60, 238. Pple. -άμενος Γ 350, Ζ 475, Κ 368, Ρ 46 : ξ 436. Infin. -ασθαι κ 533, λ 46. (1) To utter words of exultation, triumph, vaunting, derision : ἐπεύχεται αὔτως Ρ 450. Cf. Ρ 35 : ψ 59.—With complementary infin. : ἐπευξάμενος βαλέειν Κ 368.—To utter such words over a smitten foe : ὅς μ' ἔβαλε καὶ ἐπεύχεται Ε 119. Cf. Λ 449, Ν 373, 413, 445, Ξ 453, Υ 388, Φ 427, Χ 330 : χ 286.—To utter them *over* him. With dat. : τῷ ἐπεύξατο Ξ 478. Cf. Λ 431, Π 829, Φ 121, 409.—(2) To pray. With dat. : Διί Γ 350 = Ρ 46, Ζ 475. Cf. κ 533 = λ 46, υ 60. — With dat. and complementary infin. : πᾶσι θεοῖσι νοστῆσαι Ὀδυσῆα ξ 423, υ 238, φ 203.—Absol. ξ 436.

ἔπεφνον, aor. φένω.

ἐπέφραδον, redup. aor. φράζω.

ἐπεφράσατο, 3 sing. aor. mid. ἐπιφράζω.

ἐπεφράσθης, 2 sing. aor. pass. ἐπιφράζω.

ἐπέχευε, 3 sing. aor. ἐπιχέω.

ἐπέχραον, 3 pl. aor. ἐπιχράω.

ἐπέχυντο, 3 pl. aor. pass. ἐπιχέω.

ἐπέχω [ἐπ-, ἐπι- (1) (5) (11) (15) (18)]. Aor. ἐπέσχον X 83. 3 sing. ἐπέσχε Φ 244, 407, X 494, Ψ 238, Ω 792 : π 444. 2 sing. opt. ἐπισχοίης Ξ 241. Pple. ἐπισχών I 489. 3 pl. plupf. pass. ἐπώχατο M 340. (**1**) To hold, keep, rest *upon*. With dat. : θρήνυι πόδας Ξ 241 : ρ 410.—(**2**) To extend *over*, cover. With acc.: ἑπτὰ πέλεθρα Φ 407. Cf. Ψ 190, 238 = Ω 792.—(**3**) To hold out for acceptance, offer, present: κοτύλην X 494. Cf. I 489 : π 444. —Of presenting the breast to a suckling X 83.—(**4**) To set *upon*, assail, abuse. With dat. : μοι τ 71.—(**5**) To restrain or dam (a stream) Φ 244.—(**6**) To hold oneself from action, hold back, refrain: Ἀντίνοος ἔτ' ἐπεῖχε καὶ Εὐρύμαχος φ 186 (Eu. does not seem to make the attempt till 245, and A. does not seem to make it at all).—(**7**) To shut (a gate): πᾶσαι [πύλαι] ἐπώχατο M 340 (*v.l.* πάσας ἐπῴχετο).

ἐπεῴκει, 3 sing. plupf. See ἐπέοικε.

ἐπήβολος [app. with ἐπη- (with metrical lengthening) for ἐπι-, fr. ἐπιβάλλομαι. See ἐπιβάλλω (2)]. Having, having the disposal of: νηός β 319.

ἐπήγαγον, aor. ἐπάγω.

ἐπηγκενίδες, αἱ [app. ἐπ-, ἐπι- (1) + ἐνεγκέμεν. See φέρω]. Dat. ἐπηγκενίδεσσι. The pieces fitted upon the top of the ἴκρια of the σχεδίη of Odysseus, and forming the upper surface thereof ε 253.

ἐπῄεν, 3 sing. impf. ἔπειμι[1].

ἐπηετανός, -όν [prob. ἐπ-, ἐπι- (16) + ηε- = αἰεί + suff. -τανος. 'Lasting for ever']. (**1**) Never-failing, always available: γάλα δ 89.—Unfailing, constant, regularly afforded or given: κομιδή θ 233, σῖτον σ 360.—Ever-flowing, always full: πλυνοί ζ 86, ἀρδμοί ν 247.—(**2**) In neut. sing. ἐπηετανόν as adv., in never-failing abundance: ἐ. ἔχουσιν κ 427. Cf. η 99.—Ever, all the year round: γανόωσαι η 128.

ἐπήϊε, 3 sing. impf. ἔπειμι[2].

ἐπήϊξα, aor. ἐπαΐσσω.

ἐπήϊσαν, 3 pl. impf. ἔπειμι[2].

ἐπῆλθε, ἐπήλυθε, 3 sing. aor. ἐπέρχομαι.

ἐπημοιβός [ἐπαμείβω. Cf. ἐπαμοιβαδίς]. (**1**) Of a garment, kept for a change (= ἀμοιβάς): χιτῶνες ξ 513.—(**2**) Of ὀχῆες, app., crossing each other (cf. ἐπαμοιβαδίς) M 456. (The κληΐς would secure the ὀχῆες to the gate at their point of intersection, and so make of the whole a solid structure without separate play in the parts.)

ἐπήν [ἐπεὶ ἄν]. When, after that. (**1**) With subj. in **a** relative sentence corresponding to sentences with εἰ (**4**). See Table at end (II) (B) (a) (3).—(**2**) With subj. or opt. in conditional relative sentences. For the examples and constructions see Table (III) (B) (a) (3), (D) (34) (35) (36) (38) (49) (65).

ἐπήνησαν, 3 pl. aor. ἐπαινέω.

ἔπηξε, 3 sing. aor. πήγνυμι.

ἐπηπείλησε, 3 sing. aor. ἐπαπειλέω.

ἐπηπύω [ἐπ-, ἐπι- (5)]. To give one's voice in approval or assent *to*. With dat.: ἀμφοτέροισιν ἐπήπυον Σ 502.

ἐπήρατος, -ον [ἐπ-, ἐπι- (19) + ἔραμαι. 'Lovely']. An epithet of general commendation, pleasing, charming, delightful, fair, or the like: δαιτός I 228 : εἵματα θ 366, ἄντρον ν 103 = 347.—As epithet of places, fair, pleasant: πτολίεθρον Σ 512, X 121. Cf. δ 606.

ἐπήρετμος, -ον [ἐπ-, ἐπι- (2) + ἐρετμόν]. (**1**) At the oar: ἑταῖροι ἦατ' ἐπήρετμοι β 403.—(**2**) Epithet of ships, fitted or furnished with oars δ 559 = ε 16 = ρ 145, ε 141, ξ 224.

ἐπηρεφής [ἐπ-, ἐπι- (5) + ἐρέφω]. Overhanging: κρημνοί M 54.—Of cliffs, beetling κ 131, μ 59.

ἐπήρκεσε, 3 sing. aor. ἐπαρκέω.

ἐπῆρσε, 3 sing. aor. ἐπαραρίσκω.

ἐπῇσαν, 3 pl. impf. ἔπειμι[2].

ἐπήσκηται, 3 sing. pf. pass. ἐπασκέω.

ἐπητής. App., well-mannered, courteous: οὕνεκ' ἐ. ἐσσι ν 332, ἐπητῇ ἀνδρί σ 128.

ἐπήτριμοι, -α. App., in succession, one after another: πυρσοὶ φλεγέθουσιν ἐπήτριμοι Σ 211. Cf. Σ 552, T 226.

ἐπητύς, -ύος, ἡ [ἐπητής]. Courtesy, gentle usage φ 306.

ἐπήφυσε, 3 sing. aor. ἐπαφύσσω.

ἐπί. (Commonly with anastrophe when immediately following the vb. or case-form (and see γ 161).) (**I**) Adv. (**1**) Position on or upon something, thereon: ἐπὶ δ' ἀργύρεον ζυγὸν ἦεν I 187. Cf. H 223, Λ 630 (on the table): α 291, γ 9, δ 132, η 90, θ 475, etc.—(**2**) At a place, thereat: ἐπὶ σκέπας ἦν ε 443 = η 282, ζ 210, μ 336. —(**3**) Denoting an occasion or cause, thereat, thereupon: ἐπὶ δὲ Τρῶες κελάδησαν Θ 542, γέλασαν δ' ἐπὶ πάντες Ψ 840. Cf. B 148, Λ 45, N 822, Π 612, P 723, etc.: ζ 117.—(**4**) Denoting (sometimes vaguely) that action, effort or the like takes place in a specified or indicated direction or is directed to or against something or to a specified or indicated object or end: κρατερὸν δ' ἐπὶ μῦθον ἔτελλεν A 25, εἴ ποτέ τοι ἐπὶ νηὸν ἔρεψα (in thy honour) 39, ἦμος ἐπὶ κνέφας ἦλθεν (came upon them) 475, ἐπὶ φρεσὶ κέκασται (excels all) Υ 35. Cf. A 408, 528, Γ 461, Δ 384, I 539, K 99, Λ 235, etc.: ἀνέμων ἐπ' ἀΰτμένα χεῦεν γ 289, ἐπὶ χερσὶ μάσασθαι λ 591. Cf. α 273, γ 152, 161, θ 245, ξ 195, ρ 241, σ 64, etc.—(**5**) Besides, in addition, too: ἐπὶ μέγαν ὅρκον ὀμοῦμαι A 233, ἐπὶ ξύλα λέγεσθε Θ 507. Cf. E 705, O 662, Σ 529, Φ 373, etc.: μ 399 = ο 477, υ 229.—(**6**) Following, succession: πρὸ μέν τ' ἄλλ', αὐτὰρ ἐπ' ἄλλα N 799. Cf. N 800.—(**7**) Accompaniment: ἐπὶ δ' ἕψονται θεοὶ ἄλλοι Δ 63, ἐπὶ μείλια δώσω (δώσει) (with her) I 147, 289. Cf. ι 297, μ 349.—(**8**) In answer or response: ἐπὶ δὲ στενάχοντο T 301 = X 515 = Ω 746, T 338, X 429, Ω 722. Cf. Ω 776.—(**9**) Being in charge: ἐπὶ δ' ἀνὴρ ἐσθλὸς ὀρώρει Ψ 112. Cf. γ 471, ξ 104.—(**10**) To, towards, at, on, upon:

ἦλθε δ' ἐπὶ ψυχή Ψ 65. Cf. Λ 480, Ψ 232, etc. : γέροντας ἐπὶ πλέονας καλέσαντες (to the council) η 189, οἷον ἐπ' ἦμαρ ἄγῃσιν σ 137. Cf. λ 84, 90, 632, μ 427, σ 1, etc.—In hostile sense : ἐπὶ δ' ὄρνυτο Ψ 689. Cf. Δ 221, Ε 618, Θ 158, etc. : φ 100.—(**11**) On to, on, upon, over something : ἐπ' ἄρα φάρμακα πάσσεν Δ 218, δέελον δ' ἐπὶ σῆμά τ' ἔθηκεν Κ 466. Cf. Α 462, Ζ 419, Λ 639, Ν 543, Ψ 256, etc. : γ 179, 459, θ 443, κ 520, μ 47, τ 58, etc.—(**12**) Thrusting or pushing home : ἐπὶ κληῖδ' ἐτάνυσσεν α 442. Cf. Ρ 48.—(**II**) Prep. (**1**) With dat. (**a**) On, upon : ἐπὶ χθονὶ Α 88, ἐπὶ πύργῳ Γ 153. Cf. Α 219, 462, Δ 248, 470 (over his body), Ε 42, etc. : α 211, γ 5, 273, 408, etc.—With locative : ἐπ' ἰκριόφιν γ 353, ν 74, ο 283. Cf. ε 59, λ 607.—In pregnant sense : ἐξ αὐτοὶ βαῖνον ἐπὶ ῥηγμῖνι θαλάσσης Α 437. Cf. Α 486, Ε 141 (against each other), Λ 5, Ν 359, Χ 97 (against), etc. : κατέθηκεν ἐπ' ἀπήνῃ ζ 75. Cf. α 364, δ 440, κ 375, μ 362, etc.—With locative : ἐπὶ στεφάνην κεφαλῆφι θήκατο Κ 30 : τ 389.—In reference to imposing, laying or conferring something *upon* a person : ἄλγε' ἐπ' ἀλλήλοισι τιθέντες Ε 384, ἐπ' αὐτῷ κῦδος ἔθηκεν Ψ 400. Cf. Ζ 357, etc. : λ 524, τ 592, etc.—Sim. : εἰ γὰρ ἐπ' ἀρῇσιν τέλος γένοιτο ρ 496.—To bestowing a name : ἐπὶ πᾶσι τίθενται θ 554.—To attaching *to* something : δησάμενοι ἐπὶ κληῖσιν ἐρετμά θ 37.—(**b**) At, by, beside : ἐπὶ νηυσίν Α 559, πηγῇς ἔπι Κηφισοῖο Β 523. Cf. Β 472 (over against)), 788, Η 86, Μ 168, Χ 93 (app., in the hole), etc. : α 103, β 391, δ 40, ζ 52, ι 103, etc.—Sim., among, in the enjoyment of (wealth) Ι 482 : α 218.—In closer definition of something : οὔτασε χεῖρ' ἐπὶ καρπῷ Ε 458. Cf. Σ 594, etc. : ω 398, etc.—With locative in reference to position : ἐπὶ δεξιόφιν Ν 308. Cf. Ν 309.—(**c**) App., implying penetration, into, in : ἔγχος κατέπηξεν ἐπὶ χθονὶ Ζ 213. Cf. Ψ 876.—So in reference to the mind, into, in : τῷ ἐπὶ φρεσὶ θῆκεν Α 55, etc. Cf. ε 427, etc.—(**d**) For, with a view to : ᾧ ἔπι πολλὰ μόγησα Α 162. Cf. σ 44.—In consideration of : μισθῷ ἔπι ῥητῷ Φ 445. Cf. Κ 304.—In the case of, in the matter of, on the occasion of, in honour of, for : μητρὶ φίλῃ ἐπὶ ἦρα φέρων (to her) Α 572, αἴθ' οὕτως ἐπὶ πᾶσι χόλον τελέσειεν Δ 178. Cf. Δ 235, 258, Ι 492, Ξ 67, Ρ 400, Φ 585, Ω 82, etc. : τοιῷδ' ἐπ' ἀέθλῳ λ 548, ἐπὶ μηρία θέντες Ἀπόλλωνι φ 267. Cf. γ 164, π 19, σ 414, ω 91, etc.—(**e**) Besides, in addition to : ἀλλ' ἐπὶ τῇσιν Ι 639, μή τις ἐφ' ἕλκεϊ ἕλκος ἄρηται (wound on wound) Ξ 130, τόσους ἐπὶ τοῖσι χιτῶνας Ω 231. Cf. γ 113, λ 287, χ 264, etc.—In comparison with : ἐπὶ γαστέρι κύντερον η 216.—(**f**) In reference to concomitance : ἀτελευτήτῳ ἐπὶ ἔργῳ (with your task unaccomplished) Δ 175, τῷδ' ἐπὶ θυμῷ (with this . . .) Ν 485, ἐπ' ἀρωγῇ Ψ 574 : ἀνηνύστῳ ἐπὶ ἔργῳ (with no end to the business) π 111. Cf. π 99, ρ 308, 454, ω 511.—At the hands of : ἐπὶ ἴστορι Σ 501.—(**g**) After, following : τῷ δ' ἐπὶ Τυδεΐδης ὦρτο Η 163. Cf. Θ 262, etc. : η 120, υ 162, etc.—(**h**) In charge or superintendence of, over : ἐπ' ὀΐεσσιν Ε 137, υἱὸν ἐπὶ κτεάτεσσι λιπέσθαι 154. Cf. Ζ 424, etc. : σημαίνειν ἐπὶ δμῳῇσιν χ 427. Cf. ο 89, υ 209, φ 363, etc. —(**i**) To, towards, in the direction of : νηυσὶν ἔπι Ε 327, ἕλκ' ἐπὶ οἷ Λ 239. Cf. Β 6, Δ 251, Υ 53, etc. : ρ 330, χ 205, etc.—Sim. : Πατρόκλῳ ὅ γ' ἐπ' ὀφρύσι νεῦσεν Ι 620.—In reference to lighting or coming *upon* something : ἐπὶ σώματι κύρσας Γ 23. Cf. Ψ 821.—In hostile sense, against, upon : ἧκεν ἐπ' Ἀργείοισι βέλος Α 382, ἐπ' ἀλλήλοισι θορόντες Λ 70. Cf. Γ 15, Ε 124, Θ 327, Λ 294, etc. : β 316, κ 214, ν 60, χ 8, etc.—So ἐφ' ἵπποιιν μάστιγας ἄειραν Ψ 362. — Of laughing *at* or exulting *over* a person : ἐπ' αὐτῷ γέλασσαν Β 270, Ψ 784, τῷ δ' ἐπὶ μακρὸν ἄϋσεν Ε 101, etc. : υ 358 = φ 376. Cf. υ 374, χ 412.—In reference to position, in the direction of, towards : ἐπὶ οἷ τετραμμένον Ν 542. —(**j**) In reference to time. (**α**) During, for the space of : ἐπ' ἤματι δακρύσαντας Τ 229. Cf. Θ 529. —(**β**) During, on : ὅς τις ἐπ' ἤματι τῷδε μεθίῃσι μάχεσθαι Ν 234. Cf. Τ 110 : ἐπ' ἤματι μῆλον ἀγινεῖ (each day, day by day) ξ 105.—(**γ**) In the space of : τοσσάδε μέρμερ' ἐπ' ἤματι μητίσασθαι (in a single day) Κ 48 : τρὶς ἐπ' ἤματι μ 105. Cf. β 284.—(**2**) With acc. (**a**) To, towards, in the direction of : ἐπὶ νῆας Α 12, τώ οἱ ὤμω ἐπὶ στῆθος συνοχωκότε Β 218, ἀταρπιτὸς ἦεν ἐπ' αὐτήν (leading to it) Σ 565. Cf. Α 306, 440, Β 808, Δ 78, etc. : α 149, 183, 274, β 260, etc.—So ἐπὶ δεξιά Η 238, etc.—In hostile sense Ε 590, Ν 101, etc. : ρ 295. —In quest of, for : ἐπὶ Νέστορα Κ 54. Cf. Β 18, etc. : γ 421, etc.—In reference to that *to* which one turns or proceeds : ἐπὶ ἔργα τράποντο Γ 422. Cf. Β 381, etc. : θ 395, ξ 455, ω 394, etc.—To directing the sight or voice : γεγωνέμεν ἐπ' Αἴαντος κλισίας Λ 7, ἐπὶ Θρῃκῶν καθορώμενος αἶαν Ν 4, etc.—To seeing *to* something : ἐπὶ ἔργα ἰδεῖν π 144.—To being brought *into* sorrow ξ 338. —In view of, for : πᾶσαν ἐπ' ἰθύν Ζ 79 : δ 434.— (**b**) Indicating arrival at a point : ἐπὶ κλισίας ἱκέσθην Α 328. Cf. Β 17, etc. : κ 117, μ 430, etc. —In reference to time : οὐδ' ἐπὶ γῆρας ἵκετο θ 226. —(**c**) In reference to adjusting *to*, bringing *into conformity with*, something : ἐπὶ ἶσα Μ 436 = Ο 413 : ἐπὶ στάθμην ε 245, ρ 341 = φ 44, φ 121, ψ 197.—To bringing *into* a specified formation : ὅς τίς σφιν ἐπὶ στίχας ἡγήσαιτο (into their ranks) Β 687. Cf. Γ 113.—To being *in* such a formation : θρέξασκον ἐπὶ στίχας Σ 602.—Sim. : ἐπὶ πτολέμοιο γεφύρας ἥατο Θ 553.—(**d**) On, upon. In reference to placing, setting, seating or sitting *on* or *at* something : ἕζετο θῖν' ἐφ' ἁλός Α 350, θῖν' ἐφ' ἁλὸς εἰρυμέναι Ν 682. Cf. Θ 442, etc. : εἷσαν ἐπὶ σκέπας ζ 212. Cf. μ 171, etc.—Sim. : ἐπ' ἀμφοτέρους πόδας ἵζει Ν 281, ἑζόμενος ἐπὶ γοῦνα (*i.e.* with his knees on the ground, 'sitting on his heels') Ξ 437.—In reference to attaching : ἔδησαν ἐπ' ὀμφαλόν Ω 273.—To falling *on* a part of the body : ἐπὶ στόμα Ζ 43. Cf. Ε 586, etc.—To a part *by* which one is seized : ἑλὼν ἐπὶ μάστακα ψ 76.—(**e**) In reference to position, on, at : νηῶν ἐπ' ἀριστερά Ν 675. Cf. Β 526, Ε 355, etc. : γ 171, ε 277.—(**f**) On to, on : ἐπὶ πύργον ἰοῦσαν Γ 154, ἀποβάντες ἐπὶ χθόνα Θ 492. Cf. Z 375, M 448, P 504, Ψ 393, etc. : ρ 413, χ 2, etc.—(g) In reference to motion *over* or *on* something: πᾶσαν ἐπ' αἶαν I 506, ἐλάαν ἐπὶ κύματα N 27. Cf. B 159, Ξ 254, T 378, Υ 227, Ψ 320, etc. : α 97, β 364, ε 175, ζ 138, etc.—In reference to directing the sight: ὁρόων ἐπὶ πόντον A 350, etc. Cf. ε 84, etc.—(h) In reference to pouring liquid *over* or *on* something: ὕδωρ ἐπὶ χεῖρας ἔχευαν Γ 270, etc. Cf. α 146, etc.—And in gen. to diffusion, distribution, extent, existence, *over* or *on* a space or tract: Ἠὼς ἐκίδνατο πᾶσαν ἐπ' αἶαν Θ 1, κλέος κέ οἱ εἴη πάντας ἐπ' ἀνθρώπους (among them) K 213. Cf. H 63, 446, P 447, Ψ 226, 742, etc. : γ 3, δ 417, η 332, μ 386, ξ 403, ρ 386, etc.—To a surface *on* which a characteristic is displayed: ἐπὶ νῶτα δαφοινός B 308.—Sim.: [ἵππους] σταφύλῃ ἐπὶ νῶτον ἐΐσας (as measured across their backs) B 765.—(i) In reference to going *among*, *over* or *round* persons: οἰχόμενοι ἐπὶ πάντας Ξ 381. Cf. Υ 353 : γ 252.—Sim. : πόλλ' ἐπὶ ἄστε' ἀλώμενος ο 492, τ 170. Cf. π 63.—In reference to division or distribution *among* persons: δασσάμενοι ἐφ' ἡμέας π 385.—(j) In reference to extent or distance: ὅσον τ' ἐπὶ λᾶαν ἵησιν Γ 12. Cf. O 358, P 368, etc.: ε 251, λ 577 (covering), etc.—(k) In reference to a part of the body *on* which one lies: ἐπὶ πλευρὰς κατακείμενος Ω 10.—(l) In reference to time, for, during: μείνατ' ἐπὶ χρόνον B 299. Cf. I 415, etc. : μ 407, etc.—Sim. : εὗδον ἐπ' ἠῶ καὶ μέσον ἦμαρ (on through . . .) η 288.—(3) With genit. (a) On, upon : ἐπ' ὤμων A 46, ἐπ' ἠϊόνος Ψ 61. Cf. E 550, Λ 38, Υ 229 (see ἄκρος (3)), X 225, etc.: α 162, 171, ε 33, 82, κ 170, etc.—In reference to leaning *on* a part of the body: ὀρθωθεὶς ἐπ' ἀγκῶνος K 80.—To the part of a thing *on* which it stands: ἔγχε' ἐπὶ σαυρωτῆρος ἐλήλατο (*i.e.* were driven in by the butt) K 153.—In pregnant sense: ἐπ' ἠπείροιο ἔρυσσαν A 485. Cf. Γ 293, Σ 422, Ω 190, etc. : τίθει ἐπ' ἀπήνης ζ 252. Cf. η 162, ι 85, ο 547, etc.—(b) At, by, in: ἐπὶ Βουπρασίου Λ 756. Cf. Σ 557, X 153 : μύλης ἔπι η 104. Cf. α 185, ε 489, ι 140, etc.—*At* anchor: ἐπ' εὐνάων Ξ 77.—(c) Towards, in the direction of: ἐπὶ νηῶν E 700. Cf. Γ 5, Λ 546, Φ 454, Ψ 374, etc. : γ 171, ε 238, etc.—Sim., app., *to* oneself, withdrawn *into* oneself: σιγῇ ἐφ' ὑμείων H 195.—With a form in -φιν : ἐπ' αὐτόφιν ἥατο σιγῇ T 255.—(d) Along with, with : ὅσσα ἔοικεν ἐπὶ παιδὸς ἕπεσθαι α 278 = β 197.—(e) In reference to time, in the time of, in the days of: ἐπ' εἰρήνης B 797. Cf. E 637, etc.—So, app., ἐπὶ δώρων (in the time of gifts, not delaying and so missing the reward) I 602.

ἔπι [for ἔπ-εστι]. There is in a specified or indicated place, affecting or characterizing a specified or indicated person, or the like. With or without dat. : οὔ τοι ἔπι δέος A 515, καλὸν εἶδος ἔπι Γ 45. Cf. E 178, etc. : ᾧ ἔπι κώπη θ 403. Cf. β 58, λ 367, ξ 92, etc.

†**ἐπιάλλω** [ἐπ-, ἐπι- (5)]. 3 sing. ἐπίηλε. To set on foot, instigate : τάδε ἔργα χ 49.

ἐπιάλμενος, aor. pple. ἐφάλλομαι.

ἐπιανδάνω [ἐπι- (5)]. 3 sing. impf. ἐφήνδανε H 45. To please, be pleasing or acceptable. With dat. : βουλὴ θεοῖσιν H 45. Cf. ν 16, π 406 = υ 247, σ 50 = 290 = φ 143 = 269.—Impers. : ἐμοὶ ἐπιανδάνει οὕτως H 407.

†**ἐπιάχω** [ἐπι- (5)]. 3 pl. impf. ἐπίαχον (or rather (cf. under ἰάχω) aor. ἐπίϜαχον, or with augment ἐπέϜαχον, ἐπεύαχον). To shout in approval or assent H 403 = I 50.—In answer or defiance E 860 = Ξ 148, N 835.

ἐπίβαθρον [ἐπιβα-, ἐπιβαίνω]. A return made for a passage in a ship ο 449.

ἐπιβαίνω [ἐπι- (11) (12) (14)]. (A) Aor. ἐπέβην κ 347, λ 167, 482. 1 pl. -ημεν ι 83. 3 -ησαν χ 424. ἐπέβαν ψ 238. 2 dual subj. ἐπιβῆτον ψ 52. 1 pl. ἐπιβήομεν ζ 262, κ 334. Opt. ἐπιβαίην E 192 : ε 177. 2 sing. -αίης Ξ 299. 3 -αίη E 666 : μ 77. 3 pl. -αῖεν Θ 512. Pple. ἐπιβάς, -ᾶσα Δ 99, E 328, Ξ 226, O 387 : ε 50, κ 480, ν 319. Infin. ἐπιβήμεναι I 133, 275, T 176 : η 196, κ 340, 342, μ 282, ξ 229. ἐπιβῆναι ε 399, μ 434. 2 sing. fut. in mid. form ἐπιβήσεαι Θ 165. Dat. pl. masc. pple. ἐπιβησομένοισι Ψ 379. 3 sing. aor. ἐπεβήσετο (ἐπιβήσετο) Θ 44, K 513, 529, Λ 517, N 26, Ω 322 : δ 521, ζ 78. Imp. ἐπιβήσεο E 221, Θ 105, Λ 512. Acc. sing. masc. pple. ἐπιβησόμενον E 46, Π 343.—(B) Fut. infin. ἐπιβησέμεν Θ 197. 3 sing. aor. ἐπέβησε Θ 129, I 546. 3 pl. -ησαν ψ 13. 2 pl. subj. ἐπιβήσετε η 223. Imp. ἐπίβησον Θ 285. (I) *Intrans.* in all forms except those under (B). (1) With genit., to set foot *upon*, get *upon* : πύργων Θ 165. Cf. M 444.—Of horses Ψ 379.—Absol. O 387 : μ 77, 434.—To embark *upon* (a ship or raft) : νεῶν Θ 512 : σχεδίης ε 177. Cf. δ 708, ι 101, ν 319.—Of landing from a ship *upon* : πατρίδος αἴης δ 521. Cf. η 196, ι 83, λ 167, 482, μ 282.—So of coming to shore out of the sea : ἠπείρου ε 399. Cf. ψ 238.—To mount (a chariot, etc.) : ἵππων E 46. Cf. E 192, 221, Θ 44, Λ 512, Ω 322, etc. : ζ 78.—To mount (a horse) : ἵππων ἐπεβήσετο (app. meaning one of them) K 513, 529.—To mount, place oneself *upon* (a bed) : εὐνῆς I 133 = 275 = T 176 : κ 334, 340, 342, 347, 480.—Of a corpse, to take its place, be placed, *upon* (the pyre) : πυρῆς Δ 99.—(2) To make one's way *to*, proceed *to*. With genit. : πόληος Π 396 : ξ 229.—So to make one's way *to* and reach : πόλιος ζ 262.—(3) To set foot *within* ; hence, fig., with genit., to have enjoyment of : ἐϋφροσύνης ψ 52.—To embark upon a course of, give oneself up to : ἀναιδείης χ 424.—(4) To traverse by flying *over*. With acc. : Πιερίην Ξ 226 : ε 50.—(5) Absol., to go on one's own feet (as opposed to being carried) E 666.—(II) *Trans.* in forms (B). (1) With genit., to cause to embark *upon* (a ship) : Ἀχαιοὺς νηῶν ἐπιβησέμεν Θ 197.—To set on shore from a ship *upon* : ἐμῆς πάτρης η 223.—To cause to mount (a chariot) : ἵππων Θ 129.—To cause (a person) to take his place *upon* (the pyre) (*i.e.* slay him) : πολλοὺς πυρῆς ἐπέβησεν I 546.—(2) Fig., with genit., to bring *within the pale of*, bring *into the* *enjoyment of*: ἐϋκλείης Θ 285.—To bring *into a course of*, lead to adopt: σαοφροσύνης ψ 13.

ἐπιβάλλω [ἐπι- (11) (12)]. **(1)** To throw or cast upon something indicated Ψ 135.—To lay on (the lash): ἱμάσθλην ζ 320.—**(2)** In mid., to throw oneself *upon* in eagerness to possess. With genit.: ἐνάρων ἐπιβαλλόμενος Z 68.—**(3)** Of a ship, app., to head *towards*, stand for. With acc.: Φεὰς ἐπέβαλλεν ο 297.

ἐπιβάς, aor. pple. ἐπιβαίνω.

ἐπιβάσκω [ἐπι- (11)]. Like ἐπιβαίνω (II) (2). to bring *within the pale of*, involve *in*. With genit.: κακῶν υἷας Ἀχαιῶν B 234.

ἐπιβήμεναι, ἐπιβῆναι, aor. infin. ἐπιβαίνω.

ἐπιβήομεν, 1 pl. aor. subj. ἐπιβαίνω.

ἐπιβήσεαι, 2 sing. fut. mid. ἐπιβαίνω.

ἐπιβήσεο, aor. imp. mid. ἐπιβαίνω.

ἐπίβησον, trans. aor. imp. ἐπιβαίνω.

ἐπιβήτωρ, -ορος, ὁ [ἐπιβη-, ἐπιβαίνω]. **(1)** One who mounts (a chariot), a (skilled) fighter from the chariot σ 263.—**(2)** Of an animal, 'the mounter,' the male or mate λ 131 = ψ 278.

ἐπιβλής, ὁ [ἐπι- (18) + βλη-, βάλλω]. App., a movable piece of wood to secure a gate, passing through a hole in one gate-post and fitting into a socket in the other Ω 453 (no doubt identical with the κληΐς of 455).

†**ἐπιβοάω** [ἐπι- (5)]. Fut. mid. ἐπιβώσομαι α 378, β 143. 1 pl. ἐπιβωσόμεθα (*v.l.* ἐπιδωσόμεθα) K 463. In mid., with acc., to call *to* for aid: θεούς α 378 = β 143.—App., to call *to* in thanksgiving: Ἀθήνην K 463.

ἐπιβουκόλος [ἐπι- (10) + βουκόλος. Pleonastically, 'the herdsman in charge of (the herd).' Cf. ἐπιβώτωρ, ἐπίουρος, ἐπιποιμήν, μετάγγελος]. A herdsman: βοῶν γ 422, υ 235 = φ 199, χ 268, 285, 292.

ἐπιβρέμω [ἐπι- (5)]. Of wind, to roar *upon* (and fan). With acc.: πῦρ P 739.

†**ἐπιβρίθω** (ἐπι- (5)]. 3 pl. aor. ἐπέβρῖσαν M 414. 3 sing. subj. ἐπιβρίσῃ E 91, H 343, M 286. 3 pl. opt. ἐπιβρίσειαν ω 344. **(1)** To bear or press heavily upon someone: μὴ ἐπιβρίσῃ πόλεμος H 343.—To bring one's weight to bear upon the foe: μᾶλλον ἐπέβρισαν M 414.—**(2)** Of rain or snow, to fall destructively or in excessive abundance E 91, M 286.—To fall in suitable abundance ω 344.

ἐπιβώσομαι, fut. mid. ἐπιβοάω.

ἐπιβώτωρ, -ορος, ὁ [ἐπι- (10) + βώτωρ. Cf. ἐπιβουκόλος]. A shepherd or goatherd: μήλων ν 222.

ἐπιγίγνομαι [ἐπι- (7)]. To succeed, come on in due succession: [ἄλλα φύλλα] ἔαρος ἐπιγίγνεται ὥρῃ Z 148. (*V.l.* ἔαρος ἐπιγίγνεται ὥρη.)

†**ἐπιγιγνώσκω** [ἐπι- (5)]. 3 sing. aor. subj. ἐπιγνώῃ ω 217. 3 pl. ἐπιγνώωσι σ 30. **(1)** To look upon, watch, see σ 30.—**(2)** To recognize ω 217.

ἐπιγνάμπτω [ἐπι- (11)]. 3 sing. aor. ἐπέγναμψε B 14, 31, 68. Pple. ἐπιγνάμψας Φ 178. Fem. ἐπιγνάμψᾱσα A 569. **(1)** To bend towards oneself: δόρυ Φ 178.—**(2)** Fig., to bend, influence: νόον I 514.—To bend to one's purpose, bring over to one's views B 14 = 31 = 68.—**(3)** To put restraint upon, restrain, repress: κῆρ A 569.

ἐπιγνώῃ, 3 sing. aor. subj. ἐπιγιγνώσκω.

ἐπιγουνίς, -ίδος, ἡ [ἐπι- (1) + γουν-, γόνυ]. The great extensor muscle of the thigh ρ 225, σ 74.

ἐπιγράβδην [ἐπιγράφω]. Grazing, inflicting a superficial wound: πῆχυν ἐ. βάλεν Φ 166.

†**ἐπιγράφω** [ἐπι- (5)]. 3 sing. aor. ἐπέγραψε Δ 139: χ 280. Pple. ἐπιγράψας H 187, Λ 388. Infin. ἐπιγράψαι N 553. **(1)** To graze, inflict a superficial wound upon: χρόα Δ 139. Cf. Λ 388, N 553 (here, app., simply, to touch or reach): χ 280.—**(2)** To scratch a mark upon: κλῆρον H 187.

ἐπιδέδρομε, 3 sing. pf. ἐπιτρέχω.

ἐπιδέξιος, -ον [ἐπι- (11) + δεξιός]. In neut. pl. ἐπιδέξια as adv., (in sequence) from left to right, in the sun's direction (*i.e.* in the lucky order): ὄρνυσθ' ἑξείης ἐ. φ 141.—App., on the right hand (*i.e.* in the lucky quarter): ἀστράπτων B 353.

ἐπιδευής, -ές [ἐπιδεύομαι]. Contr. pl. ἐπιδευεῖς I 225, N 622. **(1)** Needy, in want E 481.—**(2)** With genit., lacking, lacking in, being without, not having: κρειῶν M 299. Cf. N 622: δ 87.—Suffering want or being stinted in the matter of: δαιτὸς ἐΐσης I 225.—Falling short of: βίης Ὀδυσῆος φ 253.—Falling short in the matter of: βίης φ 185.—Absol., lacking the necessary strength ω 171.—**(3)** In neut. ἐπιδευές as abstract sb., lack: ἵνα μή τι δίκης ἐ. ἔχησθα T 180.

ἐπιδεύομαι [ἐπι- (19) + δεύομαι. See δεύω[2]]. With genit., to lack, find or feel the want of: σεῦ Σ 77: τούτων ο 371.—To fall short of (a person): κείνων ἀνδρῶν E 636.—To be unequal to, unfitted for: μάχης Ψ 670, μάχης Ἀχαιῶν (against the . . .) Ω 385.—To stand in need of, seek to get, desire: χρυσοῦ B 229.

ἐπιδέω [ἐπι- (5)]. To make fast, secure: ἐπέδησε θύρας φ 391.

ἐπιδημεύω [ἐπι- (2) + δῆμος in sense 'town.' Cf. πανδήμιος]. To dwell or remain in the city π 28.

ἐπιδήμιος [ἐπι- (2) + δήμιος]. **(1)** Among one's people, at one's home α 194, 233.—**(2)** Having a specified character in relation to one's own people as distinguished from strangers: ἐπιδήμιοι ἁρπακτῆρες (robbing your own folk (instead of your foes)) Ω 262.—**(3)** Of war, civil: πολέμου I 64.

†**ἐπιδίδωμι** [ἐπι- (5) (8)]. 3 sing. aor. ἐπέδωκε I 148, 290. Aor. infin. ἐπιδοῦναι Ψ 559. 1 pl. fut. mid. ἐπιδωσόμεθα (*v.l.* ἐπιβωσόμεθα) K 463. 1 pl. aor. subj. ἐπιδώμεθα X 254. **(1)** To give *with* (a daughter). With dat.: [μείλια] θυγατρί I 148 = 290.—**(2)** To give by way of making up to a person: ἄλλο Ψ 559.—**(3)** In mid., with reciprocal sense, of parties to an oath, to grant to each other the sanction of the gods as witnesses: θεοὺς ἐπιδώμεθα X 254.—App. with a vague notion of mutually calling upon a god: Ἀθήνην K 463.

ἐπιδῑνέω [ἐπι- (5) (11)]. **(1)** To whirl round (in preparation for a throw): λᾶαν ἧκ' ἐπιδινήσας H 269: = ι 538. Cf. Γ 378, T 268.—**(2)** To turn over, ponder, consider. In mid.: τόδε θυμὸς πόλλ' ἐπιδινεῖται υ 218.—**(3)** In pass., of flying birds, to wheel towards each other: ἐπιδινηθέντε τιναξάσθην πτερά β 151.

ἐπιδιφριάς, -άδος, ἡ [ἐπι- (1) + δίφρος]. App. = ἄντυξ (1): ἵπποι ἐξ ἐπιδιφριάδος ἱμᾶσι δέδεντο Κ 475.

ἐπιδίφριος [as prec.]. (Put) on a chariot: εἰς ὅ κε δῶρα ἐπιδίφρια θήῃ (θείω) ο 51, 75.

ἐπιδόντα, acc. sing. masc. aor. pple. ἐπείδω.

ἐπιδοῦναι, aor. infin. ἐπιδίδωμι.

ἐπίδρομος [ἐπι- (11) + δρομ-, δραμ-. See τρέχω]. Capable of being taken by assault: τεῖχος Ζ 434.

ἐπιδώμεθα, 1 pl. aor. subj. mid. ἐπιδίδωμι.

ἐπιδωσόμεθα, 1 pl. fut. mid. ἐπιδίδωμι.

ἔπιε, 3 sing. aor. πίνω.

ἐπιείκελος [ἐπι- (19) + εἴκελος]. Like, resembling. With dat.: ἀθανάτοισιν Α 265, Δ 394, Λ 60. Cf. Ι 485, 494, Χ 279, Ψ 80, Ω 486: ο 414, φ 14, 37, ω 36.

ἐπιεικής [ἐπι- (19) + (F)εἴκω[1]]. (1) Befitting, fitting, meet, suitable: τύμβον Ψ 246.—Adequate in amount or value: ἀμοιβήν μ 382.—(2) Absol. in neut. ἐπιεικές, what is fitting, meet, right: ὡς ἐ. ὀπυιέμεν ἐστίν β 207.—With copula to be supplied: ὡς ἐ. Θ 431, Τ 147, Ψ 537: θ 389.—So with infin.: ὅν κ' ἐ. ἀκουέμεν Α 547. Cf. Τ 21, Ψ 50.

ἐπιεικτός, -όν [app. ἐπι- (4) + (F)είκω[2]. For the form cf. νεμεσητός (2)]. Always with neg., giving senses (1) Unyielding, indomitable: μένος οὐκ ἐπιεικτόν τ 493.—(2) Ungovernable, not to be restrained: μένος Ε 892.—(3) Irresistible: σθένος Θ 32.—(4) Irrepressible: πένθος Π 549.—(5) Intolerable, unendurable: ἔργα θ 307.

ἐπιείσομαι, fut. mid. ἐφίημι[2].

ἐπιέλπω [ἐπι- (19)]. In mid., to hope. With fut. infin.: ἐμοὺς μύθους εἰδήσειν Α 545.—With acc. and fut. infin.: ἐπιελπόμενος τό γε θυμῷ νευρὴν ἐντανύειν φ 126.

†**ἐπιέννυμι** [ἐπι- (12)]. 1 pl. aor. ἐπιέσσαμεν υ 143. Pf. pple. mid. ἐπιειμένος, -ου Α 149, Η 164, Θ 262, Ι 372, Σ 157: ι 214, 514. (1) In act., to put upon a person as a (bed-)covering: χλαῖναν υ 143.—(2) In pf. mid. in sense sim. to those of ἕννυμι (II) (2). Fig.: ἀναιδείην ἐπιειμένε (clothed with . . . as with a garment) Α 149, ἐπιειμένοι ἀλκήν (clad upon with . . .) Η 164 = Θ 262, Σ 157. Cf. Ι 372: ι 214, 514.

ἐπιέσσαμεν, 1 pl. aor. ἐπιέννυμι.

ἐπιζάφελος [app. ἐπι- (19) + *ζάφελος in sim. sense, poss. fr. ζα- + φελ-, to swell. Cf. ὀφέλλω[2]]. Thus, of wrath, swelling, bursting forth, furious: χόλος Ι 525.

ἐπιζαφελῶς [adv. corresponding to prec. From *ἐπιζαφελής]. Furiously Ι 516: ζ 330.

ἐπίηλε, 3 sing. aor. ἐπιάλλω.

ἐπιήρανος [ἐπι- (19) + (F)ήρ. Cf. ἐρίηρος]. Pleasing, grateful: ποδάνιπτρα τ 343.

ἐπιθαρσύνω [ἐπι- (5)]. To cheer, encourage Δ 183.

ἐπιθεῖναι, aor. infin. ἐπιτίθημι.

ἐπίθημα, -ατος, τό [ἐπι- (1) + θη-, τίθημι]. A lid or cover: φωριαμῶν Ω 228.

ἐπιθήσω, fut. ἐπιτίθημι.

ἐπίθοντο, 3 pl. aor. mid. πείθω.

ἐπιθρέξαντος, genit. sing. neut. aor. pple. ἐπιτρέχω.

ἐπιθρῴσκω [ἐπι- (12) (14)]. (1) To leap *upon*. With dat.: τύμβῳ Μενελάου (in way of insult or derision) Δ 177.—To leap *on board of* (a ship). With genit.: νηός Θ 515.—(2) To leap or bound *over* (a space). With acc.: τόσσον ἐπιθρῴσκουσιν ἵπποι Ε 772.

ἐπιθύω [ἐπ-, ἐπι- (11)]. (1) To rush to or at something π 297.—(2) With infin., to be eager, strive: [νέκυν] ἐρύσσασθαι Σ 175.

ἐπιίστωρ, -ορος, ὁ [ἐπι- (5) + (F)ισ-, οἶδα. See εἴδω (C). 'One who has knowledge in a particular line']. Thus app., one with knowledge or experience of something specified: μεγάλων ἔργων (deeds of prowess) φ 26.

ἐπικάρ, also written **ἐπὶ κάρ**. App., either headlong (as fr. ἐπὶ κάρη (ἐπί (II) (2) (d)) or (with obscure derivation) sideways: χαράδραι ῥέουσαι ἐ. Π 392.

ἐπικάρσιος, -η, -ον [ἐπικάρ]. Of ships, app., plunging their bows in the sea, or drifting sideways, making leeway ι 70.

ἐπίκειμαι [ἐπι- (12) (18)]. 3 sing. fut. ἐπικείσεται Ζ 458. (1) To be laid or imposed upon a person: ἐπικείσετ' ἀνάγκη Ζ 458.—(2) Of a door, to be shut: θύραι ἐπέκειντο ζ 19.

†**ἐπικείρω** [ἐπι- (5)]. 3 sing. aor. ἐπέκερσε. App., to cut the line of retreat of, cut off the retreat of Π 394.

ἐπικείσεται, fut. ἐπίκειμαι.

ἐπικεκλιμένας, acc. pl. fem. pf. pple. pass. ἐπικλίνω.

†**ἐπικέλλω** [ἐπι- (12)]. 3 sing. aor. ἐπέκελσε ν 114. Infin. ἐπικέλσαι ι 148. Acc. pl. masc. pple. ἐπικέλσαντας ι 138. (1) To put one's ship on shore, bring her to shore ι 138.—(2) Of a ship, to come to shore ι 148.—To come to shore *on*. With dat.: ἠπείρῳ ν 114.

†**ἐπικέλομαι** [ἐπι- (5)]. 3 sing. aor. ἐπεκέκλετο. To call upon, summon, invoke: Ἐρινῦς (*i.e.* to further his prayers) Ι 454.

ἐπικεράννῡμι [ἐπι- (5)]. Aor. infin. ἐπικρῆσαι. To mix (wine) with water η 164.

ἐπικερτομέω [ἐπι- (5)]. To make fun of, mock, jeer at Π 744: χ 194.—In Ω 649 ἐπικερτομέων is app. to be taken as absol., and as referring to Achilles' tone in what follows as to Agamemnon.

ἐπικεύθω [ἐπι- (5)]. Fut. ἐπικεύσω Ε 816, Κ 115: δ 350, 744, ε 143, ξ 467, ρ 141, 154, τ 269, ψ 265. 2 sing. aor. subj. ἐπικεύσῃς ο 263. (1) To withhold (speech) Ε 816: δ 350 = ρ 141, δ 744, π 168, σ 171.—(2) Absol., to conceal one's thoughts or knowledge, withhold speech Κ 115: ε 143, ξ 467, ο 263, ρ 154, τ 269, ψ 265.

ἐπικίδνημι [ἐπι- (15)]. In pass., of the water of a river, to be spread *over*, to flow *upon*. With acc.: αἶαν Β 850.—So of the dawn, to be spread or shed *over* (a space) Η 451, 458.

ἐπικλείω [ἐπι- (5)]. To praise, extol, applaud: ἀοιδήν α 351.

ἐπίκλησις, ἡ [ἐπι- (6) + κλη-, καλέω]. (1) In acc. with a vb. of naming, as a second or derived name: ὅν τε κύν' Ὠρίωνος ἐπίκλησιν καλέουσιν Χ 29, Ἀστυάναξ, ὃν Τρῶες ἐπίκλησιν καλέουσιν (*i.e.* name thus) 506 (cf. Ζ 402). Cf. Η 138 (as a nickname), Σ 487 := ε 273.—(2) Adverbially in acc., in name, nominally (cf. πρόφασις, χάρις (2) (b)): ἐπίκλησιν Βώρῳ [τέκεν] Π 177.

†**ἐπικλίνω** [ἐπι- (18)]. Acc. pl. fem. pf. pple. pass. ἐπικεκλιμένας. To put into position for closing a gate, put to: ἐπικεκλιμένας σανίδας καὶ ὀχῆα Μ 121.

ἐπίκλοπος, ὁ [ἐπι- (5) + κλοπ-, κλέπτω]. (1) Cunning, wily ν 291.—(2) With genit., using deceit in the matter of, cunning or wily in: μύθων Χ 281.—Cunning or skilful in the matter of: τόξων φ 397.—(3) As sb., a cozener or cheat λ 364.

ἐπίκλυον, *aor.* [ἐπι- (5)]. (1) To listen to, give ear to: ἐπεὶ αἶνον ἐπέκλυεν Ψ 652.—(2) To hear, learn. With genit.: Ζηνὸς ἀγγελιάων ε 150.

†**ἐπικλώθω** [ἐπι- (5) + κλώθω, to spin. Cf. Κλῶθες. 'To spin the thread of one's destiny']. (Cf. ἐπινέω.) 3 sing. aor. ἐπέκλωσε π 64. 3 pl. -αν γ 208, λ 139. 3 sing. subj. ἐπικλώσῃ δ 208. 3 pl. aor. mid. ἐπεκλώσαντο Ω 525: α 17, θ 579. 3 pl. subj. ἐπικλώσωνται υ 196. To assign as one's lot or portion: ὄλβον γ 208, δ 208, τά λ 139, π 64.—In mid. θ 579, υ 196.—With infin. In mid.: οἰκόνδε νέεσθαι α 17.—Absol. In mid. Ω 525.

†**ἐπικόπτω** [ἐπι- (5)]. Fut. pple. ἐπικόψων. To bring one's blow to bear upon, strike: βοῦν γ 443.

ἐπικουρέω [ἐπίκουρος]. To give one's services in aid, fight in another's cause Ε 614.

ἐπίκουρος, -ου, ὁ [no doubt a compound of ἐπι-]. (1) One who gives his services in aid, one who fights in support of another or in another's cause Γ 188, Ε 478, Φ 431.—(2) In pl., auxiliaries Δ 379.—Esp. of the allies supporting the Trojan cause Β 130, 803, 815, Γ 451, 456, Ε 473, etc.

ἐπικόψων, fut. pple. ἐπικόπτω.

ἐπικραίνω, ἐπικραιαίνω [ἐπι- (5)]. 3 sing. aor. opt. ἐπικρήνειε Ο 599. Imp. ἐπικρήηνον Α 455, Θ 242, Π 238. To grant accomplishment or fulfilment of (a wish or prayer) Α 455 = Π 238, Θ 242, Ο 599.—Absol. Β 419, Γ 302.

ἐπικρατέω [ἐπι- (5)]. (1) To hold rule: ὅτ' ἐπικρατέωσιν ἄνακτες οἱ νέοι ξ 60 (as ἄνακτες (masters), *i.e.* when the young are masters).—To give directions, keep one's rule in evidence ρ 320.—(2) With dat., to hold sway among or in: νήεσσιν Κ 214: νήσοισιν α 245 = π 122 = τ 130.—(3) To have the upper hand in battle, be victorious Ξ 98.

ἐπικρατέως [adv. fr. ἐπικρατής conn. with ἐπικρατέω]. In overwhelming force, with overpowering might Π 67, 81.—Putting forth one's strength: ἰὸν ἧκεν ἐ. Ψ 863.

ἐπικρήηνον, aor. imp. ἐπικραίνω.

ἐπικρήνειε, 3 sing. aor. opt. ἐπικραίνω.

ἐπικρῆσαι, aor. infin. ἐπικεράννυμι.

ἐπίκριον, τό [ἐπ-, ἐπι- (1) + ἴκρια]. A top or look-out place fitted to the mast at some distance above its base in the ἴκρια ε 254, 318.

†**ἐπιλάμπω** [ἐπι- (4)]. 3 sing. aor. ἐπέλαμψε. To shine or give its light on the occurrence of something specified: ἠέλιος ἐπέλαμψεν (thereupon) Ρ 650.

ἐπιλείβω [ἐπι- (12)]. To make a libation upon something specified: ἀνιστάμενοι ἐπέλειβον γ 341.

ἐπιλεύσσω [ἐπι- (14)]. To see, have vision, *over* (a space). With acc.: τόσσον ἐπιλεύσσει Γ 12.

ἐπίληθος [ἐπιλήθω]. Bringing forgetfulness. With genit.: φάρμακον κακῶν ἐπίληθον δ 221.

ἐπιλήθω [ἐπι- (19)]. 3 sing. aor. ἐπέλησε υ 85. Fut. mid. ἐπιλήσομαι Χ 387. 3 sing. -εται α 57. 3 pl. -ονται Η 452. (1) In act., to cause to forget. With genit.: ἁπάντων υ 85.—(2) In mid., with genit. (a) To forget, cease to think of: τεῖχεος τὸ πολίσσαμεν Η 452. Cf. Χ 387: α 57.—(b) To forget, fail to bethink or avail oneself of: τέχνης δ 455, σχεδίης ε 324.

ἐπιληκέω [ἐπι- (8) + ληκ-, λάσκω. 'To make a sound in accompaniment']. Hence, app., to beat time with the feet θ 379.

ἐπιλήσομαι, fut. mid. ἐπιλήθω.

ἐπιλίγδην [ἐπι- (19) + λίγδην]. In a grazing manner, so as to be wounded superficially Ρ 599.

ἐπιλλίζω [ἐπ-, ἐπι- (5) + ἰλλίζω, conn. with ἰλλός, squinting]. To make a sidelong glance *at* in order to incite to something. With dat.: ἐπιλλίζουσί μοι ἑλκέμεναι δὲ κέλονται σ 11.

ἐπιλωβεύω [ἐπι- (5)]. To mock at a person β 323.

†**ἐπιμαίνομαι** [ἐπι- (5)]. 3 sing. aor. ἐπεμήνατο. To be mad *after*. With dat.: Βελλεροφόντῃ Ζ 160.

ἐπιμαίομαι [ἐπι- (5) (11)]. 3 sing. fut. ἐπιμάσσεται Δ 190. 3 sing. aor. ἐπεμάσσατο ν 429, π 172. Pple. ἐπιμασσάμενος ι 302, 446, τ 480. Fem. -η τ 468. (1) With genit., to aim *at*, seek to get: μεγάλων δώρων Κ 401.—To strive *after*, struggle *for*: νόστου ε 344.—To steer *for*, head *for*: σκοπέλου μ 220.—(2) To strike: μάστιγι ἵππους Ε 748 = Θ 392. Cf. Ρ 430: ν 429, π 172.—(3) To seize, grasp τ 480.—(4) To handle, touch, feel: οἴων νῶτα ι 441. Cf. ι 446.—Absol. ι 302 (feeling for the mortal spot), τ 468.—To keep feeling, finger: ξίφεος κώπην λ 531.—To put the hand upon, examine (a wound) Δ 190.

ἐπιμάρτυρος, ὁ [ἐπι- (5) + μάρτυρος]. (Written also as two words.) A witness invoked in sanction of something: Ζεὺς ἄμμ' ἐ. ἔστω Η 76. Cf. α 273.

ἐπιμάσσεται, 3 sing. fut. ἐπιμαίομαι.

ἐπίμαστος [ἐπιμασ-, ἐπιμαίομαι]. App., sought out, that has been brought (*i.e.* by Eumaeus), and has not come unasked: ἀλήτην υ 377.

ἐπιμειδάω [ἐπι- (5)]. To smile at a person, look towards him with a smile of propitiation or encouragement Δ 356, Θ 38: χ 371.—With a smile of amusement or derision Κ 400.

ἐπιμεῖναι, aor. infin. ἐπιμένω.

ἐπιμέμφομαι [ἐπι- (5) + μέμφομαι in sim. sense]

To find fault, show displeasure : εὐχωλῆς (in the matter of . . .) A 65, 93, τέο ἐπιμέμφεαι ; B 225.—To find fault with, blame. With dat. : κασιγνήτοις π 97, 115.

†**ἐπιμένω** [ἐπι- (6) (19)]. Aor. imp. ἐπίμεινον Z 340, T 142 : α 309, δ 587, ρ 277. Infin. ἐπιμεῖναι λ 351. (1) To wait or tarry (a little) longer : νῦν ἐπίμεινον Z 340. Cf. T 142 : α 309, δ 587, λ 351.—(2) To remain where one is, stay behind ρ 277.

ἐπιμήδομαι [ἐπι- (5)]. To contrive (something) *against*. With dat. : δόλον ἐπεμήδετο πατρί δ 437.

ἐπιμηνίω [ἐπι- (5)]. To cherish resentment *against*. With dat. : Πριάμῳ N 460.

ἐπιμιμνήσκω [ἐπι- (5)]. 1 pl. aor. opt. mid. ἐπιμνησαίμεθα P 103 : δ 191. Aor. pple. pass. ἐπιμνησθείς α 31, δ 189. With genit. (1) In mid. and pass., to remember, think of : Αἰγίσθοιο α 31. Cf. δ 189.—To remember, bethink oneself of : χάρμης P 103.—(2) In mid., to speak about : σεῖο δ 191.

ἐπιμίμνω [ἐπι- (2)]. To remain or abide *at*. With dat. : ἔργον ᾧ ἐπιμίμνω ξ 66, ο 372.

ἐπιμίξ [ἐπι- (19) + μιξ-, μίσγω]. Mingled together, in a confused mass : πλῆτο ἐ. ἵππων τε καὶ ἀνδρῶν Φ 16. Cf. Ψ 242.—In confusion, with all order lost : ὀρίνονται Λ 525. Cf. Ξ 60.—Indiscriminately, with random rage : μαίνεται λ 537.

ἐπιμίσγω [ἐπι- (5)]. In pass., with dat., to mingle *with*, have dealings or intercourse *with* : ἄμμι ζ 205. Cf. ζ 241.—In hostile sense : ἂψ ἐπιμισγομένων (as they joined battle (app. genit. absolute and referring to the whole of the combatants)) E 505, αἰεὶ Τρώεσσ' ἐπιμίσγομαι (am always in touch with . . .) K 548.

ἐπιμνησαίμεθα, 1 pl. aor. opt. mid. ἐπιμιμνήσκω.

ἐπιμνησθείς, aor. pple. pass. ἐπιμιμνήσκω.

†**ἐπιμύζω** [ἐπι- (4) + μύζω, to murmur]. 3 pl. aor. ἐπέμυξαν. To murmur or mutter at something : ἐπέμυξαν Ἀθηναίη τε καὶ Ἥρη (thereat) Δ 20 = Θ 457.

†**ἐπινέμω** [ἐπι- (14)]. 3 sing. aor. ἐπένειμε. To distribute or give out among a company : σῖτον I 216, Ω 625 : υ 254.

ἐπινεύω [ἐπι- (5)]. To nod : κόρυθι δ' ἐπένευεν (with his . . ., *i.e.* it nodded) X 314.—To nod in sanction of a promise O 75.

ἐπινεφρίδιος [ἐπι- (1) + νεφρός, the kidneys]. On, forming part of the substance of, the kidneys : δημόν Φ 204.

ἐπινέω [ἐπι- (5) + νέω²]. (Cf. ἐπικλώθω.) To assign as one's lot or portion Υ 128.—Absol. with complementary infin. : τῷ ὡς Μοῖρ' ἐπένησε . . . κύνας ἆσαι Ω 210.

ἐπινηνέω [ἐπι- (12) + νηνέω, app. = νηέω]. To pile or heap up *upon*. With genit. : νεκροὺς πυρκαϊῆς H 428 = 431.

ἐπίξῡνος, -ον [ἐπι- (19) + ξυνός]. Common : ἀρούρῃ M 422.

ἔπιον, aor. πίνω.

ἐπιόντα, acc. sing. masc. pple. ἔπειμι².

ἐπιορκέω [ἐπίορκος]. To swear falsely, perjure oneself : οὐδ' ἐπιορκήσω T 188.

ἐπίορκος [app. ἐπι- (5) + ὅρκος. 'In violation of one's oath']. (1) Falsely sworn T 264.—(2) In neut. ἐπίορκον as adv., of swearing, falsely, so as to perjure oneself : ὅτις κ' ἐ. ὀμόσσῃ Γ 279, T 260, ἐ. ἐπώμοσεν K 332 (here of unintentional falsity, the fulfilment of the oath turning out to be impossible).

ἐπιόσσομαι [ἐπι- (5)]. To have one's eye upon ; hence, to exercise vigilance, use one's efforts, to prevent : ἐπιοσσομένω θάνατον ἑταίρων P 381.

ἐπίουρος [ἐπι- (10) + οὖρος². Cf. ἐπιβουκόλος]. (1) A guardian, protector, warder N 450.—(2) A herdsman ν 405 = ο 39.

ἐπιόψομαι, fut. See ἐφοράω.

ἐπιπείθω [ἐπι- (4)]. Fut. mid. ἐπιπείσομαι Ψ 609. 2 sing. -εαι O 178. 3 -εται O 162, P 154, Σ 296. In mid., to yield to inducement, persuasion or command, to do another's bidding, be ruled, obey : οὐ τις ἐπιπείσεται Σ 296. Cf. I 660 : β 103 = κ 466 = μ 28 = ω 138, κ 406, 475, 550 = μ 324 = τ 148.—With dat. : σοὶ ἐπιπείθονται E 878. Cf. A 218, 345 = I 205 = Λ 616, A 565, Δ 412, O 162, 178, T 305, Ψ 609 : τ 14 = χ 108 = 393.—With infin. P 154 (see under εἶμι (1) (a)).

†**ἐπιπέλομαι** [ἐπι- (11)]. Neut. aor. pple. ἐπιπλόμενον. Of time, to come on or round : ἐπιπλόμενον ἔτος (the pple. adjectivally, 'revolving') η 261 = ξ 287.

†**ἐπιπέτομαι** [ἐπι- (11)]. 3 sing. aor. ἐπέπτατο N 821 : ο 160, 525. Aor. infin. ἐπιπτέσθαι Δ 126. To fly *towards*. With dat. : εἰπόντι οἱ ἐπέπτατο ὄρνις N 821 : = ο 160 = 525.—Of an arrow, to fly or speed to its mark Δ 126.

ἐπιπίλναμαι [ἐπι- (11)]. To approach or come near to a specified place : οὐ χιὼν ἐπιπίλναται ζ 44.

†**ἐπιπλάζω** [ἐπι- (14)]. Aor. pple. pass. ἐπιπλαγχθείς. In pass., to wander or rove *over* or *upon*. With acc. : πόντον ἐπιπλαγχθείς θ 14.

ἐπιπλέω [ἐπι- (14)]. Also **ἐπιπλώω** ε 284. Aor. pple. ἐπιπλώσας Γ 47. 2 sing. aor. ἐπέπλως γ 15. Pple. ἐπιπλώς Z 291. To sail *over* or *upon*, traverse. With acc. : πόντον ἐπιπλώσας Γ 47. Cf. A 312, Z 291 : γ 15, δ 842, ε 284, ι 227, 470, ο 474.

ἐπιπλήσσω [ἐπι- (5)]. Fut. infin. ἐπιπλήξειν Ψ 580. (1) To strike K 500.—(2) To attack with words, to find fault with, chide. With dat. : μοι M 211, Ψ 580.

ἐπιπλόμενον, neut. aor. pple. ἐπιπέλομαι.

ἐπιπλώς, aor. pple. ἐπιπλέω.

ἐπιπλώω. See ἐπιπλέω.

ἐπιπνέω [ἐπι- (5)]. In pres. only in forms fr. ἐπιπνείω. 3 pl. aor. subj. ἐπιπνεύσωσι ι 139. Of wind (1) To blow upon a person E 698.—To blow *upon*. With dat. : νηΐ δ 357.—(2) To blow in a particular (*i.e.* the desired) direction ι 139.

ἐπιποιμήν, -ένος [ἐπι- (10) + ποιμήν. Cf. ἐπιβουκόλος]. A herdsman μ 131.

ἐπιπρέπω [ἐπι- (19)]. To have a specified appearance : οὐδέ τοι δούλειον ἐπιπρέπει εἶδος (shows like a slave's) ω 252.

ἐπιπροέηκα, aor. ἐπιπροΐημι.

ἐπιπροέμεν, aor. infin. ἐπιπροΐημι.

†ἐπιπροϊάλλω [ἐπι- (11) + προ- (1)]. 3 sing. aor. ἐπιπροΐηλε. To push forward towards (and for) a person: τράπεζάν σφωϊν Λ 628.

†ἐπιπροΐημι [ἐπι- (11) + προ- (1) + ἵημι[1]]. Aor. ἐπιπροέηκα Ρ 708, Σ 58, 439. 3 sing. ἐπιπροέηκε Ι 520: ο 299. Aor. infin. ἐπιπροέμεν Δ 94. (1) To send forth or let fly (an arrow) *at*. With dat.: Μενελάῳ ἰόν Δ 94.—(2) To send forth (a person) on a specified or indicated mission: ἄνδρας Ι 520, Ἀχιλλῆα νηυσὶν Σ 58 = 439 (the dat. appears to be sociative, 'with the . . .').—(3) To send forth (a person) *towards* or *to*. With dat.: κεῖνον νηυσὶν Ρ 708.—(4) To steer *for*, make *for*. With dat.: νήσοισιν ο 299.

†ἐπιπταίρω [ἐπι- (4)]. 3 sing. aor. ἐπέπταρε. To sneeze *at*, *i.e.* as giving a favourable omen *to accompany*. With dat.: πᾶσι ἔπεσσιν ρ 545.

ἐπιπτέσθαι, aor. infin. ἐπιπέτομαι.

ἐπιπωλέομαι [ἐπι- (14)]. (1) To go *round* or *among*, inspect, review. With acc.: στίχας ἀνδρῶν Γ 196, Δ 231, 250.—(2) To range *round* or *among* with hostile intent. With acc.: στίχας ἀνδρῶν Λ 264 = 540.

†ἐπιρρέζω [ἐπι- (5)]. 3 pl. pa. iterative ἐπιρρέζεσκον. To do sacrifice to an indicated divinity ρ 211.

ἐπιρρέπω [ἐπι- (5)]. To descend in the scales of fate *upon*, come *upon*. With dat.: ὄφρ' ἡμῖν ὄλεθρος ἐπιρρέπῃ Ξ 99.

ἐπιρρέω [ἐπι- (12)]. (1) To flow *over* or *on the surface of*. With acc.: Πηνειόν Β 754.—(2) Fig., of bodies of men, to stream on and on Λ 724.

†ἐπιρρήσσω [ἐπι- (18)]. 3 sing. pa. iterative ἐπιρρήσσεσκε Ω 456. 3 pl. -ον Ω 454. To thrust or drive home (the fastening of a gate): ἐπιβλῆτα Ω 454, 456.

†ἐπιρρίπτω [ἐπι- (11)] 3 pl. aor. ἐπέρριψαν. To throw or hurl *at*. With dat.: δοῦρά μοι ε 310.

ἐπίρροθος [ἐπιρροθέω, to shout to (in encouragement), fr. ἐπι- (5) + ῥοθέω, to make a sound. Cf. ῥόθιος]. A supporter, aider, helper Δ 390, Ψ 770.

ἐπιρρώομαι [ἐπι- (2) (4)]. 3 pl. aor. ἐπερρώσαντο Α 529. (1) Of hair, to ripple or flow forward on the occurrence of something: νεῦσε . . . χαῖται δ' ἐπερρώσαντο (with the nod) Α 529.—(2) To ply one's task *at*. With dat.: μύλαισιν υ 107.

ἐπίσκοπος, -ου, ὁ [ἐπι- (5) + σκοπ-, σκέπτομαι]. (1) One who watches over something, a guardian or protector Χ 255, Ω 729. — One who looks (sharply) after something, a (keen) trafficker in or snatcher of something: ὁδαίων θ 163.—(2) One who spies *upon* (something), a spy. With dat.: Τρώεσσιν Κ 38, νήεσσιν 342.

ἐπισκύζομαι [ἐπι- (4)]. 3 sing. aor. opt. ἐπισκύσσαιτο η 306. To be angry or offended at something Ι 370: η 306 (should take offence).

ἐπισκύνιον, τό [no doubt a compound of ἐπι-]. The fold of skin above the eyes. Of a lion Ρ 136.

ἐπισκύσσαιτο, 3 sing. aor. opt. ἐπισκύζομαι.

ἐπισμυγερῶς [adv. fr. ἐπισμυγερός, fr. ἐπι- (19) + σμυγερός app. = μογερός, adj. fr. μόγος]. In sad or grievous fashion, to one's cost γ 195, δ 672.

ἐπίσπαστος [ἐπισπασ-, ἐπισπάω, fr. ἐπι- (5) + σπάω]. Brought upon oneself, such as one has oneself to thank for: κακόν σ 73, ω 462.

ἐπισπεῖν, aor. infin. ἐφέπω[1].

ἐπισπέρχω [ἐπι- (5)]. (1) To urge a person or a horse on to exertion Ψ 430: χ 451.—(2) *Intrans. for reflexive*, of wind, to rush, blow furiously ε 304.

ἐπισπέσθαι, aor. infin. mid. ἐφέπω[2].

ἐπισσείω [ἐπι- (5)]. (1) To shake something (threateningly) at a person: τῇ (*sc.* αἰγίδι) ἐπισσείων φοβέειν Ἀχαιούς Ο 230 (τῇ with φοβέειν).—(2) To shake (thus) *at*. With dat.: αἰγίδα πᾶσιν Δ 167.

ἐπισσεύω [ἐπι- (5) (11)]. 3 sing. aor. ἐπέσσευε σ 256, τ 129, υ 87. 3 sing. subj. ἐπισσεύῃ ε 421. Pple. ἐπισσεύας ξ 399. 3 sing. aor. mid. ἐπέσσυτο Ε 438, 459, Ι 398, Φ 227, etc.: δ 841, ζ 20. 1 pl. ἐπεσσύμεθα δ 454. 3 sing. pf. ἐπέσσυται Α 173, Ζ 361, Ι 42. Pple. ἐπεσσύμενος, -ου Μ 143, 388, Ξ 147, Ο 395, Π 411, 511, Ρ 737, Υ 288, Χ 26: ε 314, 428, 431, χ 307, 310. (I) (1) To set on or incite against a person ξ 399.—(2) With dat., to set in motion or send *against*: κῆτός μοι ε 421. —To send or cause to operate *against*: κακά μοι σ 256 = τ 129. Cf. υ 87. — (II) In mid. (1) To hasten or speed towards a specified or indicated point: ἀγορήνδ' ἐπεσσεύοντο Β 208, ἐπεσσύμενον πεδίοιο (over the . . .) Χ 26. Cf. Β 86, Ν 757, Σ 575: ν 19.—(2) To speed *to*. With dat.: οἱ δ 841.—With acc.: δέμνια κούρης ζ 20.—(3) In hostile sense, to rush, dart, dash, spring at or against someone or something: ἐπέσσυτο δαίμονι ἶσος Ε 438 = Π 705 = 786 = Υ 447. Cf. Π 411, Υ 288, Φ 234, 601: δ 454.—Of a wave ε 314, 431.—(4) To do this *against*. With dat.: νηυσίν Ο 347, 593. Cf. Ε 459 = 884, Φ 227.—With acc.: μνηστῆρας χ 307. Cf. Μ 143, Ο 395. — Of fire Ρ 737.—With genit.: τείχεος Μ 388, Π 511.—(5) Without indication of direction, to speed, rush: ἐπεσσύμενος πεδίοιο Ξ 147.—(6) In pf. pple., putting forth an effort, making a spring: ἐπεσσύμενος λάβε πέτρης ε 428.—Speeding, running up: λάβε γούνων χ 310.—(7) To be set, bent, disposed, inclined in an indicated direction: εἴ τοι θυμὸς ἐπέσσυται Α 173.—With complementary infin.: κτήμασι τέρπεσθαι Ι 398.—With ὥς τε and infin.: ὥς τε νέεσθαι Ι 42.—With ὄφρα Ζ 361.

ἐπίσσωτρον [ἐπι- (1) + σῶτρον, felloe]. The tire of a wheel Ε 725, Λ 537, Υ 394, 502, Ψ 505, 519.

ἐπισταδόν [ἐπι- (14) + στα-, ἵστημι]. Going round and standing or stopping by each in turn: νείκεον μ 392. Cf. ν 54 = σ 425.—Attending to each detail in succession: δόρπον ὁπλίζοντο π 453.

ἐπίσταμαι. 3 sing. subj. ἐπίστηται Π 243. 3 sing. opt. ἐπίσταιτο Ξ 92: θ 240. 1 pl. -αίμεσθα Ν 238. 3 pl. fut. ἐπιστήσονται Φ 320. (1) With infin. (a) To know how *to do*, have skill, be skilled, *in doing*: δαίδαλα τεύχειν Ε 60, ἢ ἐπίστηται πολεμίζειν (will prove to be a fighter) Π 243. Cf. Β 611, Ε 222 = Θ 106, Ν 223, 238: ι 49.—(b) To be able *to do* (something difficult or puzzling): ὅστε' ἀλλέξαι Φ 320.—With neg., to be at a loss *as to doing*: οὔ πῃ θέσθαι ἐπίσταμαι ν 207.—To have the strength *to do*: πῆλαι ἔγχος Π 142 = Τ 389.—(c) To know how *to do*, have the wit, knowledge, character, turn of mind, needed *for doing*: ἄρτια βάζειν Ξ 92: = θ 240. Cf. Ρ 671, Δ 404.—(2) To know so as to have skill in: ἔργα Ψ 705: β 117 = η 111.—(3) Adjectivally in pres. pple. (a) Skilled, skilful, expert, clever, astute: ἐπιστάμενος ἄκοντι (comitative dat., with the . . .) Ο 282. Cf. Τ 80: ἰητρὸς ἐπιστάμενος δ 231. Cf. ν 313, ψ 185. —So ἐπισταμένοισι πόδεσσιν Σ 599.—(b) Skilled in or in the use of. With genit.: φόρμιγγος καὶ ἀοιδῆς φ 406.—(c) In moral sense, knowing the right, of good character or disposition ξ 359. —(4) Absol., to know, have knowledge: ἐπιστάμεναι σάφα θυμῷ δ 730.

ἐπισταμένως [adv. fr. pres. pple. of ἐπίσταμαι]. Skilfully, deftly, dexterously: μίστυλλον Η 317 = Ω 623, ὀδόντες ἔχον ἔνθα καὶ ἔνθα ἐ. (skilfully arranged or disposed) Κ 265. Cf. ε 25, 245, λ 368, μ 307, ρ 341 = φ 44, τ 422, 457, υ 159, 161, ψ 197.

ἐπιστάτης, ὁ [ἐπι- (2) + στα-, ἵστημι. 'One who stands by or beside']. A suppliant or almsman; or perh., a follower or dependant ρ 455.

ἐπιστενάχω [ἐπι- (9)]. To groan in answer. In mid.: ἐπεστενάχοντο δ' ἑταῖροι Δ 154.

ἐπιστεφής [ἐπιστέφω]. Filled to the brim: κρητῆρας ἐπιστεφέας οἴνοιο (for the genit. cf. next) Θ 232: β 431.

†**ἐπιστέφω** [ἐπι- (5) + στέφω in sense 'to pack close']. 3 pl. aor. mid. ἐπεστέψαντο. To fill to the brim: κρητῆρας ἐπεστέψαντο ποτοῖο (genit. of material, with . . .) Α 470, Ι 175: = α 148 = γ 339 = φ 271.

ἐπιστήμων [ἐπίσταμαι]. Skilful, clever, adroit: ἐ. βουλῇ τε νόῳ τε π 374.

ἐπιστήσονται, 3 pl. fut. ἐπίσταμαι.

ἐπίστιον, τό. A slip on which to haul up a ship ζ 265.

ἐπιστοναχέω [ἐπι- (4)]. To make a sound under stress of something. Of the sea Ω 79.

†**ἐπιστρέφω** [ἐπι- (11)]. Aor. pple. ἐπιστρέψας. *Intrans. for reflexive*, to turn oneself towards something: ἕλκεν ἐπιστρέψας Γ 370 (*i.e.* in pulling he turned partly round towards his friends).

ἐπιστροφάδην [as next]. Turning from one to another, taking one after another: κτεῖνεν Κ 483. Cf. Φ 20: χ 308, ω 184.

ἐπίστροφος [ἐπι- (14) + στροφ-, στρέφω]. Going about or among: ἐ. ἦν ἀνθρώπων (had intercourse or dealings with (many) men) α 177.

ἐπιστρωφάω [ἐπι- (14)]. To go about *among*, visit. With acc.: ἐπιστρωφῶσι πόληας ρ 486.

ἐπισφύριον, τό [ἐπι- (1) + σφυρόν]. Perh. a guard of metal fixed on the leg between the knee and the ankle and partly covering the κνημίς so as to supplement this in protecting against the chafing of the shield: κνημῖδας ἀργυρέοισιν ἐπισφυρίοις ἀραρυίας Γ 331 = Λ 18 = Π 132 = Τ 370. Cf. Σ 459.

ἐπισχερώ [ἐπι- (7) + σχε- = (σ)εχ-, ἔχω]. In a row, one after or beside another: εἰς ὅ κε κτεινώμεθ' ἐ. Λ 668, ἀκτὴν εἰσανέβαινον ἐ. Σ 68. Cf. Ψ 125.

ἐπισχεσίη, -ης, ἡ [ἐπι- (11) + σχε-. See prec. Cf. ἐπέχω (3)]. An offering or putting forward: μύθου φ 71.

ἐπίσχεσις, ἡ [ἐπι- (5) + σχε- as prec. Cf. ἐπέχω (6)].—Holding back, reluctance, hesitation ρ 451.

ἐπισχοίης, 2 sing. aor. opt. ἐπέχω.

ἐπίσχω [ἐπ-, ἐπι- (5) (11)]. (1) To aim or direct a missile in an indicated direction. In mid.: ἐπισχόμενος βάλεν ἰῷ χ 15.—(2) To restrain, control, manage: ἵππους Ρ 465.—To withhold or restrain from. With genit.: θυμὸν ἐνιπῆς υ 266.

ἐπισχών, aor. pple. ἐπέχω.

ἐπιτάρροθος [an unexplained word. App. conn. with ἐπίρροθος]. In sense = ἐπίρροθος Ε 808, 828, Λ 366 = Υ 453, Μ 180, Ρ 339, Φ 289: ω 182.

ἐπιτέλλω [ἐπι- (5)]. 2 sing. aor. ἐπέτειλας Ε 818. Subj. ἐπιτείλω Κ 63, Ν 753. Imp. ἐπίτειλον Ω 112. Pple. ἐπιτείλας Κ 72, Ν 213. Infin. ἐπιτεῖλαι Δ 64, Κ 56. 3 sing. aor. mid. ἐπετείλατο α 327. Dat. sing. masc. pple. ἐπιτειλαμένῳ ρ 21. (1) To lay, impose, inflict upon a person. In mid.: νόστον λυγρόν, ὃν ἐπετείλατο α 327.—With dat.: χαλεποὺς μοι ἐπετέλλετ' ἀέθλους λ 622.—(2) (a) To lay an injunction or charge upon, give an order or orders to, a person: ὣς ἐπέτελλεν Ι 259 = Λ 790. Cf. Β 10, Ι 369, Κ 56, 72, Λ 768, 782, Ρ 360, Φ 445: ρ 186.—In mid. Ρ 382: ρ 21.—(b) With dat.: υἱέϊ σῷ Ω 112, ὧδέ μ' ἐπέτελλε, μὴ . . . ((with the assurance) that he would not . . .) 780. Cf. Ε 198, Κ 63, Λ 765, Ν 213, 753: ρ 9.—In mid. Β 802, Δ 301, Κ 61: μ 217.—(c) With dat. and the injunction directly reported Λ 785, Ρ 668.—In mid. Ι 252, Π 838.—(d) With acc. of what is enjoined or ordered: συνθεσιάων ἃς ἐπέτελλε (which he bade him remember) Ε 320. Cf. Ε 818.—(e) With dat. and acc.: ἕκαστά μ' ἐπέτελλεν Ψ 107. Cf. ψ 361.—In mid.: κούροισι ταῦτ' ἐπιτέλλομαι Ι 68. Cf. Α 295, Τ 192, Ψ 95: θ 40.—(f) With dat. and infin.: 'Αθηναίῃ ἐπιτεῖλαι ἐλθεῖν Δ 64. Cf. Δ 229, Ζ 207, Ι 179, Λ 47 = Μ 84, Λ 273 = 399, Λ 783, Φ 230: γ 267, μ 268 = 273. In mid. φ 240.—(g) With infin. to be supplied: ὄφρα μῦθον ἐνίσπω, ὃν Νέστωρ ἐπέτελλεν [ἐνισπεῖν] Λ 840.

ἐπιτέρπω [ἐπι- (4)]. In mid., to take delight *in*. With dat.: ἔργοις ξ 228.

ἐπιτηδές. In sufficient number: ἐν ἐρέτας ἐ. ἀγείρομεν Α 142: μνηστήρων σ' ἐ. ἀριστῆες λοχόωσιν (in force; or perh. here rather to be taken in sense 'with set purpose') ο 28.

†**ἐπιτίθημι** [ἐπι- (5) (6) (12) (18)]. Fut. ἐπιθήσω Ψ 796. 2 sing. -εις Τ 107. 3 -ει Δ 190, Υ 369. 1 pl. -ομεν β 192. Aor. ἐπέθηκα τ 256, ψ 194. 3 -ε Δ 111, Ξ 169, Ω 589: ι 240, 243, 314, 340, κ 545, ν 370, φ 45. 3 sing. aor. opt. ἐπιθείη ι 314. 2 pl. ἐπιθεῖτε Ω 264: χ 62. Imp. ἐπίθες χ 157. Nom. dual masc. pple. ἐπιθέντε χ 201. Fem. pple. ἐπιθεῖσα α 140, δ 56, η 176, κ 372, ο 139, ρ 95.

Infin. ἐπιθεῖναι E 751, H 364, 391, Θ 395 : λ 525. **(1)** To put or place upon something : οὐκ ἂν ταῦτ' ἐπιθεῖτε; (*sc.* on the waggon) Ω 264.—To put (food) on the table : εἴδατ' ἐπιθεῖσα α 140 = δ 56 = η 176 = κ 372 = ο 139 = ρ 95.—To put or fit on something by way of completing or finishing or for ornament: ἐπέθηκε κορώνην Δ 111. Cf. τ 256, φ 45, ψ 194.—To apply (a remedy) : φάρμακα Δ 190.—**(2)** To put or place *upon*. With genit. : Ἕκτορα λεχέων Ω 589.—With dat. : κεφαλῇ καλύπτρην κ 545.—**(3)** With dat., to impose (a penalty) *upon* : σοὶ θωὴν β 192.—To give (fulfilment) *to* : οὐδὲ τέλος μύθῳ ἐπιθήσεις T 107. Cf. Υ 369.—**(4)** To put to, shut (a door) Ξ 169 : χ 157, 201.—**(5)** To put in position (something covering or closing) : νέφος E 751 = Θ 395 : θυρεὸν ι 240 = 340, 314.—App., to bring into action : λόχον λ 525 (see ἀνακλίνω (1)).—**(6)** To apply (something covering or closing) *to*. With dat. : φαρέτρῃ πῶμα ι 314. Cf. ι 243, ν 370.—**(7)** To give in addition, add : οἴκοθεν ἄλλα H 364, 391. Cf. Ψ 796 : χ 62.

ἐπιτῑμήτωρ, ὁ [ἐπι- (5) + τιμη-, τιμάω. 'One who honours']. A patron or protector ι 270.

†***ἐπιτλάω** [ἐπι- (5) + τλάω]. 3 sing. aor. imp. ἐπιτλήτω. **(1)** To be patient, to acquiesce in something proposed Ψ 591.—**(2)** To lend a patient ear *to*, let oneself be ruled *by*. With dat. : ἐπιτλήτω τοι κραδίη μύθοισιν ἐμοῖσιν T 220.

ἐπιτολμάω [ἐπι- (5)]. **(1)** To steel oneself to endure something ρ 238.—**(2)** To steel or resign oneself *to do*. With infin. : ἐπιτολμάτω κραδίη ἀκούειν α 353.

ἐπίτονος, ὁ [ἐπι- (7) + τον-, τείνω]. The backstay of a mast (cf. πρότονοι) μ 423.

ἐπιτοξάζομαι [ἐπι- (11)]. To shoot *at*, use the bow *against*. With dat. : Ἕκτορι Γ 79.

ἐπιτραπέω [ἐπι- (11) + τραπ-, τρέπω]. To commit or leave a duty *to*. With dat. and infin. : Τρωσὶ φυλάσσειν K 421.

ἐπιτρέπω [ἐπι- (11). 2 sing. aor. ἐπέτρεψας Φ 473. 3 -ε K 116. 2 sing. opt. ἐπιτρέψειας ο 24. 3 -ειε η 149. Imp. ἐπίτρεψον τ 502. Infin. ἐπιτρέψαι φ 279, χ 289. 1 pl. aor. ἐπετράπομεν K 59. Imp. pl. ἐπιτράπετε P 509. 3 sing. aor. mid. ἐπετράπετο ι 12. 3 sing. pf. pass. ἐπιτέτραπται E 750, Θ 394. 3 pl. ἐπιτετράφαται B 25, 62. **(1)** In mid., of the mind, etc., to be turned or inclined in a specified direction, to be bent or set on *doing*. With infin. : σοὶ θυμὸς ἐπετράπετο εἴρεσθαι (is set on . . .) ι 12.—**(2)** With dat. **(a)** To turn over, commit, entrust, leave *to* : ᾧ λαοί ἐπιτετράφαται B 25 = 62 : Μέντορι οἶκον β 226. Cf. E 750 = Θ 394, P 509 : ο 24, χ 289.—**(b)** To leave or bequeath *to* : παισὶ κτήματα η 149.—**(c)** To commit or leave an indicated duty *to* : τοῖσι μάλιστα K 59.—**(d)** To leave it *to* (a person) *to do* : σοὶ οἴῳ πονέεσθαι K 116.—**(e)** To leave a matter *to*, leave oneself *in the hands of* : θεοῖσιν τ 502, φ 279.—**(3)** With dat., to yield or give up *to* : Ποσειδάωνι νίκην Φ 473.—To yield or give in *to* : γήραϊ K 79.

ἐπιτρέχω [ἐπι- (11) (14)]. Genit. sing. neut. aor. pple. ἐπιθρέξαντος N 409. 3 sing. aor. ἐπέδραμε Δ 524, E 617. 3 dual ἐπεδραμέτην, ἐπιδραμέτην K 354, Ψ 418, 433, 447. 3 pl. ἐπέδραμον Ξ 421, Σ 527 : ξ 30. 3 sing. pf. ἐπιδέδρομε ζ 45, υ 357. **(1)** To run *towards* in its course, tend to approach. With dat. : ἅρμαθ' ἵπποις ἐπέτρεχον Ψ 504.—**(2)** To run towards or up to a person, etc., with hostile intent : ἐπέδραμεν ὅς ῥ' ἔβαλεν Δ 524. Cf. E 617, K 354, Ξ 421, Σ 527.—Of dogs ξ 30.—**(3)** To run after or in pursuit of a competitor in a race. Of horses Ψ 418, 447.—**(4)** To run *over* (a space). Of horses : τόσσον ἐπιδραμέτην Ψ 433.—Of a spear, to pass over (and graze) something : ἀσπὶς ἐπιθρέξαντος ἄϋσεν ἔγχεος (genit. absolute) N 409.—**(5)** In pf., of light, to play or be shed upon something : λευκὴ ἐπιδέδρομεν αἴγλη ζ 45.—Of a mist, to be spread over something υ 357.

ἐπιτρέψαι, aor. infin. ἐπιτρέπω.

ἐπιτροχάδην [ἐπιτροχ-, ἐπιτρέχω]. **(1)** Trippingly on the tongue, without stumbling : ἀγόρευεν Γ 213.—**(2)** Fluently, too fluently, with a torrent of words σ 26.

†**ἐπιφέρω** [ἐπι- (5)]. 3 sing. fut. ἐποίσει A 89 : π 438. Aor. ἐπένεικα T 261. To lay (a hand or one's hands) *upon*. With dat. : σοὶ χεῖρας A 89. Cf. T 261 : π 438.

ἐπιφθονέω [ἐπι- (5)]. To grudge something to, be disinclined to grant something to : ᾧ κ' ἐπιφθονέοις, ὁ δ' εἶσιν ὀπίσσω λ 149.

ἐπιφλέγω [ἐπι- (14) (19)]. **(1)** To burn up, consume : νεκρὸν πῦρ Ψ 52.—**(2)** To blaze or rage *over* or *through*. With acc. : ὕλην B 455.

†**ἐπιφράζω** [ἐπι- (5)]. 2 sing. aor. mid. ἐπεφράσω Φ 410. 3 ἐπεφράσατο E 665 : θ 94, 533. 3 sing. subj. ἐπιφράσσεται ο 444. 1 pl. opt. ἐπιφρασσαίμεθα N 741. 3 ἐπιφρασσαίατο B 282 : σ 94. 2 sing. aor. pass. ἐπεφράσθης ε 183. In mid. and pass. **(1)** To think of, have the wit to do : τὸ οὔ τις ἐπεφράσατο, μηροῦ ἐξερύσαι δόρυ (it did not occur to them) E 665.—**(2)** To take (counsel) : ἐπιφρασσαίμεθ' ἂν βουλήν N 741.—**(3)** To think of, have the wit to think of, devise : τὸν μῦθον ἀγορεῦσαι ε 183 (the infin. complementary).—To devise, contrive : ὑμῖν ὄλεθρον ο 444.—**(4)** To mark, note something regarding : 'Αλκίνοός μιν οἶος ἐπεφράσατο θ 94 = 533, ἵνα μή μιν ἐπιφρασσαίατ' 'Αχαιοί (lest he should betray himself) σ 94.—To mark, get into one's head. With dependent clause : οὐκ ἐπεφράσω ὅσσον ἀρείων εὔχομ' ἔμεναι Φ 410.—To get cognizance of, learn, hear : βουλήν B 282.

ἐπιφρονέω [ἐπίφρων]. To mark or discern what should be marked or discerned : ὡς σὺ ἐπιφρονέουσ' ἀγορεύεις (showing good discernment) τ 385.

ἐπιφροσύνη, -ης, ἡ [ἐπίφρων]. **(1)** Sagacity or adroitness in an emergency ε 437.—**(2)** In pl., sense or prudence leading one to do something specified : αἳ γὰρ ἐπιφροσύνας ἀνέλοιο οἴκου κήδεσθαι τ 22.

ἐπίφρων, -ονος [app. ἐπι- (5) + φρήν. 'Applying the mind to something']. **(1)** Having good sense, well-balanced in mind, shrewd, sagacious ψ 12.—

(2) Of counsel, wise, shrewd, sagacious γ 128, π 242, τ 326.

ἐπιχειρέω [ἐπι- (5) + χείρ]. To lay hands *upon*, apply oneself *to*. With dat. : δείπνῳ ω 386. Cf. ω 395.

†**ἐπιχέω** [ἐπι- (12) (15)]. 3 sing. aor. ἐπέχευε α 136, δ 52, η 172, κ 368, ο 135, ρ 91. Infin. ἐπιχεῦαι Ω 303. 3 sing. aor. mid. ἐπεχεύατο ε 257, 487. 3 pl. aor. pass. ἐπέχυντο Ο 654, Π 295. (1) To pour over a person's hands : χέρνιβα α 136 = δ 52 = η 172 = κ 368 = ο 135 = ρ 91.—(2) To pour *over* (the hands). With dat. : χερσὶν ὕδωρ Ω 303.—(3) In mid., to pile up on oneself, cover oneself with : χύσιν ἐπεχεύατο φύλλων ε 487.—To pile up or dispose against something : πολλὴν ἐπεχεύατο ὕλην ε 257 (*i.e.*, app., set it outside the wickerwork as additional protection).—(4) In pass., of persons, to stream or be spread over an indicated or specified space : τοὶ δ' ἐπέχυντο Ο 654. Cf. Π 295.

ἐπιχθόνιος [ἐπι- (1) + χθον-, χθών]. Dwelling on earth. Epithet of men Α 266, 272, Β 553, Δ 45, Ι 558, Ω 505 : α 167, θ 479, σ 136, χ 414 = ψ 65.—Absol. in pl., the dwellers on earth : ἄλλος ἐπιχθονίων Ω 220. Cf. ρ 115, ω 197.

†**ἐπιχράω** [ἐπι- (5) + χράω[2]]. 3 pl. aor. ἐπέχραον. With dat., to attack, assail, lay hands *upon* : λύκοι ἄρνεσσιν Π 352, Δαναοὶ Τρώεσσιν 356.—To assail with importunities, beset : μητέρι β 50.

ἐπιχρίω [ἐπι- (5)]. Aor. pple. ἐπιχρίσᾱσα σ 172. (1) To apply unguent to, anoint (one's person or a part thereof) : παρειάς σ 172.—In mid. : χρῶτ' ἐπιχρίεσθαι σ 179.—(2) To besmear : [τόξον] ἀλοιφῇ φ 179.

ἐπιψαύω [ἐπι- (5)]. To exercise the power of touch in an indicated direction. Fig. : ὅς τ' ὀλίγον περ ἐπιψαύῃ πραπίδεσσιν (has even a little range with his wits) θ 547.

ἐπιωγή [ἐπι- (5) + ἰωγή]. A place where ships may lie under the lee of the land, a roadstead ε 404.

ἐπιών, pple. ἔπειμι[2].

ἔπλεξε, 3 sing. aor. πλέκω.

ἔπλετο, 3 sing. aor. mid. πέλω.

ἔπληντο, 3 pl. aor. pass. πελάζω.

ἐπλήσθη, 3 sing. aor. pass. πίμπλημι.

ἔπνευσε, 3 sing. aor. πνέω.

ἐποίσει, 3 sing. fut. ἐπιφέρω.

ἐποίχομαι [ἐπ-, ἐπι- (11) (14)]. (1) With acc., to go *towards*, to go to join : μνηστῆρας ἐπῴχετο α 324.—In hostile sense, to assail, attack. Of Apollo : οὐρῆας Α 50.—So absol. : ἐποιχόμενος κατέπεφνεν Ω 759 : γ 280 = ο 411.—Of Artemis. Absol. ε 124 = λ 173 = 199.—Of a hero under the inspiration of a divinity. Of Diomedes Ε 330, Κ 487.—Of Hector Ο 279.—(2) To range, go about, go hither and thither : πάντοσε Ε 508, Μυρμιδόνας ἐποιχόμενος θώρηξεν Π 155. Cf. Ζ 81, Κ 167, 171, Π 496 = 533, Ρ 215 : ζ 282.—Of missiles Α 383.—(3) To range or go hither and thither *over*. With acc. : νηῶν ἴκρια Ο 676.—Of sound : [αὐτὴ] πάσας [πύλας] ἐπῴχετο Μ 340 (*v.l.* πᾶσαι ἐπῴχατο).—(4) To go round a company : ἐπῴχετο οἰνοχοεύων α 143. Cf. ρ 346 = 351.—(5) With acc., to range or go hither and thither *round* or *among* : πάντας ἐπῴχετο κελεύων Ρ 356.—To go *round* or *among*, inspect, review : πάσας [φώκας] δ 451.—(6) To walk *along* (the web) following the shuttle, to work at (the web). With acc. : ἱστὸν ἐποιχομένην Α 31. Cf. ε 62, κ 222, 226, 254.—(7) Hence, in gen., to ply (one's task) : ἔργον ἐποίχεσθαι Ζ 492 : α 358, ρ 227, σ 363, φ 352.—To go to see about, busy oneself about : δόρπον ν 34.—Absol., to go about a task : ἐποιχομένη ἔντυεν ἵππους Ε 720 = Θ 382.

ἐπόμνῡμι [ἐπ-, ἐπι- (4) + ὄμνυμι]. 3 sing. aor. ἐπώμοσε Κ 332. To take an oath at one's bidding : ἐπόμνυον ὡς ἐκέλευεν ο 437 = σ 58. Cf. Κ 332.

ἐπομφάλιος [ἐπ-, ἐπι- (1) + ὀμφαλός]. In neut. ἐπομφάλιον as adv., on the boss (of a shield) : βάλε σάκος ἐπομφάλιον Η 267.

ἐποπίζομαι [ἐπ-, ἐπι- (5)]. To have regard for, respect, shrink from incurring : Διὸς μῆνιν ε 146.

ἐποπτάω [ἐπ-, ἐπι- (1)]. To roast upon something indicated : ἐπώπτων ἔγκατα μ 363.

ἐποπτεύω [ἐπ-, ἐπι- (14) + ὀπτεύω, fr. ὀπ-. See ὁράω]. (διοπτεύω.) 3 sing. pa. iterative ἐποπτεύεσκε. To go over, visit, inspect : ἔργα π 140.

ἔπορε, 3 sing. aor. πόρω.

†**ἐπορέγω** [ἐπ-, ἐπι- (11)]. Aor. pple. mid. ἐπορεξάμενος. In mid., to reach towards a person in order to strike him : ἐπορεξάμενος οὔτασε χεῖρα Ε 335.

†**ἐπόρνῡμι** [ἐπ-, ἐπι- (5)]. Also **ἐπορνύω** Ο 613. 3 sing. aor. ἐπῶρσε Ρ 72, Υ 93, Χ 204 : ε 109, η 271, ι 67, χ 429. 3 pl. opt. ἐπόρσειαν Η 42. Imp. ἔπορσον Ε 765. 3 sing. aor. mid. ἐπῶρτο Φ 324. (1) To rouse to action, stir up : μένος Υ 93, Χ 204.—To incite *to do*. With infin. : πολεμίζειν Η 42.—(2) With dat. (a) To rouse or incite to action *against*, set *on* : Ἀθηναίην οἱ Ε 765. Cf. Ρ 72.—To rouse or set in motion (a natural force) *against* : νηυσὶν ἄνεμον ι 67. Cf. ε 109.—(b) To bring (something evil) *upon* : ὀϊζύν μοι η 271. Cf. Ο 613.—(c) To cause (sleep) to come *to* : τῇ ὕπνον χ 429.—(3) In mid., to rouse or bestir oneself to action *against*, rush *upon*. With dat. : ἐπῶρτ' Ἀχιλῆϊ Φ 324.

ἐπορούω [ἐπ-, ἐπι- (11)]. (1) To rush at a foe, make an attack or assault : τρὶς ἐπόρουσεν Ε 436, Π 784, Υ 445. Cf. Γ 379, Ν 541, Π 330, Υ 284, 442, Φ 33, Χ 138.—To rush up in order to strip a fallen foe : ἐπόρουσε καὶ αἴνυτο τεύχεα Λ 580. Cf. Ν 550, Ο 579.—(2) With dat. (a) To rush *at*, attack, assail : Αἰνείᾳ Ε 432. Cf. Δ 472, Λ 256, Ο 520, 525, Π 320, Φ 144, 392.—(b) To rush or speed *to* or *towards* as a helper : Τυδεΐδῃ Ε 793.—(c) Of sleep, to come irresistibly, fall, *upon* : Ὀδυσσῆϊ ψ 343.—(3) To rush *to* (and mount) (a chariot). With acc. : ἅρμ' ἐπορούσας Ρ 481.

ἔπορσον, aor. imp. ἐπόρνυμι.

ἔπος, τό (Ϝέπος). [Cf. (Ϝ)εἶπον.] Dat. sing. ἔπεϊ Ε 879. ἔπει Α 395, 504, Ο 106. Dat. pl. ἐπέεσσι Α 223, Γ 38, Μ 267, Ο 162, etc. : β 189, η 17, κ 173, π 279, etc. ἔπεσσι Ι 113, Κ 542, etc. : δ 484, ε 96, ι 258, ρ 545, etc. ἔπεσι Α 77, 150,

211, B 73, Ψ 682 : θ 170, ρ 374, ω 161. (1) Something said, an utterance or speech, a word: ἐ. ἔφατο A 361, ἅλιον ἐ. ἔκβαλον Σ 324. Cf. B 807, Γ 204, Δ 350, E 170, etc. : γ 226, 374, δ 503, θ 241, etc.—What one has to say, discourse, words: ἵν' ἐ. ἀκούσῃς ἡμέτερον λ 561.—An element of speech, a word : τά μοι ἔειπε, τῶν οὐδέν τοι κρύψω ἐ. δ 350 = ρ 141.—(2) In pl., speech, discourse, words: ἔπεα πτερόεντα προσηύδα A 201, ὄτρυνεν ἐπέεσσιν Γ 249, ἐπέεσσι καθάπτετο O 127. Cf. A 223, 304, 519, B 73, 75, etc. : β 189, 323, γ 264, δ 286, λ 99, etc.—(3) In pl., words, speech, as distinguished from action : ἔπεσιν ὀνείδισον A 211, ἐπέεσσί κ' ἀθανάτοισι μαχοίμην Υ 367. Cf. Π 628, Υ 200, 211, 256, 431 : ζ 143, 146.—Contrasted in terms with χεῖρες A 77, Π 630.—In sing. with ἔργον A 395, 504, E 879, O 234 : β 272, 304, γ 99 = δ 329, δ 163, λ 346, ο 375.—In pl. : ἐπέων ἠδὲ καὶ ἔργων Λ 703.—With βίη : ἢ ἔπει ἠὲ βίῃ O 106.—(4) The sense of the word coloured by the context A 108 (a prediction), 150 (your orders), 216 (your injunction), 419 (your prayer), 543 (your intention), B 361 (the counsel), Γ 83 (a proposal), H 375 (proposal), 394 (proposal), Θ 8 (my announced purpose, my will), I 100 (say what is in your mind and hearken to what another has to say), Λ 652 (tidings), 788 (counsel), Ξ 44 (the threat), 212 (your request), 234 (my request), O 156 (the commands), 162 (my commands), 178 (his commands), 566 (his exhortation), Π 236 (my prayer), 686 (the injunction), P 701 (tidings), Σ 273 (counsel), T 121 (a piece of news), X 454 (the thing which I say (the thing being identified with the words)), Ψ 544 (what you propose), Ω 75 (a suggestion), 92 and 224 (his injunction), 744 (counsel) : γ 243 (a question), δ 137, 420 and 461 (questions), ζ 289 (counsel, directions), θ 91 (his lays), 141 (this proposal of yours), 358 (your request), κ 178 (exhortation), 428 (orders), λ 146 (directions), 348 (this suggestion), μ 222 (exhortation), 266 (injunction), ξ 131 (a story), ο 536 = ρ 163 = τ 309 (prediction), π 469 (the news), ρ 519 (lays), 584 (cf. I 100 above), σ 166 (a warning), τ 98 (cf. I 100 above), 565 (idle promises), υ 115 (wish, prayer), 236 (prediction), φ 278 (counsel).

ἐποτρύνω [ἐπ-, ἐπι- (5)]. 2 sing. aor. ἐπότρῡνας θ 185. 3 -ε O 456. Subj. ἐποτρῡ́νω Π 525 : α 89. 2 sing. -ῃς β 189. 3 -ῃσι Π 690 : θ 45. -ῃ K 130, O 148 : ι 139. 2 dual -ητον Z 83. 3 pl. -ωσι ω 355. 3 sing. opt. ἐποτρῡ́νειε ξ 461, 498. Imp. ἐπότρῡνον O 258 : ζ 36. Pple. ἐποτρῡ́νας β 422, ι 488, κ 128, λ 44, etc. Infin. ἐποτρῦναι κ 531. 1 pl. aor. subj. mid. ἐποτρῡνώμεθα θ 31. (1) (a) To rouse or stir to action, incite, urge, press, exhort : φάλαγγας Z 83, 'Οδυσῆα Θ 92. Cf. K 130, O 43 : α 89, ε 139, θ 185, ξ 461, ρ 395.—(b) With complementary infin. : τάφρον διαβαινέμεν M 50. Cf. N 767 = P 117 = 683, O 456, Π 525, 690, P 178 : θ 45.—(c) With dat. and infin. : ἱππεῦσιν ἐλαυνέμεν ἵππους O 258. Cf. κ 531.—(d) With acc. and infin. : ἑὲ αὐτὸν μαχέσασθαι Υ 171. Cf. β 189, ζ 36, ξ 498, ο 73.—(e) With acc. of what one is urged to do : ὅττι κ' ἐποτρύνῃ O 148.—(f) Absol. : εἰς ὅ κε θυμὸς ἐποτρύνῃ ι 139. Cf. Z 439, M 442, N 94 = 480 = P 219, O 725, P 553, Υ 364, 373, Ω 297 : β 422 = ο 217 = 287, η 262, ι 488, 561, κ 128, λ 44, ξ 79, ο 208, ω 175.—(2) To hasten on with, press on. In mid. : ἐποτρυνώμεθα πομπήν θ 31.—(3) To stir up (strife) *against*. With dat. : νῶϊν ἐποτρύνει πόλεμον χ 152.—(4) To dispatch (a message) : ἀγγελίας ω 355.

ἐπουράνιος [ἐπ-, ἐπι- (2) + οὐρανός]. Dwelling in the heavens. Epithet of the gods Z 129, 131, 527.—Of a god ρ 484.

†**ἐποχέω** [ἐπ-, ἐπι- (1) + ὀχέω]. 3 sing. fut. pass. ἐποχήσεται. To carry or bear *upon*. With dat. : μὴ τοῖς ἵπποισιν ἀνὴρ ἐποχήσεται ἄλλος K 330. Cf. P 449.

ἐπόψεαι, 2 sing. fut. See ἐφοράω.

ἔπραθον, aor. πέρθω.

ἔπρηξας, 2 sing. aor. πρήσσω.

ἔπρησε, 3 sing. aor. πρήθω.

ἑπτά, *indeclinable*. Seven B 719, Z 421, I 85, 122 = 264, I 128, 149, 270, 291, T 243, 246, Φ 407 : ι 202, μ 129, ω 274.—Absol. : ἑ. παρίσχομεν I 638.—With another numeral: ἑ. καὶ δέκα ε 278, η 267, ω 63.

ἑπταβόειος [ἑπτά + βόειος]. Of seven layers of ox-hide : σάκος H 220, 222, 245, 266, Λ 545.

ἑπτάετες [ἑπτά + ἔτος]. For seven years: ἤνασσεν γ 304, μένον η 259, ξ 285.

ἑπταπόδης [ἑπτά + ποδ-, πούς, foot, as a measure of length]. Seven-foot : θρῆνυν (app. raised seven feet) O 729.

ἑπτάπυλος, -ον [ἑπτά + πύλη]. The seven-gated. Epithet of the Boeotian Thebes Δ 406 : λ 263.

ἔπταρε, 3 sing. aor. πταίρω.

ἔπτατο, 3 sing. aor. πέτομαι.

ἕπταχα [ἑπτά]. Into seven parts ξ 434.

ἔπτηξαν, 3 pl. aor. πτήσσω.

ἐπτοίηθεν, 3 pl. aor. pass. πτοιέω.

ἐπύθοντο, 3 pl. aor. πεύθομαι.

ἕπω[1] [σεπ-]. (ἀμφι-, δι-, ἐφ-, μεθ-.) (1) To handle, take into one's hands, turn over : τεύχεα Z 321.—(2) With advbs. (a) With ἀμφί. (α) To beset : ἀ. 'Οδυσῆα Τρῶες ἕπον Λ 483.—(β) To busy oneself about : ἀ. βοὸς ἕπετον κρέα Λ 776. Cf. H 316 := τ 421, θ 61.—(b) With ἐπί, to attend to : ἐ. ἔργον ἕποιεν ξ 195.—(c) With μετά, to direct, look after : μ. Τυδέος υἱὸν ἕπουσαν K 516.—(d) With περί, to pull about, handle : περὶ τεύχε' ἕπουσιν O 555.

ἕπω[2] [σεq-, σεπ-. Cf. L. *sequor*]. Only in mid. Imp. ἕπευ N 465, O 556 : ο 281, ψ 52, 78. Fut. ἕψομαι K 108 : β 287, ζ 32. 2 sing. -εαι Ω 733. 3 -εται Δ 415, Ω 182 : γ 359. 1 pl. -όμεθα N 785 : ψ 127. 3 -ονται Δ 63. Infin. ἕψεσθαι φ 104. 2 sing. aor. ἕσπεο (σέσπεο) K 285. 3 -ετο Γ 376, Δ 476, Λ 472, M 398, N 300, 492, O 559, Π 632 : α 125, δ 276, ζ 164, θ 109, ρ 53. 3 dual -έσθην Γ 239. 1 pl. -όμεθα A 158. 3 pl. subj. ἕσπωνται μ 349. Opt. ἑσποίμην τ 579, φ 77. Pple. ἑσπόμενος -ου K 246, M 395, N 570. Without reduplication, imp. σπεῖο K 285 (app. for σπέο, the lengthening being due to the first arsis). 3 sing. σπέσθω M 350, 363. Infin. σπέσθαι E 423: δ 38, χ 324. (ἐφ-, μεθ-.) (**1**) (**a**) To follow in company with, go or come with, accompany, a person or persons or something: ἀλλ' ἕπεο K 146. Cf. K 246, N 381, 465, O 556, Σ 387, 572: ἡ δ' ἕσπετ' Ἀθήνη α 125. Cf. ε 91, κ 313, 448, ξ 45, 482, ο 162, 281, 470, ψ 52, 78, ω 5.—(**b**) With dat.: υἱεῖ σῷ Γ 174. Cf. I 428, K 108, M 91, N 300, X 450, etc.: γ 376, δ 276, ζ 276, ξ 298, ο 81, τ 245.—(**c**) With ἅμα: θεοὶ ἅμα πάντες ἕποντο A 424. Cf. Γ 447, I 170, K 194, Λ 472 = O 559 = Π 632, Λ 781, Ω 327: β 287, 413 = θ 46 = 104, ζ 319, θ 109, κ 231 = 257.—With ἅμα and dat.: τοκεῦσιν ἅμ' ἕσπετο Δ 476. Cf. Γ 143, E 423, I 512, K 222, M 350, etc.: β 11, γ 359, δ 38, ζ 32, κ 425, etc.—(**d**) With μετά: μετὰ νέφος εἵπετο πεζῶν Ψ 133.—With μετά and dat.: μετά σφιν εἵπετο Σ 234.—(**e**) With σύν: σὺν δ' εἵπετ' Ὀδυσσεύς κ 436.—With σύν and dat.: σὺν ἀμφιπόλοισιν ἕπεσθαι η 304.—(**2**) Of herdsmen accompanying their herd. With ἅμα: δύω ἅμ' ἕποντο νομῆες Σ 525: ρ 214 = υ 175.—With ἅμα and dat.: ἅμ' ὕεσσιν ἑπέσθω ο 397.—Of their dogs following with them. With dat.: ἐννέα σφι κύνες ἕποντο Σ 578.—Of sheep. With μετά and acc.: ὡς εἴ τε μετὰ κτίλον ἕσπετο μῆλα N 492.—(**3**) To go with as one's wife. With dat.: σοὶ ἄλοχον σπέσθαι χ 324.—With ἅμα and dat.: ἣ ἅμ' ἕπηται (ἕπωμαι) Ἀχαιῶν [κείνῳ] ὅς τις ἄριστος π 76, τ 528, τῷ κεν ἅμ' ἑσποίμην τ 579 = φ 77. Cf. φ 104.—(**4**) To go with, fall to the lot of. With dat.: τῷ κε νικήσαντι γυνὴ ἕποιτο Γ 255.—(**5**) (**a**) To follow a person as one's chief or leader: λαοὶ ἕποντο N 492. Cf. Δ 430: γ 363.—To form part of an expedition, follow with the rest Γ 239, 240, Ω 400: λ 493.—(**b**) With dat.: παῦρός οἱ εἵπετο λαός B 675. Cf. B 619, Δ 91, I 44, Λ 228, M 78, etc.: γ 165, δ 536, ζ 164, ι 159, λ 168, etc.—(**c**) With ἅμα: ἅμα νέφος εἵπετο πεζῶν Δ 274. Cf. E 591, Λ 796, M 124, N 690, 717, etc.: ψ 127, ω 117.—With ἅμα and dat.: σοὶ ἅμ' ἑσπόμεθα A 158. Cf. B 524, 534, 542, 762, M 87, etc.: λ 372, ο 541, τ 196.—(**6**) (**a**) To follow up, hang upon, the foe: αἰὲν ἀποκτείνων ἕπετο Λ 154. Cf. Λ 165, 168, 565, 754, O 277, Π 372, P 730.—Of flowing water Φ 256.—(**b**) With ἅμα: Τρῶες ἅμ' ἕποντο P 753.—(**c**) App., with ἀμφί, to beset: ἀμφ' Ὀδυσσῆα Τρῶες ἕποντο Λ 474 (prob. ἕπον should be read. See 483 under ἕπω[1] (2) (a) (α)).—(**7**) To be in a person's service: ἓξ δρηστῆρες ἕπονται π 248.—To be at the service of, fulfil the behests of. With dat.: πρεσβυτέροισιν Ἐρινύες αἰὲν ἕπονται O 204.—(**8**) To keep up with, play one's part with. With dat.: ἕπεθ' ἵπποις ἀθανάτοισιν Π 154.—Sim. of the limbs, to keep up with one's spirit or strength, play their part: εἴθ' ὡς . . . ὥς τοι γούναθ' ἕποιτο Δ 314. Cf. υ 237 = φ 202.—(**9**) To follow the motion of, fall forward following. With dat.: ἑσπόμενος πέσε δουρί (*i.e.* as it was drawn back) M 395, ἑσπόμενος περὶ δουρί (transfixed by it and giving way before the blow; περί advbl.) N 570.—(**10**) Of an inanimate object, to follow the motion of, come away with, something: ἔπαλξις ἕσπετο πᾶσα (came away, gave way) M 398.—With dat.: προτὶ φρένες δουρὶ ἕποντο (came away with it; προτί advbl.) Π 504.—With ἅμα and dat.: τρυφάλεια ἅμ' ἕσπετο χειρί Γ 376.—(**11**) To fall in with something proposed, agree, concur: ἐπὶ δ' ἕψονται θεοὶ ἄλλοι Δ 63. Cf. μ 349.—(**12**) Of a dowry, to go with, accompany. With ἐπί and genit.: ἕεδνα ὅσσα ἔοικε φίλης ἐπὶ παιδὸς ἕπεσθαι α 278 = β 197.—(**13**) Of honour, to accompany, attend, come to. With dat.: Διὸς κούρῃσιν ἕπεσθαι τιμήν I 513.—With ἅμα and dat.: τούτῳ κῦδος ἅμ' ἕψεται Δ 415.—(**14**) Of a quality, to go with, be shown in (a person). With dat.: ὅ τοι οὐκ ἕπετ' ἀλκή Θ 140.

ἐπώμοσε, 3 sing. aor. ἐπόμνυμι.

ἐπώνυμος [ἐπ-, ἐπι- (4)) + ὄνυμα, Aeolic form of ὄνομα]. Of a name, given on account of some particular circumstance: Ἀλκυόνην καλέεσκον ἐπώνυμον, οὕνεκα . . . I 562: Ἀρήτη ὄνομ' ἐστὶν ἐπώνυμον η 54 (app. because she had been prayed for, fr. ἀρή[1]), Ὀδυσεὺς ὄνομ' ἔστω ἐπώνυμον τ 409 (the reason for the name being given in the preceding lines).

ἐπῶρσε, 3 sing. aor. ἐπόρνυμι.

ἐπῶρτο, 3 sing. aor. mid. ἐπόρνυμι.

ἐπῴχατο, 3 pl. plupf. pass. ἐπέχω.

ἐπῴχετο, 3 sing. impf. ἐποίχομαι.

ἐράασθε, 2 pl. impf. ἔραμαι.

ἔραζε. To the earth, to the ground, on the ground: πῖπτον M 156, Σ 552. Cf. Π 459, P 619, 633: ο 527, χ 20, 85, 280.

ἔραμαι. 2 pl. impf. ἐράασθε Π 208. Aor. ἠρασάμην Ξ 317. 3 sing. ἠράσατο Π 182. ἠράσσατο Υ 223: λ 238. With genit. (**1**) To love, be in love with: σεο Γ 446 = Ξ 328.—In aor., to fall in love with: ὁπότ' ἠρασάμην Ἰξιονίης ἀλόχοιο Ξ 317. Cf. Π 182, Υ 223: λ 238.—(**2**) To be fond of (something), long for, lust after (it): πολέμου I 64, φυλόπιδος Π 208.

ἐραννός, -ή, -όν [ἔραμαι. 'Lovely']. Fair, pleasant. Epithet of places I 531, 577: η 18.

ἔρανος, -ου, ὁ. A feast to which the partakers contributed in shares (cf. εἰλαπίνη) α 226, λ 415.

ἐρατεινός, -ή, -όν [ἔραμαι. 'Lovely']. (**1**) An epithet of general commendation, pleasing, charming, delightful, fair, or the like: ὁμηλικίην Γ 175. Cf. Z 156, T 347, 353, Φ 218: δαῖτα θ 61, υ 117, ἑτάροισιν ἐ. (a pleasing sight) ι 230. Cf. δ 13, ψ 300.—(**2**) As epithet of places, fair, pleasant B 532, 571, 583, 591, 607, Γ 239, 401, 443, E 210, Ξ 226, Σ 291: η 79.

ἐρατίζω [ἔραμαι]. To be greedy after. With genit.: κρειῶν ἐρατίζων Λ 551 = P 660.

ἐρατός [as ἐρατεινός]. = ἐρατεινός (1) Γ 64.

ἐργάζομαι [(F)έργον]. (**1**) To do work, work, labour: σφίσιν ἐργάζεσθαι ἀνάγκη ξ 272 = ρ 441.—Of a piece of apparatus, to do its work, operate Σ 469.—(**2**) To do, perform: ἔργα ἀεικέα Ω 733. Cf. ρ 321, υ 72 (complementary infin.), χ 422 (do.), ω 210.—(3) To work upon, work up: χρυσόν γ 435.

ἔργαθε, 3 sing. aor. ἔργω[1].

†**ἔργνῡμι** [=(*F*)έργω[1]]. 3 sing. impf. ἐέργνῡ. To shut up, confine: συφεοῖσιν (in the . . .) κ 238.

ἔργον, -ου, τό (*F*έργον) [cf. (*F*)έρδω]. (1) Something done or performed or to be done or performed, a deed: ἃ Ζεὺς μήδετο ἔργα B 38, ὑπέσχετο μέγα ἐ. N 366. Cf. Γ 130, E 757, I 595, Π 120, Σ 77, etc.: α 338, β 63, γ 275, κ 199, σ 221, etc.—For ἐ. contrasted in terms with ἔπος see ἔπος (3).—(2) One's work, the work in hand or before one: μὴ ἀμβαλλώμεθα ἐ. B 436, ἀτελευτήτῳ ἐπὶ ἔργῳ Δ 175, ὄφρ' ἐπὶ ἔργα τράπωνται Ψ 53. Cf. B 137, H 465, Σ 473, T 150, 242: β 252, ε 243, ι 250 = 310 = 343, ξ 195, ρ 227, σ 363, χ 479.—(3) Toilsome work, toil, labour: ἐ. ἀεικὲς ἔχοντα T 133.—A task: ἔργα κ' ἀεικέα ἐργάζοιο Ω 733.—(4) A kind of work or activity, a sphere of action: ἐν πάντεσσ' ἔργοισι δαήμονα Ψ 671. Cf. Δ 258: ἔργα κάκ' ἔμμαθεν ρ 226. Cf. θ 245, ξ 228, ο 320, σ 362, υ 378.—(5) The process or condition of working, work, action: ἀνηνύστῳ ἐπὶ ἔργῳ (with no end to the business) π 111.—Carrying into effect, action: πλεόνων ἐ. ἄμεινον M 412. Cf. I 374.—(6) (a) Work of war, warfare, strife. (α) With qualifying words: ἐ. Ἄρηος Λ 734. Cf. Π 208.—So πολεμήϊα ἔργα B 338, E 428, H 236, Λ 719, N 727, 730: μ 116. Cf. Θ 453.—(β) Without such words: ἐπ' αὐτῷ ἐ. ἐτύχθη Δ 470. Cf. Δ 539, M 271, 416: χ 149.—περὶ ἔργα τέτυκτο (in . . .) P 279: λ 550.—(b) One's work in war, one's prowess: παρ' ἔμ' ἵστασο καὶ ἴδε ἐ. P 179: χ 233. Cf. Z 522.—In pl., deeds of prowess: ἐπιίστορα ἔργων φ 26.—(7) Work on the land, tillage: ἔρις ἔργοιο σ 366. Cf. ξ 222, σ 369.—In pl.: ἔργων ἀνέπαυσεν P 549.—(8) A piece of work in the arts, a piece of craftsmanship: χαρίεντα ἔργα τελείει ζ 234 = ψ 161.—(9) A work, occupation, affair: θαλάσσια ἔργα B 614: ε 67.—(10) (a) The work, a piece of work, an occupation, proper to women: ἀμφίπολοι ἐπὶ ἔργα τράποντο Γ 422, ἀμφιπόλοισι κέλευε ἐ. ἐποίχεσθαι Z 492. Cf. Z 324, 490: = α 356 = φ 350, α 358, δ 683, τ 514, φ 352.—(b) In pl., their various crafts or occupations: ἀμύμονα ἔργα ἰδυίας I 128. Cf. I 270, Σ 420, T 245, Ψ 263, 705: ἔργ' ἐπίστασθαι β 117 = η 111. Cf. ν 289 = π 158, ο 418, υ 72, χ 422, ω 278.—(c) In pl., skill in such crafts, craftsmanship: οὐ χερείων ἔργα (in . . .) A 115. Cf. I 390, N 432.—(d) The materials of their work: ἀκὴν ἔμεναι παρὰ ἔργῳ (by their (your) work) φ 239, 385.—(11) A matter, affair, business, thing: εἰ σοὶ πᾶν ἐ. ὑπείξομαι (in everything) A 294, λοίγια ἔργα 518, τάδε ἔργα (these troubles) Γ 321. Cf. B 252, E 429, Z 348, Θ 9, I 228, etc.: ἐν πᾶσι ἔργοισιν η 52, μὴ ἀμφαδὰ ἔργα γένοιτο τ 391. Cf. β 280, γ 56, π 373, ρ 78, 274, τ 323.—App. in vague sense 'thing': χερμάδιον, μέγα ἐ. E 303, Υ 286.—A state of affairs: εἴσιδεν ἐ. ἀεικές Ξ 13.—(12) The result of work. (a) Something made, the work of . . .: πέπλοι ἔργα γυναικῶν Z 289. Cf. H 444, T 22: δ 617 = ο 117, η 97, κ 223, ω 75.—Something due to action, the work of . . .: τόδε ἐ. [ἐστὶν] Ἀθηναίης π 207.—(b) A device or representation: τελαμών, ἵνα θέσκελα ἔργα τέτυκτο λ 610.—(c) A piece of tilled land, a farm or estate: ἀνδρῶν πίονα ἔργα M 283, ἵκετο ἔργ' ἀνθρώπων (app. meaning 'the world of men') T 131. Cf. B 751, E 92, Π 392: πατρώϊα ἔργα β 22, οὔτε βοῶν οὔτ' ἀνδρῶν φαίνετο ἔργα (tilled with oxen or by the hand of man) κ 98, [ᾧ] θεὸς ἐ. ἀέξῃ ξ 65. Cf. β 127 = σ 288, δ 318, ζ 259, η 26, κ 147, ξ 66, 344, ο 372, 505, π 140, 144, 314, ω 388.

ἔργω[1], and, with prothetic ἐ, **ἐέργω,** contr. to **εἴργω** Ψ 72 (*F*έργω, ἐ*F*έργω). 3 pl. aor. ἔρξαν ξ 411. 3 sing. aor. ἐέργαθε E 147. ἔργαθε Λ 437. Acc. sing. masc. aor. pple. pass. ἐρχθέντα Φ 282. 3 pl. pf. ἔρχαται Π 481: κ 283. Nom. pl. fem. pple. ἐεργμέναι E 89. 3 pl. plupf. ἐέρχατο κ 241. ἔρχατο P 354: ι 221, ξ 73. (ἀνεέργω, ἀπο-, διεέργω, προεέργω, συν-.) (1) To ward or keep off: [βέλος] ἀπὸ χροὸς Δ 130.—To ward or keep off from. With genit.: παιδὸς μυῖαν Δ 131. Cf. P 571.—(2) To keep at a distance, prevent the approach of: τῆλέ με εἴργουσι ψυχαί Ψ 72.—To debar: ἀπὸ τιμῆς λ 503.—To debar from participation in. With genit.: πολέμοιο N 525.—(3) To keep apart: βόε ζυγὸν οἶον ἀμφὶς ἐέργει N 706 (*i.e.* they are as close together as the yoke admits).—To keep off or from contact with something: ἀπὸ χθονὸς ἔεργε Ξ 349.—To keep (a ship) away, head (her) off: καπνοῦ ἐκτὸς ἔεργε νῆα μ 219.—(4) To separate, sever: ἀπ' αὐχένος ὦμον E 147. Cf. Λ 437.—(5) To shut up, confine: κλαίοντες ἐέρχατο κ 241. Cf. ι 221, κ 283, ξ 73, 411.—To coop up: ἐρχθέντ' ἐν ποταμῷ Φ 282.—(6) To debar from freedom of movement, constrain to movement in a specified direction: ἂψ ἐπὶ νῆας ἔεργεν Π 395.—(7) To pack together: σάκεσσιν ἔρχατο πάντῃ (were formed into, formed, a barrier with their shields) P 354.—In reference to a dike or embankment, to draw it tight so as to form a continuous barrier in order to confine a river: γέφυραι ἐεργμέναι E 89.—To form into a fence or containing substance: ἔνθα φρένες ἔρχαται ἀμφὶ κῆρ (contains, surrounds, the heart) Π 481.—(8) To bound: ὅσον ἐκ νηῶν ἀπὸ πύργου τάφρος ἔεργεν Θ 213 (app., the space which, measuring along a line drawn (outwards at any point) from the ships, the trench bounded at a distance from the wall, *i.e.* the space between the wall and the trench).—To skirt, pass along: ἐπ' ἀριστερὰ λαὸν ἐέργων M 201 = 219 (see ἀριστερός (2) (b)).—For ἐντὸς ἐέργειν see ἐντός (1).

***ἔργω**[2]. See next.

ἔρδω, ἕρδω (*F*έρδω) [*F*εργ-, *F*έργjω. Cf. (*F*)έργον, (*F*)ρέζω]. 2 sing. pa. iterative ἔρδεσκες ν 350. 3 -ε I 540. From *ἔργω (**F*έργω) (the fut. and aor. forms written also ἑ-) Fut. ἔρξω ε 360, λ 80. Infin. ἐρξέμεν η 294. 3 sing. aor. ἔρξε κ 435, ψ 312. 3 pl. -αν θ 490. 2 sing. subj. ἔρξῃς B 364: α 293. Opt. ἔρξαιμι ν 147. Acc. sing. masc. pple. ἔρξαντα E 650: ψ 277. Fem. ἔρξᾱσα π 177, σ 197. Imp.

ἔρξον Δ 37, Χ 185 : ν 145, π 67, ω 481. Infin. ἔρξαι ε 342. 2 sing. pf. ἔοργας (Ϝέϝοργας) Γ 57, Φ 399, Χ 347. 3 -ε Β 272, Γ 351, Ε 175, Θ 356, Π 424. Pple. ἐοργώς Ι 320 : χ 318. 3 sing. plupf. ἐώργει (ϝεϜόργει) δ 693, ξ 289. (1) To do, act: ἔρξον ὅπως ἐθέλεις Δ 37. Cf. Β 364, Δ 29 = Π 443 = Χ 181, Χ 185 : ὧδ' ἔρξω ε 360. Cf. ε 342, ζ 258, η 294, κ 435, ν 145, 147, π 67, 177, σ 197, ω 481.—With acc. of person affected by the action: εὖ μιν ἔρξαντα Ε 650.—(2) To do, perform, accomplish: μυρί' ἐσθλά Β 272. Cf. Γ 57, Θ 356, Ι 320, Κ 503, Ξ 261, Ο 148, Φ 399, Χ 347 : ἔργα βίαια β 236, οἷα μενοινᾷς ἔρδειν χ 218. Cf. α 293, θ 490, λ 80, ξ 289, ο 360, τ 92, χ 318, ψ 312.—With double acc. of what is done and of the person or thing affected: ὅ με πρότερος κάκ' ἔοργε Γ 351. Cf. Ε 175 = Π 424, Ι 540 : δ 693.—(3) To do or offer (sacrifice): ἑκατόμβας Α 315, Β 306. Cf. Λ 707 : η 202, λ 132 = ψ 279, ν 350, ψ 277.

ἐρεβεννός, -ή, -όν [Ἔρεβος. Cf. ἐρεμνός]. Dark, murky: νύξ Ε 659 = Ν 580, Θ 488, Ι 474, Χ 466. Cf. Ε 864, Ν 425, Χ 309.

ἐρέβινθος, ὁ. The chick-pea Ν 589.

ἐρεείνω. (ἐξ-.) (1) To ask, inquire, make inquiry: δεύτερον ἐρέεινεν Γ 191. Cf. Γ 225 : τ 42, ω 262.—In mid.: ἐρεείνετο μύθῳ ρ 305.—(2) To ask or inquire about: ἵπποι οὓς ἐρεείνεις Κ 558. Cf. Ζ 145, Φ 153 : ω 281.—(3) To question (a person): μιν Ζ 176. Cf. ε 85, η 31, λ 234, υ 190, ψ 365.—(4) With double acc. of person questioned and of what is inquired about: πόσιν ἕκαστα δ 137. Cf. α 220.

ἐρέεσθαι, infin. mid. See εἴρομαι.

ἐρεθίζω [ἐρέθω]. (1) To irritate, provoke to anger: μή μ' ἐρέθιζε Α 32, Ω 560. Cf. ι 494.—(2) In milder sense, to tease, provoke, worry: Ἥρην Δ 5. Cf. Ε 419 : υ 374.—Absol. ρ 394.—(3) To provoke to fight, try to bring to close quarters Ρ 658.—(4) To provoke or rouse into making disclosures τ 45.

ἐρέθω. (1) = ἐρεθίζω (1) Γ 414.—(2) = ἐρεθίζω (2) Α 519.—(3) To keep from peace or rest, trouble: ὀδύναι μ' ἐρέθουσιν δ 813. Cf. τ 517.

ἐρείδω. 3 sing. aor. ἔρεισε Λ 235, Ρ 48. Pple. ἐρείσας Χ 97, 112 : θ 66, 473. Infin. ἐρεῖσαι λ 426. 3 sing. aor. mid. ἐρείσατο Ε 309, Λ 355. Pple. ἐρεισάμενος Β 109, Θ 496, Μ 457, Π 736. 3 sing. aor. pass. ἐρείσθη Η 145, Λ 144, Μ 192. Pple. ἐρεισθείς Χ 225 : ι 383. 3 pl. pf. ἐρηρέδαται Ψ 284, 329. 3 sing. plupf. ἠρήρειστο Γ 358, Δ 136, Η 252, Λ 436. 3 pl. ἐρηρέδατο η 95. (ἐν-, ἐπ-.) (1) To press closely, be in close contact with, so that mutual support is afforded: ἀσπὶς ἀσπίδ' ἔρειδεν Ν 131 = Π 215.—(2) To press, strive, carry on a contest. In mid.: μηκέτ' ἐρείδεσθον Ψ 735.—(3) With σύν, in reference to the dead, to bring together (the lips), compose (the mouth): σὺν στόμ' ἐρεῖσαι λ 426.—(4) To put one's weight or strength into a blow, thrust, etc.: ἐπὶ δ' ἔρεισεν Λ 235 = Ρ 48.—In mid. Μ 457, Π 736.—In pass. ἐρεισθεὶς δίνεον ι 383.—With instrumental dat.: ἐρείδοντες βελέεσσιν Π 108.—(5) In pass., of a missile, to force its way, pass: διὰ θώρηκος ἠρήρειστο Γ 358 = Δ 136 = Η 252 = Λ 436.—(6) To cause to lean or stand, lean, prop (against something): πύργῳ ἔπ' ἀσπίδ' ἐρείσας Χ 97. Cf. Χ 112 : θ 66 = 473, χ 450.—(7) In mid. and pass. (a) To lean or support oneself (upon or with something): τῷ ἐρεισάμενος Β 109, Θ 496, ἐρείσατο χειρὶ γαίης (on the ground with his hand) Ε 309, Λ 355. Cf. Ξ 38, Τ 49, Χ 225 : κ 170.—(b) To lean or be set against something so as to afford support: λᾶε ξύλου ἑκάτερθεν ἐρηρέδαται Ψ 329.—(c) To hang down (on to something), rest (upon it): οὔδεϊ χαῖται ἐρηρέδαται Ψ 284.—(d) To lie or be stretched out (upon something): ὕπτιος οὔδει ἐρείσθη Η 145, Λ 144, Μ 192.—(e) To stand (against something), be ranged (round about along it): θρόνοι περὶ τοῖχον ἐρηρέδατο η 95.

ἐρείκω. 3 sing. aor. ἤρικε Ρ 295. (1) To rend Ν 441.—(2) In aor., to be rent: ἤρικε κόρυς Ρ 295.

ἔρειο, imp. mid. εἴρομαι.

ἐρείομεν, 1 pl. subj. See εἴρομαι.

ἐρείπω. 3 sing. aor. ἤριπε Δ 462, Ε 47, Θ 122, Π 319, Ρ 619, Χ 330, etc.: χ 296. ἔριπε Ε 68, Υ 417. 3 sing. subj. ἐρίπῃσι Ρ 522. Pple. ἐριπών Ε 309, Θ 329, Λ 355. Fem. ἐριποῦσα Ε 357, Φ 243, 246. 3 sing. plupf. pass. ἐρέριπτο Ξ 15. (ἐξ-, κατ-, ὑπ-.) (1) To pull or throw down: ἐπάλξεις Μ 258. Cf. Ξ 15, Ο 356, 361.—(2) In aor., to fall: ἤριπεν ὡς ὅτε πύργος Δ 462. Cf. Δ 493, Ε 47, 58, 68, 75, Ν 389, Ρ 522, Φ 243, Χ 467, etc.: χ 296.

ἔρεισε, 3 sing. aor. ἐρείδω.

ἐρείσθη, 3 sing. aor. pass. ἐρείδω.

ἐρεμνός, -ή, -όν [Ἔρεβος. Cf. ἐρεβεννός]. Dark, murky: νυκτί λ 606.—Referring to the gloom of the underworld ω 106.—Dark, threatening: αἰγίδα Δ 167, λαίλαπι Μ 375, Υ 51.

ἔρεξα, aor. ῥέζω.

ἐρέοιμι, opt. See εἴρομαι.

ἐρέοντο, 3 pl. impf. mid. See εἴρομαι.

ἐρέπτομαι. (ὑπερέπτω.) To take as food, eat, munch. Of men or horses: λωτόν Β 776, κρῖ Ε 196, Θ 564 : λωτόν ι 97.—Of fishes, to gnaw away: δημόν Φ 204.—Of birds, to peck up: πυρόν τ 553.

ἐρέριπτο, 3 sing. plupf. pass. ἐρείπω.

ἐρέσθαι, aor. infin. See εἴρομαι.

ἐρέσσω. (δι-, προ-.) To ply the oar, row Ι 361 : ι 490, λ 78, μ 194.

ἐρέτης [ἐρε-, ἐρέσσω]. A rower: ἐρέτας ἀγείρομεν Α 142. Cf. Α 309, Β 719 : α 280, β 307, 319, ν 115, π 349.

ἐρετμόν, -οῦ, τό [ἐρε-τ-μόν, ἐρέσσω]. An oar: προέρεσσαν ἐρετμοῖς Α 435 : εὐῆρες ἐ. λ 121. Cf. δ 580, ζ 269, θ 37, λ 77, μ 171, ν 22, π 353, etc.

ἐρεύγομαι. 3 sing. aor. ἤρυγε Υ 403, 404. Acc. sing. masc. pple. ἐρυγόντα Υ 406. (προσ-.) (1) To roar: ἤρυγεν ὡς ὅτε ταῦρος ἤρυγεν Υ 403. Cf. Υ 406.—Of the sea Ρ 265 : ε 403, 438. (Or the passages relating to the sea may be taken in a sense sim. to (2), 'to send forth its spray, break in foam.')—(2) To belch: ἐρεύγετο οἰνοβαρείων ι 374.—To belch or spew forth: φόνον αἵματος Π 162.

ἐρεύθω [ἐρυθρός]. Aor. infin. ἐρεῦσαι Σ 329. To redden: αἵματι γαῖαν Λ 394. Cf. Σ 329.

ἐρευνάω. (1) To make search, hunt, quest Σ 321.—(2) Of dogs, to follow (the scent): ἴχνι' ἐρευνῶντες τ 436.—(3) To search for: τεύχεα χ 180.

ἐρεῦσαι, aor. infin. ἐρεύθω.

†ἐρέφω. Aor. ἔρεψα Α 39: ψ 193. 3 pl. ἔρεψαν Ω 450. To furnish with a roof, roof: νηόν Α 39 (app. referring to a temporary structure of branches), [κλισίην] Ω 450: [θάλαμον] ψ 193.

ἐρέχθω. To shatter, shiver, rend Ψ 317.—Fig.: ἄλγεσι θυμὸν ἐρέχθων ε 83 = 157.

ἔρεψα, aor. ἐρέφω.

ἐρέω[1], fut. εἴρω[2].

ἐρέω[2]. See εἴρομαι.

ἐρῆμος, -η, -ον. (1) Uninhabited, desolate: νῆσον γ 270. Cf. μ 351.—Abandoned, empty, vacant: χῶρον Κ 520.—(2) Abandoned, forsaken, left to one's own devices: τὰ δ' ἐρῆμα φοβεῖται Ε 140.

ἐρηρέδαται, 3 pl. pf. pass. ἐρείδω.

ἐρητύω. 3 sing. pa. iterative ἐρητύσασκε Β 189, Λ 567. 3 sing. aor. opt. ἐρητύσειε Α 192. 3 pl. aor. pass. ἐρήτῡθεν Β 99, 211. (κατ-.) (1) To hold back, hold in check, check, restrain, curb: φῶτα ἕκαστον Β 164, 180. Cf. Α 192, Β 75, 189, Ι 462, 635, Λ 567, Ν 280, Σ 503: ι 493 = κ 442, π 43.—In mid.: ἐρητύοντο λαόν Ο 723.—(2) To get under control, bring back to discipline: κήρυκές σφεας Β 97, ἐρήτυθεν καθ' ἕδρας (settled themselves) 99, 211.—(3) In mid. (a) To check oneself, come to a stand, stop: παρὰ νηυσὶν ἐρητύοντο Θ 345, Ο 367. Cf. Ο 3.—(b) To hold back from going, remain in a specified place: ἐρητύοντο αὖθι γ 155.

ἐριαύχην, -ενος [ἐρι- + αὐχήν]. With high-arched or with powerful neck. Epithet of horses Κ 305, Λ 159, Ρ 496, Σ 280, Ψ 171.

ἐριβρεμέτης [ἐρι- + βρέμω]. Loud-thundering. Epithet of Zeus: Ζηνὸς ἐριβρεμέτεω Ν 624.

ἐριβῶλαξ, -ακος, ὁ, ἡ [ἐρι- + βῶλος]. Having rich clods, fertile, having fertile lands: Φθίῃ Α 155. Cf. Β 841, Γ 74, Ε 44, Ν 793, Ρ 172, etc.: ν 235.

ἐρίβωλος, -ον [as prec.]. = prec. Ι 329, 363, Σ 67, Φ 154, 232, Ψ 215: ε 34.

ἐρίγδουπος, also **ἐρίδουπος,** -ον Υ 50, Ω 323: γ 399, 493, η 345, κ 515, ο 146, 191, υ 176, 189. [ἐρι- + (γ)δοῦπος.] (1) Loud-thundering. Epithet of Zeus Ε 672, Η 411, Κ 329, Μ 235, Ν 154, Ο 293, Π 88: θ 465 = ο 180, ο 112.—(2) With thundering hooves: πόδες ἵππων Λ 152.—Of sea-shores, on which the sea roars, sounding Υ 50.—Of rivers, roaring, rushing κ 515.—Echoing, resounding: αἰθούσης Ω 323: γ 493 = ο 146 = 191. Cf. γ 399 = η 345, υ 176, 189.

ἐριδαίνω [ἔρις]. Aor. infin. mid. ἐρῑδήσασθαι Ψ 792. (1) To quarrel, wrangle, dispute, contend Α 574, Β 342: σ 403.—To contend, maintain one's position: οὐ δυνήσεται ἐριδαινέμεν οἷος α 79.—(2) Of winds, to contend. With dat.: Εὖρός τε Νότος τ' ἀλλήλοιιν Π 765.—(3) To compete or contend with a person. In mid.: ἀργαλέον ποσσὶν ἐριδήσασθαι Ἀχαιοῖς (for the Achaeans to contend (*sc.* with Odysseus) in the race) Ψ 792.—To be rivals, vie with one another β 206.—To engage in rivalry or competition φ 310.

ἐριδμαίνω [ἔρις]. To irritate, enrage Π 260.

ἐρίδουπος. See ἐρίγδουπος.

ἐρίζω [ἔρις]. 3 pl. pa. iterative ἐρίζεσκον θ 225. 3 pl. aor. subj. ἐρίσωσι σ 277. 3 sing. opt. ἐρίσειε ψ 126. ἐρίσσειε Γ 223: ο 321, τ 286. 3 pl. ἐρίσσειαν Ο 284. Nom. dual masc. pple. ἐρίσαντε Α 6. Pl. ἐρίσαντες Ν 109. 3 sing. aor. subj. mid. ἐρίσσεται δ 80. (1) To be at variance, quarrel, wrangle, dispute: διαστήτην ἐρίσαντε (having conceived offence) Α 6, περὶ ἴσης Μ 423.—With dat.: βασιλεῦσιν Β 214, 247, κείνῳ ἐρίσαντες Ν 109.—(2) To challenge. With dat. and infin.: ἀλλήλοιϊν μαχέσσασθαι σ 38.—(3) To engage in rivalry or competition: περὶ μύθων Ο 284.—To rival, compete with, vie with, a person: Νέστωρ οἶος ἔριζεν Β 555. Cf. τ 286.—With dat.: βασιλῆϊ Α 277. Cf. Γ 223, Ζ 131, Ψ 404: δ 78, θ 223, 225, 371, σ 277, ψ 126.—To match oneself with, stand up to in fight. With dat.: Κρονίωνος παισὶν Φ 185.—With dat. of that in which one vies with a person: ποσίν Ν 325.—With double dat.: δρηστοσύνῃ οὐκ ἄν μοι ἐρίσσειεν ἄλλος ο 321.—So in mid. Ε 172: δ 80.—With dat. and acc.: εἰ Ἀφροδίτῃ κάλλος ἐρίζοι (in . . .) Ι 389. Cf. ε 213.

ἐρίηρος [ἐρι- + (ϝ)ήρ. Cf. ἐπιήρανος]. Pl. ἐρίηρες. Epithet of ἑταῖρος, ἑταῖροι (and in α 346, θ 62, 471 of ἀοιδός), worthy, faithful, trusty or the like Γ 47, 378, Δ 266, Θ 332 = Ν 421, Π 363, Ψ 6: α 346, θ 62 = 471, ι 100, 172, 193, 555, κ 387, 405, 408, 471, μ 199, 397 (here merely conventional) = ξ 249, ξ 259 = ρ 428, τ 273.

ἐριθηλής, -ές [ἐρι- + θηλ-, θάλλω]. Showing good growth, flourishing: ἀλωάων ἐριθηλέων Ε 90, μυρίκης ὄζους Κ 467, ἔρνος ἐλαίης Ρ 53.

ἔρῑθος, ὁ. A labourer Σ 550, 560.

ἐρικῡδής, -ές [ἐρι- + κῦδος]. An epithet of general commendation, glorious, radiant, splendid, illustrious, sumptuous, or the like: θεῶν δῶρα Γ 65, Υ 265, ἥβης Λ 225, Λητοῦς Ξ 327, δαῖτα Ω 802: γ 66 = υ 280, κ 182, ν 26, Γαίης υἱόν λ 576, θεῶν τέκνα 631.

ἐρίμῡκος [ἐρι- + μυκ-, μυκάομαι]. Loud-bellowing. Epithet of oxen Υ 497, Ψ 775: ο 235.

ἐρῑνεός, -οῦ, ὁ. The wild fig-tree: ἐρινεὸν τάμνε νέους ὄρπηκας (double acc. of whole and part) Φ 37. Cf. μ 103, 432.—A particular tree referred to as a landmark: λαὸν στῆσον παρ' ἐρινεόν Ζ 433. Cf. Λ 167, Χ 145.

Ἐρῑνύς, -ύος, ἡ. Acc. pl. Ἐρῑνῦς Ι 454: β 135. An avenging divinity. (1) Upholding the moral order (a) As executor (in pl. as executors) of a parental curse Ι 454, 571: β 135, λ 280.—(b) As protecting the rights of an elder brother: πρεσβυτέροισιν Ἐρινύες αἰὲν ἕπονται Ο 204.—(c) As protecting beggars: πτωχῶν Ἐρινύες ρ 475.—

(d) As sending ἄτη: ἄτης, τήν οἱ ἐπὶ φρεσὶ θῆκ' Ἐρινύς ο 234. Cf. Τ 87.—(e) Invoked as guarding the sanctity of an oath Τ 259.—(f) App. regarded mainly or merely as maleficent: [Πανδαρέου] κούρας ἔδοσαν Ἐρινύσιν ἀμφιπολεύειν υ 78.—(2) Upholding the laws ordering the physical universe: Ἐρινύες ἔσχεθον αὐδὴν [ἵππου] Τ 418.—(3) App., with the idea of personality lost, meaning merely 'curses': οὕτω κεν τῆς μητρὸς ἐρινύας ἐξαποτίνοις Φ 412.

ἔριον = εἴριον.

ἐριούνης [explained as fr. ἐρι- + ὀνα-, ὀνίνημι]. Thus, the helper. Epithet of Hermes Υ 34: θ 322.

ἐριούνιος. = prec. Epithet or a name of Hermes Υ 72, Ω 360, 440, 457, 679.

ἔριπε, 3 sing. aor. ἐρείπω.

ἔρις, -ιδος, ἡ. Acc. ἔριδα Γ 7, Ε 861, Π 662, Υ 55, etc.: ζ 92, θ 210. ἔριν γ 136, 161, π 292, τ 11. (1) Strife, contention, wrangling: ἔριδι ξυνέηκε μάχεσθαι (in . . .) Α 8, λῆγ' ἔριδος 210, εἵνεκ' ἐμῆς ἔριδος (in my quarrel) Γ 100. Cf. Α 177 = Ε 891, Λ 319, Ι 257, Σ 107, Τ 58, 64, Υ 253, Ψ 490: γ 136, 161, π 292 = τ 11, σ 13, υ 267.—In pl., instances of this, quarrels, wranglings: ἔριδας καὶ νείκεα Β 376. Cf. Υ 251.—(2) The strife of battle: ἔριδος καὶ ἀϋτῆς Ε 732. Cf. Ε 861, Η 210, Λ 529, Ν 358, Ξ 389, etc.—Of the hostile action of Hephaestus against Xanthus Φ 359.—Of the hostile action of Xanthus against Achilles: τί μοι ἔριδος; (*quasi*-partitive genit.; 'what have I to do with . . ?') Φ 360.—Of the fighting of the cranes and the Pygmies Γ 7.—(3) Rivalry, competition: ἐξ ἔριδος μάχεσθαι (in pure rivalry or combativeness, making a match of it) Η 111. Cf. Η 301: ἔριδα προφέρουσαι ζ 92, ἔρις ἔργοιο (a match) σ 366. Cf. δ 343 = ρ 134, θ 210.—(4) Personified Δ 440, Ε 518, 740, Λ 3, 73, Σ 535, Υ 48.

ἐρίσ(σ)ειε, 3 sing. aor. opt. ἐρίζω.

ἐρισθενής [ἐρι- + σθένος]. Mighty. Epithet of Zeus Ν 54, Τ 355, Φ 184: θ 289.

ἔρισμα, τό [ἐρισ-, ἐρίζω]. An occasion of quarrel or strife Δ 38.

ἐριστάφυλος [ἐρι- + σταφυλή]. Of wine, the product of rich grapes, full-bodied ι 111 = 358.

ἐρίτῑμος, -ον [ἐρι- + τιμή]. Epithet of the aegis, awe-inspiring Β 447, Ο 361.—Of gold, precious, highly prized Ι 126 = 268.

ἔριφος, -ου. A kid Π 352, Ω 262: ι 220, 226, ρ 224, 242, τ 398.

ἑρκεῖος [ἕρκος]. Having his altar in the ἕρκος (see ἕρκος (2)). Of Zeus χ 335.

ἑρκίον, τό [ἕρκος]. = ἕρκος (1) (a): ἑ. αὐλῆς Ι 476: σ 102.

ἕρκος, τό. (1) (a) A fence or enclosing wall: ἕρκεα ἀλωάων Ε 90. Cf. Σ 564: ἕρκεος αὐλῆς χ 442 = 459. Cf. η 113, ω 224.—ἕρκος ὀδόντων, the (double) row formed by the teeth (as we should say, 'the lips' or 'the mouth'): ἐπεί κε [ψυχὴ] ἀμείψεται ἑ. ὀδόντων Ι 409, ποῖόν σε ἔπος φύγεν ἑ. ὀδόντων; Δ 350 = Ξ 83: α 64 = ε 22 = τ 492 = ψ 70, γ 230, φ 168. Cf. κ 328.—(b) Fig., of a person or persons: ἑ. πολέμοιο (against . . .) Α 284, ἑ. Ἀχαιῶν (their defence) Γ 229, Ζ 5, Η 211, ἑ. ἔμεν πολέμοιο (to stem the tide of war) Δ 299.—Sim. of a piece of armour, etc.: ἑ. ἀκόντων Δ 137, Ο 646. Cf. Ε 316.—So also: φράξαντο νῆας ἕρκεϊ χαλκείῳ ('with a ring of steel') Ο 567.—(2) The enclosed space in which a house stands = (or at any rate including) the αὐλή. In reference to the κλισίη of Achilles Π 231 = (in reference to Priam's palace) Ω 306.—To the house of Odysseus ψ 190.—So in pl. in reference to this house (perh. with a vague notion of separate parts making up the space): αἴθουσαί τε καὶ ἕρκεα καὶ δόμοι θ 57. Cf. π 341 = ρ 604, υ 164, φ 238 = 384 (here app. referring to the premises generally).—(3) A snare or springe χ 469.

ἕρμα¹, -ατος, τό. (1) A shore or prop put under a ship drawn up on shore in order to keep her upright: ὑφ' ἕρματα τάνυσσαν Α 486. Cf. Β 154.—Fig., of persons: ἕρμα πόληος Π 549: ψ 121 (a or the buttress or stay).—(2) App. with transference of notion from upholding to causing: ἕρμ' ὀδυνάων Δ 117.

ἕρμα², -ατος, τό [σερ-. See εἴρω¹]. An earring Ξ 182: σ 297.

ἑρμίς, -ῖνος [app. conn. with ἕρμα¹]. A bedpost θ 278, ψ 198.

ἔρνος, τό. A young tree, a sapling Ρ 53, Σ 56 = 437: ζ 163, ξ 175.

ἔρξαν¹, 3 pl. aor. ἔργω¹.

ἔρξαν², 3 pl. aor. See ἔρδω.

ἔρξε, 3 sing. aor. See ἔρδω.

ἔρξω, fut. See ἔρδω.

ἔροιτο, 3 sing. aor. opt. See εἴρομαι.

ἔρος, -ου, ὁ. In Γ 442, Ξ 294 ἔρως. [ἔραμαι.] (1) Love, desire: ἔρως με φρένας ἀμφεκάλυψεν Γ 442. Cf. Ξ 294, 315: σ 212.—(2) Desire, inclination, or appetite (for something): μολπῆς καὶ ὀρχηθμοῖο Ν 638, γόου Ω 227.—See also under ἵημι¹ (9).

ἑρπετός [ἕρπω]. Having the power of movement: ὅσσ' ἐπὶ γαῖαν ἑρπετὰ γίγνονται δ 418.

ἑρπύζω [ἕρπω]. Of a man broken by grief or suffering, to move slowly and heavily: ἑρπύζων παρὰ πυρκαϊήν Ψ 225. Cf. α 193, ν 220.

ἕρπω [σερπ-. Cf. L. *serpo*]. To exercise the power of movement proper to a living being, to move: ὅσσα τε γαῖαν ἔπι πνείει τε καὶ ἕρπει Ρ 447: = σ 131. Cf. μ 395, ρ 158.

ἐρράδαται, 3 pl. pf. pass. ῥαίνω.

ἐρραίσθη, 3 sing. aor. pass. ῥαίω.

ἔρρεε, ἔρρει, 3 sing. impf. ῥέω.

ἔρρεξε, 3 sing. aor. ῥέζω.

ἔρρηξε, 3 sing. aor. ῥήγνυμι.

ἔρρῑγα, pf. ῥιγέω.

ἐρρίγησε, 3 sing. aor. ῥιγέω.

ἐρρίζωσε, 3 sing. aor. ῥιζόω.

ἔρριψε, 3 sing. aor. ῥίπτω.

ἐρρύσατο, 3 sing. aor. mid. ἐρύω².

ἔρρω (Fέρρω). (1) To go, come, move (connoting mischance, difficulty or the like): ἐνθάδε ἔρρων (on this ill-omened journey, this fool's quest) Θ 239, Ι 364 : οἴῳ ἔρροντι (wandering about in desperation) δ 367.—Of the movement of the halting Hephaestus Σ 421.—(2) In imp., be off, let him be off, take yourself off, let him take himself off (more or less in way of imprecation) Θ 164, Ι 377 (let him go his own way to bane), Υ 349 (let him go for what I care), Χ 498, Ψ 440 (go your own mad way), Ω 239 : ε 139 (let him go if he chooses), κ 72, 75.

ἐρρώσαντο, 3 pl. aor. ῥώομαι.

ἔρση, -ης, ἡ (Ϝέρση). Except in ι 222 with prothetic ἐ, **ἐέρση.** (1) Dew Ψ 598 : ε 467, ν 245.—(2) In pl., drops of water from a cloud, rain-drops : ὑψόθεν ἧκεν ἐέρσας Λ 53. Cf. Ξ 351. —(3) A young lamb or kid newly yeaned ι 222.

ἐρσήεις, -εντος [ἔρση]. With prothetic ἐ, **ἐερσήεις** Ω 419. (1) Dew-besprent, dewy Ξ 348.—(2) Of a corpse, fresh, with the look of health Ω 419, 757.

ἐρύγμηλος [app., with -ηλος (cf. ὑψηλός) fr. ἐρυγμός, sb. fr. ἐρυγ-, ἐρεύγομαι]. Bellowing Σ 580.

ἐρυγόντα, acc. sing. masc. aor. pple. ἐρεύγομαι.

ἐρυθαίνω [ἐρυθ-, ἐρυθρός]. To make red, redden : ἐρυθαίνετο γαῖα Κ 484. Cf. Φ 21.

ἐρυθρός. Red : χαλκόν Ι 365, νέκταρ Τ 38 : ε 93, οἶνον 165, ι 208, μ 19, 327, ν 69, π 444, οἶνος ι 163.

†ἐρῡκανάω [frequentative fr. ἐρύκω]. 3 pl. ἐρῡκανόωσι. To hold in restraint, detain α 199.

ἐρῡκάνω. =next. (κατ-.) To restrain, keep from going : ἐρύκανεν ἑταίρους κ 429.

ἐρύκω. Fut. ἐρύξω ο 68. 3 sing. -ει Θ 178, Φ 62, Ω 156, 185 : η 315, θ 317. Aor. ἔρυξα ρ 515. 3 sing. -ε Κ 527. 3 pl. -αν Γ 113. 1 pl. subj. ἐρύξομεν Ο 297. Pple. ἐρύξας Ζ 217 : π 82. Imp. ἔρυξον τ 16. 3 sing. aor. ἠρύκακε Ε 321, Υ 458, Φ 594. ἐρύκακε Λ 352, Μ 465, Ο 450, Ρ 292, Υ 268, Φ 165, 384 : φ 227. 3 sing. opt. ἐρῡκάκοι Η 342. Imp. ἐρύκακε Ν 751. Pl. ἐρῡκάκετε Ζ 80. Infin. ἐρῡκακέειν Ε 262 : γ 144, λ 105, υ 313. (ἀπ-, κατ-.) (1) To restrain from doing or continuing to do something, to curb, keep or hold back, check : μηδέ μ' ἔρυκε μάχης (from . . .) Σ 126. Cf. Θ 206, Φ 384, Ω 156=185 : ἕτερός με θυμὸς ἔρυκεν ι 302. Cf. λ 105, ξ 283, υ 313, φ 227.—To restrain from action, keep inactive : λαόν Ω 658.—(2) To confine, shut up, keep from egress or escape, detain : πόντος, ὃ πολέας ἐρύκει Φ 59. Cf. Π 369, Φ 62, 63 : ἔρυξον ἐνὶ μεγάροισι γυναῖκας τ 16. Cf. α 14, δ 466, θ 317, ι 29.—In mid. : ἐν νήσῳ ἐρύκεαι (let yourself be . . .) δ 373.—(3) To detain or keep with one in hospitality or in a friendly way : ξείνισ' ἐείκοσιν ἤματ' ἐρύξας Ζ 217. Cf. δ 594, 599, η 315, ο 68, π 82, ρ 515.—Sim., in pass., to be kept or looked after in an indicated place : οὐδ' αὐτὸς ἐρύκεσθαι μενεαίνω ρ 17.—(4) To separate or lie between two bodies of men : ὀλίγος χῶρος ἐρύκει Κ 161.—(5) In reference to troops, to rally, get together : λαὸν ἐρυκάκετε Ζ 80. Cf. Ν 751.—(6) To keep assembled or in an indicated place : λαόν Ψ 258 : γ 144.—(7) In reference to horses, etc., to pull up, rein in Γ 113, Κ 527.—To hold in, keep in hand Λ 48=Μ 85, Μ 76.—To tether Ε 262, 321.—To hold, stand by the heads of Ω 470.—(8) To stop a person in his career or course : δουρὶ βαλὼν ἠρύκακεν Υ 458.—In mid., to check oneself in one's course : μὴ ἐρύκεσθον Ψ 443.—(9) To prevent the passage or progress of, check, stop : τάφρον, ἢ χ' ἵππον ἐρυκάκοι Η 342. Cf. Θ 178, Μ 465, Ο 297, Φ 7 : χ 138.—In mid. Μ 285.—(10) To debar from approach, keep aloof : τρεῖς κέ μιν μῆνας οἶκος ἐρύκοι ρ 408.—(11) To ward off, keep off, guard from : [χαλκὸν] ἐρύκακε τρυφάλεια Λ 352. Cf. Υ 268=Φ 165, Φ 594.—With dat. : κακόν, τό οἱ οὔ τις ἐρύκακεν Ο 450=Ρ 292. Cf. ε 166.

ἔρυμα, τό [ἐρύω²]. A means of protection, a defence or guard : χροός Δ 137.

ἐρύξω, fut. **ἔρυξα,** aor. ἐρύκω.

ἐρύσαντο, 3 pl. aor. mid. ἐρύω¹.

ἐρυσάρματες [ἐρυσ-, ἐρύω¹ + ἁρματ-, ἅρμα]. Chariot-drawing. Epithet of horses Ο 354, Π 370.

ἐρύσατο, 3 sing. aor. mid. ἐρύω².

ἔρυσε, 3 sing. aor. ἐρύω¹.

ἔρυσθαι, non-thematic pres. infin. mid. ἐρύω².

ἐρυσίπτολις. *V.l.* for ῥυσίπτολις.

ἔρῡσο, 2 sing. non-thematic impf. mid. ἐρύω².

ἔρυσσαν, 3 pl. aor. ἐρύω¹.

ἐρύσσεαι, 2 sing. aor. subj. mid. ἐρύω².

ἐρύσσεται, 3 sing. fut. mid. ἐρύω².

ἔρῡτο, 3 sing. non-thematic impf. mid. ἐρύω².

†ἐρύω¹ (Ϝερύω). Pres. pple. ἐρύων, -οντος Δ 467, 492, Ο 464, Χ 493. 3 pl. impf. ἔρυον Μ 258, Σ 540. 3 pl. fut. ἐρύουσι Λ 454, Ο 351, Χ 67. Infin. ἐρύειν Ρ 235, 287, 396. 3 sing. aor. εἴρυσε (ἐϜέρυσε) Π 863 : β 389. εἴρυσσε Γ 373, Σ 165 : θ 85. ἔρυσε Ν 598, Ρ 581. 1 pl. ἐρύσσαμεν δ 577, λ 2. 3 εἴρυσαν Θ 226, Λ 9, Ξ 32. ἔρυσαν Ε 573, Ξ 35 : χ 187, 193. ἔρυσσαν Α 485, Π 781 : δ 780, θ 51, π 325, 359. 2 sing. subj. ἐρύσσῃς Ε 110. 3 ἐρύσῃ Ρ 230. 1 pl. ἐρύσσομεν Α 141, Ξ 76, Ρ 635, 713 : θ 34, κ 423, π 348. 3 ἐρύσσωσι ρ 479. Opt. ἐρύσαιμι Θ 24. 2 pl. ἐρύσαιτε Θ 21. Imp. pl. ἐρύσσατε κ 403. Pple. ἐρύσας Ψ 21, Ω 16 : κ 303. ἐρύσσας ι 99. Pl. ἐρύσαντες Σ 232 : ι 77, μ 14, 402. Acc. ἐρύσαντας θ 508. Fem. ἐρύσᾱσα Ε 836. Infin. ἐρύσαι Ρ 419 : ξ 134, χ 176. ἐρύσσαι Θ 23, Φ 175. **Mid.** 3 pl. impf. ἐρύοντο Ρ 277. Fut. infin. ἐρύεσθαι Ξ 422. Aor. εἰρυσάμην κ 165. 3 sing. εἰρύσσατο Χ 306 : χ 79. ἐρύσσατο Δ 530, Φ 200, Χ 367 : τ 481. 3 pl. ἐρύσαντο Α 466, Β 429, Δ 506, Η 318, Ρ 317, Σ 152, Ω 624 : γ 65, 470, θ 504, ξ 431, υ 279. 2 sing. opt. ἐρύσαιο Ε 456. 1 pl. ἐρυσαίμεθα Ξ 79, Ρ 104, 159, 161. 3 pl. ἐρυσαίατο Ε 298. Pple. ἐρυσσάμενος Α 190, Γ 271, 361, Μ 190, Ν 610, Ξ 496, Ρ 127, Τ 252, Υ 284, Φ 116, 173 : δ 666, ι 300, κ 126, 294, 321, 535, λ 24, 48. Infin. ἐρύσασθαι Χ 351. ἐρύσσασθαι Σ 174, Φ 176 : φ 125. 3 sing. aor. εἴρῡτο χ 90. **Pass.** 3 pl. pf. εἰρύαται (ϜεϜερυ-) Ξ 75. εἰρύαται Δ 248 : ζ 265. 3 pl. plupf. εἰρύατο Ξ 30, Ο 654. εἴρυντο Σ 69. Nom. pl. fem. pple. εἰρῡμέναι Ν 682. (αὐερύω, εἰσ-, ἐξ-, ἐπ-, κατ-, προ-.) (1) To drag, haul, pull : κοῖλον δόρυ ἐρύσαντας ἐπ' ἄκρης θ 508. Cf. Γ 373, Ω 16 : ι 99, μ 14, ρ 479, χ 187.—In mid.

θ 504.—Of dragging the body of a foe from the fight: νεκρὸν ἐρύοντα ἰδών Δ 467. Cf. Δ 492, Π 781, Ρ 230, 235, 287, 396, 419, Σ 165, 540, Ψ 21.—In mid. Δ 506 = Ρ 317, Ε 298, Ξ 422, Ρ 127, 159, 161, 277, Σ 174.—Of so dragging the body of a friend Ε 573, Ρ 581, 635 = 713, Σ 232.—In mid. Ρ 104, Σ 152.—(**2**) To draw or pull in a specified direction: ἐξ ὤμοιο ὀϊστόν Ε 110. Cf. Θ 21, 23, 24, Ν 598, Π 863, Φ 175: κ 303.—In mid. Φ 176, 200, Χ 367: κ 165, τ 481.—To draw (a person) away, cause (him) to quit something. In mid.: οὐκ ἂν τόνδ' ἄνδρα μάχης ἐρύσαιο; (from the . . .) Ε 456.—To draw or pull (a person) from a specified position: ἀφ' ἵππων ὦσε χειρὶ ἐρύσασα Ε 836.—(**3**) To draw (a part of one's clothing) into a specified position: φᾶρος κὰκ κεφαλῆς εἴρυσσεν θ 85.—To pluck (a person by part of his clothing): ἄλλον χλαίνης ἐρύων Χ 493.—(**4**) To pull or tear at with a view to demolishing: κρόσσας πύργων Μ 258.—To pull about, tear (a corpse) Λ 454, Ο 351, Χ 67.—To tear (the skin from the bones): ῥινὸν ἀπ' ὀστεόφιν ξ 134.—(**5**) In mid., to draw (cooked food) off the spits: ἐρύσαντο πάντα Α 466 = Β 429 = Η 318 = Ω 624 : = ξ 431. Cf. γ 65 = 470 = υ 279.—(**6**) To draw (a ship) up out of the water: νῆ' ἐπ' ἠπείροιο ἔρυσσαν Α 485, ἔνθα Μυρμιδόνων εἴρυντο νέες Σ 69. Cf. Δ 248, Θ 226 = Λ 9, Ν 682, Ξ 30, 32, 35, 75, Ο 654: νῆες ὁδὸν εἰρύαται ζ 265 (app., along, *i.e.* on each side of, the way; cf. ἀγρούς 259). Cf. κ 403, 423, π 325, 359.—(**7**) To draw down (a ship) in order to launch her: νῆα ἐρύσσομεν εἰς ἅλα Α 141. Cf. Ξ 76: β 389, δ 577, 780, θ 34, 51, λ 2, π 348.—In mid. Ξ 79: δ 666.—(**8**) To draw a bow: ἐπὶ τῷ ἐρύοντι Ο 464.—To bend (a bow) in order to string it. In mid.: ἐρύσσασθαι [τόξον] μενεαίνων φ 125.—(**9**) In mid., to draw (a sword): φάσγανον ἐρυσσάμενος Α 190. Cf. Γ 361 = Ν 610, Δ 530, Μ 190, Ξ 496, Υ 284, Φ 116, 173, Χ 306 : = χ 79, ι 300, κ 126, 294, 321, 535 = λ 48, λ 24, χ 90.—To draw up, take into one's hand (a knife worn by one) Γ 271 = Τ 252.—(**10**) To pull up so as to suspend: κίον' ἂν' ὑψηλὴν ἐρύσαι (ἔρυσαν) χ 176, 193.—With ἀνά, to hoist (sails): ἂν' ἱστία ἐρύσαντες ι 77, μ 402.—(**11**) To weigh. In mid.: εἴ κέν σ' αὐτὸν χρυσῷ ἐρύσασθαι ἀνώγοι (to weigh your body with or against gold, *i.e.* pay your weight in gold) Χ 351.

†**ἐρύω**[2] (σερύω. Cf. L. *servo*). [(σ)ερῠ-, (σ)ρῡ-, fr. which the forms come with varying quantity due to the mutual influence of the stems]. Only in mid. Pres. ῥύομαι Ο 257. ῥῠομαι ξ 107. 3 sing. ῥῠεται Κ 259, 417: ο 35. 1 pl. εἰρῠόμεσθα Φ 588 (app. due to the analogy of the pf.). 3 ῥῠονται Ι 396. 3 sing. impf. ἐρύετο Ζ 403. ῥύετο Π 799. 3 sing. opt. ῥύοιτο Μ 8. 2 pl. ῥύοισθε Ρ 224. 2 sing. non-thematic impf. ἔρῡσο Χ 507. 3 sing. ἔρῡτο Δ 138, Ε 23, 538, Ν 555, Ρ 518, Ψ 819: ω 524. 3 pl. ῥύατο Σ 515: ρ 201. Infin. ἔρυσθαι ε 484, ι 194, κ 444, ξ 260, ρ 429. ῥῦσθαι Ο 141. 2 sing. pa. iterative ῥύσκευ Ω 730. 3 sing. fut. ἐρύσσεται Κ 44. 3 pl. εἰρύσσονται Σ 276 (app. due to the analogy of the pf.). Infin. ἐρῠ́εσθαι Ι 248, Υ 195. Aor. ῥῡσάμην Ο 29. 2 sing. εἰρῠ́σαο (ἐσερυ-) Φ 230. 3 εἰρῠ́σατο Δ 186, Ο 274, Υ 93. ἐρῠ́σατο Β 859, Ε 344, Λ 363, Υ 450: ξ 279, χ 372. ἐρρῠ́σατο Ο 290, Υ 194: α 6. ῥύσατο ψ 244. 3 dual ῥῡσάσθην Ξ 406. 2 sing. subj. ἐρύσσεαι Υ 311. 3 sing. opt. ἐρῠ́σαιτο Ω 584. ῥύσαιτο ζ 129, μ 107. εἰρύσσαιτο Θ 143: π 459 (app. due to the analogy of the pf.). 2 pl. εἰρύσσαισθε Ρ 327. Imp. ῥῦσαι Ρ 645, Ω 430. Infin. εἰρύσσασθαι Α 216. 3 pl. pf. εἰρῠ́αται (σεσρυ-) Α 239. εἰρύαται π 463. 3 sing. plupf. εἴρῡτο Π 542, Ω 499: ψ 229. 3 pl. εἰρῠ́ατο Χ 303. εἴρυντο Μ 454. Infin. εἴρυσθαι γ 268, ψ 82, 151. (**1**) To keep from harm, keep safe, guard, protect: ὄφρα νῆας ῥύοιτο Μ 8, σανίδων, αἳ πύλας εἴρυντο (gave it its strength) 454. Cf. Κ 44, 259, Ν 555, Ξ 406, Ο 257, Π 799, Ρ 224, 327, Σ 276, Φ 588, Χ 303, Ψ 819, Ω 430: γ 268, ο 35.—With dat.: μίτρης, ἣ οἱ πλεῖστον ἔρυτο Δ 138.—(**2**) To tend (a herd) ξ 107.—To keep, tend, see to (a house) ψ 151.—(**3**) To protect from inclemency of weather ε 484.—To cover (one's nakedness): μήδεα ζ 129.—(**4**) To keep back, detain: Ἠῶ ἐπ' Ὠκεανῷ ψ 244.—(**5**) In sinister sense, of foes, to lie in wait for: οἴκαδέ μ' ἰόντα π 463.—(**6**) To keep watch and ward over, guard: τεῖχος Σ 515. Cf. Κ 417: ι 194 = κ 444, ξ 260, ρ 201, 429, ψ 229.—(**7**) To be the guardian, defender or protector of (a city, etc.): οἵ τε πτολίεθρα ῥύονται Ι 396. Cf. Ζ 403, Π 542, Χ 507, Ω 499, 730.—(**8**) To bring out of danger or trouble, save, rescue: ἐρύσατό σ' Ἀπόλλων Λ 363 = Υ 450. Cf. Ε 23, 344, Ι 248, Ο 274, 290, Ρ 645, Υ 93, 194, 195, 311: α 6, μ 107, ξ 279, χ 372.—To rescue from troubles: Ἡρακλῆα Ο 29.—(**9**) In reference to immaterial things (**a**) To have in one's keeping, be the depositary of: θέμιστας Α 239.—(**b**) In reference to wrath, to keep (it within the breast), not to allow (it) to break out: μὴ κραδίῃ χόλον οὐκ ἐρύσαιτο Ω 584.—In reference to something known, to keep it (in the mind), refrain from uttering it: μηδὲ φρεσὶν εἰρύσσαιτο π 459.—(**c**) To be in possession of, comprehend: θεῶν δήνεα ψ 82.—(**d**) To observe, not to run counter to, obey: σφωΐτερον ἔπος Α 216.—To carry out (another's will, something resolved upon): βουλὰς Κρονίωνος Φ 230.—(**e**) App., to pay constant attention to, keep always in mind: πάντων ἀνθρώπων γενεήν Ο 141.—(**10**) To ward off: κῆρα Β 859, ἔγχος Ε 538 = Ρ 518 : = ω 524.—To arrest (a missile weapon) in its course: βέλος εἰρύσατο ζωστήρ Δ 186.—App., sim., in reference to something immaterial: ἀνήρ κεν οὔ τι Διὸς νόον εἰρύσσαιτο Θ 143.

ἔρχαται, 3 pl. pf. pass. ἔργω[1].

†**ἐρχατάω** [ἐρχ-, ἔργω[1]]. 3 pl. impf. pass. ἐρχατόωντο. To shut up, confine ξ 15.

ἔρχατο, 3 pl. plupf. pass. ἔργω[1].

ἐρχθέντα, acc. sing. masc. aor. pple. pass. ἔργω[1].

ἔρχομαι. Imp. ἔρχευ Ζ 280, Ψ 893: ζ 69, λ 251, ρ 22, 282, ψ 20, etc. From *ἐλεύθω fut. ἐλεύσομαι Ζ 365, Μ 369, Ν 753: δ 381, 470. 2 sing -εαι δ 390, 424, κ 267, 540. 3 -εται Α 425, Θ 12, Φ 62: κ 538, λ 135, ξ 167, π 8, υ 232, etc. 1 pl. -όμεθα Μ 225.

3 -ονται Ψ 497 : κ 530. Infin. ἐλεύσεσθαι Ο 180, Τ 129 : α 168, β 176, ι 514, ν 132, ψ 72, etc. Aor. ἦλθον Α 207, Ζ 519, Η 35, Ο 175, Ω 401 : α 194, δ 82, λ 166, ο 270, etc. 2 sing. -ες Η 25, Ν 250 : δ 274, λ 57, π 23, ρ 41, etc. 3 -ε Α 12, Ε 658, Ζ 54, Ν 91, Σ 2, Τ 51, etc. : α 16, γ 194, ε 40, ν 221, σ 1, φ 17, etc. 1 pl. ἤλθομεν δ 439, ι 262, ξ 496, ψ 249, etc. 2 -ετε Ω 240 : δ 146. 3 ἦλθον Β 249, Γ 189, Η 275, Ρ 532, Ψ 116, etc. : α 144, γ 34, η 325, μ 438, τ 60, χ 446, etc. 1 sing. ἤλυθον Α 152 : δ 317, ξ 278, π 206, ω 322, etc. 2 -ες Γ 428, Ν 252, Ω 104 : β 262, δ 810, λ 94. 3 -ε Γ 205, Ε 803, Π 478, Ψ 532, etc. : γ 306, η 284, ν 161, π 453, etc. 3 pl. -ον Δ 221, Ε 607, Ν 174, Υ 47, etc. : λ 226, ο 415. Subj. ἔλθω Φ 567, Χ 113 : ν 412, ο 543, π 138, ρ 56. 2 sing. -ῃς Κ 62, 510 : γ 316, δ 478, ο 13. 3 -ῃ Λ 194, Ο 57, Υ 130, Φ 231, etc. : η 33, μ 288, ρ 230, τ 84, etc. -ῃσι Ε 132, 821, Τ 191 : α 77, γ 422, ξ 398, etc. 2 dual -ητον Κ 444. 1 pl. -ωμεν Ν 744 : ζ 296, χ 77. 2 -ητε Ο 147. 3 -ωσι Ι 166, Φ 532 : τ 564, 566. Opt. ἔλθοιμι λ 501. 2 sing. -οις Ω 556. 3 -οι Ε 301, Η 415, Χ 43, etc. : α 403, β 54, ο 423, ψ 102, etc. Imp. ἐλθέ Δ 70, Ν 810, Ψ 770, Ω 112 : α 284. Pl. ἔλθετε ω 214. Pple. ἐλθών, -όντος Α 269, Ε 220, Ζ 435, Λ 140, Ξ 504, Τ 70, Φ 46, 444, etc. : α 115, γ 390, δ 171, θ 6, ο 156, σ 8, ψ 7, ω 267, etc. Fem. ἐλθοῦσα, -ης Α 394, 401, Β 387, Γ 162, Ο 33, Σ 135, 190 : ε 317, κ 411, ψ 22. Infin. ἐλθέμεναι Α 151, Ο 55, Ρ 67, 69, Υ 175 : γ 233, ε 220, θ 466. ἐλθέμεν Δ 247, Κ 18, Ο 146, Ω 203, etc. : γ 188, ε 99, σ 183, ω 307, etc. ἐλθεῖν Β 413, Ε 118, Μ 301, Φ 150, etc. : α 422, δ 786, κ 152, σ 402, etc. Pf. εἰλήλουθα Ε 204, Φ 81, 156, Ω 460 : ν 257, π 131, τ 549. 2 sing. -ας Α 202, Ζ 128, 254, Ψ 94 : ε 87, ι 273, ν 237, ο 42, χ 45, ω 300. 3 -ε Ο 131 : γ 318, η 199, etc. 1 pl. εἰλήλουθμεν Ι 49 : γ 81. Pple. εἰληλουθώς τ 28, υ 360. ἐληλουθώς Ο 81. 3 sing. plupf. εἰληλούθει Δ 520, Ε 44, Λ 230, Ν 364, Ρ 350, Υ 485. (ἀμφ-, ἀν-, ἀπ-, δι-, εἰσ-, ἐξ-, ἐπ-, κατ-, μετ-, παρ-, παρεξ-, ὑπ-.) **(1)** To go, go or take one's way, proceed : ἐς στρατὸν ἐλθέ Δ 70. Cf. Α 168, Γ 394, Ζ 280, Λ 839, Ο 81, etc. : εἰς σπέος ἤλυθεν ε 77. Cf. γ 318, η 40, κ 154, 320, ξ 373, etc.—Absol. Ι 649, Μ 343, Υ 167, etc. : δ 826, ζ 40, κ 152, etc.—With cognate acc. : ὁδὸν ἐλθέμεναι Α 151 : πολλὴν ὁδὸν ἦλθεν φ 20. Cf. γ 316 = ο 13, π 138.—In aor. pple. with finite vb., to go and . . . (cf. ἄγω (I) (9)): ἐλθοῦσ' ὑπελύσαο Α 401, ἐλθὼν εἴσομαι Ξ 8 (referring εἴσομαι to ἵημι[2]). Cf. Θ 11, Π 521, etc. : ο 24.—**(2)** To have movement, move, walk : χαμαὶ ἐρχομένων ἀνθρώπων Ε 442.—**(3)** To set out, depart, go : ἐρχομένῳ μοι ἐπέτελλεν Ε 198. Cf. Ε 150, Ι 43.—**(4)** To come : ἦλθεν ἐπὶ νῆας Α 12. Cf. Α 194, Γ 205, Δ 247, Η 219, Ο 131, etc. : νέον ἄλλοθεν εἰλήλουθεν γ 318. Cf. β 262, γ 426, ζ 296, ι 273, ξ 496, etc.—Absol. Α 202, Ι 49, Κ 62, etc. : α 144, ε 87, ο 543, etc.—With acc. of space : ἄλλην ὁδὸν ἤλθομεν ι 262.—In aor. pple. as under (1), to come and . . . : ἐλθὼν ἐκάκωσεν Λ 690. Cf. Ζ 257, Τ 140, etc. : α 255, ε 24, ο 410, σ 8, etc.—**(5)** To approach, draw near, come up : εἰ μὴ κήρυκες ἦλθον Η 275. Cf. Κ 540, etc. : γ 34, etc.—With ἐπί : ἦλθε δ' ἐπὶ ψυχή Ψ 65 : λ 84, 90. Cf. σ 1, etc.—Of hostile approach : ἐρχομένων ἄμυδις Ν 343. Cf. Ζ 435, Θ 89, etc.—Sim. : τῶν ὁμόσ' ἦλθε μάχη Ν 337.—With ἐπί : ἐπὶ Τρώων στίχες ἤλυθον Δ 221, Ρ 107. Cf. Ε 220, etc.—With (ἐν)αντίος, -ον : Ἕκτορος ἀντίον ἐλθεῖν Η 160, ἀντίος οἱ ἦλθεν Ο 584. Cf. Λ 219, Ο 454, etc. : ξ 278, etc.—With ἄντα Π 622.—With ἀγχίμολον Δ 529, etc. : ξ 410, etc.—With ἐναντίβιον Υ 130.—With κατεναντίον Φ 567.—**(6)** To present oneself : ὅς κε μόρσιμος ἔλθοι π 392 = φ 162. Cf. β 54.—**(7)** To return, to come back or home : ἐλθόντ' ἐκ πολέμοιο Ε 409. Cf. Θ 12, Κ 337, 444, 510, Ξ 504, Φ 57, etc. : περιφραζώμεθα νόστον, ὅπως ἔλθῃσιν α 77. Cf. α 168, γ 188, δ 82, ε 40, χ 45, etc.—With acc. of space : ἐλευσόμεθ' αὐτὰ κέλευθα Μ 225.—With αὖτις : ἐλεύσομαι αὖτις Μ 369, Ν 753. Cf. Α 425, Τ 129 : δ 478.—With ἄψ : ἄψ κ' εἰς ἡμέας ἔλθοι Κ 211. Cf. Ν 175 = Ο 550 : κ 244, τ 544, etc.—With πάλιν : πάλιν ἐλθεῖν Ι 408 : τ 533.—**(8)** To go or come for a purpose expressed by the fut. pple. : ἦλθον παύσουσα τὸ σὸν μένος Α 207. Cf. Ν 256, Ξ 301, Ο 180, etc. : α 281, β 265, etc.—**(9)** Of the coming on of a period of time : κνέφας ἦλθεν Θ 500. Cf. Β 387, Ξ 77, Φ 231 : ἐπὴν ἔλθῃσι θέρος λ 192. Cf. α 16, ζ 48, τ 515, etc.—With ἐπί : ἐπί τ' ἤλυθε νύξ δ 429. Cf. Α 475, Β 413, Λ 194 = 209 = Ρ 455, etc. : α 422, 423, γ 329, η 284, etc.—**(10)** **(a)** Of the motion of birds : ὥς τε ψαρῶν νέφος ἔρχεται Ρ 755. Cf. Θ 251, Μ 218 : υ 242.—**(b)** Of bees : μελισσάων ἐρχομενάων Β 88.—**(c)** Of wind : ἦν ἔλθῃ ἀνέμοιο θύελλα μ 288. Cf. Β 147, 395, Ι 6, Ρ 57 : ε 317, μ 407, 427.—**(d)** Of a cloud Δ 276, Π 364.—**(e)** Of a river Ε 91.—**(f)** Of blood : αὐλὸς ἀνὰ ῥῖνας ἦλθεν αἵματος χ 18. Cf. σ 97.—**(g)** Of sound : περὶ φρένας ἤλυθ' ἰωή Κ 139. Cf. π 6, ρ 261, τ 444.—**(h)** Of fire : ὅσσον ἐπὶ φλὸξ ἦλθεν Ψ 251.—**(i)** Of a heavenly body ν 94.—**(j)** Of a spear or arrow : δι' ἀσπίδος ἦλθ' ἔγχος Γ 357. Cf. Δ 482, Ε 16, Η 247, Λ 97, etc. : διὰ δ' ἀμπερὲς ἦλθεν ἰός φ 422. Cf. χ 16.—**(k)** Of a leaden weight Ω 82.—**(11)** **(a)** Of death or old age coming upon one : εἰς ὅ κε γῆρας ἔλθῃ καὶ θάνατος ν 60. Cf. λ 135, ψ 282.—**(b)** Of the intoxicating influence of wine : περὶ φρένας ἤλυθεν οἶνος ι 362.—**(c)** Of bane, etc. : ἄγχι τοι ἦλθε κακόν Λ 363 = Υ 450. Cf. Λ 439, Ο 450 = Ρ 292 : υ 368.—**(d)** Of tidings coming : ὅτ' ἀγγελίη ποθὲν ἔλθῃ ξ 374. Cf. α 414.—**(e)** Of pain shooting : ὀδύνη διὰ χροὸς ἦλθεν Λ 398.—Of pain departing Χ 43, Ω 514.—**(f)** Of something spoken of as passing, coming, appearing : γέρας μοι ἔρχεται ἄλλῃ Α 120, ὄφρα κε δῶρα ἔλθῃσιν Τ 191 : ἦλθον [ἱστὸς καὶ τρόπις] μ 438.—**(12)** To take place : πρὶν γάμον ἐλθεῖν ζ 288.—**(13)** To come (under one's hand) : χρυσόν, ὅτις χ' ὑποχείριος ἔλθῃ ο 448.—**(14)** Of coming to be in a specified condition : αἴ κέν τι νέκυς ᾐσχυμμένος ἔλθῃ Σ 180.—**(15)** Of a place taken in estimation : μὴ δεύτερος ἔλθοι (should come second) Χ 207. Cf. Κ 368.—Sim. Ψ 547, 779.

ἐρωδιός, ὁ. Perh. the night heron Κ 274.

ἐρωέω[1] [ἐρωή[1]]. (ἀπ-.) (1) To hold or draw back, refrain: μηδ' ἔτ' ἐρώει B 179, X 185.—To hold or draw back from. With genit.: ἐρωῆσαι πολέμοιο N 776. Cf. Ξ 101, P 422, T 170.—(2) To slacken speed, give ground to a competitor Ψ 433. —(3) Of a cloud, to retire, pass away μ 75.—(4) To drive or force back: ἐρωήσαιτέ κέ [μιν] ἀπὸ νηῶν N 57.

ἐρωέω[2] [ἐρωή[2]]. (ἐξ-, ὑπ-.) Of blood, to spirt out: αἷμ' ἐρωήσει περὶ δουρί A 303: π 441.

ἐρωή[1], -ῆς, ἡ. Pause, cessation: πολέμου Π 302, P 761.

ἐρωή[2], -ῆς, ἡ. (1) Swing, effort, impetus: λικμητῆρος ἐρωῇ N 590. Cf. Γ 62.—(2) A rush or attack: οὐχ ὑπέμεινεν ἐρωὴν Πηνελέωο Ξ 488.—(3) The rush or flight (of missiles) Δ 542, P 562. —(4) The throw or flight (of a spear): μετὰ δούρατος ᾤχετ' ἐρωήν (followed it up to recover it) Λ 357, λείπετο δουρὸς ἐρωήν (by a spear's throw) Ψ 529. Cf. O 358, Φ 251.

ἐρώμεθα, 1 pl. aor. subj. See εἴρομαι.

ἔρως. See ἔρος.

ἐς. See εἰς.

ἐσαγείρω [ἐσ-, εἰσ- (1)]. In mid. (1) To gather or come together to an indicated place: ἐσαγείρετο λαός ξ 248.—(2) To recover (consciousness): ἐσαγείρετο θυμόν (was coming to himself) O 240, Φ 417.

ἐσάγω. See εἰσάγω.

ἐσαθρέω [ἐσ-, εἰσ- (4)]. To catch sight of: εἰ ἐσαθρήσειεν 'Αλέξανδρον Γ 450.

ἐσακούω [ἐσ-, εἰσ- (4)]. To hearken, give ear: οὐδ' ἐσάκουσεν 'Οδυσσεύς Θ 97.

†**ἐσάλλομαι** [ἐσ-, εἰσ- (1)]. 3 sing. aor. ἐσήλατο M 438, Π 558. ἐσᾶλτο M 466, N 679. To leap or spring *at*. With acc.: τεῖχος M 438, Π 558. Cf. M 466, N 679.

ἔσαν, 3 pl. impf. εἰμί.

ἕσαν, 3 pl. aor. See ἕζομαι.

ἐσάντα. See εἰσάντα.

ἕσασθαι, aor. infin. mid. ἕννυμι.

ἕσατο, 3 sing. aor. mid. ἕννυμι.

ἐσάωσα, aor. σαόω.

ἐσβαίη, 3 sing. aor. opt. **ἐσβάντες,** nom. pl. masc. aor. pple. ἐσβαίνω. See εἰσβαίνω.

ἔσβεσε, ἔσβη, 3 sing. aorists σβέννυμι.

†**ἐσδέρκομαι** [ἐσ-, εἰσ- (4)]. Aor. ἐσέδρακον Ω 223. 3 sing. -ε ι 146, τ 476. (1) To have sight of, see: τὴν νῆσον ι 146. Cf. Ω 223.—(2) To direct the sight *to*, look *towards*. With acc.: Πηνελόπειαν τ 476.

†**ἐσδύω** [ἐσ-, εἰσ- (2)]. 2 sing. fut. mid. ἐσδύσεαι. To engage in, take part in. In mid. Ψ 622.

ἐσέδρακον, aor. ἐσδέρκομαι.

ἐσελεύσομαι, fut. ἐσέρχομαι. See εἰσέρχομαι.

ἔσελθε, aor. imp. ἐσέρχομαι. See εἰσέρχομαι.

ἐσεμάσσατο, 3 sing. aor. ἐσμαίομαι.

ἐσέρχομαι. See εἰσέρχομαι.

ἐσέχυντο, 3 pl. aor. pass. ἐσχέω.

ἐσήλατο, 3 sing. aor. ἐσάλλομαι.

ἐσημήναντο, 3 pl. aor. mid. σημαίνω.

ἔσηνε, 3 sing. aor. σαίνω.

ἕσθην, 3 dual plupf. mid. ἕννυμι.

ἐσθής, -ῆτος, ἡ [Fέσ-νυμι, ἕννυμι]. (1) Clothing, raiment α 165, β 339, ε 38 = ψ 341, ζ 192, θ 440, ν 136 = π 231, ξ 510, ο 207, ω 67.—Of bed-clothing ψ 290.—(2) Articles of clothing, clothes: ἐσθῆτα ἔσφερον η 6. Cf. ζ 74, 83.

ἐσθίω [ἔσθω]. (κατ-.) (1) To eat (food): βρώμην κ 460 = μ 23, μ 302. Cf. α 9, ξ 80, 109, υ 348.—Absol., to take food, eat β 305, ξ 443, ρ 358, 478. —(2) Of the cannibal Cyclops, to devour ι 292, υ 19, ψ 313.—Of the action of consuming fire Ψ 182.—(3) To eat up, devour, consume: τόδε δῶμα φ 69. Cf. δ 318.

ἐσθλός, -ή, -όν. (1) Well-born, noble ζ 284.—(2) Warlike, soldierly, stout, skilful in fight B 366, Δ 458, Z 444, Ω 167, etc.: θ 582, 585, χ 204. —Absol.: ἐσθλὰ [τεύχεα] ἐ. ἔδυνεν Ξ 382. Cf. E 176 = Π 425, I 319, X 158.—(3) Passing into (4): πατέρ' ἐσθλόν α 115. Cf. β 46, 71, γ 98 = δ 328, γ 379, δ 236, 724 = 814, δ 726 = 816, π 214, τ 395, ψ 360.—(4) Good, worthy, serviceable, skilled: ἀγορηταί Γ 151. Cf. E 51, H 126, Υ 396, Ψ 112, 546, 636: ἑταῖροι β 391. Cf. β 33, γ 471, ε 110 = 133 = η 251, θ 110, λ 7 = μ 149, ξ 104, ο 310, 557, π 263, ρ 381, τ 334, ψ 331, ω 427.—Of horses Ψ 348.—Absol.: ἐσθλοῖς ἠδὲ κακοῖσιν ζ 189. Cf. θ 553, χ 415 = ψ 66.—(5) In moral sense, good, of right feeling. Absol.: φρένες ἐσθλῶν N 115, O 203. Cf. I 514.—Of the mind, showing discretion, good judgment or discernment, well-balanced: νόον N 733. Cf. P 470: β 117 = η 111, η 73, λ 367. —(6) Of things or abstractions, good of their kind, good, excellent, fine, helpful, in place, or the like: ἔπος (promising good fortune) A 108, φάρμακα Λ 831. Cf. A 576, E 3, K 213, Ξ 382, Σ 313, etc.: κτήματα β 312, ὁμοφροσύνην ζ 182. Cf. ζ 30, ι 242, μ 347, τ 547 (boding well), etc.—Morally good or fitting. Absol.: ἐσθλά τε καὶ τὰ χέρεια σ 229 = υ 310.—(7) Absol. in neut. ἐσθλόν (a) A good thing. With infin.: ἐ. [ἐστι] Διὶ χεῖρας ἀνασχέμεν Ω 301.—(b) What is good, good: ἄλλοτε κακῷ κύρεται ἄλλοτ' ἐσθλῷ Ω 530. Cf. ο 488.—(8) (a) Absol. in neut. pl. ἐσθλά in sense (7) (b): μυρί' ἐσθλὰ ἔοργε (has done much good service) B 272, ἐσθλὰ φραζομένῳ M 212. Cf. K 448: ἔσθλ' ἀγορεύοντες (fair words) ρ 66. Cf. υ 86.—(b) Good or valuable material things: πολλὰ καὶ ἐσθλά δ 96. Cf. κ 523 = λ 31.

ἔσθορε, 3 sing. aor. ἐσθρώσκω.

ἔσθος, τό [Fέσ-νυμι, ἕννυμι]. A garment Ω 94.

†**ἐσθρώσκω** [ἐσ-, εἰσ- (1) (2)]. 3 sing. aor. ἔσθορε. (1) To leap or spring at something M 462.—(2) To leap or spring into something Φ 18.

ἔσθω [ἔδθω, ἔδω]. (1) To eat (food). Of men and beasts: κρέα Θ 231: βάλανον ν 409.—Absol., to take food, eat Ω 476: ε 94, 197, ζ 249 = η 177, η 220, κ 272, 373, π 141, υ 337.—(2) Of the cannibal Cyclops, to devour: ξείνους ι 479.—Of a woman fiercely desiring vengeance Ω 213.—Of worms, to eat, gnaw Ω 415.—(3) To eat up, devour, consume: κειμήλιά τε πρόβασίν τε β 75.

ἔσιδε, 3 sing. aor. ἐσείδω. See εἰσείδω.

ἐσιδέσθην, 3 dual aor. mid. ἐσείδω. See εἰσείδω.

ἐσίδεσκε, 3 sing. pa. iterative ἐσείδω. See εἰσείδω.

ἐσίζω [ἐσ-, εἰσ- (2)]. In mid., to take one's place *in* or *among*. With acc.: ἐπειδὰν ἐσίζηται λόχον N 285.

ἐσίημι [ἐσ-, εἰσ- (1) + ἵημι²]. In mid., to speed *to* or *towards*. With acc.: αὖλιν ἐσιέμεναι χ 470.

ἐσκαταβαίνω [ἐσ-, εἰσ- (1) + κατα- (1)]. To go or proceed down *to*. With acc.: ὄρχατον ἐσκαταβαίνων ω 222.

ἐσκέδασε, 3 sing. aor. σκεδάννυμι.

ἔσκον, pa. iterative εἰμί.

†ἐσμαίομαι [ἐσ-, εἰσ- (1)]. 3 sing. aor. ἐσεμάσσατο. To touch, affect: θυμόν P 564, Υ 425.

ἔσομαι, fut. εἰμί.

ἐσοράω. See εἰσοράω.

ἐσόψομαι, fut. ἐσοράω. See εἰσοράω.

ἔσπασε, 3 sing. aor. σπάω.

ἔσπεισαν, 3 pl. aor. σπένδω.

ἔσπεο, 2 sing. aor. mid. ἕπω².

ἕσπερα, metaplastic neut. pl. ἕσπερος.

ἑσπέριος [(Ϝ)έσπερος]. **(1)** At even, with the evening (constructed with a sb. or pronoun, but in sense qualifying the verb): ἑ. ἂν προτὶ Ἴλιον ἀπονεοίμην Φ 560: ἑσπερίους ἀγέρεσθαι ἀνώγει β 385. Cf. β 357, ι 336, 452, ξ 344, ο 505, π 452.—**(2)** Of the west, dwelling in the west, western: ἀνθρώπων θ 29.

ἕσπερος, ὁ (Ϝέσπερος. Cf. L. *vesper*). **(1)** Evening α 422 = σ 305, α 423 = σ 306, δ 786.—ἀστὴρ ἕσπερος, the evening-star X 318.—**(2)** Metaplastic neut. pl. ἕσπερα with collective sense, evening-time: ποτὶ ἕσπερα ῥίγιον ἔσται ρ 191.

ἔσπετε, imp. pl. ἐννέπω.

ἕσπετο, 3 sing. aor. mid. ἕπω².

ἕσσα, aor. ἕννυμι.

ἕσσαι¹, aor. infin. ἕννυμι.

ἕσσαι², 2 sing. pf. mid. ἕννυμι.

ἕσσατο, 3 sing. aor. mid. ἕννυμι.

ἐσσείοντο, 3 pl. impf. pass. σείω.

ἐσσεῖται, 3 sing. fut. εἰμί.

ἔσσευα, aor. σεύω.

ἐσσί, 2 sing. pres. indic. εἰμί.

ἕσσο, 2 sing. plupf. mid. ἕννυμι.

ἔσσο, imp. εἰμί.

ἔσσομαι, fut. εἰμί.

ἔσσυμαι, pf. mid. σεύω.

ἐσσύμενος, pf. pple. mid. σεύω.

ἐσσυμένως [adv. fr. ἐσσύμενος. See σεύω (II) (2)]. With speed, eagerness, alacrity, zeal, vehemence Γ 85, Ο 698, Φ 610, Ψ 55, 172, 364, 511, Ω 124: ι 73, ξ 347, ο 288, π 51.

ἔσσυο, 2 sing. aor. mid. σεύω.

ἔσσυται, 3 sing. pf. mid. σεύω.

ἔσσυτο, 3 sing. aor. mid. σεύω.

ἕσσω, fut. ἕννυμι.

ἐστάθη, 3 sing. aor. pass. ἵστημι (B).

ἕσταθι, pf. imp. ἵστημι (C).

ἔσται, 3 sing. fut. εἰμί.

ἕσταμεν, 1 pl. plupf. ἵστημι (C).

ἑστάμεν, ἑστάμεναι, pf. infin. ἵστημι (C).

ἔσταν, 3 pl. aor. ἵστημι (B).

ἑσταότ-, pf. pple. ἵστημι (C).

ἔστασαν, 3 pl. aor. ἵστημι (A).

ἕστασαν, 3 pl. plupf. ἵστημι (C).

ἑστᾶσι, 3 pl. pf. ἵστημι (C).

ἔστε, 2 pl. imp. εἰμί.

ἐστέ, 2 pl. pres. indic. εἰμί.

ἕστηκε, 3 sing. pf. ἵστημι (C).

ἑστήκει(ν), 3 sing. plupf. ἵστημι (C).

ἔστην, aor. ἵστημι (B).

ἐστήρικτο, 3 sing. plupf. pass. στηρίζω.

ἐστήριξε, 3 sing. aor. στηρίζω.

ἔστησαν¹, 3 pl. aor. ἵστημι (A).

ἔστησαν², 3 pl. aor. ἵστημι (B).

ἔστησε, 3 sing. aor. ἵστημι (A).

ἔστι, ἐστί, 3 sing. pres. indic. εἰμί.

ἔστιχον, 3 pl. aor. στείχω.

ἐστιχόωντο, 3 pl. impf. στιχάομαι.

ἕστο, 3 sing. plupf. mid. ἕννυμι.

ἐστόρεσε, 3 sing. aor. στορέννυμι.

ἐστρατόωντο, 3 pl. impf. στρατόομαι.

ἔστρωτο, 3 sing. plupf. pass. στορέννυμι.

ἔστυγον, 3 pl. aor. στυγέω.

ἐστυφέλιξε, 3 sing. aor. στυφελίζω.

ἔστω, ἔστων, 3 sing. and pl. imp. εἰμί.

ἕστωρ, -ορος. A peg fitting into a hole in the pole of a chariot Ω 272.

ἐσφαγμένα, nom. pl. neut. pf. pple. pass. σφάζω.

ἔσφαξαν, 3 pl. aor. σφάζω.

ἐσφέρω [ἐσ-, εἰσ- (2)]. **(1)** To carry into a specified place: ἐσθῆτα εἴσω η 6.—**(2)** In mid., of a river, to draw into its current and carry along with it: πολλὰς πεύκας Λ 495.

ἐσφήκωντο, 3 pl. plupf. pass. σφηκόω.

ἐσφορέω [ἐσ-, εἰσ- (2)]. **(1)** To carry into an indicated place τ 32.—**(2)** To carry *into*. With acc.: εἵματα μέλαν ὕδωρ ζ 91.

ἐσχάρη, -ης, ἡ. Ablative ἐσχαρόφιν η 169. Locative ἐσχαρόφιν ε 59, τ 389. **(1)** The fire-place or hearth of the μέγαρον, app. in or about the middle and surrounded by columns (σταθμοί, κίονες): ἧσται ἐπ' ἐσχάρῃ κίονι κεκλιμένη ζ 305, ἷζεν ἐπ' ἐσχαρόφιν τ 389 (*v.l.* ἀπ' ἐσχαρόφιν, at a distance from the . . ., taking ἐσχαρόφιν as ablative). Cf. ζ 52, η 153, 160, 169, υ 123, ψ 71.—Of the fire-place in Calypso's cave ε 59.—Of that in Eumaeus's hut ξ 420.—**(2)** In pl., πυρὸς ἐσχάραι, app., hearths, families: ὅσσαι Τρώων πυρὸς ἐσχάραι K 418 (cf. Τρῶας ἐφέστιοι ὅσσοι ἔασιν B 125).

†ἐσχατάω [ἔσχατος]. Acc. sing. masc. pres. pple. ἐσχατόωντα K 206. Nom. fem. ἐσχατόωσα, -ης B 508, 616. **(1)** To be situated on the verge or border of an indicated region. In pres. pple. in adjectival use: Ἀνθηδόνα ἐσχατόωσαν B 508. Cf. B 616.—**(2)** To stray on the border of an indicated region: δηΐων τινὰ ἐσχατόωντα K 206.

ἐσχατιή, -ῆς, ἡ [ἔσχατος]. The extremity, the furthest or most remote part, the edge or border: Φθίης I 484, πολέμοιο (the skirts) Λ 524, Υ 328, [πυρῆς] Ψ 242: λιμένος (the mouth) β 391, Γόρτυνος γ 294, ἀγροῦ δ 517, ε 489, σ 358, ω 150, νήσου ε 238, ἐπ' ἐσχατιῇ σπέος εἴδομεν (*i.e.* in the first part of the land they came to) ι 182, ἢ ἐπ' ἐσχατιῆς ἢ σχεδόν (in a remote part) ι 280, ἐπ' ἐσχατιῇ (at the mouth of the harbour) κ 96, αἰπόλια ἐσχατιῇ βόσκονται (in the most remote part of the island) ξ 104.

ἔσχατος, -ον. (**1**) The extreme, furthest, most remote: ἔσχατοι ἀνδρῶν (dwelling in the uttermost parts of the earth) α 23, οἰκέομεν ἀπάνευθε, ἔσχατοι (the last or outermost of civilized communities) ζ 205, θάλαμόνδε ἔσχατον (to the innermost θ.) φ 9.—With genit.: ἔσχατοι ἄλλων K 434 (the most remote from the centre as compared with all others, holding the most advanced post).—(**2**) In neut. pl. ἔσχατα as adv.: ἔσχατα νῆας εἴρυσαν (at the extremities of the line) Θ 225 = Λ 8.

ἔσχε, 3 sing. aor. ἔχω.

ἔσχεθε, 3 sing. aor. ἔχω.

†ἐσχέω [ἐσ-, εἰσ- (2)]. 3 pl. aor. pass. ἐσέχυντο. In pass., of persons, to pour or stream into an indicated or specified place: κατὰ πύλας M 470, ἐς πόλιν Φ 610.

ἔσχισε, 3 sing. aor. σχίζω.

ἔσω. See εἴσω.

ἑταιρίζω. See ἑταρίζω.

ἑταῖρος. See ἕταρος.

ἐτάλασσας, 2 sing. aor. τλάω.

ἐτάνυσσα, aor. τανύω.

ἐτάραξε, 3 sing. aor. ταράσσω.

†ἑταρίζω, ἑταιρίζω [ἕταρος, ἑταῖρος]. Aor. infin. ἑταιρίσσαι Ω 335. 3 sing. aor. opt. mid. ἑταρίσσαιτο N 456. (**1**) To be companion to, associate with: ἀνδρί Ω 335.—(**2**) In mid., to take with one as a companion N 456.

ἕταρος, ἑταῖρος, -ου, ὁ. (The forms about equally common.) Fem. ἑτάρη Δ 441. ἑταίρη I 2. Acc. ἑταίρην ρ 271. A companion, comrade, associate, fellow, in various uses. (**1**) A comrade in arms, implying various degrees of connexion from a close comradeship between or among equals or a relationship resembling that of knight and squire to mere common participation in warfare: ἑτάρων εἰς ἔθνος ἐχάζετο Γ 32, Πάτροκλον, ὃν ἑταῖρον I 220. Cf. A 179, 345, E 514, Z 6, K 151, M 379, N 767, Π 195, P 150, Ω 123, etc.: α 237, θ 217, 584, 586, λ 371, 382, 520, ν 266, ξ 480, ψ 324, ω 79.—One taking part with another in a particular enterprise: λοχησάμενος σὺν ἑταίρῳ ν 268. Cf. K 235, 242: δ 408, 433.—(**2**) A comrade in a sea voyage or expedition: ξὺν νηῒ ἠδ' ἑτάροισιν α 182. Cf. Γ 47, Π 170: α 304, β 212, γ 167, δ 367, λ 331, etc.—Esp. of the comrades of Odysseus in his wanderings α 5, β 174, ε 110, κ 33, λ 51, μ 33, τ 276, etc.—(**3**) A follower of or attendant on a king or chief: ἐκέλευσεν ἑταίρους ἵππους ζευγνύμεναι Γ 259. Cf. γ 32, δ 536, λ 412.—(**4**) (**a**) A companion, comrade, associate, friend, in gen.: πόλλ' ἑταῖροι [ἐλλίσσοντο] I 585. Cf. Σ 251, X 492, Ω 63: β 225, ι 367, ξ 462, π 354, σ 350, etc.—Fem.: Ἔρις, Ἄρεος ἑτάρη Δ 441.—(**b**) Of relationship with a protecting divinity: πάντων φίλταθ' ἑταίρων ω 517 (said by Athene).—(**c**) A boon-companion: ἑταῖρος εἰλαπιναστής P 577.—(**d**) Of fellow-servants: οἷς ἑτάροισιν ἐκέκλετο ὑφορβός ξ 413. Cf. ξ 407, 460, ο 309, 336, π 8, 84.—(**5**) Fig.: οὖρον, ἐσθλὸν ἑταῖρον λ 7 = μ 149.—Fem.: φύζα, φόβου ἑταίρη I 2: φόρμιγξ, ἣν δαιτὶ θεοὶ ποίησαν ἑταίρην ρ 271.

ἐταρπήτην, 3 dual aor. pass. τέρπω.

ἐτέθαπτο, 3 sing. plupf. pass. θάπτω.

ἐτεθήπεα, plupf. τέθηπα.

ἔτεινε, 3 sing. aor. τείνω.

ἔτεισε, 3 sing. aor. τίω.

ἐτειχίσσαντο, 3 pl. aor. τειχίζομαι.

ἔτεκε, 3 sing. aor. τίκτω.

ἐτελέσθη, 3 sing. aor. pass. τελέω.

ἐτέλεσσα, aor. τελέω.

ἐτεός [cf. ἔτυμος, ἐτήτυμος]. (**1**) In accordance with truth, true: εἰ ἐτεόν περ (whether (what I say) is true) Ξ 125.—Absol.: πόλλ' ἐτεά τε καὶ οὐκί (true things, truth) Υ 255.—(**2**) In neut. ἐτεόν as adv., truly, really, in fact. Always with εἰ: εἰ ἐ. παρὰ ναῦφιν ἀνέστη Σ 305. Cf. E 104, H 359 = M 233, Θ 423, M 217, N 153, 375: εἰ ἐ. ἐμός ἐσσι π 300. Cf. γ 122, ι 529, ν 328, π 320, τ 216, ψ 36, 107, ω 259, 352.—Truly expressing one's feelings: εἰ ἐ. ἀγορεύεις O 53.—With true insight into the future: εἰ ἐ. Κάλχας μαντεύεται B 300.

ἑτεραλκής [ἕτερος + ἀλκή]. Of νίκη (connecting with ἕτερος (2)), bringing success to the other (and previously unsuccessful) side, turning the tide of war; or perh. (connecting with ἕτερος (5)), won by another's might, *i.e.* by divine interposition H 26, Θ 171, Π 362, P 627: χ 236.—Sim.: ἑτεραλκέα δῆμον O 738 (a reserve available for turning the tide of war, or simply as a reinforcement).

ἑτερήμεροι [ἕτερος + ἡμέρη]. Being in a specified condition on alternate days: ἄλλοτε μὲν ζώουσ' ἑτερήμεροι, ἄλλοτε δ' αὖτε τεθνᾶσιν λ 303 (the adj. app. qualifying both members of the expression, the sense being that they were in life and in death (presumably both together) on alternate days).

ἕτερος, -η, -ον. Instrumental fem. ἑτέρηφι Π 734, Σ 477, X 80. (**1**) One of two: χωλὸς ἕτερον πόδα B 217, χειρὶ λαβὼν ἑτέρῃ (*i.e.* the left) M 452. Cf. κ 171.—Absol. (in pl. of one of two bodies or pairs): εἰ ἕτερος φύγῃσιν E 258, ἑτέροισι κῦδος ἔδωκαν N 303, ἕτερόν γε πέδησε (one or the other of the parties to a quarrel) T 94. Cf. E 288, H 292 = 378 = 397, Υ 210, X 266.—With neg., neither of two bodies: οὐδ' ἕτεροι μνώοντ' ὀλοοῖο φόβοιο Λ 71 = Π 771.—(**2**) The other of two: (**a**) ἑτέροιο διὰ κροτάφοιο πέρησεν αἰχμή Δ 502. Cf. Υ 473.—(**b**) With the article: τοίχου τοῦ ἑτέροιο (by the opposite . . .) I 219, Ω 598, τὴν ἑτέρην πόλιν Σ 509. Cf. μ 101, ψ 90.—(**3**) Repeated: (**a**) ἑ. (ἕτεροι) . . . ἑ. (ἕτεροι) . . ., one (some) . . . the other(s) . . .: ἕτερον μὲν δῶκε, ἕτερον δ' ἀνένευσεν Π 250. Cf. Γ 103: ἕτερον μὲν . . . ἑτέρας δὲ . . . η 123.—Sim.: ἐξ ἑτέρων ἕτερ' ἐστίν ρ 266 (see ἐκ (II) (4)).—With ellipse in the first member: νέκυάς τ' ἀγέμεν, ἕτεροι δὲ μεθ' ὕλην H 418, 420. Cf. Ω 528 : η 126. —In the second: ἑ. ῥίπτασκε . . . ὁ δὲ . . . θ 374. Cf. υ 132.—(b) With the article: χειρὶ τῇ ἑτέρῃ . . . τῇ δ' ἑτέρῃ . . . Ξ 272. Cf. χ 183.— With ellipse in the first member: τὸν μὲν . . . τὸν δ' ἕτερον . . . E 146. Cf. X 151 : ι 430, ν 68. —With the article in one member only: ἑτέρῳ μὲν . . . τῷ δ' ἑτέρῳ . . . Φ 164. Cf. ε 266.— (c) With ἄλλος as correlative: ὅς χ' ἕτερον μὲν κεύθῃ, ἄλλο δὲ εἴπῃ I 313. Cf. I 472, N 731 : η 123, ν 68.—(4) In correlative clauses, the second. With the article: οἱ μὲν . . . τῶν δ' ἑτέρων . . . τῶν δὲ τρίτων . . . M 93. Cf. Π 179 : κ 354.— (5) Another: ὅς χ' ἕτερ' ἅρμαθ' ἵκηται Δ 306 : ἑ. με θυμὸς ἔρυκεν ι 302 (see θυμός (I) (8)).—With the article: τοὺς ἑτέρους Κρηθῇϊ τέκεν (these besides) λ 258.—Absol., another, others: ἀρξάντων ἑτέρων Φ 437 : ἔς κε δεκάτην γενεὴν ἕτερόν γ' ἔτι βόσκοι (another (and so on), *i.e.* one after another) ξ 325 = τ 294.—(6) In dat. or instrumental fem. ἑτέρῃ, ἑτέρηφι (sc. χειρί), with or without the article, with the other hand: σκαιῇ ἔγχος ἔχων· ἑτέρηφι δὲ λάζετο πέτρον Π 734 : χειρὶ λάβε δεξιτερῆφι, τῇ δ' ἑτέρῃ . . . τ 481. Cf. Σ 477.—Repeated: τῇ ἑτέρῃ μὲν . . . τῇ δ' ἑτέρῃ . . . (with one hand . . . with the other . . .) Φ 71.—With ellipse in the first member X 80 : γ 441.

ἐτέρφθησαν, 3 pl. aor. pass. τέρπω.

ἑτέρωθεν [ἕτερος + -θεν (1) (2)]. (1) From the other side or quarter: αὖεν Ἄρης Υ 51, Πηλεΐδης ὦρτο (to meet him) 164 : ἡ δὲ [κρήνη] ὑπ' αὐλῆς οὐδὸν ἵησιν (sheds its waters in this direction from its situation over against the other) η 130. —(2) On the other side, in the opposite quarter: Ἰδομενεὺς ἕστηκεν Γ 230, Τρῶες [κόσμηθεν] (facing them) Λ 56 = Υ 3. Cf. Z 247, I 666, Λ 215 = M 415, Π 763, P 138: εἴδωλον ἀγόρευεν (*i.e.* beyond the range of the sword) λ 83.—(3) The local sense obscured, on the other hand, on his or their side or part: Ἀτρεΐδης ἐμήνιεν A 247, Τρῶες ὁπλίζοντο Θ 55, Πάτροκλος ἀναίνετο Λ 647. Cf. E 668, H 311, 419, 430, N 489, 835, Ξ 388, O 501, Π 427, 733, 755, Σ 32, 243, X 79 : π 43, φ 368, χ 211.

ἑτέρωθι [ἕτερος + -θι]. (1) On the other side, opposite μ 235 (see ἔνθεν (2)).—In another quarter, elsewhere: ὃν ἂν ἐγὼν ἑ. νοήσω (shirking the fight) O 348 : εἶσε λόχον, ἑ. δ' ἀνώγει δαῖτα πένεσθαι (in another part of the palace) δ 531.—(2) Anywhere: εἴ χ' ἑ. πύθηαι E 351.

ἑτέρως [adv. fr. ἕτερος]. To the opposite effect, otherwise: ἑ. ἐβόλοντο θεοί α 234.

ἑτέρωσε [ἕτερος + -σε]. (1) To or towards the other or opposite side or quarter: νέκυν ἑ. ἐρύοντα (off, away) Δ 492 : ἑ. φόβηθεν π 163.—To one side: κάρη βάλεν Θ 306. Cf. Θ 308, N 543, Ψ 697 : ἐκλίθη [λέβης] (turned over) τ 470. Cf. χ 17.— Aside: λιασθεὶς Ψ 231.—Sim.: βάλ' ὄμματα π 179. —Opposed to πρό, aside: οὐ προκυλίνδεται [πέλαγος] οὐδ' ἑ. Ξ 18 (*v.l.* οὐδετέρωσε).—(2) In the opposite quarter: καθῖζον Υ 151.

ἐτέταλτο, 3 sing. plupf. pass. τέλλω.

ἐτετεύχατο, 3 pl. plupf. pass. τεύχω.

ἔτετμε, 3 sing. aor. τέμω.

ἐτέτυκτο, 3 sing. plupf. pass. τεύχω.

ἔτευξα, aor. τεύχω.

ἔτης, ὁ. App. expressing some such relationship as that of fellow-townsman: σοὺς ἔτας καὶ ἑταίρους H 295. Cf. Z 239, 262, I 464, Π 456 = 674 : δ 3, 16, ο 273.

ἐτήτυμος [cf. ἐτεός, ἔτυμος]. (1) True: ὅδε μῦθος ψ 62.—Bringing the truth, sure: ἄγγελος X 438.—Real, actual: κείνῳ οὐκέτι νόστος ἐ. (one cannot believe in it) γ 241.—(2) In neut. ἐτήτυμον as adv., truly: τοῦτ' ἀγόρευσον ἐ. α 174, etc.— Truly, really, in fact: εἰ ἐ. αἴτιός ἐστιν N 111. Cf. δ 157.—Of a truth, verily: ταῦτ' ἐ. οὐ κακόν ἐστιν Σ 128.—Of promising, faithfully A 558.

ἔτι. (1) (a) In reference to the present or past, now (then) as formerly, still, yet; with neg., no more, no longer: οὐ γὰρ ἔτ' ἀμφὶς φράζονται B 13, ἔτ' ἐκολῴα 212, ἔτι μοι μένος ἔμπεδόν ἐστιν E 254. Cf. B 641, I 675, Λ 172, M 199, etc.: α 233, 404, β 210, δ 833, etc.—(b) With neg. in sense corresponding to οὐκέτι (2): λοίγια ἔργα τάδ' ἔσσεται οὐδ' ἔτ' ἀνεκτά (will come to the point of being . . .) A 573. Cf. β 63 (twice).— (2) In reference to the future, yet, further, still; with neg., no more, no longer, no further: ἠδ' ἔτι δώσει A 96, οὐδ' ἔτι φασὶ σχήσεσθαι I 234. Cf. B 141, 260, E 465, H 447, etc.: α 315, β 230, ζ 33, η 270, etc.—Further, as the next step: ὄφρα κ' ἔτι γνῶμεν . . . X 382.—(3) In the future, hereafter: οὐ γὰρ ἔτ' ἄλλη ἔσται θαλπωρή Z 411. Cf. X 86 : σ 22.—At or before some future time, yet: ἔτι που Τρώων ἡγήτορες κονίσουσιν πεδίον Ξ 144. Cf. ε 290.—Preceding πρίν: οὐδέ κεν ὧς ἔτι πείσειε, πρὶν . . . I 386. Cf. χ 63.—After all, in spite of all, yet: ἔτι κε καὶ ὧς ἵκοισθε λ 104. Cf. κ 269, etc.—(4) Again, once more: δός μοι ἔτι ι 355. Cf. A 455, B 258, T 70, etc.: μ 428, etc.—(5) At the time in question in contrast with the future, still, yet: ἀήθεσσον ἔτ' αὐτῶν K 493. Cf. Z 222, H 433, etc.: β 313, γ 401, etc.—(6) Too, also, further, besides, still: ἠμὲν πάλαι ἠδ' ἔτι καὶ νῦν I 105. Cf. E 621, Υ 269, etc.: γ 60, λ 623, π 305, etc.—(7) Strengthening ἐξ in temporal sense (cf. ἐξέτι): ἐξ ἔτι τοῦ ὅτε . . . (ever since the time when . . .) I 106.—Strengthening νῦν I 111, Λ 790, etc.—πρίν ν 336.—With οὐδέ, nor yet O 709.—(8) With adjectives and adverbs, yet, still: οὐδ' ἄρ' ἔτι δὴν ἦν Z 139, ἔτι ζωόν 500, etc. Cf. α 197, β 296, etc.—Sim.: ἔτι τοσαῦτα (as much again) ν 258.—(9) Strengthening comparatives, yet, still, even: ἔτι πλέονας E 679, ἔτι μᾶλλον I 678. Cf. O 121, etc.: α 322, ε 417, θ 203, etc.—Sim.: ἦ κ' ἔτι πολλοὶ γαῖαν ὀδὰξ εἷλον (more) X 16.

ἐτίναξε, 3 sing. aor. τινάσσω.

ἔτῖσε, 3 sing. aor. τίω.

ἔτλην, aor. τλάω.

†ἑτοιμάζω [ἑτοῖμος]. 3 sing. aor. imp. ἑτοιμασάτω T 197. 2 pl. ἑτοιμάσατε A 118. 3 pl. aor. mid. ἑτοιμάσσαντο ν 184. 3 pl. opt. ἑτοιμασσαίατο K 571.

To get ready, prepare, provide: ἐμοὶ γέρας Α 118. Cf. Τ 197.—In mid. Κ 571 : ν 184.

ἑτοῖμος, -η, -ον. (1) Ready, prepared : ὀνείατα Ι 91 = 221 = Ω 627 : = α 149 = δ 67 = 218 = ε 200 = θ 71 = 484 = ξ 453 = ο 142 = π 54 = ρ 98 = υ 256.—(2) Awaiting one : αὐτίκα τοι μεθ' Ἕκτορα πότμος ἑ. Σ 96.—(3) Brought to fulfilment or reality : ταῦτά γ' ἑτοῖμα τετεύχαται Ξ 53. Cf. θ 384.—Sim. : οὔ σφισιν ἥδε γε [μῆτις] ἑτοίμη (successful, realized) Ι 425.

ἔτορε, 3 sing. aor. τορέω.

ἔτος, τό (Ϝέτος. Cf. L. *vetus*). A year (1) Considered as a space of time : τοσσαῦτ' ἔτεα πτολεμίξομεν Β 328, τῶν προτέρων ἐτέων (in former years) Λ 691.—(2) Considered as a point or unit of time or as one of a series : ἐεικοστὸν Ω 765 : ὅτε δὴ ἐ. ἦλθε τῷ . . . α 16. Cf. β 89, 107, δ 82, η 261, λ 295, π 206, ω 288, etc.

ἔτραπε, 3 sing. aor. τρέπω.

ἔτραφε, 3 sing. aor. τρέφω.

ἔτραφεν, 3 pl. aor. pass. τρέφω.

ἔτρεσε, 3 sing. aor. τρέω.

ἔτρεψε, 3 sing. aor. τρέπω.

ἔτυμος [cf. ἐτεός, ἐτήτυμος]. (1) True. Absol. : ψεύδεα ἐτύμοισιν ὁμοῖα (truths) τ 203, οἱ (*sc.* ὄνειροι) ἔτυμα κραίνουσιν (come true) 567.—(2) In neut. ἔτυμον as adv., rightly, correctly : οὔ σ' ἐ. φάμεν πεπνῦσθαι (*i.e.* we were wrong in thinking . . .) Ψ 440, ἐ. ἐρέω ; Κ 534 : = δ 140.—Truly, really, in fact : ἐ. ἦλθεν ψ 26.

ἐτύπη, 3 sing. aor. pass. τύπτω.

ἔτυχες, 2 sing. aor. τυγχάνω.

ἐτύχησε, 3 sing. aor. τυγχάνω.

ἐτύχθη, 3 sing. aor. pass. τεύχω.

ἐτώσιος. Vain, fruitless. (1) Of missile weapons, launched in vain : ἔγχος ἤϊχθη ἐτώσιον Γ 368. Cf. Ε 854, Ξ 407 = Χ 292, Ρ 633 : χ 256, 273.—(2) Of gifts, given in vain ω 283.—(3) Useless, idle : ἐτώσιον ἄχθος ἀρούρης Σ 104.

ἐΰ, εὖ [neut. of ἐΰς]. (1) Well, with skill, address or knowledge, deftly : εὖ τις δόρυ θηξάσθω Β 382. Cf. Β 777, Δ 111, Ε 466, Μ 458, Ψ 761, etc. : ἐὺ κρίνασθαι ἑταίρους δ 408, φρίξας εὖ λοφιήν (so that it stood well up) τ 446. Cf. ε 236, ζ 318, θ 37, τ 460, ψ 193, etc.—(2) In reference to knowledge, well, fully, thoroughly : ὄφρ' ἐὺ εἰδῇς Α 185. Cf. Α 385, Β 301, Ψ 240, etc. : α 174, β 170, δ 494, λ 442, τ 501, etc.—(3) (a) Duly, rightly, well, in accordance with usage, rule, one's duties, obligations or instructions : εὖ δάσσαντο Α 368. Cf. Γ 72, Κ 63, Λ 779, Π 223, etc. : εὖ κατάλεξον γ 97. Cf. γ 357, δ 589, ξ 108, etc.—Strengthening an expression of sim. force : εὖ κατὰ κόσμον Κ 472, Λ 48, etc.—(b) In reference to hospitality, well : ἐὺ ἐξείνισσα τ 194. Cf. ξ 128, etc.—(c) To benefiting or favouring : εὖ μιν ἔρξαντα (when he had done well by him) Ε 650 : οἷσιν εὖ φρονέῃσιν η 74. Cf. σ 168.—For ἐὺ φρονέων see ἐϋφρονέων.—(d) To speaking *well* of a person : ἵνα τίς σ' ἐὺ εἴπῃ α 302 = γ 200.—(4) (a) In good case, in safety, in good condition : εὖ ἐλθέμεν γ 188. Cf. Α 19, etc. : θ 427, σ 260, etc.—(b) With good results for oneself : τάχ' οὐκ εὖ πᾶσι πιθήσεις (you will not do well to . . .) φ 369.—(c) In reference to living, well, at ease ρ 423 = τ 79.—To feasting, well, sumptuously Ω 802 : κ 452, σ 408.—Sim. : εὖ πᾶσι παρέξω θ 39, εὖ εἱμένοι ο 331, εὖ θαλπιόων τ 319.—(d) For εὖ ναιόμενον πτολίεθρον and the like see ναίω[1] (4), ναιετάω (2).

εὑ. See ἑέ.

εὐαγγέλιον, τό [εὐ- (5) + ἀγγελίη]. A reward for bringing good tidings ξ 152, 166.

εὔαδε, 3 sing. aor. ἁνδάνω.

εὐανθής [εὐ- (5) + ἄνθος]. Of hair, showing fine growth, sprouting luxuriantly λ 320.

εὔβοτος, -ον [εὐ- (5) + βοτά]. Having goodly cattle : νῆσος ο 406.

εὖγμα, -ατος, τό [εὐγ-, εὔχομαι]. A boast or vaunt : κενὰ εὔγματα εἰπών χ 249.

ἐΰγναμπτος, -ον [ἐΰ- (1) + γνάμπτω. 'Well bent or curved']. Fashioned with art : κληῖσιν σ 294.

εὐδείελος, -ον [app. for εὐδέελος, εὔδηλος, fr. εὐ- (4) + δῆλος]. Thus, bright, shining. Epithet of islands : Ἰθάκην β 167. Cf. ι 21, ν 212, 234, 325, ξ 344, τ 132.

εὐδικίη, -ης, ἡ [εὐ- (5) + δίκη]. Good laws, even justice. In pl. : ὅς τ' εὐδικίας ἀνέχῃσιν τ 111.

εὔδμητος, ἐΰδμητος, -ον [εὐ-, ἐΰ- (1) + δμη-, δέμνω]. Well-constructed, well-built. Epithet of walls, etc. Α 448, Μ 36, 137, 154, Π 700, Φ 516, Χ 195 : η 100, υ 302, χ 24, 126.

εὕδω. 3 sing. pa. iterative εὕδεσκε Χ 503. [ἐν-, καθ-.) (1) To be asleep, sleep, slumber : τὸν κίχανεν εὕδοντα Β 19. Cf. Β 2, 23, 24, Κ 83, Ξ 334, 352, 358, etc. : εὗδον παννύχιος η 288. Cf. δ 804, θ 317, ι 428, κ 12, ν 74, ο 5, etc.—With ὕπνον as cognate acc. θ 445.—Of animals : ὅθι σύες εὗδον ξ 533.—(2) To lay oneself down to sleep, go to bed, go to sleep : οὐδὲ Τρῶας εἴασεν εὕδειν Κ 300. Cf. Ι 663 = Ω 675, Χ 503 : εὕδειν ὄρνυντο β 397. Cf. γ 359, δ 794 = σ 189, λ 331, 374, ο 396, σ 328.—Of animals, to lie down and sleep δ 405.—(3) Of the sleep of death Ξ 482.—(4) Of the winds, to be hushed or stilled Ε 524.

εὐειδής [εὐ- (5) + εἶδος]. Fair to see, beauteous : γυναῖκ' εὐειδέα Γ 48.

εὐεργεσίη, -ης, ἡ [sb. corresponding to two next]. (1) Well-doing, the doing of what is right χ 374.—(2) A service done, a benefit conferred χ 235.

εὐεργής, -ές [εὐ- (1) (3) + ἔργω[2]]. (1) Well or skilfully made, constituted or fashioned with art. Epithet of chariots, ships, etc. : δίφρον Ε 585, Ν 399, Π 743, νηῦς Ω 396 : μ 166, π 322, νῆα θ 567, ι 279, λ 70, 106, 159, μ 305, ο 33, ψ 234, λώπην ν 224.—Of gold, app., fine ι 202, ω 274.—(2) Done by way of service or benefit. Absol. in neut. pl., services, benefits : χάρις εὐεργέων (for . . .) δ 695, χ 319.

εὐεργός, -όν [εὐ- (2) + ἔργω[2]]. Doing what is right, of good walk and conversation λ 434 = ο 422 = ω 202.

εὐερκής [εὐ- (5) + ἕρκος]. Well fenced or walled. Epithet of αὐλή Ι 472 : φ 389, χ 449.—Of doors or gates, securely barring passage, stout: θύραι ρ 267.

ἐΰζυγος, -ον [ἐϋ- (5) + ζυγόν]. With goodly ζυγά (see ζυγόν (2)). Epithet of ships ν 116, ρ 288.

ἐΰζωνος, -ον [ἐϋ- (5) + ζώνη]. Well girdled. Epithet of women Α 429, Ζ 467, Ι 366 = Ψ 261, Ι 590, 667, Ψ 760.

εὐηγενής [app. εὐ- (1) + γεν-, γίγνομαι. But the -η- cannot be explained. See εὐηφενής]. Well-born, of noble race Λ 427, Ψ 81.

εὐηγεσίη, -ης, ἡ [εὐ- (5) + ἡγεσ-, ἡγέομαι]. Good leadership τ 114.

εὐήκης [εὐ- (5) + *ἀκή, point]. Well-pointed, sharp: αἰχμῆς εὐήκεος Χ 319.

εὐήνωρ, -ορος [εὐ- (3) + ἀνήρ]. That is of service or benefit to men. Epithet of οἶνος ('that maketh glad the heart of man') δ 622.—Of χαλκός ν 19.

εὐήρης, -ῆρες [εὐ- (1) + ἀρ-, ἀραρίσκω]. Well fitted or balanced. Epithet of oars λ 121, 125 = ψ 272, λ 129, μ 15, ψ 268.

εὐηφενής [εὐ- (5) + ἄφενος]. Wealthy, rich. Prob. to be read for εὐηγενής (q.v.).

ἐΰθριξ, ἐΰτριχος [ἐϋ- (5) + θρίξ]. With flowing mane. Epithet of horses Ψ 13, 301, 351.

ἐΰθρονος, -ον [ἐϋ- (5) + θρόνος]. With beautiful seat, fair-seated. Epithet of Ἠώς Θ 565: ζ 48, ο 495, ρ 497, σ 318, τ 342.

εὔθῡμος [εὐ- (5) + θυμός]. Well-disposed, bountiful: ἄναξ ξ 63.

εὐκαμπής, -ές [εὐ- (1) + κάμπτω]. Curved into due form, fashioned with art or skill σ 368, φ 6.

εὐκέατος, -ον [εὐ- (1) + κεάζω]. Readily cleft or split, or perh., deftly split (into billets for burning): κέδρου ε 60.

εὔκηλος [app. ἐϝέκηλος, ἔϝκηλος. Cf. (ϝ)έκηλος]. = ἕκηλος (1): εὐ. τὰ φράζεαι ἅσσα θέλησθα (without interference on my part) Α 554, πολέμιζον Ρ 371. Cf. γ 263, ξ 479.

ἐϋκλεής, -ές [ἐϋ- (5) + κλέος]. Acc. pl. ἐϋκλεῖας (for ἐϋκλεέας) Κ 281: φ 331. (1) Honoured, distinguished Κ 281.—In good odour or repute: κατὰ δῆμον φ 331.—(2) Absol. in neut. ἐϋκλεές with infin.: οὐχ ἧμιν ἐϋκλεὲς ἀπονέεσθαι (it will do us little credit, will be to our disgrace, to . . .) Ρ 415.

ἐϋκλείη, -ης, ἡ [ἐϋκλεής]. Honour, good repute Θ 285: ξ 402.

ἐϋκλειῶς [adv. fr. ἐϋκλεής. Doubtless for ἐϋκλεεῶς]. Gloriously: ὀλέσθαι Χ 110.

ἐϋκνήμις, -ῖδος [ἐϋ- (5) + κνημίς]. Equipped with good κνημῖδες. Epithet of the Achaeans Α 17, Β 331, Γ 86, Δ 414, etc.: β 72, γ 149, λ 509, σ 259, υ 146.—Applied also to ἑταῖροι (of this race) β 402, ι 60, 550, κ 203, ψ 319.

εὐκόσμως [adv. fr. εὔκοσμος, fr. εὐ- (5) + κόσμος]. In due wise, according to accepted convention φ 123.

ἐϋκτίμενος, -η, -ον [ἐϋ- (1) + κτίμενος, pf. pple. pass. fr. κτι-, κτίζω]. (1) Epithet (a) Of cities, etc. Well-built, or furnished with fair buildings Β 570, 712, Δ 33, Ε 543, Ζ 13, Ρ 611, Φ 40, 433, etc.: γ 4, δ 342 = ρ 133, θ 283, χ 52, ω 377.—Applied to streets Ζ 391.—(b) Of buildings, well-built, fair δ 476 = ζ 315 = κ 474 = ο 129 = ψ 259, ι 533, ω 214.—(c) Of a threshing-floor, well constructed Υ 496.—(d) Of gardens, orchards or vineyards, well laid out Φ 77: ω 226, 336.—(2) App., put into profitable condition, 'developed': νῆσον ι 130 (see κάμνω (2)).

ἐΰκτιτος [ἐϋ- (1) + κτι- as in prec.]. = prec. (1) (a) Β 592.

εὐκτός [vbl. adj. fr. εὔχομαι]. In neut. pl. εὐκτά, matter for boasting Ξ 98.

εὔκυκλος, -ον [εὐ- (5) + κύκλος]. Epithet (1) Of a waggon, well-wheeled ζ 58, 70.—(2) Of shields, made of plates skilfully rounded Ε 453 = Μ 426, Ε 797, Ν 715, Ξ 428.

εὐλείμων [εὐ- (5) + λειμών]. Having fair meadows δ 607.

εὐλή, -ῆς, ἡ. A worm or maggot preying on dead bodies Τ 26, Χ 509, Ω 414.

εὔληρα, τά. Reins Ψ 481.

εὐμενέτης [εὐ- (5) + μένος]. A well-wisher: χάρματ' εὐμενέτῃσιν ζ 185.

εὔμηλος, -ον [εὐ- (5) + μῆλον[1]]. Having goodly sheep or goats: νῆσος ο 406.

ἐϋμμελίης [ἐϋ- (5) + μελίη]. Genit. ἐϋμμελίω Δ 47, 165, Ζ 449. Of the good ashen spear, wielder of the stout spear. Epithet of Priam Δ 47 = 165 = Ζ 449.—Of the sons of Panthus Ρ 9, 23, 59.—Of Peisistratus γ 400.

εὐνάζω [εὐνή]. Fut. εὐνάσω δ 408. (κατ-, παρ-.) (1) In pass., to be laid or retire to rest, go to bed, lie down to sleep: ἐν προδόμῳ εὐνάζετο υ 1. Cf. ψ 299.—Of seals δ 449.—Of birds ε 65.—Connoting sexual intercourse: παρ ἀνδράσιν εὐνάζεσθαι ε 119.—(2) To cause to couch in a manner suitable for something contemplated: εὐνάσω ἑξείης δ 408.

εὐνάω [εὐνή]. (κατ-.) (1) To still (lamentation) δ 758.—(2) In pass. as prec. (1). Of winds being hushed or stilled ε 384.—Connoting sexual intercourse: θεὰ βροτῷ εὐνηθεῖσα (with . . .) Β 821. Cf. Γ 441, Ξ 314, 331, 360, Π 176: δ 334 = ρ 125, θ 292, κ 296.—(3) = prec. (2): ἑξείης εὔνησεν δ 440.

εὐνή, -ῆς, ἡ [εὐδνή, εὕδω]. Ablative εὐνῆφι(ν) Ο 580: β 2, γ 405, δ 307. (1) Properly, bedding as distinguished from the bedstead (δέμνια, λέκτρον, λέχος): ἐκθεῖσα λέχος ἐμβάλετ' εὐνήν ψ 179. Cf. γ 403, η 347, θ 269.—But app. including bed and bedding: κάτθετ' εὐνήν, δέμνια καὶ χλαίνας τ 317.—So in pl. λ 188.—(2) A bed, bed, one's bed: ὄρνυτ' ἐξ εὐνῆφιν β 2, γ 405, δ 307. Cf. Ι 618, Κ 75, Χ 504 (but perh. the last passage should come under (1); cf. λέκτροισιν 503): α 427, δ 294, η 342, θ 2, 249, ξ 519, ο 58, 96, ρ 102 = τ 595, υ 130, χ 196.—(3) Couching, going to bed: ἐπεί τοι εὔαδεν εὐνή Ξ 340. Cf. ψ 257.—(4) (a) The marriage-bed: ἀλλήλων ἀπέχονται εὐνῆς καὶ φιλότητος Ξ 207 = 306. Cf. Ξ 209, 336, Σ 85: γ 403, δ 333 = ρ 124, η 347, θ 269, π 34, 75 = τ 527, ψ 226, 289, 349, 354.—Fig., wedlock: ἔτλην ἀνέρος εὐνήν Σ 433.—(b) With reference to intercourse outside of wedlock: τῆς εὐνῆς ἐπιβήμεναι (the bed of her, her bed) I 133 = 275 = T 176. Cf. Ξ 296 : Κίρκης ἐπέβην εὐνῆς κ 347. Cf. κ 334, 340, 342, 480.—(c) Fig., sexual intercourse : ἐμίγην φιλότητι καὶ εὐνῇ Γ 445. Cf. Z 25, O 32, T 262, Ω 130 : α 433, ε 126, κ 297, 335, ο 421, ψ 219, 346.—Sim. in pl. : εὐναὶ ἀθανάτων (the embraces) λ 249.—(5) A place for rest or sleep in gen., a lair : εὐνὴν ἐπαμήσατο ε 482.—In pl. λ 194.—(6) In pl., a dwelling or abode : Τυφωέος εὐνάς (where he lies couched beneath the earth) B 783. Cf. Ω 615.—(7) A bivouac : Τρώων εὐναί K 408. Cf. K 464.—(8) A lurking-place, a place of ambush δ 438.—(9) The lair of a deer Λ 115, O 580, X 190.—Of a lion δ 338 = ρ 129.—A place in which to keep swine ξ 14.—(10) In pl., stones with hawsers attached thrown out to anchor the bows of a ship : ἐξ εὐνὰς ἔβαλον A 436, ἐπ' εὐνάων (at anchor) Ξ 77. Cf. ι 137, ο 498.

εὐνῆθεν [εὐνή + -θεν (1)]. From one's bed υ 124.

εὖνις. Reft or bereaved of. With genit. : υἱῶν X 44 : ψυχῆς τε καὶ αἰῶνος ι 524.

ἐΰννητος [ἐΰ- (1) + νη-, νέω²]. Of fine spun work : χιτῶνας Σ 596. Cf. Ω 580 : η 97.

εὐνομίη, -ης, ἡ [εὐ- (5) + νόμος, usage, custom]. Good order or governance ρ 487.

εὔξατο, 3 sing. aor. εὔχομαι.

εὔξεστος, ἐΰξεστος, -η, -ον, also -ος, -ον [εὐ-, ἐΰ- (1) + ξεσ-, ξέω]. Epithet of the products of the art of the carpenter or other craftsman, fashioned with skill or curious art : ἀσαμίνθους K 576, δίφρῳ Π 402. Cf. H 5, N 613, Σ 276, Ω 271, 275, 280, 578 (*v.l.* here ἐϋσσώτρου), 590 : ἀπήνῃ ζ 75, χηλῷ ν 10. Cf. δ 48, ξ 225, ο 333, ρ 87, 602 = ω 408, τ 101, φ 137 = 164.

ἐΰξοος, -ον [ἐΰ- (1) + ξέω]. = prec. B 390, Δ 105, Λ 629, N 594, 706 : α 128, δ 590, ε 237, θ 215, τ 586, φ 92, 281, 286, 326, 336, χ 71.

ἔϋξος [as prec.]. = prec. : δουρός K 373.

εὔορμος [εὐ- (5) + ὅρμος²]. Affording good holding-ground, moorings, or shelter. Epithet of harbours Φ 23 : δ 358, ι 136.

εὐπατέρεια, -ης [εὐ- (5) + πατήρ]. Daughter of divine or noble sire. Epithet of Helen Z 292 : χ 227.—Of Tyro λ 235.

εὔπεπλος, ἐΰπεπλος, -ον [εὐ-, ἐΰ- (5) + πέπλος]. Wearer of the fair robe. Epithet of women E 424, Z 372, 378, 383, Ω 769 : ζ 49, φ 160.

εὐπηγής [εὐ- (1) + πηγ-, πήγνυμι]. Compact of bodily frame, well-knit φ 334.

εὔπηκτος, ἐΰπηκτος, -ον [εὐ-, ἐΰ- (1) + πηκ-, πήγνυμι]. Well built or constructed. Epithet of buildings or chambers B 661, I 144, 286, 663 = Ω 675 : ψ 41.

ἐΰπλειος, -ον [ἐΰ- (4) + πλεῖος]. Well-filled ρ 467.

ἐϋπλεκής [ἐΰ- (1) + πλέκω]. (1) Braided or twisted with curious art : θύσανοι B 449.—(2) Epithet of chariots, app., having a cunningly plaited platform (cf. E 727) Ψ 436.

εὔπλεκτος, ἐΰπλεκτος, -ον [as prec.]. (1) Skilfully twisted Ψ 115.—(2) = prec. (2) Ψ 335.

εὐπλοίη, -ης, ἡ [εὐ- (5) + πλέω]. A good or successful voyage I 362.

ἐϋπλόκαμος, -ον [ἐΰ- (5) + πλόκαμος]. As fem. pl. ἐϋπλοκαμῖδες β 119, τ 542. Having goodly locks, fair-tressed. Epithet of women and goddesses Z 380 = 385, Λ 624, Ξ 6, Σ 48, X 442, 449 : α 86, β 119, ε 125, ζ 135, η 41, κ 136, etc.

ἐϋπλυνής, -ές [ἐΰ- (1) + πλύνω]. Well or freshly washed, fair : φᾶρος θ 392, 425, ν 67, π 173.

εὐποίητος, -η, -ον, also -ος, -ον [εὐ- (1) + ποιέω]. (Cf. ποιητός (2).) Epithet of various products of art, well made, constructed, woven : φάλαρα Π 106, βοῶν 636 : πυράγρην γ 434, εἵματα ν 369, θρόνοις υ 150.

εὔπρηστος, -ον [εὐ- (1) + πρησ-, πρήθω]. Of wind from bellows, puffed out duly so as to suit the work in hand Σ 471.

εὔπρυμνος, -ον [εὐ- (5) + πρύμνη]. With goodly stern. Epithet of ships Δ 248.

εὔπυργος, -ον [εὐ- (5) + πύργος]. Well fortified. Epithet of Troy H 71.

εὔπωλος, -ον [εὐ- (5) + πῶλος]. Abounding in fine foals. Epithet of Troy E 551, Π 576 := ξ 71, β 18, λ 169.

εὐράξ [εὖρος. For the termination cf. μουνάξ. Perh. orig. a naval term, 'on the broadside']. On one side : στῆ Λ 251, O 541.

εὑρίσκω. Aor. εὗρον κ 408, ψ 45. 3 sing. -ε A 498, Δ 89, E 794, Σ 372, Ω 83, etc. : α 106, β 299, ξ 5, ο 4, ψ 55, etc. 1 pl. -ομεν Λ 771 ; ι 217, κ 252. 3 -ον A 329, E 753, M 127, Ω 98, etc.: β 408, δ 3, κ 113, ω 15, etc. 3 sing. subj. εὕρῃ X 192, ω 462. -ησι M 302. 1 pl. -ωμεν I 49 : μ 300. 2 -ητε λ 108. 3 -ωσι H 31. Opt. εὕροιμι ν 43. 3 sing. -οι ι 535. Pple. εὑρών Γ 24. Infin. εὑρέμεναι B 343 : δ 374, 467, μ 393. εὑρεῖν I 250. 3 sing. aor. mid. εὕρετο Π 472 : φ 304. Opt. εὑροίμην ι 422. Imp. εὕρεο τ 403. (ἐξ-, ἐφ-.) (1) To find, to light or come upon : ἔλαφον Γ 24. Cf. E 169, Θ 127, Λ 473, Ω 98 ; μνηστῆρας α 106. Cf. δ 450, ζ 277, 282, κ 113, 210, 252, μ 300, ω 15, 222.—Of immaterial things : ἐν πήματα οἴκῳ ι 535.—Absol. : ὄφρα κεν εὕρῃ X 192.—(2) To find or come upon in a specified place or condition or doing something specified : παρὰ κλισίῃ ἥμενον A 329. Cf. B 169, Γ 125, Z 321, H 382, I 186, M 121, etc. : ἐν μεγάροισιν β 299. Cf. β 408, δ 3, ε 151, η 136, κ 408, λ 108, etc.—(3) To find out, discover, hit upon, devise, contrive : μῆχός τι B 343, ἄκος I 250. Cf. δ 374, 467, μ 393, τ 158.—In mid. : τοῖο εὕρετο τέκμωρ (for this state of things, this confusion) Π 472. Cf. ι 422.—To find out or discover by experience : τέκμωρ Ἰλίου H 31, I 49 (see τέκμωρ (1)).—To think of or hit upon as fitting or suitable. In mid. : ὄνομ' εὕρεο ὅττι κε θῆαι τ 403.—(4) To bring upon oneself, incur : μή τις κακὸν εὕρῃ ω 462.—In mid. φ 304.

Εὖρος, ὁ. The east wind B 145 (app. here, from the sing. vb., the wind of east and south), Π 765 : ε 295, 332, μ 326, τ 206.

εὖρος, τό [εὐρύς]. Width, breadth λ 312.

ἐΰρραφής [ἐΰ- (1) + ῥαφ-, ῥάπτω]. Well or strongly stitched : ἐϋρραφέεσσι δοροῖσιν β 354, 380.

ἐΰρρεής [ἐϋ- (1) + ῥέω]. Genit. ἐϋρρεῖος (for ἐϋρρεέος) in passages cited. Flowing with fair streams. Epithet of rivers Z 508 = O 265, Ξ 433 = Φ 1 = Ω 692.

ἐϋρρείτης [as prec.]. = prec. Z 34 : ξ 257.

ἐΰρροος [as ἐϋρρεής]. = ἐϋρρεής H 329, Φ 130.

εὐρυάγυια [εὐρύς + ἄγυια]. With wide streets. Epithet of cities. Of Troy B 12, 29 = 66, 141 = I 28, B 329, Ξ 88 : δ 246, χ 230.—Of Mycene Δ 52.—Of Athens η 80.—In gen. : πτόλις ο 384.

εὐρυκρείων. See εὐρύς (2) (b).

εὐρυμέτωπος, -ον [εὐρύς + μέτωπον]. Broad-fronted. Epithet of oxen Υ 495, K 292 : = γ 382, λ 289, μ 262, 355, υ 212.

†εὐρύνω [εὐρύς]. 3 pl. aor. εὔρῡναν. To make wide or broad : εὔρυναν ἀγῶνα (marked off an ample space) θ 260.

εὐρυόδεια [εὐρύς + ὁδός]. With wide ways, wide-stretching. Epithet of the earth or the surface thereof : χθονός Π 635 : γ 453, κ 149, λ 52.

εὐρύοπα [εὐρύς + either (F)όψ or ὀπ- (for which see ὁράω)]. Voc. εὐρύοπᾰ Π 241. Acc. εὐρύοπᾰ A 498, Θ 206, Ξ 265, O 152, Ω 98, 331. Prob. orig. a voc. and turned into nom. and acc. Either far-sounding, far-thundering, or far-seeing. Epithet of Zeus A 498, E 265, Θ 206, 442, I 419 = 686, N 732, Ξ 203, 265, O 152, 724, Π 241, P 545, Ω 98, 296, 331 : β 146, γ 288, δ 173, λ 436, ξ 235, ρ 322, ω 544.

εὐρύπορος, -ον [εὐρύς + πόρος]. With wide ways, on which one may roam far and wide : θαλάσσης O 381 : δ 432, μ 2.

εὐρυπυλής, -ές [εὐρύς + πύλη]. Wide-gated. Epithet of the house or realm of Hades : εὐρυπυλὲς Ἄϊδος δῶ Ψ 74 : λ 571.

εὐρυρέεθρος [εὐρύς + ῥέεθρον]. Flowing with wide streams, broad-channelled. Epithet of a river : Ἀξιός Φ 141.

εὐρύς, -εῖα, -ύ. Acc. sing. masc. εὐρέα Z 291, I 72, Σ 140, Φ 125 : δ 435, ω 118. εὐρύν A 229, Γ 364, H 178, T 196, etc. : α 67, δ 378, ζ 150, π 183, etc. **(1) (a)** Wide, broad, spacious : στρατὸν Ἀχαιῶν A 229, ὤμους Γ 210, τάφρον H 441, τεῖχος (thick) M 5, αἰγιαλός Ξ 33, ἀγῶνα (numerous) Ψ 258. Cf. K 29, Λ 527, Ξ 145, O 358, Σ 542, etc. : θάλαμον β 338, σπέος ε 77. Cf. δ 603, 605, ε 163, 483, ν 243, σ 385, etc.—Comp. εὐρύτερος, -η Γ 194, Ψ 427.—**(b)** Of places : Ἑλίκην εὐρεῖαν B 575. Cf. Z 173, N 433, 453, Σ 591, etc. : α 62, λ 460, ν 256, etc.—**(c)** As epithet of the sea Z 291, I 72 : α 197, β 295, δ 498, etc.—Sim. : εὐρέα νῶτα θαλάσσης B 159, Θ 511, Υ 228 : γ 142, δ 313, 560, etc.—θαλάσσης κόλπον Σ 140 : δ 435.—ἁλὸς κόλπον Φ 125.—**(d)** Of the earth : χθών Δ 182, Θ 150, Λ 741, Φ 387.—**(e)** Of the heavens Γ 364, E 867, Θ 74, O 36, etc. : α 67, δ 378, ε 169, ζ 150, etc.—**(2)** In neut. sing. εὐρύ as adv. **(a)** εὐρὺ ῥέων = εὐρυρέεθρος B 849, Π 288, Φ 157, 186, 304.—Sim. : Ἀλφειοῦ, ὅς τ' εὐρὺ ῥέει E 545.—**(b)** εὐρὺ κρείων (written also εὐρυκρείων), whose rule stretches far and wide, lord of wide lands. Epithet of Agamemnon A 102, 355, Γ 178, H 107, etc. : γ 248.—Of Poseidon Λ 751.—**(3)** Wide-spread, far-spreading : κλέος α 344, γ 83, 204, δ 726 = 816, τ 333, ψ 137.

εὐρυσθενής [εὐρύς + σθένος]. Whose might reaches far and wide. Epithet of Poseidon Θ 201, H 455 : = ν 140.

εὐρυφυής, -ές [εὐρύς + φύω]. Broad-eared : κρῖ δ 604 (the grains of barley not being set so close round the central stem of the ear as in wheat).

εὐρύχορος, -ον [εὐρύς + χορός]. With spacious dancing-places. Epithet of cities. Applied also to countries, app. merely in sense 'spacious' (perh. by confusion of the second element with χῶρος) : Μυκαλησσόν B 498, Ἑλλάδος I 478. Cf. Ψ 299 : δ 635, ζ 4, λ 256, 265, ν 414, ο 1, ω 468.

εὐρώεις, -εντος [εὐρώς, mould]. Dank : οἰκία [Ἄϊδος] Υ 65. Cf. κ 512, ψ 322, ω 10.

εὑρών, aor. pple. εὑρίσκω.

ἐΰς, ἐΰ. Acc. masc. ἐΰν Θ 303 : σ 127. Also **ἠΰς, ἠΰ.** Acc. masc. ἠΰν E 628, Z 8, 191, Υ 457. From ἑεύς, genit. masc. ἑῆος A 393, O 138, T 342, Ω 422, 550 : ξ 505, ο 450. **(1)** Epithet of persons, good, goodly, serviceable or the like A 393, B 653, Z 191, N 246, 691, T 342, etc. : ι 508, ξ 505, ο 450, σ 127.—**(2)** Such as may serve some end or confer benefit, good, excellent : μένος ἠΰ P 456, Υ 80, Ψ 524, Ω 6, 442 : β 271.

εὗσε, 3 sing. aor. εὕω.

ἐΰσκαρθμος [ἐϋ- (1) + σκαίρω]. Bounding with nimble feet, swift. Epithet of horses N 31.

ἐΰσκοπος, -ον [ἐϋ- (1) + σκοπ-, σκέπτομαι]. Sharp-sighted. Epithet of Hermes Ω 24, 109 : α 38, η 137.—Aiming well. Epithet of Artemis λ 198.

ἐΰσσελμος, -ον [ἐϋ- (5) + σέλματα, rowing-benches]. Having goodly rowing-benches. Epithet of ships B 170, H 84, I 231, Λ 193, Ξ 97, etc. : β 390, δ 409, ι 127, μ 358, ν 101, etc.

ἐΰσσωτρος, -ον [ἐϋ- (5) + σῶτρον, felloe]. Having goodly felloes. Epithet of a waggon : ἀπήνης Ω 578 (*v.l.* ἐϋξέστου).

ἐϋσταθής, -ές [ἐϋ- (1) + σταθ-, ἵστημι]. Well-based, well-built. Epithet of chambers Σ 374 : υ 258, χ 120, 127, 257 = 274, 441, 458, ψ 178.

ἐϋστέφανος, -ον [ἐϋ- (5) + στέφανος]. **(1)** With fair crown. Epithet of Artemis Φ 511.—Of Aphrodite θ 267, 288, σ 193.—Of Mycene (the heroine) β 120.—**(2)** Well crowned with walls. Epithet of Thebes T 99.

ἐΰστρεπτος [ἐϋ- (1) + στρεπ-, στρέφω]. = next : βοεῦσιν β 426 = ο 291.

ἐϋστρεφής, -ές [ἐϋ- (1) + στρέφω]. Twisted or plaited with art or skill : ἐϋστρεφεῖ οἰὸς ἀώτῳ N 599, 716, νευρήν O 463 (*v.l.* in N ἐϋστρόφῳ). Cf. ι 427, κ 167, ξ 346, φ 408.

ἐΰστροφος [ἐϋ- (1) + στροφ-, στρέφω]. *V.l.* for and = ἐϋστρεφής in N 599, 716.

εὖτε [another form of ἠΰτε]. **(1)** When, at the time when. **(a)** With indic. : εὖτε πύλας ἵκανεν Z 392. Cf. Θ 367, Λ 735, etc. : γ 9, ν 93, υ 56, etc.—Introducing a simile Γ 10.—Correlative with τῆμος. See τῆμος (2).—**(b)** With subj. in conditional relative sentences. For the examples and constructions see Table at end, (III) (B) (a) (1) (3), (D) (34) (35).—(2) Like, as: εὖτε πτερὰ γίγνετο Τ 386.

εὐτείχεος, -ον [εὐ- (5) + τεῖχος]. Well-walled. Epithet of Troy Α 129, Β 113 = 288 = Ε 716 = Ι 20, Θ 241.—Acc. εὐτείχεα Π 57.

ἐΰτμητος [ἐϋ- (1) + τμη-, τάμνω]. Cut or made with art or skill. Epithet of articles of leather: τελαμῶνι Η 304 = Ψ 825. Cf. Κ 567, Φ 30, Ψ 684.

ἐϋτρεφής [ἐϋ- (1) + τρέφω]. Well-fed, plump: ὄϊες ι 425, αἰγός ξ 530.

ἐΰτρητος [ἐϋ- (1) + τρη-, τετραίνω]. Skilfully pierced: λοβοῖσιν Ξ 182.

ἐΰτριχας, acc. pl. ἐΰθριξ.

ἐΰτροχος, -ον [ἐϋ- (5) + τροχός]. Having good wheels. Epithet of chariots and waggons Θ 438, Μ 58, Ω 150 = 179, 189, 266, 711: ζ 72.

εὔτυκτος, -ον [εὐ- (1) + τυκ-, τεύχω]. Well made or constructed. Epithet of various products of art or skill: ἱμάσθλην Θ 44 = Ν 26, κλισίην Κ 566, Ν 240. Cf. Γ 336 = Ο 480 = Π 137: = χ 123, δ 123, ξ 276.

εὐφημέω [εὐ- (1) + φημί]. (ἐπ-.) Either, to speak words of good omen, or, to keep (ritual) silence: εὐφημῆσαι κέλεσθε Ι 171.

εὐφραδέως [adv. fr. εὐφραδής, fr. εὐ- (1) + φραδ-, φράζω]. In clear or well-chosen terms: εὐ. πεπνυμένα πάντ' ἀγορεύεις τ 352.

εὐφραίνω, ἐϋφραίνω [εὔφρων]. Fut. ἐϋφρανέω Η 297. Infin. εὐφρανέειν Ε 688. 3 sing. aor. εὔφρηνε Ω 102. 2 sing. subj. ἐϋφρήνῃς Η 294. Infin. εὐφρῆναι Ρ 28. (1) To gladden, rejoice, cheer, comfort Ε 688, Η 294, 297, Ρ 28, Ω 102 (gave her kindly welcome): ν 44, υ 82.—(2) In pass., to have pleasure, make merry, enjoy oneself: εὐφραίνεσθαι ἔκηλον β 311.

ἐϋφρονέων [pres. pple. fr. *ἐϋφρονέω, fr. ἐϋ- (1) or (3) + φρονέω]. Also written ἐῢ φρονέων. Either, with good intent, or, with good sense: ἀγορήσατο Α 73, etc.: β 160, etc.

εὐφροσύνη, ἐϋφροσύνη, -ης, ἡ [εὔφρων]. Gladness, happiness, joy, mirth, merriment ι 6, κ 465, υ 8, ψ 52.—In pl. in sim. sense: θυμός σφισιν ἐϋφροσύνῃσιν ἰαίνεται ζ 156.

εὔφρων, ἐΰφρων, -ονος [εὐ-, ἐϋ- (5) + φρήν]. (1) Mirthful, merry, taking one's pleasure: δαίνυται εὔφρων Ο 99. Cf. ρ 531.—(2) Giving joy, bringing mirth. Epithet of οἶνος Γ 246.

εὐφυής [εὐ- (1) + φύω. 'Well-grown']. Well-shaped, goodly: μηροί Δ 147.—Of a tree, showing good growth, well-developed: πτελέην Φ 243.

εὔχαλκος, -ον [εὐ- (5) + χαλκός]. Finely wrought of bronze Η 12, Ν 612: ο 84.—With sharp point of bronze: μελίην Υ 322.

†εὐχετάομαι [in form frequentative fr. εὔχομαι]. 3 pl. εὐχετόωνται δ 139, μ 98. 3 pl. impf. εὐχετόωντο Θ 347, Λ 761, Ο 369, Χ 394: α 172, μ 356, ξ 189, π 58, 223. Opt. εὐχετοῴμην θ 467, ο 181. 3 sing. εὐχετόῳτο Μ 391. Infin. εὐχετάασθαι Ζ 268, Ρ 19, Υ 348: χ 412. (1) To avouch or declare oneself *to be*, etc. With infin.: τίνες ἔμμεναι εὐχετόωντο; α 172 = ξ 189 = π 58 = 223. Cf. δ 139.—(2) To boast vaunt Ρ 19, Υ 348.—With complementary infin.: ἀκήριοι παρφυγέειν μ 98.—(3) To exult, triumph Μ 391.—With ἐπί and dat., to exult or triumph *over* (a fallen foe): κταμένοισιν ἐπ' ἀνδράσιν χ 412.—(4) To pray. With dat.: Κρονίωνι Ζ 268. Cf. Θ 347 = Ο 369: μ 356.—(5) To give glory, make thanksgiving. With dat.: Ἕκτορι θεῷ ὣς Χ 394. Cf. Λ 761: θ 467 = ο 181.

εὐχή, -ῆς, ἡ [εὔχομαι]. A prayer κ 526.

εὔχομαι. 3 sing. aor. εὔξατο Θ 254: ε 444, ρ 239, υ 97. 3 pl. εὔξαντο Α 458, Β 421: γ 447, μ 359. 2 sing. subj. εὔξεαι γ 45. Opt. εὐξαίμην μ 334. Pple. εὐξάμενος, -η Α 381, 453, Ν 417, Π 236, Τ 257, etc.: ζ 280, ν 51, ξ 463, φ 211, ω 518, 521. (ἐπ-.) (1) With infin., to avouch or declare oneself, claim, *to be*, etc. (sometimes tending to pass into sense (2)): ἄριστος Ἀχαιῶν εἶναι Α 91, Β 82, ταύτης γενεῆς εἶναι Ζ 211. Cf. Δ 264, Ε 173, 246, Ζ 231, Θ 190, Ι 60, Ξ 113, etc.: Μέντης εἶναι α 180, ἱκέτης τοι εἶναι ε 450. Cf. α 187, γ 362, ε 211, ι 263, ξ 199, ο 425, χ 321, etc.—To claim *to do* as a matter of right: πάντ' ἀποδοῦναι Σ 499.—(2) To boast, vaunt: εὐχόμενος μετέφη Τ 100. Cf. Α 397, Β 597, Θ 198, Ξ 366, Υ 424: εὐξάμενός τι ἔπος ἐρέω (will 'show off' a little) ξ 463.—With complementary infin.: ἄντα Ποσειδάωνος πολεμίζειν Φ 476. Cf. Γ 430, Θ 254, 526, Φ 501.—(3) To exult, triumph: μεγάλ' εὔχεο Π 844. Cf. Ε 106, Λ 379, 388, Ν 417 = Ξ 458 = 486, Ν 447, 619 = Ρ 537 = Φ 183, Ξ 500, Υ 393.—(4) To pray. With dat.: Ἀπόλλωνι Α 87. Cf. Γ 296, Ζ 312, Η 194, Ψ 547, Ω 290, etc.: β 261, γ 43, μ 334, ν 51, 231, ω 518, etc.—With complementary infin.: θάνατον φυγεῖν Β 401. Cf. Ξ 484, Ο 374, Σ 75, Ω 287: φ 211.—With dat. and infin.: Διὶ θυμὸν φθίσθαι ο 353. Cf. Ι 183.—Absol.: ὣς ἔφατ' εὐχόμενος Α 43, εὐξαμένου ἤκουσεν 381. Cf. Α 458, Ζ 304, Ι 509, Ο 371, etc.: β 267, γ 45, ε 444, ζ 280, ο 222, ρ 239, etc.—(5) To give glory, make thanksgiving: αἴ τέ μοι εὐχόμεναι θεῖον δύσονται ἀγῶνα Η 298 (like εὐχετάομαι (5); or perh. μοι should be taken as ethic dat., 'on my account').—(6) To vow. With complementary infin.: Ἀπόλλωνι ῥέξειν ἑκατόμβην Δ 101, 119. Cf. ρ 50, 59.

εὖχος, τό [εὔχομαι]. Subject of exultation or triumph, triumph, glory: ἐμοὶ μέγ' εὖχος ἔδωκας Ε 285. Cf. Ε 654 = Λ 445, Η 81, 154, 203, Λ 288, 290, Μ 328, Ν 327, Ο 462, Π 625, 725, Φ 297, 473, Χ 130: ι 317, φ 338, χ 7.

ἐΰχροής, -ές [ἐϋ- (5) + χρο-, χρώς]. Of fresh colour, fresh, in good condition: δέρμα ξ 24.

εὐχωλή, -ῆς, ἡ [εὔχομαι]. (1) A boast or vaunt: πῇ ἔβαν εὐχωλαί; Θ 229.—(2) Shouting in exultation or triumph: οἰμωγή τε καὶ εὐχωλή Δ 450 = Θ 64.—A subject of exultation or triumph: κατά κεν εὐχωλὴν Πριάμῳ λίποιεν Ἑλένην Β 160. Cf. Β 176, Δ 173, Χ 433.—(3) A prayer: θεοὺς εὐχωλῇς παρατρωπῶσ' ἄνθρωποι Ι 499: εὐχωλῇσι λιτῇσί τε ἐλλισάμην (the two words hardly to be distinguished) λ 34.—(4) A thanksgiving. In pl.: εὐχωλῇς χαίρετε ν 357.—(5) A vow: εὐχωλῆς ἐπιμέμφεται (*i.e.* a vow unperformed) Α 65, 93.

εὕω. 3 sing. aor. εὗσε ι 389, ξ 75. 3 pl. εὗσαν ξ 426. (**1**) To singe ι 389.—(**2**) To singe off the bristles of (swine) in the process of cooking them: σιάλους εὕοντας β 300. Cf. I 468 = Ψ 33: ξ 75, 426.

εὐώδης, εὐῶδες [εὐ- (5) + ὀδ-, ὄζω]. Sweet-smelling, fragrant: θαλάμῳ Γ 382. Cf. β 339, ε 64.

εὐῶπις, -ιδος [εὐ- (5) + ὦπα]. Fair, comely: κούρην ζ 113, 142.

ἔφαγον, aor. See φάγον.

†ἐφάλλομαι [ἐφ-, ἐπι- (11) (12)]. 3 sing. aor. ἐπᾶλτο N 643, Φ 140. Pple. ἐπιάλμενος ω 320. ἐπάλμενος H 260, Λ 421, 489, M 404, N 529, 531: ξ 220. Acc. masc. ἐπιάλμενον H 15. Pl. masc. ἐπάλμενοι χ 305. (**1**) To leap or spring to or towards a person: κύσσε μιν ἐπιάλμενος ω 320.—(**2**) In hostile sense, to leap or spring at or upon a foe: οὔτασεν ἐπάλμενος Λ 421. Cf. H 260, M 404, N 529, 531: ξ 220.—Of birds of prey χ 305.—(**3**) To leap or spring *at* or *upon* (a foe). With dat.: Μενελάῳ N 643. Cf. Λ 489, Φ 140.—(**4**) To leap or spring *on to*, mount. With genit.: ἵππων ἐπιάλμενον (just as he had . . .) H 15.

ἔφαλος, -ον [ἐφ-, ἐπι- (2) + ἅλς¹]. On the seashore. Epithet of cities B 538, 584.

ἐφάμην, impf. mid. φημί.

ἔφαν, 3 pl. impf. φημί.

ἐφάνη, 3 sing. aor. pass. φαίνω.

†ἐφάπτω [ἐφ-, ἐπι- (3) (5)]. 2 sing. aor. subj. mid. ἐφάψεαι ε 348. 3 sing. pf. pass. ἐφῆπται B 15, 32, 69, H 402, M 79, Φ 513: χ 41. 3 sing. plupf. ἐφῆπτο Z 241: χ 33. (**1**) To fasten *upon*; hence, fig., in pass., with dat., to be the lot or portion of: ἀθανάτοισιν ἔρις ἐφῆπται Φ 513.—To impend inevitably *over*, be fated *to*: Τρώεσσι κήδε' ἐφῆπται B 15 = 32 = 69. Cf. Z 241, H 402, M 79: χ 33, 41.—(**2**) To lay hold of, touch. In mid., with genit.: ἐπὴν ἐφάψεαι ἠπείροιο ε 348.

†ἐφαρμόζω [ἐφ-, ἐπι- (19)]. 3 sing. aor. opt. ἐφαρμόσσειε. To fit well, be well adapted to. With dat.: εἰ οἷ ἐφαρμόσσειεν [ἔντεα] T 385.

ἔφασαν, 3 pl. impf. φημί.

ἐφάψεαι, 2 sing. aor. subj. mid. ἐφάπτω.

ἐφέζομαι [ἐφ-, ἐπι- (12)]. Aor. infin. act. ἐφέσσαι ν 274. Fut. infin. mid. ἐφέσσεσθαι I 455. Aor. imp. ἔφεσσαι ο 277. Pple. ἐφεσσάμενος π 443. (**1**) In pres. and impf. (or non-sigmatic aor. (see ἕζομαι)). (**a**) To seat oneself in a specified position: ἔνθα δ' ἐφέζετο ρ 334.—(**b**) To seat or set oneself *on*. With dat.: Περγάμῳ E 460. Cf. Φ 506: δ 509, 717.—Of cicadas Γ 152.—Of a bird Ψ 878.—(**2**) In aor. act. and fut. and sigmatic aor. mid. (**a**) To set, seat, place *on*. With dat.: γούνασιν οἷσιν ἐφέσσεσθαι υἱόν I 455. Cf. π 443.—(**b**) To put on board a ship: Πύλονδέ με καταστῆσαι καὶ ἐφέσσαι (to put on board for Pylos and land there (with a prothysteron)) ν 274.—(**c**) To put *on board* (a ship). With genit.: νηός μ' ἔφεσσαι ο 277.

ἐφέηκα, aor. ἐφίημι¹.

ἐφείω, aor. subj. **ἐφείην,** aor. opt. ἐφίημι¹.

ἐφέλκω [ἐφ-, ἐπι- (5) (8)]. (**1**) To draw on or induce to an indicated course of action. In mid.: αὐτὸς ἐφέλκεται ἄνδρα σίδηρος π 294 = τ 13.—(**2**) In pass., to be dragged, to drag or trail along: τὸ δ' ἐφέλκετ' ἔγχος (along with the wounded man) N 597. Cf. Ψ 696.

ἐφέπω¹ [ἐφ-, ἐπι- (5) (11) + ἕπω¹]. 3 pl. pa. iterative ἐφέπεσκον μ 330. 2 sing. fut. ἐφέψεις Φ 588. Infin. ἐφέψειν ω 471. Aor. ἐπέσπον λ 197. 3 sing. -ε γ 16, δ 714. 3 pl. -ον T 294: γ 134, λ 372, 389, χ 317, 416, ω 22. 2 sing. subj. ἐπίσπῃς Z 412, X 39. 3 -ῃ B 359, O 495, Υ 337: δ 196. 3 sing. opt. ἐπίσποι β 250. Infin. ἐπισπεῖν H 52, Φ 100: δ 562, ε 308, μ 342, ξ 274, ω 31. (**1**) To direct or drive (horses): ἵππους ἐφέπων κέλευεν Ω 326.—(**2**) To direct or drive (horses) *against* (a foe). With dat.: Πατρόκλῳ ἔφεπε ἵππους Π 724. Cf. Π 732.—(**3**) To deal with, take in hand (foes): τοσσούσδ' ἀνθρώπους Υ 357. Cf. Υ 359.—Absol., to drive off, keep back, the foe O 742.—(**4**) To drive before one in flight: Τρῶας Λ 177, πεδίον 496 (app. meaning the men and horses flying over it (cf. πεδίον μετεκίαθον 714 cited under μετεκίαθον)). Cf. Υ 494, X 188.—Absol.: σφεδανὸν ἔφεπεν Φ 542.—(**5**) To go in quest of or pursue (game): ἄγρην μ 330.—To 'drive' (a place, *i.e.* the game found there): κορυφὰς ὀρέων ι 121.—(**6**) With notion of reaching a point, to meet or encounter (one's fate or the like): ἐπεὶ ἂν σύ γε πότμον ἐπίσπῃς Z 412, ἐπισπεῖν αἴσιμον ἦμαρ Φ 100. Cf. B 359, H 52, O 495, T 294, Υ 337, Φ 588, X 39: β 250, γ 16, 134, δ 196, 562, 714, ε 308, λ 197, 372, 389 = ω 22, μ 342, ξ 274, χ 317 = 416, ω 31, 471.

†ἐφέπω² [ἐφ-, ἐπι- (8) + ἕπω²]. Only in mid. Aor. pple. ἐπισπόμενος, -ου N 495: γ 215, ξ 262, π 96, 426, ρ 431, ω 183, 338. Infin. ἐπισπέσθαι Ξ 521. (**1**) To follow in company with, go with, accompany, a person ω 338.—With dat.: ἑοῖ αὐτῷ N 495. Cf. π 426.—(**2**) To follow up, hang upon, a flying foe: οὔ οἵ τις ὁμοῖος ἐπισπέσθαι ἦεν ἀνδρῶν τρεσσάντων (genit. absol.) Ξ 521.—(**3**) With dat., to follow the guidance of, be influenced by (something immaterial): θεοῦ ὀμφῇ γ 215 = π 96.—To give oneself up to, yield to (passion): μένεϊ σφῷ ξ 262 = ρ 431, ω 183.

ἐφέσσαι, aor. infin. See ἐφέζομαι.

ἔφεσσαι, aor. imp. mid. See ἐφέζομαι.

ἐφέσσεσθαι, fut. infin. mid. See ἐφέζομαι.

ἐφεστᾶσι, 3 pl. pf. ἐφίστημι.

ἐφεστήκει, 3 sing. plupf. ἐφίστημι.

ἐφέστιος [ἐφ-, ἐπι- (2) + ἑστίη = ἱστίη. 'At the hearth']. At home, in one's home: ἀπολέσθαι ἐ. γ 234, ἦλθεν ἐ. (has come home) ψ 55.—In the home of another: ἔμ' ἐφέστιον ἤγαγε δαίμων (brought me to be her guest) η 248.—Τρῶας ἐφέστιοι ὅσσοι ἔασιν (who have homes, are householders (in the city)) B 125.

ἐφετμή, -ῆς, ἡ [ἐφ-, ἐπι- (5) + ἑ-, ἵημι¹]. (**1**) An injunction, charge, behest: οὐ λήθετ' ἐφετμέων A 495, τεὴ ἐπίνυσσεν ἐ. (*i.e.* the consequences of carrying it out) Ξ 249. Cf. E 508, 818, O 593, Σ 216, Φ 299: δ 353.—(**2**) In pl. in generalized sense, the laws (of Ζεὺς ἱκετήσιος) Ω 570, 586.

†**ἐφευρίσκω** [ἐφ-, ἐπι- (19)]. 1 pl. aor. ἐφεύρομεν β 109, κ 452, ω 145. Subj. ἐφεύρω ε 417. 3 sing. opt. ἐφεύροι Β 198, Δ 88, Ε 168, Ν 760 : ε 439. (**1**) To find, to light or come upon Δ 88, Ε 168, Ν 760 : ε 417, 439.—(**2**) To come upon and find doing something specified : βοόωντα Β 198. Cf. β 109 = ω 145, κ 452.

ἐφέψειν, fut. infin. ἐφέπω[1].

†**ἐφεψιάομαι** [ἐφ-, ἐπι- (5)]. 3 pl. ἐφεψιόωνται τ 331. 3 pl. impf. ἐφεψιόωντο τ 370. To jeer *at*, make fun of, mock. With dat. : τεθνεῶτι τ 331, κείνῳ 370.

ἐφῆκα, aor. ἐφίημι[1].

ἔφημαι [ἐφ-, ἐπι- (1) (2)]. To be seated, sit, *on* or *by*. With dat. : θρόνῳ ζ 309, κλητ̈δεσσιν μ 215.

ἐφημέριος [ἐφ-, ἐπι- (16) + ἡμέρη]. During the day, for that day : οὔ κεν ἐ. βάλοι δάκρυ δ 223.—Absol. in neut. pl. : ἐφημέρια φρονέοντες (thinking only of things of the day, limited in outlook) φ 85.

ἐφημοσύνη, -ης, ἡ [ἐφίημι[1]]. (**1**) = ἐφετμή (1) Ρ 697 : μ 226.—(**2**) A message given in charge to deliver : ἐπεὶ πᾶσαν ἐφημοσύνην ἀπέειπεν π 340.

ἔφην, impf. φημί.

ἐφήνδανε, 3 sing. impf. ἐπιανδάνω.

ἔφηνε, 3 sing. aor. φαίνω.

ἐφῆπται, 3 sing. pf. pass. ἐφάπτω.

ἐφήσω, fut. ἐφίημι[1].

ἔφθη, 3 sing. aor. φθάνω.

ἐφθίατο, 3 pl. plupf. pass. φθίω.

ἔφθιθεν, 3 pl. aor. pass. φθίω.

ἔφθιται, 3 sing. pf. pass. φθίω.

ἐφιζάνω [ἐφ-, ἐπι- (1) (11)]. (**1**) To sit in a specified position. Fig. of sleep Κ 26.—(**2**) To sit down *to* (a meal). With dat. : δείπνῳ ἐφιζανέτην Κ 578.

ἐφίζω [ἐφ-, ἐπι- (1)]. 3 sing. pa. iterative ἐφίζεσκε ρ 331. To sit upon something indicated : δίφρον, ἔνθα δαιτρὸς ἐφίζεσκεν ρ 331. Cf. γ 411, τ 55.

†**ἐφίημι**[1] [ἐφ-, ἐπι- (5) (11) + ἵημι[1]]. Imp. pl. ἐφίετε χ 251. Pple. ἐφιείς Α 51. Fut. ἐφήσω Ω 117 : τ 550, 576, υ 39. 2 sing. ἐφήσεις Α 518 : ν 376. 3 -ει δ 340, ρ 131, υ 29, 386. Aor. ἐφέηκα Υ 346. ἐφῆκα Ε 188, 206. 3 sing. ἐφέηκε Σ 108 : ι 38, ξ 464. ἐφῆκε Α 445, Δ 396, Π 812, Φ 170, 524 : δ 339, ρ 130, ψ 37. Aor. subj. ἐφείω Α 567. Opt. ἐφείην Σ 124. 3 sing. ἐφείη α 254. Imp. ἔφες Ε 174. From ἐφιέω 3 sing. impf. ἐφίει Ο 444. ἐφίει ω 180. Pres. pple. mid. ἐφιέμενος ν 7. Dat. sing. fem. ἐφιεμένῃ Ω 300. Fut. ἐφήσομαι Ψ 82. (**1**) To send, launch, discharge (a spear) at the foe : μὴ ἅμα πάντες ἐφίετε δούρατα χ 251.—(**2**) To shoot, let fly, launch an arrow or spear *at*. With dat. : φῶτα, τῷ ἐφέηκα Υ 346. Cf. Ε 206.—To shoot, let fly, launch (an arrow or spear) *at*. With dat. : τῷδ' ἔφες ἀνδρὶ βέλος Ε 174. Cf. Α 51, Ε 188, Ο 444, Π 812, Φ 170 : ω 180.—(**3**) To send or dispatch as a messenger *to*. With dat. Ω 117.—(**4**) To send (evil, bane, ill fortune, etc.) *upon*. With dat. : Ἀργείοισι κήδε' ἐφῆκεν Α 445. Cf. Δ 396, Φ 524 : δ 339 = ρ 130, δ 340 = ρ 131, ι 38, τ 550.—(**5**) To lay (hostile hands) *upon*. With dat. : ὅτε κέν τοι χεῖρας ἐφείω Α 567. Cf. α 254, ν 376, υ 29, 39, 386, ψ 37.—(**6**) To bring into the position of *doing something*, set on or incite *to do something*. With infin. : ὅς τ' ἐφέηκε πολύφρονά περ χαλεπῆναι Σ 108. Cf. Α 518, Σ 124 : ξ 464.—(**7**) To lay or enjoin *upon*. With dat. : μνηστήρεσσιν ἄεθλον τ 576.—(**8**) In mid., to lay an injunction or charge *upon*. With dat. : ἀνδρὶ ἑκάστῳ ἐφιέμενος ν 7.—With acc. of what is enjoined : τόδε Ω 300.—With dat. and acc. : ἄλλο τοι ἐφήσομαι Ψ 82.

†**ἐφίημι**[2] [ἐφ-, ἐπι- (11) + ἵημι[2]]. Only in mid. Fut. ἐπιείσομαι (ἐπιϝίσομαι) Λ 367, Υ 454 : ο 504. Aor. pple. fem. ἐπιεισαμένη Φ 424. (**1**) To hurry up to an indicated spot Φ 424.—(**2**) To hasten or speed *to*. With acc. : ἀγρούς ο 504.—To go *against*, attack (a foe). With acc. : τοὺς ἄλλους Λ 367 = Υ 454.

†**ἐφικνέομαι** [ἐφ-, ἐπι- (5)]. 3 pl. aor. ἐφΐκοντο. To reach, bring one's blow to bear upon. With genit., of what is reached (cf. τυγχάνω (2)) : ἀλλήλων Ν 613.

ἐφίλατο, 3 sing. aor. mid. φιλέω.

ἐφίστημι [ἐφ-, ἐπι- (2) (5) (11)]. 3 sing. aor. ἐπέστη Κ 124, 496, Ψ 201. 3 pl. pf. ἐφεστᾶσι Μ 326. 3 sing. plupf. ἐφεστήκει Ζ 373, Ψ 106. 3 pl. ἐφέστασαν Ε 624, Ν 133, Ο 703, Π 217, Σ 554 : χ 203. Genit. sing. masc. pple. ἐφεσταότος Ρ 609. Nom. pl. ἐφεσταότες Μ 52, 199, Σ 515. Infin. ἐφεστάμεναι ω 380. ἐφεστάμεν α 120. (**1**) In aor. and mid. (**a**) To come up and take one's stand in a specified position : θύρῃσιν ἐφίστατο (in the . . .) Λ 644, ἐπέστη βηλῷ ἔπι Ψ 201.—(**b**) To come up *to*, come *to*. With dat. : ἐπέστη μοι Κ 124.—With locative Κ 496.—(**2**) In pf. and plupf. (**a**) To have one's stand, stand, in a specified or indicated position : τεῖχος ῥύατ' ἐφεσταότες Σ 515. Cf. Μ 52, 199 : α 120.—(**b**) With dat., to stand *upon* : πύργῳ ἐφεστήκει Ζ 373. Cf. Ρ 609.—To stand *by* or *beside* : ψυχή μοι ἐφεστήκει Ψ 106. Cf. Ν 133 = Π 217.—(**c**) To stand facing the foe Ε 624 : χ 203, ω 380.—(**d**) To stand *facing* (the foe). With dat. : ἐφέστασαν ἀλλήλοισιν Ο 703.—(**e**) Of bane figured as ready to pounce upon one : κῆρες ἐφεστᾶσιν Μ 326.—(**f**) To stand ready for or at one's work : ἀμαλλοδετῆρες ἐφέστασαν Σ 554.

ἐφόλκαιον, τό [ἐφ-, ἐπι- (12) + ὁλκ-, ἕλκω]. Prob., a ship's lading-plank : ἐφόλκαιον καταβάς ξ 350.

ἐφομαρτέω [ἐφ-, ἐπι- (5)]. To come along with a person, come on, in an indicated direction : ἐφομαρτεῖτον καὶ σπεύδετον Θ 191, Ψ 414. Cf. Μ 412.

ἐφοπλίζω [ἐφ-, ἐπι- (5)]. 3 pl. fut. ἐφοπλίσσουσι ζ 69. 1 pl. aor. subj. ἐφοπλισόμεσθα Θ 503, Ι 66. 3 ἐφοπλίσσωσι ω 360. 2 sing. opt. ἐφοπλίσσειας ζ 57. 2 pl. ἐφοπλίσσαιτε Ω 263. Pl. pple. ἐφοπλίσσαντες Ψ 55 : β 295. Infin. ἐφοπλίσαι ζ 37. ἐφοπλίσσαι τ 419. (**1**) To get ready for use, prepare, equip : ἅμαξαν Ω 263. Cf. ζ 37, 57, 69.

—Absol., to fit out a ship for a voyage β 295.—(2) To make ready, prepare (a meal) Δ 344, Θ 503, Ι 66, Ψ 55 : τ 419, ω 360.

ἐφοράω [ἐφ-, ἐπι- (5) (14)]. From ὀπ- fut. in mid. form ἐπιόψομαι Ι 167 : β 294. 2 sing. ἐπόψεαι Ξ 145 : υ 233. Pple. ἐποψόμενος, -ου η 324, τ 260, 597, ψ 19. **(1)** To look upon, behold, survey. Of the sun : ὃς πάντ' ἐφορᾷς Γ 277. Cf. λ 109 = μ 323.—**(2)** To regard with attention, watch, observe ν 214, ρ 487.—**(3)** To have sight of, see, behold : φεύγοντας Ξ 145. Cf. υ 233.—**(4)** To visit, go to see, see η 324, τ 260 = 597 = ψ 19.—**(5)** To select or choose after inspection or holding in review : τοὺς ἂν ἐγὼ ἐπιόψομαι, οἱ δὲ πιθέσθων (whomsoever I select, let them . . .) Ι 167. Cf. β 294.

ἐφορμάω [ἐφ-, ἐπι- (5) (11)]. **(1)** To stir to action, put in action, stir up, *against*. With dat. : οἵ μοι ἐφώρμησαν πόλεμον Γ 165. Cf. η 272.—**(2)** In mid. and pass. **(a)** To be stirred, stir oneself, to hostile action, to rush with hostile intent, make attack, in a specified or indicated direction : πάντες ἐφορμηθέντες Ζ 410. Cf. Π 313, Ρ 465, 489, Σ 282, Υ 461, Ω 800 : μ 122.—Of the gadfly χ 300.—**(b)** To pounce *upon*, attack. With acc. : ὥς τ' ὀρνίθων αἰετὸς ἔθνος ἐφορμᾶται Ο 691.—**(c)** To rush in an indicated direction for an indicated purpose : τρὶς ἐφορμήθην λ 206.—**(d)** With infin., to be disposed, have in mind, intend, *to do* : ποιησέμεν φ 399.—Of the mind or spirit, to be stirred or inclined *to do* : πολεμίζειν Ν 74. Cf. α 275, δ 713.

ἐφορμή, ἡ [ἐφορμάω]. A way of attack χ 130.

ἐφράσ(σ)ατο, 3 sing. aor. mid. φράζω.

ἐφράσθης, 2 sing. aor. pass. φράζω.

ἔφριξε, 3 sing. aor. φρίσσω.

ἔφῡ, 3 sing. aor. φύω.

ἐφυβρίζω [ἐφ-, ἐπι- (5)]. To treat a person with insult or outrage : ἐφυβρίζων ἕλετο Ι 368.

ἔφυγες, 2 sing. aor. φεύγω.

ἔφυδρος [ἐφ-, ἐπι- (8) + ὕδωρ]. Coming with, bringing, rain : Ζέφυρος ξ 458.

ἐφύπερθε(ν) [ἐφ-, ἐπι- (1) + ὕπερθε]. **(1)** On or upon something, thereon : στορέσαι ἐ. τάπητας Ω 645 : = δ 298 = η 337. Cf. Ι 213 : ι 383, ρ 210.—**(2)** Above : κρηδέμνῳ ἐ. καλύψατο Ξ 184. Cf. δ 150, ε 232.

ἔχαδε, 3 sing. aor, χανδάνω.

ἐχάρη, 3 sing. aor. pass. χαίρω.

ἔχεαν, 3 pl. aor. χέω.

ἐχέθῡμος, -ον [ἔχω + θυμός. See θυμός (I) (4) (b)]. Controlling one's passions, continent θ 320.

ἐχεπευκής, -ές [ἔχω + πευκ- as in πευκεδανός. 'Having sharpness']. Sharp, piercing : βέλος Α 51, Δ 129.

ἔχεσκον, pa. iterative ἔχω.

ἔχευε, 3 sing. aor. χέω.

ἐχέφρων, -ονος [ἔχω + φρήν]. Having good sense, sensible, discreet Ι 341 : ν 332.—Epithet of Penelope δ 111, ν 406, π 130, 458, ρ 390, ω 198, 294.

ἐχθαίρω [ἔχθος]. 3 sing. aor. ἤχθηρε Υ 306. Also (as *v.l.* for ἔχθαιρε (impf.)) λ 437, 560, τ 364. 3 sing. opt. ἐχθήρειε Ι 452. (ἀπ-.) To regard with disfavour, dislike or enmity, dislike, hate : οὐδὲ Μενοιτιάδην ἤχθαιρε πάρος γε Ρ 270, Πριάμου γενεὴν ἤχθηρε (has taken into disfavour) Υ 306. Cf. Ι 452 : γ 215 = π 96, δ 692, λ 437, 560, τ 364.—Absol. ο 71.

†ἐχθάνομαι [ἔχθος]. 3 sing. aor. ἤχθετο ξ 366, τ 338. Pple. ἐχθόμενος δ 502. Infin. ἐχθέσθαι δ 756. (ἀπ-.) **(1)** To incur the disfavour or enmity of. With dat. : ἤχθετο θεοῖσιν ξ 366. Cf. δ 502, 756.—**(2)** Sim. of things, to become distasteful to τ 338.

ἔχθιστος [superl. fr. ἐχθ-, ἐχθρός]. (The) most disliked or hated, (the) most hateful or detestable : ἐ. μοί ἐσσι Α 176, Ε 890. Cf. Β 220, Ι 159.

ἐχθοδοπέω [ἐχθοδοπός, hateful, app. related to ἔχθος as ἀλλοδαπός to ἄλλος]. To incur the enmity of, get into a quarrel with. With dat. : ἐχθοδοπῆσαι Ἥρῃ Α 518.

ἔχθος, τό. **(1)** Disfavour, enmity : Διὸς ἐ. ἀλευάμενος ι 277.—**(2)** A taking of offence, a falling into enmity : μὴ μέσσῳ ἀμφοτέρων μητίσομαι ἔχθεα λυγρά Γ 416.

ἐχθρός, -ή, -όν [ἔχθος]. **(1)** Hated, hateful, detested, detestable Ι 312, Π 77 : ξ 156, ρ 499.—**(2)** Of things and abstractions, distasteful, disliked, loathed : δῶρά μοι Ι 378. Cf. φ 147.—**(3)** In neut. with infin. in impers. construction, to be distasteful or displeasing *to do* : ἐχθρόν μοί ἐστιν αὖτις εἰρημένα μυθολογεύειν μ 452.

ἔχμα, -ατος [ἔχω]. **(1)** A buttress or support : πύργων Μ 260.—Something holding a thing in place : πέτρης (*i.e.* the support afforded to the stone by the πέτρη) Ν 139.—App., a prop for a ship = ἕρμα[1] (1) Ξ 410.—**(2)** An obstruction or impediment Φ 259.

ἔχραε, 3 sing. aor. χράω[2].

ἔχυτο, 3 sing. aor. pass. χέω.

ἔχω [σ(ε)χ-]. Impf. εἶχον (ἔσεχον), -ες Γ 123, Η 217, Μ 456, Ρ 354, Χ 474, etc. : γ 444, θ 285, λ 584, μ 362, 433, etc. Without augment ἔχον, -ες Α 463, Β 2, Ι 209, Σ 378, Φ 441, etc. : α 104, γ 182, δ 459, ζ 179, χ 128, etc. Pa. iterative ἔχεσκον, -ες Γ 219, Ε 126, 472, Ι 333, Ν 257, Χ 458 : η 99. Fut. ἕξω, -εις Ι 609, Ν 51, Ρ 232, Σ 274, Υ 27, Ψ 833 : ζ 281, σ 73, τ 494. Infin. ἑξέμεν Ε 473. ἕξειν ο 522. Fut. σχήσω, -εις Λ 820, Ν 151, Ξ 100, Ρ 182, Ω 670 : λ 70, χ 70, 171, 248. Infin. σχήσειν Μ 4, 166. 2 sing. aor. ἔσχες ι 279. 3 ἔσχε Β 275, Ε 300, Λ 848, Ν 520, Π 740, Φ 58, etc. : ε 451, ρ 291. 3 pl. ἔσχον γ 454, δ 352, λ 24. 1 pl. subj. σχῶμεν Φ 309. Pple. σχών α 157, δ 70, ρ 592. Infin. σχέμεν Θ 254. σχεῖν Π 520, Φ 341, Ψ 50. Aor. σχέθον κ 95. 3 sing. ἔσχεθε Μ 184, Ν 608, Π 340, Υ 398 : δ 284, π 430, φ 129, χ 409, ω 530. σχέθε Α 219, Λ 96, Ν 163, Τ 119 : δ 758, ξ 490, 494, ψ 243. 3 dual ἐσχεθέτην Μ 461. 3 pl. ἔσχεθον Ο 653, Τ 418 : τ 458. σχέθον Δ 113, Η 277, Ξ 428, Π 506. 3 sing. imp. σχεθέτω θ 537, 542. Infin. σχεθέειν Ψ 466. **Mid.** 3 sing. fut. ἕξεται Ι 102. 2 pl. fut. σχήσεσθε Ν 630.

Infin. σχήσεσθαι I 235, 655, M 107, 126, N 747, P 503, 639. 3 sing. aor. ἔσχετο M 294, N 368, P 696, Υ 262, 272, Φ 581, Ψ 397: δ 525, 705, μ 204, ρ 238, τ 472. σχέτο H 248, Φ 345. 3 pl. ἔσχοντο Γ 84: λ 334, ν 2, ω 57. 3 pl. subj. σχῶνται ν 151. 3 pl. opt. σχοίατο B 98. Imp. σχέο H 110, Φ 379. Pl. σχέσθε X 416: β 70. Pple. σχόμενος, -η M 298: α 334, ζ 141, λ 279, π 416, σ 210, φ 65. Infin. σχέσθαι δ 422. (ἀμπέχω, ἀν-, ἀπ-, δι-, ἐπ-, κατ-, παρ-, περι-, προ-, συν-, ὑπερ-, ὑπ-.) **(I)** Trans. **(1)** To hold in the hand or hands, the arms, the claws, etc.: στέμματ' ἔχων ἐν χερσίν A 14, νεβρὸν ἔχοντ' ὀνύχεσσιν Θ 248, ἔχεν ἀγκὰς ἄκοιτιν Ξ 353. Cf. A 603, E 230, 593, Z 400, N 600, Ω 284, etc.: α 104, δ 300, ε 49, ν 67, ο 527, φ 59, ψ 232, etc.—Absol. I 209.—In mid. M 294, P 355, Υ 262, etc.: α 334 = π 416 = σ 210 = φ 65.—**(2)** To have or keep hold of, hold: χειρὸς ἔχων Μενέλαον (by the hand) Δ 154, ἔχεν ἔγχος Φ 72, αἵ ἑ μετὰ σφίσιν εἶχον (supported her) X 474. Cf. Λ 488, O 717, Π 763, Σ 33, 536, 580, Ψ 136, etc.—**(3)** **(a)** To hold, maintain, keep, cause to be, in a specified position or condition: ὑψοῦ κάρη ἔχει Z 509 = O 266, πεπταμένας πύλας ἔχετε Φ 531. Cf. Λ 72, M 122, N 200, etc.: ἄγχι σχὼν κεφαλήν α 157 = δ 70 = ρ 592, κενεὰς σὺν χεῖρας ἔχοντες (holding the palms together with nothing between them, empty-handed) κ 42. Cf. ζ 107, ξ 494, χ 471.—**(b)** To hold ready for action in a specified or indicated direction: χεῖράς τε καὶ ἔγχεα ἀντίον ἀλλήλων E 569. Cf. Ψ 871.—**(4)** To hold up, support: κίονας α 53, σεῖον ζυγὸν ἀμφὶς ἔχοντες (supporting it at either end) γ 486 = ο 184, ὅθι φρένες ἧπαρ ἔχουσιν ι 301 (or perh., enfolds, surrounds (see (10)).—Absol. γ 454.—**(5)** To hold apart: ἣ κληῖδες ἀπ' ὤμων αὐχέν' ἔχουσιν X 324.—Sim.: κίονας, αἳ γαῖάν τε καὶ οὐρανὸν ἀμφὶς ἔχουσιν α 54.—**(6)** To hold, occupy, inhabit (cities, houses, etc.): 'Ολύμπια δώματ' ἔχοντες A 18, οἵ τ' 'Ελεῶν' εἶχον B 500. Cf. B 504, E 404, 710, Π 68, 261, etc.: α 67, β 336, δ 756, ζ 123, 177, κ 283, ω 282, etc.—To occupy, lie upon: νέκυες οὖδας ἔχοντες ψ 46.—**(7)** **(a)** To hold in possession, have or keep possession of, keep, retain, have: πολλὰ δ' ἔχεσκεν I 333, ἔχουσι τεύχεα κεῖνοι Σ 188. Cf. A 113, E 271, T 148, Ω 115, etc.—In pass.: ἔντεα μετὰ Τρώεσσιν ἔχονται Σ 130. Cf. Σ 197.—Sim.: νίκης πείρατ' ἔχονται ἐν θεοῖσιν H 102.—**(b)** To withhold from the rightful owner: ἑλὼν ἔχει γέρας A 356 = 507 = B 240. Cf. I 111, 336: ο 231, φ 30.—**(8)** To detain or keep with one in hospitality: τρεῖς μιν νύκτας ἔχον ρ 515.—To keep as an inmate of one's house υ 377.—**(9)** To compel to a course of action: χαλεπὴ ἔχε δήμου φῆμις ξ 239—**(10)** To enfold, surround: τεῖχος νῆας ἐντὸς ἔχον M 8. Cf. O 653.—To contain: ποτόν β 341.—**(11)** To cover, reign over, envelop: οὐδέ ποτ' αἴθρη κείνου ἔχει κορυφήν μ 76. Cf. ν 245.—**(12)** To guard, keep safe: πόλιν E 473, Διὸς αἴσῃ, ἥ μ' ἕξει I 609 (app. with admixture of sense 'to abide with'; cf. (42) and αἶσα (6)). Cf. X 322, Ω 730.—To have in charge: πύλας E 749 = Θ 393.—**(13)** To hold fast, secure (a gate, etc.): θύρην ἔχεν ἐπιβλής Ω 453. Cf. M 456.—To secure (a passage) χ 128.—To hold together: οὐ σάρκας ἶνες ἔχουσιν λ 219.—**(14)** App., to husband or keep in reserve: εἰν ἀγορῇ σθένος ἕξομεν (husband our strength (by keeping together) in the . . .) Σ 274.—**(15)** To retain (something in the mind): ἔχετ' ἐν φρεσὶ μῦθον ο 445.—To retain (something) in the mind: ἔχε σιγῇ μῦθον τ 502.—To retain something (in the mind): σῇσιν ἔχε φρεσίν B 33, 70.—**(16)** To cherish or harbour (resentment) A 82, N 517.—**(17)** To take hold of (in one's mind), contrive: νόον σχέθε τόνδ' ἐνὶ θυμῷ ξ 490.—**(18)** In sailing, to keep (a place or celestial object) in a specified quarter: νῆσον ἐπ' ἀριστέρ' ἔχοντες γ 171. Cf. ε 277.—**(19)** To hold back, hold in check, resist: Ἕκτορα Λ 820, N 687. Cf. M 166, N 51, 151, Υ 27, Φ 309: χ 171.—**(20)** To debar from freedom, confine, keep, hold fast: οὐδέ μιν ἔσχε πόντος Φ 58: εἰ δέσματ' ἔχῃσιν α 204. Cf. α 198, δ 289, 352, 360, 416, 419, 459, θ 340, κ 339, λ 24.—**(21)** To stay, stop: 'Ερινύες ἔσχεθον αὐδήν T 418. Cf. A 219, Λ 96, 848, Φ 341: ε 451, τ 458.—To suspend (hostilities): πόλεμον Ω 670.—To cease from playing, hush (a musical instrument): σχεθέτω φόρμιγγα θ 537.—Absol. θ 542.—**(22)** To keep back from action, stay, restrain: παρὰ νηυσὶν ἑταίρους Π 204. Cf. T 119: δ 284, π 430, φ 129, χ 70, 248, 409.—To restrain, keep quiet: γέροντα X 412.—**(23)** To restrain or stop from. With genit.: ἀγοράων B 275. Cf. δ 758.—With infin.: ἀμυνέμεναι P 182.—**(24)** To keep, delay: νύκτα ψ 243.—**(25)** To manage, keep in hand: ἵππων ἐχέμεν δμῆσίν τε μένος τε P 476 (as regards δμῆσιν with an admixture of sense (28)).—**(26)** To hold (horses) in hand: ἵππους ἔχε φυσιόωντας Δ 227. Cf. Δ 302, Λ 341, N 386, Π 506, 712.—**(27)** To moor (a ship): σχέθον ἔξω νῆα κ 95. Cf. ι 279.—**(28)** To have, possess: γέρας A 163, βασιλῆας ἀνὰ στόμ' ἔχων (making them the subject of discourse) B 250, ὑπερδέα δῆμον P 330, ἔγχος X 293. Cf. A 168, Λ 271, N 714, Ξ 11, P 232, Ψ 51, Ω 212, etc.: α 311, δ 97, ζ 179, ι 196 (took with me), κ 427, ο 281, π 388, σ 142 (accept), υ 293, etc.—To have in a specified place or condition: ὑπὸ κρασὶν ἔχον ἀσπίδας K 152. Cf. δ 186.—**(29)** Of animals or inanimate objects, to be furnished, supplied, infested with: ἵπποι ἡνίοχον ἔχοντες N 537 = Ξ 431. Cf. P 436: ἠλακάτη εἶρος ἔχουσα δ 135, εὐνὴ ἀράχνι' ἔχουσα π 35. Cf. θ 558, ι 426.—Sim.: πήληξ καναχὴν ἔχεν (kept up, gave forth) Π 105, τρίποδες τόσσον ἔχον τέλος (were so far finished) Σ 378. Cf. Π 794, Σ 495.—Of a state of things, to have in it, bring with it, involve: τὸ ἀνεκτὸν ἔχει κακόν υ 83.—**(30)** To wear, bear, carry, on one's person or about one: τόξ' ὤμοισιν ἔχων A 45. Cf. B 872, Γ 17, H 137, 150, Λ 527, Ξ 376, P 473, Σ 132, 538, 595, 597, 598: εἵματα ζ 61, πολλὴν ἠέρα η 140. Cf. α 256, ζ 64, ν 224, 225, υ 206, ω 231, etc.—**(31)** To have to wife: τὴν 'Αντηνορίδης εἶχεν Γ 123. Cf. Γ 53, Λ 740, N 173, 697 = O 336, Φ 88: δ 569 η 313, λ 270, 603.—In pass., to be the wife of.

With dat.: τοῦ θυγάτηρ ἔχεθ' Ἕκτορι Z 398.—To have one as a husband: ἕξει μιν ἤματα πάντα ζ 281.—**(32)** In reference to mental or bodily faculties, characteristics or conditions, to have or be characterized by: κυνὸς ὄμματα A 225, [γῆρας] Δ 316, τλήμονα θυμόν E 670. Cf. Δ 430, E 245, I 497, N 484, Π 752, Ω 282, etc.: α 368, γ 128, δ 14, κ 239, υ 171, ψ 15, etc.—**(33)** To have, suffer, be afflicted or affected by (something evil or painful): ἄχεα Γ 412, πόνον E 667, πένθος Ω 105. Cf. E 895, Z 362, I 305, O 109 (accept, endure), T 133, etc.: α 34, δ 650, η 218, θ 529, λ 167, ν 423, σ 73, etc.—Sim.: ἕλκος ἔχοντα (suffering from it) Λ 834. Cf. Π 517, T 49, 52.—**(34)** To hold, manage: οἰήϊα T 43. Cf. γ 281.—**(35)** To set in array: λαόν I 708.—**(36)** To carry on, wage (war) Ξ 57, 100.—Sim. in reference to strife: δῆριν ἔχουσιν ω 515.—**(37)** To manage, carry on, attend to, keep: πατρώϊα ἔργα β 22. Cf. δ 737, ζ 183, η 68.—**(38)** To keep (watch or guard): φυλακὰς ἔχον I 1, 471. Cf. K 515, N 10, Ξ 135: θ 285, 302.—**(39)** To drive (horses): πεδίονδ' ἔχον ἵππους Γ 263. Cf. E 230, 240, 752=Θ 396, E 829, 841, Θ 139, 254, Λ 127, 513, 760, M 124, O 354, T 424, Ψ 398, 423, 516.—Absol., to drive: ἔχει ἀσφαλέως Ψ 325. Cf. N 326, 679, O 448, Π 378, Ψ 401, 422, 466.—**(40)** To steer (a ship) κ 91, λ 70.—Absol., to steer or hold for a specified point: Πύλονδ' ἔχον γ 182.—**(41)** With infin., to have the power, ability, means, wherewithal *to do*: οὐδὲ πόδεσσιν εἶχε στηρίξασθαι Φ 242. Cf. H 217, Π 110: λ 584, μ 433, σ 364.—Absol.: οὔ πως εἶχεν (could effect nothing) P 354.—**(42)** Of feelings, mental or bodily states or characteristics, or the like, to hold, affect, come to or upon, take hold of, possess, oppress: Δία οὐκ ἔχεν ὕπνος B 2, Μενέλαον ἔχε τρόμος K 25, οὓς ἔχε γῆρας Σ 515, ἄγη μ' ἔχει Φ 221. Cf. Γ 342, I 2, 675, Λ 269, Φ 543, X 458, etc.: γ 123, θ 344, ι 295, κ 160, ξ 215, π 310, ω 244, etc.—Sim.: αὔτως σε κλέος ἔχει (attends upon you) P 143. Cf. α 95 =γ 78.—Of the operation of wine: οἶνός σ' ἔχει φρένας σ 331=391.—In pass. construction: ἔχετ' ἄσθματι O 10, Π 109. Cf. X 409: θ 182, ρ 318, σ 123=υ 200, τ 168.—**(II)** Intrans. **(1)** To hold on, hold out, hold fast, hold or stand firm, persist: οὐκ ἐδύναντο φόβον ποιῆσαι Ἀχαιῶν, ἀλλ' ἔχον M 433. Cf. M 4, 184, 461, N 608, Π 340, 740, Υ 398, Ψ 720, Ω 27.—Sim.: ἔκτοσθε ὀδόντες ἔχον (were fastened) K 264: σανίδες ἔχον (were in place, *i.e.* barred the way) ψ 42.—With pple.: σοὶ χρὴ ἀρχοὺς λισσομένῳ ἐχέμεν E 492.—**(2)** To bear up, remain firm, retain outward composure: πάρος ἔχε νωλεμὲς αἰεί π 191. Cf. τ 494.—**(3)** To hold its way: δι' ὤμου ἔγχος ἔσχεν N 520=Ξ 452.—**(4)** To make an attack: ἐπ' αὐτῷ ἔχωμεν χ 75 (cf. ἐπέχω (4)).—**(5)** To hold, reign: ὅτ' ἐϋφροσύνη ἔχῃ κατὰ δῆμον ι 6.—**(6)** To stretch, extend: ῥίζαι ἑκὰς εἶχον μ 435, κίονες ὑψόσ' ἔχοντες (lofty) τ 38.—**(7)** To remain in a specified condition: οὐδέ οἱ ἔγχος ἔχ' ἀτρέμας N 557. Cf. ξ 416.—As copula: εὖ τοι κομιδὴ ἔχει ω 245.—**(III)** Middle (see also (I) (1)). **(1)** To cling or stick: ἔχετ' ἐμπεφυυῖα A 513. Cf. ε 329, 433, μ 433, 437, ω 8.—To cling to. With genit.: πέτρης ἔχετο ε 429. Cf. ι 435.—**(2)** To hinge or depend: τοῦ δ' ἐκ Φαιήκων ἔχεται κάρτος ζ 197. Cf. λ 346.—To hinge or depend upon. With genit.: σέο δ' ἕξεται ὅττι κεν ἄρχῃ (you will have the credit of it) I 102.—**(3)** **(a)** To be stopped or stayed: ἔσχετό οἱ φωνή P 696=Ψ 397: =δ 705 =τ 472.—To come to a stand, halt, stop: στῆ ἄντα σχομένη ζ 141.—Of a ship μ 204.—**(b)** To be stopped in one's or its course, to be held back or in check: σχέτο [ἔγχος] H 248, οὐδ' ἔτι φασὶ (ἔφαντο) σχήσεσθαι I 235, M 107 (but in these two passages the word may refer to the Greeks in sense (6)): οὐδ' ἔτι φασὶν Ἕκτορος μένος σχήσεσθαι P 639. Cf. Υ 272, Φ 345.—**(4)** To put constraint on oneself, refrain, forbear, cease, let be: σχέο Φ 379. Cf. X 416: β 70, ν 151, ρ 238.—To restrain oneself from, refrain, forbear, cease from. With genit.: εἴ ποτ' ἀϋτῆς σχοίατο B 98. Cf. Γ 84, I 655, N 630, 747, Ξ 129, P 503: δ 422, ω 57.—To restrain (one's hands from evil): κακῶν ἄπο χεῖρας ἔχεσθαι χ 316.—**(5)** To be held or absorbed (cf. the pass. use under (I) (42)): κηληθμῷ ἔσχοντο λ 334=ν 2. Cf. λ 279.—**(6)** To hold out, hold one's ground: ἔφαντ' οὐκέτ' Ἀχαιοὺς σχήσεσθαι M 126. Cf. Π 501=P 559.—See also (3) (b).—**(IV)** With adverbs. **(1)** With ἀνά. **(a)** To lift up, raise: ἂν κεφαλὴν ἔσχεν ρ 291 (cf. ἀνέχω (I) (1)).—**(b)** In mid., to restrain oneself, refrain from action: ἀνὰ δὲ σχέο H 110 (cf. ἀνέχω (II) (8)).—**(2)** With κατά. **(a)** To cover, enfold: ἔχεν κάτα γαῖα B 699 (cf. κατέχω (6)).—**(b)** To contain, enfold, bound: κατὰ κόλπον ἐχούσας B 560.—**(c)** To restrain: κατὰ δ' ἔσχεθε λαόν ω 530 (cf. κατέχω (2)).—**(d)** To hold down, oppress, afflict: κατά μιν γῆρας ἔχει λ 497.—**(3)** With παρά, to provide: παρά τε σχεῖν ὅσσα . . . Ψ 50 (cf. παρέχω (1)).—**(4)** With ὑπό, in mid., to promise: ὑπό τ' ἔσχετο καὶ κατένευσεν N 368 (cf. ὑπίσχομαι (1)). Cf. δ 525 (cf. ὑπίσχομαι (2)).

ἐχώσατο, 3 sing. aor. χώομαι.

†ἑψιάομαι [from a sb. *ἕψις conn. with L. *jocus*]. 3 pl. imp. ἑψιαάσθων ρ 530. Infin. ἑψιάασθαι φ 429. (ἐφ-, καθ-.) To sport, play: καθήμενοι ἑψιαάσθων ρ 530, ὥρη ἑψιάασθαι φ 429.

ἕψομαι, fut. mid. ἕπω[2].

ἐῶ. =ἐάω.

ἔω, subj. εἰμί.

ἐῷ, 3 sing. opt. ἐάω.

ἔωθε, 3 sing. pf. ἔθω.

ἐῴκει, 3 sing. plupf. εἴκω[1].

ἐώλπει, 3 sing. plupf. ἔλπω.

ἔωμεν, 1 pl. subj. See ἄω.

ἐῷμι, opt. ἐάω.

ἐών, pple. εἰμί.

ἐῳνοχόει, 3 sing. impf. οἰνοχοέω.

ἐώργει, 3 sing. plupf. ἔρδω.

ἕως. See ἦος.

ἔωσε, 3 sing. aor. ὠθέω.

ἔωσι, 3 pl. subj. εἰμί.

ἑωσφόρος, ὁ [ἕως=ἠώς + -φορος, φέρω. 'Bringing the dawn']. The morning-star Ψ 226.

ζᾱής [ζα- + ἡ-, ἄημι]. Acc. ζᾱῆν μ 313. Blowing strongly, furious, blustering M 157 : ε 368, μ 313.

ζάθεος, -η [ζα- + θεῖος]. Holy, sacred. Like ἠγάθεος, epithet of places A 38 = 452, B 508, 520, I 151 = 293, O 432.

ζάκοτος [ζα- + κότος]. Surly, cross-grained. Absol. Γ 220.

ζατρεφής [ζα- + τρέφω]. Well-nourished, goodly δ 451, ξ 19, 106.—Of, prepared from, such an animal : σάκος ταύρων ζατρεφέων H 223.

ζαφλεγής [ζα- + φλέγω]. Full of fire or life. Of men Φ 465.

ζαχρηής, ζαχρειής [ζα- + (perh.) χράω². 'Fierce in attack']. (**1**) Furious or formidable in fight M 347 = 360, N 684.—(**2**) Of winds, furious, blustering E 525.

ζειαί, αἱ. Some kind of grain δ 41.—The growing plant δ 604.

ζείδωρος, -ον [ζειαί + δωρέομαι]. Grain-giving. Epithet of the earth B 548, Θ 486, Υ 226 : γ 3 = μ 386, δ 229, ε 463, η 332, ι 357, λ 309, ν 354, τ 593.

ζέσσε, 3 sing. aor. ζέω.

ζεύγλη, -ης, ἡ [ζευγ-, ζεύγνυμι]. A cushion fastened under the yoke to prevent chafing, a yoke-cushion P 440, T 406.

†**ζεύγνῡμι** [ζυγόν]. Infin. ζευγνύμεναι Γ 260. ζευγνῦμεν O 120. ζευγνῦμεν Π 145. 3 pl. impf. ζεύγνυον T 393. ζεύγνυσαν Ω 783. 3 sing. aor. ζεῦξε Ω 690 : ζ 253. 3 pl. ἔζευξαν γ 478. ζεῦξαν Ω 277 : ζ 73. 3 sing. subj. ζεύξῃ Υ 495. 3 sing. opt. ζεύξειε Ω 14. Imp. ζεῦξον ο 47. Pl. ζεύξατε γ 476. Fem. pple. ζεύξᾱσα ζ 111. Infin. ζεῦξαι Ψ 130. Pres. infin. mid. ζεύγνυσθαι ψ 245. 3 dual impf. ζευγνύσθην Ω 281. 3 pl. (ἐ)ζεύγνυντο γ 492, ο 145, 190. Nom. pl. fem. pf. pple. pass. ἐζευγμέναι Σ 276. (ὑπο-.) (**1**) To yoke (horses, mules, or oxen) Γ 260, O 120, Π 145, T 393, Υ 495, Ψ 130, Ω 14, 277, 690, 783 : γ 476, 478, ζ 73, 111, 253, ο 47.—In mid., to have one's beasts yoked : τὼ ζευγνύσθην Ω 281.—To have (one's beasts) yoked : ἵππους ἐζεύγνυντο γ 492 = ο 145 = 190. Cf. ψ 245.—(**2**) To join together, secure together in position : σανίδες ἐζευγμέναι Σ 276.

ζεῦγος, τό [ζεύγνυμι]. A team of draught-animals : ζεύγεα ἐλάστρεον Σ 543.

Ζεφυρίη, ἡ [fem. of adj. fr. next]. = next η 119.

Ζέφυρος, -ου, ὁ. The west wind B 147, Δ 276, 423, H 63, I 5, Λ 305, T 415, Φ 334, Ψ 195, 200, 208 : β 421, δ 402, 567, ε 295, 332, κ 25, μ 289, 408, 426, ξ 458, τ 206.—Joined with ἄνεμος Π 150.

ζέω. 3 sing. aor. ζέσσε Σ 349 : κ 360. Of water, to boil up, boil : ἐπεὶ ζέσσεν ὕδωρ (had come to the boil) Σ 349 : = κ 360.—Of the containing caldron : ὡς λέβης ζεῖ ἔνδον Φ 362.—Of the waters of a river exposed to fire Φ 365.

ζηλήμων, -ονος [ζῆλος, jealousy]. Jealous, envious : σχέτλιοί ἐστε, θεοί, ζηλήμονες ε 118.

ζητέω [cf. δίζημαι, δίζω]. To seek, seek for : ἐμ' ἔξοχα πάντων ζήτει Ξ 258.

ζόφος, -ου, ὁ. Darkness, gloom. (**1**) The gloom of the nether world : ἀναστήσονται ὑπὸ ζόφου Φ 56. Cf. Ψ 51 : λ 57, 155, υ 356.—The nether world : Ἀΐδης ἔλαχε ζόφον O 191.—(**2**) The gloom into which the sun appears to set γ 335.—The region of darkness, the quarter of the setting sun, the west : σπέος πρὸς ζόφον εἰς Ἔρεβος τετραμμένον (*i.e.*, app., facing west with an internal downward direction) μ 81.—Contrasted with ἠώς κ 190.—With ἠώς τ' ἠέλιός τε M 240 : ι 26, ν 241.

ζυγόδεσμον, τό [ζυγόν + δεσμός]. A yoke-fastening, the rope or thong by which the yoke was secured to the pole Ω 270.

ζυγόν, -οῦ, τό [cf. L. *jugum*, Eng. *yoke*]. Ablative ζυγόφι(ν) T 404, Ω 576. (**1**) A yoke for draught-animals E 730, 731, Θ 543, Π 470, Ω 268, etc. : γ 383, 486 = ο 184, δ 39.—(**2**) In pl., oarsmen's benches extending from side to side of a ship : ὑπὸ ζυγὰ δῆσα [ἑτάρους] ι 99. Cf. ν 21.—(**3**) The cross-bar which joined the horns of a lyre and to which the strings were fastened I 187.

ζωάγρια, τά [ζωγρέω¹. App. orig. the price paid for sparing a prisoner's life]. The price of one's life, a reward for preserving one's life by care or help Σ 407 : θ 462.

ζωγρέω¹ [ζωός + ἀγρέω]. To take alive, spare a prisoner's life Z 46 = Λ 131, K 378.

ζωγρέω² [ζωή + ἀγείρω or ἐγείρω]. To re-assemble or rouse the vital forces of, revive E 698.

ζωή, -ῆς, ἡ [ζώω]. Life ; hence, the means of living, means, substance ξ 96, 208, π 429.

ζῶμα, τό [ζώννυμι. 'That which is girded about one']. (**1**) A waist-cloth or apron, prob. of leather, worn in warfare Δ 187, 216 : ξ 482.—(**2**) Something of the same kind, but doubtless of lighter material, worn in an athletic contest Ψ 683.

ζώνη, -ης, ἡ [ζώννυμι]. (**1**) A girdle worn by a goddess or a woman : ζώσατο ζώνῃ Ξ 181. Cf. ε 231 = κ 544.—Fig. : λῦσε παρθενίην ζώνην (her maiden girdle) λ 245.—(**2**) The waist or loins of a man B 479, Λ 234.

ζώννῡμι. Nom. pl. masc. aor. pple. ζώσαντες σ 76. App. as 3 pl. pres. subj. mid. ζώννυνται ω 89. 3 sing. pa. iterative ζωννύσκετο E 857. 3 sing. aor. ζώσατο Ξ 181 : σ 67. Imp. ζῶσαι σ 30. Nom. dual masc. pple. ζωσαμένω Ψ 685, 710. (**1**) To gird up (a person) for action σ 76.—(**2**) In mid. (**a**) To gird oneself : ζώσατο ζώνῃ Ξ 181 (*v.l.* ζώνην, put on her . . .).—(**b**) To gird oneself up for action : ζώννυσθαι ἄνωγεν Λ 15. Cf. E 857, K 78, Ψ 685, 710 : σ 30, 67, ω 89.—With acc. of what is girded on : κέλευσε χαλκὸν ζώννυσθαι Ψ 130 (cf. *v.l.* under (a) and μίτρην, *v.l.* for μίτρῃ E 857).

ζῶντος, contr. genit. sing. masc. pres. pple. ζώω.

ζωός, -ή [ζώω]. (**1**) Alive, living : ζωόν τε καὶ ἀρτεμέα E 515, ζωὸν ἕλεν (took prisoner) Z 38. Cf. B 699, Z 50, M 10, Σ 418, Ψ 77, etc. : α 197, γ 256, λ 78, 86, ξ 272, τ 272, ψ 55, etc.—(**2**) Absol. in pl. (**a**) The living, those not slain : ζωοὺς σάω Φ 238.—(**b**) Those yet in life : χαλεπὸν τάδε ζωοῖσιν ὁρᾶσθαι λ 156.—(**c**) The living, men : ὄφρ' ἂν ζωοῖσιν μετέω X 388. Cf. Ψ 47 : κ 52, ξ 487.

ζωρός. Of wine, strong, unmixed. In comp. : κρητῆρα ζωρότερον κέραιε I 203.

ζώς. Acc. ζών. =ζωός (1) E 887, Π 445.

ζώσατο, 3 sing. aor. mid. ζώννυμι.

ζωστήρ, -ῆρος, ὁ [ζωσ-, ζώννυμι]. (1) A warrior's belt Δ 132, 134, 135, 186, 213, 215, E 539, 615, Z 219, H 305, K 77, Λ 236, M 189, P 519, 578, Υ 414. —(2) A belt or girdle worn in ordinary life ξ 72.

ζῶστρον, τό [as prec.]. =prec. (2) ζ 38.

ζώω. Contr. genit. sing. masc. pres. pple. ζῶντος A 88. (1) To be alive, live: ζώειν φασὶ Μενοίτιον Π 14. Cf. A 88, E 157, Σ 10, T 327, X 49, etc. : β 132, γ 354, λ 303, μ 21, ρ 391, χ 38, etc.—(2) Absol. in pres. pple. pl., the living, men : ἀγαυότατον ζωόντων ο 229. Cf. κ 72.—(3) To pass a life or existence of a specified kind : θεοὶ ῥεῖα ζώοντες Z 138. Cf. Ω 526 : θεοὶ ὄλβια δοῖεν ζωέμεναι (prosperity that they may pass their lives therein) η 149. Cf. δ 805, ε 122, ρ 423= τ 79.—With cognate acc. : ζώεις ἀγαθὸν βίον ο 491.

ἦ[1], 3 sing. impf. ἠμί.

ἦ[2]. (1) Affirmative or emphasizing particle (a) ἦ μέγα πένθος Ἀχαιΐδα γαῖαν ἱκάνει A 254. Cf. A 78, 232, 240, 255, 293, 342, etc. : ἦ μάλα δή σε διδάσκουσιν θεοὶ αὐτοί α 384. Cf. β 60, δ 81, 663, 770, ζ 278, κ 465, etc.—With an ironical tone A 229 : β 325.—With concessive force, it is true that, yet, although : ἦ καὶ γένει ὕστερος ἦεν Γ 215. —(b) Combined with other particles (α) ἦ μάν B 370, N 354, etc.—(β) ἦ μέν Γ 430, E 197, I 57 (yet to be sure you are young (heightening the preceding qualified praise)), etc.: κ 65, λ 447, ν 425, etc.—This combination introducing an oath A 77, Ξ 275, T 109, etc. : ξ 160=τ 305.—ἦ μήν : ἦ μὴν Τρῶές γε κέλονται (I assure you, virtually= although) H 393. Cf. B 291.—(γ) ἦ τε Γ 56, 366, E 201, K 450, etc. : α 288, β 62, μ 138, etc.—(δ) ἦ τοι (ἤτοι) A 68, 140, 211, B 813, etc. : α 155, 267, 307, 394, etc.—(2) Interrogative particle (a) Introducing a direct question (α) ἦ ἐθέλεις . . . ; A 133. Cf. A 203, B 229, E 349, Θ 140, O 18, T 343, Υ 17, etc.: ἦ καί μοι νεμεσήσεαι; α 158. Cf. α 391, γ 251, δ 682, θ 336, ι 405, κ 284, λ 160, etc.—(β) In the first clause in questions in disjunctive form (cf. ἠέ (2)) : ἦ πού τις νήσων ἦε . . . ; ν 234, etc.—(γ) Introducing a question with disjunctive force : ἦ ἀνθρώπων εἰμὶ σχεδόν ; ζ 125, etc.—(b) Introducing an indirect question: τόδε εἰπέ, ἦ . . . π 138.

ἦ[3]. See ἠέ (2).

ἤ. See ἠέ.

ἦα, impf. εἰμί.

ἦα. See ἤϊα.

ἥαται, 3 pl. pres. **ἥατο,** 3 pl. impf. ἧμαι.

ἠβαιός, -ή, -όν. (1) Little, inconsiderable, of small worth, few in number: οὔ οἱ ἔνι τρίχες οὐδ' ἠβαιαί σ 355. Cf. Ξ 141 : φ 288.—(2) Absol. in neut. sing. ἠβαιόν (a) A little space, a short distance: ἐλθόντες ἠ. ἀπὸ σπείους ι 462. Cf. N 702. —(b) For a short space of time, for a little: οὐκ ἀνάβλησις ἔσσεται οὐδ' ἠ. B 380. Cf. B 386, N 106. —(c) A little, to a small or trifling extent: οὔ σε χρὴ αἰδοῦς οὐδ' ἠ. γ 14. Cf. Υ 361.

ἡβάω [ἥβη]. Acc. sing. masc. pres. pple. ἡβώοντα I 446. Nom. pl. ἡβώοντες Ω 604 : κ 6. Nom. fem. ἡβώωσα ε 69. Opt. ἡβώοιμι H 157, Λ 670, Ψ 629 : ξ 468, 503. Contr. ἡβῷμι H 133. 3 sing. aor. subj. ἡβήσῃ α 41. Pple. ἡβήσας τ 410. Dual masc. ἡβήσαντε E 550. (1) To be in one's youthful prime, in the vigour of early manhood : ἀνὴρ μάλ' ἡβῶν M 382. Cf. H 133, 157=Λ 670, I 446, Ψ 629, Ω 565, 604 :=κ 6, ξ 468, 503, ψ 187. —Of a flourishing vine ε 69.—(2) In aor., to have attained this stage of growth: ἡβήσαντε ἅμ' Ἀργείοισιν ἑπέσθην E 550. Cf. α 41, τ 410.

ἥβη, -ης, ἡ. (1) Youthful prime, early manhood : ἥβης μέτρον Λ 225, τοῦ περ χαριεστάτη ἥ. (in whom youthful manhood shows most . . .) Ω 348. Cf. N 484, Π 857=X 363, P 25 : δ 668, κ 279, λ 317, σ 217, τ 532, ψ 212.—(2) The vigour or strength proper to this stage of growth : ὄφρ' ἥβη πεποίθεα θ 181. Cf. Ψ 432.—In reference to an elderly man, bodily vigour, suppleness of frame: οὐδέ τι ἥβης δεύεται θ 136, δέμας ὤφελλε καὶ ἥβην π 174 (in both cases of Odysseus).—(3) Manhood viewed as a stage attained or to be attained : ἥβην ἵξεσθαι Ω 728. Cf. ο 366.

ἡβώοιμι, opt. ἡβάω.

ἠγάασθε, 2 pl. impf. ἄγαμαι.

ἤγαγον, aor. ἄγω.

ἠγάθεος, -η, -ον [app. ἠγα-=ἀγα- + θεῖος]. Holy, sacred. Like ζάθεος, epithet of places A 252, B 722, Z 133, Φ 58, 79: β 308, δ 599, 702=ε 20, θ 80, ξ 180.

ἠγάσσατο, 3 sing. aor. ἄγαμαι.

ἤγγειλε, 3 sing. aor. ἀγγέλλω.

ἤγειρα[1], aor. ἀγείρω.

ἤγειρα[2], aor. ἐγείρω.

ἡγεμονεύω [ἡγεμών]. (1) To act as guide or pilot, show the way: θεός τις ἡγεμόνευεν ι 142, κ 141. Cf. ρ 194.—With dat., to guide (a person), show (him) the way: δεῦρό οἱ ἡγεμόνευεν ρ 372. Cf. κ 445.—With cognate acc., to show (the way): ὁδὸν ἡγεμονεύσω ζ 261, η 30. Cf. κ 501.—(2) To lead the way, act as leader, take the lead : Τηλέμαχος πρόσθ' ἡγεμόνευεν χ 400.—With dat. : τοῖσιν ἡγεμόνευεν γ 386, θ 4=421, ψ 293.—With dat. and cognate acc. : τοῖσιν ὁδὸν ἡγεμόνευεν ω 225.—Sim. : ὅτ' ἀνὴρ ὀχετηγὸς ὕδατι ῥόον ἡγεμονεύῃ (guides the flow) Φ 258.—(3) To lead the way, give a lead, in a course of action : τῇ ἴμεν ᾗ κε σὺ ἡγεμονεύῃς O 46.—(4) To precede a person by an interval of time : Ὀδυσσεὺς ὕστερος, αὐτὰρ Τηλέμαχος πρόσθ' ἡγεμόνευεν ω 155.—(5) To be the leader, commander or chief of. (a) With genit. : Λοκρῶν B 527, τῆς ἑτέρης [στιχός] Π 179. Cf. B 540, 552, 645, 657, etc.—(b) With dat. : Τρωσίν B 816.—(6) Absol., to act as chief or leader, lead one's men N 53, Π 92.

ἡγεμών, -όνος, ὁ [ἡγέομαι]. (1) A guide or pilot, one who shows the way: ἅμ' ἡγεμόν' ἐσθλὸν ὄπασσον ο 310. Cf. κ 505.—(2) A leader, commander or chief: κέλευεν οἷσιν ἕκαστος ἡγεμόνων Δ 429. Cf. B 365, Γ 1, E 38, I 85, M 87, etc.

ἡγέομαι. Fut. ἡγήσομαι Ξ 374. 3 sing. aor. ἡγήσατο A 71, B 867, M 251, Υ 144, etc.: β 405, ε 192, ξ 48, ω 469, etc. 3 dual -άσθην B 620, 678, 864, 870. Subj. ἡγήσομαι ο 82. 2 sing. opt. ἡγήσαιο η 22. 3 -αιτο B 687: ζ 114, 300. 3 sing. imp. ἡγησάσθω I 168. Infin. ἡγήσασθαι X 101: κ 263, ξ 238. (ἐξ-.) (1) To act as guide or pilot, show the way: καὶ ἂν πάϊς ἡγήσαιτο ζ 300. Cf. ν 65, ο 82.—With dat., to guide (a person), show (him) the way: ἥ οἱ πόλιν ἡγήσαιτο (to the city) ζ 114. Cf. A 71: η 22.—With cognate acc., to show (the way): τὸν ἠνώγεα αὐτὴν ὁδὸν ἡγήσασθαι (to take me by the way by which he had come) κ 263.—(2) To lead the way, act as leader, take the lead: ὣς φωνήσας ἡγήσατο Υ 144. Cf. I 168, 192, M 28, Ω 96: α 125, β 405 = γ 29 = η 37, β 413 = θ 46 = 104, ε 192, ξ 48.—(3) To lead the way, give a lead, in a course of action. With dat.: τοῖσιν Εὐπείθης ἡγήσατο νηπιέῃσιν (in their . . .) ω 469.—To give a lead, cause a start to be made. With dat. and genit. of that in which a start is made: ἀοιδὸς ἡμῖν ἡγείσθω ὀρχηθμοῖο ψ 134.—(4) To be the leader, commander or chief of. (a) With genit.: ἐπικούρων M 101. Cf. B 567, 620, 638, 678, 731, 851, 867, 870.—(b) With dat.: Μῄοσιν B 864, νῆες, ᾗσιν Ἀχιλλεὺς ἐς Τροίην ἡγεῖτο (brought to Troy under his command) Π 169. Cf. B 687, E 211: ξ 238.—(5) Absol., to act as chief or leader, lead one's men M 251 = N 833, N 802, Ξ 374: ξ 470.—To lead a person on, induce him to follow: κερδοσύνῃ ἡγήσατο X 247.—(6) To lead or lead on (one's men). With genit.: ἡγήσατο λαῶν O 311.—With dat.: Τρωσὶ ποτὶ πτόλιν ἡγήσασθαι X 101.—(7) To take the lead, be the leading person, among. With dat.: ἡγεῖτο μνηστῆρσιν π 397.

ἠγερέθομαι [ἀγείρομαι. Cf. ἠερέθομαι beside ἀείρομαι]. (1) To come or gather together, assemble: ἀμφ' Ἀτρεΐωνα ἠγερέθοντο Ψ 233. Cf. B 304, K 127, T 303, Ω 783: περὶ ἑταῖροι ἠγερέθοντο β 392. Cf. γ 412, λ 228, ρ 34, 65, σ 41, τ 542, ω 468.—(2) To be or remain gathered together or in a body: ἀμφί μιν Κρητῶν ἀγοὶ ἠγερέθονται Γ 231. Cf. M 82.

ἤγερθεν, 3 pl. aor. pass. ἀγείρω.

ἡγηλάζω [*ἡγηλός, apt to lead, fr. ἡγέομαι]. (1) To play the leader or fugleman to: κακὸς κακὸν ἡγηλάζει ρ 217.—(2) To lead (a specified kind of existence), endure (a specified fate): κακὸν μόρον ἡγηλάζεις λ 618.

ἡγήσομαι, fut. ἡγέομαι.

ἡγήτωρ, -ορος, ὁ [ἡγέομαι]. A leader, commander or chief: δύω ἡγήτορες ἦσαν Δ 393. Cf. B 79, Γ 153, K 181, O 330, Υ 383, etc.: Ταφίων α 105. Cf. η 98, 136, 186 = θ 26 = 97 = 387 = 536, θ 11, λ 526, ν 186, 210.—With ἀνήρ: Πυλίων ἡγήτορες ἄνδρες Λ 687. Cf. Π 495, 532.

ἠγνοίησε, 3 sing. aor. ἀγνοιέω.

ἠγοράασθε, 2 pl. impf. ἀγοράομαι.

ἠγορόωντο, 3 pl. impf. ἀγοράομαι.

ἠδέ [ἤ² δέ]. And: ταύρων ἠδ' αἰγῶν A 41. Cf. A 96, 251, B 27, 79, 118, etc.: α 13, 95, 135, 170, 182, 231, etc.—So ἠδὲ καί: Διὸς ἄγγελοι ἠδὲ καὶ ἀνδρῶν A 334, etc. Cf. β 209, etc.—Correlative with ἠμέν. See ἠμέν.

ᾔδεα, plupf. εἴδω (C).

ᾔδεε, ᾔδη, 3 sing. plupf. εἴδω (C).

ἤδη [ἤ² δή]. (1) Previously to some specified or indicated time, by or before this (or that) time, by now, now, already, ere this: ἤδη οἱ ἐφῆκα βέλος E 188. Cf. A 250, 260, 590, B 699, Γ 56, 184, etc.: ἤδη Ἀϊδόσδε βεβήκει γ 410. Cf. β 164, 211, 402, 410, γ 241, 335, etc.—Reinforcing νῦν O 110, etc.: ξ 213, etc.—(2) In reference to the future, now: ἢ ἤδη με δαμόωσιν Z 368. Cf. Λ 821, Π 438, Ψ 20, Ω 635, etc.: ἤδη σχεθέτω φόρμιγγα θ 537. Cf. α 303, δ 294, ν 151, τ 300, χ 101, ω 506, etc.—Reinforcing νῦν A 456, etc.: κ 472, etc.

ᾔδησθα, 2 sing. plupf. εἴδω (C).

†ἥδομαι [ἡδύς]. 3 sing. aor. ἥσατο ι 353. Aor. pple. ἁσμενος, -ου Ξ 108, Υ 350: ι 63, 566, κ 134. (1) In aor., to conceive delight or pleasure. With pple., expressing the occasion: ἥσατο πίνων ι 353.—(2) In aor. pple., having conceived or conceiving pleasure, well-pleased, glad: ἐμοὶ κεν ἀσμένῳ εἴη (I should be glad . . .) Ξ 108, φύγεν ἄσμενος ἐκ θανάτοιο (was glad to flee . . .) Υ 350: προτέρω πλέομεν ἄσμενοι ἐκ θανάτοιο (glad to have escaped . . .) ι 63 = 566 = κ 134.

ἦδος, τό [cf. ἡδύς]. Pleasure, profit, satisfaction: μίνυνθα ἡμέων ἔσσεται ἦ. (we shall profit our friends little) Λ 318, τί μοι τῶν ἦ.; (what satisfaction have I in that?) Σ 80. Cf. A 576: = σ 404, ω 95.

ἡδυεπής [ἡδύς + ἔπος]. Sweet-speaking, silver-tongued. Of Nestor A 248.

ἥδυμος. See under νήδυμος.

ἡδύποτος [ἡδύς + πο-, πίνω]. Sweet to drink. Of wine β 340, γ 391, ο 507.

ἡδύς, ἡδεῖα, ἡδύ. Also fem. ἡδύς μ 369 [σϝαδ- as in ἀνδάνω]. (1) Sweet or pleasant. (a) To the taste. Of wine β 350, γ 51, δ 746, η 265, ι 162, etc.—Of a meal: δεῖπνον υ 391.—(b) To the sense of smell: ὀδμή ι 210. Cf. μ 369.—(c) To the ear: ἀοιδήν θ 64.—(2) Of sleep or rest, sweet, grateful, balmy, refreshing Δ 131: α 364 = π 451 = τ 604 = φ 358, ο 44, τ 510, ψ 17.—Superl. ἥδιστος: ὕπνος ν 80.—(3) Pleasing, agreeable, such as commends itself to one: εἴ πως τόδε πᾶσι φίλον καὶ ἡδὺ γένοιτο Δ 17. Cf. H 387: ω 435.—(4) In neut. ἡδύ as adv. (a) So as to gratify the sense of smell, sweetly: ἀμβροσίην ἡδὺ πνείουσαν δ 446.—(b) Of sleeping, sweetly: ἡδὺ κνώσσουσα δ 809.—(c) Of laughing, merrily, heartily: ἡδὺ γελάσσας Λ 378. Cf. B 270, Φ 508, Ψ 784: = υ 358 = φ 376, π 354, σ 35, 111.

ἠε. See ἠέ (2).

ἠέ (ἠϝέ), ἤ. (1) Disjunctive particle. (a) Or: ἐγὼ ἢ ἄλλος Ἀχαιῶν B 231. Cf. A 40, 515, B 800, Γ 394, Δ 83, 142, etc.: εἰλαπίνη ἠὲ γάμος; α 226. Cf. α 162, 282, β 375, γ 94, δ 45, 396, etc.—So ἤ τε (ἤτε) T 148.—(**b**) ἠὲ (ἤ) . . . ἠὲ (ἤ) . . ., either . . . or . . .: ἢ νῦν δηθύνοντ' ἢ ὕστερον αὖτις ἰόντα A 27. Cf. A 138, 395, E 484, I 78, 537, K 370, etc.: ἠὲ δόλῳ ἢ ἀμφαδόν α 296. Cf. γ 99, 217, δ 546, ε 484, ζ 103, κ 228, etc.—Thrice or four times A 145, H 179, K 6, etc.: κ 433, ο 84, etc.—So ἤ τε (ἤτε) . . . ἤ τε (ἤτε) . . . I 276 = T 177, Λ 410, P 42.—ἤ . . . τε B 289.—(**2**) In questions in disjunctive form (the second particle written ἦε, ἦ). (**a**) Direct: ἤέ τι βέβληαι, ἦε . . .; N 251. Cf. O 735, etc.: γ 72, ω 109, etc.—Thrice N 308, etc.—Without the particle in the first clause O 203, etc.: υ 130, φ 194, etc.—(**b**) Indirect, whether . . . or . . .: μερμήριξεν, ἤ . . . ἦε . . . A 190. Cf. B 238, Δ 15, E 86, Θ 377, N 327, Σ 308 (and see whether . . .), etc.: ὄφρ' ἐῢ εἰδῶ, ἠὲ . . . ἦ . . . α 175. Cf. α 268, γ 170, δ 28, ζ 142, λ 175, π 260, τ 525, etc.—Without the particle in the first clause K 546, etc.: δ 837, etc.—With εἰ or αἴ in the first clause B 368, Z 368, Θ 533, X 246: ω 218.—With change of construction ρ 275.—(**3**) After comparatives, than: ἀρείοσιν ἠέ περ ὑμῖν A 260. Cf. E 531, Θ 190, Π 688, etc.: νεώτεροι ἢ πάρος ἦσαν κ 395. Cf. α 322, θ 154, etc.—So ἤ τε (ἤτε) π 216.—After ἄλλος K 404, etc.—After ἀλλοῖος π 181, τ 267.—After verbs implying comparison: βούλομαι . . . ἢ . . . A 117, etc.: ἔφθης . . . ἢ . . . λ 58, etc.

ἦε, ἤει, 3 sing. impf. εἶμι.

ἠείδη, 3 sing. plupf. εἴδω (C).

ἤειρε, 3 sing. aor. ἀείρω.

ἠέλιος, -ου, ὁ. Also **Ἥλιος** θ 271. Ἠέλιος as voc. Γ 277. (**1**) The sun. (**a**) ἅμ' ἠελίῳ καταδύντι (at sunset) A 592, ἠ. ἐπέλαμψεν P 650. Cf. A 475, Δ 44, E 267, Θ 485, 538, K 547, Ξ 185, etc.: β 181, δ 45, ζ 98, η 124, κ 160, ο 404, υ 356, etc.—(**b**) ὑπ' αὐγὰς ἠελίοιο, in the upper world, among the living λ 498, 619, ο 349.—Of seeing the sun, *i.e.* of living: δηρὸν ἔτ' ὄψεσθαι φάος ἠελίοιο E 120. Cf. Σ 61 = 442, Ω 558: δ 540 = κ 498, δ 833, ξ 44 = υ 207.—Sim. of being born: ἠελίου ἴδεν αὐγάς Π 188.—Of leaving the sun, *i.e.* of dying: λείψειν (λιπὼν) φάος ἠελίοιο Σ 11: λ 93.—(**2**) The quarter of the rising sun, the east: πρὸς ἠῶ τ' ἠέλιόν τε M 239: ι 26, ν 240.—(**3**) The sun-god: Ἠ. ὃς πάντ' ἐφορᾷς Γ 277. Cf. Γ 104, Θ 480, Ξ 344, T 197, etc.: βοῦς Ὑπερίονος Ἠελίοιο α 8. Cf. γ 1, θ 271, κ 138, λ 16, 109, μ 133, τ 276, ω 12, etc.

ἦεν, 3 sing. impf. εἰμί.

ἠερέθομαι [ἀείρομαι. Cf. ἠγερέθομαι beside ἀγείρομαι]. (**1**) To take wing: ὡς ἀκρίδες ἠερέθονται Φ 12.—(**2**) To wave about, flutter: θύσανοι ἠερέθονται B 448.—Fig., of the mind, to be blown about by passion or caprice, to be unsteady or untrustworthy Γ 108.

ἠέριος, -η (ἠϝέριος) [ἀϝερ-. Cf. ἠώς, ἄριστον, αὔριον, ἦρι, L. *aurora*]. With the early morning: ἠερίη ἀνέβη οὐρανόν A 497. Cf. A 557, Γ 7: ι 52.

ἠεροειδής, -ές [ἠερ-, ἀήρ + εἶδος]. (**1**) Epithet of the sea, misty, melting into the haze of distance Ψ 744: β 263, γ 105, 294, δ 482, ε 164, 281, θ 568 = ν 150 = 176, μ 285.—In neut. ἠεροειδές as adv., through the haze, in the haze of distance: ὅσσον ἠ. ἀνὴρ ἴδεν E 770.—(**2**) Of a rock, shrouded in mist μ 233 (cf. 74).—(**3**) Epithet of caves, dim, dusky, shadowy μ 80, ν 103 = 347, 366.

ἠερόεις, -εντος [ἠερ-, ἀήρ]. (**1**) Hazy, gloomy, dark: Τάρταρον Θ 13, ζόφον M 240, O 191, Φ 56, Ψ 51: λ 57, 155, ν 241.—(**2**) Hazy, misty: κατ' ἠερόεντα κέλευθα (through the paths of the clouds) υ 64.

ἠέρος, genit. ἀήρ.

ἠεροφοῖτις [ἠερ-, ἀήρ + φοιτάω]. Walking in darkness. Epithet of Erinys I 571, T 87.

ἠερόφωνος [perh. fr. ἀείρω + φωνή. Cf. ἠερέθομαι, μετ-ήορος. 'Lifting up the voice']. Thus, loud-voiced. Epithet of heralds Σ 505.

ἦην, 3 sing. impf. εἰμί.

ἠθεῖος, -η. In voc. ἠθεῖε as a form of address to an elder or a master Z 518 (Paris to Hector), K 37 (Menelaus to Agamemnon), X 229, 239 (the supposed Deïphobus to Hector).—Sim. in the periphrasis ἠθείη κεφαλή Ψ 94 (Achilles to the shade of Patroclus. Patroclus was the senior Λ 787).—In ξ 147 (ἠθεῖόν μιν καλέω) Eumaeus means that he mentally addresses his absent master as ἠθεῖε.

ἤθελον, impf. ἐθέλω.

ἦθος, τό [conn. with ἔθω and orig. σϝῆθος]. In pl., the accustomed haunts of animals: ἤθεα ἵππων Z 511 = O 268.—The sties of swine ξ 411.

ἤϊα[1], τά. Contr. ἦα ε 266, ι 212. (**1**) Provisions for a voyage: ὅπλισσον ἤϊα β 289, ἤϊα φερώμεθα 410, ἤϊά κε πάντα κατέφθιτο δ 363, ἐν καὶ ἦα κωρύκῳ ε 266, ι 212, νηὸς ἐξέφθιτο ἤϊα πάντα μ 329.—(**2**) Prey: θώων ἤϊα πέλονται N 103.—(**3**) Chaff (in this sense perh. a different word): ὡς ἄνεμος ζαὴς ἠΐων (disyllable) θημῶνα τινάξῃ ε 368.

ἤϊα[2], impf. εἶμι.

ἤϊθεος, -ου, ὁ. An unmarried youth Δ 474, Λ 60, Σ 567, 593, X 127, 128: γ 401, ζ 63, λ 38.

ἤϊκτο, 3 sing. plupf. mid. εἴκω[1].

ἤϊξε, 3 sing. aor. ἀΐσσω.

ἠϊόεις, -εντος. Epithet of a river, of unknown meaning: ἐπ' ἠϊόεντι Σκαμάνδρῳ E 36.

ἤϊον, 3 pl. impf. εἶμι.

ἤϊος. Epithet of Apollo, of unknown meaning: ἤϊε Φοῖβε O 365, Υ 152.

ἤϊσαν, 3 pl. impf. εἶμι.

ἤϊσκε, 3 sing. impf. ἐΐσκω.

ἤϊσσον, 3 pl. impf. ἀΐσσω.

ἠΐχθη, 3 sing. aor. pass. ἀΐσσω.

ἠϊών, -όνος, ἡ. Dat. pl. ἠϊόνεσσι ε 156. (**1**) A beach or shore of the sea: ἠϊόνος προπάροιθε βαθείης B 92. Cf. H 462, M 31, Ξ 36, Υ 148, Ψ 61.—(**2**) In pl. (**a**) Portions of the shore, beaches, shores: ἀμφ' ἄκραι ἠϊόνες βοόωσιν (to their furthest points) P 265 (*v.l.* ἄκραι ἠϊόνος, taking ἄκραι as sb. (see ἄκρη (3)) and ἠϊόνος in sense (1), 'the headlands of the shore'), ἠὼς φαινομένη ὑπεὶρ ἅλα τ' ἠϊόνας τε Ω 13. Cf. ε 156.—(**b**) Beaches or spits projecting into the sea: ἠϊόνας παραπλῆγας ε 418 = 440. Cf. ζ 138.

ἦκα. (**1**) Of action, gently, without effort:

ψύξασα Υ 440. Cf. Ψ 336 : σ 92, 94, υ 301.—Gently, without violence: ἀπώσατο γέροντα Ω 508.—(2) Of journeying, softly, at a foot-pace ρ 254.—(3) Of speaking, softly, in an undertone Γ 155.—(4) Of the soft play of light on a glossy surface: χιτῶνας ἧκα στίλβοντας ἐλαίῳ Σ 596.

ἧκα, aor. ἵημι[1].

ἤκαχε, 3 sing. aor. ἀχέω.

ἠκέσατο, 3 sing. aor. ἀκέομαι.

ἤκεστος, -η [doubtfully explained as fr. ἠ-= ἀ-[1] + -κεστος. See κεστός]. Thus, untouched by the goad: βοῦς ἠκέστας Ζ 94 = 275, 309.

ἥκιστος [superl. fr. ἧκα. Cf. ἥσσων]. The slowest or weakest: ἥ. ἐλαυνέμεν (in driving) Ψ 531.

ἠκόντισαν, 3 pl. aor. ἀκοντίζω.

ἥκω. To have come Ε 478 : ν 325.

ἠλάκατα, τά [ἠλακάτη]. The yarn spun off from the distaff ζ 53, 306, η 105, ρ 97, σ 315.

ἠλακάτη, -ης, ἡ. A distaff Ζ 491 := α 357 = φ 351, δ 131, 135.

ἤλασα, aor. ἐλαύνω.

ἠλασκάζω [cf. next]. (1) To wander aimlessly about Σ 281.—(2) To go about or skulk in order to avoid (danger): ὅππῃ ἐμὸν μένος ἠλασκάζει ι 457.

ἠλάσκω [ἄλη]. To rove or flit about: ἔλαφοι καθ' ὕλην αὔτως ἠλάσκουσαι Ν 104. Cf. Β 470.

ἠλᾶτο, 3 sing. impf. ἀλάομαι.

ἤλδανε, 3 sing. aor. ἀλδαίνω.

ἠλέ. See ἠλεός.

ἤλειψε, 3 sing. aor. ἀλείφω.

ἤλεκτρον, τό. (1) Amber δ 73.—(2) In pl., beads of amber: ὅρμον ἠλέκτροισιν ἐερμένον σ 296. Cf. ο 460.

ἠλέκτωρ. The sun Ζ 513, Τ 398.

ἠλεός [app. conn. with ἀλάομαι, ἠλάσκω]. Voc. ἠλέ Ο 128. (1) Crazed, distraught: φρένας ἠλέ (in your . . .) Ο 128. Cf. β 243.—(2) That takes away one's wits or discretion: οἶνος ξ 464.

ἠλεύατο, 3 sing. aor. ἀλέομαι.

ἠλήλατο, 3 sing. plupf. pass. ἐλαύνω.

ἦλθον, aor. ἔρχομαι.

ἠλίβατος, -ον. Of unknown meaning. Epithet of πέτρη Ο 273, 619, Π 35 : ι 243, κ 88, ν 196.

ἤλιθα [poss. conn. with ἅλις]. Strengthening πολλός: ἤλιθα πολλήν Λ 677. Cf. ε 483, ι 330, ξ 215, τ 443.

ἡλικίη, -ης, ἡ [ἧλιξ]. (1) Time of life: ἥν πως ἡλικίην αἰδέσσεται (may respect my age) Χ 419.—(2) Those of the same age as oneself, one's fellows in years, one's contemporaries: ἡλικίην ἐκέκαστο Π 808.

ἧλιξ, -ικος. Of the same age: βόες σ 373.

Ἥλιος. See ἠέλιος.

ἤλιτε, 3 sing. aor. ἀλιταίνω.

ἠλιτόμηνος [ἀλιτ-, ἀλιταίνω + μήν. 'Failing in (the due number of) months']. Untimely born Τ 118.

ἧλος, -ου, ὁ [Ϝῆλος. Cf. L. *vallus*]. A nail or stud used for ornament Α 246, Λ 29, 633.

ἤλυθον, aor. ἔρχομαι.

ἤλυξα, aor. ἀλύσκω.

Ἠλύσιος [said to be for ἠλύθ-τιος, fr. ἠλυθ- (see ἔρχομαι). 'To which . . . go']. Ἠλύσιον πεδίον, an abode of everlasting bliss assigned to mortals favoured by the gods δ 563.

ἦλφον, aor. ἀλφάνω.

ἧλω, 3 sing. aor. ἁλίσκομαι.

ἠλώμην, impf. ἀλάομαι.

ἧμα, -ατος, τό [ἡ-, ἵημι[1]]. A throwing or hurling. In pl.: ὅσσον ἥμασιν ἔπλευ ἄριστος (in throwing the spear) Ψ 891.

ἠμαθόεις, -εντος [ἄμαθος]. Abounding in sand, sandy, by the sandy shore. Epithet of Pylus Β 77, Ι 153 = 295, Λ 712 : α 93, β 214 = 359, β 326, δ 633, λ 257, 459, ω 152.

†**ἧμαι** [ἡσ-]. 1 sing. pres. ἧμαι Σ 104, Ω 542 : θ 157, ξ 41. 2 ἧσαι Β 255, Ο 245. 3 ἧσται Τ 345 : ζ 305, λ 142, π 145, σ 240, etc. 1 pl. ἥμεθα Ο 740. 2 ἧσθε β 240. 3 pl. ἧαται (ἧσ-αται), also written εἵαται Β 137, Κ 100, 161, 422 : β 403, ζ 307. ἕαται Γ 134, Ι 628. 1 sing. impf. ἥμην Ζ 336 : κ 374, λ 49. 3 ἧστο Α 512, Ζ 324, Ν 11, Ο 393, Ψ 451, etc.: α 114, γ 32, ζ 52, ρ 68, ψ 91, etc. 3 dual ἥσθην Δ 21, Θ 445, 458 : η 232. 1 pl. ἥμεθα γ 263, ι 78, 162, λ 10, 82, ψ 42, etc. 3 ἧατο (ἧσ-ατο), also written εἵατο Γ 149, Η 61, Θ 554, Ο 10, Σ 504, Ω 99, etc.: α 326, β 398, γ 8, ι 545, υ 106, etc. ἕατο Η 414. ἧντο Γ 153. Imp. ἧσο Β 200, Γ 406, Δ 412 : π 44, σ 105, υ 262. Pple. ἥμενος, -η Α 330, 358, Ε 771, Η 100, Ο 153, Φ 389, etc.: α 108, δ 596, η 106, ι 8, κ 375, ρ 506, φ 100, etc. Infin. ἧσθαι Α 134, 416, Ν 253, 280 : η 160, κ 507, 536, τ 120, ψ 365. (ἀφ-, ἐν-, ἐφ-, καθ-, μεθ-, παρ-.) (1) To sit, be seated: παρὰ κλισίῃ ἥμενον Α 330, ἕαται σιγῇ Γ 134. Cf. Β 200, Δ 21, Ζ 324, Θ 445, Ι 190, Ν 11, etc.: ἥμενοι ἐν ῥινοῖσιν α 108. Cf. α 114, β 36, γ 8, 32, ζ 52, θ 157, κ 374, etc.—(2) To sit idle, doing nothing: ἥμενοι αὖθι ἕκαστοι ἀκήριοι Η 100. Cf. Α 134, Ν 253 : οἷον ἧσθ' ἄνεῳ β 240. Cf. κ 375, π 145.—Requiring to do nothing: ἱστία ἐρύσαντες ἥμεθα ι 78 = ξ 256. Cf. κ 507, λ 10 = μ 152.—(3) To sit, abide, be, remain, doing something specified or in a specified condition or place: ἀδάκρυτος ἧσθαι Α 416, ἧαται ποτιδέγμεναι Β 137, τηλόθι πάτρης ἧμαι ἐνὶ Τροίῃ Ω 542. Cf. Β 255, Δ 412, Θ 480, Ι 628, Κ 100, 161, 422, Ο 740, Σ 104 : γ 263, ν 337, 424, ξ 41, τ 120, φ 425.—(4) Of an army, to be set down or encamped: τὴν πόλιν ἀμφὶ δύω στρατοὶ ἥατο Σ 509.—Of a sentinel or scout, to be at his post Κ 182.—To be posted: δύω σκοποὶ ἥατο Σ 523. Cf. Ω 799.—(5) Of a thing, to be set, fixed, placed: ἔνθα μύλαι ἥατο υ 106.

ἦμαρ, -ατος, τό [cf. ἡμέρη]. (1) Day, the day, the period of daylight: μέσον ἦ. Φ 111, ὄφρ' ἀέξετο ἦ. Θ 66 = Λ 84 := ι 56. Cf. η 288, κ 86, 470, ρ 191, σ 367 = χ 301.—For δείελον ἦ. see δείελος (2).—(2) A day considered as a space of time. (a) As a period of daylight: πᾶν ἦ. Α 592, νύκτας τε καὶ ἦ. Ε 490. Cf. Α 601, Ι 326, Σ 340, 453, Τ 162, Χ 432, Ψ 186, Ω 73, 713, 745 : β 345, ε 156, 388, ι 74, 161 = 556 = κ 183 = 476 = μ 29 = τ 424, κ 11, 28, 80 = ο 476, κ 142, λ 183 = ν 338 = π 39, π 365, ρ 515, τ 513, υ 84, ω 41, 63.—(b) As embracing both daylight and dark: ἐείκοσιν ἤματα Z 217, ἤματα πάντα Θ 539 (for ever), M 133 (ever), N 826, Ξ 235 (all my days), 269, 276, Π 499, Ψ 594, Ω 491: β 205, δ 209, 592, ε 136 = η 257 = ψ 336, ε 210, 219, ζ 46, 281, η 94, θ 431, ι 123, κ 467, ο 54, φ 156, ψ 6, ω 25. Cf. Φ 45: δ 360, ε 278, η 267, τ 199.—(3) A day considered as a point or unit of time or as one of a series: ἤματι κείνῳ (on that day, that day) B 37, 482, Δ 543, Σ 324, Φ 517, τρίτῳ ἤματι Λ 707, ἤματα πάντα (during or on each day, every day) T 226. Cf. B 351, 743, Γ 189, Δ 164 = Z 448, E 210, Z 345, 422, Θ 475, I 253 = 439 = Λ 766, I 363, Λ 444, M 279, N 98, 335, Ξ 250, O 76, 252, 719, Π 385, P 401, Σ 85, T 60, 89, 98, Φ 5, 77, 584, X 359, 471, Ψ 87: β 55 = ρ 534, γ 180, ε 34, 262, 309, 390 = ι 76 = κ 144, ζ 170, η 326, θ 468, μ 399 = ο 477, σ 137, τ 153 = ω 143, υ 19, 116, ψ 252.—ἐπ' ἤματι K 48 (in a single day), T 229 (for the day (and no longer)): β 284 (in one day), μ 105 (in the day, a day), ξ 105 (each day, day by day). Cf. N 234, T 110.—(4) With an adj., expressing periphrastically the substantival notion implicit in the adj. (a) αἴσιμον ἤ. (the fatal day, the fate, one's fate) Θ 72, Φ 100, X 212: π 280.—(b) ἤ. ἀναγκαῖον (the day that brings compulsion, slavery) Π 836.—(c) δούλιον ἤ. (the day that brings slavery, slavery) Z 463: ξ 340, ρ 323.—(d) ἐλεύθερον ἤ. (the day or time of freedom, freedom) Z 455, Π 831, Υ 193.—(e) κακὸν ἤ. (the day that brings bane, bane) I 251, 597, Υ 315 = Φ 374: κ 269, 288, ο 524.—(f) μόρσιμον ἤ. (the fatal day, one's fate) O 613: κ 175.—(g) νηλεὲς ἤ. (the day of pitiless fate, fate, bane) Λ 484, 588, N 514, O 375, P 511, 615, Φ 57: θ 525, ι 17.—(h) νόστιμον ἤ. (the day that brings one's home-coming, one's home-coming) α 9, 168, 354, γ 233 = ε 220 = θ 466, ζ 311, π 149, ρ 253, 571, τ 369.—(i) ὀλέθριον ἤ. (the day that brings bane, bane) T 294, 409.—(j) ἤ. ὀρφανικόν (the day that brings orphanhood, orphanhood) X 490.

ἦμας, acc. ἡμεῖς.

ἠμάτιος, -η [ἠματ-, ἦμαρ]. (1) By day, in the day-time: ἠματίη ὑφαίνεσκεν β 104 = ω 139. Cf. τ 149.—(2) Day by day, daily I 72.

ἥμβροτον, aor. ἁμαρτάνω.

ἡμεῖς. Nom. ἡμεῖς B 126, 305, 320, etc.: α 37, 76, γ 81, etc. Genit. ἡμείων E 258, Υ 120: ω 159, 170. ἡμέων Γ 101, Λ 318, Φ 458: α 33, ι 498, ξ 271, etc. Dat. ἡμῖν A 67, 147, 214, etc.: α 10, 166, β 31, etc. ἧμιν (ἥμιν) B 339, P 415, 417: θ 569, κ 563, λ 344, ν 177, ρ 376, υ 272. Acc. ἡμέας Θ 211, 529, K 211, etc.: β 86, 244, 330, etc. ἦμας π 372. Pron. of the 1st person pl., we A 583, B 328, 324, Λ 695, N 114, etc.: β 95, γ 276, δ 294, η 202, π 185, etc.—App. sing. π 44.

ἠμείψατο, 3 sing. aor. mid. ἀμείβω.

ἡμείων, genit. ἡμεῖς.

ἦμεν, 1 pl. impf. εἰμί.

ἠμέν [ἦ² μέν]. Correlative with ἠδέ. ἠμὲν . . . ἠδὲ . . ., both . . . and . . .: ἠμὲν νέοι ἠδὲ γέροντες B 789. Cf. E 751, I 36, Λ 7, M 159, O 226, etc.: ἠμὲν ἀπείλησας . . . ἠδὲ . . . (you boasted that . . . and lo . . .) θ 383. Cf. α 97, β 68, γ 105, κ 22, ξ 193, etc.—So ἠμὲν . . . ἠδὲ . . . ἠδὲ . . . Δ 258, etc.—ἠμὲν . . . δὲ . . . M 428.—ἠμὲν . . . τε . . . θ 575.—Retaining something of the original emphasis (surely . . . and even so . . .) A 453, etc.

ἡμέρη, -ης, ἡ [cf. ἦμαρ]. = ἦμαρ (3): ἡ. ἥδε Θ 541 = N 828. Cf. λ 294 = ξ 293, ξ 93, ω 514.

ἡμερίς, ἡ [ἥμερος. Cf. κραταιός, κραταιΐς]. The cultivated vine, the vine ε 69.

ἥμερος, -ον. Tame, domestic: χῆνα ο 162.

ἡμέτερόνδε [acc. of ἡμέτερος + -δε (1)]. To our (my) house: ἡ. ἐλθόντες θ 39. Cf. ο 513, ω 267.

ἡμέτερος, -η, -ον [ἡμεῖς]. (1) Our B 374, Γ 233, Z 58, K 342, Λ 720, etc.: α 45, β 26, ζ 191, λ 33, ν 181, etc.—With the article: αἱ ἡμέτεραι ἄλοχοι B 136.—Absol.: εἰς ἡμέτερον (sc. δῶμα) β 55 = ρ 534.—ἐφ' ἡμέτερα (sc. δώματα) (to our homes, home) I 619.—(2) My A 30, Z 151 = Υ 214, H 363, I 108, O 224, Π 244, T 73, Φ 60, Ω 567: α 397, γ 186, δ 101, θ 255, κ 334, λ 562, π 45, 117, 300, 442, τ 344, φ 375, χ 464, ω 216.—Absol.: ἐς ἡμέτερον (sc. δῶμα) η 301.—ἐφ' ἡμέτερα (sc. δώματα) (home) ο 88. (Sometimes, esp. in uses with οἶκος and the like, it is difficult to say which sense should be preferred.)

ἡμέων, genit. ἡμεῖς.

†**ἠμί.** Only in 3 sing. impf. ἦ. To utter speech, speak, say: ἦ καὶ . . . A 219. Cf. A 528, Γ 292, 310, 355, etc.: β 321, γ 337, ζ 198, ι 371, etc.

ἡμιδαής [ἡμι- + δα(F)-, δαίω¹]. Half-burnt Π 294.

ἡμίθεος [ἡμι- + θεός]. Half-divine, of divine parentage on one side: ἀνδρῶν M 23.

ἡμῖν, ἧμιν, ἥμιν, dat. ἡμεῖς.

ἡμιόνειος, -η, -ον [ἡμίονος]. (1) Drawn by mules Ω 189, 266: ζ 72.—(2) For, worn by, mules Ω 268.

ἡμίονος, -ου, ὁ, ἡ [ἡμι- + ὄνος. 'A half-ass']. (1) A mule (doubtless including the hinny) H 333, K 352, P 742, Ψ 121, Ω 150, etc.: δ 636, ζ 37, η 2, θ 124, ο 85, ρ 298, etc.—In B 852 (ἡμιόνων ἀγροτεράων) app. not strictly mules but some species intermediate between the horse and the ass.—(2) Like ἵππος (3): ἐφ' ἡμιόνων κείμενον (*i.e.* on the waggon) Ω 702.

ἡμιπέλεκκον, -ου, τό [ἡμι- + πέλεκκον in sense 'axe']. A half-axe, an axe with a single cutting edge Ψ 851, 858, 883.

ἥμισυς, -υ [ἡμι-]. (1) Half, half of: ἡμίσεες λαοί γ 155.—(2) Absol., half of what is specified or indicated. (a) ἡμίσεες εἰλεῦντο Φ 7. Cf. γ 157, ω 464.—(b) In neut. ἥμισυ: τιμῆς ἡ. Z 193. Cf. I 580 (following τὸ ἡ. 579 (see below)), P 231 (twice): ι 246 (twice), ν 114, ρ 322.—With the article: τὸ δ' ἡ. κεῖτ' ἐπὶ γαίης N 565. Cf. I 579 —(3) In neut. as adv., to the extent of a half: ἡ. μείρεο τιμῆς I 616.

ἡμιτάλαντον, τό [ἡμι- + τάλαντον]. A half-talent: χρυσοῦ Ψ 751, 796.

ἡμιτελής [ἡμι- + τελέω]. Half-finished, half-built: δόμος B 701.

ἧμος. When, at the time when. **(1)** With indic.: ἦμος δ' ἠέλιος κατέδυ A 475. Cf. A 477, Π 779, etc.: β 1, ι 58, 168, etc.—Introducing a simile μ 439. —Correlative with τῆμος. See τῆμος (2).—**(2)** With subj. in a conditional relative sentence. See Table at end (III) (B) (a) (1).

ἤμῡνε, 3 sing. aor. ἀμύνω.

ἠμύω. (ὑπεμνήμυκε.) **(1)** To cause to bend, bow, droop: κάρη Θ 308.—**(2)** To bend, bow, droop: λήϊον ἠμύει ἀσταχύεσσιν (with its ears) B 148, ἤμυσε καρήατι T 405.—Of a city nodding or tottering to its fall B 373 = Δ 290.

ἤμων, -ονος, ὁ [ἡ-, ἵημι[1]]. One skilled in throwing (the spear): ἤμονες ἄνδρες Ψ 886.

ἤμων, 3 pl. impf. ἀμάω[1].

ἦν, 3 sing. impf. εἰμί.

ἤν [εἰ ἄν]. With subj. **(1)** Introducing in protasis one of two opposed clauses, even if, even though, though, granted that = εἰ (4). For the examples see (II) of Table at end.—**(2)** Introducing the protasis of conditional sentences, if, on condition that, supposing that = εἰ (5). For the examples see (III) of Table.—**(3)** In final clauses, if haply, in the hope that = εἰ (9) (b): ἐμὲ πρόες, ἤν πού τι φόως Δαναοῖσι γένωμαι Π 39. Cf. H 39, Ξ 78, P 245, Υ 172, X 419: ἤν που ἀκούσῃ (ἀκούσω) α 94, β 360, γ 83. Cf. α 282, β 216, ε 417.—**(4)** In an object clause, whether = εἰ (10) (b): ὄφρα ἴδῃ ἤν τοι χραίσμῃ φιλότης O 32.

ἠναίνετο, 3 sing. impf. ἀναίνομαι.

ἤνασσε, 3 sing. impf. ἀνάσσω.

ἥνδανε, 3 sing. impf. ἁνδάνω.

ἤνεικε, 3 sing. aor. φέρω.

ἠνεμόεις, -εσσα [ἄνεμος]. Blown upon or vexed by the winds: ἄκριας ι 400, π 365. Cf. X 145: τ 432.—Epithet of places. Of Troy Γ 305, Θ 499 = M 115, N 724, Σ 174, Ψ 64, 297.—Of Enispe B 606.—Of Mimas γ 172.

ἤνησε, 3 sing. aor. αἰνέω.

ἡνία, τά. The reins used in driving a chariot Γ 261, E 226, 262, 365, Θ 121, Π 404, P 619, Ψ 337, etc.: γ 483, ζ 81.

ἠνίκα. When: ἠ. ἀγινεῖς αἶγας χ 198.

ἡνιοχεύς, ὁ. **(1)** = ἡνίοχος (1) E 505, Θ 312, Π 737.—**(2)** Used loosely of the παραιβάτης (cf. ἡνίοχος (2)) T 401.

ἡνιοχεύω [ἡνίοχος]. **(1)** To act as ἡνίοχος of a war-chariot, drive it Λ 103, Ψ 641, 642.—**(2)** To drive a waggon ζ 319.

ἡνίοχος, -ου, ὁ [ἡνία + ὀχ-, ἔχω. 'He that holds the reins']. **(1)** The driver of a war-chariot as distinguished from the παραιβάτης or fighting man: παραιβάται ἡνίοχοί τε Ψ 132. Cf. E 231, 580, Θ 119, 124 = 316, Θ 126, Λ 47 = M 84, Λ 161, 273 = 399, Λ 280, M 111, N 386, 394, 537 = Ξ 431, P 427, 439, 610, Σ 225, Ψ 280.—**(2)** Used loosely of the παραιβάτης (cf. ἡνιοχεύς (2)): θρασὺν ἡνίοχον φορέοντες Ἕκτορα Θ 89 (Eniopeus was driving, see 119, where he also is called ἡ.).—In pl. including both the ἡ. proper and the παραιβάτης: σὺν ἡνιόχοισι κακοῖσιν P 487.—**(3)** One who drives his chariot in a race: μήτι ἡ. περιγίγνεται ἡνιόχοιο Ψ 318. Cf. Ψ 460, 465, 502.

ἠνίπαπε, 3 sing. aor. ἐνίπτω.

ἦνις [doubtfully explained as fr. ἕνος, cited in sense 'year']. Thus, one year old, that is a yearling: δυοκαίδεκα βοῦς ἤνις Z 94 = 275, 309, βοῦν ἦνιν K 292 := γ 382.

ἦνον, 3 pl. impf. ἄνω[1].

ἠνορέη, -ης, ἡ [ἀνήρ]. Instrumental ἠνορέηφι Δ 303. Manliness, valour, mettle, prowess: ἠνορέηφι πεποιθώς Δ 303. Cf. Z 156, Θ 226 = Λ 9, P 329: ω 509.

ἦνοψ, -οπος. Of unknown meaning. Perh. glittering, gleaming, or the like: ἤνοπι χαλκῷ Π 408, Σ 349 := κ 360.

ἤντεον, 3 pl. impf. See ἀντάω.

ἤντετο, 3 sing. aor. ἄντομαι.

ἦντο, 3 pl. impf. ἧμαι.

ἤνυσε, 3 sing. aor. ἀνύω.

ἠνώγεα, plupf. ἀνώγω.

ἠνώγεον, 3 pl. impf. See ἀνώγω.

ἤνωγον, 3 pl. impf. ἀνώγω.

ἦξε, 3 sing. aor. ἄγνυμι.

ἠοῖος, -η, -ον [ἠώς]. **(1)** Of the east, dwelling in the east, eastern θ 29.—**(2)** In fem. as sb., the morning: πᾶσαν ἠοίην μένομεν δ 447.

ἤομεν, 1 pl. impf. εἶμι.

ἧος. Also **ἕως** β 78. This form scanned as a monosyllable P 727. **(1)** While, so long as: ἧος ζώει ρ 390. Cf. τ 530.—Correlative with τόφρα. See τόφρα (3).—**(2)** While, during the time that: ἧος ὁ ταῦθ' ὥρμαινεν A 193 := δ 120 = ε 365, ἧός μοι πάρ' ὀϊστοί (while I still have them) χ 106. Cf. ν 315 = ο 153, ρ 358.—Correlative with τόφρα. See τόφρα (3).—With τῆος. See τῆος (2).—**(3)** For a time, up to a certain point of time: ἕως μὲν θέουσιν P 727. Cf. M 141, N 143, O 277, P 730: β 148, γ 126 (all that time).—**(4)** Until. **(a)** With indic.: ἧος ὄλεσε θυμόν Λ 342 = Υ 412. Cf. Λ 488: ε 429, η 280, ι 233, ν 321, ο 109.—**(b)** With subj. **(α)** Pure: ἧος ἵκηται ἰσόπεδον N 141.—**(β)** With κεν: ἧός κε τέλος κιχείω Γ 291. Cf. P 622, Ω 154, 183.—**(c)** With opt. **(α)** Pure: ἧος θερμαίνοιτο (to remain there till it should . . .) ι 376. Cf. ψ 151.—**(β)** With κεν: ἕως κ' ἀπὸ πάντα δοθείη β 78.—Correlative with τόφρα. See τόφρα (3).—**(5)** In order that. With opt.: ἧος χυτλώσαιτο ζ 80. Cf. δ 800, ε 386.—After a vb. of praying, that. With opt.: ἀρώμενος ἧος ἵκοιο γῆρας τ 367.

ἧπαρ, -ατος, τό. The liver Λ 579 = N 412 = P 349, Υ 469, 470, Ω 212: ι 301, λ 578, χ 83.

ἤπαφε, 3 sing. aor. ἀπαφίσκω.

ἠπεδανός [prob. for ἀ-πεδ-ανός fr. ἀ-[1] + πεδ-, ποδ-, πούς. 'Not firm on the feet.' Cf. ἔμπεδος]. Thus, weakly, feeble Θ 104: θ 311.

ἠπειρόνδε [acc. of next + -δε (1)]. **(1)** To or on to the land as opposed to the sea: ἐκ πόντου βὰς ἠ. ε 56. Cf. ε 438, ι 73, 485, κ 403, 423, ν 116, ψ 236.—**(2)** To the mainland as opposed to an island: πέμψω σ' ἠ. σ 84, ἀνάξομέν μιν ἠ. 115 (in both cases said in Ithaca).

ἤπειρος, -ου, ἡ. **(1)** The land as opposed to

the sea: νῆ' ἐπ' ἠπείροιο ἔρυσσαν Α 485: εἴτ' ἐπ' ἠπείρου . . . εἴτ' ἐν πελάγει γ 90. Cf. α 162, ε 348, 350, 399, 402, ι 85 = κ 56, ι 496, ν 114, ξ 136, π 325, 359, 367.—(2) Inland parts as opposed to the coast ι 49.—(3) The mainland, as opposed to an island or islands: οἳ ἤπειρον ἔχον Β 635 (the coast of the mainland opposite the islands): οὔτ' ἠπείροιο οὔτ' αὐτῆς Ἰθάκης ξ 97. Cf. ν 235, ξ 100, φ 109, ω 378.

ἠπεροπεύς, ὁ [ἠπεροπεύω]. A cheat, deceiver, cozener, beguiler: ἠπεροπῆά τε καὶ ἐπίκλοπον λ 364.

ἠπεροπευτά, *voc.* [ἠπεροπεύω]. Beguiler (of women) Γ 39 = Ν 769.

ἠπεροπεύω. (1) To deceive, cozen: ἵν' ἐμὰς φρένας ἠπεροπεύσῃς ν 327.—Absol. ξ 400.—To trick, take unfair advantage of Ψ 605.—(2) To beguile the heart of, lead astray (a woman) Ε 349: ο 419.—So τά τε φρένας ἠπεροπεύει γυναιξὶν ο 421.—With direct and cognate acc.: τί με ταῦτα λιλαίεαι ἠπεροπεύειν; (to beguile me thus) Γ 399.

ἠπιόδωρος, -ον [ἤπιος + δῶρον]. App., generous in giving, bountiful in supplying her children's needs, grudging them nothing: μήτηρ Ζ 251.

ἤπιος, -η, -ον. (1) Well or kindly disposed, kindly, gentle, mild, not harsh or rigorous: ἤπια δήνεα οἶδεν (is well disposed towards me) Δ 361 (see εἴδω (III) (12)), ἐθέλω τοι ἠ. εἶναι Θ 40 = Χ 184. Cf. Ω 770, 775: β 47, 230 = ε 8, β 234 = ε 12, κ 337, λ 441, ν 314, ξ 139, ο 152, 490.—Absol. in neut. pl.: εἴ μοι ἤπια εἰδείη (were well disposed towards me) Π 73: ὁμῶς τοι ἤπια οἶδεν (is at one with you in loyalty of heart) ν 405 = ο 39, ἀνάκτεσιν ἤπια εἰδώς (loyal to them) ο 557. See in reference to these εἴδω (III) (12).—(2) Giving kindly tendance, solicitous for the well-being of what is committed to one Ψ 281.—(3) Of speech, tending to effect reconcilement or bring peace υ 327.—(4) Of medicinal applications, soothing, allaying pain Δ 218, Λ 515, 830.

ἠπύτα [ἠπύω. Prob. orig. a voc. turned into a nom.]. Loud-voiced: κῆρυξ Η 384.

ἠπύω. (ἐπ-.) (1) To call to (a person): Κύκλωπας ι 399. Cf. κ 83.—(2) Of the wind, to roar Ξ 399.—Of the lyre, to sound ρ 271.

ἦρ (Fῆρ) [referred to *var*, to choose, wish]. What is pleasing or agreeable. Only in acc. sing. ἦρα in phrase ἦρα φέρειν, to do acceptable service, make oneself agreeable, show oneself well disposed: μητρὶ φίλῃ ἐπὶ ἦρα φέρων Α 572. Cf. Α 578: γ 164, π 375, σ 56.—Sim.: θυμῷ ἦρα φέροντες (yielding to it, giving in to it) Ξ 132.

ἤραρε, 3 sing. aor. ἀραρίσκω.

ἠράσ(σ)ατο, 3 sing. aor. ἔραμαι.

ἤρατο, 3 sing. contr. aor. mid. ἀείρω.

ἠρᾶτο, 3 sing. impf. ἀράομαι.

ᾕρεε, ᾕρει, 3 sing. impf. αἱρέω.

ἠρήρει, 3 sing. plupf. ἀραρίσκω.

ἠρήρειστο, 3 sing. plupf. pass. ἐρείδω.

ἦρι [ἀFερ-. See ἠέριος]. Early in the morning Ι 360: τ 320, υ 156.

ἠριγένεια, -ης [ἦρι + γεν-, γίγνομαι]. Early-born. Epithet of Ἠώς Θ 508, Α 477 = Ω 788: = β 1 = γ 404 = 491 = δ 306 = 431 = 576 = ε 228 = θ 1 = ι 152 = 170 = 307 = 437 = 560 = κ 187 = μ 8 = 316 = ν 18 = ο 189 = ρ 1 = τ 428, δ 195, μ 3, ν 94.—Without Ἠώς, the dawn: οὐδέ σέ γ' ἠ. λήσει χ 197. Cf. ψ 347.

ἤρικε, 3 sing. aor. ἐρείκω.

ἠρίον, τό. A grave-mound, a barrow Ψ 126.

ἤριπε, 3 sing. aor. ἐρείπω.

ἤρκεσε, 3 sing. aor. ἀρκέω.

ἥρμοσε, 3 sing. aor. ἁρμόζω.

ἥρπασε, ἥρπαξε, 3 sing. aor. ἁρπάζω.

ἠρτύναντο, 3 pl. aor. mid. ἀρτύνω.

ἤρυγε, 3 sing. aor. ἐρεύγομαι.

ἠρύκακε, 3 sing. aor. ἐρύκω.

ἠρῶ, 2 sing. impf. ἀράομαι.

ἥρως, -ωος. Genit. ἥρως ζ 303. Dat. ἥρωϊ Ι 613, Ν 582, Ρ 137, Ψ 151, etc.: β 99, τ 144, ω 134. ἥρῳ Η 453: θ 483. (1) A warrior: στίχας ἡρώων Υ 326. Cf. Α 4, Β 483, 579, Π 144 = Τ 391, Σ 56 = 437, Ψ 645: λ 329, φ 299.—With ἄνδρες: στίχας ἀνδρῶν ἡρώων Ε 747 = Θ 391. Cf. Ι 525, Ν 346: α 101, δ 268, λ 629, ω 25, 88.—(2) Prefixed to an ethnic name, of a body of the same race in arms together: ὦ φίλοι ἥρωες Δαναοὶ Β 110 = Ζ 67 = Ο 733 = Τ 78. Cf. Β 256, Μ 165, Ν 629, Ο 219, 230, 261, 702, Τ 34, 41: ω 68.—(3) Prefixed or added as a sort of title to the name or patronymic of a warrior: ἥ. Ἀτρεΐδης Α 102 = Η 322 = Ν 112, Λήϊτος ἥ. Ζ 35. Cf. Β 708, 844, Δ 200, Ζ 63, Η 453, Ι 613, Λ 339, 771, Μ 95, Ν 92, 384, 428, 439, 575, 582, Π 751, 781, Ρ 137, 706, Σ 325, Φ 163, Χ 298, Ψ 151, 747, 893, Ω 474, 574: λ 520.—(4) In voc. as a form of address to a warrior Κ 416, Υ 104.—With a proper name: Εὐρύπυλ' ἥρως Λ 819, 838.—(5) Applied to warriors, but signifying little more than 'the man,' 'the wight': ἔτρεψεν ἀδελφειοῦ φρένας ἥ. Ζ 61. Cf. Γ 377, Η 120 = Ν 788, Κ 179, Ψ 824.—In apposition: ὅ γ' ἥ. ἔστη Ε 308. Cf. Ε 327, Θ 268, Κ 154, Λ 483, Ν 164, Ψ 896.—(6) As an honourable appellation of others than warriors: ἐπὶ φᾶρος βάλετ' ὤμοις ἥ. ο 62. Cf. η 44, θ 242.—With ἄνδρες ξ 97.—With an ethnic name: ἥρωας Ἀχαιούς α 272.—(7) Prefixed or added as a sort of title to the name or patronymic of another than a warrior: Λαέρτην ἥρωα α 189. Cf. β 15, 99 = τ 144 = ω 134, β 157 = ω 451, γ 415, δ 21 = 303, 617 = ο 117, ζ 303, η 155, θ 483, λ 342, ξ 317, ο 52, 121, 131, σ 423, χ 185.—(8) In voc. as a form of address to another than a warrior δ 423, η 303, κ 516.—With a proper name: Τηλέμαχ' ἥρως δ 312.

ἦσαν, 3 pl. impf. εἰμί.

ἥσατο, 3 sing. aor. ἥδομαι.

ἥσει, 3 sing. fut. ἵημι[1].

ἦσθα, 2 sing. impf. εἰμί.

ἧσι, 3 sing. aor. subj. ἵημι[1].

ἦσι, 3 sing. subj. εἰμί.

ἤσκειν, 3 sing. impf. ἀσκέω.

ἧσο, imp. ἧμαι.

ἥσσων, -ονος [for ἡκjων. Comp. fr. ἦκα. Cf.

ἥκιστος]. (1) Of less worth or merit, inferior Π 722, Ψ 322, 858.—(2) In neut. ἧσσον as adv., less: ὀλίγον τί μ' ἧ. ἐτίμα ο 365.

ἧσται, 3 sing. ἧμαι.

ἤστην, 3 dual impf. εἰμί.

ἡσυχίη, ἡ [ἡσύχιος]. Peace, freedom from disturbance: ἡ. ἂν ἐμοὶ καὶ μᾶλλον ἔτ' εἴη σ 22.

ἡσύχιος. At peace, undisturbed Φ 598.

ᾐσχυμμένος, pf. pple. pass. αἰσχύνω.

ᾔσχῡνε, 3 sing. aor. αἰσχύνω.

ἥσω, fut. ἵημι[1].

ἦτε, 2 pl. impf. εἰμί.

ἦτε. See ἠέ.

ᾐτιάασθε, 2 pl. impf. αἰτιάομαι.

ἠτίμασε, 3 sing. aor. ἀτιμάζω.

ᾐτιόωντο, 3 pl. impf. αἰτιάομαι.

ἤτοι. See ἤ[2].

ἦτορ, τό. Only in nom. and acc. sing. (1) The heart: πάλλεται ἦ. ἀνὰ στόμα Χ 452. Cf. Κ 93.—(2) The 'heart,' breast,' soul, mind. As the seat or a seat (a) (α) Of life, vitality, the vital powers, strength (cf. θυμός (I) (1) (a)): εἰ χάλκεόν μοι ἦ. ἐνείη Β 490: τετιημένος ἦ. η 287. Cf. δ 703 = ψ 205, τ 136, ω 345.—Hence (β) The animating principle, the vital spirit, the soul, the life, life, one's life (cf. θυμός (I) (1) (b)): μὴ ἦ. ὀλέσσῃς Ε 250. Cf. Λ 115 (of fawns), Ο 252, Π 660, Ρ 535, Φ 201, Ω 50: ἀπορραῖσαι ἦ. π 428.—(b) Of spirit, courage, stoutness, resolution, endurance: ἄλκιμον ἦ. Ε 529. Cf. Γ 31, Π 209, 242, 264 (of wasps), Ρ 111 (of a lion), Τ 169, Υ 169 (of a lion), Φ 114, 425, 571, Ω 205, 521: μινύθει τοι ἦ. ἑταίρων δ 374. Cf. δ 467, 481 = κ 496, ε 297 = 406 = χ 147, ι 256, κ 198 = 566 = μ 277, χ 68.—(c) Of anger, wrath, passion: κεχολωμένος ἦ. (in his heart) Ξ 367. Cf. Κ 107, Ω 585.—(d) Of desire or appetite: σίτοιο ἄσασθαι ἦ. Τ 307.—(e) Of volition: τί σφῶϊν μαίνεται ἦ.; Θ 413. Cf. Ο 166, 182: δῶρον ὅττι κέ μοι δοῦναι ἦ. ἀνώγῃ α 316.—(f) Of feelings, emotions, moods: τετιημέναι ἦ. Θ 437, χαίρει μοι ἦ. Ψ 647. Cf. Ε 364, 670, Ι 9, 705, Κ 575 (their tired hearts), Λ 556, Ν 84, Ο 554, Π 450, 509, Τ 366, Φ 389, Χ 169: ἦ. οἱ ἰάνθη δ 840, τάφος οἱ ἦ. ἵκανεν ψ 93. Cf. α 48, 60, 114, β 298, δ 538, 804, η 269, θ 303, ι 62 = 105 = 565 = κ 77 = 133, κ 313, ν 286, 320, ο 481, π 92, ρ 46, 514, σ 153, υ 22, 84, ψ 53.—(g) Of the faculty of deliberating or considering: ἦ. οἱ μερμήριξεν Α 188.—Of recollection: ὥς μοι ἰνδάλλεται ἦ. τ 224.—(h) Of one's character or disposition: ἀμείλιχον ἦ. ἔχουσα Ι 572. Cf. Ι 497: ψ 172.

ἠϋγένειος [ἠΰ-, εὐ- (5) + γενειάς]. Well-bearded. Epithet of lions Ο 275, Ρ 109, Σ 318: δ 456.

ηὔδα, 3 sing. impf. αὐδάω.

ἠΰκομος, -ον [ἠΰ-, εὐ- (5) + κόμη]. With beautiful hair, fair-tressed. Epithet of goddesses and women. Of Leto Α 36, Τ 413: λ 318.—Of Thetis Δ 512, Π 860.—Of Athene Ζ 92, 273, 303.—Of Here Κ 5.—Of Calypso θ 452, μ 389.—Of Briseïs Β 689.—Of Helen Γ 329 = Η 355 = Θ 82, Ι 339, Λ 369, 505, Ν 766.—Of Niobe Ω 602.—μητέρος Ω 466.

ἠΰς. See ἐΰς.

ἤϋσε, 3 sing. aor. αὔω[2].

ἠΰτε [cf. εὖτε]. (1) As when, introducing similes. With indic. Β 87, 455, 480, Γ 3, Π 487, Φ 573, Χ 139.—With subj. Ρ 547.—Without expressed vb. Β 469, Ο 618, Ρ 737: φ 48.—(2) Like, as: ἠΰτ' ὀμίχλη Α 359. Cf. Β 754, Δ 243, Η 219, Τ 374, etc.: θ 280, 518, λ 222, ρ 463, etc.—(3) After a comp., than: μελάντερον ἠΰτε πίσσα Δ 277.

Ἥφαιστος [use of the proper name]. A fire: σπλάγχν' ὑπείρεχον Ἡφαίστοιο Β 426.

ἦφι, instrumental fem. See ἑός.

ἤφυσε, 3 sing. aor. ἀφύσσω.

ἠχή, -ῆς, ἡ (Ϝηχή) [cf. (Ϝ)ι(Ϝ)άχω, (Ϝ)ι(Ϝ)αχή]. Sound, noise: ἠχῇ θεσπεσίῃ Θ 159 = Ο 590, Μ 252, Ν 834, Ο 355, Π 769, Ψ 213: γ 150, λ 633. Cf. Β 209, Ν 837.

ἠχήεις, -εσσα (Ϝηχήεις) [(Ϝ)ηχή]. Sounding. Epithet of the sea Α 157.—Of a house, echoing δ 72.

ἤχθετο[1], 3 sing. impf. ἄχθομαι.

ἤχθετο[2], 3 sing. aor. ἐχθάνομαι.

ἤχθηρε, 3 sing. aor. ἐχθαίρω.

ἧχι [ἧ (see ὅς[2] (II) (6)) + advbl. suff. -χι]. Where: ἧ. ἑκάστῳ δῶμα Ἥφαιστος ποίησεν Α 607. Cf. Γ 326, Ε 774, Θ 14, Λ 76: γ 292, ζ 94, τ 553.—In an object clause: ἄλλους πευθόμεθ', ἧ. ἕκαστος ἀπώλετο γ 87.

ἤχλῡσε, 3 sing. aor. ἀχλύω.

ἥψατο, 3 sing. aor. mid. ἅπτω.

ἠῶθεν [ἠώς + -θεν (1)]. From the dawn; hence, at dawn, in the morning. Referring to the next morning: ἠ. ἴτω ἐπὶ νῆας Η 372. Cf. Η 381, Λ 555 = Ρ 664, Σ 136, Ψ 49, Ω 401: ἠ. ἀγορήνδε καθεζώμεσθα κιόντες α 372. Cf. γ 153, 366, δ 214, η 189, μ 293, ξ 512, ο 308, 506, ρ 600, σ 248, τ 320, φ 265, 280, ω 72.

ἠώς, -οῦς, ἡ (ἠϜώς) [αϜοσ-. Cf. ἠέριος]. Dat. ἠοῖ (ἠόϊ) Η 331, Λ 685, Ν 794, Ω 600, etc.: δ 407, μ 24, ξ 266, π 2, etc. Acc. ἠῶ (ἠόα) Ε 267, Θ 565, Ι 240, Σ 255, etc.: β 434, η 288, π 368, ψ 243, etc. Locative ἠῶθι Λ 50: ε 469, ζ 36. (1) Dawn, the dawn, the daybreak: ἅμ' ἠοῖ Η 331, Ι 618, 682, Λ 685, Ω 600, ὅσον τ' ἐπικίδναται ἠ. Η 451, 458, ἠῶθι πρό (in front of the dawn, with the dawn) Λ 50: ε 469, ζ 36. Cf. Ε 267, Η 433, Θ 1, 508, Κ 251, Ψ 227, Ω 12, 695: δ 194, 407, ζ 31, η 222, μ 24, ξ 266 = ρ 435, ο 50, 396, π 2, 270.—(2) A dawning or morning considered as a space of time: ὄφρ' ἠ. ἦν Θ 66 = Λ 84, ἠοῦς ὄψεαι (in the morning) Θ 470, τὸν [μῦθον] ἠοῦς (the morrow's) 525. Cf. Φ 111: νηῦς ἠῶ πεῖρε κέλευθον (through the morning) β 434. Cf. η 288, ι 56.—(3) A morning considered as a point or unit of time or as one of a series: δυωδεκάτη Α 493 = Ω 31, Φ 80, Ω 413. Cf. Ν 794, Φ 156, Ω 781, 785: τ 192, 571.—(4) The quarter of the dawn, the east: πρὸς ἠῶ τ' ἠέλιόν τε Μ 239: ι 26, ν 240. Cf. κ 190.—(5) The dawn personified: ῥοδοδάκτυλος Ἠ. Α 477 = Ω 788, Ζ 175, Ι 707, Ψ 109, Ἠ. ἐκ λεχέων ὄρνυτο Λ 1. Cf. Β 48, Θ 565, Ι 240, 662, Λ 723, Σ 255, Τ 1,

Ω 417 : Ἠοῦς υἱός δ 188. Cf. β 1, ε 1, 121, 390, ζ 48, ι 151, κ 541, μ 3, ψ 243, etc.

θαάσσω [cf. θόωκος, θῶκος]. To sit, be seated: ἕδος ἔνθα θάασσεν Ι 194. Cf. Ο 124 : δηθὰ θεῶν ἐν δαιτὶ θαασσέμεν γ 336.

θαιρός, ὁ. App. vertical (presumably metal) pegs at the top and bottom of a side of a gate working in stone sockets and governing the opening and shutting Μ 459.

θαλάμη, -ης, ἡ [cf. θάλαμος]. A den or hole ε 432.

θαλαμηπόλος, ἡ [θάλαμος + -πολος, conn. with πολεύω]. A female servant in charge of the sleeping-rooms, a chamber-maid η 8, ψ 293.

θάλαμόνδε [acc. of next + -δε (1)]. To the θάλαμος (in sense (4)) β 348, φ 8, χ 109, 161.

θάλαμος, -ου, ὁ. A room or chamber. **(1) (a)** A sleeping-chamber, a bed-room: πρόσθεν θαλάμοιο θυράων Ι 473 (app. a room built in the αὐλή and opening into the αἴθουσα near the πρόδομος; or perh. a portion of the αἴθουσα next the πρόδομος walled off). Cf. Ι 475 : ὅθι οἱ θ. αὐλῆς δέδμητο α 425 (αὐλῆς app. local genit., 'in the . . .'; cf. Ι 473 above), ἐς θάλαμον ᾧ ἔνι κούρη κοιμᾶτο ζ 15. Cf. α 436, 441, β 5 = δ 310, γ 413, η 7, κ 340, τ 48.—**(b)** A bridal chamber: γήμας ἐκ θαλάμοιο μετὰ κλέος ἵκετ' Ἀχαιῶν (leaving his just wedded wife) Λ 227.—**(c)** The sleeping-chamber occupied by a married pair: θάλαμον λιποῦσα (*i.e.* the bed of Menelaus) Γ 174. Cf. Γ 382, 391, 423, Ζ 244, 248, Ι 582, 588, Ρ 36 : νοσφισσαμένην θάλαμόν τε πόσιν τε δ 263. Cf. ψ 178, 192, 229, 295.—Of such a room in the palace of Zeus Ξ 166, 188, 338.—In the palace of Hephaestus θ 277.—**(2)** A chamber appropriated to the lady of a house and her maidens: ὡρμᾶτ' ἐκ θαλάμοιο Γ 142 (the same as the μέγαρον of 125). Cf. Ζ 316, 321, 336 : ἐξ Ἑλένη θαλάμοιο ἤλυθεν δ 121. Cf. δ 718, 802, ρ 36 = τ 53, ρ 506.—In pl. of the women's apartments generally: νύμφας ἐκ θαλάμων ἠγίνεον Σ 492 (cf. χ 143 cited under (4); or this may be the pl. of indefiniteness like νύμφας in this line and γάμοι and εἰλαπίναι in the prec. line) (*v.l.* ἐς θαλάμους, which would go under (1) (b)): μυχῷ θαλάμων ἥμεθα ψ 41.—**(3)** A work-room Δ 143.—**(4)** A room for storage or safe custody, a store-room, a treasure-chamber: θύρη θαλάμοιο ἀνέρος ἀφνειοῖο Ω 317 : χηλὸν ἐξέφερεν θαλάμοιο θ 439, ἀνέβαινε ἐς θαλάμους χ 143 (app. meaning a single room; cf. Σ 492 cited under (3)). Cf. Ζ 288, Χ 63, Ω 191, 275 : β 337, γ 441, ζ 74, ο 99, π 285, τ 17, 256, φ 42, χ 140, 155, 157, 166, 174, 179, 180, ω 166.

θάλασσα, -ης, ἡ. **(1)** The sea: πολυφλοίσβοιο θαλάσσης Α 34. Cf. Α 157, 437, 496, Β 159, 294, Δ 248, etc.: πεφευγότες θάλασσαν α 12. Cf. α 50, 52, β 260, 407, γ 142, δ 435, 501, 504, ε 401, 413, 418, ζ 95, 272, etc.—**(2)** Distinguished in terms from the land: γαίης νέρθε καὶ θαλάσσης Ξ 204. Cf. Θ 24.—From the land and the heavens Σ 483 : μ 404 = ξ 302.—From other waters Φ 196.—**(3)** Personified: γλαυκή σε τίκτε θ. Π 34.—**(4)** Sea-water: θ. κήκιε πολλή ε 455. Cf. Κ 572.

θαλάσσιος [θάλασσα]. Of or pertaining to the sea: ἔργα Β 614 : ε 67.

θαλέθω [θάλλω]. In pres. pple., flourishing, luxuriant: θάμνος ἐλαίης ψ 191.—Of youths, lusty, in prime of vigour ζ 63.—Of swine: θαλέθοντες ἀλοιφῇ (swelling with fat) Ι 467, Ψ 32.

θαλερός, -ή, -όν [θάλλω]. **(1)** Lusty, in prime of vigour: αἰζηοί Γ 26. Cf. Δ 474, Ζ 430, Θ 156, 190, Κ 259, Ξ 4, etc.—**(2)** Of a woman, blooming, in pride of beauty: παράκοιτιν Γ 53.—**(3)** Of marriage, app. giving the notion of the union of a pair in prime of youth ζ 66, υ 74.—**(4)** Of parts of the body, well-developed, stout: μηρώ Ο 113.—Of a horse's mane, long, flowing Ρ 439.—**(5)** Of the voice, full, rich Ρ 696 = Ψ 397 : = δ 705 = τ 472.—**(6)** Of tears, big Β 266, Ζ 496, Ω 9, 794 : δ 556, κ 201, 409, 570, λ 5, 391, 466, μ 12, π 16, χ 447.—**(7)** Of lamentation, loud, vehement κ 457.—**(8)** Of fat, thick, abundant θ 476.

θαλίη, -ης, ἡ [θάλλω]. Abundance, plenty Ι 143, 285.—In pl.: τέρπεται ἐν θαλίῃς λ 603.

θαλλός, ὁ [θάλλω]. Green stuff, fodder: θαλλὸν ἐρίφοισι φορῆναι ρ 224.

†**θάλλω.** Pf. pple. τεθηλώς μ 103. Fem. τεθαλυῖα, -ης Ι 208 : ζ 293, λ 192, 415, ν 245, 410. 3 sing. plupf. τεθήλει ε 69. **(1)** Of vegetation, to grow profusely, flourish, be luxuriant: ἡμερὶς τεθήλει σταφυλῇσιν (flourished with its . . .) ε 69.—**(2)** In pf. pple. **(a)** Growing profusely, flourishing, luxuriant: ἐρινεὸς φύλλοισι τεθηλώς μ 103.—Sim. of a garden, etc.: τέμενος τεθαλυῖά τ' ἀλωή ζ 293.—Of autumn (the season of 'mellow fruitfulness') λ 192.—**(b)** Of the fat or lard of swine, rich ν 410.—Sim.: συὸς ῥάχιν τεθαλυῖαν ἀλοιφῇ (rich with . . .) Ι 208.—**(c)** Of dew, copious ν 245.—**(d)** Of a feast, sumptuous, affording good cheer λ 415.

θάλος, τό [θάλλω]. A young shoot or branch. Fig. of a youthful person Χ 87 : ζ 157.

†**θαλπιάω** [θάλπω]. Pres. pple. θαλπιόων. To be warm: εὖ θαλπιόων τ 319.

θάλπω. To warm, to make flexible by the application of heat φ 179, 184, 246.

θαλπωρή, ἡ [θάλπω]. Warmth; hence **(1)** Comfort, consolation, cheering: οὐκ ἄλλη ἔσται θ. Ζ 412. Cf. α 167.—**(2)** Heartening, confidence: μᾶλλον θ. ἔσται Κ 223.

θάλυς, -εια, -υ [θάλλω]. **(1)** Of a feast, sumptuous, affording good cheer Η 475 : γ 420, θ 76, 99.—**(2)** Absol. in neut. pl., good cheer: θαλέων ἐμπλησάμενος κῆρ Χ 504.

θαλύσια, τά [θάλλω]. A sacrifice of first fruits: χωσαμένη ὅ οἱ οὔ τι θ. ῥέξεν Ι 534.

θαμά [adv. answering to θαμέες]. Often: ταῦτά με θ. ἐβάζετε Π 207. Cf. Ο 470 : α 143, 209, δ 178, 686, ο 516, π 27, τ 521.

θαμβέω [θάμβος]. **(1)** To wonder, be struck with wonder or astonishment: θάμβησεν Ἀχιλεύς Α 199. Cf. Γ 398, Θ 77, Ψ 728 = 881, Ω 483, 484 : θαμβήσασα βεβήκει α 360 = φ 354. Cf. α 323, δ 638, κ 63, ω 101.—(**2**) To wonder or marvel at: *ὄρνιθας* β 155. Cf. π 178, ρ 367.

θάμβος, *τό.* Genit. *θάμβευς* ω 394. Wonder, astonishment, amazement: *θ. ἔχεν εἰσορόωντας* Γ 342. Cf. Δ 79, Ψ 815, Ω 482: γ 372, ω 394.

θαμέες. Nom. pl. fem. *θαμειαί.* Acc. *θαμειάς.* (**1**) Set or standing closely together: *ἔνθα θαμειαὶ εἴρυντο νέες* Σ 68. Cf. K 264, M 296, T 383 = X 316: *ἀραρὼν θαμέσι σταμίνεσσιν* ε 252. Cf. μ 92, ξ 12.—(**2**) Coming, flying, falling, thick and fast: *θαμέες ἄκοντες ἀΐσσουσιν* Λ 552 = P 661, *ὥς τε νιφάδες πίπτωσι θαμειαί* M 278. Cf. M 44, 287, Ξ 422.—(**3**) Occurring at short intervals over a space, numerous: *πυραὶ καίοντο θαμειαί* A 52.

θαμίζω [*θαμά*]. (**1**) To come often to, frequent, an indicated place: *πάρος γε μὲν οὔ τι θαμίζεις* Σ 386 = 425: ε 88.—(**2**) To go about, ply one's vocation: *ἅμα νηῒ θαμίζων* θ 161.—(**3**) With pass. pple., to be accustomed to treatment of an indicated kind: *οὔ τι κομιζόμενός θάμιζεν* (was not wont to be (so) cared for) θ 451.

θάμνος, ὁ [cf. *θαμέες*]. (**1**) A bush, shrub, small tree: *θάμνῳ ὑπ' ἀμφικόμῳ* P 677. Cf. Λ 156, X 191: *δοιοὺς ὑπήλυθε θάμνους* ε 476, *θάμνος ἐλαίης* (consisting of . . .) ψ 190. Cf. χ 469 —(**2**) In pl., a thicket: *θάμνων ὑπεδύσετο* ζ 127. Cf. ε 471, η 285.

θανατόνδε [acc. of *θάνατος* + -δε (1)]. To one's death: *ὡς εἰ θ. κιόντα* Ω 328. Cf. Π 693, X 297.

θάνατος, -ου, ὁ [*θαν-*, *θνήσκω*]. (**1**) Death A 60, B 302, Γ 101, E 68, I 571, etc.: β 100, γ 236, δ 180, ι 467, λ 488, etc.—(**2**) Personified: *Ὕπνῳ κασιγνήτῳ Θανάτοιο* Ξ 231. Cf. Π 454, 672 = 682.—(**3**) A kind or mode of death: *λευγαλέῳ θανάτῳ ἁλῶναι* Φ 281 := ε 312, *πάντες στυγεροὶ θάνατοί [εἰσιν]* μ 341. Cf. λ 412, ο 359, σ 202, χ 462, ω 34.

θανέεσθαι, fut. infin. *θνήσκω.*

θάνον, aor. *θνήσκω.*

†**θάομαι**[1] [*θαϝ-*. Cf. *θαῦμα, θηέομαι*]. 3 pl. aor. opt. *θησαίατο.* To admire, look at with admiration σ 191.

†**θάομαι**[2] [*θη-* as in *τι-θή-νη*]. Non-thematic pres. infin. *θῆσθαι* δ 89. 3 sing. aor. *θήσατο* Ω 58. (**1**) To suck (the breast): *γυναῖκα θήσατο μαζόν* (double acc. of whole and part, 'a woman's breast') Ω 58.—(**2**) To suck (milk): *παρέχουσι γάλα θῆσθαι* (for their young to suck) δ 89.

θάπτω. 3 pl. aor. *θάψαν* Ω 612. 3 sing. plupf. pass. *ἐτέθαπτο* λ 52. (*κατα-*.) To pay funeral rites to (a corpse): *ὁππότ' Ἀμαρυγκέα θάπτον Ἐπειοί* Ψ 630. Cf. Φ 323, Ψ 71, Ω 612, 665: *οὐ πω ἐτέθαπτο* λ 52. Cf. γ 285, μ 12, ω 417.

θαρσαλέος, -η, -ον [*θάρσος*]. (**1**) Bold, stout, courageous, spirited, confident: *πολεμιστὴν* E 602 = Π 493 = X 269. Cf. T 169, Φ 430, 589: η 51.—Neut. comp. *θαρσαλεώτερον* in impers. construction: *θ. ἔσται* (one would feel more confidence, have better heart) K 223.—(**2**) Over-bold, audacious, presuming: *θαρσαλέος τις προΐκτης* ρ 449. Cf. τ 91.

θαρσαλέως [adv. fr. prec.]. (**1**) Boldly, confidently: *ἀγόρευεν* α 382 = σ 411 = υ 269. Cf. α 385.—(**2**) Too boldly or confidently: *ἀγορεύεις* σ 330 = 390.

θαρσέω [*θάρσος*]. 3 pl. pf. *τεθαρσήκᾱσι* I 420, 687. (**1**) To be of good heart or courage, of good cheer: *θαρσῶν μάχεσθαι* E 124, *τεθαρσήκασι λαοί* (are (now) of good heart) I 420 = 687.—In imp. *θάρσει* Δ 184, Θ 39 = X 183, K 383, O 254, Σ 463, Ω 171: β 372, δ 825, θ 197 (*τόνδε γ' ἄεθλον*, as touching this . . .), ν 362 = π 436 = ω 357, τ 546, χ 372.—(**2**) In aor., to take heart, pluck up courage: *θαρσήσας εἰπέ* A 85. Cf. A 92, Υ 338: γ 76, 252.

θάρσος, *τό* [= *θράσος*]. Genit. *θάρσευς* P 573. (**1**) Boldness, courage, spirit, confidence: *σῷ θάρσει* Z 126. Cf. E 2, H 153, P 570, 573, Φ 547: α 321, γ 76, ζ 140, ι 381, ξ 216.—(**2**) Excessive boldness or confidence: *θ. ἄητον ἔχουσα* Φ 395.

θάρσυνος, -ον [*θάρσος*]. Having plucked up courage: *Τρώων πόλις ἐπὶ πᾶσα βέβηκεν θ.* Π 70.—Taking courage: *θ. οἰωνῷ* (from the . . .) N 823.

θαρσῡ́νω [*θάρσος*]. 3 sing. pa. iterative *θαρσύνεσκε* Δ 233. 2 sing. aor. *θάρσῡνας* ν 323. 3 -ε K 190. Subj. *θαρσύνω* γ 361. Imp. *θάρσῡνον* Π 242. (*ἐπι-*.) To encourage, hearten, cheer, put spirit into: *τοὺς θάρσυνε μύθῳ* K 190. Cf. Δ 233, N 767 = P 117 = 683, Π 242, Σ 325, Ψ 682: γ 361, ι 377, ν 323, π 448, ω 448.

θάσσων, -ονος [for *θακίων*. Comp. of *ταχύς* with transference of aspirate]. (**1**) Swifter: *ποσὶν θ.* (with the feet, in running) O 570. Cf. N 819.—(**2**) In neut. *θᾶσσον* as adv. (**a**) The quicker, the speedier, the sooner: *ὄφρα κε θ. ἐγείρομεν Ἄρηα* B 440. Cf. Z 143 = Υ 429, M 26, Ψ 53: β 307, κ 33.—(**b**) Quickly rather than slowly, quickly, with speed: *θ. Ἀθηναίῃ ἐπιτεῖλαι* Δ 64. Cf. N 115, Π 129, P 654, T 68, Υ 257: *ἔρρ' ἐκ νήσου θ.* κ 72. Cf. η 152, κ 44, 192, 228, 268, ο 201, π 130, υ 154, ω 495.

θαῦμα, *τό* [*θαϝ-* as in *θάομαι*[1]]. (**1**) Wonder, amazement: *θ. μ' ἔχει* κ 326.—(**2**) A wonder or marvel: *θ. ἰδέσθαι* (to behold) E 725, K 439, Σ 83, 377, *μέγα θ. τόδ' ὁρῶμαι* (this is a great wonder that I see) N 99 = O 286 = Υ 344 = Φ 54. Cf. Σ 549: ζ 306, η 45, θ 366, ι 190, λ 287, ν 108, ρ 306, τ 36.

θαυμάζω [*θαῦμα*]. 3 pl. pa. iterative *θαυμάζεσκον* τ 229. 3 sing. fut. in mid. form *θαυμάσσεται* Σ 467. (*ἀπο-*.) (**1**) To wonder, marvel, to feel or be struck with wonder, astonishment or admiration: *γυναῖκες ἱστάμεναι θαύμαζον* Σ 496. Cf. Ω 394: *θαύμαζεν ὁ γεραιός* γ 373. Cf. δ 44, η 145, θ 265, ν 157, π 203.—With dependent clause: *θαυμάζομεν οἷον ἐτύχθη* B 320.—(**2**) To wonder or marvel at, look upon with wonder or eager curiosity: *πτόλεμόν τε μάχην τε* N 11. Cf. K 12, Σ 467: *λιμένας καὶ νῆας* η 43. Cf. α 382 = σ 411 = υ 269, δ 655, ι 153, τ 229, ω 370.—With infin.: *οἷον θαυμάζομεν* (impf.) *Ἕκτορα αἰχμητὴν ἔμεναι* (thinking that he was . . .) E 601.—To look upon or behold (a person) with respectful wonder and admiration: *Πρίαμος θαύμαζ' Ἀχιλῆα* Ω 629. Cf. Ω 631: θ 459.

†**θαυμαίνω** [as prec.]. Nom. pl. masc. fut. pple.

θαυμανέοντες. To witness or watch with eager interest: ἀέθλια θαυμανέοντες θ 108.

θάψαν, 3 pl. aor. θάπτω.

θεά, -ᾶς, ἡ [fem. of θεός]. Dat. pl. θεῇσι Θ 305. Λ 638, Τ 286: η 291. θεῇς Γ 158. θεαῖς ε 119. (**1**) A female divine (or semi-divine) being, a goddess: εἰ θεά σε γείνατο μήτηρ Α 280 (Thetis). Cf. Α 1, Β 182, Γ 396, Θ 305, Σ 429, etc.: Καλυψώ, δῖα θεάων α 14, θεά οἱ ἔκλυεν ἀρῆς δ 767 (Athene). Cf. β 392, ε 215, κ 222, μ 131, υ 393, etc.—(**2**) A goddess as distinguished in terms from a god: εἰρωτᾷς με θεὰ θεόν ε 97. Cf. Κ 50.—From a woman: θεᾶς οὐδὲ γυναικός Ξ 315.—(**3**) With the name of a particular goddess. With Ἥρη Α 55, Ε 711, Θ 350, etc.—With Ἀθήνη Α 206, Β 166, Ε 405, etc.: α 44, β 382, γ 13, etc.—With Ἠώς Β 48.—With Θέτις Ι 410, Ο 76, Σ 127, etc.—With Θέμις Ο 93.—With Ἶρις Ο 206, Σ 182.—With Ἐρινύς ο 234.

θέαινα, ἡ [fem. as prec. Cf. λέαινα, lioness]. A goddess as distinguished from a god: πάντες τε θεοὶ πᾶσαί τε θέαιναι Θ 5 = Τ 101, Θ 20. Cf. θ 341.

θέειον, -ου, τό. Also **θήϊον** χ 493. Sulphur. (**1**) In reference to the sulphurous smell associated with a thunderbolt: δεινὴ θεείου γίγνεται ὀδμή Ξ 415. Cf. Θ 135: μ 417, ξ 307.—(**2**) Used for cleansing by fumigation: ἐκάθηρε θεείῳ Π 228. Cf. χ 481, 493.

θεειόω [θέειον] (διαθειόω.) To cleanse with the fumes of sulphur χ 482.—In mid. ψ 50.

θείην, aor. opt. τίθημι.

θειλόπεδον, τό [app. θείλη = εἵλη, the sun's warmth + πέδον, the ground]. A warm spot in a vineyard in which the grapes were left to be dried by the sun, a 'sun-trap' η 123.

θεῖναι, aor. infin. τίθημι.

θείνω. 3 sing. aor. ἔθεινε Φ 491. θεῖνε Π 339. 3 sing. subj. θείνῃ σ 63. Pple. θείνας Υ 481. To strike, smite: μή σε ἴδωμαι θεινομένην Α 588. Cf. Ζ 135, Κ 484, Π 339, Ρ 430, Υ 481, Φ 21, 491: ὅς κέ σε θείνῃ σ 63. Cf. ι 459, χ 443.

θείομεν, 1 pl. aor. subj. τίθημι.

θεῖος, -η, -ον [θεός]. (**1**) Partaking of the nature of the gods, divine, immortal: θείοιο γέροντος (Proteus) δ 395.—(**2**) Consisting of gods: ἀγῶνα (see ἀγών (1) (a)) Η 298, Σ 376.—(**3**) Connected with the gods, sacred: ἁλός Ι 214 (perh. as used for purifying sacrifices): χορόν θ 264 (app. from the dance being regarded as a matter of ritual).—(**4**) Of divine origin, from a divine source, divine: Ὄνειρος Β 22, 56, ὀμφή Β 41, γένος Ζ 180, πύργου Φ 526 (app. as god-built; see 446 and cf. Η 452, Θ 519): ὄνειρος ξ 495.—Applied to persons of divine descent: Ἴλου Κ 415 (he was descended from Zeus; see Υ 215-232), Ἡρακλῆος Ο 25, Υ 145, ἀνδρὸς θείοιο Ἀχιλλῆος Π 798, Πηλεΐδαο Ρ 199, Ἀχιλλῆος Τ 279, 297: Ἐνιπῆος λ 238 (since all rivers spring from Zeus).—(**5**) Applied to kings as holding their office from Zeus δ 621, 691, π 335.—To heralds as under his special protection Δ 192, Κ 315.—To bards as singing by divine inspiration Σ 604: = δ 17, α 336, θ 43, 47, 87, 539, ν 27, π 252, ρ 359, ψ 133, 143, ω 439.—(**6**) Applied as a mere epithet of honour to Odysseus Β 335, Ι 218, Κ 243, Λ 806: α 65, β 233, 259, γ 398, δ 682, etc.—To Oïleus Ν 694 = Ο 333.—To Thoas Ξ 230.—To Munes Τ 296.—(**7**) Denoting a superlative degree of excellence or beauty: ποτόν β 341, ι 205, δόμον δ 43.

θεῖσα, aor. pple. fem. τίθημι.

θείω[1]. See θέω.

θείω[2], aor. subj. τίθημι.

θέλγω. 3 sing. pa. iterative θέλγεσκε γ 264. 3 fut. θέλξει π 298. 3 sing. aor. ἔθελξε Ο 322: κ 318. Pple. θέλξας Ν 435. Infin. θέλξαι κ 291. 2 sing. aor. pass. ἐθέλχθης κ 326. 3 pl. ἔθελχθεν σ 212. (κατα-.) (**1**) To work upon by spells or enchantment, bewitch, charm Ω 343: = ε 47, κ 291, 318, 326, ω 3.—Sim. of the operation of passion: ἔρῳ θυμὸν ἔθελχθεν σ 212.—(**2**) Of divine interference, to lay a spell upon, bind up from activity: Ἀχαιῶν νόον Μ 255. Cf. Ν 435, Ο 322, 594: π 298.—(**3**) To work upon by wiles, cajole, lead on to one's hurt, prejudice, or dishonour: Ἀγαμεμνονέην ἄλοχον γ 264. Cf. α 57, μ 40, 44, σ 282.—(**4**) To beguile, deceive, cheat: δόλῳ [μιν] ἔθελγεν Φ 604. Cf. Φ 276: ξ 387, π 195.—(**5**) To charm, delight, ravish ρ 521.—In mid.: οἷα μυθεῖται, θέλγοιτό κέ τοι ἦτορ ρ 514.

θελκτήριον, τό [θέλγω]. (**1**) A means of enchantment, a spell Ξ 215.—(**2**) A means of propitiating or placating: θεῶν θελκτήριον θ 509.—(**3**) Something that charms or delights α 337.

θέλξαι, aor. infin. θέλγω.

θέλω. See ἐθέλω.

θέμεθλα, τά [θε-, τίθημι]. (**1**) The root or bed (of the eye) Ξ 493.—(**2**) The lower part (of the throat) Ρ 47.

θεμείλια, τά [as prec.]. Supports, consisting of stakes or stones, set to contain the face of an earthwork or mound (cf. στήλη (1)) Μ 28, Ψ 255.

θέμεναι, θέμεν, aor. infin. τίθημι.

θέμις, -ιστος, ἡ [θε-, τίθημι] (**1**) In pl., a body of traditionary rules or precedents: βασιλεύς, ᾧ δῶκε Κρόνου πάϊς θέμιστας Β 206. Cf. Α 238, Ι 99: ι 112, 215 (see δίκη (2)).—In sing.: ὃς οὔ τινα οἶδε θέμιστα Ε 761 (has no regard for any usage of decency; see εἴδω (III) (12)).—(**2**) What is established or sanctioned by custom or usage: ἣ θ. ἐστίν Β 73 (as is my right), Ι 33 (do.), Ψ 581 (as usage requires), Ω 652 (as the custom is), ἣ θ. ἀνθρώπων πέλει (as is the way of . . .) Ι 134, ἣ θ. ἐστὶν ἤ τ' ἀνδρῶν ἤ τε γυναικῶν (as is the way of . . .) 276 = Τ 177, ξείνια παρέθηκεν, ἅ τε ξείνοις θ. ἐστίν (which by the customs of hospitality one . . .) Λ 779, ἄορ ἔχων· τῷ δ' οὐ θ. ἐστὶ μιγῆναι (mortal must not encounter it) Ξ 386, πάρος γ' οὐ θ. ἦεν . . . (it was not permitted . . .) Π 796, οὐ θ. ἐστὶ . . . (it must not be that . . .) Ψ 44: ἣ θ. ἐστίν γ 45 (as the custom is), 187 (as is your due), λ 451 (as it is his privilege to do), ἣ τε ξείνων θ. ἐστίν (as . . . use to do) ι 268, οὔ μοι θ. ἐστὶ . . . (I may not . . .) κ 73, ξ 56, ἣ θ. ἐστὶ γυναικός (as a woman's way ever is) 130, ἐπεί μοι

. . . θ. ἐστίν (since it is my right to . . .) π 91, ἡ γὰρ θ. ὅς τις . . . (for that is due to him who . . .) ω 286.—(3) A judgment or doom Π 387.—(4) An ordinance or decree Ι 156, 298.—(5) An oracular reply (in answer to an inquiry as to what is right to be done) π 403.—(6) A place of judgment Λ 807.—(7) As proper name, a goddess with such functions as may be gathered from the name and the context Ο 87, 93, Υ 4 : β 68.

θεμιστεύω [θέμις]. To pronounce judgments, act as judge λ 569.—(2) With genit. (like ἀνάσσω (3) (a)), to rule over, be master of: παίδων ι 114.

θεμόω [θε-, τίθημι]. To drive or carry in a specified direction: νῆα χέρσον ἱκέσθαι ι 486, 542.

θέναρ, -αρος, τό. App., the palm of the hand Ε 339.

θέντες, nom. pl. masc. aor. pple. τίθημι.

θέντων, 3 pl. aor. imp. τίθημι.

θέο, aor. imp. mid. τίθημι.

θεόδμητος [θεός + δμη-, δέμω]. God-built: πύργων Θ 519 (cf. Φ 526 cited under θεῖος (4)).

θεοειδής (θεοϜειδής) [θεός + (Ϝ)εἶδος]. Divine of form, godlike. Epithet of persons Β 623, 862, Γ 16, Μ 94, Ρ 494, 534, Τ 327, Ω 217, etc. : α 113, δ 628, ζ 7, η 231, κ 205, ο 271, φ 277, etc.

θεοείκελος (θεοϜείκελος) [θεός + (Ϝ)είκελος]. Like the gods, godlike. Epithet of persons Α 131 = Τ 155 : γ 416, δ 276, θ 256.

θεόθεν [θεός + -θεν (1)]. From, at the hands of, the gods : θ. οὐκ ἔστ' ἀλέασθαι [θάνατον] π 447.

θεοπροπέω [θεοπρόπος]. To reveal the divine will Α 109, Β 322 : β 184.

θεοπροπίη, -ης, ἡ [θεοπρόπος]. A disclosure of the divine will, the divine will as disclosed to a seer: οὐ θεοπροπίης ἐμπάζομαι Π 50. Cf. Λ 794, Π 36 : α 415, β 201.—In pl. Α 87, 385.

θεοπρόπιον, -ου, τό [as prec.]. =prec. : εἰπὲ θεοπρόπιον ὅ τι οἶσθα Α 85.—In pl. Ζ 438.

θεοπρόπος [app., 'one who prays to a god,' fr. θεός + προπ-, perh. conn. with L. *precor*]. One who reveals the divine will, a seer Μ 228 : α 416.—Joined with οἰωνιστής Ν 70.

θεός, -οῦ, ὁ, ἡ. Instrumental θεόφιν. With a word expressing likeness Η 366, Ξ 318, Ρ 477 : γ 110, 409. This form as ablative Ρ 101, Ψ 347. (1) A divine being, a god Α 28, Β 318, Γ 230, Ε 177, Θ 200, Ξ 168, Π 531, Τ 3, Χ 10, Ω 460, etc. : α 323, β 5, δ 236, θ 177, μ 88, ρ 475, τ 396, φ 258, ω 445, etc.—(2) A god as distinguished in terms from a goddess: εἰρωτᾷς με θεὰ θεόν ε 97. Cf. Κ 50.—From a mortal: ἠμὲν θεὸν ἠδὲ καὶ ἄνδρα Ε 128. Cf. Τ 417, Χ 9, Ω 259, etc. : δ 397, 654, etc. —(3) Without reference to any particular god, the divine power, heaven: θεός που σοὶ τό γ' ἔδωκεν Α 178. Cf. Β 436, Ζ 228, Η 4, Ι 49, Ρ 327, Φ 47, etc. : οὐκ ἄνευ θεοῦ β 372. Cf. γ 131, θ 170, ι 158, λ 292, ρ 399, σ 265, etc.—(4) A goddess Α 516, Γ 381, Δ 58, Ε 331, 339, 839, Ζ 380 = 385, Θ 7, Σ 394, Ω 223 : α 420, β 297, 406 = γ 30 = ε 193 = η 38, δ 831 (twice), ε 194, 459, ζ 149, 150, η 41, 71, 246, 255, θ 467 = ο 181, κ 136 = λ 8 = μ 150, κ 297, μ 449, ν 189, υ 47.—(5) A goddess as distinguished in terms from a woman: ἢ θεὸς ἠὲ γυνή κ 228, 255.—(6) In pl., the gods: τίς θεῶν; Α 8, θεοί μοι αἴτιοί εἰσιν Γ 164. Cf. Α 18, Β 321, Δ 1, Ζ 138, Η 360, Ι 485, Μ 8, etc. : α 17, β 66, δ 379, ε 335, η 132, λ 276, μ 394, etc.—(7) In pl., the gods as distinguished in terms from the goddesses: πάντες τε θεοὶ πᾶσαί τε θέαιναι Θ 5 = Τ 101, Θ 20. Cf. θ 341. —From mortals: πρός τε θεῶν πρός τ' ἀνθρώπων Α 339. Cf. Α 403, Ι 239, Ξ 233, Φ 264, etc. : α 338, β 211, π 265, ω 64, etc.

θεουδής (θεοδϜής) [for θεοδϜεής fr. θεός + δϜ-, δείδοικα]. Acc. sing. θεουδέα (for θεουδεέα) τ 364. God-fearing, reverencing the gods ζ 121 = ι 176 = ν 202, θ 576, τ 109, 364.

θεραπεύω [θεράπων]. To do service to, serve. With dat. : ᾧ πατρί ν 265.

θεράπων, -οντος, ὁ. (1) A follower, retainer or henchman: θεράποντες ἀπ' ὤμων τεύχε' ἕλοντο Η 122. Cf. Α 321, Ε 48, Ζ 53, Λ 843, Ν 600, Ο 401, Π 272 = Ρ 165, Τ 143, 281, Ω 396, 406, 573 : ἴσθμιον ἤνεικεν θ. σ 300. Cf. α 109, δ 23 = 217, δ 38, 784, π 253, 326 = 360, σ 297, 424.—Fig. of warriors: θεράποντες Ἄρηος Β 110 = Ζ 67 = Ο 733 = Τ 78. Cf. Η 382, Θ 79, Κ 228, Τ 47.—Of kings: θεράποντε Διός λ 255.—(2) A warrior in honourable personal attendance on another, the relation of the two resembling generally that of squire and knight: ἠΰς θ. Ἀχιλῆος (Patroclus) Π 653. Cf. Η 149, Λ 322, 620, Ν 246, 331, Ο 431, Π 165 = Ρ 388, Π 244, 279, 464, 865, Ρ 164, 271, Σ 152, Ψ 90, 113 = 124, 528, 860 = 888.—(3) Applied to a warrior's ἡνίοχος: ἵππους θ. ἀπάνευθ' ἔχεν Δ 227, ἡνίοχον θεράποντα Ε 580. Cf. Ζ 18, Θ 104, 109, 113, 119, Λ 341, 488, Μ 76, 111, Ν 386, Υ 487.

θερμαίνω [θερμός]. 3 sing. aor. subj. θερμήνῃ Ξ 7. (ὑπο-.) To heat Ξ 7 : ι 376.

θερμός [θέρω]. Warm, hot: λοετρά Ξ 6, Χ 444. Cf. Η 426, Λ 266, Π 3, Ρ 438, Σ 17, 235 : δ 523, θ 249, 451, ι 388, ξ 77, τ 362, 388, ω 46.

†θέρμω [θέρω]. 2 pl. aor. imp. θέρμετε θ 426. 3 sing. aor. mid. θέρμετο Σ 348, Ψ 381 : θ 437. (1) To warm, heat: ὕδωρ θ 426.—(2) In mid., to become warm or hot: θέρμετο δ' ὕδωρ Σ 348 : = θ 437. Cf. Ψ 381.

θέρος, τό [θέρω. 'The hot season']. Genit. θέρευς η 118. Summer : θέρεϊ (in summer) Χ 151 : χείματος οὐδὲ θέρευς (in winter or summer) η 118. —As distinguished from ὀπώρη, early summer λ 192, μ 76, ξ 384.

θέρω. Fut. pple. mid. θερσόμενος τ 507. Aor. subj. pass. θερέω ρ 23. (1) In mid., to warm oneself: φόως ἔμεν ἠδὲ θέρεσθαι τ 64. Cf. τ 507. —(2) In pass., to be warmed: ἐπεί κε πυρὸς θερέω (genit. of material) ρ 23.—To be burnt: μὴ ἄστυ πυρὸς θέρηται Ζ 331. Cf. Λ 667.

θές, aor. imp. τίθημι.

θέσαν, 3 pl. aor. τίθημι.

θέσθαι, aor. infin. mid. τίθημι.

θέσκελος [the first element seems to be the same as in θέσ-φατος]. (1) App., marvellous, wondrous, or the like : ἔργα Γ 130 : λ 374, 610.—

(2) So in neut. θέσκελον as adv., marvellously, in wondrous wise: ἔϊκτο θέσκελον αὐτῷ Ψ 107.

θεσμός, ὁ [θεσ-, τίθημι]. Place, site ψ 296.

θεσπέσιος, -η, -ον [θε-, θεός + σ(ε)π-. See ἐννέπω]. (1) Absol. in fem., sentence pronounced by a god, the will of heaven: εἰ καὶ θεσπεσίῃ πόλιν οὐκ ἀλαπάξεις B 367.—(2) Of song, befitting a god, divinely sweet B 600.—Of singers, heavenly sweet of voice: Σειρήνων μ 158.—(3) (a) Of shouting or lamentation, such as might come from a god's throat, immense, deafening: ἠχῇ Θ 159 = O 590, M 252, N 834, O 355. Cf. Π 295, Σ 149: βοή ω 49. Cf. γ 150, λ 43, 633.—(b) Of inarticulate sounds. Of the sound of branches of trees smiting each other Π 769.—Of that of rushing winds N 797, Ψ 213.—(4) The force of the second element lost (a) Of or pertaining to the gods, divine: βηλοῦ A 591.—(b) Indicating a high degree of some quality such as abundance, greatness, greatness of extent, completeness, swiftness, beauty, sweetness or the like: πλοῦτον B 670. Cf. B 457, I 2, O 669, P 118, Υ 342: ὀδμή ι 211. Cf. β 12 = ρ 63, η 42, θ 19, ι 68 = μ 314, ι 434, ν 363, υ 289, ω 6.

θεσπεσίως [adv. fr. prec.]. In sense corresponding to prec. (4)(b): θ. ἐφόβηθεν (in panic rout) O 637.

θεσπιδαής, -ές (θεσπιδαFής) [θε-σπ- as in θεσπέσιος (with the force of the second element lost) + δα(F)-, δαίω[1]]. Epithet of fire, defying human efforts, devouring, consuming M 177, 441, O 597, Υ 490, Φ 342, 381, Ψ 216: δ 418.

θέσπις [θε-σπ- as in θεσπέσιος]. = θεσπέσιος (2). Of song α 328, θ 498.—Of a singer ρ 385.

θέσφατος, -ον [the second element φα-, φημί. The first explained as θεσ-, θεός]. (1) Pronounced or ordained by a god or by the divine will. Neut. in impers. construction: ὡς γὰρ θέσφατόν ἐστιν Θ 477.—With infin.: θανέειν δ 561. Cf. κ 473.—(2) Absol. in neut. pl. θέσφατα, divine ordinances or decrees: οὔ τι θεῶν ἐκ θ. ἤδη E 64. Cf. ι 507 = ν 172, λ 151, 297, μ 155.—(3) = θεσπέσιος (4) (b): ἀήρ η 143.

θέτο, 3 sing. aor. mid. τίθημι.

θεύσεαι, 2 sing. fut. θέω.

θέω [θεF-]. Also **θείω** [prob. for θή(F)ω, fr. θηF-, long form of θεF-]. 3 pl. pa. iterative θέεσκον Υ 229. 2 sing. fut. in mid. form θεύσεαι Ψ 623. Infin. θεύσεσθαι Λ 701. (ἀμφι-, προ-, συν-, ὑπεκπρο-.) (1) Of men, horses, etc., to run, speed: θέεις ἀκίχητα διώκων P 75, ἵπποι βάρδιστοι θείειν Ψ 310. Cf. B 183, Δ 244, Z 54, O 442, T 415, Ψ 387, etc.: γ 112, 370, δ 202, θ 123, 247, ξ 501, ρ 308, χ 99, 106.—To run a race, contend in a race Λ 701, Ψ 623.—(2) Of the motion of a ship: νηῦς ἔθεεν κατὰ κῦμα A 483: = β 429. Cf. γ 281, μ 407, ν 86, 88, ξ 299, ο 294.—Of a person in a ship: ὅτε κεῖνος ἐν νηυσὶ Μαλειάων ὄρος ἶξε θέων γ 288.—Of a rolling stone N 141.—Of a δίσκος θ 193.—Of a potter's wheel Σ 601.—(3) Of things, to run or extend: ἄντυξ ἣ πυμάτη θέεν ἀσπίδος Z 118. Cf. Z 320 = Θ 495, N 547, Υ 275: περὶ κλίσιον θέε πάντῃ ω 208.

θέωμεν, 1 pl. aor. subj. τίθημι.

θεώτερος, -η [comp. fr. θεός] Holy as distinguished from common: [θύραι] ν 111.

θῆαι, 2 sing. aor. subj. mid. τίθημι.

θήγω. 3 sing. aor. imp. mid. θηξάσθω B 382. (1) To sharpen, whet. In mid.: δόρυ B 382.—(2) Of a boar whetting his tusks Λ 416, N 475.

†θηέομαι [θαF-. Cf. θάομαι[1]]. 2 sing. opt. θηοῖο Ω 418. 3 sing. impf. θηεῖτο ε 75, ζ 237, η 133, θ 265. 1 pl. ἐθηεύμεσθα ι 218. 3 θηεῦντο H 444, K 524, Ψ 728, 881: β 13, ρ 64. 2 sing. aor. θηήσαο ω 90. 3 θηήσατο ε 76, η 134, ο 132. 3 pl. ἐθηήσαντο τ 235. θηήσαντο O 682, X 370: θ 17, κ 180. 2 sing. opt. θηήσαιο ρ 315. 3 -αιτο ε 74. (1) To look or gaze upon, view, behold, with interest, curiosity, wonder, admiration: πολέες ἑ θηήσαντο O 682. Cf. H 444, K 524, X 370: μαρμαρυγὰς ποδῶν θ 265. Cf. β 13 = ρ 64, ε 76 = η 134, ι 218, κ 180, ο 132, τ 235.—(2) To look about one with wonder or admiration: στὰς θηεῖτο ε 75, η 133.—To look upon something with wonder, to wonder, marvel, be astonished: λαοὶ θηεῦντο Ψ 728 = 881: θηεῖτο κούρη ζ 237. Cf. ε 74, θ 17, ρ 315, ω 90.—With dependent clause: θηοῖό κεν οἷον . . . Ω 418.

θήῃ, 3 sing. aor. subj. τίθημι.

θηητήρ [θηέομαι]. An admirer, fancier φ 397.

θηΐον = θέειον.

θῆκε, 3 sing. aor. τίθημι.

θηλέω [θη-, θάλλω]. (ἀνα-.) To teem with, abound in. With genit.: ἴου ε 73.

θῆλυς [θη-, θάομαι[2]]. Also in regular fem. form θήλεια B 767, Θ 7, Λ 681, Υ 222: δ 636, ι 439, ξ 16, φ 23. (1) Female: θήλεια θεός Θ 7, ὄϊν θῆλυν K 216. Cf. B 767, E 269, Λ 681, T 97, Υ 222, Ψ 409: δ 636 = φ 23, ι 439, κ 527, 572, ξ 16.—Comp. θηλυτέρη, female as opposed to male: θεαί θ 324, γυναικῶν λ 386. Cf. Θ 520: λ 434 = ο 422 = ω 202, ψ 166.—(2) Characteristic of women, feminine: θῆλυς ἀϋτή ζ 122.—(3) Of dew, copious: θῆλυς ἐέρση ε 467.

θημών, -ῶνος, ὁ [θη-, τίθημι]. A heap ε 368.

θην. Enclitic affirmative particle: οὔ θην δηρὸν βέῃ Π 852. Cf. I 394, Λ 365 = Υ 452, O 288, P 29, Φ 568: γ 352, π 91.—With mocking or ironical force: οὔ θήν μιν ἀνήσει θυμὸς νεικείειν B 276. Cf. Θ 448, K 104, N 620, 813, Ξ 480: οὐ μέν θην κείνης γε χερείων εὔχομαι εἶναι ε 211.

θηξάσθω, 3 sing. aor. imp. mid. θήγω.

θήρ, θηρός, ὁ. Dat. pl. θήρεσσι ε 473, ξ 21. θηρσί ω 292. A wild beast, wild creature Γ 449, Θ 47, K 184, Λ 119, 546, Ξ 283, O 151, 324, 586, 633, Φ 470, 485: ε 473, λ 573, ξ 21, ω 292.

θηρευτής, ὁ [θηρεύω]. A hunter M 41.—With κύων, a hunting dog: ἐν κυσὶ θηρευτῇσιν Λ 325.

θηρεύω [θήρ]. To hunt, engage in hunting: ὥς μιν θηρεύοντ' ἔλασεν σῦς τ 465.

θήρη, -ης, ἡ [θήρ]. (1) Hunting, the chase: αἵμονα θήρης E 49. Cf. K 360: τ 429.—(2) The quarry: ἔδωκε θεὸς μενοεικέα θήρην ι 158.

θηρητήρ, -ῆρος, ὁ [θηράω = θηρεύω]. A hunter E 51, Λ 292, O 581, P 726, Φ 574.—Of a bird of prey: αἰετοῦ, τοῦ θηρητῆρος Φ 252. Cf. Ω 316.—Of despoilers of a wasps' nest Μ 170.

θηρήτωρ, -ορος, ὁ. =prec. Ι 544.

θηρίον, τό [prob. θήρ + suffix distinguishing an individual from a class]. A wild beast: μάλα μέγα θηρίον ἦεν κ 171, 180.

θής, θητός, ὁ. A labourer for hire δ 644.

θησαίατο, 3 pl. aor. opt. θάομαι[1].

θήσατο, 3 sing. aor. θάομαι[2].

θῆσθαι, non-thematic pres. infin. θάομαι[2].

θήσω, fut. τίθημι.

θητεύω [θητ-, θής]. To serve as a hired labourer: θητεύσαμεν μισθῷ ἔπι ῥητῷ Φ 444. Cf. λ 489, σ 357.

θίς, θινός, ὁ. (1) The beach or shore of the sea: ἐπὶ θινὶ β 408. Cf. η 290, ι 46, 551.—The beach or shore (of the sea): παρὰ θῖνα θαλάσσης Α 34. Cf. Α 316, 327, 350, Δ 248, Ι 182, Λ 622, Ν 682, Ξ 31, Τ 40, Ψ 59, Ω 12: β 260, γ 5, δ 432, 779, ζ 94, 236, θ 49, κ 154, 179, 402, 407 = μ 367, κ 569, λ 75, ν 65, 220, ξ 347, ο 205, π 358.—App., a piece of the shore covered by shallow water: ὡς δ' ὅτ' ἀναπάλλεται ἰχθὺς θῖν' ἐν φυκιόεντι Ψ 693.—(2) A heap: ὀστεόφιν θὶς μ 45.

†**θλάω**. 3 sing. aor. ἔθλασε σ 97. θλάσσε Ε 307, Μ 384. To smash, crush: κοτύλην Ε 307, κυνέην Μ 384, ὀστέα σ 97.

†**θλίβω**. 3 sing. fut. mid. θλίψεται. To press or rub: πολλῇς φλιῇσι θλίψεται ὤμους ρ 221.

θνήσκω. Fut. infin. in mid. form θανέεσθαι Δ 12, Ο 728: υ 21. Aor. θάνον λ 412. 2 sing. θάνες Χ 486: ω 37. 3 ἔθανε Φ 610: γ 248, θ 226. θάνε Β 642: α 396, β 96, ο 253, τ 141, ω 131. 3 pl. θάνον Μ 13: ι 66, λ 389, ω 22. Subj. θάνω Λ 455, Σ 121. 2 sing. θάνῃς Δ 170, Χ 55. 3 θάνῃσι Τ 228: δ 196, λ 218. 1 pl. θάνωμεν μ 156. 3 θάνωσι Η 410. 3 sing. opt. θάνοι ο 359. 3 pl. θάνοιεν χ 472. Imp. θάνε Φ 106. Pple. θανών, -όντος Η 80, Θ 476, Λ 453, Ο 350, Π 457, 675, Ρ 120, 182, 379, 538, 564, Σ 195, Φ 28, Χ 73, 343, 389, Ψ 9, 70, 223, Ω 16, 575: α 236, γ 258, δ 553, ε 310, λ 486, 554, ρ 115, 312, ω 77, 79, 93, 190, 296, 436. Infin. θανέειν Ο 289, Χ 426: α 59, δ 562, ε 308, μ 342, ξ 274. θανεῖν Η 52. 3 sing. pf. τέθνηκε Σ 12: α 196, β 132, δ 110, 199, 834, 837, λ 461, 464, υ 208, ω 264. 3 pl. τεθνᾶσι Η 328, Χ 52: λ 304, ο 350. Opt. τεθναίην Σ 98. 2 sing. τεθναίης Ζ 164. 3 τεθναίη Γ 102. Imp. τέθναθι Χ 365. 3 sing. τεθνάτω Ο 496. Pple. τεθνηώς Ρ 161. Genit. τεθνηῶτος Ι 633, Ν 659, Σ 173, Τ 210, Ψ 192, Ω 244: α 289, β 220. τεθνηότος Ρ 435: ο 23, ω 56. Dat. τεθνηῶτι κ 494. τεθνεῶτι τ 331. Acc. τεθνηῶτα Ζ 464, Π 858, Ρ 229, 341, Σ 537, Τ 289, 403, Χ 364: μ 10. τεθνηότα Ρ 402, Τ 300, Ω 20. Genit. pl. τεθνηώτων Π 16. Acc. τεθνηῶτας Ζ 71. τεθνηότας ψ 84. Acc. sing. fem. τεθνηυῖαν δ 734. Infin. τεθνάμεναι Ω 225. τεθνάμεν Ο 497, Ρ 405, Τ 335: π 107, υ 317, φ 155. (ἀπο-, ἐκ-, κατα-.) (1) To die: θνήσκων ἔλιπε Θυέστῃ Β 106. Cf. Α 56, 383, Δ 12, 170, Η 52, 410, Λ 455, Ο 728, Σ 121, Τ 228, Φ 106, Χ 55, Ω 743: θανέειν ἱμείρεται α 59. Cf. δ 196, 562, ε 308, θ 526, λ 218, μ 22, 156, 342, ξ 274, ο 359, υ 21, χ 472.—(2) In a *quasi*-passive sense of being slain in battle: χερσὶν ὑπ' Αἴαντος θανέειν Ο 289. Cf. Α 243, Χ 426.—(3) In aor. indic. (a) In strict aor. sense: αἶψ' ἔθανεν Εὔρυτος θ 226. Cf. γ 248, ι 66, λ 389 = ω 22, λ 412, ω 37.—In pple.: ἀνδρὸς τῆλε θανόντος (that met his death . . .) ρ 312, θανὼν φθιμένοισι μετείην (may I die and . . .) ω 436.—(b) To have died, be dead: θάνε Μελέαγρος Β 642. Cf. Μ 13, Φ 610, Χ 486: ἐπεὶ θάν' Ὀδυσσεύς α 396, β 96 = τ 141 = ω 131. Cf. ο 253.—In pple.: ὄφρα πυρός με λελάχωσι θανόντα (in death) Η 80 = Χ 343, περὶ Πατρόκλοιο θανόντος (the dead . . .) Θ 476, Ρ 120, 182, Σ 195, Μενοιτιάδαο θανόντος ἄχεος (for the death of . . .) Ρ 538, οὔ μεν ζώοντος . . ., ἀλλὰ θανόντος (now that I am dead) Ψ 70. Cf. Λ 453, Ο 350, Ρ 379, 564, Φ 28, Χ 73, Ψ 223, Ω 16, 575: οὔ κε θανόντι περ ὧδ' ἀκαχοίμην (if he were dead) α 236, ζωὸς ἠὲ θανών (alive or dead) δ 553, μή τι θανὼν ἀκαχίζευ (let not thy death grieve thee) λ 486. Cf. γ 258, ε 310, λ 554, ρ 115, ω 77, 79, 93.—Absol. in pl. pple., the dead: γέρας θανόντων Π 457 = 675, Ψ 9: ω 190, 296. Cf. Χ 389.—(4) In pf. (a) To be dead: τεθναίη (let him lie dead) Γ 102, πολλοὶ τεθνᾶσιν Η 328, οὔ ποτε ἔλπετο τεθνάμεν (that he was dead) Ρ 405. Cf. Ζ 164, Ο 496, 497, Σ 12, 98, Τ 335, Χ 52, 365, Ω 225: ζώει ὅ γ' ἦ τέθνηκεν β 132, δ 110, 837 = λ 464. Cf. δ 199, 834 = ω 264, λ 304, ο 350, π 107, υ 208, 317, φ 155.—In pple., dead: νεκροὺς τεθνηῶτας (the dead bodies) Ζ 71. Cf. Ζ 464, Ι 633, Ν 659, Π 16, 858, Ρ 161, 229, 341, 402, 435, Σ 173, 537, Τ 210, 289, 300, 403, Χ 364, Ψ 192, Ω 20, 244: εἴ κε τεθνηῶτος ἀκούσῃς (hear of his death) α 289. Cf. β 220, δ 734, κ 494, μ 10, ο 23, τ 331, ψ 84, ω 56.—(b) In strict pf. sense: οὔ πω τέθνηκεν Ὀδυσσεύς (Ὀρέστης) α 196, λ 461.

θνητός, -ή [θνη-, θνήσκω]. (1) Mortal, liable to death Α 339, Κ 403, Ν 322, Π 622, Φ 569, etc.: α 219, γ 3, λ 244, μ 118, υ 46, etc.—(2) Absol., a mortal man, a man: ἕνεκα θνητῶν Α 574, τί δόμεν Πηλῆϊ θνητῷ; (to Peleus, to a mortal) Ρ 444. Cf. Μ 242, Ρ 547, Υ 64: τ 593.—Fem.: θνητὰς ἀθανάτῃσιν ἐρίζειν ε 213.

θοινάω [θοίνη, a meal]. To entertain at table: ἐς αὐτοὺς προτέρω ἄγε θοινηθῆναι δ 36.

θόλος, -ου. A building, app. of no great size, within the αὐλή, of unknown nature and use χ 442 = 459, 466.

θοός, -ή, -όν [θεϝ-, θέω]. (1) Quick in movement, nimble, swift, fleet: θοός περ ἐὼν πολεμιστής Ε 571. Cf. Ε 536, Μ 306, Ο 585, Π 422, 494.—(2) (a) Epithet of Ares Ε 430, Θ 215, Ν 295 = 328, 528, Π 784, Ρ 72, 536.—Of warriors Β 542, 758, Ε 462.—(b) Of ships Α 12, 300, 308, Β 619, Ι 332, Μ 112, etc.: α 260, 303, γ 61, δ 173, 255, 779, etc.—(c) Of night (app. thought of as a body of darkness passing swiftly over the earth) Κ 394, 468, Μ 463, Ξ 261, Ω 366 = 653: μ 284.—(d) Of a chariot Λ 533 = Ρ 458.—(e) Of a whip, quickly making itself felt Ρ 430.—(f) Of a meal, perh., deftly served θ 38.—(g) Of a missile χ 83.—(3) νήσοισιν ἐπιπροέηκε θοῇσιν ο 299. Doubtfully explained (cf. *θοόω*) as the 'sharp' or 'pointed islands,' supposed to form part of the group called the Echinades.

θοόω [poss. conn. with prec. and meaning orig. 'to make quick or active,' acquiring the sense of sharpening when applied to weapons, etc.]. To sharpen, put a point upon: *ἐθόωσα* [*ῥόπαλον*] ι 327.

θόρε, 3 sing. aor. *θρῴσκω*.

θοῦρος, and in fem. form **θοῦρις,** -*ιδος*, with acc. -*ιν* [*θορ-*, *θρῴσκω*]. Rushing, impetuous, eager for the fray. Epithet (1) Of Ares E 30, 35, 355, 454, 507, 830, 904, O 127, 142, Φ 406, Ω 498.—(2) Of *ἀλκή* Δ 234, Z 112, H 164, Λ 313, Σ 157, etc.: δ 527.—(3) Of a shield, app. by transference of epithet from the bearer to the shield: *ἀσπίδα θοῦριν* Λ 32, Υ 162.—Sim. of the aegis O 308.

θόωκος. See *θῶκος*.

θοῶς [adv. fr. *θοός*]. Quickly, speedily Γ 325, 422, E 533, 722, 748 = Θ 392, Θ 219, Π 145: ε 243, ζ 92, θ 443, 447, ι 469, ξ 72, 248, ο 216, 447, π 350, φ 46, 241, χ 19, ψ 372, ω 220.

θράσος, *τό* [= *θάρσος*]. Boldness, courage: *οὐκ ἔχει θράσος ὅς κεν ἴδηται* Ξ 416.

θρασυκάρδιος [*θρασύς* + *καρδίη*]. Stout of heart K 41, N 343.

θρασυμέμνων, -*ονος* [*θρασύς* + *μεμ-*, *μάω*]. Of bold spirit, stout of heart E 639: λ 267.

θρασύς, -*εῖα* [cf. *θράσος*]. (1) Bold, stout: *ἡνίοχον* Θ 89, 126, *ἡνιοχῆα* 312.—Epithet of Hector M 60 = 210, N 725, X 455, Ω 72, 786.—Of other heroes Θ 128, Π 604: κ 436.—(2) Of hands, stout, strong Λ 553 = P 662, Λ 571, N 134, O 314, Ψ 714: ε 434.—(3) Epithet of war, carried on with spirit, strenuous Z 254, K 28: δ 146.

θρέξασκον, 3 pl. pa. iterative *τρέχω*.

θρέπτρα, *τά* [*θρεπ-*, *τρέφω*]. Recompense for rearing due by a child to his parents: *οὐδὲ τοκεῦσι θ. ἀπέδωκεν* Δ 478 = P 302.

θρέψα, aor *τρέφω*.

θρηνέω [*θρῆνος*]. To sing a dirge, wail Ω 722: ω 61.

θρῆνος, *ὁ* [cf. *θρόος*]. A funeral-song, a dirge: *θρήνων ἐξάρχους* Ω 721.

θρῆνυς, *ὁ*. (1) A foot-stool Ξ 240, Σ 390: = κ 315 = 367, α 131, δ 136, ρ 409, 462, 504, τ 57.—(2) Prob. a plank or gangway connecting the forward and after *ἴκρια* of a ship: *ἀνεχάζετο θρῆνυν ἐφ' ἑπταπόδην, λίπε δ' ἴκρια* O 729.

θριγκός, *ὁ*. (1) An uppermost course in a wall, a coping ρ 267.—(2) A frieze running along the upper part of the inner walls of a house η 87.

θριγκόω [*θριγκός*]. To finish off the upper part of the wall of (an enclosure) with something intended to give protection or to prevent exit: *ἐθρίγκωσεν* [*αὐλήν*] *ἀχέρδῳ* ξ 10.

θρίξ, *τριχός*, *ἡ*. Always in pl. (1) The hair of the head: *πολιὰς τρίχας* X 77. Cf. Ψ 135 (locks of hair): ν 399, 431, σ 355.—The hair on the limbs: *ὀρθαὶ τρίχες ἔσταν ἐνὶ μέλεσσιν* Ω 359.—(2) The hairs of the mane of a horse Θ 83.—The hairs of a horse's tail Ψ 519.—The hair on the head of an ox γ 446.—Of the wool of sheep Γ 273.—Of the bristles of swine T 254: κ 239, 393, ξ 422.

θρόνα, *τά*. Figures or designs in woven work: *ἐν θρόνα ἔπασσεν* (*i.e.* in the web) X 441.

θρόνος, -*ου*, *ὁ*. A seat or chair: *καθέζετ' ἐπὶ θρόνου* A 536. Cf. Θ 199, 442, Λ 645, Ξ 238, O 124, 142, 150, Σ 389, 422, Υ 62, Ω 515, 522, 553: *κατὰ κλισμούς τε θρόνους τε* (the two words hardly to be distinguished) α 145. Cf. α 130, δ 51, ε 86, ζ 308, θ 65, ρ 32, υ 96, χ 23, etc.

θρόος, *ὁ*. Sound, noise; hence, speech Δ 437.

†**θρυλίσσω.** 3 sing. aor. pass. *θρυλίχθη*. To crush, bruise: *θρυλίχθη μέτωπον* Ψ 396.

θρύον, *τό*. Collectively, rushes Φ 351.

θρῴσκω. 3 sing. aor. *ἔθορε* Δ 79, H 182, O 573: κ 207. *θόρε* Θ 320, O 582, Υ 381, Ψ 353, 509. 3 pl. *θόρον* Θ 252, Ξ 441, O 380. 3 pl. subj. *θόρωσι* χ 303. Pple. *θορών*, -*όντος* E 161, K 528, Λ 70, O 580, Π 770, 773. Fem. *θοροῦσα* ψ 32. (*ἀνα-*, *ἀπο-*, *ἐκ-*, *ἐν-*, *ἐπι-*, *ἐσ-*, *προ-*, *ὑπερ-*.) To leap, spring, bound, dart: *κὰδ δ' ἔθορ' ἐς μέσσον* Δ 79. Cf. E 161, Θ 252 = Ξ 441, Θ 320 = Ψ 509, K 528, Λ 70 = Π 770, O 380, 573, 580, 582, 684, Υ 381, Φ 126: *ἀπὸ λέκτροιο θοροῦσα* ψ 32. Cf. χ 303.—Of inanimate objects: *ἐκ δ' ἔθορε κλῆρος κυνέης* H 182. Cf. N 589, O 314, 470, Π 773, Ψ 353: κ 207.

θρωσμός [*θρῴσκω*]. Only in phrase *ἐπὶ θρωσμῷ πεδίοιο*, a piece of ground rising from, and somewhat above the general level of, the plain K 160, Λ 56 = Υ 3.

θυγάτηρ, *ἡ* [cognate with Eng. *daughter*, German *tochter*]. Genit. *θῠγατέρος* Φ 504: τ 400. *θυγατρός* δ 4, η 290, λ 421. Dat. *θῠγατέρι* κ 106, ο 364. *θυγατρί* I 148, 290. Acc. *θῠγατέρα* E 371, Z 192, Λ 626, Φ 88, etc. *θύγατρα* A 13, 95, 372, Λ 740: β 53, λ 260, 269, σ 276. Voc. *θύγατερ* E 348, H 24, Ξ 194, etc.: α 10, θ 464, υ 61, etc. Nom. pl. *θῠγατέρες* B 492, Λ 271, Ω 166, 604: γ 451, κ 6. *θύγατρες* Z 238, I 144, 286, X 155: λ 227. Genit. *θυγατρῶν* B 715, Z 252, N 365, Φ 142, etc.: γ 452. Dat. *θῠγατέρεσσι* O 197. Acc. *θῠγατέρας* κ 7. *θύγατρας* X 62: λ 329, χ 222. A daughter, one's daughter A 13, 538, B 548, 715, Z 238, 398, etc.: α 52, β 53, γ 452, 465, δ 4, η 290, etc.

θύελλα, -*ης*, *ἡ* [*θύω*[1]]. (1) A rushing or violent wind or storm: *φλογὶ ἶσοι ἠὲ θυέλλῃ* N 39. Cf. Z 346, M 253, O 26, Φ 335: *ἀναρπάξασά μιν θ. φέρεν* δ 515, ψ 316. Cf. δ 727, ε 317, 419, ζ 171, η 275, κ 48, 54, μ 288, 409, υ 63, 66.—(2) Of a dust-storm: *κονίη ἵσταθ' ὥς τε νέφος ἠὲ θ.* Ψ 366.—App. of volcanic fire: *πυρὸς ὀλοοῖο θύελλαι* μ 68.

θυήεις [*θύος*. Cf. *θυόεις*]. Fragrant with the savour of sacrifice: *βωμός* Θ 48, Ψ 148: θ 363.

θυηλαί, *αἱ* [*θύω*[2]]. App., firstlings of meat given to the gods: *ἐν πυρὶ βάλλε θυηλάς* I 220.

θῡμαλγής [*θυμός* + *ἄλγος*]. Paining or burdening the heart, painful, distressing, grievous Δ 513, I 260, 387, 565: θ 272, π 69, σ 347 = υ 285, υ 118, χ 189, ψ 64, 183, ω 326.

θῡμᾱρής, -ές [θυμός + ἀρ-, ἀραρίσκω. 'Fitted to the heart']. Neut. in form θῡμῆρες κ 362. (**1**) Such as to inspire affection, lovely, beauteous: ἄλοχον Ι 336: ψ 232.—(**2**) Suited to one's taste, grateful to the senses: [ὕδωρ] θυμῆρες κεράσασα (till it became . . .) κ 362.—(**3**) Suited to one's needs, serviceable: σκῆπτρον ρ 199.

θῡμηγερέων [θυμός + ἀγερ-, ἀγείρω]. Endeavouring to rally one's spirit, making a fight for life: ἐκ δ' ἔπεσον θυμηγερέων η 283.

θῡμηδής, -ές [θυμός + ἡδύς]. Pleasing to the heart, desirable, choice: χρήματα π 389.

θῡμῆρες. See θυμαρής.

θῡμοβόρος, -ον [θυμός + βορ-, βι-βρώσκω]. Eating the heart, that will not leave the heart in peace. Epithet of ἔρις Η 210, 301, Π 476, Τ 58, Υ 253.

θῡμοδακής [θυμός + δακ-, δάκνω]. Biting the heart, stinging to action: μῦθος θ 185. (Cf. δάκε φρένας μῦθος Ε 493.)

θῡμολέων, -οντος [θυμός + λέων]. Lion-hearted: πόσιν δ 724 = 814.—Epithet of Heracles Ε 639: λ 267.—Of Achilles Η 228.

θῡμοραϊστής [θυμός + ῥαίω]. Life-destroying: θάνατος Ν 544, Π 414 = 580. Cf. Π 591, Σ 220.

θῡμός, -οῦ, ὁ. The 'heart,' 'breast,' soul, mind (cf. ἦτορ, καρδίη, κραδίη, κῆρ, φρήν). (**I**) As the seat or a seat (when coupled with φρήν, φρένες, κραδίη hardly to be distinguished therefrom) (**1**) Of life; hence (**a**) Vitality, the vital powers, strength (cf. ἦτορ (2) (a) (α), κῆρ (2) (a)): ὀλίγος ἔτι θ. ἐνῆεν Α 593. Cf. Γ 294 (of sacrificial victims), Δ 152, Ξ 439, Ο 240, Π 540, Υ 472, Φ 417, Χ 475: εἰς ὅ κεν αὖτις θυμὸν λάβητε κ 461. Cf. ε 458, κ 78, τ 263, ω 349.—(**b**) The animating principle, the vital spirit, the soul, the life, life, one's life (cf. αἰών (3), ἦτορ (2) (a) (β), μένος (7), ψυχή (1)): τάχ' ἂν θυμὸν ὀλέσσῃ Α 205. Cf. Δ 524, 531, Ε 155, 317, 673, 698, Λ 334, Μ 150 (of wild boars), Ρ 17, Φ 296, etc.: κεκαφηότα θυμόν ε 468. Cf. λ 201, 203, μ 350, ν 270, ξ 405, ο 354, ρ 236, υ 62, φ 154, 171, χ 388 (of fishes), 462.—(**c**) The spirit or soul thought of as distinct from the body and as leaving it at death (cf. ψυχή (4)): θ. ᾤχετ' ἀπὸ μελέων Ν 671 = Π 606. Cf. Δ 470, Η 131, Μ 386, Π 469 (of a horse), 743, Υ 406, Ψ 880 (of a bird): λίπ' ὀστέα θ. γ 455 (of a sacrificial victim), μ 414. Cf. κ 163 (of a deer) = τ 454 (of a wild boar), λ 221.—(**2**) Of spirit, courage, stoutness, resolution, endurance: ὅν τινα θ. ἐμοὶ μαχέσασθαι ἀνώγει Η 74. Cf. Α 228, Β 276, Γ 9, Δ 289, Ε 470, Ζ 439, Κ 205, Ν 73, 487, Ο 321, Ρ 68, Χ 252, etc.: ἀέξεταί μοι θ. β 315. Cf. α 320, 353, δ 447, 459, 713, ε 222, ι 435, λ 181 = π 37, π 99, ρ 284, σ 61, 135, ψ 100 = 168, ω 163, 511.—In reference to animals or insects Μ 300 (a lion), Ν 704 (oxen). Cf. Π 162, 266, etc.—(**3**) (**a**) Of anger, wrath, indignation: θυμὸν χολώθη (in his heart) Δ 494, Ν 660, ἀπειλήσω τό γε θυμῷ (from my heart, in earnest) Ο 212. Cf. Α 192, 217, 243, 429, Β 196, 223, Ζ 326, Ι 109, 255, 436, 496, 587, 629, 635, 675, Ξ 50, 207 = 306, Ο 155, Π 206, 616, Σ 113 = Τ 66, Τ 271, Υ 29: μὴ χόλον ἔνθεο θυμῷ ω 248. Cf. η 306, λ 562, υ 266.—Hence, anger, wrath: σοὶ ἄλληκτον θυμὸν ἐνὶ στήθεσσι θεοὶ θέσαν Ι 637. Cf. ν 148.—Evil passions: ὑμέτερος θ. καὶ ἀεικέα ἔργα φαίνεται δ 694.—(**b**) Of madness, rage, fury, wild excitement: ἀλύσσοντες περὶ θυμῷ Χ 70 (of dogs) (see Φ 65, etc., under (4) (a)). Cf. Ψ 468: φ 302.—(**4**) (**a**) Of desire, longing, appetite: ἵμερον ἔμβαλε θυμῷ Γ 139, περὶ δ' ἤθελε θυμῷ . . . Φ 65, Ω 236 (περί advbl., 'exceedingly in his heart'; cf. Χ 70 under (3) (b) and ξ 146 under (6)), αἴ γάρ με μένος καὶ θ. ἀνείη . . . (desire for vengeance) Χ 346. Cf. Α 468 = 602 = Β 431 = Η 320 = Ψ 56, Β 589, Δ 263, Θ 301 = 310, 322, Ι 177, Κ 401, Ν 386, Π 255, Σ 176, Υ 77, Φ 177, Ω 198, 288: ἐπεὶ ἔπιον ὅσον ἤθελε θ. γ 342 = 395 = η 184 = 228 = σ 427, φ 273. Cf. β 248, ε 95 = ξ 111, θ 70, 98, 450, λ 105, 206, 566, ν 40, ξ 28, 46, ο 66, π 141, 479 = τ 425, ρ 603, σ 164, τ 198, 343, ψ 257.—In reference to animals Θ 189 (of horses), Χ 142 (of a hawk).—One's wishes or liking: ἄρσαντες κατὰ θυμόν Α 136. Cf. Ι 645.—(**b**) Of the sexual impulse: τῇ θυμὸν ὄρινεν (sought to excite . . .) Γ 395. Cf. Ξ 316: ᾧ θυμῷ εἴξασα μίγη . . . ε 126. Cf. σ 212.—(**5**) Of volition: οὐκ Ἀτρεΐδῃ ἥνδανε θυμῷ Α 24 = 378, εἴ τοι θ. ἐπέσσυται Α 173, ἑκὼν ἀέκοντί γε θυμῷ Δ 43. Cf. Ε 676, Η 68, Θ 39, Ι 398, Κ 534, Μ 174, Σ 90, Υ 32, Φ 386, Χ 78, etc.: ἐπεπείθετο θ. β 103, τελέσαι με θ. ἄνωγεν ε 89. Cf. δ 140, η 187, 258, θ 45, ν 145, ξ 445, σ 409, φ 194, etc.—In reference to animals: οὐδὲ λύκοι τε καὶ ἄρνες ὁμόφρονα θυμὸν ἔχουσιν Χ 263. Cf. Κ 531 = Λ 520 (horses).—Inclination, 'a mind': ἐπεί τοι θ. [ἐστιν] αἰτιάασθαι Ν 775. Cf. Υ 349.—(**6**) Of feelings, emotions, moods, such as joy, grief, affection, dislike, pity, hope, fear, resentment, reverence, regard, solicitude, wonder, etc.: θυμῷ φιλέουσα Α 196 = 209, κεχαροίατό κε θυμῷ 256, ἄχος κραδίην καὶ θυμὸν ἵκανεν Β 171, σεβάσσατο τό γε θυμῷ Ζ 167, 417. Cf. Β 142, Γ 438, Δ 208, Η 189, Θ 138, Ι 8, 343 (from the bottom of my heart), 639, Κ 69, 355, Ν 82, 163, Ξ 104, Ο 561, Ρ 254, 625, Τ 229, Φ 456, Ψ 62, etc.: θάμβησεν κατὰ θυμόν α 323, ὃ οὔ ποτε ἔλπετο θυμῷ γ 275, κότον ἔνθετο θυμῷ λ 102, δείσασ' ἐνὶ θυμῷ π 331. Cf. α 4, β 79, 138, δ 71, ε 83, θ 15 (their curiosity), κ 63, 248, λ 39, ξ 146 (see Φ 65, etc., under (4) (a)), σ 161, 330, τ 71, υ 59, φ 87, 218, ω 90, etc.—In reference to animals Κ 492 (horses), Λ 555 = Ρ 664 (a lion): κ 217 (dogs).—One's good will or favour (cf. ἀποθύμιος): ἀπὸ θυμοῦ μᾶλλον ἐμοὶ ἔσεαι Α 562, σοὶ ἐκ θυμοῦ πεσέειν Ψ 595.—(**7**) Of the faculty of perception or knowledge: ᾔδεε κατὰ θυμὸν ὡς . . . Β 409. Cf. Δ 163 = Ζ 447, Η 44, Μ 228, Π 119, Σ 224 (of horses), Υ 264: οὐδὲ θυμῷ ὠΐσθη δόλον εἶναι δ 452. Cf. β 112, δ 730, κ 374, ν 339, ο 211, σ 154, 228, τ 485 = ψ 260, χ 373, ω 391.—(**8**) Of the faculty of thinking, deliberating, judging, considering, devising, conjecturing: ταῦθ' ὥρμαινε κατὰ φρένα καὶ κατὰ θυμόν Α 193 = Λ 411 = Ρ 106 = Σ 15, ἥδε οἱ κατὰ θυμὸν ἀρίστη φαίνετο βουλή Β 5 = Κ 17 = Ξ 161, κακὰ μήσατο θυμῷ Ζ 157, οὔ ποτε ἔλπετο θυμῷ . . . Ρ 404.

Cf. B 36, Δ 309, E 671, Θ 169, 430, I 101, 459, 537, K 447, 491, Λ 340, 403 = P 90 = Σ 5 = Υ 343 = Φ 53 = 552 = X 98, Λ 407 = P 97 = Φ 562 = X 122 = 385, N 8, Ξ 253, O 163, 566, Π 646, P 200, 442, 603, Σ 4, Υ 195, Φ 137, Ψ 313, Ω 680: μῦθον ἔνθετο θυμῷ (laid it to heart) α 361 = φ 355, ἕτερός με θ. ἔρυκεν (as if a second inward voice admonished him) ι 302, νόον σχέθε τόνδ' ἐνὶ θυμῷ ξ 490. Cf. α 200, 294, β 116, 156, γ 128, δ 117 = ω 235, δ 120 = ε 365 = 424, ε 285 = 376, ε 298 = 355 = 407 = 464, ζ 118, ι 213, 295, 299, 318 = 424 = λ 230, κ 50, 151, 317, 415, μ 58, 217, ν 154, ξ 150, 219, 391, ο 27, 172, 202, π 73, 237, ρ 595, τ 283, 312, 390, 524, υ 5, 10, 38, 93, 217, 304 (app., you did well in not hitting . . .), χ 11, ψ 72, 223, 345.—**(9)** Of memory or recollection: μνήσατο κατὰ θυμὸν Αἰγίσθοιο ('Αντιλόχοιο) α 29, δ 187, ἔπος μοι ἔμπεσε θυμῷ (came into my mind) μ 266.—**(10)** Of one's character or disposition: ὥς τοι θ. ἤπια δήνεα οἶδεν Δ 360, οἷος κείνου θ. ὑπερφίαλος O 94. Cf. Σ 262, etc.: ἐμὸν θυμὸν γνώσεαι (what manner of man I am) π 309. Cf. ε 191, ι 272 = 368, ι 287, ο 20, 212, τ 364, ψ 97, etc.—**(II)** Vaguely as the seat of κῆρ (2) (g): ἐμὸν κῆρ ἄχνυται ἐν θυμῷ Z 524.—**(III)** One's inward self as a region in which something takes place without outward manifestation: εὔχεθ' ὃν κατὰ θυμόν (in to himself) Ψ 769: θυμῷ ἐλέαιρε γυναῖκα (without letting any outward sign appear) τ 210. Cf. ε 444, υ 301, χ 411.—**(IV)** In a more or less physical sense: ὃν θυμὸν κατέδων Z 202. Cf. H 216, N 280, O 280, Ψ 370: οὐκέτι κεύθετε θυμῷ βρωτὺν σ 406. Cf. ι 75 = κ 143, κ 379.

θυμοφθόρος [θυμός + φθορ-, φθείρω]. Life-destroying: φάρμακα (poisons) β 329, ἄχος (heart-breaking, crushing) δ 716, κάματον (that crushes the spirit) κ 363, ὅς κε τοῦτον ἀνιάζῃ θ. (molesting or annoying beyond endurance) τ 323.—Absol.: γράψας ἐν πίνακι θυμοφθόρα πολλά (much matter that was to be his death-warrant) Z 169.

θύνω [θύω¹]. To run, run about, rush B 446, E 87, 96, 250, K 524, Λ 73, 188 = 203, 342 = Υ 412, Λ 570, Υ 493: ω 449.

θυόεις, -εν [θύος. Cf. θυήεις]. Sweet-smelling, fragrant: θυόεν νέφος O 153.

θύον, τό. A tree not identified, the wood of which emits (sweet) odour when burnt ε 60.

θύος, τό [θύω²]. Dat. pl. θυέεσσι Z 270, I 499. **(1)** A making of sacrifice, a sacrifice or offering I 499.—In pl. of a single offering: λίσσομ' ὑπὲρ θυέων ο 261.—**(2)** What is sacrificed or offered: πρὸς νηὸν ἔρχεο σὺν θυέεσσιν Z 270.

θυοσκόος, -ου, ὁ [θυ-, θύος + σκο- as in σκοπός]. App. a religious adviser skilled in divination from sacrifices, perh. from observation of the smoke thereof φ 145, χ 318, 321.—Joined with μάντις Ω 221.

†θυόω [θύος. Cf. θυήεις, θυόεις]. Neut. pf. pple, pass. τεθυωμένον. To impart fragrance to: ἐλαίῳ, τό ῥά οἱ τεθυωμένον ἦεν (which she had by her in (full) fragrance) Ξ 172.

θύραζε [θύρη]. **(1)** Out through a door, out of a room or house: βῆ θ. (from his smithy) Σ 416. Cf. Ω 572: ἢν ἕλκωσι θ. π 276. Cf. ζ 53, ο 62, 451, τ 69, φ 238 = 384.—Of leaving a cave ι 418, 444, 461.—Of passing the gates of dreams τ 566.—With ἐκ: ἐκ θ. ἔδραμον (out of doors) Σ 29: δόμων ἐξῆγε θ. ο 465. Cf. σ 386, τ 68, υ 179, 361, 367, φ 89, 299, 388.—In pregnant sense: ἐξελθόντες μεγάρων ἕζεσθε θ. (out of doors) χ 375. Cf. υ 97, χ 456.—**(2)** Forth from a specified or indicated space or region: [ἰχθὺν] ἔρριψε θ. (out of the sea) μ 254, διὰ δ' ἀμπερὲς ἦλθε θ. ἰός (through and out from the axe-heads) φ 422.—With ἐκ: οὐδὲ θ. εἴων ἐξιέναι (from the line of the ships) Σ 447. Cf. E 694, Π 408, Φ 29, 237: ε 410.

θυρωρός [θύρη + ὀρ-, ὄρομαι]. Watching the door, watch(-dogs): κύνας θυρωρούς X 69.

θυρεός, -οῦ, ὁ [θύρη]. Something (in the passages cited a huge stone) placed to block up a door ι 240 = 340, ι 313.

θύρετρα, τά [θύρη]. A door (cf. θύρη (1) (b)) B 415: αὐλῆς θ. (app., a door leading to the αὐλή from the λαύρη) χ 137. Cf. σ 385, φ 49.

θύρη, -ης, ἡ. Locative θύρηφι(ν) ι 238, χ 220. **(1)** **(a)** The door of a room: θαλάμοιο Ω 317. Cf. α 441, χ 155, 157, 201, 258 = 275, 394.—**(b)** In pl. (properly of a double or folding door; cf. ρ 267), the door of a house or room: ἐπὶ Πριάμοιο θύρῃσιν B 788. Cf. Z 89, 298, H 346, I 473, 475, Λ 644, Ξ 167 = 339, 169, X 66: προπάροιθε θυράων (*i.e.* the main door of the μέγαρον) α 107, θύρας ὤϊξεν (*i.e.* of the house) κ 230. Cf. α 255, 436 (the same as the θύρην of 441), ζ 19, η 88, ρ 530 (outside), χ 76, etc.—Of the entrance to the cave of the Cyclops ι 243, 304, 416, 417.—To the cave of Scylla μ 256.—Of the entrances to the cave of the Naiads ν 109, 370.—Of the door of a pigsty κ 389.—**(2)** **(a)** The gate of the αὐλή: αὐλὴν ποίησαν· θύρην δ' ἔχε μοῦνος ἐπιβλὴς Ω 453.—**(b)** In pl.: κληῗδα θυράων Ω 455. Cf. Ω 567 (the same as the θύρην of 453): ἔκτοσθεν αὐλῆς ὄρχατος ἄγχι θυράων η 112, αἰθούσης θύρας (see αἴθουσα (2)) σ 102, ἐπ' αὐλείῃσι θύρῃσιν (see αὔλειος) 239, ψ 49. Cf. α 120, π 344, ρ 267, φ 191, 240, 389, 391, ψ 370.—**(3)** In locative 'at the door.' Hence, outside ι 238.—Out of doors, abroad: κτήματα, τά τ' ἔνδοθι καὶ τὰ θύρηφιν (*i.e.* cattle, sheep, etc.) χ 220.

θύρηθι [θύρη + -θι]. Like θύραζε (2): ὦκα θύρηθ' ἔα (out of the water) ξ 352.

θύσανος, -ου, ὁ. A tassel or pendant. Attached to the aegis: παγχρύσεοι εὐπλεκέες B 448 (app. of twisted wire).—To Here's girdle Ξ 181.

θύσθλα, τά. App., mystic implements borne in the rites of Dionysus: θ. χαμαὶ κατέχευαν Z 134.

θυσσανόεις, -εσσα [θύσανος]. Furnished with tassels or pendants. Epithet of the aegis E 738, O 229, P 593, Σ 204, Φ 400.

θύω[1] [cf. θύνω]. **(1)** To run, rush: ἔγχεϊ (spear in hand) Λ 180, Π 699, X 272.—Of a river Φ 234, 324.—Of the sea Ψ 230: ν 85.—Of the wind μ 400, 408, 426—Fig.: ὀλοιῇσι φρεσὶ θύει A 342.—**(2)** To run or flow (with a liquid): δάπεδον ἅπαν αἵματι θῦεν λ 420, χ 309 = ω 185.

θύω[2]. **(1)** To offer in sacrifice portions of a

meal before partaking: θεοῖσι θῦσαι ἀνώγει I 219. Cf. ι 231, ο 222, 260.—(2) To offer (such portions to the gods): ἄργματα θῦσε θεοῖς ξ 446.

θυώδης [θύος (cf. θυήεις)+ὀδ-, ὄζω]. Sweet-smelling, fragrant δ 121, ε 264, φ 52.

θωή, -ῆς, ἡ. (1) A fine or penalty: σοὶ θωὴν ἐπιθήσομεν β 192.—(2) Specifically, a fine in place of personal service in war: ἀργαλέην θωὴν ἀλέεινεν Ἀχαιῶν N 669 (cf. Ψ 296).

θῶκόνδε [acc. of next+-δε (2)]. For or with a view to a sitting or assembly: θ. καθίζανον ε 3.

θῶκος, -ου, ὁ. Also **θόωκος** β 26, μ 318 [θο-, θα-, θαάσσω]. (1) A seat β 14, μ 318.—(2) A sitting, session, assembly: οὔθ' ἡμετέρη ἀγορὴ γένετ' οὔτε θόωκος β 26 (the two words hardly to be distinguished). Cf. ο 468.—Sim. in pl.: θεῶν ἐξίκετο θώκους (the assembled gods) Θ 439.

θωρηκτής [θωρήσσω]. Wearing the breastplate. Epithet of the Lycians M 317.—Of the Trojans O 689, 739, Φ 277.—Of the Greeks Φ 429.

θώρηξ, -ηκος, ὁ. A breastplate or corslet, consisting of two γύαλα (see γύαλον) B 544, Γ 332, Δ 133, E 99, Λ 234, N 265, O 529, T 361, etc.

θωρήσσω [θώρηξ]. 3 sing. aor. θώρηξε Π 155. 1 pl. subj. θωρήξομεν B 72, 83. Infin. θωρῆξαι B 11, 28, 65. Fut. mid. θωρήξομαι H 101, T 23. Aor. subj. θωρήξομαι Θ 376. 3 pl. aor. pass. θωρήχθησαν Γ 340, Ψ 813. Nom. pl. masc. pple. θωρηχθέντες Θ 530, Λ 49, 725, M 77, N 699, Π 257, Σ 277, 303. Infin. θωρηχθῆναι A 226, Π 40: χ 139. (ὑπο-.) (1) In act., to cause to arm for the fray, get under arms: Ἀχαιούς B 11, 28=65. Cf. B 72=83, Π 155.—(2) In mid. and pass. (a) To arm oneself for the fray, get under arms, don one's harness: τῷδε θωρήξομαι (to meet him) H 101, δός μοι τὰ σὰ τεύχεα θωρηχθῆναι (to arm myself withal) Π 40. Cf. A 226, Γ 340, Θ 54, Λ 715, Σ 189, etc.: μ 227, χ 139, ψ 369.—(b) App. meaning little more than to have one's station, post oneself, stand, be: ἐπ' ἀριστερὰ θωρήσσοντο B 526, πρὸ Φθίων θωρηχθέντες (acting as their leaders) N 699, ἅμα Πατρόκλῳ θωρηχθέντες (following him) Π 257. Cf. B 587, 818, Δ 252, Λ 709, Π 218.

θώς. Genit. pl. θώων N 103. A beast of prey, perh. the jackal Λ 474, 479, 481, N 103.

ἴᾰ, -ῆς. See εἷς.

ἰά. See ἰός.

ἰαίνω. 3 sing. aor. subj. ἰήνῃ Ω 119, 147, 176, 196. Impl. pl. ἰήνατε θ 426. 2 sing. aor. pass. ἰάνθης ψ 47. 3 ἰάνθη O 103, Ψ 598. ἰάνθη Ψ 600, Ω 321: δ 549, 840, ο 165. 2 sing. subj. ἰανθῇς T 174. 3 ἰανθῇ (beginning a line) χ 59. (1) To warm, heat: χαλκὸν ἰήνατε θ 426. Cf. κ 359, μ 175.—(2) To gladden, rejoice, cheer, comfort, placate: ἵνα φρεσὶ σῇσιν ἰανθῇς T 174, τοῖο θυμὸς ἰάνθη ὡς εἴ τε περὶ σταχύεσσιν ἐέρση ληΐου Ψ 598 (app., was gladdened as the dew upon the ears is warmed (sense (1)). *V.l.* ἐέρσῃ, 'as (the heart) of the corn is gladdened with the dew upon the ears'). Cf. Ψ 600, Ω 119=147=176=196, 321: εἰς ὅ κε σὸν κῆρ ἰανθῇ χ 59. Cf. δ 549, 840, ζ 156, ο 165, 379, τ 537, ψ 47.—To unbend (the brow): οὐδὲ μέτωπον ἰάνθη O 103.

ἰάλλω. Aor. ἴηλα O 19. 3 sing. ἴηλε θ 447. Subj. ἰήλω β 316. Imp. ἴηλον θ 443. Infin. ἰῆλαι φ 241. (ἐπ-, ἐπιπρο-, προ-.) (1) To shoot, discharge, let fly (a missile): ὀϊστόν Θ 300, 309.—(2) Hence, to send, let loose (bane): ὥς κ' ὔμμι ἐπὶ κῆρας ἰήλω β 316.—To send (a wind) ο 475.—To throw on, put on (a bond or manacle): περὶ χερσὶ δεσμὸν ἴηλα O 19.—Sim. of a means of fastening a gate φ 241.—To apply or tie (a knot): ἐπὶ δεσμὸν ἴηλον θ 443. Cf. θ 447.—To put forth (the hands) I 91=221=Ω 627: =α 149=δ 67=218=ε 200=θ 71=484=ξ 453=ο 142=π 54=ρ 98=υ 256, κ 376.—In hostile sense ι 288.—(3) To fling at, assail: ἀτιμίῃσιν (with . . .) ν 142.

ἰάνθη, 3 sing. aor. pass. ἰαίνω.

ἰάομαι. To heal, cure, make whole, tend: Παιήονά [μιν] ἀνώγειν ἰήσασθαι E 899. Cf. E 904, M 2: ι 520, τ 460.—With the injured part as object: ὀφθαλμόν ι 525.

ἰάπτω [app. distinct fr. (F)ι(F)άπτω. See ἐάφθη, προϊάπτω]. To hurt, mar β 376, δ 749.

ἴᾱσι, 3 pl. εἶμι.

ἰαύω (ἰάFω) [redup. fr. ἀF-, ἄ(F)ημι]. 3 sing. pa. iterative ἰαύεσκε ε 154. 3 pl. -ον ι 184. Aor. infin. ἰαῦσαι λ 261. Aor. ἄεσα (ἄFεσα) τ 342. 1 pl. ἀέσαμεν γ 151. Contr. ἄσαμεν π 367. 3 ἄεσαν γ 490, ο 188. Infin. ἀέσαι ο 40. (ἐν-, παρ-.) (1) To lie, rest, pass the night (not necessarily implying sleeping): Ζηνὸς ἐν ἀγκοίνῃσιν ἰαύεις Ξ 213. Cf. λ 261, χ 464, ω 209.—Of sheep, goats or swine ι 184, ξ 16.—(2) To pass (the night): ἀΰπνους νύκτας ἴαυον I 325. Cf. I 470: γ 151, 490, ε 154, ο 40, 188, π 367, τ 340, 342.—(3) To bivouac Σ 259, T 71.—To keep night-watch. Of dogs ξ 21.

ἰαχή, -ῆς, ἡ (FιFαχή) [ἰάχω]. A shouting Δ 456, M 144=O 396, Ξ 1, O 275, 384, Π 366, 373, P 266: λ 43.

ἰάχω (FιFάχω). [For the impf. forms, 3 sing. ἴαχε and 3 pl. ἴαχον (with ἴαχον Ψ 766), should prob. be read Fάχε, ἔFαχε, εὔαχε (cf. εὔαδε) and Fάκον, ἔFακον, εὔαχον, as aorists. But ἴαχον in Δ 506=P 317 seems to be for FίFαχον, impf.] (ἀμφ-, ἐπ-.) (1) To shout, cry, call. In battle or for the fight Δ 506=P 317, E 302=Θ 321=Υ 285, Λ 463, N 834, Ξ 421, Π 785, P 213, 723, Σ 160, 228, T 41, 424, Υ 382, 443: χ 81.—In rushing from an ambush δ 454.—In assent or approval: Ἀργεῖοι μέγ' ἴαχον B 333, 394.—In encouragement Ψ 766.—On seeing an encouraging omen N 822.—In pain or grief E 343, Σ 29.—In terror or affright Υ 62: κ 323.—In giving a signal Φ 341.—Of the cry of a frightened infant Z 468.—(2) Of inanimate objects. Of water, to plash: κῦμα μεγάλ' ἴαχεν A 482:=β 428.—Of fire, to roar Ψ 216.—Of a bow-string, to twang Δ 125.—Of a trumpet, to sound Σ 219.—Of heated metal plunged in water, to hiss ι 392.—Of something re-echoing sound: περὶ δ' ἴαχε πέτρη ι 395. Cf. Φ 10.

ἰγνύη, -ης, ἡ. The hollow of the knee, the ham: κατ' ἰγνύην βεβλημένος N 212.

ἴδε[1], 3 sing. aor. εἴδω (A).

ἴδε[2], aor. imp. εἴδω (A).

ἰδέ. And: ὤμοισιν ἰδὲ στέρνοισιν Γ 194, κνῆμαί τε ἰδὲ σφυρά Δ 147. Cf. B 511, 697, Δ 382, E 3, 171, etc.: δ 604, ι 186, λ 337, 431, 626, etc.

ἴδεσκε, 3 sing. pa. iterative εἴδω (A).

ἴδετο, 3 sing. aor. mid. εἴδω (A).

ἰδέω, pf. subj. εἴδω (C).

Ἴδηθεν (ῑ) [-θεν (1)]. From Ida Δ 475, Θ 397, 438.—App. as genit.: Ἴδηθεν μεδέων Γ 276 = 320 = H 202 = Ω 308.

ἴδιος, -η, -ον [conn. with (ϝ)ε, ἑ. See ἑέ]. Private, personal: πρῆξις ἥδ' ἰδίη, οὐ δήμιος γ 82.—Absol.: δήμιον ἢ ἴδιον δ 314.

ἰδίω [σϝιδ-. Cf. Eng. *sweat*]. To sweat υ 204.

ἴδμεν, 1 pl. pf. εἴδω (C).

ἴδμεναι, pf. infin. εἴδω (C).

†ἰδνόομαι. 3 sing. aor. ἰδνώθη B 266, N 618. Pple. ἰδνωθείς M 205: θ 375, χ 85. **(1)** To bend or double up one's body, curl oneself up: ὁ δ' ἰδνώθη (in pain) B 266, ἰδνώθη πεσών (in the death-struggle) N 618. Cf. χ 85.—**(2)** To bend the body for an upward throw: ἰδνωθεὶς ὀπίσω θ 375.—Sim., of an eagle bending back his head in order to use his beak M 205.

ἰδόμην, aor. mid. εἴδω (A).

ἴδον, aor. εἴδω (A).

ἰδρείη, -ης, ἡ (ϝιδρείη) [ἴδρις]. Skill: ἰδρείῃ πολέμοιο (in . . .) Π 359. Cf. H 198.

ἴδρις (ϝίδρις) [(ϝ)ιδ-, οἶδα. See εἴδω (C)]. Skilled, skilful ζ 233 = ψ 160.—With infin.: ἴδριες νῆα ἐλαυνέμεν (in propelling . . .) η 108.

†ἰδρόω [ἱδρώς]. Acc. sing. pres. pple. ἱδρώοντα Σ 372. Acc. pl. ἱδρώοντας Θ 543: δ 39. Fem. ἱδρώουσα Λ 119. Contr. pl. ἱδρῶσαι Λ 598. 3 sing. fut. ἱδρώσει B 388, 390. Aor. ἴδρωσα Δ 27. **(1)** To sweat B 390, Λ 119, 598, Σ 372, Θ 543: = δ 39.—With cognate acc.: ἱδρῶ ὃν ἴδρωσα Δ 27.—**(2)** To be covered with sweat: ἱδρώσει τευ τελαμών B 388

ἱδρύω [(σ)ιδ-, σδ-, ἵζω]. 3 pl. aor. pass. ἱδρύνθησαν Γ 78, H 56. (καθ-.) **(1)** To cause to be seated: ἵδρυε λαούς B 191. Cf. O 142: γ 37, ε 86.—**(2)** In pass., to be seated. In aor., to sit down: τοὶ δ' ἱδρύνθησαν ἅπαντες Γ 78 = H 56.

ἱδρώς, ὁ [ἰδίω]. Dat. ἱδρῷ P 385, 745. Acc. ἱδρῶ Δ 27, K 572, 574, Λ 621, Φ 561, X 2. Sweat Δ 27, E 796, K 572, 574, Λ 621, 811, N 705, 711, O 241, Π 109, P 385, 745, Φ 51, 561, X 2, Ψ 507, 688, 715: λ 599.

ἰδυῖα, fem. pf. pple. εἴδω (C).

ἰδών, aor. pple. εἴδω (A).

ἴε, 3 sing. impf. εἶμι.

ἵει (ῐ), 3 sing. impf. See ἵημι[1].

ἰείη, 3 sing. opt. εἶμι.

ἱεῖσι, 3 pl. ἵημι[1].

ἱέμεναι, infin. ἵημι[1].

ἴεν, 3 pl. impf. ἵημι[1].

ἰέναι, infin. εἶμι.

ἱέρεια, ἡ [fem. of next]. A priestess attached to the service of a particular goddess: Ἀθηναίης ἱέρειαν Z 300.

ἱερεύς, ὁ. Also **ἱρεύς** E 10, Π 604: ι 198. [ἱερός.] A priest attached to the service of a particular god: ἱερεὺς Ἀπόλλωνος A 370. Cf. A 23 = 377, A 62, E 10, I 575, Π 604, Ω 221: ι 198.

ἱερεύω. Also **ἱρεύω** ξ 94, ρ 181, τ 198, υ 3, 251. [ἱερός.] 3 pl. pa. iterative ἱρεύεσκον υ 3. ἱέρευντο Ω 125 is prob. to be taken as impf. pass. assimilated to forms like σπεῦτο. **(1)** To sacrifice (an animal to a god): Ἀθηναίῃ βοῦς Z 94 = 275, 309. Cf. Φ 131, Ψ 147: ν 182.—To the spirit of a deceased man: Τειρεσίῃ ὄϊν κ 524 = λ 32.—**(2)** To kill (an animal) for a meal, parts being offered as firstlings to a god or the gods: τοῖσι βοῦν ἱέρευσε Κρονίωνι H 314. Cf. B 402, Z 174, Σ 559, Ω 125: δεῖπνον συῶν ἱερεύσατε ὅς τις ἄριστος (for the meal) ω 215. Cf. β 56 = ρ 535, θ 59, ν 24, ξ 28, 74, 94, 414, π 454, ρ 180 = υ 250, ρ 181 = υ 251, υ 3, 391.—In mid.: δῶκα βοῦς ἱερεύσασθαι τ 198.

ἱερήϊον, τό [ἱερεύω]. **(1)** An animal for sacrifice λ 23.—**(2)** An animal to be killed as under prec. (2): ἑταῖροι δαίνυντ'· αὐτὰρ ἐγὼν ἱερήϊα πολλὰ παρεῖχον ξ 250. Cf. ρ 600.—So doubtless οὐχ ἱ. ἀρνύσθην X 159 (*i.e.* as a prize).—As object to prec. (2): οὔ ποθ' ἓν ἱρεύουσ' ἱ. ξ 94.

ἱερός, -ή, -όν. Also **ἱρός,** -ή, -όν B 420, Δ 46, Z 96, P 193, Φ 128, etc.: α 66, γ 278, ι 553, ρ 293, etc. Sacred, holy, set apart. **(1)** Of sacrifices A 99, 431, 443, 447, Ψ 146: γ 144, δ 478, λ 132 = ψ 279, υ 276.—Of altars B 305: γ 273.—Of a temple: θύρας ἱεροῖο δόμοιο Z 89.—Of the site of a sacred grove: Ὀγχηστὸν ἱερόν, Ποσιδήϊον ἄλσος B 506.—**(2)** Epithet of places: Ἴλιος ἱρή Δ 46. Cf. A 366, B 535, 625, Δ 103, E 446, etc.: Πύλου ἱερῆς φ 108. Cf. α 2, γ 278, ι 165, λ 86, 323, ρ 293.—Sim.: ἱερὰ τείχεα Θήβης Δ 378. Cf. Π 100.—Of rivers (as sprung from Zeus): ἱερὸν ῥόον Ἀλφειοῖο Λ 726. Cf. κ 351.—**(3)** Epithet of natural periods of time half-personified as divine controlling powers: κνέφας Λ 194 = 209 = P 455, ἦμαρ Θ 66 = Λ 84: = ι 56.—**(4)** Of things regarded as divine by connexion or relation: ἀλωάς (as being consecrated to Demeter) E 499, ἀλφίτου (as being the gift of Demeter) Λ 631, κύκλῳ (justice, the care of Zeus, being there dispensed) Σ 504. Cf. O 39, Π 658: βήσσας (as being about the dwelling of Circe) κ 275, ἐλαίης (as being near the nymph-haunted cave) ν 372. Cf. κ 426, 445, 554.—Sim.: ἰχθύν (perh. referring to a religious scruple against eating fish) Π 407, δίφρῳ (app. as drawn by divine steeds) P 464.—**(5)** Of persons regarded as divine by connexion or relation. Epithet of King Alcinous (as holding office from Zeus) η 167, θ 2, 4 = 421, θ 385, ν 20, 24.—Applied also to Antinous σ 34.—Of Telemachus (as being under the special protection of Athene) β 409 = σ 405 = φ 101, π 476, σ 60 = φ 130, χ 354.—Applied to persons dignified by being charged with a special function: πυλαωρούς Ω 681.—Sim. applied to the post occupied by such persons: φυλάκων τέλος K 56.—Extended to a whole host (perh. as being engaged in a pious work): Ἀργείων στρατός ω 81.—(6) Absol. in neut. (a) A sacred place or haunt: ἄλσος, ἱρὸν Ἀθηναίης ζ 322, ἄντρον, ἱρὸν νυμφάων ν 104 = 348.—(b) App., a sacrifice = (c): ὄφρ' ἱρὸν ἑτοιμάσσαίατ' Ἀθήνῃ (a sacrifice at which the arms were to be dedicated) K 571.—(c) In pl., offerings, a sacrifice, sacrifices: ὑπίσχετο ἱερά Ψ 195. Cf. A 147, B 420, E 178, I 357, K 46, Λ 707, 727, Ψ 207, 209: ἱερὰ ῥέζον γ 5. Cf. α 61, 66, γ 159, 436, δ 473, ε 102, η 191, ι 553, λ 130, π 184, ψ 277. —The actual burnt-offering: σπένδων οἶνον ἐπ' αἰθομένοις ἱεροῖσιν Λ 775. Cf. μ 362.

ἱζάνω [σι-σδ-άνω. Cf. next]. (ἀμφ-, ἐν-, ἐφ-, καθ-.) (1) To cause to be seated: ἀγῶνα Ψ 258.—(2) To sit: ἐν τῷ ἵζανον ω 209 (*i.e.* used it as a sitting-room).—Fig. of sleep: οὔ μοι ἐπ' ὄμμασιν ὕπνος ἱζάνει K 92.

ἵζω [σι-σδ-, redup. fr. σ(ε)δ-, the rough breathing representing the first σ. Cf. ἕζομαι, ἱδρύω]. 3 sing. pa. iterative ἵζεσκε Ω 472: γ 409. Imp. mid. ἵζευ Γ 162, H 115. (ἐσ-, ἐφ-, καθ-, μετα-, παρ-, προκαθ-.) (1) To cause to seat oneself, bid be seated: μή μ' ἐς θρόνον ἵζε Ω 553.—To cause (an assembly) to sit for business: βουλήν B 53.—(2) To seat oneself, sit down: ἀντίον ἷζεν Ὀδυσσῆος I 218. Cf. B 96, I 13, 87, N 281, Σ 422, Υ 15, Φ 520, Ψ 28: ἐπ' οὐδοῦ ἷζεν δ 718, ρ 339, ἵζ' ἐπὶ δεῖπνον (sit down to . . .) ω 394. Cf. ε 198, 338, θ 469, ξ 79, π 53, ρ 96, τ 389.—In mid.: πάροιθ' ἵζευ ἐμεῖο Γ 162. Cf. Γ 326, H 115, Σ 522, T 50: χ 335.—(3) To have one's seat, be seated, sit: ὅς οἱ πλησίον ἷζεν η 171. Cf. Ω 472: γ 409, λ 449, φ 146.—Of a scout, to be posted: σκοποὶ ἷζον ἐπ' ἄκριας π 365. Cf. B 792.

ἴῃ, 3 sing. subj. εἶμι.

ἴηλα, aor. ἰάλλω.

†**ἵημι**[1] (σί-σημι) [redup. fr. ση-]. 3 sing. ἵησι Γ 12, Φ 158: η 130, ι 499, λ 239. 3 pl. ἱεῖσι Γ 152. Pl. pple. ἱέντες B 774: δ 626, ρ 168. Fem. ἱεῖσαι μ 192. Infin. ἱέμεναι X 206. 3 pl. impf. ἵεν M 33. Fut. ἥσω (σήσω) P 515. 3 sing. ἥσει Ξ 240. Infin. ἥσειν θ 203. Aor. ἧκα E 125, O 19: μ 442. 3 sing. ἕηκε (ἔσηκε) A 48. ἧκε A 195, Δ 75, E 513, etc.: ζ 231, ι 481, π 191, etc. 3 sing. aor. subj. ᾗσι O 359. Opt. εἵην Ω 227. 3 sing. εἵη Γ 221. Infin. εἶναι N 638. From ἱέω. 3 sing. impf. ἵει Π 152. ἵει A 479, Δ 397, K 71, M 25, N 650, T 383, X 316: β 420, λ 7, μ 149, ο 292. Imp. ἵει Φ 338. **Mid.** 3 pl. aor. ἕντο A 469, H 323, I 92, Ψ 57, etc.: α 150, δ 68, ξ 454, ρ 99, etc. **Pass.** 3 pl. pres. ἵενται Δ 77. (ἀν-, ἀποπρο-, ἀφ-, ἐν-, ἐξ-, ἐξαν-, ἐπιπρο-, ἐφ-, καθ-, μεθ-, παρ-, προ-, συν-, ὑπερ-, ὑφ-.) (1) To send forth, throw, hurl, launch, let fly (a missile): ὀϊστόν N 650, δόρυ Π 608. Cf. A 48, 382, B 774, Γ 12, Δ 498 = O 575, H 269, Θ 134, Π 736, X 206, Ψ 840, 863: δίσκον θ 189. Cf. δ 626 = ρ 168, θ 203, ι 481, 538, φ 420.—Absol., to throw, make a throw, make one's throw: ἥσω καὶ ἐγώ P 515. Cf. O 359: ι 499.—To shoot one's arrow: διὰ δ' ἧκε σιδήρου φ 328, ω 177.—(2) In gen., to throw, send, cause to fall: ἐέρσας ἐξ αἰθέρος Λ 53. Cf. N 204, Φ 120.—(3) To send from oneself, let fall from one's grasp: φάσγανον ἧκε χαμᾶζε χ 84. Cf. M 205, P 299.—To let (oneself) fall: ἧκα καθύπερθε πόδας καὶ χεῖρε μ 442.—(4) To shed (tears) π 191, ψ 33.—(5) To send forth (the voice): ἱεῖσαι ὄπα κάλλιμον μ 192. Cf. Γ 152, 221, Ξ 151.—(6) To cause (waters) to flow: ἐς τεῖχος ἵει ῥόον M 25.—Of a river, to send or roll (its waters): ᾗ πρόσθεν ἵεν [ποταμοὶ] ὕδωρ M 33. Cf. Φ 158.—Absol.: Ἐνιπῆος, ὃς κάλλιστος ποταμῶν ἐπὶ γαῖαν ἵησιν λ 239.—So of a fountain: δύω κρῆναι ἡ μὲν . . . ἡ δ ὑπ' αὐλῆς οὐδὸν ἵησιν η 130.—(7) To send or dispatch as a messenger, on a specified or indicated mission, for some purpose, to a specified destination: πρὸ γὰρ ἧκέ μιν Ἥρη Σ 168. Cf. A 195, 208, Δ 397, Σ 182, Ω 375: ἄγγελον ἧκαν ο 458. Cf. κ 159, φ 21.—To cause (a person) to come forth, bring (him) forth: Αἰνείαν ἐξ ἀδύτοιο E 513.—To send (a wind): ἴκμενον οὖρον ἵει A 479: β 420 = ο 292, λ 7 = μ 149. —To send (evil): κακότητα K 71.—(8) In gen., to send forth, cause to appear: δράκοντα φόωσδε B 309, τοῦ πολλοὶ ἀπὸ σπινθῆρες ἵενται Δ 77. Cf. Δ 75, Θ 76, 247 = Ω 315, K 274: φ 415.—(9) To expel by satiety, put thus away (desire, inclination or appetite, thought of as something physical): ἐπὴν γόου ἐξ ἔρον εἵην Ω 227.—Cf. N 638.—In mid.: ἐπεὶ πόσιος καὶ ἐδητύος ἐξ ἔρον ἕντο A 469 = B 432 = H 323 = I 92 = 222 = Ψ 57 = Ω 628: = α 150 = γ 67 = 473 = δ 68 = θ 72 = 485 = μ 308 = ξ 454 = ο 143 = 303 = 501 = π 55 = 480 = ρ 99, ἐπεὶ σίτοιο ἐξ ἔρον ἕντο ω 489.—(10) To cause to be in a specified place or position, set, place, put, hang, throw: ἐν ἕρματα ἧκε λοβοῖσιν Ξ 182, ὑπὸ θρῆνυν ἥσει 240, ἐκ ποδοῖιν ἄκμονας ἧκα O 19, ἐν αὐτὸν ἵει πυρί (set him on fire) Φ 338. Cf. Σ 612, T 383 = X 316: κατὰ κάρητος οὔλας ἧκε κόμας ζ 231 = ψ 158, ὑπ' ἔμβρυον ἧκεν ἑκάστῃ ι 245 = 309 = 342. Cf. κ 317, τ 57, φ 47.—Of harnessing a horse: ἐν παρηορίῃσι Πήδασον ἵει Π 152.—Of applying fire: ἐν πυρὸς μένος ἧκεν Ψ 177.—(11) To inspire or infuse (spirit, panic): ἔν τοι στήθεσσι μένος ἧκα E 125, ἐν κυδοιμὸν ἧκεν Λ 539. Cf. O 327, Π 291, 730, Ψ 400.

ἵημι[2] (Ϝίημι). Only in mid. Fut. εἴσομαι (Ϝίσομαι) Ξ 8, Φ 335, Ω 462: χ 7. 3 sing. εἴσεται ο 213. 3 sing. aor. ἐείσατο (ἐϜίσατο) O 415: χ 89. εἴσατο Δ 138, E 538, M 118, N 191, P 518: ω 524. 3 dual ἐεισάσθην O 544. (ἐσ-, ἐφ-, καθ-, μεθ-.) (1) To aim at, take one's aim at. With genit.: Ὀδυσσῆος ἐείσατο χ 89.—With acc.: σκοπὸν ἄλλον εἴσομαι χ 7 (or the word may be referred to εἴδω (III) (10)).—(2) To desire, be eager or anxious, long, to do something specified or indicated, be set on doing it: τό οἱ οὔ τις ἐρύκακεν ἱεμένων περ O 450 = P 292. Cf. Π 396, P 276: ἵεται αἰνῶς β 327. Cf. α 6, δ 284, κ 246, π 430, φ 129, χ 256, 273, 409, ψ 353.—With complementary infin.: ἵετ' Αἰνείαν κτεῖναι E 434, ἱέμενος Τροίην ἐξαλαπάξαι (in my eagerness to . . .) Θ 241. Cf. B 589, Θ 301 = 310, Λ 537, M 68, N 386, 424, 501 = Π 761, N 585, Π 359, 383 = 866, Π 507, Σ 501, 547, Υ 469, 502: ἱέσθην ἐπὶ νῆα νέεσθαι γ 344, ἐμὲ ἱέμενοι γῆμαι φ 72. Cf. α 58, δ 823=ν 426=ο 30, ξ 142, 282, ο 201.—To be eager to go or make one's way in a specified direction: οἴκαδε ἱεμένων Β 154. Cf. γ 160, ι 261, ρ 5, τ 187.—Of a missile weapon checked in its eager course: ἐγχείη ἐνὶ γαίῃ ἔστη ἱεμένη Υ 280.—So with complementary infin.: ἐγχείη ἐνὶ γαίῃ ἔστη ἱεμένη χροὸς ἄμεναι Φ 70.—**(3)** To be eager for, strive for, be set upon. With genit.: νίκης ἱεμένων Ψ 371. Cf. Ψ 718, 767: ἱέμενον νόστοιο ο 69.—**(4)** To hasten, speed, rush, press, make one's way: πρόσω ἵεσθε Μ 274, τάχα εἴσομαι Ξ 8 (or the word may be referred to εἴδω (III) (1)), πάλιν εἴσομαι Ω 462. Cf. Θ 313, Μ 118, Ν 291, 707, Ο 415, Π 382: ἱεμένων Ἔρεβόσδε υ 356. Cf. χ 304.—With genit. of the point aimed at: ἱέμενοι πόλιος Λ 168: ἱέμενος ποταμοῖο ῥοάων (moving towards the river) κ 529.—With fut. pple. indicating purpose: Ζεφύροιο εἴσομαι ὄρσουσα θύελλαν Φ 335. Cf. ο 213.—So with fut. infin.: ἐεισάσθην τεύχεα συλήσειν Ο 544.—With aor. infin.: ἄλλος κ' ἀνὴρ ἵετο ἰδέειν παῖδας ν 334.—Of a weapon, to take its way: διαπρὸ εἴσατο χαλκός Ε 538=Ρ 518 := ω 524. Cf. Δ 138, Ο 543, Υ 399.—**(5)** App., to reach. With genit.: οὔ πῃ χροὸς εἴσατο Ν 191 (for the sense with *v.l.* χρώς see εἴδω (II) (1)).

ἰήνῃ, 3 sing. aor. subj. ἰαίνω.

ἴῃσι, 3 sing. subj. εἶμι.

ἵῃσι, 3 sing. pres. ἵημι[1].

ἰητήρ, -ῆρος [ἰάομαι]. A healer, a surgeon and physician: ἕλκος ἰ. ἐπιμάσσεται Δ 190. Cf. Β 732, Δ 194, Λ 518, 835: ρ 384.

ἰητρός, -οῦ [as prec.]. =prec. Λ 514, 833, Ν 213, Π 28: δ 231.

ἰθᾰγενής, ἰθαιγενής [ἰθύς[1] + γεν-, γίγνομαι]. Born in wedlock, legitimate. Absol.: ἶσόν μ' ἰθαγενέεσσιν ἐτίμα ξ 203.

ἴθι, imp. εἶμι.

ἴθμα, -ατος [ἰθ-, εἶμι]. Gait: πελειάσιν ἴθμαθ' ὁμοῖαι (app., with short, quick steps) Ε 778.

ἰθύ(ς) [ἰθύς[1]]. **(1)** Straight, straight on, without turning aside: μένος χειρῶν ἰθὺς φέρον Ε 506, ἰθὺς πρὸς τεῖχος ἔκιον Μ 137. Cf. Θ 118, Λ 95, Μ 124, 330, Ν 135, Ρ 168, 492, Υ 79, 99, 108, 172, 386, Χ 143, 243, 284: γ 10, ρ 33, ψ 207, ω 101, 397.—**(2)** Of position, straight, direct: τέτραπτο πρὸς ἰθύ οἱ Ξ 403 (straight towards him, *i.e.* he had him right in the line of his throw): ἰθὺς τετραμμένος (facing the foe) Ρ 227.—**(3)** Straight towards, to, at. With genit.: ἰθὺς Μενελάου ἤϊεν Ν 601. Cf. Ε 849, Λ 289, Μ 254, 453, Π 584, Φ 540, etc.: βῆ δ' ἰθὺς προθύροιο α 119. Cf. β 301, γ 17, ο 511, ρ 325, ω 241.

ἰθύντατα. See ἰθύς[1].

ἰθύνω [ἰθύς[1]]. Aor. ἴθῡνα ψ 197. 3 sing. ἴθῡνε Δ 132, Ε 290, Ψ 871: ε 245, ρ 341, φ 44, 121. 1 pl. subj. ἰθύνομεν Θ 110, Λ 528. 2 ἰθύνετε μ 82. 3 dual aor. pass. ἰθυνθήτην Π 475. (ἐξ-.) **(1)** To make straight or even: ἐπὶ στάθμην ἴθυνε [δοῦρα] ε 245. Cf. ρ 341=φ 44, φ 121, ψ 197.—**(2)** To aim, let fly (a missile). In mid.: ἐπ' Ἀντινόῳ ἰθύνετ' ὀϊστόν χ 8.—**(3)** To direct the course of (a missile): βέλος ἴθυνε ῥῖνα παρ' ὀφθαλμόν, λευκοὺς δ' ἐπέρησεν ὀδόντας Ε 290 (to the . . ., the head app. being bent forward to avoid the blow). Cf. Δ 132, Ρ 632.—App., to direct (an arrow) towards the mark (preparatory to putting it on the bow): ὀϊστὸν ἔχεν πάλαι, ὡς ἴθυνεν Ψ 871 (had long been holding it ready as he had directed it. App. he slips the bow under the arrow thus held).—**(4)** To direct the course of (a horse, mule, chariot, waggon), drive (it): κεῖσ' ἵππους τε καὶ ἅρμ' ἰθύνομεν, ἔνθα . . . Λ 528. Cf. Θ 110, Ω 149, 178, 362.—To bring (a horse) back to its proper direction, turn its head the right way: τὼ ἰθυνθήτην Π 475.—**(5)** To keep (a ship) on her course, steer (her): μῆτι κυβερνήτης νῆα θοὴν ἰθύνει Ψ 317. Cf. ι 78=ξ 256, λ 10=μ 152, μ 82.—Absol., to steer one's course: πηδάλιον ποιήσατο, ὄφρ' ἰθύνοι ε 255.—So in mid. ε 270.—**(6)** In mid., of combatants, to direct their course against, charge. With genit.: ἀλλήλων ἰθυνομένων Ζ 3.

ἰθυπτίων, -ωνος [ἰθύς[1] + π(ε)τ-, πέτομαι]. Flying straight to the mark. Epithet of a spear Φ 169.

ἰθύς[1], -εῖα [ἰθ-, εἶμι]. Straight. Hence just, fair, right: ἰθεῖα ἔσται [δίκη] Ψ 580.—In superl. in neut. pl. ἰθύντατα as adv., most justly or fairly: ὃς δίκην ἰθύντατα εἴποι Σ 508.

ἰθῠς[2], ἡ [as prec.]. **(1)** A straight course: ἐπεὶ σφαίρῃ ἀν' ἰθὺν πειρήσαντο (in throwing straight upwards) θ 377.—**(2)** One's course: ἀΐσσοντος ἀν' ἰθύν ((steadily) pursuing his course) Φ 303.—The course which one may be expected to take: γυναικῶν γνώομεν ἰθύν (how they are inclined, their disposition) π 304.—**(3)** An enterprise, undertaking: πᾶσαν ἐπ' ἰθύν Ζ 79. Cf. δ 434.

ἰθύς[3]. See ἰθύ(ς).

ἰθῡ́ω [ἰθύς[1]]. (ἐπ-.) **(1)** To reach or stretch towards. With genit.: τῶν ὁπότ' ἰθύσειεν λ 591.—**(2)** In fighting, to direct one's course, advance, charge: ἴθυσαν πολὺ προτέρω Δ 507. Cf. Μ 443, Π 582, Ρ 281, 353, 725.—Sim.: ἔνθα καὶ ἔνθ' ἴθυσε μάχη πεδίοιο (swayed along the plain) Ζ 2.—Of a beast of prey Λ 552=Ρ 661, Μ 48.—With genit. of the objective: ἴθυσε νεός Ο 693.—**(3)** To set oneself, begin, offer, *to do*. With infin.: ἴθυσεν ὀλολύξαι χ 408.

ἱκάνω [ἱκ- as in ἱκνέομαι, ἵκω]. (ἀφ-, εἰσαφ-.) **(1)** To present oneself to: ἦ ἄλλον πέμπωμεν ἱκανέμεν δ 29.—**(2)** To approach as a suppliant: ἱκάνω σε ε 445. Cf. ε 449, η 147, ν 231.—In mid. Σ 457 := γ 92=δ 322.—**(3)** To extend to, reach: σκόπελος οὐρανὸν ἱκάνει μ 73. Cf. Ν 547, Ξ 288, Τ 406.—Sim.: σέλας αἰθέρ' ἵκανεν Σ 214, Τ 379. Cf. Ο 686: κλέος σευ οὐρανὸν ἱκάνει τ 108. Cf. θ 74.—**(4) (a)** To be in the condition of having come to, arrived at, reached, to find oneself at, be at, a specified place (in impf. in sense 'arrived at,' 'reached,' 'found himself at'): ἵκανον ὅθι . . . Γ 145, Δ 210, Ε 780, Κ 526, Σ 520: ο 101. Cf. Ν 449: ζ 206, η 24, λ 160, ν 278, ο 492, π 31, ω 328.—Absol., to have come, present oneself:

φίλοι ἄνδρες ἱκάνετον I 197. Cf. φ 209.—With advbl. acc. defining the action of the vb.: πῇ μεμαυῖα τόδ' ἱκάνεις; (hast come thus) Ξ 298. Cf. Ξ 309, Ω 172: α 409, κ 75, τ 407.—(b) With preps. (a) ἐπί: ἐπὶ νῆας B 17 = 168.—(β) ἐς: ἐς Χρύσην ἵκανεν A 431 (here prob. in proper impf. sense, 'was approaching'), ὅσον ἐς Σκαιὰς πύλας ἵκανεν I 354 (in iterative sense, 'used to come so far'). Cf. T 3: τέων βροτῶν ἐς γαῖαν ἱκάνω; ζ 119 = ν 200. Cf. θ 362, λ 13, ν 328, τ 435.—(γ) ποτί: Διὸς ποτὶ δῶ Φ 505.—(c) With acc. of the place reached: ἵκανε θεῶν ἕδος E 868. Cf. Z 237, 242, 297, 370 = 497, 392, Θ 47, N 240, O 151, Σ 369, 385 = 424, Φ 505, X 147, Ψ 138, 214, Ω 346, 501: ἐπεὶ ἡμετέρην πόλιν ἱκάνεις ζ 191. Cf. δ 139, η 3, θ 362, ο 216, ρ 28, 255, τ 432, χ 231, ω 281.—In mid.: οἶκον ἱκάνεται ψ 7, 27, 36, 108.—Of a person using a weapon: οὐδὲ χρό' ἵκανεν Ψ 819.—Of coming up to a person: Πηλεΐωνα X 214.—Of coming to or reaching a person in the course of making a round H 186.—Sim. of an inanimate object: ὅτε χεῖρας ἵκανεν 'Οδυσσῆος τόξον ω 172.—Of attaining a period of life: ἥβης μέτρον σ 217, τ 532.—(5) Of feelings or mental or bodily states, to have come upon or seized, affect (in impf. in sense 'had come upon'): ἄχος μιν κραδίην ἵκανεν B 171, ἐμὲ κῆδος ἱκάνει Π 516. Cf. A 254 = H 124, Γ 97, Θ 147 = O 208 = Π 52, Λ 117, N 464, O 245, T 307: γῆρας ἱκάνει λ 196, τάφος οἱ ἦτορ ἵκανεν ψ 93. Cf. β 41, ε 289, 457, ζ 169, σ 81, 274.—Sim. of need: χρειὼ ἵκανεν ζ 136.—So in mid.: χρειὼ ἱκάνεται K 118, Λ 610.—Of sleep A 610, K 96: ι 333, τ 49.—Of fate Σ 465: ι 507 = ν 172.

ἴκελος, -η, -ον (Ϝίκελος) [ἰκ-, εἴκω¹]. = εἴκελος (1): ὄμματα ἴκελος Διί (in . . .) B 478. Cf. Δ 86, E 450, Λ 467, Π 11, Σ 591, T 282, Ω 80, 699, 758: δ 249, ε 54, μ 418 = ξ 308, ν 157, ρ 37 = τ 54.

ἱκέσθαι, aor. infin. ἱκνέομαι.

ἱκετεύω [ἱκέτης]. (1) To come as a suppliant: ἐς Πηλῆ' ἱκέτευσε Π 574 (of a fugitive homicide).—(2) To approach and entreat as a suppliant η 292, 301, ο 277 (of a homicide), ρ 573.—(3) To entreat, beg. With complementary infin.: πολλά μ' ἱκέτευεν ἱππόθεν ἐξέμεναι λ 530.

ἱκέτης, ὁ [ἵκω]. A suppliant (and as such bearing a sacred character): ἀντί τοι εἰμ' ἱκέταο αἰδοίοιο Φ 75. Cf. Ω 570: οὐδ' ἱκέτας ἐμπάζεαι π 422 (app., the order or class of suppliants, the relation of suppliant and protector and the obligations arising therefrom, referring to the story she proceeds to tell). Cf. ε 450, ζ 193 = ξ 511, η 165 = 181, θ 546, ι 269, 270, π 67, τ 134.—With ἀνήρ: ἱκέτεω πεφιδήσεται ἀνδρὸς Ω 158 = 187.

ἱκετήσιος [ἱκέτης]. Epithet of Zeus as protector of suppliants ν 213.

ἵκετο (ῐ), 3 sing. aor. ἱκνέομαι.

ἰκμάς, ἡ. The natural moisture (of a hide): ἄφαρ ἰ. ἔβη P 392 (see βαίνω (I) (1)).

ἴκμενος. Epithet of οὖρος. App., favourable or the like A 479: β 420 = ο 292, λ 7 = μ 149.

†**ἱκνέομαι** [ἰκ- as in ἱκάνω, ἵκω]. Nom. pl. fem. pres. pple. ἱκνεύμεναι ι 128. 1 pl. impf. ἱκνεύμεσθα ω 339. Fut. ἵξομαι Z 367. 3 sing. ἵξεται A 240, Ψ 47: θ 198, τ 20. Infin. ἵξεσθαι Z 502, Λ 182, O 252, 505, Ω 728: δ 515, κ 276. Aor. ἱκόμην Ξ 260: δ 84, ζ 176, π 233, ρ 121, etc. 2 sing. ἵκεο I 56, K 448: θ 573. ἵκευ ν 4. 3 ἵκετο (ῐ) A 362, Θ 149, Λ 88, 225, 352, N 837, Σ 64, Ω 708, etc.: γ 368, η 80, μ 2, π 57, τ 451, ψ 224, etc. 2 dual ἵκεσθον Θ 456. 3 ἱκέσθην (ῐ) A 328, I 185, Ξ 283, Ψ 215: β 150, κ 117. 1 pl. ἱκόμεθα δ 34, ι 107, μ 262, ψ 354, etc. ἱκόμεσθα B 138, Λ 726, 769: γ 61, κ 13, ξ 257, 290, etc. 3 ἵκοντο (ῐ) A 432, Γ 264, Δ 383, Λ 170, Σ 67, Ψ 2, etc.: γ 388, ζ 85, η 46, ο 109, ρ 85, ω 13, etc. Subj. ἵκωμαι A 139, E 360, I 393, Φ 558, etc.: ξ 140, ο 509. 2 sing. ἵκηαι Z 143, Θ 478, P 622, Υ 429: β 307, ε 168, η 319, ρ 448, etc. 3 ἵκηται A 166, E 129, N 141, Σ 207, etc.: γ 355, ζ 202, κ 39, μ 66, τ 319, etc. 1 pl. ἱκώμεθα ζ 296. 2 ἵκησθε Υ 24. 3 ἵκωνται O 233, Π 455, Σ 213: ν 101. Opt. ἱκοίμην Δ 171, I 363, Ξ 247, Ω 437: η 333, λ 480. 2 sing. ἵκοιο γ 117, δ 474, κ 65, ο 518, τ 367. 3 ἵκοιτο Γ 233, N 711, Π 247, T 354: ε 34, ι 351, ρ 497, ψ 151, etc. 1 pl. ἱκοίμεθα I 141, 283: κ 33. 2 ἵκοισθε λ 104, 111, μ 138. 3 ἱκοίατο Σ 544: κ 416. 3 imp. ἱκέσθω Σ 178: ο 447. Infin. ἱκέσθαι A 19, B 115, M 221, X 417, Ω 287, etc.: α 21, δ 475, ε 41, ο 66, π 59, ω 430, etc. (ἀφ-, δι-, εἰσαφ-, ἐξ-, ἐφ-, καθ-.) (1) (a) To go, proceed, take one's way: Ζηνὸς ἄσσον (approach) Ξ 247: οἴκαδε ο 66, ἐμὲ χρεὼ ἱκέσθαι (to be off) 201.—(b) With preps. (a) ἐπί: ἐπὶ νῆας Z 69, X 417. Cf. ι 128.—(β) ἐς: ἐς Ὄλυμπον E 360. Cf. κ 490.—(γ) μετά: μετὰ κλέος 'Αχαιῶν Λ 227.—(δ) πρός: τὰ ἃ πρὸς δώματα O 58.—(c) With acc.: φοβεύμενος ἵκετο νῆας (fled to the . . .) Θ 149. Cf. O 252, Σ 150: ο 509.—(d) With the prepositional and accusatival constructions combined: ἄλλων ἵκετο δῆμον, Ἄργος ἐς (fled to . . .) ο 238. Cf. υ 219.—(2) To walk about, stroll: διὰ δενδρέων ἱκνεύμεσθα ω 339.—(3) (a) To come to a specified or indicated place: δεῦρο B 138. Cf. Γ 233, E 129, Z 367, 502, Σ 213: πόθεν ἵκετο; π 57. Cf. γ 61, η 239, ι 267 (have come in supplication), μ 66, ν 303, π 233, 424, τ 379.—Of something inanimate: λοετρά Ψ 44.—Of sound: ἀμφί μ' 'Οδυσσῆος ἵκετ' ἀϋτή Λ 466.—Of a message ο 447.—With advbl. acc. defining the action of the vb.: δεῦρο τόδ' ἵκετο (has come as he has done) ρ 524.—(b) With preps. (a) ἐς: 'Ιθάκης ἐς δῆμον ξ 126.—(β) ποτί: ἐμὸν ποτὶ δῶ ν 4.—(γ) προτί: προτὶ ἄστυ ν 180, ω 154.—(c) With acc. of the place: Ἄργος ἱκέσθαι B 115 = I 22. Cf. Δ 171, Z 225, Ω 29: γ 368, δ 170, θ 13, 28, ι 351 (will visit thee), κ 435, etc.—Of something inanimate: δόρυ δ' ἂψ ἵκεθ' Ἕκτορα Υ 440.—(4) To present oneself to: ἄλλον φῶτα ὅν κεν ἵκοιο ο 518. Cf. ρ 516, ψ 314, 333.—With ἐς: ἵκετ' ἐς Πείραιον υ 372.—In unfriendly sense: κεχολώσεται ὅν κεν ἵκωμαι A 139.—To come or fall into (one's hands): ὅ τι χεῖρας ἵκοιτο μ 331.—With ἐς K 448.—(5) To approach as a suppliant: Νύκθ' ἱκόμην φεύγων Ξ 260. Cf. X 123.—With ἐς ζ 176.—Absol.: αἰδοῖός ἐστιν ὅς τις ἵκηται ε 448.—(6) Of an event,

to come on, take place: ἥν ποτε δασμὸς ἵκηται Α 166.—(7) (a) With the notion of attainment prominent, to come to, arrive at, reach, find oneself at, be at, a specified or indicated place: οἴκαδε Α 19 (reach home), λιμένος ἐντός 432. Cf. Ι 393, Σ 532, Ω 287, 338: ἧος ἵκοιτο (till he should return) ψ 151. Cf. α 173 = ξ 190 = π 224, δ 34, 520, ι 530, λ 104 (reach home), ο 210, π 59, 324, φ 211, χ 35.—Of fire π 290 = τ 9, τ 20.—(b) With preps. (α) ἐπί: ἐπὶ κλισίας Α 328 = Ι 185. Cf. Ι 652, Π 247, Ρ 622: ι 466, κ 117.—(β) εἰς, ἐς: ἐς Ὄλυμπον Θ 456. Cf. Δ 446 = Θ 60: β 307, γ 488, δ 474, ι 79, 107, etc.—Of sound: ἐς πόλιν ἵκετ' ἀϋτή ξ 265 = ρ 434.—Of smoke Φ 522.—Of perfume Ξ 174.—(γ) κατά: κατὰ στρατόν Α 484. Cf. ω 13.—(δ) μετά Γ 264, Υ 24.—(ε) ποτί γ 488 = ο 186, ξ 472.—(ζ) πρός τ 458.—(η) ὑπό Λ 182.—(c) With acc.: δόμον Γ 421, Ἀσωπόν Δ 383. Cf. Ε 367, Θ 478, Λ 170, Μ 221, Π 455, Τ 131, Φ 44, etc.: α 21, δ 515, 558, ζ 85, 304 (the place where she sits), η 83, κ 13, ο 109, ψ 296, 333, etc.—Of sound Ν 837.—Of smoke Σ 207.—Of inanimate objects: ὡς ἂν πλήμνη δοάσσεται ἄκρον ἱκέσθαι Ψ 339. Cf. Ν 141.—(d) With the prepositional and accusatival constructions combined: ἱκέσθαι οἶκον καὶ σὴν ἐς πατρίδα γαῖαν δ 475. Cf. ε 34, ζ 314 = η 76, ι 532, κ 473.—(8) In various applications in senses and constructions similar to those of (7) (a) Of getting within reach of, in hostile sense: ὅς κ' ἀνὴρ ἕτερ' ἅρμαθ' ἵκηται Δ 306.—(b) Of reaching (a mark, etc.) with a missile θ 198. Cf. ι 483 = 540.—(c) Of a weapon: οὐδ' ἵκετο χρόα Λ 352.—Of a boar's tusk τ 451.—(d) Of attaining a period of life: ἥβης μέτρον Λ 225. Cf. Ω 728: δ 668, λ 317, ο 246, 366, τ 367, ψ 212.—With ἐπί: ἐπὶ γῆρας θ 227.—Of attaining a period of time: Ἠῶ ρ 497, τ 319.—(e) Of encountering fate: ὀλέθρου πείρατα Ζ 143 = Υ 429.—(f) In discourse, to proceed to, reach: οὐ τέλος ἵκεο μύθων Ι 56.—(9) Of feelings or mental or bodily states, to come upon, seize, affect: ποθὴ ἵξεται υἷας Ἀχαιῶν Α 240, ὁππότε μιν κάματος γούναθ' ἵκοιτο Ν 711. Cf. Α 362 = Σ 73, Λ 88, Σ 64, 178, Τ 348, 354, Ψ 47, Ω 708: ο 345, ψ 224.

ἱκόμην, aor. ἱκνέομαι.

ἴκρια, τά. Locative ἰκριόφιν γ 353, ν 74, ο 283. This form as ablative μ 414, ο 552. Each of two platforms, one in the forward, and the other in the after part of a ship, the first prob. having the mast passing through it, and the second being the post of the steersman. (1) The forward one: εἰς ἴκρια νηὸς ἔβαινον πρῴρης μ 229.—(2) The after: λίπε δ' ἴκρια νηός Ο 729 (the ships were drawn up stern first): κυβερνήτης κάππεσ' ἀπ' ἰκριόφιν μ 414.—In this sense in reference to several ships: νηῶν ἴκρι' ἐπῴχετο Ο 676. Cf. Ο 685.—Doubtless the reference is also to the after platform in the following passages γ 353, ν 74, ο 283, 552.—(3) Of a similar contrivance on the σχεδίη of Odysseus ε 163, 252.

ἵκω [cf. ἵκανω, ἱκνέομαι]. Subj. ἵκωμι Ι 414 (*v.l.* ἴωμι). 3 dual impf. ἰκέτην β 152 (*v.l.* ἰδέτην). 3 sing. aor. ἶξε Β 667, Ζ 172, Λ 807, Υ 320, 328, Χ 462, Ω 122, 160: γ 288, ε 442. 3 pl. ἶξον Ε 773, Κ 470, Ξ 433, Φ 1, Ψ 38, Ω 692: γ 5, 31, 495, δ 1, ε 194. (1) To go, proceed, take one's way: εἴ κεν οἴκαδ' ἵκωμι Ι 414.—With ἐς, of birds, app., to fly (or seem to fly) *for*: ἐς δ' ἰκέτην πάντων κεφαλάς β 152.—(2) (a) To be in the condition of having come to, arrived at, reached, to find oneself at, be at, a specified place (in aor., in sense 'arrived at,' 'reached,' 'found himself at'): ἶξεν ὅθι . . . Υ 320.—With advbl. acc. defining the action of the vb.: δεῦρο τόδ' ἵκω (have come as you see) ρ 444.—(b) With preps. (α) ἐπί: ἐπὶ Θρῃκῶν τέλος Κ 470. Cf. Υ 328.—(β) ἐς: ἐς Ῥόδον Β 667. Cf. Ω 122, 160: γ 31, 495, σ 353.—(γ) κατά Λ 807: ε 442.—(c) With acc. of the place: ἡμέτερον δόμον Σ 406. Cf. Ε 773, Ζ 172, Ξ 433 = Φ 1 = Ω 692, Χ 462, Ψ 38: γ 5, 288, δ 1, ε 194.—Sim. of merchandise: πολλὰ Φρυγίην κτήματα περνάμεν' ἵκει Σ 292.—(3) To extend to, reach. (a) With εἰς, ἐς: ὥς κε σέλας εἰς οὐρανὸν ἵκῃ Θ 509. Cf. ν 248.—(b) With acc.: κνίση οὐρανὸν ἶκεν Α 317. Cf. Β 153, 458, Θ 192, Μ 338, Ξ 60, Ρ 425, Τ 362: ι 20, ο 329 = ρ 565.—(4) Of a mental state, to have come upon or seized, affect: ὅτε κέν τινα χόλος ἵκοι Ι 525. Cf. Ρ 399.—Sim. of need: τίνα χρειὼ τόσον ἵκει; β 28. Cf. Κ 142: ε 189.—Of a mental quality, to have come to, show itself in: πινυτή τοι φρένας ἵκει υ 228.

ἰλαδόν [ἴλη, εἴλη, a crowd, conn. with εἴλω]. In crowds or throngs: ἐστιχόωντο εἰς ἀγορήν Β 93.

ἱλάομαι = ἱλάσκομαι: Ἐρεχθῆα Β 550.

ἵλαος. In Α 583 ἵλᾱος. Propitious, gracious, benign Α 583, Ι 639, Τ 178.

ἱλάσκομαι [ἵλαος]. Aor. subj. ἱλάσσομαι γ 419. 2 sing. ἱλάσσεαι Α 147. 1 pl. ἱλασόμεσθα Α 444. Nom. pl. aor. pple. ἱλασσάμενοι Α 100. To propitiate, seek to win favour or grace from (a divinity): ἄνακτα (*i.e.* Apollo) Α 444. Cf. Α 100, 147, 386, 472, Ζ 380 = 385: γ 419.

ἱλήκω [as prec.]. To be propitious, lend a gracious ear: εἴ κεν ἡμῖν ἱλήκῃσιν φ 365.

ἵλημι. = prec. Imp. ἵληθι γ 380, π 184.

Ἰλιόθεν (ῑ) (Ϝιλιόθεν) [-θεν (1)]. From Ilios Ξ 251: ι 39.

Ἰλιόθι (ῑ) (Ϝιλιόθι) [-θι]. As locative of Ἴλιος: Ἰλιόθι πρό (to the front in, *i.e.* before, in front of, Ilios) Θ 561, Κ 12, Ν 349: θ 581.

Ἰλιόφι (ῑ). As genit. of Ἴλιος Φ 295.

ἰλλάς [εἴλω]. A twisted rope of thongs or withies: ἰλλάσι δήσαντες Ν 572.

ἰλύς. Mud, slime: ὑπ' ἰλύος κεκαλυμμένα Φ 318.

ἱμάς, -άντος, ὁ. Dat. pl. ἱμᾶσι Ε 727, Κ 262, 475, 499, 567, Φ 30, Ψ 324, 363. ἱμάντεσσι Θ 544. (1) A thong or strap: δῆσε χεῖρας ἱμᾶσιν Φ 30 (doubtless the belts with which the χιτῶνες of 31 were girt), βοέους Χ 397. Cf. ψ 201.—(2) In special applications. (a) In pl., straps for guiding or securing a horse, reins, haltering straps: ἵππους δῆσαν ἱμάντεσσιν Θ 544, ὅππως τανύσῃ ἱμᾶσιν Ψ 324. Cf. Κ 475, 499, 567.—(b) In pl., straps, interplaited and strained tight, forming the platform of a chariot: δίφρος ἱμᾶσιν ἐντέταται E 727.—(c) In pl., a series of straps so treated inserted in a helmet to strengthen it: [κυνέη] ἱμᾶσιν ἐντέτατο K 262.—App., the straps forming the τελαμών of a shield: ῥαφαὶ ἐλέλυντο ἱμάντων χ 186.—(d) The lash of a whip: μάστιγας ἄειραν, πέπληγόν θ' ἱμᾶσιν Ψ 363.—(e) The chin-strap of a helmet Γ 371, 375.—(f) A thong wound round the knuckles of a boxer Ψ 684.—(g) The κεστὸς ἱμάς, the love-charm, consisting of a pierced (*i.e.* embroidered) strap, carried by Aphrodite Ξ 214, 219.—(h) A strap passing through a slit in a door by which the bar or bolt (κληΐς, ὀχεύς) could be drawn from without so as to secure the door: ἐπὶ κληῗδ' ἐτάνυσσεν ἱμάντι α 442, παρὰ κληῗδος ἱμάντα (*i.e.* through the slit) δ 802. Cf. φ 46.—(i) The strap round the shaft of a τρύπανον ι 385.

ἱμάσθλη, -ης, ἡ [ἱμάς]. A whip (but see μάστιξ) Θ 43 = N 25, Ψ 582: ζ 320, ν 82.

†**ἱμάσσω** [ἱμάς]. 3 sing. aor. ἵμασε E 589, Λ 280, 531, P 624: ε 380, ζ 316. Subj. ἱμάσσω O 17. 3 sing. ἱμάσσῃ B 782. To lash, scourge: εἴ σε πληγῇσιν ἱμάσσω O 17.—To whip up (horses or mules) E 589, Λ 280, 531, P 624: ε 380, ζ 316.—Fig., of Zeus, to lash or afflict (the earth): ὅτε γαῖαν ἱμάσσῃ B 782.

ἱμείρω [ἵμερος]. Also as deponent ἱμείρομαι. 2 sing. ἱμείρεαι Ξ 269. 3 sing. aor. subj. ἱμείρεται α 41. 3 sing. opt. ἱμείραιτο Ξ 163. (1) To wish, desire. With infin.: παραδραθέειν φιλότητι Ξ 163. Cf. α 59, ε 209.—(2) With genit., to long for, sigh after: Πασιθέης Ξ 269.—To bethink oneself of, turn one's mind to: ἧς αἴης α 41.—To let one's mind dwell upon, set one's thoughts upon: κακῶν τούτων κ 431.—To be in quest of: ψύχεος ἱμείρων κ 555.

ἴμεν[1], 1 pl. εἶμι.

ἴμεν[2], **ἴμεναι**, infin. εἶμι.

ἱμερόεις, -εσσα, -εν [ἵμερος]. (1) Answering to the desires, lovely, delightsome, charming, ravishing Γ 397, E 429, Ξ 170, Σ 603: α 421 = σ 304, ρ 519, σ 194.—(2) To which one feels a tendency or inclination: πᾶσιν ἱμερόεις ὑπέδυ γόος (a yearning for weeping came upon them) κ 398.—(3) In neut. ἱμερόεν as adv., ravishingly: κιθάριζεν Σ 570.

ἵμερος, -ου, ὁ. (1) Desire, longing, yearning. With genit., of what is desired: ἀνδρὸς προτέρου Γ 139. Cf. Λ 89: ψ 144.—Sexual desire: ἵ. μ' αἱρεῖ Γ 446 = Ξ 328. Cf. Ξ 198, 216.—(2) Impulse, tendency, inclination. With genit.: γόου Ψ 14. Cf. Ψ 108, 153, Ω 514, 507: = δ 113, 183, π 215, τ 249, χ 500, ψ 231.

ἱμερτός, -όν [vbl. adj. fr. ἱμείρω]. Delightful, charming: Τιταρησσόν B 751.

ἴμμεναι, infin. εἶμι.

ἵνα. (1) Where, in which place, in the place where: ἵν' Ἀθηναίων ἵσταντο φάλαγγες B 558. Cf. B 604, E 360, K 127 (see γάρ (4)), Λ 807, Ω 382, etc.: ἵν' ἄρ' ἕζετο ζ 322. Cf. δ 85, 272, ι 136, λ 610 (in which), τ 20, etc.—After a vb. of seeing: ὄψεσθ', ἵνα τώ γε καθεύδετον (see where ...) θ 313.—(2) In reference to occasion rather than to place: σοὶ γάμος σχεδόν ἐστιν, ἵνα χρὴ ... ζ 27. Cf. ω 507.—So app. ἵνα μὴ ῥέξομεν ὧδε H 353 (in the case where ..., *i.e.* unless ...).—(3) To which place, whither, where: ἵνα μιν κάλεον ζ 55. Cf. δ 821.—So prob. ἵνα οἱ σὺν φόρτον ἄγοιμι ξ 296.—(4) In final clauses, in order that, so that. (a) With subj. (α) Pure: ἵνα ὕβριν ἴδῃ A 203. Cf. A 302, 363, 410, B 232, etc.: ἵν' εἰδῇς β 111. Cf. α 95, 302, 373, β 307, etc. —(β) With κεν μ 156.—(b) With opt. (α) Pure: ἵν' ἔκδηλος γένοιτο E 2. Cf. E 564, I 452, K 367, Λ 2, etc.: ἵνα μιν ἔροιτο α 135. Cf. γ 2, 438, δ 70, 584, etc.—(β) With κεν μ 156.

ἰνδάλλομαι. (1) To appear, show oneself, make one's appearance, come into view: ἰνδάλλετό σφισι πᾶσιν P 213. Cf. Ψ 460.—(2) To appear, seem: ὥς τέ μοι ἀθάνατος ἰνδάλλεται γ 246.—(3) App., to think (cf. the double sense 'seem' and 'think' in δοκέω): ὥς μοι ἰνδάλλεται ἦτορ τ 224 (as my mind pictures to itself).

ἰνίον (Fινίον) [ἰν-, ἴς]. The double tendon running up the back of the neck (the τένοντε (τένοντας) of K 456, Ξ 466, Π 587): βεβλήκει κατὰ ἰνίον E 73. Cf. Ξ 495.

ἴξαλος. Epithet of the wild goat. App., bounding, nimble, or the like: ἰξάλου αἰγὸς ἀγρίου Δ 105.

ἷξε, 3 sing. aor. ἵκω.

ἵξομαι, fut. ἱκνέομαι.

ἰξύς, ἡ. Dat. ἰξυῖ. The waist: περὶ ζώνην βάλετ' ἰξυῖ ε 231 = κ 544.

ἰοδνεφής, -ές (Fιοδνεφής) [ἴον + δνεφ-, δνοφ-, δνόφος. See δνοφερός]. Violet-dark; of wool, app., merely dark in colour. Prepared from the fleeces of 'black' sheep δ 135.—Growing on such a sheep ι 426.

ἰοδόκος, -ον [ἰός + δοκ-, δέχομαι]. Serving to hold arrows. Epithet of quivers O 444: φ 12, 60.

ἰοειδής [ἴον + εἶδος]. Violet-like. Epithet of the sea. Blue, or perh. merely, dark Λ 298: ε 56, λ 107.

ἰόεις, -εντος (Fιόεις) [ἴον]. = prec. Epithet of iron. App., dark: σίδηρον Ψ 850.

ἴοι, 3 sing. opt. εἶμι.

ἴομεν (ἴ), 1 pl. subj. εἶμι.

ἰόμωρος [app. ἰο-, ἰός. Cf. ἐγχεσίμωρος, ὑλακόμωρος]. App., eager or active with arrows Δ 242, Ξ 479.

ἴον, -ου, τό (Fίον. Cf. L. *vio-la*). The blue violet. Collectively: ἴου ἠδὲ σελίνου θήλεον ε 72.

ἰονθάς, -άδος. Epithet of the wild goat of unknown meaning ξ 50.

ἰόντες, nom. pl. masc. pple. εἶμι.

ἰός, -οῦ, ὁ. Acc. pl. ἰά Υ 68. An arrow A 48, Γ 80, Δ 94, Θ 514, Π 773, T 59, Ψ 862, etc.: α 262, υ 62, φ 423, χ 3, 15, 75, 82, 116, 119, 246. —In pl. ἰά denoting rather vague quantity than plurality: ἔχων ἰά (a quiverful) Υ 68.

ἰότης, -ητος, ἡ. (1) Will, ordinance, determination, working to an end: μὴ δι' ἐμὴν ἰότητα ... (it is not my doing that ...) O 41. Cf. E 874, Σ 396, T 9: η 214 = ξ 198, λ 341, 384, μ 190 =

ρ 119, π 232.—(2) App., will, wish, desire: οὐ μῶλος ἐτύχθη μνηστήρων ἰότητι (did not turn out as they wished) σ 234 (though they are represented as impartial).

ἴουλοι, οἱ. Hair on the cheeks, whiskers λ 319.

ἰοχέαιρα (ἰοχέϝαιρα) [ἰός + χεϝ-, χέω]. Shedder of arrows (cf. χέω (6) (a)). Epithet or a name of Artemis E 53, 447, Z 428, I 538, Υ 39, 71, Φ 480, Ω 606: ζ 102, λ 172, 198, ο 478.

ἱππάζομαι [ἵππος]. To drive one's chariot: ἀφραδέως ἱππάζεαι Ψ 426.

ἵππειος, -η, -ον [ἵππος]. Of, pertaining to, intended for, a horse or horses: ζυγοῦ (the horses' . . .) E 799, φάτνῃ K 568. Cf. Λ 536 = Υ 501, O 537 (of horse-hair) Ψ 392: δ 40.

ἱππεύς, ὁ [ἵππος]. (1) A warrior who fights with the aid of a chariot: πεζοί θ' ἱππῆές τε B 810 = Θ 59 := ω 70. Cf. Δ 297, 301, 322, Λ 151, 529, 720, 724, 746, M 66, O 258, 270, Ψ 133.—In voc. as epithet of Patroclus: Πατρόκλεες ἱππεῦ Π 20, 744, 812, 843.—(2) App. = ἡνίοχος: φθὰν ἱππήων Λ 51 (*i.e.* app., having left their chariots they advanced on foot in front of them), ἱππῆες μετεκίαθον 52.—(3) One who drives his chariot in a race Ψ 262, 273, 287.—(4) A charioteer in gen.: πολέες παρήϊον ἠρήσαντο ἱππῆες φορέειν Δ 144.

ἱππηλάσιος, -η [ἵππος + ἐλα-, ἐλαύνω]. Fit to be traversed by chariots: ὁδός H 340 = 439.

ἱππηλάτα [as prec. Prob. orig. a voc. turned into a nom.]. Driver of the chariot. Epithet of heroes. Of Tydeus Δ 387.—Of Peleus H 125, I 438, Λ 772, Σ 331.—Of Phoenix I 432, Π 196, T 311.—Of Oeneus I 581.—Of Nestor γ 436, 444.

ἱππήλατος, -ον [as prec.]. Affording good ground for driving δ 607, ν 242.

ἱππιοχαίτης [ἵππος + χαίτη]. Of horse-hair: λόφον Z 469.

ἱππιοχάρμης [ἵππος + χάρμη]. = ἱππεύς (1). Epithet of Troïlus Ω 257.—Of Amythaon λ 259.

ἱππόβοτος, -ον [ἵππος + βοτ-, βόσκω]. Grazed, suitable for being grazed, by horses. Of Ithaca δ 606.—Epithet of places. Of Argos B 287, Γ 75 = 258, Z 152, I 246, O 30, T 329: γ 263, δ 99, 562, ο 239, 274.—Of Tricē Δ 202.—Of Elis φ 347.

ἱππόδαμος [ἵππος + δαμ-, δαμάζω]. Tamer or breaker-in of horses. Epithet of heroes. Of Atreus B 23 = 60.—Of Castor Γ 237 := λ 300.—Of Tydeus Δ 370, Ψ 472.—Of Diomedes E 415, 781, 849, H 404 = I 51 = 711, Θ 194: γ 181.—Of Antenor Z 299, Ξ 473.—Of Hector H 38, Π 717, X 161, 211, Ω 804.—Of Hippasus Λ 450.—Of Thrasymedes Ξ 10.—Of Hyperenor P 24.—Of Nestor γ 17.—In pl. as epithet of the Trojans B 230, Γ 127, Δ 333, Z 461, Θ 110, M 440, P 230, Υ 180, etc.

ἱππόδασυς, -εια [ἵππος + δασύς]. With bushy horse-hair crest. Epithet of helmets Γ 369, Δ 459 = Z 9, N 614, 714, O 535, P 295: χ 111, 145.

ἱππόδρομος, ὁ [ἵππος + δρομ-, δραμ-. See τρέχω]. Ground that can be traversed by chariots Ψ 330.

ἱππόθεν [ἵππος + -θεν (1)]. From or out of the (Trojan) horse: ἐκχύμενοι θ 515. Cf. λ 531.

ἱπποκέλευθος [ἵππος + κέλευθος. 'One who fares with horses']. = ἱππεύς (1). In voc. as epithet of Patroclus Π 126, 584, 839.

ἱππόκομος, -ον [ἵππος + κόμη]. With horse-hair crest. Epithet of helmets M 339, N 132 = Π 216, Π 338, 797.

ἱπποκορυστής [ἵππος + κορυστής. Cf. χαλκοκορυστής]. Marshaller of chariots. In pl., epithet of heroes and peoples B 1 = Ω 677, K 431, Π 287, Φ 205.

ἱππόμαχος [ἵππος + μάχομαι]. = ἱππεύς (1). In pl., epithet of the Phrygians K 431.

ἱπποπόλος [ἵππος + -πολος, conn. with πολεύω]. Busied with horses. In pl., epithet of the Thracians N 4, Ξ 227.

ἵππος, -ου, ὁ, ἡ. (1) A horse or mare: εὖ τις ἵπποισιν δεῖπνον δότω B 383, παρήϊον ἔμμεναι ἵππων (for a horse) Δ 142, παρ' ἵππων ὠκειάων 500 (app. from a stud-farm where brood mares were kept). Cf. A 154, B 763, E 195, Z 506, etc.: γ 324, δ 8, 635, ε 371, ν 81, etc.—Of the Trojan horse δ 272, θ 492, 503, 512, λ 523.—Fig.: νηῶν, αἵ θ' ἁλὸς ἵπποι ἀνδράσι γίγνονται δ 708.—(2) In dual and pl., the horses and their chariot forming one conception, 'horses and chariot': κοσμῆσαι ἵππους B 554, ἠέρι ἔγχος ἐκέκλιτο καὶ ἵππω E 356. Cf. Γ 113, H 240, 342 (*v.l.* ἵππον see (4)), I 708, Λ 339, M 111, Σ 153, Υ 157, etc.: ξ 267 = ρ 436, ξ 278.—(3) Hence, in dual and pl., the horses neglected, passes into the sense 'chariot' simply: ἐξ ἵππων ἀποβάντες Γ 265, ἑσταότ' ἔν θ' ἵπποισι καὶ ἅρμασιν (hendiadys) Δ 366 = Λ 198, ἐφ' ἵπποιιν ἀνόρουσεν T 396. Cf. E 13, 19, 46, 111, 163, 227, 249, 255, 328, Z 232, H 16, Λ 94, 192, M 82, Ξ 435, Π 749, etc.: ι 49.—In this sense even with adjectives properly applicable only to the horses: ἵππων ὠκυπόδων ἐπέβησεν Θ 128, ἐπὶ καλλίτριχε βήμεναι ἵππω P 504. Cf. H 15, Σ 531: σ 263.—(4) Chariots and horses collectively, the horse force of an army: τάφρον, ἥ χ' ἵππον ἐρυκάκοι H 342 (*v.l.* ἵππους; see (2)).

ἱπποσύνη, -ης, ἡ [ἵππος]. Horsemanship, skill in driving or using the chariot: ἱπποσύνῃ ἐκέκαστο Ψ 289. Cf. Δ 303, Λ 503, Π 809.—In pl. in sim. sense Π 776, Ψ 307: ω 40.

ἱππότα [ἵππος. Prob. orig. a voc. turned into a nom.]. = ἱππεύς (1). Epithet of heroes. Of Nestor B 336, Δ 317, H 170, Θ 112, I 52, K 102, etc.: γ 68, 102 = 210 = 253, 386, 397, 405, 417 = 474, δ 161.—Of Phyleus B 628.—Of Tydeus E 126.—Of Oeneus Ξ 117.—Of Peleus Π 33, Ψ 89.

ἵππουρις [ἵππος + οὐρή]. Bearing a horse's tail as a crest. Of helmets Z 495, T 382, Γ 337 = Λ 42 = O 481 = Π 138 := χ 124.

†ἵπτομαι. 3 sing. fut. ἴψεται B 193. 2 sing. aor. ἴψαο A 454, Π 237. To bear hard upon, smite: λαὸν Ἀχαιῶν A 454 = Π 237, υἷας Ἀχαιῶν B 193.

ἱρεύς. See ἱερεύς.

ἱρεύω. See ἱερεύω.

ἴρηξ, -ηκος, ὁ. A bird of the falcon kind, a falcon or hawk: ὥς τ' ἴ. ὦρτο πέτεσθαι N 62. Cf.

N 819, O 237, Π 582, Σ 616, Φ 494: ε 66.—*ἴρηξ κίρκος* ν 86 (*κίρκος* being app. the more specific word).

ἶρις, *ἡ*. Dat. pl. *ἴρισσι* Λ 27. The rainbow: *ἴρισσιν ἐοικότες* Λ 27. Cf. P 547.

ἱρός. See *ἱερός*.

ἴς, *ἰνός*, *ἡ* (*Fίς*) [*ἴς*, *ἶφι*, *ἴφιος* show resemblances, but it is difficult to say whether, or to what extent, they are connected with each other]. Dat. pl. *ἴνεσι* Ψ 191. (**1**) A tendon or sinew: *χρόα ἴνεσιν* (the flesh on the . . .) Ψ 191. Cf. λ 219.—(**2**) Specifically, the double tendon at the back of an ox's neck P 522 (cf. *ἰνίον*).—(**3**) Bodily strength or vigour: *ἶν' ἀπέλεθρον ἔχοντας* E 245, *οὐ γὰρ ἐμὴ ἲς ἔσθ' οἵη πάρος ἔσκεν* Λ 668. Cf. M 320, Ψ 720: *οὐδ' ἲς οὐδὲ βίη* (the two hardly to be distinguished) σ 3. Cf. λ 393, μ 175, φ 283.—Of the wind, strength, force O 383, P 739: ι 71, ν 276, τ 186.—(**4**) Force exerted, strength put into an effort: *ἐπέρεισεν ἶν' ἀπέλεθρον* H 269 := ι 538.—(**5**) *ἴς τινος*, periphrasis for a person (cf. *βίη* (5)): *ἱερὴ ἲς Τηλεμάχοιο* β 409 = σ 405 = φ 101, π 476, σ 60 = φ 130, χ 354.—Sim.: *καλέετο ἲς ποταμοῖο* (the mighty river) Φ 356.

ἰσάζω (*Fισάζω*) [*ἶσος*]. 3 sing. pa. iterative mid. *ἰσάσκετο* Ω 607. (**1**) To make equal: *σταθμὸν ἔχουσα καὶ εἴριον ἀμφὶς ἀνέλκει ἰσάζουσα* (*i.e.* putting on wool till it balances the weight) M 435.—(**2**) In mid., to liken oneself to, compare oneself with. With dat.: *οὕνεκα Λητοῖ ἰσάσκετο* Ω 607.

ἴσαν[1], 3 pl. plupf. *εἴδω* (C).

ἴσαν[2], 3 pl. impf. *εἶμι*.

ἴσᾱσι (ῐ), 3 pl. pf. *εἴδω* (C).

ἴσθι, imp. *εἴδω* (C).

ἴσθμιον, *τό* [*ἰσθμός*, neck]. A necklace σ 300.

ἴσκω (*Fίσκω*) [app. for *Fίκσκω*, fr. *Fικ-*, *εἴκω*[1]. Cf. *ἐΐσκω*]. (**1**) To make like. With dat.: *πάντων Ἀργείων φωνὴν ἴσκουσ' ἀλόχοισιν* (*i.e.* *ἀλόχων φωναῖσιν*) δ 279 (imitating their voices).—(**2**) To liken to, deem like, take for. With dat.: *τῷ σε* (*ἐμὲ σοί*) *ἴσκοντες* Λ 799, Π 41 (*v.l.* *εἴσκοντες*).—(**3**) To speak feigningly: *ἴσκε, ψεύδεα πολλὰ λέγων* τ 203.—(**4**) To conjecture, guess: *ἴσκεν ἕκαστος ἀνήρ* χ 31 (*i.e.* so spoke from conjecture, under misapprehension).

ἰσόθεος (*Fισόθεος*) [*ἶσος* + *θεός*]. Godlike, like the gods: *φώς* Γ 310, Δ 212, Λ 472 = O 559 = Π 632, Ψ 569: α 324.—With *φώς* in apposition to the name of a hero B 565, H 136, I 211, Λ 428, 644, Ψ 677: υ 124.

ἰσόμορος [*ἶσος* + *μόρος*]. Equally favoured by destiny. Absol. O 209.

ἰσόπεδον, *τό* [*ἶσος* + *πέδον*, the ground]. A piece of level ground: *ἧος ἵκηται ἰ.* N 142.

ἶσος, *-η*, *-ον* (*Fῖσος*). Also (always in fem. and only in senses (1) (a) and (5)) with prothetic *ἐ* *ἐΐσος* *-η*, *-ον* (*ἐFισος*). (**1**) (**a**) Equal in height: [*ἵππους*] *ἐΐσας* B 765.—(**b**) Even, in line: *ἴσας ὑσμίνη κεφαλὰς ἔχεν* Λ 72.—(**c**) The same in amount or value, equal: *ἴσην βίην καὶ κῦδος* H 205. Cf. I 318, Ψ 736, 823.—With dat.: *οὐ σοί ποτε ἶσον ἔχω γέρας* (*i.e.* *σῷ γέρᾳ*) A 163.—(**2**) (**a**) Fair, one's fair . . . : *μοῖραν* υ 282, 294.—Such as to afford favour to neither side, even, fair: *πολέμου τέλος* (see *τέλος* (3)) Υ 101.—(**b**) Absol. in fem., one's fair share: *ἀτεμβόμενος ἴσης* Λ 705: ι 42 = 549.—One's allotted portion, one's allotment: *ᾧ τ' ἐρίζητον περὶ ἴσης* M 423.—(**c**) Absol. in neut. pl., fair dealing, the right (cf. *πιστός* (2) (b), *φυκτός*): *οὐδέ ποτ' ἶσα ἔσσεται, ὄφρα* . . . β 203.—(**3**) The same in quality, producing the same effects, the like: *θυμόν* N 704, P 720: *κακόν* ο 72.—(**4**) Like, resembling, comparable with. With dat.: *δαίμονι ἶσος* E 438. Cf. Λ 297, 747, M 130, N 39, Σ 56, X 132, 460, etc.: *ἶσος ἀναύδῳ* κ 378. Cf. γ 290, θ 115, λ 243, ξ 175, σ 27.—(**5**) In the *ἐϊσ-* forms epithet (**a**) Of ships, well balanced, swinging evenly on the keel, trim A 306, B 671, E 62, Θ 217, O 729, etc.: γ 10, δ 358, η 43, λ 508, etc.—(**b**) Of shields, well balanced: *ἀσπίδα πάντοσ' ἐΐσην* (so balanced as to answer freely to every movement of the arm) Γ 347, E 300, Λ 61, N 405, etc.—(**c**) Of the intelligence or one's wits, well balanced, sound, sane: *φρένας* λ 337 = σ 249, ξ 178.—(**d**) Of a meal, in which each gets his due share of the good things: *δαιτός* A 468, I 225, etc. Cf. λ 185, π 479, etc.—Sim. of the gods' share of a sacrifice: *οὔ μοί ποτε βωμὸς ἐδεύετο δαιτὸς ἐΐσης* (app. implying that the proper parts of the victim are offered, so that the god and the mortals share fairly) Δ 48 = Ω 69.—(**6**) (**a**) In neut. sing. *ἶσον* as adv., even as, in like manner or measure with. With dat.: *ἶσον ἐμοὶ φάσθαι* A 187, *ἶσόν σφιν ἀπήχθετο κηρί* Γ 454. Cf. E 467, I 142, 284, 603, 616, O 50, 167, 183, Σ 82: λ 557, ξ 203.—(**b**) So in neut. pl. *ἶσα*: *ἔτρεφε ἶσα τέκεσσι* E 71. Cf. E 441, N 176 = O 551, O 439, Φ 315: α 432, λ 304, 484, ο 520.—*κατὰ ἶσα*, on equal terms, without advantage to either side: *κατὰ ἶσα μάχην ἐτάνυσσεν* Λ 336.—So *ἐπὶ ἶσα* M 436 = O 413.

ἰσοφαρίζω [*ἶσος* + *φέρω*]. To rival, contend with, cope with, vie with. With dat.: *μένος οἱ* (in . . .) Z 101. Cf. I 390, Φ 194, 411.

ἰσοφόρος [as prec.]. Of oxen, drawing the plough with equal strength (and so cutting an even furrow): *βόες* σ 373.

ἰσόω [*ἶσος*]. In mid., to liken oneself to. With dat.: *τοῖσίν κεν ἐν ἄλγεσιν ἰσωσαίμην* η 212.

ἴστε, 2 pl. pf. *εἴδω* (C).

†**ἵστημι** [*στα-*. Cf. L. *sto*, Eng. *stand*]. (**A**) 3 pl. pres. *ἱστᾶσιν* N 336. 3 pl. impf. *ἵστασαν* (*v.l.* *ἔστασαν* (see below)) B 525, M 56, Σ 346: γ 182, θ 435, σ 307. Imp. *ἵστη* Φ 313. 3 sing. pa. iterative *ἵστασκε* τ 574. Fut. infin. *στήσειν* λ 314. Aor. *στῆσα* δ 582, ξ 258, ρ 427. 3 sing. *ἔστησε* E 368, 523, 775, Θ 49, N 34, O 126, Ψ 852: α 127, ι 248, μ 405, ξ 303, ρ 29. *στῆσε* B 558, Δ 298, Π 199: β 391, η 4, τ 188, φ 120, 123. 1 pl. *στήσαμεν* μ 305. 3 *ἔστησαν* A 448: ξ 420. *στῆσαν* Ψ 745, Ω 350: β 425, ο 290. *ἔστασαν* (traditionally explained as for *ἔστησαν*. *V.l.* *ἵστασαν* (see above)). 3 pl. subj. *στήσωσι* X 350. Imp. *στῆσον* Z 433. Pple. *στήσας* T 247, Ω 232: ε 252, κ 506. Pl.

στήσαντες π 292, τ 11. Fem. στήσᾱσα Ε 755, Υ 114: υ 111. Infin. στῆσαι Σ 344, Χ 443, Ψ 40 : θ 434. **Mid.** 3 pl. aor. στήσαντο Α 480 : β 431. Pl. pple. στησάμενοι Σ 533 : ι 54, 77, μ 402. Fem. sing. στησαμένη β 94, τ 139, ω 129. Infin. στήσασθαι Ζ 528.—**(B)** Aor. ἔστην κ 97, 148, 310. στῆν Λ 744. 2 sing. ἔστης Υ 179. 3 ἔστη Β 101, Ε 108, Ζ 43, Κ 354, etc. : θ 304, ξ 270, π 12, ρ 439, χ 332. στῆ Α 197, Β 20, Η 46, Μ 353, etc. : α 103, β 37, η 21, ο 150, etc. 3 dual στήτην Α 332, Γ 344, Ο 155, Φ 285 : ρ 261. 1 pl. στῆμεν Λ 777. 2 ἔστητε Δ 243, 246. 3 ἔστησαν Λ 593, Ν 488 : κ 391, ω 58. στῆσαν δ 22. ἔσταν Α 535, Β 467, Χ 473, Ω 359, etc. : ζ 211, θ 118, χ 115, ω 392, etc. στάν Ι 193, Λ 216, Π 601, Ψ 358, 757. 2 sing. subj. στήῃς Ρ 30. 3 στήῃ Ε 598. 1 pl. στήομεν Ο 297. στέωμεν Λ 348, Χ 231. 3 sing. opt. σταίη α 256. 3 pl. σταίησαν Ρ 733. Imp. στῆθι Χ 222, Ψ 97 : ν 387, ρ 447. Pl. στῆτε Ζ 80, Λ 588 : ζ 199, 218. Pple. στάς, -άντος Γ 210, Ε 112, Λ 622, Π 231, Ρ 490, Ψ 141, etc.: α 120, ε 75, η 133, τ 575, ω 234, etc. Fem. στᾶσα Δ 129, Ε 784, Λ 10, Ξ 154, Υ 49 : δ 370, ζ 56, κ 400, 455, μ 20. Infin. στήμεναι Ρ 167, Χ 253 : ε 414. στῆναι Φ 266 : ρ 439, σ 241. 3 sing. pa. iterative στάσκε Γ 217, Σ 160. **Mid.** 1 sing. pres. ἵσταμαι Δ 54, Ε 809, Ν 271. 3 ἵσταται Κ 173, Ο 293, Χ 318. 3 pl. ἵστανται Μ 44. 3 sing. impf. ἵστατο Β 151, Η 136, Ι 14, Ν 333, 702, Π 166, Τ 250, Υ 68, Φ 240, 327, Ψ 366 : α 129, ν 56, ξ 433, ο 257, ω 422. 3 pl. ἵσταντο Β 473, 558, Λ 171, 574, Ν 126, Ο 317, Ψ 839 : η 5, θ 110, 263, ι 381. 2 sing. imp. ἵστα(σ)ο Λ 314, Ν 448, Ρ 31, 179, Υ 197, Χ 85 : χ 233. Pl. ἵστασθε Λ 591. Pple. ἱστάμενος, -η Β 172, Δ 203, Μ 341, Ν 768, Σ 496, etc. : δ 25, ε 159, η 83, ι 402, ξ 162, etc. Infin. ἵστασθαι τ 201. Fut. στήσομαι Σ 308, Υ 90. 1 pl. στησόμεθα Σ 278. Infin. στήσεσθαι Θ 234, Λ 609, Φ 482. **Pass.** 3 sing. aor. ἐστάθη ρ 463.—**(C)** 2 sing. pf. ἕστηκας Ε 485. 3 ἕστηκε Γ 231, Δ 263, Ε 186, Σ 172, Ψ 327 : α 185, ω 299, 308. 3 dual ἕστατον Ψ 284. 3 pl. ἑστήκᾱσι Δ 434. ἑστᾶσι Δ 245, Ε 196, Ι 44, Μ 64, Ξ 308. 3 sing. plupf. ἑστήκει(ν) Δ 329, Ε 587, Μ 446, Σ 557, Τ 117, Ψ 691, etc.: θ 505, σ 344, φ 434, ω 446. 1 pl. ἕσταμεν λ 466. 3 ἕστασαν Β 777, Δ 331, Κ 520, Μ 55, Ρ 267, Ψ 370, etc. : β 341, δ 426, η 89, τ 211, φ 52, etc. 3 sing. subj. ἑστήκῃ Ρ 435 : χ 469. Imp. ἕσταθι χ 489. 2 dual ἕστατον Ψ 443. 2 pl. ἕστατε Υ 354. Pple. ἑσταότ- Β 170, 320, Δ 90, Μ 336, Ν 438, Σ 246, Τ 79, Ψ 283, etc. : θ 380, ι 442, λ 571, 583, ν 187, χ 130, ψ 46, ω 204. Infin. ἑστάμεναι Κ 480, Λ 410, Ν 56, Ο 666, Σ 374 : χ 121. ἑστάμεν Δ 342, Μ 316, Ο 675 : φ 261. (ἀμφ-, ἀνθ-, ἀν-, ἀφ-, δι-, ἐξυπαν-, ἐπαν-, ἐφ-, καθ-, μεθ-, παρ-, προ-, συν-, ὑφ-.) **(I)** In pres. and impf. act. and the other forms (A). **(1)** To set, place, put, cause to be, in a specified or indicated place or position: ἑκατόμβην ἔστησαν περὶ βωμόν Α 448, σκολόπεσσιν, τοὺς ἵστασαν (had set) Μ 56. Cf. Β 558, Ε 523, Ο 126 (cf. α 127 below), Σ 344, 346, Φ 313, Χ 443, Ψ 40, 852 : ἔγχος ἔστησε δουροδόκης ἔντοσθεν α 127, ἴκρια στήσας (setting it up) ε 252, ἥμισυ ἔστησεν ἐν ἄγγεσιν ι 248. Cf. θ 434, 435, μ 405 = ξ 303, ξ 420, ρ 29, σ 307, τ 574, φ 120, 123.—In mid. : κρητῆρα στήσασθαι Ζ 528. Cf. β 431.—**(2)** To set up (a mast) β 425 = ο 290, κ 506.—In mid. Α 480 : ι 77, μ 402.—To set up (the warp of a web). In mid. β 94 = ω 129, τ 139.—**(3)** To bring (together), assemble : ἄμυδις στήσασα θεούς Υ 114.—Sim. of a natural agency : ἀνέμων, οἵ τ' ἄμυδις κονίης ἱστᾶσιν ὁμίχλην Ν 336.—**(4)** To station, post : πεζούς Δ 298. Cf. Ζ 433.—**(5)** To draw up, set in array (troops) : Φωκήων στίχας Β 525. Cf. Π 199.—To set (a battle) in array. In mid. : στησάμενοι ἐμάχοντο μάχην Σ 533 : ι 54.—**(6)** To bring about, cause, set going : φυλόπιδα λ 314. Cf. π 292 = τ 11.—**(7)** To bring to a stand, stop, halt (horses, etc.) Ε 755, Ω 350.—Absol., to halt one's beasts : στῆσεν ἐν προθύροισιν η 4.—To tether (horses) Ε 368, 775, Θ 49, Ν 34.—**(8)** To moor (a ship) β 391.—To bring (a ship) to land : στήσαμεν ἐν λιμένι νῆα μ 305. Cf. γ 182, δ 582, ξ 258 = ρ 427.—Absol., to bring one's ship to land : στῆσεν ἐν Ἀμνισῷ τ 188. Cf. Ψ 745.—**(9)** To stop the motion of, stop : μύλην υ 111.—**(10)** To weigh out : χρυσοῦ δέκα τάλαντα Τ 247, Ω 232. Cf. Χ 350.—**(II)** In pres. and impf. mid. and the other forms (B). **(1)** To take up a specified or indicated position, to take one's stand, come and stand, in a specified or indicated place or position : στῆ ὄπιθεν (came up behind him) Α 197, ἀγχοῦ ἱσταμένη Β 172, ἵν' Ἀθηναίων ἵσταντο φάλαγγες (were taking up their position) 558. Cf. Β 20, Ε 108, Ζ 43, Η 136 (stood forth), Θ 234, Λ 314, Ξ 154, etc. : στῆ ἐπὶ προθύροις α 103, ἀμφὶ κοῦροι ἵσταντο θ 263. Cf. α 333, γ 449, ζ 218, η 5, ι 402, μ 20, ν 387, ρ 447, υ 128, etc.—Of inanimate objects : κονίη ἵστατ' ἀειρομένη Β 151. Cf. Φ 240, 327, Ψ 366.—**(2)** Of a period of time, to set in, begin : ἔαρος νέον ἱσταμένοιο τ 519. Cf. ξ 162 = τ 307.—Of a star, to appear in its place Χ 318.—**(3)** To be brought about, be set on foot : ἵστατο νεῖκος Ν 333.—**(4)** To be, stand, in a specified position : τάων οὐ πρόσθ' ἵσταμαι (protect) Δ 54, ἑκὰς ἱστάμενος Ν 263. Cf. Ε 809, Ν 271.—Impers. Fig. : ἐπὶ ξυροῦ ἵσταται ἀκμῆς ἢ . . . ἠὲ . . . Κ 173.—Of inanimate objects, to stand, be : ἔνθ' ἄλλα ἔγχεα ἵστατο α 129.—Of abstractions : περὶ κακὰ πάντοθεν ἔστη ξ 270, ρ 439.—**(5)** To remain standing, keep one's legs : ἐστάθη ἔμπεδον ρ 463. —**(6)** To make a stand, stand firm : στήομεν Ο 297. Cf. Λ 348 = Χ 231.—To stand firmly (on one's feet) : οὔ πως ἔστι πόδεσσι στήμεναι ε 414.—**(7)** To come to a stand, stand still, stop, halt : ταρβήσαντε στήτην Α 332, ἔστη δοῦπον ἀκούσας Κ 354. Cf. Ε 598, Κ 374, Λ 545, Π 806, Σ 160, Φ 551, Χ 222, 225, 293, Ω 360 : στῆτέ μοι, ἀμφίπολοι ζ 199, κῆρ οἱ ὅρμαιν' ἱσταμένῳ (halting ever and anon) η 83. Cf. ζ 211, ω 392.—Of inanimate objects : πολλὰ [δοῦρα] ἐν γαίῃ ἵσταντο (stopped short of their aim) Λ 574 = Ο 317, ἐγχείη ἐνὶ γαίῃ ἔστη Υ 280, Φ 70.—Hence, app., in aor., to (lose heart for action and) check oneself : τίφθ' οὕτως ἔστητε τεθηπότες; Δ 243, ὣς ἔστητε τεθηπότες 246 (in both passages implying continuance of the result; hence virtually 'stand idle').—**(8)** To come to a stand in face of a pressing foe, make a stand: ἐναντίοι ἔσταν Ἀχαιῶν Ε 497 = Ζ 106 = Λ 214 = Ρ 343, θῦνεν ἱστάμενος (making a stand at intervals) Λ 571. Cf. Ζ 80, Λ 171, 588, 591, 595 = Ο 591 = Ρ 114, Ρ 733.—(9) To come to a standing posture, stand up: ἀντίοι ἔσταν ἅπαντες Α 535. Cf. Γ 210, Ο 6, Υ 282, Ψ 271 = 456 = 657 = 706 = 752 = 801 = 830: στῆ μέσῃ ἀγορῇ β 37. Cf. ν 197.—So with ἀνά: ἀν' Ἀγαμέμνων ἔστη Β 101. Cf. Β 279, Ι 14, Τ 250: ἂν δ' ἵσταντο νέοι (*i.e.* for the contest) θ 110. Cf. θ 118, ν 56, ξ 433, ω 422.—Of hair, to stand on end: ὀρθαὶ τρίχες ἔσταν ἐνὶ μέλεσσιν Ω 359.—(10) To stand, remain standing: στάσκεν, ὕπαὶ δὲ ἴδεσκεν Γ 217: οὐδ' [ἄνεμος] εἴα ἵστασθαι τ 201.—To stand up (on one's feet): οὐδ' ὀρθὸς στῆναι δύναται ποσίν σ 241.—(III) In forms (C). (1) To have one's stand, stand, be, in a specified or indicated place or position: ἑσταότες θαυμάζομεν (stood and . . .) Β 320, ἵπποι παρ' ἅρμασιν ἕστασαν 777, εὗρε Λυκάονος υἱὸν ἑσταότα (in his place) Δ 90, ἑσταότ' νύξεν (as he stood facing him) Ε 579, ὅθι πλεῖστοι ἕστασαν (were gathered together) 781. Cf. Γ 231, Ε 186, Λ 600, Ο 434, Ρ 133, Σ 557, Φ 526, etc.: ἑσταότ' ἐν λίμνῃ λ 583, πὰρ λαμπτῆρσιν ἑστήκειν σ 344. Cf. γ 149, θ 380, ν 187, φ 434, χ 489, ω 446, etc.—Of inanimate objects: σὸν πλεῖον δέπας αἰεὶ ἕστηκεν Δ 263. Cf. Ι 44, Μ 55, 64, 446 (was lying), Ν 261, Ρ 435, Σ 374, 563 (was set up with . . .), Ψ 327: ἐν πίθοι ἕστασαν β 341. Cf. α 185 = ω 308, δ 426, η 89, 101, θ 505, φ 52, 261, χ 121, 469, ω 299.—(2) To remain in an indicated position: δηθὰ μάλ' ἑστήκειν Ε 587.—(3) Of a period of time, to have begun, be running: ἕβδομος ἑστήκει μείς Τ 117.—(4) To have been brought about, be on foot: φύλοπις Σ 172.—(5) To stand firm, show a bold front: σφῶϊν ἐπέοικε (χρὴ) ἑστάμεν Δ 342 = Μ 316. Cf. Λ 410, Μ 132, Ν 56, 708, Ο 666, Ρ 267.—To stand (without motion): ἀτρέμας ἑσταότα Ν 438.—Sim. of a part of the body: ὀφθαλμοὶ ὡς εἰ κέρα ἕστασαν ἀτρέμας τ 211.—(6) To stand idle, doing nothing, helpless: εὗρεν Ὀδυσῆα ἑσταότα Β 170, αἵ τ' ἐπεὶ ἔκαμον ἑστᾶσιν Δ 245. Cf. Δ 328, 329, 331, 334, 366, 367, Ε 485, Κ 480, Ν 293, Υ 245, etc.—(7) To be in a standing posture, stand: ὀρθῶν ἑσταότων ἀγορὴ γένετο Σ 246, ἑσταότος ἀκούειν (him who is on his legs, one speaking) Τ 79 (rejecting 77; if it be retained the sense must be 'to listen to one standing,' *i.e.* 'one ought to stand up to speak'). Cf. ι 442, λ 571.—To remain standing, keep one's legs: οὐδ' ἔτι δὴν ἑστήκειν Ψ 691.

ἱστίη, -ης, ἡ. A hearth: ἴστω Ζεὺς ἱ. τ' Ὀδυσῆος ξ 159 = ρ 156 = τ 304 = υ 231.

ἱστίον, -ου, τό [ἱστός]. A sail Α 481, Ο 627: β 427, δ 578, ι 70, 77, 149.—In pl. of the sail of a single vessel: ἱστία στείλαντο Α 433. Cf. Α 480: ἀν' ἱστία ἐρύσαντες μ 402. Cf. β 426 = ο 291, γ 10, δ 781, 783, ε 259, 269, θ 52, 54, κ 506, λ 3, 11, μ 170, ο 496, π 353.

ἱστοδόκη, -ης, ἡ [ἱστός + δοκ-, δέχομαι]. A crutch in the after part of a ship to receive the mast when lowered Α 434.

ἱστοπέδη, -ης, ἡ [app. ἱστός + πεδ-, ποδ-, πούς]. A mast-step (prob. = μεσόδμη) μ 51 = 162, 179.

ἱστός, -οῦ, ὁ [ἵστημι]. (1) A ship's mast Α 434, 480, Ψ 852, 878: β 424, δ 578, ε 254, ι 77, λ 3, μ 409, ο 496, etc.—(2) A loom for weaving Ζ 491: = α 357 = φ 351, ν 107 (of natural formations in a cave).—(3) The warp of a web: στησαμένη μέγαν ἱστόν β 94 = ω 129, τ 139.—(4) The web: ἱστὸν ἐποιχομένην Α 31. Cf. Γ 125, Ζ 456, Χ 440: β 104 = ω 139, β 109 = ω 145, ε 62, η 105, κ 222, 226, 254, ο 517, τ 149, ω 147.—(5) In pl., the art of weaving: ἱστῶν τεχνῆσσαι η 110.

ἴστω, 3 sing. imp. εἴδω (C).

ἴστωρ, -ορος, ὁ (Ϝίστωρ) [ἱστ-, οἶδα. See εἴδω (C) 'One who knows']. A referee or umpire Σ 501, Ψ 486.

ἰσχαλέος. Dried, desiccated: κρομύοιο τ 233.

†ἰσχανάω[1] [σισχανάω, (σ)ίσχω]. 2 sing. ἰσχανάᾳς ο 346. 3 pl. ἰσχανόωσι Ε 89. 3 pl. pa. iterative ἰσχανάασκον Ο 723. 3 pl. pres. mid. ἰσχανόωνται η 161. 3 sing. imp. ἰσχαναάσθω Τ 234. 3 pl. impf. pass. ἰσχανόωντο Μ 38. (1) To keep back from action, restrain: αὐτόν [μ'] ἰσχανάασκον Ο 723.—To debar from freedom of action, hold: Ἀργεῖοι ἐελμένοι ἰσχανόωντο Μ 38.—(2) To detain or keep with one in hospitality ο 346.—(3) To hold back, withstand, sustain the pressure of: ποταμὸν οὐ γέφυραι ἰσχανόωσιν Ε 89.—(4) In mid., to put constraint on oneself, to hold back or refrain from action: μηδέ τις ἰσχαναάσθω Τ 234. Cf. η 161.

†ἰσχανάω[2] [better ἰχανάω]. 3 sing. ἰσχανάᾳ Ρ 572. Pple. ἰσχανόων θ 288. Acc. sing. fem. ἰσχανόωσαν Ψ 300. To be eager for, yearn for. With genit.: φιλότητος θ 288. Cf. Ψ 300.—To be eager *to do*. With infin.: δακέειν Ρ 572.

ἰσχάνω [σισχάνω, (σ)ίσχω]. (1) = ἰσχανάω[1] (1): δέος ἰσχάνει ἄνδρας Ξ 387.—Sim.: κατὰ σὸν νόον ἴσχανε (check it; κατά advbl.) τ 42.—(2) = ἰσχανάω[1] (3): ὄπισθεν ἰσχανέτην, ὥς τε πρὼν ἰσχάνει ὕδωρ Ρ 747.

ἰσχίον, -ου, τό. The socket of the hip-joint, the hip-joint: βάλε κατ' ἰσχίον Ε 305. Cf. Ε 306, Λ 339: ρ 234.—Of beasts Θ 340, Υ 170.

ἴσχω [σίσχω. Redup. fr. σ(ε)χ-, ἔχω]. (ἀν-, ἀντ-, ἀπ-, ἐξ-, ἐπ-, κατα-, παρ-, ὑπίσχομαι.) (I) (1) To hold in a specified position: ἐφ' αἵματι φάσγανον ἴσχων λ 82. Cf. Ε 798, Ψ 762.—(2) To debar from freedom, keep within limits: ἥ μιν ἀνάγκῃ ἴσχει δ 558 = ε 15 = ρ 144. Cf. κ 413.—To lay restraint upon: θυμόν Ι 256.—To hold back, hold in check Ι 352.—(3) To keep back from action, stay, restrain: οὐδέ μιν ἴσχε ποταμός Φ 303. Cf. Ο 657, Υ 139: υ 330.—To keep back, stay, restrain from. With genit.: πολέμου Ω 404.—(4) To hold (horses) in hand Ο 456, Ρ 501.—(5) To hold back, withstand, sustain the pressure of: ποταμῶν ῥέεθρα Ρ 750. Cf. Ε 90.—(6) Of a feeling, to hold, affect, possess: δέος σ' ἴσχει Ε 812. Cf. Ε 817, Ν 224.—(7) To hold out, stand firm: ἴσχον πυργηδὸν ἀρηρότες Ο 618.—(II) In mid. (1) To put constraint on oneself, refrain, forbear, cease, let be: *σὺ δ' ἴσχεο* Α 214. Cf. Β 247, Γ 82: λ 251, χ 356, 367, 411, ω 54, 543.—To restrain oneself from, refrain, forbear, cease from. With genit.: *λώβης* σ 347 = υ 285. Cf. ω 323, 531.—(2) To stop or stay oneself in one's course: *οὐδ' ἔθελε προρέειν, ἀλλ' ἴσχετο* Φ 366.

ἴτε, imp. pl. *εἶμι*.

ἰτέη, -ης, ἡ (*Fιτέη*. Cf. L. *vitex*, Eng. *withy*). The willow Φ 350: κ 510.

ἴτην, 3 dual impf. *εἶμι*.

ἴτυς, ἡ (*Fίτυς*) [conn. with *ἰτέη*]. The felloe of a wheel (app. orig. one of willow) Δ 486, Ε 724.

ἴτω, 3 sing. imp. *εἶμι*.

ἰυγμός, -οῦ, ὁ [*ἰύζω*]. Shouting, shout: *μολπῇ τ' ἰυγμῷ τε* Σ 572.

ἰύζω. To shout Ρ 66: ο 162.

ἴφθῑμος, -ον, and (in sense (2)) -η, -ον [prob. not conn. with (*F*)*ίς*, (*F*)*ῖφι*, (*F*)*ίφιος*]. (1) Epithet of warriors, etc., and their adjuncts, noble, goodly, valiant, sturdy, or the like: *ψυχάς* Α 3, *Μενέλαον* Ρ 554. Cf. Γ 336, Δ 534, Θ 114, Λ 55, Μ 376, Π 620, etc.: *ἑτάρους* υ 20. Cf. κ 119, π 89, 244, τ 110, χ 123, ψ 313, ω 26.—Applied to divinities: *Πρωτέος* δ 365. Cf. κ 534 = λ 47.—To rivers Ρ 749.—In reference to animals: *βοῶν ἴφθιμα κάρηνα* Ψ 260.—(2) Of women, goodly, comely, or the like Ε 415, Τ 116: κ 106, λ 287, μ 452, ο 364, π 332, ψ 92.

ἶφι (*Fῖφι*) [see *ἴς*]. With or by might, power, force: *ἶφι ἀνάσσεις* Α 38 = 452, *βοὸς ἶφι κταμένοιο* (as opposed to death by disease) Γ 375. Cf. Α 151, Β 720, Δ 287, Ε 606, Ζ 478, Μ 367, Σ 14, Τ 417, Φ 208, 486: λ 284, ρ 443, σ 57, 156.

ἴφιος (*Fίφιος*) [see *ἴς*]. Epithet of sheep, well-grown, fat, goodly, or the like: *ἴφια μῆλα* Ε 556, Θ 505, 545, Ι 406, 466 = Ψ 166: λ 108, μ 128, 263, 322, σ 278, υ 51, ψ 304.

ἰχανάω. See *ἰσχανάω*[2].

†ἰχθυάω [*ἰχθύς*]. 3 sing. *ἰχθυάᾳ* μ 95. 3 pl. pa. iterative *ἰχθυάασκον* δ 368. To fish, angle δ 368.—To fish for: *δελφῖνάς τε κύνας τε* μ 95.

ἰχθυόεις, -εντος [*ἰχθύς*]. Breeding, peopled by, fish: *πόντον* Ι 4, Τ 378, *Ἑλλήσποντον* Ι 360, *Ὕλλῳ* Υ 392. Cf. Π 746: γ 177, δ 381 = 470, δ 390 = 424 = κ 540, δ 516 = ψ 317, ε 420, ι 83, κ 458.

ἰχθύς, ὁ. Acc. pl. *ἰχθῦς* ε 53, κ 124, μ 331, τ 113. A fish Π 407, Τ 268, Φ 22, 122, 127, 203, 353, Ψ 692, Ω 82: ε 53, κ 124, μ 252, 331, ξ 135, ο 480, τ 113, χ 384, ω 291.

ἴχνιον, -ου, τό [cf. next]. (1) A footprint: *μετ' ἴχνια βαῖνε θεοῖο* β 406 = γ 30 = ε 193 = η 38. Cf. Ψ 764.—In reference to a lion or dogs tracking by scent Σ 321: τ 436.—(2) App., in pl., outlines, fashion: *ἴχνια ποδῶν ἠδὲ κνημάων* Ν 71.

ἴχνος, τό [cf. prec.]. A scent-track: *ἴχνεσι περιήδη* (in tracking by scent) ρ 317.

ἰχώρ, ὁ. Acc. *ἰχῶ* Ε 416. The blood of the gods: *αἷμα θεοῖο, ἰχώρ* Ε 340. Cf. Ε 416.

ἴψ. Some kind of worm: *μὴ κέρα ἶπες ἔδοιεν* φ 395.

ἴψεται, 3 sing. fut. **ἴψαο,** 2 sing. aor. *ἴπτομαι*.

ἴω, subj. *εἶμι*.

ἰῷ. See *εἷς*.

ἰωγή, -ῆς, ἡ. Shelter: *Βορέω ὑπ' ἰωγῇ* (from the . . .) ξ 533.

ἰωή, -ῆς, ἡ. Rush, sweep. Of wind: *ὑπὸ Ζεφύροιο ἰωῆς* Δ 276. Cf. Λ 308.—Of fire Π 127.—Of sound: *ἰωὴ φόρμιγγος* ρ 261. Cf. Κ 139.

ἰωκή, -ῆς, ἡ. Acc. *ἰῶκα* Λ 601. Pursuit and flight: *Τρώων ἰωκάς* (their rushes) Ε 521, *εἰσορόων ἰῶκα δακρυόεσσαν* Λ 601.—Personified Ε 740.

ἴωμι, subj. *εἶμι*.

ἰών, pple. *εἶμι*.

ἰωχμός, -οῦ, ὁ. = *ἰωκή*. In concrete sense, the chasing and fleeing throng: *ἀν' ἰωχμόν* Θ 89, 158.

κάββαλε, 3 sing. contr. aor. *καταβάλλω*.

κάγ. See *κατά*.

κάγκανος. Dry: *ξύλα* Φ 364: σ 308.

†καγχαλάω. 3 pl. *καγχαλόωσι* Γ 43. Pple. *καγχαλόων* Ζ 514, Κ 565. Fem. *καγχαλόωσα* ψ 1, 59. To laugh. In exultation Κ 565: ψ 1, 59.—In self-satisfaction Ζ 514.—In derision Γ 43.

κάδ. See *κατά*.

καδδραθέτην, 3 dual contr. aor. *καταδαρθάνω*.

καδδῦσαι, nom. pl. fem. contr. aor. pple. *καταδύω*.

κάη, 3 sing. aor. pass. *καίω*.

†καθαιρέω [*καθ-*, *κατα-* (1) (5)]. 3 pl. fut. *καθαιρήσουσι* Λ 453. 1 pl. aor. *καθείλομεν* ι 149. 3 sing. subj. *καθέλῃσι* β 100, γ 238, τ 145, ω 135. Fem. pple. *καθελοῦσα* ω 296. (1) To lower (a sail) ι 149.—(2) To close (the eyes of the dead) Λ 453: ω 296.—(3) To seize, take. Of fate β 100 = γ 238 = τ 145 = ω 135.

καθαίρω [*καθαρός*]. 3 sing. aor. *ἐκάθηρε* Π 228. *κάθηρε* Ξ 171: σ 192. 3 pl. *κάθηραν* ζ 93. Imp. *κάθηρον* Π 667. Pl. *καθήρατε* υ 152. Nom. pl. masc. pple. *καθήραντες* ω 44. Infin. *καθῆραι* ζ 87. (*ἐκ-*.) (1) To clean, cleanse: *κρητῆρας* υ 152. Cf. ζ 87, χ 439, 453, ω 44.—To purify by fumigation: *δέπας ἐκάθηρε θεείῳ* Π 228.—Of the application of a cosmetic: *κάλλεϊ οἱ προσώπατα κάθηρεν* σ 192.—(2) To cleanse away, remove (impurities) Ξ 171: ζ 93.—(3) The constructions of (1) and (2) combined. With double acc.: *αἷμα κάθηρον Σαρπηδόνα* Π 667.

καθάλλομαι [*καθ-*, *κατα-* (1)]. To rush down Of a stormy wind Λ 298.

καθάπαξ [*καθ-*, *κατα-* (5) + *ἅπαξ*]. Once for all, outright, for good: *δόμεναι* φ 349.

καθάπτω [*καθ-*, *κατα-* (5)]. In mid., to address, accost: *γέροντα καθαπτόμενος προσέειπεν* β 39. Cf. Α 582, Ο 127, Π 421: β 240, γ 345, κ 70, σ 415 = υ 323, υ 22, ω 393.

καθαρός. (1) Clean, spotless: *εἵματα* δ 750 = ρ 48, δ 759 = ρ 58, ζ 61.—(2) Of a mode of death, clean, such as befits the innocent or chaste χ 462.—(3) Absol., a clear or vacant space: *ἐν καθαρῷ* Θ 491 = Κ 199, Ψ 61.

καθέζομαι [*καθ-*, *κατα-* (1)]. 3 sing. aor. act. *καθεῖσε* Ε 36, Ξ 204, Σ 389: δ 524. (I) In pres.

and in impf. (or aor.; see ἕζομαι). (1) To sit down, seat oneself, take one's seat: πάροιθ' αὐτοῖο καθέζετο Α 360. Cf. Α 405, Ι 570, Λ 81, Ο 100, Υ 136, etc.: ἔνθα καθεζόμενος ζ 295. Cf. ε 195, ι 417, ν 372, ο 285, τ 98, etc.—Of a bird perching τ 520.—(2) To come to a sitting from a recumbent posture, sit up: ἐν λέκτροισι καθεζομένη υ 58.—(II) In aor. act. (1) To cause to seat oneself, bid be seated: ἐπὶ θρόνου Σ 389. Cf. Ε 36.—(2) To cause to be somewhere, set, place: γαίης νέρθεν Ξ 204.—To post, station: σκοπὸς ὃν καθεῖσεν δ 524.

καθέηκα, aor. καθίημι[1].

καθείατο, 3 pl. impf. κάθημαι.

καθείλομεν, 1 pl. aor. καθαιρέω.

καθεῖσε, 3 sing. aor. act. καθέζομαι.

καθέλησι, 3 sing. aor. subj. καθαιρέω.

κάθεμεν, 1 pl. aor. καθίημι[1].

καθέξει, 3 sing. fut. κατέχω.

καθεύδω [καθ-, κατα- (5)]. (1) To be asleep, sleep, slumber θ 313.—(2) To lay oneself down to sleep, go to bed, go to sleep: ἔνθα καθεῦδ' ἀναβάς Α 611. Cf. γ 402, δ 304, ζ 1 = η 344, υ 141.

†**καθεψιάομαι** [καθ-, κατα- (2)]. 3 pl. καθεψιόωνται. To jeer at, mock. With genit.: σέθεν τ 372.

καθήατο, 3 pl. impf. κάθημαι.

κάθημαι [καθ-, κατα- (1)]. 3 sing. impf. καθῆστο Α 569: δ 628. 3 pl. καθήατο, καθείατο Λ 76, Υ 153, Ω 473. Imp. κάθησο Α 565, Β 191. (1) To sit, be seated: ἀκέουσα κάθησο Α 565. Cf. Δ 1, Λ 76, Ξ 5, Υ 153, Ω 161, etc.: ἐν ψαμάθοισι καθήμενος δ 539. Cf. γ 186, κ 497, ρ 478, φ 89, 420, etc.—(2) To sit idle, doing nothing: ἀσχαλόωσι καθήμενοι Ω 403. Cf. β 255, δ 628, π 264.—(3) To abide, be: βουσὶν ἐπ' ἀλλοτρίῃσι καθήμενον υ 221. Cf. β 369.

κάθηρε, 3 sing. aor. καθαίρω.

καθῆστο, 3 sing. impf. κάθημαι.

καθιδρύω [καθ-, κατα- (1)]. To cause to sit down: Ὀδυσῆα καθίδρυε ἐντὸς μεγάρου υ 257.

καθιζάνω [καθ-, κατα- (1)]. To sit down, take one's seat: θεοὶ θῶκόνδε καθίζανον ε 3.

καθίζω [καθ-, κατα- (1)]. 3 pl. aor. κάθισαν Τ 280: δ 659. Imp. κάθισον Γ 68, Η 49. Pple. καθίσσας Ι 488. Fem. καθίσᾱσα ρ 572. (1) To cause to seat oneself, bid be seated: μή με κάθιζε Ζ 360. Cf. Γ 68 = Η 49: δ 659, ρ 572.—To cause (an assembly) to sit for business, bring (it) together β 69.—(2) To set, place: ἐπ' ἐμοῖσι γούνεσσι καθίσσας Ι 488.—To seat or settle in an appointed place: κάθισαν γυναῖκας (brought them to their new home) Τ 280.—(3) To seat oneself, sit down: ἔνθα καθῖζ' Ἑλένη Γ 426. Cf. Θ 436, Λ 623, Υ 151: ἐπὶ κλῃῖσι καθῖζον β 419 = δ 579, ι 103 = 179 = 471 = 563 = λ 638 = μ 146 = ο 549, ν 76, ο 221. Cf. ε 326, θ 6, 422, π 408, ρ 90, 256.—(4) To have one's seat, be seated, sit: ἂμ πέτρῃσι καθίζων ε 156. Cf. Γ 394, Ο 50.

†**καθίημι**[1] [καθ-, κατα- (1) + ἵημι[1]]. 2 pl. pres. καθίετε Φ 132. Aor. καθέηκα Ω 642. 1 pl. aor. κάθεμεν ι 72. (1) To let down, lower: ἐν δίνῃσι ἵππους Φ 132.—To lower (sails) ι 72.—(2) To allow to pass *down*. With genit.: οἶνον λαυκανίης Ω 642.

†**καθίημι**[2] [καθ-, κατα- (1) + ἵημι[2]]. 3 sing. aor. mid. καταείσατο. Of a missile weapon, to take its eager course, speed, *down upon*. With genit.: ὅθι οἱ καταείσατο [δόρυ] γαίης Λ 358.

†**καθικνέομαι** [καθ-, κατα- (5)]. 2 sing. aor. καθίκεο Ξ 104. 3 καθίκετο α 342. (1) Of a speaker, to touch, affect, bring something home to (a hearer): μάλα πώς με καθίκεο θυμὸν ἐνιπῇ Ξ 104.—(2) Of a feeling, to come upon, seize, affect: μάλιστά με καθίκετο πένθος α 342.

κάθισαν, 3 pl. aor. καθίζω.

†**καθίστημι** [καθ-, κατα- (1)]. Aor. imp. κατάστησον μ 185. Infin. καταστῆσαι ν 274. From καθιστάω imp. καθίστα Ι 202. (1) To set down, place: μείζονα κρητῆρα Ι 202.—(2) To set on shore, land: Πύλονδέ με ν 274 (see under ἐφέζομαι (2) (b)).—(3) To bring (a ship) to land μ 185.

καθοράω [καθ-, κατα- (1)]. To look down, direct one's look downward: ἐξ Ἴδης Λ 337.—In mid.: ἐπὶ Θρῃκῶν καθορώμενος αἶαν Ν 4.

καθύπερθε(ν) [καθ-, κατα- (1) (5) + ὕπερθε]. (1) Down from above, from above: εἴ πώς οἱ κ. ἀλάλκοιεν (from the walls) Χ 196. Cf. Φ 269: ἧκα κ. πόδας μ 442. Cf. θ 279.—(2) Above, on top: Πηνειὸν κ. ἐπιρρέει (on the surface) Β 754, λαοῖσιν κ. πεποιθότες (their comrades on the wall) Μ 153. Cf. Γ 337 = Λ 42 = Ο 481 = Π 138 := χ 124, κ 353.—In reference to covering: ἄλλα πάντα εἴλυται κ. Μ 286. Cf. Σ 353, Φ 321, Ω 450, 646 := δ 299 = η 338, ψ 193.—(3) In geographical and navigational contexts (a) App., from a higher or dominating position: [ὅσσον] Φρυγίη κ. [ἐντὸς ἐέργει] (as forming part of the tableland of Central Asia Minor) Ω 545 (or perh., (approximately) to the north. Cf. (c)).—(b) To seaward of. With genit.: κ. Χίοιο (leaving the shelter it afforded) γ 170.—(c) App., to the north of. With genit.: νῆσος Συρίη Ὀρτυγίης κ. ο 404 (cf. ὑπέρ (2) (a)).

καί. (1) Connecting particle, and Α 15, 28, 31, 33, 50, 73, etc.: α 3, 19, 56, 89, 109, 110, etc.—καὶ . . . καὶ . . ., both . . . and . . .: καὶ ἓν καὶ εἴκοσι (not only one but twenty) Ν 260, καὶ σῖτον πασάμην καὶ οἶνον λαυκανίης καθέηκα Ω 641. Cf. Ν 636: ψ 55.—(2) Expressing sequence or consequence, and so, so, and then, then, accordingly, therefore, consequently: τὸν καὶ ὑπέδεισαν θεοὶ Α 406, καί μιν προσηύδα Β 7. Cf. Α 92, 411, 478, Γ 166, Ζ 353, Η 214, Κ 224, Λ 382, etc.: τάχ' ἄν ποτε καὶ τίσις εἴη β 76, καὶ τότ' Ὀδυσσῆος λύτο γούνατα ε 297. Cf. β 60, 104, δ 415, ι 131, κ 17, λ 99, μ 330, ν 79, etc.—(3) Introducing an explanation, reason, amplification, or analysis of something previously said (often with γάρ; cf. γάρ (2)): τοῦ καὶ ἀπὸ γλώσσης μέλιτος γλυκίων ῥέεν αὐδή Α 249, καὶ γάρ τε Λιταί εἰσιν Ι 502. Cf. Β 377, Δ 43, Ι 524, Λ 111, Ξ 173, Ο 251, etc.: πὰρ δ' ἄρ' ἔην καὶ ἀοιδὸς γ 267. Cf. α 434, η 24, ι 190, κ 5, λ 429, etc.—(4) As a strengthening or emphasizing particle. (a) Even, just, surely, or the like: πρίν μιν καὶ γῆρας ἔπεισιν Α 29, καὶ ὡς

116, ταῦτα μεταφρασόμεσθα καὶ αὖτις (will e'en . . .) 140, καὶ ἅπαντες H 281. Cf. A 63, 113, 174, 213, 260, B 119, Δ 406 (we *did* take it), Θ 23 (in my turn), P 647, etc. : καὶ αὐτοὶ α 33, ἦ καί μοι νεμεσήσεαι; (will you at least not be angry ?) 158, ἀνδράσι καὶ πλεόνεσσιν (who in fact outnumber us) β 245. Cf. α 58, 302, 318, β 48, 255, γ 27 (the god himself), 44, λ 441 (on your part), etc.—(b) Also, too : πίθεσθε καὶ ὔμμες A 274. Cf. A 63, 455, Γ 97, 143, Δ 138, etc. : α 10, 47, 260, 301, γ 46, δ 519, ο 488 (καί with ἐσθλόν), etc.—(5) With εἰ in various constructions. (a) εἰ καί in sense of εἰ (4), even if, or the like : εἰ καὶ καρτερός ἐστιν E 410. Cf. N 58, Π 748, etc. : εἰ καὶ χαλεπαίνοι ε 485. Cf. ζ 312, η 52, ν 6, etc.—Strengthened by περ O 117 : α 389, η 321, ι 35.—(b) καὶ εἰ (α) In sim. sense : καὶ εἰ καρτερός ἐστιν N 316, καὶ εἰ πυρὶ χεῖρας ἔοικεν Υ 371. Cf. O 51 : ν 292, π 98, φ 260, etc.—Strengthened by περ Λ 391.—(β) If even, even supposing or granting that : καὶ εἴ χ' ἑτέρωθι πύθηαι E 351. Cf. Δ 347.—(6) καί . . . περ. (a) Though, even though : καὶ μάλα περ κεχολωμένον A 217, καὶ αὐτῇ περ νοεούσῃ (though she hardly needs my counsel) 577. Cf. B 270, I 247, Λ 721, N 57, P 104, etc. : καὶ ἀθάνατός περ (even though it should be a god) ε 73. Cf. δ 502, 549, 733, κ 441, υ 271, etc.—So καί περ : καί περ πολλὰ παθόντα η 224.—(b) Intensifying without sense of opposition : καὶ πρίν περ μεμαώς E 135. Cf. H 204, K 70, etc.—(7) Coordinating words and to be translated 'or' : ἕνα καὶ δύο B 346 : αἰνότερον καὶ κύντερον λ 427. Cf. γ 115.—In two co-ordinate sentences : εἴ περ γάρ τε χόλον γε καὶ αὐτῆμαρ καταπέψῃ, ἀλλά τε καὶ . . . A 81. Cf. Δ 160 : θ 581.—(8) Marking an alternative or distinction : ἢ ἔπει ἠὲ καὶ ἔργῳ A 395. Cf. B 238, Λ 573, O 137, Π 591, etc. : ἢ . . . ἦε καὶ οὐκί α 268. Cf. γ 91, δ 712, ι 267, etc.

καίνυμαι. 2 sing. pf. (in pres. sense) κέκασσαι τ 82. 3 κέκασται Υ 35. 1 pl. κεκάσμεθα ω 509. Acc. sing. masc. pple. κεκασμένον δ 725, 815. Voc. κεκασμένε Δ 339. Infin. κεκάσθαι Ω 546. 3 sing. plupf. (in impf. sense) ἐκέκαστο B 530, E 54, N 431, Π 808, Ψ 289, Ω 535 : β 158, ι 509, τ 395. κέκαστο Ξ 124 : η 157. (ἀπο-.) (1) To excel, surpass, be superior to (another or others). With dat. of that in which one excels : ἐγχείῃ ἐκέκαστο Πανέλληνας B 530. Cf. N 431, Ξ 124, Π 808 : τ 395.—Sim. with infin. : ὁμηλικίην ἐκέκαστο ὄρνιθας γνῶναι β 158. Cf. γ 282.—(2) To excel, be pre-eminent. With dat. : ἐκηβολίαι, ᾗσιν τὸ πρίν γ' ἐκέκαστο E 54, ὃς ἐπὶ φρεσὶ κέκασται (ἐπί advbl.) Υ 35. Cf. Δ 339, Ψ 289, Ω 535 : παντοίῃς ἀρετῇσι κεκασμένον ἐν Δαναοῖσιν δ 725 = 815. Cf. η 157, ι 509, τ 82, ω 509.—With genit. of those whom one excels and dat. : τῶν σε πλούτῳ κεκάσθαι Ω 546.

καίριος [perh. properly κήριος, fr. κήρ. Cf. ἀκήριος[1]]. Deadly, fatal. In impers. construction : μάλιστα καίριόν ἐστιν Θ 84, 326.—Absol., a fatal spot : οὐκ ἐν καιρίῳ πάγη βέλος Δ 185.

καιρουσσέων, καιροσ(σ)έων, *genit. fem. pl.* [contr. fr. καιροεσσέων, genit. pl. of καιρόεσσα, fr. καῖρος, the loop supporting each vertical thread of the warp]. Close-woven : ὀθονέων η 107.

καίω (καϝ-, κηϝ-, καυ-). Aor. ἔκηα (ἔκηϝα) A 40, Θ 240. 3 sing. ἔκηε X 170, Ω 34. κῆε Φ 349 : γ 273, δ 764, ρ 241, τ 366. 3 pl. ἔκηαν χ 336. 1 pl. subj. κήομεν H 377, 396. 3 sing. opt. κήαι Φ 336. 3 pl. κήαιεν Ω 38. Imp. κῆον φ 176. Nom. pl. masc. pple. κήαντες ι 231, ν 26. Infin. κῆαι ο 97. 3 pl. aor. mid. κήαντο I 88. Pple. κηάμενος, -ου I 234 : π 2, ψ 51. 3 sing. aor. pass. (ἐ)κάη A 464, B 427, I 212 : γ 461, μ 13, 364. Infin. καήμεναι Ψ 198, 210. (ἀνα-, κατα-.) (1) To set on fire, kindle ; in pass., to burn, blaze : ὁππότ' ἂν Τροίη πυρὶ δάηται καιομένη, καίωσι δὲ υἷες Ἀχαιῶν Υ 317 = Φ 376. Cf. Θ 135, I 602, Λ 554 = P 663, O 600, Υ 491, Φ 350, 351 : ι 390.—(2) To light (a fire) ; in pass., of a fire, to burn, blaze : πυραὶ νεκύων καίοντο A 52. Cf. Θ 509, 521, 554, 561, 562, I 77, K 12, T 376 : πῦρ κήαντες ι 231. Cf. ε 59, ο 97, φ 176.—In mid. : πῦρ κήαντο I 88. Cf. I 234 : πῦρ κηάμενος (having caused it to be lighted) ψ 51. Cf. π 2.—In pass., of a fire, to light, begin to burn : οὐδὲ πυρὴ ἐκαίετο Ψ 192. Cf. Ψ 198, 210.—With κατά, in pass., of a fire, to burn itself out : ἐπεὶ κατὰ πῦρ ἐκάη I 212.—(3) To burn, consume with fire : νεκρούς H 377 = 396, Φ 343, 349. Cf. Ξ 397, Φ 336, 338, Ψ 222, 224, 242, Ω 38 : μ 13, ω 67, 69.—Fig. : καίετο 'ις ποταμοῖο (was mastered by the fire) Φ 356.—Sim. : φῆ πυρὶ καιόμενος Φ 361.—(4) To burn (a sacrifice), offer (it) by burning : μηρία A 40, Θ 240, Λ 773, O 373, X 170, Ω 34, καῖεν ἐπὶ σχίζῃς A 462. Cf. A 464 = B 427 : γ 9, 273, 461 = μ 364, γ 459, δ 764, ι 553, ν 26, ρ 241, τ 366, 397, χ 336.

κάκ. See κατά.

κακίζομαι [κακός]. To play the coward : οὔ ε κακιζόμενόν γε κατέκτα Ω 214.

κακίων, comp. κακός.

κακκείοντες, contr. pl. pple. κατακείω.

κακκῆαι, contr. aor. infin. κατακαίω.

κακοείμων, -ονος [κακός + εἷμα]. Wearing foul or ragged raiment : πτωχούς σ 41.

κακοεργίη, -ης, ἡ [κακοεργός]. Evil-doing, the doing of what is wrong χ 374.

κακοεργός, -όν [κακός + ἔργω[2]]. Evil-doing, bringing one into evil : γαστήρ σ 54.

κακομήχανος, -ον [κακός + μηχανή = μῆχος]. That plans or contrives evil Z 344 : π 418.—As epithet of ἔρις I 257.

κακόξεινος [κακός + ξεῖνος]. Unlucky in one's guests. Comp. κακοξεινώτερος υ 376.

κακορραφίη, -ης, ἡ [κακός + ῥαφ-, ῥάπτω]. Planning or contriving of evil : ἵνα μή τι κακορραφίῃ ἀλγήσετε (app. referring to her subsequent warning as to the oxen of the sun) μ 26. Cf. O 16.—In pl. β 236.

κακός, -ή, -όν. Comp. κακώτερος T 321, X 106 : ζ 275, θ 138, ο 343, φ 324. κακίων ξ 56. Neut. κάκιον I 601 : σ 174, τ 120. Nom. pl. masc. κακίους β 277. Superl. κάκιστος Π 570 : α 391, δ 199, ρ 415. (1) Of mean birth or extraction : οὐ κακὸς εἴδεται Ξ 472. Cf. Ξ 126.—Absol.: οὔ τι κακῷ ἐῴκει α 411. Cf. Ξ 472: δ 64.—(2) Spiritless, cowardly, craven, unmanly: ὃς κακὸς ἤδ' ὅς κ' ἐσθλὸς ἔῃσιν Β 365. Cf. Ε 643, Ζ 489, Θ 153, Π 570, Ρ 180: β 270, 278, γ 375.—Deficient in or deprived of strength, powerless, feeble: κακὸν καὶ ἀνήνορα κ 301, 341. Cf. φ 131.—Absol., a coward or poltroon: κακὸν ὥς Β 190, Ο 196. Cf. Δ 299, Ζ 443, Θ 94, Ι 319, Λ 408, Ν 279, Ρ 632.—(3) In reference to the bodily frame, ill-shapen, of mean appearance: εἶδος ἔην κακός Κ 316. Cf. θ 134.—(4) Not serviceable, worthless, sorry, of no account, good for nothing: κακὰ τέκνα Ω 253. Cf. Β 235, Ε 787 = Θ 228, Θ 164, Ν 623, Χ 106: ὁ κάκιστος Ἀχαιῶν ρ 415. Cf. β 277, δ 199, ζ 187, 275, ι 453, κ 68, ξ 56, ρ 246, 578, υ 227, φ 324.—Absol.: κακὸς κακὸν ἡγηλάζει ρ 217. Cf. Ω 63: ζ 189, θ 553, χ 415 = ψ 66.—Sim.: ἔργα κακά (suited to a vagabond) ρ 226, σ 362.—(5) Unskilled, inexperienced: ἡνιόχοισιν Ρ 487. Cf. θ 214.—(6) Ill to deal with, driving a hard bargain: ἐεδνωταί Ν 382.—(7) Baleful, maleficent: δαίμων κ 64, ω 149. Cf. μ 87.—Doing or contriving evil: γυναικός λ 384.—Sim.: νόῳ ν 229.—(8) Bad of its kind: νῆσος (unproductive, barren) ι 131.—Of raiment, foul, ragged δ 245, λ 191, ν 434, ξ 342, 506, ρ 24, τ 72, ψ 95, 115, ω 156.—Absol.: κακὰ εἱμένος τ 327.—Of discourse: κακόν τι (unseemly) Δ 362, μύθῳ (outrageous) Ε 650, ἔπος (grievous, woeful) Ρ 701, ἐπέεσσιν (ἔπος) (unseemly, unmannerly) Ψ 493, Ω 767: ἔπεσιν (insulting, abusive) ω 161.—In regard to weather, bad, foul, trying: νύξ ξ 457, 475.—Epithet of night as restricting activity or observation Κ 188.—(9) (a) Bringing or entailing evil, bane, harm or misfortune, evil, ill, baneful, disastrous, harmful: νοῦσον Α 10, ἕλκεϊ Β 723. Cf. Α 284, Β 114, Ζ 346, Ν 812, Ρ 401, Σ 8, Ψ 176, Ω 219 (boding ill), 532, etc.: μόρον α 166, κήδεα 244, ἄνεμον ε 109. Cf. γ 161, ε 467, κ 46, μ 300, ξ 269, υ 87, 357, ψ 217, etc.—For κακὸν ἦμαρ see ἦμαρ (4) (e).—Of sound, of evil import, betokening calamity: κόναβος κ 122.—(b) Producing evil effects, defiling, destroying: φάρμακα Χ 94 (maddening): κ 213 (working enchantment). Cf. ν 435, π 35.—(10) Of deeds, in ethical sense, evil, wrongful, violent: ἔργα β 67, θ 329, ι 477, ξ 284, π 380, ρ 158, υ 16, ψ 64, ω 199, 326.—(11) Absol. in neut. sing. κακόν. (a) Evil, bane, harm, misfortune, mischance, destruction, trouble, an instance of these: μή τι ῥέξῃ κ. υἷας Ἀχαιῶν Β 195. Cf. Ε 63, 374, Θ 541, Ι 250, Λ 363, Ξ 80, Ο 586, Τ 290, Χ 453, etc.: κ. μοι ἔμπεσεν οἴκῳ β 45, πῆμα κακοῖο (woe of evil, evil and woe) γ 152. Cf. β 166, δ 237, ζ 173, ι 423, ν 46, ο 178, ρ 567, υ 83, φ 304, etc.—In reference to persons: τυκτὸν κ. Ε 831. Cf. Φ 39: γ 306, δ 667, μ 118, π 103.—In milder sense ο 72.—(b) A hard thing, something putting a strain on one's resources: κ. με πόλλ' ἀποτίνειν β 132.—(c) In reference to action, a bad thing, something unworthy, undesirable or unprofitable: ταῦτ' οὐ κ. ἐστιν Σ 128: οὔ τι κ. βασιλευέμεν α 392. Cf. δ 837 = λ 464, υ 218.—In comp.: κάκιόν κεν εἴη . . . Ι 601.—Also in comp., not a good thing, a bad thing: κάκιον πενθήμεναι αἰεί σ 174, τ 120.—In superl.: ἦ φῂς τοῦτο κάκιστον τετύχθαι; α 391.—(12) Absol. in neut. pl. κακά. (a) In senses similar to those of (11) (a): μάντι κακῶν Α 106, κ. Πριάμῳ φέρουσαι Β 304, πολλὰ κάκ' ἄνσχεο Ω 518. Cf. Α 107, Β 234, Γ 57, 99, Δ 21, Ι 540, Ρ 105, Φ 442, etc.: ἐξ ἡμέων φασὶ κάκ' ἔμμεναι α 33, κάκ' ἔρεξεν β 72. Cf. β 134, γ 113, δ 221, ζ 175, ι 460, κ 286, μ 208, ρ 287, σ 123, ψ 287, etc.—(b) Violent efforts or strivings: μηδὲ τρίβεσθε κακοῖσιν Ψ 735.—(c) Evil devices: κακῶν ἔμπαιος φ 400.—(d) Plans ill-contrived, ill-judged courses: κακὰ μητιόωντι Σ 312.—(e) Diseases, maladies, injuries: ἰητῆρα κακῶν ρ 384.—(f) Things ill-done, excesses, wrongs: ἐπὶ προτέροισι κακοῖσιν χ 264. Cf. γ 213, φ 298, χ 316, etc.—(g) Things that defile, defilement, pollution: θέειον κακῶν ἄκος χ 481.

κακότεχνος [κακός + τέχνη]. Planned or contrived with evil intent: δόλος Ο 14.

κακότης, -ητος, ἡ [κακός]. (1) Cowardice, want of spirit or enterprise: ἡγεμόνος κακότητι Ν 108. Cf. Β 368, Ο 721: ω 455.—(2) Evil, bane, harm, destruction, ill fortune, trouble, suffering, misery, danger: κακότητα φέροντες Μ 332. Cf. Κ 71, Λ 382: ὄφρ' ὑπὲκ κακότητα φύγοιμεν γ 175. Cf. δ 167, ε 290, θ 182, τ 360, υ 203, ψ 238, etc.—(3) Wrong done to one: τείσασθαι Ἀλέξανδρον κακότητος Γ 366.

κακοφραδής [κακός + φραδ-, φράζομαι]. Dull of perception Ψ 483.

κακόω [κακός]. (1) To subject to violence or outrage: ὡς ἡμεῖς κεκακωμένοι ἦμεν· ἐλθὼν γὰρ ἐκάκωσε βίη Ἡρακληείη Λ 689.—(2) To bring into trouble or suffering: ἐπεί μ' ἐκακώσατε λίην υ 99.—To trouble, vex, distress: μηδὲ γέροντα κάκου κεκακωμένον (*i.e.* he has troubles enough as it is) δ 754.—(3) To make unsightly, disfigure: ἡμὲν κυδῆναι βροτὸν ἠδὲ κακῶσαι π 212.—To disfigure, befoul: κεκακωμένος ἅλμῃ ζ 137.

κάκτανε, contr. aor. imp. κατακτείνω.

κακῶς [adv. fr. κακός]. (1) In evil case or plight, miserably, with suffering: νοστήσομεν Β 253. Cf. Ε 698, Φ 460: ι 534, λ 114 = μ 141.—Intensifying a vb. indicating suffering: κ. πάσχοντος π 275.—Sim.: αὐχμεῖς κ. ω 250.—In impers. construction of being in evil case, of things going badly with one: Κουρήτεσσι κ. ἦν Ι 551. Cf. Ι 324.—(2) So as to bring suffering or sore trouble upon one: ἐξ ἵππων βῆσε κ. Ε 164. Cf. σ 75 (sorely).—(3) With evil intent, with malice in one's heart: κ. φρονέουσιν σ 168.—With disregard of right, with violence, abuse, insult: κ. ἀφίει Α 25 = 379. Cf. β 203, 266, δ 766, ρ 394.—κ. ῥέζειν τινά, to treat one with despite, do him wrong: κ. οἵ πέρ μιν ἔρεζον μνηστῆρες ψ 56.—(4) So as to bring trouble on oneself, in an evil hour: κ. τοξάζεαι χ 27.

καλάμη, -ης, ἡ. (1) The straw of corn Τ 222.—(2) A straw left standing after reaping. Applied to a worn-out man ξ 214.

καλαῦροψ, -οπος, ἡ [perh. fr. κάλος in sense 'string' (referring to a loop used as an aid in casting) + (F)ρέπω]. A herdsman's staff thrown to bring back errant members to the herd Ψ 845.

καλέω. Nom. pl. masc. pres. pple. καλεῦντες κ 229, 255, μ 249. Non-thematic pres. infin. καλήμεναι K 125. 3 sing. pa. iterative καλέεσκε Z 402. 3 pl. καλέεσκον I 562. Fut. pple. καλέων δ 532, ο 213. Fem. καλέουσα Γ 383 : ν 413. Aor. κάλεσσα Ω 106. 2 sing. (ἐ)κάλεσσας Υ 16 : ρ 379. 3 κάλεσσε ψ 43, ω 388. 3 pl. κάλεσσαν Π 693, X 297. Subj. καλέσσω Z 280 : ρ 52. 3 sing. opt. καλέσειε K 111, 171, Ω 74 : δ 735. Imp. κάλεσον χ 391. κάλεσσον Δ 193, K 53, M 343, O 54 : ρ 529, 544. Pple. καλέσας, -αντος O 303, T 34 : α 90, 272, η 189, ρ 330, 342. καλέσσας β 348, λ 410, ο 529. Fem. καλέσᾱσα A 402 : α 416, ρ 507. Infin. καλέσσαι Γ 117, Υ 4 : ψ 44, 51. **Mid.** 3 sing. aor. (ἐ)καλέσσατο A 54, Γ 161, O 143, P 507, Ω 193. 3 pl. καλέσαντο A 270. Imp. pl. καλέσασθε θ 43. Pple. καλεσσάμενος, -ου E 427 : γ 137, τ 15, φ 380, χ 436. Fem. καλεσσαμένη Ξ 188. **Pass.** 3 pl. impf. καλεῦντο B 684. 3 sing. pa. iterative καλέσκετο O 338. 2 sing. fut. pf. κεκλήσῃ Γ 138. Pf. κέκλημαι Δ 61, Σ 366. 3 sing. κέκληται K 259, Λ 758. 3 pl. plupf. κεκλήατο K 195. Pple. κεκλημένος B 260 : ζ 244. Infin. κεκλῆσθαι Ξ 268. (ἐκ-, ἐκπρο-, προ-, προκαλίζομαι, συγ-.) **(1)** To call, call to, summon, to bid, invite or request to come or appear: Μαχάονα δεῦρο κάλεσσον Δ 193, ὅσοι κεκλήατο βουλήν (to the . . .) K 195. Cf. A 402, Γ 117, K 53, N 740, Υ 4, Ψ 203, Ω 74, etc. : τὴν θάλαμόνδε καλέσσας β 348. Cf. α 90, δ 735, ζ 55, κ 114, ο 529, χ 391, etc.—With infin. denoting the purport of the summons: ἐς πεδίον καταβῆναι Γ 250. Cf. Γ 390, K 197, O 54.—In mid. καλεσσαμένη 'Αφροδίτην Ξ 188, ἐς ἄλοχον ἐκαλέσσατο (to his presence) Ω 193. Cf. A 54, 270, Γ 161, E 427, O 143, P 507 : γ 137, θ 43, τ 15 = φ 380, χ 436.—To call to for aid in extremity: ἐμὲ φθέγγοντο καλεῦντες μ 249.—**(2)** To bid or invite to a feast or meal or to one's house: πάντες [μιν] καλέουσιν λ 187. Cf. δ 532, λ 410, ο 213.—**(3)** To call by *such and such a name*, to name, call, speak of as, *so and so*: ὃν Βριάρεων καλέουσι θεοί A 403, 'Αλησίου ἔνθα κολώνη κέκληται (where is the hill called A.) Λ 758. Cf. A 293, E 306, Z 402, K 259, Ξ 210, Σ 487, Ω 316, etc. : ὄνομ' ὅττι σε κεῖθι κάλεον θ 550. Cf. ε 273, κ 305, μ 61, ν 104 = 348, ξ 147.—**(4)** In pass., to bear the name of *so and so*, be known as, have the reputation of being, be, *so and so*: σὴ παράκοιτις κέκλημαι Δ 61 = Σ 366. Cf. B 260, Γ 138, Ξ 268 : ἀφνειοὶ καλέονται ο 433, ρ 423 = τ 79. Cf. ζ 244, η 313.

καλήτωρ, -ορος, ὁ [καλέω]. One who summons, a crier: κήρυκα καλήτορα Ω 577.

καλλείπειν, contr. infin. καταλείπω.

καλλιγύναιξ, -αικος [καλλι-, καλός + γυναικ-, γυνή]. Abounding in fair women. Epithet of 'Ελλάς B 683, I 447.—Of 'Αχαιΐς Γ 75 = 258.—Of Σπάρτη ν 412.

καλλίζωνος, -ον [καλλι-, καλός + ζώνη]. With fair girdles. Epithet of women H 139, Ω 698 : ψ 147.

καλλίθριξ, -τριχος [καλλι-, καλός + θρίξ]. **(1)** Epithet of horses, with fair or flowing mane E 323, Θ 348, Λ 280, N 819, Σ 223, Ψ 525, etc. : γ 475, ε 380, ο 215.—Applied to ἵππω in sense 'chariot' (see ἵππος (3)) P 504.—**(2)** Epithet of sheep, with fair or thick wool: μῆλα ι 336, 469.

καλλίκομος, -ον [καλλι-, καλός + κόμη]. Bright-haired. Epithet of women I 449 : ο 58.

καλλικρήδεμνος, -ον [καλλι-, καλός + κρήδεμνον]. With fair head-covering. Epithet of women δ 623.

κάλλιμος, -ον [καλός]. **(1)** Fair, beauteous: χρόα λ 529.—**(2)** Splendid, magnificent: δῶρα δ 130, θ 439, ο 206.—**(3)** Of the voice, sweet, ravishing μ 192.—Of a wind, blowing sweetly λ 640.

κάλλιον, neut. comp. καλός.

καλλιπάρῃος, -ον [καλλι-, καλός + παρήϊον]. Fair-cheeked. Epithet of goddesses and women A 143, 184, Z 298, I 665, O 87, Ω 607, etc. : ο 123, σ 321.

καλλιπλόκαμος, -ον [καλλι-, καλός + πλόκαμος]. Bright-tressed. Epithet of goddesses and women Ξ 326, Σ 407, 592, Υ 207 : κ 220, 310.

κάλλιπον, contr. aor. καταλείπω.

καλλιρέεθρος, -ον [καλλι-, καλός + ῥέεθρον]. Sweetly flowing: κρήνην κ 107.—With fair streams: Χαλκίδα ο 295.

καλλίρ(ρ)οος, -ον [καλλι-, καλός + ῥέω]. Sweetly flowing B 752, M 33, X 147 : ε 441, ρ 206.

κάλλιστος, superl. καλός.

καλλίσφυρος, -ον [καλλι-, καλός + σφυρόν]. With beautiful ankles. Epithet of goddesses and women I 557, 560, Ξ 319 : ε 333, λ 603.

καλλίτριχος, genit. καλλίθριξ.

καλλίχορος [καλλι-, καλός + χορός]. With fair dancing-places. Epithet of a city λ 581.

καλλίων, comp. καλός.

κάλλος, -εος, τό [καλός]. **(1)** Beauty. **(a)** Of men Γ 392, Z 156, Υ 235 := ο 251, ζ 237, σ 219, ψ 156.—**(b)** Of women I 130, 272, 389, N 432 : ζ 18, θ 457, λ 282.—**(c)** Of a thing: κάλλει ἐνίκα [κρητήρ] Ψ 742.—**(2)** App., some kind of cosmetic: κάλλεϊ οἱ προσώπατα κάθηρεν σ 192.

κᾱλός, -ή, -όν. Formed fr. κάλλος nom. neut. comp. κάλλιον Ω 52 : γ 69, ζ 39, ρ 583, σ 255, etc. Nom. pl. masc. καλλίονες κ 396. Superl. κάλλιστος, -η, -ον B 673, Z 294, I 140, Φ 158, etc. : δ 614, ι 11, λ 239, ο 107, etc. (Often used merely as a more or less conventional epithet.) **(1)** In reference to personal beauty **(a)** Of a god or a man, well-favoured, shapely, goodly: κάλλιστος ἀνήρ B 673. Cf. Γ 169, Υ 233, Φ 108 : καλός τε καὶ ἀρτίπος θ 310. Cf. α 301 = γ 199, ζ 276, ι 513, κ 396, λ 310, 522.—Sim. : καλὸν εἶδος Γ 44.—Of parts or appanages of the body, shapely, goodly, beauteous: σφυρά Δ 147, χρόα E 858, ὄμματα Ψ 66. Cf. Λ 352, Φ 398, X 321, Ψ 805 : α 208, θ 85, ν 398, 430, ο 332, π 15 = ρ 39, σ 68, τ 417, ω 44.—**(b)** Of a goddess or a woman, fair, lovely, beauteous, comely: χορῷ καλὴ Πολυμήλη (in the dance) Π 180. Cf. Θ 305, I 140 = 282, 556, Π 175, Σ 383, X 155 : ἀλοσύδνης δ 404. Cf. γ 464, ζ 108, θ 320, λ 271,

321, ν 289 = π 158, ο 418.—Of parts or appanages of the body, fair, lovely, beauteous: χρόα E 354, πλοκάμους Ξ 177, πρόσωπα T 285. Cf. Ξ 175: β 376, δ 749, σ 192, τ 208, 263.—(c) Of a god and goddess: Ἄρης καὶ Παλλὰς Ἀθήνη . . . καλὼ καὶ μεγάλω Σ 518.—(d) Of the Dawn, bright I 707.—(2) Of animals, goodly, shapely, well-formed, well-grown: καλλίστους ἵππους K 436: βόες μ 262, 355. Cf. ι 426, ρ 307.—Sim.: πώεα καλὰ οἰῶν Σ 528: λ 402, μ 129, ω 112.—(3) Of places, fair, delightful, pleasant to dwell in I 152 = 294, Σ 491: τ 173.—(4) Of things of use, buildings, constructions, etc., well-made, well-constructed, fair, goodly, fine, beauteous, or the like: χιτῶνα B 43, τεύχεα Γ 89, δίφροι E 194, τεῖχος Φ 447. Cf. Γ 331, 388, Z 294, Λ 629, Ξ 185, X 3, Ψ 268, etc.: πέδιλα α 96, δώματα γ 387, εἵματα ζ 111. Cf. α 131, γ 63, 351, ε 232, θ 69, ξ 7, τ 18, φ 7, ω 3, etc.—Sim. absol.: καλὰ ἕννυσθαι ζ 27.—(5) In various applications as an epithet of general commendation, fair, goodly, fine, beauteous, calculated to win acceptance or give satisfaction, or the like: πλατανίστῳ B 307, ἱερά Λ 727, ἄλσεα Υ 8. Cf. E 92, Z 195, 218, Ξ 351, P 55, etc.: δῶρον α 312, κειμήλια κ 40, ἀγρόν ω 206. Cf. δ 473, ο 76, ρ 600, etc.—Of a star, fair, bright Z 401, X 318.—Of waters, fair, bright, gleaming B 850, Π 229, Φ 158, 238, 244, etc.: ζ 87, λ 239, 240.—Of the voice, sweet, ravishing A 604: ε 61, κ 221, ω 60.—Of a wind, fair ξ 253, 299.—Becoming, gracing: πάντα καλὰ θανόντι περ X 73.—Pleasing, delightsome: τό γε καλὸν ἀκουέμεν ἐστὶν ἀοιδοῦ α 370. Cf. ι 3, 11.—Conferring distinction, bringing honour or fame: ἀέθλια φ 117. Cf. λ 184, σ 255 = τ 128.—(6) Absol. in neut. καλόν, a fitting or seemly thing, fitting, seemly, well, proper. With infin.: οὐ γὰρ ἔμοιγε κ. [ἄρχειν] Φ 440. Cf. I 615, P 19, T 79: οὐ κ. ἀτέμβειν . . . υ 294, φ 312. Cf. σ 287.—(7) Absol. in neut. comp. κάλλιον, a more fitting or seemly thing, more fitting, seemly or proper, better: ἐπεὶ πολὺ κ. οὕτως γ 358, θ 543. Cf. γ 69, ζ 39, ρ 583.—Fitting, seemly, well (rather than the reverse): οὔ οἱ τό γε κ. Ω 52. Cf. η 159, θ 549.—(8) In neut. καλόν as adv. (a) Well, in seemly wise: οὐ κ. ἔειπες θ 166.—(b) Sweetly, ravishingly: κ. ἀοιδιάει κ 227. Cf. A 473, Σ 570: α 155, θ 266, τ 519, φ 411.—(9) In neut. pl. καλά as adv. (a) Well, in becoming, seemly or fitting wise: οὐ κ. χόλον τόνδ' ἔνθεο θυμῷ (you do not well in this) Z 326. Cf. N 116: οὐ κ. ἔβαλες ἀλήτην (it was ill in you to . . .) ρ 483. Cf. ρ 381, 397.—(b) Well, with good consequences, in favouring circumstances: οὐ κ. συνοισόμεθα πτόλεμόνδε (it will be ill for some of us) Θ 400: οὐκέτι κ. ἀναχωρήσειν ρ 460 (*i.e.* the impunity you have enjoyed is now to cease).—(c) With prudence or good judgment: οὐκέτι κ. δόμων ἄπο τῆλ' ἀλάλησαι ο 10 (*i.e.* it is time to make for home).—(d) Sweetly, with sympathy: ὥς μοι κ. τὸν οἶτον παιδὸς ἔνισπες Ω 388.

κάλος, ὁ. In pl., tackle for raising a sail, halyards ε 260.

κάλπις, ἡ. A pitcher η 20.

κάλυμμα, τό [καλυμ-, καλύπτω]. = καλύπτρη Ω 93.

κάλυξ, -υκος, ἡ. Some kind of ornament or fastening Σ 401.

καλύπτρη, -ης, ἡ [καλύπτω]. A woman's or goddess's head-covering X 406: ε 232, κ 545.

καλύπτω. Fut. καλύψω Φ 321. Aor. κάλυψα Ξ 359. 3 sing. (ἐ)κάλυψε Γ 381, Δ 503, E 310, Λ 250, M 31, N 580, P 591, X 466, etc.: ε 293, θ 85, ι 68, σ 201, τ 507, ω 315, etc. 3 pl. (ἐ)κάλυψαν A 460, B 423, Σ 352, Ψ 254: γ 457, μ 360. 3 sing. subj. καλύψῃ M 281. Pple. καλύψας E 23, Λ 752, P 132: ρ 241. Pl. καλύψαντες Ω 796. Infin. καλύψαι H 462, N 425. **Mid.** 3 sing. aor. καλύψατο Ξ 184: ε 491. Pple. καλυψάμενος, -η Γ 141: θ 92, κ 53, 179. **Pass.** Aor. pple. καλυφθείς δ 402. Pf. pple. κεκαλυμμένος, -η, -ον Π 360, 790, Φ 318, Ω 163: α 443, θ 503, 562, λ 15. 3 sing. plupf. κεκάλυπτο N 192, Φ 549. (ἀμφι-.) (1) To cover up or envelop for protection, preservation or concealment: ἠέρι πολλῇ Γ 381 = Υ 444. Cf. E 23, K 29, N 192, Σ 352, Ω 20, 163 (hiding his face in his garment), etc.: κεκαλυμμένος οἰὸς ἀώτῳ α 443. Cf. δ 402, θ 85, 503, 562, τ 507.—In mid. θ 92.—(2) In gen., to cover, envelop, enclose, enfold, overlay, shroud: μηροὺς κατὰ κνίσῃ ἐκάλυψαν A 460, χυτή με κατὰ γαῖα καλύπτοι Z 464. Cf. H 462, M 281, Π 735, P 136, Φ 318, Ψ 168, 189, etc.: σὺν δὲ νεφέεσσι κάλυψε γαῖαν ε 293. Cf. γ 457, ε 353, 435, λ 15, ρ 241, etc.—Of night K 201.—Of grief: τὸν ἄχεος νεφέλη ἐκάλυψεν P 591 = Σ 22: = ω 315. Cf. Λ 250.—Of sleep σ 201.—Of death or the darkness of death or swoon: τὸν σκότος ὄσσε κάλυψεν Δ 461, τὼ τέλος θανάτοιο κάλυψεν E 553. Cf. E 310, 659, N 425, Ξ 439, Π 325, etc.—(3) In mid. without expressed object, to cover oneself up for protection: φύλλοισι καλύψατο ε 491.—To cover or veil oneself: καλυψαμένη ὀθόνῃσιν Γ 141. Cf. Ξ 184: καλυψάμενος κείμην (hiding my face) κ 53.—With ἐκ, to uncover oneself (cf. ἐκ (I) (2)): ἐκ δὲ καλυψάμενοι θηήσαντο (showing their faces) κ 179.—(4) To put or place (something) so as to afford protection, for or in way of protection: ἀμφὶ Μενοιτιάδῃ σάκος καλύψας P 132. Cf. E 315, X 313.—Of covering or overlaying: τόσσην οἱ ἄσιν καλύψω Φ 321.—Of enveloping or shrouding: ἀμφὶ νύκτ' ἐκάλυψεν E 507.—To shed (sleep): αὐτῷ ἐγὼ περὶ κῶμα κάλυψα Ξ 359.

κᾱλῶς [adv. fr. καλός]. In becoming or seemly wise β 63.

κάμ. See κατά.

κάμαξ, -ακος, ἡ. A vine-pole Σ 563.

κάματος, -ου, ὁ [καμ-, κάμνω]. (1) Toil, labour: καμάτῳ καὶ ἱδρῷ (the sweat of toil) P 385. Cf. η 325.—(2) The result of one's labour or toil, the work of one's hands: ἄλλοι ἡμέτερον κάματον ἔδουσιν ξ 417. Cf. O 365.—(3) Weariness, exhaustion, distress, fatigue: κ. γυῖα δέδυκεν E 811. Cf. Δ 230, H 6, K 98, 312 = 399, 471, N 85, 711, P 745, Φ 52: α 192, ε 457, 472, 493, ζ 2, ι 75 = κ 143, κ 363, μ 281, ξ 318, υ 118.

κάμε, 3 sing. aor. *κάμνω*.

καμῖνώ, ἡ [*κάμινος*, furnace]. A furnace-woman: *γρηῒ καμινοῖ ἶσος* σ 27.

καμμονίη, -ης, ἡ [*καμ-, κατα-* (5) + *μονή*, sb. fr. *μένω*]. Power of endurance or outlasting, *i.e.* victory: *αἴ κεν ἐμοὶ Ζεὺς δώῃ καμμονίην* Χ 257. Cf. Ψ 661.

κάμμορος [*καμ-, κατα-*(2)) + *μόρος*]. Fate-ridden, ill-fated, wretched: *κεῖνον τὸν κάμμορον* β 351. —In voc. ε 160, 339, λ 216, υ 33.

κάμνω. 3 sing. fut. in mid. form *καμεῖται* Β 389. Aor. *ἔκαμον* φ 426. *κάμον* ψ 189. 3 sing. *κάμε* Β 101, Ε 735, Σ 614, Φ 26, Ω 613, etc.: λ 523, ο 105, φ 150. 2 dual *κάμετον* Θ 448. 3 *καμέτην* Δ 27. 3 pl. *ἔκαμον* Δ 244: μ 232. *κάμον* Δ 187, 216, Ε 338. Subj. *κάμω* Α 168. 3 sing. *κάμῃσι* Ρ 658: ξ 65. 3 pl. *κάμωσι* Η 5. 2 pl. opt. *κάμοιτε* Θ 22. 3 *κάμοιεν* ι 126. Pple. *καμών, -όντος* Γ 278, Ψ 72, 444: λ 476, ω 14. 2 sing. pf. *κέκμηκας* Ζ 262. Pple. *κεκμηώς* Ψ 232. Dat. sing. *κεκμηῶτι* Ζ 261. Acc. *κεκμηῶτα* κ 31, ν 282. Acc. pl. *κεκμηότας* Λ 802, Π 44. 1 pl. aor. mid. *καμόμεσθα* Σ 341. 3 *ἐκάμοντο* ι 130. **(1)** To toil, strive, exert oneself: *οὐδ' εἰ μάλα πολλὰ κάμοιτε* Θ 22. Cf. ξ 65.—**(2)** To produce by work, make, fabricate, construct: *σκῆπτρον, τὸ μὲν Ἥφαιστος κάμεν* Β 101. Cf. Δ 187, 216, Ε 338, 735 = Θ 386, Η 220, Θ 195, Σ 614, Τ 368: *πέπλοι, οὓς κάμεν* ο 105. Cf. ι 126, λ 523, ψ 189.—So in mid.: *νηῶν τέκτονες, οἵ κέ σφιν* (sc. *Κυκλώπεσσιν*) *καὶ νῆσον ἐϋκτιμένην ἐκάμοντο* (would have made them a fine place of it) ι 130. —In mid., to win or acquire by toil or exertion: *Τρῳαί, τὰς καμόμεσθα* (*i.e.* as captives) Σ 341.—**(3)** To grow weary, become exhausted or fatigued; in pf. to be weary, exhausted or fatigued: *περὶ ἔγχεϊ χεῖρα καμεῖται* (in his . . .) Β 389. Cf. Ε 797, Ζ 261, Λ 802 = Π 44, Τ 170, Ψ 232, 444: *ἐμὲ ὕπνος ἐπήλυθε κεκμηῶτα* κ 31 = ν 282. Cf. μ 280.—In aor. pple. pl., that have succumbed to the toils of life, *i.e.* have died: *καμόντας ἀνθρώπους* (the dead) Γ 278. Cf. λ 476.—Absol.: *εἴδωλα καμόντων* Ψ 72: ω 14.—**(4)** To wear oneself out, incur weariness, exhaustion or fatigue, become wearied, exhausted or fatigued, *in doing something*. With pple.: *πολεμίζων* Α 168. Cf. Δ 244, Ζ 262, Η 5, Θ 448, Π 106, Ρ 658, Φ 26, Ψ 63, Ω 613: φ 150, 426.—Sim.: *καμέτην μοι ἵπποι λαὸν ἀγειρούσῃ* Δ 27. Cf. μ 232.

†κάμπτω. Fut. infin. *κάμψειν* Η 118, Τ 72. 3 sing. aor. *ἔκαμψε* ε 453. 3 pl. *ἔκαμψαν* Ω 274. 3 sing. subj. *κάμψῃ* Δ 486. **(1)** To bend so as to put in a desired position: *ὑπὸ γλωχῖνα δ' ἔκαμψαν* (tucked it in (see *γλωχίς*)) Ω 274.—**(2)** To form or make by bending: *ἴτυν* Δ 486.—**(3)** To bend (the knee), *i.e.* to take rest: *ἀσπασίως γόνυ κάμψειν* Η 118, Τ 72.—To bend (the knees) in exhaustion: *ἄμφω γούνατ' ἔκαμψε χεῖράς τε* ε 453 (*i.e.* they gave way under him. The idea of bending is not strictly applicable to the arms, which would drop by his side).

καμπύλος [*κάμπτω*]. Bent, curved. Epithet **(1)** Of bows Γ 17, Ε 97, Κ 333, Μ 372: ι 156, φ 359, 362.—Applied to the whole archery equipment Φ 502 (see *τόξον* (4)).—**(2)** Of wheels: *κύκλα* Ε 722.—**(3)** Of a chariot (referring doubtless to the curved *ἄντυξ*) Ε 231.

καναχέω [*καναχή*]. To give forth a sound, ring: *κανάχησε χαλκός* τ 469.

καναχή, -ῆς, ἡ. A sound. The ring of metal Π 105, 794.—The gnashing of teeth Τ 365.—The tramp of mules or the clatter of their trappings ζ 82.

καναχίζω [*καναχή*]. To give forth a sound, resound: *κανάχιζε δούρατα πύργων* Μ 36.

κάνεον, -ου, τό. Also **κάνειον** κ 355. **(1)** A bread-basket, app. of wicker-work Ι 217 = Ω 626: α 147, θ 69, π 51, ρ 335, 343 (the meat presumably from another basket; see (2)), σ 120, υ 255.—**(2)** A similar basket for meat υ 300.—**(3)** A similar basket for sacrificial meal γ 442, δ 761.—**(4)** A bread-basket of metal: *χάλκειον κάνεον* Λ 630. Cf. κ 355.

καννεύσας, contr. aor. pple. *κατανεύω*.

κανών, -όνος, ὁ. Dat. pl. *κανόνεσσι* Ν 407. **(1)** App., each of two pieces set inside a shield to keep it in shape, one running from top to bottom and the other placed horizontally, the middle portion of the latter forming a handle: [*ἀσπίδα*] *δύω κανόνεσσ' ἀραρυῖαν* Ν 407. Cf. Θ 193. —**(2)** In weaving, app., each of two horizontal rods to which the lower ends of the threads of the warp (*μίτος*) were attached, the even threads to one and the odd to the other Ψ 761.

κάπ. See *κατά*.

κάπετος, -ου, ἡ [app. (*σ*)*κάπετος*, fr. *σκάπτω*, to dig]. **(1)** A ditch surrounding a vineyard Σ 564. —**(2)** A ditch in fortification Ο 356.—**(3)** A grave Ω 797.

κάπη, -ης, ἡ. A horse's crib or manger: *ἵππους κατέδησαν ἐπὶ κάπῃσιν* Θ 434: δ 40.

καπνίζω [*καπνός*]. To raise a smoke, *i.e.* to make fire: *κάπνισσαν καὶ δεῖπνον ἕλοντο* Β 399.

καπνός, -οῦ, ὁ. **(1)** Smoke: *κ. ἰὼν ἐξ ἄστεος* Σ 207. Cf. Α 317, Θ 183, Ι 243, Σ 110, Φ 522, Ψ 100: *καπνὸν ἀπὸ χθονὸς ἀΐσσοντα* κ 99. Cf. α 58, ι 167, κ 149, 152, 196, μ 202, 219, ν 435, π 288 = τ 7, τ 18.—**(2)** Steam: *ἀμφὶ κ. γίγνεται ἐκ πηγῆς* Χ 149.

κάππεσον, contr. aor. *καταπίπτω*.

κάπριος, -ου, ὁ [= next]. A wild boar Λ 414, Μ 42.—Joined with *σῦς* Λ 293, Ρ 282.

κάπρος, -ου, ὁ [= prec.]. **(1)** A wild boar: *κάπρω μέγα φρονέοντε* Λ 324. Cf. Ρ 725: ζ 104 —Joined with *σῦς*: *συσὶ κάπροισιν* Ε 783 = Η 257. Cf. Ρ 21. —**(2)** A boar as a sacrificial victim Τ 197, 251, 254, 266: λ 131 = ψ 278.

καπύω [cf. *καπνός*]. 3 sing. aor. *ἐκάπυσσε* Χ 467. From the same stem (*καπ-* = *καφ-*) acc. sing. masc. pf. pple. *κεκαφηότα* Ε 698: ε 468. To breathe or pant forth: *ἀπὸ ψυχὴν ἐκάπυσσεν* Χ 467, *κεκαφηότα θυμόν* (panting it forth) Ε 698: ε 468.

κάρ¹, *καρός* [perh. conn. with *κείρω*]. Thus, a chip or shaving. As the type of something worthless: *τίω μιν ἐν καρὸς αἴσῃ* Ι 378.

κάρ². See ἐπικάρ.

κάρ³. See κατά.

καρδίη, -ης, ἡ [cf. κραδίη, κῆρ]. =κραδίη (3) (b): ἐν σθένος ὦρσεν (σθένος ἔμβαλ') ἑκάστῳ καρδίῃ B 452 = Λ 12 = Ξ 152.

κάρη, τό. **(a)** Genit. καρήατος Ψ 44. κάρητος ζ 230, ψ 157. Dat. καρήατι T 405, X 205. κάρητι O 75. Nom. pl. καρήατα Λ 309. Acc. καρήατα P 437. **(b)** Genit. κράατος Ξ 177. Dat. κράατι χ 218. Acc. pl. κράατα T 93. **(c)** Genit. κρᾱτός A 530, Z 472, N 189, P 205, X 468, etc.: ε 323, κ 288, λ 600, ν 102, ξ 276, etc. Dat. κρᾱτί Γ 336, E 743, K 335, T 381, etc.: ι 490, μ 99, χ 123. Acc. κρᾶτα θ 92. Genit. pl. κράτων χ 309, ω 185. Dat. κρᾱσί K 152. **(d)** An anomalous locative form κράτεσφι K 156. **(1)** The head: ἀπ' ἐμεῖο κ. τάμοι ἀλλότριος φώς E 214. Cf. A 530, B 259, Γ 336, Z 472, K 152, etc.: κὰδ δὲ κάρητος οὔλας ἧκε κόμας ζ 230. Cf. ε 285, ζ 107, θ 92, ι 490, λ 600, etc.—For κάρη κομόωντες see κομάω.—Of horses: ὑψοῦ κ. ἔχει Z 509 = O 266. Cf. P 437, T 405.—**(2) (a)** The top of a mountain: κρατὸς ἀπ' Οὐλύμποιο Υ 5.—**(b)** The head of a harbour: ἐπὶ κρατὸς λιμένος ι 140, ν 102, 346.

κάρηνον, -ου, τό [κάρη]. Only in pl. **(1)** = κάρη (1) (but never in the strict literal sense): ὣς πῖπτε κάρηνα Τρώων Λ 158. Cf. Λ 500.—Periphrastically: ἵππων ξανθὰ κάρηνα I 407. Cf. Ψ 260: νεκύων ἀμενηνὰ κάρηνα κ 521, 536, λ 29, 49.—**(2)** = κάρη (2) (a) A 44, B 869, H 19, Υ 58, B 167 = Δ 74 = X 187 = Ω 121: = α 102 = ω 488, ζ 123, ι 113.—**(3)** In reference to cities, the topmost part, the citadel (cf. κρήδεμνον (2)): πολλάων πολίων κάρηνα B 117 = I 24. Cf. B 735.

κάρητος, genit. κάρη.

καρκαίρω [imitative]. To quake, tremble: κάρκαιρε γαῖα πόδεσσιν (with, under, the feet) Υ 157.

καρπάλιμος [καρπ- = κραιπ- as in κραιπνός]. Swift. Epithet of the feet Π 342, 809, X 166.

καρπαλίμως [adv. fr. prec.]. **(1)** Swiftly, at speed, nimbly: κ. ἤϊξε διὰ δρυμά Λ 118. Cf. Υ 190, X 159, Ψ 408, Ω 327: μεθ' ἡμιόνους κ. ἔρχεσθαι ζ 261. Cf. θ 122, κ 146.—**(2)** Swiftly, speedily, quickly, soon, at once, without loss of time, smartly: κ. ἀνέδυ πολιῆς ἁλός A 359. Cf. A 435, B 17, Γ 117, E 868, Θ 506, etc.: κ. ἔζευξαν ἵππους γ 478. Cf. β 406, γ 418, ζ 312, θ 16, ι 216, etc.

καρπός¹, -οῦ, ὁ. **(1)** Fruit in general: τάων οὔ ποτε κ. ἀπόλλυται η 117, δένδρεα κατὰ κρῆθεν χέε καρπόν (their fruit) λ 588. Cf. τ 112.—**(2)** Specifically of the fruit of the vine, grapes Σ 568.—Of the fruit of the lotus ι 94.—Of that of the cornel κ 242.—Of that of the poppy Θ 307.—Of the ears or grains of growing corn: ἀνθερίκων καρπόν Υ 227.—Grain as distinguished from chaff: ὅτε Δημήτηρ κρίνῃ καρπόν τε καὶ ἄχνας E 501.—Grain to be ground: ἀλετρεύουσι μύλῃς ἔπι μήλοπα καρπόν η 104.—**(3)** Collectively, the fruits of the earth, the produce of one's land: οὔ ποτ' ἐν Φθίῃ καρπὸν ἐδηλήσαντο A 156.—**(4)** ἀρούρης καρπός, of corn or grain Z 142, Φ 465.—Of wine Γ 246.

καρπός², -οῦ, ὁ. The wrist: οὔτασε χεῖρ' ἐπὶ καρπῷ E 458. Cf. E 883, Θ 328, P 601, Σ 594, Φ 489, Ω 671: ἐπὶ καρπῷ ἑλὼν ἐμὲ χεῖρα (taking me by the hand at the wrist) σ 258. Cf. χ 277, ω 398.

καρρέζουσα, contr. fem. pres. pple. καταρρέζω.

καρτερόθῡμος [καρτερός + θυμός]. Stout-hearted N 350, Ξ 512: φ 25.—Absol. in voc. E 277.

καρτερός, -ή, -όν [κάρτος. Cf. κρατερός]. **(1)** Strong, mighty, powerful, stout, staunch: πολέμῳ ἔνι κ. ἐσσι I 53. Cf. A 178, 280, E 410, 592, 645, 806, N 124, 127, 316: κ. ἀνήρ δ 242, 271, υ 393. Cf. θ 139, χ 13.—With infin. indicating that in which stoutness is displayed: κ. μάχῃ ἔνι φῶτας ἐναίρειν N 483.—**(2)** Powerful, influential: ὑμεῖς καρτεροὶ αἰεί ο 534. Cf. ξ 116.—**(3)** Violent, of violence: ἔργα E 757, 872.—**(4)** Of a wound, deep-struck Π 517, 523.—**(5)** Of an oath, mighty, potent T 108, 127: δ 253, κ 381, μ 298, σ 55.

κάρτιστος, -η, -ον [superl. (with metathesis) of κρατύς]. **(1)** In superl. sense of καρτερός (1): κάρτιστον 'Αχαιῶν Z 98. Cf. A 266, 267, H 155, Θ 17, I 558.—Of an eagle Φ 253.—Absol. A 267.—In superl. sense of καρτερός (2) Υ 243.—**(2)** Of a battle, the most hotly contested, the most desperate Z 185.—**(3)** Absol. in neut. κάρτιστον, the best course to take, the best thing to do: φυγέειν κ. [ἐστιν] μ 120.

κάρτος, τό [cf. κράτος]. **(1)** Physical strength, might, stoutness, prowess: εἰ γὰρ δοίη κ. ἐμοί P 562, ὅ τ' οὐκέτι κ. 'Αχαιῶν (that there is no fight left in them) 623. Cf. Θ 226 = Λ 9, I 254, O 108, P 322, 329: γ 370, δ 415, ν 143, σ 139.—**(2)** National strength or power: Φαιήκων κ. τε βίη τε (the two words hardly to be distinguished) ζ 197.

†**καρτῡ́νω** [κάρτος]. 3 pl. aor. mid. ἐκαρτύναντο. To strengthen. In mid.: ἐκαρτύναντο φάλαγγας (pulled their ranks together) Λ 215 = M 415, Π 563.

καρφαλέος [κάρφω]. **(1)** Dried up, parched: ἠϊὼν ε 369.—**(2)** In neut. καρφαλέον as adv., with a dry, *i.e.* a harsh or grating sound (cf. αὖος (2)): κ. οἱ ἀσπὶς ἄϋσεν N 409.

†**κάρφω**. Fut. κάρψω ν 398. 3 sing. aor. κάρψε ν 430. To dry up, make withered or shrivelled: χρόα ν 398, 430.

καρχαλέος [app. conn. with κάρχαρος. See next]. Thus, rough (in the throat): δίψῃ καρχαλέοι Φ 541.

καρχαρόδους, -όδοντος [κάρχαρος, sharp-pointed + ὀδούς]. With sharp or jagged teeth. Epithet of dogs K 360, N 198.

κασιγνήτη, -ης, ἡ [fem. of κασίγνητος]. A sister I 584, K 317, Π 432, Σ 52, 139, 356, Υ 71, Φ 470: δ 810.—Of Eris and Ares: "Αρεος κ. ἑτάρη τε Δ 441.

κασίγνητος, -ου, ὁ [κάσις, brother + γνη- = (with metathesis) γεν-, γίγνομαι]. **(1) (a)** A brother, whether of the full or of the half blood: οἷο (*sc.* 'Αλεξάνδροιο) κασιγνήτοιο Λυκάονος Γ 333 (sons of Priam, A. by Hecabe, while L.'s mother was Laothoë (X 46)), ἡ (*sc.* 'Αφροδίτη) κασιγνήτοιο (sc. Ἄρηος) ἤτεεν ἵππους E 357 (they were children of Zeus, Ares by Here (E 892), Aphrodite by Dione (E 370)), σὺν γαμβροῖσι κασιγνήτοισί τε σοῖσιν 474 (sons of Priam by various mothers), Ἕκτωρ οὔ τι κασιγνήτῳ (sc. Ἑλένῳ) ἀπίθησεν Z 102 (both sons of Priam and Hecabe), οὔτ' αὐτῆς Ἑκάβης . . . οὔτε κασιγνήτων 452, κασίγνητός τοί εἰμι H 48 (Helenus to Hector), Αἴας οὐκ ἀμέλησε κασιγνήτοιο (sc. Τεύκροιο) πεσόντος Θ 330 (they appear to have been full brothers (O 439); but see Θ 284 and also M 371 cited under (b), which imply no more than their having the same father), πένθος ἑ ὀφθαλμοὺς ἐκάλυψε κασιγνήτοιο (sc. Ἰφιδάμαντος) πεσόντος Λ 250 (brother of Coon; see 257 cited under (b). Both were sons of Antenor), Ἀκάμας ἀμφὶ κασιγνήτῳ (sc. Ἀρχελόχῳ) βεβαώς Ξ 477 (both were sons of Antenor (B 823, M 100)), Ἕκτωρ δ' ὡς ἐνόησε κασίγνητον Πολύδωρον Υ 419 (P.'s mother was Laothoë (X 46)). Cf. Δ 155, E 359, Z 239, 421, 430, I 567, 632, Ξ 473, 483, O 436, 466, Π 320, 326, 456 = 674, T 293, Ω 793: γ 39, ζ 155, η 4, θ 546, 585, ο 16, 237, 273, π 97, 115, σ 140, φ 216, ω 434, 484.—Of Sleep and Death Ξ 231.—Of two rivers Φ 308.—(b) With words defining the nature of the tie: Ἰφιδάμαντα κασίγνητον καὶ ὄπατρον Λ 257 (either, son of the same mother and father, or, taking ὄπατρος epexegetically, his brother, the son of his father), Τεῦκρός οἱ (sc. Αἴαντι) ἅμ' ᾔε κ. καὶ ὄπατρος M 371 (see Θ 330 cited under (a)), ἠὲ κασίγνητον ὁμογάστριον ἠὲ καὶ υἱόν Ω 47.—(2) App. in a wide sense, including cousins: Ἕκτωρ κασιγνήτοισι κέλευσε, πρῶτον δ' Ἱκεταονίδην ἐνένιπε, Μελάνιππον O 545 (Hicetaon was brother to Priam (Υ 237)).

κασσίτερος, -ου, ὁ. Tin: χαλκὸν κασσίτερόν τε Σ 474. Cf. Λ 25, 34, Σ 565, 574, 613, Υ 271, Φ 592, Ψ 503, 561.

κασσορνῦσα, contr. fem. pres. pple. See καταστορέννυμι.

κάσχεθε, 3 sing. contr. aor. κατέχω.

κατά. (Commonly with anastrophe when immediately following the vb. or case-form). Also in assimilated forms κάγ, κάδ, κάκ, κάμ, κάπ, κάρ. (I) Adv. (1) Down, downwards: κατ' ἄρ' ἕζετο A 68, ὅς τε Τροίην κατὰ πᾶσαν ὁρᾶται (sees it from on high) Ω 291. Cf. A 413, B 549, Λ 676, N 653, P 619, Ψ 700, etc.: κατὰ φρόνιν ἤγαγεν (from the city) δ 258, κὰδ δ' ἔβαλεν 344. Cf. θ 67, κ 567, λ 426, 599, ο 496, τ 599, ω 540, etc.—In reference to getting into or putting on armour: αὖτις κατὰ τεύχε' ἔδυν Δ 222.—(2) Down upon or over something: κὰδ δέ οἱ ὕδωρ χεῦαν Ξ 435. Cf. Θ 50, T 282: κεφαλῇ κατὰ ῥάκος ἀμφικαλύψας ξ 349. Cf. η 286, λ 433, etc.—(3) Against or affecting a person: πείσεται ἅσσα οἱ αἶσα κατὰ Κλῶθές τε γεινομένῳ νήσαντο λίνῳ η 197.—(4) In intensive senses (a) In reference to fastening down, binding or securing: κατὰ πρυμνήσι' ἔδησαν A 436. Cf. T 94, etc.: θεοῦ κατὰ μοῖρα πέδησεν λ 292. Cf. β 425, ο 498, τ 42, etc.—Sim. in reference to drawing reins tight: κατὰ δ' ἡνία τεῖνεν (τεῖναν) Γ 261, 311, T 394.—Also κατὰ συφεοῖσιν ἐέργνυ κ 238.—(b) In reference to covering or spreading over something: κατὰ κνίσῃ ἐκάλυψαν (as we say, 'up') A 460. Cf. B 699, Z 464, Θ 441, Π 325, etc.: κατὰ κρᾶτα καλυψάμενος θ 92. Cf. γ 457, τ 507, etc.—So in a geographical expression in reference to containing or enfolding, about, round: βαθὺν κατὰ κόλπον ἐχούσας B 560.—(c) To destruction or extinction: μὴ κατὰ χρόα σαπήῃ T 27, κατὰ δ' ᾕρεε Πηλεΐωνα (was bent on his utter destruction) Φ 327. Cf. A 40, B 317, Δ 157, Z 416, Θ 403, T 334, Ψ 237, etc.: οἳ κατὰ βοῦς ἤσθιον α 8. Cf. β 376, γ 307, 315, μ 364, τ 539, etc.—(d) With λείπω: τὸν κατ' αὐτόθι λεῖπεν Φ 201. Cf. B 160, K 273, P 91, 535, etc.: κατὰ δ' ἄμμε λίπον ὄπισθεν κ 209. Cf. σ 257, φ 90, etc.—(e) In general intensive sense: τὸν κατ' ὄσσε ἔλλαβε θάνατος E 82. Cf. Ψ 623, etc.: κατὰ δ' ἔσχεθε λαόν ω 530. Cf. α 192, ι 372, 459, κ 113, λ 151, 497, ρ 323, υ 109, etc.—(II) Prep. (1) With genit. (a) Down from: κατ' Οὐλύμποιο A 44. Cf. E 111, Z 128, I 15, Λ 811, N 772, etc.: κατὰ παρειῶν δ 223. Cf. α 102, δ 680, ε 313, θ 508, σ 355, etc.—With ablative Δ 452, etc.—In reference to a point *from* which action takes place: κατ' ἀκροτάτης πόλιος κελεύων Υ 52.—(b) Down upon: πνείοντε κατ' ὤμων N 385. Cf. Γ 217, E 659, Σ 24, Ψ 765, etc.: κατὰ κρατός κ 362. Cf. θ 85, etc.—Down into: κατὰ χθονὸς ᾤχετο Ψ 100. Cf. Φ 172.—Down through: ἀμβροσίην στάξε κατὰ ῥινῶν T 39.—(c) In reference to extent down or in from an opening: μέσση κατὰ σπείους δέδυκεν μ 93. Cf. ι 330.—(2) With acc. (a) Down through or along: αἷμα κατὰ ῥῖνας πρῆσεν Π 349. Cf. M 33, etc.: ὁδὸν κάτα (down the track) ρ 204. Cf. ε 461, σ 97.—So in reference to a wound: ἔρρει αἷμα κατ' ὠτειλήν P 86.—Sim.: ψυχὴ κατ' ὠτειλὴν ἔσσυτο Ξ 518.—In reference to motion downwards and inwards: μυῖαι καδδῦσαι κατ' ὠτειλάς T 25. Cf. T 209.—Without notion of actual downward movement, through, along: λαοφόρον καθ' ὁδόν O 682. Cf. M 469, etc.: κατ' ἠερόεντα κέλευθα υ 64. Cf. ξ 254, etc.—καθ' ὁδόν (by the way) θ 444.—(b) Down into: ἁλὸς κατὰ κῦμα Z 136. Cf. δ 510.—So of going *into* a place: κατὰ σταθμοὺς δύεται E 140. Cf. Φ 559.—Sim.: καθ' ὅμιλον ἔδυ Γ 36.—(c) Through, throughout, among, over, in, on: κατὰ στρατὸν Ἀχαιῶν A 229, ἔβη κατὰ νῆας B 47. Cf. B 345, 470, Γ 151, E 162, Z 201, etc.: Ἰθάκην κάτα α 247. Cf. α 116, β 383, γ 302, ε 52, ι 6, κ 122, τ 233, etc.—In reference to the sight: πάπτηνε κατὰ στίχας P 84. Cf. Π 646: χ 381.—To piercing, through: κατὰ κύστιν ἤλυθ' ἀκωκή E 67. Cf. N 652.—To position in or within (a space): κατ' ἀντίθυρον π 159.—(d) In reference to motion *over* something: ἔθεεν κατὰ κῦμα A 483. Cf. Δ 276, N 737, T 93, Ψ 230, etc.: οἵη Ἄρτεμις εἶσι κατ' οὔρεα ζ 102. Cf. β 429, ε 377, etc.—(e) In the region of, about, by: κατὰ βωμούς B 305. Cf. A 409, M 340.—Sim.: [ξυστὰ] κατὰ στόμα εἱμένα χαλκῷ (at the point) O 389.—Also: [ἑανὸν] κατὰ στῆθος περονᾶτο (on her . . .) Ξ 180.—In reference to arriving *at* a spot: ὅτε κατὰ νῆας ἵξεν Λ 806. Cf. N 329: ω 13.—Over against, opposite: ὅτε κατ' αὐτοὺς σταίησαν P 732.—Sim.: κατ' ἐνῶπα ἰδὼν Δαναῶν (in the face of the . . .) O 320. Cf. P 167.—In nautical sense, abreast of, off: ἐπεί ῥ' ἵκοντο κατὰ στρατόν A 484. Cf. ε 441.—In reference to wounding or striking, in the region of, in: κατὰ δεξιὸν ὦμον E 46. Cf. E 66, 73, 305, 579, Z 64, Θ 83, etc.: πρυμνότατον κατὰ νῶτον ρ 463. Cf. κ 161, τ 452, χ 15, etc.—Sim. in reference to a shield, etc., struck, on: κατ' ἀσπίδα νύξεν Ψ 818. Cf. Γ 347, E 537, Λ 351, Π 106, etc.—(f) Of position, on, upon: κατὰ βοὸς κέρας ἐμβεβαυῖα Ω 81. Cf. X 133: ἕζοντο κατὰ κλισμούς α 145. Cf. κ 233, ρ 86, etc.—(g) In reference to the mind, etc., in: χωόμενον κατὰ θυμόν A 429. Cf. A 193, 555, B 3, E 406, etc.: θάμβησεν κατὰ θυμόν α 323. Cf. α 4, 29, 294, etc.—(h) According to, in accordance or consonance with: ἄρσαντες κατὰ θυμόν A 136. Cf. A 286, B 214, Γ 59, I 108, Λ 336, etc.: κατὰ μοῖραν β 251. Cf. γ 138, etc.—Sim.: κατ' ἄντηστιν υ 387.—(i) In the matter of, with a view to, for, with, on: κατὰ δαῖτα A 424. Cf. O 447: κατὰ πρῆξιν γ 72. Cf. γ 106, λ 479, etc.—(j) Distributively, by: κατὰ φῦλα, κατὰ φρήτρας B 362: κατ' οἴκους α 375 = β 140.—So ἐρήτυθεν καθ' ἕδρας (in their several seats) B 99, 211.—(k) In reference to being *in* a specified formation: ἵζοντο κατὰ στίχας Γ 326.—(l) With personal pronouns, by (oneself): μαχόμην κατ' ἔμ' αὐτόν A 271. Cf. B 366.

καταβαίνω [κατα- (1)]. Aor. κατέβην ψ 252. 3 pl. κατέβησαν K 541. κατέβαν Ω 329: ω 205. 1 pl. subj. καταβήομεν K 97. Imp. κατάβηθι ψ 20. Pple. καταβάς Λ 184: ζ 281, ξ 350. Fem. καταβᾶσα P 545: υ 31. Infin. καταβήμεναι M 65, Ξ 19: κ 432. καταβῆναι Γ 252: κ 558, λ 63. 3 sing. aor. mid. κατεβήσετο Z 288, N 17, Ω 191: α 330, β 337, κ 107, ο 99. 3 sing. subj. καταβήσεται O 382. Imp. καταβήσεο E 109. (1) To go or come down, descend: ἐς πεδίον Γ 252. Cf. Λ 184, M 65, N 17, P 545: οὐρανόθεν ζ 281, υ 31. Cf. κ 107, 558 = λ 63, ψ 20 (go downstairs), 252, ω 205.—App. on the analogy of going down from a city: ἐς τοὺς φύλακας καταβήομεν (*sc.* from the ships) K 97.—Of something inanimate: ὥς τε κῦμα νηὸς ὑπὲρ τοίχων καταβήσεται O 382.—Of a wind, to come upon something, come on to blow: πρίν τινα κεκριμένον καταβήμεναι οὖρον Ξ 19.—(2) To come down or descend *from*. With genit.: πόλιος Ω 329.—To quit by descending, come down from: ὑπερώϊα σ 206, ψ 85.—To descend or come down (a means of descent): κλίμακα α 330, ἐφόλκαιον ξ 350.—(3) To descend from horseback, alight K 541.—To dismount *from* (a chariot). With genit.: καταβήσεο δίφρου E 109.—(4) In reference to entering a room (cf. κατά (II) (2) (b)): ἐς θάλαμον Z 288, Ω 191: ο 99. Cf. κ 432.—Sim.: ὅτ' εἰς ἵππον κατεβαίνομεν (the Trojan horse) λ 523.—To enter (a room): θάλαμον κατεβήσετο β 337.

καταβάλλω [κατα- (1)]. 3 sing. contr. aor. κάββαλε (καβ- = κατα-) E 343, Θ 249, I 206, M 206: ζ 172, ρ 302. (1) To throw down, let fall: κάββαλεν [αἰετὸς] νεβρόν Θ 249. Cf. M 206.—To set down, place: κρεῖον I 206.—To thrust from oneself, let go one's hold of: ἀπὸ ἕο κάββαλεν υἱόν E 343.—Of a dog throwing back his ears ρ 302.—(2) To throw down in way of destruction: ὄχθας καπέτοιο O 357.—(3) To cast ashore: ἐνθάδε [με] κάββαλε δαίμων ζ 172.

καταβάς, aor. pple. καταβαίνω.

καταβήμεναι, καταβῆναι, aor. infin. καταβαίνω.

καταβήσεται, 3 sing. aor. subj. mid. καταβαίνω.

καταβλώσκω [κατα- (1) (3)]. To go down *through*. With acc.: ἄστυ καταβλώσκοντα π 466.

†**καταβρόχω** [κατα- (5) + βρόχω, to swallow]. 3 sing. aor. opt. καταβρόξειε. (ἀνα-.) To swallow down, swallow: ὃς φάρμακον καταβρόξειεν . . . δ 222.

καταγηράσκω [κατα- (5)]. From καταγηράω 3 sing. impf. κατεγήρα ι 510. (1) To pass one's days and reach old age: μαντευόμενος κατεγήρα Κυκλώπεσσιν (among the . . .) ι 510.—(2) To show signs of age, age: αἶψ' ἐν κακότητι βροτοὶ καταγηράσκουσιν τ 360.

καταγῑνέω [κατ-, κατα- (1)]. To fetch, bring, carry, down: ἀπ' ὀρέων ὕλην κ 104.

†**κατάγνῡμι** [κατ-, κατα- (5)]. 3 sing. aor. κατέαξε ι 283. 1 pl. κατεάξαμεν N 257. To break in pieces, shiver: ἔγχος N 257.—To wreck (a ship): νέα ι 283.

κατάγω [κατ-, κατα- (1)]. Aor. infin. καταξέμεν Z 53. 3 sing. aor. κατήγαγε λ 164, τ 186. 1 pl. aor. mid. κατηγαγόμεσθα κ 140. (1) To lead or conduct down: ψυχὰς μνηστήρων ω 100.—Of a compelling cause: χρειώ με κατήγαγεν εἰς 'Αΐδαο λ 164.—(2) To lead or take from inland towards the shore: ἐπὶ νῆας E 26, Z 53, Φ 32: τρεῖς σιάλους κατάγων (*i.e.* from the pasture to the city) υ 163.—(3) To bring from the sea to land: τὸν Κρήτηνδε κατήγαγεν ἲς ἀνέμοιο τ 186.—*Intrans.*, to bring one's ship to land, make one's landfall: οἱ δ' ἰθὺς κάταγον γ 10 (*v.l.* κατάγοντο as below).—So in mid.: ἐπ' ἀκτῆς νηῒ κατηγαγόμεσθα (instrumental dat., 'with the ship') κ 140.—(4) In mid., of ships, to come to land: 'Ιθάκηνδε κατήγετο νηῦς π 322. Cf. γ 178.

καταδάπτω [κατα- (5)]. 3 pl. aor. κατέδαψαν γ 259. Infin. καταδάψαι X 339. To devour. Of dogs X 339.—Of dogs and birds of prey γ 259.—Fig., in pass., to be torn or distressed: καταδάπτεταί μευ ἦτορ π 92.

†**καταδαρθάνω** [κατα- (5)]. Aor. κατέδραθον η 285, ψ 18. 3 pl. κατέδραθον θ 296. Contr. 3 dual καδδραθέτην ο 494. Subj. καταδράθω ε 471. (1) To go to sleep, compose oneself to sleep: εἴ κε θάμνοις ἐν καταδράθω ε 471. Cf. η 285, θ 296.—(2) To sleep: καδδραθέτην οὐ πολλὸν ἐπὶ χρόνον ο 494. Cf. ψ 18.

καταδέρκομαι [κατα- (1)]. To look down upon: οὐδέ ποτ' αὐτοὺς 'Ηέλιος καταδέρκεται (never shines upon them) λ 16.

καταδεύω [κατα- (5) + δεύω[1]]. To wet through: πολλάκι μοι κατέδευσας χιτῶνα I 490.

καταδέω [κατα- (5)]. (1) To tie up or secure: [ἀσκὸν] μέρμιθι κ 23.—(2) To tie or secure (a rope)

Ω 274.—(3) To bind or secure (a person), put (him) in bonds ξ 345, ο 443.—Sim.: τῶν ἄλλων ἀνέμων κελεύθους ε 383. Cf. κ 20.—Fig.: κατέδησέ [με] κελεύθου (hindered me from . . .) η 272.—(4) To halter or secure (a horse) Θ 434, K 567: δ 40.—In reference to a mule Ψ 654.—To sheep κ 572.—To goats υ 176.—To a cow and goats υ 189.

καταδημοβορέω [κατα- (5) + δημοβορ-, δημοβόρος]. To consume as part of the common stock: λαοῖσι δότω καταδημοβορῆσαι Σ 301.

καταδράθω, aor. subj. καταδαρθάνω.

†**καταδύω** [κατα- (1)]. 3 sing. aor. κατέδῡ A 475, 605, Z 504: δ 246, 249, ι 168, 558, κ 185, 478, μ 31, ν 33, τ 426. Pple. καταδύς, -δύντος A 592, 601, K 545, Σ 210, T 162, 207, Ω 713: γ 138, ι 161, 556, κ 183, 476, μ 29, 228, π 366, ρ 570, 582, τ 424. Fem. καταδῦσα Θ 375. Contr. pl. καδδῦσαι T 25. Infin. καταδύμεναι Γ 241. καταδῦναι K 231, 433, N 307, O 299: ο 328. 1 pl. fut. mid. καταδῡσόμεθα κ 174. 3 sing. aor. κατεδύσετο Δ 86, H 103, K 517. Imp. καταδύσεο Σ 134. (1) In mid., to go down, descend: εἰς 'Αΐδαο δόμους κ 174.—(2) In act., to enter, go into, make one's way into: καταδῦσα Διὸς δόμον Θ 375. Cf. δ 246, 249.—Of flies making their way into a dead body T 25.—(3) In act. and mid., to enter, mingle with (a throng, etc.): Τρώων κατεδύσεθ' ὅμιλον Δ 86. Cf. Γ 241, K 231, 433, 517, 545, N 307, O 299, Σ 134: μνηστήρων καταδῦναι ὅμιλον ο 328.—(4) In act. and mid., to get into, put on (armour): ἐπεὶ κατέδυ τεύχεα Z 504, κατεδύσετο τεύχεα H 103. Cf. μ 228.—(5) In act., of the sun, to enter Ocean, set: ἦμος ἠέλιος κατέδυ A 475. Cf. A 592, 601, 605, Σ 210, T 162, 207, Ω 713: ἅμ' ἠελίῳ καταδύντι π 366. Cf. γ 138, ι 168, ν 33, etc.

καταείσατο, 3 sing. aor. mid. καθίημι².

†**καταέννῡμι** [κατα- (5)]. 3 pl. impf. καταείνυσαν (-Ϝεσνυ-) (v.l. καταείνυον) Ψ 135. Neut. pf. pple. pass. καταειμένον ν 351. Acc. sing. καταειμένον τ 431. To cover as with clothing: θριξὶ πάντα νέκυν καταείνυσαν Ψ 135.—In pass., to be so covered: ὄρος καταειμένον ὕλῃ ν 351, τ 431.

†**καταζαίνω** [κατ-, κατα- (5) + ἀζαίνω = ἄζω]. 3 sing. pa. iterative καταζήνασκε. To dry up: [γαῖαν] λ 587.

καταθάπτω [κατα- (5)]. Contr. aor. infin. κατθάψαι Ω 611. To pay funeral rites to (a corpse): τὸν καταθάπτειν ὅς κε θάνῃσιν T 228. Cf. Ω 611.

καταθεῖναι, aor. infin. κατατίθημι.

καταθείομεν, 1 pl. aor. subj. κατατίθημι.

καταθείς, aor. pple. κατατίθημι.

†**καταθέλγω** [κατα- (5)]. 3 sing. aor. κατέθελξε. To work upon by spells or enchantment, to bewitch, charm κ 213.

καταθήσω, fut. κατατίθημι.

καταθνήσκω [κατα- (5)]. Contr. 3 aor. κάτθανε I 320, Φ 107. 3 pl. pf. κατατεθνήκᾱσι O 664. 3 sing. opt. κατατεθναίη δ 224. Pple. κατατεθνηώς, -ῶτος H 89, 409, K 343, 387, Π 526, 565, P 369, Σ 540, X 164, Ψ 331: κ 530, λ 37, 147, 541, 564, 567, χ 448. Genit. sing. fem. κατατεθνηυίης λ 84, 141, 205. (1) To die: κάτθανε καὶ Πάτροκλος Φ 107. Cf. I 320, X 355.—(2) In pf., to be dead: ἡμὲν ὅτεῳ ζώουσι καὶ ᾧ κατατεθνήκασιν O 664: εἴ οἱ κατατεθναίη μήτηρ (should lie dead) δ 224.—In pple., dead: ἀνδρὸς σῆμα κατατεθνηῶτος H 89. Cf. H 409 (the dead bodies), K 343, 387, Π 526, 565, P 369 (the dead . . .), Σ 540, X 164, Ψ 331: ψυχὴ μητρὸς κατατεθνηυίης λ 84. Cf. κ 530, λ 37, 141, 147, 205, 541, 564, χ 448.—Absol., the dead, the departed: τῶν ἄλλων ψυχὰς κατατεθνηώτων λ 567.

καταθνητός [κατα- (5) + θνητός]. Mortal, liable to death: οὔ τι καταθνητὸς τέτυκτο E 402 = 901. Cf. Z 123, K 440: γ 114, ι 502, ρ 587, τ 285, υ 76, ψ 126.

καταθύμιος [κατα- (1) + θυμός]. Weighing on the heart, troubling: οὔ τί τοι θάνατος καταθύμιός ἐστιν (thou thinkest not of it) P 201. Cf. K 383: ἔπος τό μοι καταθύμιόν ἐστιν (that craves utterance) χ 392.

καταιβατός, -ή, -όν [καται-, κατα- (1) + βα-, βαίνω]. Affording access for descent, leading to a downward passage: θύραι ν 110.

†**καταικίζω** [contr. fr. καταεικίζω. κατα- (5)]. 3 sing. pf. pass. κατῄκισται. To mar, spoil, befoul: [τεύχεα] κατῄκισται π 290 = τ 9.

καταισχύνω [κατ-, κατα- (5)]. 2 pl. aor. subj. καταισχύνητε π 293, τ 12. To bring shame upon, act unworthily of: πατέρων γένος ω 508. Cf. ω 512.—To act unworthily in the matter of, mar the seemliness of: δαῖτα καὶ μνηστύν π 293 = τ 12.

καταΐσχω, κατίσχω [κατα- (1) (5) + (σ)ίσχω]. 2 sing. subj. mid. κατίσχεαι B 233. (1) To keep under control: [ἵππους] Ψ 321.—(2) To retain, keep. In mid.: ἥν ἀπονόσφι κατίσχεαι B 233.—(3) To occupy: οὔτε ποίμνῃσι καταΐσχεται [νῆσος] οὔτ' ἀρότοισιν (no flocks browse there nor does corn sprout) ι 122.—(4) To bring a (ship) to land: ἐς πατρίδα γαῖαν νῆα κατισχέμεναι λ 456.

καταῖτυξ. A kind of helmet described in K 258.

κατακαίριος [κατα- (5) + καίριος]. Deadly, fatal Λ 439.

κατακαίω [κατα- (5)]. 3 sing. aor. κατέκηε Z 418. 1 pl. subj. κατακήομεν H 333. Infin. κατακῆαι κ 533, λ 46. Contr. κακκῆαι λ 74. (1) To burn, consume with fire Z 418, H 333, 408: λ 74.—(2) To burn (a sacrifice), offer (it) by burning B 425: κ 533 = λ 46.

κατάκειμαι [κατα- (1)]. 3 pl. κατακείαται Ω 527. (1) To lie, lie outstretched Ω 10.—(2) To lie, be, in a specified condition: μῆλα, τὰ δὴ κατάκειτ' (κατέκειτ') ἐσφαγμένα κ 532, λ 45.—(3) To lie hidden, lie close, lurk: ἐν λόχμῃ κατέκειτο σῦς τ 439. Cf. P 677.—(4) Fig., of grief, to be hushed or stilled: ἄλγε' ἐν θυμῷ κατακεῖσθαι ἐάσομεν Ω 523.—(5) Of things, to be laid or set down, be, in a specified place: δοιοὶ πίθοι κατακείαται ἐν Διὸς οὔδει Ω 527.

κατακείρω [κατα- (5)]. 3 pl. aor. κατέκειραν ψ 356. To ravage, pillage: οἶκον χ 36.—To seize upon, make away with, consume: βίοτον πολλόν δ 686, μῆλα ψ 356.

κατακείω, *fut.* [κατα- (1)]. Contr. pl. pple. κακκείοντες Α 606, Ψ 58: α 424, γ 396, η 229, ν 17. To go to rest: κακκείοντες ἔβαν οἶκόνδε ἕκαστος Α 606: = γ 396 = η 229 = ν 17. Cf. Ψ 58: α 424, η 188 (fut. as imp.), σ 408, 419.

κατακῆαι, aor. infin. κατακαίω.

†**κατακλάω** [κατα- (5)]. 3 pl. impf. κατέκλων Υ 227. 3 sing. aor. pass. κατεκλάσθη Ν 608: δ 481, 538, ι 256, κ 198, 496, 566, μ 277. To break, snap short off: κατεκλάσθη ἐνὶ καυλῷ ἔγχος Ν 608.—To break off, snap off: ἄκρον ἐπ' ἀνθερίκων καρπὸν θέον οὐδὲ κατέκλων Υ 227.—In pass., fig., of the heart or spirit, to be broken: κατεκλάσθη φίλον ἦτορ δ 481 = 538 = κ 496, ι 256, κ 198 = 566 = μ 277.

†**κατακλίνω** [κατα- (1)]. Aor. pple. κατακλίνας. To lay down: δόρυ κατακλίνας ἐπὶ γαίῃ κ 165.

κατακοιμάω [κατα- (5)]. In pass., to lay oneself down to sleep, go to sleep: παρ' ἄμμι μένων κατακοιμηθήτω Ι 427. Cf. Β 355, Λ 731.

κατακοσμέω [κατα- (5)]. **(1)** To set in due order, order duly. In mid.: ἐπὴν πάντα δόμον κατακοσμήσησθε χ 440.—**(2)** To fit (an arrow to the string): ἐπὶ νευρῇ κατεκόσμει ὀϊστόν Δ 118.

κατακρῆθεν. See under κρῆθεν.

κατακρύπτω [κατα- (5)]. Fut. infin. κατακρύψειν Χ 120. Aor. pple. κατακρύψας ι 329. Fem. κατακρύψᾱσα ο 469, ψ 372. **(1)** To hide, hide away, conceal: τρί' ἄλεισα ὑπὸ κόλπῳ ο 469. Cf. Χ 120: ι 329.—**(2)** To cover up or shroud for concealment: νυκτί ψ 372.—**(3)** *Intrans. for reflexive*, to conceal oneself, shroud oneself from sight: οὔ τι κατακρύπτουσι [θεοί] η 205.—To dissemble one's person, disguise oneself: ἄλλῳ δ' αὐτὸν φωτὶ κατακρύπτων ἤϊσκεν δ 247.

κατακτείνω [κατα- (5)]. 3 sing. fut. κατακτενεῖ Ψ 412. 3 pl. fut. κατακτανέουσι (for which prob. κατακτενέουσι should be read) Ζ 409. 3 sing. aor. subj. κατακτείνῃ Υ 302: χ 73. 3 pl. κατακτείνωσι ο 278. 3 sing. opt. κατακτείνειε Υ 465, Ω 226, 586: χ 53. Pple. κατακτείνας Λ 432, Χ 245, Ω 481: ψ 118. Acc. sing. κατακτείναντα Ρ 505, Χ 109. Infin. κατακτεῖναι Λ 141: χ 32. Aor. κατέκτανον Ψ 87: ν 259, 271. 2 sing. κατέκτανες χ 29. 3 κατέκτανε Ε 608, Ζ 204, Η 90: δ 535, λ 411, φ 27. 1 pl. κατεκτάνομεν ω 66. 3 sing. subj. κατακτάνῃ Χ 86. Imp. κατάκτανε δ 743. Contr. κάκτανε Ζ 164. Aor. κατέκταν Δ 319. 3 sing. κατέκτα Β 662, Μ 378, Ν 170, Ξ 514, Ο 432, Σ 309, Ω 214. Pple. κατακτάς Ν 696, Ο 335, Ρ 187, Χ 323: ο 224, 272. Infin. κατακτάμεναι Γ 379, Ε 436, Υ 346, 442, Φ 140, 170. κατακτάμεν Ι 458, Μ 172, Ο 557, Τ 59, Φ 484: δ 700. Aor. pple. mid. (in sense of pf. pass.) κατακτάμενος π 106. 2 pl. fut. pass. κατακτενέεσθε Ξ 481. 3 pl. aor. κατέκταθεν Ε 558, Ν 780: γ 108. To kill, slay: πατρὸς ἑοῖο μήτρωα Β 662. Cf. Γ 379, Ε 558, Μ 172, Ν 780, Ρ 187, Ψ 87, etc.: α 75, γ 108, δ 535, ν 259, π 106, χ 29, etc.

†**κατακύπτω** [κατα- (1)]. 3 sing. aor. κατέκυψε. To bend down, stoop: πρόσσω κατέκυψεν Π 611 = Ρ 527.

†**καταλέγω**[1] [κατα- (1) + λέγω[1]]. 3 sing. fut. mid. καταλέξεται γ 353. 3 sing. aor. κατελέξατο Ι 690: κ 555. Imp. κατάλεξαι τ 44. 3 sing. aor. κατέλεκτο Ι 662: ν 75, ξ 520. Pple. καταλέγμενος λ 62, χ 196. Infin. καταλέχθαι ο 394. In mid. and pass., to lay oneself down, lie down to rest, go to rest: ἔνθ' ὁ γέρων κατέλεκτο Ι 662. Cf. Ι 690: Κίρκης ἐν μεγάρῳ καταλέγμενος λ 62. Cf. γ 353, κ 555, ν 75, ξ 520, ο 394, τ 44, χ 196.

†**καταλέγω**[2] [κατα- (5) + λέγω[2]]. Fut. καταλέξω Ι 262 (or aor. subj.), Κ 413, 427: γ 80 (or aor. subj.), ι 14, ξ 99 (or aor. subj.), π 226, τ 497, ω 123, etc. 1 pl. -ομεν ο 156. Aor. κατέλεξα η 297, κ 16, μ 35, ρ 122. 2 sing. -ας Ι 115, Τ 186: γ 331, λ 368, ξ 508, ψ 225. 3 -ε Ι 591: δ 256, κ 250, τ 464, ψ 321. 2 sing. subj. καταλέξῃς θ 496. 3 -ῃ δ 738. Imp. κατάλεξον Κ 384, 405, Ω 380, 407, 656: α 169, γ 97, δ 832, κ 421, π 235, χ 417, etc. Infin. καταλέξαι ψ 309. **(1)** To enumerate, tell of in order: μνηστῆρας π 235. Cf. τ 497, χ 417.—Absol. ξ 99.—**(2)** To tell over, recount, relate, touch upon in order, go through, deal with, make communication of, put before one: ἐμὰς ἄτας Ι 115. Cf. Ι 591, Τ 186: πάντα νόον Ἀχαιῶν δ 256, τῶν ἄλλων ἑτάρων ὄλεθρον κ 250, 421, ἀληθείην π 226 = χ 420, ρ 108, 122, φ 212. Cf. γ 331, δ 239, 738, η 297, θ 496, ι 14, κ 16, λ 368, μ 35, ξ 508, ο 156, υ 334, ψ 225, 309, 321, ω 123, 303.—**(3)** To tell, tell of or about, give information about, explain: ταῦτα Κ 413, 427. Cf. Κ 384 = 405: = α 169 = 224 = λ 170 = ω 256 = 287, λ 140.—With dependent clause δ 832.—Absol. γ 80.—**(4)** With dependent clause, to say, tell: ὅσσα . . . Ι 262: ὅπως . . . γ 97 = δ 327, ρ 44. Cf τ 464, ψ 321.—With acc. and clause: τόδε κατάλεξον, ποσσῆμαρ . . . Ω 656. Cf. Ω 380, 407: α 206, δ 486, θ 572, λ 370, 457, ο 383, π 137.

καταλείβω [κατα- (1)]. In pass., to drop down: μέλιτος καταλειβομένοιο Σ 109.

καταλείπω [κατα- (5)]. Contr. infin. καλλείπειν Κ 238. Fut. καλλείψω ν 208. Infin. καλλείψειν Ξ 89. Aor. κάλλιπον Ι 364: χ 156. 2 sing. -ες Ρ 151, Φ 414. 3 -ε Ζ 223, Κ 338, Μ 92: α 243, γ 271, λ 279, φ 33. Imp. κάλλιπε ε 344. Infin. καλλιπέειν π 296. **(1)** To leave behind one on going from a place: ἐν δώμασ' ἐμοῖσιν Ζ 221. Cf. Ζ 223, Ι 364, Μ 92: οὖρον ἐπὶ κτεάτεσσιν ἐμοῖσιν ο 89. Cf. λ 174, ν 208.—**(2)** To leave as a heritage: παιδὶ [τόξον] φ 33. Cf. α 243, λ 279.—**(3)** To leave in a specified condition: σῶμα ἐν Κίρκης μεγάρῳ ἄκλαυτον λ 53. Cf. λ 72, 86, 447, ο 348, π 289 = τ 8, ρ 314, χ 156.—**(4)** To leave, not to take away: δύο φάσγανα π 296.—To leave, not to take or choose: τὸν ἀρείω Κ 238.—**(5)** To leave, abandon, forsake: Ἀχαιούς Φ 414.—Of retreating and abandoning slain or wounded comrades Μ 226.—With complementary infin.: Ἀργείοισιν ἕλωρ γενέσθαι Ρ 151. Cf. γ 271, ε 344.—**(6)** To leave, depart from, abandon (a place), quit: Τρώων πόλιν Ξ 89. Cf. Κ 338, Χ 383, Ω 383.

καταλέχθαι, aor. infin. mid. καταλέγω[1].

καταλήθω [κατα- (5)]. In mid., with genit., to forget, cease to think of: θανόντων Χ 389.

καταλοφάδεια [an acc. pl. neut., used adverbially, formed fr. κατα- (3) + λόφος]. On one's neck: φέρων [ἔλαφον] κ 169.

καταλύω [κατα- (5)]. (1) To loose, unyoke (horses) δ 28.—(2) To bring to ruin, destroy: πολίων κάρηνα Β 117 = Ι 24.

καταμάρπτω [κατα- (5)]. To make up upon (a person), catch (him) up Ζ 364.—To make up upon, catch (a fleeing foe) Ε 65, Π 598.

καταμάω [κατ-, κατα- (5) + ἀμάω[2]]. To gather or scrape up. In mid.: κόπρον καταμήσατο Ω 165.

†**καταμύσσω** [κατ-, κατα- (5)]. 3 sing. aor. mid. καταμύξατο. To tear, scratch. In mid.: καταμύξατο χεῖρα Ε 425.

κατανεύω [κατα- (1)]. Fut. in mid. form κατανεύσομαι Α 524. Contr. aor. pple. καννεύσας ο 464. (1) To depress the chin, nod, in token or sanction of assent, come under an undertaking or promise, give a promise (cf. ἀνανεύω): φημὶ κατανεῦσαι Κρονίωνα (that he promised his favour) Β 350, ὡς τὸ πρῶτον κατένευσα Δ 267. Cf. Α 514, 524, Ο 374: ν 133.—(2) With infin. of what one promises to do: δωσέμεναι Κ 393, Ν 368: δ 6.—Of what one promises to grant or bring about: κατένευσεν Ἴλιόν [μ'] ἐκπέρσαντ' ἀπονέεσθαι Β 112, Ι 19.—With dependent clause: ὡς . . . Α 558.—(3) To undertake to give or grant, promise: νίκην Θ 175. Cf. Α 527: ω 335.—To promise to perform or bring about: βουλέων, ἅς τέ μοι κατένευσεν (*i.e.* promised to carry his will into effect) Μ 236.—(4) To convey an order or give a sign by making the motion: κρατὶ κατανεύων ι 490. Cf. ο 463, 464.

κάταντα [app. formed fr. κατά as ἄναντα fr. ἀνά]. Downhill Ψ 116.

καταντῑκρύ [κατ-, κατα- (1)]. Right *down from*. With genit.: τέγεος πέσεν κ 559. Cf. λ 64.

κατάνω [κατ-, κατα- (5)]. To waste, consume: τὰ πολλὰ κατάνεται β 58 = ρ 537.

καταξέμεν, aor. infin. κατάγω.

κατάπαυμα, τό [καταπαύω]. A means of stopping or stilling: γόου Ρ 38.

καταπαύω [κατα- (5)]. (1) To put a stop to, bring to an end: πόλεμον καταπαυσέμεν Η 36.—To lay aside (wrath) Π 62.—To appease (wrath) δ 583.—(2) To put a stop to the activities of, lay restraint upon (a person): Ζῆνα Ο 105. Cf. β 168, 241 (*v.l.* κατερύκετε), 244.—Contextually, to kill, slay: ἔγχος κέ σ' ἐμὸν κατέπαυσεν Π 618.—(3) To stop or restrain from. With genit.: ἀγηνορίης μιν Χ 457. Cf. ω 457.

†**καταπέσσω** [κατα- (1)]. 3 sing. aor. subj. καταπέψῃ. To digest so as to keep down (wrath): εἴ περ χόλον καὶ αὐτῆμαρ καταπέψῃ (swallows it down) Α 81.

καταπέφνῃ, 3 sing. aor. subj. καταφένω.

†**καταπήγνῡμι** [κατα- (5)]. 3 sing. aor. κατέπηξε Ζ 213, Ι 350. 3 pl. -αν Η 441. 3 sing. aor. pass. κατέπηκτο Λ 378. To fix, stick, plant: ἔγχος ἐπὶ χθονὶ Ζ 213. Cf. Η 441, Ι 350.—In pass. of an arrow entering the earth: ἰὸς ἐν γαίῃ κατέπηκτο Λ 378.

†**καταπίπτω** [κατα- (1)]. Contr. aor. κάππεσον Λ 593. 3 sing. -ε Δ 523, Μ 386, Ν 549, Ο 280, 538, Π 290, 311, 414, 580, 743, Ψ 251, 728, 881: ε 374, μ 414, χ 85. 3 dual -έτην Ε 560. 3 pl. -ον Μ 23, Π 662, Ψ 731. (1) To fall or drop from a high or relatively high position: ἀφ' ὑψηλοῦ πύργου Μ 386, ἀπὸ δίφρου Π 743. Cf. Λ 593: μ 414.—Of a dead bird Ψ 881.—(2) To let oneself fall: πρηνὴς ἁλὶ κάππεσεν (plunged into the sea) ε 374. —(3) To fall from one's own height, come to the ground: ἐπὶ στήθεσσιν Ψ 728, ἐπὶ χθονὶ 731.—Of slain or wounded men Δ 523 = Ν 549, Ε 560, Μ 23, Π 290, 311, 414 = 580, 662: χ 85.—Sim. of the equipment of slain warriors Μ 23.—(4) In gen., of inanimate objects, to fall: βαθεῖα κάππεσε τέφρη Ψ 251. Cf. Ο 538.—Fig.: πᾶσι παραὶ ποσὶ κάππεσε θυμός Ο 280.

καταπλέω [κατα- (1)]. To sail to land, put in: ἔνθα κατεπλέομεν ι 142.

†**καταπλήσσω** [κατα- (5)]. 3 sing. aor. pass. κατεπλήγη. In pass., to be struck with dismay: κατεπλήγη φίλον ἦτορ Γ 31.

καταπρηνής [κατα- (1) + πρηνής]. Of the hand, down-turned, so turned that the flat of it is brought to bear upon something: χερσὶ καταπρηνέσσιν (with the flat of his hands) Ο 114 = 398: = γ 199. Cf. Π 792: ν 164, τ 467.

†**καταπτήσσω** [κατα- (1)]. Aor. pple. καταπτήξας Χ 191. 3 dual aor. καταπτήτην Θ 136. To crouch down or cower in fear. Of horses: ὑπ' ὄχεσφιν Θ 136.—Of a fawn: ὑπὸ θάμνῳ Χ 191.

καταπτώσσω [κατα- (1)]. = prec.: τίπτε καταπτώσσοντες ἀφέστατε; Δ 340. Cf. Δ 224, Ε 254, 476.

καταπύθω [κατα- (5)]. In pass., to rot, decay: οὐ καταπύθεται ὄμβρῳ Ψ 328.

κατᾱράομαι [κατ-, κατα- (1)]. (1) To call down (evil upon one): τῷ καταρῶνται ἄλγεα τ 330.—(2) To pray for a curse upon a person. With fut. infin. indicating the nature of the curse: μή ποτε γούνασιν οἷσιν ἐφέσσεσθαι φίλον υἱὸν ἐξ ἐμέθεν γεγαῶτα Ι 454.

κατᾱρῑγηλός [κατα- (5)] + (F)ριγηλός in sim. sense, fr. (F)ριγέω]. Causing shuddering, regarded with aversion, dreaded, feared ξ 226.

†**καταρρέζω** [app., κατα- (1) + (F)ρέζω, though it is difficult to trace the sense-development]. Contr. fem. pres. pple. καρρέζουσα Ε 424. 3 sing. aor. κατέρεξε Α 361, Ε 372, Ζ 485, Ω 127: δ 610, ε 181, ν 288. To stroke, caress: Ἀχαιϊάδων τινά Ε 424, χειρί μιν Α 361 = Ε 372 = Ζ 485 = Ω 127: = δ 610 = ε 181, ν 288.

καταρρέω [κατα- (1) + (σ)ρέ(F)ω]. To flow down: αἷμα καταρρέον ἐξ ὠτειλῆς Δ 149, Ε 870.

κατάρχω [κατ-, κατα- (5)]. In mid., as a word of ritual, to take up and hold in readiness (sacrificial materials) (cf. ἄρχω (1) (b)): χέρνιβά τ' οὐλοχύτας τε κατάρχετο γ 445.

†**κατασβέννῡμι** [κατα- (5)]. 3 sing. aor. κατέσβεσε. To extinguish, quench (fire) Φ 381.

†**κατασεύω** [κατα- (1)]. 3 sing. aor. mid. κατέσσυτο. In mid., to flow *down in the course or direction of.* With acc.: ἄψορρον κῦμα κατέσσυτο ῥέεθρα Φ 382.

κατασκιάω [κατα- (5)]. To cast a shadow over, overshadow: ὄζοι κατεσκίαον Χάρυβδιν μ 436.

καταστῆσαι, aor. infin. καθίστημι.

†**καταστορέννῡμι** [κατα- (5)]. Contr. fem. pple. καστορνῦσα (fr. καστόρνυμι) ρ 32. 3 pl. aor. κατεστόρεσαν Ω 798. (1) To spread: κώεα θρόνοις ἔνι ρ 32.—(2) To cover up: λάεσσιν Ω 798.

†**καταστυγέω** [κατα- (5)]. 3 sing. aor. κατέστυγε. To be struck with horror, sicken: κατέστυγε μῦθον ἀκούσας Ρ 694.

κατάσχῃ, 3 sing. aor. subj. κατέχω.

κατατεθναίη, 3 sing. pf. opt. καταθνήσκω.

κατατεθνήκᾱσι, 3 pl. pf. καταθνήσκω.

κατατεθνηῶτος, genit. sing. masc. pf. pple. καταθνήσκω.

κατατήκω [κατα- (5)]. 3 sing. aor. κατέτηξε τ 206. (1) To cause to melt, melt, dissolve: χιόνα τ 206.—In pass., to be melted, melt, dissolve: ὡς χιὼν κατατήκεται τ 205.—(2) In pass., to waste or pine away: φίλον κατατήκομαι ἦτορ τ 136.

†**κατατίθημι** [κατα- (1)]. Fut. καταθήσω τ 572. 3 sing. -ει π 45. Aor. κατέθηκα ι 329, π 288, τ 7. 3 sing. -ε Γ 293, 425, Δ 112, Ζ 473, Ψ 267: ζ 75, ι 247, ν 20, 370, ρ 333, 356, τ 100, υ 96, φ 82, χ 340, ω 91, 166. 3 pl. -αν Ω 271. 1 pl. contr. aor. κάτθεμεν ω 44. 3 κάτθεσαν Π 683, Σ 233, Ψ 139: β 415, ν 135, 284, π 230, τ 55. 1 pl. subj. καταθείομεν φ 264. Contr. imp. pl. κάτθετε τ 317, φ 260. Pple. καταθείς υ 259. Nom. dual masc. καταθέντε Ψ 381. Infin. καταθεῖναι π 285. Contr. κατθέμεν τ 4. **Mid.** 3 dual contr. aor. κατθέσθην χ 141. 1 pl. κατθέμεθα σ 45. 3 pl. κατέθεντο Γ 114: ν 72, ρ 86, 179, υ 249. Subj. καταθείομαι Χ 111: τ 17. Contr. nom. pl. masc. pple. κατθέμενοι ω 190. Infin. καταθέσθαι τ 20. (1) To set down, set, lay, put, deposit, in a specified or indicated place or position: ἄρνας ἐπὶ χθονός Γ 293, τῇ δίφρον κατέθηκεν 425. Cf. Δ 112, Ζ 473, Π 683, Σ 233, Ψ 139, 381, Ω 271: πάντ' ἐπὶ νηΐ β 415. Cf. ζ 75, ι 247, 329, ν 20, 135, 284, π 45, 230, ρ 333, 356, τ 55, 100, 317, υ 96, 259, φ 82, χ 340, ω 44.—In mid. Γ 114: ν 72.—In mid., to lay out (a corpse) for funeral rites: οἵ κε κατθέμενοι γοάοιεν ω 190.—(2) To set down or propose as a prize Ψ 267: ω 91.—To set down (the material for a contest): ἄεθλον τ 572.—(3) To put down, lay aside: κάτθετε [τόξα] φ 260. Cf. φ 264.—In mid. Χ 111: ρ 86 = 179 = υ 249.—(4) To set aside for some purpose. In mid.: γαστέρες αἰγῶν, τὰς ἐπὶ δόρπῳ κατθέμεθα σ 45.—(5) To put or stow away: τεύχεα ἐς μυχὸν θαλάμου π 285. Cf. ν 370, π 288 = τ 7, τ 4, ω 166.—In mid. τ 17, 20, χ 141.

κατατρύχω [κατα- (5)]. To wear out, reduce to straits, put too great a strain on the resources of: λαούς Ρ 225. Cf. ο 309, π 84.

†**καταφένω** [κατα- (5)]. Aor. κατέπεφνον ω 325. 3 sing. -ε Ζ 183, 186, 190, 423, Ω 759: γ 252, 280, δ 534, ε 124, 128, λ 173, 199, 574, ο 411. 3 pl. -ον ψ 329. 3 sing. subj. καταπέφνῃ Γ 281. Pple. καταπεφνών Ρ 539. To kill, slay: Μενέλαον Γ 281. Cf. Ζ 183, 186, 190, 423, Ρ 539, Ω 759: γ 252, 280 = ο 411, δ 534, ε 124 = λ 173 = 199, ε 128, λ 574, ψ 329, ω 325.

†**καταφέρω** [κατα- (1)]. 3 sing. fut. mid. κατοίσεται (κατ-, κατα-). To bring down (to death): οὔ μ' ἄχος κατοίσεται Ἄϊδος εἴσω Χ 425.

†**καταφθίω** [κατα- (5)]. 3 sing. fut. καταφθίσει ε 341. 3 sing. aor. pass. κατέφθιτο δ 363. Pple. καταφθίμενος, -ου Χ 288: γ 196, λ 491. Infin. καταφθίσθαι β 183. (1) In act., to cause to perish, destroy: οὔ σε καταφθίσει ε 341.—(2) In pass., to perish, die: σεῖο καταφθιμένοιο Χ 288: ὡς καὶ σὺ καταφθίσθαι ὤφελες β 183. Cf. γ 196, λ 491.—Of inanimate objects, to perish, fail: ἤϊά κε πάντα κατέφθιτο δ 363.

†**καταφλέγω** [κατα- (5)]. Fut. καταφλέξω. To burn, consume: τάδε πάντα πυρί Χ 512.

καταφῡλαδόν [κατα- (4) + φῦλον]. By races or tribes: τριχθὰ ᾤκηθεν κ. Β 668.

†**καταχέω** [κατα- (1)]. 2 sing. aor. κατέχευας ξ 38. 3 -ε Β 670, Γ 10, Ε 734, Θ 385, Μ 158, Π 459, Ψ 282: β 12, ζ 235, η 42, θ 19, ρ 63. 3 pl. -αν Ζ 134. 3 sing. subj. καταχεύῃ Ψ 408: τ 206. Infin. καταχεῦαι Η 461. 3 pl. aor. pass. κατέχυντο μ 411. (1) To pour (a liquid) *upon.* With genit.: ἔλαιον χαιτάων Ψ 282.—(2) In gen., to shed, let fall: νιφάδας Μ 158. Cf. Π 459: τ 206.—To shed or spread (mist) Γ 10: η 42.—(3) To let fall all together or in a mass: θύσθλα Ζ 134.—In pass., to fall all together or in a mass: ὅπλα πάντα εἰς ἄντλον κατέχυντο μ 411.—To let (a robe) fall from one's person Ε 734 = Θ 385.—(4) To sweep away in destruction: τεῖχος εἰς ἅλα Η 461.—(5) Fig., to shed, pour, cause to come, bring: πλοῦτον Β 670. Cf. Ψ 408: β 12 = ρ 63, ζ 235, θ 19, ξ 38.

καταχθόνιος [κατα- (1) + χθον-, χθών]. Of the world below. Epithet of Zeus regarded (in this passage only) as ruler of the underworld Ι 457.

κατέαξε, 3 sing. aor. κατάγνυμι.

κατέβην, aor. καταβαίνω.

κατεβήσετο, 3 sing. aor. mid. καταβαίνω.

κατέδαψαν, 3 pl. aor. καταδάπτω.

κατέδραθον, aor. καταδαρθάνω.

κατέδῡ, 3 sing. aor. καταδύω.

κατεδύσετο, 3 sing. aor. mid. καταδύω.

κατέδω [κατ-, κατα- (5)]. 3 pl. subj. mid. (in fut. sense) κατέδονται Χ 89: φ 363. (1) To eat (one's heart): ὃν θυμὸν κατέδων Ζ 202.—(2) Of beasts, to devour Χ 89: φ 363.—Of worms, to eat, gnaw Ω 415.—Sim. of flies Τ 31.—(3) To eat up, devour, consume, make away with: οἶκον Ὀδυσσῆος β 237. Cf. λ 116, ν 396 = 428 = ο 32, ρ 378, τ 159, 534.

κατέθελξε, 3 sing. aor. καταθέλγω.

κατέθεντο, 3 pl. aor. mid. κατατίθημι.

κατέθηκα, aor. κατατίθημι.

κατείβω [κατ-, κατα- (1)]. (1) To shed (a tear)

φ 86.—(2) In pass., of tears, to fall *from*. With genit.: κατείβετο δάκρυ παρειῶν Ω 794.—Of water, to flow: ὕδωρ κατειβόμενον κελαρύζει Φ 261. Cf. O 37: = ε 185.—Of time, to pass away: κατείβετο αἰών ε 152.

†**κάτειμι** [κατ-, κατα- (1) + εἶμι]. 1 sing. κάτειμι ο 505. 3 κάτεισι Λ 492, Υ 294. Acc. sing. masc. pple. κατιόντα ν 267. Nom. fem. κατιοῦσα, -ης Δ 475: π 472. Infin. κατίμεν Ξ 457. 3 sing. impf. κατήϊε κ 159. (1) To come down, descend: Ἰδηθεν Δ 475: ποταμόνδε κ 159.—Of coming from the field to the town: ἀγρόθεν ν 267.—Of a river, to flow down Λ 492.—(2) To come from the sea to land, come in. Of a ship: νῆα κατιοῦσαν π 472.—(3) In pres. with fut. sense, to go or come down, descend: κατίμεν δόμον Ἄϊδος εἴσω Ξ 457. Cf. Υ 294: ο 505.

κατείρυσε, 3 sing. aor. κατερύω.

κατείρυσται, 3 sing. pf. pass. κατερύω.

κατέκειραν, 3 pl. aor. κατακείρω.

κατέκηε, 3 sing. aor. κατακαίω.

κατεκλάσθη, 3 sing. aor. pass. κατακλάω.

κατέκτα, 3 sing. aor. κατακτείνω.

κατέκταθεν, 3 pl. aor. pass. κατακτείνω.

κατέκτανον, aor. κατακτείνω.

κατέκυψε, 3 sing. aor. κατακύπτω.

κατέλεκτο, 3 sing. aor. mid. καταλέγω[1].

κατέλεξα, aor. καταλέγω[2].

κατελέξατο, 3 sing. aor. mid. καταλέγω[1].

κατελεύσομαι, fut. κατέρχομαι.

κατελθέμεν, aor. infin. κατέρχομαι.

†**κατεναίρω** [κατ-, κατα- (5)]. 3 sing. aor. mid. κατενήρατο. To kill in fight. In mid. λ 519.

κατεναντίος [κατ-, κατα- (5) + ἐναντίος]. In neut. sing. κατεναντίον as adv., facing, opposing, against. With dat.: οἱ Φ 567.

κατενήρατο, 3 sing. aor. mid. κατεναίρω.

κατεπάλμενος, aor. pple. κατεφάλλομαι.

κατεπᾶλτο, 3 sing. aor. κατεφάλλομαι.

κατέπεφνον, aor. καταφένω.

κατέπηκτο, 3 sing. aor. pass. καταπήγνυμι.

κατέπηξε, 3 sing. aor. καταπήγνυμι.

κατεπλήγη, 3 sing. aor. pass. καταπλήσσω.

†**κατερείπω** [κατ-, κατα- (5)]. 3 sing. aor. κατήριπε Ε 92. 3 sing. pf. κατερήριπε Ξ 55. To fall, be destroyed: τεῖχος κατερήριπεν Ξ 55.—To suffer destruction, be ruined: ἔργα κατήριπεν αἰζηῶν Ε 92.

κατέρεξε, 3 sing. aor. καταρρέζω.

κατερήριπε, 3 sing. pf. κατερείπω.

κατερητύω [κατ-, κατα- (5)]. (1) To check, restrain τ 545 (checked her tears).—(2) To hold, keep, detain: ἐν μεγάροισιν Ι 465: ι 31.

κατερῡκάνω [κατ-, κατα- (5)]. = next (1): μή μ' ἐθέλοντ' ἰέναι κατερύκανε Ω 218.

κατερῡ́κω [κατ-, κατα- (5)]. (1) To restrain from doing something, keep or hold back, stop, check: καί τ' ἐσσυμένην κατερύκει Π 9, εἰ μὴ Ἀχιλλεὺς κατέρυκεν Ψ 734. Cf. Θ 412, Ω 771: β 241 (*v.l.* καταπαύετε), γ 345, δ 284, π 430, χ 409, ω 51.—To delay, keep waiting: ἦ σ' ἐσσύμενον κατερύκω; Ζ 518.—(2) To confine, shut up, keep from egress or escape, detain: οὔ τι ἑκὼν κατερύκομαι (mid., let myself be . . .) δ 377, ἥ μιν κατέρυκεν ψ 334. Cf. α 55, 197, δ 498, 552.—(3) To detain or keep with one in hospitality or in a friendly way: αὐτοῦ μιν κατέρυκεν Ζ 192 = Λ 226. Cf. α 315, ο 73.

†**κατερύω** [κατ-, κατα- (1) + ἐρύω[1]]. 3 sing. aor. κατείρυσε ε 261. 3 sing. pf. pass. κατείρυσται θ 151. Infin. κατειρύσθαι ξ 332, τ 289. To draw (a ship) down to the water: νηῦς κατείρυσται θ 151, νῆα κατειρύσθαι ξ 332 = τ 289.—Of launching Odysseus's σχεδίη ε 261.

κατέρχομαι [κατ-, κατα- (1)]. Fut. κατελεύσομαι α 303. 3 sing. aor. κατῆλθε κ 560, λ 65. 1 pl. -ομεν Υ 125: δ 573, λ 1. 3 -ον Η 330. 1 sing. κατήλυθον α 182, δ 428, μ 391, ω 115. 3 pl. κατήλυθον β 407, θ 50, ν 70. Acc. sing. masc. pple. κατελθόντα Ζ 284. Infin. κατελθέμεν Ζ 109: λ 475. (1) To go or come down, descend: ἐξ οὐρανοῦ Ζ 109. Cf. Ζ 284, Η 330: κ 560 = λ 65, λ 475.—Of an inanimate object: κατερχομένης ὑπὸ πέτρης ι 484 = 541.—(2) To come down or descend *from*. With genit.: Οὐλύμποιο Υ 125.—(3) To go or come from inland towards the shore: ἐπὶ νῆα α 303, β 407 = θ 50 = ν 70, δ 428 = μ 391, δ 573 = λ 1, πόλινδε λ 188.—(4) To come from the sea to land, put in: ξὺν νηῒ κατήλυθον α 182.—Sim. of a journey to Ithaca: ὅτε κεῖσε κατήλυθον ὑμέτερον δῶ (to . . .) ω 115.

κατέσβεσε, 3 sing. aor. κατασβέννυμι.

κατεσθίω [κατ-, κατα- (5)]. Of a beast of prey, to devour Γ 25.—Sim. of a dolphin Φ 24.—Of a serpent Β 314.—Of Scylla μ 256.

κατέσσυτο, 3 sing. aor. mid. κατασεύω.

κατεστόρεσαν, 3 pl. aor. καταστορέννυμι.

κατέστυγε, 3 sing. aor. καταστυγέω.

κατέσχε, 3 sing. aor. κατέχω.

κατέτηξε, 3 sing. aor. κατατήκω.

†**κατευνάζω** [κατ-, κατα- (5)]. 3 pl. aor. pass. κατεύνασθεν. In pass., to be laid or retire to rest Γ 448.

κατευνάω [κατ-, κατα- (5)]. (1) To lay to rest, cause to sleep: ἄλλον κε θεῶν κατευνήσαιμι Ξ 245. Cf. Ξ 248.—(2) In pass., to be laid, lie down, to rest: τὸν ἐπὴν κατευνηθέντα ἴδησθε δ 414. Cf. δ 421.

†**κατεφάλλομαι** [κατ-, κατα- (1) + ἐφ-, ἐπι- (5) (11)]. 3 sing. aor. κατεπᾶλτο Τ 351. Pple. κατεπάλμενος Λ 94. To spring down in order to meet a foe: ἐξ ἵππων Λ 94.—To spring down for an indicated purpose: οὐρανοῦ ἐκ κατεπᾶλτο Τ 351 (*v.l.* οὐρανοῦ ἐκκατεπᾶλτο).

κατέφθιτο, 3 sing. aor. pass. καταφθίω.

κατέχευε, 3 sing. aor. καταχέω.

κατέχυντο, 3 pl. aor. pass. καταχέω.

κατέχω [κατ-, κατα- (1) (5)]. 3 sing. fut. καθέξει Ο 186, Π 629, Σ 332: ν 427, ο 31. 3 sing. aor. κατέσχε λ 549. 3 sing. subj. κατάσχῃ ο 200. 3 sing. contr. aor. κάσχεθε Λ 702. 3 sing. aor. mid. κατέσχετο γ 284, τ 361. Fem. pple. κατασχομένη Γ 419. (1) To hold down, keep in a lowered position: κεφαλήν ω 242.—(2) To lay restraint upon: εἴ με καθέξει Ο 186.—In mid., to pause in one's course, make a stop: ἔνθα κατέσχετο γ 284.—(3) To detain in hospitality ο 200.—(4) To seize, detain, withhold from the rightful owner: ἵππους Λ 702.—(5) To fill (with sound): ἀλαλητῷ πᾶν πεδίον κατέχουσιν Π 79.—(6) To cover, shroud, veil: νὺξ κάτεχ' οὐρανόν ν 269.—Cf. Ρ 368, 644: ι 145.—In mid., to cover up (a part of oneself): κατέσχετο χερσὶ πρόσωπα τ 361.—In mid. without expressed object, to cover or veil oneself: κατασχομένη ἑανῷ Γ 419.—To cover up, enfold, hold: τοὺς κάτεχεν αἶα Γ 243. Cf. Π 629, Σ 332: λ 301, 549, ν 427 = ο 31.

κατήγαγε, 3 sing. aor. κατάγω.

κατήϊε, 3 sing. impf. κάτειμι.

κατῄκισται, 3 sing. pf. pass. καταικίζω.

κατῆλθε, 3 sing. aor. κατέρχομαι.

κατήλυθον, aor. κατέρχομαι.

†**κατηπιάω** [κατ-, κατα- (5) + ἠπιάω in sim. sense, fr. ἤπιος]. 3 pl. impf. pass. κατηπιόωντο. To assuage, allay: ὀδύναι κατηπιόωντο Ε 417.

κατηρεφής, -ές [κατ-, κατα- (5) + ἐρέφω]. (1) Roofed: κλισίας Σ 589.—With (lofty) roof: σπέος ν 349.—Embowered: σπέος δάφνῃσι κατηρεφές (in . . .) ι 183.—(2) Of a wave, overhanging, curled ε 367.

κατήριπε, 3 sing. aor. κατερείπω.

κατηφείη, -ης, ἡ [κατηφής]. A cause of shame or disgrace, a disgrace Γ 51, Π 498, Ρ 556.

κατηφέω [κατηφής]. To have one's spirits dashed, become downcast: στῆ κατηφήσας Χ 293. Cf. π 342.

κατηφής. Subject to shame, disgraced: κατηφέες ἐσσόμεθ' αἰεί ω 432.

κατηφών, -όνος, ὁ [κατηφής]. A shame or disgrace. Of persons: σπεύσατέ μοι, κατηφόνες Ω 253.

κάτθανε, 3 sing. contr. aor. καταθνήσκω.

καθθάψαι, contr. aor. infin. καταθάπτω.

κάτθεμεν, 1 pl. contr. aor. κατατίθημι.

καθθέμεν, contr. aor. infin. κατατίθημι.

κάτθεσαν, 3 sing. contr. aor. κατατίθημι.

κατίμεν, infin. κάτειμι.

κατιόντα, acc. sing. masc. pple. κάτειμι.

κατίσχω. See καταΐσχω.

κατοίσεται, 3 sing. fut. mid. καταφέρω.

κατόπισθε(ν) [κατ-, κατα- (5) + ὄπισθε(ν)] (1) Behind, in the track of something: οὐδὲ πολλὴ γίγνετ' ἁρματροχιὴ κ. Ψ 505.—(2) Behind, in the back: βαλών χ 92.—Behind, by the back parts: ὡς ὅτε κύων συὸς ἅπτηται κ. Θ 339.—(3) (Left) behind, remaining where one is: ὅτ' ἐγὼ κ. λιποίμην φ 116.—(4) With genit., behind, following: νεός λ 6 = μ 148.—(5) In time to come: νέμεσιν κ. ἔσεσθαι χ 40.—Thereafter: ὅρκια κ. ἔθηκεν ω 546.

κάτω [κατά]. Downwards, down: ἕλκεται Ρ 136: ὀρόων ψ 91.

κατωμάδιος [κατ-, κατα- (1) + ὦμος. 'Down from the shoulder']. Swung from the shoulder: δίσκου Ψ 431.

κατωμαδόν [as prec.]. With the full swing of the arm: μάστιγι κ. ἤλασεν ἵππους Ο 352. Cf. Ψ 500.

κατωρυχής [κατ-, κατα- (1) + ὀρυχ-, ὀρύσσω]. Embedded, partly sunk, in the ground: λάεσσιν ζ 267, λίθοισιν ι 185.

καυλός, -οῦ, ὁ. (1) In a spear, either (a) A tongue of metal continuing the head and let into the wooden shaft (cf. πόρκης), or (b) The end of the shaft let into a hollow in the head (αὐλός; see αὐλός (3)): ἐν καυλῷ ἐάγη δόρυ (at the . . .) Ν 162, Ρ 607. Cf. Ν 608, Π 115.—(2) In a sword, a tongue of metal continuing the blade and secured between the wooden pieces forming the handle: ἀμφὶ καυλὸν φάσγανον ἐρραίσθη Π 338.

καῦμα, -ατος, τό [καϜ-, καυ-, καίω]. Heat, hot weather: καύματος ἔξ (after . . .) Ε 865.

καύστειρα, -ης [fem. of *καυστήρ, fr. καϜ-, καυ-, καίω]. Blazing, that scorches the participants. Epithet of battle: μάχης Δ 342 = Μ 316.

καὐτός, crasis of καὶ αὐτός.

κε(ν), *enclitic*. Conditional or limiting particle. (Cf. ἄν[1].) For the uses in protasis and apodosis see (6). (1) With subj.: σύ κεν κακὸν οἶτον ὄληαι Γ 417. Cf. Α 184, Θ 405, Ι 619, Κ 282, Λ 433, Μ 226, etc.: τῶν κέν τις τόδ' ἔχῃσιν α 396. Cf. β 213, δ 80, ι 356, κ 539, ξ 183, σ 265, etc.—In other examples (*e.g.* ὑποείξω Ο 211, καταλέξω Ι 262: γ 80) the form may be taken as aor. subj. or fut. indic.—(2) With fut. indic.: οἵ κέ με τιμήσουσιν Α 175. Cf. Δ 176, Θ 404, Ξ 267, Ρ 515, Χ 70, etc.: τούς κε θέλξει π 297. Cf. ε 36, κ 432, ο 524, π 260, ρ 540, σ 265, etc.—(3) With opt. in potential or fut. sense: νῦν γάρ κεν ἕλοι πόλιν Β 12. Cf. Α 64, 100, Β 160, 373, Γ 53, etc.: ἐμοί κε κέρδιον εἴη β 74. Cf. α 266, 380, β 86, γ 117, 365, δ 560, etc.—(4) In potential sense in suppositions contrary to fact. (a) In reference to the past (α) With impf., aor. or plupf. indic.: καί κεν πολὺ κέρδιον ἦεν Γ 41, ἦ τέ κεν ἤδη λάϊνον ἕσσο χιτῶνα 56. Cf. Δ 421, Ε 22, 885, Θ 454, Ι 545, Λ 382, etc.: τῷ κέν οἱ τύμβον ἐποίησαν α 239, ἤ κεν Ὀρέστης κτεῖνεν (will have slain him) δ 546. Cf. γ 258, δ 174, 178, ε 311, η 278, ι 79, etc.—(β) With pres. or aor. opt.: φαίης κε ζάκοτόν τιν' ἔμμεναι Γ 220. Cf. Γ 41, Δ 429, Μ 58, 381, 447, Ν 127, Ο 697, Ρ 366, Τ 90: οὐ κε κακοὶ τοιούσδε τέκοιεν δ 64. Cf. ε 73, θ 280, ν 86.—(b) In reference to the present with pres. opt.: οὔ κε Τηλέμαχον ὧδ' ἀνιείης (would not be setting him on) β 185.—(5) Repeated δ 733.—Joined with ἄν[1] in various constructions Λ 187, 202, Ν 127, Ω 437: ε 361, ζ 259, ι 334.—(6) For uses in protasis with εἰ (αἴ) and in the corresponding relative sentences see Table at end (II) (B) (a) (2) (subj.), (D) (4) (5) (6) (11) (subj.), (18) (19) (20) (21) (22) (opt.), (III) (B) (a) (2) (subj.), (b) (2) (opt.), (C) (a) (2) (aor. indic.), (D) (8) (9) (10) (fut.), (20) (21) (22) (23) (24) (25) (26) (27) (28) (29) (30) (31) (32) (33) (43) (44) (subj.), (47) (48) (60) (61) (62) (63) (64) (opt.).—For uses in apodosis see (II) (C) (a) (1) (aor. indic.), (3) (opt.), (D) (12) (16) (21) (opt.), (III) (C) (a) (1) (aor. or impf. indic.), (2) (aor. indic.), (4) (5) (opt.), (b) (opt.), (c) (1) (opt.), (D) (5) (16) (opt.), (22) (fut.), (25) (subj.), (29) (41) (opt.), (46) (48) (fut.), (51) (subj.), (56) (62) (opt.).—For αἴ κεν (not in protasis) see αἴ (3) (4).—For εἴ κεν (not in prot.) see εἰ (9) (10).—For ἧός κεν see ἧος (4).—For ἵνα κεν see ἵνα (4).—For ὅ κεν (not in prot.) see ὅ (4) (c).—For ὅς κεν (not in prot.) see ὅς[2] (II) (3) (a), (5), (9) (a).—For ὅπως κεν (not in prot.) see ὅπως (2) (b) (c).—For ὅς τίς κεν (not in prot.) see ὅς τις (2)—For ὅτε κεν (not in prot.) see ὅτε (4).—For ὄφρα κεν (not in prot.) see ὄφρα (1) (b), (5)(a)(b).—For ὡς κεν (not in prot.) see ὡς (6) (b), (7) (a), (8) (a) (β), (b) (β), (13).—(7) With infin. Χ 110.

†**κεάζω.** 3 sing. aor. ἐκέασσε ε 132, η 250. κέασε ξ 418. κέασσε Π 347. 3 pl. κέασαν υ 161. Aor. κεάσαιμι μ 388. Infin. κεάσσαι ο 322. 3 sing. aor. pass. κεάσθη Π 412, 578, Υ 387. Acc. pl. neut. pf. pple. κεκεασμένα σ 309. (1) To split, cleave: κεφαλὴ ἄνδιχα κεάσθη Π 412 = Υ 387, 578.—(2) To splinter, shiver, break in pieces: ὀστέα Π 347: νῆα ε 132 = η 250, μ 388.—(3) To produce (firewood) by splitting or chopping: ξύλα ξ 418, ο 322, υ 161, ξύλα κεκεασμένα σ 309.

κέαται, 3 pl. κεῖμαι.

κέατο, 3 pl. impf. κεῖμαι.

†**κεδάννυμι** [(σ)κεδ-. = σκεδάννυμι]. 3 sing. aor. ἐκέδασσε Ε 88, Ρ 283, 285: γ 131, ν 317, ξ 242. 3 pl. aor. pass. κέδασθεν Ο 657. Nom. pl. masc. pple. κεδασθέντες Β 398, Ν 739. Genit. sing. fem. κεδασθείσης Ο 328, Π 306. (1) To scatter, disperse: κύνας αἰζηούς τε Ρ 283: Ἀχαιούς γ 131 = ν 317, ξ 242.—To break (ranks): Τρώων φάλαγγας Ρ 285.—Cf. Ο 328 = Π 306.—(2) To scatter, carry away in destruction: γεφύρας Ε 88.—(3) In pass., to separate, scatter, take each his own way: οὐδὲ κέδασθεν ἀνὰ στρατόν Ο 657. Cf. Β 398, Ν 739.

κεδνός, -ή, -όν. (1) Affectionately solicitous, giving loving tendance, loving, devoted: τοκῆας Ρ 28. Cf. Ω 730: ἀμφίπολος α 335 = σ 211 = φ 66. Cf. α 432, κ 8, χ 223—In superl.: ἑταῖροι, οἵ οἱ κεδνότατοι ἦσαν (the most attached or devoted) Ι 586. Cf. κ 225.—(2) Considerate, thoughtful for the welfare of others: ἄνακτος ξ 170.—(3) Absol. in neut. pl.: κεδνὰ ἰδυῖα (ἰδυῖαν), having her heart bent to loving care, full of affectionate solicitude, devoted (see εἴδω (III) (12)) α 428, τ 346, υ 57, ψ 182, 232.

κέδρινος [κέδρος]. Fragrant with the wood of the κέδρος: θάλαμον Ω 192.

κέδρος, -ου, ἡ. Prob. a variety of juniper: ὀδμὴ κέδρου τε θύου τε δαιομένων ε 60.

κείατο, 3 pl. impf. κεῖμαι.

κεῖθεν [-θεν (1). Cf. κεῖνος]. (1) From that place, thence: ἐξ οὗ κ. ἔβην Ω 766. Cf. Φ 42, 62: κ. σφεας ἀπώσατο ἐς ἀνέμοιο ν 276. Cf. α 285, δ 519, ν 278, ρ 53, τ 223 = ω 310.—(2) From a specified point in a sequence of events: κ. δ' αὐτὸς ἐγὼ φράσομαι ἔργον τε ἔπος τε Ο 234.

κεῖθι [-θι. Cf. κεῖνος, ἐκεῖθι]. In that place, there: καὶ κ. μεμνήσομ' ἑταίρου Χ 390. Cf. Γ 402, Μ 348, 358: ὅσα κ. πάθον κακά γ 116. Cf. γ 262, θ 467 = ο 181, θ 519, 550, μ 106, ξ 297, ο 281, τ 216.

κεῖμαι [cf. κείω, κοιμάω]. 3 pl. κέαται Λ 659, 826, Π 24, Τ 203: σ 44. κέονται Χ 510: λ 341, π 232. 3 sing. subj. κεῖται (κέεται for κείεται) (also written κῆται) Τ 32, Ω 554: β 102, ε 395, τ 147, ω 137. 3 pl. impf. κείατο Λ 162: φ 418, ψ 47. κέατο Ν 763, Ω 168, 610. Imp. κεῖσο Σ 178, Φ 122, 184. 3 sing. pa. iterative κέσκετο φ 41. Fut. κείσομαι, -εαι Θ 537, Σ 121, 338, Φ 318, Χ 71: χ 319. (ἐγ-, ἐπι-, κατα-, παρα-, περι-, προ-, προσ-.) (1) To be in a prostrate or recumbent position, lie: ἥμενον, οὐδ' ἔτι κεῖτο Ο 240, πυρήν, ᾗ ἔνι κεῖται Πάτροκλος Ψ 210. Cf. Ε 848, Ι 556, Λ 162, Ο 9, Σ 236, Χ 71, Ψ 60, etc.: ὑπερωΐῳ κεῖτ' ἄσιτος δ 788. Cf. ι 372, κ 54, λ 577, ν 284, ξ 354, ρ 291, υ 6, etc.—(2) To lie low, lie dead: οὐκ ἄτιτος κεῖτ' Ἄσιος Ν 414. Cf. Δ 175, Ε 467, Π 541, Ρ 92, etc.: ἐοικότι κεῖται ὀλέθρῳ α 46. Cf. β 102, γ 109, χ 48, 319, etc.—(3) To lie down to rest: ἀποβάντες ἐκείμεθα νηὸς ἅπαντες ν 281. Cf. ι 298.—(4) To lie, be, remain, in a specified condition: ἐν νήσῳ κεῖτ' ἄλγεα πάσχων Β 721. Cf. Β 724, Λ 659, Σ 435, Τ 203, Χ 386, etc.: κείμεθα θυμὸν ἔδοντες ι 75 = κ 143. Cf. ε 13, 395, 457, λ 195, ρ 296, etc.—Fig.: κεῖται ἐν ἄλγεσι θυμός φ 88.—(5) To be idle: ἄνα, μηδ' ἔτι κεῖσο Σ 178. Cf. Β 688, 694, 772, Η 230.—(6) Of things, to be laid, set, placed, to lie, stand, be, in a specified or indicated place or position: τεύχεα κεῖται ἐπὶ χθονὶ Γ 195, [πέπλος] ἔκειτο νείατος ἄλλων Ζ 295. Cf. Η 265, Κ 75, Μ 381, Ο 388, Φ 364, etc.: φόρμιγγα, ἥ που κεῖται ἐν ἡμετέροισι δόμοισιν θ 255. Cf. α 162, θ 277, ι 319, ξ 136, σ 44, etc.—Of a part of a dead man: κάρη ἐν κονίῃσι κεῖτο Χ 403. Cf. Ρ 300.—Of a dead or dying serpent Μ 209.—Fig.: ταῦτα θεῶν ἐν γούνασι κεῖται Ρ 514 = Υ 435: = α 267 = π 129, α 400, παιδός οἱ ἐνὶ φρεσὶ πένθος ἔκειτο ω 423.—(7) To be set down or proposed as a reward: κεῖτ' ἐν μέσσοισι δύω χρυσοῖο τάλαντα Σ 507.—Of a prize, to be set down or proposed: τάδ' ἄεθλα κεῖτ' ἐν ἀγῶνι Ψ 273. Cf. Χ 163.—(8) Of places, to lie, be situated: Ὠγυγίη ἀπόπροθεν εἰν ἁλὶ κεῖται η 244. Cf. ι 25, ν 235.—Sim.: οἶκον, ὃς ὀρχάτου ἐγγύθι κεῖται ω 358.—To lie, be: νῆσος χθαμαλὴ κεῖται κ 196.—(9) Of things, to lie, be, remain, in a specified condition: αἴγειρος ἀζομένη κεῖται Δ 487. Cf. Ι 335: εἵματά τοι κεῖται ἀκηδέα ζ 26. Cf. ζ 59, π 35, ω 187.—(10) To lie unused: βιὸν ἔα κεῖσθαι (let it be) Ο 473. Cf. χ 186.—(11) To be laid away, laid up, stored, bestowed: πόλλ' ἐν ἀφνειοῦ πατρὸς κειμήλια κεῖται Ζ 47. Cf. Α 124, Β 777, Δ 143, 144, Ι 382, Λ 132, Χ 510: ἰδὼν εὖ κείμενα δῶρα θ 427. Cf. β 338, δ 613, κ 9, ν 11, ο 128, π 232, ρ 532, χ 109, etc.

κειμήλιον, -ου, τό [κεῖμαι]. (1) Something to be treasured up, a valuable: μή τί μοι ἐκ μεγάρων κ. ἐσθλὸν ὄληται ο 91.—A keepsake: σοὶ τοῦτο κ. ἔστω Ψ 618: δῶρον, ὅ τοι κ. ἔσται ἐξ ἐμεῦ α 312. Cf. δ 600.—(2) In pl., treasures, valuables, goods of price: πόλλ' ἐν ἀφνειοῦ πατρὸς κειμήλια κεῖται Ζ 47. Cf. Ι 330, Λ 132, Σ 290, Ω 381: ὅσσ' ἐν ἐμῷ οἴκῳ κειμήλια κεῖται δ 613 = ο 113. Cf. β 75, κ 40, ξ 326, ο 101, 159, ρ 527, τ 272, 295, φ 9.

κεῖνος, -η, -ο [cf. ἐκεῖνος, ἐκεῖθι, κεῖθεν, κεῖθι, κεῖσε].

(1) That person or thing, the person or thing referred to, he, she, it (with backward reference): κάρτιστοι δὴ κεῖνοι ἐπιχθονίων τράφεν ἀνδρῶν Α 266. Cf. Α 271, Β 330, Γ 440, Ε 894, Ζ 200, Θ 430, Ι 678, etc.: ἐκ τοῦ δ' οὔτ' Ὀδυσῆα ἐγὼν ἴδον οὔτ' ἐμὲ κεῖνος α 212, περὶ κεῖνα (about those parts) δ 90. Cf. α 46, β 124, γ 88, δ 182, ε 24, ζ 166, η 69, κ 18, etc.—(2) As antecedent to a relative: κεῖνος ὅς κε . . . Ι 312. Cf. ζ 158, ξ 156, ο 21, ω 90.—(3) In deictic sense: κεῖνος ὅ γ' ἐν θαλάμῳ (yonder he is in the . . .) Γ 391, νῦν οἱ πάρα κεῖνος Ἄρης (there is Ares . . .) Ε 604, κεῖνος ὅ γ' ἧσται (there he sits) Τ 344, ἔτι κεῖνος κεῖται (there he lies) Ω 412: ὡς νῦν Ἶρος κεῖνος ἧσται (is sitting there) σ 239.—(4) In contrast with a clause with ἐνθάδε: σύας καὶ κεῖνα (matters with the herd) φυλάξων· σοὶ δ' ἐνθάδε πάντα (matters here) μελόντων ρ 593.—(5) With sb., that: ἤματι κείνῳ Β 37, 482, Δ 543, Σ 324, Φ 517. Cf. Ξ 250, Ω 90: α 233, δ 145, λ 614, ρ 243=φ 201.—(6) With sb. forming the antecedent to a relative: κείνων ἀνδρῶν οἳ . . . Ε 636. Cf. Ν 232: θ 209.—(7) With sb. in deictic sense: κεῖνος αὖτ' ἀνὴρ ἔρχεται ἐς θάλαμον (there he goes) χ 165.—(8) In dat. fem. κείνῃ, by that way: κείνῃ παρέπλω Ἀργώ μ 69. Cf. ν 111.

κεινός, -ή, -όν [κενϝός] Γ 376, Δ 181, Λ 160, Ο 453. Also **κενεός** Β 298: κ 42, ο 214, and **κενός** χ 249. (1) Empty, containing nothing: σὺν κεινῇσιν νηυσίν Δ 181. Cf. κ 42.—Empty, lacking the usual contents: κεινὴ τρυφάλεια ἅμ' ἕσπετο χειρί (*i.e.* separated from the head) Γ 376, κείν' ὄχεα (masterless) Λ 160, Ο 453.—(2) Empty, idle, vain: εὔγματα χ 249.—(3) In neut. sing. κενεόν as adv., empty-handed, without success, having effected nothing: κ. νέεσθαι Β 298: ἂψ ἰέναι κ. ο 214.

κείρω. Fut. infin. κερέειν Ψ 146. 3 sing. aor. ἔκερσε Ν 546, 548. κέρσε Κ 456, Ξ 466. Nom. pl. masc. pple. κέρσαντες Ω 450. 3 pl. aor. mid. κείραντο ω 46. Infin. κείρασθαι Ψ 46: δ 198. (ἀπο-, δια-, ἐπι-, κατα-.) (1) To cut through, sever: ἀπὸ δ' ἄμφω κέρσε τένοντε Κ 456, Ξ 466. Cf. Ν 546, 548.—To cut (the hair): σοὶ κόμην κερέειν Ψ 146.—In mid.: κείραντο χαίτας ω 46. Cf. Ψ 46, 136: δ 198.—(2) To cut into shape: δοῦρ' ἐλάτης Ω 450.—(3) To tear, rend, devour: γῦπέ μιν ἧπαρ ἔκειρον λ 578.—To bite at, nibble Φ 204.—(4) To ravage, lay waste: λήϊον Λ 560.—(5) To consume, devour, make away with: [βίοτον] α 378=β 143, κτήματα β 312, σ 144, χ 369, ω 459.—(6) Fig., to thwart, defeat: μάχης μήδεα Ο 467, Π 120.

κεῖσε [-σε. Cf. κεῖνος]. (1) Thither: κ. οὐκ εἶμι Γ 410. Cf. Κ 289, Λ 528, Μ 356, 368 = Ν 752, Ξ 313, Ψ 145, Ω 199: οἴχετο κ. α 260. Cf. δ 262, 274, 619=ο 119, ζ 164, κ 266, μ 221, ν 423, ο 311, π 85, σ 339, ω 115.—(2) Up to a specified point: αἳ κεῖσέ γε φέρτεραι ἦσαν (referring to αὐτοῦ in the prec. line) Ψ 461.

κεῖσο, imp. κεῖμαι.

κείσομαι, fut. κεῖμαι.

κείω, *fut.* [cf. κεῖμαι]. Also **κέω** η 342. (κατα-.) (1) To go to rest: ἔνθ' ἴομεν κείοντες Ξ 340: ὄρσο κέων η 342, σχίζῃ δρυός, ἣν λίπε κείων (when he went to bed) ξ 425, κείω δ' ὡς τὸ πάρος περ ἀΰπνους νύκτας ἴαυον τ 340. Cf. ξ 532, σ 428, τ 48, ψ 292.—(2) To take rest, lie: οὐ μέν σφεας ἔτ' ἔολπα μίνυνθά γε κείεμεν οὕτω θ 315.

κεκαδήσει, 3 sing. fut. χάζω.

κεκαδησόμεθα, 1 pl. fut. mid. κήδω.

κεκαδών, aor. pple. χάζω.

κεκάλυπτο, 3 sing. plupf. pass. καλύπτω.

κέκασται, 3 sing. pf. καίνυμαι.

κεκαφηότα, acc. sing. masc. pf. pple. See καπύω.

κεκεασμένα, acc. pl. neut. pf. pple. pass. κεάζω.

κέκευθε, 3 sing. pf. κεύθω.

κέκλετο, 3 sing. aor. κέλομαι.

κεκλήγοντες, nom. pl. masc. thematic pf. pple. κλάζω.

κεκληγώς, pf. pple. κλάζω.

κέκλημαι, pf. pass. καλέω.

κεκλήσῃ, 2 sing. fut. pf. pass. καλέω.

κεκλίαται, 3 pl. pf. pass. κλίνω.

κέκλιτο, 3 sing. plupf. pass. κλίνω.

κέκλοντο, 3 pl. aor. κέλομαι.

κέκλυθι, κέκλυτε, pf. imp. sing. and pl. κλύον.

κέκμηκας, 2 sing. pf. κάμνω.

κεκμηώς, pf. pple. κάμνω.

κεκόνῖτο, 3 sing. plupf. pass. κονίω.

κεκοπώς, pf. pple. κόπτω.

κεκορήμεθα, 1 pl. pf. pass. κορέννυμι.

κεκορηότε, nom. dual masc. pf. pple. κορέννυμι.

κεκορυθμένος, pf. pple. pass. κορύσσω.

κεκοτηότι, dat. sing. masc. pf. pple. κοτέω.

κεκράανται, 3 pf. pass. κραίνω.

κεκριμένος, pf. pple. mid. and pass. κρίνω.

κεκρυμμένον, acc. sing. neut. pf. pple. pass. κρύπτω.

κεκρύφαλος, ὁ. App. some kind of hood or cap Χ 469.

κεκύθωσι, 3 pl. redup. aor. subj. κεύθω.

κελαδεινός, -ή [κέλαδος]. (1) Epithet of a wind, blustering: Ζέφυρον Ψ 208.—(2) (She) in whose train din follows. Epithet or a name of the huntress Artemis Π 183, Υ 70, Φ 511.

κελαδέω [κέλαδος]. To shout in approval or applause: ἐπὶ Τρῶες κελάδησαν Θ 542=Σ 310. Cf. Ψ 869.

κέλαδος, -ου, ὁ. Noise, din, disturbance: κέλαδον καὶ ἀϋτήν Ι 547. Cf. Σ 530: σ 402.

κελάδω [κέλαδος]. Of water, to flow with a rushing sound, murmur: πὰρ ποταμὸν κελάδοντα Σ 576. Cf. Φ 16.—Of a wind, to bluster, roar β 421.

κελαινεφής, -ές [app. for κελαινονεφής fr. κελαινός + νέφος]. (1) (The) god of the black cloud. Epithet or a name of Zeus Α 397, Β 412, Ζ 267, Λ 78, Ο 46, Φ 520, Χ 178, Ω 290: ι 552=ν 25, ν 147.—(2) With the force of the second element lost, dark in hue, black (=κελαινός): αἷμα Δ 140, Ε 798, Ξ 437, Π 667, Φ 167: λ 36, 153.

κελαινός, -ή, -όν. Dark in due, black or nearly black: αἷμα Α 303, Η 329, Λ 829, 845, δέρμα Ζ 117, κῦμα Ι 6, χθών (darkened by the clouds)

Π 384: αἷμα λ 98, 228, 232, 390, π 441, τ 457.—Bringing darkness in its train: λαίλαπι Λ 747. —In fig. use, of night, dark, enveloping in its shades, hiding from the light: ἀμφὶ δὲ ὄσσε κελαινὴ νὺξ ἐκάλυψεν Ε 310 = Λ 356.

κελαρύζω. To trickle, trickle along, flow or fall fitfully or in drops: ἀφ' ἕλκεος αἷμα κελάρυζεν Λ 813. Cf. Φ 261: ἄλμην, ἥ οἱ ἀπὸ κρατὸς κελάρυζεν ε 323.

κέλευθος, -ου, ἡ. Acc. pl. (besides the regular form) κέλευθα Α 312, Μ 225, Ξ 17, Ο 620: γ 71, 177, δ 842, ι 252, 261, κ 20, ο 474, υ 64, ω 10. (1) A way, road, path: πολλαὶ ἀνὰ στρατόν εἰσι κέλευθοι Κ 66. Cf. Ν 335, Ο 357: ἄλσος ἄγχι κελεύθου ζ 291. —In reference to natural phenomena: ἐγγὺς νυκτός τε καὶ ἤματός εἰσι κέλευθοι (the outgoings) κ 86.—(2) Collectively, the paths, haunts or resorts (of . . .) (cf. πάτος (2)): θεῶν ἀπόεικε κελεύθου Γ 406 (v.l. ἀπόειπε κελεύθους).—(3) A means of passage, a passage, access, opening: πολέεσσι θῆκε κέλευθον Μ 399. Cf. Μ 411, 418, Ο 260.—Sim.: χάζεσθαι κελεύθου, to get out of the way, *i.e.* to yield passage to the foe: οὐδ' ἄν πω χάζοντο κελεύθου Ἀχαιοί Λ 504. Cf. Μ 262.—(4) A going, journey, voyage, course: διαπρήσσουσα κέλευθον Α 483. Cf. Ξ 282, Ψ 501: τὸν θεοὶ βλάπτουσι κελεύθου α 195. Cf. β 213, 429, 434, δ 380 = 469, δ 389 = κ 539, η 272, ν 83.—Sim.: τῶν ἄλλων ἀνέμων κατέδησε κελεύθους (restrained each from its accustomed blowing) ε 383.—(5) In pl. in form κέλευθα denoting rather vague number or a group than plurality: οὐ κόσμῳ παρὰ ναῦφιν ἐλευσόμεθ' αὐτὰ κέλευθα (following the same general lines) Μ 225: ἄλλην ὁδόν, ἄλλα κέλευθα ἤλθομεν ι 261. —ὑγρὰ κέλευθα (the watery ways) Α 312: γ 71 = ι 252, δ 842, ο 474.—So ἰχθυόεντα κέλευθα γ 177, ἠερόεντα κέλευθα υ 64, εὐρώεντα κέλευθα ω 10.—Sim. in sense corresponding to (4): ἀνέμων λαιψηρὰ κέλευθα (the rush) Ξ 17, Ο 620: βυκτάων ἀνέμων κατέδησε κέλευθα (put restraint on the whole group) κ 20.

†**κελευτιάω** [frequentative from κελεύω]. Pple. κελευτιόων Ν 125. Nom. dual masc. κελευτιόωντε Μ 265. To play the leader: Αἴαντε κελευτιόωντ' ἐπὶ πύργων πάντοσε φοιτήτην Μ 265. Cf. Ν 125.

κελεύω [cf. κέλομαι]. Aor. infin. κελευσέμεναι δ 274. (1) Of persons, to command, order, bid, enjoin, give orders or injuctions. (a) With acc. and infin.: ἑταίρους ἵππους ζευγνύμεναι Γ 259. Cf. Β 11, Ε 823, Θ 318, Σ 469, Υ 4, etc.: αὐτὸν αἰτίζειν ρ 345. Cf. ε 384, η 48, ι 177, μ 193, etc. —(b) With acc. alone Δ 286, 359: ο 209, ρ 22, φ 175, ω 175.—(c) With dat. and infin.: κηρύκεσσι κηρύσσειν Β 50. Cf. Ε 485, Ι 658, Π 727, Ψ 39, etc.: ἑτάροισιν ὅπλων ἅπτεσθαι β 422. Cf. δ 296, η 163, ι 488, λ 44, ο 93, etc.—(d) With this dat. and acc. of what is enjoined: ἀμφιπόλοισι ἔργα κέλευεν Ζ 324. Cf. π 136 = ρ 193 = 281.—(e) With dat. alone: πῶς μοι κελεύεις; Κ 61. Cf. Δ 428, Λ 154, Ο 545, 717, Π 684, etc.: ζ 198, ο 217.—(f) With infin. alone: ἄρνε οἰσέμεναι Γ 119. Cf. Ζ 179, Υ 6: δ 233, ι 326, 469, μ 53, 163.—(g) Absol.: ἐν πυμάτοισι κελεύων Λ 65, Ζεὺς ἥμενος ὕψι κέλευεν (was supreme over them) Υ 155. Cf. Δ 322, Ε 528, Ζ 519, Ν 91, Ξ 248, etc.: β 415, κ 251, 443, μ 303, χ 255, etc.—(2) Passing into milder sense, to bid, exhort, charge, desire, urge, recommend, counsel, invite. (a) With acc. and infin.: σίτοιό μ' ἄσασθαι ἦτορ Τ 306. Cf. Ε 199, Η 284, Λ 781, Σ 13, Χ 101, etc.: οἴκαδέ μ' ἀποστείχειν ψ 276. Cf. β 263, η 262, 304, ν 274, ο 305, ψ 264.—With neg., to counsel against a course: πόλεμον οὐκ ἄμμε κελεύω δύμεναι Ξ 62.—(b) With this acc. and acc. of what one bids to be done: τί με ταῦτα κελεύετε; θ 153. Cf. Υ 87: θ 350.—(c) With acc. alone Ω 220: δ 274, η 28, κ 516, λ 507.—(d) With dat. and infin.: ἀλόχῳ δεῖπνον τετυκεῖν ο 93. Cf. Β 151.—(e) With this dat. and acc. as under (b): σοὶ τόδε κελεύω Τ 192.—(f) With dat. alone: φωτὶ ἑκάστῳ Ν 230, σπεύδοντι κέλευον (cheered him on) Ψ 767. Cf. Ε 463: ζ 211. —(g) With infin. alone: φεύγειν σὺν νηυσίν Β 74. Cf. Λ 641, Μ 237, Υ 95, Ψ 404: η 226 = ν 47, κ 17, 339, 373, 386, υ 341.—(h) Absol. Δ 380, Ξ 278, Φ 223, Ψ 96, 539, Ω 599, 669: δ 485, 673 = θ 398, δ 745, θ 347, 402, ι 339, κ 345, ο 437, σ 58.—(3) In sim. constructions with senses as under (2) of mental faculties and impersonal agencies: ὅππῃ σε κραδίη θυμός τε κελεύει Ν 784, τά με θυμὸς κελεύει Η 68 = 349 = 369 = Θ 6: = η 187 = θ 27 = ρ 469 = σ 352 = φ 276, εἰ μὴ θυμός με κελεύοι ι 278. Cf. θ 204, ξ 517 = ο 339, π 81 = φ 342, φ 198.—χόλος καὶ τὰ κελεύει Υ 255.—γαστέρι, ἥ τ' ἐκέλευσεν ἕο μνήσασθαι η 217.—(4) Of driving horses: τοὺς ἐφέπων μάστιγι κέλευεν Ω 326.—Absol.: μάστιγι κέλευεν Ψ 642.

κέλης, -ητος, ὁ [κελ- as in κέλλω]. With ἵππος, a riding-horse: κέληθ' ὡς ἵππον ἐλαύνων ε 371.

κελήσεται, 3 sing. fut. κέλομαι.

κελητίζειν [κέλης]. To ride: ἵπποισι κελητίζειν εὖ εἰδώς (on . . .) Ο 679.

†**κέλλω.** 1 pl. aor. ἐκέλσαμεν ι 546, λ 20, μ 5. Dat. pl. fem. pple. κελσάσῃσι ι 149. Infin. κέλσαι κ 511. (ἐπι-.) (1) To bring (a ship) to shore: νῆ' ἐκέλσαμεν λ 20. Cf. ι 546 = μ 5, κ 511. —(2) Of a ship, to come to shore: κελσάσῃσι νηυσὶ καθείλομεν ἱστία ι 149.

κέλομαι [cf. κελεύω]. 3 sing. fut. κελήσεται κ 296. 3 sing. redup. aor. (ἐ)κέκλετο Δ 508, Ζ 66, 287, Θ 184, Λ 285, Ν 489, Π 268, Σ 343, Χ 442, Ψ 402, etc.: δ 37, ζ 71, η 335, ξ 413, τ 418, υ 147. 3 pl. κέκλοντο Ψ 371. Pple. κεκλόμενος, -ου Θ 346, Λ 91, 460, Ν 332, Ο 353, 368, Π 525. (ἐπι-.) (1) Of persons, to command, order, bid, enjoin, give orders or injunctions. (a) With acc. and infin.: μυθήσασθαί με Α 74. Cf. Ο 146, Π 657, Ω 582: θεράποντας ἅμα σπέσθαι δ 37. Cf. γ 425, ι 100, 193, ξ 259 = ρ 428, υ 213, φ 265, 381.—(b) With dat. and infin.: Τρώεσσι τεῖχος ὑπερβαίνειν Μ 467. Cf. Σ 343, Χ 442: υἱοῖσι δεῖπνον ἐφοπλίσσαι τ 418. Cf. η 335.—(c) With dat. alone: ἀμφιπόλοισι κέκλετο Ζ 287. Cf. Δ 508, Ζ 66, Ο 353, Π 525, Ρ 183, Ψ 371, etc.: ζ 71, ξ 413, υ 147.—(d) With infin. alone: ἵππους ζευγνύμεν Ο 119. Cf. Ι 171: β 114, ο 16, σ 12.—(2) Of a compelling physical force or natural agency. Absol.: ἐπεὶ κέλετο μεγάλη ἴς Ἠελίου τ' αὐγή μ 175.—(3) Passing into milder sense, to bid, exhort, charge, desire, urge, recommend, counsel, invite. (a) With acc. and infin.: Τρῶας τεύχε' ἀποθέσθαι Γ 88. Cf. Α 134, Γ 434, Ε 810, Ι 517, Ν 69, Ο 138, Σ 286, Ω 297, 434: θεούς με δειδίμεν ι 274. Cf. δ 812, ε 174, κ 296, 299, 337, λ 71, ο 513, π 433.—(b) With dat. and infin.: φυλασσέμεναι κέλονται ἀλλήλοις Κ 419.—(c) With dat. alone: ἀλλήλοισιν Θ 346 = Ο 368. Cf. Λ 91, 312, Μ 274, Φ 307.—(d) With infin. alone: ἐς χορὸν ἐλθέμεν Ο 508. Cf. Α 386, Μ 235, Ξ 96, Σ 254: γ 317.—(e) Absol.: Τρῶές γε κέλονται Η 393, κεκλόμενοι καθ' ὅμιλον (cheering each other on) Λ 460 = Ν 332. Cf. Ψ 894: ε 98, ρ 400.—(4) In sim. constructions with senses as under (3) of appetites or mental faculties: κέλεταί ἑ θυμὸς (γαστήρ) ἐς δόμον ἐλθεῖν Μ 300: ζ 133. Cf. ρ 555.—κέλεταί με θυμός Τ 187, Κ 534: = δ 140.—γαστὴρ ἐσθέμεναι κέλεται η 220.—ἐφ' Ἕκτορι κέκλετο θυμός Π 382.—(5) To call, call to, summon (= καλέω (1)): Ἥφαιστον Σ 391.

κέλσαι, aor. infin. κέλλω.

κεμάς, -άδος, ἡ. A young deer Κ 361.

κεν. See κε(ν).

κενεαυχής [κενεός + αὐχέω, to boast]. Idly boasting: κενεαυχέες ἠγοράασθε Θ 230.

κενεός. See κεινός.

κενεών, -ῶνος, ὁ [κενός]. The hollow under the ribs on each side, the flank Ε 284, 857, Λ 381, Π 821: χ 295.

κενός. See κεινός.

†κεντέω. Aor. infin. κένσαι. To whip or goad on: ἵππον Ψ 337.

κεντρηνεκής [κέντρον + ἐνεκ-. See φέρω]. App., carried along, kept at speed, by the κέντρον: κεντρηνεκέας ἔχον ἵππους Ε 752 = Θ 396.

κέντρον, -ου, τό [κεντέω]. Prob. a pliant rod with a metal point serving both as whip and goad (see μάστιξ) Ψ 387, 430.

κέντωρ, -ορος, ὁ [κεντέω]. One who applies the κέντρον, a (skilful) driver Δ 391, Ε 102.

κέονται, 3 pl. κεῖμαι.

κεράασθε, imp. pl. mid. κεράω.

κεραΐζω [cf. κείρω]. Fut. infin. κεραϊξέμεν Π 830. (1) To cut down, slay Β 861.—Absol.: ὑμεῖς μὲν φεύγοντες, ἐγὼ δ' ὄπιθεν κεραΐζων Φ 129.—(2) To ravage, lay waste Ε 557, Π 752, Χ 63.—To sack (a city) Π 830, Ω 245: θ 516.

κεραίω [κερασ-jω. Cf. κερασ-, κεράννυμι]. To mix (a bowl): [κρητῆρα] ζωρότερον κέραιε Ι 203.

κεραμεύς, ὁ [κέραμος]. A potter Σ 601.

κέραμος, -ου, ὁ. An earthenware vessel, a wine-jar Ι 469.—A vessel large enough to confine a person in: χαλκέῳ ἐν κεράμῳ δέδετο Ε 387.

†κεράννῡμι. 3 sing. aor. κέρασσε γ 390, ε 93. Nom. sing. fem. pple. κεράσᾱσα κ 362. 3 sing. aor. mid. κεράσσατο γ 393, σ 423. Pple. κερασσάμενος η 179, ν 50. From κέραμαι 3 pl. subj. mid. κέρωνται Δ 260. (ἐγ-, ἐπι-.) (1) To mix, temper: θυμῆρες κεράσασα [ὕδωρ] κ 362.—To mix (wine) with water. In mid.: ὅτε οἶνον ἐνὶ κρητῆρι κέρωνται Δ 260.—Sim. in reference to nectar ε 93.—(2) To mix (a bowl): ἀνὰ κρητῆρα κέρασσεν οἴνου γ 390 (ἀνά advbl.).—In mid. γ 393, η 179 = ν 50, σ 423.

κεραοξόος [κερα(σ)-, κέρας + ξο-, ξέω]. Working in horn: τέκτων Δ 110.

κεραός [κέρας]. Horned δ 85.—Epithet of deer: ἔλαφον Γ 24, Λ 475, Ο 271, Π 158.

κέρας, τό. Dat. κέρᾳ Λ 385. Nom. pl. κέρα (for κέραα) Δ 109: τ 211, φ 395. Genit. κεράων Ρ 521: γ 439, τ 566. Dat. κεράεσσι Ν 705: τ 563. κέρασι Κ 294: γ 384, 426, 437. (1) A horn of an animal. Of a wild goat Δ 109.—Of oxen Ν 705, Ρ 521, Ψ 780, Κ 294: = γ 384, 426, 437, 439.—In a simile: ὀφθαλμοὶ ὡς εἰ κέρα ἕστασαν τ 211.—(2) In pl., horn as a material: αἱ μὲν [πύλαι] κεράεσσι τετεύχαται τ 563. Cf. τ 566.—(3) Each of two horns or pieces of horn forming a bow and joined by the πῆχυς φ 395.—(4) App., one's hair brought into a peak or topknot: κέρᾳ ἀγλαέ Λ 385 (adorned with, pluming yourself upon . . .).—(5) In an angling context: βοὸς κέρας Ω 81: μ 253. The sense is much disputed, and cannot be ascertained. Perh. after all it is simply a hook of horn that is meant.

κέρασσε, 3 sing. aor. κεράννυμι.

κεραυνός, -οῦ, ὁ. A thunderbolt Θ 133, 405, 419, 455, Ξ 417, Ο 117, Φ 198, 401: ε 128, 131, η 249, μ 387, 415 = ξ 305, μ 416 = ξ 306, ψ 330, ω 539.

κεράω [cf κεράννυμι]. Imp. pl. mid. κεράασθε γ 332. 3 pl. impf. κερόωντο θ 470, υ 253. κερῶντο ο 500. To mix (wine) with water ω 364.—In mid. γ 332, θ 470, ο 500, υ 253.

κερδαλέος, -η, -ον [κέρδος]. (1) Of a person, cunning, clever, wily: κερδαλέος κ' εἴη ὅς σε παρέλθοι ν 291.—Of a child, sharp, quick-witted, clever ο 451.—(2) Of counsel, shrewd, sage: βουλῆς Κ 44.—Of thoughts or designs, cunning, wily, guileful: νοήμασιν θ 548.—Of speech, cunning, wilily composed ζ 148.

κερδαλεόφρων [κερδαλέος + φρήν]. Cunning of heart, wily. In voc.: κερδαλεόφρον Α 149 (or here perh. rather, greedy, self-seeking), Δ 339.

κέρδιστος [superl. fr. κέρδος]. The craftiest, the most wily: κ. ἀνδρῶν Ζ 153.

κερδίων [comp. fr. κέρδος]. Only in neut. κέρδιον. (1) More or most profitable or advantageous, better, best: τό κεν πολὺ κ. εἴη Η 28. Cf. Ο 226, Ρ 417: υ 304, 331, 381.—Absol.: πολύ κε κ. ἦεν Γ 41. Cf. Ε 201 = Χ 103: = ι 228, β 320.—With infin., the better or best course to take, the better or best thing to be done or that can happen: ἐμοί κε κ. εἴη χθόνα δύμεναι Ζ 410: τό γε κ. εἴσατο, χρήματ' ἀγυρτάζειν τ 283. Cf. Χ 108, Ν 458 = Ξ 23: = σ 93 = χ 338 = ω 239, β 74, ζ 145, κ 153, λ 358 = υ 316.—Sim. with ὄφρα Π 652.—With a statement of the course taken ε 474, ο 204.—(2) Profitable rather than the reverse, profitable, good: ἔπος, τό κε κ. εἴη σ 166. Cf. Τ 63.—Absol.: τῶ οὔ νύ τι κ. ἡμῖν ἔλπομαι ἐκτελέεσθαι (no good)

Η 352.—With infin.: οὔ σφιν ἐφαίνετο κ. εἶναι μαίεσθαι προτέρω (it seemed useless to do it) ξ 355.

κέρδος, τό. (1) In pl., gains, profits: ἐπίσκοπος κερδέων ἁρπαλέων θ 164.—(2) Good, advantage, profit, service: ὅππως κ. ἔῃ Κ 225. Cf. π 311.—(3) A device or plan: κακὰ κέρδεα βουλεύουσιν ψ 217. Cf. ψ 140.—(4) In pl., cunning arts, cunning, craft, guile: κέρδεσιν, οὔ τι τάχει γε Ψ 515. Cf. β 88.—(5) In pl., shrewd or sage counsel or devices, sagacity, astuteness, intelligence: φρένας ἐσθλὰς κέρδεά τε β 118, κέρδεα νωμῶν (and so having the wit to play up to his father) υ 257. Cf. ν 297, 299, σ 216, τ 285.—(6) In pl., skill: ὅς κε κέρδεα εἰδῇ Ψ 322. Cf. Ψ 709.

κερδοσύνη, -ης, ἡ [κέρδος]. Cunning, craft: κερδοσύνῃ ἡγήσατο Χ 247. Cf. δ 251, ξ 31.

κερέειν, fut. infin. κείρω.

κερκίς, -ίδος, ἡ. In weaving, app., the shuttle, a rod carrying the πηνίον Χ 448: ε 62.

κερόωντο, 3 pl. impf. mid. κεράω.

κέρσε, 3 sing. aor. κείρω.

κερτομέω [κέρτομος = κερτόμιος]. (ἐπι-.) (1) To make fun of, make game of, subject to ridicule, mock, jeer at: μή τίς [μιν] κερτομέοι ἐπέεσσιν (should use uncivil speech to him) η 17, κερτομέων Ὀδυσῆα σ 350. Cf. π 87.—Absol.: σὺ δὲ κερτομέων ἀγορεύεις Β 256. Cf. β 323, θ 153, ν 326.—(2) App., to enrage, irritate by action: [σφῆκας] Π 261.

κερτομίαι, αἱ [cf. next]. Mocking or abusive speech, jeers, taunts, abuse: κερτομίας μυθήσασθαι Υ 202 = 433: κερτομίας τοι ἀφέξω υ 263.

κερτόμιος [perh. fr. κερ-, κείρω]. Mocking, teasing, making fun or game of a person: ἐπέεσσιν Δ 6, Ε 419: ω 240.—Absol. in neut. pl., mocking, taunting or abusive speech: Κύκλωπα προσηύδων κερτομίοισιν ι 474. Cf. υ 177.—Reproachful speech Α 539.

κέρωνται, 3 pl. subj. mid. See κεράννυμι.

κερῶντο, 3 pl. impf. mid. κεράω.

κέσκετο, 3 sing. pa. iterative κεῖμαι.

κεστός [app. for κενστός, κενττός, fr. κεντέω]. Pierced: κεστὸν ἱμάντα Ξ 214 (see ἱμάς (2) (g)).

κευθάνω [κεύθω]. To hide, keep out of sight: οὐκ ἐκεύθανον, εἴ τις ἴδοιτο (made no attempt to hide him if or when they saw him) Γ 453.

κευθμός, -οῦ, ὁ [κεύθω]. A hiding-place, a hole: ἄταλλε κήτεα πάντοθεν ἐκ κευθμῶν Ν 28.

κευθμών, -ῶνος, ὁ [κεύθω]. A remote or innermost part, a recess: μαιομένη κευθμῶνας ἀνὰ σπέος ν 367.—Applied to pigsties κ 283.

κεῦθος, τό [κεύθω]. A lower part: ὑπὸ κεύθεσι γαίης (below earth's depths, in the deepest depths of the earth) Χ 482: ω 204.

κεύθω. Fut. κεύσω γ 187, ψ 273. 3 sing. aor. κύθε γ 16. 3 pl. redup. aor. subj. κεκύθωσι ζ 303. 3 sing. pf. κέκευθε Χ 118: γ 18. 3 sing. plupf. ἐκεκεύθει ι 348. (ἐπι-.) (1) To cover up, envelop, enclose, enfold: εἰς ὅ κεν αὐτὸς ἐγὼν Ἄϊδι κεύθωμαι (in . . . (the only instance of the local use of Ἀΐδης)) Ψ 244. Cf. γ 16.—Sim. in reference to one entering a building: ὁπότ' ἄν σε δόμοι κεκύθωσι καὶ αὐλή ζ 303.—(2) To hold, contain, have in it: ὅσα τε πτόλις ἥδε κέκευθεν (all there is therein) Χ 118: οἷόν τι ποτὸν τόδε νηῦς ἐκεκεύθει (what manner of . . . was this that it bore) ι 348.—Of something immaterial: τί νύ τοι νόος ἔνδοθι κεύθει; (how art thou minded?) ω 474.—So, to have within one: ἥν τινα μῆτιν ἐνὶ στήθεσσι κέκευθεν γ 18.—(3) To keep from sight, hide, conceal: δάκρυα τ 212.—In a *quasi*-immaterial sense: οὐκέτι κεύθετε θυμῷ βρωτὺν οὐδὲ ποτῆτα (thought of as reappearing in violence and insolence) σ 406.—In reference to thoughts, speech, etc., to hide, conceal, withhold: ὅς χ' ἕτερον μὲν κεύθῃ ἐνὶ φρεσίν, ἄλλο δὲ εἴπῃ Ι 313. Cf. θ 548, φ 194, ψ 30.—Absol., to conceal one's thoughts, withhold speech: ἐξαύδα, μὴ κεῦθε Σ 74. Cf. Α 363 = Π 19.—(4) To make concealment from (a person), keep (him) in the dark: οὐδέ σε κεύσω γ 187, ψ 273.

κεφαλή, -ῆς, ἡ. Locative κεφαλῆφι Κ 30, 257, 261, 496: υ 94. This form as ablatival genit. Κ 458. As true genit. Λ 350, Π 762. (1) The head: κεφαλῇ κατανεύσομαι Α 524, κεφαλὴν ἴκελος Διί (in face) Β 478. Cf. Β 20, Ε 73, Κ 15, Λ 72, Μ 385, Ν 202, etc.: ἄγχι σχὼν κεφαλήν α 157. Cf. α 208, ε 232, ζ 226, θ 68, ι 498, ν 29, etc.—In reference to the Gorgon Ε 741: λ 634.—To Ate Τ 126.—(2) In reference to one's height: κεφαλῇ μείζονες ἄλλοι ἔασιν (in stature) Γ 168. Cf. Γ 193, 227 (by his . . .).—(3) The head as typifying the life: ἀπέτεισαν σὺν σφῇσιν κεφαλῇσιν Δ 162. Cf. Ρ 242: β 237, τ 92.—(4) In an oath or adjuration: λίσσομ' ὑπὲρ σῆς αὐτοῦ κεφαλῆς ο 262. Cf. Ο 39.—(5) As periphrasis for a person: Τεῦκρε, φίλη κεφαλή Θ 281, πολλὰς ἰφθίμους κεφαλὰς Ἄϊδι προϊάψειν Λ 55. Cf. Σ 82, 114, Φ 336, Χ 348, Ψ 94, Ω 276, 579: τοίην κεφαλὴν γαῖα κατέσχεν, Αἴαντα λ 549. Cf. α 343, λ 557.—Sim.: αἲ ἐμῇ κεφαλῇ κατ' ὀνείδεα χεῦαν χ 463.—(6) Of animals. Of sheep Γ 273—Of a wild goat Δ 109.—Of a wild boar Ι 548.—Of swine κ 239, ξ 422.—Of a serpent (represented in art) Λ 39.—Of horses Ψ 381.—Of an ox γ 446.—Of a dog ρ 291.

κεχάνδει, 3 sing. plupf. χανδάνω.

κεχαρηότα, acc. sing. masc. pf. pple. χαίρω.

κεχαρησέμεν, fut. infin. χαίρω.

κεχαρισμένος, pf. pple. χαρίζομαι.

κεχάροντο, 3 pl. aor. mid. χαίρω.

κεχηνότα, acc. sing. masc. pf. pple. χαίνω.

κεχολώσομαι, fut. mid. χολόω.

κεχρημένος, pf. pple. mid. χράω[1].

κέχρητο, 3 sing. plupf. mid. χράω[1].

κέχυται, 3 sing. pf. pass. χέω.

κέω. See κείω.

κῆαι, aor. infin. καίω.

κήδειος [κῆδος]. To whom one is bound by family ties, dear, beloved: κασιγνήτους Τ 294.

κηδεμών, -όνος [κήδω]. In pl., mourners bound to the dead man by family ties, kindred mourners Ψ 163, 674.

κήδεος [κῆδος]. That is matter of family grief: οἷσι κήδεός ἐστι νέκυς Ψ 160.

κήδιστος [superl. fr. κῆδος]. Dearest as being, or as if being, bound by family ties: κήδιστοι μεθ' αἷμά τε καὶ γένος αὐτῶν θ 583. Cf. Ι 642: κ 225.

κῆδος, τό [cf. next]. (1) Trouble, pain: ἦ πού τί σε κ. ἱκάνει; Ο 245. Cf. Π 516.—Matter for trouble or care: τῶν ἄλλων οὐ κ. (we need not mind about them) χ 254.—Trouble or grief occasioned by a family loss: χρή σε γαμβρῷ ἀμυνέμεναι εἴ πέρ τί σε κ. ἱκάνει Ν 464.—(2) In pl., troubles, woes, sorrows, sufferings, cares: Ἀργείοισι κήδε' ἐφῆκεν Α 445. Cf. Β 15, Δ 270, Ι 592, Κ 106, Τ 302, Ω 617, etc.: κήδεα πόλλ' Ὀδυσῆος ε 5, εἴροντο κήδε' ἑκάστη (app., those who were dear to them in the world above) λ 542, ὁππόσα κήδε' ἀνέτλης ξ 47. Cf. α 244, δ 108, η 242, θ 149, ν 307, ο 399, etc.—Trouble or grief occasioned by a family loss: πατέρι γόον καὶ κήδεα λεῖπεν Ε 156. Cf. Ζ 241.

κήδω [cf. prec.]. 3 pl. pa. iterative κήδεσκον ψ 9. Nom. pl. masc. fut. pple. κηδήσοντες Ω 240. 3 sing. pa. iterative mid. κηδέσκετο χ 358. 1 pl. fut. κεκαδησόμεθα Θ 353. (περι-.) (1) To cause trouble or pain to, trouble, pain, distress, vex, lay a heavy hand upon: ἀνάσχεο κηδομένη περ Α 586, τὸν κήδειν ὅς κ' ἐμὲ κήδῃ Ι 615. Cf. Ε 400, Η 110, Π 516, Ρ 550, Ω 542, etc.: εἴροντο ὅττι ἑ κήδοι ι 402. Cf. γ 240, η 215, τ 511.—Sim.: οἵ θ' ἑὸν οἶκον κήδεσκον ψ 9.—(2) In mid., to trouble oneself about, be solicitous for the welfare of, care for, take thought for. With genit.: σεῦ κήδεται Β 27. Cf. Α 56, Ζ 55, Θ 353, Ω 422, etc.: ἦ μευ πατὴρ ὣς κήδεαι υἷος ρ 397. Cf. ξ 461, χ 358.—Sim.: οἴκου κήδεσθαι τ 23, 161. Cf. ξ 4.—The genit. not expressed: ἄλοχον φιλέει καὶ κήδεται [αὐτῆς] Ι 342. Cf. Α 196=209: γ 223, ξ 146.—So μὴ ταῦτα παραύδα, κηδομένη περ (though it is in care for me that thou dost it) σ 178.

κῆε, 3 sing. aor. καίω.

κηκίω. (ἀνα-.) To ooze or trickle ε 455.

κήλειος [prob. for κανάλεος or κηάλεος fr. καϜ-, καίω]. Burning, blazing. Epithet of fire: πυρί Ο 744.

κήλεος. =prec.: πυρί Θ 217, 235, Σ 346, Χ 374, 512: θ 435, ι 328.

κηληθμός, -οῦ, ὁ [κηλέω, to bewitch. Cf. ἀκήλητος]. Charm, spell, glamour λ 334=ν 2.

κῆλον, -ου, τό. A missile. Of the arrows of Apollo Α 53, 383.—Of snow: Ζεὺς πιφαυσκόμενος τὰ ἃ κῆλα Μ 280.

κήξ, ἡ. Some kind of sea-bird: εἰναλίη κήξ ο 479.

κῆπος, -ου, ὁ. A piece of prepared ground, a garden or orchard: κρήνη ἀνὰ κῆπον ἅπαντα σκίδναται η 129. Cf. Θ 306, Φ 258: δ 737, ω 247, 338.

κήρ, κηρός, ἡ. (1) Bane, death: τό τοι κὴρ εἴδεται εἶναι Α 228, κῆρ' ἀλεείνων Γ 32. Cf. Β 352, 859, Γ 360, 454, Ε 22, Ν 665, Π 47, Σ 115, Ω 82, etc.: κηρὶ δαμείς γ 410. Cf. β 165, 283, δ 502, ρ 500, σ 155, χ 330, etc.—So κὴρ θανάτοιο (consisting in . . .) Π 687.—(2) One's destined fate: ἐμὲ κὴρ ἀμφέχανε, ἥ περ λάχε γιγνόμενόν περ Ψ 78.—(3) Figured as a weight put in the balance and typifying death or one's fate: ἐν δὲ τίθει δύο κῆρε θανάτοιο Θ 70=Χ 210. Cf. Θ 73.—(4) More or less distinctly personified as agent of death: τίς νύ σε κὴρ ἐδάμασσε θανάτοιο; λ 171=398.—In pl.: οὓς κῆρες φορέουσιν Θ 528. Cf. Δ 11, Μ 113, 402, Ν 283, Ο 287, Φ 565: β 316, 352=ε 387, δ 512, ρ 547=τ 558, χ 66, ψ 332.—So κῆρες θανάτοιο Β 302, 834=Λ 332, Ι 411, Μ 326, Φ 548, Χ 202: ξ 207.—(5) Fully personified: ἐν δ' Ἔρις ἐν δὲ Κυδοιμὸς ὁμίλεον, ἐν δ' ὀλοὴ Κήρ Σ 535.

κῆρ, τό [app. for κηρ-δ, καρδίη, κραδίη]. Only in nom. and acc. sing. and in dat. sing. κῆρι. (Cf. ἦτορ, θυμός, καρδίη, κραδίη, φρήν.) (1) The heart: ἔνθα φρένες ἔρχαται ἀμφὶ κ. Π 481.—(2) The 'heart,' 'breast,' soul, mind, as the seat or a seat (a) Of life; hence vitality, the vital powers, strength (cf. θυμός (I) (1) (a)): φθινύθεσκε κ. Α 491, κ. ἀπινύσσων (in his heart) Ο 10. Cf. ε 454, κ 485.—(b) Of the intelligence, of the faculty of thinking, deliberating, considering: πολλά οἱ κ. ὅρμαινεν η 82, ψ 85. Cf. σ 344.—(c) Of spirit, courage, stoutness, endurance: σὸν κ. τετλάτω ἐν στήθεσσιν π 274. Cf. Ν 713.—Periphrastically with genit. of proper name to denote a warrior: Πυλαιμένεος λάσιον κ. Β 851. Cf. Π 554: δ 270.—(d) Of anger, wrath, passion: χωόμενος (χωόμενον) κ. (in his heart) Α 44, Ι 555, Ψ 37, ὑμῖν νεμεσσῶμαι περὶ κῆρι Ν 119 (περί doubtless to be taken as adv. and κῆρι as locative; lit. 'exceedingly in my heart'; cf. under (g)). Cf. Ν 206, Π 585: η 309, μ 376.—Of rage or fury: λύσσα οἱ κ. ἔχεν Φ 542.—(e) Of desire, longing, appetite: θαλέων ἐμπλησάμενος κ. Χ 504. Cf. Τ 319: ἐμὸν κ. ἤθελ' ἀκουέμεναι μ 192.—(f) Of volition: ἐπιγνάμψασα κ. Α 569. Cf. Ξ 208, Ο 52: οὐδέ νύ μοι κ. ἤθελ' ἔτι ζώειν δ 539, κ 497.—(g) Of feelings, emotions, moods, such as joy, grief, affection, dislike, fear, reverence, regard, solicitude, etc.: τάων μοι περὶ κῆρι τιέσκετο Ἴλιος Δ 46 (περί doubtless to be taken with τάων and κῆρι as locative; lit. 'beyond these in my heart'), ὅτ' ἄν τοι ἀπέχθωνται περὶ κῆρι 53 (see above under (d)), γηθόσυνος κ. (in his heart) 272=326, Σ 557, κ. ἀχέων Ε 399, ἐμὸν κ. ἄχνυται ἐν θυμῷ (my heart within me) Ζ 523. Cf. Η 428, Ι 117, Κ 16, Λ 274, Ν 430, Ξ 139, Ρ 539, Ω 61, 435, etc.: τεταρπόμενος κ. α 310, ἀοιδῆς, ἥ τέ μοι ἐνὶ στήθεσσι κ. τείρει 341. Cf. δ 259, ε 36, ζ 158, η 69, ι 413, 459, κ 247, ρ 216, τ 516, χ 58, etc.—In reference to animals Μ 45, Ψ 284, 443.—(h) Of one's character or disposition: κ. ἀτέραμνον ἔθηκαν ψ 167.

κηρεσσιφόρητος [κήρεσσι, dat. pl. of κήρ + φορέω]. Borne on (to doom) by the κῆρες Θ 527.

κηρόθι [κῆρ + -θι]. In the heart, heartily. Always in phrase κηρόθι μᾶλλον, right heartily, from the bottom of one's heart (see μᾶλλον (3)): (ἐ)χολώσατο Φ 136: ι 480, ρ 458, σ 387, χ 224, φίλει με ο 370. Cf. Ι 300: ε 284, λ 208.

κηρός, -οῦ, ὁ. Bees-wax μ 48, 173, 175, 199.

κῆρυξ, -ῦκος, ὁ. One of a class of attendants on kings or chiefs found sometimes discharging the general duties of a θεράπων (1) (Β 184, Δ 198, Ι 174, Μ 342, 351, Σ 558, Ψ 39, 897, Ω 149, 178,

282, 352, 674, 689; and *passim* in the Odyssey (in A 321 : σ 424 κῆρυξ and θεράπων conjoined)), or executing a special commission (A 391), and sometimes discharging public functions (τ 135) (in this capacity regarded as being under the special protection of Zeus (Δ 192, K 315), and thus as affording a measure of protection by their presence (ι 90, κ 59, 102)), *i.e.* delivering formal messages (A 334, H 274, 384), making proclamations or announcements (Θ 517, Λ 685, Ψ 39, Ω 577, 701), conducting ceremonials (Γ 116, 245, 248, 268, 274 : υ 276), accompanying formal missions (I 170, 689), superintending the drawing of lots (H 183), regulating combats (H 274, 278), summoning to the field (B 437, 442), summoning to the assembly (B 50, I 10 : β 6, θ 8) or regulating the proceedings at the assembly (B 97, 280, Σ 503, 505, Ψ 567 : β 38) A 321, 334, 391, B 50, 97, 184, 280, 437, 442, Γ 116, 245, 248, 268, 274, Δ 192, 198 = M 351, H 183, 274, 278, 384, Θ 517, I 10, 170, 174, 689, K 315, Λ 685, M 342, P 324 (see κηρύσσω (1)), Σ 503, 505, 558, Ψ 39, 567, 897, Ω 149, 178, 282 = 674, 352, 577, 689, 701 : α 109, 143, 146 = γ 338 = φ 270, α 153, β 6, 38, δ 301, 677 = π 412, δ 681, 707, η 163, 178 = ν 49, θ 8, 47, 62 = 471, θ 69, 107, 256, 261, 399 = σ 291, θ 418, 474, 477, 482, ι 90 = κ 102, κ 59, ν 64, π 252, 328, 333, 336, 469, ρ 173, 334, σ 424, τ 135, 244, υ 276, χ 357.

κηρύσσω [κῆρυξ]. **(1)** To discharge the various duties of a κῆρυξ : ὃς κηρύσσων γήρασκεν P 325.—**(2)** To summon to the assembly : ἀγορήνδε Ἀχαιούς B 51 : = β 7.—Absol. B 52 : = β 8.—**(3)** To summon to the field : πόλεμόνδ' Ἀχαιούς B 443. Cf. B 438.—Absol. B 444.

κῆται, 3 sing. subj. κεῖμαι.

κῆτος, τό [καϜ-. Cf. L. *cavus* and κοῖλος. Orig. sense 'gulf']. A sea-monster : ὄφρα τὸ κῆτος ὑπεκπροφυγὼν ἀλέαιτο Υ 147. Cf. N 27 : ε 421, μ 97.—Applied to seals δ 443, 446, 452.

κητώεις, -εσσα [κῆτος]. Lying among rifted hills. Epithet of Lacedaemon B 581 : δ 1.

κηώδης [*κῆϜος, incense, fr. κηϜ-, καίω + ὀδ-, ὄζω]. Fragrant, sweet-smelling Z 483.

κηώεις, -εντος [*κῆϜος. See prec.]. = prec. Γ 382, Z 288, Ω 191 : = ο 99.

κίδνημι [(σ)κιδ-, (σ)κεδ-. = κεδάννυμι]. (ἐπι-.) In pass., of the dawn, to be spread or shed : ἠὼς ἐκίδνατο πᾶσαν ἐπ' αἶαν Θ 1, Ω 695. Cf. Ψ 227.

κιθαρίζω [κίθαρις]. To play or accompany oneself on the κίθαρις Σ 570.

κίθαρις, ἡ. **(1)** A lyre (hardly to be distinguished from the φόρμιγξ ; cf. Σ 569 with 570 and α 153 with 155) α 153.—**(2)** The music of the κίθαρις : κ. τε χοροί τε θ 248. Cf. α 159.—**(3)** The art of playing the κίθαρις (= κιθαριστύς) : κ. τά τε δῶρ' Ἀφροδίτης Γ 54. Cf. N 731.

κιθαριστύς, ἡ [κιθαρίζω]. The art of playing the κίθαρις : ἐκλέλαθον κιθαριστύν B 600.

κικλήσκω [with reduplication fr. κλη-, καλέω]. **(1)** To summon (= καλέω (1)) : γέροντας B 404. Cf. I 11, Λ 606, P 532, Ψ 221 : χ 397.—In mid. K 300.—With infin. denoting the purport of the summons : παιδὶ δόμεν θάνατον I 569.—**(2)** To call by *such and such a name*, name *so and so* (= καλέω (3)) : τὸν κορυνήτην ἄνδρες κίκλησκον H 139. Cf. B 813, Ξ 291 : Οὖτιν με κικλήσκουσιν ι 366, νῆσός τις Συρίη κικλήσκεται (there lies an island called . . .) ο 403. Cf. δ 355, σ 6.

κῖκυς, ἡ. Power, vigour λ 393.

κῑνέω [cf. next]. (ἀπο-.) **(1)** To move, put into motion, impart movement to Π 298 : θ 298.—To shake (the head) : κινήσας κάρη P 200, 442 : = ε 285 = 376. Cf. ρ 465 = 491 = υ 184.—To stir up (persons) to motion, cause (them) to move onwards : ῥάβδῳ ἄγε κινήσας ω 5.—In pass., to move, address oneself to motion : αὐτοῦ κινηθέντος A 47.—**(2)** To disturb, rouse to action, irritate : σφῆκας Π 264.—To disturb the surface of, ruffle : βαθὺ λήϊον B 147.—To raise (waves) : [κῦμα] B 395, Δ 423.—To rouse from rest, stir up : λὰξ ποδὶ κινήσας K 158 : ο 45.—To shake (a door) in order to attract attention χ 394.—In pass., to be moved or troubled, be put into commotion : κινήθη ἀγορή B 144, 149. Cf. Π 280.—**(3)** To move from one position to another : [Αἴαντα] τυτθὸν ἀπὸ χθονός Ψ 730.

κίνῡμι [cf. prec.]. **(1)** In pass., to move, address oneself to motion, get into movement, make a start : ἐς πόλεμον κίνυντο φάλαγγες Δ 281. Cf. Δ 332, 427, K 280 : κινυμένων ἑτάρων κ 556.—**(2)** To stir, shake up : ἐλαίου κινυμένοιο Ξ 173.

κινυρός, -ή. Uttering a plaintive cry. Of a cow P 5.

κίον, with augment **ἔκιον,** *aor.* [κι- as in κινέω, κίνυμι]. (μετεκίαθον.) **(1)** To go or come, take or make one's way, proceed, be on foot : ἀπάνευθε κιών A 35. Cf. A 348, Γ 423, Δ 251, Z 399, I 504, N 658, etc. : ἰθὺς κίε Τηλεμάχοιο β 301. Cf. α 311, γ 168, δ 427, ζ 84, κ 574, ν 125, etc.—Pleonastically : βήτην κιόντε χ 378.—Of mules Ψ 115.—Of ships B 509 : ι 64.—**(2)** In pple. with a finite vb., to go and . . . (cf. ἄγω (I) (9)) : στῆ παρ' Αἰάντεσσι κιών M 353. Cf. I 511, T 50 : ἀπαγγέλλεσκε κιών (went with messages) σ 7. Cf. θ 254, ρ 508.—**(3)** To be brought into a specified condition : μή τίς οἱ (μοι) ἀτεμβόμενος κίοι ἴσης (should go without his due) Λ 705 : ι 42 = 549.

κίρκος, -ου, ὁ. A bird of the falcon kind, a falcon or hawk P 757, X 139 : ο 526.—ἴρηξ κ. See ἴρηξ.

κιρνάω [cf. κεράννυμι]. To mix (wine) with water : οἶνον ἐκίρνα η 182 = ν 53, κ 356.

κίρνημι. = prec. ξ 78 = π 52, π 14.

κισσύβιον, -ου, τό [κισσός, ivy. App. orig. a vessel of ivy-wood]. **(1)** A mixing-bowl : ἐν κισσυβίῳ κίρνη οἶνον ξ 78 = π 52.—**(2)** A drinking-cup ι 346.

κίστη, -ης, ἡ. A box or chest ζ 76.

κιχάνω. Non-thematic pres. subj. κιχείω A 26, Γ 291, Z 228, Λ 367, Σ 114, Υ 454. 1 pl. κιχείομεν Φ 128. 3 sing. opt. κιχείη B 188, I 416 : ρ 476. Pple. κιχείς Π 342. Infin. κιχήμεναι O 274. κιχῆναι π 357. 3 dual impf. κιχήτην K 376. 1 pl.

ἐκίχημεν π 379. 2 sing. thematic impf. (fr. κιχέω) ἐκίχεις ω 284. 3 sing. aor. ἔκιχε γ 169. κίχε Ω 160. 3 pl. κίχον Σ 153. 3 sing. subj. κίχησι μ 122. Pple. κιχών ο 157. **Mid.** Nom. sing. neut. non-thematic pres. pple. κιχήμενον Λ 451. Acc. κιχήμενον Ε 187. Fut. κιχήσομαι Β 258, Κ 370 : ξ 139. 2 sing. κιχήσεαι δ 546, η 53. 3 κιχήσεται Σ 268. 1 pl. κιχησόμεθα Κ 126. Infin. κιχήσεσθαι Ζ 341, Φ 605 : ι 477. 3 sing. aor. κιχήσατο Δ 385, Ζ 498, Κ 494, Φ 263, Χ 226 : ζ 51, τ 400. **(1)** To come to, reach, find oneself at, a specified place : εἰς ὅ κεν ἄστυ κιχείομεν Φ 128.—**(2)** To come up to, present oneself to (a person). In mid. : κιχήσαθ' Ἕκτορα Χ 226.—**(3)** To come up to, reach, get within reach of (a person, etc.) : ὅν κε κιχείω Ζ 228, Λ 367 = Υ 454. Cf. Κ 376, Ο 274, Π 342, Σ 114, 153.—To reach (a person with a weapon). In mid. : δουρί σε κιχήσομαι Κ 370.—To reach, stretch as far as to (a person) : μή σε κίχησι τόσσησιν κεφαλῇσιν μ 122.—To come to or reach (a person) in the course of making a round or of going over a number : ὅν τινα βασιλῆα κιχείη Β 188.—In mid. Κ 494.—**(4)** To make up upon, overtake, catch up : θέων ἐκίχανεν ἑταίρους Ρ 189. Cf. Ψ 407, 524 : γ 169, π 357.—In mid. Ζ 341, Φ 263, 605.—Absol., to succeed in one's design : φόνον οἱ ἐράπτομεν οὐδ' ἐκίχημεν π 379.—**(5)** To come or light upon, fall in with, find (a person) : ἔνθα σφέας ἐκίχανε Μελανθεύς ρ 212.—In mid. : οὐκ ἔτ' ἄλλον ἤπιον ὧδε ἄνακτα κιχήσομαι ξ 139. Cf. η 53.—To come upon or find (a person) in a specified place or condition : μή σε παρὰ νηυσὶ κιχείω Α 26, εὕδοντα Β 18. Cf. Γ 383, Κ 150 : εἴ μιν ζωὸν ἐκίχεις (had found him . . .) ω 284. Cf. κ 60, ο 157, 257.—In mid. Β 258, Δ 385, Ζ 498, Κ 126, Σ 268 : δ 546, ζ 51.—**(6)** To come upon, find (a state of things) : κίχεν ἐνοπήν τε γόον τε Ω 160.—In mid. τ 400.—**(7)** To attain (an end) : ἧός κε τέλος πολέμοιο κιχείω Γ 291.—**(8)** Of a missile, to reach its mark : ὅς τούτου (from him) βέλος κιχήμενον ἔτραπεν ἄλλῃ (on the point of striking) Ε 187.—**(9)** Of something immaterial, to come upon, seize : οὐδέ κέ μ' ὦκα τέλος θανάτοιο κιχείη Ι 416. Cf. ρ 476.—In mid. : ἔμελλέ σε κιχήσεσθαι κακὰ ἔργα (*i.e.* retribution for them) ι 477. Cf. Λ 451.—**(10)** To be in the condition of having reached (something), find oneself in a specified position. In mid.: κιχανόμενοι τὰ σὰ γοῦνα (*i.e.* in supplication) ι 266.—**(11)** To be in the condition of having overtaken (a person) : ὅτ' ἐκίχανε [Κύπριν] πολὺν καθ' ὅμιλον ὀπάζων (had made up on her) Ε 334. Cf. θ 329.—**(12)** To be in the condition of having come upon or fallen in with (a person) : ἐπεί σε πρῶτα κιχάνω τῷδ' ἐνὶ χώρῳ ν 228.—**(13)** To be in the condition of having come upon or found (a person) in a specified condition : ἐπεί σε θύοντα κιχάνω ο 260.—In mid. Τ 289.—**(14)** Of bodily states, to have come upon, affect : κιχάνει [μιν] δίψα τε καὶ λιμός Τ 165.—Of death, fate, bane Ρ 478 = 672 = Χ 436, Χ 303.—In mid. Λ 441.

κίχλη, ἡ. A bird of the thrush kind χ 468.

κίχον, 3 pl. aor. κιχάνω.

κίων, -ονος, ὁ, ἡ. A supporting beam, a pillar or column : ἔγχος ἔστησε πρὸς κίονα α 127 = ρ 29, κίονι κεκλιμένη ζ 307. Cf. θ 66 = 473, τ 38, χ 176, 193, 466, ψ 90, 191.—κίονες μακραί, the pillars supporting the heavens α 53.

κλαγγή, -ῆς, ἡ [κλαγ-, κλάζω]. A sharp piercing sound. The cry of birds : γεράνων Γ 3, 5.—The cry of the shades of the dead likened to that of birds : κλαγγὴ νεκύων ἦν οἰωνῶν ὥς λ 605.—The squealing of swine ξ 412.—The cry or shouting of men : κλαγγῇ ἴσαν Γ 2. Cf. Β 100, Κ 523.—The twang of a bow Α 49.

κλαγγηδόν [κλαγγή]. Uttering their cry. Of birds : κλαγγηδὸν προκαθιζόντων Β 463.

†κλάζω. Nom. dual pres. pple. κλάζοντε Π 429. 3 pl. aor. ἔκλαγξαν Α 46. Pple. κλάγξας, -αντος Κ 276, Μ 207. Pf. pple. κεκληγώς Λ 168, Ρ 88 : μ 408. Thematic pf. pple. (in pres. sense) κεκλήγων (*v.l.* κεκληγώς) Β 222, Ε 591, Λ 344, Ν 755. Nom. pl. κεκλήγοντες (*v.l.* κεκληγῶτες) Μ 125, Π 430, Ρ 756, 759 : ξ 30. Acc. κεκλήγοντας (*v.l.* κεκληγῶτας) μ 256. To utter or emit a sharp piercing sound. **(1)** Of the cry of birds : αἰετὸς κλάγξας πέτετο Μ 207. Cf. Κ 276, Π 429, Ρ 756.—**(2)** Of the barking of dogs ξ 30.—**(3)** Of the cry or shouting of men : ὣς οἱ κεκλήγοντες ὄρουσαν Π 430. Cf. Β 222, Ε 591 = Λ 344, Λ 168, Μ 125, Ν 755, Ρ 88, 759 : κατήσθιε κεκλήγοντας μ 256.—**(4)** Of the singing of a high wind : ἦλθε κεκληγὼς Ζέφυρος μ 408.—**(5)** Of the rattling of arrows striking against each other Α 46.

κλαίω [κλαϝ-]. Dat. pl. masc. pple. κλαιόντεσσι μ 311. 3 sing. pa. iterative κλαίεσκε Θ 364. 3 sing. aor. κλαῦσε γ 261, ω 293. Pple. κλαύσας Ω 48. Fut. in mid. form κλαύσομαι Χ 87. 3 pl. -ονται Σ 340, Υ 210. (μετα-.) **(1)** To weep, wail, make lament : τί κλαίεις ; Α 362, κλαιοντά [σ'] ἀφήσω (in pitiable plight) Β 263. Cf. Γ 176, Η 427, Λ 136, Ρ 427, Τ 5, Χ 427, Ψ 252, etc. : μηκέτι κλαῖε δ 544. Cf. β 376, δ 184, 541, θ 523, ι 98, κ 241, τ 541, etc. —To lift up one's voice in distress : κλαίεσκε πρὸς οὐρανόν Θ 364.—**(2)** To lament, bewail : σφῶν αὐτῶν κήδεα Τ 301. Cf. Ω 85 : ψ 352.—To bewail (oneself) : κλαίω ἔμ' ἄμμορον Ω 773.—**(3)** To mourn the loss of, weep for, lament (a person) : ἄμοτόν σε κλαίω τεθνηότα Τ 300, ἑὸν πατέρα (fearing or anticipating the loss of him) Ω 511. Cf. Τ 301, Υ 210, Ω 773 : Ὀδυσῆα, φίλον πόσιν α 363 = π 450 = τ 603 = φ 357. Cf. δ 196, μ 309, τ 209.—**(4)** To pay dues of mourning or lament to : παῖδά κε κλαίοισθα Ω 619. Cf. Χ 87, Ψ 9 : οὐδέ κέ τίς μιν κλαῦσεν Ἀχαιϊάδων γ 261. Cf. ω 64, 293.

κλάσε, 3 sing. aor. κλάω.

κλαυθμός, -οῦ, ὁ [κλαϝ-, κλαυ-, κλαίω]. Weeping, wailing, lamentation : ἔπειτα ἄσεσθε κλαυθμοῖο Ω 717. Cf. δ 212, 801, ρ 8, φ 228, χ 501, ω 323.

†κλάω. 3 sing. aor. κλάσε ζ 128. 3 sing. aor. pass. ἐκλάσθη Λ 584. (δια-, ἐνι-, κατα-.) **(1)** To break, break off short : ἐκλάσθη δόναξ Λ 584.—**(2)** To break off : ἐξ ὕλης πτόρθον κλάσεν ζ 128.

κλεηδών, -όνος, ἡ [κλέω]. Also **κληηδών** δ 317.

(1) News, tidings: εἴ τινά μοι κληηδόνα πατρὸς ἐνίσποις δ 317.—(2) An omen or presage, something said which bears a significance of which the speaker is unconscious, a speech that serves as an omen (=φήμη): χαῖρε κλεηδόνι σ 117, υ 120.

κλειτός, -ή, -όν [κλείω]. (1) Famous, renowned. Epithet of the Ithacan chiefs: μετὰ κλειτοὺς βασιλῆας ζ 54.—Of the Trojan allies: Τρώων κλειτῶν τ' ἐπικούρων Γ 451, Ρ 14. Cf. Ζ 227, Λ 220, Ρ 212, Σ 229.—Of auxiliaries in gen. Δ 379.—Of a place: Πανοπῆϊ Ρ 307.—(2) Of sacrifices, goodly, befitting the occasion Δ 102 = 120 = Ψ 864 = 873, Η 450 = Μ 6.

κλείω [κλεϝέω, fr. κλέ(ϝ)ος]. Also **κλέω**. Fut. κλείω ρ 418. 2 sing. impf. pass. ἔκλεο (for ἐκλέεο) Ω 202. (ἐπι-.) To tell of, sing of, celebrate: ἔργα, τὰ κλείουσιν ἀοιδοί α 338. Cf. ρ 418.—In pass., to be famed or celebrated: ἧς ἔκλε' ἐπ' ἀνθρώπους (for which) Ω 202. Cf. ν 299.

κλέος, τό (κλέϝος). Acc. pl. κλέα (for κλέεα) Ι 189, 524: θ 73. (1) A report or rumour: πεύθετο μέγα κ., οὕνεκα . . . Λ 21, μετὰ κ. ἵκετ' Ἀχαιῶν (following up the rumour of the expedition) 227. Cf. Ν 364: ψ 137.—With an admixture of sense (2): σεῖο μέγα κ. αἰὲν ἄκουον, χεῖρας αἰχμητὴν ἔμεναι π 241. Cf. Θ 192: σ 126. — Report, rumour, tidings: τί κ. ἔστ' ἀνὰ ἄστυ; π 461. Cf. α 283 = β 217, γ 83, ν 415.—As opposed to knowledge or certainty: κ. οἶον ἀκούομεν οὐδέ τι ἴδμεν Β 486.—(2) Good report or repute, fame, glory, honour (sometimes with ἐσθλόν): ἵνα κ. ἐσθλὸν ἄροιτο Ε 3, τὸ δ' ἐμὸν κ. οὔ ποτ' ὀλεῖται Η 91. Cf. Ζ 446, Ι 413, Κ 212, Ρ 16, Σ 121, etc.: παιδί κε μέγα κ. ἤρατο α 240. Cf. α 95, β 125, γ 204, η 333, ι 20, σ 255, ω 94, etc.—High reputation for skill in something: ποῦ τοι τόξον καὶ κ.; Ε 172.—In pl., famous deeds, high achievements, notable conduct: κλέα ἀνδρῶν Ι 189, 524: θ 73.—(3) In reference to things, fame, celebrity: τεῖχος, τοῦ κ. ἔσται ὅσον τ' ἐπικίδναται ἠώς Η 451. Cf. Β 325: θ 74. — (4) Something that brings fame or honour or confers distinction: τῷ μὲν κ. ἄμμι δὲ πένθος Δ 197 = 207, τοῖον κ. ἀπώλεσαν ἡνιόχοιο (glory of, consisting in, a . . .) Ψ 280. Cf. Ρ 131, 232, Χ 514: δ 584.

κλέπτης, ὁ [κλέπτω]. A thief Γ 11.

κλεπτοσύνη, -ης, ἡ [κλέπτω]. Unscrupulous dealing, sharp practice τ 396.

κλέπτω. 3 sing. aor, ἔκλεψε Ε 268, Ξ 217. Infin. κλέψαι Ω 24, 71, 109. (ἐκ-, ὑποκλοπέομαι.) (1) To take away by stealth, filch, purloin: τῆς γενεῆς ἔκλεψεν Ἀγχίσης (filched (a strain) from that . . .) Ε 268, κλέψαι [Ἕκτορα (*i.e.* his corpse)] ὀτρύνεσκον Ἀργειφόντην Ω 24. Cf. Ω 71, 109.—(2) To cozen, beguile, lead astray: μὴ κλέπτε νόῳ Α 132. Cf. Ξ 217.

κλέω. See κλείω.

κλήδην [κλη-, καλέω]. By name: κλήδην εἰς ἀγορὴν κικλήσκειν ἄνδρα ἕκαστον Ι 11.

κληηδών. See κλεηδών.

κλήθρη, ἡ. The alder ε 64, 239.

κληΐς, -ῖδος, ἡ [κληΐω]. Dat. pl. κληΐδεσσι(ῑ) μ 215. κληῗσι Π 170, Ω 318: β 419, ι 103, ο 221, etc. (1) A bar or bolt securing a gate or door within: θύρας σταθμοῖσιν ἐπῆρσε κληῗδι κρυπτῇ Ξ 168. Cf. Ω 318, 455 (here app. identical with the ἐπιβλής of 453): ἐπὶ κληῗδ' ἐτάνυσσεν ἱμάντι α 442, σταθμοῖο παρὰ κληῗδα λιάσθη (*i.e.* through the slit for the ἱμάς) δ 838. Cf. δ 802, φ 241.—App., a pin securing the ὀχῆες of a gate at their point of intersection Μ 456 (see ἐπημοιβός (2)).—(2) An instrument for pushing back from without the bar or bolt of a door: οἴξασα κληῗδι θύρας Ζ 89: ἐν κληῗδ' ἧκεν (*i.e.* into an aperture made for the purpose) φ 47. Cf. φ 6, 50.—(3) In pl., rowlocks or thole-pins (to which the oars were secured by the τροποί); also explained as oarsmen's benches (as passing from side to side of, and stiffening, the framework of a ship = ζυγά. See ζυγόν (2)); but θ 37 cited below seems to be decisive against this: πεντήκοντ' ἔσαν ἄνδρες ἐπὶ κληῗσιν ἑταῖροι Π 170: δησάμενοι δ' εὖ πάντες ἐπὶ κληῗσιν ἐρετμὰ ἔκβητε θ 37. Cf. β 419 = δ 579, ι 103 = 179 = 471 = 563 = λ 638 = μ 146 = ο 549, μ 215, ν 76, ο 221.—(4) The collar-bone (as joining the breast and neck): τὸν ἕτερον κληῗδα παρ' ὦμον πλῆξεν Ε 146. Cf. Ε 579, Θ 325, Ρ 309, Φ 117, Χ 324 (in pl.).—(5) A tube or sheath to receive a pin of a περόνη: περόναι κληῗσιν ἀραρυῖαι σ 294 (= the αὐλοῖσιν of τ 227: see αὐλός (4)).

κληϊστός, -ή, -όν [κληΐω]. That can be secured, fitted with a bar or bolt: σανίδες β 344.

†κληΐω. 3 sing. aor. ἐκλήϊσε ω 166. κλήϊσε τ 30, φ 387, 389. Infin. κληῗσαι φ 236, 241, 382. (1) To secure (a gate or door) τ 30 = φ 387, φ 236 = 382, φ 241, 389.—(2) To put to or secure (a bar or bolt): ἐκλήϊσεν ὀχῆας ω 166.

κλῆρος, -ου, ὁ. (1) An object used in an appeal to the divine agency supposed to be concerned in the results of chance, a lot: κλήρους ἐν κυνέῃ πάλλον Γ 316. Cf. Γ 325, Η 175, 182, 189, 191, Ψ 352, 353, 861: ἐπὶ κλήρους ἐβάλοντο ξ 209. Cf. κ 206, 207.—(2) Such an object viewed abstractedly, the lot: κλήρῳ πεπάλασθε Η 171. Cf. ι 331.—Decision by lots, the lot: πρῶτος κλήρῳ λάχεν Ψ 862. Cf. Ω 400.—(3) A piece of land that has fallen to one's lot, a piece of land allotted to one: οἶκόν τε κλῆρόν τε ξ 64. Cf. Ο 498.

κλητός [κλη-, καλέω]. (1) Invited, made welcome ρ 386.—(2) Absol. in pl., men called or chosen for a mission: κλητοὺς ὀτρύνομεν, οἵ κε . . . Ι 165.

κλιθῆναι, aor. infin. pass. κλίνω.

κλῖμαξ, -ακος, ἡ [κλίνω]. A ladder or staircase: κλίμακα κατεβήσετο οἷο δόμοιο α 330. Cf. κ 558 = λ 63, φ 5.

κλίνθη, 3 sing. aor. pass. κλίνω.

κλιντήρ, -ῆρος, ὁ [κλίνω]. App. = κλισμός: λύθεν οἱ ἅψεα πάντα αὐτοῦ ἐνὶ κλιντῆρι (as she sat) σ 190.

κλίνω. 3 sing. aor. ἔκλῑνε Ξ 510: χ 121. κλῖνε Ψ 510. 3 pl. ἔκλῑναν Ε 37, Θ 435: δ 42. κλῖναν ι 59. 3 sing. subj. κλίνῃσι Τ 223. Pple. κλίνας φ 137, 164. Pl. κλίναντες Λ 593, Ν 488, Χ 4. Fem. sing. κλίνᾱσα Γ 427. Aor. pple. mid. κλῑνάμενος ρ 340. 3 sing. aor. pass. ἐκλίνθη Γ 360, Ζ 468, Η 254, Ν 543: χ 17. κλίνθη Ψ 232.

ἐκλίθη τ 470. 3 dual κλινθήτην Κ 350. Infin. κλινθῆναι Ψ 335. κλιθῆναι α 366, σ 213. 3 pl. pf. κεκλίαται Π 68: δ 608. Pple. κεκλιμένος, -η Γ 135, Ε 709, Λ 371, Ο 740, Φ 18, 549, Χ 3: ζ 307, λ 194, ν 235, ρ 97. 3 sing. plupf. ἐκέκλιτο Ε 356. κέκλιτο Κ 472. (ἀνα-, ἀπο-, ἐγ-, ἐπι-, κατα-, μετα-, παρα-, προσ-, ὑπο-.) (1) To turn (the eyes): ὄσσε πάλιν κλίνασα Γ 427.—(2) To cause (a foe) to give way, put (him) to flight: Τρῶας ἔκλιναν Δαναοί Ε 37. Cf. ι 59.—(3) To turn the fortune of (a battle): ἐπεί ῥ' ἔκλινε μάχην ἐννοσίγαιος Ξ 510.—To cause (the balance) to incline or turn. Fig. of deciding a battle: ἐπὴν κλίνῃσι τάλαντα Ζεύς Τ 223.—(4) To cause to lean, set, support (against something): σάκε' ὤμοισι κλίναντες (*i.e.* so holding the shields that the lower edges touched or nearly touched the ground and the upper rested against the shoulders) Λ 593 = Ν 488, Χ 4, κλῖνε μάστιγα ποτὶ ζυγόν Ψ 510. Cf. Ψ 171, Θ 435: = δ 42, φ 137 = 164, χ 121.—In mid., to lean or support oneself (against something): κλινάμενος σταθμῷ ρ 340.—(5) In pass., to incline oneself or lean in a specified direction: κλινθῆναι ἐπ' ἀριστερά Ψ 335.—To incline oneself aside, bend or turn aside or away: ἐκλίνθη καὶ ἀλεύατο κῆρα Γ 360 = Η 254. Cf. Ζ 468.—Sim. of a part of the body: ἐκλίνθη ἑτέρωσε κάρη Ν 543.—To move or go aside: παρὲξ ὁδοῦ κλινθήτην Κ 350.—(6) In pass., to lay oneself down, sink down: κλίνθη κεκμηώς Ψ 232.—To lay oneself down, couch: παραὶ λεχέεσσι κλιθῆναι (παραί advbl.) α 366 = σ 213.—To lie back, recline: κλισμῷ κεκλιμένη ρ 97.—To fall from an upright position, come down: ἐκλίνθη ἑτέρωσε χ 17.—(7) In pass., to lean or support oneself (upon or against something): ἀσπίσι κεκλιμένοι Γ 135. Cf. Λ 371, Φ 549, Χ 3: κίονι κεκλιμένη (*i.e.* her seat resting against it) ζ 307.—Of things, to lean or be supported (against something): ἠέρι δ' ἔγχος ἐκέκλιτο (was leaning) Ε 356. Cf. Φ 18.—To lie, be placed, be: ἔντεά σφι χθονὶ κέκλιτο Κ 472.—To lie, be shed or strewn: φύλλων κεκλιμένων λ 194.—To be turned over or upset: ἐκλίθη [λέβης] τ 470.—(8) In pass., of places, to slope (towards the sea), lie (on the shore of the sea): νήσων, αἵ θ' ἁλὶ κεκλίαται δ 608. Cf. ν 235.—Sim. of a person dwelling or being on the shore of a lake or of the sea: λίμνῃ κεκλιμένος Κηφισίδι Ε 709, ἐν Τρώων πεδίῳ πόντῳ κεκλιμένοι (*i.e.* having no other support or base) Ο 740. Cf. Π 68.

κλισίη, -ης, ἡ [κλίνω. 'A place for lying down'] Locative κλισίηφι Ν 168. A hut or cabin. (1) Of the huts erected by the Greeks on the Trojan shore beside the drawn-up ships: κατὰ κλισίας τε νέας τε Α 487. Cf. Α 322, Β 9, Θ 220, Λ 618, Μ 155, Ν 144, Ξ 392, Ο 409, Ψ 112, Ω 122, etc.: δ 255, θ 501.—In pl. of a group of huts appropriated to a particular chief: πλεῖαί τοι χαλκοῦ κλισίαι [εἰσίν] Β 226. Cf. Α 306, Θ 224 = Λ 7, Ι 71, Τ 263, etc.—And even, app., of a single such hut Η 313 = Ι 669, Ι 263, Λ 834, Μ 1, Ν 253, 256, Ο 478, Τ 141, 179, Ψ 254, 810.—(2) Of a herdsman's hut: σταθμούς τε κλισίας τε Σ 589.—Of the hut of Eumaeus ξ 194, 404, 408, ο 301 = π 1, ο 398, π 159, 178, ρ 516.—(3) App. = κλισμός: τῇ κλισίην ἔθηκεν δ 123. Cf. τ 55.

κλισίηθεν [κλισίη + -θεν (1)]. From one's hut: τὴν κλισίηθεν ἔβαν ἄγοντες Α 391, Ἀχιλῆος κλισίηθεν ἀπούρας (from his hut) Ι 107. Cf. Μ 336, Ν 296, Τ 288, Ψ 564.—In reference to hearing: κλισίηθεν ἀκούσας Λ 603.

κλισίηνδε [acc. of κλισίη + -δε (1)]. To one's hut: ἔβαν κλισίηνδε ἕκαστος Ι 712. Cf. Α 185, Κ 148, Ν 294, Ψ 58, 275, 662: ξ 45, 48.

κλίσιον, τό [as κλισίη]. App., outbuildings about a house: ἔνθα οἱ οἶκος ἔην, περὶ δὲ κλίσιον θέε πάντῃ ω 208.

κλισμός, -οῦ, ὁ [κλίνω]. A seat on which one can recline, an easy chair: εἷσεν ἐν κλισμοῖσιν Ι 200. Cf. Θ 436, Λ 623, Ω 597: ἕζοντο κατὰ κλισμούς τε θρόνους τε (the two words hardly to be distinguished) α 145 = γ 389 = ω 385. Cf. α 132, δ 136, κ 233, ο 134, ρ 86 = 179 = υ 249, ρ 90, 97.

κλῑτύς, ἡ [κλίνω]. Acc. pl. κλιτῦς Π 390. A slope, a hill-side: πολλὰς κλιτῦς ἀποτμήγουσι χαράδραι Π 390: ἐς κλιτὺν ἀναβάς (to higher ground) ε 470.

κλονέω [κλόνος]. (συγ-, ὑπο-.) (1) To drive (foes) in confusion, strike (them) with panic, throw (them) into disorder or disorderly flight: φάλαγγας Ε 96. Cf. Λ 496, 526, Ξ 14 = Ο 7, Φ 533.—Of beasts of prey attacking a herd or flock Ο 324.—Of wind driving flame: πάντῃ κλονέων ἄνεμος φλόγα εἰλυφάζει Υ 492.—Of winds driving clouds Ψ 213.—To strike (a person) with panic, put (him) to headlong flight: Ἕκτορα κλονέων ἔφεπεν Χ 188.—(2) In pass., to be driven in confusion, be in confusion, be panic-stricken, be in disorder or disorderly flight: ὅθι πλεῖστοι κλονέοντο Ε 8, Π 285. Cf. Ε 93, Λ 148, Ξ 59, Ο 448, Σ 7, Φ 528, 554.—To get oneself entangled or impeded: μηδὲ κλονέεσθαι ὁμίλῳ Δ 302.

κλόνος, -ου, ὁ. (1) Confusion, panic, disorder: ἐν κλόνον Ἀργείοισιν ἧκεν Π 729.—(2) A confused or agitated throng, the press of battle: ἰόντα κατὰ κλόνον Π 789. Cf. Ε 167, Π 331, 713, Υ 319, Φ 422.

κλόπιος [κλοπ-, κλέπτω]. Artful, guileful: μύθων ν 295.

κλοτοπεύω. App., to talk idly, chatter, or the like: οὐ χρὴ κλοτοπεύειν Τ 149.

κλύδων, ὁ [κλυδ-, κλύζω]. The surge of the sea: ὄφρ' ἀπὸ τοίχους λῦσε κ. τρόπιος μ 421.

†κλύζω. 3 pl. pa. iterative κλύζεσκον Ψ 61. 3 sing. aor. pass. ἐκλύσθη Ξ 392: ι 484, 541. (1) Of waves, to wash up, break Ψ 61.—(2) In pass., of the sea, to wash up, rise or surge up: ἐκλύσθη θάλασσα ποτὶ κλισίας τε νέας τε Ξ 392. Cf. ι 484 = 541.

κλύον, with augment **ἔκλυον**, *aor.* Imp. κλῦθι Α 37, 451, Ε 115, Κ 278, Π 514, Ψ 770: β 262, γ 55, δ 762, ε 445, ζ 324, ι 528. Pl. κλῦτε Β 56, Σ 52: δ 722, ζ 239, ξ 495, ο 172. Pf. imp. κέκλυθι Κ 284: ξ 462, ο 307. Pl. κέκλυτε Γ 86, 97, 304,

456, H 67, 348, 368, Θ 5, 497, P 220, T 101 : β 25, η 186, κ 189, ρ 370, σ 43, φ 68, ω 443, etc. (ἐπι-.) (1) To hear. With acc. of what is heard: Εκτορος αὐδήν N 757. Cf. Δ 455, O 270 : β 297.—With genit. : ἐκυρῆς ὀπός X 451. Cf. Π 76 : δ 831, κ 311.—With genit. of person heard : τοῦ μεγάλ' ἔκλυεν αὐδήσαντος δ 505.—(2) To learn by hearing, hear: ἀγγελίην τινά Π 13 : β 30, 42. Cf. ξ 89, τ 93.—Without expressed object: μάλιστα δέ τ' ἔκλυον αὐτοί (app., their happiness comes home to themselves most of all) ζ 185 (cf. N 734).—With genit. of person from whom a thing is heard and infin.: οὐδ' ἔκλυον αὐδήσαντος ἄνδρ' ἕνα τοσσάδε μητίσασθαι K 47.—(3) To listen, hearken, give ear: κλῦτε, φίλοι (hearken to me) B 56. Cf. P 220, Σ 52: δ 722, η 186 = θ 26 = 97 = 387 = 536, ξ 462 = ο 307, ξ 495.—With genit. of person : κέκλυτέ μευ Γ 86, 456, Θ 5, etc. Cf. Γ 97: κλῦτέ μευ ζ 239, ο 172. Cf. β 25, σ 43, φ 68, ω 443, etc.—With genit. of what is listened to: κέκλυτέ μευ μύθων (my words) κ 189 = μ 271 = 340. Cf. κ 481.—(4) To listen to in sense of yielding or obeying. With genit. of person: τοῦ μάλα κλύον ἠδ' ἐπίθοντο H 379. Cf. I 79, etc. : ἔκλυον αὐδησάσης γ 337, Cf. γ 477, etc.—With a request in acc. : ἐμὸν ἔπος ἔκλυες Ξ 234.—(5) Of a divine power, to lend a favourable ear to one's prayer: κλῦθι, ἄναξ Π 514. Cf. Ψ 770 : γ 55, ε 445, ι 528.—With genit. of the person praying: κλῦθί μευ, ἀργυρότοξε A 37. Cf. A 43, 218, 453, E 115, I 509, K 284, N 303, etc. : τοῦ ἔκλυεν Ἀθήνη γ 385 = ζ 328. Cf. δ 762 = ζ 324, ι 536, υ 102.— With dat. : κλῦθί μοι β 262. Cf. Ω 335.—With the prayer in acc. : ἐμὸν ἔπος ἔκλυες εὐξαμένοιο Π 236.—In genit. : θεά οἱ ἔκλυεν ἀρῆς δ 767.

κλυτοεργός [κλυτός + ἔργω[2]]. Famed for his handiwork. Epithet of Hephaestus θ 345.

κλυτόπωλος [κλυτός + πῶλος]. With splendid foals. Epithet of Hades E 654 = Λ 445, Π 625.

κλυτός, -όν [κλύον. 'Heard of']. (1) Famed, famous, renowned. Epithet of persons : πατέρα α 300 = γ 198 = 308, ζ 36.—With proper names: Ἱπποδάμεια B 742, Ἀχιλλεύς Υ 320. Cf. Ω 789: ε 422, κ 114, λ 310, ω 409.—With the name of a place : Ἄργος Ω 437.—Epithet of Poseidon Θ 440, I 362, Ξ 135, 510, O 173, 184 : ε 423, ζ 326, ι 518. —Of Hephaestus Σ 614.—In the most general and undefined sense : κλυτὰ φῦλ' ἀνθρώπων Ξ 361: κλυτὰ ἔθνεα νεκρῶν κ 526.—(2) Famed for his skill, skilful: τέκτων Ψ 712.—With dat. indicating that in which one excels: Πηλεγόνα κλυτὸν ἔγχεϊ Φ 159.—(3) Epithet of things, goodly, fine, excellent, splendid, noble, or the like : δώματα B 854, τεύχεα E 435, τείχεα Φ 295, δῶρα Ω 458, etc. : δώματα ε 381, εἵματα ζ 58, ἄλσος 321, δῶρα θ 417, λιμένα κ 87, τεύχεα μ 228, ἔργα υ 72, etc.—Applied to animals: μῆλα ι 308.—To one's 'lordly name' : ὄνομα ι 364, τ 183.

κλυτοτέχνης [κλυτός + τέχνη]. Famed for his art. Epithet of Hephaestus A 571, Σ 143, 391 : θ 286.

κλυτότοξος [κλυτός + τόξον]. Famed for the bow. Epithet of Apollo Δ 101, 119, O 55 : ρ 494, φ 267.

Κλῶθες, αἱ [κλώθω, to spin]. (ἐπικλώθω.) The Spinners, figured as agents of αἶσα and as spinning the thread of men's destinies : πείσεται ἅσσα οἱ αἶσα κατὰ Κλῶθές τε γεινομένῳ νήσαντο λίνῳ (κατά advbl., 'against him,' 'for him') η 197.

κλωμακόεις, -εσσα. Explained as rugged, hilly. Epithet of a place : Ἰθώμην B 729.

†κνάω. 3 sing. non-thematic impf. κνῆ. To reduce to small particles, grate : τυρόν Λ 639.

κνέφας, -αος, τό. The evening dusk, the shades of night: ἐπὶ κ. ἦλθεν A 475. Cf. B 413, Θ 500, Λ 194 = 209 = P 455, Ω 351 : γ 329 = ε 225, ι 168 = 558 = κ 185 = 478 = μ 31 = τ 426, σ 370.

κνῆ, 3 sing. non-thematic impf. κνάω.

κνήμη, -ης, ἡ. The lower leg : κνημῖδας περὶ κνήμῃσιν ἔθηκεν Γ 330 = Λ 17 = Π 131 = T 369. Cf. Δ 147, 519, K 573, N 71, Ξ 468, P 386, Σ 411 = Υ 37, Φ 591 : μηρούς τε κνήμας τε θ 135. Cf. τ 469, ω 228.

κνημίς, -ῖδος, ἡ [κνήμη]. (1) A gaiter or legging, doubtless of leather or stuff (in Σ 613, Φ 592 tin being used as the most pliable metal) worn by warriors on the lower leg as a protection against chafing by the edge of the shield: κνημῖδας περὶ κνήμῃσιν ἔθηκεν Γ 330 = Λ 17 = Π 131 = T 369. Cf. Σ 459, 613, Φ 592.—(2) A gaiter or legging worn in agricultural work: περὶ κνήμῃσι βοείας κνημῖδας δέδετο ω 229.

κνημός, -οῦ, ὁ [app. conn. with κνήμη]. A spur or projecting lower part of a mountain : Ἴδης ἐν κνημοῖσιν B 821, Λ 105, Φ 449. Cf. Φ 559, Ψ 117: δ 337 = ρ 128.

κνῆστις, ἡ [κνη-, κνάω]. Dat. κνήστῑ (no doubt for κνήστιϊ). An instrument for grating, a grater: κνῆ τυρὸν κνήστι χαλκείῃ Λ 640.

κνίση, -ης, ἡ. (1) Fat: κνίσην μελδόμενος σιάλοιο Φ 363. Cf. σ 45, 119, υ 26.—(2) The fat of burnt sacrifice : μηροὺς κατὰ κνίσῃ ἐκάλυψαν A 460 = B 423 : = μ 360, γ 457.—(3) The savour of burning or roasting flesh : κνίση οὐρανὸν ἷκεν A 317. Cf. A 66, Δ 49 = Ω 70, Θ 549, I 500 : μ 369, ρ 270.

κνισήεις [κνίση]. Neut. κνισῆεν. Full of the savour of roasting meat: δῶμα κ 10.

κνυζηθμός, -οῦ, ὁ [κνυζάομαι, to whine]. A whining or whimpering: κνυζηθμῷ [κύνες] φόβηθεν π 163.

κνυζόω. To disfigure, mar ν 401, 433.

κνώδαλον, τό. A wild beast ρ 317.

κνώσσω. To sleep, slumber δ 809.

κοῖλος, -η, -ον (κόϝιλος. Cf. L. *cavus* and κῆτος). (1) Having a cavity inside, hollow: δόμον (a nest of wasps or bees) M 169 : λόχον (*i.e.* the Trojan horse) δ 277, θ 515, δόρυ (the same) θ 507, φαρέτρης φ 417.—Of caves μ 84, 93, 317.—(2) Showing a cavity or cleft, fissured : πέτρην Φ 494.—Formed with a cavity into which something is to fit: μεσόδμης β 424 = ο 289.—(3) Fashioned in concave form, hollow. Epithet of ships A 26, E 791, H 78, Θ 98, K 525, etc.: α 211, β 18, γ 344, δ 817, κ 447, ο 420, etc.—Joined with ἐΐσῃ λ 508.—With μέλαινα γ 365, δ 731, κ 272.—(4) Depressed below the surrounding surface, forming a depression, sunken: χαράδρης Δ 454, ὁδοῦ Ψ 419.—Of a grave: κάπετον Ω 797.—Epithet of a place, lying in a hollow, low-lying: Λακεδαίμονα B 581: δ 1.—(5) Concave as viewed in section from the opening, forming an indentation or bay: λιμένος κ 92, αἰγιαλόν χ 385.

κοιμάω [cf. κεῖμαι]. (κατα-.) (1) To cause to sleep, lull to sleep: εἴς μ' ἄτην κοιμήσατε ὕπνῳ μ 372. —To furnish with the means of sleeping, entertain for the night: τὸν αὐτοῦ κοίμησεν γ 397.—Of a beast, to lay (its young) to rest δ 336 = ρ 127.—To cause (the eyes) to close in sleep: κοίμησόν μοι Ζηνὸς ὄσσε Ξ 236.—To hush or still (winds or waves) M 281: μ 169.—To still or allay (pangs): κοίμησον ὀδύνας Π 524.—(2) In mid. and pass., to take one's rest, be laid or retire to rest, lie down to sleep: κοιμήσαντο παρὰ πρυμνήσια νηός A 476. Cf. A 610, Z 246, 250, H 482, I 705, 713, Ω 636, 673: ἀσπαστὸν ἐείσατο κοιμηθῆναι η 343. Cf. δ 295, ζ 16, κ 479, μ 32, ξ 523, τ 49, υ 4, etc.—Of animals: σύας ἔρξαν κοιμηθῆναι ξ 411.—To go to sleep (when one ought to be awake): μὴ φύλακες κοιμήσωνται K 99.—Of the sleep of death: κοιμήσατο χάλκεον ὕπνον Λ 241.—Not implying resting: τίς κ' εἰναλίῳ παρὰ κήτεϊ κοιμηθείη; (*i.e.* lie in ambush) δ 443. —Connoting sexual intercourse: τῇ ἀσπαστὸν ἐείσατο κοιμηθῆναι θ 295.

κοιρανέω [κοίρανος]. (1) To act as leader or chief, play the leader or chief: κοιρανέων δίεπε στρατόν B 207. Cf. Δ 230, 250, E 332, 824.—(2) To be chief, rule, bear rule, hold sway: Λυκίην κάτα M 318: Ἰθάκην κάτα α 247 = π 124, ο 510, φ 346.—To lord it, play the master: μνηστῆρας, οἳ ἐνθάδε κοιρανέουσιν υ 234. Cf. ν 377.

κοίρανος, -ου, ὁ. A leader or chief: εἷς κοίρανος ἔστω B 204. Cf. B 487, 760, H 234 = I 644 = Λ 465, Θ 281.—In sarcasm of Irus: ξείνων καὶ πτωχῶν κοίρανος σ 106.

κοίτη, -ης, ἡ [= next]. A resting-place, a bed or couch: ἀεικελίῳ ἐνὶ κοίτῃ ἄεσα τ 341.

κοῖτος, -ου, ὁ [cf. κεῖμαι, κοιμάω]. (1) A resting-place. In reference to birds χ 470.—(2) Taking of rest, rest, sleep: ὄφρα κοίτοιο μεδώμεθα γ 334. Cf. β 358, η 138, ξ 455, 525, π 481, τ 510, υ 138.—(3) Desire for rest, sleepiness: ἐπεὶ ἕλῃσι κ. ἅπαντας τ 515.

κολεόν. See κουλεόν.

κολλήεις, -εντος [κόλλα, glue. Cf. next]. Made of pieces joined side by side and so arranged as to overlap each other lengthwise and thus give strength: ξυστά O 389.

κολλητός, -ή, -όν [κολλάω, to glue. Cf. prec.]. Having the pieces composing it (closely or skilfully) held or joined together: ξυστὸν κολλητὸν βλήτροισιν O 678 (*i.e.*, app., made as explained under prec. and held together by the βλῆτρα).—Epithet of chariots Δ 366 = Λ 198, T 395, Ψ 286: ρ 117.—Of doors I 583: φ 137 = 164, ψ 194.

κόλλοψ, -οπος, ὁ. A peg holding stretched a string of a lyre φ 407.

κολοιός, -οῦ, ὁ. A jackdaw Π 583, P 755.

κόλος [cf. κολούω]. Having a part lopped off, reduced to a stump: πῆλε κόλον δόρυ Π 117.

κολοσυρτός, -οῦ, ὁ. A troop, band, rout: ἀνδρῶν ἠδὲ κυνῶν M 147, ἀνδρῶν N 472.

κολούω [cf. κόλος]. To cut short (1) Fig., to cause to fail, disappoint, bring to nothing: τὸ μὲν τελέει, τὸ δὲ κολούει Υ 370. Cf. θ 211.—(2) To give in scanty measure, stint: δῶρα λ 340.

κόλπος, -ου, ὁ. (1) A fold formed by the upper part of a woman's πέπλος falling loosely down over the girdle, the bosom of the robe: παῖδ' ἐπὶ κόλπῳ ἔχουσα Z 400. Cf. Z 136, 467, 483, Ξ 219, 223, Σ 398, X 80: κατακρύψασ' ὑπὸ κόλπῳ ο 469.—In pl. in reference to a single person: δεύοντο δάκρυσι κόλποι I 570.—The loose breast of a man's χιτών: αἷμα κόλπον ἐνέπλησεν Υ 471.—(2) A gulf or bay B 560.—(3) The 'bosom' (of the sea): δῦτε θαλάσσης κόλπον Σ 140. Cf. Φ 125: δ 435.—In pl., the hollows or troughs (of the sea): κόλπους ἁλός ε 52.

κολῳάω [κολῳός]. To make an unseemly noise, scold, rail: ἔτι μοῦνος ἐκολῴα B 212.

κολώνη, -ης, ἡ. A hill or mound: αἰπεῖα B 811, Λ 711, Ἀλησίου κολώνη 757.

κολῳός, -οῦ, ὁ [cf. κολοιός]. Unseemly noise, din, disturbance: εἰ ἐν θεοῖσι κολῳὸν ἐλαύνετον Λ 575.

†**κομάω** [κόμη]. Only in pres. pple. in acc. dual and nom. and acc. pl. κομόωντε, -ωντες, -ωντας. (1) To have abundant hair: κάρη κομόωντες, covered as to the head with hair, *i.e.* wearing a full head of hair. Epithet of the Achaeans B 11, Γ 43, Δ 261, H 85, Θ 53, I 45, N 310, Σ 6, T 69, etc.: α 90, β 7, υ 277.—Sim.: κάρη κομόωντας ἑταίρους β 408.—In reference to horses: ἐθείρῃσιν (instrumental dat.) κομόωντε (having flowing manes) Θ 42 = N 24.—(2) ὄπιθεν κομόωντες, wearing the hair long behind, *i.e.* having it cut short or shaved off in front. Epithet of the Abantes B 542.

κομέω. 3 sing. pa. iterative κομέεσκε ω 212, 390. To tend, minister to, relieve the wants of: τὸν χρὴ κομέειν ζ 207.—To look after, care for, provide for, see to the welfare of, keep supplied the wants of: τέκνα λ 250, με μ 450, γέροντα ω 212, 390.—To look after, attend to (horses) Θ 109, 113.—To look after, bestow care upon, tend (dogs) ρ 310, 319.

κόμη, -ης, ἡ. (1) The hair, one's hair: κόμης ἕλε Πηλεΐωνα (by the hair) A 197. Cf. Γ 55, Σ 27, X 406, Ψ 46: δ 198.—In pl. κόμαι Χαρίτεσσιν ὁμοῖαι (like that of the . . .) P 51. Cf. ζ 231 = ψ 158.—(2) A lock dedicated to a divinity: σοὶ κόμην κερέειν Ψ 146 (κόμην = χαίτην 141). Cf. Ψ 151, 152.—(3) Leaves, foliage (app. including the boughs): ἐλαίης ψ 195.

κομιδή, -ῆς, ἡ [κομίζω]. (1) Tendance, ministrations: κ. οἱ θεῷ ὣς ἔμπεδος ἦεν θ 453.—Being looked after or cared for: αὐτόν σ' οὐ κ. ἔχει ω 249. —Entertainment, relief of wants: κομιδῆς κεχρημένοι ξ 124.—Tendance or care bestowed on horses Θ 186, Ψ 411.—On plants ω 245, 247.—(2) Supply of necessaries or comforts, supplies: οὐ κ. κατὰ νῆα ἦεν ἐπηετανός θ 232.

κομίζω [κομέω]. Fut. κομιῶ ο 546. Aor. κόμισσα Λ 738. 3 sing. κόμισε Ξ 456, 463. (ἐ)κόμισσε Β 183, 875, Ν 579: σ 322, υ 68. 3 pl. κόμισαν Γ 378, Ν 196, Ψ 699. 3 sing. subj. κομίσσῃ κ 298. Imp. κόμισσον π 82. 3 sing. aor. mid. (ἐ)κομίσσατο Θ 284: ζ 278, ξ 316. 3 pl. κομίσαντο Α 594. 2 sing. opt. κομίσαιο Χ 286. Imp. κόμισαι Ε 359. (1) To tend, care for, minister to: οὐ κομιζόμενος θάμιζεν θ 451.—(2) To look after, care for, provide for, see to the welfare of, keep supplied the wants of: τὸν γηράσκοντα Ω 541. Cf. σ 322, υ 68, ω 251.—In mid.: κομίσσατό σ' ᾧ ἐνὶ οἴκῳ Θ 284.—(3) To entertain hospitably ο 546, π 82, ρ 113.—(4) To come to the aid of, supply the needs of: οὔ μοι θέμις ἐστὶ κομιζέμεν ἄνδρα τὸν ὅς κε . . . κ 73. Cf. κ 298.—In mid. Ε 359.—To pick up, rescue, come to the relief of, relieve the wants of. In mid.: Σίντιές μ' ἄνδρες κομίσαντο Α 594. Cf. ζ 278, ξ 316.—(5) To attend to, ply (one's work): τὰ σ' αὐτῆς ἔργα κόμιζε Ζ 490 := α 356 = φ 350.—(6) To pick up, take up from the ground: τρυφάλειαν Γ 378. Cf. Β 183, Ν 579.—To carry off as prize, seize upon: χρυσόν Β 875, ἵππους Λ 738.—To carry off, take rightful possession of: δέπας (*i.e.* as a prize) Ψ 699.—To carry off (corpses) from the enemy Ν 196.—To carry, take with one, convey: χηλόν ν 68.—(7) To receive (a missile in one's flesh): κόμισε χροΐ [ἄκοντα] Ξ 456.—In mid. Χ 286.—Sim.: κόμισεν [ἄκοντα] Ἀρχέλοχος Ξ 463.—(8) To guard, see to, look after, watch over: δῶμα π 74, υ 337, κτήματα ψ 355.

κομόωντες, nom. pl. masc. pres. pple. κομάω.

κομπέω [κόμπος]. To emit a sharp sound, to ring, clash: κόμπει χαλκός Μ 151.

κόμπος, ὁ. A noise or din. The sound produced by the whetting of a boar's tusks Λ 417, Μ 149.—By feet beating the ground θ 380.

κοναβέω [κόναβος]. To emit a sharp sound. (1) To ring, clash: ἀμφὶ πήληξ κονάβησεν Ο 648, ἀμφὶ κνημὶς κασσιτέροιο κονάβησεν Φ 593 (a strange expression in reference to so soft a material).—(2) To resound, re-echo: ἀμφὶ νῆες κονάβησαν Β 334 = Π 277. Cf. ρ 542.

κοναβίζω [κόναβος]. = prec. (1) To ring, clash: χαλκὸς κονάβιζεν Ν 498, Φ 255.—Of the din produced by feet beating the ground Β 466.—(2) To resound, re-echo: ἀμφὶ δῶμα κονάβιζεν κ 399.

κόναβος, ὁ. A noise or din: κόναβος κατὰ νῆας ὀρώρει κ 122.

κονίη, -ης, ἡ (ῐ) [κόνις]. (1) Dust: ἀπὸ χαιτάων κονίην βαλόντε Ρ 457. Cf. Λ 282, Ψ 502, 732, 739.—So in pl.: κεῖσθαι μεθ' αἵματι καὶ κονίῃσιν Ο 118. Cf. Π 639, 796, 797: χ 383.—(2) Dust as commonly lying on the ground or on a floor, the dust: ἤριπ' ἐν κονίῃ Ε 75. Cf. Ψ 506.—So in pl.: ἐν κονίῃσιν ὀδὰξ λαζοίατο γαῖαν Β 418. Cf. Γ 55, Δ 536, Ε 588, Ζ 453, Κ 457, Π 471, Σ 26, Ψ 26, etc.: κὰδ δ' ἔπεσ' ἐν κονίῃσιν κ 163 = τ 454, σ 98, 398, χ 329.—(3) Earth, soil: κονίην ὑπέρεπτε ποδοῖιν Φ 271.—(4) Dust stirred up or blown about, a cloud of dust: ὑπό σφισιν ὦρτο κονίη Λ 151. Cf. Β 150, Λ 163, Μ 254, Ψ 365: κονίη ἐκ κρατὸς ὀρώρει λ 600.—So κονίης ὁμίχλην Ν 336, ἐν (μετὰ) στροφάλιγγι κονίης Π 775, Φ 503: ω 39.—(5) In pl., ashes: ἕζετ' (ἧσθαι) ἐπ' ἐσχάρῃ ἐν κονίῃσιν η 153, 160.

κόνις, ἡ. Dat. κόνι Ω 18: λ 191. (1) = κονίη (2): κόνιος δεδραγμένος Ν 393 = Π 486. Cf. Ψ 764, Ω 18.—The particles considered separately with reference to their number: ὅσα ψάμαθός τε κ. τε Ι 385.—(2) = κονίη (4): ὅτε πλείστη κ. ἀμφὶ κελεύθους Ν 335.—(3) = (in sing.) κονίη (5): κόνιν αἰθαλόεσσαν χεύατο κὰκ κεφαλῆς Σ 23: = ω 316 (in Σ doubtless from an altar in front of the hut; but in ω hard to say whence), ἐν κόνι ἄγχι πυρός λ 191.

κονίσαλος, -ου, ὁ [κόνις]. Raised dust, a cloud of dust: ὑπὸ ποσσὶ κ. ὄρνυτο Γ 13. Cf. Ε 503, Χ 401.

κονίω [κόνις]. 3 pl. fut. κονίσουσι Ξ 145. 3 sing. aor. ἐκόνῑσε Φ 407. Nom. pl. masc. pf. pple. pass. κεκονῑμένοι Φ 541. 3 sing. plupf. κεκόνῑτο Χ 405. (1) To cover or befoul with dust: χαίτας Φ 407. Cf. Φ 541, Χ 405.—(2) To raise dust, leave a cloud of dust behind in one's motion: κονίοντες πεδίοιο (in traversing the plain) Ν 820, Ψ 372, 449: θ 122.—To raise a cloud of dust over, fill with dust: πεδίον Ξ 145.

κοντός, -οῦ, ὁ. A pole ι 487.

κοπρέω [κόπρος]. To manure: τέμενος κοπρήσοντες ρ 299.

κόπρος, ἡ. (1) Dung: κυλινδόμενος κατὰ κόπρον Χ 414, Ω 640. Cf. Ω 164: ι 329, ρ 297, 306.—(2) A farm-yard: βοῦς ἐλθούσας ἐς κόπρον κ 411. Cf. Σ 575.

κόπτω. Aor. ἔκοψα κ 127. 3 sing. κόψε Κ 513, Μ 204, Ν 203, Ψ 690, 726: ξ 425. Pple. κόψας Λ 146, Ρ 521. Pf. pple. κεκοπώς σ 335 (app. formed direct fr. κόπος, a striking. Cf. ἀρημένος, δεδουπότος, πεφυζότες). Thematic pf. pple. κεκόπων Ν 60 (*v.l.* κεκοπώς). 3 sing. aor. mid. κόψατο Χ 33. (ἀνα-, ἀπο-, ἐπι-.) (1) To strike, smite: [ἵππους] τόξῳ Κ 513, σκηπανίῳ ἀμφοτέρω κεκόπων (striking them) Ν 60, κόψ' ὄπιθεν κώληπα (kicked) Ψ 726. Cf. Ρ 521, Ψ 690: θ 528, ξ 425, σ 28, 335.—Of a snake Μ 204.—In mid., to smite (one's head) in grief Χ 33.—(2) To strike or dash (against the ground): ποτὶ γαίῃ κόπτεν ι 290.—(3) With ἀπό, to strike *off from* (something): κεφαλὴν ἀπὸ δειρῆς κόψεν Ν 203.—So χεῖράς τ' ἠδὲ πόδας κόπτον χ 477 (app. with continuation of the force of ἀπό in 475).—To cut through, sever: ἀπ' αὐχένα κόψας Λ 146. Cf. κ 127.—(4) To hammer, form, fashion: δεσμούς Σ 379: θ 274.

†**κορέννῡμι**. 2 sing. fut. κορέεις Ν 831. 3 κορέει Θ 379, Ρ 241. 3 sing. aor. opt. κορέσειε Π 747. Nom. dual masc. pf. pple. κεκορηότε σ 372. **Mid.** 3 sing. aor. (ἐ)κορέσσατο Λ 87, 562: υ 59. 1 pl. κορεσσάμεθα Χ 427. 3 pl. subj. κορέσωνται Χ 509: κ 411. 3 pl. opt. κορεσαίατο ξ 28. Pple. κορεσσάμενος Τ 167: ξ 46. Infin. κορέσασθαι Ν 635.

Pass. Aor. (ἐ)κορέσθην δ 541, κ 499. 1 pl. pf. κεκορήμεθα θ 98, ψ 350. 2 κεκόρησθε Σ 287. Nom. pl. masc. pple. κεκορημένοι ξ 456. **(1)** To sate, satiate, satisfy: Τρώων κύνας Θ 379, Ν 831, Ρ 241. Cf. Π 747.—**(2)** In pf. act. and in mid. and pass., to take, in pf. to have, one's fill of something material or immaterial: ἐπεί κε κύνες κορέσωνται Χ 509.—With genit.: φυλόπιδος κορέσασθαι Ν 635. Cf. Λ 562, Τ 167: δαιτὸς κεκορήμεθα φόρμιγγός τε (have had our fill of . . .) θ 98. Cf. κ 411, ξ 28, 46, 456, σ 372.—In reference to misfortune, etc.: πολέων κεκορήμεθ' ἀέθλων (have had troubles enough, app. implying that they had now come to an end) ψ 350.—With pple.: ἦ οὔ πω κεκόρησθε ἐελμένοι ἔνδοθι πύργων; (had enough of being . . .) Σ 287. Cf. Χ 427: ἐπεὶ κλαίουσα κορέσσατο υ 59. Cf. δ 541 = κ 499.—**(3)** In mid., to become wearied or worn out. With pple.: ἐπεί τ' ἐκορέσσατο χεῖρας τάμνων δένδρεα (as to his hands, when his hands have grown weary) Λ 87.

κορέω. To cleanse by sweeping, sweep, sweep out: δῶμα κορήσατε υ 149.

κορθύω [κορθ-, κορυθ-, κόρυς]. In mid., of the sea, to rise into crests: κῦμα κορθύεται Ι 7.

κορμός, -οῦ, ὁ [κορ-, κείρω]. The (bare) trunk of a tree: κορμὸν ἐκ ῥίζης προταμών ψ 196.

κόρος, -ου, ὁ [κορέννυμι]. Satiety, one's fill: πάντων κόρος ἐστὶν Ν 636. Cf. Τ 221: δ 103.

κόρση, -ης, ἡ. One of the temples of the head (= κρόταφος (1)): τὸν βάλε δουρὶ κόρσην Δ 502, ξίφει ἤλασε κόρσην Ε 584, Ν 576.

κορυθάϊξ, -ῖκος [κορυθ-, κόρυς + ἀϊκ-, ἀΐσσω]. = next. Epithet of Enyalius Χ 132.

κορυθαιόλος [κορυθ-, κόρυς + αἰόλος]. With glancing helm. Epithet of Hector Β 816, Γ 83, Ε 680, Ζ 263, Η 158, Λ 315, Μ 230, Ο 246, Ρ 96, Σ 21, Τ 134, Υ 430, Χ 249, etc.—Of Ares Υ 38.

κόρυμβον, τό [κορ- as in κορυφή]. App. = ἄφλαστον: νηῶν κόρυμβα Ι 241.

κορύνη, -ης, ἡ. A club used as one's weapon Η 141, 143.

κορυνήτης, ὁ [κορύνη]. The club-bearer, he who fights with the club. Of Areïthous Η 9, 138.

κόρυς, -υθος, ἡ [cf. κορυφή]. Acc. κόρυν Ν 131, Π 215. κόρυθα Ζ 472, Λ 351, Ν 188, Ο 125, Σ 611, etc. Dat. pl. κορύθεσσι Η 62, Ξ 372, Ρ 269. A helmet, helm Γ 362, Ε 4, Ζ 470, Η 62, Λ 351, Μ 160, etc.: τ 32, ω 523.

κορύσσω [κορύθ-σω. κορυθ-, κόρυς]. Aor. pple. mid. κορυσσάμενος Τ 397. Pf. pple. pass. κεκορυθμένος, -ου Γ 18, Δ 495, Λ 43, Ν 305, Π 802, Ρ 3, Υ 117, etc.: φ 434, χ 125. **(1)** To arm, equip. In pf. pple. pass., armed, equipped: αἴθοπι χαλκῷ Δ 495, Ν 305, Υ 117, etc.: φ 434.—Of spears, armed, headed (with . . .): δοῦρε κεκορυθμένα χαλκῷ Γ 18, Λ 43: = χ 125.—So the pple. alone: ἔγχος κεκορυθμένον Π 802.—**(2)** In mid., to arm or equip oneself: κορύσσετ' Ἀχιλλεύς Τ 364. Cf. Η 206, Κ 37, Π 130, Ρ 199, Τ 397: μ 121.—Implying getting oneself into motion for the fight: τὼ κορυσσέσθην, ἅμα δὲ νέφος εἵπετο πεζῶν Δ 274.—**(3)** To marshal, set in array: πόλεμον Β 273.—**(4)** In mid., to rear the head. Of Eris: ὀλίγη πρῶτα κορύσσεται Δ 442.—**(5)** To cause (water) to rise into crests: κόρυσσε κῦμα ῥόοιο Φ 306.—In mid., to rise into crests: πόντῳ κορύσσεται [κῦμα] Δ 424.

κορυστής, ὁ [κορύσσω]. A marshaller of men, a commander or chief: ἄνδρα κορυστήν Δ 457. Cf. Θ 256, Ν 201, Π 603, Σ 163.

κορυφή, -ῆς, ἡ [cf. κόρυς]. **(1)** The head. Of a horse Θ 83.—**(2)** The top or a top of a mountain or rock (but the pl., when used of a single mountain, gen. hardly to be distinguished from the sing.): ἀκροτάτῃ κορυφῇ Οὐλύμποιο Α 499 = Ε 754 = Θ 3, ἐν κορυφῇσι καθέζετο Θ 51. Cf. Β 456, Γ 10, Λ 183, Μ 282, Ξ 157, 228, Π 144, Υ 60, etc.: β 147, ι 121, 481, κ 113, μ 74, 76.—The highest point of a mountainous island: ἐπ' ἀκροτάτης κορυφῆς Σάμου Θρηϊκίης Ν 12.

κορυφόω [κορυφή]. In mid., of waves, to come to a head, break: κορυφοῦται [κῦμα] Δ 426.

κορώνη, -ης, ἡ [for the sense-development cf. Eng. *crow* in sense 'crow-bar' and in the (now obsolete) sense 'door-knocker.'] **(1)** Some kind of sea-bird, commonly translated 'sea-crow': κορῶναι εἰνάλιαι ε 66. Cf. μ 418 = ξ 308.—**(2)** A tip at one end of a bow with a notch to receive the loop of the string: χρυσέην ἐπέθηκε [τόξῳ] κορώνην Δ 111.—**(3)** A curved projection on a door serving as a handle and as a means of securing the end of the bolt-strap: θύρην ἐπέρυσσε κορώνῃ α 441, ἱμάντ' ἀπέλυσε κορώνης φ 46. Cf. η 90, φ 138 = 165.

κορωνίς [κορώνη]. Curved. Epithet of ships (referring to the upward curve at bow and stern): νηυσὶ (νήεσσι) κορωνίσιν Α 170, Β 297, 392, 771 = Η 229, Ι 609, Λ 228, Ο 597, Σ 58 = 439, Σ 338, Υ 1, Χ 508, Ω 115, 136: τ 182, 193.

κοσμέω [κόσμος]. (ἀπο-, κατα-.) **(1)** To set in order, draw up, marshal, array, be in charge of: κοσμῆσαι ἵππους τε καὶ ἀνέρας ἀσπιδιώτας Β 554. Cf. Β 704, 727, Γ 1, Λ 51, Μ 87, Ξ 379, 388.—In mid.: κοσμησάμενος πολιήτας Β 806.—**(2)** To divide into communities or bodies: Ῥόδιοι διὰ τρίχα κοσμηθέντες Β 655. Cf. ι 157.—**(3)** To prepare, make ready: δόρπον η 13.

κοσμητός, -ή, -όν [κοσμέω]. (Well-)ordered, trim: πρασιαί η 127.

κοσμήτωρ, -ορος, ὁ [κοσμέω]. A marshaller of men, a commander or chief: κοσμήτορε λαῶν Α 16 = 375, Γ 236: κοσμήτορι λαῶν σ 152.

κόσμος, -ου, ὁ. **(1)** An ornament or adornment: κ. ἵππῳ Δ 145.—Array, dress: ἐπεὶ πάντα περὶ χροῒ θήκατο κόσμον Ξ 187.—**(2)** Preparation, contrivance: ἵππου κόσμον ἄεισον (*i.e.* tell of the stratagem) θ 492.—**(3)** Order, due order: κατὰ κόσμον, in order, duly, as one would have a thing done, aright Κ 472, Λ 48 = Μ 85, Ω 622: θ 489, ξ 363.—So κόσμῳ (in due order) ν 77.—With negative, unduly, in unseemly wise, not in accordance with decency, right feeling or regard for established usage: οὐ κατὰ κόσμον Β 214. Cf. Ε 759, Θ 12 (with πληγείς, 'with no measured stroke'), P 205 : γ 138, θ 179, υ 181.—So οὐ κόσμῳ (in rout) M 225.

κοτέω [κότος]. Dat. sing. masc. pf. pple. κεκοτηότι Φ 456 : ι 501, τ 71, χ 477. 3 sing. aor. mid. κοτέσσατο Ψ 383. 3 sing. subj. κοτέσσεται E 747, Θ 391 : α 101. Pple. κοτεσσάμενος E 177, Π 386 : ε 147. Fem. κοτεσσαμένη Ξ 191, Σ 367 : τ 83. To bear resentment, cherish wrath, be in wrath (in aor., to conceive resentment, grow wroth) : οὐδ' ὄθομαι κοτέοντος A 181, μετ' Ἀδμήτου υἱὸν κοτέουσα βεβήκει Ψ 391, κεκοτηότι θυμῷ (with resentment, rancour, rage, in their hearts) Φ 456 : ι 501, τ 71, χ 477.—With dat.: ἀλλήλοισιν κοτέοντε Γ 345. Cf. K 517, Ξ 143.—In mid., with dat. : τῷ Ἀχαιοὶ κοτέοντο B 223, κοτεσσάμενος Τρώεσσιν E 177. Cf. E 747, Π 386, Σ 367, Ψ 383, Θ 391 : = α 101, ε 147, τ 83.—With genit. of the cause: τῆσδ' ἀπάτης κοτέων Δ 168. —With the cause expressed by an acc. In mid. : κοτεσσαμένη τό γε, οὕνεκα . . . Ξ 191.

κοτήεις [prob. for κοτέσϝεις fr. κοτεσ-, κοτέω]. Bearing resentment or a grudge, in wrath : θεός νύ τίς ἐστι κοτήεις E 191.

κότος, -ου, ὁ. Resentment, a grudge, rancour, jealousy, wrath (cf. χόλος (2)) : μετόπισθεν ἔχει κότον A 82, αἴ κε μὴ κότῳ ἀγάσησθε (look on him with grudging jealousy) Ξ 111. Cf. Θ 449, N 517, Π 449 : λ 102, ν 342.

κοτύλη, -ης, ἡ. (1) A cup X 494 : ο 312, ρ 12. —(2) The socket of the hip-joint (resembling a shallow cup) (= ἰσχίον) E 306, 307.

κοτυληδών, -όνος [κοτύλη]. Locative pl. κοτυληδονόφιν. In pl., the suckers of the cuttle-fish (so called from their cup-like shape) : πρὸς κοτυληδονόφιν [πουλύποδος] λάϊγγες ἔχονται ε 433.

κοτυλήρυτος [app. κοτύλη + ῥυ-, ῥέω]. Thus, (caught in cups and) poured out from them on the ground : ἀμφὶ νέκυν κοτυλήρυτον ἔρρεεν αἷμα Ψ 34.

κουλεόν, -οῦ, τό. Also **κολεόν.** The sheath or scabbard of a sword : ἕλκετ' ἐκ κολεοῖο ξίφος A 194. Cf. A 220, Γ 272 = T 253, H 304 = Ψ 825, Λ 30, M 190 : θ 404, κ 333, λ 98.

κούρη, -ης, ἡ [fem. of κοῦρος]. (1) A girl or young woman (commonly translatable 'maid,' 'maiden,' but not in itself implying maidenhood) A 98, 111, 336, B 872, I 637, Π 56, T 272, Ω 26, etc. : ζ 15, 20, 47, 74, η 2, θ 468, κ 105, σ 279, υ 74, ω 518, etc.—(2) A daughter, one's daughter : κούρην Βρισῆος A 392. Cf. B 598, E 875, I 388, N 173, Ξ 321, Φ 506, etc. : κ. Διός β 296. Cf. α 329, β 433, δ 10, ζ 22, λ 283, ν 356, ο 233, τ 518, ω 58, etc.

κούρητες, οἱ [κοῦρος]. = κοῦρος (1) : δῶρα φέρον κούρητες Ἀχαιῶν T 248. Cf. T 193.

κουρίδιος, -η, -ον [perh. fr. κείρω, referring to a custom of cutting a bride's hair before marriage]. (1) Of a wife, wedded, lawful : ἀλόχου A 114. Cf. H 392, Λ 243, N 626, T 298 : ν 45, ξ 245, ο 356.—Applied to a husband : πόσιν E 414. Cf. λ 430, τ 266, ψ 150, ω 196, 200.—Absol. in masc., a husband : κουριδίοιο τεθνηότος ο 22.—(2) Belonging to a wedded pair, nuptial : λέχος O 40, δῶμα τ 580 = φ 78.

κουρίζω [κοῦρος]. To be a κοῦρος : σάκος, ὃ κουρίζων φορέεσκεν (in his youth) χ 185.

κουρίξ [κουρή, a cutting of the hair, fr. κείρω]. By the hair : ἔρυσάν μιν κ. χ 188.

κοῦρος, -ου, ὁ [perh. fr. κείρω, referring to a cutting of a lock from a boy's head at the age of puberty]. (1) A young man, a youth A 470, Δ 321, I 175, O 284, Υ 405, Φ 27 : α 148, β 96, δ 643, η 100, θ 35, ο 151, π 248, χ 30, etc.—With a qualifying sb. (cf. ἀνήρ (1) (d)) : κούρων θηρητήρων (hunters) P 726, κούρῳ αἰσυμνητῆρι (a youth that is a . . ., a youthful . . .) Ω 347. Cf. Σ 494.—With an adj. reinforcing the idea of youthfulness : πρωθῆβαι θ 262. Cf. Ω 347.—So in voc. : κοῦροι νέοι (boys that you are) N 95.—(2) One in youthful vigour, one fit to bear arms, a warrior : κούρους Καδμείων προκαλίζετο E 807, κούροισι ταῦτ' ἐπιτέλλομαι I 68 (the general body of the host as opposed to the γέρουσιν of 70). Cf. Δ 393, I 86, M 196.—(3) A male as opposed to a female : ὅν τινα γαστέρι μήτηρ κοῦρον ἐόντα φέροι Z 59.—(4) A son : κοῦρον Ζήθοιο τ 523.—κοῦροι Ἀχαιῶν (like υἷες Ἀχαιῶν), the Achaeans, Achaeans A 473, B 562, Γ 82, 183, Ξ 505, P 758, X 391 : ω 54. Cf. ἐείκοσι κοῦροι Ἀχαιῶν (here app. implying youth) π 250.—Sim. : κοῦροι Βοιωτῶν B 510, κοῦροι Ἀθηναίων B 551.

κουρότερος [comp. fr. prec.]. (1) Younger, more youthful : μηδ' ἐρίδαινε μετ' ἀνδράσι κουροτέροισιν φ 310.—(2) Youthful rather than old. Absol. : σὺ δὲ κουροτέροισι μετεῖναι (the class of youths, the young) Δ 316.

κουροτρόφος, -ον [κοῦρος + τροφ-, τρέφω]. Rearing youths, nursing-mother. Of Ithaca ι 27.

κοῦφος. Light. (1) In neut. pl. κοῦφα as adv., nimbly : ποσὶ προβιβάς N 158.—(2) In neut. sing. comp. κουφότερον as adv., with lighter heart : μετεφώνεε Φαιήκεσσιν θ 201.

κόψε, 3 sing. aor. κόπτω.

κράατα, acc. pl. κάρη.

κράατος, genit. sing. κάρη.

κραδαίνω [κραδάω]. In pass., to quiver, shake : αἰχμὴ κραδαινομένη κατὰ γαίης ᾤχετο N 504 = Π 614 (app. referring to vibration after the spear's entering the ground). Cf. P 524.

κραδάω. To shake, brandish : ἔγχος H 213. Cf. N 583, Υ 423 : τ 438.

κραδίη, -ης, ἡ [cf. καρδίη, κῆρ]. (Cf. ἦτορ, θυμός, καρδίη, κῆρ, φρήν.) (1) The heart : κ. μοι ἔξω στηθέων ἐκθρῴσκει K 94. Cf. N 282, 442, X 461, Ω 129.—(2) Vaguely as the seat of ἦτορ (2) (b) : ἐν οἱ κραδίῃ στένει ἦτορ Υ 169.—(3) The 'heart,' 'breast,' soul, mind. As the seat or a seat (when coupled with θυμός hardly to be distinguished therefrom) (a) Of the intelligence : ὡς ἄνοον κραδίην ἔχες Φ 441.—(b) Of spirit, courage, stoutness, endurance : ἔμ' ὀτρύνει κ. καὶ θυμὸς ἀγήνωρ K 220, ἐν οἱ κραδίῃ θάρσος βάλεν Φ 547. Cf. A 225, K 244, 319, M 247, N 784 : σοὶ ἐπιτολμάτω κ. καὶ θυμὸς ἀκούειν α 353. Cf. δ 293, σ 61, υ 17, 18, 23.—Of insects Π 266.—(c) Of anger, wrath, passion :

οἰδάνεταί μοι κ. χόλῳ I 646. Cf. ι 635, Ω 584.—(d) Of volition: διχθά μοι κ. μέμονε φρεσίν Π 435. Cf. T 220, Ψ 591: δ 260, θ 204, ξ 517 = ο 339, ο 395, π 81 = φ 342, υ 327, φ 198.—(e) Of feelings, emotions, moods, such as joy, grief, fear, apprehension, regard for others, etc.: ἄχος μιν κραδίην καὶ θυμὸν ἵκανεν B 171. Cf. A 395, Θ 147 = O 208 = Π 52, K 10, Φ 551, Ψ 47: πολλά οἱ κ. προτιόσσετ' ὄλεθρον ε 389. Cf. δ 427 = 572 = κ 309, δ 548, ρ 489, σ 274, 348 = υ 286, υ 13.—(f) Of one's character or disposition: αἰεί τοι κ. ἐστὶν ἀτειρής Γ 60. Cf. ψ 103.

κραίνω, also **κραιαίνω** (app. properly κρᾱαίνω, κραίνω and κρααίνω being related as κρᾱτ- and κρᾱατ-, for which see κάρη). Aor. imp. κρῆνον υ 115. κρήηνον A 41, 504. Pl. κρηήνατε γ 418, ρ 242. Infin. κρῆναι ε 170. κρηῆναι I 101. **Pass.** Fut. infin. κρανέεσθαι I 626. 3 pf. pass. (app. sing.) κεκράανται δ 616, ο 116. 3 plupf. (app. sing.) κεκράαντο δ 132. (ἐπι-.) (1) To accomplish, fulfil, carry out, bring to pass: ἐφετμάς E 508. Cf. I 626: τ 567.—Absol.: κρηῆναι καὶ ἄλλῳ (act on his advice) I 101. Cf. ε 170.—(2) To grant accomplishment or fulfilment of (a wish or prayer): τόδ' ἐέλδωρ A 41, 504: γ 418, ρ 242, ἔπος υ 115.—(3) To finish off or complete the fashioning of (with something): χρυσῷ ἐπὶ χείλεα κεκράαντο (κεκράανται) (the rim thereon, thereof, was (is) finished off with gold) δ 132, 616 = ο 116.—(4) To hold sway, rule θ 391.

κραιπνός, -ή, -όν [cf. καρπάλιμος]. (1) Moving with speed, swift Π 671, 681.—Of winds, rushing, blustering ε 385, ζ 171.—Of the feet, swift, nimble Z 505, P 190, Φ 247, X 138, Ψ 749: ξ 33.—Of the mind, hasty, rash. In comp.: κραιπνότερος νόος [ἐστίν] (hasty rather than the opposite) Ψ 590.—(2) In neut. pl. κραιπνά as adv., with speed, swiftly: κ. προβιβάς N 18: ρ 27. Cf. E 223 = Θ 107.

κραιπνῶς [adv. fr. prec.]. (1) With speed, swiftly: διέπτατο O 83, 172. Cf. Ξ 292: θ 247.—(2) Quickly, speedily, soon: ἐξ ὕπνοιο ἀνόρουσεν K 162.

κραναός, -ή, -όν. Rugged, rocky. Epithet of Ithaca Γ 201: α 247 = π 124, ο 510, φ 346.

κρανέεσθαι, fut. infin. pass. κραίνω.

κράνεια, -ης, ἡ. The cornel-tree Π 767: κ 242.

κρᾱνίον, -ου, τό [app. fr. κρᾱ-. See κάρη]. The head. Of horses Θ 84.

κρᾱσί, dat. pl. κάρη.

κρᾶτα, acc. sing. κάρη.

κραταιγύαλος [κραταιός + γύαλον]. With solid plates: θώρηκες T 361.

κραταιΐς, ἡ [κραταιός. Cf. ἥμερος, ἡμερίς]. An inherent power or force: τότ' ἀποστρέψασκε [λᾶαν] κραταιΐς (*i.e.* the tendency of the stone to move towards a lower level) λ 597. Cf. Κράταιϊς (also accented Κραταιΐς), the mother of Scylla μ 124 (a personification of the wild forces of nature).

κραταιός, -ή, -όν [κράτος]. Strong, mighty, powerful: Κρόνου υἷε N 345. Cf. ο 242, σ 382.—Of a wild beast Λ 119.—Epithet of μοῖρα, compelling, resistless E 83 = Π 334 = Υ 477, E 629, Π 853 = Ω 132, T 410, Φ 110, Ω 209.

κραταίπεδος [κραταιός + πέδον, the ground]. Solid, firm: οὖδας ψ 46.

κρατερός, -ή, -όν [κράτος. Cf. καρτερός]. Instrumental fem. κρατερῆφι Φ 501: ι 476, μ 210. (1) Strong, mighty, powerful, stout, staunch: αἰχμητής Γ 179. Cf. Γ 429, Δ 87, E 244, Z 97, N 90, O 164, Π 716, P 204, Φ 566, etc.: ἐμὸς υἱός, ἅμα κρατερὸς καὶ ἀμύμων γ 111. Cf. λ 255, 265.—Absol.: γῆ, ἥ τε κατὰ κρατερόν περ ἐρύκει Φ 63.—Of a lion δ 335 = ρ 126.—Of parts of the body: ὀδοῦσιν (of a lion) Λ 114, 175 = P 63: χερσίν δ 288.—Sim.: πρόφερε κρατερὸν μένος K 479, κρατερῆφι βίηφιν Φ 501, κρατερὴ ἲς Ὀδυσῆος Ψ 720. Cf. N 60, P 742.—In bad sense, that abuses his power, violent: κύνας ἆσαι, ἀνδρὶ πάρα κρατερῷ Ω 212.—(2) Epithet of heroes, etc. B 622, Δ 89, 401, E 385, 392, Z 130, H 38, M 129, 366, 387, Π 189, Φ 546, 553, Ψ 837, etc.: δ 11, ι 407, 446, ο 122.—Of Ares B 515.—Of Φόβος N 299.—Of Hades N 415: λ 277.—Of Ἔρις Υ 48.—(3) Of things, capable of resisting force, stout: ἀσπίδι Γ 349, P 45.—Capable of producing an intended effect, stout: βέλος E 104. Cf. Θ 279, Σ 477: ω 170.—Of fire, against which nothing can stand, devouring λ 220.—Of bonds, restraining tightly, strict E 386: θ 336, 360.—(4) Of feelings, mental or bodily states, or the like, taking strong hold of one, overpowering, overmastering: ἄλγεα B 721, τρόμος Z 137, λύσσα I 239. Cf. Λ 249, Φ 543: δέος ξ 88. Cf. ε 13, 395, κ 376, λ 593, ο 232, ρ 142.—Of necessity, compelling, resistless: ἀνάγκη Z 458: κ 273.—Of rebuke, that bears heavily upon one, oppresses the heart: ἐνιπήν E 492.—Of an injunction, stern, harsh: μῦθον A 25 = 379.—Strict, requiring implicit obedience: μῦθον A 326, Π 199.—Of speech, bold, defiant: μῦθον O 202.—Of fighting, hotly contested, fierce. Epithet of ὑσμίνη: διὰ κρατερὰς ὑσμίνας B 40. Cf. Δ 462, E 84, Ξ 448, Π 447, 567, etc.: λ 417.—Of ἔρις N 358, Π 662.—Of φύλοπις Σ 242: π 268.—Of defence, stout, determined: ἀμφίβασιν E 623.—Strengthening βίηφι (βίη (6) (b)) ι 476, μ 210.

κρατερόφρων, -ονος [κρατερός + φρήν]. Stout-hearted Ξ 324: δ 333 = ρ 124, λ 299.—Of a beast K 184.

κρατερῶνυξ, -υχος [κρατερός + ὄνυξ]. With solid hooves, strong-hoofed. Epithet of horses and mules E 329, Π 724, 732, Ω 277: ζ 253, φ 30.—Epithet of wolves, with powerful claws, strong-clawed κ 218.

κρατερῶς [adv. fr. κρατερός]. With or by the exercise of strength or force, violently, with violence: ἐμάχοντο M 152: κὰδ δ' ἔβαλε κ. δ 344 = ρ 135.—In reference to speech, with vehemence, right out, without weighing one's words: ἀγόρευσεν Θ 29 = I 694. Cf. I 431.—To defence or resistance, stoutly, staunchly Λ 410, N 56, O 666, Π 501 = P 559.—To indignation, highly, intensely: κ. ἐνεμέσσα N 16 = 353.

κράτεσφι, locative κάρη.

κρατευταί, *αἱ*. Supports on each side of a fire-place on which to rest the ends of spits, 'dogs': ὀβελοὺς κρατευτάων ἐπαείρας Ι 214.

κρατέω [κράτος]. (ἐπι-.) (1) To hold sway, rule, have power: μέγα κρατέων ἤνασσεν Π 172. Cf. ν 275, ο 298, ω 431.—To rule the fight, have the upper hand, hold the issues of war in one's hands, show matchless prowess: ὅς τις ὅδε κρατέει Ε 175 = Π 424. Cf. Φ 214, 315.—(2) To be ruler over, hold sway or exercise power among, be lord of. With genit.: Ἀργείων Α 79. Cf. Α 288: ο 274.—With dat.: νεκύεσσιν λ 485. Cf. π 265.

κράτος, *τό* [cf. κάρτος]. (1) Physical strength, might, stoutness, prowess: δόλῳ, οὔ τι κράτεϊ γε Η 142. Cf. Ν 484, Π 524, Υ 121: α 70, φ 280.—(2) Might, power, authority, influence: σὸν κ. αἰὲν ἀέξειν Μ 214. Cf. Β 118 = Ι 25, Ι 39, Π 54: ε 4.—The power of rule, the leading voice, 'the say': τοῦ κ. ἔστ' ἐνὶ οἴκῳ (δήμῳ) α 359 = φ 353, λ 353.—(3) Of a bird of omen, app., efficacy in boding, significance Ω 293 = 311.—(4) That which gives a thing its peculiar excellence: τὸ (*i.e.* the process described) σιδήρου κ. ἐστὶν ι 393.—(5) Mastery, victory, the upper hand: ἐπὶ Τρώεσσι τίθει κ. Α 509. Cf. Ζ 387, Λ 192, 207, 319, 753, Ν 486, 743, Ο 216, Ρ 206, Σ 308.—A signal success or achievement, a triumph: Τρωσί κε μέγα κ. ἐγγυάλιξεν Ρ 613.

κρᾱτός, genit. κάρη.

κρατύς [κράτος]. = κρατερός (2). Epithet of Hermes Π 181, Ω 345: = ε 49, 148.

κράτων, genit. pl. κάρη.

κρέας, *τό*. Pl. κρέα (for κρέαα) μ 395, χ 21. Genit. κρειῶν (prob. for κρεάων) Λ 551, Μ 300, Ρ 660: α 141, δ 88, ι 9, ξ 28, π 49, ρ 258, etc. κρεῶν ο 98. Dat. κρέασι Θ 162, Μ 311. Acc. κρέα Δ 345, Θ 231, Ι 217, Λ 776, Χ 347, Ω 626: α 112, γ 33, ι 162, ξ 109, ο 140, ρ 331, ω 364, etc. (1) Flesh: κ. ὀπτόν π 443. Cf. ρ 344.—A piece of flesh: τοῦτο πόρε κ. θ 477.—(2) In pl. in collective sense, flesh: ὀπταλέα κρέα ἔδμεναι Δ 345. Cf. Θ 162 = Μ 311, Θ 231, Ι 217 = Ω 626, Λ 551 = Ρ 660, Λ 776, Μ 300, Χ 347: κρειῶν πίνακας α 141. Cf. α 112, γ 33, δ 88, ι 9, μ 19, ο 98, ρ 258, υ 348, ω 364, etc.

κρεῖον[1], *τό* [κρέας]. A block on which to chop or cut flesh Ι 206.

κρεῖον[2], voc. κρείων.

κρείσσων, -ονος [for κρετίων, comp. fr. κρατ-ύς]. Neut. κρεῖσσον ζ 182. (1) Physically stronger or mightier: κ. εἰς ἐμέθεν ἔγχει (with the . . .) Τ 217. Cf. Υ 334, Φ 190, 191: χ 353.—Absol. Φ 486.—(2) Proving the stronger, victorious, having the upper hand: ὁππότερός κε κ. γένηται Γ 71 = 92: = σ 46. Cf. σ 83, χ 167.—(3) Mightier, more powerful or potent, having more authority: κ. βασιλεύς [ἐστιν] Α 80. Cf. Π 688, Ρ 176, Ψ 578: φ 345.—(4) Absol. in neut., anything better or more excellent: οὐ τοῦ γε κ. [ἐστιν] ζ 182.

κρείων, -οντος, *ὁ* [cf. κραίνω]. Voc. κρεῖον θ 382. ι 2, λ 355, etc. Fem. κρείουσα Χ 48. (1) A ruler or lord: ὕπατε κρειόντων Θ 31: = α 45 = 81 = ω 473.—(2) Epithet of Agamemnon, lordly, august Α 130, Β 100, Γ 118, Δ 153, Ε 537, Ζ 63, Ι 62, Λ 126, Ξ 41, Π 58, Ψ 110, etc.—Applied to Alcinous θ 382 = 401 = ι 2 = λ 355 = 378 = ν 38.—To Agapenor Β 609.—To Helicaon Γ 123.—To Haemon Δ 296.—To Elephenor Δ 463.—To Eumelus Ψ 354.—To Amaryncеus Ψ 630.—Even to Eteoneus, Menelaus's θεράπων δ 22.—Epithet also of Poseidon Θ 208, Ν 10, 215, Ξ 150, Φ 435: ε 282, 375.—And of a river: Ἀχελώϊος Φ 194.—(For εὐρὺ κρείων, εὐρυκρείων, see εὐρύς (2) (b).)—Applied to offspring: παίδων κρειόντων (app., who might have grown up to be chiefs among the people) Ω 539.—(3) In fem.: Λαοθόη, κρείουσα γυναικῶν Χ 48 (pre-eminent among women (partitive genit.), pearl of women).

κρειῶν, genit. pl. κρέας.

†κρεμάννῡμι. Fut. κρεμόω (for κρεμάω) Η 83. 3 sing. aor. κρέμασε θ 67, 105. Nom. pl. masc. pple. κρεμάσαντες Θ 19. 2 sing. impf. pass. (fr. κρέμαμαι) ἐκρέμω (for ἐκρέμαο) Ο 18, 21. (ἀγ-, ἀπο-, παρα-.) (1) To hang, suspend: σειρὴν ἐξ οὐρανόθεν Θ 19.—In pass., to hang, be suspended: ὅτε τ' ἐκρέμω ὑψόθεν Ο 18. Cf. Ο 21.—(2) To hang up, suspend: ἐκ πασσαλόφι φόρμιγγα θ 67 = 105. Cf. Η 83.

κρεῶν, genit. pl. κρέας.

κρήγυος. Good. Absol.: τὸ κρήγυον, that which is good or to be desired Α 106.

κρήδεμνον, -ου, *τό* [κρη-, κάρη + δέω]. (1) A woman's or goddess's head-covering (app. = κάλυμμα, καλύπτρη): κρηδέμνῳ καλύψατο Ξ 184. Cf. Χ 470: ἀπὸ κρήδεμνα βαλοῦσαι ζ 100. Cf. ε 346, 351, 373, 459.—In pl. in the same sense: ἄντα παρειάων σχομένη κρήδεμνα α 334 = π 416 = σ 210 = φ 65.—(2) Like κάρηνον (3) in reference to cities, 'the diadem of towers': Τροίης ἱερὰ κρήδεμνα Π 100. Cf. ν 388.—(3) App., the string securing the cover of a wine-jar γ 392.

κρηῆναι, aor. infin. κραίνω.

κρῆθεν [κρη-, κάρη + -θεν (1)]. Only in phrase κατὰ κρῆθεν (also written κατακρῆθεν). (1) Down from the head, from head to foot. Fig.: Τρῶας κατὰ κρῆθεν λάβε πένθος (κατά advbl.) Π 548.—(2) App. on the analogy of κατά with genit. (κατά (II) (1) (b)), down on the head, on to the head: δένδρεα κατὰ κρῆθεν χέε καρπόν λ 588.

κρημνός, -οῦ, *ὁ* [κρημ-, κρεμάννυμι]. A steep bank of a river (overhanging or having the appearance of overhanging): πτῶσσον ὑπὸ κρημνούς Φ 26. Cf. Φ 175, 200, 234, 244.—A similar face of a ditch Μ 54.

κρῆναι, aor. infin. κραίνω.

κρηναῖος, -η, -ον [κρήνη]. Of or pertaining to a spring or fountain: νύμφαι ρ 240.

κρήνη, -ης, *ἡ*. (1) A spring of water Β 305, 734, Ι 14, Π 3, 160, Φ 197, 257: ζ 292, ι 141, κ 350, ν 408.—(2) Such a spring built about and furnished with a basin in which the water collects and can overflow, a fountain: ὅτ' ἐπὶ κρήνην ἀφίκοντο τυκτήν ρ 205. Cf. ε 70, η 129, κ 107, ο 442, υ 158, 162.

κρήνηνδε [acc. of prec. + -δε (1)]. To the fountain: μεθ' ὕδωρ ἔρχεσθε κρήνηνδε υ 154.

κρητήρ, -ῆρος, ὁ [κρη-, κεράννυμι]. (1) A large bowl in which wine was mixed with water for drinking (the drinking being commonly preceded by libation), a mixing-bowl: κρητῆρας ἐπεστέψαντο ποτοῖο Α 470, Ι 175. Cf. Δ 260, Ζ 528, Ι 202, Ψ 741, 778: οἶνον ἔμισγον ἐνὶ κρητῆρσι καὶ ὕδωρ α 110. Cf. α 148, β 330, δ 222, ι 9, κ 356, λ 419, ν 105 (of natural formations in a cave), υ 152, φ 145, etc.—Libation specially referred to: ἀπὸ κρητῆρος Ἀθήνῃ ἀφυσσόμενοι λεῖβον οἶνον Κ 578. Cf. Γ 247, 269, 295, Ψ 219.—A bowl in which nectar was mixed (cf. ε 93): νέκταρ ἀπὸ κρητῆρος ἀφύσσων Α 598.—(2) Referring rather to the contents than to the bowl: πίνοντες κρητῆρας οἴνοιο Θ 232, ζωρότερον κέραιε [κρητῆρα] Ι 203: ἀνὰ κρητῆρα κέρασσεν οἴνου γ 390. Cf. γ 393, η 179 = ν 50, σ 423.

κρῖ, τό [= κριθαί]. Barley Ε 196, Θ 564, Υ 496: δ 41, μ 358.—The growing plant δ 604.

†**κρίζω.** 3 sing. aor. κρίκε. To creak: κρίκε ζυγόν (*i.e.* with the strain) Π 470.

κρῖθαί, αἱ [for κρσ-θαι. Cf. L. *hordeum*]. Barley. The growing plant. In pl.: ἄρουραν πυρῶν ἢ κριθῶν Λ 69. Cf. ι 110, τ 112.

κρίκε, 3 sing. aor. κρίζω.

κρίκος, -ου, ὁ. A ring attached to the boss (ὀμφαλός) on the yoke of a chariot and passed over the ἕστωρ on the pole Ω 272.

κρίνω [cf. L. *cerno*]. 3 sing. aor. ἔκρῖνε Α 309. 3 pl. ἔκρῖναν σ 264. Pple. κρίνας Ζ 188, Π 199: δ 666, ι 90, 195, κ 102, ξ 108. 3 sing. aor. mid. ἐκρίνατο Ε 150: δ 778. 3 pl. imp. κρῖνάσθων θ 36. Pple. κρῖνάμενος Ι 521, Λ 697, Τ 193: δ 530, ω 108. Infin. κρίνασθαι δ 408. Nom. dual masc. aor. pple. pass. κρινθέντε θ 48. Nom. pl. κρινθέντες Ν 129. Pf. pple. mid. and pass. κεκριμένος, -η Κ 417, Ξ 19: ν 182, π 248, ω 107. (ἀπο-, δια-, ὑποκρίνομαι.) (1) To sift, separate: καρπόν τε καὶ ἄχνας Ε 501.—(2) To pick out, select, choose: συῶν τὸν ἄριστον ξ 108.—In mid. Λ 697.—Absol. in mid. ω 108.—In pf. pple. pass., the best, choicest, noblest: κοῦροι κεκριμένοι π 248. Cf. ν 182, ω 107.—(3) To pick out, select, detail, for some service or mission: ἐρέτας ἐείκοσιν Α 309, οὔ τις κεκριμένη [φυλακὴ] ῥύεται στρατόν (having the special duty assigned to them) Κ 417. Cf. Ζ 188: ἀνὰ δῆμον ἀρίστους δ 666, κούρω κρινθέντε δύω καὶ πεντήκοντα βήτην (forming the body detailed for the service) θ 48. Cf. ι 90 = κ 102, ι 195, ξ 217.—Sim. in reference to a wind: πρίν τινα κεκριμένον καταβήμεναι ἐκ Διὸς οὖρον (blowing steadily in one direction, decided, as if dispatched by Zeus on a mission) Ξ 19.—In mid. Ι 521, Τ 193: δ 408, 530, 778.—In mid., to present oneself, get oneself ready for some service: κούρω δύω καὶ πεντήκοντα κρινάσθων θ 36.—(4) To divide, class, arrange: κρῖν' ἄνδρας κατὰ φῦλα (by . . .) Β 362.—(5) To marshal or arrange (troops): ἐπεὶ πάντας στῆσεν ἐῢ κρίνας Π 199, οἱ ἄριστοι κρινθέντες Τρῶας ἔμιμνον (having got themselves together) Ν 129.—Absol., to marshal one's troops Β 446.—(6) In mid. (from the notion of two parties standing in opposition), to measure oneself, pit oneself, against the foe: ὥς κε πανημέριοι κρινώμεθ' Ἄρηϊ (in . . .) Β 385. Cf. Σ 209: ω 507.—(7) To decide (a combat), bring (it) to an issue: οἵ κ' ἔκριναν μέγα νεῖκος πολέμοιο σ 264 (would have decided it (in a case which has not happened), app. implying that they would therefore always do so).—Sim.: ὁπότε μνηστῆρσι καὶ ἡμῖν μένος κρίνηται Ἄρηος (is brought to an issue) π 269.—To settle (a dispute): κρίνων νείκεα πολλά μ 440.—To give (a judgment or doom): οἳ σκολιὰς κρίνωσι θέμιστας Π 387.—(8) In mid., to interpret, expound (cf. ὑποκρίνομαι (1)): τοῖς οὐχ ὁ γέρων ἐκρίνατ' ὀνείρους Ε 150.

κριός, -οῦ, ὁ. A ram ι 447, 461.

κριτός [κρίνω]. Picked out, detailed, or appointed, for some purpose: λαός Η 434: αἰσυμνῆται θ 258.

κροαίνω. Of a horse, to beat the ground with the hoofs, clatter Ζ 507 = Ο 264.

κροκόπεπλος, -ον [κρόκος + πέπλος]. In saffron robe. Epithet of Ἠώς Θ 1, Τ 1, Ψ 227, Ω 695.

κρόκος. The crocus (from a variety of which saffron is obtained; see prec.). Collectively Ξ 348.

κρόμυον, τό. An onion Λ 630: τ 233.

κρόσσαι, αἱ. Applied to some part of the Greek wall protecting the ships (but there is nothing to show what part is meant): κρόσσας πύργων ἔρυον Μ 258, κροσσάων ἐπέβαινον 444.

κροταλίζω [κρόταλον, a rattle, conn. with κροτέω]. To cause to rattle, rattle along: ἵπποι κείν' ὄχεα κροτάλιζον Λ 160.

κρόταφος, -ου, ὁ. (1) One of the temples of the head (= κόρση): τὸν βάλε δουρὶ κόρσην· ἡ δ' ἑτέροιο διὰ κροτάφοιο πέρησεν αἰχμή Δ 502. Cf. Υ 397.—(2) In pl., the temples: κόρυθα κροτάφοις ἀραρυῖαν Ν 188, Σ 611. Cf. Ν 805, Ο 609, 648, Π 104: ὑπὸ κροτάφοισιν ἰούλους ἀνθῆσαι λ 319. Cf. σ 378, χ 102.

κροτέω. To cause to rattle, rattle along: ἵπποι κείν' ὄχεα κροτέοντες Ο 453.

κρουνός, -οῦ, ὁ. A spring of water: κρουνῶν ἐκ μεγάλων Δ 454. Cf. Χ 147, 208.

κρύβδα [κρύπτω]. Without the knowledge of. With genit.: κρύβδα Διός Σ 168.

κρύβδην [as prec.]. Avoiding, so as to avoid, notice, secretly: κρύβδην, μηδ' ἀναφανδά, νῆα κατισχέμεναι λ 455. Cf. π 153.

κρυερός [κρύος, cold, chill]. Chilling, freezing, numbing. Fig. as epithet of φόβος Ν 48.—Of γόος Ω 524: δ 103, λ 212.

κρυόεις, -εντος. Fem. -εσσα. [As prec.] Fig. as epithet of Ἰωκή Ε 740.—Of φόβος Ι 2.

κρυπτάδιος, -η, -ον [κρύπτω]. (1) Secret, clandestine: φιλότητι Ζ 161.—(2) Absol. in neut. pl. κρυπτάδια, secret or veiled designs or purposes: κ. φρονέοντα Α 542.

κρυπτός, -ή, -όν [κρύπτω]. Secret, private, such as cannot be used without special knowledge: κληῗδι Ξ 168.

κρύπτω. 3 sing. pa. iterative κρύπτασκε Θ 272. Fut. κρύψω δ 350, ρ 141. 3 sing. aor. κρύψε λ 244. 3 pl. ἔκρυψαν ξ 357. Subj. κρύψω ν 304. Nom. pl. masc. pple. κρύψαντες Ξ 373. Infin. κρύψαι Σ 397. 3 sing. aor. pass. κρύφθη N 405. Acc. sing. neut. pf. pple. κεκρυμμένον λ 443. Acc. pl. κεκρυμμένα ψ 110. (ἀπο-, ἐγ-, κατα-, ὑπο-.) (1) To hide, hide away, conceal, put away or keep from view or knowledge: ἥ μ' ἐθέλησε κρύψαι χωλὸν ἐόντα Σ 397. Cf. Φ 239: λ 244, ν 304, ξ 357.—(2) To keep private or secret, keep to oneself: σήματα κεκρυμμέν' ἀπ' ἄλλων ψ 110.—(3) To withhold (speech or a communication): ἔπος δ 350 = ρ 141. Cf. λ 443.—(4) To cover up for protection, shield or shelter from harm: σάκεϊ μιν κρύπτασκεν Θ 272. Cf. N 405, Ξ 373.

κρύσταλλος, -ου, ὁ [cf. κρυερός, κρυόεις]. Ice: σακέεσσι περιτρέφετο κρύσταλλος ξ 477. Cf. X 152.

κρυφηδόν [κρύπτω]. Avoiding notice, secretly: ἢ ἀμφαδὸν ἦε κ. ξ 330 = τ 299.

κρύφθη, 3 sing. aor. pass. κρύπτω.

κρύψω, fut. κρύπτω.

κτάμεναι, aor. infin. κτείνω.

κτανέοντα. See κτείνω.

κτάνον, aor. κτείνω.

κτάομαι [cf. κτίζω]. (1) To become the owner of, get, gain, acquire: κτήμασι, τὰ γέρων ἐκτήσατο Πηλεύς I 400.—In reference to slaves: οἰκήων, οὓς κτήσατ' Ὀδυσσεύς ξ 4. Cf. ξ 450.—To found and stock (a house): ἐμοὶ ἐκτήσατο κεῖνος [οἶκον τόνδε] υ 265.—To win (a bride) ω 193.—(2) In pf., to possess, hold, have: ὅσα φασὶν Ἴλιον ἐκτῆσθαι I 402.

κτάσθαι, aor. infin. mid. κτείνω.

κτέαρ, τό [κτάομαι]. Only in dat. pl. κτεάτεσσι. In pl. (1) Possessions, goods, effects, property: υἱὸν ἐπὶ κτεάτεσσι λιπέσθαι E 154. Cf. Z 426 (spoils), I 482, Σ 300, Ψ 829: τοῖσδε κτεάτεσσιν ἀνάσσω δ 93. Cf. α 218, ο 89, ρ 471, υ 289.—(2) Possessions viewed as applied to some end, means, resources: τὴν πρίατο κτεάτεσσιν ἑοῖσιν α 430. Cf. ξ 115, 452, ο 483.

†**κτεατίζω** [κτεατ-, κτέαρ]. Aor. κτεάτισσα Π 57. 3 sing. κτεάτισσε ω 207. Pple. κτεατίσσας β 102, τ 147, ω 137. To become the owner of, get, gain, acquire, win: δουρί [μιν] ἐμῷ κτεάτισσα Π 57. Cf. β 102, τ 147 = ω 137.—To make (a farm), bring (land) into cultivation: ἀγρόν, ὃν Λαέρτης κτεάτισσεν ω 207.

κτείνω. App. acc. sing. masc. secondary pres. pple. in desiderative sense κτανέοντα Σ 309. 3 sing. pa. iterative κτείνεσκε Ω 393. Fut. κτενέω π 404. 2 sing. κτενέεις X 13. 3 κτενέει X 124, Ω 156, 185. κτενεῖ O 65, 68. Infin. κτενέειν N 42, O 702, P 496. 2 sing. aor. κτεῖνας Ω 500. 3 ἔκτεινε Π 594, T 296: δ 188, ψ 8, ω 429. κτεῖνε O 651: δ 547, λ 422, τ 523, ψ 63. 3 pl. ἔκτειναν μ 379. Subj. κτείνω Θ 182. 2 sing. κτείνῃς Υ 186: α 296, λ 120. 3 κτείνῃ Γ 284, E 236. Opt. κτείναιμι ξ 405, υ 42. Pple. κτείνας Z 481, Λ 759, O 587, Π 292: γ 305, 309, δ 257, ξ 380. Pl. κτείναντες ρ 80. Fem. κτείνᾱσα ω 200. Infin. κτεῖναι E 261, 435, Z 167, N 629, Ξ 47, Φ 279: δ 823, ν 426, ξ 282, ο 30, υ 50, 315, ψ 79. Aor. ἔκτανον ψ 363. κτάνον H 155, Λ 672. 2 sing. ἔκτανες X 272. 3 ἔκτανε B 701, Z 416, K 560, Π 849, P 589, Σ 456, T 414, Ω 151, 180, 736: α 30, 36, 299, β 19, γ 307, θ 228, τ 539, 543. κτάνε E 679, P 60, Φ 211, 236, 344: γ 250. 3 pl. ἔκτανον α 108. κτάνον Ω 479. 3 sing. aor. ἔκτα Z 205, M 46: α 300, γ 198, 308, λ 324, 410. 1 pl. ἔκταμεν μ 375. 3 pl. ἔκταν K 526: τ 276. 1 pl. subj. κτέωμεν χ 216. Infin. κτάμεναι E 301, P 8: κ 295, 322. Aor. infin. mid. κτάσθαι O 558. Aor. pple. mid. (in sense of pf. pass.) κτάμενος, -η Γ 375, E 21, 28, N 262, O 554, Π 757, Σ 337, X 75, Ψ 23: χ 401, 412, ψ 45. 3 pl. aor. pass. ἔκταθεν Λ 691: δ 537. (ἀπο-, κατα-.) To kill, slay: τὸν ἔκτανε Δάρδανος ἀνήρ B 701. Cf. A 410, Γ 375, E 301, Λ 691, N 110 (mid., 'let themselves be slain'), Π 292, etc.: ἔκταθεν ἐν μεγάροισιν δ 537. Cf. α 30, β 19, γ 250, κ 295, μ 375, τ 523, etc. —In mid. O 558.—With the corpse as object: νεκρόν, τὸν ἔκταν' Ἀχιλλεύς Ω 151, etc.—Sim.: μετὰ κταμένοισι νέκυσσιν χ 401, ψ 45.—Absol. K 483, Λ 193, N 145, P 454, Φ 220, etc.

κτέρας, τό [κτάομαι]. (1) Something possessed, a possession, chattel, thing: δέπας, μέγα κ. Ω 235. Cf. K 216.—(2) In pl. κτέρεα, a man's favourite possessions burnt on his pyre or placed in his grave; hence κτέρεα κτερίζειν, κτερεΐζειν, to burn or place thus, and so, to perform funeral rites: ἐπί κε κτέρεα κτερίσαιεν Ω 38: ἐπὶ κτέρεα κτερεΐξαι α 291. Cf. β 222, γ 285.—(3) So κτέρεα, funeral rites: ἔλαχόν κε κτερέων ε 311.

κτερεΐζω [κτέρας]. Aor. subj. κτερεΐξω β 222. Infin. κτερεΐξαι α 291. (1) κτέρεα κτερεΐζειν, see prec. (2).—(2) To pay funeral rites to, honour with funeral rites, perform the obsequies of: σὸν ἑταῖρον ἀέθλοισι κτερέϊζε Ψ 646. Cf. Ω 657.

†**κτερίζω** [as prec.]. Fut. κτεριῶ Σ 334. 3 pl. κτεριοῦσι Λ 455, X 336. 3 sing. aor. opt. κτερίσειε γ 285. 3 pl. κτερίσαιεν Ω 38. (1) κτέρεα κτερίζειν, see κτέρας (2).—(2) = prec. (2) Λ 455, Σ 334, X 336.

κτέωμεν, 1 pl. aor. subj. κτείνω.

κτῆμα, -ατος [κτάομαι]. (1) Something possessed, a piece of property, a chattel or thing: μή τι δόμων ἐκ κ. φέρηται ο 19.—(2) In pl. possessions, goods, effects, property, wealth, chattels, things: ὅθι πλεῖστα δόμοις ἐν κτήματα κεῖται I 382. Cf. Γ 70, E 481, H 350, N 626, Σ 292, etc.: πολλὰ κτήματ' ἄγων γ 312. Cf. α 375, β 123, γ 314, δ 175, κ 404, ξ 92, ρ 532, φ 214, etc.

κτῆσις, ἡ [κτάομαι]. Possessions, goods, effects, property, wealth, chattels, things: χηρωσταὶ διὰ κτῆσιν δατέοντο E 158. Cf. Ξ 491, O 663, Σ 512, X 121, T 333: = η 225 = τ 526, δ 687, ξ 62, τ 534.

κτητός [κτάομαι]. That may be acquired or won: κτητοὶ τρίποδές [εἰσιν] I 407.

κτίδεος, -η [(ἰ)κτιδ-, (ἰ)κτίς, the polecat or martin]. Of the skin of the ἰκτίς: κυνέην K 335, 458.

†**κτίζω.** 3 sing. aor. κτίσσε Υ 216. 3 pl. ἔκτισαν λ 263. To people (a tract of country): Δαρδανίην Υ 216.—To found (a city): Θήβης ἕδος λ 263.

κτίλος, -ου, ὁ. A ram Γ 196, Ν 492.

κτίσσε, 3 sing. aor. κτίζω.

κτυπέω [κτύπος]. 3 sing. aor. ἔκτυπε Θ 75, Ο 377, Ρ 595 : φ 413. κτύπε Θ 170. To give forth a sound. Of crushed or falling trees, to crash Ν 140, Ψ 119.—Of Zeus, to thunder Η 479, Θ 75, 170, Ο 377, Ρ 595 : φ 413.

κτύπος, -ου, ὁ. A sound or noise : κτύπον ἀΐεν Κ 532, Διὸς κτύπον (the thunder) Ο 379. Cf. Κ 535, Ρ 175, Τ 363 : π 6, τ 444, φ 237 = 383.—Sound, noise : τόσσος κ. ὦρτο Υ 66. Cf. Μ 338.

κύαμος, -ου, ὁ. A bean Ν 589.

κυάνεος, -η, -ον [κύανος]. (1) Represented in κύανος : δράκοντες Λ 26. Cf. Λ 39, Σ 564.—(2) Dark in hue, dark : φάλαγγες Δ 282 (app. not so much an epithet of φάλαγγες as a reflection in the poet's mind from the preceding storm simile), Τρώων νέφος Π 66 (likening the encircling foes to a threatening storm-cloud), νεφέλη (the darkness of death) Υ 418. Cf. Ε 345, Χ 402, Ψ 188, Ω 94 : νεφέλη μ 75, γαῖα ψάμμῳ κυανέη (dark with sand, showing dark sand) 243. Cf. μ 405 = ξ 303, π 176.—Of divine eyebrows : κυανέῃσιν ἐπ' ὀφρύσι νεῦσε Κρονίων Α 528 = Ρ 209. Cf. Ο 102.

κυανόπεζα [κύανος + πέζα]. Having the feet ornamented with designs in κύανος : τράπεζαν Λ 629.

κυανοπρῴρειος, -ον. [As next.] = next γ 299.

κυανόπρῳρος, -ον [κύανος + πρῴρη]. Having the prow ornamented with designs in κύανος. Epithet of ships Ο 693, Ψ 852, 878 : ι 482, 539, κ 127, λ 6 = μ 148, μ 100, 354, ξ 311, χ 465.

κύανος, -ου, ὁ. Glass paste or enamel coloured with a pigment doubtless to be identified with the pigment of brilliant cobalt hue largely used in the palace at Cnossus (see Sir Arthur Evans's *The Palace of Minos*, 1921, vol. i. p. 534) : θριγκὸς κυάνοιο η 87. Cf. Λ 24, 35.

κυανοχαίτης [κύανος + χαίτη]. Voc. κυανοχαῖτα Ο 174, 201 : ι 528. Nom. κυανοχαῖτα (prob. orig. the voc. turned into a nom.) Ν 563, Ξ 390. Dark-haired. Epithet or a name of Poseidon Ν 563, Ξ 390, Ο 174, 201, Υ 144 : γ 6, ι 528, 536.—As epithet of a horse, dark-maned Υ 224.

κυανῶπις, -ιδος [κύανος + ὦπα]. Dark-eyed. Epithet of Amphitrite μ 60.

κυβερνάω. To steer (a ship), keep (her) on her course : νῆα κυβερνῆσαι γ 283.

κυβερνητήρ, -ῆρος, ὁ. [As next.] = next : οὐ Φαιήκεσσι κυβερνητῆρες ἔασιν θ 557.

κυβερνήτης, ὁ [κυβερνάω]. The steersman of a ship : νῆας ἄνεμός τε κυβερνῆταί τ' ἴθυνον ι 78 = ξ 256. Cf. Τ 43, Ψ 316 : γ 279, λ 10 = μ 152, μ 217, 412.

κυβιστάω. To tumble, throw a somersault : ὡς ῥεῖα κυβιστᾷ Π 745, 749.—Of fishes jumping out of the water Φ 354.

κυβιστητήρ, -ῆρος, ὁ [κυβιστάω]. A tumbler, acrobat, posturer Π 750, Σ 605 : = δ 18.

κυδαίνω [κῦδος]. 3 sing. aor. κύδηνε Ψ 793. Infin. κυδῆναι π 212. (1) In reference to one's appearance, to confer splendour or beauty : Αἰνείαν ἀκέοντό τε κύδαινόν τε Ε 448. Cf. π 212.—(2) To do honour to, bring into honour or triumph, exalt Ν 348, 350, Ο 612.—(3) To treat with marks of respect or distinction, address in complimentary terms Κ 69.—To gratify by marks of distinction ξ 438.—To flatter Ψ 793.

κυδάλιμος [κῦδος]. Glorious, renowned, famous. (1) As a vague epithet of commendation : ἀνέρε Ρ 378 : υἱάσιν ξ 206. Cf. ο 358, ρ 113, τ 418.—(2) Epithet of Menelaus Δ 100, Η 392, Ν 591, Ρ 69, etc. : δ 2, 16, 23 = 217, δ 46, ο 5, 141.—Of Capaneus Δ 403.—Of Aias Ο 415.—Of Nestor Τ 238.—Of Achilles Υ 439.—Of Odysseus γ 219, χ 89.—Of Telemachus χ 238.—Of the Solymi Ζ 184, 204.—Of a man's heart Κ 16, Σ 33 : φ 247.—Of a lion's or a boar's Μ 45.

κυδάνω [κῦδος]. (1) To do honour to, bring into honour or triumph, exalt Ξ 73.—(2) To be triumphant, exult : Ἀχαιοὶ μέγα κύδανον Υ 42.

κύδηνε, 3 sing. aor. κυδαίνω.

κυδιάνειρα, -ης [κῦδος + ἀνήρ]. That brings men honour. Epithet of μάχη Δ 225, Ζ 124, Η 113, Θ 448, Μ 325, Ν 270, Ξ 155, Ω 391.—Of ἀγορή Α 490.

†**κυδιάω** [frequentative fr. κῦδος]. Pres. pple. κυδιόων Β 579, Ζ 509, Ο 266. Pl. κυδιόωντες Φ 519. To bear oneself proudly or triumphantly : ἐδύσετο χαλκὸν κυδιόων Β 579. Cf. Φ 519.—Of a horse Ζ 509 = Ο 266.

κύδιστος, -η [superl. fr. κῦδος]. Most glorious or renowned. Epithet of Athene Δ 515 : γ 378.—In voc. as epithet of Zeus Β 412, Γ 276, 298, etc.—Of Agamemnon Α 122, Β 434, Θ 293, etc. : λ 397 = ω 121.

κυδοιμέω [κυδοιμός]. To drive in confusion or uproar, make havoc of : ἡμέας εἶσι κυδοιμήσων Ο 136.—Absol. : ἂν' ὅμιλον ἰόντε κυδοίμεον Λ 324.

κυδοιμός, -οῦ, ὁ. Confusion, uproar, panic : ἐν κυδοιμὸν ὦρσε Κρονίδης Λ 52. Cf. Κ 523, Λ 538, Σ 218.—In concrete sense, the hurrying throng of battle : ἐκ κυδοιμοῦ Λ 164.—Personified Σ 535.—Figured as a symbol : Ἐνυὼ ἔχουσα Κυδοιμόν Ε 593.

κῦδος, τό. (1) The outward splendour of a divinity : κύδεϊ γαίων Α 405, Ε 906, Θ 51, Λ 81.—(2) Honour, glory, renown, distinction : ᾧ τε Ζεὺς κ. ἔδωκεν Α 279, οἴσεσθαι μέγα κ. Ἀχαιοῖσι προτὶ νῆας (bring the Achaeans glory, or perh., win glory in the eyes of the Achaeans) Χ 217. Cf. Γ 373, Δ 95, Θ 176, Ι 303, Π 84, Ρ 251, Ω 110, etc. : γ 57, ο 320, τ 161.—(3) The glory of victory, victory, triumph, the upper hand : ὁπποτέροισι Ζεὺς κ. ὀρέξῃ Ε 33, [ἶσον] κ. ὄπασσον (*i.e.* make the fight a drawn one) Η 205. Cf. Ε 225, Θ 141, Μ 407, Ο 595, Ρ 321, Ψ 400, etc. : δ 275, χ 253.—So κ. ὑπέρτερον Μ 437, Ο 491, 644.—(4) A source of honour, something which confers honour or distinction : κόσμος θ' ἵππῳ ἐλατῆρί τε κ. Δ 145. Cf. ο 78 (see ἀγλαΐη (2)).—Of a person : μέγα σφι κ. ἔησθα Χ 435.—So μέγα κ. Ἀχαιῶν. Of Odysseus Ι 673 = Κ 544 : μ 184.—Of Nestor Κ 87 = 555 = Λ 511 = Ξ 42 : = γ 79 = 202.

κυδρός, -ή [κῦδος]. =κυδάλιμος (1): Διὸς κυδρὴ παράκοιτις Σ 184. Cf. λ 580, ο 26.

κυέω [cf. κῦμα]. (ὑποκύομαι.) To bear in the womb, be pregnant with: ἐκύει υἱόν Τ 117.—Of a mare: βρέφος ἡμίονον κυέουσαν Ψ 266.

κύθε, 3 sing. aor. κεύθω.

κυκάω. Dat. sing. masc. pres. pple. κυκόωντι Ε 903. (1) To stir, mix: [γάλα] Ε 903.—(2) To stir and mix (ingredients with wine) so as to make a κυκεών: τυρόν σφι καὶ ἄλφιτα καὶ μέλι οἴνῳ ἐκύκα κ 235.—Without expressed object: κύκησέ σφι οἴνῳ Λ 638.—(3) To stir or trouble (waters): [Σκάμανδρος] ὄρινε ῥέεθρα κυκώμενος Φ 235. Cf. Φ 240, 324.—Of Charybdis μ 238, 241.—(4) To throw into disorder or confusion, strike with panic: κυκήθησαν Τρῶες Σ 229. Cf. Λ 129, Υ 489.

κυκεών, ὁ [κυκάω]. Acc. κυκεῶ κ 290, 316. κυκειῶ Λ 624, 641. A semi-liquid mess compounded of wine and other ingredients (called σῖτος κ 235, 290, but app. intended to be drunk Λ 641: κ 237, 316, 318) (cf. κυκάω (2)): τεύξει τοι κυκεῶ κ 290. Cf. Λ 624, 641: κ 316.

†**κυκλέω** [κύκλος]. 1 pl. aor. subj. κυκλήσομεν. To convey by means of wheels, carry in waggons: νεκρούς Η 332.

κύκλος, -ου, ὁ. Acc. pl. (besides the regular form) κύκλα Ε 722, Σ 375. A ring or circle. (1) Each of a number of concentric circular pieces of metal forming a shield: ἔντοσθεν βοείας ῥάψε θαμειὰς χρυσείῃς ῥάβδοισι διηνεκέσιν περὶ κύκλον (corresponding with each circle, but no doubt covering the joints) Μ 297 (the pieces of leather being sewed together with the wire), ἀσπίδα, ἣν πέρι κύκλοι δέκα χάλκεοι ἦσαν Λ 33.—Sim. of both an outer circle of metal and the corresponding inner circle of leather: διὰ δ' ἀμφοτέρους ἕλεν [ἐγχείῃ] κύκλους ἀσπίδος (tore apart the metal facing and the leather backing) Υ 280.—(2) A chariot-wheel Ψ 340.—In pl. κύκλα denoting rather vague quantity than plurality, a set of chariot-wheels: ἀμφ' ὀχέεσσι βάλε κύκλα Ε 722.—So of wheels under a tripod Σ 375.—(3) A semi-circular range of seats for judges: ἥατ' ἐπὶ ξεστοῖσι λίθοις ἱερῷ ἐνὶ κύκλῳ Σ 504.—(4) A cordon of men drawn round a hunted beast δ 792.—(5) In dat. κύκλῳ, in a circle, round about: χέε δέσματα κύκλῳ ἀπάντῃ θ 278.

κυκλόσε [κυκλο-, κύκλος + -σε]. Coming into a circle, in a circle: ἀγηγέρατο Δ 212, διαστάντες Ρ 392.

κυκλοτερής,-ές [app. κύκλος + τερ-, τείρω. 'Rubbed or worn into a circle,' but with the force of the second element obscured]. Round, circular: ἄλσος ρ 209.—Sim.: ἐπεὶ κυκλοτερὲς τόξον ἔτεινεν (predicatively, 'into a (semi-) circle') Δ 124.

κύκνος, -ου. A swan Β 460 = Ο 692.

κυκόωντι, dat. sing. masc. pres. pple. κυκάω.

κυλίνδω. 3 sing. aor. pass. κυλίσθη Ρ 99. (ἐκ-, προ-, προπρο-.) (1) To put into rolling motion, roll along. Of the sea: γαίῃ Θεσπρωτῶν πέλασεν μέγα κῦμα κυλίνδον ξ 315. Cf. α 162.—Of a wind, to roll (billows) before it: Βορέης μέγα κῦμα κυλίνδων ε 296.—So in pass.: πολλὸν τρόφι κῦμα κυλίνδεται Λ 307.—Fig.: γιγνώσκειν ὅτι πῆμα θεὸς Δαναοῖσι κυλίνδει Ρ 688.—So in pass.: νῶϊν τόδε πῆμα κυλίνδεται (is coming on us) Λ 347. Cf. Ρ 99: β 163, θ 81.—(2) In mid. or pass., to be rolled down, roll down: πέδονδε κυλίνδετο λᾶας λ 598.—To roll along, roll about: ὅλμον δ' ὣς ἔσσευε κυλίνδεσθαι δι' ὁμίλου Λ 147. Cf. Ν 142, 579, Ξ 411, Π 794.—Of breaking waves ι 147.—To roll oneself about, wallow: κυλινδόμενος κατὰ κόπρον Χ 414, Ω 640. Cf. Ω 165: δ 541 = κ 499.—Of a horse, to roll himself about, writhe, in the death-struggle Θ 86.

κυλλοποδίων [app. a pet-form fr. κυλλοποδ-, fr. κυλλός, crooked + ποδ-, πούς]. Voc. κυλλοπόδιον Φ 331. Little crook-foot. A name of Hephaestus Σ 371, Υ 270, Φ 331.

κῦμα, -ατος, τό [κυ-, to swell, as in κυέω]. (1) A wave of the sea: ὡς τε μέγα κ. θαλάσσης νηὸς ὑπὲρ τοίχων καταβήσεται Ο 381. Cf. Β 144, Μ 28 (comitative dat., 'to be carried by the . . .'), Ν 27, Ο 621, Ψ 61, etc.: κύματα τροφόεντα, ἶσα ὄρεσσιν γ 290. Cf. γ 91, 299, ε 54, 109, 224, 313, 320, 366, η 278, θ 232, ι 147, 485 (the wash of the thrown rock), κ 93, μ 419, ν 88, etc.—A wave of a river λ 243.—(2) Collectively, the wave or waves of the sea, the swell or surge of the sea, the swelling or heaving surface of the sea: ἀμφὶ κ. στείρῃ ἴαχεν Α 481. Cf. Α 483, Δ 422, Ι 6, Μ 285, Ξ 16, Ρ 264, etc.: κύματι πηγῷ πλάζετο (on the . . .) ε 388. Cf. α 162, γ 295, ε 402, ζ 171, η 273, μ 202 (breakers), ν 99, etc.—(3) In reference to the flowing surface of a river: θρῴσκων τις κατὰ κ. ἰχθύς Φ 126. Cf. Φ 240, 263, 268, 306, 313, 326, 382: ἔσχε κ. (stayed his flow) ε 451. Cf. ε 461.—So in reference to Ocean λ 639.

κυμαίνω [κῦμα]. Of the sea, to swell or surge: πόντον κυμαίνοντα Ξ 229: δ 425, 510, 570 = λ 253, ε 352.

κύμβαχος. (1) Headlong: ἔκπεσε δίφρου κ. Ε 586.—(2) As sb., app., the crown (of a helmet): κόρυθος κύμβαχον νύξεν Ο 536.

κύμινδις, ἡ. The name given by mortals to a bird not identified (cf. χαλκίς) Ξ 291.

κυνάμυια, κυνόμυια [κυν-, κύων + μυῖα. 'Dog-fly']. As a term of abuse, one who unites in her person the shamelessness of the dog and the boldness of the fly Φ 394, 421.

κυνέη, -ης, ἡ [commonly taken as fem. of κύνεος (sc. δορά, hide) in sense 'a helmet,' originally of dogskin]. A helmet Γ 316, Ε 743, 845 (the cap of darkness, the name 'Αΐδης ('ΑϜίδης) here preserving its orig. sense 'the Invisible,' fr. α-[1] + (Ϝ)ιδ-, εἴδω), Κ 261, Μ 384, Π 793, etc.: κ 206, ξ 276, χ 111, 123, 145.—With adjectives of material: ταυρείην Κ 257, κτιδέην 335, 458: πάγχαλκος σ 378, πάγχαλκον χ 102.—A cap worn in ordinary life: αἰγείην ω 231.

κύνεος [κυν-, κύων]. Having the characteristics of the dog, shameless: κύνεός περ ἐών Ι 373.

κυνέω. Aor. κύσα ξ 279. 3 sing. ἔκυσε ψ 208. κύσε Ζ 474, Ω 478: ε 463, ν 354, π 21, 190, ω 398.

ἔκυσσε Θ 371 : φ 225. κύσσε π 15, ρ 39, τ 417, ω 320. 3 sing. opt. κύσσειε ψ 87. Infin. κύσσαι ω 236. To kiss Z 474, Θ 371, Ω 478 : δ 522, ε 463, ν 354, ξ 279, π 15 = ρ 39, π 21, 190, ρ 35 = χ 499, τ 417, φ 224, 225, ψ 87, 208, ω 236, 320, 398.

κυνηγέτης, ὁ [κυν-, κύων + ἄγω. 'One who leads dogs']. A hunter ι 120.

κυνόμυια. See κυνάμυια.

κυνοραιστής [κυν-, κύων + ῥαίω]. A dog-tick : κεῖτ' Ἄργος, ἐνίπλειος κυνοραιστέων ρ 300.

κύντατος [superl. fr. κυν-, κύων. 'Most like what a dog might do']. Most outrageous or offensive : μερμήριζε ὅ τι κύντατον ἔρδοι K 503.

κύντερος [comp. fr. κυν-, κύων. 'More like a dog']. More lost to all sense of shame or decency, more reckless or outrageous : οὐ σέο κύντερον ἄλλο Θ 483. Cf. λ 427.—Applied to the belly η 216.—Of a deed, more outrageous or offensive υ 18.

κυνώπης [κυν-, κύων + ὦπα. 'Dog-eyed']. Lost to all sense of shame or decency, shameless, reckless, outrageous. In voc. κυνῶπα A 159.

κυνῶπις, -ιδος [as prec.]. = prec. : κυνώπιδος εἵνεκα κούρης θ 319. Cf. Σ 396 : λ 424.—In self-depreciation : δαὴρ ἐμὸς ἔσκε κυνώπιδος Γ 180. Cf. δ 145.

κυπαρίσσινος [κυπάρισσος]. Of cypress-wood : σταθμῷ ρ 340.

κυπάρισσος, ἡ. The cypress ε 64.

κύπειρον, τό. A plant difficult to identify, perh. galingale. Collectively Φ 351 : δ 603.

κύπελλον, -ου, τό. A drinking-cup : παιδὸς ἐδέξατο κ. A 596. Cf. Γ 248, Δ 345, I 670, Ω 305 : α 142 = δ 58, κ 357, β 396, υ 253.

†**κύπτω.** 3 sing. aor. opt. κύψειε λ 585. Pple. κύψας P 621, Φ 69. Dat. sing. masc. κύψαντι Δ 468. (κατα-.) To stoop, stoop or bend down : ὁσσάκι κύψει' ὁ γέρων λ 585. Cf. Δ 468, P 621, Φ 69.

κύρμα, τό [κύρω. 'That which one lights upon']. An object of prey, prey : δηΐων κυσὶ κύρμα γενέσθαι P 272. Cf. E 488, P 151 : γ 271, ε 473, ο 480.

κύρσας, aor. pple. κύρω.

κυρτός. Curved. Of waves, arched, curling Δ 426, N 799.—Of the shoulders, round, humped B 218.

†**κυρτόω** [κυρτός]. Nom. sing. neut. aor. pple. pass. κυρτωθέν. To cause to take a curved form : κῦμα κυρτωθέν (arching over the pair) λ 244.

κύρω. Aor. pple. κύρσας Γ 23, Ψ 428. (ἐγ-, συγ-.) (1) To come upon, light upon. With ἐπί and dat. : ἐπὶ σώματι κύρσας Γ 23.—Sim., app. : αἰὲν ἐπ' αὐχένι κῦρε δουρὸς ἀκωκή (kept constantly grazing it) Ψ 821.—(2) To come against, come into (violent) contact with. With dat. : ἅρματι κύρσας (*i.e.* Menelaus's chariot) Ψ 428.—(3) To meet with, experience. In mid. With dat. : κακῷ κύρεται Ω 530.

κύσ(σ)ε, 3 sing. aor. κυνέω.

κύστις, ἡ. The bladder E 67, N 652.

κῡφός [κυφ-, κύπτω]. Bent, stooping β 16.

κύψας, aor. pple. κύπτω.

κύων, κυνός, ὁ, ἡ. Voc. κύον Θ 423, Λ 362, Υ 449, Φ 481, X 345 : σ 338, τ 91. Dat. pl. κυσί Λ 325, M 303, P 127, Σ 179, Ψ 21, etc. : σ 87, χ 476. κύνεσσι A 4, M 41, P 725, Ψ 183. (1) A dog A 4, B 393, Θ 379, N 233, X 42, Ψ 21, etc. : β 11, γ 259, η 91, κ 216, ρ 291, σ 105, υ 14, etc.—(2) Specifically (a) A hunting-dog : ταχέες τε κύνες θαλεροί τ' αἰζηοί Γ 26. Cf. E 476, Θ 338, I 545, Λ 325, X 189, etc. : τ 228, 429, 436, 438, 444.—(b) A sheep-dog or a dog guarding cattle, goats or swine K 183, M 303, N 198, O 587, P 65, 110, 658, Σ 578, 581, etc. : ξ 21, 29, 35, 37, π 4, 6, 9, 162, ρ 200, φ 363.—(c) The dog of Hades : ἄξοντα κύν' Ἀΐδαο Θ 368. Cf. λ 623.—The dog of Orion, Sirius : κύν' Ὠρίωνος X 29.—(3) As a type of shamelessness : κυνὸς ὄμματ' ἔχων (cf. κυνώπης) A 225.—(4) As a term of abuse or depreciation : δμῳάς, κύνας οὐκ ἀλεγούσας τ 154. Cf. Θ 299, 527 : ρ 248, τ 372.—In voc. : κύον ἀδεές Θ 423, Φ 481, κύον Λ 362 = Υ 449, X 345, κακαὶ κύνες N 623 (the fem. app. conveying a special taunt). Cf. σ 338, τ 91, χ 35.—As a term of self-depreciation : δᾶερ ἐμεῖο κυνὸς κακομηχάνου Z 344. Cf. Z 356.—(5) Some kind of marine animal, a sea-dog μ 96.

κῶας, τό. Dat. pl. κώεσι γ 38, υ 142. A prepared fleece used (1) As bedding : χλαῖναν καὶ κώεα, τοῖσιν ἐνεῦδεν υ 95. Cf. I 661 : υ 3, 142, ψ 180.—(2) For sitting upon : ἵδρυσε κώεσιν ἐν μαλακοῖσιν γ 38. Cf. π 47, ρ 32, τ 58, 97, 101, φ 177, 182.

κώδεια, ἡ. A poppy-head Ξ 499.

κωκῡτός, -οῦ, ὁ [κωκύω]. A crying out in grief or distress : κωκυτῷ εἴχοντο X 409. Cf. X 447.

κωκύω. (1) To cry out in grief or distress : κώκυσέν τ' ἄρ' ἔπειτα Σ 37. Cf. Σ 71, T 284, X 407, Ω 200, 703 : β 361, δ 259, θ 527, τ 541.—(2) To make lament for : ἑὸν πόσιν ω 295.

κώληψ, -ηπος. App., the hollow behind the knee : κόψ' ὄπιθεν κώληπα Ψ 726.

κῶμα, τό [κω-, κοιμάω]. Sleep, slumber : αὐτῷ περὶ κῶμα κάλυψα Ξ 359. Cf. σ 201.

κώπη, -ης, ἡ. A handle. (1) The handle of a sword : ἄορ, ᾧ ἔπι κώπη ἀργυρέη θ 403. Cf. A 219 : λ 531.—(2) The handle of a κληΐς in sense (2) φ 7.—(3) The handle of an oar, and hence, an oar : ἐμβαλέειν κώπης ι 489 = κ 129. Cf. μ 214.

κωπήεις, -εντος [κώπη]. Fitted with a handle, handled. Epithet of swords O 713, Π 332, Υ 475.

κώρυκος, -ου, ὁ. A bag or wallet : ἐν δὲ καὶ ᾖα [θῆκε] κωρύκῳ ε 267. Cf. ι 213.

κωφός, -ή, -όν. (1) Blunt : βέλος Λ 390.—(2) Without sensibility, senseless : γαῖαν Ω 54.—(3) Of the wave of the sea in a ground-swell, making no plash, heaving without breaking : ὅτε πορφύρῃ πέλαγος κύματι κωφῷ Ξ 16.

λᾶας, ὁ Δ 521 : λ 598. Genit. λᾶος M 462 : θ 192. Dat. λᾶϊ Π 739. Acc. λᾶαν B 319, Γ 12, H 268, M 445, 453 : ι 537, λ 594, 596, ν 163.

Nom. dual λᾶε Ψ 329. Genit. pl. λάων Μ 29, Φ 314. Dat. λάεσσι Γ 80 Ω 798 : ζ 267, κ 211, 253, ξ 10. (1) A stone : ὅσον τ' ἐπὶ λᾶαν ἵησιν Γ 12. Cf. Γ 80, Δ 521, Η 268, Μ 445, 453, 462, Π 739, Φ 314, Ψ 329 : λᾶος ὑπὸ ῥιπῆς θ 192. Cf. ι 537, λ 594, 596, 598.—(2) In pl., stones used in construction : θεμείλια φιτρῶν καὶ λάων Μ 29. Cf. Ω 798 : ῥυτοῖσιν λάεσσιν ἀραρυῖα ζ 267. Cf. κ 211=253, ξ 10.—(3) Something of stone : λᾶάν μιν ἔθηκεν (turned it to stone) Β 319 : ν 163.

λάβε, 3 sing. aor. λαμβάνω.

λαβραγόρης, ὁ [λάβρος + ἀγορεύω]. A rash talker : οὐδέ τί σε χρὴ λαβραγόρην ἔμεναι Ψ 479.

λαβρεύομαι [λάβρος]. To pour out words without consideration, talk rashly Ψ 474, 478.

λάβρος. Of wind, rushing, blustering : Ζέφυρος λάβρος ἐπαιγίζων Β 148. Cf. ο 293.—Of water, rushing, overwhelming : ποταμὸς λάβρος ὕπαιθα ῥέων Φ 271. Cf. Ο 625.—Of rain, pouring, torrential. In superl. : ὅτε λαβρότατον χέει ὕδωρ Ζεύς Π 385.

λαγχάνω. Aor. ἔλαχον Ι 367, Ο 190 : ε 311. λάχον Ω 400. 3 sing. ἔλαχε Ο 191, 192. λάχε Ψ 79, 354, 356, 357, 862. 1 pl. λάχομεν Δ 49, Ω 70. 3 ἔλαχον Κ 430 : ι 334. 3 sing. subj. λάχῃσι Η 171. λάχῃ Ω 76. Pple. λαχών ε 40, ν 138. Acc. sing. masc. λαχόντα Σ 327. Infin. λαχεῖν Η 179. 2 pl. subj. redup. aor. λελάχητε Ψ 76. 3 pl. λελάχωσι Η 80, Ο 350, Χ 343. 3 pl. pf. λελόγχᾱσι λ 304. (1) To get, receive, have assigned to one, as one's lot or portion : ἅσσ' ἔλαχόν γε Ι 367. Cf. Δ 49=Ω 70, Σ 327 : λαχὼν ἀπὸ ληΐδος αἶσαν ε 40=ν 138, τιμὴν λελόγχασιν ἶσα θεοῖσιν (enjoy) λ 304. Cf. ξ 233.—With genit. : κτερέων ε 311.—Absol. : ὡς αὐτοί περ ἐλάγχανον υ 282.—Of one's fate, to have power over (one) given to it, be destined to (one) : κήρ, ἥ πέρ [με] λάχε γιγνόμενόν περ Ψ 79.—To have a specified post or position assigned to one : πρὸς Θύμβρης ἔλαχον Λύκιοι Κ 430.—(2) To agree to receive, receive, accept. With genit. : δώρων Ω 76.—(3) To get or have assigned to one by lot : ἔλαχον ἅλα ναιέμεν (wherein to dwell) παλλομένων Ο 190. Cf. Ο 191, 192.—To have it fall on or be assigned to one by lot *to do*. With infin. : τῷ δ' ἐπὶ Μηριόνης λάχ' ἐλαυνέμεν Ψ 356. Cf. Ψ 357, Ω 400.—Absol., to have the lot fall upon one : μετὰ τὸν λάχ' Εὔμηλος Ψ 354. Cf. Η 171, 179, Ψ 862 : ι 334.—(4) To fall to one's lot : ἐς ἑκάστην [νῆα] ἐννέα λάγχανον αἶγες ι 160.—(5) In redup. aor., to give (one) his due of. With genit. : ὄφρα πυρός με λελάχωσιν Η 80=Χ 343. Cf. Ο 350, Ψ 76.

λαγωός, ὁ. A hare Κ 361 : ρ 295.—Joined with πτώξ : πτῶχα λαγωόν Χ 310.

λᾶε nom. dual, **λάεσσι** dat. pl. λᾶας.

λάζομαι. To grasp, seize, take hold of : ὀδὰξ λαζοίατο γαῖαν (bite the dust) Β 418, ἡνία χερσὶν Ε 365, Ρ 482=Ω 441. Cf. Ε 371, 745=Θ 389, Ε 840, Π 734 : γ 483.—In reference to speech : πάλιν ὅ γε λάζετο μῦθον Δ 357 (took back his words) : ν 254 (restrained himself in speech, left the truth unsaid).

λαθικηδής [λαθ-, λανθάνω + κῆδος]. Soothing, pacifying : μαζόν Χ 83.

λάθον, aor. λανθάνω.

λάθρῃ [λαθ-, λανθάνω]. (1) By stealth, clandestinely, secretly, so as to escape notice : παρελέξατο Β 515, Π 184, βαλέειν (taking you at unawares) Η 243. Cf. Ν 352, 357 : δ 92, θ 269, ο 430, ρ 43, 80 (by secret contrivance), χ 445.—Imperceptibly, so as to affect one by slow degrees : γυῖα βαρύνεται Τ 165.—(2) With genit., without the knowledge of, so as to escape the notice of : Λαομέδοντος Ε 269. Cf. Ω 72.

λᾶϊ, dat. λᾶας.

λᾶϊγξ, -ϊγγος, ἡ [λᾶας]. A pebble : ἧχι λάϊγγας ἀποπλύνεσκε θάλασσα ζ 95. Cf. ε 433.

λαῖλαψ, -απος, ἡ. (1) A furious wind, a storm of wind, a tempest : βαθείῃ λαίλαπι τύπτων Λ 306. Cf. Λ 747, Μ 375, Π 384, Υ 51 : ω 42.—(2) Furious wind, storm, tempest : ἄγει λαίλαπα πολλήν Δ 278. Cf. Ρ 57 : ἄνεμος (Ζέφυρος) λαίλαπι θύων (in storm) μ 400, 426. Cf. ι 68=μ 314, μ 408.—(3) App., an accompaniment of a storm, a storm-cloud : ὅτε τε Ζεὺς λαίλαπα τείνῃ Π 365.

λαιμός, -οῦ, ὁ. The throat : Ἀφαρῆα λαιμὸν τύψεν Ν 542. Cf. Ν 388, Σ 34 : χ 15.—More specifically, the gullet Τ 209.

λᾱΐνεος [λᾶας]. Of stone : πλυνοί Χ 154.

λάϊνος [λᾶας]. Of stone : τεῖχος Μ 178. Cf. ν 106 (of natural formations in a cave)—λάϊνος οὐδός Ι 404 : θ 80 (in both cases app. referring to the threshold of a temple built of stone), π 41 (in the hut of Eumaeus), ρ 30, υ 258, ψ 88 (in these three cases at the entrance to the μέγαρον of Odysseus, app. a massive and broad stone threshold on which the μέλινος οὐδός rested (see μέλινος (2)).—Fig. : λάϊνόν χ' ἕσσο χιτῶνα Γ 57 (would have been stoned).

λαισήϊον, -ου, τό [app. conn. with λάσιος]. Thus, a light shield of skin with the hair left on Ε 453 =Μ 426.

λαῖτμα, τό [cf. λαιμός]. The gulf of the sea : τόδε λαῖτμα διατμήξας ε 409. Cf. η 35, 276, ι 323.—With ἁλός : ἁλὸς ἐς μέγα λαῖτμα Τ 267. Cf. θ 561.—With θαλάσσης : ὑπὲρ μέγα λαῖτμα θαλάσσης ι 260. Cf. δ 504, ε 174.

λαῖφος, τό. A ragged garment, rags ν 399.—So in pl. : τοιάδε λαίφε' ἔχοντα υ 206.

λαιψηρός [=αἰψηρός; or perh. conn. with λαῖλαψ]. Swift, rushing : ἀνέμων λαιψηρὰ κέλευθα Ξ 17, Ο 620.—Of the arrows of Apollo, quickly reaching the mark, swift Φ 278.—Of a person, swift, nimble Φ 264.—Epithet of the knees Κ 358, Ο 269, Υ 93, Χ 24, 144, 204.

λάκε, 3 sing. aor. λάσκω.

λακτίζω [λάξ]. To apply the foot to, kick : λακτίζων ποσὶ γαῖαν σ 99. Cf. χ 88.

†λαμβάνω. 3 sing. aor. ἔλαβε Δ 463, Ε 328, Ρ 620, Ψ 100 : ζ 81, ρ 326. ἔλλαβε Γ 34, Ε 83, Θ 371, Ξ 475, Π 599, Ω 170, etc. : α 298, σ 88, 394, χ 71, ω 49. λάβε Α 500, Ε 159, Ζ 166, Λ 126, Ν 470, Ρ 695, Υ 418, Ω 478, etc. : δ 704, ε 428, θ 186, ο 102, φ 148, χ 310, etc. 2 dual λάβετον

K 545. 3 λαβέτην Z 233, Ψ 711. 3 pl. λάβον ο 387. 3 sing. subj. λάβῃ Δ 230, Ω 480. λάβῃσι I 324, Φ 24, Ω 43 : α 192. 1 pl. λάβωμεν Θ 191. 2 λάβητε κ 461. Opt. λάβοιμι O 22. 3 sing. λάβοι Π 30 : ι 418. 1 pl. λάβοιμεν E 273, Θ 196. Imp. λαβέ A 407, O 229, Ω 465. 3 λαβέτω φ 152. Pple. λαβών, -όντος B 261, Z 45, Λ 106, M 452, N 235, P 678, Φ 286, Ψ 275, etc. : ζ 142, 147, ι 41, λ 4, ο 269, ω 398, etc. Fem. λαβοῦσα Γ 385, E 853, Φ 504 : η 255, τ 390, 467, ψ 87. **Mid.** 3 sing. aor. ἐλλάβετο ε 325. Redup. aor. infin. λελαβέσθαι δ 388. **(1)** To grasp, seize, lay or take hold of, lay hands upon : σε B 261, χερμάδιον E 302. Cf. Z 233, K 328, Λ 842, O 22, P 620 (picked up), Υ 418 (pressed them back towards their place), Φ 24, Ψ 100 (it eluded him), Ω 465, etc. : ζ 81, θ 186, ι 418, σ 394, τ 390, etc.—In mid. δ 388.—With genit. : λάβε πέτρης ε 428. Cf. Ψ 711 : χ 310.—In mid. : ἐλλάβετο σχεδίης ε 325.—With genit. of part grasped : τὸν ποδῶν ἔλαβεν (by the feet) Δ 463. Cf. A 407, B 316, Γ 369, Θ 371, Σ 155, etc. : ζ 142, σ 101, τ 480, χ 342, etc.—So with a form in -φιν : κεφαλῆφιν ἐπεὶ λάβε [νέκυν] Π 762.—Sim. : πρύμνηθεν ἐπεὶ λάβε [νῆα] O 716.—**(2)** To take, capture, seize, make spoil of : ἀσπίδα Νεστορέην Θ 191, εἴ πως εὐ πεφίδοιτο λαβών (making him his prisoner) Υ 464. Cf. E 273, K 545, Λ 106, Φ 36 : ι 41, ο 387.—To catch (a fish) μ 254.—**(3)** To kill, slay : υἷας Πριάμοιο δύω E 159. Cf. Θ 196, Λ 126.—**(4)** To get hold of, get : [μάστακα] I 324.—To take for use, take to oneself : λαβὼν ἐρετμόν λ 121. Cf. N 235 : υ 300, φ 148, 152, χ 71. —Sim. : ἑτάρους τε λαβὼν καὶ νῆα ο 269.—**(5)** In various uses. **(a)** To take as one's due : τὰ πρῶτα Ψ 275.—**(b)** To take, exact : ἄποινα Z 427.—**(c)** To win (fame) : κλέος α 298.—**(d)** To take (out of a receptacle) : δέπας ἐκ χηλοῖο Π 228.—Sim. : δέπας λάβεν (to make a present of it) ο 102. —**(e)** To make (a meal) : δαῖτα Ω 43.—**(f)** To take under one's care η 255.—**(g)** To recover (one's strength) : εἰς ὅ κεν αὖτις θυμὸν λάβητε κ 461.—**(6)** Of feelings, bodily or mental states, or the like, to come to or upon, seize, affect, take hold of : Ἀτρεΐωνα χόλος λάβεν A 387, ὑπὸ τρόμος ἔλλαβε γυῖα Γ 34. Cf. Δ 230, E 394, Λ 402, Ξ 475, P 695, Ψ 468, Ω 480, etc. : εὖτ' ἄν μιν κάματος κατὰ γυῖα λάβῃσιν α 192. Cf. δ 704, σ 88, ω 49.—Of death, etc. : τὸν ἔλλαβε θάνατος καὶ μοῖρα E 83 = Π 334 = Υ 477. Cf. ρ 326.—**(7)** In aor. pple. with a finite vb., to take and . . . (cf. ἄγω (I) (9)) : ἕλκε γλυφίδας λαβὼν Δ 122. Cf. ι 328, λ 4, 35, φ 359, ψ 87, ω 398.

†**λαμπετάω** [frequentative fr. λάμπω]. Dat. sing. neut. pres. pple. λαμπετόωντι. To gleam, flash : πυρὶ λαμπετόωντι A 104 := δ 662.

λαμπρός, -ή, -όν [λάμπω]. **(1)** Bright, radiant, refulgent, flashing, glittering, glistening : φάος ἠελίοιο A 605, κορύθεσσιν P 269. Cf. Δ 77, E 120, Θ 485, N 132 = Π 216 : τ 234.—In superl. : λαμπρότατος ὅ γ' ἐστίν (*i.e.* Sirius) X 30.—**(2)** In neut. sing. λαμπρόν as adv., brightly, with radiance, glitteringly : ἀστέρ', ὅς τε μάλιστα λαμπρὸν παμφαίνῃσιν E 6. Cf. N 265, T 359.

λαμπτήρ, -ῆρος, ὁ [λάμπω]. A brazier for giving light and heat σ 307, 343, τ 63.

λάμπω. (ἀπο-, ἐπι-.) To shed beams of bright light, to shine, flash, glitter, glisten : τεύχεα ποικίλ' ἔλαμπεν Δ 432. Cf. K 154, Λ 45, 66, M 463, N 245 = X 32, N 474.—In mid. : λάμπετο δουρὸς αἰχμή Z 319 = Θ 494. Cf. N 341, O 608, 623, Π 71, P 214, Σ 492, 510, T 366, Υ 46, 156, X 134 : δαΐδων ὕπο λαμπομενάων τ 48, ψ 290.

λανθάνω, λήθω. 3 sing. pa. iterative λήθεσκε Ω 13. 2 sing. fut. λήσεις ν 393. 3 λήσει Ψ 326, 416 : λ 126, χ 198. Infin. λήσειν λ 102. Aor. λάθον ν 270. 3 ἔλαθε Ξ 1, P 1, 626, 676, Υ 112, Ω 477. λάθε Γ 420, O 583, Π 232, P 89, X 277, Ψ 388 : ι 281, μ 182. 3 dual λαθέτην χ 179. 3 pl. λάθον Ω 331. 3 sing. subj. λάθῃσι X 191 : μ 220. 3 sing. opt. λάθοι K 468, Ω 566 : δ 527. Pple. λαθών I 477, Λ 251, M 390, O 541, Ω 681 : ρ 305. 3 sing. subj. redup. aor. λελάθῃ O 60. **Mid.** Fut. λήσομαι α 308. Infin. λήσεσθαι λ 554. 3 sing. aor. λάθετο I 537. 3 pl. λάθοντο N 835, O 322, Π 357. Subj. λάθωμαι Z 265, X 282. 3 sing. λάθηται ι 102. 3 pl. λάθωνται K 99. Opt. λαθοίμην K 243 : α 65. 3 pl. λαθοίατο κ 236. Infin. λαθέσθαι M 235 : ι 97. 3 pl. redup. aor. λελάθοντο Δ 127. 3 sing. imp. λελαθέσθω Π 200. Infin. λελαθέσθαι T 136. 3 sing. pf. λέλασται E 834. 1 pl. λελάσμεθα Λ 313. Pple. λελασμένος Π 538, 776, Ψ 69 : ν 92, ω 40. Acc. sing. masc. λελασμένον N 269. (ἀπεκ-, ἐκ-, ἐπιλήθω, καταλήθω.) **(1)** To escape, elude, avoid, to manage or fail to attract the observation, notice or attention of : οὐδέ σε λήθω (nothing that I do escapes thee) A 561, πάσας Τρῳὰς λάθεν Γ 420, λαθὼν φύλακας I 477, οὐδέ σε λήθω τιμῆς ἧς . . . (app., thou art mindful of me in the matter of the . . .) Ψ 648, οὐδέ με λήθεις (I know it right well) Ω 563. Cf. K 468, Λ 251, Ξ 296, O 461, 583, Π 232, P 676, X 191, 193, 277, Ψ 326, Ω 566, 681 : ἔμ' οὐ λάθεν (I saw what he was driving at) ι 281, παρέσσομαι, οὐδέ με λήσεις (thou wilt not look in vain for aid) ν 393. Cf. λ 102, 126, ρ 305, χ 179.—Without expressed object : ἀπὸ τείχεος ἆλτο λαθών M 390. Cf. O 541 : β 106 = ω 141, τ 151.—With pple. expressing the action which is unnoticed : οὐδέ σε λήθω κινύμενος (my setting forth is not hidden from thee) K 279, ἄλλον τινὰ μᾶλλον λήθω μαρνάμενος (others may not mark my prowess) N 273, βάλλοντες ἐλάνθανον (shot from a concealed position) 721, οὐδ' ἔλαθ' Ἥρην ἰών Υ 112. Cf. N 560, P 89, Ψ 388, Ω 331, 477 : μή ἑ λάθοι παριών δ 527, μή σε λάθῃσι [νηῦς] κεῖσ' ἐξορμήσασα (sheer off before thou art aware of it) μ 220, λάθον ἑ θυμὸν ἀπούρας (took him at unawares and slew him) ν 270. Cf. θ 93 = 532, μ 17, 182, π 156, τ 88, 91.—With a clause with sim. force : οὐδ' ἔλαθ' Αἴαντα Ζεύς, ὅτε . . . P 626.—With a pple. expressing a circumstance : οὐδ' ἔλαθ' Ἀτρέος υἱὸν Πάτροκλος δαμείς P 1.—Of a natural phenomenon : οὐδέ μιν ἠὼς λήθεσκεν Ω 13. Cf. χ 198.—Of sound Ξ 1.—Impers. : οὐδέ με λήσει (I shall know well how to do it) Ψ 416.—With clause : οὐδέ ἑ λήθει ὅππως . . . (he knows well how to . . .) Ψ 323.—(2) To cause to forget or lose consciousness of. With genit.: ὄφρ' [Ἕκτορα] λελάθῃ ὀδυνάων Ο 60.—(3) In mid., with genit., to forget, with various shades of meaning. (a) To lose the recollection of, cease to remember: οὐδ' ὣς τοῦ λήθετο β 23. Cf. κ 236.—(b) To lose the recollection of, cease to be afflicted or affected by: λελασμένος [τῶν] ὅσσ' ἐπεπόνθει ν 92.—(c) To lose the power of displaying or putting in practice: ἀλκῆς Z 265.—In reference to a dead man, for whom all thought of something is over: λελασμένος ἱπποσυνάων Π 776: ω 40.—(d) To let slip from the memory: οὔ ποτε λήσομαι αὐτῶν (what has been said) α 308.—(e) To put out of one's mind, cease to be influenced by: χόλου λ 554.—(f) To put out of one's mind, remove oneself from the operation of: Ἄτης Τ 136.—(g) To fail to do due honour to: θεῶν Ω 427. Cf. ξ 421.—(h) To neglect, take no thought for the welfare or well-being of, care nothing for: οὐδὲ σέθεν θεοὶ λελάθοντο Δ 127, τῶν (sc. Ἀχαιῶν) λέλασται (has no care for them) E 834. Cf. Π 538, Ψ 69: πῶς ἂν Ὀδυσῆος λαθοίμην; α 65.—(i) To pass over: πῶς ἂν Ὀδυσῆος λαθοίμην; Κ 243.—(j) To let slip from one's mind, care no longer about, cease to strive for, depart from: νόστου ι 97, 102, ἀπειλάων ν 126.—(k) To neglect, put from one's thoughts, omit, fail or neglect to carry out, exercise, display or put in practice: οὐ λήθετ' ἐφετμέων παιδὸς ἑοῦ Α 495, μὴ φυλακῆς λάθωνται Κ 99, τί παθόντε λελάσμεθ' ἀλκῆς; (do we forget our . . . ?) Λ 313. Cf. E 319, M 203, 393, N 269, 835, Ο 322, Π 200, 357, P 759, X 282, Ψ 725: μ 227.—Without expressed object: ἢ λάθετ' ἢ οὐκ ἐνόησεν Ι 537. Cf. Ι 259 = Λ 790. (l) To forget, not to consider or put confidence in: Ζηνὸς βουλέων Μ 235.

λάξ. With the foot: προσβάς (setting his foot upon the corpse) E 620, ἐν στήθεσι βάς Z 65. Cf. N 618, Π 503, 863: ἔνθορεν ἰσχίῳ (kicked it) ρ 233.—Joined with ποδί: λὰξ ποδὶ κινήσας Κ 158: ο 45.

λαός, -οῦ, ὁ (λαFός). (1) The folk or people of a king or chief: Πριάμοιο Δ 47 = 165 = Z 449. Cf. Θ 246, Ω 28: η 60.—In pl.: ἄτερ λαῶν πόλιν ἑξέμεν ἠδ' ἐπικούρων (without either your own folk or strangers) E 473, πολλῶν λαῶν ἐσσι ἄναξ Ι 98. Cf. Ξ 93, P 145, Φ 458, Ω 37: β 234 = ε 12, δ 176, η 323, ν 62, χ 54.—In pl., subjects, folk: λαοὶ Ἀγαμέμνονος εὐχόμεθ' εἶναι ι 263.—(2) A band or following, followers, folk: πολὺν λαὸν ἀγείρας B 664. Cf. B 675, Ι 483, Σ 452: ζ 164, ξ 248.—Sim.: ἄλλος λ. Μυρμιδόνων Λ 796.—In pl.: ἅμα τῷ γε πολὺ πλεῖστοι καὶ ἄριστοι λαοὶ ἕποντο B 578. Cf. B 580, 708, 773, 818, Γ 186, Δ 91, 202, E 643, Κ 170, N 710, Π 551, Υ 383.—In pl., one's men or people, one's servants: ὡς ὅτ' ἀνὴρ βοὸς βοείην λαοῖσιν δώῃ τανύειν P 390.—(3) The general body of a community, the people in general: κήρυκες λαὸν ἐρήτυον Σ 503. Cf. Ω 665, 789: β 41, 81, γ 305, ω 530.—In pl.: καταρτρύχω λαούς P 226. Cf. Σ 301, 497, 502, X 408, Ω 611, 715, 740, 777: τὸν πάντες λαοὶ θηεῦντο β 13 = ρ 64. Cf. β 252, γ 214, ζ 194, η 71, λ 136, ν 156, π 375, χ 133, etc.—(4) In gen., folk, people: ἐπεὶ πολὺν ὤλεσα λαόν B 115 = Ι 22. Cf. E 758: λ 500, 518.—In pl.: λαοὶ περίτρεσαν ἀγροιῶται Λ 676. Cf. ι 265, ω 428.—(5) In pl., the bystanders, the crowd: λαοὶ γέροντα μόγις ἔχον X 412. Cf. θ 125.—(6) In the most gen. sense, men. In pl.: πάντων ἀριδείκετε λαῶν θ 382 = 401 = ι 2 = λ 355 = 378 = ν 38. Cf. Ι 117.—(7) The general body of a host, the host in general: ἅμα λαῷ θωρηχθῆναι Α 226. Cf. Α 54, B 99, Δ 287, E 465, N 349, Ψ 258, etc.: γ 140, 144.—In pl.: ὀλέκοντο λαοί Α 10. Cf. Α 16, 263, Γ 318, Ι 420, M 229, Σ 523, Ψ 53, etc.: γ 156, δ 156, σ 152, etc.—Distinguished in terms from the leaders: ἡγήσατο . . . ἐπὶ δ' ἴαχε λαὸς ὄπισθεν N 834. Cf. Ο 695, 723, Ω 658.—In pl.: ὅς θ' ἡγεμόνων κακὸς ὅς τε λαῶν B 365. Cf. N 108, 492, Ο 15, Σ 519.—Including the leaders: ἐπιπροέηκεν ἀρίστους κρινάμενος κατὰ λαὸν Ἀχαιϊκόν Ι 521.—(8) In gen., a host or army: ὅτ' ἐν Θήβῃσιν ἀπώλετο λαὸς Ἀχαιῶν Z 223. Cf. B 120, 799, Δ 28, 377, 407, 430, Ι 338, Λ 716, 770.—Of a part or section of a host: ᾗ πλεῖστον ὀρινόμενον ἴδε λαόν (where he perceived the greatest confusion) Π 377.—(9) In pl., fighters, fighting men, warriors: στρατῷ εὐρέϊ λαῶν Δ 76, λαοῖσιν καθύπερθε πεποιθότες M 153. Cf. Σ 509.—Foot-soldiers as distinguished from fighters using chariots: ἵππον καὶ λαόν H 342. Cf. Ι 708, Σ 153.—A body detailed for some purpose: κριτὸς λαὸς Ἀχαιῶν H 434.

λᾶος, genit. λᾶας.

λᾱοσσόος, -ον [λαός + σο-, συ-, σεύω]. Urger of hosts. Epithet of Athene N 128: χ 210.—Of Ares P 398.—Of Eris Υ 48.—Of Apollo Υ 79.—Of Amphiaräus ο 244.

λᾱοφόρος, -ον [λαός + φορ-, φέρω. 'Carrying people']. Of a road, that is a highway, full of traffic: λαοφόρον καθ' ὁδόν Ο 682.

λαπάρη, -ης, ἡ. The hollow under the ribs on each side, the flank: οὖτα κατὰ λαπάρην Z 64. Cf. Γ 359 = H 253, Ξ 447, 517, Π 318, X 307.

†λάπτω [cf. L. *lambo*, Eng. *lap*]. Nom. pl. masc. fut. pple. λάψοντες. To lap up with the tongue: ἀπὸ κρήνης λάψοντες ὕδωρ Π 161.

λάρναξ, -ακος, ἡ. (1) A chest or coffer: ὅπλα λάρνακ' ἐς συλλέξατο Σ 413.—(2) A cinerary urn (= σορός) Ω 795.

λάρος, -ου. Some kind of sea-bird ε 51.

λᾱρός (prob. λα(σ)ερός, fr. λασ-, desire. Cf. λιλαίομαι). Pleasant to the taste P 572.—Epithet of δεῖπνον Τ 316.—Of δόρπον μ 283, ξ 408.—Superl. λαρώτατος β 350.

λάσιος, -η, -ον. Hairy, shaggy (as indicating strength): στήθεσσιν Α 189.—Applied to κῆρ used periphrastically (see κῆρ (2) (c)) B 851, Π 554.—In reference to a sheep or a part thereof, covered with thick wool, woolly Ω 125: ι 433.

†λάσκω. 3 sing. aor. λάκε N 616, Ξ 25, Υ 277. Pf. pple. λεληκώς X 141. Fem. λελακυῖα μ 85. (ἐπιληκέω.) To emit a sharp or piercing sound. Of bones breaking with a crack N 616.—Of the ring of struck metal: λάκε χαλκός Ξ 25. Cf. Υ 277.—Of the cry of a bird of prey in pursuit of its quarry: κίρκος ὀξὺ λεληκώς (with shrill cry) Χ 141.—Of the yell of Scylla μ 85.

λαυκανίη, -ης, ἡ (cf. ἀσφάραγος, φάρυξ). The throat: ᾗ κληῗδες ἀπ' ὤμων αὐχέν' ἔχουσι, λαυκανίην (in 'whole-and-part' apposition with αὐχένα) Χ 325.—More specifically, the gullet: οἶνον λαυκανίης καθέηκα Ω 642.

λαύρη, -ης, ἡ. A passage leading from front to back on the outside of one of the side walls of the μέγαρον χ 128, 137.

λαφύσσω [λαπ- as in λάπτω]. 3 sing. dual impf. λαφύσσετον Σ 583. To gulp down, swallow greedily. Of lions Λ 176=Ρ 64, Σ 583.

λάχε, 3 sing. aor. λαγχάνω.

λάχεια, *fem. adj.* [perh. fr. λαχ- as in λάχνη]. Thus, overgrown with brushwood, rough: νῆσος ι 116, ἀκτή κ 509 (*v.l.* in both cases ἐλάχεια, fem. of ἐλαχύς, small).

λάχνη, -ης, ἡ. (1) Hair, down: πυκάσαι γένυς λάχνῃ λ 320. Cf. Β 219.—(2) The nap or pile of cloth: οὔλη ἐπενήνοθε (*sc.* χλαίνῃ) λάχνη Κ 134.

λαχνήεις, -εντος [λάχνη]. Covered with hair, hairy, shaggy: Φῆρας Β 743, στήθεα Σ 415.—Bristly: συὸς δέρματι Ι 548.—Of a vegetable product, covered with down, downy: ὄροφον Ω 451.

λάχνος, -ου, ὁ [=λάχνη]. Wool ι 445.

λάχον, aor. λαγχάνω.

λάψοντες, nom. pl. masc. fut. pple. λάπτω.

λάω. Of a dog, app., to grip or pin: ἀσπαίροντα [ἐλλὸν] λάων τ 229. Cf. τ 230.

λάων, genit. pl. λᾶας.

λέβης, -ητος, ὁ. (1) A vessel of metal in which to boil water (app. distinguished from the τρίπος only by the shape) Ι 123=265=Τ 244, Φ 362, Ψ 259, 267, 485, 613, 885, Ω 233: μ 237, ν 13, 217, ο 84, ρ 222.—(2) Such a vessel to contain water for washing and in which the water was caught again after being poured over a part of the body: χέρνιβ' ἐπέχευεν ὑπὲρ ἀργυρέοιο λέβητος α 137=δ 53=η 173=κ 369=ο 136=ρ 92, λέβητα, τοῦ (with water from which) πόδας ἐξαπένιζεν τ 386. Cf. γ 440, τ 469.

†**λέγω**[1] [λεχ-]. Aor. ἔλεξα Ξ 252. Imp. λέξον Ω 635. Fut. mid. λέξομαι ρ 102, τ 595. 2 sing. λέξεαι η 319. 3 λέξεται δ 413. 3 sing. aor. ἐλέξατο Ι 666: δ 305. 3 dual λεξάσθην Ξ 350. Subj. λέξομαι ψ 172. 3 sing. λέξεται Δ 131. Opt. λεξαίμην γ 365, τ 598. 3 pl. imp. λεξάσθων Ι 67. Infin. λέξασθαι Θ 519. 3 sing. aor. ἔλεκτο τ 50. λέκτο δ 453, ε 487, η 346. Imp. λέξο Ω 650: κ 320. λέξεο Ι 617: τ 598. (κατα-, παρα-, παρακατα-, προσ-.) To lay. (1) To cause to lie down or take rest: λέξον με τάχιστα Ω 635.—Hence, to lull, soothe to rest: ἔλεξα Διὸς νόον Ξ 252.—(2) In mid., to lay oneself down, lie down, take rest: αὐτόθι λέξεο μίμνων Ι 617. Cf. Ι 666, Ξ 350, Ω 650: παρ' Ἑλένῃ ἐλέξατο δ 305, λέξομαι εἰς εὐνήν (will go to my bed and lay me down) ρ 102=τ 595. Cf. γ 365, δ 413, 453, ε 487, η 346, κ 320, τ 50, 598, ψ 172.—To bivouac, take up one's station: φυλακτῆρες λεξάσθων παρὰ τάφρον Ι 67. Cf. Θ 519.—(3) In mid., to lie, be at rest: ὅτε λέξεται ὕπνῳ (in sleep) Δ 131. Cf. η 319.

λέγω[2] [λεγ-]. Nom. pl. masc. fut. pple. λέξοντες ω 224. 3 sing. aor. ἔλεξε λ 151. 3 sing. aor. mid. λέξατο Φ 27. 3 sing. opt. λέξαιτο ω 108. Infin. λέξασθαι Β 125. Aor. ἐλέγμην ι 335. 3 sing. λέκτο δ 451. Aor. pass. ἐλέχθην Γ 188. (ἀλ-, διαλέγομαι, κατα-, προ-, συλ-.) (1) To gather up, pick up: ἀν' ἔντεα λέγοντες Λ 755.—To collect, gather, get together: αἱμασιὰς λέγων (λέξοντες) σ 359, ω 224.—To collect, get together a stock of. In mid.: ξύλα πολλὰ λέγεσθε (λέγοντο) Θ 507, 547.—To pick out, collect, bring together, out of a mass: ὀστέα Πατρόκλοιο λέγωμεν Ψ 239: λέγομέν τοι ὀστέα οἴνῳ ἐν ἀκρήτῳ (collected them and put them in . . .) ω 72.—In mid.: ὀστέα λέγοντο Ω 793.—(2) In mid., to pick out, choose, select: δυώδεκα λέξατο κούρους Φ 27. Cf. ω 108.—(3) To number, count: ἐν ἡμέας πρώτους λέγε κήτεσιν δ 452.—To reckon up, count (a number). In mid.: λέκτο δ' ἀριθμόν δ 451.—In mid., to number themselves, tell themselves off singly: εἴ κ' ἐθέλοιμεν Ἀχαιοί τε Τρῶές τε . . . Τρῶας μὲν λέξασθαι . . . Β 125.—(4) In mid., to number or reckon oneself (among others), add oneself (to their number): πέμπτος μετὰ τοῖσιν ἐλέγμην ι 335.—Sim. in pass.: μετὰ τοῖσιν ἐλέχθην (was numbered among them) Γ 188.—(5) To tell off or detail for some duty: ἐς λόχον Ν 276.—(6) To tell over, recount, relate, touch upon in order, go through, deal with, make communication of, put before one, explain: κήδεα πόλλ' Ὀδυσῆος ε 5, ἐπεὶ κατὰ θέσφατ' ἔλεξεν λ 151. Cf. λ 374, μ 165, ξ 197, 362, ο 487, τ 203, ψ 308.—(7) To utter a string of: λέγ' ὀνείδεα Β 222.—In mid.: τί σε χρὴ ταῦτα λέγεσθαι; (why string together words about that?) Ν 275.—(8) In mid., with reciprocal force, to talk together: μηκέτι νῦν δήθ' αὖθι λεγώμεθα (let us lose no more time in talk) Β 435.—Sim. with acc. of what is said: μηκέτι ταῦτα λεγώμεθα Ν 292=Υ 244: γ 240, ν 296.

†**λειαίνω** [λεῖος]. Fut. λειανέω Ο 261. 3 pl. aor. λείηναν θ 260. Pple. λειήνας Δ 111. To make smooth, polish Δ 111.—To make smooth, remove all obstacles or irregularities of surface from: κέλευθον πᾶσαν Ο 261. Cf. θ 260.

λείβω [cf. εἴβω]. Nom. dual masc. aor. pple. λείψαντε Ω 285: ο 149. Nom. pl. masc. λείψαντες σ 426. Infin. λεῖψαι Η 481: μ 362. (ἀπο-, ἐπι-, κατα-.) (1) To shed (tears): δάκρυα Ν 88, 658, Σ 32: ε 84=158, θ 86, 93=532, π 214.—(2) To pour forth (wine) in way of libation: Διὶ λείβειν οἶνον Ζ 266. Cf. Κ 579, Π 231=Ω 306, Α 463:=γ 460.—Absol., to make libation: πρὶν λεῖψαι Κρονίωνι Η 481, ὄφρα λείψαντε κιοίτην (might make libation before going) Ω 285: οὐδ' εἶχον μέθυ λεῖψαι (to make libation therewith) μ 362. Cf. β 432, ο 149, σ 426.

λείηναν, 3 pl. aor. λειαίνω.

λειμών, -ῶνος, ὁ [λείβω]. A tract of low well-watered ground, a meadow: Ἀσίῳ ἐν λειμῶνι,

Καϋστρίου ἀμφὶ ῥέεθρα B 461. Cf. B 463, 467, Π 151: δ 605, ε 72, ζ 292, ι 132, λ 539, 573, μ 45, 159, φ 49, ω 13.

λειμωνόθεν [λειμών + -θεν (1)]. From the meadows: ὄροφον λ. ἀμήσαντες Ω 451 (*i.e.* cutting them in the meadows and bringing them away).

λεῖος, -η, -ον (λεῖϝος. Cf. L. *lēvis*). Smooth, free from obstacles or irregularities of surface, with unbroken surface: ἱππόδρομος Ψ 330. Cf. Ψ 359: ι 134, κ 103.—Not obstructed by, free from. With genit.: λεῖος πετράων ε 443 = η 282.—App., in neut. pl. λεῖα in *quasi*-substantival use, a smooth state of things, a stretch of ground with smooth or unbroken surface: λεῖα δ' ἐποίησεν παρ' Ἑλλήσποντον M 30.—Of a poplar, having the branches of the stem cut close, trimmed Δ 484.

λείπω. Fut. λείψω δ 602. 3 sing. λείψει O 136. 1 pl. λείψετε N 620. Infin. λείψειν Σ 11. Aor. ἔλιπον E 480. λίπον E 204, I 447, Λ 759. 2 sing. λίπες K 406. 3 ἔλιπε B 35, 106: ξ 426. λίπε A 428, Δ 292, E 696, K 287, Λ 99, Ξ 225, Σ 65, Ω 470, etc.: γ 455, η 79, μ 1, π 341, ρ 254, etc. 3 dual λιπέτην K 273, Ξ 284: γ 485. 1 pl. λίπομεν δ 488. 3 ἔλιπον Ω 580. λίπον B 722, Π 371, 507, P 535: ζ 317, κ 209, χ 119. Subj. λίπω P 91. 3 sing. λίπῃ Π 453: λ 221. 3 sing. opt. λίποι E 685: η 224, σ 91. 1 pl. λίποιμεν Δ 173. 2 λίποιτε B 176. 3 λίποιεν B 160, P 667. Imp. λίπε κ 266, ο 199. 3 sing. λιπέτω γ 424. 2 pl. λίπετε K 443, T 403. Pple. λιπών, -όντος Δ 181, E 20, Z 254, N 250, Ξ 281, P 612, etc.: γ 1, η 65, λ 93, σ 257, φ 90, etc. Fem. λιποῦσα Γ 174, Π 857, X 363, Ω 144: σ 270. Acc. λιποῦσαν τ 531. Infin. λιπεῖν M 111. 3 sing. pf. λέλοιπε A 235: ξ 134, 213. **Mid.** Aor. λιπόμην Λ 693: ι 316, ν 286, ο 481. 3 sing. λίπετο Π 294, Ω 707: δ 536. 3 pl. (ἐ)λίποντο M 14: δ 495, θ 125, υ 67. 3 sing. subj. λίπηται T 235: δ 710. 2 dual λίπησθον Ψ 407. 2 pl. λίπησθε Ψ 248. 3 λίπωνται T 230: γ 354 Opt. λιποίμην I 437: φ 116. 3 sing. λίποιτο Γ 160. Infin. λιπέσθαι E 154, Ξ 485: γ 196, ρ 187. **Pass.** 3 sing. fut. pf. λελείψεται Ω 742. 3 sing. pf. λέλειπται K 253, N 256, Ω 260. Plupf. λελείμμην X 334. 3 sing. ἐλέλειπτο B 700: θ 475. λέλειπτο K 256, N 168, Ψ 523: κ 447, χ 200. Pple. λελειμμένος ι 448. Nom. pl. masc. λελειμμένοι Ω 687. Infin. λελεῖφθαι Ω 256, 494. (ἀπο-, ἐκπρο-, κατα-, προ-, ὑπο-.) **(1)** To leave behind, not to take or bring with one: ὡς λίπον [ἵππους] E 204, τὸ δ' ἐὸν [φάσγανον] παρὰ νηῒ λέλειπτο K 256. Cf. K 443, M 111, N 168, T 339 (had left), Φ 17, 496: δ 602, ι 238, 338, ξ 425, 480, φ 90, χ 95.—**(2)** To leave behind while taking other things or the rest: κὰδ δ' ἔλιπον δύο φάρεα Ω 580: ἐπὶ πλεῖον ἐλέλειπτο (was left) θ 475. Cf. ν 258.—**(3)** To leave remaining; in pass., to remain, be left: τριτάτη ἔτι μοῖρα λέλειπται (is all that is left us for our work (not implying that the whole of it remained)) K 253. Cf. N 256, Ψ 640.—**(4)** To leave (a person) behind while one departs, to leave, quit, withdraw from (often with specification of the place or state in which the person is left): τὸν δὲ λίπ' αὐτοῦ χωόμενον A 428, ὅθι μιν λίπον υἷες Ἀχαιῶν B 722. Cf. B 35, Δ 181 (his corpse), I 445, K 273, Σ 468, T 288, X 213, etc.: ὃν λεῖπε νέον γεγαῶτ' ἐνὶ οἴκῳ δ 112, οὐδὲ παρὰ νηῒ λέλειπτο (stayed behind) κ 447. Cf. γ 424, κ 209, λ 68, ν 403, χ 200, etc.—Sim.: κατά κεν εὐχωλὴν Πριάμῳ λίποιεν Ἑλένην B 160. Cf. B 176, Δ 173.—**(5)** To leave, forsake, abandon, leave to one's own devices or to one's (or its) fate: ἔνθ' ἄλοχον ἔλιπον καὶ νήπιον υἱόν E 480, λίπε λαὸν Ἀχαιϊκόν O 218. Cf. Γ 174, Π 368, P 13, 535, T 403, etc.—**(6)** To leave (a disposed-of foe) without taking further action, let (him) lie: ἄνδρα κτείνας πύματον λίπον Λ 759. Cf. Λ 99, Φ 201.—**(7)** Of the life leaving the body: τὸν λίπε θυμός Δ 470. Cf. E 685, 696, M 386, Π 857, etc.: γ 455, η 224, λ 221, μ 414, ξ 426, σ 91.—Absol.: ψυχὴ λέλοιπεν ξ 134.—**(8)** To leave, quit, withdraw from (a place): Ἑλλάδα I 447. Cf. Ξ 225, 281, Σ 65, X 137, etc.: ποταμοῖο ῥέεθρα ζ 317. Cf. γ 1, η 79, θ 452, κ 462, ξ 301, τ 531, etc.—Sim.: λιπὼν δίφρον E 20, λίπε νῆας Λ 229, λιπέτην ἅλα Ξ 284. Cf. I 194, O 124, 729, etc.: λιπὼν φάος ἠελίοιο λ 93.—Of a severed tree: ἐπεὶ πρῶτα τομὴν λέλοιπεν A 235.—**(9)** To leave, cease to take part in (the fight): λιπὼν πόλεμον (quitting the field) Z 254, Ξ 43. Cf. N 250.—**(10)** To let be, leave in peace, cease to vex: σκόπελον οὔ ποτε κύματα λείπει B 396. Cf. O 136.—**(11)** To leave behind one as heir, successor, avenger: ἀοσσητὴρ μετόπισθε λελείμμην X 334: μίαν οἴην παῖδα λιπόντα η 65.—**(12)** To leave alive; in pass., to be left living, survive (cf. (18) (d)): τῶν οὔ τινά φημι λελεῖφθαι Ω 256 = 494. Cf. Ω 260.—**(13)** To leave as an inheritance or bequest: Ἀτρεὺς θνήσκων ἔλιπε [σκῆπτρον] Θυέστῃ B 106. Cf. B 107.—**(14)** To leave behind one at one's death in a specified state or condition: κατὰ με χήρην λείπεις Ω 726. Cf. B 700, X 483.—**(15)** To cause (a future of woe) to be another's lot: πατέρι (*i.e.* the father of his victims) γόον καὶ κήδεα λεῖπεν E 157, ἐμοὶ λελείψεται ἄλγεα (will be my lot) Ω 742.—**(16)** To leave behind, outdistance; in pass., to come behind, be outdistanced by. With genit.: λείπετο Μενελάου δουρὸς ἐρωήν Ψ 529. Cf. Ψ 523 (where the word occurs again without construction): λελειμμένος οἰῶν ι 448.—In mid., to let oneself be left behind or outdistanced (see also (18) (e)): τίη λείπεσθε; Ψ 409.—**(17)** To fail, cease to be available to: ἐπεὶ λίπον ἰοὶ ἄνακτα χ 119.—*Intrans.*, to fail, come to nothing: νῦν ἤδη πάντα λέλοιπεν ξ 213.—**(18)** In aor. mid. **(a)** To be left behind while another departs, be left: ὅς κε λίπηται νηυσὶν ἐπ' Ἀργείων (shall tarry) T 235, οὐδέ τις αὐτόθι λίπετ' ἀνήρ Ω 707. Cf. I 437: λιπόμην ἀκαχήμενος ἦτορ ν 286, αὐτοῦ λιπέσθαι (to stay here) ρ 187. Cf. ι 316, φ 116.—Sim.: μηδ' ἡμῖν πῆμα λίποιτο Γ 160.—**(b)** To be left after the occurrence of something in a specified state or condition: ἡμιδαὴς νηῦς λίπετο Π 294: λιπόμην ἀκαχήμενος ἦτορ ο 481. Cf. υ 67.—**(c)** To be left as heir, successor, protector, avenger: υἱὸν οὐ τέκετ' ἄλλον ἐπὶ κτεάτεσσι λιπέσθαι E 154, γνωτὸν ἀρῆς ἀλκτῆρα λιπέσθαι Ξ 485. Cf. γ 196, 354.—(d) To be left living, survive: οἱ μὲν δάμεν, οἱ δὲ λίποντο M 14. Cf. Λ 693, T 230, Ψ 248: οὐδέ τις ἑτάρων λίπετο δ 536. Cf. δ 495.—Sim.: ἵνα μηδ' ὄνομ' αὐτοῦ λίπηται δ 710.—(e) To be left behind or outdistanced: οἱ δ' ἐλίποντο θ 125.—To let oneself be left behind or outdistanced (see also (16)): ἵππους Ἀτρεΐδαο κιχάνετε, μηδὲ λίπησθον Ψ 407.

λειριόεις, -εντος. Fem. -εσσα [λείριον, lily]. (1) Lily-white: χρόα λειριόεντα N 830.—(2) Epithet of the thin voice of the cicada, to which the 'chirruping' of old men is likened Γ 152 (the tenuity of the sound app. suggesting the tenuity of the flower's form).

λεϊστός, by-form of ληϊστός.

λεῖψαι, aor. infin. λείβω.

λείψω, fut. λείπω.

λέκτο[1], 3 sing. aor. mid. λέγω[1].

λέκτο[2], 3 sing. aor. mid. λέγω[2].

λέκτρον, -ου, τό [λεκ-, λεχ-, λέγω[1]]. A bedstead, a bed: ἕζετ' ἐν λέκτρῳ α 437. Cf. τ 516, ψ 32, 296.—In pl. in the same sense: εὕδεσκ' ἐν λέκτροισιν X 503. Cf. θ 337, υ 58, 141.

λέκτρονδε [prec. + -δε (1)]. To bed: λέκτρονδε εὐνηθέντες (going to bed) θ 292. Cf. ψ 254.

λελαβέσθαι, redup. aor. infin. mid. λαμβάνω.

λελάθῃ, 3 sing. subj. redup. aor. λανθάνω.

λελάθοντο, 3 pl. redup. aor. mid. λανθάνω.

λελακυῖα, fem. pf. pple. λάσκω.

λελασμένος, pf. pple. mid. λανθάνω.

λελάχωσι, 3 pl. subj. redup. aor. λαγχάνω.

λελειμμένος, pf. pple. pass. λείπω.

λέλειπται, 3 sing. pf. pass. λείπω.

λελεῖφθαι, pf. infin. pass. λείπω.

λελείψεται, 3 sing. fut. pf. pass. λείπω.

λεληκώς, pf. pple. λάσκω.

λελίημαι, *pf.* Only in pple. Showing eager haste, using eager speed: βὰν ἰθὺς Δαναῶν λελιημένοι M 106, Π 552.—With ὄφρα (instead of infin.): λελιημένος ὄφρα τάχιστα τεύχεα συλήσειεν (eager to . . .) Δ 465. Cf. E 690.

λελόγχᾱσι, 3 pl. pf. λαγχάνω.

λέλοιπε, 3 sing. pf. λείπω.

λελουμένος, pf. pple. mid. λούω.

λέλυται, 3 sing. pf. pass. λύω.

λελῦτο, 3 sing. pf. opt. pass. λύω.

λέξασθαι[1], aor. infin. mid. λέγω[1].

λέξασθαι[2], aor. infin. mid. λέγω[2].

λέξεο, λέξο, aor. imp. mid. λεγω[1].

λέξομαι[1], fut. mid. λέγω[1].

λέξομαι[2], aor. subj. mid. λέγω[1].

λέξον, aor. imp. λέγω[1].

λέξοντες, nom. pl. masc. fut. pple. λέγω[2].

λέπαδνον, τό. The breast-strap against which a chariot-horse pulled. Only in pl. (perh. so used to include the girth): ἐν λέπαδνα κάλ' ἔβαλεν E 730. Cf. T 393.

λεπταλέος, -η [λεπτός]. Of a boy's singing-voice, small, soft Σ 571.

λεπτός, -ή, -όν [λέπω]. (1) Shelled out from the husk, peeled. Absol. in neut. pl.: ῥίμφα λέπτ' ἐγένοντο (it, *i.e.* the barley, becomes peeled grain (the vb. assimilated in number to the predicate)) Υ 497.—(2) Of small thickness, thin. In superl. λεπτότατος, -η: ᾗ λεπτότατος θέε χαλκός Υ 275. Cf. Υ 276.—Small in section, slender, thin: μηρίνθῳ Ψ 854.—Small in width, narrow: εἰσίθμη ζ 264.—In or consisting of fine threads or fibres: ἀράχνια θ 280. Cf. β 95 = ω 130, ρ 97, τ 140.—Of fine texture, delicately woven: λίνοιο λεπτὸν ἄωτον I 661, ὀθόνας Σ 595. Cf. X 511: ε 231 = κ 544, η 97, κ 223 (in reference to the web).—In a state of fine division, powdery: κονίῃ Ψ 506.—(3) Of a mental faculty, narrow in range, of small reach: μῆτις K 226, Ψ 590.

†**λέπω**, 3 sing. aor. ἔλεψε. (ἀπο-.) To strip or peel off: περί ἑ χαλκὸς ἔλεψε φύλλα τε καὶ φλοιόν (double acc. of whole and part) A 236.

λέσχη, -ης, ἡ. App., some place of public resort: εὕδειν ἐς λέσχην [ἐλθών] σ 329.

λευγαλέος, -η, -ον [cf. λυγρός]. (1) Suffering wretchedness, wretched, in sorry case: πτωχῷ π 273 = ρ 202 = ω 157, ρ 337.—(2) As a term of contempt, sorry, pitiful, wretched, weak: φρεσίν I 119. Cf. β 61.—App., inferring contempt, contemptuous, abusive: ἐπέεσσιν Υ 109.—(3) Bringing or inferring wretchedness or woe, wretched, woeful, miserable, baleful: θανάτῳ Φ 281 := ε 312, ο 359. Cf. ο 399, υ 203.—As epithet of war: πολέμοιο N 97, δαΐ Ξ 387.

λευγαλέως [adv. fr. prec.]. In sorry case, in pitiful plight: λ. κε Τρῶες ἐχώρησαν N 723.

λευκαίνω [λευκός]. (ὑπο-.) To make white, whiten: λεύκαινον ὕδωρ ἐλάτῃσιν μ 172.

λεύκασπις, -ιδος [λευκός + ἀσπίς]. With bright shield. Epithet of Deïphobus X 294.

λευκός, -ή, -όν [λυκ- as in λύχνος. Cf. L. *luceo*]. (1) Bright, resplendent, shining: ὀμφαλοί Λ 35. Cf. Ξ 185, Ψ 268: ζ 45, κ 94.—(2) Bright or light in colour, often to be translated 'white,' but of very indefinite application (often a mere epithet): ἱστία A 480, πόλιν Ὀλοοσσόνα B 739, γάλα Δ 434, E 902, κρῖ E 196, Θ 564, Υ 496, ὀδόντας E 291, πήχεε 314. Cf. B 735, Γ 103, E 503, 583, K 263, Λ 416, 573 = O 316, Λ 640, Π 347, P 56, Σ 353, 560, Ψ 252, 282, 329, 455, Ω 231, 793: ὀστέα α 161, λ 221, ω 72, 76, ἱστία β 426 = ο 291, δ 783 = θ 54, ι 77, κ 506, μ 402, [λίθοι] γ 408, κρῖ δ 41, 604, μ 358, ὕδατι ε 70, γάλακτος ι 246, ἄλφιτα κ 520, λ 28, ξ 77, ὀδόντι τ 393 = ψ 74, τ 465, φ 219, ω 332, πήχεε ψ 240.—Comp. λευκότερος, -η K 437: σ 196.

λευκώλενος, -ον [λευκός + ὠλένη, the lower arm]. White-armed. Epithet of Here and of women. Of Here A 55, 195, 208, 572, 595, E 711, Θ 350, O 92, Φ 377, Ω 55, etc.—Of Helen Γ 121: χ 227.—Of Andromache Z 371, 377, Ω 723.—Of Nausicaa ζ 101, 186, 251, η 12.—Of Arete η 233, 335, λ 335.—ἀμφίπολοι ζ 239, σ 198.—δμωαί τ 60.

λευρός [λεϝ-ρός. Cf. λεῖος]. With even surface, level: χώρῳ η 123.

λεύσσω. (ἐπι-.) (1) To discern with the eye, have sight of, see, perceive, behold: πυρὸς ἰωήν

Π 127. Cf. Π 70, Υ 346 : πυρπολέοντας κ 30. Cf. ζ 157, θ 200.—(2) To look at, inspect, examine : δαίδαλα Τ 19.—(3) To direct one's sight, look, gaze : ἐπὶ πόντον Ε 771. Cf. θ 171, ι 166.—(4) To see mentally, see, perceive : λεύσσετε τό γε, ὃ . . . Α 120.—(5) To direct one's mind to an end, take thought, consider : λεύσσει ὅπως . . . Γ 110.—To take thought for, consider : ταῦτά γε λεῦσσε ψ 124.

λεχεποίη [λεχ-, λέγω¹ + ποίη]. With beds of grass, with fair meadows, grassy. Epithet of a city : Πτελεόν Β 697.

λεχεποίης [= prec.]. With grassy banks. Epithet of a river : Ἀσωπόν Δ 383.

λέχος, τό [λεχ-, λέγω¹]. Dat. λεχέεσσι Γ 448, Σ 233, Χ 87, Ψ 25, Ω 600, etc. : α 366, γ 399, κ 497, ω 44, etc. λέχεσσι Γ 391 : α 440, κ 12. (1) Properly, a bedstead as distinguished from the bedding (εὐνή) : ἐκθεῖσαι λέχος ἐμβάλετ' εὐνήν ψ 179. Cf. ψ 184, 189, 199, 203. (Cf. λ. καὶ εὐνήν γ 403, η 347, θ 269 cited under (3) (a).)—In pl. of a single bed : ἐν δινωτοῖσι λέχεσσιν Γ 391. Cf. Γ 448 : α 440, γ 399 = η 345, κ 12.—(2) A bed, one's bed : πρὸς ὃν λέχος ἤϊεν Α 609. Cf. Ι 621, 659, 660, Ω 648 : η 340 = ψ 291, ψ 171, 177.—In pl. of a single bed : οὐ μοι θνήσκων λεχέων ἐκ χεῖρας ὄρεξας Ω 743 : ἐκ λεχέων μ' ἀνεγεῖραι (my bed) δ 730. Cf. κ 497.—(3) (a) The marriage-bed : νωΐτερον λέχος αὐτῶν Ο 39. Cf. Γ 411 : ἄλοχος λέχος πόρσυνε καὶ εὐνήν γ 403. Cf. η 347, θ 269.—In pl. : παραὶ λεχέεσσι κλιθῆναι (παραί advbl.) α 366 = σ 213. Cf. Λ 1 : = ε 1.—(b) With reference to intercourse outside of wedlock : ἤ κέν τοι ὁμὸν λ. εἰσαναβαίνοι Θ 291. Cf. Α 31.—(4) A litter used for carrying a dead body from the field. In pl. : Πάτροκλον κάτθεσαν ἐν λεχέεσσιν Σ 233.—A stand on which a dead body was placed to await the funeral rites or on which it could be carried, a bier. In pl. : οὔ σε κλαύσομαι ἐν λεχέεσσιν Χ 87, τὸν λεχέων ἐπέθηκεν Ω 589. Cf. Σ 352, Φ 124, Χ 353, Ψ 25, 171, Ω 600, 702, 720 : ω 44, 295.

λέχοσδε [prec. + -δε (1)]. To bed Γ 447 : ψ 294.

λέων, -οντος, ὁ. (Referring to the female Ζ 181, Ρ 133, Φ 483 (though in Ρ 133 in masc. construction).) Dat. pl. λέουσι Χ 262. λείουσι Ε 782, Η 256, Ο 592. A lion Γ 23, Ε 161, Ζ 181, Μ 299, Ρ 133, Σ 579, Χ 262, etc. : δ 335 = ρ 126, δ 456, 791, ζ 130, ι 292, κ 212, 218, 433, λ 611, χ 402 = ψ 48.

λήγω. Fut. λήξω Ι 97, Τ 423, Φ 224. Infin. λήξειν ν 294. 3 pl. aor. λῆξαν Ζ 107. Opt. λήξαιμι χ 63. 3 sing. λήξειε Ι 191 : θ 87. (ἀπο-, μεταλλήγω.) (1) To cease, give over, desist, stop : οὐδ' ἔληγε θεός Φ 248. Cf. Ι 97, Τ 423.—(2) To cease or desist from. With genit. : ἔριδος Α 210, 319, Ι 257, Φ 359, χοροῖο νέον λήγοντα (pple. of the impf., 'having just . . .') Γ 394. Cf. Α 224, Ζ 107, Κ 164 : ν 294.—With complementary pple. : ὁπότε λήξειεν ἀείδων Ι 191. Cf. Φ 224 : θ 87.—(3) To cause to cease from something, put restraint upon : οὐ λῆγε μένος μέγα Ν 424. Cf. Φ 305.—With genit. indicating that from which one restrains : φόνοιο χ 63.

ληθάνω [λήθω]. To cause to forget. With genit. : ἔκ με πάντων ληθάνει η 221.

λήθη, ἡ [λήθω]. Forgetfulness Β 33.

λήθω. See λανθάνω.

ληϊάς, -άδος [ληΐς]. Captured, taken Υ 193.

ληϊβότειρα, -ης [λήϊον + βοτ-, βόσκω]. Crop-consuming. Epithet of the wild boar σ 29.

†ληΐζομαι [ληΐς]. Fut. ληΐσσομαι ψ 357. 3 sing. aor. ληΐσσατο Σ 28 : α 398. To get by rapine, carry off as captives or spoil : δμῳαὶ ἃς ληΐσσατο Σ 28 : πολλὰ ληΐσσομαι ψ 357. Cf. α 398.

λήϊον, -ου, τό. Standing corn : βαθὺ λ. Β 147, Λ 560. Cf. Ψ 599 : ι 134.

ληΐς, -ΐδος, ἡ. Spoil, booty : ὅτε κεν δατεώμεθα ληΐδα Ι 138 = 280. Cf. Λ 677, Μ 7, Σ 327 : μενοεικέα σφι ληΐδα δῶκα (booty which he had in hand) ν 273. Cf. γ 106, ε 40 = ν 138, κ 41, ν 262, ξ 86.

ληϊστήρ, -ῆρος, ὁ [ληΐζομαι]. One who sails the sea in quest of spoil, a rover : οἷά τε ληϊστῆρες [ἀλόωνται] ὑπεὶρ ἅλα γ 73 = ι 254. Cf. π 426, ρ 425.

ληϊστός, -ή, -όν [ληΐζομαι]. Also **λεϊστός.** That may be carried off as spoil or booty : ληϊστοὶ βόες [εἰσὶ] καὶ μῆλα Ι 406. Cf. Ι 408.

ληΐστωρ, -ορος, ὁ [as ληϊστήρ]. = ληϊστήρ : Τάφιοι ληΐστορες ἄνδρες ο 427.

ληῖτις, -ιδος [ληΐς]. That dispenses the spoil. Epithet of Athene Κ 460.

λήκυθος, -ου, ἡ. An oil-flask ζ 79, 215.

λήξω, fut. λήγω.

λήσει, 3 sing. fut. λήθω. See λανθάνω.

λιάζομαι. 2 sing. aor. λιάσθης Χ 12. 3 (ἐ)λιάσθη Ο 520, 543 : δ 838. 3 pl. λίασθεν Ψ 879. Pple. λιασθείς Α 349, Λ 80, Υ 418, Φ 255, Ψ 231 : ε 462. (1) To bend and slip away from danger : ὁ δ' ὕπαιθα λιάσθη Ο 520. Cf. Φ 255.—(2) To sink down, droop, fall : πρηνὴς ἐλιάσθη Ο 543. Cf. Υ 418, 420.—Of the drooping of a dying bird's wings Ψ 879.—(3) To slip or glide away : παρὰ κληῖδα λιάσθη δ 838.—(4) To go aside or apart, retire : ἑτάρων νόσφι λιασθείς Α 349. Cf. Λ 80, Ψ 231 : ε 462.—To turn aside from one's proper course : σὺ δεῦρο λιάσθης Χ 12.—(5) To part, open so as to afford passage : λιάζετό σφι κῦμα θαλάσσης Ω 96.

λιαρός. Warm : ὕδατι Λ 830, 846, Χ 149. Cf. Λ 477 : ω 45.—Of a warm soft wind : οὖρον ε 268 = η 266.—Of balmy sleep Ξ 164.

λιάσθη, 3 sing. aor. λιάζομαι.

λίγα [λιγυρός. Cf. λίπα]. In clear or loud tones, loudly, with full voice : λίγ' ἐκώκυεν Τ 284. Cf. δ 259, θ 527, κ 254.

λιγαίνω [λιγύς]. To use the full voice, make proclamation. With infin. indicating the purport : κήρυκες λίγαινον τοὺς ἴμεν οἷσι . . . Λ 685.

†λίγγω. 3 sing. aor. λίγξε. To twang Δ 125.

λίγδην. With a glancing blow, grazing the flesh : Τηλέμαχον βάλε χεῖρα λ. χ 278.

λιγέως [adv. fr. λιγύς]. In clear tones, with a clear flow of words : [ἀγόρευεν] Γ 214.—In loud tones, loudly : κλαίοντα Τ 5. Cf. κ 201, λ 391, π 216, φ 56.—Of blowing winds, whistling : φυσῶντες λ. Ψ 218.

λιγυρός, -ή, -όν [λιγύς]. Clear-sounding: ἀοιδῇ μ 44. Cf. μ 183.—Of winds or the blowing thereof, whistling E 526, N 590, Ψ 215.—So of a whip whistling in the air Λ 532.—Of a bird, that utters a shrill cry Ξ 290.

λιγύς, λίγεια, λιγύ. Emitting a clear or shrill sound. (1) Speaking in clear tones, whose words flow clearly forth: λ. ἀγορητής Α 248. Cf. Β 246, Δ 293, Τ 82: υ 274.—Epithet of Μοῦσα ω 62.—Of winds, whistling N 334, Ξ 17, Ο 620: γ 176, 289, δ 357.—(2) In neut. λιγύ as adv., with whistling sound δ 567.—(3) Emitting a clear note, resonant. Epithet of the 'sounding lyre' Ι 186, Σ 569: θ 67 = 105, 254, 261, 537, χ 332, ψ 133.

λιγύφθογγος [λιγύς + φθογγή]. Clear-voiced. Epithet of heralds B 50, 442, I 10, Ψ 39: β 6.

λιγύφωνος, -ον [λιγύς + φωνή]. Of a bird, that utters a shrill cry: ἅρπη Τ 350.

λίην (ῑ). (1) Exceedingly, very, very much: λ. φύλλοισιν ἐοικότες Β 800: νήπιός εἰς λ. τόσον; (so very . . . as this would seem to show thee to be) δ 371. Cf. θ 231, 489, κ 552, ν 238, 243, ο 405 (not so very . . .).—With notion of excess: λ. πολλοί (too many for that) Τ 226. Cf. Ι 229, Φ 566: λ. πινυτή (too much so for any fear of that) λ 445, λ. ἑκὰς ἤλθομεν ξ 496. Cf. γ 227, ν 421, π 243.—(2) With verbs, exceedingly, greatly: κεχολώατο λ. ξ 282, π 425. Cf. ξ 461, υ 99.—With notion of excess: λ. ἄχθομαι ἕλκος (I can bear it no longer) E 361, λ. μαίνεται (his rage passes all bounds) Ζ 100. Cf. Ζ 486, Ν 284, Ξ 368 (we can make shift to do without him), Φ 288: μηδὲ δείδιθι λ. δ 825. Cf. θ 205 (I can contain myself no longer), π 86 (too much to let me think of that), σ 20 (do not provoke me too far), ψ 175 (unduly).—(3) καὶ λίην, truly, verily, of a surety: καὶ λίην κεῖνός γε ἐοικότι κεῖται ὀλέθρῳ α 46. Cf. Α 553, Τ 408: γ 203, ι 477, λ 181 = π 37, ν 393, ο 155, ρ 312.—Strengthening a wish: καὶ λ. οὗτός γε μένος ὀλέσειεν Θ 358.

λίθαξ, -ακος [λίθος]. Of a rock, app., studded with projecting stones, rough ε 415.

λιθάς, -άδος, ἡ [λίθος]. In dat. pl. λιθάδεσσι. (1) A stone: σεῦεν κύνας πυκνῇσιν λιθάδεσσιν ξ 36. —(2) In pl., stones used in construction ψ 193.

λίθεος [λίθος]. Of stone Ψ 202: ν 107.

λίθος, -ου, ὁ. Fem. M 287: τ 494. (1) A stone E 308, H 264, Θ 327, M 287, 459, Π 740, Φ 403, Ψ 340: θ 190, ι 305, 416, ν 370, τ 494.—A large stone used as or shaped into a seat: ἧατ' ἐπὶ ξεστοῖσι λίθοις Σ 504. Cf. θ 6.—In pl. app. of several stones forming or shaped into a seat γ 406.—A large stone embedded in the ground, or perh. a rock projecting above the ground, pierced for the securing of a cable ν 77.—(2) In pl., stones used in construction: ὡς ὅτε τοῖχον ἀνὴρ ἀράρῃ πυκινοῖσι λίθοισιν Π 212. Cf. ι 185. —(3) Stone as a material: θάλαμοι ξεστοῖο λίθοιο Ζ 244, 248. Cf. Δ 510: ψ 103.—(4) Something of stone: λαοὺς λίθους ποίησεν (turned them to stone) Ω 611, λίθος περ ἐοῦσα (stone though she be) 617. Cf. ν 156.—(5) A rock or reef γ 296.

λικμάω. To winnow grain, etc., by throwing it against the wind E 500.

λικμητήρ, -ῆρος, ὁ [λικμάω]. A winnower N 590.

λικριφίς. Obliquely, sideways: λ. ἀΐξας Ξ 463: τ 451.

λιλαίομαι [λι-λάσομαι, fr. λασ-, desire. Cf. λαρός]. (1) To desire or be anxious *to do something* or *for something to happen*, be bent or set on *doing something*. With infin.: εἰ ἐν φιλότητι λιλαίεαι εὐνηθῆναι Ξ 331. Cf. Γ 399, N 253, Π 89, Υ 76: εἰ ἀκουέμεναι λιλαίεαι λ 380. Cf. α 15 = ι 30, ι 32, 451, ο 308, 327, υ 27, χ 349 (find it not in thy heart to . . .), ψ 334.—Of inanimate objects Λ 574 = Ο 317, Φ 168.—(2) To desire, be eager for. With genit.: πολέμοιο Γ 133: βιότοιο (tendering, in fear for, their lives) μ 328, ω 536. Cf. α 315, ν 31.—φόωσδε λιλαίεο (make thy way with all speed to . . .) λ 223.

λιμήν, -ένος, ὁ. Dat. pl. λιμένεσσι Ψ 745. λιμέσι M 284: τ 189. A harbour or haven A 432, M 284, Φ 23: α 186, β 391, ε 404, ν 96, ξ 1, π 324, etc.—In pl. in the same sense: στῆσαν ἐν λιμένεσσιν Ψ 745. Cf. τ 189.

λίμνη, -ης, ἡ. A piece or sheet of water. (1) A pool: Τάνταλον ἐσταότ' ἐν λίμνῃ λ 583.—(2) A lake B 711, 865, E 709, Υ 390.—Of the water spread by a river overflowing its banks Φ 317.—(3) The sea N 21, 32, Ω 79: γ 1 (the Ocean stream), ε 337.

λῑμός, -οῦ, ὁ. Hunger (in Τ 348, 354: ε 166, κ 177 app. used to include thirst) Τ 166, 348, 354: δ 369 = μ 332, ε 166, κ 177, μ 342.

λῖν, acc. λίς[1].

λινοθώρηξ [λίνον + θώρηξ]. Wearing a stout tunic of linen by way of corslet B 529, 830.

λίνον, -ου, τό. Flax; things made thereof. (1) A cord, a fishing-line Π 408.—The thread of destiny: τὰ πείσεται ἅσσα οἱ Αἶσα γιγνομένῳ ἐπένησε λίνῳ Υ 128. Cf. Ω 210: η 198.—(2) Something made of cords, a net E 487.—(3) Linen; app. a sheet of linen wherewith to cover oneself in bed (cf. ῥῆγος): Ὀδυσσῆϊ στόρεσαν ῥῆγός τε λίνον τε ν 73. Cf. ν 118.—λίνοιο ἄωτος. See ἄωτος (2) (a).

λίνος, -ου, ὁ. A song sung at the vintage (see Frazer, *Golden Bough*, 3rd ed. pt. v. vol. i. pp. 216, 257) Σ 570.

λίπα [prob. related to λιπαρός as λίγα to λιγυρός]. In reference to anointing, richly, plenteously: ἐπεὶ ἔχρισεν λίπ' ἐλαίῳ γ 466 = κ 364. Cf. K 577, Ξ 171, Σ 350: ζ 96, 227, κ 450, τ 505.

λιπαροκρήδεμνος, -ον [λιπαρός]. With bright head-dress. Epithet of Χάρις Σ 382.

λιπαροπλόκαμος, -ον [λιπαρός]. With tresses glossy with oil: κεφαλῆς Τ 126.

λιπαρός, -ή, -όν. (1) Anointed with oil: αἰεὶ λιπαροὶ κεφαλὰς καὶ πρόσωπα ο 332.—(2) Bright as with oil, bright, glossy (or perh. shining with actual oil; cf. χιτῶνας ἧκα στίλβοντας ἐλαίῳ Σ 596): καλύπτρην Χ 406: κρήδεμνα α 334 = π 416 = σ 210 = φ 65.—Of a 'diadem of towers,' bright, glittering: Τροίης λιπαρὰ κρήδεμνα ν 388.—Of the feet, smooth, fair, goodly Ξ 241, B 44 = K 22 = 132 = Ξ 186 : = β 4 = δ 309 = υ 126, ν 225, ρ 410.—(3) Gentle in incidence or operation, pleasant: θέμιστας I 156, 298 : γήρᾳ λ 136 = ψ 283, τ 368.

λιπαρῶς [adv. fr. prec.]. Of a gentle decline into the vale of years, gently, imperceptibly: γηρασκέμεν δ 210.

λίπον, aor. λείπω.

λίς[1], ὁ [not conn. with λέων]. (Referring to the female Σ 318 (though in masc. construction).) Acc. λῖν Λ 480. A lion Λ 239, 480, O 275, P 109, Σ 318.

λίς[2]. Only in dat. λῖτί Σ 352, Ψ 254. Acc. λῖτα Θ 441 : α 130. This form app. as acc. pl. neut. κ 353. A cloth or covering Θ 441.—Used for covering a corpse laid out to await funeral rites Σ 352.—For covering a cinerary urn Ψ 254.—A cloth whereon to sit: ὑπὸ λῖτα πετάσσας α 130, κ 353.

λίς[3] = λισσός: πέτρη μ 64, 79.

λίσσομαι [λίτ-σομαι]. 3 sing. impf. ἐλ(λ)ίσσετο Z 45, M 49 (*v.l.* εἰλίσσετο, see ἑλίσσω (6)), Φ 71 : κ 264. 3 pl. ἐλλίσσοντο I 585. 3 sing. pa. iterative λισσέσκετο I 451. Aor. ἐλλισάμην λ 35, ν 273. 2 sing. subj. λίσῃ κ 526. Imp. λίσαι A 394. Aor. opt. λιτοίμην ξ 406. Infin. λιτέσθαι Π 47. (1) To make entreaty or petition to, entreat, supplicate: πάντας Ἀχαιούς A 15, Δία λίσαι 394. Cf. B 15, Z 45, I 465, M 49, O 660, Φ 71, X 35, etc. : β 68, ζ 142, θ 157, μ 53, ο 261, χ 311, etc.—With complementary infin.: λίσσεται ἔμπεδον εἶναι [πομπήν] θ 30.—(2) To beg, entreat, pray *to do*. With infin.: μένειν σε A 174. Cf. A 283, Δ 379, Θ 372 = O 77, I 451, 574, T 304, X 240 : Εὐρύμαχον παῦσαι τόξον φ 278.—Sim.: ἔμ' ἕταροι λίσσοντο τυρῶν αἰνυμένους ἰέναι πάλιν (to let the party . . .) ι 224.—With dependent clause: λίσσεθ' Ἥφαιστον ὅπως λύσειεν Ἄρηα θ 344. Cf. γ 19.—With acc. of the subject of entreaty: οἷ αὐτῷ θάνατον λιτέσθαι Π 47.—With double acc. of the person entreated and of the subject: ταῦθ' ἅ με λίσσεαι δ 347 = ρ 138. Cf. β 210.—(3) To pray to (a divinity): θεοὺς παρατρωπῶσ' ἄνθρωποι λισσόμενοι I 501 : πρόφρων κε Δία λιτοίμην (make my peace with him (*i.e.* with Ζεὺς ξείνιος)) ξ 406.—With infin.: τῷ Ἄτην ἅμ' ἕπεσθαι I 511.—Of addressing the shades of the dead κ 526, λ 35.

λισσός, -ή, -όν. With unbroken surface, smooth: πέτρη γ 293, ε 412, κ 4.

λιστρεύω [λίστρον]. To dig round about: φυτόν ω 227.

λίστρον, -ου, τό. A spade or shovel χ 455.

λῖτα, acc. λίς[2].

λιτανεύω [λιτ-, λίσσομαι]. Aor. ἐλλιτάνευσα κ 481. 1 pl. subj. λιτανεύσομεν Ω 357. (1) To make entreaty or petition to, entreat, supplicate: μιν I 581. Cf. X 414, Ω 357 : η 145, κ 481.—(2) To pray to (a divine power). With infin.: πολλὰ λιτάνευεν [ἀνέμους] ἐλθέμεν Ψ 196.

λιτέσθαι, aor. infin. λίσσομαι.

λιτή, -ῆς, ἡ [λιτ-, λίσσομαι]. A prayer: εὐχωλῇσι λιτῇσί τε ἐλλισάμην (the two words hardly to be distinguished) λ 34.—Personified: Λιταί εἰσι (there are such beings as . . .) Διὸς κοῦραι I 502 (*i.e.* prayers of repentance, for forgiveness, addressed by an offender to the person injured).

λῖτί, dat. λίς[2].

λιτοίμην, aor. opt. λίσσομαι.

λοβός, -οῦ, ὁ. The lobe of the ear Ξ 182.

λόγος, ὁ [λέγω[2]]. In pl., talk, discourse: τὸν ἔτερπε λόγοις O 393. Cf. α 56.

λόεον, impf. See λούω.

λοέσσατο, 3 sing. aor. mid. See λούω.

λοετρόν, τό (λοϝετρόν) [λοϝ-, λούω]. In pl., water for washing or bathing Ξ 6, X 444, 445, Ψ 44 : θ 249, 451.—Fig.: λοετρῶν Ὠκεανοῖο (the baths of ocean) Σ 489 : = ε 275.

λοετροχόος, ὁ [λοετρόν + χο-, χέω]. An attendant who poured out water for the bath υ 297.—λ. τρίπος, a caldron in which to heat water for the bath Σ 346 : θ 435.

λοιβή, -ῆς, ἡ [λείβω]. Libation: λοιβῆς τε κνίσης τε Δ 49 = Ω 70. Cf. I 500.—Applied ironically to the wine brought for the Cyclops ι 349.

λοίγιος [λοιγός]. Baneful: λοίγια ἔργα, sad work, a bad business A 518, 573.—Absol. in neut. pl. λοίγια in same sense: οἴω λοίγι' ἔσεσθαι Φ 533, Ψ 310.

λοιγός, -οῦ, ὁ. Bane, evil, death, destruction: λοιγὸν ἀμῦναι A 67. Cf. A 456, E 662, Θ 130, N 426, Π 32, Φ 134, etc.

λοιμός, ὁ. Plague, pestilence A 61.

λοισθήϊος [λοῖσθος]. Of a prize, for the last, the last Ψ 785.—Absol. in neut. pl. λοισθήϊα, the last prize Ψ 751.

λοῖσθος. The last, coming last Ψ 536.

λοπός, -οῦ, ὁ [λέπω]. A husk or skin: σιγαλόεντα, οἷόν τε κρομύοιο λοπὸν κάτα ἰσχαλέοιο τ 233 (glistening as (there is glistening) over the skin of . . ., *i.e.* glistening like the skin of . . .).

†λούω (λόϝω) [λοϝ-. Cf. L. *lavo*]. 3 sing. aor. λοῦσε E 905, Π 679 : γ 464, 466, η 296, κ 364, 450, ψ 154, ω 366. 3 pl. λοῦσαν Σ 350, Ω 587 : δ 49, θ 364, ρ 88. 3 sing. subj. λούσῃ Ξ 7. 3 pl. opt. λούσειαν Σ 345. Imp. λοῦσον Π 669. Pl. λούσατε ζ 210. Nom. sing. fem. pple. λούσᾱσα ε 264. Infin. λοῦσαι Ω 582. 3 sing. aor. λόε (λόϝε) κ 361. Infin. mid. λούεσθαι Z 508, O 265. λοῦσθαι ζ 216. 3 pl. aor. λούσαντο K 576 : δ 48, ρ 87, ψ 142. 3 sing. opt. λούσαιτο ω 254. Imp. pl. λούσασθε ψ 131. Infin. λούσασθαι Ψ 41 : θ 449. Pf. pple. λελουμένος E 6. From λοέω (λοϝέω) impf. λόεον δ 252. Aor. pple. λοέσσας Ψ 282. Infin. λοέσσαι τ 320. Fut. mid. (or aor. subj.) λοέσσομαι ζ 221. 3 sing. aor. λοέσσατο ζ 227. Pple. λοεσσάμενος, -η K 577, Φ 560 : α 310, ζ 96, θ 427. (ἀπο-.) (1) To wash the body of, cause to bathe: Τηλέμαχον λοῦσε Πολυκάστη γ 464. Cf. E 905 : δ 49, ε 264, ζ 210, θ 364, τ 320, ψ 154, etc.—In reference to cleansing a corpse Π 669, 679, Σ 350, Ω 582, 587.—In reference to horses: λοέσσας [ἵππους] ὕδατι Ψ 282.—(2) With ἀπό, to wash away or off: εἰς ὅ κε λούσῃ ἄπο βρότον Ξ 7.—With double acc.

of what is cleansed and of what is washed away: ὄφρα Πάτροκλον λούσειαν ἄπο βρότον Σ 345.—(3) In mid., to wash one's body, bathe oneself: ἐς ἀσαμίνθους βάντες λούσαντο Κ 576, λοεσσάμενος ποταμοῖο (genit. of space or material, 'in the . . .') Φ 560. Cf. Κ 577: α 310, δ 48, ζ 96, θ 427, ψ 131, ω 254, etc.—Of a horse: εἰωθὼς λούεσθαι ποταμοῖο Ζ 508 = Ο 265.—Fig. of a star: λελουμένος Ὠκεανοῖο Ε 6.—(4) In mid., with ἀπό, to wash away or off from one's body: λούσασθαι ἄπο βρότον Ψ 41.

λοφιή, -ῆς, ἡ [λόφος]. The bristly back of a wild boar: φρίξας εὖ λοφιήν τ 446.

λόφος, -ου, ὁ. (1) The neck Κ 573.—Of horses Ψ 508.—(2) A crest or plume on a helmet: δεινὸν λόφος καθύπερθεν ἔνευεν Γ 337 = Λ 42 = Ο 481 = Π 138, κόρυθος φάλον ἤλασεν ὑπὸ λόφον αὐτόν (just at the base of it) Ν 615. Cf. Ζ 469, Ο 537, Σ 612, Τ 383 = Χ 316: χ 124.—(3) The crest or summit of a hill λ 596.—An eminence or ridge: ὅθι Ἕρμαιος λ. ἐστίν π 471.

λοχάω [λόχος]. 3 pl. λοχόωσι ν 425, ο 28. λοχῶσι ξ 181. Nom. pl. masc. pple. λοχόωντες δ 847, π 369. To lie in wait for, lie in ambush for: λοχόωσί μιν νέοι ν 425. Cf. δ 847, ξ 181, ο 28, π 369, χ 53.—In mid. δ 388, 463, 670, ν 268.—Absol.: ὅθι σφίσιν εἶκε λοχῆσαι Σ 520.

λόχμη, -ης, ἡ [λοχ- as in λόχος]. The lair of a wild beast: ἐν λόχμῃ κατέκειτο σῦς τ 439.

λόχονδε [acc. of λόχος + -δε (2)]. For, to take part in, with a view to, an ambush: λόχονδ' ἰέναι Α 227. Cf. ξ 217.

λόχος, -ου, ὁ [λεχ-, λέγω[1]]. (1) A body of men lying in wait or in ambush or detailed for such a purpose: εἷσε λόχον Ζ 189, μὴ λόχος εἰσέλθῃσι πόλιν (a body detailed to effect a surprise) Θ 522. Cf. Δ 392, Ν 285: δ 531, ξ 469.—(2) A lying in wait, an ambush: λόχῳ ὑπεθωρήσσοντο (for . . .) Σ 513, μὴ δείσητ' Ἀργείων λόχον (any attempt at surprise on their part) Ω 779. Cf. Ν 277: δ 395, 441, λ 525, π 463.—(3) A place of concealment with a view to hostile action, a lurking-place: ἐκ λόχου ἀμπήδησεν Λ 379.—Applied to the Trojan horse δ 277, θ 515.—(4) App. a band or troop: εἴ περ πεντήκοντα λόχοι ἀνθρώπων νῶϊ περισταῖεν υ 49.

λοχόωσι, 3 pl. pres. λοχάω.

λύγος, -ου, ἡ [cf. L. *ligo*]. A pliant twig, a withy Λ 105: ι 427, κ 166.

λυγρός, -ή, -όν [cf. λευγαλέος, L. *lugeo*]. (1) As a term of contempt, sorry, pitiful, good for nothing, of no account: ὅς τις πολέμοιο μεθείη λ. ἐών Ν 119. Cf. Ν 237: ι 454, σ 107.—(2) Bringing or inferring wretchedness or woe, wretched, woeful, miserable, painful, distressing, baleful, disastrous: ὄλεθρον Β 873, γήραϊ Ε 153, ἀγγελίης Ρ 642. Cf. Ζ 16, Ν 346, Χ 242, etc.: νόστον α 327, πένθεϊ β 70, κήδεα λ 369. Cf. α 341, γ 87, ψ 224, ω 250, etc.—As epithet of war: δαΐ Ν 286, Ω 739.—Of the belly ρ 473.—Bringing evil consequences, ill-wrought: ἀνδροκτασίης Ψ 86.—Carrying bale, deadly, fatal: σήματα Ζ 168.—Of drugs, working evil effects, bringing to ill δ 230, κ 236.—Of a wound, deep-struck, sore Ο 393, Τ 49.—Of garments, foul, sorry, evil π 457, ρ 203 = ω 158, ρ 338, 573.—(3) Absol. in neut. pl., things of ill, evils: πόλεμοι καὶ ἄκιντες καὶ ὀϊστοί, λυγρά ξ 226.—Evil fortune, ill: ᾧ κε τῶν λυγρῶν δώῃ Ω 531. Cf. σ 134.—Bane, evil: ταῦτ' ἐμήσατο λυγρά γ 303.—In ethical sense, evil, mischief: λυγρὰ ἰδυῖα (cherishing evil in her heart) λ 432 (see εἴδω (III) (12)).

λυγρῶς [adv. fr. prec.]. So as to inflict pain, sorely: πεπληγυῖα Ε 763.

λύθρον, -ου, τό. Gore: λύθρῳ παλάσσετο χεῖρας Λ 169. Cf. Ζ 268, Υ 503: χ 402 = ψ 48.

λυκάβας, -αντος, ὁ [λυκ-, light, as in λύχνος + βα-, βαίνω. 'The going of light']. Thus, prob., the period of time in which daylight goes and comes again: τοῦδ' αὐτοῦ λυκάβαντος (within a day's space, ere the sun shall set again) τ 306. (This interpretation involves bracketing ξ 161-162 (= τ 306-307); but is obviously superior to the interpretation 'a year.')

λυκέη [fem. adj. fr. λύκος (*sc.* δορά)]. A wolf-skin Κ 459.

Λυκηγενής [prob. λύκος + γεν-, γίγνομαι]. Thus, wolf-born. Epithet of Apollo Δ 101, 119.

λύκος, -ου, ὁ. A wolf Δ 471, Κ 334, Λ 72, Ν 103, Π 156, 352, Χ 263: κ 212, 218, 433.

λῦμα, -ατος, τό [λυ-, λούω]. In pl., defilement, impurities: ἀπὸ χροὸς λύματα πάντα κάθηρεν Ξ 171. Cf. Α 314.

λύμην, aor. pass. λύω.

λυπρός, -ή, -όν [λυπ- as in λύπη, distress]. Poor, sorry, worthless: γαῖα ν 243.

λῡσιμελής [λυσ-, λύω + μέλος]. That relaxes the limbs. Epithet of sleep υ 57, ψ 343.

λύσις, ἡ [λυσ-, λύω]. A releasing or ransoming: ἀνάβλησις λύσιος Ω 655.—A means of release from the toils of something, a means of escape: θανάτου λύσιν ι 421.

λύσσα, ἡ. Rage, fury, lust of battle: λύσσαν ἔχων ὀλοήν Ι 305. Cf. Ι 239, Φ 542.

λυσσητήρ, -ῆρος [λυσσάω, vb. fr. prec.] One who is raging mad: τοῦτον κύνα λυσσητῆρα (that mad dog) Θ 299.

λυσσώδης [app. for λυσσοϝείδης, fr. λύσσα + (ϝ)εἶδος]. Raging, consumed with lust of battle. Absol.: ὁ λυσσώδης, Ἕκτωρ Ν 53.

λύτο, 3 sing. aor. pass. λύω.

λύχνος, -ου, ὁ [λυκ-, light. Cf. L. *luceo*]. A lamp: χρύσεον τ 34.

λύω (ῡ). 3 sing. aor. pass. λύθη Ε 296, Θ 123, 315, Ρ 298. 3 pl. λύθεν Π 805, Σ 31: δ 794, θ 360, σ 189, 341. Aor. λύμην Φ 80. 3 sing. λύτο Φ 114, 425: δ 703, ε 297, 406, σ 212, χ 68, 147, ψ 205, ω 345. λῦτο Ω 1. 3 pl. λύντο Η 12, 16, Ο 435. 3 sing. pf. λέλυται Θ 103, Ω 599. 3 pl. λέλυνται Β 135, Η 6: θ 233, σ 242. 3 sing. opt. λελῦτο σ 238. 3 pl. plupf. ἐλέλυντο χ 186. λέλυντο Ν 85. (ἀνα-, ἀπο-, ἐκ-, ἐξανα-, κατα-, ὑπεκπρο-, ὑπο-.) (1) To loosen, undo, unfasten, untie: ζωστῆρα Δ 215. Cf. Π 804: πρυμνήσια β 418. Cf. γ 392, ε 459, ν 77, etc.—In mid.: λύοντο τεύχε' ἀπ' ὤμων P 318.—In proper mid. sense of unfastening something from oneself: ἀπὸ στήθεσφιν ἐλύσαθ' ἱμάντα Ξ 214.—Of loosening the maiden girdle λ 245.—To undo the fastening of: ἀσκόν κ 47.—To strike (sail): λύον ἱστία ο 496.—(2) To set free from bonds or confinement, to release, relax one's hold upon: λῦσαι γέροντα δ 422, ἐπεὶ ἐκ δεσμοῖο λύθεν θ 360. Cf. θ 345, 347, κ 298, 387, λ 296, μ 53, 163, 193.—In mid., to set oneself free ι 463.—To rescue from bonds, effect the release of O 22.—In mid.: ἢ τοὺς λυσόμενος δεῦρ' ἔρχεαι; κ 284. Cf. κ 385.—To release (from trouble or sickness): θεοὶ κακότητος ἔλυσαν ε 397. Cf. ν 321.—To save (from imminent danger) π 364.—(3) To set free (a captive) for ransom: παῖδ' ἐμοὶ λύσαιτε Α 20. Cf. Α 29, Φ 80.—With genit. of price: ἔλυσεν ἀποίνων Λ 106.—Of restoring a corpse Ω 76, 116, 137, 555, 561, 593, 599.—Of restoring the armour of a slain foe P 163.—In mid., to effect the ransoming of: ξεῖνός μιν ἐλύσατο Φ 42. Cf. Α 13 = 372, Κ 378.—So of effecting the restoration of a corpse Ω 118 = 146 = 195, 175, 237, 502, 685.—(4) To unyoke (horses, etc.): λῦσαν ἵππους Θ 433. Cf. Ε 369, Λ 620, Σ 244, Ψ 27, Ω 576, etc.: δ 35, 39, η 6.—In mid. Ψ 7, 11.—To untether (horses) Κ 480, 498.—(5) To settle or compose (a dispute, quarrel or difference): καὶ ἀνδράσι νείκεα λύει η 74. Cf. Ξ 205 = 304.—(6) To dissolve or dismiss (an assembly), allow or cause (it) to disperse: λῦσαν ἀγορήν Α 305. Cf. Β 808, Τ 276, Ω 1: β 69, 257.—(7) To disperse (cares): λύων μελεδήματα θυμοῦ Ψ 62: = υ 56, ψ 343.—(8) With notion of destruction, to resolve into the component parts, disintegrate, cause to part: σπάρτα λέλυνται (lie in decay) Β 135: ὄφρ' ἀπὸ τοίχους λῦσε κλύδων τρόπιος μ 421.—To cause (stitches) to give way or come undone: ῥαφαὶ ἐλέλυντο ἱμάντων χ 186.—To bring to ruin, destroy: ὄφρα Τροίης κρήδεμνα λύωμεν Π 100. Cf. Β 118 = Ι 25: ν 388.—(9) To break up or dissipate (the vital forces), to break up, dissipate or suspend the vital forces or the strength in (the limbs, the heart, etc.), to cause (the limbs, etc.) to give way or collapse. (a) By the application of force to fatal or nearly fatal effect: οὔτησε ξυστῷ, λῦσε δὲ γυῖα Δ 469, τοῦ λύθη ψυχή τε μένος τε Ε 296. Cf. Ε 176, Η 12, Ν 360, Π 332, Ρ 29, etc.: ξ 69, 236, σ 238, 242, ω 381.—In reference to an animal: λῦσεν βοὸς μένος γ 450.—(b) By strong emotion, fear, stupor: τὸν ἄτη φρένας εἷλε, λύθεν δ' ὑπὸ γυῖα Π 805. Cf. Σ 31, Φ 114, 425: Ὀδυσσῆος λύτο γούνατα καὶ ἦτορ ε 297 = 406 = χ 147. Cf. δ 703, σ 212, 341, χ 68, ψ 205, ω 345.—(c) By weariness, exhaustion, hardship: καμάτῳ ὑπὸ γυῖα λέλυνται Η 6. Cf. Ν 85: θ 233, υ 118.—Sim. of the effects of old age Θ 103.—Of relaxation of the limbs in sleep δ 794 = σ 189.

λωβάομαι [λώβη]. To treat without regard to right or decency, commit outrage upon. With direct and cognate acc.: λώβης, ἣν ἐμὲ λωβήσασθε Ν 623.—Absol. Α 232 = Β 242.

λωβεύω [λώβη]. (ἐπι-.) To play a trick upon, mock, make game of: τίπτε με λωβεύεις; ψ 15. Cf. ψ 26.

λώβη, -ης, ἡ. (1) Treatment without regard to right or decency, despiteful usage, outrage: πρίν γ' ἀπὸ πᾶσαν ἐμοὶ δόμεναι λώβην Ι 387. Cf. Λ 142, Ν 622, Τ 208: σ 347 = υ 285, τ 373, υ 169, ω 326.—(2) A cause or occasion of reproach or opprobrium: λώβη τάδε γ' ἔσσεται, εἰ . . . Η 97. Cf. Σ 180: σ 225, ω 433.—(3) A mark for mockery, an object of ridicule Γ 42.

λωβητήρ, -ῆρος, ὁ [λωβάομαι]. One who utters despiteful or scurrilous words, an insulter, a foul-mouthed fellow Β 275, Λ 385.—A good-for-nothing person, a worthless fellow Ω 239.

λωβητός [λωβάομαι]. App., despitefully used by fortune, wretched, miserable Ω 531.

λωΐτερος [cf. next]. Better, more profitable or advisable: τόδε λωΐτερον ἔμμεναι α 376 = β 141.

λωΐων, λώϊον [cf. prec.]. Always in neut. Better. Absol.: χρή σε δόμεναι καὶ λώϊον ἠέ περ ἄλλοι σίτου (a larger portion) ρ 417.—Better, more profitable or advisable: τόδε σφιν λ. ἐστιν β 169.—Absol. with infin.: λ. ἐστι δῶρ' ἀποαιρεῖσθαι Α 229.—So with ὧδε: δοκέει μοι ὧδε λ. ἔσσεσθαι Ζ 339.—As adv., better, more fully: γνωσόμεθ' ἀλλήλων καὶ λ. ψ 109.

λώπη, -ης, ἡ [λέπω]. A garment ν 224.

λωτόεις, -εντος [λωτός (1)]. Contr. acc. pl. neut. λωτοῦντα. Overgrown with λωτός: πεδία λωτοῦντα Μ 283. (*V.l.* λωτεῦντα (λωτέοντα) fr. λωτέω, to teem with λωτός.)

λωτός, -οῦ, ὁ. (1) A plant, perh. some kind of trefoil or clover. Collectively: ἵπποι λωτὸν ἐρεπτόμενοι Β 776. Cf. Ξ 348, Φ 351: δ 603.—(2) A fruit of some kind, described as having an irresistibly seductive taste ι 93, 97, 102.—The tree producing the fruit ι 94.

Λωτοφάγοι, οἱ [λωτός (2) + φάγον]. The lotus-eaters ι 84, 91, 92, 96, ψ 311.

λωφάω. To make pause, cease, give over: ὅδε τάχα λωφήσει Φ 292.—To find respite or relief from. With genit.: κακῶν ι 460.

μά. A particle used in affirmations or strong protestations, followed by acc. of a deity or thing invoked. Affirmatively with ναί: ναὶ μὰ τόδε σκῆπτρον (by this . . .) Α 234.—With οὐ in negation: οὐ μὰ Ζῆνα Ψ 43. Cf. Α 86: υ 339.

μαζός, -οῦ, ὁ. One of the breasts. (1) In women: γυναῖκα θήσατο μαζόν Ω 58. Cf. Ε 393, Χ 80, 83: πάϊς οἱ ἦν ἐπὶ μαζῷ λ 448. Cf. τ 483.—(2) In men, the mammilla: βάλε στῆθος παρὰ μαζὸν δεξιόν Δ 480. Cf. Δ 123, 528, Ε 145, Θ 121, 313, Λ 108, 321, Ο 577, Ρ 606: χ 82.

μάθον, aor. μανθάνω.

μαῖα, ἡ [perh. fr. μα-, μήτηρ]. A word of address to a woman older than the speaker, good mother, dame, gossip β 349, 372, ρ 499, τ 16, 482, 500, υ 129, ψ 11, 35, 59, 81, 171.

μαιμάω [redup. fr. μα-, μάω]. 3 pl. μαιμώωσι Ν 75. μαιμῶσι Ν 78. Pple. μαιμώων Ο 742.

Fem. μαιμώωσα E 661, O 542. (ἀνα-, περι-.) To be eager or quiver for action, show eager alacrity in action: μαίμησέ οἱ ἦτορ E 670, μαιμώων ἔφεπ' ἔγχεϊ O 742. Cf. N 75, 78.—Of the eager course of a weapon E 661, O 542.

μαινάς, -άδος, ἡ [μαίνομαι]. A madwoman: μεγάροιο διέσσυτο μαινάδι ἴση X 460.

μαίνομαι. (ἐπι-.) (1) To rage, act like a madman, be in unreasoning rage or fury: σὺ δὲ μαίνεαι οὐκέτ' ἀνεκτῶς ι 350. Cf. Θ 360: σ 406, φ 298.—Of the Bacchic frenzy Z 132.—Of the raging of fire: ὡς ὅτε πῦρ οὔρεσι μαίνηται O 606. —(2) Of martial frenzy: εἰ οὕτω μαίνεσθαι ἐάσομεν Ἄρηα E 717. Cf. Z 101, Θ 355, I 238, O 605, Π 245, Φ 5: λ 537.—With cognate acc.: οὐχ ὅ γ' ἄνευθε θεοῦ τάδε μαίνεται (makes this wild work) E 185.—In pple., a madman: τοῦτον μαινόμενον E 831.—Of a weapon: εἰ καὶ ἐμὸν δόρυ μαίνεται Θ 111. Cf. Π 75.—(3) To be distracted or out of one's wits. In pple., a madman: μαινόμενε, φρένας ἠλέ O 128.—In fem., a madwoman: μαινομένῃ ἐϊκυῖα Z 389.—Of the wits, etc.: τί σφῶϊν μαίνεται ἦτορ; Θ 413. Cf. Ω 114 = 135.

μαίομαι, 3 sing. fut. μάσσεται I 394. Aor. infin. μάσασθαι λ 591. (ἀμφι-, ἐπι-, ἐσ-.) (1) To make search, search, seek: μαίεσθαι προτέρω ξ 356.—To search through, examine: κευθμῶνας ν 367.—(2) To seek out, get: Πηλεύς μοι γυναῖκά γε μάσσεται αὐτός I 394 (*v.l.* γαμέσσεται (γαμέω)). —(3) To seize, grasp λ 591.

μάκαρ, -αρος [μακ-, μακρός]. (1) Having great resources, great, powerful, influential, wealthy: ἀνδρὸς μάκαρος κατ' ἄρουραν Λ 68. Cf. α 217.— (2) Happy, fortunate: ὦ μάκαρ Ἀτρεΐδη Γ 182. Cf. Ω 377.—Superl. μακάρτατος: σεῖο μακάρτατος (beyond thee, in reference to thee) λ 483. Cf. ζ 158.—(3) As epithet of the gods, happy, blessed, living at ease, dwelling serene A 339, 406, 599, etc.: α 82, ε 7, θ 281, etc.—Absol. in pl., the blessed gods, the gods κ 299.

μακαρίζω [μάκαρ]. To pronounce blessed, esteem fortunate ο 538 = ρ 165 = τ 311.

μακεδνός, -ή, -όν [μακ-, μακρός]. Tall, high: αἰγείροιο η 106.

μάκελλα, ἡ. A mattock Φ 259.

μακρός, -ή, -όν. (1) Long (as applied to weapons commonly a mere epithet): ἔγχεα Γ 135. Cf. Γ 137, E 297, N 497, etc.: οὐρῇσιν κ 215. Cf. μ 229, φ 121, χ 149, 251, 279, 293.—In superl.: τὰ μακρότατ' ἔγχεα Ξ 373.—(2) High, tall, lofty (sometimes, doubtless, with connotation of sense (3)): τείχεα Δ 34, X 507, δένδρεα I 541, Λ 88, οὔρεα N 18: κίονας α 54, δένδρεα ε 238, τείχεα η 44, πίτυσσιν ι 186, κλίμακα κ 558, ἐρινεόν μ 432, ὄζοι 436, etc.—Epithet of Olympus A 402, B 48, E 398, Θ 199, O 21, Σ 142, Ω 468, etc.: κ 307, ο 43, υ 73, ω 351.—In superl.: ἐλάτην, ἣ μακροτάτη πεφυυῖα αἰθέρ' ἵκανεν Ξ 288.—Tall in person. In comp.: μακρότερόν μιν θῆκεν θ 20. Cf. σ 195.— (3) Great, thick, stout: ἕρματα A 486, ὀχῆα M 121, 291, N 124, σανίδες Σ 276: δούρατα ε 162, 370, ἐπηγκενίδεσσιν ε 253.—Of waves, great, big, swollen B 144: ε 109, ι 147, ω 110.—(4) Wide, broad, spacious: ἠϊόνος στόμα Ξ 36. Cf. O 358.— (5) Of great content, great, capacious: φρείατα Φ 197.—(6) In reference to periods of time, long: ἤματα κ 470, σ 367 = χ 301. Cf. λ 373.—(7) Of a desire, great, of one's heart: τόδε μακρὸν ἐέλδωρ ψ 54.—(8) In neut. sing. μακρόν as adv. In reference to the utterance of sound, loudly, with full voice, at the top of one's voice: μ. ἄϋσεν Γ 81. Cf. E 101, Z 66, Λ 285, Υ 50, etc.: ζ 117.— (9) So in neut. pl. μακρά: βοῶν B 224.—Of a bull: μ. μεμυκώς Σ 580.—In reference to one's gait or movement, with long strides or steps, striding along or about, strutting along: μ. βιβάντα Γ 22. Cf. H 213, N 809, O 307, 676, 686, Π 534: λ 539. —Of a ram ι 450.

μακών, aor. pple. μηκάομαι.

μάλα. (1) Intensively with adjectives and adverbs, very, exceedingly, quite, just, altogether, or the like: μ. ὦκα B 52, μ. νήπιος H 401. Cf. A 156, Γ 204, E 710, I 360, M 382, N 152, Σ 254, etc.: μ. ἀτρεκέως α 179, μ. καλόν 301. Cf. β 200, γ 20, δ 169, 439, ε 26, 161, 342, κ 111, σ 370, etc. —Strengthening πᾶς B 10, N 741, O 546, etc.: β 306, ε 216, etc.—Strengthening ἀμφότερος Θ 67, etc.—With comp., by far: πρότερος μ. K 124.— (2) Intensively with verbs and participles, much, greatly, in large measure, deeply, heartily, with good will, earnestly, eagerly, strongly, or the like: θαρσήσας μ. A 85, φεῦγε μ. (by all means) 173, μ. ἔκλυον 218. Cf. A 217, Γ 25 (greedily), Δ 225, 379, E 471 (bitterly), H 286, I 75 (they sorely need . . .), 318, 419, K 229, 251 (quickly), Λ 710 (well), M 51 (loudly), N 146 (to close quarters), 463 (the need is dire), 708 (keeping closely together), Ξ 58 (closely), P 502 (from close at hand), 571 (carefully), Ψ 63, Ω 663, etc.: μ. ἀσχαλόωσιν α 304, μ. χατέουσα β 249. Cf. δ 472 (clearly), ε 341, ζ 44, 319 (skilfully), η 32 (willingly), θ 316, 413 (with all my heart), μ 108 (very close), ξ 361, σ 381, ω 400, etc.—(3) Emphasizing an expression generally rather than attaching itself to particular words, of a surety, surely, verily: ἦ μ. δή σε κιχάνεται ὄλεθρος Λ 441. Cf. B 241, E 278, Z 255, I 40, P 34, Σ 12, etc.: ἀλλὰ μ. οὔ πως ἔστι Διὸς νόον παρεξελθεῖν ε 103. Cf. α 384, β 325, ε 286, ξ 391, π 8, τ 40, etc.

μαλακός, -ή, -όν. (1) Yielding to the touch, soft, into or upon which one sinks or settles down comfortably: εὐνῇ I 618, K 75, X 504. Cf. Ξ 349: κώεσιν γ 38. Cf. δ 124, υ 58, χ 196 (in sarcasm), ψ 290, 349.—Soft or yielding in texture, readily adapting itself to one's form or to what it covers: χιτῶνα B 42, πέπλοισιν Ω 796. Cf. α 437, τ 234.—Of meadows, yielding to the tread, covered with rich grass, grassy: λειμῶνες ε 72, ι 133.—Of cultivated land, yielding readily to the plough, easily cultivable: νειόν Σ 541.— (2) Of speech, gentle, winning, conciliatory: ἐπέεσσιν A 582, Z 337. Cf. α 56, κ 70, 422, π 286 = τ 5.—Of sleep, stealing gently upon one, sweet K 2 = Ω 678, Ξ 359: ο 6, σ 201.—So of a gentle or painless death: θάνατον σ 202.—Easy to deal with. In comp.: μαλακώτερος ἀμφαφάασθαι Χ 373.

μαλακῶς [adv. fr. prec.]. In reference to sleeping, softly, at ease: ἐνεύδειν γ 350. Cf. ω 255.

μαλερός. Epithet of fire. App., consuming, devouring Ι 242, Υ 316=Φ 375.

μαλθακός. Faint-hearted, remiss Ρ 588.

μάλιστα [superl. of μάλα]. (1) With adjectives and adverbs, in the highest degree, most: μ. λαμπρόν Ε 5, ἄγχι Ξ 460. Cf. Ζ 433, Θ 84, 326, Ν 568, 683, Ξ 399, Χ 410.—With a vb., in a very high degree, greatly, much: ὅπως πετάσειε μ. θυμόν σ 160.—(2) In general intensive use, most, especially, principally, chiefly: Ἀτρεΐδα μ. [λίσσετο] Α 16, τὸν μ. τῖεν Β 21. Cf. Β 589, Γ 97, Δ 96, Θ 500, etc.: ὅσσαν, ἥ τε μάλιστα φέρει κλέος α 283. Cf. α 342, 359, δ 434, θ 582, etc.—In reference to something on the point of happening, nearly: μέμβλωκε μ. ἦμαρ ρ 190.

μᾶλλον [comp. of μάλα]. (1) With adjectives, in a higher degree, more: τιμήεσσα σ 162.—More, rather: μ. ἐπήρατος ἱπποβότοιο (rather . . . than . . .) δ 606.—Strengthening a comp.: ῥηΐτεροι Ω 243.—(2) In general intensive use (a) More, yet more, rather: Ἑκτορέοις ἄρα μ. ἐπὶ φρένα θῆχ' ἱεροῖσιν Κ 46, μή μοι μ. θυμὸν ὀρίνῃς Ω 568. Cf. Θ 470, Ν 272, 638, 776, Τ 200: μ. ἔτ' ἢ τὸ πάροιθεν α 322. Cf. α 89, 351, δ 819, θ 154, ο 198, σ 216, υ 166.—Better, in better wise: μ. ἅρμα οἴσετον Ε 231.—Better, preferably, for choice: ἀμφοτέρω μ. Μ 344=357.—(b) The more, all the more, the better, all the better: ἀπὸ θυμοῦ μ. ἐμοὶ ἔσεαι Α 563, ὄφρ' ἔτι μ. μαχώμεθα Τ 231. Cf. Β 81, Ε 208, Ι 257, 700, Τ 16, Φ 305, etc.: μ. πιέζειν δ 419. Cf. β 202, ι 13, σ 22, τ 117, 249, etc.—(3) Much (rather than little). See κηρόθι.

μάν [cf. μέν, μήν[2]]. Affirmative particle: οὐ μὰν οὐδ' Ἀχιλεὺς μάρναται Δ 512, ἄγρει μάν (nay come!) Ε 765, ἔσται μὰν ὅτ' ἂν . . . (the time will yet come when . . .) Θ 373. Cf. Θ 512, Ν 414, etc.: οὐ μὰν ἡμῖν ἀπὸ σκοποῦ μυθεῖται λ 344. Cf. ρ 470.—With ἤ. See ἤ[2] (1) (b) (α).

†μανθάνω. Aor. μάθον Ζ 444. 2 sing. ἔμμαθες σ 362. 3 ἔμμαθε ρ 226. To learn. In aor., to have learned, know: ἔργα κακά ρ 226, σ 362.—With infin., to have been brought up or trained *to be*: ἐπεὶ μάθον ἔμμεναι ἐσθλός Ζ 444.

μαντεύομαι [μάντις]. (1) To utter prophecy or divination, prophesy, divine: ἦ ἐτεὸν μαντεύεται Β 300: νῦν τοι ἐγὼ μαντεύσομαι α 200. Cf. β 170, 178, ο 172, ρ 154, υ 380, ψ 251.—To be seer, act as seer: μαντευόμενος κατεγήρα Κυκλώπεσσιν ι 510. Cf. ο 255.—(2) To prophesy in regard to: ταῦτα μαντεύεσθαι β 180.—To foretell, prophesy, presage: ὄλεθρον Π 859. Cf. Α 107, Τ 420.

μαντήϊον, τό [μαντεύομαι]. A prophetic warning: μαντήϊα Τειρεσίαο Κίρκης τε μ 272.

μάντις, ὁ. Genit. μάντηος (*v.l.* μάντιος) κ 493, μ 267. A seer or diviner Α 62, 92, 106, 384, Ν 69, 663, Ω 221: α 202, ι 508, κ 493, 538, λ 99, 291, μ 267, ο 225, 252, ρ 384.

μαντοσύνη, -ης, ἡ [μάντις]. The art of divination: ὃς μαντοσύνῃ ἐκέκαστο ι 509. Cf. Α 72.—In pl., app. referring to the various means of divination: ὃς περὶ πάντων ᾔδεε μαντοσύνας Β 832=Λ 330.

μαραίνω. 3 sing. aor. pass. ἐμαράνθη Ι 212. To quench (fire): ἐπεὶ φλὸξ ἐμαράνθη (had died down) Ι 212, πυρκαϊὴ ἐμαραίνετο Ψ 228.

μαργαίνω [μάργος]. To behave like a madman, rage: μαργαίνειν ἐπὶ θεοῖσιν Ε 882.

μάργος, -η. Out of one's wits, beside oneself ψ 11.—Absol. in voc., 'madman!' π 421.—Applied to the belly, raging, unappeasable σ 2.

μαρμαίρω [μαρ- as three next]. To be bright, to glitter, flash, gleam, sparkle: ἔντεα μαρμαίροντα Μ 195. Cf. Ν 22, 801, Π 279, 664, Σ 131, 617, Ψ 27.—Of the eyes: ὄμματα μαρμαίροντα Γ 397.

μαρμάρεος, -η, -ον [μαρ- as prec. and two next]. Bright, glittering, gleaming Ξ 273, Ρ 594, Σ 480.

μάρμαρος, -ου, ὁ [μαρ- as two prec. and next]. A stone of some such substance as quartz Μ 380: ι 499.—With πέτρος Π 735.

μαρμαρυγή, -ῆς, ἡ [μαρ- as three prec.]. A twinkling or flickering: μαρμαρυγὰς ποδῶν θ 265.

μάρναμαι. 2 sing. impf. ἐμάρναο χ 228. Imp. μάρναο Ο 475, Π 497. (1) To fight, do battle, take part in the fight: οὐδ' Ἀχιλεὺς μάρναται Δ 513. Cf. Ε 33, Η 301, Λ 74, Π 195, Σ 453, etc.: πρόπαν ἦμαρ ἐμαρνάμεθα ω 41. Cf. γ 85, λ 513, π 98=116, ω 39, 507.—With cognate acc.: ὅσα μαρνάμεθα γ 108.—To fight, do battle, with. With dat.: μαρνάμενον Μενελάῳ Γ 307, μάρναντο Τρωσὶν τε καὶ Ἕκτορι Ν 720. Cf. Ζ 204, Ι 327, Λ 190=205, Ο 475, 557: ι 50, χ 228.—With ἐπί: μάρνασθαι δηΐοισιν ἐπ' ἀνδράσιν Ι 317=Ρ 148.—(2) Of fighting otherwise than with arms, to box σ 31.—(3) To fight with words, quarrel, wrangle, dispute: εἰ σφῶϊν πυθοίατο μαρναμένοιϊν Α 257.

μάρπτω. 3 sing. fut. μάρψει Ο 137. 3 sing. aor. ἔμαρψε ω 390. 3 sing. subj. μάρψῃ Φ 564. Pple. μάρψας ι 289, 311, 344, κ 116. Infin. μάρψαι Χ 201. (κατα-, συμ-.) (1) To lay hold of, seize, clasp Ξ 346, Ο 137, Φ 489: ι 289, 311, 344, κ 116.—With cognate acc. ἕλκεα, ἅ κεν μάρπτῃσι κεραυνός (which the thunderbolt shall make by fastening upon . . .) Θ 405=419.—(2) To catch up, overtake Φ 564, Χ 201.—(3) To bring oneself in contact with, touch: οὐδὲ χθόνα μάρπτε ποδοῖιν Ξ 228.—(4) Of sleep, to come upon: οὐχ Ἑρμείαν ὕπνος ἔμαρπτεν Ω 679. Cf. Ψ 62: =υ 56.—So of old age: ἐπεὶ κατὰ γῆρας ἔμαρψεν ω 390.

μαρτυρίη, -ης, ἡ [μάρτυρος]. A giving of information, a denouncing. In pl. λ 325.

μάρτυρος, -ου, ὁ. (1) One who is to bear or can bear testimony, a witness: τὼ αὐτὼ μάρτυροι ἔστων Α 338. Cf. Β 302.—(2) A witness invoked in sanction of something (cf. ἐπιμάρτυρος): ὑμεῖς μάρτυροι ἔστε Γ 280. Cf. Η 76, Ξ 274, Χ 255: μάρτυροι ἀμφοτέροισι θεοὶ [ἔστων] ξ 394. Cf. α 273.—(3) An ever-present witness, a protector or guardian: ἱκέτας, οἷσι Ζεὺς μ. [ἐστιν] π 423.

μάρψει, 3 sing. fut. μάρπτω.

μάσασθαι, aor. infin. *μαίομαι.*

μάσσεται, 3 sing. fut. *μαίομαι.*

μάσσων, *μᾶσσον* [comp. fr. *μακρός*]. In neut. *μᾶσσον* as adv., further: *ἧσειν* θ 203.

μάσταξ, *-ακος, ἡ.* (1) The mouth: *μάστακα χερσὶ πιέζεν* δ 287. Cf. ψ 76.—(2) A mouthful, a morsel I 324.

†**μαστίζω** [*μάστιξ*]. 3 sing. aor. *μάστιξε.* To apply the *μάστιξ* to, touch up (horses or mules): *μάστιξεν ἵππους* E 768 = K 530 = Λ 519. Cf. Θ 117, E 366 = Θ 45 = X 400 : = γ 484 = 494 = ο 192, ζ 82.

μάστιξ, *-ῑγος, ἡ.* A whip (following the indications of Λ 532, O 352, Ψ 362 : ζ 316 ; see also Ψ 500 under *μάστις* and Υ 171 under *μαστίω*) ; but *μάστιξ* in Ψ 384 and *κέντρον* in 387 are evidently represented as identical, and seem to be the same as the *ἱμάσθλη* of 582, and there are grounds for explaining all as a pliant rod with a metal point serving both as whip and goad (which involves taking *ἱμάντες* in Ψ 363 in sense 'reins'): *μάστιγι θοῶς ἐπεμαίεθ' ἵππους* E 748 = Θ 392. Cf. (besides as above) E 226, 840, K 500, P 430, 479, 482 = Ω 441, T 395, Ψ 390, 510, 642, Ω 326 : ζ 81, 316.—Fig. of the 'lash' of Zeus: *Διὸς μάστιγι δαμέντες* (*ἐδάμημεν*) M 37, N 812.

μάστις, *ἡ.* Dat. *μάστῑ* Ψ 500. = prec.: *μάστι ἔλαυνε κατωμαδόν* Ψ 500. Cf. ο 182.

μαστίω [*μάστις*]. To apply the *μάστιξ* to, touch up, one's horses: *μάστιε νῦν* P 622.—In mid. of a lion lashing himself with his tail Υ 171.

ματάω. To do ineffective work, show oneself clumsy or unskilful: *ἀπέκοψε παρήορον οὐδὲ μάτησεν* Π 474.—To idle, lose time Ψ 510.—Of horses, to shirk their work, grow restive E 233.

ματεύω [app. conn. with prec.]. To be at a loss or at fault: *οὐ δηθὰ ματεύσομεν* Ξ 110.

ματίη, *-ης, ἡ* [*ματάω*]. Ill directed or ill judged action, folly κ 79.

μάχαιρα, *-ης, ἡ.* A knife Γ 271 = T 252, Λ 844. —App. a dagger: *μαχαίρας χρυσείας ἐξ ἀργυρέων τελαμώνων* Σ 597.

μαχειόμενος, pple. See *μάχομαι.*

μαχεῖται, 3 sing. fut. *μάχομαι.*

μαχέοιτο, 3 sing. opt. *μάχομαι.*

μαχέονται, 3 pl. fut. *μάχομαι.*

μαχεούμενον, acc. sing. masc. pple. See *μάχομαι.*

μαχεσ(σ)αίμην, aor. opt. *μάχομαι.*

μαχέσ(σ)ασθαι, aor. infin. *μάχομαι.*

μάχη, *-ης, ἡ* [*μαχ-* as in *μάχομαι*]. (1) War, battle, armed conflict, fighting: *μάχῃ Τρώεσσιν ἀρήγειν* A 521, *ἔσχοντο μάχης* Γ 84. Cf. Δ 225, E 157, H 290, Λ 409, N 483, O 15, P 142, X 218, Ω 385, etc.: δ 497.—(2) A battle, armed conflict, fight: *μάχην ἐμάχοντο* M 175, *ἀντιόωντες τῆσδε μάχης* Υ 126. Cf. A 177, E 456, 763, Λ 336, M 436, N 789, P 261, Υ 18, etc.: ι 54, λ 612.—*μάχη τινός,* a fighting with a person: *Αἴαντος ἀλέεινε μάχην* (did not care to engage him) Λ 542.—(3) In concrete sense, a force engaged in fighting, an embattled host, a battle array, a fighting throng: *ἀρτύνθη μάχη* (the lines were re-formed) Λ 216, *μάχη ἐπὶ πᾶσα φαάνθη* P 650. Cf. E 167, 824, N 337, Ξ 155, Ω 402, etc.—(4) In local sense, a field of battle: *μάχης ἐπ' ἀριστερά* E 355. Cf. P 368, etc.—(5) The art of war, war, fighting: *μάχης εὖ εἰδότε πάσης* B 823 = M 100, E 11, 549. Cf. E 634, N 811.

μαχήμων [*μάχομαι*]. Warlike M 247.

μαχήσασθαι, aor. infin. *μάχομαι.*

μαχήσομαι, fut. *μάχομαι.*

μαχητής, *ὁ* [*μάχομαι*]. A warrior: *νέοι σε τείρουσι μαχηταί* Θ 102.—With implied notion of stoutness or skill: *μικρὸς δέμας, ἀλλὰ μ.* E 801. Cf. Π 186 : γ 112, δ 202, σ 261.

μαχητός [*μάχομαι*] With whom one may fight, to be fought with μ 119.

μαχλοσύνη, *-ης, ἡ.* Lust; app., satisfaction or scope for the satisfaction thereof: *ἥ οἱ πόρε μαχλοσύνην ἀλεγεινήν* Ω 30.

μάχομαι. 3 sing. opt. *μαχέοιτο* A 272. 3 pl. *μαχέοιντο* A 344. 2 dual imp. *μάχεσθον* H 279. Pple. *μαχειόμενος* (lengthened fr. *μαχεόμενος*) ρ 471. Acc. sing. masc. *μαχεούμενον* λ 403. Nom. pl. masc. *μαχεούμενοι* ω 113. 3 sing. pa. iterative *μαχέσκετο* H 140. 3 sing. fut. *μαχεῖται* Υ 26. 3 pl. *μαχέονται* B 366. Fut. *μαχήσομαι* A 298, Γ 290, I 32, Φ 498. 2 sing. *μαχήσεαι* Ψ 621. 3 *μαχήσεται* I 702, Σ 265 : σ 63. 1 pl. *μαχησόμεθα* Z 84, H 291, 377, 396, I 48, P 719. 3 pl. *μαχήσονται* Γ 137, 254, H 30. Pple. *μαχησόμενος, -ου* A 153, B 801, M 216, P 146, Σ 59, 440, T 157. Infin. *μαχήσεσθαι* E 833, P 604. 3 sing. aor. *μαχέσσατο* Z 184. 1 pl. *μαχεσσάμεθα* B 377. Opt. *μαχεσσαίμην* N 118. 2 sing. *μαχέσαιο* Z 329. 3 *μαχέσαιτο* Ω 439. Acc. sing. masc. pple. *μαχεσσάμενον* Γ 393. Nom. dual masc. *μαχεσσαμένω* A 304. Infin. *μαχέσασθαι* Γ 20, E 496, H 74, Θ 168, Υ 171, X 223, etc. *μαχέσσασθαι* O 633 : σ 39. *μαχήσασθαι* E 483 : β 245. (*ἀμφι-, προ-.*) (1) To fight, do battle, take part in the fight, engage in fight: *μαχόμην κατ' ἔμ' αὐτόν* A 271, *μετὰ πρώτοισι μάχεσθαι* E 536. Cf. A 153, Γ 290, H 140, M 2, O 698, Υ 408, X 243, etc.: *οἳ ἄστυ πέρι Πριάμοιο μάχοντο* ε 106. Cf. λ 403, ξ 491, π 171, ρ 471, χ 65, 245, ω 113.—Of single combat: *Ἀλέξανδρος καὶ Μενέλαος μαχήσονται περὶ σεῖο* Γ 137. Cf. Γ 20, H 40, Υ 88, Φ 160, etc. —To box: *ὁ ξεῖνος καὶ Ἶρος ἐρίζετον ἀλλήλοιϊν χερσὶ μαχέσσασθαι* σ 39. Cf. Ψ 621.—(2) To fight, engage in fight, do battle, with. With dat.: *Τρωσίν* Δ 156. Cf. A 151, E 130, N 238, Π 520, Φ 429, Ω 439 (will attack thee), etc.: β 245, 251, λ 169, ν 390, ξ 71, π 244, σ 63, χ 214.—With *ἐπί*: *ἐπὶ Τρώεσσιν* E 124, Λ 442, Υ 26. Cf. E 244.—With *πρός*: *πρὸς Τρῶας* P 471.—Of single combat. With dat.: *μενοινώω καὶ οἴος Ἕκτορι μάχεσθαι* N 80. Cf. A 298, Γ 435, H 74, Υ 179, etc.—Of boxing Ψ 554 : σ 31, 52.—(3) With cognate acc.: *μάχην ἐμάχοντο* M 175. Cf. B 121, Γ 435, Σ 533, etc.: ι 54.—(4) To contend with in manly sports. With dat.: *τίς ἂν φιλέοντι μάχοιτο;* θ 208.—(5) Of fighting with a beast: *θηρὶ μαχέσσασθαι* O 633.—Of a beast attacking or fighting with men: ὡς κύων ὑλάει μέμονέν τε μάχεσθαι υ 15. Cf. Υ 171.—Of beasts or birds fighting: ὥς τ' αἰγυπιοὶ μεγάλα κλάζοντε μάχωνται Π 429. Cf. Π 758, 824.—(6) To fight with words, quarrel, wrangle, dispute, contend: ἀντιβίοισι μαχεσσαμένω ἐπέεσσιν Α 304. Cf. Α 8, Β 377.—(7) To oppose, set oneself against, thwart. With dat.: οὐκ ἐθέλησα Ποσειδάωνι μάχεσθαι ν 341.—(8) To be up in arms against (a person), assume an attitude of protest in regard to (him), find fault with or upbraid (him). With dat.: σοὶ πάντες μαχόμεσθα· σὺ γὰρ . . . Ε 875. Cf. Ζ 329, Ι 32, Ν 118.

μάψ. (1) In vain, to no purpose, fruitlessly: μ. ἄπρηκτον πόλεμον πολεμίζειν Β 120.—For no good reason, without aim or object so far as one is concerned: μ. ἕνεκ' ἀλλοτρίων ἀχέων Υ 298.—(2) In unseemly wise, without regard for right, decency or established usage: μ., ἀτὰρ οὐ κατὰ κόσμον Β 214, Ε 759. Cf. Ν 627: γ 138.—(3) Without justification or good reason, idly, thoughtlessly, frivolously, lightly: μ. αὔτως εὐχετάασθαι Υ 348. Cf. Ο 40: π 111.

μαψιδίως [adv. fr. μαψίδιος, adj. fr. μάψ]. (1) =μάψ (3): τίς νύ σε τοιάδ' ἔρεξε, μ.; Ε 374= Φ 510. Cf. β 58=ρ 537, η 310, ξ 365, ρ 451.—(2) Without determined course, idly: ἦ μ. ἀλάλησθε; γ 72=ι 253.

†***μάω.** 2 dual pf. μέματον Θ 413, Κ 433. 1 pl. μέμαμεν Ι 641, Ο 105. 2 μέματε Η 160. 3 μεμάᾱσι Κ 208, 236, 409, Υ 165, Χ 384: δ 700, 740, ε 18, ρ 520, υ 215, χ 263. 3 imp. μεμάτω Δ 304, Υ 355. Pple. μεμᾰώς Δ 40, Ε 135, Λ 239, Ν 137, Σ 156, Φ 65, Χ 36, etc.: ε 375, τ 231, 449. μεμᾱώς Π 754. Genit. μεμᾰῶτος Θ 118. Dat. μεμᾰῶτι Ν 80, 317, Χ 284. Acc. μεμᾰῶτα Α 590, Η 261, Θ 327, Λ 95, Ξ 375, Ρ 181, Υ 256, Ω 298, etc.: δ 351, 416, λ 210. Nom. dual μεμᾰῶτε Ε 569, Ζ 120, Υ 159, Χ 243, Ψ 814. μεμᾰότε Ν 197. Acc. μεμᾰῶτε Ε 244, Ν 46, Π 555, Ρ 531. Nom. pl. μεμᾰῶτες Β 473, Γ 9, Ν 40, Ρ 727, etc.: ο 183, υ 50, ω 395. μεμᾰότες Β 818. Dat. μεμᾰῶσι Μ 200, 218. Acc. μεμᾰῶτας Ι 361, Ο 276: χ 172. Fem. μεμαυῖα Δ 440, Ε 518, Ξ 298, Ο 83, etc.: ν 389, π 171. Acc. μεμαυῖαν Δ 73, Τ 349, Χ 186: ρ 286, ω 487. Nom. pl. μεμαυῖαι Ε 779, Λ 615. 3 pl. plupf. μέμασαν Β 863, Η 3, Θ 56, Μ 89, 197, Ν 135, 337: λ 315. Pf. μέμονα Ε 482. 2 sing. μέμονας Η 36, Ι 247, Ν 307, Ξ 88, Φ 481, Ω 657. 3 μέμονε Μ 304, Π 435, Σ 176, Φ 315: ο 521, υ 15. (For the forms cf. γέγαα, γέγονα under γίγνομαι (A).) (ἐμ-.) (1) To be eager, anxious or ready: ἐπεὶ μεμάασί γε πολλοί (are ready to volunteer) Κ 236, μέμονεν ἶσα θεοῖσιν (his heart swells like that of a god) Φ 315.—(2) To be eager, anxious or ready, show eagerness, anxiety or readiness. strive or struggle, *to do something*, to be bent or set on *doing something*. With pres. or aor. infin.: μέμασαν μάχεσθαι Β 863, διαπραθέειν μεμαῶτες Ι 532. Cf. Α 590, Δ 40, 304 (be carried away by his eagerness), Ε 852, Ν 182, Σ 156, Χ 413, etc.: δ 351, ε 18, λ 210, ρ 520, υ 15, etc.—With fut. infin.: μέμασαν τεῖχος ῥήξειν Μ 197. Cf. Β 543, Μ 200, 218: ο 521, ω 395.—(3) To be eager for. With genit.: μεμαῶτα μάχης Ι 655, μεμαότε ἀλκῆς (eager to display . . .) Ν 197. Cf. Ε 732, Ρ 181, Υ 256.—(4) In pple. without construction (a) Eager to be doing, keen for action, in eager course, pressing on, bent or set on doing something: μεμαότες ἐγχείῃσιν (with their spears, *i.e.* eager to use them) Β 818, Ἔρις ἄμοτον μεμαυῖα Δ 440, στυφέλιξέ μιν μεμαῶτα (checked his fury) Η 261. Cf. Δ 73, Θ 327, Ν 46, Ο 604, Ω 298, etc.: δ 416 (struggling), ν 389, χ 172, ω 487.—Applied to the insistent hungry belly ρ 286.—(b) Eagerly, with eager haste, speed, alacrity or zeal: βῆ ῥ' ἀν' ὁδὸν μεμαώς Κ 339. Cf. Ε 143, Λ 239, 258, Ν 40, Ο 83, Π 754, Φ 174, etc.: ἤϊξαν πεδίονδε μεμαῶτες ο 183.—(5) To hasten, speed: πῇ μέματον; (whither away so fast?) Θ 413. Cf. Λ 615, Ξ 298.—(6) To be minded or inclined, to purpose, design: διχθά μοι κραδίη μέμονεν (I am in two minds) Π 435.—With pres. or aor. infin.: πῇ μέμονας καταδῦναι ὅμιλον; Ν 307, ἧε μένειν μεμάασιν Χ 384. Cf. Η 160, Κ 208=409, Κ 433, Μ 304, Ω 657: λ 315.—With fut. infin.: πῶς μέμονας πόλεμον καταπαυσέμεν; Η 36. Cf. Ι 247, Ξ 88, Ο 105, Φ 481 (presume to . . .).

με. See ἐμέ.

μεγάθῡμος, -ον [μέγας + θυμός]. Great-hearted. Epithet of heroes, etc. Β 518, 706, Δ 479, Ε 25, 565, Ζ 145, Ξ 454, Ο 440, Π 818, Ρ 214, Ψ 694, etc.: γ 189, 364, 423, η 62, ο 2, 229, 243, τ 180, φ 296.—Of Athene θ 520, ν 121.—Of the royal councillors: βουλὴν μεγαθύμων γερόντων Β 53.—Of peoples Α 123, Β 541, Ε 27, Ι 549, Ν 699, etc.: γ 366, η 16, ω 57.—Applied to a bull Π 488.

μεγαίρω [μέγας. 'To think too great']. 3 sing. aor. μέγηρε Ψ 865. 2 sing. subj. μεγήρῃς γ 55. Pple. μεγήρας Ν 563, Ο 473. To be unwilling to give or allow, to grudge. With acc. and dat.: μέγηρέ οἱ τό γ' Ἀπόλλων Ψ 865.—With dat. alone: Δαναοῖσι μεγήρας Ο 473.—With genit. indicating that in respect of which grudging takes place and dat.: τάων οὔ τοι ἐγὼ πρόσθ' ἵσταμαι οὐδὲ μεγαίρω Δ 54.—With this genit. alone: βιότοιο μεγήρας (grudging him the taking of his foe's life) Ν 563. —With dat. and infin. indicating what is grudged: μηδὲ μεγήρῃς ἡμῖν τελευτῆσαι τάδε ἔργα γ 55.—With prepositional clause and infin.: ἀμφὶ νεκροῖσι κατακαιέμεν οὔ τι μεγαίρω Η 408.—With infin. and acc. of person concerned as subject of it: μνηστῆρας οὔ τι μεγαίρω ἔρδειν ἔργα βίαια (I say nothing against their doing so) β 235.—Without construction θ 206.

μεγακήτης [μέγας + κῆτος]. Epithet of the sea, with mighty deeps γ 158.—Epithet of ships, with mighty hollow, capacious Θ 222=Λ 5, Λ 600. —Epithet of the dolphin, with mighty maw Φ 22.

μεγαλήτωρ, -ορος [μεγαλ-, μέγας + ἦτορ]. Great-hearted. Epithet of heroes, etc. Β 547, Ε 468, Ζ 283, Ν 189, Π 257, Υ 175, etc.: γ 432, δ 143, ζ 17, η 58, λ 85, etc.—Of peoples Θ 523, Ν 302, 656, Τ 278, Φ 55: τ 176.—Applied to θυμός (my, thy, his, great heart) I 109, Λ 403, etc. : ε 298, ι 299, etc.

μεγαλίζομαι [μεγαλ-, μέγας]. To bear oneself proudly, be haughty ψ 174.—To be too proud to do something K 69.

μεγάλως [μεγαλ-, μέγας]. Greatly, in a high degree, to a great extent : ἐμὲ μ. ἀκαχίζεις π 432. Cf. P 723.

μεγαλωστί [as prec.] = prec. Strengthening μέγας by reduplication (cf. αἰνόθεν αἰνῶς, οἰόθεν οἶος) Π 776, Σ 26 : ω 40.

μέγαρον, -ου, τό. (1) The chief room of a house, the general living-room, the hall : ἐνὶ μεγάροισιν ἑκάστῃ πῦρ καιόντων Θ 520 : μέθυ νεῖμον πᾶσιν ἀνὰ μ. η 180. Cf. δ 37, 300, η 230, λ 420, π 343, φ 229, etc.—In pl. in the same sense : ὁμάδησαν ἀνὰ μέγαρα α 365. Cf. δ 238, θ 242, λ 334, ο 77, σ 183, χ 172, etc.—Such a room in the abode of a god Σ 374.—In the hut of Achilles Ω 647.—Of the chief room in the hut of Eumaeus π 165.—So in pl. : παρήμενος ἐν μεγάροισιν ρ 521. —In pl. of such a room in the modest dwelling of Laertes ω 392, 396, 412.—(2) The house itself, one's house or home : τρεῖς μοί (οἵ) εἰσι θύγατρες ἐνὶ μεγάρῳ I 144, 286. Cf. B 661, Z 91, 272, 377, N 431, Ω 209 (at home) : ἴτω ἐς μ. πατρός α 276. Cf. α 270, δ 744, η 65, ν 377, π 341, χ 370, etc.—In pl. in the same sense : πατρὸς ἐν μεγάροισιν Z 428. Cf. A 418, B 137, Z 421, N 667, O 439, Ω 219, etc. : τρέφε Ναυσικάαν ἐν μεγάροισιν η 12. Cf. α 269, γ 213, ζ 62, λ 68, ο 231, φ 30, etc.—In pl. app. including the αὐλή : χῆνες ἐκέχυντο ἀθρόοι ἐν μεγάροις τ 540. Cf. τ 552.—In pl. of the abodes of the gods Λ 76, Φ 475 : α 27.—(3) A chamber or a set of chambers appropriated to the lady of a house and her maidens, the women's quarters (cf. ὑπερώϊον (2)) : τὴν εὗρ' ἐν μεγάρῳ Γ 125 (the same as the θάλαμος of 142), μεγάροιο διέσσυτο X 460 (the same as the μυχὸς δόμου of 440) : ἐς μ. καλέσασα α 416, ἦλθον ἀμφίπολοι ἐκ μεγάροιο (*i.e.* from the part of it from which they had been summoned) σ 198. Cf. σ 185, 316, τ 60, υ 6, φ 236 = 382, χ 497, ψ 43. —In pl. in the same sense : Πηνελόπειαν ἐνὶ μεγάροισιν ἄνωχθι μεῖναι ρ 569. Cf. Z 286 : β 94 = ω 129, τ 16, 30 = φ 387, τ 139, χ 399.

μεγαρόνδε [prec. + -δε (1)]. To the μέγαρον (in sense (1)) : βῆ δ' ἰέναι μ. π 413. Cf. φ 58, ψ 20.

μέγας, μεγάλη, μέγα. Comp. μείζων, -ονος. Neut. μεῖζον. Superl. μέγιστος, -η, -ον. (1) Of great longitudinal extent, long (as applied to weapons commonly a mere epithet) : ξίφος A 194, τάφρον H 441, I 350. Cf. Γ 272, Δ 124, O 677, X 307, etc. : ἔγχος α 100. Cf. κ 262, φ 74, ω 172, etc.—(2) Of great upward extent, high, tall, lofty : πύργον Z 386. Cf. O 619, Π 297, Φ 243 : ἐρινεός μ 103. Cf. δ 501, θ 569, μ 71, χ 466, etc. —Epithet of Olympus A 530, Θ 443.—(3) Of persons, tall, of large build, goodly : ἠΰς τε μέγας τε B 653. Cf. Δ 534, E 628, Σ 518, Φ 108, etc. : καλόν τε μέγαν τε α 301. Cf. ι 508, ν 289, σ 4, 382, φ 334, etc.—In comp. : κεφαλῇ μείζονες ἄλλοι ἔασιν Γ 168. Cf. ζ 230 = ψ 157, κ 396, ω 369. —Of parts of the body, well developed, stout, strong : μηρούς σ 68. Cf. O 695 : ρ 225.—Of the voice, great, full : ὄπα Γ 221.—Of horses or oxen, stout, goodly B 839 = M 97, Ψ 750. Cf. σ 372. —In superl. K 436.—Grown-up, come to man's estate β 314, σ 217, τ 532.—(4) Wide, broad, spacious, extensive : τέμενος M 313. Cf. B 210, 332, Δ 483, E 448, H 462, N 588, Σ 588, Φ 239, Ω 452, etc. : ὄρχατος η 112. Cf. γ 107, ε 461, ξ 7, ρ 299, τ 178, etc. —Of flocks : οἰῶν μέγα πῶϋ Γ 198, Λ 696, O 323 : μ 299.—Of garments, wide, flowing : φᾶρος B 43, Θ 221 : ε 230, θ 84. Cf. ξ 521, σ 292, etc.—In superl. Z 90, 271, 294 := ο 107.—Covering a wide space : ὁμίχλην N 336.—Sim. : κεῖτο μέγας μεγαλωστί Π 776. Cf. Σ 26 : ω 40.—Epithet of οὐρανός A 497, E 750 = Θ 394, Φ 388.—Of the sea (no doubt sometimes with notion of depth also) Ξ 16, T 267 : γ 179, δ 504, etc.—(5) Of great size, great, large : λίθον H 265. Cf. Γ 23, E 213, Λ 265, Π 158, Σ 344, 476, etc. : ἀσκόν ε 266. Cf. β 94, ε 234, ι 240, μ 173, ξ 530, σ 118, φ 177, ω 80, etc.—Sim. : Λυκίων μέγα ἔθνος M 330.—In comp. : μείζονα κρητῆρα I 202. Cf. H 268 : θ 187, ι 537, μ 96.—Of waves, big, swollen O 381, P 264, Φ 268, 313 : γ 295, ε 320, κ 94, μ 60, etc.—Of springs, great, welling forth in abundance : κρουνῶν Δ 454.—Of a meal, abundant, sumptuous : δόρπον T 208.—(6) Of sound, mighty, loud, resounding, far-sounding : ἀλαλητῷ M 138, Ξ 393. Cf. O 384, Φ 9, 256, 387 : ω 463.—In comp. Ξ 4.—In reference to a report or rumour or to fame, wide-spread, known far and wide : κλέος Z 446, κῦδος Θ 176, etc. Cf. γ 79, etc.—In comp. : μεῖζον κλέος θ 147. Cf. σ 255 = τ 128.—In superl. ι 264.—(7) Great, thick, stout, strong : σάκος ('his ponderous shield') Γ 335, κληῗδα Ω 455. Cf. M 57, 134, 257, etc. : τειχίον π 165. Cf. μ 436, etc. —In comp. Ξ 377.—In superl. Ξ 371.—Of fire, etc., with powerful blaze, blazing strongly or fiercely : πῦρ Θ 521, I 211, σέλαϊ P 739. Cf. ε 59, ψ 51.—Of wind, blustering μ 408, ξ 458, τ 200.—(8) Of the heart, great, distended with pride, full of spirit or daring, swollen, swelling : δάμασον θυμὸν μέγαν I 496. Cf. B 196, H 25, I 184, Φ 395.—In superl. P 21.—(9) Of great power or influence, of might, of power, mighty, powerful : θεός (θεόν) E 434, Θ 200, Π 531, T 410, Ω 90.—Sim. of the Scamander Υ 73, Φ 192, 248, 282, 329.—Epithet of gods and heroes, mighty, the mighty B 134, 816, Δ 295, E 39, 610, 721, H 427, Λ 501, M 136, etc. : δ 27, θ 226, etc.—Distinguishing the Salaminian from the lesser Aias : Αἴας ὁ μέγας Π 358.—In superl. B 412, Γ 276 = 320 = H 202 = Ω 308, Γ 298.—(10) (a) Of occurrences, emotions, qualities, etc., of great weight, efficacy, effect, significance, importance or value, great, mighty, weighty, heavy, potent, important, serious, significant of much : ὅρκον A 233, πένθος 254, σθένος Λ 11, etc. Cf. Δ 38, E 285, I 9, K 282, N 122, Π 208, T 270, etc. : πῆμα β 163, ἔργων φ 26, ἀρετῇ ω 193. Cf. γ 275, ε 289, θ 136, λ 195, χ 149, ψ 188, etc.—In comp. I 498, N 120, O 121 : β 48, λ 474, π 291, etc.—In superl. A 525, B 118, O 37, X 288, etc. : α 70, ε 4, 185.—Of great value, price or amount, valuable, costly, precious : δῶρον I 576, χρεῖος Λ 698. Cf. K 304, 401, X 163, etc. : ἄγαλμα θ 509.—In comp. A 167, Ψ 551, 593.—In superl. Ψ 640.—Absol. : σὺν μεγάλῳ ἀπέτεισαν (with a heavy penalty, at a grievous rate) Δ 161 : λίην μέγα εἶπες (too great a thing to be looked for) γ 227, etc.—(b) In bad sense, violent, outrageous, audacious, evil : ἔργον γ 261, λ 272, μ 373, τ 92, ω 426, 458.—(11) In neut. sing. μέγα as adv. (a) Greatly, much, in a high degree, to a great extent, far : μ. κεν κεχαροίατο A 256. Cf. A 103, B 27, Z 261, I 509, Σ 162, Ψ 682, etc. : μ. δυναμένοιο α 276. Cf. δ 30, 503, ο 376, π 139, φ 247, etc.—With power or might : μ. πάντων Ἀργείων ἤνασσεν K 32, μ. ἔξιδεν (with all his might) Υ 342. Cf. A 78, Π 172 : λ 485, ο 274.—μ. φρονέων, with great things in the mind, at a high pitch of resolve or endeavour Θ 553, Λ 296, 325, N 156, Π 258, 758, 824, X 21.—μ. εἰπεῖν, to talk big χ 288.—(b) Strengthening an adj. or adv., in a high degree, exceedingly, very : μ. νήπιος Π 46, ἄνευθε μ. νῶϊν X 88. Cf. A 158, etc. : ι 44, etc.—Strengthening a comp. or superl., by much, by far, much : μ. ἄριστος B 82, μ. ἀμείνονες Δ 405. Cf. B 239, T 216, X 158, etc. : λ 478, χ 374, ψ 121, etc.—Sim. : μ. ἔξοχος B 480. Cf. ο 227, φ 266.—(c) In reference to sound, loudly, with a loud voice or sound : μ. ἴαχον B 333. Cf. B 784, Ξ 147, 399, P 334, Υ 260, X 407, etc. : μ. ἔπταρεν ρ 541. Cf. ι 395, κ 323, ρ 239, etc.—(12) In neut. pl. μεγάλα as adv. (a) Strengthening other words : μ. ἤλιθα πολλή ι 330.—(b) In reference to sound, loudly, with a loud voice or sound : μεγάλ' εὔχετο A 450. Cf. A 482, Θ 75, 347, Π 391, 429, Ψ 119, etc. : μεγάλ' αὐδήσαντος (app. connoting boastfulness) δ 505. Cf. β 428, ι 392, 399, ξ 354, υ 113, φ 413.—Sim. in reference to the loud beating of the heart in agitation : κραδίη μ. πατάσσει N 282.

μέγεθος, τό [μέγας]. Tall stature, goodly build (cf. μέγας (3)) : εἶδός τε μ. τε φυήν τε B 58. Cf. H 288, Ψ 66 : ε 217, ζ 152, λ 337 = σ 249, σ 219, ω 253, 374.

μέγηρε, 3 sing. aor. μεγαίρω.

μέγιστος, superl. μέγας.

μεδέων, ὁ [μεδ- as in μέδομαι. Cf. μέδων]. A ruler or lord Γ 276 = 320 = H 202 = Ω 308, Π 234.

μέδομαι [cf. μήδομαι]. Fut. μεδήσομαι I 650. (1) To devise, plan, contrive, meditate : κακά Δ 21 = Θ 458.—(2) To bethink oneself of, think of, take thought for, remember, make arrangements for. With genit. : πολέμοιο B 384, ἀλκῆς Δ 418 = E 718. Cf. I 622, 650, Σ 245, Ω 2, 618 : δείπνοιο τ 321. Cf. β 358, γ 334, λ 110 = μ 137.

μέδων, -οντος, ὁ [μεδ- as in μέδομαι. Cf. μεδέων]. (1) A ruler or lord : ἁλὸς μέδοντος α 72.—(2) A leader, commander or chief B 79, K 301, Λ 816, M 376, Π 164, etc. : η 136, 186 = θ 26 = 97 = 387 = 536, θ 11, λ 526, ν 186, 210.

†**μεθαιρέω** [μεθ-, μετα- (7)]. 3 sing. pa. iterative (formed fr. the stem ἑλ- of the aor. (see αἱρέω)) μεθέλεσκε. To catch in one's turn : [σφαῖραν] θ 376.

†**μεθάλλομαι** [μεθ-, μετα- (1)]. Aor. pple. μετάλμενος. To spring or rush in pursuit of a foe or of a competitor, to spring or rush upon him : οὔτασε μετάλμενος E 336. Cf. Λ 538, M 305, N 362, Ξ 443, Ψ 345.

μεθέηκα, aor. μεθίημι[1].

μεθείω, aor. subj. μεθίημι[1].

μεθέλεσκε, 3 sing. pa. iterative μεθαιρέω.

μεθέμεν, aor. infin. μεθίημι[1].

μεθέπω[1] [μεθ-, μετα- (1) + ἕπω[1]]. Aor. pple. μετασπών P 190 : ξ 33. To direct or drive (one's horses in quest of or to join a person). With acc. of the person : Τυδεΐδην μέθεπεν ἵππους E 329. —So without the direct object : ἡνίοχον μέθεπεν (drove in quest or search of . . .) Θ 126.—To direct one's course towards, make for, an indicated object : [ἑταίρους] P 190. Cf. ξ 33.—To come to pay a visit : ἠὲ νέον μεθέπεις, ἦ . . . α 175.

†**μεθέπω**[2] [μεθ-, μετα- (1) + ἕπω[2]]. Only in mid. Aor. pple. μετασπόμενος. To follow up a foe : ἀπιόντα μετασπόμενος βάλεν N 567.

μεθήῃ, 3 sing. aor. subj. μεθίημι[1].

μεθῆκε, 3 sing. aor. μεθίημι[1].

μέθημαι [μεθ-, μετα- (3)]. To sit *among.* With dat. : μνηστῆρσι μεθήμενος α 118.

μεθημοσύνη, -ης, ἡ [as next]. Slackness in action, remissness N 121.—In pl. N 108.

μεθήμων, -ονος [μεθίημι[1]]. Slow to take action, remiss, careless B 241 : ζ 25.

μεθήσω, fut. μεθίημι[1].

†**μεθίημι**[1] [μεθ-, μετα- (1) (the senses app. developed through the notion of sending forth from oneself) + ἵημι[1]]. 1 pl. μεθίεμεν Ξ 364. 2 μεθίετε M 409, N 116. 3 sing. subj. μεθίῃσι N 234. 2 pl. imp. μεθίετε Δ 234. Acc. sing. masc. pple. μεθιέντα Δ 516, Z 330, M 268, N 229. Acc. pl. μεθιέντας Δ 240. Infin. μεθϊέμεναι N 114. μεθϊέμεν Δ 351. 3 pl. impf. μέθιεν φ 377. Fut. μεθήσω Λ 841. 3 sing. -ει α 77, ο 212. 1 pl. -ομεν O 553, P 418. 2 -ετε N 97. Infin. μεθησέμεναι π 377. -έμεν Υ 361. Aor. μεθέηκα P 539. 3 sing. μεθέηκε Ψ 434, Ω 48. μεθῆκε Φ 177 : ε 460, φ 126. Aor. subj. μεθείω Γ 414. 3 sing. μεθήῃ ε 471 (*v.l.* μεθείῃ, see below). 1 pl. μεθῶμεν K 449. 3 sing. opt. μεθείη N 118 : ε 471 (*v.l.* here μεθήῃ, see above). Infin. μεθέμεν A 283, O 138. From μεθιέω 2 sing. pres. μεθιεῖς Z 523 : δ 372. 3 μεθιεῖ K 121. 3 sing. impf. μεθίει O 716, Π 762, Φ 72. (1) To relax one's hold of something, let it go : ἐπεὶ λάβεν οὐχὶ μεθίει O 716, Π 762. Cf. Φ 72 : ἐς ποταμὸν μεθῆκεν (let it fall into the . . .) ε 460.—(2) To let go or release (a captive) K 449. —Sim. in reference to a guest : οὔ σε μεθήσει (will not hear of thy going) ο 212.—(3) App., to relax, relieve, free (from a burden) : κῆρ ἄχεος μεθέηκα (have lightened it of my grief) P 539.—Of a state or condition, to relieve (a person) of its

presence, quit (him): εἴ με μεθήῃ ῥῖγος ε 471.—(4) To let go or dismiss from one's mind: Ἀχιλλῆϊ μεθέμεν χόλον A 283. Cf. O 138: α 77.—So, to let go, depart from. With genit.: χόλοιο φ 377.—To dismiss from one's thoughts, cease to care for, no longer interest oneself in: μὴ χωσαμένη σε μεθείω Γ 414.—(5) To yield, give: νίκην Ξ 364.—With infin., to yield the doing of something, to suffer, allow, permit: εἰ τοῦτον Τρώεσσι μεθήσομεν ἄστυ πότι ἐρύσαι P 418.—(6) To relax one's efforts, lose resolution, grow slack or faint-hearted, in the matter of, relax, cease, refrain, hold back, from. With genit.: ἀλκῆς Δ 234, M 409, N 116, πολέμοιο Δ 240, 351, Z 330, N 97, 114, 118, μάχης M 268, βίης (relaxed from his effort) (*v.l.* βίῃ, 'in his effort') Φ 177: φ 126.—Sim. with infin.: μάχεσθαι N 234. Cf. Ψ 434.—So κλαύσας καὶ ὀδυράμενος μεθέηκε [κλαίειν καὶ ὀδύρεσθαι] (ceases to weep) Ω 48.—To refrain from rendering friendly offices to, neglect. With genit.: σεῖο τειρομένοιο (in thy trouble) Λ 841.—(7) Absol., to relax one's efforts, become slack, cease to exert oneself, lose heart: ὅθι μεθιέντα ἴδοιτο Δ 516. Cf. Z 523, K 121, N 229, O 553, Υ 361: δ 372, π 377 (will not be idle).

†**μεθίημι**[2] [μεθ-, μετα- (1) + ἵημι[2]]. Only in mid. Aor. pple. μετεισάμενος (μετα(ϝ)ισάμενος). To speed or make in an indicated direction for some purpose: μετεισάμενος ὄτρυνε φάλαγγας N 90. Cf. P 285.

μεθίστημι [μεθ-, μετα- (3) (6)]. Fut. μεταστήσω δ 612. (1) In act., to set in a different manner, to change: ταῦτα μεταστήσω (will give another gift instead) δ 612.—(2) In mid., to take one's stand, come and stand, *among*. With dat.: ἑτάροισι μεθίστατο E 514.

μεθομῑλέω [μεθ-, μετα- (3)]. To consort *with*. With dat.: τοῖσιν μεθομίλεον A 269.

μεθορμάω [μεθ-, μετα- (1)]. In pass., to set out with an indicated object, start on an expedition: Λυρνησσὸν πέρσα μεθορμηθεὶς Υ 192.—To make a dart or effort towards an indicated object: μεθορμηθεὶς ἐλλάβετο σχεδίης ε 325.

μέθυ, τό. Wine H 471, I 469: δ 746, η 179, ι 9, μ 362, ξ 194, ρ 533, etc.

μεθύω [μέθυ]. To be drunken: μεθύοντι ἐοικώς σ 240.—To drip, be soaked: βοείην μεθύουσαν ἀλοιφῇ (with . . .) P 390.

μεθῶμεν, 1 pl. aor. subj. μεθίημι[1].

μειδάω. (ἐπι-.) To smile A 595 = Φ 434, A 596, E 426 = O 47, Z 404, Ξ 222, 223, Ψ 555: δ 609, ε 180, ν 287, π 476, υ 301, ψ 111.

†**μειδιάω** = prec. Only in pres. pple. μειδιόων, -ωσα: μειδιόων βλοσυροῖσι προσώπασιν (a grim smile of anticipated triumph) H 212. Cf. Φ 491, Ψ 786.

μείζων, comp. μέγας.

μείλανι, dat. sing. masc. See μέλας.

μείλια, τά [cf. μειλίσσω]. Presents given with a bride by her father I 147, 289.

μείλιγμα, -ατος, τό [μειλίσσω]. A sweet morsel, a titbit: μειλίγματα θυμοῦ (such as delight their hearts) κ 217.

μείλινος. See μέλινος.

μειλίσσω. To soften, to soothe: πυρὸς μειλισσέμεν [νέκυας] (as to giving them the consolation of fire (genit. of material)) H 410.—In mid., to speak comfortably, mince one's words: μή μ' αἰδόμενος μειλίσσεο γ 96 = δ 326.

μειλιχίη, -ης, ἡ [μειλίσσω]. Slackness or backwardness in action O 741.

μειλίχιος, -η, -ον [μειλίσσω]. (1) Winning, pleasing: αἰδοῖ θ 172.—(2) Of speech, winning, pleasing, mild, gentle, kindly, conciliatory: μύθοισιν Z 343. Cf. I 113, K 288, 542, Λ 137, M 267, Φ 339: ζ 143, 148, κ 173, λ 552, σ 283, etc.—Absol. in pl., such speech: προσηύδα μειλιχίοισιν Δ 256, Z 214, P 431: υ 165.

μείλιχος [= prec.]. (1) Of persons, winning, mild, gentle, kindly P 671, T 300, Ω 739.—(2) = prec. (2) ο 374.

μεῖνα, aor. μένω.

μεῖξαι, aor. infin. **μείξεσθαι**, fut. infin. pass. μίσγω.

μείρομαι. 3 sing. pf. ἔμμορε A 278, O 189: ε 335, λ 338. 3 sing. plupf. pass. εἵμαρτο Φ 281: ε 312, ω 34. (1) To receive a share of, take one's part of. With genit.: ἥμισυ μείρεο τιμῆς I 616.—(2) In pf., to have one's share of, to have, hold, be entitled to. With genit.: τιμῆς A 278, O 189: ε 335, λ 338.—(3) In pass. in impers. construction, to be allotted as one's portion, be fated: λευγαλέῳ με θανάτῳ εἵμαρτο ἁλῶναι (it was the fate assigned me) Φ 281: = ε 312. Cf. ω 34.

μείς, ὁ [μήνς, μένς]. = μήν[1] T 117.

μείων, comp. μικρός.

μελαγχροιής [μέλας + χροιή]. Of dark or swarthy complexion, tanned π 175.

μέλαθρον, -ου, τό. Ablative μελαθρόφιν θ 279. (1) A roof-beam or rafter θ 279, λ 278, χ 239.—App., a free end of such a beam projecting outside: κατ' ἄρ' ἕζετ' ἐπὶ προὔχοντι μελάθρῳ τ 544.—(2) Such a beam as typifying the house, one's 'roof': κατὰ πρηνὲς βαλέειν Πριάμοιο μέλαθρον B 414. Cf. I 204, 640 (the obligations of hospitality): σ 150.

μελαίνω [μέλας]. To make dark; in pass., to grow dark: μελαίνετο χρόα καλόν (her flesh grew livid) E 354, νειὸς μελαίνετ' ὄπισθεν (was represented as darkened in hue by some process of shading) Σ 548.

μελάνδετος [μέλας + δέω. 'Bound in black']. App., having the hilts bound round with dark bands. Epithet of swords O 713.

μελανόχροος [μέλας + χρώς]. = μελαγχροιής τ 246.

μελανόχρως [as prec.]. Dark-hued N 589.

μελάντερος, comp. μέλας.

μελάνυδρος, -ον [μέλας + ὕδωρ]. In which the water wells up from dark depths. Epithet of springs I 14, Π 3, 160, Φ 257: υ 158.

μελάνω [μέλας]. To grow dark H 64.

μέλᾱς, μέλαινα, μέλᾰν. Dat. sing. masc. μείλανι Ω 79. Comp. μελάντερος. (1) Dark in hue, dark (not necessarily implying the absence of colour, but sometimes to be translated 'black'): [ἄρνα] μέλαιναν Γ 103, κυάνοιο Λ 24, 35, τέφρη Σ 25, αἰετοῦ Φ 252. Cf. Η 265 = Φ 404, Κ 215, Σ 562: οἴνοιο ε 265, ι 196, 346, ὄϊν κ 527, 572. Cf. ε 488, κ 304.—In comp.: μελάντερον ἠΰτε πίσσα Δ 277. Cf. Ω 94.—Applied to the φρένες thought of as darkened by deep emotion: μένεος φρένες ἀμφὶ μέλαιναι πίμπλαντο Α 103 := δ 661 (*i.e.* the double organ (see ἀμφί (I) (1) (b)) was filled with fury (so as to be) black in both parts). Cf. Ρ 83, 499, 573. (In all these cases also written, with sim. sense, ἀμφιμέλαιναι.)—Absol.: τὸ μέλαν δρυός (the dark heart) ξ 12.—(2) Epithet (a) Of ships Α 141, 300, Β 524, Ε 550, etc.: β 430, γ 61, δ 781, ζ 268, etc.—(b) Of the earth: γαῖα μέλαινα Β 699, Ο 715, Ρ 416, Υ 494: λ 365, 587, τ 111.—So ἠπείροιο μελαίνης ξ 97, φ 109.—(c) Of blood Δ 149, Η 262, Ν 655, etc.: γ 455, ω 189.—(d) Of water (app. referring to the dark hue of water as seen by transmitted light with little or no reflection from the surface): μέλαν ὕδωρ Β 825, Π 161, Φ 202: δ 359, ζ 91, μ 104, ν 409.—So of the sea: μείλανι πόντῳ Ω 79.—And of waves Ψ 693: ε 353.—Of the surface of the sea rippled by a breeze: μέλαιναν φρῖκα Φ 126. Cf. δ 402.—(e) Of night Θ 486, 502, Ξ 439, etc.: η 253 = ξ 314, μ 291.—Of evening: μέλας ἕσπερος α 423 = σ 306.—Sim.: θανάτου μέλαν νέφος Π 350. Cf. Ρ 591 = Σ 22 := ω 315, δ 180.—(f) Of κήρ Β 859, Γ 360, 454, etc.: β 283, γ 242, ρ 500, ω 127, etc.—Of death Β 834 = Λ 332, Π 687: μ 92, ρ 326.—(g) Applied also to pain: μελαινέων ὀδυνάων Δ 117. Cf. Δ 191, Ο 394.

μέλδομαι. To cause to melt, melt Φ 363.

μελέδημα, -ατος, τό [μέλω]. In pl., cares, anxieties, grief: μελεδήματα θυμοῦ Ψ 62 := υ 56, ψ 343, μελεδήματα πατρός (for his . .) ο 8. Cf. δ 650.

μελεδώνη, -ης, ἡ, or **μελεδών,** -ῶνος [as prec.]. = prec. In pl.: ὀξεῖαι μελεδῶναι (μελεδῶνες) τ 517.

μελεϊστί [μέλος]. Limb-meal, limb by limb: ταμών Ω 409: ι 291. Cf. σ 339.

μέλεος, -η, -ον. (1) Vain, useless, idle, empty: εὖχος (because got without fighting) Φ 473, οὔ τοι μέλεος εἰρήσεται αἶνος (in vain) Ψ 795. Cf. ε 416.—(2) In neut. sing. μέλεον as adv., in vain, idly: ἑστάμεναι μ. σὺν τεύχεσιν (doing nothing) Κ 480, μ. ἠκόντισαν (without result, each making a miss) Π 336.

μελήσει, 3 sing. fut. μέλω.

μέλι, -ιτος, τό [cf. L. *mel*]. Honey Α 249, Λ 631, Σ 109, Ψ 170: κ 234, ν 69, ω 68.

μελίγηρυς [μέλι + γῆρυς]. Honey-toned, honey-flowing: μελίγηρυν ὄπα μ 187.

μελίη, -ης, ἡ. (1) The ash: φηγόν τε μελίην τε Π 767. Cf. Ν 178.—(2) A spear with shaft of ash, a spear in gen. Β 543, Π 143 = Τ 390, Υ 277, 322, Φ 162, 169, 174, Χ 133, 225, 328: ξ 281, χ 259 = 276.

μελιηδής [μέλι + ἡδύς]. Honey-sweet. Epithet of wine Δ 346, Ζ 258, Κ 579, Μ 320, Σ 545: γ 46, ι 208, ξ 78 = π 52, σ 151, 426, φ 293.—Of wheat Κ 569.—Of fruit Σ 568: ι 94.—Of clover or grass ζ 90.—Of bees-wax μ 48.—Applied to one's life or soul: θυμόν Κ 495, Ρ 17: λ 203.—To sleep τ 551.—To one's home-coming: νόστον λ 100.

μελίκρητον, τό [μέλι + κρη-, κεράννυμι]. A mixture of honey and (prob.) milk κ 519 = λ 27.

μέλινος, also **μείλινος** [μελίη]. Of ash. (1) Epithet of spears, with shaft of ash Ε 655, 666, Ν 715, etc.—(2) μέλινος οὐδός, app., a threshold of wood set upon the λάϊνος οὐδός at the entrance to the μέγαρον ρ 339 (see λάϊνος).

μέλισσα, ἡ [cf. μέλι]. A bee: σφῆκες ἠὲ μέλισσαι Μ 167. Cf. Β 87: ν 106.

μελίφρων, -ονος [μέλι + φρήν]. Honey-hearted. Epithet of wine Ζ 264, Θ 506, 546, Ω 284: η 182 = ν 53, κ 356, ο 148.—Of wheat: πυρόν Θ 188.—Of σῖτος ω 489.—Applied to sleep Β 34.

μέλλω. (1) To be about, be going, *to do something*, to be on the point of *doing it* (sometimes tending to pass into (2)). With fut. infin.: θήσειν ἔτ' ἔμελλεν ἄλγεα Β 39, ἔμελλέ μιν δώσειν Ζ 52. Cf. Ζ 393, Λ 22, Ο 601, Τ 98, Ψ 544, etc.: ὅτ' ἔμελλε πάλιν οἰκόνδε νέεσθαι ζ 110, Ἀγαμέμνονος φθίσεσθαι κακὸν οἶτον ἔμελλον (I have just escaped his fate) ν 384. Cf. δ 514, η 18, ι 378, λ 596, ρ 364, υ 393, χ 9, etc.—With pres. infin.: ἔμελλε λίσσεσθαι Κ 454. Cf. τ 94.—With aor. infin.: ὅτ' ἔμελλον ἐπαΐξασθαι ἄεθλον Ψ 773.—(2) To be destined or fated *to be* or *to do*. With fut. infin.: ἅ ῥ' οὐ τελέεσθαι ἔμελλον Β 36, ὣς ἄρ' ἐμέλλετ' ἄσειν κύνας (fate destined you to . . .) Λ 817. Cf. Β 694, Ε 205, Κ 336, Μ 3, Ο 612, Υ 466, Φ 47, Ω 85, etc.: μέλλον ἔτι ξυνέσεσθαι ὀϊζυῖ η 270, οὐκ ἄρ' ἔμελλες λήξειν ἀπατάων (it could not be that you should . . .) ν 293. Cf. β 156, ζ 165, ι 230, 477, λ 553, φ 98, ψ 221, ω 28, etc.—Impers.: τῇ τελευτήσεσθαι ἔμελλεν (it was fated) θ 510.—With pres. infin.: οὐκ ἄρ' ἔμελλες ἀνάλκιδος ἀνδρὸς ἑταίρους ἔδμεναι ι 475.—With aor. infin.: ἔμελλεν οἷ αὐτῷ θάνατον λιτέσθαι (he was fated to find that his prayer had been to his own death) Π 46. Cf. Σ 98.—(3) To be likely *to be* or *to be doing* or *to do*, to be presumably *so and so* or *doing so and so*. With pres. infin.: ὅθι που μέλλουσι βουλὰς βουλεύειν (where it is likely they are conferring) Κ 326, ᾧ μέλλεις εὔχεσθαι (to whom you must pray) Λ 364 = Υ 451, τὰ μέλλετ' ἀκουέμεν (no doubt you know) Ξ 125: μέλλε ποτὲ οἶκος ὅδ' ἀφνειὸς ἔμμεναι (all know how flourishing it was) α 232, ὄλβον θεοὶ μέλλουσιν ὀπάζειν (surely you know that it is the gods who . . .) σ 19, καὶ ἐγώ ποτ' ἔμελλον ὄλβιος εἶναι (I too in my day was . . .) 138, πολλάκι που μέλλεις ἀρήμεναι (no doubt you prayed) χ 322. Cf. δ 94, 200.—Impers.: ἐμοὶ μέλλει φίλον εἶναι (you may be sure that it is) Α 564. Cf. Β 116 = Ι 23 = Ξ 69, Ν 226.—With aor. infin. of something likely to have taken place or that presumably has taken place: ἄλλοτε δή ποτε μᾶλλον ἐρωῆσαι πολέμοιο μέλλω (may have done so (but cannot be accused of doing so now)) Ν 777, μέλλει τις τελέσσαι (is likely to have done so, *i.e.* may be expected to do so) Σ 362. Cf. Φ 83, Ω 46: δ 274, 377, ξ 133.—With fut. infin.: τά που μέλλεν ἀγάσσεσθαι θεὸς αὐτός (app., it must have been that he was to do so) δ 181.

μέλος, τό. Dat. pl. μελέεσσι ν 432. μέλεσσι Λ 669, Ψ 191, Ω 359 : λ 394, ν 398, 430, σ 77, φ 283. A limb. In pl., one's limbs, one's bodily frame : θυμὸν ἀπὸ μελέων δῦναι δόμον Ἄϊδος Η 131, γναμπτοῖσι μέλεσσιν Λ 669, Ω 359. Cf. Ν 672 = Π 607, Π 110, Ρ 211, Ψ 191, 689 : θ 298, κ 393, λ 201, 394, 600, ν 398, 430, 432, ο 354, σ 70 = ω 368, σ 77, φ 283.—In reference to a bird Ψ 880.—To a sacrifice : πάντων ἀρχόμενος μελέων ξ 428.

μέλπηθρον, -ου, τό [μέλπω]. That which affords sport. In pl. : κυνῶν μέλπηθρα γένοιτο (a sport for . . .) Ν 233. Cf. Ρ 255 = Σ 179.

μέλπω. To sport or play. **(1)** With special reference to dancing. In mid. : ἰδὼν μετὰ μελπομένῃσιν ἐν χορῷ Ἀρτέμιδος Π 182.—App., to dance the war-dance. Fig. : οἶδα δ' ἐνὶ σταδίῃ δηΐῳ μέλπεσθαι Ἄρηϊ (in honour of Ares) Η 241. —**(2)** With special reference to singing. In mid. : μετά σφιν ἐμέλπετ' ἀοιδός Σ 604 := δ 17 = ν 27. —To honour or celebrate in song : μέλποντες ἑκάεργον Α 474.

μέλω. 3 sing. fut. μελήσει Ε 430, Ζ 492, Ρ 515, Υ 137, Ψ 724 : α 358, λ 332, 352, ρ 601, φ 352. 3 pl. μελήσουσι Ε 228, Κ 481. Infin. μελησέμεν Κ 51. 3 sing. aor. subj. μελήσῃ Κ 282. 3 sing. pf. (in pres. sense) μέμηλε Β 25, 62, Ε 876, Ι 228, Τ 213 : ε 67, ζ 65, μ 116. 3 sing. subj. μεμήλῃ Δ 353, Ι 359. Pple. μεμηλώς Ε 708, Ν 297, 469. 3 sing. plupf. (in impf. sense) μεμήλει Β 614 : α 151. **Mid.** 3 sing. fut. μελήσεται Α 523. 3 sing. thematic pf. (in pres. sense) μέμβλεται Τ 343. 3 sing. plupf. (in impf. sense) μέμβλετο Φ 516 : χ 12. **(1)** In act. and mid., to be an object of care, concern, solicitude, anxiety or interest, to, to concern, be the concern of, to make anxious, interest, trouble : ἐμοί κε ταῦτα μελήσεται (I will make it my care) Α 523, ᾧ τόσσα μέμηλεν (who has so many responsibilities) Β 25 = 62, οὔ σφι θαλάσσια ἔργα μεμήλει 614, τά κεν Διὶ μελήσει (the issue is in his hands) Ρ 515. Cf. Δ 353, Ε 228, 490, 876, Ζ 441, 492, Ι 228, Κ 51, Ο 231, Τ 213, Φ 516, Ω 152, etc. : τοῖσιν ἄλλα μεμήλει (they turned to . . .) α 151, μέλε οἱ ἑὼν ἐν δώμασι νύμφης ε 6, μή τί τοι ἡγεμόνος γε ποθὴ μελέσθω κ 505, Ἀργὼ πᾶσι μέλουσα (at whose name all hearts stir, the storied . . .) μ 70 (*v.l.* πασιμέλουσα). Cf. α 358, β 304, δ 415 (bethink you of your . . .), ζ 65, 270, η 208, ι 20, ν 362, ρ 594, σ 421, χ 12, etc.—Impers. : οὐκ ἔμελέν μοι ταῦτα μεταλλῆσαι (I cared not to . . .) π 465. Cf. α 305.—**(2)** To be concerned with, busied about. With genit. : πλούτοιο μεμηλώς Ε 708, πτολέμοιο μεμηλώς (his mind set on it) Ν 297 = 469.

μεμάᾱσι, 3 pl. pf. μάω.

μεμακυῖαι, fem. pl. pf. pple. μηκάομαι.

μέμασαν, 3 pl. plupf. μάω.

μεμαώς, pf. pple. μάω.

μέμβλεται, 3 sing. thematic pf. μέλω.

μέμβλωκε, 3 sing. pf. βλώσκω.

μεμηκώς, pf. pple. μηκάομαι.

μέμηλε, 3 sing. pf. μέλω.

μεμιγμένος, pf. pple. pass. μίσγω.

μέμνημαι, pf. mid. μιμνήσκω.

μεμνήσομαι, fut. pf. mid. μιμνήσκω.

μέμονα, pf. μάω.

μεμορυγμένα, acc. pl. neut. pf. pple. pass. μορύσσω.

μέμῡκε, 3 sing. pf. μύω.

μεμύκει, 3 sing. plupf. μυκάομαι.

μεμῡκώς, pf. pple. μυκάομαι.

μέν [cf. μάν, μήν[2]]. **(1)** Affirmative particle : οὐ μέν σοί ποτε ἶσον ἔχω γέρας Α 163. Cf. Α 211, 216, 234, 269, 273, 514, Β 145, 203, etc. : οὐ μὲν γάρ τι κακὸν βασιλευέμεν α 392. Cf. α 78, 173, 208, 222, 411, β 318, γ 14, 236, etc.—In less emphatic use, serving to bring out a new point Β 101, Σ 84, Ψ 328, etc. : ι 159, 320, etc.—μέν τοι Δ 318, etc. : δ 157, etc.—μέν τε Ν 47, etc. : ε 447, etc.—With ἦ. See ἦ[2] (1) (b) (β).—**(2)** In adversative use : οὐδέ τι θυμὸς ἐδεύετο δαιτὸς ἐΐσης, οὐ μὲν φόρμιγγος (nor yet) Α 603, πόθεόν γε μὲν ἀρχόν (but they . . .) Β 703. Cf. Ι 57 (under ἦ[2] (1) (b) (β)), Λ 813, etc. : οὐ μέν σ' οὐδὲ ἐῶσι θεοὶ κλαίειν δ 805. Cf. κ 65 (under ἦ[2] (1) (b) (β)), etc.—**(3)** Marking an alternative : οὐ . . . οὐδὲ μὲν . . . Α 154, οὐδὲ . . . οὐδὲ μὲν . . . Ι 374, etc. Cf. θ 553, χ 415, etc.—**(4)** Anticipating and answered by δέ Α 18, 53, 135, 140, 183, etc. : α 11, 22, 24, 66, 110, etc.—ἀλλά Α 22, Γ 213, Δ 7, etc. : α 262, 307, γ 265, etc.—αὐτάρ, ἀτάρ Α 50, 127, 165, etc. : α 215, β 125, δ 31, etc.—αὖτε Β 816, Ν 195, Φ 190.

μενεαίνω [μένος]. 1 pl. aor. μενεήναμεν Τ 58 : δ 282. **(1)** To be eager, show eagerness or ardour, strive : μάλα περ μενεαίνων Ο 617. Cf. Χ 10 : ε 341.—Of mental struggling : κτεινόμενος μενέαινεν (faced his fate) Π 491.—**(2)** To desire, be eager or anxious, long, strive, be minded, *to do something,* be set on *doing it.* With infin. : κατακτάμεναι Γ 379, μηδὲ θεοῖς μενεαινέμεν ἶφι μάχεσθαι (let not your spirit carry you away so as to . . .) Ε 606. Cf. Δ 32, Ν 628, Ο 507, Φ 33, 543, etc. : δ 282, κ 295, 322, λ 392, 585, ν 30, ρ 17, 185, υ 315, φ 125.—In reference to the eager course of a missile : ἆλτ' ὀϊστός, καθ' ὅμιλον ἐπιπτέσθαι μενεαίνων Δ 126.—**(3)** To be enraged, to show or be filled with rage or bitterness, to rage : νήπιοι, οἳ Ζηνὶ μενεαίνομεν (against Zeus) Ο 104, Ἕκτορ' ἀεικίζεν μενεαίνων (in his rage) Ω 22. Cf. Τ 58, 68, Ω 54 : α 20, ζ 330.—Of martial rage : Τρωσὶν μενεαίνων Τ 367.

μενεδήϊος, -ον [μένω + δήϊος[2]. 'Withstanding the foe']. Stout, staunch Μ 247, Ν 228.

μενεήναμεν, 1 pl. aor. μενεαίνω.

μενεπτόλεμος [μένω + πτόλεμος]. Stout in the fight, staunch. Epithet of heroes, etc. Β 740, 749, Δ 395, Ζ 29, Κ 255, Ν 693, Τ 48, Ψ 836, 844 : γ 442.

μενεχάρμης [μένω + χάρμη]. = prec. Ι 529, Λ 122, 303, Ν 396, Ο 582, Ψ 419.

μενέχαρμος [as prec.]. = prec. Ξ 376.

μενέω, fut. μένω.

μενοεικής, -ές [μένος + εἴκω¹. 'Fitted to, satisfying, the spirit']. Abundant, plentiful, satisfying, contenting, in abundance or plenty: δαῖτα I 90. Cf. Ψ 29, 139, 650: ληΐδα ν 273. Cf. ε 166, 267, ζ 76, ι 158, ν 409, π 429, υ 391.—Absol.: πάρα μενοεικέα πολλὰ δαίνυσθαι (abundance, to feast thereon to our heart's desire) I 227. Cf. Τ 144: ξ 232.

μενοινάω. 1 sing. pres. μενοινώω Ν 79. 3 sing. subj. μενοινάᾳ Τ 164. μενοινήῃσι Ο 82. From μενοινέω 3 pl. impf. μενοίνεον Μ 59. (1) To wish, desire, be bent upon: ὅ τι φρεσὶ σῇσι μενοινᾷς Ξ 221, ὡς δ' ὅτ' ἂν ἀΐξῃ νόος ἀνέρος . . . μενοινήῃσί τε πολλά (forms many wishes, *i.e.* wishes himself in this place or that) Ο 82. Cf. β 34, 275, 285, δ 480, ζ 180, ο 111, ρ 355.—To turn over in one's mind, to design, purpose: νόος οἱ ἄλλα μενοινᾷ β 92 = ν 381. Cf. λ 532, σ 283.—To turn over (in one's mind) with anxiety: τίη δὲ σὺ ταῦτα μετὰ φρεσὶ σῇσι μενοινᾷς; (why let that trouble thee?) Ξ 264.—To show eagerness or ardour. With dependent clause: μενοίνεον εἰ τελέουσιν Μ 59.—Absol.: ὧδε μενοινῶν Ο 293.—(2) To desire, be eager or anxious, long, be minded, *to do something*. With infin.: μάχεσθαι Κ 101. Cf. Ν 79, 214, Τ 164: β 36, 248, φ 157, χ 217.

μένος, τό. (1) Passion, vehement or commanding feeling or emotion in general: μ. ἄσχετε (whose passion defies restraint) β 85 = ρ 406, β 303, ὄτρυνε μ. ἑκάστου (desire to see the marvel) θ 15. Cf. ξ 262 = ρ 431.—In pl.: ἐμῶν μενέων ἀπερωεύς (of my desires, of what I have set my heart upon) Θ 361.—In a more or less concrete sense: ἀνὰ ῥῖνας δριμὺ μ. προὔτυψεν ω 319.—(2) One's spirit, the spirit within one: αὐτόν με μ. ἄνωγε κεῖσ' ἰέναι Ω 198. Cf. Ε 892, Ν 634.—(3) Specifically, fury, rage: μένεος φρένες πίμπλαντο Α 103, μ. Ἄρηος (the fury of battle) Σ 264. Cf. Α 207, 282, Η 210, Ι 679, Τ 202, Φ 305, Χ 346: δ 661, ι 457, λ 562, ω 183.—In a more or less concrete sense: εἰ μὴ νὺξ διακρινέει μ. ἀνδρῶν (the eager fighters) Β 387: μ. Ἄρηος (the combat) π 269.—Distraction, frenzy. In reference to horses Ψ 468.—(4) Spirit, courage, stoutness: ἐν τοι στήθεσσι μ. πατρώϊον ἧκα Ε 125. Cf. Ε 2, 470, Θ 335, Ν 424, Ο 594, Π 529, Τ 159, Χ 96, 459, Ω 6, etc.: ὄφρα οἱ μ. ἐν φρεσὶ θείω α 89. Cf. α 321, β 271, γ 104, λ 270, 515, μ 279, ν 387, τ 493.—In reference to beasts Ρ 20, Υ 172.—(5) Might, vigour, power, strength: ἔτι μοι μ. ἔμπεδόν ἐστιν Ε 254. Cf. Ζ 101, Η 457, Ι 706, Ο 60, Π 621, Φ 482, etc.: μ. καὶ χεῖρας λ 502. Cf. υ 19, φ 426, χ 226, ω 520.—In reference to horses, etc.: σφῶϊν ἐν γούνεσσι βαλῶ μ. ἠδ' ἐνὶ θυμῷ Ρ 451 (the word as connected with θυμῷ coming under (4)). Cf. Ρ 456, 742, Ψ 390, 400, 524, Ω 442.—In reference to inanimate objects: πυρὸς μ. Ρ 565. Cf. Ν 444 = Π 613 = Ρ 529, Υ 372.—In a more or less concrete sense: μ. χειρῶν ἰθὺς φέρον Ε 506. Cf. Ζ 127, 502, Θ 178, Μ 166, Ο 510, Υ 374, etc.: μ. πνείοντες χ 203.—In pl.: μένεα πνείοντες (πνείοντας) Β 536, Γ 8, Λ 508, Ω 364. Cf. Δ 447 = Θ 61.—Might or strength in exercise: μένεος σχήσεσθαι Ρ 503. Cf. Ρ 638, Φ 340.—In reference to horses Ρ 476.—(6) μ. τινός, periphrasis for a person (cf. βίη (5)): Λεοντῆος μ. Ψ 837. Cf. Η 38, Λ 268, 272, Ξ 418, Π 189, Φ 383: μ. Ἀλκινόοιο η 167, 178 = ν 49, θ 2, 4 = 421, θ 385, 423, ν 20, 24, 64. Cf. θ 359, σ 34.—With sim. periphrasis: κούρην φέρεν μ. ἡμιόνοιϊν η 2.—Also μένος Βορέαο Ε 524, ἀναπνείουσα πυρὸς μένος (breathing fire) Ζ 182. Cf. Μ 18, Ψ 177, 190, 238 = Ω 792: ε 478, κ 160, λ 220, τ 440.—(7) The animating principle, the vital spirit, the soul, the life, life, one's life (cf. θυμός (I) (1) (b)): τοῦ λύθη ψυχή τε μ. τε Ε 296 = Θ 123 = 315. Cf. Γ 294, Ζ 27, Θ 358, Π 332, Ρ 29, 298: ἦϊά κε κατέφθιτο καὶ μένε' ἀνδρῶν δ 363.—In reference to an animal γ 450.

μένω. 3 pl. pa. iterative μένεσκον Τ 42. Fut. μενέω Λ 317, Π 239, Τ 308, Υ 22, Ψ 279: ε 362, π 132. 2 sing. μενέεις κ 285. 3 pl. μενέουσι Ι 45, Μ 79, Φ 310. Infin. μενέειν Ξ 375. Aor. ἔμεινα κ 53, ξ 244. μεῖνα ξ 292. 2 sing. ἔμεινας Ζ 126. 3 ἔμεινε Ξ 286. μεῖνε Ε 571, Ν 564, Ξ 119, Ο 585: δ 508, 733. 1 pl. ἐμείναμεν ι 151, 306, 436, μ 7. μείναμεν Λ 723. 3 pl. ἔμειναν Ο 656. 3 sing. subj. μείνῃ Θ 536. 2 sing. opt. μείνειας Γ 52. Imp. pl. μείνατε Β 299. Infin. μεῖναι Α 535, Ν 830, Ο 165, Π 147, Φ 609, Χ 5, 252: ζ 295, ι 138, ν 204, ξ 270, ο 305, 346, ρ 570, 582. (ἀνα-, ἐπι-, παρα-, ὑπο-.) (1) To remain where one is, to remain, stay, tarry, abide, continue to be, in a specified or indicated place: οὐδέ σε λίσσομαι μένειν Α 174, ἴση μοῖρα μένοντι (for him who stays behind) Ι 318, ἔνθ' ἔμεινε (stayed his course, stopped) Ξ 286, ὄφρα μένω (remain quiescent, take no action) Ω 658. Cf. Α 492, Β 298, Ζ 258, Κ 370, Π 239, Ρ 721 (sticking together), Σ 64, Τ 42, Υ 22, Χ 5, etc.: μέν' αὖθι β 369. Cf. γ 427, δ 447, ζ 295, η 259, ι 97, μ 373 (the comrades whom I left behind me), ξ 244, ο 51, ρ 20, τ 199, υ 330, etc.—Of something inanimate: [ἔγχος] αὐτοῦ μεῖνεν Ν 564. Cf. Ι 610 = Κ 90: δ 508.—To remain as one is, refrain, wait: δύντα δ' ἐς ἠέλιον μενέω Τ 308. Cf. ρ 582.—(2) To remain, continue, be, in a specified condition: ἕνα μῆνα μένων ἀπὸ ἧς ἀλόχοιο Β 292. Cf. Τ 263: υ 23.—To stand firm, stand without motion, stand still: ὥς τε στήλη μένει ἔμπεδον Ρ 434. Cf. Ρ 436: ρ 235.—Sim. of ships lying without motion ν 100.—(3) To await the coming, approach or return of (a person): ὄφρα μένοιεν νοστήσαντα ἄνακτα Ν 37. Cf. Υ 480, Φ 609: α 304, δ 439, 847, ι 232, ο 346, χ 181.—To await in an indicated posture the approach of: οὐδέ τις ἔτλη μεῖναι ἐπερχόμενον (to remain seated on his approach) Α 535.—To await (an occurrence) or the coming or coming on of (a period of time): Ἠῶ Λ 723. Cf. Ο 599: ι 151 = μ 7, ι 306 = 436.—Absol.: ἔνθ' ἔμενεν (bided his time) ν 161.—With infin.: Τρῶας σχεδὸν ἐλθέμεν Δ 247. Cf. α 422 = σ 305, δ 786, ζ 98.—With dependent clause: ὁππότε πύργος Ἀχαιῶν ἄλλος Τρώων ὁρμήσειεν (waiting till . . .) Δ 333. Cf. Λ 666.—(4) To await the attack of, stand up to: Μενέλαον Γ 52, Τρῶας Ε 527=Ο 622. Cf. Ν 476, 836, Ο 165, 406, Φ 571, Χ 252: ι 57.—Sim.: Τρώων μένει Ἄρηα Λ 836.—Also ἐμὸν ἔγχος Ζ 126. Cf. Θ 536, Ν 830, Ο 709, Π 147.—Of a beast: σῦς, ὅς τε μένει κολοσυρτὸν ἀνδρῶν Ν 472. Cf. Χ 93.—Of something inanimate: πέτρη, ἥ τε μένει ἀνέμων κέλευθα Ο 620.—Of facing the attack of a beast: μένουσι [κάπριον] Λ 418.—Absol., to await the foe, stand firm, stand one's ground: μενέμεν καὶ ἀμυνέμεναι ὥρεσσιν Ε 486, Αἰνείας οὐ μεῖνεν 571. Cf. Ε 522, Λ 317, Μ 79, Ξ 375, Ο 539, Π 659, Φ 310, etc.: οἴη Ἀλκινόου θυγάτηρ μένεν ζ 139. Cf. ξ 270.—Of wasps Μ 169.

μέρμερος [μερ- as in next]. Such as to cause anxiety, baneful, evil: ἔργα Θ 453, Κ 289, 524.—Absol. in neut. pl., baneful deeds: μέρμερα ῥέζων (ῥέζεν) Λ 502, Φ 217. Cf. Κ 48.

μερμηρίζω [μερ- as in prec.]. Aor. μερμήριξα κ 50, 151, 438. 3 sing. -ε Α 189, Ε 671, Ξ 159, etc.: β 93, δ 791, ρ 235, etc. Subj. μερμηρίξω π 261. Pple. μερμηρίξας λ 204, π 237. Infin. μερμηρίξαι π 256. (**1**) To turn (a thing) anxiously over in one's mind, to ponder or consider (it), meditate (it), have (it) in view: πολλά α 427, φόνον ἡμῖν β 325. Cf. Υ 17: δ 533, τ 2=52, υ 38, 41.—Of a lion δ 791.—To think out or contrive: δόλον τόνδε β 93, ω 128.—To think of, find: ἀμύντορά τινα π 256, 261.—(**2**) Absol., to ponder, consider, deliberate, meditate: τρὶς μερμήριξεν Θ 169, ἔτι μερμήριζον (were hesitating) Μ 199. Cf. ε 354, λ 204, π 237, υ 93.—With dependent clause. (**a**) With relative: ὅ τι κύντατον ἔρδοι Κ 503.—(**b**) With clause introduced by ὡς (how) Β 3.—(**c**) By ὅπως Ξ 159: ι 554, ο 169, υ 28, 38.—(**d**) With alternatives introduced by ἤ . . . ἤ . . . Α 189, Ε 671, Ν 455, Π 647: δ 117, ζ 141, κ 50, π 73, ρ 235, σ 90, υ 10, χ 333.—With the first alternative expressed by an infin. and the second introduced by ἤ: μερμήριξε κύσσαι . . . ἤ . . . ω 235.—With infin. expressing only one of the alternatives: διάνδιχα μερμήριξεν ἵππους στρέψαι (had half a mind to . . .) Θ 167. Cf. κ 151, 438.

μέρμις, -ῑθος, ἡ [cf. μηρύομαι]. A cord or string: κατέδει μέρμιθι κ 23.

μέροπες. Epithet of ἄνθρωποι and βροτοί of unknown meaning: μερόπων ἀνθρώπων Α 250, μερόπεσσι βροτοῖσιν Β 285. Cf. Γ 402, Ι 340, Λ 28, Σ 288, 342, 490, Υ 217: υ 49, 132.

μεσαιπόλιος [μέσος + πολιός]. Half-grey, grizzled: μ. περ ἐών Ν 361.

μεσηγύ, μεσσηγύ, μεσσηγύς [μέσ(σ)ος]. (**1**) Adv., in the space separating two objects, between, midway: πολλὰ [δοῦρα] μεσσηγὺ ἐν γαίῃ ἵσταντο (in mid career) Λ 573=Ο 316. Cf. Ψ 521: μηδέ τι μεσσηγύς γε κακὸν πάθῃσιν (by the way) η 195.—In such a space in reference to abstractions: τὸ μὲν τελέει, τὸ δὲ καὶ μεσσηγὺ κολούει (short of fulfilment) Υ 370.—(**2**) Prep. with genit. (**a**) In local sense, between: ὤμων μεσσηγύς Ε 41, μεσηγὺ νηῶν καὶ ποταμοῦ καὶ τείχεος (in the space separating the ships and the river from the (city) wall) Π 396. Cf. Ε 769, Ζ 4, Ν 33, Ω 78, etc.: δ 845, ο 528, χ 93, 341, 442=459.—(**b**) Of reciprocal relation or action, between: κέλαδον καὶ ἀϋτὴν Κουρήτων τε μεσηγὺ καὶ Αἰτωλῶν Ι 549.

μεσήεις [μέσος]. Holding an intermediate position in a scale of excellence, neither good nor bad Μ 269.

μεσόδμη, -ης, ἡ [μέσος + δμ-, δέμω]. (**1**) In a ship, a sort of box in which the mast was set (prob.=ἱστοπέδη): ἱστὸν κοίλης ἔντοσθε μεσόδμης στῆσαν β 424=ο 289.—(**2**) In a house, prob., a base or pedestal supporting a column τ 37, υ 354.

μέσος, -η, -ον. Also **μέσσος**, -η, -ον. (**1**) The middle or midmost part of the . . ., the middle or midst of the . . .: μέσον ἱστίον Α 481, Ἄργεϊ μέσσῳ (in the heart of . . .) Ζ 224. Cf. Γ 78, Ε 582, Η 258, 267, Θ 68, Λ 167, Π 231, Υ 254, Ψ 241, etc.: πέλαγος μέσον γ 174. Cf. α 344, β 37, δ 400, μ 80 (halfway up), 93 (waist-deep), etc.—In reference to a period of time: μέσον ἦμαρ (noon) Φ 111: η 288.—In pl., the midst of the . . .: μέσσῃσι μετὰ δμῳῇσιν π 336. Cf. Ν 312, Σ 569.—(**2**) Absol.: δουρὶ μέσον περόνησεν (in his middle) Η 145, Ν 397, μέσσῃ δ' ἐνὶ πῖλος ἀρήρει (app. so as to form a lining to protect the head from chafing) Κ 265, σφῆκες μέσον αἰόλοι (about the middle) Μ 167. Cf. Ν 534, Π 623, Υ 413, 486, Ψ 875: ἐν μέσσῃ καθῖζεν ε 326. Cf. ε 487, κ 196, υ 306.—In pl.: στὰς ἐν μέσσοισιν Η 384, ἕλκε μέσσα λαβών (grasping the middle of it) Θ 72, Χ 212, ἐνὶ μέσσῃς κλαῖεν Ω 84. Cf. Δ 212, Λ 35, 413, Μ 457, Ν 308, Ο 635, Σ 606, Τ 77, Ψ 134, etc.: δ 19, 281, 413, ω 441.—(**3**) (**a**) μέσσῳ, in the midst: μέσσῳ ποταμοί [εἰσιν] λ 157.—(**b**) μέσσῳ= μεσηγύ (2) (a): μέσσῳ ἀμφοτέρων σκῆπτρα σχέθον Η 277: μέσσῳ δαιτυμόνων (among the . . .) θ 66 =473.—(**c**) μέσσῳ=μεσηγύ (2) (b): μέσσῳ ἀμφοτέρων μητίσομαι ἔχθεα Γ 416.—(**4**) (**a**) ἐν μέσ(σ)ῳ, in the middle space, in the midst: ἔμ' ἐν μέσσῳ καὶ Μενέλαον συμβάλετε μάχεσθαι Γ 69. Cf. Γ 90, Κ 474, Ρ 375, Σ 264: ἐν μέσσῳ στᾶσα μ 20. Cf. ι 429.—Sim. after a compound of ἐν: ἔνθορε μέσσῳ Φ 233. Cf. Δ 444: μ 443.—(**b**) ἐς μέσ(σ)ον, into the middle space, in the midst: ἐς μέσσον ἰών Γ 77=Η 55. Cf. Δ 79, 299, Ο 357, Ψ 704, 814: θ 144, 262, ρ 447, σ 89.—With genit.: ἐς μέσον ἀμφοτέρων Ζ 120 = Υ 159. Cf. Γ 266 = 341.—ἐς μέσον ἀμφοτέροισι δικάσσατε (impartially) Ψ 574.—(**c**) κατὰ μέσσον, through the midst: ἀντικρὺ κατὰ μέσσον Π 285. Cf. Δ 541, Ε 8.—(**5**) In neut. sing.: μέσ(σ)ον as adv., in the middle: νηῦς ἔθεεν μέσσον ὑπὲρ Κρήτης (app., taking the mid-sea course) ξ 300.— =μεσηγύ (2) (a): κὰδ δὲ μέσον τάφρου καὶ τείχεος ἷζον Ι 87.

μέσσατος [superl. fr. μέσσος]. Like μέσος (4) (a): ἐν μεσσάτῳ ἔσκεν (just in the middle) Θ 223=Λ 6.

μέσσαυλος, ὁ [μέσ(σ)ος + αὐλή]. Etymologically, the middle part of the αὐλή, but used simply as=αὐλή. (**1**) In sense (1) (a): ἀέκων ἔβη [λίς] ἀπὸ μεσσαύλοιο Ρ 112. Cf. Λ 548, Ρ 657: ὅτε οἱ μέσσαυλον ἵκοντο ἡμέτεροι ἕταροι κ 435 (app.=the αὐλή of ι 184, etc.).—(2) In sense (2) Ω 29.

μεσσηγύ(s). See μεσηγύς.

μεσσοπαγής, -ές [μέσ(σ)ος + παγ-, πήγνυμι]. Planted or driven in up to the middle: ἔγχος Φ 172.

μέσσος. See μέσος.

μέσφα. Until. With genit.: μέσφ' ἠοῦς Θ 508.

μετά. (I) Adv. (1) Towards, in the direction of, something: μετὰ δ' ἰὸν ἕηκεν Α 48.—Sim. indicating that action is directed in a particular way: μετὰ Τυδέος υἱὸν ἔπουσαν (directing, looking after, him) Κ 516.—(2) Among, in company with, others: μετὰ δ' ἀνέρες οὓς ἔχε γῆρας Σ 515. Cf. Β 446, 477.—Among others, in a company: μετὰ μῦθον ἔειπεν Γ 303, etc. Cf. μ 319, σ 2.—With, in addition to, others: μετὰ δ' ἔσσεται κούρη Βρισῆος Ι 131, 273. Cf. Ο 67.—(3) Coming after, following: μετὰ νέφος εἵπετο πεζῶν Ψ 133.—(4) After in time, afterwards, in succession: πρῶτος ἐγώ, μετὰ δ' ὔμμες φ 231.—Afterwards, in after days: μετὰ γάρ τε καὶ ἄλγεσι τέρπεται ἀνήρ ο 400.—(5) So as to face the rear or reverse one's position, round: μετὰ δ' ἐτράπετο Α 199. Cf. Θ 94.—(6) In reference to change of position in a course or path: μετὰ δ' ἄστρα βεβήκει (had crossed the meridian) μ 312, ξ 483.—(7) At intervals: μετὰ δ' [ὅρμος] ἠλέκτροισιν ἔερτο ο 460.—(II) Prep. (commonly with anastrophe when immediately following the case-form). (1) With dat. (a) Between (α) In reference to the hands, arms or feet: μετὰ χερσίν (in . . .) Ε 344, μετὰ ποσσίν Τ 110. Cf. Λ 4, Ο 717, etc.: γ 281, δ 300, ε 49, φ 245, etc.—To the jaws: μετὰ γένυσσιν Λ 416. Cf. Ν 200.—Sim. in reference to the φρένες regarded as having a double character: μετὰ φρεσίν (in . . .) Δ 245, Ι 434, Σ 419, etc.: δ 825, κ 438, π 436, etc.—(β) Of position or relations *between* two persons or groups: ἢ φιλότητα μετ' ἀμφοτέροισι βάλωμεν Δ 16. Cf. Γ 110, Δ 38, Η 66, etc.: γ 136, ω 476, etc.—(b) Among, amid, in the midst of, with: μετά σφισιν Β 93. Cf. Α 252, Γ 85, Δ 2, Θ 525, Σ 234, Φ 122, etc.: α 19, β 310, δ 254, ι 335, 418, κ 204, etc.—In reference to things: μετ' ἀστράσιν Χ 28, 317, μετὰ πνοιῇς ἀνέμοιο (on the . . .) Ψ 367. Cf. Ν 579, 668, Ο 118: β 148, γ 91, δ 499, ε 224 = ρ 285.—With sing. sb. in collective sense: μεθ' αἵματι Ο 118, μετὰ στροφάλιγγι κονίης (in . . .) Φ 503. Cf. Τ 50, Χ 49: θ 156, λ 449.—Of division or distribution: δάσσαντο μετὰ σφίσιν Α 368.—(2) With acc. (a) Between (with notion of motion): ἔφερον ἅρμα μετὰ Τρῶας καὶ Ἀχαιούς (between the fighting lines) Λ 533 = Ρ 458.—(b) So as to be among or with, to, towards, to join: βεβήκει μετὰ δαίμονας ἄλλους Α 222. Cf. Α 423, Γ 264, Ε 264, Ρ 149, etc.: ἄνδρας μέτα οἰνοποτῆρας ἤϊεν θ 456. Cf. γ 168, ζ 115, λ 563, ψ 83, etc.—In hostile sense Ε 152, Ζ 21, Ν 301 (or perh. here simply 'to join'), Ρ 460, etc.: ζ 133.—In reference to things: μετὰ νῆας Ε 165, Μ 123. Cf. Β 376, Ζ 511, etc.: μετὰ δαῖτας (to share in them) χ 352.—With sing. sb. in collective sense: ἀνάγοντο μετὰ στρατὸν Ἀχαιῶν Α 478. Cf. Ε 573, Η 115, Ξ 21, Υ 33, etc.—(c) Without notion of motion, among: θυμὸν ὄρινε πᾶσι μετὰ πληθύν Β 143. Cf. Ι 54: οἳ ἀριστεύουσι μεθ' ἡμέας δ 652 (or this might come under (f)). Cf. π 419.—(d) Going after or behind, following, following up: μετὰ κλέος ἵκετ' Ἀχαιῶν (following up the rumour of the expedition) Λ 227. Cf. Λ 357, Ν 364, 492, 513, Σ 321: μεθ' ἡμιόνους ἔρχεσθαι ζ 260. Cf. β 406, etc.—(e) Following, after, in succession to: τὸν δὲ μετ' Ἀτρεΐδαι [ἦλθον] Θ 261. Cf. Θ 289, Σ 96, Ψ 227, 354, etc.: λ 260, ο 147, etc.—(f) In comparisons, after, next to: κάλλιστος μετὰ Πηλεΐωνα Β 674. Cf. Η 228, Ι 140, Μ 104, Π 146, etc.: β 350, θ 117, 583, λ 310, etc.—(g) Following, taking the line of, in consonance with: μετὰ σὸν καὶ ἐμὸν κῆρ Ο 52. Cf. Σ 552.—(h) After, for, in order to find or get, in quest or search of: βῆ ῥ' ἰέναι μετὰ Νέστορα Κ 73. Cf. Η 418, Λ 700, Ν 247, 252, Π 536, etc.: πλέων μετὰ χαλκόν α 184. Cf. β 206, ν 415, π 151, υ 153, φ 17 (to recover it), etc.—Sim.: πόλεμον μέτα (for . . .) Υ 329. Cf. Η 147, Ν 291.—In reference to looking: σκεψάμενος μεθ' ἑταίρους (for . . .) μ 247.—(3) With genit., among, along with, with: μετὰ Βοιωτῶν ἐμάχοντο Ν 700, τῶν μέτα παλλόμενος Ω 400. Cf. Φ 458: κ 320, π 140.

μέτα [for μέτ-εστι]. There is among specified persons: οὐ γάρ τις μέτα τοῖος ἀνὴρ ἐν τοῖσδεσιν φ 93.

μεταβαίνω [μετα- (6)]. Aor. imp. μετάβηθι. Fig., to choose a fresh theme θ 492.

μεταβουλεύω [μετα- (6)]. To adopt changed or different counsels: μετεβούλευσαν ἄλλως ε 286.

μετάγγελος, ὁ, ἡ [μετ-, μετα- (1). Pleonastically, 'a messenger who goes in quest.' Cf. ἐπιβουκόλος]. A messenger: θεοῖσι μ. Ο 144. Cf. Ψ 199.

μεταδαίνυμαι [μετα- (3)]. 3 sing. fut. μεταδαίσεται σ 48. Aor. subj. μεταδαίσομαι Ψ 207. To take a meal, take one's meals, *with*. With dat.: αἰεὶ ἡμῖν μεταδαίσεται σ 48. Cf. Χ 498.—To partake of with others: ἵνα δὴ καὶ ἐγὼ μεταδαίσομαι ἱρῶν (partitive genit.) Ψ 207.

μεταδήμιος [μετα- (3) + δῆμος]. Among the (*i.e.* one's own) people, at home: οὐ γὰρ ἔθ' Ἥφαιστος μ. θ 293.—Among, afflicting, the people: κακὸν μεταδήμιον ν 46.

μεταδόρπιος [app. μετα- (3) + δόρπον (the apparatus of the meal, rather than the meal, being thought of)]. Thus, in the middle of, at, δόρπον: οὐ γὰρ ἐγώ γε τέρπομ' ὀδυρόμενος μ. (in the midst of good cheer) δ 194.

μεταδρομάδην [μετα- (1) + δρομ-, δραμ-. See τρέχω]. Running in pursuit Ε 80.

μεταΐζω [μετα- (3) + ἵζω]. To take one's seat among a company π 362.

μεταΐσσω [μετ-, μετα- (1)]. Aor. pple. μεταΐξας Φ 564: ρ 236, υ 11. To rush at or upon a person: κτεῖνε μεταΐσσων Π 398. Cf. Φ 564: ρ 236, υ 11.

†μετακλαίω [μετα- (5)]. Fut. infin. μετακλαύσεσθαι. To make lament afterwards (*i.e.* when the opportunity for action has gone) Λ 764.

†**μετακλίνω** [μετα- (6)]. Genit. sing. masc. aor. pple. pass. μετακλινθέντος. To turn the fortune of (war): πολέμοιο μετακλινθέντος (if the tide of battle should turn and set against them) Λ 509.

μεταλλάω. (**1**) To ask, inquire, make inquiry, ask questions: μετάλλησάν γε μὲν οὔ τι Ε 516: παίδων οὐκέτι μέμνηται οὐδὲ μεταλλᾷ (asks anything about them) ο 23. Cf. ξ 378, ο 362, ψ 99.—(**2**) To ask or inquire about: οὓς σὺ μεταλλᾷς Κ 125, Ν 780. Cf. Α 550: ξ 128, π 465, ρ 554, τ 190 (inquired him out), ω 321.—(**3**) To question (a person): σε Α 553: π 287 = τ 6.—With indirect question: ξείνους οἵ τινές εἰσιν γ 69.—With cognate acc.: ἔπος ἄλλο μεταλλῆσαι Νέστορα γ 243.—(**4**) With double acc. of person questioned and of what is asked about: ὅ με μεταλλᾷς Γ 177: = η 243 = ο 402, τ 171. Cf. α 231 = ο 390, τ 115, ω 478.

†**μεταλλήγω** [μετα- (6)]. Dat. sing. masc. aor. pple. μεταλλήξαντι. To cease, desist, from. With genit.: χόλοιο Ι 157, 261, 299.

μετάλμενος, aor. pple. μεθάλλομαι.

μεταμάζιος [μετα- (2) + μαζός]. In neut. sing. μεταμάζιον as adv., between the breasts Ε 19.

μεταμίσγω [μετα- (3)]. 1 pl. fut. μεταμίξομεν χ 221. To throw into one mass or sum with, lump with. With dat.: κτήματα τοῖσιν Ὀδυσσῆος χ 221.—To set or place among other objects: δαΐδας μετέμισγον σ 310.

μεταμώνιος. App., of none effect, coming to nothing, vain, idle, or the like: τὰ πάντα θεοὶ μεταμώνια θεῖεν Δ 363. Cf. β 98 = τ 143 = ω 133.—Absol.: μεταμώνια βάζεις σ 332 = 392.

μετανάστης, ὁ [μετα- (6) + ναστ-, ναίω[1]]. One who has changed his home, an exile, an outcast: ὡς εἴ τινα μετανάστην Ι 648 = Π 59.

μετανίσ(σ)ομαι [μετα- (6) + νίσσομαι]. Of a heavenly body in its path, to change its position, pass: ἦμος δ' ἠέλιος μετενίσ(σ)ετο βουλυτόνδε Π 779: = ι 58.

μεταξύ [μετά]. Between (= μεσηγύ (1)): μάλα πολλὰ μεταξύ [ἐστιν] Α 156.

μεταπαύομαι [μετα- (7)]. To give oneself intervals of rest: μεταπαυόμενοι μάχοντο Ρ 373.

μεταπαυσωλή, ἡ [μεταπαύομαι]. A turn of rest, an interval (cf. παυσωλή) Τ 201.

μεταπρεπής [μεταπρέπω]. Conspicuous or eminent *among*. With dat.: δόμον μεταπρεπέ' ἀθανάτοισιν (admired even where gods gather together) Σ 370.

μεταπρέπω [μετα- (3)]. To be conspicuous, eminent, distinguished, distinguish oneself, be the best or finest, *among*. With dat.: ἱππεῦσι μετέπρεπον ἡμετέροισιν Λ 720. Cf. Β 481, 579, Ν 175 = Ο 550, Π 596, 835, Ψ 645: ζ 109, κ 525, λ 33, ρ 213 = υ 174.—With infin. expressing that in which one is distinguished: πᾶσι μετέπρεπε ἔγχεϊ μάρνασθαι Π 194.

μετασπόμενος, aor. pple. mid. μεθέπω[2].

μετασπών, aor. pple. μεθέπω[1].

μέτασσαι, αἱ [μετά. 'The later born']. The later (lambs) ι 221 (*i.e.* those born after the πρόγονοι and before the ἕρσαι).

μετασσεύομαι [μετα- (1)]. 3 sing. aor. μετέσσυτο Φ 423, Ψ 389. To set off, take one's way, after or in the train of another Ζ 296.—To start off in pursuit of, make for, a person Φ 423.—To make for, make up to (a person): ποιμένα λαῶν Ψ 389.

μεταστένω [μετα- (5)]. To lament afterwards, look back upon with grief: ἄτην δ 261.

μεταστήσω, fut. μεθίστημι.

μεταστοιχί [μετα- (1) + στοῖχος, row, line, fr. στείχω (app. with the notion of following the line with the eye). Cf. τριστοιχί]. In line, side by side: στὰν μ. Ψ 358 = 757.

†**μεταστρέφω** [μετα- (6)]. 2 sing. fut. μεταστρέψεις Ο 203. 3 sing. aor. subj. μεταστρέψῃ Κ 107. 3 pl. μεταστρέψωσι β 67. 3 sing. opt. μεταστρέψειε Ο 52. Aor. pple. pass. μεταστρεφθείς, -έντος Θ 258, Λ 447, 595, Ν 545, Ο 591, Ρ 114, 732. (**1**) In pass., to turn oneself about, wheel round, for flight: Θόωνα μεταστρεφθέντα οὔτασεν Ν 545. Cf. Θ 258 = Λ 447.—So as to face the foe: στῆ μεταστρεφθεὶς Λ 595 = Ο 591 = Ρ 114. Cf. Ρ 732.—(**2**) To change (one's temper or mood): εἴ κε μεταστρέψῃ ἦτορ Κ 107. Cf. Ο 52.—Absol., to change one's mind Ο 203.—(**3**) To work a change: μή τι μεταστρέψωσι [θεοί] (bring some evil to pass) β 67.

†**μετατίθημι** [μετα- (3)]. 3 sing. aor. μετέθηκε. To set or cause among a company: οὔ κέ τι τόσον κέλαδον μετέθηκεν (among us) σ 402.

μετατρέπομαι [μετα- (1)]. 'To turn oneself so as to follow with one's view']. To have regard for, care for, trouble oneself about. With genit.: τῶν οὔ τι μετατρέπῃ Α 160. Cf. Ι 630, Μ 238.

μετατροπαλίζομαι [μετα- (7) + τροπ-, τρέπω]. (ἐντροπαλίζομαι.) To keep turning round: τότ' οὔ τι μετατροπαλίζεο φεύγων (turned to face me in thy flight) Υ 190.

μεταυδάω [μετα- (3)]. (**1**) To speak *among*, address. With dat.: πᾶσι μετηύδα Ο 103. Cf. Σ 139, Τ 269, Χ 449, Ψ 5, Ω 32, 715: δ 721, ζ 217, θ 96, μ 153, 376, υ 291, etc.—Absol.: ἐν μέσσῳ στᾶσα μετηύδα μ 20.—To speak among a company in address to one of them: μετηύδα· "Ἀντίλοχε . . ." Ψ 569.—(**2**) To say, speak, utter (words) *among*, address in words. With dat.: ἔπε' Ἀργείοισι μετηύδα Β 109. Cf. Θ 496, Ι 16: α 31.

†**μετάφημι** [μετα- (3)]. 3 sing. impf. μετέφη. To speak *among*, address. With dat.: τοῖσιν Α 58 = Τ 55. Cf. Τ 100: τοῖσιν δ 660. Cf. θ 132, σ 51, 312, etc.—To speak *among* a company in address to one of them. With dat.: τοῖς μετέφη . . . "φίλε κασίγνητε . . ." Δ 153.—To speak *among*, be spokesman of (in prayer to a god). With dat.: τοῖσιν εὐχόμενος μετέφη Β 411.

μεταφράζομαι [μετα- (5)]. To consider afterwards: ταῦτα μεταφρασόμεσθα καὶ αὖτις (will go into this later) Α 140.

μετάφρενον, -ου, τό [μετα- (4) + φρήν. 'The part behind the midriff']. The back Β 265, Ε 40, Θ 95, Κ 29, Π 791, Ρ 502, Υ 488, Ψ 380, etc.: θ 528.—So in pl.: ὅτεῳ στρεφθέντι μετάφρενα γυμνωθείη Μ 428.

μεταφωνέω [μετα- (3)]. To speak *among*, address. With dat.: Μυρμιδόνεσσιν Σ 323. Cf. Η 384: θ 201, π 354, σ 35, χ 69.—Absol. κ 67.—To speak *among* a company in address to one of them. With dat.: τοῖσι μετεφώνεεν . . . "Τυδεΐδη . . ." Ι 52.

μετέᾱσι, 3 pl. μέτειμι[1].

μετέειπον, *aor.* [μετα- (3)]. To speak *among*, address. With dat.: Ἀργείοισιν Η 123. Cf. Β 336, Γ 96, Η 170, Κ 241, Ξ 109, etc.: β 95, 157, δ 773, λ 342, ο 439, φ 130, etc.—Absol.: ἀνίστατο καὶ μετέειπεν Η 94. Cf. Η 399, etc.: β 24, υ 321, etc.—To speak *among* a company in address to one of them. With dat.: τοῖσι μετέειπε . . . "Νέστορ . . ." Κ 219. Cf. Ψ 889, etc.: γ 330, ρ 151, etc.—To speak among a company in address to one of them: ὀψὲ μετέειπε Διομήδης· "Ἀτρεΐδη . . ." Ι 31. Cf. Θ 30, etc.: η 155.

μετέῃσι, 3 sing. subj. μέτειμι[1].

μετέθηκε, 3 sing. aor. μετατίθημι.

μετείην, opt. μέτειμι[1].

†**μέτειμι**[1] [μετ-, μετα- (3) (7) + εἰμί]. 3 pl. μετέᾱσι Η 227. 1 sing. subj. μετέω Χ 388. μετείω Ψ 47. 3 μετέῃσι Γ 109. 1 sing. opt. μετείην κ 52, ω 436. 3 μετείη Ε 85, Υ 235: ο 251. Infin. μετέμμεναι Σ 91. μετεῖναι Δ 316. Fut. μετέσσομαι Δ 322: ξ 487. 3 sing. μετέσσεται Β 386. To be *among* or *with*, to have one's being or station, abide, dwell, *among* or *with*, consort *with*. With dat.: οἷς ὁ γέρων μετέῃσιν Γ 109. Cf. Δ 316, 322, Ε 85, Η 227, Σ 91, Υ 235, Χ 388, Ψ 47: ἢ ἔτι ζωοῖσι μετείην κ 52. Cf. ξ 487, ο 251, ω 436.—Of something coming in in an interval: οὐ πανσωλὴ μετέσσεται Β 386.

†**μέτειμι**[2] [μετ-, μετα- (1) + εἶμι]. 1 sing. μέτειμι Ζ 341. 3 μέτεισι Ν 298. (**1**) To go, take one's way, on an indicated errand: πόλεμόνδε Ν 298.—(**2**) With fut. sense, to follow after a person: ἴθ', ἐγὼ δὲ μέτειμι Ζ 341.

μετεῖναι, infin. μέτειμι[1].

μετεισάμενος, aor. pple. mid. μεθίημι[2].

μέτεισι, 3 sing. μέτειμι[2].

μετείω, subj. μέτειμι[1].

μετεκίαθον, *aor.* [μετα- (1) + κι-, κίον]. To go in quest or pursuit of, make for: Τρῶας καὶ Λυκίους Π 685. Cf. Σ 581.—So app.: ὅτε πᾶν πεδίον μετεκίαθον Λ 714 (had chased or swept the plain (cf. ἔφεπε πεδίον Λ 496 cited under ἐφέπω[1] (4))).—Without expressed object: ἐφ' ἵππων βάντες μετεκίαθον (went off to see what the matter was) Σ 532.—To follow after: ἱππῆες ὀλίγον μετεκίαθον (app., came up close) Λ 52.—To go to visit: Αἰθίοπας α 22.

μετελεύσομαι, fut. μετέρχομαι.

μετελθών, aor. pple. μετέρχομαι.

μετέμμεναι, infin. μέτειμι[1].

μετέπειτα [μετ-, μετα- (5) + ἔπειτα]. (**1**) Afterwards, in after time: ἅμα τ' αὐτίκα καὶ μ. ξ 403. Cf. Ξ 310.—(**2**) Then, next: πρῶτα . . . μ. . . . κ 519 = λ 27, λ 640.

μετέρχομαι [μετ-, μετα- (1) (3)]. Fut. μετελεύσομαι Ζ 280. 3 sing. opt. μετέλθοι α 229. Imp. μέτελθε Φ 422. Pple. μετελθών Δ 539, Ε 456, 461, Ν 127, 351, Ξ 334, Π 487: α 134, ζ 222. (**1**) To go in quest of: Πάριν Ζ 280.—To seek for (tidings) γ 83.—To go to see, visit: ἔργα π 314.—To go and attend to (one's affairs): μετέρχεο ἔργα γάμοιο Ε 429.—(**2**) To go, take one's way, on a specified or indicated errand or for a specified or indicated purpose: οὐκ ἂν τόνδ' ἄνδρ' ἐρύσαιο μετελθών; (go and . . .) Ε 456. Cf. Ε 461, Ζ 86, Ν 351, Φ 422 (go after her).—(**3**) To go or come, make one's way, present oneself, find oneself, *among*. With dat. or locative: θεοῖσι πᾶσι μετελθών Ξ 334, λέων ἀγέληφι μετελθών Π 487. Cf. α 134, ζ 132, 222.—Without construction, to come upon the scene, present oneself: ὅς τις πινυτός γε μετέλθοι α 229. Cf. Δ 539, Ν 127.

μετέσσομαι, fut. μέτειμι[1].

μετέσσυτο, 3 sing. aor. μετασσεύομαι.

μετέφη, 3 sing. impf. μετάφημι.

μετέω, subj. μέτειμι[1].

μετήορος [μετ-, μετα- (2) + ἀείρω]. In mid-air, in air, into the air, off the ground: τά κε μετήορα πάντα γένοιτο Θ 26. Cf. Ψ 369.

μετοίχομαι [μετ-, μετα- (1)]. (**1**) To go in quest or pursuit of: ἀοιδόν θ 47. Cf. Ε 148.—(**2**) = μετέρχομαι (2): ἀνὰ ἄστυ μετῴχετο θ 7. Cf. Κ 111 (go and summon): τ 24.

μετοκλάζω [μετ-, μετα- (7) + ὀκλάζω, to squat]. To squat now on one ham now on the other Ν 281.

μετόπισθε(ν) [μετ-, μετα- (4) (5)]. (**1**) In or from a position behind or in the rear: ὅσοι μ. ἀφέστασαν Ο 672, μ. μιν ποδῶν λάβεν Σ 155. Cf. Κ 490, Ρ 261, Ψ 346.—In a geographical sense: ὅσσοι μ. [ναίουσιν] (in the quarter in which the day ends) ν 241.—With genit., behind: μ. νεός ι 539. Cf. Ι 504.—With a vb. of remaining or leaving, behind: μή τις μ. μιμνέτω Ζ 68. Cf. Χ 334, Ω 687.—(**2**) In the back or rearward part of something, behind: ἴχνια μ. ποδῶν Ν 71. Cf. Χ 396.—(**3**) Changing one's position to a position facing rearwards: στρεφθεὶς μ. (turning his back) Ο 645.—(**4**) Afterwards, in after time, later: μ. τοι ἄχος ἔσσεται Ι 249. Cf. Α 82, Υ 308, Ω 111, 436: δ 695, ε 147, θ 414, λ 224, 382, χ 319, 345, ω 84.—(**5**) Then, next Χ 119.

†**μετοχλίζω** [μετ-, μετα- (6)]. 3 sing. aor. opt. μετοχλίσσειε. To remove, change the position of: [λέχος] ψ 188.—To thrust back (the fastening of a gate): ὀχῆα Ω 567.

μετρέω [μέτρον]. (ἀνα-, δια-.) To measure, traverse: πέλαγος μέγα μετρήσαντες γ 179.

μέτρον, -ου, τό. (**1**) Something wherewith to measure, a graduated rule or cord Μ 422. —(**2**) A unit of capacity determined by context or usage; a quantity of anything indicated by such a unit: δῶκε μέθυ, χίλια μέτρα Η 471, τέσσαρα μέτρα κεχανδότα Ψ 268. Cf. Ψ 741: β 355, ι 209.—(**3**) A stage of development or growth: ἥβης μ. Λ 225: δ 668, λ 317, σ 217, τ 532.—A point at the end of and measuring a course to be traversed: ὅρμου μ. (the anchorage) ν 101.—(**4**) The measurement or length of anything. In pl.: *μέτρα κελεύθου* δ 389 = κ 539.

μετώπιος [*μέτωπον*]. In neut. sing. *μετώπιον* as adv., on the forehead: *βάλε μ.* Π 739. Cf. Λ 95.

μέτωπον, -ου, τό [*μετ-*, *μετα-* (2) + *ὦπα*. 'The part between the eyes']. The forehead or brow Δ 460 = Z 10, N 615, O 102, Π 798, Ψ 396: χ 86, 94, 296.—In pl.: *πασάων δ' ὑπὲρ κάρη ἔχει ἠδὲ μέτωπα* ζ 107.—Of a horse: *ἐν μετώπῳ λευκὸν σῆμα τέτυκτο* Ψ 454.—The front (of a helmet) Π 70.

μευ. See *ἐμέ*.

μέχρι(ς). With genit. (1) As far as, to: *μέχρι θαλάσσης* N 143.—(2) Until: *τέο μέχρις;* (how long?) Ω 128.

μή. Negative particle, commonly used with the moods expressive of command or wish, *i.e.* the imperative, the subjunctive and the optative (cf. *οὐ*). (1) In prohibitions or dehortations. (a) With imp. (α) Pres. or pf.: *μή μ' ἐρέθιζε* A 32, *μή τις ὀπίσσω τετράφθω* M 272. Cf. A 295, B 354, Γ 82, etc.: α 315, β 230, 303, γ 313, etc. —(β) Aor.: *μή τις ἀκουσάτω* π 301. Cf. Δ 410, Π 200, Σ 134: ω 248.—(b) With infin. as imp.: *μή τι διατρίβειν τὸν ἐμὸν χόλον* Δ 42. Cf. Ψ 83, etc.: λ 441, χ 287, etc.—(c) With subj. (α) Aor.: *μή με ἕλωρ Δαναοῖσιν ἐάσῃς κεῖσθαι* E 684. Cf. Δ 37, I 33, O 115, etc.: μ 300, etc.—(β) Pres. in 1st pers.: *μὴ ἴομεν* M 216. Cf. A 26, etc.: β 404, π 389, etc.—(2) In wishes. With opt.: *μὴ ἐμέ γ' οὖν οὗτος λάβοι χόλος* Π 30. Cf. N 232, etc.: α 386, δ 699, η 316, μ 106, ν 46, etc.—(3) In deprecations and expressions of apprehension. With subj. (a) Aor.: *μή τι ῥέξῃ κακόν* (may it not be that . . .) B 195, *μὴ νεμεσσηθέωμέν οἱ* (let him beware lest we . . .) Ω 53. Cf. E 487, Π 128, Φ 563, etc.: ε 415, ο 12, π 255, σ 334, φ 370, etc.—(b) Pres.: *μή μιν κερτομέωσιν* π 87. Cf. ε 356, ο 19.—(4) After vbs. of fearing, lest. (a) With aor. subj. (α) Referring to the future: *δείδοικα μή οἱ ἀπειλὰς ἐκτελέσωσιν* I 244. Cf. K 39, N 52, 745, etc.: δ 820, θ 230, μ 122, etc.—(β) To the past: *δείδοικα μή τι πάθωσιν* K 538. Cf. A 555, X 455, etc.—(b) With pres. subj. Referring to the future: *μή με φέρῃ* ε 419. Cf. ρ 188.—(c) With opt. Referring to the future: *δείσας μή πώς οἱ ἐρυσαίατο νεκρόν* E 298. Cf. Λ 509, etc.: λ 634, π 179, etc.—(d) With indic. Referring to the past: *δείδω μὴ νημερτέα εἶπεν* ε 300.—(5) In subordinate clauses expressing apprehension not preceded by such a vb., lest. (a) With aor. subj. (α) Referring to the future: *ἀπόστιχε, μή τι νοήσῃ* A 522, *οὐδέ τι ἴδμεν μή πως μενοινήσωσι . . .* (whether they will not . . .) K 101. Cf. A 28, 587, Γ 414, E 250, etc.: β 98, γ 315, δ 396, θ 444, κ 301, etc.—(β) To the past: *ἐς φύλακας καταβήομεν μὴ κοιμήσωνται* K 98.—(b) With pres. subj. (α) Referring to the future: *φραζέσθω, μή τίς οἱ ἀμείνων μάχηται* E 411, etc. Cf. β 179, etc.—(β) To the present: *ἴδοι τις μὴ . . . ὦσιν* ω 491. Cf. ν 216.—(c) With opt. Referring to the future: *σάκεα σχέθον, μὴ πρὶν ἀναΐξειαν* Δ 114. Cf. E 202, Λ 705, etc.: α 133, δ 527, φ 395, etc.—(d) With fut.: *ἀγάγωμεν, μή πως κεχολώσεται* Υ 301. Cf. ω 544.—(6) In protasis with *εἰ* (*αἴ*), *ἤν*. (a) With subj.: *εἰ δέ κε μὴ δώωσιν* A 137. Cf. Ξ 111, etc.: *ἢν μή τις ἔχῃ νῆα* λ 159. Cf. ξ 398, etc.—(b) With opt.: *εἰ μὴ Μοῦσαι μνησαίατο* B 491. Cf. E 215, I 515: ε 178, ι 278, κ 343, π 103.—(c) With indic., when the protasis follows the apodosis: *ἔνθα χ' ὑπέρμορα νόστος ἐτύχθη, εἰ μὴ ἔειπεν* B 156. Cf. B 261, Γ 374, I 231, etc.: β 71, δ 364, ε 427, ν 385, τ 346, χ 359, etc.—With no expressed apodosis: *εἰ μή τις θεός ἐστιν* E 177.—For the converse construction see *οὐ* (3) (a).—(7) In final clauses. (a) With subj.: *ὡς μὴ πάντες ὄλωνται* Θ 37. Cf. A 118, I 614, etc.: β 376, ε 490, etc.—(b) With opt.: *ἵνα μή τις ἀθρήσειεν* M 390. Cf. E 24, etc.: α 157, ι 42, etc.—(8) In conditional relative sentences (cf. *οὐ* (4)). (a) With subj.: *ᾧ μὴ ἀοσσητῆρες ἔωσιν* δ 165, ψ 119, *ᾧ μὴ πάρα* (*i.e.* *παρέωσι*) *γείτονες* ε 489.—(b) With opt.: *ὅτε μὴ κελεύοι* Ξ 248. Cf. N 319: λ 289, 490, π 197, ψ 185. —(c) With indic.: *οὓς μὴ κῆρες ἔβαν φέρουσαι* B 302. —(9) With indic. (a) In oaths (cf. (11) (b)): *ἴστω νῦν τόδε Γαῖα . . . μὴ δι' ἐμὴν ἰότητα πημαίνει* O 41. Cf. K 330, T 261.—(b) In questions expecting a neg. answer: *ἦ μή πού τινα δυσμενέων φάσθ' ἔμμεναι ἀνδρῶν;* ζ 200, etc.—(10) With pple.: *μὴ μνηστεύσαντες μηδ' ἄλλοθ' ὁμιλήσαντες ὕστατα νῦν δειπνήσειαν* δ 684 (*μή* with *ὁμιλήσαντες* and *μνηστεύσαντες* parenthetical, 'may they after their wooing and having no meeting elsewhere eat now for the last time.' See *μηδέ* (5), and for the parenthetical pple. and re-echoing neg. cf. *μὴ τεχνησάμενος μηδ' ἄλλο τι τεχνήσαιτο* λ 613).—(11) With infin. (see also (1) (b)). (a) After a vb. of saying, promising, knowing, etc.: *εἴσεαι μή τι καταισχύνειν γένος* ω 508. Cf. I 455, Ξ 46, Σ 255, etc.: ι 530, etc.—(b) In oaths: *ὅρκον ὀμοῦμαι μή ποτε τῆς εὐνῆς ἐπιβήμεναι* I 133. Cf. Υ 315, etc.: β 373, δ 254, ε 187, etc.—(c) In a prayer B 413.—(d) With *ὀφέλλω*. See *ὀφέλλω¹* (2) (3) (5).

μηδέ [*μή δέ*]. Negative particle, in general use corresponding to *μή* as *οὐδέ* to *οὐ*. (1) Adversatively, but not (cf. *δέ* (1)): *τὰ μὲν ἄλλα μετάλλα, μηδ' ἐμὸν ἐξερέεινε γένος* τ 116.—(2) In continuation, and not, nor (cf. *δέ* (2)): *λῆγ' ἔριδος, μηδὲ ξίφος ἕλκεο* A 210. Cf. Γ 407, 434, Ξ 85, etc.: α 289, 369, γ 96, δ 754, etc.—(3) Preceded by a negative, nor (sometimes rather to be translated 'or'): *μή τι σὺ ταῦτα διείρεο μηδὲ μετάλλα* A 550, *μηκέτι λεγώμεθα, μηδ' ἔτι δηρὸν ἀμβαλλώμεθα ἔργον* B 435. Cf. I 523, etc.: β 231, ε 160, etc.—(4) Not even: *μηδ' ὅν τινα γαστέρι μήτηρ φέροι* Z 58. Cf. K 239, etc.: δ 710, etc.—To be translated 'neither': *μηδὲ σὺ κεῦθε ὅττι κέ σ' εἴρωμαι* θ 548.—(5) Re-echoing a negative for emphasis. See under *μή* (10) and cf. *οὐδέ* (5).—(6) Introducing a prohibition: *μηδέ τις οἷος μεμάτω μάχεσθαι* Δ 303.

μήδεα¹, τά. Counsels, arts, plans, devices, schemes: *εἰδὼς μ. πυκνά* Γ 202, *ὅτε μ. ὕφαινον* Γ 212. Cf. B 340, Γ 208, H 278, O 467, Π 120, P 325 (see *φίλος* (5) (c)), Σ 363, Ω 88, 282 = 674: β 38, ζ 12, λ 202, 445, ν 89, τ 353, υ 46.

μήδεα[2], τά. The genitals, the testicles, the private parts ζ 129, σ 67, 87, χ 476.

μηδείς. Neut. μηδέν [μηδέ + εἷς]. Absol. in neut., nothing: ἀναίνετο μηδὲν ἑλέσθαι (double neg., 'refused to accept anything') Σ 500 (the μή implying that the will was concerned).

μήδομαι [μήδεα[1]. Cf. μέδομαι]. 2 sing. fut. μήσεαι λ 474. 2 sing. aor. μήσαο Ξ 253. 3 (ἐ)μήσατο Z 157, K 52, 289: γ 194, 249, 261, 303, κ 115, λ 429, χ 169, ω 96, 199, 426, 444. (ἐπι-.) **(1)** To take counsel, devise measures B 360.—**(2)** To devise, plan, contrive, meditate, intend, have in view: ἔργα B 38. Cf. Z 157, H 478, K 289, Ξ 253, Φ 19, 413, Ψ 176: Ζεὺς οὔ πω μήδετο νόστον γ 160, ἄλλο τι τόδε μήδεαι οὐδέ τι πομπήν (it is not of a safe journey for me that you are here thinking but of something else) ε 173. Cf. γ 132, 166, 194, ε 189, λ 429, χ 169, ω 199, etc.—With double acc. of what is devised, etc., and of the person aimed at: Ἕκτορα ἀεικέα μήδετο ἔργα X 395 = Ψ 24. Cf. K 52: ω 426.

†μηκάομαι. Aor. pple. μακών Π 469: κ 163, σ 98, τ 454. Pf. pple. μεμηκώς K 362. Fem. pl. μεμακυῖαι Δ 435. 3 pl. thematic plupf. (in impf. sense) ἐμέμηκον ι 439. Of sheep or goats, to bleat: ὄϊες ἀζηχὲς μεμακυῖαι (bleating) Δ 435. Cf. ι 439.—In reference to the cry of a hunted creature K 362.—Of a wounded and dying horse or other animal: κὰδ δὲ πέσε μακών (with a cry) Π 469 := κ 163 = τ 454.—Of Irus when knocked down by Odysseus σ 98.

μηκάς, -άδος [μηκάομαι]. Bleating. Epithet of goats Λ 383, Ψ 31: ι 124, 244 = 341.

μηκέτι [μὴ ἔτι, app. on the analogy of οὐκέτι]. In general use corresponding to μή as οὐκέτι to οὐ. **(1)** In reference to the present, no more, no longer. In a conditional relative sentence: εὖτ' ἂν μ. ἐπικρατέωσιν ἄνακτες ρ 320.—**(2)** In reference to the future, no more, no longer, no further: μ. δηθὰ λεγώμεθα B 435. Cf. B 259, H 279, N 292 = Τ 244, Σ 295, Τ 354, 376, Ψ 492, 735, Ω 560: μ. κλαῖε δ 543. Cf. γ 240, κ 297, 457, 489, 548, ν 296, σ 203, τ 263, 584, υ 314.

μήκιστος [superl. fr. next]. The tallest: τὸν μήκιστον κτάνον ἄνδρα H 155: οὓς μηκίστους θρέψεν λ 309.—In neut. pl. μήκιστα as adv., at long last, in the issue: τί νύ μοι μ. γένηται; ε 299, 465.

μῆκος, τό. **(1)** Length ι 324.—**(2)** In reference to stature, height λ 312.—Tallness of stature as an element of womanly beauty: μ. ἔπορ' Ἄρτεμις υ 71.

μήκων, ἡ. A poppy Θ 306.

μηλέη, -ης, ἡ [μῆλον[2]]. An apple-tree: ὄγχναι καὶ ῥοιαὶ καὶ μηλέαι η 115 = λ 589. Cf. ω 340.

μηλοβοτήρ, -ῆρος, ὁ [μῆλον[1] + βοτ-, βόσκω]. A shepherd: κτεῖνον μηλοβοτῆρας Σ 529.

μῆλον[1], -ου, τό. **(1)** In pl., small cattle, sheep or goats B 696, Δ 476, E 556, K 485, M 301, etc.: α 92, δ 622, θ 59, ι 298, ν 222, etc.—**(2)** Referring specifically **(a)** To sheep: ὡς εἴ τε μετὰ κτίλον ἕσπετο μῆλα N 492. Cf. δ 86, 413, κ 85, 525, 532, λ 4, 20, 33, 35, 45, 108 (see μ 129), μ 128, 136, 263, 322.—In sing., a sheep: ἢ βοῦν ἠέ τι μ. μ 301.—**(b)** To goats: ὑπὸ σπέος [αἰπόλος] ἤλασε μῆλα Δ 279. Cf. ρ 246.—In sing., a goat: μ. αἰγῶν ὅς τις φαίνηται ἄριστος ξ 105.

μῆλον[2], -ου, τό. **(1)** A fruit: ἄνθεσι μήλων (fruit-blossom) I 542.—**(2)** Specifically, an apple η 120.

μῆλοψ, -οπος [μῆλον[2] + ὀπ-. See ὁράω]. Apple-hued, yellow. Epithet of grain η 104.

μήν[1], μηνός, ὁ [cf. μήνη]. A (lunar) month. **(1)** Considered as a space of time: ἕνα μῆνα μένων B 292. Cf. E 387: κ 14, μ 325, ξ 244, ρ 408, ω 118.—**(2)** Considered as a point or unit of time or as one of a series: ὅτε μῆνες ἐξετελεῦντο λ 294 = ξ 293, τοῦ φθίνοντος μηνός ξ 162 = τ 307. Cf. κ 470, τ 153 = ω 143.

μήν[2] [cf. μάν, μέν]. Affirmative particle: εἰ δ' ἄγε μὴν πείρησαι (do but . . .) A 302, καὶ μὴν οἱ τότε . . . (even they) T 45. Cf. Ω 52, Ψ 410 := π 440 = τ 487, καὶ μὴν . . . εἰσεῖδον (and . . . too I saw) λ 582, 593.—With ἦ. See ἦ[2] (1) (b) (β).

μήνη, -ης, ἡ [cf. μήν[1]]. The moon: τοῦ σέλας γένετ' ἠΰτε μήνης T 374. Cf. Ψ 455.

μηνιθμός, -οῦ, ὁ [μηνίω]. Wrath, ire: μηνιθμὸν καταπαυσέμεν Π 62. Cf. Π 202, 282.

μήνῑμα, τό [μηνίω]. A cause or occasion of wrath: μή μ. γένωμαι X 358: λ 73.

μῆνις, ἡ. **(1)** Wrath, ire: μῆνιν ἄειδε Ἀχιλῆος A 1. Cf. A 75, E 178, I 517, O 122, T 35, 75, Φ 523: γ 135.—**(2)** The operation or effect of wrath: Διὸς ἀλεώμεθα μῆνιν E 34. Cf. E 444 = Π 711, N 624: β 66, ε 146, ξ 283.

μηνίω (μηνίω B 769). [μῆνις.] (ἀπο-, ἐπι-.) **(1)** To be wrathful or angry, feel or harbour wrath or anger: μήνι' Ἀχαιοῖσιν (against the . . .) A 422, ἱρῶν μηνίσας (having conceived wrath in the matter of . . .) E 178. Cf. A 488, B 769, M 10, Σ 257: ρ 14.—**(2)** To show wrath or anger outwardly, rage: Ἀτρεΐδης ἑτέρωθεν ἐμήνιεν A 247.

μῆρα, τά. Also in dual μῆρε. = next A 464 = B 427 := γ 461 = μ 364, γ 179, ν 26.

μηρία, τά [μηρός]. As a word of ritual, the thigh bones of a victim with the flesh adhering A 40, Θ 240, Λ 773, O 373, X 170, Ω 34: γ 9, 273, 456, δ 764, ι 553, ρ 241, τ 366, 397, φ 267, χ 336.

μήρινθος, -ου, ἡ [cf. μηρύομαι]. A cord or string Ψ 854, 857, 866, 867, 869.

μηρός, -οῦ, ὁ. **(1)** The thigh: φάσγανον ἐρυσσάμενος παρὰ μηροῦ A 190. Cf. Δ 146, E 305, K 573, Λ 583, M 162, etc.: θ 135, ι 300, κ 439, ν 198, σ 67, etc.—**(2)** In pl. = μηρία A 460 = B 423 := μ 360.

μηρύομαι [cf. μέρμις, μήρινθος]. To lower (a sail): ἱστία μηρύσαντο μ 170.

μήσατο, 3 sing. aor. μήδομαι.

μήστωρ, -ωρος, ὁ [μησ-, μήδομαι]. **(1)** A counsellor or adviser, one versed in counsel or devices H 366, Ξ 318, P 477: γ 110, 409.—Of Zeus Θ 22, P 339.—**(2)** One who devises or brings about something. In reference to warriors: μήστωρες (μήστωρας) ἀϋτῆς (raisers of the battle-shout) Δ 328, N 93 = 479, Π 759. Cf. Z 97 = 278, M 39, Ψ 16.—Of horses E 272, Θ 108.

μήτε. In general use corresponding to μή as οὔτε to οὐ: μήτε . . . μήτε . . . , neither . . . nor . . . (after a negative, either . . . or . . .) A 275, E 827, H 400, Θ 7, K 249, Ξ 342, Π 98, Φ 288, Ω 337: α 39, ν 308, ξ 387, π 302, ρ 401, σ 79, 416 = υ 324.—μήτε . . . τε . . . N 230.

μήτηρ, -έρος, ἡ [cognate with L. *mater*, Eng. *mother*, German *mutter*]. Genit. μητρός E 371, I 566, P 408, Σ 216, Φ 412, etc.: α 368, γ 310, ζ 287, λ 84, ο 347, ω 334, etc. Dat. μητρί A 351, E 555, I 555, Ξ 502, Π 8, etc.: β 373, ζ 51, ο 127, υ 334, etc. Voc. μῆτερ A 352, 586, Z 264, Σ 79, T 21: α 346, λ 164, ρ 46, σ 227, φ 344, etc. (1) A mother, one's mother A 280, 357, Γ 238, Δ 130, E 248, etc.: α 215, β 135, γ 95, δ 224, θ 550, etc. —In reference to birds or animals B 313 = 327, B 315, E 555, P 4: κ 414.—(2) Applied to districts, etc., in reference to what they produce: Ἴτωνα μητέρα μήλων B 696. Cf. Θ 47, I 479, Λ 222, Ξ 283, O 151: ο 226.

†**μητιάω** [μῆτις]. 3 pl. μητιόωσι K 208, 409. Dat. sing. masc. pple. μητιόωντι Σ 312. Nom. pl. μητιόωντες Υ 153: α 234. Dat. μητιόωσι H 45. Nom. sing. fem. μητιόωσα O 27: ζ 14, θ 9. 3 pl. impf. μητιόωντο M 17. Imp. pl. mid. μητιάασθε X 174. (συμ-.) (1) To deliberate, take counsel, concert measures H 45. — To take (counsel): μητιόωντες βουλάς Υ 153.—With dependent clause. In mid.: μητιάασθε ἠὲ . . . ἦε . . . (consider whether . . .) X 175.—(2) To meditate, purpose, propose to oneself, have in mind: ἅσσα τε μητιόωσι μετὰ σφίσιν K 208 = 409. Cf. Σ 312.—To devise, plan, contrive, scheme to bring about: κακά O 27. Cf. α 234, ζ 14 = θ 9.—With infin. expressing what is planned or contrived: τεῖχος ἀμαλδῦναι M 17.

μητίετα [μῆτις]. As voc. A 508. Elsewhere as nom. (prob. orig. the voc. turned into a nom.) The counsellor or deviser. Epithet of Zeus A 175, B 197, Z 198, H 478, Θ 170, etc.: ξ 243, π 298, υ 102.

μητιόεις, -εντος [μῆτις]. Skilful in attaining one's ends. Applied to drugs: φάρμακα μητιόεντα (helpful, bringing relief) δ 227.

†**μητίομαι** [μῆτις]. Fut. μητίσομαι Γ 416, O 349. 3 pl. aor. ἐμητίσαντο μ 373. 1 sing. opt. μητῖσαίμην σ 27. Infin. μητίσασθαι K 48, Ψ 312: ι 262. (1) To exhibit skill or address: οὐδὲ πλείονα ἴσασι μητίσασθαι (know better how to . . ., are more skilful) Ψ 312.—(2) To devise, plan, contrive, scheme to bring about Γ 416, K 48, O 349: μ 373.—With double acc. of what is devised, etc., and of the person aimed at: ὄν ἂν κακὰ μητισαίμην σ 27.—Absol. ι 262.

μητιόωσι, 3 pl. μητιάω.

μῆτις, ἡ. Dat. μήτῖ Ψ 315, 316, 318: ν 299. (1) Skill, address Ψ 313, 315, 316, 318.—(2) Skill in counsel or device, astuteness, shrewdness: ὄφρα σε μ. ἐξάγαγ' ἐξ ἄντροιο υ 20. Cf. B 169, 407, 636, H 47 = Λ 200, K 137: β 279, γ 120, ν 299, ψ 125. —(3) Contrivance, scheming: διὰ μῆτιν Ἀθήνης K 497.—(4) Counsel, concerting of measures: ὑφαίνειν μῆτιν H 324 = I 93. Cf. δ 678, ι 422, ν 303, 386, τ 326.—(5) A course of action, scheme, plan: ὄφρ' ἄλλην φράζωνται μῆτιν ἀμείνω I 423. Cf. K 19, Ξ 107, O 509, P 634, 712: δ 739, ι 414, κ 193, τ 158.—(6) What one proposes to effect, one's intention or purpose, what one has in one's mind: ἥν τινα μῆτιν κέκευθεν γ 18. Cf. H 447.—(7) The faculty of deliberation or weighing in the mind: λεπτὴ μῆτις [ἐστιν] K 226, Ψ 590.

μητίσομαι, fut. μητίομαι.

μητροπάτωρ, ὁ [μητρ-, μήτηρ + πατήρ]. The father of one's mother, one's maternal grandfather Λ 224.

μητρυιή, -ῆς, ἡ. A stepmother E 389 (*i.e.*, app., of the sons of Aloeus), N 697 = O 336.

μητρώϊος [μητρ-, μήτηρ]. Of one's mother: μητρώϊον ἐς δῶμα (*i.e.* her old home) τ 410.

μήτρως, ὁ. A maternal uncle B 662, Π 717.

†**μηχανάομαι** [μηχανή = μῆχος]. 2 pl. μηχανάασθε υ 370. 3 μηχανόωνται γ 207, δ 822, π 134, φ 375, etc. 3 sing. opt. μηχανόῳτο π 196. Acc. pl. masc. pple. μηχανόωντας σ 143. Infin. μηχανάασθαι γ 213, π 93. 3 pl. impf. μηχανόωντο Θ 177, Λ 695: υ 394, χ 432. (περι-.) (1) To construct, put together Θ 177.—(2) To devise, contrive, put in practice: ἀτάσθαλα Λ 695: γ 207, π 93, ρ 588, σ 143, υ 170, 370. Cf. γ 213, π 134, 196, ρ 499, υ 394, φ 375, χ 432.—Absol., to lay plans, form devices, plot: πολλοὶ ἐπ' αὐτῷ μηχανόωνται δ 822.

μῆχος, τό. A means, device or expedient for carrying out one's wishes or remedying a state of matters: οὐδέ τι μ. εὑρέμεναι δυνάμεσθα B 342. Cf. μ 392.—With infin.: ἄκος εὑρεῖν I 249. Cf. ξ 238.

μίᾰ, -ῆς. See εἷς.

μιαίνω. 3 sing. aor. subj. μιήνῃ Δ 141. 3 pl. aor. pass. μιάνθησαν Π 795, Ψ 732. A form μιάνθην Δ 146 explained as 3 pl. aor. pass. or as a 3 dual (for μιάν-σθην). (1) To stain, colour: ἐλέφαντα φοίνικι Δ 141. — (2) To stain, defile, sully, soil Δ 146, Π 795, 797, P 439, Ψ 732.

μιαιφόνος [μιαίνω + φόνος]. Blood-stained. Epithet of Ares E 31 = 455, 844, Φ 402.

μιάνθην. See μιαίνω.

μιάνθησαν, 3 pl. aor. pass. μιαίνω.

μιαρός [μιαίνω]. Stained, sullied Ω 420.

μιγάζομαι [μιγ-, μίσγω]. To have sexual intercourse: μιγαζομένους φιλότητι θ 271.

μίγδα [μιγ-, μίσγω]. Mingled, in one mass, with something ω 77.—With dat., among: μ. ἄλλοισι θεοῖσιν Θ 437.

μίγη, 3 sing. aor. pass. μίσγω.

μιγήσεσθαι, fut. infin. pass. μίσγω.

μιήνῃ, 3 sing. aor. subj. μιαίνω.

μικρός. (1) Of small size: λίθος γ 296.—(2) In reference to stature, short: μικρὸς δέμας (in . . .) E 801.—Comp. μείων B 528, 529, Γ 193.

μίκτο, 3 sing. aor. pass. μίσγω.

μιλτοπάρηος, -ον [μίλτος, cinnabar + παρήϊον. Cf. φοινικοπάρῃος]. Red-prowed. Epithet of ships B 637: ι 125.

μιμνάζω [μίμνω]. To tarry, loiter: παρὰ νηυσίν B 392, K 549.

μιμνήσκω [redup. fr. *μνη-, μνάομαι*]. Fut. *μνήσω* O 31. 3 sing. *-ει* μ 38. 2 sing. aor. *ἔμνησας* γ 103. 3 sing. subj. *μνήσῃ* ξ 170. Fem. pple. *μνήσᾱσα* A 407. **Mid.** 3 sing. pa. iterative *μνησάσκετο* Λ 566. 1 pl. fut. *μνησόμεθα* η 192. 3 *-ονται* Δ 172. Infin. *-εσθαι* B 724, T 64: μ 212. 3 sing. aor. *(ἐ)μνήσατο* Ω 602, 613: α 29, δ 187. 3 pl. *μνήσαντο* Δ 222, Θ 252, Ξ 441, O 380, Π 357: π 481. Subj. *μνήσομαι* I 647. 2 sing. *μνήσῃ* θ 462. 1 pl. *μνησόμεθα* κ 177. *μνησώμεθα* O 477, T 148, Ω 601: δ 213, υ 246, χ 73. 3 sing. opt. *μνήσαιτο* δ 527. 3 pl. *μνησαίατο* B 492: η 138. Imp. *μνῆσαι* K 509, O 375, X 84, Ω 486: γ 101, δ 331, 765, χ 208. 3 sing. *μνησάσθω* P 671. 2 pl. *μνήσασθε* Z 112, H 371, O 662, etc. Pple. *μνησάμενος, -η* N 48, T 314, 339, Ω 504, 509: ε 6, κ 199, μ 309, τ 118, υ 205. Infin. *μνήσασθαι* η 217, λ 71. Pf. *μέμνημαι* E 818, Z 222, I 527: ω 122. 2 sing. *μέμνηαι* Φ 442. *μέμνῃ* O 18, Υ 188, Φ 396: ω 115. *μέμνησαι* Ψ 648. 3 *μέμνηται* Θ 362: β 233, ε 11, ο 23. 1 pl. subj. *μεμνώμεθα* ξ 168. Opt. *μεμνῄμην* Ω 745. 3 sing. *μεμνέῳτο* (app., with metathesis of quantity, for *μεμνῄοιτο*) Ψ 361. Pple. *μεμνημένος, -η* E 263, T 153, Ω 4, 129, 216: α 343, δ 151, 592, θ 244, 431, κ 464. Infin. *μεμνῆσθαι* T 231: δ 353, σ 267. 3 sing. plupf. *μέμνητο* ω 195. 3 pl. *μέμνηντο* P 364. Fut. pf. *μεμνήσομαι* X 390. Infin. *μεμνήσεσθαι* τ 581, φ 79. **Pass.** Aor. infin. *μνησθῆναι* δ 118. (*ἀνα-, ἀπο-, ἐπι-, ὑπο-*.) (**1**) To remind (a person): *μνήσει σε καὶ θεὸς αὐτός* μ 38.—To remind (a person) of (something). With genit.: *τῶν νῦν μιν μνήσασα* A 407. Cf. O 31: γ 103, ξ 169, 170. —(**2**) In mid. and (in (c)) in pass. (the pf. in pres. and the plupf. in impf. sense). (**a**) With genit., to recall to or bear in mind, remember, recollect, bethink oneself of: *μνήσονται πατρίδος αἴης* Δ 172, *οὐδέ τι τῶν μέμνηται, δ . . .* Θ 362. Cf. B 724, I 647, O 662, T 64, X 390, Ω 486, etc.: *μνήσατ' Αἰγίσθοιο* α 29, *ὡς εὖ μέμνητο Ὀδυσῆος* ω 195. Cf. β 233, δ 187, κ 199, μ 212 (survive to look back upon them), ο 23 (thinks no more of them), χ 208, etc.—With acc.: *Τυδέα δ' οὐ μέμνημαι* Z 222. Cf. I 527: ω 122.—With dependent clause: *ἦ οὐ μέμνῃ ὅτε . . .;* (the time when . . ., how . . .) O 18, Υ 188, Φ 396: ω 115.—With infin.: *ἀλλήλοις ἀλεξέμεναι φόνον* P 364.—Absol.: *ἐπαΐξαι μεμνημένος ἵππων* (make a rush for them—do not forget) E 263. Cf. T 153, 314: *μεμνημένος μυθεόμην* (as my memory prompted me) δ 151. Cf. α 343, ε 6, μ 309, τ 118.—(**b**) With genit., to remember or bear in mind so as to put in practice or use or bring about, not to neglect, to bethink oneself of, turn one's mind to: *μνήσασθε ἀλκῆς* Z 112, *σέων μέμνημαι ἐφετμέων* E 818. Cf. Δ 222, H 371, Π 357, T 231, X 268, Ω 129, etc.: *νόστου μιμνήσκεσθαι* γ 142, *ὅτε μνησαίατο κοίτου* η 138. Cf. δ 213, 353, 527, κ 177, π 481, υ 138, 246, χ 73.—To bear in mind the interests of, watch over, attend to: *πατρὸς* σ 267.—With acc., to note and bear in mind, observe, watch: *δρόμους* Ψ 361 (*v.l. δρόμου*).—To take thought (for something), consider: *περὶ πομπῆς μνησόμεθα* η 192.—(**c**) With genit., to tell or speak about: *πατρὸς μνησθῆναι* δ 118. Cf. θ 244.—So with acc.: *ἄλλα μεμνώμεθα* (change our discourse) ξ 168.—With dependent clause: *εἰ μὴ Μοῦσαι μνησαίαθ' ὅσοι . . .* B 492.

μίμνω [redup. fr. *μν-, μεν-, μένω*]. Dat. pl. masc. pple. *μιμνόντεσσι* B 296. (*ἀνα-, ἐπι-, παρα-*.) (**1**) To remain where one is, to remain, stay, tarry, abide, continue to be, in a specified or indicated place: *μή τις μετόπισθε μιμνέτω* Z 69. Cf. B 296, 331, Z 431, I 552, 617, N 747, O 689, Σ 263, T 189, 190, X 439, Ω 470: *αὐτόθι μίμνει ἀγρῷ* (has his abode at the farm) λ 187. Cf. ζ 245, ι 172, κ 489, λ 356, μ 161, ο 545, ψ 38, ω 396, 464.—(**2**) To remain or be in a specified condition: *ἵνα περ τάδε τοι σόα μίμνῃ* Ω 382: ν 364. —(**3**) To await the coming or approach of (a person): *ἄλλους* Δ 340: *τί μ' οὐ μίμνεις ἑλέειν μεμαῶτα;* (stay for my embrace) λ 210.—To await the coming or coming on of (a period of time): *Ἠῶ* Θ 565, I 662, Σ 255: π 368, σ 318, τ 50.—To await an occurrence. With dependent clause: *μίμνετ' εἰς ὅ κε . . .* (wait till . . .) β 97 = τ 142 = ω 132.—(**4**) To await the attack of, stand up to: *οὐδέ μιν μίμνον* E 94. Cf. I 355, M 136, N 129, X 38, 92.—Sim.: *μίμνομεν Ἄρηα* P 721. Cf. N 106. —Of something inanimate: *δρύες, αἵ τ' ἄνεμον μίμνουσιν* M 133.—Absol., to await the foe, stand firm, stand one's ground: *οὐκ Ἰδομενεὺς τλῆ μίμνειν* Θ 78, *Νέστωρ οἶος ἔμιμνεν* (here hardly more than sense (1)) 80. Cf. N 713, O 727 = Π 102.

μιν, *enclitic*. Acc. pron. of the 3rd person. (**1**) Him A 100, 290, 332, 361, 407, etc.: α 71, 95, 135, 192, 194, etc.—(**2**) Her A 29, 201, 585, Γ 386, 388, etc.: α 97, 432, β 113, δ 375, 704, etc, —(**3**) Referring to things, it A 237, Δ 143, etc.. ι 120, κ 305, etc.—The antecedent a neut. pl.: κ 212, ρ 268.—(**4**) With *αὐτός* in reflexive sense: *αὐτόν μιν πληγῇσι δαμάσσας* δ 244.

μινύθω [cf. L. *minuo*]. 3 pl. pa. iterative *μινύθεσκον* ξ 17. (**1**) To diminish, make smaller, take from. In reference to abstractions: *Ἀργείων μένος* O 493. Cf. Υ 242.—To deprive (a person) of power or spirit, take the heart out of (him): *ὅτινας μινύθῃ* [*Ζεύς*] O 492.—(**2**) To diminish in number, make fewer: *ἄρσενας σύας μινύθεσκον ἔδοντες* ξ 17.—(**3**) To waste or decay away: *περὶ ῥινοὶ μινύθουσιν* μ 46.—To suffer destruction, be destroyed or ruined Π 392, P 738.—Of the heart or spirit, to waste or pine away: *μινύθει ἦτορ ἑταίρων* δ 374. Cf. δ 467.

μίνυνθα [cf. prec.]. For a short time, for a little while: *ἐπεί τοι αἶσα μ. περ* A 416. Cf. Δ 466, Λ 317, 539, M 356, N 573, Ξ 358, P 277, Υ 27, Ψ 97: θ 315, λ 501, ο 494, χ 473.

μινυνθάδιος [*μίνυνθα*]. Lasting but a short time, short: *αἰών* Δ 478 = P 302.—In comp.: *μινυνθαδιώτερον ἄλγος ἔσσεται* X 54.—Of persons, short-lived A 352, O 612, Φ 84: λ 307, τ 328.

μινυρίζω. To make lament in a low tone,

weep softly δ 719.—To whimper, make whimpering complaint, whine E 889.

μῖξαι, aor. infin. μίσγω.

μίξεσθαι, fut. infin. pass. μίσγω.

μισγάγκεια, ἡ [μίσγω + ἄγκος]. A place where two glens join their streams Δ 453.

μίσγω. 3 pl. aor. ἔμιξαν, ἔμειξαν, δ 41. Infin. μῖξαι, μεῖξαι O 510. **Pass.** 2 sing. subj. μίσγεαι B 232. 3 sing. pa. iterative μισγέσκετο σ 325. 3 pl. ἐμισγέσκοντο υ 7. Fut. infin. μιγήσεσθαι K 365. μίξεσθαι, μείξεσθαι ζ 136, ω 314. 3 sing. aor. (ἐ)μίχθη E 134, Θ 99, K 457, N 642, O 457, Υ 374 : χ 329. 3 pl. ἔμιχθεν Γ 209, K 180, Ψ 687. Pple. μιχθείς Γ 48. Infin. μιχθήμεναι Λ 438. Aor. ἐμίγην Γ 445. 2 sing. ἐμίγης O 33. 3 (ἐ)μίγη E 143, Z 25, Φ 143 : ε 126, η 61, ο 420, ψ 219. 3 pl. μίγεν ι 91. μίγησαν θ 268. 2 sing. subj. μιγήῃς ε 378. 3 pl. μιγέωσι B 475. Opt. μιγείην ο 315. 2 sing. μιγείης Γ 55. 3 μιγείη δ 222, ε 386. Acc. sing. masc. pple. μιγέντα Δ 354 : σ 379. Nom. dual μιγέντε κ 334. Nom. sing. fem. μιγεῖσα α 73, λ 268, τ 266. Infin. μιγήμεναι Z 161, 165, N 286, O 409, Φ 469. μιγῆναι I 133, 275, Ξ 386, T 176 : λ 306, υ 12. 3 sing. aor. ἔμικτο α 433. μίκτο Λ 354, Π 813. Pf. pple. μεμιγμένος, -η, -ον K 424 : δ 230, θ 196, λ 123, τ 175, ψ 270. 3 sing. plupf. ἐμέμικτο Δ 438. (ἀνα-, ἐπι-, μετα-, προ-, συμ-.) (**1**) To mix together : οἶνον καὶ ὕδωρ α 110.—(**2**) To mix with something : ἀνὰ κρῖ ἔμιξαν δ 41. Cf. δ 222.—To mix (wine) with water Γ 270.—With that with which a thing is mixed in dat. : ἅλεσσι μεμιγμένον εἶδαρ λ 123 = ψ 270. — Sim. : Τρώεσσι μεμιγμένοι (sharing quarters with them) K 424.—Also θ 196, υ 203 (to bring into trouble).—(**3**) To mix together in confusion or without distinction : ἐπεί κε νομῷ μιγέωσιν [αἶγες] B 475. Cf. δ 230.—Sim. : γλῶσσ' ἐμέμικτο Δ 438. Cf. τ 175.—(**4**) To bring together (in fight) : αὐτοσχεδίῃ μεῖξαι χεῖρας O 510.—In pass., to come together in fight : μιγήμεναι ἐν δαΐ N 286. Cf. Δ 456, Υ 374, Φ 469.—So χεῖρες ἔμιχθεν Ψ 687.—Sim. : μισγομένων ἀνέμων θύελλα ε 317.—(**5**) In pass., to mingle with, to set oneself, take one's place or stand, find or get oneself, among, visit, join, reach. With dat. : προμάχοισιν ἐμίχθη E 134, Θ 99, N 642, O 457. Cf. Γ 48, Δ 354, E 143, K 365, Λ 354, Π 813, Ω 91 : κούρῃσιν ἔμελλε μίξεσθαι ζ 136. Cf. ε 378, 386, ι 91, ο 315.—Sim. : μιχθήμεναι [ἔγχος] ἔγκασιν (to penetrate) Λ 438, ἀλὶ μίσγεται [ἀέλλη] (comes upon and ruffles) N 797. Cf. Ξ 386 (to encounter), O 409 (to get among), K 457 := χ 329 (rolled in the dust).—With ἐν or ἐνί : ἐνὶ προμάχοισι μιγέντα σ 379. Cf. Γ 209, K 180.—Sim. Γ 55.—With ἐς Σ 216.—Absol. : οὐ μίσγεσθαι ἐῶσιν Ψ 73. Cf. σ 49.—(**6**) In pass., to associate or be intimate with. With dat. : ἐμισγόμεθ' ἀλλήλοισιν α 209. Cf. ζ 288, η 247.—Absol. δ 178, ω 314.—(**7**) In pass., to have sexual intercourse : τῆς εὐνῆς ἐπιβήμεναι ἠδὲ μιγῆναι I 133 = 275 = T 176. Cf. B 232, Γ 445, Z 25, 161, Ξ 295 : α 433, θ 268, κ 334, λ 268, ο 430, τ 266, χ 445, ψ 219.—With dat. of person : γυναικί περ ἐν φιλότητι μίσγεσθαι Ω 131. Cf. Z 165, Φ 143 : α 73, ε 126, η 61, λ 306, ο 420, σ 325, υ 7, 12.—With cognate acc. : φιλότης τε καὶ εὐνή, ἣν ἐμίγης O 33.

μισέω. With infin., to dislike or shrink from the idea of *something happening* : μίσησέ μιν δηΐων κυσὶ κύρμα γενέσθαι P 272.

μισθός, -οῦ, ὁ. (**1**) An inducement held out to one, a reward : μισθὸς οἱ ἄρκιος ἔσται K 304. Cf. δ 525.—(**2**) A return for one's work or labour, hire, wages M 435, Φ 445, 450, 451, 457 : κ 84 (double wages), σ 358.

μιστύλλω. To cut up (flesh) for cooking H 317 = Ω 623, I 210, A 465 = B 428 := γ 462 = μ 365 = ξ 430, ξ 75, τ 422.

μίτος, ὁ. The warp in weaving Ψ 762.

μίτρη, -ης, ἡ. App. some kind of metal guard worn round the waist under the ζωστήρ, ζῶμα and θώρηξ Δ 137, 187, 216, E 857.

μίχθη, 3 sing. aor. pass. μίσγω.

μνάομαι [cf. μιμνήσκω]. 2 sing. μνᾷ π 431. Dat. sing. masc. pple. μνωομένῳ δ 106. Nom. dual μνωομένω ο 400. Infin. μνάασθαι α 39. μνᾶσθαι ξ 91. 3 pl. impf. ἐμνώοντο B 686. μνώοντο Λ 71, Π 697, 771 ; λ 288. 3 sing. pa. iterative μνάσκετο υ 290. (ὑπο-.) (**1**) = μιμνήσκω (2) (a). Absol. : κήδεσιν ἀλλήλων τερπώμεθα μνωομένω ο 400. Cf. δ 106. (**2**) = μιμνήσκω (2) (b) : οὐ πολέμοιο ἐμνώοντο B 686. Cf. Λ 71 = Π 771.—Sim. : φύγαδε μνώοντο (turned their minds to flight, turned to flight) Π 697.—(**3**) To seek or woo for one's bride, court : ἤδη σε μνῶνται ἀριστῆες ζ 34. Cf. α 248 = π 125, ζ 284, λ 117 = ν 378, λ 288, π 431, τ 133, υ 290, φ 161, 326, ω 125.—Absol., to do one's wooing, make court ξ 91, π 77, 391, τ 529.—To make illicit suit to, seek to debauch (the wife of another) α 39.

μνῆμα, τό [μνη-, μνάομαι]. Something serving to remind, a memento or remembrancer : τάφου μ. Ψ 619. Cf. ο 126, φ 40.

μνημοσύνη, ἡ [as prec.]. A bearing in mind (in the sense of μιμνήσκω (2) (b)), thought or care for something : πυρός Θ 181.

μνήμων [as prec.]. Having a good memory, clear in recollection φ 95.—Mindful or heedful of something, keeping a careful eye on something : φόρτου θ 163.

μνήσαντο, 3 pl. aor. mid. μιμνήσκω.

μνησάσκετο, 3 sing. pa. iterative mid. μιμνήσκω.

μνηστεύω [μνη-, μνάομαι]. To seek or woo for one's bride, court : ἀγαθὴν γυναῖκα σ 277.—Absol., to do one's wooing, make court δ 684.

μνηστή, -ῆς [as prec.]. Wooed (and won), wedded. Epithet of ἄλοχος Z 246, I 399, 556, Λ 242 : α 36, λ 177.

μνηστήρ, -ῆρος, ὁ [as prec.]. Dat. pl. μνηστήρεσσι α 91, β 395, ο 315, τ 2, φ 3, etc. μνηστῆρσι α 114, β 21, δ 790, υ 5, χ 4, etc. A wooer or suitor : μνηστήρων δίκη σ 275. Cf. σ 247.—Of the suitors for Penelope in the absence of Odysseus : α 91, β 21, γ 206, δ 625, ε 27, λ 119, ν 193, etc.

μνῆστις, ἡ [as prec.]. A bearing in mind (in the sense of μιμνήσκω (2) (b)), thought or care for something : δόρπου ν 280.

μνηστύς, -ύος, ἡ [as prec.]. A wooing or courting: παύσεσθαι μνηστύος β 199. Cf. π 294 = τ 13.

μνήσω, fut. μιμνήσκω.

μνώοντο, 3 pl. impf. μνάομαι.

μογέω [μόγος]. To suffer toil, hardship, distress, to toil, labour: πολλὰ μόγησα Α 162, ἄλλος μογέων ἀποκινήσασκε [δέπας] (with trouble or difficulty, could just . . .) Λ 636. Cf. Β 690, Ι 492, Μ 29, Ψ 607: ἄλγεα πολλὰ μογήσας (after sore toil and distress) β 343, μογέοντες (tired, weary) ω 388. Cf. δ 106, ε 223, ζ 175, η 214, μ 190, π 19, ψ 307, etc.

μόγις [μόγος]. With difficulty, hardly, just, only just Ι 355, Φ 417, Χ 412: γ 119 (only after long years), τ 189.

μόγος, -ου, ὁ. Toil, labour Δ 27.

μογοστόκος, -ον [μογοσ- (to be taken as a relic of the acc. pl. of μόγος; cf. δικασπόλος) + τοκ-, τίκτω. Hence 'pangs-generating,' 'that brings on the woman's pains.' Or perh. μογο-, μόγος + στακ-, to stay. Hence 'pangs-staying,' 'that brings the woman relief from her pains']. Epithet of Εἰλείθυια or the Εἰλείθυιαι Λ 270 (which seems to point to the first explanation), Π 187, Τ 103.

μόθος, -ου, ὁ. The press of battle, battle Η 117, 240, Σ 159, 537, Φ 310.

μοι. See ἐμέ.

μοῖρα, -ης, ἡ. (**1**) (Due) measure. κατὰ μοῖραν, duly, fitly, properly, in the proper way, in seemly wise: ἔειπες Α 286. Cf. Ι 59, Ο 206, Π 367, Τ 256, etc.: πάντα κατὰ μοῖραν γ 457. Cf. β 251, γ 331, θ 496, ο 170, ρ 580, etc.—So ἐν μοίρῃ: πέφαται (has met his deserts) χ 54. Cf. Τ 186.—παρὰ μοῖραν, unduly, in unseemly wise ξ 509.—(**2**) A part, portion, division: παρῴχωκεν πλέων νὺξ τῶν δύο μοιράων (more of it than two (of the three) watches), τριτάτη δ' ἔτι μοῖρα λέλειπται (see under λείπω (3)) Κ 253. Cf. δ 97.—(**3**) A share or portion allotted or available: ἴση μοῖρα μένοντι (the same share of the spoil) Ι 318. Cf. Ο 195, Π 68: σπλάγχνων μοίρας γ 40, υ 260. Cf. γ 66 = υ 280, θ 470, λ 534, ξ 448, ο 140, ρ 258, 335, τ 423, υ 281, 293.—(**4**) One's portion or lot in life, one's fate or destiny, what is allotted by fate: οὔ πώ τοι μ. [ἐστι] θανεῖν Η 52. Cf. Ο 117, Π 434, Ρ 421, Σ 120, Ψ 80: δ 475, ε 41, 114, 345, ι 532.—Sim.: ἐφ' ἑκάστῳ μοῖραν ἔθηκαν ἀθάνατοι (its place or use) τ 592, οὐδ' αἰδοῦς μοῖραν ἔχουσιν (have no room in their hearts for it) υ 171.—(**5**) Good fortune: μοῖράν τ' ἀμμορίην τε υ 76.—(**6**) Fate that comes upon or overtakes one, evil fate, death, doom: μ. μιν ἀμφεκάλυψεν Μ 116. Cf. Δ 517, Ε 83, Ζ 488, Ν 602, Π 849, Ρ 478, Φ 83, Χ 303, etc.: μ. θανάτοιο (fate consisting in death, *i.e.* death) β 100. Cf. λ 292, φ 24, χ 413, ω 29, etc.—(**7**) Fate or destiny as decreed by the gods: μ. θεῶν γ 269.—So μ. alone, the decrees of fate (cf. αἶσα (6), μόρος (3)): ὑπὲρ μοῖραν Υ 336.—(**8**) Fate personified Τ 87, 410, Ω 209.—In pl., the Fates Ω 49.

μοιρηγενής [μοῖρα + γεν-, γίγνομαι]. Child of (good) fortune Γ 182.

μοιχάγρια, τά [μοιχός, adulterer + ἄγρη. 'Spoils exacted from an adulterer']. Compensation levied for adultery: μοιχάγρι' ὀφέλλει θ 332.

μόλιβος, ὁ. Lead Λ 237.

μολοβρός, ὁ. A term of abuse or depreciation of unknown meaning. Of a beggar ρ 219, σ 26.

μολπή, -ῆς, ἡ [μέλπω]. Sport, play. (**1**) With special reference to dancing: μολπῆς ἐξάρχοντες ἐδίνευον Σ 606 := δ 19. Cf. Σ 572: ζ 101, φ 430.—(**2**) To singing: μολπῇ θεὸν ἱλάσκοντο καλὸν ἀείδοντες παιήονα Α 472. Cf. Ν 637 := ψ 145, α 152.

μολύβδαινα, -ης, ἡ [μόλυβδος = μόλιβος]. A leaden weight Ω 80.

μολών, aor. pple. βλώσκω.

μονόω [= μουνόω]. To leave alone or without aid: ἐνὶ Τρώεσσι μονωθείς Λ 470.

μόριμος [μόρος]. Decreed by fate. Absol. in neut. sing. in impers. construction: μόριμόν οἵ ἐστ' ἀλέασθαι Υ 302.

μορμύρω. (ἀνα-.) Of water, to flow with noise, rush, roar Ε 599, Σ 403, Φ 325.

μορόεις, -εντος [perh. fr. μόρον, mulberry]. Thus, as if consisting of berries, berry-like, clustering: ἕρματα μορόεντα Ξ 183 := σ 298.

μόρος, -ου, ὁ. (**1**) One's portion or lot in life, one's fate or destiny, what is allotted by fate: μόρος μοί [ἐστιν] ἐνθάδ' ὀλέσθαι Τ 421. Cf. Ζ 357, Χ 280 (*i.e.* that I was doomed), Ω 85: λ 618.—(**2**) Fate that comes upon or overtakes one, evil fate, death, doom: ἀλλὰ καὶ ὣς ὀλέεσθε κακὸν μόρον Φ 133. Cf. Σ 465: α 166, ι 61, λ 409, π 421, υ 241.—(**3**) The decrees of fate (cf. μοῖρα (7)): ὑπὲρ μόρον (also written ὑπέρμορον), beyond, contrary to, in defiance of, fate: μὴ καὶ τεῖχος ὑπέρμορον ἐξαλαπάξῃ Υ 30. Cf. Φ 517: α 34, 35, ε 436.

μόρσιμος [= μόριμος]. Of or pertaining to fate: μόρσιμον ἦμαρ. See ἦμαρ (4) (f).—Destined to endure a specified fate: οὔ με κτενέεις, ἐπεὶ οὔ τοι μ. εἰμι Χ 13.—Destined or marked out by fate to achieve something: ἤ κε γήμαιθ' ὅς κε μόρσιμος ἔλθοι π 392 = φ 162.—Absol. in neut. sing. in impers. construction, decreed by fate: σοὶ αὐτῷ μόρσιμόν ἐστι δαμῆναι Τ 417. Cf. Ε 674.

†**μορύσσω**. Acc. pl. neut. pf. pple. pass. μεμορυγμένα. To sully, make foul: μεμορυγμένα καπνῷ ν 435.

μορφή, -ῆς, ἡ. Beauty, grace: μ. ἐπέων (honied speech) λ 367. Cf. θ 170.

μόρφνος, ὁ. Of uncertain meaning: αἰετόν, μόρφνον θηρητῆρα Ω 316 (perh. (comparing αἰετοῦ μέλανος, τοῦ θηρητῆρος Φ 252) the dark one, the hunter).

μόσχος, -ον. App., young, slender, pliant: δίδη μόσχοισι λύγοισιν Λ 105.

μουνάξ [μοῦνος. For the termination cf. εὐράξ]. Alone, by oneself, singly θ 371, λ 417.

μοῦνος, -η, -ον. (**1**) Alone, by oneself, without others near, without aider or helper: μοῦνος ἐὼν μετὰ Καδμείοισιν Δ 388. Cf. Κ 225, Λ 406, 467, Μ 411, Ο 611, Ρ 94, 472, Υ 188, Χ 456: γ 217, η 204, κ 157, μ 297, π 105, 239, υ 30, 40, χ 13, 107, ψ 38.—(**2**) Alone, only, the only one in the same predicament: Θερσίτης μοῦνος ἐκολῴα B 212. Cf. I 335, 340, 482, K 317 (*i.e.* the only son), Ξ 492, Φ 443: β 365 (an only child), δ 496, λ 68, π 19, 118, 119, 120.—Strengthening εἷς: ἀμφίπολος μία μούνη ψ 227.—A single: ἐπιβλής Ω 453.

μουνόω [μοῦνος]. (1) To isolate, leave alone or without aid: μουνωθέντα σε λάβον ο 386.—(2) To make single: ὧδε ἡμετέρην γενεὴν μούνωσε Κρονίων (*i.e.* allowed but one son in a generation) π 117.

Μοῦσαι, αἱ. The Muses, the goddesses of song and poetry A 604, B 484 = Λ 218 = Ξ 508 = Π 112, B 491, 594, 598: ω 60.—In sing., the Muse B 761: α 1, θ 63, 73, 481, 488, ω 62.

μοχθέω [μόχθος, toil]. To be afflicted, be troubled or vexed K 106.

μοχθίζω [as prec.]. = prec. B 723.

μοχλέω [μοχλός]. To displace by means of bars or levers: στήλας ἐμόχλεον M 259.

μοχλός, -οῦ, ὁ. A bar or lever for moving weights ε 261.—Of the bar of wood applied to the eye of the Cyclops ι 332, 375, 378, 382, 387, 394, 396.

μῡδαλέος, -η, -ον. Wet, dripping Λ 54.

μῡελόεις, -εντος [μυελός]. Full of marrow, marrowy. Epithet of bones: ὀστέα ι 293.

μῡελός, -οῦ, ὁ. Marrow Υ 482, X 501.—Fig.: ἄλφιτα, μυελὸν ἀνδρῶν β 290. Cf. υ 108.

μῡθέομαι [μῦθος]. 2 sing. μῡθεῖαι (μυθέεαι) θ 180. μῡθέαι β 202. 3 pl. pa. iterative μῡθέσκοντο Σ 289. (ἀπο-, παρα-, προτι-.) (1) To utter speech, speak, declare, say: ὥς οἱ ἐμυθεόμην β 172. Cf. H 76, Θ 40 = X 184, P 200, Ψ 305, P 442: = ε 285 = 376, θ 79, 180, λ 345, τ 287, ψ 265.—(2) In indirect discourse. With acc. and infin. Φ 462.—With ὡς θ 497, ξ 151, τ 269.—With indirect question: μυθήσεαι ὅττεό σε χρή α 124. Cf. δ 152.—(3) To give utterance to, utter, speak, say, tell, declare: νημερτέα μυθήσασθε Z 376. Cf. A 291, Z 382, H 284, I 645, Λ 201, Υ 202 = 433, Υ 246: β 202, γ 125, 140, δ 829, λ 507, ξ 125, π 339, ρ 15, 514, 580, σ 342, φ 193.—(4) To tell, declare, reveal, make known: οὔνομά κε μυθησαίμην Γ 235. Cf. β 373, ι 16, μ 155, ν 191.—To tell of, declare the meaning or significance of, expound: μῆνιν Ἀπόλλωνος A 74. Cf. β 159.—(5) To speak of, mention μ 223.—To speak of, tell of, describe: πληθὺν οὐκ ἂν ἐγὼ μυθήσομαι B 488. Cf. γ 114, δ 240, η 213, λ 328, 376, 517, μ 451, τ 245, 500.—To speak of or describe as being *so and so*: πόλιν μυθέσκοντο πολύχρυσον Σ 289.

μῡθολογεύω [μῦθος + λέγω[2]]. To speak of, tell of, describe: τάδε μ 450. Cf. μ 453.

μῦθος, -ου, ὁ. (1) Something said, an utterance or speech: μῦθον ἀκούσας Γ 76. Cf. B 335, Δ 357, H 404, Θ 492, etc.: θ 185, 272, ν 254, υ 271, etc.—(2) What one has to say, speech, discourse, words: ἄλλων μῦθον ἄκουε B 200. Cf. B 199, 282, K 61, 190, Λ 781, Π 631, etc.: ἵνα μῦθον ἀκούσῃς ἡμέτερον λ 561. Cf. α 273, β 77, γ 94, ξ 379, ρ 57, etc.—Contrasted in terms with ἔργον T 242: α 358.—(3) In pl., speech, discourse, words: μύθων ἦρχεν B 433. Cf. B 796, Γ 171, 212, Z 343, Λ 643, O 284, Σ 252, X 281, etc.: μύθοις τέρπεσθε δ 239. Cf. α 28, β 83, γ 23, 124, δ 214, 774, η 157, κ 189, ο 53, φ 291, etc.—Contrasted in terms with ἔργα I 443.—(4) The sense of the word coloured by the context A 25 = 379, A 33 = Ω 571, A 221, 326, Π 199 (a charge or injunction), A 273 (counsel), 388 (a threat), 545 (counsels, intentions), 565 (my charge), B 16 (the charge or commission), Γ 87 (the proposal), Δ 323 (counsel), 412 (my injunction), E 715 (our promise), H 358 = M 232 (counsel), H 374 = 388 (what he is prepared to agree to), H 406 (their answer), Θ 412 (his message), 524 (the order), I 62 (my counsel), 309 (my mind), 522 (their mission), 625 (our charge), 627 (the answer), K 288 (a message or communication), 337 (word, information), Λ 186 (this injunction), 839 (the exhortation), M 80 = N 748 (his recommendation), Ξ 127 (my counsel), O 202 (this reply), Π 83 (of my charge), T 85 (this reproach), 107 (thy boast), 220 (my counsel), Υ 295 (his counsel), 369 (his vaunts), Ψ 157 (thy counsel): α 271, 305 (my counsel), 361 = φ 355 (his injunction), α 373 (an order or command), β 137 (injunction), 412 (my purpose), δ 676 (the plots), 744 (the matter), 777 (the purpose), ε 98 (the matter), η 161 (the word from thee), θ 302 (the matter), λ 368 (thy story), 442 (give her all thy confidence), 492 (his story, how it is with him), ν 16, π 406 = υ 247, σ 50 = 290 = φ 143 = 269 (the proposal or suggestion), ν 298, π 420 (counsel), ο 196 (my request), 445 (the matter), π 387 (what I propose), ρ 177 (the proposal or suggestion), 399 = υ 344 (a command or order), τ 502 (what I say), φ 71 (of a plea or defence), χ 289 (the thing that you would say, the matter), ψ 62 (this story of yours), 349 (a charge), ω 465 (the counsel or recommendation).

μυῖα, -ης, ἡ. A fly: ὡς ὅτε μήτηρ παιδὸς ἐέργῃ μυῖαν Δ 131. Cf. B 469, Π 641, P 570, T 25, 31.

μῡκάομαι. 3 sing. aor. μύκε Υ 260. 3 pl. μύκον E 749, Θ 393, M 460. Pf. pple. (in pres. sense) μεμῡκώς Σ 580, Φ 237. 3 sing. plupf. (in impf. sense) μεμῡκει μ 395. (ἀμφι-.) Of cattle, to low or bellow Σ 580: κ 413, μ 395.—So μεμυκὼς ἠΰτε ταῦρος Φ 237.—Of gates, to grate or groan in opening E 749 = Θ 393.—Sim. of a gate being burst open M 460.—Of a struck shield, to sound or ring Υ 260.

μῡκηθμός, -οῦ, ὁ [μυκάομαι]. A lowing or bellowing: μυκηθμοῦ βοῶν μ 265. Cf. Σ 575.

μύκον, 3 pl. aor. μυκάομαι.

μύλαξ, -ακος, ὁ [μύλη]. Dat. pl. μυλάκεσσι. A stone like the stone of a quern, a large stone M 161.

μύλη, -ης, ἡ. A handmill or quern: ἀλετρεύουσι μύλης ἔπι καρπὸν η 104. Cf. υ 106, 111.

μυλήφατος [μύλη + φα-, φένω]. Mill-crushed: ἀλφίτου β 355.

μυλοειδής [μύλη + εἶδος]. Like the stone of a quern, of large size: μυλοειδέϊ πέτρῳ H 270.

μύνη, -ης, ἡ [perh. conn. with ἀ-μύνω, 'a defence, a means of parrying or evading']. Thus, an excuse or pretext: μή μύνησι παρέλκετε φ 111.

μυρίκη, -ης, ἡ (ῐ). The tamarisk K 466, 467, Φ 18, 350.

μυρίκινος [μυρίκη]. Of the tamarisk Z 39.

μῡρίος, -η, -ον. (1) Numberless, countless, endless, measureless A 2, B 272, Δ 434, O 632, etc.: θ 110, κ 9, λ 282, μ 97, etc.—Absol. in neut. pl.: μυρία ἤδη β 16, μυρί' ἕλοντο (sc. ἕδνα) ο 367. Cf. ω 283.—(2) With sing., measureless, infinite, immense: πένθος Σ 88. Cf. Υ 282: ο 452.—With a collective sb., in measureless quantity, an immensity of . . .: χέραδος Φ 320.

μύρομαι. To shed tears, weep Z 373, P 438, 441, Σ 234, T 6, 213, 340, X 427, Ψ 14, 106, 109, Ω 794: κ 202=568, τ 119.

μύσαν, 3 pl. aor. μύω.

μυχμός, -οῦ, ὁ. Groaning, moaning ω 416.

μυχοίτατος [superl. fr. *μύχοι, locative adv. fr. μυχός] Innermost, furthest from the door: ἷζεν φ 146.

μυχόνδε [acc. of μυχός + -δε (1)]. To the innermost part: μεγάροιο μ. χ 270.

μυχός, -οῦ, ὁ. The innermost or most removed part: μυχῷ Ἄργεος (in a nook of . .) Z 152, μυχῷ θαλάμοιο P 36, μυχοὺς λιμένος (the creeks or recesses) Φ 23, μυχῷ δόμου X 440 (the same as the μέγαρον of 460; see μέγαρον (3)). Cf. I 663 =Ω 675: μυχῷ δόμου (app.=θάλαμος (1) (c)) γ 402, δ 304, η 346. Cf. γ 263, ε 226, η 87, 96, ι 236, ν 363, π 285, χ 180, ψ 41, ω 6.

†**μύω**. 3 pl. aor. μύσαν Ω 637. 3 sing. pf. μέμῡκε Ω 420. Of the eyes, to close Ω 637.—Sim. of wounds Ω 420.

μυών, -ῶνος, ὁ. A muscle Π 315, 324.

μῶλος, -ου, ὁ. Struggle, contest, fight: μ. ὀρώρει P 397. Cf. B 401, H 147, Π 245, Σ 134, 188: σ 233.

μῶλυ, τό. A magic plant described in κ 304.

μωμάομαι [μῶμος]. To blame, censure, reproach: Τρῳαί με μωμήσονται Γ 412.

μωμεύω [as prec.]. =prec. ζ 274.

μῶμος, -ου, ὁ. Blame, blameworthiness β 86.

μώνυχες [(σ)μώνυχες, fr. σμ=σεμ-, εἷς + ὄνυξ in sense 'hoof']. With single, *i.e.* not cloven, hoofs. Epithet of horses E 236, Θ 139, K 392, Λ 708, etc.: ο 46.

ναί. Emphasizing affirmative particle, truly, of a surety. Followed by δή A 286=Θ 146= Ω 379, K 169, Σ 128, Ψ 626: δ 266, σ 170, υ 37, χ 486.—In an affirmation, followed by μά A 234.

ναιετάω [in form frequentative fr. ναίω¹]. Fem. pple. ναιετάουσα, -ης, ναιετόωσα, -ης B 648, Γ 387, Z 415: α 404, θ 574. 3 sing. pa. iterative ναιετάασκε Λ 673, P 308: ο 385. 3 pl. ναιετάασκον B 539, 841. (περι-.) (1) To live, dwell, abide, have one's home: Λακεδαίμονι ναιετοώσῃ (in . . .) Γ 387. Cf. H 9, Λ 673: ζ 153, 245, ο 255, 360, 385, ρ 523.—(2) Of cities, by a sort of personification, to stand, have their place: Ἰθάκης ἔτι ναιεταούσης (while . . . stands) α 404. Cf. Δ 45.—So of islands, to lie ι 23.—Sim. with εὖ, of cities, houses, etc., to have a fair exposure or aspect, be pleasant to dwell in: πόλεις εὖ ναιετοώσας B 648, δόμους εὖ ναιετάοντας Z 370=497, Λ 769. Cf. Z 415: β 400, δ 96, θ 574, ρ 28, 85= 178, 275, 324=φ 242, τ 30=φ 387, υ 371, χ 399, ω 362.—(3) To live in, dwell in, have one's home in, inhabit, hold, have: Ἰθάκην ι 21. Cf. B 539, 841, P 172, 308.

ναίω¹ [νασ-]. 3 sing. pa. iterative ναίεσκε E 708, Π 719. 3 pl. -ον B 758. Aor. νάσσα δ 174. 3 sing. aor. pass. νάσθη Ξ 119. (ἀπο-.) (1) To live, dwell, abide, have one's home: ἔναιεν ἐνὶ Φηρῇ E 543. Cf. B 130, Z 13, I 154, N 176, Π 233, etc.: γ 292, δ 98, ε 58, ν 240, ο 96, etc.—(2) Of a house, by a sort of personification, to stand, be situated: δόμον δείξω, ἐπεί μοι πατρὸς ἐγγύθι ναίει η 29.—So of islands, to lie: νήσων, αἳ ναίουσι πέρην ἁλός B 626.—(3) To live in, dwell in, have one's home in, inhabit, hold, have: Ἀσπληδόνα B 511. Cf. B 593, Γ 74, Z 15, I 484, O 190, etc.: α 51, δ 555, ι 36, 49, 113, etc.—(4) In pres. pple. pass. with εὖ, of places, well inhabited, holding a goodly people: εὖ ναιόμενον πτολίεθρον A 164, B 133, I 402, N 380. Cf. Γ 400, E 489, I 149, 291, N 815, Ξ 255=O 28, Π 572: ν 285.—(5) In aor., to establish or settle (a city): Ἄργεϊ κέ οἱ νάσσα πόλιν δ 174.—(6) In aor. pass. in mid. sense, to establish oneself, settle, take up one's abode: Ἄργεϊ νάσθη Ξ 119.

ναίω² [=νάω]. To flow, be filled to overflowing: ναῖον ὀρῷ ἄγγεα ι 222.

νάκη, -ης, ἡ. A covering of skin: νάκην αἰγός (of goatskin) ξ 530.

νάπη, -ης, ἡ. A valley or glen: ἔκ τ' ἔφανεν νάπαι Θ 558=Π 300.

ναρκάω. To become numbed or deadened: νάρκησε χείρ Θ 328.

νάσθη, 3 sing. aor. pass. ναίω¹.

νάσσα, aor. ναίω¹.

†**νάσσω**. 3 sing. aor. ἔναξε. To press or stamp down, tread hard: γαῖαν φ 122.

ναύλοχος [ναυ-, νηῦς + λοχ-, λεχ-, λέγω¹]. Of harbours, in which ships may lie safely, safe, well sheltered δ 846, κ 141.

ναύμαχος [ναυ-, νηῦς + μάχομαι]. Intended to be used in sea-fighting O 389, 677.

ναυσικλειτός [ναυσί, as dat. of νηῦς + κλειτός]. Famed for his ships: Δύμαντος ζ 22.

ναυσικλυτός, ναυσίκλυτος [as prec. + κλυτός]. Famed for ships. Epithet of the Phaeacians η 39, θ 191=369=ν 166, π 227.—Of the Phoenicians ο 415.

ναύτης, ὁ [ναυ-, νηῦς]. A seaman or sailor Δ 76, H 4, O 627, T 375: α 171=ξ 188, θ 162, ι 138, μ 98, ο 435, π 57, 222.

ναυτιλίη, -ης, ἡ [ναύτης]. Seamanship θ 253.

ναυτίλλομαι [ναύτης]. 3 sing. aor. subj. ναυτίλλεται (ναυτίλεται) δ 672. To sail, go a voyage: Αἴγυπτόνδε ναυτίλλεσθαι ξ 246. Cf. δ 672.

ναῦφι, locative and ablative νηῦς.

νάω (σνάϜω). To flow Φ 197 : ζ 292.

νέα, acc. νηῦς.

νεαρός [νέος]. Young : παῖδες B 289.

νέατος, νείατος, -η [superl. Cf. νείαιρα, νειόθεν, νειόθι. App. not conn. with νέ(Ϝ)ος]. (1) Lowest, the lowest : ἔκειτο νείατος ἄλλων Z 295 : =ο 108. Cf. B 824, Θ 478.—The lowest part of : παρὰ νείατον ἀνθερεῶνα E 293. Cf. E 857, Λ 381, O 341, Π 821, P 310.—(2) Extreme, outermost, the extreme or outermost : [πόλεις] νέαται Πύλου I 153 =295. Cf. Λ 712 : παρὰ νείατον ὅρχον η 127.—Forming the extremity of a row, the extreme or last : τὸν ἔβαλεν νείατον ἀστράγαλον Ξ 466 (here, contextually, the highest).

νεβρός, ὁ, ἡ. The young of the deer, a fawn Δ 243, Θ 248, 249, O 579, Φ 29, X 1, 189 : δ 336= ρ 127, τ 230.

νέες, nom. pl. νηῦς.

νεηγενής [νέος + γεν-, γίγνομαι]. New-born : νεβρούς δ 336=ρ 127.

νεήκης [νέος + *ἀκή = ἀκωκή]. Newly sharpened : πελέκεσσι νεήκεσιν N 391=Π 484.

νέηλυς, -υδος [νέος + ἐλυ(θ)-, ἔρχομαι]. Newly come, a new-comer K 434, 558.

νεηνίης, ὁ [νέος]. A youth. With ἀνήρ : νεηνίῃ ἀνδρὶ ἐοικώς κ 278. Cf. ξ 524.

νεῆνις, -ιδος, ἡ [νέος]. A young woman, a maiden : παρθενικῇ ἐϊκυῖα νεήνιδι η 20. Cf. Σ 418.

νεῖαι, contr. 2 sing. pres. νέομαι.

νείαιρα, -ης [comp. Cf. νέατος, νείατος]. The lower part of : νειαίρῃ ἐν γαστρί E 539=P 519, E 616. Cf. Π 465.

νείατος. See νέατος.

νεικέω [νεῖκος]. Also **νεικείω** (νεικεσίω, fr. νεικεσ-, νεῖκος). 3 pl. νεικεῦσι Υ 254. 3 sing. pa. iterative νεικείεσκε B 221, Δ 241. 3 pl. -ον Υ 86. Fut. νεικέσω K 115. 2 sing. aor. ἐνείκεσας Γ 59, Z 333. 3 νείκεσε E 471, K 158, Φ 470, 480 : θ 158, 239, ρ 239. νείκεσσε Γ 38, Δ 336, 368, Z 325, H 161, Ω 29 : ρ 215, 374, χ 225. (1) To quarrel, contend, dispute : εἵνεκα ποινῆς Σ 498.—To set quarrel abroach, create a disturbance : ὄφρα μὴ νεικείῃσι πατήρ A 579.—(2) To use words of reproach, speak in blame : ὣς νείκεσσ' ὁ γέρων H 161.—(3) With dat., to throw reviling words at, throw blame upon, revile, abuse, reproach : μή μοι ὀπίσσω νεικείῃ ρ 189. Cf. Υ 252, 254.—(4) To revile, abuse, reproach, use despiteful language to, blame : μήτε μ' αἴνεε μήτε νείκει K 249. Cf. A 521, B 221, Γ 59, M 268, Φ 470, Ω 29 (flouted, humiliated), etc. : η 303, θ 158, μ 392, σ 9, τ 108, etc.

νεῖκος, τό. (1) A quarrel, contention, dispute : τοῦ εἵνεκα ν. ὄρωρεν Γ 87=H 374=388. Cf. B 376, Δ 37, Ξ 205=304, Σ 497, X 116, Ω 107 : η 74, θ 75, μ 440.—Contention, strife : ν. ἄριστε(in . . .) Ψ 483. Cf. υ 267, φ 303.—(2) The strife of war, lust of battle : ν. σφ' ὁμοίϊον ἔμβαλε μέσσῳ Δ 444.—A fight or battle : ὣς ἄγε ν. Ἀθήνη Λ 721. Cf. Λ 671, 737, N 122, 271, 333, O 400, P 544 : π 98=116, σ 264.—Fighting, battle : πόνος καὶ ν. M 348, ἔριδος μέγα ν. (battle-strife) P 384. Cf. M 361, Υ 140, Φ 513 : ω 543.—The tide of battle, the battle : ν. ἀπωσαμένους M 276.—(3) A reproach, a reviling or abusing : φεύγων νείκεα πατρός I 448. Cf. Υ 251.—Reproach : νείκει ὀνειδίζων (in . . .) H 95.

νεῖμε, 3 sing. aor. νέμω.

νειόθεν [-θεν (1). Cf. νέατος, νείατος]. From the bottom : ν. ἐκ κραδίης (from the bottom of his heart) K 10.

νειόθι [-θι. Cf. νέατος, νείατος]. At the bottom of. With genit. : ν. λίμνης Φ 317.

νειός, -οῦ, ἡ [νέος]. A fallow field (in process of being ploughed up) : ἑλκέμεναι νειοῖο ἄροτρον (genit. of space) K 353. Cf. N 703, Σ 541, 547 : ε 127, θ 124, ν 32.

νεκάς, ἡ [cf. νέκυς]. Dat. pl. νεκάδεσσι. A heap of slain : ἐν αἰνῇσιν νεκάδεσσιν E 886.

νεκρός, -οῦ, ὁ [cf. νέκυς]. (1) A dead body, a corpse Δ 467, E 620, H 332, N 194, P 13, Φ 235, etc. : μ 10, 13.—(2) The spirit of a dead man conceived of as departing from the body : ὅσσ' ἐπιεικὲς νεκρὸν ἔχοντα νέεσθαι ὑπὸ ζόφον Ψ 51.—In pl., the shades of the departed, the dead : ἔθνεα νεκρῶν κ 526, λ 34, 632. Cf. λ 475.

νέκταρ, -αρος, τό. The drink of the gods A 598, Δ 3 : ε 93, 199, ι 359.—Introduced by divine agency into the corpse of Patroclus T 38.—Into Achilles T 347, 353.

νεκτάρεος [νέκταρ]. App., fragrant. Epithet of garments Γ 385, Σ 25.

νέκυς, -υος, ὁ [cf. νεκρός]. Dat. pl. (besides νεκύεσσι) νέκυσσι λ 569, χ 401, ψ 45. Acc. pl. (besides νέκυας) νέκυς H 420 : ω 417. (1) A dead body, a corpse A 52, Δ 492, E 397 (cf. 886 cited under νεκάς, and O 118), H 84, Λ 534, Π 526, Σ 152, Ψ 168, etc. : χ 271, 401, 407, 437, 448, ψ 45, ω 417.—(2) In pl., the shades of the departed, the dead : νέκυας καὶ δῶμ' Ἀΐδαο ἵξεσθαι O 251. Cf. κ 518, 521, 530, 536, λ 26, 29, 37, 49, 94, 147, 485, 491, 541, 564, 569, 605, μ 383.

νεμέθω [νέμω]. In mid., of birds, to take their food, peck : πελειάδες νεμέθοντο Λ 635.

νεμεσάω, νεμεσσάω [νέμεσις]. (1) To be righteously indignant or vexed, to conceive, feel or express blame or censure, utter reproach Δ 507, Θ 198, K 145=Π 22, N 293 : ρ 481=φ 285.—With dat. : ἄλλῃ νεμεσῶ ζ 286. Cf. N 16=353, Ψ 494 : β 101=τ 146=ω 136, φ 147.—With dat. and with the cause expressed by a pple. : οὐ νεμεσῶ Ἀγαμέμνονι ὀτρύνοντι μάχεσθαι Δ 413.—By an acc. : μή μοι τόδε νεμέσσα, οὕνεκα . . . ψ 213.—By an infin. : μή μοι νεμεσήσετε τείσασθαι . . . O 115.—(2) So in mid. and in aor. pass. in mid. sense : πᾶσι νεμεσσηθεῖσα μετηύδα (her feelings getting the better of her) O 103, νεμεσσηθεὶς χ' ὑποείξω (though indignant, repressing my indignation) 211. Cf. O 227 : νεμεσσῶμαι δέ τ' ἀκούων φ 169. Cf. α 228, τ 264.—The cause expressed by an acc. : ὃς νεμεσσᾶται κακὰ ἔργα ξ 284.—By acc. and infin. : νεμεσσήθη ξεῖνον δηθὰ θύρῃσιν ἐφεστάμεν α 119. Cf. σ 227.—By infin. alone : νεμεσσῶμαί γ' οὐδὲν κλαίειν . . . (I say nothing against it) δ 195.—With dat. : τῷ νεμέσσηθεν B 223. Cf. K 115, 129,

N 119, P 93, 100, Ω 53 : α 158, ο 69, τ 121.—(3) In sim. forms, to be dissatisfied or displeased with oneself : νεμεσσήθητε θυμῷ (think shame (to stand idle)) Π 544. Cf. β 64.—With infin. δ 158.

νεμεσητός, νεμεσσητός [νεμεσ(σ)άω]. (1) Absol. in neut. sing. νεμεσσητόν, something worthy of indignation or blame, a shame or disgrace : ν. κεν εἴη Γ 410, Ξ 336 : χ 489.—With infin. : κεχολῶσθαι Ι 523. Cf. Τ 182, Ω 463 : χ 59.—(2) App., capable of or inclined to anger, easily roused to wrath (for the form cf. ἐπιεικτός) : νεμεσητὸς [ἐστιν] ὅ με προέηκεν Λ 649.

νεμεσίζομαι [νέμεσις]. (1)=νεμεσάω (1) Ε 872.—With the cause expressed by acc. and infin. : οὐ νεμεσίζομ' Ἀχαιοὺς ἀσχαλάαν (I cannot blame them) Β 296.—With dat. : Ἥρῃ Θ 407, 421. Cf. β 239.—With dat. and the cause expressed by an acc. : οὐ νεμεσίζῃ Ἄρῃ τάδε ἔργα ; Ε 757.—(2)=νεμεσάω (3) : ὑμέτερος εἰ θυμὸς νεμεσίζεται αὐτῶν (if you can see your conduct in its true light) β 138.—Sim. with infin. : νεμεσιζέσθω Πάτροκλον κυσὶν μέλπηθρα γενέσθαι (let the thought sting him) Ρ 254.—(3) To fear the wrath of, stand in awe of, reverence : θεούς α 263.

νέμεσις, ἡ. Dat. νεμέσσι Ζ 335. (1) Righteous indignation or vexation, blame, censure, reproach : ἐν φρεσὶ θέσθε νέμεσιν (*i.e.* the fear of it) Ν 122. Cf. Ζ 335, 351 : ν. μοι ἐξ ἀνθρώπων ἔσσεται β 136. Cf. χ 40.—(2) Something worthy of righteous indignation or of blame, censure or reproach. With infin. (cf. χάρις (4) (b)) : οὐ ν. Τρῶας καὶ Ἀχαιοὺς ἄλγεα πάσχειν (small blame to them if they . . .) Γ 156. Cf. Ξ 80 : α 350, υ 330.

νεμεσσάω. See νεμεσάω.

νεμεσσητός. See νεμεσητός.

νέμος, τό. A glade or dell Λ 480.

νέμω. 3 sing. aor. ἔνειμε ξ 449. νεῖμε Ι 217, Ω 626 : ξ 436, υ 253. 3 pl. ἔνειμαν ξ 210. νεῖμαν Γ 274. Imp. νεῖμον η 179, ν 50. (ἀμφι-, ἐπι-.) (1) To give as one's lot or portion, assign : οἰκία ξ 210.—In reference to one's fortune : Ζεὺς αὐτὸς νέμει ὄλβον ζ 188.—To distribute or give out among a company : κρέα Ι 217=Ω 626. Cf. η 179=ν 50, θ 470, κ 357, ξ 436, 449, ο 140, υ 253.—Without expressed object : κήρυκες νεῖμαν ἀρίστοις Γ 274.—(2) In mid., to get as one's lot or portion, to hold, occupy, possess, enjoy (places, lands, etc.) : τέμενος νεμόμεσθα Μ 313. Cf. Β 496, 504, 531, Ζ 195, Υ 8, etc. : οἳ νεμόμεσθ' Ἰθάκην β 167. Cf. η 26, λ 185, υ 336.—To have one's abode, dwell, be settled : ἀμφ' Ἄρμ' ἐνέμοντο Β 499.—(3) To drive one's flock : ἐπῆλθε νέμων ι 233.—(4) In mid., of domestic animals, to feed, crop the herbage, graze : σύες νέμονται πὰρ Κόρακος πέτρῃ ν 407. Cf. Ο 631 : υ 164.—To feed on, crop, graze : νέμεαι ἄνθεα ποίης ι 449. Cf. Ε 777.—Of fire : πυρὸς μένος ἧκε, ὄφρα νέμοιτο (might consume the corpses) Ψ 177.—In pass. of something consumed by fire : ὡς εἴ τε πυρὶ χθὼν νέμοιτο Β 780.

νένιπται, 3 sing. pf. pass. νίζω.

νεοαρδής [νέος + ἄρδω, to water. Cf. ἀρδμός]. Newly watered : ἀλωήν Φ 346.

νεογιλός, -η [νέος + an uncertain second element]. App., newly born : σκύλακος μ 86.

νεόδαρτος [νέος + δαρτός fr. δέρω]. Newly stripped off : δέρμα χ 363. Cf. δ 437.

νεοθηλής [νέος + θηλ-, θάλλω]. Freshly sprouting : ποίην Ξ 347.

νεοίη, ἡ [obscurely formed fr. νέος]. App., the fire or impulsiveness of youth Ψ 604.

νέομαι [conn. with νόστος]. Contr. νεῦμαι Σ 136. 2 sing. νεῖαι (νέεαι) λ 114, μ 141. (ἀν-, ἀπο-.) (1) To go or come back or home, return : σαώτερος ὥς κε νέηαι Α 32, ἐς πατρίδα γαῖαν Β 453. Cf. Β 236, Γ 74, Ε 907, Ι 42, Σ 377, etc. : α 17, 87, γ 60, δ 351, ι 95, μ 334, ο 3, ψ 23, etc.—(2) To take one's way, proceed upon one's way, proceed, go, come, depart : βουλῆς ἐξ Β 84. Cf. Σ 240, Τ 6, Φ 48, 598, Ψ 51, 662 : ταῦτα τελευτήσας νεόμην δ 585, ρ 148. Cf. β 52, γ 170, δ 8, μ 188, ν 30, 206, ξ 261=ρ 430, ξ 498, ο 72, σ 186=χ 434=496, φ 374, χ 484.—Of rivers, to take their way, run, flow Μ 32.—(3) In pres. with fut. sense, to go or come back or home, return : ἐπεὶ οὐ νέομαί γε φίλην ἐς πατρίδα γαῖαν Σ 101=Ψ 150. Cf. Γ 257, Ξ 221, Ρ 497, Σ 136, Τ 330 : β 238, δ 633, ζ 110, λ 114=μ 141, λ 176, ξ 152, υ 156, ω 460.—To take one's way, go, depart : αὐτὰρ ἐγὼ νέομαι ν 61.

νεοπενθής [νέος + πένθος]. Having its sorrow still fresh : θυμόν λ 39.

νεόπλυτος [νέος + πλύνω]. Newly washed ζ 64.

νεόπριστος [νέος + πρίω, to saw]. Newly sawn, preserving its freshness : ἐλέφαντος θ 404.

νέος, -η, -ον (νέϜος). (1) (a) Young, youthful Θ 102, Ι 57, Λ 684, Ν 95, Ψ 306, 589, Ω 368, 725 : α 395, β 29, γ 24, 376, δ 665, 720, θ 58, ν 222, ξ 61, π 71, 99, 210, ρ 294.—(b) In comp. : νεωτέρω ἐμεῖο Α 259. Cf. Κ 165, 176, Φ 439, Ψ 587, Ω 433 : β 188, κ 395, σ 31, 52.—Young rather than old, of the younger generation γ 49, 125, 363, φ 132.—More full of youthful vigour : οὔ τις σεῖο νεώτερος Ο 569.—In superl. : νεώτατος ἔσκον ἁπάντων Η 153. Cf. Ξ 112, Υ 409, Ψ 476 : κ 552.—(2) Absol., a young man, a youth : νέον ἠὲ γέροντα π 198. Cf. Ι 446, Ξ 108, Χ 71.—In pl. Α 463, Β 789, Ι 36, 258, Λ 503, Ψ 756 : β 324, 331, γ 460, θ 110, ν 425, ο 331, σ 6, ω 89, etc.—In comp., a young man as opposed to an older, one of the younger generation η 293.—In pl. Δ 324, Ψ 643 : η 294.—(3) New, newly made, constructed, composed : θαλάμοιο Ρ 36. Cf. β 293, φ 407.—In superl. : ἀοιδήν, ἥ τις νεωτάτη ἀμφιπέληται α 352.—(4) Fresh, young, newly grown or sprouted : φοίνικος ἔρνος ζ 163. Cf. Φ 38.—(5) Of recent date : χρεῖος, οὔ τι νέον γε γ 367. Cf. Ι 527.—Having but lately attained a specified condition : νύμφην (a young wife) λ 447.—(6) A fresh . . ., another : γυναῖκα Β 232. Cf. Ζ 462.—(7) In neut. sing. νέον as adv., newly, lately, recently, just now, but now, just : χοροῖο ν. λήγοντα (pple. of the impf., 'just come from the dance') Γ 394, ὃς ν. εἰληλούθει Ν 364. Cf. Α 391, Δ 332, Η 64, 421, Λ 663, Μ 336, Ν 211, Ο 240, Ω 444, 475 : α 175, γ 318, δ 112, 144, θ 13, 289, π 26, 181, 199, ρ 112, σ 309, τ 400, 433, 519, υ 191, 360, χ 426.—Freshly, recently: ν. φοίνικι φαεινός (its fresh colour not yet dimmed) O 538.—Freshly, anew: αἰεὶ ν. ἐρχομενάων (ever in fresh swarms) B 88.

νεός, genit. νηῦς.

νεόσμηκτος [νέος + σμήχω]. Newly burnished or polished: θωρήκων N 342.

νεοσσός, -οῦ, ὁ [νέος]. A young bird, a nestling: στρουθοῖο νεοσσοί B 311. Cf. I 323.

νεόστροφος, -ον [νέος + στροφ-, στρέφω]. Newly twisted: νευρήν O 469.

νεότευκτος [νέος + τευκ-, τεύχω]. Newly wrought: κασσιτέροιο Φ 592.

νεοτευχής [νέος + τεύχω]. Newly made or constructed, new: δίφροι E 194.

νεότης, -ητος, ἡ [νέος]. (1) Youth Ξ 86.—(2) Youthful vigour: ἀτέμβονται νεότητος Ψ 445.

νεούτατος, -ον [νέος + οὐτάω]. Newly wounded, just wounded: χειρός N 539. Cf. Σ 536.

νέποδες. App., offspring, brood δ 404.

νέρθε(ν). See ἔνερθε(ν).

νεῦμαι, contr. form of νέομαι.

νευρή, -ῆς, ἡ [cf. next]. Locative νευρῆφι λ 607. This form as ablative Θ 300, 309, N 585, O 313, Π 773, Φ 113.—A bowstring Δ 118, 123, 125, Θ 300, 309, 324, 328, Λ 476, 664, N 585, O 313, 463, 469, Π 773, Φ 113: λ 607, τ 587, φ 97 = 127, 410, 419, ω 171.

νεῦρον, -ου, τό [cf. prec.]. (1) A tendon: νεῦρα διεσχίσθη Π 316.—(2) In pl. with collective sense = prec.: ἕλκε νεῦρα βόεια Δ 122.—(3) A string whipping the head of an arrow to the shaft: ν. τε καὶ ὄγκους Δ 151.

νευστάζω [frequentative fr. νεύω]. (1) To make a quick inclination (with the head), nod σ 154.—Of one sitting in a state of helplessness: νευστάζων κεφαλῇ (letting his head drop forwards) σ 240.—Sim. of the accommodation of a helmet to the wearer's motion: νευστάζων κόρυθι Υ 162.—(2) To convey an order by a motion of the head: ὀφρύσι νευστάζων (with my brows, bending the head forward) μ 194.

νεύω. (ἀνα-, ἐπι-, κατα-.) (1) To make a quick inclination of the head, bend the head: ψαῦον κόρυθες νευόντων (genit. with κόρυθες, 'as the men bent their heads') N 133 = Π 217.—Of the nodding of the crest of a helmet Z 470, Γ 337 = Λ 42 = O 481 = Π 138 := χ 124.—To bend (the head). Of persons on whom destruction has come: νεύοιεν κεφαλὰς δεδμημένοι σ 237.—(2) To nod in token or sanction of a promise, promise, undertake, vouchsafe: ἐπ' ὀφρύσι νεῦσεν (with his brows, bending the head forward) A 528 = P 209.—With infin.: νεῦσέ οἱ λαὸν σόον ἔμμεναι Θ 246.—(3) To convey an order or make a sign by a motion of the head: νεῦσ' Αἴας Φοίνικι I 223: ἐπ' ὀφρύσι νεῦσεν π 164. Cf. π 283, ρ 330, φ 431.—With infin.: στορέσαι λέχος I 620.—With ἀνά, to make a sign in prohibition (cf. ἀνανεύω (3)): ἀνὰ δ' ὀφρύσι νεῦον ι 468.

νεφέλη, -ης, ἡ [cf. νέφος]. A cloud: ἐν αἰθέρι καὶ νεφέλῃσιν O 20, 192. Cf. B 146, E 522, Π 298: ε 291, μ 74, 405 = ξ 303.—A cloud or body of mist, mist: νεφέλῃ εἰλυμένος ὤμους E 186. Cf. E 345, Ξ 350, O 308, P 551, Υ 150: θ 562, λ 15.—Fig.: ν. μιν ἀμφεκάλυψεν (the mist of death) Υ 417. Cf. P 591 = Σ 22 := ω 315.

νεφεληγερέτα [νεφέλη + ἀγείρω]. (Prob. orig. a voc. turned into a nom., from which the genit. νεφεληγερέταο (E 631, 736, Θ 387, O 154, Υ 10, Φ 499) is formed.) The cloud-gatherer. Epithet of Zeus A 511, 560, E 631, H 280, Λ 318, O 154, etc.: α 63 = ε 21 = ω 477, ι 67, μ 313, 384 = ν 139 = 153.

νέφος, τό [cf. νεφέλη]. Dat. pl. νεφέεσσι E 867, P 594: ε 293, 303, ι 68, π 264, etc. νέφεσσι N 523. A cloud: ν. ἐρχόμενον κατὰ πόντον Δ 275, νέφεα σκιόεντα E 525. Cf. E 751, Λ 28, 62, O 170, P 372, Ψ 213, etc.: ε 293, 303, θ 374, ι 68 = μ 314, ι 145, λ 592, π 264, υ 104, 114, χ 304.—A cloud or body of mist: τοῖόν τοι ν. ἀμφικαλύψω Ξ 343. Cf. O 153, 668, Σ 205, Ψ 188.—Fig.: θανάτου ν. Π 350. Cf. P 243: δ 180.—Also ν. εἵπετο πεζῶν Δ 274, Ψ 133. Cf. Π 66, P 755.

νέω[1] [σνυ-]. 3 pl. impf. ἔννεον (ἔσνεϝον) Φ 11. To swim: χείρεσσι νέων ε 344. Cf. Φ 11: ε 442.

νέω[2]. (ἐπι-.) To spin. In mid. η 198.

νεῶν, genit. pl. νηῦς.

νῆάδε [acc. of νηῦς + -δε (1)]. To or towards the ship: ν. ἐπεσσεύοντο ν 19.

νηγάτεος. Of unknown origin and meaning: χιτῶνα B 43, κρηδέμνῳ Ξ 185.

νήγρετος [νη- + ἐγείρω. 'From which one is not (readily) roused']. Of sleep, deep, sound ν 80.—In neut. sing. νήγρετον as adv., of sleeping, soundly, fast: ἵνα ν. εὕδοι ν 74.

νήδυια, τά [νηδύς]. The bowels P 524.

νήδυμος [no doubt (ϝ)ήδυμος = ἡδύς (cf. καλός, κάλλιμος) with adhesion of final ν transferred from preceding words. Cf. Eng. *newt* (for *ewt*, with *n*- fr. *an*), and *nickname* (for *eke-name*, with sim. *n*-)]. Epithet of sleep, sweet, grateful, refreshing (= ἡδύς (2)) B 2, K 91, 187, Ξ 242, 253, 354, Π 454, Ψ 63: δ 793, μ 311, 366, ν 79.

νηδύς, -ύος, ἡ. The belly N 290, Υ 486: ι 296.—The womb Ω 496.

νηέω. (ἐπινηνέω, παρανηνέω.) To heap or pile up: ὕλην Ψ 139, 163. Cf. Ψ 169, Ω 276: ξύλα πολλά τ 64.—To heap up (a fire), make a good (fire): πῦρ εὖ νηῆσαι ο 322.—To heap (a ship) full, give (her) a full cargo I 358.—In mid. I 137, 279.

νηϊάς, -άδος. = νηΐς. Defining νύμφη ν 104 = 348, 356.

νήϊος [νηῦς]. Of or for a ship: δόρυ O 410, P 744: ι 384. Cf. ι 498.—Absol. in neut. νήϊον, a piece of ship-timber Γ 62, N 391 = Π 484.

νηΐς [νάω]. A Naiad, a nymph of a spring or river. Defining νύμφη Z 22, Ξ 444, Υ 384.

νῆις, -ιδος [νη- + (ϝ)ιδ-, εἴδω]. Lacking knowledge, unskilled H 198.—Lacking knowledge of, unskilled in. With genit.: ἀέθλων θ 179.

νηκερδής, -ές [νη- + κέρδος]. That brings no gain or profit, profitless: βουλήν P 469: ἔπος ξ 509.

νηκουστέω [νη- + ἀκούω]. To neglect the behest or summons of. With genit.: θεᾶς Υ 14.

νηλεής, -ές [νη- + ἔλεος]. With hyphaeresis νηλής Ι 632. Dat. νηλέϊ Γ 292, Ε 330, Ν 501, Π 345, Τ 266, etc.: δ 743, θ 507, ι 272, μ 372, χ 475, etc. Acc. νηλέα Τ 229. Pitiless, ruthless, relentless, showing no feeling for others, hard: ἦτορ Ι 497. Cf. Ι 632: ι 272 = 368, ι 287.—Absol. in voc.: νηλεές Π 33, 204.—So νηλέα θυμὸν ἔχοντας (steeling our hearts) Τ 229.—Applied to δεσμός Κ 443.—To ὕπνος (as bringing mischief upon one) μ 372.—For νηλεὲς ἦμαρ see ἦμαρ (4) (g). —Epithet of χαλκός Γ 292, Δ 348, Ε 330, Μ 427, Ν 501 = Π 761, Ν 553, Π 345, 561, Ρ 376, Τ 266: δ 743, θ 507, κ 532, λ 45, ξ 418, σ 86, φ 300, χ 475.

νηλῑτις, νηλεῖτις, -ιδος [νη- + ἀλιτ-, ἀλιταίνω]. Guiltless: αἵ νηλίτιδές εἰσιν π 317 = τ 498, χ 418.

νῆμα, -ατος, τό [νέω[2]]. Yarn for spinning δ 134.—In pl., a weaver's work, woven work: μή μοι νήματ' ὄληται β 98 = τ 143 = ω 133.

νημερτέως [adv. fr. next]. Truly ε 98, τ 269.

νημερτής, -ές [νη- + ἁμαρτ-, ἁμαρτάνω]. (1) Unerring, having or speaking with perfect knowledge δ 349 = ρ 140, δ 384, 401, 542.—Infallibly purposed, that shall not fail: βουλήν α 86, ε 30. —(2) Consonant with reality, true: μὴ πάντα νημερτέα εἶπεν (that it was all true that she said) ε 300. Cf. Γ 204: λ 137, ρ 549, 556, 561.—(3) Absol. in neut. pl. νημερτέα, the truth: νημερτέα μυθήσασθε Ζ 376. Cf. γ 19, λ 96, ο 263.—(4) In neut. sing. νημερτές as adv. (a) Clearly, plainly, so that no mistake may be made: ἐνίσπες χ 166.—(b) Truly: ὑπόσχεο Α 514. Cf. Ξ 470: γ 101 = δ 331, γ 327, δ 314, 642, λ 148, μ 112, ψ 35.—(5) In neut. pl. νημερτέα as adv., with certainty, clearly: ἐπεὶ τῶν νόον νημερτέ' ἀνέγνω φ 205.

νηνεμίη, -ης [νήνεμος]. A stillness of the air, a calm: νηνεμίης (in a time of calm) Ε 523.

νηνέμιος, -η, -ον [νήνεμος]. With no wind stirring, breathless: γαλήνη ε 392, μ 169.

νήνεμος, -ον [νη- + ἄνεμος]. Windless: ὅτε τ' ἔπλετο νήνεμος αἰθήρ Θ 556.

νήξομαι, fut. mid. νήχω.

νηός, -οῦ, ὁ. A temple: εἴ ποτέ τοι νηὸν ἔρεψα (app. here a temporary structure of branches) Α 39, νηὸν Ἀθηναίης Ζ 88. Cf. Β 549, Ε 446, Ζ 93 = 274, Ζ 269 = 279, Ζ 297, 308, Η 83: ζ 10, μ 346.

νηπενθής, -ές [νη- + πένθος]. Banishing grief and pain: φάρμακον δ 221.

νηπιάη, -ης, ἡ [νήπιος]. Childish thoughts or ways. In pl.: νηπιάας ὀχέειν α 297.

νηπιαχεύω [νηπίαχος]. Of a child, to sport or play: ὅτε παύσαιτο νηπιαχεύων Χ 502.

νηπίαχος [νήπιος]. Young, of tender years: παισίν Β 338. Cf. Ζ 408, Π 262

νηπιέη, -ης, ἡ [νήπιος]. (1) Childishness, childish ways: ἐν νηπιέῃ Ι 491.—In pl.: ἐπεὶ ποιήσῃ ἀθύρματα νηπιέῃσιν Ο 363.—(2) Folly, thoughtlessness. In pl.: νηπιέῃσι ποδῶν ἀρετὴν ἀναφαίνων Υ 411.—Foolish or thoughtless action. In pl.: τοῖσιν Εὐπείθης ἡγήσατο νηπιέῃσιν ω 469.

νήπιος, -η, -ον. (1) Young, of tender years: τέκνα Β 136. Cf. Δ 238, Ε 480, Ζ 400, Ι 440, Π 8, etc.: β 313, δ 818, ζ 301, λ 449, τ 530, etc.—In reference to the young of a bird or animal Β 311, Λ 113.—Absol. in neut. pl. νήπια, the young of an animal: λέων, ᾧ νήπι' ἄγοντι . . . Ρ 134.—(2) Such as a child's is, feeble: βίη νηπίη [ἐστίν] Λ 561.—(3) Childish, foolish, thoughtless, senseless, credulous: φῆ αἱρήσειν πόλιν, ν. Β 38. Cf. Β 873, Ε 406, Η 401, Π 46, Σ 311, Χ 445 (fond heart), etc.: α 8, γ 146, δ 31, ι 44, φ 85, etc.—In voc. νήπιε Π 833, Σ 295, Φ 99, Χ 333.—Absol. in masc., a fool: ῥεχθὲν ν. ἔγνω Ρ 32 = Υ 198.—In neut. pl., foolish things, folly: νήπια βάζεις δ 32.

νήποινος [νη- + ποινή]. (1) With no compensation or penalty exacted in respect of one, unavenged: νήποινοί κ' ὄλοισθε α 380 = β 145.—(2) In neut. sing. νήποινον as adv., without making compensation or recompense, without compensation or recompense made: βίοτον ν. ἔδουσιν α 160. Cf. α 377 = β 142, ξ 377, 417, σ 280.

νηπύτιος [νη- + ἠπύω. Cf. L. *infans*]. Childish, foolish, senseless. In voc. νηπύτιε Φ 410, 441, 474, 585.—In reference to speech: ἐπέεσσι νηπυτίοισιν Υ 211.—Absol., a fool: νηπύτιοι ὥς Ν 292 = Υ 244. Cf. Υ 200, 431.

Νηρηΐς, -ΐδος [fem. patronymic fr. Νηρεύς]. A daughter of Nereus, a Nereïd or sea-nymph Σ 38, 49, 52.

νῆσος, -ου, ἡ. An island: Ἐχινάων ἱεράων νήσων Β 626. Cf. Β 108, 677, 721, Γ 445, Σ 208, Φ 454, Χ 45: εἶδον νῆσον (that it was an island on which I was) κ 195. Cf. α 50, γ 171, δ 368, ε 13, ι 130, κ 3, μ 143, ν 95, etc.

νῆστις [νη-εδ-τις, νη- + ἐδ-, ἔδω]. Without eating, fasting Τ 156, 207: σ 370.

νητός [νηέω]. Heaped or piled up β 338.

νηῦς, ἡ [cf. L. *navis*]. Genit. νηός (νηϝός) Α 439, Θ 515, Π 1, Ψ 852, etc.: α 171, ι 60, ν 74, τ 243, etc. νεός Ο 423, 693, 704: η 252, ι 482, μ 100, φ 390, etc. Dat. νηΐ. Acc. νῆα Α 141, Ι 137, Ο 417, Τ 277, etc.: α 280, β 212, ν 65, ψ 330, etc. νέα ι 283. Nom. pl. νῆες Β 303, Δ 247, Ν 14, Υ 60, etc.: β 292, ζ 264, ι 64, ρ 288, etc. νέες Β 509, 516, Ν 174, Σ 69, etc.: γ 312, η 9, 36, ι 125. Genit. νηῶν Β 152, Ε 550, Ν 57, Ω 141, etc.: δ 361, ζ 268, κ 123, φ 39, etc. νεῶν Α 48, Θ 490, Ξ 146, Υ 33, etc.: ζ 271, μ 67. Dat. νηυσί Α 26, Ι 47, Ν 1, Χ 89, etc.: α 61, β 18, ο 387, σ 181, etc. νήεσσι Α 71, Δ 239, Μ 112, Ψ 248, etc.: γ 131, λ 399, ξ 260, ω 109, etc. νέεσσι Γ 46, Ν 333, Ο 409, Τ 135, etc.: ξ 230. Acc. νῆας Α 12, Β 8, Μ 7, Σ 14, etc.: γ 180, η 43, ξ 247, ω 43, etc. νέας Α 487, Ν 96, Ξ 392, Ρ 612, etc.: γ 153, κ 15, λ 124, ξ 258, etc. Locative ναῦφι Θ 474, Π 281, Σ 305. This form as ablative Β 794, Μ 225, Ν 700, Π 246: ξ 498. A ship Α 71, 141, 170, 308, 439, 476, etc.: α 171, 211, 260, 280, β 307, 390, etc.—In pl. of the Greek ships drawn up on the Trojan shore and with the κλισίαι forming the camp Α 12, 48, 487, Β 398, 794, Ζ 69, etc.: α 61, δ 248, 255, λ 545, ξ 496, 498, 501, ω 43.—In pl. of the ships of a particular chief Α 306, Ι 185, etc.

νήχω [νέω¹]. Fut. mid. νήξομαι ε 364. (παρα-.) To swim ε 375, 399, 439, η 280.—In mid. : ἐπήν μοι σχεδίην διὰ κῦμα τινάξῃ, νήξομαι ε 364. Cf. η 276, ξ 352, ψ 233, 237.

νίζω. Fut. νίψω τ 376. 3 sing. νίψει τ 356. 3 sing. aor. ἔνιψε Π 229. νίψε Κ 575 : τ 505. Aor. νίψον τ 358. 3 sing. aor. mid. νίψατο Π 230. Pple. νιψάμενος Ω 305 : β 261, μ 336. Pl. νιψάμενοι κ 182. Infin. νίψασθαι α 138, δ 54, η 174, κ 370, ο 137, ρ 93. 3 sing. pf. pass. νένιπται Ω 419. (ἀπο-, ἐξαπο-.) (**1**) To wash, cleanse : σπόγγοισι τραπέζας νίζον α 112. Cf. Π 229.—(**2**) To wash the feet of : νίψον σοῖο ἄνακτος ὁμήλικα τ 358. Cf. τ 374, 392, 505.—With double acc. of person and part : ἥ σε πόδας νίψει τ 356. Cf. τ 376.—(**3**) To wash away or off : ἐπεί σφιν κῦμα θαλάσσης ἱδρῶ νίψεν ἀπὸ χρωτὸς Κ 575. Cf. Λ 830, 846, Ω 419.—With ἀπό, off : ὕδατι νίζοντες ἄπο βρότον Η 425.—(**4**) In mid., to wash (one's hands) : νίψατο αὐτὸς χεῖρας Π 230 : χεῖρας νιψάμενος ἁλός (genit. of material, 'in the . . .') β 261. Cf. κ 182, μ 336.—To wash (one's body). With second acc. of what is washed away or off : χρόα νίζετο ἅλμην ζ 224.—To wash one's hands : νιψάμενος κύπελλον ἐδέξατο Ω 305. Cf. α 138= δ 54=η 174=κ 370=ο 137=ρ 93.

νῑκάω [νίκη]. 1 pl. pa. iterative νῑκάσκομεν λ 512. (**1**) To overcome, vanquish, get the better of, in fight or in a contest : δοκέω νικησέμεν Ἕκτορα Η 192, ἀνδρὶ νικηθέντι γυναῖκ' ἔθηκεν (as a prize for the loser) Ψ 704. Cf. Γ 404, Ν 318, Π 79, Υ 410, Φ 501, Ψ 634, 680, 756 : ν 261, σ 83, 333=393.—(**2**) Absol., to be the conqueror, prove the winner, in fight or in a contest Γ 439, Δ 389, Ε 807, Υ 102, Ψ 669, Γ 71=92 : =σ 46, θ 520, λ 548.—In aor. pple., the winner : τῷ κε νικήσαντι κεκλήσῃ ἄκοιτις Γ 138. Cf. Γ 255, Ψ 702.—In aor. pple. pass., the loser : τῷ νικηθέντι τίθει δέπας Ψ 656. Cf. Ψ 663.—(**3**) In gen., to overcome, get the better of : νόον νίκησε νεοίη (overcame your better judgment) Ψ 604. Cf. σ 319. —With cognate acc. : νίκης, τήν μιν ἐγὼ νίκησα (*i.e.* I won the cause) λ 545.—(**4**) To excel, be first or preeminent among, bear away the palm from : ἀγορῇ ἑ παῦροι νίκων Ο 284. Cf. Ι 130, 272 : λ 512.—(**5**) Absol., to be first or pre-eminent, bear the palm Β 370, 597, Σ 252 : γ 121.—Of an inanimate object : κάλλει ἐνίκα [κρητήρ] (in . . .) Ψ 742.—Of abstractions, to prevail, rule, carry it away : βουλὴ κακὴ νίκησεν κ 46. Cf. Α 576 : =σ 404.

νίκη, -ης, ἡ. (**1**) Victory, the upper hand, in fight or in a contest Γ 457, Δ 13, Ζ 339, Θ 176, Ν 166 (the victory which had eluded his grasp), Ξ 364, Π 689, etc. : χ 236.—(**2**) In gen., victory, getting the better of someone λ 544.

νίσσομαι, νίσομαι [for νι-νσ-ομαι, redup. fr. νσ-, νεσ-, conn. with νέομαι]. (μετα-, ποτι-.) (**1**) To go or come back, return : ἐκ πεδίου νίσοντο Μ 119. Cf. δ 701=ε 19.—(**2**) To take one's way, go, come : πόλεμόνδε Ν 186, Ο 577. Cf. Σ 566.—(**3**) In pres. with fut. sense, to go or come back, return : οὐ γὰρ ἔτ' αὖτις νίσομαι ἐξ Ἀΐδαο Ψ 76. Cf. κ 42.

νιφάς, -άδος, ἡ [νίφω]. Dat. pl. νιφάδεσσι Γ 222. (**1**) A snowflake Γ 222, Μ 156, Τ 357.—So νιφάδες χιόνος Μ 278.—(**2**) Snow : ν. ἠὲ χάλαζα Ο 170.

νιφετός, ὁ [νίφω]. Snow Κ 7 : δ 566.

νιφόεις, -εντος [νίφω]. Snowclad, snowcapt : ὄρεϊ Ν 754. Cf. Ξ 227, Σ 616, Υ 385 : τ 338.

νίφω [cf. L. *niv-*, *nix*, Eng. *snow*]. To snow Μ 280.

νίψω, fut. νίζω.

νοέω [νόος]. (εἰσ-, προ-.) (**1**) To perceive with the eye, see, discern, mark, observe (often with complementary pple. or adj.) : τὸν ὡς ἐνόησεν ἐρχόμενον Γ 21, τῶν οὔ τιν' ἰδέειν δύναμ' οὐδὲ νοῆσαι Ε 475. Cf. Β 391, Γ 30, 396, Δ 200, Ε 95, Ζ 470, Μ 143, Ο 348, Φ 49, etc. : α 58, δ 116, 653, ζ 163, θ 271, μ 248, π 5, τ 232, etc.—Absol. Γ 374, Ε 669, Θ 91, Μ 393, Ρ 483, etc. : δ 148, π 160, τ 478, χ 162, etc.—(**2**) To perceive with the mind, see, mark, understand : οὔ τι δολοφροσύνην ἐνόησεν Τ 112. Cf. Α 522 : ζ 67, σ 228, υ 309, 367.—With dependent clause : τὸ νήπιος οὐκ ἐνόησεν, ὡς . . . ι 442. Cf. χ 32.—Absol. Κ 225 : α 322, φ 257.—With dependent clause : νοῆσαι ὅππως . . . Α 343. Cf. Κ 224, Υ 264, Χ 445.—In pres. pple., not lacking perception, recognizing quickly the calls of expediency or propriety, intelligent, of good sense : καὶ αὐτῇ περ νοεούσῃ Α 577. Cf. Ψ 305 : π 136=ρ 193=281.—(**3**) To think of, propose to oneself, purpose : μή μοι ταῦτα νόει φρεσίν Ι 600. Cf. Ψ 140=193 : β 382=393=δ 795 =ζ 112=σ 187, δ 219, ε 188, 382, ζ 251, π 409, ρ 576 (taken this into his head), ψ 242, 344.—(**4**) To turn over in one's mind, think out, plan, contrive, devise : τοῦτό γ' ἐναίσιμον οὐκ ἐνόησεν β 122, η 299. Cf. Α 543, 549, Η 358=Μ 232, Ι 104, 105, Ψ 415.—Absol. : περίοιδε νοῆσαι Κ 247. Cf. ε 170.—(**5**) To think of, have the wit to say or do : ἀλλ' αὐτὸς νοήσεις γ 26. Cf. σ 230. —With complementary infin. : τὸ οὔ τις ἐνόησε, μηροῦ ἐξερύσαι δόρυ Ε 665.—Followed directly by infin. : οὐκ ἐνόησα καταβῆναι ἰὼν ἐς κλίμακα λ 62.—In mid. : οὐ μάστιγα νοήσαθ' ἑλέσθαι Κ 501.—Absol. : ὅππως οἱ κατὰ μοῖραν ὑποκρίναιτο νοήσας (should hit upon the right interpretation) ο 170.—(**6**) To think of a thing, have it occur to one : ἢ λάθετ' ἢ οὐκ ἐνόησεν Ι 537.—(**7**) To think, with the thought directly reported Ο 81.—(**8**) To be minded or disposed, have one's mind made up. With infin. : νοέω καὶ αὐτὸς Ἕκτορα λῦσαι Ω 560. Cf. Χ 235.—(**9**) To consider the case of, make up one's mind as to : νόησον Αἰνείαν, ἢ . . . ἦ . . . Υ 310.

νόημα, -ατος, τό [νοέω]. (**1**) A thought, idea, notion : τίπτε τοι ἐνὶ φρεσὶ τοῦτο ν. ἔπλετο ; β 363. Cf. Η 456, Σ 295 : η 36, ο 326, ρ 403.—(**2**) The mind : οὐκέτι τοι φρένες ἔμπεδοι [εἰσιν] οὐδὲ ν. σ 215. Cf. σ 220, υ 82, 346.—(**3**) Mental power or reach, intelligence : σεῖο κε νοήματι προβαλοίμην (in . . .) Τ 218.—(**4**) One's mind, nature, disposition: αἰεί τοι τοιοῦτον ἐνὶ στήθεσσι ν. ν 330. Cf. Ω 40: ζ 183.—(5) What one has in one's mind, a purpose, design, intention: οὐχ Ἕκτορι πάντα νοήματ' ἐκτελέει K 104. Cf. Σ 328: θ 559, ψ 30.—In collective sense: Διὸς νόημα (his purposes) P 409.—(6) A device or contrivance: νοήμασι κερδαλέοισιν θ 548. Cf. β 121.—(7) What comes into one's mind or occurs to one: οὔ τι νοήματος ἤμβροτεν ἐσθλοῦ (the right thing to do) η 292. Cf. ξ 273.

νοήμων, -ονος [νοέω]. Right-thinking: οὔ (τι) νοήμονες οὐδὲ δίκαιοι β 282, γ 133, ν 209.

νόθος, -η. Not born in wedlock, bastard, illegitimate B 727, Δ 499, E 70, Θ 284, Λ 102, 490, N 173, 694 = O 333, Π 738.—Absol., a bastard: ὁ νόθος ἡνιόχευεν Λ 103.

νομεύς, ὁ [νομ-, νεμ-, νέμω]. A herdsman or shepherd Λ 697, O 632, Σ 525, 577, 583: δ 413, π 3, 27, ρ 214 = υ 175, ρ 246, φ 19.—Joined with ἄνδρες P 65.

νομεύω [νομεύς]. To tend or drive (one's flock): ἐνόμευε μῆλα ι 217. Cf. ι 336, κ 85.

νομόνδε [acc. of next + -δε (1)]. To the pasture: ν. ἐξέσσυτο μῆλα ι 438. Cf. Σ 575.

νομός, -οῦ, ὁ [νομ-, νεμ-, νέμω]. A pasture or grazing-ground B 475, Z 511 = O 268, Σ 587: ι 217, κ 159.—ἐπέων πολὺς ν. ἔνθα καὶ ἔνθα Υ 249, app., much room to roam hither and thither, wide scope.

νόος, -ου, ὁ. Contr. νοῦς κ 240. (1) The mind: μὴ κεῦθε νόῳ A 363, ν. ἔμπεδος ἦεν Λ 813. Cf. A 132, I 514, K 122, M 255, O 52, etc.: α 347, β 92, η 263, ν 255, υ 366, etc.—(2) Mental power or reach, intelligence: περὶ νόον ἐστὶ βροτῶν (in . . .) α 66. Cf. K 226, N 732, O 643, Σ 419: κ 494.—(3) Sense, good sense, judgment, discretion: ν. ἀπόλωλε καὶ αἰδώς O 129. Cf. K 391, Υ 133: ζ 320, η 73.—(4) One's mind, spirit, nature, disposition: σοὶ ἀτάρβητος ν. ἐστίν Γ 63. Cf. Π 35, Ψ 484: α 3, ε 190, ζ 121 = ι 176 = ν 202, θ 576, σ 136, 332 = 392, σ 381.—(5) One's mind, will, liking: ὅπῃ τοι ν. ἔπλετο X 185. Cf. I 108 (not by my good will), Υ 25.—(6) What one has in his mind, his mind, purpose, design, intent, what he has in view: ὄφρα κ' ἔτι γνῶμεν Τρώων νόον X 382. Cf. B 192, H 447, Θ 143: β 124, 281, δ 256, ε 103, 137, λ 177, ν 229, φ 205, χ 215.—(7) A plan, design, device, a scheme, system or method of action: τόνδε νόον ἔχοντες Δ 309. Cf. I 104, O 509, Ω 367: νόον σχέθε τόνδ' ἐνὶ θυμῷ ξ 490. Cf. ε 23 = ω 479.—(8) Counsel, concerting of measures, contriving, planning, scheming: νόῳ καὶ ἐπίφρονι βουλῇ γ 128. Cf. Ξ 62: δ 267, μ 211, ν 305, π 197, 374, τ 326.—(9) What one has in his mind, his expectation, hope, desire: τοῖσιν ὅδ' ἦν ν. O 699. Cf. Ψ 149.—(10) What one has in his mind, what he knows or can tell: δαῆναι ἐμὸν νόον δ 493.

νοστέω [νόστος]. (ἀπο-.) (1) To come to or reach a specified place, arrive: κεῖσέ με νοστήσαντα δ 619 = ο 119.—(2) To return, come back: ὄφρα μένοιεν νοστήσαντα ἄνακτα N 38.—Implying a safe return E 157, K 247, N 232, P 207, 239, 636, Σ 238, X 444, Ω 705: κ 285, 419.—(3) To return home, reach one's home: ἢ εὖ ἦε κακῶς νοστήσομεν B 253.—Implying more or less a happy or safe return E 212, O 374, Σ 330, Ψ 145: α 36, 163, 268, ν 43, τ 463, ω 400, etc.—With οἴκαδε Δ 103 = 121, Σ 60 = 441, Σ 90: β 343, θ 102, μ 43, etc.—With οἰκόνδε E 687.—With ὅνδε δόμονδε α 83, υ 329, etc.

νόστιμος [νόστος]. (1) Of or pertaining to one's home-coming: νόστιμον ἦμαρ. See ἦμαρ (4) (h).—(2) Destined, that may be expected, to return safe home: οὐκέτι ν. ἐστιν τ 85, υ 333. Cf. δ 806.

νόστος, -ου, ὁ [cf. νέομαι]. (1) A coming to or reaching a specified place, a getting to it: νέων ἐπιμαίεο νόστου γαίης Φαιήκων (to the land of the . . .) ε 344.—(2) A returning or going back: νῆας ἔπι K 509. Cf. I 622.—(3) A going home, one's return home or home-coming, one's journey home α 326, γ 132, 142, δ 497, ε 108, ι 37, 97, 102, κ 15, λ 110 = μ 137, λ 384, ο 3, σ 242, ψ 351, etc.—Implying more or less a happy or safe return B 155, 251, I 413, 434, Π 82: α 5, 13, 77, 94 (to seek for tidings of his homeward bound father), 287 (learn that he has so far safely accomplished the homeward journey), γ 160, δ 519, ζ 14, μ 419, ξ 61, χ 323, etc.

νόσφι(ν). (I) Adv. (1) Away, far away: ν. ἐόντες γ 193.—At a distance, away, absent: ὅτε σὺ ν. γένηαι κ 486. Cf. X 332: ξ 147, 527.—(2) Apart, aloof, by himself or themselves: ν. καθήμεναι Δ 9. Cf. E 322, K 416, O 244, P 382, 408: λ 544.—(3) Away, off, to a distance, apart, aloof: ν. κιόντα Λ 284, Ξ 440. Cf. Λ 80, Ω 583: δ 289, θ 286, ν 164.—In reference to direction, away, aloof: ν. ἰδών ρ 304. Cf. N 4.—(II) Prep. with genit. (1) Far from: ν. φίλων πάντων Ξ 256. Cf. T 422, X 508.—In the absence of: οὓς ἐπέφνετε ν. ἐμεῖο Φ 135.—(2) Apart or aloof from, at a distance from: ν. πόληος α 185 = ω 308, π 383, ω 212. Cf. Z 443, Σ 465: δ 367.—Apart from, having separated oneself from or left: ὅτε τ' ἤλυθε ν. Ἀχαιῶν E 803.—Without reference to place: τοί κεν Ἀχαιῶν ν. βουλεύωσιν B 347.—(3) Away from, to a distance from: ἑτάρων ν. λιασθεὶς A 349. Cf. Θ 490, Ψ 365.—(4) Apart from, without the help or countenance of: πολλὰ πονήσατο νόσφιν ἐμεῖο I 348. Cf. ξ 9 = 451.—(5) Apart from, except: ν. θεῶν M 466. Cf. Υ 7: α 20.

νοσφίζομαι [νόσφι]. Aor. νοσφισάμην τ 339. 3 sing. νοσφίσατο λ 425. Nom. sing. fem. pple. νοσφισσαμένη τ 579, φ 77, 104. Acc. νοσφισσαμένην δ 263. Aor. pple. in pass. form νοσφισθεὶς λ 73. (1) To turn away in incredulousness, disdain or aversion: ψεῦδός κεν φαῖμεν καὶ νοσφιζοίμεθα μᾶλλον B 81 = Ω 222. Cf. λ 425.—With genit.: πατρός ψ 98.—(2) To turn one's back, depart: μή μ' ἄκλαυτον καταλείπειν, νοσφισθεὶς λ 73.—(3) To turn one's back upon, leave, quit: τόδε δῶμα τ 579 = φ 77, φ 104. Cf. δ 263, τ 339.

νοτίη, -ης, ἡ [Νότος]. A shower Θ 307.

νότιος [Νότος]. (1) Flowing, running: ἱδρώς Λ 811, Ψ 715.—(2) Absol. as sb., the part towards the south: ὑψοῦ ἐν νοτίῳ νῆ' ὅρμισαν δ 785, θ 55 (*i.e.* just outside the haven (which is thought of as facing south) to await the evening land-breeze).

Νότος, -ου, ὁ. (1) The south wind B 145 (see under Εὖρος), B 395, Γ 10, Λ 306, Π 765, Φ 334: γ 295, ε 295, 331, μ 289, 325, 326, 427.—(2) The south: πρὸς Νότου ν 111.

νοῦς. See νόος.

νοῦσος, -ου, ἡ. A disease, illness, ailment A 10, N 667, 670: ε 395, ι 411, λ 172, 200, ο 408.

νυ, *enclitic* [shortened form of νῦν]. (1) In temporal sense like νῦν (1) (2) (3): ἤ νύ σέ που δέος ἴσχει E 812. Cf. A 28, B 258, Ξ 340, O 440, etc.: τόθι γάρ νύ οἱ αἴσιμον ἦεν ναιέμεναι ο 239. Cf. α 244, β 327, ζ 275, κ 562, etc.—In past suppositions contrary to fact: καί νύ κεν εἴρυσσεν Γ 373. Cf. E 311, etc.: δ 363, ι 79, etc.—Strengthening δή T 95, etc.—(2) Like νῦν (5): ἦ ῥά νύ μοί τι πίθοιο Δ 93, etc.—(3) As affirmative particle: θεοί νύ μοι αἴτιοί εἰσιν (it is the gods that . . .) Γ 164, θεός νύ τίς ἐστι κοτήεις (it must be . . .) E 191. Cf. Γ 183, Θ 32, O 128, Π 622, T 169, etc.: α 32, 347, μ 280, τ 501, υ 114, etc.—(4) In questions: τί νύ σ' ἔτρεφον; A 414. Cf. Δ 242, Φ 474, etc.: δ 462, ζ 25, 149, υ 193, etc.—In indirect questions: γνώσῃ ὅς θ' ἡγεμόνων κακὸς ὅς τέ νυ λαῶν B 365. Cf. α 407.

νυκτερίς, -ίδος, ἡ [νυκτ-, νύξ]. A bat: τῷ ἐχόμην ὡς νυκτερὶς μ 433. Cf. ω 6.

νύμφη, -ης, ἡ. Voc. νύμφα Γ 130: δ 743. (1) A young woman, a maiden I 560.—(2) A nymph, one of a class of semi-divine female beings imagined as inhabiting the sea, fountains, islands, caves, etc.: νυμφάων, αἵ τ' ἄλσεα νέμονται καὶ πηγὰς ποταμῶν καὶ πίσεα Υ 8. Cf. Ω 616: α 71, ζ 105, 123, ι 154, μ 132, 318, ν 107, 350, 355, ξ 435, ρ 211, 240.—Of Calypso α 14, 86, δ 557 =ε 14=ρ 143, ε 6, 30, 57, 149, 153, 196, 230 =κ 543, ψ 333.—Defined by νηΐς Z 21, Ξ 444, Υ 384.—By ὀρεστιάς Z 420.—By νηϊάς ν 104=348, 356.—(3) A bride, a woman about to be married Σ 492.—(4) A bride, a woman not long married λ 38, 447.—Applied to matrons. To Helen Γ 130.—To Penelope δ 743.

νυμφίος [νύμφη]. Not long married: παιδὸς νυμφίου Ψ 223. Cf. η 65.

νῦν. (1) At the present time, now: οἷοι νῦν βροτοί εἰσιν E 304. Cf. A 109, B 254, H 129, M 271, etc.: α 82, γ 69, ρ 245, σ 239, etc.—At the present time, on the present occasion, now, as opposed in terms to the past or future: ἢ νῦν δηθύνοντ' ἢ ὕστερον αὖτις ἰόντα A 27. Cf. A 455, Γ 439, Δ 321, etc.: τὸ πρίν· ἀτὰρ μὲν νῦν γε . . . δ 32. Cf. α 369, γ 366, ζ 243, etc.—(2) In the time following more or less directly the present, now: νῦν δ' εἶμι Φθίηνδε A 169. Cf. A 59, 421, B 12, H 226, etc.: α 200, β 314, γ 359, δ 685, etc.—(3) Looking back to an occurrence in the past, now: ὃς νῦν Ἀργείοισι κήδε' ἐφῆκεν A 445. Cf. A 506, B 274, Δ 12, N 772, etc.: α 35, 43, β 28, ζ 172, etc.—So in a past supposition contrary to fact: νῦν ἂν ὕστατα λωβήσαιο A 232 =B 242.—(4) νῦν δέ, but as it is: τιμήν μοι ὄφελλεν ἐγγυαλίξαι· νῦν δ' οὐδέ με τυτθὸν ἔτεισεν A 354. Cf. A 417, B 82, I 519, M 326, etc.: α 166, β 79, ξ 371, σ 403, etc.—(5) In sentences expressing a command, request, exhortation or wish, with the temporal sense weakened or effaced, now: νῦν ἐμέθεν ξύνες ὦκα B 26. Cf. A 407, E 129, Ξ 219, Φ 428, etc.: νῦν μήτ' εἴης μήτε γένοιο σ 79. Cf. α 271, β 281, δ 395, θ 202, κ 320, λ 441, etc.—(6) Continuing an enumeration, now, and now: νῦν αὖ τοὺς ὅσσοι . . . τῶν αὖ ἦν ἀρχὸς Ἀχιλλεύς B 681.—(7) In a question, well now: πῶς γὰρ νῦν . . . ; K 424. Cf. σ 223.

νυν, *enclitic.* (1) =νῦν (1) K 105.—(2) =νῦν (5) Ψ 485.

νύξ, νυκτός, ἡ [cf. L. *nox*, Eng. *night*]. (1) Night, the night, the period of darkness: ἐπήλυθε ν. Θ 488. Cf. A 47, B 57, Γ 11, H 282, Ξ 78, Ω 366, etc.: νύκτα διὰ δνοφερήν ο 50. Cf. δ 429, ε 294, ι 143, κ 86, τ 66, ψ 243, etc.—(2) A night considered as a space of time: πολλὰς ἀΰπνους νύκτας ἴαυον I 325. Cf. E 490, Θ 529, I 470, K 188, 251, 252, 312=399, Σ 274, 340, X 432, Ψ 186, Ω 73, 745: β 105, 345, γ 151, ε 466, μ 312, ρ 515, τ 340, υ 85, χ 195, etc.—(3) A night considered as a point or unit of time or as one of a series: δεκάτῃ ν. I 474. Cf. I 78, K 497, Σ 251, X 102: τῇδε νυκτὶ υ 88. Cf. η 253=ξ 314, μ 447, ξ 93, σ 272.—(4) Night personified Ξ 259, 261.—(5) Darkness, a pall or cloud of darkness: Ζεὺς ἐπὶ νύκτα τάνυσεν ὑσμίνῃ Π 567. Cf. E 23, 506: λ 19, υ 351, 362, ψ 372.—The darkness of death or of stupor: ὄσσε ν. ἐκάλυψεν E 310=Λ 356. Cf. E 659=N 580, N 425, Ξ 439, X 466.

νύξε, 3 sing. aor. νύσσω.

νυός, -οῦ, ἡ. A daughter-in-law: νυὸν ἀνδρῶν αἰχμητάων (Helen being regarded as having contracted affinity with her husband's nation) Γ 49, θυγατέρες ἰδὲ νυοί Ω 166. Cf. X 65: γ 451.

νύσσα, -ης, ἡ [νύσσω. 'The scratch']. (1) The starting-line in a race: τοῖσιν ἀπὸ νύσσης τέτατο δρόμος Ψ 758: θ 121.—(2) The turning-post: ἐν νύσσῃ τοι ἵππος ἀριστερὸς ἐγχριμφθήτω Ψ 338. Cf. Ψ 332, 344.

νύσσω. 3 sing. aor. νύξε E 46, Λ 96, M 395, O 536, Π 404, Ψ 819, etc. Pple. νύξας ξ 485. (1) To wound, pierce or strike by a thrust with a pointed weapon, make a thrust at with such a weapon: τὸν ἔγχεϊ νύξε κατὰ δεξιὸν ὦμον E 46. Cf. Λ 96, O 536, Π 346, Υ 397, etc.—Without expressed object Λ 235=P 48, N 147=O 278=P 731, Ψ 819.—Sim. in mid. of reciprocal action Ξ 26= Π 637.—(2) App. implying no more than striking with the hand: χείρεσσ' ἀσπίδα νύσσων Π 704.—(3) To give one a nudge (with the elbow): ἀγκῶνι νύξας ξ 485.

νώ. See νῶϊ.

νωθής. Obstinately lazy, refractory Λ 559.

νῶϊ. Genit. and dat. νῶϊν. This form as

nom. Π 99. Acc. νῶϊ. Also νώ Ε 219: ο 475. Pron. of the 1st person dual, we: καὶ νῶϊ μεδώμεθ' ἀλκῆς Δ 418, νῶϊν ἐπέντυε μώνυχας ἵππους Θ 374. Cf. Θ 428, Χ 88, etc.: δ 160, 172, ο 475, etc.

νωΐτερος, -η, -ον [νῶϊ]. Our (of two persons): λέχος Ο 39: ὅπα μ 185.

νωλεμές (cf. next). Without cease, cessation, pause, relaxation of effort, blenching: μάχην ἔχουσιν Ξ 58. Cf. Ρ 413.—Strengthened by αἰεί Ι 317 = Ρ 148, Ρ 385, Τ 232: π 191, χ 228.

νωλεμέως [cf. prec.] = prec.: κίνυντο φάλαγγες Δ 428. Cf. Ε 492, Ν 3, 780: πίεζεν δ 288. Cf. ι 435, λ 413, μ 437, υ 24.

νωμάω [νέμω]. (1) To distribute or give out among a company: σπλάγχνα υ 252.—Without expressed object Α 471 = Ι 176 := γ 340 = φ 272, η 183, ν 54 = σ 425.—(2) To handle, wield, move, control: σκῆπτρον Γ 218. Cf. Ε 594, Η 238, Ο 677: κ 32, μ 218, φ 245, 393, 400, χ 10.—To put in motion, ply (the limbs, etc.): γούνατ' ἐνώμα Κ 358, Χ 144. Cf. Ο 269, Χ 24.—In reference to the mind, to apply it (skilfully) to the matter in hand, have it in (constant) practice or readiness: νόον πολυκερδέα νωμῶν ν 255.—Sim. in reference to the contents of the mind: κέρδε' ἐνώμας σ 216. Cf. υ 257.

νώνυμνος, -ον [= next]. (1) = next (1) Μ 70 = Ν 227 = Ξ 70. —(2) Undistinguished, obscure, inglorious: γενεήν α 222.

νώνυμος, -ον [νη- + ὄνυμα, Aeolic form of ὄνομα]. (1) Nameless, the very name lost: ὅπως ἀπὸ φῦλον ὄληται νώνυμον ξ 182.—(2) Unknown, little known, obscure: οὐδέ τι λίην οὕτω νώνυμός ἐστιν [ἥδε γαῖα] ν 239.

νῶροψ, -οπος. App., gleaming, glancing, or the like. Epithet of χαλκός Β 578, Η 206, Λ 16, Ν 406, Π 130, Ξ 383 := ω 467 = 500.

νῶτον, -ου, τό. (1) The back: οὐκ ἂν ἐν αὐχένι πέσοι βέλος οὐδ' ἐνὶ νώτῳ Ν 289. Cf. Ε 147, Υ 279, Φ 69, Ψ 714: ρ 463.—Of horses Β 765.—Of sheep ι 441.—Of a wild boar Ν 473.—The back of an animal cut off for use as food, the chine Ι 207: θ 475.—In pl., app., slices cut from the back: νώτοισι γέραιρεν Η 321: ξ 437. Cf. δ 65.—(2) In pl. in sing. sense: μετὰ νῶτα βαλών Θ 94. Cf. Ν 547, Υ 414: ζ 225.—Of a ram ι 433.—Of a deer κ 161.—Of a serpent Β 308.—Of the surface of the sea: ἐπ' εὐρέα νῶτα θαλάσσης Β 159, Θ 511, Υ 228: γ 142, δ 313, 362, 560 = ε 17 = 142 = ρ 146.

νωχελίη, -ης, ἡ. Remissness, supineness, tardiness in action: βραδυτῆτί τε νωχελίῃ τε Τ 411.

ξαίνω. To comb or card (wool) χ 423.

ξανθός, -ή, -όν. Yellow. Of horses, bay or chestnut Ι 407, Λ 680.—Of hair, yellow, fair Α 197, Ψ 141: ν 399, 431.—As a personal epithet, of the fair hair, fair-haired. Of Meleager Β 642.—Of Menelaus Γ 284, 434, Δ 183, 210, etc.: α 285, γ 168, 257, 326, etc.—So κάρη ξανθὸς Μενέλαος ο 133.—Of Demeter Ε 500.—Of Agamede Λ 740.—Of Rhadamanthus δ 564, η 323.

ξεινήϊος [ξεῖνος]. (1) Such as may fitly be given by a host to a guest: δῶρα ω 273.—(2) Absol. in neut., a present given by a host to a guest, or given one to the other by persons between whom the ξεῖνος relationship exists (see ξεῖνος (2)): ἀλλήλοισι πόρον ξεινήϊα Ζ 218. Cf. Κ 269, Λ 20: θ 389, ι 267.—Sarcastically: τοῦτό (*i.e.* the stroke with the spear) τοι ἀντὶ ποδὸς ξεινήϊον [ἔσται] χ 290. Cf. ι 370.—(3) Absol. in neut. pl., fare or good things put before a guest: παράθες οἱ ξεινήϊα Σ 408. Cf. γ 490, δ 33.

ξεινίζω [ξεῖνος]. 1 pl. fut. ξεινίσσομεν η 190. Aor. ἐξείνισσα Γ 207: τ 194, ω 266, 271. 2 sing. ξείνισας τ 217. ξείνισσας ω 288. 3 ξείνισε Ζ 217. ξείνισσε Γ 232, Ζ 174. Infin. ξεινίσαι ξ 322. To receive or entertain hospitably, treat as an honoured guest Γ 207, 232, Ζ 174, 217: γ 355, η 190, ξ 322, τ 194 = ω 271, τ 217, ω 266, 288.

ξείνιος [ξεῖνος]. (1) That guards the obligations arising from the relationship of guest and host and the claim of strangers to protection. Epithet of Zeus Ν 625: ι 271, ξ 284.—(2) Absol. in neut., a present given by a host to a guest ι 229, 365, τ 185.—Sarcastically ι 356, υ 296.—(3) Absol. in neut. pl., fare or good things put before a guest Λ 779, Σ 387 := ε 91, ξ 404, ο 188.—Sarcastically ι 517.

ξεινοδόκος, -ου, ὁ [ξεῖνος + δοκ-, δέχομαι]. A host, one's host Γ 354: θ 210, 543, ο 55, 70, σ 64.

ξεῖνος, -ου, ὁ. (1) A foreigner or stranger. (a) A foreigner, one belonging to another land: ἐπ' ἀνθρώπους ξείνους ἠδ' οἷσιν ἀνάσσεις Ω 202.—One not of one's own immediate folk: ξεῖνοί τε καὶ αὐτοῦ βώτορες ξ 102. Cf. ρ 382.—(b) A stranger, one who comes into, or finds himself in, a land not his own: εἰσῆλθε Μυκήνας ξ. Δ 377. Cf. Δ 387: η 24, σ 106 (wanderers or vagabonds), τ 333 (travellers), φ 292.—Such a person regarded as being under the guardianship of Zeus, as entitled to protection and aid: πρὸς Διός εἰσι ξεῖνοί τε πτωχοί τε ζ 208 = ξ 58. Cf. θ 546, ι 270, 478, ξ 57, π 108, σ 222, etc.—(c) A stranger, a person whom one has not seen before, an unknown person who presents himself before one: πόθεν τοι ξ. ὅδ' ἵκετο; π 57. Cf. α 120, δ 26, ζ 209, θ 28, ξ 414, ρ 10, σ 401, υ 129, etc.—Vocatively α 123, γ 71, δ 371, ζ 187, etc.—Vocatively by a ξ. to one of those among whom he has come θ 166, ξ 53.—(2) One of two persons (in pl. the persons) dwelling at a distance from each other between whom there exists a special tie of friendship and mutual hospitality: ξ. μοι πατρώϊός ἐσσι Ζ 215. Cf. Ζ 224, 231, Ν 661, Ο 532, Ρ 150, 584, Φ 42: ξ. ἐμός ἐστιν λ 338. Cf. α 105, 176, 187, 313, ι 18, ο 196, τ 191, ω 104, etc.—(3) A host, one's host: ξείνια παρέθηκεν, ἅ τε ξείνοις θέμις ἐστίν Λ 779. Cf. θ 208, ι 268, τ 371.—(4) A guest, one's guest: ξεινοδόκοι καὶ ξ. θ 543. Cf. γ 350, ο 54, 73, 74, υ 295 = φ 313, φ 27.

ξεινοσύνη, -ης, ἡ [ξεῖνος]. The ξεῖνος relationship (see ξεῖνος (2)) φ 35.

ξενίη, -ης, ἡ [ξεν-, ξεῖνος]. Hospitable bounty:

μίξεσθαι ξενίῃ (in mutual hospitality) ω 314. Cf. ω 286.

ξένιος, -η, -ον [=ξείνιος]. (**1**) That serves as a symbol of the obligations of a guest in reference to his host or of the claims of a stranger to protection: ἴστω ξενίη τράπεζα ξ 158=ρ 155=υ 230.—(**2**)=ξείνιος (1) ξ 389.—(**3**) Absol. in neut. pl. =ξείνιος (3) ο 514, 546.

ξερός. Dry. Absol. in neut., the dry land, the shore: ποτὶ ξερὸν ἠπείροιο ε 402.

ξεστός, -ή, -όν [ξεσ-, ξέω]. Smoothed, smooth, wrought, polished: αἰθούσῃσιν (of wrought stone) Ζ 243, Υ 11, λίθοιο 244, 248. Cf. Σ 504: α 138=δ 54=η 174=κ 370=ο 137=ρ 93, γ 406, θ 6, κ 211 =253, μ 172, ξ 350, π 408, σ 33, τ 566, χ 72.—Of the Trojan horse: ἵππῳ ἔνι ξεστῷ δ 272.

ξέω. 3 sing. aor. ἔξεσε Ε 81. ξέσσε ε 245, ρ 341, φ 44. (ἀμφι-.) (**1**) To remove roughness or irregularities from the surface of, smooth, work up ε 245, ρ 341=φ 44, ψ 199.—(**2**) With ἀπό, to slice off: ἀπὸ δ' ἔξεσε χεῖρα Ε 81.

†**ξηραίνω** [ξηρός=ξερός]. 3 sing. aor. pass. ἐξηράνθη. (ἀγ-.) To dry up Φ 345, 348.

ξίφος, -εος, τό. Dat. pl. ξιφέεσσι Η 273, Π 337, Ρ 530. ξίφεσι Ν 147, Ξ 26, Ο 712, Π 637, etc.: χ 443, ω 527. A sword Α 194, 210, 220, Β 45, Γ 18, etc.: β 3, θ 406, λ 531, π 80, χ 326, etc.

ξύλον, -ου, τό. (**1**) A piece of wood, a post Ψ 327.—(**2**) In pl., wood for burning, firewood: ξύλα πολλὰ λέγεσθε Θ 507. Cf. Θ 547, Σ 347, Φ 364, Ω 778: γ 429, θ 436, ξ 418, ο 322, etc.

ξύλοχος, -ου, ἡ [ξύλον]. A wood, coppice, thicket Ε 162, Λ 415, Φ 573: δ 335=ρ 126, τ 445.

ξύμβλητο, 3 sing. aor. mid. See συμβάλλω.

ξύν. See σύν. **ξυμ-, ξυν-.** See συμ-, συν-.

ξυνέαξε, 3 sing. aor. See συνάγνυμι.

ξυνέηκε, 3 sing. aor. See συνίημι.

ξυνελάσσαι, aor. infin. See συνελαύνω.

ξύνες, aor. imp. See συνίημι.

ξυνέσεσθαι, fut. infin. See σύνειμι[1].

ξύνεσις. See σύνεσις.

ξύνετο, 3 sing. aor. mid. See συνίημι.

ξῡνήϊος [ξυνός]. In common: τεύχε' ἀμφότεροι ξυνήϊα ταῦτα φερέσθων Ψ 809.—Absol. in neut. pl. ξυνήϊα, a common store: οὔ τί που ἴδμεν ξυνήϊα κείμενα πολλά (laid up in abundance) Α 124.

ξυνίει, imp. See συνίημι.

ξύνιεν, 3 pl. impf. See συνίημι.

ξύνισαν, 3 pl. impf. See σύνειμι[2].

ξυνιών, pres. pple. See σύνειμι[2].

ξῡνός, -ή, -όν. Common: γαῖ' ἔτι ξυνὴ [ἐστιν] Ο 193. Cf. Π 262.—Impartial Σ 309.

ξυνοχή. See συνοχή.

ξυρόν, -οῦ, τό. A razor. Fig.: ἐπὶ ξυροῦ ἵσταται ἀκμῆς ἢ . . . ἠὲ . . . Κ 173.

ξυστόν, -οῦ, τό [neut. of ξυστός, vbl. adj. from next. 'That which is worked smooth']. (**1**) A spear Δ 469=Λ 260, Λ 565, Ν 497.—(**2**) Some kind of long pole used in sea-fighting Ο 388, 677.

ξύω. (ἀπο-.) To remove irregularities from the surface of, scrape smooth: λίστροισιν δάπεδον ξῦον χ 456.—To treat so as to produce a smooth surface upon: ἑανόν, ὅν οἱ Ἀθήνη ἔξυσ' ἀσκήσασα Ξ 179.

ὁ, ἡ, τό. Genit. τοῦ, τῆς, τοῦ. Genit. masc. and neut. τοῖο Α 380, 493, etc.: γ 334, 388, etc. Genit. dual τοῖϊν Λ 110, etc.: σ 34. Nom. pl. τοί Α 447, Β 52, etc.: α 112, 250, etc. Fem. ταί Γ 5, etc.: ζ 90, etc. Genit. pl. fem. τάων Δ 46, Ε 320, etc.: β 119, η 117, etc. Dat. τῇσι Ζ 298, etc.: ζ 101, etc. τῇς Ε 750, etc.: δ 721, etc. (**1**) The substantival article. (**a**) As anaphoric pronoun of the 3rd person, he, she, it: ὁ γὰρ νοῦσον ἀνὰ στρατὸν ὦρσεν Α 9. Cf. Α 12, 29, 43, 58, 221, etc.: α 9, 13, 31, 113, 249, 277, etc.—ὁ (οἱ) μὲν . . . ὁ (οἱ) δὲ . . ., one (some) . . . the other ((the) others) . . . : οἱ μὲν δάμεν, οἱ δὲ λίποντο Μ 14. Cf. Β 90, Σ 499, etc.: α 24, ε 477, η 104, κ 85, etc.—With γε Α 65, 261, 548, etc.: α 4, 195, etc.—So in resumption in a second clause: νῆας ἔπηξε, πολὺν δ' ὅ γε λαὸν ἀγείρας βῆ Β 664. Cf. Γ 409, etc.: β 327, etc.—Of the 1st person: ὁ δ' ἀλλοδαπῷ ἐνὶ δήμῳ πολεμίζω Τ 324.—(**b**) Sometimes to be translated 'this,' 'that,' in pl. 'these (those) things, matters, etc.': τό τοι κὴρ εἴδεται εἶναι Α 228, τῶν οὐκ ἄν τι φέροις 301. Cf. Α 318, Ρ 228, etc.: α 10, 74 (from that time), ι 393, ξ 444, ω 255, etc.—With γε: εἰ τό γ' ἄμεινον Α 116, etc.: μὴ μητέρ' ἄξευ τό γε (to that point) ρ 401, etc.—(**c**) In dat. sing. fem. τῇ, in that place or spot, there: τῇ τόν γε μένον δ 847. Cf. Θ 327, Λ 520, etc.: μ 62, etc.—Thither: τῇ γ' ἐλθόντες Ζ 435. Cf. Ο 360, etc.: θ 556.—So Ο 46.—(**2**) The attributive article. With sb. or proper name in apposition: ἡ δ' ἅμα τοῖσι γυνὴ κίεν Α 348, τοὺς δὲ κατὰ πρύμνας ἔλσαι Ἀχαιούς 409. Cf. Δ 20, 391, 502, Ε 449, etc.: α 439, β 365, γ 450, δ 353, ε 94, etc.—(**3**) Passing into the definite article. (**a**) The article of contrast: παῖδα δ' ἐμοὶ λύσαιτε, τὰ δ' ἄποινα δέχεσθαι (and on the other side accept the ransom) Α 20, ἢ τῶν πλεόνων Λυκίων ἀπὸ θυμὸν ἕλοιτο (more Lycians instead) Ε 673. Cf. Α 340, Β 217, 278, Δ 399, etc. Also in *Od. passim.*—With adjectives, numerals, genitives, etc.: τῇ δεκάτῃ Α 54, τὸν ἐμὸν χόλον Δ 42, τοὺς τέσσαρας Ε 271, τὴν αὐτοῦ Ι 342. Cf. Α 6, 165, 198, Ζ 201, 435, Θ 525, Ι 320, Λ 613, Π 358, Ψ 265, etc. Also in *Od. passim.*—(**b**) The defining article: ὁ γέρων Α 33, τὸν ὄνειρον Β 80. Cf. Α 35, 552, Β 275 (conveying a hostile or contemptuous tone), 351, Ε 265, 308, 320, Η 412, Κ 97, Λ 142, Ξ 280, Υ 147, Ψ 75, etc. Also in *Od. passim.*—With an infin.: τὸ φυλάσσειν υ 52.—(**4**) As relative (accented throughout; except in Α 125, Ι 167: δ 349=ρ 140 following the antecedent, and most commonly referring to a definite antecedent). (**a**) μῆνιν, ἣ μυρί' Ἀχαιοῖς ἄλγε' ἔθηκεν Α 2. Cf. Α 36, 72, 234, 319, 321, 336, etc.: ἔτος, τῷ οἱ ἐπεκλώσαντο νέεσθαι α 17. Cf. α 23, 97, 344, 430, etc.—(**b**) With τε: συσί, τῶν τε σθένος οὐκ ἀλαπαδνόν Ε 783. Cf. Β 262, etc.: α 338, γ 73, etc.—(**c**) With final force. With subj. and κεν: δῶρα φερέμεν, τά κε θυμὸν ἰήνῃ Ω 119.—(d) (α) With fut., subj. or opt. in conditional relative sentences. For the examples and constructions see Table at end (III) (B) (a) (1), (b) (1), (D) (11) (20) (26) (32). —(β) With subj. in a simile: ἐκ νήσου, τὴν δήϊοι ἀμφιμάχωνται Σ 208.—(e) (α) In dat. sing. fem. τῇ, in or at the place or spot in which, in or at which place or spot, where: τῇ ἔμελλε διεξίμεναι Z 393. Cf. Λ 499, Ψ 775, etc.: δ 565, ε 442, etc.—In which way or manner, as: τῇ περ δὴ καὶ ἔπειτα τελευτήσεσθαι ἔμελλεν θ 510.—To the place or spot in which, to where: εἴ κε φεύγω τῇ περ κλονέονται Φ 554.—(β) In acc. sing. neut. τό, wherefore: τὸ καὶ κλαίουσα τέτηκα Γ 176, τό μοι ἔστι ταλαύρινον πολεμίζειν H 239. Cf. M 9, P 404, etc.: θ 332.

ὄαρ, -αρος, ἡ. Contr. dat. pl. ὤρεσσι E 486. A wife E 486, I 327.

ὀαρίζω. To hold converse with. With dat.: ἣ γυναικί Z 516. Cf. X 127 (of lovers' converse and dalliance), 128.

ὀαριστής, ὁ [ὀαρίζω]. One who holds familiar converse, is admitted to intimacy, with another: Μίνως Διὸς ὀαριστής τ 179.

ὀαριστύς, ἡ [ὀαρίζω]. Familiar converse, lovers' dalliance Ξ 216.—Of the commerce of foemen P 228.—Of grappling with the foe N 291.

ὀβελός, -οῦ, ὁ. A spit: ἀμφ' ὀβελοῖσιν ἔπειραν (ἔπειρεν) (ἀμφί advbl.) A 465 = B 428, I 210. Cf. H 317 = Ω 623, I 213: γ 462 = μ 365 = ξ 430, γ 463, μ 395, ξ 75, 77, τ 422.

ὀβριμοεργός [ὄβριμος + ἔργω²]. That does deeds of violence, violent: ἀνέρα X 418. Cf. E 403.

ὀβριμοπάτρη [ὄβριμος + πατρ-, πατήρ]. Daughter of a mighty sire. Epithet or a name of Athene E 747 = Θ 391: = α 101, γ 135, ω 540.

ὄβριμος [app. βρι- as in βρίθω, βριαρός]. (1) Heavy: ἄχθος ι 233. Cf. ι 241, 305.—(2) Mighty, powerful. Of water Δ 453.—Epithet of Ares E 845, N 444 = Π 613 = P 529, N 521, O 112.—Of Hector Θ 473, K 200, Λ 347, Ξ 44.—Of Achilles T 408.—Epithet of spears Γ 357, Δ 529, E 790, Λ 456, etc.

ὀγδόατος, -η, -ον [ὄγδοος + superl. suff.]. The eighth T 246: γ 306, δ 82.

ὄγδοος [ὀκτώ]. As a disyllable η 261, ξ 287. = prec. H 223, 246: η 261 = ξ 287.

ὀγδώκοντα [ὀκτώ]. Eighty B 568 = 652.

ὄγκιον, τό (poss. fr. ἐνεκ-. See φέρω]. Thus, a box or tray for carrying things φ 61.

ὄγκος, -ου, ὁ. A barb of an arrow Δ 151, 214.

ὄγμος, -ου, ὁ [ἄγω]. (1) In ploughing, a furrow Σ 546.—(2) In reaping, the line taken by a reaper advancing through the field: δράγματα μετ' ὄγμον πῖπτον (following the line of the reaper, in line on his left) Σ 552, βασιλεὺς ἑστήκει ἐπ' ὄγμου 557 (*i.e.* watching the reapers from the line of the nearest). Cf. Λ 68.

ὄγχνη, -ης, ἡ. (1) A pear-tree η 115 = λ 589, ω 234, 247, 340.—(2) A pear η 120.

ὀδαῖα, τά [ὁδός]. Cargo taken in for the return voyage, a home-cargo (opposed to φόρτος): ἐπείγετ' ὦνον ὀδαίων ο 445. Cf. θ 163.

ὀδάξ [δακ-, δάκνω]. With the teeth: ὀ. ἕλον οὖδας (bit the dust) Λ 749, T 61, Ω 738. Cf. B 418, X 17: α 381 = σ 410 = υ 268, χ 269.

ὅδε, ἥδε, τόδε [-δε (3)]. Genit. τοῦδε, τῆσδε, τοῦδε. Dat. pl. masc. and neut. τοίσδεσσι K 462: β 47, 165, ν 258. Masc. τοίσδεσι κ 268, φ 93. (1) This person or thing (in reported speech generally (and properly) referring to what belongs to or concerns the speaker; cf. οὗτος): τοῦδ' ἕνεκα A 110, τήνδε θεῷ πρόες 127. Cf. A 257, 275, 302, B 5, 236, etc.: α 169, 371, 396, β 162, 191, etc.—(2) With sb., etc., this: τόδ' ἐέλδωρ A 41. Cf. A 214, 234, 287, B 252, etc.: α 232, β 93, 280, 317, etc.—(3) In deictic or predicative sense = here: Ἕκτορος ἥδε γυνή (this is . . .) Z 460. Cf. E 175, I 688, O 286, T 140, etc.: ξείνω δή τινε τώδε (here are . . .) δ 26. Cf. α 185, ζ 206, λ 141, π 205, etc.—(4) In dat. sing. fem. τῇδε, here: τῇδε τετεύξεται ὄλεθρος M 345. Cf. P 512, Ω 139: ε 113, ζ 173, μ 186.

ὁδεύω [ὁδός]. To go, find passage, make one's way: ἐπὶ νῆας Λ 569.

ὁδίτης, ὁ [ὁδός + ι-, εἶμι]. A journeyer, wayfarer, passenger, passer-by Π 263: η 204, λ 127, ν 123, ρ 211, ψ 274.

ὀδμή, -ῆς, ἡ [ὀδ-, ὄζω]. A smell or scent Ξ 415: δ 406, 442, 446, ε 59, ι 210.

ὁδοιπόριον, τό [ὁδοιπόρος]. A reward for bearing one company ο 506.

ὁδοιπόρος, -ου, ὁ [app. a locative fr. ὁδός + πορ- as in πόρος]. A journeyer or wayfarer Ω 375.

ὁδός, -οῦ, ἡ [σεδ-. See ὄζος (2)]. The first syllable lengthened metrically οὐδός ρ 196. (1) A way, path, track, passage, road: ἐπεὶ πρὸ ὁδοῦ ἐγένοντο (local genit., 'forward on their way') Δ 382, παρὲξ ὁδοῦ κλινθήτην K 349, ἀμφὶς ὁδοῦ δραμέτην (local genit., 'apart on their way') Ψ 393. Cf. Z 15, 391, H 143, Π 374, etc.: ε 237, ζ 264, θ 107, ι 261, κ 103, etc.—(2) A going, journey, voyage, course: τὴν ὁδὸν ἣν Ἑλένην ἀνήγαγεν (on that voyage on which . . .) Z 292. Cf. A 151, I 626: ἐπειγόμενός περ ὁδοῖο α 309. Cf. α 444, β 285, γ 316, δ 393 (in your absence on a long journey), ζ 165, θ 444, π 138, φ 20, etc.—(3) Means of journeying or passage, facilities for a journey: πάρ τοι ὁδός (your way lies open) I 43: ὁδὸν ἤτεον κ 17. Cf. μ 334.

ὀδούς, -όντος, ὁ. Dat. pl. ὀδοῦσι E 75, Λ 114, etc. In pl., the teeth Δ 350, E 74, K 375, Π 348, P 617, etc.: α 64, μ 91, σ 28, 98, etc.—Of lions Λ 114, 175 = P 63, Υ 168.—A boar's tusk; in pl., his tusks K 263, Λ 416, 417, M 149, N 474: τ 393 = ψ 74, τ 450, 465, φ 219, ω 332.

ὀδύνη, -ης, ἡ. (1) In reference to bodily pain, a pain or pang: ὀδύνη διὰ χροὸς ἦλθεν Λ 398.—In pl., pains, pangs: ἀχθομένην ὀδύνῃσιν E 354. Cf. Δ 117, E 399, M 206, O 60, etc.: ι 415, 440, ρ 567.—(2) In reference to mental pain, grief, sorrow, distress: ἀζηχὴς ὀ. Ἡρακλῆος (for . .) O 25.—In pl., griefs, sorrows, distresses: ἐμοὶ ὀδύνας κάλλιπεν α 242. Cf. β 79, δ 812, τ 117.

ὀδυνήφατος, -ον [ὀδύνη + φα-, φένω. 'That kills

pain']. Stilling or allaying pain, soothing: φάρμακα E 401 = 900, ῥίζαν Λ 847.

ὀδύρομαι. 3 sing. aor. subj. ὀδύρεται Ψ 222: δ 740. Pple. ὀδῡράμενος Ω 48. (1) To make lament, weep, wail, mourn, sorrow, grieve: ὀδύρετο δάκρυα λείβων Σ 32. Cf. I 591, 612, X 79, Ψ 154, 222, 224, Ω 48, 128, 166, 549: α 55, δ 194, ε 160, θ 33, ξ 129, σ 203, ψ 241, etc.—With genit. of person mourned for: τῶν πάντων οὐ τόσσον ὀδύρομαι ὡς ἑνός X 424: = δ 104. Cf. δ 819, ξ 40, 142, 174, ο 355.—With genit. of something not attained mourned for: γάμου φ 250.—(2) To make lament or complaint, set forth one's wrongs: εἴ που κεῖνος ἐξελθὼν λαοῖσιν ὀδύρεται δ 740.—(3) To lament, weep for, mourn: ἕταρον T 345. Cf. Ω 714, 740: α 243, δ 100, 110.—Of a bird: [στρουθὸς] ὀδυρομένη τέκνα B 315.—(4) To long for in sorrow, be sick for to the point of tears: πατρίδα γαῖαν ν 219. Cf. ε 153, ν 379.—With infin., to express by lamentation one's longing to do something: οἰκόνδε νέεσθαι B 290.

†**ὀδύσσομαι.** 2 sing. aor. ὠδύσαο α 62. 3 ὠδύσατο Σ 292: ε 340. 3 pl. ὀδύσαντο Z 138: τ 275. Pple. ὀδυσσάμενος τ 407. Genit. sing. masc. ὀδυσσαμένοιο Θ 37, 468. 3 sing. pf. ὀδώδυσται ε 423. To be angry, wroth, incensed, to rage: ὀδυσσαμένοιο τεοῖο (in thy wrath) Θ 37 = 468, ἐπεὶ ὠδύσατο Ζεύς (has conceived wrath against us) Σ 292.—With dat. of person: τί νύ οἱ τόσον ὠδύσαο; α 62. Cf. Z 138: ε 340, 423 (cherishes wrath), τ 275, 407.

ὀδώδει, 3 sing. plupf. ὄζω.

ὄεσσι, dat. pl. ὄϊς.

ὄζος, -ου, ὁ. (1) A branch or shoot: φύλλα καὶ ὄζους A 234. Cf. B 312, Δ 484, Z 39, K 467, Ξ 289, Π 768, Φ 245: μ 435.—(2) A scion or child (but in this sense perh. another word ὀ- = ἀ-² + ζ- = σδ-, σεδ-, root of ὁδός, 'a companion or follower'): ὄζος Ἄρηος B 540, 704, 745, 842, M 188, Ψ 841, Ω 474. Cf. B 663, Γ 147 = Υ 238.

†**ὄζω.** 3 sing. plupf. (in impf. sense) ὀδώδει ε 60, ι 210. To have a certain scent, smell; of a scent, to spread, come, reach the sense: τηλόθ' ὀδμὴ κέδρου τε θύου τ' ὀδώδει ε 60. Cf. ι 210.

ὅθεν [ὁ-, ὅς² + -θεν (1)]. (1) From which place or spot, whence: ὅθεν ῥέεν ὕδωρ B 307. Cf. K 200, Λ 758: γ 319, 321, δ 358 (see ἀπό (II) (1) (a)), χ 460.—Sim.: ἐς Σικελούς, ὅθεν κέ τοι ἄξιον ἄλφοι υ 383.—In reference to a starting-point: τοῦ χώρου ὅθεν τέ περ οἰνοχοεύει (the spot from which the round is begun) φ 142.—(2) In reference to source, origin or birth, whence: γένος μοι ἔνθεν ὅθεν σοί Δ 58. Cf. B 852, 857.—To a source from which one draws: ὅθεν ἱδρεύοντο η 131, ρ 206.—To a source of (imagined) light λ 366 (see εἴδω (I) (1)).

ὅθι [as prec. + -θι]. (1) In or at the place or spot in which, in or at which place or spot, where: Λήμνῳ ἔν, ὅθι μιν λίπον B 722. Cf. B 572, Γ 145, Δ 41, 217, E 8, Θ 83, etc.: ἐν δαπέδῳ, ὅθι περ πάρος δ 627. Cf. α 50, β 338, γ 326, δ 127, 426, ε 280, ι 50, etc.—With subj. or opt. in conditional relative sentences. For the examples and constructions see Table at end (III) (B) (a) (1), (b) (1).—(2) To the place or spot in which, to where: ἴθυνεν ὅθι ζωστῆρος ὀχῆες σύνεχον Δ 132, etc. Cf. α 425, etc.

ὄθομαι. (1) With neg., not to care for, trouble oneself about, have regard for. With genit.: οὐδ' ὄθομαι κοτέοντος (I care not for your wrath) A 181.—Absol. O 107.—(2) With infin., to hesitate *to do something*, shrink from *doing it*: οὐκ ὄθεται ἦτορ ἶσον ἐμοὶ (ἶσόν οἱ) φάσθαι O 166, 182.—Sim. with pple.: οὐκ ὄθετ' αἴσυλα ῥέζων E 403.

ὀθόνη, -ης, ἡ. A cloth (prob. of linen) η 107.—In pl., clothes or wrappings (prob. of linen): ἀργεννῇσι καλυψαμένη ὀθόνῃσιν Γ 141. Cf. Σ 595.

ὄθριξ, ὄτριχος [ὀ- = ἀ-² + θρίξ]. Of horses, having hair of the same colour, one in coats B 765.

οἷ, οἱ. See ἑέ.

†**οἴγνῡμι.** 3 sing. aor. ὤϊξε Z 298, Ω 446: α 436, γ 392, κ 230, 256, 312, χ 399. ᾦξε Ω 457. 3 pl. ὤϊξαν ψ 370, ω 501. Aor. pple. fem. οἴξᾱσα Z 89. 3 pl. impf. pass. ὠΐγνυντο B 809, Θ 58. (ἀναοίγω.) (1) To open, set open (a gate or door): ὤϊξε πύλας Ω 446. Cf. B 809 = Θ 58, Z 89, 298: α 436, κ 230 = 256 = 312, χ 399, ψ 370, ω 501.—To draw back (a bar in order to open a door): [κληῗδα] Ω 457.—(2) To broach or draw (wine): οἴνου, τὸν ὤϊξεν ταμίη γ 392.

οἶδα, pf. εἴδω (C).

οἰδάνω [οἰδέω]. To cause to swell. Fig.: χόλος, ὅς τε καὶ ἄλλων οἰδάνει νόον I 554.—Sim. in pass.: οἰδάνεται μοι κραδίη χόλῳ (swells with . . .) I 646.

οἰδέω. To swell: ᾤδεε χρόα πάντα (acc. of part affected, his flesh became swollen) ε 455.

οἶδμα, -ατος, τό [οἰδέω]. A swelling. Of water: ποταμὸς οἴδματι θύων (in flood) Φ 234. Cf. Ψ 230 (with swelling surface).

οἰέτης [ὀ = ἀ-² + -ι- (app. representing lengthening before ϝ) + (ϝ)έτος]. Of horses, of the same age, one in years B 765.

ὀϊζῡρός, -ή, -όν [ὀϊζύς]. (1) Wretched, miserable, unhappy, ill-starred: ὀ. περὶ πάντων ἔπλεο A 417. Cf. N 569: γ 95 = δ 325, δ 197, 832.—Absol.: ὀ. τις υ 140.—Comp. ὀϊζυρώτερος. Absol. P 446.—Superl. ὀϊζυρώτατος ε 105.—(2) Causing, bringing in its train, pain or grief, sorrowful, woful: πολέμοιο Γ 112. Cf. θ 540, λ 182 = π 38, ν 337.

ὀϊζύς, -ύος, ἡ. (1) Sorrow, grief, woe, distress, hardship: πόνον τ' ἐχέμεν καὶ ὀϊζύν N 2. Cf. Z 285, Ξ 480: γ 103, δ 35, ε 289, η 211, 270, etc.—(2) The result of pains or painful toil O 365.

ὀϊζύω [ὀϊζύς]. To suffer grief, distress, anxiety, hardship Γ 408: δ 152, ψ 307.—With cognate acc., to suffer: ἧς εἵνεκ' ὀϊζύομεν κακὰ πολλά Ξ 89.

οἰήϊον, -ου, τό. The steering-oar of a ship T 43: ι 483 = 540.—In pl. app. of a single oar: ἐπεὶ νηὸς οἰήϊα νωμᾷς μ 218.

οἴηκες [app. conn. with prec.]. Perh., guides on the yoke for the reins Ω 269.

οἴκαδε [cf. οἰκόνδε]. To one's house or home, home, homewards: οἰ. ἴμεν A 170, οἰ. δόμεναι πάλιν (hand over to be borne to my home) H 79 = X 342. Cf. A 19, B 154, Γ 72, Δ 103, H 335, etc.: β 176, δ 520, ε 108, θ 102, κ 35, etc.

οἰκεύς, ὁ [οἶκος]. A house servant, a servant in gen.: ὅ οἱ βιότοιο μάλιστα κήδετο οἰκήων ξ 4. Cf. E 413, Z 366: δ 245, ξ 63, π 303, ρ 533.

οἰκέω [οἶκος]. (1) To live, dwell, abide, have one's home: οἴκεον ἐν Πλευρῶνι Ξ 116. Cf. ζ 204, ι 200, 400.—(2) To live in, dwell in, inhabit: ὑπωρείας ᾤκεον Ἴδης Υ 218.—In pass., of a city, to be a habitation, continue in being, stand: οἰκέοιτο πόλις Πριάμοιο Δ 18.—(3) In aor. pass. in mid. sense, of a people, to settle, organize or dispose themselves: τριχθὰ ᾤκηθεν καταφυλαδόν B 668.

οἰκίον, τό [οἶκος]. (1) A house or abode: οἵ περὶ Δωδώνην οἰκί' ἔθεντο B 750. Cf. β 154, φ 215.—(2) In pl. in the same sense: οἰκία ναίων (dwelling) Z 15, H 221, N 664, Π 595, P 584. Cf. P 308: β 335, δ 555, 798, ι 505=531, ξ 210, π 385, υ 288, ω 104.—Of the house or realm of Hades Υ 64.—Of the home of the Dawn μ 4.—Of a wasps' nest M 168, Π 261.—Of an eagle's nest M 221.

οἴκοθεν [οἶκος + -θεν (1)]. (1) From one's house or home: δέπας, ὅ οἱ. ἧγεν Λ 632.—(2) From one's store, from one's own resources (cf. οἶκος (3)): καὶ οἴκοθεν ἄλλ' ἐπιθεῖναι H 364, 391. Cf. Ψ 558, 592.

οἴκοθι [οἶκος + -θι]. At one's house or home, at home: τοιαῦτα καὶ αὐτῷ οἱ. κεῖται φ 398. Cf. Θ 513: γ 303, τ 237.

οἴκοι [locative of οἶκος]. At one's house or home, at home: οἱ. ἔσαν α 12. Cf. A 113, Ω 240: θ 324, ν 42, ο 15, 178.

οἰκόνδε [acc. of οἶκος + -δε (1)]. (1) To one's house or home, home, homewards: ἔβαν οἰκόνδε ἕκαστος A 606. Cf. B 158, 290, Δ 180, Z 189, Ψ 856, etc.: α 17, 317, ε 204, ζ 159, λ 410 (here, app., simply 'to the palace'), ν 125, ψ 221, etc.—(2) To the part of a house allotted to one, to one's own quarters (cf. οἶκος (2)): ἡ θαμβήσασα πάλιν οἰκόνδε βεβήκει α 360=φ 354. Cf. γ 396, ψ 292.

οἶκος, -ου, ὁ (Ϝοῖκος. Cf. L. *vicus*). (1) A house or abode (sometimes, as in Eng. 'house,' thought of along with the inhabitants or contents): ἡμετέρῳ ἐνὶ οἴκῳ A 30. Cf. Γ 233, Z 56, 490, 500, H 127, Θ 284, I 147, 289, O 498, P 738, Ω 471, 572: μέλλε ποτὲ οἶκος ὅδ' ἀφνειὸς ἔμμεναι α 232. Cf. α 248, 251, 258, β 45, δ 4, ζ 9, η 314, ι 35, λ 389, etc.—App. including the curtilage of the house: χῆν' ἀτιταλλομένην ἐνὶ οἴκῳ ο 174. Cf. τ 536.—In pl. in the same sense as the sing.: ἐκ νέκυς οἴκων φόρεον ω 417.—(2) Applied to a particular part of a house (cf. τ 598 and οἰκόνδε (2)). (a) To Penelope's quarters: εἰς οἶκον ἰοῦσα α 356 =φ 350. Cf. δ 717.—(b) App. to a detached building appropriated to mill-workers: φήμην ἐξ οἴκοιο γυνὴ προέηκεν ἀλετρίς υ 105.—(3) One's store (cf. οἴκοθεν (2)): οὐ σύ γ' ἂν ἐξ οἴκου οὐδ' ἅλα δοίης ρ 455.

οἰκτίρω, οἰκτείρω [οἶκτος]. 3 sing. aor. ᾤκτειρε Λ 814, Π 5, Ψ 534. To pity, take pity on, feel pity for, feel sorry for: τὸν ἰδὼν ᾤκτειρεν Λ 814, Π 5=Ψ 534. Cf. Ψ 548, Ω 516.

οἴκτιστος [superl. fr. οἶκτος]. (1) The most pitiable, miserable or wretched: θανάτῳ λ 412, ω 34. Cf. ψ 79.—Absol.: τοῦτ' οἴκτιστον πέλεται δειλοῖσι βροτοῖσιν X 76. Cf. μ 258, 342.—(2) In neut. pl. οἴκτιστα as adv., in the most miserable or wretched wise: ὅπως οἴκτιστα θάνοιεν χ 472.

οἶκτος, ὁ. Pity, compassion, sympathy with one in trouble or distress β 81, ω 438.

οἰκτρός [οἶκτος]. (1) Pitiable: κοιμήσατο χάλκεον ὕπνον οἰκτρός Λ 242.—Comp. οἰκτρότερος: οἰκτρότερ' ἄλλ' ἀγορεῦσαι (more moving) λ 381.—Superl. οἰκτρότατος λ 421.—(2) In neut. pl. οἰκτρά as adv., pitiably, so as to move compassion, expressing great grief: ὀλοφυρομένη δ 719. Cf. κ 409, τ 543, ω 59.

οἰκωφελίη, ἡ [οἶκος + ὀφέλλω[2]]. Care or thought for one's house or worldly estate ξ 223.

οἶμα, -ατος, τό. Rush, spring, swoop Π 752.—Sim. in pl.: αἰετοῦ οἴματ' ἔχων Φ 252.

οἰμάω [οἶμα]. To spring, swoop, pounce: οἴμησεν ὥς τ' αἰετός X 308:=ω 538. Cf. X 140, 311.

οἴμη, -ης, ἡ. A lay or poem: θεός μοι ἐν φρεσὶν οἴμας παντοίας ἐνέφυσεν χ 347. Cf. θ 74, 481.

οἶμος, -ου, ὁ. A stripe: οἶμοι κυάνοιο Λ 24.

οἰμωγή, -ῆς, ἡ [οἰμώζω]. A crying out in distress or pain, weeping, wailing Δ 450=Θ 64, X 409, 447, Ω 696: υ 353.

†οἰμώζω. 3 sing. aor. ᾤμωξε Γ 364, M 162, Σ 35, X 33, Ψ 178, etc.: ι 395, ν 198. 3 pl. ᾤμωξαν Ψ 12. 3 sing. opt. οἰμώξειε H 125. Pple. οἰμώξας E 68, Π 290, Υ 417, Φ 529, X 34: ι 506, λ 59, μ 370, σ 398. To cry out in or express grief, distress, pain or disappointment: γνὺξ ἔριπ' οἰμώξας (with a cry of pain) E 68. Cf. Γ 364, H 125, M 162, Π 290, X 33, etc.: ι 395, 506=λ 59, μ 370, ν 198, σ 398.

οἰνίζομαι [οἶνος]. To get (wine) for oneself, to supply oneself with wine H 472, Θ 506, 546.

οἰνοβαρείων [a ppl. form fr. οἶνος + βαρύς]. Heavy with wine, drunken, in one's drunkenness: ἐρεύγετο οἰνοβαρείων ι 374. Cf. κ 555, φ 304.

οἰνοβαρής [οἶνος + βαρύς]. Heavy with wine, drunken. Absol. in voc. A 225.

οἰνόπεδος, -ον [οἶνος + πέδον, the ground]. With soil fit for producing wine, vine-bearing: ἀλωῆς α 193, λ 193.—In neut. as sb., vineyard land I 579.

οἰνοπληθής [οἶνος + πλῆθος]. Full of wine, bearing wine in abundance: νῆσος ο 406.

οἰνοποτάζω [οἶνος + πο-, πίνω (as in ἐκπέποται)]. To drink one's wine: ἃς ὑπίσχεο οἰνοποτάζων (sitting over your wine) Υ 84. Cf. ζ 309, υ 262.

οἰνοποτήρ, -ῆρος, ὁ [as prec.]. A drinker of wine: ἄνδρας μέτα οἰνοποτῆρας ἤϊεν (to join the company at their wine) θ 456.

οἶνος, -ου, ὁ (Ϝοῖνος. Cf. L. *vinum*, Eng. *wine*). Wine A 462, Γ 246, Z 261, H 467, I 224, etc.: α 110, β 340, γ 40, ι 347, λ 61, etc.

οἰνοχοεύω [as next]. =next (1) B 127, Υ 234: α 143, φ 142.

οἰνοχοέω [οἶνος + χοή]. Nom. pl. masc. pres. pple. οἰνοχοεῦντες γ 472. 3 sing. impf. ἐοινοχόει, ἐῳνοχόει (ἐϜοινοχόει) Δ 3: υ 255. οἰνοχόει A 598:

ο 141. (**1**) To pour out wine for drinking, act as cup-bearer: ἐοινοχόει Μελανθεύς υ 255. Cf. δ 233, ο 141, 323.—(**2**) To pour out (wine) for drinking: οἶνον οἰνοχοεῦντες γ 472.—Of nectar Α 598, Δ 3.

οἰνοχόος, -ου, ὁ [οἶνος + χέω]. One who pours out wine for drinking, a cup-bearer: οἰνοχόος ἐπαρξάσθω δεπάεσσιν σ 418, φ 263. Cf. Β 128: ι 10, σ 396.

οἶνοψ, -οπος [οἶνος + ὀπ-. See ὁράω]. Dark in hue like wine. (**1**) Epithet of πόντος, wine-dark, purple Β 613, Ε 771, Η 88, Ψ 143, 316: α 183, β 421, γ 286, δ 474, ε 132, etc.—(**2**) Epithet of oxen, app., of the characteristic dark hue of most of the species, *i.e.* dark brown Ν 703: ν 32.

οἰνόω [οἶνος]. To make drunk; in pass., to become drunk: μή πως οἰνωθέντες ἀλλήλους τρώσητε (in an access of drunkenness) π 292 = τ 11.

οἴξᾱσα, aor. pple. fem. οἴγνυμι.

οἰόθεν. Strengthening οἶος by reduplication (cf. αἰνόθεν αἰνῶς, μέγας μεγαλωστί). App., man to man: οἰόθεν οἶος μαχέσασθαι Η 39. Cf. Η 226.

ὀΐομαι, οἴομαι. 3 sing. impf. ὠΐετο (ῑ) κ 248, υ 349. 3 sing. aor. ὀΐσατο (ῑ) α 323, ι 213, τ 390. Pple. ὀϊσάμενος ι 339, κ 232, 258, ο 443. Aor. in pass. form ὠΐσθην π 475. 3 sing. ὠΐσθη δ 453. Pple. ὀϊσθείς Ι 453. Also 1st pres. in act. form ὀΐω (ῑ) Α 558, Ε 894, Κ 551, Ν 153, Φ 399, etc.: β 255, ν 427, ο 31. ὀΐω (ῐ) Α 59, Ε 284, Ζ 341, Θ 536, Ρ 503, Φ 92, Ω 355, etc.: α 201, γ 27, ν 5, σ 259, τ 215, φ 91, ψ 261, etc. οἴω Ε 252, Κ 105, Ο 298, Ρ 709, Ψ 310, etc. (**1**) To think, deem, fancy, imagine, suspect, expect: αἰεὶ ὀΐεαι (are always suspecting something) Α 561. Cf. Ι 453: τῷ ἑπόμην ὀϊόμενός περ (though boding that no good would come of it) ξ 298. Cf. ι 339, ο 443, ρ 586, ω 401 (beyond our hopes).—To bethink oneself of something to be avoided: ὀΐσατο μὴ . . . τ 390.—ὀΐω parenthetically, 'I ween' Θ 536, Ν 153: β 255, π 309, ψ 261.—So ὀΐομαι χ 140.—Prob. also in ξ 363.—Impers., to appear, seem: ὧδέ μοι ὀΐεται, ὡς ἔσεταί περ τ 312.—(**2**) With acc. (**a**) To think of, have occur to one: ἅ πέρ κ' οἴοιτο καὶ ἄλλος ρ 580.—(**b**) To bode, dwell on the thought of: κῆρας Ν 283.—(**c**) To be full of the thought of, be impelled to: γόον κ 248 = υ 349.—(**d**) To imagine, figure to oneself. With dependent clause: τόδε καὐτὸς ὀΐεαι, ὥς κεν ἐτύχθη (can imagine for yourself how . . .) γ 255.—(**e**) To suspect the existence of: δόλον κ 380.—(**f**) To expect, look for the coming of: κεῖνον β 351. Cf. υ 224.—(**g**) To intend, purpose, have in view: τά γ' οὐκ ὀΐω (I will see that that does not happen) ν 427 = ο 31.—(**3**) With infin. (**a**) With pres., pf. or aor. infin., to think, suppose, surmise, deem, suspect: καταvεῦσαί σε Α 558, τὸν ἐνὶ κλισίῃσι κεῖσθαι Λ 834, Πηλῆα τεθνάμεν Τ 334. Cf. Ε 894, Κ 551, Ν 262, 273, Ξ 454, Ρ 641, 687, Ψ 467: α 173, γ 27, δ 453, 754, κ 193, ξ 214, τ 568, etc.—(**b**) With fut. infin., to think, expect, deem, ween: ἄμμε παλιμπλαγχθέντας ἂψ ἀπονοστήσειν Α 59. Cf. Α 78, Δ 12, Ε 252, Ζ 341, Ι 315, Λ 609, Μ 66, etc.: α 201, β 198, γ 226, ζ 173, θ 203, ι 213, λ 101, etc.—To intend, propose, have a mind, be minded: οὐδέ σ(οι) ὀΐω ἄφενος ἀφύξειν (I have no notion of doing anything of the sort) Α 170. Cf. Α 296: νῦν σευ ὀΐω πειρήσεσθαι (am going to . . .) τ 215.

οἰόπολος [οἶος. Cf. ἀκρόπολος]. Lonely, solitary, remote Ν 473, Ρ 54, Τ 377, Ω 614: λ 574.

οἶος, -η, -ον (scanned ⏑⏑ Ν 275, Σ 105: η 312, υ 89). (**1**) (**a**) Of such nature, kind or sort as, such as: οἷος πάρος εὔχεαι εἶναι Δ 264. Cf. Ε 126, 304, Η 208, Ι 105, 447, etc.: ἀνὴρ οἷος Ὀδυσσεὺς ἔσκεν β 59. Cf. β 118, γ 480, ε 422, ο 379, τ 255, etc.—Correlative with τοῖος. See τοῖος (1) (a). See also τοιόσδε (1) (a), τοιοῦτος.—(**b**) With infin., such as to . . .: οἷός τε πατρὸς ἀέθλια ἀνελέσθαι φ 117. Cf. τ 160, φ 173.—Introducing similes Δ 75, Ε 554, Η 63, Λ 62, etc.: ζ 102.—(**2**) With subj. in conditional relative sentences. For the examples and constructions see Table at end (III) (B) (a) (1), (D) (20) (31).—(**3**) In causal sense (= ὅτι τοῖος): τὸν χόλος λάβεν οἷον ἄκουσε (because of what he had heard) Ζ 166, οἷ' ἀγορεύεις (since you say such things) Σ 95. Cf. Β 320, Ε 758, Ξ 95, Ω 630, etc.: οἷ' ἀγορεύεις (to judge by what you say) δ 611, οἷος κεῖνος ἔην βουλευέμεν (for such a man he was to . . .) ξ 491. Cf. ε 183, 303, ρ 479, σ 143, 338, χ 217, etc.—Giving a reason in anticipation: οἷος κείνου θυμὸς ὑπέρβιος, οὔ σε μεθήσει ο 212. Cf. Θ 450, Σ 262: ρ 514.—(**4**) Exclamatory in advbl. and other constructions: οἷον δὴ θαυμάζομεν Ἕκτορα (to think how we . . .!) Ε 601, οἷόν τινά φασι βίην Ἡρακληείην εἶναι (what a man they say he was!) 638, οἷον ἔειπες (what a thing is this that you have said!) Η 455. Cf. Ν 633 (even as now . . .), Ο 287, Ρ 471, 587 (if now you . . .), Φ 57, etc.: α 32 (to think how . . .!), 410, δ 242, λ 429, 519, ρ 248, etc.—(**5**) In object clauses, of what nature, kind or sort, what kind of a . . ., what: γνοίης χ' οἵου φωτὸς ἔχεις παράκοιτιν Γ 53. Cf. Β 192, 194 (what he said), Ε 222, Λ 653, Ο 94, 97, etc.: οὐκ ἀΐεις οἷον κλέος ἔλλαβεν; α 298. Cf. δ 689, θ 244, ι 348, ο 20, τ 219, etc.—(**6**) In neut. οἷον as adv. (see also (4)). (**a**) Even as, as: οἷον ὅτε πρῶτόν περ ἐμισγέσθην φιλότητι Ξ 295. Cf. τ 233.—(**b**) In what manner, how: οὐχ ὁράᾳς οἷον . . .; Ο 555.—With an adj., how: οἷον ἐερσήεις κεῖται Ω 419. Cf. τ 494.—(**c**) Seeing that: οἷον ἔθ' εὕδεις Ω 683. Cf. β 239, ξ 392.—(**7**) In neut. pl. οἷα as adv. (**a**) Even as, as: οἷα θεάων λεπτὰ ἔργα πέλονται κ 222. Cf. θ 365.—With τε θ 160, ι 128, λ 364, 536, ο 324.—(**b**) Even as, like. With τε: οἷά τε φύλλα η 106. Cf. γ 73 = ι 254.

οἶος, -η, -ον. (**1**) With no one near, unaccompanied, alone, by oneself: καθήμενος οἶος Θ 207. Cf. Β 822, Γ 143, Θ 444, Ι 438, Μ 349, etc.: α 331, β 11, 70, δ 367, ι 188, κ 281, etc.—(**2**) Without countenance, support or aid, from one's own resources, alone, by oneself: οἶον μάχεσθαι Δ 156. Cf. Δ 304, Ε 304, Η 42, Ν 481 (in my need), Π 100, 243, etc.: ὃν αὐτὸς κτήσατο οἶος ξ 450. Cf. α 79, ι 410.—For οἰόθεν οἶος see οἰόθεν.—(**3**) With no one or nothing in the same predicament or case or doing the same thing, with no one having the same ability, alone, only, nothing but: ὄφρα μὴ οἶος ἀγέραστος ἔω A 118, κλέος οἶον ἀκούομεν B 486, ὅς μοι οἶος ἔην (*i.e.* the others count for nothing) Ω 499. Cf. A 198, 398, B 247, E 641, Z 403, I 190, 638, Λ 74, etc.: α 13, 354, β 84, γ 424, ζ 139, θ 230, κ 95, ξ 244, 482, π 133, χ 130, etc.—**(4)** In neut. οἶον as adv., only, solely, exclusively: οὐδ' ἔτι κεῖνον στεναχίζω οἶον, ἐπεὶ . . . (I have not only to mourn my loss, for . . .) α 244. Cf. I 355.

οἰοχίτων, -ωνος [οἶος + χιτών]. Clad only in a χιτών ξ 489.

οἰόω [οἶος]. To leave alone, leave by himself or to itself: Τρώων οἰώθη καὶ Ἀχαιῶν φύλοπις (*i.e.* by the departure of the gods) Z 1. Cf. Λ 401.

ὄϊς, ὁ, ἡ (ὄϜις. Cf. L. *ovis*). Genit. ὄϊος I 207: δ 764. οἰός M 451, N 599, 716, O 373: α 443, φ 408. Acc. ὄϊν K 215, Ω 621: κ 524, 527, 572, λ 32. Nom. pl. ὄϊες Δ 433, Ψ 31: ι 184, 425, 431. Genit. ὀΐων ι 167, 441, 443, ξ 519, υ 3. οἰῶν Γ 198, Λ 678, 696, O 323, Σ 529, 588, X 501: ι 448, λ 402, μ 129, 266, 299, ξ 100, υ 142, ω 112. Dat. ὀΐεσσι E 137, Z 424, K 486: ζ 132, ρ 472. οἴεσι ο 386. ὄεσσι Z 25, Λ 106: ι 418. Acc. ὄϊς Λ 245: β 56, ι 244, 341, ρ 180, 535, υ 250. A sheep Γ 198, Δ 433, Z 25, Λ 245, O 373, etc.: α 443, δ 764, ζ 132, ι 167, κ 524, etc.

ὀΐσατο, 3 sing. aor. ὀΐομαι.

οἶσε, aor. imp. φέρω.

οἰσέμεν[1], fut. infin. φέρω.

οἰσέμεν[2], aor. infin. φέρω.

οἰσέμεναι, aor. infin. φέρω.

οἴσετε, aor. imp. pl. φέρω.

οἰσέτω, 3 sing. aor. imp. φέρω.

οἶσθα, 2 sing. pf. εἴδω (C).

ὀϊσθείς, aor. pple. ὀΐομαι.

ὀϊστεύω [ὀϊστός]. (δι-.) To shoot an arrow or arrows Δ 196 = 206, Θ 269: θ 216, μ 84, χ 119.—With genit. of person aimed at: ὀΐστευσον Μενελάου Δ 100.

ὀϊστός, -οῦ, ὁ. An arrow A 46, Δ 118, E 110, Θ 300, Λ 478, N 650, etc.: θ 229, λ 607, ξ 225, σ 262, τ 575, φ 12, 60, 98, 173, 416, 420, χ 3, 8, 106, ω 178.

οἶστρος, ὁ. The gad-fly or breeze χ 300.

οἰσύϊνος, -η, -ον [οἰσύα, osier]. Of osier, wattled: ῥίπεσσιν οἰσυΐνῃσιν ε 256.

οἴσω, fut. φέρω.

οἶτος, -ου, ὁ. One's fate, fate that comes upon one: κακὸν οἶτον ἀναπλήσαντες Θ 34 = 354 = 465. Cf. Γ 417, I 563, Ω 388: α 350, γ 134, θ 489, 578, ν 384.

†οἰχνέω [οἴχομαι]. 3 pl. οἰχνεῦσι γ 322. 3 sing. pa. iterative οἴχνεσκε O 640. 3 pl. οἴχνεσκον E 790. (εἰσ-, ἐξ-.) To go or come, take or make one's way E 790, O 640: γ 322.

οἴχομαι. (ἀπ-, ἐξ-, ἐπ-, μετ-, παρ-.) **(1)** To go or come, take or make one's way, proceed: ᾠχόμεθ' ἐς Θήβην A 366. Cf. A 380, E 495, Λ 357, X 223 (will go and . . .), Ψ 564, etc.: πότ' ᾤχετο; δ 642. Cf. α 260, β 383, ι 47, ν 415, ω 333 (when I journeyed thither), etc.—Of inanimate objects: ἀνὰ στρατὸν ᾤχετο κῆλα θεοῖο A 53. Cf. N 505 = Π 615.—So of a wind: ὥς μ' ὄφελ' οἴχεσθαι προφέρουσα κακὴ ἀνέμοιο θύελλα Z 346. Cf. υ 64.—Of something immaterial: Ὄσσα κατὰ πτόλιν οἴχετο πάντῃ ω 413.—**(2)** With the notion of leaving a place prominent, to go away or off, depart, take one's departure, leave: ὅτ' ἂν (εἴ κεν) Ἀχαιοὶ οἴχωνται ἐς πατρίδα γαῖαν H 460 = O 499. Cf. B 71, N 627, Ξ 311, 361, T 356: εἴ κεν Ἄρης οἴχοιτο θ 353. Cf. θ 356, ν 286, π 24 = ρ 42, π 142, ρ 104, 294, τ 183, 260 = 597 = ψ 19.—Of immaterial things: θυμὸς ᾤχετ' ἀπὸ μελέων N 672 = Π 607. Cf. X 213, Ψ 101.—**(3)** To have gone, be gone: ἐπεὶ ᾤχοντο (had gone) Δ 382, γαιήοχος οἴχεται εἰς ἅλα δῖαν O 223. Cf. E 511, Λ 288, N 782, P 588, T 346, Ψ 577: α 242, 410, δ 166, 634, 639, 665, 707, 821, θ 294, ν 216, ξ 25, τ 193 (since he had left for . . .), ω 225.—Of a heavenly body: φάος οἴχετ[αι] ὑπὸ ζόφον γ 335.—Of immaterial things: πῇ τοι μένος οἴχεται; E 472. Cf. N 220, Ω 201.—In pple., absent, away: πατρὸς δὴν οἰχομένοιο α 281, β 215, 264, ο 270. Cf. δ 164, 393, ξ 144, 376, ο 355, σ 313, υ 216, 290, ω 125.

ὀΐω, οἴω. See ὀΐομαι.

οἰωνιστής, ὁ [οἰωνίζομαι fr. οἰωνός]. One skilled in drawing omens from the behaviour of birds, an augur B 858, P 218.—Joined with θεοπρόπος N 70.

οἰωνοπόλος, -ου, ὁ [οἰωνός + -πολος, conn. with πολεύω]. = prec. A 69, Z 76.

οἰωνός, -οῦ, ὁ. **(1)** A bird: πέλαγος, ὅθεν τέ περ οὐδ' οἰωνοὶ αὐτόετες οἰχνεῦσιν γ 321. Cf. λ 605, π 216.—**(2)** Distinguished as **(a)** A bird of prey: ἑλώρια κύνεσσιν οἰωνοῖσί τε πᾶσιν A 5. Cf. B 393, Θ 379, Λ 395, 453, N 831, P 241, X 335, 354, Ω 411: γ 259, 271, ξ 133, ω 292.—**(b)** A bird of omen: οἰωνοῖσι πείθεσθαι M 237. Cf. Ω 292, 293 = 311, Ω 310: ο 532, ρ 160.—Applied to an omen drawn from such a bird: οὐκ οἰωνοῖσιν ἐρύσατο κῆρα B 859. Cf. M 243, N 823: α 202.

ὀκνέω. Also **ὀκνείω** (ὀκνεσίω) [ὄκνος]. To shrink from *doing something*, hesitate *to do it*. With infin.: ἀρχέμεναι πολέμοιο ὄκνεον Y 155. Cf. E 255.

ὄκνος, -ου, ὁ. Shrinking from action, hesitation: ὄκνῳ εἴκων K 122, N 224. Cf. E 817.

†ὀκριάομαι [ὀκριόεις]. 3 pl. impf. ὀκριόωντο. App. 'to deal in sharps'; hence, to squabble, quarrel: πανθυμαδὸν ὀκριόωντο σ 33.

ὀκριόεις, -εντος [ὄκρις, a jagged point]. Jagged, rough: χερμαδίῳ Δ 518. Cf. Θ 327, M 380, Π 735: ι 499.

ὀκρυόεις, -εντος. Fem. -εσσα [no doubt for κρυόεις, the form suggested by prec.]. Causing shuddering. Fig.: δᾶερ ἐμεῖο κυνὸς κακομηχάνου ὀκρυοέσσης (κακομηχάνοο κρυοέσσης) Z 344, πολέμου ἐπιδημίου ὀκρυόεντος (ἐπιδημίοο κρυόεντος) I 64.

ὀκτάκνημος [ὀκτ-, ὀκτώ + -α- (on analogy of numerals in -α) + κνήμη]. Eight-spoked: κύκλα E 723.

ὀκτώ, *indeclinable.* Eight B 313 = 327, Θ 297 : θ 60, χ 110.

ὀκτωκαιδέκατος, -η, -ον [ὀκτώ + καί + δέκατος]. The eighteenth : ὀκτωκαιδεκάτῃ (*sc.* ἡμέρῃ), on the eighteenth day ε 279 = η 268, ω 65.

ὀλβιοδαίμων [ὄλβιος + δαίμων]. Happy in the protection and aid of a δαίμων, happy, fortunate. In voc. ὀλβιόδαιμον Γ 182.

ὄλβιος [ὄλβος]. **(1)** Happy, fortunate, prosperous : ἀμφὶ λαοὶ ὄλβιοι ἔσσονται λ 137. Cf. λ 450, ρ 354, σ 218, ψ 284, ω 36, 192.—Bringing good luck : δῶρα, τά μοι θεοὶ ὄλβια ποιήσειαν ν 42. —In neut. pl. ὄλβια, happiness, good fortune, prosperity : θεοὶ ὄλβια δοῖεν η 148, θ 413, ω 402.— **(2)** With special reference to material prosperity, wealthy, rich, of great power or influence : σὲ τὸ πρὶν μὲν ἀκούομεν ὄλβιον εἶναι Ω 543. Cf. ρ 420 = τ 76, σ 138.

ὄλβος, -ου, ὁ. **(1)** Happiness, good fortune, prosperity : οὔ μοι τοιοῦτον ἐπέκλωσαν θεοὶ ὄλβον γ 208. Cf. δ 208, ζ 188, σ 19, 123 = υ 200, σ 273. —**(2)** With special reference to material prosperity, wealth, riches, much substance, great power or influence : ὄλβῳ τε πλούτῳ τε μετέπρεπε Μυρμιδόνεσσιν Π 596. Cf. Ω 536 : ξ 206.

ὀλέθριος [ὄλεθρος]. Fatal, baneful, deadly : ὀλέθριον ἦμαρ. See ἦμαρ (4) (i).

ὄλεθρος, -ου, ὁ [ὄλλυμι]. Destruction, bane, death, evil fate : οὐδέ τί οἱ τό γ' ἐπήρκεσεν ὄλεθρον B 873. Cf. Z 16, Λ 120, N 773, Σ 129, etc. : α 11. Cf. β 152, θ 579, κ 250, ξ 300, π 411 (the fate intended for him), etc.—A kind or mode of death K 174, X 325, Ω 735 : γ 93, κ 115, ο 268, etc.

ὀλεῖται, 3 sing. fut. mid. ὄλλυμι.

ὀλέκω [ὀλε-, ὄλλυμι]. 3 sing. pa. iterative ὀλέκεσκε T 135. To destroy, kill, slay E 712 = H 18, Θ 279, Λ 150, 326, 530, O 249, Σ 172, T 135, 152, Φ 521 : κ 125, χ 305.—In pass., to perish, die : ὀλέκοντο λαοί A 10. Cf. Π 17.

ὄλεσ(σ)ε, 3 sing. aor. ὄλλυμι.

ὀλέσω, fut. ὄλλυμι.

ὀλετήρ, -ῆρος, ὁ [ὀλε-, ὄλλυμι]. A destroyer or slayer : φίλης κεφαλῆς ὀλετῆρα Σ 114.

ὀλιγηπελέων, -ουσα [a ppl. form fr. ὀλιγη-, ὀλίγος + πέλω. App. 'little moving']. Thus, hardly able to stir, with little life in one's limbs, weak, feeble : ἄπνευστος καὶ ἄναυδος κεῖτ' ὀλιγηπελέων ε 457. Cf. O 24, 245 : τ 356.

ὀλιγηπελίη, -ης, ἡ [cf. prec.]. Weakness, feebleness : μή με στίβη ἐξ ὀλιγηπελίης δαμάσῃ ε 468.

ὀλιγοδρανέων [a ppl. form fr. ὀλίγος + δράω. 'Able to do little']. Showing weakness or feebleness, with feeble utterance: τὸν ὀλιγοδρανέων προσέφη O 246 = X 337. Cf. Π 843.

ὀλίγος, -η, -ον. **(1)** Not much, little : ὀλίγος ἔτι θυμὸς ἐνῆεν A 593.—Absol. Λ 801 = Π 43 = Σ 201 (see ἀνάπνευσις).—Superl. : ἄμητος ὀλίγιστός [ἐστιν] T 223.—**(2)** Of small extent : ὀλίγη ἦν ἀμφὶς ἄρουρα Γ 115. Cf. K 161, M 423, Π 68, P 394.— **(3)** Of no great size, small : σάκος Ξ 376. Cf. Π 825 : μ 252, υ 259.—Of a wave, not rising high, inconsiderable κ 94.—Of utterance, carrying no great volume of sound, small : ὀπί ξ 492.—Of persons, of small stature, short, of small build : ὀλίγος τε καὶ οὐτιδανὸς καὶ ἄκικυς ι 515. Cf. B 529. —Sim. of Eris : ἥ τ' ὀλίγη πρῶτα κορύσσεται (rears her head but a little way) Δ 442.—**(4)** In reference to time, of no great duration, short : ἐπιδραμέτην ὀλίγον χρόνον Ψ 418. Cf. T 157.— **(5)** Of small value : δόσις ὀλίγη τε φίλη τε ζ 208, ξ 58 (see δόσις).—Absol. : ὀλίγον τε φίλον τ' ἔχων A 167.—Of small amount : χρεῖος γ 368.—**(6)** In neut. sing. ὀλίγον as adv., not much, little : ὀ. τί μ' ἧσσον ἐτίμα ο 365. Cf. E 800, M 452.—A little, slightly : καὶ εἴ κ' ὀ. περ ἐπαύρῃ [βέλος] Λ 391. Cf. P 538, T 217, Ψ 424, 789 : στιβαρώτερον οὐκ ὀλίγον περ θ 187. Cf. θ 547, κ 24, τ 244.—App., leaving a small interval : ἱππῆες ὀ. μετεκίαθον (came up close) Λ 52.—Slowly, taking one's time, without haste : ὀ. γόνυ γουνὸς ἀμείβων Λ 547.—**(7)** In genit. ὀλίγου, all but, nearly, almost : ὀλίγου σε κύνες διεδηλήσαντο ξ 37.

†ὀλισθάνω. 3 sing. aor. ὄλισθε. To miss one's footing, slip : ὄλισθε θέων Ψ 774.—To slip out of position : ἐκ οἱ ἧπαρ ὄλισθεν (*i.e.*, app., the edge projected through the wound) Υ 470.

ὄλλῡμι. **(A)** Fut. ὀλέσω ν 399. 2 sing. ὀλέσσεις M 250. 3 ὀλέσσει β 49. Aor. ὤλεσα B 115, I 22, X 104 : ι 40. 2 sing. ὤλεσας ω 93. 3 ὤλεσε Λ 342, Π 753, P 616, Υ 412, X 107, Ω 638 : η 60, τ 274, φ 88, ψ 68, ω 428. ὄλεσε λ 318, ν 431. ὄλεσσε Θ 90, 270 : δ 446, φ 284. 3 pl. ὤλεσαν H 360, M 234 : σ 181, 252, τ 125. ὄλεσαν ψ 319, ω 528. ὄλεσσαν Ω 609. 2 sing. subj. ὀλέσῃς A 559. ὀλέσσῃς E 250, K 452, Λ 433 : τ 81. 3 ὀλέσῃ B 4. ὀλέσσῃ A 205, Σ 92 : β 330. 3 pl. ὀλέσωσι X 360. 3 sing. opt. ὀλέσειε Θ 358 : δ 668. Imp. ὄλεσσον P 647. Pple. ὀλέσας, -αντος Θ 498, N 763, O 66, Ω 168 : β 174, ι 63, 534, 566, κ 134, λ 114, μ 141, ν 340. ὀλέσσας I 188, T 60. Fem. ὀλέσᾱσα τ 265. Infin. ὀλέσαι Ω 242 : μ 349, τ 482. ὀλέσσαι Π 861, Φ 216, Ω 46 : μ 350.—**(B)** 2 sing. pf. ὄλωλας Ω 729. 3 ὄλωλε K 186, O 111, Π 521, Ω 384 : γ 89, δ 318. 3 sing. subj. ὀλώλῃ Δ 164, Z 448. 3 sing. plupf. ὀλώλει K 187. **Mid.** 3 sing. fut. ὀλεῖται B 325, H 91 : ω 196. 2 pl. ὀλέεσθε Φ 133. Infin. ὀλέεσθαι O 700, Φ 278. Aor. ὀλόμην λ 197. 2 sing. ὤλεο Ω 725. 3 ὤλετο I 413, 415, N 772, Π 489, P 411, 642, 655, Σ 80 : α 168, β 183, 365, γ 235, δ 489, ε 436, η 60, ρ 319, ψ 68. ὄλετο ξ 68, ο 247. 3 pl. ὤλοντο ι 61. ὄλοντο Δ 409, Λ 693, Π 546, 848, Σ 230, Ω 603 : α 7, 355, δ 98, ε 306, κ 132, 437, λ 382, 629, τ 277, φ 22. Subj. ὄλωμαι ο 90. 2 sing. ὄληαι Γ 417. 3 ὄληται Λ 764, Υ 303 : β 98, ξ 130, 181, ο 91, τ 143, ω 133. 3 pl. ὄλωνται Θ 34, 37, 354, 465, 468. 2 pl. opt. ὄλοισθε α 380, β 145. Infin. ὀλέσθαι Γ 428, N 349, T 421, X 110, Ω 764 : α 377, β 142, 284, ε 113, ι 496, ξ 68, ο 327, σ 401. (ἀπ-, δι-, ἐξ-, ἐξαπ-.) **(I)** In pres. and aor. act. **(1)** **(a)** To destroy, cause the destruction of, kill, slay, cause the death of, make away with : πολέας 'Αχαιῶν A 559, B 4, εὐχωλὴ ἀνδρῶν ὀλλύντων Δ 451 = Θ 65. Cf. Θ 449, 472, 498, K 201, Λ 83, O 66, P 647, Φ 216, X 360, Ω 609 : β 330, ι 40, λ 318, ψ 319, ω 528.—To bring down destruction or ruin on the head of, be the death of: μαῖα, τίη μ' ἐθέλεις ὀλέσαι; τ 482.—Sim.: ἐή τέ μιν ὤλεσεν ἀλκή Π 753.—(b) In reference to inanimate objects, to destroy, bring to nothing: νῆας Θ 498. Cf. μ 349, ν 399, 431, ψ 319.—(c) To destroy, lay waste (a city) Ι 188, Τ 60.—(d) To consume, bring to nothing (goods or substance): βίοτον ἀπὸ πάμπαν ὀλέσσει β 49.—(e) In reference to faculties or qualities, to cause to perish, destroy, deprive one of: ἔκ τοι θεοὶ φρένας ὤλεσαν Η 360=Μ 234. Cf. δ 668, σ 181, 252=τ 125, φ 284.—(f) To counteract, be a remedy against: ὄλεσσε κήτεος ὀδμήν δ 446.—(2) To lose, incur the loss of, be deprived of: θυμόν Α 205. Cf. Ε 250, Θ 358, Ν 763, Ω 46, 242, etc.: ἑταίρους β 174. Cf. μ 350, τ 81, 265, 274, φ 88, ψ 68, ω 93, etc.—To incur the loss of under one's leadership, lose, throw away: πολὺν λαόν Β 115=Ι 22. Cf. Χ 104, 107: η 60, ω 428.—(II) In pf. and plupf. act. and in mid. and pass. (1) (a) To be destroyed, perish, die: κεῖνοι σφετέρῃσιν ἀτασθαλίῃσιν ὄλοντο Δ 409, ὀλλυμένων Δαναῶν Θ 202, ἀνὴρ ὤριστος ὄλωλεν Π 521. Cf. Γ 428, Δ 451, Θ 34, Λ 83, Ν 349, etc.: α 7, 380, γ 89, κ 123, ξ 68, ο 90, ρ 319, τ 277, etc.—With cognate acc.: σύ κεν κακὸν οἶτον ὄλῃαι Γ 417. Cf. Φ 133.—(b) In reference to inanimate objects, to be destroyed, perish, come to nothing, disappear: μή μοι νήματ' ὄληται β 98=τ 143=ω 133. Cf. κ 132, ο 91.—(c) Of a city, to be destroyed or laid waste: ὅτ' ἄν ποτ' ὀλώλῃ Ἴλιος Δ 164=Ζ 448. Cf. Ν 772.—(d) Of goods, substance or the like, to be consumed, destroyed, brought to nothing: ἀνδρὸς ἑνὸς βίοτον νήποινον ὀλέσθαι α 377=β 142, ὄλωλε πίονα ἔργα δ 318.—(e) Of abstractions, to perish, be lost, vanish: ὅου κλέος οὔ ποτ' ὀλεῖται Β 325, ὤλετό μοι νόστος Ι 413, ὕπνος ὄλωλεν (ὀλώλει) Κ 186, 187. Cf. Η 91, Ι 415: α 168, ω 196.—(2) To be lost, go astray: ἵππους, αἵ οἱ ὄλοντο φ 22.

ὅλμος, -ου, ὁ (Fόλμος) [Fελ-, (F)είλω]. App., a cylindrical piece of wood for use as a roller: ὅλμον ὣς ἔσσευεν (sc. the mutilated body) Λ 147.

ὀλοιός. See ὀλοός.

ὀλολῡγή, -ῆς, ἡ [ὀλολύζω]. An ecstatic religious shout of women Ζ 301.

ὀλολύζω. 3 sing. aor. ὀλόλυξε δ 767. 3 pl. ὀλόλυξαν γ 450. Infin. ὀλολύξαι χ 408. To shout in exultation or triumph (always of women) χ 408, 411.—Sim. of an ecstatic shout of women at a religious ceremony γ 450, δ 767.

ὀλόμην, aor. mid. ὄλλυμι.

ὀλοοίτροχος, ὁ [app. for FολοF-οί-τροχος, fr. Fελυ-, FελF-, (F)είλω+τρέχω. The -οι- not explained]. A rolling stone Ν 137.

ὀλοός, -ή, -όν [ὄλλυμι]. Also **ὀλοιός** Α 342, Χ 5. Destructive, baneful, deadly, painful, mischievous, bringing mischief Γ 133, Ι 305, Λ 71, Ν 629, 665, Ξ 139, Π 567, 849, Χ 65, Ψ 10, Ω 487, etc.: β 100, γ 135, ι 82, λ 276, μ 68, 113, χ 200, etc.—Comp. ὀλοώτερος Γ 365, Ψ 439: υ 201.—Superl. ὀλοώτατος Χ 15: δ 442 (here of two terminations).—Absol. in neut. pl. ὀλοά, mischief: τῷ ὀλοὰ φρονέων Π 701.

ὀλοόφρων, -ονος [ὀλοός+φρήν]. Having mischief in his mind, malign α 52, κ 137, λ 322.—Applied to animals Β 723, Ο 630, Ρ 21.

ὀλοφυδνός [cf. next]. Lamentable, piteous, tearful: ἔπος Ε 683 (or here perh. rather, beseeching (cf. next (6)), Ψ 102: τ 362.

ὀλοφύρομαι. 2 sing. aor. ὀλοφύραο λ 418. 3 ὀλοφύρατο Θ 245, Ρ 648: δ 364, κ 157. (1) To make lament, sorrow, weep, mourn, grieve: ὀλοφυρόμενος (ὀλοφυρομένη) ἔπεα προσηύδα Ε 871=Λ 815, Σ 72. Cf. Ο 114=398, Φ 106: β 362, δ 719, κ 418, λ 418, ν 199, χ 447, etc.—(2) To lament, weep for, mourn: παῖδα τ 522. Cf. Ω 328.—(3) To feel pity or compassion. With genit. of person pitied: Δαναῶν Θ 33=464. Cf. Θ 202, Π 17, Χ 169.—(4) To feel for, pity, take pity upon, compassionate, be touched by the plight of: τὸν πατὴρ ὀλοφύρατο δάκρυ χέοντα Θ 245=Ρ 648. Cf. Λ 656, Π 450: δ 364, κ 157.—(5) With infin., app., to bewail the necessity of doing something: πῶς ἄντα μνηστήρων ὀλοφύρεαι ἄλκιμος εἶναι; (why not pluck up heart to face them?) χ 232.—(6) App., to beseech. Parenthetically: καί μοι δὸς τὴν χεῖρ', ὀλοφύρομαι Ψ 75.

ὀλοφώϊος. (1) Crafty, cunning, malign: δήνεα Κίρκης κ 289.—(2) Absol. in neut. pl. ὀλοφώϊα, wiles, craft, cunning: ὀλοφώϊα τοῖο γέροντος δ 410, ὀλοφώϊα εἰδώς (with craft or cunning in his heart) δ 460 (see εἴδω (III) (12)).—Connoting malignity ρ 248.

ὄλῡραι, αἱ. Some kind of grain (perh. the same as ζειαί) Ε 196, Θ 564.

ὄλωλε, 3 sing. pf. ὄλλυμι.

ὄλωμαι, aor. subj. mid. ὄλλυμι.

ὁμαδέω [ὅμαδος]. To make a common din or murmur of voices, burst into uproar: μνηστῆρες ὁμάδησαν α 365=δ 768=σ 399, ρ 360, χ 21.

ὅμαδος, -ου, ὁ [ὁμός]. (1) A throng, concourse, company: ἐς Τρώων ὅμαδον κίεν Η 307, ἐνὶ πρώτῳ ὁμάδῳ μάχεσθαι (in the forefront of the battle) Ρ 380. Cf. Ο 689.—(2) A roar or murmur of voices, uproar: ὅμαδος ἦν Β 96. Cf. Ι 573, Κ 13, Μ 471=Π 296, Π 295, Τ 81, Ψ 234: κ 556.—Of the roaring of wind Ν 797.

ὁμαλός [ὁμός]. Smooth ι 327.

ὁμαρτέω [ὁμοῦ+ἀρ-, ἀραρίσκω]. (ἐφ-.) (1) To do something together or at the same moment, coincide in action: ἐξ οἴκου βῆσαν ὁμαρτήσαντες ἅμ' ἄμφω φ 188. Cf. Μ 400.—(2) To act as a companion or attendant Ω 438.—To keep up with something, vie with it in speed: οὐδέ κεν ἴρηξ κίρκος ὁμαρτήσειεν ν 87.

ὁμαρτήδην [ὁμαρτέω]. Doing something together or at the same moment, acting coincidently Ν 584.

ὄμβρος, -ου, ὁ. Rain Γ 4, Ε 91, Κ 6, Λ 493, Ν 139 (with its rain-swollen stream), Ψ 328: α 161, δ 566, ε 480, ζ 43, ι 111=358, ν 245, τ 442.—Of snow Μ 286.

ὀμεῖται, 3 sing. fut. ὄμνυμι.

ὁμηγερής [ὁμοῦ + ἀγείρω]. Gathered together, assembled: ἐπεὶ ὁμηγερέες ἐγένοντο Α 57, Ω 790. Cf. Β 789, Η 415, Ο 84, Ω 84, 99: β 9 = θ 24 = ω 421.

ὁμηγυρίζομαι [ὁμήγυρις]. To call together, assemble: ὁμηγυρίσασθαι Ἀχαιοὺς εἰς ἀγορήν π 376.

ὁμήγυρις, ἡ [ὁμοῦ + ἄγυρις]. An assembled company: θεῶν μεθ' ὁμήγυριν ἄλλων Υ 142.

ὁμηλικίη, -ης [ὁμῆλιξ]. (1) One of the same age as another, his fellow in years: ὁμηλικίη μοί ἐσσι χ 209. Cf. Υ 465: γ 49, ζ 23.—(2) In reference to two persons, of like age or years: εἰ ὁμηλικίη γε γενοίμεθα Ν 485.—(3) In collective sense, those of the same age as another, his fellows in years or contemporaries: πᾶσαν ὁμηλικίην ἐκέκαστο Ν 431. Cf. Γ 175, Ε 326: β 158, γ 364.

ὁμῆλιξ, -ικος [ὁμός + ἧλιξ]. Of the same age, of like years: ὁμήλικές εἰμεν ο 197. Cf. ω 107.—Absol., one of the same age as another, his fellow in years: νίψον σοῖο ἄνακτος ὁμήλικα τ 358.—In pl., those of the same age as another, his fellows in years or contemporaries: μετὰ πάντας ὁμήλικας ἔπλεν ἄριστος Ι 54. Cf. π 419.

ὁμηρέω. To meet with, encounter. With dat.: ὡμήρησέ μοι παρ' ἑταίρων ἄγγελος π 468.

ὁμῑλαδόν [ὅμιλος]. In a body: ἕποντο Ο 277, Ρ 730.—Keeping close together, maintaining close contact: ἐμάχοντο Μ 3.

ὁμῑλέω [ὅμιλος]. 3 pl. impf. ὡμίλευν Σ 539. (μεθ-.) (1) To come together, gather together, assemble, meet δ 684, φ 156.—To be gathered together, form a band or company: περὶ κεῖνον ω 19.—(2) To associate, consort, keep company with. With dat.: μνηστῆρσιν β 21, 288, 381, π 271, σ 167. Cf. Α 261.—With παρά: οὕνεκα πὰρ παύροισιν ὁμιλεῖς σ 383.—(3) To keep (with others), countenance or support them: μετὰ Τρώεσσιν ὁμιλεῖ Ε 834.—(4) To company (with the foe), engage in fight, carry on the fight, take part in the battle, join battle: ἐνὶ πρώτοισιν ὁμιλεῖ Σ 194. Cf. Λ 502, Π 641, 644, Σ 535, 539, Τ 158.—With dat.: Δαναοῖσιν Λ 523, Ν 779. Cf. α 265 = δ 345 = ρ 136.—(5) Senses (4) and (3) united: Τυδεΐδην οὐκ ἂν γνοίης ποτέροισι μετείη, ἠὲ μετὰ Τρώεσσιν ὁμιλέοι ἦ μετ' Ἀχαιοῖς Ε 86.

ὅμῑλος, -ου, ὁ. (1) An assembly, concourse, company: πολλὸς χορὸν περιίσταθ' ὅ. Σ 603. Cf. Η 183, 186, Χ 462, Ψ 651, 804, 813, Ω 712: α 225, θ 109, ο 328, π 29, ρ 67, 564, 590, ψ 303.—In dat. ὁμίλῳ, in a body: ἦλθον ὁμίλῳ προτὶ ἄστυ Φ 606. Cf. Ν 50, 87.—In reference to inanimate objects: οὔ τι μεμιγμένον ἐστὶν ὁμίλῳ [σημάτων] (the mass of . . .) θ 196.—(2) A throng gathered for or engaged in battle, the battle-throng: ἐρχόμενον προπάροιθεν ὁμίλου Γ 22. Cf. Δ 86, Ε 334, Λ 516 (in the direction of his friends), Μ 191, Ρ 149 (to his friends), 471, Τ 402, Υ 178 (so far forth from the . . .), etc.: θ 216, λ 514.—Sim.: μνηστήρων ἐς ὅμιλον ἀκοντίσαι (ἀκόντισαν) χ 263, 282.—So of a host in bivouac Κ 231, 338, 433, 499, 517, 545.—Of a body of men gathered to attack or attacking a beast: λέων ἀνδρῶν ἐν ὁμίλῳ δ 791. Cf. Ο 588, Υ 173.

ὁμίχλη, -ης, ἡ. A mist Α 359, Γ 10, Ρ 649.—Of a cloud of dust: κονίης ὁμίχλην Ν 336.

ὄμμα, -ατος, τό [ὀπ-. See ὁράω]. The eye. Always in pl.: ὄμματα καὶ κεφαλὴν ἴκελος Διί Β 478. Cf. Α 225, Γ 397, Θ 349, Κ 91, Ψ 66, Ω 343: = ε 47, α 208, ε 492, π 179, ω 3.—The face or countenance: οὐκ ἴδον ὄμματα φωτός Λ 614. Cf. Γ 217 (keeping his face turned to the earth).

ὄμνῡμι, ὀμνύω. Fut. in mid. form ὀμοῦμαι Α 233, Ι 132, Φ 373: υ 229. 3 sing. ὀμεῖται Ι 274. Aor. ὤμοσα δ 253. 3 sing. ὤμοσε Τ 127: ξ 331. ὄμοσε Ξ 280, Τ 113: β 378, κ 346. ὄμοσσε Κ 328, Ψ 42. 1 pl. ὠμόσσαμεν Υ 313. 3 ὄμοσαν μ 304, ο 438, σ 59. 3 sing. subj. ὀμόσσῃ Γ 279, Τ 260. Opt. ὀμόσαιμι Ο 40. Imp. ὄμοσον β 373. ὄμοσσον Α 76, Κ 321, Ξ 271, Τ 108. 2 pl. ὀμόσσατε μ 298, σ 55. Pple. ὀμόσας ξ 392. ὀμόσσας Τ 265. Infin. ὀμόσαι Τ 187. ὀμόσσαι ε 178, κ 299, 343. (ἀπ-, ἐπ-.) (1) To make an affirmation, give an undertaking, indicate a resolve, under the sanction of an oath, to swear: σκῆπτρον λάβε καί οἱ ὄμοσσεν Κ 328. Cf. Γ 279, Ξ 278, 280, Τ 260, 265: β 378 = κ 346, μ 304 = ο 438 = σ 59, ξ 392.—With cognate acc.: μέγαν ὅρκον Α 233. Cf. Ι 132, Τ 108, Υ 313, etc.: δ 253, ε 178, κ 299, υ 229, etc.—(2) To swear to the truth of (something): ταῦτ' ἐγὼν ἐθέλω ὀμόσαι Τ 187.—To swear to (an undertaking): τόδ' ὀμοῦμαι Φ 373.—(3) With pres., aor. or pf. infin. indicating what is affirmed: μή ποτε τῆς εὐνῆς ἐπιβήμεναι Ι 132, 274, Τ 175: νῆα κατειρύσθαι καὶ ἐπαρτέας ἔμμεν ἑταίρους ξ 331, τ 288.—With μὴ μέν Ψ 585.—(4) With ἦ μέν and fut. infin. indicating what is undertaken or resolved: ἦ μέν μοι πρόφρων ἀρήξειν Α 76. Cf. Κ 321, etc.—Without ἦ μέν: μή ποτ' ἐς Οὔλυμπον αὖτις ἐλεύσεσθαι Ἄτην Τ 127. Cf. Υ 313, Φ 373: ε 178 = κ 343, κ 299.—With μὴ μέν and aor. infin.: μὴ μὲν πρὶν Ὀδυσῆ' ἀναφῆναι, πρίν γε . . . δ 253.—Without μέν: μὴ μητρὶ τάδε μυθήσασθαι, πρίν γε . . . β 373.—With clause: μή τις ἐμὲ χειρὶ βαρείῃ πλήξῃ σ 55. Cf. μ 298.—(5) To invoke in sanction of an oath, swear by: Στυγὸς ὕδωρ Ξ 271. Cf. Ο 40.

ὁμογάστριος [ὁμός + γαστήρ]. Born of the same mother: κασίγνητον ὁμογάστριον Ω 47. Cf. Φ 95.

ὁμόθεν [ὁμός + -θεν(1)]. From the same point. With ἐξ: δοιοὺς θάμνους ἐξ ὁμόθεν πεφυῶτας (from the same root or stem) ε 477.

ὁμοίιος. Of unknown origin and meaning. Epithet of γῆρας Δ 315.—Of νεῖκος Δ 444.—Of πόλεμος: ὁμοιΐου π(τ)ολέμοιο (ὁμοιΐο͜ο πτολέμοιο) Ι 440, Ν 358, 635, Ο 670, Σ 242, Φ 294: σ 264, ω 543.—Of θάνατος γ 236.

ὁμοῖος, -η, -ον. (1) Like, the like, resembling: οὔ ποθ' ὁμοίης ἔμμορε τιμῆς (*i.e.* very different (from that of common men)) Α 278, οὔ πω πάντες ὁμοῖοι ἀνέρες ἐν πολέμῳ Μ 270. Cf. Δ 410, Ε 441: χρώς τοι οὐκέθ' ὁμοῖος (like what it was) π 182, παῦροι Ἀχαιῶν ἦσαν ὁμοῖοι (like him) τ 240.—Absol.: ὁππότε τὸν ὁμοῖον ἀνὴρ ἐθέλῃσιν ἀμέρσαι (one as good as himself) Π 53: ὡς αἰεὶ τὸν ὁμοῖον ἄγει θεὸς ὡς τὸν ὁμοῖον (as heaven brings one like, so it brings his like) (ὥς seems to be better read than ὡς) ρ 218.—With dat.: τρήρωσι πελειάσιν Ε 778, κόμαι Χαρίτεσσιν ὁμοῖαι (like the Graces' . . .) Ρ 51. Cf. Β 553, Ι 305, Κ 216, 437, Ξ 521, Ρ 475, Ψ 632: β 121, 276, γ 468, ζ 16, 231 = ψ 158, θ 14, τ 203, ψ 163.—With complementary infin.: τῷ οὔ πώ τις ὁμοῖος γένετ' ἀνὴρ κοσμῆσαι ἵππους Β 553. Cf. Κ 437, Ξ 521, Ρ 475.—(2) The same, one and the same: εἴ μοι ὁμοίη μοῖρα τέτυκται Σ 120. Cf. Σ 329.

ὁμοιόω [ὁμοῖος]. In pass., to be made like, to liken oneself to, vie with. With dat.: ἶσον ἐμοὶ φάσθαι καὶ ὁμοιωθήμεναι ἄντην Α 187. Cf. γ 120.

ὁμοκλέω, ὁμοκλάω [ὁμοῦ + καλέω]. 3 sing. pa. iterative ὁμοκλήσασκε Β 199. (1) To shout together in encouragement, urge comrades to action with shouts: ὁμόκλεον ἀλλήλοισιν Ο 658.—To shout together in rebuke, reproach or menace: πάντες ὁμοκλήσαντες ἔχον ἵππους (raising a shout to daunt the foe) Ο 354: μνηστῆρες πάντες ὁμόκλεον φ 360. Cf. τ 155, φ 367, χ 211, ω 173.—(2) Of a single person, to shout an order. With acc. and infin.: ἦ λαοὺς ἐς τεῖχος ὁμοκλήσειεν ἀλῆναι Π 714.—To shout in encouragement or with a view to urging on to action: μέγα Τρώεσσιν ὁμόκλα Σ 156. Cf. Υ 365, Ψ 337, 363.—In rebuke or reproach: δεῖν' ὁμοκλήσας προσέφη 'Απόλλων Ε 439. Cf. Β 199, Ζ 54, Π 706, Ω 248, 252.—In menace: τῇ ῥ' ἔχ' ὁμοκλήσας (raising a shout to daunt the foe) Π 378. Cf. Υ 448: ξ 35.

ὁμοκλή, -ῆς, ἡ [cf. ὁμοκλέω]. (1) A rebuke or reproach: ἄνακτος (πατρὸς) ὑποδείσαντες ὁμοκλήν Μ 413 = Ψ 417 = 446, Ω 265. Cf. ρ 189.—(2) A menacing or threatening shout: ἔχε τρόμος ἀνδρὸς ὁμοκλῇ Ζ 137, μάχῃ ἔνι μεῖναι ὁμοκλήν (to stand up to the shouting foe) Π 147.

ὁμοκλητήρ, -ῆρος, ὁ [ὁμοκλέω]. A shouter. In encouragement: τοῖο ἄνευθεν ἐόντος ὁμοκλητῆρος ἀκούσας (*i.e.* he heard his voice as he urged on his horses) Ψ 452.—In menace: μή τις ὀπίσσω τετράφθω ὁμοκλητῆρος ἀκούσας (before the shouts of the foe) Μ 273.

ὀμόργνῡμι. *Aor. pple. mid. ὀμορξάμενος, -η Σ 124: θ 88, λ 530. (ἀπ-.) To wipe off or away: ἀπ' ἰχῶ χειρὸς ὀμόργνυ Ε 416.—In mid., to wipe away from one's face: δάκρυ' ὀμορξάμενος θ 88. Cf. Σ 124: λ 527, 530.

ὁμός, -ή, -όν. The same, one and the same: οὐ πάντων ἦεν ὁμὸς θρόος Δ 437. Cf. Ν 354, Ο 209, Ψ 91, Ω 57: κ 41, ρ 563.—The same as. With dat.: ἤ κέν τοι ὁμὸν λέχος εἰσαναβαίνοι Θ 291.—Common, in which all take part: τῶν ὁμὸν ἵστατο νεῖκος Ν 333.

ὁμόσε [ὁμός + -σε]. To the same spot: τῶν ὁμόσ' ἦλθε μάχη (they joined battle) Ν 337. Cf. Μ 24.

ὄμοσ(σ)ε, 3 sing. aor. ὄμνυμι.

ὁμοστιχάω [ὁμοῦ + στιχ-, στείχω]. To go with, accompany. With dat.: βόεσσιν Ο 635.

ὁμότῑμος [ὁμός + τιμή]. Entitled to be held in the same estimation, equally to be honoured: εἴ μ' ὁμότιμον ἐόντα καθέξει Ο 186.

ὁμοῦ [ὁμός]. (1) In the same place, together Ψ 84.—Into the same place, together: θῆρας ὁμοῦ εἰλεῦντα λ 573.—(2) At the same time, together, both at once: εἰ ὁμοῦ πόλεμός τε δαμᾷ καὶ λοιμὸς 'Αχαιούς Α 61. Cf. Δ 122, Λ 127, 245, Ρ 362, 745, Υ 499: ε 294 = ι 69 = μ 315, ι 75 = κ 143, μ 67, 178, 424.—(3) With dat., along with, with, among: νεφέεσσιν Ε 867. Cf. Ο 118: δ 723, ο 365.

ὁμοῦμαι, fut. ὄμνυμι.

ὁμοφρονέω [ὁμόφρων]. To be of like mind with another ζ 183.—To feel with another, sympathize with him ι 456.

ὁμοφροσύνη, -ης, ἡ [ὁμόφρων]. Oneness or likeness of mind, concord: ὁμοφροσύνην ὀπάσειαν ζ 181.—So in pl.: ἧδ' ὁδὸς καὶ μᾶλλον ὁμοφροσύνῃσιν ἐνήσει ο 198.

ὁμόφρων, -ονος [ὁμός + φρήν]. In reference to the mind, like that of another, having the same inclinations. Of animals: οὐδὲ λύκοι τε καὶ ἄρνες ὁμόφρονα θυμὸν ἔχουσιν Χ 263.

ὁμόω [ὁμός]. To unite Ξ 209.

ὀμφαλόεις, -όεσσα, -όεν [ὀμφαλός]. (1) Furnished with a boss. Epithet of shields (cf. ὀμφαλός (2)) Δ 448, Ζ 118, Μ 161, Χ 111, etc.: τ 32.—(2) Of the yoke of a chariot, furnished with a boss (cf. ὀμφαλός (3)) Ω 269.

ὀμφαλός, -οῦ, ὁ. (1) The navel: οὖτα παρ' ὀμφαλόν Δ 525. Cf. Ν 568, Υ 416, Φ 180.—Fig., the centre: νήσῳ ἐν ἀμφιρύτῃ, ὅθι τ' ὀ. ἐστι θαλάσσης α 50.—(2) A boss on a shield Λ 34, Ν 192.—(3) A boss on the yoke of a chariot Ω 273.

ὄμφαξ, -ακος, ἡ. An unripe grape η 125.

ὀμφή, -ῆς, ἡ. A voice. Always of a divine voice or inspiration: ἐπισπόμενοι θεοῦ ὀμφῇ γ 215 = π 96. Cf. Β 41, Υ 129.

ὁμώνυμος [ὁμός + ὄνυμα, Aeolic form of ὄνομα]. Bearing the same name Ρ 720.

ὅμως [ὁμός]. All the same, nevertheless: ὅμως δ' οὐ λήθετο χάρμης Μ 393. Cf. λ 565.

ὁμῶς [ὁμός]. (1) Alike, equally, likewise: ἄμφω ὁμῶς φιλέουσα Α 196 = 209. Cf. Ο 98, Ρ 422: νυκτὶ ὁμῶς πλείειν (*i.e.* as well as by day) ο 34, ὁμῶς ἐφοίτων (with one consent) ω 415. Cf. δ 775, θ 542, ψ 332.—(2) Preceding clauses joined by . . . τε . . . τε, τε καί, alike: πλῆθεν ὁμῶς ἵππων τε καὶ ἀνδρῶν Θ 214, κάτθαν' ὁμῶς ὅ τ' ἀεργὸς ἀνὴρ ὅ τε . . . Ι 320. Cf. Λ 708, Ο 257, Ρ 644, Φ 521, Ω 73: κ 28, 80 = ο 476, ω 63.—(3) In the same manner, to the same degree: οὐκέθ' ὁμῶς τιμῆς ἔσεαι Ι 605. Cf. Φ 62.—(4) With dat., equally with, like as: ὁμῶς τοι ἤπια οἶδεν ν 405 = ο 39. Cf. Ε 535, Ξ 72, Ι 312: = ξ 156.

ὄναρ, τό [cf. ὄνειρος]. A vision seen in sleep, a dream: οὐκ ὀ., ἀλλ' ὕπαρ ἐσθλόν τ 547. Cf. Κ 496: υ 90.—In generalized sense, dreams: καὶ γάρ τ' ὀ. ἐκ Διός ἐστιν Α 63.

ὄνδε [acc. sing. masc. of ὅς[1] + -δε (1)]. To his . . . (with the -δε doubled): ὄνδε δόμονδε Π 445: α 83 = ξ 424 = υ 239 = φ 204, γ 272, ρ 527, υ 329.

ὄνειαρ, -ατος, τό [ὀνίνημι]. (1) Something that

benefits, a means of aid, an aid, benefit, help: *ἐφράσατο μέγ' ὄνειαρ* δ 444. Cf. ο 78.—Of a person: *πᾶσιν ὄνειαρ* Χ 433. Cf. Χ 486.—**(2)** In pl., good things, good cheer: *παρά σφιν ὀνείατα μυρία κεῖται* κ 9. Cf. ο 316.—See also under *ἑτοῖμος* (1).—**(3)** In pl., goods, substance: *τοσσάδ' ὀνείατ' ἄγοντα* Ω 367.

ὀνείδειος [*ὄνειδος*]. Conveying blame or censure, reproachful, reviling, abusive: *μῦθον* Φ 393, 471. Cf. Α 519, Β 277, Π 628, Φ 480: σ 326.—Absol. in neut. pl., reviling, abuse: *ὀνειδείοισιν ἐνίσσων* Χ 497.

ὀνειδίζω [*ὄνειδος*]. 2 sing. aor. *ὀνείδισας* Ι 34. Imp. *ὀνείδισον* Α 211. **(1)** To use words of blame or censure, speak in abuse or reviling: *μετέειπε νείκει ὀνειδίζων* Η 95.—**(2)** To make matter of blame or reproach, cast in one's teeth: *ἀλκήν μοι ὀνείδισας* (*i.e.* the want of it) Ι 34: *τὴν γαστέρ' ὀνειδίζων* σ 380.—With dependent clause: *ὀνείδισον ὡς ἔσεταί περ* (speak out to him and tell him how it will be) Α 211, *ἧσαι ὀνειδίζων ὅτι . . .* (casting in his teeth that . . .) Β 255.

ὄνειδος, τό. **(1)** In pl., words of blame, censure, reproach, abuse, reviling: *λέγ' ὀνείδεα* Β 222. Cf. Α 291, Β 251, Γ 242, 438, Ι 460, Υ 246: ρ 461.—**(2)** In pl., shame, disgrace: *αἳ ἐμῇ κεφαλῇ κατ' ὀνείδεα χεῦαν* χ 463.—**(3)** A cause or source of reproach or blame: *ἐμοί κ' ὀνείδεα ταῦτα γένοιτο* ζ 285. Cf. Π 498, Ρ 556.

ὀνείρειος, -η, -ον [*ὄνειρος*]. Of dreams: *πύλῃσιν* δ 809.

ὀνειροπόλος, -ου, ὁ [*ὄνειρος* + *-πολος*, conn. with *πολεύω*]. One busied with dreams, one skilled in the interpretation of dreams Α 63, Ε 149.

ὄνειρος, ὁ. Also **ὄνειρον, τό** δ 841. Acc. pl. (besides *ὀνείρους*) *ὀνείρατα* υ 87. **(1)** A vision seen in sleep, a dream: *θεῖός μοι ἐνύπνιον ἦλθεν ὄ.* ξ 495. Cf. Β 80, Ε 150: δ 841, ζ 49, λ 207, 222, τ 535, 555, 560, 562, 568, υ 87, ω 12.—Personified Β 6, 8, 16, 22, 56.—**(2)** The state of one who is dreaming, a dream, the land of dreams: *ἐν περ ὀνείρῳ* τ 541, 581 = φ 79. Cf. Χ 199.

ὀνήμενος, aor. pple. mid. *ὀνίνημι*.

ὀνήσει, 3 sing. fut. *ὀνίνημι*.

ὄνησις, ἡ [*ὀνίνημι*]. Good, profit φ 402.

ὄνθος, -ου, ὁ. Dung Ψ 775, 777, 781.

ὀνίνημι. 3 sing. fut. *ὀνήσει* Η 172, Θ 36, 467: ψ 24. Infin. *ὀνήσειν* Ε 205. Aor. *ὄνησα* Α 503. 2 sing *ὤνησας* Α 395. 3 *ὤνησε* ξ 67. 3 pl. *ὤνησαν* Ι 509. **Mid.** 2 sing. fut. *ὀνήσεαι* Ζ 260. 3 *ὀνήσεται* Η 173, Π 31. 1 pl. *ὀνησόμεθα* ξ 415. Aor. imp. *ὄνησο* τ 68. Pple. *ὀνήμενος* β 33. (*ἀπ-*.) **(1)** To be of service to, confer benefit upon, benefit, profit, help: *'Αχαιούς* Η 172. Cf. Α 395, 503, Ε 205, Ι 509, Ω 45: *σὲ τοῦτό γε γῆρας ὀνήσει* (will benefit you so far, you may thank your years for that) ψ 24. Cf. ξ 67.—Without expressed object: *βουλήν, ἥ τις ὀνήσει* Θ 36 = 467.—**(2)** In mid., to get good, benefit, profit, help or enjoyment from something, be the better for it: *καὐτὸς ὀνήσεαι* Ζ 260. Cf. Η 173: *πρὸς δ' αὐτοὶ ὀνησόμεθα* (will get some enjoyment for ourselves) ξ 415.—With genit. of that from which good is derived: *τί σευ ἄλλος ὀνήσεται;* Π 31: *δαιτὸς ὄνησο* (make the best of it, be thankful for what you have got) τ 68.—In aor. pple., blessed (cf. *οὐλόμενος*): *ἐσθλός μοι δοκεῖ εἶναι, ὀνήμενος* β 33.

ὄνομα, -ατος, τό. Also **οὔνομα** Γ 235, Ρ 260: ζ 194, ι 355. A name, one's name Γ 235, Ρ 260: δ 710, ζ 194, θ 550, ι 16, ο 256, etc.—The name or fame of a person or of something: *'Ιθάκης γε καὶ ἐς Τροίην ὄ. ἵκει* ν 248. Cf. ω 93.

ὀνομάζω [*ὄνομα*]. 2 sing. aor. *ὠνόμασας* ω 339. **(1)** To address by name: *πατρόθεν ἐκ γενεῆς ὀνομάζων ἄνδρα ἕκαστον* Κ 68. Cf. Χ 415: δ 278.—In the recurring formula *ἔπος τ' ἔφατ' ἔκ τ' ὀνόμαζεν* app. meaning no more than 'to address' (the name is often not given in the reported speech, and in ζ 254 and κ 319 is not known to the speaker. In θ 194 the name cannot have been used, as it was not then known to the Phaeacians. In ρ 215 Melantheus cannot have known any name by which to address the disguised Odysseus. In ξ 52 the disguised Odysseus knew Eumaeus's name, but cannot be supposed to have used it) Α 361, Γ 398, Ζ 253, Η 108, etc.: β 302, γ 374, δ 311, η 330, etc.—**(2)** To speak of or mention by name, utter the name of: *τὸν καὶ οὐ παρεόντ' ὀνομάζειν αἰδέομαι* ξ 145.—**(3)** To name, tell the name of δ 551.—**(4)** To name, specify, detail, enumerate: *δῶρα* Σ 449. Cf. Ι 515, ω 339.

†ὄνομαι. 2 sing. *ὄνοσαι* ρ 378. 3 pl. *ὄνονται* φ 427. 3 sing. opt. *ὄνοιτο* Ν 287: θ 239. 3 sing. fut. *ὀνόσσεται* Ι 55. Infin. *ὀνόσσεσθαι* ε 379. Aor. *ὠνοσάμην* Ξ 95, Ρ 173. 3 sing. *ὤνατο* Ρ 25. 2 pl. *ὀνόσασθε* Ω 241. 3 sing. opt. *ὀνόσαιτο* Δ 539, Ν 127, Ρ 399. Pple. *ὀνοσσάμενος* Ω 439. Here app. should come as 2 pl. pres. *οὔνεσθε*, *v.l.* in Ω 241 (see above). To think little of, make light of, look upon or treat with contempt or scorn, disparage: *ἔργον* Δ 539. Cf. Ι 55, Ν 127, 287, Ξ 95 = Ρ 173, Ρ 25, 399, Ω 439: θ 239, φ 427.—With genit.: *κακότητος* ε 379.—With dependent clause: *ἦ ὀνόσασθ' ὅτι . . . ;* (seems it so light a thing that . . . ?) Ω 241: *ἦ ὄνοσαι ὅτι . . . ;* (is it not enough that . . . ?) ρ 378.

†ὀνομαίνω [*ὄνομα*]. 2 sing. aor. *ὀνόμηνας* ω 341. 3 *ὀνόμηνε* Κ 522, Ξ 278, Π 491, Ψ 90, 178, Ω 591. Subj. *ὀνομήνω* Β 488, Ι 121: δ 240, λ 328, 517. 2 sing. *ὀνομήνῃς* λ 251. (*ἐξ-*.) **(1)** To address or call to by name, call upon by name: *ἑταῖρον* Κ 522, Π 491, Ψ 178, Ω 591.—To call upon by name in adjuration: *θεούς* Ξ 278.—**(2)** To name, tell the name or names of, enumerate by name: *πληθύν* Β 488. Cf. λ 328, 517.—**(3)** To disclose a person's name λ 251.—**(4)** To name, appoint: *σόν με θεράποντ' ὀνόμηνεν* Ψ 90.—**(5)** To name, specify, detail, enumerate: *δῶρα* Ι 121. Cf. δ 240.—With a promise implied. With fut. infin.: *ὄρχους μοι ὀνόμηνας δώσειν πεντήκοντα* ω 341.

ὀνομακλήδην [*ὄνομα* + *κλη-*, *καλέω* (cf. *ἐξονομακλήδην*)]. By name Χ 415: δ 278.

ὀνομάκλυτος [*ὄνομα* + *κλυτός*]. Of famous name: *Ἄλτης* Χ 51.

ὀνομαστός, -ή, -όν [ὀνομάζω]. To be named: Κακοΐλιον οὐκ ὀνομαστήν τ 260=597=ψ 19.

ὀνόμηνε, 3 sing. aor. ὀνομαίνω.

ὄνος, ὁ. An ass Λ 558.

ὄνοσαι, 2 sing. pres. ὄνομαι.

ὀνόσαιτο, 3 sing. aor. opt. ὄνομαι.

ὀνόσσεται, 3 sing. fut. ὄνομαι.

ὀνοστός [ὀνοσ-, ὄνομαι]. To be made light of or treated with indifference: δῶρα I 164.

ὄντας, acc. pl. masc. pple. εἰμί.

ὄνυξ, ὁ. Dat. pl. ὀνύχεσσι in passages cited. In pl., an eagle's talons: νεβρὸν ἔχοντ' ὀνύχεσσιν Θ 248. Cf. M 202=220: β 153, ο 161.

ὀξυβελής [ὀξύς + βέλος. The force of the second element app. obscured]. Sharp, pointed. Epithet of an arrow: ὀϊστός Δ 126.

ὀξυόεις, -εντος [ὀξύς]. Sharp, pointed. Epithet of spears E 50, 568, H 11, Ξ 443, etc.: τ 33, υ 306.

ὀξύς, -εῖα, -ύ. (1) Sharp, keen, with sharp point or edge: δοῦρε δύω ὀξέα Λ 44. Cf. K 135, Λ 392, M 56 (pointed), 447 (coming to a point), O 711, etc.: α 99, γ 443, ε 411 (jagged), μ 74 (rising to a point), etc.—Epithet of weapons or parts thereof A 190, Δ 185, 214, 490, 530, etc.: β 3, δ 700, κ 145, ξ 271, χ 265, etc.—Sim. of cutting instruments: ἐρινεὸν ὀξέϊ χαλκῷ τάμνεν Φ 37. Cf. Ψ 412: μ 173.—(2) Fig. of the beams of the sun, piercing, penetrating P 372.—In reference to perception with the eye, quick. In superl., with infin.: ὀξύτατον εἰσοράασθαι Ξ 345. Cf. P 675.—Of sound, shrill, piercing: ἀϋτή O 313.—Of pain or grief, sharp, piercing: ὀδύναι Λ 268, 272. Cf. Λ 269, Π 518, T 125, X 425: λ 208, τ 517.—As epithet of Ares, eager, impetuous H 330.—As epithet of battle, keen, fierce: ὀξὺν Ἄρηα B 440, Δ 352=T 237, Θ 531=Σ 304, Λ 836, P 721.—(3) In neut. sing. ὀξύ as adv. (a) Of perceiving with the eye, with keen glance, quickly: νόησεν Γ 374=E 312, E 680, Θ 91, 132, Λ 343, O 649, Υ 291. Cf. ε 393.—Sim. of perceiving with the ear, quickly (the exercise of the power of hearing being thought of as keen like a glance): ἄκουσεν P 256.—(b) In reference to sound, shrilly, piercingly: βοήσας P 89. Cf. Σ 71, Υ 52, X 141.—(4) In neut. pl. ὀξέα as adv., in reference to sound, shrilly, piercingly: κεκλήγων B 222. Cf. M 125, P 88.—(5) In neut. sing. superl. ὀξύτατον as adv., of perceiving with the eye, with keenest glance, most quickly: οὔτ' ὀξύτατον δέρκεται ὄσσε Ψ 477.

ὀπάζω. Fut. ὀπάσσω θ 430, φ 214. 3 sing. ὀπάσσει ω 201. 1 pl. ὀπάσσομεν Ω 153. Aor. ὤπασα N 416. ὄπασσα κ 204. 3 sing. ὤπασε I 483, X 51: θ 498. ὄπασσε Ξ 491, P 196, Σ 452, Ω 461: δ 131, ν 68, ξ 62. 3 pl. ὤπασαν Z 157: ν 121, 305. Opt. ὀπάσαιμι Ψ 151. 3 pl. ὀπάσειαν ζ 181, ν 45. Imp. ὄπασσον H 205, Π 38: ο 310. Pple. ὀπάσσας ι 90, κ 102. Infin. ὀπάσσαι δ 619, ο 119. 3 sing. aor. mid. ὀπάσσατο T 238. 2 sing. subj. ὀπάσσεαι K 238. Pple. ὀπασσάμενος κ 59. (1) To cause to go with, accompany or attend, a person, send with him: ὤπασά οἱ πομπόν N 416. Cf. Π 38, Σ 452, Ω 153, 461: ι 90=κ 102, κ 204, ν 68, ο 310, υ 364.—To cause to follow a person as chief, give a person rule over: πολύν μοι ὤπασε λαόν I 483.—In mid., to attach to oneself, take with one, as companion: κήρυκα καὶ ἑταῖρον κ 59. Cf. K 238, T 238.—(2) To make over, give as a present, give, present: Πατρόκλῳ κόμην ὀπάσαιμι φέρεσθαι (I am ready to . . ., I can do no better than . . .) Ψ 151. Cf. P 196: χρυσέην ἠλακάτην δ 131. Cf. δ 619=ο 119, θ 430, ν 121, 305, ω 283.—(3) With less definite object, to cause to attend upon a person, attach to him, give, grant, bestow: κάλλος Z 157. Cf. H 205, Θ 141, M 255, Ξ 358, 491, O 327, Π 730, P 566, Φ 570, X 51 (*i.e.* as a dowry): ὁμοφροσύνην ζ 181. Cf. γ 57, θ 498, ν 45, ξ 62, ο 320, σ 19, τ 161, φ 214, ψ 210, ω 201.—(4) To press hard upon, chase, pursue: Ἀχαιούς Θ 341. Cf. E 334, P 462.—In pass.: [ποταμὸς] ὀπαζόμενος Διὸς ὄμβρῳ (driven onwards) Λ 493.—Of an abstraction, to bear hard upon, oppress: γῆράς μ' (σ') ὀπάζει Δ 321, Θ 103.

ὄπατρος [ὀ-=ἀ-[2] + πατρ-, πατήρ]. Having the same father Λ 257, M 371. (See κασίγνητος (1) (b).)

ὀπάων, -ονος, ὁ [cf. ὀπάζω]. (1) =θεράπων (1) Ψ 360.—(2) =θεράπων (2) H 165=Θ 263, K 58, P 258.—(3) Like θεράπων (3) P 610.

ὅπῃ, ὅππῃ. (1) In whichever direction, whithersoever: ἄρχ', ὅππῃ σε κραδίη κελεύει N 784. Cf. Υ 25 and X 185 (as . . .): α 347, ξ 517=ο 339, π 81=φ 342, σ 242.—With subj. or opt. in conditional relative sentences. For the examples and constructions see Table at end (III) (B) (a) (1), (b) (1), (D) (15) (17).—(2) In what direction, whither: πάπτηνεν ἕκαστος ὅπῃ φύγοι ὄλεθρον (to see where he could turn to escape . . .) Ξ 507=Π 283, εἰσορόων χρόα, ὅπῃ εἴξειεν (to see where he might find an opening) X 321. Cf. θ 573, χ 43.—(3) In what spot, where: εἴφ' ὅπῃ ἔσχες νῆα ι 279. Cf. ι 457.—In what direction or quarter: οὐ γὰρ ἴδμεν ὅπῃ ζόφος οὐδ' ὅπῃ ἠώς, οὐδ' ὅπῃ . . . οὐδ' ὅπῃ . . . κ 190.

ὀπηδέω [cf. ὀπάζω]. (1) To be in attendance on a person, attend him as a follower, retainer or henchman B 184, Ω 368.—Of an inanimate object, to be carried or borne by a person, accompany him: ἀνεμώλιά μοι ὀπηδεῖ [τόξα] E 216.—Of a divinity, to cause his protecting or favouring power to go with or attend on a person, act as his protector or guardian: Διί, ὅς θ' ἱκέτῃσιν ἅμ' αἰδοίοισιν ὀπηδεῖ η 165=181. Cf. ι 271, τ 398.—(2) Of abstractions, to attend upon a person, be attached to him, be given, granted, bestowed on him: ἀρετὴν σήν, ἥ τοι ὀπηδεῖ θ 237. Cf. P 251.

ὀπίζομαι [ὄπις]. (ἐπ-.) To regard with awe or reverence, stand in awe of, observe: μητρὸς ὠπίζετ' ἐφετμήν Σ 216. Cf. ν 148, ξ 283.—To pay regard or heed to, direct one's thoughts to, think of: ἔμ' οὐδὲν ὀπίζεο X 332.

ὄπιθε(ν). See ὄπισθε(ν).

ὀπῑπεύω [ὀπ-. See ὁράω]. To eye: τί ὀπιπεύεις πολέμοιο γεφύρας; (instead of advancing to the fight) Δ 371, οὔ σ' ἐθέλω βαλέειν ὀπιπεύσας (holding you in talk and looking out for a weak spot) H 243: ὀπιπεύσεις γυναῖκας (will be ogling the maids) τ 67.

ὄπις, -ιδος, ἡ [ὀπ-. See ὁράω]. Acc. ὄπιδα ξ 82, υ 215. ὄπιν Π 388: φ 28. The watch (kept by the gods) on the deeds of men, their regard for righteousness and reprobation of evil-doing: θεῶν ὄπιν οὐκ ἀλέγοντες Π 388. Cf. υ 215, φ 28.—So without θεῶν: οὐκ ὄπιδα φρονέοντες ξ 82. Cf. ξ 88.

ὄπισθε(ν), ὄπιθε(ν) [-θε(ν) (2). Cf. ὀπίσσω]. (I) (1) Of place. (a) Behind, in rear, in the hinder part: στῆ ὄπιθεν Α 197, πρόσθε λέων, ὄπιθεν δὲ δράκων Ζ 181. Cf. Β 542, Λ 397, Ν 289, Ρ 718 (covering the rear), Τ 397 (following him), etc.: σανίδας ἐκδῆσαι ὄπισθεν χ 174 (*i.e.* his feet and hands were to be bound together behind him and were to be made fast to the boards). Cf. δ 357, ε 167, ζ 307, θ 527, ν 84, ο 34, τ 436.—τὰ ὄπισθεν, the hinder parts Λ 613.—(b) Behind, remaining behind, while another departs or others depart: ὄπισθε μένων Ι 332. Cf. κ 209, λ 72, ο 88, ρ 201.—τοὺς ὄπιθεν Ἀχαιούς Ν 83 (the laggards).—Absent: τῶν ὄπιθεν λ 66 (those left at home).—(c) Towards the rear: ὄπιθεν σάκος βάλεν (behind his back) Λ 545.—(2) Of time, afterwards, hereafter, thereafter, in the future, in time to come, later: ταῦτ' (τὰ) ὄπισθεν ἀρεσσόμεθα Δ 362, Ζ 526. Cf. Ι 515 and 519 (for the future), Μ 34: κακῶς ὄπιθεν φρονέουσιν (*i.e.* they are awaiting their opportunity) σ 168. Cf. β 270, 278, ξ 393, χ 55, ψ 249, 261.—(II) With genit., of place, behind, in rear of: ὄπισθε μάχης Ν 536=Ξ 430. Cf. Ε 595, Ρ 468, Ω 15.

ὀπίσσω, ὀπίσω [cf. ὄπισθε]. (1) Of direction, backwards, back: ἀνεχάζετο τυτθὸν ὀπίσσω Ε 443. Cf. Γ 218, 261, Μ 205, Υ 119, etc.: θ 375, λ 149, μ 410.—In reference to the exercise of a mental faculty: πρόσσω καὶ ὀπίσσω (see πρόσσω (1)).—Back to the same place, back again: ὀπίσω κίε π 150. Cf. η 326.—Sim.: ὄφρ' ἐξεμέσειεν ὀπίσσω ἱστὸν αὖτις μ 437.—(2) Of place, behind, in rear: ἑξακέονται ὀπίσσω (follow and . . .) Ι 507, αὐτὰρ ὀπίσσω ἡ πληθὺς ἐπὶ νῆας ἀπονέοντο (behind the screen covering their retreat) Ο 304. Cf. Ο 735, Ρ 752, Φ 30, Χ 137.—Sim.: τῷ ἄλγεα κάλλιπ' ὀπίσσω (left behind her) λ 279. Cf. Γ 160: ψ 119.—(3) Of time, afterwards, hereafter, thereafter, in the future, in time to come, later: Τρῳαί μ' ὀπίσσω μωμήσονται Γ 411. Cf. Δ 37, Ζ 352, 450, Ο 497, etc.: α 222 (for the time to come), β 179, ζ 273, λ 433, ξ 137, σ 132, etc.—As *quasi*-sb.: ἐς ὀπίσσω σ 122=υ 199.

ὀπίστατος [superl. fr. ὄπισθε]. The hindmost, the last. Absol. Θ 342=Λ 178.

ὀπίσω. See ὀπίσσω.

ὁπλέω [ὅπλον]. Here prob. should come pres. infin. mid. ὅπλεσθαι Τ 172, Ψ 159 (for ὁπλεῖσθαι). To get ready, make ready, prepare: ἄμαξαν ζ 73.—In mid., to make ready (a meal) for oneself, prepare oneself (a meal): δεῖπνον ὅπλεσθαι Τ 172, Ψ 159.

ὁπλή, -ῆς, ἡ. A hoof Λ 536=Υ 501.

ὁπλίζω [ὅπλον]. 3 sing. aor. ὥπλισσε Λ 641. Imp. ὅπλισσον β 289. Infin. ὁπλίσαι Ω 190. 3 sing. aor. mid. ὡπλίσατο (ὁ-) Ψ 301, 351. ὡπλίσσατο Λ 86. ὁπλίσσατο β 20, ι 291, 311, 344, κ 116. 1 pl. ὁπλισάμεσθα δ 429, 574. 1 pl. subj. ὁπλισόμεσθα μ 292. 3 pl. aor. pass. ὅπλισθεν ψ 143. (ἀφοπλίζομαι, ἐφ-.) (1) To deck, array: ὅπλισθεν γυναῖκες (came in their finery) ψ 143.—(2) To get ready, make ready, prepare: κυκειῶ Λ 641: νῆες ὁπλίζονται πόντον ἔπι (are set their courses over . . .) ρ 288. Cf. Ω 190: β 289.—(3) In mid. (a) To get or make oneself ready, make one's preparations: ἔξω ἰὼν ὁπλίζετο ξ 526.—With infin.: ὁπλίζοντο νέκυας ἀγέμεν Η 417.—(b) To get ready, harness (one's horses) Ψ 301, 351.—(c) To make ready (a meal) for oneself, prepare oneself (a meal): δεῖπνον Λ 86: ι 311, κ 116, δόρπον β 20, δ 429=574, ι 291, 344, μ 292, π 453.—(d) To don one's harness, make ready or prepare for the fray: Τρῶες ἀνὰ πτόλιν ὁπλίζοντο Θ 55. Cf. ω 495.

ὅπλον, -ου, τό. (1) An implement, appliance, tool: ὅπλ' ἐν χερσὶν ἔχων γ 433. Cf. Σ 409, 412.—Specifically, a rope or cable: ἐμὲ κατέδησαν ὅπλῳ ξ 346. Cf. φ 390.—(2) In pl., the tackle of a ship landed from her when not in use and taken on board before putting to sea: πάντ' ἐν νηῒ ὅπλ' ἐτίθει β 390. Cf. ζ 268, κ 404, 424, μ 410.—Specifically, the running tackle: ὅπλων ἅπτεσθαι β 423, δησάμενοι ὅπλα 430. Cf. λ 9, μ 151, ο 288.—(3) In pl., warlike array, harness, armour: ὅπλοισιν ἔνι δεινοῖσιν ἐδύτην Κ 254, 272. Cf. Σ 614, Τ 21.

ὁπλότερος, -η, *comp.* Younger: ὁπλότερος γενεῇ Β 707. Cf. Δ 325: τ 184, φ 370.—Youthful rather than old: αἰεὶ ὁπλοτέρων ἀνδρῶν φρένες ἠερέθονται (the younger generation, the class of youths) Γ 108, Χαρίτων μίαν ὁπλοτεράων (one of the youthful . . .) Ξ 267, 275.—Superl. **ὁπλότατος**, -η. Youngest, the youngest: Νέστορος ὁπλοτάτη θυγάτηρ γ 465. Cf. Ι 58: η 58, λ 283, ο 364.

ὁποῖος, ὁπποῖος, -η, -ον. (1) As relative, of whatever sort or kind. With subj. or opt. in conditional relative sentences (with τοῖος as correlative). For the examples and constructions see Table at end (II) (B) (b), (III) (D) (29).—(2) In object clauses, of what sort or kind: ὁπποίης ἐπὶ νηὸς ἀφίκεο α 171=ξ 188.—With the indefinite ἄσσα: εἰπέ μοι ὁπποῖ' ἄσσα εἵματα ἕστο τ 218.

ὀπός, ὁ. Fig-juice used to curdle milk for cheese Ε 902.

ὁπόσ(σ)ος, ὁππόσος. (1) As relative, as many as: κτήμαθ' ὁπόσσα τοί ἐστιν (all your possessions) χ 220.—As much as. Absol.: ὁπόσσον ἐπέσχε πυρὸς μένος (the space that the fire covered) Ψ 238=Ω 792.—(2) In object clauses, how many or great, what: ὄφρ' εἴπῃς ὁππόσα κήδε' ἀνέτλης ξ 47.—Absol.: ποθέων ὁπόσα τολύπευσεν Ω 7.

ὁπότε, ὁππότε. (1) When, at the time when. (a) With indic.: ὁππότε μιν ξυνδῆσαι ἤθελον Α 399. Cf. Θ 230, Λ 671, Ξ 317, etc.: δ 731, ε 125, σ 409, ψ 345.—Introducing a simile Λ 492.—(b) (α) With subj. or opt. in relative sentences corresponding to sentences with εἰ (4). For the examples and constructions see Table at end (II) (B) (a) (1), (b), (D) (7).—(β) In conditional relative sentences. See Table (III) (B) (a) (1) (2) (3) (5), (b) (1), (D) (12) (16) (20) (26) (31) (34) (35) (37) (54)(59).—(γ) With subj. introducing similes: ὡς ὁπότε . . . Λ 305 : δ 335 = ρ 126. — (2) Against the time when: δέγμενος ὁππότ' ἀφορμηθεῖεν (watching for the time when . . .) Β 794. Cf. Δ 229, Κ 189, etc. : υ 386.—(3) At which time, when: ἔσσεται ἠώς, ὁππότε τις καὶ ἐμεῖο Ἄρῃ ἐκ θυμὸν ἕληται Φ 112. Cf. Ν 817.—(4) In an object clause: ἴδμεν ὁππότε νεῖτ' ἐκ Πύλου; δ 633.

ὅπου. In object clauses, in what place, where: δμώων κέ τεο πειρηθεῖμεν, ὅπου τις νῶϊ τίει π 306 (*i.e.* at the various ἔργα of 314). Cf. γ 16.

ὅππῃ. See ὅπῃ.

ὁππόθεν. In indirect questions and object clauses, whence: ἐρέσθαι, ὁ. οὗτος ἀνήρ (where he comes from) α 406. Cf. γ 80, ξ 47.—In reference to origin: εἰπὲ τεὸν γένος, ὁ. ἐσσί τ 162.

ὁππόθι. (1) As relative, where: ὁππόθι πιότατον πεδίον Καλυδῶνος Ι 577.—(2) In an object clause: σάφα εἰπέμεν ὁππόθ' ὄλωλεν γ 89.

ὁπποῖος. See ὁποῖος.

ὁππόσε. Whithersoever. With subj. in a relative sentence corresponding to sentences with εἰ (4): ὁππόσ' ἐπέλθω ξ 139 (see Table at end (II) (D) (3)).

ὁππόσος. See ὁπόσος.

ὁππότε. See ὁπότε.

ὁππότερος, -η, -ον. (1) As relative, whichever of the two. (a) With indic.: ἡμέων ὁπποτέρῳ θάνατος τέτυκται Γ 101. Cf. Γ 321.—(b) With subj. in conditional relative sentences. For the examples and constructions see Table at end (III) (D) (20) (26).—(c) In pl. in reference to two bodies of men. With opt. in a conditional relative sentence. See Table (III) (D) (54).—(2) In object clauses, which of the two: Ζεὺς τό γε οἶδεν, ὁπποτέρῳ θανάτοιο τέλος πεπρωμένον ἐστίν Γ 309. Cf. Γ 317, Χ 130 : μ 57. — In pl. in reference to two bodies of men Ε 33.—So in reference to two pairs of horses Ψ 487.

ὁπποτέρωθεν [-θεν (1)]. In an object clause, from which quarter: οὐδ' ἂν ἔτι γνοίης ὁπποτέρωθεν Ἀχαιοὶ κλονέονται Ξ 59.

ὅππως. See ὅπως.

ὀπταλέος [ὀπτός]. Roasted, roast: κρέα Δ 345 : μ 396, κρειῶν π 50.

ὀπτάω [ὀπτός]. (ἐπ-.) To roast: κρέ' ὤπτων γ 33. Cf. γ 65 = 470 = υ 279, ξ 76, ο 98, υ 27, 252. —Without expressed object Ι 215, Α 466 = Β 429 = Η 318 = Ω 624 : = ξ 431, γ 463, ο 323, τ 423.

ὀπτήρ, -ῆρος, ὁ [ὀπ-. See ὁράω]. A scout: ὀπτῆρας ὄτρυνα νέεσθαι ξ 261 = ρ 430.

ὀπτός. Roasted, roast δ 66, π 443, χ 21.

ὀπυίω. To take or have to wife, marry: ὅς [μιν] ἀναφανδὸν ὄπυιεν Π 178, τὴν ὤπυιε ἀμφιγυήεις Σ 383. Cf. Ν 379, 429, Ξ 268 : β 207, 336, δ 798, ο 21, π 386.—Absol. in pres. pple., a married man: οἱ δύ' ὀπυίοντες ζ 63.—In pass., of the woman, to be taken to wife, be married: ἐξ Αἰσύμηθεν ὀπυιομένη Θ 304.

ὄπωπα, pf. ὁράω.

ὀπωπή, -ῆς, ἡ [ὄπωπα. See ὁράω]. (1) The presentation of something to the sight, sight of something: ὅπως ἤντησας ὀπωπῆς γ 97 = δ 327, ρ 44.—(2) The faculty of sight, vision: ἁμαρτήσεσθαι ὀπωπῆς ι 512.

ὀπώρη, -ης, ἡ. Late summer, harvest-time: ἀστέρ', ὅς τ' ὀπώρης εἶσιν (in . . .) Χ 27.—Distinguished from θέρος λ 192, μ 76, ξ 384.

ὀπωρινός [ὀπώρη]. Of, that comes in, late summer or harvest-time: ἀστέρι Ε 5. Cf. Π 385, Φ 346 : ε 328.

ὅπως, ὅππως. (1) In such way or manner as, as. (a) With indic.: ἔρξον ὅπως ἐθέλεις Δ 37 : ν 145. Cf. ξ 172, ο 111, etc.—(b) With subj. or opt. in conditional relative sentences. For the examples and constructions see Table at end (III) (B) (a) (1) (2), (b) (1).—(2) In object clauses, in what way or manner, how. (a) With indic.: κατάλεξον ὅπως ἤντησας ὀπωπῆς γ 97. Cf. Κ 545, etc. : δ 109 (thinking how . . .), etc.—With fut.: οὐδ' ἴδμεν ὅπως ἔσται τάδε ἔργα Β 252. Cf. Δ 14, etc. : ν 376, 386, τ 557, etc.—After a past tense: ἑλίσσετο μερμηρίζων ὅππως χεῖρας ἐφήσει υ 29.—(b) With subj., pure or with κεν : οὐδέ ἑ λήθει ὅππως τανύσῃ Ψ 324. Cf. Γ 110, Κ 225, Ρ 144, etc. : φράζεσθαι ὅππως κε μνηστῆρας ἀπώσεαι α 270. Cf. α 77, etc. —(c) With opt.: μερμήριξεν ὅππως ἐξαπάφοιτο Ξ 160. Cf. Α 344, etc. : γ 129, ι 554, etc.—With κεν Ι 681.—(3) In final clauses, so that, in order that. (a) With fut.: ὅπως ἀντάξιον ἔσται Α 136. Cf. α 57.—(b) With subj.: λοχῶσιν ὅπως ἀπὸ φῦλον ὄληται ξ 181. Cf. γ 19.—(c) With opt.: ὅπως κῆρας ἀλάλκοι Φ 548. Cf. ζ 319, ν 319, etc.—(4) When: ὅπως ἴδον αἷμα Λ 459. Cf. Μ 208 : γ 373, χ 22.

ὁράω. 1 sing. pres. ὁρόω Ε 244, Λ 651, Ω 355 : α 301, γ 199, λ 141, σ 143. 2 ὁράᾳς Η 448, Ο 555, Φ 108 : ρ 545. 2 pl. opt. ὁρόῳτε Δ 347. Pple. ὁρόων Α 350, Γ 325, Υ 23, etc. : α 229, θ 314, ψ 91. Pl. ὁρόωντες Ρ 637, Ω 633 : η 145, ι 295, υ 373. Fem. ὁρόωσα τ 514. Pres. infin. mid. ὁράασθαι π 107, σ 4, υ 317. From ὄρημαι (cf. δίζημαι) 2 sing. pres. mid. ὄρηαι ξ 343. From ὀπ- 2 sing. fut. in mid. form ὄψεαι Δ 353, Θ 471, Ι 359, Ω 601 : ω 511. ὄψει μ 101. ὄψῃ Ψ 620. 3 ὄψεται λ 450, ο 516, ρ 7. Pple. ὀψόμενος ψ 360. Fem. ὀψομένη Ξ 200, 205, 301, 304. Pl. ὀψόμεναι Σ 141. Infin. ὄψεσθαι Ε 120, Ξ 343, Ω 492 : ν 357, π 24, ρ 42. Aor. imp. ὄψεσθε Ω 704 : θ 313. Pf. ὄπωπα Β 799, Ζ 124, Ω 392 : ρ 371, φ 94. 2 sing. ὄπωπας γ 93, δ 323. 3 sing. plupf. ὀπώπει φ 123, ψ 226. (εἰσ-, ἐφ-, καθ-.) (1) In act. and mid., to look, gaze: θαύμαζον ὁρόωντες η 145. Cf. Υ 23 : δ 47 = κ 181. —To direct one's sight, look, gaze, in a specified direction: θεοὶ ἐς πάντες ὁρῶντο Χ 166. Cf. Α 350, Γ 325, Π 646, Ρ 637, Ω 633 : ε 439, σ 344, υ 373, ψ 91.—(2) To look at or upon, gaze upon. In act. and mid.: αἰεὶ τέρμ' ὁρόων (keeping his eyes upon it) Ψ 323 : τὸν ὁρῶντο ο 462. Cf. θ 459.—(3) To look to something, consider it, judge by it. In act. and mid. : ἐς γενεὴν ὁρόων Κ 239 : ἐς μέγεθος ὁρώμενος σ 219.—(4) To look to, attend to, something : ἐς ἐμὰ ἔργ' ὁρόωσα τ 514.—(5) In act. and mid., to have sight of, see, behold : τῶν ἄλλων οὔ τις ὁρᾶτο [αὐτήν] Α 198, οὐ πω τοιόνδε λαὸν ὄπωπα Β 799. Cf. Γ 234, Ε 120, Λ 651, Ν 99, Ξ 343, etc. : α 229, γ 93, λ 156, 450, ν 357, ξ 343, etc.—With indefinite object : ὁρόων ἀκάχημαι θ 314. Cf. δ 226, φ 123.—With complementary pple. or adj. : ὅτι θνήσκοντας ὁρᾶτο Α 56. Cf. Γ 306, Ε 244, Θ 471, Ι 359, etc. : μάλα σ' ὁρόω καλόν τε μέγαν τε α 301 = γ 199. Cf. σ 143, ω 511.—With complementary clause : οὐχ ὁράᾳς ὅτι . . . ; Η 448. Cf. Δ 347, Ο 555, Φ 108 : θ 313, ρ 545.—The infin. used epexegetically : εἶδος μάλα μέγας ἦν ὁράασθαι σ 4.—(6) To visit, go to see, see. In mid. : ὀψόμεναί τε γέρονθ' ἅλιον καὶ δώματα πατρός Σ 141. Cf. Ξ 200, 205 = 304, 301 : ψ 360.—(7) To admit to one's presence, see : οὐδέ σε μήτηρ ὄψεται ο 516.—(8) Of mental vision : ὁρόων θάνατον Υ 481, οἷος ὅρα πρόσσω καὶ ὀπίσσω Σ 250 : ω 452.

ὄργυια, ἡ [ὀργ-, ὀρέγω]. The length of the outstretched arms, a fathom Ψ 327 : ι 325, κ 167.

ὀρέγω. Pres. pple. (fr. ὀρέγνυμι) ὀρεγνύς Α 351, Χ 37. Fut. ὀρέξω Ρ 453. 1 pl. ὀρέξομεν Μ 328, Ν 327. Infin. ὀρέξειν Ο 602. 2 sing. aor. ὄρεξας Ω 743. 3 ὤρεξε Ψ 406, Ω 102. 2 sing. subj. ὀρέξῃς Χ 57. 3 ὀρέξῃ Ε 33, 225, 260, Χ 130 : ο 312. 3 pl. opt. ὀρέξειαν ρ 407. Infin. ὀρέξαι Λ 79, Μ 174, Ο 596 : δ 275. **Mid.** 3 sing. aor. ὠρέξατο Ε 851, Ψ 99. ὀρέξατο Ζ 466, Ν 20, 190. 3 sing. imp. ὀρεξάσθω Δ 307. Pple. ὀρεξάμενος Π 314, 322, Ψ 805. Fem. ὀρεξαμένη φ 53. Infin. ὀρέξασθαι λ 392. 3 pl. pf. ὀρωρέχαται Π 834. 3 pl. plupf. ὀρωρέχατο Λ 26. (ἐπ-.) (1) To hold or stretch out (a hand or the hands) : χεῖρας ὀρεγνύς Α 351, Χ 37. Cf. Ο 371, Ω 743 : ι 527, μ 257, ρ 366.—So in mid. : ἀνδρὸς παιδοφόνοιο ποτὶ στόμα χεῖρ' ὀρέγεσθαι Ω 506 (but χεῖρ' (*i.e.* χειρί) may be read, bringing the passage under (3) (a). Cf. Ψ 99 there cited).—(2) To hold out, offer for acceptance, bestow, give : Θέτις ὤρεξε [δέπας] πιοῦσα (*i.e.* held it out to return it) Ω 102 : αἴ κέν τις κοτύλην καὶ πύρνον ὀρέξῃ ο 312. Cf. ρ 407.—With immaterial object, to yield, grant, bestow, give : κῦδος Ε 33, εὖχος Μ 328, τάχος Ψ 406, etc. : κῦδος δ 275.—(3) In mid. (a) To stretch out one's limbs, make a stretch, stretch, reach : τρὶς ὀρέξατ' ἰών (made three strides) Ν 20 : ὀρέξασθαι μενεαίνων (to reach out a hand to me) λ 392. Cf. φ 53.—So κυάνεοι δράκοντες ὀρωρέχατο (were astretch, *i.e.* were represented with heads outstretched) Λ 26.—With genit. of that towards which one reaches out : οὗ παιδὸς ὀρέξατο Ζ 466.—With dat. of the part employed : ὠρέξατο χερσίν Ψ 99.—So ἵπποι ποσσὶν ὀρωρέχαται (are astretch, are in their full stride) Π 834.—(b) To make a lunge or thrust. With dat. of the weapon : ὠρέξατ' ἔγχεϊ Ε 851. Cf. Δ 307.—With this dat. and genit. of the person attacked : ὀρέξατο δουρὶ Ἕκτορος Ν 190.—With acc. of part reached : ἔφθη ὀρεξάμενος σκέλος (ὦμον) (app. a construction *ad sensum*, 'got his blow in first and struck . . .') Π 314, 322. Cf. Ψ 805.

ὀρεῖται, 3 sing. fut. mid. ὄρνυμι.

ὀρεκτός, -ή, -όν [ὀρεκ-, ὀρέγω]. Of spears, held out or presented for action : μελίῃσιν Β 543.

ὀρέξω, fut. ὀρέγω.

ὀρέοντο, 3 pl. aor. mid. ὄρνυμι.

ὀρεσίτροφος [ὄρεσι, dat. pl. of ὄρος + τροφ-, τρέφω]. Bred in the mountains, mountain-bred. Of lions Μ 299, Ρ 61 : ζ 130, ι 292.

ὀρεσκῷος [ὀρεσ-, ὄρος + (poss.) a second element conn. with κοῖτος, κεῖμαι]. Thus, couching in the mountains : Φηρσίν Α 268 : αἶγας ι 155.

ὀρέστερος [comp. fr. ὀρεσ-, ὄρος. 'Of the mountains' (as opposed to the valleys)]. Mountain-bred : δράκων Χ 93 : λύκοι ἠδὲ λέοντες κ 212.

ὀρεστιάς, -άδος [ὀρεσ-, ὄρος]. A mountain-nymph. Defining νύμφη Ζ 420.

ὄρεσφι, locative, ablative and genit. ὄρος.

ὀρεχθέω [perh. conn. with ὀρέγω]. Thus, of oxen, to stretch themselves out, plunge Ψ 30.

ὄρηαι, 2 sing. pres. mid. See ὁράω.

ὄρηται, 3 sing. aor. subj. mid. ὄρνυμι.

ὄρθαι, aor. infin. mid. ὄρνυμι.

ὄρθιος [ὀρθός]. In neut. pl. ὄρθια as adv., in shrill tones : ἤϋσεν Λ 11.

ὀρθόκραιρος, -η [ὀρθός + κραῖρα = κέρας]. (1) Epithet of oxen, with upright horns Θ 231, Σ 573 : μ 348.—(2) Epithet of ships, with sterns running up into a tall ornamental projection (ἄφλαστον, κόρυμβον), with tall sterns Σ 3, Τ 344.

ὀρθός, -ή, -όν. Upright, erect : ἔγχεά σφιν ὄρθ' ἐλήλατο Κ 153. Cf. Ω 359.—In or to an upright posture, upright, erect : ὀρθῶν ἑσταότων Σ 246. Cf. Ψ 271 = 456 = 657 = 706 = 752 = 801 = 830, Ω 11 : μ 51 = 162, 179, σ 241, φ 119.—Of sheep ι 442.

ὀρθόω [ὀρθός]. To set upright, set on one's legs again Η 272, Ψ 695.—In pass., to stand up, rise up : ὀρθωθεὶς ἔνδυνε χιτῶνα Κ 21.—To assume from a recumbent a partially upright posture, raise oneself : ἕζετο ὀρθωθείς Β 42, Ψ 235. Cf. Κ 80.

ὀρίνω [ὀρ- as in ὄρνυμι]. Aor. ὄρῑνα δ 366. 2 sing. ὤρῑνας θ 178. ὄρῑνας ξ 361, ο 486. 3 ὤρῑνε Τ 272 : η 273. ὄρῑνε Β 142, Δ 208, Φ 235, Ω 760, etc. : ρ 150, 216. Subj. ὀρίνω Ο 403. 2 sing. ὀρίνῃς Ω 467, 568. 2 sing. opt. ὀρίναις Λ 792. **Pass.** 3 sing. aor. ὠρίνθη Π 509. ὀρίνθη Ε 29, Π 280, Σ 223. 3 sing. opt. ὀρινθείη Ω 585. Nom. pl. masc. pple. ὀρινθέντες χ 23. (συν-.) (1) To put into a state of commotion, stir, agitate, trouble : ὀρινομένη θάλασσα (raised in billows) Β 294. Cf. Ι 4, Λ 298 : η 273.—To put into violent motion : ῥέεθρα (brought them down in spate) Φ 235.—With personal object, to throw into confusion or disorder, strike with panic : μνηστῆρας ω 448.—In pass., of men, to be thrown into confusion or disorder, be put to disorderly rout, be struck with panic : ὀρινομένους ὑπὸ καπνοῦ Ι 243. Cf. Λ 521, 525, Ξ 14 = Ο 7, Ξ 59, Π 377 : ὀρινθέντες κατὰ δῶμα (rushing in confusion) X 23.—Sim. of a single person: σοὶ ὀρινομένῳ κατὰ δῶμα (rushing in your rage) χ 360.—(2) With immaterial object, to stir up, bring about, cause: ὀρυμαγδόν Φ 313. Cf. Ω 760.—In reference to the heart or mind, to stir, rouse, agitate, trouble, touch: θυμόν B 142. Cf. E 29, I 595, Π 509, Ω 585, etc.: δ 366, ρ 47, 216, σ 75, etc.

ὅρκιον, -ου, τό [app. neut. of ὅρκιος, adj. fr. ὅρκος]. (1) In pl., sacrificial victims or other offerings in sanction of an oath, oath-offerings: κήρυκες ἀνὰ ἄστυ θεῶν φέρον ὅρκια (the gods being to be invoked as witnesses) Γ 245. Cf. Γ 269.—(2) In sing., an oath-sacrifice: οὐχ ἅλιον πέλει ὅρκιον (our . . .) Δ 158.—(3) ὅρκια τάμνειν, to make a compact with the sanction of an oath, enter into a solemn treaty or agreement B 124, Γ 73 = 256, Γ 94, 105, 252, Δ 155, T 191: ω 483.—(4) Hence, in pl., a compact, treaty, agreement: συνθεσίαι τε καὶ ὅρκια B 339. Cf. Γ 107, 280, 299, 323, Δ 67 = 72, 157, 236, 269, 271, H 69, 351, 411, X 262, 266: ω 546.—(5) In pl., an oath: ὅρκια τοι δώσω τ 302.

ὅρκος, -ου, ὁ. (1) Something invoked in sanction of an oath, something by which one swears: ὅ τοι μέγας ἔσσεται ὁ. A 239. Cf. B 755, O 38: = ε 186.—(2) An oath: μέγαν ὅρκον ὀμοῦμαι (ὀμεῖται) A 233, I 132, 274. Cf. Ξ 280, T 108, 113, 127, 175, Υ 313 (oaths by many different objects), X 119, Ψ 42, 441: β 377, 378 = κ 346, δ 253, 746, ε 178 = κ 343, κ 299, 381, μ 298, 304 = ο 438 = σ 59, ξ 151, 171, ο 436, σ 55, υ 229.—(3) The taking of an oath, swearing: ἀνθρώπους ἐκέκαστο κλεπτοσύνῃ θ' ὅρκῳ τε (i.e. false swearing) τ 396.

ὁρμαθός, -οῦ, ὁ [ὅρμος¹]. A chain or string of objects ω 8.

ὁρμαίνω [ὁρμάω]. 3 sing. aor. ὅρμηνε Φ 137. 3 pl. ὅρμηναν β 156. (1) To stir up, bring about: πόλεμον K 28: δ 146.—(2) To turn over, revolve, ponder, consider, debate, have in contemplation, meditate: ταῦτα A 193 = Λ 411 = P 106 = Σ 15, K 507. Cf. K 4: δολιχὸν πλόον γ 169. Cf. γ 151, δ 120 = ε 365 = 424, δ 732, 793, 843, η 83, σ 345, ψ 86.—Absol.: ὣς ὁ γέρων ὥρμαινεν Ξ 20. Cf. Π 435, Φ 64, X 131: ζ 118.—With dependent clause. With ἤ . . . ἤ . . . γ 169, δ 789, ο 300, ψ 86.—With ὅπως Φ 137, Ω 680.—With relative: ὅρμηναν ἅ περ . . . β 156.

ὁρμάω [ὁρμή]. (ἀφ-, ἐξ-, ἐφ-, μεθ-.) (I) (1) To incite, urge, spur on: ὅρμησέ μ' ἐς πόλεμον Z 338.—(2) To stir up, bring about: πόλεμον σ 376.—(3) *Intrans. for reflexive.* (a) To make onslaught, attack. With genit. of what is attacked: ὁππότε πύργος Ἀχαιῶν Τρώων ὁρμήσειεν Δ 335.—(b) To put oneself in act or motion *to do something.* With infin.: ὁσσάκι ὁρμήσειε στῆναι ἐναντίβιον Φ 265. Cf. N 64, X 194.—(II) In mid. and pass. (1) To address oneself to motion, take one's way, proceed, speed, start, start up to do something: ὁρμᾶτ' ἐκ θαλάμοιο Γ 142. Cf. I 178, N 754, Ξ 313: οὐδ' ὁρμηθέντος ἄκουσα (that he had gone) δ 728. Cf. δ 282, ν 82.—Sim.: ὁρμηθεὶς θεοῦ (starting from (the inspiration of) the god, stirred by the god) θ 499.—(2) In hostile sense, to rush, make a rush, make onslaught, attack: ἐναντίω οἱ ὁρμηθήτην E 12, δεύτερος ὡρμᾶτ' ἔγχεϊ 855. Cf. N 496, 512, 526, 559, 562, O 529, Π 402, 467, P 530, 605, Σ 269, T 236, X 312, Ψ 817: μ 126.—Of animals κ 214.—With genit. of the person attacked: ὁρμήθη Ἀκάμαντος Ξ 488. Cf. Φ 595.—To make a rush in order to strip a fallen foe: ὡρμήθη μεμαὼς ἀπὸ τεύχεα δῦσαι N 182, ὁρμηθέντος ἀκόντισεν N 183. Cf. N 188, 190.—(3) To put oneself in act or motion *to do something.* With infin.: διώκειν ὁρμήθησαν K 359. Cf. Θ 511.—To be eager *to do something.* With infin.: ἦτόρ οἱ ὁρμᾶτο πτολεμίζειν Φ 572.

ὅρμενος, aor. pple. mid. ὄρνυμι.

ὁρμή, -ῆς, ἡ. (1) An inciting, urging, starting: ἐμὴν ποτιδέγμενος ὁρμήν (waiting on the word from me) K 123, θηρὸς ὑφ' ὁρμῆς (in terror of the beast) Λ 119. Cf. β 403.—(2) A rush, onset, starting: πυρὸς ὁρμῇ (the rage of the . . .) Λ 157: ὑπὸ κύματος ὁρμῆς (the shock of the . . .) ε 320, μελέῃ μοι ἔσσεται ὁρμή (my endeavour) 416.—Sim.: ἐς ὁρμὴν ἔγχεος ἐλθεῖν (that I may come within spear-cast of him) E 118.—In hostile sense, a rush or attack: μόγις μευ ἔκφυγεν ὁρμήν I 355.—A rush to strip a fallen foe Δ 466.

ὅρμημα, -ατος, τό [ὁρμάω]. In pl., struggles of war, fighting, battling: Ἑλένης ὁρμήματα (about . . ., for the sake of . . .) B 356, 590.

ὅρμηνε, 3 sing. aor. ὁρμαίνω.

†ὁρμίζω [ὅρμος²]. 1 pl. aor. ὁρμίσαμεν μ 317. 3 ὅρμισαν γ 11, δ 785, θ 55. 1 pl. subj. ὁρμίσσομεν Ξ 77. To bring (a ship) to anchor, moor (her) Ξ 77: γ 11, δ 785, θ 55.—To draw up (a ship) on shore μ 317.

ὅρμος¹, -ου, ὁ [εἴρω¹]. A chain worn round the neck Σ 401: ο 460, σ 295.

ὅρμος², -ου, ὁ. An anchorage, moorings, a landing-place A 435: = ο 497, ν 101.

ὄρνεον, τό [cf. next]. A bird N 64.

ὄρνῑς, -ῑθος, ὁ, ἡ. ὄρνῖς Ω 219. Dat. pl. ὀρνίθεσσι P 757: χ 303. ὄρνισι H 59. (1) A bird B 459, 764, Γ 2, I 323, etc.: α 320, β 181, ε 65, μ 331, χ 303.—With a specific name added: ὄρνισιν αἰγυπιοῖσιν H 59. Cf. ε 51, τ 548.—(2) Distinguished as a bird of omen: ὅ τ' ἐκ Διὸς ἤλυθεν ὁ. Θ 251, ὁ. σφιν ἐπῆλθεν M 200. Cf. K 277, M 218, N 821: = ο 160 = 525, β 155, 159, ο 531, υ 242, ω 311.—Applied to a person: μή μοι αὐτὴ ὁ. κακὸς πέλευ Ω 219.

ὄρνῡμι. Also ὀρνύω M 142: φ 100. Imp. ὄρνυθι Z 363, O 475, T 139: ρ 46. Infin. ὀρνύμεναι P 546. ὀρνύμεν I 353: κ 22. 3 sing. pa. iterative ὄρσασκε P 423. Fem. fut. pple. ὄρσουσα Φ 335. 3 sing. aor. ὦρσε A 10, B 451, E 8, Λ 53, N 83, T 41, Ψ 14, etc.: γ 161, η 169, π 154, τ 249, ψ 144, etc. 3 pl. ὦρσαν Λ 152: ι 154. 3 sing. subj. ὄρσῃ I 703, Ξ 522. 1 pl. ὄρσομεν Δ 16. ὄρσωμεν H 38. 2 ὄρσητε Ψ 210. Pple. ὄρσας X 190: λ 400, 407, ω 110. Fem. ὄρσᾱσα Ξ 254. 3 sing. redup. aor. ὤρορε B 146, N 78: δ 712, θ 539, τ 201, ψ 222.

3 sing. pf. ὄρωρε B 797, Γ 87, H 374, M 348, O 400, Ω 107, etc. 3 sing. subj. ὀρώρῃ I 610, K 90, Λ 477, X 388 : σ 133. 3 sing. plupf. ὀρώρει B 810, Δ 436, Λ 500, M 177, N 169, P 384, Ω 512, etc. : ε 294, θ 380, κ 122, λ 600, ω 70, etc. ὠρώρει Σ 498. **Mid.** 3 sing. fut. ὀρεῖται Υ 140. 3 sing. aor. ὤρετο M 279, Ξ 397, X 102. ὦρτο E 590, H 162, Λ 129, N 62, Υ 48, Φ 248, Ω 515, etc. : γ 176, θ 3, ξ 412, π 215, ψ 348, etc. 3 pl. ὀρέοντο B 398, Ψ 212. 3 sing. subj. ὄρηται π 98, 116, υ 267. 3 sing. opt. ὄροιτο ξ 522. Imp. ὄρσο Δ 204, E 109, Ω 88 : η 342, χ 395. ὄρσεο Γ 250, Π 126, Σ 170, Φ 331 : ζ 255. ὄρσευ Δ 264, T 139. Pple. ὄρμενος, -ου Λ 326, 572, P 738, Φ 14. Infin. ὄρθαι Θ 474. 3 sing. thematic pf. ὀρώρεται τ 377, 524. 3 sing. subj. ὀρώρηται N 271. (ἀπ-, ἐν-, ἐπ-, ὑπ-.) (I) (1) To set in motion, stir up, raise, send : κύματα B 146, κονίην Λ 152. Cf. M 253, Ξ 254, Φ 335 : ε 366, 385, κ 22, λ 400 = 407, μ 313, τ 201, ω 110.—To rouse, startle, cause to flee : [νεβρὸν] ἐξ εὐνῆς X 190.—To start (game) ι 154.—To raise, cause to rise or stand up : Ὀδυσῆα ἀπ' ἐσχαρόφιν η 169.—(2) To rouse, cause to bestir oneself, incite to action, spur on, urge on, set on, send : Σαρπηδόνα ἐπ' Ἀργείοισιν M 293. Cf. Δ 439, E 8, H 38, I 539, K 518, etc. : γ 167, δ 712, π 154, φ 100, ψ 348, 367.—To rouse, incite, set on, *to do something*. With infin. : μάχεσθαι N 794. Cf. M 142, P 273 : ψ 222.—With inanimate object : πυρὴν καήμεναι Ψ 210.—(3) In general, to stir up, bring about, set going, raise, send, inspire : νοῦσον ἀνὰ στρατόν A 10, ἐν σθένος ὦρσεν ἑκάστῳ B 451. Cf. Δ 16, Θ 335, I 353, 533, Λ 53, 544, N 362, Ξ 522, O 718, P 423, Σ 218, Ψ 14, 108, 153, Ω 507 : γ 161, δ 113, 183, κ 457, ρ 46, τ 249, υ 346, ψ 144, 231.—(II) In mid., in pf. and plupf. act., and also (N 78 : θ 539) in redup. aor. act. (1) To be set in motion, stirred up, raised, to rise, spring up : ὡς ὅτε κῦμα θαλάσσης ὄρνυται Δ 423. Cf. Γ 13, E 865, H 64, Λ 151, Ξ 395, Ψ 214 : κονίη ἐκ κρατὸς ὀρώρει (rose) λ 600.—(2) To rouse or bestir oneself, address oneself to motion, set to work, speed, rush, be moved, move : ὦρτο διὲκ προθύρου O 124, ὅτε τ' ὤρετ' Ἀχιλλεύς (shook off his inactivity) X 102. Cf. B 398, Δ 421, Θ 474, T 2, Ψ 759, etc. : ἐξ οὗ ὤρορ' ἀοιδός (was moved to song) θ 539. Cf. α 347, ξ 499, τ 377 (is torn), 524, χ 364, ω 496.—Of the limbs : εἰς ὅ κε γούνατ' ὀρώρῃ (play their part) I 610 = K 90. Cf. Λ 477, X 388 : σ 133.—Sim. : μένος μοι ὤρορεν (is roused) N 78. Cf. Λ 827.—Of weapons Λ 572.—Of a ship μ 183.—Of night ε 294 = ι 69 = μ 315.—With infin. indicating a purpose : ὦρτο πόλινδ' ἴμεν η 14. Cf. M 279, N 62, Ψ 488 : β 397.—So of inanimate objects : ὦρτο δ' ἐπὶ λιγὺς οὖρος ἀήμεναι γ 176. Cf. Ξ 397.—With fut. pple. : ὦρτ' ἀγγελέουσα Θ 409 = Ω 77 = 159. Cf. θ 256.—In imp., rouse, bestir yourself (yourselves) ! speed ! up ! come ! come forward ! Γ 250, Δ 204, 509, E 109, etc. : φ 141, χ 395.—With infin. ζ 255.—With fut. pple. η 342.—(3) To stand up or forth : ὤρνυτ' Ἀγαμέμνων Γ 267. Cf. H 162, 163, Ψ 288, etc. : θ 111.—(4) To rise or start up from a recumbent or sitting position : ἀπὸ θρόνου ὦρτο Λ 645. Cf. Λ 2, Ω 515 : ὄρνυτ' ἐξ εὐνῆφιν β 2. Cf. γ 405, δ 307, ε 2, θ 2, 3, ψ 348.—(5) In hostile sense, to rush, make a rush, spring, make onslaught, attack : δεύτερον ὄρνυτο χαλκῷ Γ 349. Cf. E 13, 17 = Π 479, E 590, Λ 129, 343, P 45, Υ 158, 164, Φ 248, Ψ 689.—(6) In general, to be stirred up, brought about, set going, raised, to be on foot, come into being, spring up, rise, be manifested, seen, heard : πόλεμος ἀλίαστος ὄρωρεν (is on foot) B 797, πολὺς ὀρυμαγδὸς ὀρώρει 810 = Θ 59 : = ω 70. Cf. Γ 87, Δ 436, E 532, Θ 135, I 573, M 177 (raged), P 397, T 363, etc. : θ 343, 380, κ 122, ξ 412, 522, π 98 = 116, 215, υ 267, χ 308, ω 48, 184.

ὀροθύνω [ὀρ- as in ὄρνυμι]. 3 sing. aor. ὀρόθῡνε K 332, N 351, O 572, 595 : ε 292. Imp. ὀρόθῡνον Φ 312. (1) To set in motion, stir up, raise, send : ὀρόθυνον ἐναύλους (bring them down in flood) Φ 312 : ἀέλλας ε 292.—(2) To rouse, incite to action, spur on, urge on K 332, N 351, O 572, 595 : σ 407.

ὄροιτο, 3 sing. aor. opt. mid. ὄρνυμι.

ὄρομαι [ὀρ-, ὁράω. Cf. οὖρος², ἐπίουρος, θυρᾱωρός, πυλᾱωρός]. 3 sing. plupf. ὀρώρει Ψ 112. To keep an eye on something, watch : ἐπὶ δ' ἀνὴρ ἐσθλὸς ὀρώρει (superintended the work) Ψ 112 : ἐπὶ δ' ἀνέρες ἐσθλοὶ ὄροντο (did watchful service) γ 471, ἐπὶ δ' ἀνέρες ἐσθλοὶ ὄρονται (tend the flocks) ξ 104.

ὄρος, οὖρος, τό. Dat. pl. ὄρεσσι A 235, E 523, Π 353, P 282, etc. : γ 290, λ 574, τ 205. οὔρεσι Δ 455, E 52, M 132, N 390, O 606, Ω 614, etc. Locative ὄρεσφι Λ 474, T 376, X 139, 189. This form as ablative Δ 452, Λ 493. As genit. K 185. A mountain or hill : οὔρεα σκιόεντα A 157, ἀπ' Ἰδαίων ὀρέων Θ 170. Cf. B 456, Γ 34, Δ 452, M 146, N 17, etc. : β 147, γ 287, ε 283, ζ 102, θ 569, λ 243, etc.

ὀρός, -οῦ, ὁ. Whey ι 222, ρ 225.

ὀρούω. (ἀν-, ἀπ-, ἐν-, ἐπ-.) (1) To rush, speed, spring, dart : ἐς δίφρον ὀρούσας Λ 359, 743. Cf. B 310, M 83, Υ 327, Φ 182, Ω 80.—Of an inanimate object : ἐκ κλῆρος ὄρουσεν (jumped out) Γ 325.—Of the flight or course of a weapon N 505 = Π 615, Φ 593.—Of sleep : ἐφ' ὕπνος ὄρουσεν Ψ 232.—Of the winds κ 47.—(2) In hostile sense, to rush, spring, make onslaught, attack : ἐν πρώτοις ὄρουσεν Λ 92, 217. Cf. Ξ 401, O 726, Π 258, 430.—Of a beast of prey O 635.

ὀροφή, -ῆς, ἡ [ἐρέφω]. A roof χ 298.

ὄροφος, -ου, ὁ [as prec.]. Reeds used for thatching, thatch : ὄροφον ἀμήσαντες Ω 451.

ὀρόω. See ὁράω.

ὄρπηξ, -ηκος, ὁ. A branch : ἐρινεὸν τάμνεν ὄρπηκας (double acc. of whole and part) Φ 38.

ὄρσας, aor. pple. ὄρνυμι.

ὄρσεο, ὄρσευ, ὄρσο, aor. imp. mid. ὄρνυμι.

ὀρσοθύρη, -ης, ἡ [*ὄρσος = ὄρρος, rump + θύρη]. A back or subsidiary door (in the passages cited app. giving access from the μέγαρον to the λαύρη) χ 126, 132, 333.

ὄρσουσα, fut. pple. fem. ὄρνυμι.

ὀρυκτός, -ή, -όν [ὀρυκ-, ὀρύσσω]. Formed by digging: τάφρον Θ 179, Ι 67, Κ 198, Υ 49. Cf. Μ 72, Ο 344, Π 369.

ὀρυμαγδός, -οῦ, ὁ. (1) A sound or noise: δρυτόμων ἀνδρῶν Π 633.—A noise or din caused by clashing or striking: ὀρυμαγδὸν φιτρῶν καὶ λάων Φ 313. Cf. ι 235.—In reference to a river, a roaring or rushing Φ 256.—(2) Din, noise, shouting, tumult: πολύς Β 810=Θ 59, Δ 449=Θ 63, Κ 185: ω 70.—A din, noise, shouting, tumult: ἀνιηθεὶς ὀρυμαγδῷ α 133. Cf. Ρ 424, 741.—(3) The tumult of battle. With the notion of noise obscured: ἐρύεσθαι ὑπὸ Τρώων ὀρυμαγδοῦ (from the hands of the . . .) Ι 248. Cf. Κ 539, Ρ 461.

ὀρύσσω. Aor. ὄρυξα λ 25. 3 pl. ὄρυξαν Η 440. 1 pl. subj. ὀρύξομεν Η 341. Pple. ὀρύξας φ 120. Infin. ὀρύξαι κ 517. (1) To form by digging, dig: τάφρον Η 341, 440: φ 120, βόθρον κ 517, λ 25.—(2) To dig up, get out of the ground κ 305.

ὀρφανικός [ὀρφανός]. Orphan, fatherless Ζ 432, Λ 394.—ἦμαρ ὀρφανικόν. See ἦμαρ (4) (j).

ὀρφανός, -ή. Orphan, deprived of one's parents: ἐλίποντο ὀρφαναὶ ἐν μεγάροισιν υ 68.

ὀρφναῖος, -η, -ον [ὄρφνη, darkness]. Dark, murky: νύκτα Κ 83=386, 276: ι 143.

ὄρχαμος, -ου, ὁ. A leader or chief. Applied to heroes Β 837, Ζ 99, Ξ 102, Ρ 12, etc.: γ 400, δ 156, κ 538, ο 167, etc.—To Eumaeus ξ 22, 121, ο 351=389=π 36, ρ 184.—To Philoetius υ 185, 254.

ὄρχατος, -ου, ὁ [ὄρχος]. (1) A row: φυτῶν ὄρχατοι Ξ 123.—(2) An orchard η 112, ω 222, 245, 257, 358.

ὀρχέομαι [ὄρχος]. 3 pl. impf. ὠρχεῦντο Σ 594. To dance Σ 594: θ 371, 378, ξ 465.

ὀρχηθμός, -οῦ, ὁ [ὀρχέομαι]. Dancing, the dance Ν 637:=ψ 145, θ 263, ψ 134, 298.

ὀρχηστήρ, -ῆρος, ὁ [ὀρχέομαι]. A dancer: κοῦροι ὀρχηστῆρες Σ 494.

ὀρχηστής, ὁ [as prec.]. =prec.: ὀρχηστήν περ ἐόντα (tauntingly in reference to the agility of Meriones) Π 617. Cf. Ω 261.

ὀρχηστύς, ἡ [ὀρχέομαι]. (1) Dancing, the dance α 152, 421=σ 304, ρ 605—(2) Dancing, skill in the dance: ὅσσον περιγιγνόμεθ' ἄλλων ὀρχηστυῖ θ 253. Cf. Ν 731.

ὄρχος, -ου, ὁ. A row (of vines) η 127, ω 341.

ὄρωρε, 3 sing. pf. ὄρνυμι.

ὀρώρει[1], 3 sing. plupf. ὄρνυμι.

ὀρώρει[2], 3 sing. plupf. ὄρομαι.

ὀρώρεται, 3 sing. thematic pf. mid. ὄρνυμι.

ὀρωρέχαται, 3 pl. pf. mid. ὀρέγω.

ὅς[1]. See ἑός.

ὅς[2], ἥ, ὅ. Genit. masc. ὅου α 70. Fem. ἕης Π 208. Neut. ὅου Β 325. Dat. pl. fem. ᾗς Β 341, etc. ᾗσι Ε 54, etc.: ζ 272, etc. (I) Demonstrative pronoun, he, etc. οὐδ' οἳ ἄναρχοι ἔσαν Β 703. Cf. Ζ 59, Φ 198, etc.: δ 389, 653.—Of the second person Η 160.—(II) As relative. (1) (a) ὃς Χρύσην ἀμφιβέβηκας Α 37, ᾧ ἔπι πολλὰ μόγησα 162, ἄντυγες αἳ περὶ δίφρον [ἦσαν] Λ 535. Cf. Α 94, 289, 603, 604, Β 73, etc.: α 1, 54, 69, 108, 161, 191, etc.—(b) With τε: οἵ τε θέμιστας εἰρύαται Α 238. Cf. Α 86, Β 470, etc.: α 52, δ 826, ε 4, etc.—For ὃς γάρ see γάρ (4).—(2) In causal sense: τόδε μέγ' ἄριστον ἔρεξεν, ὃς τὸν λωβητῆρ' ἔσχ' ἀγοράων (seeing that he has . . ., for he has . . .) Β 275. Cf. Ε 403, Θ 34, Μ 235, Π 204, Χ 236, etc.: α 8, δ 724, ι 274, κ 338, μ 281, σ 114, etc.—(3) With final force. (a) With subj., pure or with κεν: τιμὴν ἀποτινέμεν, ἥ τε καὶ ἐσσομένοισι μετ' ἀνθρώποισι πέληται Γ 287, κλητοὺς ὀτρύνομεν, οἵ κ' ἔλθωσι Ι 165. Cf. Φ 127, etc.: δ 29, ν 400, etc.—(b) With opt. ο 458.—(4) (a) With subj. or opt. in relative sentences corresponding to sentences with εἰ (4). For the examples and constructions see Table at end (II) (B) (a) (2), (D) (4) (16).—In conditional relative sentences. See Table (III) (B) (a) (1) (2) (3), (b) (1) (3), (C) (a) (5), (D) (13) (19) (20) (21) (22) (24) (26) (29) (30) (31) (32) (34) (45) (47) (54) (56) (57) (58) (62) (64).—(b) With subj. in similes: ἀστέρ', ὅς τε μάλιστα λαμπρὸν παμφαίνῃσιν Ε 5. Cf. Κ 184, Π 387, etc.: ν 31, etc.—(5) In object clauses: γνώσῃ ὅς θ' ἡγεμόνων κακὸς ὅς τέ νυ λαῶν, ἠδ' ὅς κ' ἐσθλὸς ἔῃσιν Β 365. Cf. Η 171, Υ 21, Φ 609, Ψ 498, etc.: οὐδέ τι οἶδα οἵ τ' ἐσάωθεν οἵ τ' ἀπόλοντο γ 185. Cf. β 156, θ 576, κ 110, etc.—(6) In dat. sing. fem. ᾗ. (a) In or at the place or spot in which, in or at which place or spot, where: ᾗ ῥ' ἴδε γυμνωθέντα βραχίονα Μ 389. Cf. Μ 33, Ν 53, 679, Ο 448, 616, Π 377, Υ 275, Χ 324, Ψ 420: χῶρον, ᾗ οἱ πέφραδ' ὑφορβόν ξ 2.—(b) Whither: ὄφρ' ἀφίκοντο, ᾗ μιν ἀνώγει Ν 329. Cf. Ζ 41, Φ 4: μ 81.—With subj. in a conditional relative sentence. See Table (III) (D) (26).—(c) In such way or manner as, as: ᾗ τελέει περ Θ 415. Cf. Ι 310.—With subj. in conditional relative sentences. See Table (III) (D) (31) (34).—(7) In neut. ὅ. (a) Because, since, seeing that, in that: χωσαμένη ὅ . . . Ι 534. Cf. Ι 564, Ν 166, Υ 283, Φ 150, etc.: α 382, β 45, δ 206, etc.—So ὅ τε Α 244, Δ 32, Ζ 126, Ο 468, etc.: ε 357, θ 78, ξ 90, etc.—(b) That, how: λεύσσετε τό γε πάντες ὅ μοι γέρας ἔρχεται ἄλλῃ Α 120. Cf. Ε 433, Θ 32, 362, Ι 493, etc.: γ 146, δ 771, μ 295, ν 340, etc.—So ὅ τε Α 412, Ε 331, Θ 251, Π 433, etc.: θ 299, ξ 366, etc.—(8) In neut. pl. ἅ with τε, in such manner as, as: ἅ τε παρθένος ἠΐθεός τ' ὀαρίζετον Χ 127.—(9) In neut. ὅ with prepositions in temporal expressions. (a) εἰς ὅ κε with subj. (α) Till, until (cf. εἰς (II) (1) (i) (α)): εἰς ὅ κεν ἄστυ ἕλωμεν Β 332. Cf. Γ 409, Ε 466, Η 30, Ι 46, etc.: β 97, ζ 295, θ 318, ι 138, λ 122, etc.—With opt.: τεύχοιμι διαμπερές, εἰς ὅ κ' Ἴλιον ἕλοιεν Ο 70.—(β) As long as, while. With subj. in conditional relative sentences. See Table at end (III) (B) (a) (2), (D) (20).—(b) ἐξ οὗ. (α) From the time when, since (cf. ἐκ (II) (12) (a)): ἐξ οὗ διαστήτην (taking up the tale from the point when . . .) Α 6. Cf. Θ 295, Ν 778, Ω 638, 766: ἐξ οὗ ἔβη β 27. Cf. β 90, λ 168, π 142, σ 181, etc.—(β) Since which time: ἐξ οὗ Κενταύροισι καὶ ἀνδράσι νεῖκος ἐτύχθη φ 303.

ὁσίη, ἡ. That which is right or permitted. With infin.: οὐδ' ὁσίη κακὰ ῥάπτειν ἀλλήλοισιν π 423. Cf. χ 412.

ὅσος, ὅσσος, -η, -ον. **(1)** Such in number, quantity or volume as, as many or much as, such as: ὅσοι θεοί εἰσ' ἐν Ὀλύμπῳ (all the gods in . . .) A 566 (θεοί attracted into the relative clause), ὅσοι οὐ βουλῆς ἐπάκουσαν B 143, ἀγηγέραθ' ὅσσοι ἄριστοι [ἦσαν] (as many as were . . ., the whole number of the . . .) Δ 211. Cf. B 125, 249 (of all who . . .), 468, 681, Γ 57, E 267, I 55 (of all the . . .), 401, etc.: α 11, 278, β 209, γ 108, 186, 312, η 68 (of all the women who . . .), θ 36, 214 (in all contests that are practised), λ 329, μ 86, etc.—Introducing a simile δ 791.—Correlative with τόσος. See τόσος (4).—With τοσόσδε. See τοσόσδε (1).—**(2)** With subj. or opt. in conditional relative sentences. For the examples and constructions see Table at end **(III) (B) (a)** (1) (2) (3), (D) (12) (13) (14) (56).—**(3)** In reference to magnitude or extent, of such magnitude, size, extent or importance as: ὅσον τ' ἐπὶ λᾶαν ἵησιν (as far as . . .) Γ 12, ὅση δύναμίς γε πάρεστιν (as far as my strength goes) Θ 294. Cf. B 616, H 451, Θ 213, K 351, P 368, Ψ 190, etc.: τοῦ ὅσον τ' ὄργυιαν ἀπέκοψα (*i.e.* τόσον ὅση ὄργυια γίγνεται) ι 325, ὅσον τ' ἐπὶ ἥμισυ (*i.e.* ἐφ' ὅσον τὸ ἥμισυ γίγνεται) ν 114. Cf. ι 322, κ 113, 517, etc.—In reference to stature B 528.—Introducing similes Π 589, Ψ 431, 845, Ω 317.—With subj.: ὅσσον τίς τ' ἔδαφος νηὸς τορνώσεται ε 249.—Correlative with τόσος. See τόσος (4).—**(4)** With infin. in this sense ε 484 (such a thing as might . . .).—**(5)** In causal sense (=ὅτι τόσος): κεχολωμένοι ὅσσοι ὄλοντο (because so many . . .) Π 546. Cf. Ω 630: δ 75, χ 46.—**(6)** In object clauses, how many, who, what, how much, how great: οὐδέ τι οἶδε πένθεος, ὅσσον ὄρωρεν Λ 658. Cf. B 492, etc.: μυθεόμην ὅσ' ἐμόγησεν δ 152. Cf. γ 105, δ 241, κ 45, etc.—**(7)** In neut. ὅσ(σ)ον as adv. **(a)** To such an extent as, as greatly as, as much as, as far as: ὅσσον γιγνώσκω N 222. Cf. E 860 (as loudly as . . .), I 177, Ψ 327, etc.: γ 395, η 108, etc.—**(b)** In reference to distance, as far as: ὅσσον ἀνὴρ ἴδεν E 770. Cf. I 354 (and no further), Ψ 517, etc.: ε 400, θ 229, π 290, etc.—Introducing a simile Ψ 517.—**(c)** In object clauses, to how great an extent, how much, how greatly: ὅσσον φέρτερός εἰμι A 186. Cf. A 516, etc.: η 327, θ 102, etc.—**(d)** Correlative with τόσον. See τόσος (5) (d).—With τοσόνδε. See τοσόσδε (3).

ὄσσα, ἡ. **(1)** A rumour or report α 282, β 216.—**(2)** Rumour personified B 93: ω 413.

ὁσσάκι [ὅσ(σ)ος]. As often as, each time. With opt. in conditional relative sentences (with τοσσάκι as correlative). See Table at end (III) (B) (b) (1).

ὁσσάτιος = ὅσ(σ)ος. How much. In causal sense: ὁσσάτιον ἀπώλεσε λαὸν Ἀχαιῶν (seeing that he has smitten so much . . .) E 758.

ὄσσε, *neut. dual.* The eyes, one's eyes: ὄσσε οἱ πυρὶ ἐΐκτην A 104. Cf. A 200, Γ 427, Δ 461, Λ 453, N 3, etc.: δ 186, 704, ε 151, μ 232, ν 401, etc.—In reference to lions: ὄσσε καλύπτων P 136: ἐν οἱ ὄσσε δαίεται ζ 131.

ὄσσομαι [ὄσσε]. (ἐπι-, προτι-.) **(1)** To look, glance. With *quasi*-cognate acc.: κάκ' ὀσσόμενος (looking bale, with baleful look) A 105.—**(2)** To look at, look for: ὀσσόμενος πατέρ' ἐνὶ φρεσίν (keeping his father's image before his mind's eye) α 115.—So Ὀδυσῆα ὀσσομένη υ 81.—Of something inanimate: πέλαγος, ὀσσόμενον ἀνέμων κέλευθα (watching for, biding) Ξ 17.—**(3)** To bode, portend, betoken: κακὸν ὀσσομένη Ω 172. Cf. β 152.—**(4)** To bode, forbode, have a presentiment of, apprehend: κάκ' ὄσσετο θυμός κ 374. Cf. σ 154.—Of horses Σ 224.

ὅσσος. See ὅσος.

ὀστέον, -ου, τό. Locative ὀστεόφι π 145. This form as ablative ξ 134. As genit. (or perh. as instrumental of material; see below) μ 45. A bone: πέρησεν ὀ. αἰχμή Δ 460. Cf. Δ 174, E 67, H 334, Λ 97, M 185, etc.: πολὺς ἀμφ' ὀστεόφιν θίς (there is a great heap of bones; or perh., taking ὀστεόφιν as instrumental of material, 'a heap (is made) of bones') μ 45. Cf. α 161, ε 426, ι 293, λ 219, σ 96, etc.—In pl., the osseous bodily framework as typifying the body: λίπ' ὀστέα θυμός M 386, Π 743, Υ 406: μ 414. Cf. λ 221.—In reference to an animal γ 455.

ὅς τις, ἥ τις, ὅ τι. Nom. sing. masc. ὅτις Γ 279, T 260, etc.: α 47, β 350, ε 445, etc. The two elements separated by an enclitic ὅ κέν τις π 257. Neut. ὅττι X 73: κ 44. Genit. sing. neut. ὅτευ ρ 421, τ 77. ὅττεο α 124, χ 377. ὅττευ ρ 121. Dat. sing. masc. ὅτεῳ M 428, O 664: β 114. Acc. sing. masc. ὅτινα θ 204, ο 395. Neut. ὅττι A 294, 543, B 361, etc.: α 158, 316, β 161, etc. Nom. pl. neut. ὅτινα X 450 (elsewhere ἄσσα *q.v.*). Genit. pl. masc. ὅτεων κ 39. Dat. pl. masc. ὁτέοισι O 491. Acc. pl. masc. ὅτινας O 492. **(1)** Who, which, with an indefinite force, 'whoever (whatever) he (it) may be': θεοπρόπιον ὅ τι οἶσθα A 85, τίπτ' ἀλᾶσθε, ὅ τι δὴ χρειὼ τόσον ἵκει; (on what account do you wander thus, in respect of which . . .?) K 142. Cf. Γ 286, E 175, Φ 103, Ψ 43, etc.: ἥ τις σύ πέρ ἐσσι θεάων δ 376. Cf. β 114, ε 445, η 150, θ 550, ρ 53, etc.—With τε Ψ 43: β 114 cited above.—**(2)** With final force: ὄνομ' εὕρεο ὅττι κε θῆαι τ 403. Cf. P 640: π 257.—**(3) (a)** With subj. in relative sentences corresponding to sentences with εἰ (4). For the examples and constructions see Table at end (II) (B) (a) (1), (D) (6).—**(b)** With subj. or opt. in conditional relative sentences. See Table **(II) (B) (b), (III) (B) (a) (1) (2) (5),** (b) (1), (C) (a) (5), (D) (12) (13) (14) (15) (17) (19) (20) (26) (28) (29) (45) (54) (55) (56) (57) (58) (61).—**(4)** In object clauses, who, what: ὅς κ' εἴποι ὅ τι τόσσον ἐχώσατο (why) A 64, ἔσπετε οἵ τινες ἡγεμόνες ἦσαν B 487. Cf. Γ 192, K 503, Λ 612, Ξ 195, Π 424, etc.: α 124, 401, γ 16, δ 61, η 17, θ 28, χ 450, etc.

ὅτε. **(1)** When, at the time when. **(a)** With

indic. (a) ὅτε Τρώεσσιν ἐν ἀγρομένοισιν ἔμιχθεν Γ 209. Cf. Α 397, Β 303, 471, etc.: α 16, β 314 (now that I am . . .), γ 180, δ 145, etc.—(β) So ᾔδεα μὲν ὅτε . . . οἶδα δὲ νῦν ὅτε . . . (I knew what it meant when . . .) Ξ 71: ἦ οὐκ οἶσθ' ὅτε . . . ; (what happened when . . .) π 424.—(γ) Introducing similes: ὡς ὅτε . . . Β 209, Γ 33, Δ 275, etc.: ε 432, μ 251, ν 31, etc.—ὡς ὅτ' ἂν . . . Μ 41: κ 410.—(δ) With πρίν. See πρίν (6) (a).—(b) (a) ὅτ' ἄν with subj. like (1) (a) (β): ὄφρα ἰδῇ (ἴδῃς) ὅτ' ἂν ᾧ (σῷ) πατρὶ μάχηται (μάχηαι) (i.e. what it is to fight with . . .) Θ 406, 420.—(β) With subj. in a relative sentence corresponding to sentences with εἰ (4). See Table at end (II) (B) (a) (1).—(γ) With fut., subj. or opt. in conditional relative sentences. For the examples and constructions see Table (III) (B) (a) (1) (2) (3), (b) (1) (2) (3), (C) (a) (6), (D) (9) (12) (17) (20) (26) (32) (34) (35) (37) (45) (51) (52) (54) (55) (56) (57) (58).—(δ) With subj. introducing similes: ὡς ὅτε Β 147, Δ 130, 141, Ε 597, Ζ 506, etc.: ε 328, ζ 232 = ψ 159, ι 391, τ 518, υ 25.—With ἄν: ὡς ὅτ' ἂν Κ 5, Λ 269, Ο 80, 170, Ρ 520, Τ 375, Ω 480: ε 394, κ 216, χ 468, ψ 233.—With opt.: ὡς ὅτε ι 384.—(ε) With πρίν with subj. and ἄν or opt. See πρίν (6) (b) (c).—(2) Introducing similes without expressed vb.: ὡς ὅτε Β 394, Δ 462, Μ 132, Ν 471, 571, Ο 362, 679, Π 406, Σ 219, Ψ 712: ε 281, λ 368, τ 494.—(3) Against the time when: ποτιδέγμενον ἀγγελίην, ὅτ' ἀποφθιμένοιο πύθηται (waiting for the tidings which shall tell him that . . .) Τ 337.—(4) At which time, when: ἔσσεται ἦμαρ ὅτ' ἄν ποτ' ὀλώλῃ Ἴλιος Δ 164. Cf. Β 351, Θ 373 (the day will come when . . .), 475, etc.: σ 272.—So ἦ οὐ μέμνῃ ὅτε . . . (the time when . . . how . . .) Ο 18, Υ 188, Φ 396: ω 115.—εἰς ὅτε κε . . . (against the time when . . .) β 99 = τ 144 = ω 134.—(5) When, after that, as soon as: ὅτε δὴ σχεδὸν ἦσαν Γ 15. Cf. Α 432, 493, Ζ 191, etc.: α 332, γ 269, 286, etc.—(6) Since, from the time when: ἐμοὶ χλαῖναι καὶ ῥήγεα ἤχθεθ', ὅτε Κρήτης ὄρεα νοσφισάμην τ 338. Cf. Φ 81, 156: ω 288.—(7) While: ὅτε δὴ ῥ' ἐπὶ νῆ' ᾔομεν, τόφρα . . . κ 569.—(8) When, whereas: ὅτε τ' ἄλλοι ἅπαξ θνήσκουσιν μ 22.—(9) Since, seeing that: ὅτ' ὀνείδεα βάζεις ρ 461. Cf. ν 129.—(10) ὅτε μή without expressed vb., unless, except: ὅτε μὴ Διὶ πατρί Π 227.—(11) Written oxytone, ὀτέ. With ἄλλοτε. See ἄλλοτε (2).—ὀτέ alone, at another time, again Π 690, Ρ 178.

ὅτι, ὅττι [neut. of ὅς τις]. (1) Because, since, seeing that, in that: ὅτι ῥα θνήσκοντας ὁρᾶτο Α 56. Cf. Β 255, Ε 326, Ξ 407, Π 35, Φ 411, etc.: ὅττι μιν ὧς ὑπέδεκτο ξ 52. Cf. ε 340, θ 238, ο 342, χ 36, ψ 115, etc.—(2) That: οὐδέ μιν ἠγνοίησεν ὅτι . . . Α 537. Cf. Ε 349, Ζ 231, Η 448, etc.: οὐκ ἀΐεις ὅτι . . . ; σ 11. Cf. ν 314, π 131, etc.—(3) Strengthening a superl. See τάχιστα (2).

ὀτραλέως [cf. next]. Quickly, featly, deftly: δεῖπνον ἔθηκας Τ 317. Cf. Γ 260: τ 100.

ὀτρηρός, -ή [cf. prec.]. Deft, rendering ready service Α 321, Ζ 381: α 109, δ 23 = 217, δ 38.

ὀτρηρῶς [adv. fr. prec.]. Quickly δ 735.

ὄτριχας, acc. pl. ὄθριξ.

ὀτρυντύς, ἡ [ὀτρύνω]. A summons: ἄλλην ὀτρυντὺν ποτιδέγμενος Τ 234. Cf. Τ 235.

ὀτρύνω. 3 pl. pa. iterative ὀτρύνεσκον Ω 24. Fut. ὀτρυνέω Κ 55. 2 sing. ὀτρυνέεις Κ 38. 3 ὀτρυνέει β 253. Pple. ὀτρυνέων Ν 209: ω 116. Fem. ὀτρυνέουσα ο 3, σ 186, χ 434, 496. Aor. ὄτρῦνα ξ 261, ρ 430. 3 sing. ὤτρῦνε (ὄτρῦνε) Γ 249, Δ 73, Ε 461, Θ 398, Λ 185, Ν 44, Ο 560, Ψ 111, Ω 143, etc.: β 392, ζ 254, θ 15, λ 214, 226, ρ 362, χ 241, ω 487. Subj. ὀτρύνω Ο 402: ι 518. 3 sing. ὀτρύνῃσι Ο 59: ξ 374. 1 pl. ὀτρύνομεν Ι 165: α 85, π 355. 3 sing. opt. ὀτρύνειε ο 306. 3 pl. ὀτρύνειαν θ 90. Imp. ὄτρῡνον Π 495, Ρ 654, Τ 69: ρ 75, χ 484. Genit. sing. masc. pple. ὀτρύναντος Κ 356, Ο 744. Infin. ὀτρῦναι Θ 219: ο 37, 40. (ἐπ-.) (1) To rouse to action, urge on, stir up, set on, encourage, urge, press, incite, exhort, summon, call upon, dispatch, send, to do something or to proceed somewhither for some purpose: ὀτρύνων πόλεμόνδε Β 589, πυμάτας ὤτρυνε φάλαγγας Δ 254. Cf. Γ 249, Δ 73, Κ 38 (to play the . . .), 356, Ο 59, Τ 349, Ω 143, etc.: α 85, β 74, ζ 254, λ 226, ο 37, ρ 75, χ 241, ω 405, etc.—To rouse or stir (a person's spirit): ὄτρυνε μένος ἑκάστου Ε 470. Cf. Ε 563, Μ 266, etc.: θ 15.—With infin.: ἰέναι Β 94, μάχεσθαι Δ 294, ἀνδρῶν δυσμενέων δῦναι στρατόν Κ 220. Cf. Ε 496, Π 495, Ρ 654, Ψ 49, Ω 24, etc.: β 244, θ 90, ι 518, ξ 261, σ 61, etc.—With fut. pple.: ἀγγελέουσαν Θ 398 = Λ 185. Cf. Τ 156: ο 40.—(2) To hasten on, speed, bring about: πομπήν η 151, λ 357. Cf. β 253.—To send, cause to appear: εἴδωλον λ 214.—To dispatch or send (a message) π 355.—(3) To press for, urge one's claim to, importune for: πομπήν θ 30.—(4) In mid., to rouse oneself to action, take action, to put oneself in motion, bestir oneself, set oneself, get ready, to do something: ὑμεῖς ὀτρύνεσθαι ἅμ' ἠοῖ η 222.—With infin.: ὀτρύνοντο νέκυς ἀγέμεν Η 420. Cf. Ξ 369: κ 425, ρ 183.

ὅττι. See ὅτι.

οὐ. Before a vowel **οὐκ** (**οὐχ**). Also **οὐκί** Β 238, Ο 137, etc.: α 268, λ 493, etc. **οὐχί** Ο 716, Π 762. Negative particle, commonly denying a predication (cf. μή). (1) In gen. negation: τὴν οὐ λύσω Α 29. Cf. Α 24, 152, Β 2, 238, etc.: οὐκ οἶδα α 216. Cf. α 42, 236, γ 14, ω 29, etc.—Repeated Α 114, Ψ 43, etc.: γ 27, etc.—With participles Δ 224, Η 185, etc.: β 50, λ 66, etc.—With adjectives, adverbs or adverbial expressions Β 214, Ε 366, Θ 360, etc.: β 251, δ 846, ρ 153, etc.—(2) Not merely negativing a verb but expressing the opposite meaning. See ἐάω (4), ἐθέλω (3), φημί (6).—(3) In protasis with εἰ. (a) With indic. when the protasis precedes the apodosis (the only exception to the rule being ι 410): εἰ δέ τοι οὐ δώσει ἑὸν ἄγγελον, . . . Ω 296. Cf. Δ 160, Ο 162, Υ 129: β 274, μ 382, ν 144.—For the converse construction see μή (6) (c).—(b) With subj.: εἰ δ' ἂν ἐμοὶ τιμὴν τίνειν οὐκ ἐθέλωσιν, . . . Γ 289. Cf. Υ 139.—(4) In conditional relative sentences (cf. μή (8)). (a) With subj.: ὅτινας οὐκ ἐθέλῃσιν . . . O 492.—(b) With indic.: ὅσοι οὐ βουλῆς ἐπάκουσαν B 143. Cf. H 236, Σ 363, etc.: γ 349.—(5) After μή (cf. οὐδέ (6), οὐκέτι (3)): μὴ χόλον οὐκ ἐρύσαιτο Ω 584. Cf. A 28, 566, K 39. —(6) With infin. after vbs. of saying, thinking, etc.: ἅ τιν' οὐ πείσεσθαι ὀΐω A 289. Cf. P 174, etc.: γ 28, ε 342, etc.—(7) (a) In questions expecting an affirmative answer: οὐ νεμεσίζῃ; E 872. Cf. B 194, H 448, etc.: α 60, β 312, ε 23, etc.—(b) With opt. and ἄν in questions constituting a form of polite or affectionate imperative: οὐκ ἂν δή μοι ἐφοπλίσσειας ἀπήνην; ζ 57. Cf. Γ 52, E 32, K 204, etc.: η 22.—(8) With other particles. (a) οὔ ποτε, οὐ . . . ποτε, at no time, never A 163, 234, B 325, 396, E 441, K 164, N 556, etc.: α 308, 433, β 256, γ 275, δ 693, η 258, λ 528, etc. —(b) οὔ πω, οὐ . . . πω. (α) In no wise, not at all, by no means A 224, Γ 306, M 270, Ξ 143, etc.: θ 540, μ 208, π 143, etc.—(β) Not yet, never yet A 106, 262, B 122, 553, Γ 169, Δ 331, I 148, K 293, etc.: α 196, β 118, γ 160, δ 269, ι 455, κ 502, λ 52, μ 66, etc.—In reference to the future ε 358, κ 174.—(c) οὔ πώ ποτε, οὐ . . . πώ ποτε, never yet A 106, 154, Γ 442, Ξ 315: μ 98, φ 123, ψ 328.—(d) οὔ πως, οὐ . . . πως, in no wise, not at all, by no means Δ 158, H 217, M 65, N 114, Ξ 63, etc.: β 130, ε 103, λ 158, ο 49, π 196, etc. —(e) (α) οὔ τις, οὔ τι, οὐ . . . τις, οὐ . . . τι, no one, nothing: οὔ τις σοὶ χεῖρας ἐποίσει A 88, τῶν οὐκ ἄν τι φέροις 301. Cf. A 271, 511, 547, 562, Γ 365, E 475, H 197, etc.: β 121, 191, 199, 411, γ 192, δ 106, ε 11, ζ 176, etc.—With sb., no: οὔ τις ἀνήρ N 222. Cf. E 761, Σ 192, etc.: κ 202, ν 423, etc.—(β) οὔ τι, οὐ . . . τι as adv., in no wise, not at all: οὔ τί μοι αἴτιοί εἰσιν A 153, οὐ μὲν γάρ τι καταθνητός γε τέτυκτο E 402. Cf. A 588, B 338, Γ 11, Δ 286, Z 102, etc.: α 75, 78, 173, β 235, 240, 282, γ 367, δ 199, etc.

οὖας, -ατος, τό. Also **οὖς** Λ 109, Υ 473. Dat. pl. οὔασι M 442. ὠσί μ 200. (1) The ear K 535, Λ 109, M 442, N 177, O 129, etc.: μ 47, 177, 200, σ 86, 96, υ 365, φ 300, χ 475.—Of a dog ρ 291, 302.—(2) An ear or handle of a drinking vessel (cf. ὠτώεις) Λ 633.—Of a tripod Σ 378.

οὖδας, τό. (1) The surface of the earth, the earth, the ground: ὕπτιος οὔδει ἐρείσθη H 145. Cf. Λ 749, M 448, Ξ 468, Π 612, Ψ 283, etc.: θ 376, ι 135, 242, 459, ν 395, χ 269, 467.—(2) A floor or pavement: πέπλον κατέχευεν πατρὸς ἐπ' οὔδει E 734 = Θ 385. Cf. Ω 527: ψ 46.

οὖδάσδε [prec. + -δε (1)]. To the ground: οὐ. πελάσσαι κ 440. Cf. P 457.

οὐδέ [οὐ δέ]. Negative particle, in general use corresponding to οὐ as μηδέ to μή. (1) Adversatively, but not, yet not (cf. δέ (1)): βάλεν, οὐδ' ἔρρηξεν χαλκός Γ 348. Cf. B 419, 753, Γ 302, Δ 127, 477, E 621, etc.: β 182, γ 143, δ 675, ε 81, θ 344, ι 230, etc.—(2) In continuation, and not, nor (cf. δέ (2)): ὃν ἠτίμησ' Ἀγαμέμνων, οὐδ' ἀπέλυσε θύγατρα A 95. Cf. A 97, 170, 173, 220, 330, 406, etc.: α 166, 296, 410, β 36, 82, 203, 296, etc.—(3) Preceded by a negative, nor (sometimes rather to be translated 'or'): οὐ δέμας οὐδὲ φυήν A 115. Cf. A 132, 154, 155, 160, 181, 262, etc.: οὔ τι νοήμονες οὐδὲ δίκαιοι β 282. Cf. β 44, 63, 185, 210, 270, δ 201, 240, ζ 201, etc.—(4) Not even: οὐδέ με τυτθὸν ἔτεισεν A 354, οὐδ' οἳ τόσοι ἦσαν Γ 190, ὅ γ' ἄρ' οὐδὲ θεὸν μέγαν ἅζετο E 434. Cf. Δ 387, I 351, etc.: α 6, 18, γ 115, μ 62, etc.—Preceded by a negative: οὔ τις . . . οὐδ' ἤν . . . A 90, οὐκέτ' ἔπειτα . . . οὐδ' ἠβαιόν B 380. Cf. B 489, Γ 443, etc.: α 204, β 118, γ 14, etc.—To be translated 'neither': οὐδὲ γὰρ αὐτῷ ὕπνος ἐπὶ βλεφάροισιν ἐφίζανεν K 25. Cf. Π 852, etc.: οὐδ' ὄπιθεν κακὸς ἔσσεαι β 270. Cf. ρ 273, etc.—(5) Re-echoing a negative for emphasis (cf. μηδέ (5)): οὐ μὰν οὐδ' Ἀχιλεὺς μάρναται Δ 512, etc.: οὐ μέν σ' οὐδὲ ἐῶσι κλαίειν δ 805. Cf. ε 212, θ 159, etc.—(6) After μή: μὴ ματήσετον, οὐδ' ἐθέλητον . . . E 233. Cf. O 164, Ω 569.—(7) With infin.: ἐπεὶ οὐδέ σε πεισέμεν οἴω E 252, etc. Cf. ν 335, etc.—(8) Giving a reason or explanation, for not (cf. δέ (3)): οὐδέ τί που ἴδμεν ξυνήϊα κείμενα πολλά A 124, οὐδέ τί πω σάφα ἴδμεν B 252. Cf. Z 360, I 613, M 113, Π 60, etc.: β 369, γ 23, ι 143, λ 463, ν 238, etc.—Sim. with γάρ: οὐδὲ γὰρ ἡμετέρῃ βραδυτῆτι Τρῶες . . . T 411.—With ἐπεί: ἐπεὶ οὐδὲ ἔοικεν (for it is not fitting) A 119. Cf. E 252, P 270, etc.—(9) Introducing a negative principal clause after a temporal protasis (cf. δέ (4)): ὅτε δὴ . . . οὐδὲ μὲν εὕδοντας εὗρον K 181. Cf. κ 18.—(10) Repeated, the first connecting in one of the foregoing constructions with what precedes and the second attaching itself to a particular word: οὐδὲ μὲν οὐδ' οἳ ἄναρχοι ἔσαν B 703, 726, οὐδὲ μὲν οὐδὲ Τρῶας εἴασεν εὕδειν (did not let them sleep either) K 299. Cf. P 24, etc.: οὐδέ κεν ἄλλως οὐδὲ θεὸς τεύξειεν θ 176, οὐδὲ μὲν οὐδ' ἔνθεν περ ἀπήμονας ἦγον ἑταίρους (not even thence) κ 551.—Repeated for emphasis: οὐδὲ γὰρ οὐδέ κεν αὐτὸς ὑπέκφυγε κῆρα (not even he) E 22, ἐπεὶ οὐδὲ μὲν οὐδὲ ἔοικε . . . (for of a surety it is not seemly) M 212, οὐδὲ γὰρ οὐδ' ἐμέ φημι λελασμένον ἔμμεναι ἀλκῆς (neither do I . . .) N 269. Cf. Z 130, Σ 117: οὐδὲ γὰρ οὐδέ τις ἄλλος . . . (for never yet did . . .) θ 32, κ 327. Cf. φ 319.

οὐδείς, -ενός. Neut. οὐδέν. [οὐδέ + εἷς.] (1) Not any, no: κτέρας K 216. Cf. X 513: δ 350 = ρ 141. —Absol. in masc., no one: οὐδενὶ εἴκων X 459: = λ 515.—In neut., nothing: οὐδὲν ἑοργώς χ 318. Cf. ι 34, σ 130.—(2) In neut. as adv., not at all, in no wise, by no means: οὐ. ἔτεισας A 244. Cf. A 412 = Π 274, X 332, Ω 370: δ 195, 248, ι 287, λ 563, τ 264, υ 366, χ 370.

οὐδενόσωρος [οὐδενός, genit. of prec. + ὥρη, care]. Not worth caring for, not worth a thought Θ 178.

οὐδετέρωσε [οὐδέτερος, neither of two (fr. οὐδέ + ἕτερος) + -σε]. Opposed to οὐ πρό, nor aside Ξ 18 (*v.l.* οὐδ' ἑτέρωσε. See ἑτέρωσε).

οὐδός[1], -οῦ, ὁ. (1) A threshold, a block or row of blocks standing more or less above the surrounding level and forming the lower part of a doorway or gateway, in the case of the *μέγαρον* raised considerably and of considerable width, and so affording room for sitting or standing (see *αὔλειος*, *λάϊνος*, *μέλινος* (2), *χάλκεος*): *ἔστη ἐπ' οὐδὸν ἰών* Z 375. Cf. I 404, 582: *τὸν κατ' οὐδοῦ βάντα προσηύδα Πηνελόπεια* δ 680 (no doubt the threshold of the *μέγαρον*. App. he has followed the suitors into the *μ.*, and as he is coming out again P. sees him from her quarters, addresses him, and comes down (cf. 760) to speak to him), *ἐπ' οὐδοῦ ἷζε θαλάμοιο* 718 (app., a block of wood or stone at the foot of the stairs leading to the *θ.* (P. is below; cf. 760)), *ἐς μυχὸν ἐξ οὐδοῦ* η 87, *ὑπ' αὐλῆς οὐδόν* 130 (= *οὐδὸν αὔλειον*). Cf. η 135, κ 62, ρ 575 (*sc.* *θαλάμοιο*; see 506), σ 17, φ 43, χ 2, etc.—A verge or edge ascribed to the gulf of Tartarus Θ 15.—(2) Fig.: *γήραος οὐ.*, app. not so much the threshold as the stage of old age, old age itself (the threshold being thought of as within the room as in ρ 339) X 60, Ω 487: ο 246, 348, ψ 212.

οὐδός[2]. See *ὁδός*.

οὖθαρ, *-ατος, τό* [cf. L. *uber*, Eng. *udder*]. The udder of an animal ι 440.—Fig, in reference to richness of soil: *Ἄργος, οὖθαρ ἀρούρης* I 141 = 283.

οὐκ, οὐκί. See *οὐ*.

οὐκέτι [*οὐκ ἔτι*]. In general use corresponding to *οὐ* as *μηκέτι* to *μή*. (1) In reference to the present or past, no more, no longer: *ἔνθ' ἐμοὶ οὐκέτ' ἐρητύετο θυμός* I 462, *οὐκέτι δῶρ' ἐτέλεσσαν* (*i.e.* they changed their minds) 598, *οὐκέτι δύναμαι παρμενέμεν* O 399. Cf. N 515, 701, 761, O 727 = Π 102, P 238, 603, 623, T 343, Φ 391, X 384: α 189, 297, γ 241, δ 12, ε 153, λ 456, μ 205, 223 (*i.e.* he gave up the idea), ο 23, σ 215, υ 137, χ 226, etc.—(2) Indicating the reaching of a limit, point, pitch: *Ἀχαιΐδες, οὐκέτ' Ἀχαιοί* (whom I can now no longer call . . .) B 235, H 96, *μαίνεται οὐκέτ' ἀνεκτῶς* (he has come to the point of being unbearable) Θ 355. Cf. Δ 539, H 357, Θ 427, I 164, K 118, Λ 610, M 73, 231 = Σ 285, N 116: *οὐκέτι καλὰ διὲκ μεγάροιό γ' ὀΐω ἂψ ἀναχωρήσειν* (your insolence is such that . . .) ρ 460. Cf. ι 350, ο 10, υ 223.—(3) In reference to the future, no more, no longer, no further: *οὐκέτ' ἀνάβλησις ἔσσεται* B 379. Cf. Θ 352, I 418 = 685, I 605, Λ 823, M 125, N 747, Φ 565: β 238, 285, θ 150, λ 176, μ 56, ν 128, σ 145, τ 166, υ 180, χ 27, ω 460.—After *μή*: *μὴ οὐκέτι φυκτὰ πέλωνται* Π 128.—Never more, never in the future: *οὐκέτι πῆμά ποτ' ἔσσεαι* K 453.

οὐλαί, *αἱ*. Barley grains sprinkled at a sacrifice: *ἑτέρῃ ἔχεν οὐλὰς ἐν κανέῳ* γ 441.

οὐλαμός, *-οῦ, ὁ* (*Fουλαμός*) [*Fελ-*, *εἴλω*]. A throng (of warriors) Δ 251, 273, Υ 113, 379.

οὐλή, *-ῆς, ἡ*. A wound scarred over, a scar τ 391, 393 = ψ 74, τ 464, 507, φ 219, 221, ω 331.

οὔλιος [= *οὖλος*[2]]. Deadly, baleful: *ἀστήρ* Λ 62 (app. Sirius as in X 27).

οὐλοκάρηνος [*οὖλος*[3] + *κάρηνον*]. Curly-headed, with crisp or curly hair τ 246.

οὐλόμενος, *-η, -ον* [metrical variant of *ὀλόμενος*, aor. pple. mid. of *ὄλλυμι*. For the sense cf. *ὀνήμενος* under *ὀνίνημι* (2)]. Accursed, unblest: *μῆνιν* A 2. Cf. E 876, T 92: *φάρμακον* κ 394. Cf. δ 92, λ 410, 555, ο 344, ρ 287, 474, σ 273, ω 97.—In voc. masc. Ξ 84: ρ 484.

οὖλος[1] [*ὀλ-Fος* = the later *ὅλος*]. Whole, entire: *ἄρτον* ρ 343, *μηνί* ω 118.

οὖλος[2] [app. conn. with *ὀλοός*]. Baneful, destructive B 6, 8, E 461, 717, Φ 536.—In neut. sing. *οὖλον* as adv.: *οὖλον κεκλήγοντες* P 756, 759 (app., shrieking a cry of destruction, uttering a death-shriek; or perh. the word should be referred to next, in sense 'close in texture,' and thus 'in full, unbroken, cry').

οὖλος[3], *-η* [for *Fολ-νος*. Cf. L. *vellus*, Eng. *wool*]. Woolly: *λάχνη* K 134.—Woolly, close or thick in texture, thick: *ταπήτων* Π 224. Cf. Ω 646: δ 50 = ρ 89, δ 299 = η 338, κ 451, τ 225.—Of hair, crisp, curly ζ 231 = ψ 158.

οὐλοχύται, *αἱ* [*οὐλαί* + *χυ-*, *χέω*]. = *οὐλαί* A 449, B 410, A 458 = B 421: = γ 447, γ 445, δ 761.

οὔλω. To be sound or well. In voc. *οὖλε* as a salutation ω 402 (health be to thee).

οὑμός = *ὁ ἐμός* Θ 360.

οὖν. (1) Affirmative particle: *φημὶ γὰρ οὖν κατανεῦσαι Κρονίωνα* (for I do declare that . . .) B 350: *τλήτω ἔμπης οὖν ἐπιμεῖναι ἐς αὔριον* (for all his impatience to be gone) λ 351.—For *γ' οὖν* see *γε*.—(2) In the first of correlative clauses: *μήτ' οὖν . . . μήτε* . . . Θ 7, *οὔτ' οὖν . . . οὔτε . . . οὔτε* . . . P 20. Cf. Υ 7, etc.: α 414, π 302, etc.—In the second: *οὔ τις . . . οὐδ' οὖν* . . . ι 147, *οὔτε . . . οὔτ' οὖν* . . . λ 200.—(3) Particle of transition, so, then, now: *οἱ δ' ἐπεὶ οὖν ἤγερθεν* A 57. Cf. Γ 21, I 550, O 232, X 475, etc.: *πρῶτ' οὖν λούσαντο* ψ 142. Cf. β 123, γ 34, δ 49, 780, π 478, ρ 226, φ 57, etc.

οὕνεκα [*οὗ ἕνεκα*]. (1) In the sense of *οὗ ἕνεκα*: *πρήξαντα* [*τοῦτο*] *οὕνεκα δεῦρ' ἱκόμεσθα* γ 61.—(2) Wherefore, so that: *ἡ δ' Ἄτη σθεναρή, οὕνεκα πάσας ὑπεκπροθέει* I 505.—(3) Because, since, seeing that, in that: *οὕνεκα τὸν Χρύσην ἠτίμασεν* A 11. Cf. A 111, B 580, Z 386, H 140, Ξ 192, etc.: γ 53, δ 482, η 10, 300, θ 200, ν 332, etc.—Correlative to *τοὔνεκα*. See *τοὔνεκα*.—(4) That, to the effect that: *ἀγγελίην ἐρέοντα οὕνεκά οἱ σῶς ἐσσι* ο 42. Cf. Λ 21: ε 216, ν 309, etc.

οὔνεσθε. See *ὄνομαι*.

οὔνομα, *-ατος*. See *ὄνομα*.

οὐραῖος, *-η* [*οὐρή*]. Of the tail Ψ 520.

Οὐρανίωνες, *οἱ* [*οὐρανός*. App. a patronymic in form. Cf. *Ὑπερίων*]. The heavenly gods E 373 = Φ 509, E 898 (here app. the sons of Uranus, *i.e.* the Titans; cf. O 225), Φ 275, Ω 547.—*θεοὶ Οὐρανίωνες* A 570, P 195, Ω 612: η 242 = ι 15, ν 41.

οὐρανόθεν [*οὐρανός* + *-θεν* (1)]. From heaven or the heavens: *ἦλθεν οὐ.* A 195, *οὐ. ὑπερράγη αἰθήρ* Θ 558 = Π 300 (the action thought of as wrought from the firmament, the phenomena of the clouds being ascribed to Zeus). Cf. A 208, Λ 184, P 545, Ψ 189: ε 294 = ι 69 = μ 315, ζ 281, ι 145, υ 31.—

With preps. With ἀπό Θ 365, Φ 199: λ 18, μ 381. —With ἐξ Θ 19, 21, P 548.

οὐρανόθι, locative οὐρανός.

οὐρανομήκης [οὐρανός + μῆκος]. Reaching the heavens, very tall: ἐλάτη ε 239.

οὐρανός, -οῦ, ὁ. Locative οὐρανόθι Γ 3. (**1**) The firmament, heaven, the heavens: κνίση οὐρανὸν ἷκεν A 317, οὐρανόθι πρό (in the front of heaven) Γ 3. Cf. B 153, Δ 44, H 423, Θ 16, Ξ 174, etc.: α 54, δ 400, ι 20, μ 404, ν 269, etc.—Personified O 36: = ε 184.—(**2**) The heavens as the abode of the gods: [Θέτις] ἀνέβη οὐρανὸν Οὔλυμπόν τε A 497. Cf. E 749, 750, Z 108, T 128, 130, 351, etc.: ἀθανάτοισι τοὶ οὐρανὸν εὐρὺν ἔχουσιν α 67. Cf. η 199, λ 316, etc.

οὐρεύς, ὁ. A mule A 50, K 84, Ψ 111, 115, Ω 716.

οὐρή, -ῆς, ἡ. The tail of an animal: οὐρῇσι περισσαίνοντες κ 215. Cf. Υ 170: ρ 302.

οὐρίαχος, -ου, ὁ. The butt-end: ἔγχεος N 443, Π 612 = P 528.

οὖρον, -ου, τό. (**1**) A limit or boundary, a boundary-stone: οὖρον ἀρούρης Φ 405.—Cf. M 421. —(**2**) (The distance between) the side limits of an area ploughed by such and such an animal in a given time, the length of the furrow being regarded as constant: ὅσσον ἐν νειῷ οὖρον πέλει ἡμιόνοιϊν (this ploughing-range of mules being taken as a rough standard of distance) θ 124.— So in pl. K 351.—(**3**) The regular range of the δίσκος taken as a sim. standard. In pl.: ὅσσα δίσκου οὖρα πέλονται Ψ 431. (Cf. δισκουρα.)

οὐρός, -οῦ, ὁ. A trench by which ships drawn up on land could be dragged down to the sea, a launching-way: οὐροὺς ἐξεκάθαιρον B 153.

οὖρος[1], -ου, ὁ. A fair wind, a favouring breeze: τοῖσιν ἴκμενον οὖρον ἵει Ἀπόλλων A 479. Cf. H 5: ὅτ' ἂψ θεοὶ οὖρον στρέψαν (*i.e.* caused the wind to veer to a favourable direction) δ 520. Cf. β 420, γ 176, δ 357, ε 167, λ 7, etc.—A wind, without implication of a particular direction: πρίν τινα κεκριμένον καταβήμεναι οὖρον Ξ 19.

οὖρος[2], -ου, ὁ [cf. ὅρομαι]. A guardian, protector, warder, watcher: οὖρος Ἀχαιῶν Θ 80, Λ 840, O 370 = 659: γ 411. Cf. ο 89.

οὖρος[3], τό. See ὄρος.

οὖς. See οὖας.

οὔσης, genit. sing. fem. pple. εἰμί.

οὐτάζω [cf. next]. 3 sing. aor. οὔτασε E 56, H 258, Λ 338, N 438, O 523, Π 467, P 344, etc. 3 sing. subj. οὐτάσῃ Φ 576. Infin. οὐτάσαι Ξ 424, Π 322. 3 sing. pf. pass. οὔτασται Λ 661, Π 26. Pple. οὐτασμένος λ 536. (**1**) To strike or wound by a thrust or lunge: οὔτασε χεῖρα δουρί E 336. Cf. E 56, Λ 338, M 427, Ξ 424, etc.: λ 536.—With cognate acc.: ἕλκος, ὅ με βροτὸς οὔτασεν ἀνήρ E 361.—In mid. of reciprocal action: καί νύ κε δὴ ξιφέεσσ' αὐτοσχεδὸν οὐτάζοντο H 273.—(**2**) To wound by the cast of a weapon Π 467.—(**3**) To thrust a weapon into, pierce (a shield): μέσον σάκος οὔτασε δουρί H 258. Cf. N 552, 607, 646, O 528.

οὐτάω [cf. prec.]. 3 sing. pa. iterative οὐτήσασκε X 375 οὔτασκε O 745. 3 sing. aor. οὖτα Δ 525, E 376, Z 64, Λ 490, Ξ 447, Π 311, T 53, Υ 455, etc.: χ 293, 294. Nom. pl. masc. pple. of this aor. in pass. sense οὐτάμενοι Λ 659, N 764, Ξ 128, 379, etc.: λ 40. Acc. sing. fem. in sim. sense οὐταμένην Ξ 518, P 86. Infin. οὐτάμεναι Φ 68, 397: ι 301, τ 449. οὐτάμεν E 132, 821. (**1**) To strike or wound by a thrust or lunge: πλευρὰ οὔτησε ξυστῷ Δ 469. Cf. E 132, Z 64, Λ 659, Ξ 128, etc.: ι 301, λ 40, τ 449, 452, χ 293, 294, 356.— In pass. construction with cognate acc.: ψυχὴ κατ' οὐταμένην ὠτειλὴν ἔσσυτο (the wound thus inflicted) Ξ 518. Cf. P 86.—(**2**) To thrust a weapon into, pierce (a shield): ἀσπίδος ὀμφαλὸν οὖτα N 192. Cf. N 561.—To thrust (at a shield), deliver a blow (upon it): οὔτησε κατ' ἀσπίδα Λ 434 = P 43. Cf. Φ 400.

οὔτε. In general use corresponding to οὐ as μήτε to μή. (**1**) οὔτε . . . οὔτε . . ., neither . . . nor . . . (after a negative, either . . . or . . .) A 93, 108, 115, 299, 490, 548, 553, B 202, Γ 218, Δ 359, etc.: α 202, 212, 249, 414, β 26, 42, 127, 200, γ 127, δ 142, etc.—(**2**) οὔτε . . . οὐδὲ . . . ν 207.—(**3**) οὔτε . . . δὲ . . . H 433, Ω 368.— (**4**) οὔτε . . . τε . . . Ω 156 = 185.—(**5**) οὐ . . . οὔτε . . . λ 483.—(**6**) With infin.: οὔτ' ἐς δαῖτ' ἰέναι I 487, etc. Cf. π 203, etc.

οὐτιδανός [οὔ τις]. Of no account, worthless, sorry, good for nothing: δειλός τε καὶ οὐτιδανός A 293. Cf. Λ 390: θ 209 (useless, blind to his own interests), ι 460, 515.—Absol.: ἐπεὶ οὐτιδανοῖσιν ἀνάσσεις (men of nought) A 231. Cf. σ 383 (*v.l.* οὐκ ἀγαθοῖσιν).

οὗτος, αὕτη, τοῦτο. Genit. τούτου, ταύτης, τούτου. (**1**) This person or thing (in reported speech generally (and properly) referring to what belongs to or concerns the person spoken to; cf. ὅδε): λαοὺς οὐκ ἐπέοικε παλίλλογα ταῦτ' ἐπαγείρειν A 126, ἐθέλοιμ' ἂν τοῦτο γενέσθαι M 69 (here referring to the speaker's own wish). Cf. A 140, 286, 525, 564, B 326, 760, Γ 177, 178, Δ 415, E 187, 257, I 617, etc.: α 82, 159, 174, 179, 350, 390, β 74, 253, γ 46, 47, 359, δ 551, etc.—(**2**) With sb., etc., this: τοῦτο ἔπος A 419. Cf. E 761, H 456, Ξ 471, Π 30, etc.: α 340, β 124, μ 219, π 263 (these champions of yours), etc.—In much the sense of the definite article: οὐκ ἔσθ' οὗτος ἀνήρ, ὅς κε . . . (the man who . . .) ζ 201. —(**3**) In deictic or predicative sense = here: τίς δ' οὗτος ἔρχεαι οἶος; K 82. Cf. K 477, Λ 650, etc.: η 48, υ 377, etc.

οὕτως, οὕτω [adv. of οὗτος]. (**1**) In this or that way or manner, thus, so (often (and properly) referring to what concerns the person spoken to; cf. ὧδε): οὕτω Διὶ μέλλει φίλον εἶναι B 116. Cf. A 131, 564, Δ 189, E 218, N 309 (app., so much as on the left), 825 (as surely), etc.: γ 223, 358, δ 485, ε 146, θ 465, ι 262, etc.—Correlative with ὡς Δ 178, etc.: δ 148, etc.—(**2**) In that case, in consequence, thus, then: οὕτως οὔ τίς οἱ νεμεσήσεται K 129. Cf. Λ 382, Φ 412: β 334, σ 255 = τ 128, etc.—

(3) Introductory, so, so then: οὕτω δὴ μεθήσομεν; O 553. Cf. B 158, etc.: ε 204.—Sim.: ταῦτα μὲν οὕτω πάντα πεπείρανται μ 37.—Thus we see that . . ., so true it is that . . .: οὕτως οὐ πάντεσσι θεοὶ χαρίεντα διδοῦσιν θ 167.—(4) With imp., as you are, as I tell you, without more ado, straightway, at once: στῆθ' οὕτως ἐς μέσσον ρ 447. Cf. X 498.—In milder sense, app. little more than 'prithee': ἀμφίπολοι, στῆθ' οὕτω ἀπόπροθεν ζ 218.—(5) Qualifying an adj., pple. or adv. (a) Thus, so: καλὸν οὕτω Γ 169. Cf. H 198 (so . . . as that would imply), I 40, etc.: οὕτω χρηΐζοντι λ 340. Cf. γ 315, δ 543, ν 239 (not so very . . . as to justify that), etc.—(b) Quite, wholly: μὰψ οὕτω B 120.

οὐχί. See οὐ.

ὀφέλλω¹, ὀφείλω. Aor. ὄφελον Λ 380, Σ 367: α 217, δ 97, ε 308, λ 548, ν 204, ξ 274. 2 sing. ὤφελες Γ 428: β 184. ὄφελες Α 415, Γ 40, I 698, Σ 86: ω 30. 3 ὤφελε Ψ 546. ὄφελε Γ 173, Δ 315, Z 345, K 117, T 59, Φ 279, X 426. 2 pl. ὠφέλετε Ω 254. (1) To owe, be liable for or indebted in: χρεῖος Λ 688. Cf. θ 332, 462, φ 17.—In pass., to be owing or due: οἷσι χρεῖος ὀφείλετο Λ 686. Cf. Λ 698: γ 367.—(2) In impf. or aor. with infin. of what one ought to do or be doing: νῦν ὄφελεν κατὰ πάντας ἀριστῆας πονέεσθαι K 117. Cf. Σ 367 (why should I not . . .?), T 200: δ 472 (what you should do is to . . .).—Of what one ought to have done: τιμήν πέρ μοι ὄφελλεν ἐγγυαλίξαι Α 353, μὴ ὄφελες λίσσεσθαι I 698 (ὄφελες μὴ . . .). Cf. Ψ 546.—(3) In impf. or aor. with infin. expressing a vain wish that something were the case: ἀνδρὸς ὤφελλον ἀμείνονος εἶναι ἄκοιτις (would that I were . . .) Z 350. Cf. δ 97.—Expressing a wish that something had been the case: ἀγγελίης, ἣ μὴ ὤφελλε γενέσθαι Σ 19. Cf. P 686, T 59: β 184, θ 312.—(4) So with αἴθε in the same tenses expressing a wish in reference to the present: αἴθ' ὄφελες παρὰ νηυσὶν ἀδάκρυτος ἧσθαι (would that you were sitting . . .) Α 415. Cf. Γ 40, Ξ 84, Σ 86.—In reference to the past: αἴθ' ὤφελλ' ὁ ξεῖνος ἄλλοθ' ὀλέσθαι (would that he had . . .) σ 401. Cf. Γ 40, Σ 86, Ω 254: ν 204.—(5) So with ὡς in reference to the present: ὡς ὄφελέν τις ἀνδρῶν ἄλλος ἔχειν (would that it were another's lot) Δ 315. Cf. α 217.—To the past: ὡς ὤφελες αὐτόθ' ὀλέσθαι (would that you had . . .) Γ 428. Cf. Γ 173, Z 345, H 390, Λ 380, Φ 279, X 426, 481, Ω 764: ε 308, λ 548, ξ 68, 274, ω 30.

ὀφέλλω². 3 sing. aor. opt. ὀφέλλειε Π 651: β 334. (ἐξ-.) To increase, add to, cause to wax, intensify: πόνον B 420, Π 651, οὔ τι χρὴ μῦθον ὀφέλλειν (to make long speeches) Π 631. Cf. Γ 62, Δ 445, Υ 242: β 334, π 174.—In pass., to become greater, wax great: ὀφέλλετο μένος Ψ 524.—To cause (waves) to swell: μάλιστα κύματ' ὀφέλλει O 383.—To make (a house) rich, store (it) with substance ο 21.—In pass., of a house, to wax rich, grow great: αἶψα οἶκος ὀφέλλετο ξ 233.—With personal object, to exalt, magnify: ὄφρ' ἂν 'Αχαιοὶ ὀφέλλωσί ἑ τιμῇ Α 510 (or perh. 'make rich'; see under τιμή (6)).

ὄφελος, τό [ὀφέλλω²]. Good, use, help: αἴ κ' ὄ. τι γενώμεθα N 236. Cf. P 152, X 513.

ὀφθαλμός, -οῦ, ὁ [ὀπ-. See ὁράω]. The eye Α 587, Γ 28, E 127, I 503, Λ 250, etc.: α 69, β 155, δ 115, θ 64 (sight), λ 426, etc.—Of wild boars N 474: τ 446.

ὄφις, ὁ. A serpent or snake M 208 (the lengthening of the first syllable unexplained).

ὄφρα. (1) Till, until. (a) With indic.: ὄφρ' ἀφίκοντο N 329. Cf. E 588, K 488, Ξ 429, etc.: α 363, η 276, λ 152, μ 420, ξ 290, etc.—(b) With subj., pure or with κεν or ἄν: ὄφρα τελέσσῃ Α 82, ὄφρα κε οἶνον ἐνείκω Z 258, ὄφρ' ἂν ἵκηται O 23. Cf. M 281, Π 10, X 192, Ω 431, etc.: δ 588, ζ 304, etc.—(c) With opt.: ὄφρ' ἐξεμέσειεν μ 437. Cf. K 571.—With ἄν: ὄφρ' ἂν ἄγοιεν ρ 298.—(2) While, so long as. (a) With indic.: ὄφρα μήνιεν B 769. Cf. E 788, Λ 266, etc.: α 233, θ 181, υ 136, etc.—(b) With subj. in conditional relative sentences. For the examples and constructions see Table at end (III) (B) (a) (1) (2), (D) (12) (13) (20) (34) (43) (44).—(3) While, during the time that. (a) With indic.: ὄφρ' ἀμφεπένοντο Δ 220. Cf. Λ 357, Ξ 358, etc.: κ 125.—(b) With subj. in conditional relative sentences. See Table (III) (B) (a) (1), (D) (26) (35).—(4) For a time: ὄφρα μὲν βοῦς βόσκεν, αὐτὰρ ἐπεὶ . . . O 547.—(5) In final clauses, in order that, so that. (a) With subj.: ὄφρα μὴ οἶος ἀγέραστος ἔω Α 118. Cf. Α 133, 147, 158, 185, 524, etc.: α 85, 88, 174, 310, β 329, γ 15, etc.—With κεν: ὄφρα κε γνῶμεν X 382. Cf. B 440: γ 359, κ 298, π 234, τ 45, etc.—With ἄν: ὄφρ' ἂν ἐκεῖθι δαῖτα πτωχεύῃ ρ 10. Cf. σ 364, χ 377.—(b) With opt.: ὄφρα πολεμίζοι Δ 300. Cf. E 666, Z 170, 195, H 340, etc.: α 261, γ 175, 285, δ 463, 473, etc.—With κεν: ὄφρα χ' ἀλίπλοα τείχεα θείη M 26.—With ἄν: ὄφρ' ἂν ἵκοιο κ 65. Cf. ω 334.—(c) With fut.: ὄφρ' εἴσεται Θ 110, Π 242. Cf. δ 163, ρ 6, σ 419.—(6) A clause with ὄφρα instead of infin.: λελιημένος ὄφρα τάχιστα τεύχεα συλήσειεν Δ 465. Cf. E 690, Z 361, Π 653.—(7) Correlative with τόφρα. See τόφρα (3).

ὀφρυόεις, -εσσα [ὀφρύς]. Set on the brow of a hill, mountain-built. Epithet of Ilius X 411.

ὀφρύς, ἡ. Acc. pl. ὀφρῦς Π 740. (1) One of the eyebrows; in pl., the eyebrows: ἐπ' ὀφρύσι νεῦσεν Α 528, τὸν ὑπ' ὀφρύος οὗτα Ξ 493. Cf. N 88, Ξ 236, O 102, Ψ 396, etc.: δ 153, θ 86, μ 194, π 164, etc.—(2) In pl., the brow or edge of a hill: καθῖζον ἐπ' ὀφρύσι Καλλικολώνης Υ 151.

ὄχα [connexion with ἔξοχος uncertain]. Intensive, strengthening ἄριστος, by far, the very Α 69, B 761, Γ 110, etc.: γ 129, θ 123, ι 420, etc.

ὄχεα, τά [Ϝεχ-. Cf. L. *veho*]. Instrumental (in 'comitative' use) ὄχεσφι Δ 297, E 219, Θ 290, I 384, Λ 699, M 114, 119, Π 811, Σ 237, X 22, Ψ 518: δ 533. The same form as locative E 28, 794, Θ 41, 136, 565, M 91, N 23, O 3, Ψ 130. As ablative Ψ 7. As genit. E 107. (1) In sing. sense, a chariot (viewed as including all the parts thereof): ἐξ ὀχέων ἅλτο Γ 29. Cf. Δ 306, E 28, 107, 219, 369, etc.—(2) In pl. sense, chariots : κεῖν' ὄχεα κροτάλιζον Λ 160. Cf. Δ 297, Θ 504, 565, Ι 384, Μ 119, Ο 3, Π 379, Σ 224, 231, Ψ 7, 130 : δ 533.

ὀχετηγός, ὁ [ὀχετός, conduit (Ϝεχ- as in prec.) + ἄγω]. One who conducts water in a conduit or ditch Φ 257.

ὀχεύς, ὁ [ὀχ-, ἔχω]. Something that holds. (1) A means of securing a helmet on the head Γ 372.—(2) In pl., the fastenings of a belt: ζωστῆρος ὀχῆες Δ 132, Υ 414.—(3) A bar or bolt for securing a gate or door within : οὐδ' ἐρρήξαντ' ἂν πύλας καὶ μακρὸν ὀχῆα Μ 291 (here and in Ν 124 app. the same as the ὀχῆες of Μ 455). Cf. Μ 121, 455, 460, Ν 124, Φ 537, Ω 446, 566 (in Ω app. identical with the ἐπιβλής of 453) : φ 47, ω 166.

ὀχέω [Ϝεχ- as in ὄχεα]. Pa. iterative ὀχέεσκον λ 619. (ἐπ-.) (1) In pass., to be carried or borne : ἵπποι ἀλεγεινοὶ ὀχέεσθαι (for being carried, *i.e.* they are hard to drive) Κ 403 = Ρ 77, νηυσὶν ὀχήσονται (will be carried off in . . .) Ω 731.—Sim. in mid. : πολέεσσιν ὀχήσατο κύμασιν (rode) ε 54.—(2) To carry (an affliction) with one, be unable to flee from (it) : ἣν ἄτην φ 302.—To have laid upon one, endure : ὀϊζύν η 211. Cf. λ 619.—To indulge in, practise : νηπιάας α 297.

ὀχθέω [Ϝεχ- as in prec. Cf. L. *vehe-mens*]. To be moved in mind or spirit, be troubled or agitated, express or manifest emotion, trouble or agitation : τὴν μέγ' ὀχθήσας προσέφη Α 517, ὄχθησαν θεοὶ 570. Cf. Λ 403, Ψ 143, etc. : δ 30, φ 248, ψ 182, etc.

ὄχθη, -ης, ἡ. A river-bank Φ 17, 171, 172.—In pl., the banks of a river : παρ' ὄχθας Σαγγαρίοιο Γ 187. Cf. Δ 475, 487, Ζ 34, Λ 499, Μ 313, Ξ 445, Σ 533, Φ 10, 337 : ζ 97.—The shore of the sea ι 132.—The sides of a ditch Ο 356.

†**ὀχλέω** [Ϝεχ- as in ὄχεα]. 3 pl. pres. pass. ὀχλεῦνται. To move, disturb Φ 261.

†**ὀχλίζω.** 3 pl. aor. opt. ὀχλίσσειαν. (μετ-.) To raise, lift : ἐπ' ἄμαξαν ἀπ' οὔδεος Μ 448. Cf. ι 242.

ὀχός, -οῦ, **ὄχος,** -ου, ὁ [ὀχ-, ἔχω]. Something that affords safety or security : λιμένες νηῶν ὀχοί ε 404.

ὄψ, ὀπός, ἡ (Ϝόψ). A voice : ἄειδον ἀμειβόμεναι ὀπὶ καλῇ Α 604. Cf. Γ 221, Ξ 150, Π 76, Σ 222, Χ 451 : ἤκουσα ὄπα Πριάμοιο θυγατρός λ 421. Cf. ε 61, κ 221, μ 52, 160, 185, 187, 192, ξ 492, υ 92, ω 60.—Of lambs Δ 435.—Of the cicada Γ 152.—With special reference to what is uttered : ξυνέηκε θεᾶς ὄπα Β 182 = Κ 512. Cf. Η 53, Λ 137, Υ 380, Φ 98 : ω 535.

ὀψέ. (1) Not early, late : ὀψὲ δύοντα Βοώτην ε 272. Cf. Φ 232.—(2) Long after, after a long interval : ὀψὲ μετὰ νῶϊ κίεν γ 168.—(3) After the lapse of a long time, late : ὀψέ περ ἐλθών ψ 7. Cf. ι 534, λ 114 = μ 141.—At length, at last : ὀψὲ τελεῖ Δ 161. Cf. Η 94, 399 = Ι 31 = 696, Θ 30, Ι 432, Ρ 466 : δ 706, ε 322, η 155, μ 439, υ 321.—(4) At a late stage, late in the day : καὶ ὀψέ περ υἷας 'Αχαιῶν ἐρύεσθαι Ι 247.

ὄψεαι, ὄψει, ὄψῃ, 2 sing. fut. mid. See ὁράω.

ὀψείω [ὀπ-σείω. Desiderative fr. ὀπ-. See ὁράω]. To desire to see, go to view. With genit. : αὐτῆς καὶ πολέμοιο Ξ 37.

ὄψεται, 3 sing. fut. mid. See ὁράω.

ὀψίγονος [ὀψέ + γον- = γεν-, γίγνομαι]. Of a generation later than one's own, late-born : τί σευ ἄλλος ὀνήσεται ὀ. περ; Π 31.—Absol. in pl., the men of the generations to come, posterity α 302 = γ 200.—So with ἄνθρωποι Γ 353, Η 87.

ὄψιμος [ὀψέ]. Having reference to a date in the far future, pointing far forward : τέρας Β 325.

ὄψις, ἡ [ὀπ-. See ὁράω]. (1) Exercise of the power of vision : ὄψει οὔ πω σὺ ἐμοὺς ἴδες (with your eyes) Υ 205. Cf. ψ 94.—(2) The fact of seeing something, the sight of . . . : πατρὸς ὄψιν ἀτυχθεὶς Ζ 468.—(3) Appearance, outward seeming : ἀγαθήν Ω 632.

ὀψιτέλεστος [ὀψέ + τελεσ-, τελέω]. To be fulfilled in the far future : τέρας Β 325.

ὄψον, -ου, τό [ὀπ- as in ὀπτός]. (1) A piece of cooked meat Ι 489.—In pl., such meat : σῖτον καὶ οἶνον ὄψα τε γ 480. Cf. ε 267, ζ 77.—(2) A relish : κρόμυον ποτῷ ὄψον Λ 630.

πάγη, 3 sing. aor. pass. πήγνυμι.

πάγος, -ου, ὁ [παγ-, πήγνυμι]. App., a reef in the sea ε 405, 411.

παγχάλκεος [παν-, πᾶς + χάλκεος]. All of bronze : ἄορ θ 403. Cf. Υ 102 : λ 575.

πάγχαλκος, -ον [παν- as in prec. + χαλκός]. = prec. : κυνέη σ 378. Cf. χ 102.

παγχρύσεος [παν-, πᾶς + χρύσεος]. All of gold : θύσανοι Β 448.

πάγχυ [παν-, πᾶς]. Wholly, altogether, entirely, quite, to the full (in negative statements and injunctions commonly rather strengthening the negation than attaching itself closely to the verb, etc., and to be translated 'at all,' 'by any means,' 'in any wise,' or the like ; cf. πάμπαν) : π. ἀκαχήμενος (bereft of all comfort) Ε 24, σοὶ οὔ πω π. θεοὶ κοτέουσιν Ξ 143. Cf. Κ 99, Μ 67, Ν 747, Ξ 95, Ο 196, Π 538, etc. : οἶκον π. διαρραίσει β 49, μηδὲ π. δείδιθι δ 825. Cf. β 279, δ 755, κ 236, ν 133, ο 327, χ 236, etc.—Of a surety, verily : π. νύκτα φυλάξεις χ 195. Cf. ρ 217.

πάθον, aor. πάσχω.

παιδνός, ὁ [παιδ-, παῖς]. A boy : παιδνὸς ἐών φ 21, ω 338.

παιδοφόνος [παιδ-, παῖς + φον-, φένω]. Slayer of one's sons Ω 506.

παίζω [παιδ-, παῖς]. Aor. imp. παίσατε θ 251. To play, sport ζ 100, 106, η 291, θ 251 (show us your skill in sport), ψ 147 (dancing).

παιήων, -ονος, ὁ. (1) A song of propitiation addressed to Apollo in his character of healer (cf. Π 514-529), and app. as thus identified with Παιήων, the Healer, who, however, appears to be represented as a separate person (cf. Ε 401, 899, 900 : δ 232) : καλὸν ἀείδοντες παιήονα Α 473.—(2) A song of rejoicing Χ 391.

παιπαλόεις, -εντος. Fem. -εσσα, -ης. Rugged,

rocky N 17 : κ 97 = 148, 194.—Of islands : Ἴμβρου N 33, Ω 78 : Χίοιο γ 170, Σάμοιο δ 671 = ο 29, δ 845, Ἰθάκην λ 480.—Of roads, rough, stony M 168, P 743 : ρ 204.

πάϊς, also **παῖς,** παιδός, ὁ, ἡ. Voc. πάϊ ω 192. παῖ λ 553. Genit. pl. παίδων Θ 57, O 663, Υ 304, Ω 539, etc. : γ 401, η 70, ο 22, ω 434, etc. Dat. παίδεσσι γ 381, ε 394, λ 431. παισί B 337, Z 283, M 435, Φ 185, etc. : η 149, ν 62, 258. A child. (1) In reference to age, a boy : μή τί μευ ἠΰτε παιδὸς πειρήτιζε H 235. Cf. B 289, Z 467, Θ 271, Λ 558, 710, Π 260, etc. : δ 32, 665, 688, ζ 300, σ 216, φ 95, χ 358.—(2) In reference to relationship. (a) A son : Πριάμοιο παῖδες A 255. Cf. A 393, B 205, E 386, Z 26, K 170, Λ 783, etc. : παῦροι παῖδες ὁμοῖοι πατρὶ πέλονται β 276. Cf. α 207, γ 196, δ 164, η 149, ι 519, λ 299, etc.—(b) A daughter : παῖδ' ἐμοὶ λύσαιτε φίλην A 20. Cf. A 443, 447, Γ 175, E 880, X 51 : ὅσσα ἔοικε φίλης ἐπὶ παιδὸς ἕπεσθαι α 278 = β 197. Cf. δ 13, 263, η 65, 300, 313, θ 488, κ 139, λ 604, σ 323.—(c) Without distinction of gender : ἵνα παισὶν ἀεικέα μισθὸν ἄρηται M 435. Cf. Δ 131, E 408, H 334, Θ 57, K 422, O 497, etc. : γ 381, ε 394, η 70, ι 115, κ 5, λ 431, ν 62, etc.—(d) Used by elders in addressing younger persons : μηκέτι, παῖδε φίλω, πολεμίζετε H 279.

παιφάσσω. (ἐκ-.) To make oneself conspicuous : παιφάσσουσα διέσσυτο λαόν (dazzling) B 450.

πάλαι. (1) Long ago, long ere this : π. κ' ἦσθα ἐνέρτερος Οὐρανιώνων E 898. Cf. Φ 432 : τ 282, υ 222, ψ 29.—(2) Long, of old (referring to time long past or comparatively recent) : π. πολέμων ἐῢ εἰδώς Δ 310, ὀϊστὸν ἔχεν π. Ψ 871. Cf. H 89, Π 441 = X 179, X 301, Ψ 331 : ε 240, ρ 366, σ 309.—With pres. : μοῖραν ἔχει π. (has long had it) υ 293.—(3) In the past, formerly : ἡμὲν π. ἠδ' ἔτι καὶ νῦν I 105.—(4) With sb. in adjectival use, of olden days : τόδε ἔργον π., οὔ τι νέον γε I 527.

παλαιγενής [πάλαι + γεν-, γίγνομαι]. Old in years, aged, old Γ 386, P 561 : χ 395.

παλαιός, -ή, -όν [cf. πάλαι]. (1) Old in years, aged, old Ξ 136 : α 395, δ 720, θ 58, ν 432, τ 346.—Absol., an old man : ἢ νέος ἠὲ π. Ξ 108.—In comp., old rather than young, of the older generation : ὡς ἀθάνατοι τιμῶσι παλαιοτέρους ἀνθρώπους Ψ 788.—(2) Of the days of old, that lived long ago, old : Ἴλου Λ 166. Cf. Λ 372.—Of long standing, old : ξεῖνος Z 215.—The old, the accustomed : λέκτροιο ψ 296.—Absol. in pl., those of old : οὐδὲ παλαιῶν, τάων αἳ . . . (the women of old days) β 118.—Absol. in neut. pl., things of old, the wisdom of ancient days : παλαιά τε πολλά τε εἰδώς β 188, η 157, ω 51.—(3) Constructed long ago, long in use, old : νῆες β 293.—That has been long stored up, old : οἴνοιο β 340.

παλαισμοσύνη, -ης, ἡ [παλαίω]. Wrestling Ψ 701 : θ 103, 126.

παλαιστής, ὁ [παλαίω]. A wrestler θ 246.

παλαίφατος, -ον [πάλαι + φα-, φαν-, φαίνω]. Put forth long ago, old : θέσφατα ι 507 = ν 172.—Of old renown, old-world : δρυός τ 163.

παλαίω [πάλη]. To wrestle : Φιλομηλεΐδῃ ἐπάλαισεν (with . . .) δ 343 = ρ 134. Cf. Ψ 621, 733.

παλάμη, -ης, ἡ [cf. L. *palma*]. Locative παλάμηφι Γ 338, Π 139 : ρ 4. This form as ablative Γ 368. The hand (thought of in reference to its grasp) : ἐν παλάμῃς φορέουσιν A 238. Cf. Γ 128, 338, E 558, Θ 111, O 677, etc. : α 104, β 10, ε 234, ρ 4, 231, τ 577 = φ 75.

παλάσσω. Fut. infin. παλαξέμεν ν 395. Pf. pple. pass. πεπαλαγμένος, -ου Z 268 : χ 184, 402, ψ 48. 3 sing. plupf. πεπάλακτο Λ 98, 535, M 186, Υ 400, 500 : χ 406. (1) To spatter, sprinkle : ἐγκέφαλος ἔνδον ἅπας πεπάλακτο Λ 98 = M 186 = Υ 400.—(2) To bespatter, besprinkle, wet, befoul : παλάσσεθ' αἵματι θώρηξ E 100. Cf. Z 268, Λ 169, 535 = Υ 500, P 387, Υ 504 : ν 395, χ 184, 402 = ψ 48, χ 406.

πάλη, -ης, ἡ. Wrestling Ψ 635 : θ 206.

παλίλλογος [πάλιν + λογ-, λέγω[2]]. Brought together again A 126 (till they be . . .).

παλιμπετής [πάλιν + πετ-, πίπτω. 'Falling back']. In neut. παλιμπετές as adv., to where one came from, back : ὥς κε π. ἀπονέωνται ε 27.—In the direction contrary to that desired, back : ἂψ ἐπὶ νῆας ἔεργε π. Π 395.

†παλιμπλάζω [πάλιν + πλάζω]. Aor. pple. pass. παλιμπλαγχθείς, -έντος. To drive back from one's goal, foil, baffle A 59 : ν 5.

πάλιν. (1) To where one came from, back again, back : π. ᾤχετο A 380, π. κίε θυγατέρος ἧς (app. genit. of point attained, returned to . . .) Φ 504. Cf. Z 189, Θ 399, I 408, Π 87, Ω 462, etc. : α 360, ζ 110, η 280, ι 95, π 467, τ 533 (*i.e.* to her father's), etc.—Sim. : ἐξελκομένοιο π. (drawn back the way it had entered) Δ 214.—Strengthened by αὖτις E 257, P 533, Ψ 229 : ξ 356, ο 431.—By ἄψ Σ 280.—(2) Away from an object, away, aside : ὦσε π. κλίνασα Γ 427. Cf. N 3, Φ 415, 468.—With genit. : π. τράπεθ' υἱος (from . . .) Σ 138. Cf. Υ 439.—(3) In a backward direction, backwards : χειρὶ π. ἐρύσασα E 836.—(4) With notion of contradiction, against a person : οὔ τις π. ἐρέει (will gainsay you) I 56.—(5) With notion of repetition, again. Strengthened by αὖτις : οὔ μιν π. αὖτις ἀνήσει θυμὸς νεικείειν . . . B 276.—(6) With notion of restoration, back : δόμεναι π. A 116, H 79 = X 342. Cf. X 259.—Sim. : π. ὅ γε λάζετο μῦθον Δ 357 : ν 254 (see λάζομαι).—So in reference to restoration to a state : π. ποίησε γέροντα π 456.—With genit. : αὐτοῖο π. χύτ' ἀήρ (left him so that he again became visible) η 143.

παλινάγρετος [πάλιν + ἀγρέω]. To be taken back, revocable : οὐκ ἐμὸν παλινάγρετον A 526.

παλίνορσος [πάλιν + (perh.) ἐρσ-, L. *erro*. Cf. ἄψορρος]. Turning away Γ 33.

παλίντιτος [πάλιν + τίω]. Consisting in paying back or requital : παλίντιτα ἔργα (works of vengeance, revenge) α 379 = β 144.

παλίντονος [πάλιν + τον-, τείνω]. Of bows, curving back, *i.e.* bent back in the centre to form a handle ; or perh. a general epithet, springing back, elastic Θ 266, K 459, O 443 : φ 11, 59.

παλιρρόθιος [πάλιν + ῥόθιος]. Flowing back, with backward flow: παλιρρόθιόν μιν πλῆξε [κῦμα] ε 430. Cf. ι 485.

παλίωξις, ἡ [for παλι-ίωξις, fr. παλι-, πάλιν + ἰωκ-, ἰωκή]. A pursuit back, a retreat: εἴ κε π. γένηται M 71. Cf. O 69, 601.

παλλακίς, -ίδος, ἡ. A concubine: ἔμ' ὠνητὴ τέκε μήτηρ, π. ξ 203. Cf. I 449, 452.

πάλλω, 3 sing. aor. πῆλε Z 474, Π 117. Infin. πῆλαι Π 142, T 389. 3 sing. aor. pass. πάλτο O 645. App. imp. pl. aor. mid. πεπάλασθε H 171. Infin. πεπαλάσθαι ι 331. (For these two forms prob. πεπάλεσθε, πεπαλέσθαι should be read.) (ἀνα-, ἐκ-.) (**1**) To shake, poise, sway, brandish, wield (a spear or missile): δοῦρε δύω πάλλων Γ 19. Cf. E 304, Π 117, 142, X 320, etc. —To dandle (a child) Z 474.—(**2**) In pass., to throb, vibrate, beat: πάλλεται ἦτορ X 452. Cf. X 461.—App., to be tripped up, trip: ἐν ἀσπίδος ἄντυγι πάλτο O 645.—(**3**) To shake (lots) together: κλήρους ἐν κυνέῃ πάλλον (πάλλομεν) Γ 316 = Ψ 861 : κ 206.—Absol., to shake the lots Γ 324, H 181, Ψ 353.—(**4**) In mid., to cast lots: κλήρῳ πεπάλασθε H 171, ἐγὼν ἔλαχον ἅλα παλλομένων (partitive genit., 'of us when we cast lots') O 191, τῶν μέτα (with them) παλλόμενος κλήρῳ λάχον . . . Ω 400. Cf. ι 331.

παλύνω. 3 sing. aor. ἐπάλῦνε K 7. Pple. παλύνας ξ 429. (**1**) To sprinkle, scatter, strew: ἐπ' ἄλφιτα πάλυνεν Λ 640, ἄλφιτα πάλυνον (app. in water to make porridge) Σ 560. Cf. κ 520, λ 28, ξ 77.—(**2**) To sprinkle, besprinkle, powder, cover lightly: ὅτε χιὼν ἐπάλυνεν ἀρούρας K 7. Cf. ξ 429.

παμμέλᾱς, -ανος [παμ-, παν-, πᾶς + μέλας]. All black, black all over γ 6, κ 525, λ 33.

πάμπαν [παν-, πᾶς reduplicated with assimilation of the ν]. Wholly, altogether, entirely, quite (in negative statements and injunctions commonly rather strengthening the negation than attaching itself closely to the verb, etc., and to be translated 'at all,' 'by any means,' 'in any wise,' or the like ; cf. πάγχυ): πολέμου ἀποπαύεο π. A 422, οὐδ' ὅ γε π. χάζετο M 406. Cf. I 435, N 111, 761, Ξ 91, P 406, Υ 376, etc. : βίοτον ἀπὸ π. ὀλέσσει β 49, οὐδ' Ἀγαμέμνονι π. ἑήνδανεν γ 143. Cf. δ 693, θ 552, λ 528, π 375, υ 140, etc.

παμποίκιλος [παμ-, παν-, πᾶς + ποικίλος]. All-variegated, many-coloured Z 289 : ο 105.

πάμπρωτος [παμ-, παν-, πᾶς + πρῶτος]. The first of all, taking the lead: π. ὑφαίνειν ἤρχετο μῆτιν H 324 = I 93.—In neut. sing. πάμπρωτον as adv., first of all, as the first thing, to start with: νῆας π. ἐρύσσαμεν δ 577. Cf. δ 780, κ 403, 423, λ 2.—Sim. in neut. pl. πάμπρωτα, first of all, before all others: τοῦ κε π. παρὰ δῶρα φέροιο Δ 97. Cf. P 568.

παμφαίνω [reduplicated fr. φαίνω]. To shine, gleam, glitter: ἀστέρα, ὅς τε μάλιστα λαμπρὸν παμφαίνῃσιν E 6, στήθεσι παμφαίνοντας (app., their (naked) breasts glistening (instead of their armour)) Λ 100. Cf. Z 513, Λ 30, 63, Ξ 11, T 398, X 26.

†**παμφανάω** [reduplicated fr. φαν-, φαίνω]. Pres. pple. παμφανόων, -ωντος. Fem. παμφανόωσα. To shine, gleam, glitter: τεύχεα παμφανόωντα E 295. Cf. B 458, E 619, Z 473, Σ 206, Ψ 613, etc. : δ 42, ν 29, τ 386, χ 121.

πάναγρος [παν-, πᾶς + ἄγρη]. That catches all: λίνοιο E 487.

πάναιθος, -η [παν-, πᾶς + αἴθω]. Gleaming all over: κορύθεσσιν Ξ 372.

παναίολος [παν-, πᾶς + αἰόλος]. Glancing or gleaming all over: ζωστήρ Δ 186, K 77. Cf. Δ 215, Λ 236, 374, N 552.

πανάπαλος [παν-, πᾶς + ἁπαλός]. Quite tenderly reared, delicately nurtured ν 223.

πανάποτμος [παν-, πᾶς + ἄποτμος]. That has ill fortune to the full, dogged by evil fate Ω 255, 493.

πανάργυρος [παν-, πᾶς + ἄργυρος]. All of silver: κρητῆρα ι 203, ω 275.

παναφῆλιξ, -ικος [παν-, πᾶς + ἀφ-, ἀπο- (1) + ἧλιξ]. App., cut off from his equals in years X 490.

παναώριος [παν-, πᾶς + ἀ-[1] + ὥρη]. Destined to be cut off untimely, shortlived Ω 540.

πανδαμάτωρ [παν-, πᾶς + δαμάζω]. All-subduing (cf. δμήτειρα). Epithet of sleep Ω 5 : ι 373.

πανδήμιος [παν-, πᾶς + δῆμος, in sense 'town.' Cf. ἐπιδημεύω]. Roving through all the town, vagabond: πτωχός σ 1.

πανῆμαρ [παν-, πᾶς + ἦμαρ]. All the day long: ᾧ τε π. ἕλκητον βόε πηκτὸν ἄροτρον ν 31.

πανημέριος, -η [παν-, πᾶς + ἡμέρη]. All the day long: πανημέριοι θεὸν ἱλάσκοντο (*i.e.* all the rest of the day) A 472, ὥς κε πανημέριοι κρινώμεθ' Ἄρηϊ B 385. Cf. Λ 279, P 180, 384, Σ 209, T 168 : γ 486 = ο 184, δ 356 (in a day's sail), λ 11, μ 24.

πανθυμαδόν [παν-, πᾶς + θυμός]. With all spirit, *i.e.* fiercely, bitterly: ὀκριόωντο σ 33.

παννύχιος, -η [παν-, πᾶς + νυχ-, νύξ]. All the night long: εὗδον παννύχιοι B 2. Cf. B 24 = 61, H 476, 478, Θ 508, 554, K 2 = Ω 678, Σ 315, 354, Ψ 105, 217 : α 443, β 434 (*i.e.* all the rest of the night), η 288, μ 429.

πάννυχος [as prec.]. = prec. Λ 551 = P 660, Ψ 218 : ξ 458, υ 53.—In neut. sing. πάννυχον as adv.: τί π. ἀωτεῖς ; K 159.

πανομφαῖος [παν-, πᾶς + ὀμφή]. From whom proceed all omens by voices or sounds: Ζηνί Θ 250.

πάνορμος [παν-, πᾶς + ὅρμος[2]]. Ever affording anchorage: λιμένες ν 195.

πανόψιος [παν-, πᾶς + ὀπ-. See ὁράω. Cf. ὑπόψιος]. Seen by all, conspicuous: πανόψιον ἔγχος ἑλοῦσα Φ 397.

πανσυδίῃ [παν-, πᾶς + συ-, σεύω. Cf. ἐπασσύτερος]. Coming all together, in a body, in full force B 12, 29 = 66, Λ 709, 725.

πάντῃ [παντ-, πᾶς]. (**1**) In all directions,

every way: κατὰ στρατὸν ᾤχετο π. E 495. Cf. A 384, Z 81, Λ 156, Ξ 413, Ψ 463, etc.: β 383, μ 233, φ 394, 405, ω 355, 413.—(2) On every side, all about, all round: π. ὀρώρει πῦρ M 177. Cf. E 739, M 430, N 736, Π 111, P 354, Ψ 34, 127, Ω 799: π. οἱ βεβλήαται εὐναί (*i.e.* now in one place, now in another) λ 193. Cf. ω 208.

πάντοθεν [παντο-, πᾶς + -θεν (1) (2)]. (1) From all quarters, directions, parts, from every side: π. ἐκ κευθμῶν N 28. Cf. Π 110, Φ 364, Ψ 112, 689: ρ 171.—(2) = πάντῃ (2): λαμπόμενος πυρὶ π. (all about him) O 623. Cf. ξ 270, ρ 439.

παντοῖος, -η, -ον [παντ-, πᾶς]. Of all sorts or kinds: ἀνέμων (blowing from all quarters, all the winds) B 397, P 56, δόλους Γ 202, δρόμου (in all directions and at all speeds) Σ 281, ἀϋτμήν (of every desired degree of force) 471. Cf. O 642, Υ 249, X 268, Ψ 308, 314: α 142, γ 119, δ 725, ζ 77, 234, ο 246, ρ 486 (taking all forms), etc.

πάντοσε [παντο-, πᾶς + -σε]. In all directions, every way: π. ἐποιχόμενος E 508, π. ἀκούειν Π 515 (the power of hearing being thought of as projected towards the source of the sound; cf. Δ 455 cited under τηλόσε). Cf. M 266, N 649, P 674, 680, Σ 479: λ 606, ρ 209, 366, χ 24, 380.—For ἀσπὶς π. ἐΐση see ἴσος (5) (b).

πάντως [παντ-, πᾶς]. By all means. Strengthening a negative: π. οὐκ ἄν με τρέψειαν (the whole band of them shall not . . .) Θ 450: π. οὔ τί με λήθεις (of a surety you do not . . .) τ 91. Cf. υ 180.

πανυπέρτατος, -η [παν-, πᾶς + ὑπέρτατος]. Furthest out to sea ι 25.

πανύστατος [παν-, πᾶς + ὕστατος]. The last of all: π. ἤλυθεν ἄλλων Ψ 532. Cf. Ψ 547: ι 452.

πάππα, *voc.* [a child's word for 'father']. Used by a daughter in affectionate address ζ 57.

παππάζω [πάππα]. To call one '(dear) father': οὐδέ τί μιν παῖδες παππάζουσιν E 408.

παπταίνω. 3 sing. aor. πάπτηνε M 333, Ξ 507, Π 283, P 84: χ 43, 381. Pple. παπτήνας, -αντος Δ 497, Θ 269, Λ 546, O 574, P 603, Ψ 690: ρ 330. Fem. παπτήνᾶσα X 463: τ 552. (ἀπο-.) (1) To look narrowly about one, peer, throw one's glance round, glance: ἀμφὶ ἓ παπτήνας Δ 497 = O 574. Cf. Θ 269, Λ 546, N 551, P 84, 603, 674, X 463, Ψ 464, 690: λ 608, μ 233, ρ 330, τ 552, χ 24, 380, ω 179.—With dependent clause: πάπτηνεν ἕκαστος ὅπῃ φύγοι ὄλεθρον Ξ 507 = Π 283 := χ 43. Cf. M 333, N 649: χ 381.—(2) To look about for, throw one's glance round in quest of: Μαχάονα Δ 200. Cf. P 115.

πάρ. See παρά, πάρα.

παρά. (Commonly with anastrophe when immediately following the vb. or case-form (and see Γ 440)). Also in forms πάρ, παραί (which does not suffer anastrophe). (I) Adv. (1) Beside, by, near, someone or something: παρὰ νύκτας ἴαυον I 470. Cf. A 611, Γ 135, Δ 330, E 112, Λ 512, etc.: παραὶ λεχέεσσι κλιθῆναι α 366. Cf. α 132, γ 267, δ 305, ε 196, ζ 18, etc.—At hand, ready to aid, at command: πάρα θεοί εἰσι καὶ ἡμῖν Γ 440.—Sim.: παρά τε σχεῖν ὅσσα . . . Ψ 50.—For παρ' αὐτόθι see αὐτόθι (1).—(2) Past, passing by, something: παρά τις κιών Π 263. Cf. μ 82.—(3) Aside, away: παραί οἱ ἐτράπετ' ἔγχος Λ 233 = N 605.—Denoting turning or bending of a person's mind: παρά μ' ἤπαφε δαίμων ξ 488.—(II) Prep. (1) With dat. (a) Beside, by, near, in the company of: παρὰ νηυσίν A 26. Cf. A 329, 358, B 355, H 135, Υ 53, etc.: παρ' Ἀτρεΐδῃ γ 156. Cf. δ 443, 595, ε 119, η 203, λ 178, ο 386, etc.—With locative: παρὰ ναῦφιν Θ 474. Cf. M 302, etc.—Among: ἤειδε παρὰ μνηστῆρσιν α 154.—In pregnant sense: πὰρ δέ οἱ ἔστη Φ 547. Cf. A 405, Γ 262, N 617, etc.: α 142, γ 37, ν 122, ρ 572, etc.—(b) In the house, establishment or land of, in the hands or power of: ἐπεὶ φιλέεσθε παρ' αὐτῇ N 627. Cf. Δ 1, P 324, T 148, Ψ 411, Ω 212, etc.: παρὰ μητρὶ κεῖσθαι ο 127. Cf. α 123, θ 420, λ 175, 460, 490, ν 204, etc.—(c) Set alongside in contemplation, beside, along with: παρὰ καὶ κακῷ ἐσθλὸν ἔθηκεν ο 488.—(2) With acc. (a) In reference to motion ending beside or near a person or thing, beside, by, near: ἐς δίφρον ἔβαινε παραὶ Διομήδεα E 837. Cf. Γ 406, H 190, Λ 314, etc.: στῆ παρὰ σταθμόν α 333. Cf. θ 469, ρ 96, χ 333, etc.—Sim. in reference to striking with a weapon, missile, etc.: παρὰ οὖς ἔλασε ξίφει Λ 109. Cf. Δ 480, 518, E 146, M 204, Φ 491, etc.: χ 82.—So in reference to a weapon struck Π 115.—In reference to visiting a person, to: πὰρ Μενέλαον οἴχετο ν 414. Cf. Σ 143: α 285.—(b) In reference to motion alongside of a thing, along, by: βῆ παρὰ θῖνα θαλάσσης A 34. Cf. A 347, K 54, Λ 558, P 297, Σ 576, Ψ 225, etc.: παρὰ Μίμαντα γ 172. Cf. δ 432, ο 295, ω 11, etc.—(c) Without notion of motion in reference to action or existence in a region alongside of a person or thing, along, by: ἔρδον ἑκατόμβας παρὰ θῖν' ἁλός A 316. Cf. A 463, B 522, 604, Γ 272, Δ 487, M 313, P 290, etc.: πρασιαὶ παρὰ νείατον ὄρχον πεφύασιν η 127. Cf. ζ 89, μ 32, ξ 347, τ 553, χ 127, etc.—(d) In reference to motion past something, past, passing: παρ' Ἴλου σῆμ' ἐσσεύοντο Λ 166, οὖτα παρ' ἀσπίδα (getting within the guard of the shield) Π 312. Cf. E 293, Z 42, etc.: δ 802, etc.—(e) Beyond, in excess of: πὰρ δύναμιν N 787. Cf. ξ 509.—(3) With genit. (a) From beside, or simply, from: φάσγανον ἐρυσσάμενος παρὰ μηροῦ A 190, πλευρά, τά οἱ παρ' ἀσπίδος ἐξεφαάνθη (beyond it, outside its shelter) Δ 468. Cf. B 596, 787, Θ 533, Λ 1, N 211, etc.: ἀνιόντα παρ' Ἴλου α 259. Cf. γ 347, 431, θ 289, μ 70, ο 58, etc.—With ablative: παρὰ ναῦφιν M 225: ξ 498.—(b) With vbs. of taking, receiving, bringing or the like, from, at the hands of: ὅττι ῥά οἱ γαμβροῖο πάρα φέροιτο Z 177. Cf. Δ 97, Λ 795, Σ 137, Ω 429, 502, etc.: ὄφρα πομπῆς τύχῃς παρὰ πατρὸς ἐμοῖο ζ 290. Cf. ξ 452, ο 158, etc.—(c) In reference to source or origin: ἄλλος κε πὰρ Διὸς χόλος ἐτύχθη O 122.—To a point *from* which action takes place: φθεγξάμενος παρὰ νηός Λ 603.

πάρα [for πάρ-εστι, πάρ-εισι]. Also in form πάρ. (1) There is (are) by or present: πάρα γὰρ καὶ ἀμείνονες ἄλλοι Ψ 479.—(2) There is (are) available or at one's command or disposal, there is (are) here or there for or aiding one. With or without dat. : πάρ' ἔμοιγε καὶ ἄλλοι Α 174. Cf. Ε 603, 604, Ι 43, 227, Υ 98, Φ 192 : πάρα τοι δίφρος τε καὶ ἵπποι, πὰρ δέ τοι υἷες ἐμοί γ 324. Cf. γ 351, δ 559 = ε 16 = ρ 145, ε 141, 489 (here for παρέωσιν), ι 125, π 45, ρ 452, χ 106.—(3) It is possible : ἐπεὶ οὐ μέν τι πάρα προνοῆσαι ἄμεινον ε 364.

†**παραβαίνω** [παρα- (2)]. Pf. pple. παρβεβαώς (παρ-, παρα-) Λ 522. Nom. dual παρβεβαῶτε Ν 708. To take one's way *beside*. With dat. : παρβεβαῶτ' ἕστασαν ἀλλήλοιιν (fronted the foe holding united course) Ν 708.—Sim. of accompanying another in a chariot : Ἕκτορι παρβεβαώς (standing beside him (as charioteer)) Λ 522.

παραβάλλω [παρα- (2)]. In mid., to set down (a stake) beside others or by the side of an umpire ; hence, to set at hazard, risk (cf. παρατίθημι (2)) : αἰὲν ἐμὴν ψυχὴν παραβαλλόμενος Ι 322.

παραβάσκω [παρα- (2)]. To act as παραιβάτης : Ἄντιφος παρέβασκεν Λ 104.

παραβλήδην [παραβάλλω]. App., 'risking the experiment' : ἐπειρᾶτ' ἐρεθιζέμεν Ἥρην, παραβλήδην ἀγορεύων ('drawing her fire,' provoking a retort, provokingly) Δ 6.

†**παραβλώσκω** [παρα- (2)]. 3 sing. pf. παρμέμβλωκε (παρ-, παρα-) Δ 11, Ω 73. To go *beside*. With dat. : τῷ Ἀφροδίτη αἰεὶ παρμέμβλωκεν (attends, protects) Δ 11. Cf. Ω 73.

παραβλώψ, -ῶπος [παρα- (4) + βλέπω, to look]. With sidelong or furtive glance Ι 503 (of the Λιταί (see λιτή) as figuring an offender, who cannot look the injured person in the face).

παραγίγνομαι [παρα- (2)]. To be *beside*, be *in attendance upon*. With dat. : παρεγίγνετό σφι δαιτί (attended upon them at the . . .) ρ 173.

†**παραδαρθάνω** [παρα- (2)]. 3 sing. aor. παρέδραθε υ 88. Infin. παραδραθέειν Ξ 163. To sleep, go to sleep, take one's rest, *beside*. With dat. : παρέδραθέ μοι υ 88. Cf. Ξ 163.

†**παραδέχομαι** [παρα- (1)]. 3 sing. aor. παρεδέξατο. To receive from another : σῆμα Ζ 178.

παραδραθέειν, aor. infin. παραδαρθάνω.

παραδραμέτην, 3 dual aor. παρατρέχω.

†**παραδράω** [παρα- (2)]. 3 pl. παραδρώωσι. To do work *in attendance upon*, serve. With dat. : οἷά τε τοῖς ἀγαθοῖσι παραδρώωσι χέρηες ο 324.

†**παραδύω** [παρα- (3)]. Aor. infin. παραδύμεναι. To slip past Ψ 416.

παραείδω [παρ-, παρα- (2)]. To sing *beside* or *to*. With dat. : ἔοικά τοι παραείδειν χ 348.

†**παραείρω** [παρ-, παρα- (2)]. 3 sing. aor. pass. παρηέρθη. In pass., to hang down by the side, on one side : παρηέρθη κάρη Π 341.

παραθείμην, aor. opt. mid. παρατίθημι.

παράθες, aor. imp. παρατίθημι.

παραθήσομεν, 1 pl. fut. παρατίθημι.

παραί. See παρά.

παραιβάτης, ὁ [παραι- (2) + βα-, βαίνω. 'He that goes beside']. The fighting man in a war-chariot as distinguished from the ἡνίοχος or driver : παραιβάται ἡνίοχοί τε Ψ 132.

παραιπεπίθῃσι, 3 sing. aor. subj. παραπείθω.

παραίσιος [παρ-, παρα- (5) + αἴσιος]. Boding ill : σήματα Δ 381.

παρᾱΐσσω [παρ-, παρα- (3)]. 3 sing. aor. παρήϊξε Ε 690, Θ 98. 3 pl. παρήϊξαν Λ 615. To dart past Ε 690, Θ 98, Υ 414.—To dart *past*. With acc. : ἵπποι με παρήϊξαν Λ 615.

παραιφάμενος, pres. pple. mid. παράφημι.

παραίφασις, πάρφασις, ἡ [παραι- (4) + φα-, φημί]. Persuasion : ὀαριστὺς πάρφασις Ξ 217 (winning dalliance). Cf. Λ 793 = Ο 404.

†**παρακαταβάλλω** [παρα- (2) + κατα- (1)]. 3 sing. aor. παρακάββαλεν (καβ-, κατα-) Ψ 683. 3 pl. παρακάββαλον Ψ 127. To throw down in readiness : ὕλην Ψ 127.—In Ψ 683 (ζῶμά οἱ παρακάββαλεν) the sense required seems to be 'put about him.'

†**παρακαταλέγω** [παρα- (2) + κατα- (1) + λέγω[1]]. 3 sing. aor. mid. παρκατέλεκτο (παρ-, παρα-). In mid., to lie down *beside*, lie *with*. With dat. : τῇ παρκατέλεκτο Ι 565. Cf. Ι 664.

παράκειμαι [παρα- (2)]. 3 sing. pa. iterative παρεκέσκετο ξ 521. To be beside one, at one's hand or laid up, in readiness or for use, be there : ὀϊστόν, ὅ οἱ παρέκειτο τραπέζῃ φ 416. Cf Ω 476 : ξ 521.—Fig., to lie before one as a matter of choice. Impers. : νῦν ὑμῖν παράκειται ἐναντίον ἠὲ μάχεσθαι ἢ φεύγειν χ 65.

παρακλιδόν [παρα- (4) + κλι-, κλίνω. 'Bending aside']. Shirking the question δ 348 = ρ 139.

†**παρακλίνω** [παρα- (4)]. Aor. pple. παρακλίνας. (1) To bend or turn (something) aside : κεφαλήν υ 301.—(2) To turn aside, deviate from the course, swerve Ψ 424.

παρακοίτης, ὁ [παρ-, παρα- (2) + ἀκοίτης]. A husband Ζ 430, Θ 156.

παράκοιτις, ἡ [παρ-, παρα- (2) + ἄκοιτις]. Dat. sing. παρακοίτῑ γ 381. A wife Γ 53, Δ 60 = Σ 365, Ι 590, Ξ 346, Σ 184, Φ 479, Ω 60 : γ 381, 451, δ 228, λ 298, 305, 580, ο 26, φ 158, ψ 92.

†**παρακρεμάννῡμι** [παρα- (2)]. Aor. pple. παρακρεμάσας. To let hang by one's side Ν 597.

†**παραλέγω** [παρα- (2) + λέγω[1]]. 3 sing. aor. mid. παρελέξατο Β 515, Ζ 198, Π 184, Υ 224, Ω 676 : λ 242. Subj. παραλέξομαι Ξ 237. In mid., to lie *with*. With dat. : Λαοδαμείῃ Ζ 198. Cf. Β 515, Π 184 : λ 242.—In reference to Here and Zeus Ξ 237.—To Briseïs and Achilles Ω 676.—To Boreas and the mares of Erichthonius Υ 224.

†**παραμείβω** [παρ-, παρα- (3)]. Aor. pple. mid. παραμειψάμενος. In mid., to go past, pass by : τόν ζ 310.

παραμένω, παρμένω [παρα- (2)]. 3 sing. aor. παρέμεινε Λ 402. To remain *with* (a person), keep (him) company. With dat. : οὐκέτι τοι δύναμαι παρμενέμεν Ο 400.—So to stand *by* in the fight : οὐδέ τις αὐτῷ Ἀργείων παρέμεινεν Λ 402. Cf. Ν 151.

παραμίμνω [παρα- (2)]. To remain or abide with a person γ 115.—To stay, tarry, delay β 297.

παραμῡθέομαι [παρα- (4)]. To urge, advise, counsel. With dat. and infin.: τοῖς ἄλλοισιν οἴκαδ' ἀποπλείειν I 417, 684. Cf. O 45.

παρανηνέω [παρα- (2) + νηνέω, app. = νηέω]. To heap or pile up in readiness for use: σῖτον παρενήνεον ἐν κανέοισιν α 147. Cf. π 51.

†**παρανήχω** [παρα- (3)]. Aor. subj. mid. παρανήξομαι. To swim, make one's way by swimming, along the shore. In mid. ε 417.

πάραντα [app. formed fr. παρά as ἄναντα fr. ἀνά]. Along-hill Ψ 116.

†**παραπαφίσκω** [παρ-, παρα- (4)]. 3 sing. aor. παρήπαφε. To beguile, trick Ξ 360.

†**παραπείθω** [παρα- (4)]. 3 sing. aor. παρέπεισε H 120, N 788, Ψ 606. 3 sing. aor. subj. παραιπεπίθῃσι (παραι-, παρα-) χ 213. Pple. παρπεπιθών (παρ-, παρα-) ξ 290. Nom. pl. παρπεπιθόντες Ψ 37: ω 119. Nom. sing. fem. παραιπεπιθοῦσα Ξ 208. To induce to an act or a course of action, persuade, prevail upon, win over H 120 = N 788, Ξ 208, Ψ 37, 606: ξ 290, χ 213, ω 119.

†**παραπέμπω** [παρα- (3)]. 3 sing. aor. παρέπεμψε. To conduct or pilot (safely) past a danger μ 72.

†**παραπλάζω** [παρα- (4)]. 3 sing. aor. παρέπλαγξε ι 81, υ 346. Fem. pple. παραπλάγξᾱσα τ 187. 3 sing. aor. pass. παρεπλάγχθη O 464. (1) To cause to deviate from the proper course: παρεπλάγχθη οἱ ἄλλῃ ἰός (went wide) O 464.—To drive from one's course and *away from.* With genit.: Κυθήρων ι 81. Cf. τ 187.—(2) To disturb or derange (the mind) υ 346.

παραπλήξ, -ῆγος [παρα- (4) + πλήσσω]. Of spits projecting from the shore, on which the seas break aslant: ἠϊόνας ε 418 = 440.

†**παραπλώω** [παρα- (3)]. 3 sing. aor. παρέπλω. To sail past a place μ 69.

†**παραπνέω** [παρα- (3)]. 3 sing. aor. opt. παραπνεύσειε. Of wind, to blow past something: ἵνα μή τι παραπνεύσει' ὀλίγον περ κ 24 (*i.e.* so that none of the winds might slip past the fastening of the bag).

παραρρητός [παρα- (4) + ῥη-, εἴρω[2]]. Open to persuasion I 526.—Absol. in pl., words of persuasion: παραρρητοῖσι πιθέσθαι N 726.

παρασταδόν [παρα- (2) + στα-, ἵστημι]. Standing by O 22: κ 173 = 547 = μ 207.

παρασταίης, 2 sing. aor. opt. παρίστημι.

παραστάς, aor. pple. παρίστημι.

παραστήσεσθαι, fut. infin. mid. παρίστημι.

†**παρασφάλλω** [παρα- (4)]. 3 sing. aor. παρέσφηλε. To balk or thwart a person: παρέσφηλεν γὰρ Ἀπόλλων (caused him to miss his aim) Θ 311.

παρασχέμεν, παρασχεῖν, aor. infin. παρέχω.

†**παρατεκταίνομαι** [παρα- (5)]. 2 sing. aor. opt. παρατεκτήναιο ξ 131. 3 παρατεκτήναιτο Ξ 54. To make or order differently: οὐδέ κεν ἄλλως Ζεὺς αὐτὸς παρατεκτήναιτο (could help us) Ξ 54: ἔπος κε παρατεκτήναιο (tell a story differing from the truth, a cozening tale) ξ 131.

†**παρατίθημι** [παρα- (2)]. 1 pl. fut. παραθήσομεν Ψ 810. Aor. παρέθηκα ι 326. 3 sing. παρέθηκε Λ 779: α 139, 141, δ 133, ξ 76, σ 120, φ 29, etc. 3 pl. aor. πάρθεσαν (παρ-, παρα-) δ 66. Imp. παράθες Σ 408. Aor. opt. mid. παραθείμην ο 506, τ 150. 3 sing. παραθεῖτο β 105, ω 140. Nom. pl. masc. pple. παρθέμενοι β 237, γ 74, ι 255. From παρτιθέω 3 sing. pres. παρτιθεῖ α 192. (1) To set or place beside a person: ἐπεὶ δαΐδας παραθεῖτο (παραθείμην) (had had them set) β 105 = ω 140, τ 150. Cf. ε 92.—To set or place *beside.* With dat.: τράπεζαν, τὴν ἥν οἱ παρέθηκεν φ 29. Cf. δ 133, ι 326.—To set (food or drink) before a person: ξείνιά τ' εὖ παρέθηκεν Λ 779. Cf. α 139, 141, σ 120, etc.—To set (food or drink) *before.* With dat.: ἀμφιπόλῳ, ἥ οἱ βρῶσίν τε πόσιν τε παρτιθεῖ α 192. Cf. Σ 408, Ψ 810: δ 66, ξ 76, π 49.—In mid. ο 506.—(2) In mid., to set at hazard, risk (cf. παραβάλλω): σφὰς παρθέμενοι κεφαλάς β 237. Cf. γ 74 = ι 255.

†**παρατρέπω** [παρα- (4)]. Aor. pple. παρατρέψας. To turn aside: ἵππους Ψ 398, 423.

†**παρατρέχω** [παρα- (3)]. Aor. παρέδραμον Ψ 636. 3 sing. παρέδραμε K 350. 3 dual παραδραμέτην X 157. (1) To run past a point, pass a point at a run K 350, X 157.—(2) To run *past,* outstrip in a race. With acc.: Ἴφικλον παρέδραμον Ψ 636.

†**παρατρέω** [παρα- (4)]. 3 pl. aor. παρέτρεσσαν. To rush aside in affright: παρέτρεσσάν οἱ ἵπποι E 295.

παρατροπέω [παρα- (4)]. To turn away from the point, put off: παρατροπέων με δ 465.

παρατρωπάω [παρα- (4)]. To bend the mind of, win over: θεοὺς θυέεσσι παρατρωπῶσιν I 500.

παρατυγχάνω [παρα- (2)]. To be present *with.* With dat.: παρετύγχανε μαρναμένοισιν Λ 74.

παραυδάω [παρ-, παρα- (4)]. (1) To use persuasion to, endeavour to induce to an act or a course of action, urge π 279, σ 178 (talk me not into this).—(2) To speak in comfortable terms to: μέν' εἰς ὅ κε μύθοις ἀγανοῖσι παραυδήσας ἀποπέμψῃ (cheer you on your way) ο 53.—To speak comfortably of, minister false comfort in regard to: θάνατον λ 488.

†**παραφεύγω** [παρα- (3)]. Aor. infin. παρφυγέειν (παρ-, παρα-). To pass a point in safety μ 99.

παράφημι [παρα- (4)]. Pres. pple. mid. παραιφάμενος (παραι-, παρα-) Ω 771. παρφάμενος (παρ-, παρα-) M 249: β 189. Infin. παρφάσθαι π 287, τ 6. (1) To give counsel or advice. With dat. and infin.: μητρὶ παράφημι πατρὶ ἐπὶ ἦρα φέρειν A 577.—(2) To induce to a course of action, persuade, prevail upon, win over. In mid.: παρφάμενος ἐπέεσσιν M 249. Cf. Ω 771: β 189.—(3) To use evasive speech to, put off. In mid.: μνηστῆρας μαλακοῖς ἐπέεσσι παρφάσθαι π 287 = τ 6.

†**παραφθάνω** [παρα- (3)]. 3 sing. aor. opt. παραφθαίῃσι (app. formed on the analogy of subjunctives in -ῃσι) K 346. Pple. παραφθάς X 197. Aor. pple. mid. παραφθάμενος Ψ 515. To outstrip, get ahead of: ἄμμε K 346. Cf. X 197.—In mid. Ψ 515.

παρβεβαώς, pf. pple. παραβαίνω.

παρδαλέη, -ης, ἡ [fem. adj. fr. next (*sc.* δορά)]. The skin of a panther Γ 17, K 29.

πάρδαλις, ἡ. A panther N 103, P 20, Φ 573: δ 457.

παρέᾱσι, 3 pl. πάρειμι[1].

παρεδέξατο, 3 sing. aor. παραδέχομαι.

παρέδραθε, 3 sing. aor. παραδαρθάνω.

παρέδραμον, aor. παρατρέχω.

παρέζομαι [παρ-, παρα- (2)]. In pres. and in impf. (or non-sigmatic aor.; see ἕζομαι). **(1)** To seat oneself, sit down, take one's seat, beside a person: παρέζεο καὶ λαβὲ γούνων A 407.—**(2)** To seat oneself, sit down, take one's seat, *beside*. With dat.: σοὶ παρέζετο A 557. Cf. E 889: δ 738, υ 334.

παρέθηκα, aor. παρατίθημι.

παρειαί, αἱ [cf. παρήϊον]. The cheeks: ὦχρός μιν εἷλε παρειάς Γ 35. Cf. Λ 393, Σ 123, X 491, Ω 794: α 334, δ 198, θ 522, λ 529, σ 172, etc.—In reference to eagles: δρυψαμένω ὀνύχεσσι παρειάς β 153.

παρείη, 3 sing. opt. πάρειμι[1].

παρείθη, 3 sing. aor. pass. παρίημι.

†**πάρειμι**[1] [παρ-, παρα- (2) + εἰμί]. 3 sing. πάρεστι Θ 294, N 786: ξ 80, 444, ρ 457, ψ 128. 2 pl. πάρεστε B 485. 3 παρέᾱσι E 192, Ξ 299: ν 247. 3 sing. opt. παρείη X 20: β 62, σ 370. Pple. παρεών, -όντος O 325, 665, Ω 475: α 140, θ 491, λ 66, ξ 145, ο 74, 335, etc. Infin. παρέμμεναι Σ 472: δ 640. παρεῖναι X 298: ε 105, 129, ρ 347. 2 sing. impf. παρῆσθα δ 497. 3 παρῆεν θ 417. 3 pl. πάρεσαν Λ 75. Fut. παρέσσομαι ν 393. 3 sing. παρέσσεται A 213, I 135, 277, Σ 466. παρέσται K 217. **(1)** To be by or present, be in a specified or indicated place, be present at something, be with one, be here or there: πάρεστέ τε, ἴστε τε πάντα (are present (at all that happens)) B 485, ἐν δαίτῃσι παρέσται K 217. Cf. O 325, 665, X 298, Ω 475 (in attendance): θ 491, λ 66, ξ 145, ο 74, 335.—With dat., to be present or in company *with*, be *with*: ἄγασθέ μοι ἄνδρα παρεῖναι ε 129, ἐγώ γέ τοι παρέσσομαι (shall be found at your side) ν 393. Cf. Λ 75: δ 640, ε 105.—To be present *at*: μάχῃ δ 497.—**(2)** To be available or at one's command or disposal, be here or there for one: ἵπποι οὐ παρέασιν E 192, Ξ 299. Cf. Θ 294, I 135 = 277, N 786: ν 247, ξ 444, ρ 457, σ 370, ψ 128.—In neut. pple. pl., one's resources, one's store: χαριζομένη παρεόντων (genit. of material, 'from her store') α 140 = δ 56 = η 176 = κ 372 = ο 139 = ρ 95.—With dat., to be available *to*, be there or at command *for*: εἴ μοι δύναμίς γε παρείη X 20. Cf. A 213, Σ 466, 472: β 62, θ 417, ξ 80.—Of a quality, to be present *in*, be found *in*: αἰδὼς οὐκ ἀγαθὴ κεχρημένῳ ἀνδρὶ παρεῖναι ρ 347.

†**πάρειμι**[2] [παρ-, παρα- (3) + εἶμι]. Pple. παριών. To pass a point, go past or by: μή ἑ λάθοι παριών δ 527. Cf. ρ 233.

πᾰρεῖπον, *aor.* [παρ-, παρα- (4) + (F)εῖπον]. **(1)** To use persuasion, endeavour to induce a person to a course of action, urge (something) upon him: αἴσιμα παρειπών Z 62, H 121. Cf. Λ 793 = O 404.—**(2)** To persuade, win over, talk over: μή σε παρείπῃ A 555. Cf. Z 337.

παρέκ, παρέξ [παρά + ἐκ, ἐξ]. **(I)** Adv. **(1)** Out along: νῆχε π. (along the shore) ε 439.—**(2)** Passing a point, past: π. ἐλάαν μ 47, 109.—**(3)** Aside from the straight line, diverging: π. ἀγορευέμεν (app., to wrong purpose) M 213: οὐκ ἂν ἄλλα π. εἴποιμι (away from the point) δ 348 = ρ 139, ἄλλα π. μεμνώμεθα (passing from him) ξ 168, ταῦτα π. ἐρέουσα (to bring me this false news) ψ 16.—**(4)** Out beside something: στῆ π. (forth beside him) Λ 486.—**(5)** Out, off: ὦσα [νῆα] π. ι 488 (perh. implying a sidelong movement).—**(II)** Prep. **(1)** With genit. **(a)** Along and outside of: νῆσος π. λιμένος τετάνυσται (*i.e.* across the mouth) ι 116.—**(b)** Aside from: π. ὁδοῦ K 349.—**(2)** With acc. **(a)** Along, alongside of: π. ἅλα I 7.—**(b)** Past, leaving on one side or behind, passing, beyond: σῆμα π. Ἴλοιο Ω 349. Cf. Ψ 762: μ 55, 276, 443 (on the further side of), ο 199.—Sim.: π. νόον (in defiance of . . .) K 391, Υ 133, δῶρα π. Ἀχιλῆα δέχεσθαι (behind his back) Ω 434.—**(c)** Out beyond: π. τειχίον αὐλῆς π 165, 343.

παρεκέσκετο, 3 sing. pa. iterative παράκειμαι.

†**παρεκπροφεύγω** [παρ-, παρα- (3) + ἐκ- (1) + προ- (1)]. 3 sing. aor. subj. παρεκπροφύγῃσι. To slip past, elude (a person): μή σε π. ἄεθλα Ψ 314.

†**παρελαύνω** [παρ-, παρα- (3)]. 3 sing. aor. παρήλασε μ 186. παρέλασσε Ψ 382, 527. 3 pl. παρήλασαν Ψ 638: μ 197. Infin. παρελάσσαι Ψ 427. **(1)** **(a)** To drive one's chariot past another, outstrip him in the race: ἤ κε παρέλασσ' ἢ ἀμφήριστον ἔθηκεν Ψ 382. Cf. Ψ 427.—**(b)** To sail past a specified point: οὔ πώ τις τῇδε παρήλασεν μ 186.—**(2)** With acc. **(a)** To drive *past*, outstrip, in the chariot-race: παρέλασσέ κέ μιν Ψ 527. Cf. Ψ 638.—**(b)** To sail *past*: Σειρῆνας μ 197.

παρελέξατο, 3 sing. aor. mid. παραλέγω.

παρελεύσεαι, 2 sing. fut. παρέρχομαι.

παρέλθῃ, 3 sing. aor. subj. παρέρχομαι.

παρέλκω [παρ-, παρα- (4)]. To use shifts, evade the issue φ 111.—In mid., to draw off to oneself, gain by trickery: δῶρα σ 282.

παρέμεινε, 3 sing. aor. παραμένω.

παρέμμεναι, infin. πάρειμι[1].

παρέξ. See παρέκ.

†**παρεξελαύνω** [παρ-, παρα- (3) + ἐξ- (1)]. 2 sing. aor. subj. παρεξελάσῃσθα. = παρελαύνω (1) (a) Ψ 344.

†**παρεξέρχομαι** [παρ-, παρα- (3) + ἐξ- (1)]. Aor. pple. fem. παρεξελθοῦσα κ 573. Infin. παρεξελθεῖν K 344: ε 104, 138. To pass by, slip past, make good one's passage: παρεξελθεῖν πεδίοιο (local genit.) K 344: ῥεῖα παρεξελθοῦσα κ 573.—To get oneself *past*, defeat, frustrate. With acc.: Διὸς νόον ε 104 = 138.

παρέξω, fut. παρέχω.

παρέπεισε, 3 sing. aor. παραπείθω.

παρέπεμψε, 3 sing. aor. παραπέμπω.

παρέπλαγξε, 3 sing. aor. παραπλάζω.

παρέπλω, 3 sing. aor. παραπλώω.

παρέρχομαι [παρ-, παρα- (3)]. 2 sing. fut. παρελεύσεαι Α 132. 3 sing. aor. παρῆλθε ε 429. 3 sing. subj. παρέλθῃ Ψ 345 : θ 230. 3 sing. opt. παρέλθοι ν 291. Infin. παρελθέμεν Θ 239. (1) To pass, make good one's passage μ 62, π 357.—In reference to the passage of a wave ε 429.—(2) With acc., to go *past*, pass, leave on one side or behind: τεὸν βωμόν Θ 239.—To outstrip Ψ 345 : θ 230.—To overreach, get the better of, outwit Α 132 : ν 291.

πάρεσαν, 3 pl. impf. πάρειμι[1].

παρέσσομαι, fut. πάρειμι[1].

παρέσται, 3 sing. fut. πάρειμι[1].

παρεστάμεναι, pf. infin. παρίστημι.

παρέστασαν, 3 pl. plupf. παρίστημι.

παρέστη, 3 sing. aor. παρίστημι.

παρέστηκε, 3 sing. pf. παρίστημι.

πάρεστι, 3 sing. pres. πάρειμι[1].

παρέσφηλε, 3 sing. aor. παρασφάλλω.

παρέτρεσσαν, 3 pl. aor. παρατρέω.

παρευνάζω [παρ-, παρα- (2)]. In pass., to lie *with*. With dat. : δμῳῇσι γυναιξίν χ 37.

παρέχω [παρ-, παρα- (2)]. 3 sing. subj. πᾱρέχῃ (παρσέχῃ) τ 113. Fut. παρέξω θ 39, σ 317. 3 sing. παρέξει Ψ 835. 3 sing. aor. subj. παράσχῃ Γ 354 : ο 55. Infin. παρασχέμεν Τ 140, 147. παρασχεῖν ζ 28. (1) To furnish, provide, supply, present, give, grant: δῶρα Τ 140, 147. Cf. Σ 556, Ψ 835 : ἀρετήν σ 133. Cf. δ 89, ζ 28, θ 39, ξ 250, ο 490, σ 317, 360, τ 113, υ 8.—(2) To afford, show, manifest: φιλότητα Γ 354 : ο 55.

παρεών, pple. πάρειμι[1].

παρῆεν, 3 sing. impf. πάρειμι[1].

παρηέρθη, 3 sing. aor. pass. παραείρω.

παρήϊξε, 3 sing. aor. παραΐσσω.

παρήϊον, τό [cf. παρειαί]. (1) The cheek Ψ 690 : τ 208.—In reference to wolves Π 159.—To a lion χ 404.—(2) A cheek ornament for a horse: παρήϊον ἔμμεναι ἵππων (general pl., 'for some horse') Δ 142.

παρήλασε, 3 sing. aor. παρελαύνω.

παρῆλθε, 3 sing. aor. παρέρχομαι.

πάρημαι [παρ-, παρα- (2)]. (1) To sit by or beside a person : ὡς μή μοι τρύζητε παρήμενοι Ι 311. Cf. Ω 652 : α 339, ν 411, ξ 375, ρ 521, σ 231, τ 209. —In reference to birds λ 578.—With dat., to sit *by* or *beside* : παρήμενός μοι τέρπειν τ 589.—To sit *at*, *by*, *in the enjoyment of*: δαιτὶ παρήμενος α 26. Cf. ρ 456.—To abide, be, *by* or *with* : σύεσσιν ν 407.—(2) To sit idle, doing nothing, *by* or *beside*. With dat. : νηυσὶ παρήμενος Α 421, 488.

παρηορίαι, αἱ [παρήορος]. The traces attaching the παρήορος (see next (2)) Θ 87, Π 152.

παρήορος [παρ-, παρα- (2) + ἠορ-, ἀείρω. 'Hung on at the side,' 'dangling loosely.' Cf. συνήορος, τετράοροι]. (1) Sprawling Η 156.—Loose or uncontrolled in mind, flighty Ψ 603.—(2) As sb., an extra trace-horse attached to a chariot Π 471, 474.

παρήπαφε, 3 sing. aor. παραπαφίσκω.

παρῆσθα, 2 sing. impf. πάρειμι[1].

παρθέμενοι, nom. pl. masc. aor. pple. mid. παρατίθημι.

παρθενική, -ῆς, ἡ = παρθένος Σ 567 : η 20, λ 39.

παρθένιος, -η [παρθένος]. (1) Of a maiden : ζώνην λ 245.—(2) Born out of wedlock Π 180.

παρθενοπίπης [παρθένος + ὀπιπεύω]. One who ogles girls. Voc. παρθενοπῖπα Λ 385.

παρθένος, -ου, ἡ. A young unmarried woman, a maid, a maiden, a girl Β 514, Σ 593, Χ 127, 128 : ζ 33, 109, 228.

πάρθεσαν, 3 pl. aor. παρατίθημι.

παριαύω [παρ-, παρα- (2)]. To lie *with*. With dat. : τῇ παριαύων Ι 336.

παρίζω [παρ-, παρα- (2)]. To sit down *beside*. With dat. : Τηλεμάχῳ παρῖζεν δ 311.

†**παρίημι** [παρ-, παρα- (2) + ἵημι[1]]. 3 sing. aor. pass. παρείθη (for παρ-ε-σέ-θη). In pass., to hang down by the side of something, to hang down loosely : παρείθη μήρινθος Ψ 868.

παρίστημι [παρ-, παρα- (2)]. 2 sing. aor. παρέστης Γ 405, Ε 116, Κ 290. 3 παρέστη Ο 442, 483, 649, Χ 371, Ω 303 : α 335, ι 52, ρ 73, σ 211, φ 66. 3 dual subj. παρστήετον σ 183. 2 sing. opt. παρασταίης ν 389. 3 παρσταίη Υ 121. 3 pl. παρασταῖεν θ 218. 2 pl. imp. πάρστητε Π 544. Pple. παραστάς Β 189, Ζ 75, Λ 261, Π 114, Υ 375, Ψ 155, etc. : θ 238, ι 325, π 338, ρ 221, φ 379, etc. παρστάς Κ 157. Fem. παρστᾶσα ψ 87. 3 sing. pf. παρέστηκε Π 853, Ω 132. 3 pl. plupf. παρέστασαν Η 467. Infin. παρεστάμεναι Ο 255, Ρ 563, Φ 231 : δ 827, υ 94. **Mid.** Imp. παρίσταο Κ 291. Fut. infin. παραστήσεσθαι ω 28. (I) In aor. and mid. (1) To take up a position, take one's stand, come and stand, by or beside a person or thing, come up to or approach a person : τὸν ἐρητύσασκε παραστάς Β 189. Cf. Γ 405 (have come here), Δ 212, Η 188, Μ 60, Ρ 119, Ω 303 (presented herself), etc. : πέλεκυν ἔχων παρίστατο γ 443. Cf. η 341, θ 218, κ 109, ο 123, ρ 73 (went up to him), ψ 87, etc.—To take up a position, take one's stand, come and stand, *by* or *beside*, come up to, approach. With dat. : τῷ παρίστατ' Ὀδυσσεύς (came up to him) Β 244. Cf. Ζ 75, Ο 442, Π 2, Ρ 338, Ψ 155, etc. : ἀμφίπολός οἱ ἑκάτερθε παρέστη α 335. Cf. β 384, μ 43, ο 104, ρ 221, σ 183, etc.—(2) To come and stand by a person as a helper, to come to his aid or support : ἀλλά, φίλοι, πάρστητε Π 544.—To come and stand *by* as a helper, to come to the aid or support of, aid, succour, support, protect. With dat. : ἡμείων τις Ἀχιλῆϊ παρσταίη Υ 121. Cf. Ε 116, 570, Κ 279, Ο 442, Ψ 783, etc. : γ 222, ν 301, 389.—(3) Of fate, to come *upon*. With dat. : Διὸς αἶσα παρέστη ἡμῖν ι 52. Cf. π 280, ω 28.—(II) In pf. and plupf. (1) To have one's stand, stand, be, *by* or *beside*. With dat. : δόκησέ οἱ παρεστάμεναι κεφαλῆφιν υ 94.—(2) To stand by a person as a helper, to aid, succour, support, protect him δ 827.—To stand *by* as a helper, to aid, succour, support. With dat. : παρεστάμεναι καὶ ἀμύνειν Πατρόκλῳ Ρ 563. Cf. Ο 255, Φ 231.—(3) Of fate, to be at hand, impend *over*. With dat. : ἄγχι τοι παρέστηκεν θάνατος καὶ μοῖρα Π 853 = Ω 132.—(4) To be in an indicated place, be present, be there : νῆες ἐκ Λήμνοιο παρέστασαν Η 467.

παρίσχω [παρ-, παρα- (2)]. (1) To hold in readiness, keep at hand : [ἵππους] Δ 229.—(2) To hold at one's disposal, offer : ἑπτὰ [κούρας] I 638.

παριών, pple. πάρειμι².

παρκατέλεκτο, 3 sing. aor. mid. παρακαταλέγω.

παρμέμβλωκε, 3 sing. pf. παραβλώσκω.

παρμένω. See παραμένω.

πάροιθε(ν) [*πάροι, locative adv. (cf. πάρος) + -θε(ν) (2)]. (1) In front, before : π. λάμπετο δουρὸς αἰχμή (before him as he went) Z 319 = Θ 494. Cf. Υ 437 (at the point), Ψ 213 (before them) : η 125 (in the foreground), τ 33 (going before them), 227 (app., on the face of the περόνη).—Leading in a race Ψ 498.—With genit., in front of, before : π. αὐτοῖο καθέζετο A 360, 500. Cf. Γ 162, Ξ 427, O 154 (into his presence), Π 255 : δ 625 = ρ 167, π 166.—(2) In temporal sense. (a) Before the happening of something : π. εἰρύσατο ζωστήρ (before the arrow got so far) Δ 185. Cf. O 227 (before it came to that) : ζ 174 (ere that).—(b) In time past, formerly : ἀλλοῖος ἠὲ π. π 181. Cf. Ψ 20 = 180 : ρ 294.—So τὸ π. : μᾶλλον ἔτ' ἢ τὸ π. α 322. Cf. β 312, σ 275.

παροίτερος, -η [comp. fr. *πάροι. See prec.]. More forward, in front, leading : ἄλλοι μοι δοκέουσι παροίτεροι ἔμμεναι ἵπποι Ψ 459. Cf. Ψ 480.

παροίχομαι [παρ-, παρα- (3)]. 3 sing. pf. παρῴχωκε, παροίχωκε K 252 (v.l. παρῴχηκε, as if fr. *παροιχέω). (1) To pass on, go on one's way : παρῴχετο γηθόσυνος κῆρ Δ 272 = 326.—(2) Of time, to pass, go by K 252.

πάρος. (1) Before, heretofore, theretofore, in time past, formerly, on a former occasion : ἐμεῦ π. ἔκλυες A 453, ἔνθα π. κοιμᾶτο 610. Cf. Λ 111, 825, Π 557, X 403, etc. : β 119, δ 627, ζ 325, κ 395, λ 394, σ 36, etc.—So τὸ π. N 228, X 233 : ω 486.—With pres. of a state of things continuing up to the time of speaking : τί π. λαβρεύεαι ; (why have you ever been a rash talker ?) Ψ 474. Cf. Δ 264 : ὅσοι π. εἰσὶν ἄριστοι θ 36. Cf. ν 401, 433.—Cf. also under (2) and (3).—(2) (τὸ) π. γε, before (not now (then)) (whatever may be (have been) the case now (then)) : π. γέ σ' οὐκ εἴρομαι A 553. Cf. N 465, Π 796, P 270, 587, Σ 386, X 302, etc. : τὸ π. γε θεοὶ φαίνονται ἐναργεῖς η 201. Cf. δ 810, ι 448, σ 164, etc.—(3) (τὸ) π. περ. (a) Before (not merely now (then)) (even as now (then)) : ὅς σε π. περ ῥύομαι O 256. Cf. E 806, H 370, M 346, Ξ 131, X 250, etc. : νοῦς ἦν ἔμπεδος ὡς τὸ π. περ κ 240. Cf. β 305, ε 82, ν 358, ω 508, etc.—(b) In the sense of π. γε (see (2)) : οἳ τὸ π. περ ἐλάφοισιν ἐοίκεσαν N 101. Cf. Ω 201.—(4) Before the arrival of a specified time, past or future, earlier, sooner : π. οὐκ ἔσσεται ἄλλως, πρίν γε . . . E 218. Cf. Θ 166 (before that), etc. : πάρος μιν ἔκτα λ 324. Cf. β 127, ρ 293, etc.—Already, as it was : π. μεμαυῖαν Δ 73 = T 349 = X 186 : = ω 487.—(5) With aor. infin., before . . . ing . . . : π. Διὸς ὅσσε ἰδέσθαι Ξ 286. Cf. Z 348, Λ 573, M 221, etc. : μενέαινεν Ὀδυσῆϊ π. ἣν γαῖαν ἱκέσθαι (in the period before his reaching it, *i.e.* until he reached it) α 21. Cf. θ 376, π 218, etc.—With pres. infin. : π. δόρποιο μέδεσθαι Σ 245.—(6) In local sense, before, in front of. With genit. : Τυδεΐδαο π. σχέμεν ἵππους Θ 254.

παρπεπιθών, aor. pple. παραπείθω.

παρστάς, aor. pple. παρίστημι.

παρτιθεῖ. See παρατίθημι.

παρφάσθαι, infin. mid. παράφημι.

πάρφασις. See παραίφασις.

παρφυγέειν, aor. infin. παραφεύγω.

παρῴχωκε, παρῴχηκε, 3 sing. pf. παροίχομαι.

πᾶς, πᾶσα, πᾶν. Genit. παντός, πάσης, παντός. Genit. pl. fem. πᾱσάων ζ 107. πᾱσέων I 330, Σ 431 : δ 608, υ 70, etc. Dat. pl. masc. and neut. (besides πᾶσι) πάντεσσι A 288, K 173, Σ 521, etc. : β 166, θ 21, ν 292, etc. (1) In sing. (a) All the, the whole, the whole of the : ἦμαρ A 592. Cf. B 149, 780, 823, Γ 50, Λ 714, etc. : θαλάσσης α 53. Cf. δ 447, ε 455 (all his . . .), ν 193, ξ 267, etc.—So with a collective pl. : πάντες λαοί β 13. Cf. δ 176, θ 382, etc.—Predicatively : πᾶς κεκάλυπτο N 191. Cf. O 537, etc. : μ 238, ν 169, etc.—(b) All, the whole of : Τηλέμαχον πάντα κύσεν π 21. Cf. B 108, 575, etc. : τ 475, etc.—A whole : μῆνα κ 14, etc.—Of all sorts : βουλήν N 741, etc. : ἐδωδήν ε 196, etc.—(c) Each, every : πᾶν ἔργον A 294. Cf. Z 79 : δ 434.—Absol., every one : πρόσσω πᾶς πέτεται Π 265. Cf. ν 313.—(d) Absol., the whole of a specified thing : πᾶν εὖ λειήνας Δ 111. Cf. π 351.—(2) In pl. (a) All the : ἀρίστους Γ 19. Cf. A 5, 15, 22, 78, 424, B 579, 809, etc. : ἀγυιαί β 388, πελεκέων οὐκ ἤμβροτε πάντων στειλειῆς (did not miss the στειλειή of any of them) φ 421. Cf. α 71, 78, β 174 (all his . . .), γ 254, etc.—(b) All : πάντων ἐκπαγλότατ' ἀνδρῶν A 146. Cf. A 257, 286, 545, 597, B 285, Γ 95, E 60 (all kinds of . . .), etc. : ἤματα πάντα (every day) β 55. Cf. α 76 (all of us), β 176, γ 430, etc.—(c) With numerals, in all : ἐννέα πάντες H 161. Cf. Σ 373, T 247, etc. : ε 244, θ 258, etc.—(d) Absol., the whole number of specified or indicated persons or things : λεύσσετε τό γε πάντες A 120. Cf. A 122, 288, 367, 471, B 480, 485, etc. : ἕως κ' ἀπὸ πάντα δοθείη β 78, ἐπεὶ πάντα λοέσσατο (his whole body) ζ 227. Cf. α 43, 273, β 91, 152, 175, 284, etc.—(3) In neut. pl. πάντα as adv., altogether, wholly, quite : π. ἐνίκα (in all the contests) Δ 389, Τυδεΐδῃ μιν ἔγωγε π. ἐΐσκω E 181. Cf. Λ 613, Φ 600, X 491, etc. : δ 654, ν 209, etc.—With neg. : μὴ π. μνηστῆρσιν ὁμιλεῖν (not in any wise to . . .) σ 167 (cf. πάγχυ, πάμπαν).

πασάμην, aor. πατέομαι.

πασιμέλουσα [πᾶσι, dat. pl. masc. of πᾶς + μέλουσα, pres. pple. fem. μέλω]. (Written also πᾶσι μέλουσα.) At whose name all hearts stir, the storied : Ἀργὼ πασιμέλουσα μ 70.

πάσσαλος, -ου, ὁ. Ablative πασσαλόφι Ω 268 : θ 67, 105. A peg on which to hang something E 209, Ω 268 : α 440, θ 67 = 105, φ 53.

πάσσασθαι, aor. infin. πατέομαι.

πάσσω. (ἐμ-.) (1) To let fall in shreds or small particles, sprinkle : φάρμακα Δ 219, E 401,

900, Λ 515, 830, Ο 394, ἁλός (partitive genit.) Ι 214.—(2) In weaving, to insert in a web Χ 441.

πάσσων, comp. παχύς.

πάσχω [for πάθ-σκω]. Fut. in mid. form πείσομαι β 134. 3 sing. -εται Υ 127 : η 197. Infin. -εσθαι σ 132. Aor. ἔπαθον Ι 492 : η 221. πάθον Ι 321, Π 55, Σ 397 : δ 95, ε 223, θ 155, ν 263. 2 sing. ἔπαθες Ψ 607. πάθες ξ 362, ο 487. 3 πάθε Ω 7 : α 4, ν 90, ξ 32. 1 pl. πάθομεν Φ 442 : γ 113. 2 πάθετε κ 458. 3 ἔπαθον : θ 490, ψ 67. πάθον Ξ 67, γ 116. Subj. πάθω Λ 404 : ε 465, ζ 173. 2 sing. -ῃς ρ 596. -ῃσθα Ω 551. 3 -ῃ ο 401. -ῃσι Λ 470, Ρ 242, Υ 126, Χ 505 : δ 820, η 195. 1 pl. -ωμεν Ν 52 : μ 321. 3 -ωσι Κ 538. Opt. πάθοιμι Τ 321, Φ 274. 3 sing. -οι Ε 567, Ν 670, Χ 220 : σ 224, τ 464. 1 pl. -οιμεν ι 53. 3 -οιεν Κ 26. Pple. παθών, -όντος Λ 313, Φ 82 : β 174, δ 81, ε 377, η 224, θ 184, μ 27, ν 131, ο 176, π 205, ω 106. Fem. παθοῦσα Χ 431. Infin. παθέειν Ρ 32, Σ 77, Υ 198 : ε 347. Pf. πέπονθα ρ 284. 2 sing. πέπονθας ν 6. 2 pl. πέποσθε ψ 53. πέπασθε (for πέπαθ-τε : cf. πεπαθυίῃ below) Γ 99 : κ 465. Dat. sing. fem. pple. πεπαθυίῃ ρ 555. 3 sing. plupf. ἐπεπόνθει ν 92. (1) To suffer, endure, undergo, to have laid upon one, be called upon to bear : ἄλγεα Β 667. Cf. Γ 99, 128, Ε 886, Ι 492, Ρ 32, Υ 127, etc. : κακόν τι β 179. Cf. α 4, 49, β 174, δ 81, 95, η 221, θ 490, ν 90, ξ 416, etc.—Absol. : κακῶς πάσχοντος ἐμεῖο (sore though my plight be) π 275.—(2) To have (something) come upon, happen to, or befall one : τί παθόντε λελάσμεθ' ἀλκῆς ; (why do we thus . . ?) Λ 313, τί πάθω ; (what is to become of me ?) 404 : ἐξερέεινον ἅπαντα, οὐλὴν ὅττι πάθοι (about the wound, what befell him, *i.e.* how he got the wound) τ 464. Cf. ε 465, υ 351, ω 106 (what has brought you here ?).—(3) With indefinite object, to have (something evil) come upon one, encounter (mischance), meet (one's death) : μή τι πάθοι Ε 567. Cf. Κ 26, 538, Λ 470, Ν 52, Ρ 242, Υ 126, Φ 274 : οὐδέ τί τοι παθέειν δέος ε 347. Cf. δ 820, μ 321, ρ 596, σ 224.

πάταγος, -ου, ὁ. A sound or noise. A chattering (of the teeth) Ν 283.—Of the cracking of breaking branches Π 769.—Of the splash with which persons fall into a river Φ 9.—Of noise or din in battle Φ 387.

πατάσσω. (ἐκ-.) Of the heart, to beat, knock at the ribs Η 216, Ν 282, Ψ 370.

†**πατέομαι.** Aor. πασάμην Φ 76, Ω 641. 1 pl. ἐπασσάμεθα ι 87, κ 58. 3 πάσαντο Α 464, Β 427 : γ 9, 461, μ 364. Pple. πασσάμενος, -ου α 124, δ 61. Infin. πάσασθαι Ι 487, Τ 160 : ι 93. πάσσασθαι κ 384. Plupf. πεπάσμην Ω 642. To partake of, taste : σπλάγχνα Α 464 = Β 427 : = γ 461 = μ 464, γ 9. Cf. Φ 76.—With partitive genit. : σίτου καὶ οἴνοιο Τ 160. Cf. Ω 641, 642 : α 124, δ 61, ι 87 = κ 58, ι 93 (gave them of it to eat (thereof)), κ 384. —Absol., to partake of food or drink, eat or drink : ἐν μεγάροισι πάσασθαι Ι 487.

πατέω [πάτος]. To trample under foot. Fig. : καθ' ὅρκια πάτησαν Δ 157.

πατήρ, -έρος, ὁ [cf. L. *pater*, Eng. *father*, German *vater*]. Genit. πατρός Α 396, Β 146, Ζ 47, Ξ 11, Φ 36, Ω 265, etc. : α 94, β 14, ε 395, ν 173, ρ 43, ψ 30, etc. Dat. πατρί Α 98, Γ 50, Θ 283, Ν 454, Π 143, Ω 100, etc. : β 276, ζ 51, ν 51, τ 14, ω 518, etc. Voc. πάτερ Α 503, Β 371, Θ 31, Μ 164, Χ 178, Ω 362, etc. : α 45, δ 341, η 28, π 222, τ 36, ω 511, etc. Genit. pl. πατρῶν δ 687, θ 245. (1) A father, one's father Α 98, 358, Β 260, Γ 50, Δ 219, etc. : α 94, 135, β 14, γ 16, δ 94, etc.—(2) Of Zeus as the father of gods and men : π. ἀνδρῶν τε θεῶν τε Α 544. Cf. Α 503, Β 146, 371, Γ 350, Δ 235, etc. : α 28, δ 341, η 316, μ 65, ν 51, etc.—(3) In voc. as a form of respectful address to an elder Ω 362 : η 28, θ 408, etc. —(4) In pl., one's fathers or forefathers : γένος πατέρων Ζ 209. Cf. θ 245, ω 508.

πάτος, -ου, ὁ. (1) A beaten way ; hence, the beaten track, the space through which men usually pass : κιόντες ἐκ πάτου ἐς σκοπιήν Υ 137. —(2) The haunts (of men) (cf. κέλευθος (2)) : πάτον ἀνθρώπων ἀλεείνων Ζ 202.—Frequenting, coming and going (of men) : οὐ π. ἀνθρώπων ἀπερύκει ι 119.

πάτρη, -ης, ἡ [πατρ-, πατήρ]. (1) One's fatherland, birthplace, home : τηλόθι πάτρης Α 30. Cf. Μ 243, Ω 480, 766, etc. : β 365, η 223, ρ 318, τ 168, etc.—(2) One's parentage : ἀμφοτέροισιν ὁμὸν γένος ἠδ' ἴα π. Ν 354.

πατρίς, -ίδος [πατρ-, πατήρ]. Of one's fathers. (1) With αἶα, γαῖα, ἄρουρα, one's fatherland, birthplace, home (= prec. (1)) : ἐς πατρίδα γαῖαν Β 140, ἀπὸ πατρίδος αἴης 162. Cf. Γ 244, Δ 172, Η 335, Λ 817, etc. : π. ἄρουρα α 407. Cf. α 75, 290, δ 521, κ 29, etc.—(2) Absol. in the same sense : ἐς πατρίδα Ι 428, 691, Μ 16. Cf. Ε 213 : δ 474, 522, η 151, ι 34, etc.

πατρόθεν [πατρ-, πατήρ + -θεν (1)]. By the name of one's father Κ 68 (see γενεή (1)).

πατροκασίγνητος, -ου, ὁ [πατρ-, πατήρ + κασίγνητος]. A father's brother, an uncle on the father's side, one's uncle Φ 469 : ζ 330, ν 342.

πατροφονεύς, ὁ [πατρ-, πατήρ + φον-, φένω]. The slayer of another's father α 299, γ 197, 307.

πατροφόνος, ὁ [as prec.]. The slayer of one's own father, a parricide : ὡς μὴ π. καλεοίμην Ι 461.

πατρώϊος, -η, -ον [πατρ-, πατήρ]. Of, pertaining to, inherited or derived from, one's fathers or one's father, hereditary : σκῆπτρον Β 46, 186. Cf. Ε 125, Ζ 215, 231, Τ 387, Υ 391, Φ 44 : ξεῖνος α 175, 417, ρ 522. Cf. α 187, 387, β 22 (the family . . .), 254, 286, μ 136, ν 188 and 251 (his fatherland), ρ 69.—Absol. in neut. pl., one's inheritance : ἔχειν πατρώϊα πάντα π 388. Cf. ρ 80, υ 336, χ 61.

παῦρος, -ον. (1) Small in number, consisting of few : λαός Β 675.—Comp. παυρότερος : λαόν Δ 407.—(2) In pl., few in number, few : βροτοῖσιν Ι 545. Cf. Λ 689 : β 241 (few as they are), 276, 277.—In comp. : παυροτέρους περ ἐόντας Ο 407. Cf. Β 122, Ε 641, Θ 56, Ν 739 : ξ 17.—(3) Absol. in masc. pl., few : παῦροι 'Αχαιῶν Ο 283. Cf. σ 383, τ 240, ψ 236.—In comp. : παυρότεροι φθίνυθον Ρ 364.—In neut. pl., few things, not much, little : διὰ παῦρα δασάσκετο I 333. Cf. Γ 214 : ξ 210.

παυσωλή, ἡ [παυσ-, παύω]. A period of rest, an interval (cf. μεταπαυσωλή) B 386.

παύω. Pa. iterative παύεσκον χ 315. 1 pl. aor. subj. παύσωμεν H 29. 3 sing. pa. iterative mid. παυέσκετο Ω 17. 1 pl. aor. subj. παυσώμεσθα H 290. (ἀνα-, ἀπο-, κατα-, μεταπαύομαι.) (I) (1) To cause to cease from action, stop the activities of, give pause to, lay restraint upon, stop : παῦσεν ἀριστεύοντα (stopped him in his career as he was . . .) Λ 506. Cf. Φ 314 : χ 315.—Contextually, to kill, slay υ 274.—With inanimate object : [ποταμὸς] παῦσεν ἐὸν ῥόον ε 451. Cf. κ 22.—Sim. : παῦσαι τόξον (no longer let it go round, lay it aside) φ 279.—With genit. of that from which one is stopped or restrained : ἀοιδῆς B 595. Cf. Γ 150, E 909, M 389, O 15, Φ 294, etc. : δ 659, 801, ψ 298, ω 42.—With infin. : ἔμ' ἔπαυσας μάχεσθαι Λ 442.—(2) To cause to cease, bring to an end, stop, restrain, curb : χόλον A 192, πόλεμος πέπαυται Γ 134. Cf. A 207, 282, H 29, 331, I 459, O 72, Π 528, T 67 : ω 543.—(3) To give relief or deliverance (from something). With genit. : αἴ κέ ποθι Ζεὺς παύσῃ ὀϊζύος δ 35. Cf. Δ 191 : ε 492, ο 342.—(II) In mid. (1) To cease from action, give up or abandon a course of action, make pause, desist, give over : παύσατο χωόμενός περ Ξ 260. Cf. Θ 295, I 260, Φ 373, 384, Ψ 823 : εὖτ' ἐπαύετ' ἀοιδός ρ 359. Cf. β 169, δ 103, ζ 174, π 405, 433, υ 110.—Of conditions or inanimate things, to cease, abate : παύσαθ' αἷμα (ceased to flow) Λ 267, 848, ασθμα καὶ ἱδρὼς παύετο O 242. Cf. Ψ 228 : ε 384, 391, μ 168.—To refrain from action, pause : παύεσθαί σε κέλομαι (to think twice about it) Γ 434.—With genit. of that from which one desists : ἐπεὶ παύσαντο πόνου A 467. Cf. B 100, H 290, Σ 125, Υ 43, etc. : παύσεσθαι μνηστύος β 198, παυομένῳ δόρποιο (rising from table) τ 402. Cf. δ 683, 812, θ 540, ν 180, π 278, etc.—With pple. : ὅτε παύσαιτο νηπιαχεύων X 502. Cf. μ 400, 426.—(2) To rest : ἐνὶ κλισίῃ παυέσκετο Ω 17.—To find relief or deliverance, get rest (from something). With genit. : ἐλπόμενοι παύσασθαι πολέμοιο Γ 112. Cf. Φ 432.

παφλάζω. Of waves, to splash or dash : κύματα παφλάζοντα N 798.

πάχετος [app. a by-form of παχύς. Cf. περιμήκετος]. Thick, stout : δίσκον θ 187. Cf. ψ 191.

πάχιστος, superl. παχύς.

πάχνη, ἡ [παγ-, πήγνυμι]. Hoar-frost, rime : ὕπερθε χιὼν γένετ' ἠΰτε πάχνη ξ 476.

παχνόω [as prec.]. To freeze, chill. Fig. : ἦτορ παχνοῦται (loses its courage) P 112.

πάχος, τό [as prec.]. Thickness ι 324.

παχύς, -εῖα, -ύ [as prec.]. Comp. πάσσων, -ονος (for παχ-ίων). Superl. πάχιστος. (1) Clotted : αἷμα Ψ 697.—(2) Thick, stout : σκῆπτρον Σ 416. Cf. M 446.—Sim. : αὐλὸς αἵματος χ 18.—(3) In reference to the person, of large build, of goodly presence : μείζονα καὶ πάσσονα ζ 230 = ψ 157, ω 369. Cf. θ 20, σ 195.—(4) In reference to parts of the body, well developed, stout, strong : χειρὶ παχείῃ Γ 376. Cf. Π 314, 473, etc. : ζ 128, ι 372, etc.

πέδαι, αἱ [πεδ-, ποδ-, πούς]. Shackles : ἀμφὶ ποσσὶν [ἵππων] πέδας ἔβαλεν N 36.

πεδάω [πέδαι]. 3 sing. πεδάᾳ δ 380, 469. 3 pl. pa. iterative πεδάασκον ψ 353. To put in bonds : θεοῦ κατὰ μοῖρα πέδησε, δεσμοί τε βουκόλοι τε λ 292.—Hence, to hold, shackle, trammel, to hold back, keep back, detain, stop : Διώρεα μοῖρα πέδησε (*i.e.* prevented his escape) Δ 517, πέδησε γυῖα (took from him the power of movement) N 435, καθ' ἕτερόν γ' [Ἄτη] πέδησεν (gets in her grip) T 94, μὴ ἑκὼν τὸ ἐμὸν δόλῳ ἅρμα πεδῆσαι (got in the way of it) Ψ 585. Cf. δ 380 = 469, λ 292, ν 168, ψ 17, 353.—To constrain *to do something*. With infin. : Ἕκτορ' αὐτοῦ μεῖναι μοῖρα πέδησεν X 5.—Of one fate-bound to death or ruin : ὅτε μιν μοῖρ' ἐπέδησε δαμῆναι γ 269. Cf. σ 155.

πέδιλα, τά [πεδ-, ποδ, πούς]. Sandals : ποσσὶ δ' ὑπὸ λιπαροῖσιν ἐδήσατο καλὰ πέδιλα B 44 = K 22 = 132 = Ξ 186 : = β 4 = δ 309 = υ 126. Cf. Ω 340 : α 96, ν 225, ξ 23, π 80, etc.

πεδίον, -ου, τό. (1) The ground : λίθον κείμενον ἐν πεδίῳ H 265 = Φ 404. Cf. E 82, O 9, Π 749, P 621 : γ 260.—(2) (a) A stretch or tract of low-lying and more or less level ground, a plain : πολέος πεδίοιο θέουσαι (local genit., 'along . . .,' 'over . . .') Δ 244, τέμενος πεδίοιο ταμέσθαι (on the . . .) I 580, πεδία λωτοῦντα M 283. Cf. Z 507, Λ 677, 714, P 748, etc. : γ 431, 485, δ 602, ε 329, θ 122, ξ 267, etc.—(b) A particular plain. With defining words : π. τὸ Ἀλήϊον Z 201. Cf. I 577, Φ 558 : δ 563.—Referring especially to the Trojan plain B 473, Γ 133, 252, Z 2, H 66, Λ 496, etc.—Defined by accompanying words : Σκαμάνδριον B 465, Τρωϊκόν Ψ 464. Cf. K 11, O 739 : λ 513.

πεδίονδε [prec. + -δε (1)]. (1) To the earth : ἐξ οὐρανόθεν π. Θ 21. Cf. Ψ 189.—(2) To or towards the plain : ἔχον ἵππους Γ 263. Cf. Z 393, K 188, Λ 492, Ξ 31, P 750, Υ 148, Φ 3, 563, X 309, 456, Ω 401 : γ 421, ο 183.

πεδόθεν [πέδον, the ground + -θεν (1). 'From the ground (upwards)']. Wholly ; hence, constantly, ever : μύθων κλοπίων, οἵ τοι π. φίλοι εἰσίν ν 295.

πέδονδε [πέδον, the ground + -δε (1)]. To the (lower) ground : ἀνέμων ἀέλλῃ, ἥ τ' εἶσι πέδονδε (*i.e.* from the mountain-tops down upon the sea) N 796. Cf. λ 598.

πέζα, -ης, ἡ [for πέδja, fr. πεδ-, ποδ-, πούς]. The extremity of the pole of a chariot, app. curved to receive the yoke Ω 272.

πεζός [for πεδjός, fr. πεδ-, ποδ-, πούς]. (1) On foot : ὄρνυτο π. E 13. Cf. Δ 231, E 204, I 329 (in forays by land), Λ 230 (as a foot-soldier), 341, 721, N 385, P 612, Ω 438 : α 173 = ξ 190 = π 224, γ 324 (by land), ζ 319, ι 50, λ 58, 159, π 59.—(2) Absol. in pl., fighters on foot, footmen : πεζοί θ' ἱππῆές τε B 810 = Θ 59 : = ω 70. Cf. Δ 274, 298, Λ 150, 529, 724, M 59, Ψ 133 : ξ 267 = ρ 436.

πείθω. 2 sing. fut. πείσεις A 132, Z 360, Λ 648,

Σ 126, Ω 219, 433 : ξ 363. 3 πείσει I 345. Infin. πεισέμεν Ε 252, I 315. πείσειν Χ 357. 2 sing. fut. πιθήσεις φ 369. Fut. πεπιθήσω Χ 223. 3 sing. aor. opt. πείσειε I 386 : ξ 123. 1 pl. aor. subj. πεπίθωμεν I 112. 1 pl. opt. πεπίθοιμεν Α 100. 3 πεπίθοιεν I 181, Ψ 40. Fem. pple. πεπιθοῦσα Ο 26. Infin. πεπιθεῖν I 184. Aor. pple. πιθήσας Δ 398, Ζ 183, I 119, Λ 235, Ν 369, Ρ 48, Χ 107 : φ 315. Pf. πέποιθα Ν 96 : π 71, φ 132. 3 sing. πέποιθε Ψ 286 : π 98, 116. 3 pl. πεποίθᾱσι Δ 325. Subj. πεποίθω ω 329. 2 sing. πεποίθῃς Α 524 : ν 344. 1 pl. πεποίθομεν κ 335. Pple. πεποιθώς, -ότος Β 588, Δ 303, Ζ 505, Μ 135, Π 624, Ρ 329, Σ 158, Ψ 319, etc. : ζ 130, η 34, ι 107, υ 289. Plupf. πεποίθεα δ 434, θ 181. 3 sing. ἐπεποίθει Π 171. 1 pl. ἐπέπιθμεν Β 341, Δ 159, Ξ 55. **Mid.** Imp. πείθευ Ξ 235. Fut. πείσομαι Η 286, Ψ 96 : ε 358. 2 sing. πείσεαι I 74. 3 πείσεται Λ 789. 3 pl. πείσονται Θ 154, Ψ 157 : π 280. Infin. πείσεσθαι Α 289, 296, 427, Υ 466 : γ 146. Aor. πιθόμην Ε 201, I 453, Χ 103 : ι 228. 3 dual πιθέσθην Ο 156. 3 pl. (ἐ)πίθοντο Γ 260, Η 379, I 79, Μ 109, 468, Ξ 133, 378, Ο 300, Ψ 54, 249, 738 : γ 477, ζ 71, 247, ι 44, κ 178, 428, μ 222, ο 220, 288, υ 157, χ 178, ψ 141. 2 sing. subj. πίθηαι Α 207, Φ 293, Ψ 82 : α 279. 3 πίθηται Α 420, Λ 791. 1 pl. πιθώμεθα Σ 273. 2 sing. opt. πίθοιο Δ 93, Η 28, 48, Ξ 190 : δ 193, υ 381. 3 pl. πιθοίατο Κ 57. Imp. pl. πίθεσθε Α 259, 274, Σ 266 : λ 345, ω 461. 3 πιθέσθων I 167. Infin. πιθέσθαι Η 282, 293, Ν 726 : ρ 21. 3 sing. aor. opt. πεπίθοιτο Κ 204. (ἐπι-, παρα-.) (1) To induce or win over to an act or a course of action, to persuade, win over, prevail upon, urge successfully, to do or refrain from doing something : οὐδέ με πείσεις Α 132. Cf. Δ 104, Ε 252, Ζ 51, Ο 26, Χ 78, etc. : ἔπειθεν (ἔπειθον) Ἀχαιούς β 106 = ω 141, τ 151. Cf. α 43, η 258 = ι 33, ι 500, ψ 337.—With complementary infin. : τόνδε πεπιθήσω μαχέσασθαι Χ 223. Cf. Ψ 40.—(2) To induce to regard one with favour, win or bring over, prevail with : τότε κέν μιν ἱλασσάμενοι πεπίθοιμεν Α 100. Cf. I 112, 181, 184, 315, 345, 386, Μ 173.—(3) To induce to believe in the truth of something, win to a belief or assurance, convince : πείθεις μεν θυμόν ψ 230. Cf. ξ 123, 363, 392.—(4) In mid. and in fut. πιθήσω. (a) To yield to inducement, persuasion or command, yield, submit oneself, be ruled, obey, hearken to another, follow his lead, be guided by him, do his bidding : ἀλλὰ πίθεσθε Α 259. Cf. Α 207, 274, 427, Β 139, Γ 260, Ε 201, Η 121, 379, etc. : δμώεσσιν ἐκέκλετο, τοὶ δ' ἐπίθοντο ζ 71. Cf. α 279, γ 146, 477, ε 358, ι 44, μ 213, ο 288, etc. —With dat. of the person to whom or that to which one yields or submits oneself : ἐπείθετο μύθῳ Α 33, πείθονταί οἱ Ἀχαιοί Α 79. Cf. Α 150, 214, 273, Β 85, Δ 93, I 74, Μ 109, etc. : οὐκ εὖ πᾶσι πιθήσεις φ 369. Cf. β 227 (to humour him), γ 358, δ 193, κ 178, ο 541, ρ 21, etc.—With dat. and infin. : ἐῷ θυμῷ ἐλθεῖν Κ 204. Cf. ω 456.—Sim., to yield or resign oneself to something coming upon one in the course of nature. With dat. : ἀγαθὸν καὶ νυκτὶ πιθέσθαι Η 282 = 293. Cf. Ψ 48, 645, Θ 502 = I 65 : = μ 291.—(b) To bring oneself to believe in the truth of something, be convinced. With infin. : οὔ πω ἐπείθετο ὃν πατέρ' εἶναι π 192. Cf. Θ 154.—To believe in, be convinced by. With dat. : ἀγγελίῃ α 414.—(5) In pf. and plupf. and in the aor. pple. πιθήσας (these forms occurring only in this sense), and also (twice Δ 408 : υ 45) in mid. (a) To feel assurance or confidence, be satisfied : κεφαλῇ τοι κατανεύσομαι, ὄφρα πεποίθῃς Α 524. Cf. ν 344, ω 329.—(b) To put one's trust in, trust to, rely upon, commit oneself to, have trust or confidence in, be emboldened by. With dat. or instrumental : δεξιαί, ᾗς ἐπέπιθμεν Β 341, ἱπποσύνῃ τε καὶ ἠνορέηφι πεποιθώς Δ 303, θεῶν τεράεσσι πιθήσας 398, ἡγεμόνας τοῖς ἐπεποίθει Π 171. Cf. Ζ 505 (committing his going to his . . .), 510 (letting himself be carried away by it, exulting in it), I 119 (committing myself to the guidance of . . .), Λ 235 (giving it its way, following it up), Μ 135, Ν 96 (I look to you to . . .), 369, Ξ 55, Ρ 329, etc. : δ 434, ζ 130, η 34, θ 181, ι 107, κ 335, π 71 (feel confident of . . .), 98 = 116, υ 45, 289, φ 132, 315.

πείκω [app. a metrical lengthening of πέκω]. To comb or card (wool) : εἴρια πείκετε σ 316.

†πεινάω [πείνη]. Pres. pple. πεινάων, -οντος Γ 25, Π 758, Σ 162. Non-thematic infin. πεινήμεναι υ 137. To be hungry, suffer the pangs of hunger Γ 25, Π 758, Σ 162.—With genit., to hunger after : σίτου υ 137.

πείνη, ἡ. Famine, scarcity ο 407.

πειράζω [cf. πειράω]. To make proof or trial of (a person). With genit. : ἀνδρῶν π 319, ἐμέθεν ψ 114.—To make trial of a person's sagacity, try to elicit information from him, pump him : ὣς φάτο πειράζων ι 281.

†πειραίνω [πεῖραρ]. Dual masc. aor. pple. πειρήναντε χ 175, 192. 3 sing. pf. pass. πεπείρανται μ 37. (1) To attach (a cord) : σειρήν χ 175 = 192.—(2) To bring to an end, accomplish : ταῦτα πάντα πεπείρανται μ 37.

πεῖραν, 3 pl. aor. πείρω.

πεῖραρ, -ατος, τό. (1) A rope or cord : ἐξ αὐτοῦ πείρατ' ἀνήφθω (ἀνῆπτον) μ 51 = 162, 179.—Fig. of the rope of strife (see ἐπαλλάσσω) Ν 359.—(2) In derived senses (app. coming through the notion of a measuring-rope, but the original sense in the end quite lost sight of). (a) An end, limit, boundary : πείρατα γαίης Ξ 200, 301. Cf. Θ 478 : δ 563, ι 284, λ 13.—(b) The end or termination of something. In pl. : οὔ πω ἐπὶ πείρατ' ἀέθλων ἤλθομεν ψ 248.—(c) The coming to pass, the crisis or supreme moment, of something (cf. τέλος (5)). In pl. : ὡς κεν θᾶσσον ὀλέθρου πείραθ' ἵκηαι Ζ 143 = Υ 429. Cf. Η 402, Μ 79 : χ 33, 41. —(d) An extreme stage or crisis of something : μέγα π. ὀϊζύος ε 289.—(e) A decision or determination : ἐπὶ ἵστορι π. ἑλέσθαι Σ 501.—(f) The issue or event in respect of something. In pl. : νίκης πείρατα Η 102.—(g) In pl., the final or essential points, the sum or substance, of something (cf.

τέλος (7)): ἐπεὶ ᾧ παιδὶ ἑκάστου πεῖρατ' ἔειπεν Ψ 350.—So, app.: ὅπλα, πείρατα τέχνης (in which the exercise of art lies) γ 433.

πειράω. Also in mid. and pass. as deponent. (1) To make a trial or test: αἰγανέης, ἥν ἀνὴρ ἀφέῃ πειρώμενος (for practice) Π 590.—To make trial of, try, test. With genit.: πειρήθη ἕο αὐτοῦ Τ 384. Cf. Ο 359, Ψ 432: φ 282, 410.—With acc.: τροχόν Σ 601.—(2) In hostile sense, to make an attempt upon a person or place, try one's fortune, try conclusions: πρίν γε νὼ σὺν ἔντεσι πειρηθῆναι Ε 220, τρὶς τῇ γ' ἐλθόντες ἐπειρήσαντο (delivered an assault) Ζ 435. Cf. Ε 129, 279, Λ 386, Ν 457, 806, Χ 381 (make a demonstration), Ψ 553. —With dependent clause. With ἤ . . . ἤ . . . Φ 225.—Of trying one's fortune in a contest θ 205, 213.—With genit., to make an attempt upon, try conclusions with: μήλων Μ 301, Ἀχιλῆος Φ 580. Cf. Τ 70, Υ 349, 352, Ψ 804: ζ 134.—(3) To make trial of a person, tempt him, lead him on Β 73, 193.—With genit.: πειρᾷ ἐμεῖο Ω 390, 433. Cf. Ι 345.—(4) To try, test, put to the proof, in regard to veracity, knowledge, fidelity, ability, or the like. With genit.: ἀέθλους, τοὺς (cognate acc., 'in which') Φαίηκες ἐπειρήσαντ' Ὀδυσῆος θ 23, νῦν σευ ὀΐω πειρήσεσθαι τ 215. Cf. Κ 444: ν 336, π 305, ψ 181, ω 216.—Absol. δ 119 = ω 238, ω 240.—(5) To try to find out about something, go in quest of information: πειρήσομαι ἠδὲ ἴδωμαι ζ 126.—With genit.: τῶνδ' ἀνδρῶν πειρήσομαι, οἵ τινές εἰσιν ι 174.—So, to examine: τόξον ἐνώμα, πειρώμενος [αὐτοῦ] φ 394.—(6) To find out about to one's cost, experience. With genit.: τῶν ἔμελλον Ἀχαιοὶ πειρήσεσθαι φ 418.—(7) To make trial, try what one can do, make an attempt, try one's skill: εἰ δ' ἄγε μὴν πείρησαι (try it) Α 302. Cf. Θ 18: ἐπειρήσαντο πόδεσσιν θ 120. Cf. γ 23 (am not practised in . . .), δ 417 (will try to escape), θ 149, 377, φ 184.—To attempt, try one's hand at or on, set one's hand to. With genit.: ἵνα πειρησαίμεθα ἔργου σ 369. Cf. Ψ 707, 753 = 831: θ 100, 126, 145, 184, φ 113, 135, 159, 180 = 268. —(8) To endeavour, do one's endeavours, try, attempt, set oneself, *to do something*. With infin.: τῷ πειρήσω ἀλαλκεῖν ἄγρια φῦλα Τ 30. Cf. Δ 5, Θ 8, Μ 341.—With dependent clause. With ὡς: πειρᾶν ὡς πεπίθοιεν Πηλεΐωνα Ι 181. Cf. Δ 66 = 71, Φ 459: β 316.—With ὅπως δ 545.

πεῖρε, 3 sing. aor. πείρω.

πειρήναντε, dual masc. aor. pple. πειραίνω.

πειρητίζω [πειράω]. (1) To make trial of, try, test, put to the proof. With genit.: σθένεός τε καὶ ἀλκῆς χ 237.—To make trial of, make an experiment with. With genit.: τόξου πειρήτιζεν (*i e.* tried to string it) φ 124 = 149.—(2) In hostile sense, to make an attempt upon a person, make an assault or attack: ἔθελεν ῥῆξαι στίχας ἀνδρῶν πειρητίζων Ο 615.—To make an attempt upon, assault, attack: στίχας ἀνδρῶν πειρητίζων Μ 47.— (3) To try, test, put to the proof in regard to courage, good will, fidelity, or the like. With genit.: μή μευ ἠΰτε παιδὸς πειρήτιζε (*i.e.* try to frighten me) Η 235: συβώτεω ξ 459 = ο 304. Cf. π 313.—(4) To pursue a quest, make investigation or search: ἄσσον ἴεν ἀλωῆς πειρητίζων ω 221. —(5) To endeavour, try, attempt, *to do something.* With infin.: ῥήγνυσθαι τεῖχος Μ 257.

πείρινς, -ινθος, ἡ. A receptacle of some kind fixed upon a waggon Ω 190, 267: ο 131.

πείρω. 3 sing. aor. ἔπειρε Ι 210, Υ 479: ξ 75. πεῖρε Π 405: β 434. 3 pl. ἔπειραν Α 465, Β 428: γ 462, μ 365, ξ 430. πεῖραν Η 317, Ω 623: τ 422. **Pass.** Pf. pple. πεπαρμένος -η, -ον Α 246, Ε 399, Λ 633, Φ 577. (ἀμ-.) To drive something pointed through, pierce, transfix: ἥλοισι πεπαρμένον (studded with . . .) Α 246, Λ 633, τὸν διὰ χειρὸς ἔπειρεν αἰχμῇ Υ 479. Cf. Φ 577: ἰχθῦς ὣς πείροντες (spearing) κ 124.—Fig.: ὀδύνῃσι πεπαρμένος Ε 399. —To drive (something through something): διὰ δ' αὐτοῦ πεῖρεν [ἔγχος] ὀδόντων Π 405.—To spit (meat) Α 465 = Β 428, Η 317 = Ω 623, Ι 210: γ 33, 462 = μ 365 = ξ 430, ξ 75, τ 422.—To cleave (waves): ἀνδρῶν τε πτολέμους κύματά τε πείρων (app. with a zeugma) Ω 8: = θ 183 = ν 91 = 264.—With cognate acc.: νηῦς πεῖρε κέλευθον (cleft her way) β 434.

πεῖσα, -ης, ἡ [prob. as πεῖσμα]. Obedience, subjection: ἐν πείσῃ κραδίη μένεν υ 23.

πείσεσθαι[1], fut. infin. mid. πείθω.

πείσεσθαι[2], fut. infin. mid. πάσχω.

πεῖσμα, -ατος, τό [πενθ-, to bind. Cf. πενθερός]. A ship's cable ζ 269, ι 136, κ 96, 127, ν 77, χ 465. —A rope or fastening in general κ 167.

πείσομαι[1], fut. mid. πείθω.

πείσομαι[2], fut. mid. πάσχω.

†**πέκω** [cf. πείκω]. Aor. pple. fem. mid. πεξαμένη. To comb: χαίτας Ξ 176.

πέλαγος, τό. The deep sea, the high sea Ξ 16: γ 91, 174, 179, 321, ε 330.—Joined with ἅλς: ἁλὸς ἐν πελάγεσσιν (app., in the depths of the sea) ε 335.

πελάζω [πέλας]. Aor. ἐπέλασσα ξ 350. 3 sing. πέλασε Δ 123, Θ 277, Μ 112, 194, Π 418: ξ 315. ἐπέλασσε Ο 418, Φ 93: γ 291, 300, δ 500, η 277, ο 482. πέλασσε Β 744, Ν 1: ε 111, 134, ι 39. 3 pl. πέλασαν Α 434, Ξ 435: η 254, μ 448, χ 193. ἐπέλασσαν ξ 358. 2 sing. subj. πελάσῃς λ 106. 3 πελάσῃ μ 41. πελάσσῃ Ν 180, Ω 154, 183. 1 pl. πελάσσομεν κ 424. Infin. πελάσαι χ 176. πελάσσαι Ψ 719: κ 440. Imp. pl. πελάσσατε κ 404. Dual aor. imp. πελάσσετον Κ 442. **Mid.** 3 pl. aor. opt. πελασαίατο Ρ 341. **Pass.** 3 sing. aor. πελάσθη Ε 282. 3 pl. πέλασθεν Μ 420. 3 sing. aor. πλῆτο Ξ 438. 3 pl. ἔπληντο Δ 449, Θ 63. πλῆντο Ξ 468. Pf. pple. πεπλημένος μ 108. (προσ-.) (1) To bring into contact with, cause to touch. With dat.: ἱστὸν ἱστοδόκῃ (lowered it to the . . .) Α 434, νευρὴν μαζῷ Δ 123, πάντας χθονί (brought them to the ground) Θ 277 = Μ 194 = Π 418. Cf. Ν 180, Ξ 435 (laid him on the ground), Ψ 719 (to throw him): ξ 350 (entered the water on my breast), χ 176, 193.—With οὖδάσδε κ 440.—Fig.: ὀδύνῃσί ἑ πελάζειν (to bring . . . upon him) Ε 766.—(2) In more general sense, to bring, carry, conduct, to a specified or indicated place, to bring or take into a specified or indicated position or neighbourhood: ἐπεί ῥ' ἐπέλασσέ γε δαίμων O 418, Φ 93. Cf. ε 111=134, η 254=μ 448, κ 404, 424.—With dat.: Τρῶας νηυσὶν N 1. Cf. B 744, K 442, Ω 154 and 183 (bring into his presence): γ 291, 300, δ 500, η 277, ι 39, λ 106, ξ 315, 358, ο 482.—In mid. P 341.—(3) *Intrans. for reflexive*, to draw near, approach: ὅς τις ἀϊδρείῃ πελάσῃ μ 41.—To draw near to, approach. With dat.: πέλασεν νήεσσιν M 112.—(4) In pass. (a) To come near to or in contact with, to touch. With dat.: ἀσπίδες ἔπληντ' ἀλλήλῃσιν Δ 449= Θ 63, ἐξοπίσω πλῆτο χθονί (fell back on the ground) Ξ 438. Cf. E 282, Ξ 468: μ 108 (skirting it).—(b) To come into an indicated position or neighbourhood: ἐπεὶ τὰ πρῶτα πέλασθεν (when once they had made good their approach) M 420.

πέλας. Near, close: χριμφθεὶς κ 516.—Close to, near, beside. With genit.: Τηλεμάχου ο 257.

πέλασ(σ)ε, 3 sing. aor. πελάζω.

πέλεθρον, -ου, τό. A measure (app. considerable) of length or area: ἐπ' ἐννέα κεῖτο πέλεθρα λ 577. Cf. Φ 407.

πέλεια, ἡ. A wild dove or pigeon Φ 493: ο 527, χ 468.—Joined with τρήρων X 140, Ψ 853, 855, 874: μ 62, υ 243.

πελειάς, -άδος, ἡ. =prec. Λ 634.—Joined with τρήρων E 778.

πελεκκάω [πέλεκυς]. To shape with the axe: πελέκκησε [δοῦρα] χαλκῷ ε 244.

πέλεκκον, -ου, τό [cf. πέλεκυς]. An axe-handle: ἀξίνην, ἐλαΐνῳ ἀμφὶ πελέκκῳ N 612.

πέλεκυς, ὁ. Dat. pl. πελέκεσσι N 391, O 711, Π 484. An axe (referred to both as in peaceful and in warlike use (cf. ἀξίνη); distinguished from ἡμιπέλεκκον Ψ 851): πίτυς, τὴν τέκτονες ἄνδρες ἐξέταμον πελέκεσσιν N 391=Π 484, πελέκεσσι καὶ ἀξίνῃσι μάχοντο (the two words hardly to be distinguished) O 711. Cf. Γ 60, P 520, Ψ 114, 851, 856, 882: γ 442, 449, ε 234, ι 391, τ 573, 578=φ 76, φ 120, 260, 421.

πελεμίζω. 3 sing. aor. πελέμιξε Φ 176: φ 125. Infin. πελεμίξαι Π 108. 3 sing. aor. pass. πελεμίχθη Δ 535, E 626, N 148, Π 612, P 528. (1) To cause to quiver or vibrate, shake: ὕλην Π 766. Cf. N 443.—To shake or force out of position: [σάκος] Π 108.—To shake in impatience of effort, apply violent force to: τρὶς πελέμιξε μελίην (τόξον) ἐρύσσασθαι μενεαίνων Φ 176: φ 125.—(2) In pass., to quiver, vibrate, shake: πελεμίζετ' Ὄλυμπος Θ 443. Cf. Π 612=P 528.—To reel, lose one's footing, stagger Δ 535=E 626=N 148.

πελέσκεο, 2 sing. pa. iterative mid. πέλω.

πέλλα, ἡ. A milk-pail Π 642.

πέλω, and in mid. form **πέλομαι** (without distinction of sense) [orig. sense 'to turn']. 3 sing. aor. ἔπλε M 11. **Mid.** Imp. πέλευ Ω 219. 2 sing. pa. iterative πελέσκεο X 433. 2 sing. aor. ἔπλεο A 418, X 281. ἔπλευ I 54, Π 29, Ψ 69, 891. 3 ἔπλετο A 506, B 480, Δ 479, M 271, N 677, T 57, X 116, Ω 94, etc.: α 225, β 364, ε 392, κ 273, ν 145, ρ 57, σ 113, χ 48, etc. (ἀμφι-, ἐπιπέλομαι, περιπέλομαι.) (1) To turn out to be, come to be, become, come into being, and simply, to be: ὃς ἕρκος Ἀχαιοῖσιν πέλεται (is) A 284, ἠΰτε κλαγγὴ γεράνων πέλει (is to be heard, goes up) Γ 3, μινυνθάδιός οἱ αἰὼν ἔπλετο Δ 479. Cf. Γ 287, Δ 158, E 729 (stood out), I 592 (come upon them), K 351, 531, Λ 392, N 237, 632 (are your doing), Ξ 158, Π 128, T 221, 365, X 443 (might be ready), Ω 524 (comes of . . .), etc.: δῶ οἱ ἀφνειὸν πέλεται α 393, γαλήνη ἔπλετο ε 392, ἐν γυνὴ πέλεν ω 211. Cf. β 276, δ 45, ε 79, ζ 108, θ 169, λ 125, ν 60 (come upon them), ξ 20 (numbered), ρ 57, σ 367 (come round), τ 192, χ 48, etc.—(2) In aor. also, to have turned out to be, have come to be; hence, to be: ὠκύμορος περὶ πάντων ἔπλεο (art) A 418, ἔνθα μάλιστ' ἐπίδρομον ἔπλετο τεῖχος (is) Z 434. Cf. A 506, H 31, I 54, M 271, Ξ 337, O 227, Π 29, T 57, Ψ 69, Ω 94, etc.: τίς ὅμιλος ὅδ' ἔπλετο; (is) α 225, κρατερὴ μοι ἔπλετ' ἀνάγκη (has come upon me) κ 273. Cf. β 364 (has come), η 217, θ 571, ν 145, σ 113, υ 304, φ 397, etc.

πέλωρ, τό. A being of uncommon size or strength or of peculiarly daunting or portentous aspect (cf. πέλωρον). Of Hephaestus Σ 410.—Of the Cyclops ι 428.—Of Scylla μ 87.

πελώριος [πέλωρ]. Of uncommon size or strength, great, huge, prodigious, wondrous: ἄνδρα (Agamemnon) Γ 166, Αἴας (Αἴαντα) 229, H 211, P 174, 360, Ἀΐδης E 395, ἔγχος 594, Θ 424, Περίφαντα E 842, 847, Ἄρης H 208, τεύχεα K 439, Σ 83, Ἕκτορα Λ 820, Ἀχιλῆα Φ 527, X 92: κύματα γ 290, ἀνήρ (the Cyclops) ι 187, θαῦμα 190, Ὠρίωνα λ 572, λᾶαν 594.

πέλωρον, τό. =πέλωρ. Of the portents that appeared at Aulis B 321.—Of the Gorgon E 741: λ 634.—Of the Cyclops ι 257.—Of the deer taken by Odysseus in Circe's island κ 168.—Of the creatures transformed by Circe κ 219.

πέλωρος, -ον [πέλωρ]. =πελώριος: δράκοντα M 202=220: χῆνα ο 161.

†πεμπάζομαι [πέμπε, Aeolic form of πέντε]. 3 sing. aor. subj. πεμπάσσεται. To count, reckon up: ἐπὴν πάσας πεμπάσσεται δ 412.

πεμπταῖος [as prec.]. On the fifth day: πεμπταῖοι Αἴγυπτον ἱκόμεσθα ξ 257.

πέμπτος, -η, -ον [as prec.]. The fifth Π 197, Ψ 351 (was the fifth who . . .), 615: ε 263, ι 335 (made the fifth), ω 309.—Coming fifth in a contest. Absol.: πέμπτῳ φιάλην ἔθηκεν Ψ 270.

πέμπω. Fut. πέμψω A 184: α 93, δ 589, ε 140, 167, π 81, 83, σ 84, φ 342. 3 sing. -ει ξ 517, ο 34, 339. 1 pl. -ομεν φ 309. 3 -ουσι δ 564, ε 37, ξ 333, τ 290. Infin. πέμψειν Φ 48. πεμψέμεναι κ 484. 2 sing. aor. πέμψας O 27. 3 ἔπεμψε A 442: λ 623, 626. πέμψε Σ 240, Φ 43. 3 pl. ἔπεμψαν δ 586, ρ 149. πέμψαν ψ 340. Subj. πέμψω β 133, ζ 255. 2 sing. -ῃς Π 445. 1 pl. -ωμεν υ 383. Opt. πέμψαιμι φ 374. 2 sing. -ειας ι 350. 3 -ειε λ 635. Imp. πέμψον K 464, Ω 310, 430: γ 369, ε 25. Pple. pl. πέμψαντες α 38. Infin. πέμψαι B 6: ι 524, ξ 336, 396. (ἀπο-, ἐκ-, παρα-, προ-.) (1) To send, send forth, cause to go, dispatch: αἴ κε ζῶν πέμψῃς Σαρπηδόνα ὅνδε δόμονδε Π 445. Cf. Ο 27, Π 447, 671, 681, Σ 240, Φ 48, Ψ 137: δόμον Ἄϊδος εἴσω ι 524. Cf. δ 8, 29, 564, ι 461, λ 635, σ 84, υ 383, φ 309, 374, ω 419.—To send away or back: αἴ κ' ἀπὸ μητέρα πέμψω β 133. Cf. Α 184, Φ 43.—(2) To send or dispatch on an errand or mission or for some specified or indicated purpose (the purpose sometimes expressed by an infin. or fut. pple.): πρό μ' ἔπεμψεν Ἀγαμέμνων παῖδα σοὶ ἀγέμεν Α 442, πέμψαι ἐπ' Ἀγαμέμνονι Ὄνειρον Β 6. Cf. Γ 116, Ζ 168, 207, Ι 253 = 439 = Λ 766, Ι 438, 575, Π 240, 454 (to bear him), 575, Σ 237, 452, Ω 310: Ἑρμείαν πέμψαντες α 38, ἐνθάδε μ' ἔπεμψε κύν' ἄξοντα λ 623. Cf. δ 5 (*i.e.* as his bride), 799, ν 66.—(3) In reference to inanimate objects, to send, cause to go: ἐκ θεμείλια κύμασι πέμπεν Μ 28: οὖρον ε 167. Cf. ο 34.—To send or dispatch by an intermediary: εἵματ' ἐνθάδε καὶ σῖτον π 83. Cf. δ 623.—To send (evil upon a person) Ο 109.—(4) To dispatch on one's way, speed, arrange for or preside over the departure of: σὺ δὲ τοῦτον πέμψον σὺν δίφρῳ καὶ υἱέϊ γ 369. Cf. Ω 780: δ 589, ε 140, 263, η 227 = ν 48, η 264, ι 350, κ 18, 484, ν 39, 52, 206, ξ 396, 517 = ο 339, ο 15, 74, π 81 = φ 342, τ 461, ψ 315.—(5) To conduct, convoy, convey, take with one, bring, escort, see safe: Χρυσηΐδα ἐς Χρύσην Α 390. Cf. Κ 464, Ω 430: ὄφρα σε πέμψω πατρὸς ἐμοῦ πρὸς δῶμα ζ 255. Cf. α 93, δ 560 = ε 17 = 142 = ρ 146, δ 586 = ρ 149, ε 25, 37, θ 556, λ 626, ξ 333 = τ 290, ξ 336, π 228 = υ 188, τ 281, ψ 340.

πεμπώβολον, -ου, τό [πέμπε as in πεμπάζομαι + ὀβελός]. A five-pronged sacrificial fork Α 463: = γ 460.

πέμψω, fut. πέμπω.

πενθερός, -οῦ, ὁ [πενθ-, to bind]. A father-in-law, one's father-in-law Ζ 170: θ 582.

πενθέω [πένθος]. Also **πενθείω** (πενθεσίω, fr. πενθεσ-, πένθος). Non-thematic pres. infin. πενθήμεναι σ 174, τ 120. 3 dual impf. πενθείετον Ψ 283. To mourn, sorrow, grieve σ 174, τ 120. —To mourn for Ψ 283.—To pay mourning rites to: νέκυν Τ 225.

πένθος, τό. (1) Pain of the mind, sorrow, grief, woe, trouble, distress: τί σε φρένας ἵκετο πένθος; Α 362. Cf. Α 254, Ι 3, Λ 249, Ρ 37, Ω 105, etc.: α 342, β 70, ζ 169, η 218, σ 324 (feeling for her), ω 231, etc.—(2) A cause of sorrow or grief: τῷ μὲν κλέος ἄμμι δὲ π. Δ 197 = 207.

πενίη, -ης, ἡ [πένομαι]. Poverty, want, need: πενίῃ εἴκων ξ 157.

πενιχρός [πένομαι]. Poor, destitute of the comforts and conveniences of life. Absol. γ 348.

πένομαι [cf. πόνος]. (ἀμφι-.) (1) To work at something, be busy, busy oneself: περὶ δεῖπνον δ 624 = ω 412. Cf. Ω 124: κ 348.—(2) To direct one's energies to, attend to, be busied, busy oneself, about, trouble oneself about: ὣς οἱ τὰ πένοντο Α 318. Cf. Σ 558, Τ 200: β 322, γ 428, δ 531, 683, ν 394, ξ 251, π 319, χ 199, ω 407.

πεντάετες [πεντ-, πέντε + -α- (on the analogy of numerals in -α) + ἔτος]. For five years: παραμίμνων γ 115.

πενταέτηρος [as prec.]. Five years old: βοῦν Β 403, Η 315: τ 420, ὗν ξ 419.

πένταχα [πέντε]. In five divisions Μ 87.

πέντε, *indeclinable* [cf. L. *quinque*, Eng. *five*]. Five Κ 317, Π 171, Σ 481, Υ 270, Ψ 833: γ 299, ζ 62.

πεντήκοντα, *indeclinable* [πέντε]. Fifty Β 509, 556, 685, 719, Δ 393, Ε 786, Ζ 244, Λ 678, 748, Π 168, 170, Ψ 147, Ω 495: η 103, μ 130, ξ 15, υ 49, χ 421, ω 342.—Absol.: παρ' ἑκάστῳ ἥατο π. Θ 563. —With another numeral: ἑκατὸν καὶ π. Λ 680: δύω καὶ π. θ 35, 48, π 247.

πεντηκοντόγυος [πεντήκοντα + γύης, a measure of land. Cf. τετράγυος]. Containing fifty measures Ι 579.

πεντηκόσιοι [πέντε + ἑκατόν]. Five hundred. Absol.: πεντηκόσιοι ἐν ἑκάστῃ ἥατο γ 7.

πεξαμένη, aor. pple. fem. mid. πέκω.

πεπαθυίῃ, dat. sing. fem. pf. pple. πάσχω.

πεπαλαγμένος, pf. pple. pass. παλάσσω.

πεπάλακτο, 3 sing. plupf. pass. παλάσσω.

πεπαλάσθαι, aor. infin. mid. πάλλω.

πεπάλασθε, imp. pl. aor. mid. πάλλω.

πεπαρμένος, pf. pple. pass. πείρω.

πέπασθε, 2 pl. pf. πάσχω.

πεπάσμην, plupf. πατέομαι.

πεπείρανται, 3 sing. pf. pass. πειραίνω.

πεπερημένος, pf. pple. pass. περάω[2].

πέπηγε, 3 sing. pf. πήγνυμι.

πεπιθεῖν, aor. infin. πείθω.

πεπιθήσω, fut. πείθω.

πέπληγον, 3 pl. thematic plupf. πλήσσω.

πεπληγώς, pf. pple. πλήσσω.

πεπλημένος, pf. pple. pass. πελάζω.

πέπλος, -ου, ὁ. (1) A cloth or cover: ἀμφὶ [δίφροις] πέπλοι πέπτανται Ε 194. Cf. Ω 796.—A cloth put on a seat for ease in sitting η 96.—(2) A woman's (or goddess's) robe Ε 315, 338, 734 = Θ 385, Ζ 90, 271, 289, 302, Ω 229: ζ 38, ο 105, 124, σ 292.

πέπνῡμαι, *pf.* [prob. fr. πνῡ-, to be vigorous, and conn. with ἐμπνύνθη, πινύσσω, πινυτός, ποιπνύω]. (1) To be in full mental vigour, have one's mental powers unimpaired: τῷ νόον πόρε Περσεφόνεια οἴῳ πεπνῦσθαι κ 495.—To be of sound understanding, have good sense: οὔ σ' ἔτυμόν γε φάμεν πεπνῦσθαι Ψ 440. Cf. Ω 377: ψ 210.—(2) In pple. πεπνυμένος, wise, of sound understanding, of good sense, astute, shrewd, sagacious: Οὐκαλέγων τε καὶ Ἀντήνωρ, πεπνυμένω ἄμφω Γ 148. Cf. Η 276, Ι 689, Ψ 570: γ 20 = 328, γ 52, δ 190, 204, θ 388, σ 65, 125, τ 350.—Epithet of Antenor Γ 203, Η 347.—Of Meriones Ν 254 = 266.—Of Poulydamas Σ 249.—Of Antilochus Ψ 586.—Of Telemachus α 213, 367, 388, χ 461, etc.—Of Laertes ω 375.—Applied to discourse or counsel: μήδεα Η 278. Cf. α 361 = φ 355, β 38, σ 230, τ 352. —Absol.: πεπνυμένα βάζεις Ι 58: δ 206, πεπνυμένα εἰδώς 696, 711, χ 361, ω 442, ὅς κεν πεπνυμένα εἰδῇ θ 586.

πέποιθα, pf. πείθω.

πεπόλιστο, 3 sing. plupf. pass. πολίζω.

πέπονθα, pf. πάσχω.

πέποσθε, 2 pl. pf. πάσχω.

πεπότηται, 3 sing. pf. ποτάομαι.

πέπρωται, 3 sing. pf. pass. πόρω.

πέπταται, 3 sing. pf. pass. πετάννυμι.

πεπτεῶτας, acc. pl. masc. pf. pple. πίπτω.

πεπτηώς, pf. pple. πτήσσω.

πεπύθοιτο, 3 sing. aor. opt. πεύθομαι.

πεπυκασμένος, pf. pple. pass. πυκάζω.

πέπυσμαι, pf. πεύθομαι.

πέπων [πεπ-, πέσσω. 'Ripened, softened']. Only in voc. sing. and pl. πέπον, πέπονες. (1) Used in courteous or affectionate address: πέπον Καπανηϊάδη (good . . .) E 109. Cf. O 437, Π 492.—Applied by the Cyclops to his ram: κριὲ πέπον (my pet) ι 447.—Absol. in courteous or affectionate address or remonstrance: ὦ πέπον, ὦ Μενέλαε (good brother of mine) Z 55, (ὦ) πέπον (gentle sir, good friend or brother or brother in arms) I 252, Λ 314, 765, M 322, O 472, Π 628, P 120, 179, 238: ν 154, χ 233.—(2) Used in reproach. Absol.: ὦ πέπονες (weaklings) B 235, N 120.

περ, *enclitic* [shorter form of περί]. (1) Intensive particle, very, even, indeed, just, or the like: ἀγαθός περ ἐών (you the great warrior, *i.e.* implying that he should be content with that) A 131, ὡς ἔσεταί περ 211, τιμήν πέρ μοι ὄφελλεν ἐγγυαλίξαι (honour, surely, he ought to have . . .) 353, οἴκαδέ περ νεώμεθα (let us not stop short of home) B 236, ἀλλά περ οἶος ἴτω (even if he come alone) M 349. Cf. A 260, 416, Γ 201, Δ 263, Λ 391, 789, N 72, Ξ 295, O 604, etc.: σοί περ (thee whom it might be expected to touch) α 59, οὔ κε θανόντι περ ὧδ' ἀκαχοίμην (if I had just his death to mourn) 236, κηδόμενοί περ (in our sore trouble) γ 240. Cf. α 315, β 305, γ 236, δ 819, θ 360, 547, ν 294, etc.—With εἰ, ἤν A 81, 580, B 123, T 32, X 487, etc.: α 167, 188, 204, β 246, θ 355, etc.—With relatives: ὅς περ, ὅ περ B 318, I 367, N 638, etc.: β 156, η 55, λ 630, etc.—οἷός περ E 340, etc.: λ 394, etc.—ὅθι περ B 861, etc.: δ 627, etc.—ὅθεν περ γ 321, φ 142.—ἔνθα περ Z 379, etc.: α 128, etc.—ἔνθεν περ φ 243 = 392.—(2) With a sense of opposition, though, even though (gen. in ppl. construction): ἀχνύμενός περ (however much . . .) A 241, μινυνθάδιόν περ ἐόντα (short-lived though I be) 352, σύ πέρ μιν τεῖσον (since Agamemnon will not) 508, ἀνάσχεο κηδομένη περ 586. Cf. A 546, B 246, Γ 159, E 94, I 301 (if not him), Ξ 375, Φ 185, etc.: ἱέμενός περ α 6. Cf. α 288, 309, β 249, ε 209, ζ 136, ι 57, λ 111, etc.—For καὶ . . . περ, καί περ see καί (6).—With ἔμπης. See ἔμπης (4).

περάᾱν[1], pres. infin. περάω[1].

περάᾱν[2], pres. infin. περάω[2].

περαιόω [cf. περάω[1]]. To convey across; in pass., to pass over, cross, the sea: μὴ φθέωσι περαιωθέντες ω 437.

πέρασαν, 3 pl. aor. περάω[2].

περάτη, -ης, ἡ [app. fr. περάω[1]]. Thus, the passage of night, the space which darkness traverses in the course of a night ψ 243.

περάω[1] [cf. πόρος]. 3 pl. pres. περόωσι δ 709, ε 176, ζ 272, ι 129. Infin. περάᾱν B 613, M 63: ε 174. 3 sing. pa. iterative περάασκε ε 480, τ 442. Fut. infin. περήσειν E 646. περησέμεναι M 200, 218. 3 sing. aor. ἐπέρησε E 291, Φ 594. πέρησε Δ 460, 502, Z 10. 1 pl. περήσαμεν ω 118. Subj. περήσω Ψ 71. 2 sing. περήσῃς κ 508. Infin. περῆσαι M 53: λ 158. (ἐκ-.) (1) To pass, make one's or its way: ἐπὶ πόντον B 613, διὰ κροτάφοιο πέρησεν αἰχμή Δ 502. Cf. Π 367: δ 709, ε 176, κ 508.—(2) To cross, get to the other side of (an obstacle): τάφρος, οὐ περῆσαι ῥηϊδίη M 53. Cf. M 63, 200, 218, Φ 283: λ 158.—To traverse, make one's way over the surface of or across: λαῖτμα θαλάσσης ε 174. Cf. ζ 272, ι 129, ω 118.—(3) To pass into or through, penetrate: πέρησεν ὀστέον εἴσω αἰχμή Δ 460 = Z 10. Cf. E 291: ε 480, τ 442.—Absol. Φ 594.—To pass through (an opening): πύλας 'Αΐδαο E 646, Ψ 71.

†**περάω**[2] [cf. πέρνημι]. Pres. infin. περάᾱν Φ 454. Aor. πέρασσα Φ 102. 2 sing. πέρασσας Φ 78. 3 ἐπέρασσε Φ 40. 3 pl. ἐπέρασσαν ο 387. πέρασαν ο 428. 2 pl. subj. περάσητε ο 453. 3 sing. opt. περάσειε ξ 297. **Pass.** Pf. pple. πεπερημένος Φ 58. To sell into slavery: Λῆμνόν μιν ἐπέρασσεν (to one dwelling in Lemnos) Φ 40. Cf. Φ 58, 78, 102, 454: ξ 297, ο 387, 428, 453.

πέρην [cf. περάω[1]]. Beyond, on or to the other side of. With genit.: οἳ ναίουσι πέρην Εὐβοίης B 535 (*i.e.* to one looking from Asia; by others taken as 'over against'). Cf. B 626, Ω 752.

πέρησε, 3 sing. aor. περάω[1].

πέρθω [cf. πορθέω]. Fut. infin. πέρσειν Φ 584. Aor. πέρσα Υ 192. 3 sing. ἔπερσε α 2. πέρσε Z 415, Λ 625, T 296, Υ 92. 3 pl. opt. πέρσειαν Φ 517. Pple. πέρσας B 660, Π 57. Pl. πέρσαντες ε 107, ξ 241. Aor. ἔπραθον ι 40. 3 pl. ἔπραθον Σ 454. **Pass.** 3 sing. fut. πέρσεται Ω 729. Non-thematic aor. infin. πέρθαι (for πέρθ-σ-σθαι) Π 708. (δια-, ἐκ-.) To sack or ravage (a town): πέρσας ἄστεα πολλά B 660. Cf. B 374, Z 415, M 15, Π 57, Σ 342, T 296, etc.: α 2, ε 107, ι 40, ξ 241.

περί. (Commonly with anastrophe when immediately following the vb. or case-form or beginning a sentence. Also often written πέρι in sense (I) (3).) (I) Adv. (1) Round, about, round about, someone or something: περί ἑ χαλκὸς ἔλεψεν A 236, πολλοὶ περὶ κτείνοντο Δ 538. Cf. B 19, 43, E 776, Z 320, Λ 395, N 570, P 243, Σ 402, etc.: β 391, δ 719, η 87, ι 141, 395, ν 189, ρ 439, σ 201, etc.—In reference to seasons coming round: περὶ δ' ἔτραπον ὧραι κ 469. Cf. κ 470, τ 153 = ω 143.—With notion of protection: πέρι Ποσειδάων Νέστορος υἱὸν ἔρυτο N 554.—Joined with ἀμφί Φ 10, Ψ 191.—(2) In reference to spinning or twirling motion, round and round: περὶ σχεδίην ἐλέλιξεν ε 314. Cf. Ξ 413.—(3) Beyond measure, exceedingly, very much: περὶ κῆρι Δ 53,

N 119, πέρι πολέμῳ ἔνι καρτερός ἐσσι I 53. Cf. H 289, Θ 161, I 100 (more than others), N 727, P 22, etc.: ἅ οἱ πέρι δῶκεν β 116. Cf. α 66, β 88, γ 95, θ 44, μ 279, ξ 146, χ 96, etc.—Especially, in particular: πέρι δ' αὖ Πριάμοιό γε παίδων Φ 105.—(4) In reference to survivance, beyond something: πόλεμον περὶ τόνδε φυγόντε M 322. Cf. T 230.—(5) In the matter of, in regard to, something: περὶ τεύχε' ἕπουσιν O 555.—(II) Prep. (1) With dat. (a) Round, about, round about: περὶ Σκαιῇσι πύλῃσιν Σ 453. Cf. A 303, B 389, Γ 330, Λ 559, M 148, Ψ 561, etc.: περὶ ζώνην βάλετ' ἰξυῖ ε 231. Cf. β 3, ι 144, 394, ο 60, φ 407, etc.—In reference to a transfixing or piercing weapon: κυλινδόμενος περὶ χαλκῷ Θ 86. Cf. N 441, Π 315, Φ 577, etc.: λ 424.—Joined with ἀμφί λ 609.—(b) With notion of protection: ἑσταότες περὶ Πατρόκλῳ P 355, etc. Cf. ρ 471, etc.—For βαίνειν περί τινι see βαίνω (I) (6) (a) and cf. περιβαίνω.—(c) In reference to contention *over* something: ὄφρα περὶ παιδὶ πόνος εἴη Π 568. Cf. ε 310.—(d) In reference to motion *about the inside of* something: κνίση ἑλισσομένη περὶ καπνῷ A 317. Cf. X 95.—(e) About, concerning, for: περὶ γὰρ δίε ποιμένι λαῶν E 566. Cf. I 433, K 240, etc.: β 245.—(2) With acc. (a) Round, about, round about: μαρνάμενοι περὶ ἄστυ Z 256. Cf. A 448, B 750, Δ 211, Λ 535, M 177, Ψ 309, etc.: ἣν πέρι πύργος ζ 262. Cf. γ 107, δ 792, θ 282, ι 402, λ 42, ρ 261, etc.—In reference to the φρένες: τὸν περὶ φρένας ἤλυθ' ἰωή K 139, etc. Cf. ι 362.—Round or about and upon: ἣν περὶ Φόβος ἐστεφάνωται E 739, etc.—Joined with ἀμφί B 305, P 760.—(b) Round about the inside of: ἑλισσόμενοι περὶ δίνας Φ 11.—Round about on the inside of: ἑστάμεναι περὶ τοῖχον μεγάροιο Σ 374. Cf. M 297 (see κύκλος (1)): η 95.—So κρημνοὶ περὶ πᾶσαν [τάφρον] ἕστασαν ἀμφοτέρωθεν M 54.—So also of concentric circles of metal forming a whole Λ 33 (see κύκλος (1)).—(c) About, over: περὶ κεῖνα ἠλώμην δ 90. Cf. δ 368.—(d) About, concerning, for, in the matter of: περὶ δόρπα πονέοντο Ω 444. Cf. Γ 408: δ 624 = ω 412.—(3) With genit. (a) Round, about, round about: ἡ τετάνυστο περὶ σπείους ἡμερίς ε 68. Cf. ε 130 (see βαίνω (I) (3) (a)). (b) Beyond, excelling, superior to: ὃς περὶ πάντων ᾔδεε μαντοσύνας B 831. Cf. A 258, 287, Δ 46, 375, E 325, Θ 27, N 374, etc.: ὃς περὶ νόον ἐστὶ βροτῶν α 66. Cf. α 235, δ 201, 608, λ 216, etc.—(c) About, concerning, for, touching, in the matter of: μαχήσονται περὶ σεῖο Γ 137. Cf. H 301, Λ 700, M 216, 423, O 284, Σ 265, etc.: ἵνα μιν περὶ πατρὸς ἔροιτο α 135. Cf. η 191, θ 225, ι 423, λ 403, π 234, ρ 563, 571, etc.—With notion of protection: ἀμύνονται περὶ τέκνων M 170. Cf. Θ 476, M 142, 243, Π 497, P 147, etc.: ω 39.

περιάγνῡμι [περι- (1)]. In pass., of sound, to break about one, echo round: Ἕκτορος [ὄψ] περιάγνυται Π 78.

†**περιβαίνω** [περι- (1)]. 3 sing. aor. περίβη Θ 331, N 420. 3 pl. περίβησαν Ξ 424. Pple. περιβάς P 80. Acc. sing. masc. περιβάντα P 313. Infin. περιβῆναι E 21. To bestride and protect a fallen friend (cf. βαίνω (I) (6) (a)): θέων περίβη Θ 331 = N 420. Cf. Ξ 424.—With genit.: ἀδελφειοῦ E 21.—With dat.: Πατρόκλῳ P 80. Cf. P 313.

περιβάλλω [περι- (1) (3)]. (1) To throw *round*. With genit.: πεῖσμα περίβαλλε θόλοιο χ 466.—In mid., to put about oneself, put on: περιβαλλομένους τεύχεα χ 148.—(2) To excel, be preeminent, be first: ὅσσον ἐμοὶ ἀρετῇ περιβάλλετον ἵπποι Ψ 276.—To excel, outrival, surpass: περιβάλλει ἅπαντας μνηστῆρας δώροισιν ο 17.

περίβη, 3 sing. aor. περιβαίνω.

περιγίγνομαι [περι- (3)]. To excel, outrival, surpass. With genit.: ὅσσον περιγιγνόμεθ' ἄλλων θ 102 = 252.—To prove superior to, get the better of, beat. With genit.: μῆτι ἡνίοχος περιγίγνεται ἡνιόχοιο Ψ 318.

περιγλαγής [περι- (4) + γλάγος]. Overflowing with milk: πέλλας Π 642.

περιγνάμπτω [περι- (2)]. To round (a promontory): περιγνάμπτοντα Μάλειαν ι 80.

†**περιδείδια**, *pf. with pres. sense* K 93, N 52, P 240, 242 [περι- (5) (6) + δείδια. See δείδοικα]. 3 pl. aor. περίδεισαν (περίδϝεισαν) Λ 508. Nom. pl. masc. pple. περῑδείσαντες Ψ 822. Nom. sing. fem. περῑδείσᾱσα O 123, Φ 328. (1) To be greatly afraid N 52.—(2) To feel fear *on account of*, fear *for*. With genit.: Δαναῶν K 93. Cf. P 240.—With dat.: ἐμῇ κεφαλῇ P 242. Cf. Λ 508, O 123, Φ 328, Ψ 822.

περιδέξιος [περι- (1) + δεξιός. App., 'righthanded on both sides']. Thus, ambidextrous Φ 163.

†**περιδίδωμι** [περι- (with what force is not clear) + δίδωμι]. Fut. mid. περιδώσομαι ψ 78. 1 dual aor. subj. περιδώμεθον Ψ 485. To stake, wager, hazard. With genit. of what is staked or hazarded: ἐμέθεν περιδώσομαι αὐτῆς ψ 78. Cf. Ψ 485.

περίδραμον, 3 pl. aor. περιτρέχω.

περίδρομος, -ον [περι- (1) (2) + δρομ-, δραμ-. See τρέχω]. (1) Running round, set round, surrounding: ἄντυγες E 728.—(2) Running round, rotating: πλῆμναι E 726.—(3) Such as one can run round, standing apart: κολώνη B 812: αὐλή (*i.e.* with a cleared space round it) ξ 7.

†**περιδρύπτω** [περι- (1)]. 3 sing. aor. pass. περιδρύφθη. To tear all round, lacerate: ἀγκῶνας περιδρύφθη (had his elbows all torn) Ψ 395.

†**περιδύω** [περι- (1)]. 3 sing. aor. περίδῡσε. App., to strip off from round one: χιτῶνας Λ 100.

περιδώμεθον, 1 dual aor. subj. mid. περιδίδωμι.

περιδώσομαι, fut. mid. περιδίδωμι.

περίειμι [περι- (3) + εἰμί]. 2 sing. περίεσσι σ 248. To be superior to, excel, surpass. With genit.: εἴ τι γυναικῶν ἀλλάων περίειμι νόον τ 326. Cf. σ 248.

†**περιέχω** [περι- (1)]. 1 pl. aor. mid. περισχόμεθα ι 199. Imp. περίσχεο A 393. In mid., to throw one's arms *round*; hence, to protect, come to the aid of. With genit.: παιδὸς ἑῆος A 393.—With acc.: μιν ι 199.

περιῄδη, 3 sing. plupf. περίοιδα.

περιηχέω [περι- (1) + ἠχέω, fr. ἠχή]. To ring all round: περιήχησε χαλκός H 267.

περιθεῖεν, 3 pl. aor. opt. περιτίθημι.

περιίδμεναι, infin. περίοιδα.

†**περιίστημι** [περι- (1)]. 3 pl. aor. περίστησαν Δ 532. 3 pl. subj. περιστήωσι P 95. 3 pl. opt. περισταῖεν υ 50. 3 sing. impf. mid. περιίστατο Σ 603. 3 pl. aor. περιστήσαντο B 410: μ 356. 3 sing. aor. pass. περιστάθη λ 243. To take one's stand round about: περίστησαν ἑταῖροι Δ 532.—In pass., of an arching wave, to remain stationary round something, enfold it, cover it from view: κῦμα περιστάθη κυρτωθέν λ 243.—In mid. and non-sigmatic aor., to stand *round*, surround. With acc.: μή με περιστήωσιν P 95, πολλὸς χορὸν περιίσταθ' ὅμιλος Σ 603: εἴ περ πεντήκοντα λόχοι νῶϊ περισταῖεν υ 50.—So in mid. in sigmatic aor.: βοῦν περιστήσαντο B 410. Cf. μ 356.

περικαλλής, -ές [περι- (6) + κάλλος]. (Like καλός often used merely as a more or less conventional epithet.) (1) In reference to personal beauty. (a) Of a woman, fair, lovely, beauteous, comely E 389, Π 85: λ 281.—(b) Of parts of the body, fair, lovely, beauteous, goodly: δειρήν Γ 396: ὄσσε ν 401, 433.—(2) Of things of use, buildings, constructions, etc., well-made, well-constructed, fair, goodly, fine, beauteous, or the like: φόρμιγγος A 603, δίφρον Γ 262, δόμον Γ 421. Cf. Z 321, Θ 238, Λ 632, Ψ 897, Ω 229, etc.: αὐλῆς α 425, στειλειόν ε 236, χηλόν θ 438. Cf. α 153, γ 481, κ 347, ν 149, ρ 343, χ 438, etc.—(3) In various applications as an epithet of general commendation, fair, goodly, fine, or the like: φηγῷ E 693, τέμενος I 578: ἔργα β 117 = η 111, λίμνην γ 1, ποταμοῖο ῥόον ζ 85, ἀγρούς ξ 263 = ρ 432.—Of light, fair, bright: φάος τ 34.

περίκειμαι [περι- (1) (3)]. (1) To be set *about*, enclose, cover. With dat.: γωρυτῷ, ὃς τόξῳ περίκειτο φ 54.—So, to lie upon and embrace: Πατρόκλῳ T 4.—(2) To be laid up for one in excess of others, *i.e.* to remain as profit: οὐδέ τί μοι περίκειται (it profits me nothing) I 321.

περικήδω [περι- (5)]. In mid., to be solicitous for the welfare or good of, care *for*, take thought *for*. With genit.: Ὀδυσσῆος γ 219, βιότου ξ 527.

περίκηλος [περι- (6) + an uncertain second element]. Very dry: δένδρεα ε 240, ξύλα σ 309.

περικλυτός [περι- (6) + κλυτός]. (1) Famed, famous, renowned. Epithet of persons: υἱόν Σ 326: ἀοιδός α 325, θ 83 = 367 = 521.—With a proper name: Ἄντιφος Λ 104.—Of towns: Μυρμιδόνων ἄστυ δ 9, ἄστυ π 170, ω 154.—Of Hephaestus A 607, Σ 383, 393 = 462, 587, 590: θ 287, 300, 349, 357, ω 75.—(2) Epithet of things, fine, splendid, noble: ἔργα Z 324, δῶρα H 299, I 121, Σ 449.

περικτίονες [περι- (1) + κτι-, κτίζω]. Dat. pl. περικτιόνεσσι Σ 212, T 104, 109. Dwelling round about: ἀνθρώπους β 65. Cf. P 220.—Absol., the dwellers round about: πάντεσσι περικτιόνεσσιν ἀνάξει (ἀνάξειν) T 104, 109. Cf. Σ 212.

περικτῖται, οἱ [as prec.]. = prec. Absol.: τὴν πάντες μνώοντο περικτῖται λ 288.

†**περιμαιμάω** [περι- (1)]. Fem. pres. pple. περιμαιμώωσα. To quest *round*. With acc.: σκόπελον μ 95.

περίμετρος [περι- (6) + μέτρον]. Very long: ἱστόν (consisting of long threads) β 95 = ω 130, τ 140.

περιμήκετος, -ον [as next]. Of great height, lofty: ἐλάτην Ξ 287: Τηΰγετον ζ 103.

περιμήκης, -ες [περι- (6) + μῆκος]. (1) Of great length, long: κοντόν ι 487. Cf. κ 293, μ 90, 251, 443.—(2) Of great height, lofty: πέτρης N 63. Cf. ν 183.—Of great upward size, standing high: ἱστοὶ λίθεοι ν 107.

†**περιμηχανάομαι** [περι- (5)]. 3 pl. pres. περιμηχανόωνται η 200. 3 pl. impf. περιμηχανόωντο ξ 340. To contrive (something) in regard to someone or to someone's prejudice: ἄλλο τόδε θεοὶ περιμηχανόωνται η 200.—To contrive (something) *in regard to* or *to the prejudice of*. With dat.: δούλιον ἦμαρ ἐμοὶ περιμηχανόωντο ξ 340.

περιναιέται, οἱ [περι- (1) + ναίω[1]]. The dwellers round about: κεῖνον π. τείρουσιν Ω 488.

περιναιετάω [περι- (1)]. To dwell round about: οἳ κατὰ ἄστυ [εἰσὶ] καὶ οἳ περιναιετάουσιν θ 551. Cf. β 66, ψ 136.—Of cities, by a sort of personification, to have their place or lie round about: μίαν πόλιν, [τάων] αἳ περιναιετάουσιν δ 177.

περιξεστός, -ή [περι- (6) + ξεστός]. Highly polished, very smooth μ 79.

περίοιδα, *pf. with pres. sense* [περι- (3) (6) + οἶδα. See εἴδω (C)]. Infin. περιίδμεναι N 728. 3 sing. plupf. περιῄδη ρ 317. (1) To have great skill, be highly skilled: ἴχνεσι περιῄδη ρ 317.—With infin.: νοῆσαι K 247.—(2) To have greater skill than, excel, surpass. With genit.: καὶ βουλῇ περιίδμεναι ἄλλων N 728.

†**περιπέλομαι** [περι- (1) (2)]. Aor. pple. περιπλόμενος, -ου. (1) To be *round about*, encircle, compass about. With acc.: ἄστυ Σ 220.—(2) In aor. pple. of the revolving year (cf. περιτέλλομαι): πέντε περιπλομένους ἐνιαυτούς Ψ 833. Cf. α 16, λ 248.

περιπευκής, -ές [περι- (6) + πευκ- as in πευκεδανός]. Exceeding sharp, piercing Λ 845.

†**περιπλέκω** [περι- (1)]. 3 sing. aor. pass. περιπλέχθη ψ 33. Pple. περιπλεχθείς ξ 313. In pass. with dat., to put one's arms *round*, grasp in one's arms: ἱστῷ περιπλεχθείς ξ 313.—To embrace: γρηῒ περιπλέχθη ψ 33.

περιπληθής [περι- (6) + πλῆθος]. Having many inhabitants, populous: νῆσος ο 405.

περιπλόμενος, aor. pple. περιπέλομαι.

περιπρό [περι- (6) + πρό]. Ever forward, with constant rush: ἔγχεϊ θῦεν Λ 180, Π 699.

†**περιπροχέω** [περι- (1) + προ- (1)]. Aor. pple. pass. περιπροχυθείς. In pass., fig., of passion, to come upon one, invade the mind: ἔρος περιπροχυθείς Ξ 316.

περιρρέω [περι- (2)]. To flow *about*. With acc.: μοχλὸν αἷμα περίρρεεν ι 388.

περιρρηδής [περι- (1) + (perh.) ῥηδ-, ῥαδ- as in

ῥαδινός]. Thus, doubled *round*, sprawling *over*. With dat. : τραπέζῃ χ 84.

περίρρυτος, -ον [περι- (1) + ῥυ-, ῥέω]. Flowed round (by the sea), sea-girt : Κρήτῃ τ 173.

περισθενέω [περι- (6) + *σθενέω, fr. σθένος]. To be exceeding strong : μή με περισθενέων δηλήσεται (in his might) χ 368.

περίσκεπτος [περι- (1) + σκεπ-, σκέπτομαι]. Exposed to view from every side, open, clear (cf. περιφαίνομαι (2)) : χώρῳ α 426, κ 211 = 253, ξ 6.

περισσαίνω [περι- (1)]. Of animals, to move about a person and fawn upon him κ 215, π 10. —To move *about* and fawn upon. With acc. : Τηλέμαχον περίσσαινον κύνες π 4.

περισσείω [περι- (1)]. In pass., to wave or float about something : περισσείοντ' ἔθειραι Τ 382, Χ 315.

περισταδόν [περι- (1) + στα-, ἵστημι]. Standing round : Τρῶες π. οὔταζον σάκος Ν 551.

περιστάθη, 3 sing. aor. pass. περιίστημι.

περισταῖεν, 3 pl. aor. opt. περιίστημι.

περιστείλᾱσα, aor. pple. fem. περιστέλλω.

†**περιστείχω** [περι- (2)]. 2 sing. aor. περίστειξας. To walk or pace *round*. With acc. : κοῖλον λόχον δ 277.

†**περιστέλλω** [περι- (1)]. Aor. pple. fem. περιστείλᾱσα. To dress or lay out (a corpse) : οὐδέ ἑ μήτηρ κλαῦσε περιστείλασα ω 293.

περιστεναχίζομαι [περι- (1)]. To resound or re-echo *about*. With dat. : δῶμα περιστεναχίζεται αὐλῇ κ 10. Cf. ψ 146.

περιστένω [περι- (6) + στένω = στείνω]. In pass., to be glutted : περιστένεται γαστήρ Π 163.

περιστέφω [περι- (1)]. To enwreathe, cover up : νεφέεσσι περιστέφει οὐρανὸν Ζεύς ε 303.

περίστησαν, 3 pl. aor. περιίστημι.

περιστήσαντο, 3 pl. aor. mid. περιίστημι.

περιστήωσι, 3 pl. aor. subj. περιίστημι.

†**περιστρέφω** [περι- (2)]. Aor. pple. περιστρέψας. To whirl round (before a throw) Τ 131 : θ 189.

περισχόμεθα, 1 pl. aor. mid. περιέχω.

περιτάμνω [περι- (1)]. To surround and cut off (cattle) in order to make booty of them (cf. τάμνω (9)). In mid. λ 402, ω 112.

περιτέλλομαι [περι- (2)]. In pple. of the revolving year (cf. περιπέλομαι (2), περιτροπέω (2)) : περιτελλομένων ἐνιαυτῶν Β 551. Cf. Θ 404 = 418 : λ 295 = ξ 294.

†**περιτίθημι** [περι- (1)]. 3 pl. aor. opt. περιθεῖεν. To put *about*. Fig., to endow (one) with. With dat. : αἲ γὰρ ἐμοὶ θεοὶ δύναμιν περιθεῖεν γ 205.

περίτρεσαν, 3 pl. aor. περιτρέω.

περιτρέφω [περι- (1)]. In pass., to become curdled, curdle : ὦκα [γάλα] περιτρέφεται Ε 903. —Of ice, to be deposited, grow thick, *about*. With dat. : σακέεσσι περιτρέφετο κρύσταλλος ξ 477.

†**περιτρέχω** [περι- (1)]. 3 pl. aor. περίδραμον. To run up and stand round Χ 369.

†**περιτρέω** [περι- (1)]. 3 pl. aor. περίτρεσαν. To flee on all sides : λαοὶ περίτρεσαν Λ 676.

περιτρομέω [περι- (1)]. To tremble or quiver *round* or *about*. With dat., in mid. : σάρκες περιτρομέοντο μέλεσσιν σ 77.

περιτροπέω [περι- (1) (2)]. **(1)** To surround and drive (into a compact flock) : μῆλα ι 465.—**(2)** In pple. of the revolving year (cf. περιτέλλομαι) : εἴνατος περιτροπέων ἐνιαυτός Β 295.

περίτροχος [περιτρέχω]. Round, circular : σῆμα Ψ 455.

περιφαίνομαι [περι- (1)]. In pple. **(1)** Seen from all round, conspicuous : ὄρεος περιφαινομένοιο Ν 179.—**(2)** = περίσκεπτος. Absol. : ἐν περιφαινομένῳ (in, bordering upon, a clearing) ε 476.

περιφραδέως [adv. fr. περιφραδής, fr. περι- (6) + φραδής]. With great care, carefully : ὤπτησαν Α 466 = Β 429 = Η 318 = Ω 624 : = ξ 431, τ 423.

περιφράζομαι [περι- (5)]. To take counsel concerning (something), devise, contrive : περιφραζώμεθα νόστον α 76.

περίφρων, -ονος [περι- (6) + φρήν]. Voc. περίφρον π 435, σ 245, 285, φ 321. Of great good sense, wise, sage, prudent. Epithet of women. Of Aegialeia Ε 412.—Of Penelope α 329, δ 787, ε 216, ξ 373, etc.—Of Arete λ 345.—Of Eurycleia τ 357, 491 = υ 134, φ 381.

†**περιφύω** [περι- (1)]. Aor. pple. περιφύς π 21, ω 320. Fem. περιφῦσα τ 416. Infin. περιφῦναι ω 236. To grow round ; hence, to throw one's arms round a person, embrace him : Τηλέμαχον κύσεν περιφύς π 21. Cf. ω 320.—To throw one's arms *round*, embrace. With dat. : περιφῦσ' Ὀδυσῆϊ τ 416.—With acc. : κύσσαι καὶ περιφῦναι ἐὸν πατέρα ω 236.

†**περιχέω** [περι- (1)]. 3 sing. aor. περίχευε γ 437, η 140, ψ 162. 3 sing. subj. περιχεύῃ γ 426. Pple. περιχεύας Κ 294, Φ 319 : γ 384. 3 sing. aor. subj. mid. περιχεύεται ζ 232, ψ 159. **(1)** To shed or spread something round or over another thing : χέραδος περιχεύας Φ 319.—To shed *round*. With dat. : ἠέρ', ἥν οἱ περίχευεν Ἀθήνη η 140.—So of something immaterial : τῷ περίχευε χάριν ψ 162. —**(2)** To spread *round*, put *round* as a covering or adornment. With dat. : χρυσὸν κέρασιν περιχεύας Κ 294 : = γ 384. Cf. γ 426, 437.—So of spreading one metal on the ground of another in, app., some process of enamel : ὡς ὅτε τις χρυσὸν περιχεύεται ἀργύρῳ ζ 232 = ψ 159.

†**περιχώομαι** [περι- (5)]. 3 sing. aor. περιχώσατο. To be angered or wroth, conceive anger or wrath, *about* or *on account of*. With genit. : παλλακίδος μοι περιχώσατο Ι 449. Cf. Ξ 266.

περιωπή, -ῆς, ἡ [περι- (1) + ὀπ-. See ὁράω]. A spot commanding a view on all sides, a look-out place : ἀνήϊον ἐς περιωπήν κ 146. Cf. Ξ 8, Ψ 451.

περιώσιος [περι- + an uncertain second element]. In neut. sing. περιώσιον as adv., beyond measure : θαυμάζειν π 203. Cf. Δ 359.

περκνός (ὑποπερκάζω). App., dappled, spotted with dark : αἰετόν, ὃν καὶ περκνὸν καλέουσιν Ω 316.

πέρνημι [cf. περάω[2]]. 3 sing. pa. iterative πέρνασκε Ω 752. To export for sale, sell to foreign buyers : πολλὰ Φρυγίην κτήματα περνάμεν' ἵκει Σ 292.—To sell into slavery: περνὰς νήσων ἔπι τηλεδαπάων Χ 45. Cf. Ω 752.

περονάω [περόνη]. (1) To pierce, transfix Η 145, Ν 397.—(2) In mid., to fasten (a garment) about one with a περόνη (or ἐνετή): ἐνετῇσι κατὰ στῆθος περονᾶτο [ἑανόν] Ξ 180. Cf. Κ 133.

περόνη, -ης, ἡ [πείρω]. Something for piercing; a clasp, buckle, or brooch for fastening a garment about one. In connexion with a woman's dress Ε 425: σ 293.—With a man's τ 226, 256.

περόωσι, 3 pl. pres. περάω[1].

πέρσα, aor. πέρθω.

περῶντα, acc. sing. masc. pres. pple. περάω[1].

πέσε, 3 sing. aor. πίπτω.

πεσέονται, 3 pl. fut. πίπτω.

πεσσός, -οῦ, ὁ. A pebble or 'man' used in playing a game the rules of which are unknown: πεσσοῖσι θυμὸν ἔτερπον α 107.

πέσσω [πεπ-. Later πέπτω. Cf. πέπων]. (κατα-.) (1) To ripen, bring to maturity η 119.—(2) To digest. Fig.: γέρα πεσσέμεν (to brood over them, enjoy them) Β 237, χόλον πέσσει (πέσσων) (nurses (nursing) it, keeps (keeping) it warm) Δ 513, Ι 565, ὥς τις βέλος πέσσῃ (may hug his wound) Θ 513, κήδεα πέσσει (πέσσω) (broods (brood) upon them, dwells (dwell) upon them) Ω 617, 639.

πεσών, aor. pple. πίπτω.

πέταλον, -ου, τό. A leaf Β 312: τ 520.

†πετάννῡμι. 3 sing. aor. πέτασε ε 269. 3 pl. πέτασαν ζ 94. πέτασσαν Α 480: δ 783, θ 54. 3 sing. opt. πετάσειε σ 160. Pple. πετάσσας Δ 523, Θ 441, Ν 549, Ξ 495, Φ 115: α 130, ε 374, ι 417, κ 506, ω 397. **Pass.** 3 pl. aor. πετάσθησαν φ 50. Nom. pl. fem. pple. πετασθεῖσαι Φ 538. 3 sing. pf. πέπταται ζ 45. 3 pl. πέπτανται Ε 195. Acc. pl. fem. pple. πεπταμένας Φ 531. 3 sing. plupf. πέπτατο Ρ 371. (ἀνα-.) (1) To spread, spread out, spread wide: ἀν' ἱστία πέτασσαν Α 480. Cf. Δ 523 = Ν 549, Ε 195, Θ 441, Ξ 495, Φ 115: ὑπὸ λῖτα πετάσσας α 130. Cf. δ 783, ε 269, 374, ζ 94, θ 54, ι 417, κ 506, ω 397.—Fig., app., to flutter or set agog: θυμὸν μνηστήρων σ 160.—(2) Of a gate or door, to open, throw open, open wide: πεπταμένας πύλας ἔχετε Φ 531. Cf. Φ 538: φ 50.—(3) In pass., of clear sky, to be outspread over something: αἴθρη πέπταται ζ 45.—Of light, to be shed, play: πέπτατ' αὐγὴ ἠελίου Ρ 371.

πετεηνός, -όν [πετ-εσ-ηνός, fr. πέτομαι]. (1) Able to fly, fledged π 218. — Winged. Epithet of birds Β 459, Ο 690.—(2) Absol., in neut. pl., winged creatures, birds: αἰετόν, τελειότατον πετεηνῶν Θ 247 = Ω 315. Cf. Ο 238, Ρ 675, Φ 253, Χ 139: ν 87.

πέτομαι [cf. πίπτω]. 3 sing. aor. ἔπτατο Ε 99, Ν 587, 592, Π 469: κ 163, λ 208, μ 203, ο 531, τ 454, ω 534. πτάτο Ψ 880. 3 sing. subj. πτῆται (app. for πτάεται) Ο 170. Pple. fem. πταμένη Ε 282, Π 856, Χ 362. (ἀπο-, δια-, εἰσ-, ἐπι-, ὑπερ-.) To fly. (1) Of winged creatures: βοτρυδὸν [μέλισσαι] πέτονται Β 89, κλαγγῇ γέρανοι πέτονται Γ 5. Cf. Μ 207 (flew off), Ν 62, Π 265: β 147, 148, ο 531.—(2) Of the flight through the air of divine horses Ε 366 = Θ 45, Ε 768.—Of gods Ο 150.—Of the flight of Poseidon's horses on the water Ν 29.—Of rapid motion of mortal horses Κ 530, Ο 684, Π 149, Ψ 381, etc.: γ 484 = 494 = ο 192.—(3) Of the flight of the soul of men, etc., from the body: ψυχὴ ἐκ ῥεθέων πταμένη Π 856 = Χ 362. Cf. Ψ 880, Π 469: = κ 163 = τ 454.—(4) Of rapid motion of men: ἐμμεμαὼς ἰθὺς πέτετο Χ 143. Cf. Ν 755, Φ 247, Χ 198, Ω 345: = ε 49, θ 122.—Sim.: τρίς μοι ἐκ χειρῶν ἔπτατο [μητρὸς ψυχή] λ 208.—(5) Of an arrow or a thrown spear: διὰ δ' ἔπτατ' ὀϊστός Ε 99, τῆς διαπρὸ αἰχμὴ πταμένη 282. Cf. Ν 587, 592, Υ 99.—Sim. of a καλαῦροψ Ψ 846.—(6) Of other inanimate things: [ὀλοοίτροχος] πέτεται Ν 140. Cf. Ο 170: μ 203, ω 534.

πετραῖος, -η [πέτρη]. That dwells in a rock: Σκύλλην μ 231.

πέτρη, -ης, ἡ [cf. πέτρος]. (1) A rock or cliff on land or in or bordering upon the sea: πέτρης ἐκ γλαφυρῆς Β 88. Cf. Β 617, Δ 107, Ι 15, Ν 137, Ω 614, etc.: πέτρης ἐκ πείσματα δήσας κ 96. Cf. γ 293, δ 501, ε 443, θ 508, μ 59, 241, ν 408, ψ 327, etc.—(2) The rock forming the walls of a cave: περὶ δ' ἴαχε πέτρη ι 395, ὁρμαθοῦ ἐκ πέτρης (attached at each end to the walls) ω 8.—(3) A large detached mass of stone, a rock: κατερχομένης ὑπὸ πέτρης ι 484 = 541. Cf. ι 243.—(4) For οὐκ ἀπὸ δρυὸς οὐδ' ἀπὸ πέτρης see δρῦς (3).

πετρήεις, -εσσα [πέτρη]. Rocky, rugged: νῆσος δ 844 —Epithet of places Β 496, 519, 640, Ι 405.

πέτρος, -ου, ὁ [cf. πέτρη]. A stone: βάλε πέτρῳ Π 411. Cf. Η 270, Π 734, Υ 288.

πεύθομαι. Also **πυνθάνομαι** β 315, ν 256. Fut. πεύσομαι ψ 262. 2 sing. -εαι Σ 19. 3 -εται Υ 129: β 256. Pple. πευσόμενος, -ου α 94, 281, β 215, 264, 360, ν 415, ο 270. Aor. πυθόμην δ 732, ξ 321, ψ 40. 3 dual πυθέσθην Ρ 427. 3 pl. ἐπύθοντο Ε 702, Ο 224, 379, Σ 530. 2 sing. subj. πύθηαι Ε 351, Ρ 685, Ω 592: γ 15, δ 494. 3 -ηται Τ 337: δ 713, τ 486. 2 pl. -ησθε θ 12. 3 -ωνται Η 195. Opt. πυθοίμην Ρ 102, Τ 322: β 43, κ 147. 3 -οιτο Κ 207, 211: β 31. 3 pl. -οιατο Α 257. Infin. πυθέσθαι Β 119, Ζ 465, Κ 308, 320, 395, Λ 649, Χ 305: κ 152, 155, 537, λ 50, 76, 89, ν 335, ο 377, φ 255, ω 433. 3 sing. aor. opt. πεπύθοιτο Ζ 50, Κ 381, Λ 135. Pf. πέπυσμαι λ 505. 2 sing. πέπυσσαι λ 494. 3 πέπυσται β 411, ρ 510. Infin. πεπύσθαι Ρ 641. 3 sing. plupf. ἐπέπυστο Ν 674. πέπυστο Ν 521, Χ 437. 3 dual πεπύσθην Ρ 377. (1) To hear. Absol. or with object: σιγῇ, ἵνα μὴ Τρῶές γε πύθωνται Η 195, Διὸς κτύπον Ο 379. Cf. Ε 351, Κ 207, Σ 530: α 157 = δ 70 = ρ 592, κ 147, τ 486, ψ 40.—In reference to a report or rumour: πεύθετο Κύπρονδε μέγα κλέος Λ 21 (*i.e.* the report came as far as to Cyprus).—To overhear: βουλάς δ 677 = π 412.—With genit., to hear: σῆς βοῆς Ζ 465. Cf. Ο 224.—So in reference to tidings: λυγρῆς ἀγγελίης Ρ 641, 685, Σ 19. Cf. β 256.—(2) To hear of, learn of, come to know of or about, something. Absol. or with object (sometimes with complementary adj. or pple.): καὶ ἐσσομένοισι πυθέσθαι B 119, X 305, εἴ κεν ἐμὲ ζωὸν πεπύθοιτο Z 50 = K 381, κλέα ἀνδρῶν I 524. Cf. E 702, Λ 135, N 674, T 322 (the object in 326), Υ 129: νῦν δὲ πυνθάνομαι (learn the story, am getting to realize what is going on) β 315, ὅσσα πεύθομαι (what I hear from time to time) γ 187, εἰ πυθόμην ταύτην ὁδὸν ὁρμαίνοντα δ 732. Cf. β 31, 43, 411 (knows nothing of the matter), δ 494, λ 76, π 134, ρ 158, φ 255, ψ 262, ω 433.—With genit. of the person about whom something is heard: οὔ πω πεπύσθην Πατρόκλοιο θανόντος P 377. Cf. A 257, N 521, P 102, 427, T 322, 337, X 437: θ 12, λ 494, 505, ξ 321, ρ 510.—With genit. of the person from whom something is heard: τό γε μητρὸς ἐπεύθετο P 408.—With genit. of a thing heard about: Ἰθάκης ν 256.—With clause: ὅτι . . . Ω 592.—(3) To have heard, have learned, know (cf. ἀκούω (5)): οὐδέ πω Ἕκτωρ πεύθετο Λ 498.—With acc. of the person or thing known about: πεύθετο οὗ παιδὸς ὄλεθρον π 411.—With acc. and clause: ἄλλους πάντας πευθόμεθα, ἧχι . . . γ 87.—(4) To find out about something, seek or get information about it. Absol. or with object: ταῦτα πάντα K 211, νηῶν σχεδὸν ἐλθέμεν ἔκ τε πυθέσθαι (to get what information I can) K 320. Cf. α 94, β 215, 264, 360, δ 713, κ 152 (spy out the land), 155, ν 335, 415, ο 377.—With genit. of the person about whom something is to be found out: πατρὸς δὴν οἰχομένοιο α 281. Cf. γ 15, ο 270.—With genit. of the person from whom something is to be found out: πρὶν Τειρεσίαο πυθέσθαι (before getting directions from . . .) κ 537 = λ 50 = 89.—With clause: ἠὲ . . . ἦ . . . K 308, 395. Cf. Λ 649: δ 713, ι 88 = κ 100.

πευκάλιμος, -η. Wise, shrewd, astute: φρεσὶν Θ 366, Ξ 165, O 81, Υ 35.

πευκεδανός [πευκ-, sharp, prob. conn. with L. *pug-*, *pungo*. Cf. ἐχεπευκής, περιπευκής, πικρός]. Sharp, piercing. Epithet of war K 8.

πεύκη, -ης, ἡ. A pine-tree Λ 494.—A felled pine or a piece thereof: ξύλον πεύκης Ψ 328.

πεύσομαι, fut. πεύθομαι.

πέφανται[1], 3 sing. pf. pass. φαίνω.

πέφανται[2], 3 pl. pf. pass. φένω.

πεφάσθαι, pf. infin. pass. φένω.

πεφασμένον, acc. sing. masc. pf. pple. pass. φαίνω.

πέφαται, 3 sing. pf. pass. φένω.

πεφεύγοι, 3 sing. pf. opt. φεύγω.

πεφήσεαι, 2 sing. fut. pass. φένω.

πεφήσεται[1], 3 sing. fut. pass. φαίνω.

πεφήσεται[2], 3 sing. fut. pass. φένω.

πεφιδέσθαι, aor. infin. φείδομαι.

πεφιδήσεται, 3 sing. fut. φείδομαι.

πέφνον, aor. φένω.

πεφοβήατο, 3 pl. plupf. pass. φοβέω.

πέφραδε, 3 sing. redup. aor. φράζω.

πεφρίκᾱσι, 3 pl. pf. φρίσσω.

πεφύᾱσι, 3 pl. pf. φύω.

πεφυγμένος, pf. pple. mid. φεύγω.

πεφυζότες, nom. pl. masc. pf. pple. φεύγω.

πεφύκασι, 3 pl. pf. φύω.

πεφυλαγμένος, pf. pple. mid. φυλάσσω.

πεφυρμένος, pf. pple. pass. φύρω.

πεφυῶτας, acc. pl. masc. pf. pple. φύω.

πῇ. (1) Whither? where? πῇ ἔβη Ἀνδρομάχη; Z 377. Cf. B 339, E 472, Θ 94, 229, 413, K 385, Ξ 298, Ω 201, 362: κ 281, ν 203, ο 509, ρ 219, υ 43, φ 362.—(2) At what point? where? πῇ μέμονας καταδῦναι ὅμιλον; N 307.—(3) In what way? how? πῇ κέν τις ὑπεκφύγοι ὄλεθρον; μ 287. Cf. β 364.

πῃ, *enclitic*. (1) Somewhither: ἠέ πῃ ἐκπέμπεις κειμήλια Ω 381. Cf. Γ 400, Z 378.—With neg., nowhither, not anywhither: πέμψω μὶν οὔ πῃ ε 140. Cf. Z 383: β 127 = σ 288.—(2) In some region, somewhere: ἀλλά πῃ ἄλλῃ πλάζετο γ 251.—With neg., nowhere, not anywhere: ἔκβασις οὔ πῃ φαίνεται ε 410. Cf. N 191, P 643, Ψ 463: μ 232, ν 207, χ 140.—(3) In some wise, somehow: οὕτω πῃ τάδε γ' ἐστὶν Ω 373.—With neg., in no wise, not in any wise: οὐδέ πῃ ἔστι . . . Z 267. Cf. Π 110, Φ 219, Ω 71: μ 433.

πηγή, -ῆς, ἡ. (1) The head waters of a river, a spring: ἔνθα πηγαὶ δοιαὶ ἀναΐσσουσι Σκαμάνδρου X 147. Cf. Φ 312, Υ 9: = ζ 124.—(2) In pl., the waters of a river, its streams: πηγῇς ἔπι Κηφισοῖο B 523. Cf. Ψ 148.

πηγεσίμαλλος [πηγεσι-, πήγνυμι + μαλλός, a lock of wool]. Thick-fleeced Γ 197.

πήγνῡμι. 2 sing. fut. πήξεις X 283. 3 sing. aor. ἔπηξε B 664, N 570. πῆξε Δ 460, E 40, Z 10, Θ 258, Λ 447, N 372, 398, O 650: χ 83. 1 pl. πήξαμεν μ 15. 3 sing. subj. πήξῃ Θ 95. Pple. πήξας, -αντος Γ 217: λ 129, ψ 276. Infin. πῆξαι Σ 177: ε 163, λ 77. 3 sing. pf. πέπηγε Γ 135. 3 sing. plupf. (ἐ)πεπήγει N 442, Π 772. **Pass.** 3 sing. aor. ἐπάγη K 374, X 276. πάγη Δ 185, 528, E 616, Υ 283, 486, Ψ 877. 3 pl. πάγεν Λ 572. 3 pl. aor. πῆχθεν Θ 298. (ἐγκατα-, κατα-, συμ-.) (1) To set firmly, fix, stick: κεφαλὴν ἀνὰ σκολόπεσσιν Σ 177. Cf. λ 77, 129, μ 15, ψ 276.—To stick (a spear) in the earth when not in use. In pf. in pass. sense: παρ' ἔγχεα πέπηγεν Γ 135.—(2) To set or direct (the countenance): κατὰ χθόνος ὄμματα πήξας Γ 217.—(3) To stick, plunge, plant (a spear) into a foe or his shield, send (an arrow) into him (in pass. sense in plupf.): μεταφρένῳ ἐν δόρυ πῆξεν E 40, δόρυ ἐν κραδίῃ ἐπεπήγει N 442. Cf. Δ 185, 460, 528, E 616, Θ 298, N 372, etc.: χ 83.—In pass. and plupf., of a spent spear or arrow, to be stuck (in the earth), enter (it) and remain standing: ἐν γαίῃ ἐπάγη K 374, X 276. Cf. Ψ 877.—So without mention of the earth: πολλὰ Κεβριόνην ἀμφὶ δοῦρα πεπήγει Π 772, ταρβήσας ὅ οἱ ἄγχι πάγη βέλος Υ 283.—(4) In pass., of the limbs, to be deprived of the power of movement, become stiffened: νέρθε γοῦνα πήγνυται X 453.—(5) To put together, construct, build: νῆας B 664: ἴκρια ε 163.

πηγός [πηγ-, πήγνυμι]. Of horses, of compact bodily frame, stout I 124 = 266.—Of the wave of the sea, big, mighty ε 388, ψ 235.

πηγυλίς [πηγ-, πήγνυμι]. Icy-cold ξ 476.

πηδάλιον, -ου, τό [πηδόν]. A steering-oar: π. μετὰ χερσὶ νηὸς ἔχοντα γ 281. Cf. ε 255, 270, 315, θ 558.

πηδάω. (ἀμ-.) To spring, bound, leap: ὑψόσε ποσσὶν ἐπήδα Φ 269. Cf. Φ 302.—Of a dart Ξ 455.

πηδόν, -οῦ, τό, or **πηδός**, -οῦ, ὁ. An oar: ἀναρρίπτειν ἅλα πηδῷ η 328, ν 78.

πηκτός [πηκ-, πήγνυμι]. Put together, the work of man's hands. Epithet of a work of mechanical skill: ἄροτρον K 353, N 703: ν 32.

πῆλε, 3 sing. aor. πάλλω.

πήληξ, -ηκος, ἡ. A helmet Θ 308, N 527, 805, Ξ 498, O 608, 647, Π 105, 797, Υ 482: α 256.

πῆμα, -ατος, τό. (**1**) Bane, mischief, destruction, evil, woe, misery: κατένευσε Κρονίων Δαναοῖσι π. Θ 176. Cf. Λ 347, 413, O 110, P 688: ὅπως ἔτι π. φύγοιμι ξ 312. Cf. γ 152, η 195, θ 81, μ 27, 231, ξ 275, 338, ο 345.—(**2**) An instance of this; with pl.: πήματά κ' ἔπασχον E 886, λίην μέγα π. εἰσορόωντες I 229. Cf. O 721, P 99, Ω 547: α 49, β 163, γ 100, ε 33, 179, ι 535, φ 305, etc.—(**3**) A cause of bane, mischief, destruction, evil, woe or misery. Of persons: πατρί σῷ μέγα π. Γ 50. Cf. Γ 160, Z 282, K 453, X 288, 421: μ 125, ρ 446, 597.—Of inanimate things λ 555.

πημαίνω [πῆμα]. Fut. infin. πημανέειν Ω 781. 3 pl. aor. opt. πημήνειαν Γ 299. 3 sing. aor. pass. πημάνθη ξ 255. Infin. πημανθῆναι θ 563. To bring bane or mischief upon: Τρῶας O 42.—Absol., to take hostile action, take the offensive, attack: ὁππότεροι πρότεροι πημήνειαν Γ 299. Cf. Ω 781.—In pass., to suffer harm or damage: οὔ τι πημανθῆναι ἔπι δέος θ 563. Cf. ξ 255.

πηνίον, τό. In weaving, the spool on which the woof was wound (cf. κερκίς) Ψ 762.

πῆξε, 3 sing. aor. πήγνυμι.

πηός, -οῦ, ὁ. A kinsman by marriage Γ 163: θ 581, κ 441, ψ 120.

πήρη, -ης, ἡ. A wallet or scrip: πλῆσαν πήρην ρ 411. Cf. ν 437, ρ 197 = σ 108, ρ 357, 466.

πηρός. Explained as 'maimed' or 'helpless': πηρὸν θέσαν [Θάμυριν] B 599.

πῆχθεν, 3 pl. aor. pass. πήγνυμι.

πῆχυς, ὁ. (**1**) (**a**) The elbow: πῆχυν βάλε χειρὸς δεξιτερῆς Φ 166.—(**b**) The arm: ἀμφ' ἑὸν υἱὸν ἐχεύατο πήχεε E 314. Cf. ρ 38, ψ 240, ω 347.—(**2**) The middle piece or handle of a bow: τόξου πῆχυν ἄνελκεν Λ 375, N 583. Cf. φ 419.

πῖαρ, τό [cf. πίων]. Fatness. Hence, rich, fertile soil: μάλα πῖαρ ὑπ' οὖδας [ἐστιν] ι 135.—The cream or flower of something: βοῶν ἐκ πῖαρ ἑλέσθαι Λ 550 = P 659.

πῖδαξ, -ακος, ἡ. A spring Π 825.

πῖδήεις, -εσσα [cf. prec.]. With many springs, many-fountained. Epithet of Mount Ida Λ 183.

πίε, 3 sing. aor. πίνω.

πιέειν, aor. infin. πίνω.

πιέζω. Aor. pple. pass. πιεσθείς θ 336. (**1**) To press, squeeze, compress: βραχίονα Π 510. Cf. δ 287, μ 174.—(**2**) To grip, grasp: ἀστεμφέως ἐχέμεν μᾶλλόν τε πιέζειν δ 419.—(**3**) To load (with bonds), secure tightly: ἐν δεσμοῖς πιεσθείς θ 336. Cf. μ 164, 196.

πιεῖν, **πῑέμεν**, aor. infin. πίνω.

πῑειρα, fem. πίων.

πιεσθείς, aor. pple. pass. πιέζω.

πίῃ, 3 sing. aor. subj. πίνω.

πιθήσας, aor. pple. πείθω.

πιθόμην, aor. mid. πείθω.

πίθος, -ου, ὁ. A large jar: πίθοι οἴνοιο β 340. Cf. Ω 527: ψ 305.

πικρόγαμος [πικρός + γάμος]. Finding a bitter marriage (*i.e.* not marriage but death), ruing one's wooing α 266 = δ 346 = ρ 137.

πικρός, -ή, -όν (in δ 406 of two terminations) [prob. πικ-, πευκ-. Cf. πευκεδανός]. (**1**) Sharp-pointed, sharp, keen, piercing: ὀϊστόν Δ 118. Cf. Δ 134, X 206, etc.: χ 8.—(**2**) Of pain, acute, piercing, darting: ὠδῖνας Λ 271.—(**3**) Pungent or bitter to the taste: ῥίζαν Λ 846. Cf. ε 323.—Pungent to the smell: ὀδμήν δ 406.—(**4**) Fig.: μὴ πικρὴν Αἴγυπτον ἵκηαι ρ 448 (you prate of Egypt. You will find yourself in a sorry sort of Egypt, *i.e.* in trouble).

πίλναμαι [cf. πελάζω]. (ἐπι-, προσ-.) To be brought into contact with, touch. With dat.: ἅρματα χθονὶ πίλνατο Ψ 368.—With prep.: οὐκ ἐπ' οὔδει πίλναται (makes contact (so as to be) upon the . . ., touches it) T 93.

πῖλος, ὁ. Felt K 265.

πιμπλάνω [cf. next]. To fill I 679.

πίμπλημι [redup. (with euphonic μ) fr. πλα-, πλη-]. 3 sing. aor. πλῆσε N 60, P 573. 3 pl. πλῆσαν Ξ 35, Π 374, Σ 351: ρ 411. 3 pl. opt. πλήσειαν Π 72. Aor. pple. fem. πλήσᾱσα Π 223: ε 93. **Mid.** 3 pl. aor. opt. πλησαίατο τ 198. Pple. πλησάμενος, -ου I 224: ξ 87, 112, ρ 603. **Pass.** 3 sing. aor. ἐπλήσθη Υ 156. 3 pl. πλῆσθεν P 211, 696, Ψ 397: δ 705, τ 472. 3 sing. aor. πλῆτο P 499, Σ 50, Φ 16, 300, Ψ 777: μ 417, ξ 267, 307, ρ 436. 3 pl. πλῆντο θ 57. (ἀνα-, ἐμπίπλημι.) To fill. (**1**) (**a**) To fill (a receptacle or the like) by pouring or putting something into it. With genit. of material: πλῆσαν πήρην σίτου ρ 411. Cf. Π 223, Σ 351.—In mid.: πλησάμενος δῶκε σκύφος ξ 112. Cf. ξ 87.—With genit.: πλησάμενος οἴνοιο δέπας I 224.—Of satisfying the appetite. In mid.: ἵνα πλησαίατο θυμόν τ 198.—With genit.: πλησάμενος θυμὸν ἐδητύος ρ 603.—In pass., to be filled, be full. With genit. or instrumental: ὄνθου πλῆτο στόμα (had his mouth filled with . . .) Ψ 777, ὄσσε οἱ δακρυόφι πλῆσθεν P 696 = Ψ 397: = δ 705 = τ 472. Cf. κ 248 = υ 349.—(**b**) In immaterial sense. With genit.: ἀμφοτέρω πλῆσεν μένεος N 60. Cf. P 573.—In pass., to be filled, be full. With genit.: πλῆσθέν οἱ μέλε' ἀλκῆς P 211. Cf. P 499, A 104: = δ 662.—(**2**) (**a**) To fill or occupy the whole extent or capacity of: πλῆσαν ἠϊόνος στόμα Ξ 35. Cf. Π 374, Φ 23.—With genit.: ἐναύλους κε πλήσειαν νεκύων Π 72. Cf. ε 93 (loading it).—In pass., to be filled, be full. With genit.: τῶν πλῆτο σπέος Σ 50. Cf. Υ 156,

Φ 16, 300: θ 57, ξ 267 = ρ 436.—(b) In immaterial sense: ἐν δὲ θεείου πλῆτο μ 417, ξ 307.

πίναξ, -ακος, ὁ. (1) A plank or board μ 67.—(2) A platter: κρειῶν πίνακας α 141 = δ 57, π 49.—(3) A writing-tablet Z 169.

πινύσσω [prob. fr. πνῡ-. See πέπνυμαι]. To make wise; hence, to teach one a lesson, teach one better: ἤδη μ' ἄλλο τεὴ ἐπίνυσσεν ἐφετμή Ξ 249.

πινυτή, -ῆς, ἡ [cf. next]. Wisdom, sound understanding, good sense H 289: υ 71, 228.

πινυτός, -ή [prob. fr. πνῡ-. See πέπνυμαι]. Wise, of sound understanding, of good sense: ὅς τις π. γε μετέλθοι α 229. Cf. δ 211, λ 445, υ 131, φ 103, ψ 361.

πίνω. 3 sing. pa. iterative πίνεσκε Π 226. Aor. ἔπιον ο 373. 3 sing. ἔπιε σ 151. πίε δ 511, λ 98, 153, 390. 3 pl. ἔπιον I 177: γ 342, 395, η 184, 228, σ 427, φ 273. πίον X 2: σ 426. Subj. πίω λ 96. 2 sing. πίῃσθα Z 260. 3 πίῃ κ 328. Opt. πίοιμι κ 316. 3 sing. πίοι χ 11. 3 pl. πίοιεν Ω 350. Imp. πίε ι 347. Pple. πιών κ 326. Pl. πιόντες X 70. Fem. πιοῦσα Ω 102. Infin. πιέμεν ο 378. πῑέμεν Π 825: π 143, σ 3. πιέειν Δ 263, H 481: λ 232, 584, 585. πιεῖν Θ 189: θ 70, κ 386. **Mid.** Fut. pple. πῑόμενος κ 160. Nom. pl. neut. πῑόμενα N 493. (ἐκ-.) To drink. (1) To drink (liquid): οἶνον E 341. Cf. B 825, Δ 262, Θ 189, I 177, Ξ 5, Π 226, X 70: α 340, θ 70, ι 249, 297, κ 316, λ 98, ρ 225, etc.—Of a drowning man drinking the brine: ἐπεὶ πίεν ἁλμυρὸν ὕδωρ δ 511.—With partitive genit.: αἵματος λ 96. Cf. ο 373, χ 11.—Absol. Δ 263, Z 260, H 481, Λ 641, 642, N 493, Ξ 1, Π 825, P 250, X 2, Ω 102, 350, 476: α 258, β 305, ε 197, η 99, κ 160, λ 584, etc.—(2) To drink the contents of (a vessel): κύπελλα οἴνου Δ 346. Cf. Θ 232.—(3) In pass., to be drunk up, consumed: πολλὸν μέθυ πίνετο I 469: τόδε δῶμα φ 69. Cf. ι 45, υ 312.

πίον, 3 pl. aor. πίνω.

πίπτω [redup. fr. π(ε)τ-. Cf. πέτομαι]. 3 pl. fut. in mid. form πεσέονται Λ 824. Infin. πεσέεσθαι I 235, M 107, 126, P 639. Aor. ἔπεσον η 283. πέσον λ 64. 3 sing. ἔπεσε Δ 134, Θ 485, Λ 297, 676, N 178, etc.: κ 163, σ 98, τ 454, ω 540. πέσε Δ 482, E 82, H 16, M 395, N 181, etc.: ε 315, ι 371, κ 559, μ 410, σ 398, etc. 3 dual πεσέτην Ψ 216. 3 pl. ἔπεσον H 256, Φ 9, 387, Ψ 687: ε 295, ω 526. πέσον E 583, Λ 311, N 617, O 714, Π 276, 741, P 760: μ 417, ξ 307, π 13. 3 sing. subj. πέσῃ T 110. -ῃσι O 624: θ 524, χ 254. 3 dual -ητον Λ 325. 1 pl. -ωμεν N 742. 3 -ωσι O 63. 3 sing. opt. πέσοι N 289. 3 pl. -οιεν Z 453, Ψ 437. Pple. πεσών, -όντος A 594, B 175, Γ 289, Δ 504, Θ 270, Λ 241, etc.: κ 51, ξ 475, σ 91, χ 22, 94, ω 525. Fem. πεσοῦσα N 530, Π 118: ο 479, σ 397. Infin. πεσέειν Z 82, 307, Ψ 595. Acc. pl. masc. pf. pple. πεπτεῶτας χ 384. Acc. pl. neut. πεπτεῶτα Φ 503. (ἀμφι-, ἀπο-, ἐκ-, ἐμ-, κατα-, προ-.) To fall. (1) To fall or drop from a high or relatively high position: πέσε δὲ λίθος εἴσω M 459. Cf. A 594, E 82, M 156, O 435, P 760, Φ 9, etc.: τέγεος πέσεν (from the . . .) κ 559. Cf. λ 64, μ 239, ξ 129, ο 479, π 13, σ 397, τ 469, ω 535, 540.—(2) To be hurled or thrown from such a position: φῶτες ἔπιπτον πρηνέες ἐξ ὀχέων Π 378. Cf. H 16, Ψ 437: ε 315, μ 417, ξ 307.—(3) To let oneself fall, throw oneself: ἐν γούνασι πῖπτε Διώνης E 370. Cf. κ 51.—(4) Of a missile, to light, find its mark: ἐν δ' ἔπεσε ζωστῆρι ὀϊστός Δ 134. Cf. N 289.—Of a missile that misses its mark, to fall, light, in a specified way: ἡμῖν ἐτώσια [βέλεα] πίπτει ἔραζε P 633. Cf. χ 259 = 276, 280.—(5) In immaterial senses. Of sleep: ἐπεί σφισιν ὕπνος ἐπὶ βλεφάροισιν ἔπιπτεν β 398. Cf. ε 271, ν 79, ψ 309.—Of fear: τοῖς δέος ἐν φρεσὶ πίπτει ξ 88.—Of falling out of favour: σοὶ ἐκ θυμοῦ πεσέειν Ψ 595.—Of strife: ἐν ἄλλοισι θεοῖσιν ἔρις πέσεν Φ 385.—(6) Uses with adverbs and prepositions. (a) With ἐν. (α) To rush into, in among, upon, something: ἐν νήεσσι πεσόντες B 175. Cf. Λ 297, O 624, Ψ 216.—Sim. of a breaking wave O 624.—Of a rushing stream Φ 241.—(β) To fall upon a foe, rush upon a specified objective, make assault upon it: οὐδ' ἔτι φασὶ [Τρῶες] σχήσεσθ', ἀλλ' ἐν νηυσὶ πεσέεσθαι I 235, βάν ῥ' ἰθὺς Δαναῶν, οὐδ' ἔτ' ἔφαντο σχήσεσθ', ἀλλ' ἐν νηυσὶ πεσέεσθαι M 107 (but in these two passages it is possible to take σχήσεσθαι as referring to the Greeks in sense (III) (6) of ἔχω, and πεσέεσθαι in sense (γ) below). Cf. Λ 325, N 742, Π 276, P 639: ἐν δ' ἔπεσον προμάχοις ω 526.—(γ) To fall back in rout upon something, rush or flee in disorder to a specified objective: ἐν χερσὶ γυναικῶν φεύγοντας πεσέειν (take refuge in our wives' arms) Z 82, ἔφαντ' οὐκέτ' Ἀχαιοὺς σχήσεσθ', ἀλλ' ἐν νηυσὶ πεσέεσθαι M 126. Cf. Λ 311, 824, O 63.—(b) With σύν. (α) To rush together for some purpose, make united effort: σὺν Εὖρός τε Νότος τ' ἔπεσον ε 295.—(β) To rush together with hostile intent, engage in fight with each other: σύν ῥ' ἔπεσον λείουσιν ἐοικότες H 256. Cf Φ 387, Ψ 687.—(7) To fall from one's or its own height. (a) To lose the erect position, come to the ground: θάμνοι πρόρριζοι πίπτουσιν Λ 157, πέσεν ὕπτιος O 647. Cf. Ξ 418, O 648, Φ 407, Ψ 120: η 283 (app., coming out of the water I sank down), ι 371, μ 410, σ 91, 98, 398.—Of corn that is being cut Λ 69, Σ 552.—(b) To drop down wounded, be wounded: οὐκ ἀμέλησε κασιγνήτοιο πεσόντος Θ 330.—(c) To fall in battle or fight, drop down dead, be slain: τὸν πεσόντα ποδῶν ἔλαβεν Δ 463. Cf. A 243, Γ 289, Δ 482, 504, E 561, Θ 67, K 200 (app. pple. of the impf., 'that had fallen'), M 395, etc.: θ 524, χ 22, 94, 118, 254, 384, ω 181, 449, 525.—Of slain animals Π 469: κ 163 = τ 454.—(8) To come to a lower from a higher level, sink. Of the setting sun Θ 485.—Of wind, to fall, abate ξ 475, τ 202.

πῖσος, τό. A water-meadow: πίσεα ποιήεντα Υ 9: = ζ 124.

πίσσα, ἡ. Pitch Δ 277.

πιστός, -όν [πιθ-τός, fr. πιθ-, πείθω]. (1) Of persons: trusty, faithful, true O 331, 437, P 500, 575, 589, Σ 235, 460: ο 539.—In superl. πιστότατος

Π 147.—(2) (a) In which one may feel confidence, such as to beget trust, sure, faithful: ὅρκια B 124, Γ 73=256, Γ 94, 245, 252, 269, 280, 323, Δ 157, H 351, T 191, X 262: ω 483.—(b) Absol. in neut. pl., trustworthiness, faith (cf. ἶσος (2) (c), φυκτός): ἐπεὶ οὐκέτι πιστὰ γυναιξίν (in . . .) λ 456.

πιστόω [πιστός]. To make trustworthy. (1) In pass., to give assurance, bind oneself surely. With infin.: ὅρκῳ πιστωθῆναι ἀπήμονά μ' οἴκαδ' ἀπάξειν ο 436.—In mid., to give assurance to a person, give him confidence; ἐπιστώσαντ' ἐπέεσσιν Φ 286.—(2) In pass., to feel assurance, be convinced: ὄφρα πιστωθῆτον φ 218.—(3) In mid., to give mutual pledges, exchange troth: χεῖράς τ' ἀλλήλων λαβέτην καὶ πιστώσαντο Z 233.

πίσυνος [πιθ-, πείθω]. Trusting in, relying upon, emboldened by, something. With dat.: τόξοισιν E 205. Cf. Θ 226=Λ 9, I 238, Ω 295, 313: σ 140.

πίσυρες [Aeolic form of τέσσαρες]. Four O 680, Ψ 171, Ω 233: ε 70, χ 111.—With another numeral: π. καὶ εἴκοσι π 249.

πίτνημι [cf. πετάννυμι]. From πιτνάω 3 sing. impf. πίτνᾱ Φ 7. To spread, spread out: χεῖρας λ 392.—To cause (mist) to be outspread over something, spread or shed (it) Φ 7.—In pass., to be outspread, flutter: ἀμφὶ χαῖται πίτναντο X 402.

πίτυς, ἡ. Dat. pl. πίτυσσι ι 186. A pine-tree N 390=Π 483.—A felled pine or a piece thereof: δέδμητο πίτυσσιν ἰδὲ δρυσίν ι 186.

πῐφαύσκω [with reduplication fr. φα-, φαίνω]. (1) To make manifest to the sight, display, show. In mid.: πιφαυσκόμενος τὰ ἃ κῆλα M 280. Cf. O 97, Φ 333.—(2) To tell of, indicate, point out: ἵπποι, οὓς πίφαυσκε Δόλων K 478.—In mid. ο 518.—(3) To give a signal: ῥοίζησε πιφαύσκων Διομήδεϊ K 502.—(4) To bring forward, propose, tender. In mid.: μή μοι ἄποινα πιφαύσκεο Φ 99.—(5) To set forth, communicate, disclose, make known, declare: μῦθον ἅπαντα λ 442.—In mid.: ἤέ τι Μυρμιδόνεσσι πιφαύσκεαι; (have you anything to . . . ?) Π 12. Cf. β 32, 44, φ 305 (prophesy), ψ 202.—(6) To set forth or utter (words or discourse): ἔπεα K 202. Cf. χ 131=247.—(7) To make declaration, state one's case, one's wishes, what one sees or knows: δήμῳ πιφαύσκων Σ 500. Cf. μ 165.—In mid. β 162, ν 37.

πιών, aor. pple. πίνω.

πίων, -ονος. Fem. πίειρα. Superl. πῑότατος I 577. (1) Of beasts, fat, plump B 403, I 207, M 319, Ψ 750: β 56=ρ 535, ι 217, 237, 312, 315, 337, 464, ξ 419, ρ 180=υ 250, υ 186, ω 66.—Rich with fat: μηρία A 40, Λ 773, O 373. Cf. δ 65, 764, τ 366.—Of fat, rich, thick: καλύψας πίονι δημῷ ρ 241. Cf. X 501: ξ 428.—(2) Of land or a country, rich, fertile E 710, I 577, M 283, Π 437, Σ 541, etc.: β 328, δ 318, ν 322, ξ 329, τ 173, etc.—Of cities or a house, full of substance, rich: πιείρας πόλεις Σ 342: οἶκον ι 35.—Of a temple or a part thereof, rich with offerings: νηῷ B 549, ἀδύτοιο E 512: νηόν μ 346.—Of a meal, plentiful, sumptuous: δαιτὶ πιείρῃ T 180.

πλαγκτός [πλαγκ-, πλάζω. 'Sent adrift']. Unsettled, crazy. Absol. in voc. φ 363.

πλαγκτοσύνη, -ης, ἡ [as prec.]. Wandering, a roving life: πλαγκτοσύνης κακώτερον ο 343.

πλάζω [πλαγ-. Cf. πληγή, πλήσσω]. 3 sing. aor. πλάγξε ω 307. Fut. mid. πλάγξομαι ο 312. 3 sing. aor. pass. πλάγχθη Λ 351: α 2. Pple. πλαγχθείς, -έντος Ξ 120: ζ 278, ν 278. (ἀπο-, ἐπι-, παρα-, προσ-.) (1) To beat upon: κῦμα πλάζ' ὤμους Φ 269: δύω νύκτας κύματι πλάζετο (was beaten upon, tossed, by the waves) ε 389.—(2) To drive or turn from one's or its course, cause to take another or an undesired course: δαίμων με πλάγξ' ἀπὸ Σικανίης δεῦρ' ἐλθέμεν ω 307. Cf. P 751: α 2 (was tossed about), 75, ν 278.—To drive back from one's goal, foil, baffle: ἐπίκουροι, οἵ με μέγα πλάζουσιν B 132.—To drive, force to flee, from a place: Ἀργεϊ νάσθη πλαγχθείς Ξ 120.—To daze: πλάζε [μνηστῆρας] πίνοντας β 396.—(3) In mid. and pass., to wander, rove, roam: εἰ ἄλλου μῦθον ἀκούσας πλαζομένου [Ὀδυσσῆος] (have heard from some one else the story of his wanderings) γ 95=δ 325, πλαζόμενοι κατὰ ληΐδα γ 106. Cf. K 91: γ 252, ν 204, ξ 43, ο 312, π 64, 151.—To stray, lose one's way: πλαγχθέντα ἧς ἀπὸ νηός ζ 278.—Of a missile, to glance off: πλάγχθη ἀπὸ χαλκόφι χαλκός Λ 351.

†**πλανάομαι**. 3 pl. πλανόωνται. To deviate from the straight course, go deviously: ἵπποι πλανόωνται ἀνὰ δρόμον (run all over the course) Ψ 321.

πλατάνιστος, -ου, ἡ. A plane-tree: καλῇ ὑπὸ πλατανίστῳ B 307, πρὸς πλατάνιστον ὄρουσεν 310.

πλατύς, -ύ. Wide, broad: τελαμῶνος E 796. Cf. H 86, N 588, P 432: ω 82.—Of flocks, broad, extensive: αἰπόλια B 474, Λ 679: =ξ 101, 103.

πλέες, nom. pl. See πλείων.

πλεῖος, -η, -ον [πλη-, πίμπλημι]. Also **πλέος** υ 355. Comp. πλειότερος λ 359. (1) Filled to the utmost capacity, full: δεπάεσσιν Θ 162=M 311. Cf. K 579, Λ 637: λ 359.—With contents undiminished, still full: σὸν πλεῖον δέπας αἰεὶ ἕστηκεν Δ 262.—(2) With genit., full of, filled with: πλεῖαί τοι χαλκοῦ κλισίαι B 226. Cf. I 71: δ 319 (crowded with . . .), μ 92, ο 446, ρ 605, υ 355.

πλεῖστος, -η, -ον, *superl.* [πλε-ῖστος. Cf. πλείων]. (1) The most numerous, in greatest number: πλεῖστοι καὶ ἄριστοι λαοί B 577, 817. Cf. B 580, Γ 185, I 382, Λ 148, M 89=197, O 448: ὅθι πλεῖστα κτήματα κεῖται δ 127. Cf. δ 229, ε 309.—With nouns of multitude: ὅμιλον O 616, λαόν Π 377.—Absol.: ὅθι πλεῖστοι κλονέοντο E 8. Cf. E 780, Z 69, Ξ 520, Π 285: π 77, 392=φ 162, υ 335.—(2) The most, the most in quantity or abundance: κόνις N 335, καλάμην T 222.—(3) The greatest, the most serious: κακόν δ 697.—(4) In neut. sing. πλεῖστον as adv., the most, to the greatest extent, in the highest degree: ἥ οἱ πλεῖστον ἔρυτο Δ 138. Cf. T 287.

πλείω. See πλέω.

πλείων, -ονος, *comp.* Neut. πλεῖον [πλε-ίων. Cf. πλεῖστος]. Also **πλέων**, -ονος. Nom. pl. masc. πλείους ω 464. πλέες Λ 395. Dat. pl. πλείοσι K 106: μ 196, τ 168. πλεόνεσσι A 281, 325, N 739, O 611,

Π 651 : β 245, 251, μ 54, 164, π 88, σ 63, χ 13. Acc. πλέας Β 129. (1) More, more numerous, in greater number: πλέας ἔμμεναι υἷας Ἀχαιῶν Τρώων Β 129. Cf. Ε 673, Κ 106, 506, Λ 395, Ο 611, etc.: ἀνήϊξαν ἡμίσεων πλείους ω 464. Cf. β 245, η 189, ι 48, μ 54, τ 168, etc.—Absol.: ἐπεὶ πλεόνεσσιν ἀνάσσει Α 281, οὐδὲ πλείονα ἴσασι μητίσασθαι (have more knowledge so as to . . ., know better how to . . .) Ψ 312. Cf. Α 325, Ε 531, Ν 355, Π 651, etc.: β 251, μ 188, ξ 498, π 88, σ 63, χ 13.—(2) Many rather than few. Absol.: πλεόνων ἔργον ἄμεινον Μ 412.—(3) Greater in quantity or amount: πλέων νύξ (more of the night) Κ 252.—Absol.: ἐπὶ πλεῖον ἐλέλειπτο θ 475. Cf. Α 165.

πλεκτός, -ή, -όν [πλεκ-, πλέκω]. Formed by plaiting or twisting, plaited, twisted: ταλάροισιν (*i.e.* of wicker-work) Σ 568. Cf. Χ 469: ι 247, χ 175 = 192.

†**πλέκω**. 3 sing. aor. ἔπλεξε Ξ 176. Aor. pple. mid. πλεξάμενος κ 168. (περι-.) (1) To plait, twist, braid: πλοκάμους Ξ 176.—(2) To form by plaiting or twisting, plait, twist: πεῖσμα κ 168.

πλέος. See πλεῖος.

πλευρά, τά [cf. next]. In collective sense, the side of the body: πλευρὰ οὔτησε ξυστῷ (in the side) Δ 468. Cf. Λ 437.

πλευραί, αἱ [cf. prec.]. The ribs, the sides of the body: σμώδιγγες ἀνὰ πλευρὰς ἀνέδραμον Ψ 716. Cf. Υ 170, Ω 10: ρ 232.

πλέω. Also **πλείω** ο 34, π 368. **πλώω** Φ 302: ε 240. 2 pl. fut. in mid. form πλεύσεσθε μ 25. (ἀναπλέω, ἀποπλείω, ἐπιπλέω, καταπλέω, παραπλώω.) (1) To go or make one's way by sea, sail the seas, sail: πλέων ἐπὶ πόντον Η 88. Cf. α 183, γ 276, ε 278, ι 62, κ 28, etc.—Of ships: Ἑλλήσποντον ἐπ' ἰχθυόεντα πλεούσας νῆας ἐμάς Ι 360. Cf. γ 158, μ 70.—To set sail, sail: ἅμ' ἠοῖ πλεύσεσθε μ 25. Cf. Γ 444, Ξ 251: ξ 253.—(2) To sail over or upon, traverse: πόθεν πλεῖθ' ὑγρὰ κέλευθα; γ 71 = ι 252.—(3) In gen., to be borne on the surface of water, float: πολλὰ τεύχεα πλῶον καὶ νέκυες Φ 302. Cf. ε 240.

πλέων, -ονος. See πλείων.

πληγή, -ῆς, ἡ [πληγ- as in πλήσσω]. A blow or stroke: ὑπὸ πληγῆς πατρὸς Διός (*i.e.* his lightning) Ξ 414. Cf. Β 264, Λ 532, Ο 17, Π 816: ὑπὸ πληγῇσιν ἱμάσθλης ν 82. Cf. δ 244, ρ 283, σ 54.

πλήγη, 3 sing. aor. pass. πλήσσω.

πλῆθος, τό [πλη-, πίμπλημι]. Numerical strength or superiority, numbers: πεποιθότας πλήθεϊ σφετέρῳ Ρ 330.—So, app., πλήθει πρόσθε βαλόντες (by being two to one) Ψ 639.

πληθύς, -ύος, ἡ [πλη-, πίμπλημι]. (1) The whole number, the body, the multitude: πληθύος ἐκ Δαναῶν Ι 641.—(2) The general or common body, the host: ἡγεμόνας ἕλεν, αὐτὰρ ἔπειτα πληθύν Λ 305. Cf. Β 143, 278, 488, Ο 295, 305.—(3) A throng gathered for or engaged in battle: κατὰ πληθὺν Λυκίων Ε 676. Cf. Λ 360, Ρ 31 = Υ 197, Υ 377, Χ 458: λ 514.—(4) Numerical strength, numbers: οὐ πληθὺν διζήμενος (not wishing merely to swell the array) Ρ 221.—Numerical superiority, numbers, a being outnumbered, an outnumbering: πληθὺν ταρβήσας Λ 405. Cf. π 105.

πλήθω [πλη-, πίμπλημι]. (1) To be filled or occupied to the whole extent or capacity: τραπέζας πληθούσας (loaded) λ 419.—With genit.: πλήθει μοι νεκύων ῥέεθρα Φ 218. Cf. Θ 214: ι 8.—(2) Of a river, to be brimming, be in flood: ποταμοὶ πλήθουσιν Π 389. Cf. Ε 87, Λ 492: τ 207.—Of the moon, to be at the full, be full: σελήνην πλήθουσαν Σ 484.

πληκτίζομαι [πληκτ-, πλήσσω]. To bandy blows with. With dat.: πληκτίζεσθ' ἀλόχοισι Διός Φ 499.

πλήμνη, -ης, ἡ. The nave of a wheel: πλῆμναι ἀργύρου Ε 726. Cf. Ψ 339.

πλημυρίς. A swell or heave (of the sea): πλημυρὶς ἐκ πόντοιο ι 486.

πλήν. Excepting, except, save. With genit.: πλήν γ' αὐτοῦ Λαοδάμαντος θ 207.

πλῆντο[1], 3 pl. aor. pass. πελάζω.

πλῆντο[2], 3 pl. aor. pass. πίμπλημι.

πλῆξα, aor. πλήσσω.

πλήξιππος [πληξ-, πλήσσω + ἵππος]. Smiter of horses. Epithet of Pelops Β 104.—Of Menestheus Δ 327.—Of Orestes Ε 705.—Of Oïleus Λ 93.

πλῆσε, 3 sing. aor. πίμπλημι.

πλῆσθεν, 3 pl. aor. pass. πίμπλημι.

πλησίος, -η, -ον [πέλας]. (1) Near, close: πλησίαι αἵ γ' ἥσθην (close to each other) Δ 21 = Θ 458. Cf. Λ 593 = Ν 488, Β 271 (his neighbour) = Δ 81 = Χ 372: = θ 328 = κ 37 = ν 167 = σ 72 = 400 = φ 396, κ 93.—Near to, close to. With genit.: ἀλλήλων ε 71.—With dat.: ἀλλήλοισιν Ψ 732: β 149.—(2) In neut. sing. πλησίον as adv., near, close, close by: ἑστήκει Δ 329. Cf. Σ 422: θ 7 (in a body), υ 106 (from near at hand).—Near to, close to. With genit.: ἀλλήλων Γ 115, Ζ 245, 249. Cf. μ 102, ξ 14.—With dat.: οἱ η 171.

πλησίστιος [πλησ-, πίμπλημι + ἱστίον]. Swelling the sail: οὖρον λ 7 = μ 149.

πλήσσω. Aor. πλῆξα κ 162. 3 sing. πλῆξε Β 266, Γ 362, Ε 147, Λ 240, Μ 192, Π 115, 791, Ρ 294: ε 431, μ 412. 3 sing. subj. πλήξῃ σ 57. 3 sing. opt. πλήξειε Κ 489. Pple. πλήξας, -αντος Ε 588, Π 332: υ 17, χ 20. Pf. pple. πεπληγώς Χ 497. Fem. πεπληγυῖα Ε 763: κ 238, 319, π 456. Thematic pf. pple. πεπλήγων (*v.l.* πεπληγώς) Β 264. Infin. πεπληγέμεν Π 728, Ψ 660. 3 pl. thematic plupf. (in impf. sense) ἐπέπληγον Ε 504. πέπληγον Ψ 363: θ 264. **Mid**. Aor. pple. πληξάμενος Π 125. 3 sing. thematic plupf. (in impf. sense) πεπλήγετο Μ 162, Ο 113, 397: ν 198. 3 pl. πεπλήγοντο Σ 31, 51. **Pass**. 3 sing. aor. πλήγη Ν 394, Π 403. Pple. πληγείς, -έντος Θ 12, 455, Ο 117, Ψ 694: φ 50. Fem. πληγεῖσα Ρ 296: μ 416, ξ 306. (δια-, ἐκ-, ἐνι-, ἐπι-, κατα-.) (1) To administer a blow to, strike, hit, smite, beat: σκήπτρῳ Β 266, πὺξ πεπληγέμεν (to fall to with their fists) Ψ 660. Cf. Π 791, Χ 497, Ψ 363, 694: θ 264, κ 238, 319, π 456, σ 57, υ 17, φ 50, χ 20.—In mid.: ὣ πεπλήγετο μηρώ Μ 162. Cf. Ο 113, Π 125, Σ 31, 51, Ο 397: = ν 198.—To drive away with blows:

ἀγορῆθεν B 264.—To whip up (horses) Π 728.—Of horses, to kick E 588.—Of inanimate objects: ἱστὸς πλῆξε κυβερνήτεω κεφαλήν μ 412. Cf. ε 431.—(2) With ἐκ, to drive out of one's wits or one's mind (cf. ἐκπλήσσω): ἔκ οἱ ἡνίοχος πλήγη φρένας (lost his wits) N 394. Cf. Π 403: σ 231.—(3) To strike, hit, smite, with a weapon Γ 362, E 147, 763, K 489, Λ 240, M 192, Π 115, 332, P 294, 296: κ 162.—Of Zeus and his lightning: πληγέντε κεραυνῷ Θ 455. Cf. Θ 12, O 117: μ 416 = ξ 306.—(4) To set in motion by striking or beating: κονισάλῳ, ὃν οὐρανὸν ἐς πολύχαλκον ἐπέπληγον πόδες ἵππων E 504.

πλῆτο[1], 3 sing. aor. pass πελάζω.

πλῆτο[2], 3 sing. aor. pass. πίμπλημι.

πλίσσομαι. Of mules, app., to prance along: εὖ πλίσσοντο πόδεσσιν ζ 318.

πλόκαμος, -ου, ὁ [πλέκω]. A lock or tress of hair: πλοκάμους ἔπλεξεν Ξ 176.

πλόος, ὁ [πλέω]. A voyage or course: δολιχὸν πλόον ὁρμαίνοντας γ 169.

πλοῦτος, -ου, ὁ. Wealth, riches, abundance of substance A 171, B 670, E 708, Π 596, Ω 536, 546: ξ 206, ω 486.

πλοχμός, -οῦ, ὁ [πλέκω]. A lock of hair: πλοχμοί, οἳ χρυσῷ τε καὶ ἀργύρῳ ἐσφήκωντο P 52.

πλυνός, -οῦ, ὁ [πλύνω]. A place for washing clothes, a washing-trough: λαΐνεοι X 153. Cf. ζ 40, 86.

πλύνω. 3 pl. pa. iterative πλύνεσκον X 155. Fut. pple. fem. πλυνέουσα ζ 59. Pl. πλυνέουσαι ζ 31. 3 pl. aor. πλῦναν ζ 93. Pple. fem. πλύνᾱσα ω 148. (ἀπο-.) To wash clothes: ἴομεν πλυνέουσαι ζ 31. Cf. ο 420.—To wash (clothes): ὅθι εἵματα πλύνεσκον X 155. Cf. ζ 59, 93, ω 148.

πλωτός, -ή [πλώω]. Floating κ 3.

πλώω. See πλέω.

πνείω. See πνέω.

πνεύμων, -ονος, ὁ [πνευ-, πνεϝ-, πνέω]. One of the lungs: πάγη ἐν πνεύμονι χαλκός Δ 528.

πνέω (πνέϝω). Also **πνείω.** 3 sing. aor. ἔπνευσε Ω 442. 3 sing. subj. πνεύσῃ T 159. (ἀναπνέω, ἀποπνείω, ἐμπνέω, ἐπιπνέω, παραπνέω.) (1) To breathe N 385.—(2) To draw the breath of life, live, exist: ὅσσα τε γαῖαν ἔπι πνείει P 447: = σ 131.—(3) To breathe forth. Fig.: μένεα πνείοντες (πνείοντας) B 536, Γ 8, Λ 508, Ω 364. Cf. χ 203.—(4) To breathe or inspire into a person, etc.: ἐν δ' ἔπνευσ' ἵπποισι μένος Ω 442. Cf. T 159.—(5) Of wind or a breeze, to breathe, blow δ 361, 567, ε 469, η 119.—(6) To emit an odour, smell: ἀμβροσίην ἡδὺ πνείουσαν δ 446.

πνοιή, -ῆς, ἡ [πνέω]. (1) A breathing, the breath: πνοιῇ [ἵππων] μετάφρενον θέρμετο Ψ 380.—A breath: δόρυ πνοιῇ ἔτραπεν Υ 439.—(2) Of the breath or blast of fire Φ 355.—(3) In reference to wind, a breathing, blowing, breeze, blast E 526, 697, Λ 622, M 207, N 590, Ξ 395, Π 149, P 55, T 415, Ψ 215, 367, Ω 342: = α 98 = ε 46, β 148, δ 402, 839, ζ 20, κ 25, 507.

ποδάνιπτρα, τά [πόδα, acc. of πούς + νιπ-, νίζω]. Water for washing the feet τ 343, 504.

ποδάρκης [ποδ-, πούς + an uncertain second element]. Swift-footed. Epithet of Achilles A 121, B 688, Z 423, Λ 599, Π 5, Σ 181, etc.

ποδηνεκής, -ές [ποδ-, πούς + ἐνεκ-. See φέρω]. Reaching to the feet: δέρμα λέοντος K 24 = 178, ἀσπίδα (*i.e.* such as to cover the whole of the bearer when the rim rested on the ground) O 646.

ποδήνεμος, -ον [ποδ-, πούς + ἄνεμος. 'Like the wind in feet']. Windswift. Epithet of Iris B 786, E 353, 368, Λ 195 = O 168, O 200, Σ 166, 183 = 196, Ω 95.

ποδώκεια, -ης, ἡ [ποδώκης]. Swiftness of foot. In pl.: ποδωκείῃσι πεποιθώς B 792.

ποδώκης, -εος [ποδ-, πούς + ὠκύς]. Swift-footed: ἵππους B 764, P 614. Cf. K 316, Ψ 262 (app. with transference of epithet from horses to drivers), 376.—Epithet of Achilles B 860, Θ 474, N 113, Π 134, P 486, Σ 234, etc.: λ 471, 538.

πόθεν [-θεν (1)]. Whence? (1) In local sense: τίς π. εἰς ἀνδρῶν; Φ 150: α 170 = κ 325 = ξ 187 = ο 264 = τ 105 = ω 298, η 238 (or poss. these passages may be referred to (2)). Cf. γ 71 = ι 252, π 57.—In indirect construction: εἰρώτα (εἴροντο) τίς εἴη καὶ π. ἔλθοι ο 423, ρ 368.—(2) In reference to race or origin. In indirect construction: οὐκ οἶδα π. γένος εὔχεται εἶναι (whence in the matter of race, *i.e.* of what stock he claims to be) ρ 373.

ποθέν, *enclitic* [cf. prec.]. (1) From some or any place or quarter: ἐλθών ποθεν α 115, υ 224. Cf. α 414, β 351, η 52, ξ 374, σ 376, φ 195, ω 149.—In reference to finding, somewhere: εἴ ποθεν ἐξεύροι Σ 322.—(2) From any source: εἴ ποθεν ἄλλα γένοιτο I 380. Cf. ε 490, χ 62.

ποθέω [ποθή]. Non-thematic pres. infin. ποθήμεναι μ 110. 3 sing. pa. iterative ποθέεσκε A 492. 3 pl. aor. πόθεσαν O 219. Infin. ποθέσαι β 375, δ 748. (1) To feel the want of, long for, yearn for, mourn for, a person or thing absent or lost: ἀϋτήν τε πτόλεμόν τε A 492. Cf. E 414, Ψ 16, Ω 6: τοίην κεφαλήν α 343. Cf. ι 453, λ 196 (sick with hope of it deferred), μ 110, σ 204, τ 136.—(2) To miss, to feel the want of, be at a loss on account of or distressed by the absence or want of: ἀρχόν B 703 = 726, 778. Cf. B 709, E 234, Λ 161, O 219: χ 387.—(3) To miss, remark the absence or loss of: πρίν [μ'] αὐτὴν ποθέσαι β 375. Cf. δ 748, ν 219, π 287 = τ 6.

ποθή, -ῆς, ἡ (cf. πόθος). (1) A longing, yearning or mourning for a person or thing absent or lost: σῇ ποθῇ (through mourning for you) T 321.—(2) A missing a person or thing, a feeling at a loss or in distress on account of his or its absence or loss: Ἀχιλλῆος A 240. Cf. Z 362, Λ 471, Ξ 368, P 690, 704: β 126, θ 414, κ 505.—(3) Lack, want, scarcity: ξενίων ο 514, 546.

πόθι. In what place? where? π. τοι πόλις; α 170 = κ 325 = ξ 187 = ο 264 = τ 105 = ω 298.

ποθί, *enclitic* [cf. prec.]. (1) Somewhere: ἠέ ποθι πτολέμοιο μέγα στόμα [τεύχων] K 8.—(2) In negative or conditional contexts, anywhere: οὐδέ ποθι νέφος ἐστίν υ 114. Cf. N 309: ρ 195.—In any part: οὐδέ ποθι μιαρός Ω 420.—(3) Somehow, haply:

αἴ κέ ποθι Ζεὺς δῷσι . . . Α 128. Cf. Ζ 526 : α 379 = β 144, δ 34, μ 96, 215, ξ 118, ρ 51 = 60, χ 252.—(4) Qualifying an expression, haply, I ween, no doubt, as it would seem : ἀλλά ποθι Ζεὺς αἴτιος α 348. Cf. Ν 630, Τ 273, Ω 209.

πόθος, -ου, ὁ [cf. ποθή]. = ποθή (1) Ρ 439 : δ 596, λ 202 (mourning for you), ξ 144.

ποιέω. Impf. mid. ποιεύμην Ι 495. (ἐμ-.) (1) To make, construct, form, fabricate, fashion, prepare: δῶμα Α 608, σάκος Η 222. Cf. Ζ 316, Η 339, 435, Ο 363, Υ 12, etc. : α 239, δ 796, ε 253, ζ 10, θ 373, ρ 207, etc.—In mid. Ε 735 = Θ 386, Μ 5, 168, Σ 371 : ε 251, 255, 259.—To make or prepare (a bed) : πεποίηταί τοι εὐνή η 342.—(2) To make, bring about, cause, cause to come into existence or take place : φόβον Μ 432, αἴθρην Ρ 646. Cf. Μ 30, Ν 120 : α 250 = π 127, ε 452, τ 34.—In mid. Θ 2, 489 : β 126.—To make (a bargain). In mid. : ῥήτρην ποιησόμεθα ξ 393. —(3) To put (into a person's mind), suggest : ἐνὶ φρεσὶν ὧδε νόημα ποίησεν ξ 274. —With infin. : ἑστάμεναι Ν 55.—(4) To appoint, nominate : ταμίην κ 21.—In mid. : πέντε ἡγεμόνας ποιήσατο Π 171.—(5) To make, cause to be (so and so). With complementary adj. : ἄφρονα ποιῆσαι καὶ ἐπίφρον' ἐόντα ψ 12. Cf. Α 461 = Β 424 : = γ 458 = μ 361, α 235, ι 327, 524, ν 42.—With sim. sb. : μή σέ γε βασιλῆα ποιήσειεν α 387. Cf. Ω 537, 611 : π 456, ρ 271.—In mid. Γ 409, Ι 397, 495 : ε 120, η 66, κ 433.—To cause *to do something*. With infin. : ἐπεί σε θεοὶ ποίησαν ἱκέσθαι οἶκον ψ 258.—(6) To do, effect, perform : ἦ σοὶ ἄριστα πεποίηται ; Ζ 56.—In mid. : οὐδέ τιν' ἄλλην μύθου ποιήσασθαι ἐπισχεσίην ἐδύνασθε (could put forward no other plea) φ 71.

ποίη, -ης, ἡ. Grass Ξ 347 : ι 449, σ 368, 370, 372.

ποιήεις, -εντος. Fem. -εσσα [ποίη]. Grassy, grass-clad : ἄγκεα δ 337 = ρ 128. Cf. Υ 9 : = ζ 124.—Of places, grassy, with grassy meadows Β 503, Ι 150 = 292 : π 396.

ποιητός, -ή, -όν [ποιέω]. (1) Made, constructed, fabricated : σάκεος πύκα ποιητοῖο Σ 608. Cf. Ε 466 : α 333 = θ 458 = π 415 = σ 209 = φ 64, α 436, χ 455.—(2) Epithet of various products of art, well made, constructed or fabricated (= εὐποίητος) : δόμοις Ε 198, τρίποδος Ψ 718. Cf. Κ 262, Μ 470, Ψ 340 : ν 306.

ποικίλλω [ποικίλος]. To make, form, fashion, with curious art Σ 590.

ποίκιλμα, τό. In pl., broidery, ornamental variegated work in wool : κάλλιστος ποικίλμασιν Ζ 294 : = ο 107.

ποικιλομήτης [ποικίλος + μῆτις]. Of many and various devices or wiles. Epithet of Odysseus Λ 482 : γ 163, η 168, χ 115, 202, 281.—Absol. in voc. addressed to Odysseus : ποικιλομῆτα ν 293.

ποικίλος, -η, -ον. (1) Parti-coloured, marked with patches of a different colour or shade, dappled : παρδαλέῃ Κ 30 : ἐλλόν τ 228. —(2) Wrought or ornamented with curious art, elaborately wrought or ornamented. With reference to broidery or ornamental variegated work in wool, etc. : πέπλον Ε 735 = Θ 386. Cf. Ξ 215, 220, Χ 441 : σ 293.—Of various products of art : ἅρματα ποικίλα χαλκῷ (with . . ., *i.e.* having the metal parts curiously wrought) Δ 226, Κ 322, 393, θώρηκα Π 134. Cf. Γ 327, Δ 432, Ε 239, Ζ 504, Κ 75, 149, 501, 504, Μ 396, Ν 181, 537 = Ξ 431, Ξ 420 : κλισμόν α 132. Cf. γ 492 = ο 145 = 190.—(3) Elaborately contrived, intricate, complicated : δεσμόν θ 448.

ποιμαίνω [ποιμήν]. 3 sing. pa. iterative ποιμαίνεσκε ι 188. To tend (a flock) : μῆλα ι 188.—Absol., to tend one's flock, act as shepherd : ποιμαίνων (ποιμαίνοντ') ἐπ' ὀέσσιν Ζ 25, Λ 106.—In pass., of flocks, to roam the pastures : αἶγας καὶ ὄϊς, τά οἱ ἄσπετα ποιμαίνοντο Λ 245.

ποιμήν, -ένος, ὁ. (1) A shepherd (in κ 82 app. including 'herdsman'; and this sense is possible in all the passages except Ε 137, Μ 451, Ν 493 and Π 354, where the sense 'shepherd' (in Π 354 including 'goatherd') is required) Γ 11, Δ 455, Ε 137, Θ 559, Μ 451, Ν 493, Π 354, Σ 162, Ψ 835 : δ 87 κ 82.—(2) Of kings and chiefs, π. λαῶν, shepherd of the host. Applied to Agamemnon Β 243, 254, 772 = Η 230, Δ 413, Κ 3, Λ 187, 202, Ξ 22, Τ 35, 251, Ω 654 : γ 156, δ 532, ξ 497.—To Menelaus Ε 566, 570 : δ 24.—To Nestor Β 85, Κ 73, Ψ 411 : γ 469, ο 151, ρ 109.—To Atreus Β 105.—To Aeneas Ε 513, Υ 110.—To Glaucus Ζ 214.—To Hector Κ 406, Ξ 423, Ο 262, Χ 277.—To Diomedes Λ 370, Ψ 389.—To Machaon Λ 506, 598, 651.—To Achilles Π 2, Τ 386.—To Aegisthus δ 528.—To Odysseus σ 70, υ 106.—To Laertes ω 368.—To Mentor ω 456.—To various minor heroes Α 263, Δ 296, Ε 144, Η 469, Ι 81, Λ 92, 578, 842, Ν 411, 600, Ξ 516, Ρ 348.

ποίμνη, -ης, ἡ [ποιμαίνω]. A flock ι 122.

ποιμνήϊος [ποίμνη]. Of or pertaining to a flock : σταθμὸν ποιμνήϊον (a sheep-farm) Β 470.

ποινή, -ῆς, ἡ. (1) A blood-price, a sum paid as compensation and satisfaction by a homicide to the family of the slain man : εἵνεκα ποινῆς ἀνδρὸς ἀποφθιμένου Σ 498. Cf. Ι 633, 636.—In reference to requital or vengeance for men slain in battle Ν 659, Ξ 483, Π 398, Φ 28 (to pay the price of his blood in their persons).—So of the vengeance taken on the Cyclops ψ 312.—(2) Something given in recompense for loss or deprivation, amends : ποινὴν Γανυμήδεος (for the loss of . . .) Ε 266. Cf. Ρ 207.—A sum to be paid by an enemy as compensation for loss or damage, an indemnity : μαχήσομαι εἵνεκα ποινῆς Γ 290 (= τιμήν 286, 288).

ποῖος, -η, -ον. (1) Of what nature, kind, or sort? ποῖοί κ' εἶτ' Ὀδυσῆϊ ἀμυνέμεν ; (what sort of helpers would he find you ?) φ 195.—(2) Without special reference to nature, etc., what? ποίῃ νηΐ σ' ἤγαγον ; π 222. —Carrying on an indirect question : ἐρέσθαι ὁππόθεν οὗτος ἀνήρ, ποίης δ' ἐξ εὔχεται εἶναι γαίης α 406.—(3) Rather exclamatory than interrogative, expressing surprise or anger : ποῖον τὸν μῦθον ἔειπες (what a word is this that you have said !) Α 552. Cf. Δ 350, Θ 209, etc. : α 64, γ 230, φ 168, etc.—Absol. : ποῖον ἔειπες Ν 824. Cf. Ψ 570 : β 85 = ρ 406, β 243.

ποιπνύω [prob. fr. πνῡ-. See πέπνυμαι]. To show activity, exert oneself, be busy: διὰ δώματα ποιπνύοντα (bustling about) A 600. Cf. Θ 219 (to bestir himself and . . .), Ξ 155 (showing himself everywhere), Σ 421 (nimbly played their part), Ω 475 (were doing busy service): γ 430 (busied themselves), υ 149 (bestir yourselves and . . .).

πόκος, -ου, ὁ [πέκω]. A fleece M 451.

πολέες, nom. pl. πολύς.

πολεῖς, nom. pl. πολύς.

πόλεις, acc. pl. πόλις.

πολεμήϊος [πόλεμος]. Of or for war, warlike: ἔργα B 338, E 428, H 236, Λ 719, N 727, 730, τεύχεα H 193: ἔργα μ 116.

πολεμίζω, πτολεμίζω [πόλεμος]. Fut. πτολεμίξω Φ 463. 1 pl. πολεμίξομεν Ω 667. πτολεμίξομεν B 328. Pple. πολεμίξων K 451, O 179. πτολεμίξων N 644. Infin. πολεμίξειν Υ 85. (1) To fight, do battle, take part in the fight, engage in fight: ἐπεί κε κάμω πολεμίζων A 168, πολεμίζειν οὐκ εἴασκον E 802. Cf. B 328, Δ 300, E 520, Θ 428, I 318, etc.: ν 315 = ο 153, ξ 240.—Of horses Π 834. —Of single combat Γ 67, H 152, O 179, Υ 85, etc. —(2) To fight, engage in fight, do battle, with. With dat.: πολεμιζέμεναι Τρώεσσιν I 337. Cf. B 121, Λ 279, Π 89, T 168, 325: γ 86.—With the dat. suppressed: ῥηΐτεροι πολεμίζειν (to fight with) Σ 258.—Of single combat. With dat.: εἰ σοὶ πτολεμίξω Φ 463. Cf. Γ 435, H 42, 169, I 356, O 539.—With cognate acc.: πόλεμον πολεμίζειν B 121, Γ 435.

πολεμιστής, ὁ. **πτολεμιστής** X 132. [πολεμίζω.] A fighter, warrior E 289 = Υ 78 = X 267, E 571, 602 = Π 493 = X 269, K 549, N 300, O 585, P 26, Φ 589, X 132: ω 499.—With implied notion of stoutness: πολεμιστὰ μετ' ἀνδράσιν Π 492.

πόλεμόνδε, πτόλεμόνδε Θ 400. [Acc. of πόλεμος + -δε (1).] (1) To the fight: κηρύσσειν B 443, ὀτρύνων 589. Cf. B 872, Δ 264, H 209, N 186, Σ 452, etc.: φ 39.—(2) To the war λ 448.

πόλεμος, -ου, **πτόλεμος**, -ου, ὁ. (1) War, battle, armed conflict, fighting: πόλεμος καὶ λοιμός A 61, αὐτήν τε πτόλεμόν τε 492. Cf. A 422, B 384, E 388, Z 328, 492, Θ 35, etc.: α 12, δ 146, ε 224, κ 553, λ 537, ξ 222, etc.—(2) A war: πόλεμον περὶ τόνδε φυγόντε M 322. Cf. A 177 = E 891, B 121, Γ 291, N 364, Ξ 87, Ω 8: = θ 183 = ν 91 = 264, α 238 = δ 490 = ξ 368, λ 493, ξ 225, ω 95.—(3) A battle, armed conflict, fight (in some of the passages more or less of a local sense ('field of battle') may be discerned): ἐς πόλεμον θωρηχθῆναι (for the fray) A 226, ὁππότ' ἄρξειαν πολέμοιο Δ 335, ἐκφερέμεν πολέμοιο E 234, λιπὼν πόλεμον Z 254. Cf. A 491, Γ 435, E 132, Z 480, Λ 524, M 436, N 11, P 735, Φ 610, etc.: θ 519, ω 43.—(4) In concrete sense, a fighting force or throng, an army or host: πόλεμον κορύσσων (setting the battle in array) B 273. Cf. I 604, N 536, etc.—(5) The art of war, war, fighting: ἰδρείῃ πολέμοιο Π 359. Cf. I 440, Π 811.—In pl.: πολέμων ἐῢ εἰδώς Δ 310.

πολέος, genit. sing. πολύς.

πόλεος, genit. sing. πόλις.

πολέσ(σ)ι, dat. pl. πολύς.

πολεύω [cf. πωλέομαι]. To go about, go to and fro: κατὰ ἄστυ χ 223.

πόληος, genit. sing. πόλις.

πόλιες, nom. pl. πόλις.

†**πολίζω** [πόλις]. 1 pl. aor. πολίσσαμεν H 453. 3 sing. plupf. pass. πεπόλιστο Υ 217. (1) To found (a city): οὔ πω Ἴλιος ἐν πεδίῳ πεπόλιστο Υ 217.—(2) To build (a wall): τεῖχος H 453.

πολιήτης, ὁ. = πολίτης: κοσμησάμενος πολιήτας (the men of his own city) B 806.

πόλινδε [acc. of πόλις + -δε (1)]. To or towards the city E 224, Z 86, K 209 = 410, N 820: α 189, ζ 255, η 14, λ 188, ξ 26, 372, ο 306, π 155, ρ 182, 185, 375.

πολιοκρόταφος [πολιός + κρόταφος]. Grey-headed: γέροντας Θ 518.

πολιός, -ή, -όν, also -ός, -όν. (1) Of an indeterminate lightish hue (app. without reference to colour), grey, greyish. Epithet of iron I 366 = Ψ 261: φ 3 = 81 = ω 168.—Of a wolf: λύκοιο K 334. —Of the sea (app. referring orig. to the light hue of shallow water) A 350, Δ 248, O 190, Υ 229, etc.: β 261, δ 580, ε 410, ζ 272, λ 75, etc.—(2) In reference to hair, of the hue assumed in old age, grey or white X 77.—In reference to the head or chin, covered with grey or white hair: κάρη, γένειον X 74, Ω 516: κεφαλῆς ω 317.—In reference to men, grey- or white-headed ω 499.

πόλιος, genit. sing. πόλις.

πόλις, πτόλις, ἡ. Genit. πόλιος B 811, E 791, Λ 168, etc.: ζ 262, θ 524, ι 41, etc. πτόλιος Δ 514, P 147, Σ 265, etc.: ζ 294, λ 403, ν 156, etc. πόλεος Φ 567. πόληος Π 395, 549, Φ 516, X 110, 417: α 185, ζ 40, π 383, ψ 121, ω 212, etc. Dat. πόλει E 686, Z 88, H 345, etc.: ζ 9, θ 569, ν 152, etc. πτόλεϊ P 152, Ω 707. πόληϊ Γ 50. Nom. pl. πόλιες ο 412. πόληες Δ 45, 51: τ 174. Genit. πολίων A 125, B 117, Γ 400, etc.: ω 418. Dat. πολίεσσι φ 252, ω 355. Acc. pl. πόλιας θ 560, 574. πόλεας Δ 308. πόλεις B 648, I 328, Σ 342, 490. πόληας ρ 486. (1) A town or city (cf. ἄστυ) A 19, B 12, Δ 4, E 473, etc.: α 170 (your native city), β 154, γ 85, ε 101, etc.—With the name of a particular town in apposition: πόλιν Τροίην A 129. Cf. B 739, Z 152, I 530, Λ 711: λ 510.—In genit.: Ἰλίου πόλιν E 642. Cf. H 345: κ 416.—(2) πόλις ἄκρη (ἀκροτάτη), the highest part of a city, the citadel: ἐν πόλει ἄκρῃ Z 88, 297, 317, H 345, ἐν πόλει ἀκροτάτῃ X 172. Cf. Z 257, Υ 52, X 383.—So without ἄκρη: ὢς φάτ' ἀπὸ πτόλιος θεός Δ 514. Cf. P 144 (see ἄστυ).—(3) With special reference to the inhabitants or community: Τρώων πόλις ἐπὶ πᾶσα βέβηκεν (the whole cityful of them) Π 69, ὄφελος πτόλεϊ τε καὶ αὐτῷ P 152. Cf. Γ 50, Ω 706.

πολίτης, ὁ [πόλις]. In pl., the dwellers in a town or city, the citizens: ὅθεν ἱδρεύοντο πολῖται η 131, ρ 206. Cf. O 558, X 429.

πολλάκι(ς) [πολλός]. Often, many a time A 396, Γ 232, Θ 362, I 490, K 121, N 666, P 408, T 85, Ψ 281: δ 101, π 443, ρ 420 = τ 76, χ 322.

πολλός, -ή, -όν, **πολύς**, -ύ, **πουλύς** (the last fem. E 776, Θ 50, K 27 : δ 709). From πολύς genit. πολέος Δ 244, E 597, Ψ 475, 521, 562 : β 126, θ 405, υ 25. Nom. pl. πολέες B 417, Δ 143, Z 452, etc. : γ 134, ζ 284, χ 204. πολεῖς Λ 708. Genit. πολέων E 691, O 680, Π 398, etc. : δ 267, ι 352, λ 379, etc. Dat. πολέεσσι E 546, I 73, M 399, etc. : ε 54, θ 137, σ 123, υ 200. πολέσι Δ 388, K 262, Λ 688, etc. : β 166, λ 495, υ 30. πολέσσι N 452, P 236, 308. Acc. πολέας A 559, B 4, E 804, etc. : γ 262, δ 170, ω 427. (1) In pl., of great number, many : πολλὰς ψυχάς (many a . . .) A 3, πολέες περ ἐόντες E 94. Cf. B 91, Γ 99, Δ 143, E 383 (many a one of us), Z 296, etc. : πολλῶν ἀνθρώπων α 3, τὰ πολλὰ κατάνεται (these things, many as they are, are wasted, our great substance dwindles away) β 58 = ρ 537.. Cf. α 4, β 166, γ 262, δ 3, θ 217, ι 352 (of the multitudes of men), etc.—(2) In sing. with nouns of multitude, consisting of many individuals, numerous, great, vast : πολὺν ὅμιλον E 334. Cf. Θ 472, N 472, etc. : θ 109, ρ 67, etc.—(3) (a) Absol. in masc. and fem. pl. πολλοί (πολλαί), πολέες, many men or women, many a man or woman, many : ὡς ὀλέσῃς πολέας A 559, ἐκπρεπέ' ἐν πολλοῖσιν (in the multitude) B 483, πολλῇσι κήδε' ἐφῆπτο Z 241. Cf. A 242, B 161, Δ 230, E 176, I 73, etc. : δ 257, θ 17, ν 239, υ 30, φ 367, etc.—(b) οἱ πολλοί, the greater part of an indicated number, most of them (cf. (4) (b)) : τῶν πολλῶν Ἄρης ὑπὸ γούνατ' ἔλυσεν Ω 498.—(4) (a) Absol. in neut. pl. πολλά, many things, much : ὅτι οἱ π. διδοῦσιν B 255. Cf. A 156, I 320, K 4, Λ 684, Ξ 67, etc. : α 427, β 102, δ 81, ζ 174, λ 83, etc.—(b) τὰ πολλά in sense sim. to that of (3) (b) : τὰ π. ἐτώσια θῆκεν χ 273.—(5) In sing., of great amount, quantity, abundance or volume, much : πολὺν λαόν B 115, πολὺς ὀρυμαγδός 810, πολλὸν φῦκος I 7. Cf. Γ 381, Z 525, I 469, K 6, N 804, etc. : β 126, δ 258, ε 323, ζ 86, ξ 136, etc.—Absol. : πολέος ἄξιος (ἄξιον) Ψ 562 : θ 405.—So in pl. with sb. in collective sense : κρέα πολλά Θ 231. Cf. Θ 507, I 97 (much folk), 116 (many men), Σ 560, Ω 556, etc. : ἔεδνα πολλά (a great dowry) α 278, ὄψα πολλά ε 267. Cf. α 112, ι 266, λ 379, τ 64, etc.—(6) In sing. (a) In reference to extension in space, wide, broad, far-stretching : πολέος πεδίοιο Δ 244, πολλός τις ἔκειτο (like some monster 'extended long and large') H 156. Cf. K 27, Υ 249, etc. : β 364, etc.—Absol. : ἐπὶ πολλὸν ἑλίσσεται (wheels wide) Ψ 320.—(b) Of great size, large : τύμβον οὐ πολλόν Ψ 245. Cf. μ 45.—(c) Of great length, long : πολλὴν ὁδόν φ 20.—So of time, long : πολὺν χρόνον B 343, Γ 157, M 9 : β 115, δ 543, 594, etc. Cf. μ 407, etc.—(7) In neut. sing. πολλόν, πολύ, as adv. (a) Greatly, much, in a high degree, to a great extent, far : πολὺ πρίν I 250. Cf. T 113, etc. : β 167.—(b) In reference to position or motion, far : πολὺ πρὸ ἑτάρων Δ 373, πολλὸν ἀποπλαγχθείς N 592. Cf. Z 125, Ξ 30, P 342, X 459, etc. : πολλὸν διήφυσε σαρκός (partitive genit., making an extensive wound) τ 450. Cf. δ 811, ε 350, ζ 40, λ 515, ξ 339, etc.—(c) With a vb. of preference, much, far : πολὺ βούλομαι A 112. Cf. P 331 : ρ 404.—(d) With vbs. of excelling, rivalling or falling short, much, far, by much, by far : πολλὸν κείνων ἐπιδεύεαι ἀνδρῶν E 636, πολλὸν ἐνίκα Σ 252. Cf. I 506, N 815, P 142, T 219, etc. : α 253, γ 121, φ 185, etc.—(e) With comparatives and superlatives, much, far, by much, by far : πολλὸν ἄριστος A 91, πολὺ μεῖζον 167. Cf. A 169, Γ 41, Δ 51, Z 479, Λ 162, etc. : α 113, γ 250, η 321, θ 129, λ 239, etc.—(f) Often, oft, time and again : πολλόν μοι ἐπέσσυτο θυμός I 398.—(8) In neut. pl. πολλά as adv. (a) Greatly, much, in a high degree, intensely, to a great extent : π. μόγησα A 162, π. ἀεκαζομένη Z 458, π. μετακλαύσεσθαι (bitterly) Λ 764. Cf. Θ 22, I 348, Λ 557, Π 826, P 66 (loudly), Ψ 116 (with much play of the heels), Ω 328, etc. : π. μοι κραδίη πόρφυρεν δ 427. Cf. α 1, ν 221, 277, ξ 65, 67, ρ 393 (in many words), etc.—In great numbers : ἄθλων οἷά τε π. πέλονται θ 160.—(b) With vbs. of entreating, enjoining or persuading, repeatedly, with anxious iteration, with insistence or assiduity, earnestly, pressingly, strongly : π. ἠρᾶτο A 35, π. ἐπέτελλεν Δ 229, π. ἀπεμυθεόμην I 109. Cf. E 358, 528, I 183, Λ 782, P 431, etc. : γ 54, 264, 267, δ 433, κ 521, etc.—Sim. : π. κεν ἀθανάτοισιν ἀνὰ χεῖρας ἀείραι H 130.—(c) Often, oft, time and again : π. πρὸς ἠέλιον κεφαλὴν τρέπεν ν 29. Cf. B 798, I 568, P 430, Ω 391, 755 : ε 389, ι 128, λ 536.—(d) Far and wide : π. ἴθυσε μάχη Z 2.

πολύαινος [πολυ-, πολύς + αἶνος]. App., much praised, illustrious. Epithet of Odysseus I 673 = K 544, Λ 430 : μ 184.

πολυάϊξ, -ῖκος [πολυ-, πολύς + ἀϊκ-, ἀΐσσω]. Much rushing, impetuous, violent. Epithet of war or battle : πολέμοιο A 165, Υ 328 : λ 314.—So κάματος πολυάϊξ, the weariness of many assaults E 811.

πολυανθής [πολυ-, πολύς + ἄνθος]. Much blossoming, flowery : ὕλης ξ 353.

πολυάρητος [πολυ-, πολύς + ἀράομαι]. The object of many prayers, called upon in many prayers : θεός ζ 280.—The subject of many prayers, longed for in many prayers : [πάϊς] τ 404.

πολύαρνι, *dat.* [πολυ-, πολύς + ἄρνα. Cf. πολύρρην]. Rich in sheep : Θυέστῃ B 106.

πολυβενθής, -έος [πολυ-, πολύς + βένθος]. With many deeps or recesses : λιμένος A 432 : = π 324, κ 125, π 352, ἁλός δ 406.

πολύβουλος, -ον [πολυ-, πολύς + βουλή]. Of many devices. Epithet of Athene E 260 : π 282.

πολυβούτης [πολυ-, πολύς + βοῦς]. Rich in oxen : ἄνδρες πολυβοῦται I 154 = 296.

πολυγηθής [πολυ-, πολύς + γηθέω]. Bringing the glad changes of the year. Epithet of ὧραι Φ 450.

πολυδαίδαλος, -ον [πολυ-, πολύς + δαίδαλον]. (1) Displaying much curious workmanship, elaborately or richly wrought or adorned : θώρηκος Γ 358, ἀσπίδα Λ 32, κλισμῷ Ω 597, etc. : θάλαμον ζ 15, χρυσός ν 11, ὅρμον σ 295.—(2) Skilled in curious arts : Σιδόνες Ψ 743.

πολυδάκρυος, -ον [πολυ-, πολύς + δάκρυον]. =next: μάχης P 192.

πολύδακρυς [πολυ-, πολύς + δάκρυ]. Bringing many tears, woeful, baleful. Epithet of war or battle: Ἄρηα Γ 132, Θ 516 = Τ 318, πόλεμον Γ 165, Χ 487, ὑσμίνη P 544.

πολυδάκρῡτος [πολυ-, πολύς + δακρύω]. The subject of many tears, much to be wept for Ω 620.—Accompanied by many tears, tearful: γόοιο τ 213 = 251 = φ 57.

πολυδειράς, -άδος [πολυ-, πολύς + δειράς, rock]. Rocky. Epithet of Olympus A 499 = E 754 = Θ 3.

πολυδένδρεος [πολυ-, πολύς + δένδρεον]. Abounding in trees, treey δ 737, ψ 139, 359.

πολύδεσμος, -ον [πολυ-, πολύς + δεσμός]. Having many bands or cords, held together by much cordage: σχεδίης ε 33, η 264.

πολυδίψιος [πολυ-, πολύς + δίψα]. Dry, waterless. Epithet of Argos Δ 171.

πολύδωρος, -ον [πολυ-, πολύς + δῶρον]. Bringing (her parents) a great bride-price (cf. ἀλφεσίβοιος); or perh., bountiful (cf. ἠπιόδωρος): ἄλοχος Z 394, Χ 88: ω 294.

πολύζυγος, -ον [πολυ-, πολύς + ζυγόν]. Having many benches: νηΐ B 293.

πολυηγερής [πολυ-, πολύς + ἀγείρω]. Gathered together from many quarters: ἐπίκουροι Λ 564.

πολυήρατος, -ον [πολυ-, πολύς + ἔραμαι]. Much desired or to be desired, lovely, charming, sweet: ἥβην ο 366. Cf. ο 126, ψ 354.—Epithet of a place: Θήβη λ 275.

πολυηχής [πολυ-, πολύς + ἠχή]. Much resounding, roaring: αἰγιαλῷ Δ 422.—Much trilling: φωνήν τ 521.

πολυθαρσής, -ές [πολυ-, πολύς + θάρσος]. Bold, dauntless: μένος P 156, Τ 37: ν 387.

πολυϊδρείη, -ης [πολύϊδρις]. Great prudence or shrewdness. In pl.: νόου πολυϊδρείῃσιν β 346.

πολύϊδρις [πολυ-, πολύς + (F)ιδ-, οἶδα. See εἴδω (C)]. Very shrewd or astute ο 459, ψ 82.

πολύϊππος [πολυ-, πολύς + ἵππος]. Rich in horses: Μέντορος N 171.

πολυκαγκής [πολυ-, πολύς + καγκ- as in κάγκανος]. Parching: δίψαν Λ 642.

πολύκαρπος, -ον [πολυ-, πολύς + καρπός[1]]. Bearing much fruit, fruitful: ἀλωή η 122. Cf. ω 221.

πολυκερδείη, -ης [πολυκερδής]. Great shrewdness, astuteness or cunning. In pl.: πολυκερδείῃσι νόοιο ψ 77. Cf. ω 167.

πολυκερδής [πολυ-, πολύς + κέρδος]. Very shrewd, astute or cunning: νόον ν 255.

πολύκεστος [πολυ-, πολύς + κεστός]. Much embroidered: ἱμάς Γ 371.

πολυκηδής [πολυ-, πολύς + κῆδος]. Troublous, grievous: νόστον ι 37, ψ 351.

πολυκλήϊς, -ῖδος. Written also **πολυκληΐς**, -ῖδος [πολυ-, πολύς + κληΐς]. App., having many row-locks (cf. κληΐς (3)). Epithet of ships B 74, 175, H 88, Θ 239, N 742, O 63, Ψ 248: θ 161, υ 382, φ 19, ψ 324.

πολύκληρος [πολυ-, πολύς + κλῆρος (3)]. Owning much land, wealthy ξ 211.

πολύκλητος [πολυ-, πολύς + κλη-, καλέω]. Called together from many quarters Δ 438, K 420.

πολύκλυστος [πολυ-, πολύς + κλύζω]. Much surging or dashing. Epithet of the sea: πόντῳ δ 354, ζ 204, τ 277.

πολύκμητος [πολυ-, πολύς + κμη-, κάμνω]. Much or elaborately wrought Z 48 = K 379 = Λ 133: = φ 10, ξ 324. — Elaborately or richly adorned: θαλάμοιο δ 718.

πολύκνημος [πολυ-, πολύς + κνημός]. With many mountain-spurs, hilly: Ἐτεωνόν B 497.

πολυκοιρανίη, ἡ [πολυ-, πολύς + κοίρανος]. The rule of many B 204.

πολυκτήμων [πολυ-, πολύς + κτῆμα]. Having many possessions, wealthy E 613.

πολυλήϊος [πολυ-, πολύς + λήϊον]. Having much corn-land E 613.

πολύλλιστος [πολυ-, πολύς + λίσσομαι]. Greatly longed for ε 445.

πολύμηλος [πολυ-, πολύς + μῆλον[1]]. Rich in sheep or goats B 705, Ξ 490.—Of a place B 605.

πολύμητις [πολυ-, πολύς + μῆτις]. Of many counsels or devices. Epithet of Odysseus A 311, Γ 200, Δ 329, etc.: β 173, δ 763, ε 214, etc.—Of Hephaestus Φ 355.

πολυμηχανίη, -ης, ἡ [πολυμήχανος]. Skill or cunning in contrivance ψ 321.

πολυμήχανος [πολυ-, πολύς + μηχανή = μῆχος]. Of many devices, resourceful, never at a loss: ἐπεὶ π. ἐστιν α 205.—Epithet of Odysseus (always in voc.) B 173, etc.: ε 203, ω 192, etc.

πολυμνήστη, *fem. adj.* [πολυ-, πολύς + μνάομαι]. Wooed by many δ 770, ξ 64, ψ 149.

πολύμῡθος [πολυ-, πολύς + μῦθος]. Of many words, having a flow of language Γ 214: β 200.

πολυπαίπαλος [πολυ-, πολύς + παιπάλη, fine flour, fig. of subtlety or wiliness]. Full of wiles, crafty: Φοίνικες ο 419.

πολυπάμων, -ονος [πολυ-, πολύς + πάομαι, to acquire]. Of many possessions, wealthy Δ 433.

πολυπενθής, -έος [πολυ-, πολύς + πένθος]. Full of sorrows, sorrowful, woeful I 563: ξ 386, ψ 15.

πολυπῖδαξ, -ακος [πολυ-, πολύς + πῖδαξ]. With many springs, many-fountained. Epithet of Mount Ida Θ 47, Ξ 157, O 151, etc.

πολύπικρος [πολυ-, πολύς + πικρός]. In neut. pl. as adv., in right bitter fashion π 255.

πολύπλαγκτος [πολυ-, πολύς + πλαγκτός]. Tossed about or roving from shore to shore ρ 425, υ 195.—Absol. ρ 511.—Of the wandering wind Λ 308.

πολύπτυχος, -ον [πολυ-, πολύς + πτυχ-, πτύξ]. With many clefts or glens. Epithet of Olympus Θ 411, Υ 5.—Of Mount Ida Φ 449, Χ 171.

πολύπῡρος, -ον [πολυ-, πολύς + πυρός]. Rich in wheat: νῆσος ο 406.—Of places Λ 756, O 372: ξ 335 = τ 292, π 396.

πολύρρην (πολύFρην) [πολυ-, πολύς + *Fρήν. See ἄρνα. Cf. πολύαρνι]. Rich in sheep I 154 = 296.

πολύρρηνος. = prec. λ 257.

πολύς. See πολλός.

πολύσκαρθμος, -ον [πολυ-, πολύς + σκαίρω]. Far-bounding: Μυρίνης B 814.

πολυσπερής [πολυ-, πολύς + σπείρω]. Widely dispersed, spread over the face of the earth: *ἀνθρώπων* B 804. Cf. λ 365.

πολυστάφυλος, -ον [πολυ-, πολύς + σταφυλή]. Rich in grapes B 507, 537.

πολύστονος, -ον [πολυ-, πολύς + στόνος]. Much sighing, full of sorrows τ 118.—Causing many sighs, grievous, baneful A 445, Λ 73, O 451.

πολύτλας [πολυ-, πολύς + τλάω]. Much enduring, stout, unflinching. Epithet of Odysseus Θ 97, I 676 = K 248, Ψ 729, 778: ε 171, ζ 1, η 1, θ 446, etc.

πολυτλήμων [as prec.]. = prec.: *θυμός* H 152: *πολυτλήμων εἰμί* σ 319.

πολύτλητος [as prec.]. That has suffered much, torn by suffering: *γέροντες* λ 38.

πολυτρήρων, -ωνος [πολυ-, πολύς + τρήρων]. Haunted by pigeons B 502, 582.

πολύτρητος [πολυ-, πολύς + τρη-, τετραίνω]. Full of holes: *σπόγγοισιν* α 111, χ 439, 453.

πολύτροπος [πολυ-, πολύς + τροπή]. Of many devices, resourceful. Epithet of Odysseus α 1, κ 330.

πολυφάρμακος, -ον [πολυ-, πολύς + φάρμακον]. (**1**) Conversant with drugs or medicaments Π 28. —(**2**) Knowing many charms or spells κ 276.

πολύφημος, -ον [πολυ-, πολύς + φήμη]. (**1**) Where many voices are heard, voiceful: *ἀγορήν* β 150. —(**2**) Knowing many tales or songs: *ἀοιδός* χ 376.

πολύφλοισβος, -ον [πολυ-, πολύς + φλοῖσβος]. Loud sounding, voiceful. Epithet of the sea A 34, B 209, Z 347, I 182, N 798, Ψ 59: ν 85, 220.

πολύφορβος, -ον, and -η, -ον [πολυ-, πολύς + φορβή]. That feeds many. Epithet of the earth: *γαῖαν πολυφόρβην* I 568, *πολυφόρβου γαίης* Ξ 200, 301.

πολύφρων, -ονος [πολυ-, πολύς + φρήν]. Of great intelligence or sense, sensible, discreet. Absol.: *ἐφέηκε πολύφρονά περ χαλεπῆναι* Σ 108. Cf. ξ 464. —As epithet of Hephaestus, of high intellectual capacity, ingenious, skilful Φ 367: θ 297, 327.—In sim. sense as epithet of Odysseus α 83 = ξ 424 = υ 239 = φ 204, υ 329.

πολύχαλκος, -ον [πολυ-, πολύς + χαλκός]. (**1**) Rich in bronze K 315.—Of places Σ 289: ο 425.—(**2**) Fig. of the heavens (cf. *χάλκεον οὐρανόν* P 425) E 504: γ 2.

πολύχρυσος, -ον [πολυ-, πολύς + χρυσός]. Rich in gold K 315.—Of places H 180, Λ 46, Σ 289: γ 304.

πολυωπός [πολυ-, πολύς + ὀπ-, ὄπωπα. See ὁράω]. With many openings or meshes. Epithet of a net: *δικτύῳ* χ 386.

πομπεύς, ὁ [πομπή]. One who conducts, escorts, sees safe, a guide, escort, protector: *οἵ τοι πομπῆες ἔσονται* γ 325. Cf. γ 376, δ 362, ν 71, υ 364.

πομπεύω [πομπεύς]. To conduct, escort, see safe: *αὐτή μιν πόμπευον* ν 422.

πομπή, -ῆς, ἡ [πέμπω]. (**1**) (**a**) Conduct, escort, guidance, seeing safe: *θεῶν ὑπὸ πομπῇ* Z 171. Cf. ε 32, η 193, ν 151, 180.—(**b**) A conducting, escorting, seeing safe: *ἐκ πομπῆς ἀνιοῦσαν* θ 568 = ν 150 = 176.—(**2**) A dispatching or speeding on one's way, an arranging for or presiding over one's departure: *ὄφρα πομπῆς τύχῃς* ζ 290, *οὐκέτι φαίνετο π.* (*i.e.* they had lost their favouring wind) κ 79. Cf. ε 173, 233, η 151, 191, 317, θ 30, 31, 33, 545, ι 518, κ 18, λ 332, 352, 357, ν 41, τ 313.

πομπός, -οῦ, ὁ, ἡ [πέμπω]. One who conducts, conveys, escorts, sees safe, a guide, escort, protector: *τῷ ἅμα πομπὸν ἕπεσθαι* δ 162. Cf. N 416, Π 671, 681, Ω 153, 182, 437, 439, 461: δ 826, θ 566 = ν 174.

πονέομαι [πόνος]. Pres. pple. *πονεύμενος*, -ου Δ 374, N 288. (ἀμφι-.) (**1**) To labour or work with one's hands, work, toil: *ὅπλα, τοῖς ἐπονεῖτο* Σ 413. Cf. H 442: π 13, υ 159 (did their work). —(**2**) To work at: *ὄφρα ταῦτα πονεῖτο* Σ 380.—To produce by work, make, construct: *τύμβον* Ψ 245. —(**3**) To be busy, be much occupied, busy oneself, have or engage in toil or labour, exert oneself: *ᾔδεε ἀδελφεὸν ὡς ἐπονεῖτο* B 409. Cf. I 12, 348, K 70, 116, 117, 121: ι 250 = 310 = 343, ρ 258 and υ 281 (the attendants).—(**4**) To be busied or engaged, busy oneself (with or about something): *πεπόνητο καθ' ἵππους* (*i.e.* they were taking up all his attention) O 447. Cf. Ω 444.—(**5**) To busy oneself about, be engaged or engage oneself in, see to: *τάδ' ἀμφὶ πονησόμεθα* Ψ 159. Cf. ο 222, χ 377.—To attend to, look to, set in order: *ὅπλα* λ 9, μ 151.—(**6**) To be engaged in the toil and moil of war, take part in the fight, fight: *οἵ μιν ἴδοντο πονεύμενον* (at work with his spear) Δ 374, *πονέοντο καθ' ὑσμίνην* E 84 = 627. Cf. N 288, Υ 359.

πόνος, -ου, ὁ [cf. πένομαι]. (**1**) Labour, toil, work, trouble: *ἐπεὶ παύσαντο πόνου* A 467 = B 430 = H 319. Cf. Δ 26, 57, E 567 (all they had gone through), 667 (they were too busy), Z 77 (the chief burden), K 164: β 334, θ 529, λ 54 (they had so many other things to attend to), π 478 = ω 384, ψ 249.—In pl., toils, troubles, difficulties: *τὸν Ζεὺς ἐνέηκε πόνοισιν* K 89. Cf. K 245, 279: δ 818, ν 301, υ 48.—(**2**) Hardship, suffering, distress: *ἄνευθε πόνου καὶ ἀνίης* η 192. Cf. X 488: ν 423.—So, app., *πότε κέν τις ἀναπνεύσειε πόνοιο;* T 227 (referring to the hardship of fasting).—(**3**) Referring specially to the toil and moil of war, war, fighting: *καὶ πόνος ἐστὶν ἀνιηθέντα νέεσθαι* (we have e'en had fighting enough to disgust a man and send him home) B 291, *ἰαχή τε π. τε* Δ 456. Cf. B 420, E 517, Z 525 (have to bear this heavy burden of war), Λ 430, M 348, N 2, Ξ 480, O 416 (fought their fight), Φ 137, X 11 (app., the slaughtering of them), etc.: μ 117.—(**4**) In concrete sense, a fighting throng: *ἔβη ἂμ πόνον ἀνδρῶν* N 239 = Π 726 = P 82.—The field of battle: *φέρον ἐκ πόνου* Ξ 429. Cf. P 718. —(**5**) The result of toil, weariness Z 355.

ποντόθεν [πόντος + -θεν (1)]. From the open sea: *κῦμα ποντόθεν ὀρνύμενον* Ξ 395.

πόντονδε [acc. of πόντος + -δε (1)]. Towards the open sea, seawards: *φέρεν π. θύελλα* κ 48.—Into the sea: *π. βαλὼν βέλος* ι 495.

ποντοπορεύω [ποντοπόρος]. To traverse the sea, sail the sea ε 277, 278, η 267.

ποντοπορέω. =prec. Of a ship λ 11.

ποντοπόρος, -ον [πόντος + -πορος, πείρω]. Cleaving the seas. Epithet of ships A 439, B 771, Γ 46, etc.: μ 69, ξ 339, ο 284, etc.

πόντος, -ου, ὁ. Ablative ποντόφιν ω 83. The sea, the deep sea, the high sea, the open sea A 350, B 145, 665, Γ 47, Δ 276, etc.: α 4, β 263, γ 15, δ 359, η 109, etc.—With ἅλς: π. ἁλός (the deep of the sea) Φ 59.—Distinguished in terms from the land: πείρατα γαίης καὶ πόντοιο Θ 479. Cf. δ 821, ε 294, π 367, etc.—From the heavens: ἐξ αἰθέρος ἔμπεσε πόντῳ ε 50. Cf. Ξ 258.

πόποι. Always with ὢ (ὤ), expressing contextually surprise, a being struck by something, grief, anger, remonstrance, rebuke, disappointment, a being balked of something, a drawing of special attention to something, or the like A 254, B 272 (look you now!), Θ 427 (ah well!), N 99, O 467 (ah me!), Π 745 (see now!), P 171, X 373 (why, look you!), etc.: α 32 (to see now how . . .!), δ 169, 333, ε 286, ι 507, κ 38, etc.

πόρε, 3 sing. aor. πόρω.

πορθέω [cf. πέρθω]. (δια-.) To sack or ravage (a town or land) Δ 308: ξ 264 = ρ 433.

πορθμεύς, ὁ [πορθμός]. A ferryman υ 187.

πορθμός, -οῦ, ὁ [πόρος]. A narrow strip of water, a channel: ἐν πορθμῷ Ἰθάκης τε Σάμοιό τε (between . . . and . . .) δ 671 = ο 29.

πόρις, ἡ = πόρτις κ 410.

πόρκης, ὁ. In a spear, a metal ferrule, or perh. a lashing of wire, securing the tongue of the head (see καυλός (1) (a)) in the shaft Z 320 = Θ 495.

πόρον, aor. πόρω.

πόρος, -ου, ὁ [πορ-, περάω[1]]. A place where a river may be passed, a ford B 592, Ξ 433 = Φ 1 = Ω 692.—πόροι ἁλός, the paths of the sea μ 259.

πόρπη, -ης, ἡ [πορ-, πείρω]. App. = περόνη Σ 401.

πορσαίνω [πόρω]. Nom. sing. fem. fut. pple. πορσανέουσα Γ 411. Also **πορσύνω.** Of a wife, to prepare (and share) (her husband's bed): κείνου πορσανέουσα λέχος Γ 411: τῷ ἄλοχος λέχος πόρσυνεν γ 403. Cf. η 347.

πόρταξ, -ακος. =next P 4.

πόρτις, ἡ [cf. πόρις]. A calf E 162.

πορφύρεος, -η, -ον [cf. next]. (1) Of disturbed water, gleaming, glancing: πορφύρεον κῦμα ποταμοῖο Φ 326, ἀμφὶ κῦμα στείρῃ πορφύρεον μεγάλ' ἴαχεν (flashing as it fell off on each side of the cutwater) A 482: = β 428. Cf. Π 391: λ 243, ν 85 (the white wake).—So in reference to the light reflected from (the irregular surface of) a cloud: πορφυρέῃ νεφέλῃ πυκάσασα ἓ αὐτήν P 551.—Applied to the sinister gleam figured to play on (the cloud or mist of) death: πορφύρεος θάνατος E 83 = Π 334 = Υ 477.—To the lurid gleam of the rainbow set against a storm-cloud: πορφυρέην ἶριν P 547.—To the warm hue of blood: αἵματι πορφυρέῳ P 361.—(2) Of bright hue, bright, brilliant, gay: δίπλακα Γ 126, X 441, φᾶρος Θ 221, τάπησιν I 200, ῥήγεα Ω 645, πέπλοισιν 796: χλαῖναν δ 115 = 154, τ 225, ῥήγεα δ 298 = η 337, κ 353, φᾶρος θ 84, σφαῖραν 373, δίπλακα τ 242, τάπητας υ 151.

πορφύρω [redup. fr. φύρω). Of the disturbed sea, to heave Ξ 16.—Fig., of the heart, to be troubled, moved, stirred: πολλά οἱ κραδίη πόρφυρεν Φ 551. Cf. δ 427 = 572 = κ 309.

*†**πόρω.** Aor. πόρον Ω 60: δ 745, ι 360, τ 255, ω 273. 3 sing. ἔπορε (πόρε) A 72, Δ 219, Z 168, Λ 353, O 441, T 21, Ψ 92, 277, Ω 30, etc.: δ 130, ε 321, ζ 228, ι 201, κ 7, λ 282, μ 302, τ 512, υ 71, etc. 3 pl. ἔπορον P 196: π 230. πόρον Z 218, Ω 234. 3 sing. subj. πόρῃ Z 228: χ 7. πόρῃσι β 186, π 77, υ 335. 1 pl. πόρωμεν Ψ 893. 3 πόρωσι Π 86. 2 sing. opt. πόροις ι 267. 3 πόροι ξ 460, π 392, σ 202, τ 413, φ 162. Imp. πόρε I 513: θ 477. Pple. πορών Π 178, Φ 80: τ 529. Pl. πορόντες τ 460. **Pass.** 3 sing. pf. πέπρωται Σ 329. Pple. πεπρωμένος, -ου Γ 309, O 209, Π 441, X 179. **(1)** To give, put into another's hands, hand to him: σήματα λυγρά Z 168.—**(2)** To give, make another the owner of, present, make a present of: ξεινήϊα Z 218, τεύχεα H 146. Cf. K 546, Λ 353, O 441, Π 86, 143 = T 390, P 196, T 21, Ψ 92, 277, 540, 893, Ω 234: β 186, δ 130, 617, ι 267, π 77, etc.—To cause (a woman) to conceive (a child): πόρεν οἱ ἀγλαὸν υἱόν Π 185.—**(3)** To pay (a bride-price or ransom): ἀπερείσια ἕδνα Π 178, λύμην τρὶς τόσσα πορών Φ 80. Cf. Π 190, X 472: λ 282, τ 529.—**(4)** To give in marriage: ἀνδρὶ πόρον παράκοιτιν Ω 60. Cf. κ 7.—Sim. in reference to a concubine I 667.—**(5)** To give, furnish, supply, to another for his use or to meet his needs: φάρμακα Δ 219: δ 228, σῖτον καὶ μέθυ 745. Cf. ε 321, 372, ζ 228, θ 477, ι 360, κ 302, μ 302, ξ 460, τ 255.—To administer (a drug): φάρμακον κ 394.—**(6)** Of immaterial things, to give, grant, allow, bestow, confer: μαντοσύνην A 72. Cf. Ω 30: κ 494, υ 71, χ 7.—To inflict or send (evil): κακά ι 460, πένθος τ 512.—To send (death) σ 202.—**(7)** With infin., to grant, allow: πόρε Διὸς κούρῃσιν ἕπεσθαι τιμήν (let them have their meed of honour) I 513.—With the infin. suppressed: κτείνειν ὅν κε θεός γε πόρῃ Z 228.—**(8)** In pf. pass., to be decreed by fate, to be fated or destined: ὁπποτέρῳ θανάτοιο τέλος πεπρωμένον ἐστίν Γ 309.—Impers. with acc. and infin.: ἄμφω πέπρωται ὁμοίην γαῖαν ἐρεῦσαι Σ 329.—Of a person, to be fated, to have his lot or portion fixed, in a specified way (see αἶσα (4)): ὁμῇ πεπρωμένον αἴσῃ O 209. Cf. Π 441 = X 179.

πόσε [-σε]. Whither? πόσε φεύγετε; Π 422: ζ 199, πόσ' ἴμεν; κ 431.

ποσί, dat. pl. πούς.

Ποσιδήϊος. Of Poseidon: ἄλσος B 506.—In neut., a temple of Poseidon ζ 266.

πόσις[1], ὁ [cf. δέσποινα]. A husband Γ 163, E 71, Z 240, H 411, Θ 190, N 766, etc.: α 15, δ 137, ζ 277, κ 115, λ 430, ξ 130, etc.

πόσις[2], ἡ [πο- as in ποτόν]. Drink: οὐ π. οὐδὲ βρῶσις T 210. Cf. T 231, 320: α 191, ζ 209 = 246,

248, κ 176, μ 320, ν 72, ο 490.—See also under ἵημι[1] (9).

ποσσῆμαρ [πόσ(σ)ος, how many ? + ἦμαρ]. For how many days ? In indirect question Ω 657.

ποσσί, dat. pl. πούς.

πόστος [πόσος, how many ?]. Which in a series of numbers ? πόστον ἔτος ἐστίν, ὅτε . . .; (how many years is it since . . . ?) ω 288.

ποταμόνδε [acc. of ποταμός + -δε (1)]. To, towards or into the or a river Φ 13, 120 : κ 159.

ποταμός, -οῦ, ὁ. (1) A river B 861, E 87, Z 508, M 18, O 691, etc. : δ 477, ε 441, ζ 59, η 281, κ 351, etc.—With the name of a particular river added, the river . . . : ποταμὸν Κηφισόν B 522. Cf. B 659, E 544, Λ 499, etc. : ξ 258 = ρ 427.—Of ocean : ποταμοῖο ῥέεθρα Ὠκεανοῦ Ξ 245. Cf. Σ 607, Υ 7 : λ 639, μ 1.—(2) Personified, a river-god : ποταμοὶ καὶ γαῖα, ὑμεῖς μάρτυροι ἔστε Γ 278. Cf. E 544, Υ 7, Φ 136, etc. : λ 238.

ποτάομαι, ποτέομαι [πέτομαι]. 3 sing. pf. πεπότηται λ 222. 3 pl. πεποτήαται B 90. (ἀμφιποτάομαι, ἐκποτέομαι.) To fly about, fly hither and thither : αἱ μέν τ' ἔνθα ἅλις πεποτήαται, αἱ δέ τε ἔνθα (are on the wing) B 90, ἔνθα καὶ ἔνθα ποτῶνται 462 : ψυχὴ ἀποπταμένη πεπότηται (hovers about) λ 222, ὡς ὅτε νυκτερίδες ποτέονται ω 7.

πότε. When ? πότ' ᾤχετο ; δ 642. Cf. T 227.

ποτέ, *enclitic.* (1) (a) In time past, in days of old, formerly, once, once upon a time : ὥς ποτ' ἐπ' εἰρήνης B 797. Cf. A 39, 260, 453, B 547, Γ 180, 205, Δ 106, etc. : τήν ποτε πρίατο α 430. Cf. γ 84, δ 342, ζ 162, η 9, 59, θ 76, etc.—(b) In reference to the future, at some time, some day, in days to come, yet : ἦ ποτ' Ἀχιλλῆος ποθὴ ἵξεται υἷας Ἀχαιῶν A 240. Cf. A 205, 213, Δ 164, 182, etc. : τάχ' ἄν ποτε καὶ τίσις εἴη β 76. Cf. β 342, γ 216, θ 461, 567, etc.—(2) In negative or conditional contexts, at any time, ever : εἴ ποτε δὴ αὖτε χρειὼ ἐμεῖο γένηται A 340. Cf. A 155, 166, 490, B 202, Δ 410, E 700, K 453, etc. : οὐδέ ποτ' ἔσβη οὖρος γ 182. Cf. β 26, 203, γ 127, δ 360, 566, ε 39, 151, θ 562, etc.—With οὐ. See οὐ (8) (a) and (c).

πότερος. In pl. in an indirect question, which of two groups : οὐκ ἂν γνοίης ποτέροισι μετείη E 85.

ποτή, ἡ [πέτομαι]. App., flight : ποτῇ ἀνεδύσετο λίμνης (flew up from . . .) ε 337.

ποτής, -ῆτος, ἡ [πο- as in ποτόν]. Drink : ἐδητύος ἠδὲ ποτῆτος Λ 780. Cf. T 306 : δ 788, ε 201, ι 87 = κ 58, κ 379, 384, ρ 603, σ 407.

ποτητός [ποτάομαι]. Winged. Absol. in neut. pl., birds : τῇ οὐδὲ ποτητὰ παρέρχεται μ 62.

ποτί [cf. προτί, πρός]. (I) Adv. Besides, in addition, too : ποτὶ δ' ἄσπετα δῶρα δίδωμι υ 342. Cf. K 108, Π 86.—(II) Prep. (With anastrophe when immediately following the case-form.) (1) With dat. (a) On, upon, against : οὐδέ μιν παῖδες ποτὶ γούνασι παππάζουσιν E 408 : νῆάς γε ποτὶ σπιλάδεσσιν ἔαξαν κύματα γ 298. Cf. ε 401, θ 378.—In pregnant sense : ποτὶ σκῆπτρον βάλε γαίῃ A 245. Cf. Δ 112, Υ 420 : μή με βάλῃ ποτὶ πέτρῃ ε 415. Cf. β 80, ζ 310, θ 190, ι 289, λ 423, —(b) In the direction of, towards : τὸν ποτί οἷ εἷλεν ω 347.—(2) With acc. (a) To, towards, in the direction of : εἶμι Διὸς ποτὶ δῶ A 426. Cf. Z 286, M 240, 273, O 295, T 395, X 101, Ω 506, etc. : γ 295, ζ 95, θ 321, 374, μ 432, ρ 75, τ 389, etc.—Indicating arrival at a point : ἄστυ πότι P 419 : ἐπεὶ ἵκευ ἐμὸν ποτὶ δῶ ν 4. Cf. Φ 505 : γ 488, ζ 297, etc.—Sim. : ἐξ ἱστὸν ἄραξε ποτὶ τρόπιν (right (down) to the keel, at the keel) μ 422.—In reference to sitting *on* something : ἢ ποτὶ βωμὸν ἵζοιτο χ 334. Cf. χ 379.—(b) In reference to speech : ποτὶ Πρίαμον φάτο Ω 353. Cf. Ω 598.—In reference to the sight : παπταίνοντες ποτὶ τοίχους χ 24.—(c) In reference to the direction in which action takes place, towards, against : ἐκλύσθη θάλασσα ποτὶ κλισίας Ξ 392. Cf. Ξ 394, 396 (app. with an object to be supplied), P 264 : ε 402, μ 71.—(d) In reference to placing or leaning *against* something : ποτὶ τοῖχον ἀρηρότες β 342. Cf. Ψ 510 : σ 102.—To placing *beside* something : ποτὶ τύμβον δείμομεν πύργους (τεῖχος ἔδειμαν) H 337, 436 (*i.e.*, app., including the mound in the fortification, the wall starting from each side of it). Cf. M 64 (*i.e.* the wall comes next).—(e) In reference to position, in the direction of, towards : ὅσσοι [ναίουσι] ποτὶ ζόφον ν 241. Cf. Λ 622, Ψ 869.—(f) In reference to time, at the approach of, towards : ποτὶ ἕσπερα ρ 191.—(3) With genit. In reference to position maintained by one moving person in relation to another, towards, on the side of (something) : αὐτὸς δὲ ποτὶ πτόλιος πέτετ' αἰεί (kept on the city side of him) X 198.

ποτιδέρκομαι. See προσδέρκομαι.

†ποτιδέχομαι [ποτι-, προσ- (3)]. Aor. pple. ποτιδέγμενος, -ου H 415, I 628, K 123, T 234, 336 : β 186, 205, 403, η 161, ι 545, φ 156, χ 380, ψ 91, ω 396. Nom. pl. fem. -αι B 137.—(1) To wait for (a coming or expected event or person), await, look out for : ἐμὴν ὁρμήν K 123. Cf. T 234 : ἡμέας ι 545. Cf. β 403, η 161, ω 396.—With clause : ποτιδέγμενοι ὁππότ' ἄρ' ἔλθοι H 415. Cf. ψ 91.—Absol. : ποτιδέγμενοι ἤματα πάντα (waiting on here indefinitely) β 205, φ 156. Cf. B 137 and I 628 (looking for our coming).—To await or anticipate with apprehension : ἀγγελίην T 336. Cf. χ 380.—(2) To expect, look for, the receipt of (something) : δῶρον β 186.

ποτιδόρπιος [ποτι-, προσ- (3) + δόρπον]. Available for, ready to be taken at or to be used in connexion with, one's evening meal ι 234, 249.

ποτικέκλιται, 3 sing. pf. pass. See προσκλίνω.

ποτινίσ(σ)ομαι [ποτι-, προσ- (2)]. To come, be brought, to a specified place : ἐς Ὀρχομενόν I 381.

†ποτιπτήσσω [ποτι-, προσ- (1)]. Nom. pl. fem. pf. pple. ποτιπεπτηυῖαι. To crouch down *towards.* With genit. : ἀκταὶ λιμένος ποτιπεπτηυῖαι (sinking down in front of it and so closing it in) ν 98.

ποτιπτύσσω. See προσπτύσσω.

ποτιτέρπω [ποτι-, προσ- (3)]. To engage agreeably the attention of, entertain O 401.

ποτιφωνήεις [ποτι-, προσ- (3) + φωνήεις in sim.

sense fr. φωνή]. Endowed with speech: εἰ ποτιφωνήεις γένοιο ι 456.

πότμος, -ου, ὁ. (1) What befalls one, one's lot or fate: ὃν πότμον γοόωσα Π 857 = Χ 363. Cf. κ 245.—(2) Evil fate or destiny, bane, death: θάνατον καὶ πότμον Β 359, Ο 495, Υ 337, εἰ πότμον ἀναπλήσῃς βιότοιο (a fate that ends thy life) Δ 170. Cf. Δ 396, Ζ 412, Η 52, Λ 263, Σ 96, Φ 588, Χ 39: β 250, γ 16 (the manner of his death), δ 196, 339, 562, λ 197, τ 550, ω 471, etc.

πότνα. =next. πότνα θεά, mighty goddess ε 215, ν 391, υ 61.

πότνια [ποτ- as in δεσπότης, master. Cf. δέσποινα]. (1) Mistress, queen: πότνια θηρῶν, Ἄρτεμις Φ 470.—(2) As a title of honour. (a) Given to goddesses. To Here Α 551, 568, Θ 198, Ν 826, Ξ 159, Ο 34, Σ 239, etc.: δ 513.—To Hebe Δ 2.—To Enyo Ε 592.—To Athene Ζ 305.—To Calypso α 14, ε 149.—To Circe θ 448, κ 394, 549, μ 36.—(b) Joined with μήτηρ, lady mother Α 357, Ζ 264, Ι 561, Ν 430, Σ 35, Τ 291, etc.: ζ 30, λ 180, μ 134, ο 385, σ 5, τ 462, etc.

ποτόν, -οῦ, τό [πο-, πίνω. See ἐκπέποται under ἐκπίνω]. Something drunk or to be drunk, drink, liquor Α 470, Λ 630, Ι 175 : = α 148 = γ 339 = φ 271, β 341, ι 205, 348, 354.

ποῦ. (1) In what place? where? ποῦ τοι τόξον; Ε 171. Cf. Κ 406, 407 (twice), Ν 770, 772, Ο 440, Υ 83: γ 249, ζ 277, υ 193, ω 299.—Carrying on an indirect question: ἐρέσθαι ὁππόθεν οὗτος ἀνήρ . . . ποῦ δέ νύ οἱ γενεή α 407.—(2) Whither? where? ποῦ τοι ἀπειλαὶ οἴχονται; Ν 219.

που, *enclitic.* (1) Somewhere: εἴ που ἐφεύροι Δ 88. Cf. Ε 168, Κ 206, Π 514, etc.: α 94, 197, δ 639, ε 417, ζ 278, υ 340, etc.—(2) In negative or conditional contexts, anywhere: οὐδέ τί που ἴδμεν ξυνήϊα Α 124. Cf. Ζ 330, Τ 327, etc.: εἴ που ὄπωπας γ 93. Cf. η 320, λ 458, ξ 44, etc.—(3) Somehow, haply: ἤν πού τι φόως γένωμαι Π 39. Cf. Η 39, Ο 571, etc.: δ 512, ν 418, etc.—(4) In negative or conditional contexts, in any way, haply: εἴ τί που ἔστιν δ 193, μή πού τις ἐπαγγείλῃσιν 775. Cf. Ι 371, Κ 511, Λ 366, Ν 293, etc.: β 71, κ 486, μ 300, ο 403, etc.—(5) Qualifying an expression, haply, I ween, no doubt, as it would seem: θεός που σοὶ τό γ' ἔδωκεν Α 178, οὕτω που Διὶ μέλλει φίλον εἶναι Β 116. Cf. Γ 43, Ζ 438, Ι 628, Κ 326, etc.: οἵ πού μ' ἀσχαλόωσι μένοντες α 304, Ζηνός που τοιήδε γ' αὐλή δ 74. Cf. β 164, δ 756, ζ 155, θ 255, λ 139, etc.—Sim. in questions, direct and indirect, can it be that? haply, it may be that: οὕτω που ἔλπεαι υἷας Ἀχαιῶν ἀπτολέμους ἔμεναι; Ι 40, ἦ ῥ' ἔτι που σχήσουσιν Ἕκτορα Λ 820. Cf. Ν 456, etc.: ζ 125, 200, θ 584, ν 234, etc.

πουλυβότειρα, -ης [πουλυ-, πουλύς + βοτ-, βόσκω]. That feeds many. Epithet of the earth Γ 89, 265, Ζ 213, Θ 73, 277, Μ 158, etc.: θ 378, μ 191, τ 408.—Of Achaeïs Λ 770.

πουλύπους, -ποδος [πουλυ-, πουλύς + πούς]. The sea-polypus, the octopus or cuttle-fish ε 432.

πουλύς. See πολλός.

πούς, ποδός, ὁ [πό(δ)ς. Cf. L. *ped-, pes*]. Genit. and dat. dual ποδοῖϊν (-οῖιν) Ξ 228, 477, Ο 18, Σ 537, Φ 271, Ψ 770: π 6, τ 444. Dat. pl. πόδεσσι Γ 407, Κ 346, Π 809, Ρ 27, etc.: ε 413, ζ 39, θ 103, ν 261, etc. ποσί Ε 745, Ζ 505, Θ 339, Ν 18, etc.: α 131, δ 136, θ 206, λ 595, etc. ποσσί Β 44, Γ 13, Η 212, Ν 19, Ο 356, etc.: α 96, β 4, ε 44, θ 148, etc. (1) One of the feet, one's foot; in dual and pl., the feet, one's feet: χωλὸς ἕτερον πόδα Β 217, ὑπὸ ποσσὶν Θ 443, οὐδὲ χθόνα μάρπτε ποδοῖϊν Ξ 228. Cf. Α 591, Β 44, Ι 523 (*i.e.* their coming hither), Ν 205, Τ 92, etc.: α 96, δ 149, ζ 39 (on foot), ο 45, υ 365, χ 20, etc.—Of animals. Of horses Β 466, Ε 504, Ι 124, Ν 36, Π 794, etc.—Of mules Ψ 121: ζ 318.—Of dogs τ 228 (in his paws). Cf. Θ 339: τ 444.—Of oxen Υ 497: υ 299, χ 290.—Of deer Λ 476: κ 168, τ 231.—Of birds Ψ 854, 866: ο 526 (in its claws).—(2) With special reference to speed in running or in the race: ποσὶν οὔ πως ἔστιν ἐρίζειν (in swiftness of foot) Ν 325. Cf. Ο 642, Υ 410, Χ 160, Ψ 444, 792, etc.: θ 103, 206 (in the race), 230, etc.—(3) πόδας ὠκύς, swift-footed. Epithet of Achilles Α 58, 84, 148, 215, 364, 489, Ι 196, Λ 112, etc.—Of Orsilochus ν 260.—Sim.: πόδας ταχύς. Of Achilles Ν 348, Ρ 709, Σ 354, 358.—Of Meriones Ν 249.—Of Aeneas Ν 482.—Of Antilochus Σ 2.—πόδας ὠκέα as epithet of Iris Β 790, 795, Θ 425, etc.—Epithets of animals. Of the hare: πόδας ταχὺς πτώξ Ρ 676.—Of the dog: κύνες πόδας ἀργοί Σ 578: β 11.—Of the horse: πόδας αἰόλος ἵππος Τ 404.—(4) A projecting spur of a hill: ὑπαὶ πόδα νείατον Ἴδης Β 824. Cf. Υ 59.—(5) A sheet of a sail, a rope or strap attached to one of the lower corners of it and used to extend it or alter its direction ε 260, κ 32.

πραπίδες, αἱ. (1) The midriff: βάλ' (ἔβαλ') ἧπαρ ὑπὸ πραπίδων Λ 579 = Ν 412 = Ρ 349.—(2) The 'heart,' 'breast,' soul, mind, as the seat or a seat (a) Of the faculty of perception or knowledge, of the wits: ὅς τ' ὀλίγον περ ἐπιψαύῃ πραπίδεσσιν θ 547.—(b) Of the faculty of contriving, devising, designing, of ingenuity: ποίησεν ἰδυίῃσι πραπίδεσσιν Α 608. Cf. Σ 380, 482, Υ 12: η 92.—(c) Of the emotions, of grief or sorrow: ἦ κέ μοι αἰνὸν ἀπὸ πραπίδων ἄχος ἔλθοι Χ 43. Cf. Ω 514.

πρασιή, -ῆς, ἡ [πράσον, leek. 'Leek-bed']. A bed of herbs η 127, ω 247.

πρέπω. (ἐπι-, μετα-.) To be pre-eminent, conspicuous, distinguished, noted: ἔπρεπε καὶ διὰ πάντων Μ 104. Cf. θ 172, σ 2 (was noted for his . . .).

πρέσβᾰ, ἡ [fem. of πρέσβυς]. (1) The eldest: π. Διὸς θυγάτηρ Ἄτη Τ 91. Cf. γ 452.—(2) That is senior in dignity. Of Here: π. θεά, queen of heaven Ε 721 = Θ 383, Ξ 194 = 243.

πρεσβήϊον, τό [πρέσβυς]. A meed of honour: πρώτῳ τοι μετ' ἐμὲ π. ἐν χερὶ θήσω Θ 289.

πρεσβυγενής [πρέσβυς + γεν-, γίγνομαι]. The first-born: π. Ἀντηνορίδης (the first-born son of . . .) Λ 249.

πρέσβυς. Only in comp. and superl. (1) Comp. πρεσβύτερος, the elder: πρεσβύτερος σύ ἐσσι Λ 787.—Absol. in pl., the elders, the seniors: πρεσβυτέροισιν Ἐρινύες αἰὲν ἕπονται Ο 204.—(2) Superl. πρεσβύτατος, the first-born, the eldest: πρεσβυτάτην με τέκετο Κρόνος (app. with an admixture of the sense 'senior in dignity') Δ 59, πρεσβύτατος γενεῇ Ζ 24. Cf. Λ 740.—Absol.: πρεσβυτάτην ὤπυιε θυγατρῶν Ν 429. Cf. Φ 143: ν 142 (he must mean, after himself. He is represented as the elder in Ο 204 cited under (1)).

†**πρήθω.** 3 sing. aor. ἔπρησε β 427. πρῆσε Α 481, Π 350. Nom. pl. masc. pple. πρήσαντες Η 429, 432. Infin. πρῆσαι Β 415. (ἀνα-, ἐμ-.) (1) Of wind, to blow into, swell by blowing: ἔπρησεν ἄνεμος ἱστίον β 427. Cf. Α 481.—(2) To eject by blowing, spirt out: αἷμ' ἀνὰ στόμα Π 350.—(3) To burn, consume (with or in fire): πυρὸς θύρετρα (genit. of material) Β 415. Cf. Η 429, 432.

πρηκτήρ, -ῆρος, ὁ [πρηκ-, πρήσσω]. (1) A doer: ἔργων Ι 443.—(2) A trader or trafficker θ 162.

πρηνής, -ές [προ- (1)+ἠν-, face. Cf. ἀπηνής, ὑπηνήτης. 'With the face forward']. On the face or belly, prone (opposed to ὕπτιος): ἤριπε πρηνής Ε 58. Cf. Β 418, Δ 544, Ζ 43, 307, Λ 179, Μ 396, Ο 543, Π 310, 379, 413, 579, Ρ 300, Φ 118, Ψ 25, Ω 11: ε 374, χ 296.—Of inanimate objects, to utter ruin or destruction: πρηνὲς βαλέειν Πριάμοιο μέλαθρον Β 414.

πρῆξις, ἡ [πρήσσω]. (1) Accomplishment, result, issue: οὔ τις πρῆξις πέλεται γόοιο (no profit comes of it) Ω 524: οὔ τις πρῆξις ἐγίγνετο μυρομένοισιν (their weeping profited them nothing) κ 202 = 568.—(2) An affair or business γ 72 = ι 253, γ 82.

πρῆσε, 3 sing. aor. πρήθω.

πρήσσω. 3 pl. pa. iterative πρήσσεσκον θ 259. 2 sing. fut. πρήξεις Ω 550. 3 πρήξει τ 324. 2 sing. aor. ἔπρηξας Σ 357. Acc. sing. masc. pple. πρήξαντα γ 60. Infin. πρῆξαι Α 562: β 191, π 88. (δια-.) (1) To pass over, traverse: ἅλα ι 491.—To traverse a space, pass, advance, make one's way: ἵνα πρήσσωμεν (ἵνα πρήσσῃσιν) (ὄφρα πρήσσωμεν) ὁδοῖο (local genit., may get upon our (his) way) Ω 264: γ 476, ο 47, 219.—To accomplish (a journey or course): κέλευθον Ξ 282, Ψ 501: ν 83.—(2) To accomplish, do, carry out, effect, perform: πρῆξαι οὔ τι δυνήσεαι Α 562, οὔ τι πρήξεις ἀκαχήμενος υἷος (it will profit you nothing to mourn for him) Ω 550. Cf. Λ 552 = Ρ 661: εὖ πρήσσεσκον ἕκαστα (were charged with the due arrangements) θ 259. Cf. β 191, γ 60, π 88, τ 324.—Absol.: ἔπρηξας καὶ ἔπειτα (you have got your way after all) Σ 357.

†**πρίαμαι.** 3 sing. aor. πρίατο. To buy, acquire by purchase α 430, ξ 115, 452, ο 483.

πρῐν. (1) Before, heretofore, theretofore, in time past, formerly: ὡς πρίν Β 344, καὶ πρίν περ μεμαώς Ε 135, μένος δ πρὶν ἔχεσκες 472. Cf. Γ 132, 430, Ε 127, Ι 523, etc.: γ 408, δ 212, 724, ε 334, ζ 4, κ 393, λ 484, etc.—So τὸ πρίν Ε 54, Ζ 125, Ι 403, Ν 105, etc.: δ 32, 518.—(2) Before the arrival of a specified or indicated time past or future, earlier, sooner: πρίν μιν καὶ γῆρας ἔπεισιν (ere that) Α 29, πρὶν ὑποφθὰς δουρὶ περόνησεν (before he could use his club) Η 144, πρὶν κνέφας ἦλθεν Θ 500. Cf. Η 390, Ι 250, Ξ 424, Σ 283, Ψ 190 (before the due time), Ω 551, etc.: β 198, γ 117, λ 632, ν 427, ξ 334, φ 36, etc.—So τὸ πρίν Ο 72.—(3) With or without τό, up to a point of time, so long: τὸ πρὶν μὲν ἀναίνετο γ 265, πρὶν οὔ τι νεμεσσητὸν κεχολῶσθαι χ 59.—(4) With aor. infin., before . . . ing . . .: πρὶν γνώμεναι Β 348, πρὶν ἐλθεῖν υἷας Ἀχαιῶν (before their coming) Ι 403. Cf. Α 98, Δ 115, Ζ 81, Θ 453, Μ 172, Ο 588, etc.: α 210, β 128, δ 255, ζ 288, κ 385, ν 124, ο 210, etc.—So with ἤ: πρίν γ' ἢ ἕτερόν γ' αἵματος ἆσαι Ἄρηα Ε 288, Χ 266.—With pres. infin.: πρὶν . . . ἄγειν θ' ἑκατόμβην Α 98. Cf. τ 475.—(5) With subj.: πρίν γ' ἐμ' ἴδηαι Σ 135. Cf. Σ 190, Ω 781: κ 175, ν 336, ρ 9.—Cf. πρὶν ὥρη [ἔῃ] ο 394.—With opt.: πρὶν πειρήσαιτ' Ἀχιλῆος Φ 580.—(6) With ὅτε. (a) With indic.: πρίν γ' ὅτε δὴ θάλαμος ἐβάλλετο Ι 588. Cf. Μ 437: δ 180, ν 322, ψ 43.—(b) With ἄν and subj.: πρίν γ' ὅτ' ἂν ἑνδεκάτη γένηται β 374. Cf. δ 477.—(c) With opt.: πρίν γ' ὅτε σ' ὄψου ἄσαιμι Ι 488.—(7) In two co-ordinate clauses, anticipatory in the first and resuming in the second: οὐδ' ὅ γε πρὶν λοιγὸν ἀπώσει, πρίν γ' ἀπὸ πατρὶ δόμεναι κούρην Α 97. Cf. Β 348, Η 481, Σ 189, Ω 781, etc.: δ 254, 475, τ 475, etc.

πριστός [πρίω, to saw]. Sawn, cut or fashioned with the saw: ἐλέφαντος σ 196, τ 564.

πρό. (I) Adv. (1) Forward, forwards, forth: πρὸ γὰρ ἧκεν Ἥρη Α 195. Cf. Α 208, 442, Δ 382 (see ὁδός (1)), Ο 360, Π 188, etc.: φ 21.—(2) In front, before: πρὸ δούρατ' ἔχοντο Ρ 355. Cf. Ν 799, 800: ε 385.—(3) In temporal sense, before: πρὸ ἐόντα (the past) Α 70.—Beforehand: ἐπεὶ πρό οἱ εἴπομεν α 37.—(II) Prep. with genit. (1) In front of, before: πρὸ ἄστεος Ο 351. Cf. Ε 96, 789, Ι 708, Τ 292, etc.: κ 105, ω 468.—With locative: ἠῶθι πρό (see ἠώς (1)). Ἰλιόθι πρό (see Ἰλιόθι). οὐρανόθι πρό (see οὐρανός (1)).—In reference to chieftainship: πρὸ Φθίων Ν 693. Cf. Ν 699.—Before the face of, in subjection to: ἀθλεύειν πρὸ ἄνακτος ἀμειλίχου Ω 734.—Under compulsion of: πρὸ φόβοιο Ρ 667.—(2) In front of, in advance of: πρὸ ἑτάρων μάχεσθαι Δ 373.—In advance of, preceding: πρὸ δ' ἄρ' αὐτῶν κύνες ἤϊσαν τ 435. Cf. Κ 286, Ρ 726, Ψ 115.—(3) In defence of, defending, protecting: πρὸ Τρώων ἑσταότα Ω 215. Cf. Θ 57, Χ 110.—In reference to a champion, on behalf of Δ 156.—(4) In temporal sense, before, sooner than: καί τε πρὸ ὁ τοῦ ἐνόησεν Κ 224. Cf. ο 524, ρ 476.

προαλής [app. a compound of προ-]. Sloping, forming a declivity: χώρῳ Φ 262.

†**προβαίνω** [προ- (1) (2)]. 2 sing. pf. προβέβηκας Ζ 125, Ψ 890. 3 προβέβηκε Κ 252. 3 sing. subj. προβεβήκῃ Π 54. (1) To go forward: ἄστρα προβέβηκεν (have got far forward in their course) Κ 252.—(2) To go *before*, advance *in front of*. With genit.: πολὺ προβέβηκας ἁπάντων Ζ 125.—In pf. of the state or condition of going before; hence, to be pre-eminent, to excel, surpass: ὅ τε κράτεϊ προβεβήκῃ (in . . .) Π 54.—With genit.: ὅσον προβέβηκας ἁπάντων Ψ 890.

†**προβάλλω** [προ- (1) (2)]. 3 sing. pa. iterative

προβάλεσκε ε 331. Nom. pl. masc. aor. pple. προβαλόντες Λ 529. 3 pl. aor. mid. προβάλοντο A 458, B 421, Ψ 255 : γ 447. Opt. προβαλοίμην T 218. (1) To throw forward or forth : Νότος Βορέῃ προβάλεσκε [σχεδίην] (surrendered it) ε 331.—In mid. : ἐπεὶ οὐλοχύτας προβάλοντο (had sprinkled them) A 458 = B 421 : = γ 447.—Fig. : ἔριδα προβαλόντες (app., throwing it forward, dashing forward in combat) Λ 529 (cf. Γ 7 cited under προφέρω (2)).—(2) To throw before or in front. In mid. : θεμείλια προβάλοντο (set them in the face of the mound) Ψ 255.—Hence, in mid., to excel, surpass. With genit. : σεῖό κε νοήματι προβαλοίμην (in . . .) T 218.

πρόβασις, ἡ [as next]. = next β 75.

πρόβατα, τά [προ- (1) + βα-, βαίνω]. Cattle, flocks and herds Ξ 124, Ψ 550.

προβέβηκε, 3 sing. pf. προβαίνω.

προβέβουλα, pf. προβούλομαι.

προβιβάω [προ- (1)]. To advance : ὑπασπίδια προβιβῶντι (προβιβῶντος) N 807, Π 609. (With προβιβάντι, προβιβάντος from next as *vv. ll.*)

προβίβημι [προ- (1)]. To stride along forwards, make one's way or advance with a stride : κραιπνὰ ποσὶ προβιβάς N 18. Cf. N 158 : ο 555, ρ 27. (And see prec.)

προβλής, -ῆτος [προ- (1) + βλη-, βάλλω]. Projecting, jutting out : σκοπέλῳ B 396, στήλας M 259, πέτρῃ Π 407 : ἀκταί ε 405, κ 89, ν 97.

προβλώσκω [προ- (1)]. 3 pl. aor. πρόμολον ο 468. Imp. πρόμολε Σ 392. Pple. προμολών Φ 37 : δ 22. Fem. προμολοῦσα Σ 382 : ω 388. To go or come forward or forth : τὴν ἴδε προμολοῦσα Χάρις Σ 382. Cf. Σ 392, Φ 37 (making a descent upon it) : δ 22, ο 468, τ 25 (to leave their quarters), φ 239 = 385, ω 388.

προβοάω [προ- (2)]. To shout in front : προβοῶντε μάχην ὤτρυνον Ἀχαιῶν (cheering their followers on) M 277.

πρόβολος, -ου, ὁ [προ- (1) + βολ-, βάλλω]. A projecting rock : ἐπὶ προβόλῳ μ 251.

†**προβούλομαι** [προ- (2)]. Pf. προβέβουλα. To rank *before*, prefer. With genit. : Κλυταιμνήστρης [μιν] προβέβουλα (prefer her to . . .) A 113.

προγενέστερος [comp. of προγενής, fr. προ- (3) + γεν-, γίγνομαι. 'Born before']. (1) Older : ὁ γὰρ προγενέστερος ἦεν B 555. Cf. I 161, Ψ 789 : β 29, δ 205, τ 244.—(2) Old rather than young : ὃς Φαιήκων προγενέστερος ἦεν (was an elder among the . . .) η 156 = λ 343, οὐδ' οἱ προγενέστεροι ἦσαν (the elders among us) ω 160.

†**προγίγνομαι** [προ- (1)]. 3 pl. aor. προγένοντο. To come forward, appear, come in sight Σ 525.

πρόγονοι [προ- (3) + γον-, γεν-, γίγνομαι. 'Those born before']. The firstlings (of the lambs) ι 221.

†**προδάω** [προ- (3)]. Aor. pple. προδαείς. To know something beforehand : μή πώς με προδαεὶς ἀλέηται (forming a suspicion) δ 396.

προδοκή, -ῆς, ἡ [προ- (1) + δοκ-, δέχομαι]. A place where one may lie in wait, a lurking-place. In pl. : δεδεγμένος ἐν προδοκῇσιν Δ 107.

πρόδομος, -ου, ὁ [προ- (2) + δόμος]. A space in front of the door of the μέγαρον, app. the part of the line of the αἴθουσα into which the door opened : εὗρεν ἐνὶ προδόμῳ δέπα ο 466. Cf. I 473 (see θάλαμος (1) (a)).—Used as a sleeping-place for visitors Ω 673 (Priam and the herald in Achilles's dwelling) : = δ 302 (Telemachus and Pisistratus in Menelaus's house) (cf. Ω 644 : = δ 297). Cf. ο 5, υ 1 (the disguised Odysseus in his own house), 143 (the same in the same).—A space in front of the door of the dwelling of Eumaeus ξ 5.

προεέργω [προ- (2)]. To stand in front of someone and debar (him from doing something). With infin. : πάντας προέεργε ἐπὶ νῆας ὁδεύειν Λ 569.

προέηκα, aor. προΐημι.

†**προείδω** [προ- (1) (3)]. 3 pl. aor. subj. προΐδωσι P 756. Pple. προϊδών X 275 : δ 396, ε 393. Pl. προϊδόντες Σ 527. 3 pl. aor. subj. mid. προΐδωνται ν 155. (1) To direct one's glance forward, look forward or before one : ὀξὺ μάλα προϊδών ε 393. Cf. X 275.—(2) To catch sight of, descry, see : τὰ προϊδόντες Σ 527. Cf. P 756.—In mid. ν 155.—(3) To catch sight of beforehand : μή πώς με προϊδὼν ἀλέηται (catching sight of me before the time) δ 396.

προέμεν, aor. infin. προΐημι.

†**προερέσσω** [προ- (1)]. 1 pl. aor. προερέσσαμεν ι 73, ν 279. 3 προέρεσσαν A 435 : ο 497. To row one's ship forward, row it to a specified place ν 279.—To row (one's ship) forward, row (it) to a specified place : νῆ' εἰς ὅρμον προέρεσσαν A 435 : = ο 497. Cf. ι 73.

†**προερύω** [προ- (1) + ἐρύω[1]]. 3 sing. aor. προέρυσσε A 308. Subj. προερύσσω I 358. To draw down (a ship) in order to launch her A 308, I 358.

πρόες, aor. imp. προΐημι.

πρόεσαν, 3 pl. aor. προΐημι.

προέχω [προ- (1) (2)]. Also **προὔχω**. (1) To project, jut out : πύργῳ ἐπὶ προὔχοντι (a projecting angle of the wall) X 97. Cf. ζ 138, κ 90, μ 11, τ 544, ω 82.—(2) In mid., to have in front of one : προὔχοντ' ἐννέα ταύρους (*i.e.* they faced the sea with the bulls in front of them) γ 8.—(3) To be in front in a race : τὸν προὔχοντα δοκεύει Ψ 325, φράσσαθ' ἵππον προὔχοντα 453.

προῆκε, 3 sing. aor. προΐημι.

προήκης [προ- (2) + *ἀκή, point, edge]. With sharp, *i.e.* thin, blades. Epithet of oars μ 205.

προθέλυμνος, -ον [προ- (1) + θέλυμνα, foundations. Cf. τετραθέλυμνος.] (1) App., from the foundations onwards, *i.e.* by the roots (cf. πρόρριζος) : προθέλυμνα χαμαὶ βάλε δένδρεα I 541. Cf. K 15. —(2) App., with base advanced : σάκεϊ N 130.

προθέω [προ- (1) (2)]. 3 sing. pa. iterative προθέεσκε X 459 : λ 515. (1) To flee before a pursuer K 362.—To rush to the fray in front of others : πολὺ προθέεσκεν X 459 : = λ 515.—(2) Fig., of speech, to dash forward (for utterance) A 291.

†**προθρῴσκω** [προ- (1)]. Aor. pple. προθορών. To leap or spring forward Ξ 363, P 522, 523.

προθῡμίη, -ης, ἡ [προ- (1) + θυμός]. Zeal, alacrity. In pl.: ᾗσι προθυμίῃσι πεποιθώς (his heart full of ardour for the fray) B 588.

πρόθυρον, -ου, τό [προ- (2) + θύρη]. (1) The gateway of the αὐλή Ω 323: α 119, γ 493 = ο 146 = 191.—So in pl. (cf. θύρη (2) (b)): στῆμεν ἐνὶ προθύροισιν Λ 777. Cf. Σ 496, Χ 71: α 103, δ 20, η 4.—Of the gate of the steading of Eumaeus ξ 34.—In pl. π 12.—(2) The doorway of the μέγαρον: κεῖται ἀνὰ πρόθυρον τετραμμένος (*i.e.* the doorway of the chief room of the hut) Τ 212: εἶκε προθύρου σ 10. Cf. σ 101, 386, υ 355, φ 299, χ 474.—Of such a doorway in the palace of Zeus Ο 124.—In the palace of Hephaestus. In pl. θ 304, 325.—In the dwelling of Circe. In pl. κ 220.

προϊάλλω [προ- (1)]. To send forth or dispatch on a mission or errand or to take up an occupation: ἐμὲ Ζεὺς τῷ ἐπαλεξήσουσαν προΐαλλεν Θ 365. Cf. Λ 3: ο 370.—To send away or dispatch for use: σιάλων τὸν ἄριστον ξ 18.

†**προϊάπτω** [προ- (1) + (ϝ)ι-(ϝ)άπτω, to throw. Cf. ἀπτοεπής, ἐάφθη]. 3 sing. fut. προϊάψει Ζ 487. Infin. προϊάψειν Ε 190, Λ 55. 3 sing. aor. προΐαψε Α 3. To send, dispatch: πολλὰς ψυχὰς Ἄϊδι Α 3. Cf. Ε 190, Ζ 487, Λ 55.

προϊδών, aor. pple. προείδω.

†**προΐημι** [προ- (1) + ἵημι[1]]. 3 sing. προΐησι μ 253. 3 pl. προϊεῖσι Λ 270. Fem. pple. προϊεῖσα β 92, ν 381. Aor. προέηκα Θ 297, Κ 125. 3 sing. προέηκε Δ 398, Ε 290, Η 468, Λ 201, etc.: β 147, γ 183, ε 268, ξ 466, etc. προῆκε Ρ 545. 3 pl. aor. πρόεσαν δ 681, θ 399, π 328, σ 291. Imp. πρόες Α 127, Π 38, 241. 3 sing. προέτω Λ 796. Infin. προέμεν κ 155. From προϊέω. 3 sing. pres. προϊεῖ Β 752. Impf. προΐειν ι 88, κ 100, μ 9. 2 sing. προΐεις ω 333. 3 προΐει Α 326, Γ 118, Ε 15, Η 249, etc.: ν 64, ω 519, 522. (1) To send forth, throw, hurl, launch, let fly (a missile): ἔγχος Γ 346. Cf. Γ 355, Θ 297, Ν 662, Υ 438, etc.: ω 519 = 522.—Absol., to throw, make a throw, make one's throw: ὣς φάμενος προέηκεν Ε 290.—To throw or let fall (fishing tackle) μ 253.—(2) To send from oneself, let fall from one's grasp: πόδα τ 468. Cf. ε 316.—(3) To let fall (a word), send forth or utter (speech) ξ 466, υ 105.—(4) Of a river, to send or roll (its waters): Τιταρησσόν, ὅς ῥ' ἐς Πηνειὸν προϊεῖ ὕδωρ Β 752.—(5) To send forth or dispatch on a specified or indicated mission or to a specified destination: Βρισηΐδος εἵνεκα κούρης Α 336, Ταλθύβιον νῆας ἔπι ἰέναι Γ 118. Cf. Α 326, Η 468, Ι 442, Κ 125, Λ 201, Μ 342, etc.: β 147, δ 161, θ 399, μ 9, π 328, etc.—To let go, surrender: τήνδε θεῷ πρόες Α 127.—(6) To send (a wind) γ 183, ε 268 = η 266, κ 25.—(7) Of something immaterial, to send: ἀγγελίας β 92 = ν 381. Cf. Λ 270, Π 241.

προικός [genit. of προίξ, gift. 'Of one's bounty,' 'as a free gift' (genit. of material)]. Without repayment or reimbursement: χαρίσασθαι ν 15.—App., without paying for it, with impunity: γεύσεσθαι Ἀχαιῶν ρ 413.

προΐκτης, ὁ. A beggar ρ 352, 449.

†**προΐστημι** [προ- (2)]. Aor. pple. προστήσας. To set in front, put forward Δ 156.

προκαθίζω [προ- (1) + καθ-, κατα- (1)]. Of birds, to keep settling (ever) forwards Β 463.

†**προκαλέω** [προ- (1)]. 3 sing. aor. mid. προκαλέσσατο Η 218, 285, Ν 809. 3 sing. subj. προκαλέσσεται Η 39. Imp. προκάλεσσαι Γ 432, Η 50: θ 142. In mid., to summon or invite to the fight or to a contest, challenge, defy, dare: μαχέσασθαι ἐναντίον Γ 432. Cf. Η 39, 50, 218, 285, Ν 809: θ 142.

προκαλίζομαι [προ- (1) + καλέω]. = prec. Γ 19, Δ 389, Ε 807, Η 150: θ 228, σ 20 (to fisticuffs).

πρόκειμαι [προ- (2)]. To be set before one, be set to one's hand: ὀνείαθ' ἑτοῖμα προκείμενα. See Ι 91, etc., cited under ἑτοῖμος (1).

πρόκλυτος [προ- (1) or (3) + κλυτός]. Of report or fame, heard of old; or perh., heard forwards, handed on by tradition Υ 204.

πρόκροσσοι, -αι [προ- + (app.) the obscure κρόσσαι]. App., row after row, in rows or ranks: [νῆας] προκρόσσας ἔρυσαν Ξ 35.

προκυλίνδω [προ- (1)]. In mid., of the sea, to roll forward Ξ 18.

†**προλέγω** [προ- (2) + λέγω[2]]. Absol. in pf. pass. pple. pl., the picked men, the flower: Ἀθηναίων προλελεγμένοι Ν 689.

†**προλείπω** [προ- (1)]. Aor. pple. προλιπών γ 314, ο 11, ψ 120. Pl. προλιπόντες Ρ 275. Infin. προλιπεῖν ν 331. 3 sing. pf. προλέλοιπε β 279. (1) To leave, forsake, abandon, leave to one's own devices or to one's (or its) fate: κτήματα γ 314 = ο 11 (with ἄνδρας in the same lines simply 'leaving behind you'). Cf. Ρ 275: ν 331.—Of a quality, to forsake (one), fail (him): οὐδέ σε μῆτις Ὀδυσσῆος προλέλοιπεν β 279.—(2) To leave, quit, withdraw from: πηοὺς καὶ πατρίδα γαῖαν ψ 120.

προμαχίζω [πρόμαχος]. To act or pose as champion Γ 16.—To fight with in front of the others. With dat.: μηκέτ' Ἀχιλλῆϊ προμάχιζε Υ 376.

προμάχομαι [προ- (2)]. To fight in front of the others Ρ 358.—To fight *in front of.* With genit.: ἁπάντων (to advance beyond them) Λ 217.

πρόμαχος [προ- (2) + μάχομαι. 'He who fights in front']. In pl., the front rank, the fighting line, the forefront of the battle: ἐν προμάχοισι φανέντα Γ 31. Cf. Δ 253, 495, Ε 134, 250, Λ 188, 358, etc.: σ 379, ω 526.

†**προμίσγω** [προ- (3)]. Aor. infin. pass. προμιγῆναι. In pass., to have sexual intercourse with in anticipation of another. With dat.: παλλακίδι προμιγῆναι Ι 452 (app., to take an opportunity of anticipating his father and so making felt the contrast between the two).

προμνηστῖνοι, -αι [perh. formed fr. *πρόμνηστις, abstract noun fr. προ- (1) + μένω. Cf. ἀγχιστῖνοι]. Each waiting his turn before going forward, one after another: ἐπήϊσαν λ 233, ἐσέλθετε φ 230.

πρόμολον, 3 pl. aor. προβλώσκω.

πρόμος [a superl. of πρό]. Leading, chief: ἄνδρα Ε 533.—Absol., a leading fighter, a champion:

ἐκ πάντων πρόμος ἔμμεναι Ἕκτορι (against Hector) Η 75. Cf. Γ 44, Η 116, 136, Ο 293, Χ 85 : λ 493.

προνοέω [προ- (3)]. (1) To perceive or detect beforehand, have an inkling of: δόλον Σ 526.—(2) To think of, devise ε 364.

πρόξ, προκός. Some kind of deer ρ 295.

προπάροιθε(ν)[προ-(4) + πάροιθε(ν)]. (1) In front, before: π. κιών Ο 260. Cf. Ο 355 (going before them), Π 319 (at his feet): δ 225 (before his eyes).—With genit. in geographical sense: νῆσος Αἰγύπτου π. (lying off . . .) δ 355.—In front of, before: π. πυλάων Μ 131, στῆ αὐτῆς π. Ξ 297. Cf. Β 92, 811, Δ 348, Ζ 307, Ν 205, Ο 66, Σ 615 (at her feet), etc. : α 107, ι 482, κ 354, ο 122, ρ 357, ω 416, etc.—(2) In temporal sense (a) Before, sooner than, someone else: π. ἰδών Κ 476.—Before another, preceding him in time: εἶμι π. (will go first) ρ 277. Cf. ρ 282.—(b) Before the happening of something: π. σφι φάνη μέγα ἔργον Ἄρηος (ere that) Λ 734. Cf. Χ 197.—(c) In time past, formerly: οὔ τις ἀνὴρ π. μακάρτατος οὔτ' ἄρ' ὀπίσσω λ 483.

πρόπᾱς, -ᾶσα, -αν [προ-(4) + πᾶς]. Strengthened form of, but hardly to be distinguished from, πᾶς. (1) In sing., all the, the whole: πρόπαν ἦμαρ (all the day long) Τ 162, Ω 713, Α 601: = ι 161 = 556 = κ 183 = 476 = μ 29 = τ 424, ω 41.—(2) In pl., all the: νῆας προπάσας Β 493.

†**προπέμπω** [προ- (1) (2)]. Aor. προὔπεμψα ρ 54, ω 360. 3 sing. -ε Θ 367 : ρ 117. (1) To send or dispatch on an errand. With complementary fut. pple.: ἄξοντα κύνα Θ 367.—(2) To dispatch on one's way, arrange for the departure of: ἐς Μενέλαον ρ 117.—(3) To send on ahead of oneself: τὸν προὔπεμψα σὺν ἑτάροισιν ρ 54. Cf. ω 360.

προπέφανται, 3 sing. pf. pass. προφαίνω.

†**προπίπτω** [προ- (1)]. Nom. pl. masc. aor. pple. προπεσόντες. To bend the body forward (so as to swing to the oar): προπεσόντες ἔρεσσον ι 490, μ 194.

προποδίζω [προ- (1) + ποδίζω, fr. ποδ-, πούς]. To set the foot forward, to advance, march along Ν 158, 806.

προπρηνής, -ές [προ- (4) + πρηνής]. (1) On the face, prone Ω 18.—(2) Stooping forwards χ 98.—(3) In neut. sing. προπρηνές as adv., forwards: σκῆπτρον οὔτ' ὀπίσω οὔτε π. ἐνώμα Γ 218.

προπροκυλίνδω [προ- (1) (doubled) (2) (4) + κυλίνδω]. (1) In pass., of a wanderer, to be rolled on and on, be tossed ever onwards: δεῦρ' ἵκετο προπροκυλινδόμενος ρ 525.—(2) In mid., to grovel *before the face of*. With genit.: πατρὸς Διός Χ 221 (the genit. app. depending on one προ- (προ- (2)), the other προ- strengthening the vb. (προ- (4))).

προρέω [προ- (1)]. Of rivers, streams, etc., to flow forward or forth, flow, send their waters: ἅλαδε Ε 598, Μ 19. Cf. Φ 260, 366, Χ 151 : ε 444, κ 351.

πρόρριζος, -ον [προ- (1) + ῥίζα]. From the roots onwards, by the roots, roots and all (cf. προθέλυμνος): ὡς ὅτ' ἐξερίπῃ δρῦς π. Ξ 415. Cf. Λ 157.

πρός [cf. προτί, ποτί]. (I) Adv. (1) For, to equip, something: πρὸς δ' ἄρα πηδάλιον ποιήσατο ε 255.—(2) Besides, in addition, too: πρὸς δ' ἄμφω ῥῆξε τένοντε Ε 307. Cf. Μ 102, Ν 678, Χ 59: ξ 415, π 291, τ 10, υ 41.—(II) Prep. (1) With dat. (a) Making contact with, upon, against: πρὸς περόνῃ καταμύξατο χεῖρα Ε 425 : πρὸς ἀλλήλῃσιν ἔχονται ε 329. Cf. ε 434.—With locative: ὡς ὅτε πρὸς κοτυληδονόφιν λάϊγγες ἔχονται ε 433.—In pregnant sense: πέτρῃς πρὸς μεγάλῃσι βαλόν η 279. Cf. ι 284, 459.—(b) In reference to position, in the direction of, towards: τέτραπτο πρὸς ἰθύ οἱ Ξ 403.—(c) Besides, in addition to: πρὸς τοῖσί τε ὕπνος κ 68.—(2) With acc. (a) To, towards, in the direction of: εἶμ' αὐτὴ πρὸς Ὄλυμπον Α 420. Cf. Α 609, Β 310, Ε 398, Ζ 41, Θ 74, Ο 58, etc. : β 258, 298, η 131, ι 315, κ 278, etc.—In hostile sense, against: ἐστρατόωντο πρὸς τείχεα Θήβης Δ 378. Cf. Μ 332, Ρ 471.—Sim.: πρὸς ῥόον ἀΐσσοντος Φ 303.—Indicating arrival at a point: πρὸς τεῖχος ἀφικάνει Ζ 388. Cf. τ 458, etc.—In opposition to, against the will of: πρὸς δαίμονα φωτὶ μάχεσθαι Ρ 98. Cf. Ρ 104.—(b) In reference to speech or directing the voice, to: καί με πρὸς μῦθον ἔειπεν Β 59. Cf. Β 156, Γ 155, Ε 274, Θ 364, etc. : δ 803, ε 298, κ 34, etc.—Sim. in reference to swearing: ὤμοσε πρὸς ἔμ' αὐτόν ξ 331, τ 288.—In reference to conversation, with: πρὸς ἀλλήλους ἐνέποντες Λ 643. Cf. ψ 301.—In reference to the sight, to, towards: παπταίνοντι πρὸς πέτρην μ 233. Cf. ν 29, etc.—(c) In reference to the direction in which action takes place, towards, against: πρὸς κῦμα χανών μ 350. Cf. ρ 237.—(d) In reference to wounding or striking a part of the body, in: βεβλήκει πρὸς στῆθος Δ 108. Cf. Λ 144, Φ 424, etc. : ι 301, etc.—(e) In reference to placing or leaning *against* something: ἅρματ' ἔκλιναν πρὸς ἐνώπια Θ 435 := δ 42. Cf. Χ 112, Ψ 171, etc. : α 127, χ 120, etc.—Sim.: Ἀμφινόμου πρὸς γοῦνα καθέζετο (sat down leaning against . . .) σ 395. Cf. ψ 90.—(f) In reference to position, in the direction of, towards: πρὸς Τρῶας τετραμμένοι Ε 605. Cf. ι 26, ν 240, etc.—(g) In reference to exchanging things *with* a person: ὃς πρὸς Διομήδεα τεύχε' ἄμειβεν Ζ 235.—(3) With genit. (a) In reference to position or to the taking place of some phenomenon, in the direction of, towards: πρὸς ἁλὸς Κᾶρες . . . πρὸς Θύμβρης δ' ἔλαχον Λύκιοι Κ 428, φόως γένετ' ἠμὲν πρὸς νηῶν καὶ πολέμοιο Ο 670. Cf. ν 110, 111, φ 347.—(b) In reference to coming *from* a specified quarter: ἀλώμενος ἵκετ' ἐμὸν δῶ, ἠὲ πρὸς ἠοίων ἢ ἑσπερίων ἀνθρώπων θ 29.—Sim.: πρὸς Διός εἰσι ξεῖνοι ζ 207, ξ 57.—(c) At the hands of, from, by: τιμὴν ἀρνύμενοι πρὸς Τρώων Α 160, ἦ σοι ἄριστα πεποίηται πρὸς Τρώων; Ζ 57. Cf. Ζ 525, Π 85, etc. : λ 302, σ 162.—By the commission of: οἵ τε θέμιστας πρὸς Διὸς εἰρύαται Α 239.—(d) Before the face of: οὐδ' ἐπιορκήσω πρὸς δαίμονος Τ 188. Cf. Α 339, 340.—In entreaty, in the name of, by: νῦν σε πρὸς πατρὸς γουνάζομαι ν 324. Cf. λ 67.—At the bidding of: πρός κ' ἄλλης ἱστὸν ὑφαίνοις Ζ 456.

†**προσάγω** [προσ- (2)]. 3 sing. aor. προσήγαγε. To bring to an indicated place: τίς δαίμων τόδε πῆμα προσήγαγεν; (has brought hither) ρ 446.

†**προσαΐσσω** [προσ- (2)]. Aor. pple. προσαΐξας. To rush in an indicated direction: ἤ λίσσοιτο προσαΐξας 'Οδυσῆα (run up to him and . . .) χ 337. Cf. χ 342, 365.

προσαλείφω [προσ- (1)]. To rub (something) *upon*, apply (it) *to*. With dat.: προσάλειφεν ἑκάστῳ φάρμακον ἄλλο κ 392.

προσαμύνω [προσ- (3)]. Aor. infin. προσαμῦναι Π 509. (1) To bring help or succour to, help, aid. With dat.: ἤ τί οἱ χήμεῖς προσαμύνομεν Β 238. —(2) Absol, to bring succour, make defence, show fight for someone or something Ε 139, Π 509.

†**προσαραρίσκω** [προσ- (1)]. Nom. pl. neut. pf. pple. προσαρηρότα. In pf., to be fitted to something: ἐπίσσωτρα προσαρηρότα Ε 725.

προσαυδάω [προσ- (3)]. 3 dual non-thematic impf. προσαυδήτην Λ 136, Χ 90. (1) To speak to, address, accost: κερτομίοισι Διὰ προσηύδα Α 539. Cf. Δ 192, 256, Ε 30, Ζ 144, Λ 136, etc.: α 252, γ 41, ι 345, λ 99, ξ 484, etc.—Without expressed object, to make address, speak Δ 24, Η 225, Μ 353, etc.: κ 400, ξ 79, ο 62, etc.—(2) To say in way of address, speak, utter: ἔπεα πτερόεντα Δ 92, 203, Ε 871, Π 706, etc.: β 362, δ 25, κ 377, π 22, etc.—(3) With double construction of (1) and (2), to address words to: ἔπεά μιν πτερόεντα προσηύδα Α 201. Cf. Δ 69, Ε 242, Μ 365, Ν 94, etc.: α 122, δ 77, κ 265, π 7, etc.

†**προσβαίνω** [προσ- (1) (2)]. 3 sing. aor. προσέβη ξ 1. 3 pl. προσέβαν Ψ 117: τ 431. Pple. προσβάς Ε 620, Π 863. 3 sing. aor. mid. προσεβήσετο Β 48, Ξ 292: φ 5, 43. (1) To go one's way, proceed, in a specified direction: προσέβη τρηχεῖαν ἀταρπόν (advbl. acc., 'by a . . .') ξ 1.—(2) To go *to* or *towards*, approach. With acc.: κνημοὺς Ἴδης Ψ 117. Cf. τ 431.—In mid.: Ὄλυμπον Β 48. Cf. Ξ 292.—(3) To step *upon*, set foot *upon*. With acc. In mid.: κλίμακα φ 5, οὐδόν 43.—Without expressed object: λὰξ προσβάς (setting his foot upon the corpse) Ε 620, Π 863.

προσβάλλω, προτιβάλλω [προσ- (3)]. (1) To smite. Of the rays of the sun: Ἠέλιος νέον προσέβαλλεν ἀρούρας Η 421 := τ 433.—(2) In mid., to give heed to, direct one's attention to: ταύτην οὐ προτιβάλλεαι Ε 879.

προσδέρκομαι, ποτιδέρκομαι [προσ- (2)]. To direct the sight *to*, look *towards*. With acc.: πατέρα προσεδέρκετο υ 385. Cf. Π 10: ρ 518.

προσέειπον, προτιεῖπον (Χ 329), *aor.* [προσ- (3)]. To speak to, address, accost: Κάλχαντα Α 105. Cf. Α 206, Θ 138, Λ 602, Π 432, Ρ 11, etc.: α 178, β 39, δ 461, ζ 56, θ 144, etc.—Without expressed object, to make address, speak Ω 361: δ 234, ω 350, 393.—With double acc. of the person addressed and of what is said: ὄφρα τί μιν προτιείποι Χ 329.

προσέθηκε, 3 sing. aor. προστίθημι.

†**πρόσειμι** [προσ- (2) + εἶμι]. Pres. pple. προσιών, -όντος. To approach, draw near, draw up: ζωὸν προσιόντα Ε 515 = Η 308. Cf. Ε 682, Κ 339, Λ 742, Ν 615: π 5.

προσέλεκτο, 3 sing. aor. mid. προσλέγω.

προσερεύγομαι [προσ- (2)]. Of the sea, to roar, or, perh., to break in foam, *against*. With acc.: κύματα, τά τε προσερεύγεται αὐτήν Ο 621.

προσέστιχε, 3 sing. aor. προσστείχω.

προσέφην, impf. πρόσφημι.

προσήγαγε, 3 sing. aor. προσάγω.

πρόσθε(ν). (1) Of place (a) In front of, before, preceding, someone or something (often with the notion of defence): π. σάκεα σχέθον Δ 113, π. στᾶσα 129. Cf. Ε 300, 315, Ζ 17, Ν 440, etc.: π. δέ οἱ ποίησε γαλήνην ε 452. Cf. χ 400, ω 155.—With genit.: τάων οὔ τοι ἐγὼ π. ἵσταμαι Δ 54. Cf. Ε 56, 107, Η 224, Ι 473, etc.: στῆ π. αὐτοῦ η 21. Cf. θ 524, ο 164, χ 4, ω 540.—(b) Before, in the front part: π. λέων Ζ 181.—(c) In front or in advance of others: ὁππότεροι π. ἵπποι Ψ 487. Cf. Ψ 572, etc.—With genit.: οἷος π. ἄλλων Δ 304.—(2) Of time (a) Before, in time past, in days of old: οὗ καὶ π. ἀρίστη φαίνετο βουλή Η 325. Cf. Α 251, Μ 33, Υ 28, Ψ 570, etc.: π. μοι ἀεικέλιος δέατ' εἶναι ζ 242. Cf. ρ 371, χ 432, ω 52.—So τὸ π.: ὡς τὸ π. Μ 40. Cf. Ψ 583: δ 688, λ 629.—In adjectival use: τῶν π. ἀνδρῶν Ι 524.—(b) Before another or others, first: ἔγνω π. Ν 66, Ω 698. Cf. Γ 317, 346, Ε 851: ι 370.—With genit., before, sooner than: ὄφρα π. ἄλλων θάνατον ἐπίσπῃ (that he may be the foremost to perish) Β 359.—(c) Before the arrival of a specified or indicated time past or future, earlier, sooner: π. μιν μοῖρ' ἀμφεκάλυψεν (ere that) Μ 116: μὴ π. κλέος γένηται, πρὶν . . . ψ 137. Cf. ρ 7, ψ 223.

προσιών, pres. pple. πρόσειμι.

πρόσκειμαι [προσ- (1)]. To be put upon something, be put in position: οὔατ' οὔ πω προσέκειτο Σ 379.

προσκηδής [προσ- (3) + κῆδος]. Involving a close tie, that binds closely together φ 35.

†**προσκλίνω, ποτικλίνω** [προσ- (1)]. 3 sing. aor. προσέκλῖνε φ 138, 165. 3 sing. pf. pass. ποτικέκλιται ζ 308. To cause to lean, set, support, *against*. With dat.: βέλος προσέκλινε κορώνῃ φ 138 = 165.—In pass., to lean or be supported (so as to be) *close to*. With dat.: πατρὸς ἐμοῖο θρόνος ποτικέκλιται αὐτῇ (is set close to the queen's) ζ 308.

†**προσλέγω** [προσ- (1) + λέγω[1]]. 3 sing. aor. mid. προσέλεκτο. In mid., to lay oneself down, recline, beside or at the feet of another: εἶσέ τέ [με] καὶ προσέλεκτο μ 34.

†**προσπελάζω** [προσ- (3)]. Aor. pple. προσπελάσας. To bring into contact with, cause to touch. With dat.: ἄκρῃ προσπελάσας [νῆα] (dashing it against a . . .) ι 285.

προσπίλναμαι [προσ- (3)]. To be brought into contact with, touch. With dat.: νήσῳ προσεπίλνατο νηῦς (made the island) ν 95.

προσπλάζω [προσ- (2)]. Of water, to beat up against something: κῦμα χιόνα προσπλάζον ἐρύκεται Μ 285.—To dash up *against*. With dat.: λίμνῃ προσέπλαζε γενείῳ λ 583.

προσπτύσσω, ποτιπτύσσω [προσ- (1)]. 3 sing. fut. mid. προσπτύξεται λ 451. 3 sing. aor. προσπτύξατο δ 647. Subj. προσπτύξομαι γ 22, θ 478, ρ 509. In mid. **(1)** To fold to one's bosom, embrace λ 451.—**(2)** To greet, convey good wishes to θ 478.—**(3)** To speak to, address γ 22.—Without expressed object β 77, δ 647.—With double acc. of the person addressed and of what is said: ὄφρα τί μιν προσπτύξομαι ρ 509.

πρόσσοθεν [-θεν (2). Cf. πρόσσω]. Before one: ἐλαύνων πρόσσοθεν ἵππους Ψ 533.

†**προσστείχω** [προσ- (2)]. 3 sing. aor. προσέστιχε. To make one's way *to*, proceed *to*. With acc.: προσέστιχεν Ὄλυμπον υ 73.

πρόσσω, πρόσω. **(1)** Of the direction of motion, forwards, onwards, on: δοῦρ' ὅρμενα πρόσσω Λ 572. Cf. Λ 615, Μ 274, Ν 291, Ο 543, Π 265 (straight for his object), 382, Ρ 734, Σ 388: νῆα πρόσω φέρε κῦμα ι 542. Cf. φ 369.—In reference to the exercise of a mental faculty: νοῆσαι ἅμα πρόσσω καὶ ὀπίσσω (to look before and after, be capable of reasoning from the past to the future) Α 343. Cf. Γ 109, Σ 250: ω 452.—**(2)** Of change of position, forwards: πρόσσω κατέκυψεν Π 611 = Ρ 527.—Of position, forwards, facing one's front: πρόσω τετραμμένος Ρ 598.

προστήσας, aor. pple. προΐστημι.

†**προστίθημι** [προσ- (1)]. 3 sing. aor. προσέθηκε To set or place in an indicated position: λίθον, ὃν προσέθηκεν ι 305.

προσφάσθαι, pres. infin. mid. πρόσφημι.

πρόσφατος [προσ-, app. with sense 'before one's very eyes,' 'in one's view' + φα-, φαν-, φαίνω. '(As if) newly revealed']. Fresh, unsullied: πρόσφατος κεῖσαι Ω 757.

†**πρόσφημι** [προσ- (2)]. Impf. προσέφην ι 282, 501, κ 422. 2 sing. -ης Π 20, 744, 843: ξ 55, ο 325, ρ 512, χ 194, etc. 3 -η Α 84, Β 172, Δ 183, Ζ 520, etc.: α 63, β 348, δ 30, ε 214, etc. Pres. infin. mid. προσφάσθαι ψ 106. **(1)** To speak *to*, address, accost. With acc.: Σθένελον Ε 108. Cf. Α 84, Β 795, Η 405, Ι 196, etc.: α 63, β 399, δ 59, ζ 24, etc.—Without expressed object, to make address, speak Β 172, Ε 439, Κ 369, etc.: κ 422, λ 565, ο 9.—**(2)** To say in way of address, speak, utter. In mid.: ἔπος ψ 106.—**(3)** With double construction of (1) and (2): τὴν οὔ τι προσέφη Α 511. Cf. Δ 401, Ε 689 = Ζ 342, Θ 484, Φ 478: υ 183.

προσφυής [προσφύω]. Attached to, forming part of, something: θρῆνυν προσφυέ' ἐκ κλισίης τ 58.

†**προσφύω** [προσ- (1)]. Aor. pple. προσφύς μ 433. Fem. προσφῦσα Ω 213. To grow to; hence, to attach oneself to something: τοῦ μέσον ἧπαρ ἔχοιμι ἐσθέμεναι προσφῦσα (burying my teeth in it) Ω 213.—To attach oneself *to*, seize, grasp. With dat.: ἐρινεῷ προσφύς μ 433.

προσφωνέω [προσ- (2)]. To speak *to*, address, accost. With acc.: Ὀδυσσῆα Λ 346. Cf. Β 22, Γ 389, Λ 464, etc.: δ 69, θ 381, ξ 401, ο 539, etc.—Without expressed object, to make address, speak ε 159, κ 109.—With double acc. of the person addressed and of what is said: οὐδέ τί μιν προσεφώνεον Α 332, Θ 445.

πρόσω. See πρόσσω.

πρόσωπον, τό [προσ- (1) + ὦπα. 'The part beside the eyes,' 'the region of the eyes']. Dat. pl. προσώπασι Η 212. Acc. προσώπατα σ 192. The face, visage, countenance: χαρίεν Σ 24. Cf. ο 332, υ 352.—In pl. in the same sense: πρόσωπα καὶ χεῖρ' ἀπομόργνυ Σ 414. Cf. Η 212, Τ 285: θ 85, σ 173 (ἀμφί advbl., πρόσωπα acc. of part affected), 192, τ 361.

†**προτάμνω** [προ- (1) (2) (3)]. Aor. pple. προταμών Ι 489: ψ 196. Aor. opt. mid. προταμοίμην σ 375. **(1)** To carry a cutting process forward in a specified direction: κορμὸν ἐκ ῥίζης προταμών (cutting it into shape) ψ 196.—**(2)** In reference to priority in time, to cut off something before: πρίν γ' ὅτε σ' ὄψου ἄσαιμι προταμών (cutting thee off the first morsel) Ι 489.—**(3)** In mid., to cut (a furrow) before or in front of one σ 375.

πρότερος, -η, -ον [comp. fr. πρό]. **(1)** That is in front: ἐν προτέροισι πόδεσσιν (his fore-paws) τ 228.—**(2)** Sooner, earlier: οὔ τις π. τόν γ' εἴσεται (before you) Α 548, π. γεγόνει (had been born before him, was the elder) Ν 355. Cf. Ρ 14, Τ 219, Φ 440: β 31, 43.—With genit., sooner than, before: ἐμέο π. ἐπέγρετο Κ 124.—With πρίν: οὐκ εἴων προτέρην αἵματος ἆσσον ἴμεν, πρὶν . . . (to do so before . . ., until I should . . .) λ 88.—**(3)** In neut. sing. πρότερον as adv., sooner Ξ 467.—**(4)** **(a)** Doing, succeeding in doing, something before another, anticipating him, taking the lead or initiative, assuming the aggressive, commencing, first (cf. πρῶτος (5) (a)): ὁππότεροι πρότεροι πημήνειαν Γ 299, πρότερος προΐει ἔγχος Ε 15. Cf. Γ 351, Δ 67, Ε 276, Θ 253 (cutting in), Π 569, Τ 183, etc.: γ 13, π 460, υ 394, ω 23, etc.—**(b)** Sim. in oblique cases of one to whom action is directed before another, first (cf. πρῶτος (5) (b)): ὑμῖν πὰρ προτέροισι πυρὸν ἔθηκεν Θ 188. Cf. Ο 157: γ 50, 53.—**(5)** Belonging to time past: ἐπὶ προτέρων ἀνθρώπων (in the days of the men of old) Ε 637, Ψ 332. Cf. Λ 691, Φ 405: θ 223, λ 630.—Absol. in pl., the men of old: οἱ πρότεροι Δ 308.—**(6)** Born sooner, older: π. καὶ ἀρείων Β 707, Ψ 588: τ 184. Cf. Ο 166, 182.—**(7)** Belonging to the past as opposed to the present, the former . . ., one's former . . .: ἀνδρός Γ 140. Cf. Γ 163, 429: ο 22, τ 504, χ 264 (to add to the former wrongs).—The preceding . . .: ἠοῖ τῇ προτέρῃ Ν 794. Cf. Φ 5, Ψ 790 (of the last generation and the men who lived then).—Absol.: τῇ προτέρῃ (*sc.* ἡμέρῃ), the day before π 50.

προτέρω [πρότερος]. **(1)** Further, further on, to a greater distance: ἦ πῄ με π. πολίων ἄξεις; (local genit., 'among the cities') Γ 400. Cf. Ε 672: ε 417.—**(2)** Forwards, towards one's front, onwards, on: ἴθυσαν Δ 507.—**(3)** Forward, on (contextually, in reference to persons entering or advancing into a house, 'in'): βάτην (entered)

Ι 192, ἄγε (brought them in) 199, βάτην (pursued their way) Κ 469, ἔπεο (come in) Σ 387 : = ε 91, ἐς δ' αὐτοὺς προτέρω ἄγε δ 36, πλέομεν (pursued our course) ι 62 = 105 = 565 = κ 77 = 133, νῆες κίον (set sail) ι 64, βὰν ἰέναι ο 109.—(4) In reference to prolongation or continuance of action or a state of things, further, yet further, longer: προτέρω κ' ἔτ' ἔρις γένετο (would have gone yet further) Ψ 490, εἴ κ' ἔτι προτέρω γένετο δρόμος (had continued) 526. Cf. δ 667 (see ἄρχω (1) (a)), ξ 356, ω 475.

†**προτεύχω** [προ-(1)]. Pf. infin. pass. προτετύχθαι. To cause to go forth, let go forth : τὰ προτετύχθαι ἐάσομεν (regard these things as gone on their way, put them out of our minds, let bygones be bygones) Π 60, Σ 112 = Τ 65.

προτί [cf. πρός, ποτί]. (I) Adv. Besides, in addition, too : ἐκ χροὸς ἕλκε δόρυ, προτὶ δὲ φρένες αὐτῷ ἕποντο (*i.e.* the spear drew out the midriff with it) Π 504. Cf. ρ 379.—(II) Prep. (1) With dat. (a) On, upon, in pregnant sense : βαλλόμενα προτὶ γαίῃ Χ 64.—(b) In the direction of, towards : τὴν προτὶ οἷ εἷλεν Φ 507. Cf. Υ 418.—(2) With acc. (a) To, towards, in the direction of : ἔρχονται προτὶ ἄστυ Β 801. Cf. Γ 116, Η 310, Κ 336, Λ 26, etc. : δ 9, η 2, θ 517, ι 147, etc.—Indicating arrival at a point : ἵκοντο προτὶ ἄστυ ω 154. Cf. ν 181.—In reference to attaching or suspending : κρεμόω [τεύχεα] προτὶ νηόν (*i.e.* will carry them there and hang them up) Η 83.—(b) In reference to speech, to : προτὶ ὃν μυθήσατο θυμόν Ρ 200, 442 : = ε 285 = 376.—(c) In reference to the direction in which action takes place, towards, against : προτὶ πέτρας κῦμα ῥοχθεῖ μ 59.—(3) With genit. In reference to that *from* which one derives something : τά σε προτί φασιν Ἀχιλλῆος δεδιδάχθαι Λ 831.

προτιάπτω [προτι-, προσ- (1)]. To attach *to*. With dat. Of something immaterial : τόδε κῦδος Ἀχιλλῆϊ προτιάπτω (grant it to him) Ω 110.

προτιβάλλω. See προσβάλλω.

προτιειλέω [προτι-, προσ- (3)]. To force to take, drive into, a specified course : ἐπὶ νῆας ἀπὸ στρατόφι Κ 347.

προτιεῖπον. See προσέειπον.

†**προτίθημι** [προ- (2)]. 3 pl. impf. πρότιθεν α 112. 3 sing. aor. προὔθηκε Ω 409. To set or place before one : ἦέ μιν ἦσι κυσὶ προὔθηκεν Ω 409 : τραπέζας (set ready for the feast) α 112.

προτιμῡθέομαι [προτι-, προσ- (2)]. To speak *to*, address. With acc. : ἑὸν υἱὸν προτιμυθήσασθαι λ 143.

προτιόσσομαι [προτι-, προσ- (2)]. (1) To direct the eyes towards, look at η 31, ψ 365.—(2) To bode, forebode, have a presentiment of, apprehend : ὄλεθρον ε 389, θάνατον ξ 219.—Absol., to see one's fate before one, forebode it Χ 356.

πρότμησις, ἡ [προ- (2) + τμη-, τάμνω]. App., the cut place in front, *i.e.* the navel Λ 424.

πρότονοι, οἱ [προ- (2) + τον-, τείνω]. The forestays of a mast (cf. ἐπίτονος) Α 434 : β 425 = ο 290, μ 409.

προτρέπω [προ- (1)]. 3 sing. aor. subj. mid. προτράπηται λ 18. Opt. προτραποίμην μ 381. Infin. προτραπέσθαι Ζ 336. In mid. (1) To go forward or take one's way in a specified direction. Of the sun : ὅτ' ἂν ἂψ ἐπὶ γαῖαν ἀπ' οὐρανόθεν προτράπηται λ 18. Cf. μ 381.—(2) To turn and flee in a specified direction : ἐπὶ νηῶν Ε 700.—(3) Fig., to betake oneself to something, yield oneself up to it : ἄχεϊ προτραπέσθαι Ζ 336.

προτροπάδην [προ- (1) + τροπ-, τρέπω]. Turning right away in an indicated direction, in downright flight, headlong (cf. prec. (2)) : φοβέοντο Π 304.

†**προτύπτω** [προ- (1)]. 3 sing. aor. προὔτυψε ω 319. 3 pl. προὔτυψαν Ν 136, Ο 306, Ρ 262. To dash or press forwards : Τρῶες προὔτυψαν ἀολλέες Ν 136 = Ο 306 = Ρ 262.—Of passion : ἀνὰ ῥῖνας δριμὺ μένος προὔτυψεν (burst forth) ω 319.

προὔθηκε, 3 sing. aor. προτίθημι.

προὔπεμψα, aor. προπέμπω.

προὔτυψε, 3 sing. aor. προτύπτω.

προὔφαινον, impf. προφαίνω.

προὔχω. See προέχω.

προφαίνω [προ- (1)]. Impf. act. and pass. προὔφαινον, προὐφαινόμην. Acc. sing. masc. aor. pple. pass. προφανέντα ω 160. Nom. dual προφανέντε Ω 332. Acc. προφανέντε Θ 378, Ρ 487. 3 sing. pf. προπέφανται Ξ 332. (1) To show forth, show, display : τέραα μ 394.—(2) *Intrans.*, to give forth light, be visible : οὐδὲ σελήνη προὔφαινεν ι 145.—(3) In pass., to come into view, appear, make one's appearance, present oneself : προφανέντε ἀνὰ πτολέμοιο γεφύρας Θ 378, τὰ προπέφανται ἅπαντα (lie open to view) Ξ 332. Cf. Ρ 487, Ω 332 : ν 169, ω 160.—*Impers.* : οὐδὲ προὐφαίνετ' ἰδέσθαι (there was not light enough to see) ι 143.

πρόφασις, ἡ [προ- (1) + φα-, φημί]. A profession or declaration. Adverbially in acc., as the cause that moves one, as the occasion (cf. ἐπίκλησις (2), χάρις (2) (b)) : κλαίουσα, ἐπὶ δὲ στενάχοντο γυναῖκες, Πάτροκλον πρόφασιν, σφῶν δ' αὐτῶν κήδε' ἑκάστη Τ 302 (*i.e.* his death was the immediate occasion, and each had her own griefs as well).—With genit. : εὐνῆς πρόφασιν (for the sake of . . .) Τ 262.

προφερής [προφέρω (with προ- (2)). 'Borne in front']. Comp. προφερέστερος, -η, better, more skilled or serviceable : ἐμεῖο προφερέστεροι φ 134. Cf. Κ 352 : θ 221.—Superl. προφερέστατος, the best, the most skilled : ἅλματι πάντων προφερέστατος ἦεν (at . . ., in . . .) θ 128.

προφέρω [προ- (1)]. (1) To bear or carry in a specified or indicated direction or to a specified or indicated destination : ὡς ὄρνις νεοσσοῖσι προφέρῃσι μάστακα Ι 323. Cf. Ζ 346, Ρ 121 : υ 64.—(2) To put forth, display : κρατερὸν μένος Κ 479.—To bring forth, utter (abuse) : ὀνείδεα Β 251.—To cast in one's teeth : δῶρ' Ἀφροδίτης Γ 64.—To offer (battle) (cf. Λ 529 cited under προβάλλω (1)). In mid. : ἔριδα προφέρονται Γ 7.—To display, engage in (rivalry) : ἔριδα προφέρουσαι ζ 92.—So in mid. θ 210.

†**προφεύγω** [προ- (1)]. 3 sing. aor. subj. προφύγῃ Ξ 81. 2 sing. opt. προφύγοισθα χ 325. Pple. προφυγών, -όντος Z 502, H 309 : λ 107. Infin. προφυγεῖν Λ 340. (1) To flee Λ 340.—(2) To flee from, escape from, escape, elude: μένος καὶ χεῖρας Ἀχαιῶν Z 502. Cf. H 309, Ξ 81 : λ 107, χ 325.

προφρονέως [adv. fr. next]. Zealously, earnestly, seriously E 810, 816, Z 173, H 160, P 224.

πρόφρων, -ονος [προ- (1) + φρήν. 'With forward mind']. Fem. (besides πρόφρων) πρόφρασσα. Displaying zeal, eagerness, earnestness : ὄμοσσον ἦ μέν μοι π. ἀρήξειν (zealously) A 77, πῶς τίς τοι π. ἔπεσιν πείθηται; (with alacrity) 150. Cf. A 543 (readily gratifying me), Θ 23 (with a will), 175 (really meaning it), I 480 (with hearty hospitality), K 290 (with zealous solicitude), Ξ 71, 357 (with all your energies), P 353 (with good spirit), Φ 500 (boldly), X 303, Ψ 647 (gladly) : β 230 = ε 8 (with honest zeal), β 387 (willingly), ε 143 (with sincere thought for his good), 161 (without grudging), θ 498 (in full measure), ι 355 (give me more and plenty), κ 386 (in good earnest), ν 359 (take thought for me and . . .), 391, ξ 54 (with hearty hospitality), 406 (should be fain to . . .), τ 398 (solicitously), υ 372, ψ 314.—Of the heart, zealous, eager, earnest : θυμῷ πρόφρονι (in earnest, really meaning it) Θ 40 = X 184, Ω 140. Cf. K 244 : π 257.

προφυγών, aor. pple. προφεύγω.

προχέω [προ- (1)]. To pour forth Φ 219.—In pass., of bodies of men, to pour or stream in a specified direction : τῇ προχέοντο πεφυζότες Φ 6. Cf. B 465, O 360.

πρόχνυ. App., utterly : ὀλέσθαι ξ 69. Cf. Φ 460.—App., of sitting, full on the ground, with limbs extended on the ground : καθεζομένη I 570.

προχοαί, αἱ [προχέω]. The place where a river flows into the sea, its mouth : ἐπὶ προχοῇσι ποταμοῖο P 263. Cf. ε 453, λ 242.—In reference to Ocean, app., its stream : ἐν προχοῇς Ὠκεανοῖο υ 65.

πρόχοος, -ου, ἡ [προχέω]. (1) A vessel for holding water to be poured on the hands Ω 304 : α 136 = δ 52 = η 172 = κ 368 = ο 135 = ρ 91.—(2) A vessel from which to pour wine into the cups σ 397.

πρυλής. (1) On foot : πρυλέες ῥώοντο (Ἕκτορι ἑπώμεθα) Λ 49 = M 77.—(2) Absol. in pl., fighters on foot, footmen : ἡγεμόνα πρυλέων O 517.—With the notion 'on foot' not prominent, fighters in gen. : τὸν πρώτοισι μετὰ πρυλέεσσι δάμασσας Φ 90. Cf. E 744.

πρύμνη, ἡ [πρυμνός]. (1) The stern (of a ship) : τῆς (sc. νηός) πρύμνη ἀείρετο ν 84.—Without νηός, a ship's stern : ἐν πρύμνῃ καθέζετο ο 285. Cf. A 409, Θ 475, Ξ 32, O 385, Π 124, Σ 76, 447.—(2) In apposition with νηῦς : νηῒ πάρα πρύμνῃ Ἀγαμέμνονος (by the stern of . . .'s ship) H 383. Cf. K 35, 570, Λ 600, M 403, N 333, 762, Ξ 51, 65, O 248, 435, 704, 722, Π 286, T 135 : β 417, μ 411, ν 75 (at the stern), ο 206, 223.

πρύμνηθεν [πρύμνη + -θεν (1)]. From, in the direction from, beginning with, the stern : πρύμνηθεν ἐπεὶ λάβε [νῆα] (by the stern) O 716.

πρυμνήσια, τά [πρύμνη]. Cables for mooring a ship's stern to the shore : κατὰ πρυμνήσι' ἔδησαν A 436. Cf. A 476 : β 418, ι 137, 178 = 562 = λ 637 = μ 145 = ο 548, μ 32, ο 286, 498, 552.

πρυμνός, -ή, -όν. (1) The hindmost or endmost part of the . . ., the base or root of the . . . (in the case of a part of the body denoting the end next the body) : γλῶσσαν πρυμνήν E 292, ἄγνυτον ὕλην πρυμνὴν ἐκτάμνοντες (at the bases of the boles) M 149, ἐξέρυσε πρυμνοῖο βραχίονος ἔγχος N 532. Cf. N 705, Π 314, 323 : ρ 504.—Superl. πρυμνότατος : πρυμνότατον κατὰ νῶτον (*i.e.* where the back and shoulder join) ρ 463.—At the base : λᾶας πρυμνὸς παχύς M 446.—(2) App. in neut. as sb., the root (of the . . .) : πρυμνὸν ὕπερ θέναρος E 339.—(3) App. in neut. as adv., by the root : ἐξ ὀδόντας ὦσε δόρυ πρυμνόν P 618.

πρυμνωρείη, -ης, ἡ [πρυμνός + ὄρος]. The base or foot of a mountain : ἐν πρυμνωρείῃ Ἴδης Ξ 307.

πρῴην [πρώϊος]. Lately, recently, the other day : τὸν σὺ π. κτεῖνας Ω 500. Cf. E 832.

πρωθήβης [πρῶτος + ἥβη]. In the first bloom of youth : κοῦροι πρωθῆβαι θ 263. Cf. Θ 518.

πρώθηβος, -η [as prec.]. = prec. α 431.

πρῶϊ. Early : π. ὑπηοῖοι Θ 530 = Σ 277 = 303.—Too early, untimely : σοὶ π. παραστήσεσθαι ἔμελλε μοῖρα ω 28.

πρωϊζός [πρῶϊ]. In neut. pl. πρωϊζά as adv., just before : χθιζά τε καὶ π. B 303 (see χθιζός (3)).

πρώϊος [πρῶϊ]. In neut. sing. πρώϊον as adv., early this morning : νευρήν, ἣν ἐνέδησα π. O 470.

πρών, πρώονος, ὁ. A rock, cliff, bluff Θ 557 = Π 299, M 282, P 747.

πρῴρη, -ης, ἡ [πρό]. A ship's bow or prow. In apposition with νηῦς : ἴκρια νηὸς πρῴρης μ 230.

πρώτιστος [an anomalous superl. form fr. πρῶτος]. Strengthened form of, but gen. hardly to be distinguished from, πρῶτος. (1) (a) Like πρῶτος (5) (a) : νηὸς ἀποθρῴσκοντα πολὺ πρώτιστον Ἀχαιῶν B 702. Cf. Ξ 442 : ξ 220, τ 447.—(b) Like πρῶτος (5) (b) : ἅς τοι πρωτίστῳ δίδομεν B 228. Cf. Π 656.—(2) In neut. sing. πρώτιστον as adv. (a) Like πρῶτος (6) (b). First, in the first place, first of all : πῦρ μοι π. γενέσθω χ 491.—(b) Like πρῶτος (6) (c) (β) : Ἀρτέμιδι π. ἐπεύξατο υ 60.—(c) Like πρῶτος (6) (j) : οἷον ὅτε π. ἐλείπετε πατρίδα γαῖαν (when first you . . .) κ 462.—(3) In neut. pl. πρώτιστα as adv. (a) Like πρῶτος (6) (b) : π. λέων γένετο δ 456.—(b) Like πρῶτος (6) (c) (α) : π. δύσετο χαλκόν χ 113. Cf. I 168.—(c) Like πρῶτος (6) (c) (β) : Κάλχαντα π. προσέειπεν (addressed him first) A 105. Cf. B 405, Σ 478 : γ 57, 419, ν 404 = ο 38 (go to him first of all).—(d) Like πρῶτος (6) (i) : ἐμὲ π. ἕταροι λίσσοντο ι 224.—(e) Like πρῶτος (6) (l) : ἐξ οὗ τὰ π. ἑπόμην Ἀγαμέμνονι (ever since . . .) λ 168.

πρωτόγονος [πρῶτος + γον-, γεν-, γίγνομαι]. First-born (of the year) : ἀρνῶν (the firstlings) Δ 102 = 120 = Ψ 864 = 873.

πρωτοπαγής [πρῶτος + παγ-, πήγνυμι]. Nom. pl. masc. *πρωτοπαγεῖς* E 194. App., put together for the first time, newly made: *δίφροι* E 194, *ἅμαξαν* Ω 267.

πρωτόπλοος, -ον [πρῶτος + πλέω]. Of a ship, app., making her first voyage θ 35.

πρῶτος, -η, -ον [πρόατος, superl. fr. πρό]. **(1)** In reference to position, the most advanced in a specified or indicated direction, the first or foremost: *οἱ πρῶτοί τε καὶ ὕστατοι* B 281. Cf. Δ 480 (in the forefront of the fray), Z 445, Θ 83, M 260 (against the face of the works), 315, 321, Ξ 31 (next the plain), 75 (next the sea), O 634, 654 (next the plain), 656, Π 394, Σ 579, Φ 90: θ 197, ο 36 (the first in your course), σ 379.—**(2)** The foremost or front part of the . . ., the front of the . . .: *ἐν πρώτῳ ῥυμῷ* Z 40, Π 371. Cf. Θ 411 (just in front of the gate, at the entrance to it), O 340 (in the front of the fight), P 380, 471, T 50, Υ 173, 275 (the edge), 395, X 66 (before the house-door), Ω 272: α 255 (just within the door), φ 422 (the top of the . . .), χ 250.—**(3)** Absol., the winner in a contest: *ἄεθλα τῷ πρώτῳ* Ψ 265.—In neut. pl. *τὰ πρῶτα*, the first prize Ψ 275, 538.—**(4)** Absol. in pl. **(a)** Those who stand or advance in or to the front of the fray, the front rank: *ἐνὶ πρώτοισι μάχεσθαι* I 709. Cf. Δ 341, E 536, Θ 337, Λ 61, etc.—**(b)** The most prominent in some sphere of activity: *μετὰ πρώτοισι πονεῖτο* (with the best) I 12.—**(c)** The first in social rank, the leading men ζ 60.—**(d)** Gen., the most distinguished, the first: *ἐν πρώτοισιν ὀΐω ἔμμεναι* θ 180. Cf. O 643.—**(5)** **(a)** Being the first to do something, first, giving a lead, showing the way, taking the initiative, doing something before another, anticipating him (cf. πρότερος (4) (a)): *πρῶτος κελόμην* A 386, *οὐδὲ σέθεν θεοὶ λελάθοντο, πρώτη δὲ Διὸς θυγάτηρ* (*i.e.* she was the first to bethink her of you) Δ 128, *πρώτῳ στρεφθέντι* (*i.e.* he was the first to flee) E 40. Cf. Δ 343, 459, 457, E 38, Z 5, K 532, N 809, Π 812, Υ 161 (leaving his fellows the first), etc.: α 113, γ 36, θ 216, λ 51, χ 212, etc.—**(b)** Sim. in oblique cases of that to which action is first directed or which is first affected in some way, first (cf. πρότερος (4) (b)): *τίνα πρῶτον ἐξενάριξαν;* E 703, *πὰρ σοὶ πρώτῳ πασάμην ἀκτήν* (*i.e.* formed thus a tie with you first of the Greeks) Φ 76. Cf. E 829, K 18, N 46, P 553, etc.: β 39, δ 452, ζ 176, η 237 (I will begin by asking you), θ 462, ι 14, λ 235, φ 304, etc.—**(6)** In neut. sing. (*τὸ*) *πρῶτον* and pl. (*τὰ*) *πρῶτα* as adv. **(a)** In front. (i) *πρῶτον ἀντιάσαντες* (forming a screen to cover the retreat) O 297.—(ii) *ἱππῆας πρῶτα στῆσεν* Δ 297, *πρῶτα περὶ τέρμα βαλούσας* (leading) Ψ 462.—**(b)** First, in the first place, first of all, to begin with (as opposed to subsequent action). (i) *βουλὴν πρῶτον ἷζεν* B 53, *πρῶτον Μίνωα τέκεν* (this was the beginning of the race) N 450. Cf. Γ 315, Z 179, Λ 628, Ξ 170, Ψ 237, etc.: β 190, δ 411, θ 120, μ 39, ν 117, π 173, ω 240, etc.—(ii) *αὐέρυσαν πρῶτα* A 459. Cf. B 73, Γ 330, E 458, I 32, Λ 244, Φ 343, etc.: *Γυρῇσίν μιν πρῶτ' ἐπέλασσε* δ 500 (taken up by 502; this was the first stage of his fate), *Ναυσίθοον πρῶτα Ποσειδάων γείνατο* (this was the beginning of the race) η 56. Cf. κ 154, 519, λ 158, σ 192, ψ 131, etc.—**(c)** In advbl. use corresponding **(a)** To the adjectival use (5) (a), first. (i) *οἱ ἐξ πρῶτον ἀκοντίσατε* χ 252.—(ii) *ἴστω Ζεὺς πρῶτα* T 258: = τ 303, ξ 158 = ρ 155 = υ 230, *ἢ πρῶτ' ἐξερέοιτο* (anticipate him, begin the conversation) δ 119.—**(β)** To the adjectival use (5) (b), first. (i) *οὐρῆας πρῶτον ἐπῴχετο* (they were the first to be attacked) A 50.—(ii) *Ὀρσίλοχον πρῶθ' ἕλεν* (he was the first man slain) Θ 274. Cf. Λ 301, Π 694, Ψ 262: *πρῶτ' ἐς Πύλον ἐλθέ* (let Pylus be your first goal) α 284, *δέσποιναν πρῶτα κιχήσεαι* η 53, *αὐτόν σε πρῶτα σάω* (let your own safety be your first care) ρ 595. Cf. ν 228, ρ 573.—Sim.: *ἔνθεν μιν ἐδέγμην πρῶτα φανεῖσθαι* μ 230 (*i.e.* he thought he should catch sight of her from that position sooner than from elsewhere).—**(d)** In reference to the first doing or occurrence of something, for the first time, first. (i) *ὅθι πρῶτον λιπέτην ἅλα* Ξ 284 (they did not leave it till they reached that point), *πρῶτον ὑπηνήτῃ* (newly) Ω 348: κ 279. Cf. Ξ 295, Π 113.—(ii) *ἐλθὼν τὸ πρῶτον* δ 159.—(iii) *ὅθι πρῶτ' ἐμβασίλευεν* (had his first period of kingship) B 572, *οὐ νῦν πρῶτ' ἄντ' Ἀχιλῆος στήσομαι* Υ 89. Cf. Π 811: ο 420.—(iv) *τοῖος οἷόν μιν τὰ πρῶτ' ἐνόησα* α 257. Cf. θ 268.—**(e)** With a temporal conjunction, when first, as soon as: *ἐπὴν δὴ πρῶτα κατευνηθέντα ἴδησθε* δ 414.—**(f)** At first, to begin with (implying a subsequent change). (i) *πρῶτον ἀτίζων ἔρχεται* Υ 166.—(ii) *πόντῳ πρῶτα κορύσσεται* [*κῦμα*] Δ 424. Cf Δ 442: λ 640.—(iii) *πεζὸς τὰ πρῶτ' ἤλυθεν* P 612. Cf. Ψ 523.—**(g)** Before doing something, as a preliminary, first. (i) *ἄλλην χρὴ πρῶτον ὁδὸν τελέσαι* κ 490.—(ii) *πρῶτα θεῶν εἰρώμεθα βουλάς* π 402. Cf. K 344.—**(h)** In reference to preference or choice, first, before anything else: *πρῶτον τοῦ πατρὸς ἑλοίμεθα νόστιμον ἦμαρ* π 149.—**(i)** At once, straightway: *οὕνεκά σ' οὐ τὸ πρῶτον, ἐπεὶ ἴδον, ὧδ' ἀγάπησα* ψ 214.—**(j)** Marking the time of an action or occurrence as a point of departure, a beginning, an opening of a new era. (i) *ὅτε σε πρῶτον ἔπλεον ἁρπάξας* (since first I . . .) Γ 443, *ὅθι πρῶτον ἐξαίνυτο θυμόν* (where he began by slaying him) E 848, *ὅτε με πρῶτον τέκε μήτηρ* (and so brought me into all this woe) Z 345, *ἀλκήν μοι πρῶτον ὀνείδισας* (you began it by reflecting on my valour) I 34, *ὅτε πρῶτον λίπον Ἑλλάδα* (when first I . . .) 447: *ὁππότε κε πρῶτον πελάσῃς νῆα Θρινακίῃ* (then will come the time for prudence) λ 106, *ὅθι πρῶτον γενόμην* (where I had my first being) ξ 141, *ὅτε μιν πρῶτον τέκε μήτηρ* τ 355.—(ii) *τὸ πρῶτον ἀάσθη* (and so brought his fate upon him) δ 509.—(iii) *ἐξ ἧς πρῶτα καὶ ἡμέας ἵκετο πένθος* (first came upon us) ψ 224.—(iv) *μῆνιν ἄειδε . . . ἐξ οὗ τὰ πρῶτα διαστήτην* (take up the tale from the point when first . . ., *i.e.* from the beginning of the quarrel) A 6, *ἢ τὰ πρῶτα πύλας ἐσᾶλτο* (began the attack) N 679.—**(k)** Denoting fixity of determination, purpose or condition, or that something is done or brought about finally or completely, once for all. (i) ὥς οἱ ὑπέστην πρῶτον O 75, ὥς σφιν πρῶτον ἀπήχθετο Ἴλιος Ω 27, ἐπεί με πρῶτον ἔασας 557. Cf. A 319, T 136 : δ 6, ν 127, 133.—(ii) ὡς τὸ πρῶτον ὑπέστην Δ 267, ὅππως τὸ πρῶτον τανύσῃ [ἵππους] (from the start) Ψ 324.—(iii) ὥς οἱ πρῶτα δόσαν γέρας A 276, ἐπεὶ δὴ πρῶτα δαμάσθη (let us accept that and make the best of it) T 9.—(l) Denoting inevitability of consequence or of the continuance of a state or condition on the doing or occurrence of something, (when) once . . ., (since) once . . ., (who) once . . . (i) εὖτ' ἂν πρῶτον ὁμιλήσωσι φάλαγγες T 158. Cf. N 285 : ὅτε πρῶτον Κρήτης ὄρεα νοσφισάμην (ever since . .) τ 338. Cf. γ 320, κ 328.—(ii) ἐπεὶ δὴ τὸ πρῶτον ἐγείνατο παῖδα δ 13, ἐπεὶ τὸ πρῶτον ἀνέκραγον (and so committed myself) ξ 467.—(iii) ἐπεὶ δὴ πρῶτα τομὴν λέλοιπεν A 235. Cf. P 427 : ἐπεί κε πρῶτα λίπῃ ὀστέα θυμός λ 221. Cf. γ 183.—(iv) ἐπὴν τὰ πρῶτα γένηται Z 489. Cf. M 420 : θ 553.

πρωτοτόκος, -ον [πρῶτος + τοκ-, τίκτω]. Having borne offspring for the first time. Of a cow P 5.

†**πταίρω**. 3 sing. aor. ἔπταρε. (ἐπι-.) To sneeze : Τηλέμαχος μέγ' ἔπταρεν ρ 541.

πταμένη, aor. pple. fem. πέτομαι.

πτάτο, 3 sing. aor. πέτομαι.

πτελέη, -ης, ἡ. An elm Z 419, Φ 242, 350.

πτέρνη, -ης, ἡ. The heel X 397.

πτερόεις, -εντος [πτερόν]. Feathered, winged. Epithet of arrows Δ 117, E 171, Π 773, Υ 68.—Of λαισήϊα, fluttering E 453 = M 426.—Of words, fig., winged : ἔπεα πτερόεντα A 201, Γ 155, Δ 69, E 242, etc. : α 122, β 269, δ 25, ι 409, etc.

πτερόν, τό [π(έ)τομαι]. (1) A feather Λ 454 : β 151, ε 53, ο 527.—(2) In pl., a bird's wings : σὺν πτερὰ πυκνὰ λίασθεν Ψ 879. Cf. T 386, Ω 319. —App. in sing. in the same sense : ὠκεῖαι ὡς εἰ πτερὸν ἠὲ νόημα η 36.—Fig. of oars λ 125 = ψ 272.

πτέρυξ, -υγος, ἡ [πτερόν]. A bird's wing : ὑπὸ πτέρυγος βάλεν Ψ 875. Cf. B 316, 462 : β 149.

†**πτήσσω** [πτηκ-. Cf. πτώσσω]. 3 sing. aor. πτῆξε Ξ 40. 3 pl. ἔπτηξαν θ 190. Pf. pple. πεπτηώς ξ 354, χ 362. Pl. πεπτηῶτες ξ 474. (κατα-, ποτι-, ὑπο-.) (1) To crouch, cower : κείμην πεπτηώς (cowering for concealment) ξ 354. Cf. ξ 474, χ 362.—To cower, stoop, bend low, in apprehension θ 190.—(2) To strike with dismay : πτῆξε θυμὸν Ἀχαιῶν Ξ 40.

πτῆται, 3 sing. aor. subj. πέτομαι.

†**πτοιέω**, 3 pl. aor. pass. ἐπτοίηθεν. (δια-.) To terrify, scare, dismay χ 298.

πτολεμίζω, πτολεμιστής, πτόλεμος. See πολεμίζω, πολεμιστής, πόλεμος.

πτολίεθρον, τό. = πτόλις, πόλις (1) A 164, B 228, 501, I 149, etc. : γ 4, θ 283, ι 165, κ 81, ω 377.—With the name of a particular town in genit. : Ἰλίου εὖ ναιόμενον π. B 133. Cf. B 538, Δ 33 = Θ 288, N 380, Φ 433 : α 2, γ 485, ο 193.

πτολιπόρθιος. = next. Epithet of Odysseus ι 504.

πτολίπορθος, -ον [πτόλις + πορθέω]. Sacker of cities. Epithet of Odysseus B 278, K 363 : θ 3, ι 530, ξ 447, π 442, σ 356, χ 283, ω 119.—Of Oïleus B 728.—Of Enyo E 333.—Of Achilles Θ 372 = O 77, Φ 550, Ω 108.—Of Ares Υ 152.—Of Otrynteus Υ 384.

πτόλις. See πόλις.

πτόρθος, -ου, ὁ. A branch of a tree or shrub : ἐξ ὕλης πτόρθον κλάσε φύλλων ζ 128.

πτύγμα, τό [πτύσσω]. The parts brought together in folding, a fold : πρόσθε οἱ πέπλοιο πτύγμ' ἐκάλυψεν (folded the loose part of her robe about him) E 315.

πτυκτός [πτύσσω]. Of a writing-tablet, folding, *i.e.* double, made of two hinged pieces which could be closed on each other and (no doubt) in some way secured : πίνακι Z 169.

πτύξ, πτυχός, ἡ [πτυχ-, πτύσσω]. (1) A 'fold' or cleft in the furrowed side or top of a hill : κατὰ πτύχας Οὐλύμποιο Λ 77. Cf. Υ 22 (in a cleft) : τ 432.—(2) One of the layers of hide or metal forming a shield H 247, Σ 481, Υ 269, 270.

πτύξᾱσα, aor. pple. fem. πτύσσω.

πτύον, τό. Ablative πτυόφιν. A shovel by which grain, etc., to be winnowed was thrown against the wind (= ἀθηρηλοιγός) N 588.

πτύσσω [πτυχ-]. Aor. pple. fem. πτύξᾱσα α 439, ζ 111, 252, τ 256. (προσ-.) To fold (clothes) α 439, ζ 111, 252, τ 256.—In pass. : ἔγχεα πτύσσοντο θρασειάων ἀπὸ χειρῶν σειόμενα N 134, doubtfully explained as 'bent to the strain' as they were brandished, or 'formed a serried mass' (presenting the appearance of folds or layers).

πτύω. (ἀπο-, ἐκ-.) To spit out : αἷμα Ψ 697.

πτώξ, πτωκός, ὁ [πτωκ-, πτώσσω. 'The cowering or timid animal']. A hare P 676.—Joined with λαγωός : πτῶκα λαγωόν X 310.

πτωσκάζω [πτώσσω]. = next (1) Δ 372.

πτώσσω [πτωκ-. Cf. πτήσσω]. (κατα-.) (1) To cower or crouch in fear or from cowardice, shrink from the fray Δ 371, E 634, H 129, Φ 26. —Of locusts Φ 14.—With acc. of the person from whom one shrinks : οὐδ' ἂν ἔτι δὴν ἀλλήλους πτώσσοιμεν Υ 427.—Sim. of birds : νέφεα πτώσσουσαι (shrinking from the region of the clouds, flying low) χ 304.—(2) To cringe in humility ; hence, to go about begging : πτώσσων (πτώσσειν) κατὰ δῆμον ρ 227, σ 363.

πτωχεύω [πτωχός]. 3 sing. pa. iterative πτωχεύεσκε σ 2. To go about begging, beg one's bread : προτὶ ἄστυ ἀπονέεσθαι πτωχεύσων ο 309. Cf. σ 2, τ 73.—To beg (one's bread) : ὄφρ' ἂν ἐκεῖθι δαῖτα πτωχεύῃ ρ 11. Cf. ρ 19.

πτωχός, -οῦ, ὁ [πτώσσω (2)]. A beggar ζ 208, ξ 400, π 209, σ 1, etc.—With ἀνήρ : ἄλλος τις π. ἀνήρ φ 327.

πυγμαχίη, -ης, ἡ [πυγμάχος]. Fighting with the fists, boxing : πυγμαχίης ἄεθλα (for . . .) Ψ 653. Cf. Ψ 665.

πυγμάχος [πυγ-, πύξ + μάχομαι]. One who fights with the fists, a boxer θ 246.

πυγμή, -ῆς, ἡ [πυγ-, πύξ]. = πυγμαχίη Ψ 669.

πυγούσιος [πυγών, a measure of length derived from the forearm, a cubit]. Of a cubit's length κ 517, λ 25.

πύελος, -ου. A trough or box holding grain for feeding poultry τ 553.

πυθέσθαι, aor. infin. πεύθομαι.

πυθμήν, -ένος, ὁ. **(1)** A base or support: δύω ὑπὸ [δέπαϊ] πυθμένες ἦσαν Λ 635 (app. the base of the hollow part ran out again after contraction to form a foot).—A leg of a tripod: χρύσεά σφ' ὑπὸ κύκλα ἑκάστῳ πυθμένι θῆκεν (fitted a wheel under each leg) Σ 375.—**(2)** The base of a tree, the part of the trunk next the ground ν 122, 372, ψ 204.

πυθόμην, aor. πεύθομαι.

πύθω, 3 sing. fut. πύσει Δ 174. (κατα-.) **(1)** To affect with decomposition, make rotten, rot: ὀστέα Δ 174.—**(2)** In pass., to suffer decomposition, decompose, rot, decay: οὗ ὀστέα πύθεται ὄμβρῳ α 161. Cf. Λ 395: μ 46.

πύκα. **(1)** In reference to construction, closely, without breaks or interstices, so as to give good shelter or protection: πύλας π. στιβαρῶς ἀραρυίας (both closely fitted and strong) Μ 454, σάκεος π. ποιητοῖο Σ 608. Cf. α 333 = θ 458 = π 415 = σ 209 = φ 64, α 436, χ 455.—In reference to complete protection afforded by armour: Λυκίων (Τρώων) π. θωρηκτάων (wearing the goodly breastplate) Μ 317, Ο 689, 739.—**(2)** In reference to things coming thick and fast: πρίν γ' ὅτε δὴ θάλαμος π. ἐβάλλετο (was struck by many a dart) Ι 588.—**(3)** In reference to the exercise of mental faculties, with close devotion to the subject in hand, shrewdly, astutely: νόον π. περ φρονεόντων Ι 554, Ξ 217.—**(4)** In reference to attention or care, with close attention, with anxious care: π. [μιν] ἔτρεφεν Ε 70.

πυκάζω [πύκα]. 3 sing. aor. πύκασε Θ 124, 316, Κ 271, Ρ 83. Pple. πυκάσας Ω 581. Fem. πυκάσᾱσα Ρ 551. Infin. πυκάσαι λ 320. Pf. pple. pass. πεπυκασμένος Ξ 289: χ 488. Nom. pl. neut. πεπυκασμένα Β 777, Ψ 503. **(1)** To put something round or about (something), cover, cover up, for protection, concealment or decency: νέκυν πυκάσας Ω 581. Cf. Β 777, Ξ 289, Ρ 551: ῥάκεσιν πεπυκασμένος χ 488.—To protect, shield: πύκασεν κάρη [κυνέῃ] Κ 271.—To shelter or conceal (oneself): μή πως ἐντὸς πυκάζοιεν σφέας αὐτούς μ 225.—To cover the surface of by way of ornamentation: ἅρματα χρυσῷ πεπυκασμένα Ψ 503.—In reference to something growing upon and covering a surface: πρίν σφωϊν ἰούλους πυκάσαι γένυς λάχνῃ λ 320.—**(2)** Of grief overwhelming (a person): Ἕκτορ' ἄχος πύκασε φρένας Θ 124 = 316, Ρ 83.

πυκιμηδής [πύκα + μήδεα [1]]. Shrewd in counsel, clever: γραίης α 438.

πυκινός, -ή, -όν, **πυκνός,** -ή, -όν [πύκα]. **(1)** Close in texture, dense, thick: πυκινὸν νέφος Ε 751 = Θ 395, νεφέλην Π 298.—**(2)** Of things placed close together or at short intervals, close-set, thick: πυκινοῖσι λίθοισιν Π 212. Cf. Μ 57, Ν 133 = Π 217, Φ 245, Ω 453, 798: ὀδόντες πυκνοί μ 92. Cf. ε 329, 433, 480, ξ 12, τ 520, ψ 193.—Of things appearing together in a limited space, numerous, many: πυκναὶ σμώδιγγες ἀνέδραμον Ψ 716.—**(3)** In reference to construction, closely constructed or made, well fitted together, without breaks or interstices, affording good shelter, protection or security: πυκινὸν δόμον Κ 267, Μ 301, ἀσπίδα ῥινοῖσιν πυκινήν (made of closely fitted . . .) Ν 804. Cf. Ξ 167 = 339, Ο 529, Τ 355: ζ 134, η 81, 88, ν 68, ξ 521, 529, ψ 229.—Sim. of something natural, thick, affording close covert: ἐν λόχμῃ πυκινῇ τ 439. Cf. τ 442.—Sim. of a bed, such as to afford good protection, warm, cosy: πυκινὸν λέχος Ι 621, 659: η 340 = ψ 291, ψ 177, 179.—Letting nothing escape from within, holding its contents, tight, well-fenced: δέρμασιν ἐν πυκινοῖσιν β 291, πυκινοὺς κευθμῶνας κ 283.—**(4)** Of grief, overwhelming: πυκινὸν ἄχος Π 599. Cf. τ 516.—Sim. of ἄτη, overpowering Ω 480.—**(5)** Consisting of many individual persons or things, dense, close, thick: πυκιναὶ φάλαγγες Δ 281, Ε 93. Cf. Η 61, Λ 118, Ν 145, 199, 680, Ξ 349, Σ 320, Ψ 122, 879: ἐκ πυκινῆς ὕλης ζ 128. Cf. ε 53, 471, κ 150, 197, ξ 473.—**(6)** Doing something at short intervals, thick-coming, coming thick and fast: πυκινοῖσι βελέεσσιν Λ 576. Cf. ξ 36.—Falling quickly one after the other, falling fast or in a shower: ὣς πυκνὰ καρήατα δάμνατο λαῶν Λ 309. Cf. Λ 454: τιναξάσθην πτερὰ πυκνά β 151. Cf. δ 153.—**(7)** Of the mind, or mental faculties, shrewd, astute, sagacious, wise: Διὸς πυκινὸν νόον Ο 461. Cf. Ξ 294 (though . . .).—**(8)** Displaying shrewdness, astuteness, sagacity, or wisdom, shrewd, astute, sagacious, wise, shrewdly or cunningly devised or contrived: πυκινὴν βουλήν Β 55 = Κ 302, Ι 76, πυκινὸν λόχον Δ 392, Ω 779: λ 525. Cf. Γ 202, 208, Ζ 187, Η 375, Λ 788, Σ 216, Ω 75, 282 = 674, 744: γ 23, τ 353.—Absol. in neut. pl. πυκινά, shrewdness, astuteness: πυκινὰ φρονέοντι ι 445.—**(9)** In neut. sing. πυκινόν as adv., in reference to grief which overwhelms one, heavily, sorely: πυκινόν περ ἀχεύων λ 88.—**(10)** In neut. pl. πυκινά, πυκνά, as adv. **(a)** With short intervals between: πήρην, πυκνὰ ῥωγαλέην (full of rents) ν 438 = ρ 198 = σ 109.—**(b)** At short intervals, often, much: ὣς πυκίν' ἀναστενάχιζεν Κ 9. Cf. Σ 318, Φ 417.

πυκινῶς [adv. fr. πυκινός]. **(1)** In reference to construction, closely, without breaks or interstices, so as to give good shelter or protection: θύρας π. ἀραρυίας Ι 475. Cf. Φ 535: β 344, φ 236 = 382, χ 155, 258 = 275, ψ 194.—**(2)** In reference to grief which overwhelms one, heavily, sorely: π. ἀκαχήμενον Τ 312. Cf. τ 95, υ 84, ψ 360.—**(3)** Shrewdly, wisely: π. τοι ὑποθησόμεθα (for your good) Φ 293. Cf. α 279.

πυκνός. See πυκινός.

πυλάρτης [πύλη + ἀρ-, ἀραρίσκω]. The gate-fastener, the gate-keeper. Epithet of Hades Θ 367, Ν 415: λ 277.

πυλαωρός, ὁ [πύλη + ὀρ-, ὄρομαι]. He that watches the gate, a gate-keeper Φ 530, Ω 681.

πύλη, -ης, ἡ. (1) (a) A gate of a city or other place B 809, Δ 34, E 466, Z 80, I 573, M 175, etc. —(b) In pl. of a single gate (as consisting of two wings): πυλέων ἐξέσσυτο H 1. Cf. Γ 145, E 646, 749, Θ 15, M 120, N 124, X 99, Ω 709, etc.: ξ 156.—(2) Of the gates of dreams: ἐν ὀνειρείῃσι πύλῃσιν δ 809. Cf. τ 562.—Of the gates of the sun ω 12.

Πυλοιγενής [locative of Πύλος + γεν-, γίγνομαι]. Born at Pylus, sprung from Pylus: βασιλῆος B 54, ἵπποι Ψ 303.

πύματος, -η, -ον. (1) Of position, the last, the hindmost: φάλαγγας Δ 254.—Absol. in pl., those in the rear, the rear rank: ἐν πυμάτοισι κελεύων Λ 65.—(2) That is at the extremity of something: ἄντυξ ἣ πυμάτη θέεν ἀσπίδος (at its edge) Z 118.—The extreme part of the . . ., the extremity of the . . .: ἐξ ἐπιδιφριάδος πυμάτης (its edge) K 475, ῥινὸς ὕπερ πυμάτης (the top of it) N 616, ἄντυγα πὰρ πυμάτην σάκεος (the edge of the rim) Σ 608.—(3) The last in sequence or time: δρόμον Ψ 373, 768. Cf. β 20.—In oblique cases of that to which action is last directed or which is last affected in some way, last: Οὖτιν πύματον ἔδομαι ι 369. Cf. Λ 759, X 66: η 138.—(4) (a) In neut. sing. πύματον as adv., for the last time. With ὕστατον in the same sense: π. τε καὶ ὕστατον X 203: υ 116.—(b) So in neut. pl. πύματα. With ὕστατα in the same sense: ὕστατα καὶ π. δ 685, υ 13.

πυνθάνομαι. See πεύθομαι.

πύξ. With the fist: πὺξ ἀγαθόν (the great boxer) Γ 237, οὐ πύξ γε μαχήσεαι (will never box again) Ψ 621. Cf. Ψ 634 (at boxing), 660 (to box): θ 103, 130, 206, λ 300.

πύξινος [πύξος, the box-tree]. Of box-wood: ζυγόν Ω 269.

πῦρ, πυρός, τό [cf. Eng. *fire*, Germ. *feuer*]. (1) Fire: ὄσσε οἱ πυρὶ λαμπετόωντι ἐΐκτην A 104. Cf. B 340 (to the flames with . . .), 415 (genit. of material, 'with fire'), E 4, 215 (commit to the flames), Z 182, M 177, Ξ 396, etc.: δ 418, ε 490, ι 390, μ 68, π 290, ρ 23, τ 39, etc.—Funeral-fire, the flames of the pyre: ὄφρα πυρός με λελάχωσιν H 79. Cf. O 350, Ψ 76, etc.: ω 65.—(2) The result of the application of fire to prepared combustible material, fire; when a particular mass of fire is referred to, a fire: ἐν πυρὸς αὐγῇ I 206, ἐν νηυσὶ πῦρ βαλέειν N 629. Cf. Θ 521, 563, I 211, O 420, Π 122, Σ 344, T 376, etc.: γ 341, ε 59, ζ 305, θ 426, 501, ξ 518, ρ 572, χ 481, etc.—Of watch-fires: ἔνθα πῦρ κήαντο I 88 (*i.e.* each band lighted its fire).—A funeral-pyre Ψ 45.

πυρά, τά [cf. prec.]. Watch-fires Θ 509, 554, 561, 562, I 77, 234, K 12.

πυράγρη, -ης, ἡ [πῦρ + ἄγρη]. A smith's tongs: γέντο πυράγρην Σ 477. Cf. γ 434.

πυρακτέω [app. fr. *πυράζω, vb. fr. πῦρ]. To bring the influence of fire to bear upon, harden by fire: [ῥόπαλον] ι 328.

πυργηδόν [πύργος]. In line: π. σφέας αὐτοὺς ἀρτύναντες M 43 (in line of battle). Cf. N 152, O 618.

πύργος, -ου, ὁ. (1) A fortified wall securing a city or strong place; in pl., walls, ramparts: ἧντ' ἐπὶ πύργῳ Γ 153, δείμομεν πύργους H 338. Cf. Z 373, H 437 (hardly to be distinguished from τεῖχος), Θ 165, I 574, M 36, 332 (the part of the wall under his charge), O 737, Π 700, Σ 274, X 97 (a projecting angle of the wall), Ω 443, etc.: ζ 262.—Fig. of a person: τοῖος σφιν π. ἀπώλεο (so mighty a wall of defence was lost in thee) λ 556.—(2) A tower erected for defence on such a wall: φέρων σάκος ἠΰτε πύργον H 219 = Λ 485 = P 128. Cf. Δ 462.—(3) A body of troops formed in line: δέκα πύργοι Ἀχαιῶν Δ 347, πάπτηνεν ἀνὰ πύργον Ἀχαιῶν (the line of defenders) M 333. Cf. Δ 334.

πυργόω [πύργος]. To surround with a wall, fortify: Θήβης ἕδος πύργωσαν λ 264.

πυρετός, -οῦ, ὁ [πῦρ]. Fever X 31.

πυρή, -ῆς, ἡ [πῦρ]. (1) A funeral-pyre: πυραὶ νεκύων καίοντο θαμειαί A 52. Cf. Δ 99, H 336, 434, I 546, Σ 336, Ψ 22, 141, 164, 165, 167, 172, 174, 192, 194, 210, 216, 217, 241, 256, Ω 787, 879: ω 69.—(2) The fire of a sacrifice: πυρὴν ἐμπλησέμεν ἐσθλῶν κ 523 = λ 31.

πῡρηφόρος [πυρός + -φορος, φέρω. Cf. πυροφόρος]. Wheat-bearing: πεδίον γ 495.

πυριήκης [πυρί, dat. of πῦρ + *ἀκή, point]. Sharpened by fire: μοχλόν ι 387.

πυρίκαυστος [πυρί, dat. of πῦρ + καυ-, καίω]. Charred (at the end to prevent rotting) N 564.

πυρκαϊή, -ῆς, ἡ [πῦρ + καίω. 'A place where fire is kindled']. A funeral-pyre: νεκροὺς πυρκαϊῆς ἐπενήνεον H 428 = 431. Cf. Ψ 158, 225, 228, 231, 237, 250 = Ω 791.

πύρνον, -ου, τό [πύρινος, adj. fr. πυρός]. A wheaten cake or loaf ο 312, ρ 12, 362.

πῡρός, -οῦ, ὁ. Wheat Θ 188, K 569: τ 536, 553, υ 109.—The growing plant. In pl.: πυροί τε ζειαί τε δ 604. Cf. Λ 69: ι 110, τ 112.

πῡροφόρος, -ον [πυρός + -φορος, φέρω. Cf. πυρηφόρος]. Wheat-bearing: ἀρούρης M 314. Cf. Ξ 123, Φ 602.

πυρπολέω [πῦρ + -πολος, conn. with πολεύω]. To attend to, keep up, a fire. Absol. in pres. pple. pl.: πυρπολέοντας ἐλεύσσομεν (could see men tending their fire) κ 30.

πυρσός, -οῦ, ὁ [πῦρ]. A beacon-fire or signal-fire: πυρσοὶ φλεγέθουσιν Σ 211.

πύσει, 3 sing. fut. πύθω.

πω, *enclitic*. (1) With negative, in no wise, not at all: μὴ δή πω χάζεσθε O 426. Cf. Δ 184, 234, P 422, X 279: ψ 59.—With οὐ. See οὐ (8) (b) (α).—(2) With negative, not yet, never yet: ἐσθλὸν δ' οὔτε τί πω εἶπας ἔπος οὔτ' ἐτέλεσσας A 108. Cf. A 542, B 419, H 433, Λ 497, Π 76, X 9, Ψ 73, etc.: οὐδέ πω ὥρη εὕδειν λ 373. Cf. γ 23, λ 161, ψ 315, etc.—In reference to the future: μὴ δή πω λυώμεθ' ἵππους Ψ 7. Cf. Σ 134, Ω 553: χ 431.—With οὐ. See οὐ (8) (b) (β), 8 (c).

πωλέομαι [cf. πολεύω]. 2 sing. pres. πωλέαι

δ 811. Nom. pl. masc. pres. pple. πωλεύμενοι β 55, ρ 534. Impf. πωλεύμην χ 352. 3 sing. pa. iterative πωλέσκετο Α 490, Ε 788 : λ 240. (ἐπι-.) To go or come habitually or regularly, use or be wont to go or come : εἰς ἀγορήν Α 490. Cf. Ε 350, 788 : δεῦρο (frequents this spot) δ 384, οὔ τι πάρος γε πωλέαι (it has not been your wont to come hither) 811, ἐπ' Ἐνιπῆος ῥέεθρα (haunted them) λ 240. Cf. β 55 = ρ 534, ι 189, χ 352.

πῶλος, -ου, ὁ, ἡ [cf. Eng. *foal*, Germ. *fohlen*]. A foal Λ 681, Υ 222, 225 : ψ 246.

πῶμα, -ατος, τό. A means of protecting or securing the contents of something : ἴδε π. (the lid) θ 443. Cf. Δ 116 (the top), Π 221 (the lid) : β 353 (with stoppers), θ 447, ι 314.

πῶς. (1) How? in what way or manner? by what means? πῶς τοι δώσουσι γέρας; Α 123, πῶς κε κῆρας ὑπεξέφυγεν; Χ 202. Cf. Η 36, Κ 61 (in what sense?), 243, Λ 838, Ρ 327, Σ 188, Τ 81, Ω 519 : α 171, γ 22, θ 352, κ 64, ο 195, σ 31, υ 129, etc.—(2) How? why? for what cause, inducement or reason? on what ground or pretext? πῶς τίς τοι πείθηται; Α 150, πῶς ἐθέλεις ἄλιον θεῖναι πόνον; Δ 26. Cf. Δ 351, Ι 437 (how could I bring myself to stay?), Ρ 149 (how can we look to you to . . .?), Σ 364, Φ 481, Ω 203 (what can induce you to . . .?) : α 65, ι 351 (what will bring anyone here?), κ 337, χ 231.—(3) How? in what state or condition? πῶς αἱ φυλακαί; Κ 408. Cf. Ξ 333 (how would it be?) : σ 223.—πῶς γὰρ νῦν; how then? Κ 424.—How? of what nature or kind? πῶς ὔμμιν ἀνὴρ ὅδε φαίνεται εἶναι; λ 336.

πως, *enclitic*. (1) Somehow, haply : αἴ κέν πως θωρήξομεν υἷας Ἀχαιῶν Β 72. Cf. Α 66, 408, Ν 807, Χ 346, etc. : ι 317, κ 147, μ 113, χ 91, etc. —(2) In negative or conditional contexts, in any way, haply : εἴ πως τόδε πᾶσι φίλον γένοιτο Δ 17. Cf. Γ 436, Ε 250, Π 60, etc. : δ 388, μ 224, 288, π 148, etc.—With οὐ. See οὐ (8) (d).—(3) Qualifying an expression, I ween, it would seem : ἀεί πώς μοι ἐπιπλήσσεις Μ 211. Cf. Ξ 104.

πωτάομαι [πέτομαι. Cf. ποτάομαι]. To fly. Of missiles : λίθοι πωτῶντο θαμειαί Μ 287.

πῶϋ, τό. A flock (of sheep) : πώεα οἰῶν Λ 678. Cf. Γ 198, Λ 696, Ο 323, Σ 528 : νομεὺς ὣς πώεσι μήλων δ 413. Cf. λ 402, μ 129, 299, ξ 100, ω 112.

ῥα. See ἄρα.

ῥάβδος, -ου, ἡ (an initial consonant app. lost). (1) A rod or wand. (a) A fishing-rod μ 251.—(b) A magic wand. Of that of Hermes Ω 343 := ε 47, ω 2.—Of that of Circe κ 238, 293, 319, 389.—Such a wand used by Athene in effecting transformations of Odysseus ν 429, π 172, 456.—(2) App. to be taken as = ῥαφή : βοείας ῥάψε χρυσείης ῥάβδοισιν (*i.e.* with wire) Μ 297.

ῥαδινός, -ή, -όν (an initial consonant app. lost). Pliant : ἱμάσθλην χερσὶν ἔχε ῥαδινήν Ψ 583.

ῥαθάμιγγες, αἱ [app. fr. ῥαίνω]. Sprinklings or drops (of blood) Λ 536 = Υ 501.—Sprinklings (of dust) Ψ 502.

ῥαίνω. Aor. imp. pl. ῥάσσατε υ 150. 3 pl. pf. pass. ἐρράδαται υ 354. 3 pl. plupf. ἐρράδατο Μ 431. To sprinkle, besprinkle : ῥαίνοντο κονίῃ Λ 282, αἵματ' ἐρράδατο Μ 431. Cf. υ 150 (*i.e.* with water), 354.

ῥαιστήρ, -ῆρος, ἡ [ῥαίω]. A smith's hammer : γέντο ῥαιστῆρα κρατερήν Σ 477.

ῥαίω. 3 sing. impf. ἔρραιε ζ 326. Fut. infin. ῥαισέμεναι ν 177. 3 sing. aor. subj. ῥαίσῃ ψ 235. Infin. ῥαῖσαι ν 151. Fut. infin. mid. ῥαίσεσθαι θ 569. 3 sing. aor. pass. ἐρραίσθη Π 339. (ἀπορραίω, διαρραίω.) (1) To smite, break in pieces, shiver : φάσγανον ἐρραίσθη Π 339.—To disintegrate, scatter: ἐγκέφαλός κε ῥαίοιτο πρὸς οὔδεϊ ι 459.—(2) To smite, afflict, shipwreck (a person) ε 221, ζ 326.—To smite, wreck (a ship) ν 151, 177, ψ 235.—In mid. θ 569.

ῥάκος, τό (Ϝράκος). (1) An old or worn piece of cloth ζ 178.—(2) An old or tattered garment ν 434, ξ 342, 349.—In pl., tattered garments, rags : ζώσατο ῥάκεσιν σ 67. Cf. ξ 512, σ 74, τ 507, φ 221, χ 1, 488.

ῥαπτός, -ή, -όν [ῥάπτω]. Mended with patches, patched : χιτῶνα ω 228, κνημῖδας 229.

ῥάπτω. 3 sing. aor. ῥάψε Μ 296. Infin. ῥάψαι Σ 367. (1) To sew or stitch together, stitch : βοείας Μ 296.—(2) To devise, contrive, plan, plot : κακά Σ 367 : γ 118, π 423. Cf. π 379, 422.

ῥάσσατε, aor. imp. pl. ῥαίνω.

ῥαφή, -ῆς, ἡ [ῥάπτω]. A stitch or seam : ῥαφαὶ ἐλέλυντο ἱμάντων χ 186.

ῥάχις, ἡ. The backbone and immediately adjoining flesh, the chine : συὸς ῥάχιν Ι 208.

ῥάψε, 3 sing. aor. ῥάπτω.

ῥέα, ῥεῖα (Ϝρέα, Ϝρεῖα) (ῥέα in *Iliad* only. A monosyllable in Μ 381, Ν 144, Ρ 461, Υ 101, 263). (1) Easily, with ease, without effort or difficulty, readily : ῥέα πάλλεν Ε 304, ὅπως ἵπποι ῥεῖα διέλθοιεν (without giving the driver trouble, without shying) Κ 492. Cf. Β 475, Γ 381, Θ 179, Λ 802, Μ 381, Ν 90 (with effortless stride), 144 (without check), Π 745 (nimbly), Ρ 461, Σ 600 (smoothly), Υ 263 (without check, straight), Ω 567, etc. : β 322 (without more ado), γ 231, δ 207, ζ 108, 300, κ 573, ρ 265, 273 (you saw it at once), 305, ψ 188.—(2) At ease, at one's ease : θεοὶ ῥεῖα ζώοντες Ζ 138 : δ 805, ε 122.—(3) Without thinking of the consequences, lightly, readily : ἄλλον κεν θεῶν ῥεῖα κατευνήσαιμι Ξ 245.—Sim. : τούτοισι ταῦτα μέλει ῥεῖα (they enjoy themselves with no thought for the morrow) α 160.

ῥέεθρον, τό [ῥέω]. (1) A stream : ποταμοὶ καὶ ῥέεθρα λ 157.—(2) In pl., the streams or waters (of a river) : Καϋστρίου ἀμφὶ ῥέεθρα Β 461. Cf. Η 135, Θ 369, Ξ 245, Ρ 749, Φ 9, Ψ 205, etc. : γ 292, ζ 317, λ 240.—(3) In pl., the flow or course of a river : ἄψορρον κῦμα κατέσσυτο ῥέεθρα (*i.e.* in the proper channel) Φ 382.

ῥέζω (Ϝρέζω) [Ϝρεγ-, Ϝρέγjω. Cf. (Ϝ)έρδω]. Pa. iterative ῥέζεσκον χ 209. 3 pl. ῥέζεσκον Θ 250 :

χ 46. Fut. ῥέξω K 292, 294, Ω 370 : γ 382, 384. 3 sing. ῥέξει Ξ 62. 1 pl. ῥέξομεν H 353 : η 191. Infin. ῥέξειν Δ 102, 120, Υ 186, Ψ 146, 864, 873 : κ 523, λ 31, ρ 51, 60. Aor. ἔρεξα I 453 : δ 352, 582, σ 139. 2 sing. ἔρεξας Ψ 570 : ι 352. 3 ἔρρεξε I 536, K 49, X 380. ἔρεξε B 274, E 373, I 647, K 51, Φ 509 : β 72, δ 242, 271, λ 272, φ 298. ῥέξε I 535. 1 pl. ἐρέξαμεν γ 159. 3 ἔρεξαν ω 458. 2 sing. subj. ῥέξῃς δ 478. 3 ῥέξῃ B 195 : θ 148. 1 pl. ῥέξομεν Λ 838 : μ 344. 3 pl. ῥέξωσι π 381. Opt. ῥέξαιμι T 90. 3 sing. ῥέξειε δ 205, 649. Pple. ῥέξας, -αντος A 147, I 357, K 282, 525, Λ 727, O 586, Σ 455, X 305 : δ 473, 690, ι 553, λ 130, ρ 567. Infin. ῥέξαι A 444, B 802, Γ 354 : γ 144, χ 314, ψ 222. Aor. pple. neut. pass. ῥεχθέν, -έντος I 250, P 32, Υ 198. (ἐπιρρέζω, καταρρέζω.) (1) To do, act : ὧδε ῥέξαι B 802. Cf. H 353, I 453 (did as she bade me), X 259, Ω 661 : ι 352.—With acc. of person affected by the action : κακῶς οἵ πέρ μιν ἔρεζον ψ 56.—(2) To do, perform, accomplish : τόδε μέγ' ἄριστον B 274, ῥεχθέντος κακοῦ I 250. Cf. E 374, K 51, Λ 502, Ξ 62, O 586, T 90, X 305, Ψ 494, etc.: α 47, β 232, δ 205, θ 148 (wins), λ 272, π 381, υ 314, χ 46, ψ 222, etc.—Absol. in aor. pple. neut. pass. : ῥεχθὲν δέ τε νήπιος ἔγνω (*i.e.* is wise after the event) P 32 = Υ 198. —With double acc. of what is done and of the person affected : ξεινοδόκον κακὰ ῥέξαι Γ 354. Cf. B 195, Δ 32, E 373 = Φ 509, I 647, K 49, Ω 370 : β 72, 73, δ 690, σ 15, χ 209, 314.—(3) To do or offer (sacrifice), sacrifice (a victim) : ἱερὰ ῥέξας A 147. Cf. A 444, Δ 102 = 120 = Ψ 864 = 873, I 357, 535, K 292, 294, Λ 727, Ψ 146, 206 : α 61, γ 159, 144, 382, ι 553, κ 523, etc.—Without expressed object, to do or offer sacrifice : ἄλλος ἄλλῳ ἔρεζε θεῶν B 400. Cf. Θ 250, I 536 : μ 344, ξ 251.

ῥέθεα, τά. Explained as, the limbs : ψυχὴ ἐκ ῥεθέων πταμένη Π 856 = X 362. Cf. X 68.

ῥεῖα. See ῥέα.

ῥέξω, fut. ῥέζω.

ῥέπω (Ϝρέπω). (ἐπιρρέπω.) To incline or sink downwards : ῥέπεν αἴσιμον ἦμαρ Ἀχαιῶν Θ 72. Cf. X 212.

ῥερυπωμένα, nom. pl. neut. pf. pple. pass. ῥυπάω.

ῥεχθέν, aor. pple. neut. pass. ῥέζω.

ῥέω (σρέϜω). 3 sing. impf. ἔρρεε Δ 140, N 539, Π 110, Ψ 34, 688 : λ 600. ἔρρει P 86. 3 pl. ἔρρεον κ 393. 3 sing. aor. pass. ῥύη γ 455. (ἐπιρρέω, καταρρέω, περιρρέω, προ-, ὑπεκπρο-.) (1) Of a river or stream, to flow, run : ποταμοὶ κατ' ὄρεσφι ῥέοντες Δ 452. Cf. E 88, 773, Z 172, Π 389, 391, P 751, Σ 403, Φ 256, 271 : κ 513, τ 207.—For εὐρὺ ῥέω, εὐρὺ ῥέων see εὐρύς (2) (a).—Of streaming blood : ἀμφὶ νέκυν ἔρρεεν αἷμα Ψ 34.—Of streaming sweat : κατὰ νότιος ῥέεν ἱδρώς (streamed down) Λ 811, Ψ 715. Cf. Π 110, Ψ 688 : λ 600. —Of the rain of thick-coming missiles : τῶν ἐκ χειρῶν βέλεα ῥέον M 159.—Of bristles dropping off all together : τῶν ἐκ μελέων τρίχες ἔρρεον κ 393.—With dat. of that which flows : ῥέεν αἵματι γαῖα (ran with blood) Δ 451 = Θ 65, O 715, Υ 494.—(2) To flow, run, flow or run forth, gush forth : ὅθεν ῥέεν ὕδωρ B 307. Cf. Γ 300, Δ 140, E 339, 340 (*i.e.* when a god is wounded), N 539, 655 = Φ 119, P 86, 438 : ι 140, 290, λ 36, ρ 209, τ 204.—So in aor. pass. : ἐπεὶ ἐκ μέλαν αἷμα ῥύη γ 455.—Of speech : ἀπὸ γλώσσης ῥέεν αὐδή A 249. —With dat. of that which flows : ἡ μὲν [πηγὴ] ὕδατι λιαρῷ ῥέει (runs with . . .) X 149. Cf. ε 70.

ῥηγμίς, -ῖνος, ἡ [ῥήγνυμι]. (1) The broken water or surf beside the beach : ἐπὶ ῥηγμῖνι θαλάσσης (at the edge of the breakers) A 437, Θ 501. Cf. B 773, Π 67 : δ 430 = 575 = ι 169 = 559 = κ 186, δ 449, ι 150 = 547 = μ 6, ο 499.—(2) The surf or broken surface (of the sea) : ἄκρον ἐπὶ ῥηγμῖνος ἁλὸς Υ 229 (see ἄκρος (3)). Cf. μ 214.

ῥήγνῡμι (Ϝρήγνυμι). 3 pl. ῥηγνῦσι P 751. 3 sing. pa. iterative ῥήγνυσκε H 141. Fut. ῥήξω Ψ 673. Infin. ῥήξειν B 544, M 198, 262. 3 sing. aor. ἔρρηξε Γ 348, H 259, N 124, P 44 : μ 409. ῥῆξε Γ 375, E 307, Z 6, Θ 328, O 464, Π 310, Υ 399, etc. Pple. ῥήξας I 476, N 139. Nom. pl. masc. ῥήξαντες M 341. Infin. ῥῆξαι Λ 538, O 615, 617. **Mid.** 3 pl. aor. ἐρρήξαντο M 291. ῥήξαντο Λ 90. 1 pl. subj. ῥηξόμεθα M 224. Pple. ῥηξάμενος, -ου M 90, 411, 418, N 680, O 409. Infin. ῥήξασθαι M 308. (ἀναρρήγνυμι, ἀπορρήγνυμι, ἐκ-, συρρήγνυμι, ὑπορρήγνυμι.) (1) To smash, crush : ὀστέον M 185, Π 310, Υ 399.—To rend, tear : χρόα Ψ 673.—(2) In pass., of the sea, to break, become surf : περί σφισι κῦμα ῥήγνυτο Σ 67. Cf. Δ 425.—(3) To rend, rive, penetrate, perforate : θώρηκας B 544. Cf. Γ 348 = H 259 = P 44, N 439, 507 = P 314, Υ 268 = Φ 165.—(4) To break asunder or in two, sever, cause to part, snap or give way : ἱμάντα Γ 375, ἔχματα πέτρης N 139. Cf. E 307, Θ 328, M 459, O 464, Π 587 : ἱστοῦ προτόνους μ 409.—With ἀπό, to break off, cause to part from a fastening : ῥῆξεν ἀπὸ λόφον O 537.—(5) To break (opposed ranks) : φάλαγγα Z 6. Cf. H 141, Λ 538, O 615, 617.—In mid. : ῥηξάμενος Δαναῶν στίχας N 680. Cf. Λ 90, N 718, O 409.—(6) To lay open by breaking, break or make a way through (a barrier) : θαλάμοιο θύρας I 476. Cf. M 198, 262, 341, N 124, P 751.—In mid. : τεῖχος ῥηξάμενοι M 90. Cf. M 224, 257, 291, 308, 418, 440.—Absol., to break a way through a barrier. In mid. : ἀργαλέον μοί ἐστι μούνῳ ῥηξαμένῳ θέσθαι κέλευθον M 411.—(7) To cause (strife) to break out. In mid. : ἐν αὐτοῖς ἔριδα ῥήγνυντο Υ 55.

ῥῆγος, τό. (1) App., a cloth, prob. of wool, laid on the rough bedding for the comfort of the sleeper (cf. λίνον (3)) : κώεά τε ῥῆγός τε λινοιό τε λεπτὸν ἄωτον I 661. Cf. Ω 644 : = δ 297 = η 336, γ 349, 351, ζ 38, λ 189, ν 73 (here app. simply laid on the deck of the ship), 118, τ 318, 337, υ 141, ψ 180.—(2) App., a similar cloth thrown over the back of a chair : ἔβαλλε θρόνοις ἔνι ῥήγεα καθύπερθ', ὑπένερθε δὲ λῖθ' ὑπέβαλλεν κ 352.

ῥηθέντι, dat. sing. neut. aor. pple. pass. εἴρω[2].

ῥηΐδιος, -η, -ον [ῥεῖα]. Easy. With complementary infin. : τάφρος οὐχ ὑπερθορέειν ῥηϊδίη (easy to . . .) M 54. Cf. Υ 265.—So in impers. use :

ῥηΐδιόν [ἐστι] θεοῖσι κυδῆναι βροτόν π 211.—Easy to understand or follow: ἔπος λ 146.

ῥηϊδίως [adv. fr. prec.]. (1) Easily, with ease, without effort or difficulty: ἐνίκα ῥ. Δ 390. Cf. I 184, Λ 114, M 448, Π 690 (*i.e.* by his divine power), P 283, X 140 (with smooth flight), etc.: ῥ. ἀφελὼν θυρεόν ι 313. Cf. θ 376, ξ 196 (could go on relating . . .), π 198, φ 92, 407, etc.—(2) Without thinking of the consequences, lightly: τοὺς σάωσας ῥ., ἐπεὶ οὔ τι τίσιν γ' ἔδεισας ὀπίσσω X 19.

ῥήϊστος, -η, -ον [superl. fr. ῥεῖα]. The easiest or happiest, the most free from care: βιοτή δ 565.

ῥήΐτατος [superl. fr. ῥεῖα]. In neut. pl. ῥηΐτατα as adv., with the greatest ease, with the least effort: ὅς κε ῥ. ἐντανύσῃ βιόν τ 577 = φ 75.

ῥηΐτερος [comp. fr. ῥεῖα]. Easier. With complementary infin.: ῥηΐτεροι πολεμίζειν (to fight with) Σ 258. Cf. Ω 243.

ῥηκτός [ῥηκ-, ῥήγνυμι]. That may be rent or torn: ἀνδρί, ὃς χαλκῷ ῥηκτὸς [εἴη] N 323.

ῥῆξε, 3 sing. aor. ῥήγνυμι.

ῥηξηνορίη, -ης, ἡ [ῥηξήνωρ]. Might to break the ranks of the foe ξ 217.

ῥηξήνωρ, -ορος [ῥηξ-, ῥήγνυμι + ἀνήρ]. That breaks the ranks of the foe (cf. ῥήγνυμι (5)). Epithet of Achilles H 228, N 324, Π 146, 575: δ 5.

ῥήξω, fut. ῥήγνυμι.

ῥῆσις, ἡ [ῥη-, εἴρω²]. Discourse, talk: ἀκούεις μύθων ἡμετέρων καὶ ῥήσιος φ 291.

ῥήσσω [ἀ-ράσσω]. (ἐπιρρήσσω.) To beat time: ῥήσσοντες ἁμαρτῇ ἕποντο Σ 571.

ῥητήρ, -ῆρος, ὁ [ῥη-, εἴρω²]. A speaker: μύθων ῥητῆρα I 443.

ῥητός [ῥη-, εἴρω²]. Stated, specified, agreed upon: μισθῷ ἔπι ῥητῷ Φ 445.

ῥήτρη, -ης, ἡ [ῥη-, εἴρω²]. A (verbal) agreement, a bargain or covenant ξ 393.

ῥῑγεδανός, -ή [ῥῖγος]. Horrible, a thing to shudder at: Ἑλένης T 325.

ῥῑγέω (Fριγέω) [ῥῖγος]. 3 sing. aor. ἐρρίγησε O 466. ῥίγησε Γ 259, Δ 148, Λ 254, O 34, 436, Π 119, etc.: ε 116, 171. 3 pl. ἐρρίγησαν M 208. Pf. ἔρρῑγα P 175. 3 sing. ἔρρῑγε H 114. 3 sing. subj. ἐρρίγῃσι Γ 353. 3 sing. plupf. ἐρρίγει ψ 216. (ἀπορριγέω.) (1) To be physically affected by fear as if by cold, shudder with fear, dread or apprehension: ῥίγησεν Ἀγαμέμνων Δ 148. Cf. Δ 150, 279, E 596 = Λ 345, Λ 254, M 208, 331, O 34, 436, 466, Π 119.—Sim.: αἰεί μοι θυμὸς ἐρρίγει μὴ . . . (was in constant terror lest . . .) ψ 216.—(2) To shudder at, dread, shrink from: πόλεμον E 351, οὐκ ἔρριγα μάχην (it is not my wont to shrink from the fight) P 175.—(3) To shrink from *doing something.* With infin.: ὄφρα τις ἐρρίγῃσι ξεινοδόκον κακὰ ῥέξαι Γ 353, τούτῳ ἔρριγ' ἀντιβολῆσαι (does not care to meet him) H 114.—(4) To be physically affected by a sudden summons or announcement, be fluttered or thrown into agitation: ὣς φάτο, ῥίγησεν δ' ὁ γέρων Γ 259. Cf. ε 116, 171.

ῥίγιον [neut. comp. fr. ῥῖγος]. (1) Colder: ποτὶ ἕσπερα ῥ. ἔσται ρ 191.—(2) More to be feared or dreaded, worse: τό οἱ (τοι) καὶ ῥίγιον ἔσται (it will be the worse for him (you)) A 325, 563. Cf. Λ 405: υ 220.

ῥίγιστος [superl. fr. ῥῖγος]. The most to be feared or dreaded. Absol. in neut. pl.: ῥίγιστα τετληότες εἰμέν (the worst extremities) E 873.

ῥῖγος, τό (Fρῖγος). Cold: εἴ με μεθήῃ ῥῖγος ε 472.

ῥιγόω [ῥῖγος]. To be cold, feel cold: οὐκ ἐφάμην ῥιγωσέμεν ξ 481.

ῥίζα, -ης, ἡ (Fρίζα). (1) The root of a tree or plant: δρύες ῥίζῃσιν μεγάλῃσιν ἀραρυῖαι M 134. Cf. I 542, Φ 243: κ 304, μ 435, ψ 196.—(2) The prepared root of a plant used medicinally: ἐπὶ δὲ ῥίζαν βάλε πικρήν Λ 846.—(3) In pl., the 'roots' of the eye, the attachments of the eye within the orbit: σφαραγεῦντο [γλήνης] πυρὶ ῥίζαι ι 390.

†**ῥιζόω** [ῥίζα]. 3 sing. aor. ἐρρίζωσε ν 163. 3 sing. pf. pass. ἐρρίζωται η 122. To furnish with roots: ἔνθα οἱ ἀλωὴ ἐρρίζωται (there grows his vineyard with its trees) η 122.—Fig.: νῆ' ἐρρίζωσεν ἔνερθεν (fixed immovably) ν 163.

ῥίμφα [ῥίπτω]. (1) With speed or velocity, swiftly, fast: θέων K 54, Ψ 766. Cf. Z 511 = O 268, Λ 533 = P 458, N 30, 515, Ξ 282, X 163, Ψ 501, Ω 691: θ 193, μ 182, ν 83, 88, 162.—(2) Speedily, quickly, with haste: δεῖπνον ἕλοντο Θ 54. Cf. Ω 799.—(3) In short space, soon: λέπτ' ἐγένοντο Υ 497.

ῥῑνός, -οῦ, ἡ, also **ῥῑνόν,** τό K 155: ε 281 (Fρινός, Fρινόν). (1) The stripped-off skin of a beast, a hide: ἕρπον ῥινοί μ 395. Cf. H 474.—(2) A prepared hide. Used for sleeping or sitting upon: ὑπὸ δ' ἔστρωτο ῥινὸν βοός K 155: ἥμενοι ἐν ῥινοῖσι βοῶν α 108.—For wearing: ἕσσατο ῥινὸν λύκοιο K 334.—(3) A layer of leather forming part of a shield H 248, N 406, 804.—(4) Leather: κυνέην ῥινοῦ K 262, δοῦπος . . . ῥινοῦ τε βοῶν τε (of leather and the shields thereof, *i.e.* of the leather shields) Π 636. Cf. Υ 276: μ 423.—(5) A shield: σύν ῥ' ἔβαλον ῥινούς Δ 447 = Θ 61, ῥινοῖσι βοῶν φράξαντες ἐπάλξεις (of ox-leather) M 263. Cf. E 308: ε 281.—(6) The skin of a man: περὶ ῥινοὶ μινύθουσιν (their skins) μ 46. Cf. ξ 134, χ 278.—So in pl.: ἔνθα κ' ἀπὸ ῥινοὺς δρύφθη (would have had his skin stripped off) ε 426. Cf. ε 435.

ῥῑνοτόρος [ῥινός + τορέω]. Piercer of shields. Epithet of Ares Φ 392.

ῥίον, -ου, τό (an initial consonant app. lost). (1) A peak or pinnacle of a mountain Θ 25, Ξ 154, 225 = T 114: ι 191.—(2) A rock or reef projecting into the sea γ 295.

ῥῑπή, -ῆς, ἡ [ῥίπτω]. (1) The rush or rapid or impetuous flight of a missile: λᾶος ὑπὸ ῥιπῆς M 462: θ 192.—The range or 'carry' of a missile: ὅσση αἰγανέης ῥ. τέτυκται Π 589.—(2) The rush of wind O 171, T 358.—Of fire Φ 12.—(3) The rush or furious onset of a warrior: οἵ κ' ὄλωνται ἀνδρὸς ἑνὸς ῥιπῇ Θ 355.

ῥιπτάζω [frequentative fr. ῥίπτω]. To throw to and fro, toss: ῥιπτάζων κατὰ δῶμα θεούς Ξ 257.

†**ῥίπτω** (*Fρίπτω*). Pa. iterative *ῥίπτασκον* Ο 23. 3 sing. *ῥίπτασκε* Ψ 827 : θ 374, λ 592. Fut. *ῥίψω* Θ 13. 3 sing. *ῥίψει* Ω 735. 3 sing. aor. *ἔρριψε* Τ 130, Χ 406, Ψ 842, 845 : ζ 115, ι 398, μ 254, υ 299. *ῥῖψε* Α 591, Γ 378, Τ 268. (*ἀναρρίπτω, ἀπορρίπτω, διαρρίπτω, ἐπιρρίπτω.*) (1) To throw, cast, hurl : *τρυφάλειαν ῥῖψ' ἐπιδινήσας* Γ 378. Cf. Α 591, Θ 13, Ο 23, Τ 130, 268, Χ 406, Ψ 827, 845, Ω 735 : ζ 115, θ 374, ι 398, υ 299.—Absol., to make one's throw : *τὸ τρίτον ἔρριψεν Αἴας* Ψ 842.—Of the operation of wind : *τὰς ἄνεμος ῥίπτασκε ποτὶ νέφεα* λ 592.—(2) To jerk or pull in a specified direction : [*ἰχθὺν*] *θύραζε* μ 254.

ῥίς, *ῥινός, ἡ* (an initial consonant app. lost). (1) The nose : *ἀμβροσίην ὑπὸ ῥῖνα θῆκεν* δ 445. Cf. Ε 291, Ν 616 : σ 86.—(2) So in pl., the nose (as containing the two nostrils) : *ἀπ' οὔατα ῥῖνάς τ' ἀμήσαντες* φ 301. Cf. Ξ 467, Π 503, Ψ 395 : χ 475.—With special reference to the nostrils : *αἷμ' ἀνὰ στόμα καὶ κατὰ ῥῖνας πρῆσεν* Π 349. Cf. Τ 39, Ψ 777 : ε 456, χ 18, ω 318.

ῥίψ, *ῥιπός, ἡ.* In pl., wicker-work : *φράξε σχεδίην ῥίπεσσι οἰσυΐνῃσιν* ε 256.

ῥίψω, fut. *ῥίπτω.*

ῥοδανός (an initial consonant app. lost) [app. =*ῥαδινός*]. Thus, waving : *δονακῆα* Σ 576.

ῥοδοδάκτυλος, -*ον* [*ῥόδον*, rose + *δάκτυλος*, finger]. Epithet of the dawn, rosy-fingered, spreading rosy rays : *Ἠώς* Ζ 175, Ι 707, Ψ 109, Α 477 = Ω 788 : = β 1 = γ 404 = 491 = δ 306 = 431 = 576 = ε 228 = θ 1 = ι 152 = 170 = 307 = 437 = 560 = κ 187 = μ 8 = 316 = ν 18 = ο 189 = ρ 1 = τ 428, ε 121, ψ 241.

ῥοδόεις, -*εντος* [*ῥόδον*, rose]. Rose-scented : *ἐλαίῳ* Ψ 186.

ῥοή, -*ῆς, ἡ* [*ῥέω*]. In pl., the streams or waters (of a river) : *Μαιάνδρου ῥοάς* Β 869. Cf. Γ 5, Δ 91, Ε 774, Ζ 4, Θ 560, Λ 732, Π 669, 679, 719, Σ 240, Τ 1 : ζ 216, ι 450, κ 529, χ 197, ω 11.—Of a stream of water poured over something : *ἔνιψ' ὕδατος ῥοῇσιν* Π 229.

ῥόθιος [*ῥόθος*, a rushing noise]. Of waves, rushing, breaking in uproar : *κῦμα* ε 412.

ῥοιβδέω. (*ἀναρροιβδέω.*) To swallow down μ 106.

ῥοιζέω [*ῥοῖζος*]. To whistle Κ 502.

ῥοῖζος, -*ου, ἡ.* Whistling : *πολλῇ ῥοίζῳ πρὸς ὄρος τρέπε μῆλα* ι 315.—The whizzing of missiles in flight : *ὀϊστῶν ῥοῖζον* Π 361.

ῥοιή, -*ῆς, ἡ.* A pomegranate-tree : *ὄγχναι καὶ ῥοιαὶ καὶ μηλέαι* η 115 = λ 589.

ῥόος, -*ου, ὁ* [*ῥέω*]. (1) The stream or waters (of a river) : *ἱκόμεσθα ῥόον Ἀλφειοῖο* Λ 726. Cf. Μ 25, Π 151, Σ 402, Φ 16, 147, 219, 241, 263, 306, 369 : ε 449, ζ 85, λ 21, μ 1.—(2) The moving waters of a river, its current : *βέβρυχεν μέγα κῦμα ποτὶ ῥόον* (as it meets the current) Ρ 264, *πρὸς ῥόον ἀΐσσοντος* (against the current) Φ 303 : *νῆα κατ' Ὠκεανὸν ποταμὸν φέρε κῦμα ῥόοιο* (the moving stream of its current) λ 639. Cf. ε 451.—(3) The flow or wash of the sea : *βόμβησαν ἐρετμὰ κατὰ ῥόον* μ 204. Cf. ε 327.—A current or set of the sea : *κῦμά με ῥόος τ' ἀπέωσεν* ι 80. Cf. ξ 254.—(4) The flow or course of a river : *ποταμοὺς ἔτρεψε νέεσθαι κὰρ ῥόον* (*i.e.* in their proper channels) Μ 33, *πᾶσι* [*ποταμοῖσι*] *ῥόον πεδίονδε τίθησιν* (turns their course to the . . .) Ρ 750 : *ἂψ ἔφερε* [*κρήδεμνον*] *κῦμα κατὰ ῥόον* (down its stream) ε 461.—Sim. in reference to water used in irrigation : *ὡς ὅτ' ἀνὴρ ὀχετηγὸς ὕδατι ῥόον ἡγεμονεύῃ* (guides its flow) Φ 258.

ῥόπαλον, -*ου, τό* (*Fρόπαλον*) [(*F*)*ρέπω*]. A club or cudgel. Used for beating an ass Λ 559, 561.—In the hunt λ 575.—A stick or staff for support in walking : *δός μοι, εἴ ποθί τοι ῥ. τετμημένον ἐστί, σκηρίπτεσθαι* ρ 195.—Such a stick used as a weapon of offence : *ἠὲ μεταΐξας ῥοπάλῳ ἐκ θυμὸν ἕλοιτο* ρ 236.—Of the stick carried by the Cyclops ι 319.

ῥοχθέω. Of the sea, to roar, dash in uproar : *ῥόχθει μέγα κῦμα* ε 402. Cf. μ 60.

ῥύατο, 3 pl. non-thematic impf. mid. *ἐρύω*^{2}.

ῥυδόν [*ῥυ-, ῥέω*]. In a stream : *ῥ. ἀφνειοῖο* (on whom riches flowed) ο 426.

ῥύη, 3 sing. aor. pass. *ῥέω.*

ῥυμός, -*οῦ, ὁ* [*ἐ-ρύω*^{1}]. The pole of a chariot Ε 729, Ζ 40, Κ 505, Π 371, Ψ 393, Ω 271.

ῥύομαι. See *ἐρύω*^{2}.

ῥύπα, *τά.* Impurities, dirt ζ 93.

†**ῥυπάω** [*ῥύπα*]. Acc. sing. masc. pres. pple. *ῥυπόωντα* ω 227. Acc. pl. neut. *ῥυπόωντα* ζ 87, ν 435. Nom. pl. neut. pf. pple. pass. *ῥερυπωμένα* ζ 59. To be dirty or squalid : *ῥυπόωντα ἕστο χιτῶνα* ω 227. Cf. ζ 87, ν 435.—So in pf. pass. : *εἵματα, τά μοι ῥερυπωμένα κεῖται* ζ 59.

ῥυπόω = prec. : *ὅτι ῥυπόω* τ 72, ψ 115.

ῥυσάμην, aor. mid. *ἐρύω*^{2}.

ῥύσατο, 3 sing. aor. mid. *ἐρύω*^{2}.

ῥῦσθαι, non-thematic pres. infin. mid. *ἐρύω*^{2}.

ῥύσια, *τά* [*ἐ-ρύω*^{1}]. Cattle, etc., driven off by way of reprisal : *ῥύσι' ἐλαυνόμενος* Λ 674.

ῥυσίπτολις [*ῥυσι-, ἐρύω*^{2} + *πτόλις*]. That guards the city : *Ἀθηναίη ῥυσίπτολι* Ζ 305 (*v.l. ἐρυσίπτολι*).

ῥύσκευ, 2 sing. pa. iterative mid. *ἐρύω*^{2}.

ῥυσός, -*ή* [*ἐ-ρύω*^{1}]. Drawn, wrinkled Ι 503 (of the *Λιταί* (see *λιτή*) as figuring an offender with his face wrinkled by the mental struggle caused by his reluctance to ask pardon).

ῥυστάζω [frequentative fr. *ἐ-ρύω*^{1}]. 3 sing. pa. iterative *ῥυστάζεσκε* Ω 755. To drag, haul Ω 755.—To haul or pull about, maltreat : *δμῳάς* π 109 = υ 319.

ῥυστακτύς, -*ύος, ἡ* [*ῥυστάζω*]. A hauling or pulling about, maltreatment σ 224.

ῥυτήρ^{1}, -*ῆρος, ὁ* [*ἐ-ρύω*^{1}]. (1) A (skilful) drawer (of the bow or of arrows) : *ῥυτῆρα βιοῦ καὶ ὀϊστῶν* φ 173. Cf. σ 262.—(2) In pl., the reins of a chariot : [*ἵπποι*] *ἐν ῥυτῆρσι τάνυσθεν* (pulled in the governance of, pulled at, the reins) Π 475.

ῥυτήρ^{2}, -*ῆρος, ὁ* [*ῥύομαι, ἐρύω*^{2}]. A keeper or guard : *σταθμῶν ῥυτῆρα* ρ 187, 223.

ῥυτός [*ἐ-ρύω*^{1}]. Prob., drawn out of the earth, dug, quarried : *λάεσσιν* ζ 267, ξ 10.

ῥωγαλέος, -*η,* -*ον* [*ῥήγνυμι*]. Full of rents or

holes, rent, torn : Ἑκτόρεον χιτῶνα δαΐξαι ῥωγαλέον (so as to pierce it with many a hole) B 417. Cf. ν 435, 438 = ρ 198 = σ 109, ξ 343.

ῥώξ, ῥωγός [perh. fr. ῥήγνυμι. 'Clefts']. In pl., app., passages forming continuations or branches of the λαύρη : ἀνὰ ῥῶγας μεγάροιο χ 143.

ῥώομαι. 3 pl. impf. ἐρρώοντο Ψ 367. 3 pl. aor. ἐρρώσαντο Ω 616 : ψ 3, ω 69. (ἐπιρρώομαι.) To move nimbly, speed along : ὑπ' ἀμφίπολοι ῥώοντο ἄνακτι Σ 417.—Of nimble motion of the limbs : ὑπὸ κνῆμαι ῥώοντο Σ 411 = Υ 37. Cf. ψ 3. —Of movement in the dance Ω 616.—Of rhythmical movement as part of a ceremony ω 69.—To rush to the fray : αὐτοὶ πρυλέες ῥώοντο Λ 50. Cf. Π 166.—Of a horse's mane, to stream (with the wind) Ψ 367.

ῥῶπες, αἱ. Growing twigs κ 166.—Cut brushwood used for sitting upon : ῥῶπας ὑπέχευε δασείας ξ 49. Cf. π 47.

ῥωπήϊα, τά [ῥῶπες]. Small growing trees and shrubs, brushwood N 199, Φ 559, Ψ 122 : ξ 473.

ῥωχμός, ὁ [ῥήγνυμι]. A break or sudden dip (in the ground) : ῥωχμὸς ἔην γαίης Ψ 420.

σαίνω. 3 sing. aor. ἔσηνε ρ 302. (περισσαίνω.) Of dogs, etc., to show delight or fondness, fawn : νόησε σαίνοντας κύνας π 6. Cf. κ 217, 219, ρ 302 (wagged his tail).

σακέσπαλος [σακεσ-, σάκος + πάλλω]. Wielder of the shield. Epithet of Tydeus E 126.

σάκος, -εος, τό. Dat. pl. σακέεσσι ξ 477. σάκεσσι P 354 : π 474. σάκεσι Δ 282, P 268 : ξ 479. A shield Γ 335, H 219, Λ 545, M 339, N 130, etc. : ξ 277, 477, 479, 482, π 474, σ 377, χ 101, 110, 122, 144, 184, 279.

σάλπιγξ, ἡ. A trumpet Σ 219.

†σαλπίζω [σάλπιγξ]. 3 sing. aor. σάλπιγξε. To sound the trumpet. Fig.: ἀμφὶ σάλπιγξεν οὐρανός (re-echoed as with the trumpet's sound) Φ 388.

σανίς, -ίδος, ἡ. **(1)** A board or plank : σανίδας ἐκδῆσαι ὄπισθεν χ 174.—One of the boards fixed on the framework and forming the face of a gate : πύλαι σανίδες τ' ἐπὶ τῇς ἀραρυῖαι Σ 275. Cf. M 453, 461.—**(2)** In pl., the two wings of a gate or door, a gate or door : σείων κολλητὰς σανίδας I 583. Cf. M 121, Φ 535 : β 344, φ 137 = 164 (against the . . .), χ 128, ψ 42.—**(3)** Boarding ; in the passage cited, app. a wooden stage or platform raised above the earthen floor of a room : ἐφ' ὑψηλῆς σανίδος βῆ· ἔνθα δὲ χηλοὶ ἕστασαν φ 51.

σάος, σόος, -η, -ον, **σῶς** (the first only in comp. σαώτερος A 32). **(1)** Free from harm, safe, unharmed, unhurt, safe and sound, in good case : σαώτερος ὥς κε νέηαι (the safer) A 32, λαὸν σῶν ἔμμεναι 117. Cf. E 531 = O 563 (find safety), H 310, Θ 246, O 497, Π 252 : δ 98, ο 42, π 131, τ 300. —Of things, safe, unharmed, whole, intact : οὔτ' ἠέλιον σῶν ἔμμεναι οὔτε σελήνην P 367.—**(2)** Free from danger, in safety, safe, not liable to be harmed : ὅππως σόοι μαχέοιντο (*i.e.* with the least risk possible) A 344. Cf. X 332.—So of things : ἵνα περ τάδε τοι σόα μίμνῃ Ω 382 : ν 364.—**(3)** Sure to come or happen, inevitable : σῶς τοι (μοι) ὄλεθρος N 773 : ε 305, χ 28.

σαοφροσύνη, -ης, ἡ [σαόφρων]. Soundness of sense, good sense, discretion, prudence ψ 13.—So in pl. : σαοφροσύνῃσι νοήματα πατρὸς ἔκευθεν ψ 30.

σαόφρων, -ονος [σάος + φρήν]. Of sound or good sense, discreet Φ 462 : δ 158.

†σαόω [σάος]. 3 pl. subj. σαῶσι I 393. 2 sing. opt. σαῷς (σαόοις) I 681. 3 σαῷ (σαόοι) I 424. Non-thematic imp. σάω ν 230, ρ 595. Nom. pl. masc. pple. σώοντες (σαόοντες) ι 430. 3 sing. non-thematic impf. σάω Π 363, Φ 238. Pa. iterative σώεσκον (σαόεσκον) Θ 363. Fut. σαώσω κ 286. 2 sing. -εις A 83. 3 -ει I 78, K 44. 3 dual -ετον E 224. 1 pl. -ομεν T 408. Aor. ἐσάωσα ε 130. 2 sing. σάωσας X 18. 3 ἐσάωσε Θ 500, Λ 752, N 734, Ξ 259, O 290, Σ 395 : δ 444, ε 452, χ 372. σάωσε E 23 : δ 288, 513. 3 pl. ἐσάωσαν Σ 405. 2 sing. subj. σαώσῃς P 144, X 56. 3 σαώσῃ P 692. 2 dual σαώσετον P 452. 1 pl. σαώσομεν E 469, X 175 : χ 357. 2 sing. opt. σαώσειας P 149. 3 σαώσαι Φ 611 : γ 231, δ 753. 3 pl. σαώσειαν M 123. Imp. σάωσον Λ 828 : δ 765. Pl. σαώσατε O 427. Infin. σαῶσαι Φ 274, Ω 35. Aor. imp. pl. σαώσετε N 47. Infin. σαωσέμεναι N 96. σαωσέμεν I 230, T 401. 2 sing. fut. mid. σαώσεαι φ 309. 3 pl. aor. pass. ἐσάωθεν γ 185. 3 sing. imp. σαωθήτω P 228. Infin. σαωθῆναι O 503 : κ 473. (ἐκ-, ὑπεκ-.) **(1)** To save from imminent or present danger, bring off safely, rescue from or bring safe through peril or trouble : τὼ νῶϊ πόλινδε σαώσετον (bring us off in safety to the city) E 224, ἐκ πολέμου Λ 752. Cf. E 23, Θ 363, I 78, M 123 (give him way to the ships and safety), O 503, T 401, Φ 238, etc. : γ 185, 231 (bring him safe home), δ 288, 444, 513, 753, 765, ε 130, 452, ι 430, κ 286, 473, χ 357, 372.—In reference to things : νῆας I 230, πόλιν καὶ ἄστυ P 144. Cf. I 424, 681, K 44, N 96.—In mid., to bring oneself off safely, get off unharmed : ἔνθεν οὔ τι σαώσεαι φ 309.—**(2)** To rescue from the foe, bring or carry off from hostile hands : τὸν νέκυν περ ἐόντα σαῶσαι Ω 35. Cf. E 469, O 427, P 149, 692.—**(3)** To preserve from danger, keep from harm, see safe, stand by : φράσαι εἴ με σαώσεις A 83. Cf. X 56 : αὐτόν σε σάω (look after yourself) ρ 595. Cf. ν 230.—In reference to things : ταῦτα ν 230.

σαπήῃ, 3 sing. aor. subj. pass. σήπω.

σαρδάνιος, -όνιος. In neut. sing. σαρδάνιον as adv., of smiling, app. scornfully, bitterly υ 302.

σάρξ, σαρκός, ἡ. The flesh of the body : διήφυσε σαρκός (partitive genit.) τ 450.—In pl. : σάρκες περιτρομέοντο μέλεσσιν σ 77. Cf. Θ 380 = N 832 : ι 293, λ 219.

σαυρωτήρ, -ῆρος, ὁ. The butt-end (of a spear) (app. = οὐρίαχος) K 153.

σάφα. **(1)** In reference to knowledge, with full understanding, clearly, with certainty, well : οὔ πω σ. οἶσθ' οἷος νόος Ἀτρεΐωνος B 192. Cf. B 252, E 183, H 226, M 228, O 632, Υ 201 = 432 : α 202, β 108 = ω 144, δ 730, ρ 153, 307, 373, ω 404.

—(2) In reference to speech, with clearness of exposition, plainly, fully, without concealment: ἀγγελίην, ἥν χ' ἡμῖν σ. εἴποι β 31. Cf. β 43, ρ 106. —With certainty or clear knowledge: σ. εἰπέμεν ὁππόθ' ὄλωλεν γ 89.—App., truly, correctly: μὴ ψεύδε' ἐπιστάμενος σ. εἰπεῖν Δ 404.

σάω[1], non-thematic imp. σαόω.

σάω[2], 3 sing. non-thematic impf. σαόω.

σαῷς, σαῷ, 2 and 3 sing. opt. σαόω.

σαώσω, fut. σαόω.

σαώτερος, comp. σάος.

†**σβέννῡμι.** 3 sing. aor. ἔσβεσε Π 293. 3 pl. σβέσαν Ψ 250, Ω 791. Imp. pl. σβέσατε Ψ 237. Infin. σβέσσαι Ι 678, Π 621. 3 sing. aor. ἔσβη Ι 471: γ 182. (κατα-.) (1) To put out, quench (fire) Π 293, Ψ 237, 250 = Ω 791.—To quell, destroy, crush: πάντων ἀνθρώπων μένος Π 621. —To put away (wrath) Ι 678.—(2) Intrans. in non-sigmatic aor., of a fire, to go out: οὐδέ ποτ' ἔσβη πῦρ Ι 471.—Of wind, to cease to blow, fall: οὐδέ ποτ' ἔσβη οὖρος γ 182.

†**σεβάζομαι** [σέβας]. 3 sing. aor. σεβάσσατο. To be restrained from doing (something) by sensitiveness to the opinion of others, shrink from doing (it), think shame to do (it) (cf. αἰδέομαι (2)): σεβάσσατο τό γε θυμῷ Ζ 167, 417.

σέβας, τό [σέβομαι]. (1) Sensitiveness to the opinion of others, fear of what others may think or say, shame (= αἰδώς (2)): σέβας σε θυμὸν ἱκέσθω Σ 178.—(2) Wonder: σέβας μ' ἔχει εἰσορόωντα (εἰσορόωσαν) γ 123, δ 75, 142, ζ 161, θ 384.

σέβομαι. To be moved by respect for the opinion of others, fear what others may think or say, think shame (cf. αἰδέομαι (4)): οὔ νυ σέβεσθε; Δ 242.

σειρή, -ῆς, ἡ [(σ)είρω, εἴρω[1]]. A cord or rope Θ 19, 25, Ψ 115: χ 175 = 192.

σείω (prob. σϝείω). 3 pl. impf. pass. ἐσσείοντο Υ 59. (ἐπισσείω, περισσείω, ὑποσσείω.) (1) To shake, cause to quiver or vibrate: σανίδας Ι 583. Cf. Ο 321: γ 486 = ο 184.—To shake or brandish (a spear): σείων ἐγχείην Ε 563. Cf. Γ 345, Ν 135, 558, Χ 133.—In pass., to shake or quiver: ἀμφί οἱ κροτάφοισι σείετο πήληξ Ν 805. Cf. Ξ 285, Υ 59. —(2) In mid., to change one's position suddenly, start: σείσατ' εἰνὶ θρόνῳ Θ 199.

σέλας, τό. Dat. σέλαϊ Ρ 739. σέλᾳ Θ 563: φ 246. Blaze, glow, brightness: ἧατο σέλᾳ πυρός Θ 563. Cf. Θ 509, Ο 600, Ρ 739, Σ 214, Τ 17 (*i.e.* of fire), 366, 374, 375, 379: δαΐδων σ. σ 354. Cf. φ 246.—A thunderbolt: δαιόμενον ἧκε σ. Θ 76.

σελήνη, -ης, ἡ [σέλας]. The moon Θ 555, Ρ 367, Σ 484: δ 45 = η 84, ι 144, ω 148.

σέλῑνον, -ου, τό. Prob. water-parsley (wild celery), smallage. Collectively Β 776: ε 72.

σέσηπε, 3 sing. pf. σήπω.

†**σεύω** (prob. σϝεύω). Aor. ἔσσευα Ε 208. σεῦα Υ 189. 3 sing. ἔσσευε Λ 147, Ξ 413, Υ 325. σεῦε Ζ 133, Λ 294: ξ 35. 3 pl. σεῦαν ζ 89. 3 sing. subj. σεύῃ Λ 293. Pple. σεύας Ο 681. **Mid.** 3 pl. impf. ἐσσεύοντο Β 150, 808, Ι 80, Λ 167, 419, Χ 146: ξ 456, ω 466. 3 sing. aor. σεύατο Ζ 505, Η 208, Ξ 227: ε 51. 3 pl. ἐσσεύαντο Λ 549, Ο 272. 3 pl. subj. σεύωνται Γ 26, Λ 415. 3 sing. opt. σεύαιτο Ρ 463, Υ 148, Ψ 198. Pple. σευάμενος Χ 22. 2 sing. aor. ἔσσυο Π 585: ι 447. 3 ἔσσυτο Β 809, Θ 58, Ξ 519, Ρ 678: ξ 34, τ 448. σύτο Φ 167. Pf. ἔσσυμαι Ν 79. 3 sing. ἔσσυται κ 484. Pple. ἐσσύμενος, -ου Ζ 518, Λ 554, 717, Ν 57, 142, 315, 630, 787, Ρ 663, Ω 404: δ 416, 733, ο 73. Acc. sing fem. ἐσσυμένην Π 9. (ἀνα-, ἀπο-, δια-, ἐκ-, ἐπισσεύω, κατα-, μετασσεύομαι.) (I) To set in motion: ἐξ ἀμφοτέροιιν αἷμ' ἔσσευα (caused it to spirt forth) Ε 208, Διωνύσοιο τιθήνας σεῦε κατὰ Νυσήϊον (chased them) Ζ 133, ὅλμον ὥς [ϝ'] ἔσσευεν (hurled the body) Λ 147. Cf. Λ 293 (sets on), 294, Ξ 413 (sent him spinning), Ο 681 (urging them on), Υ 189 (chased you), 325 (caused him to shoot up): ζ 89 (drove them), ξ 35 (scattered them).—In mid.: εἴ περ ἂν αὐτὸν σεύωνται κύνες (seek to drive him off) Γ 26. Cf. Λ 549 (drive off) = Ο 272 (chase), Υ 148 (should chase him).—(II) In mid. (1) To set oneself in motion, to hasten, speed, rush: νῆας ἔπ' ἐσσεύοντο Β 150, σεύατ' ἔπειτα (made eager way) Η 208. Cf. Β 808, 809 = Θ 58, Ζ 505, Ι 80, Λ 167 (were in flight), 415 (are afoot, bestir themselves), 419, Ξ 227, 519, Π 585, Ρ 678, Φ 167 (spirted forth), Χ 22 (at full speed), 146: ε 51 (made his way), ι 447 (bring up the rear), ξ 34, 456, τ 448, ω 466.—To set oneself *to do something.* With infin.: ὅτε σεύαιτο διώκειν Ρ 463.—Of something inanimate, to begin *to do something.* With infin.: ὄφρ' ὕλη σεύαιτο καήμεναι Ψ 198.—(2) In pf., to be in a state of eagerness or excitement: ποσσὶν ἔσσυμαι ἀμφοτέροισιν (with both my feet, I cannot keep my feet still) Ν 79: θυμός μοι ἔσσυται ἤδη (is eager to be off) κ 484.—In pple., in a state of eagerness, eager, set or bent upon something: ἦ σε καὶ ἐσσύμενον κατερύκω; (delay you in your haste) Ζ 518. Cf. Λ 554 = Ρ 663, Ν 57, 142, 315, 630, 787, Π 9, Ω 404: ο 73.—With complementary genit.: καὶ ἐσσύμενός περ ὁδοῖο δ 733.—With complementary infin.: ἐσσυμένους πολεμίζειν Λ 717. Cf. δ 416.

σηκάζω [σηκός]. To coop up in or as in a pen: σήκασθέν κε κατὰ Ἴλιον Θ 131.

σηκοκόρος, -ου, ὁ [σηκός + κορέω]. One who sweeps out pens ρ 224.

σηκός, -οῦ, ὁ. A pen or fold for sheep, goats or cattle Σ 589: ι 219, 227, 319, 439, κ 412.

σῆμα, -ατος, τό. (1) A distinguishing mark: γνῶ κλήρου σ. ἰδών Η 189.—(2) A spot or patch of white hair on the forehead of a horse, a star Ψ 455.—(3) A peg or something similar stuck in the ground to mark the distance of a throw (cf. τέρμα (2)): ὑπέρβαλε σήματα πάντων Ψ 843. Cf. θ 192, 195.—(4) A guiding mark Κ 466.— (5) A sign or token. (a) Something indicating that a stage or point has been reached λ 126, ψ 273.—(b) Something indicated to a person for guidance of his action Ψ 326.—(c) A signal for action φ 231.—(d) Something adduced as proof, an evidence: σ. ἀριφραδὲς ἄλλο τι δείξω φ 217. Cf. τ 250 = ψ 206, ψ 73, 110, 188, 202, 225, ω 329, 346.—(e) A guest-token, the credentials brought by a guest to satisfy his host as to his identity: ᾔτεε σ. ἰδέσθαι Z 176. Cf. Z 178.—So in pl.: πόρε σήματα λυγρά Z 168.—(6) A sign from heaven, a portent or omen: ἔνθ' ἐφάνη μέγα σ. B 308. Cf. B 353, Δ 381, Θ 171, I 236, N 244, X 30: φ 413.—An omen or presage of human origin υ 111.—(7) A mound of earth or stones erected over and marking a grave, a grave-mound or barrow (=τύμβος): παρὰ σήματι Ἴλου K 415. Cf. B 814, Z 419, H 86, 89, Λ 166, Φ 322, Ψ 45, 255, 257, Ω 16, 51, 349, 416, 755, 799, 801: α 291, β 222, λ 75.—A wooden post erected on and marking a grave: ξύλον . . . σῆμά τευ βροτοῖο πάλαι κατατεθνηῶτος Ψ 331.

σημαίνω [σῆμα]. Fut. σημανέω μ 26. 3 sing. aor. σήμηνε Ψ 358, 757. 3 pl. aor. mid. ἐσημήναντο H 175. (1) To put a distinguishing mark upon, mark. In mid.: κλῆρον ἐσημήναντο ἕκαστος H 175.—(2) To point out, show, indicate: τέρματα Ψ 358=757.—To indicate, tell about: ἕκαστα μ 26.—(3) To give one's orders to. With dat.: πᾶσι A 289. Cf. A 296, B 805.—(4) To take command, act as leader: πένθ' ἡγεμόνας ποιήσατο σημαίνειν Π 172.—To act as master: ἐπὶ δμῳῇσι γυναιξὶν χ 427.—To be in command of, command, be in charge of. With genit.: στρατοῦ ἄλλου Ξ 85.—With dat.: φυλάκεσσιν K 58. Cf. P 250.—(5) To superintend work, act as superintendent or overseer: σήμαινεν Ὀδυσσεύς χ 450. Cf. Φ 445.—(6) To guide or direct the actions of, act as counsellor to. With dat.: οἱ Λ 789.

σημάντωρ, -ορος, ὁ [σημαίνω]. (1) A commander or captain Δ 431.—(2) A master ρ 21, τ 314.—(3) He who guides the horses, a charioteer (=ἡνίοχος (1)) Θ 127.—He who drives the cattle or sheep, a herdsman or shepherd O 325.

σήμερον. To-day, this day: τούτῳ Ζεὺς κῦδος ὀπάζει σ. Θ 142. Cf. Λ 431, T 103, Υ 127, 211: ρ 186, 252, σ 377.—For to-day: παύσωμεν πόλεμον H 30. Cf. H 291.

σήμηνε, 3 sing. aor. σημαίνω.

σήπω. 3 sing. pf. σέσηπε B 135. 3 sing. aor. subj. pass. σαπήῃ T 27. In pf. and pass., to undergo natural decomposition or decay, rot: οὐδέ τί οἱ χρὼς σήπεται Ω 414. Cf. B 135 (lie rotted away), T 27.

σθεναρός, -ή [σθένος]. Strong, of might I 505.

σθένος, -εος, τό. (1) Physical strength, power, might, vigour: ἐν σ. ὦρσεν ἑκάστῳ B 451. Cf. Θ 32, I 351, Λ 827, M 224, Π 542, Σ 274 (see ἔχω (I) (14)), Υ 361, etc.: θ 136, φ 282, χ 237.—Of animals: λέοντος σ. E 139. Cf. E 783, M 42, P 22, etc.: σ 373.—Of inanimate objects: οὐδέ τι πρώονα σθένεϊ [ποταμοὶ] ῥηγνῦσι ῥέοντες P 751.—(2) σ. τινός, like βίη (5), periphrasis for a person: σ. Ἰδομενῆος N 248. Cf. Ψ 827.—Sim.: σ. Ὠρίωνος (the constellation) Σ 486, σ. Ὠκεανοῖο 607, Φ 195.—(3) The strength of life, vital force: αὐδὴ καὶ σ. Σ 420.

σίαλος, -ου, ὁ. A (fattened and full-grown) domestic swine or pig Φ 363: β 300, κ 390, ξ 19, υ 163.—Joined with σῦς I 208: ξ 41, 81, ρ 181 =υ 251.

σῖγαλόεις, -εντος. Bright, shining, glittering, glistening, glossy. Epithet of various things: ἡνία E 226, 328, Θ 116, 137, Λ 128, P 479, εἵματα X 154, δέσματα 468: θρόνῳ ε 86, εἵματα ζ 26, ῥήγεα 38, λ 189, τ 318, 337, ψ 180, ἡνία ζ 81, ῥήγεϊ ν 118, χιτῶνα ο 60, τ 232, ὑπερώϊα π 449, σ 206, τ 600, χ 428.

σῖγάω [σιγή]. To be silent. In imp. σίγα, be silent! hush! Ξ 90: ξ 493, ρ 393, τ 42, 486.

σῖγή, -ῆς, ἡ. Silence. In dat. σιγῇ, in silence, keeping silence, without speech, restraining the lips: ἴσαν Γ 8. Cf. Γ 134, 420, Δ 431, H 195, T 255: δ 776, η 30, ν 76, ο 391, σ 142, τ 502, φ 388.—Without construction: σιγῇ νῦν (let no more be said) ο 440.

σιδήρεος, -η, -ον, **σιδήρειος**, -η, -ον (H 141, 144, Θ 15, P 424, Ω 205, 521). [σίδηρος.] (1) Of iron: ἄξονι E 723. Cf. H 141, 144, Θ 15: α 204.—Epithet of the heavens regarded as a vault of burnished metal, the iron . . . ο 329=ρ 565.—(2) As if of iron: ὀρυμαγδός (unwearying, ceaseless, incessant) P 424, θυμός (hard as iron, inflexible) X 357, πυρὸς μένος (relentless) Ψ 177, ἦτορ (not to be turned from its course, daring all) Ω 205, 521: κραδίη (stout as iron) δ 293, θυμός (not open to compassion or sympathy) ε 191, σοὶ σιδήρεα πάντα τέτυκται (you are all of iron) μ 280, ἦτορ (unfeeling) ψ 172.

σίδηρος, -ου, ὁ. (1) Iron Δ 510, H 473, I 366, Υ 372, Ψ 834: α 184, ι 393.—(2) Various things made of iron. The point of an arrow: τόξῳ [πέλασε] σίδηρον Δ 123.—An axe Δ 485.—A knife or sword Σ 34.—A knife Ψ 30.—A bar of iron or something of the sort: ὀφθαλμοὶ ὡς εἰ κέρα ἕστασαν ἠὲ σίδηρος τ 211. Cf. τ 494.—(3) Collectively, implements or weapons of iron: πολιὸν σίδηρον (*i.e.* the articles of iron proposed as prizes) Ψ 261, τίθει ἰόεντα σίδηρον 850 (defined in the next line): διοϊστεῦσαι (διοϊστεύσειν) (εἴ κε διοϊστεύσω) σιδήρου (*i.e.* the axe-heads set up to be shot through by the suitors) τ 587, φ 97=127, φ 114. Cf. Z 48= K 379=Λ 133: =φ 10, ξ 324, π 294=τ 13, φ 3= 81=ω 168, φ 61, 328, ω 177.

σίζω. To hiss ι 394.

σῖνομαι. 3 pl. pa. iterative σινέσκοντο ζ 6. (1) To hurt, harm, do mischief to: εἴ κε σίνηαι [βόας] λ 112=μ 139. Cf. Ω 45.—(2) To harry, despoil: οἵ σφεας σινέσκοντο ζ 6.—To lay violent hands upon, carry off to destruction: ἑταίρους μ 114.

σίντης [σίνομαι]. Ravening: λῖν σίντην Λ 481, λύκοι σίνται Π 353. Cf. Υ 165.

†σῖτέομαι [σῖτος]. 3 pl. pa. iterative σιτέσκοντο. To take one's meals, eat: ἐν τῷ σιτέσκοντο ω 209.

σῖτος, -ου, ὁ. (1) Food other than flesh-meat (definitely in this sense or distinguished in terms from meat): σῖτον ἐπένειμε, ἀτὰρ κρέα νεῖμεν Ἀχιλλεύς I 216, Ω 625: σῖτον ὄψα τε γ 479, ἀνέμισγε σίτῳ φάρμακα λυγρά κ 235. Cf. α 139=δ 55 =η 175=κ 371=ο 138=ρ 94=259, α 147, δ 623, ι 9, κ 290, 375, μ 19, ξ 449, 456, ο 334, π 51, ρ 335, 412, υ 254, χ 21.—(2) Food distinguished in terms from drink: οὐ σῖτον ἔδουσ', οὐ πίνουσι οἶνον Ε 341. Cf. Θ 507, 547, Ι 706 = Τ 161, Τ 306, Ω 641: α 139 = δ 55 = η 175 = ο 138 = ρ 94, α 147, γ 479, δ 623, 746, ε 165, η 265, 295, ι 9, 87 = κ 58, μ 19, 327, ν 69, 244, ξ 46, ο 334, π 51, 110, ρ 533, τ 61, υ 137, 254, 313, 378.—(3) Food in general without these distinctions: σίτου ἵμερος Λ 89. Cf. Τ 44, 163, Ω 129, 602, 613, 619: ἐπὶ χθονὶ σῖτον ἔδοντες θ 222, ι 89 = κ 101. Cf. δ 60, ζ 99, ξ 455 (the leavings of the meal), π 83, ρ 418, 457, 558, σ 360, υ 130, ω 395, 489.

σῖτοφάγος [σῖτος + φάγον]. Food-eating ι 191.

σιφλόω. App., to injure or harm in some way: θεός ἑ σιφλώσειεν Ξ 142.

σιωπάω [σιωπή]. To be silent, cease from talking: σιωπᾶν λαὸν ἀνώγει Β 280. Cf. Ψ 568: εἰ γὰρ σιωπήσειαν 'Αχαιοί (cease their clamour) ρ 513.

σιωπή, -ῆς, ἡ. Silence. In dat. σιωπῇ. (1) In silence, keeping silence, without speech, restraining the lips: ἰδὼν ἐς παῖδα σ. Ζ 404. Cf. Δ 412, Η 427, Ι 190, 620, Ξ 310 (without telling of my intention), Σ 556: α 325, 339, κ 140, ν 309, ο 463. —(2) Silent. With ἀκήν: ἀκὴν ἐγένοντο σ. See ἀκήν (2).

σκάζω. To limp, halt, walk lame: σκάζων ἐκ πολέμου Λ 811. Cf. Τ 47.

σκαιός, -ή, -όν. (1) That is on the left side, the left . . . In fem. σκαιή (sc. χείρ), the left hand: σκαιῇ ἔγχος ἔχων Π 734. Cf. Α 501, Φ 490. —(2) That lies to the left of a spectator: ῥίον γ 295.

σκαίρω. To frisk, gambol, skip along: ποσὶ σκαίροντες Σ 572. Cf. κ 412.

σκαφίς, -ίδος, ἡ. Some kind of vessel for milk ι 223.

†σκεδάννῡμι [cf. κεδάννυμι, σκίδναμαι]. 3 sing. aor. ἐσκέδασε Η 330. σκέδασε Ρ 649, Υ 341, Ψ 162: ν 352. Imp. σκέδασον Τ 171, Ψ 158: θ 149. (ἀπο-, δια-.) (1) To shed in drops: αἷμα Η 330.—(2) To cause (a body of men) to disperse, dismiss (it): λαόν Τ 171. Cf. Ψ 158, 162.—(3) To disperse or scatter (mist) Ρ 649, Υ 341: ν 352.—To scatter, dismiss (cares): σκέδασον ἀπὸ κήδεα θυμοῦ θ 149.

σκέδασις, ἡ [σκεδάννυμι]. A (disorderly) scattering, a rout: μνηστήρων σκέδασιν α 116, υ 225.

†σκέλλω. 3 sing. aor. opt. σκήλειε. To dry up, shrivel up, parch: χρόα Ψ 191.

σκέλος, τό. The leg: πρυμνὸν σ. Π 314.

σκέπαρνον, τό. An adze ε 237, ι 391.

σκέπας, τό. Shelter, protection, cover: ἀνέμοιο (from the . . .) ε 443 = η 282, ζ 210, μ 336.—A place affording shelter, protection or cover: εἶσαν ἐπὶ σ. ζ 212.

†σκεπάω [σκέπας]. 3 pl. σκεπόωσι. To afford shelter from, ward off: κῦμα ν 99.

σκέπτομαι. Aor. pple. σκεψάμενος μ 247. (1) To look, look about: σκέπτεο νῦν, αἴ κεν ἴδηαι . . . Ρ 652.—(2) To look, turn one's eyes, in a specified direction: ἐς νῆα μ 247.—(3) To look out for, watch: ὀϊστῶν ῥοῖζον Π 361.

σκήλειε, 3 sing. aor. opt. σκέλλω.

σκηπάνιον, -ου, τό [σκήπτομαι]. A staff: σκηπανίῳ ἀμφοτέρω κεκόπων Ν 59. Cf. Ω 247.

σκήπτομαι. (ἐνισκίμπτω.) To lean or support oneself in walking (upon something): ἄκοντι σκηπτόμενον Ξ 457.—To lean upon a staff for support in walking, walk with a staff: ἐδύσετο δώματα σκηπτόμενος ρ 338. Cf. ρ 203 = ω 158.

σκηπτοῦχος [σκηπτ-, σκῆπτρον + ἔχω]. Bearing a staff of office. Epithet of βασιλῆες Α 279, Β 86: β 231 = ε 9, δ 64, θ 41.—Absol. in the sense of βασιλεύς: τοὶ ἅμ' ἕποντο σκηπτοῦχοι θ 47. Cf. Ξ 93.

σκῆπτρον, -ου, τό [σκήπτομαι]. (1) A stick or staff for support in walking: ἕλε σ. παχύ, βῆ δὲ θύραζε Σ 416. Cf. ν 437, ξ 31, ρ 199, σ 103 (*i.e.* to be used in defence).—(2) A staff of office. Borne (a) By a priest: σ. καὶ στέμμα θεοῖο Α 28. Cf. Α 15 = 374.—(b) By a king or chief: Ζεύς οἱ ὑπὸ σκήπτρῳ ἐδάμασσεν ['Αργείους] Ζ 159. Cf. Β 46, 101, 186, 199, 206, 265, 268, Η 412, Ι 38, 99, 156, 298, Σ 557: γ 412, λ 569.—(c) By heralds Η 277.—(d) By a seer λ 91.—(3) A staff in the custody of a herald and handed by him to one wishing to speak in an assembly in token of his right to a hearing: ἐν κῆρυξ χειρὶ σ. ἔθηκεν Ψ 568. Cf. Α 234, 245, Β 279, Γ 218, Κ 321 (the speaker offering the staff which he holds), 328, Σ 505 (app. a single staff held by the speakers in succession is meant): β 37, 80.

σκηρίπτομαι. (1) To lean, apply oneself, apply one's weight: σκηριπτόμενος χερσίν τε ποσίν τε (pushing with his hands and scrambling with his feet) λ 595.—(2) To support oneself in walking ρ 196.

σκιάζω [σκιή]. To throw shadow over, bring into darkness, darken: ἄρουραν Φ 232.

†σκιάω [as prec.]. 3 pl. impf. pass. σκιόωντο. (κατα-.) = prec.: σκιόωντο πᾶσαι ἀγυιαί β 388 = γ 487 = 497 = λ 12 = ο 185 = 296 = 471.

σκίδναμαι [cf. σκεδάννυμι]. (διασκίδνημι.) (1) To be scattered or dispersed: ὑψόσ' ἄχνη σκίδναται Λ 308. Cf. Π 375.—(2) Of men, to disperse, go each his own way: κατὰ κλισίας τε νέας τε Α 487. Cf. Τ 277 = Ψ 3, Ω 2: α 274, β 252, 258.—(3) Of water, to run dispersed: κρῆναι, ἡ μὲν ἀνὰ κῆπον σκίδναται η 130.

σκιερός [σκιή]. Shadowy, shady: νέμεϊ Λ 480: ἄλσος υ 278.

σκιή, -ῆς, ἡ. A shadow: σκιῇ εἴκελον ἢ καὶ ὀνείρῳ λ 207. Cf. κ 495 (like shadows).

σκιόεις, -εντος [σκιή]. (1) On which shadows fall or play, having the surface diversified with patches of dark or shadow, shadowy: οὔρεα Α 157, νέφεα Ε 525, Λ 63, Μ 157: θ 374, λ 592. Cf. ε 279 = η 268.—(2) Faintly lighted, shadowy, dim: μέγαρα α 365 = δ 768 = σ 399, κ 479, λ 334 = ν 2, ψ 299.

σκιόωντο, 3 pl. impf. pass. σκιάω.

σκιρτάω [σκαίρω]. To frisk or gambol Υ 226, 228.

σκολιός, -ή, -όν. Crooked. Fig., unjust, inequitable: θέμιστας Π 387.

σκόλοψ, -οπος, ὁ [cf. σκῶλος]. In pl., palisades, pales or stakes fixed in the ground in a close row, vertical or inclined, as a defence: ὕπερθε σκολόπεσσιν ἠρήρει [τάφρος] Μ 55. Cf. Η 441, Θ 343 = Ο 1, Ι 350, Μ 63, Ο 344, Σ 177 (app. those on the wall of the city; cf. the next passage): η 45.

σκόπελος, -ου, ὁ. A natural prominence, a rock or crag Β 396: μ 73, 80, 95, 101, 108, 220, 239, 430.

σκοπιάζω [σκοπιή]. (διασκοπιάομαι.) To direct one's look to something, observe it: μάλα περ σκοπιάζων Ξ 58.—To look out for something, watch: δηρὸν καθήμενος ἐσκοπίαζον κ 260.—To spy upon: ἄνδρας δυσμενέας Κ 40.

σκοπιή, -ῆς, ἡ [σκοπός]. (1) A spot from which one can command a view, a look-out place: ἥμενος ἐν σκοπιῇ Ε 771. Cf. Δ 275, Υ 137, Χ 145: δ 524, κ 97 = 148, 194, ξ 261 = ρ 430.—A mountain peak: σκοπιαὶ καὶ πρώονες Θ 557 = Π 299.—(2) A looking out, a look-out or watch: σκοπιὴν ἔχεν θ 302.

σκοπός, -οῦ, ὁ, ἡ [σκοπ-, σκέπτομαι]. (1) One stationed to look out or watch, a look-out: τὸν ἀπὸ σκοπιῆς εἶδε σ. δ 524. Cf. Β 792, Σ 523, Ω 799: π 365, χ 156.—One stationed to keep an eye on the competitors in a race Ψ 359.—(2) One set to watch the actions of others, an overseer: δμῳάων σ. ἔσσι χ 396.—(3) One who goes to observe the movements or dispositions of an enemy, a spy Κ 324, 526, 561.—(4) A mark or aim: οὐδέ τι τοῦ σκοποῦ ἥμβροτον φ 425. Cf. χ 6.—ἀπὸ σκοποῦ, wide of the mark: οὐκ ἀπὸ σκοποῦ μυθεῖται λ 344.

σκότιος [σκότος]. Not born in open wedlock, conceived in stealth: σκότιόν ἑ γείνατο μήτηρ Ζ 24.

σκοτομήνιος, -ον [σκότος + μήν]. In the dark (part of the) month, *i.e.* moonless: νύξ ξ 457.

σκότος, -ου, ὁ. Darkness: ποτὶ σκότον ἐτράπετο (away from the light) τ 389.—The darkness of death: τὸν σ. ὄσσε κάλυψεν Δ 461 = 503 = Ζ 11, Δ 526 = Φ 181, Ν 575, Ξ 519, Ο 578, Π 316, Υ 393, 471. Cf. Ε 47, Ν 672 = Π 607, Π 325.

σκυδμαίνω [σκύζομαι]. (ἀπο-.) To be angry or wroth with, feel resentment against. With dat.: μή μοι σκυδμαινέμεν Ω 592.

σκύζομαι. (ἐπι-.) To be angry or wroth, bear resentment Θ 483, Ι 198.—To be angry or wroth with, feel resentment against. With dat.: Διὶ πατρί Δ 23 = Θ 460. Cf. Ω 113, 134: ψ 209.

σκύλαξ, -ακος (fem. when the gender is indicated). A puppy: κύων ἀμαλῇσι περὶ σκυλάκεσσι βεβῶσα υ 14. Cf. ι 289, μ 86.

σκύμνος, -ου. A (lion's) cub Σ 319.

σκῦτος, τό. A piece of leather ξ 34.

σκυτοτόμος, -ου, ὁ [σκῦτος + τομ-, τάμνω]. A worker in leather: σκυτοτόμων ὄχ' ἄριστος Η 221.

σκύφος, τό. A cup ξ 112.

σκώληξ, ὁ. A worm Ν 654.

σκῶλος, ὁ [cf. σκόλοψ]. A stake Ν 564.

σκώψ, σκωπός. Some kind of owl ε 66.

σμαραγέω. To give forth a loud sound: σμαραγεῖ πόντος (roars) Β 210. Cf. Β 463 (re-echoes with the cries of the birds), Φ 199 (crashes).

σμερδαλέος, -η, -ον [cf. next and L. *mordeo*, to bite]. (1) Terror-striking, awe-inspiring, dread, terrible, daunting: δράκων Β 309. Cf. Μ 464, Ν 192, Σ 579, Υ 65, 260, Φ 401: σ. αὐτῇσι φάνη ζ 137. Cf. λ 609, μ 91.—(2) In neut. sing. σμερδαλέον as adv. (a) Terribly, dauntingly: δέδορκεν Χ 95: ἐβόησεν ω 537. Cf. ι 395.—Violently: ἀμφὶ πήληξ σ. κροτάφοισι τινάσσετο Ο 609.—(b) Loudly, piercingly, vehemently, with ringing or re-echo: νῆες κονάβησαν Β 334 = Π 277. Cf. Β 466, Θ 92, Ν 498, Ο 648, Σ 35, Τ 399, Φ 255, 593: ἐβόησεν θ 305. Cf. κ 399, ρ 542.—(3) In neut. pl. σμερδαλέα as adv. (a) = (2) (a): ἰάχων Ε 302 = Θ 321 = Υ 285, Π 785, Υ 382, 443: χ 81. Cf. Η 479.—(b) = (2) (b): ἰάχων Τ 41.

σμερδνός, -ή, -όν [cf. prec.]. (1) = prec. (1): Γοργείη κεφαλή Ε 742.—(2) In neut. sing. σμερδνόν as adv. = prec. (2) (b): βοόων Ο 687, 732.

σμήχω. To wipe off: ἁλὸς χνόον ζ 226.

σμικρός, -ή, -όν [= μικρός]. Small Ρ 757.

σμύχω. Aor. infin. σμῦξαι Ι 653. To consume (with fire), burn: πυρὶ νῆας Ι 653.—In pass., to be consumed (with fire), blaze: ὡς εἰ ἅπασα Ἴλιος πυρὶ σμύχοιτο Χ 411.

σμῶδιξ, -ιγγος, ἡ. A weal Β 267, Ψ 716.

σόλος, -ου, ὁ. A mass or lump of iron. Used for distance-throwing as a trial of strength or skill Ψ 826, 839, 844.

σόος. See σάος.

σορός, ἡ. A cinerary urn (= λάρναξ (2)): ὡς ὀστέα νῶϊν ὁμὴ σ. ἀμφικαλύπτοι Ψ 91.

σός, σή, σόν [σοῦ, a genit. of σύ]. Genit. pl. fem. σέων (scanned as one syllable) Ε 818. Thy, your (cf. τεός) Α 42, 179, 297, Γ 50, 174, Δ 60, 262, etc.: α 195, 402, β 112, 178, γ 117, etc.—With the article: τὸ σὸν γέρας Α 185. Cf. Π 40, etc.: β 403, ξ 512, etc.—Absol.: ἐπὶ σοῖσι καθήμενος (where your heritage is) β 369. Cf. Ψ 83.—With the article Ψ 572.—As predicative adj., thine: εἰ σός εἰμι ι 529.

σοφίη, -ης, ἡ. Skill Ο 412.

σπάρτα, τά [app. fr. σπάρτος, broom (*i.e.* the common, hardly the Spanish, broom)]. Ropes or cables (properly of broom) Β 135.

†σπάω. 3 sing. aor. ἔσπασε Μ 395, Ν 178. σπάσε Ε 859. Aor. mid. σπασάμην κ 166. 3 sing. (ἐ)σπάσατο Δ 530, Ε 621, Ν 510, Τ 387: β 321. σπάσσατο Λ 240. Imp. pl. σπάσσασθε χ 74. Pple. σπασσάμενος Π 473: κ 439, λ 231. Genit. sing. neut. aor. pple. pass. σπασθέντος Λ 458. (ἀνα-, ἐκ-.) (1) To draw, pull, pluck, in a specified direction: ἐκ δόρυ σπάσεν αὖτις Ε 859. Cf. Λ 458, Μ 395, Ν 178.—In mid. Δ 530, Ε 621 = Ν 510, Λ 240: β 321.—(2) In mid., to draw (one's sword): σπασσάμενος ἄορ παρὰ μηροῦ Π 473: = κ 439 = λ 231. Cf. χ 74.—Sim. of drawing a spear from its σῦριγξ: ἐκ σύριγγος ἐσπάσατ' ἔγχος Τ 387.—(3) To pull off or pluck (something growing). In mid.: σπασάμην ῥῶπάς τε λύγους τε κ 166.

σπεῖο. Aor. imp. mid. ἕπω[2].

σπεῖος. See σπέος.

σπεῖρον, -ου, τό. (1) In pl., clothes, clothing,

articles of attire: σπεῖρα κάκ' ἀμφ' ὤμοισι βαλών δ 245. Cf. ζ 179.—(2) A covering wherewith to honour a dead body β 102, τ 147 = ω 137.—(3) The sail of a ship ε 318, ζ 269.

σπένδω. 2 sing. subj. σπένδῃσθα δ 591. 3 sing. pa. iterative σπένδεσκε Π 227. 3 pl. σπένδεσκον η 138. 3 sing. pa. iterative σπείσασκε θ 89. 3 pl. aor. ἔσπεισαν ν 55. σπεῖσαν Ι 177: γ 342, 395, η 184, 228, σ 427, φ 273. 2 sing. subj. σπείσῃς Ζ 259: γ 45. 1 pl. σπείσομεν η 165, 181. Imp. σπεῖσον Ω 287. Pple. σπείσας Π 253: ξ 447, σ 151. Pl. σπείσαντες Ι 657, 712: γ 334, ν 39, σ 419, φ 264. Infin. σπεῖσαι γ 47. (ἀπο-.) To pour out wine as a drink-offering, make libation: Διὶ πατρί Ζ 259, Ω 287. Cf. Ι 177, 657, 712, Π 227, 253, Ψ 196: σπείσας ἔπιεν οἶνον σ 151. Cf. γ 45, 342, δ 591, η 137, μ 363, ν 39, φ 264, etc.—To pour out (wine) in way of libation: σπείσας οἶνον ξ 447. Cf. Λ 775.

σπέος, σπεῖος (ε 194), τό. Genit. σπείους ε 68, 226, ι 141, 330, 462, μ 93. Dat. σπῆϊ Σ 402, Ω 83: β 20, ι 476, μ 210. Dat. pl. σπέσσι α 15, 73, δ 403, ε 155, ι 30, 114, ψ 335. σπήεσσι ι 400, κ 404, 424, π 232. A cave, cavern, grotto: ὑπὸ σπέος ἤλασε μῆλα Δ 279. Cf. Ν 32, Σ 50, 65, 402, Ω 83: β 20, ε 57, 63, ι 141, 400, κ 404, μ 80, ν 366, τ 188, etc.—In pl. of a single cave α 15 = ι 30, α 73, δ 403, ε 155, π 232, ψ 335.

σπέρμα, τό [σπείρω, to sow]. Seed. Fig.: σπέρμα πυρὸς σώζων ε 490.

σπέρχω. (ἐπι-.) To set in rapid motion. **(1)** In mid., to put oneself in eager motion, be in act, *to do something*. With infin.: ὁπότε σπερχοίατ' Ἀχαιοὶ φέρειν Ἄρηα Τ 317.—**(2)** In mid., to put forth one's efforts, exert oneself: σπερχομένοιο γέροντος (giving his impetuosity way) Ω 248: ὁπότε σπερχοίατ' ἐρετμοῖς (should ply their oars) ν 22.—**(3)** In mid. pple., with speed, in haste, hastily, without loss of time: σπερχόμενος ἐσύλα τεύχεα Λ 110. Cf. Ψ 870, Ω 322: ι 101, ο 60.—Sim. of the eager motion of a ship: νηῦς ἠπείρῳ ἐπέκελσε σπερχομένη ν 115.—**(4)** *Intrans. for reflexive*, of wind, to rush, blow furiously: ὁπότε σπέρχοιεν ἄελλαι γ 283. Cf. Ν 334.

σπέσθαι, aor. infin. mid. ἕπω².

σπέσσι, dat. pl. σπέος.

σπεύδω. Dat. pl. masc. pres. pple. σπευδόντεσσιν Ρ 745. 3 sing. aor. σπεῦσε ι 250, 310, 343. 1 pl. subj. σπεύσομεν Ρ 121. Imp. pl. σπεύσατε Ω 253. Fut. mid. σπεύσομαι Ο 402. **(1)** To hasten on with (something), lose no time in getting (it) done, accomplish (it) with speed: ταῦτα χρὴ σπεύδειν Ν 236: ἐπεὶ σπεῦσε τὰ ἃ ἔργα ι 250, 310, 343.—To press, urge, the accomplishment of (something): γάμον σπεύδουσιν τ 137.—**(2)** In mid., to speed, hasten, hurry: σπεύσομαι εἰς Ἀχιλῆα Ο 402.—So *intrans. for reflexive*: ἤϊξε σπεύδουσα Λ 119.—**(3)** *Intrans. for reflexive*, to put oneself in eager motion for some end, show eagerness, zeal, or alacrity: σπεύδοντα μάχην ἐς κυδιάνειραν Δ 225, οὓς σπεύδοντας ἴδοι (eager for the fray) 232. Cf. Θ 293.—**(4)** *Intrans. for reflexive*, to put forth one's efforts, exert oneself: τὸ οὔ τις ἐπεφράσατο σπευδόντων (such was their haste) Ε 667, ἐφομαρτεῖτον καὶ σπεύδετον (show your speed) Θ 191, Ψ 414, περὶ Πατρόκλοιο θανόντος σπεύσομεν Ρ 121, τὸν εὗρε σπεύδοντα (hard at work) Σ 373, τὼ σπεύδοντε πετέσθην (at the top of their speed) Ψ 506, σπεύσατέ μοι (get to work) Ω 253. Cf. Ρ 745, Σ 472, Ψ 767: ω 324.

σπήεσσι, dat. pl. σπέος.

σπῆϊ, dat. sing. σπέος.

σπιδής. Of unknown meaning. Commonly explained as 'wide': διὰ σπιδέος πεδίοιο Λ 754.

σπιλάς, -άδος, ἡ. A rock or reef in or projecting into the sea: νῆας ποτὶ σπιλάδεσσιν ἔαξαν κύματα γ 298, σπιλάδες τε πάγοι τε ε 405 (the two words difficult to distinguish). Cf. ε 401.

σπινθήρ, -ῆρος, ὁ. A spark Δ 77.

σπλάγχνα, τά. The entrails (such as the heart, liver and spleen) of an animal killed as under ἱερεύω (1) or (2): ἐπεὶ σπλάγχνα πάσαντο Α 464 = Β 427: = γ 461 = μ 364. Cf. Β 426: γ 9, 40, υ 252, 260.

σπόγγος, -ου, ὁ. A sponge: σπόγγῳ ἀμφὶ πρόσωπ' ἀπομόργνυ Σ 414. Cf. α 111, υ 151, χ 439, 453.

σποδιή, -ῆς, ἡ [σποδός]. Smouldering ashes, embers: ὡς ὅτε τις δαλὸν σποδιῇ ἐνέκρυψεν ε 488.

σποδός, -οῦ, ἡ. Smouldering ashes, embers: μοχλὸν ὑπὸ σποδοῦ ἤλασα πολλῆς ι 375.

σπονδή, -ῆς, ἡ [σπένδω]. In pl., an agreement ratified by libations: σπονδαί τ' ἄκρητοι καὶ δεξιαί Β 341 = Δ 159.

σπουδή, -ῆς, ἡ [σπεύδω]. **(1)** Exertion, effort: ἄτερ σπουδῆς τάνυσε τόξον φ 409.—ἀπὸ σπουδῆς, in earnest, seriously: εἰ τοῦτον [μῦθον] ἀπὸ σπουδῆς ἀγορεύεις Η 359 = Μ 233.—**(2)** In dat. σπουδῇ **(a)** With haste or speed, without loss of time: ἀνάβαινε ο 209.—**(b)** With much ado, with difficulty: ἐξήλασσαν [ὄνον] Λ 562. Cf. Β 99 (*i.e.* they could hardly be got to do so), Ε 893, Ν 687, Ψ 37: ἤλυξαν ὄλεθρον γ 297. Cf. ν 279, ω 119.

στάδιος, -η, -ον [στα-, ἵστημι]. (αὐτοστάδιος.) **(1)** Of fighting, stand-up, close (as opposed to the use of missiles): ἄριστος τοξοσύνῃ, ἀγαθὸς δὲ καὶ ἐν σταδίῃ ὑσμίνῃ Ν 314. Cf. Ν 713.—**(2)** Absol. in fem. (*sc.* ὑσμίνη), stand-up fighting: ἐνὶ σταδίῃ μέλπεσθαι Ἄρηϊ Η 241. Cf. Ν 514.—Such fighting as opposed to the use of missiles: ἐπιστάμενος μὲν ἄκοντι, ἐσθλὸς δ' ἐν σταδίῃ Ο 283.

†στάζω. 3 sing. aor. στάξε Τ 39, 354. Imp. στάξον Τ 348. (ἐν-.) To introduce into something in drops: Πατρόκλῳ ἀμβροσίην καὶ νέκταρ στάξε κατὰ ῥινῶν Τ 39 (the word applying strictly to νέκταρ only). Cf. Τ 348, 354.

στάθμη, -ης, ἡ [στα-, ἵστημι]. A device employed by carpenters, etc., a line rubbed with chalk or the like and drawn tight along a surface so as to leave on its removal a straight line marked thereon for the workman's guidance: ὥς τε σ. δόρυ νήϊον ἐξιθύνει Ο 410: ἐπὶ στάθμην ἴθυνε [δοῦρα] (to the line) ε 245. Cf. ρ 341 = φ 44, φ 121, ψ 197.

σταθμόνδε [acc. of next + -δε (1)]. To the steading: σ. ἀπονέεσθαι ι 451.

σταθμός, -οῦ, ὁ [στα-, ἵστημι]. (1) The establishment of a shepherd or herdsman, a farm-house with its outbuildings: λίς, ὃν κύνες ἀπὸ σταθμοῖο δίωνται Ρ 110. Cf. Β 470, Μ 304, Π 642, Τ 377: ξ 32, 358, ο 306, π 45, 66, 156, 163, 318, ρ 26, 200. —Sim. in pl.: κατὰ σταθμοὺς δύεται Ε 140. Cf. Ε 557, Π 752, Σ 589: ξ 504, π 82, ρ 20, 187, 223.—(2) A door-post: θύρας σταθμοῖσιν ἐπῆρσεν Ξ 167 = 339. Cf. δ 838, ζ 19, η 89, κ 62, ρ 340, φ 45, χ 120, 181, 257 = 274.—(3) In the μέγαρον, one of a group of columns surrounding the hearth and supporting the roof: στῆ παρὰ σταθμὸν τέγεος α 333 = θ 458 = π 415 = σ 209 = φ 64. Cf. ρ 96.—(4) A weight: σταθμὸν ἔχουσα καὶ εἴριον Μ 434.

σταίη, 3 sing. aor. opt. ἵστημι (Β).

σταμῖνες [στα-, ἵστημι]. Dat. σταμίνεσσι. The uprights of the ἴκρια of the σχεδίη of Odysseus ε 252.

στάν, 3 pl. aor. ἵστημι (Β).

στάξε, 3 sing. aor. στάζω.

στάς, aor. pple. ἵστημι (Β).

στάσκε, 3 sing. pa. iterative ἵστημι (Β).

στατός [στα-, ἵστημι]. Of a horse, that has been confined in a stall, stalled Ζ 506 = Ο 263.

σταυρός, -οῦ, ὁ [στα-, ἵστημι]. A stake or pale: σταυροὺς ἐκτὸς ἔλασσεν ξ 11. Cf. Ω 453.

σταφύλη, -ης, ἡ. A level, a plummet used for determining levels: [ἵππους] σταφύλῃ ἐπὶ νῶτον ἐΐσας (*i.e.* of equal height as measured by a level across their backs) Β 765.

σταφυλή, -ῆς, ἡ. A bunch or cluster of grapes Σ 561: ε 69, η 121, ω 343.

στάχυς [cf. ἄσταχυς]. An ear of corn Ψ 598.

στέαρ, στέᾱτος, τό. Stiff fat, tallow or suet: ἐκ δὲ στέατος ἔνεικε μέγαν τροχόν φ 178 = 183 (scanned as a disyllable, or the vowel before στ- allowed to be short).

στείβω. To trample under foot: νέκυας Λ 534. Cf. Υ 499.—To tread or tramp (clothes) in washing ζ 92.

στεῖλα, aor. στέλλω.

στειλειή, -ῆς, ἡ. The handle of an axe φ 422.

στειλειόν, τό. = prec. ε 236.

στεῖνος, τό [στείνω]. (1) A narrow or confined space in which a body of persons is cooped up: εἴλεον [δμῳὰς] ἐν στείνει χ 460.—A narrow or confined space within which free movement is impossible: στεῖνος γάρ, ὅθι τρώσεσθαι ὀΐω Μ 66.—A narrow part (of a track) Ψ 419.—(2) A position or state of difficulty, a strait or pass: μή πω χάζεσθε μάχης ἐν στείνεϊ τῷδε Ο 426. Cf. Θ 476.

στείνω and (in sense (4)) **στένω**. (μετα-, περι-.) (1) To confine within a narrow space, coop up: στείνοντο λαοὶ Ξ 34.—To make narrow: θύρετρά κέ τοι φεύγοντι στείνοιτο (would seem all too narrow) σ 386.—(2) To impede the freedom of movement of, cumber: ἀρνειὸς λάχνῳ στεινόμενος ι 445.—(3) To fill to the point of overcrowding or oppression. With genit.: στείνοντο σηκοὶ ἀρνῶν ι 219. —With dat.: οὐ δύναμαι προχέειν ῥόον στεινόμενος νεκύεσσιν Φ 220.—(4) *Intrans.*, to be oppressed by a feeling of fulness: μέγ' ἔστενε κῆρ (he was oppressed as to the heart, his heart was full to bursting) Κ 16. Cf. Σ 33: φ 247.—With ἦτορ as subject: ἔν οἱ κραδίῃ στένει ἦτορ Υ 169.—Hence, to give audible vent to the feeling, to groan or moan: ἐπὶ δ' ἔστενε δῆμος Ω 776.—Of the moaning of the swelling sea Ψ 230.

στεινωπός, -όν [στεῖνος + ὦπα. 'Narrow-looking']. Narrow, strait: ὁδῷ Η 143, Ψ 416 (in the latter passage 'a narrow part of the track'). Cf. Ψ 427. —Absol., a narrow passage, a strait: στεινωπὸν ἀνεπλέομεν μ 234.

στεῖρα[1], -ης, ἡ. The stem or cutwater of a ship: ἀμφὶ κῦμα στείρῃ ἴαχεν Α 482 : = β 428.

στεῖρα[2]. Of a cow, that has not calved: βοῦν κ 522 = λ 30, υ 186.

στείχω. 3 pl. aor. ἔστιχον Π 258. (ἀπο-, περι-, προσ-.) To go, take or make one's way, proceed: ἐνθάδε στείχοντες Β 287. Cf. Β 833 = Λ 331, Ι 86, Π 258: η 72, ι 418, 444, λ 17, ρ 204, ψ 136.

στέλλω. Fut. στελέω β 287. Aor. στεῖλα ξ 248. 3 pl. στεῖλαν Δ 384 : γ 11. Acc. sing. masc. aor. pple. στείλαντα ξ 247. 3 pl. aor. mid. στείλαντο Α 433. (περι-.) (1) To get ready, equip, fit out: νῆα β 287. Cf. ξ 247, 248.—In mid., to get oneself ready, array oneself: ἄλλοι στέλλεσθε Ψ 285. —To set in array: οὓς ἑτάρους στέλλοντα Δ 294.—(2) To furl (a sail): ἱστία στεῖλαν ἀείραντες γ 11. —To lower (a sail): ἱστία στέλλοντας π 353.—So in mid. Α 433.—(3) To dispatch, send: ἀγγελίην ἐπὶ Τυδῆ στεῖλαν Δ 384 (see ἀγγελίη).—To urge, incite: μάχην ἐς κυδιάνειραν Μ 325.

στέμμα, -ατος, τό [στέφω]. A fillet or chaplet of wool borne by a priest: σκῆπτρον καὶ στέμμα θεοῖο Α 28.—In pl. in the same sense: στέμματ' ἔχων ἐν χερσὶν Ἀπόλλωνος χρυσέῳ ἀνὰ σκήπτρῳ (to denote his being a suppliant) Α 14 = 373.

στεναχίζω [στενάχω]. (ἀνα-, περιστεναχίζομαι, ὑπο-.) (1) To be oppressed by a feeling of fulness. In mid.: μέγα στεναχίζετο θυμῷ (his heart was full to bursting) Η 95.—To groan or moan: ἠρνεῖτο στεναχίζων Τ 304. Cf. Ψ 172, 225: α 243, ι 13, λ 214, π 188, 195, ω 317.—(2) To give forth a heavy sound under repeated pressure, rumble. In mid.: ὑπὸ δὲ στεναχίζετο γαῖα λαῶν ἰζόντων Β 95. Cf. Β 784.—To resound, re-echo. In mid.: περὶ δὲ στεναχίζετο δῶμα κ 454.

στενάχω [στένω, στείνω]. 3 sing. pa. iterative στενάχεσκε Τ 132. (ἀνα-, ἐπι-.) (1) To groan or moan: βαρὺ στενάχων Α 364. Cf. Θ 334, Σ 70, 318, Φ 417, Ω 123, 639, etc.: δ 516, ε 429, η 274, ι 306, 415, ξ 354, etc.—In mid. Τ 301 = Χ 515 = Ω 746, Τ 338, Χ 429, Ψ 1, Ω 722: κ 55.—Of the roaring of a beast Π 489.—Of the roaring of rushing water Π 391.—Of the rushing sound of horses in rapid motion. In mid.: ὣς ἵπποι μεγάλα στενάχοντο θέουσαι Π 393.—(2) To mourn for, lament, bewail. In mid.: τοὺς στενάχοντο γοῶντες ι 467.—To recall with grief the doings of (a person), bewail the consequences of his actions: Ἄτην αἰεὶ στενάχεσκεν Τ 132.

στένω. See στείνω.

στερεός, -ή, -όν. (1) Resisting force, rigid, stout: βοέης Ρ 493.—Fig., of the heart, hard, unyielding. In comp.: σοὶ αἰεὶ κραδίη στερεωτέρη ἐστὶ λίθοιο ψ 103.—(2) Firmly fixed, not to be displaced: ὡς ὅτε τις στερεὴ λίθος τ 494.—(3) Of speech, stern, harsh Μ 267.

†**στερέω.** Aor. infin. στερέσαι. To deprive of. With genit.: στερέσαι με τῆς ληΐδος ν 262.

στερεῶς [adv. fr. στερεός]. (1) So as to give rigidity or power of resistance: [κυνέη] ἱμᾶσιν ἐντέτατο σ. Κ 263.—(2) So as to prevent movement, tight, fast: ἐμὲ κατέδησαν σ. ξ 346.—Without relaxation of pressure, with constant strain: νῶτα ἑλκόμενα σ. Ψ 715.—(3) Resisting persuasion, inflexibly, sternly: ἠρνεῖτο σ. Ψ 42. Cf. Ι 510.

στέρνον, -ου, τό. (1) The breast or chest: τὸν βάλε σ. ὑπὲρ μαζοῖο Δ 528. Cf. Β 479, Δ 530, Η 224, Λ 842, Ο 542, Π 312=400, Υ 163, Χ 313: ε 346, 373.—Of animals Δ 106, Ψ 365, 508: ι 443.—(2) In pl. in the same sense: εὐρύτερος στέρνοισιν (in the . . .) Γ 194. Cf. Ν 282, 290.

στεροπή, -ῆς, ἡ [cf. ἀστεροπή]. (1) Lightning, the lightning flash Κ 154, Λ 66.—(2) Flash, gleam: χαλκοῦ Λ 83, Τ 363: δ 72, ξ 268=ρ 437.

στεροπηγερέτα [στεροπή + ἀγείρω]. (Prob. orig. a voc. turned into a nom.) Gatherer of lightnings. Epithet of Zeus Π 298.

στεῦμαι. (1) To press forward, essay eagerly: στεῦτο διψάων (in his thirst) λ 584.—(2) To put oneself forward *to do something*, make as though one would do it. With infin.: στεῦταί τι ἔπος ἐρέειν Γ 83.—(3) To hold oneself out as willing or able *to do something*, promise *to do it*. With infin.: στεῦτο Τρωσὶ μαχήσεσθαι Ε 832. Cf. Σ 191.—(4) To declare boastingly, boast, vaunt. With infin.: στεῦτο νικησέμεν Β 597. Cf. Ι 241.—(5) To declare threateningly, threaten. With infin.: στεῦτ' ἀπολεψέμεν οὔατα Φ 455.—(6) To declare positively, assert with confidence, insist. With infin.: στεῦται Ὀδυσῆος ἀκοῦσαι ρ 525.

στεφάνη, -ης, ἡ [στέφω]. (1) A circlet for the head, a coronal Σ 597.—(2) A helmet Η 12, Κ 30, Λ 96.—(3) The brow of a hill Ν 138.

στέφανος, ὁ [as prec.]. An encircling ring: πολέμοιο Ν 736.

στεφανόω [στέφανος]. (1) To set or dispose round or about something: τείρεα, τά τ' οὐρανὸς ἐστεφάνωται (is set round with them, has them set around it as a crown) Σ 485: νῆσον, τὴν πέρι πόντος ἐστεφάνωται κ 195. Cf. Ε 739.—(2) To set upon something as a central figure: ἀσπίδι δ' ἐπὶ Γοργὼ ἐστεφάνωτο Λ 36.—(3) To set round something so as to envelop it: ἀμφί μιν νέφος ἐστεφάνωτο Ο 153.

στέφω. (ἀμφιπερι-, ἐπι-, περι-.) To set round something so as to envelop it: ἀμφί οἱ κεφαλῇ νέφος ἔστεφεν Σ 205.—In reference to something immaterial, to put round as a crown or so as to adorn: μορφὴν ἔπεσι στέφει θ 170.

στέωμεν, 1 pl. aor. subj. ἵστημι (B).

στῇ, 3 sing. aor. ἵστημι (B).

στῆθι, aor. imp. ἵστημι (B).

στῆθος, τό. Dat. pl. στήθεσι Δ 430, Ζ 65, Λ 100, Ν 618, Π 163, 503, Υ 20, Χ 452. στήθεσσι Α 83, Γ 63, Δ 152, Ζ 51, Λ 19, Ν 73, Ρ 22, Φ 182, etc.: α 341, β 90, γ 18, η 258, λ 566, ο 20, υ 9, φ 87, etc. Locative στήθεσφι Β 388. This form as ablative Λ 374, Ξ 150, 214. As genit. Ε 41, 57, Θ 259, Λ 448, Χ 284: χ 93. (1) The breast or chest Β 218, Γ 221, Δ 430, 480, Ε 19, Λ 374, etc.: ι 301, ξ 351, σ 21, υ 17, χ 82, 93, 286.—Of animals Δ 108, Λ 282, Μ 204, Π 753: χ 404.—(2) In pl. in reference to a single person: χιτῶνα περὶ στήθεσσι δαΐξαι Β 416. Cf. Γ 332, Δ 420, Ε 317, Ζ 65, Ι 490, Κ 9, etc.: λ 609, π 174, σ 69, υ 62.—(3) The breast as a seat (a) Of spirit, courage, boldness. In pl. as above: ἐν στήθεσσι μένος βάλεν Ε 513. Cf. Ε 125, Ρ 570.—(b) Of wrath or resentment: Ἥρῃ οὐκ ἔχαδε σ. χόλον Δ 24=Θ 461. Cf. Σ 110.—In pl. as above: εἰ χόλον αὐτῆμαρ καταπέψῃ, ἀλλ' ἔχει κότον ἐν στήθεσσιν ἑοῖσιν Α 83.—Sim. of rage: ὁππότε μένος οὐ τόσον ἧσιν ἐνὶ στήθεσσιν ἐμοῖσιν Τ 202.—(c) Of grief. In pl. as above: πένθος ἐνὶ στήθεσσιν ἀέξων Ρ 139.—(d) Of care or anxiety. In pl. as above: μή τί τοι ἄλλο ἐν στήθεσσι κακὸν μελέτω ἔργον β 304.—(e) Of hope. In pl. as above: οὐ τοῦτο ἐνὶ στήθεσσιν ἔολπεν φ 317.—(f) In pl. as above of βουλή: ἔγνως ἐμὴν ἐν στήθεσι βουλήν Υ 20. Cf. Ρ 470.—Of μῆτις: ἥν τινα μῆτιν ἐνὶ στήθεσσι κέκευθεν γ 18.—Of a purpose, etc.: τοῦτον νόον, ὅν τινά οἱ νῦν ἐν στήθεσσι τιθεῖσι θεοὶ β 125. Cf. Δ 309.—Of an idea or notion: οὔ τοι τοιοῦτον ἐνὶ στήθεσσι νόημα ρ 403.—(4) The breast as the seat (a) Of ἦτορ. In pl. in reference to a single person: ἐν ἐμοὶ αὐτῇ στήθεσι πάλλεται ἤ. Χ 452. Cf. Α 189: ρ 47, υ 22.—(b) Of κῆρ. In pl. as above: Ἀχιλλῆος κ. γηθεῖ ἐνὶ στήθεσσιν Ξ 140. Cf. α 341, η 309, π 275.—(c) Of κραδίη. In pl. as above: ἐμοὶ κ. ἐνὶ στήθεσσιν ἰάνθη δ 549.—(d) Of θυμός: δαΐζετο θ. ἐνὶ στήθεσσιν Ἀχαιῶν Ι 8=Ο 629. Cf. Β 142, Δ 289, Ν 808, Ο 322, etc.: β 90, κ 461, υ 328.—Of wolves Π 163.—In pl. as above: ἄψορρόν οἱ θ. ἐνὶ στήθεσσιν ἀγέρθη Δ 152. Cf. Γ 395, Δ 313, 360, Ζ 51, Η 68, Ι 256, 629, Ν 73, etc.: δ 549, ε 191, 222, η 187, 258, θ 178, λ 566, ξ 169, etc.—Of a wild boar Ρ 22.—(e) Of νόος: ὅς τε καὶ ἄλλων οἰδάνει ἐν στήθεσσι νόον Ι 554.—In pl. as above: σοὶ ἐνὶ στήθεσσιν ἀτάρβητος ν. ἐστίν Γ 63. Cf. Ν 732: κ 329, ν 255, υ 366.—(f) Of νόημα. In pl. as above: αἰεί τοι τοιοῦτον ἐνὶ στήθεσσι ν. ν 330. Cf. Ω 41.

στήλη, -ης, ἡ. (1) A block of wood or a stake set in the ground to contain the face of an earthwork (cf. θεμείλια): στήλας προβλῆτας ἐμόχλεον Μ 259.—(2) A post or a block or pillar of stone set upon a sepulchral mound: στήλῃ κεκλιμένος ἐπὶ τύμβῳ Ἴλου Λ 371. Cf. Ν 437, Π 457=675, Ρ 434: μ 14.

στήμεναι, στῆναι, aor. infin. ἵστημι (B).

στήομεν, 1 pl. aor. subj. ἵστημι (B).

†στηρίζω [στερεός]. 3 sing. aor. ἐστήριξε Δ 443. στήριξε Λ 28. Infin. στηρίξαι μ 434. Aor. infin. mid. στηρίξασθαι Φ 242. 3 sing. plupf. pass. ἐστήρικτο Π 111. (ἐν-.) (**1**) To set, fix: οὐρανῷ ἐστήριξε κάρη Δ 443. Cf. Λ 28.—In pass., to be propped against something, lean upon it. Fig.: πάντῃ κακὸν κακῷ ἐστήρικτο (one trouble followed closely on another) Π 111.—(**2**) In mid., to plant oneself firmly, find firm footing: οὐδὲ πόδεσσιν εἶχε στηρίξασθαι Φ 242.—So *intrans. for reflexive*: οὐδέ πῃ εἶχον στηρίξαι ποσὶν μ 434.

στῆσα, aor. ἵστημι (A).

στῆσαν[1], 3 pl. aor. ἵστημι (A).

στῆσαν[2], 3 pl. aor. ἵστημι (B).

στῆτε, aor. imp. pl. ἵστημι (B).

στήτην, 3 dual aor. ἵστημι (B).

στιβαρός, -ή, -όν [στείβω]. (**1**) Thick, stout. In comp.: δίσκον στιβαρώτερον ἢ οἵῳ Φαίηκες ἐδίσκεον θ 187.—(**2**) Of parts of the body, well-knit, stout, strong, powerful: ὤμῳ Ε 400, χερσὶν Μ 397, Ψ 686, 711. Cf. Ν 505 = Π 615, Ξ 455, Ο 126, Σ 415, Ψ 843: χερσὶν δ 506. Cf. ε 454, θ 84, 136, 189, μ 174, ξ 528, ο 61, σ 69, 335.—Of weapons, strongly made, stout: ἔγχος Π 141 = Τ 388, Π 802, Ε 746 = Θ 390 := α 100. Cf. Χ 307.—(**3**) Strong, stout, capable of resisting great force: σάκος Γ 335 = Π 136 = Τ 373, Σ 478, 609.

στιβαρῶς [adv. fr. prec.]. Strongly, stoutly, so as to be capable of resisting great force: πύλας πύκα στιβαρῶς ἀραρυίας Μ 454.

στίβη, ἡ. Frost ε 467, ρ 25.

στίλβω. (ἀπο-.) To be bright or resplendent, shine: κάλλεϊ τε στίλβων καὶ εἵμασιν Γ 392, χιτῶνας ἧκα στίλβοντας ἐλαίῳ (glossy) Σ 596. Cf. ζ 237.

στιλπνός, -ή, -όν [στίλβω]. Shining, bright, glistening: ἔερσαι Ξ 351.

***στίξ,** ἡ [στιχ-, στείχω]. Genit. στιχός Π 173, Υ 362. Elsewhere only in nom. pl. στίχες and acc. στίχας. (**1**) A line or rank of foot-soldiers or charioteers: Φωκήων στίχας ἵστασαν Β 525, ἵππους ἔρυξαν ἐπὶ στίχας Γ 113. Cf. Γ 196, Δ 90, Η 61, Λ 91, Ο 279, Ρ 84, Υ 362 (*i.e.* the enemy's line of battle), etc.: α 100.—Of hunters drawn up in line Μ 47, 48.—Sim. of dancers Σ 602.—(**2**) A regiment or detachment of troops: τῆς ἰῆς στιχὸς ἦρχε Μενέσθιος Π 173.

†στιχάομαι [στιχ-, στείχω]. 3 pl. impf. ἐστιχόωντο. To go, take or make one's way, proceed, march: εἰς ἀγορήν Β 92. Cf. Γ 266 = 341, Δ 432, Σ 577.—Of a ship, to make her way, sail Β 516 = 680 = 733, Β 602.

στόμα, -ατος, τό. (**1**) The mouth: βασιλῆας ἀνὰ σ. ἔχων Β 250, εἴ μοι δέκα στόματ' εἶεν 489. Cf. Ζ 43, Κ 375, Ξ 91, 467, Ο 607, Π 345, 349, 410, Χ 452, Ψ 395, 777, Ω 506: ε 322, 456, λ 426, μ 187, σ 97.—(**2**) In transferred senses. (**a**) The mouth of a harbour, the entrance to it κ 90.—(**b**) The mouth of a passage, the opening by which one enters or leaves it: σ. λαύρης χ 137.—(**c**) The mouth or outfall of a river: ὅτε δὴ ποταμοῖο κατὰ σ. ἷξεν ε 441. Cf. Μ 24.—(**d**) The front, *i.e.* the point, of a weapon: ξυστὰ κατὰ σ. εἱμένα χαλκῷ Ο 389.—(**e**) ἠϊόνος στόμα Ξ 36 (the two containing capes being app. likened to jaws, and the curving shore to the hollow of the mouth).—(**f**) πτολέμοιο σ. Κ 8 (war being app. likened to the jaws of a devouring monster). Cf. Τ 313, Υ 359.

στόμαχος, -ου, ὁ [στόμα]. The throat: κατὰ στομάχοιο θέμεθλα Ρ 47.—Of animals Γ 292, Τ 266.

στοναχέω [στοναχή]. (ἐπι-.) To groan or moan: ἀδινὸν στοναχῆσαι Σ 124.

στοναχή, -ῆς, ἡ [στενάχω]. A groaning or moaning: τῶν σ. ὀρώρει Ω 512. Cf. Β 39, 356, 590, Ω 696: ε 83 = 157, ξ 39, π 144, φ 237 = 383, χ 501, ω 416.

στονόεις, -εσσα, -εν [στόνος]. (**1**) Causing groanings, woeful, pitiable: κήδεα ι 12.—Carrying woe, bringing bale. Epithet of missile weapons: βέλεα Θ 159 = Ο 590, Ρ 374: ω 180. Cf. φ 12, 60.—Sim. of battle: Τρώων ἀϋτήν λ 383.—(**2**) Marked by or associated with groanings: ἀοιδήν (dolorous) Ω 721: εὐνήν, ἥ μοι στονόεσσα τέτυκται (whereon I lie and make lament) ρ 102 = τ 595.

στόνος, -ου, ὁ [στένω, στείνω]. A groaning or moaning: τῶν σ. ὄρνυτο Κ 483, Φ 20: χ 308, ω 184. Cf. ψ 40.—The agony of strife or conflict: ὀφέλλουσα στόνον ἀνδρῶν Δ 445. Cf. Τ 214.

†στορέννῡμι. 3 sing. aor. (ἐ)στόρεσε γ 158, ξ 50, υ 2. 3 pl. στόρεσαν Ι 660, Ω 648: δ 301, η 340, ν 73, ψ 291. Imp. στόρεσον ψ 171, 177. Pple. στορέσας Ι 213: τ 599. Infin. στορέσαι Ι 621, 659, Ω 645: δ 298, η 337. 3 sing. plupf. pass. ἔστρωτο Κ 155. (κατα-, ὑπο-.) (**1**) To give a smooth or level surface to, dispose evenly: ἀνθρακιήν Ι 213.—To lay (the sea) γ 158.—(**2**) To spread (bedding): εὗδ', ὑπὸ δ' ἔστρωτο ῥινὸν βοός Κ 155. Cf. Ω 645 := δ 298 = η 337, ν 73, υ 2.—Sim. of spreading something to sit upon: δέρμα αἰγός ξ 50.—(**3**) To prepare (a bed) by spreading the bed-clothes, make (it) up: λέχος Ι 621, 659, 660. Cf. Ω 648: δ 301, η 340 = ψ 291, ψ 171, 177.—Absol., to make one's bed: χαμάδις στορέσας τ 599.

†στρατόομαι [στρατός]. 3 pl. impf. ἐστρατόωντο. (ἀμφι-.) To be on a campaign, be in the field: παρ' ὄχθας Σαγγαρίοιο Γ 187. Cf. Δ 378.

στρατός, -οῦ, ὁ. Ablative στρατόφι Κ 347. An army or host, encamped, on the move, or in the field: νοῦσον ἀνὰ στρατὸν ὦρσεν Α 10, ἄλιον στρατὸν ἤγαγεν ἐνθάδ' Ἀχαιῶν Δ 179, ἐπὶ δεξιόφιν παντὸς στρατοῦ Ν 308. Cf. Α 53, Β 207, Ε 495, Ι 78, Λ 730, Ν 38, Π 73, Τ 352, Ω 112, etc.: β 30, 42, λ 559, υ 89, ω 81.—Including the hosts on both sides of a conflict: ἐς στρατὸν ἐλθὲ μετὰ Τρῶας καὶ Ἀχαιούς Δ 70.—A number or host (of men): ὀλλύντ' Ἀργείων πουλὺν στρατόν Θ 472.

στρεπτός, -ή, -όν [στρεπ-, στρέφω]. (**1**) Turning easily: στρεπτὴ γλῶσσ' ἐστὶ βροτῶν (capable of uttering all kinds of speech, voluble, glib) Υ 248.—(**2**) Yielding to movement, pliant. Epithet of the χιτών E 113, Φ 31.—(3) Yielding to influence, open to entreaty or reason: στρεπταὶ φρένες ἐσθλῶν O 203. Cf. I 497.

στρεύγομαι. To be subjected to continual pressure or adverse influence, be pressed or squeezed to exhaustion: δηθὰ στρεύγεσθαι ἐν δηϊοτῆτι O 512.—Of a slow death by starvation μ 351.

στρεφεδῑνέω [στρέφω + δινέω]. To cause to whirl round; in pass., of the eyes, to go wheeling round (in dizziness): στρεφεδίνηθεν ὄσσε Π 792.

στρέφω. 3 pl. pa. iterative στρέψασκον Σ 546. 3 sing. aor. στρέψε ο 205. 3 pl. στρέψαν δ 520. Pple. στρέψας, -αντος Σ 544, Υ 488: κ 528. Infin. στρέψαι Θ 168, N 396. Fut. infin. mid. στρέψεσθαι Z 516. Aor. pple. pass. στρεφθείς, -έντος E 40, 575, M 428, O 645, Π 308, 598: ι 435, π 352. Fem. στρεφθεῖσα Σ 139. (ἀνα-, ἀπο-, ἐκ-, ἐν-, ἐπι-, μετα-, περι-, ὑπο-.) (1) To turn, bend, deflect: εἰς Ἔρεβος στρέψας [ὄϊας] (*i.e.* bending their necks downwards) κ 528.—(2) To turn or guide (one's horses) in a specified direction: ἵππους ἐπὶ νῆα ο 205.—(3) To wheel (one's horses) round: ἵππους στρέψαι (so as to face the foe) Θ 168. Cf. N 396 and Υ 488 (in flight).—Absol., to wheel one's team round: ὁπότε στρέψαντες ἱκοίατο τέλσον ἀρούρης Σ 544. Cf. Σ 546.—Absol., to guide one's horses round something: αἰεὶ τέρμ' ὁρόων στρέφει ἐγγύθεν Ψ 323.—To wheel or turn (one's horses) so as to keep them in a desired relative position: ὅς οἱ σχεδὸν ἔστρεφε ἵππους P 699.—Absol.: ὑπὸ δ' ἔστρεφον ἡνιοχῆες E 505.—(4) To cause (a wind) to veer: ὅτ' ἂψ θεοὶ οὖρον στρέψαν δ 520.—(5) In mid. and pass. (a) To turn oneself about, turn round: πρώτῳ στρεφθέντι μεταφρένῳ ἐν δόρυ πῆξεν (*i.e.* turning his horses to flight) E 40, εὖτ' ἔμελλε στρέψεσθ' ἐκ χώρης ὅθι . . . Z 516. Cf. E 575, M 428, O 645, Π 308, 598, Σ 139: π 352.—To turn one's body so that it lies face upwards: ἀώτου στρεφθεὶς ἐχόμην ι 435.—(b) To turn oneself hither and thither: ὡς ὅτ' ἂν κάπριος στρέφεται M 42. Cf. M 47.—To turn one's recumbent body (this way and that), lie tossing: ἐστρέφετ' ἔνθα καὶ ἔνθα Ω 5.—(c) Of a heavenly body, to revolve: Ἄρκτον, ἥ τ' αὐτοῦ στρέφεται Σ 488 := ε 274.

στρόμβος, -ου, ὁ. Explained as 'a whipping-top': στρόμβον ὣς ἔσσευε βαλών Ξ 413.

στρουθός, -οῦ, ὁ, ἡ. A sparrow B 311, 317, 326.

στροφάλιγξ, -ιγγος, ἡ [στρέφω]. A whirl or whirling cloud (of dust): ἐν (μετὰ) στροφάλιγγι κονίης Π 775, Φ 503: ω 39.

στροφαλίζω [στρέφω]. To twist (yarn) into threads, spin (it): ἠλάκατα σ 315.

στρόφος, ὁ [στρέφω]. A rope or cord: ἐν στρόφος ἦεν ἀορτήρ (serving as a shoulder-strap) ν 438 = ρ 198 = σ 109.

στρωφάω [στρέφω]. (ἀμφιπερι-, ἀνα-, ἐπι-.) (1) To twist (yarn) into threads, spin (it): ἠλάκατα στρωφῶσα ζ 53, 306, ρ 97. Cf. η 105.—(2) In mid., to turn oneself hither and thither, go about, move about: πατρὸς κατὰ μέγαρα στρωφᾶσθαι I 463. Cf. N 557, Υ 422.

στυγερός, -ή, -όν [στυγέω]. (1) To be shuddered at, causing dread, loathing, aversion or distaste, dreadful, loathsome, hateful, distasteful: ἐμέ Γ 404, στυγερὸς οἱ ἔπλετο (she sickened at the sight of him) Ξ 158. Cf. Ψ 48: γάμον α 249 = π 126, πάντες στυγεροὶ θάνατοι βροτοῖσι [γίγνονται] μ 341. Cf. γ 288, 310, λ 81 = 465, λ 326, μ 278, ξ 235, σ 272, χ 470, ω 126, 200, 414.—(2) As a general (and more or less conventional) epithet of discommendation, hated, dreaded, dread, direful, baleful, chilling or the like: Ἄρηϊ B 385, Σ 209, νοῦσον N 670. Cf. Δ 240, E 47, Z 330, Θ 368, I 454, N 672 = Π 607, T 230, 336, X 483, Ψ 79: ἐρινῦς β 135, γαστέρι η 216, κλαυθμοῦ ρ 8. Cf. ε 396, λ 201, ο 408, υ 78, 81.

στυγερῶς [adv. fr. prec.]. In dire wise, so as to entail bitter consequences, so as to make a person rue his presumption or his falling short in something: σ. κε πολέμου ἀπερωήσειας Π 723: σ. κέ τινα πέμψαιμι νέεσθαι φ 374. Cf. ψ 23.

στυγέω. Aor. opt. στύξαιμι λ 502. 3 pl. aor. ἔστυγον κ 113. (κατα-.) (1) To regard with dread and loathing, shrink from the sight of: οἰκία ['Αϊδωνῆος], τά τε στυγέουσι θεοί περ Υ 65.—To be aghast at, sicken at the sight of: κατὰ δ' ἔστυγον αὐτήν κ 113.—To regard with aversion, shrink from contact with: λαῖφος, ὅ κε στυγέῃσιν ἰδὼν ἄνθρωπος ἔχοντα ν 400.—To regard with disfavour, treat slightingly: ἐμέ Θ 370.—(2) To fear, dread, go in fear of: τόν τε στυγέουσι καὶ ἄλλοι H 112, O 167, 183.—(3) To shrink from doing something, hesitate *to do it*. With infin.: ἶσον ἐμοὶ φάσθαι A 186. Cf. Θ 515.—(4) In sigmatic aor., to make bitter or heavy: στύξαιμί κέ τεῳ μένος λ 502.

στυφελίζω. 3 sing. aor. (ἐ)στυφέλιξε E 437, H 261, M 405, Φ 512, X 496: ρ 234. 3 pl. ἐστυφέλιξαν Π 774. 3 sing. subj. στυφελίξῃ Λ 305. Infin. στυφελίξαι A 581. (ἀπο-.) (1) To strike, smite: ἀσπίδα οἱ E 437. Cf. Λ 305, Π 774, Φ 512.—Absol., to bandy blows with another, measure one's strength against him: οὐκ ἔοικε θεὸν βροτῶν ἕνεκα στυφελίζειν Φ 380.—(2) To strike or smite so as to check the course of: στυφέλιξέ μιν μεμαῶτα H 261 = M 405.—(3) To drive away or from a specified position with blows, etc.: ἐξ ἑδέων A 581. Cf. X 496: ρ 234.—(4) To strike wantonly, treat roughly, misuse, maltreat: ξείνους στυφελιζομένους π 108 = υ 318. Cf. σ 416 = υ 324.

σύ. Nom. σύ A 76, 83, 86, 127, etc.: α 220, 301, β 183, 201, etc. Genit. σεῖο Γ 137, 365, E 411, I 60, etc.: δ 191, ε 216, ζ 156, λ 482, etc. σέο B 201, Δ 174, Z 328, etc.: β 180, λ 369, τ 363. σεό (encl.) A 396, Γ 446. σεῦ B 27, Γ 206, Z 409, etc.: ι 278, ο 19, etc. σευ (encl.) E 811, Θ 482, Ξ 95, etc.: ι 405, ν 231, τ 108, etc. σέθεν A 180, Δ 169, Z 524, H 231, etc.: γ 213, δ 160, ε 177, ξ 56, etc. Dat. σοί A 89, 158, 163, 178, etc.: α 59, 279, 305, 318, β 87, etc. σοι (encl.) A 170 (with elision): γ 359, λ 381. Acc. σέ K 43, Λ 772, Υ 187, Ω 288, etc.: α 223, 269, 386, β 275, etc. σε (encl.) A 26, 173, 280, 362, etc.: α 124, 171, 173, 225, etc. Pron. of the 2nd person sing., thou, you A 26, 89, 180,

H 111, 114, I 437, etc.: α 59, 124, β 251, ζ 27, λ 556, π 31, etc.—Strengthened by γε: σύ γε E 350, 812, etc.: θ 180, κ 486, etc.—σοί γε A 557, I 252, etc.: β 126, ζ 154, etc.—σέ γε K 96, Υ 187, etc.: α 223, β 275, etc.

συβόσῑον, -ου, τό [σῦς + βόσκω]. A herd of swine: τόσσα συῶν συβόσια Λ 679 := ξ 101.

συβώτης, ὁ [σῦς + βόσκω]. A swineherd. Of Eumaeus δ 640, ν 404, ξ 7, ο 351, π 12, ρ 5, etc.

†**συγκαλέω** [συγ-, συν- (3)]. Aor. pple. συγκαλέσας. To call together, convoke: τοὺς συγκαλέσας B 55 = K 302.

συγκλονέω [συγ-, συν- (4)]. To throw into confusion or disorder: συνεκλόνεον ὀϊστοί N 722.

†**συγκύρω** [συγ-, συν- (2)]. 3 pl. aor. opt. συγκύρσειαν. To come together, collide: μὴ συγκύρσειαν ἵπποι Ψ 435.

συγχέω [συγ-, συν- (3). 'To pour together,' 'to confound' (cf. χέω (9))]. 2 sing. aor. σύγχεας O 366. 3 συνέχευε O 364, 473. Infin. συγχεῦαι θ 139. 3 sing. aor. pass. σύγχυτο Π 471. **(1)** To bring into a state of entanglement, put into a tangle: ἡνία σφι σύγχυτο Π 471.—**(2)** To destroy, bring to nothing: [ἀθύρματα] O 364. Cf. O 366. —To make of no effect: βιὸν καὶ ἰούς O 473.—**(3)** To shatter the physical powers of, unstring: ἄνδρα θ 139.—**(4)** To work upon, confound, trouble, upset (the feelings or spirit): μή μοι σύγχει θυμόν I 612. Cf. N 808.

σῡκέη, -ης, ἡ [σῦκον]. A fig-tree: συκέαι καὶ ἐλαῖαι η 116 = λ 590. Cf. ω 246, 341.

σῦκον, -ου, τό. A fig η 121.

σῡλάω. 3 dual non-thematic impf. συλήτην N 202. **(1)** To take off, remove: πῶμα φαρέτρης Δ 116.—**(2)** To strip off (the armour and trappings of a fallen foe): τεύχεα Δ 466, E 164, 618, Z 28, H 78, 82, Λ 110, N 202, O 524, 545, 583, X 368, ἔντεα N 641.—**(3)** To lay bare, take out of its cover: τόξον Δ 105.—**(4)** To strip or despoil (a fallen foe): νεκύων τινά K 343 = 387.—**(5)** With double acc. of the armour, etc., and the person despoiled: ἔναρα νεκροὺς συλήσετε Z 71. Cf. O 428 = Π 500, P 60, X 258.

σῡλεύω [cf. prec.]. **(1)** = prec. (4) E 48.—**(2)** To rob (a person) of his due, wrong (him): τὸν αἰδέομαι συλεύειν Ω 436.

†**συλλέγω** [συλ-, συν- (3) + λέγω²]. Aor. pple. συλλέξας Σ 301. Fut. mid. συλλέξομαι β 292. 3 sing. aor. συλλέξατο Σ 413. To collect, get together, put away (in a receptacle). In mid.: ὅπλα λάρνακ' ἐς Σ 413.—To collect, bring or gather together from various quarters: [κτήματα] Σ 301. —To collect, cause to assemble, bring together into a body. In mid.: ἑταίρους β 292.

συμβάλλω, ξυμβάλλω [συμ-, συν- (2)]. 3 pl. aor. σύμβαλον Π 565, Υ 55. Imp. pl. συμβάλετε Γ 70. **Mid.** 2 sing. fut. συμβλήσεαι Υ 335. 3 sing. aor. ξύμβλητο Ξ 39, 231: ζ 54. 3 dual ξυμβλήτην φ 15. 3 pl. ξύμβληντο Ξ 27, Ω 709: κ 105. 3 sing. subj. ξύμβληται η 204. Pple. ξυμβλήμενος λ 127, ο 441, ψ 274, ω 260. Infin. ξυμβλήμεναι Φ 578. **(1)** Of waters, to unite (their streams): ὡς ὅτε χείμαρροι ποταμοὶ συμβάλλετον ὕδωρ Δ 453. Cf. E 774.—**(2)** To set together (in fight), match or pit one against another: ἐμὲ καὶ Μενέλαον συμβάλετε μάχεσθαι Γ 70. Cf. Υ 55.—*Intrans. for reflexive,* to join (in fight), join battle: σύμβαλον ἀμφὶ νέκυι μάχεσθαι Π 565.—**(3)** In mid. **(a)** To meet or encounter another: πρίν γ' ἠὲ ξυμβλήμεναι ἠὲ δαμῆναι (get to close quarters with his foes) Φ 578. Cf. Ξ 39: εἴ τις ξύμβληται ὁδίτης η 204. Cf. ο 441.—**(b)** To fall in *with*, meet, encounter. With dat.: Νέστορι ξύμβληντο βασιλῆες Ξ 27. Cf. Ξ 231, Υ 335, Ω 709: ζ 54, κ 105, λ 127, φ 15, ψ 274, ω 260.

†**συμμάρπτω** [συμ-, συν- (3)]. Aor. pple. συμμάρψας. To grasp and bring together or make a bundle of: δόνακας μυρίκης τ' ὄζους K 467.

†**συμμητιάω** [συμ-, συν- (1)]. Pres. infin. mid. συμμητιάασθαι. To join in taking counsel or concerting measures. In mid.: κάλεον συμμητιάασθαι K 197.

συμμίσγω [συμ-, συν- (2)]. In pass., to be mingled *with*, mingle *with*. With dat.: οὐδὲ Τιταρησσὸς Πηνειῷ συμμίσγεται B 753.

σύμπᾱς, ξύμπᾱς, -αντος [συμ-, συν- (4) + πᾶς]. Strengthened form of, but hardly to be distinguished from, πᾶς. In pl. **(a)** All the: συμπάντων Δαναῶν A 90. Cf. A 241, X 380: ὅσσα ξύμπαντα μόγησα (from first to last) η 214 = ξ 198. Cf. γ 59, 217.—**(b)** Absol., the whole number of indicated persons: συμπάντων ἡγεῖτο Διομήδης B 567.

†**συμπήγνῡμι** [συμ-, συν- (3)]. 3 sing. aor. συνέπηξε. To curdle (milk): γάλα E 902.

συμπλαταγέω [συμ-, συν- (2) + πλαταγέω, to make a sharp sound]. To make a sharp sound (with the palms of the hands): χερσὶ συμπλατάγησεν (clapped his hands) Ψ 102.

συμφερτός, -ή, -όν [συμφέρω]. Brought together, united: συμφερτὴ ἀρετὴ πέλει N 237 (see under ἀρετή (1)).

συμφέρω [συμ-, συν- (2)]. 1 pl. fut. mid. συνοισόμεθα Θ 400. In mid., to come together (in fight): συμφερόμεσθα μάχῃ (joined battle) Λ 736. —Sim.: οὐ καλὰ συνοισόμεθα πτόλεμόνδε Θ 400.

συμφράδμων, -ονος, ὁ [συμφράζω]. A counsellor: τοιοῦτοι δέκα μοι συμφράδμονες εἶεν B 372.

†**συμφράζω** [συμ-, συν- (1)]. Fut. mid. συμφράσσομαι I 374. 3 sing. aor. συμφράσσατο A 537, 540: δ 462, ο 202. In mid. **(1)** To join *with* in counsel or in concerting measures, devise, concert or contrive *in common with.* With dat.: ὅτι οἱ συμφράσσατο βουλὰς Θέτις (cognate acc., that they had been taking counsel together) A 537. Cf. A 540, I 374: δ 462.—**(2)** To take counsel with oneself, consider, ponder: ὅππως . . . ο 202.

σύν. Also ξύν Z 372, O 26, Π 248, 864: α 182, γ 105, 302, κ 268, ο 410. **(I)** Adv. **(1)** With another or others, in company: σὺν δ' ὁ θρασὺς εἵπετ' Ὀδυσσεύς κ 436. Cf. K 224: ω 387.—With another, lending aid: σὺν δ' ἕταροι ἤειραν Ω 590. —**(2)** Together, denoting joining, union, contact, proximity: σύν ῥ' ἔβαλον ῥινούς, σὺν δ' ἔγχεα Δ 447 = Θ 61, σὺν δ' ἤειρεν [ἵππους] K 499. Cf.

Η 256, Μ 181, 377, Φ 387, 453, Ψ 687, 879, Ω 420 : κενεὰς σὺν χεῖρας ἔχοντες κ 42, σὺν πόδας χεῖράς τε δέον χ 189. Cf. ε 295, λ 426, σ 98.—(3) Together, in a body or mass, in confusion: ἐπεὶ σύν γ' ὅρκι' ἔχευαν Δ 269, σὺν δὲ γέροντι νόος χύτο Ω 358: σὺν δύω μάρψας ι 289, 311, 344.—(4) Altogether, utterly, completely: ὄφρα μὴ σὺν δαῖτα ταράξῃ Α 579. Cf. Θ 86, Μ 384, Ψ 467, 673, Ω 467: σὺν δ' ὀστέ' ἄραξεν μ 412. Cf. ε 426, ι 498.—(II) Prep. with dat. (1) With, along with, together with, in company with, accompanied by: ἀριστήεσσιν Α 227, κολεῷ Η 304. Cf. Α 307, 325, Ζ 418, Ι 346, 615, Κ 19, Ρ 57, etc.: γρηῒ σὺν ἀμφιπόλῳ α 191. Cf. α 362, β 183, γ 32, η 304, ι 199, ν 118, ο 410, etc.—In reference to something added or adjected: σὺν ὅρκῳ ξ 151.—(2) With, having, taking or bringing with one: νηυσίν Α 170, σκήπτρῳ Β 47, ἀγγελίῃ 787. Cf. Α 183, Β 450, Γ 29, Ε 220, 297, Ζ 270, Ι 194, Λ 251, Ο 744, etc.: δίφρῳ γ 369, πλειοτέρῃ σὺν χειρί λ 359. Cf. α 182, γ 105, δ 175, μ 408, ν 258, ω 193, etc.—With instrumental in 'comitative' use: σὺν ὄχεσφιν Δ 297, Ε 219, Μ 119, Π 811, Χ 22, Ψ 518, etc.—(3) With, by means of: σὺν μεγάλῳ ἀπέτεισαν, σὺν σφῇσιν κεφαλῇσιν Δ 161. Cf. Θ 530, Π 156, etc.: σὺν δὲ νεφέεσσι κάλυψε γαῖαν ε 293, ι 68 = μ 314.—(4) With the aid of, by the help of: Ἀθήνῃ Γ 439. Cf. Ε 474, Ζ 314, Λ 792, Ο 26, etc.: θ 493, ι 454, λ 410, ν 391, etc. —Under the auspices of: σὺν θεῷ εἰλήλουθμεν Ι 49.

συναγείρω, ξυναγείρω [συν- (3)]. Aor. ξυνάγειρα Υ 21. 3 sing. aor. mid. ξυναγείρατο ξ 323, τ 293. Nom. pl. masc. aor. pple. συναγρόμενοι Λ 687. (1) To gather together, cause to assemble, summon: ὧν ἕνεκα ξυνάγειρα [ὑμέας] Υ 21.—(2) In mid., to come or gather together, assemble: συναγρόμενοι δαίτρευον Λ 687. Cf. Ω 802.—(3) In reference to things, to get together, collect: πολὺν βίοτον δ 90. — In mid.: κτήμαθ' ὅσα ξυναγείρατο ξ 323 = τ 293.

†**συνάγνῡμι, ξυνάγνῡμι** [συν- (4)]. 3 sing. aor. συνέαξε Λ 114. ξυνέαξε Ν 166. 3 pl. ξυνέαξαν ξ 383. To break in pieces, shiver: χῶσατ' ἔγχεος ὃ ξυνέαξεν Ν 166.—To damage severely or shatter (a ship) ξ 383.—To tear in pieces, rend: ὡς λέων ἐλάφοιο τέκνα συνέαξεν Λ 114.

συνάγω, ξυνάγω [συν- (3)]. (1) To drive or lead (beasts) in a body Γ 269.—(2) To gather or bring together, cause to assemble: γεραιάς Ζ 87. —In reference to inanimate objects: νεφέλας ε 291.—(3) To join or join in (battle or strife): ἵνα ξυνάγωμεν Ἄρηα Β 381 = Τ 275. Cf. Ε 861 = Ξ 149, Ξ 448 = Π 764.

†**συναείρω** [συν- (2). See ἀείρω (I) (5)]. 3 sing. aor. subj. mid. συναείρεται. To harness (horses) together. In mid.: ὅς τ' ἐπεὶ πίσυρας συναείρεται ἵππους Ο 680.

συναίνυμαι [συν- (3)]. To gather up, collect, pick up: τόξα Φ 502.

†**συναιρέω** [συν- (3)]. 3 sing. aor. σύνελε Π 740. Pple. συνελών υ 95. (1) To put together, make into a bundle: χλαῖναν καὶ κώεα υ 95.—(2) To take together, crush into one; hence, to crush, smash: ὀφρῦς Π 740.

†**συναντάω** [συν- (2)]. 3 dual non-thematic impf. συναντήτην π 333. 3 pl. aor. subj. mid. συναντήσωνται Ρ 134. (1) To meet together, meet, encounter: τὼ συναντήτην π 333.—(2) To meet with, fall in with, encounter. With dat. In mid.: ᾧ νήπι' ἄγοντι συναντήσωνται ἄνδρες ἐπακτῆρες Ρ 134.

†**συνάντομαι** [συν- (2)]. 3 sing. aor. συνήντετο Φ 34: δ 367, φ 31. 3 dual συναντέσθην Η 22. Pple. συναντόμενος ο 538, ρ 165, τ 311. (1) To meet or fall in with another, encounter him: ὥς ἄν τίς σε συναντόμενος μακαρίζοι ο 538 = ρ 165 = τ 311.—(2) To meet with, fall in with, encounter. With dat.: υἷι Πριάμοιο συνήντετο Φ 34. Cf. Η 22: δ 367, φ 31.

συνδέω, ξυνδέω [συν- (2)]. (1) To tie or secure together: συνέδησα πόδας πελώρου κ 168.—(2) To tie up, bandage: χεῖρα ξυνέδησεν Ν 599.—(3) To bind or secure (a person), put (him) in bonds: ὁππότε μιν ξυνδῆσαι ἤθελον Α 399.

συνέαξε, 3 sing. aor. συνάγνυμι.

συνέδραμον, 3 pl. aor. συντρέχω.

συνεείκοσι, *indeclinable* [συν- (3)]. In form ξυνεείκοσι. Twenty together, twenty ξ 98.

†**σύνειμι**[1] [συν- (1) + εἰμί]. In form ξύνειμι. Fut. infin. ξυνέσεσθαι. To be or dwell *with*, to be linked or joined *with*. With dat.: ὀϊζυῖ η 270.

†**σύνειμι**[2], **ξύνειμι** [συν- (2) + εἶμι]. Pple. ξυνιών, -όντος Δ 446, Θ 60, Υ 66, Φ 390. 3 dual impf. συνίτην Ζ 120, Π 476, Υ 159, Ψ 814. 3 pl. ξύνισαν Ξ 393. In dual and pl., to come together as foes, advance upon one another: ἐς μέσον συνίτην μεμαῶτε μάχεσθαι Ζ 120 = Υ 159, Ψ 814. Cf. Δ 446 = Θ 60, Ξ 393, Π 476, Υ 66, Φ 390.

†**συνελαύνω, ξυνελαύνω** [συν- (2) (3)]. 2 sing. pres. ξυνελαύνεις Φ 394. Infin. ξυνελαυνέμεν Χ 129. 1 pl. aor. συνελάσσαμεν Λ 677. 1 pl. subj. ξυνελάσσομεν σ 39. Infin. ξυνελάσσαι Υ 134. (1) To drive together, drive in: ληΐδα ἐκ πεδίου Λ 677.—(2) To set together (in fight), match or pit one against another: θεοὺς ἔριδι ξυνελάσσαι Υ 134. Cf. Φ 394: σ 39.—*Intrans. for reflexive,* to join (in fight), join battle: ἔριδι ξυνελαυνέμεν Χ 129.

σύνελε, 3 sing. aor. συναιρέω.

συνεοχμός, -οῦ, ὁ [app. fr. συνέχω]. A joining or joint: κεφαλῆς τε καὶ αὐχένος ἐν συνεοχμῷ Ξ 465.

συνέπηξε, 3 sing. aor. συμπήγνυμι.

συνέργω [συν- (2) + ἔργω[1]]. 3 pl. aor. συνεέργαθον Ξ 36. (1) To secure or bind together: ὄϊας ι 427, τρόπιν ἠδὲ καὶ ἱστόν μ 424.—(2) To gird up (a garment): ζωστῆρι συνέεργε χιτῶνα ξ 72.—(3) To enclose, shut in, bound: ὅσον συνεέργαθον ἄκραι Ξ 36.

συνέρῑθος, ἡ [συν- (1) + ἔριθος]. A fellow-labourer, a companion in work ζ 32.

συνέρρηκται, 3 sing. pf. pass. συρρήγνυμι.

σύνεσις, ἡ [συνίημι]. In form ξύνεσις. A

confluence or joining (of waters) (cf. ἵημι[1] (6)) κ 515.

συνεσταότος, genit. sing. masc. pf. pple. συνίστημι.

συνέχευε, 3 sing. aor. συγχέω.

σῡνεχής [συν(σ)έχω]. In neut. sing. σῡνεχές as adv., continuously, without remission or break: ὗε Ζεὺς συνεχές Μ 26. Cf. ι 74.

συνέχω, ξυνέχω [συν- (2)]. Nom. dual masc. pf. pple. συνοχωκότε Β 218. *Intrans.*, to hold or join together, join, meet: τώ οἱ ὤμω ἐπὶ στῆθος συνοχωκότε (stooping together) Β 218, ὅθι ζωστῆρος ὀχῆες σύνεχον Δ 133 = Υ 415. Cf. Υ 478.

συνημοσύνη, -ης, ἡ [συνίημι]. A covenant, agreement or compact Χ 261.

συνήορος, ὁ [συναείρω. Cf. παρήορος, τετράοροι]. Something linked or associated with something else, an accompaniment: φόρμιγγος, ἣ δαιτὶ συνήορός ἐστιν θ 99.

σύνθεο, aor. imp. mid. συντίθημι.

συνθεσίη, -ης, ἡ [συντίθημι]. A covenant, agreement or compact Β 339, Ε 319.

σύνθετο, 3 sing. aor. mid. συντίθημι.

†**συνθέω** [συν- (3)]. 3 sing. fut. in mid. form συνθεύσεται. To run keeping together or all in a piece; hence, to go smoothly, succeed: οὐχ ἡμῖν συνθεύσεται ἥδε γε βουλή υ 245.

†**συνίημι, ξυνίημι** [συν- (2) + ἵημι[1]]. 3 pl. impf. ξύνιεν Α 273. 3 sing. aor. ξυνέηκε Α 8, Β 182, Η 210, Κ 512, Ο 442: σ 34. Aor. imp. ξύνες Β 26, 63, Ω 133. From ξυνιέω imp. ξυνίει α 271, ζ 289, θ 241, ο 391, τ 378. **Mid.** 3 sing. aor. ξύνετο δ 76. 1 pl. subj. συνώμεθα Ν 381. (**1**) To set together (in fight), match or pit one against another: τίς σφωε θεῶν ἔριδι ξυνέηκε μάχεσθαι; Α 8. Cf. Η 210.—(**2**) In mid., to come together in agreement, come to terms: ὄφρα συνώμεθα ἀμφὶ γάμῳ Ν 381.—(**3**) To catch, mark, hear (a sound): θεᾶς ὄπα Β 182 = Κ 512.—To hear the voice of, hear (a person). With genit.: τοῖϊν ξυνέηκεν σ 34.—So in mid.: τοῦ ἀγορεύοντος ξύνετο δ 76.—(**4**) To hearken to, give ear to, mark, heed: ἐμέθεν ξυνίει ἔπος ζ 289, θ 241. Cf. τ 378.—With genit.: βουλέων μευ ξύνιεν Α 273.—To hearken to (a person), attend to (him), mark his words. With genit.: ἐμέθεν ξύνες ὦκα Β 26 = 63, Ω 133.—Absol.: ξυνέηκε, θέων δέ οἱ ἄγχι παρέστη Ο 442. Cf. α 271, ο 391.

†**συνίστημι** [συν- (2)]. Genit. sing. masc. pf. pple. συνεσταότος. In pf., to be in the state of having been brought together; hence, of battle, to be joined: πολέμοιο συνεσταότος Ξ 96.

συνίτην, 3 dual impf. σύνειμι[2].

συνοισόμεθα, 1 pl. fut. mid. συμφέρω.

συνορίνω [συν- (3)]. To put into common motion, launch in a body: συνορινόμενοι κίνυντο φάλαγγες Δ 332.

συνοχή, -ῆς, ἡ [συνέχω]. In form ξυνοχή. A joining. In pl.: ἐν ξυνοχῇσιν ὁδοῦ Ψ 330 (app., at the point where the outward and home tracks of the race-course met at the turn).

συνοχωκότε, nom. dual masc. pf. pple. συνέχω.

†**συντίθημι** [συν- (3)]. 3 sing. aor. mid. σύνθετο Η 44: α 328, υ 92. Imp. σύνθεο Α 76, Ζ 334: ο 27, 318, π 259, ρ 153, σ 129, τ 268, ω 265. Pl. σύνθεσθε Τ 84. In mid., to put together in one's mind; hence (**1**) To mark, hear: τῆς ὄπα σύνθετο υ 92. Cf. Η 44: α 328.—(**2**) To hearken to, give ear to, mark, heed: ἐμεῖο σύνθεο μῦθον ρ 153, τ 268.—To hearken to a person, attend to him, mark his words: σὺ δὲ σύνθεο Α 76, Ζ 334: ο 27, 318 = ω 265, π 259, σ 129. Cf. Τ 84.

σύντρεις [συν- (3)]. Three together, three at a time: σύντρεις αἰνύμενος [ὄϊας] ι 429.

†**συντρέχω** [συν- (2)]. 3 pl. aor. συνέδραμον. To rush together in order to encounter each other Π 335, 337.

συνώμεθα, 1 pl. aor. subj. mid. συνίημι.

σῦριγξ, -ιγγος, ἡ. (**1**) A pipe, a musical wind-instrument consisting of a tube of reed or other material: τερπόμενοι σύριγξιν Σ 526. Cf. Κ 13 (see αὐλός (1)).—(**2**) App., a socket in which to set a spear: ἐκ σύριγγος ἐσπάσατ' ἔγχος Τ 387.

†**συρρήγνῡμι** [συρ-, συν- (4)]. 3 sing. pf. pass. συνέρρηκται. To shatter the strength of: κακοῖσι συνέρρηκται (is broken down by . . .) θ 137.

σῦς, συός, ὁ, ἡ [cf. L. *sus*, Eng. *sow*, *swine*]. Also **ὗς,** ὑός. Acc. σῦν Ι 539, Π 823: ξ 27, π 454. ὗν ξ 419. Dat. pl. σύεσσι Μ 146: ν 407, ξ 25, π 3. ὕεσσι ν 410, ξ 8, 372, ο 397, φ 363. συσί Ε 783, Η 257: ξ 14. Acc. pl. σύας ξ 41, 81, ρ 181, 593, σ 105, υ 251. ὗας θ 60, π 341, ρ 604. σῦς κ 338, 433, ξ 107. (**1**) A wild boar Δ 253, Ι 548, Κ 264, Ν 471, Π 823: δ 457, σ 29, τ 393 = ψ 74, τ 439, 449, 465, φ 219, ω 332.—Qualified by ἄγριος: συὸς ἀγρίου Θ 338. Cf. Ι 539.—By ἀγρότερος: ἀγροτέροισι σύεσσιν ἐοικότε Μ 146. Cf. Λ 293: λ 611.—Joined with κάπρος: συσὶ κάπροισιν Ε 783 = Η 257. Cf. Ρ 21.—With κάπριος: συῒ καπρίῳ Λ 293, Ρ 281.—(**2**) The domestic swine or pig Ι 467, Λ 679, Ψ 32: θ 60, κ 239, λ 413, ν 407, ξ 8, ο 397, etc.—Joined with σίαλος: συὸς σιάλοιο ῥάχιν Ι 208. Cf. ξ 41, 81, ρ 181 = υ 251.

σύτο, 3 sing. aor. mid. σεύω.

συφειός, -οῦ, ὁ [σῦς. Cf. συφεός]. A pigsty: θύρας ἀνέῳξε συφειοῦ κ 389.

συφεόνδε [acc. of next + -δε (1)]. To the sty: ἔρχεο νῦν συφεόνδε κ 320.

συφεός, -οῦ, ὁ [σῦς. Cf. συφειός]. = συφειός κ 238, ξ 13, 73.

συφορβός, -οῦ, ὁ [σῦς + φέρβω, to feed]. Also **ὑφορβός.** A swineherd: ὡς παῖδα συφορβόν Φ 282. Cf. ξ 410, 504.—Of Eumaeus. In form συφορβός π 154, ρ 348, φ 189, etc.—In form ὑφορβός ξ 3, ο 301, π 20, etc.

σφάζω. 3 sing. aor. σφάξε Ω 622: γ 454. 3 pl. ἔσφαξαν Α 459, Β 422: μ 359. σφάξαν ξ 426. Nom. pl. neut. pf. pple. pass. ἐσφαγμένα κ 532, λ 45. To cut the throat of (a beast), slaughter (it) by cutting the throat Ι 467, Ψ 31, Ω 622: α 92 = δ 320, γ 454, ι 46, κ 532, λ 45, ξ 426, υ 312, ψ 305.—Absol. Α 459 = Β 422: μ 359.

σφαῖρα, -ης, ἡ. A ball: σφαίρῃ παῖζον ζ 100. Cf. ζ 115, θ 372, 377.

σφαιρηδόν [σφαῖρα]. Like a ball N 204.

†σφάλλω. 3 sing. aor. σφῆλε ρ 464. Infin. σφῆλαι Ψ 719. (ἀπο-, παρα-.) To cause to reel or fall: σφῆλαι οὔδει τε πελάσσαι Ψ 719. Cf. ρ 464.

†σφαραγέομαι. 3 pl. impf. σφαραγεῦντο. (**1**) To crackle (under the action of heat): σφαραγεῦντο πυρὶ ῥίζαι [γλήνης] ι 390.—(**2**) To be ready to burst, be full to bursting: οὔθατα σφαραγεῦντο ι 440.

σφέας. Acc. σφέας B 366, M 43, etc.: η 40, θ 480, etc. σφεάς (encl.) B 96, Δ 284, E 151, Λ 128, etc.: δ 77, ζ 6, θ 315, ν 213, etc. σφας (encl.) E 567. σφε (encl.) Λ 111, T 265: θ 271, φ 192, etc. Genit. σφείων Δ 535, N 148, etc. σφέων υ 348, ω 381. σφεών (encl.) Σ 311: γ 134. σφῶν M 155, T 302. Dat. σφίσι A 368, I 99, K 208, Λ 413, M 148, etc.: δ 683, κ 415, ξ 272, etc. σφισί (encl.) B 93, Δ 2, Θ 204, I 425, K 186, etc.: β 398, γ 150, ζ 155, η 35, θ 371, etc. σφι (encl.) A 73, 110, B 251, 614, 670, etc.: α 142, 339, β 169, 173, 284, etc. (**1**) In the encl. (and sometimes in the accented) forms anaphoric pron. of the 3rd person pl. masc. and fem., them: ἐννέα δέ σφεας κήρυκες ἐρήτυον B 96, ἵνα σφίσι βουλεύησθα I 99. Cf. A 73, 110, B 93, 704, Δ 2, 331, E 567, Λ 111, M 416, O 594, etc.: α 142, 339, β 398, γ 118, 150, ζ 6, θ 271, 480, ν 276, ξ 300, π 475, ρ 212, etc.—(**2**) In the accented forms commonly reflexive: τὰ δάσσαντο μετὰ σφίσιν A 368, ὦσαν ἀπὸ σφείων Δ 535. Cf. B 366, K 208, Λ 413, M 148, N 688, etc.: κ 415, ξ 272, π 228, etc.—So with αὐτός: σφέας αὐτοὺς ἀρτύναντες M 43, 86, N 152. Cf. M 155, T 302: δ 683, μ 225.—An encl. form thus: κέλονταί μ' ἀγινέμεναί σφισιν αὐτοῖς ἔδμεναι υ 213.

σφεδανός. In neut. σφεδανόν as adv., vehemently, eagerly, impetuously: κελεύων Λ 165, Π 372. Cf. Φ 542.

σφέλας, τό. Acc. pl. σφέλα (for σφέλαα) ρ 231. A foot-stool: σ. ἔλλαβεν σ 394. Cf. ρ 231.

σφενδόνη, -ης, ἡ. A sling N 600.

σφέτερος, -η, -ον [σφέας]. Their Δ 409, I 327, P 287, 322, 330, 419, Σ 210: α 7.—Absol.: ἐπὶ σφέτερα (*sc.* δώματα) (to their own homes) α 274, ξ 91.

†σφηκόω [σφήξ]. 3 pl. plupf. pass. ἐσφήκωντο. To make slender like a wasp's waist: πλοχμοί, οἳ χρυσῷ τε καὶ ἀργύρῳ ἐσφήκωντο P 52 (*i.e.* were pinched in with spirals of gold and silver).

σφῆλε, 3 sing. aor. σφάλλω.

σφήξ, σφηκός, ὁ. A wasp M 167, Π 259.

σφοδρῶς. Putting forth one's powers, with vigour: σ. ἐλάαν μ 124.

σφονδύλιος, -ου, ὁ. One of the vertebrae of the neck: μυελὸς σφονδυλίων ἔκπαλτο Υ 483.

σφός, -ή, -όν [σφέας]. Their A 534, Δ 162, 302, Λ 76, 90, Ξ 202=303, Π 18, Σ 231: α 34, β 237, ξ 262=ρ 431, ω 183, 411.

σφῦρα, ἡ. A hammer γ 434.

σφυρόν, τό. The ankle Δ 147, 518, Z 117, P 290, X 397.

σφωέ, *enclitic.* Acc. σφωέ A 8, K 546, Λ 751, etc.: θ 317. Dat. σφωΐν A 338, Θ 402, Λ 628, etc.: δ 28, λ 319, etc. Pron. of the 3rd person dual, they: τίς τ' ἄρ σφωε θεῶν ἔριδι ξυνέηκε μάχεσθαι; A 8. Cf. A 338, O 155, P 531, etc.: δ 28, θ 317, λ 319, etc.

σφῶϊ. Nom. σφῶϊ Λ 776, M 366, etc.: χ 173. σφώ A 574, Λ 782, etc. Genit. σφῶϊν A 257: π 171. Dat. σφῶϊν Δ 341, Θ 413, N 55, etc.: φ 209, 212. This form as nom. ψ 52. Dat. σφῷν δ 62. Acc. σφῶϊ A 336, Δ 286, E 287, etc. σφώ O 146. Pron. of the 2nd person dual, you: εἰ δὴ σφὼ ἐριδαίνετον ὧδε A 574. Cf. A 257, 336, Δ 341, etc.: δ 62, π 171, ψ 52, etc.

σφωΐτερος [σφῶϊ]. Of you two, your A 216.

σχεδίη, -ης, ἡ. A raft. Of the raft which Odysseus constructed on Calypso's island and on which he passed to Phaeacia ε 33, 163, 174, 177, 251, 314, 315, 324, 338, 343, 357, 363, η 264, 274.

σχέδιος [σχεδόν]. Hand to hand. Adv. of acc. fem. form σχεδίην, from close at hand, at close quarters: τύψον σχεδίην E 830.

σχεδόθεν [σχεδόν + -θεν (1) (2)]. (**1**) From close at hand, at close quarters: βάλεν Π 807.—(**2**) At close quarters, hand to hand: μάχεσθαι P 359.—Near, near to, close to. With genit.: στῆ ῥ' αὐτῶν σ. τ 447.—With dat.: σ. οἱ ἦλθεν 'Αθήνη β 267, ν 221, υ 30. Cf. Π 800: ο 223.

σχεδόν [σχε-, ἔχω]. (**1**) To, within, or at a short distance, near, close by, nigh: ὅτε σ. ἦσαν Γ 15, σ. ἤλασεν ἵππους Λ 488. Cf. Δ 247, K 100, Λ 116, N 268, O 456, Ψ 334 (close to the point indicated), etc.: σ. εἴσιδε γαῖαν ε 392, ι 280, ν 161, π 157, σ 146, ω 491, 493.—(**2**) To, within, or at a short distance from, near, near to, close to. With genit.: σ. ἤλυθον αὐτῶν E 607. Cf. K 308=320, 395, N 402, Υ 363: δ 439, ε 288, 475, ζ 125, ι 117, κ 156=μ 368, λ 142, 166=481, ν 162.—With dat.: ἐπεὶ ἄν τοι σ. ἔλθοι I 304. Cf. P 699, Φ 64, X 131: ι 23.—(**3**) From close at hand, at close quarters: σ. οὔτασεν E 458, 883, P 601. Cf. N 559, 576, Π 828, Υ 290, 378, 462, Φ 179, Ψ 817.—(**4**) App., right over, at a bound: ὑπερθορέειν M 53.—(**5**) Of an occurrence, impending or coming upon, coming or drawing near to. With dat.: θάνατος, ὅς τοι σ. εἶσιν P 202. Cf. β 284, ζ 27.—Sim. in impers. construction: σ. φημι ἔμμεναι, ὁππότε . . . (the time is near at hand when . . .) N 817.—(**6**) In reference to affinity, closely connected, near: καὶ πηῷ περ ἐόντι μάλα σ. κ 441.

σχέθον, aor. ἔχω.

σχεῖν, σχέμεν, aor. infin. ἔχω.

σχέσθαι, aor. infin. mid. ἔχω.

σχέτλιος, -η, -ον (σχε-, ἔχω). (**1**) Holding out, tough, unwearying: σ. εἰς, 'Οδυσεῦ μ 279. Cf. K 164.—(**2**) Hard to move, hard-hearted, cruel, pitiless, merciless: Ζεύς μ' ἄτῃ ἐνέδησε, σ. B 112, I 19. Cf. E 403, Θ 361, I 630, Π 203, P 150, Ω 33: γ 161, δ 729, ε 118, ι 351, 478, φ 28, ψ 150.—Obstinate, stubborn, self-willed Γ 414.—(**3**) In a tone of affectionate or friendly remonstrance, rash, foolhardy, irrepressible: σχέτλιε, τίπτ' ἐθέλεις ἐρεθιζέμεν ἄγριον ἄνδρα; ι 494. Cf. Σ 13, X 41, 86: λ 474, μ 21, 116.—Hard to turn from one's ways, ever bent on something ν 293.—Hard to convince, of little faith: σχέτλιε, καί τίς τε χερείονι πείθεθ' ἑταίρῳ υ 45.—(4) Of things, cruel, bringing hardship, evil: ἔργα ι 295, ξ 83, χ 413, ὕπνος κ 69.

σχέτο, 3 sing. aor. mid. ἔχω.

σχήσω, fut. ἔχω.

σχίζα, -ης, ἡ. A piece of cleft wood, a billet: κόψε σχίζῃ δρυός ξ 425.—In pl., wood cleft for fuel: καῖεν ἐπὶ σχίζῃς Α 462 := γ 459. Cf. Β 425.

†σχίζω [σχίζα]. 3 sing. aor. ἔσχισε. (δια-.) To cleave or split: ἀπὸ δ' ἔσχισε πέτρην δ 507.

σχοίατο, 3 pl. aor. opt. mid. ἔχω.

σχοῖνος, -ου, ὁ. A place where rushes grow, a bed of rushes: σχοίνῳ ὑπεκλίνθη ε 463.

σώεσκον, pa. iterative σαόω.

σώζω [cf. σαόω]. To preserve, keep, guard: σπέρμα πυρὸς σώζων ε 490.

σῶκος. Perh., the strong, the mighty: σῶκος ἐριούνιος Ἑρμῆς Υ 72.

σῶμα, -ατος, τό. A dead body, a corpse Η 79 = Χ 342: λ 53, μ 67, ω 187.—The carcase of an animal Γ 23, Σ 161, Ψ 169.

σώοντες, nom. pl. masc. pres. pple. σαόω.

σῶς. See σάος.

τάθη, 3 sing. aor. pass. τείνω.

ταλαεργός [ταλα-, τλάω + (F)έργον]. Enduring labour, patient in toil. Epithet of mules Ψ 654, 662, 666: δ 636 = φ 23.

τάλαντον, τό. (1) In pl., a pair of scales, a balance: ὥς τε τάλαντα γυνὴ χερνῆτις [ἔχει] Μ 433.—The scales of Zeus: χρύσεια πατὴρ ἐτίταινε τάλαντα Θ 69 = Χ 209. Cf. Π 658 (figuratively), Τ 223.—(2) A definite weight (of gold) of uncertain amount, a talent (of gold): δέκα χρυσοῖο τάλαντα Ι 122 = 264. Cf. Σ 507, Τ 247, Ψ 269, 614, Ω 232: δ 129, 526, θ 393, ι 202, ω 274.

ταλαπείριος [ταλα-, τλάω + πεῖρα, a trial. Cf. πειράω]. Sorely tried, much-suffering: ἱκέτην ζ 193 = ξ 511. Cf. η 24, ρ 84, τ 379.

ταλαπενθής [ταλα-, τλάω + πένθος]. Bearing up against trouble: θυμόν ε 222.

τάλαρος, -ου, ὁ. A basket: πλεκτοῖς ἐν ταλάροισι φέρον καρπόν Σ 568. Cf. δ 125, 131, ι 247 (here app. the same as the ταρσοί of 219).

τάλας [ταλα-, τλάω]. Voc. τάλαν in passages cited. Wretched, miserable. In abuse: ξεῖνε τάλαν σ 327.—Absol.: ἔξελθε, τάλαν (wretch!) τ 68.

ταλασίφρων, -ονος [ταλασι-, τλάω + φρήν]. Stout-hearted, steadfast in mind. Epithet of Odysseus Λ 466: α 87 = ε 31, δ 241, ρ 34, σ 311, etc.—Absol. Δ 421.

ταλάσσῃ, 3 sing. aor. subj. τλάω.

ταλαύρῑνος [ταλα-, τλάω + (F)ρινός]. Shield-enduring, steady under the shield. Epithet of Ares Ε 289 = Υ 78 = Χ 267.—In neut. ταλαύρινον as adv.: τό μοι ἔστι τ. πολεμίζειν (wherefore it is that I can wield the shield stoutly) Η 239.

ταλάφρων, -ονος [ταλα-, τλάω + φρήν]. = ταλασίφρων: πολεμιστήν Ν 300.

τἆλλα, crasis of τὰ ἄλλα.

ταμεσίχρως, -οος [ταμεσι-, τάμνω + χρώς]. Cutting the flesh, piercing: χαλκόν Δ 511, Ψ 803. Cf. Ν 340.

ταμίη, -ης, ἡ [τάμνω]. A female servant in general charge of the house, a housekeeper Ζ 381: α 139 = δ 55 = η 175 = κ 371 = ο 138 = ρ 94 = 259, γ 392, η 166, θ 449, ι 207, ρ 495 = σ 169, τ 96, ψ 154.—Joined with γυνή Ζ 390: β 345, γ 479.—With ἀμφίπολος Ω 302: π 152.

ταμίης, ὁ [τάμνω]. One of those to whom the charge of the food supplies of an army is committed, a controller or dispenser of supplies: ταμίαι, σίτοιο δοτῆρες Τ 44.—In gen., a controller, manager, or dispenser: ταμίην ἀνέμων κ 21. Cf. Δ 84 = Τ 224.

τάμνω. Also **τέμνω** γ 175. 3 sing. aor. τάμε Γ 292, Ε 74, 292, Ρ 618, Τ 266, Χ 328, Ψ 867. 3 pl. τάμον Ζ 194, Υ 184. 3 sing. subj. τάμῃ Ρ 522. τάμῃσι σ 86, 339. 1 pl. τάμωμεν Γ 94, Τ 191. 2 τάμητε Γ 252. 3 sing. opt. τάμοι Ε 214, Ρ 126: π 102. Pple. ταμών, -όντος Β 124, Γ 73, 256, Σ 177, Ω 409: ε 162, ι 291, μ 11, ψ 204, ω 483. Infin. ταμέειν Ν 501, Π 761, Τ 197. Aor. infin. mid. ταμέσθαι Ι 580. Nom. sing. neut. pf. pple. pass. τετμημένον ρ 195. (ἀποπρο-, ἐκ-, περι-, προ-.) (1) To cut, cut into, gash. Of wounding or piercing with the point of a spear: ὑπὸ γλῶσσαν τάμε χαλκός Ε 74. Cf. Ε 292, Ν 501 = Π 761, Ρ 618.—(2) To slay (a sacrificial victim): [κάπρον] ταμέειν Διί Τ 197.—For ὅρκια τάμνειν see ὅρκιον (3).—(3) To cut off, sever: ἀρνῶν ἐκ κεφαλέων τάμνε τρίχας Γ 273. Cf. Ρ 126, Σ 177, Ε 214 := π 102, σ 86, χ 476.—To cut or lop off for use: φιτρούς μ 11, ῥόπαλον τετμημένον ρ 195.—(4) To cut out, remove (with the knife): ἐκ μηροῦ τάμνε μαχαίρῃ βέλος Λ 844.—To cut out, remove by severing a joint: ἐκ μηρία τάμνον γ 456.—(5) To cut, cut in two, sever, divide: ἀπὸ στόμαχον κάπρου τάμεν Τ 266. Cf. Γ 292, Ρ 522, Χ 328, Ψ 867: ταμὼν ὕπο πυθμέν' ἐλαίης ψ 204.—To cleave (the sea): πέλαγος μέσον τέμνειν γ 175. Cf. ν 88.—(6) To cut (in pieces): μελεϊστὶ ταμών Ω 409. Cf. ι 291, σ 339.—To cut up, cut in pieces, for sacrifice: γλώσσας γ 332.—To cut up or carve (meat). In mid.: ταμνομένους κρέα πολλά ω 364.—Absol. Ι 209.—(7) To fell (trees): δένδρεα Λ 88. Cf. Ν 180, Ψ 119.—(8) To cut into shape, form by cutting or hacking: δούρατα ε 162. Cf. Φ 38: ξ 24.—In mid.: τάμνετο δοῦρα ε 243.—(9) With ἀμφί, to surround and cut off (cattle, etc.) in order to make booty of them (cf. περιτάμνω). In mid.: τάμνοντ' ἀμφὶ βοῶν ἀγέλας καὶ πώεα οἰῶν Σ 528.—(10) To mark off, designate: τέμενος Ζ 194, Υ 184.—In mid. Ι 580.

ταναήκης [ταναός + *ἀκή, point, edge. Cf. τανυήκης]. With slender or tapering point. Epithet of spears Η 77, Ω 754.—Having a fine edge, sharp. Epithet of an axe Ψ 118.—In one of these senses as epithet of a piercing or cutting weapon not clearly defined: χαλκῷ δ 257.

ταναός, -όν (ταναϜός) [τείνω]. Long. Epithet of a hunting-spear : αἰγανέης Π 589.

ταναύπους, -ποδος [τανα(Ϝ)ός + πούς]. Long-striding, stepping boldly out : μῆλα ι 464.

τανηλεγής [ταναός + ἀλεγ- as in ἀλεγεινός]. Bringing long woe. Epithet of death Θ 70 = Χ 210 : β 100 = γ 238 = τ 145 = ω 135, λ 171 = 398.

τανύγλωσσος, -ον [τανύω + γλῶσσα]. With long or outstretched tongue, loud crying : κορῶναι ε 66.

τανυγλώχις, -ῑνος [τανύω + γλωχίς, in sense 'barb.' Cf. χαλκογλώχις]. With long barbs : ὀϊστούς Θ 297.

τανυήκης [τανύω + *ἀκή, point, edge. Cf. ταναήκης]. Neut. τανύηκες. (1) Having a fine edge, sharp. Epithet of swords Ξ 385, Π 473 : = κ 439 = λ 231, χ 443.—(2) With slender points : ὄζους Π 768.

τάνῡμι [= τανύω]. To stretch : τάνυται [βοείη] πᾶσα διαπρό Ρ 393.

τανύπεπλος, -ον [τανύω + πέπλος]. With long robe. Epithet of Helen Γ 228 : δ 305, ο 171.—Of Thetis Σ 385 = 424.—Of Lampetië μ 375.—Of Ctimene ο 363.

τανυπτέρυξ, -υγος [τανύω + πτέρυξ]. Long-winged : οἰωνοῖσι τανυπτερύγεσσιν Μ 237. Cf. Τ 350.

τανυσίπτερος, -ον [τανυσι-, τανύω + πτερόν]. = prec. : ὄρνιθες ε 65, κίχλαι χ 468.

τανυστύς, -ύος [τανύω]. A stringing (of a bow) : τόξου φ 112 (*i.e.* the attempt to string it).

τανύφλοιος, -ον [τανύω + φλοιός]. With smooth bark : κράνειαν Π 767.

τανύφυλλος, -ον [τανύω + φύλλον]. Long-leaved : ἐλαίη ν 102, 346. Cf. ψ 190, 195.

τανύω [cf. τείνω]. Fut. τανύω φ 152. 3 pl. τανύουσι φ 174. Aor. ἐτάνυσσα ψ 201. 3 sing. (ἐ)τάνυσσε Ι 213, Λ 336, Π 662, Ρ 401 : α 138, 442, δ 54, ε 373, η 174, κ 370, ο 137, ρ 93, φ 128, 328, 407, ω 177. τάνυσε Π 567 : ο 283, φ 409. 3 pl. τάνυσσαν Α 486, Ν 359, Ξ 389. 3 sing. subj. τανύσῃ Ψ 324. τανύσσῃ Ρ 547, Ψ 761. 3 sing. opt. τανύσσειε σ 92. Pple. τανύσσας Ψ 25. Infin. τανύσσαι φ 171, 254. **Mid.** Aor. imp. τάνυσσαι ε 346. Pple. τανυσσάμενος Δ 112 : ι 298. **Pass.** 3 pl. aor. τάνυσθεν Π 475 : π 175. Pple. τανυσθείς Ν 392, Π 485, Σ 26, Υ 483. 3 sing. pf. τετάνυσται ι 116. 3 sing. plupf. τετάνυστο Κ 156 : δ 135, ε 68. (ἐκ-, ἐν-, ἐπεν-.) (1) To stretch, draw out, expand, by the application of force : ὡς ὅτ' ἀνὴρ βοείην λαοῖσιν δώῃ τανύειν Ρ 390, τανύουσι [βοείην] 391.—(2) To bend (a bow) into the position required for stringing it, to string (it) (cf. ἐντανύω (1), τιταίνω (1)) : τόξον φ 254, 409, 426, βιόν φ 328, ω 177. Cf. φ 128, 152, 171, 174.—In mid. Δ 112.—(3) To stretch and fit (a string of a lyre) : περὶ κόλλοπι χορδήν φ 407.—(4) To draw or pull in a desired direction : κανόνα Ψ 761.—(5) To shoot (the bolt of a door) : κληῗδα α 442.—(6) In reference to a natural feature, to cause to assume full proportions, fill out : γναθμοὶ τάνυσθεν π 175.—(7) To stretch, strain, draw tight, fix under tension : ἱμάντα ψ 201.—Fig., in reference to the rope of strife (cf. ἐπαλλάσσω, τείνω (2)) : πεῖραρ ἐπ' ἀμφοτέροισι τάνυσσαν Ν 359.—Sim. : κατὰ ἶσα μάχην ἐτάνυσσε Λ 336. Cf. Ξ 389, Π 662, Ρ 401.—(8) To stretch (a horse), put (him) to his pace and cause (him) to pull in the desired direction : ὅππως τὸ πρῶτον τανύσῃ [ἵππους] ἱμᾶσιν (how to . . .) Ψ 324.—In mid., of horses or mules, to stretch themselves in the energy of motion, run at full stride : ἡμίονοι ἄμοτον τανύοντο ζ 83. Cf. Π 375.—In pass., of horses, to pull in the desired direction : [ἵπποι] ἐν ῥυτῆρσι τάνυσθεν Π 475.—(9) To stretch, lay, dispose, arrange, put, set, place : ἕρματα Α 486, ὑπὸ κράτεσφι τάπης τετάνυστο Κ 156 (app., rolled up to form a pillow). Cf. Ι 213, Ψ 25 : τράπεζαν (drew it up) α 138 = δ 54 = η 174 = κ 370 = ο 137 = ρ 93. Cf. δ 135, ε 373, ο 283.—In mid. ε 346.—Of something immaterial : νύκτα Π 567, ἶριν Ρ 547.—(10) To stretch (a person on the ground), lay (him) low : ἠέ μιν τανύσσειεν ἐπὶ γαίῃ σ 92.—In mid. and pass., to stretch oneself out, lie stretched out, be outstretched : κεῖτο τανυσθείς Ν 392 = Π 485, Σ 26, Υ 483 : κεῖτο τανυσσάμενος ι 298. Cf. Ι 468 = Ψ 33.—Sim., of a plant, to stretch or spread itself, stretch, spread : τετάνυστο περὶ σπείους ἡμερίς ε 68.—(11) In geographical sense, in pass., to stretch, lie : νῆσος παρὲκ λιμένος τετάνυσται ι 116.

τάπης, -ητος, ὁ. A rug or blanket used as bedding or for covering a seat : εἷσεν ἐν κλισμοῖσι τάπησί τε Ι 200. Cf. Κ 156, Π 224, Ω 230, 645 : = δ 298 = η 337, εὕδουσ' ἐν τάπησιν κ 12. Cf. δ 124, υ 150, ω 276.

ταρ, *enclitic*. See ἄρα (8).

†ταράσσω. 3 sing. aor. ἐτάραξε Θ 86 : ε 291, 304. 3 sing. subj. ταράξῃ Α 579. Pf. pple. fem. τετρηχυῖα Η 346. 3 sing. plupf. τετρήχει Β 95. (1) To stir up, trouble : πόντον ε 291, 304.—(2) To throw into disorder, strike with panic : σὺν ἵππους ἐτάραξεν Θ 86.—To throw into disorder, mar the seemliness of : δαῖτα Α 579.—(3) In pf. and plupf., to be in disorder or confusion : τετρήχει ἀγορή Β 95. Cf. Η 346.

ταρβέω. (ὑπο-.) (1) To be in fear or terror, be frightened, terrified, alarmed : ταρβήσαντε στήτην (struck with terror) Α 331, οὐ τάρβει Δ 388. Cf. Β 268, Ε 286 = Λ 384, Κ 374, Μ 46, Ν 285, Ο 280, Υ 262, 283, 380, 430, Φ 288, 575, Ω 171 : η 51, π 179, σ 331 = 391.—(2) To fear, dread, feel terror or alarm at : χαλκόν Ζ 469. Cf. Λ 405, Ρ 586.

τάρβος, τό. Fear, alarm Ω 152, 181.

ταρβοσύνη, -ης, ἡ [τάρβος]. = prec. σ 342.

τάρπησαν, 3 pl. aor. pass. τέρπω.

ταρπώμεθα, 1 pl. aor. subj. mid. τέρπω.

ταρσός, -οῦ, ὁ. (1) App., some kind of basket or stand of wickerwork : ταρσοὶ τυρῶν βρῖθον ι 219 (app. the same as the τάλαροι of 247).—(2) App., the flat upper surface (of the foot) : βάλε ταρσὸν δεξιτεροῖο ποδός Λ 377. Cf. Λ 388.

ταρφέες, -έα [τάρφος]. Nom. fem. ταρφειαί Τ 357, 359. Acc. ταρφειάς Μ 158. Coming, flying, falling, appearing, thick and fast or at short intervals: *τὰ δράγματα* Λ 69, *ἰοί* 387, *νιφάδες* Τ 357. Cf. Μ 158, Ο 472, Τ 359: χ 246.—In neut. pl. *ταρφέα* as adv., at short intervals, without remission, continually, constantly: *στρέφεται* Μ 47. Cf. Ν 718, Χ 142: θ 379.

τάρφθη, 3 sing. aor. pass. *τέρπω.*

τάρφος, *τό.* A thicket Ε 555, Ο 606.

ταρχύω. To pay funeral rites to (a corpse), honour (it) by funeral rites: *ὄφρα ἑ ταρχύσωσιν* Η 85. Cf. Π 456=674.

ταύρειος, *-η, -ον* [*ταῦρος*]. Of bull's-hide: *κυνέην* Κ 258, *ἀσπίδα* Ν 161, 163. Cf. Π 360.

ταῦρος, *-ου, ὁ.* (1) A bull Α 41, 316, Β 550, Λ 728, Π 487, Ρ 542, Σ 580, Υ 403, Φ 131, 237: α 25, γ 6, 8, 178, λ 131=ψ 278, ν 181, 184, φ 48.—Joined with *βοῦς*: *βοῦς τ.* Β 481. Cf. Ρ 389.—(2) A bull's hide: *σάκος ταύρων ζατρεφέων* Η 223.

ταφήϊος [*τάφος*[1]]. Of or pertaining to a funeral: *ταφήϊον* (*sc. φᾶρος*), a robe wherewith to honour a dead body: *Λαέρτῃ ἥρωϊ ταφήϊον* β 99=τ 144=ω 134.

τάφος[1], *-ου, ὁ* [*θάπτω*]. Funeral rites, a funeral, a funeral feast, funeral games: *τάφον δαίνυ* Ψ 29, *Πατρόκλοιο τάφου μνῆμα* 619. Cf. Ψ 680, Ω 660, 804: *τάφου κ' ἀντιβολήσαις* δ 547. Cf. γ 309, υ 307, ω 87.

τάφος[2], *τό* [*ταφ-, τέθηπα*]. (1) Wonder, amazement, astonishment: *τ. ἕλε πάντας* φ 122. Cf. ω 441.—(2) Stupefaction: *τ. οἱ ἦτορ ἵκανεν* ψ 93.

τάφρος, *-ου, ἡ.* (1) A narrow excavation in the ground, a trench: *πελέκεας στῆσε, διὰ τάφρον ὀρύξας* φ 120.—(2) A ditch or fosse protecting a fortified place. Of the ditch dug about the Greek camp Η 341, Θ 179, Ι 67, Λ 48, Μ 4, etc.

ταφών, aor. pple. See *τέθηπα.*

τάχα [*ταχύς*]. (1) Swiftly, quickly, fast, at speed: *ἐγγύθεν ἦλθον* Ε 275: *εἰσὶ τέταρτον* [*ἔτος*] β 89.—(2) In short space, soon, before long, quickly, speedily, shortly: *τάχ' ἂν ποτε θυμὸν ὀλέσσῃ* Α 205. Cf. Β 193, Γ 436, Ζ 52 (was just on the point of doing so), Ι 573, Λ 654 (*i.e.* is as likely as not to do so), Ξ 8 (referring *εἴσομαι* to *εἴδω* (III) (1)), Π 71, Τ 131, Ψ 606 (easily), etc.: α 251, β 40, δ 514 (was just on the point of doing so), θ 202, ξ 265, τ 69, υ 393, φ 369 (you will soon find that it is ill to . . .), χ 78 (will soon find that this is the last of his shooting), etc.—(3) Without delay or loss of time, with all speed, at once, forthwith, straightway: *τάχα δ' ἄμμε διαρραίσεσθαι ὀΐω* Ω 355. Cf. Ξ 8 (referring *εἴσομαι* to *ἵημι*[2] (4)): *τάχα Τηλεμάχῳ ἐρέω* σ 338. Cf. μ 387, σ 115, 389, φ 374, ψ 23.

ταχέως [adv. fr. *ταχύς*]. With speed, swiftly: *διέπρησσον πεδίοιο τ.* Ψ 365.

τάχιστα [neut. pl. of *τάχιστος*, superl. of *ταχύς*, as adv.]. (1) At full speed, with great speed, swiftly: *ἐς νῆας ἔχε ἵππους* Λ 513. Cf. θ 561, ο 293.—(2) With the least delay or loss of time, as speedily as may be, at once, forthwith, straightway: *ὄφρα τ. μαχώμεθα* Δ 269. Cf. Γ 102, Θ 9, Ι 165, Ν 286, Ο 453, Ρ 640, Φ 311, Ω 263, etc.: α 85, γ 175, δ 473, ζ 32, ξ 407, π 349, σ 263, ω 360, etc.—*ὅττι τάχιστα*, losing not a moment, with all speed: *Μαχάονα δεῦρο κάλεσσον* Δ 193. Cf. Ι 659, Ο 146, Χ 129, Ψ 71, 403, 414: ε 112, θ 434, π 152.

τάχος, *τό* [*ταχύς*]. Swiftness, speed, fleetness: *ἵπποισιν, οἷσιν ὤρεξε τάχος* Ψ 406. Cf. Ψ 515.

ταχύπωλος [*ταχύς* + *πῶλος*]. Having fleet horses. Epithet of the *Δαναοί* Δ 232, 257, Ε 316, 345, Θ 161, Ν 620, Ξ 21, Ο 320, Ω 295, 313.—Of the *Μυρμιδόνες* Ψ 6.

ταχύς, *-εῖα, -ύ.* (For comp. and superl. see *θάσσων, τάχιστα.*) Acc. sing. masc. *ταχύν.* Voc. *ταχύ.* Nom. dual *ταχέε.* Nom. pl. *ταχέες.* Dat. *ταχέεσσι.* Acc. *ταχέας.* Quick in movement, nimble, swift, fleet (often a merely conventional epithet): *κύνες* Γ 26, *ἰόν* Δ 94. Cf. Ε 356, 885, Θ 248, 339, Π 186, etc.: γ 112, ν 261, ξ 133, ο 526, χ 3, etc.—Epithet of the Telamonian Ajax Κ 110, 175.—Of the Lesser Ajax Β 527, Ν 66, 701, Ξ 442, 520, Ρ 256, Ψ 473, 488=754.—Of Achilles Σ 69.—Of Iris Θ 399, Λ 186, Ο 158, Ω 144.—For *πόδας ταχύς* see *πούς* (3).

ταχυτής, *-ῆτος, ἡ* [*ταχύς*]. Swiftness, speed: *ταχυτῆτος ἄεθλα* (for swiftness in the race) Ψ 740. Cf. ρ 315.

τε, *enclitic.* (1) Repeated in and connecting correlative clauses: *εἴ περ γάρ τε χόλον γε καὶ αὐτῆμαρ καταπέψῃ, ἀλλά τε καὶ μετόπισθεν ἔχει κότον* Α 81, *σύν τε δύ' ἐρχομένω, καί τε πρὸ ὁ τοῦ ἐνόησεν* Κ 224, etc.: *ὄρνιθες δέ τε πολλοὶ φοιτῶσ', οὐδέ τε πάντες ἐναίσιμοι* β 181, etc.—(2) Connecting particle, and Α 5, 38, 45, 57, 66, 128, etc.: α 171, 321, β 65, 118, 153, 300, etc.—(3) . . . *τε* . . . *τε*: *λυσόμενός τε θύγατρα φέρων τ' ἀπερείσι' ἄποινα* Α 13, *ἑκατόν τε διηκοσίων τε* (not only one hundred but two) Θ 233. Cf. Α 157, 167, 196, 263, 339, etc.: *ἀνδρῶν τε θεῶν τε* α 28, *ἐνδεκάτῃ τε δυωδεκάτῃ τε* (the eleventh or twelfth) β 374. Cf. α 145, 152, 165, 191, 242, etc.— . . . *τε* . . . *τε* . . . *τε* Α 70, 177, Β 58, etc.: β 120, ε 260, ζ 152, etc.—(4) . . . *τε καὶ* . . ., . . . *τε* . . . *καὶ* . . .: *Ἀτρεΐδης τε ἄναξ ἀνδρῶν καὶ δῖος Ἀχιλλεύς* Α 7, *χθιζά τε καὶ πρωϊζά* (yesterday or the day before) Β 303, *τριχθά τε καὶ τετραχθά* (in three or four pieces) Γ 363, *δεκάκις τε καὶ εἰκοσάκις* (not ten times but twenty) Ι 379. Cf. Α 17, 23, 61, 179, 237, etc.: α 5, 25, 54, 291, 293, etc.— . . . *τε* . . . *τε καὶ* . . . Α 264, etc.: α 246, etc.—(5) . . . *τ' ἠδὲ* (*ἰδὲ*) . . ., . . . *τε* . . . *ἠδὲ* (*ἰδὲ*) . . . Α 400, Β 500, Δ 147, etc.: α 12, δ 604, etc.—(6) . . . *τε* . . . *δὲ* . . . Ε 359, Ι 519, etc.: ο 546, π 432, etc.— . . . *τε, μηδὲ* . . . φ 310.—(7) Marking an assertion as general or indefinite, in frequentative meaning of habitual action, characteristic attribute, fixed condition, permanent significance: *ὃν Βριάρεων καλέουσι θεοί, ἄνδρες δέ τε πάντες Αἰγαίωνα* Α 403, *ἐν δαίθ', ὅτε πέρ τε οἶνον κέρωνται* Δ 259, *σφῶϊν μέν τ' ἐπέοικεν ἑστάμεν* 341, *τρεῖς γάρ τ' ἐκ Κρόνου εἰμὲν ἀδελφεοί* Ο 187, *καί τέ με νεικείεσκον* Τ 86. Cf. Α 521, Β 754,

Ε 306, 340, Ι 410, Ν 279, etc.: ἔχει δέ τε κίονας α 53, ἄλλοτε μέν τε γόῳ τέρπομαι δ 102, Ἰθάκῃ δέ τε καὶ περὶ πασέων 608, κνισῆεν δέ τε δῶμα περιστεναχίζεται κ 10, ἕκαθεν δέ τε ἄστυ φάτ' εἶναι ρ 25. Cf. α 215, δ 387, 497, ε 29, ι 26, λ 123, μ 64, etc.—(8) Thus in gnomic utterances and maxims: καὶ γάρ τ' ὄναρ ἐκ Διός ἐστιν Α 63, μάλα τ' ἔκλυον αὐτοῦ 218, ληϊστοὶ μὲν γάρ τε βόες Ι 406, στρεπτοὶ δέ τε καὶ θεοὶ αὐτοί 497, ῥεχθὲν δέ τε νήπιος ἔγνω Ρ 32, etc.: τὰ γάρ τ' ἀναθήματα δαιτός α 152, οὐ γάρ τ' αἶψα θεῶν τρέπεται νόος γ 147, θεοὶ δέ τε πάντα ἴσασιν δ 379, μάλιστα δέ τ' ἔκλυον αὐτοί ζ 185, etc.—And in similes Β 210, 456, Γ 11, 25, Δ 77, 277, Ε 137, Θ 338, Κ 362, etc.: δ 535, etc.—(9) With relatives: ἅσσα τε Κ 208 = 409.—ἔνθα τε Δ 247, Ξ 215, etc.: θ 363, λ 475, etc.—ἐπεί τε Λ 87, 562, Μ 393.—ἵνα τε Ι 441, Χ 325, etc.: δ 85, κ 417, etc.—ὅθεν τε γ 321, δ 358, etc.—ὅθι τε Θ 83, etc.: α 50, ε 280, etc.—οἷός τε Η 208, Ρ 157: ε 422, ο 379, etc.—ὅσ(σ)ος τε Β 468, Γ 12, etc.: ε 484, κ 113, etc.—ὅτε τε Β 471, Ξ 522, etc.: σ 257, χ 301, etc.—For ὅ τε, ὅς τε, ὅς τίς τε see ὁ (4) (b), ὅς[2] (II) (1) (b), ὅς τις (1).—For ὥς τε see ὡς (1) (2) (3) (10).—For ὡς εἴ τε see εἰ (6) (7).—(10) With τις Β 292, Ξ 90, Ρ 542, etc.: ε 120, τ 486, etc.—(11) For τ' ἄρα, τ' ἄρ see ἄρα (8).—For ἦ τε see ἦ[2] (1) (b) (γ).—For ἤ τε (ἤτε) see ἠέ (1) (3).—(12) With εἴ περ Δ 261, etc.: α 188, etc.—(13) In definite statements, etc., app. by intrusion or corruption: δὸς δέ τέ μ' ἄνδρα ἑλεῖν, ὅς . . . Ε 118, δέελον δ' ἐπὶ σῆμά τ' ἔθηκεν Κ 466, τοὺς μέν τ' ἰητροὶ ἀμφιπένονται Π 28, σὲ δέ τ' ἐνθάδε γῦπες ἔδονται 836, οὐδέ τ' ἔληγεν Φ 248, οὐ μήν οἱ τό γε κάλλιον οὐδέ τ' ἄμεινον Ω 52, etc.: ἐν δέ τε φάρμακον ἧκεν κ 317, οὐδέ τ' ἀοιδήν μ 198, πέρασαν δέ τε δεῦρ' ἀγαγόντες ο 428, νεμεσσῶμαι δέ τ' ἀκούων φ 169, etc.

τέγεος [τέγος]. App., furnished with a roof (to sleep upon): θάλαμοι Ζ 248.

τέγος, τό. A roof: τέγεος πέσεν (πέσον) (from the . . .) κ 559, λ 64.—See also σταθμός (3).

τεθαλυῖα, pf. pple. fem. θάλλω.

τεθαρσήκᾱσι, 3 pl. pf. θαρσέω.

τεθηλώς, pf. pple. θάλλω.

τέθηπα. Plupf. (in impf. sense) ἐτεθήπεα ζ 166. Aor. pple. ταφών Ι 193, Λ 545, 777, Π 806, Ψ 101, Ω 360: π 12. (1) To be lost in wonder or amazement, marvel: ὡς κεῖνο ἰδὼν ἐτεθήπεα θυμῷ ζ 166, ἕσταν τεθηπότες (in amazement) ω 392. Cf. ζ 168, ψ 105 (here passing into sense (2)).—In aor. pple., struck with amazement, in an access of wonder: ταφὼν ἀνόρουσεν Ι 193, Λ 777, Ψ 101: π 12.—(2) To be deprived of one's power of mind, be bewildered, stunned, stupefied: τίπτ' (ὣς) ἕστητε τεθηπότες (helpless) Δ 243, 246, ἐξῆγε θύραζε τεθηπότας Φ 29. Cf. Φ 64.—In aor. pple., struck with stupor or bewilderment, one's wits or vigour gone: στῆ ταφών Λ 545, Π 806, Ω 360.

τεθνάμεν, τεθνάμεναι, pf. infin. θνήσκω.

τεθνεῶτι, dat. sing. masc. pf. pple. θνήσκω.

τέθνηκε, 3 sing. pf. θνήσκω.

τεθνηώς, pf. pple. θνήσκω.

τεθυωμένον, neut. pf. pple. pass. θυόω.

τεΐν. See τοι[1].

†**τείνω.** 3 sing. aor. ἔτεινε Δ 124. τεῖνε Γ 261, 311. 3 pl. τεῖναν Τ 394. 3 sing. subj. τείνῃ Π 365. 3 sing. opt. τείνειε Υ 101. Pple. τείνας Ε 262, 322. 3 sing. aor. pass. τάθη Ψ 375. Pple. ταθείς Ν 655, Φ 119: χ 200. 3 sing. pf. τέταται λ 19. 3 sing. plupf. τέτατο Γ 372, Μ 436, Ο 413, Ρ 543, 736, Χ 307, Ψ 758: θ 121, λ 11. 3 dual τετάσθην Δ 536, Ξ 404. 3 pl. τέταντο Δ 544. (ἐν-.) (1) To stretch, put strain upon: τέταθ' ἱστία λ 11.—(2) To draw or pull tight: ἡνία Γ 261, 311, Τ 394.—Fig., with a reference to the rope of strife (cf. τανύω (7)): τῶν ἐπὶ ἶσα μάχη τέτατο Μ 436 = Ο 413. Cf. Ρ 543, 736, Υ 101.—Sim.: ἵπποισι τάθη δρόμος (the pace was forced) Ψ 375. Cf. Ψ 758: θ 121.—To pull upon the string of (a bow), draw the string of (it) towards one, bend (it) (cf. τιταίνω (2)): ἐπεὶ τόξον ἔτεινεν Δ 124.—(3) To draw tight and secure, fasten in a state of tension: ἐξ ἄντυγος ἡνία τείνας Ε 262, 322.—(4) To stretch out (a person), secure (him) outstretched: ταθεὶς ὀλοῷ ἐνὶ δεσμῷ χ 200.—(5) To stretch, dispose, arrange, put, set, place: φάσγανον, τό οἱ ὑπὸ λαπάρην τέτατο Χ 307. Cf. Γ 372, Ξ 404.—Sim.: ὅτε τε Ζεὺς λαίλαπα τείνῃ Π 365. Cf. λ 19.—(6) To stretch (a person) on the ground, lay (him) low. In pass., to lie stretched out, be outstretched: τὼ ἐν κονίῃσι τετάσθην Δ 536. Cf. Δ 544, Ν 655 = Φ 119.

τείρεα, τά. App., stars or constellations Σ 485.

τείρω. To wear out, distress, afflict, exhaust, bear hard upon, put to sore straits, reduce to extremity: γῆράς σε τείρει Δ 315, ἤδη τειρόμενον (in extremity) Ε 391, τείρουσί [σ'] υἷες Ἀχαιῶν Ζ 255. Cf. Ε 153, 352 (was in sorry plight), Ζ 387, Θ 81 (was at the last gasp), 102 (are too much for you), 363 (in his extremity), Ι 248, Λ 801 (find respite from their distress), 841 (in your trouble), Ν 251, Π 510, Φ 353, Ω 489, etc.: α 342, β 71 (to pine), δ 369 = μ 332, δ 441, ε 324 (in his extremity), η 218, ι 441, κ 78, ω 233.

τείσω, fut. τίω.

τειχεσιπλήτης [τείχεσι, dat. pl. of τεῖχος + πλη-, πελάζω. 'That comes near to walls' (in hostile sense). Cf. δασπλῆτις]. Sacker of walled cities. Epithet of Ares. In voc. τειχεσιπλῆτα Ε 31 = 455.

†**τειχίζομαι** [τεῖχος]. 3 pl. aor. ἐτειχίσσαντο. To build (a wall): ὅτι τεῖχος ἐτειχίσσαντο Η 449.

τειχιόεις, -εσσα [τεῖχος]. Walled, high-walled: Τίρυνθα Β 559, Γόρτυνα 646.

τειχίον, τό [τεῖχος]. A wall. Of the wall of an αὐλή: παρὲκ μέγα τ. αὐλῆς π 165, 343.

τεῖχος, τό. Dat. pl. τείχεσσι Η 135. (1) A wall for protection or defence: πᾶσαν νῆσον πέρι τ. [ἐστιν] κ 3. Cf. Ο 736, Υ 145.—In sing. and pl., a city-wall, the walls of a city: τείχεα Θήβης Β 691, Δ 378, λαὸν ἀγαγόνθ' ὑπὸ τεῖχος ἄρειον Δ 407. Cf. Δ 308, Η 135, Ι 552, Σ 514: ζ 9, η 44.—(2) Applied in sing. and pl. (a) To the walls of Troy: περὶ πτόλιν αἰπύ τε τεῖχος Ζ 327, κατὰ Ἰλιόφι τείχεα λαὸν ἐέλσαι Φ 295. Cf. Δ 34, Ζ 388,

N 764, Π 397, Σ 256, X 4, 99, etc.: ξ 472.—(b) To the wall built to protect the Greek camp: ποτὶ τύμβον τεῖχος ἔδειμαν Η 436, οἳ τάδε τείχεα μηχανόωντο Θ 177. Cf. I 67, M 4, 26, N 50, Ξ 15, O 345, Σ 215, etc.

τεκμαίρομαι [τέκμαρ = τέκμωρ]. 3 sing. aor. τεκμήρατο κ 563. 3 pl. τεκμήραντο Ζ 349. (1) To ordain, appoint, decree: τάδε κακά Ζ 349, [Κρονίδης] τεκμαίρεται ἀμφοτέροισιν, εἰς ὅ κεν ἢ . . . ἢ . . . (app., settles an appointed time against which either . . . or . . .) Η 70. Cf. η 317, κ 563.—(2) To foretell: ὄλεθρον λ 112 = μ 139.

τέκμωρ, τό. (1) An end or limit: εἰς ὅ κε τ. Ἰλίου εὕρωσιν (εὕρωμεν) (till they (we) find out the limit set for it by fate, *i.e.* witness its end) Η 30, Ι 48.—So ἐπεὶ οὐκέτι δήετε τ. Ἰλίου (it is not your lot to witness its end) I 418 = 685.—(2) A bringing to a conclusion or end, a conclusion or end: τοῖο εὕρετο τέκμωρ (*i.e.* found a remedy for this state of things, this confusion) Π 472: οὐδέ τι τέκμωρ εὑρέμεναι δύνασαι (δύναμαι) (any end to the business) δ 373, 466.—(3) One's goal: ἵκετο τ., Αἰγάς N 20.—(4) A sign or token: κεφαλῇ κατανεύσομαι· τοῦτο γὰρ ἐξ ἐμέθεν γε μέγιστον τ. [γίγνεται] A 526.

τέκνον, τό [τεκ-, τίκτω]. (1) In pl., offspring, children: νήπια τέκνα Β 136, σὰ τέκνα Ω 542. Cf. B 871, Z 196, I 594, Σ 337, etc.: λ 249, μ 42, ν 45, ξ 223, τ 266, etc.—Of the offspring or young of a bird, animal or insect: στρουθοῖο τέκνα Β 311. Cf. Λ 113, M 170, T 400, etc.: π 217.—(2) In voc. sing. and pl. (a) In address by a parent to his or her child or children: φίλε τέκνον X 84, κακὰ τέκνα Ω 253. Cf. A 362, 414, Φ 379, etc.: α 64, γ 418, π 226, etc.—(b) In affectionate address by an elder not a parent K 192: β 363, γ 254, δ 78, τ 492, ψ 26, etc.

τέκον, aor. τίκτω.

τέκος, τό [τεκ-, τίκτω]. Dat. pl. τεκέεσσι Γ 160, Δ 162, M 222: θ 525, ξ 244. τέκεσσι Ε 71, 535, N 176, etc.: β 178, θ 243, κ 61. (1) Offspring, a child: Διὸς τέκος A 202, ἡμῖν τεκέεσσί τε πῆμα Γ 160. Cf. Γ 301, Δ 162, E 71, Σ 63, Ω 36, etc.: β 178, δ 175, 762 = ζ 324, θ 243, 525, κ 61, ξ 244.—Of the offspring or young of a bird, animal or insect: τ. ἐλάφοιο Θ 248. Cf. M 222, Π 265, P 133.—(2) In voc. (a) In address by a parent to his or her child: φίλον τέκος Ε 373. Cf. Θ 39, Σ 95, Φ 331, etc.: ζ 68.—By a father-in-law to his daughter-in-law Γ 162, 192.—(b) In affectionate address by an elder not a parent I 437, Ξ 190, Ψ 626, Ω 425, etc.: δ 611, η 22, σ 170, etc.

†τεκταίνομαι [τέκτων]. 3 sing. aor. τεκτήνατο Ε 62. 3 sing. opt. τεκτήναιτο Κ 19. (παρα-.) (1) To construct, build: νῆας Ε 62.—(2) To devise, contrive, think out: μῆτιν Κ 19.

τεκτοσύνη, -ης, ἡ [τέκτων]. The art of the carpenter or shipwright. In pl.: εὖ εἰδὼς τεκτοσυνάων ε 250.

τέκτων, -ονος, ὁ. (1) A skilled worker in wood, a joiner, carpenter or shipwright E 59, Z 315, N 390 = Π 483, O 411, Ψ 712: ι 126, ρ 340, τ 56, φ 43.—So τέκτονα δούρων ρ 384.—(2) With a qualifying word indicating another material in which a man works: κεραοξόος τέκτων Δ 110.

τελαμών, -ῶνος, ὁ. A baldrick supporting (a) A sword or dagger: δῶκε ξίφος (φάσγανον), σὺν κολεῷ τε φέρων καὶ τελαμῶνι Η 304 = Ψ 825, μαχαίρας ἐξ ἀργυρέων τελαμώνων Σ 598. Cf. λ 610 (see ἀορτήρ (1)), 614.—(b) A shield: ἀσπὶς σὺν τελαμῶνι Π 803. Cf. B 388, E 796, 798, Λ 38, M 401, Σ 480.—The two baldricks mentioned together: δύω τελαμῶνε, ὁ μὲν σάκεος, ὁ δὲ φασγάνου Ξ 404.—Doubtful which is meant: δησάμενος τελαμῶνι P 290.

τελέθω. (1) Of a period of time, to revolve, come round: νὺξ ἤδη τελέθει (is coming upon us) Η 282 = 293.—(2) To turn out to be, prove to be *so and so*: θαρσαλέος ἀνὴρ ἐν πᾶσιν ἀμείνων ἔργοισιν τελέθει η 52.—(3) To become *so and so*: ἀγορέων, ἵνα τ' ἄνδρες ἀριπρεπέες τελέθουσιν (win honour) I 441, ἵνα τ' ἄρνες ἄφαρ κεραοὶ τελέθουσιν (*i.e.* their horns begin to sprout immediately after birth) δ 85, παντοῖοι τελέθοντες (taking all forms) ρ 486.—(4) To come into being, be brought about, arise: οἶσθ' οἷαι νέου ἀνδρὸς ὑπερβασίαι τελέθουσιν (from, in the case of, a young man, *i.e.* what offences he will be led to commit) Ψ 589.—(5) To be: οἳ τὸ πάρος περ ζαχρηεῖς τελέθουσι καθ' ὑσμίνας (showed themselves . . .) M 347 = 360. Cf. Φ 465: ἄνθρωποι μινυνθάδιοι τελέθουσιν τ 328. Cf. θ 583.

τέλειος [τέλος]. (1) Sure, certain. In superl.: αἰετόν, τελειότατον πετεηνῶν (bringing the surest presage of fulfilment) Θ 247 = Ω 315.—(2) Perfect, without spot or blemish: αἰγῶν τελείων A 66, Ω 34.

τελείω. See τελέω.

τέλεσε, 3 sing. aor. τελέω.

τελεσφόρος [τελεσ-, τέλος + -φορος, φέρω]. That brings completion, that completes the cycle of the seasons and of the stages of vegetation. Epithet of ἐνιαυτός T 32: δ 86, κ 467, ξ 292, ο 230.

τελευτάω [τελευτή]. (1) To bring to completion, carry through, carry out, bring about, accomplish, perform: τάδε ἔργα Θ 9. Cf. N 375, T 90: α 293, β 275, 280, γ 62, η 331, ω 126, etc.—(2) In pass., to be accomplished or fulfilled, be brought to pass, come to pass: θαῦμα, ὃ οὔ ποτ' ἔγωγε τελευτήσεσθαι ἔφασκον (never thought to see) N 100: τῇ τελευτήσεσθαι ἔμελλεν (as it was fated to be) θ 510. Cf. β 171, ι 511.—(3) To accomplish, fulfil, carry out, bring to fruition or consummation (a wish or purpose): πρίν γε τὸ Πηλεΐδαο τελευτηθῆναι ἐέλδωρ O 74, νοήματα Σ 328. Cf. φ 200.—(4) To bring about, bring upon a person: κακὸν ἦμαρ ο 524.—(5) To take (an oath) in full and binding form: τὸν ὅρκον Ξ 280: = β 378 = κ 346, μ 304 = ο 438 = σ 59.—(6) To complete one's work, finish off (with something): μακρῇσιν ἐπηγκενίδεσσι τελεύτα ε 253.

τελευτή, -ῆς, ἡ [τελέω]. (1) An end or conclusion: βιότοιο Η 104, Π 787: τελευτὴν ποιῆσαι (bring matters to a conclusion, *i.e.* get rid of the suitors) α 249 = π 126.—(2) An accomplishment or fulfilment: μύθοιο I 625.

†**τελέω** [τέλος]. Also **τελείω** (τελεσίω, fr. τελεσ-, τέλος). 3 sing. pres. τελέει Υ 370. τελεῖ Δ 161. τελείει ζ 234, ψ 161. 1 pl. subj. τελέωμεν δ 776. 3 pl. opt. τελέοιεν ι 127. Nom. pl. masc. pple. τελέοντες γ 262. 3 pl. impf. (ἐ)τέλειον I 456, Ο 593. τέλεον Ψ 373, 768. Fut. τελέω Ψ 20, 180: δ 485, σ 389. τελέσσω Ψ 559. 3 sing. τελέει Θ 415: β 256, τ 557. 3 pl. τελέουσι I 156, 298, Μ 59: ζ 174, ψ 286. Aor. ἐτέλεσσα ε 409, ψ 192, 199. 2 sing. ἐτέλεσσας Α 108, Ψ 149. 3 (ἐ)τέλεσσε Δ 160, Η 69, Μ 222, Φ 457: γ 119, λ 246, χ 51. τέλεσε ε 390, ι 76, κ 144. 3 pl. ἐτέλεσσαν I 598: ν 212. τέλεσσαν η 325. Subj. τελέσω λ 352. τελέσσω Α 523. 2 sing. τελέσσῃς Ψ 543. 3 τελέσῃ Ξ 44. τελέσσῃ Α 82: ρ 51, 60. 3 pl. τελέσωσι Σ 8: σ 134. Opt. τελέσαιμι I 157. 2 sing. τελέσειας ο 195. 3 τελέσειε Δ 178, I 299, Κ 303: β 34, δ 699, θ 570, ο 112, 203, ρ 399, υ 236, 344. 1 pl. τελέσαιμεν Ν 377. Imp. τέλεσον κ 483. Infin. τελέσαι Ξ 195, 196, Σ 116, 426, 427, Χ 366, Ω 660: β 272, ε 89, 90, κ 490, λ 77. τελέσσαι Ξ 262, Σ 362, Τ 22: δ 644, ψ 250. **Pass.** 3 sing. pres. τελεῖται Β 330, Ξ 48: β 176, ε 302, ν 178, σ 271. τελείεται ξ 160, τ 305, 561. 3 sing. impf. ἐτελείετο Α 5: λ 297. Fut. infin. τελέεσθαι Α 204, Β 36: α 201, β 156, γ 226, δ 664, ο 173, π 347, χ 215. τελεῖσθαι ψ 284. 3 sing. aor. ἐτελέσθη δ 663, τ 153, ω 143. τελέσθη Ο 228: κ 470. 3 sing. pf. τετέλεσται Σ 74: ν 40, π 346. Pple. τετελεσμένος, -ου Α 212, 388, Β 257, Θ 286, 401, 454, I 310, Ξ 196, Σ 4, 427, Ψ 410, 672: β 187, ε 90, ο 536, π 440, ρ 163, 229, σ 82, τ 309, 487, 547, φ 337. 3 sing. plupf. τετέλεστο Η 465, Τ 242: ε 262, χ 479. (ἐκ-.) (1) To bring to completion, carry through, carry out, bring about, accomplish, perform: τετέλεστο ἔργον Η 465, τελέσαι με θυμὸς ἄνωγεν Ξ 195. Cf. Α 523, Κ 303, Ξ 262, Σ 8, Τ 22, Ψ 373, Ω 660, etc.: Ζεὺς ἀγαθὸν τελέσειεν, ὅ τι μενοινᾷ β 34, ὁδόν 256. Cf. β 272, γ 262, δ 663, λ 246, ν 40, ρ 51, χ 51, ψ 286, etc.—Absol.: μενοίνεον εἰ τελέουσιν (make good their passage) Μ 59. Cf. Δ 160, 161, Θ 415, Ο 228, Σ 352 (to work his will): μόγις ἐτέλεσσε Κρονίων (granted us our ends) γ 119. Cf. ε 409 (have accomplished my journey), η 325, ν 212, ο 203 (might do his bidding), τ 557 (what his purpose is), ψ 192, 199.—(2) In pass. (sometimes in impers. use), to be accomplished or fulfilled, be brought to pass, come to pass, be: τὸ καὶ τελέεσθαι ὀΐω Α 204, ὡς καὶ τετελεσμένον ἔσται Θ 286. Cf. Α 212, Β 36, 330 (are coming true), I 310, Ψ 410, etc.: α 201, β 156, 176, γ 226, ξ 160, π 440, ψ 284, etc.—(3) In pf. pple. pass., capable of accomplishment: εἰ τετελεσμένον ἐστίν Ξ 196 = Σ 427: = ε 90.—(4) To succeed *in doing something*. With infin.: δόμεναι τεκέεσσιν Μ 222. —(5) To make full or perfect: εἰς ὅ κε πᾶσαν δωτίνην τελέσω (make up the full tale) λ 352.—(6) To accomplish, fulfil, carry out, bring to fruition or consummation (a purpose, design, prediction, ordinance, wish, imprecation, charge, etc.): Διὸς ἐτελείετο βουλή Α 5, ἐπαράς I 456, Διὸς ἐφετμάς Ο 593. Cf. Α 82, 108, Δ 178, Η 69, I 156, 298, Ξ 44, Ψ 149, etc.: ὑπόσχεσιν κ 483. Cf. β 272, δ 776, λ 297, ο 195, τ 547, υ 236, etc.—(7) In reference to a period of time, to bring round in its course, bring on: περὶ ἤματα μακρὰ τελέσθη (came round) κ 470, περὶ ἤματα πόλλ' ἐτελέσθη (had come round, had passed) τ 153 = ω 143. Cf. ε 390 = ι 76 = κ 144.—(8) To pay: μισθόν Φ 457.—Sim.: οὐκέτι δῶρ' ἐτέλεσσαν (withheld the promised gifts) I 598.

τελήεις, -εντος. Fem. -εσσα [τέλος]. Of sacrifices, such as win accomplishment, acceptable: ἑκατόμβας Α 315, Β 306: δ 352, 582, ν 350, ρ 50, 59.

τέλλω. 3 sing. plupf. pass. ἐτέταλτο Β 643: λ 524. (ἀνα-, ἐπι-, περιτέλλομαι.) To cause to take a particular direction. With ἐπί, to lay (an injunction or charge upon a person), give (an order to him): κρατερὸν ἐπὶ μῦθον ἔτελλεν Α 25 = 379, Α 326, Π 199, τῷ δ' ἐπὶ πάντ' ἐτέταλτο ἀνασσέμεν Αἰτωλοῖσιν (*i.e.* he bore the whole burden of the leadership) Β 643: ἐμοὶ δ' ἐπὶ πάντ' ἐτέταλτο (*i.e.* I had sole responsibility) λ 524. Cf. ψ 349.

τέλος, τό. (1) An end or conclusion: γνῶ ὅ οἱ οὔ τι τ. κατακαίριον ἦλθεν (that it was not a fatal end that had come to him) Λ 439.—(2) The completion or finishing of something: [τρίποδες] τόσσον ἔχον τ. Σ 378.—(3) The accomplishment of something, the bringing it to a conclusion or final decision, the issue of it: τ. οὔ πώ τι πέφανται Β 122, ἐν χερσὶ τ. πολέμοιο Π 630, εἰ θεός περ ἶσον τείνειεν πολέμου τ. (*i.e.* should pull fairly or evenly at, stretch fairly, the rope of strife) (cf. πεῖραρ (1)) Υ 101. Cf. Γ 291.—(4) The accomplishment, carrying out, fulfilment, of something: οὐδὲ τ. μύθῳ ἐπιθήσεις Τ 107. Cf. Υ 369: εἰ γὰρ ἐπ' ἀρῇσιν τ. ἡμετέρῃσι γένοιτο ρ 496.—(5) The coming to pass, the crisis or supreme moment, of something (cf. πεῖραρ (2)(c)): τ. θανάτοιο Γ 309, Ε 553, I 416, Λ 451, Π 502 = 855 = Χ 361, μισθοῖο τ. (the moment for the payment of the wage) Φ 450: τ. γάμοιο (the longed-for day of marriage) υ 74, νόστοιο τέλος (the day when I should set foot on my native shore) χ 323. Cf. ε 326, ρ 476, ω 124.—(6) The final stage or consummation of something: οὐ τ. ἵκεο μύθων (have not said the last word, all that is to be said) I 56.—Sim.: οὔ τί φημι τ. χαριέστερον εἶναι ἢ ὅτε . . . (I say that there can be no higher perfection of happiness) ι 5.—(7) The essential points, the sum or substance, of something (cf. πεῖραρ (2)(g)): μύθου τ. Π 83.—(8) A post or position occupied by soldiers: δόρπον εἵλοντο (ἑλόμεσθα) (ἕλεσθε) κατὰ στρατὸν ἐν τελέεσσιν (in their (our) (your) respective quarters) Η 380, Λ 730, Σ 298, ἐς φυλάκων τ. Κ 56. Cf. Κ 470.

τέλοσδε [τέλος + -δε (1)]. In phrase θανάτοιο τέλοσδε (see prec. (5)), to the . . . I 411, Ν 602.

τέλσον, τό. In ploughing, the headland (of a field), the strip at each end of the furrows at the edge of which the plough is turned: τ. ἀρούρης Ν 707, Σ 544. Cf. Σ 547.

τέμενος, τό [τέμνω]. (1) A piece of land marked off from common land and held in severalty, *i.e.* as private enclosed property: τ. τάμον Z 194, Υ 184, τ. βασιλήϊον Σ 550. Cf. I 578, M 313, Υ 391: ζ 293, λ 185, ρ 299.—(2) A piece of land similarly marked off and dedicated to the service of a god or goddess: Πύρασον, Δήμητρος τ. (*i.e.* Pyrasus with its . . .) B 696. Cf. Θ 48, Ψ 148: θ 363.

τέμνω. See τάμνω.

τέμω. 3 sing. aor. ἔτετμε Δ 293, Z 515: α 218, γ 256, ε 81. τέτμε Z 374: ε 58. 2 sing. subj. τέτμῃς ο 15. (1) To reach, touch: τέμει [ἄροτρον] τέλσον ἀρούρης N 707.—(2) To light or come upon, find: Ἕκτορα Z 515.—To find or come upon in a specified place or condition, or doing something specified: οὓς ἑτάρους στέλλοντα Δ 293, ἔνδον Z 374: ε 81. Cf. γ 256, ε 58, ο 15.—Of a stage of life, to come upon (one): ὃν γῆρας ἔτετμεν α 218.

τένων, -οντος, ὁ [τείνω]. Always in dual or pl. A tendon (in K 456, Ξ 466, Π 587 = ἰνίον): χερμαδίῳ βλῆτο παρὰ σφυρὸν· ἀμφοτέρω δὲ τένοντε λᾶας ἀπηλοίησεν Δ 521. Cf. E 307, K 456, Ξ 466, Π 587, P 290, Υ 478, X 396.—Of an ox γ 449.

τέξεις, 2 sing. fut. τίκτω.

τεοῖο. See τοι[1].

τεός, -ή, -όν. Thy, your (cf. σός) A 138, 282, E 230, 234, Θ 238, etc.: α 295, β 123, γ 94, 122, η 290, etc.

τέρας, τό. Genit. pl. τεράων M 229. Dat. τεράεσσι Δ 398, 408, Z 183, M 256. Acc. τέραα μ 394. (1) A significant sign or token, an omen or portent: τόδ' ἔφηνε τ. Ζεύς B 324. Cf. Δ 76, 398, 408, Z 183, Λ 28 (for men), M 209, 229, 256, P 548: ἠτέομεν θεὸν φῆναι τ. γ 173. Cf. μ 394, ο 168, π 320, υ 101, 114, φ 415.—(2) Something borne as a symbol: Ἔριδα, πολέμοιο τ. μετὰ χερσὶν ἔχουσαν Λ 4 (the nature of the object seems to be beyond conjecture).—(3) Something endowed with malign mystic power: Γοργείη κεφαλή, Διὸς τ. E 742.

τέρετρον, -ου, τό [cf. τετραίνω]. A borer or gimlet: ἔνεικε τέρετρα· τέτρηνεν δ' ἄρα πάντα ε 246. Cf. ψ 198.

τέρην, -ενος. Neut. τέρεν, -ενος. [Cf. L. *teres*.] (1) Of spheroidal form, round. Epithet of tears Γ 142, Π 11, T 323: π 332.—(2) Of flesh, showing firm rounded contours Δ 237, N 553, Ξ 406.—(3) Of vegetation, swelling with sap, full of fresh life: φύλλα N 180: μ 357, ἄνθεα ποίης ι 449.

τέρμα, -ατος, τό. (1) The outward goal or turning-point in a race over a double course: αἰεὶ τέρμ' ὁρόων Ψ 323. Cf. Ψ 462, 466.—In pl. in the same sense: ὡς ὅτε περὶ τέρμαθ' ἵπποι τρωχῶσιν X 162. Cf. Ψ 309, 333, 358 = 757.—(2) In pl. = σῆμα (3): ἔθηκε τέρματα θ 193.

τερμιόεις, -εντος. Fem. -εσσα [app. 'with a τέρμις,' explained as 'fringe']. Thus, fringed: ἀσπίς Π 803: χιτῶνα τ 242.

τερπικέραυνος [τερπ-, metathesis of τρεπ-, τρέπω + κεραυνός]. Hurler of the thunderbolt. Epithet of Zeus A 419, B 478, 781, Θ 2, Λ 773, M 252, Π 232, Ω 529: η 164, 180, ξ 268 = ρ 437, τ 365, υ 75, ω 24.

τέρπω. Fut. **Mid.** τέρψομαι Υ 23. Aor. subj. τέρψομαι π 26. Pple. τερψάμενος μ 188. 1 pl. aor. subj. ταρπώμεθα Ω 636: δ 295, ψ 255. 3 sing. redup. aor. τετάρπετο T 19, Ω 513. 1 pl. subj. τεταρπώμεσθα Ψ 10, 98: λ 212. Pple. τεταρπόμενος α 310, ξ 244. Pl. τεταρπόμενοι I 705. **Pass.** 2 pl. aor. ἐτέρφθητε ρ 174. 3 ἐτέρφθησαν θ 131. 3 sing. opt. τερφθείη ε 74. 3 sing. aor. τάρφθη τ 213, 251, φ 57. 3 pl. τάρφθεν ζ 99. 3 dual aor. ἐταρπήτην ψ 300. 1 pl. τάρπημεν Λ 780. 3 pl. τάρπησαν Ω 633: γ 70, δ 47, ε 201, κ 181. 1 pl. subj. τραπείομεν (metathesis of ταρπείομεν) Γ 441, Ξ 314: θ 292. Infin. ταρπήμεναι Ω 3: ψ 346. ταρπῆναι ψ 212. (ἐπι-, ποτι-.) (I) (1) To cheer, solace, refresh. In mid.: τεταρπόμενος κῆρ α 310.—To cheer in sorrow, comfort: τέρποντες πυκινῶς ἀκαχήμενον T 312.—(2) To engage agreeably the thoughts or attention of, entertain, amuse: τὸν ἔτερπε λόγοις O 393. Cf. I 189: α 107, σ 315, τ 590.—In mid.: φρένα τερπόμενον φόρμιγγι I 186. Cf. Υ 23.—Absol.: ἀοιδόν, ὅ κεν τέρπῃσιν ἀείδων ρ 385. Cf. α 347, θ 45.—In mid. with reciprocal force: τερπέσθην μύθοισιν ψ 301. Cf. Λ 643: δ 179, 239.—(3) To satisfy. With genit. In mid.: τεταρπόμενοι ἦτορ σίτου καὶ οἴνοιο I 705.—(II) In mid. and pass. (1) To have joy or delight, give oneself up to pleasure or enjoyment, take one's pleasure or ease, enjoy oneself: φρένα τέρπετ' ἀκούων (in his heart) A 474, φιλότητι τραπείομεν εὐνηθέντε Γ 441. Cf. H 61, I 337, 400, Ξ 314, Σ 604, T 18, Φ 45 (with his . . .), Ψ 298 (live at ease): α 26, δ 17, ε 74, ζ 46, θ 91, ξ 244, ο 391, φ 105, etc.—With genit.: ὄφρα τέρπηται ἀοιδῆς (have joy in it) θ 429. Cf. ψ 212.—In reference to solacing oneself with lamentation or with the recalling of past sorrow: γόῳ φρένα τέρπομαι δ 102, κήδεσιν ἀλλήλων τερπώμεθα, μνωομένω ο 399. Cf. ο 400, τ 513.—(2) To be filled with satisfaction or exultation, exult: οἱ ἔκηλοι τέρπονται E 760. Cf. Δ 10.—(3) To be cheered or gladdened: οὔτ' αὐγῆς Ἠελίοιο τέρποντ' οὔτ' ἀνέμοισιν Θ 481. Cf. T 313.—(4) To entertain or amuse oneself: δίσκοισιν τέρποντο B 774. Cf. Σ 526: α 422 = σ 305, α 423 = σ 306, δ 626 = ρ 168, ρ 606.—(5) To satisfy one's desire (for something), take one's fill (of it). With genit.: ἐπεὶ σίτου τάρφθεν ζ 99. Cf. Λ 780: γ 70, ε 201, ψ 300, 346.—With instrumental dat.: ἐπεὶ ἐτέρφθησαν φρέν' ἀέθλοις θ 131. Cf. ρ 174.—With complementary pple.: ἐπεὶ τετάρπετο δαίδαλα λεύσσων T 19. Cf. Ω 633: δ 47 = κ 181.—Without construction: δόρποιο μέδοντο ὕπνου τε ταρπήμεναι (to have their fill thereof) Ω 3. Cf. Ω 636: = δ 295 = ψ 255.—In reference to lamentation, to take one's fill (of it), indulge oneself (in it) to the full. With genit.: ἐπεί κε τεταρπώμεσθα γόοιο Ψ 10. Cf. Ψ 98, Ω 513: λ 212, τ 213 = 251 = φ 57.

τερπωλή, -ῆς, ἡ [τέρπω]. A joy or delight: οἵην τερπωλὴν θεὸς ἤγαγεν ἐς τόδε δῶμα σ 37.

†**τερσαίνω** [cf. next]. 3 sing. aor. τέρσηνε Π 529.

Non-thematic pres. infin. pass. τερσήμεναι ζ 98. τερσῆναι Π 519. To cause to become dry, dry: εἵματ' ἠελίοιο μένον τερσήμεναι αὐγῇ ζ 98.—To check the flow of (blood): ἀφ' ἕλκεος αἷμα τέρσηνεν Π 529. Cf. Π 519.

τέρσομαι [cf. prec.]. To become dry: οὐδέ ποτ' ὄσσε δακρυόφιν τέρσοντο ε 152. Cf. η 124 (bakes in the sun).—Of a wound, to dry up, have the flow of blood checked Λ 267, 848.

τερψίμβροτος [τερψ-, τέρπω + (μ)βροτός]. That brings delight to men. Epithet of Ἠέλιος μ 269 = 274.

τέρψομαι, fut. and aor. subj. mid. τέρπω.

τεσσαράβοιος, -ον [τεσσαρ-, τέσσαρες + -α- (on analogy of numerals in -α) + βοῦς]. Of the value of four oxen: τίον ἑ τεσσαράβοιον (as being of the value of . . ., at the value of . . .) Ψ 705.

τεσσαράκοντα, *indeclinable* [τέσσαρες]. Forty Β 524 = 747, Β 534 = 545 = 630 = 644 = 710 = 737 = 759: ω 341.

τέσσαρες, -α. Four: τέσσαρες ἀρχοί Β 618, οὔατα τέσσαρα Λ 634. Cf. Ε 271, Λ 699, Σ 578, Ψ 268: δ 436, ι 335, κ 349, ξ 22, χ 110, 204, ω 279, 497.

τέταγον, *aor.* [redup. fr. ταγ-. Cf. L. *ta(n)go*]. To grasp, seize: ῥῖψε ποδὸς τεταγών (by the . . .) Α 591. Cf. Ο 23.

τέταντο, 3 pl. plupf. pass. τείνω.

τετάνυσται, 3 sing. pf. pass. τανύω.

τετάρπετο, 3 sing. redup. aor. mid. τέρπω.

τέταρτος. See τέτρατος.

τέταται, 3 sing. pf. pass. τείνω.

τετέλεσται, 3 sing. pf. pass. τελέω.

τετεύξεται, 3 sing. fut. pass. τεύχω.

τετεύχαται, 3 pl. pf. pass. τεύχω.

τετεύχημαι, *pf. pass.* [app. formed fr. τεύχεα, though the stem is τευχεσ-]. To have one's harness on: τετευχῆσθαι γὰρ ἄμεινον χ 104.

τετευχώς, pf. pple. τεύχω.

τέτηκα, pf. τήκω.

τετίημαι, *pf.* Pple. in act. form τετιηώς, -ότος Ι 13, 30, 695, Λ 555, Ρ 664, Ω 283. To be sorrowful, grieved, vexed, sore, troubled, heavy: τετιημέναι ἦτορ (dashed in spirits) Θ 437, ἶζον εἰν ἀγορῇ τετιηότες Ι 13. Cf. Θ 447, Ι 30 = 695, Λ 555 = Ρ 664, Λ 556, Ω 283: α 114, β 298, δ 804, θ 303, σ 153.—In a more physical sense: τετιημένος ἦτορ (his spirit crushed, with little life in him) η 287.

τετῑμένος, pf. pple. pass. τίω.

τέτλαθι, pf. imp. τλάω.

τετλαίη, 3 sing. pf. opt. τλάω.

τέτληκε, 3 sing. pf. τλάω.

τετληότες, nom. pl. masc. pf. pple. τλάω.

τετληυῖα, pf. pple. fem. τλάω.

τέτμε, 3 sing. aor. τέμω.

τετμημένον, nom. sing. neut. pf. pple. pass. τάμνω.

τετράγυος [τετρα-, τέσσαρες + γύης, a measure of land. Cf. πεντηκοντόγυος]. Consisting of four measures: ὄρχατος η 113.—In neut. without sb., a space of four measures: τετράγυον εἴη (let us have four measures to cover) σ 374.

τετραθέλυμνος [τετρα-, τέσσαρες + θέλυμνα, foundations. Cf. προθέλυμνος]. With four layers of hide: σάκος Ο 479: χ 122.

†τετραίνω [cf. τείρω]. Aor. τέτρηνα ψ 198. 3 sing. τέτρηνε Χ 396: ε 247. To perforate, pierce: τένοντε Χ 396.—To treat with the gimlet, make the needful perforations in: πάντα ε 247, ψ 198.

τετράκις [τετρα-, τέσσαρες]. Four times: τρισμάκαρες καὶ τετράκις ε 306.

τετράκυκλος, -ον [τετρα-, τέσσαρες + κύκλος]. Four-wheeled: ἕλκον τε̄τρᾰκυκλον ἀπήνην Ω 324: ἅμαξαι ἐσθλαὶ τε̄τρᾰκυκλοι ι 242.

τετραμμένος, pf. pple. pass. τρέπω.

τετράοροι [contr. fr. τετραήορος, fr. τετρα-, τέσσαρες + ἠορ-, ἀείρω. Cf. παρήορος, συνήορος]. Yoked four together: ἵπποι ν 81.

τετραπλῇ [contr. dat. sing. fem. of τετραπλόος, fr. τετρα-, τέσσαρες. For the second element cf. διπλόος]. Fourfold: ἀποτείσομεν Α 128.

τέτραπτο, 3 sing. plupf. pass. τρέπω.

τέτρατος, -η, -ον. Also **τέταρτος** [τετρα-, τέσσαρες]. (1) The fourth: τ. ὁπλίσαθ' ἵππους (was the fourth to . . .) Ψ 301, ἀνάειρε δύω χρυσοῖο τάλαντα τ. (taking the fourth prize) 615. Cf. β 107 = τ 152 = ω 142, γ 180, ε 262.—With ellipse of sb.: τῶν τετάρτων ἦρχε . . . (the fourth body) Β 623, Μ 98, τῆς τετάρτης [στιχὸς] ἦρχε . . . Π 196, τῷ τετάρτῳ θῆκε δύω χρυσοῖο τάλαντα (for the man running fourth) Ψ 269. Cf. β 89, κ 358, ξ 26.—(2) τὸ τέταρτον (τέτρατον), for the fourth time: ὅτε τὸ τέταρτον ἐπέσσυτο Ε 438 = Π 705 = 786 = Υ 447. Cf. Χ 208: φ 128.—On the fourth occasion: τὸ τέτρατον ἵκετο τέκμωρ (at the fourth stride) Ν 20. Cf. Φ 177.

τετραφάληρος, -ον [τετρα-, τέσσαρες + φάλαρον]. With four φάλαρα: κυνέην Ε 743 = Λ 41.

τετράφαλος, -ον [τετρα-, τέσσαρες + φάλος]. With four φάλοι: κυνέην Μ 384, κόρυθι Χ 315.

τετράφατο, 3 pl. plupf. pass. τρέπω.

τετράφθω, pf. imp. pass. τρέπω.

τετραχθά [τετρα-, τέσσαρες]. In four pieces Γ 363: ι 71.

τέτρηνα, aor. τετραίνω.

τετρήχει, 3 sing. plupf. ταράσσω.

τετρῖγει, 3 sing. plupf. τρίζω.

τέτροφε, 3 sing. pf. τρέφω.

τέττα. App. a form of courteous address: τέττα, σιωπῇ ἧσο Δ 412.

τέττιξ, -ῑγος, ὁ. The cicada Γ 151.

τετυγμένος, pf. pple. pass. τεύχω.

τετύγμην, plupf. pass. τεύχω.

τετυκεῖν, aor. infin. τεύχω.

τετύκοντο, 3 pl. aor. mid. τεύχω.

τέτυκται, 3 sing. pf. pass. τεύχω.

τετυμμένω, nom. dual masc. pf. pple. pass. τύπτω.

τετύχηκε, 3 sing. pf. τυγχάνω.

τεῦξε, 3 sing. aor. τεύχω.

τεύξεσθαι[1], fut. infin. mid. and pass. τεύχω.

τεύξεσθαι[2], fut. infin. mid. τυγχάνω.

τεύξῃ, 2 sing. fut. mid. τυγχάνω.

τεύξω, fut. τεύχω.

τεύχεα, τά. Dat. τεύχεσι Γ 29, Δ 419, Ε 450, Λ 49, Π 156, Υ 46, Χ 381, etc.: λ 74, 546, ξ 474, ω 69. τεύχεσσι Ψ 131: ω 496. Armour, harness, warlike trappings or array (app. sometimes, as in δ 784, ο 218, π 284 (cf. τ 33), π 326, 360, τ 4 (cf. 33), ω 534, etc., including arms) (cf. ἔντεα): τεύχε' ἀποθέσθαι Γ 89, ἀμφ' ὤμοισιν ἐδύσετο τεύχεα 328. Cf. Β 808, Δ 222, 466, 504, Ε 435, Ζ 230, Η 146, etc.: λ 41, μ 13, ξ 474, ο 218 (doubtless referring to some light pieces which he had taken with him rather as a matter of ceremony than for use), χ 109, 114, 139, etc.

τεύχω. [This and τυγχάνω believed to be different forms of the same word.] 3 sing. dual impf. ἐτεύχετον Ν 346. Fut. τεύξω ν 397. 2 sing. τεύξεις ω 476. 3 τεύξει κ 290. 1 pl. τεύξομεν μ 347. 3 pl. τεύξουσι α 277, β 196, ω 197. Infin. τεύξειν χ 14. Aor. ἔτευξα δ 174. 3 sing. ἔτευξε Ζ 314, Ξ 166, 338, Σ 483. τεῦξε Ε 449, Σ 609, 610, 611, 613: η 92, 235, θ 276. 3 pl. ἔτευξαν α 244. τεῦξαν Φ 538: θ 579. 3 sing. opt. τεύξειε Ξ 240: θ 177, ν 191, υ 11. Pple. τεύξας λ 409. Fem. τεύξᾱσα λ 430. Redup. aor. infin. τετυκεῖν ο 77, 94. Pf. pple. τετευχώς μ 423. **Mid.** Fut. infin. τεύξεσθαι Τ 208. 3 pl. redup. aor. τετύκοντο Α 467, Β 430, Η 319: θ 61, μ 307, π 478, υ 390, ω 384. 1 pl. opt. τετυκοίμεθα μ 283, ξ 408. Infin. τετυκέσθαι φ 428. **Pass.** Fut. infin. τεύξεσθαι Ε 653. 3 sing. fut. τετεύξεται Μ 345, 358, Φ 322, 585. 3 sing. aor. ἐτύχθη Β 155, 320, Δ 470, Λ 671, Μ 471, Ο 122, 696, Π 296, Ρ 410, 704: γ 255, δ 212, σ 36, 221, 233, φ 303, ω 124. 2 sing. pf. τέτυξαι Π 622. 3 τέτυκται Γ 101, Δ 84, Ξ 246, Ο 207, Π 589, Ρ 690, Σ 120, Τ 224, Φ 191, Χ 30, 420, 450, Ψ 240, Ω 317, 354: δ 392, 771, ζ 301, θ 544, 546, μ 280, ν 243, ρ 102, τ 595, ψ 188. 3 pl. τετεύχαται Ν 22, Ξ 53, 220: β 63, ξ 138, τ 563. 3 sing. imp. τετύχθω β 356, φ 231. Pple. τετυγμένος, -ου Ζ 243, Ξ 9, 66, Π 225, Χ 511, Ψ 741: δ 615, ι 223, κ 210, π 185, υ 366, χ 335, etc. Infin. τετύχθαι Ο 110: α 391. Plupf. τετύγμην ξ 234. 2 sing. ἐτέτυξο Μ 164. τέτυξο Θ 163. 3 (ἐ)τέτυκτο Ε 78, 402, 446, 901, Ζ 7, Λ 77, Μ 8, Ξ 215, Ο 337, 643, Π 605, Ρ 279, Σ 549, Ψ 332, 455: δ 772, θ 5, 281, 384, ι 190, λ 550, 610, ν 170, ρ 210, σ 275, τ 226, υ 110, ψ 152. 3 pl. ἐτετεύχατο Λ 808. τετεύχατο Σ 574. (προ-) (**1**) To make, construct, build, form, fabricate, fashion, prepare: εἴδωλον Ε 449, δώματα, τά ῥ' αὐτὸς ἔτευξεν Ζ 314, θεῶν ἀέκητι [τεῖχος] τέτυκτο Μ 8. Cf. Β 101, Ε 61, Ξ 166, Σ 373, 483 (wrought, represented), 609, Φ 322, Χ 511 (woven), etc.: εἶδος θ 177, νηόν μ 347. Cf. δ 174, η 92, 235, θ 276, φ 215.—With genit. of material: βόες χρυσοῖο τετεύχατο (were wrought or represented in . . .) Σ 574: περόνη χρυσοῖο τέτυκτο τ 226.—With dat.: δόμον αἰθούσῃσι τετυγμένον (built with . . .) Ζ 243. Cf. τ 563.—In pf. pple. in pass. sense, made: ἐπίτονος, βοὸς ῥινοῖο τετευχώς μ 423.—(**2**) To make, cause to be *so and so*: αὐτοὺς ἑλώρια τεῦχε κύνεσσιν Α 4: ὄφρα μιν αὐτὸν ἄγνωστον τεύξειεν ν 191. Cf. ν 397.—(**3**) In pf. pple. pass., that is a work of craftsmanship, wrought, (well or curiously) made, fashioned or constructed (cf. τυκτός): σάκος τετυγμένον Ξ 9. Cf. Ξ 66, Π 225, Ψ 741: δέπα τετυγμένα υ 153, ἀγρὸν τετυγμένον (brought into a high state of cultivation) ω 206. Cf. δ 615 = ο 115, ι 223, κ 210, 252, π 185, χ 335.—Sim. of the mind, steady, well balanced υ 366.—(**4**) To make ready, prepare (a meal or the like): τεύξει τοι κυκεῶ κ 290, δεῖπνον τετυκεῖν ο 77 = 94. Cf. Λ 624: κ 316.—In mid. Α 467 = Β 430 = Η 319, Τ 208: θ 61, κ 182, μ 283, 307, ξ 408, π 478 = ω 384, υ 390, φ 428.—Sim.: ἄλφιτα τεύχουσαι (τευχούσῃ) (grinding it) υ 108, 119.—(**5**) To make, bring about, arrange, cause, cause to come into existence or take place: ἄλγεα Α 110, ὄμβρον Κ 6. Cf. Ν 209, 346, Ο 70, Φ 538: γάμον α 277 = β 196, τάδε τέτυκται θ 544, βοήν κ 118. Cf. α 244, θ 579, κ 18, σ 350, υ 11, χ 14, ω 197, 476.—(**6**) In pass., to be brought about or to pass, to take place, be done, occur, happen, be: νόστος κ' ἐτύχθη Β 155, θαυμάζομεν οἷον ἐτύχθη 320, ὅμαδος ἐτύχθη (rose up) Μ 471 = Π 296. Cf. Δ 470, Ε 653, Λ 671, Μ 345, 358, Ο 110, 122, 696, Ρ 410, 690, 704, Φ 585, Χ 450, Ω 354 (app., matters have happened which call for, this is a matter which calls for, a wary mind): ὅττι τοι κακόν τ' ἀγαθόν τε τέτυκται δ 392. Cf. β 63, γ 255, δ 212, ξ 138, σ 36, 221, 233 (turned out), φ 303, ω 124.—In reference to the workings of fate, to be fated or decreed: ὁπποτέρῳ θάνατος τέτυκται Γ 101. Cf. Σ 120.—(**7**) To plan, contrive, plot: τεύξας θάνατον λ 409. Cf. δ 771, λ 430.—(**8**) In pf. and plupf. pass. (**a**) Signifying merely being or existence: ὅθι οἱ νηός γε τέτυκτο (stood) Ε 446, τό γε νύσσα τέτυκτο (served as . . .) Ψ 332, ἐν μετώπῳ λευκὸν σῆμα τέτυκτο 455. Cf. Λ 77, 808, Ν 22, Ξ 215, 220: οὐχ ἥδε δίκη τὸ πάροιθε τέτυκτο (this was not the custom) σ 275, τόδε σῆμα τετύχθω (let this be the signal) φ 231. Cf. θ 5, λ 610, ρ 210, ψ 188.—(**b**) As the copula (sometimes with the notion of becoming): Ζεύς, ὅς τ' ἀνθρώπων ταμίης πολέμοιο τέτυκται Δ 84 = Τ 224, οὔ τι καταθνητός γε τέτυκτο Ε 402 = 901, γυναικὸς ἄρ' ἀντὶ τέτυξο (you were not what we thought you were, you are after all no better than a woman) Θ 163, ἦ ῥά νυ καὶ σὺ φιλοψευδὴς ἐτέτυξο (so then thou art . . .) Μ 164. Cf. Ε 78, Ζ 7, Ξ 53, 246, Ο 207, 337, 643, Π 589, 605, 622, Ρ 279, Σ 549, Φ 191, Χ 30, 420, Ψ 240, Ω 317: τὰ δ' οὐ ἴσαν ὡς ἐτέτυκτο (how matters really were) δ 772 = ν 170 = ψ 152, εὐνήν, ἥ μοι στονόεσσα τέτυκται ρ 102 = τ 595. Cf. α 391, β 356, ζ 301, θ 281, 384, 546, ι 190, λ 550, μ 280, ν 243, ξ 234 (found myself), υ 110.

τέφρη, ἡ. Ashes Σ 25, Ψ 251.

τεχνάομαι [τέχνη]. (**1**) To make, fashion: εὖ τεχνήσατο καὶ ἱστία ε 259, μὴ τεχνησάμενος μηδ' ἄλλο τι τεχνήσαιτο (app., would that he had never made it, and (having made it) may he never make another of the same (*i.e.* so terrible) (see under μή (10)) λ 613.—(**2**) To contrive, devise: ταῦτ' αὐτὸς τεχνήσομαι Ψ 415.

τέχνη, -ης, ἡ. (**1**) Skill, art, craftsmanship,

cunning of hand: ἀνέρος, ὅς ῥά τε τέχνῃ νήϊον ἐκτάμνῃσιν Γ 61. Cf. γ 433, ζ 234 = ψ 161, λ 614.—Cunning, craft, wiles: οὐδ' ὁ γέρων δολίης ἐπελήθετο τέχνης δ 455.—(2) A plot, a dark design: δολίην ἐφράσσατο τέχνην δ 529.—(3) In concrete sense, something cunningly contrived, a contrivance: τέχνας εἰσορόωσιν Ἡφαίστοιο θ 327. Cf. θ 332.

τεχνήεις, -εντος [τέχνη]. Nom. pl. fem. τεχνῆσσαι (contr. fr. τεχνήεσσαι) η 110. (1) Skilled, skilful: ἱστῶν τεχνῆσσαι (in . . .) η 110.—(2) Skilfully or cunningly contrived or fashioned: δεσμοί θ 297.

τεχνηέντως [adv. fr. prec.]. With skill, skilfully: πηδαλίῳ ἰθύνετο τ. ε 270.

τεχνῆσσαι. See τεχνήεις.

τέως. See τῆος.

τῆ. There! come! With imp.: τῆ νῦν, τοῦτον ἱμάντα τεῷ ἐγκάτθεο κόλπῳ Ξ 219. Cf. Ψ 618, Ω 287: ε 346, θ 477, ι 347, κ 287.

τῆθος, τό. App., some kind of shell-fish: τήθεα διφῶν Π 747.

τηκεδών, -όνος, ἡ [τήκω]. A wasting or pining away: τηκεδόνι ἐξείλετο θυμόν λ 201.

τήκω. Pf. τέτηκα Γ 176. (κατα-.) (1) To cause to melt, melt, dissolve. In pass., to be melted, melt, dissolve: τηκομένης χιόνος τ 207.—(2) To cause to waste or pine away: μηδέ τι θυμὸν τῆκε τ 264.—In pass., to waste or pine away: ὃς ἐν νούσῳ κεῖται τηκόμενος ε 396.—So in pf. act.: κλαίουσα τέτηκα (I pine away) Γ 176.—To melt into tears: Ὀδυσσεὺς τήκετο θ 522.—To be bedewed with tears: ῥέε δάκρυα, τήκετο δὲ χρώς τ 204. Cf. τ 208.

τῆλε [cf. τηλοῦ]. (1) Far, far away, at a distance: τῆλ' ἀπὸ Λαρίσης Ρ 301. Cf. Π 117, Ρ 190, Σ 395, Ψ 72, 880: ὤλετο τῆλε β 183. Cf. γ 313, ε 315, ο 10, ρ 312.—With genit., far away from, far from: τῆλε φίλων Λ 817, Π 539. Cf. Χ 445: β 333, μ 354, τ 301, υ 340, ω 290.—(2) From far away, from afar: ἦγε τῆλ' ἐξ Ἀσκανίης Β 863.—(3) To far away, to a distance, afar, far: ῥίψω ἐς Τάρταρον, τῆλε μάλα Θ 14. Cf. Κ 153, Λ 44, 358, Υ 482, Χ 291, 468.—With genit., to far away from, far from: ἄξω τῆλ' Ἰθάκης ρ 250.

τηλεδαπός, -ή, -όν [τῆλε]. (1) Lying far off, remote: νήσων Φ 454, Χ 45.—Dwelling far off: ξείνων τ 371.—(2) From a far country: ἀνδρῶν ζ 279. Cf. ξ 415, ο 224, τ 351 = ω 268.

τηλεθάω [in form frequentative fr. θαλέθω]. Fem. pres. pple. τηλεθόωσα Ζ 148: ε 63. Acc. τηλεθόωσαν Ψ 142. Nom. pl. τηλεθόωσαι η 116, λ 590. Nom. pl. neut. τηλεθόωντα η 114. In pres. pple., of vegetation, growing profusely, flourishing, luxuriant: ὕλη τηλεθόωσα Ζ 148. Cf. Ρ 55: ε 63, η 114, 116 = λ 590, ν 196.—Of a lock of hair, luxuriant: χαίτην τηλεθόωσαν Ψ 142.—Of persons, in the bloom of youth: παῖδας τηλεθάοντας Χ 423.

τηλεκλειτός [τῆλε + κλειτός]. Far renowned, famous. Epithet of the Trojan allies Ε 491, Ζ 111 = Ι 233, Μ 108.—Of the father of Europa Ξ 321.—Of Ephialtes λ 308.—Of Icarius τ 546.

τηλεκλυτός [τῆλε + κλυτός]. = prec. Epithet of Orestes α 30.—Of horses Τ 400.

τηλεφανής [τῆλε + φαν-, φαίνω]. Far-seen, conspicuous: τύμβος ω 83.

τηλίκος. Of an age indicated by the context, of such an age: πατρὸς σοῖο, τηλίκου ὥς περ ἐγών (of my own years) Ω 487: οὐδέ τί σε χρὴ νηπιάας ὀχέειν, ἐπεὶ οὐκέτι τ. ἐσσί (you are too old for that) α 297, οὐκ ἐπὶ σταθμοῖσι μένειν ἔτι τ. εἰμί (it does not befit my years) ρ 20, ἤδη μὲν γάρ τοι παῖς τ. (the thought that he is grown up should keep you from that) σ 175, ἐπεὶ οὐκέτι τ. ἐστίν (he is old enough to know what goes on) τ 88.

τηλόθεν [τηλοῦ + -θεν (1)(2)]. (1) From far away, from afar: τ. ἐξ ἀπίης γαίης Α 270. Cf. Β 849, 857, 877, Ε 478, 651, Σ 208: γ 231, ε 283, ζ 312, η 25, 194, ι 273 = ν 237, τ 28.—(2) Far, far away, at a distance: τ. ἐν λείῳ πεδίῳ Ψ 359.

τηλόθι [τηλοῦ + -θι]. (1) Far, far away, at a distance: τ. ναίων Π 233. Cf. Θ 285, Φ 154, Ω 662: α 22, ε 55, λ 439, μ 135.—With genit., far away from, far from: τ. πάτρης Α 30, Π 461, Σ 99, Ω 86, 541: β 365.—(2) To far away, afar: τ. ὀδμὴ ἀνὰ νῆσον ὀδώδει ε 59.

τηλόσε [τηλοῦ + -σε]. To far away, to a distance, afar: τηλόσε δοῦπον ἔκλυεν Δ 455 (the power of hearing being thought of as projected towards the source of the sound; cf. Π 515 cited under πάντοσε). Cf. Χ 407.

τηλοτάτω [superl. fr. τηλοῦ]. The farthest off, the most remote: Εὐβοίης, τήν περ τηλοτάτω φάσ' ἔμμεναι η 322.

τηλοῦ [cf. τῆλε]. Far, far away, at a distance: τ. ἐπ' Ἀλφειῷ Λ 712. Cf. Ε 479, Ψ 853: ε 318, 431, ν 257, ρ 253, χ 323, ψ 68.—With genit., far away from, far from: τ. Ἀχαιΐδος αἴης ν 249.

τηλύγετος, -η [perh. fr. *τῆλυς, great (cf. τῆλε, τηλοῦ). 'Grown big']. Thus, that is entering, or has just entered, on manhood or womanhood, grown, 'great,' 'big': λιποῦσα παῖδα τηλυγέτην Γ 175 (*i.e.* just at the age when she most needed a mother's care), βῆ μετὰ Φαίνοπος υἷε, ἄμφω τηλυγέτω· ὁ δὲ τείρετο γήραϊ Ε 153 (of course the older the boys the less their father could hope for other heirs; cf. Ι 482: π 19 below), Ὀρέστῃ, ὅς μοι (οἱ) τηλύγετος τρέφεται θαλίῃ ἔνι πολλῇ (a big boy by now) Ι 143, 285, ὡς εἴ τε πατὴρ ὃν παῖδα φιλήσῃ μοῦνον τηλύγετον πολλοῖσιν ἐπὶ κτεάτεσσιν 482 (cf. Ε 153 above): ὃς οἱ τηλύγετος γένετο (was now a grown youth; see under γίγνομαι (I) (9)) δ 11, ὡς πατὴρ ὃν παῖδ' ἀγαπάζῃ μοῦνον τηλύγετον π 19 (cf. Ε 153 above).—Absol., a stripling: οὐκ Ἰδομενῆα φόβος λάβε τηλύγετον ὥς Ν 470.

τῆμος. (1) Then, at that time: τῆμος λέξεαι η 318.—(2) Correlative with ἦμος Η 434, Λ 90, Ψ 228, Ω 789: δ 401, μ 441.—With εὖτε ν 95.

τῆος. Also written τέως and scanned as ⏑– Ω 658: σ 190. (1) Meanwhile, the while: μιμνέτω αὐτόθι τῆος Τ 189, ὄφρα τέως μένω Ω 658. Cf. κ 348, ο 127, 231, π 370, σ 190.—(2) Correlative with ἧος Υ 42: δ 91.—(3) For a time, up to a certain point of time: τῆος μὲν ἔργ' ἐποπτεύεσκεν π 139. Cf. ω 162.

τηΰσιος, -η, -ον. App., idle, serving no good purpose: μὴ τηϋσίην ὁδὸν ἔλθῃς (lest your journey prove to have been a mistake) γ 316 = ο 13.

τίη [τί + ἦ²]. Strengthened form of τί (see τίς (3) (b)). For what reason? why? τίη τοι ταῦτ' ἀγορεύω; Α 365. Cf. Ζ 55, Κ 432, Ν 810, etc.: ο 326, π 421, ρ 375, τ 482, 500.

τιθαιβώσσω. App., of bees, to deposit their honey: ἔνθα τιθαιβώσσουσι μέλισσαι ν 106.

†**τίθημι** [redup. fr. θη-]. 2 sing. pres. τίθησθα ι 404, ω 476. 3 τίθησι Δ 83, Λ 392, Ρ 750, Χ 490: θ 245. 3 pl. τιθεῖσι Π 262: β 125. Pple. τιθείς Θ 171. Pl. τιθέντες Ε 384, Λ 413: ω 419. Infin. τιθήμεναι Ψ 83, 247. 3 pl. impf. τίθεσαν χ 449, 456. From τιθέω 3 sing. pres. τιθεῖ Ν 732. 3 sing. impf. (ἐ)τίθει Α 441, Θ 70, 441, Σ 541, Χ 210, Ψ 170, etc.: α 142, β 390, γ 51, ζ 76, θ 69, ρ 335, etc. Imp. τίθει Α 509: φ 177. Fut. θήσω Θ 289, Τ 121: λ 146, φ 74. 2 sing. θήσεις Π 90. 3 θήσει Υ 182: λ 101. 2 pl. θήσετε Ω 57. 3 θήσουσι Π 673. Infin. θησέμεναι Μ 35, Ο 602: υ 394. θήσειν Β 39, Ι 446, Τ 298: ε 136, η 257, ψ 336. Aor. ἔθηκα Ι 485: ν 302, ξ 276. 2 sing. ἔθηκας Ρ 37, Τ 316, Ω 741: κ 338. 3 ἔθηκε Α 2, Β 319, Γ 321, Ε 122, Ι 207, Μ 450, Ρ 470, Τ 12, Φ 524, Χ 368, etc.: γ 136, ε 265, θ 193, ι 235, λ 560, ξ 312, ο 488, σ 152, χ 123, etc. θῆκε Α 55, Ε 445, Ζ 357, Θ 324, Κ 46, Μ 399, Σ 375, Φ 145, Ψ 263, Ω 538, etc.: α 153, γ 77, ε 427, θ 20, μ 399, ρ 467, σ 195, υ 97, φ 102, etc. 3 pl. ἔθηκαν Ζ 300: ε 199, ζ 214, τ 592, ψ 167, ω 528. θῆκαν Ω 795: α 223, ν 122, σ 308. 1 pl. aor. ἔθεμεν γ 179. 3 ἔθεσαν (θέσαν) Α 290, 433, Ι 637, Μ 29, Ο 721, Τ 249, Φ 405, Ψ 631, Ω 49, etc.: ζ 248, θ 420, λ 274, 555, ν 119, ρ 258, υ 281, ψ 11. Subj. θείω Π 83, 437, Σ 387: α 89, ε 91, ι 517, ο 75. 2 sing. θήῃς Ζ 432, Π 96: κ 341. 3 θήῃ κ 301, ο 51. θῆσι π 282. 1 pl. θείομεν Α 143, Ψ 244, 486: ν 364. θέωμεν ω 485. Opt. θείην Ε 215. 2 sing. θείης Ω 661. 3 θείη Μ 26: α 116, θ 465, ο 180, π 198, υ 225, ψ 186. 1 pl. θεῖμεν μ 347. 3 θεῖεν Δ 363. Imp. θές Ζ 273: θ 425. 3 pl. θέντων τ 599. Nom. pl. masc. pple. θέντες Σ 352, Ψ 254: φ 267. Nom. sing. fem. θεῖσα φ 55. Infin. θέμεναι Β 285, Δ 57, Ψ 45, Ω 644: δ 297, η 336, φ 235. θέμεν λ 315, φ 3, 81, ω 168. θεῖναι Δ 26, Ζ 92: ν 156. **Mid.** 2 pl. pres. τίθεσθε φ 333. 3 τίθενται θ 554, ρ 269. Imp. pl. τίθεσθε τ 406. Acc. sing. masc. pple. τιθήμενον Κ 34. 1 pl. impf. τιθέμεσθα δ 578, λ 3. 3 ἐτίθεντο θ 52. τίθεντο Η 475, Ι 88: δ 781. 3 pl. fut. θήσονται Ω 402. Infin. θήσεσθαι φ 316. 3 sing. aor. θήκατο Κ 31, Ξ 187. 3 sing. aor. ἔθετο δ 761, θ 274. θέτο Γ 310, Ε 743, Ι 629, Κ 149, Λ 41, Ο 479, Τ 381: α 132, β 3, δ 308, θ 416, ξ 500, ο 241, σ 5, υ 125, φ 118, 119, χ 122. 2 pl. ἔθεσθε Θ 449. θέσθε δ 729. 3 ἔθεντο Β 750, Ι 232, Ρ 158. 2 sing. subj. θῆαι τ 403. 3 sing. opt. θεῖτο ρ 225. Imp. θέο κ 333. 3 sing. θέσθω Β 382. 2 pl. θέσθε Ν 121, Ο 561, 661. Pple. θέμενος Σ 317, Ψ 18: ι 171, κ 188, μ 319. Fem. θεμένῃ υ 387. Infin. θέσθαι Μ 411, 418: ν 207, φ 72. (ἀμφι-, ἀνα-, ἀπο-, ἐγκατα-, ἐκ-, ἐν-, ἐπανα-, ἐπι-, κατα-, μετα-, παρα-, περι-, προ-, προσ-, συν-, ὑπο-.) (**1**) (**a**) To put, set, place: ἐς ἑκατόμβην θείομεν (embark it) Α 143, ἐν χερσὶ τίθει 441. Cf. Α 433, Ε 215, Ι 207, Μ 29, Π 223, Ρ 750 (turns their course to the . . .), Σ 541, Φ 82 (has thrown me into . . .), Ω 644, etc.: ἐν νηῒ ὅπλ' ἐτίθει β 390, πόλλ' ἐπὶ μῆρ' ἔθεμεν γ 179 (*i.e.* on the altar). Cf. α 142, γ 51, δ 445, ζ 76, θ 65, λ 315, ν 119, ξ 436 (set it aside), ο 357 (brought him to it), υ 97, φ 366 (set it down), ψ 186, etc.—In mid.: οἳ περὶ Δωδώνην οἰκί' ἔθεντο (had established themselves) Β 750, ἐς δίφρον ἄρνας θέτο Γ 310, αὖλιν ἔθεντο (have established their . . .) Ι 232. Cf. Σ 317 = Ψ 18: θέτο δῶμα (*i.e.* built it) ο 241, μεγάλην κ' ἐπιγουνίδα θεῖτο (would get him a . . .) ρ 225. Cf. α 132, δ 578, θ 274, κ 333, etc.—To set (a host) in array. In mid.: θήσονται περὶ ἄστυ μάχην Ω 402.—(**b**) In sim. senses in reference to immaterial things: σοὶ ἄλληκτον θυμὸν ἐνὶ στήθεσσι θεοὶ θέσαν (wrath) Ι 637, ἐν στήθεσσι τιθεῖ νόον Ν 732. Cf. Π 83, Ρ 470, Τ 121, Ω 57, etc.: α 89, 321, β 125, γ 77, ζ 140, ο 234.—In mid.: ἐν φρεσὶ θέσθε ἕκαστος αἰδῶ Ν 121. Cf. Ο 561 = 661.—To give (a name to a child). In mid.: ὄνομ' εὕρεο ὅττι κε θῆαι παιδὸς παιδὶ τ 403. Cf. σ 5, τ 406.—Absol.: ἐπὶ πᾶσι τίθενται τοκῆες θ 554.—To apply (the mind): Ἑκτορέοις μᾶλλον ἐπὶ φρένα θῆχ' ἱεροῖσιν (paid attention to them, received them) Κ 46.—(**2**) To set down (a prize), propose as a prize: ἀγλά' ἄεθλα Ψ 263, ἵππον 265. Cf. Ψ 269, 270, 631, 653, 656, etc.: ἄεθλα ω 86.—As a subject of contest [τεύχε' Ἀχιλλῆος] λ 546.—As the material of a contest: θήσω τόξον φ 74. Cf. φ 3 = 81 = ω 168. —(**3**) To put on or about a person, endue him with: ἀμφί οἱ κυνέην κεφαλῆφιν ἔθηκεν Κ 257, 261. Cf. π 174.—To put on or about one's own person, endue oneself with: κνημῖδας περὶ κνήμῃσιν ἔθηκεν Γ 330 = Λ 17 = Π 131 = Τ 369. Cf. Γ 336 = Ο 480 = Π 137: = χ 123.—So in mid.: κρατὶ δ' ἐπὶ κυνέην θέτο Ε 743 = Λ 41. Cf. Κ 31, 34, 149, Ξ 187, Ο 479, Τ 381: β 3 = δ 308 = υ 125, θ 416, χ 122.—Of taking something (off one's person): ἀπὸ κρατὸς κυνέην ἔθηκα ξ 276.—In mid.: ἀπὸ χλαῖναν θέτο ξ 500. Cf. φ 118, 119.—(**4**) To set out (a meal), put (it before a person): παρά σφι τίθει δαῖτα Ι 90. Cf. Σ 387, Τ 316: δόρπον θησέμεναι υ 394. Cf. ε 91, 196, ζ 248, ι 517, etc.—In mid.: δαῖτα τίθενται ρ 269. Cf. Η 475, Ι 88.—In reference to horses, to put food and drink before them: ἵπποισι πυρὸν ἔθηκεν οἶνόν τε Θ 188.—(**5**) To put (into a person's mind or heart), suggest, communicate (cf. ὑποτίθημι): τῷ ἐπὶ φρεσὶ θῆκεν Α 55. Cf. Θ 218, Ι 460: ῥηΐδιόν τι ἔπος ἐνὶ φρεσὶ θήσω λ 146. Cf. ε 427, ξ 227, π 282, 291, σ 158 = φ 1.—In mid., to take into one's mind: τοῖσιν κότον ἔθεσθε Θ 449: οὐδ' ὑμεῖς περ ἐνὶ φρεσὶ θέσθε μ' ἀνεγεῖραι (never thought of it) δ 729.—(**6**) (**a**) To lay, impose, inflict, bring (evil upon a person): Ἀχαιοῖς ἄλγε' ἔθηκεν Α 2. Cf. Β 39, Ε 384, Ζ 357, Ο 721, Π 262, Ρ 37 = Ω 741, Φ 524, 525, Χ 422, Ω 538:

λ 560, ψ 306.—In mid. P 158.—(b) To bestow (upon a person, etc.), give, grant: ἐπὶ Τρώεσσι τίθει κράτος A 509. Cf. Ψ 400, 406: οἷα ἡμῖν Ζεὺς ἐπὶ ἔργα τίθησι (*i.e.* what excellence therein) θ 245. Cf. ο 488, τ 592.—(7) To bring about, make, cause, cause to come into being or to take place: φιλότητα Δ 83, φόως ἑτάροισιν Z 6, σῆμα τιθεὶς (showing) Θ 171. Cf. Γ 321, I 547, M 399, O 602, Π 96, Υ 95, Ω 661 (will do . . .): μνηστήρων σκέδασιν α 116, υ 225, ὅτε δὴ ἕβδομον ἦμαρ ἐπὶ Ζεὺς θῆκεν (in addition to the six, *i.e.* added it to the tale of the six) μ 399 = ο 477. Cf. γ 136, ι 235, λ 274, ω 476, 485, 546.—In mid.: θέσθαι κέλευθον M 411, 418: ἀγορὴν θέμενος (having called it) ι 171 = κ 188 = μ 319.—Absol.: ὣς ἔμελλον θησέμεναι (all this they were to do) M 35: οὕτω νῦν Ζεὺς θείη, οἴκαδ' ἐλθέμεναι (may Zeus so order it that I may . . .) θ 465 = ο 180.—(8) To make, cause to be *so and so.* (a) With complementary adj.: πηρὸν θέσαν B 599. Cf. B 285, Δ 26, E 122, Λ 392, M 26, Π 90, Φ 172 (drove it in up to the middle), Ψ 382 (would have made it a dead heat), Ω 531, etc.: νόστον ἀργαλέον θήσει θεὸς λ 101. Cf. α 223, γ 88, ε 136, ζ 229, ι 404, ν 302, σ 195, φ 102, χ 256, ψ 11, etc.—In mid.: ἄγριον θέτο θυμόν I 629.—Sim. in mid.: εὖ ἀσπίδα θέσθω (let him see well to it) B 383.—(b) With sim. sb.: εἴ μιν αἰχμητὴν ἔθεσαν A 290. Cf. B 319, I 446, T 298, Φ 484, Ψ 333: ἤ μοι σῦς ἔθηκας ἑταίρους κ 338, δέρμα παλαιοῦ θῆκε γέροντος (that of a . . .) ν 432. Cf. λ 555, ν 156, 163, ο 253, π 198.—In mid.: ἐμὲ θέσθαι γυναῖκα φ 72, τί ἐλέγχεα ταῦτα τίθεσθε; (make this into a reproach) 333. Cf. φ 316.—To appoint, nominate, make: τὴν ἔθηκαν Ἀθηναίης ἱέρειαν Z 300. Cf. Ψ 486.

τιθήνη, -ης, ἡ [redup. fr. θη-, θάομαι[2]]. A female servant in charge of a child, a nurse: φέρει ἅμα παῖδα τιθήνη Z 389. Cf. Z 467, X 503.—Applied to the attendants of Dionysus (as typifying the nymphs who nursed him at his birth) Z 132.

τίκτω [for τι-τκ-ω, redup. fr. τ(ε)κ-]. 2 sing. fut. τέξεις λ 249. Aor. τέκον A 418, Σ 55, X 87, Ω 210, 255, 493. 2 sing. ἔτεκες A 352. τέκες E 875. 3 ἔτεκε B 728, Z 196, 199, H 469, Π 150, Ω 562: β 131, η 63, λ 262, 307. τέκε A 36, B 313, E 313, Z 22, Θ 304, K 404, N 450, Ξ 492, Π 175, T 413, Υ 240, Φ 159, Ω 540, etc.: α 71, γ 95, η 198, κ 139, μ 125, ξ 174, ο 364, π 119, τ 355, etc. 1 pl. τέκομεν X 485, Ω 727. 3 ἔτεκον Υ 225. τέκον η 55. 3 sing. subj. τέκῃ τ 266. 3 pl. τέκωσι θ 554. 3 sing. opt. τέκοι N 826. 3 pl. τέκοιεν δ 64. Pple. τεκών π 120. Fem. τεκοῦσα A 414: μ 134. Infin. τεκέειν Ω 608. **Mid.** Fut. infin. τέξεσθαι T 99. 3 sing. aor. τέκετο B 741, Δ 59, E 154, Z 154, N 451, Ξ 434, Υ 215, X 48, etc.: ο 249. 1 pl. τεκόμεσθα X 53: ψ 61, ω 293. Infin. τεκέσθαι X 481: δ 387, χ 324. To give existence to (living beings). (1) Of the father, to beget: ὃν τίκτε Φυλεύς B 628. Cf. E 547, Z 155, Λ 224, N 450, etc.: δ 64, η 63, ξ 174, ο 243, etc.—In mid.: πρεσβυτάτην με τέκετο Κρόνος Δ 59. Cf. B 741, E 154, Z 154, etc.: δ 387, ο 249.—Of Zeus as the father of rivers. In mid.: Ξάνθου, ὃν τέκετο Ζεύς Ξ 434 = Φ 2 = Ω 693.—Of a river: Ἀξιοῦ, ὃς τέκε Πηλεγόνα Φ 159. Cf. γ 489 = ο 187.—In mid.: Ἀλφειοῦ, ὃς τέκετ' Ὀρτίλοχον E 546.—Of Ocean: τὴν Ὠκεανὸς τέκεν κ 139.—(2) Of the mother (a) To conceive: ἥ μιν ὑπ' Ἀγχίσῃ τέκεν E 313. Cf. B 513, 714, 728, 820, H 469, Ξ 444, etc.: α 71, τ 266.—In mid. B 742.—Of Ποδάργη Π 150.—(b) To bear: τὸν τέκε Λητώ A 36. Cf. A 352, B 658, Z 196, K 404, N 826 (be called my mother), Ξ 318, etc.: β 131, γ 95, η 198, λ 249, ξ 202, ο 364, etc.—Absol.: τί νύ σ' ἔτρεφον αἰνὰ τεκοῦσα; A 414.—In mid. O 187, T 99, X 48: χ 324.—Of a bird: μήτηρ [νεοσσῶν] ἐνάτη ἦν, ἣ τέκε τέκνα B 313 = 327.—Of mares Υ 225.—Of sheep δ 86, τ 113.—Of the earth B 548.—Of the sea Π 34.—Of a lake B 865.—(3) Of both parents, to engender, give life to: ὃν τέκομεν σύ τ' ἐγώ τε X 485. Cf. X 234, Ω 727: η 55, θ 554.—In mid. X 53: ψ 61, ω 293.

τίλλω. (1) To pluck out or tear (one's hair): πολιὰς τρίχας τίλλων ἐκ κεφαλῆς X 78. Cf. X 406.—In mid. κ 567.—(2) To tear one's hair in sorrow for. In mid.: τὸν τιλλέσθην Ω 711.—(3) To pluck or tear the feathers from: τίλλε πέλειαν ο 527.

τῑμάω [τιμή]. (1) To hold in or treat with honour, regard or esteem, show or pay honour to, honour: ἄλλοι, οἵ κέ με τιμήσουσιν A 175, τιμῆς ἧς τέ μ' ἔοικε τετιμῆσθαι Ψ 649 (ἧς app. genit. of price, 'the degree of honour in the measure of which I should be esteemed,' 'the honour which is my due'). Cf. A 454, I 38, M 310, Π 460, Ψ 788, etc.: οἵ κέν μιν θεὸν ὣς τιμήσουσιν ε 36, ὡς κείνη τετίμηταί τε καὶ ἔστιν (*i.e.*, app., τετίμηταί τε καί ἐστι [τιμήεσσα, worthy of honour]) η 69. Cf. γ 379, ξ 203, ο 365.—In mid. X 235: τ 280 = ψ 339, υ 129.—(2) To bring into honour, exalt, glorify: τίμησόν μοι υἱόν A 505. Cf. A 559, B 4, Θ 372 = O 77, O 612, Π 271, P 99.

τῑμή, -ῆς, ἡ [τίω]. (1) Recompense, compensation, indemnity; a recompense, compensation, indemnity: τιμὴν ἀρνύμενοι A 159, τιμὴν ἀποτινέμεν Γ 286, ὃς κεῖται ἐμῆς ἕνεκα τιμῆς (has lost in life in striving to win me . . .) P 92: Ἀγαμέμνονος εἵνεκα τιμῆς (to win . . . for . . .) ξ 70, (in striving to win . . . for . . .) 117. Cf. Γ 288, 459, E 552: χ 57.—(2) The value or estimation in which a person is held, position in a scale of honour, estimation, regard: μή μοι πατέρας ὁμοίῃ ἔνθεο τιμῇ Δ 410. Cf. I 319, Ψ 649 (see λανθάνω (1)), Ω 57, 66.—(3) Due estimation or regard, respect, honour: πόρε καὶ σὺ Διὸς κούρῃσιν ἕπεσθαι τιμήν I 514.—(4) Dignity, honour, worship: θεοί, τῶν περ καὶ μείζων τιμή I 498. Cf. A 278, P 251: ε 335, θ 480, λ 302, 304.—(5) The dignity, honour or prerogative attaching to an office or position: τιμῆς βασιληΐδος ἥμισυ Z 193. Cf. B 197, I 616, O 189 (his share of dignity or prerogative), Υ 181: α 117, λ 495, 503, ω 30.—(6) Honour, distinction, esteem, renown: τιμήν μοι ἐγγυαλίξαι A 353, ὄφρ' ἂν 'Αχαιοὶ υἱὸν ἐμὸν τείσωσιν ὀφέλλωσίν τέ ἑ τιμῇ 510 (or perh. this should come under (1), 'make him rich with recompense'). Cf. I 608, Π 84.—Honour or distinction conferred by some particular circumstance: ξεῖνος ἐμός ἐστιν, ἕκαστος δ' ἔμμορε τιμῆς (shares the honour of entertaining him) λ 338.

τῑμήεις, -εντος. Fem. τῑμήεσσα. Neut. τῑμῆεν [τιμή]. Contr. nom. sing. masc. τῑμῆς I 605. Acc. τῑμῆντα Σ 475. **(1)** Held in or treated with honour, regard or esteem, honoured: οὐκέθ' ὁμῶς τιμῆς ἔσεαι I 605. Cf. ν 129, σ 161.—In comp.: αἶψα τιμηέστερος πέλεται α 393.—**(2)** Precious, prized, of price: χρυσόν Σ 475. Cf. α 312, θ 393, λ 327.—In superl.: δώρων ὃ τιμηέστατόν ἐστιν δ 614 = ο 114.

τῑ́μιος [as prec.]. = prec. (1) κ 38.

τινάσσω. 3 sing. aor. ἐτίναξε Γ 385, N 243, P 595, Υ 57. 3 sing. subj. τινάξῃ ε 363, 368. 3 dual aor. mid. τιναξάσθην β 151. 3 pl. aor. pass. τίναχθεν Π 348. **(1)** To cause to vibrate, shake or quiver, shake: ἐκ δὲ τίναχθεν ὀδόντες (*i.e.* were forced out of their sockets) Π 348, αἰγίδα P 595. Cf. Γ 385, Υ 57: ὡς ἄνεμος ἠΐων θημῶνα τινάξῃ (*i.e.* blows it hither and thither) ε 368, οὐκ ἀνέμοισι τινάσσεται ζ 43. Cf. χ 88.—In mid. in reciprocal sense: τιναξάσθην πτερὰ πυκνά (shook out of each other) β 151.—With διά, to shake in pieces, break up: ἐπήν μοι σχεδίην διὰ κῦμα τινάξῃ ε 363.—In pass., to vibrate, shake, quiver: ἀμφὶ πήληξ κροτάφοισι τινάσσετο (*i.e.* with the violence of the conflict) O 609.—**(2)** To brandish or flourish (a weapon): δύο δοῦρε M 298. Cf. Υ 163, X 311: χ 149.—In reference to lightning: ἀστεροπῇ ἐναλίγκιος, ἥν τε Κρονίων ἐτίναξεν N 243.

τίνυμαι [τίνω]. (ἀπο-.) **(1)** To chastise, punish: ὅς τίνυται ὅς τις ἁμάρτῃ ν 214. Cf. Γ 279, T 260.—**(2)** To take vengeance for, punish (a transgression): λώβην τινύμενος ω 326.

τίνω. See τίω.

τίπτε [τί ποτε]. Before an aspirate τίφθ'. **(1)** What?: τίπτε με κεῖνος ἄνωγεν; Ω 90: τίπτε σε χρεώ; α 225. Cf. X 85: δ 312 (for what purpose?).—With a sb.: τίπτ' ἔτι μεῖζον μήσεαι ἔργον; λ 474.—**(2)** Why? how? A 202, B 323, Δ 243, Z 254, H 24, Θ 447, etc.: β 363, δ 681, ε 87, ι 403, κ 378, λ 93, etc.

τίς, τί. Genit. τίνος. Genit. τέο B 225, Ω 128: δ 463. τεῦ Σ 192: ο 509, ω 257. Genit. pl. τέων Ω 387: ζ 119, ν 200, υ 192. **(1)** Who? which? in neut., what?: τίς θεῶν ξυνέηκε μάχεσθαι; A 8: τέο ἐπιμέμφεαι; B 225, τί μοι ἔριδος; (what part have I in . . . ? what have I to do with . . . ?) Φ 360. Cf. Γ 226, E 465, 703, Λ 313, Σ 192 (see εἴδω (III) (8)), etc.: τίνες ἔμμεναι εὐχετόωντο; α 172, τί κεν ῥέξειε καὶ ἄλλος; δ 649. Cf. β 28, 332, δ 443, ε 299, ζ 276, κ 573, etc.—Joined with another interrogative: τίς πόθεν. See πόθεν (1).—In indirect construction: τίς τῶν ἄριστος ἔην, σύ μοι ἔννεπε B 761: εἰρώτα (εἴροντο) τίς εἴη ο 423, ρ 368.—**(2)** With sb., etc., what?: τίς τοι ἀνάγκη πτώσσειν; E 633: τίς τοι ἄλλος ὁμοῖος; P 475. Cf. P 586, Ω 367, 387: τίνα δ' αὐτῷ μήσατ' ὄλεθρον; γ 249, τί κακὸν τόδε πάσχετε; (what . . . is this that you . . . ?) υ 351. Cf. α 225, δ 642, κ 64, λ 171, ν 233, etc.—**(3)** Adverbially in neut. τί. **(a)** In respect of what? in what? how? why?: τί δέ σε φρένας ἵκετο πένθος; A 362. Cf. Δ 31, Λ 606, N 275, Π 31, Σ 80, etc.: τί σε χρὴ ψεύδεσθαι; ξ 364. Cf. φ 110, ω 95, etc.—**(b)** For what reason? why?: τί κλαίεις; A 362. Cf. A 414, Γ 399, Δ 371, Θ 293, I 337, etc.: τί νύ οἱ τόσον ὠδύσαο; α 62. Cf. δ 465, θ 153, ι 447, κ 431, μ 450, etc.

τις, τι, *enclitic*. Genit. τινός. Genit. τεο π 305. τευ B 388, E 897, N 252, etc.: α 217, δ 264, ι 497, etc. Dat. τεῳ Π 227: λ 502, υ 114. τῳ A 299, etc.: κ 32, etc. **(1)** Someone, one, a man, something: ὅν κέ τις οἴσει Τρώων B 229, ὡς δ' ὅτε τις . . . Γ 33. Cf. Δ 196, E 185, Θ 95, 269, K 84, etc.: ἤν τίς τοι εἴπῃσι βροτῶν α 282, καί τι φέρεσθαι ο 378. Cf. α 396, β 67, 101, δ 637, 735, ξ 373 (for some reason), etc.—**(2)** With sb., etc., some, a: μάντιν τινά A 62, κακόν τι B 195. Cf. Γ 83, E 191, Z 506, K 207, etc.: μάκαρός τευ ἀνέρος α 217, δήμιόν τι ἄλλο β 32. Cf. α 408, β 326, γ 348, δ 26, ε 421, λ 479, etc.—**(3)** **(a)** Some sort or kind of, some: μνημοσύνη τις γενέσθω Θ 181. Cf. Θ 521, Ψ 103.—**(b)** With an adj., etc., giving a notion of indefiniteness: πολλός τις (like some monster) H 156, μάλα τις θρασυκάρδιος ἔσται (a stout-hearted kind of fellow) K 41. Cf. E 638, etc.: ὅσσος τις χρυσὸς ἔνεστιν (how much there may be in it) κ 45. Cf. ι 348, κ 329, ξ 391, ρ 449, σ 327, etc.—**(4)** A certain person or thing: ἅ τιν' οὐ πείσεσθαι ὀΐω (meaning himself) A 289, ἦ ῥά νύ μοί τι πίθοιο Δ 93, etc.: εἰ μή τίς με θεῶν ὀλοφύρατο, Εἰδοθέη δ 364, πλυνούσῃ τις μίγη ο 420, etc.—**(5)** With sb., a certain, a: αἰπεῖά τις κολώνη B 811. Cf. Λ 711, 722, O 174, etc.: νῆσός τις δ 354. Cf. γ 293, δ 384, ι 508, ν 96, ξ 463, etc.—With a proper name: Δάρης τις E 9. Cf. K 314, etc.: κ 552.—**(6)** The general body, each man, every one, men, 'they': ὧδέ τις εἴπεσκεν B 271, ὄφρα τις ἐρρίγῃσιν Γ 353, ἀλλά τις αὐτὸς ἴτω P 254. Cf. B 355, 382, Δ 176, 300, Z 459, 479, H 91, M 317, Π 209, P 227, 420, Σ 466, T 153, etc.: ἵνα τίς σ' εὖ εἴπῃ α 302, πρίν τινα τῶν ἑτάρων ἀῦσαι ι 65. Cf. ο 538, π 305, ψ 135, etc.—With ἄλλος: ἵνα τις στυγέῃσιν ἄλλος Θ 515.—With ἀνήρ Ξ 484.—**(7)** Many a one, many a man: ἱδρώσει τευ τελαμών B 388, πάρος τινὰ γαῖα καθέξει Π 629. Cf. Θ 379, 513, Σ 122, etc.: τῶ κέν τις ἐκλελάθοιτο γάμοιο γ 224, ἀλλά τιν' οὐ φεύξεσθαι ὀΐομαι ὄλεθρον (*i.e.* not a man of you shall escape) χ 67. Cf. λ 502, ν 394, 427, φ 157, etc.—**(8)** Anyone, one, a man, anything: πῶς τίς τοι πείθηται; A 150, οὐδέ τί μιν προσεφώνεον 332. Cf. A 534, B 354, 486, Δ 303, 362, etc.: α 167, β 230, γ 184, 260, δ 489, 690, ε 80, 120, etc.—For οὔ τις see οὐ (8) (e) (α).—**(9)** With sb., etc., any, a: ἔπος τι A 108, ἄλλῳ τῳ 299. Cf. B 342, Γ 45, E 817, Σ 362, etc.: α 166, β 303, δ 373, 544, ε 101, ζ 68, etc.—For οὔ τις . . . see οὐ (8) (e) (α).—**(10)** Adverbially in neut. τι. (a) In any wise, at all: οὐδέ τί που ἴδμεν . . . A 124. Cf. A 115, 394, 468, 550, 575, B 238, E 762, I 238, 435, etc.: εἴ τί που ἔστιν δ 193. Cf. α 202, 296, β 71, 283, γ 72, δ 632, etc.—For οὔ τι see οὐ(8)(e)(β).—(b) In some wise, in some way, somehow, in a way, so to speak: πάντα τί μοι κατὰ θυμὸν ἐείσαο μυθήσασθαι I 645. Cf. I 197, Φ 101, etc.: τοῦτό τί μοι κάλλιστον εἴδεται εἶναι ι 11. Cf. ο 365, etc.

τίσις, ἡ [τίω]. (1) Repayment, indemnity β 76.—(2) Retribution, vengeance, chastisement: ἐπεὶ οὔ τι τίσιν γ' ἔδεισας X 19. Cf. α 40, ν 144.

τίσω, fut. τίω.

τιταίνω [τείνω]. Aor. pple. τιτήνας N 534. (1) To bend (a bow) into the position required for stringing it, to string (it) (cf. τανύω (2)): τόξα Θ 266.—In mid. φ 259.—(2) To pull upon the string of (a bow), draw the string of (it) towards one, bend (it) (cf. τείνω (2)). In mid.: ἐπὶ Τυδεΐδῃ ἐτιταίνετο τόξα E 97. Cf. Λ 370.—(3) In mid., to stretch oneself in the energy of motion, put forth all one's strength: ἂψ ὤσασκε τιταινόμενος λ 599.—Sim., of horses, to run at full stride, draw at full strength: ἵππος, ὅς ῥά τε ῥεῖα θέῃσι τιταινόμενος X 23. Cf. Ψ 518.—Of the rapid flight of birds: τιταινομένω πτερύγεσσιν (straining forward on the wing) β 149.—So, app., *intrans. for reflexive*, of horses: τιταίνετον ὅττι τάχιστα (get into your stride) Ψ 403.—(4) To pull, draw: ἵππος ἅρμα τιταίνων B 390, M 58, ἄροτρον N 704.—(5) To stretch, dispose, arrange, put, set, place: ἐτίταινε τάλαντα (*i.e.* held them out clear of his person) Θ 69 = X 209, περὶ μέσσῳ χεῖρε τιτήνας N 534: προπάροιθε θρόνων ἐτίταινε τραπέζας (drew them up) κ 354.

τιτός [τίω]. Consisting in paying back or requital: τότ' ἂν τιτὰ ἔργα γένοιτο Ω 213 (for *v.l.* see ἄντιτος).

τιτύσκομαι [τι-τύκ-σκομαι or τι-τύχ-σκομαι, τυκ-, τυχ-, τυγχάνω]. (1) To make ready, prepare: πῦρ Φ 342.—In reference to getting horses ready, to yoke Θ 41, N 23.—(2) To take aim, direct one's weapon, shoot, throw: ἰοῖσιν τιτυσκόμενοι Γ 80, τιτυσκόμενος καθ' ὅμιλον N 560. Cf. φ 421, χ 118, 266, ω 181.—With genit. of what is aimed at: αὐτοῖο τιτύσκετο δουρί N 159, 370. Cf. Λ 350, N 498, Φ 582.—(3) To direct the course of something, thrust it in a specified direction: ἐν κληῗδ' ἧκεν, ἄντα τιτυσκομένη φ 48.—(4) In reference to the operation of the mind, to be set *on doing something*, be eager *to do it*. With infin.: τιτύσκετο φρεσὶν ᾗσιν ἢ τευ ἀκοντίσσαι, ἠὲ . . . N 558.—In reference to the mind attributed to the Phaeacian ships: τιτυσκόμεναι φρεσί (finding their way) θ 556.

τίφθ. See τίπτε.

†τίω, τίνω. (The pres. τίω, τίομαι, and the impf. and pa. iterative therefrom only in senses (1) and (2). τίνω only in pple. τίνων β 193 and infin. τίνειν Γ 289, Σ 407 in sense (4)). (The fut. and aor. written both τῑ- (τῖ-) and τει- (τεῖ-).) 1 sing. pres. τΐω Δ 257, I 378. 3 τίει I 238. τΐει ν 144, π 306, υ 132. 3 pl. τίουσι ξ 84. τΐουσι ν 129. Infin. τῑέμεν ο 543, ρ 56. 1 sing. impf. τῖον Σ 81. 2 τῖες ω 78. 3 τῖε B 21, E 326, Z 173, Π 146, Ω 575. τΐε N 176, O 551, P 576: α 432, τ 247. 1 pl. ἐτίομεν E 467, I 631, O 439: λ 484. 3 pl. ἔτῑον χ 370. τῖον E 536, Ψ 703. τΐον Θ 161, Ψ 705. 3 pl. subj. τίωσι I 258. Nom. pl. fem. pple. τίουσαι χ 425. 3 sing. pa. iterative τΐεσκε N 461. 3 pl. τίεσκον χ 414, ψ 65. Fut. τίσω I 142: θ 356, ξ 166. 2 sing. τίσεις P 34: χ 218. 3 τίσει I 284. 2 pl. τίσετε Λ 142. 3 τίσουσι I 303, 603: μ 382. Infin. τίσειν θ 348. 2 sing. aor. ἔτῑσας A 244. 3 ἔτῑσε A 354, 412, I 118, Π 274: η 67. 3 pl. ἔτῑσαν I 110: ω 352. 2 pl. subj. τίσετε Φ 134. 3 τίσωσι A 510. 3 pl. opt. τίσειαν A 42. Imp. τῖσον A 508. **Mid.** 3 sing. fut. τίσεται ξ 163, ο 177. 1 pl. τῑσόμεθα ν 15, ω 435. Infin. τίσεσθαι Γ 28: ω 470. 3 sing. aor. ἐτίσατο B 743: γ 197, 203, ο 236, ψ 57, ω 482. τίσατο ι 479. Opt. τῑσαίμην X 20: ι 317. 3 sing. τίσαιτο ν 213, ψ 31. 1 pl. τῑσαίμεθα T 208. 3 τῑσαίατο υ 169. Imp. τῖσαι μ 378. Infin. τίσασθαι B 356, 590, Γ 351, 366, O 116: γ 206, υ 121. **Pass.** 3 sing. pres. τίεται Θ 540, N 827: η 67. Opt. τιοίμην Θ 540, N 827. 3 sing. impf. τίετο E 78, K 33, Λ 58, N 218, Π 605: ξ 205. 3 sing. pa. iterative τῑέσκετο Δ 46. Pf. pple. τετῑμένος Ω 533: ν 28. Acc. sing. masc. τετῑμένον Υ 426: θ 472. (ἀποτίνω, ἐξαποτίνω.) (1) To value, estimate: τίω μιν ἐν καρὸς αἴσῃ I 378, τρίποδα δυωδεκάβοιον τῖον (at . . .) Ψ 703. Cf. Ψ 705.—(2) To hold in or treat with honour, regard, esteem or respect, show or pay honour to, honour, esteem, respect: ὅ τ' ἄριστον Ἀχαιῶν οὐδὲν ἔτεισας A 244. Cf. A 354, B 21, Δ 46, E 78, Θ 161, etc.: ἶσά μιν ἀλόχῳ τίεν α 432. Cf. η 67, θ 472, λ 484, ν 129, π 306, etc.—With immaterial object: δίκην τίουσιν ξ 84.—In pf. pple. pass. in adjectival sense: ἑταῖρον τετιμένον Υ 426.—(3) To bring into honour, exalt, glorify: τεῖσόν μιν, Ζεῦ A 508. Cf. I 118.—(4) To pay: ζωάγρια τίνειν Σ 407. Cf. Γ 289: τίσειν αἴσιμα πάντα θ 348. Cf. β 193, θ 356, μ 382, ξ 166.—(5) To pay for, pay the penalty for, make recompense for: τείσειαν Δαναοὶ ἐμὰ δάκρυα A 42, τείσεις γνωτὸν ἐμόν (*i.e.* pay for the slaying of him, pay me his blood-price (in kind)) P 34. Cf. Λ 142, Φ 134: ω 352.—Absol.: σῷ αὐτοῦ κράατι τίσεις (pay the penalty) χ 218.—(6) In mid. (a) To repay or indemnify oneself: ἀγειρόμενοι κατὰ δῆμον τισόμεθα ν 15.—(b) To exact a penalty or recompense for, take vengeance for: τείσασθαι φόνον υἷος O 116. Cf. B 356, 590, T 208: υ 169, ψ 31, ω 470.—(c) To exact a penalty, retribution, requital or vengeance from, to chastise, punish: φάτο τείσεσθαι ἀλείτην Γ 28. Cf. B 743, Γ 351, X 20: ἐτίσατο πατροφονῆα γ 197. Cf. ι 479, μ 378, ν 213, ξ 163, υ 121, ψ 57, ω 435, 482.—Absol.: καὶ λίην ἐτίσατο (took his vengeance) γ 203, εἴ πως τισαίμην ι 317. Cf. ο 177.—(d) To take vengeance upon, chastise, punish (for a wrong). With genit.: τίσασθαι μνηστῆρας ὑπερβασίης γ 206. Cf. Γ 366.—(e) With double acc.: ἐτίσατο ἔργον ἀεικὲς Νηλῆα ο 236.

†***τλάω.** Fut. in mid. form τλήσομαι Γ 306, Λ 317, Τ 308 : ε 222, 362. 2 sing. aor. ἐτάλασσας Ρ 166. 2 sing. subj. ταλάσσῃς Ν 829. 3 ταλάσσῃ Ο 164. Aor. ἔτλην Σ 433, Χ 251, Ω 505 : θ 182, κ 53. 2 sing. ἔτλης Ρ 153, Φ 150, Χ 236, Ω 519 : λ 475, ρ 104, 456, υ 18. 3 ἔτλη Α 534, Ε 21, Η 151, 480, Ρ 733, Σ 246, Τ 14, Υ 421, Χ 136 : β 82, δ 242, 271, 716, λ 143, 425, ξ 269, ρ 438, ψ 150. τλῆ Ε 385, 392, 395, Θ 78. 1 pl. τλῆμεν Ε 383. 2 ἔτλητε Ω 35. 3 ἔτλαν Φ 608. Opt. τλαίην β 219, κ 52. 2 sing. τλαίης Δ 94 : α 288, ε 178, κ 343, λ 376. 3 τλαίη Κ 307, Ω 565 : κ 384. 3 pl. τλαῖεν Ρ 490. 3 sing. imp. τλήτω λ 350. 2 pl. τλῆτε Β 299. 2 sing. pf. τέτληκας Α 228, 543. 3 τέτληκε τ 347. 1 pl. τέτλαμεν υ 311. 3 sing. opt. τετλαίη Ι 373. Imp. τέτλαθι Α 586, Ε 382 : υ 18. 3 sing. imp. τετλάτω π 275. Dat. sing. masc. pple. τετληότι δ 447, 459, ι 435, λ 181, π 37, σ 135, ψ 100, 168, ω 163. Nom. pl. masc. τετληότες Ε 873. Nom. sing. fem. τετληυῖα υ 23. Infin. τετλάμεναι ν 307. τετλάμεν γ 209, ζ 190. (ἀνα-, ἐπι-.) (**1**) To undergo evil, have evil laid upon one, suffer : πολλοὶ τλῆμεν ἐξ ἀνδρῶν Ε 383. Cf. Ε 385, 392.—(**2**) To undergo (evil), have (it) laid upon one, suffer (it) : τλῆ 'Αΐδης ὀϊστόν Ε 395, ῥίγιστα τετληότες εἰμέν (we go on suffering . . .) 873. Cf. Σ 433 : θ 182, τ 347, υ 18.—(**3**) To endure evil with fortitude, resolution or patience, to bear up, hold out, submit : τέτλαθι καὶ ἀνάσχεο Α 586, Ε 382, τλῆτε, φίλοι (have patience) Β 299. Cf. Τ 308 : χρὴ τετλάμεν ἔμπης γ 209, ζ 190. Cf. α 288, β 219, ε 222, 362, κ 52, 53, ν 307, π 275, υ 18, 311.—(**4**) In pf. pple. in adjectival sense, enduring, steadfast, patient : τετληότι θυμῷ δ 447, 459, ι 435, λ 181 = π 37, σ 135, ω 163, κραδίη τετληυῖα υ 23.—In bad sense, not to be moved or touched, hard : τετληότι θυμῷ ψ 100 = 168.—(**5**) To exhibit resolution or fortitude, show a firm front, stand firm : μενέω καὶ τλήσομαι Λ 317.—(**6**) To take (a deed) upon oneself, dare (it), brace or nerve oneself to (it) : ἔτλην οἷ' οὔ πώ τις βροτὸς ἄλλος Ω 505. Cf. δ 242, 271.—App., to stand up to, face (the foe) : οὐκ ἂν ἐφορμηθέντε γε νῶϊ τλαῖεν μαχέσασθαι (to endure our onset so as to fight with us, to stand up to us and fight with us) Ρ 490.—(**7**) With infin. (**a**) To have the spirit, courage or resolution *to do something*, venture or dare *to do it* : τλαίης κεν Μενελάῳ ἐπιπροέμεν ἰόν (would pluck up spirit and . . .) Δ 94, οὐδ' ἔτλη περιβῆναι ἀδελφειοῦ Ε 21. Cf. Α 228, Η 480, Ι 373, Ν 829, Ο 164, etc. : λ 475, ξ 269, ρ 438.—Absol. : οὐδέ τις ἔτλη Η 151.—(**b**) To have the hardihood or boldness *to do something* : οὐδέ τις ἔτλη μεῖναι ἐπερχόμενον (*i.e.* awe made them rise) Α 534.—(**c**) With neg., not to have the heart *to do something*, not to endure *to do it* : οὔ πω τλήσομ' ὁρᾶσθαι μαρνάμενον φίλον υἱόν Γ 306. Cf. Υ 421 : β 82.—Sim. in interrogative form : τίς κεν ἀνὴρ πρὶν τλαίη πάσσασθαι ἐδητύος πρὶν λύσασθ' ἑτάρους ; κ 384.—(**d**) To make up one's mind *to do something*, bring, induce, steel or prevail upon oneself *to do it* : οὐδέ τί πώ μοι πρόφρων τέτληκας εἰπεῖν ἔπος Α 543, τὸν οὐκ ἔτλητε σαῶσαι (could not find it in your hearts to . . .) Ω 35 : οὐδ' ἔτ' ἔτλη δίφρῳ ἐφέζεσθαι (had not the heart to . . .) δ 716. Cf. ε 178 = κ 343, λ 143, 350, 376, 425, ρ 104, 456, ψ 150.

τλήμων, -ονος [τλη-, τλάω]. Enduring, stout, unflinching : θυμόν Ε 670. Cf. Φ 430.—Epithet of Odysseus Κ 231, 498.

τλήσομαι, fut. τλάω.

τλητός [τλη-, τλάω]. = τλήμων Ω 49.

†**τμήγω** [τ(ε)μ-, τέμνω]. Aor. pple. τμήξας Λ 146. 3 pl. aor. pass. τμάγεν Π 374. (ἀπο-, δια-.) To cut, sever : χεῖρας ἀπὸ ξίφεϊ τμήξας Λ 146.—To cut up (**a** body of the foe), scatter (it) : ἐπεὶ ἂρ τμάγεν Π 374.

τμήδην [τμη-, τμήγω]. So as to cut or wound : τ. αὐχέν' ἐπῆλθεν [ἐγχείη] Η 262.

τμήξας, aor. pple. τμήγω.

τόθι [correlative to ὅθι]. There, in that place : τόθι οἱ αἴσιμον ἦεν ναιέμεναι ο 239.

τοι,[1] *enclitic.* Also τεΐν Λ 201 : δ 619, 829, λ 560, ο 119. Genit. τεοῖο Θ 37, 468. = σοι (see σύ) Α 28, 39, 40, 107, 123, 173, etc. : α 170, 179, 200, 214, 222, 282, etc.

τοι[2], *enclitic.* Affirmative particle : αἰσχρόν τοι δηρὸν μένειν Β 298, μητρός τοι μένος ἐστὶν ἀάσχετον (*i.e.* I admit it) Ε 892. Cf. Β 361, Δ 29, 405, Ε 801, 873, Ζ 211, etc. : α 203, β 88, 372, δ 93, ζ 33, ι 27, etc.—In maxims : οὔ τοι ἀπόβλητ' ἐστὶ θεῶν δῶρα Γ 65. Cf. Ι 158, etc. : β 276, θ 329, etc.—For ἤ τοι, ἤτοι see ἤ[2] (1) (b) (δ).—For μέν τοι see μέν (1).

τοιγάρ [τοι[2] + γάρ]. So then, accordingly, therefore : τοιγὰρ ἐγὼν ἐρέω Α 76. Cf. Κ 413, 427 : α 179, δ 612, η 28, θ 402, etc.

τοῖος, -η, -ον. (**1**) (**a**) Of such nature, kind or sort, such : τοῖον 'Ατρεΐδην θῆκε Ζεύς Β 482, τοῖοι ἧντ' ἐπὶ πύργῳ (such were they who sat . . .) Γ 153, τοῖοί τοι μιάνθην μηροί (in such fashion) Δ 146. Cf. Δ 289, 399, 488 (so he lay slain), Ε 7, Η 211, etc. : ἐπεὶ σέ γε τοῖον ἐγείνατο Πηνελόπεια α 223, ἀνέγνων μιν τοῖον ἐόντα (recognized him for what he was) δ 250. Cf. α 343, δ 206, 227, ν 115, π 307, etc. — Correlative with οἷος. (**α**) τοῖος . . . οἷος . . ., such . . . as . . . Α 262, Ε 483, etc. : α 257, σ 136, etc.—(**β**) οἷος . . . τοῖος . . ., such as, as . . . so . . . Ε 864, Ζ 146, etc. : ω 377.—With ὁποῖος Υ 250 : ρ 421, τ 77.—With ὅς[2] : Η 231, Ρ 164 : β 286, δ 826.—(**b**) With infin. : ἡμεῖς δ' οὔ νύ τι τοῖοι ἀμυνέμεν β 60.—(**2**) In causal sense : τοίη οἱ ἐπίρροθος ἦεν Δ 390. Cf. Ε 828, Ξ 343, Ο 254, etc.—(**3**) With an adj., denoting that the adj. is to be taken in its full or exact sense, quite, just (cf. (4) (b)) : οὐ μάλα πολλόν, ἀλλ' ἐπιεικέα τοῖον (just befitting) Ψ 246 : θάνατος ἀβληχρὸς μάλα τοῖος (full gentle) λ 135, ψ 282, παῖδα κερδαλέον δὴ τοῖον (quite sharp) ο 451.—(**4**) In neut. τοῖον as adv. (**a**) To such an extent, so much, so greatly, so : τοῖον ὑποτρομέουσιν Χ 241. Cf. γ 496, ω 62.—Qualifying an adj. with ὅθεν as correlative : πέλαγος μέγα τοῖον, ὅθεν . . . (so wide that thence . . .)

γ 321.—(b) With force corresponding to sense (3): θαμὰ τοῖον (quite often) α 209, σιγῇ τοῖον (without a word more) δ 776, η 30, σαρδάνιον μάλα τοῖον (surely quite . . .) υ 302.

τοιόσδε, -ήδε, -όνδε [-δε (3)]. Strengthened form of prec. **(1)** **(a)** Of such nature, kind or sort, such: τοιῇδ' ἀμφὶ γυναικὶ Γ 157. Cf. B 120, 799, Γ 46, Λ 432, Τ 324, Χ 420: δ 74, 149, ζ 157, λ 501, 548, ο 330, π 205 (such as you see me), τ 359, υ 206.—Absol.: τίς νύ σε τοιάδ' ἔρεξεν; Ε 373 = Φ 509. Cf. δ 64, ζ 244.—Correlative with οἷος Ω 375: α 371 = ι 4, ρ 313. —**(b)** With infin.: χήτεϊ τοιοῦδ' ἀνδρὸς ἀμύνειν . . . Ζ 463.—**(2)** In neut. τοιόνδε as adv., to such an extent, so: οὔ πω τοιόνδε κατέδραθον (so soundly) ψ 18.

τοιοῦτος, -αύτη, -οῦτον. Strengthened form of τοῖος. Of such nature, kind or sort, such: τοιοῦτοι συμφράδμονες Β 372. Cf. Η 242, Ψ 644, etc.: γ 208, δ 650, ν 330, ξ 118, τ 74, etc.—Absol.: τοιαῦτα πρὸς ἀλλήλους ἀγόρευον Α 274, τοιοῦτοι ἐείκοσιν Π 847. Cf. Ε 274, Ρ 643, Ψ 494, etc.: α 47, δ 620, ζ 160, etc.—Correlative with οἷος δ 269, σ 36.—Followed by infin.: οὔ μοι τοιοῦτον κῆρ μαψιδίως κεχολῶσθαι η 309. Cf. ω 254.

τοῖχος, -ου, ὁ. **(1)** The wall of a house, room or courtyard: τοῖχον δώματος Π 212. Cf. Ι 219, Σ 374, Ω 598: θρόνοι περὶ τοῖχον ἐρηρέδατο η 95, ἐπήσκηταί οἱ αὐλὴ τοίχῳ καὶ θριγκοῖσιν ρ 267. Cf. β 342, η 86, τ 37, υ 302, 354, χ 24, 126, 259 = 276, ψ 90.—**(2)** In pl., the sides (of a ship): νηὸς ὑπὲρ τοίχων Ο 382. Cf. μ 420.

τοκάς, -άδος [τοκ-, τίκτω]. Kept for breeding: σύες τοκάδες ξ 16.

τοκεύς [τοκ-, τίκτω]. Genit. pl. τοκήων Γ 140, Ο 663, Χ 338, etc.: δ 62, 596, η 54, etc. τοκέων Ο 660, Φ 587. In dual and pl., one's parents: ἐπεὶ τοκεῦσιν ἅμ' ἕσπετο Δ 476. Cf. Γ 140, Ξ 296, Ο 439, Υ 203, Χ 338, etc.: α 170, δ 62, ζ 50, θ 312, ι 34, ο 382, τ 158, etc.—Applied to grandparents: Ἀρήτη ἐκ τοκήων τῶν αὐτῶν [ἐστὶν] οἵ περ τέκον Ἀλκίνοον η 54 (her husband's parents were her grandparents).

τόκος, -ου, ὁ [τοκ-, τίκτω]. **(1)** Childbearing Τ 119.—Of the bearing of offspring by an animal Ρ 5.—**(2)** Hardly to be distinguished from γενεή (1) and coupled with it in a hendiadys: πάντων Ἀργείων (ἀνθρώπων) γενεήν τε τόκον τε Η 128, Ο 141.—Sim. coupled with γενεή (6): ὅθι οἱ γενεή τε τόκος τε ο 175.

τολμάω [τλάω]. (ἐπι-.) **(1)** To endure evil with fortitude, resolution or patience, to bear up, hold out, submit (= τλάω (3)): ἐτόλμα βαλλόμενος ω 162. Cf. υ 20.—**(2)** To take (something) upon oneself, dare or boldly undertake (it) (= τλάω (6)): αἰνότατον πόλεμον τολμήσαντα θ 519.—**(3)** To have the spirit, courage or resolution *to do something*, venture or dare *to do it*. With infin. (= τλάω (7) (a)): οὐδ' ὅ γ' ἐτόλμησεν ἂψ ἵππους στρέψαι Ν 395 (*i.e.* his terror prevented him from taking the risk involved in wheeling). Cf. Ρ 68: ὅς τις τολμήσειε μοχλὸν τρῖψαι (should undertake to . . .) ι 332.—Absol.: αἰεί οἱ θυμὸς ἐτόλμα (was ready for adventure) Κ 232, οὐδέ οἱ ἵπποι τόλμων (they were daunted) Μ 51.—**(4)** To have the hardihood or effrontery *to do something*. With infin. (= τλάω (7) (b)): εἰ τολμήσεις Διὸς ἄντ' ἔγχος ἀεῖραι Θ 424.—**(5)** To make up one's mind *to do something*, bring, induce or prevail upon oneself *to do it*. With infin. (= τλάω (7) (d)): οὐ τόλμησεν ἕκαστα εἰπεῖν ω 261.

τολμήεις, -εντος [τολμάω]. **(1)** Enduring, steadfast, patient ρ 284.—**(2)** Bold, daring, adventurous Κ 205.

τολυπεύω. To carry out, carry through: πολέμους Ξ 86. Cf. Ω 7: α 238 = δ 490 = ξ 368, τ 137, ω 95.

τομή, -ῆς, ἡ [τέμνω]. The stump left after cutting a branch or sapling Α 235.

τοξάζομαι [τόξον]. (ἐπι-.) To shoot with the bow: οὐδοῦ ἄπο τοξάσσεται χ 72. Cf. θ 220, 228, χ 78 = 134.—With genit. of what is shot at: φωτῶν θ 218, ἀνδρῶν χ 27.

τοξευτής, ὁ [τοξεύω]. A bowman, archer: τοξευτῇσι τίθει σίδηρον Ψ 850.

τοξεύω [τόξον]. To shoot at with the bow. With genit.: πελείης Ψ 855.

τόξον, -ου, τό. **(1)** A bow Β 718 (the bow), Δ 105, Ε 171, Ι 559, Λ 375, Ν 594, etc.: θ 215, 225 (in contests of archery), λ 607, μ 84, φ 3, χ 71, etc.—**(2)** App., skill in archery: Πάνδαρος, ᾧ καὶ τ. Ἀπόλλων αὐτὸς ἔδωκεν Β 827 (cf. Δ 105 *sqq.*, where the making of his bow is described). Cf. Ο 441.—**(3)** In pl. of a single bow: τόξ' ὤμοισιν ἔχων Α 45, τόξοισιν πίσυνος (in my bow) Ε 205. Cf. Γ 17, Ε 97, Ζ 322, Θ 266, 370, etc.: κ 262, φ 90, 259, 264, 349, etc.—**(4)** Applied in pl. to arrows: τόξων ἀϊκάς Ο 709.—To the whole archery equipment, bow, quiver and arrows: ἀπ' ὤμων αἴνυτο τόξα . . . ἔκπιπτον δ' ὀϊστοὶ Φ 490, συναίνυτο τόξα πεπτεῶτ' ἄλλυδις ἄλλα 502. Cf. Φ 496, 504.

τοξοσύνη, -ης, ἡ [τόξον]. Skill with the bow, archery: ἄριστος Ἀχαιῶν τοξοσύνῃ Ν 314.

τοξότης, ὁ [τόξον]. A bowman, archer. In voc. τοξότᾰ Λ 385.

τοξοφόρος, -ου [τόξον + -φορος, φέρω]. One who bears a bow, an archer Φ 483.

†τορέω. 3 sing. aor. ἔτορε. (ἀντι-.) To pierce: οὐδ' ἔτορε ζωστῆρα Λ 236.

†τορνόομαι [τόρνος, a carpenter's tool, a string used for striking circles]. 3 pl. aor. τορνώσαντο Ψ 255. 3 sing. subj. τορνώσεται ε 249. To mark off the circumference of, mark out the space which something is intended to cover: τορνώσαντο σῆμα Ψ 255. Cf. ε 249.

τόσος, **τόσσος**, -η, -ον. **(1)** Such in number, quantity or volume, as many or much: τρὶς τόσσα δῶρα Α 213, τόσσον λαόν Δ 430. Cf. Β 472, Ε 136, Θ 560, Λ 678, Μ 338, Χ 423, Ω 670, etc.: α 248, β 184, θ 340, μ 123, ξ 96, 326, σ 402, τ 365, etc.—**(2)** In reference to magnitude or extent, of such magnitude, size, extent or importance: τόσσον ἐπιλεύσσει Γ 12, κακὸν τόσον Ρ 410. Cf. Β 25, Δ 32, Ω 319, etc.: τόσσον ἔπι σχεδίην ποιήσατο ε 251, τόσσην πέτρην ι 243. Cf. ι 265, 324, ρ 407, etc.—

In reference to stature: τόσος πάϊς α 207. Cf. B 528.—(3) In causal sense: τόσσην ἅσιν καλύψω Φ 321. Cf. I 546.—(4) Correlative with ὅσος. (a) τόσος . . . ὅσος . . . such, etc. . . . as . . . B 528, Γ 190, I 125, 385, Λ 741, P 410, etc.: δ 106, ζ 180, τ 169, 347, etc.—(b) ὅσος . . . τόσος . . . such as, as, etc. . . . so, etc. . . . Ω 319, etc.: α 248, ι 324, etc.—(5) In neut. τόσ(σ)ον as adv. (a) To so great an extent, so much, so greatly, by so much: ὅ τι τόσσον ἐχώσατο A 64, οὐ τόσσον χόλῳ ἧμην (it was not so much in anger that . . .) Z 335. Cf. Θ 27, 407, Ξ 394 (so loudly), etc.: α 62, β 28, δ 104, ι 403, χ 50, etc.—So in pl.: τόσ' ἔβραχεν φ 49.—With an adj. or adv.: τόσσον πλέας B 129. Cf. Υ 178, Φ 275, 370: φ 372.—For λίην τόσον see λίην (1).—In causal sense: τόσον ἔβραχεν (so loudly) E 863.—(b) In reference to distance, as or so far: τόσσον ἔνερθεν Θ 16, τόσσον ἐχώρησαν Π 592. Cf. Ψ 522, etc.: τόσσον ἄνευθεν δ 356. Cf. ε 400, ι 491, 499, etc.—(c) To a certain extent, so far: τόσον μὲν ἔεργεν ἀπὸ χροός Δ 130, τόσσον μὲν ἔχον τέλος Σ 378. Cf. X 322, Ψ 454,—(d) Correlative with ὅσον. (α) τόσον . . . ὅσον . . . E 786, Z 450, P 240, etc.: δ 356, ε 400, etc.—(β) ὅσον . . . τόσον . . . Π 722, Ψ 522, 847: θ 125.—With ὡς X 424: = δ 104.

τοσόσδε, τοσσόσδε, -ήδε, -όνδε [-δε (3)]. Strengthened form of prec. (1) Such in number or quantity, as many or much: τοσσούσδ' ἀνθρώπους Υ 357. Cf. B 120, 799, Ω 367: τοσσῶνδ' ἀέκητι δ 665.—With infin.: τοσσήνδε δύναμιν τίσασθαι μνηστῆρας γ 205.—Correlative with ὅσος: λαοὶ τοσσοίδ' ὅσσοισιν ἀνάσσεις Ξ 94. Cf. K 48, Σ 430.—(2) Of such magnitude or extent: τοσσῆσδ' ὑσμίνης Υ 359. Cf. ε 100.—(3) In neut. τοσσόνδε as adv., to so great an extent, so much, so greatly: τοσσόνδε βίης ἐπιδευέες φ 253.—Correlative with ὅσον X 41.

τοσοῦτος, τοσσοῦτος, -οῦτον. Strengthened form of τόσος. (1) Such in number or quantity, as many or much: τοσσαῦτ' ἔτεα B 328: ἄφενος τοσσοῦτον ξ 99. Cf. ν 258.—(2) Such in importance or weight, so great: τοσοῦτόν σ' ἔθηκα (*i.e.* as great as you now are) I 485.—(3) In neut. τοσοῦτον as adv. (a) To so great an extent, so much, so greatly: νεώτατος τοσοῦτον Ψ 476: οὔ τι γάμου τοσσοῦτον ὀδύρομαι, ἀλλ' εἰ . . . (I do not so much . . . but to think how it will be if . . .) φ 250. Cf. φ 402.—(b) As far: ἤσειν ἢ τοσσοῦτον ἢ ἔτι μᾶσσον θ 203.

τοσσάκι [τόσ(σ)ος]. So often, each time. Correlative with ὁσσάκι. See ὁσσάκι.

τόσσος. See τόσος.

τοσσόσδε. See τοσόσδε.

τοσσοῦτος. See τοσοῦτος.

τότε. (1) Then, at that time: καὶ τόθ' ἅμαρτεν Θ 311, τῶν τότε (of the men of that time) I 559. Cf. B 221, 699, Γ 187, Δ 321, 427, etc.: γ 219, 411, δ 98, ζ 12, θ 74, 81, etc.—(2) Then, after that, thereupon: καὶ τότε δὴ θάρσησεν A 92. Cf. A 476, Z 176, H 405, I 561, K 318, etc.: β 348, γ 132, δ 69, 480, ε 391, etc.—(3) Then, in that case or event, in those circumstances: τότε κέν μιν πεπίθοιμεν A 100. Cf. Δ 36, 182, N 344, X 108, etc.: λ 112, μ 54, etc.—(4) Written oxytone, τοτέ, afterwards, again, at another time: τοτὲ δ' αὖτις ἔδυ νέφεα Λ 63. Cf. Ω 11.—τοτὲ μὲν . . ., τοτὲ δὲ . . ., at one time . . ., at another . . . ω 447.

τοὔνεκα [demonstrative corresponding to οὕνεκα]. For that reason, therefore A 96, Δ 477, E 342, I 159, Λ 23, etc.: γ 50, 92, η 303, ν 194, ξ 388, etc.—Correlative with οὕνεκα Γ 405, N 728.—Taking up ἐπεί Z 334.—Taking up ὅττι ψ 116.—Taken up by ὄφρα γ 15.

τόφρα. (1) Up to an indicated point of time, during an indicated space of time: τ. τί μοι πεφιδέσθαι φίλτερον ἦεν Φ 101: τ. δέ μ' αἰεὶ κῦμ' ἐφόρει ζ 171. Cf. θ 453.—(2) While something is going on, in the meanwhile, meanwhile: τ. τοὺς ὦρσεν N 83. Cf. K 498, O 525, P 79, Σ 338, T 24, Φ 139: τ. ταῦτ' Αἴγισθος ἐμήσατο λυγρά γ 303. Cf. δ 435, ε 246, θ 438, μ 166, υ 77, ψ 289, etc.—(3) Correlative with ὄφρα. (a) τόφρα . . . ὄφρα . . . (α) So long . . . until . . . A 509, K 325, Λ 754, O 232: δ 289.—(β) So long . . . while . . . β 123.—(b) ὄφρα . . . τόφρα . . . (α) While . . . so long . . . Θ 67 = Λ 85, I 551, Λ 189, 204, M 12, O 319, Π 778, Σ 258: ε 362, ζ 260, ι 57, ο 362, υ 330, χ 117.—(β) While . . . meanwhile . . . Δ 221, H 194, Θ 88, Λ 359, M 196, O 343, Σ 381: κ 126.—With ἦος. (a) τόφρα . . . ἦος . . . so long . . . until . . . β 77, ε 123.—(b) ἦος . . . τόφρα . . . (α) While . . . so long . . . O 392: μ 328.—(β) While . . . meanwhile . . . K 507, Λ 412, O 540, P 107, Σ 16, Φ 606: ε 425.—With ὅτε, while . . . meanwhile . . . κ 571.

τράγος, -ου, ὁ. A he-goat: ἀρνειούς τε τράγους τε ι 239.

τράπε, 3 sing. aor. τρέπω.

τράπεζα, -ης, ἡ [τετρα- (with loss of the first syllable), τέσσαρες + πέζα. 'A thing with four feet or legs']. A table I 216, Λ 628, 636, Ω 476, 625: α 111, 138, ε 92, θ 69, ι 8, etc.

τραπεζεύς [τράπεζα]. Of or pertaining to a table; of dogs, attending their master at table X 69, Ψ 173: ρ 309.

τραπείομεν, 1 pl. aor. subj. pass. τέρπω.

τραπέω [cf. ἀτραπιτός]. To tread (grapes): ἄλλας [σταφυλὰς] τραπέουσιν η 125.

τράφε, 3 sing. aor. τρέφω.

τράφεν, 3 pl. aor. pass. τρέφω.

τραφερός, -ή, -όν [τραφ-, τρέφω]. Absol. in fem., the solid land, the dry land: ἐπὶ τραφερήν τε καὶ ὑγρήν Ξ 308: υ 98.

τράφη, 3 sing. aor. pass. τρέφω.

τραφθῆναι, aor. infin. pass. τρέπω.

τρεῖς, τρία [cf. L. *tres*, Eng. *three*]. Three B 671, Δ 51, Z 196, I 144, Λ 27, etc.: β 21, δ 409, ε 484, ι 431, ο 469, etc.—Absol.: τρεῖς ἑνὸς ἀντὶ πεφάσθαι N 447. Cf. Υ 269: ζ 63, ξ 26.

τρέμω. To tremble, shake, quiver: ὑπὸ δ' ἔτρεμε γυῖα K 390. Cf. N 18, Φ 507: λ 527.

τρέπω. Fut. τρέψω O 261. 3 sing. aor. ἔτρεψε Δ 381, Z 61, M 32, Σ 469. τρέψε Π 645, Φ 349. 3 sing. opt. τρέψειε I 601. 3 pl τρέψειαν Θ 451.

Pple. τρέψας Φ 603, X 16. 3 sing aor. ἔτραπε (τράπε) E 187, 676, Θ 157, 257, M 24, Π 657, Υ 439: τ 479. 3 pl. ἔτραπον κ 469. Imp. pl. τράπετε δ 294. **Mid.** Nom. pl. aor. pple. τρεψάμενοι α 422, σ 305. 3 sing. aor. ἐτράπετο A 199, K 45, Λ 233, 237, N 605, Π 594, P 546, Φ 468 : η 263, τ 389, φ 413. τράπετο P 733, Σ 138 : ρ 73. 3 pl. τράποντο Γ 422. 3 pl. subj. τράπωνται Ψ 53. Infin. τραπέσθαι ε 350, κ 528. **Pass.** Aor. infin. τραφθῆναι ο 80. 3 sing. pf. imp. τετράφθω M 273. Pple. τετραμμένος, -η E 605, N 542, P 227, 598, T 212 : ε 71, μ 81. 3 sing. plupf. τέτραπτο Ξ 403 : δ 260. 3 pl. τετράφατο K 189. (ἀνα-, ἀπο-, ἐν-, ἐπι-, ἐπιτραπέω, μετατρέπομαι, παρα-, προ-.) (**1**) In reference to position, to turn or direct in a specified direction : πάλιν τρέπεν ὄσσε N 3. Cf. M 24, N 7, Π 645, Σ 469, Φ 349, 415 : ν 29.—In pass. : ἀνὰ πρόθυρον τετραμμένος T 212 (see ἀνά (II) (2) (b)). Cf. ε 71, μ 81.—(**2**) To turn or direct the course of in a specified direction : φύγαδε τράπεν ἵππους Θ 157, 257. Cf. Π 657, Φ 603 : εἰς εὐνὴν τράπεθ' ἡμέας (send us off to bed) δ 294. Cf. ι 315. — To put to flight : τρέψω 'Αχαιούς O 261.—(**3**) To turn or direct to an indicated course of action : μηδέ σε δαίμων ἐνταῦθα τρέψειεν I 601.—(**4**) To turn or divert the course of : βέλος ἔτραπεν ἄλλῃ E 187, πάλιν τρέπεν ἵππους Θ 432. Cf. Θ 399, M 32, Υ 439, X 16.—In reference to the mind : κατὰ πληθὺν Λυκίων τράπε θυμόν E 676. Cf. Z 61 : τῇ νόον ἔτραπεν (diverted her attention) τ 479.—(**5**) To turn or divert from an indicated course of action : Ζεὺς ἔτρεψε παραίσια σήματα φαίνων Δ 381. Cf. Θ 451.—(**6**) In mid. and pass. (**a**) To turn oneself round, turn round or about : Γλαῦκος πρῶτος ἐτράπετο Π 594.—(**b**) To turn oneself, turn, be turned, in a specified direction : μετὰ δ' ἐτράπετο A 199, πεδίονδ' αἰεὶ τετράφατο K 189. Cf. E 605, N 542, Ξ 403, P 227, 598, Σ 138, Φ 468 : ε 350, κ 528, ρ 73, τ 389.—(**c**) To turn or direct one's course in a specified direction : μή τις ὀπίσσω τετράφθω M 273.—To take a turning or winding course, go on a roaming journey : τραφθῆναι ἀν' 'Ελλάδα ο 80.—(**d**) To betake oneself to a specified course of action : ἐπὶ ἔργα τράποντο Γ 422. Cf. Ψ 53 : α 422 = σ 305. —(**e**) To be turned or diverted from a course : παραί οἱ ἐτράπετ' ἔγχος Λ 233 = N 605. Cf. Λ 237.— Of changing one's mind or liking : ἐπεὶ Διὸς ἐτράπετο φρήν (his mind has changed) K 45. Cf. P 546 : κραδίη μοι τέτραπτο νέεσθαι δ 260. Cf. γ 147, η 263.—(**f**) Of the flesh, to change colour : τοῦ κακοῦ τρέπεται χρώς N 279. Cf. N 284, P 733 : φ 413.—(**7**) *Intrans. for reflexive* = (6) (c) : περὶ δ' ἔτραπον ὧραι (had returned on their course) κ 469.

τρέσ(σ)ε, 3 sing. aor. τρέω.

τρέφω. Aor. θρέψα Ω 60. 3 sing. ἔθρεψε (θρέψε) B 548, 766, Λ 223, N 466, Π 329 : β 131, λ 309, ξ 22, ο 363, ρ 293. 3 pl. θρέψαν ξ 175. Pple. θρέψας ι 246. Fem. θρέψᾱσα Σ 57, 438 : μ 134. 3 sing. aor. ἔτραφε Φ 279, Ψ 90. τράφε B 661. 3 dual ἐτραφέτην E 555. 1 pl. τράφομεν Ψ 84. Infin. τραφέμεν H 199, Σ 436 : γ 28. (This aor. always intrans. (see (6) (b), (7)), except in Ψ 90 (see (2)). 3 sing. pf. τέτροφε ψ 237. **Mid.** 2 sing. aor. opt. θρέψαιο τ 368. **Pass.** 3 sing. aor. τράφη Γ 201, Λ 222. 3 pl. ἔτραφεν Ψ 348 : κ 417. τράφεν A 251, 266 : δ 723, ξ 201. (περι-.) (**1**) To solidify, curdle, coagulate : ἥμισυ θρέψας γάλακτος ι 246.—In pf., to become solidified : πολλὴ περὶ χροῒ τέτροφεν ἅλμη (encrusts their flesh) ψ 237.— (**2**) To bestow a parent's or a nurse's care upon, bring up, rear, nurture : τί νύ σ' ἔτρεφον ; A 414, Πηλεύς μ' ἔτραφεν ἐνδυκέως Ψ 90. Cf. B 548, E 70, Θ 283, Λ 223, N 466, Ξ 202 = 303, Π 191, 203, Σ 57 = 438, X 421, 480, Ω 60 : σύ μ' ἔτρεφες αὐτὴ τῷ σῷ ἐπὶ μαζῷ τ 482. Cf. α 435, β 131, η 12, λ 67, μ 134, ξ 141, ο 363, τ 354, ψ 325, etc. —In mid. τ 368.—Not implying actual care or nurture : μέγα μιν 'Ολύμπιος ἔτρεφε πῆμα Τρωσίν Z 282. Cf. ξ 175.—(**3**) To supply with the necessaries of life, look after, tend : τὸν (*i.e.* Odysseus) ἐγὼ (*i.e.* Calypso) φίλεόν τε καὶ ἔτρεφον ε 135. Cf. η 256, ψ 335, ω 389.—(**4**) In reference to animals, to rear. (**a**) Of horses B 766.—In pass. : ἵππους Λαομέδοντος, οἳ ἐνθάδε γ' ἔτραφεν ἐσθλοί Ψ 348.—(**b**) Of dogs X 69 : ξ 22, ρ 293, φ 364.—(**c**) Of the fat of swine : τά θ' ὕεσσι τρέφει ἀλοιφήν ν 410. —(**d**) Of sea-monsters supposed to be reared by Amphitrite ε 422.—(**e**) Of the Chimaera Π 329.—(**5**) Of growing a lock of hair : χαίτην, τὴν Σπερχειῷ τρέφεν Ψ 142.—In reference to plant life, to bestow care upon, watch, tend : οἷον τρέφει ἔρνος ἀνὴρ ἐλαίης P 53.—(**6**) (**a**) In pass., to be brought up, grow up : οἵ οἱ ἅμα τράφεν A 251. Cf. A 266, Γ 201, I 143, 285, Λ 222, T 326 : δ 723, κ 417, ξ 201, ο 365.—(**b**) In non-sigmatic aor. act. in the same sense : ὃς ἐνθάδε γ' ἔτραφ' ἄριστος Φ 279. Cf. B 661, H 199, Σ 436, Ψ 84 : γενέσθαι τε τραφέμεν τε γ 28.— (**7**) Of animals, to rear or nurture their young. In non-sigmatic aor. act. in intrans. sense (cf. (6) (b)) : οἵω λέοντε δύω ἐτραφέτην ὑπὸ μητρί E 555.—(**8**) Of the earth, to nourish on her breast, produce, bring forth, yield : τόσα φάρμακα ἤδη ὅσα τρέφει χθών Λ 741 : οὓς μηκίστους θρέψεν ἄρουρα λ 309. Cf. σ 130.—Sim. of a forest : ἄγρια, τά τε τρέφει οὔρεσιν ὕλη E 52.—(**9**) Of something immaterial : οἰκωφελίη, ἥ τε τρέφει ἀγλαὰ τέκνα (is the mother of . . .) ξ 223.

τρέχω. 3 pl. pa. iterative θρέξασκον (fr. aor. θρέξα, for which see ἐπιθρέξαντος under ἐπιτρέχω) Σ 599, 602. 3 sing. aor. ἔδραμε E 599, Ξ 413. δράμε ψ 207. 3 dual δραμέτην Ψ 393. 3 pl. ἔδραμον Σ 30. (ἀνα-, δια-, ἐν-, ἐπι-, παρα-, περι-, συν-, ὑπο-.) (**1**) Of men or horses, to run : ἐκ θύραζε ἔδραμον Σ 30, αἵ οἱ ἵπποι ἀμφὶς ὁδοῦ δραμέτην Ψ 393. Cf. E 599, Ψ 520 : ψ 207.—Of swift motion in the dance : θρέξασκον ἐπισταμένοισι πόδεσσιν (*i.e.* wheeled in concentric circles) Σ 599. Cf. Σ 602.—(**2**) Of the motion of a drill ι 386.— (**3**) Of a spinning motion imparted to a man struck with a stone Ξ 413.

τρέψω, fut. τρέπω.

τρέω. 3 sing. aor. ἔτρεσε O 586. τρέσε O 589,

X 143. τρέσσε Λ 546, P 603. 3 pl. ἔτρεσαν Λ 745, P 729, T 15. τρέσσαν ζ 138. Genit. pl. masc. pple. τρεσσάντων Ξ 522. Infin. τρέσσαι N 515. (δια-, παρα-, περι-, ὑπο-.) (1) To be struck by fear and withdraw from that which is feared, to flee, retreat, retire: τρέσσεν ἐφ' ὁμίλου Λ 546. Cf. Λ 745, N 515, Ξ 522 (genit. absol.), O 586, 589, P 332, 603, 729, T 15, X 143: ζ 138.—(2) To shrink from or shirk the fight: τρεῖν μ' οὐκ ἐᾷ Ἀθήνη E 256. Cf. Φ 288.—(3) To shrink from, be unable to face: δεταί, τάς τε τρεῖ Λ 554 = P 663.

τρήρων, -ωνος, ἡ [τρέω. 'The timid bird']. A wild dove or pigeon. Joined with πέλεια X 140, Ψ 853, 855, 874: μ 63, υ 243.—With πελειάς E 778.

τρητός [τρη-, τε-τραίνω]. Perforated, having a hole in it: λίθοιο ν 77.—Of bedsteads, prob., pierced with holes, either for fixing on ornamentation (cf. δινωτοῖσι λέχεσσιν Γ 391) or to receive straps passed through to support the bedding Γ 448, Ω 720: α 440, γ 399 = η 345, κ 12.

τρηχύς, -εῖα. Having a rough surface. Of stones, rough, jagged E 308, H 265 = Φ 404.—So of a projection into the sea: τρηχεῖαν ἐπ' ἀκτήν ε 425.—Of a path, rough, uneven: τρηχεῖαν ἀταρπόν ξ 1.—Of Ithaca, rough, rugged ι 27, κ 417, 463, ν 242.—So of Aegilips B 633.—Of Olizon B 717.

τρία, neut. τρεῖς.

τρίαινα, ἡ [τρι-, τρεῖς]. The trident of Poseidon M 27: δ 506, ε 292.

τρίβω. Aor. infin. τρῖψαι ι 333. (ἀπο-, δια-.) To rub. Of oxen, to thresh (corn) by trampling it on a threshing-floor, tread (it): τριβέμεναι κρῖ λευκόν Υ 496.—To press (an instrument into something) and work (it) round: μοχλὸν τρῖψαι ἐν ὀφθαλμῷ ι 333.—In mid., to wear oneself out: μηδὲ τρίβεσθε κακοῖσιν Ψ 735.

τρίγληνος [τρι-, τρεῖς + γλήνη]. Having three beads or drops: ἕρματα Ξ 183 := σ 298.

τριγλώχις, -ῖνος [τρι-, τρεῖς + γλωχίς in sense 'barb']. With three barbs: ὀϊστῷ E 393, ἰῷ Λ 507.

τρίετες [τρι-, τρεῖς + ἔτος]. For three years: τ. ἔληθεν β 106 = ω 141. Cf. ν 377, τ 151.

τρίζω. Acc. pl. masc. pf. pple. τετρῑγῶτας B 314. Nom. sing. fem. τετρῑγυῖα Ψ 101. Pl. τετρῑγυῖαι ω 9. 3 sing. plupf. τετρίγει Ψ 714. To utter or emit a thin or a sharp piercing sound. Of the cry of birds B 314.—Of the cry of bats ω 7.—Of the thin cry of the shades of the dead: ψυχὴ ᾤχετο τετριγυῖα Ψ 101. Cf. ω 5, 9.—Of a part of the body: τετρίγει νῶτα θρασειάων ἀπὸ χειρῶν (creaked as the hands slipped over the skin) Ψ 714.

τριήκοντα, *indeclinable* [τρι-, τρεῖς]. Thirty B 516 = 680 = 733.

τριηκόσιοι (τρῑηκόσια Λ 697) [τρι-, τρεῖς]. Three hundred ν 390, φ 19.—Absol.: κρινάμενος τριηκόσια Λ 697.—With another numeral: τριηκόσιοί τε καὶ ἑξήκοντα ξ 20.

τρίλλιστος, -ον [τρι-, τρίς + λίσσομαι]. Thrice, *i.e.* greatly, longed for: νύξ Θ 488.

τρίπλαξ, -ακος [τρι-, τρίς. For the second element cf. δίπλαξ]. Triple: ἄντυγα Σ 480 (perh., formed of three metal bands).

τριπλῇ [τρι-, τρίς. Cf. τετραπλῇ]. Threefold: ἀποτείσομεν A 128.

τρίπολος, -ον [τρι-, τρίς + πολέω, πολεύω, in sense 'to plough']. Thrice ploughed, *i.e.*, app., ploughed thrice before being sown: νειόν Σ 542. Cf. ε 127.

τρίπος, -ποδος, ὁ [τρι-, τρεῖς + πούς]. A tripod, a pot or cauldron resting on three legs; a similar ornamented vessel, often presented as a prize, reward or gift: πρεσβήϊον, ἢ τρίποδ' ἠὲ δύω ἵππους Θ 290, ἀμφὶ πυρὶ στῆσαι τρίποδα Σ 344. Cf. I 122, Λ 700, T 243, X 164, Ψ 485, etc.: δ 129, θ 434, 435, 437, κ 359, 361, ν 13, 217, ο 84.

τρίπτυχος, -ον [τρι-, τρίς + πτυχ-, πτύξ]. Triple, made with three layers: τρυφάλεια Λ 353.

τρίς [τρεῖς]. (1) Thrice, three times in succession: τ. ἐπόρουσεν E 436. Cf. Z 435, Θ 169, Π 702, Σ 155, Ψ 13, etc.: τ. μὲν ἔδωκα, τ. δ' ἔκπιεν ι 361. Cf. γ 245 (see ἀνάσσω (2)), δ 86, λ 206, μ 105, φ 125, etc.—(2) Thrice or three times (as many or as much): τρὶς τόσσα A 213, Φ 80. Cf. E 136, Ω 686: θ 340.

τρισκαίδεκα, *indeclinable* [τρίς, τρεῖς + καί + δέκα]. Thirteen: μῆνας E 387: ὄγχνας ω 340.

τρισκαιδέκατος, -η [τρισκαίδεκα]. (1) The thirteenth: τὸν τρισκαιδέκατον θυμὸν ἀπηύρα K 495. Cf. K 561: θ 391.—(2) ἡ τρισκαιδεκάτη (sc. ἡμέρη), the thirteenth day: τῇ τρισκαιδεκάτῃ (on the thirteenth day) τ 202.

τρίσμακαρ, -αρος [τρίς + μάκαρ]. Thrice-blest ε 306, ζ 154, 155.

τριστοιχί [τρίστοιχος. Cf. μεταστοιχί]. In three rows or lines: ἔντεα χθονὶ κέκλιτο τ. K 473.

τρίστοιχος [τρι-, τρεῖς + στοῖχος, row, line, fr. στείχω]. Set in three rows or lines: ὀδόντες μ 91.

τρισχίλιοι, -αι, -α [τρίς + χίλιοι]. Three thousand: τρισχίλιαι ἵπποι Υ 221.

τρίτατος, -η, -ον [τρί-τ-ατος, τρι-, τρεῖς + ordinal suff. (cf. τρίτος) + superl. suff.]. (1) The third, the last of three: τοῖσιν ἅμα τ. κίεν B 565. Cf. I 363, K 253, Ξ 117, O 188, 195, Ω 761: ι 90 = κ 102 (as a third).—Absol. in pl.: μετὰ τριτάτοισιν ἄνασσεν (*i.e.* the third generation) A 252.—Coming third in a contest. With ellipse of sb.: τῷ τριτάτῳ κατέθηκε λέβητα Ψ 267.—(2) The third, one in every three: ὧν τριτάτην ἔχων μοῖραν (a third part) δ 97.

Τρῑτογένεια [traditionally (but doubtfully) explained as fr. a river Triton in Boeotia or Thessaly, or fr. the lake Tritonis in Libya]. Trito-born. Name or an epithet of Athene Δ 515, Θ 39 = X 183: γ 378.

τρίτος, -η, -ον [τρί-το-ς, τρι-, τρεῖς + ordinal suff.]. (1) The third, the last of three: τρίτῳ ἤματι Λ 707, τρίτα ἄεθλα (the third set of prizes) Ψ 700. Cf. M 91, 95, Π 193, 850: β 89, δ 551, ε 390 = ι 76 = κ 144, ξ 471, υ 185.—Absol.: ἡ τρίτη κ 356.—In pl.: τῶν τρίτων [ἦρχ'] Ἕλενος (the third body) M 94.—(2) τὸ τρίτον (a) In the third place. Strengthened by αὖ or αὖτε: τὸ τρίτον αὖ κατέπεφνεν Ἀμαζόνας Z 186. Cf. Ψ 842: κ 520, λ 28.—(b) For the third time. Strengthened by αὖτε or αὖτις: τὸ τρίτον αὖτ' Αἴαντα ἰδὼν ἐρέεινεν Γ 225, τό κε τρίτον αὖτις πάλαιον Ψ 733.

τρίχα [τρι-, τρεῖς]. (1) Into three bodies: διὰ τ. κοσμηθέντες B 655: ι 157.—(2) In three ways: τ. σφισὶν ἥνδανε βουλή (three courses were before them) θ 506.—(3) At the third stage: ἦμος (ὅτε) τ. νυκτὸς ἔην (when it had come to the third part in respect of the night, when it was in the third watch of the night) μ 312, ξ 483.

τριχᾶϊξ, -ῑκος [τριχ-, θρίξ + ἀϊκ-, ἀΐσσω]. With streaming hair. Epithet of the Dorians τ 177.

τρίχες, nom. pl. θρίξ.

τριχθά [as τρίχα]. (1) In three pieces: τ. τε καὶ τετραχθὰ διατρυφέν (διέσχισεν) Γ 363: ι 71.—(2) Into three portions or lots: τ. πάντα δέδασται O 189.—(3) In three bodies or communities: τ. ᾤκηθεν B 668.

τρῖψαι, aor. infin. τρίβω.

Τροίηθεν [-θεν (1)]. From Troy γ 257, 276, δ 488, ι 259, λ 160.—With ἀπό Ω 492: ι 38.

τρομέω [τρόμος]. (ἀμφι-, περι-, ὑπο-.) (1) To tremble, be affected by fear, show fear: ἐτρόμεον καὶ ἐδείδισαν H 151. Cf. K 95, O 627.—In mid. K 10, 492.—(2) To tremble before, be in fear of, dread: τὸν τρομέουσι καὶ ἄλλοι P 203. Cf. σ 80.—To hold in fear, have before one's eyes, regard: ὄπιδα θεῶν υ 215.—To be apprehensive of, fear. In mid.: θάνατον τρομέεσθαι π 446.

τρόμος, ὁ [τρέμω]. Trembling, quaking, fear or apprehension outwardly manifested: ὑπὸ τ. ἔλλαβε γυῖα Γ 34. Cf. E 862, Z 137, K 25, Λ 117, etc.: σ 88, ω 49.

τροπέω [τρέπω]. (παρα-, περι-.) To turn, wheel: ἵπποι ἂψ ὄχεα τρόπεον Σ 224.

τροπή, -ῆς, ἡ [τρέπω]. A turning-point: ὅθι τροπαὶ ἠελίοιο ο 404. (What exactly is meant by these 'turning-points of the sun' can hardly be determined.)

τρόπις, ἡ. The keel of a ship ε 130, η 252, μ 421, 422, 424, 438, τ 278.

τροπός, -οῦ, ὁ. A strap securing an oar to the rowlock (cf. κληΐς (3)) δ 782 = θ 53.

τρόφις, -ι [τρέφω]. Big, swollen: τρόφι κῦμα Λ 307.

τροφόεις, -εντος. = prec. O 621: γ 290.

τροφός, -οῦ, ἡ [τρέφω]. A nurse. Of Eurycleia, who nursed Odysseus β 361, δ 742, ρ 31, τ 15, χ 391, ψ 69, etc.

τροχάω [τρέχω. Cf. τρωχάω]. Acc. sing. masc. pres. pple. τροχόωντα. To run ο 451.

τροχός, -οῦ, ὁ [τρέχω]. (1) A wheel. (a) A chariot-wheel Z 42 = Ψ 394, Ψ 517.—(b) A potter's wheel Σ 600.—(2) A round piece or cake of something: κηροῖο (στέατος) μέγαν τροχόν μ 173, φ 178 = 183.

†**τρυγάω** [τρύγη, crop]. 3 pl. pres. τρυγόωσι η 124. 3 pl. opt. τρυγόῳεν Σ 566. (1) To vintage (a vineyard), strip (it) of grapes at the vintage: ὅτε τρυγόῳεν ἀλωήν Σ 566.—(2) To gather (grapes) at the vintage: ἑτέρας [σταφυλὰς] τρυγόωσιν η 124.

τρύζω. To make a low murmuring sound, coo: ὡς μή μοι τρύζητε (*i.e.* may not try to coax me) I 311.

τρύξοντα, acc. sing. masc. fut. pple. τρύχω.

τρῦπανον, -ου, τό [cf. next]. An instrument for boring, a drill ι 385.

†**τρῡπάω** [cf. prec.]. 3 sing. pres. opt. τρῡπῷ (app. contr. fr. τρυπάοι). To perforate with a drill, bore, drill ι 384.

τρυφάλεια, -ης, ἡ [τρυ-, a stem of τέσσαρες + φάλος. Properly an adj. (*sc.* κόρυς). Thus '(a helmet) with four φάλοι']. A helmet Γ 372, E 182, K 76, Λ 352, N 530, Σ 458, etc.: χ 183.

τρύφος, τό [θρύπτω, to break]. A part broken off: τὸ τρύφος ἔμπεσε πόντῳ δ 508.

τρύχω. Acc. sing. masc. fut. pple. τρύξοντα ρ 387. (κατα-.) To lay an intolerable burden on the resources of, consume the substance of or in, beggar, ruin: οἶκον α 248 = π 125, τ 133, πτωχὸν οὐκ ἄν τις καλέοι τρύξοντα ἓ αὐτόν (to eat him out of house and home) ρ 387.—In pass., to see one's substance wasted or consumed, be subjected to impoverishment: ἦ τ' ἂν τρυχόμενός περ ἔτι τλαίης (τλαίην) ἐνιαυτόν α 288, β 219.—In mid., to let oneself be worn out: μηδὲ τρυχώμεθα λιμῷ κ 177.

τρώγω. To nibble, crop ζ 90.

τρώκτης, ὁ [τρώγω. 'Gnawer']. A keen trafficker. Applied to Phoenicians ξ 289, ο 416.

τρωπάω [τρέπω]. 3 sing. pa. iterative mid. τρωπάσκετο Λ 568. (ἀπο-, παρα-.) (1) Of a bird, to modulate its notes, vary their cadence τ 521.—(2) In mid., to turn or betake oneself in a specified direction: τρωπάσκετο φεύγειν (to flight) Λ 568. Cf. O 666, Π 95: ω 536.

τρώσῃς, 2 sing. aor. subj. τρώω.

τρωτός [τρώω]. Capable of being wounded, vulnerable: τούτῳ τ. χρώς [ἐστιν] Φ 568.

τρωχάω [τρέχω. Cf. τροχάω]. To run X 163: ζ 318.

†**τρώω**. 3 sing. τρώει φ 293. 2 sing. aor. subj. τρώσῃς Ψ 341. 2 pl. τρώσητε π 293, τ 12. Fut. infin. pass. τρώσεσθαι M 66. (1) To wound π 293 = τ 12.—(2) To bring to grief: ἵππους Ψ 341.—In pass., to come to grief: ὅθι τρώσεσθαι ὀΐω M 66.—Of wine, to overcome, overpower, drive out of one's right mind φ 293.

†**τυγχάνω** [cf. τεύχω]. 3 sing. impf. τύγχανε ξ 231. 2 sing. aor. ἔτυχες E 287. 3 τύχε E 587, Λ 684. Subj. τύχωμι E 279, H 243: χ 7. 2 sing. τύχῃς ζ 290. 3 τύχῃ Θ 430, Ψ 857. τύχῃσι Λ 116. 2 sing. opt. τύχοις μ 106. Pple. τυχών E 98, 582, 858, N 371, 397, Π 623, Ψ 726: ο 158, τ 452. 3 sing. aor. ἐτύχησε O 581, Ψ 466. τύχησε ξ 334, τ 391. Pple. τυχήσας Δ 106, E 579, M 189, 394: φ 13. 3 sing. pf. τετύχηκε κ 88. Pple. τετυχηκώς P 748. 2 sing. fut. mid. τεύξῃ τ 314. Infin. τεύξεσθαι Π 609. (παρα-.) (1) To light or fall upon, come into contact with. With genit.: ἀμάθοιο E 587.—To fall in with or encounter a person: δῶρα τά οἱ δῶκε τυχήσας φ 13.—(2) To reach, hit, strike. With genit.: μηρίνθοιο Ψ 857.—So in mid.: ἔλπετο τεύξεσθαι προβιβῶντος Π 609.—

(3) Absol., to hit one's mark, make good one's aim, get one's blow or thrust home: ἥμβροτες οὐδ' ἔτυχες E 287. Cf. E 279, H 243, O 581: χ 7. —In aor. pple., making good one's aim, with unerring aim, getting one's blow home, with a home thrust: ὃν ὑπὸ στέρνοιο τυχήσας βεβλήκει (getting his shot home under the . . .) Δ 106, βάλ' ἐπαΐσσοντα τυχών E 98. Cf. E 579, 582, 858, M 189, 394, N 371, 397, Π 623, Ψ 726: τ 452.—(4) To have success in doing something, do it successfully. With pple.: οὐκ ἐτύχησεν ἑλίξας (in turning) Ψ 466. —(5) To get, obtain, have granted to or bestowed upon one. With genit.: ὄφρα τάχιστα πομπῆς τύχῃς ζ 290. Cf. ο 158.—In mid. τ 314.—(6) To fall to one's lot: οὕνεκά μοι τύχε πολλά Λ 684. Cf. ξ 231.—(7) To chance or happen to be somewhere or to be doing something. With complementary words: εἰ τύχησι μάλα σχεδόν Λ 116: τύχησεν ἐρχομένη νηῦς (chanced to be sailing) ξ 334 = τ 291. Cf. μ 106.—Without such word: ὅς κε τύχῃ (as his hap may be) Θ 430. —In pf., to be, lie, be set, in a specified position: ὃν πέρι πέτρῃ τετύχηκεν κ 88. Cf. P 748.

τυκτός, -ή, -όν [τυκ-, τεύχω]. = τετυγμένος (τεύχω (3)): τυκτῇσι βόεσσιν M 105: ἐπὶ κρήνην τυκτήν (*i.e.* with a basin of wrought stone) ρ 206. Cf. δ 627 = ρ 169.—Thorough, perfect, 'regular': τυκτὸν κακόν E 831.

τύμβος, -ου, ὁ. A mound of earth or stones erected over and marking a grave, a grave-mound or barrow (cf. ἠρίον, σῆμα (7)) B 604, 793, Δ 177, H 336, 435, Λ 371, Π 457 = 675, P 434, Ψ 245, Ω 666: α 239 = ξ 369, δ 584, λ 77, μ 14, 15, ω 32, 80.

τυμβοχόη, -ης, ἡ [τύμβος + χέω]. The throwing up of a grave-mound: οὐδέ τί μιν χρεὼ ἔσται τυμβοχόης Φ 323.

τύνη. A more or less emphatic form = σύ E 485, Z 262, M 237, Π 64, T 10, Ω 465.

τυπείς, aor. pple. pass. τύπτω.

τυπή, -ῆς, ἡ [τύπτω]. A blow or stroke: χαλκοῖο τυπῇσιν E 887.

τύπτω. 3 sing. aor. τύψε Δ 531, N 529, 542, P 313, T 125, Υ 446, Φ 117, 180. 3 sing. subj. τύψῃ Υ 378. Imp. τύψον E 830. Pple. τύψας Υ 462, X 68: χ 98. 3 sing. aor. pass. ἐτύπη Ω 421. 2 sing. opt. τυπείης N 288. Pple. τυπείς Λ 191, 206, 433, M 250, N 573, O 495, Π 861, Σ 92. Nom. dual masc. pf. pple. τετυμμένω N 782. (προ-.) (1) To strike or beat (with a cudgel) Λ 561.—(2) To strike or wound (app. implying that the weapon is held in the hand; but τυπείς in N 573 below resumes βάλεν in 567): δουρὶ τυπείς Λ 191, Φόρκυνα μέσην κατὰ γαστέρα τύψεν P 313. Cf. E 830, N 288, 573, O 495, Υ 378, Φ 20, etc.: χ 98, 308, 309 = ω 185, ω 527.—With the part of the body struck as object: γαστέρα μέσην Δ 531. Cf. N 529.—With double acc. of the person and of the part of the body struck: γαστέρα μιν τύψεν Φ 180. Cf. N 542.—In a pass. construction representing a construction with cognate acc.: ἕλκεα ὅσσ' ἐτύπη Ω 421.—(3) In gen., to strike or beat: ἴχνια τύπτε πόδεσσιν Ψ 764. Cf. χ 86.—To beat (the sea with oars) (cf. ἐλαύνω (8)): ἅλα τύπτον ἐρετμοῖς δ 580 = ι 104 = 180 = 472 = 564 = μ 147, μ 180. Cf. μ 215.—(4) Of the striking or beating of inanimate objects: Ζέφυρος λαίλαπι τύπτων Λ 306.—With double acc. as under (2): ἀμφί μιν σφυρὰ τύπτε δέρμα Z 117.—(5) Of grief smiting a person: τὸν ἄχος τύψεν T 125.

τῡρός, -οῦ, ὁ. Cheese Λ 639: δ 88, κ 234, υ 69. —In pl., cheeses: τυρῶν αἰνυμένους (αἰνύμενοι) (partitive genit.) ι 225, 232. Cf. ι 219.

τυτθός, -όν. Little. (1) In reference to a person in childhood or boyhood, little, of tender years, a child: ὅ σ' ἔτρεφε τυτθὸν ἐόντα Θ 283. Cf. Z 222, Λ 223, N 466, X 480, Ψ 85 (a mere boy): α 435, λ 67, ο 381, υ 210 (while yet a boy), ψ 325.—(2) In neut. sing. τυτθόν as adv. (a) Little: τ. ἔτι ζώοντα (his thread of life worn thin) T 335.—(b) A little: οὐδέ με τ. ἔτεισεν A 354: τό σ' ἔτι τ. εἰρήσομαι (I have one more thing to ask you about) τ 509. —(c) For a little, for an instant: τυτθὸν ἀνέπνευσαν (found a short respite) Π 302. Cf. X 494.—(d) To a short distance, a little: ἀνεχάζετο τ. ὀπίσσω E 443. Cf. K 345, M 406, O 728, Ψ 730.—(e) At a short distance, a little: τ. ἀποπρὸ νεῶν H 334, τ. ὑπεκπροθέοντα (keeping always a little ahead) Φ 604. Cf. ι 483 = 540.—(f) By a little, only just: ἠλεύατ' ἔγχος τ. N 185, P 306. Cf. O 628, P 609.—(g) In reference to the voice, in a low soft tone: τ. φθεγξαμένη (in still small accents) Ω 170.—(3) In acc. pl. neut. in *quasi*-advbl. sense: κηροῖο τροχὸν τυτθὰ διατμήξας (into small pieces) μ 174, νῆά κε τυτθὰ κεάσαιμι (into fragments) 388.

τυφλός. Blind Z 139.

τύχε, 3 sing. aor. τυγχάνω.

τύχησε, 3 sing. aor. τυγχάνω.

τύψε, 3 sing. aor. τύπτω.

τῶ, τώ, τῷ [το-, ὁ]. (1) Therefore, accordingly, so: τῶ οὐ νεμεσίζομαι B 296. Cf. A 418, B 250, Δ 410, E 129, Z 224, etc.: τὼ μνηστήρων ἔα βουλήν β 281, τῷ σε Ζεὺς τίσατο ι 479. Cf. γ 134, η 25, θ 226, λ 339, ν 5, etc.—(2) In that case or event, in those circumstances, then: τῶ κε τάχ' ἠμύσειε πόλις B 373. Cf. H 158, N 57, Φ 280, X 427, Ψ 527, etc.: τῷ κέν οἱ τύμβον ἐποίησαν α 239. Cf. γ 224, δ 733, θ 467, ο 537, υ 273 (if he had done so), etc.

τώς. (1) Thus, in this manner: κεῖνος τὼς ἀγόρευεν B 330 = Ξ 48: = σ 271.—(2) So, in such a degree: τὼς ἔην μαλακός τ 234.—Correlative with ὡς: μὴ τώς σ' ἀπεχθήρω ὡς νῦν φίλησα Γ 415.

ὑακίνθινος [ὑάκινθος]. Of the ὑάκινθος: κόμας ὑακινθίνῳ ἄνθει ὁμοίας ζ 231 = ψ 158 (the point of resemblance app. being in the clustering flowers with their curling petals).

ὑάκινθος. Prob. the blue-bell, the wild hyacinth. Collectively Ξ 348.

ὑββάλλω. See ὑποβάλλω.

ὑβρίζω [ὕβρις]. (ἐφ-.) (1) To show ὕβρις, act without regard to right or decency, exhibit an overbearing spirit or demeanour, bear oneself with wantonness: ὑβρίζοντες ἀτάσθαλα μηχανόωνται γ 207. Cf. α 227, ρ 245, 588, σ 381.—With cognate acc.: λώβην, ἣν οἴδ' ὑβρίζοντες . . . υ 170.—(2) To treat with wanton despite, maltreat Λ 695: υ 370.

ὕβρις, ἡ. Wanton disregard of decency or of the rights or feelings of others, an overbearing or domineering spirit or demeanour, a spirit of wanton aggression or violence, wantonness, violence: τῶν ὕβρις οὐρανὸν ἵκει ο 329 = ρ 565. Cf. α 368 = δ 321, δ 627 = ρ 169, ξ 262 = ρ 431, π 86, 410, 418, ρ 487, 581, ψ 64, ω 352.—A manifestation of such a spirit: ὕβριος εἵνεκα τῆσδε (this insult) Α 214. Cf. Α 203.

ὑβριστής [ὑβρίζω]. Having no regard for right or decency, wanton, violent Ν 633: ζ 120 = ι 175 = ν 201, ω 282.

ὑγιής. Sound, profitable: μῦθος Θ 524.

ὑγρός, -ή, -όν. (1) Fluid, liquid Ε 903.—Sim.: ὑγρὰ κέλευθα (the watery ways) Α 312: = ο 474, γ 71 = ι 252, δ 842.—Epithet of oil and water: ἔλαιον Ψ 281: ζ 79, 215, η 107, ὕδωρ δ 458.—(2) In neut. sing. ὑγρόν as adv.: ἀνέμων ὑ. ἀέντων (with rain, bringing rain) ε 478, τ 440.—(3) Absol. in fem., (the) waters, (the) sea: ἐπὶ τραφερήν τε καὶ ὑγρήν Ξ 308. Cf. Κ 27, Ω 341: = α 97 = ε 45, δ 709, υ 98.

ὑδατοτρεφής [ὑδατ-, ὕδωρ + τρέφω]. Nourished by water, loving water: αἰγείρων ρ 208.

†ὑδραίνω [ὕδωρ]. Nom. sing. fem. aor. pple. mid. ὑδρηναμένη. In mid., to apply water to one's person, wash oneself, bathe: ὑδρηναμένη εὔχε' Ἀθηναίῃ (εὔχεο πᾶσι θεοῖσιν) δ 750 = ρ 48. Cf. δ 759 = ρ 58.

ὑδρεύω [ὕδωρ]. To draw water κ 105.—In mid.: ὅθεν ὑδρεύοντο πολῖται η 131, ρ 206.

ὑδρηλός [ὕδωρ]. Well watered ι 133.

ὑδρηναμένη, nom. sing. fem. aor. pple. mid. ὑδραίνω.

ὕδρος, -ου, ὁ [ὕδωρ]. A water-snake Β 723.

ὕδωρ, -ατος, τό [cf. L. *unda*, Eng. *water*]. (The υ freq. lengthened metrically.) (1) Water Β 307, Γ 270, Ζ 457, Η 99, Ι 15, etc.: α 110, γ 429, δ 213, ε 70, ζ 86, ι 209, etc.—Of a flood of water: ἀλὲν ὑ. ἐξέρρηξεν ὁδοῖο Ψ 420.—(2) In various specific applications. (a) A river: σχεδὸν ὕδατος ε 475. Cf. Φ 14.—The waters of a river: Τιταρησσόν, ὅς ῥ' ἐς Πηνειὸν προΐει ὑ. Β 752. Cf. Β 755, 850, Θ 369, Φ 21, etc.: δ 478, ε 185, κ 514.—Of the waters of two or more rivers: ὡς ὅτε ποταμοὶ συμβάλλετον ὑ. (their waters) Δ 453, ὥς τε πρὼν ἰσχάνει ὑ. Ρ 747 (= ποταμῶν ῥέεθρα 749). Cf. Μ 33.—(b) A spring of water: ὕδατ' ἀενάοντα ν 109. Cf. μ 306.—(c) A pond: χῆνες πυρὸν ἔδουσιν ἐξ ὕδατος (coming from their . . .) τ 537.—(d) Rain: ὅτε λαβρότατον χέει ὑ. Ζεύς Π 385.—(e) The sea, the wave of the sea: Αἰγύπτῳ ἐπέλασσεν ἄνεμός τε καὶ ὑ. γ 300. Cf. η 277, ο 482.—The water of the sea: ἁλμυρὸν ὑ. δ 511. Cf. μ 104, 172, 236, etc.

ὑετός, -οῦ, ὁ [ὕω]. Rain Μ 133.

υἱός, -οῦ, ὁ. (The first syllable shortened Α 489, Δ 473, Ε 612, Ζ 130, Η 47, Ι 84, Π 21, etc.: λ 270, 478.) Also, fr. stem υἱυ-, genit. υἱέος Ω 122: γ 489, δ 4, λ 174, ο 187, σ 162. Dat. υἱέϊ Γ 174, Ο 455, Υ 81, Φ 141, Ω 112: γ 369, δ 5, 10, π 438, 452, ψ 61, ω 213. υἱεῖ Σ 144, 458: ξ 435. Acc. υἱέα Ν 350. Nom. pl. υἱέες Β 641, 666, Ε 10, Λ 138, 692, Π 449, Ω 604: κ 6, ξ 201, τ 414, 430, 437, 459. υἱεῖς ο 248, ω 387, 497. Acc. υἱέας Β 693, Ε 149, Λ 123, Ψ 175, 181, Ω 205, 521: δ 211. Voc. pl. υἱεῖς Ε 464. And fr. this stem by hyphaeresis genit. υἷος Β 230, Ε 266, Ν 522, Ξ 9, Ο 116, 138, Σ 138, Τ 324, Ψ 746, Ω 422, 550: λ 452, ρ 397, υ 218. Dat. υἷι Β 20, 791, Ν 216, Π 177, Φ 34, Χ 302, Ψ 383: δ 143, 771, λ 273. Acc. υἷα Μ 129, Ν 185, 792, Ο 419, 427: δ 765, ν 259, υ 35. Nom. dual υἷε Β 679, 822, 831, 843, 865, Μ 95, 99, Ν 345. Acc. υἷε Ε 27, 152, 542, Λ 102, 329, Υ 460: ο 242. Nom. pl. υἷες Α 162, Β 253, Δ 114, Ζ 255, Η 403, Κ 165, Ν 146, Ο 675, Π 56, Ρ 23, Σ 444, Φ 376, Ω 399, etc.: β 51, γ 104, δ 285, ζ 62, θ 514, ν 315, ψ 220, ω 38, etc. Dat. υἱάσι, Ε 463, Ο 197, Ω 248, 546: γ 32, 57, 387, κ 7, ξ 206, ρ 113, τ 466, φ 220. Acc. υἷας Α 240, Β 72, Ε 159, Ι 40, Κ 49, Μ 128, Ξ 106, Σ 76, Τ 156, Χ 62, Ω 189, etc.: β 115, 198, ξ 229, τ 394, χ 221. A son, one's son Α 9, Β 20, Γ 174, Δ 89, Ε 10, Ζ 154, etc.: α 88, β 2, γ 57, δ 4, ε 28, ζ 62, etc.—Of warriors: υἷες Ἄρηος Β 512, Ι 82.—υἷες Ἀχαιῶν, the sons of the Achaeans, the Achaeans Α 162, Β 72, Δ 114, Ζ 255, etc.: β 115, γ 104, δ 285, θ 514, etc.—Sim.: Τρώων καὶ Ἀχαιῶν υἷες ω 38.

υἱωνός, -οῦ, ὁ [υἱός]. A grandson, one's grandson Β 666, Ε 631, Ν 207: ω 515.

ὑλαγμός, -οῦ, ὁ [ὑλακ- as in ὑλακτέω]. A barking or baying Φ 575.

ὑλακόμωρος [ὑλακ- as in prec. Cf. ἐγχεσίμωρος, ἰόμωρος]. App., delighting in barking or baying. Epithet of dogs ξ 29, π 4.

ὑλακτέω [ὑλάω]. Of dogs, to bark or bay Σ 586.—Fig. of the oppressed heart seeking relief: κραδίη οἱ ἔνδον ὑλάκτει υ 13. Cf. υ 16.

ὑλάω. (1) Of dogs, to bark or bay π 9, υ 15.—In mid. π 162.—(2) To bark or bay at: οὐδ' ὕλαον προσιόντα π 5.

ὕλη, -ης, ἡ. (1) A wood or forest Γ 151, Ζ 147, Μ 148, Ο 273, Σ 320, etc.: ε 63, 470, 475, ζ 128, κ 159, ξ 353.—(2) Woodlands, woods: ἄγρια, τά τε τρέφει οὔρεσιν ὑ. Ε 52. Cf. Ε 555, Λ 118, Ν 18, 102, etc.: ὄρος καταειμένον ὕλῃ (with wood) ν 351, τ 431. Cf. ε 398, ι 120, κ 150, 197, ν 246, ρ 316.—(3) Lop, the smaller branches of felled timber: πολλὴν ἐπεχεύατο ὕλην ε 257.—Such branches used as fuel, firewood, faggot-wood: ἕτεροι μεθ' ὕλην Η 418, 420. Cf. Ψ 50, 111, 127, 139, 163, 198, Ω 662, 784: ι 234, κ 104.

ὑλήεις, -εντος. Fem. -εσσα [ὕλη]. Covered with woods, woody, (well) wooded: ὑπὸ Πλάκῳ ὑληέσσῃ Ζ 396, 425, Χ 479. Cf. Κ 362, Ν 12, Ρ 748, Φ 449: α 186, 246 = π 123 = τ 131, ι 24, 118, 191, κ 308, ξ 2.

ὑλοτόμος [ὕλη + τομ-, τάμνω]. (1) Fitted for cutting or felling wood: πελέκεας Ψ 114.—(2) As sb., a wood-cutter Ψ 123.

ὑμεῖς. Nom. ὑμεῖς B 75, 485, Γ 280, etc.: β 76, γ 347, δ 419, etc. Genit. ὑμείων Δ 348, H 195, T 153: φ 318. ὑμέων H 159, O 494: ν 7, υ 351, χ 219. Dat. ὑμῖν A 18, 260, H 73, etc.: α 373, 376, β 43, etc. Acc. ὑμέας β 75, 210, μ 163, φ 198, ω 396. Pron. of the 2nd person pl., you, ye A 18, B 75, Δ 246, H 195, I 421, etc.: α 373, β 75, δ 415, η 211, ι 16, etc.

ὑμέναιος, ὁ. A wedding or bridal song: πολὺς ὑμέναιος ὀρώρει Σ 493.

ὑμέτερόνδε [acc. of ὑμέτερος + -δε (1)]. To your house: ἤγαγέ με ὑ. Ψ 86.

ὑμέτερος, -η, -ον [ὑμεῖς]. Your E 686, Θ 455, P 222, 226, Υ 116, Ψ 84: β 138, δ 688, η 269, θ 156, κ 525, ο 441, etc.

ὔμμες. You (= ὑμεῖς) A 274, 335, Ξ 481, Ψ 469, Ω 242: φ 231. Dat. ὔμμι Δ 249, Z 77, H 387, etc.: β 316, λ 336, ο 506, etc. Acc. ὔμμε Λ 781, Ψ 412: ν 357, σ 407, ω 109.

ὕμνος, -ου, ὁ. A lay: ὕμνον ἀκούων θ 429.

ὑμός, -ή, -όν [ὑμεῖς]. Your E 489, N 815: ι 284.—Your own: κτήματα α 375 = β 140.

ὑπάγω [ὑπ-, ὑπο- (3) (8)]. **(1)** To lead away from the range or reach of something: ἐκ βελέων ὕπαγεν Λ 163.—**(2)** To lead (horses, etc.) under the yoke: ἡμιόνους ὕπαγον ζεῦξάν τε ζ 73.—To lead (them) *under* (the yoke) and yoke them. With acc.: ὕπαγε (ὕπαγον) ζυγὸν ἵππους Π 148, Ψ 291, Ω 279.

ὑπαί. See ὑπό.

ὕπαιθα [ὑπαί]. **(1)** Away from under; hence, out of reach, eluding a foe: ὑ. λιάσθη O 520. Cf. Φ 493, X 141.—**(2)** Under: ὑ. ῥέων (*i.e.* carrying him off his legs) Φ 271.—**(3)** With genit. **(a)** Away from under, out of reach of, eluding: ὕπαιθα τοῖο λιασθείς Φ 255.—**(b)** Under: ἄνακτος (*i.e.* supporting him) Σ 421.

†**ὑπαΐσσω** [ὑπ-, ὑπο- (1) (9)]. 3 sing. fut. ὑπαΐξει Φ 126. Aor. pple. ὑπαΐξας B 310. **(1)** To dart *from under*. With genit.: βωμοῦ B 310.—**(2)** To dart along *beneath*. With acc.: φρῖκα Φ 126.

ὑπακούω [ὑπ-, ὑπο- (12)]. 3 sing. aor. ὑπάκουσε ξ 485. Infin. ὑπακοῦσαι δ 283. **(1)** To listen, give ear ξ 485.—**(2)** To listen and make response, to answer, reply: ἔνδοθεν ὑπακοῦσαι δ 283. Cf. κ 83.

†**ὑπαλέομαι** [ὑπ-, ὑπο- (3)]. Aor. pple. ὑπαλευάμενος. To escape *from the power of*, get *beyond the reach of*. With genit.: τῶν ὑπαλευάμενος ο 275.

ὑπάλυξις, ἡ [ὑπαλύσκω]. A possibility or the means of escape: κακῶν ὑπάλυξιν (from . . .) ψ 287. Cf. X 270.

†**ὑπαλύσκω** [ὑπ-, ὑπο- (3)]. 2 sing. aor. ὑπάλυξας Λ 451. 3 ὑπάλυξε δ 512, ε 430, τ 189. Pple. ὑπαλύξας θ 355. Infin. ὑπαλύξαι M 327. **(1)** To keep away from, escape from, avoid, shun (impending danger): κῆρας δ 512. Cf. M 327.—**(2)** To get away, effect one's escape or release, from (danger or an obligation in which one is involved): κῦμα ε 430, χρεῖος θ 355. Cf. τ 189.—**(3)** Absol., to effect one's escape, escape, save oneself: φθῆ σε τέλος θανάτοιο κιχήμενον, οὐδ' ὑπάλυξας Λ 451.

†**ὑπαντιάω** [ὑπ-, ὑπο- (12)]. Aor. pple. ὑπαντιάσας. To meet an attacking foe: οὔ τις ἤρκεσεν ὄλεθρον πρόσθεν ὑπαντιάσας (taking his stand before him and meeting the foe) Z 17.

ὕπαρ, τό. A waking reality, the actual sight of something: οὐκ ὄναρ, ἀλλ' ὕπαρ τ 547. Cf. υ 90.

†**ὑπάρχω** [ὑπ-, ὑπο- (12)]. 3 sing. aor. subj. ὑπάρξῃ. To make a beginning, give a lead, set an example: ἡ γὰρ θέμις, ὅς τις ὑπάρξῃ (for that is due to him who has first hospitably entreated another) ω 286.

ὑπασπίδιος [ὑπ-, ὑπο- (4) + ἀσπιδ-, ἀσπίς]. In neut. pl. ὑπασπίδια as adv., under the shield, under guard of the shield: ὑ. προποδίζων N 158. Cf. N 807, Π 609.

ὕπατος, -η, -ον [in form superl. fr. ὑπό]. **(1)** The topmost part of the . . ., the top of the . . .: ἐν πυρῇ ὑπάτῃ Ψ 165, Ω 787.—**(2)** Of Zeus, (the) highest, (the) supreme: Ζῆν' ὕπατον Κρονίδην E 756, Κρονίδη, ὕπατε κρειόντων (supreme among . . .) Θ 31: = α 45 = 81 = ω 473. Cf. Θ 22, P 339, Ψ 43, T 258: = τ 303.

ὑπέᾱσι, 3 pl. pres. ὕπειμι.

ὑπεδείδισαν, 3 pl. plupf. ὑποδείδια.

ὑπέδεισαν, 3 pl. aor. ὑποδείδια.

ὑπέδεκτο, 3 sing. aor. ὑποδέχομαι.

ὑπεδέξατο, 3 sing. aor. ὑποδέχομαι.

ὑπέδραμε, 3 sing aor. ὑποτρέχω.

ὑπέδῡ, 3 sing. aor. ὑποδύω.

ὑπεδύσετο, 3 sing. aor. mid. ὑποδύω.

ὑπεθερμάνθη, 3 sing. aor. pass. ὑποθερμαίνω.

†**ὕπειμι** [ὑπ-, ὑπο- (4) + εἰμί]. 3 pl. pres. ὑπέᾱσι I 204. 3 pl. impf. ὑπῆσαν Λ 681. To be *under*. With dat.: ἐμῷ μελάθρῳ I 204, πολλῇσιν [ἵπποισι] πῶλοι ὑπῆσαν (many had sucking foals) Λ 681.

ὑπείξομαι, fut. ὑποείκω.

ὑπείρ. See ὑπέρ.

ὑπειρέβαλον, aor. See ὑπερβάλλω.

ὑπειρέχω. See ὑπερέχω.

ὑπείροχος [ὑπειρ-, ὑπερ- (5) + ὀχ-, ἔχω]. Preeminent, prominent: ὑπείροχον ἔμμεναι ἄλλων (among . . .) Z 208 = Λ 784.

ὑπέκ, before a vowel **ὑπέξ** [ὑπό + ἐκ, ἐξ]. **(1)** Adv. Out of the power, range or reach of something: ὄφρ' (ἵν') ὑπὲκ κακότητα φύγοιμεν γ 175, ι 489 = κ 129.—**(2)** Prep. with genit. **(a)** From under or beneath, away from under or beneath: ἵππους λύσαθ' ὑπὲξ ὀχέων Θ 504, τείχεος αἰὲν ὑπὲκ κατ' ἀμαξιτὸν ἐσσεύοντο (app. to get the better going afforded by the road) X 146.—Up from out of: ἀγέροντο ψυχαὶ ὑπὲξ Ἐρέβευς λ 37.—App., up away from: ἔγχος ὦσεν ὑπὲκ δίφροιο E 854.—**(b)** In reference to saving or escaping, from out of, out of the reach or range of, away from, from: ὑπὲκ βελέων Δ 465, Σ 232. Cf. N 89, O 628, 700, P 461, 581, 589, Υ 300: μ 107.—Sim. in reference to carrying off from a protector: [ἄρνας] ὑπὲκ μήλων αἰρεύμενοι Π 353.

ὑπεκλίνθη, 3 sing. aor. pass. ὑποκλίνω.

ὑπεκπροθέω [ὑπ-, ὑπο- (3) + ἐκ- (1) + προ- (1)]. To run forward out from among, outstrip: Ἄτη πάσας πολλὸν ὑπεκπροθέει I 506.—Absol.: τὸν διώκετο τυτθὸν ὑπεκπροθέοντα (keeping ever a little in front) Φ 604 : τόσσον ὑπεκπροθέων λαοὺς ἵκετο (running forward out of the ruck) θ 125.

ὑπεκπρολύω [ὑπ-, ὑπο- (1) + ἐκ- (1) + προ- (1)]. To loose *from under* and *from* something (and send) forth. With genit. : ἡμιόνους ὑπεκπροέλυσαν ἀπήνης (loosed them from under the yoke, detached them from the waggon, and turned them off to graze) ζ 88.

ὑπεκπρορέω [ὑπ-, ὑπο- (1) + ἐκ- (1) + προ- (1)]. To flow from beneath something on and out: ὕδωρ ὑπεκπρορέει (wells up from the communication of the troughs with the river, passes on, and flows out of the troughs) ζ 87.

†**ὑπεκπροφεύγω** [ὑπ-, ὑπο- (3) + ἐκ- (1) + προ-(1)]. Aor. opt. ὑπεκπροφύγοιμι μ 113, υ 43. Pple. ὑπεκπροφυγών Υ 147, Φ 44. To get away from the power or reach of, and make good one's escape: εἴ πως ὑπεκπροφύγοιμι Χάρυβδιν μ 113.—Absol., to get away from the power or reach of something or from restraint and make good one's escape: ὄφρα τὸ κῆτος ὑπεκπροφυγὼν ἀλέαιτο Υ 147. Cf. Φ 44 : πῇ κεν ὑπεκπροφύγοιμι; (*i.e.* from the relatives of the slain men) υ 43.

ὑπεκρύφθη, 3 sing. aor. pass. ὑποκρύπτω.

†**ὑπεκσαόω** [ὑπ-, ὑπο- (3) + ἐκ- (1)]. 3 sing. aor. ὑπεξεσάωσε. To remove from the reach of danger, rescue: αὐτὸν ὑπεξεσάωσεν Ἀπόλλων Ψ 292.

ὑπεκφέρω [ὑπ-, ὑπο- (3) (4) + ἐκ- (1)]. (1) To remove *from the range or area of.* With genit.: υἱὸν πολέμοιο Ε 318, 377.—(2) To move (a shield) outwards by elevating the base Θ 268.—(3) *Intrans. for reflexive,* of horses, to carry themselves forward, speed onwards (cf. ἐκφέρω (6)) γ 496.

†**ὑπεκφεύγω** [ὑπ-, ὑπο- (3) + ἐκ- (1)]. Aor. ὑπέκφυγον ι 286, μ 446. 2 sing. ὑπέκφυγες Υ 191. 3 ὑπεξέφυγε Θ 369, Χ 202. ὑπέκφυγε Ε 22, Π 687: ψ 320. 3 pl. ὑπεξέφυγον λ 383. 3 sing. opt. ὑπεκφύγοι Ζ 57 : μ 287, π 372, υ 368. Infin. ὑπεκφυγέειν Θ 243 : μ 216. (1) To keep away from the power or reach of, escape, avoid, shun (impending danger): κῆρα Ε 22, Π 687. Cf. Ζ 57, Χ 202: ι 286, μ 216, 287, 446, π 372, υ 368.—(2) To get away, effect one's escape, from (danger in which one is involved): Τρώων ἀϋτήν λ 383. Cf. Θ 369.—(3) Absol., to effect one's escape, escape, save oneself: ἐς Λυρνησσόν Υ 191. Cf. Θ 243 : ψ 320.

ὑπέλθῃ, 3 sing. aor. subj. ὑπέρχομαι.

ὑπέλυντο, 3 pl. aor. pass. ὑπολύω.

ὑπέμεινα, aor. ὑπομένω.

ὑπεμνάασθε, 2 pl. impf. ὑπομνάομαι.

ὑπεμνήμῡκε, ὑπομνήμῡκε. App. for ὑπεμήμυκε, 3 sing. pf. ὑπημύω, fr. ὑπ-, ὑπο- (4) + ἠμύω. Thus, to be bowed down, hang one's head: πάντ' ὑ. (finds humiliation everywhere) Χ 491.

ὑπέμνησε, 3 sing. aor. ὑπομιμνήσκω.

ὑπένερθε(ν) [ὑπ-, ὑπο- (4) + ἔνερθε(ν)]. (1) Beneath, below: οἳ ὑ. καμόντας ἀνθρώπους τίνυσθον (in the underworld) Γ 278. Cf. Δ 147, Ν 30, Ρ 386, Υ 61 : ὑπένερθε λίθ' ὑπέβαλλεν κ 353. Cf. μ 242.—(2) With reference to position in relation to something surrounding, below, underneath, within: εἰρύσατο ζωστὴρ ἠδ' ὑ. ζῶμα Δ 186. Cf. Δ 215.—(3) With genit. (a) Beneath, below, under: ποδῶν ὑ. Β 150.—(b) In a geographical context, under shelter of, under the lee of: ὑ. Χίοιο γ 172.

†**ὑπεξάγω** [ὑπ-, ὑπο- (3) + ἐξ- (1)]. 3 sing. aor. opt. ὑπεξαγάγοι. To remove out of danger, take in safety away σ 147.

†**ὑπεξαλέομαι** [ὑπ-, ὑπο- (3) + ἐξ- (1)]. Aor. infin. ὑπεξαλέασθαι. To keep away from the reach of, avoid: χεῖρας Ο 180.

†**ὑπεξαναδύω** [ὑπ-, ὑπο- (1) + ἐξ- (1) + ἀνα- (1)]. Aor. pple. ὑπεξαναδύς. To rise up or emerge *from out of.* With genit. : ἁλός Ν 352.

ὑπεξεσάωσε, 3 sing. aor. ὑπεκσαόω.

ὑπεξέφυγε, 3 sing. aor. ὑπεκφεύγω.

ὑπέρ [in form comp. fr. ὑπό]. Also (in phrase ὑπεὶρ ἅλα) **ὑπείρ** Ψ 227, Ω 13 : γ 73, δ 172, ι 254. (ὑπέρ commonly with anastrophe when immediately following the case-form.) Prep. with (1) Acc. (a) In reference to motion or extent *over* a space: τὸ δὲ τεῖχος ὕπερ πᾶν δοῦπος ὀρώρει Μ 289. Cf. Ψ 227, Ω 13 : ἦ μαψιδίως ἀλάλησθε ὑπεὶρ ἅλα; γ 73 = ι 254. Cf. δ 172, ι 260.—(b) In reference to passing *over* an object: ὑπὲρ ὦμον ἤλυθ' ἀκωκή Ε 16, δόρυ χροὸς ἀντετόρησε πρυμνὸν ὕπερ θέναρος 339 (app. the κόλπος of the robe is held up in defence by the hand with the palm outwards). Cf. Ε 851, Κ 373, etc. : η 135, χ 279, etc.—(c) In excess of, beyond, in violation, transgression or defiance of: αἶσαν Γ 59 = Ζ 333, Ζ 487, Π 780, ὅρκια Γ 299, Δ 67 = 72, 236, 271, Διὸς αἶσαν Ρ 321, μόρον Υ 30, Φ 517 (see ὑπέρμορον, μόρος (3)), μοῖραν Υ 336 : μόρον α 34, 35, ε 436 (see ὑπέρμορον, μόρος (3)).—In reference to a person, in spite of, with . . . against one: ὑπὲρ θεόν Ρ 327.—(2) Genit. (a) In reference to position or height *over* or *above* something: ὑπὲρ κεφαλῆς Β 20, ὅσον τ' ὄργυι' ὑπὲρ αἴης Ψ 327. Cf. Ν 200, etc. : δ 803, ζ 107, μ 406, π 471, etc.—So in reference to the position of a wound: βάλε στέρνον ὑπὲρ μαζοῖο Δ 528. Cf. Ε 145, Ν 616, Ο 433, etc. : τ 450.—To pouring water on hands held *over* a basin: χέρνιβα [χερσὶν] ἐπέχευεν ὑπὲρ ἀργυρέοιο λέβητος α 137, etc.—In a navigational context, to the north of: ὑπὲρ Κρήτης ξ 300 (cf. καθύπερθε (3) (c)).—In reference to position far away *over* a space: τηλοῦ ὑπὲρ πόντου ν 257.—(b) In reference to motion *passing over* an object: ὥς τε κῦμα νηὸς ὑπὲρ τοίχων καταβήσεται Ο 382. Cf. Μ 424. Ξ 412, Π 406, Υ 279, Ψ 73, 820, etc. : ρ 575.—To the motion of sound: ὑπὲρ τάφρου ἴαχεν Σ 228.—(c) In defence of, for the protection of: τεῖχος ἐτειχίσσαντο νεῶν ὕπερ Η 449, etc.—(d) On behalf of: ἑκατόμβην ῥέξαι ὑπὲρ Δαναῶν Α 444.—(e) On account of, concerning: ὅθ' ὑπὲρ σέθεν αἴσχε' ἀκούω Ζ 524.—(f) In adjurations, by: ὑπὲρ τοκέων γουνούμενος Ο 660. Cf. Ο 665, Χ 338, Ω 466 : ο 261.

ὑπεραής [ὑπερ- (1) + ἄημι]. (Cf. ἀκραής.) Of wind, blowing on high Λ 297.

ὑπέραι, αἱ. In pl., ropes or straps attached to and used for trimming a sail ε 260.

†**ὑπεράλλομαι** [ὑπερ- (3)]. 3 sing. aor. ὑπερᾶλτο Υ 327. Acc. sing. masc. pple. ὑπεράλμενον E 138. To leap or spring *over*. With genit.: αὐλῆς E 138. —With acc.: πολλὰς στίχας Υ 327.

ὑπερβαίνω [ὑπερ- (3)]. 3 sing. aor. ὑπέρβη θ 80, π 41, ρ 30, ψ 88. 3 pl. ὑπέρβασαν M 469. 3 sing. subj. ὑπερβήῃ I 501. (1) To pass or step *over*, pass, cross. With acc.: τεῖχος M 468, 469: λάϊνον οὐδόν θ 80, π 41, ρ 30, ψ 88.—(2) To transgress, trespass, sin: ὅτε κέν τις ὑπερβήῃ I 501.

†**ὑπερβάλλω, ὑπειρβάλλω** [ὑπερ- (3)]. Aor. ὑπειρέβαλον Ψ 637. 3 sing. ὑπέρβαλε Ψ 843, 847. Infin. ὑπερβαλέειν λ 597. (1) To topple or push *over*. With acc.: [λᾶαν] ἄκρον ὑπερβαλέειν λ 597.—(2) To throw or cast a missile, make a throw or cast, *further than* (another), outthrow (him). With genit.: τόσσον παντὸς ἀγῶνος ὑπέρβαλεν Ψ 847.—With acc.: δουρὶ ὑπειρέβαλον Φυλῆα Ψ 637. —To make a throw or cast *further than* or *beyond* (a specified distance). With acc.: ὑπέρβαλε σήματα πάντων Ψ 843.

ὑπερβασίη, -ης, ἡ [ὑπερβαίνω]. (1) A trespass, wrong, offence: ἵν' ὑπερβασίας ἀποτίσῃ χ 168. Cf. Ψ 589.—(2) Transgression, wrongdoing, evil conduct: τίσασθαι μνηστῆρας ὑπερβασίης γ 206. Cf. Γ 107, Π 18: ν 193 = χ 64.

ὑπέρβη, 3 sing. aor. ὑπερβαίνω.

ὑπέρβιος, -ον [ὑπερ- (6) + βίη]. (1) Headlong, headstrong, not to be restrained or turned aside Σ 262: ο 212.—(2) Overweening, arrogant, wanton: ὕβριν α 368 = δ 321, π 410. —In neut. ὑπέρβιον as adv., in overweening wise, wantonly, recklessly: βοῦς μευ ἔκτειναν ὑ. μ 379. Cf. P 19: ξ 92, 95, π 315.

ὑπερδεής (ὑπερδεϝής) [ὑπερ- (5) + δε(ϝ)-, δεύω²]. Acc. sing. ὑπερδέα (for ὑπερδεέα). Very scanty, very small in number: ὑπερδέα δῆμον ἔχοντας P 330.

†**ὑπερείπω** [ὑπ-, ὑπο- (4)]. 3 sing. aor. ὑπήριπε. To give way beneath one, collapse: ὑπήριπε γυῖα Ψ 691.

ὑπερέπτω [ὑπ-, ὑπο- (1)]. To eat away *from under*. With genit.: [ποταμὸς] κονίην ὑπέρεπτε ποδοῖιν Φ 271.

ὑπερέχω, ὑπειρέχω [ὑπερ- (1)]. 3 sing. aor. ὑπερέσχε I 420, 687: ν 93. 3 sing. subj. ὑπέρσχῃ Δ 249: ξ 184. 3 sing. aor. ὑπερέσχεθε Λ 735, Ω 374. (1) To hold, keep in position, *over*. With genit.: σπλάγχν' ὑπείρεχον Ἡφαίστοιο B 426.—(2) To hold or stretch (one's hand or hands) over a person in way of protection: αἴ κ' ὔμμιν ὑπέρσχῃ χεῖρα Κρονίων Δ 249. Cf. E 433: ξ 184.—To hold or stretch thus (one's hand) *over*. With genit.: ἐμεῖό τις θεῶν ὑπερέσχεθε χεῖρα Ω 374. Cf. I 420 = 687.—(3) *Intrans.* (a) To be *above*, exceed in height, overtop. With genit.: στάντων Μενέλαος ὑπείρεχεν ὤμους Γ 210 (στάντων app. referring to the whole assembly; ὤμους acc. of part concerned, 'with his . . .').—(b) Of a heavenly body, to rise ν 93.—To rise or appear *above* (the earth). With genit.: εὖτ' ἠέλιος ὑπερέσχεθε γαίης Λ 735.

ὑπερηνορέω [ὑπερ- (6) + ἀνήρ]. To act in overweening wise, display arrogance or wantonness: μνηστῆρας ἀπάλαλκε κακῶς ὑπερηνορέοντας δ 766. Cf. β 266.—In pres. pple. ὑπερηνορέων, -οντος, in adjectival use, overweening, overbearing, arrogant: Τρώων ὑπερηνορεόντων Δ 176. Cf. N 258: νέων β 324. Cf. β 331, ζ 5, etc.

ὑπερήσει, 3 sing. fut. ὑπερίημι.

ὑπερηφανέω [ὑπερ- (6) + an uncertain second element]. App., to conceive arrogance, be led on to arrogance or wantonness: ταῦθ' ὑπερηφανέοντες (ταῦτα advbl., 'by these things') Λ 694.

ὑπερθε(ν) [ὑπέρ + -θεν (1) (2)]. (1) From above: Δηϊοπίτην οὔτασεν ὦμον ὑ. (with a downward blow) Λ 421. Cf. ω 344. —(2) Above: ὑ. φοξὸς ἔην κεφαλήν B 218. Cf. E 122, 503, H 101 (in heaven above), M 4, O 36, etc.: ε 184, θ 135, π 47, υ 2, ω 230, etc.—(3) With reference to position in relation to a centre, outside, surrounding: ὑ. ἐπίσσωτρα προσαρηρότα E 724. Cf. N 682: ὑ. χιὼν γένετο (*i.e.* on the surface of objects) ξ 476.—(4) In reference to position in relation to a base, at the end or point: πρυμνὸς παχύς, αὐτὰρ ὑ. ὀξὺς ἔην M 446.

†**ὑπερθρῴσκω** [ὑπερ- (3)]. 3 pl. fut. in mid. form ὑπερθορέονται Θ 179. Aor. ὑπέρθορον I 476. 3 pl. ὑπέρθορον Π 380. Infin. ὑπερθορέειν M 53. To leap or spring *over*. With acc.: τάφρον Θ 179, Π 380. Cf. I 476.—Absol. M 53.

ὑπέρθῡμος [ὑπερ- (5) (6) + θυμός]. (1) Great-hearted, high-minded, bold, noble B 746, Δ 365, E 77, Z 111, M 128, etc.: γ 448, λ 269, ο 252.—(2) Overweening, arrogant, wanton E 376: δ 784, η 59, ξ 209, π 326 = 360.

ὑπερθύριον, τό [ὑπερ- (1) + θύρη]. The lintel of a door η 90.

†**ὑπερίημι** [ὑπερ- (3) + ἵημι¹]. 3 sing. fut. ὑπερήσει. To throw *beyond*. With acc.: τόδε [σῆμα] θ 198.

ὑπερικταίνομαι [app. ὑπ-, ὑπο- (4) + an unknown ἐρικταίνομαι]. Of the feet, perh., to hobble along beneath one: πόδες ὑπερικταίνοντο ψ 3.

Ὑπερῑονίδης [app. a double patronymic in form. See next]. = next: Ἠελίου Ὑπεριονίδαο μ 176.

Ὑπερίων, -ονος [ὑπέρ. App. a patronymic in form. Cf. Οὐρανίωνες]. He that is on high, that bestrides the heavens. A name of the sun α 24.—Joined with Ἠέλιος Θ 480: α 8, μ 133, 263, 346, 374.—With ἠλέκτωρ T 398.

†**ὑπερκαταβαίνω** [ὑπερ- (3) + κατα- (1)]. 3 pl. aor. ὑπερκατέβησαν. To pass *over* and descend from, pass, cross. With acc.: τεῖχος N 50, 87.

ὑπερκύδας, -αντος [ὑπερ- (5) + κῦδος]. Far renowned, far famed. Epithet of the Achaeans Δ 66 = 71.

ὑπερμενέων, -οντος [ὑπερμενής in bad sense]. Overweening, overbearing, arrogant: ἄνδρες τ 62.

ὑπερμενής [ὑπερ- (5) + μένος]. Of exceeding might or power, mighty, powerful. Epithet of Zeus B 116 = I 23 = Ξ 69, B 350, 403, H 315, 481, Θ 470, Λ 727, N 226.—Of kings Θ 236: ν 205, υ 222.—Of the Trojan allies P 362.

ὑπέρμορον [use as adv. of neut. sing. of ὑπέρμορος

fr. ὑπερ- (4) + μόρος. Also written ὑπὲρ μόρον]. See μόρος (3).—Neut. pl. ὑπέρμορα in the same sense: Ἀργείοισί χ' ὑ. νόστος ἐτύχθη Β 155.

†**ὑπεροπλίζομαι** [ὑπέροπλος]. 3 sing. aor. opt. ὑπεροπλίσσαιτο. To scorn, despise, look down upon ρ 268.

ὑπεροπλίη, -ης [ὑπέροπλος]. Insolence, arrogance. In pl.: ᾗς ὑπεροπλίῃσι τάχ' ἄν ποτε θυμὸν ὀλέσσῃ Α 205.

ὑπέροπλος [ὑπερ- (6) + an unknown second element]. Insolent, arrogant. In neut. sing. ὑπέροπλον as adv., insolently, arrogantly: ἔειπεν Ο 185. Cf. Ρ 170.

†**ὑπερπέτομαι** [ὑπερ- (2) (3)]. 3 sing. aor. ὑπέρπτατο. To fly over something. Of a missile: ὑπέρπτατο ἔγχος Ν 408, Χ 275: χ 280.—To fly *over* or *beyond*. With acc.: δίσκος ὑπέρπτατο σήματα πάντων θ 192.

ὑπερράγη, 3 sing. aor. pass. ὑπορρήγνυμι.

ὑπέρσχῃ, 3 sing. aor. subj. ὑπερέχω.

ὑπέρτατος [superl. fr. ὑπέρ]. In the highest position: μαρμάρῳ, ὃ κεῖτο ὑ. (on the top of a heap) Μ 381, ἧστο ὑ. (raised above the others) Ψ 451.

ὑπερτερίη, -ης, ἡ [ὑπέρτερος]. App. = πείρινς: ἀπήνην ὑπερτερίῃ ἀραρυῖαν ζ 70.

ὑπέρτερος [comp. fr. ὑπέρ]. (**1**) Relating to the upper hand or victory: εὖχος (the glory of victory) Λ 290.—So κῦδος Μ 437, Ο 491, 644.—(**2**) Of higher rank, one's superior: γενεῇ ὑ. Λ 786.—(**3**) In reference to position in relation to a centre, on the outside, the outside . . .: κρέα (the fleshy muscular parts as opposed to the entrails) γ 65 = 470 = υ 279.

ὑπερφίαλος [ὑπερ- (6) + an unknown second element]. Heedless of the rights or feelings of others, careless of the consequences of one's actions, reckless, regardless: ἐπεί οἱ παῖδες ὑπερφίαλοι [εἰσιν] Γ 106. Cf. Ε 881, Ν 621, Ο 94, Φ 224, 414, 459, Ψ 611: β 310, γ 315 = ο 12, δ 790, ζ 274, ι 106, λ 116, ν 373, ξ 27, ο 315, 376, π 271, σ 167, υ 12, 291, φ 289, ψ 356.—Absol.: ὑπερφιάλοισι μετελθών α 134.—Of speech, rash, idle: ἔπος δ 503, μύθους 774.

ὑπερφιάλως [adv. fr. prec.]. (**1**) In reckless or regardless wise: ὑβρίζοντες α 227.—(**2**) In a high-handed or striking fashion: ἦ μέγα ἔργον ὑ. ἐτελέσθη (τετέλεσται) δ 663, π 346.—(**3**) Excessively, greatly: μή τις ὑ. νεμεσήσῃ Ν 293. Cf. Σ 300: ρ 481 = φ 285, σ 71.

†**ὑπέρχομαι** [ὑπ-, ὑπο- (8) (11)]. 3 sing. aor. ὑπήλυθε Η 215, Υ 44: ε 476. 2 pl. ὑπήλθετε μ 21. 3 sing. subj. ὑπέλθῃ σ 150. To go or make one's way *under* or *beneath*, enter. With acc.: δοιοὺς θάμνους (slipped under them) ε 476, μέλαθρον σ 150. Cf. μ 21.—Fig.: Τρῶας τρόμος ὑπήλυθε γυῖα (γυῖα acc. of part affected, 'seized their limbs') Η 215 = Υ 44.

ὑπερωέω [ὑπ-, ὑπο- (12) + ἐρωέω²]. To start back under stress of something: ὑπερώησάν οἱ ἵπποι (thereat, in terror) Θ 122 = 314 = Ο 452.

ὑπερῴη, -ης, ἡ [ὑπέρ]. The upper part of the mouth, the palate Χ 495.

ὑπερωϊόθεν [ὑπερώϊον + -θεν (1)]. From the women's quarters: ὑ. σύνθετ' ἀοιδήν α 328.

ὑπερώϊον, ὑπερῷον, τό [ὑπέρ]. (**1**) An upper chamber: ὑ. εἰσαναβᾶσα Β 514.—So in pl.: εἰς ὑπερῷ' ἀναβάς Π 184.—(**2**) In pl., a raised set of chambers appropriated to the lady of a house and her maidens, the women's quarters (cf. μέγαρον (3)): εἰς ὑπερῷ' ἀναβᾶσα α 362 = τ 602 = φ 356, δ 751 = ρ 49 = ψ 364, εἰς ὑπερῷ' ἀνέβαινε δ 760 (app. the same as the θάλαμος of 718). Cf. β 358, π 449, σ 206, 302, τ 600, χ 428, ψ 1, 85.—So in sing.: ὑπερωΐῳ κεῖτο δ 787. Cf. ο 517, ρ 101, τ 594.

ὑπέστη, 3 sing. aor. ὑφίστημι.

ὑπέσχεθε, 3 sing. aor. ὑπέχω.

ὑπέσχετο, 3 sing. aor. ὑπίσχομαι.

ὑπέτρεσαν, 3 pl. aor. ὑποτρέω.

ὑπέφηνε, 3 sing. aor. ὑποφαίνω.

ὑπέχευε, 3 sing. aor. ὑποχέω.

†**ὑπέχω** [ὑπ-, ὑπο- (4) (6)]. Aor. pple. ὑποσχών Ε 269. 3 sing. aor. ὑπέσχεθε Η 188. (**1**) To hold under something: χεῖρα Η 188.—(**2**) To submit (a female) to the male: ὑποσχὼν θήλεας ἵππους Ε 269.

ὑπήλθετε, 2 pl. aor. ὑπέρχομαι.

ὑπήλυθε, 3 sing. aor. ὑπέρχομαι.

ὑπήνεικαν, 3 pl. aor. ὑποφέρω.

ὑπηνήτης [ὑπήνη, hair on the lower part of the face, fr. ὑπ-, ὑπο- (4) + ἠν-, face. Cf. ἀπηνής, πρηνής]. Having hair sprouting on the lower part of the face, getting a beard: πρῶτον ὑπηνήτῃ Ω 348: κ 279.

ὑπηοῖος, -η, -ον [ὑπ-, ὑπο- (12) + ἠώς]. (**1**) Of the dawn, the morning . . . .: στίβη ρ 25.—(**2**) With the dawn, at break of day: πρῶϊ ὑπηοῖοι ἐγείρομεν Ἄρηα (στησόμεθ' ἂμ πύργους) Θ 530 = Σ 277 = 303.—In neut. ὑπηοῖον as adv. in the same sense: χθιζὸν ὑ. δ 656.

ὑπήριπε, 3 sing. aor. ὑπερείπω.

ὑπῆσαν, 3 pl. impf. ὕπειμι.

ὑπίσχομαι [ὑπ-, ὑπο- (7) + ἴσχομαι, ἴσχω]. 2 sing. aor. ὑπέσχεο Ο 374: ν 133. 3 ὑπέσχετο Β 112, Ι 19, 263, Μ 236, Ν 366, 376, Τ 141: δ 6, λ 291, ω 335. Subj. ὑπόσχωμαι Χ 114. 3 sing. ὑπόσχηται Κ 39. 3 pl. ὑπόσχωνται Χ 350. Imp. ὑπόσχεο Α 514. Pple. ὑποσχόμενος Κ 303: ο 195, 203. Pl. ὑποσχόμενοι Ι 576, Ν 377. Infin. ὑποσχέσθαι Ζ 93, 115, 274. (Cf. ἔχω (IV) (4).)—(**1**) To come under an undertaking, give a promise, promise: ὑπόσχεό μοι Α 514. Cf. Ο 374: ὑπίσχεται ἀνδρὶ ἑκάστῳ (makes promises) β 91 = ν 380. Cf. ν 133, ο 195, 203.—With fut. infin. of what one undertakes or promises to do: δυοκαίδεκα βοῦς ἱερευσέμεν Ζ 93 = 274. Cf. Χ 114: δ 6, λ 291.—Of what one promises to grant or bring about: Ἴλιόν [μ'] ἐκπέρσαντ' ἀπονέεσθαι Β 112, Ι 19. Cf. θ 347.—(**2**) To undertake to give, promise: ἑκατόμβας Ζ 115. Cf. Ι 263, 576, Ν 376, Τ 141, Χ 350, Ψ 195, 209: ὦνον ὑπισχόμεναι (tendering it, chaffering) ο 463. Cf. ω 335.—(**3**) To promise to perform or bring about, undertake: τόδε ἔργον Κ 39, 303, βουλέων, ἅς τέ μοι ὑπέσχετο (*i.e.* promised to carry his will into effect) Μ 236, ἀπειλαί, ἃς ὑπίσχεο (undertook to make good) Υ 84. Cf. N 366, 377.

ὕπνος, -ου, ὁ. **(1)** Sleep A 610, B 2, E 413, N 636, X 502, etc.: α 363, β 398, δ 105, η 318, ι 372, etc.—Personified Ξ 231, 233, 242, 264, 270, 286, 354, Π 454, 672 = 682.—**(2)** Oppression caused by lack of sleep, heaviness, drowsiness: καμάτῳ ἀδηκότες ἠδὲ καὶ ὕπνῳ K 98. Cf. ζ 2, μ 281.

ὑπνώω. To sleep, slumber: καὶ ὑπνώοντας ἐγείρει Ω 344: = ε 48 = ω 4.

ὑπό. Also **ὑπαί** B 824, Γ 217, K 376, Λ 417, etc. (ὑπό commonly with anastrophe when immediately following the vb. or case-form.) (I) Adv. **(1)** From under or beneath something: ὑπαὶ δὲ ἴδεσκεν (looked up from under his brow) Γ 217 (cf. ὑπόδρα), ἔλυεν ὑφ' ἵππους Ψ 513. Cf. Σ 319.—**(2)** From the power, range or reach of something: ἦλθε φυγὼν ὕπο νηλεὲς ἦμαρ Φ 57. Cf. M 113, N 395: ι 17, ψ 332.—**(3)** Under or beneath something, underneath, below: ὑφ' ἕρματα τάνυσσαν A 486, ὑπὸ τρόμος ἔλλαβε γυῖα Γ 34, Ξ 506, ὑπὸ γλῶσσαν τάμεν (at the root) E 74. Cf. H 6, K 155, Λ 579, 635, Ξ 240, etc.: α 130, δ 636 (at the teat), θ 436, λ 527, π 47, ψ 204, etc.—**(4)** Indicating coming under an obligation or undertaking. See ἔχω (IV) (4).—**(5)** Indicating occasion, cause, accompaniment, thereat, therewith, thereto: ὑπό κεν ταλασίφρονά περ δέος εἷλεν Δ 421, χώρησαν δ' ὑπὸ πρόμαχοι Δ 505, ὑπὸ δ' ἔστρεφον ἡνιοχῆες (following the movement of the lines) E 505. Cf. Δ 497, Θ 4, Λ 417, Σ 570 (to the lyre), Ψ 108, etc.: δ 113, θ 380, π 215, φ 411, etc.—(II) Prep. **(1)** With genit. **(a)** From under or beneath: ὑπὸ δ' ᾔρεον ἕρματα νηῶν B 154. Cf. Θ 543, N 611, T 17, etc.: κρήνη [ῥέει] ὑπὸ σπείους ι 141. Cf. δ 39, η 5, ι 463, χ 364, etc.—So with ablative: ζυγόφιν T 404, Ω 576, ὄχεσφιν Ψ 7.—**(b)** In reference to saving or escaping, away from, from, from out of: ἐρύεσθαι ὑπὸ Τρώων ὀρυμαγδοῦ I 248. Cf. Θ 363, M 74, P 224, 645, T 73: ἀνσχεθέειν ὑπὸ κύματος ὀρμῆς ε 320.—Sim. in reference to carrying off from a protector: νεκρὸν ὑπ' Αἴαντος ἐρύειν P 235. Cf. N 198.—**(c)** In reference to position, under, beneath, underneath: ἱμάς, ὅς οἱ ὑπ' ἀνθερεῶνος τέτατο Γ 372. Cf. E 796, Θ 14, Φ 318, Ψ 874: οὔ πω ἐτέθαπτο ὑπὸ χθονὸς εὐρυοδείης λ 52.—Sim. in reference to taking hold or grasping: ὑπ' ἀνθερεῶνος ἑλοῦσα A 501. Cf. Λ 842.—**(d)** Passing into the next sense: ὑπὸ δὲ στεναχίζετο γαῖα λαῶν ἰζόντων B 95, σμῶδιξ ἐξυπανέστη σκήπτρου ὕπο 268. Cf. N 27, Ξ 285, etc.: ι 484, μ 406, π 10, etc.—**(e)** Under the influence of, under compulsion or stress of, by the power, force, agency or means of, caused by, under, because of, by reason of, by, from, before, at: εὖτ' ἂν ὑφ' Ἕκτορος πίπτωσιν A 242, μὴ ὑπ' αὐτοῦ δουρὶ δαμήῃς Γ 436, ὑπὸ Ζεφύροιο ἰωῆς Δ 276. Cf. B 334, Γ 61, 128, E 92, Z 73, H 64, Θ 149, 183, K 376, Λ 119, 391, M 462, N 140, Ξ 414, O 171, 275 (at the sound of it), Π 519, Φ 12, Ψ 86, etc.: ὑπ' ἀνάγκης β 110, ὑπὸ κύματος ἀρθείς ε 393. Cf. η 263, θ 192, ι 66, κ 78, τ 114, etc.—**(f)** In reference to accompaniment: δαΐδων ὕπο (to the light of . . .) Σ 492: τ 48, ψ 290.—**(g)** In reference to motion to a point *under* something: ὡς ὅτε κῦμ' ἐν νηῒ πέσῃσι λάβρον ὑπαὶ νεφέων (seeming to reach them) O 625. Cf. Π 375: τὸν μοχλὸν ὑπὸ σποδοῦ ἤλασα ι 375. Cf. ε 346, 373.—With verbs of striking, etc.: ὑπὸ στέρνοιο τυχήσας Δ 106. Cf. N 177, 671, Ξ 493, Ψ 875, etc.—**(h)** In reference to passing *under* something: βάλ' αὐχέν' ὑπὸ στεφάνης H 12. Cf. Λ 259, 424, 579 = N 412 = P 349, Π 339, 347, Φ 591: σ 96.—**(2)** With dat. **(a)** In reference to position, under, beneath, underneath: ὑπὸ πλατανίστῳ B 307, ἐπεὶ ζεύξειεν ὑφ' ἅρμασιν ἵππους Ω 14. Cf. Δ 44, Z 396, I 472, K 152, N 88, Π 378, Σ 244, etc.: α 186, γ 478, δ 153, θ 522, ι 443, κ 359, ξ 533, ο 469, etc.—So with locative: ὄχεσφιν Θ 41, κράτεσφιν K 156, etc.—Sim.: Βορέω ὑπ' ἰωγῇ ξ 533.—In pregnant sense: ποσσὶ δ' ὑπ' ἐδήσατο πέδιλα B 44. Cf. E 693, Θ 267, Σ 375, Ω 644, etc.: α 96, δ 297, ι 245, χ 449, etc.—**(b)** Passing into the next sense: ὑπὸ ποσσὶ στεναχίζετο γαῖα B 784. Cf. Γ 13, Λ 151, N 19, T 363, Υ 497, etc.: εἴκοι ὑπὸ βῶλος ἀρότρῳ σ 374.—**(c)** = (1) (e): χερσὶν ὑφ' ἡμετέρῃσιν ἀλοῦσα B 374, θεῶν ὑπὸ πομπῇ (under their conduct) Z 171, ὕπνῳ ὕπο Ω 636. Cf. Γ 352, E 93, Z 453, H 129, Λ 433, N 590, etc.: ὤλεθ' ὑφ' Αἰγίσθοιο δόλῳ γ 235, γήρᾳ ὕπο λιπαρῷ ἀρημένον λ 136. Cf. δ 295, 402, 790, η 193, ν 82, σ 156, τ 488, etc.—So with locative: ἐπόρνυέ οἱ μόρσιμον ἦμαρ ὑπὸ Πηλεΐδαο βίηφιν O 614.—**(d)** In subjection to, under the charge or guidance of, under: ὑφ' ἡνιόχῳ εἰωθότι E 231. Cf. Z 159, I 156, 298: δέδμητο λαὸς ὑπ' αὐτῷ γ 305. Cf. η 68.—**(e)** Indicating the subjection of the female to the male in conception and in reference to the bearing of offspring, by: ἥ μιν ὑπ' Ἀγχίσῃ τέκεν E 313. Cf. B 714, H 469, Ξ 492, etc.: ἥ ῥ' ὑπὸ Τυνδαρέῳ γείνατο παῖδε λ 299.—Sim.: Ἀφροδίτης, τὴν ἄρ' ὑπὸ μνηστῆρσιν ἔχον χ 445.—**(3)** With acc. **(a)** In reference to motion to a point *under* something: ὑπὸ Ἴλιον ἦλθεν (to the walls of . . .) B 216, ὑπὸ σπέος ἤλασε μῆλα Δ 279. Cf. Δ 407, E 731, Θ 271, Λ 181, M 264, Σ 145, X 195, Ψ 51, etc.: γ 335, δ 146, 425, 445, ε 481, ι 99, κ 191, ξ 469, υ 81, ω 234, etc.—With verbs of striking, etc.: βάλε λαιμὸν ὑπ' ἀνθερεῶνα N 388. Cf. N 615, P 309, Υ 275.—**(b)** In reference to motion passing *under* something: τρέσε τεῖχος ὕπο Τρώων X 144. Cf. E 67, N 652, Σ 281: κρήνη ὑπ' αὐλῆς οὐδὸν ἵησιν η 130. Cf. β 181.—**(c)** In reference to position, stretching, extending, lying or being under, under, beneath, underneath: οἳ δ' ἔχον Ἀρκαδίην ὑπὸ Κυλλήνης ὄρος B 603. Cf. B 824, Γ 371, E 267, T 259, X 307: μάλα πῖαρ ὑπ' οὖδάς [ἐστιν] ι 135. Cf. ι 433, λ 498, 619, ο 349, χ 362.—**(d)** In reference to time, during, throughout the time of: πάνθ' ὑπὸ μηνιθμόν Π 202.—In the course of: νύχθ' ὑπὸ τήνδε X 102.

ὑποβάλλω, ὑββάλλω [ὑπο- (8)]. **(1)** To put underneath: ὑπένερθε λῖθ' ὑπέβαλλεν κ 353.—**(2)** To throw in one's word, interrupt a speaker:

ἑσταότος μὲν καλὸν ἀκουέμεν, οὐδὲ ἔοικεν ὑββάλλειν Τ 80 (rejecting 77; if it be retained the sense must be 'to prompt another, put him up as one's mouthpiece').

ὑποβλήδην [ὑποβάλλω (2)]. Throwing in a word, interrupting: ὑ. ἠμείβετο Α 292.

ὑπόβρυξ, -υχος [ὑπο- (4) + βρέχω, to wet. Cf. ἀναβρέχω and also δίπτυξ under δίπτυχος]. Under water: τὸν ὑπόβρυχα θῆκεν ε 319.

ὑποδάμνημι [ὑπο- (5)]. To subdue under another, overcome, oppress. In mid.: ἠὲ ἑκὼν ὑποδάμνασαι (let yourself be oppressed) γ 214 = π 95.

ὑποδέγμενος, pf. pple. ὑποδέχομαι.

†**ὑποδείδια,** *pf. with pres. sense* ρ 564. [ὑπο- (12) + δείδια. See δείδοικα.] 3 pl. plupf. (with impf. sense) ὑπεδείδισαν Ε 521. 3 pl. aor. ὑπέδεισαν (ὑπέδϝεισαν) Α 406. Imp. pl. ὑποδείσατε (with the ϝ neglected) β 66. Pple. ὑποδείσας (ὑποδϝείσας) Χ 282: ι 377, π 425. Nom. pl. masc. ὑποδείσαντες Μ 413, Σ 199, Ψ 417, 446, Ω 265. Fem. ὑποδείσᾱσα κ 296. **(1)** To tremble before something, be afraid, feel fear: μή τίς μοι ὑποδείσας ἀναδύῃ (struck with fear) ι 377.—**(2)** To tremble before, be afraid of, fear, dread, stand in awe of: τόν Α 406. Cf. Ε 521, Μ 413 = Ψ 417 = 446, Σ 199, Χ 282, Ω 265: θεῶν μῆνιν β 66. Cf. κ 296, π 425, ρ 564.

ὑποδεξίη, ἡ [ὑποδέχομαι]. Hospitable entertainment, hospitality: πᾶσά τοί ἐσθ' ὑποδεξίη (it is for thee to offer all hospitality) Ι 73.

†**ὑποδέχομαι** [ὑπο- (4) (5) (7) (12)]. Fut. ὑποδέξομαι Σ 59, 440: π 70, τ 257. 2 sing. ὑποδέξεαι Σ 89. 3 sing. aor. ὑπεδέξατο Ζ 136, Σ 398: χ 470. 2 sing. aor. ὑπέδεξο ξ 54. 3 ὑπέδεκτο Ι 480: β 387, ξ 52, υ 372, ψ 314. Infin. ὑποδέχθαι Η 93. Pf. pple. ὑποδέγμενος ν 310, π 189. 3 sing. plupf. ὑπέδεκτο ξ 275. **(1)** To receive, catch: Θέτις ὑπεδέξατο κόλπῳ δειδιότα Ζ 136. Cf. Σ 398.—To receive, take in: στυγερὸς ὑπεδέξατο κοῖτος χ 470.—**(2)** To receive, welcome: τὸν οὐχ ὑποδέξομαι (ὑποδέξεαι) αὖτις οἴκαδε νοστήσαντα Σ 59 = 440, Σ 89: τ 257.—To receive hospitably, take under one's care or protection: πρόφρων μ' ὑπέδεκτο Ι 480. Cf. ξ 52, 54, π 70, υ 372, ψ 314.—**(3)** To accept or take up a challenge: δεῖσαν ὑποδέχθαι Η 93.—**(4)** To undertake to grant a request, promise something: ὅ οἱ πρόφρων ὑπέδεκτο β 387.—**(5)** In plupf. and pf. pple. **(a)** To submit to, put up with, endure: βίας ὑποδέγμενος ἀνδρῶν ν 310, π 189.—**(b)** To await, be laid up for or destined to: ἔτι με πῆμ' ὑπέδεκτο ξ 275.

ὑποδήματα, τά [ὑπο- (4) + δέω]. Sandals: ποσὶν ὑποδήματα δοῦσα ο 369. Cf. σ 361.

ὑποδμώς, ὁ [ὑπο- (5) + δμώς. 'A servant under a master']. A servant or minister δ 386.

ὑπόδρα [ὑπο- (2) + an uncertain second element]. (Looking) from beneath (the eye-brows), with a scowl: ὑπόδρα ἰδών Α 148 = Χ 260 = 344 = Ω 559, Β 245, Δ 349 = Ξ 82, Δ 411 = Ε 251 = Κ 446, Ε 888, Μ 230 = Ρ 169 = Σ 284, Ο 13, Ρ 141, Υ 428: θ 165 = σ 14 = χ 60 = 320, ρ 459 = σ 388, σ 337 = τ 70, χ 34.

†**ὑποδράω** [ὑπο- (5)]. 3 pl. ὑποδρώωσι. To serve under a master, be servant or minister: οἵ σφιν ὑποδρώωσιν ο 333.

ὑποδρηστήρ, -ῆρος, ὁ [ὑπο- (5) + δρηστήρ. 'A servant under a master']. A servant or attendant ο 330.

†**ὑποδύω** [ὑπο- (1) (3) (4) (8) (11)]. 3 sing. aor. ὑπέδῡ κ 398. Nom. dual masc. pple. ὑποδύντε Θ 332, Ν 421, Ρ 717. Nom. sing. fem. ὑποδῦσα δ 435. 2 sing. fut. mid. ὑποδύσεαι υ 53. 3 sing. aor. ὑπεδύσετο ζ 127. **(1)** In middle, with genit., to come out *from under*, emerge *from*: θάμνων ὑπεδύσετο ζ 127.—To get away *from the influence of*, get *clear of*: κακῶν ὑποδύσεαι ἤδη υ 53.—**(2)** With acc., to plunge *beneath*: ὑποδῦσα θαλάσσης κόλπον δ 435.—To get or put oneself under something so as to exert upward force: τὸν ὑποδύντε φερέτην Θ 332 = Ν 421. Cf. Ρ 717.—**(3)** Of a feeling, to come upon one: πᾶσιν ὑπέδυ γόος κ 398.

ὑποείκω [ὑπο- (12) + εἴκω[2]]. Fut. (or aor. subj.) ὑποείξω Ο 211. Fut. in mid. form ὑποείξομαι Ψ 602. ὑπείξομαι (ὑπ-, ὑπο-) Α 294. 2 sing. ὑπείξεαι μ 117. 3 sing. aor. ὑπόειξε Ο 227: π 42. 1 pl. subj. ὑποείξομεν Δ 62. **(1)** With genit., to retire or withdraw before the foe from: νεῶν ὑπόεικον Π 305.—To keep oneself withdrawn from, keep away from: ὑπόεικε μάχης Λ 204.—To withdraw from so as to make room for another: τῷ ἕδρης ἐπιόντι πατὴρ ὑπόειξεν π 42.—**(2)** To yield, give way, submit: εἰ σοὶ ὑπείξομαι Α 294. Cf. Δ 62, Ο 211: μ 117.—Of an inanimate object, to yield to a blow, give way: οὐ ῥηΐδι' ἐστὶ θεῶν δῶρ' ὑποείκειν Υ 266.—**(3)** To retire from, avoid: χεῖρας ἐμάς Ο 227.—**(4)** To cease from something, give over. With complementary pple.: ὑποείξομαί τοι χωόμενος Ψ 602.

†**ὑποζεύγνῡμι** [ὑπο- (4)]. Aor. subj. ὑποζεύξω. To yoke (horses): ἵππους ο 81.

†**ὑποθερμαίνω** [ὑπο- (12)]. 3 sing. aor. pass. ὑπεθερμάνθη. In pass., to become heated on the occurrence of something: ὑπεθερμάνθη ξίφος αἵματι (thereupon) Π 333 = Υ 476.

ὑποθέσθαι, aor. infin. mid. ὑποτίθημι.

ὑποθημοσύνη, -ης, ἡ [ὑποτίθημι]. Suggestion, instance. In pl.: ὑποθημοσύνῃσιν Ἀθήνης π 233.—Inspiration. In pl.: ὑποθημοσύνῃσιν Ἀθήνης Ο 412.

ὑποθήσομαι, fut. mid. ὑποτίθημι.

ὑποθωρήσσω [ὑπο- (12)]. To get under arms for some purpose: λόχῳ ὑπεθωρήσσοντο (for an ambush) Σ 513 (the prefix app. merely indicating vaguely the purpose already defined by λόχῳ).

†**ὑποκλίνω** [ὑπο- (4)]. 3 sing. aor. pass. ὑπεκλίνθη. In pass., to lay oneself down *under*. With dat.: σχοίνῳ ὑπεκλίνθη ε 463.

ὑποκλονέω [ὑπο- (12)]. In pass., to be driven in confusion *before* a foe. With dat.: εἰ ἂν τούτους ὑποκλονέεσθαι ἐάσω Ἀχιλῆϊ Φ 556.

ὑποκλοπέομαι [ὑπόκλοπος fr. ὑποκλέπτω fr. ὑπο- (4) + κλέπτω]. To conceal oneself in some hiding-place, keep out of sight: εἴ τις ζωὸς ὑποκλοπέοιτο χ 382.

ὑποκρίνομαι [ὑπο- (12)]. 3 sing. aor. opt. ὑποκρίναιτο Μ 228: ο 170. Imp. ὑπόκρῖναι τ 535.

Infin. ὑποκρίνασθαι τ 555. (1) To give an interpretative response in regard to, to interpret, expound (cf. κρίνω (8)): ὄνειρον τ 535, 555.—Absol.: ὧδέ χ' ὑποκρίναιτο θεοπρόπος Μ 228. Cf. ο 170 (read the sign).—(2) To respond by a declaration of one's will or purpose: μῦθον ἀκούεις, ὥς τοι ὑποκρίνονται Η 407. Cf. β 111.

†**ὑποκρύπτω** [ὑπο- (4)]. 3 sing. aor. pass. ὑπεκρύφθη. To hide or cover up *under* or *beneath*. With dat.: νηῦς ἄχνῃ ὑπεκρύφθη Ο 626.

ὑπόκυκλος [ὑπο- (4) + κύκλος]. Fitted with wheels or castors beneath: τάλαρον δ 131.

†**ὑποκύομαι** [ὑπο- (6) + κύω = κυέω]. Aor. pple. fem. ὑποκῦσαμένη Ζ 26: λ 254. Pl. ὑποκῦσάμεναι Υ 225. To conceive under the act of the male, to conceive, become pregnant: ὑποκυσαμένη διδυμάονε γείνατο παῖδε Ζ 26. Cf. λ 254.—Of mares Υ 225.

ὑπολείπω [ὑπο- (12) (the prefix app. pointing vaguely the contrast with what does not remain)]. Fut. pass. ὑπολείψομαι ρ 276, 282, τ 44. (1) To leave remaining or unconsumed; in pass., to remain, be left: πέμπτον ὑπελείπετ' ἄεθλον Ψ 615: ἃ τῇ προτέρῃ ὑπέλειπον ἔδοντες π 50.—(2) In pass., to be left behind, remain, while another departs: ἐν μεγάρῳ ὑπελείπετ' Ὀδυσσεύς η 230 = τ 1 = 51. Cf. ρ 276, 282, τ 44.

ὑπολευκαίνω [ὑπο- (12)]. In pass., to become white in consequence of something: αἱ ὑπολευκαίνονται ἀχυρμιαί (thereupon, thereat) Ε 502.

ὑπολίζων, -ονος [ὑπολιγίων, fr. ὑπο- (4) + ὀλιγίων, comp. fr. ὀλίγος]. Smaller than and under something else: λαοὶ ὑπολίζονες ἦσαν (were overtopped by the gods) Σ 519.

ὑπολύω [ὑπο- (3) (4)]. 3 pl. aor. pass. ὑπέλυντο Π 341. (1) To set free or release from something: ὑπέλυσα ἑταίρους ι 463.—To set free or release *from*. With genit. In mid.: τὸν ὑπελύσαο δεσμῶν Α 401.—(2) To break up or dissipate (the vital forces), cause (the limbs) to give way or collapse under one, by the application of force to fatal effect (the prefix app. referring in strictness only to the limbs): τῶν ὑπέλυσε μένος καὶ γυῖα Ζ 27. Cf. Π 341, Ψ 726.—In reference to an animal Ο 581.

†**ὑπομένω** [ὑπο- (12) (the prefix in the first sense app. pointing vaguely the contrast with those who do not remain)]. Aor. ὑπέμεινα κ 258. 3 sing. ὑπέμεινε Ξ 488, Π 814, Ρ 25: α 410, κ 232. 3 pl. ὑπέμειναν Ε 498, Ο 312. Infin. ὑπομεῖναι Ρ 174. (1) To remain where one is, stay behind: Εὐρύλοχος ὑπέμεινεν κ 232. Cf. κ 258.—To remain or stay for some purpose. With infin.: οὐδ' ὑπέμεινε γνώμεναι (for one to know him) α 410.—(2) To await the onset of (an attacking foe), stand up to (him): Πάτροκλον Π 814. Cf. Ρ 25, 174.—Sim.: ἐρωὴν Πηνελέωο Ξ 488.—Absol., to await the foe, stand firm, stand one's ground: Ἀργεῖοι ὑπέμειναν ἀολλέες Ε 498, Ο 312.

†**ὑπομιμνήσκω** [ὑπο- (11)]. Fut. pple. fem. ὑπομνήσουσα ο 3. 3 sing. aor. ὑπέμνησε α 321. To remind (a person) of (something), cause (him) to think or bethink himself of (it). With genit.: ὑπέμνησέ ἑ πατρός α 321. Cf. ο 3.

†**ὑπομνάομαι** [ὑπο- (12)]. 2 pl. impf. ὑπεμνάασθε. To woo or court (the wife of a living husband) (the prefix implying that the wooers seek a right concurrent, and therefore in conflict, with the husband's rights): αὐτοῦ ζώοντος ὑπεμνάασθε γυναῖκα χ 38.

ὑπομνήμῦκε. See ὑπεμνήμυκε.

ὑπομνήσουσα, fut. pple. fem. ὑπομιμνήσκω.

Ὑπονήϊος, -ον [ὑπο- (4) + Νήϊον]. Lying under Mount Neïum: Ἰθάκης γ 81.

ὑποπεπτηῶτες, nom. pl. masc. pf. pple. ὑποπτήσσω.

ὑποπερκάζω [ὑπο- (12) + περκάζω in sim. sense, fr. περκ- as in περκνός]. To assume a dark hue, colour (the prefix app. indicating that this takes place under some influence, *i.e.* that of the sun): ἕτεραι [σταφυλαὶ] ὑποπερκάζουσιν η 126.

Ὑποπλάκιος, -η, -ον [ὑπο- (4) + Πλάκος]. Lying under Mount Placus: Θήβῃ Ζ 397.

†**ὑποπτήσσω** [ὑπο- (4)]. Nom. pl. masc. pf. pple. ὑποπεπτηῶτες. To cower *under*. With dat.: νεοσσοὶ πετάλοις ὑποπεπτηῶτες Β 312.

†**ὑπόρνῡμι** [ὑπ-, ὑπο- (11)]. 3 sing. redup. aor. ὑπώρορε. To stir the heart of: τοῖον ὑπώρορε [Ἀργείους] Μοῦσα ω 62.

†**ὑπορρήγνῡμι** [ὑπο- (1)]. 3 sing. aor. pass. ὑπερράγη. To rend or cleave from beneath something: ὑπερράγη αἰθήρ Θ 558 = Π 300 (*i.e.* (the cloud-bank in) the upper air is rent away from beneath the sources of light).

ὑπόρρηνος, -ον [ὑπο- (4) + *Ϝρήν. See ἄρνα]. With a lamb at suck: ὄϊν Κ 216.

ὑποσσείω [ὑπο- (4)]. To work or keep spinning by the application of force to the lower part of: [τρύπανον] ι 385.

ὑποστάς, aor. pple. ὑφίστημι.

ὑποσταχύομαι [ὑπο- (6) + στάχυς]. To yield increase: οὐδέ κεν ἄλλως ὑποσταχύοιτο βοῶν γένος υ 212.

ὑποστεναχίζω [ὑπο- (12)]. To give forth a heavy sound, rumble, on the occurrence of something: γαῖα ὑπεστενάχιζεν (thereupon, thereat) Β 781.

ὑποστήτω, 3 sing. aor. imp. ὑφίστημι.

†**ὑποστορέννῡμι** [ὑπο- (4)]. Aor. infin. ὑποστορέσαι. To spread (a bed) for the reception of a sleeper υ 139.

ὑποστρέφω [ὑπο- (10) (12)]. 3 pl. aor. subj. ὑποστρέψωσι Μ 71. 2 sing. opt. ὑποστρέψειας Γ 407. Pple. ὑποστρέψας Λ 446: θ 301. Fut. infin. mid. ὑποστρέψεσθαι σ 23. Aor. pple. pass. ὑποστρεφθείς Λ 567. (1) To wheel (one's horses) round in flight from the foe Ε 581.—(2) In mid. and pass. (a) To turn oneself about, turn round, so as to face the foe: αὖτις ὑποστρεφθείς Λ 567.—(b) To return, come back: ὑποστρέψεσθαι ἐς μέγαρον Ὀδυσῆος σ 23.—(3) *Intrans. for reflexive* (a) = (2) (a): εἴ χ' ὑποστρέψωσιν (turn upon us) Μ 71.—(b) To turn oneself in a specified direction: φύγαδ' αὖτις ὑποστρέψας Λ 446.—(c) To turn back, turn on one's steps: αὖτις ὑποστρέψας θ 301.—(d)=(2)(b): μηδ' ἔτ' ὑποστρέψειας Ὄλυμπον (to . . .) Γ 407.

ὑποσχέσθαι, aor. infin. ὑπίσχομαι.

ὑποσχεσίη, -ης, ἡ [as next]. =next N 369.

ὑπόσχεσις, ἡ [ὑποσχ-, ὑπίσχομαι]. A promise, undertaking, engagement B 286, 349 : κ 483.

ὑποσχόμενος, aor. pple. ὑπίσχομαι.

ὑποσχών, aor. pple. ὑπέχω.

ὑποταρβέω [ὑπο- (12)]. To feel fear or dread before the face of: τοὺς ὑποταρβήσαντες (struck with terror at their appearance) P 533.

ὑποταρτάριος [ὑπο- (4)+Τάρταρος]. That is below in Tartarus: θεούς Ξ 279.

†ὑποτίθημι [ὑπο- (11)]. Fut. mid. ὑποθήσομαι α 279, β 194, ε 143. 2 sing. ὑποθήσεαι δ 163. 3 ὑποθήσεται γ 27. 1 pl. ὑποθησόμεθα Θ 36, 467, Φ 293. Aor. imp. ὑπόθευ ο 310. Infin. ὑποθέσθαι Λ 788. In mid., to put into a person's mind, suggest, communicate (cf. τίθημι (5)): ἄλλα δαίμων ὑποθήσεται γ 27. Cf. Θ 36=467, Λ 788 : δ 163.—Absol., to make a suggestion, give advice or counsel: πυκινῶς τοι ὑποθησόμεθα Φ 293. Cf. α 279, β 194, ε 143, ο 310.

†ὑποτρέχω [ὑπο- (8)]. 3 sing. aor. ὑπέδραμε. To run in under the weapon of a foe: ὑπέδραμε καὶ λάβε γούνων Φ 68 : κ 323.

ὑποτρέω [ὑπο- (12)]. 2 sing. aor. ὑπέτρεσας P 587. 3 pl. ὑπέτρεσαν O 636, P 275. Infin. ὑποτρέσαι H 217. (1) To flee from the face of danger, take to flight, retreat, retire: νεκρὸν προλιπόντες ὑπέτρεσαν P 275. Cf. H 217, O 636.—(2) To flee before the face of: Μενέλαον P 587.

ὑποτρομέω [ὑπο- (12)]. 3 pl. pa. iterative ὑποτρομέεσκον Υ 28. (1) To tremble on account of something, be affected by fear, show fear: τοῖον ὑποτρομέουσιν X 241.—(2) To tremble before, be in fear of, dread: μιν Υ 28.

ὑπότροπος [ὑπο- (10) + τρέπω]. Returning, coming back: ὑπότροπον ἐκ πολέμοιο Z 501. Cf. Z 367 : υ 332, φ 211, χ 35.

ὑπουράνιος [ὑπ-, ὑπο- (4) + οὐρανός]. Under heaven: πετεηνῶν P 675.—As far as heaven covers: μέγα κέν οἱ ὑπουράνιον κλέος εἴη K 212 : τοῦ μέγιστον ὑπουράνιον κλέος ἐστίν ι 264 (in these two passages in sense qualifying the vb.).

†ὑποφαίνω [ὑπο- (1)]. 3 sing. aor. ὑπέφηνε. To move *from under* so as to bring to the light, cause to peep *from under*. With genit.: θρῆνυν ὑπέφηνε τραπέζης ρ 409.

†ὑποφέρω [ὑπο- (3)]. 3 pl. aor. ὑπήνεικαν. To bear away out of danger E 885.

ὑποφεύγω [ὑπο- (12)]. To flee before (a foe): οὐ τὸν δύναται ὑποφεύγειν X 200.

ὑποφήτης, ὁ [ὑπο- (12)+φημί]. One who gives an interpretative response in regard to or reveals the oracles of a god, a prophet Π 235.

†ὑποφθάνω [ὑπο- (12)]. Aor. pple. ὑποφθάς H 144. Aor. pple. mid. ὑποφθάμενος δ 547. Fem. ὑποφθαμένη ο 171. In act. and mid., to anticipate: τὸν ὑποφθαμένη φάτο μῦθον (getting in her word first) ο 171.—Absol., to be beforehand in doing something: ὑποφθὰς δουρὶ περόνησεν (getting in his blow first) H 144. Cf. δ 547.

ὑποχείριος [ὑπο- (4)+χείρ]. Under one's hand: χρυσόν, ὅτις χ' ὑποχείριος ἔλθῃ (as much as I can lay my hands upon) ο 448.

†ὑποχέω [ὑπο- (4)]. 3 sing. aor. ὑπέχευε. To spread or strew under a person: βοείας Λ 843 : ῥῶπας ξ 49.

ὑποχωρέω [ὑπο- (12)]. To retire or recoil in the face of danger: Ἀργεῖοι ὑπεχώρησαν Z 107. Cf. N 476, X 96.

ὑπόψιος [ὑπ-, ὑπο- (2) + ὀπ-. See ὁράω. "Looked at from below." Cf. πανόψιος]. An object of contempt or hatred: ὑπόψιον ἄλλων (to . . .) Γ 42.

ὕπτιος [ὑπό]. On the back, supine (opposed to πρηνής): ἄλλοθ' ὕπτιος, ἄλλοτε δὲ πρηνής Ω 11. Cf. Δ 108, 522, H 145, 271, Λ 144, 179, M 192, N 548, O 434, 647, Π 289, 863, P 523 : ι 371, σ 398.

ὑπώπια, τά [ὑπ-, ὑπο- (4)+ὦπα. Cf. ἐνώπια]. App., the face: νυκτὶ θοῇ ἀτάλαντος ὑπώπια (his face like . . .) M 463.

ὑπώρεια, ἡ [ὑπ-, ὑπο- (4) + ὄρος]. A region skirting or fringing a mountain Υ 218.

ὑπωρόφιος [ὑπ-, ὑπο- (4)+ὀροφή]. Under one's roof: ὑπωρόφιοί τοι εἰμεν I 640.

ὑπώρορε, 3 sing. redup. aor. ὑπόρνυμι.

ὗς. See σῦς.

ὑσμίνη, -ης, ἡ. Dat. ὑσμῖνι (fr. *ὑσμίς) B 863, Θ 56. (1) A fight or combat: ἐνὶ κρατερῇ ὑσμίνῃ Δ 462. Cf. B 40, E 84, Λ 72, N 314, Π 567, Υ 245, etc. : λ 417, 612.—(2) In concrete sense, a fighting force, a battle array: ὑσμίνην ἤρτυνον O 303, κεδασθείσης ὑσμίνης (the ranks) 328=Π 306. Cf. Λ 297, O 340, Υ 395.

ὑσμίνηνδε [acc. of prec. + -δε (1)]. To the fight: ἴέναι B 477.

ὑσμῖνι, dat. See ὑσμίνη.

ὑστάτιος, -η, -ον [ὕστατος]. (1)=ὕστατος (1) O 634.—(2) = ὕστατος (2) (b) ι 14.—(3) In neut. sing. ὑστάτιον as adv. = ὕστατος (3) (a): οὐκέτι Δαναῶν κεκαδησόμεθ' ὑστάτιόν περ (*i.e.* it is our last chance) Θ 353.

ὕστατος [superl. Cf. ὕστερος]. (1) In reference to position, the least advanced in an indicated direction, the last: οἱ πρῶτοί τε καὶ ὕστατοι B 281. Cf. N 459.—(2) (a) Being the last to do something, last: ὕστατος λάχ' ἐλαυνέμεν ἵππους Ψ 356 (*i.e.* his lot came out last, which would give him the outside place): ὕστατος μήλων ἔστειχεν ι 444. Cf. ι 448.—(b) Sim. in oblique case of that to which action is last directed, last: τίνα ὕστατον ἐξενάριξαν; E 703. Cf. Λ 299, Π 692.—(3) (a) In neut. sing. ὕστατον as adv., for the last time: τότε γ' ὕ. μ 250.—With πύματον in the same sense: πύματόν τε καὶ ὕ. X 203 : υ 116.—(b) So in neut. pl. ὕστατα: νῦν ὕστατ' ἂν λωβήσαιο A 232=B 242. Cf. υ 119, χ 78=134.—With πύματα in the same sense: ὕστατα καὶ πύματα δ 685, υ 13.

ὕστερος [comp. Cf. ὕστατος]. (1) After another, later, second, afterwards: ὕ. ὄρνυτο χαλκῷ E 17=Π 479, ὕστερος ἐλθών Σ 320. Cf. ω 155.—With genit., later than, after: σεῦ ὕστερος Σ 333.—(**2**) In neut. sing. ὕστερον as adv. (**a**) After another, later, afterwards: ἐμὲ προτὶ ἄστυ ὑ. ἄξει π 272.—(**b**) Later, afterwards, in the future, another time or day: ὑ. αὖτις ἰόντα A 27. Cf. H 30, 291, 377 = 396, Θ 142, K 450, Λ 365 = Υ 452, Ξ 313, Υ 127: ὑ. ἄλλον ἥσειν θ 202. Cf. ι 351.—Sim. ἐς ὕστερον: ἐς ὑ. ὁρμηθῆναι (a second time, again) μ 126.—(**3**) In neut. pl. ὕστερα as adv. in the sense (2)(b): ὑ. ταῦτα πένεσθαι π 319.—(**4**) Born later, younger: γένει ὕστερος Γ 215.

ὑφαίνω [cf. ὑφάω]. Pa. iterative ὑφαίνεσκον τ 149. 3 sing. ὑφαίνεσκε β 104, ω 139. Aor. subj. ὑφήνω ν 303. Imp. ὕφηνον ν 386. Pple. ὑφήνας δ 739. Fem. ὑφήνᾱσα ω 147. (**1**) To weave: ἱστόν Γ 125, Z 456, X 440: β 94 = ω 129, β 104 = ω 139, ε 62, ο 517, τ 139, 149, ω 147, φάρεα ν 108.—(**2**) Fig., to piece together in the mind, contrive, devise, develop: ὅτε μύθους καὶ μήδεα πᾶσιν ὕφαινον (developed them in the ears of the company) Γ 212, μῆτιν H 324 = I 93. Cf. Z 187: δ 678, 739, ε 356, ι 422, ν 303, 386.

ὑφαντός, -ή, -όν [ὑφαίνω]. Woven: ἐσθῆτα ν 136 = π 231, εἵματα ν 218.

ὕφασμα, -ατος, τό [ὑφαίνω]. Something woven: ὑφάσματά τε χρυσόν τε (woven work) γ 274.

†ὑφάω. 3 pl. pres. ὑφόωσι. To weave η 105.

ὑφέλκω [ὑφ-, ὑπο- (3)]. To draw out of the reach of the foe Ξ 477.

ὑφέντες, nom. pl. masc. aor. pple. ὑφίημι.

ὑφήνας, aor. pple. ὑφαίνω.

ὑφηνίοχος, -ου, ὁ [ὑφ-, ὑπο- (5) + ἡνίοχος. 'Acting as driver under the fighting man']. = ἡνίοχος Z 19.

†ὑφίημι [ὑφ-, ὑπο- (4) + ἵημι[1]]. Nom. pl. masc. aor. pple. ὑφέντες. To lower: ἱστόν A 434.

†ὑφίστημι [ὑφ-, ὑπο- (7)]. Aor. ὑπέστην Δ 267, O 75, Ψ 20, 180. 2 sing. ὑπέστης N 375: ι 365, κ 483. 3 ὑπέστη I 519, Λ 244, T 243, Φ 273. 1 pl. ὑπέστημεν E 715, T 195. 3 ὑπέσταν B 286. 3 sing. opt. ὑποσταίη I 445. 3 sing. imp. ὑποστήτω I 160. Pple. ὑποστάς Φ 457: γ 99, δ 329. (**1**) To come under an undertaking, give a promise, promise: ὡς τὸ πρῶτον ὑπέστην Δ 267. Cf. O 75: ι 365.—With cognate acc.: ὑπόσχεσιν ἥν περ ὑπέσταν B 286. Cf. E 715: κ 483.—With infin. of what one undertakes or promises to do: δῶρ', ὅσσ' ὑπέστημεν δώσειν T 195. Cf. I 445.—(**2**) To undertake to give, promise: τὰ δ' ὄπισθεν ὑπέστη I 519. Cf. Λ 244, T 243, Φ 457.—(**3**) To promise to perform, undertake: εἰ τελευτήσεις ὅσ' ὑπέστης N 375. Cf. Ψ 20 = 180: γ 99 = δ 329.—(**4**) To make up one's mind *to do something*, bring oneself *to do it* (cf. τλάω (7)(d)): ὡς οὔ τίς με θεῶν ὑπέστη σαῶσαι (could find it in his heart to . . .) Φ 273.—(**5**) To make admission, admit: ὑποστήτω μοι, ὅσσον βασιλεύτερός εἰμι I 160.

ὑφορβός. See συφορβός.

ὑφόωσι, 3 pl. pres. ὑφάω.

ὑψαγόρης [ὕψι + ἀγορή]. Voc. ὑψαγόρη β 85, 303, ρ 406. One who talks loudly and boldly: Τηλέμαχ' ὑψαγόρη β 85 = ρ 406, β 303. Cf. α 385.

ὑψερεφής, -ές [ὕψι + ἐρέφω. Cf. ὑψηρεφής]. High-roofed, lofty: δῶμα E 213, T 333: = η 225 = τ 526, δ 15, 46, η 85, ο 241. Cf. δ 757, κ 111 = ο 424, ν 5, ο 432.

ὑψηλός, -ή, -όν [ὕψι]. (**1**) Of great upward extent, high, lofty, tall: ἀκτῇ B 395, φηγῷ H 60. Cf. Γ 384, E 560, M 131, 282, 388, Π 429, Φ 171, Ψ 247, etc.: α 126, 330, ζ 58, θ 422, ι 183, π 285, φ 51, χ 176, etc.—(**2**) Having a lofty position, high: ἀφ' ὑψηλῆς κορυφῆς ὄρεος Π 297: μελάθρου λ 278. Cf. B 855.

ὑψηρεφής [ὕψι + ἐρέφω. Cf. ὑψερεφής, ὑψόροφος]. High-roofed, lofty: θαλάμοιο I 582.

ὑψηχής [ὕψι + (app.) ἠχ- as in ἠχή]. Thus, as epithet of horses, loud-neighing E 772, Ψ 27.

ὕψι [cf. ὑψοῦ]. (**1**) On high, aloft: ὕψι καθημένω π 264. Cf. O 387, Υ 155, Ψ 874.—(**2**) To a high or relatively high position, to a great height, high: ἀναθρῴσκων N 140. Cf. Π 374, P 723.—Stepping high: βιβάντα N 371.—(**3**) Afloat (cf. ὑψοῦ(3)): ὕψι ἐπ' εὐνάων ὁρμίσσομεν [νῆας] Ξ 77.

ὑψιβρεμέτης [ὕψι + βρέμω]. High-thundering. Epithet of Zeus A 354, M 68, Ξ 54, Π 121: ε 4, ψ 331.

ὑψίζυγος [ὕψι + ζυγόν. Cf. ζυγόν (2)]. Seated aloft. Epithet of Zeus Δ 166, H 69, Λ 544, Σ 185.

ὑψικάρηνος, -ον [ὕψι + κάρηνον]. Rearing the head aloft, lofty: δρύες M 132.

ὑψίκερως [ὕψι + κέρας]. High-horned: ὑψίκερων ἔλαφον κ 158.

ὑψίκομος, -ον [ὕψι + κόμη. Cf. κόμη (3)]. Lofty and leafy (the second element being equivalent to a separate epithet; cf. οἰόζωνος Soph. *O.T.* 846, 'alone and girt up,' 'journeying alone,' πυκνόπτερος *O.C.* 17, 'many and winged.' Cf. ὑψιπέτηλος): δρυσίν Ξ 398. Cf. Ψ 118: αὐλὴ δέδμητο δρυσὶν ὑψικόμοισιν ι 186 (the second element here obscured, the reference being only to the length of the pieces of timber), δρυός μ 357 (here referring especially to the wealth of foliage). Cf. ξ 328 = τ 297.

ὑψιπετήεις = ὑψιπέτης. Epithet of the eagle: αἰετός X 308: = ω 538.

ὑψιπέτηλος [ὕψι + πέταλον]. Lofty and leafy (cf. ὑψίκομος): δένδρεον N 437: δ 458. Cf. λ 588.

ὑψιπέτης [ὕψι + πέτομαι]. High-flying, soaring. Epithet of the eagle: αἰετός M 201 = 219, N 822: υ 243.

ὑψίπυλος, -ον [ὕψι + πύλη]. With lofty gates: Θήβην Z 416, Τροίην Π 698 = Φ 544.

ὑψόθεν [ὑψ- as in ὕψι + -θεν (1)(2)]. (**1**) From a high or relatively high position, from on high, from above: βρόντησεν ὑ. Υ 57. Cf. Λ 53, M 383: ὑ. ἐξ ὀροφῆς χ 298. Cf. β 147, ρ 210, υ 104.—(**2**) On high, aloft: ἐκρέμω ὑ. O 18.

ὑψόθι [ὑψ- as in ὕψι + -θι]. On high, high up, aloft: ὑ. ἐόντι K 16. Cf. P 676, T 376.

ὑψόροφος [ὕψι + ὀροφή. Cf. ὑψηρεφής]. High-roofed, lofty: θάλαμον Γ 423. Cf. Ω 192, 317: β 337, δ 121, ε 42 = 115, η 77.

ὑψόσε [ὑψ- as in ὕψι + -σε]. To a high or relatively high position, high, up, upwards: ἀπὸ χθονὸς ὑ. ἔεργεν Ξ 349, ὑ. αὐγὴ γίγνεται Σ 211. Cf. K 461, 465, 505, Λ 307, M 138, Υ 325, Φ 269, 302, 307, 324, X 34, Ψ 501: θ 375, ι 240=340, μ 238, 249, 432, ν 83, τ 38, χ 467.

ὑψοῦ [cf. ὕψι]. (1) On high, high up, aloft: ὑψοῦ κάρη ἔχει Z 509=O 266. Cf. N 12, 200, 201. —(2) To a high or relatively high position, high: νῆα ἔρυσσαν ὑψοῦ ἐπὶ ψαμάθοις (high and dry) A 486.—So that something may have a considerable height: ἴκρια πῆξαι ὑψοῦ (make it of a good height) ε 164.—(3) Afloat (cf. ὕψι (3)): ὑψοῦ νῆ' ὅρμισαν δ 785, θ 55.

ὕω. To rain: ὗε Ζεύς M 25: ξ 457.—In pass., to be rained upon: ὑόμενος καὶ ἀήμενος ζ 131.

φαάνθη, 3 sing. aor. pass. φαίνω.

φαάντατος [app. superl. fr. φαεννός=φαεινός]. Very bright: ἀστήρ ν 93.

φάγον, with augment **ἔφαγον,** *aor.* (1) To eat (food): λωτοῖο καρπόν ι 94. Cf. δ 33, ι 232.—With partitive genit.: λωτοῖο φαγών ι 102. Cf. ο 373.—Absol., to take food, eat: πόρε κρέας, ὄφρα φάγῃσιν θ 477. Cf. κ 386, ο 378, π 143, ρ 404, σ 3, ω 254.—(2) Of beasts, etc., to eat up, devour: οὔ πω τόν γε κύνες φάγον οὐδ' οἰωνοί Ω 411. Cf. B 317, 326.—Of the cannibal Cyclops ι 347.—Of Scylla μ 310.—Of fishes, to eat, nibble at, gnaw Φ 127: ξ 135, ω 291.—(3) To eat up, devour, consume: κατὰ ζωὴν φαγέειν π 429. Cf. β 76, γ 315=ο 12.

φαέθων [φαϝ- as in φάον]. Bright, resplendent. Epithet of ἠέλιος Λ 735: ε 479, λ 16, τ 441, χ 388.

φαεινός, -ή, -όν [φαϝ- as in φάον]. Having a bright surface, of bright hue, bright, shining, resplendent (most commonly a merely conventional epithet): κρητῆρα Γ 247, δουρί Δ 496, σελήνην Θ 555. Cf. Γ 357, 419, Z 219, Λ 645, N 3, etc.: Ἠοῦς δ 188, περόνην τ 256. Cf. ζ 19, κ 23, ξ 482, φ 54, ψ 201, etc.—In comp.: θώρηκα φαεινότερον πυρὸς αὐγῆς Σ 610.

φαείνω [φαϝ- as in φάον]. To give light, shine. Of the sun γ 2, μ 383, 385.—To illuminate a chamber, afford light. Of braziers: λαμπτῆρας ἵστασαν, ὄφρα φαείνοιεν σ 308.—Of a torch-bearer σ 343.

φαεσίμβροτος, -ον [φαϝεσ-, φαϝ- as in φάον + (μ)βροτός]. That brings or gives light to men. Epithet of ἠώς Ω 785.—Of ἠέλιος κ 138, 191.

φαιδιμόεις, -εντος [φαίδιμος]. =φαίδιμος (2): Ἐπειοί N 686.

φαίδιμος [φα-. Cf. φάον]. (1) Glistening, shining, bright. Epithet of parts of the body: γυῖα Z 27, Θ 452, K 95, N 435, Π 805, Ψ 63, 691: ὤμῳ λ 128 = ψ 275.—(2) Epithet of persons, illustrious, famous, renowned, or the like Δ 505, Z 144, I 434, P 288, Φ 97, etc.: β 386, γ 189, κ 251, ξ 164, π 395, ω 76, etc.

φαίην, opt. φημί.

φαίνω [φαν-, φα-. Cf. φάον]. 3 sing. pa. iterative φάνεσκε Λ 64: λ 587, μ 241, 242. 3 sing. aor. ἔφηνε B 318, 324: ο 168. 3 pl. subj. φήνωσι ο 26. 3 sing. opt. φήνειε μ 334. Infin. φῆναι γ 173. **Pass.** Instrumental (in 'comitative' use) fem. pres. pple. φαινομένηφι I 618, 682, Λ 685, Ω 600: δ 407, ζ 31, η 222, μ 24, ξ 266, ο 396, π 270, ρ 435. 3 sing. pa. iterative φαινέσκετο ν 194. Fut. infin. φανεῖσθαι μ 230. 3 sing. fut. πεφήσεται P 155. 2 sing. aor. φάνης π 181. 3 (ἐ)φάνη A 477, B 308, Z 175, H 104, O 275, Ω 785, etc.: β 1, ε 279, ζ 137, η 268, ψ 241, etc. 3 dual φανήτην H 7. 1 pl. φάνημεν ι 466. 3 ἔφανεν Θ 557, Π 299. φάνεν σ 68. 2 sing. subj. φανήῃς ν 402. 3 φανήῃ T 375, X 73, Ω 417: ε 394, ψ 233. φανῇ I 707. 3 sing. opt. φανείη Υ 64: ψ 60. Imp. φάνηθι Σ 198. 3 sing. φανήτω υ 101. Pple. φανείς, -έντος Γ 31: ι 230. Fem. φανεῖσα π 159. Infin. φανήμεναι I 240. φανῆναι π 410, σ 160, 165. 3 sing. aor. φαάνθη P 650. 3 pl. φάανθεν A 200. 3 sing. pf. πέφανται B 122, Π 207. Acc. sing. masc. pple. πεφασμένον Ξ 127. (ἀνα-, δια-, ἐκ-, περιφαίνομαι, προ-, ὑπο-.) (I) (1) In reference to material and immaterial objects, to cause to appear or be seen, bring to light or notice, display: [δράκοντα] B 318. Cf. B 324, 353, Δ 381, I 236: ἀρετὴν σήν θ 237. Cf. γ 173, ο 168, σ 67, 74, υ 114, φ 413.—To bring to action, display: ἀεικείας υ 309.—(2) To make known, declare, set forth: μῦθον πεφασμένον Ξ 127. Cf. Σ 295.—To point out, indicate: ὁδόν μ 334, παράκοιτιν (cause to find and win her) ο 26.—To bring into hearing: ἀοιδήν (struck up) θ 499.—(3) To bring into being: 'Ελένῃ θεοὶ γόνον οὐκέτ' ἔφαινον (afforded her no further hope of offspring) δ 12.—(4) To illuminate a chamber, afford light, give one light: φαίνοντες δαιτυμόνεσσιν η 102. Cf. τ 25.—(II) In pass. (1) Of persons or material or immaterial subjects, to appear, be seen, come into view or notice, show oneself or itself, be shown, displayed, manifested, brought about: οἴῳ φαινομένη A 198, δεινὼ οἱ ὄσσε φάανθεν (gleamed terrible) 200, τέλος οὔ πώ τι πέφανται (we can find no end to the business) B 122, φαινομένων τὸν ἄριστον (of those who come forward) K 236, ἐφαίνετο πᾶσα Ἴδη N 13. Cf. B 308, E 864, H 104 (would have come upon thee), Θ 556, Λ 734 (was put before them), P 155, Σ 198 (show thyself), T 375, X 324 (an opening showed), Ψ 375, etc.: οὐδέ ποτ' οὖροι φαίνοντο δ 361, ὅτ' ἐφαίνετο νόστος (when the chance of it came) 519, ἐφάνη ὄρεα ε 279, οὔ πω φαίνετ' ἐναντίη ζ 329, οὐκέτι φαίνετο πομπή (we had now no hope of it) κ 79. Cf. δ 695, ε 394, 410 (I can see no . . .), η 201, ι 192, κ 98, μ 230, ο 517, π 410, τ 39, (shine as if with . . .), 557, υ 101, φ 73 (awaits you), ω 448, etc.—So in pa. iterative act.: πᾶσα φάνεσκεν μ 241. Cf. Λ 64: λ 587, μ 242.—(2) Of the dawn, to break: ἦμος φάνη Ἠώς A 477, ἅμ' ἠοῖ φαινομένηφιν I 618. Cf. Z 175, I 240, 707, Ψ 109, etc.: β 1, δ 407, ψ 241, etc.—(3) To be seen or prove to be *so and so.* With complementary adj.: οὗ ἀρίστη φαίνετο βουλή H 325=I 94:= ω 52.—With complementary genit.: νίκη φαίνεται Μενελάου (is declared for him) Γ 457.—(4) To appear or seem to be *so and so,* look *so and so.* With complementary adj.: ἥδε οἱ ἀρίστη φαίνετο βουλή B 5 = K 17 = Ξ 161, μέγα σφισὶ φαίνετο ἔργον (loomed grim before them) M 416. Cf. Δ 278: σμερδαλέος αὐτῇσι φάνη ζ 137. Cf. ι 318 = 424 = λ 230, ν 194, 402, ξ 106, π 181, χ 149.—With adj. and infin.: ἥ τίς τοι ἀρίστη φαίνεται εἶναι ο 25.—Sim.: πῶς ὔμμιν ἀνὴρ ὅδε φαίνεται εἶναι; λ 336.—Impers.: οὔ σφιν ἐφαίνετο κέρδιον εἶναι ξ 355.

φαλαγγηδόν [φάλαγξ]. Keeping their ranks: προχέοντο O 360.

φάλαγξ, -αγγος, ἡ. A line or array of battle: Τρώων ῥῆξε φάλαγγα Z 6.—In pl., the lines or ranks B 558, Γ 77, Δ 254, E 93, Z 83, etc.

φάλαρα, τά. Prob., bosses or knobs set round a helmet: βάλλετο [πήληξ] κὰπ φάλαρα Π 106.

†φαληριάω. Nom. pl. neut. pres. pple. φαληριόωντα. App., to be flecked with white: κύματα φαληριόωντα (i.e. flecked with foam) N 799.

φάλος, -ου, ὁ. Something on a helmet carrying the plume (app., from the hardness attributed to it, of metal; see Γ 362-363, Π 338-339): ψαῦον ἱππόκομοι κόρυθες φάλοισιν N 132 = Π 216. Cf. Γ 362, Δ 459 = Z 9, N 614, Π 338.

φαμέν, 1 pl. pres. φημί.

φάμεν, 1 pl. impf. φημί.

φάμενος, pres. pple. mid. φημί.

φάν, 3 pl. impf. φημί.

φάνη, 3 sing. aor. pass. φαίνω.

φάντο, 3 pl. impf. mid. φημί.

φάο, pres. imp. mid. φημί.

φάον, *aor.* (φάϝον). Of the dawn, to break: φάεν Ἠώς ξ 502.

φάος, τό [φαϝ- as in φάον]. Acc. pl. φάεα π 15, ρ 39, τ 417. Also **φόως**. (1) The light of day, the light of the sun: Ἠὼς προσεβήσετ' Ὄλυμπον φόως ἐρέουσα B 49, Ἠέλιος, οὗ τε καὶ ὀξύτατον πέλεται φάος εἰσοράασθαι (the emission of the sun's light being thought of as an exercise of the power of sight) Ξ 345. Cf. Λ 2 = T 2, O 669, P 647, Ψ 226: ε 2, λ 93, ν 94, φ 429, ψ 245, 348, 371.—In reference to life: λείψειν φάος ἠελίοιο Σ 11. Cf. E 120, Σ 61 = 442, Ω 558: δ 540 = κ 498, δ 833, ξ 44 = υ 207.—(2) φάος ἠελίοιο = ἠέλιος: ἐπεὶ κατέδυ φάος ἠελίοιο A 605. Cf. Θ 485, Ψ 154: = π 220 = φ 226, ν 33, 35.—So without ἠελίοιο: ἔδυ φάος Θ 487. Cf. γ 335.—(3) Of artificial light: τούτοισι φάος παρέξω σ 317. Cf. τ 34, 64.—A source of such light: τίς τοι φάος οἴσει; (a light) τ 24.—(4) Applied to a person: ἦλθες, Τηλέμαχε, γλυκερὸν φάος (sweet light of my eyes) π 23 = ρ 41.—(5) Help, succour, safety, salvation: φόως ἑτάροισιν ἔθηκεν (opened a way for them) Z 6, αἴ κέν τι φόως Δαναοῖσι γένηαι πατρί τε σῷ Θ 282 (with a zeugma, bring help to your friends and glory to your father), αἴ κέν τι φόως Δαναοῖσι γένηαι Λ 797. Cf. O 741, Π 39, 95 (*i.e.* have cleared the ships of the foe), P 615, Σ 102, Υ 95 (*i.e.* led him on), Φ 538.—(6) In pl., the eyes: κύσσε μιν ἄμφω φάεα π 15 = ρ 39, τ 417.

φαρέτρη, -ης, ἡ. A quiver for arrows A 45, Δ 116, Θ 323, K 260, O 443: ζ 270, ι 314, φ 11, 59, 233, 417, χ 2, 71.

φάρμακον, -ου, τό. (1) A medicinal preparation, a remedial, soothing or sedative drug or application: ἐφ' ἕλκεϊ φάρμακ' ἔπασσεν O 394. Cf. Δ 191, 218, E 401, 900, Λ 515, 830: ἐς οἶνον βάλε φ. δ 220. Cf. δ 227.—Referring specially to potent herbs and remedial preparations made therefrom: ἣ τόσα φάρμακα ᾔδη ὅσα τρέφει εὐρεῖα χθών Λ 741. Cf. δ 230.—(2) An evil drug or application, a poison, poison: φ. ἀνδροφόνον διζήμενος α 261. Cf. β 329.—A herb producing evil effects: δράκων βεβρωκὼς κακὰ φάρμακα X 94.—(3) A magic or enchanted drug: κατέθελξεν, ἐπεὶ κακὰ φάρμακ' ἔδωκεν κ 213. Cf. κ 236, 290, 317, 326, 327, 394.—An application undoing the effects of magic or enchantment: προσάλειφεν ἑκάστῳ φ. ἄλλο κ 392.—A herb protecting from magic or enchantment: οὐκ ἐάσει φ. ἐσθλόν κ 292. Cf. κ 287, 302.

φαρμάσσω [φάρμακον]. To temper or harden (metal): πέλεκυν φαρμάσσων ι 393.

φᾶρος, τό. (1) A mantle or cloak (always ascribed to persons of distinction) (cf. χλαῖνα) B 43, Θ 221, Σ 353, Ω 231, 580, 588: γ 467, ε 230, ζ 214, θ 84, 392, ο 61, etc.—(2) A web: εἰς ὅ κε φ. ἐκτελέσω β 97 = τ 142 = ω 132. Cf. ν 108, τ 138, ω 147.—(3) A piece of cloth: φάρε' ἕνεικεν, ἱστία ποιήσασθαι ε 258.

φάρυξ, -υγος (cf. ἀσφάραγος, λαυκανίη). The throat: φάρυγος λάβεν (by the . . .) τ 480.—More specifically, the gullet: φάρυγος ἐξέσσυτο οἶνος ι 373.

φάς, pres. pple. φημί.

φάσαν, 3 pl. impf. φημί.

φάσγανον, -ου, τό. A sword A 190, E 81, K 256, Ξ 405, O 713, etc.: κ 145, λ 82, π 295, χ 74, etc.

φάσθαι, pres. infin. mid. φημί.

φᾶσί, 3 pl. pres. φημί.

φάσκω [φα-, φημί]. (1) To say, assert, declare. With infin.: περί σε βροτῶν πεπνυμένον εἶναι φάσκεν δ 191. Cf. θ 565, κ 331, λ 306, μ 275, ν 173, ξ 321, τ 191, ω 75, 269.—With neg., to deny that one has . . ., say that one has not . . .: Ὀδυσσῆος οὔ ποτ' ἔφασκεν ἀκοῦσαι ρ 114.—(2) To say, promise, undertake. With infin.: ἔφασκές μ' Ἀχιλλῆος ἄλοχον θήσειν T 297. Cf. ε 135, η 256, ψ 335.—(3) To think, deem, expect. With infin.: οὔ μ' ἔτ' ἐφάσκετ' οἴκαδ' ἱκέσθαι χ 35. Cf. N 100.

φασσοφόνος [φάσσα, dove + φον-, φένω]. Dove-killing: ἴρηκι O 238.

φάτις, ἡ [φα-, φημί]. Talk, report, rumour: ἐκ τούτων φ. ἀνθρώπους ἀναβαίνει ἐσθλή ζ 29, αἰσχυνόμενοι φάτιν ἀνδρῶν (scandal) φ 323. Cf. ψ 362.—In reference to public opinion: δήμου φάτιν I 460.

φάτνη, -ης, ἡ. A crib or manger: ἀτίταλλ' ἐπὶ φάτνῃ E 271, Ω 280. Cf. Z 506 = O 263, K 568: δ 535 = λ 411.

φάτο, 3 sing. impf. mid. φημί.

φέβομαι [φεβ-, φόβος]. (1) To flee, to be in flight, take to flight: Τρῶας μένον οὐδὲ φέβοντο E 527 = O 622. Cf. E 223 = Θ 107, Θ 342 = Λ 178, Λ 121, 404, M 136, O 345: χ 299.—(2) To flee from, escape from: Τυδέος υἱόν E 232.

φείδομαι. 3 sing. fut. πεφιδήσεται Ο 215, Ω 158, 187. 3 sing. aor. φείσατο Ω 236. Aor. opt. πεφιδοίμην ι 277. 3 sing. πεφίδοιτο Υ 464. Infin. πεφιδέσθαι Φ 101. With genit. **(1)** To abstain from harming, keep one's hands off, have mercy upon, spare: ἱκέτεω Ω 158 = 187. Cf. Ο 215, Υ 464, Φ 101: ι 277, π 185, χ 54.—**(2)** To save from injury or inconvenience, be solicitous for, spare: ἵππων Ε 202.—**(3)** Not to have the heart to part with, to withhold, keep back, spare: δέπαος Ω 236.

φειδώ, ἡ [φείδομαι]. **(1)** Abstinence from wasting or consuming something, sparing: κτήματα δαρδάπτουσιν, οὐδ' ἔπι φ. ξ 92. Cf. π 315.—**(2)** Withholding or grudging something: οὔ τις φ. νεκύων (as touching . . .) Η 409.

φειδωλή, ἡ [φείδομαι]. Abstinence from, or half-heartedness in, the use of something, sparing: δούρων Χ 244.

φείσατο, 3 sing. aor. φείδομαι.

†***φένω.** Aor. ἔπεφνον Φ 55. πέφνον λ 500. 2 sing. ἔπεφνες Ρ 35, 204, Ω 756: χ 229. 3 ἔπεφνε (πέφνε) Δ 397, Ζ 12, Η 142, Ν 363, Ο 329, Ρ 80, Φ 96, Ψ 776, etc.: δ 91, λ 453, 516, 518, φ 29, 36, χ 268, 359, ψ 84. 1 pl. ἐπέφνομεν Κ 478, Π 547, Χ 393. 2 ἐπέφνετε Φ 135. 2 sing. subj. πέφνῃς χ 346. 3 πέφνῃ Υ 172: λ 135, ψ 282. Acc. sing. masc. pple. πεφνόντα Π 827. Infin. πεφνέμεν Ζ 180. From φα- 2 sing. fut. pass. πεφήσεαι Ν 829: χ 217. 3 πεφήσεται Ο 140. 3 sing. pf. πέφαται Ο 140, Ρ 164, 689, Τ 27: χ 54. 3 pl. πέφανται Ε 531, Ο 563. Infin. πεφάσθαι Ν 447, Ξ 471, Ω 254. (κατα-.) To kill, slay: Πήδαιον ἔπεφνεν Ε 69. Cf. Δ 397, Ε 531, Ζ 12, Ν 447, Ο 140, etc.: ἐν μοίρῃ πέφαται χ 54. Cf. δ 91, λ 135, φ 29, χ 217, 268, ψ 84, etc.

φέριστος [superl. Cf. φέρτερος, φέρτατος]. The most distinguished, the noblest: ἄνδρα Ι 110.—In voc. as a form of address, my good friend, my friend, good sir: τίς σύ ἐσσι, φέριστε; Ζ 123, Ω 387. Cf. α 405, ι 269.—Addressed to a god: τίς σύ ἐσσι, φέριστε, θεῶν; (my gracious visitant) Ο 247.—To horses: τίῃ λείπεσθε, φέριστοι; (my noble steeds) Ψ 409.

φέρτατος [superl. Cf. φέριστος, φέρτερος]. **(1)** Of the greatest physical might, the strongest or most powerful: εἴ κ' ἐθέλῃσι στυφελίξαι· ὁ γὰρ πολὺ φ. ἐστιν Α 581. Cf. μ 246.—Very warlike, exceeding soldierly: υἱόν Ο 526.—**(2)** The best, the best fitted to take the lead in war or peace, pre-eminent: μέγα φέρτατ' Ἀχαιῶν Π 21 = Τ 216: = λ 478. Cf. Β 769.—**(3)** The most skilled: ἔγχει (with the . . ., in the use of the . . .) Η 289. Cf. θ 129.—**(4)** The best, the most tolerable (of evils): κακῶν κε φέρτατον εἴη Ρ 105.

φέρτε, imp. pl. φέρω.

φέρτερος, -η, -ον [comp. Cf. φέριστος, φέρτατος]. **(1)** Of greater physical might, stronger or more powerful: Μενελάου σῇ τε βίῃ καὶ χερσὶ καὶ ἔγχεϊ φ. εἶναι (in . . ., with . . .) Γ 431. Cf. Η 105, Ο 165, 181, Π 722, 780 (had the upper hand), Ρ 168, Τ 217, Υ 135, 368, Φ 264, 488, Χ 40, Ψ 461 (had the lead): ζ 6, ι 276, π 89, σ 234, φ 371, 373.—More warlike or soldierly Β 201.—**(2)** More powerful, of greater resources, more able to work one's will, in greater place: ἐκ δήμου ἔλασσεν, ἐπεὶ φ. ἦεν Ζ 158. Cf. Α 186, 281, Δ 56, Θ 144, 211, Κ 557: ε 170, χ 289.—**(3)** In neut. in impers. construction, better, preferable: φέρτερόν ἐστιν οἴκαδ' ἴμεν Α 169. Cf. Δ 307: μ 109, φ 154.

φέρτρον, -ου, τό [φέρω]. A bier Σ 236.

φέρω. Imp. pl. φέρτε Ι 171. 3 sing. pa. iterative φέρεσκε ι 429. 3 pl. φέρεσκον κ 108. From οἰ- Fut. οἴσω Η 82: ο 448, χ 101. 3 sing. οἴσει Β 229, Φ 125: τ 24. 3 dual οἴσετον Ε 232. 1 pl. οἴσομεν Γ 104. 3 οἴσουσι Ν 820, Ξ 308, Τ 144: γ 204. Pple. οἴσων θ 257, χ 162. Infin. οἰσέμεν Σ 191. From ἐνεκ- 3 sing. aor. ἤνεικε σ 300, χ 493. ἔνεικε Ο 705, Ψ 564: δ 436, ε 246, 258, ι 285, ξ 74, σ 292, 295, 301, φ 183. 1 pl. ἐνείκαμεν ω 43. 3 ἔνεικαν Ι 306, Ν 213, 453: δ 784, θ 428, ν 12, σ 297. Subj. ἐνείκω Ζ 258: χ 139, 487. 3 sing. ἐνείκῃ β 329. 3 sing. opt. ἐνείκαι Σ 147: φ 196. Imp. pl. ἐνείκατε θ 393. Pple. ἐνείκας Ρ 39. Infin. ἐνεῖκαι Σ 334: σ 286. Aor. imp. ἔνεικε φ 178. Infin. ἐνεικέμεν (v.l. ἐνεγκέμεν) Τ 194. From οἰ- Aor. imp. οἶσε χ 106, 481. 3 sing. οἰσέτω Τ 173: θ 255. 2 pl. οἴσετε Γ 103, Ο 718: υ 154. Infin. οἰσέμεν γ 429. οἰσέμεναι Γ 120, Ψ 564: θ 399, μ 10, σ 291. **Mid.** 2 sing. fut. οἴσῃ Ψ 441. 3 οἴσεται Ψ 663, 667, 858. Pple. οἰσόμενος Ν 168, 248, 257. Fem. οἰσομένη τ 504. Infin. οἴσεσθαι Χ 217. From ἐνεκ- 3 pl. aor. ἠνείκαντο Ι 127. (ἀνα-, ἀντι-, ἀπο-, ἐκ-, ἐπι-, ἐσ-, κατα-, προ-, συμ-, ὑπεκ-, ὑπο-.) **(1)** To overcome the weight of, lift and sustain: χερμάδιον, ὃ οὐ δύο γ' ἄνδρε φέροιεν Ε 303, Υ 286.—**(2)** **(a)** To carry, bear, convey, take (in reference to material and immaterial things): ἀνὰ ἄστυ ὅρκια Γ 245, μῦθον Κ 288, τὸν ἑταῖροι ἔνεικαν (i.e. from the fight) Ν 213. Cf. Ζ 69, Η 78, Π 671, Υ 108 (bear your point right onwards), Ω 119, etc.: οἴσουσι κλέος εὐρύ (will spread it far and wide) γ 204, χαλκόν ν 19. Cf. α 428, ι 429, ο 161, τ 24, ω 43, etc.—In mid.: δόμεναι οἰκόνδε φέρεσθαι (to take home with me) α 317, δώσει δέ τι ἔν γε φέρεσθαι (to take with you) ο 83, δόμεναι τάδε τόξα φέρεσθαι (i.e. to be his own) φ 349. Cf. Λ 798, Χ 245, Ψ 275: ο 378.—**(b)** Of the limbs, etc.: ῥίμφα ἑ γοῦνα φέρει Ζ 511 = Ο 268. Cf. Ζ 514, Ν 515, Ο 405, Ρ 700, Σ 148, Ω 341: = α 97 = ε 45, ο 555.—**(c)** Of fate Ι 411.—**(3)** Of horses or mules, to draw (a chariot or waggon or a person or something therein): ἵπποι ῥίμφ' ἔφερον ἅρμα Λ 533, ἵπποι οἵ μ' οἴσουσιν Ξ 308. Cf. Β 838, Ε 232, Ν 31, etc.: [ἡμίονοι] φέρον ἐσθῆτα καὶ αὐτήν ζ 83. Cf. η 2.—**(4)** In reference to gestation, to carry, bear: ὅν τινα γαστέρι μήτηρ φέροι Ζ 59.—**(5)** Of inanimate objects, to carry, bear, bear along: κνίσην ἄνεμοι φέρον οὐρανὸν εἴσω Θ 549. Cf. Λ 156, Μ 254, etc.: ὥς σε φέρῃσι [σχεδίη] ε 164. Cf. γ 300, δ 516, ε 111, η 277, κ 26, ν 89, etc.—**(6)** In pres. pple. with a finite vb., to take and . . . (cf. (10) and ἄγω (I) (9)): δὸς ταῦτα φέρων ρ 345. Cf. α 127 = ρ 29, χ 146, etc.—**(7)** In pass., to be carried or borne along: πᾶν ἦμαρ φερόμην (fell) A 592. Cf. Υ 172, Φ 120 (to drift with the current), Ψ 151 (to go its way): ἐπὶ σχεδίης φέρεσθαι η 274. Cf. ε 331, η 253 (drifted), ι 70, μ 425, 442 (*i.e.* committed myself to chance), τ 468 (let it slip from her hands), etc.—To be borne forward, advance: ὅς τις ἐπὶ νηυσὶ φέροιτο Ο 743.—(**8**) To bring or fetch (in reference to material and immaterial things): ἄποινα A 13, οἶνον Z 258, εἰ μὴ δῶρα φέροι (were not offering them) I 515, φόως Λ 2, τεύχεα Σ 137. Cf. Γ 103, I 171, Ο 175, Σ 191, 555, etc.: α 408, β 329, γ 429, 441, δ 436, ε 246, ζ 74, ι 349, μ 10, etc.—In mid.: οἰσόμενος δόρυ Ν 168, 248. Cf. Z 177, Ν 257, X 217 (see under κῦδος (2)): β 410, τ 504.—(**9**) Of inanimate objects: οὓς ἐνθάδε νῆες ἔνεικαν I 306. Cf. Ν 453, etc.—(**10**) In pres. pple. as under (6), to bring and . . . : δίφρον κατέθηκε φέρουσα Γ 425. Cf. I 331, Μ 222, etc.: α 136, 139, δ 133, ι 361, etc.—(**11**) To win, get, gain, carry off: ἤ κε φέρῃσι μέγα κράτος Σ 308.—In mid.: τοῦ κε παρὰ δῶρα φέροιο Δ 97, αἴ κε φερώμεθα χεῖρον ἄεθλον Ψ 413. Cf. I 127, Ν 486, Σ 308, Ψ 441, etc.: δαῖτα φέροντο κ 124.—(**12**) To bear with one or it the potency of (something), to bring, bring about, bring to bear, present, work, do: μητρὶ ἐπὶ ἦρα φέρων A 572, κακὰ Πριάμῳ φέρουσαι Β 304, δεῖμα φέρων Δαναοῖσιν Ε 682. Cf. A 578, Γ 6, Ε 211, Θ 516, 541, Μ 332, X 31, etc.: γ 74, 164, δ 273, ζ 203, μ 231, ρ 289, σ 56, τ 565, etc.—(**13**) To bear as increase, produce: τῇ πλεῖστα φέρει ἄρουρα φάρμακα δ 229, φέροι κεν ὥρια πάντα ι 131. Cf. ι 357, τ 111.—Sim.: ἄμπελοι, αἵ τε φέρουσιν οἶνον ἐριστάφυλον ι 110.—(**14**) To carry off, bear or snatch away: τῶν οὐκ ἄν τι φέροις A 301, ὑπὲκ θανάτοιο φέρονται (are snatched from the jaws of death) Ο 628. Cf. Β 302, Ε 484 (see under ἄγω (I) (4)), Ρ 70: θ 409, μ 99, ξ 207, ο 19.—In mid.: ἤ κεν ἔναρα φέρωμαι Θ 534.—(**15**) To bear, endure: λυγρά σ 135.

φεύγω. 3 sing. pa. iterative φεύγεσκε Ρ 461. φύγεσκε ρ 316. Fut. in mid. form φεύξομαι Σ 307. 2 pl. φεύξεσθε Β 175. 3 φεύξονται Β 159. Infin. φεύξεσθαι Λ 590, Ν 89, Ο 700, Φ 93: χ 67. Aor. φύγον ζ 170. 2 sing. ἔφυγες Λ 362, Υ 449. 3 φύγε Δ 350, Ξ 83, Σ 117, Υ 350, Φ 493, 496: α 64, γ 230, ε 22, κ 131, μ 66, σ 155, τ 492, φ 168, ψ 70. 1 pl. φύγομεν ι 61, 467, μ 260. 3 φύγον Γ 4, Θ 137, Λ 128, Ψ 465: α 11, γ 192. 3 sing. subj. φύγῃ Σ 271, Φ 103, X 487: ξ 184. φύγῃσι Ε 258, Η 118, 173, Τ 72, Φ 296. 1 pl. φύγωμεν Ρ 714. Opt. φύγοιμι ξ 312. 3 sing. φύγοι Z 59, Ξ 507, Π 98, 283: δ 789, ο 300, χ 43. 1 pl. φύγοιμεν A 60: γ 175, ι 489, κ 129, μ 157. Pple. φυγών, -όντος Μ 322, Φ 57: ι 17, ο 277, π 21, ρ 47, ψ 238. Infin. φυγέειν Β 393, Ν 436, Ξ 80: δ 504, μ 120. φυγεῖν Β 401, Μ 327. 3 sing. pf. opt. πεφεύγοι Φ 609. Nom. pl. masc. pple. πεφευγότες α 12. Nom. pl. masc. pple. πεφυζότες (app. formed direct fr. φύζα. Cf. ἀρημένος, δεδουπότος, κεκοπώς) Φ 6, 528, 532, X 1. Pf. pple. mid. πεφυγμένος α 18. Acc. πεφυγμένον Z 488, X 219: ι 455. (ἐκ-, παρα-, παρεκπρο-, προ-, ὑπεκ-, ὑπεκπρο-, ὑπο-.) (**1**) To flee. (**a**) To flee under the influence of fear, be in flight: πρόσθεν ἔθεν φεύγοντα Ε 56, πῇ φεύγεις; Θ 94, προχέοντο πεφυζότες (in rout) Φ 6. Cf. Ε 532, Z 82, Λ 150, Μ 123, Ν 436, Ο 63, Σ 150, X 1, 157, etc.: ζ 199, μ 120, π 424 (seeking refuge from the angry people), σ 386, χ 66, ω 54.—(**b**) To quit the seat of war and flee homewards: φεύγειν σὺν νηυσίν Β 74. Cf. A 173, Β 140 = I 27, Β 159, 175, Θ 511, I 47, Κ 147 = 327. —(**c**) To leave a place and hastily take an indicated course: ξὺν τοίσδεσι φεύγωμεν (let us be off) κ 269. Cf. γ 166, 167, ι 43.—(**d**) To slip away, make off: εἴ κεν Ἄρης οἴχηται φεύγων θ 356. —(**2**) To flee from, seek to escape from, seek safety from: νείκεα πατρός I 448. Cf. Ξ 80, Σ 307: Νηλέα ο 228, θάνατον καὶ κῆρα 276. Cf. ε 446.—(**3**) To escape, evade, avoid (impending danger or trouble): θάνατον A 60, χειμῶνα Γ 4, φυγὼν ὕπο νηλεὲς ἦμαρ Φ 57. Cf. Β 393, Μ 327, Ξ 507, Φ 93, X 487, etc.: α 11, γ 175, ι 61, κ 131, ξ 312, ψ 238, etc.—In mid.: μοῖραν πεφυγμένον ἔμμεναι Z 488. Cf. X 219: ι 455.—(**4**) To get away from, effect one's escape from (danger or trouble in which one is involved): Ἕκτορα Λ 327, πόλεμον τόνδε Μ 322: πόλεμόν τε πεφευγότες ἠδὲ θάλασσαν α 12. Cf. δ 504, ζ 170.—With genit. In mid.: οὐδ' ἔνθα πεφυγμένος ἦεν ἀέθλων α 18.—(**5**) Absol., to effect one's escape, escape, save oneself, come safe away: εἰ ἕτερός γε φύγῃσιν Ε 258. Cf. Z 59, Λ 590, Ρ 461, Υ 350, Φ 609, etc.: οἳ φύγον ἐκ πολέμου γ 192. Cf. μ 66, ξ 184, ρ 316, etc.—(**6**) To flee or quit one's country, go into exile: φεύγων ἐξ Ἄργεος ἄνδρα κατακτάς ο 224. Cf. Β 665, I 478: ν 259, ο 277, υ 223, ψ 120.—To flee (one's country): πατρίδα φεύγων ο 228.—(**7**) Of immaterial or inanimate things (**a**) To make way beyond, pass: ποῖόν σε ἔπος φύγεν ἕρκος ὀδόντων; Δ 350 = Ξ 83: α 64 = ε 22 = τ 492 = ψ 70, γ 230, φ 168.—(**b**) To fly or slip from the grasp of: Νέστορα δ' ἐκ χειρῶν φύγον ἡνία Θ 137. Cf. Λ 128, Ψ 465.

φῆ. Like: φῆ κύματα θαλάσσης Β 144, φῆ κώδειαν ἀνασχὼν Ξ 499.

φῆ, 3 sing. impf. φημί.

φήγινος [φηγός]. Of oak, oaken: ἄξων Ε 838.

φηγός, -οῦ, ἡ. The oak: φηγόν τε μελίην τε Π 767.—Sacred to Zeus: εἷσαν ὑπὸ Διὸς φηγῷ Ε 693. Cf. Η 60.—An oak near the Scaean gate forming a landmark: Σκαιάς τε πύλας καὶ φηγόν Z 237. Cf. Η 22, I 354, Λ 170.—This seems to be referred to also in Φ 549.

φήμη, -ης, ἡ [φημί]. Something said which bears a significance of which the speaker is unconscious, a speech that serves as an omen (= κληηδών (2)): φήμην τίς μοι φάσθω υ 100. Cf. β 35, υ 105.

†**φημί.** (Enclitic in pres. indic. act. except 2 sing.) 1 sing. pres. φημὶ Β 129, Ε 652, Z 98, etc.: β 171, δ 141, ε 290, etc. 2 φῄς Δ 351, Ξ 265, Ρ 174: α 391, η 239. φῆσθα ξ 149. 3 φησί A 521, Ξ 366, Ο 107, etc.: α 215, ε 105, ρ 352, etc. 1 pl. φαμέν Ο 735. 2 φατέ π 93, ρ 196. 3 φασί Β 783,

Δ 375, E 635, etc. : α 33, γ 84, δ 201, etc. 3 sing. subj. *φήῃ* λ 128, ψ 275. *φῇσι* α 168. *φῇ* τ 122. Opt. *φαίην* Z 285 : υ 326. 2 sing. *φαίης* Γ 220, 392, Δ 429, O 697, P 366 : γ 124. 3 *φαίη* σ 218, ψ 135. 1 pl. *φαῖμεν* B 81, Ω 222. Pple. *φάς* I 35. Nom. pl. masc. *φάντες* Γ 44, Ξ 126. Impf. *ἔφην* Π 61, Υ 348 : δ 171, λ 430, 540, ξ 176. *φῆν* Σ 326 : β 174. 2 sing. *ἔφης* X 280, 331. *φῆς* E 473 : ξ 117. *ἔφησθα* A 397, Π 830 : γ 357, ψ 71. *φῆσθα* Φ 186. 3 *ἔφη* A 584, B 265, E 111, etc. : β 377, μ 390, ρ 409, etc. *φῆ* B 37, Φ 361, Ω 608 : δ 504, θ 567, λ 237, etc. 1 pl. *ἔφαμεν* ω 24. *φάμεν* Θ 229, Ψ 440 : δ 664, ι 496, π 347. 2 *φάτε* ρ 25. 3 *ἔφασαν* O 700 : κ 35, 46, υ 384. *φάσαν* B 278, Δ 374 : ι 500, κ 67, μ 192, φ 366, χ 31. *ἔφαν* Γ 161, 302, H 206, etc. : ι 413, κ 422, ρ 488, etc. *φάν* Z 108 : β 337, η 343, σ 342. 3 sing. fut. *φήσει* Θ 148, 153. **Mid.** 2 pl. pres. *φάσθε* ζ 200, κ 562. Imp. *φάο* π 168, σ 171. 3 sing. *φάσθω* υ 100. Pple. *φάμενος* E 290. Pl. *φάμενοι* κ 446. Fem. *φαμένη* E 835, X 247, 460 : λ 150, ν 429, σ 206, ψ 85. Infin. *φάσθαι* A 187, I 100, Λ 788, etc. : θ 549, ι 504, λ 443, etc. Impf. *ἐφάμην* Γ 366, E 190, Θ 498, etc. : δ 382, ι 272, κ 70, etc. 3 sing. *ἔφατο* A 33, B 807, Δ 326, etc. : α 42, β 267, ε 301, etc. *φάτο* A 188, B 182, Γ 28, etc. : α 420, β 296, δ 37, etc. 3 pl. *ἔφαντο* Z 510, M 106, 125, P 379 : α 194, δ 638, ν 211. *φάντο* ω 460. (*ἀπο-*, *ἐκ-*, *μετα-*, *παρα-*, *προσ-*.) In act. and mid. **(1)** To utter speech, speak, say: *ὣς ἔφη* A 584, *ὣς φάμενος* E 290. Cf. A 188, B 278, Γ 161, Φ 361, etc. : α 42, β 35, 377, δ 382, κ 46, etc. —**(2)** To utter, speak, say, tell : *ἔπος ἔφατο* A 361. Cf. I 100, Σ 17, Φ 393, etc. : *μῦθόν κε φαίην* υ 326. Cf. β 384, γ 357, π 168, etc.—**(3)** To speak out, make disclosure θ 549, φ 194.—To say, communicate, reveal, disclose : *τὸ μὲν φάσθαι, τὸ δὲ καὶ κεκρυμμένον εἶναι* λ 443.—**(4)** To say, state, assert, declare : *ὡς φάσαν οἵ μιν ἴδοντο πονεύμενον* Δ 374.—With infin. : *Κρονίωνι λοιγὸν ἀμῦναι* A 397, *ἄτερ λαῶν πόλιν ἑξέμεν* E 473. Cf. B 129, Δ 351, Z 206, Θ 229, P 174, etc. : α 33, β 171, δ 504, η 239, θ 567, ι 504, λ 540, etc.—With omission of the infin. : *εἴ σε κακὸν φήσει* Θ 153.—**(5)** In 3 pl. pres. with indefinite subject understood, they say, men say, it is said. With infin. : *περὶ ἄλλων φασὶ γενέσθαι* Δ 375, *ζώειν ἔτι φασὶ Μενοίτιον* Π 14. Cf. B 783, E 635, Z 100, I 401, etc. : α 189, γ 188, δ 387, ζ 42, ν 249, etc.—Sim. in 3 pl. impf. mid. : *ἔφαντό μιν ἐπιδήμιον εἶναι* α 194.—**(6)** With neg., to declare that . . . not . . . (cf. *φάσκω* (1)) : *ἡμίονον δ' οὔ φημί τιν' ἀξέμεν ἄλλον* Ψ 668. Cf. Ψ 579, etc. : θ 138, etc.—To refuse : *οὔ φησιν δώσειν* H 393.—**(7)** To deem, suppose, think. With infin. : *αἱρήσειν πόλιν* B 37, *ἀθανάτων τίν' κατελθέμεν* Z 108, *Δηΐφοβον παρεῖναι* X 298. Cf. Γ 44, 366, Δ 429, E 190, Θ 498, etc. : α 391, δ 171, ζ 200, ι 496, λ 430, ν 357, etc.—With omission of the infin. : *ψευδός κεν φαῖμεν* B 81 = Ω 222. Cf. E 184, Ξ 126. —Without construction : *ἦ τοι ἔφης γε* X 280.—**(8)** To have such and such an opinion of oneself, think so and so of oneself, be minded so and so : *ἶσον ἐμοὶ φάσθαι* A 187, O 167. Cf. Ξ 366, O 183.

φῆμις, *ἡ* [*φημί*]. **(1)** What is said, speech, talk : *ἤ τινα φῆμιν ἐνὶ Τρώεσσι πύθοιτο* K 207 : *χαλεπὴ ἔχε δημοῦ φ.* ξ 239. Cf. ζ 273, π 75 = τ 527.—**(2)** Fame, reputation ω 201.—**(3)** The place of talking (= *ἀγορή* (3)) : *ἐς θῶκον πρόμολον δήμοιό τε φῆμιν* ο 468.

φῆν, impf. *φημί*.

φῆναι, aor. infin. *φαίνω*.

φήνη, *-ης*, *ἡ*. A bird not identified, commonly taken as the sea-eagle or the lammergeyer γ 372, π 217.

Φῆρες, *οἱ* [said to be an Aeolic form for *θῆρες*. Thus 'wild men']. The Centaurs (as to whom see φ 295-304) A 268, B 743.

φῆς, 2 sing. impf. *φημί*.

φῄς, 2 sing. pres. *φημί*.

φθάνω (*φθάνϜω*). 2 sing. aor. *ἔφθης* λ 58. 3 *ἔφθη* Π 314, 322. *φθῆ* Λ 451 : χ 91. 3 pl. *φθάν* Λ 51. 3 sing. subj. *φθήῃ* Π 861. *φθῇσι* Ψ 805. 1 pl. *φθέωμεν* π 383. 3 *φθέωσι* ω 437. 3 sing. opt. *φθαίη* K 368, N 815. 3 pl. fut. mid. *φθήσονται* Ψ 444. Aor. pple. *φθάμενος* E 119, N 387, Φ 576, Ψ 779 : τ 449. (*παρα-*, *ὑπο-*.) In act. and mid. **(1)** To be first or beforehand in doing something, anticipate another in doing it : *ὅς μ' ἔβαλε φθάμενος* (getting in his blow first) E 119, *ὡς ἦλθε φθάμενος* Ψ 779. Cf. N 387, Φ 576 : τ 449.—With *ἤ* : *ἔφθης πεζὸς ἰὼν ἢ ἐγὼ σὺν νηῒ μελαίνῃ* (you have got here before me) λ 58.—With complementary pple. expressing that in which one is beforehand or in which one anticipates another : *φθάνει βλάπτουσ' ἀνθρώπους* I 506, *ἵνα μή τις φθαίη ἐπευξάμενος βαλέειν* (should be able to boast that he had first . . .) K 368, *φθῆ σε τέλος θανάτοιο κιχήμενον* (caught you before you could ward it off ; *σε* with *κιχήμενον*) Λ 451, *φθαίη κε πόλις ὑμὴ ἁλοῦσα* (will be taken before you destroy the ships) N 815, *ἔφθη ὀρεξάμενος σκέλος* (*ὦμον*) Π 314, 322 (see under *ὀρέγω* (3)(b) and cf. Ψ 805), *εἴ κε φθήῃ τυπεὶς ἀπὸ θυμὸν ὀλέσσαι* (whether before that he may not be struck so as to . . .) 861 : *φθέωμεν ἑλόντες* (take the initiative and . . .) π 383. Cf. χ 91, ω 437.—With complementary pple. and *ἤ* : *φθήσονται τούτοισι πόδες καὶ γοῦνα καμόντα ἢ ὑμῖν* Ψ 444.—With genit. of the person anticipated and complementary pple. : *φθὰν ἱππήων ἐπὶ τάφρῳ κοσμηθέντες* Λ 51 (see *ἱππεύς* (2)).—**(2)** To outstrip, outdistance : *τὸν ἄγοντα* Φ 262.

φθέγγομαι. 3 sing. aor. *φθέγξατο* Σ 218, Φ 213. Subj. *φθέγξομαι* Φ 341. Pple. *φθεγξάμενος, -ου* K 139, Λ 603 : ι 497, ξ 492, φ 192. Fem. *φθεγξαμένη* Ω 170. To utter a sound, lift up one's voice, speak, call out : *φθεγξάμενος παρὰ νηός* Λ 603. Cf. K 67, Σ 218, Φ 213, Ω 170, etc. : ι 497, κ 228, μ 249, ξ 492, φ 192, etc.

φθείρω. (*δια-*.) To destroy : *μῆλα κακοὶ φθείρουσι νομῆες* (are their destruction) ρ 246.—In pass., to perish : *φθείρεσθε* Φ 128.

φθέωσι, 3 pl. aor. subj. *φθάνω*.

φθῇ, 3 sing. aor. *φθάνω*.

Φθίηφι [locative of *Φθίη*]. At Phthia T 323.

φθίμενος, aor. pple. pass. *φθίω*.

φθινύθω [φθινυ-, φθι-, φθίω]. 3 sing. pa. iterative φθινύθεσκε A 491. (ἀπο-.) (**1**) To cause to perish or to waste or pine away, destroy, consume: φίλον κῆρ A 491. Cf. κ 485, σ 204.—(**2**) To bring to nothing, waste, consume: οἶκον ἐμόν α 250 = π 127. Cf. ξ 95.—(**3**) To perish, to waste or pine away: λαοὶ φθινύθουσιν Z 327. Cf. B 346, P 364, Φ 466: θ 530, μ 131, π 145.

φθίνω. See φθίω.

φθῑσήνωρ, -ορος [φθισ-, φθίω + ἀνήρ]. Destroying men. Epithet of war: πόλεμον B 833 = Λ 331, I 604, K 78, Ξ 43.

φθίσθαι, aor. infin. pass. φθίνω.

φθῑσίμβροτος, -ον [φθισ-, φθίω + (μ)βροτός]. Destroying men. Epithet of μάχη N 339.—Of the aegis χ 297.

φθίσονται, 3 pl. fut. pass. φθίω.

φθῖτο, 3 sing. aor. opt. pass. φθίω.

†**φθῑ́ω, φθῑ́νω.** 3 sing. impf. ἔφθῐεν Σ 446. 2 sing. subj. φθῐ́ῃς β 368. 3 sing. fut. φθῑ́σει Z 407, X 61. Infin. φθῑ́σειν Π 461. 3 pl. aor. φθῖσαν υ 67. **1** pl. subj. φθῑ́σωμεν π 369. Infin. φθῖσαι δ 741, π 428. **Pass.** 3 pl. fut. φθῑ́σονται Λ 821. Infin. φθῑ́σεσθαι T 329, Ω 86: ν 384. 3 pl. aor. ἔφθῐθεν ψ 331. 3 sing. aor. subj. φθῐ́εται Υ 173. 1 pl. φθῐόμεσθα Ξ 87. 3 sing. opt. φθῖτο λ 330. Pple. φθῐ́μενος, -ου Θ 359, Π 581: λ 558, ω 436. Infin. φθίσθαι I 246, N 667: ξ 117, ο 354. 3 sing. pf. ἔφθῐται Σ 100: υ 340. 3 pl. plupf. ἐφθῐ́ατο A 251. From φθῑ́νω 3 pl. pres. φθῑ́νουσι λ 183, ν 338, π 39. 3 sing. imp. φθῑνέτω ε 161. Pple. φθῑ́νων, -οντος κ 470, ξ 162, τ 153, 307, ω 143. (ἀποφθίω, ἐκφθίω, καταφθίω.) (**1**) In fut. and aor. act. (and once in impf. ἔφθιεν), to cause to perish, destroy: φθίσει σε τὸ σὸν μένος (will be your death) Z 407, φρένας ἔφθιεν Σ 446. Cf. Π 461, X 61: ἵνα φθίσωμεν αὐτόν π 369. Cf. δ 741, π 428, υ 67.—(**2**) In pass. (and once in subj. act. φθίῃς), to perish, die: φθίσθαι ἐνὶ Τροίῃ I 246. Cf. A 251, Θ 359, Λ 821, N 667, Ξ 87, Π 581, Σ 100, T 329, Υ 173, Ω 86: ὥς κε δόλῳ φθίῃς β 368. Cf. λ 558, ν 384, ξ 117, ο 354, υ 340, ψ 331.—Of time, to pass, pass away: πρίν κε νὺξ φθῖτο λ 330.—So in imp. act. φθινέτω, to waste or pine away: μηδέ τοι αἰὼν φθινέτω ε 161.—In aor. pple. pl. pass. in adjectival sense, absol., the dead: θανὼν φθιμένοισι μετείην ω 436.—(**3**) In act. forms fr. φθίνω, of time, to pass, pass away: ὀϊζυραὶ οἱ φθίνουσιν νύκτες λ 183 = ν 338 = π 39. Cf. κ 470, τ 153 = ω 143, ξ 162 = τ 307.

φθογγή, -ῆς, ἡ [φθέγγομαι]. A voice or cry Π 508: ι 167.—The voice: εἴσατο φθογγὴν Πολίτῃ (in voice) B 791. Cf. N 216.

φθόγγος, -ου, ὁ [φθέγγομαι]. A voice: τεὸν φθόγγον ποθέοντε E 234. Cf. ι 257, μ 41, 159, 198, σ 199 (obeying the call), ψ 326.

φθονέω (ἐπι-). (**1**) To dislike the idea of something, be dissatisfied at the prospect of it, be reluctant to allow or do it, begrudge the doing of it: εἴ περ φθονέω . . . οὐκ ἀνύω φθονέουσα Δ 55: οὔ τοι φθονέω (I make no objection) ρ 400.—With complementary infin.: δόμεναί τινα σ 16. Cf. α 346, λ 381, τ 348.—(**2**) To be reluctant to give or grant or to see given or granted, begrudge, be grudging of. With genit.: ἡμιόνων ζ 68, ἀλλοτρίων σ 18.

φιάλη, -ης, ἡ. A jar: ἐν χρυσέῃ φιάλῃ Ψ 243. Cf. Ψ 253, 270, 616.

φιλέω [φίλος]. Acc. pl. masc. pres. pple. φιλεῦντας γ 221. Non-thematic pres. infin. φιλήμεναι X 265. 3 sing. pa. iterative φιλέεσκε Γ 388, Z 15, I 450: α 264, 435, η 171, ρ 257, σ 325. 3 sing. aor. mid. ἐφίλατο E 61. φίλατο Υ 304. Imp. φῖλαι E 117, K 280. 2 sing. fut. pass. φιλήσεαι α 123, ο 281. (**1**) To hold in affection, favour or regard, hold dear, love, regard: μάλιστά μιν φιλέεσκεν Γ 388, τὴν περὶ κῆρι φίλησε πατήρ N 430, οὐκ ἔστ' ἐμὲ καὶ σὲ φιλήμεναι (*sc.* each other) X 265. Cf. Z 360, I 340, 342, 343, 481, 486, 614, Σ 126: α 264, 435, δ 171, 692, η 171, ν 406, ξ 62, 146, ο 370, ρ 257, ω 485.—Absol. δ 179, ο 70.—(**2**) With special reference to sexual love: παλλακίδος, τὴν αὐτὸς φιλέεσκεν I 450. Cf. θ 309, 316, σ 325.—(**3**) With reference to divine regard for mortals (in which sense alone the aor. mid. occurs): ἄμφω ὁμῶς φιλέουσα A 196 (of Here), ἐφίλατό μιν Ἀθήνη E 61, ἐμὲ φῖλαι (φῖλαί μ'), Ἀθήνη 117, K 280. Cf. B 197, 668, H 204, I 117, K 245, Ξ 491, etc.: γ 218, 221, 223, θ 63, 481, ο 245.—(**4**) To treat with hospitality or kindness, entertain hospitably: τοὺς ἐν μεγάροισι φίλησα Γ 207. Cf. Z 15, N 627: τίς ἂν φιλέοντι μάχοιτο; (his host) θ 208. Cf. α 123, δ 29, ε 135, η 33, θ 42, μ 450, etc.—(**5**) To take pleasure in, view with complacency or approval, love: σχέτλια ἔργα ξ 83.

φιλήρετμος [φιλ-, φίλος + ἐρετμόν]. To whom the oar is dear. Epithet of the Phaeacians ε 386, θ 96 = 386 = 535 = ν 36, λ 349.—Of the Taphians α 181, 419.

φιλοκέρτομος [φιλ-, φίλος + κερτομίαι]. Full of jeers or jibes: ὦ Πολυθερσεΐδη φιλοκέρτομε χ 287.

φιλοκτέανος [φιλ-, φίλος + κτέανον = κτῆμα]. Greedy of gain. In superl.: φιλοκτεανώτατε πάντων A 122.

φιλομμειδής [φιλ-, φίλος + μειδ-, μειδάω]. Ever smiling. Epithet of Aphrodite Γ 424, Δ 10, E 375, Ξ 211, Υ 40: θ 362.

φιλόξεινος [φιλ-, φίλος + ξεῖνος]. Well disposed to strangers, hospitably given ζ 121 = ι 176 = ν 202, θ 576.

φιλοπαίγμων, -ονος [φιλ-, φίλος + παιγ-, παίζω]. Tending to or promoting play, sportive: ὀρχηθμοῖο ψ 134.

φιλοπτόλεμος [φιλ-, φίλος + πτόλεμος]. Loving war, warlike: ἑτάροισιν Ψ 5.—Epithet of the Myrmidons Π 65, Ψ 129.—Of the Trojans Π 90, 835, P 194.—Of the Greeks P 224, T 269, Υ 351.—Of the Leleges Φ 86.

φίλος, -η, -ον. The first syllable lengthened Δ 155, E 359, Φ 308. φίλος as voc. Δ 189, I 601, K 169, etc.: α 301, γ 199, θ 413, etc. Comp.

φιλίων τ 351, ω 268. φίλτερος Λ 162, Υ 334, Φ 101, Χ 301, Ω 46 : λ 360. Superl. φίλτατος, -η, -ον Δ 51, Ε 378, Ι 198, Ν 249, Ο 111, Π 433, Σ 118, Ω 334, etc. : θ 284, π 445, ω 517. (**1**) Held in affection or regard, dear, beloved, loved : παῖδα φίλην Α 20, ἐπεὶ μάλα οἱ φίλος ἦεν 381. Cf. Α 98, Β 110, Γ 130, Δ 238, Ε 71, etc. : α 94, β 2, γ 237, ε 88, ζ 57, etc.—For Διὶ φίλος see διίφιλος.—In comp. : γύπεσσι φίλτεροι ἢ ἀλόχοισιν Λ 162. Cf. Υ 334, Ω 46 : οὔ τις φιλίων ἐμὸν ἵκετο δῶμα τ 351 = ω 268. Cf. λ 360.—In superl. : ἐμοὶ τρεῖς φίλταταί εἰσι πόληες Δ 51, πάντων φίλτατος Ε 378. Cf. Ι 198, Ν 249, Ο 111, etc. : π 445, ω 517.—(**2**) As epithet of the heart and parts of the body (cf. Shakespeare's 'my dear soul,' 'my dear heart-strings,' 'my dear blood,' etc.) : κῆρ Α 491, ἦτορ Γ 31, στήθεσσιν Δ 313, θυμόν Ε 155, χεῖρας Η 130, γούνατα 271, γυῖα Ν 85, λαιμόν Τ 209, etc. : βλέφαρα ε 493. Cf. α 60, 310, ε 462, θ 178, 233, λ 211, μ 331, ν 40, 231, τ 401, etc. —Sim. : εἵματα Β 261.—(**3**) Absol., one dear to one, a friend : ταῦτά γε πάντα, φίλος, κατὰ μοῖραν ἔειπες Κ 169. Cf. Ι 601, Φ 106, Ψ 313, 343, etc. : δεῦρο, φίλη θ 292. Cf. α 301, γ 103, 375, ρ 415, etc. — In pl. : κλῦτε, φίλοι Β 56. Cf. Γ 163, Ζ 112, Ι 528, Ν 481, Ξ 256, etc. : μετὰ οἷσι φίλοισιν α 19. Cf. α 49, β 70, δ 475, ν 192, σ 145, etc.—(**4**) Loving, friendly, kindly : οὔ τίς μοι ἔτ' ἄλλος ἤπιος οὐδὲ φίλος Ω 775 : οἷα φίλοι ξεῖνοι ξείνοισι διδοῦσιν α 313.—(**5**) Of things and abstractions. (**a**) Dear, loved, prized, pleasing, acceptable, welcome : αἰεί τοι ἔρις φίλη [ἐστίν] Α 177, πατρίδα γαῖαν Β 140. Cf. Β 162, 796, Γ 11, Η 357, Χ 58, etc. : δόσις ὀλίγη τε φίλη τε ζ 208 (see δόσις), δέμνια θ 277, δῶρα 545. Cf. α 203, θ 248, ν 295, ξ 222, σ 113, etc.—Absol. : ὀλίγον τε φίλον τ' ἔχων Α 167.—In pl. : τοί οἱ φίλα ἐργάζοντο (did his will) ω 210.—In superl. : γαιάων πολὺ φιλτάτη θ 284. Cf. Ζ 91, 272.—With complementary infin. : αἰεί τοι τὰ κάκ' ἐστὶ φίλα μαντεύεσθαι Α 107. Cf. Δ 345 : ρ 15.—(**b**) In reference to one's will, purpose or inclination : εἰ τόδε πᾶσι φίλον γένοιτο Δ 17. Cf. α 82, η 316.—In comp. : τό γε φίλτερον ἦεν Ζηνὶ Χ 301.—In impers. construction : ἐμοὶ μέλλει φίλον εἶναι Α 564. Cf. Β 116, Η 31, Κ 531, Ξ 337, etc. : η 320 = κ 66, θ 571, ν 145, ξ 397.—With complementary infin. : ἐμοὶ οὐ φίλον ἐστὶ μεταλλῆσαι ξ 378. Cf. Α 541, Δ 372, Π 556 : ι 211, ν 335, ο 362.—In comp. Φ 101.—In superl. Ω 334.—(**c**) Loving, friendly, kindly. Absol. in neut. pl. : ὅς τις ἐμοί γε φίλα ἔρδοι (do me kindnesses) ο 360.—So φίλα φρεσὶ μήδεα εἰδώς (manifesting attachment in the counsels of his heart, attached, devoted) Ρ 325 (see εἴδω (III) (12)).—Absol. in neut. pl. : φίλα εἰδότες ἀλλήλοισιν (with friendliness in our hearts) γ 277 (see εἴδω (III) (12)).—So with φρονέω : φίλα φρονέων (in friendliness of heart) Δ 219. Cf. Ε 116 (with kindly intent) : α 307 (in all kindliness), ζ 313 = η 75 (be well disposed towards you), η 15 (eager to help him), 42, π 17 (with love in his heart).

φιλότης, -ητος, ἡ [φίλος]. (**1**) Love, affection, favour, regard : οὐ φιλότητί γ' ἐκεύθανον Γ 453. Cf. Ι 630, Ω 111 : φιλότητι ἕπονται γ 363. Cf. κ 43, ξ 505, ο 197, 246.—(**2**) Sexual love or intercourse : ἵνα μίσγεαι ἐν φιλότητι Β 232, μίγη φιλότητι καὶ εὐνῇ Ζ 25. Cf. Γ 441, 445, Ζ 161, Ν 636, Ξ 163, Ο 32, Ω 130, etc. : ἀμφ' Ἄρεος φιλότητος Ἀφροδίτης τε θ 267. Cf. ε 126, θ 271, κ 335, λ 248, ο 421, ψ 219, etc.—(**3**) Friendship, amity : ἐν φιλότητι διέτμαγεν ἀρθμήσαντε Η 302. Cf. Γ 73 = 256, Γ 94, 323, Δ 16, 83, Π 282 : ω 476.—(**4**) Hospitality, kind or hospitable entertainment : ἀνδρὸς ξεινοδόκου, ὅς κεν φιλότητα παράσχῃ ο 55. Cf. Γ 354 : ο 158, 537 = ρ 164 = τ 310.

φιλοτήσιος [φιλότης]. Of or pertaining to (sexual) love : ἔργα λ 246.

φιλοφροσύνη, -ης, ἡ [φιλόφρων, fr. φιλ-, φίλος + φρήν]. Regard or consideration for others, friendliness Ι 256.

φιλοψευδής [φιλ-, φίλος + ψεῦδος]. Loving deceit Μ 164.

φίλως [adv. fr. φίλος]. Gladly, fain : φίλως χ' ὁρόῳτε εἰ . . . Δ 347.

φιτρός, -οῦ, ὁ. A log or piece of wood Μ 29, Φ 314, Ψ 123 : μ 11.

φλεγέθω [φλέγω]. (**1**) To burn, blaze : πῦρ ὄρμενον ἐξαίφνης φλεγέθει Ρ 738. Cf. Σ 211, Φ 358.—(**2**) To burn, burn up, consume : ὄφρα πυρὶ φλεγεθοίατο νεκροί Ψ 197.

φλέγμα, τό [φλέγω]. Flame, blaze : φλέγμα κακὸν φορέουσα Φ 337.

φλέγω. (ἐπι-, κατα-.) (**1**) To burn, blaze : φλέγει πῦρ Φ 13.—(**2**) To subject to the action of intense heat : ὣς τοῦ καλὰ ῥέεθρα πυρὶ φλέγετο (were ablaze) Φ 365.

φλέψ, φλεβός, ἡ. A vein : ἀπὸ φλέβα πᾶσαν ἔκερσεν Ν 546 (it is not clear what is meant by this 'vein' as described in the next line).

φλιή, -ῆς, ἡ. A doorpost ρ 221.

φλόγεος [φλογ-, φλόξ]. App., flashing or sparkling (with bright metal) : ὄχεα Ε 745 = Θ 389.

φλοιός, -οῦ, ὁ. The bark of a tree : φύλλα τε καὶ φλοιόν Α 237.

φλοῖσβος, -ου, ὁ. A confused noise, the noise of battle, the surging throng of warriors : νόσφιν ἀπὸ φλοίσβου Ε 322, Κ 416 (in the latter passage app. simply 'the noise and rumour of the general body of the host'). Cf. Ε 469, Υ 377 (= οὐλαμός in 379).

φλόξ, φλογός, ἡ [φλογ-, φλεγ-, φλέγω]. Fire, a flame of fire : ἐπεὶ φλὸξ ἐμαράνθη Ι 212. Cf. Θ 135, Ι 468, Ν 39, 53, Π 123, Σ 206, Φ 333, Ψ 217, etc. : ω 71.

φλύω. To boil (up) : ἀνὰ δ' ἔφλυε ῥέεθρα Φ 361.

φοβέω [φόβος]. Pres. pple. pass. φοβεύμενος Θ 149. Fut. φοβήσομαι Χ 250. 3 pl. plupf. πεφοβήατο Φ 206. (**1**) To put to flight, cause to flee, drive or scatter in flight : ἐφόβησε λαούς Ο 15, φόβησέ σε Κρόνου πάϊς (has chased you in terror from his presence) 91. Cf. Λ 173, 406, Ν 300, Ο 230, Π 583, Φ 267 (were seeking to put him to flight, were attacking him), etc.—(**2**) In pass., to take to flight, flee : ὑπέμειναν οὐδὲ φόβηθεν Ε 498, ἀτυζόμενοι φοβέοντο Ζ 41. Cf. Ε 140, Ζ 135,

K 510 (in flight), Λ 172, M 46 (is moved to flight), O 4 (in disorder), Π 290, Φ 206 (were fleeing), X 137, etc.: π 163.—To seek to escape, flee from: οὔ σ' ἔτι φοβήσομαι X 250.

φόβονδε [acc. of φόβος + -δε (2)]. For or to flight: μή τι φόβονδ' ἀγόρευε (counsel me not to flight) E 252, φόβονδ' ἔχε ἵππους Θ 139. Cf. O 666, P 579.

φόβος, -ου, ὁ. Fleeing, flight, rout, panic: φύζα, φόβου ἑταίρη I 2 (the two words difficult to distinguish; see φύζα), οὐδὲ μνώοντο φόβοιο Λ 71, φόβος ἔλλαβε πάντας (panic seized them) 402. Cf. B 767, E 272, Λ 544, M 144, Ξ 522, O 310 (for the putting to flight of warriors), P 42, 597, 667, Ω 216, etc.: ω 57. —Personified Δ 440, E 739, Λ 37, N 299, O 119.

φοινήεις, -εντος [φοιν-, φοινός]. Red or tawny: δράκοντα M 202 = 220.

φοινῑκόεις, -εσσα [φοῖνιξ]. (Only in fem. with the third and fourth syllables contracted.) Red or purple: σμώδιγγες αἵματι φοινικόεσσαι Ψ 717. Cf. K 133: ξ 500, φ 118.

φοινῑκοπάρῃος, -ον [φοῖνιξ + παρήϊον. Cf. μιλτοπάρῃος]. Red-prowed. Epithet of ships λ 124 = ψ 271.

φοῖνιξ, -ῑκος. (1) Red or purple as a pigment or dye: ὡς δ' ὅτε τίς τ' ἐλέφαντα γυνὴ φοίνικι μιήνῃ Δ 141. Cf. Z 219, H 305, O 538: ψ 201.—(2) As adj., of a horse, bay Ψ 454.—(3) A palm-tree: φοίνικος νέον ἔρνος ζ 163.

φοίνιος [as next]. Red: αἷμα σ 97.

φοινός [φον-, φένω]. Red: πᾶσι παρήϊον αἵματι φοινόν Π 159.

φοιτάω. Non-thematic 3 dual impf. φοιτήτην M 266. (1) To go or move about, to and fro, hither and thither, to roam: φοίτων ἔνθα καὶ ἔνθα B 779, ἀν' ὅμιλον ἐφοίτα Γ 449, E 528. Cf. I 10, M 266, N 760, O 686, Υ 6, Ω 533: β 182, λ 42, μ 420, ξ 355.—Passing into next sense: φοίτα δ' ἄλλοτε μὲν πρόσθ' Ἕκτορος, ἄλλοτ' ὄπισθεν (took his way with constant change of place) E 595.—(2) To come or go, make or take one's way: ἀΐοντες ἐφοίτων (φοίτων) ἄλλοθεν ἄλλος ι 401, κ 119, ω 415, φοίτα κατὰ λειμῶνα λ 539.—(3) To betake oneself, repair or go somewhere habitually or frequently: εἰς εὐνὴν φοιτῶντε Ξ 296.

φολκός. Perh., bandy-legged B 217.

φονεύς, ὁ [φον-, φένω]. A slayer: κασιγνήτοιο φονῆος I 632. Cf. Σ 335: ω 434.

φονή, -ῆς, ἡ [φον-, φένω]. In pl. (1) Accompaniments of slaughter, blood shed abroad, gore (cf. φόνος (5) (b)): ἀσπαίροντας ἐν φονῇσιν K 521. —(2) App., a gory carcase: μαχέσσασθαι βοὸς ἀμφὶ φονῇσιν O 633.

φόνος, -ου, ὁ [φον-, φένω]. (1) Slaying, slaughter: λῆξαν φόνοιο Z 107. Cf. T 214: φ 4, χ 63, ω 169.—(2) An instance or occurrence of this, a slaughter: φόνον Ἀχαιῶν δερκομένῳ Ξ 140: πολέων φόνῳ ἀνδρῶν ἀντεβόλησας λ 416. Cf. λ 612, ψ 137, ω 484.—(3) The slaying or killing of a person: ἀχέουσα κασιγνήτοιο φόνοιο I 567. Cf. O 116, Π 647, Φ 134: υ 246, ω 470.—(4) In more general sense, death, bane: φόνον καὶ κῆρα (the two words hardly to be distinguished) B 352, Γ 6, E 652 = Λ 443, φόνον ἤμυνε Κρονίων N 783. Cf. Π 144 = T 391, P 365, 757, Σ 133: φόνον καὶ κῆρα β 165, δ 273 = θ 513, ρ 82. Cf. β 325, δ 771, 843, λ 430, 444, π 234, 379, τ 2 = 52, φ 24, χ 11, 380.—(5) (a) Shed blood, gore: ἐρευγόμενοι φόνον αἵματος (a kind of genit. of material; app. = αἱματόεντα (cf. αἱματόεις (1) (b)) Π 162. —(b) Blood shed abroad, gore (cf. φονή (1)): κέατ' ἐν φόνῳ Ω 610. Cf. K 298: χ 376.

φοξός. Explained as 'warped in burning' (of pottery); hence, distorted, deformed: φοξὸς ἔην κεφαλήν B 219.

φορβή, -ῆς, ἡ. Food, fodder, pasture: μή μοι [ἵπποι] δευοίατο φορβῆς E 202. Cf. Λ 562.

φορεύς, ὁ [φορ-, φέρω]. A bearer or carrier: τῇ νίσοντο φορῆες Σ 566.

φορέω [φορ-, φέρω]. Non-thematic pres. infin. φορήμεναι O 310. φορῆναι B 107, H 149, K 270: ρ 224. 3 sing. pa. iterative φορέεσκε N 372, 398, 407, O 646: χ 185. 3 pl. φορέεσκον B 770, Φ 31. (ἐκ-, ἐμ-, ἐσ-.) (1) To carry about with one, bear, wear: [σκῆπτρον] ἐν παλάμῃς φορέουσιν A 238, μίτρης, ἣν ἐφόρει Δ 137. Cf. B 107, Δ 144, H 147, N 372, O 310, Π 800, Φ 31, etc.: ι 320, ο 127, ρ 245, φ 32, 41, χ 185.—Of ships, to carry as equipment: ὅπλα, τὰ νῆες φορέουσιν β 390.—(2) To carry about or hither and thither: ὅτε μέθυ οἰνοχόος φορέῃσιν ι 10.—(3) To carry, bear, convey, take (in reference to material and immaterial things): θαλλὸν ἐρίφοισι φορῆναι ρ 224, τοῦ κλέος διὰ ξεῖνοι φορέουσι πάντας ἐπ' ἀνθρώπους τ 333. —(4) Of horses, to draw (a person) in a chariot: ἵπποι, οἳ φορέεσκον Πηλεΐωνα B 770. Cf. Θ 89, K 323. —(5) Of inanimate objects, to carry, bear, bear along: ὡς ἄνεμος ἄχνας φορέει E 499. Cf. Φ 337: σχεδίην ἐφόρει κῦμα κατὰ ῥόον ε 327. Cf. δ 510, ε 328, ζ 171, μ 68.—(6) To bring or fetch: ὕδωρ Z 457: κ 358. Cf. ν 368, ω 417.—(7) To bear with one the potency of (something), to bring, bring to bear, work: φόβον Ἄρηος B 767. —(8) To carry or bear away, remove: νέκυας χ 437, 448, ταὶ ἐφόρεον δμῳαί (sc. the scrapings) 456.—To carry off, bear or snatch away: οὓς κῆρες φορέουσιν Θ 528.

φόρμιγξ, -ιγγος, ἡ. (1) A lyre (hardly to be distinguished from the κίθαρις) A 603, I 186, 194, Σ 495, 569, Ω 63: θ 67 = 105, 254, 257, 261, 537, ρ 262, 270, χ 332, 340, ψ 133, 144.—(2) The music of the φόρμιγξ: κεκορήμεθα θυμὸν φόρμιγγος θ 99. Cf. φ 430.—(3) The art of playing the φόρμιγξ: φόρμιγγος ἐπιστάμενος φ 406.

φορμίζω [φόρμιγξ]. To play or accompany oneself on the φόρμιγξ Σ 605: = δ 18, α 155, θ 266.

φορτίς, -ίδος [φορ-, φέρω]. Of a ship, adapted for carrying a heavy burden: νηὸς φορτίδος (a freight-ship) ε 250, ι 323.

φόρτος, -ου, ὁ [φορ-, φέρω]. Cargo taken on the outward voyage, an outward cargo (opposed to ὀδαῖα): ἵνα οἱ σὺν φόρτον ἄγοιμι ξ 296. Cf. θ 163.

φορύνω [cf. next]. To soil, sully, defile : σῖτος κρέα τε φορύνετο χ 21.

†**φορύσσω** [cf. prec.]. Aor. pple. φορύξας. = prec. : φορύξας αἵματι σ 336.

φόως. See φάος.

φόωσδε [φόως + -δε (1)]. To the light : δράκοντ' Ὀλύμπιος ἧκε φόωσδε (manifested, displayed) B 309 : φόωσδε λιλαίεο (*i.e.* to the upper world) λ 223.—In reference to birth : ἐπεὶ τόν γ' Εἰλείθυια ἐξάγαγε πρὸ φόωσδε Π 188. Cf. T 103, 118.

φραδής [φραδ-, φράζω]. Wary, shrewd : φραδέος νόου Ω 354.

φράδμων [φραδ-, φράζω]. Observant, shrewd : ἀνήρ Π 638.

φράζω. 3 sing. aor. φράσε λ 22. Redup. aor. ἐπέφραδον K 127. 3 sing. ἐπέφραδε Λ 795, Π 37, 51 : θ 68, κ 111, 549, ο 424. πέφραδε Ξ 500, Ψ 138 : α 444, ξ 3, τ 250, 557, ψ 206, ω 346. 3 sing. opt. πεφράδοι Ξ 335. Imp. πέφραδε α 273, θ 142. Infin. πεφραδέμεν η 49. πεφραδέειν τ 477. **Mid.** Pres. imp. φράζευ I 251 : δ 395, ν 376, π 257. Fut. φράσομαι O 234 : τ 501. φράσσομαι ε 188, π 238. 3 sing. φράσεται ψ 114. φράσσεται α 205. 1 pl. φρασσόμεθα I 619 : ψ 140. 3 φράσσονται β 367. Aor. ἐφρασάμην ρ 161. φρασάμην ψ 75. 3 sing. ἐφράσατο Ψ 450 : γ 289, δ 444, ξ 236. φράσατο K 339. ἐφράσσατο Ω 352 : δ 529. φράσσατο Ψ 126, 453. 3 pl. ἐφράσσαντο I 426 : φ 222. φράσσαντο O 671 : γ 242, κ 453, ω 391. 3 sing. subj. φράσσεται ω 217. Imp. φράσαι A 83 : π 260, χ 158, ω 331. **Pass.** 2 sing. aor. ἐφράσθης τ 485, ψ 260. (ἀμφράζομαι, δια-, ἐπι-, μεταφράζομαι, περιφράζομαι, συμ-.) (I) In act. (1) To point out, indicate, show (something in sight) : δόμον η 49. Cf. Ξ 335 : κ 111 = ο 424, τ 477.—In reference to something not in sight, to indicate as an object or goal, to direct (a person) to make his way to (someone) : ἧ οἱ Ἀθήνη πέφραδ' ὑφορβόν ξ 3.—(2) To display, exhibit, show : [κάρη] Τρώεσσιν Ξ 500. — To show forth in discourse, exhibit knowledge of : σήματα τ 250 = ψ 206, ω 346.—(3) To point out, indicate, appoint (cf. (II) (5)) : χῶρον Ψ 138 (*i.e.* the spot where the body was to be set down). Cf. λ 22.—To appoint, enjoin α 444.—(4) To make known, communicate, tell of : θεοπροπίην Λ 795, Π 37. Cf. Π 51.—To make known, tell. With dependent clause : πέφραδ' ὅπως τελέει τ 557.—To set forth or utter (discourse) : μῦθον α 273, θ 142.—(5) To instruct, direct. With dat. and infin. : ἵνα γάρ σφιν ἐπέφραδον ἡγερέθεσθαι K 127.—Without infin., to give (one) his instructions : ἐπέφραδέ μοι Κίρκη κ 549.—To instruct or show how *to do something.* With infin. : χερσὶν ἑλέσθαι θ 68.—(II) In mid. and pass. (1) To mark, descry, catch sight of : πρῶτος ἐφράσαθ' ἵππους Ψ 450. Cf. O 671, Ω 352. —(2) To remark, note, observe : φράζεο χαλκοῦ στεροπήν δ 71. Cf. κ 453 (recognized), ρ 161, τ 501, φ 222, ψ 75, ω 217, 331, 391.—With complementary pple. : τὸν φράσατο προσιόντα K 339. Cf. Ψ 453.—With clause. With ἤ . . . ἤ . . . χ 158.—With ὡς Ξ 482.—Absol. : ἐπεὶ ἐφράσθης τ 485 (*i.e.* since you know me). Cf. ψ 114 (will see more clearly).—(3) To keep an eye on, watch, guard : [ὁδόν] χ 129.—(4) To think of, bethink oneself of, call to mind : ἐπεὶ ἐφράσθης [ἄεθλον] ψ 260. Cf. π 257.—(5) To point out, indicate, appoint (cf. (I) (3)) : ἔνθα φράσσατο Πατρόκλῳ ἠρίον Ψ 126 (*i.e.* the spot where it was to be constructed).—(6) To consider, think of, reflect upon : τά σε φράζεσθαι ἄνωγα ρ 279, υ 43, ψ 122.—(7) To consider, think, bethink oneself, take thought, reflect, ponder : ἀμφὶ μάλα φράζεσθε Σ 254. Cf. E 440, Ξ 470, Π 646, Ω 354 : π 312.—With clause. With εἰ A 83 : κ 192.—With ἤ (ἠέ) . . . ἤ (ἠε) . . . I 619, X 174 : ο 167, π 238, 260.—With μή E 411, O 163, Π 446, X 358 : ρ 595.—With ὅπ(π)ως Δ 14 = Ξ 61, Ξ 3, Υ 115 : α 269, ρ 274.—(8) To take (counsel), concert (measures) : ὅτε φραζοίμεθα βουλάς λ 510. — (9) To consider, plan, devise, think, arrange, how *to do something.* With infin. : φραζέσθω νήεσσιν ἀλεξέμεναι πῦρ I 347. Cf. T 401. —With clause. With ὅπ(π)ως I 251, 680, P 144 : α 294, γ 129, ν 365, 376, ψ 117.—With ὡς I 112 : α 205, β 168.—(10) To plan, devise, think out, arrange : ὄφρ' ἄλλην φράζωνται μῆτιν I 423. Cf. A 554, I 426, M 212, O 234, P 634, 712, Σ 313 : κακά τοι φράσσονται β 367. Cf. γ 242, 289, δ 395, 444, 529, 699, ε 188, ν 373, ξ 236, π 371, ψ 140, ω 127. — (11) To be minded or inclined in a specified way : οὐ γὰρ ἔτ' ἀμφὶς ἀθάνατοι φράζονται B 14 = 31 = 68.—(12) To consider, think, *to be so and so.* With infin. : οὐκ ἄλλον φράζετο τοῦδέ τί μοι χαλεπώτερον εἶναι ἄεθλον λ 624.

†**φράσσω.** 3 sing. aor. φράξε ε 256. Nom. pl. masc. pple. φράξαντες M 263, N 130. 3 pl. aor. mid. φράξαντο O 566. Nom. pl. masc. aor. pple. pass. φραχθέντες P 268. To fence, secure, protect : ῥινοῖσιν ἐπάλξεις M 263, φραχθέντες σάκεσιν P 268. Cf. N 130 : ε 256.—In mid. O 566.

φρεῖαρ, -ατος, τό. A well : κρῆναι καὶ φρείατα Φ 197.

φρήν, φρενός, ἡ. (In sing. and pl. (the organ being regarded as a double one) without distinction of sense. The pl. occurs more frequently than the sing.) (Cf. ἦτορ, θυμός, καρδίη, κραδίη, κῆρ.) (I) The midriff. In pl. : ἔνθα φρένες ἔρχαται ἀμφὶ κῆρ Π 481. Cf. Π 504 : ι 301.—(II) Vaguely as the seat of (1) (a) ἦτορ (2) (b) : θάρσυνόν οἱ ἦτορ ἐνὶ φρεσίν Π 242. Cf. P 111, T 169.—(b) ἦτορ (2) (e) : τί σφῶϊν ἐνὶ φρεσὶ μαίνεται ἦτορ; Θ 413.—(c) ἦτορ (2) (f) : φρεσὶν ᾗσιν ἔχων δεδαϊγμένον ἦτορ ν 320.—(d) ἦτορ (2) (h) ψ 172.—(2) (a) θυμός (I) (1) (a) : ἐπεὶ ἐς φρένα θυμὸς ἀγέρθη X 475 : ω 349. Cf. ε 458. —(b) θυμός (I) (2) : αἰεί οἱ ἐνὶ φρεσὶ θυμὸς ἐτόλμα K 232. Cf. N 487. — (c) θυμός (I) (5) : ἐμοὶ οὐκέτ' ἐρητύετ' ἐν φρεσὶ θυμός I 462. Cf. Φ 386.—(d) θυμός (I) (6) : οὐ σοὶ ὀλοφύρεται ἐν φρεσὶ θυμός Θ 202. Cf. T 178, Ψ 600, Ω 321 : = ο 165, 486.—(e) θυμός (I) (8) : δίχα θυμὸς ἐνὶ φρεσὶ μερμηρίζει π 73. Cf. υ 38.—(f) θυμός (I) (10) X 357.—(g) θυμός (IV) N 280.—(3) κῆρ (2) (b) : ἄλλα οἱ κῆρ ὅρμαινε φρεσὶν ᾗσιν σ 345.—(4) κραδίη (3) (d) : διχθά μοι κραδίη μέμονε φρεσίν Π 435.—(5) νόος (2) : τῆς ἐν νόος ἐστὶ μετὰ φρεσίν Σ 419.—(III) The 'heart,' 'breast,' soul, mind, as the seat or a seat (when coupled with θυμός hardly to be distinguished therefrom) (1) Of life; hence, vitality, the vital powers, strength: ἄτη φρένας εἷλεν Π 805, τῆς ἀχέων φρένας ἔφθιεν Σ 446.—(2) Of the intelligence; specifically (a) Of the faculty of perception or knowledge: ἔγνω ᾗσιν ἐνὶ φρεσίν Α 333 = Θ 446, Π 530, Χ 296. Cf. Β 301, Δ 163 = Ζ 447, Ε 406, Θ 366, Τ 121, Υ 264, Φ 61, Ω 197, 563: φρεσὶ σύνθετ' ἀοιδήν α 328. Cf. α 115, 322, 420, δ 632, ε 206, η 327, θ 448, ι 11, ν 327, 417, ο 211, χ 347, 501.—(b) Of the faculty of thinking, deliberating, judging, considering, devising: μερμήριξε κατὰ φρένα καὶ κατὰ θυμόν Ε 671, Θ 169. Cf. Α 55, 193, 297, 342, Β 3, Γ 108, Ζ 352, Ι 119, 313, 423, 600, Κ 4, Λ 794, Ν 558, Ξ 92, Ο 81, Π 83, Τ 88, Υ 116, Φ 19, etc.: ἄλλα ἐνὶ φρεσὶ σῇσι νοήσεις γ 26. Cf. α 294, 427, 444, β 93, 363, γ 132, 151, δ 117, 676, 729 (it never occurred to you), ε 427, θ 240, 273, ι 419, λ 146, 454, 474, ξ 82, 290 (by his cunning), ο 234, 421, σ 215, 216, τ 138, υ 41, 228, φ 301, χ 333, etc.—(c) Of memory or recollection: σῇσιν ἔχε φρεσίν Β 33, τῶν ἄλλων τίς κεν ᾗσι φρεσὶν οὐνόματ' εἴποι; Ρ 260 (by exerting his powers of memory). Cf. Β 70: κ 557, ο 445.—Hence (a) The faculty of thought, intelligence: φρένες οὐκ ἔνι πάμπαν Ψ 104. Cf. κ 493.—(b) Mental power or reach, intelligence, understanding, judgment, discretion, sense, wit: οὐ χερείων . . . οὔτε φρένας οὔτε ἔργα Α 115. Cf. Ν 432, 631, Ξ 141, Ρ 171, 173, Υ 35: φρεσὶ κέχρητ' ἀγαθῇσιν γ 266, ξ 421, π 398. Cf. β 117 = η 112, δ 264, θ 168, λ 337 = σ 249, λ 367, ρ 454, φ 288, ω 194.—(c) One's wits: Γλαύκῳ φρένας ἐξέλετο Ζεύς Ζ 234. Cf. Η 360 = Μ 234, Ι 377, Ν 394, Ο 128, 724, Π 403, Ρ 470, Σ 311, Τ 137, Ω 201: β 243, ξ 178, σ 327.—In reference to distraction, rage or fury: φρεσὶ μαίνεται οὐκ ἀγαθῇσιν Θ 360. Cf. Ω 114 = 135.—To intoxication: οἶνός σ' ἔχει φρένας σ 331 = 391. Cf. ι 362, 454, τ 122, φ 297.—(3) Of spirit, courage, stoutness, resolution, endurance: οὐκ ἔστι βίη φρεσὶν οὐδέ τις ἀλκή Γ 45. Cf. Ν 55, Ρ 499, 573, Υ 381, Φ 145: α 89, γ 76, ζ 140, ρ 238, τ 347, χ 298.—In reference to animals Δ 245 (of fawns), Π 157 (of wolves).—(4) Of anger, wrath, passion: μένεος φρένες πίμπλαντο Α 103. Cf. Β 241, Π 61, Τ 127: δ 661, ζ 147.—(5) (a) Of desire, longing, appetite: σίτου περὶ φρένας ἵμερος αἱρεῖ Λ 89. Cf. Ξ 221, Τ 213: β 34, ζ 180, ο 111, ρ 355, φ 157.—(b) Of the sexual impulse: οὐ πώ ποτέ μ' ὧδέ γ' ἔρως φρένας ἀμφεκάλυψεν Γ 442. Cf. Ξ 294.—(6) Of volition: τῷ (σοὶ) φρένας ἄφρονι πεῖθεν Δ 104, Π 842, οὐ Διὸς βέομαι φρεσίν (app., in company with . . ., *i.e.* at the will of Zeus) Ο 194. Cf. Ζ 61, Η 120 = Ν 788, Ι 184, Κ 45, Μ 173, Ν 115, Ο 203, Φ 101, Χ 235: α 42, δ 777, θ 559, ξ 337, ω 435, 465.—(7) Of feelings, emotions, moods, such as joy, grief, liking, hope, fear, reverence, regard, anxiety, solicitude, etc.: τί σε φρένας ἵκετο πένθος; Α 362, φρένα τέρπετο 474, δείδοικα κατὰ φρένα μὴ . . . 555. Cf. Α 107, Ε 493, Ζ 285, 481, Θ 124, Κ 10, 46, 237, Ν 121, Ξ 264, Ο 61, Ρ 83, Σ 88, 430, Τ 19, Υ 23, Φ 583, Ω 105, etc.: τοῖσιν ἐνὶ φρεσὶν ἄλλα μεμήλει α 151, γόῳ φρένα τέρπομαι δ 102, ὀδυνάων, αἵ μ' ἐρέθουσι κατὰ φρένα καὶ κατὰ θυμόν 813, δέος ἐν φρεσὶ πίπτει ξ 88. Cf. δ 825, ε 74, ζ 65, 106, η 218, θ 131, 154, λ 195, ν 362, ρ 174, σ 324, τ 471, φ 157, ω 233, etc.—(8) Of one's character or disposition: φρεσὶν οἱ ἄρτια ᾔδη Ε 326, φίλα φρεσὶ μήδεα εἰδώς Ρ 325. Cf. Β 213, 241, Ω 40, etc.: περὶ φρεσὶν αἴσιμα ᾔδη ξ 433 (περί doubtless to be taken as adv. and φρεσίν as locative; lit. 'exceedingly in his heart'). Cf. β 231 = ε 9, κ 553, λ 445, ξ 227, σ 220, etc.—(9) As the seat of sleep Κ 139, Ξ 165.—(IV) One's inward self: μηδὲ φρεσὶν εἰρύσσαιτο (keep the knowledge to himself) π 459.

φρήτρη, -ης, ἡ [no doubt conn. with L. *frater*]. Dat. φρήτρηφι Β 363. A brotherhood or clan (app. a subdivision of the tribe (φῦλον)): κρῖν' ἄνδρας κατὰ φῦλα, κατὰ φρήτρας Β 362. Cf. Β 363.

φρίξ, φρῑκός, ἡ. A ripple on water, a ruffling of the surface of water: οἵη Ζεφύροιο ἐχεύατο πόντον ἔπι φρίξ Η 63. Cf. Φ 126, Ψ 692: δ 402.

φρίσσω [φρικ-, φρίξ]. 3 sing. aor. ἔφριξε Ν 339. Pple. φρίξας τ 446. 3 pl. pf. πεφρῑκᾶσι Λ 383, Ω 775. Nom. pl. fem. pple. πεφρῑκυῖαι Δ 282, Η 62. (1) To be rough or uneven on the surface or edge, bristle: φάλαγγες σάκεσιν πεφρικυῖαι (bristling with . . .) Δ 282, ὅτε φρίσσουσιν ἄρουραι (show their bristling ears) Ψ 599. Cf. Η 62, Ν 339.—(2) To cause to be bristly, bristle up. Of wild boars: φρίξας εὖ λοφιήν τ 446. Cf. Ν 473.—(3) To shudder at, feel terror or repulsion at the sight of: οἵ τέ σε πεφρίκασι λέονθ' ὡς αἶγες (tremble before you) Λ 383, πάντες με πεφρίκασιν (shudder at my sight, cannot bear me) Ω 775.

φρονέω [φρεν-, φρήν]. (ἐπι-.) (1) To have (good) understanding or intelligence: νόον πύκα περ φρονεόντων Ι 554, Ξ 217.—To exercise the understanding: ἄριστοι μάχεσθαί τε φρονέειν τε (in fighting and counsel) Ζ 79, φρονέων πεφυλαγμένος εἶναι (taking heed) Ψ 343.—To understand something, comprehend, see: γιγνώσκω, φρονέω π 136 = ρ 193 = 281.—(2) App., to have feeling or sensibility: ἔμ' ἔτι φρονέοντ' ἐλέησον Χ 59 (he seems to mean that old as he is age has not taken away sensibility to suffering).—(3) To be minded, inclined, disposed, bent, in a specified way: φρονέω διακρινθήμεναι ἤδη Ἀργείους καὶ Τρῶας (my mind or wish is that they be . . .) Γ 98, φρονέω τετιμῆσθαι Διὸς αἴσῃ (*i.e.* I am satisfied with such honour) Ι 608, ἰθὺς φρονέων (with straight onward course) Μ 124, ἰθὺς φρόνεον (turned not aside in their purpose) Ν 135. Cf. Ι 310, Ν 345, Ο 50, Ρ 286, Ψ 305: οἷσιν εὖ φρονέῃσιν (whom she favours) η 74.—For εὖ φρονέων see ἐϋφρονέων.—(4) To have one's mind set upon, desire, will, purpose, meditate: τὰ φρονέων, ἵνα δαμείη Ε 564, κακὰ φρονέων Η 70, Κ 486, Μ 67, Π 373, 783, τὰ ἃ φρονέων (taking his own way) Θ 430, τὰ φρονέων δώροισι κατατρύχω λαούς (for that end) Ρ 225. Cf. Α 542, Η 34, Ξ 195 = Σ 426,

O 603, 703, Π 701, X 264, 320, Ω 173 : τὰ φρονέων (to carry out this) ω 241. Cf. α 43, ε 89, κ 317, ρ 596, σ 232, υ 5, χ 51.—(5) To have the mind attuned to a specified pitch, think of oneself or of what lies before one in a specified way : θεοῖσιν ἶσα φρονέειν E 441, ὅσσον Πάνθου υἷες φρονέουσιν P 23.—For μέγα φρονέων see μέγας (11) (a).—(6) To have or conceive in one's mind or heart, be endowed with or inspired by : τὰ φρονέεις ἅ τ' ἐγώ περ Δ 361, ἀγαθὰ φρονέοντα Z 162 ((for he was) of noble heart ; cf. φρεσὶ κέχρητ' ἀγαθῇσιν γ 266), ἀταλὰ φρονέοντες Σ 567 (see ἀταλός) : πυκινὰ φρονέοντι ι 445 (cf. εἰδὼς μήδεα πυκνά Γ 202), ἐφημέρια φρονέοντες φ 85 (see ἐφημέριος). Cf. η 312.—For φίλα φρονέειν see φίλος (5) (c).—(7) To occupy one's mind with, consider, debate, turn over, ponder : τὰ φρονέων, ὅπως . . . K 491, τὰ φρονέονθ' ἃ δὴ τετελεσμένα ἦεν (*i.e.* he had a foreboding of the evil that had befallen him) Σ 4. Cf. B 36, Π 715 : α 118.—(8) To consider or take counsel with oneself, debate, ponder : ὧδέ (ὣς ἄρα) οἱ (μοι) φρονέοντι δοάσσατο κέρδιον εἶναι N 458 = Ξ 23 = Π 652 : = ο 204 = σ 93 = χ 338 = ω 239, ε 474 = ζ 145, κ 153, κακῶς φρονέουσιν (they are meditating evil) σ 168.—(9) To take into consideration or account as a reason or motive, consider, regard : τὰ φρονέων, ὅ . . . I 493 : τὰ φρονέουσ' ἅ οἱ πέρι δῶκεν Ἀθήνη (*i.e.* emboldened by the consciousness of the possession of such gifts) β 116. Cf. Ψ 545 : ξ 82.

φρόνις, ἡ [φρεν-, φρήν]. (1) What is thought : φρόνιν ἄλλων (the ideas of various men) γ 244.—(2) What is learned, information, intelligence : κατὰ φρόνιν ἤγαγε πολλήν δ 258.

φῦ, 3 sing. aor. φύω.

φύγαδε [φυγή + -δε (1)]. To or in the direction of flight, to flee : φύγαδε τράπεν ἵππους Θ 157, 257. Cf. Λ 446, Π 657, 697 (see μνάομαι (2)).

φύγε, 3 sing. aor. φεύγω.

φυγή, -ῆς, ἡ [φυγ-, φεύγω]. (1) Flight : φυγῇ ἐπὶ νῆας ἱκέσθην (in flight) κ 117.—(2) A means of flight or escape : οὐδέ τις γίγνεται φυγή χ 306.

φυγοπτόλεμος [φυγ-, φεύγω + πτόλεμος]. Shunning the fight, craven ξ 213.

φύζα, ἡ [φυγ-ja, φυγ-, φεύγω]. Flight, rout, panic : φύζα, φόβου ἑταίρη I 2 (the two words difficult to distinguish. Perh. in φύζα there is more of the notion of terror). Cf. O 62, 366, P 381 : ἐν φύζαν ἐμοῖς ἑτάροισι βάλεν ξ 269 = ρ 438.—An instance or occurrence of this : φύζαν Ἀχαιῶν δερκομένῳ Ξ 140.

φυζακινός, ἡ [φύζα]. Fearful, timid : ἐλάφοισιν N 102.

φυή, -ῆς, ἡ [φυ-, φύω]. One's bodily growth or development, one's form or figure (commonly connoting comeliness) : οὐ δέμας οὐδὲ φυήν (the two words difficult to distinguish) A 115, εἶδός τε μέγεθός τε φυήν τε B 58. Cf. Γ 208, X 370 : ε 212, ζ 16, 152, η 210, θ 134, 168.

φυκιόεις, -εντος [φυκίον = φῦκος]. Abounding in, covered with, sea-weed : θινί Ψ 693.

φῦκος, τό. Sea-weed I 7.

φυκτός [φεύγω]. That may be fled from. Absol. in neut. pl. φυκτά, means or opportunity of fleeing or escape (cf. πιστός (2) (b)) : μὴ οὐκέτι φυκτὰ πέλωνται Π 128. Cf. θ 299, ξ 489.

φυλακή, -ῆς, ἡ [φυλακ-, φύλαξ]. (1) Guarding, warding, watching : φυλακῆς μνήσασθε H 371 = Σ 299. Cf. Θ 521, K 99.—In sim. sense in pl. : φυλακὰς ἔχον I 1, 471.—(2) An outpost : Τρώων φυλακαί τε καὶ εὐναί K 408. Cf. K 416.

φυλάκους, acc. pl. See φύλαξ.

φυλακτήρ, -ῆρος, ὁ [φυλακ-, φύλαξ]. = φύλαξ (2) I 66, 80, Ω 444.

φύλαξ, -ακος, ὁ. Acc. pl. φυλάκους Ω 566. (1) A watcher or guard : λαθὼν φύλακας ἄνδρας I 477.—(2) A soldier on guard or outpost duty, a sentinel I 85, K 56, 58, 97, 127, 180, 181, 365, Ω 566.

φυλάσσω [φυλακ-, φύλαξ]. 2 sing. fut. φυλάξεις χ 195. Pple. φυλάξων ρ 593. 3 sing. aor. φύλαξε Π 686. Subj. φυλάξω δ 670. 1 pl. φυλάξομεν Θ 529. Pf. pple. mid. πεφυλαγμένος Ψ 343. (1) To guard, be on guard over, watch, protect, shield, defend, keep from harm or injury : φυλάξομεν ἡμέας αὐτούς (*i.e.* maintain our position) Θ 529. Cf. K 309 = 396, 417 : πάντ' ἐφύλασσεν β 346. Cf. β 350, η 93, κ 434, μ 136, ξ 107, ρ 593, τ 23.—(2) To be on guard, keep guard or watch, be on the look-out : νύκτα φυλασσέμεναι (through the night) K 312 = 399. Cf. K 192, 419, 421, M 303 : δ 526.—In mid. : νύκτα φυλασσομένοισιν (keeping night vigil) K 188.—To be on one's guard. In mid. : πεφυλαγμένος εἶναι (use your best care) Ψ 343.—(3) To watch, to be or keep awake : εἴ κε νύκτα φυλάσσω (spend the night awake) ε 466. Cf. υ 52, χ 195.—(4) To keep, tend, look after, see to : τόδε δῶμα ε 208.—(5) To be solicitous for the continuous existence of, preserve : αἰδῶ τεὴν φυλάσσων (thy regard for me) Ω 111.—To guard the sanctity of (a treaty) : ὅρκια Γ 280.—To cherish (wrath) : χόλος, ὃν σὺ φυλάσσεις Π 30.—To observe (an injunction) : εἰ ἔπος Πηληϊάδαο φύλαξεν Π 686.—(6) To watch over the welfare of, see safe through perils or troubles, protect, succour, aid Γ 408, E 809, K 291, O 461 : ν 301, ο 35, υ 47.—(7) To keep or preserve in a specified condition : ἔμπεδα πάντα φυλάσσειν β 227. Cf. λ 178, τ 525.—(8) To be on the watch for, look out for, with hostile intent : ὄφρα μιν λοχήσομαι ἠδὲ φυλάξω δ 670.—(9) To be on the watch for, look out for a chance of : νόστον B 251.

φυλίη, -ης, ἡ. A shrub not identified ε 477.

φύλλον, -ου, τό [cf. L. *folium*]. A leaf : φύλλα καὶ ὄζους A 234. Cf. A 237, B 468, 800, Z 146, 147, N 180, Φ 464 : φύλλων χύσις ε 483, πτόρθον φύλλων (covered with leaves, leafy) ζ 129. Cf. ε 487, 491, η 106, 285, 287, ι 51, λ 194, μ 103 (with rich foliage), 357, τ 443.

φῦλον, -ου, τό. (1) A group of persons connected by common descent and forming a community, a tribe : κρῖν' ἄνδρας κατὰ φῦλα . . . ὡς φῦλα φύλοις [ἀρήγῃ] B 362. Cf. B 840.—(2) More generally, a group of persons regarded as of common origin, a race or stock: φῦλον ἀθανάτων θεῶν E 441.—(3) The race or stock descending from a person: Ἑλένης φῦλον ξ 68. Cf. ξ 181.—(4) A race or class of persons having common characteristics: φῦλον ἀοιδῶν θ 481.—(5) In pl., the groups forming a larger group of persons; hence, such persons collectively, the race of . . .: αἳ κάλλει ἐνίκων φῦλα γυναικῶν I 130, 272. Cf. Ξ 361, O 54, 161 = 177, P 220: γ 282, η 206, 307, ο 409.—In reference to flies: ἄγρια φῦλα, μυίας T 30.

φύλοπις, -ιδος, ἡ. Acc. φύλοπιν except in λ 314. (1) Battle, fighting, strife: πόλεμον καὶ φύλοπιν Δ 15, Τρώων οἰώθη καὶ Ἀχαιῶν φ. Z 1. Cf. E 379, Λ 278, N 635, Π 208, Σ 171, Υ 141, etc.: λ 314, π 268, ω 475.—(2) In local sense, a scene of fighting, a battle-field: ἐλθεῖν ἐς Τρώων φύλοπιν Δ 65. Cf. Π 677.

φύντες, nom. pl. masc. aor. pple. φύω.

φύξηλις [φύξις]. Fleeing the foe, cowardly (the fem. termination giving a sting): φύξηλιν ἐόντα P 143.

φύξιμος [φύξις]. Offering escape. In neut. in impers. construction: ὅθι μοι φάτο φύξιμον εἶναι (that I should there find refuge) ε 359.

φύξις, ἡ [φυγ-, φεύγω]. (1) Flight (= φυγή (1)): ἢ φύξιν βουλεύουσιν K 311 = 398.—(2) Escape: μὴ φύξιν ἐμβάλλεο θυμῷ K 447.

φύρω [orig. signifying agitation. Cf. πορφύρω]. Aor. subj. φύρσω σ 21. Pf. pple. pass. πεφυρμένος, -η ι 397, ρ 103, σ 173, τ 596. To affect by admixture, to moisten, to sully, mar, stain: δάκρυσιν εἵματ' ἔφυρον Ω 162: μή σε στῆθος φύρσω αἵματος (genit. of material) σ 21. Cf. ι 397, ρ 103 = τ 596, σ 173.

φῦσαι, αἱ. A pair of bellows, a bellows: ἑλισσόμενον περὶ φύσας Σ 372. Cf. Σ 409, 412, 468, 470.

φυσάω [φῦσαι]. Of bellows, to blow: φῦσαι ἐφύσων Σ 470.—Of winds Ψ 218.

†**φυσιάω** [φῦσαι]. Acc. pl. masc. pres. pple. φυσιόωντας. Of horses, to breathe hard, pant, snort: ἵππους ἔχε φυσιόωντας Δ 227. Cf. Π 506.

φυσίζοος, -ον [φυσι-, φύω + ζωή]. Life-giving. Epithet of the earth Γ 243, Φ 63: λ 301.

φύσις, ἡ [φυ-, φύω]. The nature or qualities of a thing: φύσιν φαρμάκου ἔδειξεν κ 303.

φυταλιή, -ῆς, ἡ [φυ-, φύω]. Land laid out as an orchard or vineyard: τέμενος φυταλιῆς καὶ ἀρούρης (consisting of . . .) Z 195, M 314, Υ 185.

φυτεύω [φυτός. See φυτόν]. (1) To cause to grow, plant: πτελέας Z 419: δένδρεα μακρὰ φυτεύων (trees that are to grow to be great) σ 359. Cf. ι 108.—(2) To bring about, cause, prepare: κακόν O 134. Cf. β 165, ε 340, ξ 110, 218, ο 178, ρ 27, 82, 159.

φυτόν [neut. of φυτός, vbl. adj. fr. φύω]. A tree: φυτῶν ὄρχατοι Ξ 123. Cf. Σ 57 = 438, Φ 258: ι 108, ω 227, 242, 246.

φύω. 3 sing. fut. φύσει A 235. 3 sing. aor. ἔφῦσε κ 393. 3 sing. aor. ἔφῡ ψ 190. φῦ Z 253, 406, Ξ 232, Σ 384, 423, T 7: β 302, θ 291, κ 280, λ 247, ο 530. 3 pl. ἔφῡν ε 481, κ 397. Nom. pl. masc. pple. φύντες α 381, σ 410, υ 268. 3 pl. pf. πεφύκᾱσι η 114. πεφύᾱσι Δ 484: η 128, ι 141. Acc. pl. masc. pple. πεφυῶτας ε 477. Nom. sing. fem. πεφυυῖα Ξ 288. 3 sing. plupf. πεφύκει Δ 109, 483, Φ 352: ε 63, 238, 241. (ἐκ-, ἐμ-, περι-, προσ-.) (I) In act. in pres., fut. and sigmatic aor. (1) Of a plant, etc., to put forth, produce, develop: τόδε σκῆπτρον, τὸ μὲν οὔ ποτε φύλλα φύσει A 235. Cf. Z 148.—Absol., to show growth, put forth shoots. Fig.: ἀνδρῶν γενεὴ ἡ μὲν φύει ἡ δ' ἀπολήγει Z 149.—(2) Of the earth, to bring forth, send up, produce: χθὼν φύε ποίην Ξ 347.—Of a drug, to cause to grow, produce: τρίχες, ἃς ἔφυσε φάρμακον κ 393.—Of the wind, to promote the growth of, cause to grow: Ζεφυρίη τὰ μὲν φύει ἄλλα δὲ πέσσει η 119.—(II) In pres. pass. and in act. in non-sigmatic aor. and in pf. and plupf. (in pres. and impf. sense) (1) To be put or brought forth, grow: κέρα ἑκκαιδεκάδωρα πεφύκει (were growing) Δ 109. Cf. Δ 483, 484, Ξ 288, Φ 352: ὣς πυκνοὶ [θάμνοι] ἔφυν (had grown to be, were) ε 481, ἄσπαρτα πάντα φύονται ι 109. Cf. ε 63, 238, 241, 477, η 114, 128, ι 141, ψ 190 (there grew a . . .).—(2) To grow (into something); hence, to attach oneself (to something), fix one's hold or fasten (upon it): ἔν οἱ (μοι) φῦ χειρί (clasped his (or her) hand) Z 253 = 406 = Ξ 232 = Σ 384 = 423 = T 7: = β 302 = θ 291 = λ 247 = ο 530, κ 280, ὀδὰξ ἐν χείλεσι φύντες (biting their lips) α 381 = σ 410 = υ 268, ἔφυν ἐν χερσὶν ἕκαστος (*i.e.* one clasped one hand and one another) κ 397, ἐν χείρεσσι φύοντο ω 410.

φώκη, -ης, ἡ. A seal δ 404, 411, 436, 442, 448, 450, ο 480.

φωνέω [φωνή]. (μετα-, προσ-.) (1) To lift up the voice, utter speech, speak: φωνήσας μιν προσηύδα A 201, ξυνέηκε θεᾶς ὄπα φωνησάσης B 182. Cf. A 428, K 465, Ξ 41, Υ 380, etc.: α 122, β 257, 405, 413, etc.—φώνησεν with what is said directly reported A 333, Γ 181, E 799, H 190, etc.: δ 370, θ 140, π 43, ρ 445, etc.—(2) To lift up (the voice), utter (speech): θεᾶς ὄπα φωνησάσης ω 535.

φωνή, -ῆς, ἡ. (1) A sound uttered, a shout or shouting: ὅσση Τρώων ἔπλετο φωνή Ξ 400. Cf. O 686, Σ 221.—In reference to cattle: βοῶν ὣς γίγνετο φωνή (a lowing) μ 396.—To the nightingale: ἡ χέει πολυηχέα φωνήν (her song) τ 521.—The sound emitted by a musical instrument Σ 219.—(2) Utterance, speech: ἐκαλέσσατο φωνῇ Γ 161.—Shouting: ὃν δίωνται φωνῇ P 111. Cf. ω 530.—(3) The faculty of utterance, the voice: ἔσχετό οἱ φωνή P 696 = Ψ 397: = δ 705 = τ 472.—(4) The voice considered in regard to its power, quality or characteristics: ἀτειρέα N 45, P 555, X 227, Λυκάονι εἴσατο φωνήν (in voice) Υ 81. Cf. B 490, P 696 = Ψ 397, Σ 571, Ψ 67: τῆς φωνὴ ὅση σκύλακος γίγνεται μ 86. Cf. δ 279, 705 = τ 472, τ 381, 545.—In reference to swine: συῶν ἔχον φωνήν (their cry) κ 239.

φωριαμός, -οῦ. A chest or coffer: φωριαμῶν ἐπιθήματ' ἀνέῳγεν Ω 228. Cf. ο 104.

φώς, φωτός, ὁ. (1) A person, a man, a wight:

ἐρήτυε φῶτα ἕκαστον B 164, ἡμάρτανε φωτός (his man) K 372. Cf. B 239, 565, Γ 53, 219, E 214, etc.: α 324, 355, β 384, δ 247, ζ 187, etc.—(2) Vaguely with a proper name (cf. ἀνήρ (1) (e)): φῶτ' Ἡρακλῆα φ 26.—Sim. with words denoting a person: φῶτ' Ἀσκληπιοῦ υἱόν Δ 194. Cf. Φ 546.—(3) In genit. meaning little more than the possessive pronoun, 'his': ἐπέγραψε χρόα φωτός Δ 139. Cf. Λ 438, 462, 614: ζ 129, τ 451.—(4) With emphasis on the sex: πόσε φεύγετε φῶτα ἰδοῦσαι; (a man) ζ 199.

χάδε, 3 sing. aor. χανδάνω.

χάζω. 3 sing. fut. κεκαδήσει φ 153, 170. Aor. pple. κεκαδών Λ 334. 3 pl. fut. mid. χάσσονται N 153. 3 sing. aor. χάσσατο N 193. Pple. χασσάμενος Δ 535, E 626, N 148. Infin. χάσσασθαι M 172. 3 pl. aor. κεκάδοντο Δ 497, O 574. (ἀναχάζομαι, ἀπο-.) (1) To cause to withdraw from; hence, to separate from, deprive of. With genit.: τοὺς θυμοῦ κεκαδών Λ 334. Cf. φ 153, 170.—(2) In mid., to withdraw oneself, retire, draw back, give way: ἂψ ἑτάρων εἰς ἔθνος ἐχάζετο Γ 32, χασσάμενος πελεμίχθη Δ 535. Cf. E 249, 440, M 407, N 153, Π 122, etc.—With genit.: πυλάων χάσσασθαι M 172. Cf. Δ 497, Λ 504, N 193, O 426, etc.—(3) In mid., with genit., to hold oneself from, refrain from, stand aloof from: μίνυνθα χάζετο δουρός (refrained but a little while from his spear, *i.e.* gave it little rest) Λ 539, οὐδὲ δὴν χάζετο φωτός (*i.e.* went straight at his man) Π 736.

†**χαίνω.** 3 sing. aor. opt. χάνοι Δ 182, Z 282, Θ 150, P 417. Pple. χανών Π 350, Υ 168: μ 350. Acc. sing. masc. pf. pple. κεχηνότα Π 409. (ἀμφι-.) To open the mouth wide, gape: αἷμα πρῆσε χανών Π 350, ἕλκ' ἐκ δίφροιο κεχηνότα (agape) 409. Cf. Υ 168: πρὸς κῦμα χανών (gasping open-mouthed at . . .) μ 350.—Of the earth, to open, part, yawn: χάνοι χθών Δ 182, Θ 150. Cf. Z 282, P 417.

χαίρω. Pa. iterative χαίρεσκον Σ 259: μ 380. Fut. infin. χαιρήσειν Υ 363. Fut. infin. κεχαρησέμεν O 98. Acc. sing. masc. pf. pple. κεχαρηότα H 312. **Mid.** 3 sing. fut. κεχαρήσεται ψ 266. 3 sing. aor. χήρατο Ξ 270. 3 pl. aor. κεχάροντο Π 600: δ 344, ρ 135. 3 sing. opt. κεχάροιτο β 249, γ 438. 3 pl. κεχαροίατο A 256. **Pass.** 3 sing. aor. (ἐ)χάρη Γ 23, 27, 76, E 682, H 54, N 609: ψ 32, ω 513. 1 pl. ἐχάρημεν κ 419. 3 pl. (ἐ)χάρησαν Γ 111, E 514, H 307, T 74. 3 sing. opt. χαρείη Z 481. Nom. pl. masc. pple. χαρέντες K 541. (1) In fut. κεχαρησέμεν, to make glad, rejoice: οὐδέ τί φημι πᾶσιν ὁμῶς θυμὸν κεχαρησέμεν O 98 (the speaker the subject; what she has to say will not please the hearers).—(2) In the other tenses of the act. and in mid. and pass., to become or be glad, rejoice: σοὶ ἅμ' ἑσπόμεθ', ὄφρα σὺ χαίρῃς (*i.e.* for your advantage (and not for our own)) A 158, ἄλλοι κε Τρῶες κεχαροίατο 256, ἐχάρησαν Ἀχαιοί Γ 111. Cf. A 446, Z 481, Ξ 270, Π 600, Σ 259, Ψ 647, etc.: α 311, δ 344, ζ 30, 312 (in joy), ξ 51, τ 412, ψ 32, 266, etc.—With complementary pple.: χάρη μῦθον ἀκούσας Γ 76 = H 54, T 185. Cf. Γ 23, 27, Λ 73: οἳ χαίρουσιν βίοτον ἔδοντες (take their pleasure) ξ 377. Cf. γ 438.—(3) To rejoice at, take or have pleasure in. With dat.: κεχαρηότα νίκῃ (in a state of exultation at his victory) H 312, χαῖρε τῷ ὄρνιθι K 277. Cf. K 462: ξείνιον ᾧ κε σὺ χαίρῃς ι 356. Cf. β 35, λ 248, μ 380, ν 251, 354, 358, σ 117, υ 120, χ 306, ω 312.—In reference to a person: χαίρων Ἀντιλόχῳ Ψ 556. Cf. γ 52.—With complementary pple.: χάρη οἱ προσιόντι (hailed his approach with joy) E 682. Cf. Ω 706: τῷ χαῖρον νοστήσαντι τ 463. Cf. β 249, κ 419.—(4) In imp. (a) As a general expression of salutation or well-wishing, hail, hail to thee, good be with thee: χαῖρ', Ἀχιλεῦ I 225 (pledging him), χαῖρέ μοι, ὦ Πάτροκλε, καὶ εἰν Ἀΐδαο δόμοισιν (well be it with thee) Ψ 19 = 179: χαῖρε, πάτερ ὦ ξεῖνε θ 408, σ 122. Cf. θ 413, 461.—(b) As an expression of greeting, welcome or salutation to a person arriving or on encountering a person, welcome, hail: χαίρετε, κήρυκες A 334, χαίρετον I 197: χαῖρε, ξεῖνε α 123, ἐπεί σε πρῶτα κιχάνω, χαῖρε (well met) ν 229. Cf. δ 60, υ 199, ω 402.—(c) As an expression of farewell to a person departing, fare thee well, good befall thee: σὺ δὲ χαῖρε καὶ ἔμπης ε 205. Cf. ο 151.—(d) As a similar expression to a person from whom one is departing, good remain with thee: χαῖρέ μοι, ὦ βασίλεια, διαμπερές ν 59. Cf. ν 39.

χαίτη, -ης, ἡ. (1) A lock of hair, a lock dedicated to a divinity: ξανθὴν ἀπεκείρατο χαίτην Ψ 141 (χαίτην = κόμην 146).—In pl., the hair of the head: χαίτας πεξαμένη Ξ 175. Cf. A 529, Φ 407, X 401: δ 150, κ 567, ω 46.—The hairs considered separately: πολλὰς ἐκ κεφαλῆς ἕλκετο χαίτας K 15.—(2) A horse's mane: ἐμιαίνετο χαίτη P 439. Cf. T 405.—So in pl.: ἀμφὶ χαῖται ὤμοις ἀΐσσονται Z 509 = O 266. Cf. P 457, Ψ 282, 284, 367.

χάλαζα, -ης, ἡ. Hail K 6, O 170, X 151.

χαλεπαίνω [χαλεπός]. 3 sing. aor. subj. χαλεπήνῃ Π 386, T 183, Ω 369: ε 147, π 72, φ 133, τ 83. Infin. χαλεπῆναι Σ 108. (1) To offer violence, do outrage or despite, rage: ἦρχον χαλεπαίνων B 378. Cf. I 516, Ξ 256, Σ 108, T 183, Υ 133, Ω 369: = π 72 = φ 133, β 189, σ 415 = υ 323.—With dat., to be enraged against, bear hard upon: οὔ μοι δῆμος χαλεπαίνει π 114. Cf. Π 386: ε 147, τ 83.—(2) Of wind, to bluster, rage: ἄνεμος, ὅς τε βρέμεται χαλεπαίνων Ξ 399.—Of weather, to be wild or severe: ὥρῃ χειμερίῃ, εἰ καὶ μάλα περ χαλεπαίνοι ε 485.

χαλεπός, -ή, -όν. (1) Grievous, burdensome, heavy, sore, painful: μῆνις E 178, γῆρας Θ 103, Ψ 623. Cf. E 384, 391, N 624: πένθος ζ 169, φῆμιν (evil, ill) ω 201. Cf. β 193, κ 464, λ 292, 622, φ 377, etc.—In comp.: τοῦδέ μοι χαλεπώτερον εἶναι ἄεθλον λ 624.—Absol. in neut. pl., evil, mischief: χαλεπὰ ὁρμαίνοντες ἀλλήλοις γ 151.—(2) Dangerous: χαλεποὶ θεοὶ [γίγνονται] φαίνεσθαι ἐναργεῖς (in respect of appearing, *i.e.* when they appear) Υ 131.—(3) Difficult, hard: λιμέσιν (hard to attain or reach) τ 189.—In neut. χαλεπόν with or without copula, it is difficult or hard. With infin.: χ. σε πάντων ἀνθρώπων σβέσσαι μένος Π 620. Cf. Φ 184: χ. κεν ἀνήνασθαι δόσιν εἴη δ 651. Cf. λ 156, ν 141, υ 313, ψ 81.—Without infin. Τ 80: ψ 184.—In personal construction. With infin.: χαλεπή τοι ἐγὼ μένος ἀντιφέρεσθαι (hard to set yourself against) Φ 482. Cf. κ 305. — Without infin.: χαλεποί τοι ἔσονται [μῦθοι] (you will find it hard to know them) Α 546. — (**4**) Oppressing the spirit, terrifying, daunting: κεραυνός Ξ 417.—(**5**) Of persons, violent, despiteful, malignant, hard: ἄνδρες α 198. Cf. β 232 = ε 10, θ 575, ρ 388, 564, τ 201.—(**6**) Of discourse, stern, harsh, severe, hard: μύθῳ Β 245, Ρ 141, ὀνείδεσιν Γ 438, ἐπέεσσιν Ψ 489, 492: γ 148, μύθοισιν β 83, ρ 395, δήμου φῆμις ξ 239, ἀνάκτων ὁμοκλαί ρ 189, μῦθον (hard to sit down under) υ 271.—(**7**) Of winds, blustering, roaring, raging: θύελλαν Φ 335: ἄνεμοι μ 286.

χαλέπτω [cf. χαλεπαίνω]. To bear hard upon, oppress: θεῶν ὅς τίς σε χαλέπτει δ 423.

χαλεπῶς [adv. fr. χαλεπός]. With difficulty, hardly: χ. σ' ἔολπα τὸ ῥέξειν Τ 186.—With copula in impers. construction: διαγνῶναι χ. ἦν ἄνδρα ἕκαστον (it was hard to . . .) Η 424.

χαλῑνός, -οῦ, ὁ. A bit for a horse: ἐν χαλινοὺς γαμφηλῇς ἔβαλον Τ 393.

χαλιφρονέω [χαλίφρων]. To be of light or weak mind, lack sense: χαλιφρονέοντα σαοφροσύνης ἐπέβησαν ψ 13.

χαλιφροσύνη, -ης, ἡ [χαλίφρων]. Lightness or weakness of mind, lack of sense. In pl.: οὐ χαλιφροσύναι γέ μ' ἔχουσιν π 310.

χαλίφρων [prob. χαλάω, to loosen + φρήν]. Loose-minded, of light, weak or childish mind, senseless: νήπιος ἠδὲ χαλίφρων δ 371, τ 530.

χάλκειος, -η, -ον [χαλκός]. (Cf. χάλκεος.) Of bronze: κόρυς Μ 184, Υ 398, αὐγή (*i.e.* the gleam from the polished bronze) Ν 341. Cf. Ζ 236 (studded or fitted with bronze), Κ 31, Λ 630, 640, Μ 295, Ο 567 (see ἕρκος (1) (b)), Υ 271: φ 7.—As epithet of weapons: ἔγχεϊ (*i.e.* with head of bronze) Γ 380, αἰχμή Δ 461, etc.: ἄορ τ 241.

χαλκεοθώρηξ, -ηκος [χάλκεος + θώρηξ]. With breastplate of bronze Δ 448 = Θ 62.

χάλκεος, -ον [χαλκός]. (Cf. χάλκειος.) Of bronze: κεράμῳ Ε 387, κύκλα 723, χιτῶνα (*i.e.*, app., his θώρηξ) Ν 440. Cf. Ε 725, Η 220, Θ 15, Ν 30, 372, Χ 322 (studded or fitted with bronze), etc.: πέλεκυν ε 235, οὐδός (οὐδῷ) η 83, 89 (app. the μέλινος οὐδός (see μέλινος (2)) covered with bronze plating). Cf. η 86, κ 4.—Fig.: ἦτορ Β 490, ὕπνον (that binds as with bonds of bronze, *i.e.* the sleep of death) Λ 241, οὐρανόν (the heavens being regarded as a vault of burnished metal, 'the brazen heavens') Ρ 425 (cf. πολύχαλκος (2)), ὄπα Σ 222.—As epithet of weapons: ἔγχος (*i.e.* with head of bronze) Γ 317, ξίφος 335, δόρυ Ν 247, etc.: ἔγχος α 104, δόρυ κ 162, ξίφος 262, φάσγανον χ 80, etc.—As epithet of Ares Ε 704, 859, 866, Η 146, Π 543.

χαλκεόφωνος [χάλκεος + φωνή]. With voice of bronze (cf. ἄρρηκτος (4)). Of Stentor Ε 785.

χαλκεύς, ὁ [χαλκός]. A skilled worker in copper or bronze, a smith: μίτρη, τὴν χαλκῆες κάμον ἄνδρες Δ 187. Cf. Δ 216, Μ 295, Ο 309: ι 391.—Of a worker in gold γ 432.

χαλκεύω [χαλκός]. To work or fashion in bronze or other metal: δαίδαλα Σ 400.

χαλκεών, -ῶνος, ὁ [χαλκός]. A smithy or forge: βῆ ῥ' ἴμεν ἐς χαλκεῶνα θ 273.

χαλκήϊος [χαλκεύς]. Of a smith: ὅπλα γ 433, δόμον (the house of the χαλκεύς, the smithy) σ 328.

χαλκήρης, -ες [χαλκός + ἀρ-, ἀραρίσκω]. Furnished, strengthened, tipped, with bronze: κυνέῃ χαλκήρεϊ Γ 316, Ψ 861. Cf. Ν 714, Ο 535, 544, Ρ 268: κ 206, χ 111, 145.—As epithet of weapons: χαλκήρεϊ δουρί Ε 145, χαλκήρε' ὀϊστόν Ν 650. Cf. Δ 469, Σ 534, etc.: α 262, ε 309, ι 55, λ 40, ν 267, χ 92.

χαλκίς, -ίδος, ἡ. The name given by the gods to a bird not identified (cf. κύμινδις) Ξ 291.

χαλκοβαρής, -βάρεια, -βαρές [χαλκός + βαρύς]. Heavy with bronze: στεφάνη Λ 96, ἰός Ο 465. Cf. Χ 328: λ 532, φ 423, χ 259 = 276.

χαλκοβατής, -ές [χαλκός + βα-, βαίνω]. Based on, with floor of, bronze. Of the palace of Zeus: Διὸς χαλκοβατὲς δῶ Α 426, Ξ 173, Φ 438, 505.—Of that of Hephaestus θ 321.—Of that of Alcinous ν 4.

χαλκογλώχις, -ῖνος [χαλκός + γλωχίς in sense 'point.' Cf. τανυγλώχις]. With point of bronze: μελίης Χ 225.

χαλκοκνήμις, -ῖδος [χαλκός + κνημίς]. With κνημῖδες of bronze. Epithet of the Achaeans Η 41.

χαλκοκορυστής [χαλκός + κορυστής. Cf. ἱπποκορυστής]. Marshaller of spears. Epithet of Hector Ε 699, Ζ 398, Ν 720, Ο 221, 458, Π 358, 536, 654.—Of Sarpedon Ζ 199.

χαλκοπάρῃος, -ον [χαλκός + παρήϊον]. Of helmets, with cheek-pieces of bronze Μ 183, Ρ 294, Υ 397: ω 523.

χαλκόπους, -ποδος [χαλκός + πούς]. With feet of bronze, untiring: ἵππω Θ 41, Ν 23.

χαλκός, -οῦ, ὁ. Ablative χαλκόφι Λ 351. (**1**) Copper, but commonly, esp. in reference to weapons, signifying copper hardened by an admixture of tin, *i.e.* bronze (sometimes impossible to say whether the pure metal or the alloy is meant): πλεῖαί τοι χαλκοῦ κλισίαι Β 226, δοῦρε κεκορυθμένα χαλκῷ Γ 18. Cf. Δ 226, Ζ 48, 504, Η 223, 473, Ι 137, Ν 406, Ξ 11, Ο 389, Υ 275, Χ 50, Ψ 549, etc.: ὅθι νητὸς χαλκὸς ἔκειτο β 338. Cf. α 99, 184, δ 72, ε 38, ν 19, 136, χ 125, etc.—(**2**) Applied to things made or partly made of copper or bronze. (**a**) To spears or darts: ὄρνυτο χαλκῷ Γ 349, πάγη ἐν πνεύμονι χαλκός Δ 528. Cf. Γ 348, Ε 74, 75, 538, Η 247, Λ 351, Ν 388, Π 345, Φ 593, etc.: χ 278, 295, ω 524.—Specifically to the head of the spear: τῆλε χαλκὸς λάμπεν Κ 153, Λ 44. Cf. Χ 134.—(**b**) To an arrow: κυλινδόμενος περὶ χαλκῷ Θ 86.—(**c**) To a shield: περιήχησε χαλκός Η 267.—(**d**) To helmets: ταρβήσας χαλκόν τε ἰδὲ λόφον Ζ 469. Cf. Λ 351.—(**e**) To armour or armament in general: ἀπὸ χαλκοῦ αἴγλη οὐρανὸν ἵκεν Β 457, ἐδύσετο χαλκόν 578. Cf. Δ 420, 495, Η 206, Λ 65, Μ 151, Ν 191, Π 636, Ρ 376, Σ 522, Τ 363, Ψ 130, etc. : ξ 268 = ρ 437, φ 434, χ 113, ψ 369, ω 467 = 500.—(f) To knives : στομάχους (στόμαχον) τάμε χαλκῷ Γ 292, Τ 266. Cf. Γ 294, Φ 37. —(g) To a fish-hook : λίνῳ καὶ χαλκῷ Π 408.—(h) To tripods : ἐπεὶ ζέσσεν ὕδωρ ἐνὶ χαλκῷ Σ 349 : = κ 360. Cf. θ 426. —To a λέβης : κανάχησε χαλκός τ 469.—(i) Collectively to implements in general : ὄγκιον ἔνθα κεῖτο χαλκός, ἀέθλια τοῖο ἄνακτος φ 62.—(3) In generalized sense (a) Of weapons, 'the spear,' 'the sword,' 'my, his, etc., spear or sword' : Ἕκτόρεον χιτῶνα δαΐξαι χαλκῷ Β 417, εἰ μαχοίατο χαλκῷ Δ 348, χαλκῷ δηώσας Θ 534. Cf. Δ 511, Ε 132, Η 77, Ι 458, Μ 227, Ν 323, Π 497, Ρ 126, Σ 236, Φ 568, Ω 393, etc. : δ 226, 257, λ 120, ν 271, ξ 271, τ 522, υ 315, χ 219, etc.—(b) Of cutting implements, 'the axe,' 'the knife,' etc.: περί ἑ χαλκὸς ἔλεψε φύλλα Α 236. Cf. Ν 180, Τ 222, Φ 455, Ψ 118, 412 : δούραθ' ἁρμόζεο χαλκῷ ε 162, μῆλ' ἐσφαγμένα χαλκῷ κ 532, λ 45. Cf. ε 244, θ 507, μ 173, ξ 418, σ 86, 309, φ 300, χ 475, ψ 196.

χαλκότυπος, -ον [χαλκός + τύπτω]. Inflicted with (weapons of) bronze : ὠτειλάς Τ 25.

χαλκοχίτων, -ωνος [χαλκός + χιτών]. Bronze-clad. In pl. as epithet of the Achaeans and Argives Α 371, Β 47, Γ 127, Δ 285, etc. : α 286, δ 496.—Of the Epeans Δ 537, Λ 694.—Of the Trojans Ε 180 = Ρ 485.—Of the Boeotians Ο 330. —Of the Cretans Ν 255.

χαμάδις [χαμαί]. (1) To the ground, on to, on, the ground : ἐγκέφαλός σφι χ. ῥέοι Γ 300. Cf. Ζ 147, Η 16, 190, 480, Ο 435, 714, Π 118, Ρ 438, Ψ 220 : δάκρυ χ. βάλεν δ 114. Cf. ι 290, τ 63.— (2) Without notion of motion, on the ground : στορέσας τ 599.

χαμᾶζε [χαμαί]. To the ground, on to, on, the ground : ἅλτο Γ 29, ἀπὸ πύργου βαῖνε χαμᾶζε (*i.e.* to the ground level) Φ 529. Cf. Ε 835, Θ 134, Κ 528, Ο 537, Ψ 508, etc. : π 191, φ 136, χ 84, 327, 340.

χαμαί [app. a locative form]. (1) On the ground, on the earth : χαμαὶ ἐρχομένων ἀνθρώπων Ε 442. Cf. Λ 145 : χ. ἧσθαι η 160.—(2) With notion of motion = χαμάδις (1), χαμᾶζε : χ. πέσεν Δ 482. Cf. Δ 526, Ε 583, 588, Ζ 134, Θ 320, Ν 530, Χ 448, etc. : ρ 490, σ 28, 397, χ 188.

χαμαιευνάς, -άδος. = next. Epithet of swine : σύες κ 243, ξ 15.

χαμαιεύνης [χαμαί + εὐνή]. Sleeping on the ground : Σελλοὶ χαμαιεῦναι Π 235.

χανδάνω. 3 sing. fut. in mid. form χείσεται σ 17. 3 sing. aor. ἔχαδε Δ 24, Θ 461. χάδε Λ 462. Infin. χαδέειν Ξ 34. Acc. sing. masc. pf. pple. κεχανδότα Ψ 268 : δ 96. 3 sing. plupf. κεχάνδει Ω 192. (1) To have or hold in it, contain : θάλαμον, ὃς γλήνεα πολλὰ κεχάνδει Ω 192. Cf. δ 96.—(2) To have capacity or afford room for, hold, contain : ἤϋσεν ὅσον κεφαλὴ χάδε φωτός (with as much voice as his head would hold, with his full volume of voice, *à pleine tête*) Λ 462, τέσσαρα μέτρα κεχανδότα (holding . . .) Ψ 268. Cf. Ξ 34, Ψ 742 : ὡς οἱ χεῖρες ἐχάνδανον (as much as they could hold) ρ 344. Cf. σ 17.— (3) To repress, keep in, contain : Ἥρῃ οὐκ ἔχαδε στῆθος χόλον (*i.e.* it burst out) Δ 24 = Θ 461.

χανδόν [χαν-, χαίνω]. Open-mouthed, greedily : ὃς ἂν οἶνον χ. ἕλῃ φ 294.

χανών, aor. pple. χαίνω.

χαράδρη, -ης, ἡ. (1) A mountain-stream, a torrent Π 390.—(2) The bed of a torrent, a ravine or gorge Δ 454.

χάρη, 3 sing. aor. pass. χαίρω.

χαρίεις, -εντος. Fem. χαρίεσσα. Neut. χαρίεν, -εντος. [χάρις.] Superl. χαριέστατος of two terminations κ 279. Pleasing, lovely, fine : νηόν Α 39, εἵματα Ε 905, Χ 511. Cf. Θ 204, Ι 599 : φᾶρος ε 231 = κ 544, ἔργα ζ 234 = ψ 161, κ 223.— In superl. : πέπλος χαριέστατος Ζ 90, 271.—Of parts of the body, lovely, fair : μέτωπον Π 798. Cf. Σ 24, Χ 403. — Of incorporeal things and abstractions, pleasing, delightful, acceptable : ἀμοιβήν γ 58, ἀοιδήν ω 198.—In comp. : τέλος χαριέστερον ι 5.—In superl. : τοῦ περ χαριεστάτη ἥβη Ω 348 : τοῦ περ χαριέστατος ἥβη κ 279.— Absol. in neut. pl., what makes for pleasingness : οὐ πάντεσσι θεοὶ χαρίεντα διδοῦσιν θ 167.

χαρίζομαι [χάρις]. 3 sing. aor. opt. χαρίσαιτο Ζ 49, Κ 380, Λ 134. Infin. χαρίσασθαι ν 15, ρ 452. Pf. pple. κεχαρισμένος, -ου Ε 243, 826, Κ 234, Λ 608, Τ 287, Υ 298, Ω 661 : β 54, δ 71, θ 584, π 184, τ 397. 3 sing. plupf. κεχάριστο ζ 23. (1) To make oneself agreeable or do something agreeable (to a person), to gratify, favour, seek favour in the eyes of. With dat. : χαριζόμενος βασιλῆϊ Λ 23. Cf. Ε 71, Ν 633, Ο 449 = Ρ 291 : κ 43, ν 265, ξ 387.—To honour (with sacrifice) : οὔ νύ [τοι] Ὀδυσσεὺς χαρίζετο ἱερὰ ῥέζων ; α 61.— (2) (a) Of a person, to be agreeable or pleasing to, please. With dat. : οὐ πάντεσσι χαριζόμενος τάδ' ἀείδει θ 538.—In pf., to be pleasing or dear, recommend oneself : ἐμῷ κεχαρισμένε θυμῷ Ε 243 = 826 = Κ 234. Cf. Λ 608, Τ 287 : κεχάριστό οἱ θυμῷ ζ 23. Cf. β 54, δ 71.—(b) In pf. of things, to be pleasing or acceptable : κεχαρισμένα δῶρα Υ 298. Cf. π 184, τ 397.—Absol. in neut. pl., what is pleasing or acceptable : κεχαρισμένα κέ μοι θείης (a pleasure) Ω 661 : κεχαρισμένα εἰδώς (with pleasingness in his heart, such as one can like or love) θ 584 (see εἴδω (III) (12)).—(3) To gratify, conciliate or satisfy a person by giving, bestow on him to his heart's content : τῶν κέν τοι χαρίσαιτο πατὴρ ἀπερείσι' ἄποινα Ζ 49 = Λ 134. Cf. Κ 380 : ω 283.—Absol. : ἀργαλέον ἕνα προικὸς χαρίσασθαι ν 15.—With genit. of material : χαριζομένη παρεόντων (setting good cheer before them (him) from her store) α 140 = δ 56 = η 176 = κ 372 = ο 139 = ρ 95, ἀλλοτρίων χαρίσασθαι (to give at another's cost) ρ 452.

χάρις, ἡ [χαρ-, χαίρω]. Dat. pl. χάρισι ζ 237. (1) Loveliness, charm, beauty, grace, comeliness : χάρις ἀπελάμπετο Ξ 183 : = σ 298. Cf. β 12 = ρ 63, ζ 235, θ 19, ψ 162.—In pl. : χάρισι στίλβων ζ 237.

—In reference to something immaterial: οὔ οἱ χάρις ἀμφιπεριστέφεται ἐπέεσσιν θ 175, ὃς ἀνθρώπων ἔργοισι χάριν ὀπάζει (consummation, perfection) ο 320. —(2) (a) Favour, grace, service: φέρων χάριν Ἕκτορι Ε 211. Cf. Ε 874, Ι 613, Φ 458: ε 307.—(b) Adverbially in acc. (cf. ἐπίκλησις (2), πρόφασις): χάριν Ἕκτορος (doing him service, yielding him compliance) Ο 744.—(3) Gratification, pleasure, delight, satisfaction: τῶνδ' ἀντὶ χάριν δοῖεν Ψ 650.—With genit. of the cause: ἧς οὔ τι χάριν ἴδεν (had no joy of her) Λ 243.—(4) (a) Gratitude, thanks: Τρώεσσί κε χάριν ἄροιο (among the . . ., at the hands of the . . .) Δ 95, ἰδέω τοι χάριν Ξ 235 (see εἴδω (III) (13)): οὐκ ἔστι χάρις εὐεργέων (for . . .) δ 695, χ 319.—(b) Matter of thanks. With infin. (cf. νέμεσις (2)): ἐπεὶ οὐκ ἄρα τις χάρις ἦεν μάρνασθαι (it got me (us) no thanks) Ι 316, Ρ 147.—(5) In pl., the Graces Ε 338, Ξ 267, 275, Ρ 51: ζ 18, θ 364, σ 194.

χαρίσασθαι, aor. infin. χαρίζομαι.

χάρμα, -ατος, τό [χαρ-, χαίρω]. (1) Joy, pleasure: τὴν ἅμα χάρμα καὶ ἄλγος ἕλε φρένα τ 471.—(2) A source or cause of joy, gratification or comfort, a joy or delight: δυσμενέσι χάρμα Γ 51. Cf. Ζ 82, Κ 193, Ξ 325, Ρ 636, Ψ 342, Ω 706: ζ 185.

χάρμη, -ης, ἡ. (1) Fighting, battle: προκαλέσσατο χάρμῃ Η 218, 285. Cf. Μ 389, Π 823, Ρ 602.—(2) A fight in progress: μηδ' εἴκετε χάρμης (from the fight) Δ 509. Cf. Ξ 101, Ρ 161.—(3) Spirit, stomach, ardour for the fight, one's spirit of fight: μνήσαντο χάρμης Δ 222, Θ 252 = Ξ 441, Ο 380. Cf. Μ 203, 393, Ν 82, 104, 721, Ο 477, Ρ 103, 759, Τ 148: χ 73.—(4) The art of war, war, fighting: εἰδότε χάρμης Ε 608.

χαροπός [app. a compound of ὦπα]. Epithet of lions of uncertain meaning; perh., with flashing eyes, or the like λ 611.

χάσσατο, 3 sing. aor. mid. χάζω.

χατέω [cf. next]. (1) To be in need, be in straits: Ἀργείοισιν ἀμυνέμεναι χατέουσί περ ἔμπης Ι 518. Cf. Ο 399: β 249.—(2) With genit., to have need of, stand in need of: θεῶν γ 48.—(3) With infin. (a) To have need of *doing something*: μάλα περ χατέουσιν ἐλέσθαι [δόρπον] ν 280.—(b) To desire, wish: δμῶες χατέουσιν ἀντία δεσποίνης φάσθαι ο 376.

χατίζω [cf. prec.]. With genit. (1) To have need of, stand in need of: Θέτις νύ τι σεῖο χατίζει (wishes to see you about something) Σ 392.—(2) To wish for, desire, aim at, seek: τέο αὖτε χατίζεις; Β 225. Cf. θ 156, λ 350, χ 50. — The genit. to be supplied Ρ 221.—Absol.: οὔ τι χατίζων πωλεύμην (seeking anything for myself) χ 351.

χειή, -ῆς, ἡ. A hole or lurking-place. In reference to a serpent Χ 93, 95.

χεῖλος, τό. (1) In pl., the lips: χείλεα δίηνεν Χ 495. Cf. Ο 102: α 381 = σ 410 = υ 268, σ 21.—(2) The lip or brink of something: [τάφρου] χείλει ἐφεσταότες Μ 52.—The rim of a vessel. In pl.: χρυσῷ ἐπὶ χείλεα κεκράαντο (κεκράανται) δ 132, 616 = ο 116.

χεῖμα, -ατος, τό. (1) Bitter weather, cold: χ. με δάμναται ξ 487.—(2) Winter: χείματος οὐδὲ θέρευς (in winter or summer) η 118, χ. εὕδει ὅθι . . . (during, in, winter) λ 190.

χειμάρροος, χειμάρρους [χεῖμα + ῥέω]. Flowing with winter force, in flood: ποταμός Λ 493, Ν 138.

χείμαρρος. = prec. Δ 452, Ε 88.

χειμέριος, -η, -ον [χεῖμα]. Of, proper to, coming in, winter: ἄελλαι Β 294, ὕδωρ (a winter flood) Ψ 420. Cf. Γ 222, Μ 279: ὥρῃ (storm-time) ε 485.

χειμών, -ῶνος, ὁ [χεῖμα]. (1) The weather proper to winter, bitter or inclement weather: ἐπεὶ χειμῶνα φύγον Γ 4. Cf. δ 566.—An access of bad weather, a storm or tempest Ρ 549: ξ 522.—(2) Winter: χειμῶνι περῶντα (in winter) Φ 283.

χείρ, -ός, ἡ. Dat. sing. χερί Θ 289, Υ 182, Ω 101. Dat. pl. χείρεσι Υ 468. χείρεσσι Γ 271, Ε 559, Θ 116, Μ 382, etc.: ε 344, ι 487, ξ 312, π 444, etc. χερσί Α 14, Β 374, Ε 60, Η 255, etc.: α 153, γ 35, θ 68, ι 108, etc. (1) One of the hands, one's hand; in dual and pl., the hands, one's hands: στέμματ' ἔχων ἐν χερσίν Α 14, μηδὲ ξίφος ἕλκεο χειρί 210, ἄμφω χεῖρε πετάσσας Δ 523. Cf. Α 351, 585, Γ 270, 363, Δ 249, etc.: χεῖρ' ἕλε δεξιτερήν α 121, μὴ ἔρις καὶ χερσὶ γένηται (lest it come to fisticuffs) σ 13. Cf. β 37, 321, γ 35, 51, δ 66, etc. —In pl. where the reference is to one hand: ἐρυσσάμενος χείρεσσι μάχαιραν Γ 271 = Τ 252. Cf. Γ 367, Μ 27, Π 801, Ψ 384, etc.: δ 506, ε 292, ν 225, etc.—(2) In reference to position: Ἄρκτον ἐπ' ἀριστερὰ χειρὸς ἔχοντα (to the left of his hand, on the left hand) ε 277.—(3) In pl. in reference to fighting or violence or to one's might or strength: οὔ τις σοὶ βαρείας χεῖρας ἐποίσει Α 89, χερσὶν ὑφ' ἡμετέρῃσιν ἁλοῦσα Β 374, βίῃ καὶ χερσὶ καὶ ἔγχεϊ φέρτερος Γ 431. Cf. Α 166, 567, Ζ 502, Θ 226, 344, Μ 135, etc.: α 238, 254, θ 181, ι 512, λ 502, ν 376, σ 156, etc.—Contrasted in terms with ἔπεα: ἐν γὰρ χερσὶ τέλος πολέμου, ἐπέων δ' ἐνὶ βουλῇ Π 630. Cf. Α 77.—(4) Extended to the arm or the arms: Χρυσηΐδα πατρὶ ἐν χερσὶ τίθει Α 441, νεκρός οἱ ἔκπεσε χειρός (his arms) Δ 493, ἀπὸ δ' ἔξεσε χεῖρα Ε 81, τετυμμένω ἀμφοτέρω κατὰ χεῖρα Ν 783 (in the case of the first, the arm (cf. 529), in the case of the second, the hand (cf. 593)). Cf. Ε 344, Ζ 81, Λ 252 (the forearm), Ν 534, Ο 311 (on his arm), Π 517 (cf. 510), Φ 166, Χ 426, etc.: δ 454, ε 344, 374, 454, ζ 310, ξ 351, φ 223, etc.

χειρίς, -ῖδος, ἡ [χείρ]. A covering for the hand, a glove: χειρῖδας ἐπὶ χερσὶν [ἔχεν] ω 230.

χειρότερος [double comp. Cf. χείρων. Cf. also χερειότερος]. Less warlike, soldierly or skilful in fight: χειρότερός περ ἐών Υ 436. Cf. Ο 513.

χείρων, χεῖρον, -ονος. Also **χερείων,** χέρειον, -ονος. Dat. sing. masc. χέρηϊ Α 80. Acc. χέρεια Δ 400: ξ 176. Nom. pl. χέρηες ο 324. Acc. pl. neut. χέρεια Ξ 382: σ 229, υ 310. Used as comp. of κακός. (1) Of meaner birth, of lower rank or station: ἀνδρὶ χέρηϊ Α 80, χερείονος θεοῦ Υ 106. Cf. λ 621.—Absol.: οἷά τε τοῖς ἀγαθοῖσι παραδρώωσι χέρηες ο 324.—(2) Less warlike, soldierly or skilful in fight: ἐγὼ σέθεν πολὺ χείρων Υ 434. Cf. Δ 400, Κ 238, Ξ 377, Ο 641.—Absol.: χέρεια [τεύχεα] χείρονι δόσκον Ξ 382.—(3) Inferior, of less account, less worthy, serviceable or skilful: οὐ χερείων, οὐ δέμας οὐδὲ φυήν Α 114, ἄλλον Κεβριόναο χερείονα Μ 92. Cf. Ρ 149, Ψ 572, 577: οὔ τι κασιγνήτοιο χερείων θ 585. Cf. ε 211, ξ 176, υ 45, 82, 133, φ 325.—Absol.: χερείονά περ καταπεφνών Ρ 539.—(4) Of things, inferior, less good of their kind, of less account or estimation, worse: χέρεια [τεύχεα] Ξ 382. Cf. Ψ 413.—Impers.: σοί [κ'] αὐτῷ χεῖρον [εἴη] (you would but fare the worse) ο 515.—(5) Bad rather than good. Impers.: οὔ τι χέρειον δεῖπνον ἑλέσθαι (it is no bad thing to . . .) ρ 176, αὐτίκα δ' ἐστὶ δαήμεναι οὔ τι χέρειον (I may as well know it now) ψ 262.—Absol. in neut. pl., what is bad rather than good, bad, evil: ἐπεὶ τὰ χερείονα νικᾷ Α 576 := σ 404.—(6) Morally bad or unfitting. Absol.: ἐσθλά τε καὶ τὰ χέρεια σ 229 = υ 310.

χείσεται, 3 sing. fut. χανδάνω.

χελῑδών, -όνος, ἡ. A swallow: χελιδόνι εἰκέλη αὐδήν (ἄντην) φ 411, χ 240.

χέραδος, τό. Shingle: χέραδος περιχεύας Φ 319.

χερειότερος [double comp. Cf. χερείων. Cf. also χειρότερος]. (1) Less warlike, soldierly or skilful in fight: σέο χερειότερον Β 248.—(2) Having this quality rather than the reverse, of small account in the fight: ὅς τ' ἔξοχος . . . ὅς τε χερειότερος Μ 270.

χερείων. See χείρων.

χέρηϊ, χέρηες. See χείρων.

χερμάδιον, -ου, τό. A boulder or large stone used as a missile: χερμαδίῳ βλῆτο Δ 518. Cf. Ε 302, 582, Λ 265, Μ 154, Ξ 410, Π 774, etc.: κ 121, φ 371.

χερνῆτις, ἡ [app. fr. χείρ]. A handworker: γυνὴ χερνῆτις Μ 433.

χέρνιβον, τό [χείρ + νιπ-, νίζω]. = λέβης (2): χέρνιβον πρόχοόν τ' ἔχουσα Ω 304.

†χερνίπτομαι [χέρνιψ]. 3 pl. aor. χερνίψαντο. To wash one's hands (as a matter of ritual): χερνίψαντο καὶ οὐλοχύτας ἀνέλοντο Α 449.

χέρνιψ, -ιβος, ἡ [χείρ + νιπ-, νίζω]. Water for washing the hands: χέρνιβ' ἀμφίπολος προχόῳ ἐπέχευεν α 136 = δ 52 = η 172 = κ 368 = ο 135 = ρ 91.—Used in ritual γ 440, 445.

χέρσονδε [acc. of next + -δε (1)]. To the land: νεκροὺς ἔκβαλλε [Σκάμανδρος] χέρσονδε (on to his banks) Φ 238.

χέρσος, -ου, ἡ. The dry land, the land: ἐπὶ χέρσου βήτην Ξ 284. Cf. Δ 425, Ξ 394: κύματα κυλινδόμενα ποτὶ χέρσον ι 147. Cf. ζ 95, η 278, ι 486, κ 459, ο 495, τ 278, etc.

χεῦε, 3 sing. aor. χέω.

χεῦμα, τό [χευ-, χέω]. A thin plating or coating: θώρηκα, ᾧ πέρι χεῦμα κασσιτέροιο ἀμφιδεδίνηται Ψ 561.

χέω [χεϝ-]. Aor. χεῦα δ 584. 3 sing. ἔχευε Ε 776, Θ 50, Ι 215, Τ 222, Ω 445: β 395, γ 40, δ 216, ζ 77, λ 245, etc. χεῦε Ι 7, Ρ 270, 619: β 380, γ 289, ε 492, η 15, θ 282, etc. 1 pl. χεύαμεν ω 81. 3 ἔχευαν Γ 270, Δ 269, Ε 618, Ι 174, Ψ 256: α 146, γ 258, 338 μ 338, φ 270. χεῦαν Ξ 436: χ 463. ἔχεαν Σ 347, Ω 799: θ 436. Subj. χεύω β 222. 3 sing. χεύῃ Ξ 165. 1 pl. χεύομεν Η 336. 3 χεύωσι Η 86. Imp. χεῦον β 354. 3 pl. χευάντων δ 214. Nom. pl. masc. pple. χεύαντες Ψ 257, Ω 801: μ 14. Infin. χεῦαι Ψ 45: α 291, λ 75. **Mid.** 3 sing. aor. ἐχεύατο Ε 314, Η 63, χεύατο Σ 24: ω 317. **Pass.** 3 sing. aor. opt. χυθείη τ 590. 3 sing. aor. ἔχυτο χ 88. χύτο Ν 544, Π 414, 580, Υ 282, Ψ 385, Ω 358: η 143. 3 pl. ἔχυντο θ 297, κ 415. χύντο Δ 526, Φ 181. Nom. fem. pple. χυμένη Τ 284: θ 527. 3 sing. pf. κέχυται Μ 284. 3 pl. κέχυνται Ε 141: χ 387. 3 sing. plupf. κέχυτο Β 19, Ε 696, Π 123, 344, Υ 421, Ψ 775: ι 330, ρ 298. 3 pl. ἐκέχυντο τ 539. κέχυντο χ 389. (ἀμφι-, δια-, ἐγ-, ἐκ-, ἐπι-, ἐσ-, κατα-, περι-, περιπρο-, προ-, συγ-, ὑπο-.) (1) To pour (liquid): ὕδωρ ἐπὶ χεῖρας Γ 270, Ι 174, οἶνον ἐκ δεπάων Η 480. Cf. Ι 15 = Π 4, Ξ 436, Σ 347, Ψ 220: α 146, γ 40, δ 214, θ 436, ι 210, υ 260, etc.—In mid.: χοὴν χεῖσθαι κ 518. Cf. λ 26.—In reference to rain: ὅτε λαβρότατον χέει ὕδωρ Ζεύς Π 385.—In reference to the bowels: χύντο χολάδες (gushed forth) Δ 526 = Φ 181.—(2) To shed (tears): δάκρυ χέων Α 357, κατὰ δάκρυ χέουσα 413. Cf. Ζ 405, Η 426, Θ 245, Π 3, etc.: β 24, δ 556, κ 409, λ 183, ξ 280, χ 447, etc.—In pass., of tears, to flow, well forth: χύτο δάκρυα Ψ 385. Cf. δ 523.—(3) To shed or spread (mist) (whether actual mist or in reference to blinding or the mist of death): κατ' ὀφθαλμῶν κέχυτ' ἀχλύς Ε 696, Π 344, Υ 421, ἠέρα Ε 776, Θ 50, Ρ 270. Cf. Υ 321: η 15, ν 189, χ 88.—In reference to dispersing mist, with a word indicating reversal of action: αὐτοῖο πάλιν χύτ' ἀήρ η 143.—(4) To spread (waves) on the surface of the sea: χεῦε κύματα (raised them) γ 289.—In mid., of a ripple, to spread itself: οἵη Ζεφύροιο ἐχεύατο φρίξ Η 63.—(5) In reference to granular substances. (a) To pile or heap up (earth): ἐπὶ σῆμ' ἔχεεν Ζ 419. Cf. Η 86, 336, Ψ 45, 256, 257, Ω 799, 801: α 291, β 222, γ 258, δ 584, λ 75, μ 14, ω 81.—(b) To shed (dust). In mid.: κόνιν χεύατο κὰκ κεφαλῆς Σ 24: ω 317.—(6) In reference to a number of solid or semi-solid objects, or to masses of solid acted upon together, or with a collective sb. (a) To send thick and fast or in a shower, pour: δούρατα Ε 618.—In mid.: βέλεα χέοντο Θ 159 = Ο 590.—Sim. in reference to snow: χέει [χιόνα] Μ 281. Cf. Μ 284.—(b) Generally, to shed, spread, throw, put, place: φύλλα τὰ μέν τ' ἄνεμος χαμάδις χέει (scatters them) Ζ 147, φῦκος [κῦμ'] ἔχευεν (throws it up) Ι 7, ἐπεὶ εἰν ἐλεοῖσιν ἔχευε [κρέα] 215. Cf. Τ 222, Ψ 775: ἐν μοι ἄλφιτα χεῦον δοροῖσιν β 354, χεῦε ῥῶπας καὶ κῶας π 47 (with κῶας by a slight zeugma). Cf. β 380, θ 278, 282, 297, ι 330, λ 588, ο 527, ρ 298, χ 20, 85.—Sim. of reins: καθ' ἡνία χεῦεν ἔραζε (let them drop) Ρ 619.—(7) Of persons or animals (a) In pass., to pour forth, issue forth: νεῶν ἐχέοντο (from the . . .) Τ 356. Cf. Π 267.—(b) In pass., to throw oneself or one's arms (round a person): ἀμφ' αὐτῷ χυμένη Τ 284: θ 527, ὣς ἐμὲ κεῖνοι ἔχυντο κ 415 (the force of ἀμφί in ἀμφιθέουσι 413 being app. carried on to this vb.).—(c) In mid., to throw or place (the arms round a person): ἀμφ' ἑὸν υἱὸν ἐχεύατο πῆχεε E 314.—(d) In pass., to huddle or be huddled together: [ὄϊες] ἐπ' ἀλλήλῃσι κέχυνται E 141. Cf. τ 539, χ 387, 389.—(8) In reference to immaterial or impalpable things, to shed, spread: ἀμφί οἱ θάνατος χύτο N 544, εἴ πως τῷ ὕπνον χεύῃ Ξ 165, νηὸς κάτ' ἀσβέστη κέχυτο φλόξ (enveloped it) Π 123, κατά οἱ κεφαλῆς χέ' ἀϋτμένα (i.e. his breath fell on the other's head) Ψ 765. Cf. B 19, Π 414 = 580, Υ 282, Ω 445: ἀνέμων ἐπ' ἀϋτμένα χεῦεν (sent it abroad) γ 289, κὰκ κεφαλῆς χεῦε κάλλος ψ 156. Cf. β 395, ε 492, η 286, λ 245, 433, μ 338, σ 188, τ 521, 590, υ 54, χ 463.—(9) With σύν (cf. συγχέω). (a) To set at naught, violate (a treaty): ἐπεὶ σύν γ' ὅρκι' ἔχευαν Δ 269.—(b) To confound, trouble, upset (the mind): σὺν γέροντι νόος χύτο Ω 358.

χηλός, -οῦ, ἡ. A chest or coffer Π 221, 228, 254: β 339, θ 424, 438, ν 10, 68, φ 51.

χἠμεῖς, crasis of καὶ ἡμεῖς B 238.

χήν, χηνός, ὁ, ἡ. A goose. (1) In the wild state: χηνῶν ἢ γεράνων B 460 = O 692. Cf. P 460.—(2) Domesticated: χῆνές μοι ἐείκοσι πυρὸν ἔδουσιν τ 536. Cf. ο 161, 174, τ 543, 548, 552.

χηραμός. A cleft or hollow Φ 495.

χήρατο, 3 sing. aor. mid. χαίρω.

χηρεύω [χήρη]. To lack, be without. With genit.: ἀνδρῶν ι 124.

χήρη. Bereft of one's husband, widowed: γυναῖκες B 289. Cf. Z 432, X 484, 499, Ω 725.—With genit.: ἢ τάχα χήρη σεῦ ἔσομαι Z 408.

χηρόω [χήρη]. To make a widow of, widow: γυναῖκα P 36.—To make desolate: ἀγυιάς E 642.

χηρωσταί, οἱ [χηρόω]. App., heirs who in particular circumstances came in to the exclusion of a dead man's surviving father: χηρωσταὶ διὰ κτῆσιν δατέοντο E 158.

χῆτος, τό [χατέω]. Want, lack: χήτεϊ τοιοῦδ' ἀνδρὸς Z 463. Cf. T 324: π 35.

χθαμαλός, -ή, -όν. (1) On the ground: χθαμαλαὶ βεβλήαται εὐναί λ 194.—(2) Little raised above the surrounding level, low: 'Ιθάκη ι 25 (but the application to Ithaca causes difficulty), νῆσος κ 196.—In comp.: τὸν ἕτερον σκόπελον χθαμαλώτερον ὄψει μ 101.—In superl.: ὕπερθε τεῖχος ἐδέδμητο χθαμαλώτατον N 683.

χθιζός [χθές, yesterday]. (1) Of yesterday: χρεῖος N 745.—(2) Constructed with a sb. or pronoun, yesterday: χ. ἔβη A 424, ὅσσα χ. ὑπέσχετ' 'Οδυσσεύς T 141 (really, as in 195 cited below, the day before yesterday). Cf. β 262, ζ 170, μ 451, ω 379.—(3) In neut. χθιζόν as adv., yesterday: ὅσσα χθιζὸν ὑπέστημεν δώσειν T 195 (cf. 141 cited above): χθιζὸν ὑπηοῖον δ 656.—So in neut. pl.: χθιζά τε καὶ πρωΐζ' ὅτε νῆες ἠγερέθοντο B 303 (at the time when, yesterday or the day before, the ships had been gathering, i.e. just after they had assembled).

χθών, χθονός, ἡ. (1) The earth: ἐπὶ χθονὶ δερκομένοιο A 88, χθὼν κονάβιζεν B 465. Cf. B 780, Δ 182, Z 411, Λ 741, Ξ 228, T 362, Ψ 100, etc.: οὔ πω τέθνηκεν ἐπὶ χθονί α 196. Cf. ζ 153, η 67, κ 99, μ 191, τ 408, etc.—(2) The surface of the earth, the earth, the ground: τεύχε' ἀποθέσθαι ἐπὶ χθονί Γ 89. Cf. Γ 217, 265, E 13, Z 213, Ξ 349, etc.: ἐπὶ χθονὶ πῖπτεν ω 535. Cf. γ 453, θ 375, τ 470 (i.e. the floor), χ 86, etc.

χίλιοι, -αι, -α. A thousand: χίλια μέτρα H 471. Cf. Θ 562, Λ 244.

χίμαιρα, ἡ. A she-goat Z 181.

χιτών, -ῶνος, ὁ. (1) A loosely-fitting garment, prob. of linen, worn by men next to the body, a tunic: μαλακόν B 42, χλαῖνάν τ' ἠδὲ χιτῶνα 262. Cf. B 416, Γ 57 (see λάϊνος), E 113, 736, I 490, K 21, etc.: α 437, 439, γ 467, δ 50, ζ 214, θ 441, ν 434, etc.—(2) χ. χάλκεος, app. = θώρηξ N 439.

χιών, -όνος, ἡ. Snow: ὅτε χιὼν ἐπάλυνεν ἀρούρας K 7, νιφάδες χιόνος (snowflakes) M 278. Cf. K 437, X 152: ζ 44, ξ 476, τ 205.

χλαῖνα, -ης, ἡ. (1) An outer garment of wool, app. of the nature of a mantle or cloak, worn by men over the χιτών (app. distinguished from the φᾶρος only by being of a simpler character): ἀπὸ χλαῖναν βάλεν B 183, χλαῖνάν τ' ἠδὲ χιτῶνα 262. Cf. K 133, Π 224, X 493, Ω 163, 230: δ 50, 115, ε 229, ξ 460, ρ 86, τ 225, φ 118, etc.—(2) A cloth or blanket of similar material covering a sleeper: χλαίνας ἐνθέμεναι οὔλας καθύπερθεν ἕσασθαι Ω 646: = δ 299 = η 338. Cf. γ 349, 351, λ 189, ξ 520, τ 318, 337, υ 4, 95, 143, ψ 180.

χλούνης. Of unknown meaning: χλούνην σῦν I 539.

χλωρηΐς [χλωρός]. Epithet of the nightingale. App., of the greenwood: ἀηδών τ 518.

χλωρός, -ή, -όν. An adjective of colour of somewhat indeterminate sense. (1) Applied to what we call green. Still green, freshly cut: ῥῶπας π 47. Cf. ι 320, 379.—(2) To what we call yellow: μέλι Λ 631: κ 234.—(3) In reference to the hue of the countenance, livid, pallid: χλωρὸς (χλωροί) ὑπαὶ δείους K 376, O 4.—Epithet of δέος H 479, Θ 77, P 67: λ 43, 633, μ 243, χ 42, ω 450, 533.

χνόος, -ου, ὁ. A light flaky substance, a scurf of salt left by evaporated sea-water: ἐκ κεφαλῆς ἔσμηχεν ἁλὸς χνόον ζ 226.

χόανος, -ου, ὁ [χέω]. A crucible Σ 470.

χοή, -ῆς, ἡ [χέω]. A libation: χοὴν χεῖσθαι (χεόμην) κ 518, λ 26.

χοῖνιξ, -ικος, ἡ. A dry measure: ὅς κεν ἐμῆς γε χοίνικος ἅπτηται (draws his ration) τ 28.

χοίρεος [χοῖρος]. Of or pertaining to a χοῖρος. Absol. in neut. pl.: ἔσθιε χοίρεα (sc. κρέα) ξ 81 (porker's flesh).

χοῖρος. A young fattened pig, a porker ξ 73.

χολάδες, αἱ. The bowels Δ 526 = Φ 181.

χόλος, -ου, ὁ. (1) Gall: χόλῳ σ' ἔτρεφε μήτηρ Π 203.—(2) Anger, ire, wrath, rage (commonly, but not always, to be distinguished from κότος): χόλος λάβεν A 387, χόλον κ' ἐξακέσαιο Δ 36, μή τι διατρίβειν τὸν ἐμὸν χόλον (i.e. the giving effect to it) Δ 42. Cf. A 81, B 241, Δ 23, Z 326, I 157, 525, 646, O 122, Π 30, P 399, Υ 255, Ω 584, etc.: α 78,

433, γ 145, δ 583, θ 304, λ 554, φ 377, ω 248. —In reference to a lion Σ 322.—To a snake Χ 94.

χολόω [χόλος]. Fut. mid. κεχολώσομαι Ψ 543. 2 sing. κεχολώσεαι Ε 421, 762. 3 κεχολώσεται Α 139, Υ 301: ο 214, ω 544. (**1**) To provoke to anger or wrath, anger, enrage: ἐπεί μ' ἐχολώσατε θ 205. Cf. Α 78, Σ 111: σ 20.—(**2**) In mid. and pass., to be provoked to anger, wrath or indignation, conceive anger, wrath or indignation, be angry, wroth, indignant, enraged: ὁ δέ κεν κεχολώσεται Α 139, θυμῷ κεχολωμένον 217, σὺ μή τι χολωθῇς Ι 33. Cf. Β 195, Γ 413, Δ 391, Ι 523, Π 61, Υ 253, Φ 136, Ω 114, etc.: β 185, η 310, θ 227, ι 480, λ 544, ξ 282, ο 214, σ 25, χ 59, etc. —With dat. of the person against whom one feels anger: βασιλῆϊ χολωθεὶς Α 9. Cf. Β 629, Ε 421, Θ 407, Ο 155, Ρ 710, etc.: ζ 147, θ 276, ο 254, ω 544.—With genit. of the cause: τοῦ ἀποκταμένοιο χολώθη Δ 494. Cf. Δ 501, Λ 703, Ν 203, Ο 68, Φ 146, etc.: ἀνδρῶν μνηστήρων κεχολωμένος (enraged by the memory of their deeds) χ 369. Cf. α 69, μ 348.

χολωτός [χολόω]. Full of, displaying, anger, angry: ἐπέεσσιν Δ 241, Ο 210: χ 26, 225.

χορδή, -ῆς, ἡ. A string of a musical instrument φ 407.

χοροιτυπίη, -ης, ἡ [app. a locative form from χορός + τύπτω]. Beating of the ground in the dance, the dance. In pl.: χοροιτυπίῃσιν ἄριστοι Ω 261.

χορόνδε [acc. of next + -δε (1)]. To the dance: ἔρχεσθαι Γ 393.

χορός, -οῦ, ὁ. (**1**) Dancing, the dance: χοροῖο λήγοντα Γ 394, ἐς χορὸν ἐλθέμεν Ο 508, χορῷ καλή (in the dance) Π 180. Cf. ζ 65, 157.—In pl. in sim. sense: κίθαρίς τε χοροί τε θ 248.—A particular instance: ἐν χορῷ Ἀρτέμιδος Π 183. Cf. σ 194. —A throng or company of dancers: πολλὸς χορὸν περιίσταθ' ὅμιλος Σ 603.—(**2**) A dancing-place: λείηναν χορόν θ 260. Cf. Σ 590: θ 264, μ 4, 318.

χόρτος, -ου, ὁ. An enclosed space: αὐλῆς ἐν χόρτῳ (χόρτοισιν) Λ 774, Ω 640.

†χραισμέω. 3 sing. fut. χραισμήσει Υ 296. Infin. χραισμησέμεν Φ 316. 3 sing. aor. χραίσμησε Π 837. Infin. χραισμῆσαι Λ 120, Σ 62, 443. 3 sing. aor. ἔχραισμε Ξ 66. χραῖσμε Ε 53, Η 144. 3 sing. subj. χραίσμῃ Α 28, Γ 54, Ο 32. χραίσμῃσι Λ 387. 3 pl. χραίσμωσι Α 566. Infin. χραισμεῖν Α 242, 589, Λ 117, Ο 652, Φ 193. (**1**) To ward off, keep off. With dat. of person protected: ὄλεθρόν οἱ Η 144, Υ 296. Cf. Λ 120.—With personal object: μή νύ τοι οὐ χραίσμωσιν ἆσσον [ἔμ'] ἰόντα Α 566. —(**2**) To defend, protect, succour, aid, come to the rescue of. With dat.: μή νύ τοι οὐ χραίσμῃ σκῆπτρον θεοῖο Α 28, οὔ οἱ χραῖσμ' Ἄρτεμις Ε 53. Cf. Γ 54, Λ 117, 387, Ο 32, Π 837, Σ 62 = 443.—(**3**) Absol., to afford succour or protection, come to the rescue: ἐπεὶ τεῖχος οὐκ ἔχραισμεν Ξ 66, οὐκ ἐδύναντο χραισμεῖν Ο 652. Cf. Α 242, 589, Φ 193, 316.

χραύσῃ, 3 sing. aor. subj. χράω².

†χράω¹. Pres. pple. χρείων θ 79. Mid. χρεώμενος Ψ 834. Fut. pple. χρησόμενος, -ου θ 81, κ 492, 565, λ 165, ψ 323. Pf. pple. κεχρημένος, -ου Τ 262: α 13, ξ 124, 155, ρ 347, 421, τ 77, υ 378, χ 50. 3 sing. plupf. κέχρητο γ 266, ξ 421, π 398. (**1**) To give oracular response: ὥς οἱ χρείων μυθήσατ' Ἀπόλλων θ 79.—(**2**) In mid., to consult an oracle: ὅθ' ὑπέρβη λάϊνον οὐδὸν χρησόμενος θ 81.—To consult (a seer). With dat.: ψυχῇ χρησομένους Τειρεσίαο κ 492 = 565. Cf. λ 165, ψ 323.—(**3**) In mid., to make use of something, use it: ἕξει σόλον πέντ' ἐνιαυτοὺς χρεώμενος (having it in use) Ψ 834.—To enjoy the use of, be endowed with, have. With dat.: φρεσὶ κέχρητ' ἀγαθῇσιν γ 266, ξ 421, π 398.—(**4**) In mid., to desire, long for, wish to possess or get, have one's heart set upon, seek, aim at. With genit.: οὐκ εὐνῆς πρόφασιν κεχρημένος [αὐτῆς] Τ 262: νόστου κεχρημένον ἠδὲ γυναικός α 13. Cf. ξ 124, υ 378, χ 50.—(**5**) In mid., to stand in need of, lack. With genit.: ὅτευ κεχρημένος ἔλθοι ρ 421 = τ 77.—Absol., to be in need or want: καὶ μάλα περ κεχρημένος ξ 155.—The pf. pple. in adjectival use, needy: κεχρημένῳ ἀνδρὶ ρ 347.

†χράω² [χραϜ-]. 3 sing. aor. subj. χραύσῃ Ε 138. 3 sing. aor. ἔχραε Φ 369: ε 396, κ 64. 2 pl. ἐχράετε φ 69. (ἐπι-.) To attack, assail, lay hands upon, vex: ὅν τε ποιμὴν χραύσῃ οὐδὲ δαμάσσῃ (*i.e.* wounds him, but not fatally) Ε 138.—With dat.: στυγερὸς οἱ ἔχραε δαίμων ε 396. Cf. κ 64.—With complementary infin.: τίπτε σὸς υἱὸς ἐμὸν ῥόον ἔχραε κήδειν; (to vex it) Φ 369. Cf. φ 69.

χρεῖος, χρέος, τό [χράω¹]. (**1**) App., a consulting of a seer: ἦλθον Τειρεσίαο κατὰ χρέος (to consult him) λ 479.—(**2**) Necessary affairs, business: ἑὸν αὐτοῦ χρεῖος ἐελδόμενος α 409. Cf. β 45.—(**3**) Something that one must pay, a debt: οἷσι χρεῖος ὀφείλετο Λ 686. Cf. Λ 688, 698, Ν 746: γ 367, θ 353, 355, φ 17.

χρειώ, χρεώ, ἡ [χράω¹]. (**1**) Call or demand for the presence, possession, or use of something, need. (**a**) With expressed vb.: εἰ χρειὼ ἐμεῖο γένηται Α 341, τίπτ' ἀλᾶσθε, ὅ τι δὴ χρειὼ τόσον ἵκει; (because of what do you wander, in respect of which such need has come upon you? What is this great need that you wander thus?) Κ 142. Cf. Κ 118, 172, Λ 610: β 28, δ 312, ε 189, ζ 136, ι 136, λ 164.—With acc. of the person affected: οὐδέ τί μιν χρεὼ ἔσται τυμβοχόης Φ 322. Cf. δ 634.—With complementary infin.: ἵν' οὐ χρεώ ἐστιν εὐνὰς βαλέειν ι 136.—(**b**) Without expressed vb.: ἦ τι μάλα χρεώ (it must be some sore need that has brought you) Ι 197.—Without expressed vb. and with acc. of the person affected: μάλα χρεὼ πάντας Ἀχαιοὺς ἐσθλῆς [βουλῆς] (they have much need of it) Ι 75: τίπτε σε χρεώ; (what do you want?) Κ 85, τί σε χρεὼ ἐμεῖο; (what do you want with me?) Λ 606: τίπτε σε χρεώ; (what is your part in all this?) α 225. Cf. Ι 608, Κ 43.—Without expressed vb. and with complementary infin.: διδασκέμεν σε οὔ τι μάλα χρεώ (there is no great need to . . .) Ψ 308.—Without expressed vb. and with acc. of the person affected and complementary infin. : οὐδέ τί μιν χρεὼ νηῶν ἐπιβαινέμεν (why should he . . . ?) δ 707. Cf. ο 201.—(2) Necessity, compulsion : χρειοῖ ἀναγκαίῃ Θ 57.—Without expressed vb. and with acc. of the person affected and complementary infin. : τὸν μάλα χρεὼ ἑστάμεναι κρατερῶς (he needs must . . .) Λ 409. Cf. Σ 406.

χρείων, pres. pple. χράω[1].

χρεμετίζω. Of horses, to neigh M 51.

χρέος. See χρεῖος.

χρεώ. See χρειώ.

χρεώμενος, pres. pple. mid. χράω[1].

χρή [χράω[1]]. (1) There is need of, there needs, one should have or display. With acc. of the person affected and genit. : οὐδέ τί σε χρὴ ταύτης ἀφροσύνης (this is no time for such folly) H 109 : ὅττεό σε χρή (what your business is) α 124, τί με χρὴ μητέρος αἴνου; (i.e. she needs no praise from me) φ 110, ὄφρ' ἂν πονήσομαι ὅττεό με χρή (do my work) χ 377. Cf. γ 14, δ 463.—(2) It is necessary or needful, one needs must. (a) With acc. and infin. : τί σε χρὴ ταῦτα λέγεσθαι; (why do so ?) N 275 : ἐμὲ χρὴ γήραϊ πείθεσθαι Ψ 644. Cf. A 216, T 228, X 268 : ζ 190, κ 490, ξ 364, ψ 250, ω 407.—(b) With acc. alone : οὐδέ τί σε χρή (there is no need) τ 500.—(c) With infin. alone: νῦν δὲ χρὴ τετλάμεν ἔμπης γ 209.—(3) It befits, it is fitting or proper, it behoves, one ought. (a) With acc. and infin. : οὐ χρὴ εὕδειν βουληφόρον ἄνδρα B 24 = 61, χρή σε φάσθαι ἔπος I 100. Cf. H 331, I 496, 613, K 479, M 315, N 463, Π 492, T 67, 149, Ψ 478 : α 296, β 369, δ 492, ζ 27, κ 380, μ 154, ο 393, ρ 417, σ 17, τ 118.—(b) With acc. alone : οὐδέ τί σε χρή Π 721, T 420, Υ 133. Cf. ι 50.—(c) With infin. alone : χρὴ ἐμὸν θέμεναι πόνον οὐκ ἀτέλεστον Δ 57. Cf. E 490, I 309, 627, N 235, Π 631 : ζ 207, ο 74, τ 4, ω 324.

χρηΐζω [χράω[1]]. (1) To be in need or want : οὕτω χρηΐζοντι λ 340.—(2) To stand in need of, need, want. With genit. : ἰητῆρος Λ 835 : ὅττευ χρηΐζων ἱκόμην Λακεδαίμονα (what had brought me there) ρ 121. Cf. ρ 558.

χρῆμα, -ατος, τό [χράω[1]]. In pl., possessions, goods, effects, property : χρήματ' ἀπαιτίζοντες β 78, πῇ χρήματα φέρω τάδε; ν 203. Cf. β 203, ξ 286, ο 230, π 315, τ 284, etc.

χρησόμενος, fut. pple. mid. χράω[1].

†χρίμπτω. Aor. pple. pass. χριμφθείς. (ἐγ-.) In pass., to approach, draw near : χριμφθεὶς πέλας κ 516.

χρίω. (ἐπι-.) (1) To rub, anoint : χρῖεν ἐλαίῳ Ψ 186. Cf. Π 670, 680, Ω 587 : γ 466, δ 252, θ 364, τ 320, ψ 154, etc. — Of rubbing arrows with poison. In mid. : ἰοὺς χρίεσθαι α 262.—(2) In mid., to rub or anoint oneself : χρισάμεναι ἐλαίῳ ζ 96. Cf. ζ 220, σ 194.

χροΐ, χρόα, dat. and acc. χρώς.

χροιή, -ῆς, ἡ [χρώς]. One's flesh, body, person (= χρώς (2)) : παραδραθέειν φιλότητι ἧ χροιῇ Ξ 164.

χρόμαδος, ὁ. A grinding sound Ψ 688.

χρόνιος [χρόνος]. After a long time : υἱὸν ἐλθόντα χρόνιον (long expected) ρ 112.

χρόνος, -ου, ὁ. A space of time : ἐπὶ χρόνον (for a time) B 299, πολὺν χρόνον (for a long time, long) 343, Γ 157, M 9, τόσσον χρόνον ὅσσον . . . (for such time as . . .) Ω 670. Cf. Ξ 206 = 305, T 157, Ψ 418 : χρόνον μ' ἐνθάδ' ἐρύκεις δ 599 (= πολὺν χρόνον 594), μεῖναι χρόνον (for a time) ζ 295, ι 138, ἐπὶ χρόνον (to last us long) ξ 193. Cf. β 115, μ 407, τ 169, 221, etc.—The space of time allotted in thought to the happening of something : ἀπολέσθαι ἕνα χρόνον (i.e. once for all) O 511.

χροός, genit. χρώς.

χρυσάμπυξ, -υκος [χρυσός + ἄμπυξ]. With frontlet of gold. Of horses E 358, 363, 720 = Θ 382.

χρυσάορος [χρυσός + ἄορ]. With sword of gold. Epithet of Apollo E 509, O 256.

χρύσειος, -η, -ον [χρυσός]. (Cf. next.) (1) Of gold, golden : ἥλοισιν A 246, σειρήν (made of strands of gold wire) Θ 19. Cf. Γ 248, Δ 133, E 730, 744, Θ 69, M 297, etc. : α 137, 142, γ 41, ε 62, κ 355, σ 294, etc.—In reference to the hue of a cloud Ξ 351.—Epithet of Aphrodite I 389.—(2) Studded, ornamented or fitted with gold : λέπαδνα E 731, ἱμάσθλην (app., with handle of gold) Θ 44. Cf. Ω 21, etc. : α 97, ε 232, etc.

χρύσεος, -η, -ον [χρυσός]. (Cf. prec. Often with synizesis of the second and third syllables.) (1) Of gold, golden : δαπέδῳ Δ 2, δεπάεσσιν 3, περόνῃ E 425. Cf. Δ 111, E 724, Z 320, I 670, Σ 375, Ψ 92, etc. : γ 472, δ 131, ζ 79, θ 431, ο 460, etc.—In reference to the hue of clouds N 523, Ξ 344, Σ 206.—Epithet of Aphrodite Γ 64, E 427, T 282, X 470, Ω 699 : δ 14, θ 337, 342, ρ 37 = τ 54.—(2) Studded, ornamented or fitted with gold : σκήπτρῳ A 15. Cf. E 727, Z 236, Λ 31, etc. : λ 91, 610, etc.

χρυσηλάκατος, -ον [χρυσός + ἠλακάτη in sense 'bow']. With bow of gold. Epithet or a name of Artemis Π 183, Υ 70 : δ 122.

χρυσήνιος, -ον [χρυσός + ἡνία]. With reins of gold. Epithet of Artemis Z 205.—Of Ares θ 285.

χρυσόθρονος, -ον [χρυσός + θρόνος]. Golden-seated. Epithet of Here A 611, Ξ 153, O 5.—Of Artemis I 533 : ε 123.—Of the dawn κ 541, ξ 502, ο 250, τ 319, χ 198, etc.

χρυσοπέδιλος, -ον [χρυσός + πέδιλα]. With sandals of gold. Epithet of Here λ 604.

χρυσόπτερος, -ον [χρυσός + πτερόν]. With wings of gold. Epithet of Iris Θ 398 = Λ 185.

χρυσόρραπις [χρυσός + ῥαπίς = ῥάβδος]. With wand of gold. Epithet of Hermes ε 87, κ 277, 331.

χρυσός, -οῦ, ὁ. (1) Gold : δέκα χρυσοῖο τάλαντα I 122, χρυσὸν περιχεύας (gold foil) K 294. Cf. B 229, Z 48, I 126, Λ 25, P 52, Σ 574, etc. : ὅθι νητὸς χρυσὸς ἔκειτο β 338. Cf. α 165, γ 301, δ 73, ε 38, κ 35, ν 218, etc.—(2) Applied collectively to things made of gold. (a) To golden articles or ornaments : χρυσὸν δεδεγμένος, ἀγλαὰ δῶρα Λ 124. Cf. B 872, etc. : γ 274, ο 448, etc.—(b) To golden armour : χρυσὸν ἔδυνεν Θ 43 = N 25.

χρῡσοχόος, ὁ [χρυσός + χέω. Cf. περιχέω (2)]. One who applies gold as a covering or adornment, a goldsmith γ 425.

χρώς, ὁ. Genit. χρωτός K 575. χροός Δ 130, E 337, Λ 398, N 440, etc. : ζ 220. Dat. χροΐ H 207, Θ 43, M 464, N 241, etc. : δ 750, ζ 61, λ 191, ο 60, etc. Acc. χρῶτα σ 172, 179. χρόα Δ 139, E 354, Λ 352, N 553, etc. : β 376, δ 749, ε 455, ζ 224, etc. (1) The flesh of the body : ἀκρότατον ὀϊστὸς ἐπέγραψε χρόα Δ 139, οὔ σφι λίθος χρὼς [ἐστιν] 510, οὔ πῃ χρὼς (v.l. χροὸς) εἴσατο N 191 (see εἴδω (II) (1), ἵημι² (5)). Cf. E 337, Θ 298, Λ 437, M 427, N 574, etc. : ε 455, ν 398, 430, π 145, τ 204.—(2) One's flesh, body, person : χρυσὸν ἔδυνε περὶ χροΐ Θ 43, ἀπὸ χροὸς λύματα κάθηρεν Ξ 170. Cf. Δ 130, K 575, Λ 398, N 640, P 210, etc. : ὡς ἂν μὴ χρό' ἰάπτῃ β 376. Cf. δ 750, ζ 129, λ 191, π 182, τ 232, etc.—(3) In reference to the outward appearance or hue of the flesh, i.e. to the complexion : μελαίνετο χρόα E 354. Cf. N 279, 284, P 733 : λ 529, φ 412.

χυθείη, 3 sing. aor. opt. pass. χέω.

χυμένη, nom. fem. aor. pple. pass. χέω.

χύντο, 3 pl. aor. pass. χέω.

χύσις, ἡ [χυ-, χέω]. A collection, mass or heap of scattered objects : φύλλων χύσις (χύσιν) ε 483, 487, τ 443.

χυτλόω [χυ-, χέω]. In mid., to anoint oneself : ἧος χυτλώσαιτο ζ 80.

χύτο, 3 sing. aor. pass. χέω.

χυτός, -ή, -όν [χυ-, χέω]. Piled or heaped up (cf. χέω (5)) : γαῖα Z 464, Ξ 114. Cf. Ψ 256 : γ 258.

χωλεύω [χωλός]. To walk lame, halt, limp. Of Hephaestus Σ 411 = Υ 37, Σ 417.

χωλός, -ή, -όν. Lame, halt : χωλὸς ἕτερον πόδα (lame of one foot) B 217.—Of Hephaestus Σ 397 : θ 308, 332.—Of the Λιταί I 503.

χώομαι. 3 sing. aor. ἐχώσατο A 64, Π 616 : ε 284. χώσατο Θ 397, N 165, Ξ 406, X 291. 3 sing. subj. χώσεται A 80. Pple. χωσάμενος Φ 212. Fem. χωσαμένη Γ 414, I 534. (περι-.) To be angry, wroth or indignant, conceive anger, wrath or indignation : χωόμενος κῆρ (with wrath in his heart) A 44, ὅ τι τόσσον ἐχώσατο 64. Cf. A 46, B 782, Γ 414, Θ 397, Ξ 260, Π 616, etc. : β 80, ε 284, θ 238, λ 103 = ν 343, μ 376.—In reference to self-anger : χωόμενος ὅ τε . . . A 244.—With dat. of the person against whom one feels anger : ἀνδρὶ χέρηϊ A 80. Cf. I 555, Φ 306, 413, Ω 606 : ε 215, ψ 213.—With genit. of the cause : χωόμενος ἐϋζώνοιο γυναικός A 429. Cf. B 689, N 165, 662, Π 553, Υ 29, Φ 457, Ψ 37.—With the cause in acc. : μή μοι τόδε χώεο ε 215, ψ 213.

χωρέω [χῶρος]. (ἀνα-, ὑπο-.) To withdraw, retire, give way : χώρησαν δ' ὑπὸ πρόμαχοι Δ 505 = Π 588 = P 316, χώρησε τυτθὸν ἐπάλξιος (from the . . .) M 406, οὐδ' ἂν Ἀχιλλῆϊ χωρήσειεν (give way to him, retire before him) N 324. Cf. N 724, O 655, Π 592, 629, P 101, 533, Σ 244.

χώρη, -ης, ἡ [cf. χῶρος]. (1) A place or spot : στρέψεσθ' ἐκ χώρης ὅθι . . . Z 516 : θῆκ' αὐτῇ ἐνὶ χώρῃ (in the place from which he had taken it) φ 366. Cf. ψ 186.—The place occupied by one, one's place : στρεφθεὶς ἐκ χώρης π 352. Cf. Ψ 349. —(2) A land, country, region : ἅς τινας ἵκεο χώρας ἀνθρώπων θ 573.—(3) A space or extent of ground : ὀλίγῃ ἐνὶ χώρῃ P 394.—Space, extent of ground : χώρης ὀλίγην μοῖραν Π 68. Cf. Ψ 521.

χωρίς. (1) Separately, apart, so as to be divided or parted from others: ἔρχατο, χ. μὲν πρόγονοι, χ. δὲ μέτασσαι, χ. δ' αὖθ' ἕρσαι ι 221. Cf. ω 78.—(2) Separately, so as not to be in common or shared with others or another : χ. Ἀτρεΐδης δῶκε μέθυ H 470. Cf. δ 130.—(3) Separately, besides : χ. [δῶκα] γυναῖκας ω 278.

χῶρος, -ου, ὁ [cf. χώρη]. (1) A place or spot : ἐς χῶρον ἕνα ξυνιόντες ἵκοντο Δ 446 = Θ 60, χῶρον, ὅθ' ἕστασαν ἵπποι K 520. Cf. N 473, P 54, Φ 262, Ψ 138 : α 426, ε 442, η 123, ι 181, λ 22, φ 142, etc.—(2) A space or extent of ground : ὅθι νεκύων διεφαίνετο χῶρος Θ 491 = K 199. Cf. K 161, M 423. —A space, place, region : κάλυψε (βάθυνε) χῶρον ἅπαντα Ψ 189, 421.—A space set apart for some purpose : χῶρον διεμέτρεον Γ 315. Cf. Γ 344.—(3) A tract of country, a region : χῶρον ἀν' ὑλήεντα K 362 : ξ 2.—A land, country, region : χώρου ἄϊδρις ἐών κ 282. Cf. λ 94.

χώσατο, 3 sing. aor. χώομαι.

ψάμαθος, -ου, ἡ [cf. ἄμαθος and next]. (1) Sand : ὡς ὅτε τις ψάμαθον πάϊς [ἐρείπῃ] (a 'sand-castle') O 362 : ψαμάθῳ εἰλυμένα ξ 136.—In pl. in sim. sense : αὐτόν μιν εἰλύσω ψαμάθοισιν Φ 319. Cf. H 462, M 31.—(2) Sand as commonly occurring by the sea or by rivers, the sand, the sands : ἐπὶ ψαμάθῳ ἔθεσαν ν 119.—In pl. : νῆα ἔρυσσαν ἐπὶ ψαμάθοις A 486. Cf. Φ 202, Ψ 15, 853 : γ 38, δ 426, 438, 539, ι 546 = μ 5, ν 284, χ 387.—The particles considered separately with reference to their number : ὅσα ψάμαθός τε κόνις τε I 385.—In pl. : ψαμάθοισιν [ἐοικότες] B 800.

ψάμμος, -ου, ἡ [cf. prec.]. = prec. (1) : γαῖα ψάμμῳ κυανέῃ μ 243.

ψάρ, ψήρ. A starling Π 583, P 755.

ψαύω. (ἐπι-.) (1) To be so close together as to touch, to touch : ψαῦον κόρυθες φάλοισιν N 132 = Π 216.—(2) To come into contact with, bring something into contact with, touch. With genit. : ψαύουσιν ἐπισσώτρου τρίχες Ψ 519, ὁππότερός κε ψαύσῃ ἐνδίνων 806.

ψεδνός, -ή, -όν. Sparse, scanty, thin : λάχνη B 219.

ψευδάγγελος, -ον [ψεῦδος + ἄγγελος]. Falsifying one's message O 159.

ψευδής [ψεύδομαι]. Breaking one's troth. Absol., one guilty of doing this : οὐκ ἐπὶ ψευδέσσι Ζεὺς ἔσσετ' ἀρωγός Δ 235 (v.l. ψεύδεσσιν ; see ψεῦδος (1)).

ψεύδομαι. Fut. ψεύσομαι K 534 : δ 140. Nom. pl. aor. pple. ψευσάμενοι H 352. Nom. sing. fem. ψευσαμένη Z 163. (1) To speak falsely, lie, use deceit : κομιδῆς κεχρημένοι ψεύδονται ξ 125. Cf.

Ζ 163 : ξ 365.—(2) To break (a treaty): ὅρκια ψευσάμενοι Η 352.—(3) To make an inaccurate or incorrect statement, speak erroneously, be wrong in what one says: ψεύσομαι, ἦ ἔτυμον ἐρέω; Κ 534: =δ 140. Cf. Δ 404, Ε 635.

ψεῦδος, τό [ψεύδομαι]. (1) A falsehood, lie, piece of deceit: ψ. κεν φαῖμεν Β 81 = Ω 222, γνώμεναι εἴ τε ψ. ὑπόσχεσις (whether he promised only to deceive) Β 349. Cf. Φ 276: γ 20=328, λ 366, ξ 296, 387, τ 203.—In pl., sharp practice: ψεύδεσσι βιησάμενος Ψ 576.—An oath-breaking (cf. ψεύδομαι (2)). In pl.: ψεύδεσσιν ἀρωγός (an abettor in oath-breaking) Δ 235 (v.l. ψευδέσσιν; see ψευδής).—(2) An inaccurate, incorrect or erroneous statement: οὔ τι ψ. ἐμὰς ἄτας κατέλεξας (all you have said is but the truth) Ι 115.

ψεύσομαι, fut. ψεύδομαι.

ψευστέω [ψεύστης]. =ψεύδομαι (3): ψευστήσεις (the event will falsify your boast) Τ 107.

ψεύστης, ὁ [ψευσ-, ψεύδομαι]. A liar: ψεῦσταί τ' ὀρχησταί τε Ω 261.

†ψηλαφάω. Pres. pple. ψηλαφόων. To feel or grope about: χερσὶ ψηλαφόων ι 416.

ψήρ. See ψάρ.

ψηφίς, -ῖδος, ἡ. A pebble Φ 260.

ψιάς, -άδος, ἡ. A drop Π 459.

ψιλός, -ή, -όν. Bare: ἄροσιν (freed from trees or other encumbrances, cleared) Ι 580: νῆα ψιλὴν φέρε κῦμα (her timbers gone) μ 421, δέρμα (stripped of the hair) ν 437.

ψολόεις, -εντος [ψόλος, smoke]. Accompanied by smoke, smoky: κεραυνῷ ψ 330. Cf. ω 539.

ψύξᾱσα, aor. pple. fem. ψύχω.

ψῡχή, -ῆς, ἡ. (1) The animating principle, the vital spirit, the soul, the life, life, one's life (cf. θυμός (I) (1) (b)): λύθη ψυχή τε μένος τε Ε 296 =Θ 123=315. Cf. Λ 334, Φ 569, Χ 257, 325, 338, 467, Ψ 104, Ω 754: κεκαδήσει θυμοῦ καὶ ψυχῆς φ 154, 171. Cf. ι 523.—In pl. in reference to a number of persons: ψυχὰς ὀλέσαντες Ν 763=Ω 168. Cf. χ 444.—(2) Animate existence viewed as a possession, one's life: ἐμὴν ψυχὴν παραβαλλόμενος Ι 322, ψυχῆς ἀντάξιον 401: ψυχὰς παρθέμενοι γ 74 =ι 255. —(3) Animate existence viewed with regard to its duration, one's life or continued existence: περὶ ψυχῆς θέον Ἕκτορος Χ 161: ἀρνύμενος ἥν ψυχήν α 5, ὥς τε περὶ ψυχῆς ι 423.—In pl. in reference to a number of persons: ὅσσοι περὶ ψυχέων ἐμάχοντο χ 245.—(4) The spirit or soul thought of as distinct from the body and as leaving it at death (cf. θυμός (I) (1) (c)): πολλὰς ψυχὰς Ἄϊδι προΐαψεν Α 3, τὸν δὲ λίπε ψυχή Ε 696, ψυχὴ πάλιν ἐλθεῖν οὐ λεϊστή Ι 408. Cf. Ε 654= Λ 445, Η 330, Ξ 518, Π 453, 505, 625, 856= Χ 362: ψυχὴ ἀποπταμένη πεπότηται λ 222. Cf. κ 560=λ 65, ξ 134, 426 (of a pig), σ 91.—(5) A disembodied spirit, a shade: ψυχὴ Πατροκλῆος Ψ 65, ψυχαί, εἴδωλα καμόντων 72. Cf. Ψ 100, 106, 221: ψυχῇ (ψυχή) Τειρεσίαο κ 492=565, λ 90, 165, ψ 251, 323. Cf. κ 530, λ 37, 51, 84, 141, 150, 205, 385, 387, 467, 471, 538, 541, 543, 564, 567, ω 1, 14, 15, 20, 23, 35=191, 100, 102, 105, 120.

ψῦχος, τό [ψύχω]. Coolness κ 555.

ψυχρός, -ή, -όν [ψύχω]. Cold: νιφάδες Τ 358. Cf. Ο 171, Χ 152: αὔρη ε 469. Cf. ι 392, ξ 477, ρ 209, τ 388.—Of the bronze of a weapon: ψυχρὸν ἕλε χαλκὸν ὀδοῦσιν Ε 75.

†ψῡ́χω. Aor. pple. fem. ψύξᾱσα. (ἀνα-, ἀπο-.) To breathe, blow: ἦκα ψύξασα Υ 440.

ψωμός, -οῦ, ὁ. A bit or gobbet ι 374.

ὦ, ὤ, int. O! Oh! With voc. Α 74, 158, 442, Β 79, 235, 796, etc.: α 45, β 40, γ 43, 79, δ 26, etc.—ὤ μοι, ay me! Α 149, Δ 370, Η 96, etc.: ε 408, λ 216, ν 168, etc.—ὤ μοι Ὀδυσῆος υ 209 (ay me for . . . !).—So ὤ μοι ἐγώ Λ 404, etc.: ε 299, etc.—ὤ μοι ἐγὼ σέο τ 363.—For ὢ (ὤ) πόποι see πόποι.

ὧδε. (1) In this way or manner, thus, so (often (and properly) referring to what concerns the speaker; cf. οὕτως): ἀπειλήσω τοι ὧδε Α 181, εἰ ἐριδαίνετον ὧδε 574, οὐ τότε γ' ὧδ' Ὀδυσῆος ἀγασσάμεθ' εἶδος (as much as before) Γ 224, ὧδε γὰρ ἔβρισαν (so heavily do they bear upon us) Μ 346 (or this might come under (3)). Cf. Α 212, Β 258, 271, 802, Δ 176, 308, etc.: ὧδ' ἔρξαι ε 342, ἥμενος ὧδε (sitting here quietly) σ 224, ὅρχους δέ μοι ὧδ' ὀνόμηνας δώσειν (in the same way, similarly) ω 341. Cf. α 236, β 28, 111, δ 159, ι 403, μ 217, etc.—(2) With imp., as you are, as I tell you, without more ado, straightway, at once: ὧδ' ἐπ' ἀριστέρ' ἔχε στρατοῦ Ν 326.—Sim.: οὕνεκά σ' οὐ τὸ πρῶτον, ἐπεὶ ἴδον, ὧδ' ἀγάπησα (at once) ψ 214.—(3) Hither: αἲ γὰρ ὧδ' ἄφαρ ἐλασαίαθ' ἵππους Κ 537, πρόμολ' ὧδε Σ 392: ὧδε κατήλυθον α 182. Cf. ρ 544, φ 196.—(4) Qualifying an adj., pple. or adv., thus, so: ἀθρόοι ὧδ' ἴομεν (keeping together as we are) Β 439, ὧδ' ἀΐδηλος Ε 897. Cf. Ζ 478, Φ 358, etc.: ὧδε ἐοικότα γ 125, ὧδ' ἐκπάγλως ε 339. Cf. γ 376, δ 141, ζ 25, ξ 139, τ 350, etc.—(5) Correlative with ὡς: ὧδε . . . ὡς . . ., in like manner . . . as . . . Γ 300, etc.: γ 221, etc.

ᾤδεε, 3 sing. impf. οἰδέω.

ὠδίνω [ὠδίς]. (1) To suffer pain, be in agony: στενάχων τε καὶ ὠδίνων ὀδύνῃσιν (in agony of anguish) ι 415.—(2) To suffer the pains of childbirth: ὠδίνουσαν γυναῖκα (in labour) Λ 269.

ὠδίς, -ῖνος, ἡ. In pl., pains, pangs: Εἰλείθυιαι πικρὰς ὠδῖνας ἔχουσαι Λ 271.

ὠδύσατο, 3 sing. aor. ὀδύσσομαι.

ὠθέω [Ϝοθ-]. 3 sing. pa. iterative ὤθεσκε λ 596. ὤσασκε λ 599. Aor. ὦσα ι 488. 2 sing. ὦσας Φ 398. 3 ἔωσε Π 410. ὦσε Α 220, Β 744, Ε 19, Λ 143, Ν 193, Π 863, Ρ 618, Υ 461, Φ 235, etc.: χ 20. 3 pl. ὦσαν Δ 535, Ε 626, Θ 336, Ν 148, Π 569, Ρ 274. 3 sing. subj. ὤσῃ Ν 138. 1 pl. opt. ὤσαιμεν Π 45. Infin. ὦσαι Ν 688. **Mid.** 3 sing. aor. ὤσατο Ζ 62. 1 pl. ὠσάμεθα Θ 295. 3 ὤσαντο Π 592. 3 sing. opt. ὤσαιτο Ε 691, Π 655. 2 pl. ὤσαισθε Λ 803. Infin. ὤσασθαι Μ 420, Ο 418. (ἀν-, ἀπ-, δι-.) (1) To thrust, push, force, shove: ἐς κουλεὸν ξίφος Α 220, ὦσε δ' ἀπὸ ῥινὸν λίθος (forced it aside) Ε 308, ὦσε νεκρούς (i.e. cleared his stream of them) Φ 235. Cf. Ν 138, Ξ 494, Ο 668 (dispersed it), Ρ 618: γ 295, λ 596, 599, χ 20.—Of pushing an object by force applied from a position upon it: ὦσα [νῆα] παρέξ ι 488.—To thrust (a spear) Φ 398.—With personal object: ὅτε Φῆρας ἐκ Πηλίου ὦσεν Β 744, Ἕκτορα Ζεὺς ὦσεν ὄπισθε χειρί (pushed him forwards) Ο 694. Cf. Ε 19, Π 410, 863, Λ 143, 320, Υ 461, 489.—In mid. with such an object, to thrust back, repulse (a suppliant): ἀπὸ ἕθεν ὤσατ' Ἄδρηστον Ζ 62.—(2) To thrust or force back (a foe), cause (him) to give way or retreat: μέγαν ἑ ἐόντα [Ἕκτορ'] ὦσαν ἀπὸ σφείων Δ 535 = Ε 626 = Ν 148, ἰθὺς τάφροιο ὦσαν Ἀχαιούς Θ 336. Cf. Ν 193, 688, Π 45, 569 = Ρ 274, Φ 241.—In mid.: ὄφρ' ὤσαιτ' Ἀργείους Ε 691. Cf. Θ 295, Λ 803, Μ 420, Ο 418, Π 592, 655.—(3) To pull, draw: ἐκ οἱ μηροῦ δόρυ ὦσεν Ε 694. Cf. Ε 854.—With personal object: Σθένελον ἀφ' ἵππων ὦσε χείρ' ἐρύσασα Ε 835.

ὠΐγνυντο, 3 pl. impf. pass. οἴγνυμι.

ὠΐετο, 3 sing. impf. ὀΐομαι.

ὤϊξε, 3 sing. aor. οἴγνυμι.

ὠΐσθην, aor. ὀΐομαι.

ὦκα [ὠκύς]. (1) With speed, swiftly: ὦκα διέπρησσον πεδίοιο Β 785 = Γ 14. Cf. Ε 88, Ν 671 = Π 606, Φ 261, Ψ 364: ὦκα μεγάροιο διελθέμεν ζ 304. Cf. γ 157, 176, δ 586 = ρ 149, ο 182, 472, 555, ω 413.—(2) In short space, soon, before long, quickly, speedily, shortly: οὐδέ κέ μ' ὦκα τέλος θανάτοιο κιχείη Ι 416. Cf. Ε 903, Κ 350, Ξ 418, Ρ 190, etc.: μάλα δ' ὦκα δόμους ἵκανεν ἄνακτος ρ 255. Cf. μ 427, ξ 352, υ 27, φ 50, etc.—(3) Without delay or loss of time, with all speed, at once, forthwith, straightway: ὦχ' ἑκατόγχειρον καλέσασα Α 402. Cf. Α 447, Β 26, 52, Η 337, 417, Λ 354, etc.: ὦκ' ἐνήσομεν πόντῳ β 295. Cf. β 8, ζ 289, κ 178, ξ 33, σ 39, etc.

ὠκύαλος, -ον [app. a lengthened form of ὠκύς]. Swift. Epithet of ships Ο 705: μ 182, ο 473.

ὠκύμορος [ὠκύς + μόρος]. (1) On whom fate is coming swiftly, doomed to an early death, short-lived: ὠκύμορος καὶ ὀϊζυρός Α 417. Cf. Σ 95, 458: α 266 = δ 346 = ρ 137.—In superl.: ὠκυμορώτατος ἄλλων Α 505.—(2) Carrying swift death. Epithet of arrows Ο 441: χ 75.

ὠκυπέτης [ὠκύς + πέτομαι]. Swift-flying, swift-speeding: ἵππω Θ 42 = Ν 24.

ὠκύπορος, -ον [ὠκύς + -πορος, πείρω]. Swiftly cleaving (the seas), swift-sailing. Epithet of ships Α 421, Β 351, Κ 308, Μ 156, etc.: δ 708, ε 176, ξ 230.

ὠκύπους, -ποδος [ὠκύς + πούς]. Dat. pl. ὠκυπόδεσσι Β 383, Ψ 504. Swift-footed. Epithet of horses Β 383, Ε 296, 732, Κ 535, etc.: ψ 245.—Applied to ἵπποι in sense 'chariot' (see ἵππος (3)) Θ 129: σ 263.

ὠκύπτερος [ὠκύς + πτερόν]. Swift-winged. Epithet of the falcon: ἴρηξ Ν 62.

ὠκύροος [ὠκύς + ῥέω]. Swift-flowing: ποταμῷ Ε 598. Cf. Η 133.

ὠκύς, [-εῖα], -ύ. Nom. sing. fem. always in form ὠκέα Β 786, Ε 368, Θ 425, Λ 195, etc.: μ 374. Superl. ὠκύτατος θ 331. ὤκιστος Ο 238, Φ 253, Χ 325: χ 77, 133. (1) Quick in movement, nimble, swift, fleet (often a merely conventional epithet): ὀϊστόν Ε 395, ἴρηκι Ο 238. Cf. Ε 106, Λ 397, Π 583, etc.: τῶν νέες ὠκεῖαι ὡς εἰ πτερόν η 36. Cf. ζ 104, μ 374, φ 138, 416, etc.—Absol.: κιχάνει βραδὺς ὠκύν θ 329.—In superl.: ὤκιστος πετεηνῶν Ο 238, Φ 253. Cf. θ 331.—Of immaterial things: ὠκὺς θυμὸς πτάτο (flew swiftly) Ψ 880.—In superl.: ὤκιστος ὄλεθρος Χ 325.—Epithet of horses Γ 263, Δ 500, Ε 257, Η 240, etc.: γ 478, 496, δ 28.—Applied to ἵπποι in sense 'chariot' (see ἵππος (3)) Η 15.—Of ships Θ 197: η 34, ι 101.—Epithet of Achilles Τ 295, Φ 211, Χ 188, etc.—Of Iris Β 786, Ε 368, Λ 195, etc.—For πόδας ὠκύς (ὠκέα) see πούς (3).—(2) In neut. pl. superl. ὤκιστα as adv., very soon, speedily, at once: εἴ κε βοὴ ὤκιστα γένοιτο χ 77. Cf. χ 133.

ὤλεσα, aor. ὄλλυμι.

ὠλεσίκαρπος, -ον [ὠλεσ-, ὄλλυμι + καρπός[1]]. Shedding its fruit early: ἰτέαι κ 510.

ὤλετο, 3 sing. aor. mid. ὄλλυμι.

ὦλξ [Ϝελκ-, (Ϝ)έλκω]. Only in acc. ὦλκα. A furrow: ἱεμένω κατὰ ὦλκα Ν 707. Cf. σ 375.

ὠμηστής [ὠμός + ἔδω]. Eating raw flesh, preying on carrion: οἰωνοί Λ 454, κύνες Χ 67, ἰχθύσιν Ω 82.—Applied to a human being: ὠμηστὴς ἀνὴρ ὅ γε Ω 207.

ὡμίλευν, 3 pl. impf. ὁμιλέω.

ὠμογέρων, -οντος [ὠμός in sense 'unripe' + γέρων]. In green or lusty old age Ψ 791.

ὠμοθετέω [ὠμός + θε-, τίθημι]. In sacrificing, to lay slices of raw flesh on the fat enclosing the sacrificial joints: ἐπ' αὐτῶν (i.e. on the joints so enclosed) ὠμοθέτησαν Α 461 = Β 424: = γ 458 = μ 361.—In mid.: ὠμοθετεῖτο συβώτης ἐς πίονα δημόν ξ 427.

ὠμός. (1) Uncooked, raw: ὠμὰ κρέα ἔδμεναι Χ 347: κρέ' ὀπταλέα τε καὶ ὠμά μ 396.—So εἰ ὠμὸν βεβρώθοις Πρίαμον Δ 35.—Fig.: ἐν ὠμῷ γήραϊ θῆκεν (premature) ο 357.—(2) Raw, with the skin stripped off, excoriated, bloody: ὅς κε μήδε' ἐξερύσας δώῃ κυσὶν ὠμὰ δάσασθαι σ 87. Cf. χ 476.—In neut. pl. as adv. (though in sense qualifying rather the object than the vb.): Ἕκτορα δώσειν κυσὶν ὠμὰ δάσασθαι Ψ 21.

ὦμος, -ου, ὁ. (1) One of the shoulders, one's shoulder; in dual and pl., the shoulders, one's shoulders: τόξ' ὤμοισιν ἔχων Α 45, τώ οἱ ὤμω κυρτώ Β 217, δι' ὤμου ἔγχος ἦλθεν Δ 481. Cf. Α 46, Γ 17, Ε 7, 46, 622, Η 16, Λ 593, etc.: β 3, δ 245, ζ 219, θ 416, 528, κ 170, 262, 362, etc.—Of animals. Of horses Ζ 510 = Ο 267, Π 468.—Of a wild boar τ 452.—(2) Regarded as a seat of strength: ἐν βίην ὤμοισιν ἔθηκεν Ρ 569.

ὤμοσα, aor. ὄμνυμι.

ὠμοφάγος [ὠμός + φάγον]. Eating, preying upon, raw flesh, ravening: λείουσιν Ε 782, Η 256, Ο 592, θῶες Λ 479, λύκοι Π 157.

ᾤμωξε, 3 sing. aor. οἰμώζω.

ὤνατο, 3 sing. aor. ὄνομαι.

ὤνησε, 3 sing. aor. ὀνίνημι.

ὠνητός, -ή, -όν [ὠνέομαι, to buy, fr. ὦνος].

Bought: ἐμ' ὠνητὴ τέκε μήτηρ, παλλακίς (*i.e.* a slave) ξ 202.

ὠνόμασας, 2 sing. aor. ὀνομάζω.

ὦνος, -ου, ὁ. (Ϝῶνος. Cf. L. *venum.*) That which is given or paid as an equivalent, a price: ὦνον ἔδωκεν Φ 41, υἱὸς Πριάμοιο ὦνον ἔδωκε [κρητῆρα] (as the ransom for him; referring to the same transaction) Ψ 746: ἐπείγετ' ὦνον ὁδαίων (*i.e.* your buying, your bargaining) ο 445. Cf. ξ 297, ο 388 = 429, 452, 463.

ὠνοσάμην, aor. ὄνομαι.

ᾦξε, 3 sing. aor. οἴγνυμι.

ὦπα, τό [ὀπ-. See ὁράω]. (Cf. βλοσυρῶπις, βοῶπις, γλαυκῶπις, εἰσωπός, ἑλίκωψ, ἐνῶπα, ἐνώπια, εὐῶπις, κυανῶπις, κυνώπης, κυνῶπις, μέτωπον, πρόσωπον, στεινωπός, ὑπώπια.) The eye (always with εἰς): θεῇς εἰς ὦπα ἔοικεν (looking at her in the eye, to view) Γ 158, ἔμοιγε εἰς ὦπα ἰδέσθαι (to look me in the eye) Ι 373, ἐπὴν Διὸς εἰς ὦπα ἴδησθε Ο 147. Cf. α 411, χ 405, ψ 107.

ὤπασα, aor. ὀπάζω.

ὡπλίσ(σ)ατο, 3 sing. aor. mid. ὁπλίζω.

ὥπλισσε, 3 sing. aor. ὁπλίζω.

ὤρεξε, 3 sing. aor. ὀρέγω.

ὤρεσσι, contr. dat. pl. ὄαρ.

ὤρετο, 3 sing. aor. mid. ὄρνυμι.

ὥρη, -ης, ἡ. (1) A natural season, a period of the year: ὅσσα τε φύλλα γίγνεται ὥρῃ (in their season, *i.e.* in spring) Β 468, ὥρῃ ἐν εἰαρινῇ 471 = Π 643. Cf. Ζ 148, Φ 450: βαθὺ κε λήϊον εἰς ὥρας ἀμῷεν (in due season) ι 135. Cf. β 107 = τ 152 = ω 142, ι 51, κ 469, λ 295 = ξ 294, σ 367 = χ 301.—Personified. In pl. Ὧραι Ε 749 = Θ 393, Θ 433.—A season or time marked by special characteristics: ὥρῃ χειμερίῃ (in storm-time) ε 485, ὁππότε Διὸς ὧραι ἐπιβρίσειαν (the rainy seasons, rain-showers) ω 344.—(2) The season or time for something: ὥρη εὕδειν λ 330, 373, ὥρη δόρποιο ξ 407, ἐν ὥρῃ (in the due season) ρ 176. Cf. γ 334, λ 379, ο 126, 394, τ 510, φ 428.

ὤρῖνε, 3 sing. aor. ὀρίνω.

ὥριος [ὥρη]. Proper to a season: φέροι κεν ὥρια πάντα (all things in due season) ι 131.

ὥριστος, crasis of ὁ ἄριστος.

ὤρορε, 3 sing. redup. aor. ὄρνυμι.

ὦρσε, 3 sing. aor. ὄρνυμι.

ὦρτο, 3 sing. aor. mid. ὄρνυμι.

ὠρχεῦντο, 3 pl. impf. ὀρχέομαι.

ὀρώρει, 3 sing. plupf. ὄρνυμι.

ὥς. Written also **ὣς.** (1) In this way or manner, thus, so: ὣς ἔφατο Α 33, ὣς τὰ πένοντο 318, αἲ γὰρ ἐγὼν ὣς εἴην ἀθάνατος ὡς . . . (as surely as . . .) Θ 538. Cf. Α 68, 217, Β 35, 207, Ξ 142 (by his own folly), etc.: α 42, 96, 125, 166, β 106, 320, γ 148, 228, etc.—With αὔτως. See αὔτως (2).—(2) Absol. (a) καὶ ὥς, even so, all the same, nevertheless, for all that Α 116, Γ 159, Δ 322, Ε 482, Θ 56, etc.: δ 484, ε 219, θ 184, ι 258, etc.—(b) οὐδ' ὥς, not even so, for all that Η 263, Ι 351, 386, Λ 255, Μ 432, etc.: α 6, β 23, ε 324, κ 291, etc.—(3) Qualifying an adjective or pple., thus, so: ὣς πυκνοὶ ἀλλήλοισιν ἔφυν ἐπαμοιβαδίς ε 480. Cf. ν 389, σ 202, τ 442.—(4) Thus, so, therefore, accordingly: ὣς λίπον [ἵππους] Ε 204. Cf. Α 601, Ι 597, etc.: ὣς οὐκ αἰνότερον ἄλλο γυναικός (thus we see that . . .) λ 427. Cf. β 137, δ 93, ι 161, etc.—(5) Correlative with ὡς: (a) ὣς . . . ὡς . . ., so . . . as . . . Δ 319, Θ 538, Λ 670, Ξ 265, etc.: γ 218, ζ 166, κ 416, ξ 468, ο 156, etc.—(b) ὡς . . . ὣς . . . (α) As . . . so . . . Α 513, Β 328, 464, Δ 314, 436, Ε 163, Η 7, Θ 308, Λ 70, Μ 171, etc.: δ 340, ε 330, 370, θ 531, κ 218, 414, ν 84, ρ 218 (see ὁμοῖος (1)), etc.—(β) No sooner . . . than . . . Ξ 294, Τ 16, Υ 424.

ὡς. (1) In such or the same way or manner as, even as, as. (a) (α) ὡς ἔμ' ἀφαιρεῖται Χρυσηΐδα (as he is taking her from me, (so) will I . . .) Α 182, ὡς ἔσεταί περ 211, ὡς ἐπιτέλλω Β 10. Cf. Α 276, Β 258, Δ 267, 374, Ζ 262, 519, Θ 286, etc.: δὸς ξείνιον ὥς περ ὑπέστης ι 365, αἲ γὰρ δυναίμην . . . ὡς . . . (as surely as . . .) 525. Cf. α 35, 200, β 172, 183, 305, γ 234, δ 157, etc.—So ὥς τε: ὥς τέ τευ ἢ παρὰ πάμπαν ἀνείμονος ἠὲ πενιχροῦ (as if from . . .) γ 348, ὥς τε περὶ ψυχῆς (as was natural in a matter of life and death) ι 423. Cf. ζ 122, λ 411, etc.—(β) Introducing similes: ὡς Ε 499, Η 4, Ι 4, Λ 113, etc.: τ 205, υ 14.—ὥς τε Β 459, Γ 23, Δ 433, Μ 421, etc.: ν 81.—For ὡς ὁπότε see ὁπότε (1) (a).—For ὡς ὅτε see ὅτε (1) (a) (γ).—(γ) For ὡς γάρ see γάρ (4).—(b) With subj. (α) In conditional relative sentences. For the examples and constructions see Table at end (III) (D) (13) (35).—(β) Introducing similes: ὡς Ε 161, Ι 323, Χ 93, etc.: ε 368, θ 523, π 17.—ὥς τε Β 474, Λ 67, Μ 167, Ν 198, etc.: χ 302.—For ὡς ὁπότε see ὁπότε (1) (b) (γ).—For ὡς ὅτε see ὅτε (1) (b) (δ).—(c) Introducing a simile with opt.: ὡς ὅτε ι 384.—(d) For ὡς εἰ, ὡς εἴ τε see εἰ (6) (7).—(2) Introducing similes without expressed vb.: ὡς Ρ 4, Φ 282.—ὥς τε Ε 136, Ι 14, Μ 299, Ο 630, etc.: α 308, ζ 130, χ 384, etc.—For ὡς ὅτε see ὅτε (2).—(3) Introducing a clause reduced to its subject or object, after the manner of, as in the case of, in the likeness of, like. (a) ὡς: ὥς περ Ἀχιλλεύς Ξ 50, ὡς Πάτροκλον Τ 403, etc.: ἀνέμου ὡς πνοιή ζ 20. Cf. β 333, η 206, μ 433, ο 479, υ 140, etc.—(b) ὥς τε: ὥς τε θεός (as might be expected of a goddess) Γ 381, ὥς τε λέοντα Ε 136. Cf. Β 289, Ι 14, Λ 239, Ν 564, etc.: ὥς τε κτάμεναι μενεαίνων (like one minded to . . .) κ 295, ὥς τε θεῷ χ 349. Cf. α 227, γ 246, δ 45, ε 371, etc.—(4) Following the word to which it relates and accented: κακὸν ὥς Β 190, ὄρνιθας ὥς 764. Cf. Β 781, Γ 60, 196, Ε 78, Θ 306, etc.: ἀθάνατος ὥς ζ 309. Cf. α 320, β 47, δ 32, κ 124, etc.—(5) In what way or manner, in how high a degree. In exclamatory use, how . . . ! to think how . . . ! to think that . . . ! ὡς οὔ τίς με θεῶν ὑπέστη σαῶσαι Φ 273. Cf. Φ 441, Ω 388: ὡς ὅδε πᾶσι φίλος ἐστίν κ 38, ὡς ἐπιτροχάδην ἀγορεύει σ 26. Cf. ο 381, π 364.—Sim.: ὥς μοι δέχεται κακὸν ἐκ κακοῦ (showing how . . .) Τ 290: ὡς ἀγαθὸν καὶ παῖδα λιπέσθαι (from which we see how good a thing it is) γ 196, ὡς οὐδὲν γλύκιον ἧς πατρίδος (so true it is that . . .) ι 34. Cf. χ 319.—(**6**) In object clauses, in what way or manner, to what extent, in what degree, how. (**a**) With indic. : ᾔδεε γὰρ ἀδελφεὸν ὡς ἐπονεῖτο B 409, μέμνημαι τόδε ἔργον ὡς ἦν (how it chanced) I 528. Cf. Δ 360, H 407, I 647, Λ 768, Ξ 482, O 204, Ψ 648, etc. : ἀκούσαμεν ὡς ἐβόησας δ 281, οὐ τόλμησεν ἐπακοῦσαι ἐμὸν ἔπος, ὡς ἐρέεινον . . . (*i.e.* would not stay to learn the nature of my inquiry) ω 262. Cf. γ 194, 255, δ 772, ε 423, θ 76, ν 170, χ 374, ψ 310, etc.—With fut. : εἰπέ μοι νόστον, ὡς ἐλεύσομαι δ 381. Cf. δ 390, etc.—(**b**) With subj. (here and in (c) tending to pass into sense (8)). (**α**) Pure : μερμήριζε ὡς Ἀχιλῆα τιμήσῃ B 3.—(**β**) With κεν : πειρᾶν ὥς κ' ἄρξωσιν Δ 66. Cf. I 112, O 235, Φ 459, etc. : φράσσεται ὥς κε νέηται α 205. Cf. α 87, β 168, 316, etc.—(**c**) With opt. : πειρᾶν ὡς πεπίθοιεν Πηλεΐωνα I 181.—(**7**) In such way or manner that, so that. (**a**) With subj. pure or with κεν or ἄν : ὥς τις βέλος πέσσῃ Θ 513, ὡς ἂν δοάσσεται Ψ 339 : ὥς κ' ἄλγεα πάσχῃ χ 177. Cf. π 169.—(**b**) With opt. (**α**) Pure : ὥς μιν ψυχὴ λίποι σ 91. Cf. ι 42 = 549.—(**β**) With ἄν : ὡς ἄν τίς σε μακαρίζοι ο 538 = ρ 165 = τ 311.—(**8**) In final clauses, so that, in order that. (**a**) With subj. (**α**) Pure : ὥς μοι τόνδ' ἄνδρ' ἐξονομήνῃς Γ 166. Cf. B 363, Z 259, 357, Θ 37, I 311, etc. : ε 164, ρ 76.—(**β**) With κεν : σαώτερος ὥς κε νέηαι A 32. Cf. B 385, Z 69, H 334, Θ 508, T 151, Ω 75, etc. : ὥς κ' ἔμ' ἐμῆς ἐπιβήσετε πάτρης η 223. Cf. β 368, ε 26, θ 101, τ 319, ω 532, etc —(**γ**) With ἄν : ὡς ἄν μοι τιμὴν ἄρηαι Π 84. Cf. Π 271 : ὡς ἂν μὴ κατὰ χρόα ἰάπτῃ β 376. Cf. δ 672, 749, ν 402, π 84, ω 360.—(**b**) With opt. (**α**) Pure : ὡς ἀκούσειαν B 281. Cf. E 24, I 461, Φ 605, etc. : ὡς χόλον ἐξακέσαιτο γ 145. Cf. ζ 113, 129, ξ 297.—(**β**) With κεν : ὥς κ' αὐτὸς ἐεδνώσαιτο θύγατρα β 53. Cf. θ 21, ψ 135, ω 83.—(**γ**) With ἄν : ὡς ἄν μοι παῖδα Σκυρόθεν ἐξαγάγοις T 331 : ὡς ἂν ἐπιθύσαντες ἑλοίμεθα π 297. Cf. ρ 362.—(**9**) In which way, *i.e.* wherefore, and so : ὡς ἂν ἀπὸ σεῖο οὐκ ἐθέλοιμι λείπεσθαι I 444. Cf. Φ 291.—(**10**) ὥς τε with infin., so as to . . . : οὐ γὰρ ἔτι τηλίκος εἰμί, ὥς τε σημάντορι πιθέσθαι ρ 21.—This construction where the simple infin. might be expected : εἴ τοι θυμὸς ἐπέσσυται ὥς τε νέεσθαι I 42.—(**11**) Seeing how, in what way or manner, to what extent, in what degree, seeing that thus (= ὅτι οὕτως) : ὡς ἐλέλιχθεν Z 109, ὡς ἀγορεύεις (as to judge by your speech you think them to be) I 41, ὡς πυκνοὶ ἐφέστασαν ἀλλήλοισιν (so close together did they stand) N 133. Cf. Δ 157, I 689, K 116, Λ 689, O 698, Π 17, 600 (when they saw how he had fallen), etc. : ὡς οὔ τις μέμνηται Ὀδυσσῆος β 233, ὡς δὴ δήθ' ἐνὶ νήσῳ ἐρύκεαι (seeing that so long . . .) δ 373, ὡς ὄνομ' ἐξαπάτησεν (to think how . . .) ι 414, θαῦμά μ' ἔχει ὡς . . . (to see how . . .) κ 326, ὥς οἱ ἔειπεν Ἀθηναίη (reassured by her speech) ν 251, ὡς ἐπάγοντες ἐπῇσαν (with such a din did they . . .) τ 445. Cf. δ 841, λ 419, τ 230, φ 123, ω 194, 512, etc.—(**12**) When, after that, as soon as : ὡς ἴδον A 600. Cf. B 321, Γ 21, Δ 149, Z 237, 374, Σ 222, etc. : φαῖνεν ἀοιδήν, ἔνθεν ἑλὼν ὡς ἀπέπλειον (from the point when they had . . .) θ 500, ὡς ἐνόησεν κ 375. Cf. γ 34, θ 272, χ 148, etc.—(**13**) With opt. expressing a wish : ὡς ἔρις ἀπόλοιτο Σ 107. Cf. X 286 : ὡς ἔλθοι ρ 243 = φ 201. Cf. α 47.—Anomalously with κεν : ὥς κέ οἱ γαῖα χάνοι Z 281 (app., O that the earth could gape for him).—For ὡς ὤφελον (ὄφελον), ὡς ὤφελλον, see ὀφέλλω[1] (5).—(**14**) Introducing a dependent substantive-clause, that, how : ἀγορεύεις ὡς . . . A 110. Cf. A 558, H 402, K 160, P 450, X 10, Ψ 611, etc. : ἦ οὐχ ἅλις ὡς . . . β 312. Cf. γ 347, δ 377, ε 24, ι 443, ξ 152, ρ 157, τ 94, φ 209, χ 351, ψ 60, etc.—Introducing a clause with opt. in *oratio obliqua* : ἕκαστα εἰπεῖν, ὡς ἔλθοι (that he had come) ω 237.—(**15**) In ρ 218 (ὡς αἰεὶ τὸν ὁμοῖον ἄγει θεὸς ὡς τὸν ὁμοῖον) if ὡς be read for ὥς it must app. be taken as = εἰς or πρός. See ὁμοῖος (1).—(**16**) Correlative with οὕτως. See οὕτως (1).—With τόσσον. See τόσος (5) (d).—With τώς. See τώς (2).—With ὧδε. See ὧδε (5).—With ὥς. See ὥς (5).

ὦσα, aor. ὠθέω.

ὠσί, dat. pl. See οὖας.

ὠτειλή, -ῆς, ἡ. A wound : ἔρρεεν αἷμ' ἐξ ὠτειλῆς Δ 140. Cf. Λ 266, Ξ 518, Π 862, P 297, Σ 351, etc. : κ 164, τ 456, ω 189.

ὠτώεις, -εντος [ὠτ-, οὖς, οὖας]. Furnished with ears or handles (cf. οὖας (2)) : τρίποδα Ψ 264, 513.

ὡὐτός, crasis of ὁ αὐτός. See αὐτός (3).

ὤφελε, 3 sing. aor. ὀφέλλω[1].

ὤφελλε[1], 3 sing. impf. ὀφέλλω[1].

ὤφελλε[2], 3 sing. impf. ὀφέλλω[2].

ᾤχετο, 3 sing. impf. οἴχομαι.

ὠχράω [ὦχρος]. To turn pale or pallid : ὠχρήσαντα χρόα κάλλιμον λ 529.

ὦχρος, ὁ. Paleness, pallor : ὦχρός μιν εἷλε παρειάς Γ 35.

PREFIXES AND SUFFIXES REFERRED TO FROM THE TEXT

PREFIXES

ἀ-[1]. Before a vowel ἀν-. Also in assimilated form ἀμ- (only in P 695 := δ 704). Negative or privative.

ἀ-[2]. [(σ)α- as in ἅμα.] Copulative or sociative, indicating united or continuous action; contiguity, closeness; equivalence.

ἀγα-. [ἄγαν, very, much.] Intensive.

ἀμφι-. Before a vowel ἀμφ-. Also ἀμπ-. (1) On both sides.—(2) Having two, double.—(3) Round, about; all round or about.—(4) About, concerning.

ἀν-[1]. See ἀ-[1].

ἀν-[2]. See next.

ἀνα-. Before a vowel ἀν-. Also in assimilated forms ἀγ-, ἀϝ-, ἀλ-, ἀμ-. (1) Up, upwards; also of putting to sea.—(2) On, upon.—(3) Back; in a reverse direction.—(4) Again; return to a state; repetition.—(5) Through, over, among; diffusion.—(6) Intensive, sometimes translatable by 'up,' 'on,' 'out' (in some cases not appreciably affecting the sense).

ἀντι-. Before a vowel ἀντ-. Also in assimilated form ἀνθ-. (1) Over against, opposite.—(2) Against, whether in opposition or for protection.—(3) Before one, onwards.—(4) Equal to, the equivalent of, as good as.

ἀπο-. Before a vowel ἀπ-. Also in assimilated form ἀφ-. (1) Away, off, from, away from.—(2) Far away, away, at a distance.—(3) Asunder, in two.—(4) Back, backwards; restoration.—(5) Giving notion of requiting.—(6) With negative sense; undoing or reversing action.—(7) Intensive (in some cases not appreciably affecting the sense).

ἀρι-. Intensive.

δα-. [δια- (10). Cf. ζα-.] Intensive.

δια-. Before a vowel δι-. (1) Through; piercing.—(2) Traversing.—(3) Across; crossing.—(4) In all directions.—(5) Severing, sundering; in pieces.—(6) Separation; putting, keeping or being apart.—(7) Distinguishing.—(8) Continuity; doing something constantly; continuous succession.—(9) Exhaustiveness, in full, fully.—(10) Intensive (in some cases not appreciably affecting the sense).

δισ-. [δύο.] Also in form δι-. Twice; double.

δυσ-. (1) Giving a word an unfavourable sense, or giving a sense of ill-luck or unhappiness.—(2) Intensive of words having such senses.

εἰσ-. Also ἐσ-. (1) To, towards; or reinforcing this notion when already implicit.—(2) Into, in.—(3) On, on to.—(4) Giving notion of a directing of the mind, sight, etc., in a particular way, or reinforcing this notion when already implicit.

ἐκ-. Before a vowel **ἐξ-**. (1) Out, forth, from, away.—(2) Indicating origin or source.—(3) Indicating separation; off.—(4) Indicating suspension from or attachment to something.—(5) Indicating standing out from others or prominence, or reinforcing this idea.—(6) Indicating extension as in hammering; out.—(7) Indicating excess; beyond.—(8) Of speaking, etc., indicating absence of restraint; out, right out, aloud.—(9) Intensive (often not appreciably affecting the sense).

ἐν-. Also in forms εἰν-, ἐνι-, and in assimilated forms ἐγ-, ἐμ-. (1) In (in local and immaterial senses). Also (as in ἔνορχος, ἐνῶπα) indicating the presence in something of what is indicated by the second element.—(2) Into (in local and immaterial senses).—(3) On, upon, on to; also in hostile sense.—(4) Among.—(5) Towards.—(6) Intensive (commonly not appreciably affecting the sense).

ἐξ-. See ἐκ-.

ἐπι-. Before a vowel ἐπ-. Also in assimilated form ἐφ-. (1) Position on or upon something or on or in the surface of something.—(2) At, by, in, among.—(3) Placing, fitting or attaching in a specified or indicated position.—(4) Denoting an occasion or cause, at, in, thereat, thereupon, therein.—(5) Denoting (sometimes vaguely) that action, effort or the like takes place in a specified or indicated direction or is directed to or against something or to a specified or indicated object or end.—(6) Besides, in addition.—(7) Following, succession; being behind.—(8) Accompaniment.—(9) In answer or response.—(10) Being in charge of something.—(11) To, towards, at, on, upon, for. So in hostile sense.—(12) On to, on, upon, over.—(13) Over, passing over.—(14) Going over or along a space or line or over or round persons, etc.—(15) Extension or diffusion over a space.—(16) Extension over a period of time.—(17) On, onwards.—(18) Putting to, closing, shutting; thrusting or pressing home.—(19) Intensive (commonly not appreciably affecting the sense).

ἐρι-. Intensive.

ἐσ-. See *εἰσ-*.

εὐ-, ἐϋ-. Also **ἠϋ-**. (1) In adjectives and verbs, well, excellently, skilfully, duly; denoting also goodness of birth, facility in doing something, approval.—(2) In adjectives, well or rightly in a moral sense.—(3) In adjectives, denoting the conferring of services or benefit.—(4) In adjectives, showing the quality in a high degree.—(5) In adjectives and substantives, denoting the presence, in a high degree of goodness, excellence, beauty, well-being, benevolence or amount, of what is signified by the second element of the compound.

ζα-. [*δα-*, *δια-* (10).] Intensive.

ἡμι-. [Cf. L. *semi-*.] Half-.

ἠϋ-. See *εὐ-*.

κατα-. Before a vowel *κατ-*. Also in forms *καται-*, *κα-*, and in assimilated forms *καβ-*, *καδ-*, *καθ-*, *κακ-*, *καλ-*, *καμ-*, *καν-*, *καπ-*. (1) Down, downwards, down from, down upon, down along; reinforcing the notion when already present; also of coming in from sea.—(2) Indicating that an action or agency is directed against or prejudicially affects a person.—(3) Indicating traversing a space or extension over it.—(4) According to, by.—(5) Intensive (commonly not appreciably affecting the sense).

μετα-. Before a vowel *μετ-*. Also in assimilated form *μεθ-*. (1) Motion in quest of, after, in pursuit of, following.—(2) Position between.—(3) Among, in company with, with.—(4) Position behind.—(5) After in time, after, later.—(6) Change of position, fortune, circumstances, etc.—(7) Alternation, taking turns, occurrence of intervals.

νη-. Negative or privative.

ξυν-, ξυμ-. For words with these prefixes see the same words with *συν-*, *συμ-*.

παρα-, παραι-. Also in form *παρ-*. (1) From.—(2) Beside, by, near.—(3) Past, passing by.—(4) Aside, away; denoting turning or bending of a person's mind or will.—(5) Difference; denoting the converse of something.

περι-. (1) Of position, round, about, round about.—(2) Motion round or about; revolving motion.—(3) More than others; exceeding, excelling, surpassing.—(4) Excess.—(5) On account of, touching, in regard to, for.—(6) Intensive.

ποτι-. See *προσ-*.

προ-. (1) Forward, forwards, forth.—(2) In front, before; denoting excelling or surpassing, preference or choice.—(3) In reference to time, before, beforehand.—(4) Reinforcing the notion denoted by the second element; intensive.

προσ-. Also **προτι-**, **ποτι-**. (1) At, by, beside, on, upon, against.—(2) To, towards, against. In reference to speech, to.—(3) Denoting (sometimes vaguely) that action, effort or the like takes place in a specified or indicated direction or is directed to or against something or to a specified or indicated object or end.

προτι-. See *προσ-*.

συν-, ξυν-. Also in assimilated forms *συγ-*, *συλ-*, *συμ-*, *συρ-*. (1) With, along with.—(2) Together; denoting joining, union, contact, proximity.—(3) Together; in a body or mass; in confusion.—(4) Altogether; intensive.

ὑπερ-. Also in form **ὑπειρ-**. (1) Position above or over.—(2) Passing over.—(3) Passing over and beyond.—(4) Beyond, contrary to, in defiance of.—(5) Intensive; excelling.—(6) Indicating excess.

ὑπο-. Before a vowel *ὑπ-*. Also in assimilated forms *ὑβ-*, *ὑφ-*. (1) From under something.—(2) In reference to direction, from beneath or below.—(3) From the power, reach or range of something.—(4) Under, beneath or below something.—(5) Under the power or orders of someone.—(6) In reference to conception or the bearing of offspring indicating the submission of the female to the male.—(7) Indicating coming under an obligation or undertaking.—(8) To underneath something.—(9) Motion beneath something.—(10) Returning, coming back.—(11) Indicating a coming or an instilling into the mind or heart.—(12) Indicating (sometimes vaguely) occasion, cause, purpose, correspondence, concurrence, competition, response, relationship, contrast, or the like.

Suffixes

-δε, *enclitic*. (1) Motion towards.—(2) Purpose.—(3) Intensive.

-θεν. Also *-θε*.—(1) Motion from; from in gen.—(2) Position away from; position indicated by the first element of the compound.

-θι. Place at or in which; time when.

-σε. Motion towards; place whither.

TABLE of the Uses of *εἰ* (*αἴ*), *ἤν* in Protasis with the accompanying Apodoses and of the corresponding Relative and Conditional Relative Sentences with Future, Subjunctive and Optative.

An asterisk (*) prefixed to a reference indicates a double protasis. In I 358 foll. and 379 foll. the mark indicates a triple, and in δ 222 it indicates a quadruple protasis.—Note that as, for the purpose of the Table, it has sometimes been necessary to invert the order of the protasis and apodosis, the rules under *οὐ* (3) (a) and *μή* (6) (c) will in the cases of such inversion apparently not hold.

(I.) CITING A FACT IN CORROBORATION OR AS THE GROUND OF AN APPEAL OR EXHORTATION (*εἰ* (3))

Indic.	Indic., Imp., etc.
εἴ ποτέ τοι νηὸν ἔρεψα, ἢ εἰ . . .	*τόδε μοι κρήηνον ἐέλδωρ* *A 39
(Remember how I . . .,	and now . . .)
εἴ ποτ' ἔην γε	*δαὴρ ἐμὸς ἔσκεν* Γ 180
(As surely as ever he was	he was my . . .)
εἰ τότε κοῦρος ἔα	*νῦν αὖτέ με γῆρας ὀπάζει* Δ 321
(As once I was young	so now I am old)
εἰ δὴ Τρώων νέφος ἀμφιβέβηκε νηυσίν	*ἄρχε Μυρμιδόνεσσιν* Π 66
(Seeing how . . .	lead them on)
εἰ θοός ἐσσι	*νῦν τοι ἐελδέσθω πόλεμος* Π 494
(We know your fleetness,	so do thou put war into thy heart)
εἴ ποτε ζώοντι χαίρετε	*ὄψεσθ' Ἕκτορα* Ω 705
(You joyed in him while he lived,	now see his corpse)
εἴ ποτέ τοί τι πατὴρ ἐμὸς ἔπος ἐξετέλεσσε	*τῶν νῦν μνῆσαι, καί μοι νημερτὲς ἐνίσπες* γ 98, δ 328
(Remember what he did for you	and tell me truly)
εἴ μ' ἤγετ' ἐμὴν ἐς γαῖαν	*φήμην τίς μοι φάσθω* υ 98
(You have brought me home,	and now continue your aid and . . .)

Cf. A 394, 503, E 116, Λ 762, O 372, X 83, Ω 426 : δ 763, ο 268, ρ 240, τ 315, ω 289.

(II.) INTRODUCING ONE OF TWO OPPOSED CLAUSES (*εἰ* (4), *ἤν* (1))

(A) Simple Suppositions

Indic.	Indic., Imp., etc.
εἰ μάλα καρτερός ἐσσι	*θεός που σοὶ τό γ' ἔδωκεν* A 178
εἴ περ φθονέω	*οὐκ ἀνύω* Δ 55
εἴ περ αὐτίκ' οὐκ ἐτέλεσσεν	*ὀψὲ τελεῖ* Δ 160
εἴ τοι Ἀτρεΐδης ἀπήχθετο	*σὺ δ' ἄλλους ἐλέαιρε* I 300
εἰ καί μιν Ὀλύμπιος ἐγείρει	*ἐρωήσαιτό κεν* N 58
εἰ ὣς ἀπόλωλεν	*ἀλλ' ἤδη παῖς τοῖος [ἐστιν]* τ 85

Cf. A 280, 290, E 410, 645, *H 117, K 239, N 111, 316, *O 51, 99, 117, 724, P 421, *Υ 102, *371, X 389, Ψ 832 : ε 80, ι 35, 532, ν 6.

The Apodosis in external governance

εἰ καὶ μάλα τηλόθεν ἐσσί	*ἵνα νόστιμον ἦμαρ ἴδηαι* ζ 312

Cf. η 194, 321.

(B) General Suppositions

(a) Present

(1) Subj.	Pres. or Pf. Indic.
εἴ περ χόλον καταπέψῃ	*ἀλλὰ μετόπισθεν ἔχει κότον* Α 81
εἴ περ ἄλλοι πίνωσιν	*σὸν δὲ πλεῖον δέπας ἕστηκεν* Δ 261
εἴ τις ξύμβληται ὁδίτης	*οὔ τι κατακρύπτουσιν* η 204

Cf. Κ 225, Λ 116, Τ 164, Φ 576, Χ 191 : α 167, π 98, 116.

Relative Sentences

ὅττι *φανήῃ*	*πάντα κάλ' [ἐστίν]* Χ 73
ὅτε *καὶ λυγρὰ θεοὶ τελέσωσι*	*καὶ τὰ φέρει* σ 134

Cf. **ὅς τις** ο 401. **ὁππότε** ρ 471.

(2) Subj. *κεν*	Pres. Indic.
καὶ εἴ κ' ὀλίγον περ ἐπαύρῃ	*ὀξὺ βέλος πέλεται* Λ 391
εἴ πέρ χ' εὕρῃσι βώτορας ἄνδρας	*οὐ μέμονε δίεσθαι* Μ 302

Relative Sentences

ἐπεί *κε κάμῃσιν*	*ἰθύει* Ρ 658

Cf. **ἐπεί** Φ 575. **ὅς** ο 422, ω 202.

(3) Subj. *ἄν*	Pres. Indic.
εἴ περ ἂν αὐτὸν σεύωνται	*κατεσθίει* Γ 25

Relative Sentence

ἐπὴν *γείνεαι αὐτός*	*οὐκ ἐλεαίρεις ἄνδρας* υ 202

(4) Opt.	Pres. Indic.
εἰ καί ποθεν ἄλλοθεν ἔλθοι	*θαρσαλέος ἀνὴρ ἀμείνων τελέθει* η 52

Cf. θ 139, ξ 56.

(b) Past

Relative Sentences

Opt.	Impf. or Iterative
ὁπότε *κρίνοιμι λόχονδ' ἄνδρας*	*οὔ ποτέ μοι θάνατον προτιόσσετο θυμός* ξ 217
ὁποῖος *ἔοι καὶ* **ὅτευ** *κεχρημένος ἔλθοι*	*δόσκον ἀλήτῃ* *ρ 421, *τ 77

(C) Suppositions contrary to Fact

(a) Past

(1) Aor. or Impf. Indic.	Aor. Indic. *κεν*
εἴ πέρ μοι ἐείκοσιν ἀντεβόλησαν	*πάντες κ' ὄλοντο* Π 847

The Apodosis in loose connexion with the Protasis

οὐδ' εἴ οἱ κραδίη σιδηρέη ἦεν	*οὔ τι τάδ' ἤρκησ' ὄλεθρον* (did not . . . (and would not have . . .) though . . .) δ 293

(2) Aor. Indic.	Aor. Indic. *ἄν*
εἴ περ ἀπήμων ἦλθεν	*ὅσ' ἂν οὐκ ἐξήρατο* ε 40, ν 138

(3) Opt.	Opt. *κεν*
εἰ μάλα μιν χόλος ἵκοι	*οὔ κ' ὀνόσαιτο* Ρ 399

(b) Present

Opt.	Subj. *ἄν*
εἴ μοι δέκα γλῶσσαι εἶεν	*πληθὺν οὐκ ἂν ἐγὼ μυθήσομαι οὐδ' ὀνομήνω* *Β 489

(D) Future Suppositions

Protasis	Apodosis
(1) Fut.	Fut.
εἴ πέρ σε κακὸν φήσει	*ἀλλ' οὐ πείσονται* Θ 153
(2) Fut.	Imp.
εἴ μ' ἀτιμήσουσι	*σὸν δὲ κῆρ τετλάτω* *π 274
(3) Subj.	Fut.
εἰ ἕτερός γε φύγῃσιν	*τούτω οὐ πάλιν ἀποίσετον ἵπποι* E 258
εἴ τις ῥαίῃσι θεῶν	*τλήσομαι* ε 221

Cf. K 115, M 223 : α 204.

Relative Sentence

ὁππόσ' *ἐπέλθω*	*οὐκ ἤπιον ὧδε ἄνακτα κιχήσομαι* *ξ 139
Subj.	Words implying Future
εἴ πέρ τ' ἄλλοι κτεινώμεθα	*σοὶ δ' οὐ δέος ἔστ' ἀπολέσθαι* M 245
(4) Subj. *κεν*	Fut.
εἴ πέρ κεν ἀλύξῃς	*ὀψὲ νεῖαι* λ 113, μ 140

Cf. Υ 181 : *ξ 140.

Relative Sentence

ἥ *κ' εὐεργὸς ἔῃσιν*	*αἶσχος ἐσσομένῃσιν* λ 434
Subj. *κεν*	Fut. Words
εἴ κεν δεκάκις ἄποινα στήσωσιν	*οὐκ ἔσθ' ὃς κύνας ἀπαλάλκοι* *X 349

With Apodosis suppressed

πελέκεάς γε καὶ εἴ κ' εἰῶμεν ἑστάμεν . . . . . . φ 260

(5) Subj. *κεν*	Subj.
εἴ κε τὰ νείατα πείραθ' ἵκηαι	*σέθεν οὐκ ἀλεγίζω* Θ 478
(6) Subj. *κεν*	Imp.

Relative Sentence

ὅττι *κε κακὸν πέμπῃσιν*	*ἔχετε* O 109
(7) Subj. *ἄν*	Fut.

Relative Sentence

μηδ' ***ὁππότ'*** *ἂν Τροίη δάηται*	*ὠμόσσαμεν (ὀμοῦμαι) μὴ ἀλεξήσειν* Υ 316, Φ 375
(8) *ἤν* Subj.	Fut.
ἢν Ἀγαμέμνονα εἴπῃς	*οὔ τις χεῖρας ἐποίσει* A 90

Cf. O 504, T 32, X 487.

(9) *ἤν* Subj.	Subj.
ἢν ἔνθ' ἀφίκηαι	*οὔ σευ ἀλέγω* Θ 482
(10) *ἤν* Subj.	Imp.
ἤν περ ποδῶν ἕλκωσι	*σὸν δὲ κῆρ τετλάτω* *π 276
ἤν τις στοναχῆς ἀκούσῃ	*μὴ προβλώσκειν* φ 237, 383
(11) *ἤν κε* Subj.	Fut.
ἤν πέρ κ' ἐθέλωσιν . . .	*οὔ τί με νικήσουσιν* σ 318

Protasis	Apodosis
(**12**) Subj.	Opt. κεν
εἴ πέρ μοι καὶ ἀγάσσεαι	καί κε τοῦτ' ἐθέλοιμ' ἀρέσθαι α 389
(**13**) Opt.	Fut.
εἰ 'Αφροδίτῃ ἐρίζοι	κούρην οὐ γαμέω I 389
(**14**) Opt.	Imp.
εἰ μάλα πόλλ' ἀγορεύοι	ὁμοκλέομεν τόξον μὴ δόμεναι ω 174

(**15**) Opt. subjoined to an Infin.

εἰ μάλα περ χαλεπαίνοι	ὅσσον τε δύω ἄνδρας ἔρυσθαι ε 485
(**16**) Opt.	Opt. κεν
εἰ καὶ πολλοὶ παρασταῖεν εἰ καρτερὸς εἴη	πρῶτός κ' ἄνδρα βάλοιμι θ 217 τίς κ' οἴοιτο . . . ; χ 13

Cf. *I 379, *380, *385, *δ 224, *225, λ 356, μ 78, 88, *ν 292, υ 49, *χ 61, *62.

Relative Sentence

ᾧ μὴ βίοτος πολὺς εἴη	βουλοίμην κε θητευέμεν ἄλλῳ λ 490

With Apodosis suppressed

οὐδ' εἰ πεντάετες παραμίμνων ἐξερέοις . . . . γ 115

(**17**) Opt.	Opt. ἄν
εἰ πολλὰ κάμοιτε	οὐκ ἂν ἐρύσαιτε Θ 22

Cf. *Π 748 : γ 228.

(**18**) Opt. κεν	Fut.
εἴ κεν πολὺν χρόνον μίμνοις	τόνδε κομιῶ ο 545
(**19**) Opt. κεν	Fut. Words
εἴ κεν 'Αρίον' ἐλαύνοι	οὐκ ἔσθ' ὅς κέ σ' ἔλῃσιν *Ψ 346

Cf. X 220, *351.

(**20**) Opt. κεν	Opt.
εἴ κεν τοῦ πατρὸς ἀποφθιμένοιο πυθοίμην	οὔ τι κακώτερον πάθοιμι T 322
(**21**) Opt. κεν	Opt. κεν
εἰ καί κεν ἄλλο ἐπαιτήσειας	δοῦναί κε βουλοίμην Ψ 592
(**22**) Opt. κεν	Opt. ἄν
εἴ κέν μοι ὑποσταίη . . .	οὐκ ἂν ἐθέλοιμι . . . I 445
(**23**) Opt. ἄ	Fut.
εἴ περ ἂν Μοῦσαι ἀείδοιεν	στεῦτο νικησέμεν B 597

(III.) IN THE PROTASIS OF CONDITIONAL SENTENCES (εἰ (5), αἴ (2), ἤν (2))

(A) Simple Suppositions

(**1**) Pres. Pa. or Pf. Indic.	Various Forms
εἴ τοι θυμὸς ἐπέσσυται	φεῦγε A 173
εἰ οὕτω τοῦτ' ἐστίν	ἐμοὶ μέλλει φίλον εἶναι A 564
εἴ τι κακὸν εἴρηται	ἀρεσσόμεθα Δ 362
εἰ ἀνήρ [ἐστιν] ὅν φημι	οὐκ ἄνευθε θεοῦ μαίνεται E 184
εἰ ἀπὸ σπουδῆς ἀγορεύεις	θεοί τοι φρένας ὤλεσαν H 359, M 233
εἰ ἐτεόν μ' ὦρσεν	χάσσονται N 153
εἴ με κελεύεις . . .	τό κε τελέσσω Ψ 558
εἰ οὐ κείνου ἐσσὶ γόνος	οὐ σὲ ἔολπα τελευτήσειν β 274
εἴ τί που ἔστι	πίθοιό μοι δ 193

Cf. A 116, 393, B 357, Γ 67, 402, E 104, Z 128, 142, H 204, Θ 466, I 42, 247, 434, K 96, 176, 242, 433, Λ 138, 794, M 67, 79, 217, 348, 361, N 256, 464, *Ξ 196, 337, O 53, Π 36, 450, P 488, *Σ 120, *305, *427, T 142, 264, 305, Φ 216, 372, X 49, 52, 285, *Ω 140, 224, 406, 660 : α 82, 275, 376, β 71, 138, 141, 271, γ 324, 376, δ 831, *ε 90, 139, ζ 150, 153, 179, 282, η 199, θ 146, 408, ι 529, κ 386, 443, 473, λ 380, ν 143, 238, ο 328, π 82, 256, 300, 320, 387, ρ 14, 195, 277, 475, σ 61, 80, τ 346, υ 208, 315, χ 45, 321, 359, ψ 36, 107, ω 328, 352.

Subjoined to an Infin.

εἴ που ὄπωπας	*ἐνισπεῖν γ* 93, *δ* 323

(2) Fut. (in sense 'I am going to . . .,' 'I am to . . .')	Various Forms
εἰ πάντα τελευτήσεις	*αἰνίζομαί σε* N 375
εἴ με καθέξει	*ὑπέροπλον ἔειπεν* O 186

Cf. *A 61, E 717, Θ 423, I 231, N 97, Ξ 62, O 162, 178 : ψ 286, ω 434.

(3) The Apodosis (in the construction of (1)) in loose connexion with the Protasis

εἴ δύναταί τι χραισμεῖν	*σοὶ ποταμὸς πάρα* Φ 192
εἴ που ἀκούεις	*νῆσός τις Συρίη κικλήσκεται ο* 403

Cf. T 327, Ψ 548 : γ 122, ι 410, ξ 44, ρ 106, υ 207, φ 170.

Thus with the Apodosis in external governance

εἴ τιν' ἔτι ἔλπεται ἐξαπατήσειν	*ὄφρα καὶ ἄλλοι ἐπισκύζωνται* I 371

(4) With the Apodosis (in the construction of (1)) suppressed

εἰ μή τις θεός ἐστιν . . . . E 177

Cf. Z 150, Ξ 331, Υ 213, Φ 487 : η 320, κ 66, ο 80, ρ 484, φ 253.

(B) General Suppositions

(a) Present

(1) Subj.	Pres., Aor. or Pf. Indic. or (in similes) Subj.
εἴ τις κινήσῃ	*πρόσσω πᾶς πέτεται* Π 263
εἰ μὴ ὀτρύνῃσιν	*οὐκ ἔρχομαι ξ* 373

Conditional Relative Sentences

ἅσσα *θέλῃσθα*	*τὰ φράζεαι* A 554
ὅτε *λέξεται ὕπνῳ*	*ὡς ὅτε μήτηρ παιδὸς ἐέργῃ μυῖαν* Δ 131
ὁππότ' *ἀνὴρ ἐθέλῃ πρὸς δαίμονα μάχεσθαι*	*πῆμά οἱ κυλίσθῃ* P 98
ὅπως *ἐθέλῃσιν*	*δίδωσιν α* 349
ὅσσα *γένηται*	*ἴδμεν μ* 191
ἐπεὶ *νὺξ ἔλθῃ*	*κεῖμαι τ* 515

Cf. **ἐπεί** Λ 478, O 680 : υ 86. **εὖτε** η 202. **ἦμος** δ 400. **ὅ** Θ 391, I 592, *Π 54 : α 101, τ 266. **ὅθι** N 229. **οἷος** σ 137. **ὅππῃ** M 48. **ὁππότε** A 163, Δ 344, I 646, N 271, O 359, 382, *Π 53, 245 : δ 792, ξ 170, ρ 520, τ 168, υ 196. **ὅπως** ζ 189. **ὅς** B 293, Γ 61, 109, E 407, 747, I 117, 508, Ξ 81, Π 590 : δ 165, 207, ε 489, *ζ 287, η 74, θ 161, 547, τ 109, 329, ψ 119. **ὅς τις** A 230, 543, I 341, *O 491, *492, P 62, 631, T 265 : α 352, 415, ε 448, θ 148, 210, κ 39, λ 428, μ 40, 41, 66, ν 214, ξ 106, ο 345, π 228, υ 188, ω 286. **ὅτε** A 80, B 395, 782, Δ 259, E 91, 500, Z 524, M 286, O 207, Π 365, 386, P 728, 756, T 183, Φ 199, X 74, Ω 417 : ζ 183, η 72, ι 6, κ 486, ξ 60, ο 409, π 72, φ 133. **ὄφρα** Δ 346, E 524, Λ 477.

Subjoined to an Infin.

ὁππότ' *ἐγείρομεν Ἄρηα*	*πολέμοιο μεθιέμεν* Δ 351

To another Protasis

ὅτ' *ἀγγελίη ποθὲν ἔλθῃ*	*εἰ μὴ ὀτρύνῃσιν ξ* 374

(2) Subj. κεν	Pres., Aor. or Pf. Indic. or (in similes) Subj.

Conditional Relative Sentences

ὅς κε θεοῖς ἐπιπείθηται	μάλα τ' ἔκλυον αὐτοῦ A 218
ὅτις κ' ἐπίορκον ὀμόσσῃ	οἳ καμόντας τίνυσθον Γ 279
ἐπεί κε λάβῃσιν	ὡς ὄρνις προφέρῃσι μάστακα I 324
εἰς ὅ κ' ἀϋτμὴ μένῃ	τὸν Ζεὺς ἐνέηκε πόνοισιν K 89
ὅτις κ' ἐμὰ δώμαθ' ἵκηται	οὐ μένει θ 32
ὅτε κ' ἐπεντύνονται ἄεθλα	τάφῳ ἀντεβόλησας ω 88

Cf. **ἐπεί** A 168, B 475, H 5, 410, I 409 : θ 554, λ 221, ω 7. **ὁππότε** γ 237, υ 83. **ὅππως** Υ 243. **ὅς** E 481, I 313, 510, Λ 409, Ξ 416, Π 621, T 167, Φ 24, Ψ 322, Ω 335, 529, 531 : η 33, θ 586, κ 74, 328, ξ 126, ο 21, 55, 70, τ 564, *566. **ὅσσος** Γ 66. **ὅς τις** A 527, Θ 422, T 260. **ὅτε** Z 225, I 501, Υ 167 : λ 218, *τ 567, ω 88 (if ζώννυνται be taken as subj.). **ὄφρα** θ 147.

Subjoined to an Infin.

ὅν κε θεὸς τιμᾷ	φωτὶ μάχεσθαι P 99
ὅς τίς κ' ἐμὰ δώμαθ' ἵκηται	ξείνους ξεινίζειν γ 355

Cf. **ὅς** Z 228, 229, I 615, T 228 : ο 196, υ 295, 342, φ 313. **ὅς τις** Θ 408, 422.

(3) Subj. ἄν	Pres., Aor. or Pf. Indic.

Conditional Relative Sentences

ὅτ' ἄν τινα θυμὸς ἀνώγῃ	χρή σε κρηῆναι ἄλλῳ I 101
ἐπειδὰν ἐφίζηται λόχον	οὐ τρέπεται χρώς N 285
ἐπὴν κλίνῃσι τάλαντα Ζεύς	ἧς πλείστην καλάμην χαλκὸς ἔχευεν T 223
ἐπὴν ἔλθῃσι θέρος	βεβλήαταί οἱ εὐναὶ λ 192
ὃς ἄν μιν χανδὸν ἕλῃ	οἶνος βλάπτει φ 294

Cf. **ἐπήν** Z 489 : θ 553, κ 411, ξ 130, τ 206. **εὖτε** B 228 : α 192, ρ 320, 323, σ 194. **ὁπ(π)ότε** O 209 : *λ 17. **ὅς** τ 332. **ὅσσος** T 230. **ὅτε** B 397 : *λ 18, ν 101.

(4) ἤν Subj.	Pres. Indic.
ἤν τις ποιήσετ' ἀκοίτην	ἀγάασθε ε 120

Cf. A 166 : λ 159.

(5) Opt.	Pres. Indic.
εἰ μάλα τις πολεμίζοι	[ἴση οἱ μοῖρα γίγνεται] I 318
εἴ ποθεν ἔλθοι [ἀγγελίη]	οὐ πείθομαι α 414

Conditional Relative Sentences

ἥ τις τοιαῦτά γε ῥέζοι	ἄλλῃ νεμεσῶ *ζ 286

Cf. **ἐπεί** ω 254. **ὁππότε** ω 344. **ὅς τις** Ψ 494.

(b) Past

(1) Opt.	Impf., Iterative, Aor. or Plupf.
εἴ τις ἴδοιτο	οὐκ ἐκεύθανον Γ 453
εἴ τίς μ' ἐνίπτοι	κατέρυκες Ω 768

Conditional Relative Sentences

ὅτε μιν ὕπνος ἱκάνοι	ἔνθα κοιμᾶτο A 610
ὅν τινα βασιλῆα κιχείη	ἐρητύσασκεν B 188
ὁπόθ' ἵκοιτο	ξείνισσέ μιν Γ 233
ἐπεί τινα βεβλήκοι	ἀπὸ θυμὸν ὄλεσσεν Θ 269
ὅτ' ἐς νῆας ἴδοι	ἕλκετο χαίτας K 14
ὅτε πίνοιεν	ὀδμὴ ὀδώδει ι 208
ὁσσάκι κύψειε	τοσσάχ' ὕδωρ ἀπολέσκετο λ 585

Cf. **ἐπεί** Ω 14 : β 105, τ 150, ω 140. **ὅ** ξ 221. **ὅθι** Δ 516. **ὅπῃ** γ 106. **ὁπ(π)ότε** N 711, O 284, Σ 544, T 317 : λ 591, μ 381. **ὅππως** Σ 473. **ὅς** B 198, Δ 232, O 22. **ὁσσάκι** Φ 265, X 194. **ὅς τις** Δ 240, K 489, M 268, 428, O 731, 743, Φ 611 : ι 94, μ 331, ρ 317, χ 315, 415, ψ 66. **ὅτε** Γ 216, K 11, 78, P 463, 732, Σ 566, T 132, Υ 226, 228, X 502 : δ 191, η 138, θ 87, 90, 220, λ 510, 513, 596, μ 237, 240, π 141, σ 7, τ 49, 371, υ 138.

Subjoined to an Infin.

ὁπότε σπέρχοιεν ἄελλαι	ἐκαίνυτο νῆα κυβερνῆσαι γ 283

Cf. ξ 522.

With Apodosis suppressed

ὅ τί οἱ εἴσαιτο γελοίϊον ἔμμεναι . . . . . . B 215

(2) Opt. κεν	Impf.
Conditional Relative Sentence	
ὅτε κέν τινα χόλος ἵκοι	οὕτως ἐπευθόμεθα κλέα ἀνδρῶν I 525

(3) Subj.	Impf. or Plupf.
Conditional Relative Sentences	
ὅτε Ζεὺς ἐν φόβον ὄρσῃ	οὔ οἵ τις ὁμοῖος ἦεν Ξ 522
οἳ μνηστεύειν ἐθέλωσιν	οὐχ ἥδε δίκη τέτυκτο σ 276

(C) Suppositions contrary to Fact

(a) Past

(1) Aor., Impf. or Plupf. Indic.	Aor. or Impf. Indic. κεν
εἰ μὴ μῦθον ἔειπεν	νόστος κ' ἐτύχθη B 156
εἴ τευ ἐξ ἄλλου γένευ	πάλαι κ' ἦσθα . . . E 897
εἰ μὴ ἀνίστατο καὶ φάτο μῦθον	προτέρω κ' ἔρις γένετο Ψ 491
εἰ μὴ μετηύδα	ὀδύροντό κεν Ω 715
εἰ πυθόμην	μεῖνέ κεν δ 732
εἰ αὐτόθι γῆρα	πολλά κέ μ' ὤνησεν ξ 67
εἰ ᾔδη ὅ . . .	οὔ κεν ἐμίγη ψ 220

Cf. Γ 374, E 680, Z 75, H 106, 274, Θ 91, 132, 218, Λ 312, 751, N 725, Ξ 259, O 123, 460, Π 618, 700, P 531, 614, Σ 166, 454, Υ 291, Φ 212, 545, X 203, Ψ 155, 383, 541, 734 : γ 256, δ 364, 503, ε 427, 437, ι 497, λ 317, π 221, φ 227, ψ 21, 242, ω 42, 51, 284, 529.

The Apodosis in loose connexion with the Protasis

εἰ νόστησ' Ὀδυσεύς	ἐπεὶ τόδε κέρδιον ἦεν (was the better course (and would have proved so) if . . .) υ 332

Aor.	Impf. without κεν
εἰ μὴ ἔειπες	ἔμελλον . . . ν 385

(2) Aor. κεν	Aor. κεν
εἴ κ' ἔτι προτέρω γένετο δρόμος	παρέλασσέ κέ μιν Ψ 526

(3) Aor. or Plupf. Indic.	Aor. or Impf. Indic. ἄν
εἰ τάδε ᾔδεα	οὐκ ἂν ὑπεξέφυγεν Θ 366
εἰ μὴ παῦσεν	οὐκ ἂν χάζοντο Λ 505

Cf. M 292, Π 686, Σ 398.

(4) Aor. Indic.	Aor. or Pres. Opt. κεν
εἰ μὴ νόησεν (ἐξήγγειλεν)	ἀπόλοιτό κεν E 312, 389
εἰ μὴ ἀγάσσατο	ῥεῖά κε φέροι τεύχεα P 71
εἰ δάμη	οὔ κεν ὧδ' ἀκαχοίμην α 237

(5) Opt.	Opt. κεν
Conditional Relative Sentences	
ὅς τις ἄβλητος δινεύοι	οὐκέτι κε ἔργον ὀνόσαιτο Δ 540
ὃς τότε γηθήσειεν	θρασυκάρδιός κ' εἴη N 344

(6) Opt. (in construction of (III) (B) (b) (1))	Opt. ἄν
Conditional Relative Sentence	
ὅτε ὄπα εἴη	οὐκ ἂν Ὀδυσῆΐ γ' ἐρίσσειεν ἄλλος Γ 221

(7) The Apodosis in loose connexion with the Protasis

εἰ νῶϊν νόστον ἔδωκε Ζεύς	ἔφην μιν φιλησέμεν (I thought to . . . (and should have done so) if . . .) δ 172

(b) Past in Protasis, Present in Apodosis

Aor. or Impf. Indic.	Opt. κεν
εἰ τὸν ὄνειρον ἄλλος ἔνισπεν	ψεῦδός κεν φαῖμεν B 80
εἴ τις ἄλλος ἐκέλευεν	ψεῦδός κεν φαῖμεν Ω 220

(c) Present

(1) Opt.	Opt. κεν
εἰ νῦν Τρώεσσι μένος ἐνείη	Πάτροκλόν κ' ἐρυσαίμεθα P 156
εἰ τοιόσδ' εἴη	θηήσαιό κεν ρ 313

Cf. M 322 : ε 206, π 148.

(2) Opt.	Opt. ἄν
εἰ μὴ δῶρα φέροι	οὐκ ἄν σε κελοίμην . . . I 515
εἰ ἐπ' ἄλλῳ ἀεθλεύοιμεν	ἐγὼ ἂν τὰ πρῶτα φεροίμην Ψ 274

(D) Future Suppositions

(1) Pres. Indic.	Fut.
εἰ ἐριδαίνετον ὧδε	λοίγια ἔργα τάδ' ἔσσεται A 574
εἴ τις θεῶν ἐπιτάρροθός ἐστιν	ἐξανύω σε Λ 366, Υ 453

(2) Fut.	Fut.
εἰ μαχεῖται	οὐχ ἕξουσιν Υ 26
εἴ μοι οὐ τίσουσιν	δύσομαι εἰς 'Αΐδαο μ 382

Cf. B 379, 387, H 98, M 248, P 154, Σ 268, *Υ 129, Ω 206.

(3) Fut.	Subj.
εἴ μοι οὐ τίσουσιν	ἐν νεκύεσσι φαείνω μ 382

(4) Fut.	Opt. (wish)
εἰ μὴ ἀφ' εἵματα δύσω	μηκέτι κάρη ὤμοισιν ἐπείη *B 261

(5) Fut.	Opt. κεν
εἰ ὁμὴν θήσετε τιμήν	εἴη κεν τοῦτο ἔπος Ω 57

Cf. *A 294, P 418.

(6) Fut.	Opt. ἄν
εἰ οὐ δώσει ἄγγελον	οὐκ ἄν σε κελοίμην . . . Ω 296

Cf. Φ 463.

(7) Fut. with Apodosis suppressed

εἰ ἐς πόλεμον πωλήσεαι	[you must expect wounds, nay . . .] E 350

Cf. A 135 : β 115.

(8) Fut. κεν	Fut.
εἴ κε κύνες ἑλκήσουσιν	σοὶ κατηφείη ἔσσεται P 557

(9) Fut. κεν	Imp.
αἴ κεν 'Ιλίου πεφιδήσεται	ἴστω τοῦτο O 213

Conditional Relative Sentence

ὅτε κεν συμβλήσεαι αὐτῷ	ἀναχωρῆσαι Υ 335

(10) Fut. κεν	Opt. (wish)
εἴ κ' ἔτι σε κιχήσομαι	μηκέτι κάρη ὤμοισιν ἐπείη *B 258
εἴ κε νοστήσω καὶ ἐσόψομαι . . .	ἐμεῖο κάρη τάμοι *E 212

(11) Fut. ἄν	Imp.
Conditional Relative Sentence	
τοὺς ἂν ἐγὼ ἐπιόψομαι	πιθέσθων I 167

(12) Subj.	Fut.
εἴ σε κατακτάνῃ	οὔ σε κλαύσομαι X 86
εἴ περ ἀνάγκη [ἔῃ]	πτολεμίξομεν Ω 667
Conditional Relative Sentences	
ὄφρα ζωοῖσι μετείω	οὔ μ' ἵξετ' ἄχος Ψ 47
ἥ τις ἀρίστη [ἔῃ]	βοῦν ῥέξειν κ 522, λ 30
ὀππότ' ἐθέλῃς	εὐνὴ σοὶ ἔσσεται ψ 257

Cf. **ὁπότε** π 268. **ὅσσος** ζ 257. **ὅς τις** Ξ 221, Υ 363 : β 294. **ὅτε** Φ 323. **ὄφρα** σ 133.

Subj.	Words implying Fut.
εἰ νῆ' ἐθέλῃ ὀλέσαι	βούλομ' ἅπαξ ἀπὸ θυμὸν ὀλέσσαι μ 348
Conditional Relative Sentences	
ὀππότε μεταπαυσωλὴ γένηται	ὀφέλλετε ταῦτα πένεσθαι T 201

Cf. **ὅς τις** π 76, τ 528.

(13) Subj.	Imp.
εἴ ποτε χρειὼ γένηται	μάρτυροι ἔστων A 340
Conditional Relative Sentences	
ὥς τοι μύθου τέλος ἐν φρεσὶ θείω	πείθεο Π 83
ἥ τις ἀρίστη [ἔῃ]	νῆ' ἄρσας ἔρχεο α 280

Cf. **ὅς** γ 370, δ 409, φ 266. **ὅσσος** θ 250. **ὅς τις** H 50 : β 350, θ 424, π 348, ω 215. **ὄφρα** κ 176.

(14) Subj.	Opt. (wish)
Conditional Relative Sentences	
ὅς τις μεθίῃσιν	μὴ νοστήσειεν N 234

Cf. **ὅσος** ζ 180, ρ 355. **ὅς τις** β 34.

(15) Subj.	Opt.
Conditional Relative Sentences	
ὅν τιν' ἀποσφήλωσιν ἄελλαι	ὅθεν οὐκ ἔλποιτο ἐλθέμεν γ 320
ὅπῃ περάσητε	ὦνον ἄλφοι ο 453

(16) Subj.	Opt. κεν
Conditional Relative Sentence	
ὀππότ' ἀνὴρ τοιοῦτος αἰτίζῃ	τί κεν ῥέξειε καὶ ἄλλος ; δ 650

(17) Subj. subjoined to an Infin.	
Conditional Relative Sentences	
ὅτε τις χαλεπήνῃ	ἀπαμύνασθαι Ω 369

Cf. **ὅππῃ** θ 45. **ὅς τις** υ 335.

(18) Subj. with Apodosis in loose connexion with the Protasis	
εἴ περ γέροντ' εἴρηαι	ξεῖνοι εὐχόμεθ' εἶναι α 188

(19) Subj. with Apodosis in external governance

Conditional Relative Sentences

ᾧ περ ἀρίστῳ ⌊ἔωσιν]	κελεύομεν ἀλλήλων πειρηθῆναι Ψ 802
ὅς τις ἄριστος [ἔῃ]	πρὶν γήμασθαι σ 289

(20) Subj. κεν	Fut.
αἴ κε Ζεὺς δῷσι	ἀποτείσομεν Α 128
εἴ κε τὸν ἕλω	τεύχε' οἴσω Η 81
αἴ κ' ἐθέλῃσιν	ἰήσεται ι 520
εἴ κεν ἐντανύσῃ . . .	ἕσσω μιν φ 338

Cf. Β 364, Δ 170, *353, 415, Ε 351, 762, Ζ 260, 526, Η 118, 173, Θ 142, 287, 471, Ι 255, *359, 412, 414, 604, Κ 106, 449, 452, Λ 315, 404, 405, 455, Μ 71, Ν 829, Ξ 368, Ο 498, Π 32, 499, Ρ 29, Σ 180, 278, *306, Υ 138, Φ 437, 553, Χ 99, 256, Ψ 413, 543 : β 133, 188, ζ 313, η 75, θ 355, 496, λ 348, ν 359, π 403, ρ 230, 549, 556, σ 83, τ 327, *488, 496, υ 233, φ 213, 314, 348, 364, χ 345, ω 511.

Conditional Relative Sentences

ὅττι κεν εἴπω	οὐκ ἀπόβλητον ἔπος ἔσσεται Β 361
ἥν κ' ἐθέλωμι	ποιήσομ' ἄκοιτιν Ι 397
ὄφρα κε τοῦτον ἔχῃ νόον	ἔδονται β 124
ἐπεί κε θερέω	ἔμ' ἄξει ρ 23

Cf. **εἰς ὅ κεν** Ι 609. **ἐπεί** Ζ 83, Λ 191, 206, 764, *Σ 121, 280, Τ 402, Χ 125, 258, 509, Ψ 10 : δ 494, σ 150, χ 254. **ὅ** Υ 308. **οἷος** ο 281. **ὁππότε** Ι 702, Ξ 504, Σ 115, Χ 365 : β 357, ν 394, π 282, χ 216. **ὁππότερος** Ψ 805. **ὅς** Α 547, Β 391, Ι 74, Κ 235, 306, Λ 367, Ρ 100, 229, Σ 271, 467, Τ 72, 110, 235, Υ 454, Ψ 857 : ζ 159, ρ 11, 19, 559, σ 63, τ 27, 322, φ 280. **ὅς τις** *Α 294, Ε 421, Ι 102, Ω 92 : α 158, λ 147, ξ 445, ο 448, ψ 140. **ὅτε** Κ 130, *Υ 130. **ὄφρα** β 204.

Subj. κεν	Words implying Fut.
αἴ κε κακὸς ὣς ἀλυσκάζω	αἰδέομαι Τρῶας Ζ 443
εἴ κε σίνηαι	τεκμαίρομ' ὄλεθρον λ 112, μ 139

Cf. Ι 412, 414, Ξ 110, Σ 91, *Ψ 344 : π 405, ρ 79, φ 305.

Conditional Relative Sentences

ὅτε κέν τις ἄγηται	ὅσσον σεῦ [μέλει ἄλγος] Ζ 454

Cf. **ὅς** χ 66. Also **ὅς τις** α 389.

(21) Subj. κεν	Words of Fearing
εἴ κε λίπω τεύχεα	μή τίς μοι νεμεσήσεται *Ρ 91
εἴ κε παρανήξομαι	δείδω μὴ . . . ε 417

Cf. Ρ 94 : ε 466, 470, π 254.

Conditional Relative Sentence

ὅς κεν ἴδηται	μή τίς μοι νεμεσήσεται *Ρ 93

(22) Subj. κεν — Fut. κεν

Conditional Relative Sentences

ὅν κεν ἵκωμαι	κεχολώσεταί κεν Α 139
ὅν κεν ἀγάγω	χρυσοῦ, ὅν κέ τις οἴσει υἷος ἄποινα Β 231

(23) Subj. κεν — Fut. ἄν

Conditional Relative Sentence

ἐπεί κέ τις ἐκ θυμὸν ἕληται	αὐτὸν ἄν με κύνες ἐρύουσιν Χ 67

(24) Subj. κεν	Subj.
εἴ κεν ἀκούσω	σῆμα χεύω β 220

Cf. Ν 260 : χ 167.

Conditional Relative Sentences

ὅν κε θεὸς ἐν χερσὶ βάλῃσιν	οὐκ ἔσθ' ὅς τις φύγῃ Φ 103
ὅς κε γένηται	μοῖραν οὔ τις ἀλεύεται ω 29

(**25**) Subj. κεν	Subj. κεν
εἴ κε μὴ δώωσιν	ἕλωμαί κεν Α 137

Cf. Α 324 : δ 391.

(**26**) Subj. κεν	Imp.
εἴ κεν ἔμ' ἕλῃ	τεύχεα φερέτω Η 77
εἴ κε δώῃ κῦδος ἀρέσθαι	μὴ λιλαίεσθαι . . . Π 87
αἴ κ' ἐθέλῃσθα ἀκουέμεν	δησάντων μ 49

Cf. Γ 281, 284, Ε 129, 131, 260, *Ι 135, *277, Π 445, Τ 147, Ω 592 : α 289, ι 502, μ 53, 163, ξ 395, 398, ρ 82.

Conditional Relative Sentences

ὁππότερός κε νικήσῃ	γυναῖκ' ἀγέσθω Γ 71, 92
ᾗ κεν ἴῃσθα	φθέγγεο Κ 67
ὁππότε κέ σ' ἐλάσῃ	ἐπαῖξαι κ 293

Cf. **ἐπεί** Ι 707, Ξ 237, Υ 337, Φ 534 : ξ 153. **ὅ** Β 346. **ὁππότε** Δ 40 : λ 127, ψ 274. **ὁππότερος** *σ 46. **ὅς** Α 549, Δ 306, Θ 430, Ι 140, 146, 282, 288, Ξ 376, Ο 494, Φ 296, Ψ 247, 554, 660, 855 : λ 442, *σ 47, *270, 286. **ὅς τις** *Ο 148 : α 316, β 25, 161, 229, θ 549, τ 378, 403, 406, υ 115, ω 454. **ὅτε** Θ 180, *Ι 138, *280 : δ 420, ν 180, ο 446, π 287, τ 6. **ὄφρα** Ω 553 : τ 17.

(**27**) Subj. κεν	Opt. (wish)

Conditional Relative Sentence

ἐπεί κε μάχην δίηται	ἀσκηθὴς ἵκοιτο Π 246

(**28**) Subj. κεν	Opt.

Conditional Relative Sentence

ὅττι κεν εἴπω	πίθοιό τί μοι ; Ξ 190

(**29**) Subj. κεν	Opt. κεν
αἴ κεν ἴδῃ . . .	δῶρά κε φέροιο Δ 98
εἴ κ' ἀσινέας ἐάᾳς	ἔτι κεν ἵκοισθε λ 110

Cf. Ι 362, 414, Ν 379, Ρ 39, Ω 687 : λ 105, *φ 114.

Conditional Relative Sentences

ὅς κ' ἐντανύσῃ βιόν	τῷ κεν ἅμ' ἑσποίμην τ 577, φ 75

Cf. **ὅς τις** Ξ 190. **ὁπποῖος** Υ 250.

(**30**) Subj. κεν	Opt. ἄν
εἴ κεν ἀκούσῃς (ἀκούσω)	τλαίης (τλαίην) ἄν α 287, β 218
εἴ κ' ἀσινέας ἐάᾳς	ἔτ' ἂν ἵκοισθε μ 137

Conditional Relative Sentence

ὅν κ' ἐῢ εἴπω	οὐκ ἂν μῦθον ἀτιμήσαιτε Ξ 127

(**31**) Subj. κεν subjoined to an Infin.

αἴ κέν σ' ἐξαπάφω	κτεῖναί με ψ 79

Conditional Relative Sentences

ᾗ κε σὺ ἡγεμονεύῃς	τῇ ἴμεν Ο 46
ὅν κ' ἐθέλῃσιν	παυέμεναι κ 22

Cf. **ὁππότε** λ 106, ν 155. **ὅς** Φ 484 : φ 345.

To a Participle

Conditional Relative Sentence

οἷόν κε κατευνηθέντα ἴδησθε — τοῖος ἐών δ 421

(32) Subj. κεν with Apodosis in external governance

αἴ κε σιωπῇ οἴχωμαι — μή μοι χολώσεαι Ξ 310
αἴ κεν ἐμὲ κτείνῃς — ὄφρα νέμηαι Υ 186
αἴ κε θεοί γ' ἐθέλωσιν — ὥς κε πατρίδα γαῖαν ἵκηαι ε 169

Cf. Ε 820, Υ 301 : β 102, μ 299, τ 147, ω 137

Conditional Relative Sentences

ὅτε κεν δαινύῃ — ὄφρα εἴπῃς θ 242

Cf. **ὅ** Γ 354. **ὅς** β 128. **ὅτε** Α 567.

(33) Subj. κεν with Apodosis suppressed

εἴ κ' ἐθέλῃσι στυφελίξαι . . . . Α 580

Cf. Φ 567, Χ 111.

(34) Subj. ἄν — Fut.

εἰ δ' **ἂν** τίνειν οὐκ ἐθέλωσι — μαχήσομαι Γ 288

Cf. Ε 224, 232, Σ 273.

Conditional Relative Sentences

εὖτ' ἂν πολλοὶ πίπτωσιν — οὐ δυνήσεαι χραισμεῖν Α 242
ὁππότ' ἂν ἡβήσῃ — τίσις ἔσσεται α 41

Cf. **ἐπεί** Ζ 412. **ἐπήν** Δ 239, *Ι 358, Μ 369, Ν 753, Ψ 76, Ω 155, 184, 717 : δ 412, ε 363, μ 55, ξ 515, ο 337, χ 219. **εὖτε** Τ 158. **ᾗ** Η 286. **ὅς** Θ 10, Ο 348. **ὁπ(π)ότε** Π 62 : τ 410, *489. **ὅτε** Α 519. **ὄφρα** Χ 387 : γ 353.

Subj. ἄν — Words implying Future

Conditional Relative Sentence

ἐπὴν τοῖς ἐπιτείλω — θέω μετὰ σ' αὖτις ; Κ 63

(35) Subj. ἄν — Imp.

Conditional Relative Sentences

εὖτ' ἄν σ' ὕπνος ἀνήῃ — μή σε λήθη αἱρείτω Β 34
ὡς ἂν ἐγὼ εἴπω — πειθώμεθα Β 139
ὄφρ' ἂν τεύχεα δύω — εὔχεσθε Η 193
ἐπὴν σπείσῃς — δὸς δέπας γ 45
ὁππότ' ἂν περήσῃς — νῆα κέλσαι κ 508

Cf. **ἐπήν** *Ο 147, Π 95, 453 : α 293, δ 414, ε 348, ζ 297, κ 526, λ 119, ο 36, *σ 269, φ 159, χ 440. **ὁππότε** Φ 340 : ζ 303. **ὅτε** Δ 53, Η 459. **ὄφρα** Ζ 113, Θ 375, Σ 409 : ν 412. **ὡς** Ι 26, 704, Μ 75, Ξ 74, 370, Ο 294, Σ 297 : μ 213, ν 179.

(36) Subj. ἄν subjoined to an Infin.

Conditional Relative Sentence

ἐπὴν πόλις ἀμφικαλύψῃ ἵππον — ἀπολέσθαι θ 511

(37) Subj. ἄν with Apodosis in external governance

Conditional Relative Sentences

ὅτ' ἂν νεώμεθα — ὥς κε ὀστέ' ἕκαστος ἄγῃ Η 335
ὁππότ' ἂν εὕδησθα — μὴ δηλήσεταί τις θ 444

(38) Subj. ἄν with Apodosis suppressed or lost

εἰ δ' ἂν τούτους ὑποκλονέεσθαι ἐάσω . . . φεύγω δὲ . . . Φ 556

Conditional Relative Sentence

ἐπὴν πόλιος ἐπιβήομεν . . . . ζ 262

(39) ἤν Subj. — Fut.

ἤν ἐθέλῃσθα — ὄψεαι *Δ 353

Cf. I 393, X 55.

(40) ἤν Subj. — Words of Fearing

ἤν δηθύνῃσθα — δείδω μὴ . . . μ 121

(41) ἤν Subj. — Opt. κεν

ἢν ἔλθῃ θύελλα — πῇ κέν τις ὑπεκφύγοι; μ 288

(42) ἤν Subj. with Apodosis in external governance

ἤν ἐθέλῃσιν — ὄφρα μοι (οἱ) ἕπηται I 429, 692

(43) Subj. ἄν κεν — Fut.

Conditional Relative Sentence

ὄφρ' ἄν κε δούρατ' ἀρήρῃ — μενέω ε 361

(44) Subj. ἄν κεν — Imp.

Conditional Relative Sentences

ὄφρ' ἄν κεν ὁρᾷ (ὁρᾷς) . . . — ἀναχωρείτω (ὑπόεικε) Λ 187, 202
ὄφρ' ἄν κ' ἀγροὺς ἴομεν — ἔρχεσθαι ζ 259

(45) Opt. — Fut.

εἴ τίς μοι ἕποιτο ἄλλος — θαλπωρὴ ἔσται K 222

Conditional Relative Sentences

ὅτε μὴ Κρονίων ἐμβάλοι δαλόν — αἰπύ οἱ ἐσσεῖται . . . N 319
ὅν τινα ὕπνος ἕλοι — κοίτοιο ἔσσεται ὥρη τ 511

Opt. — Words implying Future

Conditional Relative Sentence

ὅς μὴ βόας ἐλάσειεν — οὐ τῷ ἐδίδου λ 289

(46) Opt. — Fut. κεν

εἰ ἔλθοι — βίας κεν ἀποτίσεται ρ 539

(47) Opt. κεν — Fut.

Conditional Relative Sentence

ᾧ κ' ἐπιφθονέοις — εἶσιν ὀπίσσω λ 149

(48) Opt. κεν — Fut. κεν

εἴ κεν εἰς Ἰθάκην ἀφικοίμεθα — νηόν κε τεύξομεν μ 345

(49) Opt. ἄν — Fut.

Conditional Relative Sentence

ἐπὴν τεισαίμεθα λώβην — τεύξεσθαι δόρπον T 208

(50) Opt. — Subj.

εἰ ἐθέλοις — δόρυ πόρωμεν Ψ 894

(51) Opt. — Subj. κεν

εἴ τίς σε ἴδοιτο — ἀνάβλησίς κε γένηται Ω 653
εἰ δύναιο . . . — ὅς κέν τοι εἴπῃσιν ὁδὸν δ 388

Conditional Relative Sentence

ὅτε πυθοίμην — ἥν κ' εἴπω β 43

(52) Opt. — Subj. ἄν

εἰ πειρηθείης — οὐκ ἄν τοι χραίσμῃσιν Λ 386

Cf. *B 491.

Conditional Relative Sentence

ὅτ' ἐν κονίῃσι μιγείης	οὐκ ἄν τοι χραίσμῃ Γ 55

(53) Opt.	Imp.
εἰ ἄμμε παραφθαίησιν	ἐπὶ νῆας προτιειλεῖν Κ 346

(54) Opt.	Opt. (wish)
εἰ μὴ τόξ' ἐν πυρὶ θείην	ἐμεῖο κάρη τάμοι *Ε 215
εἰ μὴ κείνοισι κακὸν γενοίμην	ἀπ' ἐμεῖο κάρη τάμοι π 103

Conditional Relative Sentences

ὅτε μαχοίατο	τοιοῦτοι εἶεν Φ 429
ὅτις τοιαῦτα ῥέζοι	ὡς ἀπόλοιτο α 47
οἵ περ ἄριστοι [εἶεν]	εἰ βόες εἶεν σ 371

Cf. **ὁππότε** σ 148. **ὁππότερος** Γ 299. **ὅς** *Ω 139. **ὅς τις** Ζ 58 : α 403, ο 359, σ 142. **ὅτε** Σ 465 : μ 106.

(55) Opt.	Opt.
εἰ τόδε φίλον γένοιτο	οἰκέοιτο πόλις Δ 17

Conditional Relative Sentences

ὅτε τὸν ὕπνος ἱκάνοι	ὅς τις τολμήσειεν . . . ι 333
ὅς τις ὀπυίοι	οἰκία δοῖμεν β 336, π 386

(56) Opt.	Opt. κεν
εἰ τάδε πυθοίατο	γηθήσαι κεν Α 257
εἴ μοί τι πίθοιο	τό κε κέρδιον εἴη Η 28
εἴ ποθεν ἔλθοι	ποῖοί κ' εἶτε ; φ 195

Cf. Δ 34, 347, Ζ 284, Η 129, Λ 135, Ν 276, 485, Ξ 208, 333, *Ο 49, Π 72, 623, Ρ 102, 160, *Υ 100 : α 163, β 251, γ 223, λ 501, ξ 132, ο 435, π 105, ρ 407, σ 223, 246, 254, 357, 384, τ 127, υ 42, 381

Conditional Relative Sentences

ᾧ τόσσα γένοιτο	οὔ κεν ἀλήϊος εἴη Ι 125, 267
ὅτε πύθοιτο	ἤν κ' εἴποι β 31
ἅσσ' ἐθέλοιεν	δρώοιμί κεν ο 317

Cf. **ἐπεί** *δ 222. **ὅς** Μ 228, Ν 322 : *δ 222, κ 383, *ν 291, χ 138, ψ 101, 169. **ὅσος** λ 361. **ὅς τις** Ξ 92 : α 229. **ὅτε** Θ 23 : λ 375, μ 114, *ν 391, *φ 116, ψ 185.

(57) Opt.	Opt. ἄν
εἰ ἐν πόντῳ γένοιτο	πολλοὺς ἂν κορέσειεν *Π 746
εἰ μὴ θυμὸς κελεύοι	οὐκ ἂν πεφιδοίμην ι 278

Cf. Χ 20, Ω 366, 653 : β 62, ε 178, κ 343.

Conditional Relative Sentences

ὅν τινα μεθιέντα ἴδοις	μαχέσαιο ἂν ἄλλῳ Ζ 330
ὅτε με χρειὼ ἵκοι	ἅσσ' ἂν μηδοίμην ε 189

Cf. **ὅς** Ν 118 : δ 205, θ 240. **ὅτε** Ξ 248 : π 197.

(58) Opt. subjoined to an Infin.

Conditional Relative Sentences

ὅτε θυμὸς ἀνώγοι	πιέειν (πιεῖν) Δ 263, Θ 189 : θ 70
ὅς τις ἐλαφρότατος πέλοιτο	θῆκεν ἀέθλιον, [τῷ δόμεν] Ψ 749

Cf. **ὅς** Σ 508. **ὅς τις** Ε 301, Ρ 8.

(59) Opt. with Apodosis in external governance

Conditional Relative Sentences

ὁππότε μιν σεύαιτο	ὄφρα κῆτος ἀλέαιτο Υ 148
ὁπότε σπερχοίατο	μή τινα βλάπτοι ν 22

(60) Opt. κεν	Fut.
εἴ κεν θάνατόν γε φύγοιμεν	ἄμμε παλιμπλαγχθέντας ὀΐω ἀπονοστήσειν *A 60

(61) Opt. κεν	Imp.
Conditional Relative Sentence	
ὅττι κέ μοι δοίης	κειμήλιον ἔστω δ 600

(62) Opt. κεν	Opt. κεν
εἰ τούτω κε λάβοιμεν	ἀροίμεθά κε κλέος E 273
εἴ κε βλεῖο	στέρνων κ' ἀντιάσειε [βέλος] N 288
εἴ κε μένοις	οἶκόν κε δοίην η 315

Cf. B 123, Z 50, Θ 196, 205, I 141, 283, K 381 : β 246, μ 345, *ν 389, ρ 223, τ 589.

Conditional Relative Sentence	
ὅς κε πλεῖστα πόροι	ἥ κε γήμαιτο π 392, φ 162

(63) Opt. κεν	Opt. ἄν
εἴ κε φάγοιτε	τάχ' ἂν τίσις εἴη β 76

Cf. N 288 : θ 353.

(64) Opt. κεν with Apodosis in external governance	
Conditional Relative Sentence	
ᾧ κ' ἐθέλοι	ὥς κε δοίη β 54

(65) Opt. ἄν	Opt. (wish)
Conditional Relative Sentence	
ἐπὴν γόου ἐξ ἔρον εἴην	κατακτείνειέ με Ω 227